Catalogue of the library of the

Royal Geographical Society

Containing the titles of all works up to

December 1893

Hugh Robert Mill

Alpha Editions

This edition published in 2019

ISBN : 9789353865047

Design and Setting By
Alpha Editions
email - alphaedis@gmail.com

CATALOGUE

OF

THE LIBRARY

OF THE

Royal Geographical Society.

CONTAINING THE TITLES OF ALL WORKS UP TO DECEMBER 1893.

COMPILED BY

HUGH ROBERT MILL, D.Sc.

LONDON:
PUBLISHED FOR THE ROYAL GEOGRAPHICAL SOCIETY BY
JOHN MURRAY,
50 ALBEMARLE STREET, W.
1895.

CONTENTS.

———◆———

PREFACE.

T HE first Catalogue of the Library of the Royal Geographical Society was prepared by the Secretary, Dr Norton Shaw, in 1852. It was superseded in 1865 by a larger Catalogue, comprising 542 pages octavo, giving the contents of the Library down to that date. This was arranged in one alphabet, according to authors' names, as far as possible, but with subject headings for anonymous books, and extensive sub-divisions under "Voyages," "Transactions," &c. This Catalogue bears marks of having been rapidly compiled and not very carefully revised. In 1871 an Appendix of 136 pages was prepared by Mr Godfrey M. Evans, of the British Museum, containing the accessions up to the end of 1870. Mr Evans also prepared a Classified Catalogue brought up to 1870. The accessions for the ten years 1870-80 were catalogued by Mr E. C. Rye, at that time Librarian to the Society, and his is an admirable piece of work, the revision having been very thorough. It consists of 380 pages, and necessarily follows the classification of the main Catalogue and its first Supplement, but uniformity was introduced into the cataloguing of compound names, and some improvements were made in the manner of entering official publications.

On my appointment as Librarian in March 1892, it became my duty to prepare a third Supplement to the Catalogue, containing the accessions for the ten years ending in 1890. This was completed, with the aid of Mr Vincent S. B. Hawkins, the Assistant-Librarian, in February 1893. But after estimates had been obtained for printing the third supplement as a volume of 420 pages, the Library Committee decided to incorporate the Catalogue of 1865 and the three appendices, and to print the whole as one volume. The additional material was prepared for the printer, and after several experiments the form now adopted was arrived at as the best and most convenient ; the use of double columns being necessary in order that the whole might be contained in a single volume.

The one aim kept in view was to produce a Catalogue of the most convenient form for the use of Fellows of the Society and practical geographers. No attempt was made to give a bibliographical description of the books or a full transcript of the title-pages. Nor are the contents of books, except in the great collections of travels in Appendix I., noted, save in a few cases, and papers in journals are not catalogued. The size of the volumes is only approximately given by the terms folio, quarto, octavo, &c., and some inconsistency may be found in this respect, as it was not considered advisable to delay the Catalogue for six months in order that the size of the sheets on which each book was printed could be ascertained. When the place of publication was London it is not noted, and where no town is given London is to be understood. The names of other towns are given as currently written in English, although on the book they may be latinised or in a foreign form. The titles in their entirety or in a slightly abbreviated form, are given in the language in which the book is written, except in the case of Russian, where it seemed better to translate than to transliterate the Russian into Roman letters. The words [In Russian] are added to these titles in every case.

The present Catalogue includes all books, pamphlets, periodicals, and other printed papers, in the possession of the Royal Geographical Society in May 1895, which had been published up to 31st December 1893, but new editions of works previously catalogued are included down to 1895. The Catalogue is arranged in four divisions, obviating the difficulties of reference arising from a mixed system of Author and Subject headings in the same alphabet.

1. GENERAL ALPHABETICAL AUTHORS' CATALOGUE.—The object of this Catalogue is to show which of the works of each Author are in the Library. It is arranged in strict alphabetical order according to surnames. The names of important ships have been added to those of authors, and in most cases biographical notices have been entered under the name of the subject of the memoir as well as that of the author. Where the biographical notice is anonymous, it appears under the name of the subject only. The convenience of these transgressions of the rule will, we believe, excuse the inconsistency.

The entries are of three kinds :—(1.) Titles of books distinguished by a small circle following the number which indicates their size, e.g., 8°, for an octavo book. Papers in the *Ergänzungshefte* of "Petermann's Mittheilungen," and in the *Supplementary Papers* of the Royal Geographical Society, are included. (2.) Pamphlets of less than 100 pages, and kept unbound or in plain cardboard covers, including extracts from periodicals, reprints, and cuttings. These are distinguished by a star, e.g., 8*, for an octavo pamphlet. (3.) Cross-references to names of joint-authors, and to the authors of papers noticed in Appendices I. and II., as well as to the early travellers whose works are noticed in Appendix I.

In many cases the alphabetical arrangement of names presents serious difficulties, and in spite of much care some anomalies remain in the text. The inconvenience due to this cause is, however, minimised by the copious use of cross-references. The difficulty arises sometimes from uncertainty as to the true surname, e.g., *E. de Bourgade la Dardye*, or *A. Bouquet de la Grye*. In such cases the titles are given under the name to which it seemed most natural to refer, with cross-references under the other names. Following the rule adopted in Mr Rye's supplement, foreign names in *de, d', le, von,* or *van, e.g., De Candolle, D'Anville. Le Blanc, von Richthofen, van Noort,* are given under the initials of the main word; but names in *De la, Du, Von der, Van der,* are given under D or V. Where such names belong to Englishmen or Americans, the article or preposition is in all cases treated as part of the name, *e.g., De Rance, Le Messurier.* Where deviations from this rule escaped notice until the proof was in pages, a cross-reference is inserted in the proper place. For the sake of uniformity, names in *Mac—* appear as if fully spelled even when the authors use the form *M^c* or *Mc*; but the use of a capital or small letter following *Mac* or *Fitz*—which does not affect the alphabetical arrangement—is in accordance with the authors' usage. The contraction *St* is placed along with *Saint.* Russian names in *Ch* are sometimes given under *Tch* or *Tsch* when occurring only in French or German titles.

The military, naval, or other official designations of authors are given merely for the purpose of allowing the author to be more easily recognised. As a rule, the highest rank reached by an author is stated when this was known; but some cases may have been overlooked, and in other cases reasons, which will be apparent on reading the entry, make a deviation from the rule advisable. Every effort has been made to give the works of different authors of the same name correctly; but there are a few cases in which it was found impossible to ascertain whether certain books were by a particular author or by a contemporary of the same name. The Christian names or initials of some authors, particularly of Frenchmen, could not be discovered without an expenditure of time that seemed unjustifiable.

The 521 pages of the alphabetical Catalogue were revised carefully by Lieut.-Col. J. Dalton and Mr E. G. Ravenstein, members of the Library Committee, whose corrections were of the utmost value.

2. APPENDIX I.—COLLECTIONS OF VOYAGES AND TRAVELS.—The collections are arranged alphabetically under the names of their compilers when these are known, and the anonymous works are placed at the end in chronological order. The contents are reprinted, with corrections when necessary, and many additions, from the previous Catalogue and Supplements.

3. APPENDIX II.—GOVERNMENT, ANONYMOUS, AND OTHER MISCELLANEOUS PUBLICATIONS.—These are incapable of alphabetical arrangement, except so far as concerns the larger divisions. The continents are given in alphabetical order, the chief countries in each also arranged alphabetically; and whenever the number of publications to be catalogued is large enough the countries are subdivided, the divisions being indicated, for convenience of reference, by letters of the alphabet. The ultimate arrangement under each head is chronological. When authors' names occur, they are as a rule referred to in the alphabetical part of the Cata-

logue, to which the Appendices are subordinate and supplementary. In this Appendix the pamphlets have not been distinguished from the bound volumes.

4. APPENDIX III.—TRANSACTIONS AND PERIODICAL PUBLICATIONS.— The Library of the Society is particularly rich in sets of transactions and periodicals, and these have recently been put in thorough order by Dr James Murie, by whom this Appendix has been compiled and revised directly from the works.   The arrangement is geographical, as in the case of Appendix II.   The continents are arranged alphabetically, the countries and the towns in each country being also in alphabetical order.   Notes and comments on the sets of serials are given in a brief form when necessary.

A new Subject Catalogue of the Library is at present in course of compilation, in which the principal contents of all the geographical books and periodicals belonging to the Society will be classified, and so the Library will be made for the first time fully available for geographical study.

In preparing this Catalogue for press, I have received much helpful advice from the President, Mr Clements R. Markham, C.B., and from Mr J. Scott Keltie, as well as great assistance from Lieut.-Col. Dalton, Mr Ravenstein, Dr Murie, Mr Vincent Hawkins, and especially from Mr Edward Heawood, M.A.

HUGH ROBERT MILL,
Librarian, R.G.S.

1 SAVILE ROW, LONDON, W.,
   27th May 1895.

CATALOGUE.

A . . . Abd-el-Qader et sa Nouvelle Capitale. *Map.* 8* *Paris*, 1840

A—— K. *See* Hennessy, J. B. N.

Aa, Van der. *See* under Robidé van der Aa ; Van der Aa.

Abad, J. R. La Republica Dominicana, Reseña General Geografico-Estadistica. 8° *Santo Domingo*, 1888

—— Puerto Rico en la Feria. Exposicion de Ponce en 1882. Memoria redactada de orden de la junta directiva de la misma, por Don José Ramon Abad. 8° *Ponce*, 1885

Abbadie, Antoine d'. Notice sur les Travaux Scientifiques ; Voyage à Olinda. 4* *Paris*, 1836-37

—— Voyage en Abyssinie. 8* *Paris*, 1839

—— Note sur le haut Fleuve Blanc. 8* *Paris*, 1849

—— Réponses de Falasha dits Juifs d'Abyssinie aux questions faites par M. Luzzato. 8* *Paris*, 1850

—— Observations relatives au cours du Nil et aux lacs de l'Afrique Centrale. 8* *Paris*, 1851

—— Géodésie d'Éthiopie, ou Triangulation d'une partie de la Haute Éthiopie, exécutée selon des méthodes nouvelles. Vérifiée et rédigée par Rodolphe Radau. *Maps. Imperfect.* 4° *Paris*, 1860-73

—— Description d'un instrument pour la pratique de la Géodésie expeditive. 4* *Paris*, 1863

—— Géographie de l'Éthiopie. Ce que j'ai entendu, faisant suite à ce que j'ai vu. Premier volume. 8° *Paris*, 1890

—— **and J. A. Chaho.** Études Grammaticales sur la Langue Euskarienne. 8° *Paris*, 1836

Abbadie, Arnauld d'. Douze Ans dans la Haute Ethiopie (Abyssinie). Vol. I. *Map.* 8° *Paris*, 1868

Abbate, Enrico. Guida al Gran Sasso d'Italia, publicata per cura della Sezione di Roma del Club Alpino Italiano. *Maps, plans, and illustrations.* 12° *Rome*, 1888

Abbate Pasha, Dr. De la prétendue Sphéricité de la Terre connue des Anciens Egyptiens. 8* *Cairo*, 1893

Abbate Pasha, Dr. Il Genio e l'obbiettivo di Colombo. In rapporto alle condizione geografiche contemporanee dell' Egitto. 8* *Naples*, 1893

Abbe, Cleveland. Smithsonian Miscellaneous Collections, 843 : The Mechanics of the Earth's Atmosphere (a Collection of Translations). 8° *Washington*, 1891

—— *See* United States, H, *b* : Appendix 2.

Abbot, H. L. Reports of Explorations and Surveys to ascertain the most practicable and economical route for a Railroad from the Mississippi River to the Pacific Ocean. Vol. 6. 4° *Washington*, 1857

—— *See* Humphreys.

Abbott, Charles C. Primitive Industry ; or, Illustrations of the Handiwork, in Stone, Bone, and Clay, of the Native Races of the Northern Atlantic Seaboard of America. (Peabody Academy of Science.) *Map and illustrations.* 8* *Salem, Mass.*, 1881

Abbott, Major F. Selections from the Report of, on the Grand Trunk Road from Goorsahai Gunge to Dehlie, 1844. *Plate.* (In India Records, N.-W. Provinces, Vol. 2.) *Allahabad*, 1856

Abbott, Francis. Results of Meteorological Observations for twenty years for Hobart Town, from Jan. 1841 to Dec. 1860. 4* *Hobart*, 1861

—— Results of Five Years' Meteorological Observations for Hobart Town, with which are incorporated the results of twenty-five years' observations. 4* *Hobart*, 1872

Abbott, Capt. J. Journey from Heraut to Khiva, Moscow, and St Petersburg during the late Russian invasion of Khiva. *Map and portrait.* 2 vols. 8° 1843

—— *See* India, G : Appendix 2.

Abbott, Samuel W. On the Geographical Distribution of certain Causes of Death in Massachusetts. *Maps.* 8° *Boston, Mass.* [1893]

Abd-er-Razzak. *See* Hakluyt Soc. Publ., Vol. 22 : Appendix 1.

Abdoul-Kerim. *See* Schefer.

Abdy, E. S. Journal of a Residence and Tour in the United States of North America, from April 1833 to October 1834. 3 vols. 12°   1835

Abel, C. Narrative of a Journey in the Interior of China, and of a Voyage to and from that Country, in the years 1816 and 1817. *Maps and plates.* 4°   1818

Abel, Sir Frederick. The Work of the ·Imperial Institute. Address delivered at the Royal Institution of Great Britain . . . 22nd April 1887. *Map.* 8* 1887

Abel-Rémusat, J. P. *See* Rémusat.

Abendroth, ——. Ritzebüttel und das Seebad zu Cuxhaven. *Map and plates.* 8°   *Hamburg*, 1818

Abercrombie, Lieut. R. Rájéndranámé ; or, History of Coorg. With an English Translation by Lieut. R. Abercrombie. 4*   *Mangalore*, 1857

Abercromby, Hon. John. A Trip through the Eastern Caucasus, with a chapter on the Languages of the Country. *Maps and illustrations.* 8°   1889

Abercromby, Hon. Ralph. Principles of Forecasting by means of Weather Charts. Issued by the authority of the Meteorological Council. *Charts, &'c.* 8°   1885

—— Weather : a Popular Exposition of the Nature of Weather Changes from Day to Day. *Illustrations.* Small 8°   1887

—— Seas and Skies in many Latitudes ; or, Wanderings in Search of Weather. *Maps and illustrations.* 8°   1888

—— *See* Symons.

Abercromby, Sir Ralph. *See* Pinckard.

Aberdeen, Earl of. *See* Walpole, Travels : Appendix 1.

Abert, Col. J. J. Report on the Commerce of the Lakes and Western Rivers. 8°   *Washington*, 1841

—— Report on the subject of Rivers and Harbours. 8°   *Washington*, 1850

Abich, H. Geognostiche Reise zum Ararat und Verschüttung des Thales von Arguri, 1840. 8°   *Berlin*, N.D.

—— Meteorologische Beobachtungen in Transcaucasien. 4*   *Berlin*, N.D.

—— Ueber das Steinsalz und seine geologische Stellung im Russischen Armenien, Palæontologischer Theil. *Plates.* 4°   *St Petersburg*, 1857

—— Sur la Structure et Géologie du Daghestan. *Plate.* 4*   *St Petersburg*, 1862

—— Aperçu de mes Voyages en Transcaucasie en 1864. 8*   *Moscow*, 1865

—— Beiträge zur geologischen Kenntniss der Thermalquellen in den Kaukasischen Ländern. Lief. 1. *Map.* 4* *Tiflis*, 1865

Abich, H. Einleitende Grundzüge der Geologie der Halbinseln Kertsch und Taman. *Plates.* 4* *St Petersburg*, 1865

—— Karten und Profile zur Geologie der Halbinseln Kertsch und Taman. Als Beitrag, &c. 4*   *Tiflis*, 1866

—— Translation by A. Phyladelphyn of Abich's "Earthquakes at Shamack and Erzeroum in May 1859." [In Russian.] *Maps.* 8*   N. P., N. D.

—— Zur Geologie des südöstlichen Kaukasus. Bemerkungen von meinen Reisen im Jahre 1865. 8* *St Petersburg*, 1866

—— Report on Explorations in Naphtha districts in the Trans-Kuban District and the Peninsula of Tamand. [In Russian.] 8*   *Tiflis*, 1867

—— Bemerkungen über die Geröll- und Trümmer-ablagerungen aus der Gletscherzeit im Kaukasus. 8*   *St Petersburg*, 1871

—— Ueber die Lage der Schneegrenze und die Gletscher der Gegenwart im Kaukasus. Small 8* *St Petersburg*, 1877

—— Ein Cyclus fundamentaler barometrischer Höhenbestimmungen auf dem Armenischen Hochlande. 4*   *St Petersburg*, 1880

—— *See* Baer and Helmersen, 13.

Abney, Capt. W. de W. *See* Cunningham, C. D.

Aboulfeda (or Abulfeda, or Abû-Ufeda). Géographie de. Traduite de l'Arabe, et accompagnée de Notes, et d'éclaircissements, par M. Reinaud. *Maps.* Vol. 1 and Vol. 2, Part I. 2 vols. 4°   *Paris*, 1848

—— Géographie d'Aboulféda. Traduite de l'Arabe en Français et accompagnée de Notes par M. Stanislas Guyard. Tome II., Seconde partie, contenant la fin de la traduction du texte Arabe et l'Index général. 4°   *Paris*, 1883

—— *See* De la Roque; Pocock ; *also* Astley, Vol. 1 ; Allgemeine Historie, Vol. 1 ; Thevenot, Vol. 1 : Appendix 1.

About, E. Rome Contemporaine. 2nd edition. 8°   *Paris*, 1861

Abrahall, Chandos Hoskyns. Arctic Enterprise : a Poem. 8*   1856

—— The Career of Franklin : an Ode ; with other Poems. 12*   1860

Abu'abd Allah Baka Ad-din Al-Janadi. *See* Omàrah.

Abu Ishak-el-Farssi-el-Istachri. *See* Madini.

Abu'l Ghazi Bahâder Khan. A General History of the Turks, Moguls, and Taters, vulgarly called Tartars, together with a Description of the Countries they inhabit ; the Genealogical History of the Taters. Translated from the MS. in the Mogul Language by Abu'l Ghazi Bahâder Khan of Khowârazm. 2 vols. 8°. 2 *Maps.*   1730

Abu Riha el Biruni. *See* Alberuni.

Abu Talib Hussyny. *See* Timur.

Aby-Serour, Mordokhaï. Premier établissment des Israélites à Timbouktou. *Plate and map.* 8° Incomplete
[*Paris*, 1870]

Acerbi, Joseph. Travels through Sweden, Finland, and Lapland, to the North Cape, in 1798-99. *Maps and plates.* 2 vols. 4° 1802

Acheson, Fred. Collection and Storage of Water in Victoria. *See* Victoria, Prize Essays : Appendix 2.

Achmet, Chan. *See* Appendix 1; Purchas, Vol. 2, Book 9.

Ackermann, Dr Carl. Beiträge zur physischen Geographie der Ostsee. *Map and tables.* 8° *Hamburg*, 1883

Acland, H. W. The Plains of Troy. *Map.* Royal 8° *Oxford*, 1839

Acosta, Joaquin. Compendio Histórico del Descubrimiento y Colonizacion de la Nueva Granada, en el Siglo Décimo sexto. *Map and plates.* 8° *Paris*, 1848
—— *See* Jomard.

Acosta, Joseph. Historia natural y moral de las Indias. En que se tratan las cosas notables del cielo . . . y los ritos . . . de los Indios. Sq. 8°
Madrid, 1608
—— The Naturall and Morall Historie of the East and West Indies. Intreating of the Remarkable Things of Heaven . . . together with the Manners . . . of the Indians. Translated from the Spanish by E. G. [Edward Grimston]. Sq. 8°
1604
—— *See* Hakluyt Soc. Publ., Vols. 60, 61 ; Gottfried ; Purchas, Vol. 3, Book 5: Appendix 1.

Acosta, Dr Nicolas. *See* Rada.

Acuna, Father Christoval de. *See* Hakluyt Soc. Publ., Vol. 24 ; Allgemeine Historie, Vol. 16 : Appendix 1.

Acunha, Tristano d'. *See* Gottfried : Appendix 1.

Adalbert of Prussia, Prince. Travels in the South of Europe and in Brazil, with a Voyage up the Amazon and Xingú : with Introduction by Baron Humboldt. Translated by Sir R. H. Schomburgk and J. E. Taylor. *Plates.* 2 vols. 8° 1849

Adam, Alex. Roman Antiquities. 8°
Edinburgh, 1797
—— Summary of Geography and History, both Ancient and Modern. *Maps.* 8°
1797

Adams, Arthur. Notes from a Journal of Research into the Natural History of the Countries visited during the Voyage of H.M.S. "Samarang," &c. 8° 1848
—— Travels of a Naturalist in Japan and Manchuria. *Frontispiece.* 8° 1870

Adams, Arthur. *See* Belcher.

Adams, A. L. Field and Forest Rambles ; with Notes and Observations on the Natural History of Eastern Canada. *Maps and plates.* 8° 1873
—— On a Fossil Saurian Vertebra (Arctosaurus Osborni) from the Arctic Regions. 8* *Dublin*, 1875

Adams, Clement. *See* Purchas, Vol. 3, Book 2 : Appendix 1.

Adams, Cyrus C. Railroad Development in Africa. (From the *Engineering Magazine*, February 1893.) *Map and illustrations.* 8* 1893

Adams, Edwin. Geography Classified : a Systematic Manual of Mathematical, Physical, and Political Geography ; with Geographical, Etymological, and Historical Notes. 12° 1863

Adams, Francis. The Australians : a Social Sketch. 8° 1893

Adams, F. O. Despatches from Mr Adams, Her Majesty's Secretary of Legation at Yedo, respecting the Deterioration of Silk in Japan. (Including Report by Mr Robertson, Her Majesty's Consul at Kanagawa, on Silk Cultivation in Japan.) *Map.* Folio* *Yedo*, 1871
—— The History of Japan from the earliest period to the present times. *Maps and plans.* 2 vols. 8° 1874-75

Adams, J. The Flowers of Modern Travels : being Elegant, Entertaining, and Instructive Extracts, selected from the works of the most celebrated travellers. 3rd edition. 2 vols. 12° 1792

Adams, J. Q. Letters on Silesia, written during a tour through that Country in the years 1800, 1801. *Map.* 8° 1804

Adams, Capt. John. Remarks on the Country extending from Cape Palmas to the River Congo ; with an Account of the European Trade with the West Coast of Africa. *Maps.* 8° 1823

Adams, John. *See* Juan.

Adams, Robert. The Narrative of a Sailor, who was wrecked on the Western Coast of Africa in 1810, was detained three Years in Slavery by the Arabs of the Great Desert, and resided several months in the City of Timbuctoo ; with Notes and an Appendix. *Map.* 4° 1816

Adams, W. B. Baikie, and C. Barron. Manual of Natural History for the Use of Travellers : being a Description of the Families of the Animal and Vegetable Kingdoms, with Remarks on the Practical Study of Geology and Meteorology ; to which are appended Directions for Collecting and Preserving. 12° 1854

Adams, William. *See* Astley, Vol. 1; Hakluyt Soc. Publ., Vol. 8; Harris, Vol. 1; Kerr, Vol. 8; Purchas, Vol. 1, Book 3; Gottfried; Allgemeine Historie, Vol. 1: Appendix 1.

Adamson, John. Obituary Notice of. 8* *Newcastle-upon-Tyne*, 1856

Adanson, M. A Voyage to Senegal, the Isle of Goree, and the River Gambia. *Map.* 8° 1759
—— *See* Pinkerton, Vol. 16: Appendix 1.

Adderley, Sir Augustus. The West Indies at the Colonial and Indian Exhibition. 8* 1887

Addison, Charles G. Damascus and Palmyra: a Journey to the East, with a Sketch of the State and Prospects of Syria under Ibrahim Pasha. *Coloured plates.* 2 vols. 8° 1838

Addison, Joseph. Remarks on several parts of Italy, &c., in the years 1701, 1702, 1703. 3rd edition. 12° 1726
—— *See* "The World Displayed," Vol. 19, p. 609: Appendix 1.

Addison, Lancelot. West Barbary; or, a Short Narrative of the Revolutions of the Kingdoms of Fez and Morocco; with an Account of the Present Customs, &c. 8° *Oxford*, 1671
—— *See* Pinkerton, Vol. 15: Appendix 1.

Adelung, Friedrich von. Kritisch-literarische Uebersicht der Reisenden in Russland bis 1700, deren Berichte bekannt sind. 2 vols. 8° *St Petersburg*, 1846
—— *See* Baer and Helmersen, 4.

Adelung, J. C. Grammatisch-kritisches Wörterbuch der Hoch-Deutschen Mundart. Mit D. W. Soltau's Beyträgen; revidirt und berichtiget von F. X. Schönberger. 4 vols. 4° *Vienna*, 1811
—— **and J. S. Vater.** Mithridates; oder allgemeine Sprachenkunde, mit dem Vater Unser als Sprachprobe in beynahe fünfhundert Sprachen und Mundarten. 3 vols. Vol. 1, Asia; Vol. 2, Europe; Vol. 3, Africa. 8° *Berlin*, 1806-16

Adhémar, J. Révolutions de la Mer. *Plates.* 8° *Paris*, 1842

Adolph, J. G. B. Mathematische und physische Erdbeschreibung mit besonderer Rücksicht auf Europa. *Portrait and maps.* 8° *Mayence*, 1829

Adolphus, John Leycester. Letters from Spain, in 1856-57. 8° 1858

Adrichromius, Christianus. Theatrum Terræ Sanctæ et Biblicarum Historiarum cum tabulis geographicis. *Maps.* Folio *Cologne*, 1600

"Adventure" and "Beagle." *See* Fitzroy, King; Macdouall, John.

Affarosi, D. Cammillo. Notizie Istoriche della Città di Reggio di Lombardia. Part 1. 4° *Padua*, 1755

Agapito, Conte G. Descrizione di Trieste. 12° *Vienna*, 1830
—— Le Grotte di Adlersberg, &c. 12° *Vienna*, 1823

Agapitoff, N. Programme for the Study of Shamanism in Siberia. [In Russian.] 8* *Irkutsk*, 1884

Agas, Ralph. Civitas Londinum. a Survey of the Cities of London and Westminster, the Borough of Southwark, and parts adjacent, in the Reign of Queen Elizabeth. Facsimile by W. H. Overall and E. J. Francis. 4* 1874

Agassiz, Prof. Alexander. On the Embryology of Echinoderms. 4* 1864
—— North American Acalephæ. 4* *Cambridge, Mass.*, 1865
—— Letter (No. 1) to C. P. Patterson on the Dredging Operations of the United States Coast Survey Steamer "Blake," during parts of January and February 1878. 8* *Cambridge, Mass.*, 1878
—— Three Cruises of the United States Coast and Geodetic Survey Steamer "Blake" in the Gulf of Mexico, in the Caribbean Sea, and along the Atlantic Coast of the United States, from 1877 to 1880. 2 vols. *Charts and illustrations.* 8° *Boston, Mass.*, 1888

Agassiz, Louis. Études sur les Glaciers. *Plates.* Folio *Neuchatel*, 1840
—— Lake Superior, its Physical Character, Vegetation, and Animals, compared with those of other and similar Regions. With a Narrative of the Tour, by J. Elliot Cabot. *Plates.* 8° *Boston, Mass.*, 1850
—— Glacial Phenomena in Maine. 8* *Boston, Mass.*, 1867
—— Address delivered on the Centennial Anniversary of the Birth of Alexander von Humboldt, under the auspices of the Boston Society of Natural History. 8* *Boston, Mass.*, 1869
—— Louis Agassiz, his Life and Correspondence. Edited by Elizabeth Cary Agassiz. 2 vols. *Illustrations.* Crown 8° 1885
—— *See* Desor; Hartt.
—— **and Mrs Agassiz.** A Journey in Brazil. *Plates.* 8° 1868

Agg, Alfred J. *See* Victoria Geological Survey: Appendix 2.

Agoub. *See* Mengin.

"Agricola." Description of the Barossa Range and its Neighbourhood in South Australia. By "Agricola." Illustrated from Original Drawings . . . by G. F. Angas. *Map and plates.* 4° 1849

Agueros, F. P. G. de. *See* Molina, J.

Aguilar, Jorge d'. *See* Gottfried; Allgemeine Historie, Vol. 17: Appendix 1.

Aguirre, Lope de, and Pedro de Ursua. *See* Hakluyt Soc. Publ., Vol. 28 : Appendix 1.

Ahmid Bin Abubekr Bin Wahshih. Ancient Alphabets and Hieroglyphic Characters Explained ; with an Account of the Egyptian Priests, their Classes, Initiation, and Sacrifices, in Arabic and in English, by Joseph Hammer. 4° 1806

Ahrling, Ewald. Carl von Linnés Brefvexling. 8* *Stockholm*, 1885

Aimé, G. *See* Algeria, A : Appendix 2.

Ainsworth, Robert. Thesaurus Linguæ Latinæ Compendiarius ; or, A Compendious Dictionary of the Latin Tongue. 4° 1783

Ainsworth, W. Account of the Caves of Ballybunian, County of Kerry. 8° *Dublin*, 1834

Ainsworth, W. The Scarborough Guide. *Plan.* 18° *York*, 1811

Ainsworth, William Francis. Researches in Assyria, Babylonia, and Chaldea. *Maps.* 8° 1838

—— Travels and Researches in Asia Minor, Mesopotamia, Chaldea, and Armenia. *Maps and woodcuts.* 2 vols. 8° 1842

—— Report on the Feasibility of establishing Telegraphic Communication between the Mediterranean Sea and the Persian Gulf. 8* 1856

—— The Euphrates Valley Railway. *Map.* 8* 1872

—— A Personal Narrative of the Euphrates Expedition. 2 vols. *Maps.* 8° 1888

—— The River Karun. 12° 1890

—— *See* Petachia.

Airy, Sir G. B. Mathematical Tracts. *Plates.* 8° *Cambridge*, 1842

—— Plan of the Buildings and Grounds of the Royal Observatory, Greenwich, with Explanation and History. *Plate.* 4° 1847

—— Report of the Astronomer Royal to the Board of Visitors for 1840 and 1852. 4°

—— Treatise on Trigonometry. Revised by Hugh Blackburn. 8° 1855

—— The Transits of Venus, 1874 and 1882. On the Preparatory Arrangements for the Observation of the Transits, &c. 8* N.D.

—— Determination of the Longitude of Valentia in Ireland by Transmission of Chronometers. 4* N.D.

Aitken, John. On Oceanic Circulation. 8* *Edinburgh*, 1874

Akers, C. E. Argentine, Patagonian, and Chilian Sketches, with a few Notes on Uruguay. Crown 8° 1893

Aksakof. Memoirs of the Aksakof Family : a Sketch of Russian Rural Life Seventy Years Ago. 8° *Calcutta*, 1871

Aksakoff, M. M. Recherches sur le Commerce aux Foires de l'Ukraine. [In Russian.] 4° *St Petersburg*, 1858

Alabaster, C., and others. Reports of Journeys in China and Japan, performed by Mr Alabaster, Mr Oxenham, Mr Markham, and Dr Willis, of Her Majesty's Consular Service in those Countries. *Map.* Folio * 1869

Alamanni, Luigi. La Coltivazione ; e le Api di Giovanni Rucellai, con Annotazioni del Dr G. B. da Prato, e di R. Titi. *Portraits.* 8° *Milan*, 1804

Alarchon, Fernando. *See* Burney, Vol. 1 ; Hakluyt, Vol. 3, p. 549 ; Ramusio, Vol. 3 : Appendix 1.

Alba, Duquesa de Berwick y de. Autografos de Cristobal Colon y Papeles de America, los Publica la Duquesa de Berwick y de Alba, Condesa di Siruela. *Facsimile autograph letters.* Folio *Madrid*, 1892

Albanie, William de. *See* Arundel, Earl of ; Hakluyt, Vol. 2 : Appendix 1.

Albarracin, Santiago J. Estudios generales sobre los Rios Negro, Limay y Collon-Curá, y Lago de Nahuel Huapí. Con numerosas vistas de los parajes recorridos, desde la barra del Rio Negro, hasta el límite occidental del lago de Nahuel-Huapí, &c. Vol. 1. *Plates.* Oblong 12° *Buenos Ayres*, 1886

"Albatross." *See* United States, I : Appendix 2.

Alberdi, Juan Bautista. Organizacion de la Confederacion Argentina. 2 vols. 8° *Besançon*, 1858

—— *See* Wheelwright.

Alberius, Eug. Disquisitio de Galilei Galileii circa Jovis Satellites Lucubrationibus, quæ in J. et R. Pittianâ Palatinâ Bibliothecâ adservantur. 8* *Florence*, 1843

—— Risposta sul preteso ritrovamento delle Effemeridi Galileiane dei Satelliti di Giove. 8* *Marseilles*, 1844

—— Ultime Parole a' suoi Galileiani sui Satelliti di Giove. 8* *Bologna*, N.D.

"Albert." *See* Mohn.

Alberti, L. De Kaffers aan de Zuidkust van Afrika, Natuur en Geschiedkundig beschreven. *Maps and plates.* 8° *Amsterdam*, 1810

—— Description Physique et Historique des Cafres, sur la Côte méridionale de l'Afrique. *Map and plates.* 8° *Amsterdam*, 1811

Alberuni. An Account of the Religion, Philosophy, Literature, Geography, Chronology, Astronomy, Customs, Laws, and Astrology of India, about A.D. 1030. An English Edition, with Notes and Indices, by Dr Edward C. Sachau. 2 vols. 8° 1888

Albornoz, Mariano Martin. Breves Apuntes sobre las Regiones Amazonicas. *Map.* 8* *Lima,* 1885

Albuquerque, Affonso d'. *See* Hakluyt Soc. Publ., Vols. 53, 55, 62, 69; Astley, Vol. 1; Gottfried; Kerr, Vol. 6; Laharpe, Vol. 1; Purchas, Vol. 1, Book 2; Allgemeine Historie, Vol. 1; A General Collection of Voyages, p. 610: Appendix 1.

Alcazova, Simon de. *See* Burney, Vol. 1; Callander, Vol. 1: Appendix 1.

Alcedo, Col. Don Antonio de. Geographical and Historical Dictionary of America and the West Indies. Translated from the Spanish, with large Additions and Compilations from Modern Voyages and Travels, and from original and authentic information, by G. A. Thomson. 5 vols. 4° 1812

"Alceste." *See* Macleod, J.

Alcock, Colonel. The Relative Power of Nations. 8* 1872

Alcock, Sir Rutherford. Elements of Japanese Grammar, for the use of Beginners. Small folio *Shanghai,* 1851
—— The Capital of the Tycoon: a Narrative of a Three Years Residence in Japan. 2 vols. *Maps and plates.* 8° 1863
—— Art and Art Industries in Japan. *Plates.* 8° 1878
—— *See* Margary; Treacher.

Alcock, T. Travels in Russia, Persia, Turkey, and Greece, in 1828-29. *Map and plate.* [Not published.] 8° 1831
—— *See* Hakluyt, Vol. 1: Appendix 1.

Aldersey, Laurence. *See* Hakluyt, Vol. 2, p. 547: Appendix 1.

Alema, V. F. *See* Schmeller.

Aleman, L, Grammaire élémentaire de la Langue Quichée. 8* *Copenhagen,* 1885

"Alert" and "Discovery." *See* Nares.

"Alert," H.M. Ship. Report on the Zoological Collections made in the Indo-Pacific Ocean during the Voyage of H.M.S. "Alert," 1881-82. *Plates.* 8°

Alexander, Sir J. E. Travels from India to England, with a Visit to the Burman Empire, and a Journey through Persia, Asia Minor, European Turkey, &c., in 1825-26. *Maps and plates.* 4° 1827
—— Visit to the Cavern Temples of Adjunta, in the East Indies. *Plate.* 4* 1829

Alexander, Sir J. E. Travels to the Seat of War in the East, through Russia and the Crimea, in 1829, with Sketches of the Imperial Fleet and Army, &c. 2 vols. *Map and plates.* 8° 1830
—— Transatlantic Sketches, comprising Visits to the most Interesting Scenes in North and South America and the West Indies. *Map and plates.* 2 vols. 8° 1833
—— Narrative of a Voyage of Observation among the Colonies of Western Africa, and of a Campaign in Kaffir-Land, in 1835. Illustrated by Major Michell. 2 vols. *Maps and plates.* 8° 1837
—— Expedition of Discovery into the Interior of Africa, through the hitherto undescribed Countries of the Great Namaquas, Boschmans, and Hill Damaras. *Map.* 2 vols. 8° 1838
—— L'Acadie; or, Seven Years' Explorations in British America. *Maps and plates.* 2 vols. 8° 1849
—— Notes on the Maories of New Zealand, with Suggestions for their Pacification and Preservation. 8* N.P., N.D.

Alexander, J. H. International Coinage for Great Britain and the United States: a Note inscribed to the Hon. James A. Pearce. 8* *Baltimore,* 1855
—— International Coinage: a Note. 12* *Oxford,* 1857
—— An Inquiry into the English System of Weights and Measures. 12* *Oxford,* 1857

Alexander, Prof. W. D. A Brief History of Land Titles in the Hawaiian Kingdom. 8* *Honolulu,* 1882
—— A Brief Account of the Hawaiian Government Survey, its Objects, Methods, and Results. 8* *Honolulu,* 1889
—— The Relations between the Hawaiian Islands and Spanish America In early times. 8* [*Honolulu*], 1892

Alexander, R. Note regarding the Population of Zillah Muttra. [From Selections from the India Records, N.W. Provinces, Vol. 1] *Allahabad,* 1855

Alexander, Sir William. *See* Purchas, Vol. 4, Book 10: Appendix 1.

Alexander VI., Pope. *See* Borgia; *also* Purchas, Vol. 1, Book 2: Appendix 1.

Alexander the Great. *See* Purchas, Vol. 1, Book 1: Appendix 1.

Alexis, M. G. Méthodologie théorique et appliquée de Géographie; ou Manuel du Maitre, établissant la manière de mettre en œuvre les différents ouvrages: manuels de l'élève, Exercices cartographiques, Atlas, Cartes murales, écrites ou muettes, Tableau Carte, Reliefs, qui composent le Cours de Géographie. 1re. Partie, Théorie générale et application à la Géographie locale. New edition. 12° *Liège,* 1883

Alfano, Guiseppe Maria. Compendio portatile di tutte le Dodici Provincie che compongono il Regno di Napoli. 12°
Naples, 1798

Alfonso X., Regis Romanorum et Castelle, Tabulæ Astronomicæ. Opera et arte mirifica viri solertis Johanis Hamman de Landoia dictus Hertzog. *Blackletter.* 2nd edition. [With correspondence respecting the Astronomical Tables of King Alfonso the Tenth, of Leon and Castille, between Augustine of Olmutz and John Lucilius Santritter of Heilbrunn.] Small 4° *Venice*, 1492
—— Libros del Saber de Astronomia, copilados, anotados, y comentados por Don Manuel Rico y Sinobas. *Plates.* Vols. 1 and 2 (1863), 3 (1864), 4 (1866), 5 pt. 1 (1867). Large folio *Madrid*

Alford, C. J. Geological Features of the Transvaal, South Africa. *Maps, &c.* 8° 1891

Alfred the Great. A Description of Europe, and the Voyages of Ohthere and Wulfstan, written in Anglo-Saxon by King Alfred the Great; with his Account of the Mediterranean Islands, of Africa, and of the History of the World to the year B.C. 1413, chiefly taken from Orosius: containing a Facsimile Copy of the whole Anglo-Saxon Text from the Cotton MS., and also from the first part of the Lauderdale MS.; a Printed Anglo-Saxon Text, based upon these MSS.; and a Literal English Translation and Notes, by the Rev. Joseph Bosworth, D.D. 4° 1855
—— See Kerr, Vol. 1: Appendix 1.

Algar, F. A Hand-Book to the Colony of Victoria (Australia). 8° 1869

Algazeli, Mahomet. *See* Purchas, Vol. 2, Book 10: Appendix 1.

Alhacen. *See* Purchas, Vol. 3, Book 1: Appendix 1.

Ali Bey. Travels in Morocco, Tripoli, Cyprus, Egypt, Arabia, Syria, and Turkey, 1803-7. *Maps and plates.* 2 vols. 4° 1816

Ali Mohammed Khan. Political and Statistical History of Gujarat, translated from the Persian, with Annotations and an Historical Introduction by J. Bird. Royal 8° 1835

Alis, Harry [Hyppolite Percher]. A la Conquête du Tchad. (*Le Figaro*, Supplément Littéraire, No. 48.) *Illustrations and map.* 8* [*Paris*, 1890]
—— La Mission Paul Crampel. (Supplément du Journal des Débats du Lundi 16 Fevrier 1891.) *Map.* 8* [*Paris*, 1891]
—— A la Conquête du Tchad. *Maps and illustrations.* Large 8° *Paris*, 1891

Alishan, L. M. D. Armenian Popular Songs, translated into English. 8* *Venice*, 1852
—— Introduction to the Geography of the Physical World and the Geography of Europe. [In Armenian.] *Maps and woodcuts.* 4° *Venice*, 1853
—— Le Haygh, sa Période et sa Fète. 8* *Paris*, 1860
—— Physiographie de l'Arménie. 8* *Venice*, 1861
—— Assises d'Antioche, reproduites en Français et publiées au sixième Centenaire de la mort de Sempad le Connétable, leur ancien traducteur Arménian. Dédiées à l'Académie des Inscriptions et Belles Lettres de France, par la Société Mekhithariste de Saint-Lazare. [Translated by Prof. Léon Alishan.] 4° *Venice*, 1876
—— Schirac, Canton d'Ararat, Pays de la Grande Arménie, Description Géographique, illustrée (en Armenien). *Maps and illustrations.* 4° *Venice*, 1881
—— Sissouan, Description Physique, Géographique, Historique, et Littéraire de la Cilicie Arménienne et Histoire de Léon le Magnifique. [Prospectus.] *Illustrations.* 4* *Venice*, 1885
—— Tableau Succinct de l'Histoire et de la Littérature de l'Arménie. 8* *Venice*, N.D.

Allan, George. The Land of the Duallas. Notes of Life in the Cameroons. 12* *Newcastle-upon-Tyne*, 1885

Allan, William. Description of Direct Line Ipswich to Warwick (Brisbane to Sydney). *Map.* 4* 1890

Allart, Maurice. *See* Vsévolojsky.

Allatif, Abd. *See* Pinkerton, Vol. 15: Appendix 1.

Alleizette, C. d'. *See* Vaillant.

Allen, Charles H. A Visit to Queensland and her Goldfields. 8° 1870
—— *See* Gurney.

Allen, Grant. Science in Arcady. 8° 1892
—— Bates of the Amazons. (From the *Fortnightly Review*, for December 1892.) Large 8* 1892

Allen, John. Specimina Ichnographica; or, A Brief Narrative of several New Inventions and Experiments, particularly the Navigating a Ship in a Calm, the Improvement of the Engine to Raise Water by Fire, &c. *Plate.* Small 4° 1730

Allen, J. A. Catalogue of the Mammals of Massachusetts; with a Critical Revision of the Species. 8° *Cambridge, Mass.*, 1849
—— *See* United States, G, a: Appendix 2.

Allen, Lieut. Henry T. Report of an Expedition to the Copper, Tananá, and Koyukuk Rivers, in the Territory of Alaska, in the year 1885. *Maps and plates.* 8° *Washington*, 1887

Allen, Capt. William. The Dead Sea, a New Route for India. *Maps and plates.* 2 vols. 8° 1855
—— *See* Beck, William.

Allen, Capt. W., and Dr T. R. H. Thomson. Narrative of the Expedition to the River Niger in 1841. *Maps and plates.* 2 vols. 8° 1848

Allen, W. Pessoa. Portugal e Africa. Primeira parte. A Questão do Zaire. 8* *Lisbon*, 1884
—— O Porto de Leixões. 8* *Lisbon*, 1891

Allgemeine Historie . . . 1748-74. For full Title and Contents, *see* Appendix 1.

Allison. *See* Pinkerton, Vol. 1 : Appendix 1.

Allman, Professor. The Method and Aim of Natural History Studies : being an Introduction to a Course of Lectures on Natural History, delivered to Working Men in the Edinburgh Museum of Science and Art. 8* *Edinburgh*, 1868

Almada, André Alvares d'. Tratado breve dos Rios de Guiné do Cabo-Verde, desde o Rio do Sanagá até aos Baixos de Sant' Anna, &c., 1594. Publicado por Diogo Köpke. *Map.* 8° *Oporto*, 1841

Almagro, Diego d' (or Almagrus Didacus). *See* Gottfried ; Laharpe, Vol. 10 ; Allgemeine Historie, Vol. 15 : Appendix 1.

Almami Sanankoroh (or Almami Samodu), his Early Years and Conquests. MS. Folio N.D.

Almansor, Jacob. *See* Purchas, Vol. 2, Book 10 : Appendix 1.

Almaraz, Ramon. Memoria acerca de los Terrenos de Metlaltoyuca presentada al Ministerio de Fomento por la Comision exploradora. *Plates.* 8* *Mexico*, 1866

Almeida, A. J. P. d'. Principios de Geologia. Small folio* *Coimbra*, 1838

Almeida, A. Lopes da Costa. Roteiro Geral dos Mares, Costas, Ilhas, e Baixos recontrecidos no Globo. 8° *Lisbon*, 1845

Almeida, J. B. Ferreira d'. *See* Portugal, B : Appendix 2.

Almeida, Manuel d'. *See* Gottfried ; Thevenot, Vol. 4 : Appendix 1.

Almeida, P. Camena d'. Les Pyrénées. 8° *Paris*, 1893

Almeida, Serra R. F. de. Geographical Description of the Captaincy of Matto Grosso. MS. 12* 1797

Almeyda (or D'Almeida), Francisco de. *See* Astley, Vol. 1 ; Gottfried ; Kerr, Vol. 6 ; Allgemeine Historie, Vol. 1 ; Collection of Voyages, p. 610 : Appendix 1.

Alston, E. R. On the Mammalia of the West of Scotland. Compiled, with others, for the British Association Meeting, 1876. 12* *Glasgow*, 1876

Alt. *See* Brampton and Alt, in Eyriès, Vol. 4 : Appendix 1.

Altamirano, Padre Diego Francisco. *See* Ballivian.

Alured, Bishop. *See* Hakluyt, Vol 2 ; Kerr, Vol. 1 ; Gottfried : Appendix 1.

Alvarado, P. de. *See* Cortes ; *also* Ramusio, Vol. 3 : Appendix 1.

Alvarez, Francisco. *See* Hakluyt Soc. Publ., Vol. 64 ; Purchas, Vol. 2 ; Ramusio, Vol. 1 : Appendix 1.

Alvarez, Pedro. *See* Ramusio, Vol. 1 : Appendix 1.

Alvear, Don Diego. 1. Historical and Geographical Account of the Province of Misiones (Paraguay), by Don Diego Alvear, one of the Spanish Boundary Commissioners [MS. in Spanish]. 2. Description of various Provinces and Districts, chiefly in Upper Peru, under the Vice Roy of Buenos Aires, 1780 [MS. in Spanish]. 3. Account of the Population of the several Provinces of Chili and their Productions [MS. in Spanish]. Folio. N.P., N.D.
—— *See* Angelis, Vol. 4 : Appendix 1.

Alves, Capt. W. *See* Dalrymple, Repertory, Vol. 1 : Appendix 1.

Alviella, Comte G. d'. *See* Becker, J. ; *also see* Goblet d'Alviella.

Amadas, Philip. *See* Hakluyt, Vol. 3, p. 549 : Appendix 1.

Amat di S. Filippo, Pietro. Delle Relazioni Antiche e Moderne fra l'Italia e l'India. Memoria premiata dalla Reale Accademia dei Lincei. *Maps.* 8° *Rome*, 1886

Amante, Fedele. Considerazioni sulle formole adoperate comunemente dai Geografi, per calcolare le posizioni Geografiche dei vertici dei triangoli geodetici. *Plates.* 4° *Naples*, 1837
—— Sulle formole da usarsi ne' calcoli geodetici per la riduzione degli angoli all' orizzonte della Stazione. 4° *Naples*, 1837

Amari Michele. Bibliotheca Arabo-Sicula ossia raccolta di testi Arabici che toccano la Geografia, la Storia, le Biografie, e la Bibliografia della Sicilia. 8° *Leipzig*, 1857

Amélineau, E. La Géographie de l'Égypte à l'Époque Copte. Large 8° *Paris*, 1893

Americus Vespucius. *See* Vespucci.

Amicis, E. de. Morocco, its People and Places. Translated by C. Rollin-Tilton. *Plates.* 4° N.D.

Amico et Statella, Vitti M. Lexicon Topographicum Siculum, in quo Siciliæ Urbes, Oppida, cum vetusta, tum extantia, Montes, Flumina, Portus, adjacentes Insulæ, ac singula loca describuntur, illustrantur. *Plans.* 3 vols. in 6. 4° *Palermo*, 1757-60

Amigorena, J. F. de. *See* Angelis, Vol. 5 : Appendix 1.

Amoretti. *See* Maldonado ; Pigafetta, A.

Ampère, J. J. Voyage en Égypte et en Nubie. 8° *Paris*, 1868

Amrein, K. C. Marco Polo : Oeffentlicher Vortrag, gehalten in der Geographisch-Kommerziellen Gesellschaft in St Gallen. 8* *Zurich*, 1879
—— 1889, Weltausstellung in Paris. Schweiz, geographische und cosmographische Karten und Apparate, Klasse, 16. 8* *Zurich*, 1890

Amunategui, M. L. La Cuestion de Límites entre Chile i la República Argentina. Vols. 1-3. 4° *Santiago*, 1879-80

Anacharsis. Recueil de Cartes Géographiques, Plans, Vues, et Médailles de l'Ancienne Grèce, relatifs au Voyage du jeune Anacharsis. 2nd edition. 4° *Paris*, 1789
—— *See* Barthélémy.

Anaman, Jacob Benjamin. Anaman's Gold Coast Almanack for 1890. [1 Sheet.]

Ancelle, J. Les Explorations au Sénégal et dans les contrées voisines, depuis l'Antiquité jusqu'à nos jours ; précédé d'une Notice Ethnographique sur notre Colonie, par le Général Faidherbe. *Map.* 12° *Paris*, 1886

Anchieta, Joseph de. *See* Collecção de Noticias, Vol. 1, p. 610: Appendix 1.

Andagoya (or Andagoza), Pascual de. *See* Hakluyt Soc. Publ., Vol. 34, Appendix 1.

Anderson, Adam. Historical and Chronological Deduction of the Origin of Commerce, from the Earliest Accounts, containing an History of the Great Commercial Interests of the British Empire ; to which is prefixed an Introduction, exhibiting a view of the Antient and Modern State of Europe, and of the Foreign and Colonial Commerce, Shipping, Manufactures, Fisheries, &c., of Great Britain and Ireland, and their influence on the Landed Interest ; with Appendices on the Modern Politico-Commercial Geography of the several Countries of Europe. *Maps.* 4 vols. 4° 1801

Anderson, Dr A. *See* Dalrymple, Oriental Repertory, Vol. 1 : Appendix 1.

Anderson, Æneas. A Narrative of the British Embassy to China, in the years 1792-94. 3rd edition. 8° 1796

Anderson, A. H. Notes of a Journey to the Auriferous Quartz Regions of Southern India, with facts relating thereto. 12* 1880

Anderson, Andrew A. Twenty-five Years in a Waggon in the Gold Regions of Africa. 2 vols. *Illustrations.* 8° 1887

Anderson, Benjamin. Narrative of a Journey to Mussardu, the Capital of the Western Mandingoes. *Map.* 12* *New York*, 1870
—— *See* Blyden.

Anderson, Sir C. H. J. The Lincoln Pocket Guide : being a Short Account of the Churches and Antiquities of the County, and of the Cathedral of the Blessed Virgin Mary of Lincoln, commonly called the Minster. *Map and plan.* 12° 1880

Anderson, G. Remarks on the Husbandry and Internal Commerce of Bengal. 8° *Calcutta*, 1804

Anderson, H. L. Census of the Sawunt Waree State, for 1851. *Census Table.* [From the India Records, No. 10] *Bombay*, 1855

Anderson, Johann. Nachrichten von Island, Grönland, und der Strasse Davis. 8° *Hamburg*, 1746
—— Description Physique, Historique, Civile et Politique de l'Islande. 2 vols. 12° *Paris*, 1764

Anderson, J. W. Notes of Travel in Fiji and New Caledonia, with some Remarks on South Sea Islanders and their Languages. *Map and plates.* 8° 1880
—— The Prospector's Handbook : a Guide for the Prospector and Traveller in Search of Metal-bearing or other Valuable Minerals. *Illustrations.* 12° 1886

Anderson, James. Glaciation and Raised Beaches in Jura and Islay. (From the Trans. Geol. Soc., Glasgow, Vol. 8, Part 2.) 8* [*Glasgow*, 1888]

Anderson, John. Observations on the Restoration of Banca and Malacca to the Dutch, as affecting the Tin Trade and General Commerce of Pinang, the Result of a Political and Commercial Mission to the States of Perak, Salengore, and Colong in 1818. 4° *Prince of Wales Island*, 1824
—— Mission to the East Coast of Summatra, in 1823, under the direction of the Government of Prince of Wales Island ; including Historical and Descriptive Sketches of the Country . . . and a Visit to the Batta Cannibal States in the Interior. *Maps and plates.* 8° 1826

Anderson, John. DuraDen: a Monograph of the Yellow Sandstone and its Remarkable Fossil Remains. *Plates.* 8° 1859

Anderson, John. A Report on the Expedition to Western Yunan *viâ* Bhamô. Royal 8°   *Calcutta*, 1871
—— Mandalay to Momein : a Narrative of the Two Expeditions to Western China of 1868 and 1875 under Colonel Edward B. Sladen and Colonel Horace Browne. *Maps and plans.* 8°   1876
—— The Selungs of the Mergui Archipelago. *Plates.* 8*   1890
—— English Intercourse with Siam in the Seventeenth Century. *Map.* 8°   1890
Anderson, Richard. Lightning Conductors, their History, Nature, and Mode of Application. 3rd edition. *Illustrations.* 8°   1885
Anderson, Major William. An Attempt to Identify some of the Places mentioned in the Itinerary of Hiuan Thsang. (Extract from the *Bengal Asiatic Journal.*) 8*   *Calcutta*, 1847
Anderson, Capt. W. C. Papers relative to the Introduction of revised Rates of Assessment into the Hoongoond and part of the Uthnee Talookas and the Yadwar Mahal of the Gokak Talooka, all of the Belgaum Collectorate ; with an Appendix, bringing up the Revenue History of these Districts to 1862-63. *Map and diagrams.* [From the India Selections, No. 81.] Royal 8° *Bombay*, 1864
Andersson, Charles John. A Journey to Lake 'Ngami. 12*   1854
—— Lake 'Ngami, or Explorations and Discoveries during Four Years Warderings in the Wilds of South - Western Africa. *Map and plates.* Royal 8° 1856
—— The Okavango River : a Narrative of Travel, Exploration, and Adventure. *Plates.* 8°   1861
—— Notes of Travel in South Africa. (Edited by L. Lloyd.) *Plate.* 8° 1875
Andersson, N. J. *See* Virgin.
Andia y Varela, José de. *See* Recueil de Voyages, Vol. 4, p. 611 : Appendix 1.
Andrada, J. Paiva de. Manica. *Map.* 8*   1891
Andrade, F. d'. Mémoires sur les connaissances scientifique de Don Ioam de Castro. 8*   *Paris*, N.D.
Andrade, J. I. Memoria dos Feitos Macaenses contra los Piratas da China, e da entrada violenta dos Inglezes na Cidade de Macão. 12°   *Lisbon*, 1835
Andrade, Jeronimo Jose Nogueira d'. Descripçaõ do estado, em que ficavaõ os Negocios da Capitania de Mossambique nos fins de Novembro de 1789 ; com algumas Observaçoens e Reflexoens sobre os mesmos Negocios e sobre as causas da Decadencia do Commercio e dos Estabilecimentos Portuguezas na Costa Oriental d'Africa, escripta no anno de 1790. MS. 4°

Andrae, C. G. Den Danske Gradmaaling. Vols. 1 to 4.   4° *Copenhagen*, 1872-84
—— Problèmes de haute Géodésie.   4* *Copenhagen*, N.D.
1er Cahier : Formation et Calcul des Triangles géodésiques.
2e Cahier : Calcul des Latitudes, des Longitudes, et des Azimuts sur le Sphéroïde.   1882
3e Cahier : Détermination du Sphéroïde Terrestre par la Combinaison des Mesures Géodésiques avec les Observations Astronomiques. *Plate*   1883
Andreas, F. C. *See* Stolze.
Andree, Karl. Geographie des Welthandels : mit geschichtlichen Erläuterungen. Erster Band, zweite Auflage. Durchgesehen und ergänzt von Richard Andree. *Portrait.* 8° *Stuttgart*, 1877
—— Zweiter Band. Die aussereuropäischen Erdtheile. 8°   *Stuttgart*, 1872
—— Dritter Band. Europa, bearbeitet von H. Glogau, J. Minoprio, Lorenz Brauer, M. Haushofer, Jos. Fischer : erste Hälfte, erster Theil. 8°   *Stuttgart*, 1877
—— Dritter Band. Europa, zweite Hälfte, bearbeitet von Dr Max Haushofer. 8° *Stuttgart*, 1877
Andree, Richard. Ethnographische Parallelen und Vergleiche. *Plates.* 8° *Stuttgart*, 1878
—— **and E. Deckert.** Handels- und Verkehrs- Geographie. Lehrbuch für Handelsschulen und verwandte Lehranstalten. Bearbeitet von Emil Deckert. Zugleich zweite Auflage von Richard Andree's Handels- und Verkehrs- Geographie. 8°   *Stuttgart*, 1882
Andreossy, Comte. Voyage à l'embouchure de la Mer-Noire, ou Essai sur la Bosphore. 8°   *Paris*, 1818
Andrew, John A. Address to the Two Branches of the Legislature of Massachusetts, 8th January 1864 ; together with accompanying Documents. 8*   *Boston, Mass.*, 1864
Andrew, Sir W. P. The Scinde Railway and its Relations to the Euphrates Valley and other Routes to India. *Maps.* 8*   1856
—— Memoir on the Euphrates Valley Route to India, with Official Correspondence. *Maps.* 8°   1857
—— The Indus and its Provinces, their Political and Commercial Importance considered in connection with Improved Means of Communication. *Maps.* 8°   1857
—— Port of Kurrachee : Depth of Water, and Commerce, 1856-57. *Map.* 8* 1857
—— The Punjaub Railway : a Selection from Official Correspondence regarding the Introduction of Railways into the Punjaub. *Map.* 8*   1857

Andrew, Sir W. P. Letter to Sir Stafford H. Northcote on the Euphrates Valley Railway. Folio* 1867
—— On the Completion of the Railway System of the Valley of the Indus. A Letter to His Grace the Duke of Argyll. *Maps.* 8* - 1869
—— The Euphrates Route to India. Letters Addressed to the British and Turkish Governments, &c. 8* 1871
—— The Euphrates Valley Route to India in connection with the Central Asian Question. *Map.* 8* 1873
—— The Bolan and Khyber Railways. Reprinted from the *Times.* With a Memorandum by Sir Henry Green on Portable Railways in Military Operations. Small 8* 1879
—— Euphrates Valley Route to India. *Map.* Large 8* 1880
—— Our Scientific Frontier. *Map.* 8° 1880

Andrews, Capt. Journey from Buenos Ayres through the Provinces of Cordova, Tucuman, and Salta to Potosi, thence by the Deserts of Caranja to Arica, and to Santiago de Chili and Coquimbo. 2 vols. 8° 1827

Andrews, C. C. Brazil, its Condition and Prospects. 8° *New York,* 1887

Andrews, John. Historical Atlas of England, Physical, Political, Astronomical, Civil and Ecclesiastical, Biographical, Naval, Parliamentary, and Geographical, Ancient and Modern, from the Deluge to the Present Time. [*Imperfect, and no maps.*] 4° 1797
—— *See* Dalrymple, Oriental Repertory, Vol. 2: Appendix 1.

Andrews, J. R. Life of Oliver Cromwell, to the Death of Charles the First. 8° 1870

Andrews, W. H. C. A Pamphlet and Map of Southern Morocco; or, "Sûs" and the "Ait Bon Amaran." 8* 1884

Andros, A. C. Pen and Pencil Sketches of a Holiday Scamper in Spain. *Map and plates.* 8° 1860

Angas, George French. Australia: a Popular Account of its Physical Features, Inhabitants, Natural History, and Productions, with the History of its Colonisation. *Map.* 8° N.D.
—— Polynesia: a Popular Description of the Physical Features, Inhabitants, Natural History, and Productions of the Islands of the Pacific; with an Account of their Discovery, and of the Progress of Civilisation and Christianity amongst them. *Map.* 8° [1866]

Angel, Manuel Uribe. Geografia General y Compendio Historico del Estado de Antioquia en Colombia. *Maps and plates.* Large 8° *Paris,* 1885

Angelis, Pedro de. Biographia del Señor General Arenales y Juicio sobre la memoria histórica de su segunda Campaña á la Sierra del Peru en 1821. *Maps.* 8° *Buenos Ayres,* 1832
—— Coleccion de Obras y Documentos relativos á la Historia, Antigua y Moderna, de las Provincias del Rio de la Plata. 6 vols. Folio *Buenos Ayres,* 1836-37
For Contents, *see* Appendix 1.
—— Historical Sketch of Pepys' Island, in the South Pacific Ocean. *Plate.* 8* *Buenos Ayres,* 1842
—— Memoria Histórica sobre los Derechos de Soberania y Dominio de la Confederacion Argentina á la Parte Austral del Continente Americano, comprendida entre las Costas del Oceano Atlantico y la Gran Cordillera de los Andes, desde la Boca del Rio de la Plata, hasta el Cabo de Hornos, inclusa la Isla de los Estados, la Tierra del Fuego, y el Estrecho de Magellanes en toda su extension. Royal 8* *Buenos Ayres,* 1852
—— *See* Parish.

Angelo, M. *See* Astley, Vol. 3; Churchill, Vol. 1; Pinkerton, Vol. 16; Allgemeine Historie, Vol. 4: Appendix 1.

Angelos, Chr. *See* Purchas, Vol. 1, Book 1: Appendix 1.

Angiolello, G. M. *See* Ramusio, Vol. 2: Appendix 1.

Ankel, Otto. Grundzüge der Landesnatur des Westjordanlandes. Entwurf einer Monographie des Westjordanischen Palästina, mit einem Vorworte von Prof. Dr Th. Fischer. 8° *Frankfort,* 1887

Annandale, Charles. Scotland in Prehistoric Times : a Brief Summary of what is known regarding the Country and its Inhabitants in times anterior to the Roman Invasion. *Illustrations.* Large 8* 1892

Annenkoff, Lieut.-Gen. M. N. *See* Heyfelder.

Anrique, R. Nicolas. Diario del Comandante Benjamin Muñoz Gamero a los lagos de Llanquihue, Todos-Santos, y Nahuelhuapi en 1849; con una introducción biográfica. 8* *Valparaiso,* 1893
—— *See* Beranger.

Anselmi, T. Grande e Completo Trattato di Pronunzia Inglese. Small 8° *Naples,* 1867

Anson, George, Lord. An Authentic Account of his Expedition, &c. 8° 1744
—— Voyage Round the World, 1704-44, compiled from Papers and other Materials of Lord Anson, and published under his direction by Richard Walter, Chaplain of H.M.S. "Centurion." *Plates.* 2 vols. 4° 1748
—— Life of. By Sir John Barrow. *Portrait.* 8° 1839

Anson, George, Lord. *See* Burney, Vol. 5 ; Callander, Vol. 3; Harris, Vol. 1 ; Kerr, Vol. 11 ; World Displayed, Vol. 7; New Collection, Vol. 3 ; Laharpe, Vol. 15 ; Allgemeine Historie, Vol. 18 : Appendix 1.

Ansted, D. T. Physical Geography. 4th edition. *Maps.* 12° 1870
—— **and Robert Gordon Latham.** The Channel Islands ; with Illustrations by P. J. Naftel. 8° 1862

"Antelope." Narrative of the Shipwreck of the "Antelope," East India pacquet, on the Pelew Islands, situated on the Western Part of the Pacific Ocean, in August 1783. *Plates.* 12° *Perth,* 1788

Anthony of Armenia. *See* Haitho.

Antillon, Don Isidore. Géographie Physique et Politique de l'Espagne et du Portugal. 8° *Paris,* 1823

Antinori, Orazio. Sopra alcuni resti di Città antiche tuttora esistenti in Tunisia nella Provincia del Fas-el-Riah. Due lettere. *See* Gubernatus, E. de : Lettere sulle Tunisia, &c. 16° *Florence,* 1867
—— *See* Petermann and Hassenstein ; Inner Afrika, No. 10.

Antipow, Q. *See* Baer and Helmersen, Vol. 22.

Antonelli. *See* Italy, A : Appendix 2.

Antonescu-Remusi, P. S. Dictionar Geografic al Judetului Vlasca. 8° *Bucharest,* 1891

Anuchin, D. N. Contributions to the History of the Knowledge of Siberia before Yermak. [In Russian.] 4° *Moscow,* 1890

Anville, Jean Baptiste Bourguignon d'. Proposition d'une Mesure de la Terre, dont il résulte une diminution considérable dans sa circonference sur les Paralleles. *Map,* 12° *Paris,* 1735
—— Éclaircissemens géographiques sur la Carte de l'Inde. 4° *Paris,* 1753
—— A Geographical Illustration of the Map of India. Translated from the French of Mons. d'Anville . ; with some Explanatory Notes and Remarks by William Herbert. *Map.* 4° 1759
—— Index ad Specimen Geographicum (to facilitate reference to d'Anville's Map of Ancient Greece). 4° 1762
—— Considérations générales sur l'étude et les connoissances que demande la composition des ouvrages de Géographie. Small 8° *Paris,* 1777
—— Dissertation sur les Sources du Nil, pour prouver qu'on ne les a point encore découvertes. 4° [*Paris,* N.D.]
—— Mémoire concernant les Rivières de l'intérieur de l'Afrique, sur les notions tirées des Anciens et des Modernes. 4° [*Paris,* N.D.]
—— Mémoire sur les mésures du Schène Égyptien et du Stade qui servoit à le composer. 4° [*Paris,* N.D.]

Anville, Jean Baptiste Bourguignon d'. Discussion de la mésure de la Terre par Eratosthène. 4° [*Paris,* N.D.]
—— L'Euphrate et le Tigre. *Map.* 4° *Paris,* 1779
—— Notices des Ouvrages de, précédées de son Éloge par M. Dacier. 8° *Paris,* 1802
—— Compendium of Ancient Geography. Translated from the French, with Prolegomena and Notes by the Translator. *Maps.* 2 vols. 8° 1810
—— Œuvres. Publiées par M. de Manne. *Portrait and map.* 2 vols. 4° *Paris,* 1834
Vol. 1.—Connoissances Géographiques Générales : Traité et Mémoires sur les Mesures Anciennes et Modernes: avec Table Analytique des Matières, et cartes qui s'y rapportent.
Vol. 2.—Mémoire et Abrégé de Géographie Ancienne et Générale, avec Table et Nomenclature des Noms de Lieux Anciens et Dénominations Modernes correspondantes, suivis des cartes qui s'y rapportent.

Aoust, Virlet d'. Coup d'œil général sur la Topographie et la Géologie du Mexique et l'Amérique Centrale. 8° *Paris,* 1865
—— Les Origines du Nil. 8° *Paris,* 1872

Apel, F. H. Drei Monate in Abyssinien und Gefangenschaft unter König Theodorus II. 8° *Zurich,* 1866

Apianus, Petrus, and Gemma Frisius. Cosmographia, sive Descriptio Universi Orbis ; adjecti sunt alii, tum Gemmæ Frisii, tum aliorum Auctorum ejus argumenti Tractatus ac Libelli varii, quorum seriem versa pagina demonstrat. *Woodcuts and diagrams, some movable.* Small folio. *Antwerp,* 1584

Apollonius Rhodius, The Argonautics of. By Francis Fawkes. *Frontispiece.* 8° 1780

Apostolides, S. Our Lord's Prayer, in One Hundred different Languages, &c. 12° [1869]

Appell, J. W. Monuments of Early Christian Art. Sculptures and Catacomb Paintings. Illustrative Notes, collected in order to promote the reproduction of remains of Art belonging to the early centuries of the Christian Era. 8° 1872

Appleton's General Guide to the United States and Canada. Illustrated with Railway Maps, Plans of Cities, and Table of Railway and Steamboat Fares. 12° *Edinburgh,* 1892
—— *See* Conkling.

Appun, Carl Ferdinand. Unter den Tropen: Wanderungen durch Venezuela, am Orinoco, durch Britisch Guyana und am Amazonenstrome in den Jahren 1849-68. 2 vols. *Plates.* 8° *Jena*, 1871

Aragão, A. C. T. de. Breve Noticia sobre o Descobrimento da America. Large 8* *Lisbon*, 1892

Arago, M. F. Instructions relatives au Voyage de Circumnavigation de la Bonite. 4° *Paris*, 1835
—— Lettre à M. A. de Humboldt, sur les Précis d'Astronomie de M. de Pontécoulant, et l'Académie des Sciences. 8* *Paris*, 1840

Arago, J. Promenade autour du Monde pendant 1817-20, sur les corvettes l'Uranie et la Physicienne, commandées par M. Freycinet. 2 vols. 8° *Paris*, 1822

Aramayo, A. Extracts from a Work on Bolivia by Avelino Aramayo, published in London in 1863. 8* 1874

Aramon, D'. Le Voyage de Monsieur D'Aramon, Ambassadeur pour le Roy en Levant. Escript par Noble Homme Jean Chesneau, publié et annoté par Ch. Schefer. (Recueil de Voyages et de Documents pour servir à l'Histoire de la Géographie. . . . Publié sous la direction de Ch. Schefer et H. Cordier.) Vol. 8. *Illustrations.* Large 8° *Paris*, 1887

Arana, D. B. Historia de la Guerra del Pacífico (1879-80). *Maps.* 8° *Santiago*, 1880
—— The same. Tomo II. (1880-81). *Map and plan.* 8° *Santiago*, 1881
—— Vida e Viagens de Fernão de Magalhães. Traducção de Hespanhol de Fernando de Magalhães Villas - Boas. Com um Appendice original. *Map.* 8° *Lisbon*, 1881

Aranha, Brito. Subsidios para a Historia do Jornalismo nas Provincias ultramarinas Portuguezas. 8° *Lisbon*, 1885

Aranzadi, Telesforo de. Atenéo de Madrid: Fauna Americana. 4° *Madrid*, 1892

Arata, P. See Peragallo.

Araujo Porto Alegre, Manoel de. Colombo: Poema. Large 8° *Rio de Janeiro*, 1892

Arber, Edward. See Howell, J.

Arbousset, Thomas, and F. Daumas. Relation d'un Voyage d'exploration au Nord-est de la Colonie du Cap de Bonne-Espérance en 1836. *Map and plates.* 8° *Paris*, 1842
—— Narrative of an Exploratory Tour to the North-east of the Colony of the Cape of Good Hope. Translated by John Croumbie Brown. 8° *Cape Town*, 1846

Arbuthnot, Alex. J. Papers relating to Public Instruction, comprising a Memorandum of the Proceedings of the Madras Government in the Department of Public Instruction; with an Appendix. [From the India Records, No. 2.] Royal 8° *Madras*, 1855
—— Report on Public Instruction in the Madras Presidency for 1855-56. [From the India Selections, No. 35.] *Tables.* Royal 8° *Madras*, 1856

Arbuthnot, Lieut. G. Herzegovina, or Omer Pasha and the Christian Rebels; with a Brief Account of Servia, its Social, Political, and Financial Condition. *Maps and plates.* 8° 1862

Archbell, James. Grammar of the Bechuana Language. 8° *Grahamstown*, 1837

Archer, Gabriel. See Purchas, Vol. 4, Book 9: Appendix 1.

Archer, Lieut. Joseph. Statistical Survey of the County of Dublin, with Observations on the Means of Improvement. *Map.* 8° *Dublin*, 1801

Archer, Major. Tours in Upper India, and in Parts of the Himalaya Mountains. 2 vols. 8° 1833

Archer, W. H. Statistical Notes on the Progress of Victoria from the Foundation of the Colony, 1835-60. First Series. 4° *Melbourne*, 1861
—— Statistical Register of Victoria, from the Foundation of the Colony; with an Astronomical Calendar for 1855. 8° *Melbourne*, 1854
—— See Victoria, C: Appendix 2.

Archer, Hon. W. See Whiting.

Archer, W. J. Report of a Journey in the Vice-Consular District of Chiengmai, Siam. *Maps.* Folio* 1888
—— Extracts from a Journal kept on a Visit to Chiengtung in May and June 1888. *Map.* Folio* 1889
—— Report on a Journey in the Mē-Kong Valley. *Map.* Folio* 1892

Archer, William. See Nansen.

Archiac, Viscount d'. See Sedgwick and Murchison; Tchihatchef.

Archibald, E. D. See Symons.

Arconati, Viscount G. Diario di un Viaggio in Arabia Petrea (1865). 4°. *Maps and photographs.* Atlas. 4° *Turin*, 1872

Ardoino, A. See Cabeza de Vaca.

Ardouin, B. Études sur l'Histoire d'Haïti, suivies de la Vie du Général J. M. Borgella. 2 vols. *Portrait.* 8° *Paris*, 1853

Arenales, General. Biografia, y Juicio sobre la Memoria Histórica de su segunda campaña á la Sierra del Peru en 1821. Por P. de Angelis. *Maps.* 8° *Buenos Ayres*, 1832

Arendarenko, —. Darwaz and Karate-ghin. [Russian Abstract.] From the *Russian Military Journal,* for November and December 1883. 4*   1884

Argal (or Argoll), Sir Samuel. *See* Purchas, Vol. 4, Book 9 : Appendix 1.

Argout, Maurice d'. *See* Rees.

Argovie, J. Muller d'. *See* France, B : Appendix 2.

"Ariel." *See* Glen.

Arias, Don F. G. *See* Angelis, Vol. 6 : Appendix 1.

Arias, Juan Luis. *See* Hakluyt Soc. Publ., Vol. 25 : Appendix 1.

Aristotle, The Life and Writings of. By Frederick A. Trendelenburg ; trans-lated from the German by G. Long. 8°
                                                         N.D.

Armas, Juan Ignacio de. Les Crânes dits déformés : Memoire lu en Espagnol à la Société Anthropologique de la Havane, le 1er Novembre 1885. 8*
                                        Havana, 1885

Armenio, R. A Libertação des Raças de Cor por uma revolução na applicação das Machinas a Vapor. Relatorio das Con-ferençias Scientificas pelo rapido atraves-sador dos Desertos e das Savanas. 8°
                            Rio de Janeiro, 1873

Armentia, Padre Nicolas. Biblioteca Boliviana de Geografia e Historia. I. Navegacion del Madre de Dios. *Map.* 8°   *La Paz,* 1887
—— *See* Ballivian.

Arminjon, V. F. Il Giappone e il Viaggio della corvetta "Magenta" nel 1866. *Map.* 8°   *Genoa,* 1869

Armit, R. H. The Wind in his Circuits ; with the Explanation of the Origin and Cause of Circular Storms and Equinoctial Gales. *Diagrams and chart.* 8° 1870
—— Light as a Motive Power : a Series of Meteorological Essays. Vol 1. *Plates.* 8°   1875
—— The History of New Guinea and the Origin of the Negroid Race : a Resumé of Past Exploration, Future Capabilities, and the Political, Commercial, and Moral Aspect of the Island. 8*   1876

Armit, Capt. W. E. Armit's Expedition into New Guinea. (Cuttings from the *Melbourne Argus.*) *Maps.* 4*   1883

Armstrong, Alex. Personal Narrative of the Discovery of the North-West Passage, with Incidents of Travel and Adventure during nearly Five Years' Service in the Arctic Regions, while in Search of the Expedition under Sir John Franklin. *Map and plate.* 8°   1857

Armstrong, A. Shantung (China) : a General Outline of the Geography and History of the Province, &c. *Map and illustration.* Small 4° *Shanghai,* 1891

Armstrong, James, John Young, and David Robertson. Catalogue of the Western Scottish Fossils ; with Intro-duction by Professor Young. Compiled for the British Association Meeting, 1876. 12°   *Glasgow,* 1876

Armstrong, John, R.E. History of the Island of Minorca. *Map and plates.* 8°
                                                        1752

Arnaud, — d'. Documents et Observa-tions sur le Cours du Bahr-el-Abiad, ou du Fleuve Blanc, et sur quelques autres points de Géographie. *Map.* 8*
                                        Paris, 1843
—— *See* Jomard.

Arnold, Arthur. Through Persia by Cara-van. 2 vols. 8°   1877

Arnold, E. *See* Nicholls, K.

Arnold, Sir Edwin. Seas and Lands [Travels]. 2nd edition. *Illustrations.* 8°   1891

Arnold, R. Arthur. From the Levant, the Black Sea, and the Danube. 2 vols. 8°   1868

Arnold, Dr Thomas. History of Rome. Vol. 2. 8°   1840
—— The Second Punic War : being Chapters of the History of Rome. Edited by William T. Arnold. *Maps.* Crown 8°   1886

Arnold, Mrs William. *See* Lebon and Pelet.

Arnot, F. S. From the Zambesi to Benguella. Extracts from the Diary and Letters of Frederick Stanley Arnot, 1884. *Map.* 16*   *Glasgow* [1885]
—— Among the Garenganze in Central Africa : being the Diary and Letters of Fred. Stanley Arnot, from March to Sep-tember 1886. *Map and illustration.* 12*   [1887]
—— Garenganze, No. 2. Six Months more Among the Garenganze : Letters from September 1886 to March 1887 of Fred. Stanley Arnot. *Map and illustration.* 12*   [1887]
—— Garenganze, or Seven Years' Pioneer Mission Work in Central Africa. *Maps and illustrations.* 8°   [1889]
—— Bihé and Garenganze, or Four Years' Further Work and Travel in Central Africa. 8°   [1893]

Arnot, Sandford. *See* Asia, General : Appendix 2.

Arnott, F. S. Report on the Hill Fort of Powagur, in the Rewa Kanta, pre-pared June 1838. [From the India Records, No. 23.] Royal 8°
                                        Bombay, 1856

Arrian. Expeditionis Alexandri libri septem, et Historia Indica, ex Bonav. Vulcanii Interpretatione Latina, post variam aliorum industriam, ita lacunis vel cognitis vel ignotis etiamnum et obscuris suppletis, ita Auctoris in Græcæ Linguæ nativo usu præstantia et facultate restituta ex plurium Manuscriptorum et præsertim unius optimi collatione, ut nunc demun prodire hic autor videri debeat, opera J. Gronovii. (Gr. et. Lat.) *Portrait.* Folio *Leyden,* 1704
—— History of Alexander's Expedition. Translated by Rooke. To which is prefixed Mr Leclerc's Criticism upon Quintus Curtius. *Map.* 2 vols. 8° 1729
—— Voyage round the Euxine Sea. Translated by W. and T. Falconer. *Maps and plates.* 4° *Oxford,* 1805
—— *See* Ramusio, Vols. 1, 2 ; Vincent, Vol. 1 : Appendix 1.

Arriens, N. A. T. Aanteekeningen omtrent eenige vulkanen van den Indischen Archipel. *Map.* 8* [*Batavia,* 1865]

Arrow, Sir Frederick. A Fortnight in Egypt at the Opening of the Suez Canal. *Map.* 8* 1869

Arroyo, Jose Miguel. Reseña de los trabajos científicos de la Sociedad Mexicana de Geografía y Estadística en el año de 1865. [Sep. Cop. from Bol. Soc. Mex. Geogr. y Estad., Tom. 12, No. 1.] Large 8* *Mexico,* 1865

Artaria. *See* Grissinger.

Arteche, José Gomez de. Geografía Historico-Militar de España y Portugal. 2nd edition. 8° *Madrid,* 1859

Arthur, G. *See* Portugal, B : Appendix 2.

Arthur, King. *See* Hakluyt, Vol. 1 : Appendix 1.

Arthur, William. What is Fiji? The Sovereignty of which is offered to Her Majesty. 8* 1859

Artieda. *See* Allgemeine Historie, Vol. 16 : Appendix 1.

Arundel, Earl of. *See* Hakluyt, Vol. 2 : Appendix 1.

Arundell, Rev. F. V. J. A Visit to the Seven Churches of Asia, with an Excursion into Pisidia, containing Remarks on the Geography and Antiquities of those Countries. *Map and inscriptions.* 8° 1828
—— Discoveries in Asia Minor, including a Description of the Ruins of several Ancient Cities, and especially Antioch of Pisidia. *Map and plates.* 2 vols. 8° 1834

Arve, Stephen d'. Les Fastes du Mont Blanc. Ascensions célèbres et Catastrophes depuis M. de Saussure jusqu'à nos jours. Small 8° *Geneva,* 1876

Arzruni, Dr A. *See* Poljakow.

Arzruni, K. Die ökonomische Lage der Armenier in der Türkei. 8* *St Petersburg,* 1879

Asbjörnsen, P. C. *See* Sars, M.

Asboth, Johann von. Bosnien und die Herzegowina. Reisebilder und Studien. *Maps and illustrations.* 4° *Vienna,* 1888
—— An Official Tour through Bosnia and Herzegovina, with an Account of the History, Antiquities, Agrarian Conditions, Religion, Ethnology, Folk-Lore, and Social Life of the People. *Illustrations.* Large 8° 1890

Ascherson. P. *See* Neumayer, G. ; Rohlfs, G. ; Schweinfurth.

Asensio, José Maria. Cristóbal Colón, su Vida, sus Viajes, sus Descubrimientos. 2 vols. *Illustrations, including coloured plates.* 4° *Barcelona,* [1891]

Ashbee, H. S. A Bibliography of Tunisia, from the Earliest Times to the End of 1888 (in two parts), including Utica and Carthage, the Punic Wars, the Roman Occupation, the Arab Conquest, the Expeditions of Louis IX. and Charles V., and the French Protectorate. *Map.* Large 8° 1889
—— *See* Graham, Alexander.

Ashby H. *See* Hodgkin.

Ashburner, Charles A. The Geologic Distribution of Natural Gas in the United States. *Map and sections.* 8° [*St Louis,* 1886]

Ashe, R. P. Two Kings of Uganda ; or, Life by the Shores of Victoria Nyanza : being an Account of a Residence of Six Years in Eastern Equatorial Africa. *Map and illustrations.* 8° 1889

Ashe, Thomas. *See* Phillips [1], Vol. 10 : Appendix 1.

Asher, A. Bibliographical Essay on the Collection of Voyages and Travels edited and published by Levinus Hulsius and his Successors, from 1598 to 1660. 4° 1839

Ashmun, Jehudi, late Colonial Agent in Liberia, Life of ; with Extracts from his Journal and other Writings ; and a Sketch of the Life of the Rev. Lott Cary. *Portrait.* 8° *New York,* 1835
—— The Liberia Farmer, or Colonist's Guide to Independence and Domestic Comfort. 8* *Philadelphia,* 1835

Aspin, J. Geo-Chronologie von Europa. 8° *Kempten,* 1829

Asplazu, Dr Augustin. La Meseta de los Andes. 8* *La Paz,* 1890

Assmann, Chr. G. De Itinere per Montes Sudetos facto anno 1788. 4° *Wittenberg,* 1789

Assmann, R. *See* Germany, C., Forschungen, &c., Vol. 1. : Appendix 2.

Asta-Buruaga, F. S. Diccionario Jeográfico de la República de Chile. *Portrait.* 8° *New York,* 1867

Astafieve, N. Topographical Sketch of Upper Armenia. [In Russian.] 8*
Tiflis, 1874

Astete, Miguel de. *See* Hakluyt Soc. Publ., Vol. 47 : Appendix 1.

Astley, Thomas. New General Collection of Voyages and Travels. 4 vols. *Maps and plates.* 8°   1745-47
For full Title and Contents, *see* Appendix 1.

Aston, H. Partition Treaty of Kattywar, concluded between the Gaekwar and the Peshwa, in 1752-53 ; Extracts from Treaties concluded by the British Government with the Gaekwar and with the Peshwa ; Engagements concluded at various Periods with the Chiefs of Kattywar ; with Remarks relating to some of these Engagements, prepared in 1845 by Capt. H. Aston.

Aston, W. G. Commercial Reports by Her Majesty's Consul-General in Corea, 1882-83 ; and Report of a Journey from Söul to Sougdo in August 1884. 8* 1885

Astor, J. J. *See* Ross, A. A.

"Astrolabe" and "Zélée." *See* D'Urville, Dumont.

Athelard of Bath. *See* Hakluyt, Vol. 2 : Appendix 1.

Atkins, H. M. Ascent to the Summit of Mont Blanc, on the 22nd and 23rd of August 1837. 8*   1838

Atkins, John. *See* Astley, Vol 2 ; Laharpe, Vol. 2 ; Allgemeine Historie, Vol. 3 : Appendix 1.

Atkins, Hon. T. Astley. Indian Wars and the Uprising of 1655 : Yonkers Depopulated. Large 8*   *Yonkers,* 1892

[Atkinson, A. T.] Early Voyagers of the Pacific Ocean. Papers of the Hawaiian Historical Society, No. 4. 8*
Honolulu, N.D.

Atkinson, E. *See* Ganot.

Atkinson, E. T. *See* India, O : Appendix 2.

Atkinson, James. The Expedition into Affghanistan : Notes and Sketches descriptive of the Country, contained in a Personal Narrative during the Campaign of 1839 and 1840, up to the Surrender of Dost Mahomed Khan. *Map.* 12° 1842

Atkinson, Lewis. *See* Scott, Arthur.

Atkinson, Mrs. Recollections of Tartar Steppes and their Inhabitants. 8° 1862

Atkinson, T. Witlam. Oriental and Western Siberia: a Narrative of Seven Years' Explorations and Adventures in Siberia, Mongolia, and Kirghis Steppes, Chinese Tartary, and part of Central Asia. *Map and plates.* Royal 8° 1858

—— Travels in the Regions of the Upper and Lower Amoor, and the Russian Acquisitions on the Confines of India and China. *Map and plates.* Royal 8°
1860

Atwood, T. The History of the Island of Dominica, containing a Description of its Situation, Extent, Climate, Mountains, Rivers, Natural Productions, &c. 8°   1791

Aubel, M. L'Importance de la Question de l'Afrique et du Choix d'un Système de Colonisation. 8*   *Paris,* 1837

Aubert, L. C. M. Beiträge zur Lateinischen Grammatik. 8* *Christiania,* 1856

Aubertin, J. J. Eleven Days' Journey in the Province of Sao Paulo, with the Americans Drs Gaston and Shaw, and Major Mereweather, &c. 8*   1866

Aucapitaine, Baron Henri. Étude sur la Caravane de la Mecque, et le Commerce de l'Intérieur de l'Afrique. Royal 8*.   *Paris,* 1861

—— Mollusques Terrestres et d'Eau Douce, observés dans la Haute Kabylie. 8*
Paris, 1862

—— Les Kabyles et la Colonisation de l'Algérie. 12°   *Paris,* 1864

—— Ethnographie : Nouvelles Observations sur l'Origine des Berbers-Thamou, à propos des lettres sur le Sahara, adressées par M. le Professeur E. Desor à M. E. Liebig. 8*   *Paris,* 1867

—— Lettre à M. E. Desor sur les Origines des Berbers. 8*   N.P., N.D.

—— Notions Ethnographiques sur les Berbers Touaregs. 8*   N.P., N.D.

—— Notice sur la Tribu des Ait Fraoucen. 8*   *Algiers,* N.D.

Aucher-Eloy, Pierre Martin Remi. Relations de Voyages en Orient de 1830 à 1838. Revues et annotées par M. le Comte Jaubert. 2 vols. *Map.* 8°
Paris, 1843

Auerbach, Prof. B. Le Plateau Lorrain, Essai de Géographie regionale ; avec 24 croquis cartographiques de J. V. Barbier et 21 vues photographiques. 8°
Paris, 1893

Auerbach, Rev. M. *See* Montefiore, Sir M.

Aufrere, A. *See* Della Cella ; Salis.

Auld, Major J. W. *See* Courtney, W.

Auldjo, John. Ascent to the Summit of Mont Blanc, 1827. *Map and plates.* 4°   1828
—— Ditto. 8°   1830
—— Sketches of Vesuvius, with Accounts of its Principal Eruptions. *Plates.* 8° 1833
—— Visit to Constantinople and some of the Greek Islands in 1833. *Plates.* 8° 1835

Aumaile, Robert L. d'. Report in detail . . . of Explorations and Surveys of the Gold, Silver, Copper, and Lead Mines of the Real de la Purisima Conception, de Papigochi de Huacaivo, Gran Barranca de Tarrarecua, Canton Minas, District of Guadaloupe í Calvo, State of Chihuahua, Republic of Mexico. *Maps.* 8°
New York, 1861

Aumale, Duc d'. Campagnes en Afrique, 1840-44. 8° *Paris*, N.D.

Aumer, Joseph. Die Arabischen Handschriften der Staatsbibliothek in München. *See* Catalogues, A: Appendix 2.

Austel, H. *See* Hakluyt, Vol. 2: Appendix 1.

Austin, C. E. Undeveloped Resources of Turkey in Asia, with Notes on the Railway to India : Essay. *Map.* Small 8° 1878

Austin, Captain. *See* Franklin, Sir John.

Auteroche, Chappe d'. Voyage en Sibérie, fait par ordre du Roi en 1761 ; contenant les mœurs, les usages des Russes, et l'État actuel de cette Puissance ; la Description Géographique de la Nivellement de la Route de Paris à Tobolsk ; l'Histoire Naturelle de la même Route ; des Observations Astronomiques, et des Expériences sur l'Électricité Naturelle. 4 vols. *Maps and plates, &c.* Folio *Paris*, 1768

—— Journey into Siberia, containing an Account of the Manners and Customs of the Russians, &c. ; with a Geographical Description of their Country, and Level of the Roads from Paris to Tobolsky. *Map and plates.* 4° 1770

—— The Antidote ; or, An Inquiry into the Merits of a Book, entitled, " A Journey into Siberia, made in MDCCLXI., by the Abbé Chappe d'Auteroche. . . ." By a Lover of Truth. Translated into English by a Lady, &c. 8° 1772

—— Voyage en Californie pour l'Observation du Passage de Vénus sur le Disque du Soleil, le 3 Juin 1769, et la Description Historique de la Route de l'Auteur à travers le Mexique. Redigé par M. Cassini. *Map and plates.* 4° *Paris*, 1772

—— A Voyage to California, to Observe the Transit of Venus ; with an Historical Description of the Author's Route through Mexico, and the Natural History of that Province ; also a Voyage to Newfoundland and Sallee by Monsieur de Cassini. *Plan.* 8° 1778

—— *See* Laharpe, Vol. 8 ; Allgemeine Historie, Vol. 20 ; "The Modern Traveller," Vol. 4, p. 610 : Appendix 1.

Averill, H. K., junr. A New Geography and History of Clinton County, New York. *Maps and illustrations.* 4° *Plattsburgh, N.Y.*, 1885

Avezac, Marie Armand Pascal d'. Esquisse générale de l'Afrique. 8° *Paris*, 1837

—— Notice des Travaux de la Société de Géographie de Paris, et du Progrès des Sciences Géographiques, 1836. 8* *Paris*, 1837

—— Deux Notes sur Anciennes Cartes Historiées MS. de l'École Catalane. *Map.* 8* *Paris*, 1844

Avezac, Marie Armand Pascal d'. Description et Histoire de l'Afrique Ancienne, précédée d'une Esquisse Générale de l'Afrique. *Plates.* 8° *Paris*, 1845

—— Les Iles Fantastiques de l'Océan Occidental du Moyen Age. 8* *Paris*, 1845

—— Notice des Découvertes faites au Moyen-age dans l'Océan Atlantique, antérieurement aux Grandes Explorations Portugaises du quinzième siècle. Royal 8* *Paris*, 1845

—— Notice sur le Pays et le Peuple des Yébus en Afrique. *Map and plates.* 8* *Paris*, 1845

—— Note sur la Première Expédition de Bethencourt aux Canaries, et sur le degré d'habileté Nautique des Portugais à cette Époque. Royal 8* *Paris*, 1846

—— Note sur la véritable Situation du mouillage marqué au Sud du Cap du Bugeder. Royal 8* *Paris*, 1846

—— Note sur un Atlas Hydrographique Manuscrit exécuté à Venise dans le XVe. Siècle, et conservé aujourd'hui au Musée Britannique. *Plate.* 8* *Paris*, 1850

—— Éthicus et les Ouvrages Cosmographiques intitulés de ce nom ; suivi d'un Appendice, contenant la Version Latine abrégée, attribuée à S. Jérôme, d'une Cosmographie supposée écrite en Grec par le noble Istriote Éthicus ; publiée pour la première fois, avec les Gloses et les Variantes des Manuscrits. 4° *Paris*, 1852

—— Grands et petits Géographes Grecs et Latins : Esquisse Bibliographique des Collections qui en ont été Publiées, Entreprises ou Projetées ; et Revue Critique des petits Géographes Grecs, avec Notes et Prolégomènes de M. Müller, compris dans la Bibliothèque des auteurs Grecs de M. A. F. Didot. 8° *Paris*, 1856

—— Considérations Géographiques sur l'Histoire du Brésil, Examen critique d'une nouvelle Histoire générale du Brésil récemment publiée en Portugais à Madrid par M. F. A. de Varnhagen. *Maps.* Large 8° *Paris*, 1857

—— Les Voyages de Améric Vespuce au compte de l'Espagne, et les Mesures Itinéraires employées par les Marins Espagnols et Portugais des XVe. et XVIe. siècle, pour faire suite aux considérations géographiques sur l'Histoire du Brésil. 8° *Paris*, 1858

—— Notice sur l'Aquitaine. [From the Encyclopédie Pittoresque.] Folio* *Paris*, N.D.

—— L'Expédition Génoise des frères Vivaldi, à la Découverte de la Route Maritime des Indes Orientales au XIIIe. siècle. 8* *Paris*, 1859

B

Avezac, Marie Armand Pascal d'. Aperçus Historiques sur la Boussole, et ses applications a l'étude des Phénomènes du Magnétisme Terrestre. 8* *Paris*, 1860

—— Sur un Globe Terrestre trouvé à Laon, antérieur à la decouverte de l'Amérique. *Map.* 8* *Paris*, 1861

—— Restitution de deux passages du texte Grec de la Géographie de Ptolémée aux Chap. V. et VI. du Sept. livre. *Plate.* 8* *Paris*, 1862

—— Note sur la Mappemonde Historiée de la Cathédrale de Héréford. Détermination de sa date et de ses sources. 8* *Paris*, 1862

—— Coup d'œil Historique sur la Projection des Cartes de Géographie. *Table.* 8* *Paris*, 1863

—— Notice sur la Vie et les Travaux du Lieut.-Gen. Albert de la Marmora, et du Contre-Amiral John Washington. 8* *Paris*, 1864

—— Note sur une Mappemonde Turke du xvie siécle conservée à la bibliothèque de Saint Marc à Venise. 8* *Paris*, 1866

—— Inventaire et Classement raisonné des "Monuments de la Géographie" publiés par M. Jomard de 1842 à 1862. 8* *Paris*, 1867

—— Les Navigations Terre-Neuviennes de Jean et Sébastien Cabot. Lettre au Révérend Léonard Woods. 8* *Paris*, 1869

—— Relation Authentique du Voyage du Capitaine de Gonneville ès Nouvelles Terres des Indes. 8° *Paris*, 1869

—— Une Digression Géographique à propos d'un beau Manuscrit à Figures de la Bibliothèque d'Altamira. La Mappemonde du viiie Siècle de Saint Béat de Liébana. 8* *Plates.* 1870

—— Atlas Hydrographique de 1511 du Génois Visconte de Maggiolo. 12* *Paris*, 1871

—— Deux Bluettes Étymologiques en réponse à M. le Cte H. de Charencey. 8* *Paris*, 1872

—— Afrique. [From l'Encyclopédie Pittoresque.] 4* *Paris*, N.D.

—— Esquisse d'Alger. Folio *Paris*, N.D.

—— *See* Carpin; Varnhagen; *also* Recueil de Voyages, Vol. 4, p. 611: Appendix 1.

Aviero, Signor, or Travideani. *See* Phillips [3], Vol. 5: Appendix 1.

Avila, Pedrarias d'. *See* Davila.

Avril, Adolphe d'. L'Arabie contemporaine, avec la description du Pélerinage de la Mecque, &c. *Map.* 8° *Paris*, 1868

Ayllon, Lucas Vasquez d'. *See* Gottfried: Appendix 1.

Aymonier, E. Notice sur le Cambodge. 8° *Paris*, 1875

—— Géographie du Cambodge. *Map.* 8° *Paris*, 1876

Ayton, or Hayton, or Anthonie of Armenia. *See* Haitho.

Aytoun, Lieut. *See* India, C (Geological Papers): Appendix 2.

Ayyad, El - Tantavy Mouhammad. Traité de la Langue Arabe Vulgaire. 8° *Leipzig*, 1848

Azambuza, Diego d'. *See* General Collection, p. 610: Appendix 1.

Azara, Don Felix de. Apuntamientos para la Historia Natural de los Quadrúpedos del Paraguay y Rio de la Plata. 2 vols. 8° *Madrid*, 1802

—— Voyages dans l'Amérique Méridionale, depuis 1781-1801; contenant la Description Géographique, Politique, et Civile du Paraguay et de la Rivière de la Plata; l'Histoire de la Découverte et de la Conquête de ces Contrées, &c.; avec une notice sur la vie et les écrits de l'Auteur, par C. A. Walkenaer, et Notes par G. Cuvier et Sonnini. *Maps and plates.* 4 vols. 8° *Paris*, 1809

—— Descripcion é Historia del Paraguay y del Rio de la Plata. Tomo 1. 8° *Madrid*, 1847

—— Viajes inéditos de D. Félix de Azara desde Santa-Fè á la Asuncion, al interior del Paraguay, y á los Pueblos Misiones; con una noticia preliminar por el General D. Bartolomé Mitre, y algunas notas por el doctor D. Juan Maria Gutierrez. 8° *Buenos Ayres*, 1873

—— *See* Angelis, Vols. 2, 4, 6: Appendix 1.

Azémar, H. Dictionnaire Stieng, Recueil de 2,500 mots. 8° *Saigon*, 1887

Azoto, Ant. Ghisilieri Vescovo d'. Predizione della Cometa dell' anno 1736, con riflessioni varie sopra le Comete passate e future, ove si tratta il loro sistema e calcolo. *Plates.* 8° *Bologna*, 1735

Azurara, Gomes Eannes de. Chronica do Descobrimento e Conquista de Guiné. Transladada do manuscrito original do Visconde da Carreira, precedida de una Introducção e notas pelo Visconde de Santarem. *Portrait.* 8° *Paris*, 1841

B

B. . . ., St J. H. Four Months Abroad: Madras to London and Edinburgh, and back through France and Italy. 8* *Madras*, 1879

B. . . ., T. Two Journeys to Jerusalem, containing: 1. A Strange and True Account of the Travels of Two English Pilgrims some years since, and what admirable Accidents befel them in their Journey to Jerusalem, Gr. Cairo, &c.; 2. The Travels of Fourteen Englishmen in 1669 to Jerusalem, Bethlem, Jericho, the River Jordan, the Lake of Sodom and Gomorrah, &c.; with the Antiquities, Monuments, and Memorable Places mentioned in Scripture. By T. B. . . . 16° 1715

B. . . , — de. History of the Expedition of Three Ships sent by the Company of the East Indies of the United Provinces [Dutch East India Company], to Terra Australis in 1721, by Mons. de B. Printed at the Hague, 1739. [MS. translation from the Dutch.] 4° N.D.

B. . . , J. M. H. Itinéraire du Royaume d'Alger. 8° *Toulon,* 1830

B. . . , M. V. From London to Lahore. By M. V. B. *Map.* 8* 1868

Babbage, B. H. The Currents of the Air and the Ocean. Nos. 1, 2, 3. 4* *Adelaide,* 1869

Babbage, Charles. Tables of Logarithms of the Natural Numbers 1 to 108,000. 2nd edition. 8° 1831
—— *See* Quetelet.

Babbs, R. The Gold Fields of South Africa, and the way to reach them. 12* N.D.

Baber. Memoirs of Zehir-ed-Din Muhammed Baber, Emperor of Hindustan, written by himself, in the Jaghatai Turki. Translated by J. Leyden and W. Erskine, with Notes and a Geographical and Historical Introduction ; together with a map of the countries between the Oxus and Jaxartes, and a Memoir regarding its construction by C. Waddington. *Map.* 4° 1826

Baber, E. Colborne. Notes on the Road through Western Yunnan, from Tali to T'éng-yueh. [Foreign Office Publication.] Folio * 1877
—— Report on the Route followed by Mr Grosvenor's Mission between Tali-fu and Momein. *Map.* [Parly. Rep.] Folio * 1878
—— Report on a Journey to Ta-Chien-Lu. [Parly. Rep.] Folio * 1879
—— Travels and Researches in Western China. R. G. S. Supplementary Papers. Vol. 1. *Maps.* Large 8° 1886
—— *See* Gill, W. ; Lacouperie.

Babinet, J. Atlas Universel de Géographie, système Homalographique. *Woodcuts.* 4* *Paris,* 1855

Babington, B. G. *See* Asia, General : Appendix 2.

Babst, J. J. *See* Danckwerth.

"Bacchante" Cruise. The Cruise of Her Majesty's ship "Bacchante," 1879-82. Compiled from the Private Journals, Letters, and Note-Books of Prince Albert Victor and Prince George of Wales, with Additions by John N. Dalton. 2 vols. *Maps, charts, plans, and illustrations.* 8° 1886

Bach, J. F. Introduction à la Connaissance des Montagnes, Vallées, Lacs, et Rivières de la Suisse ; pour servir à l'Explication de la Carte en Relief de Bauerkeller. Revu par J. B. B. Eyriés. 8* *Paris,* 1842

Bach, Mauricio. Descripcion de la Nueva Provincia de Otuquis en Bolivia. *Map.* 4* *Buenos Ayres,* 1843
—— Ditto. 2nd edition. 4* *Buenos Ayres,* 1843
—— Reimpresion Publicada per el Dr Antonio Quijarro. *Map.* 8* *Buenos Ayres,* 1885

Bache, Prof. A. D. Report on an Application of the Galvanic Circuit to an Astronomical Clock and Telegraph Register in determining Local Differences of Longitude, and in Astronomical Observations generally. 8* 1849
—— Notices of the Western Coast of the United States. U.S. Coast Survey, Dec. 1850. 8* *Washington,* 1851
—— Additional Notes of a Discussion of Tidal Observations made in connection with the Coast Survey at Cat Island, Louisiana. *Plan.* 8* *New Haven, Conn.,* 1852
—— Tide Tables for the principal Seaports of the U.S. 8* *New York,* 1855
—— The Tides of the Atlantic and Pacific Coasts of the U.S., the Gulf Stream, and the Earthquake Waves of Dec. 1854. *Maps.* 8* *New Haven, Conn.,* 1856
—— Tide Tables for the Use of Navigators, prepared from the Coast Survey Observations. *Map.* 8* *New York,* 1857
—— On the Heights of the Tides of the United States, from Observations in the Coast Survey. *Plates.* 8* *Washington,* 1858
—— Lecture on the Gulf Stream. *Plans.* 8* *New Haven, Conn.,* 1860
—— On the Influence of the Moon on the Declination of the Magnetic Needle. *Plate.* 8* *New Haven, Conn.,* 1861
—— Records and Results of a Magnetic Survey of Pennsylvania and parts of adjacent States, in 1840-41. 8* *Washington,* 1863
—— On the Heights of the Tides of the United States ; on the Winds of the Western Coast ; and on the Measurement of a Base on Epping Plains, Maine, U.S. *Plates.* 8* V.P., V.D.

Bachmaier, A. Dictionnaire Pasigraphique, précédé de la grammaire. 12° *Augsburg,* 1868
—— Pasigraphisches Wörterbuch zum Gebrauche für die deutsche Sprache. *Augsburg,* 1868
—— Pasigraphical Dictionary and Grammar. 12° 1871

Bachmann, Prof. J. *See* Fellenberg.

Back, Capt. Sir G. Narrative of the Arctic Land Expedition to the Mouth of the Great Fish River and along the Shores of the Arctic Ocean, in 1833-35. *Map and plates.* 8° 1836

Back, Capt. Sir G. Narrative of an Expedition in H.M.S. " Terror," undertaken with a view to Geographical Discovery on the Arctic Shores, in 1836-37. *Map and plates.* 8°   1838

Backer, Louis de. *See* Rubriques.

Backhoff, F. I. *See* Churchill, Vol. 2: Appendix 1.

Backhouse, James. Narrative of a Visit to the Australian Colonies. *Maps and plates.* 8°   1843

Backstrom, —. Voyage to Spitzbergen. *See* Pinkerton, Vol. 1: Appendix 1.

Bacon, Francis. *See* Verulam.

Bacon, Roger. *See* Purchas, Vol. 3, Book 1: Appendix 1.

Bacon, Thomas. First Impressions and Studies from Nature in Hindostan; embracing an Outline of the Voyage to Calcutta, and Five Years' Residence in Bengal and the Doáb, from MDCCCXXXI. to MDCCCXXXVI. 2 vols. *Plates.* 8°   1837

Baddeley, P. F. H. Whirlwinds and Dust-Storms of India: an Investigation into the Law of Wind and Revolving Storms at Sea. *Plates.* 2 vols. Royal 8°   1860

Baddeley, M. J. B. Guides by. Thorough Guide Series. *Maps and plans.* 12°

The Peak District of Derbyshire and Neighbouring Counties. 3rd edition   1884

The English Lake District. 3rd edition   1884

Ditto. 5th edition   1889

The Highlands of Scotland (as far as Stornoway, Lochinver, and Lairg), with a full Description of the various Routes from England and the principal places of interest upon them, including Edinburgh, Glasgow, Melrose, and the Falls of Clyde.   1881

Scotland. Part 1. Edinburgh, Glasgow. and the Highlands as far north as Aberdeen, Inverness, Gairloch, and Stornoway, with a full Description of the various approaches and chief places of interest in the Lowlands. 1st edition   1885

Ditto. 5th edition   1887

Scotland, Part 2. The Northern Highlands. Containing a full Description of Aberdeen, Inverness, Loch Maree, and Gairloch, and of the Mainland north of those places in the Counties of Aberdeen, Banff, Elgin, and Nairn, Inverness, Ross, Cromarty, Sutherland, and Caithness. 1st and 3rd editions 1883-86

Scotland. Part 3. The "Lowlands," including Edinburgh and Glasgow and all Scotland south of those places 1886

Baddeley's Guides—*continued.*
Ireland. Part 1. Northern Counties, including Dublin and Neighbourhood.   1887

[For Part 2, *see* Ward, C. S.]

Baddeley, M. J. B., and C. S. Ward.
North Wales. Part 1. Chester, Rhyl, Llandudno, Bangor, Llanrwst, Bettws-y-Coed, Carnarvon, Llanberis, Beddgelert, and Ffestiniog Sections   1887

Part 2. Llangollen, Bala, Dolgelley, Barmouth, Oswestry, Shrewsbury, Welshpool, Llanidloes, Machynlleth, and Aberystwith Sections   1885

South Wales and the Wye District of Monmouthshire   1886

South Devon and South Cornwall, including Dartmoor and the Scilly Isles. 2nd edition   1885

Ditto. 3rd edition   1889

[For North Devon, &c., and for other Guides of the Series, *see* Ward, C. S.]

Baden-Powell, B. H. Handbook of the Economic Products of the Punjab, with a Combined Index and Glossary of Technical Vernacular words. Vol 1. Economic Raw Produce. [By " Baden H. Powell."] *Plates.* 8° *Roorkee,* 1868

—— Handbook of the Manufactures and Arts of the Punjab. Forming Vol. 2 to the " Handbook of the Economic Products of the Punjab." *Plates.* 8° *Lahore,* 1872

Baden-Powell, B. F. S. In Savage Isles and Settled Lands: Malaysia, Australasia, and Polynesia, 1888-91. *Map and illustrations.* 8°   1892

Baden-Powell, G. S. New Homes for the Old Country: a Personal Experience of the Political and Domestic Life, the Industries, and the Natural History of Australia and New Zealand. *Map. and plates.* 8°   1872

Baden-Powell, W. Canoe Travelling: Log of a Cruise on the Baltic, and Practical Hints on Building and Fitting Canoes. *Map and illustrations.* Small 8°   1871

Badger, Rev. George Percy. Description of Malta and Gozo. *Maps and plates.* 12° *Malta,* 1838

—— The Nestorians and their Rituals, with the Narrative of a Mission to Mesopotamia and Coordistan in 1842-44, and a Visit in 1850. *Maps and plates.* 2 vols. 8°   1852

—— Description of Malta and Gozo, improved on that by George Percy Badger. *Map and illustrations.* 12° *Malta,* 1858

—— Visit to the Isthmus of Suez Canal Works. *Map.* 8*   1862

—— *See* Hakluyt Soc. Publ., 44: Appendix 1.

Badgley, J. *See* Roussin.

Badia, Iodoco Del. *See* Dante, Ignatius.

Baedeker, K. Handbooks for Travellers. *Maps and plans.* 12° *Leipzig and London*

Mittel- und Nord-Deutschland 1872
Northern Germany. (5th edition) 1873
—— Ditto. (9th edition) 1886
—— Ditto. (10th edition) 1890
Süd-Deutschland und Oesterreich. (16th edition) 1873
Southern Germany and Austria, including the Eastern Alps. (3rd edition) 1873
Süd-Baiern, Tirol und Salzburg, Steiermark, Kärnthen, Krain und Istrien. (16th edition) 1874
Southern Germany and Austria, including Hungary and Transylvania. (6th edition) 1887
—— Ditto. (7th edition) 1891
The Eastern Alps, including the Bavarian Highlands, The Tyrol, Salzkammergut, Styria, and Carinthia. (4th edition) 1879
—— Ditto, with Carniola, and Istria. (6th edition) 1888
Ditto. (7th edition) 1891
Oesterreich und Ungarn. (16th edition) 1873
Les Bords du Rhin, depuis Bâle jusqu'à la frontière de Hollande.
Coblenz, 1864
Die Rheinlande von der Schweizer bis zur Holländischen Grenze. (18th edition) 1874
The Rhine from Rotterdam to Constance. (5th edition) 1873
—— Ditto. (8th edition) 1882
—— Ditto. (10th edition) 1886
—— Ditto. (11th edition) 1889
—— Ditto. (12th edition) 1892
Belgien und Holland. (12th and 13th editions) 1873-75
Belgium and Holland. (4th edition) 1875
—— Ditto. (8th edition) 1885
—— Ditto. (9th edition) ·1888
—— Ditto. (10th edition) 1891
—— Ditto. Including the grand Duchy of Luxembourg (11th edition) 1893
Die Schweiz, nebst den angrenzenden Theilen von Ober-Italien, Savoyen und Tirol. (15th and 16th editions) 1873-75
Switzerland, and the adjacent Portions of Italy, Savoy, and the Tyrol 1867
—— Ditto. (6th edition) 1873
—— Ditto. (7th and 8th editions) 1877
—— Ditto. (11th edition) 1885
—— Ditto. (13th edition) 1889
—— Ditto. (14th edition.) *Maps, plans, and panoramas.* 12° 1891
—— Ditto. (15th edition) 1893

Baedeker's Handbooks—*continued.*

Paris and its Environs, with Routes from London to Paris, and from Paris to the Rhine and Switzerland. (4th edition) 1874
Le Nord de la France jusqu'à la Loire, excepté Paris 1884
Northern France from Belgium and the English Channel to the Loire, excluding Paris and its Environs 1889
Le Midi de la France depuis la Loire et y compris la Corse 1885
Southern France 1891
Italien. Erster Theil. Ober-Italien bis Livorno, Florenz, und Ravenna, nebst Ausflug nach Nizza und nach Ajaccio (Corsica). (12th edition) 1889
—— Zweiter Theil. Mittel-Italien und Rom. (9th edition) 1889
—— Dritter Theil. Unter-Italien und Sicilien, nebst Ausflügen nach den Liparischen Inseln, Sardinien, Malta, Tunis, und Corfu. (9th edition) 1889
Italy. First Part: Northern Italy, including Leghorn, Florence, and Ancona, and the Island of Corsica. (3rd edition) 1874
—— Northern Italy, including Leghorn, Florence, Ravenna, the Island of Corsica, and Routes through France, Switzerland, and Austria. (7th edition) 1886
—— Ditto. (8th edition) 1889
—— Ditto. (9th edition) 1892
—— Second Part: Central Italy and Rome. (4th edition) 1875
—— Second Part: Central Italy and Rome. (9th edition) 1886
—— Ditto. (10th edition) 1890
Italy. Second Part: Central Italy and Rome. (11th edition.) *Maps, plans, &c.* 1893
—— Third Part: Southern Italy, Sicily, and Excursions to the Lipari Islands, Malta, Sardinia, Tunis, and Athens. (5th edition) 1875
—— Third Part: Southern Italy and Sicily. (9th edition) 1887
—— Ditto. (10th edition) 1890
Palaestina und Syrien 1875
Palestine and Syria 1876
Palestine and Syria. (2nd edition.) *Maps, plan, and panorama* 1894 [1893]
Ægypten, Erster Theil: Unter-Ægypten bis zum Fayûm, und die Sinai-Halbinsel 1877
—— Zweiter Theil: Ober-Ægypten und Nubien bis zum zweiten Katarakt 1891
Egypt. First Part: Lower Egypt, with the Fayûm and the Peninsula of Sinai 1878
—— Ditto. (2nd edition) 1885
—— Second Part: Upper Egypt 1892

Baedeker's Handbooks—*continued.*
Great Britain : England, Wales, and
Scotland as far as Loch Maree and the
Cromarty Firth   1887
—— Ditto. (2nd edition)   1890
Griechenland   1883
Greece   1889
—— Ditto. (2nd edition.) *Maps
and plans*   1894 [1893]
London and its Environs. (6th edition)
                                      1887
—— Ditto. (8th edition.) *Maps and
plans.* 12°   1892
Norway and Sweden.˙ (3rd edition)
                                      1885
—— Ditto. (4th edition)   1889
West- und Mittel- Russland   ˙1883
The United States ; with an Excursion
into Mexico.   1893
The Dominion of Canada ; with New-
foundland, and an Excursion to Alaska
                                      1894

Baer, K. E. von. Ueber den jährlichen
Gang der Temperatur in Nowaja Semlja.
8*   [*St Petersburg*] 1837
—— Ueber den täglichen Gang der
Temperatur in Nowaja Semlja. 8*
            [*St Petersburg*] 1837
—— Ueber das Klima von Nowaja-Semlja
und die mittlere Temperatur insbe-
sondere. 8*   *St Petersburg*, 1837
—— Expédition à Novaïa Zemlia et en
Lapponie. 8*   *St Petersburg*, 1837-38
—— Sur la fréquence des Orages dans les
régions Arctiques. 8*
                      St Petersburg, 1839
—— Klima der Kirgisen-Steppe. 4* 1840
—— Why are the Right Banks of our
Rivers flowing Northwards high, and
the Left depressed? [In Russian.] 8*
                      [*Moscow*, 1857]
—— Der Alte Lauf des Armenischen
Araxes. *Maps.* 8*   1857
—— Dattel-Palmen an den Ufern des
Kaspischen Meeres, sonst und jetzt. 8*
                                      1859
—— Crania Selecta ex Thesauris Anthro-
pologicis Academiæ Imperialis Petro-
politanæ : Iconibus et Descriptionibus.
Plates. 4*   *St Petersburg*, 1859
—— Ueber Papuas und Alfuren : ein Com-
mentar zu den beiden ersten Abschnitten
der Abhandlung, Crania Selecta ex
Thesauris Anthropologicis, &c.   4*
                      St Petersburg, 1859
—— Kaspische Studien. *Maps.* 8°
                      St Petersburg, 1859
—— Ditto. VIII. Ueber ein allgemeines
Gesetz in der Gestaltung der Flussbetten.
8*   1860
—— Ueber das behauptete Seichter-werden
des Asowschen Meeres. *Map.* 8* 1861
—— Das fünfzigjährige Doctor-Jubiläum
des Geheimraths, am 29th August 1864.
Portrait. 4*   *St Petersburg*, 1865

Baer, K. E. von. Nachrichten über Leben
und Schriften des Herrn Geheimrathes.
Portrait. 4*   *St Petersburg*, 1865
—— Berichte über die Anmeldung eines
mit der Haut gefundenen Mammuths
und die zur Bergung desselben ausger-
üstete Expedition. *Plates.* 8*
                      St Petersburg, 1866
—— Das neuentdeckte Wrangells-Land.
Small 8*   *Dorpat*, 1868
—— *See infra*, Baer and Helmersen, 4, 7,
9, 16, 18.
—— **and Gr. von Helmersen.** Beiträge
zur Kenntniss des Russischen Reiches
und der angränzenden Länder Asiens.
Vols. 1–26 (Atlas to 23). 8°
                      St Petersburg, 1839-71
CONTENTS.
Vol. 1.—Wrangell, Contre-Adm. von.
Statistische und ethnographische
Nachrichten über die Russischen
Besitzungen an der Nordwestküste
von Amerika. *Map.* 8°   1839
Vol. 2.—Gens, Gen.-Major. Nach-
richten über Chiwa, Buchara, Chokand,
und den nordwestlichen Theil des
Chinesischen Staates ; bearbeitet und
mit Anmerkungen versehen von Gr.
v. Helmersen. *Map.* 8°   1839
Vol. 3.—Hagemeister, Jules de. Essai
sur les Ressources Territoriales et
Commerciales de l'Asie Occidentale,
le caractère des habitans, leur indus-
trie, et leur organisation municipale.
8°   1839
Vol. 4.—Herausgegeben von K. E. von
Baer   1841
Adelung, Fried. Ueber die älteren
ausländischen Karten von Russland.
Baer. Eine alte Abbildung der Ruinen
von Madshar. *Plate.*
Hofmann, Ernst. Geognostische Beo-
bachtungen auf einer Reise von Dorpat
bis Åbo.
Schrenck, Alex. Gust. von. Skizze der
Vegetation auf der Insel Hochland im
Finnischen Meerbusen. *Map.*
Köppen, P. von. Ueber Wald- und
Wasser-Vorrath im Gebiete der obern
und mittleren Wolga. *Map.*
Baer. Neueste Nachrichten über die
nördlichste Gegend von Sibirien
zwischen den Flüssen Pjässida und
Chatanga in Fragen und Antworten
abgefasst.
Vol. 5.—Helmersen, G. von. Reise nach
dem Ural und der Kirgisensteppe, in
1833-35. Part I.   1841
Vol. 6.—Helmersen, Gr. von. Reise
nach dem Ural und der Kirgisensteppe
in den Jahren 1833 und 1835. Part 2.
Maps, profiles.   1843
Vol. 7.—Nachrichten aus Sibirien und
der Kirgissteppe, gesammelt oder
herausgegeben von K. E. von Baer. 8°
                                      1845

Baer, K. E. von, and Gr. von Helmersen.
CONTENTS—*continued.*

Vol. 24.—Helmersen, Gr. von. Der Peipus-See und die obere Narova. 1860

—— Die Geologie in Russland. 1860

Gerstfeldt, G. von. Der Verkehr Russlands mit Westasien. *Map* 1860

Vol. 25.—Schmidt, J., Glehn, P. von, und Brylkin, A. D. Reisen im Gebiete des Amurstromes und auf der Insel Sachalin. *Maps* 1868

Vol. 26.—Meinshausen, K. Nachrichten über das Wilui-Gebiet in Ostsibirien. *Map* 1871

Baffin, William. *See* Hakluyt Soc. Publ., Vol. 5; Purchas, Vol. 3, Book 4; Allgemeine Historie, Vol. 17: Appendix 1.

—— **and Bylot.** *See* Hakluyt Soc. Publ., Vol. 5: Appendix 1.

Baggallay, Henry C. Access to Liverpool, with suggested Improvements. *Map.* 8* 1884

Bagge, A. H. Report on the Settlement of the Siam and Tenasserim Boundary. [From the India Records, No. 50.] Royal 8° *Calcutta*, 1866

Bagnols, Loais du Gué. Mémoires sur l'Intendance de la Flandre. 12° *Brussels*, 1739

Baguet, A. Rio-Grande do Sul et le Paraguay. 8° *Antwerp*, 1873

Baikie, R. Observations on the Neilgherries, including an Account of their Topography, Climate, Soil, and Productions. Edited by W. H. Smoult. *Maps and plates.* Royal 8° *Calcutta*, 1834

Baikie, Dr William Balfour. Narrative of an Exploring Voyage up the Rivers Kwo'ra and Binue (commonly known as the Niger and Tsáda) in 1854. *Map and plates.* 8° 1856

—— Observations on the Hausa and Fulfúlde Languages, with Examples. Privately printed. 8* 1861

—— Reports on the Geographical Position of the Countries in the Neighbourhood of the Niger, and on other matters connected with his Expedition. *Map.* Folio 1862

—— Despatches from, relative to the Trade of the River Niger, and to the eligibility of Central Africa as a future Cotton Field. *Map.* Folio* [1862]

—— Notes of a Journey from Bida in Nupe to Kano in Hausa, performed in 1862, by Dr W. B. Baikie, R.N., extracted from portions of Dr Baikie's Journals in possession of the Foreign Office. [Foreign Office publication.] Folio* 1866

—— *See* Adams; Reichardt.

Bailey, Capt. George W. Report upon Alaska and its People, giving Statistics as to the Numbers, Location, Pursuits, and Social Condition of the Inhabitants, the Climate, Productions, and General Resources of the Country, and of the Commerce, Ocean Currents, &c. *Map and plate.* 8* *Washington*, 1880

Bailie, A. C. The Amandebele. 8* *Grahamstown*, 1885

Baillie, Alexander F. A Paraguayan Treasure: the Search and the Discovery. *Map and plans.* Crown 8° 1887

—— Kurrachee (Karachi): Past, Present, and Future. *Map, plans, and photographs.* Large 8° 1890

Baillie, Marianne. First Impressions of a Tour upon the Continent in 1818, through Parts of France, Italy, Switzerland, the Borders of Germany, and a Part of French Flanders. *Plates.* 8° 1819

—— Lisbon in 1821-2-3. *Plates.* 2 vols. 12° 1825

—— *See* Phillips [3], Vol. 1: Appendix 1.

Baily, Francis. Account of John Flamsteed. Compiled from his own MSS., and other Authentic Documents; to which is added his British Catalogue of Stars, corrected and enlarged by Francis Baily. 4° 1835

—— Supplement to the above. 4° 1837

—— The Catalogue of Stars of the British Association for the Advancement of Science, containing the Mean Right Ascensions and North Polar Distances of 8,377 Fixed Stars, reduced to January 1850, together with their Annual Precessions, Secular Variations, and Proper Motions, as well as the Logarithmic Constants for Computing Precession, Aberration, and Nutation, with a Preface explanatory of their Construction and Application. 4° 1845

—— Journal of a Tour in Unsettled Parts of North America in 1796-97, with a Memoir of the Author. 8° 1856

—— *See* Herschel, Sir John F. W.

Baily, John. Central America, describing the States of Guatemala, Honduras, Salvador, Nicaragua, and Costa Rica, the Natural Features, &c. *Plates.* 8° 1850

Baily, Lieut. J. *See* Juarros.

Baily, L. C. Ship's Course Corrector. *One leaf.* 8* N.D.

Bain, Joseph, and Charles Rogers. Liber Protocollorum M. Cuthberti Simonis, notarii publici et scribæ capituli Glasguensis, A.D. 1499-1513; also Rental Book of Diocese of Glasgow, A.D. 1509-70. Edited by Joseph Bain and the Rev. Charles Rogers. [*Grampian Club Publications.*] Vols. 1 and 2. 8° *Edinburgh*, 1875

Baines, Thomas. Explorations in South-West Africa, being an Account of a Journey in 1861-62 from Walvisch Bay to Lake Ngami and the Victoria Falls. *Maps and illustrations.* 8° 1864
—— The Gold Regions of South-Eastern Africa; accompanied by a Biographical Sketch of the Author. *Map in cover, photographs, &c.* 8° 1877
—— *See* Lord, W. B.

Baird, Major A. W. A Manual for Tidal Observations, and their Reduction by the Method of Harmonic Analysis, with an Appendix containing Auxiliary Tables to facilitate the computations. *Illustrations.* 8° 1886
—— Spirit Levelling Operations of the Great Trigonometrical Survey of India. R.G.S. Supplementary Papers, Vol. 1. Large 8° 1886
—— **and E. Roberts.** Tide-Tables for the Indian Ports for the years 1881-87. 6 vols. 12°
—— *See* Hill; Rogers.

Baird, Prof. S. F. Directions for Collecting, Preserving, and Transporting Specimens of Natural History, prepared for the use of the Smithsonian Institution. 8* *Washington*, 1852
—— Ditto. 2nd edition. 8* *Washington*, 1854
—— *See* United States, K; California: Appendix 2.

Baker, A. Southern Servia as a British Market. *Map.* 8* 1888

Baker, A. C. *See* United States, E, Hydrogr. Off. Publ., No. 35: Appendix 2.

Baker, F. Report on the Butesur Fair of 1871. [From No. 2 of Vol. 6 of India Records, N.-W. Provinces.] 8° 1872

Baker, Capt. George. *See* Dalrymple, Repertory, Vol. 1: Appendix 1.

Baker, Hon. James H. The Sources of the Mississippi, their Discoveries, Real and Pretended: a Report read before the Minnesota Historical Society, 8th February 1887. 8* *Saint Paul, Minn.*, 1887

Baker, J. Turkey in Europe. *Maps.* 8° 1877

Baker, Marcus. Boundary Line between Alaska and Siberia. *Map.* 8* *Washington*, 1882

Baker, Sir Samuel White. Eight Years' Wanderings in Ceylon. *Plates.* 8° 1855
—— The Albert N'yanza, Great Basin of the Nile, and Explorations of the Nile Sources. 2 vols. *Maps and plates.* 8° 1866
—— Ditto. New edition. *Map and illustrations.* 8° 1888
—— The Nile Tributaries of Abyssinia, and the Sword Hunters of the Hamran Arabs. *Maps and plates.* 8° 1867

Baker, Sir Samuel White. Cyprus as I saw it in 1879. *Frontispiece.* 8° 1879
—— Ismailïa: a Narrative of the Expedition to Central Africa for the Suppression of the Slave Trade, organised by Ismail, Khedive of Egypt. 2 vols. *Maps and plates.* 8° 1874
—— Another edition. *Map and illustrations.* 8° 1886
—— Wild Beasts and their Ways: Reminiscences of Europe, Asia, Africa, and America. 2 vols. *Illustrations.* 8° 1890
—— *See* James, F. L.

Baker, R. *See* Kerr, Vol. 7; Allgemeine Historie, Vol. 1: Appendix 1.

Baker, Thomas Turner. The Recent Operations of the British Forces at Rangoon and Martaban. *Plates.* 8° 1852

Baker, Valentine. Clouds in the East: Travels and Adventures on the Perso-Turkoman Frontier. 2nd edition. *Maps and plates.* 8° 1876
—— War in Bulgaria: a Narrative of Personal Experiences. 2 vols. *Maps and plans.* 8° 1879

Baker, Major W. E. Letter on the proposed Canal between Loodianah and Ferozpore, May 1847. *Map.* [From the India Records, Vol. 2. (N.-W. Provinces).] 8° *Agra*, 1856

Baker, W. G. Realistic Elementary Geography, taught by Picture and Plan, embracing Direction, the Elements of Maps, Definitions, &c.; the Pictorial Examples are derived chiefly from the Geographical Features of England. *Maps and illustrations.* 12° 1888

Bakewell, F. C. Considerations respecting the Figure of the Earth in relation to the action of Centrifugal Force, and to the attempts to determine the Ellipticity of the Globe by Pendulum Observations. 8* 1862
—— A Dynamical Theory of the Figure of the Earth, proving the Poles to be elongated. 8* 1867

Balarin de Raconis, J. *See* Varthema.

Balbi, Adriano. Essai Statistique sur le Portugal et l'Algarve. 2 vols. 8° *Paris*, 1822
—— Introduction à l'Atlas Ethnographique du Globe. 8° *Paris*, 1826
—— Abrégé de Géographie, rédigé sur un nouveau Plan d'après les derniers Traités de Paix, et les Découvertes les plus récentes. 2 vols. 8° *Paris*, 1833
—— Abrégé de Géographie, augmenté d'une Table générale alphabétique. 8° *Paris*, 1834
—— Allgemeine Erdbeschreibung. Eine systematische Encyclopädie der Erdkunde. 2 vols. in 1. Royal 8° *Budapest*, 1842

Balbi, Adriano. Élémens de Géographie Générale, ou Description abrégée de la Terre, d'après ses divisions Politiques coordonnées avec ses grandes Divisions Naturelles, selon les dernières Transactions et les Découvertes les plus récentes. *Maps.* 12° *Paris*, 1843

—— Notice sur l'Histoire Militaire des Eléphans, &c., del Cav. Armandi. 8*
Milan, 1843

—— Dell' Influenza degli Elementi Idro-Atmosferici sulle Forze di Popolazione. 8* *Milan*, 1844

—— Elementi di Geografia Generale ossia Descrizione compendiata della Terra. *Maps.* 12° *Turin*, 1844

—— Miscellanea Italiana, ragionamenti di Geografia e Statistica patria. Raccolti e ordinati da Eugenio Balbi. 8°
Milan, 1845

—— Delle Primarie Altitudini del Globo, saggio d'Ipsometria generale. 4*
Milan, 1845

—— Della Popolazione del Portogallo dall' epoca Romana ai tempi nostri. 12*
Milan, 1846

—— Degli Studii Geografici in generale, e spezialmente in Italia. 8* *Milan*, 1846
—— San Marino. 8* [*Milan*, 1846]
—— *See* Malte-Brun.

—— **and Eugenio Balbi.** L'Austria e le primarie Potenze. 12° *Milan*, 1846
—— Nuovi Elementi di Geografia, saggio d'una Descrizione Generale della Terra. *Maps.* 12° *Turin*, 1851
—— Principii generali della Geografia. 12° *Milan*, 1864

Balbi, Eugenio. Regione Britannica. (From Vol. 4 of "Gea ossia La Terra descritta"). 8* *Trieste*, 1856
—— La Nostra Patria. Brevi Notizie di Geografia Italiana. 12* *Milan*, 1861
—— Studii di Geografia Elementare. 12°
Milan, 1862
—— Mondo Antico: Parte prima, L'Europa. 12° *Milan*, 1863
—— Ditto. Parte seconda e terza. L'Asia e l'Africa. 12° *Milan*, 1864
—— Saggio di Geografia elementare fisica e politica. 2nd edition. 12°
Milan, 1867
—— Nuovo Mondo. Mondo Marittimo. 12° *Milan*, 1868
—— I Momenti della Geografia nell' Evo medio e moderno. 8* *Pavia*, 1877

Balbi, Gasparo. Viaggio dell' Indie Orientali di G. Balbi. . . . Nelquale si contiene quanto egli in detto viaggio hà veduto per lo spatio di 9 Anni consumati in esso dal 1579 fino al 1588, &c. 12° *Venice*, 1590

—— *See* Gottfried; Pinkerton, Vol. 9: Purchas, Vol. 2, Book 10: Appendix 1.

Balboa, Miguel Cavello. *See* Ternaux-Compans, Vol. 15: Appendix 1.
Balboa, V. N. de. *See* Vasco Nuñes.
Balcarce, M. Buenos-Ayres, sa Situation présente, ses lois Libérales, sa population Immigrante, ses Progrès Commerciaux et Industriels. 8* *Paris*, 1857
Balch, Samuel W. History's Misleading Chronology. Reprinted from *Education*, Jan. 1893. 8* *Yonkers, N. Y.*, 1893
Baldæus, Philippus. Naauwkeurige Beschryvinge van Malabar en Choromandel. Derzelver aangrenzende Ryken, en het machtige Eyland Ceylon. Nevens een omstandige en grondigh doorzochte ontdekking en wederlegginge van de Afgoderye der Oost-Indische Heydenen. . . . Zijnde hier by gevoeght een Malabaarsche Spraak-Konst, &c. *Maps and plates.* Folio *Amsterdam*, 1672
—— *See* Veth; Churchill, Vol. 3: Appendix 1.
Baldelli Boni, G. B. Storia delle relazioni vicendevoli dell' Europa e dell' Asia dalla Decadenza di Roma fino alla Distruzione del Califfato. 2 vols. 4°
Florence, 1827
Baldi, Bernardino. La Nautica: Poema. 8* *Milan*, 1813
Baldrich, J. Amadeo. Las Comarcas virgenes. El Chaco Central Norte. *Map.* 8* *Buenos Ayres*, 1889
Baldwin, Archbishop. Itinerary through Wales, A.D. 1588. By Giraldus de Barri; translated by Sir R. C. Hoare. *Maps and plates.* 2 vols. 4° 1806
—— *See* Hakluyt, Vol. 2: Appendix 1.
Baldwin, D. D. Catalogue: Land and Fresh Water Shells of the Hawaiian Islands. 8* *Honolulu*, 1893
Baldwin, J. D. Pre-Historic Nations; or, Inquiries concerning some of the Great Peoples and Civilizations of Antiquity, and their probable relation to a still Older Civilization of the Ethiopians or Cushites of Arabia. Small 8°
New York, 1875
Baldwin, T. *See* Lippincott.
Baldwin, William C. African Hunting from Natal to the Zambesi, including Lake Ngami, the Kalahari Desert, &c., from 1852 to 1860. *Maps and plates.* 8°
1863
Bale, W. M. Australian Museum: Catalogue of the Australian Hydroid Zoophytes. *Plates.* 8° *Sydney*, 1884
Balfour, Surgeon-General Edward. Cyclopædia of India and of Eastern and Southern Asia, Commercial, Industrial, and Scientific, &c. 8° *Madras*, 1857
—— The Timber Trees, Timber and Fancy Woods, as also the Forests, of India and of Eastern and Southern Asia. Royal 8°
Madras, 1862

Balfour, Surgeon - General Edward, The Influence exercised by Trees on the Climate and Productiveness of the Peninsula of India. Folio* 1878
—— Report upon the Government Central Museum and the Local Museums in the Provinces, for 1855-56; with Appendices. [From the India Records, No. 39.] Royal 8° *Madras,* 1857
—— The Cyclopædia of India and of Eastern Southern Asia, Commercial, Industrial, and Scientific; Products of the Mineral, Vegetable, and Animal Kingdoms, Useful Arts and Manufactures. 3 vols. 3rd edition. 8° 1885
Balfour, F. C. The Life of Sheikh Hazin Mohammed Ali. Written by himself. Translated from two Persian MSS 8* 1830
Balfour, Sir G. Trade and Salt in India Free. 8* 1875
Balfour, Prof. Isaac Bayley. Botany of Socotra. Forming Vol. 31 of the Transactions of the Royal Society of Edinburgh. *Map and plates.* 4° *Edinburgh,* 1888
Ball, E. A. Reynolds. Mediterranean Winter Resorts : a Practical Handbook to the Principal Health and Pleasure Resorts on the Shores of the Mediterranean. *Map, illustrations.* 12° 1888
—— Ditto, 2nd edition. *Map and illustrations.* 12° 1892
Ball, John. Peaks, Passes, and Glaciers : a Series of Excursions by Members of the Alpine Club. Edited by J. Ball. *Maps and plates.* 8° 1859
—— A Guide to the Eastern Alps. *Maps.* 12° 1874
—— The Central Alps, including the Bernese Oberland, and all Switzerland excepting the neighbourhood of Monte Rosa and the Great St Bernard, with Lombardy and the adjoining portion of Tyrol. *Maps.* 12° 1876
—— A Guide to the Western Alps. *Maps.* 12° 1877
—— Notes of a Naturalist in South America. *Map.* Crown 8° 1887
—— On the Measurement of Heights by the Barometer. R.G.S. Supplementary Papers. Vol. 2. Large 8° 1889
—— *See* Hooker.
Ball, Lieut. *See* Philip ; Pelham, Vol. 1 : Appendix 1.
Ball, Sir Robert S. Atlas of Astronomy. Small 4° 1892
Ball, Prof. Valentine. On the Ancient Copper Miners of Singhbúm. 8* [*Calcutta,* 1869]
—— Notes on the Geology of the Vicinity of Port Blair, Andaman Islands. 8* [*Calcutta,* 1870]

Ball, Prof. Valentine. Notes on Birds observed in the Neighbourhood of Port Blair, Andaman Islands, during the month of August 1869. 8* [*Calcutta,* 1870]
—— Names of Birds, &c., in Four of the Aboriginal Languages of Western Bengal. 8* [*Calcutta,* 1871]
—— On the Forms and Geographical Distribution of Ancient Stone Implements in India. *Map and plates.* Small 8* *Dublin,* 1879
—— Jungle Life in India, or the Journey and Journals of an Indian Geologist. *Map and plates.* 8° 1880
—— Travels in India, by Jean Baptiste Tavernier, Baron of Aubonne. Translated from the original French edition of 1676, with a Biographical Sketch of the Author, Notes, Appendices, &c. *Maps, portraits, &c.* 2 vols. Large 8° 1889
—— *See* India, C : Appendix 2.
Ballhorn, F. Grammatography. Royal 8° 1861
Ballivian, M. V. Exploraciones y Noticias Hidrográficas de los Rios del Norte de Bolivia : Primera Parte — Traducciones, reproducciones y documentos inéditos ; Segunda Parte— Diario del Viage al Madre de Dios hecho por el P. Fr. Nicolás Armentia, en los años de 1884 y 1885, en calidad de Comisionado para explorar el Madre de Dios, y su distancia al rio Acre, y para fundar algunas misiones entre las tribus araonas. Small 8° *La Paz,* 1890
—— Documentos Históricos de Bolivia Historia de la Mision de los Mójos, por el Padre Diego Francisco Altamirano, de la Compañia de Jesús. 8° *La Paz,* 1891
—— **and Eduardo Idiaquez.** Diccionario Geográfico de la República de Bolivia. Tomo Primero, Departamento de la Paz. Large 8° *La Paz,* 1890
—— Noticia Politica, Geográfica, y Comercial de Bolivia, escrita para el "Statesman's Year-Book." 8* *La Paz,* 1891
Ballou, Maturin M. Due South : Cuba, Past and Present. 8° *New York,* 1885
Balmat, J. *See* Carrier.
"Bamang-Wato." To Ophir Direct, or the South African Gold Fields ; with a Map showing the Route taken by Hartley and Mauch, in 1866-67. *Map.* 8* 1868
Banaré. *See* Chambeyron.
Banbury, G. A. Lethbridge. Sierra Leone, or the White Man's Grave. *Illustrations.* 8° 1888
Bancroft, Edward. Essay of the Natural History of Guiana, in South America ; containing a Description of many curious Productions in the Animal and Vegetable Systems of that Country, and an Account of the Religion, Manners, and Customs of several Tribes of its Indian Inhabitants. *Frontispiece.* 8° 1769

Bancroft, G.   *See* Heeren.

Bancroft, Hubert Howe.   The Native Races of the Pacific States of North America.   5 vols.   *Maps.*   8°   1875-76

—— The Works of Hubert Howe Bancroft.   39 vols. [including above].   *Portrait, maps.*   8°   *San Francisco*, 1883-90

CONTENTS.

Vol. 6.—History of Central America, vol. 1, 1501-30.
Vol. 7.—Ditto, vol. 2, 1530-1800.
Vol. 8.—Ditto, vol. 3, 1801-87.
Vol. 9.—History of Mexico, vol. 1, 1516-21.
Vol. 10.—Ditto, vol. 2, 1521-1600.
Vol. 11.—Ditto, vol. 3, 1600-1803.
Vol. 12.—Ditto, vol. 4, 1804-24.
Vol. 13.—Ditto, vol. 5, 1824-61.
Vol. 14.—Ditto, vol. 6, 1861-87.
Vol. 15.—History of the North Mexican States and Texas, vol. 1, 1531-1800.
Vol. 16.—Ditto, vol. 2, 1801-89.
Vol. 17.—History of Arizona and New Mexico, 1530-1888.
Vol. 18.—History of California, vol. 1, 1542-1800.
Vol. 19.—Ditto, vol. 2, 1801-24.
Vol. 20.—Ditto, vol. 3, 1825-40.
Vol. 21.—Ditto, vol. 4, 1840-45.
Vol. 22.—Ditto, vol. 5, 1846-48.
Vol. 23.—Ditto, vol. 6, 1848-59.
Vol. 24.—Ditto, vol. 7, 1860-90.
Vol. 25.—History of Nevada, Colorado, and Wyoming, 1540-1888.
Vol. 26.—History of Utah, 1540-1886.
Vol. 27.—History of the North - West Coast, vol. 1, 1543-1800.
Vol. 28.—Ditto, vol. 2, 1800-46.
Vol. 29.—History of Oregon, vol. 1, 1834-48.
Vol. 30.—Ditto, vol. 2, 1848-88.
Vol. 31.—History of Washington, Idaho, and Montana, 1845-89.
Vol. 32.—History of British Columbia, 1792-1887.
Vol. 33.—History of Alaska, 1730-1885.
Vol. 34.—California Pastoral, 1769-1848.
Vol. 35.—California Inter Pocula.
Vol. 36.—Popular Tribunals, vol. 1.
Vol. 37.—Ditto, vol. 2.
Vol. 38.—Essays and Miscellany.
Vol. 39.—Literary Industries.

Bandeira, Marquez de Sá da.   Faits et Considérations relatives aux Droits du Portugal sur les territoires de Molembo, de Cabinde, et d'Ambriz, et autres lieux de la côte Occidentale d'Afrique.   *Maps and plans.*   8*   *Lisbon*, 1855

—— O Trabalho rural Africano e a Administração Colonial.   8°   *Lisbon*, 1873

—— Extrait du Rapport lu dans la première séance solennelle de la Société de Géographie de Lisbonne, le 7 Mars 1877, par R. A. Pequito.   8*   *Lisbon*, 1878

Bandinel, James.   Some Account of the Trade in Slaves from Africa as connected with Europe and America, from the Introduction of the Trade into Modern Europe down to the present time, especially with reference to the efforts made by the British Government for its extinction.   Royal 8°   1842

Baness, J. F.   Index Geographicus Indicus, being a list, alphabetically arranged, of the Principal Places in Her Imperial Majesty's Indian Empire, with Notes and Statements, Statistical, Political, and Descriptive, of the several Provinces and Administrations of the Empire, the Native States, Independent and Feudatory, attached to and in political relationship with each ; and other information relating to India and the East.   *Maps.*   8°
                                              1881

Banister. T.   *See* Hakluyt, Vol. 1 : Appendix 1.

Banks, Sir Joseph.   *See* Troil, Uno von.

Bankes, Thomas.   A Modern, Authentic, and Complete System of Universal Geography, including all the late important Discoveries made by the English, and other celebrated Navigators of various Nations, in the different Hemispheres, and containing a Genuine History and Description of the whole World.   *Maps and plates.*   2 vols.   Folio   N.D.

Banning, Émile.   L'Afrique et la Conférence Géographique de Bruxelles.   *Map.*   8°   *Brussels*, 1877

—— Ditto.   2nd edition.   *Maps and plates.*   8°   *Brussels*, 1878

—— Le Partage Politique de l'Afrique d'après les Transactions Internationales les plus récentes (1885 à 1888).   *Map.*   8°
                                   Brussels, 1888

Bannister, Saxe.   Memoir respecting British Interests, and the Interests of the Native Tribes at and near Natal, in South-Eastern Africa.   *Map.*   8*   1838

—— Control of the Privy Council over the Administration of Affairs at Home, in the Colonies, and in India.   8*   1844

—— On the Right to be heard on Petitions to the Crown, and the Control of the Privy Council (by Appeal) over Indian, &c., Affairs.   8*   1844

—— Classical Sources of the History of the British Isles, or the Rise and Fall of the Romans in Britain.   *Map.*   8°   1849

—— Pictorial Maps for the Illustration of the Land, the Sea, and the Heavens, on the Walls of large Buildings and Georamas, and Lectures on Geography.   8*
                                              1849

—— Records of British Enterprise beyond Sea, from the Earliest Original Sources to the Present Time.   Vol. I, Part 1.   8*
                                              1849

Bannister, Saxe. Journal of the First French Embassy to China, 1698-1700. Translated from an unpublished MS. by Saxe Bannister; with an Essay on the Friendly Disposition of the Chinese Government and People to Foreigners. 8° 1859
—— Some Revelations in Irish History; or, Old Elements of Creed and Class Conciliation in Ireland [including T. Sheridan's Discourse on the Rise and Power of Parliaments, 1677]. Square 8° 1870
—— Prospects and Progress of British Colonisation and Foreign Commerce. 8* N.D.

Baptista, J. Renato. Africa Oriental. Caminho de Ferro da Beira a Manica, 1891. *Maps and plates.* 4° *Lisbon*, 1892

Baraban, Léopold. A Travers la Tunisie: Études sur les Oasis, les Dunes, les Forêts, la Flore, et la Géologie. *Map and illustrations.* 8° *Paris*, 1887

Baralt, Raphael M. Resúmen de la Historia de Venezuela, desde el Descubrimiento de su territoria por los Castellanos en el Siglo XV., hasta 1797; ha cooperado á él en la parte relativa a las guerras de la Conquista de la Costa-Firme el Ramon Diaz. *Portraits.* 8° *Paris*, 1841
—— **and Ramon Diaz.** Resúmen de la Historia de Venezuela, desde 1797 hasta 1830; tiene al fin un breve Bosquejo Histórico que comprende 1831 hasta 1837. *Portraits.* 2 vols. 8° *Paris*, 1841

Barante, C. J. Essai sur le Départment de l'Aude. 8* *Geneva*, 1802

Baratti, Giacomo. The late Travels of S. Giacomo Baratti, an Italian Gentleman, into the remote Countries of the Abissins, or of Ethiopia Interior. . . ; together with a Confirmation of this Relation drawn from the writings of Damianus de Goes and Jo. Scaliger. . . . Translated by G. D. 8° 1670

Barbaro, J., and A. Contarini. *See* Hakluyt Soc. Publ., Vol. 49; Kerr, Vol. 1; Ramusio, Vol. 2: Appendix 1.

Barber, G. D. Ancient Oral Records of the Cimri, or Britons, in Asia and Europe, recovered through a literal Aramitic translation of the Old Welsh Bardic Relics. 8° 1815

Barberena, S. J. Descripcion Geografica y Estadistica de la República del Salvador. 8° *San Salvador*, 1892

Barbey, William. *See* Stefani.

Barbiani, D. G. and B. A. Mémoire sur les Tremblements de Terre dans l'île de Zante; avec une introduction par Alexis Perrey. 8* [*Paris*, 1864]

Barbichon, D. M. Dictionnaire complet de tous les Lieux de la France et de ses Colonies; contenant la nomenclature et la description exacte sous les Rapports Géographiques, Statistiques, Commerciaux, Historiques et Administratifs, des Villes, Bourgs, Villages, et Hameaux composant les 37,207 communes de la France, &c. 2 vols. 8° *Paris*, 1831

Barbié du Bocage, J. G. *See* Recueil de Voyages, Vol. 2, p. 611: Appendix 1.

Barbié du Bocage, V. A. Madagascar, possession Française depuis 1642. *Map* by V. A. Malte-Brun. 8° *Paris*, 1859

Barbiellini, C. A. Nuova Descrizione Geografica d' Italia, Antica e Moderna. *Map.* 2 vols. 8° *Milan*, 1806

Barbier de Meynard, C. Dictionnaire Géographique, Historique, et Littéraire de la Perse et des Contrées adjacentes. Extrait du Mo'djem El-Bouldan de Yaqout, et complété à l'aide de documents Arabes et Persans pour la plupart inédits. 8° *Paris*, 1861
—— Dictionnaire Turc-Français; Supplément aux Dictionnaires publiés jusqu'à ce jour. 2 vols. (IIe series, Vols. 4 and 5 of Publications de l'Ecole des Langues Orientales Vivantes.) Large 8° *Paris*, 1881-86

Barbier, J. V. Essai d'un Lexique Géographique. *Table.* 8* *Paris*, 1886
—— *See* Auerbach.

Barbinais, L. G. de la. *See* Burney, Vol. 4; Callander, Vol. 3; Laharpe, Vol. 15; Allgemeine Historie, Vol. 12, p. 605: Appendix 1.

Barbosa, Da Cunha. *See* Santarem.

Barbosa, Duarte or Odoardo. *See* Hakluyt Soc. Publ., Vol. 35; Ramusio, Vol. 1; Collecção de Noticias, Vol. 2, p. 610: Appendix 1.

Barbot, J. *See* Astley, Vol. 3; Churchill, Vol. 5; Allgemeine Historie, Vols. 3, 4, p. 602: Appendix 1.

Barca, Madame C. de la. Life in Mexico during a Residence of Two Years in that Country; with a Preface by W. H. Prescott. 8° 1843

Bárcena, M. Viaje a la Caverna de Cacahuamilpa, datos para la Geologia y la Flora de los Estados de Morelos.y Guerrero. *Plates.* 8* *Mexico*, 1874
—— Description de la Ciudad de Guadalajara, capital del Estado de Jalisco. *Plans.* 8* *Mexico*, 1880
—— *See* Castillo.

Barclay, Edgar. Mountain Life in Algeria. *Illustrations.* Royal 8° 1882

Barclay, H. *See* South Australia, A: Appendix 2.

Barclay, J. G. Astronomical Observations taken at the Private Observatory, Leyton, Essex. Vols. 1-4, 1862-77. 4° 1865-78

Barclay, J. T. City of the Great King ; or, Jerusalem as it was, as it is, and as it is to be. *Maps.* 8° *Philadelphia,* 1857

Barco, Martin de el. Argentina y Conquista del Rio de la Plata [a Poem]. Folio*   *Madrid,* 1730

Bard, Samuel A. Adventures on the Mosquito Shore. *Maps and illustrations.* 12°   1857

Baretus, John. *See* Purchas, Vol. 2, Book 7 : Appendix 1.

Bardin, L. I. La Topographie enseignée par des Plans-Reliefs et des dessins . . . Introduction. 4*   *Metz,* 1859

—— La Topographie enseignée par des dessins. 4*   *Paris,* 1867

—— *See* Huber, W.

Barents, W. *See* Hakluyt Soc. Publ., Vol. 54; Purchas, Vol. 3, Book 3 ; Allgemeine Historie, Vol. 17 : Appendix 1.

Baretti, S. J. *See* "The Modern · Traveller," p. 610 : Appendix 1.

Baretti. *See* Dictionaries : Appendix 2.

Baring, Sir E. *See* Egypt, A : Appendix 2.

Baring - Gould, Sabine. Iceland, its Scenes and Sagas. *Map and plates.* Royal 8*   1863

Barker, And. *See* Hakluyt, Vol. 4 : Appendix 1.

Barker, Edmund. *See* Astley, Vol. 1 : Appendix 1.

Barker, James N. Sketches of the Primitive Settlements on the River Delaware. 8*   *Philadelphia,* 1828

Barker, T. H. On the Relative Value of Ozonometers. 8*   1856

Barker, W. Burckhardt. Lares and Penates ; or, Cilicia and its Governors, being a Short Historical Account of that Province from the Earliest Times to the Present Day. Edited by W. F. Ainsworth. *Woodcuts.* 8°   1853

—— Practical Grammar of the Turkish Language, with Dialogues and Vocabulary. 12°   1854

Barker, Capt. W. C. On the Lighting up the Entrance to Bombay Harbour, &c. 8*   *Bombay,* 1862

Barkley, George. *See* Purchas, Vol. 3, Book 3 : Appendix 1.

Barkley, H. C. Between the Danube and Black Sea, or Five Years in Bulgaria. *Map.* Small 8°   1876

—— A Ride through Asia Minor and Armenia, giving a Sketch of the Characters, Manners, and Customs of both the Mussulman and Christian Inhabitants. 8°   1891

Barlow, A. *See* Hakluyt, Vol. 3 ; Allgemeine Historie, Vol. 17 : Appendix 1.

Barlow, J, W., and D. P. Heap. Report of a Reconnaissance in Wyoming and Montana Territories, 1871 : Letters, &c. *Map.* 8*   1872

Barlow, S. L. M. *See* Catalogues, A . Appendix 2.

Barlow, Peter. Essay on Magnetic Attractions, and on the Laws of Terrestrial and Electro Magnetism ; with an Appendix containing the Result of Experiments on Shipboard from lat. 61° 5' S. to lat. 80° N. *Plates.* 8°   1824

Barlow, Peter W. On Some Peculiar Features of the Water-bearing Strata of the London Basin. Edited by Charles Manby. 8*   1855

Barnard, Lieut. A Three Years Cruise in the Mozambique Channel for the Suppression of the Slave Trade. 12° 1848

Barnard, M. R. *See* Schübeler.

Barne, Jorge. *See* Angelis, Vol. 5 : Appendix 1.

Barnes, G. C. Notes on the System of Irrigation prevailing in the Upper Valleys of the Kangra District. *Map.* [In the India Records, N. W. Provinces, Vol. 2.]   *Allahabad,* 1856

Barnes' Hawaiian Geography. *Maps and illustrations.* Small 4°   *New York,* N.D.

Barnett, Capt. E. West India Pilot. From Cape North of the Amazons to Cape Sable in Florida, with the Outlying Islands, the Caribbean Sea, from Barbadoes to Cuba ; with the Bahama and Bermuda Islands, and Florida Strait. 2 vols. 8°   1859-61

—— *See* United Kingdom, A : Appendix 2.

Baron, Rev. R. On the Flora and Geology of Madagascar ; with Two Papers on Fossils and Rock Specimens from Madagascar, by R. B. Newton and F. H. Hatch. *Maps and plate.* 8* 1889

—— *See* Madagascar : Appendix 2.

Baron, S. *See* Churchill, Vol. 6 ; Pinkerton, Vol. 9 ; Allgemeine Historie, Vol. 10 : Appendix 1.

Barr, Capt. J. T. Narrative of the Nature of the British Relations with the Native States in the Province of Kattywar, with Notes. Royal 8°
                                 Bombay, 1856

—— Information relative to the Wandering Tribes in the Province of Kattywar. [From the India Records, No. 37.] Royal 8°   *Bombay,* 1856

Barr, William. Journal of a March from Delhi to Peshâwur, and from thence to Cabul . . ; including Travels in the Punjâb, a Visit to the City of Lahore, and a Narrative of Operations in the Kyber Pass undertaken in 1839. *Plates.* 12°   1844

Barral. *See* Silas, F.

Barrande, Joachim. Défense des Colonies. [Geological.] Parts 1 and 3. *Map and plate.* 8*   *Prague,* 1861 and 1865

Barraud, C. D. *See* New Zealand : Appendix 2.

Barret, Dr Paul. Sénégambie et Guinée : la Région Gabonaise ; l'Afrique Occidentale, la Nature et l'Homme noir. 2 vols. *Maps.* 8° *Paris*, 1888

Barret, W. *See* Kerr, Vol. 8 : Appendix 1.

Barrett, Alfred. *See* Yates, James.

Barrett, C. R. B. Essex : Highways, Byways, and Waterways. *Illustrations.* Small 4° 1892

—— Ditto. 2nd series. *Illustrations.* Small 4° 1893

Barrett-Lennard, Capt. C. E. Travels in British Columbia, with the Narrative of a Yacht Voyage round Vancouver's Island. *Frontispiece.* 8° 1862

Barrington, Daines. The Probability of reaching the North Pole discussed. Small 4° 1775

—— The Possibility of approaching the North Pole asserted ; with an Appendix containing Papers on the same Subject, and on a North-West Passage, by Colonel Beaufoy. 8° 1818

Barrio, Don Paulino del. Noticia sobre el Torreno Carbonifero de Coronel i Lota. *Map and plates.* Folio* *Santiago*, 1857

Barron, C. *See* Adams.

Barron, Lieut.-Col. The Cadastral Survey of India, R.G.S. Supplementary Papers, Vol. 1. Large 8° 1886

Barros, J. de. Da Asia de João de Barros e de Diogo de Couto. Nova edição. *Plates.* 24 vols. 12° *Lisbon*, 1777-88
CONTENTS.
Da Asia de João de Barros. Dos feitos que os Portuguezes fizeram na conquista e descubrimento das terras e mares de Oriente. [4 decades, each in 2 parts] 1777
Vida de João de Barros, por Manoel Severim de Faria, e Indice geral das quatro decadas da sua Asia 1778
Continuação da Asia de João de Barros, por Diogo de Couto. Da Asia de Diogo do Couto. Dos feitos, &c. [as above]. Decada IV., 2 pts., 1778 ; V., pt. 1, 1779 ; pt. 2, 1780 ; VI., 2 pts., 1781 ; VII., pt. 1, 1782, pt. 2, 1783 ; VIII. and IX., 1786 ; X., 2 pts., XI. and XII., 1788.
Indice geral das Decadas de Couto. N.D.

—— *See* Astley, Vol. 1 ; Ramusio, Vol. 1 ; Allgemeine Historie, Vol. 1 : Appendix 1.

Barrow, Major E. G. Routes in Dárdistan and Káfiristán. 8* *Simla*, 1886
—— Report on the British Trans-Salween Districts of Indo-China. *Map and plan.* 8° *Simla*, 1890

Barrow, Sir George. Ceylon, Past and Present. *Map.* 8° 1857

Barrow, John [*Author of the Geographical Dictionary*]. A Collection of Authentic, Useful, and Entertaining Voyages and Discoveries, digested in a Chronological Series. Vol. 1. *Plates.* 12° 1765

Barrow, Sir John. Account of Travels into the Interior of Southern Africa in 1797-98, including cursory Observations on the Geology, Geography, and Natural History of the Southern part of that Continent, and Sketches of the Physical and Moral Characters of the various Tribes surrounding the Settlement of the Cape of Good Hope. *Maps and plates.* 2 vols. 4° 1801-4

—— Travels in China, containing Descriptions, Observations, and Comparisons, made and collected in the course of a Short Residence at the Imperial Palace of Yuen-Min-Yuen, and on a Journey from Pekin to Canton. *Plates.* 4° 1804

—— Voyage to Cochin-China in 1792-93 ; to which is annexed an Account of a Journey made in 1801-2 to the Residence of the Chief of the Booshuana Nation, being the remotest point in the Interior of Southern Africa to which Europeans have hitherto penetrated. *Map and plates.* 4° 1806

—— Chronological History of Voyages into the Arctic Regions, undertaken chiefly for the purpose of discovering a North-east, North-west, or Polar passage between the Atlantic and Pacific, from the Earliest Periods of Scandinavian Navigation to the Departure of the Recent Expeditions under Captains Ross and Buchan. *Map.* 8° 1818

—— The Life of George, Lord Anson, Admiral of the Fleet. 8° 1839

—— Voyages of Discovery and Research within the Arctic Regions, from the year 1818 to the Present Time, abridged and arranged from the Original Narratives, with Occasional Remarks. *Maps and portraits.* 8° 1846

—— An Autobiographical Memoir of, including Reflections, Observations, and Reminiscences at Home and Abroad, from Early Life to Advanced Age. *Portrait.* 8° 1847

Barrow, John. Excursions in the North of Europe, through parts of Russia, Finland, Sweden, Denmark, and Norway, in 1830 and 1833. *Map.* 8° 1834

—— Tour Round Ireland, through the Sea-Coast Counties, in 1835. *Map and plates.* 8° 1836

—— Visit to Iceland, by way of Tronyem, in 1834. *Plates.* 8° 1837

Barrow, John. Tour in Austrian Lombardy, the Northern Tyrol, and Bavaria, in 1840. 8°   1841
—— The Life, Voyages, and Exploits of Admiral Sir Francis Drake. 8° 1843
—— Tour on the Continent by Rail or Road, in 1852, through Northern Germany, Austria, Tyrol, Austrian Lombardy, &c. *Map.* 12°   1853
Barrow, J. Expeditions on the Glaciers; including an Ascent of Mont Blanc, Monte Rosa, Col du Géant, and Mont Muét. *Portrait.* 8°   1864
Barry, David. *See* Juan.
Barry, Frederick W. *See* Cyprus: Appendix 2.
Barry, Dr Martin. Ascent of Mont Blanc in 1834. *Plates.* 8° *Edinburgh*, 1836
Barry, John Warren. Studies in Corsica, sylvan and social. *Map and illustrations.* 8°   1893
Barth, Dr Henry. Wanderungen durch die Küstenländer des Mittelmeeres, 1845 - 7. Erster Band. Das Nordafrikanische Gestadeland. *Map.* 8° *Berlin*, 1849
—— Travels and Discoveries in North and Central Africa, being a Journal of an Expedition undertaken in 1849-55. *Maps and plates.* 5 vols. 8°   1857
—— Reise von Trapezunt durch die nördliche Hälfte Klein-Asiens nach Scutari im Herbst 1858, mit einer Karte von Dr A. Petermann (Ergänzungsheft Vol. 1, Petermann's Mittheilungen). *Maps and plates.* 4°   *Gotha*, 1860
—— Sammlung und Bearbeitung Central-Afrikanischer Vokabularien. . . . Collection of Vocabularies of Central-African Languages. . . . Part 1. Larger Vocabularies of the Kanúri, Tédá, Hausa, Ful-ful-de, Sonõai, Lógonē, Wándalā, Bágrimma, and Māba Languages. Introductory Remarks, Chap. 1-6, &c. Large 8°   *Gotha*, 1862
—— Collection of Vocabularies of Central-African Languages. Part 2.—Introductory Remarks, Chap. 7-12. Analysis of the Fulfūlde, Songai, Lógone, Wándalā, Bágrimma, and Māba Languages. Part 3, Nouns. Royal 8° *Gotha*, 1863-66
—— Travels and Discoveries in North and Central Africa, including accounts of Tripoli, the Sahara, the remarkable kingdom of Bornu, and the Countries around Lake Chad. (Minerva Library.) *Map and illustrations.* 12°   1890
—— Ditto.—(II.) Including accounts of Timbúktu, Sókoto, and the Basins of the Niger and Bénuwé. (Minerva Library). *Illustrations.* 12°   1890
—— Dr Balfour Baikie's Thätigkeit am unteren Niger, mit besonderer Berücksichtigung der Flussschwellen dieses Stromes und derjenigen des Tsād- und Nilbeckens. *Tables.* 8* *Berlin*, N.D.

Barth, Dr Henry. *See* Hodgson, W. B.; Jomard; Malte-Brun; Petermann; Schauenberg.
Bartholemæus, —. Breves in Sphæram Meditatiunculæ, includentes Methodum et Isagogen in Universam Cosmographiam; hoc est, Geographiæ pariter atque Astronomiæ initia ac Rudimenta Suggerentes. *Woodcuts.* 12° *Cologne*, 1563
[*Bound up with works by Borrhaus, Theodoricus, &c., the whole entitled* "Cosmographia."]
Barthélemy, Abbé. Voyage du Jeune Anacharsis en Grèce, dans le milieu du quatrième siècle avant l'ère vulgaire. 7 vols. and atlas vol. 4° *Paris*, 1790
—— Voyage en Italie. 12° *Paris*, 1801
Barthema, Ludovico di. *See* Varthema.
Bartholomew, Capt. D. E. Voyage to the Cape Verd Islands, Coast of Africa, and Western Islands. MS. 4° 1819
Bartholomew, John. Gazetteer of the British Isles, Statistical and Topographical, with Appendices and Special Maps and Charts. Large 8°   *Edinburgh*, 1887
—— The same, with Census Supplement, 1891, and Appendices. [Without maps.] Large 8°   *Edinburgh* [1893]
Bartholomew, J. G. The Pocket Gazetteer of the World. 16°   1888
—— Ditto. Census edition   1892
Bartlett, John Russell. Personal Narrative of Explorations and Incidents in Texas, New Mexico, California, Sonora, and Chihuahua, connected with the United States and Mexican Boundary Commission, 1850-53. *Maps and plates.* 2 vols. 8°   *New York*, 1854
—— *See* United States, E (Hydrogr. Off. Publ., No. 48): Appendix 2.
Bartlett, W. A. *See* MacArthur, W. P.
Bartlett, W. H. Syria, the Holy Land, Asia Minor, &c., illustrated by Bartlett, Purser, Allom, &c., with Descriptions by John Carne. *Maps and plates.* 3 vols. 4°   1836-38
—— Canadian Scenery Illustrated. The Literary Department by N. P. Willis. *Map and plates.* 2 vols. 4°   1842
—— The Nile Boat, or Glimpses of the Land of Egypt. *Maps and plates.* Royal 8°   1850
—— Gleanings, Pictorial and Antiquarian, on the Overland Route. *Plates.* Royal 8°   1851
—— American Scenery; or, Land, Lake, and River Illustrations of Transatlantic Nature. The Literary Department by N. P. Willis. *Maps and plates.* 2 vols. 4°   1852
—— Jerusalem Revisited. *Plates.* 8° 1855
—— Walks about the City and Environs of Jerusalem (1842). *Maps and plates.* Royal 8°   N.D.

Bartlett, W. H. Forty Days in the Desert on the Track of the Israelites, or a Journey from Cairo by Wady Feiran to Mount Sinai and Petra. 4th edition. *Map and plates.* 8° N.D.

Bartoli, D. Missione al Gran Mogor del P. Ridolfo Aquaviva della-Compagnia di Gesú, sua Vite e Morte . . . 8° *Piacenza,* 1819

Bartoli, M. E., and L. P. de Ramón. España y sus Colonias : Noticia de su Población, Agricultura, Industria, y Comercio, &c., &c. 4° *Barcelona,* 1891

Bartolini, D. Viaggio da Napoli alle Forche Caudine ed a Benevento, e di ritorno a Caserta, ed a Monte-Casino. Small 8° *Naples,* 1827

Bartolomeo, Fra Paolino da San. Viaggio alle Indie Orientali, &c. *Plates.* 4° *Rome,* 1796

—— A Voyage to the East Indies, containing an Account of the Manners, Customs, &c., of the Natives, with a Geographical Description of the Country ; collected from Observations made during a Residence of Thirteen Years, between 1776 and 1789, in Districts little frequented by the Europeans ; with Notes and Illustrations by John Reinhold Forster. Translated from the German by William Johnston. 8° 1800

Bartolozzi, Francesco. Ricerche Istorico-critiche circa alle scoperti d' Amerigo Vespucci, con l'aggiunta di una Relazione del Medesimo, fin ora inedita. 8* *Florence,* 1789

Barton, E. *See* Hakluyt, Vol. 2; Purchas, Vol. 2, Book 8 : Appendix 1.

Barton, Lieut. J. *See* Dalrymple, Repertory, Vol. 2 : Appendix 1.

Barton, Richard. Lectures in Natural Philosophy upon the Petrifications, Gems, Crystals, and Sanitive Quality of Lough Neagh in Ireland. *Maps and plates.* 4° *Dublin,* 1751

Bartram, John. Observations on the Inhabitants, Climate, Soil, Rivers, Productions, Animals, and other Matters worthy of Notice, in his Travels from Pennsylvania to Mondaga, Oswego, and the Lake Ontario, in Canada ; to which is annexed a Curious Account of the Cataracts at Niagara by P. Kalm. *Plate.* 8° 1751

Bartram, W. Travels through North and South Carolina, Georgia, East and West Florida, the Cherokee Country, the extensive Territories of the Muscogulges or Creek Confederacy, and the Country of the Chactaws, &c. *Map and plates.* 4° 1792

Bartsch, S. Rotatoria Hungariæ. *Plates.* 8° *Budapest,* 1877

Barttelot, W. G. The Life of Edmund Musgrave Barttelot, Captain and Brevet-Major Royal Fusiliers, Commander of the Rear Column of the Emin Pasha Relief Expedition : being an Account of his Services for the Relief of Kandahar, of Gordon, and of Emin, from his Letters and Diary. 2nd edition. *Maps and portrait.* 8° 1890

Baruck, Élie M. *See* Hassan.

Barwick, Captain F. M. Diary of a Voyage from Bhamo to the Upper Reaches of the Irráwaddy, in the B. G. launch "Pathfinder," and from Sinbo to Mogaung, and thence to the Indawgyi Lake by way of the Indawchaung. *Maps and plates.* Folio* *Rangoon,* 1890

Barwick, G. F. *See* Columbus.

Barzi, C. M. *See* Mosca-Barzi.

Bas, F. de. De Residentie-Kaarten van Java en Madoera. *Maps.* 4* *Amsterdam,* 1876

—— Avis Impartial dans la Question du Congo. 8* *Schiedam,* 1890

Basevi, A., and G. E. Fritzsche. La Rappresentazione Orografica a Luce Doppia nella Cartografia Moderna. *Plate.* 8* *Rome,* 1892

Basevi, Capt. J. F., and W. J. Heaviside. *See* India, F, c, Trigonom. Surveys: Appendix 2.

"Basilisk." *See* Moresby.

Basiner, T. F. J. *See* Baer and Helmersen, 15.

Bass, George. *See* Eyriès, Vol. 4: Appendix 1.

Basset, James. Persia, the Land of the Imams : a Narrative of Travel and Residence, 1871-85. *Map.* 8° 1887 [1886]

Bastiaanse, J. H. van Boudyck. Voyage à la Côte de Guinée, dans la Golfe de Biafra, à l'île de Fernando Po, l'île de St Hélène, et autres îles dans le Passage, à bord du brickgoelette "Le Lancier." 8° *The Hague,* 1853

Bastian, Adolf. Afrikanische Reisen : Ein Besuch in San Salvador, der Hauptstadt des Königreichs Congo ; ein Beitrag zur Mythologie und Psychologie. 8° *Bremen,* 1859

—— Der Mensch in der Geschichte. 3 vols. 8° *Leipzig,* 1860

—— Die Völker des östlichen Asien : Studien und Reisen. 8° *Leipzig,* 1866-68

Vol. 1. Die Geschichte der Indochinesen.

Vol. 2. Reisen in Birma in den Jahren 1861-62. 8° *Leipzig,* 1866

Vol. 3. Reisen in Siam in Jahre 1863.

Vol. 4. Reise durch Kambodja nach Cochin China. 8° *Jena,* 1868

c

Bastian, Adolf. Das Beständige in den Menschenrassen und die Spielweite ihrer Veränderlichkeit ; Prolegomena zu einer Ethnologie der Culturvölker. *Map.* 8°
Berlin, 1868

—— Die Deutsche Expedition an der Loango-Küste nebst älteren Nachrichten über die zu erforschenden Länder. 2 vols. *Map and plates.* Small 8°
Jena, 1874-75

—— Die Culturländer des alten America. 2 vols. *Maps.* 8° *Berlin,* 1878

—— Königliche Museen zu Berlin : Steinsculpturen aus Guatemala. *Plates.* 4*
Berlin, 1882

—— Inselgruppen in Oceanien : Reiseergebnisse und Studien. *Plates.* 8°
Berlin, 1883

—— Zur Kenntniss Hawaii's : Nachträge und Ergänzungen zu den Inselgruppen in Oceanien. *Plan.* 8° *Berlin,* 1883

—— Völkerstämme am Brahmaputra und verwandtschaftliche Nachbarn : Reise-Ergebnisse und Studien. *Plates.* Large 8° *Berlin,* 1883

—— Indonesien oder die Inseln des Malayischen Archipel. *Plates.* 8° *Berlin*
1. Die Molukken 1884
2. Timor und umliegende Inseln 1885
3. Sumatra und Nachbarschaft 1886
4. Borneo und Celebes 1889
5. Java und Schluss 1894

—— Der Papua des dunkeln Inselreichs im Lichte psychologischer Forschung. 8* *Berlin,* 1885

—— Zur Lehre von den geographischen Provinzen. 8° *Berlin,* 1886

—— Controversen in der Ethnologie : I. Die Geographischen Provinzen in ihren culturgeschichtlichen Berührungspuncten. 8* *Berlin,* 1893

—— *See* Humboldt, Alex. von ; and Neumayer, G.

Bastidas, Rodriguez de. *See* Gottfried : Appendix 1.

Bastos, T. A livre navegação do Amazonas. [In Nos. 22-24 of the *Jornal do Pará,* 1864.] Large folio* *Para,* 1864

Bataillard, Paul. Nouvelles Recherches sur l'apparition et la dispersion des Bohémiens en Europe. 8* *Paris,* 1849

Batchelder, H. M. *See* Osgood.

Batchelor, Rev. John. The Ainu of Japan : the Religion, Superstitions, and General History of the Hairy Aborigines of Japan. *Illustrations.* 8° 1892

—— *See* Chamberlain.

Bate, John. Emigration : Free, Assisted, and Full-Paying Passages ; together with the Conditions for obtaining Free Land Grants, &c. 8* N D.

Bate, Comm. W. J. China Pilot ; Appendix No. 9 : Sailing Directions for Palawan Island and Passage, being the Result of the Survey in H.M.S. "Royalist," made between the years 1850-54. 8° 1855

Bateman, Charles Somerville Latrobe. The First Ascent of the Kasai, being some Records of Service under the Lone Star. *Map, plan, and illustrations.* 8° 1889

—— *See* Carvalho, H. A. D. de.

Bates, C. E. *See* Central Asia, A : Appendix 2.

Bates, Henry Walter. The Naturalist on the River Amazons : a Record of Adventures, Habits of Animals, Sketches of Brazilian and Indian Life, and Aspects of Nature, under the Equator, during eleven years of Travel. *Maps and plates.* 2 vols. 8° 1863

—— The Naturalist on the River Amazons ; with a Memoir of the Author by Edward Clodd. *Maps and illustrations.* 8° 1892

—— Illustrated Travels. *See* United Kingdom : Appendix 3.

—— *See* Allen, Grant ; Koldeway ; Stanford, E. ; Somerville, Mary ; Warburton.

Bathgate, J. New Zealand, its Resources and Prospects. *Maps and illustrations.* 8° 1880

Batres, L. "Clasificación del tipo étnico de las tribus Zapoteca del Estado de Oaxaca y alcolhua del Valle de México," and "Civilización de algunas de las diferentes tribus que habitaron el territorio, hoy Mexicano, en la antigüedad." *Map and plates.* 4° [*Mexico,* 1889]

Battell, And. *See* Astley, Vol. 3 ; Gottfried ; Pinkerton, Vol. 16 ; Purchas, Vol. 2, Book 7 ; Allgemeine Historie, Vol. 4 : Appendix 1.

Battely, John. Opera Posthuma, Antiquitates Rotupinæ, et Antiquitates S. Edmundi Burgi ad annum 1272 perductæ. *Maps and plates.* 4°
Oxford, 1745

Batten, G. H. M. Information regarding the Cotton Cultivation in the N.-W. Provinces. [From the India Records, N.W. Provinces, Part 37.] Folio
Allahabad, 1862

—— Information regarding the Slackness of Demand for European Cotton Goods. [From the India Records, N.-W. Provinces, Part 40.] Folio *Allahabad,* 1864

Batten, J. H. Notes and Recollections on Tea Cultivation in Kumaon and Garwähl. 8* 1878

—— *See* India, O : Appendix 2.

Battenberg, Franz Joseph, Prinz von. Die volkswirthschaftliche Entwicklung Bulgariens von 1879 bis zur Gegenwart. Large 8° *Leipzig,* 1891

Battie, E. Report on the Khirkee and Chutturpoor Bunds near Dehlie, April 1848. [From the India Records, Vol. 2.] —— Survey Report of the Jumna River, between Delhi and Agra, 1856. [From the India Records,' N.-W. Provinces, Part 33.] 8° *Allahabad*, 1860

Baude, Baron. L'Algérie. *Maps*, 2 vols. 8° *Paris*, 1841

Baudier, —. *See* Churchill, Vol. 8 : Appendix 1.

Baudin, Capt. *See* St Vincent.

Baudot, Maurice. Le nivellement-général de la France et le nivellement de précision de la Suisse. 8* *Paris*, 1874

Bauer, Gustav. Gedächtnisrede auf Otto Hesse gehalten in der öffentlichen Sitzung der Akademie der Wissenschaften zu München, zur Feier ihres einhundert und drei und zwanzigsten Stiftungstages am 28 März 1882. 4* *Munich*, 1882

Bauerkeller. *See* Jomard.

Bauernfeind, Carl Max von. Gedächtnisrede auf Joseph von Fraunhofer zur Feier seines hundertsten Geburtstags. 4* *Munich*, 1887 —— Das Bayerische Präcisions-Nivellement. 4* [*Munich*] 1888

Baumbauer, E. H. von. Sur un Météorographe universel destiné aux Observatoires solitaires. 8° *Haarlem*, 1874

Baumann, Dr Oscar. Beiträge zur Ethnographie des Congo. *Illustrations*. 4° *Vienna*, 1887 —— Beiträge zur physischen Geographie des Congo. *Map and plate.* 8° *Vienna*, 1887 —— Eine Afrikanische Tropen - Insel : Fernando Póo und die Bube ; dargestellt auf Grund einer Reise im Auftrage der k. k. Geographischen Gesellschaft in Wien. *Map and illustrations.* 8* *Vienna*, 1888 —— In Deutsch-Ostafrika während des Aufstandes : Reise der Dr Hans Meyer' schen Expedition in Usambara. *Illustrations*. 8° *Vienna*, 1890 —— Usambara und seine Nachbargebieten. Allgemeine Darstellung des Nordöstlichen Deutsch-Ostafrika und seiner Bewohner auf Grund einer im Auftrage der Deutsch - Ostafrikanischen Gesellschaft im Jahre 1890 ausgeführten Reise. *Maps and illustrations* *Berlin*, 1891

Baumgarten, Dr Johannes. Deutsch Afrika und seine Nachbarn im schwarzen Erdteil ; eine Rundreise in abgerundeten Naturschilderungen, Sittenscenen und ethnographischen Charakterbildern ; nach den neuesten und besten Quellen, für Freunde der geographischen Wissenschaft und der Kolonialbestrebungen, sowie für den höheren Unterricht. *Map.* 8° *Berlin*, 1887

Baumgarten, Dr Johannes. Ostafrika, der Sudan und das Seengebiet ; Land- und Leute ; Naturschilderungen, charakteristische Reisebilder und Scenen aus dem Volksleben; Aufgaben und Kulturerfolge der Christlichen Mission, Sklavenhandel ; die Anti-sklavereibewegung, ihre Ziele und ihr Ausgang ; Kolonialpolitische Fragen der Gegenwart ; nach den . . . besten Quellen. 8° *Gotha*, 1890

Baumgarten, M. *See* Churchill, Vol. 1 : Appendix 1.

Bausset, Arthur de. Aërial Navigation. *Illustrations.* 12* *Chicago*, 1887

Bauzá, Don Philipp. Ueber den gegenwärtigen Zustand der Geographie von Süd-Amerika. Uebersetzt durch W. F. von Karwinsky. [German and Spanish.] 4° *Madrid*, 1814

Bavier, S. Die Strassen der Schweiz. Gedrängte Darstellung ihrer historischen Entwicklung und ihres gegenwärtigen Bestandes, mit einem Anhang über das schweizerische Postwesen. *Map and plates.* 4° *Zürich*, 1878

Bavoux, Evariste Alger. Voyage Politique et Descriptif dans le Nord de l'Afrique. 2 vols. 8° *Paris*, 1841

Bax, Capt. B. W. The Eastern Seas : being a Narrative of the Voyage of H.M.S "Dwarf," in China, Japan, and Formosa ; with a Description of the Coast of Russian Tartary and Eastern Siberia, from the Corea to the River Amur. *Map and plates.* 8° 1875

Baxter, W. Glossarium Antiquitatum Britanicarum, sive Syllabus Etymologicus Antiq. vet. Brit. atque Iberniæ temporibus Romanorum, accedunt Edvardi Luidii de Fluviorum, Montium, Urbium, &c., Adversaria Posthuma. *Portrait.* 2nd edition. 8° 1733

Bayard, F. C. English Climatology, 1881-90. (From the *Quarterly Journal of the Royal Meteorological Society*, Vol. 18, No. 84.) *Map.* 8* 1892

Bayberger, Franz. Der Inngletscher. (Ergänzungsheft, 70—Petermann's Mittheilungen.) *Map and illustrations.* 4° *Gotha*, 1882 —— Geographisch-geologische Studien aus dem Böhmerwalde. (Ergängzungsheft, 81—Petermann's Mittheilungen.) *Maps and sketches.* 4° *Gotha*, 1886

Bayer, P. W. Herrn P. Wolfgang Bayers ehemaligen Americanischen Glaubenspredigers der Gesellschaft Jesu, Reise nach Peru, von ihm selbst beschrieben. Herausgegeben von C. G. von Murr. 12° *Nuremberg*, 1776

Bayfield, G. T. *See* Pemberton ; *also* India, I (Assam) : Appendix 2.

Bayfield, Admiral H. W. Sailing Directions for the Gulf and River of St Lawrence. 2 vols. 8°   1837
—— Nova Scotia Pilot. From Mars Head to Pope Harbour, including Halifax Harbour. 8°   1856
—— Maritime Positions in the Gulf and River St Lawrence, on the South Coast of Nova Scotia, and in Newfoundland, in 1857. 8°   1857
—— Nova Scotia Pilot. South-East Coast, from Mars Head to Cape Canso, including Sable Island. 8°   1860
—— St Lawrence Pilot, comprising Sailing Directions for the Gulf and River. 2 vols. 8°   1860
—— Pilote du Golfe et du fleuve Saint-Laurent. Traduction par A. le Gros. 8°
            Paris, 1863
Bayley, F. W. N. Four Years' Residence in the West Indies. 8°   1830
Bayley, W. H. Revenue Survey of South Arcot, with Appendices. *Maps and plans.* [From the India Records, No. 9, Madras.] Royal 8°   *Madras*, 1855
Bazley, T. *See* Mackay, A.
Beadle, B. A. *See* Lacerda.
Beadon, Robert. The Solution of the Colonial Question. (From the *Asiatic Quarterly Review.*) Large 8*   1893
"Beagle." *See* Darwin; Fitzroy.
Beal, S. Travels of Fah-Hian and Sung-Yun, Buddhist Pilgrims from China to India (400 A.D. and 518 A.D.) Translated from the Chinese. *Map.* Small 8°
            1869
—— The Life of Hiuen-Tsiang. By the Shamans Hwui-Li and Yeu-Tsung. With a Preface containing an Account of the Works of I-Tsing. 8°   1888
—— Si-Yu-Ki: Buddhist Records of the Western World. Translated from the Chinese of Hiuen Tsiang (A.D. 629). 2 vols. *Map.* 8°   1890
Beardmore, Nathaniel. Hydraulic Tables, to aid the Calculation of Water and Mill Power, Water Supply, and Drainage of Towns, and Improvement of Navigable Rivers; together with the Properties and Strength of Materials, Useful Numbers and Logarithms; also Phenomena of Tidal Rivers. *Maps.* 8°   1852
—— Manual of Hydrology, containing :—
1. Hydraulic and other Tables; 2. Rivers, Flow of Water, Springs, Wells, and Percolation; 3. Tides, Estuaries, and Tidal Rivers; 4. Rainfall and Evaporation. *Maps.* 8°   1862
Beardmore, Septimus. The Globe Telegraph: an Essay on the Use of the Earth for the Transmission of Electric Signals. 8*   1859
—— Terra - Voltaism : Remarks on the Application of a Terra-Voltaic Couple to Submarine Telegraphs. 12*   1860

Beardslee, Capt. L. A. Affairs in Alaska, and the Operations of the U.S.S. "Jamestown." *Charts.* 8°
            Washington, 1882
Beatson, Major-Gen. Alex. View of the Origin and Conduct of the War with Tippoo Sultaun, comprising the Operations of the Army under General Harris, and the Siege of Seringapatam. *Map and plates.* 4°   1800
—— Tracts relative to the Island of St Helena. *Map and plates.* 4°   1816
Beattie, W. Switzerland, illustrated in a Series of Views taken on the Spot by W. H. Bartlett. 2 vols. 4°   1839
Beatty, John. Correspondence relating to Canal Clearances in the Hydrabad Collectorate in 1855-57. Royal 8°   *Bombay*, 1859
—— Ditto, in 1857-58. *Map in separate case.* Royal 8°   *Bombay*, 1859
    [From the India Records, Nos. 50 and 52, Bombay.]
Beau, C. le. Avantures du Sr. C. Le Beau . . . ou Voyage curieux et nouveau, parmi les Sauvages de l'Amérique Septentrionale ; dans lequel on trouvera une Description du Canada, &c. 2 vols. *Plates.* 12°   *Amsterdam*, 1738
Beauchamps. *See* Hakluyt, Vol. 2 : Appendix 1.
Beauchesne-Gouin, — de. *See* Burney, Vol. 4 ; Callander, Vol. 3 : Appendix 1.
Beauclerk, Capt. G. A Journey to Marocco, in 1826. *Plates.* 8°   1828
Beauclerk, W. N. Rural Italy, an Account of the present Agricultural Condition of the Kingdom. *Map.* 8°   1888
[Beaufort, Capt.] Des Montagnes de la Terre : Notice servant de Commentaire à un Tableau comparatif de la Forme et de la Hauteur des principales Montagnes du Globe ; avec un Appendice sur les Cascades les plus remarquables. Par L. B. 8°   *Paris*, 1827
Beaufort, D. A. Memoir of a Map of Ireland, illustrating the Topography of that Kingdom, with an Index to the Map. *Map.* 4°   *Dublin*, 1792
Beaufort, Emily A. Egyptian Sepulchres and Syrian Shrines, including some Stay in the Lebanon, at Palmyra, and in Western Turkey. 2nd edition. *Map and plates.* 2 vols. Small 8°   1862
Beaufort, Capt. F. Karamania ; or, A Brief Description of the South Coast of Asia Minor, and of the Remains of Antiquity. *Maps and plates.* 8°   1818
Beaufoy, Col. Mark. Mexican Illustrations, founded upon facts indicative of the present condition of Society, Manners, Religion, and Morals among the Spanish and Native Inhabitants of Mexico. *Maps and plates. Large paper.* 8°   1828

Beaufoy, Col. Mark. Nautical and Hydraulic Experiments, with numerous Scientific Miscellanies. Vol. 1. *Portrait and plates.* 4° 1834

Beaujour, Baron Felix de. De l'Expédition d'Annibal en Italie, et de la meilleure manière d'attaquer et de défendre la Péninsule Italienne. *Map.* 8° *Paris,* 1832

Beaulieu, A. de. *See* Harris, Vol. 1; Thevenot, Vol. 2; Allgemeine Historie, Vols. 10, 18; "The World Displayed," Vol. 8, p. 609 : Appendix 1.

Beaumier, A. Itinéraire de Mogador à Maroc et de Maroc à Saffy, Février 1868. *Map.* 8* *Paris,* 1868

Beaumont, Albanis. Travels through the Rhætian Alps in the year MDCCLXXXVI., from Italy to Germany, through Tyrol. *Plates.* Folio 1792

Beaumont, Élie de. Éloge Historique de Charles-François Beautemps-Beaupré. 4* *Paris,* 1860

—— Tableau des Données Numériques qui fixent 159 cercles du réseau Pentagonal. 4* *Paris,* 1863

—— Tableau des Données Numériques qui fixent les 362 points principaux du réseau Pentagonal. 4* *Paris,* 1864

—— *See* Dufrénoy.

Beaumont, H. Bouthillier de. Choix d'un Méridien Initial Unique. *Map.* 8* *Geneva,* 1880

—— Présentation, avec Cartes Nouvelles d'une Cartographie générale pour le meilleur enseignement de la Géographie. *Map.* 8* *Geneva,* 1891

Beaumont. John, junior. Considerations on a Book, entituled, The Theory of the Earth, publisht by Dr Burnet. 4* 1693

Beaumont, J. F. A. Description des Alpes Graïques et Cottiennes, ou Tableau Historique et Statistique de la Savoie. *Maps and plates.* 4 vols, 4°; and Atlas of plates, folio. *Paris,* 1802-6

Beauplan, Sieur de. *See* Churchill, Vol. 1; Harris, Vol. 2; Knox's New Collection, Vol. 4, p. 608 : Appendix 1.

Beautemps-Beaupré, M. Exposé des Travaux relatifs á la Reconnaissance Hydrographique des Côtes Occidentales de France, suivi d'un Précis des Opérations Géodésiques par M. Daussy. 4° 1829

—— Rapports sur les Rades, Ports et Mouillages de la Côte Orientale du Golfe de Venise. 8° 1849

Beauvoir, Marquis de. A Voyage round the World. 3 vols. Small 8° 1870-72

Beavan, H. J. C. Six Weeks in Ireland. By a Templar. 12° 1862

—— Observations on the People inhabiting Spain. 8* N.D.

—— *See* Pouchet, G.

Beaver, P. African Memoranda relative to an Attempt to Establish a British Settlement on the Island of Bulama, on the Western Coast of Africa, in the year 1792 ; with a brief Notice of the Neighbouring Tribes, Soil, Productions, &c., and some Observations on the Facility of Colonising that part of Africa with a view to Cultivation, and the Introduction of Letters and Religion to its Inhabitants, but more particularly as the means of gradually abolishing African Slavery. *Maps.* 4° 1805

Becher, Capt. A. B. Tables of Mast-Head Angles, for 5 feet intervals from 30 to 280 feet, and varying distances from a Cable's-length to 4 miles, with their application to Nautical Surveying, also the Determination of Distance by Sound. 16° 1854

—— The Landfall of Columbus on his First Voyage to America ; with a Translation of the Baron Bonnefoux's History of his previous Life, and a Chart showing his Track from the Landfall to Cuba. *Map.* 8° 1856

—— Tables for Reducing Foreign Lineal Measure into English, and English Measure into Foreign. Part 1. 8° N.D.

—— Navigation of the Atlantic Ocean, with an Account of the Winds, Weather, and Currents found therein throughout the year, according to the most approved authorities ; including Extensive Extracts from *The Nautical Magazine.* 4th edition. *Charts.* 8° 1883

Becher, Ernst. *See* Dorn, A.

Becher, H. C. R. A Trip to Mexico: being Notes of a Journey from Lake Erie to Lake Tezcuco and back, with an Appendix about the Ancient Nations and Races who inhabited Mexico before and at the time of the Spanish Conquest, and the Ancient Stone and other Structures and Ruins of Ancient Cities found there. *Photographs.* Square 8° *Toronto,* 1880

Béchet, Eugène. Cinq Ans de séjour au Soudan Française. *Map.* 12° *Paris,* 1889

Beck, Dr Günther Ritter von. *See* Paulitschke.

Beck, L. C. Die Aufgaben der Geographie, mit Berücksichtigung der Handelsgeographie. 8* *Stuttgart,* 1884

Beck, Lewis C., W. W. Mather, E. Emmons, T. A. Conrad, and L. Vanuxem. The New York Geological and Mineralogical Reports for 1837. 8° *Albany, N.Y.,* 1840

Beck, William. New Waterway to the East by a Valley of Passengers, N.B., suggested by Captain Allen, R.N., in 1855 : Thoughts on its Advantages and Feasibility. *Plans and section.* 8* 1882

Becker, George F. *See* United States, G, *c* (Monographs, Vol. 3) : Appendix 2.

Becker, Jerome. La Vie en Afrique, ou Trois ans dans l'Afrique Centrale ; avec Préface du Cte Goblet d'Alviella, et Appendices, &c. 2 vols. *Map and illustrations.* 8° *Paris*, 1887

Becker, M. A. Wilhelm Haidinger. 8* *Vienna*, 1871

Becker, W. G. E. Journal einer Bergmännischen Reise durch Ungarn und Siebenbürgen. *Plates.* 2 vols in 1. 12° *Freiburg*, 1815

Beckford, W. Italy ; with Sketches of Spain and Portugal, by the Author of "Vathek." 2 vols. 8° 1834

Beckwith, Lieut. E. G. Report of Exploration of a Route for the Pacific Railroad, near the 38th and 39th Parallels of Latitude, from the Mouth of the Kansas to Sevier River, in the Great Basin. *Maps* *Washington*, 1854

Beddard, F. E. *See* United Kingdom, H, Challenger : Appendix 2.

Bedeau, Lieut.-Gen. A. *See* De la Moricière.

Bedford, E. J. *See* United Kingdom, A (Sailing Directions) : Appendix 2.

Bedot, Maurice. *See* Pictet.

Beebe, Lewis H. The Dense Water of the Ocean, its Rivers and Currents. 8* [*Philadelphia*, 1884]

Beecham, John. Ashantee and Gold Coast : being a Sketch of the History, Social State, and Superstitions of the Inhabitants of those Countries. *Map.* 12° 1841

Beechey, Capt. F. W. Narrative of a Voyage to the Pacific and Behring's Strait to co-operate with the Polar Expeditions, performed in H. M. S. "Blossom," 1825-28. *Maps and plates.* 2 vols. 4° 1831

—— Zoology of Voyage, compiled from the Collections and Notes made by Capt. Beechey, the Officers, and Naturalist of the Expedition, by J. Richardson, N. A. Vigors, G. T. Lay, N. T. Bennett, R. Owen, J. E. Gray, Rev. Dr W. Buckland, and G. B. Sowerby. *Coloured plates.* 4° 1839

—— Voyage of Discovery towards the North Pole, performed in H.M.SS. "Dorothea" and "Treat," 1818 ; with a Summary of all the Early Attempts to reach the Pacific by way of the Pole. *Map and plates.* 8° 1843

—— Report on Observations on the Tidal Streams of the English Channel and the German Ocean, in 1848-50 ; with Charts and Tables giving the Direction of the Stream in all Parts of the Channel and North Sea. *Maps.* 4° 1851

Beechey, Capt. F. W. and H. W. Proceedings of the Expedition to Explore the Northern Coast of Africa from Tripoly eastward, in 1821 and 1822, comprehending an Account of the Greater Syrtis and Cyrenaica, and of the Ancient Cities composing the Pentapolis. *Maps and plates.* 4° 1828

Beeckman. *See* Pinkerton, Vol. 11 : Appendix 1.

Beele, Baron S. Van de. *See* Van der Tuuk.

Begat, P. Exposé des Opérations Géodésiques relatives aux travaux Hydrographiques exécutés sur les Côtes Septentrionales de France. 4° *Paris*, 1839

—— Traité de Géodésie à l'Usage de Marins, ou Méthodes et Formules Trigonométriques relatives au Levé et à la Construction des Cartes Hydrographiques. *Plates.* 8° *Paris*, 1839

Begg, Alexander. The Great Canadian North-West, its Past History, Present Condition, and Glorious Prospects. 8* *Montreal*, 1881

—— Canada and its National Highway. Large 8* 1886

—— The Great North-West of Canada : a Paper read at Conference, Indian and Colonial Exhibition, London, 8th June 1886. 8* 1886

—— Emigration : a Paper read at Conference, Indian and Colonial Exhibition, London, 23rd July 1886. 8* 1886

—— The Canadian Pacific Railway : a Paper read at the Birmingham Meeting of the British Association, 2nd September 1886. *Map.* 8* 1886

Beglar, J. B. *See* India, A : Appendix 2.

Behm, Dr E. Die modernen Verkehrsmittel : Dampfschiffe, Eisenbahnen, Telegraphen (Ergänzungsheft, 19 — Petermann's Mittheilungen.) 2 *coloured maps.* 4° *Gotha*, 1867

—— *See* Petermann and Hassenstein.

—— **and Dr H. Wagner** Die Bevölkerung der Erde. I. (Ergänzungsheft, 33—Petermann's Mittheilungen.) 4° *Gotha*, 1872

—— Die Bevölkerung der Erde. II. (Ergänzungsheft, 35—Petermann's Mittheilungen.) 2 *coloured maps.* 4° *Gotha*, 1874

—— Ditto. III. (Ergänzungsheft, 41—Petermann's Mittheilungen.) 4° *Gotha*, 1875

—— Ditto. IV. (Ergänzungsheft, 49—Petermann's Mittheilungen.) 2 *coloured maps.* 4° *Gotha*, 1877

—— Ditto. V. (Ergänzungsheft, 55 — Petermann's Mittheilungen.) 2 *maps.* 4° *Gotha*, 1878

Behm, Dr E. and Dr H. Wagner. Die Bevölkerung der Erde. VI. (Ergänzungsheft, 62 — Petermann's Mittheilungen.) 3 *maps.* 4° *Gotha*, 1880 — Ditto. VII. (Ergänzungsheft, 69—Petermann's Mittheilungen.) 2 *maps.* 4° *Gotha*, 1882 —— *See* also Wagner, H.

Behrens, H. The Natural History of Hartz - Forest, in His Majesty King George's German Dominions. Translated by J. Andree. 8° 1730

Behring, Capt. *See* Harris, Vol. 2 ; Allgemeine Historie, Vol. 17 : Appendix 1.

Beilby, J. W. Reasons Suggestive of Mining on Physical Principles for Gold and Coal. 12* *Melbourne*, 1875

Beke, Dr Charles T. Origines Biblicæ ; or, Researches in Primeval History. *Map.* 8° 1834
—— On the Geological Evidence of the Advance of the Land at the Head of the Persian Gulf. 8* 1835
—— On the Complexion of the Ancient Egyptians. 8* 1836
—— On the Former Extent of the Persian Gulf, and on the Non-identity of Babylon and Babel. 8* 1836
—— Additional Remarks. 8* 1837
—— Vertheidigung gegen Dr Paulus über Origines Biblicæ. 8° *Leipzig*, 1836
—— On the Passage of the Red Sea by the Israelites, and its Locality, and on the Situation of Mount Sinai. *Map.* 8* 1838
—— On the Alluvia of Babylonia and Chaldea. 8* 1839
—— Route from Ankóber to Dima. 8* 1841
—— Abyssinia : being a Continuation of Routes in that Country. 8* *Map* [1842]
—— Mémoire justificatif en réhabilitation des Pères Pierre Paez et Jérome Lobo, Missionnaires en Abyssinie, en ce qui concerne leurs visites à la Source de l'Abaï (le Nil) et à la Cataracte d'Alata. *Map.* 8* *Paris*, 1842
—— On the Countries south of Abyssinia. *Map.* 8* [1844]
—— On the Languages and Dialects of Abyssinia, and the Countries to the south. 8* 1845
—— A Statement of Facts relative to the Transactions between the Writer and the late British Political Misssion to the Court of Shoa, in Abessinia. 8* 1846
—— Christianity among the Gallas. 8* 1847
—— Description of the Ruins of the Church of Mártula Máriam, in Abessinia. *Plates.* 4* 1847
—— On the Korarima, or Cardamom of Abessinia. 8* 1847.
—— Essay on the Sources of the Nile in the Mountains of the Moon. 8* *Edinburgh*, 1848

Beke, Dr Charles T. On the Origin of the Gallas. 8* 1848
—— Remarks on the Mats'hafa Tomar, or the Book of the Letter, an Ethiopic MS. in the University of Tübingen. 8* 1848
—— On the Sources of the Nile : being an Attempt to Assign the Limits of the Basin of that River. 8* 1849
—— On the Geographical Distribution of the Languages of Abessinia and the Neighbouring Countries. *Map.* 8* *Edinburgh*, 1849
—— Ueber die Geographische Verbreitung der Sprachen von Abessinien und der Nachbarländer. *Map.* 8* 1849
—— Letter to M. Daussy, President of the Geographical Society of France. 8* 1850
—— Observations sur la Communication supposée entre le Niger et le Nil. 8* 1850
—— Enquiry into M. Antoine d'Abbadie's Journey to Kaffa to Discover the Source of the Nile. *Map.* 8* 1851
—— Reasons for Returning the Gold Medal of the Geographical Society of France, and for withdrawing from its Membership. 8* 1851
—— A Summary of Recent Nilotic Discovery. 8* 1851
—— The Sources of the Nile : being a General Survey of the Basin of that River and of its Head Streams, with History of Nilotic Discovery. *Maps.* 8° 1860
—— On the Mountains forming the Eastern Side of the Basin of the Nile, and the Origin of the Designation of " Mountains of the Moon " as applied to them. 8* *Edinburgh*, 1861
—— The French and English in the Red Sea. 8* 1862
—— A Few Words with Bishop Colenso on the subject of the Exodus of the Israelites, and the Position of Mount Sinai. 8* 1862
—— Views in Ethnography : the Classification of the Language, the Progress of Civilisation, and the Natural History of Man. 8* 1863
—— Who Discovered the Sources of the Nile ? a Letter to Sir Roderick I. Murchison, with an Appendix. 8* 1863
—— On the Sources of the Nile. 8* 1864
—— The British Captives in Abyssinia. 8* 1865
—— The same. 2nd edition. *Map.* 8* 1867
—— The Idol in Horeb. Small 8° 1871
—— The late Dr Charles Beke's Discoveries of Sinai in Arabia and of Midian. Edited by his Widow. *Map and plates.* 8° 1878
—— *See* Lacerda.

Beke, Emily. Jacob's Flight ; or, A Pilgrimage to Harran and thence in the Patriarch's Footsteps into the Promised Land. *Map and plates.* 8°   1865

—— Summary of the late Dr Beke's published Works, and of his inadequately requited public services. Small 8*
Tunbridge Wells, 1867

Belavenetz, I. Deviations of the Compass and the Compass Observatory. [In Russian.] *Plate.* 8°
St Petersburg, 1863

—— Fixing the Compass in the Submarine Boat. [In Russian.] *Plates.* 8*
St Petersburg, 1867

Belcher, Sir Edward. Treatise on Nautical Surveying: containing an outline of the Duties of the Naval Surveyor, with Cases applied to Naval Evolutions, and Miscellaneous Rules and Tables useful to the Seaman or Traveller. *Plans and plates.* 8°   1835

—— Directions for the River Gambia. 8°

—— Narrative of a Voyage round the World performed in H.M.S. "Sulphur," 1836-42, including Details of the Naval Operations in China from Dec. 1840 to Nov. 1841. *Maps and plates.* 2 vols. 8°   1843

—— Directions for the River Douro, 1833. 8°   2nd edition   1847

—— Narrative of the Voyage of H.M.S. "Samarang," during 1843-46, employed Surveying the Islands of the Eastern Archipelago ; accompanied by a brief Vocabulary of the Principal Languages, with Notes on the Natural History of the Islands by A. Adams. *Map and plates.* 2 vols. 8°   1848

—— The Zoology of the Voyage of H.M.S. "Samarang," under the command of Sir E. Belcher, during the years 1843-46, by J. E. Gray, Sir J. Richardson, A. Adams, L. Reeve, and A. White. Edited by Arthur Adams. *Plates.* 4°
1850

—— The Last of the Arctic Voyages : being a Narrative of the Expedition in H.M.S. "Assistance," in search of Sir John Franklin, during 1852-54 ; with Notes on the Natural History, by Sir John Richardson, Professor Owen, T. Bell, J. W. Salter, and Lovell Reeve. *Maps and plates.* 2 vols. Royal 8°   1855

—— *See* Smyth, Admiral W. H.

—— **and Capt. W. T. Bate.** China Pilot: Appendix, No. 2, General Observations on the Coasts of Borneo, the Sulu, and Mindoro Seas, with Sailing Directions for Palawan Passage and Island. 8°   1859

Beldam, Joseph. Recollections of Scenes and Institutions in Italy and the East. *Plates.* 2 vols. 8°   1851

Belgrand, E., and G. Lemoine. Note sur l'État probable des Eaux courantes du Bassin de la Seine dans l'été et l'automne de 1870. 8*   *Paris,* 1870

Belknap, G. E. *See* United States, E, *a* (No. 54) : Appendix 2.

Bell, Charles N. Our Northern Waters : a Report presented to the Winnipeg Board of Trade regarding the Hudson's Bay and Straits, being a Statement of their Resources in Minerals, Fisheries, Timber, Furs, Game, and other Products ; also Notes on the Navigation of these Waters, together with Historical Events and Meteorological and Climatic Data. *Maps.* 8*   *Winnipeg,* 1884

—— The Selkirk Settlement and the Settlers : a Concise History of the Red River Country, from its Discovery, including Information extracted from original documents lately discovered, and Notes obtained from Selkirk Settlement Colonists. *Illustrations.* 8*
Winnipeg, 1887

Bell, Clara. *See* Ebers.

Bell, Col. C. W. Bowdler. *See* United Kingdom, G, War Office Publications : Appendix 2.

Bell, Dugald. On the Glacial Phenomena of Scotland, with Reference to the Reports of the Boulder Committee of the Royal Society of Edinburgh. 8*
Glasgow, 1888

Bell, Horace. The Great Indian Desert. 8*   [1889]

Bell, H. C. P. The Máldive Islands : an Account of the Physical Features, Climate, History, Inhabitants, Productions, and Trade. *Maps and diagram.* Folio   *Colombo,* 1883

Bell, James. New and Comprehensive Gazetteer of England and Wales, representing under each Article respectively the Population of the Towns and Parishes, according to the Census of 1831, and the State of the Elective Franchise as fixed by the Provisions of the Reform Bill. *Maps.* 4 vols. 8°   *Glasgow,* 1837-38

—— System of Geography, Popular and Scientific ; or a Physical, Political, and Statistical Account of the World and its Various Divisions. *Maps and plates.* 6 vols. 8°   *Glasgow,* 1838

Bell, James Stanislaus. Journal of a Residence in Circassia during the years 1837, 1838, and 1839. 2 vols. *Map and plates.* 8°   1840

—— *See* Tempsky.

Bell, John. Travels from St Petersburg in Russia to Diverse Parts of Asia. 2 vols. in 1. *Map.* 4°   *Glasgow,* 1763

—— Ditto. 2 vols. *Maps.* 4°
Glasgow, 1763

Bell, John. Travels from St Petersburg in Russia to various Parts of Asia. *Maps.* 2 vols. 8° 1788
—— *See* Pinkerton, Vol. 7; Knox's New Collection, Vol. 6, p. 608: Appendix 1.

Bell, Col. Mark S. China: being a Military Report on the North-Eastern Portions of the Provinces of Chih-Li and Shan-Tung, Nanking and its Approaches, &c.; together with an Account of the Chinese Civil, Naval, and Military Administrations, &c. &c., and a Narrative of the Wars between Great Britain and China. *Maps and plates.* Vol. 1. Large 8° *Simla,* 1884
—— Afghánistán as a Theatre of Operations, and as a Defence to India. *Map.* 8° 1885
—— Imperial Strategic Communications with Special Reference to the Turko-Persic - Indian Line, and the Strategic Considerations influencing its Alignment. *Map.* 8° *Simla,* 1885
—— Turkey in Asia and Persia. Sections 2 and 3: Reconnaissances in Mesopotamia, Armenia, Kurdistan, and Azarbaijan in 1885-86. Forming Appendix 1 to Central Asia, Part 5, and Routes in Central Asia, Section 1. Compiled by Lieut.-Colonel C. M. MacGregor (1872). *Maps, plans, and plates.* Large 8° *Simla,* 1889
—— Extracts from a Letter from Colonel M. S. Bell to Major-General Chapman, Quartermaster General in India, dated Suian-fu, 18th April 1887. Folio.*
—— Letter on proposed Journey to Kashgaria. *Map.* Folio* 1887
—— Reports of proceedings in Kashgaria and Manchuria, with Sketch Map, dated from Peking, 20th March 1887. Folio.*
—— China: Reconnaissance Journey through the Central and Western Provinces, from Peking through Shansi, Shensi, Kansuh, and Sin-Kiang to Ladakh and India, together with Notes on the Districts adjoining the Route taken and the Roads traversing them. 2 vols. Vol. 1, India *viâ* Peking to Hami; Vol. 2, Hami *viâ* Yarkand to India. *Maps, plans, and plates.* Large 8° *Calcutta,* 1888
—— A Visit to the Kárún River and Kúm. (From *Blackwood's Magazine,* April 1889.) *Map.* 8* 1889
—— Isfahán to Bushire: Roads and Resources of Southern Persia. (From *Blackwood's Magazine.*) 8* 1889

Bell, Robert. Wayside Pictures through France, Belgium, and Holland. *Illustrations.* 8° 1849

Bell, Dr Robert. The "Medicine-Man," or Indian and Eskimo Notions of Medicine. 8* *Montreal,* 1886

Bell, Dr Robert. On Glacial Phenomena in Canada. 8* *Washington,* 1890
—— The Nickel and Copper Deposits of Sudbury District, Canada. *Illustrations.* Royal 8* *Rochester, U.S.,* 1891

Bell, T. L. *See* India, C (Geological Papers): Appendix 2.

Bell, Dr William. Ein Versuch den Ort Schiringsheal der fünfmal in dem Periplus von Othere und Wulfstan enthaltend in der anglosächsischen Uebersetzung von Orosius des Königs Alfred, &c. 8* 1847
—— On the Head of Janus found on a British Coin. 8* N.D.
—— *See* Lepsius.

Bell, W. Letter from Koslogir, on Forest Culture. 4* *Edinburgh,* 1868

Bell, W. A. New Tracks in North America: a Journal of Travel and Adventure whilst engaged in the Survey for a Southern Railroad to the Pacific Ocean, during 1867-68. 2 vols. *Map and plates.* 8° 1869
—— Ditto. With Contributions by General W. J. Palmer, Major A. R. Calhoun, C. C. Parry, M.D., and Captain W. F. Colton. 2nd edition. *Maps and plates.* 8° 1870

Bellasis, A. F. An Account of the Ancient and Ruined City of Brahminabad, in Sindh, situated on a branch of the Old Bed of the Indus. MS. Folio* *Kurrachee,* 1854
—— Report on the Southern Districts of the Surat Collectorate. [From the India Records, No. 2.] *Plate.* Royal 8° *Bombay,* 1854

Bellefonds, A. Linant de. Journal of a Navigation on the Bahr-el-Abiad: Description of a Journey across the Province of Atbara, in a direction from South-West to North-East. *Map.* 4° 1828
—— Mémoire sur le Lac Moeris. *Map.* 4* *Alexandria,* 1843
—— L'Etbaye, pays habité par les Arabes Bicharieh: Géographie, Ethnologie, Mines d'or. *Map and plates.* 8°. Folio Atlas *Paris,* 1858
—— Mémoires sur les Principaux Travaux d'utilité publique exécutés en Égypte. 8°. Accompanied by Folio Atlas *Paris,* 1872-73

Bellefonds, E. Linant de. Meteorological Tables, February to July 1875: Observations made in Various Localities near the Victoria Nyanza. MS. Folio* 1875

Bellemo, Vincenzo. I Viaggi di Nicolò de' Conti. *Maps.* 12° *Milan,* 1883

Bellew, Dr H. W. Journal of a Political Mission to Afghanistan in 1857 . . ; with an Account of the Country and People. *Plates.* 8° 1862

Bellew, Dr H. W. A General Report on the Yusufzais. *Map.* 8° *Lahore*, 1864
—— Record of the March of the Mission to Seistan under the command of Major-General F. R. Pollock. [From the India Records, No. 104.] *Calcutta*, 1873
—— From the Indus to the Tigris : a Narrative of a Journey through the Countries of Balochistan, Afghanistan, Khorassan, and Iran, in 1872 ; together with a Synoptical Grammar and Vocabulary of the Brahoe Language, and a Record of the Meteorological Observations and Altitudes on the march from the Indus to the Tigris. 8°   1874
—— Kashmir and Kashgar : a Narrative of the Journey of the Embassy to Kashgar in 1873-74. 8°   1875
—— The History of Káshgharia. 4°
                               Calcutta, 1875
—— Afghanistan and the Afghans : being a Brief Review of the History of the Country and Account of its People, with Special Reference to the Present Crisis and War with the Amir Sher Ali Khan. Small 8°   1879
Bellin, S. Déscription Géographique de la Guyanne : contenant les Possessions et les Établissemens des François, des Espagnols, des Portugais, des Hollandois, dans ces vastes Pays ; le Climat, les Productions de la Terre, et les Animaux ; leurs Habitans, Mœurs, Coutumes, et le Commerce qu'on y peut faire. *Maps and plates.* 4°   *Paris*, 1763
Bellingshausen, Capt. Voyage round the World in the sloops " Vostok " and " Mirnye " in 1819-21. [In Russian.] 2 vols. in 1. 4°   *St Petersburg*, 1831
Bellitti, D. Ant. Silvestro. Delle Stufe e de' Bagni di Sciacca. *Plates.* Folio
                               Palermo, 1783
Belloni, Antonio. Memoria Idrometrica sopra il Fiume Arno. *Plate.* Small folio*   *Venice*, 1778
Bellonius, Petrus. Plurimarum singularium et memorabilium rerum in Græcia, Asia, Ægypto, Judæa, Arabia, aliisq. exteris Provinciis ab ipso Conspectarum Observationes, C. Clusius Atrebas e Gallicis Latinas faciebat. *Illustrations.* 12°   *Antwerp*, 1589
Bellot, J. R. Journal d'un Voyage aux Mers Polaires, exécuté à la Recherche de Sir John Franklin, en 1851-52 ; précédé d'une Notice sur la Vie et les Travaux de l'Auteur par M. Julien Lemer. *Portrait and map.* 8°   *Paris*, 1854
—— Lines on the Loss of. 8*
                               Manchester, 1853
Belluno, G. S. da. *See* Pellegrini.
Belly, Félix. A Travers l'Amérique Centrale, le Nicaragua, et le Canal Interocéanique. 2 vols. *Map.* 8° *Paris*, 1867
—— *See* Gamond.

Belmar, A. de. Voyage aux Provinces Brésiliennes du Pará et des Amazones en 1860, précédé d'un rapide coup d'œil sur le littoral du Brésil. 8°   1861
Beloch, Dr Julius. Campanien : Topographie, Geschichte, und Leben der Umgebung Neapels im Alterthum. 8°, Atlas 4°   *Berlin*, 1879
—— Die Bevölkerung der Griechisch-Römischen Welt. Erster Theil. Historische Beiträge zur Bevölkerungslehre.
                               Leipzig, 1886
Beloe, Rev. W. *See* Herodotus.
Belon, M. *See* Ray, John : Appendix 1.
Belt, T. The Naturalist in Nicaragua : a Narrative of a Residence at the Gold Mines of Chontales, and Journeys in the Savannahs and Forests ; with Observations on Animals and Plants in reference to the Theory of Evolution of Living Forms. ' *Map.* 8°   1874
—— The Glacial Period in the Southern Hemisphere (Reprint from the *Quarterly Journal of Science*, July 1877). 8* 1877
Beltrame, Giovanni. Di un Viaggio sul Fiume Bianco nell' Africa Centrale : Lettera. *Maps.* 8*   *Verona*, 1861
—— Il Sennaar e lo Sciangàllah. 2 vols. *Map and plate.* 12°   *Verona*, 1879
—— Il Fiume Bianco e i Dénka. *Map.* 12°   *Verona*, 1881
Beltrami, Costantino. Costantino Beltrami da Bergamo : Notizie e Lettere pubblicate per cura del Municipio di Bergamo, e dedicate alla Società Storica di Minnesota. 8*   *Bergamo*, 1865
Beluacensis Vicentius. *See* Vicentius.
Belzoni, G. Narrative of the Operations and Recent Discoveries within the Pyramids, Temples, Tombs, and Excavations in Egypt and Nubia, and a Journey to the Coast of the Red Sea in Search of the Ancient Berenice, and another to the Oasis of Jupiter Ammon. *Plate.* 4°   1820
—— The same. *Map and plates.* 2 vols. 8°   1822
—— *See* Walpole, Travels : Appendix 1.
Benaduci, Lorenzo B. Idea de una Nueva Historia General de la America Septentrional. *Frontispiece.* 4°
                               Madrid, 1746
Benard, E. Nicaragua and the Interoceanic Canal. 8* *Washington*, 1874
Ben Batuta. *See* Ibn Batuta.
Beneke, F. W. On the Warm Saline Springs of Nauheim (near Frankfort-o/M). Translated and abridged from the German by S. Sutro. *Tables.* 8° 1860
Benicken, F. W. Die Elemente der Militär-Geographie von Europa. *Map.* 8°   *Weimar*, 1821
Benisch, Dr A. *See* Petachia.

Benjamin, Rabbi, of Tudela. Itinerarium Benjamini Tudelensis. Ex Hebraico Latinum factum B. A. Montano. 8° *Antwerp*, 1575
—— Itinerary. Translated and edited by A. Asher. 2 vols. 8° 1840
—— *See* Harris, Vol. 1 ; Kerr, Vol. 1 ; Pinkerton, Vol. 7 ; Purchas, Vol. 2, Book 9 : Appendix 1.

Benjamin, I. J. Empfehlungsschreiben der grössten Gelehrten Europa. 8* *Hanover*, 1862
—— Reise in den östlichen Staaten der Union und San Francisco. *Portrait.* 8° *Hanover*, 1862
—— Eight Years in Asia and Africa from 1846 to 1855 ; with a Preface by Dr B. Seemann, and the Bible Notes from Benjamin of Tudela, R. Petachia, P. Teixeira, and Ritter's Erdkunde. *Map and woodcuts.* 8° *Hanover*, 1863

Benjamin, S. G. W. Persia and the Persians. *Portrait and illustrations.* Large 8° 1887

Benko, Freiherr Jerolim von. Reise S. M. Schiffes "Zrinyi" über Malta, Tanger, und Teneriffa nach West-Indien in den Jahren 1885 und 1886. *Map.* 8° *Pola*, 1887
—— Die Reise S. M. Schiffes "Frundsberg" im Rothen Meere, und an den Küstens von Vorderindien und Ceylon in den Jahren 1885-86. *Map and plans.* 8° *Pola*, 1888
—— Reise S. M. Schiffes "Albatros," unter Commando des k. k. Fregatten-Kapitäns Arthur Müldner, nach Süd-Amerika, dem Caplande, und West Afrika, 1885-86. *Map.* 8° *Pola*, 1889
—— Das Datum auf den Philippinen. 8* *Vienna*, 1890
—— Die Schiffs-Station der k. und k. Kriegs-Marine in Ost-Asien : Reisen S. M. Schiffe "Nautilus" und "Aurora," 1884-88. *Maps.* Large 8° *Vienna*, 1892

Benmohel, N. L. Epea Pteroenta : conveying Revelations of the Past. 8° *Dublin*, 1861

Benmohel, N. L. Σαβαλαιων, סכמיוכ. Inscription de Trèves ; avec une Digression sur l'Origine du Langage. 8* *Dublin*, 1868

[Bennassuti, Dr G.] Guida e Compendio Storico della Città di Verona e cenni intorno alla sua Provincia. *Maps.* 18° *Verona*, 1825

Benndorf, Otto. Altgriechisches Brot. 8* *Vienna*, N.D.
—— *See* Turkey in Asia, A: Appendix 2.

Bennet, J. H. Winter and Spring on the Shores of the Mediterranean ; or, The Genoese Rivieras, Italy, Spain, Corfu, Greece, The Archipelago, Constantinople, Corsica, Sicily, Sardinia, Malta, Algeria, Tunis, Smyrna, Asia

Bennet, J. H.—*continued.* Minor, with Biarritz and Arcachon, as Winter Climates. (5th edition.) *Maps and plates.* Small 8° 1875

Bennet, J. W. Ceylon and its Capabilities : an Account of its Natural Resources, Indigenous Productions, and Commercial Facilities ; to which are added Details of its Statistics, Pilotage, and Sailing Directions. *Map and plates, coloured.* 4° 1843

Bennett, F. Debell. Narrative of a Whaling Voyage round the Globe, from 1833-36, comprising Sketches of Polynesia, California, the Indian Archipelago, &c.; with an Account of Southern Whales, the Sperm Whale Fishery, and the Natural History of the Climates visited. *Map and frontispiece.* 2 vols. 8° 1840

Bennett, George. Wanderings in New South Wales, Batavia, Pedir Coast, Singapore, and China ; being the Journal of a Naturalist in those Countries during 1832-34. *Frontispiece.* 2 vols. 8° 1834
—— Gatherings of a Naturalist in Australasia : being Observations principally on the Animal and Vegetable Productions of New South Wales, New Zealand, and some of the Austral Islands. *Coloured plates, &c.* 8° 1860

Bennett, James F. The South Australian Almanack and General Directory, 1841, 1842. 8° *Adelaide*, 1841

Bensengra, V. N. Instructions for the Study of Comparative Psychology. [In Russian.] 8° *St Petersburg*, 1879

Benson, Capt. George. Sketch of Christmas Island. 8* 1838

Benson, Robert. Sketches of Corsica, or a Journal written during a Visit to that Island in 1823 ; with an Outline of its History, and Specimens of the Language and Poetry of the People. *Plates.* 8° 1825

Benson, William. Universal Phonography : an attempt to select and classify the principal sounds of Human Speech, and to denote them by one Set of Symbols for Easy Writing and Printing ; with an Appendix on the Use of Phonography for the Blind. 8* 1887

Bent, J. Theodore. The Cyclades, or Life among the Insular Greeks. *Map.* Small 8° 1885
—— The Ruined Cities of Mashonaland : being a Record of Excavation and Exploration in 1891 ; with a Chapter on the Orientation and Mensuration of the Temples by R. M. W. Swan. *Map and illustrations.* 8° 1892
—— Ditto. New edition. Small 8° 1893
—— Mashonaland and its People. (From the *Contemporary Review*.) 8* 1893

Bent, J. Theodore. The Sacred City of the Ethiopians: being a Record of Travel and Research in Abyssinia in 1893 ; with a Chapter by Professor H. D. Müller on the Inscriptions from Yeha and Aksum, and an Appendix on the Morphological Character of the Abyssinians by J. G. Garson, M.D. *Map and illustrations.* 8°   1893
—— *See* Hakluyt Soc. Publ., Vol. 87 : Appendix 1.

Bent, S. An Address delivered before the St Louis Mercantile Library Association, 6th Jan. 1872, upon the Thermal Paths to the Pole. *Maps.* 8* *St Louis,* 1872

Bentham, G. *See* Orsted, A. S.

Bentley, C. S. A New Theory of the Tides. Folio*   1879

Bentley, Rev. W. Holman. Dictionary and Grammar of the Kongo Language, as spoken at St Salvador, the ancient capital of the Old Kongo Empire, West Africa. 8°   1886
—— The same. Compiled and prepared for the Baptist Mission on the Kongo River, West Africa. 8°   1887
—— Life on the Congo ; with an Introduction by the Rev. George Grenfell. *Map and illustrations.* 12°   1887

Bentley, T. Select Views in Mysore, by Mr Home. *See* Home.

Benyowsky, Count Mauritius Augustus de. Memoirs and Travels of ; consisting of his Military Operations in Poland, his Exile into Kamchatka, his Escape and Voyage from that Peninsula through the Northern Pacific Ocean, touching at Japan and Formosa, to Canton in China ; with an Account of the French Settlement he was appointed to form upon the Island of Madagascar. Written by himself; translated from the Original Manuscript. 2 vols. *Maps and plates.* 4°   1790

Benzoni, Hieronym. Novæ Novi Orbis Historiæ, id est, rerum ab Hispanis in India Occidentali hactenus gestarum, et acerbo illorum in eas gentes dominatu, libri tres ; Urbani Calvetonis opera ex Italicis commentariis descripti, &c. ; his ab eodem adjuncta est, De Gallorum in Floridam expeditione, &c., brevis historia. 12°   *Geneva,* 1600
—— *See* Gottfried ; Hakluyt Soc. Publ., Vol. 21 ; Purchas, Vol. 4 : Appendix 1.

Beranger, Don Carlos de. Relacion Jeografica de la Provincia de Chiloé. Publicada por primera vez con una Introduccion i notas esplicativas por Nicolas Anrique. Royal 8* *Santiago,* 1893

Bérard, A. Description Nautique des Côtes de l'Algérie, suivie de Notes par De Tessan. *Plates.* 8°   *Paris,* 1837

Berchet, Guglielmo. La Repubblica di Venezia e la Persia. *Photographs.* 8°   *Turin,* 1865
—— Relazione dei Consoli Veneti nella Siria. 8°   *Turin,* 1866
—— Il Planisferio di Giovanni Leardo dell' anno 1452. 4*   *Venice,* 1880

Berchtold, Count Leopold. An Essay to Direct and Extend the Inquiries of Patriotic Travellers ; to which is added a Catalogue of the most Interesting European Travels up to 1787. 2 vols. in 1. 12°   1789

Berdmore, Septimus. Report on the Inzer Estate, situate in the Government of Orenberg . . ; accompanied by Plans. Folio   1865

Bérenger-Féraud, L. J. B. Les Peuplades de la Sénégambie. 8° *Paris,* 1879

Bérengier, T. La Nouvelle-Nursie. Histoire d'une Colonie Bénédictine dans l'Australie occidentale (1846-78). *Map and plates.* 8°   *Paris* [1879]

Beresford, B. *See* Kotzebue, A.

Berg, A. Bidrag til Kundskab om Fœröerne. 8* *Nykjobin in Zeeland,* 1889

Bergen, W. C. Navigation and Nautical Astronomy. 4th edition. 8°   1876
—— Seamanship. 3rd edition. 8° 1877

Berger, Capt. Directions for the Use of the Patent Sphereometer, invented for the purpose of obviating all abstruse Calculations in Navigation, likewise for facilitating passages from one place to another. 8*   N.D.

Berger, Dr Hugo. Die Geographischen Fragmente des Eratosthenes. 8°   *Leipzig,* 1880
—— Geschichte der wissenschaftlichen Erdkunde der Griechen. Erste Abtheilung. Die Geographie der Ionier. 8°   *Leipzig,* 1887
—— The same. Zweite Abtheilung. Die Vorbereitungen für die Geographie der Erdkugel. 8°   *Leipzig,* 1889
—— The same. Dritte Abth. Die Geographie der Erdkugel. 8° *Leipzig,* 1891
—— The same. Vierte Abth. Die Geographie der Griechen unter dem Einflusse der Römer. 8°   *Leipzig,* 1893

Bergeron, P. Voyages faits principalement en Asie dans les xii., xiii., xiv., et xv. Siècles, par Benjamin de Tudèle, Jean du Plan-Carpin, N. Ascelin, Guillaume de Rubruquis, Marc Paul Vénitien, Haiton, Jean de Mandeville, et Ambroise Contarini ; accompagnés de l'histoire des Sarasins et des Tartares, et précédez d'une Introduction concernant les voyages et les nouvelles découvertes des principaux voyageurs. 2 vols. in 1. *Maps.* 4°   *The Hague,* 1735

Bergh, Augustus. An Essay on the Causes of Distant Alternate Periodic Inundations over the Low Lands of each Hemisphere, suggesting the means whereby the Earth's surface is renovated . . . 8° 1830

—— Die ersten Elemente der Erdbeschreibung. 12° *Berlin,* 1830

Berghaus, Heinrich. Asia. Geo-Hydrographisches Memoir zur Erklärung und Erläuterung der reduzirten Karte von Hinterindien, Persischer Golf, Philippinen, Sulu-Ins. Assam, und seinen Nachbar - Ländern Bhotan, Djyntia, Katschlar, Muniper; nebst Bemerkungen über die nördlichen Provinzen des Birma-Reichs, Syrien, Arabia, und dem Nil-Lande. *Maps.* 2 vols. 4° *Gotha,* 1832-35

—— Allgemeine Länder und Völkerkunde; nebst einem Abris der physikalischen Erdbeschreibung. *Frontispiece and tables.* 6 vols. 8° *Stuttgart,* 1837-44

—— Annalen der Erd-, Völker- und Staatenkunde (continuation of "Hertha"). *See* Germany, Stuttgart: Appendix 3.

—— Physikalischer Atlas. Geographisches Jahrbuch zur Mittheilung aller wichtigern neuen Erforschungen. *Maps.* Parts 1 to 4. 4* *Gotha,* 1850-52

Berghaus, Heinrich, and Hoffman. Hertha, Zeitschrift für Erd-, Völker- und Staatenkunde. *See* Germany, Stuttgart: Appendix 3.

Bergman, Torbern. Physicalische Beschreibung der Erdkugel, auf Veranlassung der Cosmographischen Gesellschaft. Aus dem Schwedischen übersetzt von L. H. Röhl. *Plates.* 2 vols. 8° *Greifswald,* 1791

Bergmann, J. Untersuchungen über die freien Walliser oder Walser in Graubünden und Vorarlberg. *Map.* 8° *Vienna,* 1844

Bergmann, Minna J. A. *See* Wissmann.

Bergner, Rudolf. Rumänien. Eine Darstellung des Landes und der Leute. *Map and illustrations.* 8° *Breslau,* 1887

Bergsma, P. A., and L. Backer Overbeek. Bijdrage tot de Kennis der Weersgesteldheid ter Kuste van Atjeh. *Maps.* 4° *Batavia,* 1877

Bergstraesser, Dr. Die Verbindung des Caspischen mit dem Schwarzen Meere. *Map.* 4* *Gotha,* 1859

—— De la Réunion de la Mer Caspienne à la Mer Noire. *Map.* 8* *Paris,* 1861

Berjeau, J. P. Calcoen: a Dutch Narrative of the Second Voyage of Vasco da Gama to Calicut, printed at Antwerp circa 1504; with Introduction and Translation. Square 8* 1874

Berkley, J. J. Surveys by the Great Indian Peninsular Railway Company of the North-Eastern extension from Munmar to Mirzapore. *Map.* Royal 8° 1855

Berkley, J. J. Extracts from a Report relating to the Nerbudda River and Valley. [From the India Records, Nos. 14 and 19.] Royal 8° *Bombay,* 1855

Berlepsch, H. A. Die Gotthard-Bahn. (Ergänzungsheft, 65—Petermann's Mittheilungen). *3 coloured maps.* 4° *Gotha,* 1881

Berlioux, Étienne Felix. La Traite Orientale: Histoire des Chasses à l'homme organisées en Afrique depuis quinze ans, pour les Marchés de l'Orient. *Map.* 8° *Paris,* 1870

—— The Slave Trade in Africa in 1872, principally carried on for the supply of Turkey, Egypt, Persia, and Zanzibar; with a Preface by Joseph Cooper. 8° 1872

—— Doctrina Ptolemæi ab injuriâ recentiorum vindicata, sive Nilus superior et Niger verus, hodiernus Eghirren, ab antiquis explorati. *Maps.* 8° *Paris,* 1874

—— André Brue, ou l'origine de la Colonie Française du Sénégal, avec une Carte de la Sénégambie. 8° *Paris,* 1874

—— La première École de Géographie Astronomique et la prochaine découverte du pays des Garamantes. 8* *Lyons,* 1878

—— Les Anciennes Explorations et les futures découvertes de l'Afrique Centrale. 2nd edition. *Map.* 8* *Lyons,* 1879

—— Lecture de la Carte de France: Le Jura. *Maps.* 8° *Paris,* 1880

—— Les Atlantes: Histoire de l'Atlantis et de l'Atlas primitif, ou introduction à l'histoire de l'Europe. Large 8° *Paris,* 1883

—— Les Chétas sont des Scythai. Small folio* *Lyons,* 1888

Bermudes, B. *See* Wertheman.

Bermudez, John. *See* Purchas, Vol. 2, Book 7: Appendix 1.

Bernard (the Wise). *See* Recueil de Voyages, Vol. 4, p. 612: Appendix 1.

Bernard, Dr. L'Algérie qui s'en va. *Illustrations.* 12° *Paris* [1887]

Bernard, Capt. F. De Lyon à la Méditerranée. *Map and illustrations.* Small 8° *Paris,* 1855

—— Quatre mois dans le Sahara: Journal d'un Voyage chez les Touareg suivi d'un aperçu sur la deuxième Mission du Colonel Flatters. *Map and plates.* 12° *Paris,* 1881

Bernard, H., and E. Tissot. Itinéraire pour l'Isthme de Suez et les grandes villes d'Egypte (Vocabulaire Francais-Egyptien). *Map.* 12° *Paris,* 1869

Bernard, W. D. *See* Hall, W. H.

Bernardin, R. J. Classification de 100 Caoutchoucs et Gutta-Perchas. 8*
Ghent, 1872
—— Les Richesses naturelles du Globe et l'Exposition Universelle de Vienne. 8*
Ghent, 1873
—— Classification de 250 Fécules. 8*
Ghent, 1876
—— L'Afrique Centrale : Étude sur ses produits commerciaux. *Map.* 8*
Ghent, 1877
Bernardine. *See* Churchill, Vol. 8 : Appendix 1.
Bernatz, John Martin. Scenes in Ethiopia, designed from nature ; with Descriptions of the Plates, and Extracts from a Journal of Travel in that Country. 2 vols in 1. Oblong folio 1852
Bernays, L. A. The Duty of States in the Teaching of the Science and Technology of Plant Life. 8* *Brisbane*, 1875
—— Acclimatisation Society of Queensland. [Report for the year 1879.] Folio*
[Brisbane] 1880
—— Economic Tropical Horticulture in Northern Queensland. Folio
[Brisbane] 1880
—— Cultural Industries for Queensland : Papers on the Cultivation of useful Plants suited to the Climate of Queensland ; their value as Food, in the Arts, and in Medicine ; and Methods of Obtaining their Products. First Series. 8°
Brisbane, 1883
Berncastle, Dr. A Voyage to China, including a Visit to the Bombay Presidency, the Mahratta Country, the Cave Temples of Western India, Singapore, the Straits of Malacca and Sunda, and the Cape of Good Hope. 2 vols. *Plan and plates.* 12° 1850
Berndt, G. Das Val d' Anniviers und das Bassin de Sierre. (Ergänzungsheft, 68—Petermann's Mittheilungen.) *Coloured map.* 4° *Gotha*, 1882
—— Der Alpenföhn. (Ergänzungsheft, 83—Petermann's Mittheilungen.) *Map.* 4° *Gotha*, 1886
Berneaud, A. T. de. A Voyage to the Isle of Elba ; with Notices of the other Islands in the Tyrrhenian Sea. Translated from the French by William Jerdan. *Map.* 8° 1814
Bernegg. *See* Sprecher von Bernegg.
Bernier, François. Travels in the Mogul Empire. Translated by Irving Brock. 2 vols in 1. 8° 1826
—— Travels in the Mogul Empire, A.D. 1656-68. A Revised edition by Archibald Constable. *Maps and illustrations.* 8° 1891
—— *See* Churchill, Vol. 8 ; Laharpe, Vol. 5 ; Pinkerton, Vol. 8 ; Allgemeine Historie, Vol. 11 : Appendix 1.

Bernier, T. Dictionnaire Géographique, Historique, Archéologique, Biographique et Bibliographique du Hainaut. 12°
Mons, 1879
Bernouilli, J. Nachrichten von Italien. Band 3. Sicilien, &c. 8° *Leipzig*, 1782
—— Description Historique et Géographique de l'Inde, &c. *Maps and plates.* 3 vols. 4° *Berlin*, 1786-89
CONTENTS.
Vol. 1.—J. Tieffenthaler. La Géographie de l'Indoustan 1786
Vol. 2.—Anquetil du Perron. Les recherches Historiques et Géographiques sur l'Inde 1787
Vol. 3.—Part 1. Memoires de Jacques Rennell ; Plan d'Administration pour l'Inde 1788
Vol. 3.—Part 2.—Divers Mémoires Historiques et Géographiques 1789
Bernouilli, Raphaël. La Souanétie Libre : Épisode d'un Voyage à la Chaine Centrale du Caucase. *Illustrations.* 4°
Paris, 1875
Bert, Paul. *See* Chailley.
Berthelot, S. *See* Webb, P.
Berthézène, Baron. Dix-huit Mois à Alger, ou récit des Événemens qui s'y sont passés 1830-31. 8° *Montpellier*, 1834
Bertius, P. Tabularum Geographicarum Contractarum, Libri Quinque cum Luculentis Singularum Tabularum Explicationibus. *Maps and illustrations.* Oblong 8° *Amsterdam*, 1606
Bertolotti, A. Passeggiate nel Canavese. Vols. 1 to 4. 8° *Ivrea*, 1867-70
Bertolotti, David. Viaggio ai tre Laghi di Como, Lugano, e Maggiore. 16°
Como, 1825
Berton, Comte de. Le Mont Hor, le Tombeau d'Aaron. Cadès : étude sur l'Itinéraire des Israélites dans le Désert. *Maps and plates.* Royal 8° *Paris*, 1860
Bertram, J. G. *See* Galton, Francis, Vacation Tourists.
Bertrand, A. Departamento de Tarapacá : Aspecto Jeneral del Terreno, su Clima i sus Producciones. *Map.* 8*
Santiago, 1879
—— Voyage au Cachemire. 8*
Geneva, 1884
—— Passage de l'est à l'ouest du Détroit de Magellan et des canaux lateraux de la Patagonie. 8* *Geneva*, 1888
—— Souvenirs de l'Exposition Africaine, Londres, 1890 : Exposé d'une Communication faite à la Société de Géographie de Genève. 8* *Geneva*, 1891
—— Exposé d'une Communication sur Tientsin, Péking, la grand muraille de Chine, Résidence Impériale de Djehol (Mongolie intérieure), les tombeaux des Mings, la Passe de Nan-Koou, faite à la Société de Géographie de Genève le 6 Janvier 1893. 8* *Geneva*, 1893

Bertrand, P. J. B. Précis de l'Histoire Physique, Civile et Politique, de la Ville de Boulogne-sur-Mer et de ses Environs, depuis les Morins jusqu'en 1814. *Maps and plates.* 2 vols. 8° *Boulogne*, 1828-29

Bertus. *See* Hakluyt, Vol. 1 : Appendix 1.

Besant, Sir Walter. Captain Cook. *Portrait.* Small 8° 1890

—— The Life and Achievements of Edward Henry Palmer, Professor of Arabic in the University of Cambridge. By Walter Besant. 4th edition. *Portrait.* Small 8° 1883

Bescherelle, E. *See* France, B (Cape Horn) : Appendix 2.

Bescherelle, M., and G. Devars. Grand Dictionnaire de Géographie Universelle, Ancienne et Moderne, &c. 4 vols. 4° *Paris*, 1857

Beschi, Père Constant. Mémoire sur la Vie, les Ouvrages, et les Travaux Apostoliques, par M. Eug. Sicé. 8* *Paris*, 1841

Beschoren, Max. São Pedro do Rio Grande do Sul. (Ergänzungsheft, 96—Petermann's Mittheilungen.) *Map.* 4° *Gotha*, 1889

Besobrasof, W. De l'Influence de la Science Economique sur la Vie de l'Europe Moderne. 4* *St Petersburg*, 1867

Besse, Jean-Charles de. Voyage en Crimée, au Caucase, en Géorgie, en Arménie, en Asie-Mineure et à Constantinople, en 1829 et 1838, pour servir à l'Histoire de Hongrie. *Plates.* 8° *Paris*, 1838

Bessel's Refraction-Tables as Employed at the Cape of Good Hope. 4° N.D.

Bessels, Emil. Die Amerikanische Nordpol-Expedition. *Map and plates.* 8° *Leipzig*, 1879

—— *See* "Polaris."

Besson, —. *See* Yule, C. B.

Best, Capt. Abel Dottin. Journal of an Excursion into the Interior of the Northern Island of New Zealand. 8* [*Auckland*, 1842]

Best, Capt. S., and Major H. C. Cotton. Irrigation Reports and Maps of the Presidency of Madras. [From the India Records, Vol. 2] 1855-64

—— Memorandum on the System of Irrigation in the Madras Presidency. [From the India Records, Vol. 2.] *Plates.* *Madras*, 1855-64

Best, Capt. Thomas. *See* Gottfried ; Kerr, Vol. 9 ; Purchas, Vol. 1, Book 4 : Appendix 1.

Betagh, William. Voyage round the World : being an Account of a Remarkable Enterprise, begun 1719, chiefly to Cruise on the Spaniards in the Great South Ocean, relating to the True Historical Facts of that whole affair. *Map.* 8° 1728

Betagh, William. *See* Harris, Vol. 1 ; Kerr, Vol. 10 ; Pinkerton, Vol. 14 : Appendix 1.

Beteta, Gregorio de. *See* Ternaux-Compans, Vol. 20 : Appendix 1.

Betham-Edwards, M. The Roof of France ; or, The Causses of the Lozère. 8° 1889

Bethencourt, J. de. *See* Avezac ; *also* Hakluyt Soc. Publ., Vol. 46 : Appendix 1.

Bethune, Adm. C. R. D. Note on a Method of Reducing the Apparent Distance of the Moon from Sun or Star to the True Distance. 8* N.D.

—— Tables for Travellers, adapted to the pocket or sextant case. 24° 1872

—— *See* Hakluyt Soc. Publ., Vols. 1, 30 : Appendix 1.

Bethune, Baron Léon. Les Missions Catholiques d'Afrique. 8° *Lille*, 1889

Bettelheim, Dr Anton. *See* Ruge ; Smith (Bishop).

Betts, John. Exercises on Interrogatory Maps : Europe, England and Wales, Scotland, Ireland. 4 parts. 18* N.D.

Beulé, —. *See* Circourt.

Beurmann, Moritz von. *See* Petermann and Hassenstein.

Bevan, G. P. Primer of the Industrial Geography of Great Britain and Ireland. 12° 1880

—— Home Geography of England and Wales for the use of Schools. *Maps.* 8° 1893

Bevan, Theodore F. [Mr Bevan's Discoveries in New Guinea.—Newspaper Cuttings.] 8* 1887

—— Mr Theodore F. Bevan's Fifth Expedition to British New Guinea. *Map and illustrations.* 8° [*Sydney*] 1888

—— Toil, Travel, and Discovery in British New Guinea. *Maps.* 8° 1890

Bevan, W. L. The Student's Manual of Ancient Geography. Edited by William Smith. *Maps and cuts.* 12° 1867

—— and **H. W. Phillott.** Mediæval Geography : an Essay in Illustration of the Hereford Mappa Mundi. 8° 1873

Beveridge, H. Annual Address to the Asiatic Society of Bengal. 8* *Calcutta*, 1891

—— Sahibganj and Rajmahal. (From the *Calcutta Review.*) 8* 1893

Beveridge, Bishop W. Institutionum Chronologicarum, Lib. II., unà cum Totidem Arithmeticis Chronologicæ Libellis. Small 4° 1669

Beverley, H. Report on the Census of Bengal, 1872. *Maps.* Folio *Calcutta*, 1872

Bevir, J. L. Visitor's Guide to Orvieto. 12* 1884

Beyer's Guide to Western Norway ; with the Coast-route to the North Cape and Overland Routes to Christiania, by Viljam Olsvig. *Maps and panoramic view.* 12° *Bergen* [1887]

Beynen, L. R. K. *See* Koolemans Beynen.

Beyrich, E. Ueber geognostische Beobachtungen G. Schweinfurth's in der Wüste zwischen Cairo und Sues. *Maps.* Large 8*   *Berlin*, 1882

Bezaure, G. de. Le Fleuve Bleu : Voyage dans la Chine Occidentale. *Map and plates.* 16°   *Paris*, 1879

Bezold, Wilhelm von. Ueber zündende Blitze im Königreich Bayern, während des Zeitraumes 1833 bis 1882. *Map.* 4*   [*Munich*, 1886]

Bezzenberger, Dr A. *See* Müller, Dr A. ; *also* Germany, C (Forschungen, &c., Vol. 3): Appendix 2.

Bháttá Bhavabhúti. The Mahá Víra Charita ; or, The History of Ráma, a Sanscrit Play. (In the Déva-Nágaré Character.) Edited by Francis H. Trithen. Royal 8°   1848

Bianchi, —. *See* Recueil de Voyages, Vol. 2, p. 611 : Appendix 1.

Bianchi, V. *See* Schrenck and Maximowicz, 4.

Bianco, Andrea. L'Atlante di Andrea Bianco dell' Anno 1436, in dieci Tavole. Facsimile Fotografico nella Grandezza dell' Originale che si conserva nella Biblioteca Marciana, con Illustrazione di Oscarre Peschel. 4*   *Venice*, 1871

Bianconi, G. Guida del Forestiere par la Città di Bologna e suoi Sobborghi. 2 vols. *Map and plates.* 12° *Bologna*, 1820
—— Guida di Bologna. *Map and plates.* 12°   *Bologna*, 1826

Bianconi, J. Joseph. De Mari olim occupante planities et Colles Italiæ, Græciæ, Asiæ Minoris, &c., et de Ætate Terreni quod Geologi appellant Marnes Bleues. *Plate.* 5 parts. 4* *Bologna*, 1846-52

Bicheno, J. E. Ireland and its Economy. 8°   1830

Bickersteth, Miss M. Japan as we saw it ; with a Preface by the Bishop of Exeter. *Map and illustrations.* 8°   1893

Bickmore, Dr Albert S. The Ainos, or Hairy Men of Yesso, Saghalien, and the Kurile Islands. 8* *New Haven*, 1868
—— Travels in the East Indian Archipelago. *Maps and plates.* 8°   1868

Biddle, John. *See* Cabot, S.

Biddlecombe, G. Directions for Entering the River Tagus. 8°   1848 and 1854

Biddulph, C. E. The "Friend of London," or the Rajputs of Meywar. 8*   1891
—— Four Months in Persia, and a Visit to the Trans-Caspian. Large 8°   1892
—— Physical Geography of Persia. (From the *Imperial and Asiatic Quarterly Review*, July 1892.) Large 8*   1892

Biddulph, J. Tribes of the Hindoo Koosh. *Map and plates.* 8° *Calcutta*, 1880

Biddulph, W. *See* Churchill, Vol. 7 ; Purchas, Vol. 2, Book 8 : Appendix 1.

Bidermann, Dr H. J. *See* Germany, C (Forschungen, &c., Vols. 1 and 2): Appendix 2.

Bidwell, C. T. The Isthmus of Panamá. *Plate.* 8°   1865
—— The Balearic Isles. *Map and plates.* 12°   1876
—— The Cost of Living Abroad : Reports and Statistics showing the Prices of House Rent, &c., at the present time, and compared with those of the year 1858, at most of the principal places in Foreign Countries ; . . with an Appendix showing Hotel Charges, &c. 12° 1876
—— Account of the Aborigines of the Island of Puerto Rico. Compiled from "La Historia Geográphica Civil y Politica de la Isla de San Juan Bautista de Puerto Rico," by Fray Iñigo Abbad ; published at Madrid in 1788. 8* 1879

Bieberstein, Marschall. *See* Reineggs, Dr J.

Biedma, Luis H. de. *See* Hakluyt Soc. Publ., Vol. 9 ; Ternaux-Compans. Vol. 20 : Appendix 1.

Biedermann, Dr W. G. A. Petrefacten aus der Umgegend von Winterthur. Die Braunkohlen von Elgg. *Plates.* 4* *Winterthur*, 1863
—— Petrefacten aus der Umgegend von Winterthur, Viertes Heft, Reste aus Veltheim. *Plates.* 4* *Winterthur*, 1873
—— Chéloniens Tertiaires des Environs de Winterthur. Traduction Française par O. Bourrit. *Plates.* 4* *Winterthur*, N.D.

Bielenstein, Dr A. Die Grenzen des Lettischen Volksstammes und der Lettischen Sprache in der Gegenwart und im 13 Jahrhundert ; ein Beitrag zur ethnologischen Geographie und Geschichte Russlands. *With atlas.* 4° *St Petersburg*, 1892

Bielz, E. A. Siebenbürgen : ein Handbuch für Reisende nach eigenen zahlreichen Reisen und Ausflügen in diesem Lande. 2nd edition. *Maps and plans.* 12°   *Vienna*, 1885

Biffart, M. *See* United Kingdom, G : Appendix 2.

Bigelow, John. Jamaica in 1850, or the Effect of Sixteen Years of Freedom on a Slave Colony. 12° *New York*, 1851

Bigelow, Poultney. Paddles and Politics down the Danube. *Illustrations.* Crown 8°   1892

Biggar, E. B. *See* Canada, B : Appendix 2.

Bigg - Wither, T. P. Pioneering in South Brazil : Three Years of Forest and Prairie Life in the Province of Paraná. 2 vols. *Map and plates.* 8° 1878

Bigsby, John J. The Shoe and Canoe ; or, Pictures of Travel in the Canadas. *Maps and plates.* 2 vols. 8°   1850

Bikkers, A. V. W. On Spelling Reform, together with Clinton's International Pronunciation Table. 8° 1877

Bilbrough, E. Ernest. *See* Brett, H.

Bilderbeck, L. von. Wegweiser für Fremde im Aachen, Burtscheid, und ihren Umgebungen, nebst einem Ausflug nach Spa. *Map.* 8* *Aix la Chapelle*, 1825

Bilgrami, Syed Hossain, and C. Willmott. Historical and Descriptive Sketch of His Highness the Nizam's Dominions. 2 vols. *Map.* Large 8°
Bombay, 1883-84

Bilioth, Edouard, and Abbé Cottret. L'Ile de Rhodes. *Map, plan, and illustrations.* Large 8° *Rhodes*, 1881

Bille, Capt. Steen. Beretning om Corvetten Galathea's Reise omkring Jorden, 1845-47. *Maps and plates.* 3 vols. 8°
Copenhagen, 1849-51

Billecocq. *See* Pallas.

Billinghurst, Guillermo E. Reconocimiento Militar del Rio Desaguadero y de la Altiplanicie Andina. *Plate.* Large 8°
Lima, 1880
—— Estudio sobre la Geographia de Tarapacá (páginas de un libro) trabajo escrito para el Ateneo de Iquique. 8*
Santiago, 1886
—— La Irrigación en Tarapacá. *Maps and plates.* Large 8* *Santiago*, 1893

Billings, Capt. *See* Sarychef; *also* Eyriès, Vol. 6: Appendix 1.

Billings, E. Catalogues of the Silurian Fossils of the Island of Anticosti, with Descriptions of some new Genera and Species. *Cuts.* 8° *Montreal*, 1866
—— *See* Canada, A: Appendix 2.

Billings, John S. *See* United States, A (Tenth Census, Vols. 11 and 12): Appendix 2.

Binder, Henry. Au Kurdistan en Mésopotamie et en Perse (Mission scientifique du Ministère de l'Instruction publique). *Map and illustrations.* 4° *Paris*, 1887

Bineteau, H. Note sur les usages des populations indigènes de la Cochinchine Française. *Map.* 8* *Paris*, 1863
—— Notice sur la Basse-Cochinchine. 8*
Paris, 1864

Binger, Capt. L. G. Du Niger au Golfe de Guinée par Kong. *Map.* 8*
Paris, 1889
—— Esclavage, Islamisme et Christianisme. 8° *Paris*, 1891
—— Du Niger au Golfe de Guinée par le pays de Kong et le Mossi (1887-89). 2 vols in 1. *Map and illustrations.* 4°
Paris, 1892

Bingham, J. Elliot. Narrative of the Expedition to China, from the Commencement of the War to the Present Period. *Map and plates.* 2 vols. 8° 1842

Binney, W. G. *See* Gould, A. A.

Binnie, A. R. On Mean or Average Rainfall. 8* 1892

Binning, Robert B. M. Journal of Two Years' Travel in Persia, Ceylon, &c. 2 vols. 8° 1857

Biolley, Paul. Costa Rica and her Future. Translated from the French by Cecil Charles. *Map.* 8°
Washington, D.C., 1889

Biondelli, B. Scoperta dell' America fatta nel Secolo X. da alcuni Scandinavi. 8*
Milan, 1839
—— Sullo Stato attuale della Sardegna. 8*
Milan, 1841

Biot, Édouard. Mémoire sur divers Minéraux Chinois appartenant à la Collection du Jardin du Roi. 8*
Paris, 1839
—— Recherches sur la Hauteur de quelques Points Remarquables du Territoire Chinois. 8* *Paris*, 1840
—— Recherches sur la Température ancienne de la Chine. 8* *Paris*, 1840
—— Études sur les Montagnes et les Cavernes de la Chine, d'après les Géographies Chinoises. 8* *Paris*, 1840
—— Dictionnaire des Noms Anciens et Modernes des Villes et Arrondissements compris dans l'Empire Chinois. *Map.* Royal 8* *Paris*, 1842
—— Mémoire sur les Changemens du cours inférieur du Fleuve Jaune. *Map.* 8*
Paris, 1843
—— Mémoire sur l'Extension Progressive des Côtes Orientales de la Chine, depuis les Anciens Temps. 8* *Paris*, 1844
—— Sur la Direction de l'Aiguille aimantée en Chine et sur les Aurores Boréales observées dans ce même pays. 4*
Paris, 1844
—— Le Tcheou-Li, ou Rites des Tcheou. Traduit du Chinois par Biot; avec Table Analytique. *Map and plates.* 3 vols. 8°
Paris, 1851

Biot, J. B. Relation du Voyage de Découvertes, éxécute par ordre des États-Unis d'Amerique, pendant 1838-1842. Rédigée par le Lieut. Charles Wilkes. *Map.* 4° *Paris*, 1849
—— Notice sur la Vie et les Travaux de, par Alfred Maury. 12* *Paris*, 1851
—— *See* Kiefer; Maury, A.

Birago, Gen. On the Projected Canal between the Danube and the Black Sea. Folio* 1839

Birch, S. *See* Ebers, G.; Wilkinson, Sir J. G.

Birch, W. De G. *See* Hakluyt Soc. Publ., Vols. 53, 55, 62: Appendix 1.

Bird, Charles. A Short Sketch of the Geology of Yorkshire. *Map and plates.* Small 8° 1881

D

Bird, Isabella L. [Mrs Bishop]. The Hawaiian Archipelago: Six Months among the Palmgroves, Coral Reefs, and Volcanoes of the Sandwich Islands. *Map and plates.* Small 8°   1875
—— Unbeaten Tracks in Japan: an Account of Travels in the Interior, including Visits to the Aborigines of Yezo and the Shrines of Nikkô and Isé. 2 vols. *Map and illustrations.* Small 8°   1880
—— Unbeaten Tracks in Japan. New edition, abridged. *Illustrations.* Crown 8°   1885
—— The Golden Chersonese, and the Way thither. *Maps and illustrations.* 8°   1883
—— Journeys in Persia and Kurdistan, including a Summer in the Upper Karun Region, and a Visit to the Nestorian Rayahs. 2 vols. *Portrait, maps, and illustrations.* 8°   1891
—— A Journey through Lesser Tibet. 8* [1892]
—— Among the Tibetans. (From the *Leisure Hour* for February and March 1893.) *Illustrations.* 4*   1893
Bird, James. Abyssinia, Eastern Africa, and the Ethiopic Family of Languages Reviewed. *Table.* 8* *Bombay,* 1845
—— Discourse on the Object and Progress of Investigation into Oriental Literature and Science. 8*   *Bombay,* 1845
Birdwood, Sir George. *See* Stevens, Henry.
—— and William Foster. The Register of Letters, &c., of the Governour and Company of Merchants of London trading into the East Indies, 1600-19. Large 8° 1893
Birkbeck, M. Tour in France in 1814. 8°   1815
Birkmyre,W. *See* Victoria, C: Appendix 2.
Birlinger, Dr A. Schwäbisch-Augsburgisches Wörterbuch. 8° *Munich,* 1864
—— *See* Germany, C (Forschungen, &c., Vol. 4): Appendix 2.
Birt, W. R. Tabulæ Anemologicæ; or, Tables of the Wind, exhibiting a New Method of Registering the Direction of the Wind, by which the Variations of the Upper and Lower Currents of the Atmosphere, at several stations, are shown at one view. Nos. 1 and 2. 4* 1835
Biscari, Ignazio Paterno [Principe di]. Viaggio per tutte le Anticheita della Sicilia. *Map and plates.* 12° *Palermo,* 1817
Bischof, Gustav. Die Gestalt der Erde und der Meeresfläche, und die Erosion des Meeresbodens. 8* *Bonn,* 1867
Bischoff, James. Sketch of the History of Van Diemen's Land, and an Account of the Van Diemen's Land Company. *Maps and plates.* 8°   1832

Biscoe, John. Journal of a Voyage towards the South Pole, on board the brig "Tula," under the command of John Biscoe, with cutter "Lively" in company, 1830-32. MS. Folio.
Bishop, Mrs. *See* Bird, Isabella L.
Bishop, N. H. Voyage of the Paper Canoe: a Geographical Journey of 2,500 miles, from Quebec to the Gulf of Mexico, during the years 1874-75. *Map and plates.* 8° *Edinburgh,* 1878
Bishop, William Henry. Old Mexico and her Lost Provinces: a Journey in Mexico, Southern California, and Arizona, by way of Cuba. *Maps and illustrations.* 8°   1883
Bissachère, M. de la. État actual du Tunkin, de la Cochinchine, et des Royaumes de Camboge, Laos, et Lac-tho. . . . Traduit d'après les Relations Originales, &c. 2 vols. 8° *Paris,* 1812
Bissel, J. Joannis Bisselii, è Societate Jesu, Argonauticon Americanorum, sive Historiæ, Periculorum Petri de Victoria, ac Sociorum eius, Libri xv. 16° *Munich,* 1647
—— Joannis Biselii è Societate Jesu, Palæstinæ, seu Terræ-Sanctæ Topothesia, secundum Regiones ac Tribus expressa. *Maps.* 12° *Amberg,* 1659
Bissell, Capt. Austin. *See* Dalrymple, A.
Bissuel, Capt. H. Les Touareg de l'Ouest. *Map.* Large 8* *Algiers,* 1888
Bissy, R. de Lannoy de. Voyage du R. P. Mercui des Missionnaires d'Alger de Quilemané au Lac Nyassa et retour, 1889-90. *Map.* 8* *Épinal,* 1892
Bizemont, Vicomte Henri de. La France en Afrique; Algérie et Tunisie; Sénégal et Dépendances; Gabon et Congo. 8* *Paris,* 1883
Blaauw, W. H. The Barons' War, including the Battles of Lewes and Evesham. 8°   1871
Black, James A. Memoir on the Roman Garrison at Mancunium, and its probable Influence on the Population and Language of South Lancashire. 8* *Edinburgh,* 1856
Black, C. B. Itinerary through Corsica by its Rail, Carriage, and Forest Roads. *Illustrated by five maps and one plan.* 12* *Edinburgh,* 1888
Black, C. E. D. A Memoir on the Indian Surveys, 1875-90. *Map and frontispiece.* Folio   1891
—— *See* Popowski.
Black, J. G. *See* Hutton and Ulrich.
Black, J. M. An Account of the Eruption of Mount Vesuvius of April 1872. *Chart and plate.* 8*   1874
Black, William George. Heligoland and the Islands of the North Sea. 12° 1888

Black's Picturesque Tourist of England and Wales. *Maps and plates.* 12°
Edinburgh, 1854

—— Picturesque Tourist of Scotland. *Maps.* 12° *Edinburgh*, 1859

Blackbourne, H. S. A and B Tables for Correcting the Longitude and facilitating Sumner's Method on the Chart. 8° 1883

Blackie, Miss C. Geographical Etymology: a Dictionary of Place-Names, giving their Derivations; with an Introduction by John Stuart Blackie. 3rd edition. 12° 1887

Blackie, Dr W. G. A Supplement to the Imperial Gazetteer, &c. 8° 1868

—— The Imperial Gazetteer: a General Dictionary of Geography, Physical, Political, Statistical, and Descriptive, with a Supplement bringing the Geographical Information down to the latest dates. Half volumes, 1 and 2. *Plates* 1872

—— On Geography and Etymology: What these Embrace. Sketch of the Present State of our Knowledge of the Island of New Guinea. *Map.* 8°
Glasgow, 1884

—— Commercial Education: an Address to the Educational Institute of Scotland, on Saturday, 17th March 1888. 8°
Glasgow, 1888

Blackwell, J. H. Report of the Examination of the Mineral Districts of the Nerbudda Valley. [From the India, Bombay, Records, No. 44.] *Map.* Royal 8°
Bombay, 1857

Blackwell, Thomas Evans. Results of a Series of Experiments on the Discharge of Water of Waterfalls or Weirs. *Plates.* 8° 1851

Blackwood, Capt. F. P. Sailing Directions for the Outer Passage from Sydney to Torres Strait. 8° 1847

Blackwood's Educational Series, edited by Professor Meiklejohn. Geographical Readers, Standards I.-VI., 6 vols. *Illustrations.* 12° 1883

Bladen, F. M. Historical Records of New South Wales, Vol. 2, 1793-95. *Plans.* 8° *Sydney*, 1893

Blaikie, Prof. W. G. The Personal Life of David Livingstone, chiefly from his unpublished Journals and Correspondence in the possession of his Family. By William Garden Blaikie. *Portrait and map.* 8° 1880

Blair, Lieut. A. Survey of the Andamans. [From the India Records, No. 24.] Royal 8° *Calcutta*, 1858

Blake, C. C. On certain "Simious" Skulls, with especial reference to a Skull from Louth, in Ireland. 8* N.D.

Blake, E. Vale. Arctic Experiences, containing Capt. George E. Tyson's wonderful Drift on the Ice-floe, a History of the "Polaris" Expedition, the Cruise of the "Tigress," and Rescue of the "Polaris" Survivors; to which is added a general Arctic Chronology. *Map and plates.* 8° *New York*, 1874

Blake, Prof. J. F. A Visit to the Volcanoes of Italy. (From Proc. Geologists' Assoc., August 1889.) 8* 1889

Blake, William P. Description of the Fossils and Shells collected in California. 8* *Washington*, 1855

—— Notice of Remarkable Strata containing the Remains of Infusoria and Polythalamia in the Tertiary Formation of Monterey, California. 8*
Washington, 1855

—— Observations on the Physical Geography and Geology of the Coast of California, from Bodega Bay to San Diego. *Maps.* 4* *Washington*, 1855

—— On the Rate of Evaporation on the Tulare Lakes of California. 8*
Washington, 1856

—— On the Grooving and Polishing of Hard Rocks and Minerals by Dry Sand, and Remarks on the Geology of California, &c. 8* *Washington*, N.D.

Blakesley, Joseph Williams. Four Months in Algeria, with a Visit to Carthage. *Maps and plates.* 8°
Cambridge, 1859

Blakiston, J. R. The Geographical Reader, in Seven Books. 7 vols. 12° N.D.

—— How to Teach Geography: an Introduction to J. R. Blakiston's Glimpses of the Globe. 12* N.D.

Blakiston, Capt. Thomas W. Report on the Exploration of two Passes through the Rocky Mountains in 1858. *Map.* 8° *Woolwich*, 1859

—— Five Months on the Yang-Tsze, with a Narrative of the Exploration of its Upper Waters; illustrated by A. Barton. *Maps and plates.* 8° 1862

Blanc, Henry. A Narrative of Captivity in Abyssinia; with some Account of the late Emperor Theodore, his Country and People. *Plates.* 8* 1868

Blanc, L. G. Handbuch des Wissenswürdigsten aus der Natur und Geschichte der Erde und ihrer Bewohner . . ; achte Auflage, durchgesehen, berichtigt, fortgesetzt, und vermehrt von Dr Henry Lange. Vol. 1. *Maps.* 8°
Brunswick, 1868

Blanc, Vincent le. Les Voyages Fameux qu'il a faits depuis l'âge de douze ans jusques à soixante, aux quatre parties du Monde; a sçavoir, aux Indes Orientales et Occidentales, en Perse et Pegu; aux Royaumes de Fez, de Maroc, et de Guinée, et dans toute l'Afrique interieure,

Blanc, Vincent le—*continued.*
depuis le Cap de Bonne Esperance jusques
en Alexandrie, par les terres de Monomotapa, du Preste Jean et de l'Egypte ;
aux iles de la Mediterranée, et aux
principales Provinces de l'Europe, &c. ;
le tout recueilly de ses Memoires par le
Sieur Coulon. Small 4°   *Paris*, 1648
—— The World Surveyed ; or, The Famous
Voyages and Travailes of V. Le Blanc. . .
Originally written in French, and faithfully rendered into English by Francis
Brooke, Gent. Folio   1660

Blanchard, Émile. Les preuves de la
dislocation de l'extremité sud-est du
Continent Asiatique pendant l'âge moderne de la Terre. 4*   *Paris*, 1890

Blanchet, A. P. Projet d'un Canal interocéanique maritime à grande Section à
travers le grand Isthme Américain par
le Nicaragua . . . 4*   *Bourges*, 1875
—— *See* Pouchet.

Blanckenhorn, Dr Max. Die geognostischen Verhältnisse von Afrika. (Ergänzungsheft, 90 — Petermann's Mittheil-
lungen). *Map.* 4°   *Gotha*, 1888

Blane, D. A. Miscellaneous Information
connected with the Districts of Jhalawar,
Kattywar, Muchoo Kanta, Hallar, Soruth,
Burda, Gohelwar, Oond Surweya, and
Babriawar. [From the India, Bombay,
Records, No. 37.] Royal 8° *Bombay*, 1856

Blanford, H. F. Report of the Meteorological Reporter to the Government of
Bengal : Meteorological Abstract for
the year 1873. 8*   *Calcutta*, 1874
—— The Rudiments of Physical Geography
for the use of Indian Schools, and a
Glossary of the Technical Terms em-
ployed. *Plates.* 12°   1874
—— Report on the Meteorology of India
in 1879, '80, '81', '82, '83, '84, '85. *Maps
and charts.* 4°   *Calcutta*, 1881-87
—— A Practical Guide to the Climates
and Weather of India, Ceylon, and
Burmah, and the Storms of Indian Seas,
based chiefly on the Publications of
the Indian Meteorological Department.
Diagrams. 8°   1889
—— An Elementary Geography of India,
Burma, and Ceylon. 12°   1890
—— *See* Gastrell, J. E. ; *also* India, C
(Palæontologica Indica) : Appendix 2.

Blanford, Dr W. T. Account of a Visit
to Puppádoung, an extinct Volcano in
Upper Burma. *Map.* 8* *Calcutta*, 1862
—— Notes on a Journey in Northern
Abyssinia. 8*   [*Calcutta*, 1868]
—— Observations on the Geology and
Zoology of Abyssinia. *Map and plates.*
8°   1870
—— On the Mineral Resources of India.
8*   1873

Blandford, Dr W. T. The First Part
(Mammalia) of a General Work on the
Fauna of British India, including Ceylon
and Burmah. 8°   1888-91
—— Address delivered at the Anniversary
Meeting of the Geological Society of
London, on the 21st of February 1890.
8*   1890
—— *See* Medlicott ; *also* India, C ; Persia :
Appendix 2.

Blanqui, M. Algérie : Rapport sur la
Situation Économique de nos Possessions dans le Nord de l'Afrique. 8°
                              Paris, 1840

Blaramberg, — de. De la position des
trois forteresses Tauro-Scythes dont parle
Strabon. *Maps, plans.* 8° *Odessa*, 1831

Blaremberg, Lieut-Gen. Catalogue of
Trigonometrical and Astronomical Positions determined in the Russian Empire
and along its Frontiers up to 1860. *Maps.*
[In Russian.] 4°   *St Petersburg*, 1863

Blasius, J. H. Reise im Europäischen
Russland in den Jahren 1840 und 1851.
2 vols. in 1. *Plates.* 8° *Brunswick*, 1844

Blatna and Rotzmital. *See* Horky.

Blazek, Gabriel. Entwurf einer Theorie
der Meeresströmungen. *Map.* 8*
                              Prague, 1876

Bleek, W. H. J. De Nominum Generibus
Linguarum Africæ Australis, Copticæ,
Semiticarum aliarumque Sexualium. 8°
                              Bonne, 1851
—— The Languages of Mosambique :
Vocabulary of the Dialects of Lourenzo
Marques, Inhambane, Sofala, Tette, Sena,
Quellimane, Mosambique, Cape Delgado,
Anjoane, the Maravi, Mudsau, &c., drawn
up from the MSS. of Dr W. Peters,
&c. Oblong 12°   1856
—— A Brief Account of Bushman Folk-
lore and other texts. Folio   1875
—— *See* Cape Colony : Appendix 2.

Blefkens, Dithmar. *See* Gottfried ; Purchas, Vol. 3, Book 3 : Appendix 1.

Bleicher, G. Les Vosges, le sol et les
habitants. *Maps and illustrations.* 12°
                              Paris, 1890

**Blennerhassett, Rose, and Lucy Slee-
man.** Adventures in Mashonaland. By
two Hospital Nurses. 8°   1893

Blerzy, H. Les Colonies Anglaises de la
Malaisie : Penang, Malacca, Singapore,
et Sarawak. 8°   *Paris*, 1865
—— La Télégraphie Océanique. 8*
                              Paris, 1866

Bligh, G. *See* Eyriès, Vol. 3 : Appendix 1.

Bligh, Lieut. William. Narrative of the
Mutiny on Board H.M.S. "Bounty,"
and the subsequent Voyage of part of the
Crew in the ship's boat from Tofoa, one
of the Friendly Islands, to Timor, a
Dutch Settlement in the East Indies.
Maps. 4°   1790

Bligh, Lieut. William. A Voyage to the South Sea, undertaken by command of His Majesty, for the purpose of conveying the Bread-fruit Tree to the West Indies, in His Majesty's ship "The Bounty," commanded by Lieut. William Bligh ; including an Account of the Mutiny on board said Ship, &c. *Plates.* 8° *Dublin*, 1792

Blink, Dr H. Het Kongo-Land en zijne Bewoners in bettrekking tot de Europeesche Staatkunde en den Handel. *Map.* 8° *Haarlem*, 1891

—— Nederland en zijne Bewoners: Handboek der Aardrijkskunde en Volkenkunde van Nederland, met Kaarten en Afbeeldingen. 3 vols. 8° *Amsterdam*, N.D.

—— *See* Germany, C (Forschungen, &c., Vol. 4): Appendix 2.

Bliss, Richard. Classified Index to the Maps in the Royal Geographical Society's Publications, 1830-83. Large 8* *Cambridge, Mass.*, 1886

Block, Eugen. Hilfstafeln zur Berechnung der Polaris-Azimute zunächst mit Rücksicht auf die Zeitbestimmung im Verticale des Polarsterns. 4* *St Petersburg*, 1875

Block, Maurice. Bevölkerung des Französischen Kaiserreichs, in ihren wichtigsten statistischen Verhältnissen. *Maps.* 12° *Gotha*, 1861

—— L'Europe, Politique et Sociale. 2nd edition. *Maps.* 8° *Paris*, 1892

Blodget, Lorin. Climatology of Pennsylvania. *Map and diagram.* 8° *Harrisburg*, 1889

Blois, John T. Gazetteer of the State of Michigan, in three parts ; containing a General View of the State, with a succinct History from the Earliest Period to the Present Time ; and an Appendix, containing the usual Statistical Tables, and a Directory for Emigrants, &c. 12° *Detroit, Mich.*, 1838

Blomberg, Albert. *See* Sweden, A, Geologiska Undersökning : Appendix 2.

Blome, R. A Description of the Island of Jamaica, with the other Isles and Territories of America to which the English are related, viz., Barbadoes, St Christophers, Nievis or Nevis, Antego, St Vincent, Dominica, Montserrat, Anguilla, Barbada, Bermudes, Carolina, Virginia, Maryland, New York, New England, Newfoundland. Taken from the Notes of Sir Thomas Linch, Knight, Governour of Jamaica, and other experienced Persons in the said places. 12° 1672

"Blonde," H.M.S. *See* Pacific Islands: Appendix 2.

Blore, W. L. Statistics of the Cape Colony. 8° *Cape Town*, 1871

Blosseville, Ernest de. Histoire des Colonies Pénales de l'Angleterre dans l'Australie. 8° *Paris*, 1831

Blount, H. A Voyage into the Levant : a Breife Relation of a Journey lately performed by Master H. B., Gentleman, from England by the way of Venice, into Dalmatia, Sclavonia, Bosnah, Hungary, Macedonia, Thessaly, Thrace, Rhodes, and Egypt, unto Gran Cairo ; with particular Observations concerning the Moderne Condition of the Turkes and other People under that Empire. 12° 1636

—— *See* Churchill, Vol. 7; Gottfried; Pinkerton, Vol. 10: Appendix 1.

Bloxam, George W. *See* Transactions, Anthropological Institute, Index to Publications: Appendix 3.

Blümcke, Kurt. Der Aufstand in Deutsch Ostafrika und seine Niederwerkung im nördlichen Theil mit einem Nachwort über die Deutsche und die Englische Emin Pascha Expedition. *Map and illustrations.* Large 8° *Berlin*, N.D.

Blume, C. L. Toelichtingen aangaande de Nasporingen op Borneo van O. Müller. 8* *Leyden*, 1842

Blumentritt, Ferdinand. Organisation Communale des Indigènes des Philippines placés sous la domination Espagnole. Traduit de l'Allemand . . . par A. Hugot. 8* *Paris*, 1881

—— Versuch einer Ethnographie der Philippinen. (Ergänzungsheft, 67 — Petermann's Mittheilungen.) *Map.* 4° *Gotha*, 1882

—— Vocabular einzelner Ausdrücke und Redensarten, welche dem Spanischen der Philippinischen Inseln eigenthümlich sind ; mit einem Anhange : Bibliotheca Philippina ; Alphabetisch geordnete Sammlung einer Anzahl von Druckschriften und Manuscripten linguistischen, geographischen, ethnographischen, historischen und naturwissenschaftlichen Inhalts die auf die Philippinen Bezug haben. 8* *[Leitmeritz*, 1882]

—— The same. II. Theil. 8* *[Leitmeritz*, 1885]

—— Die Sprachgebiete Europas am Ausgange des Mittelalters, verglichen mit den Zuständen der Gegenwart. 8* *[Prague*, 1883]

—— Breve Diccionarrio Etnográfico de Filipinas. 12* *Manila*, 1889

—— Alphabetisches Verzeichnis der eingeborenen Stämme der Philippinen und der von ihnen gesprochenen Sprachen. 8* *Berlin*, 1890

Blumhardt, C. H. [No. 1, Vol. 9, of the *Church Missionary Record*, consisting of Extracts from the Journal of C. H. Blumhardt, during his Voyage to Abyssinia.] 8* 1838

Blundell, B. The Contributions of J. L. Peyton to the History of Virginia, and of the Civil War in America, 1861-65, Reviewed. 8* 1868

Blundevile, M. His Exercises, containing Eight Treatises. [On Navigation.] 4th edition. Small 8° 1613

Blunt, Lady Anne. Bedouin Tribes of the Euphrates. 2 vols. *Maps and plates.* 8° 1879
—— A Pilgrimage to Nejd, the Cradle of the Arab Race. A Visit to the Court of the Arab Emir, and "Our Persian Campaign." 2nd edition. 2 vols. *Map, portraits, and illustrations.* Small 8° 1881

Blunt, G. W. Memoirs of the Dangers and Ice in the North Atlantic Ocean. *Maps.* 8° *New York*, 1856

Blyden, Dr E. W. Appendix to Benj. Anderson's Journey to Musadu. Small 8* *New York*, 1870
—— Report on the Falaba Expedition, 1872. *Map.* Folio* *Freetown*, 1872
—— Christianity, Islam, and the Negro Race; with an Introduction by the Hon. Samuel Lewis. 8° 1887

Blyth, Bishop. *See* Lees, G. R.

Blyth, Edward. *See* Speke.

Blytt, A. On Variations of Climate in the Course of Time. 8* *Christiania*, 1886
—— The Probable Cause of the Displacement of Beach-lines: an Attempt to compute Geological Epochs. *Plate.* 8* *Christiania*, 1889
—— Additional Note to the probable Cause of the Displacement of Beach-lines. 8* [1889]
—— The Displacement of Beach-lines: Second Additional Note (read 15th February 1889). 8* 1889

Boas, Dr Franz. Baffin Land. (Ergänzungsheft, 80—Petermann's Mittheilungen). *Maps and sketches.* 4° *Gotha*, 1885

Boblaye, E. P. de. *See* Greece (Morea): Appendix 2.

Bocage. *See* Barbié du Bocage.

Boccaccio, Giovanni. Opera, tradotta di Latt. in volgare da M. Niccolò Liburnio, doue per ordine d'Alfabeto si tratta diffusamente de' Monti, Selva, Boschi, Fonti, Laghi, Stagni, Paludi, Golfii, e Mari, dell' Universo Mondo, d'Asia, Africa, ed Europa. 12° *Florence*, 1598

Boccardo, Gerolamo. Fisica del Globo. Spazi, climi e meteore, corso completo di Geografia Fisica e di Meteorologia. *Maps.* 8° *Genoa*, 1862

Boccaro, Antonio. *See* Portuguese Conquests, p. 612: Appendix 1.

Bock, Carl. The Head Hunters of Borneo: a Narrative of Travel up the Mahakkam and down the Barito, also Journeyings in Sumatra. *Map and coloured plates.* Large 8° 1881
—— Temples and Elephants: the Narrative of a Journey of Exploration through Upper Siam and Lao. *Map, coloured plates, and illustrations.* 8° 1884 [1883]
—— Reis in Oost- en Zuid-Borneo van Koetei naar Banjermassin, ondernomen op last der Indische Regeering in 1879 en 1880; met Aanteekeningen en Bijlagen van P. J. B. C. Robidé van der Aa, eene historische Inleiding over Koetei en de Betrekkingen van dit Leenrijk tot de Regeering van Nederlandsch-Indië, door S. W. Tromp, en een Atlas van 30 ethnografische platen in Kleurendruk en Schetskaart. 4° *The Hague*, 1887

Bocthor, Ellious. Dictionnaire Français-Arabe; revu et augmenté par A. Caussin de Perceval. 2 vols. 4° *Paris*, 1828-29

Boddam-Whetham, J. W. Pearls of the Pacific. *Plates.* 8° 1876
—— Across Central America. 8° 1877
—— Roraima and British Guiana, with a Glance at Bermuda, the West Indies, and the Spanish Main. *Map and plate.* 8° 1879

Bodde, D. An Essay to show that Petroleum may be used with advantage in Manufacturing Operations for the purpose of heating Steam-boilers and generating Steam. 8* N.P., N.D.

Boddy, Rev. Alexander A. To Kairwân the Holy: Scenes in Mohammedan Africa. *Map and plates.* Crown 8° 1885
—— With Russian Pilgrims: being an Account of a Sojourn in the White Sea Monastery, and a Journey by the old Trade Route from the Arctic Sea to Moscow; Appendix, giving a full History of the Solovetsk Obitel, by the Archimandrite Meletii. *Maps and illustrations.* Small 8° [1892]

Bode, A. Notizen gesammelt auf einer Forstreise durch einen Theil des Europäischen Russlands. *Plates.* 8° *St Petersburg*, 1854
—— *See* Baer and Helmersen, 18, 19.

Bode, Baron C. A. de. Travels in Luristan and Arabistan. *Maps and plates.* 2 vols. 8° 1845
—— *See* Khanikoff, N. de.

Bode, J. E. Anleitung zur physischen, mathematischen, und astronomischen Kenntniss der Erdkugel. *Map.* Small 8° *Berlin*, 1820

Bodenham, Roger. *See* Hakluyt, Vols. 2, 3: Appendix 1.

Bodin, J. F. Recherches Historiques sur la Ville de Saumur. *Plates.* Vol. I.
8° *Saumur*, 1812

[Bodley, J. E. C.] The Portuguese in East Africa. (From *Blackwood's Magazine.*) 8* 1888

Bodmer, Albert. Terrassen und Thalstufen der Schweiz, ein Beitrag zur Erklärung der Thalbildung. *Profiles.* 4*
Zurich, 1880

Boeck, C. Bemærkninger angaaende Graptolitherne. *Plates.* 4*
Christiania, 1851
—— *See* Gaimard.

Boeck, E. van den. *See* International Congresses (Geological): Appendix 2.

Boedo, E. C. Estudios sobre la Navegacion del Bermejo y Colonizacion del Chaco. *Map.* 8° *Buenos Ayres*, 1873

Boegner, J. Die Entstehung der Quellen, und die Bildung der Mineralquellen. 12*
Frankfort-a-M., 1843
—— Das Erdbeben und seine Erscheinungen. *Map.* 12°
Frankfort-a-M., 1847

Boehmer, George H. Observations on Volcanic Eruptions and Earthquakes in Iceland within Historic Times. Translated and condensed from a History by Th. Thoroddsen. 8* *Washington*, 1886

Boelhouwer, J. C. Herinneringen van mijn verblijf op Sumatra's Westkust gedurende de Jaren 1831-34. 8*
The Hague, 1841

Boetticher, J. G. Geographical, Historical, and Political Description of the Empire of Germàny, Holland, the Netherlands, Switzerland, Prussia, Italy, Sicily, Corsica, and Sardinia, to which are added Statistical Tables of all the States of Europe, translated from the German of J. G. Boetticher . . . *Map* (in 3 sheets, by Capt. Chauchard, &c.) *and plans.* 4° 1800

Bogle, G., and T. Manning. *See* Markham, C. R.; *also* Eyriès, Vol. 14: Appendix 1.

Bogue, Adam. Steam to Australia, its General Advantages considered; the different Proposed Routes for connecting London and Sydney compared; and the expediency of forming a Settlement at Cape York, in Torres Strait, pointed out, in a Letter to Earl Grey. *Map.* 8*
Sydney, 1848

Boguslawski, Dr Georg von. Handbuch der Ozeanographie. Band I. Räumliche, physikalische und chemische Beschaffenheit der Ozeane. *Illustrations.* 8° *Stuttgart*, 1884
—— and Dr Otto Krümmel. The same. Band 2. Die Bewegungsformen des Meeres, von Dr Otto Krümmel; mit einem Beitrage von Prof. Dr K. Zöppritz. *Map and figures.* 8° *Stuttgart*, 1887

Böhm, Dr August. Die alten Gletscher der Enns und Steyr. *Map and plate.* Large 8° *Vienna*, 1885
—— *See* Penck; Penck's Abhandlungen, 1.

Böhm, Dr Richard. Von Sansibar zum Tanganjika: Briefe aus Ostafrika, nach dem Tode des Reisenden, mit einer biographischen Skizze herausgegeben von Herman Schalow. *Map and portrait.* 8°
Leipzig, 1888

Böhmert, Dr Victor. Die Ergebnisse der sachsischen Gewerbezählung vom 5 Juni 1862. Zeits. des K. Sächsischen Statistischen Bureaus 2, Supplement heft, Jahrg. 1886. 4* *Dresden*, 1886

Bohn, H. G. *See* Humboldt, Alex. von.

Bohun, Henry. *See* Hakluyt, Vol. 2: Appendix 1.

Boicoof, Saedor Jacowits. *See* Gottfried: Appendix 1.

Boid, Capt. A Description of the Azores, or Western Islands, from Personal Observation; comprising Remarks on their Peculiarities, Topographical, Geological, Statistical, &c., and on their hitherto neglected condition. *Map and plates.* 8° 1835

Boie, F. Tagebuch gehalten auf einer Reise durch Norwegen im Jahre 1817; herausgegeben mit Anmerkungen von H. Boie. *Map.* Small 8°
Schleswig, 1822

Boileau, A. H. E. Tour through the Western States of Rajwara in 1835, comprising Beekaner, Jesulmer, and Jodhpoor; with the passage of the Great Desert, and visit to the Indus and Buhawulpoor. *Map and plates.* 4°
Calcutta, 1837
—— Letter on the Elliptical Tunnel Bridge at Seonee. *Plate.* 8* 1849
—— Extract of a Letter from, on the Construction of Metalled Roads and Bridges. [From the India Records, Vol. 2, N.-W. Provinces.] *Allahabad*, 1849

Boileau, J. T. A New and Complete Set of Traverse Tables, showing the Differences of Latitude and the De partures to every minute of the Quadrant, and to five places of Decimals; together with a Table of the Lengths of each Degree of Latitude and corresponding Degree of Longitude from the Equator to the Poles. *Plates.* 8° 1839
—— A Collection of Tables, Astronomical, Meteorological, and Magnetical; also, for Determining the Altitudes of Mountains, Comparison of French and English Weights and Measures, &c., Computed in the Office of the H.E.I.C.'s Magnetic Observatory, Simla. 4* *Umballa*, 1850
—— Papers regarding Suspension Bridges in the North-Western Provinces. [From the India Records, N.-W. Provinces, Part 29.] *Agra*, 1856

Boisgelin, Louis de. Ancient and Modern Malta ; containing a Full and Accurate Account of . . . Malta and Goza, the History of the Knights of St John of Jerusalem, &c. 2 vols. *Map and plates.* 4° 1805

Boissier, Dr E., and Dr F. A. Buhse. Aufzählung der auf einer Reise durch Transkaukasien und Persien gesammelten Pflanzen. *Map and plates.* 4°
Moscow, 1860

Bokemeyer, Dr Heinrich. Die Molukken, Geschichte and quellenmässige Darstellung der Eroberung und Verwaltung der Ostindischen Gewürzinseln durch die Niederländer ; mit einem Anhange von bisher ungedruckten Aktenstücken. *Map.* 8° *Leipzig,* 1888

Boldakoff, J. M. Translation of Sir T. Smith's Voyage in Russia. [In Russian.] 8° *St Petersburg,* 1893

"Boldrewood, Ralph." Ups and Downs: a Story of Australian Life. 12° 1878

Bolduc, J. B. Z. Mission de la Colombie. Lettre et Journal, 1842-43. 8°
Quebec, N.D.

Bolet-Paraza, Don Nicanor. The Republic of Venezuela. (From *The New England Magazine.*) *Illustrations.* 8° [*Boston, Mass.*] 1892

Bolingbroke, Henry. *See* Phillips [1], Vol. 10: Appendix 1.

Bollaert, William. Antiquarian, Ethnological, and other Researches in New Granada, Equador, Peru, and Chile, with Observations on the Pre-Incarial, Incarial, and other Monuments of the Peruvian Nations. *Plates.* 8° 1860

—— Maya Hieroglyphic Alphabet of Yucatan. 8° [1865]

—— Contributions to an Introduction to the Anthropology of the New World. 8°
N.D.

—— *See* Hakluyt Soc. Publ., Vol. 28 : Appendix 1.

Bompiana, Sofia. Italian Explorers in Africa. (From the *Leisure Hour.*) *Illustrations.* 4° 1888

Bon, Dr Gustave le. Les Monuments de l'Inde. *Maps, plans, and illustrations.* Large 4° *Paris,* 1893

Bonança, João. Historia da Luzitania c da Iberia . . Vol. 1. [*Imperfect.*] *Plates.* 4° *Lisbon,* 1887

Bonany, Sebastian. Balanza General del Comercio de la Isla de Cuba en 1841-42. 2 vols. 8° *Havana,* 1842-43

Bonaparte, Prince Charles Lucien. Note sur les Oiseaux des îles Marquises ; Note sur les Salanganes et sur leurs Nids ; Espèces nouvelles d'Oiseaux d'Asie et d'Amérique, et tableaux paralléliques des Pélagiens ou Gaviæ, &c. 4°
Paris, 1855

Bonaparte, Prince Charles Lucien. Catalogue des Oiseaux d'Europe. 8*
Paris, 1857

—— Notes sur le Genre Moquinus, nouvelle forme intermédiaire aux Turnides, aux Laniides, et aux Muscicapides. *Plate.* 8*
Paris, 1857

—— Parallelismo fra la tribu' dei Cantori Fissirostri e quella dei Volucri Hianti e dei Notturni ovvero Insidenti. 8*
Turin, 1857

Bonaparte, Prince Louis Lucien. Remarques sur certaines Notes, certaines Observations, et certaines Corrections dont M. J. Vinson, à accompagné l'Essai sur la langue Basque par F. Ribary. 8°
Paris, 1877

—— Remarques diverses sur la langue Basque. 8° 1884

Bonaparte, Pierre-Napoléon. Un Mois en Afrique. 8° *Paris,* 1850

Bonaparte, Prince Roland. Les premiers Voyages des Néerlandais dans l'Insulinde (1595-1602). *Map.* 8* *Versailles,* 1884

—— Les premiers Voyages des Néerlandais dans l'Insulinde (1595-1602). *Map.* 4*
Versailles, 1884

—— Les Habitants de Suriname : Notes recueillies à l'Exposition Coloniale d'Amsterdam en 1883. *Maps and plates.* Folio *Paris,* 1884

—— Les récents Voyages des Néerlandais à la Nouvelle-Guinée. *Map.* 4*
Versailles, 1885

—— Les derniers Voyages des Néerlandais à la Nouvelle-Guinée. *Map.* 4*
Versailles, 1885

—— Note on the Lapps of Finmark. Small 4* *Paris,* 1886

—— La Nouvelle-Guinée : IIIe notice. Le Fleuve Augusta. *Map.* Small 4*
Paris, 1887

—— The same. IVe notice. Le Golfe Huon. *Maps.* Small 4* *Paris,* 1888

—— La Laponie et la Corse. 8*
Geneva, 1889

—— Le Glacier de l'Aletsch et le Lac de Märjelen. *Plates.* 4* *Paris,* 1889

—— Le premier Établissement des Néerlandais à Maurice. *Plates.* 4*
Paris, 1890

—— Une Excursion en Corse. *Plates.* 4°
Paris, 1891

Bonar, Dr Horatius. The Land of Promise : Notes of a Journey from Beersheba to Sidon. *Maps and plates.* 8°
1858

Boncarut, A. Manual de la Navigation dans le Rio de la Plata, d'après les Documents Nautiques les plus récents. 8°
Paris, 1857

Boncompagni, D. B. *See* Hugo.

Bond, H. Letters from Daeka on the Zambesi, South Africa. 8* 1874

Bond, G. P. and W. C. *See* Peirce, B.

Bone, William. Mason's Hygrometer, a Table for obtaining the Dew - point and Moisture by Inspection. Royal 8* 1843

Boner, Charles. Transylvania, its Products and its People. *Maps and plates.* 8° 1865

Boner, Robert. *See* Purchas, Vol. 1, Book 4 : Appendix 1.

"Bonite." *See* Vaillant.

Bonnell, Geo. W. Topographical Description of Texas, with an Account of the Indian Tribes. 18° *Austin, Texas,* 1840.

Bonnal, Dr F. Arcachon : Notice médicale. Deuxième édition. 12* *Bordeaux,* 1881

Bonneau, Étienne. La Gaule d'Homère. Fragments d'un livre. 8* *Paris,* 1884

Bonnemain, Captain. *See* Cherbonneau.

Bonnetain, Paul. Le Monde Pittoresque et Monumental : L'Extrême Orient. *Maps and illustrations.* 4° *Paris* [1887]

Bonney, Prof. T. G. The Glaciers of Gunversdahl (Justedal). 8* [1870]
—— The Lofoten Islands. 8* [1870]
—— The Story of our Planet. *Illustrations.* Large 8° 1893
—— The Year Book of Science. Edited for 1892 by Professor T. G. Bonney. 1893
—— *See* Symons.

Bonnycastle, Sir Richard H. Spanish America, or a Descriptive, Historical, and Geographical Account of the Dominions of Spain in the Western Hemisphere, Continental and Insular. *Maps and plate.* 2 vols. 8° 1818
—— Newfoundland in 1842 : a Sequel to "The Canadas in 1841." *Map and plates.* 2 vols. 8° 1842
—— Canada and the Canadians in 1846. 2 vols. 8° 1846

Bonola Bey, Dr F. L'Égypte et la Géographie : Sommaire historique des Travaux Géographiques exécutés en Égypte sous la Dynastie de Mohammed Aly. 8° *Cairo,* 1889
—— La Question des Noms Geographiques en Egypte. 8* *Cairo,* 1893

Bonpland, A. *See* Humboldt, Alex. von.

Bonsdorff, A. Zur Bestimmung der Constanten des Erdellipsoids aus Gradmessungen. 8* *St Petersburg,* 1888

Bontekoë, or Bontekoes, W. J. *See* Laharpe, Vol. 4 ; Thevenot, Vol. 1 ; Allgemeine Historie, Vol. 8 : Appendix 1.

Bontier, P., and J. Le Verrier. *See* Hakluyt Soc. Publ., Vol. 46 : Appendix 1.

Bonvalot, Gabriel. En Asie Centrale : De Moscou en Bactriane. *Map and illustrations.* 12° *Paris,* 1884
—— En Asie Centrale : Du Kohistan à la Caspienne. *Map and illustrations.* 12° *Paris,* 1885
—— Du Caucase aux Indes à travers le Pamir. *Map and illustrations.* 4° *Paris,* 1889 [1888]
—— Through the Heart of Asia over the Pamir to India. Translated from the French by C. B. Pitman. 2 vols. *Map and illustrations.* 4° 1889
—— A Travers le Thibet. Supplément au Journal *Le Temps,* Janvier 1891. *Map and illus·rations.* 4* *Paris,* 1891
—— Across Thibet ; with Illustrations from Photographs taken by Prince Henry of Orleans. Translated by C. B. Pitman. *Map.* 2 vols. Large 8° 1891
—— De Paris au Tonkin à travers le Tibet inconnu. *Map and illustrations.* 4° *Paris,* 1892

Bonwick, J. Geography of Australia and New Zealand. 3rd edition. 12° *Melbourne,* 1856
—— The Wild White Man and the Blacks of Victoria. 2nd edition. *Plates.* 8° *Melbourne,* 1863
—— Astronomy for Young Australians. 12° *Melbourne,* 1864
—— Daily Life and Origin of the Tasmanians. *Map and plates.* 8° 1870
—— The Last of the Tasmanians, or the Black War of Van Dieman's Land. *Plates.* 8° 1870
—— The Mormons and the Silver Mines. Small 8° 1872
—— The Resources of Queensland. *Map.* 12° 1880
—— The British Colonies and their Resources. 4 vols. *Maps.* Crown 8° 1886
—— French Colonies and their Resources. *Map.* Crown 8° 1886
—— Early Struggles of the Australian Press. *Facsimiles.* 8* 1890

Boosé, James R. Imperial Federation : Titles of Publications relating to the British Colonies, their Government, &c., in connection with Imperial Policy. 8* 1889
—— *See* Crozet's Voyage.

Booth, A. The Stranger's Intellectual Guide to London for 1839-40. 12° 1839

Booth, E. Carton. Homes Away from Home, and the Men who make them in Victoria. *Map.* 8° 1869

Booth, James C. Memoirs of the Geological Survey of the State of Delaware ; including the Application of the Geological Observations to Agriculture. 8° *Dover,* 1841

Boothby, Richard. *See* Churchill, Vol. 8 : Appendix 1.

Borchgravie, Émile de. La Serbie administrative, économique, et commerciale. 8° *Brussels*, 1883
Borchgravie, J. de. A Travers l'Afrique. *Brussels*, 1877
Borda, — de. *See* Verdun.
Bordalo, F. M. *See* Lopes de Lima.
Borde, G. P. L. Histoire de l'Ile de La Trinidad sous le gouvernement Espagnol. Première partie. 8° *Paris*, 1876
Bordier, Dr A. Bibliothèque des Sciences Contemporaines : La Géographie Médicale. *Maps.* 12° *Paris*, 1884
Bordone, Benedetto. Libro di, nel qual si Ragiona de tutte l'Isole del Mondo, con li lor nomi Antichi e Moderni, Historie, e modi del loro vivere, &c. *Maps and woodcuts.* 3 Books in 1 Folio vol. *Venice*, 1528
Borel, L. Voyage à la Gambie : Description des Rives de ce Fleuve et des Populations qui les habitent. 8* [1865]
Borelli, Jules. Divisions, Subdivisions, Langues et Races des régions Amhara, Oromo, et Sidama. 4° [*Paris*] N.D.
—— Éthiopie Méridionale : Journal de mon voyage aux pays Amhara, Oromo, et Sidama, Septembre 1885 à Novembre 1888. *Maps and illustrations.* 4° *Paris*, 1890
Borey, T. *See* Reniger and Borey, in Hakluyt, Vol. 4 : Appendix 1.
Börgen, Prof. Dr. Ueber die Berechnung eines einzelnen Hoch oder Niedrigwassers nach Zeit und Höhe. 4* *Berlin*
—— *See* Polar Regions, Arctic, G : Appendix 2.
Borges de Figueiredo, A. C. *See* Catalogues, A : Appendix 2.
Borggreve, Dr B. *See* Germany, C (Forschungen, &c., Vol. 3) : Appendix 2.
Borgia, Pope. Pope Borgia's Arbitration. [Newspaper Cuttings.] 8* N.D.
Borrhaus, Martinus. Cosmographiæ Elementa Commentatio, Astronomica, Geographica. *Woodcuts.* 12° *Basle*, 1555
—— Astronomica - Geographica. *Woodcuts.* 12° *Basle*, 1555
[*Bound up with works by Bartholemæus, Theodoricus, &c., the whole entitled* "Cosmographia."]
Borlase, W. Observations on the Ancient and Present State of the Islands of Scilly, and their Importance to the Trade of Great Britain. *Map and plates.* 4° *Oxford*, 1756
Borne, William. A Regiment for the Sea, containing verie necessarie matters for all sorts of men and trauailers; whervnto is added an Hidrographicall discourse touching the fiue seueral passages into Cattay, written by William Borne, newly corrected and amended by Thomas Hood, D. in Phisicke, who hath added a new Regiment, and Table of Declina-

Borne, William—*continued.*
tion; wherennto is also adioyned the Mariners Guide, with a perfect Sea Carde, by the said Thomas Hood. *Woodcuts.* Small 8° 1596
Borough, C. *See* Purchas, Vol. 3, Book 2; Appendix 1.
Borrer, Dawson. A Journey from Naples to Jerusalem, by way of Athens, Egypt, and the Peninsula of Sinai; with a Translation of M. Linant de Bellefond's Mémoire sur le Lac Mœris. *Map and plates.* 8° 1845
Borri, Christoforo. Relatione della nuova Missione delli pp. della Compagnia di Giesu all regno della Cocincina. 12° *Rome*, 1631
—— *See* Churchill, Vol. 2 : Appendix 1.
Borring, L. E. *See* Rafn.
Borrow, George. Zincali; or, An Account of the Gypsies of Spain. 2 vols. 8° 1843
—— The Bible in Spain, or the Journeys, Adventures, and Imprisonments of an Englishman in an Attempt to Circulate the Scriptures in the Peninsula, with a Biographical Introduction. 2nd edition. *Illustrations.* Crown 8° 1889
Borsari, Ferdinando. La Letteratura degl' indigeni Americani. 8* *Naples*, 1888
—— Una Pagina di Storia Argentina : I. La Conquista della Pampa; II. Un sessennio di Presidenza. 8* *Naples*, 1888
—— Geografia, Etnologica, e Storica della Tripolitania, Cirenaica, e Fezzan, con cenni sulla storia di queste Regione e sul silfio della Cirenaica. 8° *Turin*, 1888
—— L'Atlantide saggio di Geografia Preistorica. 8* *Naples*, 1889
—— Le Zone Colonizzabili dell' Eritrea e delle finitime regioni etiopiche. *Maps.* 8° *Milan*, 1890
—— Etnologia Italica : Etruschi, Sardi e Siculi nel XIV° secolo prima dell' era volgare. 8* 1891
Borthwick, J. D. Three Years in California. *Map.* 8° *Edinburgh*, 1857
Börtzell, A. *See* Sweden, A : Appendix 2.
Bory de Saint-Vincent. *See* Saint-Vincent.
Bos, Lambert. Antiquities of Greece, with Notes by Leisner. Translated by Stockdale. 8° 1772
Bosanquet, C. *See* Spence, Wm.
Boschini, Marco. L'Arcipelago, con tutte le Isole, Scogli Secche, e Bassi Fondi, con i Marì, Golfi, Seni, Porti, Città, e Castelli; nella Forma, che si vedono al tempo presente; con una succinta narrativa de i loro Nomi, Favole, e Historie, tanto antiche quanto moderne. *Maps.* 8° *Venice*, 1658

Bosman, W. A New and Accurate Description of the Coasts of Guinea, divided into the Gold, the Slave, and the Ivory Coasts, containing a Geographical, Political, and Natural History of the Kingdoms and Countries, with a Particular Account of the Rise, Progress, and Present Condition of all the European Settlements, &c. [Translated from the Dutch.] 2nd edition. *Maps, plates.* 8° 1872
—— *See* Pinkerton, Vol. 16 : Appendix 1.

Bossay, P. A. Poulain de. Recherches sur Tyr et Palætyr. *Maps.* 4°
[*Paris*, 1844]
—— Essais de restitution et d'interprétation d'un passage de Scylax. *Map.* 8° *Paris*, 1863
—— *See* Recueil de Voyages, Vol. 7, p. 612 ; Appendix 1.

Bossi, B. Viage Pinteresco por los Rios Paraná, Paraguay, Sn. Lorenzo, Cuyabá, y el Arino tributario del grande Amazonas ; con la descripcion de la Provincia de Mato Grosso, bajo su aspecto Fisico, Geografico, Mineralojico, y sus producciones naturales. *Illustrations.* Imperial 8° *Paris*, 1863
—— Viaje descriptivo de Montevideo á Valparaiso, por el Estrecho de Magallanes i Canales Smith, Sarmiento, Inocentes, Concepcion, Wide, i Messiers. 8* *Santiago*, 1874
—— Exploracion de la Tierra del Fuego con el Vapor Oriental Charrúa. *Map.* 8* *Montevideo*, 1882
—— La Causa Principale del Terremoti e di altre Perturbazioni della Natura. 8* *Porto Maurizio*, 1887

Bossi, Luigi. Guida di Milano. 2 vols. 8° *Milan*, 1818
—— Vita di Cristoforo Colombo, scritta e corredata di nuove osservazioni di note storico-critiche, e di un' Appendice di documenti rari o inediti. *Plates.* 8° *Milan*, 1818
—— Guide des Étrangers à Milan, et dans les Environs de cette Ville. 18° *Milan*, 1819

Bossu, —. Nouveaux Voyages aux Indes occidentales ; contenant une Relation des differens peuples qui habitent les environs du grand Fleuve Saint-Louis, appelé vulgairement le Mississipi, &c. (2 parts in 1, 2nd edition.) 12° *Paris*, 1768

Bostock, John. *See* Pliny.

Boswell, E. Civil Division of the County of Dorset methodically arranged. *Map.* 8° *Sherborne*, 1795

Boswell, J. An Account of Corsica : the Journal of a Tour to that Island ; and Memoirs of Pascal Paoli. *Map.* 8° *Glasgow*, 1768

Boswell, J. Boswelliana : the Commonplace Book of James Boswell ; with a Memoir and Annotations by the Rev. Charles Rogers, and Introductory Remarks by the Rt. Hon. Lord Houghton. *Frontispiece.* 8° 1874

Bosworth, J. A. C. A Manual of the Nellore District in the Presidency of Madras. *Map in cover.* 8° *Madras*, 1873

Bosworth, Rev. Dr J. The Origin of the Germanic and Scandinavian Languages and Nations, with a Sketch of their Literature, and short Chronological Specimens . . . ; with a Map of European Languages. 8° 1836
—— The Origin of the Dutch, with a Sketch of their Language and Literature, and Short Examples, tracing the Progress of their Tongue and its Dialects ; also a Map of European Languages, indicating not only the Oriental origin of Europeans, but that the Dutch were amongst the earliest Teutonic tribes settled in Europe. (2nd edition.) 8° 1846
—— *See* Alfred the Great.

Boteler, T. Narrative of a Voyage of Discovery to Africa and Arabia, performed in His Majesty's ships "Leven" and "Barracouta," from 1821 to 1826, under the command of Capt. F. W. Owen, R.N. 2 vols. *Plates.* 8° 1835

Botelho, Sebastião Xavier. Memoria Estatistica sobre os Dominios Portuguezes na Africa Oriental. *Maps.* 8° *Lisbon*, 1835

Botella y de Hornos, F. de. España Geografia, Morfológica y Etiológica ; observaciones acerca de la Constitución Orográfica de la Peninsula, y leyes de dirección de sus Sierras Cordilleras, Costas, y Rios Principales. *Maps.* 4° *Madrid*, 1886

Botfield, B. Shropshire, its History and Antiquities. *Plates.* 4° 1860

Böttcher, Ernst. Orographie und Hydrographie des Kongobeckens. *Map and plates.* 8° *Berlin*, 1887

Bottego. *See* V——, G. D.

Bottis, Gaetano de. Ragionamento Istorico Intorno all' Eruzione del Vesuvio che comincio il di 29 Luglio dell' anno 1779, e continuo sino al giorno 15 del seguente mese di Agosto. *Plates.* 4° *Naples*, 1779

Boucard, Adolphe. *See* Guatemala : Appendix 2.

Bouche, Pierre. Sept ans en Afrique Occidentale : la Côte des Esclaves et le Dahomey. *Map.* 12° *Paris*, 1885

Boucher de Perthes, J. Antiquités Celtiques et Antédiluviennes : Mémoire sur l'Industrie primitive et les Arts à leur origine. 3 vols. *Plates.* 8° *Paris*, 1847-64

Boucher, F. The Indian Archipelago : a Concise Account of the Principal Islands and Places of the Indian Archipelago. *Map.* 12° 1857

Bouchette, Joseph. The British Dominions in North America ; or, A Topographical and Statistical Description of the Provinces of Lower and Upper Canada, New Brunswick, Nova Scotia, the Islands of Newfoundland, Prince Edward, and Cape Breton ; with Statistical Tables and Tables of· Distances, &c. *Plates.* 2 vols. 4° 1832

—— Topographical Dictionary of the Province of Lower Canada. 4° 1832

Boudewijnse, J. *See* Catalogues, A : Appendix 2.

Boué, Ami. Turquie d'Europe, ou Observations sur la Géographie, Géologie, &c., de cet Empire. 4 vols. 8° *Paris,* 1840

—— Itinéraires dans la Turquie d'Europe. 2 vols. in 1. 8° *Vienna,* 1854

—— Ueber die Oro-Potamo-Limne (Seen) und Lekavegraphie (Becken) des Tertiären der Europäischen Türkei, und Winke zur Ausfüllung der Lücken unserer jetzigen geographischen und geognostischen Kenntnisse dieser Halbinsel. *Maps.* 8* *Vienna,* 1879

—— Autobiographie du Docteur Médécin Ami Boué né à Hambourg le 16 mars 1794 et mort comme Autrichien à Vienne. 8° *Vienna,* 1879

—— Die Europäische Türkei (La Turquie d'Europe par A. Boué, Paris, 1840) : Deutsch herausgegeben von der Boué-Stiftungs Commission der Kais. Akademie der Wissenschaften in Wien. 2 vols. *Portrait.* 4° *Vienna,* 1889

Bouet-Willaumez, Comte E. Description Nautique des Côtes de l'Afrique Occidentale comprises entre le Sénégal et l'Equateur. *Maps, plates. Paris,* 1846

Bougainville, Jean Pierre, Baron de. Mémoire sur les Découvertes et les Établissements faits le long des Côtes d'Afrique par Hannon, Amiral de Carthage. 4° [*Paris,* 1779]

Bougainville, Louis Antoine de. Voyage autour du Monde par la Frégate la "Boudeuse" et la Flûte "l'Étoile," 1766-69. *Maps.* 4° *Paris,* 1771

—— Voyage autour du Monde par la Frégate du Roi "La Boudeuse" et la Flûte "L'Étoile," en 1766, 1767, 1768, and 1769. Seconde édition, augmentée. 2 vols. *Maps.* 8° *Paris,* 1772

—— Journal de la Navigation autour du Globe de la "Thétis" et "l'Espérance," 1824-26. 2 vols. 4° *Paris,* 1837

—— *See* Burney, Vol. 5 ; Kerr, Vol. 13 ; Laharpe, Vol. 18 ; "The Modern Traveller," Vol. 4, p. 610 : Appendix 1.

Bougard, Lieut. Le Petit Flambeau de la Mer, ou le Veritable Guide des Pilotes Cotiers ; où il est clairement enseigné la maniere de naviguer le long de toutes les Côtes de France, d'Angleterre, d'Irlande, d'Espagne, . . . &c. Revû, corrigé et augmenté. Dernière edition. *Illustrations.* Square 8° *Havre,* 1731

Bouguer, Sig. Nuovo Trattato di Navigazione, che Contiene la Teoria e la Practica del Pilotaggio. Tradotto in Italiano, con Continuazione dal V. Brunacci. *Maps and plates.* 2 vols. 8° *Leghorn,* 1795

Bouguer's Voyage to Peru. *See* Pinkerton, Vol. 14 : Appendix 1.

Bouigu, Edouard de. Description de l'Invention de Voitures roulant sur des Rails mobiles tournants et parcourant toutes les Routes, les Champs et les Deserts. *Illustrations.* 4° [*Marseilles,* 1874]

Bouïnais, A., and A. Paulus. La Cochinchine Contemporaine. *Map.* 8° *Paris,* 1884 [1883]

—— L'Indo - Chine Française Contemporaine. Cochinchine. 2e édition, revue et augmentée. Cambodge, Tonkin, Annam. 2 vols. *Maps and illustrations.* Large 8° *Paris,* 1885

—— La France en Indo-Chine. (3rd edition.) *Map.* 12° *Paris,* 1890

Bouillet, M. N. Atlas Universel d'Histoire et de Géographie contenant 1e La Chronologie, 2e La Généalogie, 3e La Géographie. *Maps and plates.* 8° *Paris,* 1865

—— Dictionnaire Universel d'Histoire et de Géographie . . . Nouvelle édition. 8° *Paris,* 1867

—— Dictionnaire Universel d'Histoire et de Géographie contenant 1e l'Histoire, 2e La Biographie, 3e La Mythologie, 4e La Géographie, ancienne et moderne. Nouvelle edition, par L. G. Gourraigne. Large 8° *Paris,* 1893

Boulangier, Commandant. Essai sur les Origines de la Méditerané : Nouvelle Méthode de Géographie et de Cartographie. *Maps and illustrations.* 8° *Paris,* 1890

Boulger, D. C. The Life of Yakoob Beg, Athalik Ghazi, and Badaulet, Ameer of Kashgar. *Map.* 8° 1878

Boult, Joseph. Speculations on the former Topography of Liverpool and the Neighbourhood. Part 1. 8* *Liverpool,* 1866

—— Further Observations on the alleged Submarine Forests on the Shores of Liverpool Bay and the River Mersey. *Privately printed.* 8* *Liverpool,* 1866

Bouniceau, Prosper. De Paris au Cap, ou le Chemin de Fér Transsaharien. 8* *Paris,* 1880

Bouquet, Col. *See* Knox's New Collection, Vol. 2, p. 608 : Appendix 1.

Bouquet de la Grye, A. Pilote des Côtes Ouest de France. Tom. 1. *Maps.* 8°
Paris, 1869

Bourchier, Capt. W. Narrative of a Passage from Bombay to England, describing the Author's Shipwreck in the "Nautilus" in the Red Sea, Journeys across the Nubian Desert, &c. *Map.* 12° 1834

Bourdieu, Capit. L. du. Notes sur quelques Ports de l'île de Haïti. 8*
Paris, 1844

Bourdonnais, Comte A. Maké de la. *See* De la Bourdonnais.

Bourgade la Dardye, E. de. Paraguay. *Map and illustrations.* 12° *Paris* [1889]
—— Paraguay, the Land and the People, Natural Wealth, and Commercial Capabilities. Edited by E. G. Ravenstein. *Map and illustrations.* Crown 8° 1892

Bourgoing, J. F. Tableaux de l'Espagne Moderne. *Maps and plates.* 3 vols. 8°
Paris, 1797
—— *See* Phillips [1], Vol. 9 : Pinkerton, Vol. 5 : Appendix 1.

Bourgoing, P. de. *See* Cortambert.

Bourjolly, Gen. Projets sur l'Algérie. *Map.* 8° *Paris,* 1847

Bourke, John G. Notes upon the Gentile Organisation of the Apaches of Arizona. 8* N.P., N.D.
—— The Snake-Dance of the Moquis of Arizona : being a Narrative of a Journey from Santa Fé, New Mexico, to the Villages of the Moqui Indians of Arizona, with a Description of the Manners and Customs of this peculiar People, and especially of the revolting religious rite the Snake-Dance ; to which is added a brief Dissertation upon Serpent Worship in general, with an Account of the Tablet Dance of the Pueblo of Santo Domingo, New Mexico, &c. *Plates.* 8° 1884
—— Compilation of Notes and Memoranda bearing upon the Use of Human Ordure and Human Urine in Rites of a Religious or Semi-Religious character among various Nations. 8* *Washington,* 1888

Bourne, Benjamin Franklin. The Captive in Patagonia, or Life among the Giants : a Personal Narrative. *Plates.* 12° *Boston, Mass.,* 1853

Bourne, F. S. A. Commercial Report on a Journey through the Provinces of Ssuch'uan, Yün-nan, Kwang-si, and Kuei-chou, from 26th October 1885 to 5th May 1886. Part 1. Ch'ung-ching Fu to Pi-chieh Hsien. *Map.* Folio* 1886
—— Ditto. Part 2. Pi-chieh Hsien to Yünnan-Fu. *Map.* Folio* 1887

Bourne, F. S. A. Report of a Journey in South-Western China. *Maps.* Folio*
1888

Bourne, G. Australian Expedition : Journal of Landsborough's Expedition in Search of Burke and Wills. 8°
Melbourne, 1863

Bourne, John. Indian River Navigation : illustrating the Practicability of opening up some thousands of miles of River Navigation in India, by the use of a new kind of Steam Vessel adapted to the Navigation of Shallow and Shifting Rivers. *Map.* 8° 1849

Bourne, H. R. Fox. The Story of our Colonies. New edition. *Maps.* 8° 1888

Bournon, Comte de. Traité complet de la Chaux Carbonatée et de l'Arragonite, auquel on a joint une Introduction à la Minéralogie en général, une Théorie de la Cristallisation et son application. *Plates.* 3 vols. 4° 1808

Bourrit, O. Journey to the Glaciers in the Duchy of Savoy. Translated by Davy. 12° *Norwich,* 1776
—— Description des Vallées de Glace et des Hautes Montagnes que forment la chaîne des Alpes Pennines et Rhétiennes. *Map and plates.* 2 vols. 8°
Geneva, 1783
—— Description des Glacières et Glaciers de Savoye. *Plates.* 8° *Geneva,* 1785
—— Description des Cols, ou Passages des Alpes. 2 vols. 8° *Geneva,* 1803
—— *See* Ziegler.

Boussingault, M., and Dr Roulin. Viajes cientificos á los Andes Ecuatoriales, ó coleccion de Memorias sobre fisica, quimica é historia natural de la Nueva Granada, Ecuador, y Venezuela. Traducidas, &c., por J. Acosta. 8°
Paris, 1849

Boutroue, Alexandre. Rapport sur une Mission Archéologique en Portugal et dans le sud de l'Espagne. *Plates.* Large 8* *Paris,* 1893
—— L'Algérie et la Tunisie à travers les Ages. *Maps.* Large 8° *Paris,* 1893
—— *See* Martins, J. P.

Bouvet, Joachim. *See* Astley, Vol. 3 : Appendix 1.

Bouvet, Lozier. *See* Burney, Vol. 5 ; Callander, Vol. 3 : Appendix 1.

Bouzet, E. du. Instructions à donner aux Batiments venant en Nouvelle-Calédonie par le Cap de Bonne-Espérance. 8°
Paris, 1858

Bovallius, Carl. Antiquités céramiques trouvées dans le Nicaragua en 1882-83. *Illustrations.* 8* N.P., N.D.
—— Nicaraguan Antiquities. *Maps and plates.* 4° *Stockholm,* 1886
—— Resa i Central-Amerika, 1881-83. 2 vols. *Maps and illustrations.* 8°
Upsala, 1887

Bove, Giacomo. Expedicion Austral Argentina: Informes preliminares presentados á los Ministros del Interior y de Guerra y Marina de la República Argentina, y publicados bajo la direccion del Instituto Geografico Argentino. *Maps and plates.* 8° *Buenos Ayres*, 1883

—— Patagonia, Terra del Fuoco, Mari Australi; Rapporto del Tenente Giacomo Bove, Capo della Spedizione al Comitato Centrale per le Esplorazioni Antartiche. Parte 1. *Maps and illustrations.* Large 8° *Genoa*, 1883

Bovis's History of Cochin China. *See* Pinkerton, Vol. 9: Appendix 1.

Bowditch, Nath. Memoir. By his son N. Ingersoll Bowditch. *Portrait.* 4° *Boston, Mass.*, 1839

—— *See* Pickering, John.

Bowditch, T. Edward. Mission from Cape Coast Castle to Ashantee; with a Statistical Account of that Kingdom, and Geographical Notices of other parts of the Interior of Africa. *Map and plates.* 4° 1819

—— Essay on the Geography of North-Western Africa. *Maps.* 12° *Paris*, 1821

—— Account of the Discoveries of the Portuguese in the Interior of Angola and Mozambique, with a Note on a Geographical Error of Mungo Park. *Maps.* 8° 1824

—— Excursions in Madeira and Porto Santo, in 1823, while on his Third Voyage to Africa; to which is added a Narrative of the Voyage to its completion, with Occurrences from Mr Bowditch's arrival in Africa to his death, a Description of the English Settlements on the River Gambia, with Zoological and Botanical Descriptions, and Translations from the Arabic. *Plates.* 4° 1825

—— *See* Mollien; Eyriès, Vol. 11; Phillips [3], Vol. 1: Appendix 1.

Bowdler, Col. C. W. *See* Bell.

Bowen, C. C. *See* Galton, Vacation Tourists, 1860.

Bowen, Emanuel. A Complete System of Geography. 2 vols. *Maps.* Folio 1747

Bowen, Sir George Ferguson. Ithaca in 1850. 8° 1854

Bower, Capt. H. Diary of a Journey across Tibet. *Maps and illustrations.* 8° *Calcutta*, 1893

Bowerbank, James Scott. A History of the Fossil Fruits and Seeds of the London Clay. Part 1. *Plates.* 8° 1840

Bowie, J. *See* British South Africa, A: Appendix 2.

Bowker, Colonel J. H. Other Days in South Africa. 8* [1884]

Bowles, S. Our New West: Records of Travel between the Mississippi River and the Pacific Ocean. . . . *Map, portraits, and plates.* 8° 1869

Bowles, W. Introduccion á la Historia Natural y á la Geografia Fisica de España. Small 4° *Madrid*, 1775

Bowring, Sir John. A Visit to the Philippine Islands. *Plates.* 8° 1850

—— The Kingdom and People of Siam, with a Narrative of the Mission to that country in 1855. *Map, facsimiles, and plates.* 2 vols. 8° 1857

Bowring, J. Wýbor z BásnictwiCeského: Cheskian Anthology, being a History of the Poetical Literature of Bohemia, with translated specimens. 12° 1832

Bowring, J. *See* Phillips [3], Vol. 3: Appendix 1.

Bowyear. *See* Dalrymple, Repertory, Vol. 1: Appendix 1.

Boxhorn, M. Z. Marci Zuerii Boxhornii Theatrum, sive Hollandiæ Comitatus et Urbium nova descriptio, qua omnium Civitatum, præcipuorumq. locorum Icones, Origines, Incrementa, Res domi forisq. gestæ, Jura, Privilegia, immunitates, ipsis Principum tabulis expressa, et Viri illustres, exhibentur. *Maps.* Oblong 8° *Amsterdam*, 1632

Boyd, Major A. J. Reminiscences of the Chincha Islands. 8* *Brisbane*, 1892

Boyd, Benjamin. On the Expediency of Transferring the Unemployed Labour of Van Diemen's Land to New South Wales. 8* *Sydney*, 1847

—— Steam to Australia and New Zealand. 8* 1850

Boyd, C. R. Resources of South-West Virginia, showing the Mineral Deposits of Iron, Coal, Zinc, Copper, and Lead, also the staples of the various Counties, Methods of Transportation, Access, &c. *Map and plates.* 8° *New York*, 1881

Boyd, R. N. Chili: Sketches of Chili and the Chilians during the War 1879-80. *Map and illustrations.* Small 8° 1881

—— Opening Address, Session 1890-91, of the Civil and Mechanical Engineers' Society, read 17th December 1890. Large 8* 1890

Boyd, ——. *See* Eyriès, Vol. 13; Appendix 1.

Boyde, Capt. Henry. Several Voyages to Barbary, containing an Historical and Geographical Account of the Country, with the Hardships, Sufferings, and manner of Redeeming Christian Slaves; together with a curious Description of Meguinez, Oran, and Alcazar, with a Journal of the late Siege and Surrender of Oran; to which are added, the Maps of Barbary and

Boyde, Capt. Henry—*Continued.*
the Sea-coasts, the Prospects of Meg-
uinez and Alcazar, an exact Plan of
Oran, and a View of the Ancient Ro-
man Ruins near Meguinez,—the whole
illustrated with Notes, Historical and
Critical. 2nd edition. 8°   1736
Boyé, J. *See* Lutké.
Boyle, Frederick. Adventures among
the Dyaks of Borneo. *Plate.* 8° 1865
—— The Free Indian Tribes of Central
America. 8*   1867
—— A Ride across a Continent : a Per-
sonal Narrative of Wanderings through
Nicaragua and Costa Rica. 2 vols.
Plates. 8°   1868
Boyle, R. Vicars. Imperial Government
Railways, Japan : Report on the Routes
for the Main Trunk Lines through Cen-
tral Japan, viz., from Tokio to Kioto and
across to Niigata. *Map.* 8* *Kobe*, 1876
—— Descriptive Reports of Lines laid out
from Kioto, via Otsu and Maibara to
Tsuruga, and from Maibara to Kano,
Miya, and Doda. *Map.* 8* *Kobe*, 1876
Braam, A. E. van. An Authentic Ac-
count of the Embassy of the Dutch East
India Company to the Court of the Em-
peror of China in the years 1794 and
1795. Translated from the original of
M. L. E. Moreau de St Méry. 2 vols.
Map. 8°   1798
Brabant, Arthur Baring. *See* Popowski.
Brabner, J. H. F. The Comprehensive
Gazetteer of England and Wales. Vol. 1,
Aar-Cat. *Maps and plates.* Large 8°
1893
Vol. 2, Cau-Goa ; Vol. 3, Gob-Les 1894
Bracciolini, Francesco. Lo Scherno
degli Dei : poema Piacevole. *Portrait.*
8°   *Milan*, 1804
Brace, C. L. The Norse-Folk : a Visit
to the Homes of Norway and Sweden.
Plates. 8°   1857
Brackenbury, Major C. B. *See* United
Kingdom : Appendix 2.
Brackenbury, Major-General Henry.
The River Column : a Narrative of the
Advance of the River Column of the
Nile Expeditionary Force, and its Re-
turn down the Rapids : with maps by
Major the Hon. F. L. L. Colborne.
Crown 8°   1885
Brackenridge, H. M. Views of Louisi-
ana, containing Geographical, Statisti-
cal, and Historical Notices of that vast
and important portion of America. 12°
Baltimore, 1817
—— Voyage to South America, 1817-18,
in the Frigate "Congress." 2 vols. 8°
1820
—— *See* Eyriès, Vol. 9 ; Phillips [3],
Vol. 3 : Appendix 1.

Bradbury, John. Travels in the Interior
of America in 1809-11, including a De-
cription of Upper Louisiana, the States
of Ohio, Kentucky, Indiana, and Ten-
nessee, with the Illinois and Western
Territories. 8°   *Liverpool*, 1817
Bradford, Alex. W. American Antiquities, and Researches into the Origin
and History of the Red Race. 8°
New York, 1843
Bradley, John. A Narrative of Travel
and Sport in Burmah, Siam, and the
Malay Peninsula. 8°   1876
Bradshaw, B. Dictionary of Mineral
Waters, Climatic Health Resorts, Sea
Baths, and Hydropathic Establishments.
2nd edition. *Map and plans.* 12° 1883
—— A B C Dictionary to the United
States, Canada, and Mexico, showing
the most Important Towns and Points
of Interest ; with Maps, Routes, &c.,
also Large General Skeleton Map show-
ing the various Steamship Routes to
various points. 12°   1886
Brady, W. Glimpses of Texas, its Di-
visions, Resources, Development, and
Prospects. 12*   *Houston*, 1871
Brækstad, H. L. *See* Hovgaard.
Bragge, W. Bibliotheca Nicotiana : a
First Catalogue of Books about Tobacco.
Square 8° [Privately printed]   1874
Braim, T. H. History of New South
Wales, from its Settlement to the close
of 1844. 2 vols. *Illustrations.* 8°
1846
Braithwaite, S. Supplement to Sir John
Ross's Second Voyage in Search of a
North-West Passage. 4*   1835
Bramall, Henry. The Mineral Resources
of New Zealand. *Map.* 8°
Liverpool, 1883
Brämer, K. *See* Germany, C (For-
schungen, &c., Vol. 2) : Appendix 2.
Brampton and Alt. *See* Eyriès, Vol. 4 :
Appendix 1.
Brand, —. *See* Pinkerton, Vol. 3 : Ap-
pendix 1.
Branda, Paul. Le Haut-Mékong ou le
Laos ouvert. *Map.* 8°   *Paris*, 1887
—— The same. New edition. *Maps.*
Paris, 1889
Brandes, H. Ueber das Zeitalter des
Geographen Eudoxos und des Astrono-
men Geminos. Ueber die antiken Na-
men und die geographische Verbreitung
der Baumwolle im Alterthum. Zwei
geographisch - antiquarische Untersuch-
ungen. 8°   *Leipzig*, 1866
Brandes, Dr J. L. A. *See* Groeneveldt.
Brandis, Sir Dietrich. Report on the
Teak Forests of Pegu for 1856. *Tables.*
[From the India Records, No. 28.] 1860
—— Ditto, for 1857-60 ; with Appendix.
Tables. [From the India Records, No.
31.]   *Calcutta*, 1861

Brandis, Sir Dietrich. Progress Report of the Forests of the Tenasserim and Martaban Provinces, for 1858-60. *Map and tables.* [From the India Records, No. 29.] *Calcutta*, 1861

—— Report on the Attaran Forests for 1860; with Appendix. [From the India Records, No. 32.] *Calcutta*, 1861

—— Reports on the Teak Forests in Pegu and the Tenasserim and Martaban Provinces, 1860-61; to which is added, Correspondence regarding the opening of the Pegu Forests to Private Enterprise. *Tables.* [From the India Records, No. 35.] *Calcutta*, 1862

—— Progress Report of Forest Administration in British Burmah, 1861-62. *Map.* [From the India Records, No. 37.] 1863

—— *See* Collins, J. ; Leeds.

Brandstetter, Prof. Dr R. Charakterisirung der Epik der Malaien. Large 8* *Lucerne*, 1891

—— Malaio-Polynesische Forschungen. 2. Die Beziehungen des Malagasy zum Malaiischen. 4° *Lucerne*, 1893

Brandt, J. F. Mittheilungen über die Naturgeschichte des Mammoth oder Mamout (Elephas primigenius). *Plates.* 8* *St Petersburg*, 1866

—— *See* Baer and Helmersen, 17 ; Helmersen and Schrenck, 1.

Branner, J. C. The Æolian Sandstones of Fernando de Noronha. *Illustrations.* 8* *New Haven, Conn.*, 1890

Brash, Richard R. Inishcaltra and its Remains. 8* 1866

Brasseur de Bourbourg, Abbé E. Charles. Lettres pour servir d'Introduction à l'Histoire Primitive des Nations Civilisées de l'Amérique Septentrionale. [French and Spanish.] 4° *Mexico*, 1851

—— Aperçus d'un Voyage dans les États de San-Salvador et de Guatemala. 8* *Paris*, 1857

—— Histoire des Nations civilisées du Mexique et de l'Amérique - Centrale durant les siècles antérieurs à Christophe Colomb, &c. 4 vols. 8° *Paris*, 1857-59

Brassey, Lady. A Voyage in the "Sunbeam:" Our Home on the Ocean for Eleven Months. 9th edition. *Maps and illustrations.* 8° 1880

—— In the Trades, the Tropics, and the Roaring Forties. *Maps and illustrations.* 8° 1885

—— The Last Voyage, to India and Australia, in the "Sunbeam." *Map, chart, and illustrations.* 8° 1889

Brassey, Lord. On the Examination of Adjusters of Compasses. 4* 1871

—— *See* Grenfell, W. P.

Brauer, F. *See* "Novara."

Brauer, Lorenz. *See* Andree, Karl.

Braumüller, J. G. Der wichtigste Kanal in Europa, durch eine Vereinigung des Schwarzen Meeres mit der Ost und Nord See vertmittelst der Weichsel und des Dniesters erneuert vorgeschlagen. 4* *Berlin*, 1815

Brauns, D. Geology of the Environs of Tokio. *Plates.* 4° *Tokio*, 2541 (1881)

Bravais, A. Sur les Lignes d'Ancien Niveau de la Mer dans le Finmark. *Map.* 8* *Paris*, N.D.

—— *See* Gaimard, P.

Brawern, H. *See* Churchill, Vol. 1 : Appendix 1.

Bray, W. *See* Pinkerton, Vol. 2 : Appendix 1.

Brazza, P. Savorgnan de. Les Voyages de Savorgnan de Brazza, Ogôoué et Congo (1875-82). Par D. Neuville and C. Bréard. *Portrait and map.* 8° *Paris*, 1884

—— Conférence faite par P. Savorgnan de Brazza, le 21 Janvier 1886, en la séance extraordinaire tenue par la Société de Géographie. *Portrait and map.* 4* *Paris*, 1886

—— Texte Publié et Coordonné par Napoléon Ney : Conférences et Lettres de P. Savorgnan Brazza sur ses Trois Explorations dans l'ouest Africain de 1875 à 1886. *Map and illustrations.* Large 8° *Paris*, 1887

—— *See* Nardi.

Bréard, C. *See* Brazza ; Neuville.

Brebner, J. M. *See* India, D : Appendix 2.

Breeks, James Wilkinson. An Account of the Primitive Tribes and Monuments of the Nilagiris. *Photographs.* 4° 1873

Breen, Henry H. St Lucia, Historical, Statistical, and Descriptive. *Map.* 8° 1844

Brehm, Dr A. E. *See* Heuglin.

Bremner, Robert. Excursions in the Interior of Russia. *Portraits.* 2 vols. 8° 1839

—— Excursions in Denmark, Norway, and Sweden. *Portraits.* 2 vols. 8° 1840

Bremond, Alphonse. Le Guide Toulousain. Troisème édition. *Map and plan.* 18° *Toulouse*, 1868

Brenchley, J. L. Jottings during the Cruise of H.M.S. "Curaçoa" among the South Sea Islands in 1865. *Map and plates.* 4° 1873

Brenchley, Julius. *See* Remy.

Brennecke, —. Sir Isaac Newton : Oration. [In German.] 8* *Posen*, 1866

Brenner, Dr Oscar. Die ächte Karte des Olaus Magnus vom Jahre 1539, nach dem Exemplar der Münchener Staatshibliothek. *Map.* 8* *Christiania*, 1886

—— Olaus Magnus und seine Karte des Nordens. Small 8* *Christiania*, 1886

Brent, G. S. Notes on a Map of the World: Fasciculus I., On the Configuration of Continents. 8* 1850

Brenton, Capt. E. P. *See* St Vincent.

Brereton, Rev. C. D. An Address, with a Proposal for the Foundation of a Church, Mission House, and School at Sarāwak. *Maps.* 8* 1846

Brerewood, Edward. *See* Purchas, Vol. 1, Book 1: Appendix 1.

Breton, Lieut. Excursions in New South Wales, Western Australia, and Van Diemen's Land, during 1830-33. *Plates.* 8° 1834

Bretschneider, E. On the Study and Value of Chinese Botanical Works, with Notes on the History of Plants and Geographical Botany from Chinese Sources. *Plates.* 8° *Foochow,* 1870

—— Fu Sang; or, Who Discovered America? 8* 1870

—— On the Knowledge possessed by the Ancient Chinese of the Arabs and Arabian Colonies and other Western Countries mentioned in Chinese Books. 8* 1871

—— Notes on Chinese Mediæval Travellers to the West. 8* *Shanghai,* 1875

—— Archæological and Historical Researches on Pekin and its Environs. *Plates.* 8* *Shanghai,* 1876

—— Die Pekinger Ebene und das benachbarte Gebirgsland. (Ergänzungsheft, 46—Petermann's Mittheilungen.) *Map.* 4ᵘ *Gotha,* 1876

—— Recherches Archéologiques et Historiques sur Pékin et ses Environs. Traduction Française par V. Collin de Plancy. [No. 12 of Publ. de l'École des Langues Orient. Viv.] *Maps, plate.* 8° *Paris,* 1879

—— Mediæval Researches from Eastern Asiatic Sources: Fragments towards the Knowledge of the Geography and History of Central and Western Asia, from the 13th to the 17th Century. 2 vols. *Maps.* 8° 1888

Brett, H. Handy Guide to New Zealand. Edited by E. Ernest Bilbrough. *Maps and illustrations.* 12° *Auckland,* 1890

—— *See* Sherrin and Wallace.

Brett, W. H. The Indian Tribes of Guiana, their Condition and Habits, &c. *Map and plates.* 8° 1868

Brewer, Henry. *See* Callander, Vol. 2: Appendix 1.

Brewin, W. *See* Harvey, T.

Bricchetti-Robecchi. *See* Robecchi.

Bridel, Philippe. *See* Turkey in Asia, B: Appendix 2.

Bridge, B. A Treatise on the Construction, Properties, and Analogies of the Three Conic Sections. 8° 1831

Bridge, John. A Visit to the Isle of Wight, by Two Wights. 16° 1884

Bridge, John. From Tilbury to Torbay, 1885-87. 12° 1888

Bridges, F. D. Journal of a Lady's Travels round the World. *Map and plates.* 8° 1883

Brie, J. de. *See* Pelham, Vol. 2: Appendix 1.

Brière, A. Lettres sur le Transsaharien. 8* *Paris,* 1881

Brierley, J. *See* Casalis.

Briggs, David. Design for a Bridge over the Nurbudda, near Jubbulpoor. *Plates.* [From the India Records, Vol. 2, N.W. Provinces.] 8° *Agra,* 1856

—— Report on the Operations connected with the Hindostan and Thibet Road, from 1850 to 1855. *Maps.* [From the India Records, No. 16.] Royal 8° *Calcutta,* 1856

Briggs, Henry George. The Cities of Gujarashtra, their Topography and History illustrated in the Journal of a Recent Tour. 4° *Bombay,* 1850

—— The Parsis, or Modern Zerdusthians. 8° *Edinburgh,* 1852

Briggs, Major-Gen. John: Brief Notes relative to the History of the Rajas of Satara, commencing with 1707; and to the Satara Jageerdars. [From the India Records, No. 41.] Royal 8° *Bombay,* 1857

Brigham, W. T. Historical Notes on the Earthquakes of New England, 1638-1869. 4° *Boston, Mass.,* 1871

—— Guatemala, the Land of the Quetzal: a Sketch. *Maps and illustrations.* 8° 1887

Bright, Richard. Travels from Vienna through Lower Hungary, with some Remarks on the State of Vienna during the Congress, 1814. *Maps and plates.* 4° *Edinburgh,* 1818

Brignon, Le Hen. *See* Burney, Vol. 5; Callander, Vol. 3: Appendix 1.

Brine, Admiral Lindesay. The Taeping Rebellion in China: a Narrative of its Rise and Progress, based upon original documents and information obtained in China. *Map and plans.* 8° 1862

—— Travels amongst American Indians, their Ancient Earthworks and Temples. *Illustrations.* 8° 1894

Brine, F. Iceland and the Faroes. 8* [1881]

Brinkley, John, Bishop of Cloyne. Elements of Plane Astronomy. Edited by the Rev. Thomas Laby. *Plates.* 8° *Dublin,* 1845

Brinton, Dr Daniel G. Notes on the Floridian Peninsula, its Literary History, Indian Tribes, and Antiquities. 8° *Philadelphia,* 1859

—— The Lineal Measures of the Semi-Civilised Nations of Mexico and Central America. 8* *Philadelphia,* 1885

E

Brinton, Dr Daniel G. On the Ikono-matic Method of Phonetic Writing, with Special Reference to American Archæology.   8*   *Philadelphia*, 1886
—— A Review of the Data for the Study of the Prehistoric Chronology of America. Address before the Section of Anthropology, American Association for the Advancement of Science.   8*
    Salem, Mass., 1887
—— Were the Toltecs an Historic Nationality?   8*   *Philadelphia*, 1887
—— On Etruscan and Libyan Names: a Comparative Study. 8**Philadelphia*, 1890
—— The American Race : a Linguistic Classification and Ethnographic Description of the Native Tribes of North and South America.   8°   *New York*, 1891
—— Anthropology, as a Science, and as a branch of University Education in the United States.   8*   *Philadelphia*, 1892
—— The Tribute Roll of Montezuma . . . Part 1. The Written Language of the Ancient Mexicans. Reprinted 20th May 1892, from Trans. Amer. Philos. Soc., Vol. 17.   4*   N.P., 1892
—— Reminiscences of Pennsylvania Folk-Lore.   8*   1892
—— Analytical Catalogue of Works and Scientific Articles.   8*   N.P., 1892
—— Further Notes on the Betoya Dialects, from unpublished sources.   8*
    [*Philadelphia*] 1892
—— Further Notes on Fuegian Languages. 8*   [*Philadelphia*] 1892
—— Address delivered on Columbus Day, 21st October 1892, at the . . . University of Pennsylvania, Philadelphia.   8*
    Philadelphia, 1892
—— Studies in South American Native Languages.   8°   *Philadelphia*, 1892
—— The Etrusco-Libyan Elements in the Song of the Arval Brethren.   8*   [1893]
—— The Native Calendar of Central America and Mexico : a Study in Linguistics and Symbolism.   8*   *Philadelphia*, 1893
—— Ethnology. On various supposed relations between the American and Asian Races. Reprinted from Memoirs of the International Congress of Anthropology, Chicago.   8*   *Chicago*, 1893
—— *See* Thomas, Cyrus.

Brisbane, Captain. *See* Weddell, James.

Brisbane, General Sir Thomas Makdougall. Reminiscences of General Sir T. M. Brisbane. *Portraits and plates*. Privately printed.   4°   *Edinburgh*, 1860
—— *See* New South Wales, D : Appendix 2.

Brisse, A., and L. de Rotrou. The Draining of Lake Fucino, accomplished by His Excellency Prince Alexander Torlonia : an Abridged Account, Historical and Technical. English translation by V. de Tivoli, jun.   4°; Atlas, folio   *Rome*, 1876

Brisson, —. *See* Saugnier.

Bristowe, Lindsay W., and Philip B. Wright. The Handbook of British Honduras for 1888-89, comprising Historical, Statistical, and General Information concerning the Colony. *Map.* 8°   1888
—— The same, for 1889-90. *Map.* 8° 1889
—— The same, for 1890-91. *Map.* 8° 1890
—— The same, for 1891-92. *Map.* Large 8°   1891
—— The same, for 1892-93. *Map.* Large 8°   1892

"Britannicus." The Dominican Republic and the Emperor Soulouque : being Remarks and Strictures on the Misstatements, and a Refutation of the Calumnies, of M. D'Alaux ; preceded by a concise Account of the Historical Events of the Dominican Republic, and a glance at the Peninsula of Samana. By "Britannicus."   8*   *Philadelphia*, 1852

Brito, P. J. M. de. Memoria Politica sobre a Capitania de Santa Catharina, escripta no Rio de Janeiro em 1816.   8°
    Lisbon, 1829

Britton, J. Descriptive Sketches of Tunbridge Wells and the Calverley Estate. *Maps and plates.* 8°   1832

Broadfoot, Lieut. James S. Reports on Parts of the Ghilzi Country, and on some of the Tribes in the neighbourhood of Ghazni ; and on the Route from Ghazni to Dera Ismail Khan by the Ghwalari Pass, 1839. Edited by Major William Broadfoot. R. G. S. Supplementary Papers, Vol. 1. *Map.* Large 8°   1886

Broadfoot, Major William. The Career of Major George Broadfoot, C.B., Governor-General's Agent North-West Frontier, 1844-45, in Afghanistan and the Punjab. Compiled from his Papers, and those of Lords Ellenborough and Hardinge. *Portrait and maps.* 8°   1888

Broadhead, G. C. *See* United States, K (Missouri) : Appendix 2.

Broca, Paul. On the Phenomena of Hybridity in the genus Homo. Edited by C. C. Blake.   8°   1864

Brocchi, G. B. Giornale delle Osservazioni fatte ne' Viaggi in Egitto, nella Siria e nella Nubia. 5 vols. and Atlas.   8°
    Bassano, 1841-43

Broch, O. J. Le Royaume de Norvége et le Peuple Norvégien, ses Rapports Sociaux, Hygiène, Moyens d'Existence, Sauvetage, Moyens de Communication et Économie. Rapport au Congrès de Bruxelles. *Plate.* 8°   *Christiania*, 1876

Brockedon, W. Illustrations of the Passes of the Alps by which Italy communicates with France, Switzerland, and Germany. *Maps and plates.* 2 vols.   4°   1828

Brockett, W. E. Narrative of a Voyage from Sydney to Torres Straits in Search of the Survivors of the " Charles Eaton." *Plates.* 8°   *Sydney*, 1836

Brocklehurst, Thomas Unett. Mexico To-day : a Country with a Great Future, and a glance at the Prehistoric Remains and Antiquities of the Montezumas. *Map and illustrations.* 8°   1883

Brocklesby, J. Elements of Physical Geography, together with a Treatise on the Physical Phenomena of the United States. *Maps.* 4°   *Philadelphia*, 1868

Brocquière, Bertrandon de la. *See* Hakluyt, Vol. 4 : Appendix 1.

Brodhead, John Romeyn. Documents relative to the Colonial History of the State of New York, procured in Holland, England, and France. Edited by E. B. O'Callaghan. *Maps.* 10 vols. 4° *Albany, N.Y.*, 1856-58
— Reports of, relative to the Colonial History of New York. 8° *New York*, 1845

Brodie, Sir Benjamin C. Address to the Ethnological Society of London, 1853 ; followed by a Sketch of the Recent Progress of Ethnology, by R. Cull. 8*   1853
— Ditto. 8*   1854

Brodie, Lieut. *See* India, I : Appendix 2.

Brodie, Walter. Pitcairn's Island and the Islanders in 1850, with Extracts from his Private Journal, and a few Hints upon California ; also the Reports of all the Commanders of Her Majesty's ships that have touched at the above Island since 1800. *Portrait and plates.* 8° 1851

Brodribb, W. A. A Plain Statement of Facts, addressed to the Small and Large Capitalists, and the Labouring Classes in England and elsewhere, on the great Capabilities and Natural Advantages of the Australian Colonies, particularly New South Wales and Victoria, for Emigration. 8°   1862
— Gipps Land and its Explorers. [Extract, Australian Newspaper.] 8* N.D.
— Recollections of an Australian Squatter, or Leaves from my Journal since 1835. 8°   *Sydney* [1883]

Brögger, W. C. *See* Sweden, A : Appendix 2.

Broke, George. With Sack and Stock in Alaska. *Maps.* 12°   1891

Brongniart, A. *See* Cuvier; *also* Greece, Morea : Appendix 2.

Broniouius de Biezerfedea, Martin. *See* Purchas, Vol. 3. Book 3 : Appendix 1.

Bronner, F. J. Parallelismus der Flusssysteme Europas, Asiens, Afrikas, und Amerikas, Vergleichungen der wichtigsten Ströme dieser Erdteile. 8* *Munich*, 1885

Brooke, Sir A. de Capell. Travels through Sweden, Norway, and Finmark to the North Cape. *Maps and plates.* 4° 1823
— Winter in Lapland and Sweden. *Map and plates.* 4°   1827
— Sketches in Spain and Morocco. *Plates.* 2 vols. 8°   1831

Brooke, Francis. *See* Blanc, V. Le.

Brooke, Capt. J. C. Report of a Tour through the Districts of Ajmere and Mairwara, N.W. Provinces [India Records, Part 32, N.W. Provinces] *Calcutta*, 1858

Brooke, Sir James, Rajah of Sarawak. Letter from Borneo, with Notices of the Country and its Inhabitants. 8*   1842
— *See* Keppel ; Mundy, R.

Brooke, R. Extracts from the Journal of an Excursion to Explore the Mahavillaganga (Ceylon). 8*   *Colombo*, 1833

Brooke, T. H. History of the Island of St Helena, from its Discovery by the Portuguese to the year 1823. 2nd edition. *Plate.* 8°   1824

Brookes, R. General Gazetteer, or Compendious Geographical Dictionary, containing Descriptions of every Country in the known World, with their Towns, People, Natural Productions, &c. Revised and corrected to the present period by A. G. Findlay. *Maps.* 8°   1854

Brooks, C. W. Early Migrations : Early Maritime Intercourse of Ancient Western Nations, Chronologically arranged and Ethnologically considered. *Frontispiece.* 8*   *San Francisco*, 1876
— Japanese Wrecks, stranded and picked up adrift in the North Pacific Ocean, Ethnologically considered. *Map.* 8*   *San Francisco*, 1876
— Origin of the Chinese Race, Philosophy of their Early Development, with an Inquiry into the Evidences of their American Origin. *Map.* 8* *San Francisco*, 1876
— On the "Jeannette" Arctic Expedition and the missing Whalers. *Maps.* 8* *San Francisco*, 1880
— The Object of Arctic Explorations. (Proceedings of the California Academy of Sciences.) 8*   *San Francisco*, 1881
— Early Discoveries of Wrangel Land : some Evidence regarding conflicting Claims ; Plans of the Rodgers Expedition. (Proceedings of the California Academy of Sciences.) 8* *San Francisco*, 1881
— Arctic Drift and Ocean Currents illustrated by the discovery on an Ice-Floe off the Coast of Greenland of relics from the American Arctic steamer "Jeannette." *Chart.* 8* *San Francisco*, 1884
— *See* Pierce, H. A.

Brooks, Francis. *See* Gottfried: Appendix 1.

Brooks, H. Natal: a History and Description of the Colony, including its Natural Features, Productions, Industrial Condition, and Prospects. Edited by Dr R. J. Mann. *Photographs and coloured plates.* 8° 1876

Brooks, Shirley. Russians of the South. 12°. [Bound with M'Culloch's "Russia and Turkey."] 1854

Brooks, W. A. Euphrates, the Road to the East. *Maps.* 8* N. D.

—— Honduras and the Interoceanic Railway: Report on the Line and its Prospects. . . . 8* 1874

Brossary, Chiron du. Instructions Nautiques sur l'Atterage et la Navigation de la Plata. 8° *Paris,* 1845

Brosselard, Henri. Voyage de la Mission Flatters au pays des Touareg Azdjers. *Map and illustrations.* 12° *Paris,* 1883

Brosselard-Faidherbe, Capt. Casamance et Mellacorée: Pénétration au Soudan. *Maps and illustrations.* 4° *Paris* [1892?]

Brosses, Charles de. Histoire des Navigations aux Terres Australes. 2 vols. 4° *Paris,* 1761

—— *See* Pinkerton, Vol. 11: Appendix 1.

Brosset, F. Description Géographique de la Géorgie par le Tsarévitch Wakhoucht, publiée d'après l'original Autographe. *Maps.* 4° *St Petersburg,* 1842

—— Rapports sur un Voyage Archéologique dans la Géorgie et dans l'Arménie, exécuté en 1847-48. 8°; and Atlas, oblong 8° *St Petersburg,* 1849-51

—— Histoire de la Géorgie, depuis l'Antiquité jusqu'au xixe. Siècle. Traduite du Géorgien. 4 vols. 8° *St Petersburg,* 1849-58

Brough, Bennett Hooper. Tacheometry, or Rapid Surveying. 8* 1887

Brough, Louisa. *See* Umlauft.

Broughton, E. Six Years' Residence in Algiers. 8° 1839

Broughton, Lord. Italy: Remarks made in several Visits from 1816 to 1854. 2 vols. 8° 1859

Broughton, —. *See* Eyriès, Vol. 2: Appendix 1.

Broughton, Thomas Duer. Letters written in a Mahratta Camp during the year 1809, descriptive of the Character, Manners, Domestic Habits, and Religious Ceremonies of the Mahrattas. *Plates.* 4° 1813

Broughton, W. R. A Voyage of Discovery to the North Pacific Ocean; in which the Coast of Asia from the lat. of 35° North to the lat. of 52° North, the Island of Insu (commonly known under the name of the Land of Jesso), the North, South, and East Coasts of Japan,

Broughton, W. R.—*continued.* the Licuchieux and the Adjacent Isles, as well as the Coast of Corea, have been Examined and Surveyed. Performed in His Majesty's sloop "Providence" and her Tender, in the years 1795, '96, '97, '98. *Maps, plates.* 4° 1804

Broun, Sir Richard. European and Asiatic Intercourse viâ British Columbia by means of a Main Through Trunk Railway from the Atlantic to the Pacific. *Map.* 8* 1858

Broun, Capt. Thomas. Manual of the New Zealand Coleoptera. (N. Z. Institute.) Parts 5-7 (1 vol.) 8° *Wellington,* 1893

—— *See* New Zealand, A: Appendix 2.

Brown, Alexander. The Genesis of the United States: a Narrative of the Movement in England, 1605-16, which resulted in the Plantation of North America by Englishmen; disclosing the Contest between England and Spain for the Possession of the Soil now Occupied by the United States of America; set forth through a Series of Historical Manuscripts now first printed, together with a reissue of rare Contemporaneous Tracts, accompanied by Bibliographical Memoranda, Notes, and brief Biographies. 2 vols. *Maps and portraits.* 8° 1890

Brown, Arnold. *See* Purchas, Vol. 2, Book 10: Appendix 1.

Brown, A. Samler. Madeira and the Canary Islands: a Practical and Complete Guide for the Use of Invalids and Tourists. 2nd edition. *Maps.* 12° 1890

Brown, C. Barrington. Geological Report on the Districts bordering on the Curiebrong, Ireng, Takutu, Rupununi, and Upper Essequebo Rivers. Folio* *Demerara,* 1871

—— Canoe and Camp Life in British Guiana. *Map and plates.* 8° 1876

—— **and W. Lidstone.** Fifteen Thousand Miles on the Amazon and its Tributaries. *Map and plates.* 8° 1878

Brown, E. An Account of Several Travels through a great Part of Germany, in Four Journeys, from Norwich to Colen, &c. *Plates.* Square 8° 1677

—— Travels in Divers Parts of Europe. *Plates.* Folio 1685

Brown, Rev. G. Notes on the Duke of York Group, New Britain, and New Ireland. (From the Journal of the Royal Geographical Society, 1877.) 8* 1878

—— **and B. Danks.** A Dictionary of the Duke of York Islands Language, New Britain Group; also a Grammar of the same, and an Introduction. MS. 8° *Sydney,* 1882

Brown, H. A. A Winter in Albania. 8° 1888

Brown, H. Y. L. Western Australia: Geological Description of Country to the North-East of Champion Bay. *Map.* Folio* *Perth, W.A.*, 1871

Brown, J. A. Palæolithic Man in N.-W. Middlesex: the Evidence of his Existence, and the Physical Conditions under which he lived, in Ealing and its neighbourhood, illustrated by the condition and culture presented by certain existing savages. *Frontispiece and plates.* 8° 1887

Brown, John. The North-West Passage, and the Plans for the Search for Sir John Franklin: a Review. *Maps and plate.* 8° 1858
—— A Sequel to the North-West Passage. *Map and facsimile.* 8° 1860
—— Notice sur la Vie et les Travaux de, par M. de la Roquette. *Portrait.* 4* *Paris*, 1863

Brown, Rev. J. Croumbie. Hydrology of South Africa, or Details of the former Hydrographic condition of the Cape of Good Hope, and of Causes of its present Aridity. 8° 1875
—— *See* Arbousset and Daumas.

Brown, J. E. A Practical Treatise on Tree Culture in South Australia. 2nd edition. *Illustrations.* 8° *Adelaide*, 1881
—— *See* South Australia, A : Appendix 2.

Brown, Rev. J. T. *See* Underhill.

Brown, Capt. Lewis. Private Journal kept while in the Murree Hills, also during his Occupation of the Fort of Kahun, and during his Retreat to Poolajee, from 8th April to 1st October 1840. [From the India Records, No. 17.] Royal 8° *Bombay*, 1855
—— Report showing the number of Fortified Places within the Districts under the Pahlunpoor Superintendency, prepared in 1844. [From the India Records, No. 25.] Royal 8° *Bombay*, 1856

Brown, M. *See* Mueller, Baron Sir F.

Brown, Marie A. The Icelandic Discoverers of America, or Honour to whom Honour is Due. *Illustrations.* Small 8° 1887

Brown, P. Hume. Early Travellers in Scotland. Edited by P. Hume Brown. *Maps.* 8° *Edinburgh*, 1891
—— *See* Kirk and Thoresby.

Brown, R. Annual Report of the Munnipore Political Agency for 1868-69. [From the India Records, No. 78.] Royal 8° *Calcutta*, 1870

Brown, Richard. A History of the Island of Cape Breton, with some Account of the Discovery and Settlement of Canada, Nova Scotia, and Newfoundland. *Maps and plate.* 8° 1869
—— Notes on the Northern Atlantic, for the use of travellers. *Map.* Small 8° 1880

Brown, Dr Robert. Vancouver-Island Exploration, 1864. [With unpublished sketches.] 8* *Victoria, B.C.*, 1865
—— A Monograph of the Coniferous genus Thuja, Linn., and of the North American Species of the Genus Libocedrus, Endl. 8* 1867
—— Florula Discoana : Contributions to the Phyto-Geography of Greenland within the Parallels of 68° and 70° North Latitude. 8* *Edinburgh*, 1868
—— Notes on the History and Geographical Relations of the Pinnipedia frequenting the Spitzbergen and Greenland Seas. 8* [1868]
—— Observations on the Medicinal and Economic Value of the Oulachan. 8* 1868
—— On the Mammalian Fauna of Greenland. 8* [1868]
—— On the Nature of the Discoloration of the Arctic Seas. 8* *Edinburgh*, 1868
—— Synopsis of the Birds of Vancouver Island. 8* 1868
—— Notes on the History and Geographical Relations of the Cetacea frequenting Davis Strait and Baffin's Bay. 8* 1868
—— On the Geographical Distribution and Physical Characteristics of the Coal-Fields of the North Pacific Coast. 8° *Edinburgh*, 1869
—— On the Geographical Distribution of the Coniferæ and Gnetaceæ. 8* *Edinburgh*, 1869
—— Das Innere der Vancouver-Insel. *Map.* 4* *Gotha* [1869]
—— On Arctic Exploration. 8* *Edinburgh*, 1870
—— Physics of Arctic Ice. 8* 1871
—— Descriptions of some new or little-known Species of Oaks from North-West America. 8* 1871
—— Die geographische Verbreitung der Coniferen und Gnetaceen. *Map.* 4* *Gotha*, 1872
—— Geological Notes on the Noursoak Peninsula, Disco Island, and the country in the vicinity of Disco Bay, North Greenland. 8* *Glasgow*, 1875
—— The Countries of the World : being a Popular Description of the various Continents, Islands, Rivers, Seas, and Peoples of the Globe. 6 vols. *Maps and plates.* Small 4° [1877-81]
—— Notes on the recent Progress of Botany in Denmark. 8* N.D.
—— The Races of Mankind: being a Popular Description of the Characteristics, Manners, and Customs of the Principal Varieties of the Human Family. 4 vols. *Plates.* Small 4° N.D.
—— The Peoples of the World : being a Popular Description of the Characteristics, Conditions, and Customs of the Human Family. 6 vols. *Illustrations.* 4° 1882

Brown, Dr Robert. Our Earth and its Story: a Popular Treatise on Physical Geography. Edited by Robert Brown, Ph.D. 3 vols. *Maps, coloured plates, and illustrations.* 4° 1887-89
—— The Adventures of Thomas Pellow, of Penryn, Mariner, Three and Twenty Years in Captivity among the Moors. Written by himself; and edited, with an Introduction and Notes, by Dr Robert Brown. *Illustrations.* 8° 1890
—— The Story of Africa and its Explorers. 3 vols. *Illustrations.* 4° 1892-94
—— *See* Dickie, G.; Green, A. H.; Rink.

Brown, Lieut.-Col. R. H. The Fayûm and Lake Mœris; with a Prefatory Note by Colonel Sir Colin Scott-Moncrieff, and *illustrations* from photographs by the Author. 4° 1892

Brown, Samuel. On the Statistical Progress of the Kingdom of Italy. 8° 1866

Browne, A. H. The Political Economy of Indian Famines. 8° *Bombay*, 1877

Browne, Lieut.-Col. Edmond Charles. The Coming of the Great Queen: a Narrative of the Acquisition of Burma. *Maps and illustrations.* 8° 1888

Browne, Edward. *See* Harris, Vol. 2: Appendix 1.

Browne, Edward G. A Year amongst the Persians: Impressions as to the Life, Character, and Thought of the People of Persia, received during twelve months residence in that country in the years 1887-88. *Map.* 8° 1893

Browne, J. Ross. Report of the Debates in the Convention of California on the Formation of the State Constitution in 1849. 8° *Washington*, 1850

Browne, Lieut. R. A. Russia and the Invasion of India. (From *Journal, United Service Institution of India.*) 8° 1893

Browne, W. H. *See* Maclean, A. J.

Browne, W. G. Travels in Africa, Egypt, and Syria, from the year 1792 to 1798. *Plates.* 4° 1799
—— The same. 2nd edition. *Maps and plates.* 4° 1806
—— *See* Pinkerton, Vol. 15; Walpole, Travels: Appendix 1.

Browne, Walter Raleigh. [A Memoir.] Excerpt, Minutes of Proceedings of the Institution of Civil Engineers, Vol. 79. 8° 1885

Browning, George. The Edda Songs and Sagas of Iceland. 12° 1876

Browning, Walter Westcott. Ireland. Handbook of Railway Distances. *Map.* Large 8° 1874

Brownrigg, Rev. Canon. The Cruise of the "Freak": a Narrative of a Visit to the Islands in Bass and Banks' Straits, with some Account of the Islands. *Map and plates.* 8° *Launceston, Tasmania,* 1876

Bruce, James. Travels to Discover the Source of the Nile, in 1768-73. 5 vols. *Maps and plates.* 4° *Edinburgh,* 1790
—— Travels into Abyssinia to Discover the Source of the Nile. Abridged by S. Shaw. 12° 1790
—— Account of the Life and Writings of. By Alexander Murray. *Map and plates.* 4° *Edinburgh,* 1808
—— The Life of Bruce, the African Traveller. By F. B. Head. *Maps, plate.* 12° 1830
—— *See* Robinson, F.

Bruce, John. Annals of the Honourable East India Company, from their Establishment by the Charter of Queen Elizabeth, 1600, to the Union of the London and English East India Companies, 1707-8. 3 vols. 4° 1810

Bruce, R. B. J. Notes on the Dera Ghazee Khan Desert, North-Western Frontier of India, and its Border Tribes. [No. 9 of New Series of Selections from the Records of the Government of Panjab and its Dependencies.] Royal 8° *Lahore,* 1871

Brucker, J. Découvreurs et Missionaires dans l'Afrique Centrale au XVIᵉ et au XVIIᵉ Siècle. 8° *Lyons,* 1878
—— Découverte des grands lacs de l'Afrique Centrale et des sources du Nil et du Zaïre au seizième Siècle. *Map.* 8° *Lyons,* 1878
—— Positions Géographiques déterminées par deux Missionaires Jésuites dans le Turkestan Oriental et la Dzoungarie en 1756, d'après deux lettres inédites des PP. Amiot et Gaubil. 8° *Lyons,* 1880
—— Benoit de Goès, Missionaire Voyageur dans l'Asie Centrale, 1603-7. 8° *Lyons,* 1879

Brückner, Dr E. Das Klima der Eiszeit. 8° *Davos,* 1891
—— Ueber Schwankungen der Seen und Meere. Vortrag IX. Deutschen Geographentage in Wien, 1892. 8° *Berlin,* 1891
—— Eiszeit-Studien in den südöstlichen Alpen. 8° *Berne,* 1891
—— Ueber die angebliche Aenderung der Entfernung zwischen Jura und Alpen. Separatabdruck aus dem XI. Jahresbericht Geog. Ges. Bern, 1891-92. 8°
—— Ueber den Einfluss der Schneedecke auf das Klima der Alpen. 8° [*Berlin*] 1893
—— Bericht über das Projekt einer Erdkarte im Masstab 1 : 1,000,000. 8° *Berne,* 1893
—— *See* Penck; Penck's Abhandlungen, 1.

Brucks, Capt. George Barnes. Memoir descriptive of the Navigation of the Gulf of Persia. [From the India Records, No. 24.] *Map.* Royal 8° *Bombay,* 1856
—— *See* Jones, Felix.

Brué, André. *See* Astley, Vol. 2 ; Laharpe, 1 ; Allgemeine Historie, 2 : Appendix 1.

Brugsch Pasha, H. Reise der k. preussichen Gesandtschaft nach Persien, 1860 und 1861. *Map and illustrations.* Large 8° *Leipzig*, 1862-63

—— Dictionnaire Géographique de l'Ancienne Egypte : contenant par ordre Alphabétique la Nomenclature comparée des Noms propres Géographiques qui se Rencontrent sur les Monuments et dans les Papyrus. Folio *Leipzig*, 1879

—— A History of Egypt under the Pharaohs, derived entirely from the Monuments, to which is added a Discourse on the Exodus of the Israelites. Translated and·edited from the German by Philip Smith. 2nd edition, with a New Preface, Additions, and Original Notes by the Author. 2 vols. *Maps and illustrations.* 8° 1881

Bruguière, Louis. Orographie de l'Europe. *Map and plates.* 4° *Paris*, 1830

—— *See* Recueil de Voyages, Vol. 3, p. 611 : Appendix 1.

Bruhns, Karl. Alexander von Humboldt, eine wissenschaftliche Biographie. 3 vols. *Portraits.* 8° *Leipzig*, 1872

—— Resultate aus den meteorologischen Beobachtungen angestellt an fünfundzwanzig königl. Sächsischen Stationen im Jahre 1871. 4° *Leipzig*, 1874

Brullé, ——. *See* Greece, Morea: Appendix 2.

Brumund, Jan Frederik Gerrit. *See* Leemanns, C. ; Veth, P. J.

Brun, Cornelius le. Voyages de, par la Moscovie en Perse, et aux Indes Orientales . . . On y a ajoûté la route qu'a suivie Mr Isbrants, Ambassadeur de Moscovie, en traversant la Russie et la Tartarie, pour se rendre à la Chine ; et quelques Remarques contre MM. Chardin et Kempfer. 2 vols. *Maps and plates.* Small folio *Amsterdam*, 1718

—— Travels into Muscovy, Persia, and part of the East Indies, containing an accurate Description of what is most Remarkable in those Countries . . . ; to which is added an Account of the Journey of Mr Isbrants . . . through Russia and Tartary to China ; together with Remarks on the Travels of Sir J. Chardin and Mr Kempfer. Translated. 2 vols. *Maps and plates.* Folio 1737

Brun, Isidore le. Tableau Statistique et Politique des Deux Canadas. 8° *Paris*, 1833

Brunet, J. New Guide to Boulogne-sur-Mer and its Environs. *Map and plates.* 18° *Boulogne*, 1858

Brunet, J. C. Manuel du Libraire et de l'Amateur de Livres : contenant, I. Un Nouveau Dictionnaire Bibliographique ; II. Une Table en forme de Catalogue Raisonné. 5 vols. 8° *Paris*, 1842-44

Brunet, G., and P. Deschamps. Manuel du Libraire et de l'Amateur de Livres. Supplément, contenant 1° un complément du Dictionnaire Bibliographique de M. J.-Ch. Brunet. . . *See* Deschamps.

Brunner, Samuel. Reise nach Senegambien und den Inseln des grünen Vorgebürges, in Jahre 1838. 8° *Berne*, 1840

Brunnhofer, Dr H. Iran und Turan : historisch-geographische und ethnologische Untersuchungen über den altesten Schauplatz der Indischen Urgeschichte ; Einzelbeiträge zur allgemeinen und vergleichenden Sprachwissenschaft. Fünftes Heft. 8° *Leipzig*, 1889

Brunnmark, Gustavus. A Short Introduction to Swedish Grammar, adapted for the use of Englishmen. 2nd edition. 8° *Stockholm*, 1820

Brun-Renaud, C. le. Les possessions Françaises de l'Afrique Occidentale. *Maps.* 12° *Paris*, 1886

Brun-Rollet, M. Le Nil Blanc et le Soudan, études sur l'Afrique Centrale, mœurs et coûtumes des Sauvages. *Map and plates.* 8° *Paris*, 1855

Bruns, Paul Jacob. Neue systematische Erdbeschreibung von Afrika. 6 vols. *Maps.* 8° *Nuremberg*, 1799

Brunson, Alfred. Prairie du Chien (Wisconsin), its Present Position and Future Prospects. 12° *Milwaukee*, 1857

Brunton, John. Description of the Line and Works of the Scinde Railway. Edited by C. Manby and J. Forrest. *Maps.* 8° 1863

—— Remarks upon the Ruins of the Ancient City of Brahminabad in the Province of Scinde. MS. 4° *Kurrachee*, 1866

Brunton, Dr T. L., and J. Fayrer. On the Nature and Physiological Action of the Poison of Naja Tripudians, and other Indian Venomous Snakes. Parts 1 and 2. 8° 1873-74

Bruton, W. *See* Churchill, Vol. 8 ; Hakluyt, Vol. 5 : Appendix 1.

Bruun, P. J. Notices sur la Topographie Ancienne de la Nouvelle Russie et de la Bessarabie. 12° *Odessa*, 1857

Bruyn, C. Le. *See* Brun.

Bruyssel, Ernest van. La République Argentine, ses Ressources naturelles, ses Colonies Agricoles, son importance comme Centre d'Immigration. 8° *Brussels*, 1888

Bruyssel, Ernest van. La République Orientale del Uruguay. 8°
Brussels, 1889
—— La République du Paraguay. 8°
Brussels, 1893

Bryan, F. T. *See* United States, K, Texas : Appendix 2.

Bryan, Margaret. A Compendious System of Astronomy in a course of familiar lectures . . . : Trigonometrical and Celestial Problems, with a Key to the Ephemeris, &c. *Plates.* 4°
1797

Bryans, J. W. The Retention of Candahar, briefly considered as a Military, Civil, and Religious Question. 8* 1880

Bryant, W. C. Picturesque America : a Delineation, by Pen and Pencil, of the Mountains, Rivers, Lakes, Forests, Waterfalls, Shores, Cañons, Valleys, Cities, and other Picturesque Features of the United States, with Illustrations on Steel and Wood by eminent American Artists. Edited by William Cullen Bryant. 4 vols. 4° N.D.

Bryce, Dr James. Cyclopædia of Geography, Descriptive and Physical, forming a New General Gazetteer of the World and Dictionary of Pronunciation. *Map and illustrations.* 8° *Glasgow*, 1856
—— **and K. Johnston.** The Library Cyclopædia of Geography, Descriptive, Physical, Political, and Historical, forming a New Gazetteer of the World. New edition. *Woodcuts.* Small 4° 1880

Bryce, J. Annan. Transcaucasia and Ararat : being Notes of a Vacation Tour in Autumn of 1876. *Frontispiece and map.* Small 8° 1877

Bryce, Rev. Professor. Manitoba, its Infancy, Growth, and present condition. *Map and illustrations.* Small 8° 1882

Bryden, H. A. Kloof and Karoo : Sport, Legend, and Natural History in Cape Colony, with a Notice of the Game Birds, and of the present Distribution of the Antelopes and larger Game. *Illustrations.* 8° 1889
—— Gun and Camera in Southern Africa : a Year of Wanderings in Bechuanaland, the Kalahari Desert, and the Lake River Country, Ngamiland ; with Notes on Colonisation, Natives, Natural History, and Sport. *Maps and illustrations.* 8° 1893

Brydges, Sir Harford Jones. Account of the Transactions of H.M. Mission to the Court of Persia in 1807-11, with a brief History of the Wahauby. 2 vols. *Map and plates.* 8° 1834

Brydone, Patrick. Voyage en Sicile et à Malthe. Traduit par Demeunier. 2 vols. *Map.* 8° *Amsterdam*, 1776

Brydone, Patrick. A Tour through Sicily and Malta, in a Series of Letters to Wm. Beckford, Esq. A new edition. 2 vols. *Map.* 8° 1790
—— Ditto. New edition. *Map.* 8° 1806

Brylkin, A. D. *See* Schmidt, F. B.

Buch, Leopold von. Description Physique des Iles Canaries, suivie d'une Indication des principaux Volcans du Globe. Traduit par C. Boulanger. 8°
Paris, 1836
—— Die Bären-Insel nach M. B. Keilhau geognostisch beschrieben. *Plate.* 4*
Berlin, 1847
—— Ueber die Juraformation auf der Erdfläche. *Map.* 8* *Berlin*, 1853
—— Ueber Ceratiten, besonders von denen, die in Kreidebildungen sich finden. *Plate.* 8* N.P., N.D.

Buchan, Dr Alexander. Handy Book of Meteorology. 2nd edition. 8° 1868
—— The Mean Pressure of the Atmosphere over the Globe for the Months and for the Year. Part I. [An Extract.] 8*
[*Edinburgh*, 1858]
—— the Mean Pressure of the Atmosphere and the prevailing Winds over the Globe for the Months and for the Year. Part 2. *Plates.* 4* *Edinburgh*, 1869
—— Note on the Determination of Heights, chiefly in the Interior of Continents, from Observations of Atmospheric Pressure. 8* [*Edinburgh*, 1869]
—— The Temperature of London for 130 Years, from 1763 to 1892. (From the *Journal* of the Scottish Meteorological Society for 1892.) Large 8* 1892
—— *See* United Kingdom, H, " Challenger " : Appendix 2.

Buchan, St John. Lightning Jottings of Seringapatam. 4* *Bangalore*, 1883
[——] To the Káveri Falls. *Map.* Small 8* *Bangalore*, 1886

Buchanan, Francis. *See* Hamilton, F. ; *also* Pinkerton, Vol. 8 : Appendix 1.

Buchanan, John. The Shiré Highlands (East Central Africa) as Colony and Mission. *Map and plan.* 8° 1885

Buchanan, J. Y. On the Occurrence of Sulphur in Marine Muds and Nodules, and its bearing on their Mode of Formation. 8* [*Edinburgh*, 1890]
—— On the Composition of Oceanic and Littoral Manganese Nodules. *Map and plate.* 4* *Edinburgh*, 1891
—— On the Composition of some Deep-Sea Deposits from the Mediterranean. 8* *Edinburgh*, 1891
—— *See* United Kingdom, H, " Challenger " : Appendix 2.

Buchenroder, W. L. von. *See* British South Africa, A : Appendix 2.

Buchholz, Reinhold. *See* Heinersdorff.

Buchner, Eug. *See* Schrenck and Maximowicz. Beiträge zur Kenntniss des Russischen Reiches, Vol. 2.
—— and T. Pleske. *See* Helmersen and Schrenck, 4.
Buchner, L. A. Ueber die Beziehungen der Chemie zur Rechtspflege. 4°
Munich, 1875
Buchner, M. Reise durch den Stillen Ozean. 8° *Breslau*, 1878
Buchner, Max. Kamerun Skizzen und Betrachtungen. 8° *Leipzig*, 1887
Buchon, J. A. C., et J. Tastu. Notice d'un Atlas en Langue Catalane, Manuscrit de l'an 1375. 4° *Paris*, 1839
Buchta, Richard. Der Sudan unter ägyptischer Herrschaft : Rückblicke auf die letzten sechzig Jahre ; nebst einem Anhange : Briefe Dr Emin Pascha's und Lupton Bey's an Dr Wilhelm Junker, 1883-85. *Maps and portraits.* 8°
Leipzig, 1888
—— *See* Junker.
Buck, Walter J. *See* Chapman, A.
Buckingham, B. H. ; George C. Foulk ; Walter M'Lean. Observations upon the Korean Coast, Japanese-Korean Ports, and Siberia. *Map.* 8° *Washington*, 1883
Buckingham, J. S. Travels in Palestine, through the countries of Bashan and Gilead, east of the River Jordan. 2 vols. *Maps and plates.* 8° 1822
—— Travels among the Arab Tribes inhabiting the countries east of Syria and Palestine, including from Nazareth to the mountains beyond the Dead Sea, and through the Plains of the Hauran. *Map and illustrations.* 4° 1825
—— Travels in Mesopotamia, including a Journey from Aleppo to Bagdad ; with Researches on the Ruins of Nineveh, Babylon, and other ancient cities. 2 vols. *Map and plates.* 8° 1827
—— Travels in Assyria, Medea, and Persia, including a Journey from Bagdad by Mount Zagros to Hamadan, the Ancient Ecbatana, Researches in Ispahan and the Ruins of Persepolis. 2 vols. *Map and plates.* 8° 1830
—— America, Historical, Statistic, and Descriptive. 3 vols. *Portrait, map, and woodcuts.* 8° 1841-45
—— Autobiography of, including his Voyages, &c. (Vol. 2.) 8° 1855
Buckland, Rev. William. Reliquiæ Diluvianæ ; or, Observations on the Organic Remains contained in Caves, Fissures, and Diluvial Gravel, and on other Geological Phenomena attesting the Action of an Universal Deluge. *Maps, plates, and table.* 4° 1824
Buckle, Major C. Papers relative to the Improvement of the Forest Revenue of the Panch Mahals. [From the India Records, No. 77.] *Map* *Bombay*, 1863

Buckley, Robert Burton. Irrigation Works in India and Egypt. *Maps and plates.* Large 8° 1893
Buckman, J. *See* Murchison.
Bucquoi, Jakob de. Aanmerkelyke ontmoetingen in de zestien jaarige Reize naa de Indiën. *Map and plates.* Small 8°
Haarlem, 1744
Buddingh, D. Een Woord over het tegenwoordige Standpunt en de Wetenschappelijke Beoefening der Natuurlijke Aardrijksbeschrijving. 8°
Haarlem, 1846
Budge, E. A. Wallis. Description of : the Tombs of Mechu, Ben, and Se-Renpu, discovered by Major-General Sir F. Grenfell in 1885. 8° [1887]
—— The Nile : Notes for Travellers in Egypt. *Map and plans.* 12° 1890
Buelna, Eustaquio. Peregrinacion de los Aztecas, y nombres Geograficos Indigenas de Sinaloa. 8* *Mexico*, 1887
—— Constitución de la Atmósfera o leyes que rigen la densidad, peso, altitud y temperatura del aire. 8* *Mexico*, 1889
Buffier, P. Geografia Universale, exposta ne' differenti modi che possono abbreviare lo Studio, e facilitar l'uso di questa Scienza, col Soccorso de' Versi Artificiali, e col Trattato della Sfera. *Maps.* 12° *Venice*, 1751
Bugeaud, M. Mémoire sur notre Établissement dans la Province d'Oran par suite de la Paix. *Map.* 8° *Paris*, 1838
—— De l'Établissement de Légions de Colons Militaires dans les possessions Françaises du Nord de l'Afrique. *Map.* 8° *Paris*, 1838
Bühler, Georg. *See* India, A : Appendix 2.
Buhse, Dr F. A. Nachrichten über drei pharmacologisch-wichtige Pflanzen und über die grosse Salzwüste in Persien. 8*
[*Moscow*, 1850]
—— Eine Reise durch Transkaukasien und Persien in den Jahren 1847-49. 8*
Moscow, 1855
—— *See* Baer and Helmersen, 13 ; Boissier.
Buist, George. Outline of the Operations of the British Troops in Scinde and Afghanistan betwixt November 1838 and November 1841 ; with Remarks on the Policy of the War. *Plate.* Small 8°
Bombay, 1843
—— Result of the Comparison of the Observations of Nine Different Barometers, read every half-hour for twenty-four successive hours. 8* *Bombay*, 1843
—— Memoir of. *Plates.* 8* *Cupar*, 1846
—— Annals of India for the year 1848 : an Outline of the Principal Events which have occurred in the British Dominions in India from 1st January 1848 to the end of the second Seikh War in March 1849. 8° *Bombay*, 1849

Buist, George. Manual of Physical Research for India. Part 1. 8°
Bombay, 1852
—— Index to Books and Papers on the Physical Geography, Antiquities, and Statistics of India. 8* *Bombay*, 1852
—— Notes on a Journey through part of Kattiawar and Goozerat, in January 1855. *Plates.* 8° 1855
—— Corrections of a few of the Errors contained in Sir W. Napier's Life of his brother Sir Charles Napier, in so far as they affect the Press of India, in a Letter addressed to the Author. 8* 1857
—— *See* India, C (Geological Papers): Appendix 2.

Bulard, ——. Sur un Nouveau Système de Représentation d'Observations Météorologiques continues faites à l'Observatoire National d'Alger. 4* [*Paris*, 1873]

Bulgarin, Thomas. Russland in historischer, statistischer, geographischer, &c., Beziehung. Geschichte; Erster Band, mit 2 Karten. Statistik; Erster Band, mit 3 Karten. 8° *Riga*, 1839

Bulger, G. E. Notes of a Tour from Bangalore to Calcutta, thence to Delhi, and subsequently to British Sikkim, during the early part of 1867. 8°
Secunderabad, 1869

Bulhões, E. Lobo de. Les Colonies Portugaises, Court Exposé de leur Situation Actuelle. 8° *Lisbon*, 1878

Bulkeley, J. *See* Kerr, Vol. 17: Appendix 1.

Bulkeley, Owen T. The Lesser Antilles : a Guide for Settlers in the British West Indies, and Tourists' Companion. *Map and illustrations.* Crown 8° 1889

Bullar, John. Hints to Assist the Inquiries of Visitors : being Brief Notices of Local Antiquities in Southampton and its Neighbourhood ; also, On the Objects worthy of Attention in an Excursion round the Isle of Wight, by John Drew. *Map.* 8* *Southampton*, 1846
" **Bulldog** " Voyage. *See* Wallich.

Buller, E. W. Semi-Azimuths : a New Method of Navigation. Part 1. 8° 1893

Buller, F. P. Chowkeedaree Assessment in Shahjehanpore. [From the India Records, Vol. 1, N.W. Provinces.] 8° 1855

Buller, Sir Walter. L. New Zealand Exhibition, 1865 : Essay on the Ornithology of New Zealand. 8° *Dunedin*, 1865
—— A Classified List of Mr S. William Silver's Collection of New Zealand Birds (at the Manor-House, Letcomb Regis), with short Descriptive Notes. *Plates.* 8° 1888
—— *See* New Zealand, A : Appendix 2.

Bullo, C. La vera Patria di Nicoló de' Conti e di Giovanni Caboto. Studi e Documenti. 8° *Chioggia*, 1880

Bullo, C. Il Viaggio di M. Piero Querini e le Relazionie della Repubblica Veneta colla Svezia. 8° *Venice*, 1881

Bullock, C. J. *See* United Kingdom, A (China Sea) : Appendix 2.

Bullock, W. Six Months Residence and Travels in Mexico, containing Remarks on the Present State of New Spain, its Natural Productions, &c. 2 vols. *Plan and plates.* 12° 1825

Bullock, W. Polish Experiences during the Insurrection of 1863-64. *Map.* Small 8° 1864

Bullock, W. H. Across Mexico in 1864-65. *Map and plates.* 8° 1866

Bulychef, I. Travels in Eastern Siberia. Part I. [In Russian.] Royal 8°
St Petersburg, 1856

Bunbury, C. J. F. Journal of a Residence at the Cape of Good Hope, with Excursions into the Interior. *Plates.* 8° 1848

Bunbury, Sir Edward H. A History of Ancient Geography among the Greeks and Romans, from the Earliest Ages till the Fall of the Roman Empire. 2 vols. *Maps.* 8° 1879

Bunbury, S. A. A Summer in Northern Europe, including Sketches in Sweden, Norway, Finland, the Aland Islands, Gothland. 2 vols. 8° 1856

Bunce, Daniel. *See* Zuchold, E. A.

Bundey, W. H. Notes of a Return Voyage from England to South Australia, *via* Ceylon, Singapore, China, Japan, California, Honolulu, and New Zealand. 8° *Adelaide*, 1882

Bunge, Dr Alexander. *See* Schrenck and Maximowicz, 3.

Bunge, E. Hospicio de Inválidos para la Republica Argentina. [Supplement to No. 47 of *El Inválido Argentino*.] Fo.*

Bunsen, Ernest de. The Origin of the Saracens. 8* N.D.

Bunsen, Georgius. De Azania, Africæ Littore Orientali, Commentatio Philologica. *Map.* 8* *Bonn*, 1852

Bunnett, F. E. *See* Vambéry.

Buonanno, G. I due Rarissimi Globi di Mercatore nella Biblioteca Governativa di Cremona. 8* *Cremona*, 1890

Burat, Amédée. Description des Terrains Volcaniques de la France Centrale. *Plates.* 8° *Paris*, 1833
—— Voyages sur les Côtes de France. *Plates.* 8° *Paris*, 1880

Burbidge, F. W. The Gardens of the Sun, or a Naturalist's Journal on the Mountains and in the Forests and Swamps of Borneo and the Sulu Archipelago. *Plates.* 8° 1880
—— A Trip to the Sooloo Archipelago. 8* 1884

Burchell, W. J. Travels in the Interior of Southern Africa. 2 vols. *Map and plates.* 4° 1822

Burckhardt, C. The Wildbad Spa in the Kingdom of Württemberg. *Map and plans.* 12* *Stuttgart*, 1863

Burckhardt, John Lewis. Travels in Nubia. *Maps and portrait.* 4° 1819
—— Travels in Syria and the Holy Land. *Maps.* 4° 1822
—— Travels in Arabia in 1814-15, comprehending an Account of those territories in Hedjaz which the Mohammedans regard as sacred. 2 vols. *Maps.* 8° 1829
—— Arabic Proverbs, or the Manners and Customs of the Modern Egyptians illustrated from their Proverbial Sayings current at Cairo, Translated and Explained. 4° 1830
—— Notes on the Bedouins and the Wahábys. 2 vols. *Map.* 8° 1831
—— *See* Phillips [3], Vol. 2, New Voyages and Travels : Appendix 1.

Burdo, A. Niger et Bénué : Voyage dans l'Afrique Centrale. *Map and plates.* 12° *Paris*, 1880
—— The Niger and Benué. *Map and plates.* 8° 1880

Burdwood, J. Tide Tables for the British and Irish Ports for 1865 ; also the Times and Heights of High Water at Full and Change for the Principal Places on the Globe. Computed by J. Burdwood, Staff Commander. 8° 1864
—— A Method for Finding the Latitude by the Simultaneous Altitudes of Two Stars. 2nd edition. 8* 1869
—— Sun's True Bearing, or Azimuth Tables, computed for Intervals of Four Minutes between the Parallels of Latitude 30° and 60° inclusive. 2nd edition. 8° 1869

Burdy, —. The Life of the Rev. Philip Skelton. [Bound up with the Lives of Dr Pocock, Dr Pearce, and Dr Newton.] 2 vols. 8° 1816

Buret, Eugène. Question d'Afrique, de la double Conquête de l'Algérie par la Guerre et la Colonisation. 8° *Paris*, 1842

Buret and Desor. *See* Ritter, Carl, p. 403.

Burgess, Capt. Boughey. A brief History of the Royal United Service Institution. 8* 1887

Burgess, Dr J. On Hypsometrical Measurements by Means of the Barometer and the Boiling-point Thermometer. 8° *Calcutta*, 1859
—— Remarks on the Bombay Tidal Observations for 1861, and other Papers relative to the Tides, Weights, and Measures, &c. 8* 1863
—— Notes of a Visit to Satrunjaya Hill, near Palitana, in September 1868. 16* *Bombay*, 1868

Burgess, Dr J. The Rock-cut Temples of Ajanta ; with an Account of a Trip to Aurangabad and Elora. 12* *Bombay*, 1868
—— Notes of a Visit to Somnath, Girnar, and other places in Kathiawad, in May 1869. 16* *Bombay*, 1869
—— Memorandum on the Survey of Architectural and other Archæological Remains, with Lists of the Rock-Excavations, Temples, Mosques, &c., in the Bombay Presidency, Sindh, Berar, Central Provinces, and Haidarabad. Folio* *Bombay*, 1870
—— *See* India, A : Appendix 2.

Burgess, Richard. On the Egyptian Obelisks in Rome, and Monoliths as Ornaments of Great Cities ; with a Discussion. 4* 1858

Burgkhardt, Dr J. *See* Germany, C, Forschungen, &c., Vol. 3 : Appendix 2.

Burgo, Giovanni Battista de. Viaggio di cinque anni in Asia, Africa, et Europa del Turco . . . ; con la descrittione di Gierusalem, Gran Cairo, Alessandria, Constantinopoli, et altre Città di Turchia, &c. 12° *Milan* [1686]

Burgst, Baron Nahuijs van. Beschouwingen over Nederlandsch Indië. 8° *The Hague*, 1847

Burkart, Joseph. Aufenthalt und Reisen in Mexico in 1825 bis 1834 : Bemerkungen über Land, Produkte, Leben und Sitten der Einwohner, und Beobachtungen aus dem Gebiete der Mineralogie, Geognosie, Bergbaukunde, Meteorologie, Geographie, &c. ; mit einem Vorworte von Dr J. Nöggerath. 2 vols. in 1. *Maps and plates.* 8° *Stuttgart*, 1836

Burke and Wills. *See* Westgarth.

Bürkli, A., and A. E. von der Linth. Die Wasserverhältnisse der Stadt Zürich und ihrer Umgebung. *Map.* 8* *Zurich*, 1871

Burmeister, Dr Herman. Geologische Bilder zur Geschichte der Erde und ihrer Bewohner. Vol. 2. 2nd edition. 12° *Leipzig*, 1855
—— Anales del Museo público de Buenos Aires, &c. Entrega 1. *Plates.* Folio *Buenos Ayres*, 1864
—— Los Caballos fósiles de la Pampa Argentina. *Plates.* Folio *Buenos Ayres*, 1875
—— Physikalische Beschreibung der Argentinischen Republik, nach eigenen und den vorhandenen Fremden, Beobachtungen entworfen. 8° *Buenos Ayres*, 1875
—— Description physique de la République Argentine, d'après des observations personelles et étrangères :—
Vol. I. (Traduite par E. Maupas) and II. (Traduite par E. Daireaux). 8° *Paris*, 1876

Burmeister, Dr Herman. Description physique de la République Argentine ; d'après des observations personelles et étrangères :—
Vol. III. (Traduite par E. Daireaux), Animaux Vertébrés, 1ere ptie. 8°
Buenos Ayres, 1879
Vol. V. (Traduite par E. Daireaux), Lepidoptères, 1ere ptie. 8°
Buenos Ayres, 1878
—— Atlas, livraisons 1 and 2. 4°
Buenos Ayres, 1879-80
—— Bericht über die Feier des 50-jährigen Doctor - Jubilaeums des, begangen den 19th December 1879, in Buenos Aires. 8*
Buenos Ayres, 1880
—— Atlas de la Description Physique de la République Argentine. Le Texte traduit en Français avec le concours de E. Daireaux. Deuxième Section. Mammifères, Deuxième Livraison. Die Seehunde der Argentinischen Küsten. *Plates.* Folio
Buenos Ayres, 1883
—— The same. Troisième Livraison. Ostéologie der Gravigraden. I. Abth Scelidotherium und Mylodon. Part 1. *Plates.* Folio
Buenos Ayres, 1886
—— Los Caballos fósiles de la Pampa Argentina : Supplemento. Die fóssilen Pferde der Pampas formation, beschrieben von Dr Hermann Burmeister, Director des Museo Nacional in Buenos Aires. Nachtrags-Bericht. *Plates.* Large folio
Buenos Ayres, 1889
—— See Petermann.

Burn, Jacob Henry. Descriptive Catalogue of the London Traders', Tavern, and Coffee-house Tokens current in the Seventeenth Century ; presented to the Coporation Library by Henry Benj. Hanbury Beaufoy. *Portraits.* 8° 1855

Burnaby, Rev. Andrew. Travels through the Middle Settlements of North America, with Observations upon the State of the Colonies. 4° 1775
—— See Pinkerton, Vol. 13 : Appendix 1.

Burnaby, Capt. F. A Ride to Khiva : Travels and Adventures in Central Asia. *Map, and maps in cover.* Small 8° 1876
—— On Horseback through Asia Minor. 2 vols. *Maps.* 8° 1877

Burne, Sir Owen Tudor. British Agents in Afghanistan. 8* [1879]

Burnell, Arthur Coke. See Yule.

Burnes, Sir Alexander. A Memoir of a Map of the Eastern Branch of the Indus, giving an account of the alterations produced in it by the Earthquake of 1819, and Bursting of the Dams in 1826, &c. MS. Small 4° 1827-28
—— Travels into Bokhara : being the Account of a Journey from India to Cahool, Tartary, and Persia ; also a Narrative of a Voyage on the Indus, from the Sea to Lahore, in 1831-33. 3 vols. *Map and plates.* 8° 1834

Burnes, Sir Alexander. Leech, Lord, and Wood's Reports ; Political, Geographical, and Commercial, on Scinde, Affghanistan, and adjacent Countries, in 1835-37. By Order of Government. *Maps.* 4° *Calcutta*, 1839
—— Cabool : a Personal Narrative of a Journey to, and Residence in, that city in 1836-38. *Plates.* 8° 1843

Burnes, James. A Narrative of a Visit to the Court of Sinde ; a Sketch of the History of Cutch . . . , and some Remarks on the Medical Topography of Bhooj. *Maps.* 8° 1831
—— Medical Topography of Bhooj. [From India Records, No. 15.] *Bombay*, 1855

Burnet, Bishop Gilbert. See Harris, Vol. 2 : Appendix 1.

Burnett, G. See Murray, Hugh.

Burney, Capt. James. Chronological History of the Discoveries in the South Sea or Pacific Ocean. 5 vols. *Maps and plates.* 4° 1803-17
[For Contents, see Appendix 1.]
—— A Chronological History of North-Eastern Voyages of Discovery, and of the Early Eastern Navigations of the Russians. *Maps.* 8° 1819

Burney, W. See Falconer, W.

Burnouf, E. M. Burnouf on the History of Buddhism in India. [A Review.] 8* [1844]

Burr, G. D. Short Essay on Sketching Ground without Instruments, deriving its Principles from a few Elementary Problems in Geometry, and Showing the Practical Method of performing them. *Plates.* 8° 1830
—— Treatise on Practical Surveying and Topographical Plan Drawing, with a Short Essay on Sketching Ground without Instruments. *Plates.* 8° 1829-30

Burr, Higford. A Trip to South America. 8* 1866

Burrough, Sir John. See Astley, Vol. 1 ; Kerr, Vol. 7 ; Allgemeine Historie, Vol. 1, p. 600 : Appendix 1.

Burrough, C., Stephen, and Capt. W. See Hakluyt, Vol. 1 : Appendix 1.

Burrows, Montagu. Historic Towns : Cinque Ports. *Maps.* 12° 1888

Burslem, Capt. Rollo. Peep into Toorkisthan. *Map and plates.* 8° 1846

Burton, Lieut.-Gen. E. F. An Indian Olio. *Illustrations.* 12° [1888]

Burton, Frances B. Thoughts on Physical Astronomy, with Practical Observations. 8* 1842

Burton, Isabel, Lady. The Life of Captain Sir Richard F. Burton. 2 vols. *Portraits, illustrations, and maps.* 8° 1893
—— The Reviewer reviewed. 12* N.D.

Burton, Sir Richard F. Scinde, or the Unhappy Valley. 2 vols. 8° 1851

Burton, Sir Richard F. Goa and the Blue Mountains, or Six Months on Sick Leave. *Map and plates.* 8° 1851

—— Personal Narrative of a Pilgrimage to El-Medinah and Meccah. 3 vols. *Maps and plates.* 8° 1855

—— Notes relative to the Population of Sind, and the Customs, Language, and Literature of the People. [India Records, No. 17.] Royal 8° *Bombay*, 1855

—— First Footsteps in East Africa, or an Exploration of Harar. *Map and plates.* 8° 1856

—— The Lake Regions of Central Africa: Picture of Explorations. *Maps and plates.* 8° *New York*, 1860

—— The Lake Regions of Central Africa: a Picture of Exploration. 2 vols. *Plates.* 8° 1860

—— The Lake Regions of Central Africa, with Notices of the Lunar Mountains and the Sources of the White Nile. [Vol. 29, R.G.S. Journal.] *Map.* 8° 1860

—— City of the Saints, and across the Rocky Mountains to California. *Map and plates.* 8° 1861

—— Abeokuta and the Camaroons Mountains: an Exploration. 2 vols. *Portrait, map, and plates.* 8° 1863

—— Wanderings in West Africa, from Liverpool to Fernando Po. By a F.R.G.S. 2 vols. *Map and plate* 8° 1863

—— A Mission to Gelele, King of Dahome; with Notices of the so-called "Amazons," the Grand Customs, the Yearly Customs, the Human Sacrifices, the Present State of the Slave Trade, and the Negro's Place in Nature. 2 vols. *Plates.* 8° 1864

—— Explorations of the Highlands of the Brazil, with a full Account of the Gold and Diamond Mines; also, Canoeing down 1,500 miles of the great River São Francisco, from Sabará to the Sea. 2 vols. *Map and plates.* 8° 1869

—— Letters from the Battlefields of Paraguay. *Map and plates.* 8° 1870

—— Proverbia Communia Syriaca 8* 1871

—— Zanzibar: City, Island, and Coast. 2 vols. *Maps and plates.* 8° 1872

—— Ultima Thule; or, A Summer in Iceland. 2 vols. *Maps and plates.* 8° 1875

—— Two Trips to Gorilla Land and the Cataracts of the Congo. 2 vols. *Maps and plates.* 8° 1876

—— The Gold-Mines of Midian and the Ruined Midianitic Cities: a Fortnight's Tour in North-Western Arabia. 8° 1878

—— The Land of Midian (Revisited). 2 vols. *Map and plates.* 8° 1879

Burton, Sir Richard F. Camoens, his Life and his Lusiads. 2 vols. 12° 1881

—— *See* Burton, Isabel; Camoens; Hitchman; Lacerda; Leared; Malte-Brun; Rainy; *also* Hakluyt Soc. Publ., Vol. 51: Appendix 1.

—— **and V. L. Cameron.** To the Gold Coast for Gold: a Personal Narrative. 2 vols. *Frontispiece and maps.* Crown 8° 1883

—— **and C. F. T. Drake.** Unexplored Syria: Visits to the Libanus, the Tulúl el Safá, the Antilibanus, the Northern Libanus, and the 'Aláh. 2 vols. *Maps and plates.* 8° 1872

—— **and James M'Queen.** The Nile Basin: Part 1, Showing Tanganyika to be Ptolemy's Western Lake-Reservoir, in a Memoir read before the Royal Geographical Society, 14th November 1864, with Prefatory Remarks by R. F. Burton; Part 2, Captain Speke's Discovery of the Source of the Nile, a Review, by James M'Queen. *Maps.* 8° 1864

—— **and J. E. Stocks.** Brief Notes relative to the Division of Time, and Articles of Cultivation in Sind; with Remarks on the Modes of Intoxication in that Province. [From the India Records, No. 17.] Royal 8° *Bombay*, 1853

Burton, W. K. *See* Milne.

Burwood, John, and Commander C. B. Yule. Australia Directory:—
Vol. 1. From Cape Leeuwin to Port Stephens, including Bass Strait and Tasmania.
Vol. 2. East Coast, Torres Strait, and Coral Sea.
Vol. 3. North, North-West, and West Coasts. 8° 1853-59-63

—— Tide-Tables for the British and Irish Ports; also the Times and Heights of High Water at Full and Change for the Principal Places on the Globe, for the years 1856-64. 6 vols. 8° 1855-63

—— Tables of the Sun's True Bearing or Azimuth, from Sunrise to 10 h. A.M. and from 2 h. P.M. to Sunset, at intervals of Four Minutes, for the Parallels of 49° and 50° North. 8° 1862

Bury, Viscount. Exodus of the Western Nations. 2 vols. 8° 1865

Busbequius, A. G. The Four Epistles of, concerning his Embassy into Turkey. . . . 12° 1694

Busby, James. Authentic Information relative to New South Wales and New Zealand. 8° 1832

Büsching, Anton Friedrich. Magazin für die neue Historie und Geographie. 16 vols. in 8. *Maps.* 4° *Halle*, 1779-81

Büsching, Anton Friedrich. Neue Erdbeschreibung. 9 vols. 12° *Hamburg*, 1770-71

CONTENTS.

Vol. 1. Dänemark, Norwegen, Schweden, und das Russische Reich.
Vol. 2. Preussen, Polen, Hungarn, und die Europäische Türkey.
Vol. 3. Portugall, Spanien, und Frankreich.
Vol. 4. Italien, und Gross-Britannien.
Vol. 5. Das Deutsche Reich: Böhmen, Oestreichische, Burgundische, Westphälische, Chur-Rheinische und Ober-Rheinische Kreis.
Vol. 6. Schwabische, Bayerische, Fränkische, und Obersächsische Kreis.
Vol. 7. Niedersächsische Kreis. Unterschiedene unmittelbare Reichsländer.
Vol. 8. Niederlande, Helvetien, Schlesien, und Glatz.
Vol. 9. Länder von Asia.

Bushby, G. A., and Major Harris. Reports on the "Oothaeegeerahs," or Professional Thieves of the Tehree, Dutteah, Shahgurh, and Chundeyree, or Banpoor States. [From the India Records, N.W. Provinces, Vol. 1.] *Agra*, 1855

Bushell, S. W. Ancient Roman Coins from Shansi. 8* *Peking*, 1886

Businger, Rev. Canon. Itinéraire du Mont-Righi et du Lac des quatre Cantons, précédé de la Description de la Ville de Lucerne. *Map and plates.* 8° *Lucerne*, 1815

Busk, G. Remarks on a Collection of 150 Ancient Peruvian Skulls, presented to the Anthropological Institute by T. J. Hutchinson. *Plates.* 8* [1874]

Buss, Dr Ernst. Die ersten 25 Jahre des Schweizer Alpenclub. 12* *Glarus*, 1889

Busse, T. Literature of the Amur Region. [In Russian.] 8° *St Petersburg*, 1882

Bussy, Genty de. De l'Etablissement des Français dans la Régence d'Alger, et des moyens d'en assurer la prospérité. 2 vols. 8° *Paris*, 1839

Bustinza, Julian de. Memoria sobre Propriedad, Extension, Ubicacion, &c., de los Terrenos cedidos a la empresa del Ferro-Carril Central Argentino en la Provincia de Santa-Fe. 8* *Rosario*, 1866

Butakoff, Alexey. Survey of the Sea of Aral. *Map.* 8* 1852

Bute, Marquess of. On the Ancient Language of the Natives of Tenerife: a Paper contributed to the Anthropological Section of the British Association for the Advancement of Science. 8* 1891

Buteux, —. Notions générales sur la géologie du Department de la Somme. 8* N.P., N.D.

Butler, E. D. Az olcsó ebéd. ·The Cheap Dinner; translated from the German into Hungarian and English. With an Allegory and a Few Fables, by Fáy; translated from the Hungarian into English and German. *Plate.* 12* N. D.

Butler, G. G., and F. P. Fletcher-Vane. The Sea Route to Siberia, followed by a brief Account of the Natural Resources of the Country. *Maps.* 4* [1890]

Butler, Prof. J. D. French Fort at Prairie du Chien and Tay-cho-pe-rah: the Four Lake Country. 8* [*Madison*] N.D.

Butler, Major John. Travels and Adventures in the Province of Assam. *Map and plates.* 8° 1855

Butler, Samuel. Sketch of Modern and Antient Geography. 8° 1830

Butler, Col. Sir W. F. The Great Lone Land: a Narrative of Travel and Adventure in the North-West of America. *Map.* 8° 1872
—— The Wild North Land: being the Story of a Winter Journey, with Dogs, across Northern North America. 4th edition. *Map.* 8° 1874
—— Akim Foo: the History of a Failure. *Map, plate.* 8° 1875
—— The Campaign of the Cataracts: being a Personal Narrative of the Great Nile Expedition of 1884-85, with Illustrations from Drawings by Lady Butler; also a Map of the Nile from the Mediterranean to the Equatorial Lakes. 8° 1887

Butrigarius, G. *See* Kerr, Vol. 6: Appendix 1.

Butterworth, J. A. The Gem Geography: a New System of Elementary Geography. Part 1. England and Wales. *Maps.* 12* [1877]

Büttikofer, J. Reisebilder aus Liberia: Resultate geographischer, naturwissenschaftlicher und ethnographischer Untersuchungen während der Jahre 1879-82 und 1886-87. I. Band. Reise und Charakterbilder. *Maps and illustrations.* 8° *Leyden*, 1890

Buttmann, A. Kurzgefasste Geographie von Alt-Griechenland: ein Leitfaden für den Unterricht in der griechischen Geschichte und die griechische Lectüre auf höheren Unterrichts-Anstalten. 8° *Berlin*, 1872

Büttner, Dr Richard. Reisen im Kongolande, Ausgeführt im Auftrage der Afrikanischen Gesellschaft in Deutschland. Dritte Auflage. *Map.* 8° *Leipzig*, 1890

Button, Sir Thomas. Some Particulars of the Voyage of, for the Discovery of a North-West Passage to China, Cathay, and Japan, 1612. 8* 1853
—— *See* Hakluyt Soc. Publ., Vol. 5; Allgemeine Historie, Vol. 17: Appendix 1.

Butts, Lieut. de. Rambles in Ceylon.
8° 1841
Buxton, Edward North. Short Stalks;
or, Hunting Camps, North, South, East,
and West. *Illustrations.* 8° 1892
Buxton, Sir Thomas Fowell. The
African Slave Trade and its Remedy.
Map. 8° 1840
—— *See* Pigafetta, F.
Byam, George. Wanderings in some of
the Western Republics of America; with
Remarks upon the Cutting of the Great
Ship Canal through Central America.
Map and plates. 8° 1850
Bylot and Baffin. *See* Hakluyt Soc.
Publ., Vol. 5: Appendix 1.
Byng, Admiral Sir George. An
Account of the Expedition of the British
Fleet to Sicily, in the years 1718, '19,
and '20, under the command of Sir
George Byng, Bart. Collected from the
Admiral's Manuscripts, and other original
papers. 3rd edition. 8* 1739
Byrne, J. C. Twelve Years' Wanderings
in the British Colonies, from 1835 to
1847. *Maps.* 2 vols. 8° 1848
Byrne, Oliver. How to Measure the Earth
with the Assistance of Railroads. 8*
Newcastle, 1838
—— The Art of Dual Arithmetic. Small
4*. 1878
—— Navigation and Nautical Astronomy.
4° 1875
Byron, Commodore Hon. John. Narrative of the Loss of the " Wager ; " with
an Account of the great Distresses
suffered by Himself and his Companions
on the Coast of Patagonia, 1740-46. 8°
1832
—— *See* Callander, Vol. 3; Hawkesworth,
Vol. 1; Kerr, Vols. 12, 17; Laharpe,
Vol. 18; "The Modern Traveller," Vol.
4; p. 610: Appendix 1.

C

Cabanes, Don Franc. Xavier de. Guia
General de Correos, Postas y Caminos
del Reino de España. 8° *Madrid,* 1830
Cabeaus, Nicolaus. Philosophia Mag-
netica in qua Magnetis natura penitus
explicatur, et omnium quæ hoc Lapide
cernuntur causæ propriæ afferuntur;
nova etiam Pyxis construitur, quæ
propriam Poli elevationem, cum suo
Meridiano, ubique demonstrat. *Woodcuts.*
Folio *Ferrara,* 1629
Cabeza de Vaca, Alvar Nunez. Naufragios de Alvar Nuñez Cabeza de Vaca,
y Relacion de la Jornada que hizo á la
Florida con el Adelantado Panfilo de
Narvaez. Folio N.P., N.D.
—— Comentarios de Alvar Nuñez Cabeza
de Vaca, Adelantado y Governador del
Rio de la Plata. Folio N.P., N.D.

Cabeza de Vaca, Alvar Nunez. Exa-
men apologetico de la historica Nar-
racion de los Naufragios, Peregrin-
aciones, i Milagros de Alvar Nuñez
Cabeza de Baca en les Tierras de la
Florida i del Nuevo Mexico, contra la
incierta i mal reparada Censura del P.
Honorio Filipono . . . por Don
Antonio Ardoino. Folio *Madrid,* 1736
—— *See* Hakluyt Soc. Publ., Vol. 81;
Kerr, Vol. 5; Purchas, Vol. 4, Book 8;
Ramusio, Vol. 3; Ternaux - Compans,
Vol. 6: Appendix 1.
Cabot, J. Eliot. *See* Agassiz, Louis.
Cabot, J. and S. Jean et Sébastien Cabot,
leur origine et leurs Voyages: Étude
d'histoire critique; suivie d'une Carto-
graphie, d'une Bibliographie, et d'une
Chronologie des Voyages au Nord-Ouest
de 1497 à 1550 d'après des Documents
inédits par Henry Harrisse. (No. 1 de
Recueil de Voyages et de Documents
pour servir a l'Histoire de la Géographie
depuis le XIIIᵉ jusqu'à la fin du XVIᵉ
siècle, publié sous la direction de MM.
Ch. Schefer et Henri Cordier.) *Map.*
Large 8° *Paris,* 1882
—— *See* Stevens, H.; Tarducci, F.
Cabot, Sebastian. Memoir of; with a
Review of the History of Maritime Dis-
covery. Illustrated by Documents from
the Rolls. By John Biddle. 8° 1831
—— Review [in French] of J. F. Nicholls's
Life of, &c. 8* *Paris,* 1878
—— *See* Stevens; *also* Burney, Vol. 1; Gott-
fried; Hakluyt, Vol. 3; Hakluyt Soc.
Publ., Vol. 5; Kerr, Vol. 6; Purchas,
Vol. 3, Book 4; Ramusio, Vol. 2; Allge-
meine Historie, Vols. 13, 16, 17: Ap-
pendix 1.
Cabral, Pedro A. *See* Astley, Vol. 1;
Gottfried; Laharpe, Vol. 1; Allgemeine
Historie, Vol. 1, p. 599; General
Collection of Voyages, p. 618; The
World Displayed, Vol. 8, p. 609:
Appendix 1.
Cabral, Stefano, and Fausto del Re.
Monumenti Antichi o della Città e del
Territorio di Tivoli. *Map.* 8° *Rome,* 1776
Cabrera, A. de. *See* Allgemeine Historie,
Vol. 16, p. 605; Appendix 1.
Cabrera, P. Felix. *See* Del Rio.
Cabrillo, J. Rodriguez. *See* Burney,
Vol. 1: Appendix 1.
Cabrol, Elie. Voyage en Grèce, 1889:
Notes et Impressions. *Plans and plates.*
4° *Paris,* 1890
Cadamosto, Aluise da. *See* Astley,
Vol. 1; Kerr, Vol. 2; Laharpe, Vol. 1;
Ramusio, Vol. 1; Collecção de Noticias,
Vol. 2, p. 610; Allgemeine Historie,
Vol. 2; General Collection of Voyages,
p. 610; Appendix 1.

Cadell, Francis. Exploration in Northern Territory [South Australia]. 4° 1868

Cadell, W. A. Journey in Carniola, Italy, and France, in 1817-18. 2 vols. *Map and plates.* 8° *Edinburgh*, 1820

Caerden, P. van. *See* Allgemeine Historie, Vol. 8: Appendix 1.

Cagnazzi, Luca de S. Saggio sulla Popolazione del Regno di Puglia. Parte Prima. *Map.* 8° *Naples*, 1820

Cailliatte, C. Les Explorations Anglaises dans l'Afrique équatoriale : Samuel Baker au lac de Louta-N'zigé. 8* [*Paris*] N.D.

Cailliaud, Frédéric. Voyage à Méroé, au Fleuve Blanc, au-delà de Fâzoql dans le midi du Royaume de Sennâr, à Syouah et dans cinq autres Oasis, 1819-22. 4 vols. *Plates.* 8° *Paris*, 1826
—— Atlas to same. 2 vols. Folio *Paris*, 1823
—— *See* Phillips [3], Vol. 7: Appendix 1.

Caillié, Réné. Journal d'un Voyage à Temboctou et à Jenné, dans l'Afrique Centrale, précédé d'Observations faites chez les Maures Braknas, les Nalous et et d'autres peuples, pendant les années 1824, 1825, 1826, 1827, 1828. 3 vols. *Portrait, map, and plates.* 8° *Paris*, 1830
—— Travels through Central Africa to Timbuctoo, and across the Great Desert to Morocco, in 1824-28. 2 vols. *Maps and plates.* 8° 1830
—— Notice Historique sur la Vie et les Voyages de. Par M. Jomard. *Portrait.* 8* *Paris*, 1839

Caine, W. S. A Trip round the World in 1887-88. *Illustrations.* 8° 1888
—— Picturesque India : a Handbook for European Travellers. *Map and illustrations.* 8° 1890

Calancha, Antonio de la. Coronica moralizada del Orden de San Augustin en el Peru, con sucesos egenplares en esta Monarquia. *Plates.* Folio *Barcelona*, 1638

Caldas, Francisco José de. Semanario de la Nueva Granada, Miscelanea de Ciencias, Literatura, Artes, é Industria. Nueva edicion, . . . con el cuadro original de la Geografia de las Plantas del Baron de Humboldt. 8° *Paris*, 1849

Caldcleugh, Alex. Travels in South America during 1819-21, containing an Account of Brazil, Buenos Ayres, and Chile. 2 vols. *Map and plates.* 8° 1825

Caldecott, Alfred. English Colonisation and Empire. *Maps.* Small 8° 1891

Caldecott, R. M. The Life of Baber, Emperor of Hindostan. *Map.* 8° 1844

Calder, Mrs E. H. S. *See* Meyer.

Calder, H. Report on the General Condition of the Colony of Tasmania. MS. Folio 1867

Calder, J. E. Some Account of the Wars, Extirpation, Habits, &c., of the Native Tribes of Tasmania. 12° *Hobart*, 1875

Calderon, C., and Edward E. Britton. Colombia, 1893. *Map and illustrations.* 8° *New York*, 1893

Calderon y Arana, Salvador. Los Grandes Lagos Nicaragüenses (en la América Central). *Map.* 8* *Madrid*, 1882
—— **and F. Quiroga y Rodriguez.** Erupcion Ofitica del Ayuntamiento de Molledo (Santander). *Plate.* 8* *Madrid*, 1877

Calindri, Gabrielle. Saggio Statistico-Storico del Stato Pontificio. 4° *Perugia*, 1829

Calisch, J. M. *See* Dictionaries, Dutch : Appendix 2.

Call, R. E. *See* United States, G, *c* : Appendix 2.

Callander, J. Terra Australis Cognita ; or, Voyages to the Terra Australis or Southern Hemisphere, during the Sixteenth, Seventeenth, and Eighteenth Centuries. 3 vols. *Maps.* 8° *Edinburgh*, 1766-68
[For full Title and Contents of the three volumes, *see* Appendix 1.]

Callejo y Angulo, P. del. Description de l'Isle de Sicile, et de ses Côtes Maritimes. *Maps and plans.* 8° *Amsterdam*, 1734

Callery, J. M. The Encyclopedia of the Chinese Language. [Specimen.] 8° 1842

Callwell, Capt. C. E. *See* United Kingdom, G, War Office Publ.. Appendix 2.

Calmet, P. Antiquities, Sacred and Profane ; or, A Collection of Critical Dissertations on the Old and New Testaments. Done into English, with Notes, by N. Tindall. *Plates.* 4° 1727

Calvert, Albert F. Pearls, their Origin and Formation. 12* 1892
—— The Mineral Resources of Western Australia. 12° 1893
—— Recent Explorations in Australia (1891 Expedition). *Map, plan, and illustrations.* 8* *Taunton*, 1893
—— Western Australia and its Gold-Fields ; with Government *Map.* 12° 1893
—— The Discovery of Australia ; with *Maps* and illustrated Appendix. 4° 1893

Calvert, Frank. Contributions to the Ancient Geography of the Troad, consisting of Investigations relative to the Sites and Remains of Colonnæ and of Ophrynium ; with a Notice of a Bronze Weight found on the Site of the Hellespontic Abydos. *Map and plate.*. 8° 1861
—— Contributions towards the Ancient Geography of the Troad : On the Site of Gergis. *Plate.* 8° N.D.

Calvert, James. *See* Williams and Calvert.

Calvert, John. Gold Rocks of Great Britain and Ireland, and a General Outline of the Gold Regions of the World, with a Treatise on the Geology of Gold. 8° 1853
—— *See* Wallace, A.

Calvert, J. Vazeeri Rupi, the Silver Country of the Vazeers, in Kulu, its Beauties, Antiquities, and Silver Mines; including a Trip over the Lower Himalayah Range and Glaciers. *Map and plates.* 8° 1873

Calvo, Joaquin Bernardo. Administracion Soto. Republica de Costa Rica. Apuntamientos Geográficos, Estadísticos, é Históricos. 8°
San José de Costa Rica, 1886-87

Camara, Antonio Alves. Analyse dos Instrumentos de Sondar e Perscrutar os segredos da Naturesa Submarinha. Seguida de um Appendice contendo estudus feitos sobre as causas de variação de densidade das agoas no porto de Montevideo. *Illustrations.* Large 8°
Rio de Janeiro, 1878
—— Ensaio sobre as Construcções Navaes Indigenas do Brasil. *Illustrations.* Large 8° *Rio de Janeiro*, 1888
—— Relatorio dos Estudos feitos no Interior do Porto da Bahia relativamente aō local mais appropriado para a mudança do Arsenel de Marinha da mesma provincia e construcções de diques. *Plan.* 8* *Rio de Janeiro*, 1884

Camarda, Dimitri. Dora d' Istria: Fylétia e Arbenoré prèj Kanekate Laoshima. *Portrait.* 8* *Leghorn*, 1867

Camargo, Alonzo de. *See* Burney, Vol. 1; Callander, Vol. 1: Appendix 1.

"Cambridge," Ship. *See* Salvin.

Camden, William. Britain, or a Chorographicall Description of the most Flourishing Kingdomes, England, Scotland, and Ireland, and the Islands adjoyning, out of the depth of Antiquitie: beautified with Mappes of the severall Shires of England. Written first in Latine by William Camden, Clarenceux K. of A.; translated newly into English by Philémon Holland, Doctour in Physick; Finally Revised, Amended, and Enlarged, with sundry Additions by the said Author. Folio 1637
—— Britannia. Newly translated into English, with large Additions and Improvements, by Bishop Edmund Gibson. *Maps.* Folio 1695

Camenzind, B. La Bolivie: Lettres d'un Voyageur Suisse. 8* *Neuchatel*, 1886

Cameron, C. H. *See* Ceylon: Appendix 2.

Cameron, Col. *See* United Kingdom, G, War Office Publ.: Appendix 2.

Cameron, J. F. Aerial Navigation. 8*
New York, 1881

Cameron, John. Our Tropical Possesions in Malayan India: being a Descriptive Account of Singapore, Penang, Province Wellesley, and Malacca, &c. *Plates.* 8° 1865

Cameron, Peter. The Insecta of the West of Scotland. Published for the British Association Meeting, 1876. 12°
Glasgow, 1876

Cameron, Capt. V. L. Copies of Letters as to the outlet of Lake Tanganyika and its supposed connection with the Congo. Folio* 1874
—— Across Africa. 2 vols. *Map and plates.* 8° 1877
—— The same. New edition, with New and Original Matter and Corrected Maps. *Illustrations.* 8° 1885
—— The Trade of Central Africa, Present and Future. 8* 1877
—— Our Future Highway. 2 vols. *Map and plates.* Small 8° 1880
—— The Log of a Jack Tar; or, The Life of James Choyce, Master Mariner, now first published; with O'Brien's Captivity in France. Edited by Commander V. Lovett Cameron, with Introduction and Notes. *Illustrations.* 8° 1891
—— *See* Burton, Sir Richard.

Cameron, W. Kôla Glanggi or Klanggi, Pahang. 8* [1882]
—— On the Patani. *Maps.* 8* N.D.

Camoens, Luis de. The Lusiad; or, The Discovery of India, an Epic Poem. Translated from the original Portuguese by W. J. Mickle. 3rd edition. 2 vols. *Map.* 8° 1798
—— Os Lusiadas (The Lusiads). English by Richard Francis Burton (edited by his wife, Isabel Burton). 2 vols. 12° 1880
—— A Memoria de Luiz de Camões. 8*
Loanda, 1881

Campagnon, Sieur. *See* Astley, Vol. 2: Appendix 1.

Campana, Visconti, and W. H. Smyth. Adriatic Pilot. From the Surveys of, and the Portolano of Marieni. 8° 1861

Campbell, Allan. Report on Parana and Cordova Railway, &c. *Map.* 8* 1861

Campbell, Archibald. Voyage round the World, 1806-12, in which Japan, Kamschatka, the Aleutian Islands, and the Sandwich Islands were visited; including a Narrative of the Author's shipwreck on the Island of Sannack . . . ; with an Account of the Present State of the Sandwich Islands. *Map.* 8°
Edinburgh, 1816

Campbell, A. D. Grammar of the Teloogoo Language. 4° *Madras*, 1820

F

Campbell, A. D. Dictionary of the Teloogoo Language, commonly termed the Gentoo, peculiar to the Hindoos of the North-Eastern Provinces of the Indian Peninsula. 4° *Madras*, 1821

Campbell, A. J. *See* Campbell, F. A.

Campbell, Sir Colin. *See* Rees.

Campbell, C. W. Report of a Journey in North Corea, in September and October 1889. [Foreign Office Report.] *Map.* Folio * 1891

Campbell, Donald. A Journey over Land to India, partly by a Route never gone before by any European. 4° 1795

—— Narrative of the Extraordinary Adventures and Sufferings by Shipwreck and Imprisonment of; comprising the Occurrences of Four Years in an Overland Journey to India. *Plates.* 18° 1808

Campbell, F. Imperial Federation Series of Colonial State - Paper Catalogues. Edited by Frank Campbell. No. 1. Cape of Good Hope, 1892. 8* 1893

Campbell, F. A. A Year in the New Hebrides, Loyalty Islands, New Caledonia; with an Account of the Early History of the New Hebrides Missions, by A. J. Campbell; a Narrative of the Voyages of the "Dayspring," by D. M'Donald; and an Appendix, containing a Contribution to the Phytography of the New Hebrides, by Baron von Mueller. *Map and plates.* 12° *Geelong*, 1873

Campbell, Lord George. Log Letters from "The Challenger." *Chart.* 8° 1876

Campbell, Sir George. The British Empire. Crown 8° [1887]

Campbell, Lieut.-Col. James. Excursions, Adventures, and Field-Sports in Ceylon, its Commercial and Military Importance. 2 vols. *Maps and plates.* 8° 1843

Campbell, John. Political Survey of Great Britain : being a Series of Reflections on the Situation, Lands, Inhabitants, Revenues, Colonies, and Commerce of this Island. 2 vols. 4° 1774

—— Travels in South Africa, 1812-13, undertaken at the request of the Missionary Society. *Map and plates.* 8° 1815

—— Second Journey into South Africa, 1819. *Map and coloured plates.* 2 vols. 8° 1822

—— *See* Eyriès, Vol. 11: Appendix 1.

Campbell, J. F. Frost and Fire : Natural Engines, Tool-marks, and Chips ; with Sketches taken at Home and Abroad by a Traveller. 2 vols. *Maps.* 8° *Edinburgh*, 1865

Campbell, M. R. *See* United States, G, c: Appendix 2.

Campbell, Robert. Pilgrimage to my Motherland, or Reminiscences of a Sojourn among the Egbas and Yorubas of Central Africa in 1859-60. *Map.* 12° 1861

Campbell, Thomas. Letters from the South, written during a Journey to Algiers. 12° *Philadelphia*, 1836

—— The same. 2 vols. *Plates.* 8° 1837

Campbell, T. M. A. J. Notes on the Island of Corsica in 1868. *Plate.* 12° 1868

Campbell, W. Observations on the Discovery of Gold in Victoria, with the Report of the Select Committee on the Claims for the Discovery of Gold in Victoria. 8° *Edinburgh*, 1856

—— India in Six, and Australia in Sixteen, Days. 8* 1883

Campbell, Rev. W. A few Notes from the Pescadores. 12* *Amoy*, 1886

—— The Gospel of St Matthew in Formosan, edited from Gravius's edition of 1661. 16° 1888

—— The same. (Sinkang Dialect) with Corresponding Versions in Dutch and English, edited from Gravius's edition of 1661. 4° 1888

—— An Account of Missionary Success in the Island of Formosa, published in London in 1650, and now reprinted with copious Appendices. 2 vols. *Portraits, map, and plan.* 12° 1889

Campbell, W. M. *See* India, F, c (Account, &c.): Appendix 2.

Campbell-Johnston, A. R. South Africa, its Difficulties and Present State, suggested by a recent Visit to that Country. 8* 1877

Campe, Joachim Heinrich. Neue Sammlung merkwürdiger Reisebeschreibungen für die Jugend. 8 vols. in 4. *Plates.* 12° *Brunswick*, 1806-17

Campen, J. van. *See* Allgemeine Historie, Vol. 5: Appendix 1.

Campen, Samuel Richard van. The Dutch in the Arctic Seas. In Two volumes ; with Illustrations, Maps, and Appendix. Vol. 1. A Dutch Arctic Expedition and Route. 3rd edition. 8° 1878

—— *See* Jonge ; Tollens.

Campenhausen, Baron. *See* Phillips [2], Vol. 3 : Appendix 1.

Campense, Albert. *See* Ramusio, Vol. 2: Appendix 1.

Camper, — de Nourquer du. *See* Eyriès, Vol. 12: Appendix 1.

Camperio, Capt. Manfredo. *See* Gessi.

Campomanes, — de. "La Industria Popular" and "La Historia de los Templarios." [Reprinted by J. D. Wagener, and forming Vols. 1 and 2 of the "Coleccion de las mejores Obras Españolas."] Small 8° *Hamburg*, 1795

Campos, A. M. de. Un Congrès permanent de Géographie en Portugal au XVe Siècle. 12° *Leiria*, 1878

Campos, — Navarro y. Itinerary of a Journey performed by command of the Prince Regent of Portugal in 1808, from Bahia to Rio de Janeiro. [MS. in Portuguese.] 4° N.D.

Canale, M. G. Degli antichi Navigatori e scopritori Genovesi. 8° *Genoa*, 1846

Cañamaque, Francisco. Recuerdos de Filipinas. 2 vols. 12° *Madrid*, 1877-79

Candé, de Maussion. Notice sur le Golfe de Honduras, et la République du Centre Amérique. 8* *Paris*, 1842

Candelier, H. Rio-Hacha et les Indiens Goajires. 8° *Paris*, 1893

Candídius, G. *See* Churchill, Vol. 1 : Appendix 1.

Candish, Sir Thomas. *See* Cavendish.

Candolle, A. de. Hypsométrie des Environs de Genève. 4° *Paris*, 1839
—— La Vie et les Écrits de Sir W. J. Hooker. 8* *Paris*, 1866
—— Lois de la Nomenclature Botanique. 8° *Paris*, 1867

Candolle, A. P. de. Catalogus Plantarum Horti Botanici Monspeliensis, addito Observationum circa Species novas aut non satis cognitas fasciculo. 8° *Montpellier*, 1813
—— Notice sur la Longévité des Arbres, et les Moyens de la constater. 8* *Geneva*, 1831

Canepa, Pietro. Quale sia il limite fra le Alpi e gli Appennini. 8* *Genoa*, 1878

Canner, Thomas. *See* Purchas, Vol. 4, Book 8 : Appendix 1.

Canstein, Baron P. von. Einige Begleitworte zur Charte von der Verbreitung der nutzbarsten Pflanzen über den Erdkörper. 8° *Berlin*, 1834

Cantley, N. Memorandum of Circumstances which affect the Value of Forest Land in the Colony of Mauritius, together with the Approximate Valuation of all Private Forest Land contained therein, mere fragments of small area excepted. *Map.* Folio. N.D.
—— First Annual Report on the Forest Department, Straits Settlements, its Organisation and Working. Folio* *Singapore*, 1885
—— Straits Settlements. Report on the Forest Department, for the year 1886. Folio* *Singapore*, 1887

Canto, Ernesto do. Os Corte Reaes : Memoria historica, acompanhada de muitos documentos ineaitos. Small square 8° *Ponta Delgada*, 1883
—— J. D. do. New Pocket Dictionary of the Portuguese and English Languages, abridged from Vieyra's Dictionary, with many alterations and improvements. 18° 1826

Cantova, P. J. Antonio de. Carolines. Découverte et Description des Iles Garbanzos, d'après le Manuscrit de l'Archivo de Indias, de Séville, intitulé : Secretaria de Nueva España. Ecclesiástico. Audiencia de Filipinas. Descubrimiento y Descripcion de las islas Garbanzos. 8* *Paris*, 1881
—— *See* Burney, Vol. 5 ; Callander, Vol. 3 : Appendix 1.

Capadose, Lieut-Col. Sixteen Years in the West Indies. 2 vols. in 1. 12° 1845

Capello, Brito. Guide pour l'usage des Cartes des Vents et des Courants du Golfe de Guinée. Traduit du Portugais par West et Le Gras. *Maps.* 8° *Paris*, 1862

Capello, H., and R. Ivens. De Benguella ás Terras de Iácca : Descripçãa de uma viagem na Africa Central e Occidental, comprehendendo narrações, aventuras e estudos importantes sobre as cabeceiras dos rios Cu-nene, Cu-bango, Lu-ando, Cu-anza, e Cu-ango. . . . Expedição organisada nos annos de 1877-80. 2 vols. *Maps, portraits, and illustrations.* 8° *Lisbon*, 1881
—— From Benguella to the Territory of Yacca : Description of a Journey into Central and West Africa [*as above*]. Translated by Alfred Elwes, Ph.D. 2 vols. *Maps, portraits, and illustrations.* 8° 1882
—— De Angola á Contra-Costa. Descripção de uma viagem atravez do continente Africano comprehendendo narrativas diversas, aventuras e importantes descobertas entre as quaes figuram a das origens do Lualaba, caminho entre as duas costas, visita ás terras da Garanganja, Katanga, e ao curso do Luapula, bem como a descida do Zambeze, do Choa ao Oceano. 2 vols. *Maps and illustrations.* 8° *Lisbon*, 1886

Caplin, —. *See* Perrot.

Capo di Vacca. *See* Cabeza de Vaca.

Capocci, E. Viaggio alla Meta, al Morrone, ed alla Maiella. 4* N.P., N.D.

Capper, Benj. Pitto. Topographical Dictionary of the United Kingdom, containing Geographical, Topographical, and Statistical Accounts of every District, Object, and Place in England, Wales, Scotland, Ireland, and the various small Islands dependent on the British Empire. *Maps.* 8° 1808

Capper, James. Observations on the Passage to India through Egypt. . . . 3rd edition. *Maps and plates.* 8° 1785
—— Observations on the Winds and Monsoons, with Notes Geographical and Meteorological. *Map.* 4° 1801
—— Journal [in India]. [*Title-page wanting.*] 4° N.D.

Capper, John. The Three Presidencies of India: a History of the Rise and Progress of the British Indian Possessions, &c. *Plates [map wanting].* 8° 1853

Capper, S. J. The Shores and Cities of the Boden See: Rambles in 1879 and 1880. *Maps and plates.* 8° 1881

Capreolus, Jacobus. Sphæra Jacobi Capreoli, moderatoris Scholæ Harcurianæ, professoris philosophiæ. 12° *Paris,* 1623

Capron, E. S. History of California, from its Discovery to the Present Time; with a Journal of the Voyage from New York, *viâ* Nicaragua, to San Francisco, and back *viâ* Panama. *Map.* 12° *Boston, Mass.,* 1854

Capron, H. *See* Japan: Appendix 2.

Capus, Guillaume. The Agriculture of the Aryan Tribes in the Sub-Pamirian Region. 8° N.D.

—— A Travers le Royaume de Tamerlan (Asie Centrale), Voyage dans la Sibérie Occidentale, le Turkestan, la Boukharie, aux bords de l'Amou-Daria, à Khiva et dans l'Oust-Ourt. *Map and illustrations.* 8° *Paris,* 1892

Carabœuf, —. *See* Recueil de Voyages, Vol. 2, p. 611: Appendix 1.

"**Caracciolo.**" Viaggio di Circumnavigazione della Regia Corvetta "Caracciolo" (Commandante C. de Amezaga), negli Anni 1881-82-83-84. 4 vols. *Maps and plates.* 8° *Rome,* 1885-[1887]

Caracciolo, Henry. How was America Peopled? An Essay on the Origin of the Natives of America found by Columbus. 12° 1893

Carate, A. de. *See* Zarate.

Cardenas y Cano, Gabriel de. Ensayo cronologico, para la Historia general de la Florida . desde el año de 1512 . . . hasta el de 1722. Folio *Madrid,* 1723

Cárdenas, J. *See* Wertheman.

Carder, Peter. *See* Gottfried; Purchas, Vol. 4, Book 6: Appendix 1.

Cardiel, P. José. *See* Angelis, Vol. 5: Appendix 1.

Cardon, J. Publicazioni Geografiche stampate in Italia fra il 1800 e il 1890. Saggio di Catalogo. 8° *Rome,* 1892

Cardoso, Luiz. Diccionario Geografico, ou Noticia Historica de. todas as Cidades, Villas, Lugares, e Aldeas, Rios, Ribeiras, e Serras dos Reynos de Portugal, e Algarve, com todas as cousas raras, que nelles se encontraõ, assim antigas, como modernas. Vols. 1 and 2, A-C. 2 vols. Small folio *Lisbon,* 1747-51

Cardozo de Castellobranco e Torres, J. C. Feo. Memorias contendo a Biographia de Vice Almirante Luiz da Motta Feo e Torres, a Historia dos Governadores e Capitaens Generaes de Angola,

Cardozo—*continued.*
desde 1575 até 1825, e a Descripçaõ Geographica e Politica dos Reinos de Angola e de Benguella. *Maps.* 8° *Paris,* 1825

Careri, Dr J. F. Gemelli. *See* Astley, Vol. 3; Burney, Vol. 4; Churchill, Vol. 4; Laharpe, Vol. 15; Allgemeine Historie, Vols. 5, 12: Appendix 1.

Careri, —, and — Licata. Club Africano di Napoli: Relazione del Progetto di Spedizione ad Assab. *Map.* 8° *Naples,* 1880

Carette, E. *See* Algeria, A: Appendix 2.

Carey and Dalgleish. Journey in Chinese Turkistan and Northern Tibet; and General Prejevalsky on the Orography of Northern Tibet. R.G.S. Supplementary Papers, Vol. 3, Part 1. *Map.* Large 8° 1890

Carey, Sir George. *See* Hakluyt, Vol. 4: Appendix 1.

Carey, H. C., and J. Lea. The Geography, History, and Statistics of America and the West Indies, exhibiting a correct account of the Discovery, Settlement, and Progress of the various Kingdoms, States, and Provinces of the Western Hemisphere. *Plates.* 8° [? 1824]

Carey, Col. W. The Crustacean Diving Dress. 12° *Southampton,* 1891

Carey, William. *See* Smith, Dr G.

Carjaval, —. *See* Callander, Vol. 1: Appendix 1.

Carles, W. R. Report on a Journey in Corea. 8° [*Shanghai,* 1884]

—— Report on a Journey in two of the Central Provinces of Corea, in October 1883. 8° 1884

—— Report of a Journey in the North of Corea. 8° 1885

—— Report of a Journey from Sŏul to the Phyông Kang Gold - Washings, dated 12th May 1885. 8° 1885

—— Report of a Journey in the North of Corea. 8° 1885

—— Life in Corea. *Maps and illustrations.* 8° 1888

Carless, T. G. Memoir on the Delta of the Indus. Report upon the Portions of the River Indus, surveyed in 1836-37, accompanied by a Journal. Memoir on the Province of Lus; and Narrative of a Journey to Beyla. Memoir on the Bay, Harbour, and Trade of Kurachee. [From the India Records, No. 17] *Bombay,* 1855

Carlet, Capt. D. *See* Kerr, Vol. 7; Allgemeine Historie, Vol. 1: Appendix 1.

Carli, Denis de. *See* Astley, Vol. 3; Churchill, Vol. 1; Pinkerton, Vol. 16; Allgemeine Historie, Vol. 4: Appendix 1.

Carlieri, Jacopo. Notizie varie dell' Imperio della China, e di qualche altro Paese adiacente, con la vita di Confucio. 12° *Florence,* 1697

Carling, John. Dominion of Canada: Emigration to the Province of Ontario. *Maps.* 8* *Toronto,* 1869

Carlini, Francesco. Dell' Ampiezza dell Arco di Meridiano, che attraversando la Pianura di Lombardia, e terminato dai Paralleli di Zurigo e di Genova, premessa una Notizia sui gradi del Meridiano di Roma e di Torino. *Plan.* 8*
Milan, 1843

Carlisle, Earl of. Diary in Turkish and Greek Waters. 8° 1854

Carlisle, Nicholas. Historical Account of the Origin of the Commission appointed to inquire concerning Charities in England and Wales, and an Illustration of several Old Customs and Words. 8° 1828

Carlleyle, A. C. L. *See* India A: Appendix 2.

Carlsen, E. Optegnelser fra den österrigskungarske Polarexpedition. (1872-74.) 12* *Tromsöe,* 1875

Carlson, F. F. Minnesteckning öfver Erik Gustaf Geijer. 8* *Stockholm,* 1870

Carlsson, G. A. *See* Sweden, A: Appendix 2.

Carlyle, Professor J. D. *See* Walpole, Turkey: Appendix 1.

Carlyle, Rev. J. E. South Africa and its Mission Fields. 8° 1878
—— The Fetichism of West Africa. 8*
[1881]
—— African Colonies and Colonisation, with Notices of Recent Annexations. *Maps.* 8° *Glasgow,* 1885

Carmichael, D. F. A Manual of the District of Vizagapatam in the Presidency of Madras. *Plate, map, and plates in cover.* 8° *Madras,* 1869

Carmichael-Smyth, Major R. The Employment of the People and the Capital of Great Britain, in her own Colonies, . . . by Undertaking the Construction of a Great National Railway between the Atlantic and the Pacific, from the Harbour of Halifax, in Nova Scotia, to the Mouth of Frazer's River, in New Caledonia. *Maps.* 8* 1849

Carmoly, E. *See* Eldad.

Carnarvon, Earl of. Recollections of the Druses of the Lebanon, and Notes on their Religion. 8° 1860

Carnbee, P. M. de. *See* Siebold.

Carne, J. Letters from the East. *Plate.* 8° 1826
—— *See* Bartlett, W. H.

Carné, Louis de. Travels in Indo-China and the Chinese Empire. *Map.* 8° 1872

Carnes, J. A. Journal of a Voyage from Boston to the West Coast of Africa; with a full description of the manner of Trading with the Natives on the Coast. 8° 1853

Carneyro, Antonio de Maris. Hydrografia la mas curiosa que asta oy a luz a Salido, recopilada de varios y escogidos Authores de la Nauegacion. 4°
San Sebastian, 1675

Caron, E. De Saint-Louis au Port de Tombouktou : Voyage d'une canonnière Française, suivi d'un Vocabulaire Sonraï. *Maps.* Large 8° *Paris,* 1891

Caron, —. *See* Pinkerton, Vol. 7: Appendix 1.

Carosi, J. P. v. Reisen durch verschiedene Polnische Provinzen. 2 vols. *Plates.* 8° *Leipzig,* 1781

Carpenter, J. *See* Nasmyth.

Carpenter, Nathanael. Geographie Delineated Forth in Two Bookes, containing the Sphericall and Topicall Parts thereof. 2nd edition. Small 8° *Oxford,* 1635

Carpenter, Dr W. B. On the Temperature of the Atlantic. 8* 1874
—— Report on Scientific Researches carried on during the months of August, September, and October 1871, in H.M. Surveying Ship "Shearwater." *Tables.* 8* 1872
—— *See* Jordan, W. L. ; and Jeffreys ; *also* United Kingdom, H, "Challenger" · Appendix 2.

Carpentier, Jean le. *See* Nieuhoff.

Carpin [or Carpini], Jean du Plan de. Relation des Mongols ou Tartares : précédée d'une Notice sur les Anciens Voyages de Tartarie en Général, par M. d'Avezac. *Map.* 4° *Paris,* 1838
—— *See* Astley, Vol. 4 ; Gottfried ; Hakluyt, Vol. 1 ; Kerr, Vol. 1 ; Allgemeine Historie, Vol. 7 ; Recueil de Voyages, Vol. 4, p. 611 : Appendix 1.

Carpmael, Charles. Report of the Meteorological Service of the Dominion of Canada, for the year ending 31st December 1880. 8° *Ottawa,* 1882

Carr, John. A Synopsis of Practical Philosophy . . . ; to which are subjoined Small Tables of Logarithms . . . 2nd edition. 18° 1843

Carr, Sir J. A Tour through Holland, along the right and left banks of the Rhine, to the South of Germany, in the Summer and Autumn of 1806. *Map and plates.* 4° 1807
—— *See* Phillips [2], Vols. 3, 5, 8 : Appendix 1.

Carra, M. Histoire de la Moldavie et de la Valachie, &c. 8° *Neuchâtel,* 1781

Carrasco, Domingo Martin. Representacion . . . al Soberano Congreso de 1853 . . . en uso del derecho que la Ley le concede. Folio* *Lima,* 1853

Carrasco, E. Calendario y Guia de Forasteros de la Republica Peruana para los años de 1850, 1851, 1852. 3 vols. 12° *Lima,* 1849-51

Carrasco, Gabriel. Datos Estadisticos de la Provincia de Santa-Fé (República Argentina). *Plan.* 8° *Rosario,* 1881
—— Descripcion Geografica y Estadistica de la Provincia de Santa-Fé éscrita para la Exposicion Continental de Buenos Aires. *Plates.* 8° *Rosario,* 1882
—— Ditto. (3rd edition.) 8° *Rosario,* 1884
Carre, —. *See* Allgemeine Historie, Vol. 10 : Appendix 1.
Carrère, F., and P. Holle. De la Sénégambie Française. 8° *Paris,* 1855
Carret, Jules. Le Déplacement Polaire: Preuves des Variations de l'Axe Terrestre. *Map.* 12° *Paris,* 1877
Carrick, R. New Zealand's Lone Lands: being brief Notes of a Visit to the outlying Islands of the Colony. *Maps and illustrations.* 8° *Wellington,* 1892
Carrier, Michel. Notice Biographique sur J. Balmat, dit Mont Blanc. *Portrait.* Small 8° *Geneva,* 1854
Carrington, Richard C. A Catalogue of 3,755 Circumpolar Stars, Observed at Redhill in 1854, 1855, and 1856, and Reduced to Mean Positions for 1855-60. *Plates.* 4° 1857
Carrington, Robert C. Foreign Measures and their English Values. 8° 1864
—— Table of Mètres, Feet, and Fathoms. 8° 1873
—— Glossary for French Charts. 12° *Calcutta,* 1879
—— *See* India : Appendix 2.
Carroll, B. R. Historical Collections of South Carolina, embracing many Rare and Valuable Pamphlets, and other Documents relating to the History of that State, from its First Discovery to its Independence in 1776. 2 vols. *Map.* 8° *New York,* 1836
Carron, Wm. Narrative of an Expedition, undertaken under the Direction of the late Mr Assistant-Surveyor E. B. Kennedy, for the Exploration of the Country lying between Rockingham Bay and Cape York. *Map.* 8° *Sydney,* 1849
Carruthers, John. Report on the Triangulation of portions of the North-West of South Australia. Folio* *Adelaide,* 1892
Carruthers, W. On the Structure and Affinities of Lepidodendron and Calamites. *Plates.* 8° N.D.
—— *See* West Indies, A : Appendix 2.
Carstensen, A. Riis. Two Summers in Greenland : an Artist's Adventures among Ice and Islands, in Fjords and Mountains. *Map and illustrations.* 8° 1890
Carta, J. B. Nouvelle Description de la Ville de Milan. 12° *Milan,* 1819
Carter, Sir G. T. Report on Blue-Book for 1885 [Sierre-Leone]. 8° *Bathurst,* 1886
—— Report on the Gambia for 1885. [Parliamentary Paper.] 8° 1887

Carter, H. J. A Geographical Description of certain Parts of the South-East Coast of Arabia, with an Essay on the Comparative Geography of the whole of this Coast. 8° *Bombay,* 1851
—— Geological Observations on the Igneous Rocks of Maskat and its Neighbourhood, and on the Limestone Formation at their Circumference. 8° *Bombay,* 1850
—— Memoir on the Geology of the South-East Coast of Arabia. *Plate.* 8° *Bombay,* 1852
—— *See* India, C (Geological Papers): Appendix 2.
Carter, Lieut. Thomas T. Report on the Survey Operations, Abyssinia. 8° 1868
Carteret, Captain P. *See* Hawkesworth ; Kerr, Vol. 12 ; Laharpe, Vol. 18 ; Modern Traveller, p. 610: Appendix 1.
Carthaus, Dr E. Aus dem Reich von Insulinde, Sumatra, und dem malaiischen Archipel. 8° *Leipzig,* 1891
Cartier, Jacques. Relation originale du Voyage de Jacques Cartier au Canada en 1534. Documents inédits sur Jacques Cartier et le Canada (Nouvelle série), publiés par H. Michelant et A. Ramé ; accompagnés de deux portraits de Cartier et de deux Vues de son Manoir. (Note sur le Manoir de Jacques Cartier par M. A. Ramé.) 8° *Paris,* 1867
—— *See* Hakluyt, Vol. 3 ; Kerr, Vol. 6 ; Pinkerton, Vol. 12 ; Ramusio, Vol. 3 : Appendix 1.
Cartwright, George. A Journal of Transactions and Events during a Residence of nearly Sixteen Years on the Coast of Labrador. 3 vols. *Maps and portrait.* 4° *Newark,* 1792
Cartwright, John. *See* Churchill, Vol. 7 ; Gottfried ; Purchas, Vol. 2, Book 9 : Appendix 1.
Carus-Wilson, Cecil. Musical Sand : a Paper read before the Bournemouth Society of Natural Science, on Friday Evening, 2nd November 1888. 12° *Poole,* 1888
Carusso, C. D. Importance de la Cartographie Officielle : Etude sur l' "Ordnance Survey" du Royaume Uni de Grande Bretagne et d' Irlande. 8° *Geneva,* 1886
—— Notice sur les Cartes Topographiques de l'État-Major Général d'Autriche-Hongrie. 8° *Geneva,* 1887
Carvalho, A. Nunes de. *See* Castro, I.
Carvalho, Henrique Augusto Dias de. O Lubuco. Algumas Observações sobre O Livro do Sr Latrobe Bateman intitulado "The First Ascent of the Kasai" [with the English Translation]. 4° *Lisbon,* 1886
—— L'Influence de la Civilisation et de la Colonisation Latine et surtout Portugaise en Afrique. 8° *Lisbon,* 1889

Carvalho, Henrique Augusto Dias de. Expediçáo Portugueza ao Muatiânvua. Methodo pratico para fallar a Lingua da Lunda contendo narrações historicas dos diversos povos. 8° *Lisbon*, 1889

—— Ditto. Descripção da Viagem á Mussumba do Muatiânvua. Vol. 1. De Loanda ao Cuango. *Maps and illustrations.* 8° *Lisbon*, 1890

—— Ditto. Ethnographia e Historia Tradicional dos Povos da Lunda. *Maps and illustrations.* 8° *Lisbon*, 1890

—— Memoria. A Lunda ou os Estados do Muatiânvua, dominios da soberania de Portugal. 8° *Lisbon*, 1890

Carvalho, José Carlos de. Météorite de Bendégo : Rapport présenté au Ministère de l'Agriculture, du Commerce, et des Travaux Publics et à la Société de Géographie de Rio de Janeiro, sur le déplacement et le transport du Météorite de Bendégo de l'intérieur de la Province de Bahia au Musée National. *Plan and plates.* 4* *Rio de Janeiro*, 1888

Carvallo, ——. *See* Allgemeine Historie, Vol. 16 : Appendix 1.

Carve, T. Itinerarium Thomæ Carve Tipperariensis, sacellani majoris Anglorum, Scotorum et Hibernorum, sub exercitu Cæsareæ Majestatis militantium cum historia facti Butleri, Gordon, Lesly, et aliorum. (Nova Editio : Quaritch.) Square 8° 1859

Carver, J. Travels through the Interior Parts of North America, in the years 1766, 1767, and 1768. *Maps and plates.* 8° 1778

Cary, John. Itinerary of the Great Roads throughout England, Wales, and Scotland. *Maps.* 8° 1812

Casa, Giovanni della. Opere. 4 vols. 8° *Milan*, 1806

Casalis, E. Les Bassoutos, ou Vingt-trois années de séjour et d'observations au Sud de l'Afrique. *Map and plates.* 8° *Paris*, 1859

—— The Basutos ; or, Twenty-three Years in South Africa. *Map and plates.* 8° 1861

—— My Life in Basutoland : a Story of Missionary Enterprise in South Africa. Translated from the French, by J. Brierley. Crown 8° 1889

Casalis, Prof. G. Dizionario Geografico, Storico, Statistico, Commerciale, degli stati di S.M. il Rè di Sardegna. Vols. 6 to 14. 9 vols. 8° *Turin*, 1840-46

Casanueva, Francisco. Inmigracion Asiatica : Informe sobre si conviene a Chile la Inmigracion de los Chinos. 4° *Santiago de Chile*, 1880

Casartelli, Rev. L. C. Notes of a Course of Lectures on Commercial Geography. 12° *Manchester*, 1884

Casas, Bartolomé de Las. Historia de las Indias. 5 vols. 8° *Madrid*, 1875-76

—— Istoria ò brevissima relatione della Destruttione dell' Indie Occidentali. Trad. di Francesco Bersabita. 4° *Venice*, 1626

—— Conquista dell Indie Occidentali. Tradotta di Marco Ginammi. Square 8° *Venice*, 1645

—— *See* Laharpe, Vol. 9 ; Purchas, Vol. 4 ; Allgemeine Historie, Vol. 15 ; Cartas de Indias, p. 612 : Appendix 1.

Casati, Major G. Ten Years in Equatoria, and the Return with Emin Pasha. Translated from the original Italian Manuscript by the Hon. Mrs J. Randolph Clay, assisted by Mr J. Walter Savage Landor. 2 vols. *Maps and illustrations.* 8° 1891

Casdagli, A. S. Πωσ 'Ευρον τον Λιβιγκστωνα. [Greek Translation of "How I Found Livingstone," by H. M. Stanley.] *Map.* 8° *Smyrna*, 1877

Casoni, L. Vannicelli. Relazione alla Santitá di nostro Signore Papa Pio IX. sulla eseguita Revisione dell' Estimo rustico nelle provincie di Camerino e Perugia. *Maps.* Folio *Rome*, 1848

—— Ditto. Delle Provincie componenti la Sezione delle Marche. *Map and tables.* Folio *Rome*, 1847

Cassas, L. F. *See* Phillips [1], Vol. 1 : Appendix 1.

Cassell's Gazetteer of Great Britain and Ireland : being a complete Topographical Dictionary of the United Kingdom. [In progress.] *Maps and illustrations.* Large 8° 1893, &c.

Casseneuve, J. *See* Astley, Vol. 3 ; Allgemeine Historie (J. Barbot), Vol. 4 : Appendix 1.

Cassini, M. Voyage en 1768, pour éprouver les Montres Marines, inventées par M. le Roy ; avec le Mémoire sur la meilleure manière de mesurer le tems en mer, qui a remporté le Prix double au jugement de l'Académie Royale des Sciences ; contenant la Description de la Montre à Longitudes, 1766, par M. le Roy. *Map and plates.* 4° *Paris*, 1770

—— A Voyage to Newfoundland and Sallee, &c. *See* Auteroche, Abbé Chappe d'.

Casström, S. N. Occhiata sullo stato della Geografia nei tempi Antichi e Moderni. 8* *Pisa*, 1824

Castagnoso, Michele de. Storia della Spedizione Portoghese in Abissinia nel Secolo xvi. 8* *Rome*, 1888

Castaneda, H. L. de. *See* Kerr, Vol. 2 : Appendix 1.

Castaneda, Pedro de. *See* Ternaux-Compans, Vol. 9 : Appendix 1.

Castell, P. *See* Allgemeine Historie, Vol. 20 : Appendix 1.

88 CAS—CAU.

Castellan, A. L. Lettres sur la Morée et les Iles de Cérigo, Hydra, et Zante. 2 parts. *Plates.* 8° *Paris*, 1808
—— *See* Phillips [3], Vol. 3 : Appendix 1.

Castellani, C. *See* General, Catalogues : Appendix 2.

Castillo, Antonio del, and Mariano Bárcena. Antropología Mexicana : el Hombre del Peñon, Noticia sobre el Hallazgo de un Hombre prehistorico en el Valle de México. *Plates.* 8*
Mexico, 1885

Castillo, Capt. Bernal Diaz del. *See* Diaz.

Castillo, Rafael del. Gran Diccionario geográfico, estadistico, é historico de España, y sus Provincias de Cuba, Puerto Rico, Filipinas, y posesiones de Africa. 4 vols. *Maps and illustrations.* 4° *Barcelona*, 1889-92

Castle, Henry James. Engineering Field-Notes on Parish and Railway Surveying and Levelling, with Plans and Sections, &c., and a Traverse Table. *Maps and plates.* 8° 1847

Castle, W. *See* Churchill, Vol. 8 : Appendix 1.

Castleton, Capt. Samuel. *See* Gottfried ; Purchas, Vol. 1 ; Allgemeine Historie, Vol. 1 : Appendix 1.

Castlenau, Francis de. Vues et Souvenirs de l'Amérique du Nord. *Plates.* 4° *Paris*, 1842
—— Expédition dans les Parties Centrales de l'Amérique du Sud, de Rio de Janeiro à Lima, et de Lima au Para, exécutée par Ordre du Gouvernement Français, pendant les années 1843 à 1847. 15 vols. 8°, 4°, and folio, viz :—
Histoire du Voyage. 6 vols. 8°
Paris, 1850
Itinéraires et Coupe géologique. *Plates, partly coloured.* Folio *Paris*, 1852
Géographie. *Maps, coloured outlines.* Folio *Paris*, 1853
Vues et Scènes. *Plates, some coloured.* 4° *Paris*, 1853
Antiquités des Incas et autres Peuples Anciens. *Plates.* 4° *Paris*, 1854
Botanique. Chloris Andina. 2 vols. *Plates.* 4° *Paris*, 1855
Zoologie. Animaux Nouveaux ou Rares. 3 vols. *Coloured plates.* 4° *Paris*, 1855-57
—— Renseignement sur l'Afrique Centrale et sur une Nation d'Hommes à Queue qui s'y trouvent d'après le rapport des Nègres du Soudan, esclaves à Bahia. *Map and plates.* 8° *Paris*, 1851

Castracane, F. *See* United Kingdom, H, "Challenger" Reports : Appendix 2.

Castro, Cristóbal Vaca de. *See* Cartas de Indias, p. 612 : Appendix 1.

Castro, Don Joam de. Vida de, por J. Freye de Andrada. *Portrait.* 18°
Lisbon, 1747
—— Roteiro em que se contem a viagem que fizeram os Portuguezes no anno de 1541, partindo da nobre Cidade de Goa atee Soez, que he no fim, e stremidade do Mar Roxo, com o sitio e pintura de todo o Syno Arabico . . . tirado a luz pela primeira vez do manuscrito original e acrescentado com o itinerarium Maris Rubri, &c. . . . pelo Doutor Antonio Nunes de Carvalho. *Map and plates.* 8° *Paris*, 1833
—— Vida de, escripta por J. F. de Andrada, Impressa conforme a primeira edição de 1651. Adjuntão se algumas breves notas, auctorizadas com Documentos Originales e ineditos por D. Francisco de S. Luiz. *Portrait.* Small 4° *Lisbon*, 1835
—— Primeiro Roteiro da Costa da India ; desde Goa até Dio ; Narrando a Viagem que fez O Vice-Rei D. Garcia de Noronha em soccorro desta Ultima Cidade, 1538-39. *Plates.* 8° *Oporto*, 1843
—— Roteiro de Lisboa a Goa, annotado por João de Andrade Corvo. *Maps and plates.* 8 *Lisbon*, 1882
—— Mémoire sur les connaissances scientifiques de, par F. D'Andrade. 8*
Paris, N.D.
—— *See* Astley, Vol. 1 ; Gottfried ; Kerr, Vol. 6 ; Purchas, Vol. 2, Book 7 : Appendix 1.

Castro, Padre J. B. Mappa de Portugal. 5 vols. 12° *Lisbon*, 1745-58

Cat, E. Notice sur la Carte de l'Ogôoué. *Map.* 8* *Paris*, 1890

Catlin, George. Letters and Notes on the Manners, Customs, and Condition of the North American Indians. 2 vols. *Maps and plates.* 8° 1841
—— Notes of Eight Years' Travels and Residence in Europe. *Plates.* 2 vols. 8° 1848
—— Catalogue of Indian Collection. 8° 1848
—— Steam-Raft, suggested as a Means of Security to Human Life upon the Ocean. *Plates.* 8* *Manchester*, 1860

Catlow, A. and M. E. Sketching Rambles, or Nature in the Alps and Apennines. 2 vols. *Plates.* 8° 1861

Catrou, François. History of the Mogul Dynasty in India, from its foundation by Tamerlane in 1399 to the accession of Aurengzebe in 1657. Translated from the French. 1826

Cauce, F. *See* Tellez.

Cautley, Col. Sir Probyn T. Report on the Khirkee and Chuttupoor Bunds, December 1848. *Map and plates.* [From the India Records, N. W. Provinces, Vol. 2] *Agra*, 1856

Cautley, Col. Sir Probyn T. Memoranda on Hall and Ainslie's Brickmaking Machines, as used in the Roorkee Brickfields. [From the India Records N.W. Provinces, Vol. 2] *Agra*, 1856
—— Report on the influence of the Jumna Canals on the Jumna River. *Plate*. [From the same] *Agra*, 1856
—— Ganges Canal: a disquisition on the Heads of the Ganges and Jumna Canals, North-Western Provinces, in reply to strictures by Sir Arthur Cotton. *Maps*. 8* *Privately printed*, 1864
—— Ganges Canal: a Valedictory Note to Major-General Sir Arthur Cotton respecting the Ganges Canal. 8* *Privately printed*, 1864

Cave, Laurence Trent. The French in Africa. *Maps*. 8° 1859

Cavellat, Gulielmus. Elementale Cosmographicum, quo totius et Astronomiæ et Geographiæ rudimenta, certissimis brevissimisque docentur apodixibus; adiunximus huic libro Cosmographiæ Introductionem cum quibusdam Geometriæ ac Astronomiæ principiis ad eam rem nece sariis. *Diagrams*. 12° *Paris*, 1550-51

Cavenagh, Capt. Orfeur. Rough Notes on the State of Nepal, its Government, Army, and Resources. *Map*. 8° *Calcutta*, 1851

Cavendish [or Candish], Sir Thomas. Life and Voyages. *See* Drake, Sir F.; *also* Burney, Vol. 2; Callander, Vol. 1; Gottfried; Hakluyt, Vol. 4; Harris, Vol. 1; Kerr, Vol. 10; Laharpe, Vol. 15; Allgemeine Historie, Vol. 12: Appendix 1.

Caviezel, M. Tourists' Guide to the Upper Engadine. Translated from the German. *Map*. 12° 1877

Cayley, Arthur. Life of Sir Walter Raleigh. 2 vols. *Portrait*. 8° 1806

Cayley, Dr H. Report on the Route to the Karakash River *viâ* the Changchenmoo Valley and Pass. [From the India Records, No. 2 (Punjab)] *Lahore*, 1868
—— and **W. H. Reynolds.** Report on the Roads through Ladákh to Yarkand; with a Letter and Memorandum from Major T. G. Montgomerie on the subject. Folio* *Simla*, 1871

Cazal, P. Manoel Ayres de. Corografia Brazilica, ou Relação Historico-Geografica do Reino do Brazil. 2 vols. 8° *Rio de Janeiro*, 1817

Cazeneuve, Dr Paul. De l'Alimentation chez les peuples sauvages et les peuples civilisés. 8° *Lyons*, 1882

Cazwini, Zakarija Ben Muhammed Ben Mahmud el. Kosmographie. Herausgegeben von Ferdinand Wüstenfeld. [In Arabic.] Vols. 1 and 2. 8° *Göttingen*, 1848-49

Cecchi, A. Da Zeila alle Frontiere del Caffa: Viaggi di Antonio Cecchi, publicati a cura e spese della Societa Geografica Italiana. 2 vols. *Maps, portraits, and illustrations*. 8° *Rome*, 1885-86

Cecil, Evelyn. Notes of my Journey round the World. *Illustrations*. 8° 1889

Cécille, M. Extrait du Rapport à la Protection de la Pêche de la Baleine, pendant 1837-39. 8* *Paris*, 1840

Cella, P. Della. *See* Della Cella.

Cellarius, Christophorus. Notitia Orbis Antiqui sive Geographia Plenior, ab ortu rerumpublicarum ad Constantinorum tempora Orbis terrarum faciem declarans. 2 vols. *Maps*. 4° *Leipzig*, 1701·6
—— Geographia Antiqua. By S. Patrick. 6th edition. *Maps*. 8° 1816
—— Geographia Antiqua, recognita denuo, et ad veterum novorumque scriptorum fidem, historicorum maxime, identidem castigata; edidit Samuel Patrick. *Maps*. 8° 1821

Céloria, Giovanni. *See* Issel.

"Centurion," Ship. *See* Kerr, Vol. 7: Appendix 1.

Centurione, P. *See* Pierling.

Cernik, Josef. Technische Studien-Expedition durch die Gebiete des Euphrat und Tigris nebst Ein- und Ausgangs-Routen durch Nord-Syrien. (Ergänzungsheft, 44 — Petermann's Mittheilungen). *Maps*. 4° *Gotha*, 1875
—— Ditto (Ergänzungsheft, 45). *Maps*. 4° *Gotha*, 1875

Cernuschi, H. Mécanique de l'Échange. 8° *Paris*, 1865
—— La Monnaie bimétallique. Small 8° *Paris*, 1876
—— Bi-metallic Money, and its bearings on the Monetary Crises in Germany, France, England, and the United States. 2nd edition. Small 8° 1876
—— *See* Jacquemart.

Cerquero, Don Jose Sanchez. Memoria sobre la posicion Geografica de Sevilla. Small 8* *San Fernando*, 1832

Ceruti, Antonius. Statuta Communitatis Novariæ. 4° *Novara*, 1878

Cervati, Domenico. Studi e Considerazioni intorno ai Porti e segnatamente su quello di S. Venere, e del bisogno di costruirsi un nuovo Porto a Napoli con un Dock. *Plan*. 8° *Naples*, 1859

Cervelli, Aug. *See* Recueil de Voyages, Vol. 2, p. 611: Appendix 1.

Cesnola, L. P. di. Cyprus, its Ancient Cities, Tombs, and Temples: a Narrative of Researches and Excavations during Ten Years' Residence as American Consul in that Island. *Maps and plates*. 8° 1877

Ceuleneer, A. de. Type d'Indien du Nouveau Monde représenté sur un bronze antique du Louvre : Nouvelle Contribution à l'Interprétation d'un fragment de Cornélius Népos. *Plates.* 8*
　　　　　　　　　　　　Brussels, 1890

Cevallos, P. T. Compendio de la Historia del Ecuador. Segunda edicion. 12°　　　　　　　　*Guayaquil*, 1885

Cevasco, M. Statistique de la Ville de Gênes. 2 vols. 8°　　*Genoa*, 1838

Chabas, F. Les Pasteurs en Egypte. 4*
　　　　　　　　　　　Amsterdam, 1868

Chack, Martin. *See* Burney, Vol. 2 : Appendix 1.

Chaddock, G. A. South-Eastern Africa. Explorations by a Member of the Mercantile Marine Service Association. *Map.* 8*　　　　　　　　　　　　1885
—— Narrative of a Voyage of Exploration in the s.s. "Maud," on the East Coast of Africa, undertaken for the purpose of ascertaining the Value of Waterways hitherto unexplored, and with the object of establishing Trade thereon, in British interests. *Maps.* 8*　*Liverpool*, 1890

Chadwick, J. O. Perseverance in Arctic Exploration : an Enquiry whether the advantages which may be expected to result from a successful Expedition to the North Pole are sufficient to justify further efforts in the attempt. 8* 1877

Chaffanjon, J. L'Orénoque et le Caura : Relation de Voyages exécutés en 1886 et 1887. *Maps and illustrations.* 12°
　　　　　　　　　　　　Paris, 1889

Chagas, M. P. Os Descobrimentos Portuguezes e os de Colombo. Tentativo de Coordenação Historica. 8° *Lisbon*, 1892

Chaggi, Memet. *See* Purchas, Vol. 3, Book 1 : Appendix 1.

Chabo, J. A. Voyage en Navarre pendant l'Insurrection des Basques (1830-35). *Plates.* 8°　　　　*Paris*, 1836
—— *See* Abbadie, Antoine d'.

Chaigneau, Michel D. Souvenirs de Hué (Cochinchine). *Map, plate, and plan.* 8°　　　　*Paris*, 1867

Chaillé - Long Bey, Colonel. Central Africa : Naked Truths of Naked People. An Account of Expeditions to the Lake Victoria Nyanza and the Makraka Niam-Niam, west of the Bahr-el-Abiad (White Nile). *Photograph, map, and plates.* 8°
　　　　　　　　　　　　　　1876
—— L'Egypte et ses Provinces perdues. 8°　　　　　　　　*Paris*, 1892

Chailley, Joseph. Paul Bert au Tonkin. *Portrait.* 12°　　　　*Paris*, 1887

Chailley-Bert, J. La Colonisation de l'Indo-Chine; l'expérience Anglaise. 12°
　　　　　　　　　　　　Paris, 1892

Chaillu. *See* Du Chaillu.

Chaix, Prof. Émile. La Circulation Océanique générale. 8* *Geneva*, 1890

Chaix, Prof. Émile. Une Course à l'Etna. 12*　　　　*Geneva*, 1890
—— L'Irrigation de l'Egypte. 8*
　　　　　　　　　　　　N.P., N.D.
—— La Vallée del Bove et la Végétation de la Région supérieure de l'Etna. *Plates.* 8*　　　　　　　*Geneva* 1891
—— L'Eruption de l'Etna en 1892. *Plates.* 8*　　　　　　　*Geneva*, 1893

Chaix, Prof. Paul. Précis de Géographie Elémentaire. 12° *Geneva*, 1843
—— Histoire de l'Amérique Méridionale au Seizième Siècle, comprenant les Découvertes et Conquêtes des Espagnols et des Portugais dans cette partie du monde,—Pérou. *Map.* 2 vols in 1. 12°
　　　　　　　　　　　　Paris, 1853
—— Des Canaux qui unissent à la Néva le Bassin du Volga. *Map.* 8* *Geneva*, 1856
—— Explorations Arctiques : Le Dr Kane, MacClintock. Part 2. 8* *Geneva*, 1860
—— Esquisse Chronologique des Voyages sur le Sénégal et la Gambie. *Map.* 8°
　　　　　　　　　　　　Geneva, 1866
—— Étude sur l'Ethnographie de l'Afrique. 8*　　　　　　*Geneva*, N.D.
—— Isthme de l'Amérique Centrale. 8*
　　　　　　　　　　　　N.D.
—— Le Bassin du Mississippi au Seizième Siècle. *Maps.* 8*　N.P., N.D.

"Challenger" Voyage. Preliminary Reports, Nos. 1 to 7. *Maps.* Folio
　　　　　　　　　　　　1873-76
—— The "Challenger" Expedition Papers, by Sir Wyville Thomson, Mr Murray, Mr Moseley, Mr Buchanan, and the late Dr von Willemöes-Suhm, communicated by permission of the Lords of the Admiralty to the Royal Society, and printed in their Proceedings. *Charts, sections, and plates.* 8°　　　　　　　1876
—— Report on the Scientific Results of the Voyage of H.M.S. "Challenger" during the years 1873-76, under the command of Captain George S. Nares and Captain Frank Tourle Thomson. Prepared under the superintendence of the late Sir C. Wyville Thomson, and now of John Murray. 4° *Charts and plates :*—
　　—— Reports : Zoology. Vols. 1-32. *Plates.* Large 4°　　1880-89
　　—— Narrative of the Cruise, with General Account of the Scientific Results of the Expedition. Vol. 1 (in 2 parts)　　　　　　　1885
　　—— Narrative. Vol. 2. Magnetical Observations, &c.　　　1882
　　—— Physics and Chemistry. Vols. 1 and 2　　　　1884 and 1889
　　—— Botany. 2 vols.　　1885-86
　　—— Deep-Sea Deposits　　1891
—— Summary of Results. 2 parts 1895
[For Contents, *see* United Kingdom, H : Appendix 2.]

Challes, — **de.** *See* Allgemeine Historie, Vol. 18 : Appendix 1.

Challice, J. A. Scheme for the Effectual Suppression of the East African Slave Trade. 8* 1869
—— The same. Appendix, 1871 ; Addenda, 1872. 8* 1872

Chalmers, Andrew. Transylvanian Recollections : Sketches of Hungarian Travel and History. 12* 1880

Chalmers, Rev. James. On the Manners and Customs of some of the Tribes of New Guinea. 8* [*Glasgow*, 1886]
—— Pioneering in New Guinea. *Maps and illustrations.* 8° 1887
—— **and W. Wyatt Gill.** Work and Adventure in New Guinea, 1877-85. *Maps and illustrations.* Crown 8° 1885

Chalmers, John. The Origin of the Chinese : an attempt to trace the connection of the Chinese with Western Nations in their Religion, Superstitions, Arts, Language, and Traditions. Small 8° 1868

Chaloner, Sir Thomas. *See* Hakluyt, Vol. 2 : Appendix 1.

Chaloner, Edward, and — Fleming. The Mahogany-Tree, its Botanical Character, Qualities, and Uses, with practical suggestions for selecting and cutting it in the regions of its growth in the West Indies and Central America ; with Notices of the projected Interoceanic Communication of Panama, Nicaragua, and Tehuantepec. *Map and plates.* 8° *Liverpool*, 1850

Chambaud, Louis. Nouveau Dictionnaire François - Anglois et Anglois-François ; contenant la signification des Mots, avec leurs différens usages. Revue, corrigée, augmentée de plusieurs mille nouveaux articles, par Jean Perrin. 2 vols. 4° 1778

Chamberlain, Basil Hall. The Language, Mythology, and Geographical Nomenclature of Japan, viewed in the light of Aino Studies, including " An Ainu Grammar " by John Batchelor, and a Catalogue of Books relating to Yezo and the Ainos. (Memoirs of the Literature College, Imperial University of Japan, No. 1.) Large 8° *Tokio*, 1887

Chamberlin, T. C. *See* United States, G, *c* ; K (Wisconsin) : Appendix 2.

Chambers, Charles. The Meteorology of the Bombay Presidency. 4° 1878
—— **and F. Chambers.** Magnetical and Meteorological Observations made at the Government Observatory, Bombay, in the years 1879 to 1882. Folio *Bombay*, 1883
—— *See* Robinson, G. T.

Chambers, Capt. Report on Irrigation from the Taptee River ; with *Plans* in a separate case. [From the India Records] 8° *Bombay*, 1861

Chambers, C. H. *See* Gastaldi, B.

Chambers, F. Report on the Administration of the Meteorological Department in Western India for the year 1878-79. Folio* *Bombay*, 1879
—— *See* Robinson, G. T., and Chambers, C.

Chambers, George F. Handbook of Descriptive and Practical Astronomy. *Plates.* 12° *London*, 1861
—— The Handbook Dictionary : a Practical and Conversational Dictionary of the English, French, and German Languages, in parallel columns, for the use of Travellers and Students. 12° 1883

Chambers, Robert. Ancient Sea-Margins, as Memorials of Changes in the Relative Level of Sea and Land. *Map and plate.* 8° 1848
—— Tracings of Iceland and the Faroe Islands. 12* 1856

Chambers, Trant. *See* Myers, F.

Chambers, William. Things as they are in America. 8° 1854

Chambeyron, and — Banaré. Instructions Nautiques sur la Nouvelle-Calédonie . . ; suivies d'une Note sur les Isles Loyalty par M. Jouan. [No. 458 of the Publ. of the Dépôt des Cartes et Plans de la Marine.] *Maps.* 8° *Paris*, 1869

Chamerovzow, Louis A. Borneo Facts *versus* Borneo Fallacies : an Inquiry into the alleged Piracies of the Dyaks of Serebas and Sakarran. 8* 1851

Chamich, Father Michael. History of Armenia, from B.C. 2247 to A.D. 1780, or 1229 of the Armenian Era. Translated from the Original Armenian by J. Audall ; to which is Appended a Continuation of the History by the Translator from 1780 to the present date. 2 vols. *Map and plates.* 8° *Calcutta*, 1827

Chamier, Capt. My Travels ; or, An Unsentimental Journey through France, Switzerland, and Italy. 3 vols. 8° 1855

Chamisso, Adelbert von. Reise um die Welt mit der Romanzoffischen Entdeckungs-Expedition in 1815-18, auf der Brigg Rurik, Capt. Otto v. Kotzebue. *Maps and portraits.* 2 vols. 12° *Leipzig*, 1846

Chamondopoulon, Mena D. Γεωγραφια Φυσικη και Πολιτικη. *Illustrations.* 12° *Athens*, 1888

Champion, P. Industries Anciennes et Modernes de l'Empire Chinois d'après des notices traduites du Chinois par Stanislas Julien. *Plates.* 8° *Paris*, 1869

Champlain, S. de. Œuvres de Champlain, publiées sous la patronage de l'Université Laval par l'Abbé C.-H. Laverdière. 2nd edition. 6 vols. *Maps and plates.* 4° *Quebec,* 1870
—— *See* Marcel; *also* Hakluyt Soc. Publ., Vol. 23; Purchas, Vol. 4: Appendix 1.

Champlouis, Nau de. Notice sur la Carte de l'Afrique sous la domination des Romains . . . d'après les travaux de Fr. Lacroix. 4* *Paris,* 1864

Champollion, —. *See* Young, T.

Chancellor, Richard. *See* Hakluyt, Vol. 1; Purchas, Vol. 3, Book 2: Appendix 1.

Chandler, Dr R. Travels in Asia Minor and Greece. 2 vols. in 1. *Maps and plates.* 4° 1817

Chandless, W. Visit to the Salt Lake: being a Journey across the Plains and a Residence in the Mormon Settlements at Utah. *Map.* 8° 1857

Chandoin, E. Trois Mois de Captivité au Dahomey. *Illustrations.* 12° *Paris,* 1891

Chandra Das, Sarat. Narrative of a Journey to Lhasa in 1881-82. *Map.* Folio *Calcutta,* 1885

Chanler, W. Astor. *See* Davis, R. H.

Chanter, J. R. Lundy Island: a Monograph, Descriptive and Historical, with Notices of its Distinguishing Features in Natural History. *Map.* 12° 1877

Chantre, Ernest. Études Paléoethnologiques, ou Recherches Géologico-Archéologiques sur l'industrie et les Moeurs de l'homme des temps antéhistoriques dans le nord du Dauphiné et les environs de Lyon. *Plates.* 4° *Paris,* 1867
—— Notice Historique sur la vie et les travaux de J. J. Fournet. 8* *Lyons,* 1870
—— Recherches Anthropologiques dans le Caucase. 5 vols. 4° *Paris*
Tome Premier. Période Préhistorique. *Map and plates* 1885
Tome Second. Période Protohistorique. Texte. *Illustrations* 1886
—— The same. Atlas 1886
Tome Troisième. Période Historique. *Plates* 1887
Tome Quatrième. Populations actuelles. *Map and plates* 1887

Chantreau, P. N. Voyage Philosophique, Politique, et Littéraire, fait en Russe 1788 et 1789. 2 vols. in 1. *Maps and plates.* 12° *Hamburg,* 1794

Chanvalon, T. de. Voyage à la Martinique, contenant diverses Observations sur la Physique, l'Histoire Naturelle, l'Agriculture, les Mœurs et les Usages de cette Isle, faites en 1751 et dans les années suivantes. *Map.* 4° *Paris,* 1763

Chapin, Frederick H. Mountaineering in Colorado: the Peaks about Estes Park. *Illustrations.* Crown 8° *Boston, Mass.,* 1889
—— The Land of the Cliff-Dwellers. *Illustrations.* 8° *Boston, Mass.,* 1892

Chaplain, William. *See* Marshall, T.

Chaplin, William. Report exhibiting a View of the Fiscal and Judicial System of Administration introduced into the Conquered Territory above the Ghauts, under the Authority of the Commissioner in the Dekhan. 8° *Bombay,* 1838

Chapman, Abel, and Walter J. Buck. Wild Spain (España Agreste): Records of Sport with Rifle, Rod, and Gun; Natural History and Exploration. *Illustrations.* 8° 1893

Chapman, C. A Voyage from Southampton to Cape Town. *Plates.* 8° 1872

Chapman, F. R. Notes on the Depletion of the Fur-Seal in the Southern Seas. (Reprinted from the *Canadian Record of Science,* October 1893.) 8* 1893

Chapman, James. Travels in the Interior of South Africa, comprising Fifteen Years' Hunting and Trading, with Journeys across the Continent from Natal to Walvisch Bay, and Visits to Lake Ngami and the Victoria Falls. 2 vols. *Maps and plates.* 8° 1868

Chapman, Capt. J. J. Some Additional Remarks upon the Ancient City of Anurajapura or Anuradhapura, and the Hill Temple of Mehentele, in the Island of Ceylon. *Map and plates.* 8* N.D.

Chapman, L. *See* Hakluyt, Vol. 1: Appendix 1.

Chappe, Abbé. *See* Auteroche.

Chappell, Lieut. Voyage of H.M.S. "Rosamond" to Newfoundland and the Southern Coast of Labrador. *Map and plates.* 8° 1818

Chardin, Sir John. Travels into Persia and the East Indies; to which is added the Coronation of the Present King of Persia, Solyman the Third. *Maps and plates.* Folio 1686
—— Sir John Chardin's Travels in Persia. Never before translated into English. 2 vols. *Illustrations.* 8° 1720
—— Voyages du Chevalier Chardin en Perse, et autres lieux de l'Orient. *Portrait and plates.* 4 vols. 4° *Amsterdam,* 1735
—— Voyages en Perse et autres lieux de l'Orient. . . . Nouvelle édition, . . . par L. Langlès. 10 vols. *Plates.* 8° and Atlas, folio *Paris,* 1811
—— *See* Brun; *also* Harris, Vol. 2; Pinkerton, Vol. 9; New Collection, Vol. 6, p. 608; The World Displayed, Vols. 15, 16, p. 609: Appendix 1.

Chardon, M. Tableau Historique et Politique de Marseille, Ancienne et Moderne. 12° *Marseilles,* 1826

Charles, Cecil. *See* Biolley.

Charlevoix, Pierre-François-Xavier de. Histoire de l'Isle Espagnole ou de S. Domingue, écrite particulièrement sur des Mémoires manuscrits du P. Jean-Baptiste le Pers, et sur les Pièces originales qui se conservent au Dépôt de la Marine. 2 vols. 4° *Paris*, 1730
—— Histoire et Description Générale de la Nouvelle France, avec le journal historique d'un Voyage fait par ordre du Roi dans l'Amérique Septentrionale. 3 vols. *Maps and plates.* 4° *Paris*, 1744
—— The same. 6 vols. *Maps.* 12° *Paris*, 1744
—— Histoire du Paraguay. 6 vols. *Maps.* 12° *Paris*, 1757
—— Journal of a Voyage to North-America, undertaken by order of the French King; containing the Geographical Description and Natural History of that Country, particularly Canada, . . . in a Series of Letters. . . . Translated from the French. 2 vols. *Map.* 8° 1761
—— The History of Paraguay; containing . . . a Full and Authentic Account of the Establishments formed there by the Jesuits from among the savage Natives. . . . Written originally in French. 2 vols. 8° *Dublin*, 1769
—— *See* Allgemeine Historie, Vols. 14, 16: Appendix 1.

Charnay, Désiré. The Ancient Cities of the New World: being Travels and Explorations in Mexico and Central America, from 1857-1882. Translated from the French by J. Gonino and Helen S. Conant. *Maps and illustrations.* Large 8° 1887

Charnock, Job. *See* Hakluyt Soc. Publ., Vol. 75.

Charnock, Richard Stephen. Local Etymology: a Derivative Dictionary of Geographical Names. 8° 1859
—— Verba Nominalia, or Words Derived from Proper Names. 8° 1866

Charon, Manuel. Estado Comercial del Amazonas Peruano. 8° *Lima*, 1877

Charpentier, J. F. W. Mineralogische Geographie der Chursächsischen Lande. *Views.* 4° *Leipzig*, 1778

Chase, J. C. *See* Wilmot.

Chasseaud, G. W. The Druses of the Lebanon, their Manners, Customs, and History; with a Translation of their Religious Code. *Map.* 8° 1855

Chassinat, Dr R. *See* Denis, A.

Chaste, De. Voyage to Tercera. *See* Pinkerton, Vol. 1: Appendix 1.

Chateaubriand, F. A. de. Itinéraire de Paris à Jérusalem et de Jérusalem à Paris, en allant par la Grèce, et revenant par l'Égypte, la Barbarie, et l'Espagne. 2nd edition. 2 vols. *Map.* 8° *Paris*, 1812

Chateauvieux, F. Lillin de. *See* Phillips [3], Vol. 1: Appendix 1.

Chatelain, Héli. Die Grundzüge des Kimbundu oder der Angola-Sprache. Separatabdruck aus der Zeitschrift für Afrikanische Sprachen, 1889. Heft 4. 8° 1889

Chatterton, Lady. The Pyrenees, with Excursions into Spain. *Plates.* 2 vols. 8° 1843

Chauchard, Capt. *See* Boetticher.

Chaudouet, F. *See* Lecousturier.

Chaumont, — de. Relation de l'Ambassade à la Cour du Roi de Siam. *Plates.* 16° *Paris*, 1687
—— *See* Allgemeine Historie, Vol. 10: Appendix 1.

Chausenque, M. Les Pyrénées, ou Voyages Pédestres dans toutes les régions de ces Montagnes. 2 vols. *Map.* 8° *Paris*, 1834

Chauvenet, W. Astronomy. 2 vols. 8° 1868

Chavanne, Joseph. Der Golf- und Polarstrom im Ost-Spitzbergischen Meere. 8° *Vienna*, 1875
—— Die geographische Ausstellung auf dem zweiten internationalen Geographen-Congresse zu Paris. 8° *Vienna*, 1875
—— Central-Afrika nach dem gegenwärtigen Stande der geographischen Kenntnisse. 8° *Vienna*, 1876
—— Die Englische Nordpolexpedition 1875-76 unter Capitän Nares, und ihre Resultate. *Map.* 12° *Vienna*, 1877
—— Ueber Sonnenflecken. 12° *Vienna*, 1879
—— Die Sahara, oder Von Oase zu Oase. Bilder aus dem Natur und Volksleben in der grossen afrikanischen Wüste. *Map and plates.* 8° *Vienna*, 1879
—— Die mittlere Höhe Afrika's. *Map.* 8° *Vienna*, 1881
—— Afrika im Lichte unserer Tage. *Map.* 12° *Vienna*, 1881
—— Reisen und Forschungen im alten und neuen Kongostaate. *Maps and illustrations.* Large 8° *Jena*, 1887
—— *See* Hellwald, F. von.

Chavero, Alfredo. Calendario Azteca, ensayo arqueológico. 2nd edition. *Plate.* Small 8° *Mexico*, 1876
—— La Piedra del Sol. *Plates.* 4° *Mexico* [1880?]

Chazallon, A. M. R Annuaire des Marées des Côtes de France, pour l'an 1839. 18° *Paris*, 1839
—— Mémoire sur les divers moyens de se procurer une Base, par la Mesure directe, par la Vitesse du son, par des Observations Astronomiques; description d'un Nouvel Instrument pour mesurer la Vitesse du Vent, et formules relatives à la Résolution des Triangles Géodesiques. *Plates.* 8° *Paris*, 1857

Chazallon, A. M. R., and Liesseau. Annuaire des Marées des Côtes de France pour les ans 1849-65 [wanting 1856]. 2 vols. 16° *Paris*, 1848-65

Cheadle, Dr W. B. *See* Milton.

Cheap, Capt. David. *See* Burney, Vol. 5 : Appendix 1.

Cheever, Rev. Henry T. Life in the Sandwich Islands ; or, The Heart of the Pacific as it was and is. 8* 1851

Chelmicki, J. C. Carlos de. Corografia Cabo-Verdiana, ou Descripção Geographico-Historica de Provincia das Ilhas de Cabo-Verde e Guiné. Vol. 1. *Plan and plates.* 8° *Lisbon*, 1841

Chélu, A. De l'Equateur à la Méditerranée, le Nil, le Soudan, l'Égypte. *Maps.* 4° *Paris*, 1891

Chenery, Leonard. *See* United States, E, a : Appendix 2.

Chenier, M. The Present State of the Empire of Morocco, its Animals, Products, Climate . . . ; with the Language, Religion, . . . Customs, and Character of the Moors, the History of the Dynasties since Edris, the Naval Force and Commerce of Morocco, and the Character. . . of the reigning Emperor. Translated from the French. 2 vols. 8° 1788

Cherbonneau, M. A. Relation du Voyage de M. le Capitaine de Bonnemain à R'Dâmes, 1856-57. *Map.* 8* *Paris*, 1857

Chergé, Ch. de. Le Guide du Voyageur à Poitiers, . . . suivi de l'Itinéraire de Tours à Poitiers, &c. 12° *Poitiers*, 1851

Cherkasski, Prince A. B. A Narrative of the Russian Military Expedition to Khiva in 1717. Translated from the Russian by R. Michell. 8* 1873

Cherry, F. *See* Purchas, Vol. 3, Book 4 : Appendix 1.

Chesneau, Jean. *See* Aramon.

Chesney, General F. R. Reports on the Navigation of the Euphrates. *Plate.* Folio 1833

—— Expeditions for the Survey of the Rivers Euphrates and Tigris in 1835-37 ; preceded by Geographical and Historical Notices of the Regions situated between the Rivers Nile and Indus. *Maps and plates.* 4 vols. [Vols. 1 and 2 only.] 4° 1850

—— Remarks on the Tubular Life-Boat invented by H. Richardson, Esq. *Plate.* 12* 1853

—— Russo-Turkish Campaigns of 1828 and 1829. *Maps.* 8° 1854

—— Narrative of the Euphrates Expedition carried on by order of the British Government during the years 1835, 1836, and 1837. Appendices. *Map and plates.* 8° 1868

—— Alexander the Great's Invasion of India. (From the Journal of the U.S. Institute of India.) *Maps.* 8* 1889

Chesson, F. W. The War in Zululand. 8* 1879

Chester, Anthony. *See* Gottfried : Appendix 1.

Chester, Sir W. *See* Hakluyt, Vol. 2 : Appendix 1.

Chester, Henrietta M. Russia, Past and Present. Adapted from the German of Lankenau and Oelnitz. *Map and illustrations.* 8° 1881

Chevalier, E. *See* Vaillant.

Chevalier, M. Description of the Plain of Troy ; with a Map of that Region delineated from an actual survey. Translated, with Notes and Illustrations, by A. Dalzel. *Maps.* 4° *Edinburgh*, 1791

Chevandier, Eugène. Recherches sur la composition élémentaire des différents bois, et sur le rendement annuel d'un hectare de Forêts. 8° *Paris*, 1844

"Chevert," Ship. *See* British New Guinea : Appendix 2.

Chevillard, Abbé Similien. Siam et les Siamois. 12° *Paris*, 1889

Chewings, Charles. The Sources of the Finke River. (Reprinted from the *Adelaide Observer.*) *Map.* 8* *Adelaide*, 1886

Cheyne, J. P. An Expedition to the Arctic Regions in search of Franklin. [Voyage of H.M.S. "Enterprise," Sir James Ross, 1848-49.] 4* 1873

Cheyney, R. *See* Hakluyt, Vol. 1 : Appendix 1.

Chickering, Jesse. Statistical View of the Population of Massachusetts from 1765 to 1840. 8° *Boston, Mass.*, 1846

Chijs. *See* Van der Chijs.

Child, Theodore. The Spanish American Republics. *Illustrations.* 4° 1892

Childe, Alex. *See* Gottfried ; Purchas, Vol. 1, Book 5 : Appendix 1.

Chilton, John. *See* Hakluyt, Vol. 3 : Appendix 1.

Chimmo, Lieut. W. Voyage of H.M.S. "Torch." (From the *Nautical Magazine.*) 8* 1857

Chimmo, W. Natural History of the Euplectella Aspergillum ("Venus's Flower-Basket"), from the Philippine Islands, &c. *Plates.* 4* 1878

Chippindall, Lieut. W. W. Observations on the White Nile in 1875. MS. Folio* [1888]

Chirita, C. Dictionar Geografic al Judetului Iasi. 8° *Bucharest*, 1888

—— Dictionar Geografic al Judetului Vasluiu. 8° *Bucharest*, 1889

—— *See* Filipescu-Dubău.

Chisholm, G. G. Longman's School Geography. *Illustrations.* Crown 8° 1886

—— Longman's School Geography for Australasia. *Illustrations.* Crown 8° 1888

Chisholm, G. G. Handbook of Commercial Geography. *Maps.* 8° 1889
—— Handbook of Commercial Geography. 3rd edition. *Maps.* 8° 1892
—— A Smaller Commercial Geography. 12° 1890
—— An Examination of the Coal and Iron Production of the principal Coal and Iron producing Countries of the World, with reference to the English Coal Question. *Diagram.* 8° 1890
—— Letter addressed to the Members of Council of the Royal Geographical Society on the System of Orthography for Native Names of Places. 4° [1890]
—— Longman's School Geography for India and Ceylon. *Illustrations.* Crown 8° 1891
—— *See* Stanford, E.; White, A. G.
—— **and C. H. Leete.** Longman's School Geography for North America. *Illustrations.* 8° *New York*, 1890
—— **and Prof. J. A. Liebmann.** Longman's School Geography for South Africa. *Illustrations.* 8° 1891
Chishull, Edmund. Travels in Turkey and back to England. Folio 1747
Chittenden, G. B. *See* United States (Surveys): Appendix 2.
Chittenden, Newton H. Official Report of the Exploration of the Queen Charlotte Islands for the Government of British Columbia. *Illustrations.* 8° *Victoria, B.C.*, 1884
Chodyxo, General. [Survey of the Caucasus. In French.] *Lithographed. Map.* 4° 1857-63
Chodzko, Léonard. Tableau de la Pologne, Ancienne et Moderne. *See* Malte-Brun, V. A.
Choffat, Paul, and P. de Loriol. Matériaux pour l'Étude Stratigraphique et Paléontologique de la Province d'Angola. *Plates.* 4° *Geneva*, 1888
Chôlet, Comte de. Voyage en Turquie d'Asie, Arménie, Kurdistan, et Mésopotamie. *Map and illustrations.* 12° *Paris*, 1892
Choris, L. Voyage pittoresque autour du Monde. *Plates.* Folio *Paris*, 1822
Choroschchin, —, and von Stein. Die Russischen Kosakenheere. (Ergänzungsheft, 71—Petermann's Mittheilungen.) *Plate and map.* 4° *Gotha*, 1883
Choyce, James. *See* Cameron, V. L.
Christaller, Rev. J. G. A Grammar of the Asante and Fante Language called Tshi [Chwee Twi]; based on the Akuapem Dialect, with reference to the other (Akan and Fante) Dialects. 8° *Basle*, 1875
—— A Dictionary of the same, with a Grammatical Introduction, and Appendices on the Geography of the Gold Coast, and other subjects. 8° *Basle*, 1881

Christaller, Rev. J. G. Sprachproben aus dem Sudan. Separatabdruck aus der "Zeitschrift für Afrikanische Sprachen," 1889-90. Heft 2. 8° *Schorndorf*, 1889
—— Sprachproben vom Sudan zwischen Asante und Mittel Niger. Separatabdruck aus der "Zeitschrift für Afrikanische Sprachen," 1889-90. Heft 2. 8° *Schorndorf*, 1890
Christie, A. T. *See* India, C (Geological Papers): Appendix 2.
Christie, S. H. Discussion of Magnetical Observations made by Captain Back during his late Arctic Expedition. 4° 1836
Christison, D. Meteorological Observations at San Jorge, Central Uruguay, in 1867-68, and on Pamperos there, with the Relation of these and other Storms at San Jorge and Buenos Ayres to each other. Large 8° 1880
—— The Gauchos of San Jorge, Central Uruguay. 8° 1881
Christmas, H. Shores and Islands of the Mediterranean, including a Visit to the Seven Churches of Asia. 3 vols. 8° 1851
Christopher, J. S. Natal, a Cotton, Sugar, Grazing, and Agricultural Country; with a Map of the Colony, and a Vocabulary of the Natal or Zulu Language. 8° N.D.
Christy, H. *See* Lartet, Edouard.
Christy, T. New Commercial Plants and Drugs. Nos. 7 to 11. *Illustrations.* 8° 1884-87
—— New and Rare Drugs. 8° 1888
Chubinski, P. P. Ethnographical Expedition to Western Russia. Vol. 5. [In Russian.] Small 4° *St Petersburg*, 1874
Chuckerbutty, T. Thoughts on Popular Education. 8° *Calcutta*, 1870
Church, Col. G. E. Bolivia and Brazil in the Amazon Valley. 8° 1870
—— The Rapids of the Madeira Branch of the Amazon River: a Preliminary Report upon the Madeira and Mamoré Railway, based upon the Maps and Surveys made by the Engineers, José and Francisco Keller. *Map.* 8° 1870
—— Explorations made in the Valley of the River Madeira from 1749 to 1868. 8° 1875
—— The Route to Bolivia *via* the River Amazon: a Report to the Governments of Bolivia and Brazil. *Maps.* 8° 1877
—— Report of Mr George Earl Church upon Ecuador. 8° *Washington*, 1883
—— The Venezuela Central Railway and its Sources of Traffic. 8° 1888
—— *See* Keller, José.

Church, John A. The Great Wall of China. (From the *Engineering Maga-zine*, February 1893.) 8*   1893

Churchill, A. and J. Collection of Voyages and Travels. *Maps and plates.* 8 vols. Folio   1707-47
[For full Title and Contents of the eight volumes, *see* Appendix 1.]

Churchill, Col. C. H. Mount Lebanon : a Ten Years' Residence from 1842 to 1852, describing the Manners, Customs, and Religion of its Inhabitants, with Historical Records of the Mountain Tribes. 3 vols. 8°   1853

—— The Druzes and the Maronites under the Turkish Rule from 1840 to 1860. 8°   1862

Churchill, G. C. *See* Gilbert, J.

Churchward, William B. My Consulate in Samoa : a Record of Four Years' Sojourn in the Navigators Islands, with Personal Experiences of King Malietoa Laupepa, his Country and his Men. 8°
                    1887

Churi, Joseph H. Sea, Nile, the Desert, and Nigritia : Travels in company with Capt. Peel, R.N., 1851-52 ; with 13 Arabic Songs . . translated . . . and set to Musical Annotation, with other Arabic Songs. 8°   1853

Chydenius, K. Svenska Expeditionen till Spetsbergen år 1861 under ledning af Otto Torell. Ur Deltagarnes Anteck-ningar och andra Handlingar. *Map and plates.* Large 8° *Stockholm,* 1865

Chy Fa Hian. *See* Fa Hian.

Cialdi, Commendat. Alessandro. Navi-gazione del Tevere e della sua Foce in Fiumicino. *Plates.* 8° *Rome,* 1845

—— Sul Tevere, sulla Linea piu con-veniente per la Unione dei due Mari e sulla Marina Mercantile dello Stato Pontificio. 8*   *Rome,* 1847

—— Osservazioni Idraulico-Nautiche sui Porti Neroniano ed Innocenziano in Anzio. *Plan.* 8*   *Rome,* 1848

—— Risultati di Studi Idrodinamici, Nautici e Commerciali sul Porto di Livorno. *Plan.* 8* *Florence,* 1853

—— Appendice. *Plan.* 8* *Rome,* 1855

—— Sul Porto-Canale di Pesaro. *Plan.* 8*   *Pesaro,* 1857

—— Sul Nuovo Emissario del Lago di Bientina e sulla Botte sotto l'Arno. *Map.* 8*   *Rome,* 1857
[The above six are bound in 1 vol.]

—— Cenni sul Moto ondoso del Mare e sulle Correnti di Esso. *Plate.* 4°
                    Rome, 1856

—— Sul Moto ondoso del Mare e sulle Correnti di esso, Specialmente su Quelle Littorali. Seconda edizione. *Plates.* 8°   *Rome,* 1866

Cialdi, Commendat. Alessandro. Les Ports-Canaux. *Maps.* 8* *Rome,* 1866

—— Port - Saïd á M. Ferdinand de Lessep. . . . Lettre du Comm. A. Cialdi . . . avec un Post-scriptum. 8*
                    Rome, 1868

—— Le Phénomène du Flot Courant, à propos du Naufrage de la Frégatte Russe " Alexandre-Newski." Lettre, &c. 8*
                    Rome, 1869

—— A MS. Translation into French of part of the work " Cenni sul Moto ondoso del Mare," &c. Folio* N.P., N.D.

—— *See* Tessan.

Ciampi, Sebastiano. Viaggio in Polonia, nella state del 1830. 8° *Florence,* 1831

Cicalek, Dr Theodor. Die Colonien des Deutschen Reiches. 8* *Vienna,* 1885

—— *See* Dorn, A.

Cieça de Leon, Pedro de. Parte Primera de la Chronica del Peru, que tracta la demarcacion de sus provincias, la descrip-cion dellas, las fundaciones de las neuvas ciudades, las ritas y costumbres de los Indios, y otras cosas estrañas dignas de ser sabidas. 12° *Antwerp,* 1554

—— The Seventeen Years' Travels of Peter de Ciezo through the mighty Kingdom of Peru, and the large Provinces of Car-tagena and Popayan in South America, from the City of Panama, on the Isthmus, to the Frontiers of Chile. *Map.* Small square 8°   1709

—— *See* Hakluyt Soc. Publ., Vol. 33, 68 : Appendix 1.

Cintra, Capt. Pedro de. *See* Astley, Vol. 1 ; Kerr, Vol. 2 ; Allgemeine Historie, Vol. 2 : Appendix 1.

Circourt, Comte Adolphe de. Remarks on "Les Monnaies d'Athènes," par M. Beulé. (Extrait des Nouvelles Annales des Voyages, Novembre 1858.) 8*   *Paris,* 1858

—— Les Russes sur l'Amur. Compte Rendu. (Extrait des Nouvelles Annales des Voyages.) 8* *Paris,* 1862

Cirera, P. Ricardo. El Magnetismo Terrestre en Filipinas. 4*
                    Manila, 1893

Citus, G. F. *See* Pierling.

Civiale, A. Les Alpes au Point de Vue de la Géographie Physique et de la Géologie : Voyages photographiques dans le Dau-phiné, la Savoie, le Nord de l'Italie, la Suisse, et le Tyrol. [2 *Maps* separate.] *Plates.* 8°   *Paris,* 1882

Clain, P. Paul. *See* Burney, Vol. 5 : Appendix 1.

Clancey, J. C. Aid to Land-Surveying (Larger edition ; in English only), containing complete Sets of Logarithmic, Traverse, Levelling, and other Tables, and accompanied with 542 illustrations on the subject. Folio *Calcutta,* 1882

Clancey, J. C. Aid to Land-Surveying (in English and Burmese), accompanied by 234 illustrations on the subject. 2nd edition. Folio *Rangoon*, 1890
—— Calculating Tables for Use in Burma. Folio *Rangoon*, 1890
—— Examination Questions in Surveying. 2nd edition. *Illustrations.* Folio *Rangoon*, 1892

Claparède, Arthur de. Annuaire Universel des Sociétés de Géographie, 1892-93. 12° *Geneva*, 1893

Clapperton, Capt. Hugh. Journal of a Second Expedition into the Interior of Africa, from the Bight of Benin to Soccatoo ; to which is added the Journal of Richard Lander from Kano to the Sea Coast, partly hy a more Eastern Route. *Map and portrait.* 4° 1829
—— *See* Denham, D. ; Lander, R.

Claray, George. *See* Heusser.

Clark, Captain. *See* Lewis and Clark, Phillips [1], Vol. 6 : Appendix 1.

Clark, G. B. The Transvaal and Bechuanaland. 2nd edition. 8* [1883]

Clark, Henry James. Trinidad, a Field for Emigration. 8* *Port-of-Spain*, 1886

Clark, J. Leslie. Emigration to Venezuelan Guayana, &c. 8* 1868

Clark, Sir James. The Sanative Influence of Climate ; with an Account of the Best Places of Resort for Invalids in England, the South of Europe, &c. 8° 1841

Clark, John. Lectures on Accompts, or Book-keeping, after the Italian manner, by Double Entry of Debtor and Creditor. Small 4° 1732

Clark, John. Proposed Plan for Ocean Telegraphy. Two Papers. 8* 1861

Clark, John A. Glimpses of the Old World, or Excursions on the Continent and in Great Britain. 2 vols. 8° 1840

Clark, J. W. *See* Galton, Vacation Tourists.

Clark, Latimer. Manual of the Transit Instrument. Small 8° 1884
—— Transit Tables for 1886 ; giving the Greenwich Mean Time of Transit of the Sun and of certain Stars for every dav in the year ; with an Ephemeris of the Sun, Moon, and Planets. 12° 1886 [1885]
—— Transit Tables for 1887 ; giving the Greenwich Mean Time of Transit of the Sun and of certain Clock Stars for every day in the year. Computed from the "Nautical Almanac for Popular Use." 12° 1887

Clark, P. D. G. The Peruvian Corporation Limited : Report on the Central Territory of Peru. 4* 1891

Clark [or Clarke], Rev. W. *See* New Collection, Vol. 5, p. 608 ; The Modern Traveller, Vol. 4, p. 610 : Appendix 1.

Clark, Dr Thomas. *See* Lankester.

Clark, William B. *See* Williams, G. H.

Clark, W. G. Peloponnesus, 1856 : Notes of Study and Travel. *Map and plans.* 8° 1858
—— *See* Galton, Vacation Tourists.

Clarke, Sir A., J. R. Bell, and G. Moyle. The Kandahar Railway. 8* 1880

Clarke, Sir Andrew. *See* Hawkshaw.

Clarke, Col. A. R. Comparisons of the Standards of Length of England, France, Belgium, Prussia, Russia, India, Australia, made at the Ordnance Survey Office, Southampton, under the direction of Sir Henry James. *Plates.* 4° 1866
—— Geodesy. 8° *Oxford*, 1880
—— *See* James, Sir H.

Clarke, C. B. A Class-Book of Geography. *Maps.* 12° 1889

Clarke, E. D. The Tomb of Alexander : a Dissertation on the Sarcophagus brought from Alexandria, and now in the British Museum. *Plates.* 4° *Cambridge*, 1805
—— Travels in Various Countries of Europe, Asia, and Africa. [For Contents, *see* Appendix 1.]

Clarke, Lieut.-Col. F. C. H. Col. Sosnoffsky's Expedition to China in 1874-75. Abridged and tabulated from the Russian. (From the Journal of the Royal Geographical Society, 1877.) 8* 1878
—— Statistics and Geography of Russsian Turkestan. Folio 1879
—— *See* Fabritius ; *also* United Kingdom, G (War Office Publ.) : Appendix 2.

Clarke, Hyde. Gazetteer of Mines in Chili. MS. Folio 1856
—— Colonization, Defence, and Railways in our Indian Empire. *Map.* 8* 1857
—— On Geological Surveys. 8* 1859
—— On the Organization of the Army of India, with especial reference to the Hill Regions. *Map.* 8* 1859
—— Ottoman Railway Company : Report on the Traffic of Smyrna, with Statistics of Trade, &c. 12* 1860
—— The Imperial Ottoman, Smyrna and Aidin Railway, its Position and Prospects. *Map.* 12* *Constantinople*, 1861
—— The Warings or Waranghians. 12° *Constantinople*, N.D.
—— Memoir on the Comparative Grammar of Egyptian, Coptic, and Ude. 8* 1873
—— Serpent and Siva Worship and Mythology in Central America, Africa, and Asia. 8* 1876
—— On Prehistoric Names of Weapons. 8* 1876
—— Himalayan Origin and Connection of the Magyar Ugrian. 8* 1877
—— *See* Long and Porter.

G

Clarke, Hyde. The Early History of the Mediterranean Populations, &c., in their Migrations and Settlements, illustrated from Autonomous Coins, Gems, Inscriptions, &c. 8*   1882
—— The Iberian and Belgian Influence and Epochs in Britain. 8*   1883
—— Examination of the Legend of Atlantis in reference to Protohistoric Communication with America. 8*   1886
—— The Picts and Pre-Celtic Britain. 8*   1887

Clarke, Major H. W. The Sextant. 12*   1885
—— *See* United States, K (New York): Appendix 2.

Clarke, James. Survey of the Lakes of Cumberland, Westmorland, and Lancashire; with an Acccunt, Historical, Topographical, and Descriptive, of the adjacent Country; and a Sketch of the Border Laws and Customs. 2nd edition. *Maps.* Folio   1789
—— The Delineator; or, A Picturesque, Historical, and Topographical Description of the Isle of Wight. *Map.* 12°
                         Newport, 1812

Clarke, John. An Essay upon the Education of Youth in Grammar Schools; . . . to which is added, An Essay upon Study, &c. 12°   *Dublin*, 1736

Clarke, J. Stanier. Progress of Maritime Discovery, from the Earliest Period to the Close of the Eighteenth Century, forming an Extensive System of Hydrography. *Maps and plates.* 4°   1803
—— Naufragia; or, Historical Memoirs of Shipwrecks, and of the Providential Deliverance of Vessels. *Frontispiece.* Small 8°   1805

Clarke, R. Remarks on the Topography and Diseases of the Gold-Coast. *Map and plate.* 8*   1860

Clarke, Richard F. *See* Lavigerie.

Clarke, W. B. New South Wales Intercolonial and Philadelphia International Exhibitions. Mines and Mineral Statistics of New South Wales, and Notes on the Geological Collection of the Department of Mines . . . ; also Remarks on the Sedimentary Formations of New South Wales, and Notes on the Iron and Coal Deposits, Wallerawang, and on the Diamond Fields, by Prof. Liversidge. *Maps and plates.* 8°   *Sydney*, 1875
—— Remarks on the Sedimentary Formations of New South Wales, illustrated by references to other Provinces of Australasia. 4th edition. *Maps.* 8° *Sydney*, 1878

Clarus, Ludwig. Das Passionsspiel zu Ober-Ammergau. Zweite umgearbeitete und verbesserte Auflage. *Plate.* [*Incomplete.*] 8°   *Munich*, 1860

Clauzel, Maréchal. Nouvelles Observations sur la Colonisation d'Alger. *Map.* 8°   *Paris*, 1832

Clavering, Capt. Voyage. *See* Sabine.

Clavigero, F. Saverio. History of Mexico: Collected from Spanish and Mexican Historians' MSS., and Ancient Paintings of the Indians; to which are added, Critical Dissertations on the Land, Animals, and Inhabitants of Mexico. Translated from the Italian by C. Cullen. 2 vols. *Maps and plates.* 4°   1787
—— Storia della California. 2 vols. in 1. *Map.* 8°   *Venice*, 1789

Clavijo, Ruy Gonzalez de. *See* Hakluyt Soc. Publ., Vol. 26: Appendix 1.

Clay, Hon. Mrs J. R. *See* Casati.

Clayborne, Thomas. *See* Purchas, Vol. 1, Book 3: Appendix 1.

Clayton, J. W. Scenes and Studies; or, Errant Steps and Stray Fancies. 8°
                                        1870

Cleghorn, Dr Hugh. The Forests and Gardens of South India. *Map and plates.* 8°   1861
—— Report upon the Forests of the Punjab and the Western Himalaya. *Maps.* 8°   *Roorkee*, 1864
—— Notes on the Botany and Agriculture of Malta and Sicily. 8* *Edinburgh*, 1870

Clément, A. Souvenirs d'un Séjour en Mésopotamie. *Map.* 8°   [1865?]

Clenard, Nicolaas. *See* Gottfried: Appendix 1.

Clennell, W. J. Report of an Overland Journey from Amoy to Foochow and back. 8*   1892

Clerk, Capt. Claude. *See* Blackwood, Vol. 6: Appendix 1.

Clerk, Mrs Godfrey. *See* Frere, A. M.

Clerke, Capt. *See* Pelham, Vol. 1: Appendix 1.

Clever, Charles P. New Mexico, her Resources, her Necessities for Railroad Communication with the Atlantic and Pacific States, her Great Future. 8*
                        Washington, 1868

Clifford, H. J. *See* Hall, Capt. Basil.

Clipperton, Capt. John. *See* Burney, Vol. 4; Callander, Vol. 3; Harris, Vol. 1; Kerr, Vol. 10: Appendix 1.

Clissold, F. Narrative of an Ascent to the Summit of Mont Blanc, 18th August 1822; with Appendix upon the Sensations experienced at Great Elevations. 8* 1823

Clodd, Edward. *See* Bates, H. W.

Clogher, Robert Bishop of. A Journal from Grand Cairo to Mount Sinai, and back again. Translated from a Manuscript written by the Prefetto of Egypt, in company with some Missionaries de Propaganda Fide at Grand Cairo; to which are added, Remarks on the Origin of Hieroglyphics, and the Mythology of the Ancient Heathens. *Plates.* Small 4°   1753
—— The same. 2nd edition. *Plates.* 8° 1753.

Cloué, Capt. G. C. Renseignements Hydrographiques sur la Mer d'Azof. *Maps and plates.* 8* *Paris,* 1856
—— Pilote de Terre - Neuve. 2 vols. *Plates.* 8° *Paris,* 1869
Clover, Richardson. *See* United States, E, *a :* Appendix 2.
Clugnet, L. Géographie de la Soie : Étude géographique et statistique sur la production et la commerce de la Soie en cocon. *Map.* 8° *Lyons,* 1877
Clutterbuck, Walter J. The Skipper in 'Arctic Seas. *Map and illustrations.* Crown 8° 1890
—— About Ceylon and Borneo : being an Account of Two Visits to Ceylon and One to Borneo. *Maps and illustrations.* Crown 8° 1891
—— *See* Lees, J. A.
Cluverius, P. Introductionis in Universam Geographiam, tam veterem quam novam. Lib. VI. accessit Bertii Breviarium Orbis terrarum. *Plate.* 32° *Oxford,* 1657
—— The same. *Plate.* 32° *Amsterdam,* 1670
—— Philippi Cluverii Introductio in Universam Geographiam. *Map and plates.* 4° 1711
—— Philippi Cluverii Gedanensis. Sicilia Antiqua. *Maps and plates.* Folio *Leyden,* N.D.
Clyde, Dr James. School Geography. 10th edition. 8° *Edinburgh,* 1866
—— The same. 24th edition. *Maps.* 12° *Edinburgh,* 1890
—— Elementary Geography ; with Appendix on Sacred Geography. 25th edition. *Maps.* 12° *Edinburgh,* 1892
Coats, Capt. W. *See* Hakluyt Soc. Publ., Vol. 12 : Appendix 1.
Cobham, C. Delaval. An Attempt at a Bibliography of Cyprus. 12* *Nicosia,* 1886
Cochard, Leon. Paris, Boukara, Samarcande : Notes de Voyage. *Maps and illustrations.* Large 8° *Paris,* 1891
Cochelet, C. Narrative of the Shipwreck of the "Sophia," in 1819, on the West Coast of Africa, and of the captivity of part of the crew in the Desert of Sahara. *Map and plates.* 8° 1822
—— Phillips [3], Vol. 9 : Appendix 1.
Cochran, William. Pen and Pencil in Asia Minor ; or, Notes from the Levant. *Illustrations.* 8° 1887
Cochrane, Capt. C. S. Journal of a Residence and Travels in Colombia, during 1823-24. 2 vols. *Map and plates.* 8° 1825
Cochrane, Capt. J. Dundas. Narrative of a Pedestrian Journey through Russia and Siberian Tartary, from the Frontiers of China to the Frozen Ocean and Kamtchatka. 2 vols. *Maps and plates.* 8° 1824
—— Ditto. 2nd edition. 2 vols. 12° 1825

Cockburn, Col. Appendix to Report on Emigration. *Map.* [Parliamentary Report.] Folio* 1828
Cockerell, —. *See* Walpole, Travels : Appendix 2.
Cocks, Alfred Heneage. Notes of a Naturalist on the West Coast of Spitzbergen. 8* [1882]
Cocks, Richard. *See* Hakluyt Soc. Publ., Vols. 66, 67 ; Astley, Vol. 1 ; Purchas, Vols. 1, 2 ; Allgemeine Historie, Vol. 1 : Appendix 1.
Codazzi, Col. Rapport sur les Travaux Géographiques, &c., dans la Venezuela. 4* 1841
—— Jeografía física i política de las Provincias de la Nueva Granada. 4* *Bogota,* 1858
Codine, J. Mémoire Géographique sur la Mer des Indes. 8° *Paris,* 1868
Codrington, Dr R. H. The Melanesian Languages. *Maps.* 8° *Oxford,* 1885
—— The Melanesians : Studies in their Anthropology and Folk-Lore. *Map and illustrations.* 8° *Oxford,* 1891
Coello, Francisco. Projecto de las Lineas Generales de Navegacion y de Ferro-Carriles en la Peninsula Española. *Map.* 8° *Madrid,* 1855
—— Noticias sobre las vias, poblaciones y Ruinas Antiguas, especialmente de la época Romana, en la Provincia de Alava. *Map.* 8° *Madrid,* 1875
—— La Cuestión del Rio Muni. *Maps.* 8* *Madrid,* 1889
—— Franc. de Luxan, and Augustin Pascual. Raseñas Geográfica, Geologica, y Agrícola de España. Small folio *Madrid,* 1859
Coen, C. J. Reise van Maarten Gerritsz Vries in 1643, naar het Noorden en Oosten van Japan, volgens het Journal gehouden door C. J. Coen ; op het schip "Castricum," naar het Handschrift, met bijlagen uitgegeven door P. A. Leupe ; met Aanteekeningen over Japan en de Aino-Landen en Zeemansgids naar de Kurilen, door P. F. von Siebold. *Map and facsimile.* 8° *Amsterdam,* 1858
—— *See* Vries, M. G.
Coen, Gustavo. Le Grandi Strade del Commercio Internazionale proposte fino dal Secolo xvi. 12° *Leghorn,* 1888
Coffin, Charles Carleton. Our New Way round the World. *Map and plates.* 8° 1869
Coffin, —. *See* Pearce, N.
Cogan, Henry. *See* Pinto.
Coghlan, J. B. *See* United States, Hydrogr. Off. Publ., No. 45 : Appendix 2.
Coghlan, T. A. The Wealth and Progress of New South Wales, 1886-87, 1888-89. *Maps and tables.* 8° *Sydney,* 1887-89

Coghlan, T. A. New South Wales: Statistical Register for 1891 and previous years. Large 8° *Sydney*, 1892
—— The Wealth and Progress of New South Wales, 1892. *Map and diagrams.* 8° *Sydney*, 1893
Coincy, L. de. Quelques mots sur la Cochinchine en 1866. 8* *Paris*, 1866
Coke, E. T. A Subaltern's Furlough: Descriptive of Scenes in various parts of the United States, Upper and Lower Canada, New Brunswick, and Nova Scotia, during the Summer and Autumn of 1832. *Plates.* 8° 1833
Coke, Hon. Henry J. A Ride over the Rocky Mountains to Oregon and California, with a Glance at some of the Tropical Islands, including the West Indies and the Sandwich Isles. *Portrait.* 8° 1852
Colange, L. de. The National Gazetteer: a Geographical Dictionary of the United States, compiled from the latest Official Authorities and Original Sources; embracing a comprehensive Account of every State, Territory, County, City, Town, and Village throughout the Union, with Populations from the last National Census; with all useful information pertaining to Railroads, Navigation, &c., &c. Large 8° [1884]
Colban, Madame. *See* Hansteen.
Colbeck, James Alfred. Letters from Mandalay, 1878-88. Edited by George H. Colbeck. 12° 1892
Colborne, Major Hon. F. L. L. *See* Brackenbury.
Colby, Col. Ordnance Survey of the County of Londonderry. Vol. 1. *Maps, plans, and plates.* 4° *Dublin*, 1837
Cold, Conrad. Küstenveränderungen im Archipel. 2nd edition. *Maps.* 8* *Munich*, 1886
Colding, A. Extrait d'un Mémoire sur les lois des courants dans les conduites ordinaires et dans la mer. 4° *Copenhagen* [1873]
Cole, G. R. Fitz-Roy. Transcaucasia. 8* 1877
—— Jòn Jònsonn's Saga: the Genuine Autobiography of a Modern Icelander. 8* 1877
—— The Peruvians at Home. Crown 8° 1884
Cole, H. H. *See* Catalogues, C: Appendix 2.
Cole, J. W. Russia and the Russians; with a Sketch of the Progress and Encroachments of Russia from the Time of the Empress Catherine. 8° 1854
Cole, Nathan. The Royal Parks and Gardens of London, their history and mode of embellishment; with hints on the propagation and culture of the Plants employed, &c. *Illustrations.* 8° 1877

Cole, R. A. An Elementary Grammar of the Coorg Language. 8° *Bangalore*, 1867
Colebrooke, Lieut.-Col. *See* Ceylon: Appendix 2.
Coleman, Col. Houston Displayed; or, Who Won the Battle of San Jacinto? By a Farmer in the Army. 8* *Bastrop, Tex.*, 1841
Colenso, William. New Zealand Exhibition, 1865. Essay on the Botany of the North Island of New Zealand. 8° *Dunedin*, 1865
Coleridge, S. T. Six Months in the West Indies, in 1825. *Map.* 8° 1825
Coles, John. Summer Travelling in Iceland: being the Narrative of Two Journeys across the Island by unfrequented routes; with a Historical Introduction, and some Hints as to the Expenses and necessary Preparations for a Tour in Iceland; with a Chapter on Askja, by E. Delmar Morgan; containing also a literal translation of three Sagas. *Maps and illustrations.* Large 8° 1882
Colladon, Daniel. Résumé historique des études géologiques et des travaux d'excavation entrepris en France et en Angleterre en vue de l'exécution d'un chemin de fer sous la Manche. Renseignements et détails officiels sur les premières études pour la perforation mécanique et l'aération des longs tunnels par l'air comprimé. 8* *Paris*, 1883
Collens, J. H. Guide to Trinidad: a Handbook for the Use of Tourists and Visitors. *Map and frontispiece.* 8° *Port-of-Spain*, 1887
—— The same. 2nd edition. *Illustrations.* 8° 1888
—— The Trinidad Official and Commercial Register and Almanack, 1892. 8° *Port-of-Spain*, 1891
Collett, Capt. H. *See* Central Asia, A: Appendix 2.
Collet, Robert. *See* Norway, A (North Atlantic Expedition): Appendix 2.
Colleville, Rev. Merille de. Belgique et Congo, ou Richesse, Bienfaisance, et Gloire: Vers et Notes. 8* *Brighton*, 1886
Colin, E. Observatoire Royal de Madagascar: Résumé des Observations Météorologiques faites à Tananarive, par le R. P. E. Colin, S.J., 1889. 8* *Antananarivo*, 1890
—— Observations Météorologiques faites à Tananarive, par le R. P. E. Colin, S.J., Observatoire Royal de Madagascar. Vol. 2. 8* *Antananarivo*, 1891
Colinza, Stephen. *See* Purchas, Vol. 1, Book 1: Appendix 1.

Collier, J. P., and Capt. W. H. Smyth. Letters on Certain Passages in the Life of Admiral Sir John Hawkins. 4° 1850

Collingridge, George. The Fantastic Islands of the Indian Ocean and of Australasia in the Middle Ages, and their significance in connection with the early Cartography of Australia. 8° *Sydney*, 1892

Collingwood, Cuthbert. Rambles of a Naturalist on the Shores and Waters of the China Sea. *Illustrations.* 8° 1868

Collingwood, J. T. *See* Waitz.

Collins, David. Account of the English Colony in New South Wales; with Remarks on the Dispositions, Customs, Manners, &c., of the Native Inhabitants of that Country; to which are added some Particulars of New Zealand, compiled from the MSS. of Lieut.-Governor King. *Maps and plates.* 4° 1798

Collins, Francis. *See* Lull, E. P.

Collins, F. *See* Phillips [2], Vol. 6: Appendix 1.

Collins, J. Report on the Caoutchouc of Commerce : being Information on the Plants yielding it, their Geographical Distribution, Climatic Conditions, and the Possibility of their Cultivation and Acclimatisation in India; with a Memorandum on the same subject by Dr Brandis. *Maps and plates.* Small 4° 1872

Collins, Lewis. Historical Sketches of Kentucky, embracing its History, Antiquities, and Natural Curiosities ; Geographical, Statistical, and Geological Descriptions. *Maps, portraits, and plates.* 8° *Cincinnati*, 1847

Collins, Perry M'Donough. A Voyage Down the Amoor ; with a Land Journey through Siberia, and Incidental Notices of Manchooria, Kamschatka, and Japan. *Plates.* 12° 1860

Collinson, John. Descriptive Account of Captain Bedford Pim's project for an International Atlantic and Pacific Junction Railway across Nicaragua, Report, and Estimate of Cost. *Maps.* 8° 1866

—— **and W. A. Bell.** The Denver Pacific Railway, its Present Position and Future Prospects. *Map.* 8° 1870

Collinson, Admiral Sir R. China Pilot. East Coast, from Hongkong to Shanghai. Edited by Robert Loney. 8° 1855

—— The Coasts of China and Tartary, from Canton River to the Sea of Okhotsk, with the adjacent Islands. 8° 1858

—— Journal of H.M.S. "Enterprise," on the Expedition in Search of Sir John Franklin's Ships by Behring Strait, 1850-55, by Capt. Richard Collinson ; with a Memoir of his other services. Edited by his brother Major-General T. B. Collinson, R.E. *Frontispiece, portrait, and maps.* 8° 1889

Collinson, Admiral Sir R. *See* Galton, Vacation Tourists; *also* Hakluyt Soc. Publ., Vol. 38 : Appendix 1.

Collinson, Major Maitland, and Staff-Commander J. C. Richards. On Fog-Signals, &c. *Plates.* 8° [1876]

Colmer, J. G. The Dominion of Canada as it will appear to the Members of the British Association for the Advancement of Science in 1884. *Map.* 8° 1884

Colnett, Capt. J. Voyage to the South Atlantic and round Cape Horn into the Pacific Ocean, for the purpose of extending the Spermaceti Whale Fisheries and other objects of Commerce, by ascertaining the Ports, Bays, Harbours, and Anchoring Berths in certain Islands and Coasts in those Seas. *Maps and plates.* 4° 1798

Colomb, Sir J. C. R. Colonial Defence and Colonial Opinion. Small 8° 1877

—— The Naval and Military Resources of the Colonies. Small 8° 1879

—— *See* White.

Colon, Christoval and Fernando. *See* Columbus.

Colquhoun, Archibald R. Across Chrysê: being the Narrative of a Journey of Exploration through the South China Border Lands from Canton to Mandalay. 2 vols. *Maps and illustrations.* 8° 1883

—— The Truth about Tonquin : being the *Times* Special Correspondence. 12° [1884]

—— English Policy in the Far East : being the *Times* Special Correspondence. 8° 1885

—— Amongst the Shans ; with upwards of Fifty whole-page Illustrations, and a Historical Sketch of the Shans, by Holt S. Hallett ; preceded by an Introduction on the Cradle of the Shan Race, by Terrien de Lacouperie. *Map.* 8° 1885

—— Exploration in Southern and South-Western China. R.G.S. Supplementary Papers, Vol. 2. *Maps.* Large 8° 1889

—— **and Holt S. Hallett.** Report on the Railway Connexion of Burmah and China ; with Account of Exploration-Survey by Holt S. Hallett, accompanied by Surveys, Vocabularies, and Appendices. *Maps and illustrations.* Folio [1884]

Colquhoun, E. P. *See* Ulrichs.

Colquhoun, P. A Treatise on the Wealth, Power, and Resources of the British Empire in every quarter of the World, including the East Indies. 4° 1815

Colthurst, Capt. *See* Kerr, Vol. 8 : Appendix 1.

Colthurst, Miss. A Natural Scale of Heights, by the application of which the Measures of different Countries are reduced to a Common Measure known to all Geographers. *Table.* Folio (folded 8°) N.D.

Colton's Traveler and Tourist's Route-Book through the United States of America and the Canadas; containing the Routes and Distances on the Great Lines of Travel, by Railroads, Stage Roads, Canals, Lakes, and Rivers. *Map.* 12° *New York*, 1851

Colton, C. Tour of the American Lakes, and among the Indians of the North-West Territory, in 1830, disclosing the Character and Prospects of the Indian Race. 2 vols. 8° 1833

Columbus, Bartholomew. *See* Wieser.

Columbus, Christopher. Carta de Cristobal Cólon enviada de Lisboa á Barcelona en Marzo de 1493. Nueva edicion critica; conteniendo las variantes de los diferentes textos, juicio sobre estos, reflexiones tendentes á mostrar á quien la Carta fué escrita, y varias otras Noticias, por el Seudónimo de Valencia. *Map.* 16° *Vienna*, 1869

—— La Historia de D. Fernando Colón, en la qual se da particular y verdadera relacion de la Vida y Hechos de el Almirante D. Christoval Colón su padre, y del descubrimiento de las Indias Occidentales . . . que tradujo de Español en Italiano Alonso de Ulloa; y aora, por no parecer el Original Español, facada del traslado Italiano. Folio N.P., N.D.

—— Lettera rarissima di Cristoforo Colombo riprodotta e illustrato dal Cavaliere Ab. Morelli. Small 8° *Bassano*, 1810

—— Letter of, describing his First Voyage to the Western Hemisphere. Small 8° *New York*, 1875

—— Los Restos de Colon. Informe de la Real Academia de la Historia al Gobierno de S. M. sobre el supuesto hallazgo de los verdaderos restos de Cristóyal Colon en la Iglesia Catedral de Santo Domingo. *Plates.* 12° *Madrid*, 1879

—— Origine, patria e gioventù di Cristoforo Colombo. Studi critici e documentari con ampla analisi degli atti di Salinerio per Celsus. Large 8° *Lisbon*, 1886

—— De Insulis nuper inventis. The Letter of Christopher Columbus announcing the Discovery of the New World: a Facsimile of the Earliest Edition, with Illustrations, reproduced for John S. Kennedy, President of the Lenox Library. 12° *New York*, 1890

—— The Spanish Letter of Columbus to Luis de Sant' Angel Escribano de Racion of the Kingdom of Aragon, dated 15th February 1493. [Reprinted in facsimile.] Translated and edited from the Unique Copy of the Original Edition (printed at Barcelona early in April 1493.) 4° 1891

—— Christophe Colomb et ses Historiens Espagnols. 8° *Paris*, 1892

Columbus, Christopher. His own Book of Privileges, 1502. Photographic Facsimile of the MS. Transliteration by G. P. Barwick; Introduction by Henry Harrisse. Compiled and edited by B. F. Stevens. *Plates.* Folio 1893

—— *See* Bossi, L.; Elton, C. J.; Fox, G. V.; Harrisse; Markham, C. R.; Peragallo; Peretti; Radlinsky; Rein; Ruge; Silva; Urbani; Varnhagen; *also* Burney, Vol. 1; Churchill, Vol. 2; Gottfried; Hakluyt Soc. Publ., Vols. 2, 43, 86; Harris, Vol. 1; Kerr, Vol. 3; Knox's Collection, Vol. 1; Laharpe, Vol. 9; Navarette, Vol. 1; Pinkerton, Vol. 12; Purchas, Vol. 1; Cartas de Indias, p. 612; Allgemeine Historie, Vol. 14; A General Collection, p. 610; The World Displayed, Vol. 1, p. 609: Appendix 1.

Columbus Documents. Raccolta di Documenti e Studi pubblicati dalla R. Commissione Colombiana per quarto centenario dalla scoperta dell' America. Large 4° *Rome*

—— Part 1. Vols. 1, 2, and 3; and Supplement to Vol. 3 1894

—— Part 2. Vols. 2 and 3 1894

—— Part 3. Vols. 1 and 2 1892-93

—— Part 4. Vols. 1 and 2 1892-93

—— Part 6. Unico 1893

Columbus, Ferdinand. *See* Lazzaroni; Lollis; Peragallo.

Colvile, Col. H. E. A Ride in Petticoats and Slippers. *Map and frontispiece.* Small 8° 1880

—— The Accursed Land; or, First Steps on the Water-Way of Edom. *Map and frontispiece.* Crown 8° 1884

—— *See* United Kingdom, G: Appendix 2.

Colvile, Mrs Zélie. Round the Black Man's Garden. *Maps and illustrations.* 8° 1893

Colvin, Verplanck. State of New York: Report on the Topographical Survey of the Adirondack Wilderness of New York, for the years 1872, 1873. *Maps.* 8° *Albany, N.Y.*, 1873, 1874

Combes, Ed., et M. Tamisier. Voyage en Abyssinie, dans le Pays des Galla, de Choa, et d'Ifat; précédé d'une Excursion dans l'Arabie-Heureuse, 1835-37. 4 vols. 8° *Paris*, 1838

Combette, Ch. Géographie Commerciale des Colonies Françaises. 8° *Paris*, 1890

Comelin, Fran. Philemon de la Motte, and Jos. Bernard (Mathurin-Trinitarian Fathers). Voyage to Barbary for the Redemption of Captives in 1720; with lists of more than 400 Slaves ransomed from Mequinez, also exact draughts of that place, Alcasar, Oran, and its neighbourhood. *Maps and plates.* 8° 1735

Comnos, Dr G. Ueber Nummerirungssysteme für wissentlich geordnete Bibliotheken. 8° *Athens*, 1874

Comoy. Étude pratique sur les Marées Fluviales, et Notamment sur le Mascaret, application aux Travaux de la partie maritime des Fleuves. Text and Atlas [in one]. *Plates.* 8°   *Paris*, 1881

Compagnon, —. *See* Allgemeine Historie, Vol. 2 : Appendix 1.

Compiègne, Marquis de. L'Afrique Équatoriale, Okanda-Bangouens-Osyéba. *Map and plates.* 12°   *Paris*, 1875
—— The same. Gabonais-Pahouins-Gallois. *Map and plates.* 12° *Paris*, 1875
—— Notice Nécrologique sur M. le Marquis de Compiègne, par C. Guillemine. 8*   *Cairo*, 1877

Compte, Louis le. Memoirs and Observations . . . made in a late Journey through the Empire of China, and published in several Letters. Translated from the Paris edition, and illustrated with Figures. 8°   1697
—— Nouveaux Mémoires sur l'état présent de la Chine. 3 vols. 12° Vols. 1 and 2, 3rd edition, 1697 ; Vol. 3, 2nd edition, 1700   *Paris*
—— Memoirs and Remarks made in above Ten Years' Travels through the Empire of China. From the French. *Plates.* 8° 1738
—— *See* Allgemeine Historie, Vol. 5 ; The World Displayed, Vol. 16 : Appendix 1.

Compton, G. T. *See* Zsigmondy.

Compton, Edward. *See* Compton, Theodore.

Compton, Theodore. A Mendip Valley, its Inhabitants and Surroundings : being an enlarged and illustrated edition of Winscombe Sketches ; with original illustrations by Edward Compton, and a Chapter on the Geological History of the Mendips by Prof. C. Lloyd Morgan. 8°   1892

Comstock, Lieut.-Col. C. B. *See* United States, II, a (Professional Papers) : Appendix 2.

Conant, Helen S. *See* Charnay.

Condamine, C. M. de la. Relation abrégée d'un Voyage fait dans l'Intérieur de l'Amérique Méridionale, depuis la Côte de la Mer de Sud jusqu'aux Côtes du Brésil et de la Guiana, en descendant la Rivière des Amazones. *Map.* 8°   *Paris*, 1745
—— A Succinct Abridgment of a Voyage made within the inland parts of South America, from the Coasts of the South Sea to the Coasts of Brazil and Guiana, down the River of Amazons. *Map.* 8° 1747
—— Journal du Voyage fait par Ordre du Roi, à l'Équateur, servant d'Introduction Historique à la Mesure des trois premiers Degrés du Méridien ; avec Supplément, servant de réponse à quelques objections. 2 vols. *Maps and plates.* 4°   *Paris*, 1751-52

Condamine, M. de la. *See* Laharpe, Vol. 11 ; Pinkerton, Vol. 14 ; Allgemeine Historie, Vols. 15, 16 : Appendix 1.

Conder, Major C. R. The High Sanctuary at Jerusalem. *Plates.* 4* 1878
—— Tent Work in Palestine : a Record of Discovery and Adventure. 2 vols. *Plates.* 8°   1879
—— Heth and Moab : Explorations in Syria in 1881 and 1882. Published for the Committee of the Palestine Exploration Fund. *Map and plates.* 8° 1883
—— Syrian Stone-Lore ; or, The Monumental History of Palestine. Published for the Committee of the Palestine Exploration Fund. *Maps and illustrations.* 8°   1886
—— Altaic Hieroglyphs and Hittite Inscriptions. *Plates.* 8°   1887
—— Palestine. *Maps and illustrations.* Crown 8°   1889

Conder, Josiah. Modern Traveller : a Description of the various Countries of the Globe. 30 vols. *Maps and plates.* 12°   1831
—— Dictionary of Geography, Ancient and Modern, comprising a succinct Description of all the Countries of the Globe, and a Glossary of Geographical Terms. 12°   1834
—— *See* Pringle, T.

Condrea, Petru. Dictionar Geografic al Judetului Roman. 8° *Bucharest*, 1891

Condurăteanu, D. P. Dictionar Geografic al Judetului Dâmbovita. 8°   *Bucharest*, 1890

Coninck, Fréd. de. Du Percement de l'Isthme de Suez, nouvelles considerations. 8*   *Havre*, 1859

Coningham, W. *See* Fitz-James.

Conklin, E. Picturesque Arizona : being the Result of Travels and Observations in Arizona during the Fall and Winter of 1877. *Plates.* 8° *New York*, 1878

Conkling, A. R. Appleton's Guide to Mexico, including a Chapter on Guatemala, and an English-Mexican Vocabulary. 3rd edition. *Map and illustrations.* 8°   *New York*, 1889

Conn, W. *See* Mandat-Grancey.

Connell, Robert. St Kilda and the St Kildians. Crown 8°   1887

Connemara, Lord. *See* Rees, J. D.

Connor, Bernard. *See* Harris, Vol. 2 ; New Collection, Vol. 4 : Appendix 1.

Connor, E. J. A Table of Products, Quotients, Squares, and Roots. 4* 1867
—— Table of Sines, &c. 8° *Bombay*, 1880

Conolly, Lieut. Arthur. Journey to the North of India, Overland from England through Russia, Persia, and Affghaunistaun. 2 vols. *Map and plates.* 8°   1838

Cook, Capt. James, and Capt. James King. Voyage to the Pacific Ocean, for making Discoveries in the Northern Hemisphere, to determine the Position and Extent of the West Side of North America, its Distance from Asia, and the Practicability of a Northern Passage to Europe; under the Direction of Captains Cook, Clerke, and Gore, in H.M.S. the "Resolution" and "Discovery," 1776-80. 3 vols. *Maps and plates.* 4°. [2 copies] 1784

—— Maps and Plates to above. Large folio.

Cook, John. *See* Burney, Vol. 4; Appendix 1.

Cook, John M. The Nile Expedition, 1884-85. Mr John M. Cook's Visit to the Soudan: an Address, delivered at the Royal Normal College for the Blind, Upper Norwood. 8* [1885]

Cook, Samuel. The Jenolan Caves: an Excursion in Australian Wonderland. *Map and plates.* 4° 1889

Cook, Capt. S. E. Sketches in Spain in 1829-30-31 and 1832. 2 vols. 8° 1834

Cooke, Col. A. C. Routes to Abyssinia. *Maps.* 8* 1867

—— The same. Another edition; with a Preface by Sir H. James. 8* 1867

—— *See* United Kingdom, G, War Office Publ.: Appendix 2.

Cooke, C. Kinloch. Australian Defences and New Guinea. Compiled from the Papers of the late Major-General Sir Peter Scratchley; with an Introductory Memoir. *Portrait and maps.* 8° 1887

Cooke, G. Wingrove. China: being *The Times* Special Correspondence from China in 1857-58, with Corrections and Additions. *Map and plates.* 12° 1858

Cooke, Lieut.-Col. Philip St George. Official Journal of a March from Santa Fè, in New Mexico, to San Diego, in Upper California. 8* *Washington*, 1849

Cooke, Thomas Fothergill. Authorship of the Practical Electric Telegraph of Great Britain, or the Brunel Award Vindicated; in seven Letters, &c. 8° *Bath*, 1868

Cooke, William Fothergill. The Electric Telegraph: Was it Invented by Professor Wheatstone? 2 vols. *Cuts.* 8° 1856-57

—— The same. 4th edition. 8° 1866

Cooke, Colonel W. S. *See* United Kingdom, G, War Office Publ.: Appendix 2.

Cooley, W. Desborough. History of Maritime and Inland Discovery. 3 vols. 12° 1830-31

—— Histoire Générale des Voyages de Découvertes Maritimes et Continentales depuis le Commencement du Monde jusqu'à nos jours. Traduite de l'Anglais par Ad. Joane et Oldnick. 3 vols. 12° 1840

Cooley, W. Desborough. Negroland of the Arabs Examined and Explained; or, An Inquiry into the Early History and Geography of Central Africa. *Map.* 8° 1841

—— Inner Africa Laid Open, in an Attempt to Trace the Chief Lines of Communication across that Continent south of the Equator; with the Routes to the Muropue and the Cazembe, Moenemoezi, and Lake Nyassa; the Journeys of Krapf and Rebmann on the Eastern Coast, and the Discoveries of Oswell and Livingstone in the heart of the country. *Map.* 8° 1852

—— Claudius Ptolemy and the Nile; or, An Enquiry into that Geographer's real merits and speculative errors, his knowledge of Eastern Africa, and the authenticity of the Mountains of the Moon. *Map.* 8° 1854

—— Dr Livingstone's Reise vom Fluss Liambey nach Loanda, in 1853-54, kritisch und kommentarisch beleuchtet. *Map.* 4* *Gotha*, 1855

—— Memoir of the Lake Regions of East Africa Reviewed (in reply to Capt. R. Burton). 8* 1864

—— Dr Livingstone's Errors. 8* [1865]

—— Mémoire sur le Tacuy de Barros. 8* *Paris*, 1869

—— Notice sur P. Paez. 8* *Paris*, 1872

—— Dr Livingstone and the Royal Geographical Society. Small 8* 1874

—— Physical Geography, or the Terraqueous Globe and its Phenomena. *Maps, plate, &c.* 8° 1876

—— *See* Parrot, F.

Coolidge, Rev. W. A. B. Swiss Travel and Swiss Guide-Books. 12° 1889

—— Was ist eine "Erste Besteigung." Separatabdruck aus No. 375 vom 26 Mai 1893, der Oesterr. Alpen-Zeitung. Large 8* *Vienna*, 1893

—— Die Deutsch redenden Gmeinden im Grauen oder Oberen Bunde (Rhätien) der Schweiz. Separatabdruck aus Nos. 376-7, Oesterr. Alpen-Zeitung. Large 8* 1893

—— *See* Conway, W. M.

—— **H. Duhamel, and F. Perrin.** Guide du Haut-Dauphiné. *Map.* 12° *Grenoble*, 1887

—— The same. Supplément. 12° *Grenoble*, 1890

Coope, W. J. Swazieland as an Imperial Factor. *Maps.* 8* N.D.

Cooper, —. Method of Adjusting and Using the Hydropneumatic Baroscope, with Tables for the Direct Determination of the Difference of Level. [2 *leaves.*] *Tables.* 4* N.P., N.D.

Cooper, Augustus. The Colonies of the United Kingdom : a Descriptive and Statistical Work of Reference, containing also some Important and Serious Facts connected with the Over-Population, Distress, and Chronic Scarcity of Employment in England. 3rd edition. 8°   *Brighton*, 1888

Cooper, A. J. The Unequal Distribution of Heat over the Earth's Surface ; or, New Theory of Tropical Heat, Polar Cold, Mountain Snows, and the Earth's Diurnal Revolution. 8*   *Liverpool*, 1878

Cooper, Charlotte F. *See* Pfeiffer.

Cooper, E. J. Catalogue of Stars near the Ecliptic observed at Markree during 1848-56, and whose places are supposed to be hitherto unpublished. 4 vols. 8°
                                          Dublin, 1851-56

Cooper J. G. *See* United States, K (California) : Appendix 2.

Cooper, Joseph. The Lost Continent ; or, Slavery and the Slave Trade in Africa, 1875. *Map.* 8°   1875
—— *See* Berlioux.

Cooper, J. Rhodes. New Zealand Settler's Guide : a Sketch of the Present State of the Six Provinces, with a Digest of the Constitution and Land Regulations. *Maps.* 12°   1857

Cooper, Thomas. Men of the Time : a Dictionary of Contemporaries, containing Biographical Notices of Eminent Characters of Both Sexes. 9th edition, revised by Thomas Cooper. 8°   1875
—— The same. New eds. 1887, 1891, 1895

Cooper, T. T. Travels of a Pioneer of Commerce in Pigtail and Petticoats ; or, An Overland Journey from China towards India. *Map and plate.* 8° 1871
—— The Mishmee Hills : an Account of a Journey made in an Attempt to Penetrate Thibet from Assam to open new Routes for Commerce. *Map and plates.* 12°   1873

Cooper, W. M. Track from Katoomba to Jenolan Caves. *Map.* Large 8°
                                          Sydney, 1885

Coorengel, J. G. *See* Robidé Van der Aa.

Coote, Sir Charles. Statistical Survey of the County of Armagh, with Observations on the Means of Improvement. *Maps.* 8°   *Dublin*, 1804

Coote, C. H. Shakspere's New Map in "Twelfth Night." Small 8*   1878
—— *See* Schöner, Johann ; *also* Hakluyt Soc. Publ., Vol. 72 : Appendix 1.

Coote, Walter. Wanderings, South and East. *Charts and illustrations.* 8° 1882
—— The Western Pacific : being a Description of the Groups of Islands to the North and East of the Australian Continent. *Charts and illustrations.* 12°
                                          1883

Cope, E. D. An Examination of the Reptilia and Batrachia obtained by the Orton Expedition to Equador and the Upper Amazon, with Notes on other Species. 8*   *Philadelphia*, 1868
—— *See* United States, G, *a* (Reports, Vol. 3) : Appendix 2.

Copland, John. *See* India, C (Geological Papers) : Appendix 2.

Copland, Rev. P. *See* Purchas, Vol. 1, Book 4 : Appendix 1.

Copland, Samuel. History of the Island of Madagascar, comprising a Political Account of the Island, the Religion, &c., of its Inhabitants, and its Natural Productions. *Map.* 8°   1822

Coppinger, R. W. Cruise of the "Alert" : Four Years in Patagonian, Polynesian, and Mascarene Waters, 1878-82. *Plates.* Large 8°   1883

Coquilhat, Camille. Sur le Haut-Congo. *Maps and illustrations.* 8° *Paris*, 1888

Cora, Prof. Guido. Da Brindisi a Bombay sguardo Fisico, Politico, Etnografico, Storico ; Economico sulla Linea di Navigazione da Brindisi a Bombay attraverso il Canale di Suez. 8* *Casale*, 1869
—— Spedizione Italiana alla Nuova Guinea. 12*   *Rome*, 1872
—— Il Tanjanika, Bacino chiuso. *Map.* 4*   [*Turin*, 1873]
—— Cenni Generali intorno ad un Viàggio nella Bassa Albania (Epiro), ed a Tripoli di Barberia compiuto dal Settembre 1874 al Gennaio 1875. *Map.* 4*   *Turin*, 1875
—— Cenni sui Lavori del Comitato Polare Internazionale (Sessioni d'Amburgo, 1879, e di Berna, 1880), e sulla Progettata Stazione Scientifica Italiana nelle Emisfero Meridionale. Lettura fatta il 5 Dicembre 1880 alla Società Geografica Italiana. 8*   *Rome*, 1880
—— Sulle Progettate Stazioni per Osservazioni Fisiche Sistematiche nelle Regioni Polari. 4*   [*Rome*] 1880
—— Cenni Intorno all' Attuale Indirizzo degli Studi Geografici. 8* *Turin*, 1881
—— Note Cartografiche sulla Reggenza di Tunisi. 2nd edition. 8* *Turin*, 1881
—— Il Sahara : Appunti e Considerazioni di Geografia Fisica. *Map.* 8* *Rome*, 1882
—— l'Hegiaz Settentrionale tra El-Wigh, Medina e Bedr Honên. *Map and plans.* Small folio*   [*Turin*] 1885
—— Della Superficie Terrestre come Oggetto Precipuo della Geografia. 4*
                                          Turin, 1885
—— I Precursori di Cristoforo Colombo verso l'America, Conferenza tenteta allo Società Geografica. Italiana il 30 Marza 1885. 8*   *Roma*, 1886

Cora, Prof. Guido. Balcanica Penisola. (Dal Supplemento alla 6a Edizione della Enciclopedia Italiana.) 4* *Turin*, 1889
—— Della opportunità di costituire un comitato apposito per promuovere sistematicamente la Corografia scientific adella Regione Italiana e Proposta per l'attuazone pratica dell' Idea. 8* *Genoa*, 1892

Coraboeuf, M. Les Opérations Géodésiques des Pyrénées. *Map.* 4° *Paris*, 1831

Corbaux, Fanny. On the Comparative Physical Geography of the Arabian Frontier of Egypt, at the Earliest Epoch of Egyptian History and at the Present Time. *Maps.* 8° *Edinburgh*, 1848

Corbin, Diana Fontaine Maury. A Life of Matthew Fontaine Maury. Compiled by his daughter Diana Fontaine Maury Corbin. 8° 1888

Corcelle, J. Industries et Richesses du Bugey. 8* *Bourg*, 1885

Cordeau, A. *See* Filon.

Cordeiro, Luciano. Viagens: Hespanha e França. 12° *Lisbon*, 1874
—— Viagens: França, Baviera, Austria, e Italia. 12° *Lisbon*, 1875
—— De la part prise par les Portugais dans la Découverte de l'Amérique. 8* *Lisbon*, 1876
—— Portugal e o Movimento Geographico Moderno. 8* *Lisbon*, 1877
—— Noticia do Cunene. 12* *Lisbon*, 1878
—— L'Hydrographie Africaine au XVIᵉ Siècle, d'après les Prémières Explorations Portugaises. 8* *Lisbon*, 1878
—— Catalogos e indicis as Publicaçaões da Sociedade de Geographia de Lisboa. 8° *Lisbon*, 1889
—— Descobertas e Descobridores, Diogo Cão. Memoria apresentada á 10a sessão do Congresso Internacional dos Orientalistas. *Plates.* 8* *Lisbon*, 1892
—— *See* Figueiredo, B. de; Moraes; *also* Portugal, B : Appendix 2.

Cordero, Manuel D. *See* Segura.

Cordes, Simon de. *See* Burney, Vol. 2 : Appendix 1.

Cordier, H. A Narrative of the Recent Events in Tong-king. 8* *Shanghai*, 1875
—— Bibliotheca Sinica. Dictionnaire Bibliographique des Ouvrages relatifs à l'Empire Chinois. 2 vols. Large 8° *Paris*, 1878-85
—— Essai d'une Bibliographie des Ouvrages publiés en Chine par les Européens au XVIIᵉ et au XVIIIᵉ Siècle. 4* *Paris*, 1883
—— Le Conflit entre la France et la Chine : Étude d'Histoire Coloniale et de droit International. 8* *Paris*, 1883
—— Le Consulat de France a Hué sous la Restauration : Documents inédits tirés des Archives des Départements des Affaires Étrangères de la Marine et des Colonies. 8° *Paris*, 1884

Cordier, H. Le Colonel Sir Henry Yule. 8* *Paris*, 1890
—— *See* Odoric de Pordenone ; *also* Catalogues: Appendix 2.

Cordiner, James. Description of Ceylon, containing an Account of the Country, Inhabitants, and Natural Productions ; with a Tour round the Island in 1800, the Campaign in Candy in 1803, and a Journey to Ramisseram in 1804. 2 vols. in 1. *Plates.* 4° 1807

Cordova, A. de. *See* Phillips [3], Vol. 2 : Appendix 1.

Cordova, Franciscus Hernandez de. *See* Gottfried ; Kerr, Vol. 3 ; Laharpe, Vol. 9 ; Allgemeine Historie, Vol. 13 : Appendix 1.

Cordova, J. de. Texas, her Capabilities and Resources : the Substance of Two Lectures, &c. 8* *Manchester*, 1858

Corio, Lodovico. I Commerci dell' Africa. Pubblicazione della Società d'Esplorazione Commerciale in Africa. 12° *Milan*, 1890

Cormack, W. E. Narrative of a Journey across the Island of Newfoundland. 8° *St John's, Newfoundland*, 1856

Cornado, F. Vasquez de. *See* Burney, Vol. 1 ; Hakluyt, Vol. 3 : Appendix 1.

Cornejo, Adrian F. *See* Angelis, Vol. 4 : Appendix 1.

Cornelissen, J. E. On the Temperature of the Sea at the Surface near the Southpoint of Africa. *Tables.* 4* *Utrecht* [1868]

Cornelius, C. S. Grundriss der physikalischen Geographie. 8° *Halle*, 1851

Cornelius, Elias. Tour in Virginia. *See* Phillips [3], Vol. 3 : Appendix 1.

Cornwall, Ira, junior. St John and the Province of New Brunswick. *Maps and illustrations.* Small 8° *St John*, N.D.

Cornwall, Richard, Earl of. *See* Hakluyt, Vol. 2 : Appendix 1.

Cornwallis, Kinahan. Two Journeys to Japan, 1856-57. 2 vols. 8° 1859

Cornish, W. R. Report on the Census of the Madras Presidency, 1871 ; with Appendix containing the Results, &c. 2 vols. Folio *Madras*, 1874

Cornwell, James. A School Geography. (47th edition.) *Maps.* 8° 1870

Coronado. *See* Cornado.

Coronelli, J. Isolario dell' Atlante Veneto. Part 1. *Maps.* Folio *Venice*, 1696

Correa, Gaspar. *See* Hakluyt Soc. Publ., Vol. 42 : Appendix 1.

Corrêa da Silva, C. E. Uma Viagem ao Estabelecimento Portuguez de S. João Baptista de Ajudá na Costa da Mina, em 1865. *Plan.* 8° *Lisbon*, 1866

Correal, F. *See* Allgemeine Historie, Vol. 15 : Appendix 1.

Corry, Joseph. Observations upon the Windward Coast of Africa ; the Religion, Character, Customs, &c., of the Natives, with a System upon which they may be Civilised, and a Knowledge attained of this extraordinary quarter of the Globe, and upon the Natural and Commercial Resources of the Country, made in 1805-6 ; with an Appendix. *Plates.* 4° 1807

Corsali, Andrea. *See* Ramusio, Vol. 1 : Appendix 1.

Cortambert, E. De l'Orthographie Géographique. 8ᵛ *Paris*, 1846

—— Notice biographique du Baron C. A. Walckenaer. 8* *Paris*, 1853

—— Parallèle de la Géographie et de l'Histoire. 8* *Paris*, 1854

—— Rapport sur le Voyage dans la Turquie d'Europe, par M. Viquesnel ; et Notice Statistique sur l'Empire Ottoman. 8° *Paris*, 1857

—— Coup-d'œil Historique sur les Voyages et sur les Progrès de la Géographie depuis 1800 jusqu'en 1856. Royal 8* *Lagny*, N.D.

—— Esquisse de la Géographie, de l'Ethnographie et de l'Histoire naturelle d'une partie d'Afrique Australe Intérieure (du cours supérieur du Fleuve Orange au cours du Zambèze). Royal 8* *Paris*, 1858

—— Tableau Général de l'Amérique : Rapport sur les Progrès de l'Ethnographie et de la Géographie en Amérique pendant 1858 et 1859. 8° *Paris*, 1860

—— Dernières Explorations en Australie : Burke, 1860-61 ; Macdouall Stuart, 1861. 8* *Paris*, N.D.

—— Trois des plus Anciens Monuments Géographiques du Moyen Age, conservés à la Bibliothèque Nationale. *Maps.* 8* *Paris*, 1877

—— **and L. de. Rosny.** Tableau de la Cochin-Chine, rédigé sous les auspices de la Société d'Ethnographie . . . précédé d'une introduction par Paul de Bourgoing. *Map, plan, and plates.* 8° *Paris*, 1862

Corte-Real, Gaspar. *See* Canto ; Harrisse ; *also* Allgemeine Historie, Vol. 13 ; General Collection of Voyages, p. 610 ; Hakluyt Soc. Publ., Vol. 86 : Appendix 1.

Cortes, Hernan or Fernando. Carta de relacion . . . por . . . D. Fernando Cortes, én la qual hace relacion de las Tierras i Provincias sin cuento que a descubierto nuevamente en el Jucatán, del año de 19 à esta parte, &c. Folio *Seville*, 1522

Cortes, Hernan or Fernando. Carta tercera de relacion . . . por D. Fernando Cortes . . . de las cosas sucedidas . . . en la conquista . , . de la . . . Ciudad de Temixtitán. Folio [*Cuioacan*] 1522

—— Carta, o quarta relacion, que Fernando Cortes . embió al . . . Señor Don Carlos . . . en la qual están otras Cartas y Relaciones que los Capitanes Pedro de Alvarado y Diego de Godoy embiaron al dicho Capitan Fernando Cortès. Folio N.P., 1524

—— *See* Gayangos ; *also* Burney, Vol. 1 ; Gottfried ; Hakluyt Soc. Publ., Vol. 40 ; Harris, Vol. 2 ; Kerr, Vol. 3 ; Laharpe, Vol. 9 ; Purchas, Vol. 3, Book 5 ; Ramusio, Vol. 3 ; New Collection, Vol. 1, p. 607 ; General Collection of Voyages, p. 610 ; Allgemeine Historie, Vol. 13 ; The World Displayed, Vols. 1, 2 : Appendix 1.

Cortes, J. D. Bolivia, Apuntes jeográficos, estadisticos, de Costumbres descriptivos e históricos. Small 8° *Paris*, 1875

Corti, Siro. Le Provincie d'Italia, studiate sotto l'aspetto Geografico e Storico.

	12° *Maps and illustrations*	*Turin*
1.	Provincia di Firenze	1887
2.	—— Pisa	1886
3.	—— Livorno	1886
4.	—— Lucca	1886
5.	—— Massa Carrara	1886
6.	—— Arezzo	1886
7.	—— Siena	1886
8.	—— Grosseto	1886
9.	Regione Siciliana	1886
10.	Provincia di Palermo	1886
11.	—— Messina	1886
12.	—— Catania	1886
13.	—— Caltanissetta	1886
14.	—— Girgenti	1886
15.	—— Trapani	1886
16.	—— Siracusa	1886
17.	—— Milano	1887
18.	—— Bergamo	1887
19.	—— Como	1887
20.	—— Brescia	1887
21.	—— Cremona	1887
22.	—— Mantova	1887
23.	—— Pavia	1887
24.	—— Sondrio	1887
25.	—— Napoli	1888
26.	—— Caserta	1888
27.	—— Salerno	1888
28.	—— Avellino	1888
29.	—— Benevento	1888
30.	—— Bari	1888
31.	—— Foggia	1888
32.	—— Lecce	1889
33.	Regione Calabrese. Provincia di Potenza	1889
34.	—— —— Catanzaro	1889
35.	—— —— Cosenza	1889
36.	—— —— Reggio	1889

Corti, Siro. Le Provincie d'Italia, studiate sotto l'aspetto Geografico e Storico—
continued:—

37. Provincia di Chieti	1890
38. —— Aquila	1890
39. —— Teramo	1890
40. —— Campobasso	1890
41. —— Torino	1890
42. —— Cuneo	1890
43. —— Novara	1890
44. —— Alessandria	1890
45. —— Cagliari	1891
46. —— Sassari	1891
47. —— Genova	1891
48. —— Porto Maurizio	1891
49. —— Venezia	1892
50. —— Verona	1892
51. —— Vicenza	1892
52. —— Belluno	1892
53. —— Padova	1892
54. —— Rovigo	1892
55. —— Treviso	1892
56. —— Udine	1892
57. —— Bologna	1893
58. —— Ferrara	1893
59. —— Piacenza	1893

Corvo, J. d'Andrade. Des Lignes Iso-
goniques au Seizième Siècle. *Maps.* 8*
Lisbon, 1881

—— Estudos sobre as Provincias Ultramarinas. 4 vols. 8° *Lisbon,* 1883-87

"Corwin." Cruise of the Revenue-
Steamer "Corwin" in Alaska and the
N.-W. Arctic Ocean in 1881 : Notes
and Memoranda, Medical and Anthro-
pological, Botanical, Ornithological.
Plates. 4* *Washington,* 1883

Coryat, Thomas. Crudities. Reprinted
from the edition of 1611 ; to which are
now added his Letters from India, &c.,
and Extracts relating to him from various
authors ; being a more particular Account
of his Travels (mostly on foot) in different
parts of the Globe, with his Orations,
Character, Death, &c. 3 vols. *Plates.*
8° 1776

—— *See* Gottfried ; Kerr, Vol. 9 : Purchas,
Vols. 1, 2 : Appendix 1.

Cosa, J. de la. *See* Allgemeine Historie,
Vol. 13 : Appendix 1.

Cosmas Indopleustes. *See* Thevenot,
Vol. 1 : Appendix 1.

Cosson, E. A. de. The Cradle of the
Blue Nile : a Visit to the Court of
King John of Ethiopia. 2 vols. *Map
and plates.* 8° 1877

—— Days and Nights of Service with Sir
Gerald Graham's Field Force at Suakin.
Plan and illustrations. 8° 1886

Cosson, E. Compendium Floræ Atlanticæ
seu Expositio Methodica Plantarum omnium in Algeria necnon in regno Tune-
tano et imperio Maroccano hucusque
notarum ; ou Flore des États Barbar-

Cosson, E.—*continued.*
esques, Algérie, Tunisie, et Maroc. Vol.
1, Première partie, Historique et Géographie. *Maps.* 8° *Paris,* 1881

—— The same. Vol. 2, Supplément à la
partie Historique et Flore des États
Barbaresques, Renonculacées-Crucifères.
8° *Paris,* 1883-87

Costa, B. F. de. Notes on a Review of
"The Pre-Columbian Discovery of
America by the Northmen," in the
North American Review for July. 16*
Charlestown, 1869

—— Cabo de Baxos ; or, The Place of
Cape Cod in the old Cartology, with
Notes on the neighbouring Coasts.
Map. 8* *New York,* 1881

—— Arctic Exploration, with an Account
of Nicholas of Lynn. *Maps.* 8*
New York, 1881

—— Myvynan Archaiology : the Pre-
Columbian Voyages of the Welsh to
America. 8* *Albany, N.Y.,* 1891

Costa, Claudio Adriano da. Revisão do
Recenseamento da População de Portugal
em 1838. Small 8* *Lisbon,* 1840

Costa, E. Mendes da. *See* Troil.

Costa, Pereira da. Commissaõ Geologica
de Portugal. Molluscos Fosseis. Gas-
teropodes dos Depositos terciarios de
Portugal, com a versaõ franceza por M.
Dalhunty. *Plates.* 8° *Lisbon,* 1866

Costa, W. H. de. In Memoriam. 12*
Charlestown, 1878

Costa Riva, A. da. *See* Gama, Vasco da.

Costantini, Giuseppe - Antonio. La
Verità del Diluvio Universale vindicata
dai dubbj, e Demostrata nelle sue Testi-
monianze. 4° *Venice,* 1747

Coste, ——. Voyage d'Exploration sur le
Littoral de la France et de l'Italie. 2nd
edition. 4° *Paris,* 1861

Costello C. P. *See* India, 1 (Assam) :
Appendix 2.

Costello, Louisa S. A Pilgrimage to
Auvergne, from Picardy to Le Velay.
2 vols. *Plates.* 8° 1842

Cotteau, E. Promenade dans l'Inde et
à Ceylan. 12° *Paris,* 1880

—— Promenades dans les deux Amériques,
1876-77. *Maps.* 12° *Paris,* 1880

—— De Paris au Japon à travers la Sibérie,
Voyage exécuté du 6 Mai au 7 Août
1881. *Maps and illustrations.* 12°
Paris, 1883

—— Un Touriste dans l'Extrême Orient :
Japon, Chine, Indo-chine, et Tonkin
(4 Août 1881—24 Janvier 1882). *Maps
and illustrations.* 12° *Paris,* 1884

—— Voyage autour du Monde (1884-85) :
Malaisie—Australie—Nouvelle Calédonie
—Tahiti—Mexique. *Map.* 8°
[*Paris*] 1885

—— Voyage aux Volcans de Java. *Illustrations.* 8* *Paris,* 1886

Cotteau, E. Quelques Notes sur Sarawak (Bornéo). 8*   *Paris*, 1886
—— Les Nouvelles-Hébrides. *Map.* 8°   *Paris*, 1886
—— En Océanie : Voyage autour du Monde en 365 jours, 1884-85. *Maps and illustrations.* 12°   *Paris*, 1888
—— Voyage au Caucase et en Transcaspienne, 24 Juillet—11 Octobre 1887. *Map and illustrations.* 8*   *Paris*, 1888
—— Une Ascension au Pic de Ténériffe. *Illustration.* 8*   *Auxerre*, 1890

Cotterill H. B. African Slave Traffic. 8*   1875
—— *See* Elton, J. F.

Cotton, Sir A. Communication with the Egyptian Soudan by the Congo. In a Letter to the Postmaster-General. 8*   *Dorking*, N.D.

Cotton, Major H. C. *See* Best, Capt. S.

Cotton, Sir Sidney. Nine Years on the North-West Frontier of India, from 1854 to 1863. 8°   1868

Cottrell, Charles Herbert. Recollections of Siberia in 1840-41. *Map.* 8°   1842

Coudreau, Henri A. La France Équinoxiale : Études et Voyage à travers les Guyanes et l'Amazonie. 2 vols., and Atlas. 8°   *Paris*, 1886-87
—— Chez nos Indiens. Quatre années dans la Guyane Française (1887-91). *Map and illustrations.* Large 8° *Paris*, 1893

Coues, Dr Elliot. An Account of the various Publications relating to the Travels of Lewis and Clarke, with a Commentary on the Zoological results of their Expedition. 8° *Washington*, 1876
—— *See* United States, G, *a* : Appendix 2.

Coullier, Ph. J. Tables des Principales Positions Géographiques du Globe, recueillies et mises en ordre d'après les Authorités les plus modernes, en deux parties, renfermant les expressions de position de tous les points maritimes connus, classés par ordre alphabétique, avec les Noms des Observateurs ou des Auteurs auxquels les chiffres sont dus ; plus un Appendice. 8°   *Paris*, 1828
—— Guide des Marins pendant la Navigation Nocturne, ou Description Générale des Phares, Fanaux, &c., construits pour la sûreté de la Navigation. *Plate.* 8°   *Paris*, 1829
—— Description Générale des Phares, Fanaux, et Remarques, existant sur les Plages Maritimes du Globe, à l'usage de la Navigation. 16°   *Paris*, 1839

Coulon, —. *See* Blanc, Vincent le.

Coulter, John. Adventures in the Pacific, with Observations on the Natural Productions, Manners, and Customs of the Natives of the various Islands. 8°   *Dublin*, 1847

Coulthard, Capt. S. *See* India, C (Geological Papers) : Appendix 2.

Coulter, John M. *See* United States, G, *a* : Appendix 2.

Counsel, Edward A. Road from Marlborough to the Pieman River, Tasmania. Folio *   *Hobart*, 1878

Courcy, Marquis de. L'Empire du Milieu [China], Description Géographique, précis Historique, &c. 8°   *Paris*, 1867

Courcy, Pol de. De Rennes à Brest et à Saint Malo : Itinéraire, descriptif et historique. Small 8° *Paris*, 1864
—— De Nantes à Brest, à Saint-Nazaire, à Rennes, et à Napoléonville : Itinéraire, descriptif et historique. *Map.* Small 8°   *Paris*, 1865

Courteille, A. Pavet de. *See* Pavet de Courteille ; Ubicini.

Courthop, Nath. *See* Purchas, Vol. 1, Book 5 : Appendix 1.

Courtin, M. de. Travaux des Ponts et Chaussées depuis 1800. 8° *Paris*, 1812

Courtney, W. Memoir of the Sawunt Waree State, 1843 ; with continuation to the close of the year 1853, by Major J. W. Auld. *Map and table.* [From the India Records, No. 10] *Bombay*, 1855

Courtney, Capt. S. *See* Harris, Vol. 1 ; Kerr, Vol. 10 ; Knox's New Collection, Vol. 3 : Appendix 1.

Cousens, H. Archæological Survey of Western India, No. 12 : an Account of the Caves at Nadsur and Karsambla. *Plates.* 4*   *Bombay*, 1891

Coutinho, Fernando. *See* Gottfried : Appendix 1.

Coutinho, José J. da C. de Azevedo. Ensaio Economico sobre o Commercio de Portugal. 8°   *Lisbon*, 1816
—— Ensaio Economico sobre o Commercio de Portugal e suas Colonias. 3rd edition. Small 8° *Lisbon*, 1828

Coutinho, J. M. da Silva. Relatorio da exploração do Rio Purús. 4*   1862
—— Considerações geraes sobre os rios que descem da cordilheira dos Andes, nas proximidades du Cuzco, cachoeiras do Purús e Hyurua. 4*   1863
—— Relatorio da exploração do Rio Madeira. 4*   *Rio de Janeiro* [1864]
—— Exploraço do Rio Hyupurá. 4*   *Rio de Janeiro* [1864]

Couto, Diogo do. Da Asia. *See* Barros, J. de.

Covarrubias, Francisco Diaz. Viaje de la Comision Astronómica Mexicana al Japon, para observar el tránsito del planeta Vénus por el disco del sol, el 8 de Diciembre de 1874. *Illustrations.* Large 8°   *Mexico*, 1876

Covel, Dr John. *See* Hakluyt Soc. Publ., Vol. 87 : Appendix 1.

Coverte [or Corverte], Capt. R. *See* Astley, Vol. 1 ; Churchill, Vol. 8 ; Gott-fried ; Kerr, Vol. 8 : Appendix 1.

Covino, F. De Turin à Chambéry ; ou, Les Vallées de la Dora riparia et de l'arc et le Tunnel des Alpes Cottiennes. Tra-duction de N. Gachet. *Maps and plates.* 12°   *Turin,* 1871

Cowan, Frank. The City of the Royal Palm, and other Poems. 8*
                          Rio de Janeiro, 1884
—— Fact and Fancy in New Zealand : The Terraces of Rotomahana, a Poem ; to which is Prefixed a Paper on Geyser Eruptions and Terrace Formations, by Josiah Martin. 8*
                          Auckland, N.Z., 1885
—— A Visit in Verse to Halemaumau. 8*   *Honolulu,* 1885
—— Australia : a Charcoal Sketch. 8*
                          Greensburg, Pa., 1886

Cowan, Rev. W. D. List of Madagascar Birds, together with the Native Names among a few of the different Tribes. 8*
                          Antananarivo, 1881
—— The Bara Land : a Description of the Country and People. *Map and plates.* 8*   *Antananarivo,* 1881
—— The Tanala. *Map.* 8*
                          Faravohitra, 1881

Cowan, T. *See* Victoria, B : Appendix 2.

Cowell, J. J. *See* Galton, Vacation Tourists.

Cowen, Charles. Witwatersrand, Johan-nesburg, and other Gold Fields. 12*
                          Johannesburg, 1887

Cowley, Capt. *See* Callander, Vol. 2 ; Hacke ; Harris, Vol. 1 ; Kerr, Vol. 10 ; Allgemeine Historie, Vol. 18 : Appen-dix 1.

Cowper, B. Harris. Cyprus, its Past, Present, and Future. 12°   N.D.

Cox, —. *See* Eyriès, Vol. 13 : Appendix 1.

Cox, —. *See* New Zealand, A : Ap-pendix 2.

Cox, E. T. Third and Fourth Annual Re-ports of the Geological Survey of Indiana, made during the years 1871 and 1872. *Sections, maps separate.* 8°
                          Indianopolis, 1872
—— *See* Owen, D. D.

Cox, Guillermo E. Viaje en las Rejiones Septentrionales de la Patagonia, 1862-63. Royal 8°   *Santiago de Chile,* 1863
—— Expedition across the Southern Andes of Chili, with the object of opening a new line of communication from the Pacific to the Atlantic Ocean by the Lake of Nahuel-Huapi and the Rivers Limay and Negro. (Translated by Sir W. Parish.) *Map.* 8*   1864

Cox, Capt. Hiram. Journal of a Residence in the Burman Empire, and more par-ticularly at the Court of Amarapoorah. *Plates.* 8°   1821

Cox, Ross. Adventures on the Columbia River, including the Narrative of a Resi-dence of Six Years on the Western Side of the Rocky Mountains, among various Tribes of Indians hitherto unknown, and a Journey across the American Continent. 2 vols. 8°   1831

Coxe, Tench. A View of the United States of America, in a Series of Papers written at various times between the years 1787 and 1794. 8°   1795

Coxe, William. Travels into Poland, Russia, Sweden, and Denmark. *Maps and plates.* 2 vols. 4°   1784
—— Travels in Switzerland, and in the Country of the Grisons. *Maps and plates.* Large paper. 2 vols. Folio
                                            1794
—— The same. 6th edition. 3 vols. *Maps and plates.* 4°   1803
—— Account of the Russian Discoveries between Asia and America ; to which are added the Conquest of Siberia, and the History of the Transactions and Commerce between Russia and China. *Maps.* 8°   1804
—— *See* Pelham, Vol. 2 ; Pinkerton, Vol. 5 : Appendix 1.

Coxon, Capt. John. *See* Dalrymple, Tracts, Vol. 2 ; Appendix 1.

Cozzens, S. W. The Marvellous Coun-try ; or, Three Years in Arizona and New Mexico. 2nd edition. *Plates.* 8° 1875

Cozzika, Jean. Question d'Abyssinie au Peuple de la Grande-Bretagne. Publié [*i.e.* translated from the Greek] par S. M. Mavrogordato. Folio *
                          Constantinople, 1867

Crab, P. Van der. *See* Robidé van der Aa.

Craik, Dr Henry. Swift : Selections from his Works. Edited, with Life, Introductions, and Notes, by Henry Craik. 2 vols. Small 8° *Oxford,* 1893

Craik, Mrs. An Unsentimental Journey through Cornwall. By the Author of " John Halifax, Gentleman." *With illustrations* by C. Napier Hemy. 4° 1884

Cram, Capt. Thomas Jefferson. Re-ports of the Topographical Bureau in relation to Internal Improvements in the Territory of Wisconsin. *Maps.* 8*
                          Washington, 1840
—— Reports, Plans, and Estimates for the Improvement of the Neenah, Wiskonsin, and Rock Rivers, the Haven of Rock River, and a Pier at the Northern Extremity of Winnebago Lake. *Maps.* 8*   *Washington,* 1840

Cramer, J. A. A Geographical and Historical Description of Ancient Greece. 3 vols. *Map and plan.* 8°   1828
—— A Geographical and Historical De-scription of Asia Minor. 2 vols. *Map.* 8°   1832

Cramer, J. A. Geographical and Historical Description of Ancient Italy. 2 vols. *With a map and plan of Rome.* 8°
Oxford, 1832

Cramer, Ludwig W. Vollständige Beschreibung des Berg-, Hütten-, und Hammerwesens in den sämmtlichen hochfürstlich Nassau-Usingischen Landen. Vol. 1, Part 1. 8° *Frankfort-a-M.*, 1805

Crampel, P. *See* Alis.

Cramp, W. B. *See* Phillips [3], Vol. 9 : Appendix 1.

Crantz, D. Historie von Grönland, enthaltend die Beschreibung des Landes und der Einwohner, &c., insbesondere die Geschichte der dortigen Mission der Evangelischen Brüder zu Neu-Herrnhut und Lichtenfels. 2nd edition. 3 vols. *Plates.* 12° *Leipzig*, 1770

—— History of Greenland, including an Account of the Mission carried on by the United Brethren in that Country to the Present Time, and a Sketch of the Mission in Labrador. 2 vols. *Maps and plates.* 8° 1820

—— *See* Allgemeine Historie, Vol. 20 : Appendix 1.

Crasto, J. de. *See* Portuguese Conquests : Appendix 2.

Craufurd, G. M. *See* Fidler.

Craven, A. E. Observations sur l'Helix Ligulata, Fér., de Madras. *Plate.* 8° *Brussels* [1869]

—— Quelques Observations sur le Hyalæa Tridentata, Lamarck. *Plate.* 8° *Brussels* [1873]

—— Monographie du Genre Sinusigera, D'Orb. *Plates.* 8° *Brussels*, 1877

Craven, Hon. R. Keppel. Tour through the Southern Provinces of Naples. *Map and plates.* 4° 1821

Crawford and Balcarres, Earl of [formerly Lord Lindsay]. Bibliotheca Lindesiana : Collations and Notes, No. 3, Grands et Petits Voyages of De Bry, by Ludovic, Earl of Crawford and Balcarres. *Plates.* 4° 1884

—— Dun Echt Observatory Publications— Vols. 1 and 2. Mauritius Expedition, 1874. Division 1. 4° *Dun Echt, Aberdeen*, 1876-77

Vol. 3. Mauritius Expedition, 1874. Division 2. Determinations of Longitude and Latitude. *Map and diagram.* 4° *Dun Echt, Aberdeen*, 1885

Crawford, John Martin. Industries of Russia. Editor of the English Translation, John Martin Crawford, U.S. Consul-General to Russia. 5 vols. Large 8° *St Petersburg*, 1893

CONTENTS.

Vols. 1 and 2.—Manufactures and Trade, with a General Industrial Map by the Depart. of Trade and Manufactures, Ministry of Finance for the World's Columbian Exposition at Chicago.

Crawford, John Martin—*continued.* Vol. 3.—Agriculture and Forestry, with coloured Maps.

Vol. 4.—Mining and Metallurgy, with a set of Mining Maps by A. Heppen, &c.

Vol. 5—Siberia and the Great Siberian Railway, with a General Map by the Department of Trade, &c.

—— *See* Dokuchaev.

Crawford, Hon. J. Coutts. New Zealand Exhibition, 1865 : Essay on the Geology of the North Island of New Zealand. 8° *Dunedin*, 1865

—— Recollections of Travel in New Zealand and Australia. *Maps and plates.* 8° 1880

Crawford, Robert. Across the Pampas and the Andes. *Map and illustrations.* Crown 8° 1884

—— Reminiscences of Foreign Travel. 8° 1888

Crawford, R. W. A Letter to the Secretary of State for India on the Constitution and Management of the East Indian Railway Company. 8* 1867

Crawfurd, John. History of the Indian Archipelago ; containing an Account of the Manners, Arts, Languages, Religions, &c., of its Inhabitants. 3 vols. *Maps and plates.* 8° *Edinburgh*, 1820

—— Journal of an Embassy from the Governor-General of India to the Court of Ava in 1827 ; with an Appendix containing a Description of Fossil Remains, by Professor Buckland and Mr Clift. *Map and plates.* 4° 1829

—— Journal of an Embassy from the Governor-General of India to the Courts of Siam and Cochin-China, exhibiting a view of the actual state of those Kingdoms. 2nd edition. 2 vols. *Maps and plates.* 8° 1830

—— A Sketch of the Geography of Borneo. 8* 1852

—— A Descriptive Dictionary of the Indian Islands and adjacent Countries. *Map.* 8° 1856

—— A Few Notes on Sir Charles Lyell's "Antiquity of Man," and on Prof. Huxley's "Evidence as to Man's Place in Nature." 8* 1863

—— On the Migration of Cultivated Plants in reference to Ethnology : Articles of Food. 8° 1866

—— Naturalisation of the Bark of Peru in India. 8* 1866

—— On the Supposed Aborigines of India as distinguished from its Civilised Inhabitants. 8* 1867

—— On the Classification of the Races of Man according to the Form of the Skull. 8* 1867

—— On the Skin, the Hair, and the Eyes, as Tests of the Races of Man. 8* 1867

Crawfurd, John. On the Vegetable and Animal Food of the Natives of Australia in reference to Social Position, with a Comparison between the Australians and some other Races of Man. 8* 1867
—— On the History and Migration of Cultivated Plants yielding Intoxicating Potables and Oils. 8° 1868
—— See Murray, Hugh.

Crawfurd, Oswald. Report on the Bar and Navigation of the Douro. *Plans.* 8* 1866
—— Portugal, Old and New. *Maps and illustrations.* 8° 1880
—— Round the Calendar in Portugal. *Illustrations.* 8° 1890

Crawshay, G. The Immediate Cause of the Indian Mutiny, as set forth in the Official Correspondence. 8* [1857]

Creagh, J. Over the Borders of Christendom and Eslamiah : a Journey through Hungary, Slavonia, Servia, Bosnia, Herzegovina, Dalmatia, and Montenegro, to the North of Albania, in the Summer of 1875. 2 vols. 8° 1876

Crealock, H. Foreign Politics and England's Foreign Policy. *Map.* 8* 1873

Credner, Dr G. R. Die Deltas (Ergänzungsheft, 56 — Petermann's Mittheilungen). 3 *sheets of maps.* 4° *Gotha,* 1878
—— Die Reliktenseen (Ergänzungsheft, 88—Petermann's Mittheilungen). 2 *maps.* 4° *Gotha,* 1887
—— Die Reliktenseen (Ergänzungsheft, 89—Petermann's Mittheilungen). *Maps.* 4° *Gotha,* 1888

Crémazy, Laurent. Notes sur Madagascar. 8* *Paris,* 1883

Cremer, Leo. Ein Ausflug nach Spitzbergen. *Map and illustrations.* 8* *Berlin,* 1892

Crescentio, Bartolomeo. Nautica Mediterranea. *Map and plates.* 4° *Rome,* 1607

Crevaux, Dr J. Voyages dans l'Amérique du Sud : contenant, I. Voyage dans l'intérieur des Guyanes (1876 - 1877), exploration du Maroni et du Yary ; II. De Cayenne aux Andes (1878 - 1879) exploration de l'Oyapock, du Paron, de l'Içá, et du Yapura ; III. A travers la Nouvelle Grenade et le Venezuela (1880-1881), exploration, en compagnie de M. E. Le Janne, du Magdalena, du Guaviare, et de l'Orénoque ; IV. Excursion chez lez Guaraounos (1881). *Maps and illustrations.* 4° *Paris,* 1883
—— See Thouar.

Criado, Matías Alónso. La Republica del Paraguay. *Map.* Folio *Montevideo,* 1888

Crijalva, H. de. See Grijalva, in Burney, Vol. 1 : Appendix 1.

H

"Cringle, Tom." Australian Sand-bar Harbours and Rivers, with Hints on the Sea Defences of Melbourne. 8* *Melbourne,* 1866
—— Earthquake Waves : Are they possible ? 16* *Melbourne,* 1868

Crofutt, G. A. Crofutt's New Overland Tourist and Pacific Coast Guide. Vol. 2. *Illustrations.* 8° *Chicago,* 1879-80

Croizier, Marquis de. La Perse et les Persans : Nasr-Eddin-Schah, le Nouvel Iran et l'équilibre Asiatique. 8* *Paris,* 1873
—— L'Art Khmer : Étude historique sur les Monuments de l'Ancien Cambodge ; avec un aperçu général sur l'Architecture Khmer, et une liste complète des monuments explorés, suivi d'un Catalogue, raisonné du Musée Khmer de Compiègne. *Map and illustrations.* 8* *Paris,* 1875
—— Les Explorateurs du Cambodge. *Portraits.* Large 8* *Paris,* 1878
—— Les Monuments de l'Ancien Cambodge, classés par provinces. 12* *Paris,* 1878
—— See Legrand.

Croll, Dr James. On Ocean Currents. 8* 1870
—— On the Cause of the Motion of Glaciers. 8* 1870
—— On Ocean Currents. Part 3. On the Physical Cause of Ocean Currents. 8* 1871 and 1874
—— The "Challenger's" Crucial Test of the Wind and Gravitation Theories of Oceanic Circulation. 8* [1875]
—— The Wind Theory of Oceanic Circulation : Objections examined, and Further Remarks on the "Crucial-Test" Argument. 8* 1875
—— On the Thickness of the Antarctic Ice and its Relations to that of the Glacial Epoch. (Reprint from the *Quarterly Journal of Science,* January 1879.) 8* 1879
—— Stellar Evolution, and its Relations to Geological Time. 8° 1889

Crome, F. G. Geographisch-historische Beschreibung des Landes Syrien. Das südliche Drittheil oder das Land Palästina. *Map.* Small 8° *Göttingen,* 1834

Cronau, Rudolf. Amerika : Die Geschichte seiner Entdeckung von der ältesten bis auf die neueste Zeit. Eine Festschrift zur 400-jahrigen Jubelfeier der Entdeckung Amerikas durch Christoph Columbus. 2 vols. *Maps and illustrations.* 4° *Leipzig,* 1892

Croockewit, J. H. Banka, Malakka, en Billiton, Verslagen aan het Bestuur van Neêrlandsch Indië, in 1849-50. 8° *The Hague,* 1852

Crookes, William. The Atlantic Cable and its Teachings. (From the *Quarterly Journal of Science,* No. 1.) 8* 1864

Cronise, T. F. The Natural Wealth of California . . . together with a Detailed Description of each County. 8°
San Francisco, 1868

Cross, R. Report to the Under Secretary of State for India on the Pitayo Chinchona, and on proceedings while employed in collecting Chinchona Seeds in 1863. *Map.* 8* 1865

Cross, Whitman. *See* United States, G, *c* : Appendix 2.

Crosse, Landor R. *See* Blackwood, Vol. 5: Appendix 1.

Crouch, Archer P. On a Surf-bound Coast ; or, Cable-Laying in the African Tropics. 8° 1887
—— Glimpses of Feverland : or, A Cruise in West African Waters. *Map.* 8° 1889

Crow, Arthur H. Highways and Byeways in Japan : the Experiences of Two Pedestrian Tourists. *Map and frontispiece.* Small 8° 1883

Crowe, Eyre Evans. The Greek and the Turk, or Powers and Prospects in the Levant. 8° 1853

Crowther, J. *See* Kerr, Vol. 9 ; Purchas, Vol. 1, Book 4: Appendix 1.

Crowther, Bishop Samuel A. Vocabulary of the Yoruba Language . . . ; to which are prefixed the Grammatical Elements of the Yoruba Language. 12° 1843
—— A Grammar and Vocabulary of the Yoruba Language . . . ; together with Introductory Remarks by O. E. Vidal. 8° 1852
—— Journals and Notices of the Native Missionaries in the River Niger, 1862. 12° 1863
—— A Grammar and Vocabulary of the Nupe Language. 8° 1864
—— Niger Mission : Report of the Overland Journey from Lokoja to Bida, on the River Niger, and thence to Lagos. 8* 1872
—— The River Niger : a Paper read before the Royal Geographical Society, 11th June 1877 ; with a brief Account of Missionary Operations . . . in the Niger Territory. 8* 1877
—— Itinerant Information in the Niger Mission. 12* *Tuwon, Brass,* 1884
—— Lists of certain Places on the Niger, Binwe, the Interior Countries, and the Bight. 8* *Brass* [1884]
—— *See* Schön.
—— **and J. Christopher Taylor.** The Gospel on the Banks of the Niger : Journals and Notices of the Native Missionaries accompanying the Niger Expedition of 1857-59. *Map.* 8° 1859

Crozals, J. de. Les Peulhs : Étude d'Ethnologie Africaine. 8° *Paris,* 1883

Crozet, M. Journaux de Nouveau Voyage à la Mer du Sud, commencé sous les ordres de M. Marion. On a joint à ce Voyage un Extrait de celui de M. de Surville dans les mêmes Parages. *Maps and plates.* 8° *Paris,* 1783

Crozet's Voyage to Tasmania, New Zealand, the Ladrone Islands, and the Philippines, in the years 1771-72. Translated by H. Ling Roth ; with a Preface, and a brief reference to the Literature of New Zealand, by Jas. R. Boosé. *Map and illustrations.* 8° 1891

Cruickshank, Robert. Eighteen Years on the Gold Coast of Africa, including an Account of the Native Tribes. 2 vols. 8° 1853

Cruls, L. Instrucções para as Commissões Brazileiras que têm de observar a Passagem de Venus pelo disco do Sol em 5-6 de Dezembro de 1882. *Plates.* 4* *Rio de Janeiro,* 1882

Cruz, Gaspar da. *See* Purchas, Vol. 3, Book 1 : Appendix 1.

Cruz, Luis de la. *See* Angelis, Vol. 1 : Appendix 1.

Cubas, Antonio Garcia. The Republic of Mexico in 1876. Translated into English by George E. Henderson. *Plates.* Large 8° *Mexico,* 1876
—— Cuadro Geográfico, Estadistico, Descriptivo é Histórico de los Estados Unidos Mexicanos. 8° *México,* 1885
—— Étude Géographique, Statistique, Descriptive et Historique des États Unis Mexicains. 8° *Mexico,* 1889

Cudmore, P. The Civil Government of the States, and the Constitutional History of the United States. 2nd edition. 8° *New York,* 1875

Cuervo, Antonio B. Resúmen de la Geografia, Histórica, Política, Estadística, i Descriptiva de la Nueva Granada. 18* *De Torres Amaya,* 1852

Cuervo, Marquez Carlos. Prehistoria y Viajes : Tierradentro Los Paeces, San Augustin, El Llano, &c., &c. *Illustrations.* 8* *Bogota,* 1893

Cuinet, Vital. La Turquie d'Asie : Géographie, administrative, statistique, descriptive et raisonnée de chaque province de l'Asie Mineure. Tomes 1-3. *Maps.* 4° *Paris,* 1890-94

Culbertson, J. A New Theory of the Cause of Tides. 8* *Glasgow,* 1867

Cull, R. *See* Conolly, John.

Cullen, C. *See* Clavigero.

Cullen, Edward. Isthmus of Darien Ship Canal. *Maps.* 8* 1852
—— Isthmus of Darien Ship Canal, with a Full History of the Scotch Colony of Darien. *Maps.* 8* 1853
—— Over Darien by a Ship Canal : Reports of the mismanaged Darien Expedition of 1854. 8* 1856

Cullen, Edward. Republic of New Granada as a Field for Emigration. 8* *Dublin*, 1858

—— The Darien Indians and the Ship Canal. 8* [1867]

Cullen, E. A. Report on the Burrum River. Folio* *Brisbane*, 1888

Cumberland, Earl of. *See* Astley, Vol. 1; Gottfried; Hakluyt, Vol. 2; Kerr, Vol. 7; Pinkerton, Vol. 1; Purchas, Vol. 4; Allgemeine Historie, Vol. 1: Appendix 1.

Cumberland, Stuart. The Queen's Highway from Ocean to Ocean. *Maps and illustrations*. 8° 1887

Cumming, C. F. Gordon. At Home in Fiji. 2 vols. *Map and illustrations*. 8° 1881

—— In the Himalayas and on the Indian Plains. *Illustrations*. 8° 1884

—— Wanderings in China. 2 vols. *Portrait, map, and illustrations*. 8° 1886

—— Two Happy Years in Ceylon. 2 vols. *Map and illustrations*. 8° 1892

Cumming, J. Gordon. *See* Piassetsky.

Cumming, Rev. J. G. Isle of Man, its History, Physical, Ecclesiastical, Civil, and Legendary. *Map and plates*. 8° 1848

—— Guide to the Isle of Man, with the means of access thereto, &c. *Map*. 12° 1861

Cumming, R. Gordon. Five Years of a Hunter's Life in the Far Interior of South Africa. 2 vols. *Map and plates*. 1850

Cummings, Samuel. The Western Pilot, containing Charts of the Ohio and Mississippi Rivers; with a Gazetteer. 8° *Cincinnati*, 1840

Cummins, J. *See* Kerr, Vol. 17: Appendix 1.

Cunha. *See* Da Cunha.

Cuningham, William. The Cosmographical Glasse, conteinyng the pleasant Principles of Cosmographie, Geographie, Hydrographie, or Nauigation. *Cuts*. Folio 1559

Cuningham, W. M. Proposed Railway through Siberia. *Map*. 8* 1891

Cunningham, Sir Alexander. The Bhilsa Topes, or Buddhist Monuments of Central India; comprising a Brief Historical Sketch of the Rise, Progress, and Decline of Buddhism; with an Account of the Opening and Examination of the various groups of Topes around Bhilsa. *Map and plates*. 8° 1854

—— Ladák, Physical, Statistical, and Historical, with Notices of the surrounding Countries. *Maps and plates*. Royal 8° 1854

—— Mahabodhi, or the great Buddhist Temple under the Bodhi-tree at Buddha-Gaya. *Plates*. 4° 1892

—— *See* India, A: Appendix 2.

Cunningham, C. D., and Capt. W. de W. Abney. The Pioneers of the Alps. *Portraits*. 4° 1887

Cunningham, James. *See* Harris, Vol. 1; Kerr, Vol. 9: Appendix 1.

Cunningham, Peter. Handbook for London, Past and Present. 2 vols. 8° 1849

Cunningham, R. O. Notes on the Natural History of the Strait of Magellan and West Coast of Patagonia, made during the Voyage of H.M.S. "Nassau" in the years 1866, '67, '68, and '69. *Maps and plates*. 8° *Edinburgh*, 1871

Cunningham, W. The Growth of English Industry and Commerce during the Early and Middle Ages. 8° *Cambridge*, 1890

Cuny, Charles. Observations générales sur le Mémoire sur le Soudan de M. le Comte d'Escayrac de Lauture. 8* *Paris*, 1858

—— Journal de Voyage de Siout à El-Obéid 1857-58. Introduction par Malte-Brun. *Map*. 8° *Paris*, 186:

Cunynghame, Lieut.-Gen. Sir A T. Travels in the Eastern Caucasus, on the Caspian and Black Seas, especially in Daghestan, and on the Frontiers of Persia and Turkey, during the Summer of 1871. *Maps*. 8° 1872

"Curaçoa." *See* Brenchley.

Curioni, Giulio. Sulla successione Normale dei diversi membri del Terreno Triasico nella Lombardia. *Plates*. 4* *Milan*, 1855

Curley, E. A. Nebraska, its Advantages, Resources, and Drawbacks. *Maps and plates*. 8° 1875

Curling, J. J. Coastal Navigation. *Chart and diagrams*. 8° 1885

Curr, Edward M. The Australian Race, its Origin, Languages, Customs, Place of Landing in Australia, and the Routes by which it spread itself over that Continent. 4 vols. (Vols. 1-3, 8°; Vol. 4, folio). *Map and illustrations* *Melbourne*, 1886-87

Currie, Sir Donald. Thoughts upon the Present and Future of South Africa, and Central and Eastern Africa. 8* 1877

—— Maritime Warfare: the Importance to the British Empire of a Complete System of Telegraphs, Coaling Stations, and Graving Docks. 8* 1877

Cursetjee, Manockjee. A Few Passing Ideas for the Benefit of India and Indians. 8° *Bombay*, 1853

Curson, Cardinal Robert. *See* Hakluyt, Vol. 2: Appendix 1.

Curtis, John G. C. Tables for Correcting Lunar Distances; with Rules for Finding the Errors and Rates of Chronometers. 8° 1836

Curtis, Joseph S. *See* United States, G, c: Appendix 2.

Curtis, Richard H. *See* Scott.

Curtis, —. Smithsonian Meteorological Tables. (Based on Guyot's Meteorological and Physical Tables.) Smithsonian Miscellaneous Collections, 844. 8°   *Washington*, 1893

Curtius, E., and F. Adler. Olympia und Umgegend. *Maps and plan.* 8° *Berlin*, 1882

Curzon, Hon. George N. Russia in Central Asia in 1889, and the Anglo-Russian Question; with Appendices and an Index. *Map and illustrations.* 8° 1889
—— Persia and the Persian Question. 2 vols. *Maps and illustrations.* 8° 1892

Curzon, Hon. Robert. Armenia : a Year at Erzeroom, and on the Frontiers of Russia, Turkey, and Persia. *Map and woodcuts.* 8°   1854
—— Visits to Monasteries in the Levant. 6th edition. *Illustrations.* 8° 1881

Cushing, —. Territory of Oregon : Report in Relation to Territory of the United States beyond the Rocky Mountains. 8*   *Washington*, 1839

Cushman, J. B. Legislative Honors to the Memory of President Lincoln. Message of Gov. Fenton to the Legislature, communicating the Death of President Lincoln. Obsequies of President Lincoln in the Legislature. 8° *Albany, N.Y.*, 1865

Cusieri, Odoardo. Storia Fisica e Politica dell' Egitto, della sua remota Antichità sino all' Epoca presente 1842. 3 vols. 8°   *Florence*, 1845

Cuspinianus, J. De Turcarum Origine, Religione, &c. 16° *Leyden*, 1654

Cust, Dr R. N. A Sketch of the Modern Languages of the East Indies. 2 *maps in cover.* 8°   1878
—— Table of Languages and Dialects of the East Indies. Square 8* 1878
—— Linguistic and Oriental Essays, written from the year 1846 to 1878. *Map.* 8°   1880
—— A Sketch of the Modern Languages of Africa. 2 vols. *Map and portraits.* 8°   1883
—— The Railway over the Sahara, from Algeria to the Senegal, and the Destruction of Colonel Flatters. *Map.* 8* 1884
—— Malaisch - Polynesische Abtheilung. 7 Internationaler Orientalisten - Congress, Wien. Mittheilung über unsere gegenwärtige Kenntniss der Sprachen Oceaniens. 8* 1886
—— Linguistic and Oriental Essays, written from the year 1847 to 1887. Second series. *Maps.* 8° 1887
—— Three Lists of Bible Translations actually accomplished, corrected up to 1st August 1890 : 1. Alphabetical ; 2. Geographical ; 3. Linguistic. *Frontispiece.* Square 8° 1890

Cust, Dr R. N. L'Occupation de l'Afrique par les Missionaires Chrétiens de l'Europe et de l'Amérique du Nord. 8* *Geneva*, 1891
—— Africa Rediviva ; or the Occupation of Africa by Christian Missionaries of Europe and North America. *Maps and frontispiece.* 8°   1891
—— [Communication on the above subject.] International Geographical Congress, Bern, Switzerland: Africa Section. 8* 1891
—— The Ethics of African Geographical Explory. 8*   [1892]
—— Remarks on the Position of the British Political Interests in Eastern Equatorial Africa in 1892. *Map.* 8* *Hertford*, 1892
—— Essay on the Progress of African Philology up to the year 1893. Prepared for the Congress of the World at Chicago, U.S. With three Appendices. 8*   1893

Custer, G. A. My Life on the Plains. 8° N.D.

Custine, Marquis de. Russia. Abridged from the French. 12°   1854

Cutler, T. Notes on Spa and its Chalybeate Springs. *Frontispiece.* Small 8° *Brussels*, 1854

Cutting, H. A. Observations on Ozone, and its Relation to Disease. 8* *Vermont*, 1874

Cuvier, Baron G. Essay on the Theory of the Earth. Translated from the French of M. Cuvier by Robert Kerr ; with Mineralogical Notes and an Account of Cuvier's Geological Discoveries, by Professor Jameson. *Plate.* 8° *Edinburgh*, 1813
—— Discours sur les Révolutions de la Surface du Globe, et sur les changemens qu'elles ont produits dans le Règne Animal. *Plates.* 4° *Paris*, 1826
—— and Alex. Brongniart. Essai sur la Géographie Minéralogique des Environs de Paris. *Maps and plates.* 4° *Paris*, 1811

Cybulz, G. Anwendung der Plastik beim Unterricht im Terrainzeichnen. *Plate.* 8* *Leipzig*, 1861

"Cygnet," Ship. *See* Burney, Vol. 4 : Appendix 1.

Czerny, Dr Franz. Die Wirkungen der Winde auf die Gestaltung der Erde. (Ergänzungsheft, 48—Petermann's Mittheilungen.) *Chart.* 4° *Gotha*, 1877

D

D——, M. A. The History of Prussia, from the Times of the Knights of the Cross and Sword to the Occupation of Hanover, 1867. Compiled . . . by M. A. D. 16°   1869

Daa, Ludvig K. Om Forholdet mellem det gamle og ny Fastlands Urbeboere. 8* *Christiania*, 1857

Daalmans, Aegidius. A Belgian Physician's Notes on Ceylon in 1687-89. Translated from the Dutch by D. W. Ferguson. (Extracted from Journal, No. 35, Volume 10, of the Royal Asiatic Society, Ceylon Branch.) 8* 1887

Da Cunha, J. Gerson. Notes on the History and Antiquities of Chaul and Bassein. *Maps, plates, and photographs.* Royal 8° *Bombay*, 1876

Da Cunha, L. M. do Couto de Albuquerque. Memorias para a Historia da Praça de Mazagão, revistas pelo Levy Maria Jordão. 4* *Lisbon*, 1864

Da Cunha, Nuno and Tristano. *See* Gottfried : Appendix 1.

Dadelszen, E. J. von. The New Zealand Official Year-Book, 1893. *Map.* 8° *Wellington*, 1893

—— Report on the Results of a Census of the Colony of New Zealand, taken for the night of the 5th April 1891. *Diagrams.* 8° *Wellington*, 1893

Daendels, H. W. Brieven, betreffende het Bestuur der Koloniën, en bevattende eene beoordeling van een Werkje, over dat onderwerp uitgegeven, getiteld : Java. -8° *Amsterdam*, 1816

D'Afflitto, D. L. Guida di Napoli. 2 vols in 1. 8° *Naples*, 1834

D'Agua, Izé, and J. Almeida. Algumas considerações acerca dos productos remettidos para a Exposição de Vienna de Austria no fim de Janeiro de 1873. 8° *Lisbon*, 1873

Dahl, W. F. *See* Baer and Helmersen, 7.

Dahlgren, Madeleine Vinton. Memoir of John A. Dahlgren, Rear-Admiral, United States Navy. *Portraits, map, and illustrations.* 8° *Boston, Mass.*, 1882

Dahse, Paulus. The Gold Coast. Translated from the German by Harry Bruce Walker. *Map.* 8* *Liverpool*, 1882

Daireaux, É. Buenos-Ayres, la Pampa, et la Patagonie. *Map.* 12° *Paris*, 1877

Dairs, J. The Jews in Roumania. 8* 1872

Dairs, J. B. On the Peculiar Crania of the Inhabitants of certain Groups of Islands in the Western Pacific. 4° *Haarlem*, 1866

D'Albertis, L. M. Journal of the Expedition for the Exploration of the Fly River. [Newspaper cuttings.] 8* *Sydney*, 1877

—— The same. *Map.* 8* *Sydney*, 1877

—— New Guinea Exploration. Extract from the Log-Book of the Steam-Launch "Neva." (N. S. W. Legislative Assembly Publication.). Folio* [*Sydney*, 1877]

—— New Guinea : What I did and what I saw. 2 vols. *Map and plates.* 8° 1880

—— *See* British New Guinea : Appendix 2.

D'Albuquerque. *See* Albuquerque.

Dalby, Isaac. *See* Mudge, Capt. ; Williams, Lieut.-Col. E.

Dale, R. Notes of an Excursion to the Isthmus of Tehuantepec, in the Republic of Mexico. *Map and plates.* 8° 1851

Dale, Sir Thomas. *See* Purchas, Vol. 4, Book 9 : Appendix 1.

Dalence, José Marie. Bosquejo Estadistico de Bolivia. 8° *Chuquisaca*, 1851

Dalhunty, —. *See* Portugal, A: Appendix 2.

Dall, William H. Alaska and its Resources. *Map and plates.* 8° *Boston*, 1870

—— Harbors of Alaska, and the Tides and Currents in their Vicinity. *Plates.* 4* [*Washington*, 1873]

—— Report of Geographical and Hydrographical Operations on the Coast of Alaska. *Map.* 4° [*Washington*, 1873]

—— Report on Mount St Elias. *Map and plate.* 8* [*Washington*, 1875]

—— On the so-called Chukchi and Namollo People of Eastern Siberia. 8* [*Philadelphia*] 1881

—— Notes on Alaska and the Vicinity of Bering Strait. *Map.* 8* [*New Haven, Conn.*, 1881]

—— *See* United States, F: Appendix 2.

Dallam, Thomas. *See* Hakluyt Soc. Publ., Vol., 87 : Appendix 1.

Dallas, A. G. San Juan, Alaska, and the North-West Boundary. 8° 1873

Dallas, James. *See* Catalogues, A : Appendix 2.

Dallas, R. C. The History of the Maroons, from their Origin to the Establishment of their Chief Tribe at Sierra Leone, including the Expedition to Cuba for the purpose of procuring Spanish Chasseurs, and the State of the Island of Jamaica for the last ten years ; with a Succinct History of the Island previous to that period. 2 vols. *Maps and illustrations.* 8° 1803

Dallas, W. L. Memoir of the Winds and Monsoons of the Arabian Sea and North Indian Ocean. *Plates.* 4* *Calcutta*, 1887

—— The Climatology of Afghanistan. (From J. United Service I. of India, Vol. 20, No. 88.) 8* [*Simla*, 1891]

Dallas, W. S. *See* Humboldt, A. von.

Dalla Torre, K. W. V. *See* Switzerland, B : Appendix 2.

Dalla Vedova, G. Il Concetto Popolare e il Concetto Scientifico della Geografia. 8* *Rome*, 1880

—— Pellegrino Matteucci ed il suo Diario inedito. *Map.* 8* *Rome*, 1885

—— *See* Ragazzi.

Dallaway, J. Constantinople, Ancient and Modern, with Excursions to the Shores and Islands of the Archipelago and to the Troad. *Map and plates.* 4° 1797

Dallet, C. Histoire de l'Église de Corée, précédée d'une Introduction sur l'Histoire, les Institutions, la Langue, les Mœurs, et Coutumes Coréennes. 2 vols. *Map and plates.* 8°　　*Paris*, 1874

D'Almeida. *See* Almeida.

D'Almeida, William Barrington. Life in Java; with Sketches of the Javanese. 2 vols. 8°　　　　　　　　1864

Dalrymple, Alexander. Historical Collection of the several Voyages and Discoveries in the South Pacific Ocean. 2 vols. in 1. *Maps.* 4°　　1770-71 [For Contents, *see* Appendix I.]

—— Collection of Nautical Memoirs and Journals, mostly published originally at the charge of the East India Company, now reprinted for the use of the Royal Navy. 4°　　　　　　　　1806

CONTENTS.

Dalrymple, Alexander. Essay on Nautical Surveying.

M'Cluer, John. Description of the Coast of India, 1787-90.

Dalrymple, A. General Remarks for the use of those who have not been accustomed to Navigate unfrequented Seas.

Macaulay, Hugh. Directions for Entering the Harbour of Olinchy, on the west side of the island Hai-lin, adjacent to the S. Coast of China.

Howel, Mr. Memoir of the harbour Heong-Kong.

Bissell, Capt. Austin. Voyage from England to the Red Sea, and along the East Coast of Arabia to Bombay, 1798-99.

Inverarity, Captain David. Memoir of a Chart of the N.W. Coast of Madagascar, 1803; and Comoro Islands, by the Hon. Thomas Howe, 1766.

Dalrymple, A. Memoir of a Chart of the Passages at the Southern Extremity of Asia.

Dalrymple, A. Catalogue of Authors who have written on Rio de la Plata, Paraguay, and Chaco, 1807.

—— Tracts, from 1764 to 1808. 3 vols. [For Contents, *see* Appendix I.]

—— Tracts, from 1769 to 1793. 4°

CONTENTS.

Vox Populi Vox Dei: Lord Weymouth's Appeal to a General Court of India Proprietors considered　　　1769

Scheme of a Voyage to Convey the Conveniences of Life to New Zealand　　　　　　　　　　　　　1771

Two Letters to the Court of Directors for Affairs of the United Company of Merchants of England trading to the East Indies, concerning the proposed Supervisorship　　　　　　　　1769

Dalrymple, Alexander—*continued.*

Letter to Dr Hawkesworth, occasioned by some groundless and illiberal imputations in his Account of the late Voyages to the South　　　　　1773

Observations on Dr Hawkesworth's Preface to the 2nd edition.

Reply to a Letter from Andrew Stuart, Esq., to the Hon. the Directors of the East India Company. [Account of the subversion of the Legal Government at Madras by imprisoning the Governor, Lord Pigot, in August 1776.]

Explanation of the Map of the East India Company's Lands on the Coast of Choromandel　　　　　　1778

Memoir on Watering the Circars　1793

—— Tracts, from 1791 to 1807. Royal 8°

CONTENTS.

Memorial to the East India Company 1791

The Poor Man's Friend　　　　1795

A Fragment on the India Trade, 1791
　　　　　　　　　　　　　　1797

Thoughts of an Old Man, of Independent Mind though Dependent Fortune, on the Present High Price of Corn 1800

Longitude: a Full Answer to the Advertisement concerning Mr Earnshaw's Timekeeper in the *Morning Chronicle*, 4th February, and *Times*, 13th February　　　　　　1806

On the Catholic Question, properly Roman Catholic Question　　1807

Notes on Two Letters to Brother Abraham concerning the Roman Catholics　　　　　　　　　1807

—— Catalogue of Printed Books and Tracts by, before 1st January 1792.

—— Catalogue of Authors who have written on Rio de la Plata, Paraguay, and Chaco. [With Manuscript and other Additions by Sir Woodbine Parish to 1840.] 4°　　　1807

—— Oriental Repertory: Vol. 1, from April 1791 to January 1793; Vol. 2, concluded in 1808. *Maps and plates.* 4° 1793-1808 [For Contents, *see* Appendix I.]

Dalrymple, G. Elphinstone. On the New Settlement in Rockingham Bay, and advance of Colonisation over North-Eastern Australia, including Mr Dalrymple's Report on his Journey from Rockingham Bay to the Valley of Lagoons. 8°　　　　　　　　1865

—— The Syrian Great Eastern Railway to India, by an entirely New Route. 8* 1878

—— *See* Smith, Joseph W.

Dalton, Capt. E. T. Correspondence and Journal of his Progress in a late Visit to a Clan of Abors on the Dihing River. [From the India Records, No. 23]　　　　　　　*Bengal*, 1855

—— Descriptive Ethnology of Bengal. *Lithograph portraits.* Large 4°　　　　　　　　　　　*Calcutta*, 1872

Dalton, Henry G. The History of British Guiana . . .; together with an Account of its Climate, Geology, Staple Products, and Natural History. 2 vols. *Map and plates.* 8° 1855

Dalton, Lieut.-Col. J. C. *See* Nadarov; Goodenough.

Dalton, John N. *See* "Bacchante."

Dalton, W. H. *See* Whitaker.

Dal Verme, Conte Luchino. Giappone e Siberia: Note d'un Viaggio nell' estremo Oriente al seguito di S. A. R. il Duca di Genova. *Maps and illustrations.* Folio* *Milan*, 1885

Daly, C. P. English Arctic Expedition. *Map.* 8* *Boston, Mass.*, 1877

Daly, Mrs Dominic D. Digging, Squatting, and Pioneering Life in the Northern Territory of South Australia. *Map.* 8° 1887

Daly, Lieut. H. Reports on the Northern Shan States. Folio* *Rangoon*, 1888-90

Daly, General H. D. Report on the Political Administration of the Territories comprised within the Central India Agency, for the year 1868-69   1869
—— Ditto, for 1869-70   1870
—— Ditto, for 1870-71   1871
—— Ditto, for 1871-72   1873
—— Ditto, for 1873-74. [From the India Records, Nos. 75, 82, 86, 102, 114.]

Dalzel, A. *See* Chevalier, M.

Dalzell, Archibald. The History of Dahomy, an Inland Kingdom of Africa, compiled from Authentic Memoirs; with Introduction and Notes. *Map and plates.* 4° 1793

Dalzell, N. A. Observations on the Influence of Forests, and on the General Principles of Management as applicable to Bombay. [From the India Records, No. 76.] 8° *Bombay*, 1863

Damberger, C. F. Travels in the Interior of Africa, from the Cape of Good Hope to Morocco, from the year 1781 to 1797, through Caffraria, the Kingdoms of Mataman, Angola, Massi, Monœmugi, Muschako, &c., likewise across the Great Desert of Sahara and the Northern Parts of Barbary. 2 vols. in 1. *Map and plate.* 8° *Dublin*, 1801

Damer, Hon. Mrs G. L. Dawson. Diary of a Tour in Greece, Turkey, Egypt, and the Holy Land. 2 vols. *Plates.* 12° 1841

Dames, Dr Wilhelm. *See* Richthofen.

Dampier, Capt. William. A New Voyage round the World, describing particularly the Isthmus of America. *Maps.* 8° 1697
—— New Voyage round the World, describing particularly the Isthmus of America, several Coasts and Islands in the West Indies, the Isles of Cape Verde,

Dampier, Capt. William—*continued.* the Passage by Terra del Fuego, the South Sea Coasts of Chili, Peru, and Mexico, the Isle of Guam, one of the Ladrones, Mindanao, and other Philippine and East India Islands near Cambodia, China, Formosa, Luconia, Celebes, &c., New Holland, Sumatra, Nicobar Isles, the Cape of Good Hope, and Santa Hellena; their Soil, Rivers, Harbours, Plants, Fruits, Animals, and Inhabitants; their Customs, Religion, Government, Trade, &c. 4 vols. *Maps and plates.* 8° 1729
—— *See* Drake, Sir F.; *also* Hakluyt Soc. Publ., Vol. 25; Callander, Vol. 2; Harris, Vol. 1; Kerr, Vol. 10; Laharpe, Vol. 15; Pinkerton, Vol. 11; Allgemeine Historie, Vol. 12; New Collection, Vol. 3, p. 608; The World Displayed, Vol. 6, p. 609: Appendix 1.

Dana, E. S. Contributions to the Petrography of the Sandwich Islands. (From the *American Journal of Science*, No. 37, March 1889.) *Illustrations.* 8* [1889]

Dana, Dr James D. On an Isothermal Oceanic Chart, illustrating the Geographical Distribution of Marine Animals. *Map.* 8* *Washington*, 1853
—— 1. On Parallel Relations of the Classes of Vertebrates, and on some Characteristics of the Reptilian Birds. 2. The Classification of Animals based on the Principle of Cephalisation; on Fossil Insects from the Carboniferous Formation in Illinois. 3. Classification of Herbivores; Note on the Position of Amphibians among the Classes of Vertebrates. 8° *New Haven, Conn.*, 1863-64
—— Corals and Coral Islands. *Plates.* 8° 1872
—— The same. 3rd edition. *Maps and illustrations.* Large 8° *New York* [1890]
—— On Volcanic Eruptions of Barren Island, Vesuvius, and Kilauea. (From the *American Journal of Science*, Vol. 31, May 1886.) 8* 1886
—— A Dissected Volcanic Mountain: some of its revelations. (From the *American Journal of Science*, No. 190.) 8* *New Haven, Conn.*, 1886
—— Kilauea after the Eruption. (From the *American Journal of Science*, Vol. 33.) 8* [1887]
—— Papers on the Volcanic and Geological History of the Hawaiian Islands. (From the *American Journal of Science*, Nos. 33-37, June 1887 to March 1889.) *Maps and illustrations.* 8* [1887-89]
—— Areas of Continental Progress in North America, and the Influence of the Conditions of these Areas on the Work carried forward within them. (From the *Bull. Geol. Soc., America*, Vol. 1, 1889.) 8* [1889]

Dana, Dr James D. On the Origin of the Deep Troughs of the Oceanic Depression : Are any of Volcanic Origin? (From the *American Journal of Science.*) *Map.* 8* [*New Haven, Conn.*, 1889]

Danckelman, Dr A. von. Die meteorologischen Beobachtungen der Güssfeldt'- schen Loango-Expedition. Nebst einem Anhang, Resultate der Beobachtungen von Dr O. Lenz am Ogowe. *Plate.* 4° *Leipzig,* 1878

—— Association Internationale du Congo. Mémoire sur les Observations Météorologiques faites à Vivi (Congo Inférieur) et sur la Climatologie de la Côte sudouest d'Afrique en général. *Map and plates.* 4* *Berlin,* 1884

—— Beiträge zur Kenntniss des Klimas des Deutschen Togolandes und seiner Nachbargebiete an der Gold und Sklaven Küste. *Plan and plate.* 8* *Berlin,* 1890

Danckwerth, Caspar, and J. Meyer. Newe Landesbeschreibung der zweij Hertzogthümer Schleswich und Holstein, zusambt vielen dabeij gehörigen newen I andkarten, die auff Ihr Königl. Maijtt. zu Dennemarck, Norwegen, &c., und Ihr Fürstl. Dürchl. beeder regierenden Hertzogen zu Schleswich Holstein, &c., aller und gnadigsten befehle von dero Königl. Maijtt. bestalten Mathematico Johanne Mejero, Hus. Cimbro, Chorographice Elaborirt, dürch Casparum Danckwerth, D., zusammen getragen und verfertigt. Vorin auch das alte Teütschland kürtzlich beschrieben, mitbegriffen ist. *Maps.* Folio N.P., 1652 [Register published by J. J. Babst, Glückstat, annexed.]

Dandini, Jerom. *See* Churchill, Vol. 7 ; Pinkerton, Vol. 10 : Appendix 1.

Danenhower, Lieut. J. W. The Polar Question. *Map.* 8* *Annapolis, Md.,* 1885

Dangar, H. Index and Directory to Map of the Country bordering upon the River Hunter, the Lands of the Australian Agricultural Company ; with the Ground-Plan and Allotments of King's Town, New South Wales. *Plate.* 8° 1828

Dangerfield, Capt. *See* India, C (Geological Papers) : Appendix 2.

Daniel, H. A. Lehrbuch der Geographie für höhere Unterrichtsanstalten. (49th edition) herausgegeben von Dr A. Kirchhoff. 12° *Halle,* 1878

—— Leitfaden für den Unterricht in der Geographie. (125th edition) herausgegeben von Dr A. Kirchhoff. 12° *Halle,* 1879

—— Kleineres Handbuch der Geographie. Auszug aus des Verfassers Vierbändigem Werke. 4th edition. 8° *Leipzig,* 1883

—— *See* Ritter.

Daniell, J. F. Observations on a New Hygrometer, which Measures the Force and Weight of Aqueous Vapour in the Atmosphere, and the Corresponding Degree of Evaporation. 8* [1820]

Daniell, Samuel, and William Daniell. Sketches representing the Native Tribes, Animals, and Scenery of Southern Africa. 48 *plates.* 4° 1820

Daniell, W. F. Sketches of the Medical Topography and Native Diseases of the Gulf of Guinea, Western Africa. 8° 1849

—— Observations on the Copals of Western Africa. 8* 1857

Danielssen, D. C. *See* Norway, A (North Atlantic Expedition) : Appendix 2.

Danilowitsch, ——. *See* Baer and Helmersen, 10.

Dankovsky, Gregor. Die Griechen als Stamm- und Sprachverwandte der Slawen. Historisch und Philologisch. 8° *Pressburg,* 1828

Danks, B. *See* Brown and Danks.

Danti, Egnatio. Egnazio Danti, Cosmografo e Matematico e le sue opere in Firenze. Memoria Storica di Iodoco Del Badia. 8* *Florence,* 1881

Danvers, F. C. India (Spon's Information for Colonial Engineers, edited by J. T. Hurst, No. 3). *Map.* 8° 1877

—— Report to the Secretary of State for India in Council on the Records of the India Office. Vol. 1, Part 1. *Map.* 8° 1887

—— Bengal, its Chief Agents and Governors. 8* [1888]

—— Report to the Secretary of State for India in Council on the Portuguese Records relating to the East Indies contained in the Archivo da Torre do Tombo, and the Public Libraries at Lisbon and Evora. 8° 1892

Danvers, Juland. Report to the Secretary of State for India in Council on Railways in India to the end of the year 1859. The same, for the years 1860-61, 1861-62, 1862-63, 1863-64, 1864-65, 1865-66, 1866-67, 1867-68, 1868-69, 1879-80. *Maps.* Folio 1860-69, 1880

Dapontès, Constantin. Éphémérides Daces, ou Chronique de la Guerre de quatre ans (1736-1739). Publiée, traduite, et annotée par Émile Legrand. I, Texte Grec. [No. 14 of Publ. de l'Éc. des Langues Orient. Viv.] 8° *Paris,* 1880

—— Ditto. II. Traduction. [No. 15 of Publ. de l'Éc. des Langues Orient. Viv.] *Portrait.* Large 8° *Paris,* 1881

—— Ditto. III. [No. 20 of Publ. de l'Éc. des Langues Orient. Viv.] Large 8° *Paris,* 1888

Dapper, O. Beschryving des Keizerryks van Taising of Sina, vertoont in de Benaming, Grens-palen, Steden, Stroomen, Bergen, Gewassen, Dieren, Gods-dienst, Tale, Letteren, &c. *Plates.* Folio
Amsterdam, 1670

—— Gedenkwaerdig ·Bedryf der Nederlandsche Oost-Indische Maetschappye, op de Kuste en in het Keizerrijk van Taising of Sina ; behelzende het tweede Gezandschap aen den Onderkoning Singlamong en Veldheer Taising Lipoui ; door J. van Kampen en K. Nobel. Vervolgt met een verhael van het voorgevallen des jaers 1603, 4, en 6, op de Kuste van Sina, en ontrent d'Eilanden Tayowan, Formosa, ay en Quemuy, onder't gezag van B. Bort ; en het derde Gezandschap aen Konchy, Tartarsche Keizer van Sina en Oost-Tartarye, onder P. van Hoorn. [*Imperfect.*] *Map and plates.* Folio *Amsterdam*, 1670

—— Asia, of Naukeurige beschryving van het rijk des Grooten Mogols, en een groot gedeelte van Indiën ; behelsende de Landschappen van Kandahar, Kabul, Multan, Haïkan, Bukkar, Send of Diu, Jesselmeer, Attak, Penjab, Kaximir, Jangapore, Dely, Mando, Malva, Chitor, Utrad, Zuratte of Kambaye, Chandisch, Narvar, Gwaliar, Indostan, Sanhat, Bakar, Nagrakat, Dekan, en Visiapour ; beneffens een volkome beschryving van geheel Persie, Georgie, Mengrelie, en andere Gebuur-gewesten, vertoont in de Benamingen, Grens-palen, Steden, Gewassen, Dieren, &c. *Map and plates.* Folio *Amsterdam*, 1672

—— Naukeurige Beschryving van Asie ; behelsende de gewesten van Mesopotamie, Babylonie, Assyrie, Anatolie, of Klein Asie ; beneffens eene volkome Beschrijving van gantsch, Gelukkigh, Woest, en Petreesch of Steenigh Arabie. Vertoont in een bondigh ontwerp van's Lants benamingen, bepalingen, verdeilingen, steden, vlekken, gewassen, dieren, zeden, en aert der inwoonders, bestiering, geschiedenissen en godsdienst, inzonderheit die van d'oude Arabieren, Mahomet en Mahometanen. 2 vols. *Map and plates.* Folio *Amsterdam*, 1680

—— Description de l'Afrique, contenant les Noms, la Situation, et les Confins de toutes ses Parties, leurs Rivières, leurs Villes, et leurs Habitations, leurs Plantes et leurs Animaux ; les Coûtumes, la Langue, les Richesses, la Religion, et le Gouvernement de ses Peuples. *Maps and plates.* Folio *Amsterdam*, 1686

—— Beschryving van Eilanden der Archipel, eertijts Egeesche Zee, nu Archipel, en de Eilanden Cyprus, Rhodos, S. Stefanio, Karpathos, Kasos, Kos of Lango, Nizaria, &c. [*Imperfect.*] *Maps and plates.* Folio 1688

Dapper, O. Naukeurige beschryving van Morea eertijts Peloponnesus; en de Eilanden, gelegen onder de Kusten van Morea, en binnen en buiten de Golf van Venetien; waer onder de voornaemste Korfu, Cefalonia, Santa Maura, Zanten, en andere in grooten getale ; behelzende derzelver Lantschappen, Steden, Rivieren, Poelen, Bergen, Gewassen, Dieren, &c. *Maps and plates.* Folio *Amsterdam*, 1688

D'Aramon. *See* Aramon.

Darapsky, Dr L. Las Aguas Mineralis de Chile. *Illustrations.* 8°
Valparaiso, 1890

Darby, William. View of the United States, Historical, Geographical, and Statistical. *Maps.* 18°
Philadelphia, 1828

—— **and Theodore Dwight.** A New Gazetteer of the United States of America : containing a Copious Description of the States, Territories, Counties, Parishes, Districts, Cities, and Towns ; Mountains, Lakes, Rivers, and Canals ; Commerce, Manufactures, Agriculture, and the Arts generally, of the United States ; also the Extent, Boundaries, and Natural Productions of the Principal Subdivisions, the Latitude and Longitude of Cities and Towns, and their Bearing and Distance from Important Places, with the Population of 1830. 8°
Hartford, Conn., 1833

Dard, J. Dictionnaire Français-Wolof, Français-Bambara, suivi du Dictionnaire Wolof-Français. 8° *Paris*, 1825

—— Grammaire Wolofe, ou méthode pour étudier la Langue des Noirs qui habitent les Royaumes de Bourba-Yolof, de Walo, de Damel, de Bour-Sine, de Saloume, de Baole, en Sénégambie ; suivie d'un Appendice où sont établies les particularités les plus essentielles des Principales Langues de l'Afrique Septentrionale. 8°
Paris, 1826

Dardye. *See* Bourgade la Dardye.

Daron, Étienne Açogh'ig de. Histoire Universelle. Traduite de l'Arménien et annotée par E. Dulaurier. 1ère partie. [18 of Publ. de l'Éc. des Langues Orient. Viv.] Large 8° *Paris*, 1883

Darondeau, B. Mélanges Hydrographiques, ou Recueil de Documents relatifs à l'Hydrographie et à la Navigation ; Extraits des Annales Maritimes et Coloniales publiées par MM. Bajot et Poirré. 3 vols. in 2. *Maps.* 8°
Paris, 1846

—— Notice sur les Erreurs des Compas dues aux attractions locales à bord des Navires en Bois et en Fer, suivie d'Instructions sur les moyens de déterminer ces Erreurs et de les corriger. 8*
Paris, 1858

Darondeau, J. B. Tableau Général des Phares et Fanaux des Côtes de Hollande et de Belgique. 8°   *Paris*, 1849
—— Tableau Général des Phares et Fanaux des Côtes Orientales de l'Amérique du Nord. 8°   *Paris*, 1851
—— Tableau Général des Phares et Fanaux des Côtes de la Méditerranée, de la Mer Noire et de la Mer d'Azoff. 8°   *Paris*, 1852
—— *See* Horsburgh, J ; Kerrhallet ; Vaillant.
Darrah, H. Z. *See* India, I (Assam) : Appendix 2.
Darwin, Charles. Geological Observations on the Volcanic Islands visited during the Voyage of H.M.S. "Beagle," together with some brief Notices on the Geology of Australia and the Cape of Good Hope : being the second part of the Geology of the Voyage of the "Beagle," &c. *Map.* 8° *London*, 1844
—— Geological Observations on South America : being the third part of the Geology of the Voyage of the "Beagle" . . . 1832 to 1836. *Map.* 8°   1846
—— The Structure and Distribution of Coral Reefs. 2nd edition. *Plates.* Small 8°   1874
—— The Life and Letters of Charles Darwin, including an Autobiographical Chapter. Edited by his son Francis Darwin. 3 vols. *Portraits and illustrations.* 8°   1887
—— Journal of Researches into the Natural History and Geology of the Countries visited during the Voyage of H.M.S. "Beagle" Round the World, under the command of Capt. Fitzroy, R.N. (From the corrected and enlarged edition of 1845.) *Illustrations.* 12°   1889
—— The same. A new edition. *Illustrations.* 8°   1890
—— On the Structure and Distribution of Coral Reefs ; also Geological Observations on the Volcanic Islands and parts of South America visited during the Voyage of H.M.S. "Beagle." With . . . a Critical Introduction to each work by Prof. John W. Judd, F.R.S. *Maps and illustrations.* 12°   1890
—— *See* Fitzroy.
Darwin, Prof. G. On Maps of the World. *Plate.* 8*   1875
Darwin, Major Leonard. On the Projection and Use of Maps for Military Purposes. Folio*   1890
—— *See* United Kingdom, G, War Office Publ. : Appendix 2.
Das. *See* Chandra Das.
Dassel, T. *See* Astley, Vol. 1 ; Hakluyt, Vol. 3 ; Kerr, Vol. 7 ; Allgemeine Historie, Vol. 1 : Appendix 1.
Dassy, G. F. Notes on Sueis, with Tables of Exports and Imports. 8*   *Constantinople*, 1859

Dati, Giuliano. La Lettera dell' Isole che ha trovato nuovamente il Re di Spagna. Poemetto in ottava rima. Publicato per cura di Gustavo Uzielli. 12°   *Bologna*, 1873
Daubeny, C. A Description of Active and Extinct Volcanos, of Earthquakes and of Thermal Springs ; with Remarks on the Causes, &c. 2nd edition. *Maps.* 8°   1848
Daubeny, Henry. The Climate of San Remo as adapted to Invalids. 8*   1865
Daubrée, A. Expériences Synthétiques relatives aux Météorites. Rapprochements auxquels ces expériences conduisent, tant pour la Formation de ces Corps Planetaires que pour celle du Globe Terrestre. 8*   *Paris*, 1866
—— Rapport sur les progrès de la Géologie Expérimentale. 4*   *Paris*, 1867
—— Les Eaux Souterraines aux Époques Anciennes, rôle qui leur revient dans l'Origine et les Modifications de la Substance de l'Écorce terrestre. *Maps and illustrations.* 8°   *Paris*, 1887
—— Les Eaux Souterraines à l'Époque Actuelle, leur Régime, leur Température, leur Composition au point de vue du rôle qui leur revient dans l'Économie de l'Écorce terrestre. 2 vols. *Maps and illustrations.* 8°   *Paris*, 1887
—— Recherches expérimentales sur le rôle possible des Gaz à hautes températures donnés de très fortes pressions et animés d'un Mouvement fort rapide dans divers Phénomènes Géologiques. 8*   *Paris*, 1891
—— Application de la méthode expérimentale au rôle possible des Gaz Souterrains dans l'histoire des Montagnes Volcaniques. 8*   *Paris*, 1892
Daulphinois, Nicholas N. *See* Churchill, Vol. 8 : Appendix 1.
D'Audiffret Pasquier, Duke. *See* United Kingdom, G, War Office Publ. : Appendix 2.
Daumas, F. *See* Arbousset.
Daumas, Lieut.-Col. Le Sahara Algérien : Études Géographiques, Statistiques, et Historiques, sur la Région au sud des Établissements Français en Algérie. *Map.* Royal 8°   *Paris*, 1845
—— and — **Fabar.** La Grande Kabylie : Études Historiques. *Table.* Royal 8°   *Paris*, 1847
Daunou, P. C. F. De la America Meridional, con algunas Observaciones acerca de este importante objeto. 8*   *Buenos Ayres*, N.D.
Daussy, Pierre. Second Mémoire sur les Marées de Côtes de France. 8°   *Paris*, 1838
—— L'Influence de la Pression Atmosphérique sur le Niveau moyen de la Mer. 8*   *Paris*, 1839

Daussy, Pierre. Nouvelle Méthode pour calculer la Marche des Chronomètres. 8*   *Paris*, 1841
—— Table des Positions Géographiques des principaux lieux du Globe, 1836, '37, 40, '41, '42, '43, '44, '46, '47, '48, '50, '51, '54-56. 8*
—— Mémoire Descriptif de la Route de Téhran à Meched et de Meched a Jezd, reconnue en 1807 par M. Truilhier, suivi d'un Mémoire les Observations faites en 1807, par le Capitaine Truilhier, dans son Voyage en Perse. *Maps.* 8°
                                                 Paris, 1841
—— Notice sur la Vie et les Travaux de, par M. de la Roquette. *Portrait.* 8*
                                                 Paris, 1861
—— *See* Hell, X. H. de; Truilhier, Capt.
Davenport and Comelati. *See* Dictionaries, Italian : Appendix 2.
Davey, Thomas. *See* Canada, G : Appendix 2.
David, A. Journal de mon troisième Voyage d'Exploration dans l'Empire Chinois. 2 vols. *Maps.* Small 8°
                                                 Paris, 1875
David, T. W. Edgeworth. *See* New South Wales, B : Appendix 2.
Davids, Arthur Lumley. Grammar of the Turkish Language, with a Discourse on the Language and Literature of the Turkish Nations, a copious Vocabulary, Dialogues, a Collection of Extracts in Prose and Verse, and lithographed Specimens of various Ancient and Modern Manuscripts. 4°   1832
Davidson, Prof. George. Directory for the Pacific Coast of the United States. 8°   *Washington*, 1858
—— The Abrasions of the Continental Shores of N.W. America, and the supposed ancient Sea-levels. 8*   1873
—— The Shoaling of the Bar at the Entrance to San Francisco Harbour. 8*
                                                 [*San Francisco*, 1884]
—— Identification of Sir Francis Drake's Anchorage on the Coast of California in the year 1579. *Maps and plates.* Large 8*   [1890]
—— The Discovery of Humboldt Bay, California. *Maps and plate.* 8*
                                                 San Francisco, 1891
—— Early Voyages on the North-Western Coast of America. 8*
                                                 [*Washington*, 1894]
—— *See* United States, F, Coast and Geodetic Survey : Appendix 2.
Davidson, G. F. Trade and Travel in the Far East; or, Recollections of Twenty-one Years passed in Java, Singapore, Australia, and China. 12°   1846
Davidson, James Wood. The Florida of To-Day : a Guide for Tourists and Settlers. *Maps and illustrations.* 12°
                                                 New York, 1889

Davidson, John. Notes taken during Travels in Africa. *Plates.* 4°
                                   Privately printed, 1839
Davie, J. Constanse. Letters from Paraguay, describing the Settlements of Monte Video and Buenos Ayres, the Presidencies of Rioja Minor, Nombre de Dios, St Mary, and St John, &c. 8°
                                                          1805
Davies, E. W. L. Algiers in 1857, its Accessibility, Climate, and Resources Described, with especial reference to English Invalids. *Plates.* 8°   1858
Davies, John. *See* Olearius.
Davies, R. H. Report on the Trade and Resources of the Countries on the North-Western Boundary of British India. 8°
                                                 Lahore, 1862
—— Central Asia. Report on the Trade and Resources of the Countries on the North-Western Boundary of British India. [Parliamentary Report.] Folio*
                                                          1864
Davies, Walter. General View of the Agriculture and Domestic Economy of South Wales; containing the Counties of Brecon, Caermarthen, Cardigan, Glamorgan, Pembroke, Radnor. 2 vols. *Maps.* 8°   1815
Davies, William. The Pilgrimage of the Tiber, from its Mouth to its Source; with some account of its Tributaries. *Map and plates*   1873
Davies, William. *See* Purchas, Vol. 4, Book 6 : Appendix 1.
Davila, Gil Gonzales. *See* Gottfried : Appendix 1.
Davila, Pedrarias. *See* Hakluyt Soc. Publ., Vol. 34; Gottfried : Appendix 1.
Davis, Andrew M'Farland. The Journey of Moncacht-Apé, an Indian of the Yazoo Tribe, across the Continent, about the year 1700. 8*   *Worcester, Mass.*, 1883
Davis, Rear-Admiral Charles H. Report on Interoceanic Canals and Railroads between the Atlantic and Pacific Oceans. *Maps.* 8°   *Washington*, 1867
—— *See* "Polaris"; Schubert; *also* United States, E, *a* : Appendix 2.
Davis, C. O. The Life and Times of Patuone, the celebrated Ngapuhi Chief. *Portrait.* 12°   *Auckland*, 1876
Davis, Edw. *See* Burney, Vol. 4 : Appendix 1.
Davis, E. J. Anatolica; or, The Journal of a Visit to some of the Ancient Ruined Cities of Caria, Phrygia, Lycia, and Pisidia. *Map and plates.* 8°   1874
—— Life in Asiatic Turkey : a Journal of Travel in Cilicia (Pedias and Trachæa), Isauria, and parts of Lycaonia and Cappadocia. *Map and plates.* 8°   1879
Davis, G. G. *See* Keely.

Davis, James Davidson. Contributions towards a Bibliography of New Zealand. 12* *Wellington*, 1887

Davis, Joachin, and M. Perez. Tablero del Palenque. Traducido por J. Davis and M. Perez. (From the Anales del Museo National.) *Plates.* 4* *Mexico*, 1880

Davis, John. *See* Markham, C. R. ; *also* Astley, Vol. 1 ; Gottfried ; Hakluyt, Vols. 3, 4 ; Hakluyt Soc. Publ., Vols. 5, 59 ; Kerr, Vols. 8, 10 ; Purchas, Vol. 1, Book 4 ; Allgemeine Historie, Vols. 1, 17 : Appendix 1.

Davis, John. *See* Westgarth.

Davis, Joseph Barnard. Thesaurus Craniorum : Catalogue of the Skulls of the Various Races of Man in the Collection of J. B. D. *Plates.* 8° 1867

Davis, Capt. J. E. *See* United Kingdom, A, Miscellaneous : Appendix 2.

—— **and P. L. H. Davis.** Sun's True Bearing ; or, Azimuth Tables, computed for intervals of four minutes, &c., with Variation Chart, and Instructions in Danish, &c. *Map.* 8° 1875

Davis, Richard Harding. An American in Africa [W. A. Chanler]. (From *Harper's Magazine*, March 1893.) *Portrait.* 8* 1893

Davis, Sir J. F. Chinese Novels, translated from the Originals ; to which are added Proverbs and Moral Maxims, collected from their Classical Books, &c., with Observations on the Language and Literature of China. 8° 1822

—— Chinese Moral Maxims, with a Free and Verbal Translation. 8* *Macao*, 1823

—— The Chinese : a General Description of the Empire of China and its Inhabitants. 2 vols. *Woodcuts.* 12° 1836

—— Chusan ; with a Survey Map of the Island. 8* 1853

—— China : a General Description of that Empire and its Inhabitants ; with the History of Foreign Intercourse down to the Events which produced the Dissolution of 1857. Vol. 1 only. *Illustrations.* 8° 1857

—— Chinese Miscellanies : a Collection of Essays and Notes. 8° 1865

Davis, J. W., and F. A. Lees. West Yorkshire : an Account of its Geology, Physical Geography, Climatology, and Botany. Part 1, Geography ; Part 2, Physical Geography and Botanical Topography. *Maps and plates.* 8° 1878

Davis, N. Ruined Cities within Numidian and Carthaginian Territories. *Map and plates.* 8° *London*, 1862

Davis, Lieut. S. *See* Turner, Capt. Samuel.

Davis, William. *See* Churchill, Vol. 7 : Appendix 1.

Davis, Prof. William M. On the Classification of Lake Basins. 8* *Boston, Mass.*, 1882

—— The Little Mountains east of the Catskills. *Plate.* 8* [1882]

—— Geographic Methods in Geologic Investigation. Lecture delivered before the National Geographic Society at Washington, 27th April 1888. (From the *National Geographic Magazine*, Vol. 1, No. 1.) 8* 1888

—— The Rivers and Valleys of Pennsylvania. *Map.* 8* *Washington*, 1889

—— Structure and Origin of Glacial Sand Plains. *Plate.* 8* *Washington*, 1890

—— **and J. Walter Wood, junr.** The Geographic Development of Northern New Jersey. Large 8* *Salem, Mass.*, 1890

Davison, G. M. Traveller's Guide through the Middle and Northern States, and the Provinces of Canada. 8° *Saratoga Springs*, 1840

Davison, —. *See* Walpole, Turkey : Appendix 1.

Davy, John. An Account of the Interior of Ceylon and of its Inhabitants, with Travels in that Island. *Map and plates.* 4° 1821

—— Notes and Observations on the Ionian Islands and Malta, with Remarks on Constantinople and Turkey. *Plates.* 2 vols. 8° 1842

—— *See* Eyriès, Vol. 13 : Appendix 1.

Davy, John. *See* Purchas, Vol. 1 : Appendix 1.

Dawkins, Prof. W. Boyd. Cave Hunting : Researches on the Evidence of Caves respecting the Early Inhabitants of Europe. *Plate.* 8° 1874

—— Early Man in Britain, and his Place in the Tertiary Period. *Woodcuts.* 8° 1880

Dawson, Alfred. *See* Leyland.

Dawson, Dr George M. British North American Boundary Commission. Report of the Geology and Resources of the Region in the Vicinity of the Forty-Ninth Parallel, from the Lake of the Woods to the Rocky Mountains, with Lists of Plants and Animals collected, and Notes on the Fossils. *Maps and plates.* 8° *Montreal*, 1875

—— Notes and Observations on the Kwakiool People of Vancouver Island. (From the Transactions of the Royal Society of Canada, Vol. 5, Sec. 2, 1887.) *Plate.* 4* *Montreal*, 1888

—— Geological and Natural History. Survey of Canada : Report on an Exploration in the Yukon District, N.W.T., and adjacent Northern Portion of British Columbia, 1887. *Maps and plates.* Large 8° *Montreal*, 1888

Dawson, Dr George M. Notes on the Indian Tribes of the Yukon District, and adjacent Northern Portion of British Columbia. 8* [*Montreal*, 1889]

—— Geological and Natural History Survey of Canada : The Mineral Wealth of British Columbia, with an Annotated List of Localities of Minerals of Economic Value. Large 8° *Montreal*, 1889

—— On Some of the Larger Unexplored Regions of Canada. *Map.* 8* *Ottawa*, 1890

—— On the Later Physiographical Geology of the Rocky Mountain Region in Canada, with Special Reference to Changes in Elevation and to the History of the Glacial Period. (From the Transactions of the Royal Society of Canada, Vol. 8, sec. 4.) *Maps.* 4* 1890

—— On the Glaciation of the Northern Part of the Cordillera ; with an Attempt to Correlate the Events of the Glacial Period in the Cordillera and Great Plains. (From *The American Geologist* for September 1890.) 8* 1890

—— Notes on the Shuswap People of British Columbia. (Reprint from Trans. Roy. Soc., Canada.) *Map.* 4* 1891

—— Note on the Geological Structure of the Selkirk Range. (Bulletin of the Geological Society of America,| Vol. 2, pp. 165-176.) 8* *Rochester*, 1891

—— Notes on the Geology of Middleton Island, Alaska. (From Bulletin Geol. Soc.. Am., Vol. 4.) Large 8* 1892

—— *See* Mackenzie, A. ; Selwyn ; *also* Canada, A : Appendix 2.

—— **and A. Sutherland.** Elementary Geography of the British Colonies. *Illustrations.* 12° 1892

Dawson, Sir J. William. Observations on the Geology of the Line of the Canadian Pacific Railway. *Map and sections.* 8* [1884]

—— British Association for the Advancement of Science : Address by Sir J. William Dawson. 8* 1886

—— The Geology of Nova Scotia, New Brunswick, and Prince Edward Island ; or, Acadian Geology. 4th edition. *Map and illustrations.* Large 8° 1891

—— *See* Canada, A, Geological Survey : Appendix 2.

—— **and B. J. Harrington.** Report on the Geological Structure and Mineral Resources of Prince Edward Island. *Map and plates.* 8° *Montreal*, 1871

Dawson, Commander L. S. Memoirs of Hydrography, including brief Biographies of the Principal Officers who have served in H.M. Naval Surveying Service between the years 1750 and 1885. 2 parts. *Portraits.* Large 8° *Eastbourne*, 1885

Dawson, S. J. Rapport sur l'Exploration de la Contrée située entre le Lac Supérieur et la Colonie de la Rivière Rouge et entre ce dernier endroit et les rivières Assiniboine et Saskatchewan. *Maps.* 4° [Also in English.] *Toronto*, 1859

Day, Capt. C. R. *See* Mockler-Ferryman.

Day, David. S. *See* United States, G, *c* (Statistical Papers): Appendix 2.

Day, F. The Fishes of India : being a Natural History of the Fishes known to Inhabit the Seas and Freshwaters of India, Burma, and Ceylon. Vols. 1 and 2. *Plates.* 4° 1876-78

Day, St John V. The Iron and Steel Industries of Scotland. [Bound up with Papers by John Fergusson, John Mayer, and James Paton, for the British Association Meeting at Glasgow, 1876.] 12° *Glasgow*, 1876

Dayman, Commander Jos. Deep-Sea Soundings in the North Atlantic Ocean, between Ireland and Newfoundland, made in H.M.S. "Cyclops," in 1857. *Maps and plates.* 8° 1858

De —. For French names such as De Candolle, *see under principal word.*

Deakin, Hon. Alfred. Irrigated India : an Australian View of India and Ceylon, their Irrigation and Agriculture. *Map.* 8° 1893

Deane, A. Ceylon. (Spon's Information for Colonial Engineers, edited by J. T. Hurst, No. 1.) 8* 1875

Deane, H. S. Report on a Preliminary Survey of the State of Perak, its Position, Boundaries, Area, what Portions are Available for Plantations, the Various Means of Transport, and the Description of Survey adapted to its Present and Future Requirements. 8* *Singapore*, 1880

Debaize, Abbé, et sa Mission Géographique et Scientifique dans l'Afrique Centrale, par Alfred Rabaud. *Portrait.* 8° *Marseilles*, 1880

Debenham, J. A New Theory of the Tides, in which the Errors of the Usual Theory are Demonstrated. 8* 1846

Debes, L. J. Færœe et Færoa reserata. Det er : Færœernis oc Færœeske Indbyggeris Beskrifvelse, &c. 12° *Copenhagen*, 1673

Dechen, H. von. Anzeige der geognostischen Karte von Deutschland, England, Frankreich, und den Nachbarländern. 8* *Berlin*, 1839

—— Sammlung der Höhenmessungen in der Rhein provinz, geordnet nach den Methoden und den Linien der Nivellements, &c. 8° *Bonn*, 1852

—— Geognostischer Führer in das Siebengebirge am Rhein. Mit mineralogischpetrographischen Bemerkungen von Dr G. vom Rath. *Map.* 12° *Bonn*, 1861

Dechen, H. von. Geognostischer Führer zu der Vulkanreihe der Vorder-Eifel. 12° *Bonn*, 1861
—— Geognostischer Führer zu dem Laacher See und seiner vulkanischen Umgebung. 12° *Bonn*, 1864
Dechevrens, Marc. Recherches sur les principaux Phénomènes de Météorologie et de Physique Terrestre. 8* *Versailles*, 1877
—— Recherches sur les Variations des Vents à Zi-Ka-Wei, d'après les observation faites de 1873 à 1877. 4* *Zi-Ka-Wei*, 1877
—— La Lumière Zodiacale étudiée d'après les observations faites de 1875 à 1879. *Plate.* 4* *Zi-Ka-Wei*, 1879
——·Le Typhon du 31 Juillet 1879. 4* *Zi-Ka-Wei*, 1879
Déchy, Moriz von. Mittheilungen über Bergreisen im Kaukasus, 1884-87. Folio* *Vienna*, 1889
—— Recherches sur l'Orographie et la Glaciologie du Caucase Central. [Extrait d'une lecture donnée à la séance du 9 Août au Congres du Paris.] 8* *Paris*, 1889
—— The Ascent of Maglich. *Map and illustrations.* 8* 1889
—— Neuere Forschungen und Bergreisen im Kaukasischen Hochgebirge. 1 and 2. 12* *Vienna*, 1889-91
—— Bergfahrten in den Alpen der Herzegowina. Separatabdruck aus Nos. 350 und 351, der *Oesterr-Alpen Zeitung.* *Plate.* Large 8* *Vienna*, 1892
Decken. *See* Von der Decken.
Deckert, Emil. Die Civilisatorische Mission der Europäer unter den wilden Völkern. 8* *Berlin*, 1881
—— Die Staaten von Mitteleuropa: für kaufmännische und gewerbliche Fachschulen und Realschulen, sowie zum Selbstunterricht. 8° *Leipzig*, 1883
—— Ueber die geographischen Grundvoraussetzungen der Hauptbahnen des Weltverkehrs. Verkehrsgeographische Studie. 8* *Leipzig*, 1883
—— Die Kolonialreiche und Kolonisationsobjekte der Gegenwart : Kolonialpolitische und Kolonialgeographische Skizzen. 12° *Leipzig*, 1884
—— *See* Andree.
Decotter, N. Géographie de Maurice et de ses Dépendances. 12* *Mauritius*, 1891
—— Geography of Mauritius and its Dependencies. 12* *Mauritius*, 1892
Deflers, A. Voyage au Yemen. Excursion botanique. *Plates.* 8° *Paris*, 1889
Defoe, D. (continued by Richardson). A Tour through the Island of Great Britain. Divided into Circuits or Journies. 8th edition. 4 vols. *Maps.* 16° 1778

Defoe, D. Robinson Crusoe. New edition, revised and corrected for the advancement of nautical education. Illustrated by technical and geographical annotation. *Illustrations.* 8° 1815
Defrémery, C. *See* Ibn Batuta.
Degrandpré, L. Voyage à la Côte occidentale d'Afrique, fait dans les années 1786 et 1787 ; contenant la Description des mœurs, usages, lois, gouvernement, et commerce des États du Congo, fréquentés par les Européens, et un précis de la traite des Noirs ainsi qu'elle avait lieu avant la Révolution française ; suivi d'un Voyage fait au Cap de Bonne-Espérance, contenant la description militaire de cette colonie. 2 vols. in 1. *Plates.* 8° *Paris*, 1801
D'Hericourt. *See* Rochet d'Héricourt.
Deguignes, Joseph. *See* Guignes.
Deichmann, L. B. *See* Petersen.
De Jongh, J. J. Costa Rica. [Cutting from *Spanish Post.*] 8* N.P., 1875
De la Barca. *See* Barca.
De la Beche, Sir Henry T. A Geological Manual. 12° 1832
—— How to Observe Geology. *Woodcuts.* 12° 1835
—— Mining, Quarrying, and Metallurgical Processes and Products. 8* 1851
De la Boulaye. *See* Pallas.
De la Bourdonnais, Comte A. Maké. Un Français en Birmanie : Notes de Voyage. 3rd edition. *Map.* 12° *Paris*,1886
De la Brocquière, B. *See* Hakluyt's Voyages, Vol. 4 : Appendix 1.
De la Caille, N. L. Journal Historique du Voyage fait au Cap de Bonne-Espérance ; précédé d'un Discours sur la Vie de l' Auteur, suivi de Remarques et de Réflexions sur les Coutumes des Hottentots et des Habitans du Cap. *Map.* 12° *Paris*, 1763
De la Condamine. *See* Condamine.
De la Croix, J. Errington. Les Mines d' Étain de Pérak (Presqu' île de Malacca). *Maps and plates.* 8° *Paris*, 1882
De la Cruz, Don Luis. Viage de D. L. de la Cruz por los Indios des de Chile à Buenos Ayres, 1806. *Map.* MS. Folio
Delafield, John J. An Inquiry into the Origin of the Antiquities of America ; with an Appendix on the Causes of the Superiority of the Men of the Northern over those of the Southern Hemisphere, by James Lakey, M.D. *Plates and facsimile.* 4° *New York*, 1839
De la Gironière, P. Aventures d'un Gentilhomme Breton aux Iles Philippines, avec un aperçu sur la géologie et la nature du sol de ces îles, sur ses habitants ; sur le règne minéral, le règne végétal et le règne animal ; sur l'agriculture, l'industrie, et le commerce de cet archipel. 2nd edition. *Map and illustrations.* Small folio *Paris*, 1857

De la Grye. *See* Bouquet de la Grye.

De la Haie, —. *See* Allgemeine Historie, Vol. 8 : Appendix 1.

Delaire, A. Genève et le Mont Blanc : Notes de Science et de Voyage. 8*
Paris, 1876

De la Jonchère, L. Demonstration de l'Immobilitez de la Terre. 12* *Paris,* 1728
—— Explication du Flux et du Reflux de la Mer. 12* *Paris,* 1728

De la Lande, M. Voyage en Italie. 3rd edition. 7 vols. Small 8°
Geneva, 1790

De la Loubère. A New Historical Relation of the Kingdom of Siam, wherein a Full and Curious Account is given of the Chinese Way of Arithmetick and Mathematick Learning. Done out of French, by A. P. Gen. *Maps and plates.* Folio 1693

De la Marck. *See* Parchappe.

De la Marmora, Comte Albert. Itinéraire de l'Ile de Sardaigne, pour faire suite au Voyage en cette contrée. 2 vols. *Portrait, maps, and plates.* 8°
Turin, 1860

Delamarre, Casimir. Un Pluriel pour un Singulier et le Panslavisme est détruit dans son principe. 8° *Paris,* 1868
—— Un Peuple Européen de quinze millions oublié devant l'histoire : Pétition au Sénat de l'Empire demandant une réforme dans l'enseignement de l'histoire. 8° *Paris,* 1869
—— La situation économique de l'Espagne; nœud Gordien de sa situation politique. 8* *Paris,* 1869

De la Martinière, H. M. P. Morocco : Journeys in the Kingdom of Fez, and to the Court of Mulai Hassan ; with Itineraries constructed by the Author, and a Bibliography of Morocco from 1844 to 1887 ; with a Preface by Lieut.-Col. Trotter. *Maps.* 8° 1889

Delambre, M. Rapport fait à l'Académie des Sciences, sur les Mémoires inèdits de M. de Paravey relatifs à l'Origine Chaldéenne des Zodiaques et à l'âge qui résulte de ceux retrouvés en Égypte. 8* *Paris,* 1832

De la Moricière and Lieut. Gen. A. Bedeau. Projets de Colonisation pour les Provinces D'Oran et de Constantine. 8° *Paris,* 1847

De la Motraye, A. Travels through Europe, Asia, and into part of Africa ; containing a great variety of Geographical, Topographical, and Political Observations . . . on Italy, Turkey, Greece, Crim and Noghaian Tartaries, Circassia, Sweden, Lapland, Prussia, Russia, Poland, &c. 3 vols. *Maps and plates.* Folio 1723-32

De la Motte, —. Le Nil : Première Conférence faite le 16 Juillet 1880 à la Société de Géographie de Paris, touchant ses études sur le Bassin du Nil. 4*
Paris, 1880
—— Bassin du Nil, Soudan, Nubie, Egypte. 4* *Paris,* 1883

De la Nauze, —. Remarques sur Ératosthène, à l'occasion de la latitude de Syéné. 8* [*Paris,* 1879]

Delano, Capt. Amasa. Narrative of Voyages and Travels in the Northern and Southern Hemispheres, comprising Three Voyages round the World, together with a Voyage in the Pacific Ocean and Oriental Islands. *Map and plates.* 8° *Boston, Mass.,* 1817
—— Pitcairn's Island. 8* N.P., N.D.

De la Noë, G., and E. de Margerie. Les Formes du Terrain. *Plates.* 4°
Paris, 1888

De la Pérouse. *See* Lapérouse.

De la Peyrère, Isaac. *See* Churchill, Vol. 2 ; Hakluyt Soc. Publ., Vol. 18 : Appendix 1.

De la Peyronie. *See* Pallas.

De la Planche, H. Description Hydrographique de la Côte Orientale de la Corée et du Golfe d'Osaka. Traduite du Russe par M. H. de la Planche. *Maps.* 8° *Paris,* 1861
—— *See* Reineke.

De la Porte, L. *See* Mendoza, J. G. de ; Walckenaer ; *also* Recueil des Voyages, Vol. 2, p. 611 : Appendix 1.

De la Richarderie, G. Boucher. Bibliothèque Universelle des Voyages. 6 vols.
Paris, 1808
[For Contents, *see* Appendix 1.]

De la Richerie, E. G. Établissements français de l'Océanie. 8* *Paris,* 1865

De la Rive, A. Nouvelles Récherches sur les Auroras Boréales et Australes, et Description d'un Appareil qui les reproduit avec les Phénomènes qui les accompagnent. *Plate.* 4* *Geneva,* 1862

De la Roché, Ant. *See* Burney, Vol. 3 : Appendix 1.

De la Roche, J. F. *See* Hakluyt, Vol. 3 : Appendix 1.

De la Roche-Poncié, —. Note sur l'Évaluation des distanc en Mer. 8*
Paris, 1860

De la Rochette. *See* Vincent, Vol. 1 : Appendix 1.

De la Roque, J. Voyage dans la Palestine, vers le Grand Emir, Chef des Princes Arabes du Desert, connus sous le nom de Bedouïns, ou d'Arabes Scenites . . ; avec la Description génerale d'Arabie, faite par le Sultan Ismael Abulfeda. *Plates.* 12° *Amsterdam,* 1718
—— Voyage de Syrie et du Mont-Liban. 2 vols in 1. 12° *Paris,* 1722

De la Roque, J. A Voyage to Arabia the Happy, by way of the Eastern Ocean and the Streights of the Red Sea, performed by the French in 1708-10. *Map and plates.* 12° 1730

De la Roquette, Dezos. Sur les Découvertes faites en Groenland. 8* *Paris, 1835*
—— Recherches sur l'Origine, l'Étymologie, et la Signification Primitive de quelques Noms de lieu en Normandie. Traduites du Danois par M. de la Roquette. 8* *Paris, 1835*
—— Notice Biographique sur la Vie et les Travaux de Prof. Keilhau. 8* *Paris, 1838*
—— Notice sur les Mines de Cuivre d'Alten (Norvége). *Map.* 8* *Paris, 1839*
—— Norvége : Extrait de l'Encyclopédie Moderne, Vol. 22. 8* *Paris, 1849*
—— Le Prince Galitzin et le Lieut. Bellot, Notices Biographiques. *Portrait, map, and facsimile.* 8* *Paris, 1854*
—— Notice sur la vie et les travaux de John Brown. 4* *Paris, 1863*
—— Note sur l'Ile d'Hai-nan, sur les Religieux de la Mission de la Chine. 8* *Paris, N.D.*
—— Le Cosmographe Espagnol Martin Fernandez de Enciso : Étude Biographique. 8* *N.P., N.D.*
—— Notice Nécrologique sur. Royal 8* *Poissy, N.D.*
—— *See* Daussy; Eyriès; Franklin; Hell; Hansteen; Humboldt; Jomard; Prevost.

De la Rosa, Presb. A. Estudio de la Filosofia y riqueza de la Lengua Mexicano. 8* *Guadalajara, 1889*

De la Sagra, Ramon. Historia Económico-Política y Estadística de la Isla de Cuba, ó sea de sus progresos en la Poblacion, la Agricultura, el Comercio y las Rentas. 4° *Havana, 1831*
—— Historia fisica, politica, y natural de la Isla de Cuba. 12 vols. in 8. *Maps and plates.* Folio *Paris, 1840-56*

CONTENTS.
Primera Parte. Historia fisica y politica.
1. Introduccion, Geografia, Clima, Poblacion, Agricultura 1842
2. Comercio maritimo, Rentas y Gastos, Fuerza Armada 1842
Segunda Parte. Historia Natural.
3. Mamiferos y Aves (por Alcides D'Orbigny) 1845
4. Reptiles (por Cocteau y Bibron) y Peces 1843
5. Moluscos (por A. D'Orbigny) 1845
6. Foraminiferas (por A. D'Orbigny) 1840
7. Crustaceos, Aragnides, é Insectos (Guérin Méneville, H. Lucas, Jacquelin Duval, De Sélys Longchamps, Bigot) 1856
8. Atlas de Zoologia 1855

De la Sagra, Ramon—*continued.*
9. Botanica (Criptogamia o Plantas Cellulares, por Camilo Montagne) 1845
10. and 11. Botanica (Fanerogamia o Plantas Vasculares, por A. A. Richard) 1845-50
12. Atlas de Botanica 1855
—— Cuba en 1860, o sea Cuadra de sus Adelantos en la Poblacion, la Agricultura, el Comercio, y las Rentas Publicas. Suplemento á la primera parte de la "Historia politica y natural de la Isla Cuba." Folio *Paris, 1862*
—— *See* Poey, A.

De la Salle, R. *See* Sparks.

De la Torre, Bertrand. *See* Callander, 1 : Appendix 1.

De la Torre, Count Raymond. *See* Collecção de Noticias : Appendix 1.

De la Torre, José Maria. Nuevo Compendio de Geografia Universal, y particular de la Monarquía Española. *Plates.* 8* *Havana, 1852*
—— Nueva Tabla de Cuentas; con el sistema Métrico aplicado á todo la Monarquía Española y multitud de noticias útiles. Part 2. 18* *Havana, 1852*
—— Compendio de Geografia, Física, Política, Estadística, y Comparada de la Isla de Cuba. 8* *Havana, 1854*
—— Nuevos Elementos de Geografia e História de la Isla de Cuba. 18* *Havana, 1856*

De la Valle, Pietro. *See* Della Valle.

De la Vega, Garcilasso. Commentarios Reales, que tratan del Origen de los Yncas, Reyes que fueron del Peru, de su Idolatria, Leyes, y Govierno en Pax y en Guerra, de sus vidas y conquistas, y de todo lo que fue aquel Imperio y su Republica, antes que los Españoles passaran a el. 2 vols in 1. Small folio *Lisbon, 1609-17*
—— Historia general del Peru : Trata el descubrimiento de el ; y como lo ganaron los Españoles ; las Guerras civiles que huvo entre Pizarros y Almagros, sobre la partija de la tierra ; castigo y levantamiento de Tyranos, y otros sucesos particulares, &c. 2nd edition. Folio *Madrid, 1722*
—— Primera parte de los Commentarios Reales, que tratan del Origen de los Yncas, &c. 2nd edition. Small folio *Madrid, 1723*
—— La Florida del Inca : Historia del Adelantado, Hernando de Soto . . . y de otros heroicos Caballeros Españoles e Indios . . ; van enmendadas en esta impresion, muchas erratas de la primera : y añadida copiosa tabla de las cosas notables ; y el Ensaio Cronológico, que contiene, las sucedidas, hasta en el año de 1722. Folio *Madrid, 1723*

De la Vega, Garcilasso. *See* Hakluyt Soc. Publ., Vols. 41, 45, 60 ; Kerr, Vol. 5; Purchas, Vol. 4, Book 7 : Appendix 1.

De la Warre, Lord. *See* Purchas, Vol. 4, Book 9 : Appendix 1.

Delaporte, L. Voyage au Cambodge : L'Architecture Khmer. *Maps and plates.* 8° *Paris*, 1880

Delavaud, L. Les Portugais dans l'Afrique Centrale avant le XVIIᵉ Siècle. 8* *Rochefort*, 1879

—— La Politique Coloniale de l'Allemagne. (From " Annales de l'École Libre des Sciences Politiques.") Large 8* *Paris*, 1888

Del Badia, J. *See* Dante.

D'Elbée, Sieur. *See* Elbée.

Delcros, Comm. Notice sur les Altitudes du Mont-Blanc et du Mont-Rose, déterminées par des Mesures Barométriques et Géodésiques. Royal 8* *Versailles*, 1851

Delegorgue, Adolphe. Voyage dans l'Afrique Australe, notamment dans le territoire de Natal, dans celui des Cafres, Amazoulous, et Makatisses, et jusqu'au Tropique du Capricorne, exécuté durant les années 1838-44, &c. 2 vols. *Maps and plates.* 8° *Paris*, 1847

Delesse, A. Lithologie des Mers de France et des Mers principales du Globe. *Map.* 8° ; Atlas, folio *Paris* [1871]

—— Rapport sur un Mémoire, intitulé " Étude des déformations subies par les terrains de la France." 8* *Paris*, 1872

—— Les Oscillations des Côtes de France. *Map.* 8* *Paris*, 1872

—— Carte agricole de la France. *Map.* Small 8* *Paris*, 1874

—— Notice sur les Travaux scientifiques de M. Delesse. 4* *Paris*, 1869

Delgado, J. F. N. Noticia ácerca das Grutas de Cesareda Commissão geologica de Portugal. Opusc. 1. 1867

—— (Terrenos paleozoicos de Portugal). Sobre a existencia do terreno siluriano no Baixo Alemtejo. *Map and plates.* 4* *Lisbon*, 1876

Delhoste, Capt. E. P. Report on the Routes leading from Kurachee to Jerruk, with an Account of the Town of Jerruk ; Report on the Country between Kurachee Tatta, and Sehwan. [From the India Records, No. 17] *Bombay*, 1855

"Delight" (Ship). *See* Hakluyt, Vol. 4 : Appendix 1.

Della Casa, Giovanni. *See* Casa.

Della Cella, Paolo. Narrative of an Expedition from Tripoli in Barbary to the Western Frontier of Egypt in 1817, with Instructions for Navigating the Great Syrtis. Translated by A. Aufrere. *Map.* 8° 1822

Della Penna, H. *See* Allgemeine Historie, Vol. 7 : Appendix 1.

Della Valle, Pietro. Travels in East India and Arabia Deserta ; whereunto is added a Relation of Sir Thomas Roe's Voyage into the East Indies. *Map.* Folio. 1665

—— Viaggi di . . . il Pellegrino, . . . descritti da lui medisimo in 54 lettere familiari . . . all'erudito . . . suo amico Mario Schipano. Diuisi in trè parti, cioè, la Turchia, la Persia, e l'India. [Parte prima, La Turchia ; Parte seconda, in 2 vols., La Persia ; Parte terza, L'India, c'ol ritorno in patria.] 4 vols. 12° *Bologna*, 1672-81

—— Ditto. 4 vols. 12° *Bologna*, 1677-81

—— Les Fameux Voyages de Pietro Della Valle. 4 vols. *Plate and portraits.* 4° *Paris*, 1664-70

—— *See* Pennesi ; *also* Pinkerton, Vol. 9 ; Thevenot, Vol. 1 ; Hakluyt Soc. Publ., Vols. 84, 85 : Appendix 1.

Dellon, —. *See* Allgemeine Historie, Vol. 10 : Appendix 1.

De Long, George W. The Voyage of the "Jeannette": the Ship and Ice Journals of George W. De Long, Lieut.-Commander U.S.N., and Commander of the Polar Expedition of 1879-81. Edited by his wife Emma De Long. 2 vols. *Portraits, maps, charts, and illustrations.* 8° 1883

—— *See* Melville.

Del Re, Giuseppe. Descrizione Reali Domini di qua del Faro nel Regno delle due Sicilie. Vols. 1, 2, 3 [Part 1.] *Maps.* *Naples*, 1830-35-36

Del Rio, Capt. Antonia. Description of the Ruins of an ancient City discovered near Palenque, in the Kingdom of Gautemala in Spanish America ; followed by Teatro Crítico Americano, or a Critical Investigation and Research into the History of the Americans, by Dr P. Felix Cabrera. *Plates.* 4° 1822

Demay, Charles. Histoire de la Colonisation Allemande. 12° *Paris*, 1889

Demersay, L. Alfred. Histoire Physique, Économique, et Politique du Paraguay et des Établissements des Jésuites. 2 vols. Royal 8° *Paris*, 1860-65

Demeunier, —. *See* Brydone, P.

Demidoff, Anatole de. Travels in Southern Russia and the Crimea, through Hungary, Wallachia, and Moldavia, during 1837. 2 vols. *Map and plates.* Royal 8° 1855

Dempsey, J. M., and W. Hughes. Our Ocean Highways : Condensed Universal Hand Gazetteer and International Route Book, by Ocean, Road, or Rail ; being a Complete Book of Reference and Guide for the Traveller to every known Port and chief City in the Whole World, &c. *Maps.* 12° 1871

I

Demtchenka, Y. The Aralo-Caspian District in Relation to Climate. [In Russian.] Small 8*   *Kiev*, 1871

Denaix, —. Rapports et Notice sur les Travaux Géographiques et Historiques. 8*   *Paris*, 1833
—— Géographie Prototype de la France. *Map.* 8°   *Paris*, 1841

Dendy, W. C. The Beautiful Islets of Britaine. 8°   1857
—— Islets of the Channel. *Maps.* 8° 1858

Dénes, Franz. Wegweiser durch die Ungarischen Karpathen. Im Auftrage des Ungarischen Karpathenvereins. *Maps and illustrations.* 12° *Iglo*, 1888

Denham, Major Dixon, and Capt. Hugh Clapperton. Narrative of Travels and Discoveries in Northern and Central Africa in 1822-24, extending across the Great Desert to the Tenth Degree of Northern Latitude, and from Kouka in Bornou to Sackatoo, the capital of the Fellatah Empire; with an Appendix. *Maps and plates.* 4°   1826

Denham, Capt. H. M. Sailing Directions for the Bristol Channel. 8°   1839
—— Report on some Islands and Reefs in the South-Western Pacific Ocean. 8° 1855
—— Hydrographic Notices: Australia, East Coast, South Coast; Mediterranean Sea, Alexandria Harbour, Indian Ocean, Eastern Archipelago, Banka Strait, China Sea; Directions for the Si Kiang or West River, the Yangtze-Kiang, the Gulf of Pe-Chile, and for the Tien-Tsin Ho or Pei Ho; Japan Islands. 8°   1856-59

Deniker, —. *See* Levasseur.

Deniker, J. Essai d'une Classification des Races Humaines basée uniquement sur les Charactères Physiques. 8* *Paris*, 1889
—— *See* France, B, a: Appendix 2.

Denina, C. Tableau Historique, Statistique, et Moral de la Haute-Italie. 8° *Paris*, 1805

Denis, A. Promenade Pittoresque et Statistique dans le Département du Var, ou Études Historiques, Géologiques, Minéralogiques, Botaniques, Agricoles, Industrielles, et Manufacturières sur ce Département. *Plates.* Folio *Toulon* [1833]
—— Hyères Ancien et Moderne. Promenades Pittoresques, Scientifiques, et Littéraires sur son Territoire, ses Environs et ses Iles. Quatrième édition très augmentée et entièrement refondue par le Docteur R. Chassinat. *Frontispiece, map, and plan.* Small 8° *Hyères*, N.D.

Denis, Ferdinand. Portugal. *Plates.* 8° *Paris*, 1846

Denis, Ferdinand. Le Génie de la Navigation : Statue en Bronze, exécutée par M. Daumas pour la ville de Toulon. *Plate.* 8°   *Paris*, 1847
—— *See* Rang.

Denison, Sir W. Varieties of Vice-Regal Life. 2 vols. *Map.* 8°   1878

Denman, Commander Hon. —, R.N. Practical Remarks on the Slave Trade, and on the existing Treaties with Portugal. 2nd edition. 8*   1839

Dennett, R. E. Seven Years among the Fjort, being an English Trader's Experiences in the Congo District. *Map and illustrations.* Crown 8°   1887

Dénniée, Baron. Précis Historique et Administratif de la Campagne d'Afrique. *Plates.* 8°   *Paris*, 1830

Dennis, George. The Cities and Cemeteries of Etruria. 3rd edition. 2 vols. *Map, plans, and illustrations.* 8° 1883

Dennis, J. S. Extract from Surveyor's Report of Township Surveys in Manitoba, Keewatin, and North-West Territories. *Map.* 8*   *Ottawa*, 1877
—— Navigation of Hudson's Bay. 8* *Ottawa* [1878]

Denniston, —. *See* New Zealand, A: Appendix 2.

Dennys, N. B. Notes for Tourists in the North of China. *Maps and plans.* 8° *Hongkong*, 1866
—— Report on the Newly-opened Ports of K'uing Chow (Hoi-How) in Hainan and of Hai-Phong in Tonquin (visited in April 1876). *Maps.* 8° *Hongkong*, 1876

Denon, Vivant. Voyage dans la Basse et la Haute Égypte, pendant les Campagnes du Bonaparte. 2 vols. *Plates.* 4°; *Plates*, folio   1802
—— The same. 2 vols. in 1. *Plates.* 4° 1809
—— Travels in Upper and Lower Egypt. Translated by Arthur Aikin. 3 vols. 8°; *Plates*, 4°   1803

Dent, C. T. Mountaineering : with Contributions by W. M. Conway, D. W. Freshfield, C. E. Mathews, C. Pilkington, Sir F. Pollock, H. G. Willink, and an Introduction by Mr Justice Wills. 2nd edition. *Illustrations.* 8°   1892

Dent, Edward J. On the Errors of Chronometers, and Explanation of a New Construction of the Compensation Balance. 8°   1842
—— A Description of the Dipleidoscope, or Double Reflecting Meridian and Altitude Instrument. 8°   1844
—— On the Aneroid Barometer, a newly invented Portable Barometer. 8° 1849
—— On the Construction and Management of Chronometers, Watches, and Clocks. 8°   1850

Dent, Hastings Charles. A Year in Brazil, with Notes on the Abolition of Slavery, the Finances of the Empire, Religion, Meteorology, Natural History, &c. *Maps and illustrations.* 8° 1886

Dentrecasteaux, Vice-Admiral. Voyage de Dentrecasteaux, envoyé à la recherche de La Pérouse . . . Rédigé par M. de Rossel. 2 vols. and Atlas. *Charts, plans, &c.* 4° *Paris*, 1808

Denzler, H. H. Die Meereshöhe des Chasseral, als Grundlage des Schweizerischen Höhennetzes. 8* N.P., 1864

Depons, F. Travels in South America during 1801-4, containing a Description of the Caraccas, and an Account of the Discovery, Conquest, Topography, &c., of the Country; with a View of the Manners and Customs of the Spaniards and the Native Indians. 2 vols. in 1. *Map.* 8° 1807
—— *See* Phillips [2], Vol. 1 : Appendix 1.

Deporter, Com. V. Apropos du Transsaharien. Extrême-sud de l'Algérie : le Gourara, le Touat, In-Salah, le Tidikelt, le pays des Touareg Hoggar, l'Adrar, Tin Bouctou, Agadès, 1888-89. *Map in separate case.* 8° *Algiers*, 1890
—— La Question du Touat. Sahara Algérien, Gourara, Touat, Tidikelt, Cararanes, et Transsaharien. Deux Conférences. *Map.* 8* *Algiers*, 1891

Depping, G. B. Merveilles et Beautés de la Nature en France. *Map and plates.* 12° *Paris*, 1812

Depree, G. C. *See* India, F, *b* : Appendix 2.

De Rance, Charles E. The Water Supply of England and Wales, its Geology, Underground Circulation, Surface Distribution, and Statistics. *Maps.* 8° 1882

De Rancy, M. *See* Rancy.

Derby, Lieut. Geo. H. Report of the Reconnaissance of the Gulf of California and the Colorado River, made in 1850-51. *Map.* 8* *Washington*, 1852

Derby, Orville A. On the Carboniferous Brachiopoda of Itaitúba, Rio Tapajos, Prov. of Pará, Brazil. [Bulletin of the Cornell University (Science), Vol. 1, No. 2.] *Plates.* 8* *Ithaca, N.Y.*, 1874
—— Physical Geography and Geology of Brazil. Translated from "A Geographia Physica do Brazil," and reprinted from *The Rio News*, of 5th, 15th, and 24th December 1884. *Maps.* 8* [*Rio de Janeiro*, 1884]
—— Contribuição para o Estudo da Geographia Physico do Valle do Rio Grande. 8* [*Rio de Janeiro*, 1885]
—— Os Picos Altos do Brazil. 8* *Rio de Janeiro*, 1889

Derenbourg, J. Essai sur l'Histoire et la Géographie de la Palestine, d'après les Thalmuds et autres sources Rabbiniques. Part 1. 8° *Paris*, 1867

Derenbourg, Hartwig. Les Manuscrits Arabes de l'Escurial. Tome 1. [Publ. de l'Éc. des Langues Orient. Viv., 11e Série, Vol. 10.] *Frontispiece.* Large 8° *Paris*, 1884
—— Ousâma Ibn Mounkiah, un Émir Syrien au Premier Siècle des Croisades (1095-1188). Parts 1 and 2. [11e Series, Vol. 12, 1st and 2nd parts, of the same.] Large 8° *Paris*, 1886 and 1889

Derfelden de Hinderstein, Baron G. F. von. Mémoire Analytique, pour servir d'explication à la Carte Générale des Possessions Néerlandaises dans le Grand Archipel Indien. 4° *The Hague*, 1844

Dermer, Thomas. *See* Purchas, Vol. 4, Book 9 : Appendix 1.

De Ricci, J. H. *See* Ricci.

Dernschwam, H. *See* Kiepert, H.

De Roos, Hon. Fred. Fitzgerald. *See* Roos.

De Rossi, Stefano. *See* Issel.

Deschamps, Léon. Histoire de la Question Coloniale en France. 8° *Paris*, 1891

Deschamps, P., et G. Brunet. Manuel du Libraire et de l'Amateur de Livres. Supplément, contenant 1° un complément du Dictionnaire Bibliographique de M. J.-Ch. Brunet. . . . 2° La Table Raisonnée des Articles. i. (A—M.) 8° *Paris*, 1878
—— Supplément, ii. (N—Z.) 8° *Paris*, 1880

Deschanel, Paul. Les Intérêts Français dans l'Océan Pacifique : 1. Mission Catholique des Gambier—Archipels des Tuamotus, des Marquises, Tubuaï, Cook, Wallis — Ile Rapa, &c. ; 2. Les Nouvelles-Hébrides — Géographie—Histoire — Colonisation Française — Libérés et récidivistes — Politique de l'Australie—Négociations Anglo-Françaises. 12° *Paris*, 1888

Des Farges. *See* Allgemeine Historie, Vol. 18 : Appendix I.

Desfontaines, L. R. *See* Peyssonnel.

Desgodins, C. H. La Mission du Thibet de 1855 à 1870. *Map.* 8° *Verdun*, 1872
—— Le Thibet d'après la Correspondance des Missionnaires. 2nd edition. *Map.* 8° *Paris*, 1885

Desgraz, C. *See* Vincendon-Dumoulin.

Desiderius, H. *See* Allgemeine Historie, Vol. 7 : Appendix I.

Desjardins, Ernest. Rhône et Danube. Nouvelles Observations sur les Fosses Mariennes et le Canal du Bas-Rhône ; Embouchures du Danube comparées à celles du Rhône ; Projet de Canalisation maritime du Bas-Danube. [*Large paper.*] *Map.* 8° *Paris*, 1870

Desjardins, Ernest. Géographie Historique et Administrative de la Gaule
Romaine. Vols. 1, 2, 3, and 4. *Maps
and plates.* Large 8°   *Paris*, 1876-93

Desjobert, A. La Question d'Alger,
Politique, Colonisation, Commerce. 8°
                                Paris, 1837
—— L'Algérie en 1844. 8°   *Paris*, 1844
—— L'Algérie en 1846. 8°   *Paris*, 1846

Desmarest, Citoyen. Géographie-Phy-
sique. Encyclopédie Méthodique.   5
vols. 4°   *Paris*, 1795

Des Michels, Abel. Tam tu Kinh, ou
le livre des phrases de trois caractères,
avec le grand commentaire de Vu'o'ng
tân thăng.   Texte, transcription Annamite et Chinoise, explication littérale
et traduction complètes.   [No. 17 of
Publ. de l'Éc. des Langues Orient. Viv.]
Large 8°   *Paris*, 1882
—— Les Poèmes de l'Annam. Luc vân
Tiên ca Diên.   Texte en caractères
figuratifs, transcription en caractères
latins, et traduction.   [No. 19 of Publ. de
l'Éc. des Langues Orient. Viv.] Large
8°   *Paris*, 1883
—— The same. Kim Vân Kiêu Tân
Truyên.   Publié et traduit pour la
première fois par Abel Des Michels. Vol.
1, and Vol. 2, Pts. 1 and 2. [IIᵉ Série,
Vols. 14 and 15 (2 parts) of Publ. de
l'Ec. des Langues Orient. Viv.] Large
8°   *Paris*, 1884-85

Desmoulins, M. Renseignements Hydrographiques et Statistiques sur la Côte
de Syrie. 8*   *Paris*, 1862

Des Muss, O. *See* Abyssinia ; Voyage en
Abyssinie, 1839-43, Part 4 : Appendix 2.

Desor, E. Nouvelles Excursions et
Séjours dans les Glaciers et les hautes
régions des Alpes de M. Agassiz et de
ses compagnons de voyage.   Accompagnées d'une Notice sur les Glaciers de
l'Allée-Blanche et du Val-Ferret par
M. Agassiz, et d'un Aperçu sur la
Structure Géologique des Alpes par M.
Studer. *Maps.* 8°   *Paris*, 1845

Dessiou, J. F. Le Petit Neptune Français ; or, French Coasting Pilot for the
Coast of Flanders (Belgium) Channel,
the Bay of Biscay, and Mediterranean.
To which is added, the Coast of Italy
from the River Var to Cape Spartivento,
with the North Coast of Sicily and the
Island of Corsica. *Maps.* 4°   1805

D'Estrey, Comte Meyners. *See* Estrey.

Detcheverry, Léonce. Nossi-Bé. Large
8*   *Paris*, 1881

Devaux, Javier. Determinacion de la
Lonjitud por la observacion de las
Ocultaciones de Estrellas por la Luna.
Nuevo Metodo para predecir la oculta-
cion i calcular la Lonjitud. *Plates.* 8°
                           Santiago de Chile, 1890

De Vea, Ant. *See* Burney, Vol. 4 : Appendix 1.

De Veaux, S. The Traveller's Own
Book to Saratoga Springs, Niagara
Falls, and Canada ; containing Routes,
Distances, Conveyances, Expenses, Use
of Mineral Waters, Baths, Description
of Scenery, &c. *Maps and plates.* 18°
                                Buffalo, 1841

Deverell, F. H. All Round Spain, by
Road and Rail, with a Short Account of a
Visit to Andorra. *Map in cover.* 8° 1884

Devereux, W. C. A Cruise in the
"Gorgon"; or, Eighteen Months on
H.M.S. "Gorgon," engaged in the
Suppression of the Slave Trade on the
East Coast of Africa ; including a Trip
up the Zambesi with Dr Livingstone.
Map. 8°   1869
—— Fair Italy : The Riviera and Monte
Carlo.   Comprising a Tour through
North and South Italy and Sicily, with
a Short Account of Malta. Post 8° 1884

"De Vergulde Draeck," Ship. *See*
Hakluyt Soc. Publ., Vol. 25: Appendix 1.

Devéria, G. Histoire des Relations de
la Chine avec l'Annam - Viêtnam du
XVIᵉ au XIXᵉ Siècle. [Publ. de l'Ec.
des Langues Orient. Viv., Vol. 13.]
Map. 8°   *Paris*, 1880
—— La Frontière Sino-Annamite. Description Géographique et Ethnographique
d'après des Documents Officiels Chinois
traduits pour la première fois. [Publ.
de l'École des Langues Orientales Viv.,
IIIᵉ Série, Vol. 1.] *Maps and illustrations.* Large 8°   *Paris*, 1886

Dewar, J. Cumming. Voyage of the
"Nyanza," R.N.Y.C.: being the Record
of a Three Years' Cruise in a Schooner-
Yacht in the Atlantic and Pacific, and
her subsequent Shipwreck. *Map and
illustrations.* 8°   *Edinburgh*, 1892

D'Ewes, J. Sporting in both Hemispheres. *Plates.* 8°   1858

Dewey, G. *See* United States, E, *a*
(No. 56) : Appendix 2.

De Windt, Harry. *See* Windt.

Deydier, —. La Locomotion Aérienne.
Plate. 8*   *Oran*, 1877

D'Halloy, J. J. d'Omalius. *See* Halloy.

D'Herbelot, M. *See* Herbelot.

Diaz, Augustin. A Brief Report on the
Organisation, Objects, and Development
of the Works of the Geographical Exploring Commission in the Republic of
Mexico. 8*   *New Orleans*, 1885

Diaz (or Dias), Bartholomew. *See*
General Collection of Voyages, p. 610:
Appendix 1.

Diaz del Castillo, Conquistador Bernal.
The Memoirs of, written by himself ;
containing a True and Full Account of
the Discovery and Conquest of Mexico
and New Spain. 2 vols. 8°   1844

Diaz del Castillo, Conquistador Bernal. See Cartas de Indias, p. 612 ; Kerr, Vols. 3, 4 : Appendix 1.

Dicey, E. A Month in Russia during the Marriage of the Czarevitch. *Portraits.* 8° 1867

Dicey, Capt. W. Report on the Creek Navigation from Akyab to Toungoop. [From the India Records, No. 19, Public Works Dept.] 8° *Calcutta*, 1856

Dick, A. H. Compendium of Mathematical Geography ; with a Preface by Laurie. 12° 1863

Dick, W. A. T. Report on the Working of the Government Botanical Gardens in the N.W. Provinces, 1867-68. [From the India Records, N.W. Prov., Part 1.] 8° *Allahabad*, 1868

Dickens, Lieut. C. H. Memorandum of Experiments on, and Analysis of, Specimens of Kunkur, on the Grand Trunk Road, near Naubutpore. [From the Records of India, N.W. Prov., Vol. 2] 8° *Agra*, 1855-64

Dickenson, Jonathan. See Gottfried : Appendix 1.

Dickenson, W. B. Dudu-Masu, Coco-Reedi, or Hook Money of Ceylon. 8* 1850

Dickie, George. Notes of Algæ collected on the Coast of North-West America by Mr R. Brown. 8* [1868]
—— Notes of Mosses and Hepaticæ, collected by Robert Brown, Esq., on the North-West Coast of America. 8* [1868]
—— See Inglefield ; Lindsay.

Dickinson, John. India : its Government under a Bureaucracy. 8° 1853

Dickson, Consul J. Report on the Jaffa-Jerusalem Railway (with plans). [Foreign Office Reports, 1893 : Miscellaneous Series, No. 288, Turkey.] 8* 1893

Dickson, Walter. The Antarctic Voyage of Her Majesty's hired Barque "Pagoda" [1844-45]. (From *United Service Magazine*, June and July 1850.) 8* 1850

Dickson, W. G. Gleanings from Japan. *Illustrations.* 8° 1889

Dickson, Oscar. See Nordenskiöld.

Dickson, William P. See Mommsen.

Dictionaries. See General : Appendix 2.

Dicuil, —. See Letronne, A.

Dieffenbach, Ernest. New Zealand, and its Native Population. 8* 1841
—— Travels in New Zealand, with Contributions to the Geography, Geology, Botany, and Natural History. 2 vols. *Plates.* 8° 1843

Diego, E. de. Viajes y Descubrimientos en el Polo Norte. 12° *Madrid*, N.D.

Diehl, Charles. Excursions in Greece to recently explored Sites of Classical interest : Mycenæ, Tiryns, Dodona, Delos, Athens, Olympia, Eleusis, Epidaurus, Tanagra ; a popular Account of the results of recent Excavations. Translated by Emma R. Perkins ; with an Introduction by Reginald Stuart Poole. 8° 1893

Diemer, Dr L. Das Leben in der Tropenzone speziell in Indischen Archipel. Nach Dr van der Burg's "De Geneesheer in Nederlandsch Indie" (1 Band, 2 Auflage), mit Genehmigung des Autors. 8° *Hamburg*, 1887

"Dido," H.M.S. See Keppel.

Diener, Dr Carl. Libanon. Grundlinien der physischen Geographie und Geologie von Mittel-Syrien. *Map and photographs.* 8° *Vienna*, 1886
—— Der Gebirgsbau der Westalpen. *Maps.* 8° *Vienna*, 1891

Diest, W. von. Von Pergamon über den Dindymos zum Pontus. [Ergän-zungsheft, 94—Petermann's Mittheilungen.] *Photograph and maps.* 4° *Gotha*, 1889

Dietrich Bey, L. Ville d'Alexandrie Municipalité : Rapport sur l'assainissement de la Ville. 3 parts. Large 8° *Alexandria*, 1892-93

Dietz, Rudolph. Die Gewerbe im Grossherzogthum Baden, ihre Statistik, ihre Pflege, ihre Erzeugnisse. 8° *Karlsruhe*, 1863

Dieulafoy, Marcel. L'Acropole de Suse d'après les fouilles exécutées en 1884, 1885, 1886, sous les auspices du Musée du Louvre. *Illustrations.* Large 4° *Paris*, 1893

Diez, — de. See Sidi Aly.

Diez de Games, Gutierre. Cronica de Don Pedro Niño, Conde de Buelna. 4° *Madrid*, 1782

Dilke, Sir Charles Wentworth. Greater Britain : a Record of Travel in English-speaking Countries during 1866 and 1867. 2nd edition. Vol. 2 only. *Maps and plates.* 8° 1869
—— The same. 8th edition. With Additional Chapters on English Influence in Japan and China, and on Hong Kong and the Straits Settlements. Crown 8° 1885
—— Gerrymandering in Africa. (From *The United Service Magazine*, November 1890.) *Map.* 8* 1890
—— Problems of Greater Britain. 2 vols. *Maps.* 8° 1890

D'Illens and Funk. See Illens.

Dillon, Hon. A. A Winter in Iceland and Lapland. 2 vols. 8° 1840

Dillon, J. Talbot. Travels through Spain, with a View to Illustrate the Natural History and Physical Geography of that Kingdom. *Map and plates.* 4° 1782
—— See Pelham, Vol. 2 : Appendix 1.

Dillon, Capt. P. Narrative and Successful Result of a Voyage to the South Seas to Ascertain the Actual Fate of La Pérouse's Expedition; interspersed with Accounts of the Religion, Manners, Customs, and Cannibal Practices of the South Sea Islanders. 2 vols. *Maps and plates.* 8° 1829

Dilthey, Richard. Der wirthschaftliche Werth von Deutsch-Ostafrika. *Map.* 12* *Düsseldorf,* 1889

Dilworth, H. W. *See* Kouli Khan.

Dinarte, Sylvio. Innocencia : a Story of the Prairie Regions of Brazil. Translated from the Portuguese, and illustrated, by James W. Wells. 12° 1889

Dingelstedt, V. Le Régime Patriarcal et le droit coutumier des Kirghiz. 8° *Paris,* 1891

Dinger, W. J. De Nadeelen van onze tegenwoordige Muntregelingen. *Plate.* 8° *Batavia,* 1887

Dingman, Benjamin. Ten Years in South America. Part 2, Bolivia. 8° *Montreal,* 1876

Dionysius. Dionysii Orbis Descriptio ; cum Commentariis Eustathii, Archiepiscopi Thessalonicensis. *Maps.* Small 8° *Oxford,* 1710

Diodorus Siculus. *See* Ramusio, Vol. 1 : Appendix 1.

Diosdado, Abbate. L'Eroismo di Ferdinando Cortese confirmato contro le censure nemiche. 12° *Rome,* 1806

Disbrowe, Lieut. H. F. Historical Sketch connected with the Tribe of Amulgavine. [From the India Records, No. 24.] 8° *Bombay,* 1856
—— *See* Hennell ; Kemball.

Distant, W. L. A Naturalist in the Transvaal. *Coloured plates, &c.* 8° 1892

Disturnell's Guide through the Middle, Northern, and Eastern States ; containing a Description of the Principal Places, Canals, Railroad and Steamboat Routes, Tables of Distances, &c. *Map.* 12° *New York,* 1847

Ditmar, K. von. *See* Schrenck and Maximowicz, Beiträge zur Kenntniss des Russischen Reiches, &c., 7.

Dittenberger, Friederich. Hand- und Lehrbuch der reinen Geographie nach natürlichen Grenzen nebst einem politisch-statistischen Anhange. 2 vols. 8° *Karlsruhe,* 1818

Dix, John A. A Winter in Madeira, and a Summer in Spain and Florence. 2nd edition. *Plates.* 12° *New York,* 1851

Dixie, Lady Florence. Across Patagonia. *Illustrations.* 8° 1880
—— Memories of a Great Lone Land. (From the *Westminster Review,* March 1893.) 8* 1893

Dixon and Portlock. *See* Portlock et Dixon, in Vol. 1 of Eyriès : Appendix 1.

Dixon, Col. C. J. Sketch of Mairwara ; giving a Brief Account of the Origin and Habits of the Mairs, their Subjugation, Civilisation, and Conversion into an Industrious Peasantry. *Maps and plates.* 4° 1850
—— Report on Ajmeer and Mairwara, illustrating the Settlement of the Land Revenue and the Revenue Administration of those Districts up to the commencement of 1853. 4° *Agra,* 1853

Dixon, E. T. The Effect of the Rotation of the Earth on the Motion of Projectiles. (From the Proceedings of the Royal Artillery Institution, May 1893.) 8* 1893

Dixon, Capt. George. Voyage round the World, but more particularly to the North-West Coast of America, 1785-88. *Maps and plates.* 4° 1789

Dixon, William Hepworth. Robert Blake, Admiral and General at Sea ; based on Family and State Papers. *Plate.* 8° 1852
—— New America. 2 vols. *Plates.* 8° 1867
—— British Cyprus. *Coloured frontispiece.* 8° 1879

Dobbie, Capt. Robert Shedden. Pocket Dictionary of English and Hindústaní. 12° 1847

Dobbs, Arthur. An Account of the Countries adjoining to Hudson's Bay, in the North-West part of America . . ; with an Abstract of Captain Middleton's Journal, and Observations upon his behaviour during his voyage, and since his return, &c. *Map.* 4° 1744
—— *See* Middleton, C.

Dobell, Peter. Travels in Kamtchatka and Siberia ; with a Narrative of a Residence in China. 2 *plates.* 8° 1830

Dobree, T. S. Sketch of the Territory of Sabah, Borneo, lately ceded to a British Association ; with Report and Analysis of Soils by J. Hughes, and an Appendix. *Maps.* 4° 1879

Doberck, W. Observations and Researches made at the Hongkong Observatory, in the year 1884. Folio* *Hongkong,* 1885

Dobrizhoffer, Martin. Account of the Abipones, an Equestrian People of Paraguay. Translated from the Latin. 3 vols. 8° 1822

Dobson, George. Russia's Railway Advance into Central Asia : Notes of a Journey from St Petersburg to Samarkand. *Maps and illustrations.* 12° 1890

D'Ochoa, C. O. *See* Pemberton.

Dochard, Surgeon. *See* Gray, W.

Dodd, J. S. Traveller's Directory through Ireland. *Maps.* 8° *Dublin,* 1801

"Doddington," East Indiaman. *See* Plaisted.

Dodge, F. S. See Emersons.

Dodman, G. Sutherland. A Voyage round the World in 500 Days : giving an Account of the Principal Parts to be Visited, with a Brief Description of the Scenery, and all particulars connected with the undertaking. *Map and plates.* Small 8° 1879

Dods, P. Gazetteer of the Central Provinces. Part 1, Baitool, Belaspore, Bhundara. 8° *Nagpore*, 1867

Dodshon, Edward. The Railway and General Freighter's Protection Agency. *Diagram.* Folio* *Manchester*, 1890

Dodsworth, Edward. See Elkington in Kerr, Vol. 9 ; Purchas, Vol. 1, Book 4 : Appendix 1.

Dodwell, Edward. A Classical and Topographical Tour through Greece, during the years 1801, 1805, and 1806. 2 vols. *Map and plates.* 4° 1819

Dodwell, H. Geographiæ Veteris Scriptores Græci Minores ; cum Interpretatione Latina, Dissertationibus, ac Annotationibus, Gr. et Lat., edidit J. Hudson. 2 vols. *Oxford*, 1698-1700

CONTENTS.

VOLUME 1.

Hannonis Periplus—Scylacis Periplus—Agatharchides de Mari Rubro—Arriani Periplus Ponti Euxini—Periplus Maris Erythræi eidem vulgo adscriptus—Nearchi Peraplus ex Arriani Indicis—Marciani Heracleotæ periplus, cum fragmentis Artemidori et Menippi—Anonymi periplus Maris Euxini.

VOLUME 2.

Dicæarchi Status Græciæ — Dicæarchi Descriptio Montis Pelii—Isidori Characeni Mansiones Parthicæ — Scymni Chii, vulgo Marciani Heracleotæ, Orbis Descriptio—Scymni Fragmenta à Luca Holstenio collecta—Plutarchi Libellus de Fluviis adscriptus — Agathemeri Compendiariarum Geographiæ Expositionum—Strabonis Epitome.

Doe, F. M. Notice des Principaux Monuments de la Ville de Troyes. 12° *Troyes*, 1838

Doeller, Dr C. Ueber die Capverden, nach dem Rio Grande und Futah-Djallon, Reiseskizzen aus Nord-West-Afrika. *Map and illustrations.* 4° *Leipzig*, 1884

Doering, Oscar. Observaciones Meteorológicas practicadas en Córdoba (República Argentina) durante el año de 1884. 8* *Buenos Ayres*, 1885
—— The same, 1885. 8* *Buenos Ayres*, 1886
—— Resultados de algunas Mediciones Barométricas en la Sierra de Córdoba. 8* *Buenos Ayres*, 1886

Doering, Oscar. La Variabilidad Interdiurna de la Temperatura en algunos puntos de la República Argentina y de América del Sur en general. III. Variabilidad de la Temperatura de Ushnaiá. 8* *Buenos Ayres*, 1886
—— The same. IV. Variabilidad de la Temperatura en Concordia. 8* *Buenos Ayres*, 1887

Doering, Dr D. Adolfo. See Argentine Rep., D : Appendix 2.

Dohrandt, F. See Schmidt, C.

Dolby-Tyler, Charles H. See Peru : Appendix 2.

Dokuchaev, Prof. V. V. The Russian Steppes : Study of the Soil in Russia, its Past and Present. Published by the Department of Agriculture, Ministry of Crown Domains, for the World's Columbian Exposition at Chicago ; editor of the English translation, John Martin Crawford: Large 8° *St Petersburg*, 1893

Döllen, W. Resultate einer astronomisch-geodätischen Verbindung zwischen Pulkowa und den Ufern des Ladogasees. 8* N.P., 1858
—— Die Zeitbestimmung vermittelst des tragbaren Durchgangsinstruments im Verticale des Polarsterns. 4* *St Petersburg*, 1863
—— The same. Zweite Abhandlung. 4* *St Petersburg*, 1874
—— Zeitstern-Ephemeriden auf das Jahr 1886 für die Zeitbestimmung vermittelst des tragbaren Durchgangsinstruments im Verticale des Polarsterns. 4* *St Petersburg*, 1886
—— Stern-Ephemeriden auf das Jahr 1887 zur Bestimmung von Zeit und Azimut mittelst des tragbaren Durchgangsinstruments im Verticale des Polarsterns. Large 8* *St Petersburg*, 1886
—— The same, 1888. Large 8* *St Petersburg*, 1887
—— The same, 1889. Large 8* *St Petersburg*, 1888
—— The same, 1891. Large 8* *St Petersburg*, 1890

Dollond, George. Description of the Atmospheric Recorder, or Self-Registering Apparatus for the various Changes of the Barometer, Thermometer, &c. *Plate.* Royal 8* N.D.

Dolomieu, Déodat de. Voyage aux Iles de Lipari fait en 1781, ou Notices sur les Iles Æoliennes, pour servir à l'Histoire des Volcans. 8° *Paris*, 1783
—— See Pinkerton, Vol. 5 : Appendix 1.

"Dolphin," Cruise of. See Lee, S. P.

Dombay, Francisci de. Grammatica linguæ Mauro-Arabicæ juxta vernaculi idiomatis usum ; accessit Vocabularium Latino-Mauro-Arabicum. *Plate.* Small 4° *Vienna*, 1800

Domenech, Abbé Em. Missionary Adventures in Texas and Mexico : a Personal Narrative of Six Years' Sojourn in those Regions. Translated from the French. *Map.* 8°   1858
—— Manuscrit Pictographique Américain, précéde d'une Notice sur l'Idéographie des Peaux-Rouges. 8°   *Paris*, 1860
—— Seven Years' Residence in the Great Deserts of North America. 2 vols. *Map and plates.* 8°   1860
Domeyko, Ignacio. Viaje a las Cordilleras de Talcaide Chillan. 8*   1849
—— Memoria sobre la Colonizacion en Chile. 8*   [1850]
Dominguez, Luis L. *See* Hakluyt Soc. Publ., Vol. 81 : Appendix 1.
Domis, H. I. De Residentie Passoeroeang op het Eiland Java. *Map and plates.* 8°   *The Hague*, 1836
Donaldson, J. W. *See* Key, T. H.
Donaldson, Thomas. The Public Domain, its History, with Statistics, with References to the National Domain, Colonisation, Acquirement of Territory, the Survey, Administration, and Several Methods of Sale and Disposition of the Public Domain of the United States ; with Sketch of Legislative History of the Land States and Territories, and References to the Land System of the Colonies, and also that of several Foreign Governments. 3rd edition. *Maps and diagrams.* 8°
Washington, 1884
—— Eleventh Census of the United States, Robert P. Porter, Superintendent. Extra Census Bulletin : Indians—Eastern Band of Cherokees of North Carolina. *Maps and plates.* 4*   *Washington*, 1892
—— Extra Census Bulletin : Indians—The Six Nations of New York—Cayugas, Mohawks (Saint Regis), Oneidas, Onondagas, Senecas, Tuscaroras. *Maps and plates.* 4°   *Washington*, 1892
Doniphan's Expedition. *See* Wislizenus.
Donkin, John G. Trooper and Redskin in the Far North-West : Recollections of Life in the North-West Mounted Police, Canada, 1884-88. *Map and portrait.* 8°
1889
Donkin, Lieut.-General Sir R. Dissertation on the Course and Probable Termination of the Niger. *Maps.* 8° 1829
Doolittle, Rev. Justus. Social Life of the Chinese, with some Account of their Religious, Governmental, Educational, and Business Customs and Opinions, with special but not exclusive reference to Fuhchau. 2 vols. *Plates.* 12° 1866
Doolittle, Thomas. Earthquakes Explained and Practically Improved : occasioned by the late Earthquake on 8th September 1692, in London, many other parts in England, and beyond Sea. 18°
1693

D'Orbigny, A. Voyage dans l'Amérique Méridionale (le Brésil, la République Orientale de l'Uruguay, la République Argentine, la Patagonie, la République du Chili, la République de Bolivia, la République du Pérou), exécuté pendant les Années 1826, 1827, 1828, 1829, 1830, 1831, 1832, et 1833. 9 vols. Small folio
Paris, 1835-47
CONTENTS.
VOLS. I. AND II.—Partie Historique. *Portrait*   1835-43
VOL. III.—Pt. 1.—Historique (1844). Pt. 2.—Géographie (1846). Pt. 3.—Géologie (1842). Pt. 4.—Paléontologie (1842).
VOL. IV.—Pt. 1.—L'Homme Américain (de l'Amérique Méridionale), considéré sous ses Rapports Physiologiques et Moraux (1838-39). Pt. 2.—Mammifères [by A. D'Orbigny and P. Gervais], (1847). Pt. 3.—Oiseaux (1835-44).
VOL. V.—Pt. 1.—Reptiles (1847). Pt. 2.—Poissons [by A. Valenciennes] (1847). Pt. 3.—Mollusques (1835-43). Pt. 4.—Zoophytes (1839-46). Pt. 5.—Foraminifères (1839).
VOL. VI.—Pt. 1.—Crustacés [by A. Milne Edwards and H. Lucas] (1843). Pt. 2.—Insectes [by E. Blanchard and A. Brullé] (1837-43).
VOL. VII.—Pts. 1 and 2.—Cryptogamie ; Sertum Patagonicum ; Cryptogames de la Patagonie, et Florula Boliviensis ; Cryptogames de la Bolivia [by C. Montague] (1839). Pt. 3.—Palmiers ; Palmetum Orbignianum ; Descriptio Palmarum in Paraguaria et Bolivia creseentium [by C. F. P. von Martius] (1847).
VOL. VIII.—Atlas Historique, Géographique, Géologique, Paléontologique, et Botanique (1847).
VOL. IX.—Atlas Zoologique (1847).
—— L'Homme Américain (de l'Amérique Méridionale), considéré sous ses Rapports Physiologiques et Moraux. 2 vols. *Map.* 8°   *Paris*, 1839
Doré, Gustave. *See* Taine.
Doria, G. I Naturalisti Italiani alla Nuova Guinea e specialmente delle loro scoperte Zoologische. Part 1. 8° *Rome*, 1878
D'Orleans. *See* Orleans.
Dorn, Alexander. Die Seehäfen des Weltverkehrs, dargestellt von Josef Ritter von Lehnert, Johann Holeczek, Dr Karl Zehden, Dr Theodor Cicalek, Ernst Becher, Rudolf Pajér, Adolf Schwarz [and, in the case of Vol. 2, the following additional names], Robert Müller, Friedrich Ritter Müller von Elblein, Eduard Edlen von Friedenfels, Alfred Freiherrn von Koudelka, unter Redaction von Alexander Dorn. 1 Band.—

Dorn, Alexander—*continued.*
Häfen Europas sowie der Asiatischen und Afrikanischen Küsten des Mittelmeerbeckens. 2 Band.—Häfen ausserhalb Europas und des Mittelmeerheckens. *Plans and illustrations.* Large 8°
Vienna, 1891-92

Dorn, B. Mélanges Asiatiques. [Einige Bemerkungen zur Geographie Persiens ; Auszüge aus zwei morgenländischen Schriftstellern, betreffend das Kaspische Meer und angränzende Länder ; Morgenländische Benennungen der Fahrzeuge auf dem Kaspischen Meere.] 8°
St Petersburg, 1870
—— Inventaire des Monnaies des Khalifes Orientaux, et de plusiers autres Dynasties. 8° *St Petersburg*, 1877
—— *See* Neamet Ullah.

Dornseiffen, Dr J. *See* Holland : Appendix 2.

Dörpfeld, Dr W. *See* Schliemann.

Dorsey, James O. Omaha and Ponka Letters. [Smithsonian Institution, Bureau of Ethnology Publ.] 8°
Washington, 1891
—— *See* United States, G, *b* : Appendix 2.

D'Orsey, Rev. J. D. Portuguese Discoveries, Dependencies, and Missions in Asia and Africa. Small 8° 1893

Doucette, M. de la. Histoire, Antiquités, Usage, Dialectes des Hautes - Alpes. *Map and plates.* 8° *Paris*, 1820

Doue, J. M. Bertrand de. De la Fréquence comparée des Vents supérieurs et inférieurs sous le climat du Puy en Velay, et de leur distribution. 8°
Versailles, 1851
—— Quatrième Mémoire sur la fréquence et la capacité pluvieuse des Vents supérieurs et inférieurs sur la Station du Puy. 8° *Paris*, 1857

Dougall, John. *See* Tofiño de San Miguel.

Doughty, C. M. On the Jöstedal-bræ Glaciers in Norway. *Plate.* 8° 1866
—— Documents Épigraphiques recueillis dans le Nord de l'Arabie. [The author's account of his travels is given in English.] *Plates.* 4° *Paris*, 1884
—— Travels in Arabia Deserta. 2 vols. *Map, plates, &c.* *Cambridge*, 1888

Douglas, Lieut. C. Report on the River Jumna, between Agra and Ooreah. *Plate.* [From the India Records, N.-W. Provinces, Part 2.] 8° *Agra*, 1855-64

Douglas, Capt. *See* Eyriès, Vol. 2 : Appendix 1.

Douglas, Prof. Robert K. China. *Map and illustrations.* 8° 1882

Douglass, James Nicholas. The Wolf Rock Lighthouse ; with an Abstract of the Discussion upon the Paper. *Plates.* 8° 1870

Doull, Alex. Report and Outline of a Plan by which an Extensive Railway may be constructed in the British North American Colonies, combining its execution with an enlarged scheme of Colonisation and Reclamation of Waste Land. *Maps.* 8° 1850
—— Employment and Colonisation of the Million, based upon a proposed Railway Communication from the Atlantic to the Pacific. 8° 1851
—— Project for Opening a North-West Passage between the Atlantic and Pacific Oceans, by means of a Railway on British Territory. 8° 1852

Dounton. *See* Downton.

Douthwaite, A. W. Notes on Corea. 16* *Shanghai*, 1884

Douville, J. B. Voyage au Congo et dans l'Intérieur de l'Afrique Equinoxiale, 1828-30. 3 vols. 8° *Paris*, 1832
—— Atlas to the same. 4° *Paris* [1832]
—— Ma Défense, ou Réponse à l'Anonyme Anglais du *Foreign Quarterly Review*, sur le Voyage au Congo ; avec Projet de Voyage en Afrique. 8* *Paris*, 1832
—— Voyage au Congo et dans l'Intérieur de l'Afrique Equinoxiale, &c. [A Review of the Work, and of M. Douville's Reply, " Ma Défense," &c.] 8* 1832
—— Trente mois de ma Vie, quinze mois avant et quinze mois après mon Voyage au Congo ; suivie de détails sur les Mœurs et les Usages des Habitans du Brésil et de Buenos Ayres, et d'une Description de la Colonie Patagonia. 8°
Paris [1833]

Dove, Prof. H. W. Repertorium der Physik. Band IV. Meteorologie, specifische Wärme, strahlende Wärme. *Maps and plates.* 8° *Berlin*, 1841
—— Remarks on his recently-constructed Maps of the Monthly Isothermal Lines of the Globe, and on some of the principal conclusions in regard to Climatology deducible from them ; with an Introductory Notice by Col. Edward Sabine. 8* 1849
—— Die Verbreitung der Wärme auf der Oberfläche der Erde erläutert durch Isothermen, thermische Isanomalen, und Temperaturcurven. *Maps and tables.* 4* *Berlin*, 1852
—— The Distribution of Heat over the Surface of the Globe, illustrated by Isothermal, Thermic Isabnormal, and other Curves of Temperature. Folio 1853
—— Die Verbreitung der Wärme in der nördlichen Hemisphäre innerhalb des 40. Breitengrades, auf zwei von H. Kiepert entworfenen Karten : 1, Karte der nördlichen Hemisphäre ; 2, Karte der Nordpolarländer. 8* *Berlin*, 1855

Dove, Prof. H. W. The Law of Storms considered in connection with the Ordinary Movements of the Atmosphere. 2nd edition. Translated by R. H. Scott. *Charts.* 8°   1862
—— Die Monats- und Jahresisothermen in der Polarprojecion, &c. *Maps.* Oblong 4°   *Berlin*, 1864

Dove, Dr Karl. Das Klima des ausser-tropischen Südafrika mit Berücksichtigung der geographischen und wirtschaftlichen Beziehungen nach klimatischen Provinzen dargestellt. *Maps.* 8°
                                    Göttingen, 1888
—— Kulturzonen von Nord-Abessinien. (Ergänzungsheft, 97—Petermann's Mittheilungen). *Map.* 4°   *Gotha*, 1890
—— Studien über Ostafrika. 3. Die mutmasslichen Verbreitungsgungen der [Malaria in Ostafrika. 4*   *Stuttgart*, 1891
—— Niederschlagsmengen am Kap der Guten Hoffnung. 4*   *Gotha*, 1892
—— Ueber meteorologische und verwandte Beobachtungen in Südwestafrika. 8*

Dow, A. *See* Ferishta.

Downes, John. Occultations of Planets and Stars by the Moon during 1853. 4*   *Washington*, 1853

Downton, Lieut-General Nicholas. *See* Astley, Vol. 1; Gottfried; Kerr, Vols. 7, 8, 9; Allgemeine Historie, Vol. 1; Purchas, Vol. 1, Book 3 : Appendix 1.

Doyne, W. T. Report upon the Plains and Rivers of Canterbury, New Zealand. *Plans.* Folio *   *Christchurch*, 1864
—— Second Report upon the River Waimakariri and the Lower Plains of Canterbury, New Zealand. Folio *
                                    Christchurch, 1865

Dozon, Aug. *See* Nalivkine, V. P.

Drach, S. M. Deductions from Mr Glaisher's "Meteorological Corrections." 8*   1851
—— Observations on Base-Length of Great Pyramid, and Royal Coffer's Dimensions. 8*   1872
—— Hypothetical Phœnician Mariner's Guide, or Supposed Names on European, &c., Coasts, as derived from the Hebrew Language, on the presumption that the Phœnician Commonsense Names were distorted by their Greek successors to form the base of the Lying Legends passing current in the World as the Greek-Latin Mythology. MS.

"Drache." Die Ergebnisse der Untersuchungsfahrten S. M. Knbt, "Drache" (Kommandant Korvetten-Kapitän Holzhauer), in der Nordsee in den Sommern 1881, 1882, und 1884. *Maps, &c.* 4°
                                    Berlin, 1886

Dragovna, Marko. Pokushai za Bibliographiju o Tsornoi Gori sastalvno Marko Dragovna. 8°   *Cettinje*, 1892

Drake, C. F. Tyrwhitt. Modern Jerusalem; with a Memoir. 8°   1875
—— *See* Burton, R. F.

Drake, Sir Francis. Lives and Voyages of Drake, Cavendish, and Dampier ; including an Introductory View of earlier Discoveries in the South Sea, and the History of the Buccaneers. *Portraits.* 16°   *Edinburgh*, 1831
—— *See* Barrow ; Peralta; *also* Hakluyt Soc. Publ., Vols. 4, 16 ; Burney, Vol. 1 ; Callander, Vol. 1; Churchill, Vol. 8 ; Gottfried ; Hakluyt, Vols. 2, 3, 4 ; Harris, Vol. 1 ; Kerr, Vol. 7 ; Laharpe, Vol. 15 ; Purchas, Vol. 4, Book 6 ; World Displayed, Vol. 5 ; New Collection, Vol. 3 ; Allgemeine Historie, Vols. 1, 12 : Appendix 1.

Drake, George. *See* Hakluyt, Vol. 3 : Appendix 1.

Drake, John. *See* Hakluyt, Vol. 4 : Appendix 1.

Dralet, M. Description des Pyrénées, considérées principalement sous les Rapports de la Géologie, de l'Économie Politique, Rurale et Forestière, de l'Industrie et du Commerce. 2 vols. *Maps and tables.* 8°   *Paris*, 1813

Draper, Lyman C. Madison, the Capital of Wisconsin, its Growth, Progress, Condition, Wants, and Capabilities. 8*
                                    Madison, Wis., 1857

Drapiez, M. Notice sur l'Établissement Géographique de Bruxelles. *Plates.* 12*
                                    Brussels, 1836
—— The same. *Plate.* 12* *Brussels*, 1842

Drasche, R. von. Die Insel Réunion (Bourbon) im Indischen Ocean. Eine geologisch-petrographische Studie, mit einem Anhange über die Insel Mauritius. *Maps and plates.* 4°   *Vienna*, 1878

Drayson, Major-General Alfred W. Sporting Scenes amongst the Kaffirs of South Africa. *Plates.* 8°   1858

Drayton, Michael. [Poly-Olbion.] A Chorographicall Description of all the Tracts, Rivers, Mountains, Forests, and other parts of this Renowned Isle of Great Britain, with intermixture of the most Remarkable Stories, Antiquities, Wonders, Rarities, Pleasures, and Commodities of the same. Divided into two Bookes ; the latter containing Twelve Songs, never before Imprinted, Digested into a Poem by Michael Drayton, Esquire. With a Table added, for Direction to those Occurrences of Story and Antiquitie, whereunto the Course of the Volume easily leades not. *Frontispiece and portrait.* 12°   1622 [1876]
—— The same, continued. 12°   [1876]

Drayton, Michael. The Second Part, or a Continuance of Poly-Olbion from the Eighteenth Song. Containing all the Tracts, Rivers, Mountaines, and Forests, intermixed with the most Remarkable Stories, Antiquities, Wonders, Rarities, Pleasures, and Commodities of the East and Northern Parts of this Isle, lying betwixt the two famous Rivers of Thames and Tweed. 12° 1622 [1876]

Drew, F. The Possibility of Applying the Roman Alphabet generally to the Languages of India. 8* [1875]
—— The Jummoo and Kashmir Territories: a Geographical Account. *Maps and plates.* 8° 1875
—— The Northern Barrier of India: a Popular Account of the Jummoo and Kashmir Territories. *Map and plates.* 8° 1877

Drew, John. *See* Bullar.

Driesch, Gerard Corn. von den. Historische Nachricht von der Röm. Kaiserl. Gross-Botschaft nach Constantinopel; worinnen ganz besondere Nachrichten von der Türken Policey, Religion, Griechischen Antiquitäten, &c. *Portraits and plates.* Small 4° *Nuremberg,* 1723

Driver, J. Letters from Madeira, in 1834. 12° 1838

Drouillet, L. Les Isthmes Américains. Projet d'une Exploration Géographique Internationale des Terrains qui semblent présenter le plus de Facilités pour le Percement d'un Canale Maritime Interocéanique. *Map.* 8* *Paris,* 1876

Drouville. *See* Eyriès, Vol. 14; Appendix 1.

Drovetti, Chev. Lettre sur une Nouvelle Mesure du Coudée trouvée à Memphis. *Plate.* 4* *Paris,* 1827
—— *See* Phillips [3] New Voyages and Travels, vol. 7; Appendix 1.

Droysen, J. G. Städtegründungen Alexanders und seiner Nachfolger. 8° N.P., 1843

Drude, Dr Oscar. Die Florenreiche der Erde. (Ergänzungsheft, 74—Petermann's Mittheilungen.) *Maps.* 4° *Gotha,* 1884
—— Handbuch der Pflanzengeographie. (Bibliothek Geographischer Handbücher, herausgegeben von Prof. Dr Friedrich Ratzel.) *Maps.* 8° *Stuttgart,* 1890

Drummond, Alex. Travels through different Cities of Germany, Italy, Greece, and several Parts of Asia, as far as the Banks of the Euphrates, in a Series of Letters, containing an Account of what is most Remarkable in their Present State, as well as in their Monuments of Antiquity. *Maps and plates.* Folio 1754

Drummond, A. T. The Distribution of Canadian Forest Trees in its Relation to Climate and other Causes. 8° *Montreal,* 1885

Drummond, Major H. Report on the Deposits of Graphite near Almorah, 1850. [From the India Records, Vol. 1, N.W. Provinces.] *Plate.* 8° *Agra,* 1855

Drummond, Prof. Henry. Tropical Africa. *Maps and illustrations.* 8° 1888
—— Tropical Africa. 4th edition. *Map and illustrations.* 8° 1891

Drury, Capt. Revised Sailing Directions for the Northern Part of the Colony of New Zealand. 12° *Auckland,* 1854

Drury, Colonel Heber. Reminiscences of Life and Sport in Southern India. 12° 1890

Drury, Robert. The Pleasant and Surprising Adventures of R. D., during his Fifteen Years Captivity on the Island of Madagascar. Written by himself. 12° 1826
—— Madagascar, or Robert Drury's Journal during Fifteen Years Captivity on that Island. [*Title-page imperfect.*] Small 8° N.D.
—— *See* Lafond de Lurcy, Vol. 6: Appendix 1.

Drygalski, Dr Erich von. Die Geoiddeformationen der Eiszeit. 8* *Berlin,* 1887
—— Ueber Bewegungen der Kontinente zur Eiszeit und ihren Zusammenhang mit den Wärmeschwankungen in der Erdrinde. 8* *Berlin,* 1889
—— Grönlands Gletscher und Inlandeis. *Plates.* 8* *Berlin,* 1892

Dubail, —, and — Grièze. Cartes croquis de Géographie militaire . . . . 8° *Paris,* 1875

Dubois, Abbé J. A. Description of the Character, Manners, and Customs of the People of India, and of their Institutions, Religious and Civil. 4° 1817

Dubois, Marcel. Examen de la Géographie de Strabon: Étude Critique de la Méthode et des Sources. Large 8° *Paris,* 1891

Du Bois Reymond, Emil. Gedächtnissrede auf Paul Erman. 4* *Berlin,* 1853

Dubourdieu, Rev. John. Statistical Survey of the County of Down, with Observations on the Means of Improvement. *Map and plates.* 8° *Dublin,* 1802
—— Statistical Survey of the County of Antrim, with Observations on the Means of Improvement. *Maps and plates.* 8° *Dublin,* 1812

Dubrovin. *See* Prejevalsky.

Ducat, Lieut. W. M. Report on Project for Reclaiming Land between Bombay and Trombay; with a Memorandum by Lieut.-Col. A. De Lisle. *Maps.* [From the India Records, No. 68, Bombay.] 1863

Ducat, Lieut. W. M. Papers relating to Canal Irrigation in Sind, with Suggestions for its Improvement. *Maps.* [From the India Records, No. 69, Bombay.] 1863

Ducatel, J. T. Annual Report of the Geologist of Maryland, 1837, 1838, and 1839, and a Treatise on Lime-Burning. 3 pts. *Maps and plates.* 8* *Annapolis,* 1837-39
—— Report on the New Map of Maryland, 1834. 8* *Annapolis,* 1834
—— **and J. H. Alexander.** Reports of the Geologist and Engineer on the New Map of Maryland, 1835-36. *Maps.* 2 parts. 8* *Baltimore,* 1835-37

Du Cerceau, Father. *See* Krusinski.

Du Chaillu, Paul B. Explorations and Adventures in Equatorial Africa; with Accounts of the Manners and Customs of the People, and of the Chace of the Gorilla, Crocodile, and other Animals. *Map and plates.* 8° 1861
—— Voyages et Aventures dans l'Afrique Équatoriale, Mœurs et Coutumes des Habitans, &c. *Maps and plates.* Royal 8° *Paris,* 1863
—— A Journey to Ashango-Land, and Further Penetration into Equatorial Africa. *Map and plates.* 8° 1867
—— The Land of the Midnight Sun: Summer and Winter Journeys through Sweden, Norway, Lapland, and Northern Finland; with Descriptions of the Inner Life of the People, their Manners and Customs, the Primitive Antiquities, &c. 2 vols. *Map and illustrations.* 8° 1881

Duchemin, I. Expériences pratiques de la Boussole circulaire faites à bord des Navires de l'État en 1873, 1874, et 1875. Square 8* *Paris,* 1875

Ducket, G. *See* Hakluyt, Vol. 1: Appendix 1.

Dudley, Robert. Dell' Arcano del Mare. 3 vols. *Plates.* Folio *Florence,* 1646-47
—— *See* Hakluyt, Vol. 4: Appendix 1.

Due, Lieut. *See* Hansteen.

Dufau et Guadet. Dictionnaire Universel abrégé de Géographie Ancienne comparée. 2 vols. in 1. *Map.* 8° *Paris,* 1820

Duff, A. The Proposed Mission to Lake Nyassa . . . : Statement submitted to the Commission of the Free Church of Scotland. *Map separate.* 8* *Edinburgh,* 1875

Duff, Sir Mountstuart E. Grant. A Political Survey. *Maps.* 8* *Edinburgh,* 1868
—— Address to the Royal Historical Society. 8* 1892

Dufferin, Lord. Letters from High Latitudes: being an Account of a Voyage to Iceland, Jan Mayen, and Spitzbergen in 1856. *Maps and plates.* 8° 1857
—— Speech of, with the Comments of the English Press. 8* 1874

Duffy, Bella. The Tuscan Republics (Florence, Siena, Pisa, and Lucca), with Genoa. (The Story of the Nations Series.) *Map and illustrations.* 8° 1892

Du Fief, Prof. J. Cours gradué de Géographie, rédigé conformément au Programme du Gouvernement à l'usage de l'Enseignement moyen du degré supérieur. 4th edition. 12° *Brussels,* 1873
—— Congrés International de Géographie Commerciale. Deuxième Session. Rapport présenté à la Société Belge de Géographie, le 3 Novembre 1879. 8* *Brussels,* 1879
—— La Question du Congo depuis son origine jusqu' aujourd'hui : Explorations, Associations du Congo, État Independant du Congo, Conférence de Berlin, Géographie du Bassin du Congo. *Maps.* 8* *Brussels,* 1885
—— La Densité de la Population en Belgique et dans les autres pays du Monde. 8* *Brussels,* 1887
—— Le Partage de l'Afrique entre les puissances Européennes. *Map.* 8* *Brussels,* 1890
—— H. M. Stanley à la Société Royale Belge de Géographie de Bruxelles. 8* *Brussels* [1890]

Dufourny. A. Royaume de Belgique, Ministère de l'Agriculture, de l'Industrie, et des Travaux publics. Guide du Batelier, ouvrage publié d'après les ordres du Gouvernement. Édition de 1889. *Maps and plans.* 12° *Brussels,* 1889

Dufrenoy, —, and Élie de Beaumont. Recherches sur les Terrains Volcaniques des deux Siciles comparés à ceux de la France centrale. *Maps.* Small 8° 1838

Dufton, Henry. Narrative of a Journey through Abyssinia, in 1862-63; with an Appendix on "The Abyssinian Captives Question." *Maps.* 8° 1867

Dugdale. *See* Varenius.

Du Halde, J. B. Description Géographique, Historique, Chronologique, Politique, et Physique de l'Empire de la Chine et de Tartarie Chinoise. 4 vols. *Maps and plates.* Imp. folio *Paris,* 1735
—— Description Géographique, Historique . . . et Physique de l'Empire de la Chine et de la Tartarie Chinoise, &c. 4 vols. *Maps and plates.* 4° *The Hague,* 1736
—— A Description of the Empire of China, and Chinese Tartary, together with the Kingdoms of Korea and Tibet . . . From the French of J. B. du Halde, with Notes . . . by the translator. 2 vols. *Maps and plates.* Folio. 1738-41
—— The General History of China: containing a Geographical, Historical, Chronological, Political, and Physical Description of the Empire of China, Chinese-Tartary, Corea and Thibet, &c. 3rd edition. 4 vols. 8° 1741

Du Halde, J. B. *See* The World Displayed, Vol. 16, p. 609: Appendix 1.

Duhamel, H. *See* Conway and Coolidge.

Duke, Joshua. Ince's Kashmir Handbook: a Guide for Visitors. 12° *Calcutta*, 1888

—— Appendix to Ince's Guide to Kashmir, Rawal Pindi to Srinagar: a Detailed Account of the New Jhelum Valley Road; together with a Brief Note of Five other Routes leading into the Valley. *Maps in separate cover.* 12° *Calcutta*, 1892

Duke, Surgeon-Major O. T. A Historical and Descriptive Report on the Districts of Thal-Chotiali and Harnai, with the adjacent Country inhabited by Biluch and Pathan Tribes. *Maps.* Folio. *Calcutta*, 1883

Du Lac, Perrin. *See* Phillips [1], Vol. 6; A Collection of Modern and Contemporary Voyages and Travels: Appendix 1.

Dulaurier, E. *See* Daron.

Dulcken, H. W. *See* Peters; Pfeiffer.

Dumergue, E. Machærus, the Prison House of John the Baptist, its Geographical and Biblical Locality identified. 8° *Douglas*, 1875

—— The Chotts of Tunis; or, The Great Inland Sea of North Africa in Ancient Times. *Map.* 12* 1883

Dumont, P. J. *See* Phillips [3], Vol. 2, New Voyages and Travels: Appendix 1.

Dumoulin, V. *See* Kulczyeki, A.

Dunant, J. Henry. Notice sur la Régence de Tunis. 8° *Geneva*, 1858

Dunant, P. L. Recherches sur le Mouvement de la Population de la Ville de Genève de 1845-72. *Tables.* 4° *Geneva*, 1876

Dunbar, —. *See* Phillips [1], Vol. 6, A Collection of Modern Contemporary Voyages and Travels: Appendix 1.

"Dunbar," Ship. *See* New South Wales, E: Appendix 2.

Duncan, Charles. Campaign with the Turks in Asia. 2 vols. *Map.* 8° 1855

Duncan, Colonel F. The Nile Expedition of 1885. 8* [*Woolwich*, 1887]

Duncan, George. Geography of India . . . 4th edition. 12° *Madras*, 1868

—— The same. 10th edition. 16° 1880

Duncan, John. Travels in Western Africa in 1845 and 1846, comprising a Journey from Whydah through Dahomey to Adofoodia, in the Interior. 2 vols. *Map.* 8° 1847

Duncan, P. M. Cassell's Natural History. Vols. 1-6. *Plates.* 4° [1877-83]

—— *See* India, C (Palæontologia Indica): Appendix 2.

Dundonald, Earl of, and H. R. Fox Bourne. The Life of Thomas, Lord Cochrane, tenth Earl of Dundonald, &c. 2 vols. *Portrait.* 8° 1869

Dunér, N., and A. E. Nordenskiöld. Explanatory Remarks in illustration of a Map of Spitzbergen. 8* *Stockholm*, 1865

Dunglison, Robley. A Public Discourse in Commemoration of Peter S. du Ponceau, late President of the American Philosophical Society. 8* *Philadelphia*, 1844

Dunlop, Alexander. Notes on the Isthmus of Panama, with Remarks on its Physical Geography, and its Prospects in connection with the Gold Regions, Gold Mining, and Washing. 8* 1852

Dunlop, Charles. Brazil as a Field for Emigration, its Geography, Climate, &c. 8* [1866]

Dunlop, R. H. W. Hunting in the Himalaya; with Notices of Customs and Countries from the Elephant Haunts of the Dehra Doon to the Bunchowr Tracks in Eternal Snow. *Map and plates.* 8° 1860

Dunlop, W. B. The March of the Mongol. (Reprinted from the *Asiatic Quarterly Review* for January 1889.) 8* 1889

—— The Key of Western China. (Reprinted from the *Asiatic Quarterly Review* for April 1889.) 8* 1889

Dunmore, Earl of. The Pamirs: being a Narrative of a Year's Expedition on horseback and on foot through Kashmir, Western Tibet, Chinese Tartary, and Russian Central Asia. 2 vols. *Maps and illustrations.* Small 8° 1893

Dunn, A. J. St Louis du Rhône, the New French Port in the Mediterranean. *Map.* 8* 1880

Dunraven, Earl of. The Great Divide: Travels in the Upper Yellowstone in the Summer of 1874. *Map and plates.* 8° 1876

Dunsford, H. A. H. The Opening of the Arctic Sea. *Map.* 12* 1890

Dunsterville, Commander Edward. The Lights of the British Islands. Corrected to 1856. 8° 1856

—— The Lights of the Coasts and Lakes of British North America. Corrected to 1856. 8° 1856

—— The Lighthouses, Lighted Beacons, and Floating Lights of the United States. Corrected to 1856. 8° 1856

—— The Lights of the West India Islands and adjacent Coasts. Corrected to 1856. 8° 1856

—— Admiralty Catalogue of Charts, Plans, Views, and Sailing Directions. 8° 1860

—— The Admiralty List of the Belgian, Dutch, Hanoverian, Danish, Prussian, Russian, Swedish and Norwegian Lights. Corrected to 1860. 8° 1860

[*Also* Eleven other Admiralty Lights, published in 1860-62.]

Dunton, John. *See* Churchill, Vol. 8: Appendix 1.

Dunwoody, H. H. C. *See* United States (Signal Service): Appendix 2.

Dupaty, President. Travels through Italy in 1785. 8°   1788

Du Pays, A. J. *See* Joanne (Hollande).

Du Périer, —. General History of all Voyages and Travels throughout the Old and New World, from the First Ages to this Present Time, illustrating both the Ancient and Modern Geography; containing an accurate Description of each Country, its Natural History and Products, the Religion, Customs, Manners, Trade, &c., of the Inhabitants, and whatsoever is curious and remarkable in any kind. *Plates.* 8°   1708

Du Périer, Lieut. Notes sur l'Atterrissage du Rio de la Plata, et sur les différentes Routes que l'on peut suivre pour remonter ce Fleuve jusqu'à Buenos Ayres. 8°
Paris, 1842

Duperrey, Capit. L. I. Voyage autour du Monde, exécuté par ordre du Roi, sur la corvette "La Coquille," pendant les années 1822, 1823, 1824, et 1825. 9 vols. 5 vols., 4°, Atlas; and 4 vols., folio
Paris, 1826-30
Vol. 1.—Partie Historique [all published]   1829
Vol. 2.—Hydrographie et Physique. *Maps*   1829-30
Vol. 3. — Botanique, par D'Urville, Bory de St Vincent et Brongniart; Cryptogamie, par Bory de St Vincent, 1828; Phanérogamie, par Brongniart, 1829.
Vol. 4.—Zoologie. Vol. 1. Par Lessen et Garnot   1826
Vol. 5.—Zoologie. Vol. 2. Par Lessen et Guérin Méneville   1830
Vol. 6.—Histoire du Voyage. Atlas
1826
Vol. 7.—Hydrographie. Atlas 1827
Vol. 8.—Histoire Naturelle, Botanique. Atlas   1826
Vol. 9.—Histoire Naturelle, Zoologie. Atlas   1826
—— Magnétisme Terrestre. 8°
Paris, 1834

Du Perron, A. *See* Bernouilli, J.

Du Petit-Thouars, A. Voyage autour du Monde sur la frégate "La Vénus," pendant les années 1836-39 *Paris*
Rélation. Vols. 1-4. *Map.* 8° 1840-43
Zoologie (1855) et Botanique (1864). [Forming Vol. 5.] 8°
Physique, par U. de Tessan. Vols. 6-10. 8°   1842-44
Atlas Pittoresque. Folio   1841
—— de Zoologie. Folio   1846
—— de Botanique. Folio   1846
—— Hydrographique. Folio   1845

Dupin, Baron Charles. Canal Maritime de Suez. Deux Rapports à l'Académie des Sciences. 8*   *Paris*, 1857-58

Duponchel, A. Le Chemin de Fer de l'Afrique Centrale: Étude Géographique. *Map.* 8*   *Montpellier*, 1875
—— Commission supérieure du Chemin de Fer Trans-Saharien. Notes sur l'organisation du Service des Études et la réglementation des chantiers de construction. *Map.* 8*   *Montpellier*, 1879
—— Le Chemin de Fer Trans-Saharien, Jonction Coloniale entre l'Algérie et le Soudan. Études préliminaires du projet, et Rapport de Mission. *Maps.* 8°
Paris, 1879
—— La Circulation des Vents à la Surface du Globe: Principes fondamentaux de la Nouvelle Théorie. 4*   *Paris*, 1891
—— La Circulation des Vents et de la Pluie dans l'Atmosphère. 8* *Paris*, 1892

Dupont, E. Société Belge des Ingénieurs et des Industriels: Conférence donnée à la Société le 29 Février 1888, sur les Résultats de l'Exploration Scientifique qu'il a faite au Congo en Juillet-Décembre 1887. 8*   *Brussels*, 1888
—— Lettres sur le Congo: Récit d'un Voyage scientifique entre l'Embouchure du Fleuve et le Confluent du Kassaï. *Maps and plates.* 8°   *Paris*, 1889

Dupré Deloire, E. F. M. Voyage à la Grande-Chartreuse, 1822. 12°
Valence, 1830
—— Une Visite à la Chartreuse près de Pavie. *Plates.* 12°   *Milan*, 1861
—— Guida al Sacro Monte di Varallo. Nuova edizione. *Plates.* 12° *Varallo*, N.D.

Dupré, —. *See* Eyriès, Vol. 14: Appendix 1.

Dupuis, Hanmer L. The Holy Places: a Narrative of Two Years Residence in Jerusalem and Palestine, with Notes on the dispersed Canaanite Tribes. 2 vols. 8°   1856

Dupuis, Joseph. Journal of a Residence in Ashantee, comprising Notes and Researches relative to the Gold Coast and the Interior of Western Africa. Chiefly collected from Arabic MSS. and Information by the Moslems of Guinea. *Map and plates.* 4°   1824

Dupuis, J. L'Ouverture du Fleuve Rouge au Commerce et les Événements du Tong-Kin, 1872-73: Journal de Voyage et d'Expédition. *Map and portrait.* 4°
Paris, 1879

Dupuy, R. Geography of Mauritius, for use in Schools and Colleges. *Map.* 12°   *Port Louis*, 1892

Dupuy, —. L'état de l'enseignement de la géographie en France. 8° *Paris*, N.D.

Durand, Abbé E. J. Considérations générales sur l'Amâzone. 8*
Paris, 1871
—— Les Indiens du Brésil, et en particulier du Bassin de l'Amâzone. 8*
Bordeaux, 1872

Durand, Abbé E. J. Coup d'œil sur l'ensemble des voies navigables de l'Amérique du Sud, et du Bassin de l'Amâzone en particulier. 8*
Bordeaux, 1872
—— Le Rio Negro du Nord et son bassin. 8* *Paris*, 1872
—— L'Amâzone Brésilien. 8* *Paris*, 1873
—— Le Solimoes ou Haut Amâzone Brésilien. 8* *Paris*, 1873
—— Le Rio Doce. 8* *Paris*, 1873
—— Voyages au Chimborazo, à l'Altar, et Ascension au Tunguragua. [Stübel, translated.] 8* *Paris*, 1874
—— Les Missions Catholiques Françaises. Texte 12°, Atlas 4° *Paris*, 1874

Durand, J. P. L. *See* Phillips [1], Vol. 4; [2] Vol. 1 : Appendix 1.

Durand, T. *See* Néry.

D'Urban, Sir Benjamin. Proceedings of the Board of Relief for the Destitute in Graham Town during 1834-35. 8°
Cape Town, 1836

D'Urban, Fortia. Dissertation sur le Passage du Rhône et des Alpes par Annibal. *Map.* 8° *Paris*, 1821
—— Recueil des Itinéraires Anciens, comprenant l'Itinéraire d'Antonin, la Table de Peutinger, et un Choix des Périples Grecs. 4° *Paris*, 1845

Duret, Théodore. Voyage en Asie : Le Japon, la Chine, la Mongolie, Java, Ceylan, l'Inde. 12° *Paris*, 1874

Durham, F. A. The Lone Star of Liberia : being the Outcome of Reflections on our own People. 8° 1892

Durier, C. Le Mont-Blanc. *Maps and plates.* 8° *Paris*, 1877

Durlacher, Alfred. Report on the Condition of the Colony of Western Australia, as shown by the Census taken 31st December 1859. Folio *Freemantle*, 1860

Duro, Cesareo Fernandez. Disquisiciones Nauticas. Conformacion, adorno y armamento de Naves Antiquas. Moletias y sufrimientos de sus tripulantes. Cómo eran las Carabelas de Colón. Los colores Nacionales. Prestigio y significacion de la bandera y el fanal. Buques Coraceros en el Siglo XV., y otras noticias. 8° *Madrid*, 1876
—— La Mar descrita por los Mareados. Mas Disquisiciones, &c. 8° *Madrid*, 1877
—— Navegaciones de los Muertos, y Vanidades de los vivos. Libro Tercero de las Disquisiciones Náuticas. 8°
Madrid, 1878
—— Los Ojos en el cielo. Libro Cuarto de las Disquisiciones Náuticas. 8°
Madrid, 1879
—— Colón y Pinzón. Informe relativo á los pormenores de descubrimiento del Nuevo Mundo presentado á la Real Academia de la Historia. 4°
Madrid, 1883

Durocher, J, *See* Gaimard, Paul.

Durrant, W. *See* Galton, Vacation Tourists.

D'Urville, Dumont J. Voyage de la corvette "L'Astrolabe," executé par Ordre du Roi, pendant les années 1826, '27, '28, '29, sous le commandement de M. J. Dumont D'Urville, &c. 13 vols. in 12 8°, and 1 vol. 4°; Atlas, 3 vols. in 7 folio, and 1 vol. elephant folio
Paris, 1830-35
Histoire du Voyage, par Dumont D'Urville. 5 vols. *Illustrations*
1830-33
Philologie, par Dumont D'Urville. 2 vols. in 1 1833-34
Botanique, par A. Lesson et A. Richard 1832
Zoologie, par J. R. C. Quoy et J. P. Gaimard. 4 vols. 1830-33
Faune Entomologique de l'Océan Pacifique, par J. A. Boisduval. 1ere ptie, Lepidoptères, 1832 ; 2me ptie, Coléoptères et autres ordres, 1835 —in 1.
Observations Nautiques, Météorologiques, Hydrographiques. et de Physique. Par Dumont D'Urville. 2 parts in 1. 4° 1833-34

Atlas. Historique, 3 vols. ⎫
—— Botanique, 1 vol. ⎬ Fol. 1833
—— Zoologie, 3 vols. ⎭

—— Hydrographique. Elephant folio 1833
—— Rapport sur les Opérations de la Campagne de la corvette "l'Astrolabe." *Maps.* 8* *Paris*, 1838
—— Expédition au Pole Antarctique des corvettes "l'Astrolabe" et la "Zélée." *Maps.* 8* *Paris*, 1840
—— Notice Nécrologique, par M. de la Roquette. Royal 8* *Poissy*, N.D.
—— Voyage au Pole Austral et dans l'Océanie sur les corvettes "L'Astrolabe" et "La Zélée," exécuté par ordre du Roi pendant les années 1837, '38, '39, '40, sous le commandement de M. J. Dumont D'Urville, &c. 22 vols. in 11, 8°; Atlas, 7 vols. in 5, folio *Paris*
Histoire du Voyage, par Dumont D'Urville. 10 vols. in 5 1842-46
Anthropologie, par — Dumoutier. 8° 1854
Zoologie, par — Hombrom et Honoré Jacquinot, 5 vols. in 2, 1846-54 (Mammifères et Oiseaux, par — Pucheran ; Reptiles et Poissons, par A. Guichenot; Crustacés, par H. Jacquinot et H. Lucas ; Insectes, par E. Blanchard ; Mollusques, Coquilles, et Zoophytes, par L. Rousseau).

D'Urville, Dumont J. Voyage au Pole Sud et dans l'Océanie sur les corvettes "L'Astrolabe" et "La Zélée"—*continued.*

Botanique, par — Hombron et H. Jacquinot. 2 vols. in 1, 1845 and 1853 (Plantes cellulaires, par C. Montagne ; Plantes vasculaires, par J. Decaisne).

Hydrographie, par C. A. Vincendon Dumoulin. 2 vols. in 1. 1843 and 1851. *Tables.*

Géologie, Minéralogie, et Géographie Physique du Voyage, par J. Grange. 2 vols. in 1. 1848 and 1854

Atlas Pittoresque. 2 vols. 1846

—— Botanique   1852 ⎫
—— Anthropologie   1842-47 ⎬ in 1.
—— Géologie   1847 ⎭
—— Zoologie   1842-53
—— Hydrographique   1847

—— [South Sea Vocabularies.] Part 2 of Philology of the "Voyage de Découvertes de 'l'Astrolabe.'" 8°   *Paris,* 1834

Dutens, J. V. *See* Pelham, Vol. 2 : Appendix 1.

Duthie, J. F. Report on a Botanical Tour in Kashmir. Vol. 1. (No. 1 of Records of the Botanical Survey of India.) 8*   *Calcutta,* 1893

Duthu, J. B. Navegacion Aérea al alcance de los sabios trabajos y observaciones de 1870 á 1880. *Plate.* 8*
Madrid, 1880

Dutreuil de Rhins, J. L. Le Royaume d'Annam et les Annamites. *Maps and plates.* 16°   *Paris,* 1879

—— L'Asie Centrale (Thibet et Régions limitrophes). Text 4°, and Atlas folio
Paris, 1889

Dutrieux, —. Note sur une affection cutanée parasitaire observée dans l'Afrique orientale. 8*   [*Ghent ?*] 1879

—— La Question Africaine au point de vue commercial. 8*   *Brussels,* 1880

—— Contribution à l'Étude des Maladies et de l'Acclimatement des Européens dans l'Afrique intertropicale. 8°
Ghent, 1880

Dutt, Jogesh Chunder. The Memory of the Early Arab Trade with India. (From *The National Magazine.*) Large 8*
Calcutta, 1888

—— Old Relics in Kamrup. 12*
Calcutta, [1891]

Dutton, Capt. Clarence E. The Hawaiian Islands and People. Lectures delivered at the U.S. National Museum, 9th February and 15th March 1884, under the auspices of the Smithsonian Institution and of the Anthropological and Biological Societies of Washington. Folio*   *Washington,* 1884

—— Volcanoes. Folio* *Washington,* 1884

Dutton, Capt. Clarence E. *See* United States, G, *c* : Appendix 2.

Dutton, Francis. South Australia and its Mines, with an Historical Sketch of the Colony, under its several Administrations, to the period of Captain Grey's departure. *Maps and plates.* 8° 1846

Dutton, Hely. Observations on Mr Archer's Statistical Survey of the County of Dublin. *Maps.* 8°   *Dublin,* 1802

Du Val, P. Traité de Géographie qui donne la Connoissance et l'usage du Globe et de la Carte, avecque les Figures necessaires pour ce sujet ; et des Tables pour connoistre dans les Cartes, les Pays, les Provinces, et les principales Villes du Monde. 12°   *Paris,* 1672

Duvaucel, A. *See* Eyriès, Vol. 14 : Appendix 1.

Duveyrier, H. Exploration du Sahara ; Les Touareg du Nord. *Map and plates.* 8°   *Paris,* 1864

—— La Tunisie. 8°   *Paris,* 1881

—— Liste de Positions Géographiques en Afrique (Continent et Iles). 1er fasc. A—G. 4*   *Paris,* 1884

—— La Confrérie Musselmane de Sîdi, Mohammed Ben Alî Es-Senousî, et son domaine gèographique en l'année 1300 de l'hégire=1883 de notre ère. *Map.* 8°
Paris, 1884

Duvivier, Gén. Solution de la Question de l'Algérie. *Maps.* 8°   *Paris,* 1841

—— Algérie. Quatorze Observations sur le dernier Mémoire du Gén. Bugeaud. 8°   *Paris,* 1842

—— Abolition de l'Esclavage, Civilisation du Centre de l'Afrique. 8* *Paris,* 1845

" Dwarf." *See* Bax.

Dwight, Theodore. *See* Mosquera.

Dybowski, Jean. La Route du Tchad, du Loango au Chari. *Map and illustrations.* Large 8°   *Paris,* 1893

Dyer, A. S. Christian Liberia, the Hope of the Dark Continent. With reference to the Work and Mission of Edward S. Morris of Philadelphia. *Portrait.* 12*
1879

Dyer, Lieut. G. L. Geography of the Sea. 8*   *Washington,* 1889

—— *See* United States, E, *a* (No. 77) : Appendix 2.

Dyer, W. T. Thistleton. *See* West Indies, A : Appendix 2.

Dykes, James William Ballantine. Salem, an Indian Collectorate. 8° 1853

E

Eachard, Lawrence. The Gazetteer's or Newsman's Interpreter : being a Geographical Index of all the considerable Cities, Patriarchships, Bishopricks, Universities, Dukedoms, Earldoms ; Imperial and Hance Towns, Ports, Forts, Castles, &c., in Europe ; of all the Empires, Kingdoms, Islands, Provinces, Peninsulas, &c., in Asia, Africa, and America. 12° 1724

Eales, H. L. *See* India, B : Appendix 2.

Eardley - Wilmot, A. P. What our Transports did in the Crimea in the Embarkation of the Turkish Army from Bulgaria to Eupatoria in the Spring of 1855. 8* 1867

Earl, George Windsor. Observations on the Commercial and Agricultural capabilities of the North Coast of New Holland, and the Advantages to be derived from the establishment of a Settlement in the vicinity of Raffles Bay. 8° 1836

—— The Eastern Seas ; or, Voyages and Adventures in the Indian Archipelago in 1832-34, comprising a Tour of the Island of Java ; Visits to Borneo, the Malay Peninsula, Siam, &c. ; also an Account of the Present State of Singapore ; with Observations on the Commercial Resources of the Archipelago. *Maps.* 8° 1837

—— The Native Races of the Indian Archipelago : Papuans. *Plates.* 8° 1853

—— A Correspondence relating to the Discovery of Gold in Australia. 8* 1853

—— A Handbook for Colonists in Tropical Australia. *Maps.* 8° *Pinang,* 1863

—— *See* also Kolff, D. H.

Earnshaw's Timekeeper. *See* Dalrymple, Tracts, Vol. 3.

East, Major C. J. *See* United Kingdom, G, War Office Publ. ; Appendix 2.

East, D. J. Western Africa : its Condition, and Christianity the Means of its Recovery. 12° 1844

Eastman, J. R. Report on the Difference of Longitude between Washington and Detroit, Michigan ; Carlin, Nevada, and Austin, Nevada. 4* *Washington,* 1874

Eastwick, Edward B. Venezuela ; or, Sketches of Life in a South American Republic ; with the History of the Loan of 1864. *Map.* 8° 1868

—— *See* Murray's Handbooks, Asia.

Eastwick, R. W. Egerton. Deli, in Sumatra. (From *The Fortnightly Review,* November 1893. Bound up with " The Ice Age and its Work," by A. R. Wallace.) 8* 1893

K

Eaton, D. The Englishman's Guide to Nice. *Loose map.* 12° *Nice,* 1875

Eaton, D. C. *See* United States, H, *a* (Prof. Papers) : Appendix 2.

Ebel, J. G. Anleitung auf die nützlichste und genussvollste Art in der Schweitz zu reisen. 2 vols. *Plates.* 8° *Zurich,* 1793

—— Schilderung der Gebirgsvölker der Schweiz. 2 vols. *Plates.* 8° *Leipzig,* 1798-1802

Eberhard, L. D. Wegweiser durch die preussischen Staaten. 8° *Berlin,* 1831

Ebers, G. Egypt, Descriptive, Historical, and Picturesque. Translated from the original German, by Clara Bell ; with an Introduction and Notes by S. Birch. Vol. I. *Illustrations.* Large 4° [1878]

—— Durch Gosen zum Sinai, aus dem Wanderbuche und der Bibliothek. *Maps and illustrations.* 8° *Leipzig,* 1881

Ebn-ed-din El Eghwati, Hadji. *See* Asia (General) : Appendix 2.

Ebn Batuta. *See* Ibn Batuta.

Ebn Haukal, an Arabian Traveller of the Tenth Century. Oriental Geography, translated by Sir W. Ouseley. *Map.* 4° 1800

Ebn-Khaldoun. Histoire de l'Afrique sous la Dynastie des Aghlabites, et de la Sicile, sous la Domination Musulmane ; accompagné d'une Traduction Française et de Notes, par A. Noel des Vergers. Arabe et Français. 8° *Paris,* 1841

Ebn-Omar el-Tounsy, Cheykh Mohammed. Voyage au Darfour. Traduit de l'Arabe ; et Préface contenant des remarques sur la Région du Nil-Blanc supérieur. *Maps and plates.* 8° *Paris,* 1845

—— Voyage au Ouadây. Traduit de l'Arabe par Perron ; Préface par Jomard. *Maps and plates.* 8° *Paris,* 1851

Eckardt, H. Matthaeus Merian, Skizze seines Lebens und ausführliche Beschreibung seiner Topographia Germaniæ nebst Verzeichniss der darin enthaltenen Kupferstiche. Eine kulterhistorische Studie von H. Eckardt. *Portrait.* 8° *Basle,* 1887

Eckardt, M. Der Archipel der Neu Hebriden. *Plates.* 8° *Hamburg,* 1882

Eckeberg, Charles Gustavus. A Short Account of the Chinese Husbandry. *See* Osbeck, P., " A Voyage to China," &c. ; *also* The Modern Traveller, p. 610 : Appendix I.

Eddy, C. W. Assisted Colonisation. 8* 1870

Edelfelt, E. G. Notes on New Guinea. [Newspaper cuttings.] 8* *Melbourne,* 1884

Edelmann, M. T. Neues Hygrometer. *Plate.* 8* N.P., N.D

Eden, Hon. Ashley. Evidence of, taken before the Indigo Commission sitting in Calcutta. 8*   *Calcutta*, 1860

Eden, C. H. China, Historical and Descriptive. *Map and plates.* 12° 1877
—— Frozen Asia: a Sketch of Modern Siberia. Together with an Account of the Native Tribes inhabiting that Region. *Map.* Small 8°   1879
—— *See* Warburton.

Eden, Richarde. The History of Trauayle in the West and East Indies, and other Countreys lying eyther way, towardes the Fruitfull and Ryche Moluccaes, as Moscouia, Persia, Arabia, Syria, Ægypte, Ethiopia, Guinea, China in Cathayo, and Giapan ; with a Discourse of the North-west Passage. Small 8°   1577
—— *See* Martyr ; Varthema.

Edgcumbe, Richard. A Missing Page in Alpine History. (From *The National Review*, October 1893.) 8*   1893

Edgar. Genealogical Collections concerning the Scottish House of Edgar ; with a Memoir of James Edgar, Private Secretary to the Chevalier St George. *Frontispiece.* Small 4°   1873

Edgar, J. W. Report on a Visit to Sikhim and the Thibetan Frontier in October, November, and December 1873. *Map.* 8°   *Calcutta*, 1874

Edgar, King. *See* Hakluyt, Vols. 1, 2 : Appendix 1.

Edge, Thomas. *See* Purchas, Vol. 3, Book 3 : Appendix 1.

Edgley, J. C. The Origin and Features of Mountain Systems ; with Remarks on the Ancient Glaciers of Wales. *Plate.* 8*   [1887]

Edlund, E. Ueber die Bildung des Eises im Meere. *Plate.* 8* [*Leipzig*, N.D.]

Edrisi. *See* Hartmann.

Edmund and Edward, Princes. *See* Hakluyt, Vol. 1 : Appendix 1.

Edward the Confessor. *See* Hakluyt, Vol. 2 : Appendix 1.

Edward, David B. The History of Texas ; or, The Emigrant's Guide to the Climate, Soil, and Productions of that Country, Geographically arranged. *Map.* 12°   *Cincinnati*, 1836

Edwardes, Charles. Rides and Studies in the Canary Islands. *Illustrations.* 8°   1888
—— Sardinia and the Sardes. 8° 1889

Edwardes, Major Herbert B. A Year on the Punjab Frontier in 1848-49. 2 vols. *Maps and plates.* 8°   1851

Edwards, A. *See* Hakluyt, Vol. 1 : Appendix 1.

Edwards, Amelia B. A Thousand Miles up the Nile. *Maps and plates.* 4° 1877
—— Pharaohs, Fellahs, and Explorers. *Portrait and illustrations.* 8°   1892

Edwards, Bryan. The History, Civil and Commercial, of the British Colonies in the West Indies. 2nd edition. 2 vols. *Maps and plates.* 4°   *London*, 1794
—— The same. 3rd edition. 3 vols. *Maps and plates.* 8°   1801
—— Historical Survey of the Island of Saint Domingo, together with an Account of the Maroon Negroes in the Island of Jamaica in 1793-94; also a Tour through the Islands of Barbadoes, St Vincent, Antigua, Tobago, and Grenada, in 1791-92, by Sir W. Young. *Maps and plates.* 4°   1801

Edwards, Capt. *See* Hamilton, G. ; *also* Eyriès, Vol. 3 : Appendix 1.

Edwards, Charles. Texas and Coahuila ; with an Exposition of the last Colonization Law. 8*   *New York*, 1834

Edwards, E. Milne. Investigações Geographicas dos Portuguezes. Traducção de Rodrigo Affonso Pequito. 8*
                     Lisbon, 1879

Edwards, Lieut. —. *See* Logan, P.

Edwards, Matilda Betham. Through Spain to the Sahara. *Plate.* 8°   1868

Edwin, King. *See* Hakluyt, Vol. 1 : Appendix 1.

Eedes, J. The Coast of South Africa : Gigantic Structures or Sea-Walls superseded. 8*   *Grahamstown*, 1862

Egede, Hans. Description of Greenland, showing the Natural History, Situation, Boundaries, and Face of the Country, the Rise and Progress of the Old Norwegian Colonies, the Ancient and Modern Inhabitants, &c. *Map and plates.* 8° 1745
—— Description of Greenland, with an Historical Introduction and a Life of the Author. *Map and woodcuts.* 8° 1818

Egerton, Lady Francis. Journal of a Tour in the Holy Land in May and June 1840. *Plates.* 8°   1841

Egerton, Lady Henrietta Grey. Alaska and its Glaciers. (From *The Nineteenth Century*, December 1892.) 8*   1892

Egerton, Sir P. de M. Grey. *See* Murchison ; *also* India, C (Geological Papers) : Appendix 2.

Egerton, Hon. W. An Illustrated Handbook of Indian Arms . . .; with an Introductory Sketch of the Military History of India. *Map and plates.* 8°   1880

Egilsson, S. *See* Gröndal.

Egli, Dr J. J. Die Entdeckung der Nilquellen. 8*   *Zürich*, 1867
—— Die Schweiz. *Illustrations.* 12°
                     Leipzig, 1886
—— Geschichte der geographischen Namenkunde. *Map.* 8° *Leipzig*, 1886
—— Kleine Schweizerkunde, ein Leitfaden in genauem Anschluss an des Verfassers "Neue Schweizerkunde." 14th edition. 12*   *St Gallen*, 1886

Egli, Dr J. J. Etymologisch-geographisches Lexikon. Separat-Ausgabe des lexikalischen Theils der "Nomina Geographica, Versuch einer allgemeinen geographischen Onomatologie." Small 4° *Leipzig*, 1880
—— Nomina Geographica. Sprach- und Sacherklärung von 42,000 geographischen Namen aller Erdräume. 2nd edition. Large 8° *Leipzig*, 1893

Egmont, J. Ægidius van, and John Heyman. Travels through part of Europe, Asia Minor, the Islands of the Archipelago, Syria, Palestine, Egypt, Mount Sinai, &c. Translated from the Low Dutch. 2 vols. *Illustrations.* 8° 1759

Egui, Bernard de. *See* Burney, Vol. 5 : Appendix 1.

Eguiluz, Diego de. Historia de la Mision de Mojos en la Republica de Bolivia escrita en 1696 por el P. Diego de Eguiluz. Publicada con varios Documentos inéditos referentes á esa Misión, Biografias, y Notas, por Enrique Torres Saldamando. Entregas 1ª. y 2ª. 8* *Lima*, 1884

Ehrenberg, C. G. Natur und Bildung der Coralleninseln und Corallenbänke in Rothen Meere. 4* *Berlin*, 1834

Ehrenberg, G. *See* Rose.

Ehrenmalm, Arwid. *See* Pinkerton, Vol. 1 ; Allgemeine Historie, Vol. 20 : Appendix 1.

Ehrenreich, Dr P. Beiträge zur Völkerkunde Brasiliens. *Plates.* Folio *Berlin*, 1891

Ehrmann, T. F. Kommodore Phillip's Reise nach der Botany-Bai auf Neuholland. *Map.* 12° *Stuttgart*, 1789
—— Beiträge zur Länder- und Staatenkunde der Tartarei. Aus Russischen Berichten. Mit einer Einleitung. Bibliothek der neuesten und wichtigsten Reisebeschreibungen zur Erweiterung der Erdkunde . . . herausgegeben von M. C. Sprengel, fortgesetzt von T. F. Ehrmann. Vierzehnter Band. *Map.* 8° *Weimar*, 1804

Eichhoff, F. G. Parallèle des Langues de l'Europe et de l'Inde, ou Étude des principales Langues Romanes, Germaniques, Slavonnes, et Celtiques, comparées entre elles et à la Langue Sanscrite ; avec un Essai de Transcription générale. 4° *Paris*, 1836

Eichstadt, F. *See* Sweden, A, Geological Survey : Appendix 1.

Eichthal, G. d'. Recherches sur l'Histoire et Origine des Foulahs ou Fellans. *Map.* 8* *Paris*, 1840
—— Mémoire sur l'Histoire Primitive des Races Océaniennes et Américaines. 8* *Paris*, 1843

Eichthal, G. d'. Études sur l'Histoire Primitive des Races Océaniennes et Américaines. 8° *Paris*, 1845
—— Étude sur les Origines Bouddhiques de la Civilisation Américaine. Première partie. *Plate.* 8* *Paris*, 1865

Eichwald, E. Reise auf dem Caspischen Meere und in den Caucasus in 1825-26. 3 vols. in 4. *Maps and plates.* 8° *Stuttgart*, 1834
—— Alte Geographie des Caspischen Meeres, des Kaukasus und des südlichen Russlands. Nach Griechischen, Römischen, und andern Quellen. *Maps, &c.* 8° *Berlin*, 1838
—— Lethaea Rossica ou Paléontologie de la Russie. Premier Volume—1re Ptie. Ancienne Période. Première partie, contenant la Flore de l'ancienne periode. 8° *Stuttgart*, 1855
—— Die Lethæa Rossica und ihre Gegner. 8* *Moscow.* 1869
—— *See* Baer and Helmersen, 8.

Eigner, A. Meteorologische Beobachtungen . . . an der Lenamündung. *See* Polar Observations, Russian: Appendix 2.

Eiloart, Ernest. The Land of Death. 12* 1887

Ekman, F. L. Description of Hydrographical and Meteorological Instruments exhibited . . . at the Philadelphia Exhibition, 1876. 8* *Stockholm*, 1876
—— On the General Causes of the Ocean Currents. 4* *Upsala*, 1876
—— Appareils Hydrographiques Exposés, par le Professeur F. L. Ekman, au Congrès Géographique de Venise, 1881. 12* [*Stockholm*, 1881]

Elbée, Sieur d'. *See* Astley, Vol. 3 : Appendix 1.

Elblein, Friedrich Ritter Müller von. *See* Dorn, A.

Elcano, —. *See* Navarette, Vol. 4 : Appendix 1.

Elcum, Rev. C. C. *See* Murray, T. B.

Eldad, the Danite. Relation d'Eldad le Danite Voyageur du IXe Siècle ; traduite en Français, suivie du Texte Hébreu et d'une Lettre Chaldéene. Par E. Carmoly. 8* *Paris*, 1838

Elder Expedition. Handbook of Instructions for the Guidance of the Officers of the Elder Scientific Exploration Expedition to the unknown portions of Australia. *Map.* 8* *Adelaide*, 1891
—— The Elder Exploring Party. [Newspaper cuttings.] 8* *Adelaide*, 1891
—— Journal of the Elder Scientific Exploring Expedition, 1891-92, under command of D. Lindsay ; equipped solely at the cost of Sir Thomas Elder, for the purpose of completing the exploration of Australia. *Maps separate.* 8° *Adelaide*, 1893
—— *See* Streich.

Elderton, W. A. Maps and Map Drawing. *Maps.* 12° 1890

Eldred, John. *See* Hakluyt, Vol. 2; Kerr, Vol. 8; Purchas, Vol. 2: Appendix 1.

Elek, P. Gegö. A' Moldvai Magyar Telepekröl. *Map.* 8° *Budapest*, 1838

Elgin, Earl of. Lord Elgin's Second Embassy to China. *See* Loch.

Elias, Ney. Introductory Sketch of the History of the Shans in Upper Burma and Western Yunnan. 8*
Calcutta, 1876

Eliot, John. The Rainfall of Cherrapunji. *Map.* 8* [1882]
—— Report on the Meteorology of India in 1886. *Map and charts.* 4°
Calcutta, 1887

"Eliza Scott," Schooner. Antarctic Voyage. *See* Moore, Wm.

Elkington, Capt. T. *See* Kerr, Vol. 9; Purchas, Vol. 1, Book 4: Appendix 1.

Ellerbeck, J. H. T. A Guide to the Canary Islands, calling at Madeira: Maps of Islands, Plans of Towns, Vocabulary, Illustrations, Routes for Tourists, and Hints to Invalids. 12° [1892]

Elles, Col. E. R. Report on the Pámir Expedition of 1883. Translated from the "Izvestiya" of the Imp. Russian Geo. Soc., No. 4 of 1883. 8* *Simla*, 1884

Ellesmere, Earl of. Guide to Northern Archæology, by the Royal Society of Northern Antiquaries of Copenhagen, Edited for the use of English Readers. 8° 1848
—— Essays on History, Biography, Geography, &c., contributed to the *Quarterly Review.* 8° 1858

Elliot, Capt. *See* Plaisted.

Elliot, Lieut-Col. C. Report on the Bustar and Kharonde Dependencies of the Raepore District. *Map and plates.* [From the India Records, No. 30.] 8°
Calcutta, 1861

Elliot, G. Gold and Mineral Prospects of Western India. 8* *Bombay*, 1874
—— Indian Remounts. 8* *Bombay*, 1874

Elliot, G. F. Scott, and Miss Catharine A. Raisin. Reports on Botany and Geology in Sierra Leone. 8* 1893

Elliot, Sir Henry. Appendix to the "Arabs in Sind." Vol. 3, Part 1, of the "Historians of India." 8°
Cape Town, 1853

Elliott, Sir C. A. Report on the Influence of Caste on Rates of Rent: Effect of Proceedings at last Settlement on Permanency of Tenure and on Condition of the Cultivator. [From the India Records, Vol. 2, No. 4.] 8° *Allahabad*, 1869

Elliott, C. B. Letters from the North of Europe: Travels in Holland, Denmark, Norway, Sweden, Finland, Russia, Prussia, and Saxony. 8° 1832

Elliot, C. B. Travels in Austria, Russia, and Turkey. 2 vols. *Map and plates.* 8° 1838

Elliott, H. W. Report on the Prybilov Group, or Seal Islands, of Alaska. *Plates.* 4° *Washington*, 1873
—— History and Present Condition of the Fishery Industries: The Seal Islands of Alaska. United States (Tenth Census Publication). *Maps and plates.* 4°
Washington, 1881
—— An Arctic Province: Alaska and the Seal Islands. *Maps and illustrations.* 8° 1886
—— *See* United States, A; G, *a*: Appendix 2.

Elliott, J. Report on the Vizagapatam and Backergunge Cyclones of October 1876. Folio *Calcutta*, 1877

Elliott, John. Report on Meteorology of the N.W. Provinces. [From the India Records, No. 1] *Allahabad*, 1871

Elliott, Mrs Frances. Diary of an Idle Woman in Constantinople. *Map and illustrations.* 8° 1893

Elliott, Capt. Robert. Views in the East, comprising India, Canton, and the Shores of the Red Sea, with Historical and Descriptive Illustrations. 2 vols. *Plates.* 4° 1833

Ellis, Col. A. B. West African Islands. 8° 1885
—— The Tshi-Speaking Peoples of the Gold Coast of West Africa, their Religion, Manners, Customs, Laws, Language, &c. *Map.* 8° 1887
—— The Ewe-Speaking Peoples of the Slave Coast of West Africa, their Religion, Manners, Customs, Laws, Languages,&c. 8° 1890
—— A History of the Gold Coast of West Africa. 8° 1893

Ellis, A. J. *See* Man.

Ellis, G. E. Memoir of Sir Benjamin Thompson, Count Rumford, with Notices of his Daughter. *Portraits and plates.* 8° *Philadelphia*, N.D.

Ellis, Henry. Voyage to Hudson's Bay, by the Dobbs Galley and California, in 1746-47, for Discovering a North-West Passage; with a Survey of the Coast, and the Natural History of the Country; also Facts and Arguments from which the future finding of such a Passage is rendered probable. *Maps and plates.* 8° 1748
—— *See* Allgemeine Historie, Vol. 17; The World Displayed, Vol. 10, p. 609: Appendix 1.

Ellis, Sir Henry. Journal of the Proceedings of the late Embassy to China, the Voyage to and from China, and the Journey from the Mouth of the Pei-ho to the Return to Canton, &c. *Maps and plates.* 4° 1817

Ellis, Sir Henry. The same. 2 vols. *Maps.* 8° 1818

Ellis, Sir Henry. Description of the Province of Connaught, dated in the month of January 1612. 4* 1837
—— History of the Boat which gave Peter the Great the first thought of building the Russian Fleet. 8° 1856
—— Representation of the Siege of Therouenne, in France, A.D. 1553. *1 leaf and plan.* 4* N.D.
—— *See* Frobisher.

Ellis, John. *See* Gottfried ; Purchas, Vol. 4, Book 7 : Appendix 1.

Ellis, Robert. An Enquiry into the Ancient Routes between Italy and Gaul, with an Examination of the Theory of Hannibal's Passage of the Alps by the Little St Bernard. *Maps.* 8° 1867.
—— *See* Law, W. J.

Ellis, Samuel. The Emigrant's Guide to Texas, with a Description of the Bays, Rivers, and Towns ; with a Table of Distances. 12* *New Orleans*, 1839

Ellis, Tristram. *See* Rodd.

Ellis, William. Narrative of a Tour through Hawaii, or Owhyhee, with Remarks on the History, Traditions, Manners, Customs, and Language of the Inhabitants of the Sandwich Islands. *Map and plates.* 8° 1826
—— History of Madagascar. 2 vols. *Map and plates.* 8° 1838
—— Polynesian Researches, during a Residence of nearly Eight Years in the Society and Sandwich Islands. 4 vols. *Map and plates.* 12° 1853
—— Three Visits to Madagascar during the years 1853, 1854, 1856, including a Journey to the Capital ; with Notices of the Natural History of the Country, and the Present Civilisation of the People. *Map and plates.* 8° 1859
—— Madagascar Revisited, describing the Events of a New Reign and the Revolution which followed, &c. *Map and plates.* 8° 1867

Ellis, William. Brief Historical Account of the Barometer. 8* [1886]
—— Address Delivered to the Royal Meteorological Society. (From the *Quarterly Journal of the Royal Meteorological Society*, Vol. 13.) Large 8* 1887
—— The same, on 18th January 1888, including a Discussion of the Greenwich Observations of Cloud during the Seventy Years ending 1887. (From the *Quarterly Journal of the Royal Meteorological Society*.) 8* 1888

El Mas'ûdi. *See* Nicholson, John.

Elphinstone, Hon. Mountstuart. Account of the Kingdom of Caubul, and its Dependencies in Persia, Tartary, and India ; comprising a View of the Afghaun Nation, and a History of the Dooraunee Monarchy. *Map and plates.* 4° 1815

Elphinstone, Hon. Mountstuart. Report on the Territories conquered from the Paishwa. 8° *Bombay*, 1838
—— History of India, the Hindú and Mahometan Periods. 8° 1857
—— *See* Eyriès, Vol. 14 : Appendix 1.

"Elpis Melena." Calabria and the Liparian Islands in the year 1860. 8° 1862

Elstobb, W. Historical Account of the Great Level of the Fens, called Bedford Level, and other Fens, Marshes, and Lowlands in this Kingdom. *Map.* 8° 1793

Elton, Charles. Origins of English History. *Maps.* Large 8° 1882

Elton, Charles J. The Career of Columbus. 8° 1892

Elton, J. F. With the French in Mexico. *Maps and illustrations.* 8° 1867
—— From Natal to Zanzibar ; with Descriptive Notes of Zanzibar, Mombasah, the Slave Trade, Sir Bartle Frere's Expedition, &c. 12* *Durban*, 1873
—— Travels and Researches among the Lakes and Mountains of Eastern and Central Africa. Edited and completed by H. B. Cotterill. *Maps and plates.* 8° 1879

Elwes, Dr Alfred. *See* Capello, H. ; Pinto, A.

Elwes, Robert. Sketcher's Tour round the World. *Plates.* Royal 8° 1854

Elwood, Mrs. Journey Overland from England, by the Continent of Europe, Egypt, and the Red Sea, to India. 2 vols. *Plates.* 8° 1830

Emanuel, H. Diamonds and Precious Stones, their History, Value, and Distinguishing Characteristics. *Plates.* 4° 1865

Emanuel, Louis. Jottings and Recollections of a Bengal "Qui Hye !" *Illustrations.* 12° N.D.

Embacher, F. Die wichtigeren Forschungsreisen des neunzehnten Jahrhunderts in synchronistischer Uebersicht. 4° *Brunswick*, 1880

Embel, J. X. Schilderung der Gebirgs-Gegenden um den Schneeberg in Oesterreich. 12° *Vienna*, 1803

Emerson, J. S, Kilauea after the Eruption of March 1886. Communications to Prof. W. D. Alexander, Surveyor-General of Hawaian Islands, by Messrs J. S. Emerson, L. L. Van Slyke, and F. S. Dodge. *Plates.* 8* [1887]

Emery, Lieut. J. B. Letters to W. D. Cooley, on the Geography of Mombas, East Africa. MS. Folio* 1833-35

Emin Pasha in Central Africa : being a Collection of his Letters and Journals. Edited and Annotated by Prof. G. Schweinfurth, Prof. F. Ratzel, Dr R. W. Felkin, and Dr G. Hartlaub. Translated by Mrs R. W. Felkin. *Map and portraits.* 8° 1888

Emin Pasha. *See* Hassan.

Emmons, Samuel Franklin. *See* United States, G, *c* (Monographs and Bulletins); H, *a* (Prof. Papers): Appendix 2.

—— **and Becker, G. F.** *See* United States, A ('Tenth Census, Vol. 13): Appendix 2.

Emory, Major W. H. Notes of a Military Reconnoissance from Fort Leavenworth, in Missouri, to San Diego, in California, including Parts of the Arkansas, Del Norte, and Gila Rivers (containing the Reports of Col. Albert, Col. St George Cooke, and Capt. Johnston), made in 1846-47. *Maps and plates.* 8° *Washington,* 1848

—— Observations, Astronomical, Magnetic, and Meteorological, made at Chagres and Gorgona, Isthmus of Darien, and at the City of Panama, New Granada. 4* *Cambridge, Mass.,* 1850

—— Report on the United States and Mexican Boundary Survey. Vol. 1. Part 1.—Containing Personal Account, General Description of the Country, the Lower Rio Bravo from Mouth of Devil's River to El Pasco del Norte, &c. Part 2.—Geological Reports, by Parry and Schott ; Palæontology and Geology of the Boundary, by Hall ; and Description of Cretaceous and Tertiary Fossils, by Conrad. *Maps and plates.* 4° *Washington,* 1857

Empoli, Giovanni da. *See* Ramusio, Vol. 1 ; Collecção de Noticias, Vol. 2, p. 610: Appendix 1.

Empson, Charles. Narratives of South America, illustrating Manners, Customs, and Scenery ; containing also numerous Facts in Natural History, collected during a Four Years' Residence in Tropical Regions. 8° 1836

Encke, Prof. On the next Return of Pons' Comet in 1832, with a Survey of the Grounds on which the New Elements rest. Translated from the German by G. B. Airy. 8* *Cambridge,* 1832

Encke's Comet, Ephemeris of, 1839. 8* 1838

"Endeavour." *See* Parkinson.

Enderby, Charles. The Auckland Islands: a Short Account of their Climate, Soil, and Productions, and the Advantages of Establishing there a Settlement at Port Ross, for carrying on the Southern Whale Fisheries. *Map and view.* 8* 1849

Endlich, F. M. Catalogue of Minerals found in Colorado. 8° *Washington,* 1878

—— On the Erupted Rocks of Colorado. 8* *Washington,* 1878

Enfantin, —. Colonisation de l'Algérie. *Map.* 8° *Paris,* 1843

Engel, Carl. The Music of the Most Ancient Nations, particularly of the Assyrians, Egyptians, and Hebrews ; with Special Reference to Recent Discoveries in Western Asia and in Egypt. *Plates.* 8° 1864

—— An Introduction to the Study of National Music ; comprising Researches into Popular Songs, Traditions, and Customs. 8° 1866

Engel, —. *See* Allgemeine Historie, Vol. 20: Appendix 1.

Engelhardt, G. *See* Wrangell.

Engelhardt, Moriz von, and Friedrich Parrot. Reise in die Krym und den Kaukasus. 2 vols. in 1, and vol. of plates. *Maps and plates.* 8° *Berlin,* 1815

Engelmann, C. The Waters of Kreuznach: a Work for General Readers. *Plates.* 8° 1854

Engelmann, Dr J. B. Résumé de l'Histoire de la Ville de Francfort et des Villes principales du Rhin. *Plates.* 12° *Heidelberg,* N.D.

Engelmann, Dr J. Leitfaden bei dem Unterricht in der Handelsgeschichte, &c. 8° *Erlangen,* 1892

Engelmann, Wilhelm. Bibliotheca Geographica. 2 vols in 1. 8° *Leipzig,* 1857-58

Engeström, Laurent d'. Rapport à sa Majesté le Roi de Suède, par son Ministre d'État et des Affaires Étrangères, en date de Stockholm le 7 Jan. 1813. Small 4* *Stockholm,* 1813

Englefield, Sir H. C. A Description of the principal Picturesque Beauties, Antiquities, and Geological Phænomena of the Isle of Wight. *Maps and plates.* Folio 1816

Engler, A. Ueber die Hochgebirgsflora des tropischen Afrika ; aus den Abhandlungen der Königl. Preuss. Akademie der Wissenschaften zu Berlin vom Jahre 1891. 4° *Berlin,* 1892

Ensor, F. Sidney. Incidents on a Journey through Nubia to Darfoor. *Maps.* 8° 1881

Entrecasteaux, Admiral d'. *See* Dentrecasteaux.

Epp, F. Schilderungen aus Holländisch-Ostindien. 8° *Heidelberg,* 1852

Eratosthenes. *See* Berger ; De la Nauze.

Erbach, E. Graf zu. Wandertage eines Deutschen Touristen im Strom- und Küstengebiet des Orinoko. *Maps and illustrations.* 8° *Leipzig,* 1892

Erckert, R von. Der Kaukasus, und seine Völker. Nach eigener Anschauung. *Map, tables, and illustrations.* 8° *Leipzig,* 1887

Erdaneta (or Urdaneta), Andres de. *See* Burney, Vol. 2: Appendix 1.

Erdmann, A. Om de Iakttagelser öfver Vattenhöjdens och Vindarnes Förändringar, &c. *Map and plate.* 4° *Stockholm,* 1856

Erdmann, A. Beskrifning öfver Dalkarlsbergs Jernmalmsfält uti Nora Socken och Örebro Län. *Plates.* 4*
Stockholm, 1858
—— Exposé des Formations Quaternaires de la Suède. *Maps.* 8*; and Atlas, 4°
Stockholm, 1868
—— *See* Sweden, A : Appendix 2.

Erdmann, E. *See* Sweden. A (Geologiska Undersökning) : Appendix 2.

Erdy, Janos. De Tabulis Ceratis in Transsilvania Repertis, Commentatus est. ErdélybenTalált Viaszos Lapok. *Plates.*
Royal 8* *Budapest,* 1856
—— A Boszna és Szerb Régi Ermek. *Plate.* 4* *Budapest,* 1858
—— Numi Transilvaniæ. Erdély Ermei Képatlaszszal. 2 parts. *Plates.* 4°
Budapest, 1862

"Erebus" and "Terror." The Zoology of the Voyage of H.M.S. "Erebus" and "Terror," under the command of Capt. Sir James Clark Ross, during the years 1839 to 1843. . . . Edited by John Richardson and John Edward Gray. 2 vols. *Map and plates.* 4° 1844-75

CONTENTS.

Vol. 1.—Summary of Voyage, by J. D. Hooker ; Mammalia, by J. E. Gray ; Birds, by G. R. Gray and R. B. Sharpe.

Vol. 2.—Reptiles, by G. R. Gray and A. Günther ; Fishes, by Sir J. Richardson ; Crustacea, by E. J. Miers ; Insects, by A. White and A. G. Butler ; Mollusca, by E. A. Smith.

—— The Botany of the Voyage, &c. *See* Hooker, Sir J. D.

—— *See* Hooker, Sir J. D. ; Malte-Brun.

Eredia, Emanuel Godinho de. Malaca, l'Inde Méridionale, et le Cathay. Manuscrit Original autographe de Godinho de Eredia, appartenant à la Bibliothèque Royale de Bruxelles. Reproduit en facsimile, et traduit par M. Léon Janssen . . .; avec une Préface de M. Ch. Ruelens. *Maps and illustrations.* 4°
Brussels, 1882

Erhardt, J. Vocabulary of the Enguduk Iloigob, as Spoken by the Masai-Tribes in East-Africa. 12° *Ludwigsburg,* 1857

Erigen (or Erigena), John. *See* Hakluyt, Vol. 2 ; Kerr, Vol. 1 : Appendix 1.

Ericsson, J. Solar Heat, and the Temperature of the Surface of the Moon. [Newspaper cuttings.] 4* 1869

Erizzo, Conte Francesco Miniscalchi. Scoperte Artiche Narrate. *Maps and plates.* 8° *Venice,* 1855

Erlenmeyer, E. Ueber den Einfluss des Freiherrn Justus von Liebig auf die Entwicklung der reinen Chemie. 4°
Munich, 1874

Erman, A. Archiv für wissenschaftliche Kunde von Russland. Vols. 1 to 25. 8°
Berlin, 1841-67
—— Reise um die Erde, durch Nord-Asien und die beiden Oceane in 1828-30. 3 vols. *2 plates.* 8° 1835-48
—— Beiträge zur Klimatologie des Russischen Reiches. 12* N.P., N.D.
—— Beobachtungen der Grösse des Luftdrucks über den Meeren und von einer sehr bestimmten Beziehung dieses Phänomens zu den geographischen Coordinaten der Orte. *Table.* 12* N.D.
—— Ueber Ebbe und Fluth an den Ochozker und Kamtschatkischen Küsten des grossen Oceans. 8* 1845
—— Travels in Siberia, including Excursions northwards to the Polar Circle, and southwards to the Chinese Frontier. Translated by Cooley. 2 vols. *Map.* 8°
1848
—— Ortsbestimmungen bei einer Fahrt durch den Grossen und Atlantischen Ocean auf der Corvette Krotkoi und darauf begründete Untersuchung der Strömungen in diesen Meeren. 8* 1852
—— *See* Hoppe, J. ; Schweinfurth.

Erman, Paul. *See* Du Bois Reymond.

Ermel, Alexander. Eine Reise nach der Robinson-Crusoe-Insel. *Map and illustrations.* 8° *Hamburg,* 1889

Ernst, A. La Exposicion Nacional de Venezuela en 1883, obra escrita de orden del ilustre Americano General Guzman Blanco. *Plates.* Folio
Caracas, 1884
—— *See* Venezuela : Appendix 2.

Erpénius, Thomas. Rudiments de la Langue Arabe ; Traduits en Français, accompagnés de Notes et suivis d'un Supplément indiquant les Différences entre le Langage Littéral et le Langage Vulgaire, par A. E. Hébert. 8°
Paris, 1844

Ersch, J. S. Literatur der Mathematik, Natur- nnd Gewerbs-Kunde, &c.; neue fortgesetzte Ausgabe von F. W. Schweigger-Seidel. 4° *Leipzig,* 1828

Erskine, Anna, Lady *See* Graham, D. C.

Erskine, J. Elphinstone. Journal of a Cruise among the Islands of the Western Pacific, including the Feejees and others inhabited by the Polynesian Negro Races. *Map and plates.* 8° 1853

Erskine, St Vincent W. Original Journals of. MS. 2 cases and 1 vol. 1868-76

Escher, A. *See* Linth.

Eschricht, Prof. Om de Nordiske Hvaldyrs Geographiske Udbredelse i Nærværende og i Tidligere Tid. *Map.* 8* *Copenhagen,* N.D.

Escobari, Dr Isaac. Analogies Philologiques de la langue Aimara. 8*
Paris, 1881

Escott, A. *See* Riddle.

Esguerra, J. Diccionario Jeográfico de los Estados Unidos de Colombia. 8°
Bogotá, 1879
Espajo, Ant. de. *See* Hakluyt, Vol. 3; Purchas, Vol. 4, Book 8 : Appendix 1.
Espérandieu, Capt. Emile. Musée de Perigueux : Inscriptions Antiques. (Publications de la Société Historique et Archéologique du Périgord.) *Plates.* 8°
Paris, 1893
"Espiegle." *See* Ommanney.
Espinosa y Tello, Don Josef. Memorias sobre las Observaciones Astronómicas hechas por los Navegantes Españoles en distintos Lugares del Globo. 2 vols. *Plates.* 4° *Madrid,* 1809
Espy, Prof. James P. Second and Third Reports on Meteorology, 1843-45 ; with Directions for Mariners. *Charts and diagrams.* Oblong folio
Washington, 1850
—— Fourth Meteorological Report. Message from the President of the United States to the Senate. *Charts and plates.* 8°   *Washington,* 1857
Esquemeling, John. The Buccaneers of America : a True Account of the most remarkable Assaults committed of late years upon the Coasts of the West Indies by the Buccaneers of Jamaica and Tortuga (both English and French) ; with facsimiles of all the original engravings, &c. Reprinted from the edition of 1684. Large 8°   1893
—— *See* Burney, Vol. 4 : Appendix 1.
Essex, Earl of. *See* Hakluyt, Vol. 5; Purchas, Vol. 4, Book 10 : Appendix 1.
Estancelin, L. Recherches sur les Voyages et Découvertes des Navigateurs Normands en Afrique, dans les Indes Orientales et en Amérique ; suivies d'Observations sur la Marine, le Commerce, et les Établissemens Coloniaux des Français. 8°   *Paris,* 1832
Estrey, Dr Cte. Meyners d'. La Papouasie ou Nouvelle-Guinée Occidentale. Ouvrage accompagné de Gravures et d'une Carte dressée et gravée par K. Hausermann. 4°
Paris and Amsterdam, 1881
Etheridge, Col. A. T. Narrative of the Bombay Inam Commission and Supplementary Settlements. [From the India Records, No. 132.] Folio* *Poona,* 1873
Etheridge, R., jun. *See* New South Wales, B : Appendix 2.
Ethersey, R. Observations on the "Bore," or Rushing Tide, in the Northern parts of the Gulf of Cambay, and the entrances of the Myhee and Saburmutee Rivers. *Map.* [From the India Records, No. 26.] 8°   *Bombay,* 1856
—— *See* Powell, F. T. ; *also* India, C (Geological Papers) : Appendix 2.

Etienne, Dr E. Le Climat de Banana en 1890, suivi des Observations Météorologiques faites du 1er décembre 1889, an 16 mai 1891. [Publications de l'État Indépendant du Congo, No. 7.] Small folio*   *Brussels,* 1892
Eton, W. Survey of the Turkish Empire, in which are considered — 1. Its Government, Finances, Military and Naval Force, Religion, History, Arts, Sciences, Manners, Commerce, and Population ; 2. The State of the Provinces, including the Ancient Government of the Crim Tartars, the Subjection of the Greeks, their Efforts towards Emancipation, and the Interest of other Nations in their Success ; 3. The Causes of the Decline of Turkey ; 4. The British Commerce with Turkey, &c. 8°
1799
Ettingshausen, Baron von [Dr Constantin]. *See* New South Wales, B : Appendix 2.
"Eugenie." *See* Virgin.
Europæus, D. E. D. Vorläufiger Entwurf über den Urstamm der indoenropäischen Sprachfamilie und seine vor-indoeuropäischen Abzweigungen, namentlich die finnisch-ungarische. *Plate and tables.* 8*   *Helsingfors,* 1863
—— Die Stammverwandtschaft der meisten Sprachen der alten und Australischen Welt. 4*   *St Petersburg,* 1870
—— The same. New edition. 4*   1877
—— Ett fornfolk med långskallig afrikansk hufvudskålstyp i norden, bestämdt till språk och nationalitet. 12°
Helsingfors, 1873
—— Die finnisch-ungarischen Sprachen und die Urheimath des Menschengeschlechtes. 8°   *Helsingfors,* N.D.
Eustace J. C. Classical Tour through Italy, 1802. 4 vols. *Map.* 8°   1815
Evans, A. J. Through Bosnia and the Herzegovina on foot, during the Insurrection, August and September 1875 ; with an Historical Review of Bosnia, and a Glimpse at the Croats, Slavonians, and the Ancient Republic of Ragusa. *Map and plates.* 8°   1876
Evans, Arthur J. *See* Freeman, E. A.
Evans, Captain Sir Frederick J. Reduction and Discussion of the Deviations of the Compass observed on board of the Iron-built Ships and Wood-built Steam-Ships in H.M.'s Navy, and the "Great Eastern." *Plates.* 4*   1861
—— A Review of Oceanic or Maritime Discovery, Exploration, and Research, as made in the half century 1831-81. 8*.
—— Report on Admiralty Surveys for the year 1879. Folio*   1881
—— *See* Richards ; *also* United Kingdom, A, Hydrogr. Off. Publ. : Appendix 2.

Evans, Captain Sir Frederick J., and Archibald Smith. Admiralty Manual for Ascertaining and Applying the Deviations of the Compass caused by the Iron in a Ship. *Plates.* 8° 1862

Evans, Lieut. H. L. Letter on the Establishment of Vernacular Libraries. [From the India Records, N.W. Provinces, Vol. 1.] 8° *Agra*, 1855

Evans, Morris. Report on the proposed Abdul Médjid Railway. Folio 1855

Evans, Patrick F. From Peru to the Plate, Overland. *Map.* 8* 1889

Everard, Robert. *See* Churchill, Vol. 6 : Appendix 1.

Everest, Sir George. Account of the Measurement of an Arc of the Meridian . . . in India. 4° 1830
—— Account of the Measurement of Two Sections of the Meridional Arc of India. With vol. of *plates.* 4° 1847

Everest, Robert. A Journey through Norway, Lapland, and part of Sweden ; with some Remarks on the Geology of the Country, &c. *Maps and plate.* 8° 1829
—— A Journey through the United States and part of Canada. 8° 1855

Everett, Edward. Europe, or a General Survey of the Present Situation of the Provincial Powers. By a Citizen of the United States. 8° 1822

Everill, Capt. H. C. Exploration of New Guinea : Capt. Everill's Report. 8* *Sydney*, 1886

Eves, C. Washington. Jamaica at the Royal Jubilee Exhibition, Liverpool, 1887. *Map and portraits.* 8° 1887
—— The West Indies. Published under the Auspices of the Royal Colonial Institute. *Maps and illustrations.* 12° 1889

Evesham, John. *See* Hakluyt, Vol. 2 ; Kerr, Vol. 7 : Appendix 1.

Evliya, Effendi. Travels in Europe, Asia, and Africa, in the Seventeenth Century. Translated from the Turkish by Ritter Joseph von Hammer. 4° 1846

Ewald, A. C. A Reference-Book of Modern Geography for the use of Public Schools and Civil Service Candidates. 12° 1870

Ewart, Lieut. J. S. *See* Dalrymple, Repertory, Vol. 1 : Appendix 1.

Ewart, W. Settlement in India, and Trade with Central Asia. 8* 1858

Ewbank, Thomas. Life in Brazil, or the Land of the Cocoa and the Palm. *Woodcuts.* 8° 1856
—— North American Rock-Writing, and other Aboriginal Modes of Recording and Transmitting Thought. Large 8* *Morrisania, N.Y.*, 1866

Exner, A. H. China : Skizzen von Land und Leuten mit besonderer Berücksichtigung kommerzieller Verhältnisse. *Portrait, plan, and illustrations.* 4° *Leipzig*, 1889

Exquemelin. *See* Esquemeling.

Eydoux, —. *See* Vaillant.

Eyre, Edward John. Journals of Expeditions of Discovery into Central Australia, and Overland from Adelaide to King George's Sound, in 1840-41 ; including an Account of the Manners and Customs of the Aborigines, and the State of their Relations with Europeans. 2 vols. *Maps and plates.* 8° 1845

Eyre, Sir Vincent. The Military Operations at Cabul which ended in the Retreat and Destruction of the British Army, January 1842 ; with a Journal of Imprisonment in Affghanistan. 2nd edition. *Map.* 8° 1843
—— On Metallic Boats and Floating Waggons for Naval and Military Service, with some Observations on American Life-Preserving Cars. *Plates.* Royal 8* 1856
—— A Retrospect of the Affghan War, with Reference to Passing Events in Central Asia. *Map.* 8* 1869

Eyriès, Jean Baptiste Benoit. Abrégé des Voyages Modernes. 14 vols in 7. 8° *Paris*, 1822-24
[For full Title and Contents of the volumes, *see* Appendix 1.]
—— Recherches sur la Population du Globe Terrestre. 8* *Paris*, 1833
—— Notice Biographique, par M. Dezos de la Roquette. Royal 8* *Paris*, 1855
—— *See* Humboldt, Alex. von.

Ezquebel, Jean de. *See* Gottfried : Appendix 1.

Ezziâni, Aboulqâsem Ben Ahmed. Le Maroc de 1631 à 1812. Extrait de l'ouvrage intitulé " Ettordjemân Elmo' Arib'an Douel Elmachriq Ou Lmaghrib," de Aboulqâsem Ben Ahmed Ezziâni, publié et traduit par O. Houdas. [2nd Series, Vol. 18 of Publ. de l'Éc. des Langues Orient. Viv.] Large 8° *Paris*, 1886

F

Faber, F. (Schmidt). *See* Switzerland, B : Appendix 2.

Fabian, R. *See* Hakluyt Soc. Publ., Vol. 7 : Appendix 1.

Fabre, Citoyen. Essai sur la Théorie des Torrens et des Rivières. *Plates.* 4° *Paris*, 1797

Fabri, D. Friedrich. Bedarf Deutschland der Colonien ? Eine politisch-ökonomische Betrachtung. Dritte Ausgabe. 8° *Gotha*, 1884
—— Fünf Jahre Deutscher Kolonialpolitik. 8° *Gotha*, 1889

Fabri, Johann Ernst. Kurzer Abriss der Geographie. 8° *Halle*, 1794

Fabricius, Prof. Adam Kristoffer. La première invasion des Normands dans l'Espagne Musulmane en 844. *See* Transactions. 8° *Lisbon,* 1892
—— *See* Portugal, B : Appendix 2.

Fabricius, J. S. *See* Norway, A (Norske Lods) : Appendix 2.

Fabricius, O. Fauna Grœnlandica, systematice sistens animalia Grœnlandiæ occidentalis hactenus indagata, &c. 8° *Copenhagen,* 1780

Fabritius, W. Baku as a Central Point of the Overland Route to India. [Translated by Capt. F. C. H. Clarke.] Folio* 1876

Fabvre, Capt. Retour en France de la corvette "la Recherche ; " Rapport sur la Seconde Campagne dans les Mers du Nord et au Spitzberg. 8* *Paris,* 1839
—— *See* Gaimard.

Facius, J. F. *See* Pausanias.

Fa Hian. Fouĕ Kouĕ Ki, ou Relation des Royaumes Bouddhiques : Voyage dans la Tartarie, dans l'Afghanistan, et dans l'Inde, exécuté à la fin du IVe Siècle, par Chy Fā Hian. Traduit du Chinois et Commenté par Abel Rémusat ; revu, &c., par Klaproth et Landresse. *Maps and plans.* 4° *Paris,* 1836
—— *See* Legge.

Faidherbe, General L. Notice sur la Colonie du Sénégal, et sur les Pays qui sont en relation avec elle. *Map.* 8* *Paris,* 1859
—— Chapitres de Géographie sur le Nord-Ouest de l'Afrique. *Map.* 8* *Saint-Louis,* 1864
—— Mémoire sur les Éléphants des armées Carthaginoises. *Map.* 8* *Bonn,* 1867
—— Voyage des cinq Nasamons d'Hérodote dans l'Intérieur de la Libye. *Map.* 8* *Algiers,* 1867
—— Recherches Anthropologiques sur les Tombeaux Mégalithiques de Roknia. *Plates.* 8° *Bonn,* 1868
—— Collection complète des Inscriptions Numidiques (Libyques), avec des Aperçus Ethnographiques sur les Numides. 4° *Lille,* 1870
—— Essai sur la langue Poul, Grammaire et Vocabulaire. 8° *Paris,* 1875
—— Le Zénaga des tribus Sénégalaises. Contribution à l'Étude de la langue Berbère. 8° *Paris,* 1877
—— Le Sénégal. La France dans l'Afrique Occidentale. *Map and plans.* 8° *Paris,* 1889
—— *See* Ancelle.

Faidherbe. *See* Brosselard-Faidherbe.

Fairbairn, Henry. A Letter to Lord William Bentinck, M.P., on the Superior Advantages of a Steam Passage to the East Indies by the Gulf of Mexico and

Fairbairn, Henry—*continued.*
the Pacific Ocean, as compared with the Proposed Route by the Red and Mediterranean Seas. *Map.* 8* 1837

Fairbairn, W. On the Application of Cast and Wrought Iron to Building Purposes. *Plates.* Royal 8° 1854

Fairbridge, Charles A., and John Noble. Catalogue of Books relating to South Africa. 8* *Cape Town,* 1886

Fairman, E. St J. Geology and Agriculture. 8* *Florence,* 1867
—— Ghirghis Mahomed, or Reports of the New Egyptian Parliament. 8° [*Pisa*] 1867
—— A Treatise on the Petroleum Zones of Italy. *Map.* 8* 1868
—— I Petrolii in Italia. Estratti da Relazioni e Rapporti Scientifici sulla esistenza del Petrolio in Italia. *Maps.* 16* *Florence,* 1869
—— *See* Wassa.

Falbe, C. T. Recherches sur l'emplacement de Carthage, suivies de Renseignements sur plusieurs inscriptions Puniques inédites, de Notices Historiques, Géographiques, &c., avec le plan topographique du terrain et des ruines de la ville dans leur état actuel, &c. 8° ; Atlas, 4° *Paris,* 1833
—— Les Antiques Monnaies d'Abdera de la Bétique. *Woodcuts.* 8* N.P., 1850

"Falcon." *See* Knight, E. F.

Falconar, David. A Journey from Joppa to Jerusalem in 1758. Small 4* 1753

Falconbridge, Anna Maria. Two Voyages to Sierra Leone, during the years 1791-2-3, in a series of Letters. . . . 2nd edition. 12° 1794

Falconer, H. *See* India, C (Geological Papers) : Appendix 1.

Falconer, Hugh, and H. Walker. Descriptive Catalogue of the Fossil Remains of Vertebrata, from the Sewalik Hills, the Nerbudda, Perim Island, &c., in the Museum of the Asiatic Society of Bengal. 8° *Calcutta,* 1859

Falconer, T. Voyage of Hanno, Greek and English, explained from the accounts of Modern Travellers, and defended against the objections of Mr Dodwell, and other writers. *Maps.* 8° 1797
—— *See* Strabo.

Falconer, Thomas. Expedition to Santa Fé : an Account of its Journey from Texas through Mexico, with particulars of its capture. 8* *New Orleans,* 1842
—— On the Discovery of the Mississippi, and on the South-Western, Oregon, and North-Western Boundary of the United States ; with a translation from the Original MS. of Memoirs, &c., by R. Cavelier de la Salle and the Chevalier Henry de Tonty. *Map.* 8° 1844

Falconer, Thomas. Notes of a Journey through Texas and New Mexico in the years 1841 and 1842. 8* N.D.
—— The Oregon Question, &c. 2nd edition. (Postscript; Second Postscript.) *See* United States, K (Oregon): Appendix 2.

Falconer, W. Miscellaneous Tracts and Collections relating to Natural History, selected from the Principal Writers of Antiquity on that subject. 4°
Cambridge, 1793
—— Dissertation on St Paul's Voyage from Cæsarea to Puteoli; on the Wind Euroclydon; and on the Apostle's Shipwreck on the Island Melite. By a Layman. *Maps.* 8° *Oxford*, 1817
—— Dissertation on St Paul's Voyage from Cæsarea to Puteoli, and on the Apostle's Shipwreck on the Island Melite. 2nd edition, with Additional Notes by T. Falconer. 8° *London*, 1870
—— The same. 3rd edition, with Additional Notes by Thomas Falconer. 8°
1872
—— New and Universal Dictionary of the Marine: being a Copious Explanation of the Technical Terms and Phrases usually employed in the Construction, Equipment, Machinery, Movements, and Military as well as Naval Operations of Ships, with such parts of Astronomy and Navigation as will be found useful to Practical Navigators; to which is annexed a Vocabulary of French Sea Phrases and Terms of Art. Modernised and much enlarged by W. Burney. *Plates.* 4° 1830
—— *See* Strabo.

Falconer, W. and T. *See* Arrian.

Falkenstein, Karl. Geschichte der geographischen Entdeckungsreisen. 5 vols in 2. 12° *Dresden*, 1828-29

Falkland, Viscountess. Chow-Chow: being Selections from a Journal kept in India, Egypt, and Syria, 2 vols. 8°
1857

Falkner, Thomas. Description of Patagonia, and the adjoining parts of South America; containing an account of the Soil, Produce, Animals, Vales, Mountains, Rivers, Lakes, &c., of those Countries; the Religion, Government, Policy, Customs, Dress, Arms, and Language of the Indian Inhabitants; and some particulars relating to the Falkland's Islands. *Map.* 4° *Hereford*, 1774
—— *See* Molina, J.

Fallati, Johannes. Zur Statistik des Flächenraums und der Volkszahl von Britisch-Indien. 8* *Tübingen*, 1852

Falle, P. Cæsarea; or, An Account of Jersey . . .; with an Appendix of Records, &c., and Letter by P. Morant. *Map and plate.* 8° 1734

Fallot, Ernest. Par delà la Méditerranée, Kabylie, Aurès, Kroumirie. *Illustrations.* 12° *Paris* [1887]

Falquet, L. Fondation d'un Institut International des Sciences Géographiques: Travail présenté au Congrès International des Sciences Géographiques de Berne, du 10 au 14 août 1891. 8* *Berne*, 1891

Falzon, Giovanni Battista. Dizionario Maltese - Italiano - Inglese arricchito di nomi di botanica, ittiologia, ornitologia, e marineria. . . . Preceduto da una breve esposizione grammaticale della lingua Maltese. 8° *Malta*, 1845

Famintzin, A. Uebersicht der Leistungen auf dem Gebiete der Botanik in Russland, während des Jahres 1890. 2 vols. Large 8° *St Petersburg*, 1892-93

Fancourt, C. St J. The History of Yucatan, from its Discovery to the Close of the Seventeenth Century. *Map.* 8° 1854

Faraday, Michael. On a Peculiar Class of Acoustical Figures, and on the Forms of Fluids Vibrating on Elastic Surfaces. 4* 1831
—— Experimental Researches in Electricity: *Plates.* 4* 1832
—— On Faraday as a Discoverer. By J. Tyndall. 8* 1868

Faria y Sousa, — De. *See* Astley, Vol. 3; Allgemeine Historie, Vol. 1: Appendix 1.

Farie, R. *See* Haxthausen.

Farini, G. A. Through the Kalahari Desert: a Narrative of a Journey with Gun, Camera, and Note-book to Lake N'gami and back. *Map, plan, and illustrations.* 8° 1886

Faris, El-Shidiac. Practical Grammar of the Arabic Language; with Interlineal Reading Lessons, Dialogues, and Vocabulary. 12° 1856

Farley, J. L. The Resources of Turkey, considered with especial reference to the Profitable Investment of Capital in the Ottoman Empire; with Statistics of the Trade and Commerce of the [28] Principal Commercial Towns. 8° 1862
—— Modern Turkey. 8° 1872

Farmer. Sarah S. Tonga and the Friendly Islands; with a Sketch of their Mission History. *Maps and plates.* 12° 1855

Farrer, Richard Ridley. A Tour in Greece, 1880; with twenty-seven illustrations by Lord Windsor. *Map.* Royal 8° 1882

"Fasana." *See* Jedina.

Fasolo, Prof. Francesco. L'Abissinia, e le Colonie Italiane sul Mar Rosso. *Maps.* 12° *Caserta*, 1887

Fassig, O. L. *See* United States, C: Appendix 2.

Faucet, C. *See* Hakluyt, Vol. 1 : Appendix 1.

Fauché, —. *See* Greece (Morea) : Appendix 2.

Faujas-Saint-Fond, B. Voyage en Angleterre, en Écosse, et aux îles Hébrides. 2 vols. *Plates.* 8° *Paris,* 1797
—— Travels in England, Scotland, and the Hebrides. 2 vols. *Plates.* 8° 1799

Faulds, Henry. Nine Years in Nipon : Sketches of Japanese Life and Manners. *Illustrations.* 8°   1885

Faure, C. Notice sur la part des Suisses dans l'Exploration et la Civilisation de l'Afrique. 8*   *Geneva,* 1883
—— Notice sur Arnold Guyot, 1807-84. 8*   *Geneva,* 1884
—— La Conférence Africaine de Berlin. *Map.* 8*   *Geneva,* 1885
—— Les Progrès de l'Enseignement de la Géographie en Angleterre sous l'impulsion des Sociétés de Londres, d'Edimbourg et de Manchester. 8* *Geneva,* 1889
—— Congrès International des Sciences Géographiques tenu à Paris en 1889 : Exposé sommaire des Voyages et Travaux Géographiques des Suisses dans le cours du XIXᵉ siècle. Large 8* *Paris,* 1891
—— L'Enseignement de la Géographie en Suisse. 8*   *Berne,* 1891
—— Les Progrès de l'Enseignement de la Géographie en France. 8*
                                  Neuchâtel, 1891

Favard, —. *See* Milliroux.

Favenc, Ernest. The Great Austral Plain, its Past, Present, and Future. *Plate.* 8*   *Sydney,* 1881
—— Western Australia, its Past History, its Present Trade and Resources, its Future Position in the Australian Group. *Map.* 4°   *Sydney,* 1887
—— The History of Australian Exploration, from 1788 to 1888. Compiled from State Documents, Private Papers, and the most Authentic Sources of Information. Issued under the auspices of the Governments of the Australian Colonies. *Maps and plates.* Large 8°
                                  Sydney, 1888

"Favourite." *See* Laplace.

Favre, Alphonse. Mémoire sur les Terrains Liasique et Keupérien de la Savoie. *Plates.* 4*   *Geneva,* 1859
—— Explication de la Carte Géologique des parties de la Savoie, du Piémont, et de la Suisse voisines du Mont Blanc. 8*   *Geneva,* 1862
—— Sur la structure en éventail du Mont Blanc. 8*   [*Geneva,* 1865]
—— Recherches Géologiques dans les parties de la Savoie, du Piémont, et de la Suisse voisines du Mont Blanc ; avec un Atlas de 32 planches. 3 vols. 8°
                                  Paris, 1867

Favre, Alphonse. H.-B. de Saussure et les Alpes. 8*   *Lausanne,* 1870
—— *See* Murchison.

Favre, Ernest. Recherches Géologiques dans la partie centrale de la Chaîne du Caucase. *Map and plate.* 4°
                                  Geneva, 1875

Favre, J. le. Lettre dv R. P. Jacques le Favre de la Campagnie de Iesvs, . . . sur son arrivée à la Chine, et l'estat present de ce Royaume. 12° *Paris,* 1662
[Bound up with Joseph Tissanier's Voyage to Tonquin.]

Fawcett, E. G. Report of the Collectorate of Ahmedabad. *Map, plates, and tables.* [From the India Records, No. 5.] 8°
                                  Bombay, 1854

Fawckner, Capt. James, Travels on the Coast of Benin, West Africa. 12°
                                  1837

Fawkes, F. The Argonautics of Apollonius Rhodius. 8°   1780

Fay, Theodore S. Great Outline of Geography. 8°   *Berlin,* N.D.

Faye, Andreas. Udtog af Norges Riges Historie. 12*   *Christiania,* 1834

Fayrer, J. H.R.H. The Duke of Edinburgh in India. 4°
                    Privately printed, Calcutta, 1870
—— The Royal Tiger of Bengal, his Life and Death. *Map and plates.* 12°
                                  1875
—— *See* Brunton, T. L.

Fazakerley, J. N. *See* Walpole, Travels : Appendix 1.

Fazello, T. Historia di Sicilia. Tradotta dal Remigio ; ricorretta dal l'Abbate Lafarina. Folio   *Palermo,* 1628

Fazio, Lorenzo. Memoria Descriptiva de la Provincia de Santiago del Estero. *Portrait, plan, and illustrations.* 4°
                                  Buenos Ayres, 1889

Fea, C. Description de Rome. Vol. 1. *Plates.* 12°   *Rome,* 1821

Fea, Leonardo. Viaggio Zoologico nel Tenasserim. *Map and illustrations.* 8*
                                  Rome, 1888

Fearnside, W. G. *See* Tombleson.

Fearon, H. B. Sketches of America : a Narrative of a Journey of Five Thousand Miles through the Eastern and Western States of America . . . ; with Remarks on Mr Birkbeck's "Notes and Letters." 3rd edition. 8°   1819

Featherstonhaugh, G. W. Geological Report of an Examination made in 1834 of the Elevated Country between the Missouri and Red Rivers. *Map.* 8°
                                  Washington, 1835
—— Report of a Geological Reconaissance in 1835 from the Seat of Government by the way of Green Bay and the Wisconsin Territory to the Coteau de Prairie. *Plates.* 8°   *Washington,* 1836

Featherstonhaugh, G. W. A Canoe Voyage up the Minnay Sotoo; with an Account of the Lead and Copper Deposits in Wisconsin, of the Gold Region in the Cherokee Country, and Sketches of Popular Manners, &c. 2 vols. in I. *Maps and plates.* 8° 1847

Fechet, Eugène. Journal of the March of an Expedition in Nubia between Assouan and Abouhamid. 8* *Cairo*, 1878

Fedchenko, A. Letters from Kokand to the *Turkestan Gazette*. From the Russian, by R. Michell. Folio* N.D.
—— *See* Yule, H.

Fedchenko, O. A. Outlines of Geography, and History of the Upper Amu-Daria. [In Russian.] 8°
St Petersburg, 1873
—— *See* Yule, H.

Federici, Cesare de. *See* Frederick.

Federmann, Nicolas. *See* Ternaux-Compans, Vol. 1 : Appendix 1.

Fedorow, W. Vorläufige Berichte über die von ihm in 1832 bis 1837 in West-Sibirien ausgeführten astronomisch-geographischen Arbeiten. Herausgegeben von Struve. *Map.* 8° *St Petersburg*, 1838

Fegræus, T. *See* Sweden, A : Appendix 2.

Feilden, Eliza Whigham. My African Home ; or, Bush Life in Natal when a Young Colony [1852-57]. *Illustrations.* Crown 8° 1887

Feilden, Col. H. W. Address by the President, Major H. W. Feilden, to the Members of the Norfolk and Norwich Naturalists' Society. 8* 1886
—— Notes from an Arctic Journal. 8°
[N.D.]
—— *See* Nares ; *also* Arctic, C : Appendix 2.

Feilding, Viscount. *See* Kennedy.

Feistmantel, O. *See* India, C (Pal. Ind.) ; New South Wales, B : Appendix 2.

Felbermann, L. Hungary and its People. *Map and illustrations.* 8° [1892]

Feldborg, A. A. A Tour in Zealand in the year 1802, with an Historical Sketch of the Battle of Copenhagen. 12° 1804
—— Denmark Delineated, or Sketches of the Present State of that Country. *Plates.* 8° *Edinburgh*, 1824

Felkin, Dr Robert W. Notes on the Madi or Moru Tribe of Central Africa. (From the Proceedings of the Royal Society of Edinburgh, Vols. 1, 2, 1883-84.) *Portrait.* 8* *Edinburgh*, 1884
—— Note on a Case of Elephantiasis Arabum. *Illustrations.* 8*
Edinburgh, 1889
—— Notes on the For Tribe of Central Africa. *Plate.* 8* *Edinburgh*, 1885
—— Uganda und sein Herrscher Mtesa. 8* *Munich*, 1885

Felkin, Dr Robert W. Notes on the Waganda Tribe of Central Africa. *Plate.* 8* *Edinburgh*, 1886
—— Observations on Malaria and Enteric Fever, and on the Suitability of Tropical Highlands for European Settlement. 8* 1891
—— Uganda. (From *The Imperial and Asiatic Quarterly Review.*) 8* 1892
—— Neue ethnographische Gegenstände aus Ost-Africa. *Illustrations.* Large 8* *Berlin*, 1892
—— *See* Emin Pasha ; Wilson, Rev. C. T.
—— and Mrs R. W. *See* Emin Pasha.

Fellenberg, E. von. Ein Abstecher in die hohe Tátra. *Plates.* 12*
[*Berne*, N.D.]
—— Geologische und topographische Wanderungen im Aare und Rhonegebiet in den Jahren 1877, 1878, und 1879. *Plates.* 12* *Berne*, 1880
—— Itinerarium für das . . . Excursionsgebiet des S. A. C. für die Jahre 1882 und 1883. Die westlichen Berner Kalkalpen und der westliche Theil des Finsteraarhorn-Central Massivs. Bearbeitet und durch geologische und mineralogische Notizen vervollständigt von Edmund v. Fellenberg. Nebst geologischen und botanischen Notizen von Prof. J. Bachmann in Bern und Prof. O. Wolf in Sitten. *Map.* 12° *Berne*, 1882
—— Beilage zu Jahrbuch XXIV. S.A.C. Zweiter Nachtrag zum kritischen Verzeichniss der gesammt Literatur über die Berner Alpen. (Excursionsgebiet, 1885-87.) 12° *Berne*, 1889
—— *See* Roth, A.

Feller, F. G. *See* Nelkenbrecher.

Fellows, Sir Charles. Ascent of Mont Blanc, 1827. *Plates.* 4° 1827
—— Journal written during an Excursion in Asia Minor, 1838. *Map and plates.* 8° 1839
—— Account of Discoveries in Lycia, 1840. *Map and plates.* Royal 8° 1841
—— Account of the Ionic Trophy Monument excavated at Xanthus. *Plates.* Royal 8° 1848
—— Travels and Researches in Asia Minor, more particularly in the Province of Lycia. *Maps and plates.* 8° 1852
—— Coins of Ancient Lycia before the Reign of Alexander ; with an Essay on the relative Dates of the Lycian Monuments in the British Museum. *Map ana plates.* Royal 8° 1855

Fenn, Harry. *See* Lane-Poole.

Fenner, Capt. G. *See* Astley, Vol. 1 ; Hakluyt, Vol. 2 ; Kerr, Vol. 7 ; Allgemeine Historie, Vol. 1 : Appendix 1.

Fenner, W. Memoir of the Survey of the Tidal Channels of the River Indus. 8* 1849

Fenning, D., and J. Collyer. New System of Geography, or a General Description of the World, containing a Particular and Circumstantial Account of all the Countries, Kingdoms, and States of Europe, Asia, Africa, and America. 2 vols. *Maps and plates.* Folio 1764

Fenteman, T. Historical Guide to Leeds and its Environs. *Map.* 12° *Leeds*, 1858

Fenton, Major A. B. Diary of an Expedition to the Upper Reaches of the Irrawaddy, and subsequently to the Indawgyi Lake, in May and June 1890. *Map.* Folio* *Rangoon*, 1890

Fenton, Edward. *See* Burney, Vol. 2 ; Callander, Vol. 1 ; Hakluyt, Vol. 4 : Appendix 1.

Fenton, F. D. Observations on the State of the Aboriginal Inhabitants of New Zealand. Folio * *Auckland*, 1859
—— Suggestions for a History of the Origin and Migrations of the Maori People. *Plate.* 8* *Auckland*, 1885

Fenton, R. A Historical Tour through Pembrokeshire. *Map and plates.* 4° 1811

Fenzl, Eduard. *See* "Novara."

Ferber, —. *See* Pinkerton, Vol. 2: Appendix 1.

Ferbers, J. J., and J. B. Fischers. Physischen Erdbeschreibung von Kurland und Naturgeschichte von Liefland. *Plate.* 8° *Riga*, 1784

Ferguson, A. M. and J. The Ceylon Handbook and Directory, and Compendium of Useful Information. (Edition of 1890-91.) *Portrait.* 8° *Colombo*, 1890
—— The Ceylon Mercantile and Planting Directory . . . 1891-92. 8° *Colombo*, 1891
—— *See* Ferguson, John.

Ferguson, Donald. Captain João Ribeiro, his Work in Ceylon, and the French Translation thereof by the Abbé Le Grand. (Extracted from Journal No. 36, Vol. 10, of the Royal Asiatic Society, Ceylon Branch.) 8* 1888
—— *See* Daalmans.

Ferguson, G. E. Report on Mission to Atabubu. *Map and plates.* Folio* 1891

Ferguson, J. *See* Guthrie, W.

Ferguson, John. Uva : an Account of the Inauguration of the new Province of Uva . . . ; with Descriptions of the Divisions of the Province, and Letters on the need for Railway Extension. *Maps.* 12° *[Colombo]* 1886
—— Ceylon in the "Jubilee Year " ; with an Account of the Progress made since 1803, and of the Present Condition of its Agricultural and Commercial Enterprises, the Resources awaiting Development by Capitalists; specially prepared maps, and numerous illustrations. 3rd edition. 8° 1887

Ferguson, John. Ceylon : its Attractions to Visitors and Settlers. (From the *Journal of the Royal Colonial Institute*, April 1892.) 8* 1892
—— The Ceylon Handbook and Directory, and Compendium of Useful Information. [Edition of 1893-94.] 8° *Colombo*, 1893

Ferguson Prof. John. The Chemical Manufactures of Glasgow and the West of Scotland. [Published with other Papers for the British Association Meeting at Glasgow, 1876.] 12° *Glasgow*, 1876

Ferguson, Wm. America, by River and Rail ; or, Notes by the Way on the New World and its People. *Frontispiece.* 8° 1856

Fergusson, Lieut. E. F. T. Account of the Dimensions and Track of a Cyclone experienced at Bombay, Nov. 1862. *Map.* 8* *Bombay*, 1862

Fergusson, James. Essay on the Ancient Topography of Jerusalem. *Plans and plates.* Small folio 1847
——- The Palaces of Nineveh and Persepolis Restored : an Essay on Ancient Assyrian and Persian Architecture. *Plates.* 8° 1851
—— Tree and Serpent Worship ; or, Illustrations of Mythology and Art in India in the First and Fourth Centuries after Christ, from the Sculptures of the Buddhist Topes at Sanchi and Amravati . . . ; with Introductory Essays, and Descriptions of the Plates. *Plates and photographs.* 4° 1868
—— Rude Stone Monuments in all Countries, their Ages and Uses. *Illustrations.* 8° 1872
—— A History of Architecture in all Countries, from the Earliest Times to the Present Day. 2nd edition. 4 vols. *Illustrations.* 8° 1873-76
—— Ditto. 3rd edition, in 5 vols. Edited by R. Phené Spiers. Vols. 1 and 2. *Illustrations.* 8° 1893
—— A Short Essay on the Age and Uses of the Brochs and Rude Stone Monuments of the Orkney Islands and the North of Scotland. 8* 1877
—— On the Norwegian Origin of Scottish Brochs. Square 8* 1878
—— *See* Tristram.
—— **and J. Burgess.** The Cave Temples of India. *Map and illustrations.* Imperial 8° 1880

Ferishta, Mahommed Casim, of Delhi. The History of Hindostan. Translated from the Persian. 2nd edition. Revised, altered, corrected, and greatly enlarged, by Alexander Dow. 2 vols. *Maps and plates.* 4° 1770

Fernandex, Antonio. *See* Gottfried : Appendix 1.

Fernandez, Francisco Emilio. El Progreso del Apostadero de Iquitos. 8*
Lima, 1869
Fernandez, F. W. Navegabilidad del Rio Otuquis, Exploracion Practicada en 1886. 12* *Buenos Ayres*, 1889
Ferrand, Henri. Histoire de Mont Iseran. (Extrait du *Bulletin de la Société de Statistique, &c., de l'Isère.*) 8*
Grenoble, 1893
Ferrari, Joseph. La Chine et l'Europe, leur Histoire et leurs Traditions comparées. 8° *Paris*, 1867
Ferraro, Capt. Diego J. Project for the Exploration of the North Polar Region. 4* *Mexico*, 1890
Ferrel, Prof. Wm. The Motions of Fluids and Solids relative to the Earth's Surface, comprising Applications to the Winds and Currents of the Ocean. 4*
New York, 1860
—— Recent Advances in Meteorology. In Annual Report of the Chief Signal Officer for the year 1885. Part 2. 4*
Washington, 1886
—— See United States, F, and H, *b*: Appendix 2.
Ferrero, General A. Rapports sur les triangulations présenté à la Commission permanent, Association Géodésique Internationale. 4° 1887-92
Ferret, A., and Galinier. Voyage en Abyssinie, dans les Provinces du Tigré, du Samen, et de l'Amhara. 2 vols. *Plates*. 8°; and Atlas, fol. *Paris*, 1847-48
Ferrier, J. P. Caravan Journeys and Wanderings in Persia, Afghanistan, Turkistan, and Beloochistan, with Historical Notices of the Countries lying between Russia and India. Translated by Capt. Jesse, and edited by H. D. Seymour. *Map and woodcuts*. 8° 1857
—— History of the Afghans. Translated by Capt. Jesse. *Maps*. 8° 1858
Ferrier, Walter F. *See* Canada, A, Geol. Survey: Appendix 2.
Ferry, Jules. Le Tonkin et la Mère-Patrie. 12° *Paris*, 1890
Férussac, Baron de. Bulletin des Sciences Géographiques, &c., Économie Publique; Voyages . . . publiés sous la direction de M. le Baron de Férussac. 28 vols. 8° *Paris*, 1824-31
Feuillée, Louis. Journal des Observations Physiques, Mathématiques et Botaniques, faites sur les Côtes Orientales de l'Amérique Méridionale, &c. *Maps and plates*. 4° *Paris*, 1725
—— *See* Callander, Vol. 3; Appendix 1.
Ficalho, Conde de. Plantas uteis da Africa Portugueza. 8* *Lisbon*, 1884
Fidler, W. The East India Company: a Memorandum by W. Fidler, with some Additions and an Index by Mr G. M. Craufurd, showing the Leading Events

Fidler, W.—*continued*.
(chiefly Political) chronologically arranged, in the Company's career, from 1599 to 1858. Folio* 1875
Field, Barron. Geographical Memoirs on New South Wales, by various hands. Containing an Account of the Surveyor-General's late Expedition to two New Ports, the Discovery of Moreton Bay River . . ., a Route from Bathurst to Liverpool Plains; together with other Papers on the Aborigines, the Geology, the Botany, the Timber, the Astronomy, and the Meteorology of New South Wales and Van Diemen's Land. Edited by Barron Field. *Maps and plates*. 8°
1825
Field, Cyrus W. Statement of some of the Advantages attendant upon making St John's, Newfoundland, a Port of Call for Trans-Atlantic Steamers. *Map*. 8*
1856
Field, H. M. The Barbary Coast. *Map and illustrations*. 8° *New York*, 1893
Field, T. W. An Essay towards an Indian Bibliography, being a Catalogue of Books relating to the History, &c., of the American Indians. 8° *New York*, 1873
Fiennes, Celia. Through England on a Side-Saddle in the Time of William and Mary, being the Diary of Celia Fiennes; with an Introduction by the Hon. Mrs Griffiths. 8° 1888
Fiesco, Bartolemi. *See* Gottfried: Appendix 1.
Fife, J. G. Irrigation in Egypt. [From the India Records, Public Works Department, No. 21.] 8° *Calcutta*, 1856
—— Report on the Eastern Narra. [From the India Records, No. 60.] *Maps*. 8° *Bombay*, 1861
—— Water Supply of Poona and Kirkee: Plans and Estimates. [From the India Records, No. 3, Irrigation Series.] 8°
Bombay, 1866
—— Report on the subject of the Rainfall in the Dekhan, and the Climatic Disturbance apparent during 1861 and 1862. [From the India Records, No. 78.] 8°
Bombay, 1863
Figari Bey, Antonio. Studii Scientifici sull' Egitto e sue Adiacenze compressa la Penisola dell' Arabia Petrea, &c. 2 vols. in 3. 8° *Lucca*, 1864-65
Figueiredo, Borges de. Homenagem a Luciano Cordeiro. *Portrait*. Large 8*
Lisbon, 1887
Figuier, Bernard. *See* Pinto.
Figuredo, Juan de. Arte de la Lengua Quichua (Grammar and Vocabulary). [*Imperfect*.] 12° *Lima*, 1700
Filipescu-Dubău, Nicu. Dictionar Geographical Judetului Dorohoiŭ. Intocmit si prelucrat in formă lexiconioâ de C. Chirita. 8° *Jassy*, 1891

Filippi, F. de. Note di un Viaggio in Persia nel 1862. 8°   *Milan,* 1865

Filisola, General Vicente. Evacuation of Texas : Translation of the Representation addressed to the Supreme Government in Defence of his Honour, and Explanation of his Operations as Commander-in-Chief of the Army against Texas. 8*   *Columbia,* 1837

Fillias, Achille. Géographie de l'Algérie. 4th edition. *Map and illustrations.* 12°
                                          Paris, 1884

Filon, Francois, and Alexandre Cordeau. Exposition Universelle de 1889 : Avant-Projet, Construction d'une Sphère Terrestre Monumentale a l'Échelle de $\frac{1}{1000000}$e 40 mètres de circonférence. *Plates.* 8*   *Paris,* 1888

Finati, Giovanni. Narrative of the Life and Adventures of, who, under the assumed name of Mahomet, made the Campaigns against the Wahabees for the Recovery of Mecca and Medina, and since acted as Interpreter to European Travellers in some of the parts least visited of Asia and Africa. Translated from the Italian, and edited by W. J. Bankes. 2 vols. *Map.* 12°   1830

Finch, John. Travels in the United States of America and Canada, with some Account of their Scientific Institutions, and Notices of the Geology and Mineralogy of those Countries ; to which is added, an Essay on the Natural Boundaries of Empires. 8°   1833
—— Natural Boundaries of Empires, and a New View of Colonisation. 12° 1844

Finch, John. To South Africa and Back : being the Narrative of a Journey through Cape Colony, Natal, Orange Free State, and the Transvaal, including Visits to the Diamond and Gold Fields. *Portrait and illustrations.* 12°   1890

Finch, Richard. *See* Purchas, Vol. 3, Book 3 : Appendix 1.

Finch, Wm. *See* Gottfried ; Kerr, Vol. 8 ; Purchas, Vol. 1, Book 4 ; Allgemeine Historie, Vol. 3 : Appendix 1.

Finck, H. T. The Pacific Coast Scenic Tour from Southern California to Alaska, the Canadian Pacific Railway, Yellowstone Park, and the Grand Cañon. *Map and illustrations.* 8°   1891

Findlay, A. G. On the various Descriptions of Lighthouses and Beacons, their Construction, and the Method of Illumination employed therein. 4°   1847
—— Directory for the Navigation of the Pacific Ocean ; with Descriptions of its Coasts, Islands, &c., from the Strait of Magalhaens to the Arctic Sea, and those of Asia and Australia, its Winds, Currents, and other Phenomena. 2 vols. *Map.* 8°   1851

Findlay, A. G. Description and List of the Lighthouses of the World. *Illustrations.* 8°   1861
—— Directory for the Navigation of the South Pacific Ocean ; with Descriptions of its Coasts, Islands, &c., from the Strait of Magalhaens to Panama, and those of New Zealand, Australia, &c. ; its Winds, Currents, and Passages. *Map.* 8°   1863
—— A Directory for the Navigation of the Indian Ocean ; with Descriptions of its Coasts, Islands, &c., from the Cape of Good Hope to the Strait of Sunda and Western Australia, including also the Red Sea and the Persian Gulf, &c. *Maps.* 8°   1866
—— The same. 2nd edition   1870
—— Remarks on Dr Livingstone's Last Journey, in Relation to the Probable Ultimate Sources of the Nile. *Map.* 8*
                                          1867
—— A Sailing Directory for the Ethiopic or South Atlantic Ocean, including the Coasts of South America and Africa. 5th edition. *Maps.* 8°   1867
—— The same. 7th edition   1871
—— A Sailing Directory for the Mediterranean Sea, including the Adriatic Sea, Black Sea, the Archipelago, and the Coast of Africa. *Map and profiles.* 8°   1868
—— A Directory for the Navigation of the Indian Archipelago, China, and Japan, from the Straits of Malacca and Sunda, and the Passages East of Java, to Canton, Shanghai, the Yellow Sea, and Japan, &c. *Maps.* 8°   1870
—— The same. 3rd edition   1889
—— A Directory for the Navigation of the North Pacific Ocean ; with Descriptions of its Coasts, Islands, &c., from Panama to Behring Strait and Japan, &c. 2nd edition. *Maps.* 8°   1870
—— The same. 3rd edition   1886
—— A Directory for the Navigation of the South Pacific Ocean ; with Descriptions of its Coasts, Islands, &c., from the Strait of Magalhaens to Panama, and those of New Zealand, Australia, &c. 3rd edition. *Map.* 8°   1871
—— The same. 5th edition   1884
—— A Description and List of the Lighthouses of the World, 1872-73. 8° 1873
—— The same. 20th edition. *Plate.* 8°
                                          1880
—— *See* Brookes, R. ; Martin ; Purdy.

Finlay, George. Remarks on the Topography of Oropia and Diacria. *Map.* 8*   *Athens,* 1838
—— Παρατηρησεις επι τησεν Ελβετια και Ελλαδι προιστορικης αρχαιολογιας. 8*   *Athens,* 1869

Finlayson, George. The Mission to Siam, and Hué, the Capital of Cochin-China, in 1821-22. From the Journal of the late G. Finlayson; with a Memoir of the Author by Sir T. Stamford Raffles. *Plate.* 8° 1826

Finley, J. P Certain Climatic Features of the Two Dakotas. [Bulletin of the Weather Bureau.] *Tables, charts, and diagrams.* 4° *Washington,* 1893
—— *See* United States, H, *b* (Professional Papers, No. 4): Appendix 2.

Finnis, John. *See* India, C (Geological Papers): Appendix 1.

Finsch, Dr Otto. Neu-Guinea und seine Bewohner. *Map.* 8° *Bremen,* 1865
—— Catalog der Ausstellung ethnographischer und naturwissenschaftlicher Sammlungen. (West Sibirische Forschungsreise, 1876. *See* Ver. f. d. Deutsche Nordpolarfahrt, 1876.) 8* *Bremen,* 1877
—— Reise nach West-Sibirien im Jahre 1876. *Maps and plates.* 8° *Berlin,* 1879
—— Bemerkungen über einige Eingeborne des Atoll Ontong - Java (" Njua "). 8* *[Berlin,* 1881]
—— Ueber seine in den Jahren 1879 bis 1882 unternommenen Reisen in der Südsee. 8* *Berlin,* 1882
—— Die Rassenfrage in Oceanien. 8* *Berlin,* 1882
—— Ueber weisse Papuas. 8* *[Berlin,* 1883]
—— Ueber Naturprodukte der westlichen Südsee, besonders der deutschen Schutzgebiete. 8* *Berlin,* 1887
—— Samoafahrten. Reisen in Kaiser Wilhelms-Land und Englisch-Neu-Guinea in den Jahren 1884 u. 1885 an bord des deutschen dampfers "Samoa." *Portrait, maps, and illustrations.* 8°; Atlas, 4° *Leipzig,* 1888
—— *See* Lindeman; Sommier and Giglioli.

Fiorauante, C. *See* Ramusio, Vol. 2: Appendix 1.

Fiore, Giovanni. Della Calabria Illustrata, opera varia Istorica; in cui, non solo regolatamente si descrive con perfetta Corografia la situazione, Promontori, Porti, Seni di Mare, Città, Castella, Fortezze, nomi delle medesime, e lor Origine, mà anche con esatta Cronologia si registrano i Dominanti, l'antiche Republiche, e fatti di Armi in esse accaduti, dagli anni del Mondo 306 fin al corrente di Cristo 1690. Vol. 1. *Map.* Folio *Naples,* 1691

Fiorini, Matteo. Le projezioni delle Carte Geografiche. Text and Atlas. 8° *Bologna,* 1881
—— Sopra la projezione Cartografica isogonica. Nota. 4* *Bologna,* 1882

Fiorini, Matteo. The same. Nota Seconda. *Plate.* 4* *Bologna,* 1883
—— Misure linerari, superficiali ed angolari offerte dalle Carte Geografiche. 8* *Florence,* 1886
—— Le Projezioni quantitative ed equivalenti della Cartografia. 8* *Rome,* 1887
—— Le Projezioni Cordiformi nella Cartografia. 8* *Rome,* 1889
—— Gerardo Mercatore e le sue Carte Geografiche. 8* *Rome,* 1890
—— I globi di Gerardo Mercatore in Italia. 8* *Rome,* 1890

Fischer, Andreas. Zwei Kaukasus Expeditionen. *Map and illustrations.* 12° *Berne,* 1891

Fischer, C. A. *See* Phillips [1], Vols. 3 and 5 : Appendix 1.

Fischer, C. T. Untersuchungen auf dem Gebiet der alten Länder- und Völkerkunde. Erstes Heft. De Hannonis Carthaginiensis Periplo. 8° *Leipzig,* 1893

Fischer —. *See* Kiepert, Dr H.

Fischer, Dr G. A. Ueber die jetzigen Verhältnisse im südlichen Galla-Lande und Wito. 8* *Hamburg,* 1877
—— Das Massai-Land (Ost-aequatorial Afrika). Bericht über die im Auftrage der Geographischen Gesellschaft in Hamburg ausgeführter Reise von Pangani bis zum Naiwascha-See. *Map and illustrations.* 8° *Hamburg,* 1885
—— Mehr Licht im dunkeln Weltteil. Betrachtungen über die Kolonisation des tropischen Afrika unter besonderer Berücksichtigung des Sansibar-Gebiets. 8° *Hamburg,* 1885

Fischer, F. A. Travels in Spain in 1797 and 1798. 8° 1802

Fischer, J. *See* Andree, Karl.

Fischer, Dr Theobald. Beiträge zur physischen Geographie der Mittelmeerländer, besonders Siciliens. *Maps.* 8° *Leipzig,* 1877
—— Studien über das Klima der Mittelmeerländer. (Ergänzungsheft, 58 — Petermann's Mittheilungen.) *Maps.* 4° *Gotha,* 1879
—— Die Dattelpalme. (Ergänzungsheft, 64—Petermann's Mittheilungen.) *Maps.* 4° *Gotha,* 1881
—— Beiträge zur Geschichte der Erdkunde und der Kartographie in Italien im Mittelalter. Sammlung mittelalterlicher Welt- und Seekarten Italienischen Ursprungs und aus Italienischer Bibliotheken und Archiven. 8° *Venice,* 1886
—— Ländeskunde der drei sudeuropäischen Halbinseln. Zweite Hälfte. *Maps and illustrations.* Large 8° *Leipzig,* 1893
—— *See* Ankel.

Fisher, Alexander. A Journal of a Voyage of Discovery to the Arctic Regions in H. M. Ships " Hecla " and " Griper," in 1819-20. *Maps.* 8° 1821
—— *See* Phillips [3], Vol. 1: Appendix 1.

L

Fisher, Fred. H. Cyprus, our New Colony, and what we know about it. *Maps.* 12°   1878
—— *See* India, O (N.W. Provinces): Appendix 2.

Fisher, G. Memorials of, relating to the Expedition of General Mexia against Tampico in 1835; presented to the Congress of the Republic of Texas. 8*
Houston, Texas, 1840

Fisher, Rev. Osmond. Physics of the Earth's Crust. 8°   1881
—— The same. 2nd edition. *Frontispiece.*   1889

Fisher, R. *See* Hakluyt, Vol. 3: Appendix 1.

Fiske, John. The Discovery of America; with some Account of Ancient America and the Spanish Conquest. 2 vols. *Portrait, maps, &c.* Crown 8°   1892

Fitch, Asa. The most Pernicious Species of United States Insects and the Curculio. 8*   *Albany, N.Y.,* 1860

Fitch, Ralph. *See* Gottfried; Hakluyt, Vol. 2; Pinkerton, Vol. 9; Purchas, Vol. 2, Book 10: Appendix 1.

Fitton, W. H. A Geological Sketch of the Vicinity of Hastings. *Plate.* 12°
1833

Fitzalan, Eugène. *See* Mueller.

Fitzclarence, Colonel. Journal of a Route across India, through Egypt, to England, in the latter end of the year 1817 and the beginning of 1818. *Maps and plates.* 4°   1819
—— *See* Phillips [3], Vol. 1: Appendix 1.

Fitzgerald, C. The Gambia, and its proposed Cession to France. *Map.* 8*
1875

Fitzgerald, J. E. An Examination of the Charter and Proceedings of the Hudson's Bay Company with reference to the grant of Vancouver's Island. *Map.* 12°   1847

Fitzgerald, W. W. A. Report on the Native Cultivation, Products, and Capabilities of the Coast Lands of the Melindi District. 4*   [1891]
—— Report on the Spice and other Cultivation of Zanzibar and Pemba Islands. 8*   1892

Fitzherbert, Captain Humphrey. *See* Purchas, Vol. 1, Book 5: Appendix 1.

Fitz-James, Capt. James. The Last Journals of, of the Lost Polar Expedition. Edited by W. Coningham. 8°
Brighton. N.D.

Fitzmaurice, Hon. W. E. Cruise to Egypt, Palestine, and Greece. *Plates.* 4°   1834

Fitz-Patrick, T. An Autumn Cruise in the Ægean; or, Notes of a Voyage in a Sailing Yacht. *Maps, plan, and illustrations.* Crown 8°   1886

Fitzroy, Admiral Robert. Narrative of the Surveying Voyages of His Majesty's Ships "Adventure" and "Beagle." *See* King, P. P.
—— Zoology of the Voyage of H.M.S. "Beagle" during the years 1832 to 1836. Edited by Charles Darwin. [Fossil Mammalia, by R. Owen; Mammalia, by G. R. Waterhouse; Birds, by J. Gould; Fish, by Leonard Jenyns; Reptiles, by Thos. Bell.] 3 vols. *Coloured plates.* 4°   1840-43
—— Sailing Directions for South America. Part 2: La Plata, Patagonia, Falkland and Staten Islands, Chile, Bolivia, and Peru. 8°   1848
—— Further Considerations on the Great Isthmus of Central America. *Map.* 8*
[1853]
—— Swinging Ship for Deviation. 2 editions. 8*   1857-59
—— Meteorological Papers compiled by Authority of the Board of Trade. *See* United Kingdom, B: Appendix 2.
—— Report of the Meteorological Department of the Board of Trade, 1855, '57, '58, '62. 4 parts. 8°   1857-62
—— Great Circle Sailing. 12°   1858
—— Report of the Meteorological Department of the Board of Trade, 1858. 8°
1858
—— Barometer and Weather Guide. 1859 and 1861. 2 editions. 8*   1859-61
—— Notes on Meteorology. 8°   1859
—— Passage Table and General Sailing Directions. 8°   1859
—— Barometer Manual. 8°   1861
—— Brief Sketch of the Scientific Career of the late. By Sir R. I. Murchison. 8*
1865

Flacourt, E. de. Histoire de la grande Isle de Madagascar. 2 parts. 4°
Paris, 1758

Flagg, Edmund. Report of the Commercial Relations of the United States. 4 vols. 4°   *Washington,* 1856

Flahault, C. Nordenskiöld, Notice sur sa vie et ses Voyages. *Map and portrait.* 8°   *Paris,* 1880

Flamsteed, John. *See* Baily, Francis.

Flawes, Capt. W. *See* "Voyages," p. 597: Appendix 1.

Fleetwood, Edward. *See* Dalrymple, Repertory, Vol. 2: Appendix 1.

Flegel, E. Vom Niger-Benüe; Briefe aus Afrika. Herausgegeben von Karl Flegel. 8°   *Leipzig,* 1890

Fleischmann, C. L. Memorial of, in Relation to the Smithsonian Legacy. 8*
Washington, 1839

Fleming, A. *See* India, C (Geological Papers): Appendix 2.

Fleming and Tibbins. *See* Dictionaries (French), General: Appendix 2.

Fleming, Francis. Southern Africa : a Geography and Natural History of the Country, Colonies, and Inhabitants, from the Cape of Good Hope to Angola. *Map.* 8° 1856

Fleming, George. Travels on Horseback in Mantchu Tartary : being a Summer's Ride beyond the Great Wall of China. *Map and plates.* 8° 1863

Fleming, Sandford. Short Sunday Service for Travelling Parties. 16° *Montreal,* 1877
—— Report on Surveys and Preliminary Operations on the Canadian Pacific Railway up to January 1877. *Map.* 8° *Ottawa,* 1877
—— Canadian Pacific Railway : Reports and Documents in reference to the Location of the Line and a western Terminal Harbour. *Maps.* 8° *Ottawa,* 1878
—— Report in reference to the Canadian Pacific Railroad. *Map.* 8° *Ottawa,* 1879
—— Report and Documents in reference to the Canadian Pacific Railway, 1880. *Maps.* 8° *Ottawa,* 1880
—— Papers on Time-Reckoning and the Selection of a Prime Meridian to be Common to all Nations. *Diagrams.* 8* *Toronto,* 1879
—— England and Canada : a Summer Tour between Old and New West-minster, with Historical Notes. *Map.* Crown 8° 1884
—— Universal or Cosmic Time ; together with other Papers, &c., in the possession of the Canadian Institute respecting the Movement for reforming the Time-System of the World, &c. (From *Proc. Can. Inst.*) *Plate.* 8* *Toronto,* 1885
—— Time-Reckoning for the Twentieth Century. From the Smithsonian Report for 1886. 8* *Washington,* 1889

Flemyng, Francis P. Mauritius, or the Isle of France : being an Account of the Island, its History, &c. *Map and plates.* 16° 1862

Fletcher, Giles. *See* Hakluyt Soc. Publ., Vol. 20 ; Purchas, Vol. 3 : Appendix 1.

Fletcher, J. C., and D. P. Kidder. Brazil and the Brazilians portrayed in Historical and Descriptive Sketches. 9th edition. *Map and plates.* 8° 1879

Fletcher, Rev. J. P. Notes from Nineveh, and Travels in Mesopotamia, Assyria, and Syria. 2 vols. 8° 1850

Fletcher, Price. Queensland, its Resources and Institutions . . . Edited by Price Fletcher. *Map.* 8° 1886

Fletcher-Vane, F. P. *See* Butler, G. G.

Fleurieu, Charles Pierre Claret, Comte de. Voyage fait par Ordre du Roi en 1768-69, à différentes parties du Monde, pour éprouver en Mer les Horloges Marines inventées par M. F. Berthoud. 2 vols. *Maps.* 4° *Paris,* 1773

Fleurieu, Charles Pierre Claret, Comte de. Discoveries of the French in 1768 and 1769, to the South-east of New Guinea, with the Subsequent Visits to the same Lands by English Navigators, who gave them new names ; to which is Prefixed an Historical Abridgement of the Voyages and Discoveries of the Spaniards in the same Seas. Translated from the French. *Charts and plates.* 4° 1791
—— A Voyage round the World, performed during the years 1790-92, by Étienne Marchand. . . . Translated from the French. 2 vols. 4° 1801
—— *See* Marchand.

Fleury, A. A. de Padua. Exploração do Rio Ivahy. 4* *Rio de Janeiro* [1864]

Flicke, Capt. Robert. *See* Astley, Vol. 1 ; Hakluyt, Vol. 2 ; Kerr, Vol. 7 ; Allgemeine Historie, Vol. 1 : Appendix 1.

Flinders, Capt. Matthew. Observations on the Coasts of Van Diemen's Land, on Bass's Strait and its Islands, and on part of the Coasts of New South Wales. 4° 1801
—— Voyage to Terra Australis, undertaken for the purpose of completing the Discovery of that vast Continent, in 1801-3, in H.M.S. "Investigator," and subsequently in the " Porpoise " and "Cumberland " ; with an Account of the Shipwreck of the " Porpoise," arrival of the " Cumberland " at Mauritius, and Imprisonment of the Commander during six years and a half in that island. 3 vols. *Atlas and plates.* 4° 1814
—— *See* Eyriès, Vol. 4 : Appendix 1.

Flinn, D. Edgar. Ireland, its Health-Resorts and Watering-Places ; with Maps showing Distribution of Temperature and Rainfall throughout Ireland. *Frontis-piece.* 8° 1888

Flint, Timothy. History and Geography of the Mississippi Valley, with a con-densed Physical Geography of the Atlantic, United States, &c. 2 vols. in 1. 8° *Cincinnati,* 1832

" Florence," Cruise of the. *See* Tyson, E.

Flores Arenas, F. Obras Escogidas. I. Obras Poéticas. 8° *Cadiz,* 1878

Florianus, —. Chronica Minora (Historiæ Hungaricæ Fontes Domestici, Vol. 4.) 4° *Budapest,* 1885

Florio-Sartori, Florindo. The Island of Caprera and the Hero of the Two Worlds : a Geographical and Historical Account. *Map and illustrations.* 12° *Naples,* 1888
—— L'Isola di Caprera e l'Eroe dei due Mondi : Cenni Geografici e Storici. *Map and illustrations.* 8° *Naples,* 1888

Floris, P. W. *See* Gottfried; Astley, Vol. 1; Purchas, Vol. 1, Book 3; Thevenot, Vol. 1 : Allgemeine Historie, Vol. 10 : Appendix 1.

Flotte D'Argençon, Comte Magloire de. Nouveau Portulan de la Mediterranée, ou Guide complet du Pilote, sur toutes les Côtes, Iles, Bancs, et Ports compris depuis Cadix jusqu'à la Mer Noire. 2 vols. 8° *Toulon*, 1829

Flower, Charles E. Algerian Hints for Tourists. *Frontispiece.* 12° 1889

Flower, W. B. Illustrated Guide to Baden-Baden. Based on the German. *Maps.* 12° *Baden-Baden*, 1865

Flower, Sir W. H. *See* West Indies, A : Appendix 2.

Floyer, Ernest Ayscoghe. Unexplored Baluchistan : a Survey, with Observations Astronomical, Geographical, Botanical, &c., of a Route through Mekran, Bashkurd, Persia, Kurdistan, and Turkey. *Map and illustrations.* 8° 1882
—— Étude sur le Nord-Etbai entre le Nil et la Mer Rouge. *Maps and illustrations.* 4° *Cairo*, 1893

Flügel, Dr J. G. *See* Hermann, G.

Flügel, G. T. Courszettel der vornehmsten Handelsplätze in Europa, nebst anderen zu den Wechselgeschäfften dienlichen Nachrichten. 6th edition. 12° *Frankfurt a. M.*, 1788

"Fly," H.M.S. *See* Jukes.

Foa, Edouard. Ethnographie : Le Dahomey. 4* [*Paris*, 1891]

Fockt, C. T. *See* Hartleben.

Foderé, F. E. Voyage aux Alpes Maritimes, ou Histoire Naturelle, Agraire, Civile, ét Médicale, du Comté de Nice et pays limitrophes. 2 vols. in 1. 8° *Paris*, 1821

Foetterle, Franz. Die geologische Uebersichtskarte des mittleren Theiles von Süd-Amerika ; mit einem Vorworte von W. Haidinger. *Map.* 8* *Vienna*, 1854
—— Bericht über die Durchstechung der Landenge von Suez. 8* *Berlin* [1857]

Fogg, W. P. Arabistan, or The Land of "The Arabian Nights": being Travels through Egypt, Arabia, and Persia, to Bagdad. With an Introduction by Bayard Taylor. *Plates.* 8° 1875

Foledo, R. Geografia de Centro-América. Adoptada por el Supremo Gobierno como testo de enseñanza en la República. Small square 8° *Guatemala*, 1874

Follada, J. B. de la. *See* Burney, Vol. 3 : Appendix 1.

Folque, F. Memoria sobre os Trabalhos Geodesicos executados em Portugal. 2 vols. 4° *Lisbon*, 1841 and 1852
—— *See* Collecção de Noticias, Vol. 7, p. 611 : Appendix 1.

Fonseca, Jose G. de. *See* Collecção de Noticias, Vol. 4, p. 611 : Appendix 1.

Fontaine, W. M. *See* United States, G,c (Monographs) : Appendix 2.

Fontane, Marius. Le Canal Interocéanique et le Canal de Suez. 4* *Paris*, 1879

Fontanedo, H. d'E. *See* Ternaux-Compans, Vol. 20 : Appendix 1.

Fontaney, Jean de. *See* Astley, Vol. 3 ; Allgemeine Historie, Vol. 5 : Appendix 1.

Fontanier, V. Voyages dans l'Inde et dans le Golfe Persique, par l'Égypte et la Mer Rouge. *Map.* 8° *Paris*, 1844

Fontbonne, G. de. Projet d'un Canal Interocéanique à niveau des deux Océans dans le Darien. *Maps and plans.* Small 8* *Sancerre*, 1875

Fonte, Bartholomew de. *See* Burney, Vol. 3 ; Allgemeine Historie, Vol. 17 : Appendix 1.

Fontenay, Peter von. *See* Allgemeine Historie, Vol. 10 : Appendix 1.

Fonton, F. La Russie dans l'Asie-Mineure, ou Campagnes du Maréchal Paskévitch en 1828 et 1829 ; et Tableau du Caucase. 8° *Paris*, 1840

Fontpertuis, Ad.-F. de. La Nouvelle Guinée, sa Géographie, ses Races, et ses Explorateurs. 4* N.P., N.D.

Foote, H. Stuart. Texas and the Texans; or, Advance of the Anglo-Americans to the South-West, including a History of Leading Events in Mexico, from the Conquest by Fernando Cortes to the Termination of the Texan Revolution. 2 vols. 12° *Philadelphia*, 1841

Foote, R. Bruce. On the Distribution of Stone Implements in Southern India. *Map.* 8* 1868
—— *See* India, C (Palæont. Ind.) : Appendix 2.

Forbes, A. California : a History of Upper and Lower California, from their First Discovery to the Present Time ; comprising an Account of the Climate, Soil, Natural Productions, Agriculture, Commerce, &c. *Map and plates.* 8° 1839

Forbes, Charles. Vancouver Island, its Resources and Capabilities as a Colony. Prize Essay. 8° *Victoria, B.C.*, 1862
—— Notes on the Physical Geography of Vancouver Island. *Map.* 8* [1864]

Forbes, Charles S. Iceland, its Volcanoes, Geysers, and Glaciers. *Map and plates.* 8° 1860

Forbes, D. On the Aymara Indians of Bolivia and Peru. *Plates.* 8° 1870

Forbes, Edward. The Relations of Natural History to Geology and the Arts. 8* 1851

Forbes, Edward. The Natural History of the European Seas. Edited and continued by R. Godwin-Austen. *Map.* 12° 1859

—— *See* Seemann ; Spratt.

Forbes, Frederick. Thesis on the Nature and History of Plague, as observed in the N.-W. Provinces of India. *Map.* 8° *Edinburgh*, 1840

Forbes, Commander F. E. Five Years in China, from 1842 to 1847 ; with an Account of the Occupation of the Islands of Labuan and Borneo by Her Majesty's Forces. *Woodcuts.* 8° 1848

—— Six Months' Service in the African Blockade, 1848. *Map.* 8° 1849

—— Dahomey and the Dahomans : being the Journals of Two Missions to the King of Dahomey, and Residence at his Capital in 1849 and 1850. 2 vols. *Plates.* 8° 1851

Forbes, G. F. Report on Cotton in the Southern States of North America. Folio* 1866

Forbes, Dr H. O. On Some of the Tribes of the Island of Timor. *Plates.* 8* 1884

—— A Naturalist's Wanderings in the Eastern Archipelago : a Narrative of Travel and Exploration from 1878 to 1883. *Map and illustrations.* 8° 1885

—— On Attempts to Reach the Owen Stanley Peak : a Report to the Royal Scottish Geographical Society on the New Guinea Expedition. *Map.* 8* *Edinburgh*, 1888

—— British New Guinea as a Colony. 8* [1892]

—— The Chatham Islands and their Story. (From the *Fortnightly Review* for May 1893.) 8* 1893

—— The Chatham Islands and their Relation to a former Southern Continent. (Roy. Geo. Soc. Suppl. Papers, Vol. 3.) *Map.* Large 8° 1893

—— The Geographical Society [of Australasia] and Mr H. O. Forbes. [Newspaper cuttings.] 12* N.P., N.D.

Forbes, Mrs H. O. Insulinde : Experiences of a Naturalist's Wife in the Eastern Archipelago. *Map.* Crown 8° 1887

Forbes, James. Oriental Memoirs : a Narrative of Seventeen Years' Residence in India. 2nd edition. Revised by . . . the Countess de Montalembert. 2 vols. 8° 1834

Forbes, Prof. James D. Travels through the Alps of Savoy and other Parts of the Pennine Chain ; with Observations on the Phenomena of Glaciers. *Maps and plates.* Royal 8° *Edinburgh*, 1843

—— Norway and its Glaciers, visited in 1851 ; with Excursions to the High Alps of Dauphiné, Berne, and Savoy. *Maps and plates.* 8° *Edinburgh*, 1853

Forbes, Prof. James D. Occasional Papers on the Theory of Glaciers. *Plates.* 8° *Edinburgh*, 1859

Forbes, John. A Physician's Holiday ; or, A Month in Switzerland in the Summer of 1848. *Map and illustrations.* 8° 1850

Forbes, Litton. Two Years in Fiji. Small 8° 1875

Forbes, Major. Eleven Years in Ceylon, comprising Sketches of the Field Sports and Natural History of that Colony, and an Account of its History and Antiquities. *Plates.* 8° 1840

Forbiger, A. Handbuch der alten Geographie. 3 vols. *Maps.* 8° *Leipzig*, 1842-48

Forbin, Comte. Voyage dans le Levant en 1817 et 1818. *Plate.* 8° *Paris*, 1819

—— *See* Allgemeine Historie, Vol. 18 : Phillips [3], Vols. 1, 2, 9 : Appendix 1.

Force, Peter. Remarks on the English Maps of Arctic Discoveries in 1850 and 1851. 8* *Washington*, 1852

Forchhammer, E. Papers on Subjects relating to the Archæology of Burma. [Various sizes and dates.] *Map and plates.*

Forchhammer, G. Hans Christian Oersted. Et Mindeskrift læst i det Kong. Danske Videnskabernes Selskabs Möde, 7th November 1851. 8* *Copenhagen*, 1852

—— Bidrag til skildringen af Danmarks Geographiske Forhold i deres Afhængighed af Landets indre Geognostiske Bygning. 4* *Copenhagen*, 1858

—— Om Sövandets Bestanddele og deres Fordeling i Havet. *Map.* 4* *Copenhagen*, 1859

—— Notitser angaaende den sandsynlige Forekomst af Juraformationen i det nordlige Jylland. 8* *Copenhagen*, 1863

Forchhammer, P. W. Topographie von Athen. *Map.* 8° *Kiel*, 1841

—— Ditto, another edition. *Gottingen*, 1873

—— Die Gründung Roms. *Map.* 8* *Kiel*, 1868

—— Daduchos. Einleitung in das Verständniss der Hellenischen Mythen, Mythensprache, und mythischen Bauten. *Plates.* 8* *Kiel*, 1875

—— Das Erechtheion. *Plates.* 4* *Kiel*, 1879

—— Mykenä und der Ursprung der Mykenischen Funde. 8° *Kiel*, 1880

—— Das goldene Vliess und die Argonauten. 8* N.P., N.D.

—— Ueber das mythische und geographische Wissen des Æschylos, oder die Wanderungen der Io. *Map.* 4* N.P., N.D.

—— Erklärung der Ilias auf Grund der in der beigegebenen original Karte von Spratt und Forchhammer dargestellten topischen und physischen. Eigenthümlichkeiten der Troischen Ebene. Ein Beitrag zur Erledigung der Homerischen Frage. 4° *Kiel*, 1884

Forchhammer, P. W. Prolegomena zur Mythologie als Wissenschaft, und Lexikon der Mythensprache. Large 8°
Kiel, 1891
—— Die Kyanen und die Argonauten. *Map.* 8* *Kiel*, 1891

Ford, Francis Clare. Argentine Republic. Reports, &c. 8*
Buenos Ayres, 1866

Ford, Isaac N. Tropical America. *Illustrations.* 8° 1893

Forel, Dr F. A. Le Lac Léman : Précis Scientifique. 12*. *Basle*, 1886
—— La Capacité du Lac Léman. 8* 1888
—— Le Léman. Monographie limnologique. 2 vols. *Maps.* 8°
Lausanne, 1892-95

Foreman, Henry. The Routes to Australia considered in reference to Commercial and Postal Interests. By the Directors of the Australian Direct Steam Navigation Company *via* Panama, in a Letter to the Right Hon. Viscount Canning. *Map.* 8* 1854

Foreman, J. The Philippine Islands : a Historical, Geographical, Ethnographical, Social, and Commercial Sketch of the Philippine Archipelago and its Political Dependencies. *Map and frontispiece.* 8° 1890

Forester, T. Rambles in Norway among the Fjelds and Fjords of the Central and Western Districts. 12° 1855
—— Rambles in the Islands of Corsica and Sardinia, with their History, Antiquities, and Present Condition. *Map and plates.* Imperial 8° 1858

Forlong, F. G. R. Report on the Toungoop Mountain Road. [From the India Records, No. 19.] 8° *Calcutta*, 1856
—— *See* Fraser and Forlong.

" Forlorn Hope," Ship. *See* M'Cormick, R.

Formaleoni, Vincenzio. Saggio sulla Nautica Antica de' Veneziani ; con una illustrazione d'alcune carte Idrografiche antiche della Biblioteca di S. Marco, che dimostrano l'Isole Antille prima della scoperta di Cristoforo Colombo. *Maps.* Small 4° *Venice*, 1783

Fornando, D. *See* Peragallo.

Forni, G. Viaggio nell' Egitto e nell' Alta Nubia. 2 vols. *Plates.* 8°
Milan, 1859

Forrest, Lieut.-Col. A Picturesque Tour along the Rivers Ganges and Jumna, in India. *Map and coloured plates.* Large 4° 1824

Forrest, Alexander. Western Australia. North-West Exploration : Journal of Expedition from De Grey to Port Darwin. *Map and plates.* Folio*
Perth, W.A., 1880

Forrest, George W. *See* India, K (Bombay) : Appendix 2.

Forrest, Sir John. Newspaper cuttings referring to his Australian Explorations [*Inquirer* and *Commercial News*]. 8* 1874
—— Explorations in Australia : I. Explorations in Search of Dr Leichardt and Party : II. From Perth to Adelaide, around the great Australian Bight ; III. From Champion Bay, across the Desert to the Telegraph and to Adelaide ; with an Appendix on the Condition of Western Australia. *Maps and plates.* 8° 1875
—— Journal of Proceedings of the Western Australian Exploring Expedition through the Centre of Australia, from Champion Bay on the West Coast to the Overland Telegraph Line between Adelaide and Port Darwin. *Map and plates.* Folio*
Perth, W.A., 1875
—— Report on the Kimberley District, North-Western Australia. *Map and plates.* Folio* *Perth, W.A.*, 1883
—— The Kimberley District, North-Western Australia. Folio* [1886]

Forrest, J. *See* Longridge ; Murray, John ; Peniston.

Forrest, Thomas. Voyage to New Guinea and the Moluccas, from Balambangan ; including an Account of Magindano, Sooloo, and other Islands, and a Vocabulary of the Magindano Tongue. *Maps and plates.* 4° 1780

Forrester, Joseph James. Papers relating to the Improvement of the Navigation of the River Douro, from its mouth to the Barca de Vilvestre in Spain, and to the Maps of that River, and of the Wine District of the Alto-Douro. 8*
Oporto, 1844
—— Documents relating to Mr Forrester's Topographical Works of the Wine Districts of the Alto-Douro and River Douro, ordered to be published by the Municipal Chamber of Oporto. 8*
Oporto, 1848
—— The Oliveira Prize Essay on Portugal ; with the Evidence regarding that Country taken before a Committee of the House of Commons in May 1852, and the Author's Surveys of the Wine Districts of the Alto-Douro. *Map.* 8° 1853
—— Memoria sobre o Curativo da Molestia nas Videiras. *Map* *Oporto*, 1857

Forsell, Carl. Statistik öfver Sverige. *Map.* 8° *Stockholm*, 1833
—— Några underrättelser hörande till Kartan öfver Södra delen af Sverige och Norrige eller Skandinavien. 4*
Stockholm, 1826

Forskal, Petrus. Descriptiones Animalium, Avium, Amphbiorum, Piscium, Insectorum, Vermium, quæ in itinere Orientali observavit Petrus Forskal, Prof. Haun: Post mortem auctoris edidit Carsten Niebuhr. Adjuncta est Materia Medica Kahirina atque Tabula Maris Rubi Geographica. *Map.* 4°
Copenhagen, 1775
—— Flora Egyptiaco-Arabica, sive descriptiones Plantarum, quas per Ægyptum Inferiorum ec Arabiam Felicem detexit, illustravit Petrus Forskal, Prof. Haun: Post mortem auctoris Carsten Niebuhr. Accedit Tabula Arabiæ Felicis Geographica-Botanica. *Map.* 4°
Copenhagen, 1775

Forster, Dr A. E. Verzeichniss der in Druck veröffentlichten Arbeiten von Friedrich Simony . . . Large 8*
Vienna, 1893

Förster, Brix. Deutsch-Ostafrika, Geographie und Geschichte der Colonie. *Map.* 8° *Leipzig,* 1890

Forster, Rev. Charles. Historical Geography of Arabia, or the Patriarchal Evidences of Revealed Religion ; with an Appendix containing Translations, and an Alphabet and Glossary of the Hamyaritic Inscriptions recently discovered in Hadramaut. 2 vols. *Maps.* 8° 1844
—— The One Primeval Language traced experimentally through Ancient Inscriptions in Alphabet Characters of Lost Powers from the Four Continents, including the Voice of Israel from the Rocks of Sinai, and the Vestiges of Patriarchal Tradition from the Monuments of Egypt, Etruria, and Southern Arabia ; with Plates, Glossaries, and Translations; the Harmony of Primeval Alphabets, *in case.* 2 vols. 8° 1851
—— The Israelitish Authorship of the Sinaïtic Inscriptions vindicated against the incorrect "Observations" in the "Sinai and Palestine" of the Rev. A. P. Stanley. 8° 1856
—— Essay addressed to Lord Lyndhurst on the True Date of Korah's Rebellion, or its Date in the Margin of our English Bible, B.C. 1471, the true one ; with an Introductory Letter to the Bishop of Winchester. 8* *Privately printed,* 1864

Förster, Dr F. Statistisch-topographisch-historische Uebersicht des Preuszischen Staats. *Map.* 8° *Berlin,* N.D.
—— Vienne : Guide illustré par le Dr Fr. Förster. 10th edition. *Map and plates.* 12° *Vienna,* 1873

Forster, George. Voyage round the World in H.M. sloop "Resolution," commanded by Capt. Cook, 1772-75. *Map.* 2 vols. 4° 1777

Forster, George. Journey from Bengal to England, through the Northern Part of India, Kashmire, Afghanistan, and Persia, and into Russia, by the Caspian Sea. 2 vols. *Map.* 4° 1798
—— *See* Eyriès, Vol. 13 : Appendix 1.

Forster, J. Reinhold. Observations made during a Voyage round the World, on Physical Geography, Natural History, and Ethic Philosophy, especially on the Earth and its Strata, Water and the Ocean, the Atmosphere, the Changes of the Globe, Organic Bodies, and the Human Species. *Chart and table.* 4° 1778
—— Geschichte der Entdeckungen und Schiff-fahrten im Norden. *Maps.* Small 8° *Frankfurt,· a. d. Oder,* 1784
—— History of the Voyages and Discoveries made in the North. Translated from the German. *Maps.* 4° 1786
—— *See* Bartolomeo ; Granger ; Kalm ; Osbeck ; Riedesel ; Thunberg ; *also* Kerr, Vol. 1 ; Laharpe, Vol. 21 ; Pinkerton, Vol. 9 : Appendix 1.
—— **and George Forster.** Characteres Generum Plantarum, quas in itinere ad Insulas Maris Australis, Collegerunt, Descripserunt, Delinearunt, annis 1772-75. *Plates.* 4° 1776

Forsyth, Joseph. Remarks on Antiquities, Arts, and Letters in Italy. 2 vols. 8° 1824

Forsyth, Capt. J. The Highlands of Central India : Notes on their Forests and Wild Tribes, Natural History, and Sports. *Plates.* 8° 1872

Forsyth, Sir T. D. Memorandum on Routes from the Punjab to Eastern Turkistan. [From the India Records (Punjab), No. 2.] 8° *Lahore,* 1868
—— Trade Routes between Northern India and Central Asia. 8* [*Exeter,* 1869]
—— Report of a Mission to Yarkund in 1873, under Command of Sir T. D. Forsyth, with Historical and Geographical Information regarding the Possessions of the Ameer of Yarkund. *Map in cover, and photographs.* 4° *Calcutta,* 1875
—— Ditto, German translation in Ergänzungsheft, 52—Petermann's Mittheilungen. *Map.* 4° *Gotha,* 1877
—— Autobiography and Reminiscences of Sir Douglas Forsyth. Edited by his Daughter. *Map and portrait.* 8° 1887
—— *See* Prejevalsky.

Forsyth, W. The Rules of Evidence as applicable to the Credibility of History. 8* 1874

Fort, G. Seymour. British New Guinea. Report on British New Guinea, from Data and Notes by the late Sir Peter Scratchley, Her Majesty's Special Commissioner. Folio* *Brisbane,* 1886

Fortescue, G. K. A Subject Index of the Modern Works added to the Library of the British Museum in the years 1880-85. Compiled by G. K. Fortescue. 4° 1886

Fortescue, Hon. John W. The Influence of Climate on Race. (From the *Nineteenth Century*, May 1893.) 8* 1893

Fortescue, W. I. *See* Tudor.

Fortia. *See* Pinkerton, Vol. 6 : Appendix 1.

Fortin, P. The Straits of Belle Isle. 8* *Montreal*, 1877

Fortis, Alberto. Travels into Dalmatia : containing General Observations on the Natural History of that Country and the Neighbouring Islands . . .; to which are added, by the same Author, Observations on the Island of Cherso and Osero. Translated from the Italian, &c. *Maps and plates.* 4° 1778

Fortunat, Dantès. Nouvelle Géographie de l'Ile d'Haïte, contenant des Notions historiques et topographiques sur les autres Antilles. *Map and illustrations.* 12° *Paris*, 1888

Fortune, Robert. Journey to the Tea Countries of China, including Sung-lo and the Bohea Hills ; with a Short Notice of the East India Company's Tea Plantations in the Himalaya Mountains. *Map and plates.* 8° 1852

—— Report upon the Tea Plantations of Deyra, Kumaon, and Gurhwal, N.W. Provinces, 1851. [From the India Records, N.W. Prov., Vol. 1.] *Agra*, 1855

—— Residence among the Chinese, Inland, on the Coast, and at Sea : being a Narrative of Scenes and Adventures during a Third Visit to China, from 1853-56. *Plates.* 8° 1857

—— Yedo and Peking : a Narrative of a Journey to the Capitals of Japan and China, &c. *Map and plates.* 8° 1863

Forwood, W. H. *See* Sheridan.

Foster, Dr C. Le Neve. *See* Lock.

—— **and William Topley.** On the Superficial Deposit of the Valley of the Medway, with Remarks on the Denudation of the Weald. *Plates.* 8* 1865

Foster, Capt. *See* Tiark.

Foster, Major Hubert. Uganda. *See* United Kingdom, G, War Office Publ.: Appendix 2.

Foster, John. Fosteriana : consisting of Thoughts, Reflections, and Criticisms of John Foster, selected from Periodical Papers not hitherto published in a collective form, and edited by Henry G. Bohn. 12° 1858

Foster, J. J. The Jenolan Caves. *Map and plan.* 8° *Sydney*, 1890

Foster, J. W. The Mississippi Valley, its Physical Geography, including Sketches of the Topography, Botany, Climate, &c. *Maps and sections.* 8° 1869

Foster, J. W., and J. D. Whitney. Report on the Geology and Topography of a Portion of the Lake Superior Land District, in the State of Michigan. Part 1, Copper Lands. *Maps and plates.* 8° *Washington*, 1850

—— Report on the Geology of the Lake Superior Land District. Part 2, The Iron Region, together with the General Geology. *Plates.* 8° *Washington*, 1851

Foster, William. *See* Birdwood.

Fossett, F. Colorado, its Gold and Silver Mines, Farms and Stock Ranges, and Health and Pleasure Resorts : Tourist's Guide to the Rocky Mountains. *Maps and plates.* 8° *New York*, 1879

Fotherbye, R. *See* Purchas, Vol. 3, Book 4 : Appendix 1.

Fotheringham, L. M. Adventures in Nyassaland : a Two Years' Struggle with Arab Slave-dealers in Central Africa. *Illustrations.* 8° 1891

Foucauld, Vicomte C. de. Reconnaissance au Maroc, 1883-84. Text and Atlas. 4° *Paris*, 1888

Foulk, George C. *See* Buckingham.

Fouqué, F. Santorin et ses Eruptions. *Maps and plates.* 4° *Paris*, 1879

Fouquet, —. *See* Callander, Vol. 3 : Appendix 1.

Foureau, F. Une Mission au Tademayt (Territoire d'In-Salah) en 1890. *Map and illustrations.* 8° *Paris*, 1890

Fournel, Marc. La Tripolitaine, les Routes du Soudan. 12° *Paris*, 1887

Fournereau, L. Les Ruines Kmers du Cambodge-Siamois. 8* *Paris*, 1889

Fournet, J. J. *See* Chantre, Ernest.

Fournier, C. I. N. Guide de l'Étranger à Lyon. *Map.* 12° *Lyons*, 1826

Fowler, George. Three Years in Persia, with Travelling Adventures in Koordistan. 2 vols. *Plates.* 8° 1841

—— History of the War . . . between Turkey and Russia, and Russia and the Allied Powers of England and France . . . to the end of 1854. *Maps.* 12° 1855

Fowler, H. A Narrative of a Journey across the Unexplored Portion of British Honduras, with a Short Sketch of the History and Resources of the Colony. *Map and photograph.* 8° *Belize*, 1879

—— A Paper on a Living Ancient City said to Exist in Central America at the Present Time, in almost the same state in which the Cities were found in the Country at the time of the Conquest, with an Account of its People. 8* [*Belize*, 1880]

Fox, General C. R. Engravings of Unpublished or Rare Greek Coins, with Descriptions: Part 1, Europe; Part 2, Asia and Africa. 2 Parts. *Plates.* 4* 1862
—— On a Coin of Glauconnesus. 8* 1869

Fox, Edward. Pleasure Paths of Travel. 8° 1857

Fox, Gustavus V. The First Landfall of Columbus : Is there, extant, evidence enough to prove the First Landing-Place of Columbus in the New World? *Maps.* Large 8° *New York*, 1883

Fox, Robert W. Observations on Mineral Veins. *Plates.* 8* *Falmouth*, 1837

Fox, William. Brief History of the Wesleyan Missions on the Western Coast of Africa, including Biographical Sketches ; with some Account of the European Settlements, and of the Slave Trade. *Map and plates.* 8° 1851

Fox, Hon. W. Hot Springs District of the North Island. Folio* *Wellington*, 1874

"Fox," Ship. *See* M'Clintock, Sir F. L.; Malte-Brun.

Foxe, John. *See* Hakluyt, Vol. 2 : Appendix 1.

Foxe, Capt. Luke. North-West Fox ; or, Fox from the North-West Passage, beginning with King Arthvr, Malga, Octhvr, the two gems of Iseland, Estotiland and Dorgia ; following with Briefe Abstracts of the Voyages of Cabot, Frobisher, Davis, Waymouth, Knight, Hudson, Button, Gibbons, Bylot, Baffin, Hankridge ; together with the Courses, Distance, Latitudes, Longitudes, Variations, Depths of Seas, Sets of Tydes, Currents, Races, and Over-falls ; with other Observations, Accidents, and Remarkable Things. . . . Small 8° 1635
—— *See* Hakluyt Soc. Publ., Vol. 5 ; Allgemeine Historie, Vol. 17 : Appendix 1.

Foy, Richard. Renseignements Nautiques sur quelques Ports de l'Océanie, de la Nouvelle Hollande, et de la Mer Rouge. 8° *Paris*, 1866

Fraas, Oscar. Aus dem Orient. Geologische Beobachtungen am Nil, auf der Sinai-Halbinsel und in Syrien. *Plates.* 8° *Stuttgart*, 1867

Fracastoro, Hieronomo. *See* Ramusio, Vol. 1 : Appendix 1.

Fraissinet, É. Le Japon, Histoire et Description ; Mœurs, Coutumes et Religion. . . . Nouvelle édition augmentée . . . par V. A. Malte-Brun. 2 vols. *Map.* 12° *Paris*, 1864

Framji, Dhanjibhai. Grammar of the Huzvarash or proper Pehlvi Language, as read by the Zoroastrians of Iran and India. Royal 8° *Bombay*, 1855
—— On the Origin and Authenticity of the Arian Family of Languages, the Zand Avesta and the Huzvarash. *Inscriptions.* 8° *Bombay*, 1861

Francesetti, L. Lettres sur les Vallées de Lanzo. *Plates.* Small 4° *Turin*, 1823

Franchet, A. *See* France, B, a: Appendix 2.

Francia, Dictator. *See* Robertson, J. P. and W. P.

Francis, Francis, junr. Saddle and Mocassin. 8° 1887

Francisco, Domingo. *See* Purchas, Vol. 1, Book 4 : Appendix 1.

Francklin, William. Observations made on a Tour from Bengal to Persia, in . . . 1786-87 ; together with a Short Account of the Remains of the celebrated Palace of Persepolis, &c. 8° 1790
—— *See* Pinkerton, Vol. 9 : Appendix 1.

Francœur, L B. Géodésie, ou Traité de la Figure de la Terre et ses Parties. . . . Quatrième édition, revue et corrigée sur les manuscrits inédits de M. Francœur, par M. Francœur fils ; augmentée de Notes sur la Mesure des Bases, par M. Hossard. *Plates.* 8° *Paris*, 1865

François, Curt von. Die Erforschung des Tschuapa und Lulongo. Reisen in Centralafrika. *Maps and illustrations.* 8° *Leipzig*, 1888
—— *See* Wissmann.

Francq, F. de. De la Formation et de la Répartition des Reliefs Terrestres. MSS. 4° 1856

Frank, Guiseppe. Viaggio a Parigi e per una gran parte dell' Inghilterra e della Scozia, per quanto concerne Spedali, Carceri, Stabilimenti di Pubblica Beneficenza e d'Instruzione Medica. 2 vols. in 1. *Tables.* 8° *Milan*, 1813

Frankland, George. Report on the Transactions of the Survey Department of Van Diemen's Land, from the foundation of the Colony to the end of Col. Arthur's administration. 8° *Hobart*, 1837

Franklin, James. The Present State of Hayti (St Domingo), with Remarks on its Agriculture, Commerce, Laws, Religion, Finances, and Population, &c. 8° 1828

Franklin, Capt. Sir John. Narrative of a Journey to the Shores of the Polar Sea, in 1819-22 ; with an Appendix on various subjects relating to Science and Natural History. *Maps and plates, some coloured.* 4° 1823
—— Narrative of a Second Expedition to the Shores of the Polar Sea in the years 1825, 1826, and 1827 ; including an Account of the Progress of a Detachment to the eastward, by John Richardson. *Maps and plates.* 4° 1828
—— Report of the Committee appointed by the Lords Commissioners of the Admiralty to Inquire into the Report on the recent Arctic Expeditions in Search of Sir John Franklin ; together with the Minutes of Evidence taken before the Committee, and Papers connected with the subject. *Maps.* [Parly. Rep.] Folio 1852

Franklin, Capt. Sir John. Additional Papers relative to the Arctic Expedition under the Orders of Captain Austin and Mr William Penny. *Maps.* Folio 1852

—— Papers relative to the recent Arctic Expeditions in Search of Sir John Franklin and the Crews of H.M.S. "Erebus" and "Terror." *Maps.* Folio 1854

—— Notice Biographique, par M. de la Roquette. *Portrait, maps, and facsimile.* 4* N.P., N.D.

—— *See* Kane; Kennedy, W.; Markham, A. H.; Oshorn; Petermann; Richardson, Sir John; Seemann; Snow; *also* Eyriès, Vol. 8: Appendix 1.

Franklin, Lady. Letter to the Lords Commissioners of the Admiralty, 12th April 1856. Folio* 1856

—— Letter to Viscount Palmerston. 8* 1857

Franklin, W. *See* Pelham, Vol. 2: Appendix 1.

Franz, J. Fünf Inschriften und fünf Städte in Kleinasien. *Maps.* 4* *Berlin,* 1840

Franzoj, Augusto. Continente Nero. Note di Viaggio. *Map and illustrations.* 8° *Turin,* 1885

Fraser, Alexander. Note by the Secretary to the Chief Commissioner, British Burmah [A. F.], in the Public Works Department, on a Proposal, by Colonel Fraser, the Chief Engineer, to Promote the Construction of a Railway from Rangoon to Prome. Folio* *Rangoon,* 1867

Fraser, Capt. F. G. R., and Capt. Forlong. Proposed New Route to Siam, Saigon, China, and Japan, across the Isthmus of Kraw. MS. Folio* 1862

Fraser, James Baillie. Tour through part of the Snowy Range of the Himālā Mountains, and to the Sources of the Jumna and Ganges. *Map.* 4° 1820

—— Journey into Korasān in 1821-22, including some Account of the Countries to the North-East of Persia. *Map.* 4° 1825

—— Travels and Adventures in Persian Provinces on the Southern Banks of the Caspian Sea, with Notices on the Geology and Commerce of Persia. 4° 1826

—— Historical and Descriptive Account of Persia, from the Earliest Ages to the Present Time; with a Detailed View of its Resources, Government, Population, Natural History, and the Character of its Inhabitants, particularly the Wandering Tribes; including a Description of Afghanistan and Beloochistan. *Map and plates.* 12° *Edinburgh,* 1834

—— Travels in Koordistan, Mesopotamia, &c.; with Sketches of the Character and Manners of the Koordish and Arab Tribes. *Plate.* 8° [1835?]

Fraser, James Baillie. Winter Journey from Constantinople to Tehran, with Travels through various parts of Persia. 2 vols. 8° 1838

—— *See* Eyriès, Vol. 14: Appendix 1.

Fraser, John. *See* Threlkeld.

Fraser, Malcolm A. C. Western Australian Year-book for 1890. *Map.* 8° *Perth, W.A.,* 1891

—— Ditto, for 1892-93. *Map.* 8° *Perth, W.A.,* 1893

Fraser, Robert. General View of the Agriculture and Mineralogy, Present State and Circumstances, of the County of Wicklow, with Observations on the Means of their Improvement. *Map.* 8° *Dublin,* 1801

—— Gleanings in Ireland, particularly respecting its Agriculture, Mines, and Fisheries. 8° 1802

Fraser, T. Notes on Individual Equipment for the East. From Personal Experience. 8* 1878

Fraunhofer, Joseph von. Gesammelte Schriften, im Auftrage der mathematisch-physikalischen Classe der Königlich Bayerischen Akademie der Wissenschaften, herausgegeben von E. Lommel. *Portrait and illustrations.* 4* *Munich,* 1888

—— *See* Bauernfeind.

Frazer, J. G. Totemism. 12° 1887

—— The Golden Bough: a Study in Comparative Religion. 2 vols. *Frontispiece.* 8° 1890

Frazer, W. On Hy Brasil, a Traditional Island off the West Coast of Ireland, plotted in a MS. map written by Sieur Tassin, Geographer Royal to Louis XIII. *Map.* Small 8* 1879

Fream, Prof. W. A Report on Canada and its Agricultural Resources. *Map and illustrations.* 8* *Ottawa,* 1885

—— Across Canada. *Map and illustrations.* 8* *Ottawa,* 1886

—— Agricultural Canada: a Record of Progress. *Map.* 8* 1889

Frederick, or Frederike, or Federici, Cæsar. *See* Gottfried; Hakluyt, Vol. 2; Kerr, Vol. 7; Purchas, Vol. 2, Book 10; Ramusio, Vol. 3: Appendix 1.

Frederick VII., King of Denmark. Vestiges d'Asserbo et de Söborg, découverts par S. M. Frédéric VII., Roi de Danemark. *Plates.* 8° *Copenhagen,* 1855

—— Sur la Construction des Salles dites des Géants. *Woodcuts.* 8* *Copenhagen,* 1857

—— Om Bygningsmaaden af Oldtidens Jættestuer. *Woodcuts.* Royal 8* *Copenhagen,* 1862

—— Ueber den Bau der Riesenbetten der Vorzeit. Royal 8* *Copenhagen,* 1863

Frederickson, A. D. Ad Orientem. *Maps and illustrations.* 8° 1890

Fredholm, K. A. *See* Sweden, A, Geologiska Undersökning (C, 83): Appendix 2.

Freeden, W. von. Mittheilungen aus der Norddeutschen Seewarte. III. Ueber die Dampferwege zwischen dem Kanal und New York, nach den Journal-Auszügen der Dampfer des Norddeutschen Lloyd, 1860-67, nebst Wind und Wetter in derselben Zeit. *Maps.* 4° *Hamburg,* 1870

—— Mittheilungen aus der Norddeutschen Seewarte. IV. Die Normalwege der Hamburger Dampfer zwischen dem Kanal und New York, nach den Journal-Auszügen derselben in den Jahren 1860, 1869, 1872. *Plates.* 4° *Hamburg,* 1872

—— Jahres-Bericht der Norddeutschen Seewarte für das Jahr 1870. Large 8° *Hamburg,* N.D.

——Siebenter Jahres-Bericht der Deutschen Seewarte für das Jahr 1874. Square 8° *Hamburg,* N.D.

—— *See* Arctic, H : Appendix 2.

Freeman, Prof. Edward A. The Historical Geography of Europe. 2 vols. *Text and maps.* 8° 1881

—— Sicily : Phœnician, Greek, and Roman. ("The Story of the Nations" Series.) *Map and illustrations.* 8° 1892

—— The History of Sicily from the Earliest Times. 4 vols. *Maps.* 8° *Oxford,* 1891-94

[Vol. 4. Edited from Posthumous MSS., with Supplements and Notes by Arthur J. Evans.]

—— *See* White, A. S.

Freeman, H. Stanhope. Grammatical Sketch of the Temahuq or Towarek Language. 8° 1862

Freeman, J. J. The Kaffir War : a Letter to Earl Grey, containing Remarks on the Causes of the present War, &c. 8° 1851

—— Tour in South Africa ; with Notices of Natal, Mauritius, Madagascar, Ceylon, Egypt, and Palestine. *Map.* 12° 1851

Freeman, R. Austin. A Journey to Bontúku, in the Interior of West Africa. *Map.* Roy. Geo. Soc. Suppl. Papers, Vol. 3. Large 8° 1892

Freeman, Thomas B. Extracts from the Journal of, on a Visit from Cape Coast to Ashantee, in the Interior of Western Africa. [Wesleyan Methodist Missionary Report, 1840.] 8° 1840

Freese, A. G. F. Reise-Handbuch durch Schweden und Norwegen. *Map.* 12° *Berlin,* 1844

Freminville, —. *See* Phillips [3], Vol. 2 : Appendix 1.

Fremont, Lieut. J. C. *See* United States, E, *a* (No. 88) : Appendix 2.

Fremont, Col. John Charles. Report of the Exploring Expedition to the Rocky Mountains in 1842, and to Oregon and North California in 1843-44. *Maps and plates.* 8° *Washington,* 1854

—— Geographical Memoir upon Upper California, in illustration of his Map of Oregon and California. 8* *Washington,* 1848

—— Life of, and his Narrative of Explorations and Adventures in Kansas, Nebraska, Oregon, and California. Memoir by S. M. Smucker. *Portrait and plates.* 12° *New York,* 1856

French, S. G. *See* United States, K (Texas) : Appendix 2.

Frenzel, Carl. Deutschlands Kolonien, Kurze Beschreibung von Land und Leuten unserer aussereuropäischen Besitzungen, Nach den neuesten Quellen bearbeitet von Carl Frenzel. Zweite, vermehrte Auflage, mit einer Beschreibung der Samoa Inseln, herausgegeben von G. Wende. *Maps and illustrations.* 8° *Hanover,* 1889

Frere, A. M. [Mrs Godfrey Clerk]. The Antipodes and Round the World ; or, Travels in Australia, New Zealand, Ceylon, China, Japan, and California. *Plates.* 8° 1870

Frere, Sir H. Bartle E. Extracts from Rough Notes, containing information with reference to the relative sizes of the three Zillas into which the British Districts in Sind are divided, as compared with the older Zillas of the Bombay Presidency. [From the India Records, No. 17.] 8° *Bombay,* 1855

—— Narrative of the Early History, &c., of the Bhonslays of Satara. [From the India Records, No. 41.] *Bombay,* 1857

—— Speech of His Excellency the Right Hon. Sir Bartle Frere, Bart., and others, delivered on the occasion of the Banquet given to His Excellency upon his return to Cape Town, 11th June 1879. 8* 1879

—— Obituary Notice. By his daughter Mary E. J. Frere. 8* [1885]

—— *See* India, C (Geological Papers) ; British Africa, Zanzibar : Appendix 2.

Freshfield, Douglas W. Travels in the Central Caucasus and Bashan, including Visits to Ararat and Tabreez, and Ascents of Kazbek and Elbruz. *Maps and plates.* 8° 1869

—— Italian Alps : Sketches in the Mountains of Ticino, Lombardy, the Trentino, and Venetia. *Map and plates.* Small 8° 1875

—— Climbs in the Caucasus. 8* [1888]

—— Ostern in Afrika. 1. Die Hügelregion der Küste Kabyliens. 2. Der Jebel Jurjura. *Map and plate.* Large 8* [*Vienna*] 1888

Freshfield, Douglas W. Search and Travel in the Caucasus. (From "Proceedings" R.G.S.) *Map and plates.* 8* 1890
—— The Forests of Abkhasia. 8* 1890
—— *See* Dent.
—— **and Adm. W. J. L. Wharton.** Hints to Travellers. 7th edition. *See* United Kingdom, Transactions R.G.S. : Appendix 2.

Fresnel. *See* Jomard.

Fresnoy, Abbé Lenglet du. Geographia Antiqua et Nova, or a System of Antient and Modern Geography. 4° 1742
—— Méthode pour étudier la Géographie; avec un Discours préliminaire sur l'Étude de cette Science, et un Catalogue des Cartes, Relations, Voyages, et Descriptions nécessaries pour la Géographie. Vol. 1. 12° *Paris,* 1768

Freston, William. Report of the Conference presided over by the Duke of Manchester, on the Question whether Colonisation and Emigration may be made Self-supporting or even Profitable to those investing Capital therein ; with Appendix. 8* 1869

Frewer, Ellen E. *See* Holub, Dr E. ; Schweinfurth.

Frey, Col. H. Campagne dans le Haut Sénégal et dans le Haut Niger [1885-86]. *Maps.* 8° *Paris,* 1888
—— Côte Occidentale d'Afrique ; Vues, Scènes, Croquis. *Maps and illustrations.* 4° *Paris,* 1890

Freycinet, Louis de. Voyage autour du Monde, entrepris par Ordre du Roi . . . exécuté sur les corvettes de S.M. "L'Uranie" et "La Physicienne," pendant les années 1817, 1818, 1819, et 1820, &c. 9 vols. 4°, and 4 folio *Paris,* 1826-44

CONTENTS.

Historique. 2 vols. in 3, 4°, 1827-39 ; and Atlas, folio, 1825.
Zoologie (by J. R. C. Quoy and P. Gaimard). 4°; and Atlas, folio 1824
Botanique (by C. Gaudichaud). 4°; and Atlas, folio 1826
Observations du Pendule. 4° 1826
Magnétisme terrestre. 4° 1842
Météorologie. 4° 1844
Navigation et Hydrographie. 4°; and Atlas, folio 1826
—— *See* Péron.

Freygan, M. and Mme. Letters from the Caucasus and Georgia, with an Account of a Journey into Persia in 1812, and an Abridged History of Persia since the Time of Nadir Shah. Translated from the French. *Map and plates.* 8° 1823

Frezier, —. Relation du Voyage de la Mer du Sud aux Côtes du Chily et du Perou, fait pendant les années 1712, 1713, and 1714. Par M. Frezier. *Maps and plates.* 4° *Paris,* 1716

Frezier, —. The same. Vol. 2. *Plates and maps.* 12° *Amsterdam,* 1717
—— A Voyage to the South Sea and along the Coasts of Chili and Peru, in the years 1712, 1713, and 1714 . . . ; with a Postscript by Dr Edmund Halley, and an Account of the Settlement, Commerce, and Riches of the Jesuites in Paraguay. *Maps and plates.* Small 4° 1717
—— Relation du Voyage de la Mer du Sud aux Côtes du Chily et du Perou, 1712-14 ; avec une Réponse à la Preface Critique du livre intitulé "Journal des Observations Physiques, Mathematiques, et Botaniques du R. P. Feuillée," &c. *Maps and plates.* 4° *Paris,* 1732
—— *See* Burney, Vol. 4 ; Callander, Vol. 3 ; Allgemeine Historie, Vols. 12, 15 : Appendix 1.

Fricker. Dr Karl. Die Entstehung und Verbreitung des Antarktischen Treibeises. Ein Beitrag zur Geographie der Südpolargebiete. *Map.* 8° *Leipzig,* 1893

Frickmann, A. Instructions pour la Navigation de la Côte Ouest d'Écosse. Traduites et mises en ordre par M. Frickmann. 1re Partie. Hébrides ou Iles de l'Ouest. 8° *Paris,* 1869
—— *See* France, B, *b* (No. 501, &c.) : Appendix 2.

Friedenfels, Eduard Edler von. *See* Dorn, A.

Friederich, A. C. A. Historisch-geographische Darstellung Alt- und Neu-Polens. *Maps.* 8° *Berlin,* 1839

Friederichsen, L. Zur Kartographie der Republik Costa-Rica, in Central Amerika. 8* *Hamburg,* 1877
—— Die Deutschen Seehäfen. Ein praktisches Handbuch für Schiffskapitäne, Rheder, Assekuradeure, Schiffsmakler, Behörden, &c. Erster Theil ; Die Häfen, Lösch- und Ladeplätze an der Deutschen Ostseeküste. *Plans.* 4° *Hamburg,* 1889
—— The same. Zweiter Theil ; Die Häfen, Lösch- und Ladeplätze an der Deutschen Nordseeküste. *Maps and plans.* 4° *Hamburg,* 1891
—— *See* Sievers.

Friederici, Charles. Bibliotheca Orientalis, or a complete List of Books, Papers, Serials, and Essays published in 1881 in England and the Colonies, Germany and France, on the History, Languages, Religions, Antiquities, and Literature of the East. Compiled by Charles Friederici. 8° [1882]
—— The same. Published in 1883 in England, &c., compiled by Charles Friederici. [8th year.] 8° 1883

Friedländer, Herman. *See* Phillips [3], Vol. 5, New Voyages and Travels : Appendix 1.

Friedmann, S. Ueber die Ursache der nichtperiodischen Vorgänge in der Atmosphäre. 8* *Vienna,* 1866

Friele, Herman. See Norway, A (North Atlantic Expedition) : Appendix 2.

Friend, C. Notes of an Excursion from the Banks of the Atrato to the Bay of Cupica, on the Coast of the Pacific, in the year 1827. 8* [1853]

Fries, J. O. See Sweden, A (Geologiska Undersökning) : Appendix 2.

Frilley, G., and J. Wlahovitj. Le Monténégro Contemporain. *Map and plates.* 12° *Paris*, 1876

Frisby, Professor Edgar. See United States, D, Naval Observatory : Appendix 2.

Fritsch, Gustav. Drei Jahre in Süd-Afrika. Reiseskizzen nach Notizen des Tagebuchs zusammengestellt. *Coloured plates.* 8° *Breslau*, 1868

—— Die Eingeborenen Süd - Afrika's, ethnographisch und anatomisch beschrieben. *Map and plates.* Large 8°, and Atlas 4° *Breslau*, 1872

Fritsch, Dr K. von. Reisebilder von den Canarischen Inseln. (Ergänzungsheft, 22 — Petermann's Geographischen Mittheilungen.) *Maps.* 4° *Gotha*, 1867

—— **and others.** Tenerife geologisch topographisch dargestellt. Ein Beitrag zur Kenntniss vulkanischer Gebirge von K. v. Fritsch, G. Hartung, und W. Reiss. Eine Karte und sechs Tafeln mit Durchschnitten und Skizzen nebst erläuterndem Text. Folio *Winterthur*, 1867

—— **and W. Reiss.** Geologische Beschreibung der Insel Tenerife. Ein Beitrag zur Kenntniss vulkanischer Gebirge. 8* *Winterthur*, 1868

—— **W. Reiss, and A. Stübel,** Santorin, The Kaimeni Islands. *Maps and photographs.* 4* 1867

Fritsche, H. Geographische, magnetische und hypsometrische Bestimmungen an zwei und zwanzig in der Mongolei und dem nördlichen China gelegenen Orten, ausgeführt in den Jahren 1868 und 1869. 4* 1870

—— Geographische, magnetische, und hypsometrische Bestimmungen an 27 im nordöstlichen China gelegenen Orten . . . 1871. (From *Repert. Meteorol. St Petersburg*, Vol. 3.) 4* *St Petersburg*, 1873

—— Ein Beitrag zur Geographie und Lehre vom Erdmagnetismus Asiens und Europas. (Ergänzungsheft, 78—Petermann's Mittheilungen.) 5 *maps*. 4° *Gotha*, 1885

—— On Chronology and the Construction of the Calendar, with special regard to the Chinese Computation of Time compared with the European. 8* *St Petersburg*, 1886

—— Ueber die Bestimmung der Geographischen Länge und Breite und der

Fritsche, H.—*continued.*
drei Elemente des Erdmagnetismus durch Beobachtung zu Lande sowie erdmagnetische und geographische Messungen an mehr als tausend verschiedenen Orten in Asien und Europa ; ausgeführt in den Jahren 1867-91. *Maps.* 8° *St Petersburg*, 1893

—— Die magnetischen Localabweichungen bei Moskau und ihre Beziehungen zur dortigen Local-attraction. [Extract from B.S. imp. Naturalistes de Moscow, No. 4.] *Maps.* 8* 1893

—— See Schrenck.

Fröbel, Julius. Seven Years' Travel in Central America, Northern Mexico, and the Far West of the United States. *Plates.* 8° 1859

—— **and Oswald Heer.** Mittheilungen aus dem Gebiete der theoretischen Erdkunde. 8° *Zürich*, 1834

Frobenius, Herman. Die Heiden-Neger des Aegyptischen Sudan. *Map.* 8° *Berlin*, 1893

Froberville, M. de. Rapport sur les Races Nègres de l'Afrique Orientale au Sud de l'Équateur. 4* *Paris*, 1850

Frobin, Count de. See Forbin.

Frobisher, Sir Martin. Instructions when going on a Voyage to the North-West Parts and Cathay, in the Time of Queen Elizabeth : a Letter from Sir Henry Ellis to S. Lyons. 4* 1816

—— See Gottfried ; Hakluyt, Vol. 3 ; Hakluyt Soc. Publ., Vols. 5, 28 ; Pinkerton, Vol. 12 ; Allgemeine Historie, Vol. 17 : Appendix 1.

Frodsham, Thomas, junior. Track to Macquarie Harbour, Tasmania. Folio* *Hobart*, 1878

Froger, Sieur. See Churchill, Vol. 8 : Appendix 1.

Frölich, Erasmus. Notitia Elementaris Numismatum Antiquorum illorum, quæ Urbium liberarum, Regum et Principum, ac Personarum illustritem appellantur. *Plates.* 4° *Vienna*, 1758

Frome, Colonel. Outline of the Method of Conducting a Trigonometrical Survey, for the Formation of Geographical and Topographical Maps and Plans, Military Reconnaissance, Levelling, &c., with the most useful Problems in Geodesy and Practical Astronomy. *Plates.* 8° 1862

Fromentin, Eugène. Sahara et Sahel. I. Un été dans le Sahara ; II. Une année dans le Sahel. *Illustrations.* Imp. 8° *Paris*, 1887

Fromm, Dr E. See Weigel.

Froude, James Anthony. Oceana, or England and her Colonies. *Illustrations.* 8° 1886

—— The English in the West Indies, or the Bow of Ulysses. *Illustrations.* 8° 1888

Fry, Herbert. London in 1881. Illustrated with Bird's-eye Views of the principal Streets. *Illustrations.* 8°
1881

—— London Illustrated by Twenty Bird's-eye Views of the Principal Streets, also by a Map showing its Chief Suburbs and Environs, and by a Street-Map of Central London originally compiled by the late Herbert Fry. Crown 8°   1890

Fuchs, Edmund, and E. Saladin. The Coal and Mineral Deposits of Indo-China. Translated and abstracted by Charles Smith. 8*   1883

Fuentes, Manuel A. Biblioteca Peruana, de Historia, Ciencias, y Litteratura. Colleccion de Escritos del anterior y presente siglo de los mas acreditados autores peruanos. i. (Antiguo Mercurio Peruano, 1); ii. (do., 2); iii. (do., 3). 12°   *Lima,* 1861

—— Lima, or Sketches of the Capital of Peru, Historical, Statistical, Administrative, Commercial, and Moral. *Plates and portraits.* 8°   *Paris,* 1866

Fulcherius Carnotensis. *See* Purchas, Vol. 2, Book 8: Appendix 1.

Fulford, H. E. Report of a Journey in Manchuria. Folio*   1887

Fulljames, Major G. Geological and Statistical Notes on portions of the Rewa Kanta Districts, from the Camp of Baroda to Chota Oodepoor, East; to Nandod and Laureea Bhurr, on the Nerbudda River, South-west; and a Description of the Iron Ores of these districts. [From the India Records, No. 23.]
Bombay, 1856

—— *See* India, C (Geological Papers): Appendix 2.

Fulton, Major R. Report and Notes on the Country traversed by the Kyaing-ton-Chiengmai Mission in 1890-91. *Maps and plans.* 8°   *Simla,* 1893

Fumagalli, Giuseppe. Bibliografia Etiopica. Catalogo descrittivo e ragionato degli scritti pubblicati dalla invenzione della stampa fino a tutto il 1891 intorno alla Etiopia e regione limitrofe. 8°
Milan, 1893

Funck. *See* Illens d' and Funck.

Funnel, William. Voyage round the World, containing an Account of Capt. Dampier's Expedition into the South Seas in 1703-4, with his various Adventures, Engagements, &c. *Maps and plates.* 8°   1707

—— *See* Callander, Vol. 3; Harris, Vol. 1; Kerr, Vol. 10: Appendix 1.

Fürer, C. Christophori Füreri ab Haimendorf, . . . Itinerarium Ægypti, Arabiæ, Palæstinæ, Syriæ, aliarumque Regionum Orientalium, &c. *Portrait and plates.* Small 8° *Nuremberg,* 1621

Furneaux, Captain. *See* Cook.

Fuss, G., A. Sawitsch, and G. Sabler. Beschreibung der zur Ermittelung des Höhenunterschiedes zwischen dem Schwarzen und dem Caspischen Meere. Herausgegeben von W. Struve. *Map.* 4°   *St Petersburg,* 1849

Fyers, Col. A. B. Itinerary of Principal and Minor Roads in the Island of Ceylon. 2nd edition. Part 1, Principal Roads. Large 8*   [*Colombo,* 1881]

Fytche, Colonel Albert. Papers regarding the Coal Mines at Thatay Khyoung. [From the India Records, No. 39.] 8°
Calcutta, 1863

—— Supplement to the British Burma Gazette, 21st December 1867: Letter on the Operation of the License Tax in British Burma, from Colonel A. Fytche to E. H. Lushington. 4* *Rangoon,* 1867

—— Narrative of the Mission to Mandalay in 1867. [India Office Rep.] Folio*
Rangoon, 1867

—— Burma Past and Present, with Personal Reminiscences of the Country. 2 vols. *Map and plates.* 8°   1878

G.

G——, R. Overland Communication with Western China. By R. G. *Map.* 8*   *Liverpool,* 1872

Gabb, W. M. On the Indian Tribes and Languages of Costa Rica. 8*
Philadelphia, 1875

—— *See* United States, K (California): Appendix 2.

Gachet, N. *See* Covino.

Gadsby, John. My Wanderings: being Travels in the East in 1846-47, 1850-51, 1852-53. 2 vols. *Map.* Small 8°
1864-65

Gaetan, Juan. *See* Callander, Vol. 1; Ramusio, Vol. 1; Allgemeine Historie, Vol. 18: Appendix 1.

Gaffarel, P. Les Colonies Françaises. 8°
Paris, 1880

—— Ditto. 4th edition. 8° *Paris,* 1888

—— Les Explorations Françaises depuis 1870. *Maps and illustrations.* 12°
Paris, 1882

—— L'Algérie. Histoire, Conquête, et Colonisation. *Maps, coloured plates, and illustrations.* 4°   *Paris,* 1883

Gage, Thomas. Nouvelle Relation des Voyages dans la Nouvelle Espagne, ses Diverses Aventures, et son retour par la Province de Nicaragua, jusques à la Havane; avec la Description de la Ville de Mexique telle qu'elle estoit autrefois, et comme elle est à present. 2 vols. *Maps and plates.* 12° *Amsterdam,* 1695

Gage, Thomas. Survey of the Spanish West Indies : being a Journal of 3,300 miles on the Continent of America, giving an Account of the Spanish Navigation thither, their Government, Castles, Ports, Negros, Mulattos, Indians, &c., . . . with a Grammar of the Indian Tongue called Poconchi or Pocoman. *Map.* Small 8° 1702

—— *See* Thevenot, Vol. 4 : Appendix 1.

Gaimard, Paul. Voyage en Islande et au Groënland, exécuté pendant les années 1835 et 1836 sur la corvette "La Recherche," commandée par M. Tréhouart, dans le but de découvrir les traces de "La Lilloise"; publié sous la direction de M. Paul Gaimard. . . . 8 vols. 8°, 1 small 4°, 2 imperial folio

Paris, 1838-52

CONTENTS.

Gaimard, Paul. Histoire du Voyage. Vol. 1. 8° 1838
Robert, Eugène. The same. Vol. 2. 8° 1850
Mequet, Eugène. Journal du Voyage. 8° 1852
Marmier, Xavier. Histoire de l'Islande. 8° 1840
—— Littérature Islandaise. 8° 1843
Lottin, Victor. Physique. 8° 1838
Robert, E. Minéralogie et Géologie. 8° 1840
—— The same. Atlas. Small 4° 1838
—— Zoologie et Médicine. 8° 1851
Atlas Historique [1 and 2 in one]. Imperial folio.
Atlas Zoologique, Médical, et Géographique. Imperial folio.

—— Voyages de la Commission Scientifique du Nord en Scandinavie, en Laponie, au Spitzberg, et aux Feröe, pendant les années 1838, 1839, et 1840, sur la corvette "La Recherche," commandée par M. Fabvre; publiés sous la direction de M. Paul Gaimard. 16 vols. 8°, 3 folio *Paris*, N.D.

CONTENTS.

Marmier, Xavier. Relation du Voyage. 2 vols. *Frontispiece.* 8°
—— Histoire de la Scandinavie. 8°
—— Littérature Scandinavie. 8°
Martins, C.; Vahl, H.; Læstadius, L. L.; Bravais, A.; Durocher, J.; Siljeström, P. A.; Boeck, C.; and Robert, E. Géographie Physique, Géographie Botanique, Botanique, et Physiologie. 2 vols. 8°
Robert, E. Géologie, Minéralogie, et Métallurgie. 8°
Durocher, J. Géologie, Minéralogie, Métallurgie, et Chimie. 8°
Lottin, V.; Bravais, A.; Lilliehöök, C. B.; Siljeström, P. A.; Meyer, E. G.; Laroche - Poncié, J. De; Fabvre, Le Capitaine, et les Officers de la corvette "La Recherche." Magnétisme Terrestre. 3 vols. 8°

Gaimard, Paul—*continued.*
Lottin, V. ; Bravais, A. ; Lilliehöök, C. B. ; Siljeström, P. A. ; Martins, C. ; Laroche-Poncié, J. De ; Læstadius, L. L. ; and Pottier, E. Météorologie. 3 vols. 8°
Lottin, V.; Bravais, A.; Lilliehöök, C. B.; and Siljeström, P. A. Aurores Boréales. 8°
Lottin, V.; Bravais, A.; Lilliehöök, C. B.; Laroche-Poncié, J. De; et les Officers de la corvette "La Recherche." Astronomie et Hydrographie. 8°
Atlas Historique et Pittoresque. 2 vols. Imperial folio.
Atlas de Physique, de Géologie, et de Zoologie. Imperial folio.

—— *See* Freycinet.

Galanti, Giuseppe M. Napoli e Contorni, nuova editione, intieramente riformata dall' editore Galanti. *Maps and plates.* 8° *Naples*, 1829

Galbraith, Joseph A., and Samuel Haughton. Manual of Mathematical Tables. 12° 1860

Galbraith, William. Barometric Tables, by which the Heights of Mountains, the Difference of Levels, &c., may be Computed. 8° *Edinburgh*, 1833
—— Mathematical and Astronomical Tables, preceded by an Introduction containing the Construction of Logarithmic and Trigonometrical Tables, Plane and Spherical Trigonometry, their Application to Navigation, Astronomy, Surveying, and Geodetical Operations. 8° *Edinburgh*, 1834
—— Trigonometrical Surveying, Levelling, and Railway Engineering. 8° 1842
—— On Trigonometrical Surveying, and its Application to Correct the Maps and Charts of the Hebrides. *Map.* 8* 1844

Galiano, Pelayo Alcalá. Memoria sobre la Situacion de Santa Cruz de Mar Pequeña en la Costa Noroeste de Africa. 8* *Madrid*, 1878
—— Memoria sobre Santa Cruz de Mar Pequeña y las Pesquerías en la Costa Noroeste de Africa. *Maps.* 8* *Madrid*, 1879
—— Mas Consideraciones sobre Santa Cruz de Mar Pequeña. *Map.* 8* *Madrid*, 1879

Galiffe, J. A. Italy and its Inhabitants, an Account of a Tour in that Country in 1816-17. 2 vols. 8° 1820

Galignani's Guide through Holland and Belgium. 18° *Paris*, 1824
—— Traveller's Guide through France. 8th edition. 16° *Paris*, 1827

Galindo, Colonel Don Juan. On Central America. 8* 1836

Galinier. *See* Ferret, A., and Galinier.

Galitzin, Prince Emmanuel. La Finlande: Notes Recueillies en 1848 pendant une Excursion de St Pétersbourg à Torneo. 2 vols. in 1. *Maps and plates.* 8° *Paris*, 1852

Galland, M. Recueil des Rits et Cérémonies du Pélerinage de la Mecque, auquel on a joint divers Écrits relatifs à la Religion, Sciences, et aux Mœurs des Turcs. 8° *Amsterdam*, 1764

Gallatin, Albert. The Right of the United States of America to the North-Eastern Boundary claimed by them. *Maps.* 8° *New York*, 1840

—— Memoir on the North-Eastern Boundary, in connection with Mr Jay's Map; with a Speech on the same subject by the Hon. Daniel Webster. *Map.* 8* *New York*, 1843

Galle, Dr Andreas. Dr A. Philippson's barometrische Höhenmessungen im Peloponnes. 8* *Berlin*, 1889

Gallée, Prof. J. H. *See* Holland: Appendix 2.

Gallenga, A. Country Life in Piedmont. 8° 1858

—— The Pearl of the Antilles. 12° 1873

Gallieni, Commander. Mission d'Exploration du Haut-Niger. Voyage au Soudan Français (Haut-Niger et Pays de Ségou), 1879-81. *Maps and illustrations.* Small folio *Paris*, 1885

Gallo, L. Storia del Cristianesimo nell' Impero Barmano, preceduta dalle Notizie del Paese. 3 vols. (forming Vols. 18, 19, and 20 of the "Collezione di Vite dei più distinti Religiosi della Congregazione dei chierici RR. di S. Paoli detti Barnabiti"). 12° *Milan*, 1862

Gallo, V. Trattato di Navigazione. 2 vols. 8° *Trieste*, 1851

Gallois, L. Les Géographes Allemands de la Renaissance. *Plates.* 8° *Paris*, 1890

—— De Orontio Finneo, Gallico Geographo. *Plates.* 8° *Paris*, 1890

Galloway, John Alex. Communication with India, China, &c. Observations on the Proposed Improvements in the Overland Route *viâ* Egypt, with Remarks on the Ship Canal, the Boulac Canal, and the Suez Railroad. *Map.* 8° 1844

Galt, John. Letters from the Levant. *Map.* 8° 1813

Galton, Francis. Narrative of an Explorer in Tropical South Africa. *Maps and plates.* 8° 1853

—— The same, being an Account of a Visit to Damaraland in 1851, with a New Map, and an Appendix bringing up the History of Damaraland to a recent date, together with a Biographical Introduction by the Editor; also Vacation Tours in 1860 and 1861, by George Grove, Francis Galton, and W. C. Clark. [Minerva Library Series.] *Portrait and illustrations.* 8° 1889

Galton, Francis. Catalogue of Models and Specimens illustrative of the Art of Travel. 8* 1858

—— Art of Travel; or, Shifts and Contrivances Available in Wild Countries. *Woodcuts.* 12° 1860

—— The same. 6th edition. *Illustrations.* 12° 1876

—— Meteorographica, or Methods of Mapping the Weather. 600 *illustrations.* Oblong 4* 1863

—— On Stereoscopic Maps taken from Models of Mountainous Countries. *Photograph.* 8* 1865

—— Vacation Tours and Notes of Travel in 1860. *Maps.* 8° 1861

CONTENTS.

—— Vacation Tours in 1861. *Maps.* 8° 1862

CONTENTS.

Galton, Francis. Vacation Tours in 1862-63. 8° 1864

CONTENTS.

Tristram, Rev. H. B. Winter Ride in Palestine.
Bertram, J. G. Fish - Culture in France.
Kennedy, C. Malcolm. The Turks of Constantinople.
Gordon, Lady Duff. Letters from the Cape.
Clark, W. G. Poland.
Powell, David. The Republic of Paraguay.
Tyrwhitt, Rev. R. St John. Sinai.
Lubbock, Mrs. The Ancient Shell-Mounds of Denmark.
Mayo, Charles. The Medical Service of the Federal Army.
Greive, Rev. W. T. The Church and People of Servia.
Gordon, Hon. Arthur. Wilderness Journeys in New Brunswick.

—— On the Employment of Meteorological Statistics in determining the best course for a ship. 8* 1873

Galvano (or Galvam), Antonio. *See* Astley, Vol. 1; Churchill, Vol. 8; Hakluyt, Vol. 4; Hakluyt Soc. Publ., Vol. 30; Kerr, Vol. 2; Purchas, Vol. 2, Book 10; Allgemeine Historie, Vol. 1: Appendix 1.

Gama, Antonio de S. da. Memoria sobre as Colonias de Portugal, situadas na Costa Occidental d'Africa, em 1814, precedida de um Discurso Preliminar, augmentada de alguns additamentos e notas. 8° *Paris*, 1839

Gama e Siva, L. da. Do Amazonas ao Oyapock. Relatorio da Commissão ao norte da Costa da Provincia do Pará. 8* *Pará*, 1877

Gama, Stefano de. *See* Astley, Vol. 1; Kerr, Vol. 6; Allgemeine Historie, Vol. 1: Appendix 1.

Gama, Vasco da. Roteiro da Viagem que em Descobrimento da India, pelo Cabo da Boa Esperança, em 1497. Publicado por Diogo Köpke, e o A. da Costa Riva. *Map and portrait.* 8° *Oporto*, 1838
—— Roteiro da Viagem em 1497. Correcta e Augmentada de algumas Observações principalmente Philologicas, por A. Herculano e o Barão do Castello de Paiva. *Map, portraits, and facsimile.* 8° *Lisbon*, 1861
—— Vlämisches Tagebuch über Vasco da Gama's zweite Reise 1502-1503. Herausgegeben von. H. C. G. Stier. 12* *Brunswick*, 1890
—— Reproduction in photo-lithography of a Letter in Portuguese from Godinho de Eredia, referring to the death of Vasco da Gama. Folio * [*Lisbon*, N.D.]
M

Gama, Vasco da. *See* Berjeau; *also* Astley, Vol. 1; Gottfried; Hakluyt Soc. Publ., 42; Laharpe, Vol. 1; Purchas, Vol. 1, Book 2; Ramusio, Vol. 1; "A General Collection of Voyages," &c.; Allgemeine Historie, Vol. 1; New Collection, Vol. 2, p. 608; "The World Displayed," Vol. 8, p. 609: Appendix 1.

Gamazoff, M. Notes of a Voyage in Turkey and Persia (1848-52), by the late General Chirikoff, Russian Commissioner for defining the Turco-Persian Boundary. [In Russian.] *Map.* 8° *St Petersburg*, 1875

Gamba, Chev. Voyage dans la Russie Méridionale, et particulièrement dans les Provinces situées au delà du Caucase, fait depuis 1820 jusqu'en 1824. 2 vols. *Maps.* 8° *Paris*, 1826

Gambini, Raffaele. Dissertazioni intorno la Storia e la Fisica del Lago Trasimeno. 8° *Perugia*, 1826

Gambino, Giuseppe. Della Popolarità e Diffusione degli studi Geografici: Pensieri e Suggerimenti ad uso di chi Insegna e di chi impara Geografia. 12° *Palermo*, 1886

Gamble, J. Essay on the Different Modes of Communication by Signals, containing a History of the Progressive Improvements in this Art, from the First Accounts of Beacons to the most Approved Methods of Telegraphic Correspondence. *Plates.* 4° 1797

Gamble, John G. Catalogue of Printed Books and Papers relating to South Africa. Part 2, Climate and Meteorology. 8* *Cape Town*, 1885
—— Cape of Good Hope. Altitudes above Sea-level of Places in South Africa south of 20° S. Latitude. 8* *Cape Town*, 1886
—— *See* Cape Colony, C: Appendix 2.

Gambóa, Pedro Sarmiento de. Viage al Estrecho de Magallanes en los años de 1579 y 1580. *Plates.* 8° *Madrid*, 1768
—— *See* Burney, Vol. 2: Appendix 1.

Games, Gutierre Diez de. *See* Diez.

Gamitto, Major A. C. P. O Muata Cazembe e os povos Maraves, Chévas, Muizas, Muembas, Lundas e outros da Africa Austral. Diario da Expedição Portugueza commandada pelo Major Monteiro, 1831-32. *Map and plates.* 8° *Lisbon*, 1854
—— *See* Lacerda, F. J. M. de; Monteiro.

Gamond, Thomé de. Carte d' Etude du Canal de Nicaragua. Avec documents par Félix Belly. 4° *Paris*, 1858

Gamwell, S. C. The Official Guide and Handbook to Swansea and its District. *Map.* 12° *Swansea*, 1880

Gan, K. Notices of Ancient Greek and Roman Authors on the Caucasus. Part 1. From Homer to the 6th Century A.D. [In Russian.] 8° *Tiflis*, 1884

Gan, K. The same. Part 2. Byzantine Writers. [In Russian.] 8° *Tiflis*, 1890

Gana, Henry Sewell. British Capital and Chilian Industry : Nitrates, Gold Mines, and Coal Mines ; with a Map of the Nitrate Fields, Gold and Coal Mines. 4* 1889

Gancedo, Alejandro. Memoria Descriptiva de la Provincia de Santiago del Estero. *Map, plans, and plates.* 8° *Buenos Ayres*, 1885

Gandini, F. Itinéraire Postale et de Commerce de l'Europe. 12° *Milan*, 1828

Ganeval, A. La France dans l'Europe, Commerciale et Industrielle. 12* *Lyons*, 1875

Ganglbauer, L. *See* Paulitschke.

Gannet, Henry. On the Arable and Pasture Lands of Colorado. 8* *Washington*, 1878

—— A Dictionary of Altitudes in the United States. [U. S. Geol. Survey, Bulletin No. 5.] 8° *Washington*, 1884

—— *See* Porter ; *also* United States, G, *b*, *c* : Appendix 2.

Ganot, —. Elementary Treatise on Physics, Experimental and Applied. Translated by E. Atkinson. 7th edition. *Plates.* 8° 1875

—— Projet d'Exploration au Pole Nord. *Plate.* 8* N.P., N.D.

Ganzenmüller, Dr Konrad. Tibet, nach den resultaten geographischer Forschungen früherer und neuester Zeit (mit einer Einleitung von H. von Schlagintweit-Sakünlünski). 8° *Stuttgart*, 1878

—— How to Enliven Geographical Instruction, and to Lighten it. (Reprinted from the American Geographical Society, Bulletin No. 4, 1887.) 8* 1887

—— Erklärung geographischer Namen, zur Belebung des geographischen Unterrichts und zur Erleichterung des Studiums der Erdkunde. 8* *Vienna*, 1888

Garay, Franciscus de. *See* Gottfried : Appendix 1.

Garay, Don José de. An Account of the Isthmus of Tehuantepec, in the Republic of Mexico, with Proposals for Establishing a Communication between the Atlantic and Pacific Oceans, based upon the Surveys and Reports of a Scientific Commission. *Maps.* 8° 1844

—— Reconocimiento del Istmo de Tehuantepec, practicado en los años 1842 y 1843, con el objeto de Communicacion Oceanica. *Maps.* 8° 1844

—— Survey of the Isthmus of Tehuantepec, executed in 1842 and 1843, with the intent of establishing a Communication between the Atlantic and Pacific Oceans. *Maps.* 8° 1844

Garcia, Diego. *See* Gottfried : Appendix 1.

Garcia, J. A. Relaciones de los Vireyes del Nuevo Reina de Granada, ahora Estados unidos de Venezuela, Estados unidos de Colombia y Ecuador. 8° *New York*, 1869

—— El Monitor Rebelde "Huascar," i sus Incidentes juzgados conforme á la Autoridad de la Ciencia, de la Lei, i de la Jurisprudencia Internacional. Large 8° *Lima*, 1877

Garcia y Cubas, A. Memoria para servir á la Carta General de la República Mexicana. *Maps.* 8° *Mexico*, 1861

Garcia y Garcia, Aurelio. Derrotero de la Costa del Peru. 8° *Lima*, 1863

—— The same. 2nd edition. 8° *Lima*, 1870

—— Peruvian Coast Pilot. *Map.* 8° *New York*, 1866

Garcia, P. A. *See* Angelis, Vols. 3, 4, 6 : Appendix 1.

Garcin, F. Au Tonkin : Un an chez les Muongs, souvenirs d'un officier. *Maps and illustrations.* 12° *Paris*, 1891

Gardiner, Comm. Allen F. Narrative of a Journey to the Zoolu Country in South Africa, undertaken in 1835. *Maps and coloured plates.* 8° 1836

—— Visit to the Indians of the Frontiers of Chili. *Map and plates.* 12° 1841

—— *See* Marsh and Stirling.

Gardiner, Charles L. W. *See* Jonge.

Gardner, A. K. Paris Illustrated. *Plates.* 8° 1847

Gardner, Christopher T. Translation [with Chinese text] of Inscription on Tablet at Hang Chow, recording the changing the T'ien Chu Tang (Roman Catholic Church) into the T'ien Hao Kung. 8* N.D.

—— Appendices to Report on the Trade of Ichang for the year 1883, published in "China," No. 6 (1884). 8* *Illustrations.* Folio 1884

—— Report on the Consular District of Newchwang, by Christopher Thomas Gardner. 8* [*Newchwang*, 1885]

Gardner, G. Travels in the Interior of Brazil, principally through the Northern Provinces and the Gold and Diamond Districts, during the years 1836-41. *Plate.* 8° 1846

Gargiolli, L. F. M. G. Description de la Ville de Florence et de ses Environs. 2 vols. *Map and plates.* 8° *Florence*, 1819

Garlington, Ernest A. Report on Lady Franklin Bay Expedition of 1883, U.S. Signal Service Notes, No. 10. *Chart.* 8* *Washington*, 1883

Garneau, F. X. Histoire du Canada depuis sa Découverte jusqu'à nos jours. 3 vols. 8° . *Quebec*, 1852

Garner, Robert. The Natural History of the County of Stafford, comprising its Geology, Zoology, Botany, and Meteorology ; also its Antiquities, Topography, Manufactures, &c. *Plates.* 8° 1844

Garnier, F. Notice sur le Voyage d'Exploration effectué en Indo-Chine, par une Commission Française pendant les années 1866-68. *Map.* 8° *Paris*, 1869

—— Note sur l'Exploration du Cours du Cambodge, par une Commission Scientifique Française. *Map.* 8° *Paris*, 1869

—— Voyage d'Exploration en Indo-Chine, effectué pendant les années 1866, 1867, et 1868, &c. 2 vols. *Maps and plates, and atlas folio.* 4° *Paris*, 1873

—— De Paris au Tibet, Notes de Voyage. *Map and illustrations.* 12° *Paris*, 1882

Garnet, —. *See* Pinkerton, Vol. 3 : Appendix 1.

Garrick, H. B. W. *See* India, A, Archæological Survey : Appendix 2.

Garson, Dr J. G. *See* Bent.

Gasca, P. de la. *See* Cartas de Indias, p. 612; Allgemeine Historie, Vol. 15 : Appendix 1.

Gaspar, F. Memorias para a Historia da Capitania de S. Vicente, hoje chamada de S. Paulo, do Estado do Brazil. 8° *Lisbon*, 1797

Gaspari, Adam C. Lehrbuch der Erdbeschreibung zur Erläuterung sowohl des neuen Methodischen Schulatlasses. 8° *Weimar*, 1811

Gasparrini, Guglielmo. Descrizione delle Isole di Tremiti, e del modo come renderle coltive. 8° *Naples*, 1838

Gastaldi, Bartolomeo. Alcuni dati sulle Punte Alpini situate fra la Levanna ed il Rocciamelone. *Plates.* 8° *Turin*, 1868

—— Lake Habitations and Pre-historic Remains in the Turbaries and Marl-Beds of Northern and Central Italy. Translated from the Italian, and edited by C. H. Chambers. 8° 1865

—— *See* Martins, C. ; Vogt, C.

Gastrell, Col. J. E. *See* India, F, *a* : Appendix 2.

—— **and Henry F. Blanford.** Report on the Calcutta Cyclone of the 5th October 1864. *Table.* 8° *Calcutta*, 1866

—— Cyclone Report. *Maps and charts, without letterpress.* Folio * *Calcutta*, 1865

Gastrell, William S. H. Argentine Republic : Report for the year 1892 on the General Condition of the Argentine Republic. No. 1147, Diplomatic and Consular Reports on Trade and Finance, Foreign Office. 8* 1893

Gates, Sir Thomas. *See* Hakluyt, Vol. 5 : Appendix 1.

Gatonbe, J. *See* Churchill, Vol. 6 : Appendix 1.

Gatschet, A. S. Analytical Report upon Indian Dialects spoken in Southern California, Nevada, and on the Lower Colorado River. 8* *Washington*, 1876

—— The Numeral Adjective in the Klamath Language of Southern Oregon. 8* N.P., N.D.

Gatterer, C. W. J. Beschreibung des Harzes. Part 1. 8° *Nuremberg*, 1792

Gatterer, Johann C. Kurzer Begriff der Geographie. 12° *Gottingen*, 1793

—— An Prvssorvm, Litvanorvm ceterorumqve popvlorvm letticorvm originem a Sarmatis liceat repetere ? *Map.* Small 4° N.P., 1792-95

Gaubil, Anthony. *See* Astley, Vol. 3 ; Allgemeine Historie, Vol. 5 : Appendix 1.

Gauchez, Victor. Conférence sur l'Application du mouvement de la Mer. *Plates.* 8* *Brussels*, 1881

Gaudichaud, C. *See* Freycinet, Vaillant.

Gaume, Monsignor. *See* Horner.

Gaupillat, G. En Ballon Libre. *Plate.* 8* *Paris*, 1892

—— *See* Martel.

Gaussin, P. L. J. B. Du Dialecte de Tahiti, de celui des Iles Marquises, et en général de la Langue Polynésienne. 8° *Paris*, 1853

Gautier, J. Le Voyageur dans le Royaume des Pays-Bas. *Map.* 12° *Brussels*, 1827

Gavazzi, A. F. Meteorologijski odnosi na Sljemenn god 1888. 8* N.P., 1889

—— Ditto, for 1889. 8* N.P., 1890

—— Vransko Jezero u Dalmaciji. *Map.* 8* *Zagreb*, 1889

—— Usce Rijeke Krke 8* *Zagreb*, 1890

—— Die Regenverhältnisse Croatiens. *Maps.* 8* *Vienna*, 1891

—— Konstante sredne dnevne temperature zraka za hrvatske postaje. 8* *Zagreb*, 1893

Gawler, J. C. Sikhim. With Hints on Mountain and Jungle Warfare. *Map and plates.* 8° 1873

Gay, Claudio. Historia Fisica y Politica de Chile, segun Documentos adquiridos en esta Republica durante doce años de Residencia en ella ; y publicada bajo los auspicios del Supremo Gobierno. 23 vols. *Portrait, plates, and maps.* 8°, and 3 vols. large 4° *Paris*, 1844-54
Historia. 5 vols. 8° 1844-49
Documentos sobre la Historia, la Estadistica, y la Geografia. 2 vols. 8° 1846-52
Botanica. Vols. 2 to 8. 8° 1845-52 .
Zoologia. Vols. 2 to 8. 8° 1847-54
Plates. 3 vols. Large 4° 1854

Gay, J. Bibliographie des Ouvrages relatifs à l'Afrique et à l'Arabie. Catalogue Méthodique. 8° *San Remo*, 1875

Gayangos, Pascual de. Cartas y Relaciones de Hernan Cortés al Emperador Carlos V. Large 8°   *Paris*, 1866
—— Catalogue of the Manuscripts in the Spanish Language in the British Museum. Vol. 4. Large 8°   1893
—— *See* Hakluyt Soc. Publ., Vol. 40: Appendix 1.

Gayet, Al. Itinéraire illustré de la Haute Égypte, les anciennes capitales des bords du Nil, avec Cartes de la Haute Égypte et de la Basse Égypte. 12°   *Paris*

Gaze, Anth. Μελετιον γεωγραφια Παλαια και Νεα. 4 vols. *Maps.* 8°   *Venice*, 1807

"Gazelle," Voyage of the. Die Forschungsreise S.M.S. "Gazelle," in den Jahren 1874 bis 1876, unter Kommando des Kapitän zur See Freiherrn von Schleinitz, herausgegeben von dem hydrographischen Amt des Reichs-Marine-Amts. 5 vols. 4°   *Berlin*
  1. Der Reisebericht. *Maps and plates* 1889
  2. Physik und Chemie. *Map and diagrams* 1888
  3. Zoologie und Geologie. *Plates* 1889
  4. Botanik. *Plates*   1889
  5. Meteorologie   1890

Gazetteers and Geographical Dictionaries, *see* General : Appendix 2.

Geare, Allen. *See* Churchill, Vol. 8: Appendix 1.

Geare, Captain M. *See* Purchas, Vol. 4, Book 6 : Appendix 1.

Geary, G. Through Asiatic Turkey: Narrative of a Journey from Bombay to the Bosphorus. 2 vols. *Map and plates.* Square 8°   1878
—— Burma after the Conquest, viewed in its Political, Social, and Commercial Aspects from Mandalay. 8°   1886

Geddes, George. Rain : Evaporation and Filtration. 8* *Albany, N.Y.*, 1855
—— Report on the Agriculture and Industry of the County of Onondaga, State of New York ; with an Introductory Account of the Aborigines. *Map and plates.* 8°   *Albany, N.Y.*, 1860

Gedeonoff, D. On the Geographical Position of Fifty Points in Turkish Armenia and Kurdistan : Observations made in 1889. [In Russian.] 4*   *St Petersburg*, 1891

Geer, G. de. *See* Sweden, A : Appendix 2.

Geiger, J. L. A Peep at Mexico: Narrative of a Journey across the Republic from the Pacific to the Gulf in December 1873 and January 1874. *Maps and photographs.* 8°   1874

Geiger, Dr Wilhelm. *See* Penck's Abhandlungen, 2.

Geikie, Sir Archibald. Outlines of the Geology of the British Isles. 12°   *Edinburgh*, 1864
—— The Scenery of Scotland viewed in connection with its Physical Geology. *Maps and illustrations.* 12°   1865
—— The same, 2nd edition. 8°   1887
—— Elementary Lessons in Physical Geography. *Maps.* 12°   1878
—— Text Book of Geology. 2nd edition. *Illustrations.* 8°   1885
—— The Teaching of Geography : Suggestions regarding Principles and Methods for the use of Teachers. 12°   1887
—— An Elementary Geography of the British Isles. 18°   1888
—— Annual Report of the Geological Survey and Museum of Practical Geology for the year ending December 31, 1892. 8*   1893
—— The Work of the Geological Survey : a Paper read before the Federated Institution of Mining Engineers. (Extract from the *Transactions* of the Institution.) 8*   1893
—— *See* Galton, Vacation Tourists ; Murchison ; Symons.

Geikie, Prof. James. The Great Ice Age and its Relation to the Antiquity of Man. *Maps.* 8°   1874
—— The same. New edition. *Plates and maps.* 8°   1894
—— Fragments of Earth Lore : Sketches and Addresses, Geological and Geographical. *Maps and illustrations.* 8°   *Edinburgh*, 1893

Geilfus, Dr G. Das Leben des Geographen, Dr Jakob Melchior Ziegler ; nach handschriftlichen Quellen, ein Denkmal der Freundschaft, von Dr G. Geilfus. *Portrait.* 8°   *Winterthur*, 1884

Geinitz, Dr E. *See* Germany, C (Forschungen, &c., Vol. 1): Appendix 2.

Geiseler, —. Die Oster-Insel, eine Stätte prähistorischer Kultur in der Südsee : Bericht des Kommandantern S. M. Kbt. "Hyäne," Kapitänlieutenant Geiseler, über die ethnologische Untersuchung der Oster-Insel (Rapanui), an den Chef der Kaiserlichen Admiralität. *Map and plates.* Large 8*   *Berlin*, 1883

Geistbeck, Dr Alois. Die Seen der Deutschen Alpen. 8 *plates of diagrams.* Folio   *Leipzig*, 1885
  [Atlas to Paper in Mitt. Ver. Erdk., Leipzig, 1884.]

Geistbeck, Dr Michael. Der Weltverkehr. Telegraphie und Post, Eisenbahnen und Schiffahrt in ihrer Entwickelung dargestellt. *Maps and illustrations.* 8° *Freiburg in Breisgau*, 1887

Gelcich, József. *See* Austria-Hungary, B : Appendix 2.

Gell, Sir William. Geography and Antiquities of Ithaca. *Map and plates.* 4° 1807
—— Itinerary of Greece; with a Commentary on Pausanias and Strabo. *Plates.* 4° 1810
—— Itinerary of the Morea: being a Collection of the Routes of that Peninsula. *Map.* 8° 1817
—— Narrative of a Journey in the Morea. *Plates.* 8° 1823
—— Topography of Rome and its Vicinity. 2 vols. *Woodcuts.* 8° 1834
—— Map to Topography of Rome. [In 8° covers.]

Gemelli. *See* Careri.

Gemma Frisius. *See* Phrysius.

Gens, Major. *See* Baer and Helmersen, 2.

Gennes, M. de. *See* Burney, Vol. 4; Callander, Vol. 3: Appendix 1.

Genth, Adolphus. The Iron Waters of Schwalbach in the Duchy of Nassau. 2nd edition. 8° *Wiesbaden,* 1855

Gentil, M. le. Voyage dans les Mers de l'Inde, à l'occasion du Passage de Vénus sur le Disque du Soleil, le 6 Juin 1761, et le 3 du même mois 1769. 2 vols. *Maps and plates.* 4° *Paris,* 1779-81

Geoffroy, L. Memoir and Notice explanatory of a Chart of Madagascar and the North-Eastern Archipelago of Mauritius. *Map.* 4* 1819

George, C. Description of a Self-Replenishing Artificial Horizon. 8* 1876
—— Description of an Improved Double Sextant. *Plate.* 8* 1876
—— Description of a Mercurial Barometer. 8* 1876

George, E. S. *See* Osburn.

Georgi, J. G. Geographisch-physikalische und naturhistorische Beschreibung des Russischen Reichs. 9 vols. *Maps.* 8° *Königsburg,* 1797
—— [A Russian Translation of Georgi's "Russland: Beschreihung aller Nationen des Russichen Reiches," &c.] 2 vols., 4 parts. *Plates.* 4° [*St Petersburg*] 1799

Georgii, Ludwig. Alte Geographie, beleuchtet durch Geschichte, Sitten, Sagen der Völker, und mit vergleichenden Beziehungen auf die neuere Länder- und Völkerkunde. 8° *Stuttgart,* 1838-40

Gepp, H. M. *See* Nansen.

Gerando, A. de. La Transylvanie et ses Habitants. 2 vols. *Map and plates.* 8° *Paris,* 1845

Gerard, Capt. A. Account of Koonawur, in the Himalaya. Edited by Lloyd. *Map.* 8° 1841

Gerard, E. The Land beyond the Forest: Facts, Figures, and Fancies from Transylvania. 2 vols. *Map and illustrations.* 8° 1888

Gerard, Jules. Life and Adventures of, comprising his Ten Years Campaigns among the Lions of Northern Africa; with a History and Description of Algeria. *Plates.* 12° 1857
—— Lion Hunting and Sporting Life in Algeria. *Plates.* 12° 1857

Gerbié, Frédéric. Le Canada et l'émigration Française. 6th edition. *Maps and illustrations.* 8° *Quebec,* 1884

Gerbillon, J. F. *See* Astley, Vol. 4; Allgemeine Historie, Vol. 7: Appendix 1.

Gerland, Dr George. Beiträge zur Geophysik. Abhandlungen aus dem Geographischen Seminar der Universität Strassburg. 1. Band. *Maps and plates.* 8° *Stuttgart,* 1887
—— Geographische Abhandlungen aus den Reichslanden Elsass-Lothringen. Mit Unterstützung der kaiserl. Regierung zu Strassburg, herausgegeben von Prof. Dr G. Gerland. Erstes Heft. *Maps.* 8° *Stuttgart,* 1892

Germain, A. Note sur Zanzibar et la Côte Orientale d'Afrique. 8* [*Paris,* 1868]
—— Quelques Mots sur l'Oman et la Sultan de Maskate. 8* [*Paris,* 1868]
—— Traité des projections des cartes géographiques. *Plates.* Royal 8° *Paris,* N.D.

Gerritsz, Hessel. The Arctic North-East and West Passage: Detectio Freti Hudsoni, or Hessel Gerritsz's Collection of Tracts by himself, Massa, and De Quir, on the N.E. and W. Passage, Siberia, and Australia. Reproduced, with the maps in photo-lithography, in Dutch and Latin, after the editions of 1612 and 1613; augmented with a new English Translation by F. J. Millard, and an Essay on the Origin and Design of this Collection by S. Muller. *Maps.* Square 8° *Amsterdam,* 1878

Gerstaecker, F. Narrative of a Journey round the World, comprising a Winter Passage across the Andes to Chili, with a Visit to the Gold Regions of California and Australia, the South Sea Islands, Java, &c. 3 vols. 8° 1853

Gerstfeldt, G. von. Der Verkehr Russlands mit Westasien. 8° 1862
—— *See* Baer and Helmersen, 24.

Gesenius, W. Ueber die Himjaritische Sprache und Schrift. 8* N.P. 1841

Gesner, A. New Brunswick, with Notes for Emigrants. Comprehending the Early History, an Account of the Indians, Settlement, Topography, Statistics, Commerce, Timber, Manufactures, Agriculture, Fisheries, Geology, Natural History, Social and Political State, Immigrants, and contemplated Railways of that Province. 8° 1847

Gessi Pasha, Romolo. Setti Anni nel Sudan Egiziano. Esplorazioni Caccie e Guerra contro i Negrieri. Memorie di Romolo Gessi Pascia riunite e pubblicate da suo figlio Felice Gessi coordinate dal Cap. Manfredo Camperio. *Map and illustrations.* 8°   *Milan*, 1891
—— Seven Years in the Soudan : being a Record of Explorations, Adventures, and Campaigns against the Arab Slave Hunters. Collected and edited by his son Felix Gessi. *Map, portrait, and illustrations.* 8°   1892

Gestro, Raffaello. *See* Issel.

Gether, A. Gedanken über die Naturkraft. 8°   *Oldenburg*, 1862
—— Anmerkungen zu Gedanken über die Naturkraft. 8*   *Oldenburg*, 1863

Gevrey, A. Essai sur les Comores. 8°
                                        Pondicherry, 1870

Ghedeonov. *See* Gedeonoff.

Giacinto, P. Carlo. Saggio di Agricoltura per le Isole di Malta e Gozo. Small 8°
                                        Messina, 1811

Gibb, George D. On Canadian Caverns. *Maps and plates.* 8*   1861

Gibbins, Rev. H. de B. The History of Commerce in Europe. *Maps.* 12°   1891

Gibbon, Edward. History of the Decline and Fall of the Roman Empire ; with an Introductory Memoir of the Author. *Portrait.* Imperial 8°   1836

Gibbon, Lieut. L. *See* Herndon.

Gibbs, A., and W. I. Myers. Peruvian and Bolivian Guano, its Nature, Properties, and Results. 8*   1844

Gibbs, E. J. England and South Africa. 8°   1889

Gibbs, J. *See* Osorio.

Gibert, Eugène. Le Mouvement Économique en Portugal et le Vicomte de San Januario. Large 8*   *Paris*, 1881

Gibson, A. *See* Hove, Dr.

Gibson, Charles B. Emigration : a Paper read at the Burdett Hall, Limehouse, on 30th March 1868. 8*   1868

Gibson, Bishop Edmund. *See* Camden.

Gibson, John. Great Waterfalls, Cataracts, and Geysers Described and Illustrated. *Map and illustrations.* 8°   1887

Gibson, T. A. Etymological Geography : being a Classified List of Terms of most frequent occurrence, entering into the Composition of Geographical Names. 12°   *Edinburgh*, 1835

Gibson, Walter M. The Prison of Weltevreden, and a Glance at the East Indian Archipelago. *Plates.* 8° *New York*, 1855

Gibson, Com. William. *See* United States, E, *a* (No. 41, B) : Appendix 2.

Giedroyc, Prince Romuald. Résumé de l'Histoire du Portugal au XIXᵉ Siècle. 8°   *Paris*, 1875

Giffard, Edward. A Short Visit to the Ionian Islands, Athens, and the Morea. *Plates.* 12°   1837

Giglioli, Dr E. H. Viaggio intorno al Globo della R. pirocorvetta Italiana "Magenta" negli anni 1865, '66, '67, '68. Relazione descrittiva e scientifica ; con uno Introduzione Etnologica di Paola Mantegazza. *Maps and photographs.* 4°
                                        Milan, 1875
—— Studi sulla razza Negrita. *Plate.* 8*
                                        Florence, 1876
—— Il Brasile nel 1876. 8* *Florence*, 1877
—— La Scoperta di una Fauna abissale nel Mediterraneo, Prima Campagna talassografica del R. piroscafo "Washington" sotto il commando del capitano di vascello G. B. Magnaghi. (Luglio, Settembre 1881.) Relazione preliminare. 8*
                                        Rome, 1881
—— Avifauna Italica : Elenco delle specie di uccelli stazionarie o di passaggio in Italia colla loro, sinonimia volgare e con notizie più specialmente intorno alle migrazioni ed alla nidificazione. 8° *Florence*, 1886
—— Esposizione Coloniale ed Indiana tenuta in Londra nel 1886. 8* *Rome*, 1887
—— Primo Resoconto dei Risultati della Inchiesta Ornitologica in Italia. Parte prima. Avifauna Italica, elenco sistematico delle specie di uccelli stazionarie o di passaggio in Italia con nuovi nomi volgari e colle notizie sinqui fornite dai Collaboratori nella inchiesta Ornitologica. *Map.* 8°   *Florence*, 1889
—— The same. Parte seconda. Avifaune Locali. Risultati della inchiesta Ornitologica nelle singole Provincie. 8°
                                        Florence, 1890
—— The same. Parte terza ed ultima. Notizie d'Indole Generale, Migrazioni, Nidificazione, Alimentazione, &c. 8°
                                        Florence, 1891
—— *See* Issel ; Scaramucci ; Sommier.
—— **and A. Issel.** Proposte Generali per la Esplorazione Biologica completa del Mediterraneo e dei Mari adiacenti. 8*
                                        Rome, 1885
—— **and A. Zannetti.** Istruzioni Scientifiche pei Viaggiatori raccolte dal Prof. A. Issel. Istruzioni per fare le Osservazioni Antropologiche et Etnologiche. 8*
                                        Rome, 1880

Gilbard, Lieut.-Col. G. J. A. Popular History of Gibraltar, its Institutions, and its Neighbourhood on both sides of the Straits, and a Guide-book to their principal places and objects of interest. *Map and plate.* Small 8° *Gibraltar*, 1882

Gilbert, Capt. B. *See* Gottfried ; Purchas, Vol. 4, Book 8 : Appendix 1.

Gilbert, G. K. *See* United States, G, *b*, *c* : Appendix 2.

Gilbert, G. M. Treatise on the Aëropleustic Art, or Navigation in the Air by means of Kites or Buoyant Sails, with a Description of the Charvolant or Kite Carriage. *Plates.* Small 4*   1851

Gilbert, Sir Humphrey. *See* Hakluyt, Vol. 3 : Appendix 1.

Gilbert, J., and G. C. Churchill. The Dolomite Mountains : Excursions through Tyrol, Carinthia, Carniola, and Friuli, in 1861, '62, and '63. *Maps and coloured plates.* 8° 1864

Gilbert, Sir J. H. Remarques sur la Relation qui existe entre les Sommes de Température et la Production Agricole. 8° *Geneva*, 1886

Gilbert, P. Observations sur la Carte du Nil de M. Miani. 8° *Brussels*, N.D.

Gilbert, Dr William. Gvilielmi Gilberti Colcestrensis, medici Londinensi⸳, de Magnete, magneticisque corporibus, et de magno Magnete Tellure, Physiologia noua, plurimis et argumentis et experimentis demonstrata. *Plates.* Small folio 1600

Gilby, Dr. *See* Monson.

Gilchrist, J. Borthwick. Hindoostanee Philology, comprising a Dictionary, English and Hindoostanee, with a Grammatical Introduction ; with a Plate exhibiting a comparative view of the Roman and Oriental characters used in the Hindoostanee Language. Vol. 1. 8° 1825

Gilder, W. H. Ice-Pack and Tundra : an Account of the Search for the "Jeannette," and a Sledge Journey through Siberia. *Maps and illustrations.* 8° 1883

—— Schwatka's Search : Sledging in the Arctic in quest of the Franklin Records. *Maps and illustrations.* 8° N.D.

Giles, Ernest. Diary of Explorations in Central Australia, August to November 1872. Folio* *Adelaide*, 1873

—— Geographic Travels in Central Australia from 1872 to 1874. *Map.* 8° *Melbourne*, 1875

—— The Journal of a Forgotten Expedition. *Map.* 8° *Adelaide*, 1880

—— Australia twice Traversed, the Romance of Exploration : being a Narrative compiled from the Journals of Five Exploring Expeditions into and through Central South Australia and Western Australia, from 1872 to 1876. 2 vols. *Portrait, maps, and illustrations.* 8° [2 copies.] 1889

—— *See* South Australia, A : Appendix 2.

Giles, Geo. M. A Report of an Investigation into the Causes of the Diseases known in Assam as Kála-Azár and Beri-Beri. *Plates.* Large 8° *Shillong*, 1890

Giles, H. A. From Swatow to Canton Overland. 8° *Shanghai*, 1877

Giles, Pearce. The True Source of the Mississippi. *Maps and frontispiece.* 8° *Buffalo, N.Y.*, 1887

Gilii, Filippo Luigi. Risultati delle Osservazioni Meteorologiche fatte nell' anno 1805. 8° *Rome*, 1806

—— Osservazioni Meteorologiche, 1806-7-8. 8° *Rome*, 1807-9

Gill, David. Trigonometrical Survey of South African Colonies. 8° 1879

Gill, Diogo. *See* "General Collection of Voyages," p. 610 : Appendix 1.

Gill, George. The Student's Geography, Physical and Descriptive, Industrial and Commercial, Political and Social, Etymological and Historical. *Maps, &c.* 12° 1890

Gill, Mrs. Six Months in Ascension : an Unscientific Account of a Scientific Expedition. *Map.* Square 8° 1878

Gill, Thomas. Bibliography of South Australia. 8° 1886

Gill, Capt. W. The River of Golden Sand : the Narrative of a Journey through China and Eastern Tibet to Burmah ; with an Introductory Essay by Colonel Henry Yule. 2 vols. *Maps and plates.* 8° 1880

—— The same. Condensed by Edward Colborne Baber ; edited, with a Memoir and Introductory Essay, by Colonel Henry Yule. *Portrait, map, and illustrations.* Small 8° 1883

Gill, Rev. W. Wyatt. New Guinea Revisited : a Supplement to Mr M'Farlane's Papers in the April, May, June, and August Numbers of the *Sunday Magazine*, 1874. 8° 1874

—— Papers on New Guinea in the *Leisure Hour*. 8° 1875

—— Life in the Southern Isles, or Scenes and Incidents in the South Pacific and New Guinea. *Map and plates.* 12° 1876

—— Tristan D'Acunha. 8° 1877

—— Historical Sketches of Savage Life in Polynesia, with illustrative Clan Songs. 8° *Wellington*, 1880

—— Jottings from the Pacific. *Illustrations.* 8° 1885

—— *See* Chalmers.

Gillam, Capt. J. *See* Allgemeine Historie, Vol. 17 : Appendix 1.

Gilliéron, J. Petit Atlas Phonétique du Valais Roman (Sud du Rhone). Oblong 12° *Paris*, N.D.

Gilliss, Lieut. J. M. The United States Astronomical Expedition to the Southern Hemisphere during 1849-52. Vols. 1, 2, 3, 6. 4 vols. *Maps and plates.* *Washington*, 1855-56

Gillmore, Parker. The Great Thirst Land : a Ride through Natal, Orange Free State, Transvaal, and Kalahari Desert. *Plate.* 8° [1878]

—— Through Gasa Land, and the Scene of the Portuguese Aggression : the Journey of a Hunter in Search of Gold and Ivory. *Map.* 8° N.D.

Gilly, W. S. Narrative of an Excursion to the Mountains of Piemont in the year 1823, and Researches among the Vaudois or Waldenses, Protestant Inhabitants of the Cottian Alps. 4th edition. *Maps and plates.* 8° 1827

Gilmore, Q. A. *See* United States, H, *a*: Appendix 2.

Gilmour, Rev. James. Among the Mongols. *Map and illustrations.* 8° N.D.

—— More about the Mongols. Selected and arranged from the diaries and papers of James Gilmour, by Richard Lovett. 8° 1893

Gilpin, W. Observations, relative chiefly to Picturesque Beauty, made in the year 1772, on several parts of England, particularly the Mountains and Lakes of Cumberland and Westmorland. 3rd edition. Vol. 1. *Plates.* 8° 1792

Ginanni, Francesco. Istoria Civile, e Naturale delle Pinette Ravennati, &c. 4° *Rome,* 1774

Ginders, A. Extracts from a Report on the Hanmer Plains Sanatorium. *Map and plates.* 8* 1891

Ginsburg, Dr Christian D. The Moabite Stone : a Fac-simile of the Original Inscription, with an English Translation, and a Historical and Critical Commentary. 4* 1870

—— Report on the Exploration of Moab. 8* 1872

Giordano, F. Cenni sulle Condizioni Fisico-Economiche di Roma e suo Territorio. *Maps.* 8° *Florence,* 1871

Giovio, P. Descriptio Britanniæ, Scotiæ, Hyberniæ, et Orchadum, ex libro Pauli Jovii, episcopi Nucer, de imperiis, et gentibus cogniti orbis. 8° *Venice,* 1548

Gipps, Sir G. Report of the Progressive Discovery and Occupation of New South Wales, during the Period of his Administration of the Government. *Maps.* Folio* 1841

Girard, Charles. American Zoological, Botanical, and Geological Bibliography for 1851. 8* *Newhaven,* 1851

Girard, Jules. La Photographie appliquée aux Études Géographiques. 12* *Paris,* 1871

—— Essai d'Orographie Sousmarine de l'Océan Atlantique Septentrional. *Map.* 8* *Paris,* 1872

—— Les Explorations Sousmarines. *Illustrations.* 8° *Paris,* 1874

—— Voyage dans les Highlands et les Hébrides. *Map.* 8* *Paris,* 1878

—— La Nouvelle-Guinée. Historique de la Découverte—Description Géographique —La Race Papoue—Mœurs et Coutumes des Indigènes — Produits du Sol — Colonisation. *Map.* 8* *Paris,* 1883

Girard, M. B. Souvenirs de l'Expedition de Tunisie. 8* *Paris,* 1883

Girard, P. S. Description Générale des différens Ouvrages à exécuter pour la Distribution des Eaux du Canal de l'Ourcq dans l'intérieur de Paris, et devis détaillé de ces Ouvrages. *Map and plates.* 4° *Paris,* 1810

Giraud, Victor. Les Lacs de l'Afrique Équatoriale : Voyage d'Exploration exécuté de 1883 à 1885. *Maps and illustrations.* 4° *Paris,* 1890

Girava Tarragones, Hieronymo. Dos Libros de Cosmographia. *Map.* 4° *Milan,* 1556

Gironière. *See* De la Gironière.

Giros (or De Quir) P. F. de. *See* Quirós.

Gisborne, Lionel. Darien Ship-Navigation. Engineer's Report. *Maps.* 8* 1852

—— The Isthmus of Darien in 1852. Journal of the Expedition of Inquiry for the Junction of the Atlantic and Pacific Oceans. *Maps.* 8° 1853

Gisborne, William. The Colony of New Zealand, its History, Vicissitudes, and Progress. *Map.* 8° 1888

Gíslason, K. Dönsk Ordabók med Islenzkum Pýdingum. Small folio *Copenhagen,* 1851

Gistel, Dr Johannes. Maximilian der Erste, König von Bayern, oder des Oberstpostmeister Napoleon's Gefangenschaft, Errettung vom Tode, und Flucht. 12* *Munich,* 1854

—— Das Heilbad zum Heiligen Kreuzbrunnen bei Wartemberg. 8* *Straubing,* 1856

—— Neueste Geographie und Statistik des Königreichs Bayern. 8° *Straubing,* 1856

——— Die südwestbayerische Schweiz, oder das Algäu im allgemeinen und ein Theil von Sonthofen insbesondere, &c. 8* *Straubing,* 1857

Giustiniani, Lorenzo. Dizionario Geografico-Ragionato del Regno di Napoli. 12 vols. 8° *Naples,* 1797-1816

Givry, A. P. Pilote Français. Instructions Nautiques, Partie des Côtes de France compris entre la Pointe de Barfleur et Dunkerque, et entre les Casquets et la Pointe de Barfleur, Environs de Cherbourg. 2 vols. 4° *Paris,* 1842-45

—— Mémoire sur l'Emploi des Chronomètres à la Mer, et sur les Principales Observations de l'Astronomie Nautique. *Plate.* 8° *Paris,* 1846

Gladisheff, —, and — Muravieff. *See* Khanikoff ; *also* Central Asia, B : Appendix 2.

Gladstone, W. E. *See* Laveleye ; Mackenzie and Irby ; Schliemann.

Gladwin, Francis. A Narrative of the Transactions in Bengal during the Soobahdaries of Azeem Us Shan, Jaffer Khan, Shuja Khan, Sirafraz Khan, and Alyvirdy Khan. Translated from the Persian by Francis Gladwin. 8° *Calcutta,* 1788

Glaisher, Ernest H. A Journey on the Berbice River and Wieroonie Creek. 8* *Georgetown*, 1885

Glaisher, James. On the Meteorology of Scotland, June 1856 to Sept. 1857. 8*
—— On the Meteorology of England during the Quarters ending March, June, September, 1857; March, June, September, December, 1858; March, June, 1859. 8* 1857-59
—— On the Determination of the Mean Temperature of every Day in the Year, from all the Thermometrical Observations taken at the Royal Observatory, Greenwich, from 1814 to the end of 1856. 8* 1858
—— On the Meteorological and Physical Effects of the Solar Eclipse of 15th March 1858. *Plates.* 8* 1858

Glanius, —. *See* Struys.

Glas, George. History of the Discovery and Conquest of the Canary Islands. Translated from a Spanish MS. ; with an Enquiry into the Origin of the Ancient Inhabitants, and a Description of the Canary Islands and the Modern History of the Inhabitants. *Map.* 4° 1764
—— *See* Pinkerton, Vol. 16 : Appendix 1.

Glaser, Eduard. Von Hodeida nach San'â vom 24 April bis 1 Mai 1885. (Abdruck aus Dr A. Petermann's Mitteilungen, 1886, Heft 1.) *Map.* 4* 1886
—— The same. (Abdruck aus Dr A. Petermann's Mitteilungen, 1886, Heft 2.) 4* 1886
—— Südarabische Streitfragen. 8* *Prague*, 1887
—— — Skizze der Geschichte und Geographie Arabiens, von den ältesten Zeiten bis zum Propheten Muhammad, nebst einem Anhange zur Beleuchtung der Geschichte Abessyniens im 3 und 4 Jahrhundert n. Chr. Zweiter Band. 8° *Berlin*, 1890
—— *See* Hommel.

Glasfurd, C. L. R. Papers relating to the Dependency of Bustar. *Map and plates.* [From the India Records, No. 39] *Calcutta*, 1863

Glave, E. J. Our Alaska Expedition. (From *Frank Leslie's Illustrated Newspaper*.) 4* *New York*, 1890-91
—— Six Years of Adventure in Congo-Land ; with an Introduction by H. M. Stanley. *Illustrations.* Large 8° 1893

Glazier, Capt. Willard. Down the Great River : embracing an Account of the Discovery of the True Source of the Mississippi ; together with Views, Descriptive and Pictorial, of the Cities, Towns, Villages, and Scenery on the Banks of the River, as seen during a Canoe Voyage of over Three Thousand Miles from its Head-Waters to the Gulf of Mexico. *Portrait, maps, and illustrations.* Small 8° *Philadelphia*, 1887

Glazier, Capt. Willard. Headwaters of the Mississippi ; comprising Biographical Sketches of early and recent Explorers of the Great River, and a Full Account of the Discovery and Location of its True Source in a lake beyond Itasca. *Maps and illustrations.* Small 8° *New York*, 1893
—— *See* Harrower.

Gleerup, E. *See* Möller.

Glehn, P. von. *See* Schmidt, F. B.

Gleichen, Count. *See* United Kingdom, G, War Office Publications : Appendix 2.

Glen, J. Foundering of the H.E.I. Co.'s gun-brig " Ariel." 8* 1872

Gliddon, George R. An Appeal to the Antiquaries of Europe on the Destruction of the Monuments of Egypt. 8° 1841
—— A Memoir on the Cotton of Egypt. 8* 1841

Glogau, H. *See* Andree, Karl.

Gloucester, Duke of (Thomas of Woodstock). *See* Hakluyt, Vol. 1 : Appendix 1.

Glover, J. R. *See* Niebuhr, C.

Glover, Sir Thomas. *See* Purchas, Vol. 2, Book 1 : Appendix 1.

Glückselig, L. Prag und dessen Merkwürdigkeiten. 2nd edition. *Plates.* 12° *Prague*, 1856

Glynn, Joseph. Rudimentary Treatise on the Power of Water as applied to drive Flour Mills and to give Motion to Turbines and other Hydrostatic Engines. *Illustrations.* 12* 1853

Gmelin, S. G. Reise durch Russland zur Untersuchung der drey Naturreiche. 4 vols. *Maps and plates.* 4° *St Petersburg*, 1774-84
—— *See* Laharpe, Vol. 8 ; Allgemeine Historie, Vol. 19 : Appendix 1.

Goalen, Lieut. *See* South Australia, A : Appendix 2.

Gobanz, J. *See* Zollikofer.

Gobat, Rev. Samuel. Journal of a Three Years' Residence in Abyssinia, in furtherance of the Objects of the Church Missionary Society ; with a Brief History of the Church of Abyssinia, by Professor Lee. *Map.* 8° 1834

Gobineau, Comte de. Les Religions et les Philosophies dans l'Asie Centrale. 2nd edition. 12° *Paris*, 1866

Goblet D'Alviella, Comte. Inde et Himalaya : Souvenirs de Voyage. *Map and plates.* 12° *Paris*, 1877
—— *See* Becker, J.

Godard, Léon. Description et Histoire du Maroc. 2 vols. *Map.* 8° *Paris*, 1860

Godericus. *See* Hakluyt, Vol. 2 : Appendix 1.

Godet, Theodore L. Bermuda, its History, Geology, Climate, Products, Agriculture, Commerce, and Government . . ; with Hints to Invalids. 8° 1860

Godman, F. Du C. Natural History of the Azores or Western Islands. *Map.* 8° 1870
—— *See* America, Central, A : Appendix 2.

Godoy, Diego de. *See* Cortes ; *also* Gottfried : Ramusio, Vol. 3 : Appendix 1.

Godwin-Austen, Colonel H. H. On the Glaciers of the Mustakh Range. *Map.* 8* [1864]
—— The Evidence of past Glacial Action in the Nágá Hills, Assam. *Map and plates.* 8* *Calcutta*, 1875
—— Notes on the Geology of part of the Dafla Hills, Assam. *Plate.* 8* *Calcutta*, 1875

Goodwin-Austen, R. *See* Forbes, E.

Goebel, Claus and Bergmann. Reise in die Steppen des südlichen Russlands. 2 vols. *Maps and plates.* 4° *Dorpat*, 1838

Goebel, H. *See* Helmersen and Schrenck, 2.

Goebel, K. Gedächtnisrede auf Karl von Nägeli, gehalten in der öffentlichen Sitzung der k. b. Akademie der Wissenschaften. 4* *Munich*, 1893

Goeje, M. J. de. Das alte Bett des Oxus Amú-Darja. *Map.* Small 8° *Leyden*, 1875

Goès, Benoit de (or Benedictus). *See* Brucker, J. ; *also* Astley, Vol. 4 ; Gottfried ; Hakluyt Soc. Publ., Vol. 37 ; Pinkerton, Vol. 7 ; Purchas, Vol. 3, Book 2 ; Allgemeine Historie, Vol. 7 : Appendix 1.

Gogorza, A. de. Canal Interocéanique du Darien : Lettres à la Société de Géographie de Paris. *Map.* 4* 1870

Göhring, H. Informe al Supremo Gobierno del Perú sobre la Expedicion á los Valles de Paucartambo en 1873 al mando del Coronel D. Baltazar La-Torre. 8°, and oblong 8° vol. of photographs. *Lima*, 1877

Golberry, S. M. Xavier. Fragment d'un Voyage en Afrique pendant 1785-87, dans les Contrées Occidentales de ce Continent, comprises entre le Cap Blanc de Barbarie et le Cap de Palmes. 2 vols. *Maps and plates.* 8° *Paris*, 1802

Gold, F. *See* Ramond.

Goldmann, C. S. The Financial, Statistical, and General History of the Gold and other Companies of Witwatersrand, South Africa. *Plan.* Large 8° 1892

Goldie, Sir George Taubman. Alcohol and Civilisation in Central Africa. Folio* 1887
—— France and England on the Niger. (From the *Paternoster Review*, No. 4, January 1891.) *Map.* 4* 1891

Goldney, P. *See* Preedy.

Goldsmid, Sir Frederic J. An Historical Memoir on Shikarpoor, prior and subsequent to the Ameers of Sind. *Table.* Memoir on the Syuds of Roree and Bukkur. *Table.* [From the India Records, No. 17.] 8° *Bombay*, 1855
—— Central Asia, and its Question. 8* 1873
—— Telegraph and Travel : a Narrative of the Formation and Development of Telegraphic Communication between England and India, under the orders of Her Majesty's Government, with incidental notices of the Countries traversed by the lines. *Maps and plates.* 8° 1874
—— On Communications with British India under possible contingencies. *Map.* 8* 1878
—— James Outram, a Biography. 2 vols. *Maps and illustrations.* 8° 1880
—— Persia, its Language and Literature : a Lecture. 8* 1892
—— *See* Vaughan ; *also* Persia : Appendix 2.

Goldsmith, L. Statistics of France. 8° 1832

Golindo, Lieut. R. E. Report of the Route from Mámu to Núshkí. 8* [*Simla*, 1886]

Gölnitz, A. Itinerarium Belgico-Gallicum. 24° *Leyden*, 1631
—— Compendium Geographicum, succinctâ Methodo Adornatum. 12° *Amsterdam*, 1649

Golovin, Ivan. The Caucasus. *Map.* 8° 1854
—— The Nations of Russia and Turkey, and their Destiny. 8° 1854

Golownin, Capt. W. Recollections of Japan, comprising a particular Account of the Religion, Language, Government, Laws, &c., of the People, and Observations on the Geography, Climate, &c., of the Country. 8° 1819
—— Memoirs of a Captivity in Japan during the years 1811 to 1813, with Observations on the Country and the People. 2nd edition. 3 vols. 8° 1824

Gomara, Francisco Lopez de. Historia de las Indias, and Cronica de la Nueva-España. Folio [? *Saragoça*, 1552-53]
—— Historia de Mexico, con el Descubrimiento de la Nueva-España, conquistada por el muy illustre y valeroso Principe Don Fernando Cortes. 12° *Antwerp*, 1554
—— *See* Burney, Vol. 1 ; Purchas, Vol. 3, Book 5 : Appendix 1.

Gomez, Stephan. *See* Gottfried : Appendix 1.

Gomme, George Laurence. English Topography : Parts 1-3. (The Gentleman's Magazine Library : being a classified Collection of the chief contents of the *Gentleman's Magazine*, from 1731 to 1868.) 8° 1891-93

Gomot, F. Annuaire de l'Algérie, 1842 ; avec des Lois, 1841. 8° *Paris*, 1842

Gonda, Bela de. La Regularisation des Portes de Fer et des autres Cataractes du bas Danube. *Plates and illustrations.* Large 8* *Paris*, 1892

Gondatti, N. L. Traces of Heathen Beliefs among the nations of North-Western Siberia. [In Russian.] 8* *Moscow*, 1888

Gonino, J. *See* Charnay.

Gonville (or Gonneville), B. P. de. *See* Callander, Vol. 1 ; Allgemeine Historie, Vol. 18 : Appendix 1.

Gonzales, Manuel. *See* Churchill, Vol. 7 ; Pinkerton, Vol. 2 ; General Collection of Voyages, p. 610 : Appendix 1.

Gooch, F. A. *See* United States, G, *c* : Appendix 2.

Gooch, Fanny Chambers. Face to Face with the Mexicans : the Domestic Life, Educational, Social, and Business Ways, Statesmanship and Situation, Legendary and General History, of the Mexican People. *Illustrations.* Large 8° 1890

Good, J. B. A Vocabulary and Outlines of Grammar of the Nitlakapamuk or Thompson Tongue (the Indian language spoken between Yale, Lillooet, Cache Creek, and Nicola Lake) ; together with a Phonetic Chinook Dictionary, adapted for use in the Province of British Columbia. Small 8* *Victoria, B.C.*, 1880

Goode, Alexander. Account of the Mechitaristican Society, founded on the Island of St Lazaro. *Portrait.* 8* *Venice*, 1825

Goode, G. Brown. *See* United States, A, (Tenth Census Publication), History and Present Condition of the Fishery Industries : Appendix 2.

Goodenough, Commodore. *See* Markham, C. R.

Goodenough, Lieut.-General W. H., and Lieut.-Col. J. C. Dalton. The Army Book for the British Empire : a Record of the Development and Present Composition of the Military Forces, and their Duties in Peace and War. *Maps and portraits.* 8° 1893

Goodisson, W. Historical and Topographical Essay upon the Islands of Corfu, Leucadia, Cephalonia, Ithaca, and Zante ; with Remarks upon the Character, &c., of the Ionian Greeks. *Maps and plates.* 8° 1822

Goodman, E. J. The Best Tour in Norway. *Map and illustrations.* Small 8° 1892

Goodrich, Caspar F. *See* United States, E, *b* : Appendix 2.

Goodrich, J. King. An Account of the Progress in Geography in the year 1885. 8* *Washington*, 1886

Goodsir, R. Anstruther. Arctic Voyage to Baffin's Bay and Lancaster Sound in Search of Friends with Sir John Franklin. *Map and plate.* 8° 1850

Goos, P. The Lighting Colomne or Sea-Mirror, containing the Sea-coasts of the Northern, Eastern, and Western Navigation ; setting forth in divers necessarie Sea-cards all the Ports . . ., as also the Situation of the Northerly Countries as Island, the Strate Davids, the Isle of Jan Mayen, Bear-Island, Old-Greenland, Spitzbergen, and Nova Zembla . . . ; whereunto is added a brief instruction of the Art of Navigation, &c. *Maps and plates.* Folio *Amsterdam*, 1670

Gopcevic, Spiridion. Makedonien und Alt-Serbien. *Maps and illustrations.* 4° *Vienna*, 1889

Gordon and Gotch. The Australian Handbook (incorporating New Zealand and New Guinea) : Shippers' and Importers' Directory and Business Guides, for 1877, '78, '85, '88, '89, '90, '93. [Annual.] *Maps and plans.* Large 8°

Gordon, Hon. A. H. Wilderness Journeys in New Brunswick, in 1862-63. Small 8° *St John*, 1864

—— *See* Galton, Vacation Tourists.

Gordon, A. R. Report of the Hudson's Bay Expedition under the command of Lieut. A. R. Gordon, R.N., 1884. *Chart.* 8* N.D.

—— Report of the Second Hudson's Bay Expedition under the command of Lieut. A. R. Gordon, R.N., 1885. *Plates and charts.* 8° N.D.

—— Report of the Hudson's Bay Expedition of 1886 under the command of Lieut. A. R. Gordon, R.N. *Charts and illustrations.* 8° N.D.

—— *See* Martin.

Gordon, C. A. Our Trip to Burmah ; with Notes on that Country. *Map, plates, and photographs.* 8° 1876

Gordon, Gen. C. G. Colonel Gordon in Central Africa, 1874-79, with a *portrait*, and *map* of the Country prepared under Colonel Gordon's supervision, from original Letters and Documents. Edited by George Birkbeck Hill. 8° 1881

—— *See* Hake ; Wilson, A. ; *also* W——, C. M.

Gordon, Rev. Daniel M. Mountain and Prairie : a Journey from Victoria to Winnipeg *viâ* Peace River Pass. *Map and illustrations.* Crown 8° 1880

Gordon, Lady Duff. Letters from Egypt, 1863-65. 2nd edition. 8° 1865

—— Last Letters from Egypt, to which are added Letters from the Cape ; with a Memoir by her daughter Mrs Ross. *Plate.* Small 8° 1875

—— *See* Galton, F., Vacation Tourists.

Gordon, Col. E. S. On Fixing Positions by the more Simple Astronomical Observations. For the use of R.A. Officers engaged in Exploration. 8*
Woolwich, 1881

Gordon, Rev. G. N. The last Martyrs of Eromanga : being a Memoir of the Rev. George N. Gordon and Ellen Catherine Powell his Wife. *Plate.* 12°
Halifax, N.S., 1863

Gordon, James. Lunar and Time Tables, adapted to New, Short, and Accurate Methods for Finding the Longitude by Chronometers and Lunar Distances. *Maps.* Royal 8°   1853

Gordon, Lieut. L. C. Miranzai Expeditions, 1891. (From the " Proceedings of the Royal Artillery Institution.") *Map.* 8*   *Woolwich*, 1891

Gordon, Lewis D. B. Report on the Scheme proposed to be carried out under the " Norfolk Estuary Act, 1846." 4*
Glasgow, 1846

—— Report to the Committee of the Bedford Level Corporation, and to the Eau Brink Commissioners on the Norfolk Estuary Scheme. 8*   1849

Gordon, M. F. Report on the Trade of Sonmeeanee, and Seaport of the Province of Lus. [From the India Records, No, 17.] 8°   *Bombay*, 1855

Gordon, Peter. Fragment of the Journal of a Tour through Persia in 1820. 12° 1833
—— *See* Murray, Hugh.

Gordon, Robert. Report on the Irrawaddy River. *Maps.* Folio   *Rangoon*, 1879-80
—— Hydraulic Work in the Irawadi Delta. *Plates.* 8*   1893

Gordon, Col. T. E. Yarkund Mission : Extract from the Journal of the Party of the Kashgar Embassy detached to the Pamir and Wakhan, from 2nd to 19th April 1874. Folio*   1874
—— Yarkund Mission : Report by Lieut.- Col. T. E. Gordon, dated Yarkund, 17th May 1874. Folio*   1874
—— The Roof of the World : being a Narrative of a Journey over the high Plateau of Tibet to the Russian Frontier and the Oxus sources of Pamir. *Maps and plates.* Square 8°   1876
—— Journey to the Pamir. [In Russian.] 8*   *St Petersburg*, 1877

Gordon-Cumming. *See* Cumming.

Gore, Capt. *See* Pelham, Vol. 1 : Appendix 1.

Gore, J. Howard. Geodesy. 12°   1891
—— *See* United States, F, Coast and Geodetic Survey : Appendix 2.

Gore, Montague. *See* Valentini.

Gorges, Sir Arthur. *See* Purchas, Vol. 4, Book 10 : Appendix 1.

Gorgolione, S. Portulano del Mare Mediterraneo. 8°   *Leghorn*, 1815

"Gorgon." *See* Devereux.

Gormáz, F. Vidal. Continuacion de los Trabajos de Esploracion del Rio Valdivia i sus afluentes. *Maps.* 8*
Santiago, 1869
—— Reconocimientos de la costa comprendida entre la rada de los Vilos i el Rio Choapa, i del Rio Valdivia i costa comprendida entre el morro Bonifacio i el Rio Maullin. *Plan.* 8* *Santiago*, 1870
—— Esploracion de la Costa de Llanquihue i Archipiélago de Chiloé. *Plans.* 8°
Santiago, 1871
—— Esploracion del Seno de Reloncaví, Lago de Llanquihue i Rio Puelo. *Plans.* 8°   *Santiago*, 1872
—— Esploracion de las Costas de Colchagua i de Curicó i de la Albufera de Vichuquen. *Map and plans.* 8*   *Santiago*, 1873
—— Instrucciones sobre el litoral de Valdivia, entre Punta Galera i el Rio Tolte. *Map.* 8°   *Santiago*, 1878
—— Jeografia Nautica i Derrotero de las Costas del Peru.   *Santiago*, 1879
—— Noticias del Desierto i sus Recursos. 8*   *Santiago*, 1879
—— Jeografia Nautica de Bolivia. *Map.* 8*   *Santiago*, 1879
—— Noticias sobre las Provincias Litorales correspondientes á los Departamentos de Arequipa, Ica, Huancavelica i Lima, por la Oficina Hidrográfica. *Map.* 8*
Santiago, 1880
—— Algunos Naufragios ocurridos en las Costas Chilenas desde su descubrimiento hasta el año de 1800. 8* *Valparaiso*, 1890

Gorrie, Daniel. Summers and Winters in the Orkneys. *Plate.* 8°   1868

Gorringe, H. H. *See* United States, E, a (Nos. 37, 38, 39, 42, 43, 46, 61) : Appendix 2.

Gosnol, Capt. *See* Gottfried ; Purchas, Vol. 4, Book 8 : Appendix 1.

Gossellin, P. F. J. Géographie des Grecs analysée, ou les Systèmes d'Eratosthenes, de Strabon, et de Ptolémée comparés entre eux et avec nos connoissances modernes. *Maps.* 4°   *Paris*, 1790
—— Recherches sur la Géographie Systématique et Positive des Anciens, pour servir de base à l'Histoire de la Géographie Ancienne. 4 vols. *Maps* 4°
Paris, 1798-1813

Gottberg, E. de. Des Cataractes du Nil, et spécialement de celles de Hannek et de Kaybar. *Maps.* 4*   *Paris*, 1867

Gottfried, Johan Lodewyk. Newe Welt, und Americanische Historien, inhaltende warhasstige und volkommene Beschreibungen aller West-Indianischen Landschafften, Insulen, Königreichen, und Provinzien. Seecusten, fliessenden und stehenden Wassern, &c. (" Historia Antipodum.") *Maps and plates.* Folio
Frankfort, 1631

Gottfried, Johan Lodewyk. De aanmerkenswaardigste en alomberoemde Zee- en Landreizen der Portugeczen, Spanjaarden, Engelsen, en allerhande Natiën : zoo van Fransen, Italiaanen, Deenen, Hoogh- en Neder-Duitsen als van veele andere Volkeren. Voornaamenlyk ondernomen tot Ondekking van de Oost- en West-Indiën, midsgaders andere verafgelegene Gewesten des Aardryks. 8 vols. *Maps and plates.* Folio. *Leyden.* [Title 1727 : 1706 where dated in detail.] For Contents, *see* Appendix 1.

Gottschalck, Friedrich. Almanach der Ritter-Orden. *Plates.* 8° *Leipzig,* 1819

Gottsche, Dr C. Land und Leute in Korea. *Map.* 8* *Berlin,* 1886

Götz, Dr W. Die Verkehrswege im Dienste desWelthandels. Einehistorisch-geographische Untersuchung samt einer Einleitung für eine Wissenschaft von den geographischen Entfernungen. *Maps.* 8° *Stuttgart,* 1888

Gould, Augustus A. Report on the Invertebrata of Massachussetts, published agreeably to an order of the Legislature. 2nd edition, comprising the Mollusca. Edited by W. G. Binney. *Plates.* 8° *Boston,* 1870

Gould, Benjamin Apthorp. Report on the History of the Discovery of Neptune. 8* *Washington,* 1850
—— The Transatlantic Longitude, as Determined by the Coast Survey Expedition of 1866 : a Report to the Superintendent of the U.S. Coast Survey. 4° *Washington,* 1869

Gould, Charles. Report upon the Subject of Gold in the Colony of Van Diemen's Land, referred to in the last Report of the Governor of Tasmania, 1862. *Map.* Folio* 1864
—— An Introduction to the Birds of Australia. 8° 1848

Gould, —, and — Dowie. Instruction for making Gaspé, and Mitis and Rimouski, in the River St Lawrence. 8° 1832

Gouldsbury, V. S. Correspondence relating to the Recent Expedition to the Upper Gambia, under the Administrator V. S. Gouldsbury. *Maps.* Folio* 1881

Gourbillon, —. *See* Phillips [3], Vol. 4 : Appendix 1.

Gourdault. J. La France Pittoresque. *Illustrations.* 4° *Paris,* 1893

Gourdin, H. *See* Rhodes, A. de.

Gourgues, Dominicus. *See* Gottfried ; Hakluyt, Vol. 3 ; Ternaux-Compans, Vol. 20 : Appendix 1.

Gourdon, W. *See* Purchas, Vol. 3, Book 3 : Appendix 1.

Gourraigne, L. G. *See* Bouillet.

Gouy, E. *See* France, B, *b* : Appendix 2.

"Governor Ready," Ship. *See* Wilson, T. B.

Gowan, Lieut.-Col. W. E. The Trans-caspian Railway, its Meaning and its Future. Translated and Condensed from the Russian of I. Y. Vatslik. (From the *J. United Service I. of India,* Vol. 18, No. 75. Simla, 1889.) 4* 1889
—— *See* Kuropatkin, A. N.

Gowen, J. R. Hints on Emigration to the New Settlement on the Swan and Canning Rivers, on the West Coast of Australia. *Map and plate.* 8* 1829

Gowing, Lionel F. Five Thousand Miles in a Sledge, a Mid-Winter Journey across Siberia. *Map and illustrations.* 8° 1889

Goyer, Pierre de. *See* Nieuhoff ; *also* Allgemeine Historie, Vol. 5 : Appendix 1.

Graaf, — de. *See* Burney, Vol. 4 : Appendix 1.

Graaf, N. *See* Allgemeine Historie, Vol. 10 : Appendix 1.

Graah, W. A. Undersögelses-Reise til Ostkysten af Gröndland, efter Kongelig Befaling udfört i Aarene 1828-31. *Plates.* 4° *Copenhagen,* 1832
—— Narrative of an Expedition to the East Coast of Greenland, sent by Order of the King of Denmark, in Search of the Lost Colonies. Translated from the Danish by G. Gordon M'Dougall, for the Royal Geographical Society of London. *Map.* 8° 1867

Graberg da Hemsö, Count J. G. Annali di Geografia e di Statistica. 2 vols. *Maps.* 8°. *Genoa,* 1802
—— Leçons Élémentaires de Cosmographie, de Géographie, et de Statistique. 12° *Genoa,* 1813
—— Scandinavie vengée de l'accusation d'avoir produit les Peuples barbares qui détruisirent l'Empire de Rome. 8° *Lyons,* 1822
—— Notice Biographique, par L. J. E. G. 18* *Florence,* 1831
—— Das Sultanat Mogh'rib-ul-Aksà, oder Kaiserreich Marokko ; in Bezug auf Landes- Volks- und Staats-Kunde beschrieben. 8° *Stuttgart,* 1833
—— Specchio Geografico e Statistico dell' Impero di Marocco. *Plates.* 8° *Genoa,* 1834
—— Degli ultimi Progressi della Geografia. 8* *Milan,* 1839
—— Nota concernenta la Carta Nautica del Genovese Becario, fatta nell' anno 1435. *Map.* 16° *Florence,* N.D.
—— *See* Rafn.

Grabham, Michael C. The Climate and Resources of Madeira as regarding chiefly the necessities of Consumption and the Welfare of Invalids. *Map. and plate.* 8° 1870

Grablovitz, Giulio. Sulle osservazione mareografiche in Italia e specialmente su quelle fatti ad Ischia. 8* *Genoa*, 1893

Graça, Francisco Calheiros da. Mémoire sur l'origine et la cause de l'échauffement des eaux du Gulf Stream. Traduction par Desiré Mouren. Small 8*
Rio de Janeiro, 1875
—— Memoria sobre a Determinação das Linhas Magneticas do Brazil. 8*
Rio de Janeiro, 1882
—— Estudos sobre a Barra de laguna, Março de 1882. 2nd edition. 8*
Rio de Janeiro, 1883

Grad, A. Charles. L'Australie Interieure : Explorations et Voyages à travers le Continent Australien, 1860-62. *Map.* 8° *Paris*, 1864

Grad, C. Résultats Scientifiques des Explorations de l'Océan Glacial à l'Est de Spitzbergen en 1871. *Map.* 8*
Paris, 1873

Graf, Prof. J. H. Die kartographischen Bestrebungen Johann Rudolf Meyers von Aarau, und andere zeitgenossische Versuche einer Vermessung der Schweiz. 8* *Berne*, 1883
—— Einige bernische Pioniere der Alpenkunde aus dem XVI. bis XVIII. Jahrhundert. 8* *Berne*, 1891
—— Notice sur la plus ancienne carte connue du Pays de Neuchâtel. *Map.* 8* *Neuchâtel*, 1892
—— Beiträge zur Topographie und Geographie der Schweiz. 8* *Berne*, 1893
—— Die Karte von Gyger und Haller aus dem Jahre 1620. 8* *Berne*, 1893
—— Die Einführung der Stundenzonenzeit und ihre Bedeutung für Handel, Verkehr und das bürgerliche Leben Schweiz. 8* N.D.
—— *See* Switzerland, A (Bibl. Nat. Suisse) : Appendix 2.

Graham, Alexander, and H. S. Ashbee. Travels in Tunisia ; with a Glossary, a Map, a Bibliography, and fifty illustrations. Large 8° 1887

Graham, C. C. Additional Inscriptions from the Hauran and the Eastern Desert of Syria. Edited, with a Preface and Notes, by John Hogg. 8* 1859

Graham, Major D. C. Statistical Report on the Principality of Kolhapoor ; to which are appended Extracts from brief Notes relative to Kolhapoor and its independent Jageerdars, by Major G. Malcolm ; together with copies of the Treaties, &c., entered into between the Hon. East India Company and the Kolhapoor State, between 1766 and 1829. Edited by R. Hughes Thomas. *Maps, plates, facsimiles, and tables.* [From the India Records, No. 8.] 8°
Bombay, 1854

Graham, Major D. C. Historical Sketch of the Bheel Tribes inhabiting the Province of Khandesh ; accompanied by an Outline down to 1843, with continuation from 1843 to 1855, by Capt. J. Rose. Compiled and edited by R. H. Thomas. *Map.* [From the India Records, No. 26.] 8° *Bombay*, 1856
—— Glimpses of Abyssinia ; or, Extracts from Letters written while on a Mission from the Government of India to the King of Abyssinia in the years 1841, 1842, and 1843. Edited by his sister Anna, Lady Erskine. 12° 1867

Graham, Lieut.-Col. J. D. Observations of the Magnetic Dip, at several positions, chiefly on the South-Western, the North-Eastern, and Northern Frontiers of the United States, and of the Magnetic Declination at two positions on the River Sabine, made in 1840, 1842-45. 4* *Philadelphia*, 1846
—— Report on the Harbours of Lake Michigan. 8° *Washington*, 1857
—— Report on the Harbours, &c., in Wisconsin, Illinois, Indiana, and Michigan. 8° *Washington*, 1857
—— A Lunar Tidal Wave in Lake Michigan Demonstrated. *Plates.* 8* *Philadelphia*, 1860
—— Report on the Improvement of the Harbours of Lakes Michigan, St Clair, Erie, Ontario, and Champlain, 1860. 8° *Washington*, 1860
—— Reports in Relation to the Intersection of the Boundary Lines of the States of Maryland, Pennsylvania, and Delaware, being a portion of Mason and Dixon's Line. *Map.* 8° *Washington*, 1860
—— *See* Peirce, B.

Graham, Maria. Journal of a Voyage to Brazil, and Residence there, during part of the years 1821, '22, '23. *Plates.* 4° 1824
—— Journal of a Residence in Chile during 1822, and a Voyage from Chile to Brazil in 1823. *Plates.* 4° 1824

Graham, Lieut. S. L. *See* United States, E, *a* (No. 86) : Appendix 2.

Graham, William. The Jordan and the Rhine, or the East and the West : being the Result of Five Years Residence in Syria, and Five Years Residence in Germany. 8° 1854

Graham, William. *See* Phillips [3], Vol. 3 : Appendix 1.

Graham, W. W. Up the Himalayas : Mountaineering on the Indian Alps. [Three Papers from *Good Words.*] *Illustrations.* 8* N.D.

Gramaye, J. B. Republica Namurcensis Hannoniæ et Lutsenburgensis. 18°
Amsterdam, 1634
—— *See* Purchas, Vol. 2 : Appendix 1.

Grambcheffsky, Colonel. *See* Grom-chefsky.

Grammont, Lucien de. Onze Mois de Sous-Préfecture en Basse-Cochinchine, contenant en outre une Notice sur la langue Cochinchinoise, des Phrases usuelles Françaises-Annamites,&c. *Map.* 8° *Napoléon-Vendée,* 1863

Grand, Émile. Défense et Occupation de la Colonie d'Alger. *Map.* 8° *Toulon,* 1837

Grandidier, Alfred. Histoire Physique, Naturelle, et Politique de Madagascar. Vol. 1—Géographie Physique et Astronomique. *Atlas.* 1ʳᵉ partie. 8ᵉ fascicule. 4° *Paris,* 1878
—— Histoire de la Géographie de Madagascar. (Deuxième tirage, revu et augmenté en 1892.) *Map.* 4° *Paris,* 1885

Granel, Joaquin. Discursos pronunciados en el Senado Argentino en la discussion del Proyecto para fijar la Capital de la Nacion. 8* *Buenos Ayres,* 1867

Granger, —. A Journey through Egypt. Translated by J. R. Forster. 8° 1773

Granmont, —. *See* Burney, Vol. 4 : Appendix 1.

Grant, Charles, Viscount de Vaux. The History of Mauritius, or the Isle of France, and the Neighbouring Islands, from their First Discovery to the Present Time, composed principally from the Papers and Memoirs of Baron Grant, &c. *Maps.* 4° 1801

Grant, C. The Gazetteer of the Central Provinces of India. 2nd edition. *Map.* 8° *Nagpur,* 1870

Grant, C. Mitchell. The Gold Mines of Oriental Siberia. 8* [1870]

Grant, Charles Scovell. West African Hygiene, or Hints on the Preservation of Health and the Treatment of Tropical Diseases, more especially on the West Coast of Africa. 2nd edition. 12° 1884

Grant, Lieut.-Col. C. W. Indian Irrigation : being a short Description of the System of Artificial Irrigation and Canal Navigation in India. 8* 1854
—— *See* India, C, Geological Papers : Appendix 2.

Grant, J. *See* Eyriès, Vol. 4 : Appendix 1.

Grant, Col. James Augustus. A Walk across Africa, or Domestic Scenes from my Nile Journal. 8° 1864
—— An African Explorer : the late Colonel J. A. Grant, C.B. (From *Blackwood's Magazine,* April 1892.) 8* 1892
—— *See* Nicholls, K. ; Nardi ; Speke ; Swayne.

Grant, Robert. *See* Johnston, A. K.

Granville, A. B. St Petersburg : Travels to and from that Capital, through Flanders, &c. 2 vols. *Maps and plates.* 8° 1828

Gras, A. le. Manuel de la Navigation dans la Mer Adriatique, d'après Marieni, Beautemps-Beaupré,&c., et les documents les plus recents. *Map and plates.* 8° *Paris,* 1855
—— Sailing Directions for the Dardanelles, the Sea of Marmora, and the Bosphorus. 8° 1855
—— Routier de l'Australie : Instructions pour Naviguer, sur la Côte Sud et Est, détroit de Torrès et Mer de Corail. Traduit et annoté d'après les travaux hydrographiques les plus récents. 2 vols. *Map.* 8° *Paris,* 1855-61
—— Phares des Mers du Globe, d'après les Documents Français et Étrangers. 8° *Paris,* 1856
—— Supplément au Livre des Phares. État général des Phares allumés ou modifiés depuis la Publication du Livre des Phares. Corrigé 1857. 8° *Paris,* 1857
—— Renseignements Hydrographiques sur les Iles Formose et Lou-Tchou, la Corée, la Mer du Japon, les Iles du Japon (Ports d'Hakodadi, Nangasaki, Simoda et Yedo), et la Mer d'Okhotsk. 8° *Paris,* 1859
—— Phares de la Mer du Nord (Belgique, Holland, Hanovre, Danemark, Norvége), la Mer Baltique (Prusse, Russie, Suède), et la Mer Blanche. Corrigés 1859, '61, '62, '64, '69. 8° *Paris,* 1859-69
—— Routier de la Baie de Fundy et de la Nouvelle-Écosse. *Paris,* 1861
—— Phares des Côtes des Iles Britanniques. Corrigés 1861, '62, '63. 8° *Paris,* 1861-63
—— Phares des Côtes Orientales de l'Amérique du Sud. 1861-64. 8° *Paris,* 1861-64
—— Phares des Côtes Occidentales d'Afrique et des îles éparses de l'Océan Atlantique. Corrigés 1862-63. *Paris,* 1862-63
—— Phares de la Mer des Antilles et du Golfe du Mexique. Corrigés 1862-69. 8° *Paris,* 1862-69
—— Phares des Mers des Indes et de Chine, de l'Australie, Terre de Van-Diémen, et Nouvelle-Zélande. Corrigés 1862-63. 8° *Paris,* 1862-63
—— Phares de la Mer Méditerranée, de la Mer Noire, et de la Mer d'Azof (Espagne, France, Italie, États de l'Église, Autriche, Grèce, Turquie, et Russie). Corrigés 1862-63. 8° *Paris,* 1862-63
—— Phares des Côtes Nord et Ouest de France, et des Côtes Ouest d'Espagne et de Portugal. Corrigés 1862-69. 8° *Paris,* 1862-69
—— Phares des Côtes Orientales de l'Amérique Anglaise et des États-Unis, 1862-64. 8° *Paris,* 1862-64
—— Routier de la Côte Sud et Sud-est d'Afrique. De l'Ile Robben à Natal. 8° *Paris,* 1863

Gras, A. le. Instructions Nautiques sur la Mer Baltique et le Golfe de Finlande. 2me édition. Tom. I. *Plates.* 8°
Paris, 1864
—— Routier des Côtes N.O., Ouest, et Sud d'Espagne. *Plates.* 8° *Paris*, 1869
—— Considérations générales sur la Mer Méditerranée. Résumé des Vents, Courants, et Routes de cette Mer. Choix d'Extraits de documents nautiques empruntés a différents auteurs. 8°
Paris, 1866
—— Description des Côtes du Royaume de Portugal, &c. *Maps.* 8° *Paris*, 1869
—— *See* Spratt, J. A. B. ; *also* France, B, *b* : Appendix 2.

Grassi, Guido. *See* Issel.

Graty, Colonel Alfred M. du. Mémoire sur les Productions Minérales de la Confédération Argentine. 8° *Paris*, 1855
—— La République du Paraguay. *Maps and plates.* 8° *Brussels*, 1862

Gravier, G. Créations d'Observatoires Circumpolaires. 8* *Paris*, 1877
—— Les Normands sur la Route des Indes. Square 8* *Rouen*, 1880
—— Étude sur une Carte inconnue, la première dressée par Louis Joliet en 1674. 8* *Paris*, 1880
—— *See* Soleillet.

Gray, A. The Maldive Islands ; with a Vocabulary taken from François Pyrard de Laval, 1602-7. 8* 1878

Gray, David. Report on New Whaling Grounds in the Southern Seas. 8*
Peterhead, 1891

Gray, G. R. List of the Specimens of Birds in the Collection of the British Museum. Part 5, Gallinæ. 12° 1867
—— *See* "Erebus."

Gray, John Edward. List of the Specimens of Lepidopterous Insects in the Collection of the British Museum. 12°
1844
—— Catalogue of Shield Reptiles in the Collection of the British Museum. Part 1. Testudinata (Tortoises). *Plates.* 4° 1855
—— Synopsis of the Species of Starfish in the British Museum. *Plates.* 4° 1866
—— *See* "Erebus."

Gray, J. Errol. Diary of a Journey to the Bor Khamti country, and sources of the Irrawaddy, made by Mr J. Errol Gray, season 1892-93, from Assam. Folio*
1893

Gray, Robert. The Birds of the West of Scotland. Published for the Brit. Asso. Meeting, 1876. 12° *Glasgow*, 1876

Gray, Roderick. Tongariro, the Sacred Mountain of the Maori. 12* [1892?]

Gray, T. *See* Spence.

Gray, Major W., and Surgeon Dochard. Travels in Western Africa in 1818-21, from the River Gambia, through Woolli, Bondoo, Galam, &c., to the River Niger. *Maps and plates.* 8° 1829

Gray, Mrs. Fourteen Months in Canton. Small 8° 1880

Grazilhier, J. *See* Astley, Vol. 3 ; Allgemeine Historie (J. Barbot), Vol. 4 : Appendix 1.

Greathed, W. H. Report on the Communication between Calcutta and Dacca. [From the India Records, No. 19.] 8°
Calcutta, 1856

Greaves, John. *See* Churchill, Vol. 2 ; Ray ; Thevenot, Vol. 1 : Appendix 1.

Greely, General Adolphus W. Three Years of Arctic Service : an Account of the Lady Franklin Bay Expedition of 1881-84, and the attainment of the Farthest North. 2 vols. *Portrait, maps, and illustrations.* Large 8° 1886
—— International Polar Expedition. Report on the Proceedings of the United States Expedition to Lady Franklin Bay, Grinnell Land. 2 vols. *Maps and illustrations.* 4° *Washington*, 1888
—— Will Dr Nansen succeed ? (From *The Forum*, August 1891.) 8* 1891
—— *See* United States, H, *b* : Appendix 2.

Greely Relief Expedition. Report of Board of Officers to consider an Expedition for the Relief of Lieut. Greely and Party. 8° *Washington*, 1884

Green, A. H. On the Natural History and Hunting of the Beaver on the Pacific Slope of the Rocky Mountains. With Notes by R. Brown. 8* 1870

—— **R. Russell, J. R. Dakyns, J. C. Ward, C. Fox Strangways, W. H. Dalton, and T. V. Holmes.** The Geology of the Yorkshire Coalfield. [Mem. Geol. Survey, England and Wales.] *Frontispiece and plans.* 8° 1878

Green, A. O. A Practical Arabic Grammar. Part 1. 2nd edition. 12° *Oxford*, 1887

Green, B. R. Numismatic Atlas of Ancient History, containing a Selection of 360 Grecian Coins of Kings, disposed in Chronological Order, from the Earliest Period to the Beginning of the Fourth Century ; from the Works of Havercamp, Pellerin, Duane, Visconti, Combe, Mionnet, &c. 21 *Plates.* Folio 1829

Green, Commander F. M. An Account of the Progress in Geography in the year 1884. 8* *Washington*, 1885
—— *See* United States, E, *a* (Nos. 63 and 65) : Appendix 2.

Green, Major H. W. R. Report on the Affairs of Khelat, from 1857 to 1860. *Map.* [From the India Records, No. 34.] 8° *Calcutta*, 1861

N

Grey, Sir George. Journals of Two Expeditions of Discovery in North West and Western Australia during 1837-39, describing many newly discovered, important, and fertile Districts, with Observations on the Moral and Physical Condition of the Aboriginal Inhabitants, &c. 2 vols. *Maps and plates.* 8° 1841
—— Poems, Traditions, and Chaunts of the Maories. [In the Maori Language.] 8° *Wellington*, 1853
—— Polynesian Mythology, and Ancient Traditional History of the New Zealand Race, as furnished by their Priests and Chiefs. *Plates.* 8° 1855

Grey, H. The Classics for the Million : being an Epitome, in English, of the Works of the principal Greek and Latin Authors. 2nd edition. 12° 1881

Griado, Matias Alonso. La República del Paraguay. *Map.* Large 8° *Asuncion*, 1888

Gribble, J. D. B. A Manual of the District of Cuddapah in the Presidency of Madras. *Maps, and map in cover.* 8° *Madras*, 1875

Grieben, A. H. Uruguay ; ist dieses Land für Wollproduction und Stammschäferein für deutsche Rechnung, und deutschen Auswanderern zu empfehlen ? 8* *Berlin*, 1864
—— Uruguay ; Viehzucht und Ackerbau auf den Estancien, wie sie betrieben werden, und wie sie betrieben werden können. 8* *Berlin*, 1864

Grieben, Theobald. Zuverlässiger Wegweiser im Harz und dessen Umgegend. *Map.* 12° *Berlin*, 1857
—— Grieben's Reise-Bibliothek. No. 38. Die Böhmischen Kurorte Franzensbad, Marienbad, Carlsbad, Teplitz. Mit Berücksichtigung von Eger und Elster . . . Zweite Auflage. *Maps and cuts.* 16° *Berlin*, 1861

Grieg, James A. *See* Norway, A : Appendix 2.

Grierson, George A. An Introduction to the Maithill Language of North Bihár, containing a Grammar, Chrestomathy, and Vocabulary. Part 1. Grammar ; Part 2. Chrestomathy and Vocabulary. [Extra Numbers to Journal of the Asiatic Society, Bengal: Part 1 for 1880, and Part 1 for 1882.] 8° *Calcutta*, 1881-82
—— The Modern Vernacular Literature of Hindustan. [Special Number of Journal of Asiatic Society of Bengal : Part 1 for 1888.] *Plates.* 8° *Calcutta*, 1889

Grierson, Capt. J. M. *See* United Kingdom, G, War Office Publications : Appendix 2.

Griesbach, Carl Ludolf. Die Erdbeben in den Jahren 1867 und 1868. 8* *Vienna*, 1869

Griesbach, Carl Ludolf. On the Geology of Natal in South Africa. *Map and plate.* 8* 1871

Grieve, James. *See* Krasheninnikov, S. P.

Griffin, Appleton P. C. Discovery of the Mississippi : Bibliographical Account. Part 2. Secondary Authorities. *Map.* 8° [*New York*, 1883]

Griffin, G. W. New South Wales, her Commerce and Resources. 8° *Sydney*, 1888

Griffin, James. A Plain and Popular System of Practical Navigation and Nautical Astronomy, comprising Methods for Ascertaining the Latitude by Meridian, Single and Double Altitudes, the Longitude by Chronometer and Lunar Observations, and the Variation of the Compass by Amplitudes and Azimuths ; including a Journey from London to Madeira, a Set of requisite Tables, and an Appendix. Revised and considerably enlarged by W. Turnbull. *Map and plates.* 8° 1854

Griffin, James. Flags, National and Mercantile. *Plates.* 8° *Portsmouth*, 1883

Griffin, L. H. The Rajas of the Punjab : being the History of the Principal States in the Punjab and their Political Relations with the British Government. Large 8° *Lahore*, 1870
—— The Punjab Chiefs : Historical and Biographical Notices of the Principal Families in the Territories under the Punjab Government. Large 8° *Lahore*, 1865
—— The Burman and his Creed. (From *The Fortnightly Review.*) 8* 1890

Griffini, D. M. Della Vita di Monsignor Gio. Maria Percoto . . . . Missionario ne' Regni di Ava e di Pegu. *Plate.* 4° *Udine*, 1781

Griffis, W. E. The Mikado's Empire. *Map and plates.* 8° *New York*, 1876
—— Corea, the Hermit Nation. *Map and illustrations.* 8° 1882

Griffith, —. *See* Pemberton.

Griffith, C. Darby. Speech on the subject of the Euphrates Railway and the Suez Canal, 15th August 1857. 8* 1857

Griffith, Richard. Geological and Mining Survey of the Connaught Coal District in Ireland. *Maps.* 8° *Dublin*, 1818

Griffith, William. Journals of Travels in Assam, Burma, Bootan, Affghanistan, and the neighbouring Countries. . . . Arranged by John M'Clelland. *Plates.* 8° *Calcutta*, 1847
—— *See* India, I : Appendix 2.

Griffiths, Hon. Mrs Emily W. *See* Fiennes.

Griffiths, J. Travels in Europe, Asia Minor, and Arabia. *Map and plates.* 4° 1805

Grigorief, V. V. Geography of Central Asia : Kabul and Kafiristan. [In Russian.] *Map and plates.* 8° *St Petersburg*, 1867
—— The Bamian Route to Cabulistan from the Valley of the Oxus. Translated by R. Michell. Folio * 1878
—— *See* Ritter, Carl.

Grijalva, H. de. *See* Burney, Vol. 1 : Appendix 1.

Grijalva, Juan de. *See* Gottfried ; Allgemeine Historie, Vol. 13 : Appendix 1.

Grimes, J. Stanley. Geonomy : Creation of the Continents by the Ocean Currents. An advanced system of Physical Geology and Geography. 12° *Philadelphia*, 1885

Grimoult, —. Renseignements Nautiques sur la Nouvelle Calédonie et les Isles Loyalty. 8° *Paris*, 1859

Grimston, Edward. *See* Acosta ; *also* Hakluyt Soc. Publ., Vol. 60 : Appendix 1.

Grindlay, Capt. Melville. View of the Present State of the Question as to Steam-Communication with India, with an Appendix. *Map.* 8* 1837

Grinfield, Edward William. The Christian Cosmos : The Son of God the Revealed Creator. 12° 1857

Grisebach, A. La Végétation du Globe, d'après sa Disposition suivant les Climats. Esquisse d'une Géographie Comparée des Plantes. Ouvrage traduit de l'Allemand, avec l'autorisation et le concours de l'Auteur, par P. de Tchihatchef, avec des Annotations du traducteur. 2 vols. *Map.* 8° *Paris*, 1875-78

Grissinger, Dr Karl. Untersuchungen über die Tiefen- und Temperatur-Verhältnisse des Weissensees in Kärnten. *Map and diagram.* 4* [*Gotha*] 1892
—— Studien zur physische Geographie der Tatra-Gruppe. 8* *Vienna*, 1893
—— Artaria's Orts-Lexikon der Oesterreichisch-Ungarischen Monarchie (incl. Occupationsgebiet, 1885) nach der Zählung von 1890, enthaltend alle Orte mit mehr als 2,000 Einwohnern. 12* *Vienna*, 1893
—— Die Schneegrenze in der "Hohen Tatra." 8* *Vienna*, N.D.

Grodekoff, Col. N. The Kirghiz and Karakirghiz of the Syr-Daria Territory. Vol. 1. Juridical Customs. [In Russian.] Large 8° *Tashkent*, 1889
—— *See* Marvin.

Groeneveldt, W. P. Notes on the Malay Archipelago and Malacca. Compiled from Chinese Sources. *Map.* 8° *Batavia*, 1877
—— **and Dr J. L. A Brandes.** Catalogus der Archeologische Verzameling van het Bataviaasch Genootschap van Kunsten en Wetenschappen. Mit Aanteekeningen omtrent de op verschillende

Groeneveldt and Brandes—*continued.*
Voorwerpen voorkomende Inscripties en een voorloopigen Inventaris der beschreven Steenen. 8* *Batavia*, 1887

Grogniet, François. *See* Burney, Vol. 4 : Appendix 1.

Gromchefsky (or Grambchefsky), Capt. Report of his Journey in 1889-90. Translated by Capt. E. F. H. M'Swiney. (From the Journal of the U.S. Institution of India, Vol. 21, No. 89.) *Map.* 8* *Simla*, 1892
—— *See* Steveni.

Gröndal, B. Clavis Poetica Antiquæ Linguæ Septentrionalis, e Lexico Sveinbjörnis Egilssonii Collecta. 8° *Copenhagen*, 1864

Groome, Francis H. *See* United Kingdom, K, Scotland : Appendix 2.

Grooss, A. Geologische Specialkarte des Grossherzogthums Hessen. Section Mainz. 8* *Darmstadt*, 1867

Groot, C. de. Herinneringen aan't Blitong, Historisch, Lithologisch, Mineralogisch, Geographisch, Geologisch en Mignborwkundig. *Plates.* 8° *The Hague*, 1887

Groot, Dr J. J. M. de. Het Kongsiwezen van Borneo. Eine Verhandelung over den Grondslag en den Aard der Chineesche politicke vereenigingen in de Koloniën, mit eene Chineesche Geschiedenis van de Kongsi Lanfong. *Maps.* 8° *The Hague*, 1885

Gros, H. F. Les Boers et l'Ouverture de l'Afrique. 8* *Geneva*, 1884

Grose. *See* Grosse.

Groser, Albert. South African Experiences in Cape Colony, Natal, and Pondoland. *Portrait, maps, and illustrations.* 8* 1891

Grosier, Abbé. A General Description of China, containing the Topography of the Fifteen Provinces. which compose this vast Empire, that of Tartary, the Isles, and other tributary Countries, &c. 2 vols. *Maps and plates.* 8° 1788

Groskurd, C. G. *See* Strabo ; Thunberg.

Grosley, —. *See* "The Modern Traveller," Vol. 4, on p. 610 : Appendix 1.

Gross, Anton Johann. Handbuch für Reisende durch die Oesterreichische Monarchie, mit besonderer Rücksicht auf die Südlichen und Gebirgsländer, nämlich Oesterreich, Salzburg, Steiermark, Illirien, Tirol, das Lombardisch-Venetianische Königreiche und Dalmatien. *Plate.* 8° *Munich*, 1834

Grosse, —. *See* New Collection, Vol. 2, p. 608 ; "The World Displayed," Vol. 9, p. 609 : Appendix 1.

Grossi, Vincenzo. Relazione Sommaria del VI. Congresso Internazionale degli Americanisti. [Torino, Settembre 1886.] 8* *Rome*, 1886

Grossman, Dr Karl. Observations on the Glaciation of Iceland. (From the *Glacialist's Magazine.*) *Map and plate.* 8*   1893

"Grosvenor," Indiaman. *See* Dalrymple, Tracts, Vol. 2 : Appendix 1.

Groth, Dr Paul. Ueber die Molekularbeschaffenheit der Krystalle. Festrede gehalten in der öffentlichen Sitzung der k. b. Akademie der Wissenschaften zu München zur Feier des 129 Stiftungstages, am 28 März 1888. 4*   *Munich*, 1888

Grotius, Hugo. Hugonis Grotii de Antiquitate Republicæ Batavicæ liber singularis. [*Title-page wanting.*] 8°
                          [*The Hague*, 1610]
—— De Rebus Belgicis, or the Annals and History of the Low Countrey Warrs. 8°
                                              1665

Grouner, —. Histoire Naturelle des Glacières de Suisse. [Translated by De Kéralio.] *Maps and plates.* 4°
                                  Paris, 1770

Grout, Rev. Lewis. Zulu-land, or Life among the Zulu-Kafirs of Natal and Zulu-land, South Africa. *Map and plates.* 8°   *Philadelphia* [1864]
—— The Isizulu : a revised edition of a Grammar of the Zulu Language, with an Introduction and an Appendix. 8° 1893

Grova, Manuel de. Epitome de la Relacion del Viaje de algunos Mercaderes de Sa. Malo á Moka ó Mocca en Arabia en el Mar Bermejo, los años de 1708 y dos siguéentes ; puesto en Español de Francés. Folio   N.P., N.D.

Grove, F. C. "The Frosty Caucasus": an Account of a Walk through part of the Range and an Ascent of Elbruz in the Summer of 1874. *Plates.* Small 8° 1875

Grove, Sir George. Geography (Green's History Primer Series). 12°   1877
—— *See* Galton.

Grove, Sir W. R. On the Correlation of Physical Forces. 8°   1846
—— On certain Phenomena of Voltaic Ignition and the Decomposition of Water into its Constitutent Gases by Heat. *Plate.* 4*   1847

Grover, Rev. H. M. Changes of the Poles and the Equator considered as a Source of Error in the Present Construction of the Maps and Charts of the Globe. *Plate.* 8*   1848

Grover, Capt. J. An Appeal to the British Nation in behalf of Col. Stoddart and Capt. Conolly, now in Captivity in Bokhara. 8*   1843
—— Bokhara Victims. 8°   1845
—— Lord Aberdeen and the Ameer of Bokhara. In Reply to the *Edinburgh Review.* 8*   1845

Growse, F. S. A Supplement to the Fatehpur Gazetteer. 8° *Allahabad*, 1887

Grubb, J. H., and Capt. T. Remon. Report on the Island of Kenn, in the Persian Gulf. *Map.* [From the India Records, No. 24.] 8°   *Bombay*, 1856

Grube, Dr W. *See* Schrenck.

Gruber, C. *See* Germany, C (Forschungen, &c., Vol. 1) : Appendix 2.

Grueber, Père —. *See* Thevenot, Vol. 4 ; Allgemeine Historie, Vol. 7 : Appendix 1.

Grunow, A. *See* "Novara."

Gryalva, Jean de. *See* Grijalva.

Guagnino, Alessandro. *See* Ramusio, Vol. 2 : Appendix 1.

Gualle (or Gali), F. *See* Burney, Vol. 2, 5 ; Callander, Vol. 1 ; Hakluyt, Vol. 3 : Appendix 1.

Guarmani, Carlo. Il Neged Settentrionale. Itinerario da Gerusalemme a Aneizeh nel Cassim. *Map.* 8°
                              Jerusalem, 1866

Gubbins, C. Report on the Settlement of Pergunnah Kurnaul. *Plates.* [From the India Records, Vol. 1, N.W. Provinces, 1855-64]   *Agra*, 1855

Gubbins, J. H. A Dictionary of Chinese-Japanese Words in the Japanese Language. [In 3 parts.] 12°   1889

Gubbio, Busone da. Fortunatus Siculus ossir L'Avventuroso Ciciliano. Romanzo storico scritto nel M.CCC.XI., pubblicato da G. F. Nott. 8°   *Florence*, 1832

Gubernatis, Angelo de. Storia dei Viaggiatori Italiani nelle Indie Orientali. 12°   *Leghorn*, 1875

Gubernatis, Enrico de. Lettere sulla Tunisia e specialmente sulle province di Susa e Monastir, con aggiunta di due lettere Archeologiche di Orazio Antinori. *Map and plates.* 16°   *Florence*, 1867

Gudbrandus Thorlacius (Bishop of Holen). *See* Hakluyt, Vol. 1 : Appendix 1.

Guedes, O. L'Industrie minière au Portugal. Renseignements Statistiques. 8°   *Lisbon*, 1878

Gueluy, —. Description de la Chine Occidentale (Mœurs et Histoire). Par un Voyageur. Traduit du Chinois par M. Gueluy, Missionnaire. *Maps.* 8°
                              Louvain, 1887

Guérasimov, D. *See* Pierling.

Guérin, J. Mésures Barométriques, suivies de quelques Observations d'Histoire Naturelle et de Physique, faites dans les Alpes Françaises, et d'un Précis de la Météorologie d'Avignon. 24°
                                  Avignon, 1829

Guérin, M. Vocabulaire du dialecte Tayal ou Aborigène de l'Ile Formose. 8* 1869

Guérin, V. Description de l'Ile de Patmos et de l'Ile de Samos. *Maps.* 8°
                                    Paris, 1856

Guérin, V. Description Géographique, Historique, et Archéologique de la Palestine, accompagnée de Cartes détaillées. Judée. Vols. 1-3. *Map.* Large 8°
Paris, 1868-69
—— The same. 2ᵐᵉ partie. Samarie. Vols. 1 and 2. *Plates.* Large 8°
Paris, 1874-75
—— The same. 3ᵐᵉ partie. Galilée. Vols. 1 and 2. *Map.* Large 8°
Paris, 1880

Guérin-Menneville, —. *See* Abyssinia (Voyage en Abyssinic, 1839-43, Part 4) : Appendix 2.

Guerra, J. Alvarez. Viajes por Filipinas. De Manila á Albay (Primera edición) ; De Manila á Marianas (Segunda edición) ; De Manila á Tayabas (Segunda edición). 3 vols. 12° *Madrid,* 1887

Guéry, P. *See* Norie.

Guest, Montague J. The Tunisian Question and Bizerta. *Maps and illustrations.* 8° 1881

Guettard and Monnet. Atlas et Description Minéralogique de la France. Part 1. 4° *Paris,* 1780
—— Atlas of Maps, &c. 4° *Paris* [1766-79]

Guevara, Father. The History of Paraguay, the Rio de la Plata, and Tucuman. [An abridged translation from the inedited MS.] MS. Folio N.D.

Guglielmini, Domenico. Della Natura de' Fiumi : Trattato Fisico-Matematico ; con le Annotazioni di Eustachio Manfredi. 2 vols. *Portrait and plates.* 8°
Milan, 1821

Guicciardini, Lodovico. Descrittione di tutti i Paesi Bassi, altrimenti detti Germania Inferiore. *Maps.* Folio
Antwerp, 1567

Guichenot, —. *See* Abyssinia (Voyage en Abyssinie, 1839-43, Part 4) : Appendix 2.

Guierra, C. *See* Gottfried ; General Collection of Voyages, p. 610 : Appendix 1.

Guignes, Joseph de. Histoire Générale des Huns, des Turcs, des Mogols, et des autres Tartares Occidentaux, &c. ; avant et depuis Jesus-Christ jusqu'à présent ; précédée d'une Introduction contenant des Tables Chronol. et Historiques des Princes qui ont regné dans l'Asie. 4 vols. in 5. 4° *Paris,* 1756-58
—— *See* Pinkerton, Vol. 11 : Appendix 1.

Guigniaut, J. D. De l'Étude de la Géographie en Général et Historique en Particulier. 8* *Paris,* 1836

Guilbert, Abbé. Description Historique des Chateau, Bourg, et Forêts de Fontainebleau. 2 vols. Small 8° *Paris,* 1731

Guillain, —. Documents sur l'Histoire, la Géographie, et le Commerce de la partie occidentale de Madagascar. *Map.* 8°
Paris, 1845

Guillain, —. Documents sur l'Histoire, la Géographie, et le Commerce l'Afrique Orientale. Exposé Critique des diverses notions acquises sur l'Afrique Orientale depuis les temps les plus reculés jusqu' à nos jours. Relation du Voyage d'Exploration a la Cote Orientale d'Afrique, exécuté pendant les années 1846, 1847, et 1848, par le brick "Le Ducouèdic." 3 vols. 8°, and Atlas folio *Paris,* N.D.

Guillaume, H. The Amazon Provinces of Peru as a Field for European Emigration : a Statistical and Geographical Review of the Country and its Resources, including the Gold and Silver Mines ; together with a mass of Useful and Valuable Information. *Map and illustrations.* Crown 8° 1888

Guillemard, Dr F. H. H. The Cruise of the "Marchesa" to Kamschatka and New Guinea, with Notices of Formosa, Liu-Kiu, and various Islands of the Malay Archipelago. 2 vols. *Maps and illustrations.* 8° 1886
—— The Life of Ferdinand Magellan, and the first Circumnavigation of the Globe, 1480-1521. *Portrait, maps, and illustrations.* Crown 8° 1890

Guillemine, C. Notice sur M. de Compiègne. 8* *Cairo,* 1877

Guimet, Émile. Promenades Japonaises. Dessins d'après nature par Félix Régamey. 2 vols. *Illustrations.* 4° *Paris,* 1878-80

Guiral, Léon. Le Congo Français du Gabon à Brazzaville. *Map and illustrations.* 12° *Paris,* 1889

Gulbenkian, Calouste S. La Transcaucasie et la Péninsule d'Apchéron : Souvenirs de Voyage. *Maps.* 12° *Paris,* 1891
—— La Péninsule d'Apchéron et le Pétrole Russe. (From *Revue des Deux Mondes,* 15 May 1891.) 8* *Paris,* 1891

Guldberg, C. M., and H. Mohn. Études sur les Mouvements de l'Atmosphère. Première partie. *Plates.* 4°
Christiania, 1876
—— The same. Deuxième Partie. *Plates.* 4° *Christiania,* 1880

Gumælius, O. *See* Sweden, A : Appendix 2.

Gümbel, C. W. Geognostische Beschreibung des Ost-bayerischen Grenzgebirges, oder des Bayerischen und Oberpfälzer Waldgebirges. *Map and plates.* 8° *Gotha,* 1868
—— Vorläufige Mittheilungen über Tiefseeschlamm. 8* N.P., 1870
—— Die geognostische Durchforschung Bayerns. 4* *Munich,* 1877
—— *See* Switzerland, B : Appendix 2.

Gumpach, Johannes von. Letter to Norton Shaw, Esq., M.D., on the Subject of the True Figure and Dimensions of the Earth. 8*
Privately printed, Guernsey, 1862

Gumpach, Johannes von. The True Figure and Dimensions of the Earth, newly determined from the Results of Geodetic Measurements and Pendulum Observations. . . . In a Letter to G. B. Airy, Astronomer Royal. *Diagrams.* 8° 1862

Gumprecht, Otto. Der mittlere Isonzo und sein Verhältniss zum Natisone. Ein Beitrag zur Lösung der Frage nach dem Alter des Isonzosystems. *Map and profile.* 8* *Leipzig,* 1886

Gumprecht, T. E. Barth und Overwegs Untersuchungsreise nach dem Tschadsee und in das Innere Africa. *Maps.* Royal 8° *Berlin,* 1852
—— *See* Stein and Hörschelmann.

Gunion, R. H. *See* India, B : Appendix 2.

Gunnlaug, Björn, junior. De Mensura et delineatione Islandiæ interioris, cura Societatis Litterariæ Islandicæ his temporibus facienda. 12* *Bessastadä,* 1834

Günther, A. *See* "Erebus ;" *also* United Kingdom, II, "Challenger" : Appendix 2.

Günther, Dr Siegmund. Lehrbuch der Geophysik und Physikalischen Geographie. 2 vols. in 1. 8° *Stuttgart,* 1884-85
—— Handbuch der Mathematischen Geographie (Bibliothek Geographischer Handbücher herausgegeben von Prof. Dr Friedrich Ratzel.) *Illustrations.* 8° *Stuttgart,* 1890
—— Johannes Kepler und der tellurisch-kosmische Magnetismus. (Penck's Geogr. Abhandlungen. Band 3, Heft 2.) *Figures.* Large 8* *Vienna,* 1888
—— Lehrbuch der physikalischen Geographie. *Plates, &c.* 8° *Stuttgart,* 1891
—— Luftdruckschwankungen in ihrem Einflusse auf die festen und flüssigen Bestandtheile der Erdoberfläche. *Diagrams.* 8° 1894

Guppy, H. B. The Solomon Islands and their Natives. *Map and illustrations.* Large 8° 1887
—— The Solomon Islands, their Geology, General Features, and Suitability for Colonization. *Maps.* Large 8° 1887

Gurley, R. R. Address on African Colonization. 8* *Philadelphia,* 1839
—— Report to the Secretary of State of the United States of Information in respect to Liberia. *Map and plates.* 8* *Washington,* 1850

Gurney, Anna. Extracts from the Kongsskugg-sio, or Speculum Regale. Translated by Anne Gurney. 8* [*Norwich*] N.D.

Gurney, Henry, and C. H. Allen. Tripoli, Tunis, Algeria, and Morocco : Report to the Committee of the British and Foreign Anti-Slavery Society. 8* 1892

Gurney, John Henry. A List of the Diurnal Birds of Prey, with References and Annotations ; also a Record of Specimens preserved in the Norfolk and Norwich Museum. 8° 1884

Gurney, Matthew. *See* Hakluyt, Vol. 2 : Appendix 1.

Gusman, Nunno di. *See* Purchas, Vol. 4, Book 8 ; Ramusio, Vol. 3 : Appendix 1.

Güssfeldt, Dr Paul. Bericht über eine Reise in den Centralen Chileno-Argentinischen Andes. Large 8* *Berlin,* 1884

Guthe, H. Lehrbuch der Geographie. 4th edition [by Hermann Wagner]. 8° *Hanover,* 1879

Guthrie, Mrs Maria. Tour performed in the years 1795-96 through the Taurida or Crimea, the antient kingdom of Bosphorus, the once powerful Republic of Tauric Cherson, and all the other Countries on the North Shore of the Euxine, ceded to Russia by the Peace of Kainardgi and Jassy. *Maps and plates.* 4° 1802

Guthrie, Mrs. Through Russia, from St Petersburg to Astrakhan and the Crimea. 2 vols. 8° 1874

Guthrie, William. New System of Modern Geography, or a Geographical, Historical, and Commercial Grammar, and Present State of the several Kingdoms of the World ; the Astronomical part by J. Ferguson. 4° 1788
—— Geographical, Historical, and Commercial Grammar, and Present State of the several Kingdoms of the World ; with a Geographical Index, &c. *Maps.* 8° 1808
—— Compendio di Geografia Universale, Ragionata, Storica, e Commerciale. *Maps.* 8° *Milan,* 1810

Gutierrez, Donate. El Algodonero. 8* *Mexico,* 1885

Gutiérrez, J. M. *See* Azara.

Gutiérrez, J. P. Memorias Histórico-políticas del Jeneral. Vol. 1. 8° *Bogota,* 1865

Gutuere. *See* Hakluyt, Vol. 2 : Appendix 1.

Gutzlaff, Charles. Sketch of Chinese History, Ancient and Modern, comprising a Retrospect of the Foreign Intercourse and Trade with China. 2 vols. *Map and tables.* 8° 1834
—— China Opened, or a Display of the Topography, History, Customs, &c., of the Chinese Empire. Revised by A. Reed. 2 vols. *Map.* 12° 1838
—— **and Peter du Ponceau.** Two Letters on the Chinese System of Writing. 4* *Philadelphia,* 1840

Guy, Lieut. *See* Jones, F.

Guyot, Arnold. A Collection of Meteorological Tables, with other Tables useful in Practical Meteorology. 8° *Washington,* 1852

Guyot, Arnold. Tables, Meteorological and Physical. 8° *Washington*, 1858
—— Ditto, 4th edition. Edited by William Libbey, jr. 8° *Washington*, 1884
—— The Earth and Man, or Physical Geography in its Relation to the History of Mankind. Abridged.] 5th edition, 1860 ; and 6th edition, 1863. 8°
—— On the Appalachian Mountain System. (From the *American Journal of Science*, Vol. 31, March 1861.) *Map.* 8*
New Haven, Conn., 1861
—— Géographie Physique Comparée, considérée dans ses Rapports avec l'Histoire de l'Humanité. *Maps.* 12° *Paris*, 1888
—— *See* Faure.

Guyot, Ducloz. *See* Burney, Vol. 5 : Appendix 1.

Guzman, Alonzo Enriquez de. *See* Hakluyt Soc. Publ., Vol. 29 : Appendix 1.

Guzmán, David J. Apuntamientos sobre la Topografia Fisica de la República del Salvador, comprendiendo ; su Historia Natural, sus Producciones, Industria, Comercio e Inmigracion, Climas, Estadistica, &c. 8° *San Salvador*, 1883

Guzmán, Dr Gustave E. *See* Guatemala : Appendix 2.

Guzmán, P. Luis. Historia de las Missiones que han hecho los Religiosos de la Compañia de Jesus, en la India Oriental, y en los Reynos de la China y Japon. 2 vols. Folio *Alcala*, 1601

Guzman, Ruiz Diaz. Historia de las Provincias del Rio de la Plata. *Map.* Folio. MS. 1612

Gyatsho, Lama Serap. *See* India, F, c : Appendix 2.

Gylden, H. Untersuchungen über die Constitution der Atmosphäre und die Strahlenbrechung in derselben. 4*
St Petersburg, 1866
—— Astronomiska Iakttagelser och Undersökningar antstalda pa Stockholm's Observatorium. Vol. 1. Nos. 1 and 2. 8*
Stockholm, 1876, 1880

Gyllius, Petrus. P. Gyllii de Constantinopoleos Topographia lib IV. 16°
Leyden, 1632

Győry, Sandor. A Hangrendozer Kiszámitásárol es Zongorák Hangolásáról Mérséklet nélkül tiszta Viszonyok szerint. 4° *Budapest*, 1858.

H

H——, T. A Short Way to Know the World, or the Rudiments of Geography. By T. H. *Frontispiece.* 12° 1712

Haacke, Dr Wilhelm. Bioekographie Museenpflege und Kolonialthierkunde, Drei Abhandlungen verwandten Inhalts nebst einer Einleitung in die Biographie der Organismen. 8° *Jena*, 1886

Haafner, J. Travels on Foot through the Island of Ceylon. Translated from the Dutch. *Illustrations.* 8° 1821
—— *See* Phillips [3], Vol. 5 : Appendix 1.

Haas, H. *See* Schneider.

Haast, Sir Julius von. Report of a Topographical and Geological Exploration of the Western Districts of the Nelson Province, New Zealand. 8°
Nelson, 1861
—— Report on the Geological Survey of the Province of Canterbury. Folio*
Christchurch, 1864
—— Report on the Formation of the Canterbury Plains. *Map and geological sections.* Folio* *Christchurch*, 1864
—— Report on the Headwaters of the River Waitaki. 4* *Christchurch* [1865]
—— Report on the Headwaters of the River Rakan. *Maps and plates.* Folio*
Christchurch, 1866
—— Moas and Moa Hunters. Small 8*
Christchurch, 1871
—— Researches and Excavations carried on in and near the Moa Bone Point Cave, Sumner Road, in the year 1872. Small 8* *Christchurch*, 1874
—— Geology of the Provinces of Canterbury and Westland, New Zealand. *Maps and plates.* 8° *Christchurch*, 1879
—— The Progress of Geology. 8*
Dunedin, 1883
—— Humanism and Realism in their Relation to Higher Education. 8*
Dunedin, 1883
—— In Memoriam : Ferdinand R. Von Hochstetter. *Portraits.* Large 8*
Christchurch, 1884

Habenicht, H. Die Spuren der Schöpfungsperioden in der Oberflächengestaltung der Erde, und daraus abgeleitete Katastrophentheorie. *Map and photographs.* 8* *Gotha*, 1875
—— Einige Gedanken über die hauptsächlichsten recenten Veränderungen der Erdoberfläche. 8* *Gotha*, 1882
—— Vorschlag zur Erlangung exakter Positionen in Inner-Afrika. (From *Ausland*, Nr. 9, 1885.) 4* 1885
—— Ueber das Woher und Wohin des gegenwärtigen geophysischen Zusstandes. *Map.* 8* *Vienna*, 1888
—— Das seismische Problem. *Map.* Large 8* *Vienna*, 1889
—— Häufigkeit der Eisberge im Golfstrome und Klimaschwankungen. 4* 1892

Habersham, A. W. My Last Cruise ; or, Where we Went, and What we Saw : being an Account of Visits to the Malay and Loo-Choo Islands, the Coasts of China, Formosa, Japan, Kamtschatka, Siberia, and the Mouth of the Amoor River. *Plates.* 8° *Philadelphia*, 1857

Hacke, William. Collection of Original Voyages. [For full Title and Contents, *see* Appendix 1.]

Hacker, B. Wegweiser oder kurze Erklärung der Merkwürdigkeiten und mahlerischen Ansichten in der Stadt Salzburg und der Umgebung. 3rd edition. 12*   *Salzburg,* 1830

Hadfield, William. Brazil, the River Plate, and the Falkland Islands; with the Cape Horn Route to Australia; including Notices of Lisbon, Madeira, the Canaries, and Cape Verds. *Woodcuts.* 8°   1854

Haeckel, Prof. Ernst. A Visit to Ceylon. Translated by Clara Bell. Small 8° 1883
—— Indische Reisebriefe. 3rd edition. *Illustrations.* 8°   *Berlin,* 1893

Haefkens, J. Reize naar Guatemala. *Plates*   *The Hague,* 1827
—— Centraal Amerika, uit een Geschiedkundig, Aardrijkskundig en Statistiek Oogpunt beschouwd. *Maps and plates.* 8°   *Dordrecht,* 1832

Haensel, John Gottfried. Letters on the Nicobar Islands, their Natural Productions, and the Manners, Customs, and Superstitions of the Natives. 8*   1812

Hafiz (the Persian Poet). *See* Nott.

Haga, A. Nederlandsch Nieuw Guinea en de Papoesche Eilanden. Historische Bijdrage, 1500-1883. 2 vols. *Map.* 8°   *Batavia,* 1884

Hage, C., and H. Tegner. Ueber die Bedingungen eines Handelsverkehrs mit dem westlichen Sibirien. Bericht über eine Spezial-Untersuchungs-Reise. Aus dem Dänischen übersetzt von Dr Richard Lehmann. *Map.* Small 8*   *Halle,* 1881

Hagemeister, Jules de. Commerce of New Russia, Moldavia, and Wallachia. Translated by Triebner. *Map and tables.* 8°   1836
—— Essai sur les Ressources Territoriales et Commerciales de l'Asie Occidentale, le Caractère des Habitans, &c. 8°   *St Petersburg,* 1839
—— *See* Baer and Helmersen, 3.

Hager, Carl. Die Marshall-Inseln in Erd- und Völkerkunde, Handel und Mission. Mit einem Anhang, Die Gilbert-Inseln. *Map.* 8° *Leipzig,* 1886
—— Kaiser Wilhelms-Land und der Bismarck-Archipel. *Maps and illustrations.* Crown 8°   *Leipzig* [1886]

Hagerty, Frank H. The Territory of Dakota: The State of North Dakota; the State of South Dakota; an Official Statistical, Historical, and Political Abstract; Agricultural, Mineral, Commercial, Manufacturing, Educational, Social, and General Statements. 8°
                    Aberdeen, S.D., 1889

Haggenmacher, G. A. Reise im Somali-Lande, 1874. (Ergänzungsheft, 47—Petermann's Mittheilungen.) *Map.* 4°
                            Gotha, 1876

Hague, Arnold. *See* United States, G, *c*; H, *a*: Appendix 2.

Hahn, C. Aus dem Kaukasus: Reisen und Studien: Beiträge zur Kenntnis des Landes. 8°   *Leipzig,* 1892

Hahn, Prof. F. G. Untersuchungen über das Aufsteigen und Sinken der Küsten. 8°   *Leipzig,* 1879
—— Insel-Studien. Versuch einer auf biographische und geologische Verhältnisse gegründeten Eintheilung der Inseln. *Map.* 8°   *Leipzig,* 1883
—— *See* Kirchhoff; Levasseur; *also* Germany, C (Forschungen, &c., Vol. 1): Appendix 2.

Hahn, T. Die Sprache der Nama. 8*
                            Leipzig, 1870

Hahnzog, A. G. Lehrbuch der Militär-Geographie von Europa. 2 vols. in 1. 12°   *Magdeburg,* 1820

Hahn-Hahn, Countess Ida. Travels in Turkey, the Holy Land, and Egypt. Translated from the German. Royal 8°
                                        1845

Haidinger, W. Bericht über die geognostische Uebersichts-Karte der Oesterreichischen Monarchie. 8*
                            Vienna, 1847
—— [Preface to.] Die Geologische Uebersichtskarte des mittleren Thieles von Süd-America. *See* Foetterle.
—— Considerations on the Phenomena attending the Fall of Meteorites on the Earth. Translated by Marshall. 8*   1861
—— *See* Becker; Hauer.

Haiens, — de la. *See* De la Haiens.

Haig, General F. T. Report on the Navigation of the Godavery, 1854; with the Remarks of the Board of Public Works thereon, and a Memorandum by G. P. Tuke. *Map.* Royal 8°
                            Madras, 1857
—— Report of a Journey to the Red Sea Ports, Somali-Land, and Southern and Eastern Arabia. 8°   [1887]

Haigh, S. Sketches of Buenos Ayres, Chili, and Peru. *Map.* 8°   1831

Hain, Victor-Armand. A la Nation sur Alger. 8°   *Paris,* 1832

Haines, C. R. Gordon's Death: What is the Truth? (From *The United Service Magazine.*) 8*   1890

Haitho, Prince (Ayton or Hayton, or Anthonie of Armenia). *See* Kerr, Vol. 1; Purchas, Vol. 3, Book 1; Ramusio, Vol. 2: Appendix 1.

Hake, A. Egmont. Events in the Taiping Rebellion : being Reprints of MS. copied by General Gordon, in his own handwriting ; with Monograph, Introduction, and Notes. *Portrait and map.* 8° 1891

Hakewill, J. A Picturesque Tour of Italy, from Drawings made in 1816-17. *Plates.* Folio 1820

Hakluyt, Richard. The Principal Navigations, Voyages, Traffiques, and Discoveries of the English Nation. 5 vols. [For Title and Contents, *see* Appendix I.]

Hakluyt Society Publications. Volumes 1 to 87, from 1847 to 1893. [For Contents of volumes, *see* Appendix I.]

H. A. L., the "Old Shekarry." *See* Levison.

Haldane, R. C. Subtropical Cultivations and Climates : a Handy Book for Planters, Colonists, and Settlers. *Illustrations.* 8° 1886

Haldeman, S. S. Report on the Present State of our Knowledge of Linguistic Ethnology, 1856. 8* *Washington,* 1856
—— Investigation of the Power of the Greek Z by méans of Phonetic Laws. 8* N.P., N.D.
—— On the Relations between Chinese and the Indo-European Languages. 8* *Cambridge, Mass.,* 1857
—— Analytic Orthography : an Investigation of the Sounds of the Voice and their Alphabetical Notation, including the Mechanism of Speech and its bearing upon Etymology. 4° *Philadelphia,* 1860

Hale, Horatio. Migrations in the Pacific Ocean. From the Volume on the Ethnography and Philology of the U. S. Exploring Expedition under Charles Wilkes. *Maps.* 8* 1846
—— *See* Wilkes.

Hale, Col. Lonsdale. Analytical Index to Major Clarke's Authorised Translation of "The Franco-German War, 1870-71." 8* 1890

Halfeld, H. G. F., and J. J. von Tschudi. Die Brasilianische Provinz Minas Geraes. (Ergänzungsheft, 9 — Petermann's Mittheilungen.) *Map.* 4° *Gotha,* 1862

Halford, George Britton. Not like Man, Bimanous and Biped, nor yet Quadrumanous, but Cheiropodous. *Plates.* 8* *Melbourne,* 1863

Haliburton, R. G. The Dwarfs of Mount Atlas : Statements of Natives of Morocco and of European Residents there as to the existence of a Dwarf Race south of the Great Atlas ; with Notes as to Dwarfs and Dwarf Worship. 8* 1891
—— Racial Dwarfs in the Atlas and the Pyrenees. (Reprinted from the *Imperial and Asiatic Quarterly Review.*) 8* 1893
—— The Holy Land of Punt. (Reprinted from the *Academy,* 8th July 1893.) 8* 1893

Hall, Rev. Alfred J. A Grammar of the Kwaguitl Language. From the Transactions of the Royal Society of Canada. Vol. 6, section 2, 1888. 4* *Montreal,* 1889

Hall, Capt. Basil. Account of a Voyage of Discovery to the West Coast of Corea, and the Great Loo-Choo Island ; with a Vocabulary of the Loo-Choo Language, by H. J. Clifford. *Maps and plates.* 4° 1818
—— Extracts from a Journal written on the Coasts of Chili, Peru, and Mexico in 1820-22. 2 vols. *Map.* 8° *Edinburgh,* 1825
—— Travels in North America in 1827-28. 3 vols. *Maps.* 8° *Edinburgh,* 1829
—— Schloss Hainfeld, or a Winter in Lower Styria. 8° 1836
—— Fragments of Voyages and Travels. Royal 8° 1852

Hall, Charles Francis. Life with the Esquimaux, &c. 2 vols. *Maps and plates* 1864
—— Narrative of the Second Arctic Expedition made by Charles F. Hall, his Voyage to Repulse Bay, Sledge Journeys to the Straits of Fury and Hecla and to King William's Land, and Residence among the Eskimos during the years 1864-69. Edited by Professor J. E. Nourse. *Photograph, plates, maps, and map in pocket.* 4° *Washington,* 1879
—— *See* MacClintock, Sir F. L. ; *also* "Polaris."

Hall, Col. Francis. Colombia, in its Present State in respect of Climate, Soil, &c. *Map.* 8° 1827

Hall, C. G. Strode. Report on the Mai Cussa. *Map.* Folio* [*Brisbane*] 1888

Hall, Edward H. The Great West : Travellers', Miners', and Emigrants' Guide and Hand-Book to the Western, North-Western, and Pacific States and Territories ; with . . . complete Tables of Distances across the American Continent. *Map.* 8° 1867

Hall, E. S. *See* Whiting.

Hall, Henry. Manual of South African Geography. *Map.* 12° *Cape Town,* 1859

Hall, Henry. *See* United States, A (Tenth Census, Vols. 8 and 22): Appendix 2.

Hall, James. Contributions to the Palæontology of New York, being some of the Results of Investigations made during 1855-58. *Woodcuts.* 8* *New York,* 1858
—— Maps and Plates of the Geological Sections of the United States of America. 4* *New York,* N.D.
—— *See* United States, H, *a* (Prof. Papers) : Appendix 2.

Hall, James, and J. D. Whitney. Report on the Geological Survey of the State of Iowa, embracing the Results of Investigations made during 1855-57. Vol. 1, Part 1, Geology; Part 2, Palæontology. 2 vols. *Maps and plates.* Royal 8°　　1858

Hall, James. *See* Hakluyt Soc. Publ., Vol. 5: Appendix 1.

Hall, John. *See* Purchas, Vol. 3, Book 4: Appendix 1.

Hall, John. Proposed Settlement of Prince Albert Land. *Map.* 8° *Melbourne*, 1862

Hall, Maxwell. Observations made on the Blue Mountain Peak. 4* 　　[1887]

—— The Jamaica Rainfall from 1870 to 1889. Supplement to the *Jamaica Gazette* of 21st January 1892. Folio*

Hall, S. C., and Mrs Hall. Ireland, its Scenery, Character, &c. Vols. 1 and 3. *Maps and plates.* Imp. 8°　　N.D.

Hall, Admiral Sir W. H. Narrative of the Voyages and Services of the "Nemesis," from 1840 to 1843; and of the Combined Naval and Military Operations in China, comprising a Complete Account of the Colony of Hong Kong, and Remarks on the Character and Habits of the Chinese; with Personal Observations by W. D. Bernard. 2 vols. *Maps and plates.* 8°　　1844

—— A few Remarks relative to the Slave Trade on the East Coast of Africa. Extracted from the Voyage of the "Nemesis." 8*　　N.D.

—— Our National Defences. *Map.* 8* 1876

—— **and W. D. Bernard.** The "Nemesis" in China, comprising a History of the late War in that Country, with an Account of the Colony of Hong Kong. *Maps and plates.* 8°　　1844

Hallberg, Baron von. *See* Phillips [3], Vol. 5: Appendix 1.

Hallett, Holt S. Address of Mr Holt S. Hallett, upon New Markets and Extension of Railways in India and Burmah. 8*　　1887

—— Address of Mr Holt S. Hallett, upon Burmah, our Gate to the Markets of Western and Central China, treating with the Proposed Connection of Burmah with China by Railway. Delivered before the Birmingham Chamber of Commerce on the 26th May 1887. 8* 1887

—— A Thousand Miles on an Elephant in the Shan States. *Maps and illustrations.* 8°　　1890

—— *See* Colquhoun.

Halley, Edmund, his Life and Work. 8*　　1880

—— *See* Frezier; *also* Burney, Vol. 4: Appendix 1.

Halloran, Alfred Laurence. Wae Yàng Jin. Eight Months' Journal kept on Board one of Her Majesty's Sloops of War during Visits to Loochoo, Japan, and Pootoo. *Plates.* 8°　　1856

Halloy, J. J. D'Omalius d'. Eléments de Géologie, ou Seconde Partie des Éléments d'Inorganomie particulière. *Maps and plates.* 8°　　*Paris*, 1839

—— Coup d'Œil sur la Géologie de la Belgique. *Map.* 8°　　*Brussels*, 1842

—— Des Races Humaines, ou Éléments d'Ethnographie. 8°　　*Paris*, 1845

Halls, J. J. *See* Pearce.

Haly, Lieut.-Col. R. H. O'Grady. The Nile above the Second Cataract: Précis of Information. Compiled in the Intelligence Branch of the Quarter-Master-General's Department. Part 1. Sarras to New Dongola; Part 2. New Dongola to Abn-Hamed and Khartûm. *Maps.* 8°　　1884

Hamel, H. *See* Astley, Vol. 4; Burney, Vol. 3; Pinkerton, Vol. 7; Allgemeine Historie, Vol. 6: Appendix 1.

Hamel, J. Tradescant der Aeltere 1618 in Russland. *Map and portrait.* 4° 1847

—— Der Dodo, die Einsiedler, und der erdichtete Nazarvogel. 8* *St Petersburg*, 1848

—— England and Russia: comprising the Voyages of John Tradescant the elder, Sir Hugh Willoughby, Richard Chancellor, Nelson, and others, to the White Sea, &c. Translated by J. S. Leigh. 8°　　1854

Hamerton, Lieut.-Col. Atkins. Information on Various Points connected with his Highness the Imaum of Muskat, and the Nature of his Relations with the British Government, &c. (Bombay Records, xxiv., N.S.) 8° *Bombay*, 1856 Treaties, Engagements, &c., concluded between Her Britannic Majesty and His Highness the Imaum of Muskat, and between the Hon. East India Company and His Highness, 1798 to 1846. Treaty (concluded Sept. 1833) between the United States of America and the Imaum of Muskat. Treaty (concluded 17th Nov. 1844) between the King of the French and the Imaum of Muskat.

Hamilton, Capt. Alexander. A New Account of the East Indies. 2 vols. *Maps and plates.* 8° *Edinburgh*, 1827

—— *See* Astley, Vol. 3; Allgemeine Historie, Vol. 5: Appendix 1.

Hamilton, Archibald. On the Trade with the Coloured Races of Africa. 8°　　1868

Hamilton, A. G. A New Key to unlock every Kingdom, State, and Province in the known World. *With a table.* 12° *Leeds*, 1839

Hamilton, Charles. Sketches of Life and Sport in South-Eastern Africa. Edited by F. G. H. Price. *Plates.* 8° 1870
—— Oriental Zigzag, or Wanderings in Syria, Moab, Abyssinia, and Egypt. *Plates.* Small 8° 1875
Hamilton, Charles. Historical Relation of the Origin, Progress, and final Dissolution of the Government of the Rohilla Afgans in the Northern Provinces of Hindostan. 8° 1787
Hamilton, Lieut.-Col. D. Report on the Shevaroy Hills. 8* *Madras,* 1862
—— Report on the Pulni Mountains. 2nd series. 8* *Madras,* 1864
—— Report on the High Ranges of the Annamullay Mountains. 8* *Madras,* 1866
Hamilton, Francis [*formerly Buchanan*]. Journey from Madras, through the Countries of Mysore, Canara, and Malabar, for the express purpose of Investigating the State of Agriculture, Arts, Commerce, Religion, Manners, Customs, History (Natural and Civil), and Antiquities, in the Dominions of the Rajah of Mysore, and the Countries acquired by the Hon. East India Company from Tippoo Sultaun. 3 vols. *Plates.* 4° 1807
—— Account of the Kingdom of Nepal, and of the Territories annexed to this Dominion by the House of Gorkha. *Map and plates.* 4° *Edinburgh,* 1819
—— *See* Eyriès, Vol. 14; Pinkerton, Vol. 8: Appendix 1.
Hamilton, G. A Voyage round the World in Her Majesty's frigate "Pandora," performed under the direction of Captain Edwards in the years 1790-92; with the Discoveries made in the South Sea, and the many Distresses experienced by the Crew from Shipwreck and Famine, in a Voyage of 1,100 miles in open boats between Endeavour Straits and the Island of Timor. 8° *Berwick,* 1793
Hamilton, George. Experiences of a Colonist Forty Years Ago: a Journey from Port Phillip to South Australia in 1839, and a Voyage from Port Phillip to Adelaide in 1846. By an Old Hand. *Illustrations.* 8° *Adelaide,* 1880
Hamilton, H. C. *See* Strabo.
Hamilton, James. Wanderings in North Africa. *Map and plates.* 8° 1856
—— Sinai, the Hedjaz, and Soudan: Wanderings around the Birth-place of the Prophet, and across the Æthiopian Desert from Sawakin to Chartum. *Maps.* 8° 1857
Hamilton, Walter. Geographical, Statistical, and Historical Description of Hindostan and the adjacent Countries. 2 vols. *Map.* 4° 1820
—— The East India Gazetteer. 2 vols. *Maps.* 8° 1828

Hamilton, Rev. Wm. Letters concerning the Northern Coast of the County of Antrim, with the Antiquities, Manners, and Customs of that Country. *Map and plates.* 8° *Dublin,* 1790
Hamilton, Wm. Remarks on Several Parts of Turkey. Part 1. Ægyptiaca, or some Account of the Antient and Modern State of Egypt, as obtained in 1801-2. 4° 1809
—— *See* Pinkerton, Vol. 3: Appendix 1.
Hamilton, Wm. John. Researches in Asia Minor, Pontus, and Armenia, with some Account of their Antiquities and Geology. 2 vols. *Map and plates.* 8° 1842
Hamilton, W. R. No Mistake, or a Vindication of the Negotiators of the Treaty of 1783 respecting the North Eastern Boundary of the United States. 8* 1842
Hamley, Colonel Charles. *See* Blackwood, Vol. 4: Appendix 1.
Hamley, W. G. A New Sea and an Old Land, being Papers suggested by a visit to Egypt at the end of 1869. *Plates.* 8° 1871
Hammard, C. F. E. Reise durch Oberschlesien zur Russisch-Kayserlichen Armee nach der Ukraine. Vol. 1. *Maps.* 8° *Gotha,* 1787
Hammer, — de. *See* Recueil de Voyages, Vol. 2, p. 611: Appendix 1.
Hammer, E. Ueber die geographisch-wichtigsten Kartenprojektionen insbesondere die zenitalen Entwürfe nebst Tafeln zur Verwandlung von geographischen Koordinaten in Azimutale. *Plates.* 8° *Stuttgart,* 1889
Hammer-Purgstall, Freiherr J. von. Denkmal auf das Grab der beyden letzten Grafen von Purstall. *Plans.* 8° *Vienna,* 1821
—— Geographie von Arabien (Jahrbücher der Literatur). 8° *Vienna,* 1840
—— Abhandlung über die Siegel der Araber, Perser, und Türken. *Plate.* 4* *Vienna,* 1848
—— Bericht über die in den letzen Jahren 1845-48 zu Constantinopel gedruckten und lithographirten Werken. [In two pamphlets.] 8* *Vienna,* 1849
—— Uebersicht der Literaturgeschichte der Araber. 4* *Vienna,* 1850
—— Ueber die Namen der Araber. 4* *Vienna,* 1852
—— Das Kamel. 4* *Vienna,* 1854
—— Ueber die Arabische Geographie von Spanien. 8* *Vienna,* 1854
—— Ueber die Arabischen Wörter in Spanischen. 8* *Vienna,* 1855
—— Geschichte Wassaf's. Persisch herausgegeben und Deutsch übersetzt. Vol. 1. 4° *Vienna,* 1856
—— *See* Evliya Effendi.

Hammer - Purgstall, Freiherr J. von.
Ueber die Menschenclasse, welche von
den Arabern "Schoubije" genannt
wird. 8*   *Vienna*, N.D.

Hammond, H. W., and R. Spankie.
Reports on the Frequency of Suits for
Ouster. (Records, N.W. Provinces of
India, Part 25.) Large 8° *Agra*, 1856

Hamor, Ralph. *See* Purchas, Vol. 4,
Book 9 : Appendix 1.

Hampton, —. *See* Polybius.

Hamy, Dr E. T. La Mappemonde
d'Angelino Dulcert, de Majorque, 1339.
8*   *Paris*, 1887
—— Note sur la Mappemonde de Diego
Ribero (1529), conservée au Musée de la
Propagande de Rome. 8* *Paris*, 1887
—— Notice sur une Mappemonde Portu-
gaïse anonyme de 1502, récemment
découverte à Londres. *Maps.* 8*
Paris, 1887
—— Note sur une Carte Marine inédite de
Giacomo Russo de Messine (1557). *Map.*
8*   *Paris*, 1888
—— Les Origines de la Cartographie de
l'Europe Septentrionale. *Maps.* 8*
Paris, 1889

Hanauer, Rev. J. E. *See* Lees, G. R.

Hanbury, B. *See* Waddington, G.

Hancock, John. Observations on the
Climate, Soil, and Production of British
Guiana, and on the Advantages of Emigration to, and Colonising the Interior
of, that Country. 8*   1840

Hancock, J. On the Cause of the Appear-
ance commonly termed Heat Lightning,
and on certain Correlative Phænomena.
8*   N.D.

Hancock, Wm. Notes on the Physical
Geography, Flora, Fauna, &c., of Northern Formosa, with Comparisons between that District and Hainan, and
other Parts of China. *Map.* 4*
[*Tantui*, 1882]

Hann, Prof. Julius J. Ueber die Wär-
meabnahme mit der Höhe im Asiatischen
Monsungebiet. 8*   *Vienna*, 1873
—— Ueber gewisse beträchtliche Unregel-
mässigkeiten des Meeres-Niveaus. 8*
Vienna, 1875
—— Zur barometrischen Höhenmessung.
8*   *Vienna*, 1876
—— Zur Meteorologie der Alpengipfel. 8*
Vienna, 1878
—— Untersuchungen über die Regen-
verhältnisse von Oesterreich - Ungarn.
[Parts 1 and 2.] 8* *Vienna*, 1879, 1880
—— Ueber den täglichen Gang einiger
meteorologischen Elemente in Wien
(Stadt). 8*   1881
—— Ueber den täglichen Gang des Luft-
druckes, der Temperatur, der Feuchtig-
keit, Bewölkung und Windstärke auf den
Plateaux der Rocky Mountains. 8* 1881

Hann, Prof. Julius J. Ueber die Tem-
peratur der Südlichen Hemisphäre. 8*
Vienna, 1882
—— Handbuch der Klimatologie. *Illus-
tration.* 8°   ·*Stuttgart*, 1883
—— Ueber die klimatischen Verhältnisse
von Bosnien und der Herzegowina. 8°
[*Vienna*] 1883
—— Einige Resultate aus Major von
Mechow's meteorologischen Beobach-
tungen im Innern von Angola. 8*
[*Vienna*] 1884
—— Beiträge zur Kenntniss der Verthei-
lung des Luftdruckes auf der Erdober-
fläche. Large 8*   [*Vienna*] 1886
—— Bericht über die Fortschritte der
geographischen Meteorologie. 8* [1888]
—— Resultate der meteorologischen Beo-
bachtungen der französischen Polar-
Expedition, 1882-83, am Cap Horn.
Maps. Folio*   [*Vienna*, 1889]
—— Temperatur-Mittel aus der Periode
1851-1885 für die österreichischen Alpen
und deren Grenz gebiete. 4* N.P., N.D.
—— Ueber die Luftfeuchtigkeit als kli-
matischer Factor. 8° [*Vienna*, 1889]
—— Zur Meteorologie des Sonnblickgipfels.
8*   *Vienna*, 1889
—— Beiträge zur Arktischen Meteorologie.
Nach den "Contributions to our Know-
ledge of the Meteorology of the Arctic
Regions ;" Part 4 and Part 5. London,
1885-1888. Large 8*   [*Vienna*] 1889
—— Die meteorologischen Ergebnisse der
Lady Franklin Bay Expedition, 1881-83.
Large 8*   [*Vienna*] 1890
—— Resultate der meteorologischen Beo-
bachtungen an der finnländischen inter-
nationalen Polarstation in Sodankylae.
4°   1890
—— Die Ergebnisse der dänischen inter-
nationalen Polar-Expeditionen im Jahre
1882-83. 4°   1890
—— Resultate der meteorologischen Beo-
bachtungen auf dem Gipfel von Pike's
Peak (Colorado), 4,308 meter (14,134
feet), nach Beobachtungen von November
1874 bis inclusive Juni 1888. 4* [1891]
—— Studien über die Luftdruck- und
Temperaturverhältnisse auf dem Sonn-
blickgipfel, nebst Bemerkungen über
deren Bedeutung für die Theorie der
Cyclonen und Anticyclonen. 8*
Vienna, 1891
—— Die neue Anemometer- und Temperatur - Station auf dem Obergipfel
(2,140 M.). 4*   1893
—— Ergebnisse der meteorologischen
Beobachtungen der niederländischen internationalen Polar-Expedition, 1882-83,
in der Kara-See. Large 8°   1893
—— What additional Stations are desired
for Meteorological and for Climatological
purposes. (Extract from the Papers of
the Chicago Meteorological Congress,
August 1893.) 8*   *Chicago*, 1893

Hann, Prof. Julius J. Der tägliche Gang der Temperatur auf dem Obergipfel (2140 m.) und einige Folgerungen aus dem selben. *2 plates.* 8* *Vienna*, 1893
—— *See* Kirchhoff; Penck's Abhandlungen, 2; Rohlfs; *also* Switzerland, B : Appendix 2.

Hannah, John. Review of "Sheep Farming in Buenos Ayres," &c., by Wilfred Latham, Esq. 16* *Buenos Ayres*, 1867

Hannan, Charles. A Swallow's Wing, a Tale of Pekin. 12° 1888

Hannibal. A Dissertation on the Passage of Hannibal over the Alps. *Maps.* 8° *Oxford*, 1820
—— *See* Beaujour, Baron F. de.

Hannington, Rev. James. The Last Journals of Bishop Hannington, from 1st August 1885 to the day of his death, 29th October 1885, containing a detailed Account of his Journey through Masai Land, his Capture and Imprisonment. 8° 1886

Hanno. *See* Falconer, T.; Fischer, C. T.; Mann, Abbé; *also* Ramusio, Vol. 1 : Appendix 1.

Hannonius, Joannes Taisnier. De usu Sphaerae Materialis, hactenus ab omnibus Philosophis, et Mathematicis magno studiosorum incommodo neglecto nunc vero in lucem tradito. 4° *Cologne*, 1559

Hanoteau, A. Essai de Grammaire de la Langue Tamachek', renfermant les principes du Langage parlé par les Imouchar'ou Touareg, des Conversations en Tamachek', des Facsimile d'écriture en caractères Tifinar'. *Map.* 8° *Paris*, 1860
—— **and A. Letourneux.** La Kabylie et les Coutumes Kabyles. 3 vols. *Map and diagram.* 8° *Paris*, 1872-73

"Hansa." *See* Koldewey.

Hansen, Dr G. A. *See* Norway, A (North Atlantic Expedition): Appendix 2.

Hanson, P. T. *See* Hansteen, C.

Hanson, William. Geographical Encyclopædia of New South Wales, including the Counties, Towns, and Villages within the Colony, with the Sources and Courses of the Rivers and their Tributaries . . . *Map and diagrams.* Large 8° *Sydney*, 1892

Hansteen, C. Untersuchungen über den Magnetismus der Erde. Uebersetzt von P. T. Hanson. *Maps and plates.* 4° *Christiania*, 1819
—— Souvenirs d'un Voyage en Sibérie. Traduits du Norvégien par Mme. Colban, et revus par MM. Sédillot et De la Roquette. *Map.* 8° *Paris*, 1857
—— *See* Sabine.
—— **and Lieut. Due.** Resultate magnetischer, astronomischer, und meteorologischer Beobachtungen auf einer Reise nach dem Oestlichen Sibirien in den Jahren 1828-30. *Maps.* 4° *Christiania*, 1863

Hanway, Jonas. An Historical Account of the British Trade over the Caspian Sea, with a Journal of Travels from London through Russia into Persia, and back again through Russia, Germany, and Holland. 4 vols. in 3. *Maps and plates.* 4° 1753
—— The same. 2nd edition. 2 vols. *Maps.* 4° 1754
—— The same. 3rd edition. *Maps and plates.* 4° 1762
—— *See* P——; *also* New Collection of Travels, Vol. 4; "The World Displayed," Vols. 14, 15, p. 609 : Appendix 1.

Harant, Kristof. Gesta z Království Ceského do Benátek, odtud do země Svaté, země Judské a Dále do Egypta, a Potom na Horu Oreb, Sinai a Sv. Kateriny v Pusté Arabii. 2 vols. *Portrait and plan.* 8° *Prague*, 1854-55

Harbord, Rev. J. B. Glossary of Navigation : a Vade - Mecum for Practical Navigators of the Royal Navy, Mercantile Marine, and Yacht Squadrons, containing Explanations of the Technical Terms used in Nautical Geography, Meteorology, and Astronomy. 2nd edition. *Charts and diagrams.* 16° *Portsmouth*, 1883

Harcourt, Capt. A. F. P. The Himalayan Districts of Kooloo, Lahoul, and Spiti. *Map and plates.* Small 8° 1871
—— *See* India, P (Selections, No. 10): Appendix 2.

Harcourt, E. Vernon. Sketch of Madeira, containing Information for the Traveller or Invalid Visitor. *Maps.* 8° 1851

Harcourt, Robert. *See* Gottfried; Purchas, Vol. 4, Book 6 : Appendix 1.

Harcus, W. South Australia, its History, Resources, and Productions. *Plates and maps in cover.* 8° 1876

Hardcastle, E. L. F. *See* Smith, M. L.

Hardegger, Dr D. Kammele von. *See* Paulitschke.

Hardie, David. Notes on some of the more Common Diseases in Queensland in Relation to Atmospheric Conditions, 1887-91. *Chart.* 8° *Brisbane*, 1893

Hardine, —. *See* Hakluyt, Vol. 2 : Appendix 1.

Hardman, —. *See* Jermann.

Hardman, Frederick. Scenes and Adventures in Central America. Small 8° *Edinburgh*, 1852

Hardman, W. *See* Stuart, J. M'D.

Hardwicke, —. *See* Eyriès, Vol. 14 : Appendix 1.

Hardwicke's Annual Biography for 1857. *See* Walford.

Hardy, C. Forest Life in Acadie : Sketches of Sport and Natural History in the Lower Provinces of the Canadian Dominion. *Plates.* 8°   1869

Hare, Augustus J. C. Cities of Southern Italy and Sicily. *Illustrations.* 12° 1883
—— Cities of Central Italy. 2 vols. *Maps and illustrations.* 12°   1884
—— Days near Rome. 3rd edition. 2 vols. *Illustrations.* Crown 8°   1884
—— North-Eastern France. *Map and illustrations.* Crown 8°   1890
—— South-Eastern France. *Map and illustrations.* Crown 8°   1890
—— South-Western France. *Map and illustrations.* Crown 8°   1890

Hare, Dr. Of the Conclusion arrived at by a Committee of the Academy of Sciences of France, agreeably to which Tornados are caused by Heat ; while, agreeably to Peltier's Report to the same body, certain Insurers had been obliged to pay for a Tornado as an Electrical Storm. 8*   *Philadelphia,* 1852
—— Queries and Strictures respecting Espy's Meteorological Report to the Naval Department ; also, the Conclusion arrived at by a Committee of the Academy of Sciences of France agreeably to which Tornados are caused by Heat, &c. 8*
          Philadelphia, 1852
—— *See* Redfield.

Hare, S. *See* Hakluyt, Vol. 4: Appendix 1.

Hare, Lieut. W. A. H. *See* United Kingdom, G, War Office Publications : Appendix 2.

Hareborne, M. W. *See* Hakluyt, Vol. 2 : Appendix 1.

Hargrave, Joseph James. Red River. 8°   *Montreal,* 1871

Hariot, P. *See* France, B, *a* ; Cape Horn: Appendix 2.

Hariot, T. A Briefe and True Report of the new found Land of Virginia, of the Commodities, &c., discouered by the English Colony there. *Plates.* 4° [Reprint.]   *Frankfort o. M.* 1595

Harkness, Henry. A Description of a Singular Aboriginal Race inhabiting the Summit of the Neilgherry Hills, or Blue Mountains of Coimbatoor, in the Southern Peninsula of India. *Plates.* 8°   1832

Harkness, H. W., and J. P. Moore. Catalogue of the Pacific Coast Fungi. 8*
          [*San Francisco,* 1880]
—— Footprints found at the Carson State Prison. *Illustrations.* 8*   [1882]

Harkness, Robert. *See* Murchison.

Harman, Capt. H. J. *See* Walker, J. T.

Harmon, D. W. (de Montreal). *See* Eyriès, Vol. 8 : Appendix 1.

Harnisch, Dr Albert. Badghis, Land und Leute, nach den geographischen Ergebnissen der afghanischen Grenzkommission von 1884-88. Large 8*
          Berlin, 1891

Harrington, B. J. *See* Dawson, J. W.

Harrington, Mark W. *See* United States, C : Appendix 2.

Harris, George W. The Practical Guide to Algiers. *Map, plan, and illustrations.* 12°   [1890]
—— "The" Practical Guide to Algiers. 2nd edition. *Maps, plans, and illustrations.* 12°   1892 [1891]
—— Ditto. 3rd edition. 12° 1893 [1892]
—— Ditto. 4th edition. 12° 1894 [1893]

Harris, John. Navigantium atque Itinerantium Bibliotheca, or a compleat Collection of Voyages and Travels. The two editions of 1705 (2 vols.) and 1745 (2 vols. in 4). *Maps, plates, and portraits.* Folio. [For full Titles and Contents, *see* Appendix 1.]

Harris, Joseph. The Description and use of the Globes and the Orrery. 2nd edition. *Plates.* 8°   1732

Harris, Major. *See* Bushby, G. A.

Harris, T. M. The Journal of a Tour into the Territory Northwest of the Alleghany Mountains, made in the Spring of the year 1803 ; with a Geographical and Historical Account of the State of Ohio. *Maps, &c.* 8°
          Boston, Mass., 1805

Harris, T. W. Entomological Correspondence of (edited by S. H. Scudder) *Portrait.* 8°   *Boston,* 1869

Harris, Walter B. The Land of an African Sultan : Travels in Morocco, 1887-89. *Map and illustrations.* Crown 8°   1889
—— A Journey through the Yemen, and some General Remarks upon that Country. *Map and illustrations.* 8° 1893

Harris, Sir William Cornwallis. Narrative of an Expedition into Southern Africa in 1836-37, from the Cape of Good Hope, through the Territories of the Chief Moselekatse, to the Tropic of Capricorn. *Map and plates.* 8°
          Bombay, 1838
—— Portraits of the Game and Wild Animals of Southern Africa, delineated from Life in their Native Haunts, during a Hunting Expedition from the Cape Colony as far as the Tropic of Capricorn, in 1836 and 1837, with Sketches of the Field Sports. *Coloured plates.* Large folio   1840
—— The Highlands of Æthiopia. 3 vols. *Frontispiece.* 8°   1844
—— Illustrations of the Highlands of Æthiopia. Folio.
—— Introduction to the Second Edition of the Highlands of Æthiopia. 8* 1844

Harrison, Capt. C. W. J. Report on Katha Nuddee and the Swamps in its Valley. *Allahabad*, 1873

Harrison, J. Park. Inductive Proof of the Moon's Insolation. *Tables.* 8* 1867

—— The Hieroglyphics of Easter Island. 8* 1874

—— Rejang Manuscripts on Bamboo. *Plate.* 4* 1875

Harrison, N. Distance Tables for Objects at Sea. 8° 1893

Harrison, R. Nine Years' Residence in Russia, from 1844 to 1853. *Plates.* 8° 1855

—— *See* Catalogues, A : Appendix 2.

Harrison, W. A. A Manual of Physiography. 12° 1878

Harrison, W. H. Rough Notes connected with the Sucheen Estate in the Surat Collectorate. *Map.* Royal 8° *Bombay*, 1856

—— Rough Notes connected with the Dhurumpoor and Banda Estates in the Surat Collectorate. *Map. Bombay*, 1856

Harrisse, Henry. Bibliotheca Americana Vetustissima : a Description of Works relating to America published between the years 1492 and 1551. 4° *New York*, 1866

—— The same. Additions. 4° *Paris*, 1872

—— Notes on Columbus. *Portrait and facsimiles.* Folio *Privately printed, New York*, 1866

—— Notes pour servir à l'Histoire, à la Bibliographie et à la Cartographie de la Nouvelle-France et des Pays adjacents, 1545-1700. 8° *Paris*, 1872

—— Jean et Sébastien Cabot, leur origine et leurs voyages. Étude d'histoire critique . . . d'après des documents inedits. (Vol. 1, "Recueil de Voyages," &c.) *Map.* Large 8° *Paris*, 1882

—— Les Corte-Real et leurs Voyages au Nouveau Monde, d'après des Documents nouveaux ou peu connus, tirés des Archives de Lisbonne et de Modène, suivi du texte inédit d'un récit de la troisième Expédition de Gaspar Corte-Real, et d'une importante Carte nautique Portugaise de l'année 1502. (Vol. 3 of "Recueil de Voyages," &c.) *Frontispiece.* Large 8° *Paris*, 1883

—— Christophe Colomb, son Origine, sa Vie, ses Voyages, sa Famille, et ses Descendants, d'après des Documents inédits tirés des Archives de Gênes, de Savone, de Séville, et de Madrid. 2 vols. (Vol. 6 of the "Recueil de Voyages," &c.) *Plates.* Large 8° *Paris*, 1884

—— Christophe Colomb et Savone. Verzellino et ses Memoirs. Études d'Histoire Critique et Documentaire. 8° *Genoa*, 1887

Harrisse, Henry. Excerpta Colombiniana : Bibliographie de Quatre Cents Pièces, Gothiques, Françaises, Italiennes, et Latines, du Commencement du XVIe Siècle, non décrites jusqu'ici, précédée d'une Histoire de la Bibliothèque Colombine et de son Fondateur. 8° *Paris*, 1887

—— Christophe Colomb : les Corses et le Gouvernement Francais. Large 8* *Paris*, 1890

—— The Discovery of North America : a Critical, Documentary, and Historic Investigation, with an Essay on the Early Cartography of the New World, including Descriptionss of 250 Maps or Globes, existing · or lost, constructed before the year 1536 ; to which are added a Chronology of 100 Voyages westward, Projected, Attempted, or Accomplished between 1431 and 1504 ; Biographical Accounts of the 300 Pilots who first crossed the Atlantic ; and a copious list of the original names of American regions, caciqueships, &c. *Maps.* 4° 1892

—— *See* Cabot ; Columbus ; Peragallo.

Harrower, Henry D. Captain Glazier and his Lake : an Inquiry into the History and Progress of Exploration at the Head-waters of the Mississippi since the Discovery of Lake Itasca. *Maps.* 8* *New York*, 1886

Hart, Capt. H. Notes of a Visit to Zanzibar, 1834. [From the India Records, No. 24.] 8° *Bombay*, 1856

Hart, H. C. Some Account of the Fauna and Flora of Sinai, Petra, and Wâdy 'Arabah (Palestine Exploration Fund Publication). *Maps and plates.* 4° 1891

Hart, Capt. P. Lewis. Report on a Project for the Supply of Water to the Poona Cantonment. 2 vols. *Plans and sections.* Royal 8° *Bombay*, 1858

Hart, Capt. S. V. W. Report on the Town and Port of Kurachee, &c. *Bombay*, 1855

—— Notes of a Visit to the Port of Sonmeeanee, and the Country lying between Kurachee and Hinglaj, in the Lus Territory, in 1840. Royal 8° *Bombay*, 1855

Hart, Sir Robert. Documents relating to 1° The Establishment of Meteorological Stations in China ; and 2° Proposals for Cooperation in the Publication of Meteorological Observations and Exchange of Weather News by Telegraph along the Pacific Coast of Asia. *Map.* Folio *Peking*, 1869

Harting, J. E. *See* Mosenthal.

Hartlaub, Dr G. *See* Emin Pasha.

Hartland, W. E. *See* Quintus Curtius.

Hartleben, A. Chronik der Zeit. Ereignisse und Operationen in Süd-Dalmatien. Von C. T. Fockt. 1. Schilderung des Landes und Volkes und Vorgeschichte des Aufstandes. Zweites Heft. *Maps and illustrations.* 8* *Vienna*, 1882

Hartleben, A. The same. 2. Von Moriz B. Zimmermann. Beginn der Operationen und Vormarsch der K. K. Truppen die ersten Actionen. Die politische Lage. Drittes Heft. *Maps and illustrations.* 8*   *Vienna,* 1882

Hartley, Sir C. A. Description of the Delta of the Danube, and of the Works recently executed at the Sulina Mouth. Edited by C. Manby and J. Forrest. *Maps.* 8°   1862
—— Notes on Public Works in the United States and in Canada, including a Description of the St Lawrence and the Mississippi Rivers and their main Tributaries. 8°   1875
—— Inland Navigations in Europe : being one of the Series of Lectures delivered at the Institution of Civil Engineers, Session 1884-85. *Maps.* 8°   1885

Hartmann, J. M. Commentatio de Geographia Africæ Edrisiana. 4°
                                 Göttingen, 1691
Hartmann, R. Die Nigritier. Eine anthropologisch - ethnologische Monographie. Erster Theil. *Plates.* 8°
                                   Berlin, 1876
—— Die Völker Afrikas. *Plates.* Small 8°   *Leipzig,* 1879
—— Abyssinien und die übrigen Gebiete der Ostküste Afrikas. *Map and illustrations.* Small 8°   *Leipzig,* 1883

Hartt, C. F. Scientific Results of a Journey in Brazil. By Louis Agassiz, and his Travelling Companions. Geology and Physical Geography of Brazil. *Maps and plates.* 8°   1870
—— The Ancient Indian Pottery of Marajó, Brazil. 8*   *Salem,* 1871
—— Notes on the Lingoa Geral, or Modern Tupi of the Amazonas. (From the Transactions of the American Philological Association, 1872.) 8*   1872
—— On the Tertiary Basin on the Maranon. 8*   *New Haven, Conn.,* 1872
—— Contributions to the Geology and Physical Geography of the Lower Amazonas : The Ereré-Monte-Alegre District and the Table-Topped Hills ; with Supplement on the Devonian Brachiopoda of Ereré, by Richard Rathbun. *Plates.* Small 8* *Buffalo, N.Y.,* 1874
—— Preliminary Report of the Morgan Expedition, 1870-71. Report of a Reconnaisance of the Lower Tapajos. [Bulletin of the Cornell University (Science), Vol. I., No. 1.] *Sketch map.* 8*   *Ithaca, N.Y.,* 1874
—— Notes on the Manufacture of Pottery among Savage Races. 12*
                            Rio de Janeiro, 1875
Hartung, G. Tenerife geologisch-topographisch dargestellt. *See* Fritsch, K.
Hartwell, Abraham. *See* Pigafetta, F ; *also* Purchas, Vol. 2, Book 7 : Appendix 1.

Harvey, Rev. M. A Short History of Newfoundland, England's Oldest Colony. 2nd edition. *Map.* 12° 1890
—— *See* Hatton, J.

Harvey, Sir Robert G. *See* Willoughby.

Harvey, Thomas, and William Brewin. Jamaica in 1866 : a Narrative of a Tour through the Island, with Remarks on its Social, Educational, and Industrial Condition. *Map.* 8°   1867

Hase, H. Nachweisungen für Reisende in Italien. 12°   *Leipzig,* 1821

Hasio, J. M. Regni Davidici et Salomonæi, Descriptio Geographica et Historica, una cum Delineatione Syriæ et Ægypti pro statu Temporum sub Seleucidis et Lagidis Regibus, &c. *Maps and plates.* Folio   *Nuremburg,* 1739

Haskel, Daniel, and J. Calvin Smith. A Complete Descriptive and Statistical Gazetteer of the United States of America, containing a particular Description of the States, Territories, Counties, Districts, Parishes, Cities, Towns, and Villages, Mountains, Rivers, Lakes, Canals, and Railroads ; with an Abstract of the Census and Statistics for 1840. 8°
                                 New York, 1843

Haslewood, Edward. New Colonies on the Uplands of the Amazon. 8* 1863

Hassall, Dr A. H. San Remo and the Western Riviera, Climatically and Medically considered. *Map, plan, and woodcuts.* Small 8°   1879

Hassall, Charles. General View of the Agriculture of the County of Monmouth, with Observations on the Means of its Improvement. *Map.* 8°   1812

Hassan, Vita. Die Wahrheit über Emin Pascha, die ägyptische Aequatorial Provinz und den Ssudán von Vita Hassan unter der Mitarbeit von Elie M. Baruck. Aus dem französichen Original übersetzt und mit Anmerkungen versehen von Dr B. Moritz. *Portrait and map.* 8°
                                   Berlin, 1893

Hasse, F. C. A. Quantum Geographia Novissimis periegesibus et transmarinis Peregrinationibus profecerit. Pars 1. Generalia Continens. 4* *Leipzig,* 1837

Hassel, G. Staats- und Address-Handbuch der Teutschen Bundes-Staaten, 1816. 8°
                                   Weimar, 1816

Hassell, —. *See* Pinkerton, Vol. 2 : Appendix 1.

Hasselquist, Frederick. Voyages and Travels in the Levant in the years 1749, 1750, 1751, 1752, containing Observations in Natural History, Physic, Agriculture and Commerce, particularly on the Holy Land and the Natural History of the Scriptures. *Map.* 8°   1706

Hasselt, A. L. van. *See* Veth, P. J.

Hassenstein, Bruno. Ost-Afrika zwischen Chartum und dem Rothen Meere bis Suakin und Massaua. Anhang—Th. von Heuglin : ein arabischer Schriftsteller über die Bedja - Lander. (Ergänzungsheft, 6—Petermann's Mittheilungen.) *Map.* 4° *Gotha, 1861*
—— *See* Petermann, Dr A.

Hassenstein, D. Some Contributions to the Geographical and Cartographical Literature of the Indo-Chinese Frontier Territories; with Note by Trelawney Saunders. *Map.* Folio* [1882]

Hasskarl, J. K. *See* Junghuhn.

Hassler, F. R. Second and Third Volumes of the Principal Documents relating to the Survey of the United States, from Oct. 1834 to Nov. 1836. 8° *New York, 1835*

Hassinger, John A. Catalogue of the Hawaiian Exhibits at the Exposition Universelle, Paris, 1889. 8* *Honolulu, 1889*

Haswell, William A. The Australian Museum, Sydney : Catalogue of the Australian Stalk- and Sessile-Eyed Crustacea. *Plates.* 8° *Sydney, 1882*

Hatch, Arthur. *See* Purchas, Vol. 2, Book 10 : Appendix 1.

Hatch, F. H. *See* Baron, R.; Posewitz.

Hatch, John. *See* Purchas, Vol. 1, Book 5 : Appendix 1.

Hatchett, Charles. On the Spikenard of the Ancients. *Plate.* 4* 1836

Hatt, P. *See* France, B, *b* (No. 570) : Appendix 2.

Hatton, Frank. North Borneo: Explorations and Adventures on the Equator; with Biographical Sketch and Notes by Joseph Hatton, and Preface by Sir Walter Medhurst. *Map, portrait, and illustrations.* 8° 1885

Hatton, Joseph. " The New Ceylon : " being a Sketch of British Borneo, or Sabah, from Official and other exclusive sources of information. *Maps and frontispiece.* Crown 8° 1881
—— *See* Streeter.
—— **and Rev. M. Harvey.** Newfoundland, the Oldest British Colony, its History, its Present Condition, and its Prospects in the Future. *Illustrations.* 8° 1883

Hatton - Richards, T. H. Royal Geographical Society of Victoria : Travels with the Hon. Sir William MacGregor, Administrator of British New Guinea. 8* *Melbourne* [1890]

Hauer, Ritter F. von. Zur Erinnerung an Wilhelm Haidinger. 8* *Vienna, 1871*
—— *See* " Novara."

o

Haughton, Rev. Samuel. The Solar and Lunar Diurnal Tides on the Coasts of Ireland. 4* *Dublin, 1855*
—— Six Lectures on Physical Geography. 8° 1880
—— *See* Galbraith, J. A.; MacClintock, F. L.

Haun, Prof. *See* Forskal, P.

Hauranne, E. D. de. Cuba et Les Antilles. 2 and 3. 8* *Paris, 1865*

Haurigot, G. Le Sénégal. *Illustrations.* 8° *Paris, 1887*

Hauser, Capt. Paul. Das Klydoskop ; graphisches Tellurium. 8* *Vienna, 1882*
—— Die Aequator-Durchgänge des Mondes. Eine Untersuchungs - Probe des Mond - Einflusses auf die Witterung. *Tables.* 12* *Buccari, 1886*

Hausermann, K. *See* Estrey.

Haushofer, M. *See* Andree, Karl.

Hauslab, Ritter von. Ueber die Bodengestaltung in Mexico und deren Einfluss. auf Verkehr und militärischen Angriff und Vertheidigung. *Maps.* 8* *Vienna, 1864*
—— Ueber die Naturgesetze der äusseren Formen der Unebenheiten der Erdoberfläche. 8* *Vienna, 1874*

Havass, Rudolph. Bibliotheca Geographica Hungarica : Bibliographia librorum de regno Hungariæ, quovis sermone compositorum : itemque eorum librorum, quos scriptores Hungarici quavis lingua conscriptos et in quocunque Geographiæ argumento versantes ediderunt : cum præfatione historiam litterarum huc spectantium illustrante. Scripsit in Acroasi. Large 8° *Budapest, 1893*

Haven, Samuel F. Archæology of the United States, or Sketches, Historical and Bibliographical, of the Progress of Information and Opinion respecting Vestiges of Antiquity in the United States. 4° *Washington, 1856*

Havers, G. *See* Hakluyt Soc. Publ., Vols. 84, 85 : Appendix 1.

Haverty, Martin. The Aran Isles : Report of the Excursion of the Ethnographical Section of the British Association from Dublin to the Western Isles of Aran, in Sept. 1857. 8* *Dublin, 1859*

Haviland, Alfred. The Geographical Distribution of Disease in Great Britain. 2nd edition. *Maps.* Large 8° 1892

Hawes, Lieut. A. G. S. *See* Satow.

Hawes, Roger. *See* Gottfried ; Kerr, Vol. 9 ; Purchas, Vol. 1 : Appendix 1.

Hawkesworth, J. Account of the Voyages undertaken by the Order of his present Majesty for making Discoveries in the Southern Hemisphere. 3 vols. *Maps and plates.* Folio 1773
[For full Title and Contents, *see* Appendix 1.]

Hawkesworth, J. *See* Dalrymple.

Hawkins, Bisset. Germany: the Spirit of her History, Literature, Social Condition, and National Economy. 8° 1838

Hawkins, F. V. *See* Galton, Vacation Tourists.

Hawkins, Sir John. *See* Gottfried; Hakluyt, Vols. 3, 4; Hakluyt Soc. Publ., Vol. 57; Purchas, Vol. 4: Appendix 1.

Hawkins, Mary W. S. Plymouth Armada Heroes: the Hawkins Family. *Illustrations.* Small 4° *Plymouth*, 1888

Hawkins, Sir Richard. The Observations of, on his Voyage to the South Sea, A.D. 1593. Folio 1622
—— *See* Burney, Vol. 2; Callander, Vol. 2; Hakluyt Soc. Publ., Vol. 1; Purchas, Vol. 4, Book 7: Appendix 1.

Hawkins, Mr. *See* Walpole: Appendix 1.

Hawkins, Capt. William. *See* Gottfried; Hakluyt, Vol. 4; Kerr, Vol. 8; Purchas, Vol. 1; Thevenot, Vol. 1: Appendix 1.

Hawkridge, Capt. *See* Hakluyt Soc. Publ., Vol. 5: Appendix 1.

Hawks, F. L. *See* Perry.

Hawks, H. *See* Hakluyt, Vol. 3: Appendix 1.

Hawkshaw, Sir John. Reminiscences of South America, from two-and-a-half years Residence in Venezuela. 16° 1838
—— Report to the Egyptian Government on the Suez Canal, Feb. 1863. *Maps.* Folio* 1863
—— **and Sir Andrew Clarke.** Copy Report by Mr Hawkshaw and Sir Andrew Clarke upon the possibility of combining Naval and Military Requirements with the objects of Dover Harbour Bill. *Map.* [Parly. Rep.] Folio 1873
—— Copy of Final Report by Mr John Hawkshaw on Holyhead New Harbour. *Map.* [Parly. Rep.] Folio 1873

Hawkwood, John. *See* Hakluyt, Vol. 2: Appendix 1.

Hawtrey, Emily. *See* Weber.

Haxthausen, Baron von. Transcaucasia: Sketches of the Nations and Races between the Black Sea and the Caspian. *Plates.* 8° 1854
—— Tribes of the Caucasus, with an Account of Schamyl and the Murids. 8° 1855
—— The Russian Empire, its People, Institutions, and Resources. Translated by R. Farie. 2 vols. 8° 1856

Hay, Admiral Sir J. C. Dalrymple. The Suppression of Piracy in the China Sea, 1849. *Map.* 8* 1889

Hay, J. O. Arakan, Past, Present, Future: a Résumé of Two Campaigns for its Development. *Map.* 8° 1892

Hayden, Everett. *See* United States, F, a: Appendix 2.

Hayden, F. V. Preliminary Field Report of the United States Geological Survey of Colorado and New Mexico. 8° *Washington*, 1869
—— Sun Pictures of Rocky Mountain Scenery, with a Description of the Geographical and Geological Features, and some Account of the Resources of the Great West, containing thirty Panoramic Views along the line of the Pacific Railroad from Omaha to Sacramento. *Photographs.* 4° *New York*, 1870
—— The Hot Springs and Geysers of the Yellowstone and Firehole Rivers. (From the *American Journal of Science*, Vol. 3.) *Map and illustrations.* 8* 1872
—— The So-called Two-Ocean Pass. *Plates.* 8* *Washington*, 1879
—— The Great West, and Recent Explorations in the Yellowstone Park. *Plates.* 8° *Philadelphia*, 1880
—— *See* Stanford, E.; *also* United States, G, a: Appendix 2.

Haydn's Dictionary of Dates and Universal Information relating to all Ages and Nations. 14th edition, containing the History of the World to August 1873. By Benjamin Vincent. 8° [1873]
—— The same. 19th edition. 1889

Haydon, G. H. Five Years' Experience in Australia Felix, comprising a Short Account of its Early Settlement and its Present Position, with many particulars interesting to intending emigrants. *Plates.* Large 8° 1846

Hayes, A. A., jun. New Colorado and the Santa Fé Trail. *Map and illustrations.* Large 8° *New York*, 1880
—— Western Journeys, New and Old. (From the *United Service Magazine*, July 1885.) 8* *New York*, 1885

Hayes, Isaac I. Arctic Boat Journey in 1854. Edited, with an Introduction and Notes, by Dr Norton Shaw. *Map.* 12° 1860
—— The Open Polar Sea: a Narrative of a Voyage of Discovery towards the North Pole in the schooner "United States." *Maps and plates.* 8° 1867
—— The Land of Desolation: being a Personal Narrative of Adventure in Greenland. 8° 1871

Hayes, Robert. *See* Purchas, Vol. 1, Book 5: Appendix 1.

Haygarth, W. *See* Walpole, Turkey: Appendix 1.

Haynes, Prof. Henry W. *See* Horsford.

Haynes, Stanley L. A Ramble in the New Zealand Bush. 8° [1868]

Hayter, H. H. Notes of a Tour in New Zealand. 12° *Melbourne*, 1874
—— Notes on the Colony of Victoria, Historical, Meteorological, and Statistical. 2nd edition. 12° *Melbourne*, 1876

Hayter, H. H. Victorian Year Book, containing a Digest of the Statistics of the Colony from 1873 to 1893. *See* Victoria : Appendix 3.

Hayward, George W. Statements of Routes between Yarkand, Kashgar, Khotan, and British Territory. 8* 1869

—— I. Vocabularies of the Dialects of Dardistan, Wakhan, Shignan, and Roshnan. II. Tables of Routes. III. Instrumental Observations in the Gilgit and Yasin Valleys. IV. Re-calculated Elevations of Towns, Villages, Passes, and Encamping - grounds in Eastern Turkistan. Folio* *Lahore,* 1870

—— Account of Explorations between British India and Eastern Turkistan. Folio* *Calcutta,* 1870

Hayward, John. New England Gazetteer, containing Descriptions of all the States, Counties, and Towns in New England, also the Mountains, Rivers, Lakes, Capes, Bays, Harbours, Islands, &c. *Plates.* 8° *Concord,* 1839

Hazard, S. Santo Domingo, Past and Present, with a Glance at Hayti. *Maps and plates.* 8° 1873

Hazen, Henry A. *See* United States, H, *b* : Appendix 2.

Hazen, Major-Gen. W. B. *See* United States, II, *b* : Appendix 2.

Hazin, Sheikh Mohammed Ali. The Life of, written by himself. Translated from two Persian Manuscripts, and illustrated with Notes explanatory of the History, Poetry, Geography, &c., which occur therein, by F. C. Belfour. [Oriental Translation Fund.] 8° 1830

Head, Sir Edmund. Papers relative to the Exploration of the Country between Lake Superior and the Red River Settlement. *Maps.* Folio 1859

Head, Capt. F. B. Rough Notes taken during some Rapid Journeys across the Pampas and along the Andes. 8° 1828

—— The Life of Bruce, the African Traveller. *Maps and plates.* 12° 1830

Head, George. Forest Scenes and Incidents in the Wilds of North America : being a Diary of a Winter's Route from Halifax to the Canadas, and a Residence in the Woods on the Borders of Lakes Huron and Simcoe. 8° 1829

Headrick, Rev. Jas. View of the Mineralogy, Agriculture, Manufactures, and Fisheries of the Island of Arran, with Notices of Antiquities, &c. *Map.* 8° *Edinburgh,* 1807

Heanley, Rev. R. M. A Memoir of Edward Steere, D.D., third Missionary Bishop in Central Africa. *Portrait and maps.* Crown 8° 1888

Heap, D. P. *See* Barlow, J. W.

Heard, J. Practical Grammar of the Russian Language. 8° *St Petersburg,* 1827

Hearn, W. M. Statistical Report of the Colaba Agency. *Map, plates, diagrams, and tables.* Royal 8° *Bombay,* 1854

Hearne, Samuel. A Journey from Prince of Wales Fort in Hudson's Bay to the Northern Ocean, for the Discovery of Copper Mines, a North-West Passage, &c., 1769-72. *Maps and plates.* 4° 1795

—— *See* Eyriès, Vol. 7 : Appendix 1.

Heath, Edwin R. Dialects of Bolivian Indians : a Philological Contribution from Material gathered during Three Years Residence in the Department of Beni, in Bolivia. 8* *Kansas City,* 1883

Heath, R. Natural and Historical Account of the Islands of Scilly. *Map and plates.* 8° 1750

—— *See* Pinkerton, Vol. 2 : Appendix 1.

Heather, J. F. A Treatise on Mathematical Instruments, in which their Construction and the Methods of Testing, Adjusting, and Using them are Concisely Explained. 12° 1863

Heatherington, A. A Practical Guide for Tourists, Miners, and Investors, and all Persons interested in the Development of the Gold Fields of Nova Scotia. *Tables.* 12° *Montreal,* 1868

—— 1860-1869. The Gold Yield of Nova Scotia. *Table.* 16* 1870

Heaton, J. H. Australian Dictionary of Dates and Men of the Time, containing the History of Australasia ,from 1542 to date. 8° 1879

Heaviside, W. I. *See* India, F, *c* : Appendix 2.

Heber, Bishop. Narrative of a Journey through the Upper Provinces of India, from Calcutta to Bombay, 1824-1825 ; with Notes upon Ceylon, and a Journey to Madras and the Southern Provinces, 1826. 3 vols. *Plates.* 8° 1829

Heberer, Michiel. *See* Gottfried : Appendix 1.

Hébert, E. Nomenclature et Classification Géologiques. 8* *Paris,* 1881

Hecquard, C. Élémens de Grammaire Franco-Serbe. 12° *Belgrade,* 1875

Hector, Sir James. On the Geology of the Country between Lake Superior and the Pacific Ocean (between the 48th and 54th Parallels of Latitude) visited by the Government Exploring Expedition under Capt. J. Palliser (1857-60). 8* 1861

—— On the Physical Features of the Central Part of British North America, and on its Capabilities for Settlement. 8* *Edinburgh,* 1861

—— Report on the Petroleum found at Taranaki. Folio* *Wellington,* 1866

—— Meteorological Report, 1868 ; including Abstracts for all previous years. 8° *Wellington,* 1869

—— The same, for 1870 ; with Returns for 1869. 8° *Wellington,* 1871

Hector, Sir James. Handbook of New Zealand : Sydney International Exhibition, 1879. *Maps and plates.* 8°
Wellington, 1879
—— Colonial Museum and Geological Survey Department : Handbook of New Zealand. 4th edition. Revised. *Maps and plates.* 8° *Wellington*, 1886
—— *See* New Zealand, A, c : Appendix 2.
—— **and W. S. W. Vaux.** Notice of the Indians seen by the Exploring Expedition under Capt. Palliser. 8* N.D.

Hedde, Isidore. Description Méthodique des Produits divers recueillis dans un Voyage en Chine. *Map and plates.* Royal 8° *St Etienne*, 1848
—— De l'Industrie Sérigene en Algérie. *Plates.* 8* *Lyon*, 1851

Heddle, J. F. Memoir on the River Indus. Royal 8° *Bombay*, 1855

Hedger, Capt. T. On Sea and Shore : an Autobiography. *Portrait.* 12°
Hull, 1891

Hedges, Sir William. *See* Hakluyt Soc. Publ., Vols. 74, 75, 78 : Appendix 1.

Hedström, Herman. *See* Sweden, A (Geologiska Undersökning): Appendix 2.

Heemskerke, Jacques van. *See* Allgemeine Historie, Vol. 17 : Appendix 1.

Heer, Oswald. Flora Tertiaria Helvetiæ : Die Tertiäre Flora der Schweiz. 3 vols. *Plates.* Folio *Winterthur*, 1855-59
—— Die Pflanzen der Pfahlbauten. *Plates.* 4*
Zürich, 1865
—— Ueber die Polarländer. Vortrag. 8*
Zürich, 1867
—— Die Kreide-Flora der Arctischen Zone, gegründet auf die von den Schwedischen Expeditionen von 1870 und 1872 in Grönland und Spitzbergen gesammelten Pflanzen. *Plates.* 4° *Stockholm* [1874]
—— Nachträge zur Miocenen Flora Grönlands enthaltend die von der Schwedischen Expedition im Sommer 1870 gesammelten Miocenen Pflanzen. *Plates.* 4* *Stockholm* [1874]
—— The Primæval World of Switzerland. Edited by James Heywood. 2 vols. *Map and plates.* 8° 1876
—— Recherches sur le Climat et la Végétation du Pays Tertiaire. Traduction de C. T. Gaudin. *Map and plate.* Folio
Winterthur, N.D.

Heeren, A. H. L. Ideen über die Politik, den Verkehr, und den Handel der vornehmsten Völker der alten Welt. 2 vols. *Maps.* 8° *Gottingen*, 1793-96
—— De Ceylone Insula, per Viginti fere Sæcula Communi Terrarum Mariumque Australium Emporio. 4° *Gottingen*, 1831
—— Historical Researches into the Politics, Intercourse, and Trade of the Carthaginians, Ethiopians, and Egyptians. 2 vols. *Maps.* 8° *Oxford*, 1838

Heeren, A. H. L. The same. 2nd edition. *Maps.* 8° 1850
—— Historical Researches into the Politics, Intercourse, and Trade of the Principal Nations of Antiquity : Asiatic Nations. 2 vols. *Maps.* 8° 1846
—— A Manual of the History of the Political System of Europe and its Colonies, from its Formation at the close of the 15th Century to its Re-establishment upon the Fall of Napoleon. 8°
1846
—— Ancient Greece (translated by G. Bancroft). Also three historical treatises : 1. Political Consequences of the Reformation ; 2. The Rise, Progress, and Practical Influence of Political Theories ; 3. The Rise and Growth of the Continental Interests of Great Britain. 2nd edition. 8° 1847
—— A Manual of Ancient History, particularly with regard to the Constitutions, the Commerce, and the Colonies of the States of Antiquity. 8° 1847

Hegenitius, Godfr., and A. Ortelius. Itinerarium Frisio-Hollandicum et Gallo-Brabanticum. 32° *Leyden*, 1630

Heger, F. Barometrische Höhenmessungen in Nord-Griechenland. 4*
Vienna, 1878

Heiderich, Dr Franz. Die mittlere Höhe Afrikas. 4* *Gotha*, 1888
—— Die mittleren Erhebungsverhältnisse der Erdoberfläche, nebst einem Anhange über den wahren Betrag des Luftdruckes auf der Erdoberfläche. (Sonderabdruck aus den Geographischen Abhandlungen herausgegeben von Prof. Dr Albrecht Penck. Band 5, Heft 1.) *Profile.* Large 8* *Vienna*, 1891

Heilprin, Prof. Angelo. Explorations on the West Coast of Florida and in the Okeechobee Wilderness. (Trans. Wagner Instit.) Large 8° *Philadelphia*, 1887
—— The Geographical and Geological Distribution of Animals. *Map.* Small 8° 1887
—— The Bermuda Islands : a Contribution to the Physical History and Zoology of the Somers Archipelago ; with an Examination of the Structure of Coral Reefs. *Illustrations.* 8° *Philadelphia*, 1889
—— Explorations in Mexico : Barometric Observations among the High Volcanoes of Mexico, with a Consideration of the Culminating Point of the North American Continent. 8* *Philadelphia*, 1890
—— The Corals and Coral Reefs of the Western Waters of the Gulf of Mexico. *Charts.* 8* *Philadelphia*, 1890
—— The Geology and Palæontology of the Cretaceous Deposits of Mexico. *Plates.* Large 8* [*Philadelphia*, 1890]

Heilprin, Prof. Angelo. The Arctic Problem, and Narrative of the Peary Relief Expedition of the Academy of Natural Sciences of Philadelphia. *Map and plates.* 8° *Philadelphia*, 1893
—— The Peary Relief Expedition. (From *Scribner's Magazine.*) *Illustrations.* 8* 1893

Heim, Dr Albert. Handbuch der Gletscherkunde. (Bibliothek geographischer Handbücher herausgegeben von Prof. Dr Friedrich Ratzel.) *Maps.* 8° *Stuttgart*, 1885
—— *See* Margerie.

Heinersdorff, Carl. Reinhold Buchholz' Reisen in West Afrika. Nach seinen hinterlassenen Tagebüchern und Briefen nebst einem Lebensabriss des verstorbenen, von Carl Heinersdorff. *Portrait.* 8° *Leipzig*, 1880

Heitland, W. E., and T. E. Raven. *See* Quintus Curtius.

Hekekyan Bey. Treatise on the Chronology of Siriadic Monuments, Demonstrating that the Egyptian Dynasties of Manetho are Records of Astrogeological Nile Observations, which have been continued to the Present Time. *Plate.* 8° 1863

Hélène, Maxime. Les Nouvelles Routes du Globe; avec une lettre de M. Ferdinand de Lesseps. Canaux isthmiques et routes souterraines, Suez, Panama, Corinthe, Malacca, Saint-Gothard, Mont-Cenis, Arlberg, Simplon, Monts-Blanc, Pyrénées, le tunnel sous-marin du Pas-de-Calais, le canal maritime de Gabès (Mer d'Algérie). *Illustrations.* Large 8° *Paris* [1883]

Heley, W. *See* Purchas, Vol. 3, Book 4: Appendix 1.

Helfer, J. W. Schriften über die Tenasserim Provinzen, den Mergui-Archipel, und die Andaman - Inseln. (Translated from the English by A. von Marschall; Preface by F. Fötterle.) 4° *Vienna*, 1860
—— Travels of Doctor and Madame Helfer in Syria, Mesopotamia, Burmah, and other lands. Narrated by Pauline, Countess Nostitz (formerly Madame Helfer), and rendered into English by Mrs George Sturge. 2 vols. 8° 1878

Helfert, Joseph Alex. F. von. Bericht über die Ausstellung von Schul- und Unterrichts-Gegenständen in Wien. *Map and plates.* Royal 8° *Vienna*, 1862

Hell, Xavier Hommaire de. Les Steppes de la Mer Caspienne, le Caucase, la Crimée, et la Russie Méridionale, Voyage Pittoresque, Historique, et Scientifique. 3 vols. 8° *Paris*, 1843-45
—— Travels in the Steppes of the Caspian Sea, the Crimea, the Caucasus, &c. 8° 1847

Hell, Xavier Hommaire de, Voyageur Français : Notice Nécrologique. Par M. de la Roquette. 8* *Paris*, 1850
—— Extrait du Voyage en Turquie et en Perse pendant 1846-48. Partie Géographique, par [P.] Daussy. *Maps.* Royal 8° *Paris*, 1859

Heller, C. *See* "Novara."

Hellwald, Friedrich von. Die Amerikanische Völkerwanderung. Eine Studie. 12* *Vienna*, 1866
—— Die Russen in Centralasien. 8° *Augsburg*, 1873
—— Ueber Colonien und über die Holländischen Niederlassungen in Ostindien. Ein Beitrag zur Niederländischen Colonialfrage. 8* *Amsterdam*, N.D.
—— *See* Matham ; Stanford.
—— **and J. Chavanne,** Die Verhandlungen des Internationalen Congresses für geographische Wissenschaften in Paris. 8* *Vienna*, 1875

Hellwald, Lieut. de. Report on the Results of the Photographic Expedition into the "Höhen Tauern" (Austrian Alps). 8* *Vienna*, 1863

Helmersen, G. von. Geognostische Bemerkungen über die Steppengegend zwischen den Flüssen Samara, Wolga, Ural, und Manytsch; gesammelt auf einer Reise in 1843 von Noeschel. *Plate.* 8* *St Petersburg*, 1846
—— Nachrichten über die im 1847 von der Russischen Geographischen Gesellschaft ausgesandte Expedition zur Erforschung des Nördlichen Ural. 8* *St Petersburg*, 1847
—— Geognostische Bemerkungen über die Halbinsel Mangyschlak, am östlichen Ufer des Kaspischen Meeres. 8* *St Petersburg*, 1848
—— Geologische Bemerkungen auf einer Reise in Schweden und Norwegen. *Plates.* 4* *St Petersburg*, 1858
—— Die Salzseen Bessarabiens und der Einbruch des Schwarzen Meeres in dieselben in 1850. *Map.* 8* *St Petersburg*, 1859
—— Die geologische Beschaffenheit des untern Narovathals und die Versandung der Narovamündung. *Map and plate.* 8* *St Petersburg*, 1860
—— Die Alexandersäule zu St Petersburg. 8* *St Petersburg*, 1862
—— Der artesische Brunnen zu St Petersburg. 8* *St Petersburg*, 1864
—— Die Geologie in Russland. ·8* *St Petersburg*, 1864
—— Der Peipus-See und die obere Narova. 8* *St Petersburg*, 1864
—— Explanatory Notes on the Geological Map of Russia. [In Russian.] 8* [*St Petersburg*] 1865
—— Des gisements de Charbon de Terre en Russie. *Map.* 8* *St Petersburg*, 1866

Helmersen, G. von. Die Steinkohlenformation des Urals und deren praktische Bedeutung. 8* *St Petersburg,* 1866

—— Die Bohrversuche zur Entdeckung von Steinkohlen auf der Samarahalbinsel, und die Naphthaquellen und Schlammvulkane bei Kertsch und Taman. *Plate.* 8* 1867

—— Das Vorkommen und die Entstehung der Riesenkessel in Finnland. *Plates.* 4* *St Petersburg,* 1867

—— Zur Frage über das behauptete Seichterwerden des Asow'schen Meeres. *Plate.* 8* *St Petersburg,* 1867

—— Die Steinkohlen des mittleren Russlands, ihre Bedeutung und ihre Zukunft. 8* *St Petersburg,* 1867

—— Studien über die Wanderblöcke und die Diluvialgebilde Russlands. *Plates.* 4* *St Petersburg,* 1869

—— Ueber die Nothwendigkeit des Waldschutzes für die schiffbaren Ströme Russlands, und über neue montanistische Untersuchungen und Massnahmen in Russland. 12* *St Petersburg,* 1876

—— Zur Frage über die central-russische Steinkohle. 12* [*St Petersburg*] 1879

—— Geologische und physicogeographische Beobachtungen im Olonezer Bergrevier. *Map.* 8°; and Atlas of plates, folio *St Petersburg,* 1882

—— *See* Baer and Helmersen, 2, 5, 6, 14, 17, 20, 21, 24; and Köppen, A.; Maximowicz; Middendorf; Murchison; Nöschel, A.; Schrenck.

Helmerson, G. von, and L. von Schrenck. Beiträge zur Kenntniss des Russischen Reiches und der angrenzenden Länder Asiens. Vols. 1 to 9. 8° (Atlas to Vol. 5, 4°) *St Petersburg,* 1879-86

CONTENTS.

Vol. 1.—Brandt, J. F. Bericht über die Fortschritte, welche die zoologischen Wissenschaften den von der kaiserlichen Akademie der Wissenschaften zu St Petersburg von 1831 bis 1879, herausgegebenen Schriften verdanken. 1879

Vol. 2.—Goebel, H. Die Vögel des Kreises Uman, Gouvernement Kiew, mit besonderer Rücksicht auf ihre Zugverhältnisse und ihr Brutgeschäft. *Tables.* 1879

Vol. 3.—Köppen, F. T. Die schädlichen Insekten Russlands. *Plate.* 1880

Vol. 4.—Köppen, F. T. Zur Verbreitung des Xanthium spinosum, L., besonders in Russland. Nebst kurzen Notizen über einige andere Unkräuter Südrusslands.

Büchner, E., and T. Pleske. Beiträge zur Ornithologie des St Petersburger Gouvernements.

Köppen, F. T. Ueber einige in Russland vorkommende giftige und vermeintlich giftige Arachniden. 1881

Helmerson and Schrenck—*continued.*

Vol. 5.—Helmersen, G. von. Geologische und physico-geographische Beobachtungen in Olonezer Bergrevier. *Map and atlas* 1882

Vol. 6.—Köppen, F. T. Das Fehlen des Eichhörnchens und das Vorhandensein des Rehs und des Edelhirsches in der Krim. Nebst Excursen über die Verbreitung einiger anderer Säugethiere in Russland, und einem Anhange: zur Herpetologie der Krim.

—— Nachschrift zum Aufsatze "Das Fehlen, &c.," enthaltend einige weitere Nachträge und Berichtigungen.

—— Die Verbreitung des Elenthiers im Europäischen Russland, mit besonderer Berücksichtigung einer in den fünfziger Jahren begonnenen Massenwanderung desselben. Nebst einem Anhange, enthaltend: Das vermeintliche Vorkommen des Bison im Gouvernement Nishni Nowgorod. Mit einer Karte.

—— Notiz über die Rückwanderung der Dreissena Polymorpha, Pall. Nebst einem Anhange: Ueber künstliche Verpflanzung der Flusskrebse in Russland.

Schmidt, F. Einige Bemerkungen zu Prof. A. E. Nordenskjöld's Reisewerk: Die Umsegelung Asien's und Europa's auf der Vega, 1878-80. Mit besonderer Beziehung auf die Geschichte der Russischen Entdeckungsreisen im und am Siberischen Eismeer. *Map* 1883

Vol. 7.—Pleske, Theodor. Uebersicht der Säugethiere und Vögel der Kola-Halbinsel. Theil I. Säugetiere. *Plate* 1884

Vol. 8.—Tolstoi, Graf. D. A. Ein Blick auf das Unterrichtwesen Russland's im 18 Jahrhundert bis 1782. Aus dem Russischen übersetzt von P. von Kügelgen.

Poljakow, I. Anthropologisches und Prähistorisches aus verschiedenen Theilen des Europäischen Russlands. Aus dem Russischen übersetzt von Fr. Russow. *Plates.*

1. Anthropologische Reise durch den mittleren und östlichen Theil des Europäischen Russland's. *Plates.*

2. Untersuchungen in Bezug auf die Steinzeit im Gouvernement Olonez, im Flussthal der Oka und am oberen Laufe der Wolga. *Plates.* 1885

Vol. 9.—Pleske, Theodor. Uebersicht der Säugethiere und Vögel der Kola-Halbinsel. Theil II. Vögel und Nachträge. 1886

Helmert, F. R. *See* Germany, A: Appendix 2.

Helmreichen, Virgil von. Skizze über den Oesterreichischen Reisenden, von H. v. Sonnleithner. 8* *Vienna*, 1852

Helms, A. Z. Travels from Buenos Ayres by Potosi to Lima, with Notes by the Translator. *Map.* 12° 1806
—— *See* Phillips, Collection of Modern and Contemporary Voyages [1], Vol. 5: Appendix 1.

Helms, Henrik. Grönland und die Grönländer. Eine Skizze aus der Eiswelt. 16° *Leipzig*, 1867

Helms, L. V. Pioneering in the Far East, and Journeys to California in 1849, and to the White Sea in 1878. *Maps and illustrations.* 8° 1882

Helps, Arthur. The Life of La Casas, "the Apostle of the Indies." *Map.* 8° 1868

Hemert, A. J. Langeveldt van. *See* Robidé Van der Aa.

Hemso, J. G. da. *See* Schow.

Henchman, Thomas. Observations on the Reports of the Directors of the East India Company on the Trade between India and Europe. 4° 1801

Henderson, Rev. Archibald. Palestine, its Historical Geography. *With topographical index and maps.* Small 8° *Edinburgh* [1884]

Henderson, E. Journal of a Residence in Iceland during 1814-15. 2 vols. *Map and plates.* 8° *Edinburgh*, 1818
—— *See* Eyriès, Vol. 7: Appendix 1.

Henderson, G., and A. O. Hume. Lahore to Yãrkand: Incidents of the Route, and Natural History of the Countries traversed by the Expedition of 1870 under T. D. Forsyth. *Plates.* 8° 1873

Henderson, George E. *See* Cubas.

Henderson, James. History of Brazil, comprising its Geography, Colonisation, Aboriginal Inhabitants, &c. *Maps and plates.* 4° 1821

Hendrik, —. *See* Gottfried; Appendix 1.

Heneage, Charles. *See* Thielmann.

Henfrey, A. The Vegetation of Europe, its Conditions and Causes. *Map.* 12° 1852

Hennell, Lieut. S. Historical Sketch of the Beniyas Tribe of Arabs from 1761 to 1831; with Continuations from 1832 to 1853 by Lieuts. Kemball and Disbrowe. Royal 8° *Bombay*, 1856

Hennepin, L. Description de la Louisiane, nouvellement découverte au Sud-Ouest de la Nouvelle France. 12° *Paris*, 1688
—— Nouvelle découverte d'un très grand pays situé dans l'Amérique, entre le Nouveau Mexique et la Mer Glaciale. *Maps and plates.* 12° *Utrecht*, 1697
—— Nouveau Voyage d'un pais plus grand que l'Europe. *Plates.* 12° *Utrecht*, 1698

Hennepin, L. A new Discovery of a Vast Country in America, extending above Four Thousand Miles, between New France and New Mexico; with a Description of the Great Lakes, Cataracts, Rivers, Plants, and Animals, also the Manners, Customs, and Languages of the several Native Indians . . ; with the Advantages of a Shorter Cut to China and Japan. *Maps and plates.* Small 8° 1699

Hennessey, Henry. The Relations of Science to Modern Civilization: an Essay. 8* *Leeds*, 1862
—— On the Distribution of Temperature in the Lower Region of the Earth's Atmosphere. *Map.* 4* *Dublin*, 1867

Hennessy, J. B. N. Report on the Explorations in Great Tibet and Mongolia, made by A—K. in 1879-82, in connection with the Trigonometrical Branch, Survey of India. *Plan.* Folio *Dehra Dun*, 1884
—— *See* India, F, c: Appendix 2.

Henniker, Sir F. Notes during a Visit to Egypt, Nubia, The Oasis, Mount Sinai, and Jerusalem. *Plates.* 8° 1823
—— The same. 2nd edition. *Plates.* 8° 1824

Hennisch, A. J. V. Handbuch für Reisende: Grossherzogthum Baden. *Illustrations.* 8° *Stuttgart*, 1837

Henrici, Ernst. Das Deutsche Togogebiet und meine Afrikareise, 1887. *Map and profiles.* 8° *Leipzig*, 1888

Henriques, Dr J. A. *See* Transactions, Portugal: Appendix 2.

Henry the Fourth, King. *See* Hakluyt, Vols. 1, 2: Appendix 1.

Henry the Seventh, King. *See* Hakluyt, Vol. 3; Pinkerton, Vol. 12: Appendix 1.

Henry, B. C. Ling-Nam; or, Interior Views of Southern China, including Explorations in the hitherto untraversed Island of Hainan. *Maps and illustrations.* 8° 1886

Henry, F. *See* Salt.

Henry, Joseph. Instructions in Reference to Collecting Nests and Eggs of North American Birds: Circular in Reference to the History of North American Grasshoppers, and in collecting North American Shells. 8* *Washington*, 1860
—— Sketch of the Life and Contributions to Science of Prof. Joseph Henry. 8° *Washington*, N.D.
—— Meteorology in its connection with Agriculture. 8* [*Washington*] N.D.

Henry, Patrick. *See* Sparks.

Henry, Prince, of Portugal. *See* Major; also Kerr, Vol. 2; Purchas, Vol. 1, Book 2: Appendix 1.

Hensbrook, P. A. M. Boele van. De Beoefening der Oostersche Talen in Nederland, en zijne overzeesche Bezitzingen, 1800-74. 4° *Leyden*, 1875

Henshaw, Henry W. (Smithsonian Institution, Bureau of Ethnology.) Perforated Stones from California. *Illustrations.* 8* *Washington*, 1887

Henszlmann, I. *See* Austria-Hungary, B : Appendix 2.

Henwood, William Jory. Report on the Metalliferous Deposits of Kumaon and Gurhwal in North-Western India. *Map.* Royal 8° *Calcutta*, 1855

Hepburn, J. C. *See* Dictionaries, B : Appendix 2.

Hepites, Stefan C. *See* Rumania Transactions : Appendix 3.

" Herald." *See* Seemann.

Héraud, G. *See* France, B, *b* (617, &c.) : Appendix 2.

Herbelot, M. d'. Bibliothèque Orientale, ou Dictionnaire Universel ; contenant généralement tout ce qui regarde la Connoissance des Peuples de l'Orient ; leurs Histoires et Traditions veritables ou fabuleuses ; leurs Religions, Sectes et Politique ; leurs Gouvernements, Loix, Coûtumes, Mœurs, Guerres, et les Révolutions de leurs Empires ; leurs Sciences et Arts ; leurs Théologie, Mythologie, Magie, Physique, Morale, Médicine, Mathématiques, Histoire Naturelle, Chronologie, Géographie, Observations Astronomiques, Grammaire, et Rhétorique ; les Vies et Actions remarquables de touts leurs Saints, Docteurs, &c. Folio. *Paris*, 1697
—— Bibliothèque Orientale, ou Dictionnaire Universel ; contenant tout ce qui fait connoître les Peuples de l'Orient, leurs Histoires et Traditions tant fabuleuses que véritables, leurs Religions et leurs Sectes, les Arts et les Sciences, les Vies de leurs Saints. 4 vols. *Portrait.* 4° *The Hague*, 1777

Herberstein, Baron Sigismund von. *See* Hakluyt, Vol. 1 ; Hakluyt Soc. Publ., Vols. 10, 11 : Appendix 1.

Herbert, T. A Description of the Persian Monarchy now beinge the Orientall Indyes, Iles, and other Parts of the Greater Asia and Africa : a Relation of some Yeares Travaile, begunne anno 1626, into Africa and the Greater Asia, especially the Territories of the Persian Monarchie, &c. *Plates.* Folio 1634
—— Some Years Travel into Africa and Asia the Great, especially describing the famous Empires of Persia and Industant, as also divers other Kingdoms in the Orientall Indies and I'les adjacent. 3rd edition. *Maps, plates.* Folio 1677
—— *See* Thevenot, Vol. 1 : Appendix 1.

Herbert, W. *See* Anville, J. B. B. d'.

Herbertson, Andrew J. *See* Mill.

Herbinius, Joh. Dissertationes de Admirandis Mundi Cataractis supra et subterraneis, earumque principio, elementorum

Herbinius, Joh.—*continued.*
circulatione, ubi eadem occasione æstus Maris refluivera ac genuina causa asseritur, necnon terrestri ac primigenio Paradiso, Locus situsque verus in Palæstina restituitur, in Tabula Chorographica ostenditur, et contra Utopios, Indianos, Mesopotamios, aliosque asseritur. *Map and plates.* Small 4° *Amsterdam*, 1678

Herckemann, E. *See* Churchill, Vol. 1 : Appendix 1.

Herculano, A. *See* Gama, Vasco da.

Herder, J. G. Ideen zur Philosophie der Geschichte der Menschheit. 4 vols. in 2. Small 4° *Leipzig*, 1784-91

Herdman, Prof. W. A. *See* United Kingdom, H, Challenger Publications : Appendix 2.

Héricourt, C. Rochet d'. *See* Rochet d'Héricourt.

Heriot, George. *See* Phillips, " Collection of Modern and Contemporary Voyages and Travels " [1], Vol. 7 : Appendix 1.

Herman, Otto. Ungarns Spinnen-Fauna. Vols. 1 and 2. *Plates.* 4° *Budapest*, 1876-78

Hermann, B. F. Abriss der physikalischen Beschaffenheit der Oesterreichischen Staaten. 8° *Leipzig*, 1782

Hermann, Gottfried. Literarische Sympathien oder industrielle Buchmacherei ; ein Beitrag zur Geschichte der neueren Englischen Lexikographie von Dr J. G. Flügel. Nebst einer Vorwort von Dr Gottfried Hermann. 8° *Leipzig*, 1843

Hermansen, W. *See* Allgemeine Historie, Vol. 8 : Appendix 1.

Hermite, Jacques le. *See* Burney, Vol. 3 ; Callander, Vol. 2 ; Harris, Vol. 1 ; Kerr, Vol. 10 ; Allgemeine Historie, Vol. 12 : Appendix 1.

Hernandez, Antonio R. del Valle. Balanza General del Comercio de la Isla de Cuba en el año 1830. Folio. *Havana*, 1841

Hernandez, Juan A. *See* Angelis, Vol. 5 : Appendix 1.

Hernandez, Pero. *See* Ternaux-Compans, Vol. 6 : Appendix 1.

Herndon, Lieut. W. Lewis. Exploration of the Valley of the Amazon. *Map and plates.* 8° *Washington*, 1854
—— **and L. Gibbon.** Exploration of the Valley of the Amazon. Part 1, by Lieut. Herndon ; Part 2, by Lieut. Gibbon. *Plates.* 2 vols. 8° *Washington*, 1853-54

Hernsheim, Franz. Südsee-Erinnerungen (1875-1880). Mit einen einleitenden Vorwort von Dr Otto Finsch. *Plates.* 4° *Berlin* [1883]

Herodotus. Translated from the Greek, with Notes by the Rev. W. Beloe. 4 vols. *Map.* 8° 1806

—— Textus Schweighæuseri, cui adjectæ sunt, editionum Schweighæuseri, Reizii et Schæferi, et Wesselingii, lectiones variantes omnes; et adnotationibus Wesselingii et Valckenarii aliorumque et suis illustravit Schweighæuser; latine ex versione J. Schweighæuser, ad editionem Reizii et Schaferi emendata. 5 vols. 8° *Glasgow,* 1818

—— [Greek], from the Text of Schweighæuser. Edited by G. Long. 2 vols 8° 1830

—— The History of Herodotus. A new English Version, edited with Copious Notes and Appendices, illustrating the History and Geography of Herodotus, from the most recent Sources of Information, and embodying the chief Results, Historical and Ethnographical, which have been obtained in the Progress of Cuneiform and Hieroglyphical Discovery. By George Rawlinson; assisted by Col. Sir Henry Rawlinson and Sir J. G. Wilkinson. 4 vols. *Maps and illustrations.* 8° 1858-62

—— The same. 4th edition. 4 vols. *Maps and illustrations.* 8° 1880

—— *See* Wheeler, J. T.

Heron, Robert. *See* Niebuhr, C.

Herrada, Martin de. *See* Purchas, Vol. 3, Book 2 : Appendix 1.

Herrera, Antonio de. The General History of the vast Continent and Islands of America commonly call'd the West Indies, from the first Discovery thereof; . . . collected from the Original Relations sent to the Kings of Spain. Translated by John Stevens. 6 vols. *Maps and plates.* Small 8° 1725-26

—— Historia General de los hechos de los Castellanos en las Islas y Tierra del Mar Oceano. 2 vols. *Maps.* Folio *Madrid,* 1730

—— *See* Hakluyt Soc. Publ., Vol. 24; Kerr, Vol. 3 ; Purchas, Vol, 3, Book 5 : Appendix 1.

Herrick, C. L. *See* United States, K, Minnesota Geol. and Nat. Hist. Survey, Bulletin No. 7 : Appendix 2.

Herrlein, A. von. Aschaffenburg und seine Umgegend. Ein Handbuch für Fremde. *Plans.* 12° *Aschaffenburg,* 1857

Herschel, Sir John F. W. Instructions for Making and Registering Meteorological Observations in Southern Africa, and other Countries in the South Seas, and also at Sea. 8* *Privately printed,* 1835

—— Memoir of Francis Baily, Esq. (From the *Monthly Notices* of the Royal Astronomical Society.) 8* 1845

Herschel, Sir John F. W. Results of Astronomical Observations made during the years 1834, '35, '36, '37, '38, at the Cape of Good Hope, being the Completion of a Telescopic Survey of the whole Surface of the Visible Heavens commenced in 1825. *Plates.* 4° 1847

—— Outlines of Astronomy. 5th edition. *Plates.* 8° 1858

—— A Manual of Scientific Enquiry. . . . 3rd edition, superintended by the Rev. Robert Main. *Map and plates.* 8° 1859

—— Meteorology, from the "Encyclopædia Britannica." *Plates.* 12° *Edinburgh,* 1861

—— Physical Geography, from the "Encyclopædia Britannica." 8° *Edinburgh,* 1861

—— A Manual of Scientific Enquiry, prepared for the Use of Officers in Her Majesty's Navy, and Travellers in general. 4th edition, superintended by R. Main. *Plate.* 8° 1871

—— The same. 5th edition. Edited by Sir R. S. Ball. 8° 1886

—— *See* United Kingdom, A, Admiralty Publ.: Appendix 2.

Herschell, Sir Wm., and Caroline Herschell. Catalogue of Stars not in the British Catalogue, from Flamsteed's observations in the "Historia Cœlestis," with Index to the latter and list of Errata. Folio 1798

Hertslet, Lewis and Sir Edward. A Complete Collection of the Treaties and Conventions, and Reciprocal Regulations, at present between Great Britain and Foreign Powers; and of the Laws, Decrees, and Orders in Council concerning the same, so far as they relate to Commerce and Navigation, to the Repression and Abolition of the Slave Trade, and to the Privileges and Interests of the Subjects of the High Contracting Parties. Compiled from Authentic Documents. Vols. 1-15, 17-18. *Maps.* 8° 1840-93

Hertslet, Sir Edward. The Map of Europe by Treaty, showing the various Political and Territorial Changes which have taken place since the general Peace of 1814. 3 vols. *Maps.* 8° 1875

—— The same. With numerous Maps and Notes. Vol. 4, 1875 to 1891. Large 8° 1891

—— General Index (chronologically and alphabetically arranged) to the British and Foreign State Papers; Vol. 1 to Vol. 63 (1373 to 1873). Vol. 64. 8° 1879

—— General Index, arranged in order of Countries and Subjects, to Hertslet's Commercial Treaties, Vols. 1-15, with Notes shewing which Treaties and other Documents were in force on the 1st January 1885. 8° 1885

Hertoge, Theodoric. *See* Burney, Vol. 2 : Appendix 1.

Hertwig, Richard. Gedächtnissrede auf Carl Theodor von Siebold, gehalten in der öffentlichen Sitzung der K. b. Akademie der Wissenschaften zu München zur Feier ihres einhundert und sieben-und-zwanzigsten Stiftungstages am 29 Marz 1886. 4* *Munich*, 1886

Hertz, Charles. La Géographie Contemporaine d'après les Voyageurs, les émigrants, les commerçants (La Conquéte du Globe). *Maps and illustrations.* Royal 8° *Paris* [1880 ?]

Hervey, Major Charles. Report of Operations in the Thuggee and Dacoity Department during 1859 and 1860. Royal 8° *Calcutta*, 1861

Hervey, Maurice H. Dark Days in Chili : an Account of the Revolution of 1891. *Plates.* 8° 1892

Herz, Dr Norbert. Lehrbuch der Landkarten Projektionen. Large 8° *Leipzig*, 1885

Hespers, Karl. *See* Schynse.

Hesronita, J. *See* Purchas, Vol. 2, Book 9 : Appendix 1.

Hess, Heinrich. Hartleben's Illustrirter Führer, No. 28, Handbuch für Touristen und Alpenfreunde. Illustrirter Führer durch die Zillerthaler Alpen und die Riesenferner-Gruppe. *Maps and illustrations.* 12° *Vienna*, 1887
—— Special- Führer durch das Gesäuse und durch die Ennsthaler Gebirge zwischen Admont und Eisenerz. 2nd edition. *Illustrations.* 12° *Vienna*, 1890

Hesse, Otto. *See* Bauer.

Hesse-Wartegg, Ernst von. Nord-Amerika, seine Städte und Naturwunder, sein Land, und seine Leute. *Plates.* 4° *Leipzig*, 1880
—— Tunis, the Land and the People. *Illustrations.* 8° 1882

Hessels, J. H. *See* Ortelius.

Hessler, Carl. Die deutschen Kolonieen. Beschreibung von Land und Leuten unserer auswärtigen Besitzungen. 2nd edition. *Maps and illustrations* *Metz*, 1889

Hettner, Dr Alfred. Reisen in den Columbianischen Anden. *Map.* 8° *Leipzig*, 1888
—— Die Kordillera von Bogotá. (Ergänz., 104—Pet. Mittheil.) 4° *Gotha*, 1892
—— *See* Germany, C (Vol. 2): Appendix 2.

Heude, Lieut. William. A Voyage up the Persian Gulf, and a Journey Overland from India to England, in 1817. *Plates.* 4° 1819

Heufler, Ludwig Ritter von. Asplenii Species Europaeae : Untersuchungen über die Milzfarne Europa's. *Maps and plates.* 8° *Vienna*, 1856

Heuglin, Theodor von. Reisen in Nord-Ost-Afrika : Tagebuch einer Reise von Chartum nach Abyssinien mit besonderer Rücksicht auf Zoologie und Geographie, in 1852-53. *Maps and plates.* 8° *Gotha*, 1857
—— Die Tinnésche Expedition im westlichen Nilquellgebiet 1863-64. (Ergänzungsheft, 15 — Petermann's Mittheilungen.) *Maps.* 4° *Gotha*, 1865
—— Reise nach Abessinien, den Gala-Ländern, Ost-Sudán und Chartúm in den Jahren 1861 und 1862, mit Vorwort von Dr A. E. Brehm. *Map and plates.* 8° *Jena*, 1868
—— Reise in das Gebiet des Weissen Nil und seiner westlichen Zuflüsse in den Jahren 1862-64. Mit einem Vorworte von Dr A. Petermann. *Map and plates.* 8° *Leipzig*, 1869
—— Reisen nach dem Nordpolarmeer in den Jahren 1870 und 1871. 3 vols. *Maps and plates.* 8° *Brunswick*, 1872-74
—— Reise in Nordost Afrika : Schilderungen aus dem Gebiete der Beni Amer und Habab, nebst zoologischen Skizzen und einem Führer für Jagdreisende. 2 vols. *Map and coloured plates.* 8° *Brunswick*, 1877
——, **Theodor Kinzelbach, W. Munzinger, and — Steudner.** Die Deutsche Expedition in Ost Afrika, 1861-62. (Ergänzungsheft, 15—Petermann's Mittheilungen.) *Coloured plates and maps.* 4° *Gotha*, 1865

Heusser, J. C., and George Claraz. Beiträge zur geognostischen und physikalischen Kenntniss der Provinz Buenos Aires. *Plate.* 4* *Zurich*, 1864

Hewett, H. H. *See* Remon.

Hewett, J. P. *See* India, O, N.W. Prov.: Appendix 2.

Hewett, Sir William. *See* Wylde.

Hewitt, James. Scripture Geography : being an Account of the more Important Countries and Places mentioned in Holy Scripture. *Map.* 12° N.D.

Hewson, M. B. Notes on the Canadian Pacific Railway. Small 8° *Toronto*, 1879

Hexham, Henry. A Copious English and Nether-Dutch Dictionary, and Nether-Dutch and English Dictionary ; with an Appendix of all the Names of all kinds of Beasts, Birds, and Fishes ; as also a Compendious Grammar. New edition, enlarged by Daniel Manly. Small 4° *Rotterdam*, 1672

Hey, R. *See* Osburn, W.

Heyd, W. Geschichte des Levantehandels im Mittelalter. 2 vols. 8° *Stuttgart*, 1879

Heyes, Rev. J. F. Aspects of Imperial Federation. 8* *Oxford*, 1887
—— The Recognition of Geography. 8* *Oxford*, 1887

Heyfelder, Dr O. Transkaspien und seine Eisenbahn: nach Acten des Erbauers Generallieutenant M. Annenkow. *Maps, sections, and illustrations.* 8° *Hanover,* 1888

Heylyn, Peter. Mikrokosmos: a Little Description of the Great World. 5th edition. 4° *Oxford,* 1631
—— Cosmographie, in Four Bookes, containing the Chorographie and Historie of the whole World, and all the principall Kingdomes, Provinces, Seas, and Isles thereof. *Maps.* Folio 1652
—— Cosmography, in Four Books, containing the Chorography and History of the whole World, and all the Principal Kingdoms, Provinces, Seas, and Isles thereof; with an Accurate and Approved Index of all the Kingdoms, Provinces, &c. . . . Revised and corrected by the Author himself immediately before his death. *Maps.* Folio 1682

Heym, Jean. Nouveau Dictionnaire Russe-François et Allemand, composé d'après le Dictionnaire de l'Académie Russe. 3 vols. 4° *Moscow,* 1799-1802

Heyman, John. *See* Egmont, J. Æ. Van.

Heyne, Benjamin. Tracts, Historical and Statistical, on India; with Journals of Several Tours through various Parts of the Peninsula, also an Account of Sumatra. *Maps and plates.* 4° 1814

Heynes, Edward. *See* Gottfried; Purchas, Vol. 1, Book 5: Appendix 1.

Heywood, B. A. A Vacation Tour at the Antipodes, through Victoria, Tasmania, New South Wales, Queensland, and New Zealand, in 1861-62. *Maps and plates.* 8°. 1863

Heywood, James. *See* Heer.

Hibbert, Samuel. Description of the Shetland Islands: an Account of their Geology, Scenery, Antiquities, and Superstitions. *Map and plates.* 4° *Edinburgh,* 1822
—— History of the Extinct Volcanoes of the Basin of Neuwied, on the Lower Rhine. *Maps and plates.* 8° *Edinburgh,* 1832

Hickson, R. *See* South Australia, A: Appendix 2.

Hickson, Sydney J. A Naturalist in North Celebes: a Narrative of Travels in Minahassa, the Sangir, and Talaut Islands; with notices of the Fauna, Flora, and Ethnology of the districts visited. *Maps and illustrations.* 8° 1889

Hickson, W. E. On the Climate of the North Pole, and on Circumpolar Exploration. 8* 1865
—— Height and Orbit of the November Meteors. 8* 1867

Higginson, Col. T. W. *See* Horsford.

Hildebrand, A. H. Report on the Southern Shan States. Folio* *Rangoon,* 1887

Hildebrand, P. A. Travels in the Holy Land of Prince Radivil Sirotka in 1582-84. [In Russian.] 8° *St Petersburg,* 1879

Hildebrandsson, H. Hildebrand. Atlas des Mouvements Supérieurs de l'Atmosphère. *Maps.* 4° *Stockholm,* 1877
—— *See* Mohn.

Hilgard, Eugene W. *See* United States, A (Tenth Census, Vol. 5), and C, a: Appendix 2.

Hill, Rev. Brian. Observations and Remarks in a Journey through Sicily and Calabria in the year 1791; with a Postscript containing some account of the ceremonies of the last Holy Week at Rome, and of a Short Excursion to Tivoli. *Map.* 8° 1792

Hill, Edward S. Lord Howe Island: Official Visit by the Water Police Magistrate and the Director of the Botanic Gardens, Sydney; together with a Description of the Island. *Map.* 8* *Sydney,* 1869

Hill, G. B. *See* Gordon, C. G.

Hill, George W. Tables of Venus, prepared for the use of the American Ephemeris and Nautical Almanac. 4* *Washington,* 1872

Hill, Gray. With the Beduins: a Narrative of Journeys and Adventures in unfrequented parts of Syria. *Maps and illustrations.* 8° 1891

Hill, J., and E. Roberts. Tide-Tables for the Indian Ports for the year 1888 (also January 1889). 12° [1887]
—— The same for the year 1889 (also January 1890). Parts 1 and 2. 12°
—— The same for the year 1895 (also January 1896), 2 Parts. Part I. Western Ports, Aden to Pamban Pass; Part II. Eastern and Burma Ports, Negapatam to Port Blair. 12° 1894
—— *See* Baird; Rogers.

Hill, Richard. A Week at Port-Royal. 12° *Montego Bay,* 1855

Hill, Robert T. The Texas Section of the American Cretaceous. (From the *American Journal of Science,* Vol. 34.) 8* 1887
—— Mexico as an Iron-producing Country. (From *The Engineering Magazine.*) 8* 1893

Hill, S. S. Travels on the Shores of the Baltic, and to Moscow. 8° 1854
—— Travels in Siberia. 2 vols. *Map.* 8° 1854
—— Travels in the Sandwich and Society Islands. 8° 1856
—— Travels in Peru and Mexico. 2 vols. 8° 1860

Hillier, Walter Caine. *See* Wade.

Himly, Karl, and Dr Georg Wegener. Nord-Tibet und Lob-Nur-Gebiet in der Darstellung des Ta-Thsing i thung yü thu. *Map.* 8* *Berlin*, 1893

Hinchcliff, T. Woodbine. Summer Months among the Alps, with the Ascent of Monte Rosa. *Map and plates.* 8° 1857

—— South American Sketches, or a Visit to Rio Janeiro, the Organ Mountains, La Plata, and the Paraná. *Map and plates.* 8° 1863

—— Over the Sea and Far Away : being a Narrative of Wanderings round the World. *Plates.* 8° 1876

Hincks, Edward. Report to the Trustees of the British Museum respecting certain Cylinders and Terra-Cotta Tablets with Cuneiform Inscriptions. 12* 1854

Hind, Prof. H. Y. Return to Legislative Assembly of Copies of Reports, &c., of the Assinniboine and Saskatchewan Expedition during 1858. *Maps.* 4° *Toronto*, 1859

—— British North America. Reports of Progress, together with a Preliminary and General Report, on the Assinniboine and Saskatchewan Exploring Expedition ; made under Instructions from the Provincial Secretary, Canada. *Maps and plates.* Folio 1860

—— Explorations in the Interior of the Labrador Peninsula, the Country of the Montagnais and Nasquapee Indians. 2 vols. *Map and coloured plates.* 8° 1863

—— A Preliminary Report on the Geology of New Brunswick, together with a Special Report on the Distribution of the "Quebec Group" in the Province. 8° *Fredericton*, 1865

Hind, J. R. The Illustrated London Astronomy, for the use of Schools and Students. *Woodcuts.* 8° 1853

Hinderstein, G. F. von Derfelden de. Mémoire Analytique pour servir d'Explication à la Carte Générale des Possessions Néerlandaises dans le Grand Archipel Indien. 4° *The Hague*, 1841

Hingston, James. The Australian Abroad : Branches from the Main Routes round the World. *Maps and illustrations.* 8° 1879

—— The same. Series 2 : Ceylon, India, and Egypt. *Illustrations.* 8° 1880

Hinman, Russel. The Source of the Mississippi. (From *Science*, 13th Aug.) 4* 1886

—— Eclectic Physical Geography. *Maps and illustrations.* 12° *New York* [1888]

Hinricks, Prof. *See* Seetzen.

Hinton, J. H. The History and Topography of the United States. 2nd edition. 2 vols. *Plates.* 4° 1834

—— The same. 3rd edition. 2 vols. *Maps and plates.* 4° 1842

Hinton, R. J. The Resources and Natural Wealth of Arizona : a Handbook to its History, Towns, Mines, Ruins, and Scenery. *Illustrations.* 12° *San Francisco* [1877]

Hiouen-Thsang (or Hiuen Tsiang). Histoire de la Vie de, et de ses Voyages dans l'Inde depuis l'an 629 jusqu'en 645, par Hoeï-li et Yen-Thsong. Traduite du Chinois par S. Julien. 8° *Paris*, 1853

—— *See* Beal ; Yule, Sir H.

Hippisley, G. Narrative of the Expedition to the Rivers Orinoco and Apuré, in South America. 8° 1819

Hippocrates. *See* Ramusio, Vol. 2 : Appendix 1.

"Hirondelle." *See* Monaco.

Hippon, Capt. Anthony. *See* Astley, Vol. 1 : Gottfried ; Kerr, Vol. 8 ; Purchas, Vol. 1, Book 3 ; Allgemeine Historie, Vol. 1 : Appendix 1.

Hirsch, A., and J. Dumur. *See* Switzerland, A : Appendix 2.

—— **and E. Plantamour.** *See* Switzerland, A : Appendix 2.

Hirschfeld, G. Vorläufiger Bericht über eine Reise im südwestlichen Kleinasien. Parts 1 and 2. *Map and plates.* 8* [1874-75]

—— Gedächtnissrede auf Karl Zöppritz gehalten am 10 April 1885, vor der Geographischen Gesellschaft zu Königsberg. 8* *Königsberg*, 1885

—— Bericht über die Fortschritte in der geographischen und topographischen Kenntniss der alten griechischen Welt. 8° *Gotha*, 1890

Hirschfield, J., and W. Pichler. Die Bäder, Quellen, und Curorte Europa's. Vol. 1. Large 8° *Stuttgart*, 1875

Hirth, F. Sketch Map of the Chinese Province of Kuang Tung, with Explanatory Appendices. Square 8* *Canton*, 1872

—— Two Articles on Chinese Geography. 8* 1873-74

—— China and the Roman Orient : Researches into their Ancient and Mediæval Relations, as represented in old Chinese Records. *Map.* 8° *Leipzig*, 1885

—— The Ta-Ts'in Question. (From the *Chinese Recorder*.) 8* 1885

—— Chinesische Studien. Erster Band. *Illustrations.* Small 4° *Leipzig*, 1890

Hislop, Stephen. Papers relating to the Aboriginal Tribes of the Central Provinces [of India] . . . Edited, with Notes and Preface, by R. Temple. 8° [*Nagpore*] 1866

—— *See* Smith, Dr George ; *also* India, C (Geological Papers) : Appendix 2.

Hitchcock, C. H. First Annual Report upon the Geology and Mineralogy of the State of New Hampshire. *Map.* 8*
Manchester, N.H., 1869

Hitchcock, Edward. Report on the Geology, Mineralogy, Botany, and Zoology of Massachusetts. *Woodcuts.* 8°
Amherst, 1833

—— Report on a Re-Examination of the Economical Geology of Massachusetts. 8° *Boston, Mass.*, 1838

——Ichnology of New England : a Report on the Sandstone of the Connecticut Valley, especially its Fossil Footmarks, made to the Government of the Commonwealth of Massachusetts. *Maps and plates.* 4° *Boston, Mass.*, 1858

Hitchcock, Prof. Roswell D. *See* Merrill.

Hitchman, Francis. Richard F. Burton : his Early, Private, and Public Life, with an account of his Travels and Explorations. 2 vols. *Illustrations.* 8° 1887

Hiuen-Tsiang. *See* Hiouen-Thsang.

Hjorth, J. Description du Golfe du Finlande et de l'entrée du Golfe de Bothnie, d'après les Instructions Nautiques. *Plates.* 8° *Paris*, 1854

—— Description des Côtes de L'Esthonie, de la Livonie, de la Courlande (Russie), de la Prusse, et de la Poméranie, jusqu'au Cap Darserort, d'après les Instructions Nautiques. *Plates.* 8° *Paris*, 1855

Hoare, Charles. Mensuration made Easy, or the Decimal for the Million, with its Application to the Daily Employments of the Artisan and Mechanic. 12* 1855

Hoare, Constance. *See* Turner-Turner.

Hoare, Sir R. C. Journal of a Tour in Ireland, A.D. 1806. *Plate.* 8° 1807

—— Classical Tour in Italy and Sicily. *Map.* 4° 1819

—— *See* Phillips [3], Vol. 1, New Voyages and Travels : Appendix 1.

Hoare, William. *See* Gottfried : Appendix 1.

Hobart, R. J. Board of Revenue : Reports on the Actual Out-turn of the Cotton Crop, North-Western Provinces, for 1872-73. [Portion of the India Records, Vol. 6, N.-W. Provinces.] 8° *Allahabad*, 1873

—— *See* India, Board of Revenue : Appendix 2.

Hobbs, Giles. *See* Purchas, Vol. 1, Book 5 : Appendix 1.

Hobhouse, Sir J. C. [afterwards Lord Broughton de Gyfford]. Journey through Albania and other Provinces of Turkey in Europe and Asia to Constantinople, in 1809-10. 2 vols. *Map and plates.* 4° 1813

Hoche, Jules. Le Pays des Croisades. *Map and illustrations.* Small folio *Paris* [1886]

Hochstetter, Ferdinand R. von. Lecture on the Geology of the Province of Auckland, New Zealand. Folio*
Auckland, 1859

—— Neu-Seeland. *Maps and plates.* 4° *Stuttgart*, 1863

—— New Zealand, its Physical Geography, Geology, and Natural History, with Special Reference to the Results of Government Expeditions in the Provinces of Auckland and Nelson. Translated from the German . . . by E. Sauter. . ; with Additions up to 1866 by the Author. *Maps and plates.* 8° *Stuttgart*, 1867

—— Die geologischen Verhältnisse des östlichen Theiles der europäischen Türkei. Erste Abtheilung. *Map.* 4° *Vienna*, 1870

—— In Memoriam : Ferdinand R. von Hochstetter. By Julius von Haast. *Portraits.* Large 8* *Christchurch*, 1884

—— *See* Kirchhoff ; Mundy, D. L. ; " Novara."

Hockin, J. P. *See* Keate.

Hodder, Edwin. The History of South Australia, from its Foundation to the year of its Jubilee ; with a Chronological Summary of all the principal events of interest up to date. 2 vols. *Maps.* 8° 1893

Hodges, William. *See* Pelham, Vol. 1 : Appendix 1.

Hodgkin, John. Calligraphia Graeca et Poecilographia Graeca, exaravit J. Hodgkin, sculpsit H. Ashby. 4° 1794

Hodgkinson, Clement. Australia, from Port Macquarie to Moreton Bay ; with Descriptions of the Natives, their Manners and Customs, the Geology, Natural Productions, Fertility, and Resources of that Region. *Map and plates.* 8° 1845

Hodgkinson, W. O. Queensland : North-West Explorations. Folio*
Brisbane, 1877

—— Report upon the Palmer River Gold Field. *Plan.* Folio* *Brisbane*, 1883

Hodgson, Adam. Letters from North America, written during a Tour in the United States of Canada. 2 vols. *Maps.* 8° 1824

Hodgson, Brian Houghton. On the Physical Geography of the Himálaya. *Map.* 8* *Calcutta*, 1850

—— Papers relative to the Colonisation, Commerce, Physical Geography, &c., of the Himalaya Mountains and Nepal. *Map.* Royal 8° *Calcutta*, 1857

—— Route from Cathmandu in Nepal, to Tāzedō on the Chinese Frontier. 4* N.D.

Hodgson, Lieut. C. J. Letter on the Proposed Canal near Tihara, below Loodianah, May 1847. 8* 1847

Hodgson, William B. The Foulahs of
Central Africa, and the African Slave
Trade. 8*   *New York*, 1843
—— Notes on Northern Africa, the Sahara,
and the Soudan, in Relation to the
Ethnography, Languages, History, Poli-
tical and Social Condition of those
Countries. 8°   *New York*, 1844
—— The Gospels, written in the Negro
Patois of English, with Arabic Characters,
by a Mandingo Slave in Georgia. 8*
                       New York, 1857
—— Remarks on the Recent Travels of Dr
Barth in Central Africa or Soudan. A
Paper read before the Ethnological
Society of New York, November 1858.
8*   *New York*, 1858
—— *See* Asia (General) : Appendix 2.

Hoernes, Dr Moriz. Dinarische Wanderungen. Cultur- und Landschaftsbilder
aus Bosnien und der Hercegovina. *Map
and illustrations.* 8°   *Vienna*, 1888

Hoëvell, W. R. van. *See* Veth.

Hofer, C. E. Beschreibung von Franzens-
brunn bey Eger, Teplitz in Böhmen und
Karlsbad. 8°   *Prague*, 1799

Hoffman, David. The Fremont Estate :
an Address to the British Public respecting Col. Fremont's Leasing Powers to
the Author, from June 1850. 8*   1851
—— California : Fremont Estates and
Gold Mines ; *Non*-Sale to Mr T. D.
Sargent. 8*   1852

Hoffmann, C. F. A Winter in the Far
West. 2 vols. 8°   1835

Hoffmann, Friedrich. Hinterlassene
Werke. 2 vols. 8° *Berlin*, 1837-38
Vol. 1.—Sein Leben und Werken. Phy-
sikalische Geographie.
Vol. 2.—Geschichte der Geognosie, und
Schilderung der Vulkanischen Er-
scheinungen.

Hoffmann, G. C. *See* Canada, A :
Appendix 2.

Hoffmann, Karl F. V. Die Erde und ihre
Bewohner, ein Hand- und Lesebuch für
alle Stände. *Maps and plates.* Royal 8°
                      Stuttgart, 1835
—— Das Vaterland der Deutschen. Part
1. 8°   *Nuremberg*, 1839
—— *See* Germany, Stuttgart, "Hertha" :
Appendix 3.

Hoffmann, —. Visit to the Kinchenjunga
Glacier. [Extract from the *Indian Daily
News*, 5th and 6th October 1891.] 8*
                      Calcutta, 1891

Hoffmeister, W. Travels in Ceylon and
Continental India, including Nepal and
other Parts of the Himalayas, to the
Borders of Thibet, with some Notices of
the Overland Route; Appendices. *Maps.*
12°   *Edinburgh*, 1848

Hoffmeyer, N. Étude sur les Tempêtes
de l'Atlantique Septentrional et Projet
d'un Service Télégraphique International
relatif à cet Océan. *Diagrams.* 4*
                      Copenhagen, 1880

Hogan, Edmund. *See* Hakluyt, Vol. 2 ;
Kerr, Vol. 7 : Appendix 1.

Hofmann, E. Reise nach den Gold-
wäschen Ost-Sibiriens. *Map and plate.*
8°   *St Petersburg*, 1847
—— *See* Baer & Helmersen, Vols. 4, 12.

Hogan, J. Sheridan. Le Canada. Essai
auquel le premier prix a été adjugé par
le Comité Canadien de l'Exposition de
Paris. *Maps.* 8°   *Montreal*, 1855

Hogarth, D. G., and J. A. R. Munro.
Modern and Ancient Roads in Asia
Minor. (Roy. Geo. Soc. Suppl. Papers,
Vol. 3.) *Maps.* Large 8°   1893

Hogben, George. Various Papers on
Earthquakes in New Zealand. *Maps.*
8*   1890-91

Högbom, A. G. *See* Sweden, A, Geologiska Undersökning : Appendix 2.

Hogendorp, Comte C. S. W. de.
Coup-d'œil sur l'île de Java, et les autres
Possessions Néerlandaises. *Map.* 8°
                      Brussels, 1830

Hogendorp, Dirk van. Berigt van den
tegenwoordigen Toestand der Bataafsche
Bezittingen in Oost-Indiën en den Handel
op dezelve. 8°   [1799]

Hogg, John. Catalogue of Sicilian Plants,
with some Remarks on the Geography,
Geology, and Vegetation of Sicily. 8*
                          1842
—— Letters from Abroad to a Friend at
Cambridge. 8°   1844
—— On some Grecian Antiquities observed
in Sicily. *Plates.* 8*   1847
—— On the Geography and Geology of
the Peninsula of Mount Sinai and the
adjacent Countries. *Maps.* 8*
                      Edinburgh, 1850
—— Notice on Recent Discoveries in
Central Africa by Barth and Overweg,
and of two supposed New Languages in
that Country. 8*   1851
—— On Acræ, a Syracusan Colony in the
South of Sicily, and its principal Antiqui-
ties. Royal 8*   1852
—— Further Notice respecting the Sinaic
Inscriptions. 8*   1854
—— On Two Events which occurred in the
Life of King Canute the Dane. 8* 1855
—— On the Sicilian and Sardinian Lan-
guages. 8*   1856
—— On the History of Iceland, and the
Icelandic Language and Literature. 8*
                          1859
—— Notice of the Annals of Granius
Licinianus, as contained in a Palimpsestic
MS. brought from Egypt. 8*   1859

Hogg, John. On the Distinctions of a Plant and an Animal, and on a Fourth Kingdom of Nature. *Plate.* 8* *Edinburgh,* 1860

—— Supplemental Notes on St George the Martyr, and on George the Arian Bishop. 8* 1861

—— On some Inscriptions from Cyprus, copied by Commander Leycester. 8* 1862

—— On the supposed Scriptural Names of Baalbec, or the Syrian Heliopolis; and on the Chief Heliopolitan Inscriptions, Temples, Deities, and Sun-Worship. 8* 1862

—— Notes on the Byblus-Rush and the Byblus-Bok. [2 *leaves.*] 8* 1864

—— On some Old Maps of Africa, in which the Central Equatorial Lakes are laid down nearly in their True Positions. *Maps.* 8* 1864

—— On Some Ancient Assyrian and Egyptian Sculptures and Incriptions in Turkey. 8* N.D.

—— Further Account of Assyrian and Egyptian Antiquities in Turkey, with a Notice of the Roman Remains at Damascus. 8* N.D.

—— On some Roman Antiquities recently discovered by Dr Barth in Northern Africa. *Plate.* 8* N.D.

—— *See* Graham, C. C.; Porter; Ross, L.; Thompson, G.

Högström, Peter. *See* Allgemeine Historie, Vol. 20: Appendix 1.

Hohenbruck, A. von. Der Internationale Congress der Flachs-Interressenten abgehalten in Wien im August 1873. 8* *Vienna,* 1873

Höhnel, Lieut. Ludwig von. Ostäquatorial Afrika. (Ergänzungsheft, 99— Petermann's Mittheilungen.) *Maps.* 4° *Gotha,* 1890

—— **A. Rosiwal, F. Toula, and E. Suess.** Beiträge zur geologischen Kenntniss des östlichen Afrika. *Map, plates, &c.* 4° *Vienna,* 1891

Holcroft, Thomas. *See* Philips, Collection of Modern and Contemporary Voyages [1], Vol. 2: Appendix 1.

Holden, Edward S. Lists of Recorded Earthquakes in California, Lower California, Oregon, and Washington Territory. Compiled from Published Works, and from Private Information. 8* *Sacramento,* 1887

Holden, William C. History of the Colony of Natal, with a Brief History of the Orange-River Sovereignty, and of the various Races inhabiting it, the Great Lake N'Gami, Commandoes of the Dutch Boers, &c. *Maps and plates.* 8° 1855

Holeczek, Johann. *See* Dorn, A.

Holgate, C. W. An Account of the Chief Libraries of Australia and Tasmania. Large 8* 1886

—— An Account of the Chief Libraries of New Zealand; with an Appendix containing the Statutes relating to Public Libraries in that Colony. 8* 1886

Holinski, A. La Californie et les Routes Interocéaniques. 12° *Brussels,* 1853

Holland, H. Travels in the Ionian Isles, Albania, Thessaly, Macedonia, &c., during the years 1812 and 1813. *Map and plates.* 4° 1815

—— The same. 2nd edition. 2 vols. *Maps and plates.* 8° 1819

Holland, Lieut.-Col. J. Routes from Kurachee to Bhooj, Tatta, Jerruk, Sukkur, Kotree, Kahun, Sonmeeanee, Ferozepoor, Ramnuggu, &c. Edited by R. Hughes Thomas. Royal 8° *Bombay,* 1855

—— Routes between Bhooj and Ahmedabad. Royal 8° *Bombay,* 1855

—— Further Correspondence relative to the Introduction of a Rough Survey and Revenue Settlement in the Province of Sind. *Map.* Royal 8° *Bombay,* 1859

Holland, Philemon. *See* Camden.

Holland, Trevenen J., and Henry Hozier. Record of the Expedition to Abyssinia. Compiled by order of the Secretary of State for War. 2 vols. and vol. of *Maps.* 4° 1870

Holle, K. F. Table van Oud- en Nieuw-Indische Alphabetten. Bijdrage tot de Palaeographie van Nederlandsch-Indië. Large 8° *Batavia,* 1882

Holley, Mrs Mary Austin. Texas. *Map.* Small 8° *Lexington, Ky.,* 1836

Hollier, R. Glances at various Objects during a Nine Weeks Ramble through Parts of France, Switzerland, Piedmont, Austrian Lombardy, Venice, Carinthia, the Tyrol, Schaffhausen, the banks of the Rhine, and Holland. *Map.* 4° 1831

Hollingworth, H. G. A Short Sketch of the Chinese Game of Chess called Kh'e, also called Seang-kh'e, to distinguish it from Wei-kh'e, another Game played by the Chinese. 8* *Shanghai* [1866]

—— List of the Principal Tea Districts in China, and Notes on the Names applied to the various kinds of Black and Green Tea. Small 8* *Shanghai,* 1876

Holm, Gerhard. Den Ostgrönlandske Expedition, udfört i Aarene 1883-85. Vol. 1. *Maps, plates, and facsimiles.* 1889. Vol. 2 (*Text and plates*). 8° *Copenhagen,* 1888

—— *See* Sweden, A, Geologiska Undersökning (*Ser. C,* No. 93): Appendix 2.

Holman, James. Travels through Russia, Siberia, Poland, Cracow, Austria, Bohemia, Saxony, Prussia, Hanover, &c., undertaken during the years 1822, 1823, and 1824, while suffering from total blindness; comprising an Account of the Author being conducted a State Prisoner from the eastern parts of Siberia. 4th edition. *Plates.* 8° 1834
—— A Voyage round the World, including Travels in Africa, Asia, Australasia, America, &c., from 1827 to 1832. 4 vols. *Portrait and plates.* 8°   1834-35

Holmberg, H. J. Ethnographische Skizzen über die Völker der Russischen Amerika. Part I. *Map.* 4°
                                    Helsingfors, 1855

Holmboe, C. A. Norsk og Keltisk, om det Norske og de Keltiske Sprogs Indbyrdes Laan. 4*   *Christiana*, 1854
—— Asaland, 2. 8*   [1872]
—— *See* Schreuder.

Holmes, W. H. The Use of Gold and other Metals among the Ancient Inhabitants of Chiriqui, Isthmus of Darien. *Illustrations.* 8*   *Washington*, 1887
—— Textile Fabrics of Ancient Peru. *Illustrations.* 8*   *Washington*, 1889

Holmes's Magneto - Electric Light, as applicable to Lighthouses. *Plate.* 8*
                                            1862

Holroyd, Arthur T. Egypt and Mahomed Ali Pacha in 1837 8*   1837
—— The Quarantine Laws, their Abuses and Inconsistencies. A Letter addressed to Sir John Cam Hobhouse. 8*   1839

Holst, N. O. *See* Sweden, A, Geologiska Undersökning : Appendix 2.

Holton, I. F. New Granada : Twenty Months in the Andes. *Maps and plates.* 8°   *New York*, 1857

Holtzapffel, Charles. A New System of Scales of Equal Parts, applicable to the various Purposes of Engineering, Architectural, and General Science. *Plate.* 8°
                                            1838

Holub, Dr Emil. Few Words on the Native Question. 8*   *Kimberley*, 1877
—— Eine Culturskizze des Marutse-Mambunda - Reiches in Süd - Central-Afrika. 8°   *Vienna*, 1879
—— The Victoria Falls : a Few Pages from the Diary of Emil Holub, M.D., written during his Third Trip into the Interior of Southern Africa. 12*
                                    Grahamstown, 1879
—— Die Colonisation Afrikas : A. Die Franzosen in Tunis, vom Standpunkte der Erforschung und Civilisirung Afrikas. 8*   *Vienna*, 1881
—— The same. B. Die Engländer in Süd-Afrika, vom Standpunkte der Erforschung und Civilisirung. I. Die Eingebornen-Frage Süd-Afrikas. 8*   *Vienna*, 1882

Holub, Dr Emil—*continued.*
—— The same. 2. Der Export und Import des Caplandes. 8*   *Vienna*, 1882
—— The same. Die Stellung des Arztes in den transoceanischen Gebieten, vom Standpunkte der Erforschung und Civilisirung. 4 heft. 8*   *Vienna*, 1882
—— Die nationalökonomische Bedeutung der Afrikaforschung. 8*   *Vienna*, 1881
—— Dr E. Holub's österreichisch-ungarische Afrika - Expedition. General-Ausweis der bis zum August 1881 eingelangten Beiträge. 8*   *Vienna*, 1881
—— Die Südafrikanischen Salzseen. *Map.* 8*   *Frankfort o. M.*, 1881
—— Sieben Jahre in Süd-Afrika, Erlebnisse, Forschungen, und Jagden, auf meinen Reisen von den Diamantenfeldern zum Zambesi, 1872-79. 2 vols. *Maps and illustrations.* 8°   *Vienna*, 1881
—— Seven Years in South Africa : Travels, Researches, and Hunting Adventures, between the Diamond - Fields and the Zambesi, 1872-79. Translated by Ellen E. Frewer. 2 vols. *Map and illustrations.* 8°   1881
—— Elephanten - Jagden in Süd - Afrika. Ausserordentlicher Vortrag, gehalten im Club österreichischer Eisenbahn-Beamten am 13 April 1882. 8*   *Vienna*, 1882
—— Von der Capstadt ins Land der Maschukulumbe. Reisen im südlichen Afrika in den Jahren 1883-87. 2 vols. *Maps and illustrations.* 8° *Vienna*, 1890
—— Die Ma-Atabele. (Abstract from "Zeitschrift für Ethnologie.") 8*   1893
—— *See* Kienitz.
—— **and M. Neumayr.** Ueber einige Fossilien aus der Uitenhage-Formation in Süd-Afrika. *Plates.* 4*
                                    Vienna, 1881
—— **and A. von Pelzeln.** Beiträge zur Ornithologie Südafrikas. *Map and plates.* 8°   *Vienna*, 1882

"Holy Crosse" (Ship). *See* Hakluyt, Vol. 2 : Appendix 1.

Home, Mr. Select Views in Mysore . . . from Drawings taken on the Spot by Mr Home ; with Historical Descriptions ; the letter-press by T. Bentley. *Map and plan.* Folio   1794

Home, Major R. *See* United Kingdom, G, War Office Publ.: Appendix 2.

Hommel, Fritz. Eduard Glasers Reise nach Mârib (in Südarabien) März-April 1888. (Beilage zur *Allgemeinen Zeitung.*) 8*   *Munich*, 1888
—— Eduard Glasers historische Ergebnisse aus seinen südarabischen Inschriften. 8*
                                    Munich, 1889

Hommey, Louis. Table d'Angles Horaires, contenant plus de quarante mille angles horaires calculés pour toutes les latitudes depuis 0° jusqu'à 70° . . . 2 vols. Imperial 8°   *Paris*, 1863

Honey, William. Narrative of the Captivity and Sufferings of William Honey, and two other British Merchant Seamen, on the Island of Arguin, on the West Coast of Africa, in 1844-45. 12* 1845

Honiberger, J. Martin. Thirty-five Years in the East: Adventures, Discoveries, Experiments, and Historical Sketches relating to the Punjab and Cashmere, in connection with Medicine, Botany, Pharmacy, &c.; with an Original Materia Medica, and a Medical Vocabulary in four European and five Eastern Languages. 2 vols in 1. *Map and plates.* 8° 1852

Hood, T. H. Notes of a Cruise in H.M.S. "Fawn" in the Western Pacific in 1862. *Map and plates.* 8° *Edinburgh*, 1863

Hood, Dr Thomas. *See* Borne.

Hoogewerff, Ensign J. A. *See* United States, D, Naval Observatory: Appendix 2.

Hooke, Robert. Posthumous Works, containing . . . : 1. The Present Deficiency of Natural Philosophy; 2. The Nature, Motion, and Effects of Light, particularly that of Sun and Comets; 3. An Hypothetical Explication of Memory; 4. Explication of the Cause of Gravity, or Gravitation, Magnetism, &c.; 5. Discourse of Earthquakes, their Causes and Effects; 6. Lectures for Improving Navigation and Astronomy; with the Author's Life published by R. Walter. *Plates.* Folio 1705

Hooker, Sir Joseph Dalton. The Botany of the Antarctic Voyage of H.M. Discovery Ships "Erebus" and "Terror" in the years 1839-43, &c. 2 vols. *Map and plates.* 4° 1847

—— Notes of a Tour in the Plains of India, the Himala, and Borneo, being Extracts from the Private Letters of Dr Hooker, written during a Government Botanical Mission to those Countries. Part 1. England to Calcutta. 8* 1848

—— Observations made when following the Grand Trunk Road across the Hills of Upper Bengal, &c., in the Soane Valley, and on the Kymaon Branch of the Vindya Hills. 8* *Calcutta*, 1848

—— On the Climate and Vegetation of the Temperate and Cold Regions of East Nepal and the Sikkim Himalaya Mountains. Royal 8* 1849

—— Notes, chiefly Botanical, made during an Excursion from Darjiling to Tongló, a lofty Mountain on the confines of Sikkim and Nepal. 8* *Calcutta*, 1849

—— Elevation of the Great Table Land of Thibet. 8* 1849

—— Introductory Essay to the Flora of New Zealand. 4* 1853

—— Himalayan Journals, or Notes of a Naturalist in Bengal, the Sikkim and Nepal Himalayas, the Khasia Mountains, &c. 2 vols. *Maps and plates.* 8° 1854

P

Hooker, Sir Joseph Dalton. The Distribution of the North American Flora. 8* 1878

—— Himalayan Journals. (The Minerva Library of Famous Books.) *Portrait, maps, and illustrations.* 12° 1891

—— **and J. Ball,** Journal of a Tour in Marocco and the Great Atlas; with an Appendix, including a Sketch of the Geology of Marocco by G. Maw. *Map and plates.* 8° 1879

—— **and Thomas Thomson.** Introductory Essay to the Flora Indica; including Preliminary Observations on the Study of Indian Botany, a Summary of the Labours of Indian Botanists, a Sketch of the Meteorology of India, Outlines of the Physical Geography and Botany of the Provinces of India. *Maps.* 8° 1855

Hooker, Sir W. J. Journal of a Tour in Iceland in 1809. 2 vols. *Maps and plates.* 8° 1813

—— Directions for Collecting and Preserving Plants in Foreign Countries. 4* *Glasgow*, 1828

—— Notes on the Botany of the Antarctic Voyage conducted by Capt. James Clark Ross in H.M. Discovery ships "Erebus" and "Terror," with Observations on the Tussac Grass of the Falkland Islands. *Plate.* 8* 1843

—— Biographical Sketch of Sir William J. Hooker. Small 8* 1865

—— La Vie et les Écrits de. Par A. de Candolle. 8* *Paris*, 1866

—— *See* Murray, Hugh; *also* Eyriès, Vol. 7: Appendix 2.

Hooley, T. Journal of an Overland Journey from Perth to Port Walcott on the North-West Coast of Australia, performed by T. Hooley, Esq., with a view to finding a Practicable Route for Driving Stock to the North District of Western Australia. [Cuttings from the *Perth Gazette* of 14th December 1866.] Folio* *Perth*, 1866

Hooper, C. L. Report of the Cruise of the U.S. Revenue-steamer "Corwin" in the Arctic Ocean, 1st November 1880. *Chart.* 8° *Washington*, 1881

—— The Cruise of the "Corwin" in the Arctic. 8* *San Francisco*, 1881

—— Report of the Cruise of the U.S. Revenue-steamer "Thomas Corwin" in the Arctic Ocean, 1881. *Plates.* 4° *Washington*, 1884

Hooper, E. D. M. The Forests of the West Indies and British Honduras. Folio*

—— Report upon the Forests of Jamaica. *Map.* Folio* 1886

—— Report upon the Forests of St Vincent. Folio* 1886

—— Report upon the Forests of Honduras. Folio* *Kurnool*, 1887

Hooper, E. D. M.　Report upon the Forests of St Lucia.　Folio*
Madras, 1887
—— Report upon the Forests of Grenada and Carriacou.　Folio*　1887
—— Report upon the Forests of Tobago. *Map.*　Folio*　*Madras*, 1887
—— Report upon Antigua in relation to Forestry. *Map.* Folio* *Madras*, 1888

Hooper, W. H.　Private Journal of the Voyage of the "Isabella" in Search of a North-West Passage.　MS.　4°　1818
—— Private Journal of the Voyage of the "Hecla" and "Griper."　MS.　Folio
1819-20
—— Private Journal of the First Voyage of the "Hecla" and "Fury."　2 vols.　MS. 4°　1821-23
—— Private Journal of the Second Voyage of the "Hecla" and "Fury."　2 vols. MS.　4°　1824-25
—— Ten Months among the Tents of the Tuski, with Incidents of an Arctic Boat Expedition in Search of Sir John Franklin, as far as the Mackenzie River and Cape Bathurst. *Map and illustrations.* 8°　1853

Hoorn, Lord van.　Embassy to Kang-hi, Emperor of China and Eastern Tartary. *See* Astley, Vol. 3; Allgemeine Historie, Vol. 5: Appendix 1.

Hop, H.　Nouvelle Description du Cap de Bonne-Espérance, avec un Journal Historique d'un Voyage de Terre, fait par ordre du Gouverneur feu Mgr. Ryk. Tulbagh, dans l'Intérieur de l'Afrique. *Plates.* 8°　*Amsterdam*, 1778

Hope, C. W.　The Dehra Dun.　II. (From the *Calcutta Review*, January 1893.) 8*　1893

Hope, Rev. H.　The Canadian Settlers' Guide. *Maps.* 8°　1860

Hopkins, B. J.　Astronomy for Every-day Readers.　2nd edition. *Illustrations.* 12°　1893

Hopkins, Edward Augustus.　Memoria accompañando un Proyecto de Ley, proveyendo los medios de disponer de las tierras publicas de la Confederacion Argentina, y otros objetos.　(Traduccion.) 8°　*Buenos Ayres*, 1857

Hopkins, Evan.　On the Connexion of Geology with Terrestrial Magnetism, showing the general Polarity of Matter . . . and other Magnetic Phenomena. *Plates.* 8°　1844
—— The same. *Plates.* 8°　1851
—— On the Structure of the Crystalline Rocks of the Andes, and their Cleavage-planes. *Plate.* 8*　1850
—— On the Geology of the Gold-bearing Rocks of the World, and the Gold-Fields of Victoria. 8*　*Melbourne*, 1853

Hopkins, L. C.　Report on the Island of Formosa, dated 12th October 1884. *Map.* 8*　1885

Hopkins, Thomas.　On the Atmospheric Changes which produce Rain and Wind, and the Fluctuations of the Barometer; with additional Essays. *Chart and diagrams.* 8°　1854

Hopkins, William.　On Glacial Theories: Abstract of a Lecture delivered before the Cambridge Philosophical Society, 16th May 1859. 8*　1859

Hoppe, J.　Californiens Gegenwart und Zukunft; nebst Beiträgen von A. Erman über die Klimatologie von Californien und über die geographische Verbreitung des Goldes. *Maps.* 8°　*Berlin*, 1849

Horbye, J. C.　Observations sur les Phénomènes d'Érosion en Norvége. *Maps and plate.* 4*　*Christiania*, 1857

Horden, Rt. Rev. J.　A Grammar of the Cree Language as spoken by the Cree Indians of North America.　12°　1881

Hore, Mrs Annie B.　To Lake Tanganyika in a Bath Chair. *Maps and portraits.* Crown 8°　1886

Hore, E. C.　Tanganyika: Eleven Years in Central Africa. *Maps and illustrations.* 8°　1892

Hore, M. *See* Hakluyt, Vol. 3: Appendix 1.

Hores, W. *See* Purchas, Vol. 1, Book 5: Appendix 1.

Horky, J. E.　Des böhmischen Freiherrn Löw von Rotzmital und Blatna, Denkwürdigkeiten und Reisen durch Deutschland, England, Frankreich, Spanien, Portugal, und Italien. Ein Beitrag zur Zeit- und Sittengeschichte des fünfzehnten Jahrhunderts.　2 vols. in 1. Small 8°　*Brünn*, 1824

Horn, Capt. van. *See* Sharp, Capt. B. and others.

Hornby, Admiral.　A Summary of "The Cruize round the World of the Squadron Detached on Particular Service under the Orders of Rear-Admiral Hornby, between the 19th day of June 1869 and the 15th day of November 1870." *Map.* Folio　1871

Horne, John.　A Year in Fiji; or, An Inquiry into the Botanical, Agricultural, and Economical Resources of the Colony. *Map.* 8°　1881

Horne, John. *See* Tudor.

Hornemann, Fred.　Travels from Cairo to Mourzouk, the Capital of the Kingdom of Fezzan, in 1797-98. *Maps.* 4°　1802
—— Voyage de F. Hornemann, dans l'Afrique Septentrionale, depuis Le Caire jusqu'à Mourzouk, Capitale du Royaume de Fezzan; suivi d'Éclaircissemens sur la Géographie de l'Afrique, par M. Rennell. Traduit de l'Anglais, . . . et augmenté de Notes et d'un Mémoire sur les Oasis . . . par L. Langlès.　2 parts in 1 vol. *Map.* 8°　*Paris*, 1803

Horner, —. Voyage à la Côte Orientale d'Afrique pendant l'année 1866, par le R. P. Horner, Missionaire Apostolique, &c.; accompagné de Documents nouveaux sur l'Afrique par Mgr. Gaume. 12°
Paris, 1872

Horner, G. R. B. Medical Topography of Brazil and Uruguay, with Incidental Remarks. 8° *Philadelphia*, 1845

Horner, Leonard. Account of some recent Researches near Cairo undertaken with the view of throwing light upon the Geological History of the Alluvial Land of Egypt. 2 parts. *Plates.* 4* 1855

Hörnes, M. *See* "Novara."

Hornius, Georgius. De Originibus Americanis. Libri Quatuor. 12°
The Hague, 1652
—— *See* Nieuhoff.

Hörnlimann, J. Ueber Seetiefenmessungen. 8* [*Berne*, 1886]

Horologgi, G. *See* Tevet.

Horowitz, Victor J. Marokko: das wesentlichste und interessanteste über Land und Leute. 8° *Leipzig*, 1887

Horrocks, J. N. Meteorological Observations, taken at Assumption, Paraguay, during the year 1878. MS. 4° 1878

Horsburgh, Capt. J. India Directory; or, Directions for Sailing to and from the East Indies, China, Australia, Cape of Good Hope, Brazil, and the interjacent ports; compiled chiefly from Original Journals of the Company's Ships, and from Obervations and Remarks made during Twenty-one Years' Experience Navigating in those Seas. 4° 1836
—— Instructions Nautiques sur les Mers de l'Inde. Traduit par M. Le Prédour; revue par M. B. Darondeau et M. G. Reille. Vol. II., et Vol. III., Part 2. 4° *Paris*, 1856-60
—— Instructions Nautiques: Traversées d'Europe aux differentes Parties de l'Inde, de le l'Australie, Côte Est d'Afrique. . . . ses Vents et Courants . . . Traduction de MM. Le Predour, Darondeau, et Reille; revue par M. J. Lafont et Ch. Pigeard. 2 vols. 4°
Paris, 1864
—— *See* Taylor, A. D.

Hörschelmann, F. *See* Stein, C. G. D.

Horsey, A. F. R. de. Routier des Côtes Sud, Sud-est, et Est d'Afrique, du Cap de Bonne-Espérance au Cap Guardafui, comprenant les îles du Canal de Mozambique. . . . Traduit de l'Anglais par M. A. Mac-Dermott. 8°
Paris, 1866
—— *See* Montgomerie; *also* United Kingdom, A (Africa): Appendix 2.

Horsey, Sir Jerome. *See* Hakluyt, Vol. 1; Hakluyt Soc. Publ., Vol. 20. : Appendix 1.

Horsfield, T. Report on the Island of Banka. 8* 1848

Horsfield, Thomas. *See* Catalogues, C, General: Appendix 2.

Horsford, Eben Norton. John Cabot's Landfall in 1497, and the Site of Norumbega: a Letter to Chief-Justice Daly, President of the American Geographical Society. *Maps, plans, and plates.* 4°
Cambridge, Mass., 1886
—— Discovery of America by Northmen: Address at the Unveiling of the Statue of Leif Eriksen, delivered in Faneuil Hall, 29th Oct. 1887. *Maps and illustrations.* 4* *New York*, 1888
—— The Problem of the Northmen: a Letter to Chief-Justice Daly, President of the American Geographical Society. *Maps, plans, and plates.* 4*
Cambridge, Mass., 1889
—— The Discovery of the Ancient City of Norumbega: a Communication to the President and Council of the American Geographical Society, at their Special Session in Watertown, 21st November 1889. *Maps and illustrations.* 4*
Cambridge, Mass., N.D.
—— Ditto. [With Poem by Whittier, &c.] *Maps and illustrations.* 4°
New York, 1890
—— The Defences of Norumbega, and a Review of the Reconnaissances of Col. T. W. Higginson, Professor Henry W. Haynes, Dr Justin Winsor, Dr Francis Parkman, and Rev. Dr Edmund F. Slafter. A Letter to Judge Daly, President of the American Geographical Society. *Maps and plates.* 4° *Boston, Mass.*, 1891
—— The Landfall of Leif Erikson, A.D. 1000, and the site of his houses in Vineland. *Maps and plates.* 4° *Boston*, 1892

Horsley, John. Britannia Romana; or, The Roman Antiquities of Britain, containing . . . the Roman Geography, in which are given the Originals of Ptolemy, Antonini Itinerarium, the Notitia, the anonymous Ravennas, and Peutinger's Table, so far as they relate to this Island; . . . and Geographical Indexes of the Latin and English Names of the Roman Places in Britain, and a General Index. *Maps and plates.* Folio 1732

Horsley, Bishop S. *See* Vincent, Vol. 1: Appendix 2.

Hort, Mrs Alfred. *Via* Nicaragua: a Sketch of Travel. Crown 8° 1887
—— Tahiti: the Garden of the Pacific. *Frontispiece.* 8° 1891

Horton, James Africanus B. Physical and Medical Climate and Meteorology of the West Coast of Africa; with Valuable Hints to Europeans for the Preservation of Health in the Tropics. 8° 1867

Hortop, Job. *See* Hakluyt, Vol. 3: Appendix 1.

Horváth, G. Monographia Lygæidarum Hungariæ. *Plate.* 4° *Budapest*, 1875

Hoseason, John Cochrane. Remarks on the Abyssinian Expenditure, and on the general Inefficiency of the Over-Sea Steam-Transport for Military Purposes. *Map.* 8* 1870

Hosie, A. Itinerary of the Road from Ch'-êng-tu, the Capital of the Province of Ssŭ-ch'uan, to Chashilumbu, the Capital of Ulterior Tibet. [Foreign Office Paper.] Folio* 1884

—— Report of a Journey through the Provinces of Ssu-ch'uan, Yünnan, and Kuei Chou, 11th February to 14th June 1883. Folio* 1884

—— Report of a Journey through Central Ssu-ch'uan, in June and July 1884. Folio* 1885

—— Three Years in Western China : a Narrative of Three Journeys in Ssŭ-ch'uan, Kuei-chow, and Yün-nan. With an Introduction by Archibald Little. *Map and illustrations.* 8° 1890

—— Report by Mr Hosie on the Island of Formosa, with special reference to its Resources and Trade. *Maps.* [Collection of Photographs in separate cover.] Folio* 1893

—— *See* China, A : Appendix 2.

Hoskiær, V. Et Besög i Græenland, Ægypten og Tyrkiet. *Maps.* Small 8° *Copenhagen*, 1879

—— Rejse i China, Japan og Indien. *Maps.* Small 8° *Copenhagen*, 1880

Hoskins, G. A. Travels in Ethiopia, above the Second Cataract of the Nile, exhibiting the State of that Country and its various Inhabitants, and illustrating the Antiquities, Arts, and History of the ancient Kingdom of Meroe. *Map and plates.* 4° 1835

—— Ethiopia *versus* Egypt. 8° 1836

—— Visit to the Great Oasis of the Libyan Desert, with an Account, Ancient and Modern, of the Oasis of Amun, and the other Oases under the dominion of the Pasha of Egypt. *Map and plates.* 8° 1837

—— Spain as it is. 2 vols. 8° 1851

—— Winter in Upper and Lower Egypt. 8° 1863

Hóskold, H. D. Mémoire Général et Spécial sur les Mines, la Métallurgie, les Lois sur les Mines, les Ressources, les Avantages, &c., de l' exploitation des Mines dans la République Argentine. *Maps, plans, and illustrations.* Large 8° *Buenos Ayres*, 1889

Hoskyn, R. *See* United Kingdom, A (Coast of Ireland) : Appendix 2.

Houdas, O. *See* Ezziani ; Nozhet-Elhâdi.

Houels Reisen durch Sizilien, Malta und die Liparischen Inseln ; eine Uebersetzung aus dem grossen und kostbaren Französischen Originalwerke von J. H. Keerl. *Plates.* 8° *Gotha*, 1797

Hough, Franklin B. History of St Lawrence and Franklin Counties, New York, from the earliest period to the present time. *Maps and portraits.* 8° *Albany, N.Y.*, 1853

Hough, Major W. Narrative of the March and Operations of the Army of the Indus in the Expedition to Affghanistan in 1838-39. *Map and plates.* 8° 1841

Houghton, Bernard. Essay on the Language of the Southern Chins and its Affinities. 8° *Rangoon*, 1892

Houghton, ——. *See* Eyriès, Vol. 10 : Appendix 1.

Houlder, Rev. J. A. North-East Madagascar : a Narrative of a Missionary Tour from the Capital to Andranovelona *via* Andovoranto and the North-east Coast, and back to Antananarivo by way of Mandritsara and Ambatondrazaka. *Map.* 8* *Antananarivo*, 1877

Housman, John. A Descriptive Tour and Guide to the Lakes, Caves, Mountains, and other Natural Curiosities in Cumberland, Westmoreland, Lancashire, and a part of the West Riding of Yorkshire. 3rd edition. *Maps and plates.* 12° *Carlisle*, 1808

—— Ditto. 7th edition. 12° *Carlisle*, 1816

Houtmann, C. *See* Allgemeine Historie, Vol. 8 : Appendix 1.

Houzeau, J. C. Histoire du Sol de l'Europe. *Map.* 8° *Brussels*, 1857

—— Annales de l'Observatoire Royal de Bruxelles : Appendice à la nouvelle série des Annales Astronomiques ; Vade-Mecum de l'Astronome. 8° *Brussels*, 1882

—— **and A. Lancaster.** Bibliographie Générale de l'Astronomie, ou Catalogue Méthodique des Ouvrages, des Mémoires, et des Observations Astronomiques publiés depuis l'origine de l'imprimerie jusqu'en 1880. Tome 2. Large 8° *Brussels*, 1882

Hove, Dr. Tours for Scientific and Economical Research made in Guzerat, Kattiawar, and the Conkuns in 1787-88. Published from the MS. in the British Museum, under the care of A. Gibson. *Plates.* Royal 8° *Bombay*, 1855

Hovell, W. Hilton. Reply to "A Brief Statement of Facts, in connection with an Overland Expedition from Lake George to Port Phillip, in 1824," published by H. Hume. 8* *Sydney*, 1855

—— **and H. Hume.** Journey of Discovery to Port Phillip, New South Wales, in 1824-25. *Map.* 8° *Sydney*, 1837

Hovell-Thurlow, Hon. T. J. The Company and the Crown. 2nd edition, revised and corrected. *Map.* 8° 1867

Hovgaard, A. Nordenskiöld's Voyage round Asia and Europe: a Popular Account of the North-East Passage of the "Vega," 1878-80. Translated from the Danish by H. L. Brækstad. *Maps and illustrations.* 8° 1882

—— The Danish-Arctic Expedition proposed by A. Hovgaard. Translated from the Danish by G. Zachariae. *Circumpolar chart.* 8* *Copenhagen*, 1882

Howard, B. Douglas. Life with Trans-Siberian Savages. Small 8° 1893

Howard, F. *See* South Australia, A: Appendix 2.

Howard, Rev. G. B. *See* Philipos.

Howard, J. Eliot. Creation and Providence, with especial reference to the Evolutionist Theory. 8* 1878

Howard, J. E. Memoirs of William Watts McNair, the First European Explorer of Kafiristan. *Portraits.* Oblong 12* N.D.

Howard, John. The Stanley Geographical Questions. Standards 1 and 2. 12* *Manchester*, N.D.

—— The same. Standard 6. 12* *Manchester*, N.D.

Howard, Luke. The Climate of London, deduced from Meteorological Observations made in the Metropolis and at various places round it. 2nd edition. 3 vols. *Plates.* 8° 1833

Howard, Lord Thomas. *See* Allgemeine Historie, Vol. 1: Appendix 1.

Howard, W. Narrative of a Journey to the Summit of Mont Blanc, made in July 1819. 12* *Baltimore*, 1821

Howel, —. *See* Dalrymple, Alex.

Howell, A. P. Note on the State of Education in India during 1866-67. Royal 8° *Calcutta*, 1868

—— Note on Jails and Jail Discipline in India, 1867-68; with Extracts from the Jail Reports of the several Governments and Administrations under the Government of India, for 1867. Royal 8° *Calcutta*, 1869

Howell, E. J. Mexico, its Progress and Commercial Possibilities. *Map.* 8° 1892

Howell, G. R. African Explorations, Ancient and Modern: Sources of the Nile and Congo. 8* *New York*, 1878

Howell, James. Instructions for Foreine Travell, 1642, collated with the second edition of 1650. (English reprint, edited by E. Arber.) 12° 1869

Howgate, H. W. Polar Colonization: Memorial to Congress, and Action of Scientific and Commercial Associations. *Maps and photographs.* 8* *Washington*, 1878

—— Polar Colonization and Exploration. *Map.* 8* N.P., N.D.

Howgate, H. W. *See* Tyson, E.

Howitt, A. W. *See* Victoria, B: Appendix 2.

Howland, O. A. The New Empire: Reflections upon its Origin and Constitution, and its relation to the Great Republic. *Map.* 8° 1891

Howlett, S. B. Directions for using Aneroid and Mercurial Barometers in determining Altitudes, with Table and Examples. *Plate.* 12* 1859

Howley, J. P. Geography of Newfoundland. 2nd edition. *Map.* 12* 1877

Howorth, Sir H. H. Some Changes of Surface affecting Ancient Ethnography. 8* 1868

—— On the Westerly Drifting of Nomades, from the 5th to the 19th Century: Part 5, Hungarians; Part 6, Kirghises or Bourouts, Kazaks, Kalmucks, Euzbegs, and Nogays; Part 9, Fins and allies. 8* N.D.

—— History of the Mongols, from the 9th to the 19th Century. 4 vols. *Maps.* Large 8°

PART 1.—The Mongols proper and the Kalmuks. 1876

PART 2.—The so-called Tartars of Russia and Central Asia. Divisions 1 and 2. 2 vols. 1880

PART 3.—The Mongols of Persia. 1888

—— The Mammoth and the Flood: an Attempt to Confront the Theory of Uniformity with the Facts of Recent Geology. 8° 1887

Howse, Joseph. Grammar of the Cree Language, with which is combined an Analysis of the Chippeway Dialect. 8° 1844

—— Words and Forms of Speech, prepared with a view to obtain their Equivalents in various Indian Dialects. [2 leaves.] Folio* *Cirencester*, N.D.

Hozier, Capt. H. M. *See* Holland, T. J.; *also* United Kingdom, G: Appendix 2.

Hubbard, Gardiner G. South America. *Map.* 8* *Washington*, 1891

Hubbard, J. H. Sport in the Canadian North-West. *Map.* 8° 1886

Hübbe-Schleiden, W. Ethiopien. Studien über West Afrika. *Map.* 8° *Hamburg*, 1879

Huber, Charles. Journal d'un Voyage en Arabie (1883-84). *Maps and plates.* Large 8° *Paris*, 1891

Huber, W. Notice Biographique sur Libre-Irmond Bardin. 8* *Paris*, 1868

Hübertz, J. R. De Sindssyge i Danmark. *Map.* 4* *Copenhagen*, 1851

Hübner, Baron von. Through the British Empire. 2 vols. *Map.* Crown 8° 1886

Hübner, Johann. Kurze Fragen aus der neuen und alten Geographie bis auf gegenwärtige Zeit continuirt. . . . *Map.* 12° *Leipzig*, 1724

Huc, E. R. Recollections of a Journey through Tartary, Thibet, and China during 1844-46. Translated by Mrs Percy Sinnet. 12°   1852
—— Souvenirs d'un Voyage dans la Tartarie, le Thibet, et la Chine pendant 1844-46. 2 vols. *Map.* 8° *Paris*, 1853
—— L'Empire Chinois, faisant suite à l'ouvrage intitulé " Souvenirs d'un Voyage dans la Tartarie et le Thibet." 2 vols. *Map.* 8°   *Paris*, 1854
—— The Chinese Empire, forming a sequel to the work entitled " Recollections of a Journey through Tartary and Thibet." 2 vols. *Map.* 8°   1855
—— Christianity in China, Tartary, and Thibet. Vol. I. 8°   1857

Huddart, Joseph. Piloting Directory for Bristol Channel, St George's Channel, and all the Coasts of Ireland. Revised by John Purdy. 8°   1837

Hudleston, W. H. On Deep Sea Investigation : Presidential Address delivered at the Opening of the Session 1881-82 of the Geologists' Association. *Map and diagrams.* 8*   1882
—— and J. F. Walker. On the Distribution of the Brachiopoda in the Oolitic Strata of Yorkshire. 8*   N.P., N.D.

Hudson, Henry. *See* Read, J. M. ; *also* Hakluyt Soc. Publ., Vols. 5, 27 ; Purchas, Vol. 3, Book 3 ; Allgemeine Historie, Vol. 17 : Appendix 1.

Hudson, T. S. A Scamper through America ; or, Fifteen Thousand Miles of Ocean and Continent in Sixty Days. *Map.* Small 8°   1882

Hudson, W. H. The Naturalist in La Plata. *Illustrations.* 8°   1892
—— Idle Days in Patagonia. Illustrated by Alfred Hartley and J. Smit. 8° 1893

Hues, Robert. *See* Hakluyt Soc. Publ., Vol. 79 : Appendix 1.

Hug, Arnold. Antiochia und der Aufstand des Jahres 387 n. Chr. *Plate.* 4°   *Winterthur*, 1863

Hügel, Baron Karl A. A. von. Kaschmir und das Reich der Siek. 3 vols. 8°   *Stuttgart*, 1840-41
—— Travels in Kashmir and the Panjah. Translated, with Notes, by Major T. B. Jervis. *Maps and plates.* Royal 8°   1845
—— Das Kabul-Becken und die Gebirge zwischen dem Hindu Kosch und dem Sutlej. *Maps.* Folio   *Wien*, 1850
—— Der Stille Ocean und die Spanischen Besitzungen im Ostindischen Archipel. *Maps.* 8°   *Vienna*, 1860
—— In Memoriam. 4*   N.D.

Hughes, A. W. Outlines of Indian History, comprising the Hindū, Mahomedan, and Christian Periods. *Maps.* 12°   1871

Hughes, A. W. A Gazetteer of the Province of Sindh. *Maps and photographs.* 8°   1874
—— The Country of Balochistan, its Geography, Topography, Ethnology, and History. [Vocabulary, and Road Routes.] *Map in cover and photographs.* 12° 1877

Hughes, Edward. Outlines of Physical Geography, Descriptive of the Inorganic Matter of the Globe, and the Distribution of Organized Beings ; with *Maps*, compiled by William Hughes. 12°   1850

Hughes, G. Amoy and the surrounding Districts. *Map.* Square 8°   *Hong Kong*, 1872

Hughes, J. *See* Dobreo.

Hughes, Robert Edgar. Two Summer Cruises with the Baltic Fleet in 1854-55, being the Log of the " Pet," Yacht. *Maps and plate.* 8°   1855

Hughes, T. S. Travels in Sicily, Greece, and Albania. 2 vols. *Maps and plates.* 4°   1820
—— Travels in Greece and Albania. 2 vols. *Maps and plates.* 8°   1830

Hughes, Rev. W. Dark Africa and the Way Out, or a Scheme for Civilising and Evangelising the Dark Continent. *Maps and illustrations.* 12°   1892

Hughes, William. Principles of Mathematical Geography, comprehending a Theoretical and Practical Explanation of the Construction of Maps, with Rules for the Formation of the various kinds of Map Projections. *Plans.* 8°   1843
—— Remarks on Geography as a Branch of Popular Education, chiefly with reference to the Principles upon which it should be Taught in Normal Schools. 8*   1847
—— Manual of British Geography, embracing the Physical, Industrial, and Descriptive Geography of England and Wales, Scotland and Ireland. *Maps.* 12°   *Edinburgh*, 1851
—— Manual of European Geography, embracing the Physical, Industrial, and Descriptive Geography of the various Countries of Europe. *Maps.* 12°   *Edinburgh*, 1851
—— The Australian Colonies, their Origin and Present Condition. 12°   1852
—— Class-Book of Modern Geography, with Examination Questions. 12° 1859
—— The Study of Geography : a Lecture. 8*   1863
—— A Treatise on the Construction of Maps, comprehending an Inquiry into the Principles of Mathematical Geography and the Relations of Geography to Astronomy, with Rules for the Formation of Map-projections. *Plates.* 12°   1864

Hughes, William. The Geography of British History, a Geographical Description of the British Islands at successive Periods, from the Earliest Times to the Present Day. *Maps.* 12° 1866
—— A Class-Book of Physical Geography, with Examination Questions. New and enlarged edition. *Map.* 8° 1868
—— Geography in its Relation to History: a Lecture, delivered at the Birkbeck Institution. 8* 1870
—— Geography in its Relation to Physical Science. 8* 1870
—— A Manual of Geography, Physical, Industrial, Political. Small 8° 1873
—— A Class-Book of Modern Geography, with Examination Questions. New edition, revised by J. Francon Williams. Small 8° 1881
—— *See* Dempsey ; Maunder.
—— **and J. F. Williams.** The Advanced Class-Book of Modern Geography, Physical, Political, Commercial. 12° 1892
—— The Geography of the British Colonies and Dependencies, Physical, Political, Commercial. *Map.* Small 8° 1892
—— An Introduction to the Study of Geography, Mathematical, Physical, Political, and Commercial. *Plate.* Small 8° 1893
Hughes, Major W. Gwynne. The Hill Tracts of Arakan. *Map and frontispiece.* 8° *Rangoon,* 1881
Hughes, Lieut. W. S. *See* United States, E, a (No. 64) : Appendix 2.
Hugo, Comte Léopold. Extraits de deux Lettres addressées à D. B. Boncompagni. 4* *Rome,* 1876
Hugot, A. *See* Blumentritt, Ferdinand.
Hugues, Luigi. Alcune considerazioni sul Primo Viaggio di Amerigo Vespucci. 8* *Rome,* 1885
—— Il Quarto Viaggio di Amerigo Vespucci. 8* [*Rome,* 1886]
—— Sul Nome " America." 12* *Turin,* 1886
—— Sul Nome " America." Seconda Memorie, con un' Appendice. 8* *Rome,* 1888
—— Guida por l'Insegnamento della Geografia nelle Scuole Primarie e Secondarie. Parte Prima—La Regione Italiana, Primi Elementi di Geografia Generale. 8* *Turin,* 1888
—— Sopra due Lettere di Amerigo Vespucci (Anni 1500, 1501). 8* *Rome,* 1891
—— Di alcuni Recenti Guidizi intorno ad Amerigo Vespucci, Osservazioni Critiche. 12* *Turin,* 1891
Huhn, E. H. T. Deutsch-Lothringen, Landes-, Volks-, und Ortskunde. 8° *Stuttgart,* 1875
Huish, Robert. The Last Voyage of Capt. Sir John Ross to the Arctic Regions for the Discovery of the North-

Huish, Robert—*continued.*
West Passage, in 1829 - 33 ; with an Abridgement of the Former Voyages of Capts. Ross, Parry, &c. *Map and plates.* 8° 1835
Hull, Prof. Edward. The Coal-Fields of Great Britain, their History, Structure, and Resources ; with Notices of the Coal-Fields of other Parts of the World. 3rd edition. *Maps and plates.* 8° 1873
—— Mount Seir, Sinai, and Western Palestine, being a Narrative of a Scientific Expedition. Published for the Committee of the Palestine Exploration Fund. *Maps and illustrations.* 8° 1885
—— A Sketch of Geological History, being the Natural History of the Earth and of its Pre-Human Inhabitants ; with an Illustrative Diagram. Crown 8° 1887
—— A Text - Book of Physiography, or Physical Geography, being an Introduction to the Study of the Physical Phenomena of our Globe. *Maps and plates.* 12° 1888
—— *See* Turkey in Asia, B : Appendix 2.
Hull, Hugh M. The Experience of Forty Years in Tasmania. *Map and plates.* 12° 1859
Hull, Thomas A. Practical Nautical Surveying. 8* 1873
—— *See* Temple, G. T.
Hullett, R. W. English Sentences, with Equivalents in Colloquial Malay. Compiled for the use of Pupils at the Raffles Institution, Singapore. 12* 1887
Hulsius, Levinus. *See* Ternaux-Compans, Vol. 5 : Appendix 1.
Hultzch, E. *See* India, A : Appendix 2.
Humann, Karl, and Otto Puchstein. Reisen in Kleinasien und Nordsyrien. *Illustrations.* Text 4°, and Atlas large 4° *Berlin,* 1890
Humbert, Aimé. Le Japon Illustré. 2 vols. *Map, plans, and plates.* Large 4° *Paris,* 1870
—— La Mer Intérieure du Japon. *Map.* 8* [*Geneva,* 1866]
Humble, W. Dictionary of Geology and Mineralogy, comprising such terms in Botany, Chemistry, Comparative Anatomy, Conchology, Entomology, Palæontology, Zoology, and other branches of Natural History, as are connected with the study of Geology. 2nd ed. 8° 1843
Humboldt, Alexander von. Political Essays on the Kingdom of New Spain. 4 vols. *Maps.* 8° 1811
—— Plates to do. 8° 1811
—— Researches concerning the Institutions and Monuments of the Ancient Inhabitants of America, with Descriptions and Views of some of the most striking Scenes in the Cordilleras. Translated by Helen M. Williams. 2 vols. *Plates.* 8° 1814

Humboldt, Alexander von. Essai Politique sur le Royaume de la Nouvelle-Espagne. 2nd edition. 4 vols. *Map in cover.* 8°   *Paris,* 1825
—— Tableaux de la Nature, ou Considérations sur les Déserts, sur la Physionomie des Végétaux, sur les Cataractes de l'Orénoque, sur la Structure et l'Action des Volcans dans les différentes Régions de la Terre, &c. Traduits de l'Allemand par J. B. B. Eyriès. 2 vols. in 1. 8°
                                     Paris, 1828
—— Fragmens de Géologie et de Climatologie Asiatiques. 2 vols. *Map.* 8°
                                     Paris, 1831
—— Report upon a Letter by, to H.R.H. [the Duke of Sussex] the President of the Royal Society, respecting Terrestrial Magnetism. 8*   1836
—— Examen Critique de l'Histoire de la Géographie du Nouveau Continent et des Progrès de l'Astronomie Nautique aux quinzième et seizième Siècles. 5 vols. 8°   1836-39
—— Ueber die Hochebene von Bogota. 8*   *Berlin,* 1838
—— Notice de deux tentatives d'ascension du Chimborazo. 8*   *Paris,* 1838
—— Asie Centrale : Recherches sur les Chaînes de Montagnes et la Climatologie comparée. 3 vols. *Map.* 8° *Paris,* 1843
—— Kosmos : Entwurf einer physischen Weltbeschreibung. 5 vols. 8°
                                  Stuttgart, 1845-62
—— Cosmos : a Sketch of a Physical Description of the Universe. Translated from the German by E. C. Otté, B. H. Paul, and W. S. Dallas. 5 vols. 12°
                                        1849-58
—— Views of Nature ; or, Contemplations on the Sublime Phenomena of Creation, with Scientific Illustrations. Translated by E. C. Otté and H. G. Bohn. *Frontispiece and facsimile.* 12°   1850
—— Travels and Researches of, by W. Macgillivray ; with a Narrative of Humboldt's most recent Researches, including his Journey to the Ural Mountains and the Caspian Sea, &c. *Portrait and plates.* 12°   1853
—— Notice sur la Vie et les Travaux de, par M. de la Roquette. *Portraits and facsimile.* 4*   *Paris,* 1860
—— Festrede bei der von den naturwissenschaftlichen Vereinen Berlins veranstalteten Humboldt-Feier, von A. Bastian. 8*   *Berlin,* 1869
—— *See* Adalbert ; Bruhns ; Kelley ; Macgillivray ; Möllhausen ; Paravey ; Rose ; Schwarzenberg.
—— **and Aimé Bonpland.** Essai sur la Géographie des Plantes ; accompagné d un Tableau Physique des Régions Equinoxiales, fondé sur des mesures exécutées depuis le dixième degré de

Humboldt, A. von, and A. Bonpland—*continued.*
latitude boréale jusqu'au dixième degré de latitude australe, pendant 1799-1803. 4°   *Paris,* 1805
—— Voyage aux Régions Equinoxiales du Nouveau Continent, 1799-1804, par Al. de Humboldt et A. Bonpland. Rédigé par Alexandre de Humboldt. Première Partie : Relation Historique. Tome premier. *Map.* 4°   *Paris,* 1814
—— Voyage de Humboldt et Bonpland. Deuxième Partie : Recueil d'Observations de Zoologie et d'Anatomie comparée, faites dans l'Océan Atlantique, dans l'Intérieur du Nouveau Continent, et dans la Mer du Sud, pendant les Années 1799-1803. Prémier volume. *Plates.* 4°   *Paris,* 1811
—— Ditto. Troisième Partie : Essai Politique sur le Royaume de la Nouvelle-Espagne. [Par Alexandre de Humboldt.] 2 vols. 4°   *Paris,* 1811
—— Ditto. Quatrième Partie. Astronomie. Recueil d'Observations Astronomiques, d'Opérations Trigonométriques, et de Mesures Barométriques, faites pendant le cours d'un Voyage aux Régions Equinoxiales du Nouveau Continent depuis 1799 jusqu 'en 1803. Par Alexandre de Humboldt ; rédigées et calculées, d'après les tables les plus exactes, par Jabbo Oltmanns. 2 vols. *Plates.* 4°   *Paris,* 1810
—— Voyage aux Régions Equinoxiales du Nouveau Continent, fait en 1799, 1800, 1801, 1802, 1803, et 1804. Rédigé par Alexandre de Humboldt. 13 vols. (in 7). 8°   *Paris,* 1816-26
—— Personal Narrative of Travels to the Equinoctial Regions of the New Continent, during 1799-1804, by Alex. de Humboldt and Aimé Bonpland. Translated by Helen M. Williams. 7 vols. in 6. *Maps and plates.* 8°   1822-29
—— Personal Narrative of Travels to the Equinoctial Regions of America, during 1799-1804, by Alex. von Humboldt and Aimé Bonpland. Translated and edited by Thomasina Ross. 3 vols. (Bohn's Scientific Library.) 12°   1852-53

Hume, Rev. A. Philosophy of Geographical Names. 8*   *Liverpool,* 1851
—— Geographical Terms, considered as tending to enrich the English Language. 8*   *Liverpool,* 1859

Hume, A. O. Report on the Boureeah Gang of Robbers, 1855. [Records, N.W.P., No. 25.] Large 8°
                                     Agra, 1856
—— Report upon the State and Progress of Education in the Etawah District for 1856, and on Hulgabundee Schools, 1859. [Records, N.W.P., No. 33.] Large 8°
                                  Allahabad, 1860
—— *See* Henderson.

Hume, Hamilton. A Brief Statement of Facts in connection with an Overland Expedition from Lake George to Port Phillip, in 1824. Edited by the Rev. William Ross. 8° *Sydney*, 1855
—— The same. 2nd edition. *Portrait.* 8° *Yass*, 1873
—— *See* Hovell.

Hume, Dr. *See* Walpole : Appendix 1.

Humme, H. C. Abiasa, een Javaansch Tooneelstuk (Wajang), met een Hollandsche vertaling en toelichtende nota. 8° *The Hague*, 1878

Hummel, D. *See* Sweden, A : Appendix 2.

Hummel, Dr Karl. Physische Geographie. 8° *Graz*, 1855

Humphreys, Capt. A. A. Report on the Experiment of Sinking Artesian Wells upon the Public Lands ; Exploration of the Rio Colorado of the West ; Exploration in Nebraska, &c. 8° *Washington*, 1859
—— **and Lieut. H. L. Abbot.** Report upon the Physics and Hydraulics of the Mississipi River, upon the Protection of the Alluvial Region against Overflow, and upon the Deepening of the Mouths, based upon Surveys and Investigations. *Maps.* 4° *Philadelphia*, 1861

Hunfalvy, J. *See* Magyar.

Hunfalvy, Paul. Literarische Berichte aus Ungarn. Vols. 1-4. *Plates.* 8° *Budapest*, 1877-80
—— Die Völker des Ural und ihre Sprachen. 8* *Budapest*, 1888

Hunnewell, J. Journal of the Voyage of the "Missionary Packet," Boston to Honolulu, 1826. *Maps and plates.* 4° *Charlestown*, 1880

Hunt, C. C. Journal of an Expedition to the Eastern Interior of Western Australia. [Cuttings from a Newspaper.] Fo* 1866

Hunt, Dr. *See* Walpole, Robert : Appendix 1.

Hunt, James. Introductory Address on the Study of Anthropology. 8* 1863
—— Anniversary Address delivered before the Anthropological Society of London, Jan. 1864. 8* 1864
—— Anniversary Address delivered before the Anthropological Society of London, 1866. 8* 1866
—— Farewell Address delivered at the Fourth Anniversary of the Anthropological Society of London, 1867. 8* 1867

Hunt, J. *See* Vogt.

Hunt, Robert. On the Importance of Cultivating Habits of Observation. 8* 1851

Hunt, R. S., and J. F. Randel. Guide to the Republic of Texas. *Map.* 18° *New York*, 1839

Hunt, Dr T. Sterry. Sur la Formation des Gypses et des Dolomies. 4* *Paris*, 1867

Hunter, Archdeacon. A Lecture on the Grammatical Construction of the Cree Language, delivered on the 2nd April 1862. Large 8° 1875

Hunter, F. M. The Aden Handbook. 8* 1873
—— A Grammar of the Somali Language ; together with a short Historical Notice, and a few Exercises for Beginners ; concluding with an English-Somali and Somali-English Vocabulary. 16° *Bombay*, 1880
—— Report of a Visit made to the Amîri District in Jan. 1880. Folio* *Bombay*
—— Report on the Province of Harrar. *Map and plan.* Folio* *Aden*, 1884
—— A Statistical Account of the British Settlement of Aden, in Arabia. *Map and plan.* 8° 1887

Hunter, Henry. *See* Sonnini, C. S.

Hunter, John. An Historical Journal of the Transactions at Port Jackson and Norfolk Island, with the Discoveries which have been made in New South Wales and in the Southern Ocean, since the publication of Phillip's Voyage, compiled from the Official Papers ; including the Journals of Governors Phillip and King, and of Lieut. Ball ; and the Voyages from the first Sailing of the "Sirius" in 1787 to the Return of that ship's Company to England in 1792. *Portrait, plates, maps, and charts.* 4° 1793

Hunter, R. *See* Hislop ; *also* India, C (Geological Papers) : Appendix 2.

Hunter, Sir W. W. A Comparative Dictionary of the Non-Aryan Languages of India and High Asia, &c. 4° 1868
—— The Annals of Rural Bengal. 4th edition. 8° 1871
—— Orissa ; or, The Vicissitudes of an Indian Province under Native and British Rule. 2 vols. *Map and plates.* 8° 1872
—— A Statistical Account of Bengal. Vol. 1-20. *Maps.* 8° 1875-76
—— Preliminary List of Places, Rivers, &c., alphabetically arranged, for the Imperial Gazetteer of India. Folio 1877
—— A Statistical Account of Assam. 2 vols. *Maps.* 8° 1879
—— The Imperial Gazetteer of India. 9 vols. *Maps.* 8° 1881
—— The same. 2nd edition. 14 vols. *Maps.* 8° 1885-87
—— The Indian Empire, its History, People, and Products. *Map* 1882

Huntingdon, R. *See* Ray : Appendix 1.

Huntington, Earl of. *See* Hakluyt, Vol. 2 : Appendix 1.

Huot, J. J. N. *See* Malte-Brun.

Hurlbert, J. B. The Climates, Productions, and Resources of Canada. *Maps.* 8° *Montreal,* 1872
—— Physical Atlas, with Coloured Maps, showing the Geographical Distribution of Plants yielding Food, Climates, Flora, Soils, Regions of Summer Rains, Geological Formations, and Hydrography of the Dominion of Canada. Folio *Ottawa,* 1880

Hurlbut, William H. Pictures of Cuba. 12° 1855

Hurgronje, Dr C. Snouck. Mekka. I. Die Stadt und ihre Herren ; II. Aus dem heutigen Leben. *Plans.* [With Atlas.] 8° *The Hague,* 1888-89
—— Bilder aus Mekka. Mit kurzem erläuterndem Texte. Folio *Leyden,* 1889

Hurtado, Diego. *See* Callander, Vol. 1 : Appendix 1.

Hutchings, James M. Scenes of Wonder and Curiosity in California. *Plates.* 8° 1865

Hutchinson, Col. A. H. Try Lapland : a Fresh Field for Summer Tourists. 2nd edition. *Map and plates.* Sm. 8° 1870
—— Try Cracow and the Carpathians. *Map and plates.* Small 8° 1872

Hutchinson, C. W. Reports on the Working of the District Daks in the North-Western Provinces, for the year 1872-73 *Allahabad,* 1873

Hutchinson, E. The Best Trade Route to the Lake Regions of Central Africa. *Map.* 8° 1877
—— The Lost Continent, its Re-discovery and Recovery. 8° N.D.

Hutchinson, Capt. Gideon. Memoir on the Sawunt Waree State, prepared in 1818. Royal 8° *Bombay,* 1855

Hutchinson, Graham. A Treatise on the Causes and Principles of Meteorological Phenomena, &c. 8° *Glasgow,* 1835

Hutchinson, Margarite. *See* Pigafetta.

Hutchinson, T. J. Impressions of Western Africa, with Remarks on the Diseases of the Climate, and a Report of the Peculiarities of Trade up the Rivers in the Bight of Biafra. 8° 1858
—— Ten Years' Wanderings among the Ethiopians, with Sketches of the Manners and Customs of the Civilized and Un-civilized Tribes, from Senegal to Gaboon. 8° 1861
—— Details of a Journey through part of the Salado Valley and across some of the Argentine Provinces. *Map.* 8° 1864
—— Buenos Ayres and Argentine Gleanings ; with Extracts from a Diary of Salado Exploration in 1862 and 1863. *Map and plates.* 8° 1865
—— The Paraná ; with Incidents of the Paraguayan War, and South American Recollections, from 1861 to 1868. *Map and plates.* 8° 1868

Hutchinson, T. J. Our Meat Supply from Abroad. 8° *Liverpool,* 1871
—— Two Years in Peru, with Exploration of its Antiquities. 2 vols. *Map and plates.* 8° 1873

Hutchinson, W. Excursion to the Lakes in Westmorland and Cumberland, with a Tour through part of the Northern Counties, in 1773 and 1774. *Plates.* 8° 1776

Hutton, Charles. Philosophical and Mathematical Dictionary, containing an Explanation of the Terms, and an Account of the several Subjects, comprised under the heads Mathematics, Astronomy, and Philosophy, both Natural and Experimental . . . 2 vols. *Portrait and plates.* 4° 1815

Hutton, Capt. F. W. The Moas of New Zealand. (Extract from the *Transactions* of the New Zealand Institute, 1891.) *Plates.* 8° 1891
—— *See* New Zealand : Appendix 2.
—— **and G. H. F. Ulrich.** Report on the Geology and Gold Fields of Otago ; with Appendices by J. G. Black and J. McKerrow. *Map and plates.* 8° *Dunedin,* 1875

Hutton, William. Voyage to Africa ; including a Narrative of an Embassy to Ashantee in 1820 ; with Remarks on the Course and Termination of the Niger, and other Principal Rivers in that Country. *Maps and plates.* 8° 1821
—— *See* Eyriès, Vol. 11 : Appendix 1.

Huxley, Prof. T. H. Physiography : an Introduction to the Study of Nature. *Maps and plates.* 8° 1877
—— The Aryan Question and Pre-Historic Man. (From *The Nineteenth Century.*) 8° 1890
—— *See* India, C (Palaeont. Ind.) : Appendix 2.

Huyshe, G. L. The Red River Expedition. *Maps.* 8° 1871

Huyssen van Kattendyke, W. J. C. Uittreksel uit het Dagboek van, gedurende zijn verblijf in Japan in 1857, 1858, en 1859. *Map.* 8° *The Hague,* 1860

Hwen Thsang. *See* Hiouen Thsang.

Hwui-li. *See* Beal.

Hyades, Dr. *See* France, B, *a* : Appendix 2.

Hyatt, Thaddeus. The Dragon-Fly, or Reactive Passive Locomotion : a Vacuum Theory of Aerial Navigation, based on the Principle of the Fan-Blower ; to which is appended some Remarks on Water and its Navigation. 4° 1882

Hyde, John. Geographical Concentration : an Historic Feature of American Agriculture. An Address delivered before the International Statistical Institute, 14th September 1893. 8° *Washington,* 1893

Hyde, John. *See* Schwatka.
"Hydra." *See* Sholl; Shortland.
Hyland, J. Shearson. Ueber die Gesteine des Kilimandscharo und dessen Umgebung. *Plate.* 8* 1888
Hyndman, H. M. *See* Yule, Sir H.
Hyvernat, H. *See* Müller-Simonis.

I.

Iambulus. *See* Purchas, Vol. 1, Book 1 : Appendix 1.
Iarric, Pierre du. Troisiesme Partie de l'Histoire des Choses plus memorables Advenues tant en Indes Orientales, qu'-autres pais de la Descouverte des Portugais . . . despuis 1600 jusques à 1610. Small 4° *Bordeaux*, 1614
—— Thesaurus Rerum Indicarum. . . . Opus nunc primum a M. Matthia Martinez e gallico in latinam sermonem translatum. 4 vols. 12° *Cologne*, 1615
Ibañez é Ibañez, Cárlos. Descripcion Geodésica de las Islas Baleares. *Maps and plates.* 8° *Madrid*, 1871
Ibbetson, D. C. J. *See* India, P : Appendix 2.
Iberri, José Ignacio. Prospectus of a Navigable Canal between Vera Cruz and Alvarado. *Map.* 12* *New York*, 1827
Ibn Batuta, Travels of, in Asia and Africa, 1324-25. Translated from the abridged Arabic MS. copies preserved in the Public Library of Cambridge ; with Notes illustrative of the History, Geography, Botany, Antiquities, &c., occurring throughout the work. 4° 1829
—— Viagens Extensas e Dilatadas do Abu-Abdallah, mais conhecido pelo nome de Ben - Batuta. Traduzidas por José de Santo A. Moura. 2 vols. 8°
Lisbon, 1840-55
—— Voyages d'Ibn Batoutah ; texte Arabe, accompagné d'une traduction par C. Defrémery et le Dr B. R. Sanguinetti ; avec Index. 4 vols. 8° *Paris*, 1853-59
—— *See* Hakluyt Soc. Publ., Vol. 37 : Appendix 1.
Ibn Haukal. *See* Ebn Haukal.
Ibn Khaldûn. *See* Ebn Khaldoun and Omárah-al-Hakami.
Ibn Omar. *See* Ebn Omar.
Ibrahim Hilmy, Prince. Zeitschrift für Ægyptische Sprache und Alterthumskunde Jahrgang I.-XXIII. 1863-85. Inhaltsverzeichniss. 4* 1886
—— The Literature of Egypt and the Soudan, from the Earliest Times to the year 1885 inclusive : a Bibliography, comprising Printed Books, Periodical Writings, and Papers of Learned Societies ; Maps and Charts, Ancient Papyri, Manuscripts, Drawings, &c. 2 vols. Vol. 1, A-L, 4°; Vol. 2, M-Z. With Appendix of Additional Works to May 1887. 4° 1886-88

Ideler, J. L. *See* Ritter, Carl.
Ides, E. Ysbrant. Three Years' Travels from Moscow overland to China : thro' Great Ustiga, Siriania, Permia, Sibiria, Daour, Great Tartary, &c., to Peking. . . . To which is annex'd an accurate description of China, done originally by a Chinese Author. . . . Printed in Dutch by the Direction of Burgomaster Witzen, formerly Ambassador in England ; and now faithfully done into English. *Plates.* [*Map wanting.*] 4° 1706
—— *See* Brun ; *also* Astley, Vol. 3 ; Harris, Vol. 2 ; Allgemeine Historie, Vol. 5 : Appendix 1.
Idiaquez, E. *See* Ballivian.
Ihre, Johannis. Lexicon Lapponicum, cum interpretatione Vocabulorum Sueco-Latina et Indice Suecano-Lapponico ; . . . auctum Grammatica Lapponica a Erico Lindahl et Johanne Ohrling. 4°
Stockholm, 1780
Ijzerman, J. W. Beschrijving der Oudheden nabij de Grens der Residenties Soerakarta en Djogdjakarta ; with Atlas. *Plates.* 4° *Batavia*, 1891
Ikin, Arthur. Texas, its History, Topography, Agriculture, Commerce, and General Statistics ; with a Copy of the Treaty of Commerce entered into by the Republic of Texas and Great Britain. *Map.* 18° 1841
Illens, d', and — Funk. Plans et Journaux des Sièges de la dernière Guerre de Flandres. Rassemblés par deux Capitaines étrangers au Service de France. *Maps and plans.* 4° *Strasburg*, 1750
Imbault-Huart, Camille. Recueil de Documents sur l'Asie Centrale. I. Histoire de l'Insurrection des Tounganes sous le règne de Tao-Kouañg (1820-28) d'après les documents chinois ; II. Description Orographique du Turkestan chinois, traduite du Si yu t'ou tché ; III. Notices géographiques et historiques sur les Peuples de l'Asie Centrale, traduite du Si yu t'ou tché. [Vol. 16 of the Publ. de l'École des Langues Orient. Viv.] *Maps.* 8° *Paris*, 1881
Imbert, Louis. Congrès National des Sociétés Françaises de Géographie. XIVe session, Tours, 1893. Projet de Création d'un Bureau Colonial auprès des Sociétés de Géographie : Rapport Fait au Congrès de Tours, le 1er Août 1893. 8° *Bordeaux*, 1893
Imhaus, E. N. Les Nouvelles-Hébrides. *Maps and illustrations.* 8° *Paris*, 1890
Impey, E. Memoir on the Physical Character of the Nerbudda River and Valley ; with a Descriptive Detail of the Mineral Resources of the Nerbudda Valley, and on the Coal Beds in its Vicinity. [No. 14 of the India Records.] *Map.* Royal 8° *Bombay*, 1855

Imray, James F. Pilotage rates and regulations for the principal ports. 8° 1858
—— The Bay of Bengal Pilot. *Maps.*
8°   1879
—— *See* United Kingdom, North Pacific Pilot, Part 1: Appendix 2.
—— and **W. H. Rosser.** The Lights and Tides of the World, together with the Variation and Dip of the Magnetic Needle. *Charts.* 4°   1869

Im Thurn, Everard F. Tables of Indian Languages of British Guiana, with an Appendix of Arawak Family Names. Folio*   *Georgetown,* 1878
—— Notes on the Indians of Guiana. Nos. 1 to 8. Small 4° *Georgetown,* 1878-79
—— A Visit to the Corentyne River. Small 4*   *Georgetown,* 1879
—— A Second Journey to the Kaieteur, in February-March 1879. Small 4*
                         Georgetown, 1879
—— The Boundary between British Guiana and Venezuela. Small 4*
                         Georgetown, 1879
—— Among the Indians of Guiana : being Sketches, chiefly Anthropologic, from the Interior of British Guiana. *Map and illustrations.* 8°   1883
—— Visit of the Governor to the Pomeroon District (July 1887). (Reprinted from the *Argosy.*) 4*   *Demerara,* 1887
—— Primitive Games. (Reprinted from *Timehri.*) 8*   *Georgetown,* 1890
—— Notes on British Guiana : a Paper read before the Royal Colonial Institute. 8*   1892

Inagaki, Manjiro. Japan and the Pacific, and the Japanese View of the Eastern Question. *Maps.* 8°   1890

Inderwick, F. A. The Story of King Edward and New Winchelsea : the Edification of a Mediæval Crown. 8° 1892

Indio [do Brazil], Arthur. Memoria Descriptiva do Electro - Marégrapho Imaginado. 2nd edition. *Plate.* 8*
                    Rio de Janeiro, 1884

Ingersoll, Ernest. The History and Present Condition of the Fishery Industries : The Oyster Industry. *Plates.* 4°
                    Washington, 1881
—— *See* United States, A : Appendix 2.

Ingersoll, Joseph R. Address at the Annual Meeting of the Pennsylvania Colonisation Society, October 25, 1838 ; with the Annual Report. 8*
                    Philadelphia, 1838

Ingigi, Luca. Villeggiature de' Bizantini, sul Bosforo Tracio. Opera del P. P. Ingigi tradotta dal P. Cherubino Aznavor. *Map and plate.* 12° *Venice,* 1831

Inglefield, Sir Edward A. A New Theory of the Physical Causes of Terrestrial Magnetism, and some Remarks in connection therewith on the Aurora Borealis. 8*   1851

Inglefield, Sir Edward A. A Summer Search for Sir John Franklin, with a Peep into the Polar Basin ; with Short Notices by Professor Dickie on the Botany, and Dr Sutherland on the Meteorology and Geology. *Map and plates.* 8°   1853

Inglis, H. D. A Personal Narrative of a Journey through Norway, part of Sweden, and the Islands and States of Denmark. 12°   1835
—— The Channel Islands. *Plates.* 8° 1835

Ingram, Ant. *See* Kerr, Vol. 7: Appendix 1.

Ingulphus (Abbot). *See* Hakluyt, Vol. 2; Kerr, Vol. 1 : Appendix 1.

Inman, James. Navigation and Nautical Astronomy. Revised by the Rev. James Williams Inman. 8°   1862
—— Nautical Tables, designed for the use of British Seamen. Revised by the Rev. James Williams Inman. Royal 8° 1864
—— Ditto. New edition. 8°   1872

Innes, Emily. The Chersonese with the Gilding off. 2 vols. *Illustrations.* Crown 8°   1885

Inskip, G. H. Queen Charlotte Islands, on Western Coast of North America : Remarks for Sailing Directions, made in the year 1853. 8*   1856

Inskip, Rev. R. M. Navigation and Nautical Astronomy : containing Practical Rules, Notes, and Examples. 8°
                         Portsea, 1865
—— Appendix to the Navigation and Nautical Astronomy : containing Explanations and Proofs of the Theory, Additional Practical Rules and Examples, Local Duration, Use of Instruments, Taking Observations, Use of Charts, Definitions, &c. *Plates.* 8° *Portsea,* 1865

International Congresses and Conferences. *See* General : Appendix 2.

Introcetta, Père. *See* Thevenot, Vol. 4 : Appendix 1.

Inverarity, Capt. David. *See* Dalrymple, A.

"Investigator." *See* Osborn, S.

Inwards, Richard. The Temple of the Andes. *Plates.* 4°   1884

Ipolyi, Arnold. A Deákmonostori XIII. századi Román Basilika. Hely-és Mütörteneti Monographia. 4° *Budapest,* 1860

Iradier-Bulfy, Manuel. Primer Viaje de la Exploradora Zona de Corisco. Reconocimiento de la Zona Ecuatorial de Africa en las Costas de Occidente ; sus Montañas, sus Rios, sus Habitantes, Posesiones Españolas del Golfa de Guinea. 8°. *Map.* [Bound up with "Boletin de la Exploradora, Año 1, Tomo 1]   *Vitoria,* 1880

Irala, Domingo M. de. *See* Cartas de Indias, p. 612 : Appendix 1.

Irby, A. H. The Diary of a Hunter from the Punjab to the Karakorum Mountains. *Map.* 8° 1863

Irby, A. P. *See* Mackenzie, G. M.

Irby, Hon. C. Leonard, and James Mangles. Travels in Egypt and Nubia, Syria and Asia Minor, during 1817 and 1818. *Maps and plates.* 8°
[*Privately printed*], 1823

Irminger, C. Den Arctiske Strömning. *Map.* 8° *Copenhagen*, 1854
—— Strömninger og Iisdrift ved Island. 8° *Copenhagen*, 1861
—— Notice sur les Pêches du Danemark, des Isles Féroé, de l'Islande et du Groenland. 8° *Paris*, 1863

Irons, W. The Settlers' Guide to the Cape of Good Hope and Colony of Natal. Compiled from Original and Authentic Materials. 12° 1858

Irvine, J. The Ashantee Difficulty. 8° *Liverpool*, 1873

Irving, Dr A. Chemical and Physical Studies in the Metamorphism of Rocks, based on a Thesis (with Appendices). 8° 1889

Irving, B. A. The Commerce of India : being a View of the Routes successively taken by the Commerce between Europe and the East, and of the Political Effects produced by the several changes. 8° 1858
—— The Great Lake, Lagoon, or Bay of Triton. *Maps.* Small 8° [*Carlisle*, N.D.]

Irving, Edward. *See* Roberts, O. W.

Irving, J. Report on a Species of Palsy, prevalent in Pergunnah Khyragurh, in Zillah Allahabad, from the Use of Kessaree Dal, an Article of Food. 8° 1860
—— Report of a Species of Palsy of the Lower Limbs, prevalent in Pergunnah Barrah, Zillah ·Allahabad. [From the India Records (N.W. Provinces).] 8° *Allahabad*, 1861

Irving, Roland Duer. *See* United States, G, c (Monographs and Bulletins) : Appendix 2.

Irving, Washington. History of the Life and Voyages of Christopher Columbus. 4 vols. *Maps.* 8° 1828
—— Voyages and Discoveries of the Companions of Columbus. *Map and plates.* 12° 1831

Irwin, Eyles. A Series of Adventures in the course of a Voyage up the Red Sea, on the Coasts of Arabia and Eygpt ; and of a Route through the Desarts of Thebais, hitherto unknown to the European Traveller, in the year 1777, &c. *Maps and plates* 1780
—— The same, in the year 1777 ; with a Supplement of a Voyage from Venice to Latichea, and of a Route through the Desarts of Arabia, by Aleppo, Bagdad, and the Tygris to Busorah, in the years 1780 and 1781. 3rd edition. 2 vols. *Illustrations.* 8° 1787

Irwin, Capt. F. Chidley. State and Position of Western Australia, commonly called the Swan River Settlement. 8° 1835

Isbister, Alexander K. A Proposal for a New Penal Settlement in connection with the Colonization of the Uninhabited Districts of British North America. 8° 1850

Isbrant Ides. *See* Brun ; Ides.

Isenberg, C. W. Grammar of the Amharic Language. 8° 1842
—— *See* Krapf.
—— and J. L. Krapf. Journals, detailing their Proceedings in the Kingdoms of Shoa, and Journeys in other Parts of Abyssinia in 1839-42 ; with a Geographical Memoir of Abyssinia and South-Eastern Africa, by J. McQueen. *Maps.* 8° 1843

Ismail-Bey, Moustapha, and Colonel Moktar-Bey. Notices Biographiques de S. E. Mahmoud-Pacha el Falaki (l'Astronome). *Portrait.* 8° *Cairo*, 1886

Issaverdens, J. Armenia and the Armenians : being a Sketch of its Geography, History, Church, and Literature. Vol. 1. 12° *Venice*, 1874
—— The same. Vol. 2. Ecclesiastical History. 12° *Venice*, 1875

Issel, Arturo. Istruzioni Scientifiche pei Viaggiatori . . . in collaborazione dei Signori Giovanni Céloria, Michele Stefano de Rossi, Raffaello Gestro, Enrico Giglioli, Guido Grassi, Angiolo Manzoni, Antonio Piccone, Gustavo Uzielli, e Arturo Zannetti. *Plates.* 8° *Rome*, 1881
—— Il Terremoto del 1887 in Liguria. *Map and plates.* 8° *Genoa* [1887]
—— *See* Giglioli.

Istakhri. *See* Madini.

Ivanoff, D. L. Brief Sketch of Geological Researches on the Pamir. [In Russian.] *Map.* 8° 1885
—— What is the Pamir? [In Russian.] 8° [1885]

Ivanovsky, A. A. Anthropological Sketch of the Torguts in the Tarbagatai District of the Chinese Empire. [In Russian.] 4° *Moscow*, 1893
—— and A. D. Bozdestvensky. On Prof. N. J. Zograf's Anthropometrical Researches on the Male Population of the Vladimir, Yaroslaff, and Kostroma Governments. [In Russian.] 8° *Moscow*, 1893

Ivashintsov, Nikolai Aleksyevich. Hydrographical Researches on the Caspian Sea. Astronomical part. [In Russian.] 4° *St Petersburg*, 1866

Ivens, R. *See* Capello.

Iver-Boty. *See* Purchas, Vol. 3, Book 3 : Appendix 1.

Ives, Edward. Voyage from England to India in 1754, and an Historical Narrative of the Operations of the Squadron and Army in India under Adam Watson and Colonel Clive in 1755-57; with the Manners, Customs, &c., of several Nations of India; and a Journey from Persia to England by an unusual Route. *Maps and plates.* 4⁵   1773

Ives, Lieut. J. C. Report upon the Colorado River of the West, explored in 1857-58. *Maps and plates.* 4°
                              Washington, 1861
—— Voyage d'Exploration du Colorado en 1857 et 1858. *Map.* 8*   N.P., N.D.

Ixtlilxochitl, F. d'Alva. *See* Ternaux-Compans, Vols. 8, 12, 13 : Appendix 1.

J

Jack, Robert Logan. Report on the Bowen River Coalfield. *Map and illustrations.* Folio*   *Brisbane,* 1879
—— Report on the Geology and Mineral Resources of the District between Charters Towers Goldfields and the Coast. *Maps, &c.* Folio* *Brisbane,* 1879
—— Report on Explorations in Cape York Peninsula, 1879-80. Folio*
                              [*Brisbane*] 1881
—— Stanthorpe Tin Mining District Preliminary Report. Folio* *Brisbane,* 1882
—— Report on the Little River Coalfield near Cooktown. *Map.* Folio*
                              Brisbane, 1882
—— Report on the Tin Mines of Herberton, Western, and Thompson's Creek Districts, and the Silver Mines of the Dry River, Queensland. *Maps and plans.* Folio*   *Brisbane,* 1883
—— Report on the Hodgkinson Gold Field. *Maps and diagrams.* Folio*
                              Brisbane, 1884
—— Mount Morgan Gold Deposits. *Map and plan.* Folio*   [*Brisbane*] 1884
—— Report on the Argentine [Star] Silver Mines, Kennedy District. *Maps and section.* Folio*   [*Brisbane*] 1886
—— Handbook of Queensland Geology. 8*   *Brisbane,* 1886
—— Geological Observations in the North of Queensland, 1886-87. *Maps.* Folio*
                              [*Brisbane*] 1887
—— Report on the Geological Features of the Mackay District. *Plans.* Folio*
                              [*Brisbane*] 1887
—— Geology of the Russell River. Folio*
                              [*Brisbane*] 1888
—— The Mineral Wealth of Queensland. *Map.* 8*   *Brisbane,* 1888
—— On Some Salient Points in the Geology of Queensland. 8*
                              [*Sydney,* 1888]

Jack, Robert Logan. Limestone District, part ot the Palmer Goldfield. Preliminary Report. *Map.* Folio*
                              [*Brisbane*] 1888
—— Report on the Limestone District, part of the Palmer Goldfield. *Map.* Folio*   1888
—— Coal Discoveries on the Flinders. Folio*   [*Brisbane*] 1888
—— Report on the Sellheim Silver Mines and Surrounding District. *Maps and plan.* Folio*   [*Brisbane*] 1889
—— Mount Morgan Gold Deposits. Second Report. Folio* [*Brisbane*] 1889
—— Tarduganba Gold Mine. *Plan.* Folio*   [*Brisbane*] 1889
—— Moondilla Gold Field. Folio*
                              [*Brisbane*] 1891
—— Notes on Broken Hill. Folio*
                              Brisbane, 1891
—— Second Report on the Tin Mines near Cooktown. *Maps.* Folio*
                              Brisbane, 1891
—— Report on Chillagoe and Koorboora Mining Districts. *Maps.* Folio*
                              Brisbane, 1891
—— Report on the Kangaroo Hills Silver and Tin Mines. *Maps.* Folio*
                              Brisbane, 1892
—— Mount Morgan Gold Deposits. Third Report. *Maps, plates, and views.* Folio*   *Brisbane,* 1892
—— Second Report on the Normanby Gold Field. *Map.* Folio* *Brisbane,* 1893
—— Russell River Gold Field. *Map.* Folio*   *Brisbane,* 1893
—— Grass-Tree Gold Field, near Mackay. *Plans.* Folio*   *Brisbane,* 1893
—— *See* New South Wales, B : Appendix 2.

Jackman, E. *See* Hakluyt's Voyages, Vol. 1 : Appendix 1.

Jackson, A. J. Report relating to the Suppression of Dacoity in Bengal for 1859. [From the India Records.] Royal 8°   *Calcutta,* 1860

Jackson, Lieut.-Col. Basil. Treatises on Military Surveying, including Sketching in the Field, Plan-Drawing, Levelling, Military Reconnaissance, &c. *Plates.* 8°   1860

Jackson, C. T. On the Geology of the Public Lands belonging to the two States of Massachusetts and Maine. Second Annual Report. *Map.* 8°
                              Boston, 1838

Jackson, E. Correspondence relating to the Suppression of Dacoity in Bengal. [From the India Records.] Royal 8°
                              Calcutta, 1855

Jackson, J. *See* Pelham, Vol. 2 : Appendix 1.

Jackson, James. Adolf-Erik Nordenskiöld. 8*   *Paris,* 1880

Jackson, James. Liste Provisoire de Bibliographies Géographiques Spéciales. 8*   *Paris*, 1881
—— Tableau de Diverses Vitesses, Exprimés en Metres per Seconde. 8*
                                                                          [*Paris*, 1885]
—— Ditto. Other editions.   1886, 1892
—— Socotora : Notes Bibliographiques. Large 8*   *Paris*, 1892
—— *See* Cook.

Jackson, James Grey. An Account of the Empire of Marocco, and the District of Suse ; . . to which is added an Accurate and Interesting Account of Timbuctoo, the Great Emporium of Central Africa. *Map and plates.* 4°   1809
—— The same. 3rd edition. *Maps and plates.* 4°   1814
—— **and El Hage Abd Salam Shabeeny.** Account of Timbuctoo and Housa, Territories in the Interior of Africa : with Notes Critical and Explanatory ; to which is added, Letters descriptive of Travels through West and South Barbary, and across the Mountains of Atlas, by J. Grey Jackson. *Maps.* 8°   1820

Jackson, Col. J. R. Mémoire sur les Seiches du Lac de Genève, composé de 1803 à 1804. 4*   *Geneva*, 1804
—— Observations on Lakes : being an Attempt to explain the Laws of Nature regarding them, the Cause of their Formation and Gradual Diminution, the Different Phenomena they Exhibit, &c. *Plate.* 4°   1833
—— What to Observe, or the Traveller's Remembrancer. Revised and edited by Dr Norton Shaw. 8°   1861

Jackson, L. D'A. Hydraulic Manual. (Parts 1 and 2 in one.) 8°   1875
    Part 1. Working Tables and Explanatory Text ; Part 2. Hydraulic Statistics, and Indian Meteorological Statistics, for the Use of Engineers.
—— Canal and Culvert Tables, based on the Formula of Kutter, under a Modified Classification, with Explanatory Text and Examples. *Plates.* 8°   1878

Jackson, Sheldon. Report on Education in Alaska. *Maps and illustrations.* 8°
                                                          Washington, 1886

Jackson, T. G. Dalmatia, the Quarnero, and Istria ; with Cettigne in Montenegro and the Island of Grado. 3 vols. *Maps, plans, and illustrations.* 8° *Oxford*, 1887

Jackson, W. B. Report on Darjeeling. [From the India Records.] *Plate.* Royal 8°   *Calcutta*, 1854

Jackson, W. H. *See* United States, G, a (Miscell.) : Appendix 2.

Jacob, Sir G. Le Grand. Observations on Ancient Copper Tablets excavated in the Sawunt Waree Districts. *Facsimiles.* [Records, No. 10, N.S.] 8° *Bombay*, 1855

Jacob, Sir G. Le Grand. [Reports, &c., in the Bombay Records, No. 37, N.S.] Large 8°   *Bombay*, 1856
    Report upon the General Condition, in 1842, of the Province of Kattywar, accompanied by Various Points of Information, principally of a Geographical and Statistical Nature, connected with that Province. *Map.*
    Brief Historical, Geographical, and Statistical Memoir on Okhamundul.
    Extract from a Report on the District of Babriawar. *Map.*
    Report on the Iron of Kattywar, its Comparative Value with British Metal, the Mines, and Mode of Smelting the Ore.

Jacob, Major John. Report on the States and Tribes connected with the Frontier of Upper Sind. Royal 8° *Bombay*, 1855

Jacob, Wm. Travels in the South of Spain, in 1809-10. *Plates.* [Imperfect.] 4°   1811
—— View of the Agriculture, Manufactures, &c., of Germany, Holland, and France in 1819. 4°   1820

"Jacob," Ship. *See* Purchas, Vol. 2, Book 6 : Appendix 1.

Jacobs, Dr Julius. Eenigen tija onder de Baliëns. Eene Reisbeschrijving met aanteekeningen betreffende Hygiène Land- en Volkenbunde van de eilanden Bali en Lombok. *Map and frontispiece.* Imp. 8°   *Batavia*, 1883
—— **and J. J. Meijer.** De Badoej's. 4°
                                                      The Hague, 1891

Jacobsen, Capt. J. A. *See* Woldt.

Jacquemart, A. L'Extrême Orient au Palais de l'Industrie. Notices sur les Collections de M. H. Cernuschi. 8*
                                                                 Paris, 1874

Jacquemont, Victor. Correspondance avec sa Famille et plusieurs de ses amis pendant son Voyage dans l'Inde, 1828-32. 2 vols. *Map.* 8°   *Paris*, 1833
—— The same. Nouvelle edition. Vol. 2. 12°   *Paris*, 1841

Jacques le Hermite. *See* Hermite.

Jadrinzew N. Sibirien, Geographische, ethnographische, und historische Studien. Mit Bewilligung des Verfassers nach dem Russischen bearbeitet und vervollständigt von Dr Ed. Petri. *Illustrations.* 8°   *Jena*, 1886

Jaeger, Gustav. Dr Jaeger's Essays on Health-Culture. Translated and edited by Lewis R. S. Tomalin. 12°   1887

Jaeger, H. Kamerun und Sudan, Ein Mahnwort an das deutsche Volk. Erster Teil. 8°   *Berlin*, 1892

Jagor, F. Singapore, Malacca, Java. Reiseskizzen. *Plates.* 8° *Berlin,* 1866

—— Reisen in den Philippinen. *Map and plates.* 8° *Berlin,* 1873

—— Travels in the Philippines. *Map and plates.* 8° 1875

Jaime, Lieut. —. De Koulikoro a Tombouctou à bord du "Mage," 1889-90. *Maps and illustrations.* Large 8° *Paris*

Jäkel, Ernest. Der Germanische Ursprung der lateinischen Sprache und des römischen Volkes. [An English review of the work.] 8* [1830]

Jal, A. Archéologie Navale. 2 vols. *Woodcuts.* 8° *Paris,* 1840

Jalhay, Henry. *See* Nunez.

James the First. The Poetical Remains of King James the First, of Scotland ; with a Memoir, and an Introduction to the Poetry, by the Rev. Charles Rogers. *Frontispiece.* 8° *Edinburgh,* 1873

James, Edwin. Account of an Expedition from Pittsburgh to the Rocky Mountains, in 1819-20. Compiled from the Notes of Major Long, T. Say, &c. 3 vols. *Plates.* 8° 1823

James, F. L. The Wild Tribes of the Soudan : an Account of Travel and Sport chiefly in the Basé Country, being Personal Experiences and Adventures during Three Winters spent in the Soudan. *Maps and plates.* 8° 1883

—— The same. Second edition. With an Account of the Routes from Wady Halfah to Berber, by the author ; and a Chapter on Khartoum and the Soudan, by Sir Samuel Baker. *Map and illustrations.* Crown 8° 1884

—— The Unknown Horn of Africa : an Exploration from Berbera to the Leopard River ; with additions by J. Godfrey Thrupp. *Map and plates.* 8° 1888

—— The same. Second edition. Containing the Narrative Portion and Notes only ; with an Obituary Notice by J. A. and W. D. James. *Map, portrait, and illustrations.* Crown 8° 1890

James, Col. Sir Henry. Abstracts from the Meteorological Observations taken at the Stations of the Royal Engineers in the year 1853-54, &c. *Map and tables.* 4° 1855

—— Meteorological Observations taken during 1829-52, at the Ordnance Survey Office, Phœnix Park, Dublin ; to which is added a Series of similar Observations made at other places in Ireland. Edited by Captain Cameron. *Plate.* 4° *Dublin,* 1856

—— Account of the Observations and Calculations of the Principal Triangulation, and of the Figure, Dimensions, and Mean Specific Gravity of the Earth

James, Col. Sir Henry—*continued.* as derived therefrom. Drawn up by Capt. A. R. Clarke. 2 vols. *Maps and plates.* 4° 1858

—— Ordnance Trigonometrical Survey. Geodetical Tables, based on the Elements of the Figure of the Earth given in the Account of the Principal Triangulation. 4° 1858

—— Instructions for taking Meteorological Observations, with Tables for their Correction, and Notes on Meteorological Phenomena. *Diagrams, &c.* 8° 1860

—— Ordnance Survey Abstracts of the Principal Lines of Spirit Levelling in England and Wales. 2 vols. *Maps and plates.* 4° 1861

—— Ordnance Survey Abstracts of the Principal Lines of Spirit Levelling in Scotland. 2 vols. *Maps and plates.* 4° 1861

—— Note on the Block of Tin dredged up in Falmouth Harbour. *Plates.* 8* 1863

—— An Account of the Levelling from the Mediterranean to the Dead Sea. By Captain C. W. Wilson. (From the *Journal,* R.G.S.) *Map.* 8* 1866

—— Notes on the Parallel Roads of Lochaber, with illustrative maps and sketches from the Ordnance Survey of Scotland. 4° *Southampton,* 1874

—— **and Col. Alex. R. Clarke.** On Projections for Maps applying to a very large extent of the Earth's Surface. *Plate.* 8* 1862

James, H. E. M. The Long White Mountain, or a Journey in Manchuria ; with some Account of the History, People, Administration, and Religion of that Country. *Maps and illustrations.* 8° 1888

James, H. R. Report of a Journey to Kokan. [From the India Records.] Royal 8° *Calcutta,* 1863

James, Lieut. Hugh. Report on the Purguna of Chandookah, in Upper Sind, with Appendices. [From the India Records.] Royal 8° *Bombay,* 1855

James, Capt. Thomas. The Dangerous Voyage of, in his intended Discovery of a North-West Passage into the South Sea ; with a Map for Sailing in those Seas, and Tables of the Variation of the Compass, &c. *Map.* 8° 1740

—— *See* Churchill, Vol. 2 ; Hakluyt Soc. Publ., Vol. 5 ; Harris, Vol. 2 ; Allgemeine Historie, Vol. 17 ; "The World Displayed," Vol. 10 : Appendix 1.

James, Thomas C. Memoir of, by Job R. Tyson. 8* *Philadelphia,* 1836

James, T. Horton. Six Months in South Australia ; with some Account of Port Phillip and Portland Bay, in Australia Felix. *Maps.* 8° 1838

Jameson, J. S. Story of the Rear Column of the Emin Pasha Relief Expedition. Edited by Mrs J. S. Jameson. *Portrait, map, and illustrations.* 8° 1890

Jameson, Robt. Mineralogical Description of the County of Dumfries. *Map and plates.* 8° *Edinburgh,* 1805
—— *See* Cuvier; Murray, Hugh.

Jamieson, Alex. A Manual of Map-making and Mechanical Geography. *Map and woodcuts.* 12° 1846

Jamieson, Mrs. Topographical, Statistical, and Domestic History of France. 12° 1836

Jamieson, Robert. Is Central Africa to remain Sealed against Intercourse with the Civilised World? a few Remarks addressed to those who desire the Amelioration of Africa. 8* *Liverpool,* 1844
—— The Inefficacy of Treaties for the Suppression of the African Slave Trade, and their Injurious Influences on British Commercial Interests in Africa; with Suggestions for the Development of the Commercial Resources of Western Central Africa, and a short Notice of the Kingdom of Benin. *Map.* 8* 1859

Jancigny, Alfred de. *See* Noury.

Janin, J. Voyage de Paris à la Mer. Description Historique des bords de la Seine. *Plates.* Small 8* *Paris* [1847]

Jankó, Dr János. Das Delta des Nil, geologischer und geographischer Aufbau des Deltas. *Maps.* 4° *Budapest,* 1890
—— Magyarország Hegyvidékeinek Csoportositása. Large 8° *Budapest,* 1891
—— Kalotaszeg Magyar Népe. *Map and illustrations.* 8° *Budapest,* 1892

Jannasch, Dr R. Die Deutsche Handelsexpedition, 1886. *Maps.* 8° *Berlin,* 1887
—— *See* Roscher, W.

Jannequin, Claude. *See* Astley, Vol. 2; Allgemeine Historie, Vol. 2: Appendix 1.

Jansen, Prof. K. *See* Germany, C (Forschungen, &c., Vol. 1): Appendix 2.

Janson, J. On the Corn-trade of the Odessa area. [In Russian.] *Map.* 8° *St Petersburg,* 1870

Janson, Charles W. Stranger in America : containing Observations made during a Residence in that Country, on the Genius, Manners, and Customs of the People of the United States, with Biographical Particulars of Public Characters, and on the Slave Trade. *Plates.* 4° 1807

Jansson, J. Accuratissima Orbis Antiqui Delineatio, sive Geographia vetus, Sacra et Profana, &c. *Maps.* Large folio *Amsterdam,* 1652

Janssen, Léon. *See* Eredia.

Janvier, T. R. The Mexican Guide. *Maps.* 12° *New York,* 1886

Jaques, William H. Torpedoes for National Defence: a Practical and Concise Review of these Weapons, their usefulness, application, cost, and most efficient types ; together with the results obtained at official trials, and a description and comparison of the Sims, Whitehead, and Howell, based upon official reports. *Illustrations.* Small 8° 1886

Jardim, Major J. R. de Moraes. O Rio Araguaya. Relatorio de sua Exploração pelo Major d'Engenheiros Joaquim R. de Moraes Jardim, precedido de um Resumo Historico sobre sua Navegação pelo Tenente Colonel d'Engenheiros, Jeronimo R. de Moraes Jardim, e seguido de um estudo sobre os Indios que habitam suas margens pelo Dr Aristides de Souza Spinola. 8* *Rio de Janeiro,* 1880

Jardine, A. W. Report on Harbours and Rivers in Queensland. Folio* *Brisbane,* 1891

Jardine, Sir W. Memoirs of Hugh Edwin Strickland. *Maps and plates.* 8° 1858

Jarrad, F. W. *See* United Kingdom, A : Appendix 2.

Jarric, Pierre du. *See* Iarric.

Jarves, James Jackson. History of the Sandwich Islands, embracing their Antiquities, Mythology, Legends, Discovery by Europeans in the Sixteenth Century, Re-discovery by Cook, with their Civil, Religious, and Political History, from the earliest traditional period to the present time. *Map and plates.* 8° *Boston, Mass.,* 1843

Jarvis, E. Immigration into the United States. 8° *Boston, Mass.,* 1872
—— Infant Mortality. 8* *Boston, Mass.,* 1873

Jäschke, Dr M. *See* Germany, C (Forschungen, &c., Vol. 3): Appendix 2.

Jaubert, P. Amédée. Voyage en Arménie et en Perse, fait dans les années 1805 et 1806, &c. *Map.* 8° *Paris,* 1821
—— *See* Paradis ; *also* Eyriès, Vol. 14; Recueil de Voyages, p. 611, Vols. 2, 5, 6 : Appendix 1.

Jay, John. Statistical View of American Agriculture, its Home Resources and Foreign Markets ; with Suggestions for the Schedules of the Federal Census in 1860. 8° *New York,* 1859

Javorsky, Dr I. L. Travels of the Russian Mission in Afghanistan and the Khanate of Bokhara in 1878-79. [In Russian.] 2 vols [in one]. *Maps and illustrations.* 8° *St Petersburg,* 1882-83

Q

Javorsky, Dr I. L. Reise der Russischen Gesandtschaft in Afghanistan und Buchara in den Jahren 1878-79. Aus dem Russischen übersetzt und mit einem Vorwort und Anmerkungen versehen von Dr Ed. Petri. 2 vols. *Maps and illustrations.* 8° *Jena,* 1885

"Jeannette" Expedition. Proceedings of a Court of Inquiry, convened at the Navy Department, Washington, D.C., 5th October 1882, in Pursuance of a Joint Resolution of Congress, approved 8th August 1882, to Investigate the circumstances of the Loss in the Arctic Seas of the Exploring Steamer "Jeannette," &c. *Plates and charts.* 8° *Washington,* 1883

Jeans, H. W. Handbook for the Stars, containing Rules for Finding the Names and Positions of all the Stars of the First and Second Magnitude. Royal 8° 1848

Jedina, Leopold von. Voyage de la Frégate autrichienne "Helgoland" autour de l'Afrique. *Illustrations.* Large 8° *Paris,* 1878

—— An Asiens Küsten und Fürstenhöfen. Tagebuchblätter von der Reise Sr. Maj. Schiffe's "Fasana" und über den Aufenthalt in Asiatischen Häfen in den Jahren 1887, 1888, und 1889. *Map and illustrations.* 4° *Vienna,* 1891

Jefferson, Thomas. Notes on the State of Virginia. [*The map wanting.*] 8° 1787

Jeffreys, Dr J. Gwyn. Report of the Committee appointed for Exploring the Coasts of Shetland by means of the Dredge. 8* 1863

—— **and Dr W. B. Carpenter.** Papers on the "Valorous" Expedition. *Chart and sections.* 8* 1876

Jeffries, D. A Treatise on Diamonds and Pearls, in which their importance is considered, and plain rules are exhibited for ascertaining the value of both; and on the true method of manufacturing Diamonds. 4th edition. 12° 1871

Jencken, Johann Ferdinand. Treatise on Light, Colour, Electricity, and Magnetism. Translated and Prefaced by Historical and Critical Essays by Henry D. Jencken. 8° 1869

Jenkins, Edward. State Emigration: an Essay. (2nd edition.) 8* 1869

Jenkins, H. L. Notes on the Burmese Route from Assam to the Hookoong Valley. *Map.* 8* 1869

—— *See* India, I: Appendix 2.

Jenkins, R. Report on the Territories of the Rajah of Nagpore. 8° *Calcutta,* 1827

Jenkinson, Anthony. *See* Astley, Vol. 4; Gottfried; Hakluyt, Vol. 1; Hakluyt Soc. Publ., Vols. 72, 73; Pinkerton, Vol. 9; Purchas, Vol. 3, Book 2; Thevenot, Vol. 1; Allgemeine Historie, Vol. 7: Appendix 1.

Jenkinson, H. J. Practical Guide to the Isle of Man. *Map in cover.* 12° 1874

Jenner, T. A Book of the Names of all Parishes, Market Towns, Villages, Hamlets, and smallest places in England and Wales. Small 8° 1668

Jenner, T. Mnemonic Geography. Part I. The Provinces of China. *Map.* 8° 1869

—— That Goodly Mountain and Lebanon: being the Narrative of a Ride through the Countries of Judea, Samaria, and Galilee, into Syria. *Map and plates.* Small 8° 1873

Jenney, Walter P. *See* United States, G, *b*: Appendix 2.

Jennings, Samuel. My Visit to the Goldfields in the South East Wynaad. *Map and plates.* 8° 1881

Jensen, J. A. D. Om Indlandsisen i Grönland. Ianledning af Dr Nansen's Expedition. *Map and illustrations.* 8* *Copenhagen,* 1888

Jentzsch, A. Berichte über die geologische Durchforschung der Provinz Preussen im Jahre 1876. 4* *Königsberg,* 1877

—— Das Relief der Provinz Preussen. Begleitworte zur Höhenschichten-Karte. *Map.* 4* *Königsberg,* 1877

Jenzsch, Gustave. Considérations relatives à la Partie Minéralogique des Instructions pour l'Expédition Scientifique Brésilienne. 8* *Dresden,* 1857

Jephson, A. J. Mounteney. Emin Pasha and the Rebellion at the Equator: a Story of Nine Months' Experiences in the last of the Soudan Provinces. With the Revision and Co-operation of Henry M. Stanley. *Maps and illustrations.* 8° 1890

Jephson, John Mounteney. Narrative of a Walking Tour in Brittany; accompanied by Notes of a Photographic Expedition by Lovell Reeve. *Photographs wanting.* 8° 1859

Jeppe, Friedrich. Transvaal Book Almanac and Directory for 1879. 12° *Pretoria,* 1879

—— The same, for 1881. 12° *Maritzburg,* 1881

—— The same, for 1889. 8° *Cape Town,* 1889

—— Die Transvaalsche oder Süd-Afrikanische Republik nebst einem Anhang: Dr Wangemann's Reise in Süd-Afrika, 1866-67 (Ergänzungsheft, 24 — Petermann's Mittheilungen). *Map.* 4° *Gotha,* 1868

Jerdan, W. *See* Berneaud.

Jermann, E. Pictures from St Petersburg. Translated by Hardman. 12° 1852

Jerningham, Hubert E. H. Report of the Expedition to the Unexplored Coxcomb Mountains in British Honduras. *Plan.* Folio * *Belize,* 1888

Jerrold, W. Blanchard. A Brage-Beaker with the Swedes; or, Notes from the North in 1852. *Plates.* 12° 1854

Jersey, Countess of. Three Weeks in Samoa. (From the *Nineteenth Century*.) 8* 1893

Jervis, A. E. S. *See* Layard, Austin.

Jervis, Guglielmo [W. P.] The Mineral Resources of Central Italy, including a Description of the Mines and Marble Quarries. *Map and plates.* 8° 1862
—— Supplement to ditto : containing an Account of the Mineral Springs, accompanied by the most Reliable Analyses. 8° 1868
—— I Tesori Sotterranei dell' Italia. Descrizione Topografica e Geologica di tutte le Località nel Regno d'Italia in cui rinvengonsi Minerali. . . . Repertorio d'Informazioni utili. 4 vols. *Plates and illustrations.* 8° *Turin*, 1873-89
—— Cenni geologici sulle Montagne Poste in prossimità al Giacimento di Antracite di Demonte. 8* *Turin*, 1874
—— Sul Giacimento di Carbon fossile Antracitico di Demonte. 8* *Milan*, 1875
—— The Anthracitic Coal of Demonte, near Cuneo, in the Italian Alps. 8* 1875
—— Guida alle Acque Minerali d'Italia coll' indicazione delle proprietà fisiche, chimiche e mediche, delle singole sorgenti e cenni Storici, Geologici e Climatologici, corredata di tre specchi sinottici, contenenti le migliori analisi chimiche. Province Meridionali. *Plans and illustrations.* Large 8° *Turin*, 1876
—— Delle Cause dei Movementi Tellurici e dei possibili ripari con riguardo Speciale al Terremoto Alpino dell' Inverno dell' anno 1887. 8* *Turin*, 1887

Jervis, Lieut. H. Narrative of a Journey to the Falls of the Cavery; with an Historical and Descriptive Account of the Neilgherry Hills. *Plates.* 8° 1834

Jervis, Major T. B. Contributions to the Statistics of Western India, in 1823-30. 8° 1830
—— Expediencyand Facility of Establishing the Meteorological and Monetary Systems throughout India on a Scientific and Permanent Basis, grounded on an Analytical Review of the Weights, Measures, and Coins of India. *Tables.* 8° *Bombay*, 1834
—— Records of Ancient Science, exemplified and authenticated in the Primitive Universal Standard of Weights and Measures. 8° *Calcutta*, 1835
—— Geographical and Statistical Memoir of the Konkun. 8° *Calcutta*, 1840
—— Review of a Narrative of the Campaign of the Army of the Indus in Sindh and Kabul in 1838-39. 8° *Bombay*, 1841

Jervis, Major T. B. Address delivered at the Geographical Section of the British Association, Newcastle - on - Tyne, descriptive of the State, Progress, and Prospects of the various Surveys and other Scientific Inquiries instituted by the Honourable East India Company throughout Asia, &c. 8* *Torquay*, N.D.
—— *See* Hügel.

Jesse, Capt. *See* Ferrier, J. P.

Jesse, J. *See* Dalrymple, Repertory, Vol. 2 : Appendix 1.

Jessup, General J. S. *See* United States, H, c : Appendix 2.

Jesuits. Lettere dell' India Orientale, scritte da' Reurendi Padri della Compagnia di Giesù. 12° *Venice*, 1580
—— Travels of several Learned Missioners of the Society of Jesus into divers parts of the Archipelago, India, China, and America. Containing a General Description of the Most Remarkable Towns, with a Particular Account of the Customs, Manners, and Religion of those several Nations. . . . . Translated from the French. *Plates.* 8° 1714
—— Nouvelles des Missions Orientales, reçues à Londres par les Directeurs du Séminaire des Missions étrangères, en 1793, 1794, 1795, et 1796. Pouvant servir de suite aux Lettres Edifiantes des Missionnaires de ia Compagnie de Jésus. 12° 1797
—— Nouvelles Lettres Edifiantes des Missions de la Chine et des Indes Orientales. 8 vols. 12° *Paris*, 1818-23
—— Relations des Jésuites : contenant ce qui s'est passé de plus remarquable dans les Missions des Pères de la Compagnie de Jésus, dans la Nouvelle-France, 1611 à 1672. 3 vols. *Maps.* Royal 8° *Quebec*, 1858

Jimenez, F. Memoria sobre la Determinacion Astronómica de la Ciudad de Cuernavaca. *Map.* 8* *Mexico*, 1866.

Jiménez de la Espada, Marcos. Las Islas de los Galápagos y otras más á poniente. *Map.* 8* [*Madrid*, 1892]

Jiménez de la Romera, Waldo. España sus Monumentos y Artes, su Naturaleza é Historia : Cuba, Puerto-Rico y Filipinas. *Illustrations.* 8° *Barcelona*, 1887

Jinman, G. Winds and their Courses. 3rd edition. *Charts, &c.* 8° 1865
—— Cloud-bands and Earth-currents. 4* N.D.

Jirecek, Dr Constantin. Beiträge zur antiken Geographie und Epigraphik von Bulgarien und Rumelien. 8° [*Berlin*], 1881

Joanne, A. and P. Collection des Guides-Joanne. *Maps, plans, and illustrations.* Small 8° *Paris*
—— De Bordeaux à Toulouse, &c. [1858]

Joanne's Guides—*continued.*
—— Itinéraire Descriptif, Historique et Artistique de la Hollande, par A. J. Du Pays. 1862
—— Itineraire générale de la France. I. De Paris à la Méditerranée ; Bourgogne, Franche-Comté, Savoie, &c. 1863
— — The same. II. Auvergne, Dauphiné, Provence, Alpes-Maritimes, Corse, &c. 1865
—— Vosges et Ardennes. *Maps and plans.* 8° 1868
— — Le Nord. 1870
— — The same. 2me édn. 1878
—— Les Environs de Paris Illustrés. 2me édn. 1872
— — Normandie. 2me édn. Augmentée d'un Appendice pour les îles Anglaises de Jersey et de Guernsey. 1872
—— The same. 1887
— — Bretagne. 2me édn. 1873
— — The same. Avec un Appendice pour les îles Anglaises de Jersey et de Guernsey. 1886
—— Les Pyrénées. 4me édn. 1874
— — The same. 1885
—— Auvergne, Morvan, Velay, Cevennes. 2me édn. 1874
—— De la Loire à la Garonne. 1875
—— Paris Illustré en 1870 et 1876. 3me édn. [1876]
—— Jura et Alpes Françaises. 1877
—— Provence, Alpes Maritimes, Corse. 1877
—— Gascogne et Languedoc. 1883
— — De la Loire à la Gironde, Poitou et Saintonge. 1884
—— The same. *Maps and plans* Paris, 1891
—— Corse. 1884
— — Auvergne et Centre. 1886
—— The same. *Maps and plans* Paris, 1892
—— Franche-Comté et Jura. 1888
—— Géographie du Département des Côtes-du-Nord. *Map and illustrations.* Small 8° Paris, 1878
—— The same, du Pas-de-Calais. (4th edition) 1883
—— The same, Seine-et-Marne. (4th edition) 1883
— — The same, Seine-Inférieure. (4th edition) 1883
—— The same, de la Somme. (4th edition) 1883
—— The same, de l'Oise. (3rd edition) 1883
—— The same, d'Eure-et-Loir. (2nd edition) 1883
— — The same, de Seine-et-Oise. (4th edition) 1883
— — The same, de l'Eure. (2nd edition) 1883
—— The same, de la Marne. (3rd edition) 1883

Joanne's Guides—*continued.*
—— The same, de l'Yonne. (3rd edition) 1884
—— De Paris à Constantinople. 1886
—— Itinéraire Historique et Descriptif de l'Algérie, de Tunis, et de Tanger, par Louis Piesse. 2me édn. 1874
—— Algérie et Tunisie, par Louis Piesse. 1888
—— États du Danube et des Balkans, Hongrie, Méridionale, Adriatique, Dalmatie, Monténégro, Bosnie, et Herzégovine. 1888
—— Grèce. I. Athènes et ses Environs. 1888
—— Ditto. II. Grèce Continentale et Iles. *Maps and plans* Paris, 1891
—— Paris, par Paul Joanne. 1889
—— De Paris à Genève et à Chamonix, par Macon et par Lyon. N.D.
Joanne, Paul. Dictionnaire géographique et administratif de la France et des ses Colonies. Publié sous la direction de Paul Joanne. Vols. 1-3, and part of Vol. 4. *Maps, plans, and illustrations.* 4° Paris, 1890-95

Jobson, Capt. Richard. *See* Astley, Vol. 2 ; Gottfried ; Purchas, Vol. 2 ; Allgemeine Historie, Vol. 3 : Appendix 1.

Jocelyn, Lord. Six Months with the Chinese Expedition ; or, Leaves from a Soldier's Note-book. 7th edition. *Illustrations.* 12° 1841

Jochmus, Lieut.-Gen. A. Der Syrische Krieg und der Verfall des Osmanen-Reiches seit 1840. 8* Frankfort-a-M., 1856
—— Memorandum on India, addressed from Singapore to Prince Metternich ; with a Preface by F. M. Lewin. 8* 1858

Joest, Wilhelm. Aus Japan nach Deutschland durch Sibirien. *Map and plates.* 8° Cologne [1882]
— — Um Afrika. *Map and plates.* 8° Cologne, 1885
—— Die Minahassa. *Map.* 8* Amsterdam [1886]
—— Tätowiren, Narbenzeichnen, und Körperbemalen. Ein Beitrag zur vergleichenden Ethnologie. *Coloured plates.* Folio Berlin, 1887
—— Spanische Stiergefechte ; eine Kulturgeschichtliche Skizze. *Plates.* 8° Berlin, 1889

Johansen, A. A Geographical and Historical Account of the Island of Bulama, with Observations on its Climate, Productions, &c. *Map.* 8* 1794

Johansson, C. J. *See* Sweden, A (Ser. C, No. 108): Appendix 2.

Johnson, Commander E. J. Sailing Directions from Sunderland Point to Berwick, with the Farn Islands. 8° 1836

Johnson, Frederic. *See* Weldon's Guide to Epping Forest.

Johnson, H. C. Ross. A Long Vacation in the Argentine Alps; or, Where to Settle in the River Plate States. *Map.* 8° 1868

Johnson, Hilary R. W. Message of the President of Liberia, communicated to the Second Session of the Nineteenth Legislature. 8* *Monrovia*, 1884
—— Ditto, communicated to the First Session of the Twentieth Legislature. 8* *Monrovia*, 1885

Johnson, J. The Oriental Voyager; or, Descriptive Sketches and Cursory Remarks on a Voyage to India and China in His Majesty's ship "Caroline." . . 1803-6. 8° 1807

Johnson, Lieut.-Col. John. A Journey from India to England, through Persia, Georgia, Russia, Poland, and Prussia, in the year 1817. *Plates.* 8° 1818

Johnson, J. Y. Madeira, its Climate and Scenery: a Handbook for Invalids and other Visitors, with Chapters on the Fauna, Flora, Geology, and Meteorology. 3rd edition. *With map of the island and plans.* 12° 1885

Johnson, Manuel J. Catalogue of 606 Principal Fixed Stars in the Southern Hemisphere. 4° 1835

Johnson, R. *See* Hakluyt, Vol. 1 . Appendix 1.

Johnson, Dr Samuel. Thoughts on the late Transactions respecting Falkland's Islands. 8* 1771

Johnston, Dr Alexander Keith. Dictionary of Geography, Descriptive, Physical, Statistical, and Historical, forming a complete General Gazetteer of the World. 8° 1850
—— The Physical Atlas of Natural Phenomena. Folio 1850
—— Historical Notice of the Progress of the Ordnance Survey in Scotland. *Map.* 8* *Edinburgh*, 1851
—— Remarks on the Scale adopted for the Ordnance Map of Scotland. 8* *Edinburgh*, 1851
—— The Geographical Distribution of Material Wealth: Historical Notes regarding the Merchant Company of Edinburgh, and the Widows' Scheme and Hospitals. *Map.* Small 4° *Edinburgh*, 1862
—— Index Geographicus: being a List, Alphabetically Arranged, of the Principal Places on the Globe, with the Countries and Subdivisions of Countries in which they are situated, and their Latitudes and Longitudes. Royal 8° 1864
—— School Atlas of Astronomy. . . . New and enlarged edition, with an Elementary Survey of the Heavens. . . By Robert Grant. 8° 1869

Johnston, Dr Alexander Keith. The Half-crown Atlas of General Geography. 12° N.D.
—— The Half-crown Atlas of British History. 12° 1871
—— Handy Royal Atlas of Modern Geography. Folio 1873
—— In Memoriam. *Portrait.* Small 4° *Edinburgh*, 1873
—— A General Dictionary of Geography, Descriptive, Physical, Statistical, Historical, forming a complete Gazetteer of the World. New edition. Small 4° 1877
—— Notes on the Geographical Labours of. Square 8* N.D.
—— Atlas of the British Empire in Europe, Asia, Oceania, Africa, and America, with Descriptive Letterpress. *Maps.* 12° N.D.

Johnston. A. Keith, junr. A Map of the Lake Region of Eastern Africa, showing the Sources of the Nile recently discovered by Dr Livingstone; with Notes on the Exploration of this Region, its Physical Features, Climate, and Population. *Map.* 8* 1870
—— The Surface Zones of the Globe: a Handbook to accompany a Physical Chart. *Maps.* 12° 1874
—— Africa. [Article in the "Encyclopædia Britannica." 9th edition.] *Map.* 4* [*Edinburgh*, 1875]
—— The Book of Physical Geography (Stewart's Local Examination Series). 12° 1877
—— Atlas and Handbook of Physical Geography, from Original and Authentic Materials, with Analytical Indexes. *Maps.* 12° 1877
—— A Physical, Historical, Political, and Descriptive Geography. *Maps and illustrations.* 8° 1880
—— The same. 3rd edition. Revised by E. G. Ravenstein. *Maps and illustrations.* 8° 1885
—— The same. 4th edition. Revised by E. G. Ravenstein. *Maps and illustrations.* 8° 1890
—— A Short Geography of Africa for the Use of Candidates at the Cambridge Local and other Examinations. Edited by E. G. Ravenstein. 2nd edition. *Map.* Crown 8° 1889
—— A Short Geography of Europe. . . . Edited by E. G. Ravenstein. *Map.* Crown 8° 1890
—— A Short Geography of Asia. . . . Edited by E. G. Ravenstein. *Map.* Crown 8° 1891
—— A School Physical and Descriptive Geography. 6th edition. Revised by A. H. Keane. *Maps.* 8° 1892
—— *See* Bryce; Milner; Stanford, E.

Johnston, Charles. Travels in Southern Abyssinia, through the Country of Adal to the Kingdom of Shoa. 2 vols. *Map.* 8°   1844

Johnston, Charles. Darwaz and Karategin: an Ethnographical Sketch. 8*
                              N.P., N.D.

Johnston, H. H. The River Congo, from the Mouth to Bólóbó, with a General Description of the Natural History and Anthropology of its Western Basin. *Maps and illustrations.* 8°   1884

—— The Kilima-njaro Expedition: a Record of Scientific Exploration in Eastern Equatorial Africa, and a General Description of the Natural History, Language, and Commerce of the Kilima-njaro District. *Portrait, maps, and illustrations.* 8°   1886

—— Report on a Journey up the Cameroons River, from Bell Town to Wuri and Budiman. [Foreign Office Paper.] *Map.* Folio*   1886

—— British Missions and Missionaries in Africa. (From *The Nineteenth Century*.) 8*   1887

—— British East Africa. (From *The Fortnightly Review.*) *Map.* 8*   1888

—— The History of a Slave. *Illustrations.* 8°   1889

—— British South-Central Africa. (From *The New Review.*) *Map.* 8*   1890

—— The Development of Tropical Africa under British Auspices. (From *The Fortnightly Review.*) 8*   1890

—— The Value of Africa. (From *The Nineteenth Century.*) 8*   1890

—— Livingstone and the Exploration of Central Africa. [The World's Great Explorers and Explorations.] *Maps and illustrations.* Crown 8°   1891

Johnston, Dr James. Reality *versus* Romance in South Central Africa: an Account of a Journey across the Continent from Benguella on the West, through Bihe, Ganguella, Barotse, the Kalihari Desert, Mashonaland, Manica, Gorongoza, Nyasa, the Shire Highlands, to the mouth of the Zambesi, on the East Coast. *Maps and illustrations.* Large 8°   1893

Johnston, Lieutenant James H. Précis of Reports, Opinions, and Observations on the Navigation of the Rivers of India by Steam-Vessels. 8*   1831

Johnston, J. F. W. Notes on North America, Agricultural, Economical, and Social. 2 vols. *Map.* 8°   1851

Johnston, R. The Competitive Geography. 2nd edition. Large 12°   1874

Johnston, T. B., and J. A. Robertson. The Historical Geography of the Clans of Scotland. *Maps and plans.* 4°   1872

Johnston, Thos. Crawford. Did the Phœnicians Discover America? *Illustrations.* 8*   *San Francisco*, 1892

Johnston, W. *See* Bartolomeo.

Johnston-Lavis, Dr H. J. Account of the Eruptive Phenomena and Geology of Monte Somma and Vesuvius, in explanation of the great Geological Map of that Volcano. 12*   1891

—— The South Italian Volcanoes, by Messrs Johnston-Lavis, Platania, Sambon, Zezi, and Mme. Antonia Lavis. Small 4°   *Naples*, 1891

Johnstone, J. C. Maoria: a Sketch of the Manners and Customs of Aboriginal Inhabitants of New Zealand. Small 8°
                                          1874

Johnstone, John K. The Isle of Axholme, its Place-Names, and River Names. 12*   *Epworth*, 1886

Johnstrup, F. Indberetning om den af Professor Johnstrup foretagne Undersögelsesreise paa Island i Sommeren 1876. *Maps and plates.* 8*
                           Copenhagen, 1876

—— Om Grönsandet i Sjælland. *Plate.* 8*
                           Copenhagen, 1876

Joliet, Louis. *See* Gravier.

Joliet, Sieur. *See* Marquette; *also* Gottfried; Thevenot, Vol. 4: Appendix 1.

Jolly, William. The Realistic Teaching of Geography; its Principles, especially in regard to Initiatory Notions; the Correction of Prevalent Errors; and Examples of Simple, Demonstrative, and Dramatic Methods. 12*   N.D.

Joly, C. Note sur une Exposition de Géographie, Botanique et Horticole, organisée par la Société Centrale d'Horticulture de Nancy. 8*   [*Nancy*] 1880

Jomard, E. François. Remarques sur les Découvertes Géographiques faites dans l'Afrique Centrale. 4*   *Paris*, 1827

—— Considérations sur l'Objet et les Avantages d'une Collection Spéciale consacrée aux Cartes Géographiques et aux Diverses Branches de la Géographie. 8*
                              Paris, 1831

—— Coup-d'œil Impartial sur l'État présent de l'Égypte, comparé à sa Situation Antérieure. 8*   *Paris*, 1836

—— Jours de Pluie Observés au Caire. 4*
                              Paris, 1839

—— Études Géographiques et Historiques sur l'Arabie, avec des Observations sur l'État des Affaires et en Égypte. 8°
                              Paris, 1839

—— Notice Historique sur la Vie de Réné Caillé. 8*   *Paris*, 1839

—— Notation Hypsométrique, ou Nouvelle Manière de Noter les Altitudes. 8*
                              Paris, 1840

—— De l'Utilité qu'on peut tirer de l'Étude Comparative des Cartes Géographiques. 8*   *Paris*, 1841

Jomard, E. François. Second Voyage à la Recherche des Sources du Bahr-el-Abiad ou Nil Blanc. 8* *Paris*, 1842
—— Rapport fait à la Société d'Encouragement pour l'Industrie Nationale sur les Cartes en Relief de MM. Bauerkeller et Compagnie. 4* [*Paris*, 1842]
—— Notice Biographique de M. Venturé de Paradis. 8* *Paris*, 1844
—— Note sur les crues prématurées du Nil en 1843. 8* [*Paris*, 1844]
—— Lettre à M. Ph. Fr. de Siebold, sur les Collections Ethnographiques. 8*
Paris, 1845
—— Cartes en Relief. Rapport fait à la Société de Géographie sur le Relief du Mont-Blanc, par M. Séné. 8* *Paris*, 1845
—— Observations sur le Voyage au Darfour, suivies d'un Vocabulaire de la Langue des Habitants, et de Remarques sur le Nil-Blanc Supérieur. *Map.* Royal 8* *Paris*, 1845
—— Renseignements Géographiques sur une partie de l'Afrique Centrale, en Réponse à la Demande d'Instructions pour e Projèt de Voyage de M. Raffenel, faite à la Société de Géographie par S. E. le Ministre de la Marine et des Colonies. 8* *Paris*, 1846
—— Note sur les Botécudos, accompagnée d'un Vocabulaire de leur Langue et de quelques Remarques. 8* *Paris*, 1846
—— Note sur la Carte d'Arabie publiée en 1847. 8* *Paris*, 1847
—— Les Antiquités Américaines au point de vue des Progrès de la Géographie. 8* *Paris*, 1847
—— Fragments sur l'Uniformité à Introduire dans les Notations Géographiques, sur les Antiquités Américaines, et sur divers points de Géographie. 8* *Paris*, 1847
—— Extrait d'un Mémoire sur l'Uniformité à Introduire dans les Notations Géographiques. 8* *Paris*, 1847
—— Sur la Publication des Monuments de la Géographie. 8* *Paris*, 1847
—— Rapport sur la Carte de la Nouvelle-Grenade de M. Acosta. 8* *Paris*, 1848
—— Rapport sur le Concours pour le Prix Annuel (Voyages de 1849). Lettre sur le Haut Fleuve Blanc, communiquée par M. d'Arnaud. 8* *Paris*, 1852
—— Coup-d'œil sur l'île Formose. *Map.* 8* *Paris*, 1859
—— Classification Méthodique des Produits de l'Industrie extra-Européenne ; . . . suivie du Plan de la Classification d'une Collection Ethnographique Complète. 8* *Paris*, 1862
—— Catalogue des Objèts d'Antiquité, et de la Collection Ethnographique. 8* *Paris*, 1863
—— Notice sur la Vie et les Travaux de. Par M. de la Roquette. *Portrait.* 4* *Paris*, 1863

Jomard, E. François. Introduction à l'Atlas des Monuments de la Géographie. 8* *Paris*, 1879
—— Fragment sur les Cartes Géographiques. Royal 8* *Paris*, N.D.
—— Notices sur la Pente du Nil Supérieur et sur divers sujets de Géographie et d'Ethnographie ; précédées d'une Lettre de Carl Ritter sur le Plan de sa Géographie Comparative. 8* *Paris*, N.D.
—— Des Cartes en Relief. 8* *Paris*, N.D.
—— Le Régiment des Dromadaires à l'Armée d'Orient (1798-1801). Emploi du Chameau à la Guerre chez les Anciens. 8* *Paris*, N.D.
—— Remarques au sujet de la Notice de M. Fresnel sur les Sources du Nil. 8* *Paris*, N.D.
—— Remarques au sujet du Voyage du Docteur Barth dans l'Adamawa. 8* *Paris*, N.D.
—— Cartes Géographiques et Géographie. Extrait de l'Encyclopédie du dix-neuvième siècle. Royal 8* *Paris*, N.D.
—— Note sur le Meat-Biscuit. 8* *Paris*, N.D.
—— *See* Avezac ; Drovetti ; Mengin ; Walckenaer ; *also* Recueil de Voyages, Vol. 4, p. 611 : Appendix 1.

Jonas, A. *See* Purchas, Vol. 3, Book 3 : Appendix 1.

Jonas of Tudela. *See* Benjamin.

Jones, F. *See* Kerr, Vol. 8 : Appendix 1.

Jones, Comm. James Felix. Narrative of a Journey through parts of Persia and Kurdistan in company with Major Rawlinson. 8* *Bombay*, 1849
—— Report on the Harbour of Grange (or Koweit) and the Island of Pheleechi, in the Persian Gulf, prepared in 1830 ; with a trigonometrical Plan by Lieuts. Guy and Brucks. [From the India Records, No. 24.] Royal 8° *Bombay*, 1856
—— Memoirs by. [Bombay Records, No. 43, N.S.] Large 8° *Bombay*, 1857
1. Journal of a Steam-Trip to the North of Baghdad, in 1846 ; with Notes on the various Objects of Interest met with en route. *Plates.*
2. Narrative of a Journey, in 1848, for the Purpose of Determining the Tract of the Ancient Nahrwan Canal ; with Preliminary Remarks on the Canal, and a Glance at the Past History of the Territory of the Nahrwan. *Plans.*
3. Narrative of a Journey to the Frontier of Turkey and Persia, through part of Kurdistan, in company with Lieut.-Colonel Sir Henry C. Rawlinson. *Maps.*
4. Researches in the Vicinity of the Median Wall of Xenophon and along the Old Course of the River Tigris, and Discovery of the Site of the Ancient Opis. *Plates.*

Jones, Comm. James Felix—*continued.*
5. Memoir of the Province of Baghdad ; with a *ground-plan of the Enceinte and plates.*

—— Notes on the Topography of Nineveh and the other Cities of Assyria, and on the General Geography of the Country between the Tigris and the Upper Zab, founded upon a Trigonometrical Survey made in 1852. Edited by R. H. Thomas. [From the India Records, No. 43.] *Maps.* Royal 8°   *Bombay*, 1857
—— The Direct Highway to the East. 8*
                                    Norwood, 1872

Jones, Rev. George. *See* Perry, M. C.

Jones, Major Helsham, and Major Sanford. Routes in Egypt, Abyssinia, and adjacent Countries. Part 1.—Egypt. *Maps.* Large 8°   *Calcutta*, 1878

Jones, John. The Gospel according to St John, translated into the Chippeway Tongue. 12°   1831

Jones, Thomas. Companion to the Mountain Barometer. 8*   1842

Jones, Thomas. *See* Astley, Vol. 1 ; Allgemeine Historie, Vol. 1 : Appendix 1.

Jones, Prof. T. Rupert. On the Practical Advantages of Geological Knowledge. Small 8*   1880
—— Obituary Notice of the late Mr G. W. Stow, Geological Surveyor of Griqualand-West and the Orange Free State, &c. &c. 8*   [1883]
—— The Mineral Wealth of South Africa. 8*   [1887]
—— *See* Lartet.

Jones, Capt. W. Report on his First Operations for Improving Irrigation within the Turrai lands of Zillah Bareilly, 1847. [From the India Records, N.W. Provinces, Vol. 2.] *Map and plates*
                                    Agra, 1856

Jones, Rear-Admiral W. Gore. Extracts from his Report of Visit to the Queen of Madagascar at Antananarivo, July 1881. Folio*   1883

Jones, W. P. *See* Porter, R. P.

Jonge, J. K. J. de. Nova Zembla. Verslag over de Voorwerpen door de Nederlandsche Zeevaarders na hunne Overwintering, op Nowaja-Semlja bij hun Vertreek in 1597 achtergelaten en 1876 door Chs. Gardiner, Esq., aldaar teruggevonden. *Photograph.* 8*
                                    The Hague, 1877
—— The Barents Relics, recovered in the Summer of 1876 by Charles L. W. Gardiner, Esq., and presented to the Dutch Government. Translated, with a Preface, by Samuel Richard Van Campen. *Map and plates.* 8°   1877
—— *See* Veth.

Jonnès, A. M. Statistique de la Grande Bretagne et de l'Irlande. 2 vols. *Map.* 8°   *Paris*, 1837

Jönsson, J. *See* Sweden, A (Geologiska Undersökning, A, *C*, No. 102; *B, b*, No. 5, &c.) : Appendix 2.

Jonveaux, É. Les Russes dans l'Asie Centrale, leurs conquêtes sur les rives du Syr et de l'Amou-Daria. 8° [*Paris*, 1866]

Jordan, R. C. R. *See* Willson, T. B.

Jordan, W. Geographische Aufnahmen in der Libyschen Wüste auf der Rohlfs'-schen Expedition im Winter 1873-74. *Map.* 8°   *Carlsruhe*, 1874
—— *See* Rohlfs.

Jordan, W. L. The Elements : an Investigation of the Forces which Determine the Position and Movements of the Ocean and Atmosphere. 2 vols. *Maps, charts, and plates.* 8°   1866-77
—— A Treatise on the Action of Vis Inertiæ in the Ocean ; with Remarks on the Abstract Nature of the Forces of Vis Inertiæ and Gravitation, and a new Theory of the Tides. *Maps and charts.* 8°   1868
—— Remarks on Recent Oceanic Explorations by the British Government, and the Supposed Discovery of the Law of Oceanic Circulation by Dr W. B. Carpenter. 8*   *Buenos Ayres*, 1871
—— The Ocean, its Tides and Currents and their Causes. *Plates.* 8°   1873
—— The same. 2nd edition. *Plates.* 8°   1885
—— A Lecture on the Winds, Ocean Currents, and Tides, and what they tell of the System of the World. *Map.* 8*
                                    1877
—— The Winds, and their Story of the World. *Plate.* 8°   1877
—— The same. 3rd edition. *Plate.* Crown 8°   1885
—— Remarks on the Recent Ocean Explorations and the Current - creating Action of Vis Inertiæ in the Ocean. *Map and plates.* 8°   1877
—— Skirmishes in the Vanguard of Science, August 1880 to February 1881. 8°   *Buenos Ayres*, 1881
—— The New Principles of Natural Philosophy. *Plates.* 8°   1883
—— The "Challenger" Explorations. 8*
                                    1888
—— The Standard of Value. 5th edition. 8°   1888

Jordanus, Friar. *See* Hakluyt Soc. Publ., Vol. 31 ; Recueil de Voyages, Vol. 4, p. 611 : Appendix 1.

Jordell, D. Catalogue Général de la Librairie Française, continuation de l'ouvrage d'Otto Lorenz (Période de 1840 à 1885) ; Tome Douzième (Période de 1886 à 1890). Quatrième fasc. Mcynard-Zuine. Large 8°   *Paris*, 1892

Jordão, L. M. *See* Da Cunha, L. M.

Jorio, Andrea de. Plan de la Ville de Naples. *Map.* 8*   1826
—— Napoli e Contorni. 8° *Naples,* 1835

Joseph, Hon. S. A. Commercial Education : a Paper read before the Congress of the Australian Chambers of Commerce, November 1888. 8*   *Melbourne,* 1889

Jouan, M. Note sur les Iles Loyalty. *See* Chambeyron et Banaré. Instructions Nautiques sur la Nouvelle Calédonie, &c.

Jouët, Victor. La Société des Missionaires du Sacré-Coeur dans les Vicariats Apostoliques de la Mélanésie et de la Micronésie. *Maps and illustrations.* 8°
                Issoudun, Indre, 1887

Joukovsky, J. Review of Remarkable Events in the Province of Orenburg, chronologically arranged, 1246-1832. [In Russian.] 8°   *St Petersburg,* 1832

Jourdan, A. J. L. Dictionnaire Raisonné, Etymologique, Synonymique, et Polyglotte, des Termes usités dans les Sciences Naturelles. 2 vols. 8°
                Paris, 1834

Journet, F. L'Australie, Description du Pays, Colons et Natifs, Gouvernement, Institutions, Productions, Travaux Publiés, Mines. *Map.* 8° *Paris,* 1885 [1884]

Joutel, —. Journal Historique du dernier Voyage que feu M. de la Sale fit dans le Golfe de Mexique, pour trouver l'embouchure et le cours de la Riviere de Missicipi, nommée à present la Rivière de Saint Louis . ; où l'on voit l'histoire tragique de sa mort, et plusieurs choses curieuses du Nouveau Monde. Redigé et mis en ordre par Monsieur le Michel. 12°   *Paris,* 1713

Jovius, P. *See* Giovio; *also* Ramusio, Vol. 2 : Appendix 1.

Joyce, T. Heath. Norway Illustrated. In two parts. (From the *Graphic,* 12th and 26th June 1886.) Folio*   1886

Joyner, H. B. The Progress and Ultimate Results of Meteorology, especially considered in reference to Japan. 8*
                Yokohama, N.D.

Joyner, Mrs A. B. *See* Löher.

Juan, Jorge, and Antonio de Ulloa. Relacion Historica del Viage a la America Meridional hecho de orden de S. Mag. para medir algunos grados de Meridiano terrestre, y venir por ellos en conocimiento de la verdadera Figura y Magnitud de la Tierra, con otras varias Observaciones Astronomicas y Physicas. 5 vols. *Maps and plates.* 4°   *Madrid,* 1748
—— Voyage Historique de l'Amérique Méridionale, et qui contient une Histoire des Yncas du Perou, et les Observations Astronomiques et Physiques faites pour déterminer la Figure et la Grandeur de la Terre. 2 vols. *Maps and plates.* 4°
                Paris, 1752

Juan, Jorge, and Antonio de Ulloa. Observaciones Astronomicas y Phisicas, hechas de Orden de S. M. en los Reynos del Peru . . de las quales se deduce la Figura y Magnitud de la Tierra, y se aplica á la Navegacion. *Maps and plates.* Small folio   *Madrid,* 1773
—— Voyage to South America, describing at large the Spanish Cities, Towns, Provinces, &c., on that Extensive Continent, undertaken, by command of the King of Spain, by Don George Juan and Don Antonio de Ulloa. Translated from the original Spanish, with Notes and Observations, and an Account of the Brazils, by John Adams. *Maps and plates.* 2 vols. 8°   1806
—— Noticias Secretas de América, sobre el Estado Naval, Militar y Politico de los Reynos del Péru y Provincias de Quito, Costas de Nueva Granada y Chile, Gobierno y Régimen particular de los Pueblos de Indios, &c., por Don Jorge Juan y Don A. de Ulloa. Sacadas a Luz Para el Verdadero conocimiento del Gobierno de los Españoles en la América Meridional, por Don David Barry. *Portrait.* Folio   1826
—— *See* Knox's New Collection, Vol. 1, p. 607 : Appendix 1.

Juggarow, G. V. *See* Nursingrow.

Juarros, Domingo. A Statistical and Commercial History of the Kingdom of Guatemala, in Spanish America ; with an Account of its Conquest by the Spaniards, and of the Principal Events to the Present Time. Translated by Lieut. J. Baily. *Maps.* 8°   1823

Judd, Prof. John W. Volcanoes : What they are, and what they teach. 4th edition. *Illustrations.* 8°   1888
—— *See* Darwin ; Symons.

Juet, R. *See* Purchas, Vol. 3 : Appendix 1.

Jühlke, Karl. Die Erwerbung des Kilima-Ndscharo-Gebiets. 8*   *Cologne,* 1886

Jukes, J. Beete. Excursions in and about Newfoundland during 1839-40. 2 vols. *Map.* 8°   1842
—— Narrative of the Surveying Voyage of H.M.S. "Fly," in Torres Strait, New Guinea, and other Islands of the Eastern Archipelago, 1842-46 ; together with an Excursion into the Interior of the Eastern part of Java. 2 vols. *Maps and plates.* 8°   1847
—— A Sketch of the Physical Structure of Australia, so far as it is at present known. *Maps.* 8°   1850

Jukes-Browne, A. J. The Building of the British Isles, a Study in Geographical Evolution. *Maps and woodcuts.* 12°
                1888
—— The Geographical Evolution of the North Sea. (From the *Contemporary Review.*) *Maps.* 8*   1893

Julian, Antonio. La Perla de la America, Provincia de Santa Marta, reconocida, observada, y expuesta en discursos historicos. Small 4°   *Madrid*, 1787

Julien, Stanislas. Exercices Pratiques d'Analyse, de Syntaxe, et de Lexigraphie Chinoise. *Facsimile.* 8°   *Paris*, 1842

—— Simple Exposé d'un fait Honorable, Odieusement dénaturé dans un Libelle récent de M. Pauthier, &c.   8°
                                   Paris, 1842

—— Mémoires sur les contrées Occidentales, traduits du Sanscrit en Chinois, en l'an 648 par Hiouen-Thsang, et du Chinois en Français par M. S. J.   2 vols. *Map.*
8°   *Paris*, 1857-58

—— *See* Champion ; Hiouen - Thsang ; Pauthier.

Julius, W. A. Semmering und Reichenau. Führer für 1 oder 2 Tage. Mit einem Panorama, &c.   16°   *Vienna*, 1858

Jung, Karl Emil. Deutsche Kolonien mit besonderer Berücksichtigung der neuesten Deutschen Erwerbungen in West Afrika und Australien. Zweite vermehrte Ausgabe. 12° *Leipzig*, 1885

Junghuhn, F. Die Battaländer auf Sumatra. 2 vols. *Maps and plates.* 8°
                                   Berlin, 1847

—— Rückreise von Java nach Europa mit der sogenannten englischen Ueberlandpost im September und October 1848. . . . Aus dem Holländischen übertragen von J. K. Hasskarl. *Maps and plates.* 8°
                                  Leipzig, 1852

—— Java : seine Gestalt, Pflanzendecke, und innere Bauart (in's Deutsche übertragen von J. K. Hasskarl). 3 vols. *Maps and plates.* 8° *Leipzig*, 1854-57

—— Staat, aantoonende de Vermeerdering der Kinaplanten op Java en de onkosten daardoor veroorzaakt sedert Julij 1856 tot December 1862. 8*   1863

Junker, Dr W. Wissenschaftliche Ergebnisse von Dr. W. Junker's Reisen in Zentral Afrika, 1880-85. (Ergänzungshefte, 92 and 93—Petermann's Mittheilungen.) *Maps.* 4°   *Gotha*, 1889

—— Dr Wilhelm Junker's Reisen in Afrika, 1875-86. Erster Band (1875-78). Nach seinen Tagebüchern unter der Mitwirkung von Richard Buchta herausgegeben von dem Reisenden. *Portrait, maps, and illustrations.* 8°   *Vienna*, 1889

—— The same. Zweiter Band (1879-82). Nach seinen Tagebüchern bearbeitet und herausgegeben von dem Reisenden. *Maps and illustrations.* 8°
                                   Vienna, 1890

—— Travels in Africa, during the years 1875-78. Translated from the German by A. H. Keane. Vol. 1. *Map and illustrations.* 8°   1890

—— The same, during the years 1879-83. Vol. 2. *Map and illustrations.* 8° 1891

Junker, Dr W. The same, during the years 1882-86. Vol. 3. *Map and illustrations.* 8°   1892

—— Dr Wilh. Junker's Reisen in Afrika, 1875-86. Dritter Band (1882-86). *Maps and illustrations.* 8° *Vienna, &c.,* 1891

—— and Dr Emin Pasha. Resultate der Meteorologischen Beobachtungen, von Dr Junker und Dr Emin-Pascha im Innern des aequatorialen Ost-Afrika. Large 8*
                                   Vienna, 1890

—— *See* Buchta.

Junker von Langegg, F. A. El Dorado. Geschichte der Entdeckungsreisen nach dem Goldlande El Dorado im 16 und 17 Jahrhundert. 8°   *Leipzig*, 1888

Jurin, Dr. *See* Varenius.

Justamond, J. O. *See* Raynal, G. T.

K.

K—— P. *See* India, F, *c* : Appendix 2.

K——, R. v. Beschrijvinge van det Archipel [Greek Islands]. 8°
                               Amsterdam, 1792

Kaempfer, Engelbert. Amœnitatum Exoticarum Politico-Physico-medicarum Fasciculi v, quibus continentur variæ Relationes, Observationes, et Descriptiones rerum Persicarum et ulterioris Asiæ, multâ attentione, in peregrinationibus per universum Orientem. *Plates.*
4°   *Lemgow*, 1712

—— Histoire Naturelle, Civile, et Ecclésiastique de l'Empire du Japon. Traduit en Français sur la version angloise de J. G. Scheuchzer. 2 vols. *Maps and plates.* Folio   *The Hague*, 1729

—— An Account of Japan. Abridged and arranged from the translation of J. G. Scheuchzer. 8°   1853

—— *See* Brun ; *also* Laharpe, Vol. 8 ; Pinkerton, Vol. 7 ; Allgemeine Historie, Vol. 11 : Appendix 1.

Kahl, A. Reisen durch Chile und die westlichen Provinzen Argentiniens. Natur- und Sittenschilderungen, mit besonderer Bezugnahme auf das volkswirthschaftliche Leben jener Nationen. 8°   *Berlin*, 1866

Kalm, Peter. Travels into North America, containing its Natural History, and a Circumstantial Account of its Plantations and Agriculture in general. . . . Translated into English by J. R. Forster. 2nd edition. 2 vols. *Map and plates.* 8°
                                        1772

—— *See* Bartram, John ; *also* Pinkerton, Vol. 13 : Appendix 1.

Kaltbrunner, D. Manuel du Voyageur. *Plates.* 8°   *Zurich*, 1879 [1878]

Kaltbrunner, D. Recherches sur l'origine des Kabyles. 8* *Geneva*, 1871
—— Aide-Mémoire du Voyageur. Notions générales de Géographie Mathématique, de Géographie Physique, de Géographie Politique, de Géologie, de Biologie, et d'Anthropologie à l'usage des Voyageurs, des Étudiants et des Gens du Monde. *Maps.* 8° *Zurich*, 1881 [1880]

Kampen, N. G. van. Staat- en Aardrijkskundige Beschrijving van het Koningrijk der Nederlanden, of der XVII. Nederlandsche Provincien, benevens het Groot - Hertogdom Luxemburg. *Map.* 8° *Haarlem*, 1827

Kan, Dr C. M. Proeve eener Geographische Bibliographie van Nederlandsch Oost-Indië voor de Jaren 1865-1880. 8° *Utrecht*, 1881
—— Chronique Bibliographique Trimestrielle. Section de Géographie et d'Ethnographie. 1. Les Colonies Néerlandaises depuis 1883 ; 2. Les îsles prises séparément et les groupes d'îsles ; 3. Ile de Borneo ; 4. L'Archipel Oriental (Célèbes les Moluques, la Nouvelle Guinée, &c.). 5. Les Indes Néerlandaises Occidentales. 8° N.P., N.D.
—— Het Hooger Onderwijs in Aardrijkskunde hier te Lande. 8* *Leyden*, 1889
—— De Periplous van Hanno. *Map.* 8* *Leyden*, 1891
—— De Aardrijkskunde en de Praktijk, Rede op der Verjaardag den Universiteit van Amsterdam. 8* *Amsterdam*, 1893
—— Les Journées du 12 au 25 Septembre 1886 à Berlin, et leur intérêt pour la Science Coloniale. 8* N.P., N.D.
—— *See* Veth.

Kandelhardt, H. C. *See* Nelkenbrecher.

Kane, Elisha Kent. Access to an Open Polar Sea, in connexion with the Search after Sir John Franklin and his Companions. *Map.* 8* *New York*, 1853
—— The U.S. Grinnell Expedition in Search of Sir John Franklin : a Personal Narrative. *Map and plates.* 8° *New York*, 1853
—— Arctic Explorations. The Second Grinnell Expedition in Search of Sir John Franklin, 1853-55. 2 vols. *Maps and plates.* 8° *Philadelphia*, 1856
—— Biographical. Elisha Kent Kane. [An extract.] 8* 1858
—— Astronomical Observations in the Arctic Seas, made in 1853-55, on the North-West Coast of Greenland. Reduced and discussed by C. A. Schott. *Map.* 4* *Washington*, 1860
—— Tidal Observations in the Arctic Seas, made during the Second Grinnell Expedition in Search of Sir John Franklin, in 1853-55, at Van Rensselaer Harbour. Reduced and discussed by Charles A. Schott. *Plates.* 8* *Washington*, 1860

Kanitz, F. Donau-Bulgarien und der Balkan. Historisch-geographisch-ethnographische Reisestudien aus den Jahren 1860-78. 3 vols. *Map and plates.* 8° *Leipzig*, 1875-79

Kankrin, Count G. *See* Keyserling.

Kant, I. Immanuel Kant's Schriften zur Physischen Geographie. Herausgegeben von Friedr. Wilh. Schubert. 8° *Leipzig*, 1839

Kao, Dionysius. *See* Harris, Vol. 2 : Appendix 1.

Kappler, August. Surinam, sein Land, seine Natur, Bevölkerung und seine Kultur- Verhältnisse mit Bezug auf Kolonisation. *Map and illustrations.* 8° *Stuttgart*, 1887

Karadschitch, V. S. Les Serbes et les Croates. 8* *Belgrade*, 1861

Karaka, Dosabhai Framji. History of the Parsis, including their Manners, Customs, Religion, and present position. 2 vols. *Plates.* 8° 1884

Karlsson, V. *See* Sweden, C (Geologiska Undersökning) : Appendix 2.

Karpinski, A. *See* Schrenck and Maximowicz, Vol. 4.

Karr, G. G. Seton, and R. H. Showell. Rough Notes connected with the Petty Principality of Junieera. [From the India Records, No. 26.] *Map.* 8° *Bombay*, 1856

Karr, H. W. Seton. *See* Seton-Karr.

Karrer, F. *See* " Novara."

Karsch, F. *See* Rohlfs.

Kaswini. *See* Cazwini.

Kater, Capt. Henry. Account of Trigonometrical operations for determining the difference of Longitude between Paris and Greenwich. 4° 1828

Katibi Roumi. *See* Sidi Ali.

Katte, A. von. Reise in Abyssinien im Jahre 1836. *Map.* 8° *Stuttgart*, 1883

Kaulbars, Baron A. Soundings taken in 1873 in the lower Amu Daria. [In Russian.] 8*, and Atlas folio, *St Petersburg*, 1888

Kaulbars, Nicolas. Aperçu des Travaux Géographiques en Russie. 8° *St Petersburg*, 1889

Kaufmann, Dr W. The Egyptian State Debt and its relation to International Law. From the German of Dr Wilhelm Kaufmann, with a Synopsis, &c. &c., by Henry Wallach. 8° 1892

Kay, Henry Cassels. *See* Omārah-al-Hakami.

Kay, Stephen. Travels and Researches in Caffraria, describing the Character, Customs, and Moral Condition of the Tribes inhabiting that portion of Southern Africa ; with Historical and Topographical Remarks illustrative of the State and Prospects of the British Settlement in its Borders, the Introduction of Christianity, and the Progress of Civilisation. *Map and plates.* 12° 1883

Kaye, Lieut.-General. Proposed Line of Railway to the River Helmund. 8* N.D.

Kayser, Dr Emanuel. *See* Richthofen.

Kayser, Gabriel. Bibliographie d'ouvrages ayant trait à l'Afrique en général dans ses Rapports, avec l'Exploration et la Civilisation de ces Contrées depuis le commencement de l'Imprimerie jusqu'à nos jours, précédé d'un Indicateur. 8° *Brussels*, 1887

Kayser, Dr Paul. *See* Schück, R.

Keane, A. H. On the Relations of the Indo-Chinese and Inter-Oceanic Races and Languages. 8* 1880

—— The Lapps, their Origin, Affinities, Habits, and Customs. 8* 1885

—— Progress of Recent Geographical Exploration. Large 8* N.D.

—— Eastern Geography : a Geography of the Malay Peninsula, Indo-China, the Eastern Archipelago, the Philippines, and New Guinea. *Map.* 12° 1887

—— Eastern Geography. 2nd edition. *Map.* 12° 1892

—— *See* Junker ; Reclus ; Riebeck ; Stanford ; Streeter.

Keary, C. F. Norway and the Norwegians. *Illustrations.* 12° 1892

Keate, George. Account of the Pelew Islands, situated in the Western Part of the Pacific Ocean, composed from the Journals and Communications from Capt. Henry Wilson and some of his Officers in 1783 ; with a Supplement, compiled from the Journals of the "Panther" and "Endeavour," sent to those Islands in 1790, by J. P. Hockin. *Map and plates.* 4° 1803

Keating, W. H. Narrative of an Expedition to the Source of St Peter's River, Lake Winnepeek, Lake of the Woods, &c., in 1823. Compiled from the Notes of Major Long, Messrs Say, Keating, and Colhoun. 2 vols. *Map and plates.* 8° 1825

Keatinge, Col. Travels in Europe and Africa. *Plates.* 4° 1816

Keatinge, Lieut. R. H. Extract from Report by, 1848, regarding certain Works constructed for purposes of Irrigation in the vicinity of Mundlaisur. [From the India Records, N.W. Provinces, Vol. 2.] *Map and plate.* Large 8° *Agra*, 1855

—— Reports on the Burwai Suspension Bridge. [From the India Records, N.W. Provinces, No. 25.] *Plates.* Large 8° *Agra*, 1856

—— Report on the Nimar Roads, 1856. [From the India Records, N.W. Provinces, No. 27.] Large 8° *Agra*, 1856

Keele, Thomas William. The Alignment of the Nepean Tunnel, New South Wales. *Figures.* 8* 1888

Keeler, Charles A. Evolution of the Colors of North American Land Birds. (California Acad. Sci., Occ. Papers 3.) *Plates.* 8° *San Francisco*, 1893

Keeling, Capt. William. *See* Astley, Vol. 1 ; Gottfried ; Kerr, Vol. 8 ; Purchas, Vol. 1, Book, 3 ; Allgemeine Historie, Vol. 1 : Appendix 1.

Keely, Robert N., jun., and G. G. Davis. In Arctic Seas : the Voyage of the "Kite" with the Peary Expedition ; together with a transcript of the log of the "Kite." *Maps, portraits, and illustrations.* 8° 1893

Keerl, J. H. *See* Houel.

Keijzer, S. Kitab, Toehpah, Javaansch-Mohammedaansch Wetboek. 8° *The Hague*, 1853

Keilhau, Prof. *See* De la Roquette.

Keily, J. R. Memoir on the Mahee Kanta, prepared in 1845, with subsequent additions. [From the India Records, No. 12.] *Map. Bombay*, 1855

—— The Pahlunpur Districts. Compiled and edited by R. Hughes Thomas. [India Records, No. 25, New Series.] *Bombay*, 1856

Brief Notes relative to the several Native States comprised within the Political Superintendency of Pahlunpoor.

Lists of the Districts, Talookas, Purgunas, and Villages subject to the Jurisdiction of Pahlunpoor.

Historical Sketches of the Native States of Pahlunpoor, Radhunpoor, Warye, Terwara, Thurad and Morwara, Wao, Sooegaum, Deodur, Santulpoor and Charchut, Bhabhur and Kankruj, comprised within the charge of the Political Superintendent of Pahlunpoor ; with copies of the Engagements binding on those States. *Map.*

Keith, Sir G. M. *See* Phillips [1], Vol. 11 : Appendix 1.

Keller, Ferdinand. Die Keltischen Pfahlbauten in den Schweizerseen. *Plates.* 4° *Zurich*, 1854

—— Pfahlbauten. Zweiter und fünfter Berichte. *Plates.* 4° *Zurich*, 1858-63

—— Ditto. Siebenter Bericht *Zurich*, 1876

—— Beilage zur archæologischen Karte der Ost-Schweiz. 2nd edition. *Maps.* 8* *Zurich*, 1874

—— The Lake Dwellings of Switzerland and other parts of Europe. 2nd edition, greatly enlarged, translated and arranged by John Edward Lee. 2 vols. *Plates.* 8° 1878

Keller, F. A. E. Des Typhons de 1848, des Ouragans Obliques et des Coups de Vent fixe, &c. 8* *Paris*, 1849

Keller, F. A. E. Exposé du Régime des Courants observés depuis le XVIe siècle jusqu'à nos jours dans la Manche et la Mer d'Allemagne et de leur supputation dans la Navigation Générale à l'aide du Routier compteur. *Plate.* 8°
Paris, 1855
—— Notice sur la Carte des Environs de Cherbourg, donnant les Parcours des Courants de Flot et de Jusant et les Établissements de leurs Étales observés en Juillet, Août, et Septembre 1844. *Map.* 8° *Paris,* 1861
—— Des Ouragans, Tornados, et Tempêtes. 8° *Paris,* 1861

Keller, Heinrich, Landkarten- und Panorama-Zeichners, Das Leben des. *Portrait and coloured plate.* 4° *Zurich,* 1865

Keller, José and Francisco. Relatorio sobre a Exploração dos Valles do Parahyba e Pomba, emprehendida no intuito de abrir-se novas vias de communicação entre esses pontos e o littoral. *Maps.* 4* *Rio de Janeiro* [1864]
—— Relatorio da Exploraçao do Rio Madeira na parte comprehendida entre a cachoeira de Santo-Antonio e a barra do Mamoré. 4* *Rio de Janeiro,* 1869
—— Exploration of the River Madeira. Report made to the Imperial Government of Brazil, and published in the Government *Relatoria* of 1870. Translated from the Portuguese by George Earl Church. 8° 1873

Keller-Leuzinger, F. Vom Amazonas und Madeira. *Map and plates.* 4° *Stuttgart,* 1874

Kellett, Capt. H., Comm. T. E. L. Thomas, and Lieut. W. J. L. Pullan. The Arctic Expedition of 1849. Reprinted from *The Times* of Jan. 24th and 25th 1850. 4* 1850
—— *See* Seemann.

Kelley, Fred. M. On the Junction of the Atlantic and Pacific Oceans, and the Practicability of a Ship-Canal, without Locks, by the Valley of the Atrato. Edited by C. Manby. *Map.* 8* 1856
—— Projêt d'un Canal Maritime sans écluses entre l'Océan Atlantique et l'Océan Pacifique à l'aide des Rivières Atrato et Truando ; précédé d'une Introduction, &c., par Malte-Brun, et suivi d'une Lettre de M. le Baron Humboldt. *Map.* 8* *Paris,* 1857
—— The Union of the Oceans by Ship-Canal without Locks, viâ the Atrato Valley. *Map.* 8° *New York,* 1859

Kelley, P. A Practical Introduction to Spherics and Nautical Astronomy, comprising new Projections and Calculations for finding the Latitude and Longitude ; also an Appendix on Time, Timekeepers, and Transit Instruments. *Plates.* Royal 8° 1822

Kellgren, A. G. *See* Sweden, C, Geologiska Undersökning, 119 : Appendix 2.

Kellogg, Capt. S. C. *See* Sheridan.

Kellor, Dr Conrad. Reisebilder aus Ostafrika und Madagaskar. *Illustrations.* 8° *Leipzig,* 1887

Kelly, John W., and Roger Wells. English-Eskimo and Eskimo-English Vocabularies ; preceded by Ethnographical Memoranda concerning the Arctic Eskimos in Alaska and Siberia. By Roger Wells and John W. Kelly. (Bureau of Education Circular of Information, No. 2, 1890.) *Map.* 8* *Washington,* 1890

Kelly, W. Keating. Syria and the Holy Land, their Scenery and their People. *Illustrations.* 8° 1844

Kelsall, Charles. Classical Excursion from Rome to Arpino. *Plates.* 8° *Geneva,* 1820
—— *See* Phillips [3], Vol. 4 : Appendix 1.

Kelsall, J. Manual of the Bellary District. *Map in cover.* 8° *Madras,* 1872

Keltie, J. Scott. Geographical Education. Report to the Council of the Royal Geographical Society. Vol. 1. Roy. Geog. Suppl. Papers. 8° 1886
—— Applied Geography : a Preliminary Sketch. *Maps and diagrams.* 12° 1890
—— What Stanley has done for the Map of Africa. (From the *Contemporary Review.*) *Maps.* 8* 1890
—— The Partition of Africa. *Maps.* 8° 1893
—— The same. 2nd edition 1895
—— Statesman's Year-Book : Statistical and Historical Annual of the States of the World, for the years 1883 onward.
—— *See* Stanley.

Kelvin, Lord. *See* Thomson, Sir Wm.

Kemball, A. B. Observations on the past Policy of the British Government towards the Arab Tribes of the Persian Gulf ; with copies of Treaties, &c., between February 1806 and May 4th 1853. Memoranda on the Resources, Localities, and Relations of the Tribes inhabiting the Arabian Shores of the Persian Gulf. Chronological Table of Events connected with the Government of Muskat, from 1730 to 1843 ; with the Joasmee Tribe of Arabs, from 1765 to 1843 ; with the Uttoobee Tribe (Bahrein), from 1716 to 1844 ; with the Wahabee Tribe, from 1795 to 1844 ; with the Beniyas Tribe, from 1793 to 1843 ; and the Debaye (Boo Felaso) Tribe, from 1834 to 1843. Statistical and Miscellaneous Information connected with the Possessions, Revenues, Families, &c., of the Imaum of Muskat, of the Ruler of Bahrein, and of the Chiefs of the Maritime Arab States in the Persian Gulf. Historical Sketch of the Boo Felasa Tribe of Arabs (Debaye), from 1834 to

Kemball, A. B.—*continued.*
1841; with continuation to 1853 by Lieut. Disbrowe. Historical Sketch of the Tribe of Ejman, from 1820 to 1841; with continuation to 1853 by Lieut. Disbrowe. Slave Trade : Paper relative to the Measures adopted by the British Government, between 1820 and 1844, for effecting the Suppression of the Slave Trade in the Persian Gulf; with copies of the Engagements entered into with the British Government, 1822-51, by the Imaun of Muskat, the Arab Chiefs, and the Government of Persia. Compiled and edited by R. Hughes Thomas. [India Records, No. 24.] *Bombay*, 1856

Kempfer. *See* Kaempfer.

Kempson, M. Memorandum on certain Works received from Persia. Memorandum on Two Scientific Treatises in Oordoo. Memorandum on Meritorious Books by Native Authors. [From the India Records, No. 2, 1872, N.W. Provinces.] *Allahabad*, 1872
—— Report on the Vernacular Newspapers and Periodicals published in the North-Western Provinces during 1872. [From the India Records, No. 4, 1873, N.W. Provinces.] *Allahabad*, 1873

Kendall, Hon. Amos. Morse's Patent. Full Exposure of Dr Charles T. Jackson's Pretensions to the Invention of the American Electro-Magnetic Telegraph. 8* *Washington*, 1852

Kendall, E. N. Reports on the State and Condition of the Province of New Brunswick, with some Observations on the Company's Tract. 8* 1835

Kendall, George W. Narrative of an Expedition across the Great South-Western Prairies, from Texas to Santa Fé, &c. 2 vols. *Map and plate.* 8° 1845

Kendall, Thomas. Grammar and Vocabulary of the Language of New Zealand. 12° 1820

Kennan, George. Tent Life in Siberia, and Adventures among the Koraks and other Tribes in Kamchatka and Northern Asia. *Map.* Small 8° *New York*, 1870
—— Siberia and the Exile System. 2 vols. *Illustrations.* Large 8° 1891

Kennedy, A. Brief Narrative of a Journey from New Zealand to England, *viâ* the Sandwich Islands, to San Francisco. . . . 8° 1871
—— New Zealand. *Map.* Small 8° 1873

Kennedy, A. J. La Plata, Brazil, and Paraguay, during the Present War. *Map.* Small 8° 1869

Kennedy, A. W. M. Clark. The Birds of Berkshire and Buckinghamshire. *Coloured plates.* Small 8° 1868

Kennedy, C. M. *See* Galton, F., Vacation Tourists; Kennedy, James.

Kennedy, E. B. Blacks and Bushrangers : Adventures in Queensland. *Illustrations.* 8° 1889
—— *See* Macgillivray, John.

Kennedy, James. Essays, Ethnological and Linguistic. Edited by C. M. Kennedy. 8° 1861
—— Life and Work in Benares and Kumaon, 1839-77. With an Introductory Note by Sir Wm. Muir. *Plates.* Crown 8° 1884

Kennedy, John. Idumæa, with a Survey of Arabia and the Arabians. *Map.* 18° 1851
—— The Jordan and the Dead Sea. 18° 1851
—— The Natural History of Man ; or, Popular Chapters on Ethnography. 2 vols. in 1. 12° 1851
—— Volcanoes, their History, Phenomena, and Causes. 18° 1852

Kennedy, Capt. J. Clark. Algeria and Tunis in 1845 : an Account of a Journey made through the two Regencies by Viscount Feilding and Capt. Kennedy. 2 vols. *Plates.* 8° 1846

Kennedy, Lieut-Col. J. P. On the Mineral Districts, &c., of the Nerbudda Valley, with accompanying Reports by Jacob and Green. Edited by R. H. Thomas. [From the India Records, No. 14.] *Bombay*, 1855

Kennedy, John S. *See* Columbus.

Kennedy, Joseph C. G. Statistical View of the Extent of American Railroads, as well those in course of construction as those completed and in operation. [1 *leaf.*] 4* 1852
—— *See* United States, A : Appendix 2.

Kennedy, William. Texas: the Rise, Progress, and Prospects of the Republic of Texas. 2 vols. *Maps.* 8° 1841
—— A Short Narrative of the Second Voyage of the " Prince Albert" in search of Sir John Franklin. *Map and plates.* 8° 1856

Kennedy, Capt. W. R. Sport, Travel, and Adventure in Newfoundland and the West Indies. *Map and illustrations.* 8° 1885

"Kensingtonian." Fragments of a Journal Saved from Shipwreck. By an Old Kensingtonian. *Plate.* 12° 1868

Keppell, Major the Hon. George. Personal Narrative of a Journey from India to England, by Bussorah, Bagdad, the Ruins of Babylon, Curdistan, the Court of Persia, the Western Shore of the Caspian Sea, Astrakan, Nishney Novogorod, Moscow, and St Petersburg, 1824. *Map and plates.* 4° 1827
—— Narrative of a Journey across the Balkan, by the two Passes of Selimno and Pravadi ; also of a Visit to Azani, and other newly-discovered Ruins in Asia Minor, in 1829-30. 2 vols. *Maps.* 8° 1831

Keppell, Major the Hon. George. Expedition to Borneo of H.M.S. "Dido" for the Suppression of Piracy; with Extracts from the Journal of James Brooke, of Sarāwak. 2 vols. *Maps and plates.* 8° 1846
—— Visit to the Indian Archipelago, in H.M.S. "Mæander"; with Portions of the Private Journal of Sir James Brooke. 2 vols. *Map and plates.* Royal 8° 1853

Ker, D. On the Road to Khiva. *Map and photographs.* 8° 1874

Kerguelen Trémarec, M. de. Relation d'une Voyage dans la Mer du Nord, aux Côtes d'Islande, du Groenland, de Ferro, de Schettland, des Orcades et de Norwége, 1767-68. *Maps and plates.* 4° *Paris,* 1771
—— *See* Pinkerton, Vol. 1; Allgemeine Historie, Vol. 21: Appendix 1.

Kerhallet, Capt. Charles Philippe de. Instruction pour remonter la Côte du Brésil, depuis San-Luiz de Marahão jusqu'au Para, pour descendre la Rivière de ce nom et pour en débouquer. *Plates.* 8° *Paris,* 1841
—— Description Nautique de la Côte Occidentale d'Afrique, depuis le Cap Roxo jusqu'aux îles de Los, comprenant l'Archipel des Bissagos. 8° *Paris,* 1849
—— Description de l'Archipel des Canaries, et de l'Archipel des îles du Cap Vert. 8° *Paris,* 1851
—— Considérations Générales sur l'Océan Indien, pour faire suite à celles sur l'Océan Atlantique. *Maps.* 8° *Paris,* 1851
—— Considérations Générales sur l'Océan Pacifique, pour faire suite à celles sur l'Océan Atlantique et sur l'Océan Indien. Revue par B. Darondeau. *Maps.* 8° *Paris,* 1851
—— Manuel de la Navigation à la Côte Occidentale d'Afrique. 3 vols. *Maps.* 8° *Paris,* 1851-52
—— Considérations Générales sur l'Océan Atlantique, suivies des Prescriptions Nautiques pour échapper aux Ouragans et d'un Mémoire sur les Courants de l'Océan Atlantique. *Maps.* 8° *Paris,* 1854
—— The Atlantic Ocean (North and South) considered with reference to the Wants of Seamen : being a General View of the Winds and Weather throughout the Year on the Shores of that Sea, with Remarks by the Translator. *Charts.* 8° 1856
—— Considérations Générales sur l'Océan Pacifique, suivies des Prescriptions Nautiques pour échapper aux Ouragans. *Maps and plates.* 8° *Paris,* 1856
—— Description de l'Archipel des Azores. 8° *Paris,* 1858

Kerhallet, Capt. Charles Philippe de. Description Nautique de Madère et des Canaries. 8° *Paris,* 1858
—— Description Nautique des îles du Cap Vert. 8° *Paris,* 1858
—— Manuel de la Navigation dans la Mer des Antilles et dans le Golfe du Mexique. 2 vols. *Maps.* 8° *Paris,* 1853, 1862-63
—— *See* Vincendon - Dumoulin, C. A ; *also* France, B, *b* : Appendix 2.

Kerigan, Thomas. Complete Mathematical and General Navigation Tables, including every Table necessary to be used with the Nautical Almanack in finding the Latitude and Longitude, . . . and their direct application to Plane and Spherical Trigonometry, Navigation, Nautical Astronomy, Dialling, Practical Gunnery, Mensuration, Gauging, &c., &c. 2 vols. *Plates.* 8° 1828
—— A Practical Treatise on the Eclipses of the Sun and Moon, and the Deflection of the Moon and Planets, explaining their calculation by simple and direct methods; with Remarks on the Anomalies of the Present Theory of the Tides, the superior Attraction of the Sun over that of the Moon at the surface of the Earth. 8° 1844
—— The Anomalies of the Present Theory of the Tides, elucidated by additional facts and arguments; with Remarks on the newly-discovered Planet. 8° 1847

Kern, Prof. H. *See* Holland : Appendix 2.

Kerpely, Antal. Magyarország Vaskövei és Vasterményei. *Diagrams.* 4° *Budapest,* 1877

Kerr, J. G. The Canton Directory. *Map and plans.* 12* *Canton,* 1873

Kerr, Mrs A. *See* Ranke.

Kerr, Robert. A General History and Collection of Voyages and Travels, arranged in systematic order. . . . 18 vols. *Maps and charts.* 8° *Edinburgh,* 1811-24 [For full Title and Contents of volumes, *see* Appendix 1.]

Kerr, Walter Montagu. The Far Interior : a Narrative of Travel and Adventure from the Cape of Good Hope across the Zambesi to the Lake Regions of Central Africa. 2 vols. *Map, portrait, and illustrations.* 8° 1886

Kerrich, Thomas. Catalogue of Roman Coins collected by Thomas Kerrich, and presented by the Rev. R. E. Kerrich to the Society of Antiquaries of London. 8* 1852

Kerry-Nicholls, J. H. The King Country, or Explorations in New Zealand : a Narrative of 600 Miles of Travel through Maoriland. *Map and illustrations.* 8° 1884

Kerst, S. Gottfried. Die Plata-Staaten und die Wichtigkeit der Provinz Otuquis und des Rio Bermejo, seit der Annahme des Princips der freien Schiff-fahrt auf den Zuflüssen des Rio de la Plata. *Map.* 8* *Berlin*, 1854

Kersten, O. Ueber Colonisation in Ost-Afrika ; mit Hervorhebung ihrer Wichtigkeit für Deutschland und besonders für Oesterreich. 8* *Vienna*, 1867

Kesselmeyer, C. A. Stellbarer Universal-Kalender der Christlichen Zeitrechnung. Folio* *Dresden*, N.D.

Kessler, J. An Introduction to the Language and Literature of Madagascar ; with Hints to Travellers, and a new Map. Small 8° 1870

Kestell-Cornish, Bishop. Journal of a Tour of Exploration in the North of Madagascar, 15th June to 22nd October 1876. *Map.* Small 8* 1877

Ketenensis, Robert. *See* Hakluyt, Vol. 2 : Appendix 1.

Kettle, W. R. A Few Notes on the Island of St Michael, Azores. *Map.* 12* [1887]

—— A Report on the Artificial Harbour of Ponta Delgada, St Michael's, Azores Islands, from Observations made during a Visit to the same, November and December 1886. *Maps and plan.* 8* 1887

Key, T. Hewitt, and J. W. Donaldson. Controversy about the "Varronianus." 12° [*Privately printed*] 1845

Keymis, L. *See* Allgemeine Historie, Vol. 16 : Appendix 1.

Keyser, Jacob de. *See* Nieuhoff ; *also* Allgemeine Historie, Vol. 5 : Appendix 1.

Keyserling, A. Aus den Reisetagebüchern des Grafen Georg Kankrin, ehemaligen kaiserlich Russischen Finanzministers, aus den Jahren 1840-45. Mit einer Lebensskizze Kankrin's, nebst zwei Beilagen. (3 parts in 1.) 8° *Brunswick*, 1865

Keyserling, Count Alex. von. *See* Murchison.

Keysler, John George. *See* New Collection of Voyages, Vols. 4, 5, p. 608 ; "The World Displayed," Vol. 19, p. 609 : Appendix 1.

Keyts, J. *See* Callander, Vol. 2 : Allgemeine Historie, Vol. 18 : Appendix 1.

Khanikoff, Jaboc, and Peter Tolstoi. List of Positions in the South-Western Parts of Central Asia determined Astronomically. [In Russian.] *Tables.* 4° *St Petersburg*, 1850

Khanikoff, Nicholas de. Description of the Khanate of Bokhara. [In Russian.] *Maps and portrait.* 8° *St Petersburg*, 1843

Khanikoff, Nicholas de. Bokhara, its Amir and its People. Translated from the Russian by the Baron C. A. de Bode. *Map and portrait.* 8° 1845

—— Mémoire sur la Partie Méridionale de l'Asie Centrale. *Maps.* 4° *Paris*, 1861

—— Mémoire sur l'Éthnographie de la Perse. *Plates.* 4° *Paris*, 1866

—— Notice sur le Livre de Marco Polo. Édité et commenté par M. G. Pauthier. 8* *Paris*, 1866

—— Memoir on the Southern Part of Central Asia. (Translated from the French.) Large 8° *Calcutta*, 1883

—— *See* Yule, H. ; *also* Recueil de Voyages, Vol. 7, p. 612 : Appendix 1.

Khanikoff, Y. V. Notes Explanatory of a Map of the Lake of Aral, in the Khanate of Khiva, and its Environs. [In Russian.] 8° *St Petersburg*, 1851

—— Journey from Orsk to Khiva and back, in 1740-41, by Gladisbeff and Mouravieff. [In Russian.] 8° *St Petersburg*, 1851

Khosrau, Nassiri. *See* Schefer, C.

Kidd, S. China ; or, Illustrations to the Symbols, Philosophy, Antiquities, Customs, Superstitions, Laws, Government, Education, and Literature of Chinese. *Plates.* 8° 1841

Kidder, D. P., and J. C. Fletcher. Brazil and the Brazilians, portrayed in Historical and Descriptive Sketches. *Map, plates, and woodcuts.* 8° *Philadelphia*, 1857

—— *See* Fletcher.

Kidder, F. The Discovery of North America by John Cabot, a First Chapter in the History of North America. *Maps.* 8° *Boston, Mass.*, 1878

Kiefer, H. Biot's Tables for calculating barometric altitudes. [In German and Russian.] 4° *Tiflis*, 1874

Kieffer, J. D., and T. X. Bianchi. Dictionnaire Turc-Français, à l'usage des Agents Diplomatiques et Consulaires, des Commerçants, des Navigateurs, et autres Voyageurs dans le Levant. 2 vols. 8° *Paris*, 1835-37

Kienitz, O. Emil Holub. Separat-abdruck aus der Augsburger Allgemeinen Zeitung vom 2, 3 und 4 September 1882. 8* 1882

Kiepert, Dr H. Memoir über die Construction der Karte von Klein-Asien und Türkisch Armenien in 6 Blatt. von V. Vincke, Fischer, v. Moltke, und Kiepert. Nebst Mittheilungen über die physikalisch - geographischen Verhältnisse der neu-erforschten Landstriche. *Maps.* 8° *Berlin*, 1854

—— Ueber die geographische Anordnung der Namen arischer Landschaften im ersten Fargard des Vendidad. *Map.* 8* *Berlin*, 1856

Kiepert, Dr H. Ueber die Persische Königsstrasse durch Vorderasien nach Herodotus. *Map.* 8* *Berlin*, 1857
—— Ueber die Leleger. *Map.* 8* 1861
—— Zur Kartographie der Europäischen Türkei. 8* [*Berlin*, 1876]
—— Zur ethnographischen Karte des Europäischen Orients. *Map.* 8*
Berlin, 1876
—— Die Gruppirung der Confessionen in Bosnien und der Hertzegowina. *Map.* 4* *Brunswick*, 1876
—— Lehrbuch der alten Geographie. Erste Hälfte : Einleitung, Asien und Africa. Zweite Hälfte : Europa. 8°
Berlin, 1877-78
—— Ueber Pegolotti's vorderasiatisches Itinerar. *Map.* 8* [*Berlin*] 1881
—— A Manual of Ancient Geography. Authorised translation from the German. Small 8° 1881
—— Hans Dernschwam's Orientalische Reise, 1553-55. *Map.* 12*
Brunswick, 1887
—— Die alten Ortslagen am Südfusse des Idagebirges. *Map and plate.* 8*
Berlin, 1889
—— and R. Koldewey. Itinerare auf der Insel Lesbos. *Maps.* 8* *Berlin*, 1890
Kindberg, Prof. N. C. *See* Canada, A, Geol. and Nat. Hist. Survey : Appendix 2.
King, Clarence. Mountaineering in the Sierra Nevada. 8° 1872
—— First Annual Report of the United States Geological Survey to the Hon. Carl Schurz, Secretary of the Interior. *Map.* 4° *Washington*, 1880
—— Statistics of the Production of the Precious Metals in the United States. United States, Tenth Census Publication. *Plates.* 4° *Washington*, 1881
—— *See* United States, G, *c*, Geological Survey ; A, Tenth Census ; H, *a* (Prof. Papers) : Appendix 2.
King, C. W. *See* Japan : Appendix 2.
King, E. The Southern States of North America : a Record of Journeys in Louisiana, Texas, the Indian Territory, Missouri, Arkansas, Mississippi, Alabama, Georgia, Florida, South Carolina, North Carolina, Kentucky, Tennessee, Virginia, West Virginia, and Maryland. 3 vols in 1. *Maps and plates.* 8° 1875
King, F. D. *See* Tait.
King, G. Report on the Working of the Government Botanical Gardens at Saharunpore. Report on the Working of the Government Tea Plantations of Hawulbagh and Ayar Tolie, in Kumaon, 1868-69. [From the India Records, N.W. Provinces, Vol. 2, No. 4]
Allahabad, 1869

R

King, Capt. James. *See* Cook.
King, J. W. Channel Pilot : South-West and South Coasts of England, Coast of France, and the Channel Islands. Compiled from various sources, but chiefly from the Surveys of Captain M. White, and from the "Pilote Français" by M. Givry. 2 parts. 8°
1859-63
—— China Pilot : The Coasts of China, Korea, and Tartary ; the Sea of Japan, Gulfs of Tartary and Amúr, and Sea of Okhotsk ; and the Babuyan, Bashí, Formosa, Meiaco Sima, Lu-Chu, Ladrones, Bonin, Japan, Saghalin, and Kuril Islands. 8° 1861
—— Pilote de la Manche, Cotes Sud et Sud-Ouest d'Angleterre, du Cap Trevose au North Foreland. . . . Traduit de l'Anglais . . . par M. Sallot Des Noyers. *Plates.* 8° *Paris*, 1869
—— *See* Reed ; *also* United Kingdom, A, Admiralty Publ. : Appendix 2.
King, Moses. King's Handbook of the United States. *See* Sweetser.
—— Handbook of New York City : an Outline History and Description of the American Metropolis. Planned, edited, and published by Moses King. 2nd edition. *Illustrations.* 8°
Boston, Mass., 1893
King, Hon. Philip G. Comments on Cook's Log (H.M.S. "Endeavour," 1770) ; with Extracts, Charts, and Sketches, April 1891. 4* *Sydney*, 1891
King, Capt. Philip Parker. Narrative of a Survey of the Intertropical and Western Coasts of Australia, between 1818-22 ; with an Appendix relating to Hydrography and Natural History. 2 vols. *Maps and plates.* 8° 1827
—— Selections from a Meteorological Journal kept on board H.M.S. "Adventure" during the Survey of the Southern Coasts of South America, 1827-30. 8*
—— Abstract from a Meteorological Journal kept at Port Stephens, New South Wales, 1843-47. *Table.* 8*
Launceston, Tas., N.D.
—— Sailing Directions for the Inner Route from Sydney to Torres Strait. 8*
1847
—— and Robert Fitz-Roy. Narrative of the Surveying Voyages of H.M.S. "Adventure" and "Beagle," between 1826-36, describing their Examination of the Southern Shores of South America, and the "Beagle's" Circumnavigation of the Globe. 4 vols. *Maps and plates.* 8° 1839
Vol. 1.—King, Captain P. P. Proceedings of the First Expedition, 1826-30.
Vol. 2.—Fitz-Roy, Capt. Robert. Proceedings of the Second Expedition, 1831-36.

King, Capt. Philip Parker, and Robert Fitz-Roy. Narrative of the Surveying Voyages of H.M.S. "Adventure" and "Beagle"—*continued.*
Vol. 3.—Darwin, Charles. Journal and Remarks on the Geology and Natural History, 1832-36.
Vol. 4.—Appendix to Vol. 2.
—— Sailing Directions for South America. Part 2. La Plata, Patagonia, Magellan Strait, Tierra del Fuego, Falkland and Staten Islands, Chile, Bolivia, and Peru. 8°   1848 and 1850
—— South American Pilot. Part 2. From the Rio de la Plata to the Bay of Panama, including Magellan Strait, the Falkland and Galapagos Islands. 8°   1860
—— *See* United Kingdom, A, Admiralty, Hydrogr. Off. Publ. : Appendix 2.

King, Richard. Facts and Arguments in Favour of a New Expedition to the Shores of the Arctic Ocean. *Map.* 12*
1836
—— Narrative of a Journey to the Shores of the Arctic Ocean in 1833-35, under the Command of Capt. Back. 2 vols. *Plates.* 8°   1836
—— On the Unexplored Coast of North America. 8*   1842

King, Capt. R. W. Campaigning in Kaffirland, or Scenes and Adventures in the Kaffir War of 1851-52. *Maps and illustrations.* 8°   1855

King, S. W. Italian Valleys of the Pennine Alps. *Maps and plates.* 8* 1858

King, Hon. T. Butler. Alabama, Florida, and Georgia Railroad. 8*
Washington, 1848
—— Railroad across the Isthmus of Panama. 8*   *Washington,* 1849
—— Report on California. 8*
Washington, 1850
—— California, the Wonder of the Age : a Book for every one going to, or having an interest in, that Golden Region. 8*
New York, 1850

King, Capt. W. *See* Hakluyt's Voyages, Vol. 4 : Appendix 1.

King, W. Nephew, jun. El. Volcan Ometepe. (From *Harper's Weekly,* 28th May.) 4*   1892

King, W. Ross. The Sportsman and Naturalist in Canada, or Notes on the Natural History of the Game, Game Birds, and Fish of that Country. *Plates.* 8°   1866
—— The Aboriginal Tribes of the Nilgiri Hills. *Plates.* 8*   1870

King, Prof. W. The Reputed Fossil Man of the Neanderthal. 8*   1864
—— Preliminary Notice of a Memoir on Rock-jointing, in its Relation to Phenomena in Physical Geography and Physical Geology. 8*   *Dublin,* 1880

King-Harman, Col. M. J. Military Objections to the Hunterian Spelling of "Indian" Words. 8*   N.D.

Kinglake, A. W. Eothen. New edition. 8°   1864

Kingsford, William. The History of Canada. Vol. 1. [1608-82]. 8° 1888

Kingsley, Rev. Charles. *See* Mansfield, C. B.

Kingsley, Henry. Eyre, the South-Australian Explorer. 8°   N.D.

Kingsmill, T. W. A Sketch of the Geology of a portion of Quang-Tung Province. *Plate.* 8*   N.D.

Kingston, Sir George Strickland. Register of the Rainfall kept in Grote Street, Adelaide, from 1st January 1839 to 16th December 1879, both inclusive. Folio   *Adelaide,* 1879

Kingston, W. H. G. Lusitanian Sketches of the Pen and Pencil. 2 vols. 8°   1845

Kinloch, Arthur. The Murray River : being a Journal of the Voyage of the "Lady Augusta" Steamer, from the Goolwa, in South Australia, to Gannewarra, above Swan Hill, Victoria, a distance from the Sea of 1400 miles. 8°
Adelaide, 1853

Kinloch, Colonel A. A. A. Large Game Shooting in Thibet, the Himalayas, and Northern India, illustrated by Photogravures. *Map.* 4°   *Calcutta,* 1885

Kinnear, John. Cairo, Petra, and Damascus, in 1839 ; with Remarks on the Government of Mehemet Ali, and on the Present Prospects of Syria. 8°   1841

Kinneir, John Macdonald. A Geographical Memoir of the Persian Empire. 4°   1813
—— Journey through Asia Minor, Armenia, and Koordistan in 1813-14 ; with Remarks on the Marches of Alexander, and Retreat of the Ten Thousand. *Map.* 8°   1818

Kintore, Earl of. Report upon his Visit to Port Darwin, and upon the Affairs of the Northern Territory of South Australia. Folio*   1891

Kinzelbach, Theodor. *See* Henglin.

Kippax, John. *See* Uztariz.

Kippis, A. A Narrative of the Voyages Round the World performed by Captain James Cook ; with an Account of his Life during the previous and intervening Periods. *Illustrations.* 8°   1883

Kips' Guide to Belgium, containing 21 Maps and Plans of Belgium, Antwerp, Brussels, Bruges, Ghent, Liege, Mons, Namur, Ostend, &c. Compiled and drawn by Joseph Kips. 2nd edition. 12°   1888

Kips' Guide to Brussels (Bruxelles), containing a Route Map, Plan of Brussels, and Environs of Brussels. 12° N.D.

Kirby, Rev. W. *See* Richardson, Sir J.

Kircher, Athanasius. China Monumentis, quà Sacris quà Profanis, nec non Variis Naturæ et Artis Spectaculis, &c.; illustrata. *Maps and plates.* Small folio *Amsterdam*, 1667

—— La Chine, illustrée de plusieurs Monuments tant Sacrés que Profanes, et de Quantité de Recherchs de la Nature et de l'Art ; avec un Dictionnaire Chinois et François. Traduit par F. S. Dalquié. *Maps and plates.* Folio *Amsterdam*, 1670

Kirchhoff, Prof. Alfred. Die hydrographische Zubehör des äquatorialen Muta Nsige. 4* [*Gotha*] 1886

—— Einleitung in die Länderkunde von Europa. *Maps.* 4° *Leipzig*, 1886

—— Unser Wissen von der Erde. Allgemeine Erdkunde und Länderkunde, herausgegeben von Alfred Kirchhoff. Erster Band ; Allgemeine Erdkunde, von Dr J. Hann, Dr F. von Hochstetter, und Dr A. Pokorny. *Maps and plates.* Large 8° *Leipzig*, 1886

—— The same, II. Europa im Allgemeinen, von Prof. Dr A. Kirchhoff ; Physikalische Skizze von Mittel-Europa, von Prof. Dr A. Penck ; Das Deutsche Reich, von Prof. Dr A. Penck. *Maps and plates.* Large 8° *Vienna*, 1887

—— The same, III. Frankreich, von Prof. Dr Friedr. Hahn ; Die Britischen Inseln, von Prof. Dr Friedr. Hahn ; Das Königreich Dänemark, von Prof. Dr Friedr. Hahn ; Schweden und Norwegen, von Prof. Dr Friedr. Hahn ; Die Nordischen Inseln, von Prof. Dr Friedr. Hahn ; Finland, von Prof. Dr Joh. Rein. *Maps and illustrations.* 4° *Vienna*, 1890

—— Matthias Oeders grosses Kartenwerk über Kursachsen aus der Zeit um 1600. 8* *Dresden* [1890]

—— Stanley und Emin nach Stanley's eigenem Werke. *Portrait.* 8* *Halle*, 1890

—— Die Territoriale Zusammen-setzung der Provinz Sachsen. *Map.* 8* *Halle*, 1891

—— Geographie in höheren Schulen. 8* N.P., N.D.

—— *See* Leutemann ; Germany, C : Appendix 2.

—— **and A. Sonnenschein.** School Geography : Junior Course. *Illustrations.* Small 8° 1891

Kirchner, J. J. Bosnien in Bild und Wort. Zwanzig Federzeichnungen, mit erklärendem Texte von A. v. Schweiger-Lerchenfeld. *Plates.* 8° *Vienna*, 1879

Kirk, Sir John. Explanation of Meteorological Tables illustrating the Climate of East Tropical Africa. 8* 1864

—— Notes on Two Expeditions up the River Rovuma, East Africa. 8* [1865]

Kirk, R. Medical Report on the Kingdom of Shoa. 8* [*Bombay*, 1843]

Kirk, T., and R. Thoresby. Tours in Scotland, 1677 and 1681. Edited by P. Hume Brown. 8° *Edinburgh*, 1892

Kirkpatrick, Colonel W. An Account of the Kingdom of Nepaul : being the Substance of Observations made during a Mission to that Country in the year 1793. *Map and plates.* 4° 1811

—— *See* Eyriès, Vol. 14 : Appendix 1.

Kirsop, R. *See* Dalrymple, Repertory, Vol. 1 : Appendix 1.

Kitchin, A. *See* Hakluyt's Voyages, Vol. 1 : Appendix 1.

Kittlitz, F. H. von. Denkwürdigkeiten einer Reise nach dem Russischen Amerika, nach Mikronesien und durch Kamtschatka. 2 vols. *Plates.* 8° *Gotha*, 1858

—— Twenty-four Views of the Vegetation of the Coasts and Islands of the Pacific, with Explanatory Descriptions, taken during the Exploring Voyage of the Russian Corvette " Senjawin," under the command of Capt. Lütke, in the years 1827, 1828, and 1829. Translated from the German, and edited by Berthold Seemann. Square 8° 1861

Kitto, Dr John. Pictorial History of Palestine and the Holy Land, including a complete History of the Jews. 2 vols. *Woodcuts.* Royal 8° 1844

—— Cyclopædia of Biblical Literature, abridged. *Maps and woodcuts.* 8° *Edinburgh*, 1855

Kitts, Eustace J. Report on the Census of Berar, 1881. Folio *Bombay*, 1882

—— A Compendium of the Castes and Tribes found in India. Folio* *Bombay*, 1885

—— The Tahtar Tribes. 12° N.D.

Kjerulf, Theodor. Das Christiania-Silurbecken, chemisch geognostisch untersucht. *Map.* 4° *Christiania*, 1855

—— Veiviser ved Geologiske Excursioner i Christiania Omegn. *Map.* 4* *Christiania*, 1865

—— The Terraces of Norway. Translated from the Norsk by Marshall Hall. 8* 1870

—— Om Skuringsmærker. Glacialformationen, Terrasser, og Strandlinier samt om Grundfjeldets og Sparagmitfjeldets Mægtighed i Norge. ii. Sparagmitfjeldets. 4° *Christiania*, 1873

—— Om Stratifikationens Spor. 4° *Christiania*, 1877

Kjerulf, Theodor. Udsigt over det Sydlige Norges Geologi. 4° *Christiania,* 1879
—— Et Stykke Geografi i Norge. *Map.* 8* [*Christiania,* N.D.]
—— *See* Murchison ; Sars.

Klaproth, Julius. Travels in the Caucasus and Georgia in 1807-8, by command of the Russian Government. Translated from the German by Shoberl. 4° 1814
—— Asia Polyglotta. Sprachatlas. *Map.* Folio *Paris,* 1823
—— Mémoires relatifs à l'Asie, contenant des Recherches Historiques, Géographiques, et Philologiques sur les Peuples de l'Orient. Vol. 1. [*The plates wanting.*] 8° *Paris,* 1824
—— The same. Vol. 3. *Maps and plates.* 8° *Paris,* 1828
—— Tableaux Historiques de l'Asie, depuis la Monarchie de Cyrus jusqu'à nos jours·; Accompagnés de Recherches Historiques et Ethnographiques sur cette Partie du Monde. 4°, and Atlas folio *Paris,* 1826
—— Asiatisches Magazin . . . herausgegeben von J. Klaproth. *See* Appendix 3, "Transactions," Germany, Weimar.
—— *See* Fa Hian ; Timkowski.

Klatt, J. Bibliography of Oriental Philology. 8° [*Berlin,* 1884]

Klein, H. J. Physische Geographie. Nach dem gegenwärtigen Standpunkte der Wissenschaft. *Illustrations.* 8° *Stuttgart* [1880]

Klein, Sydney T. Thirty-Six Hours' Hunting among the Lepidoptera and Hymenoptera of Middlesex, with Notes on the Method adopted for their Capture. 8* *Bath,* 1887

Kleinschmidt, S. Den Grönlandske Ordbog. 8° *Copenhagen,* 1871

Klemenz, D. Antiquities in the Minusinsk Museum. [In Russian.] With Atlas. 8° *Tomsk,* 1886

Kleyle, F. F. Rückerinnerungen an eine Reise in Oesterreich und Steyermark im Jahre 1810. 12° *Vienna,* 1814

Klint, Admiral Gustaf. Sailing Directions for the Baltic Sea and the Gulf of Finland. 8° 1854
—— Bothnia Pilot. *Plates.* 8° 1855
—— Pilote de la Mer Baltique, augmenté des Documents Hydrographiques les plus Récents, traduit par Alex. le Gras. *Plates.* 8° *Paris,* 1856
—— Supplément au Pilote de la Mer Baltique. 8° *Paris,* 1857
—— *See* United Kingdom, A : Appendix 2.

Klöden, Gustav Adolph von. Das Stromsystem des Oberen Nil nach den neueren Kenntnissen mit Bezug auf die älteren Nachrichten. *Maps and plates.* Royal 8° *Berlin,* 1856
—— Handbuch der Erdkunde. Erster Theil. Die physische Geographie. *Illustrations.* 8° *Berlin,* 1859

Klöden, Gustav Adolph von. Das Areal der Hoch- und Tieflandschaften Europas. *Maps.* 8* *Berlin,* 1873

Klosovsky, A. Les Orages au Sud de la Russie. *Plates.* 8* *Odessa,* 1886

Klotzsch, F. Philipp Schoenlein's botanischer Nachlass auf Cap Palmas. *Plates.* 4° *Berlin,* 1857

Kluge, Emil. Ueber Synchronismus und Antagonismus von vulkanischen Eruptionen und Beziehungen derselben zu den Sonnenflecken und erdmagnetischen Variationen. *Plate.* 8* *Leipzig,* 1863

Klunzinger, C. B. Bilder aus Oberägypten, der Wüste und dem Rothen Meere...mit einem Vorwort von Dr Georg Schweinfurth. *Plate.* 8° *Stuttgart,* 1877
—— Upper Egypt, its People and its Products : a Descriptive Account of the Manners, Customs, Superstitions, and Occupations of the People of the Nile Valley, the Desert, and the Red Sea Coast, with Sketches of the Natural History and Geology ; with a Prefatory Notice by Dr Georg Schweinfurth. *Plates.* 8° 1878

Klutschak, F. Auf der Reichenberg-Pardubitzer Bahn ins Gebirge. *Map.* 12° *Prague,* 1860

Klutschak, H. W. Als Eskimo unter den Eskimos. Eine Schilderung der Erlebnisse der Schwatka' schen Franklin-Aufsuchungs Expedition in den Jahren 1878-80. *Maps and illustrations.* 8° *Vienna,* 1881

Kmety, George. Narrative of the Defence of Kars, 29th September 1855. Translated from the German. 8* 1856

Knauz, Nándor. Kortan. 4° *Budapest,* 1876

Kner, R. *See* "Novara."

Knight, C. Geography, or First Division of "The English Cyclopædia." 4 vols. in 2, and Supplement [N.D.] 4° 1854-55
—— Natural History, or Second Division of "The English Cyclopædia." Supplement. 4° 1870
—— The Land we Live in, a Pictorial and Descriptive Tour of the British Islands. Edited by C. Knight. 3 vols. *Plates.* Small folio N.D.

Knight, Captain. Diary of a Pedestrian in Cashmere and Thibet. *Plates.* 8° 1863

Knight, E. F. The Cruise of the "Falcon," a Voyage to South America in a 30-ton Yacht. *Maps and illustrations.* 2 vols. Post 8° 1884
—— The Cruise of the "Alerte :" the Narrative of a Search for Treasure on the Desert Island of Trinidad. *Maps and illustrations.* 8° 1890
—— Where Three Empires Meet : a Narrative of Recent Travel in Kashmir, Western Tibet, Gilgit, and the adjoining countries. *Map and illustrations.* 8° 1893

Knight, Francis. *See* Churchill, Vol. 8 : Appendix 1.

Knight, Henry Gally. The Normans in Sicily: being a Sequel to "An Architectural Tour in Normandy." 12° 1838
—— An Architectural Tour in Normandy, with some Remarks on Norman Architecture. 2nd edition. *Plates.* 12° 1841
Knight, Captain, J. *See* Hakluyt Soc. Publ., Vols. 5, 56; Purchas, Vol. 3, Book 4 : Appendix 1.
Knight, Sparrow. The Coals from Se-Shan (the Hills west of Peking) 4* *Shanghai*, 1867
Knight, William. Facts and Observations towards forming a New Theory of the Earth. 8° *Edinburgh*, 1819
—— A Diary in the Dardanelles, written on board the Schooner "Corsair" while beating through the Straits from Tenedos to Marmora. 12° 1849
Knight-Bruce, G. W. H. Journals of the Mashonaland Mission, 1888 - 92. Edited, with an Introduction,.by L. K. B. *Maps and illustrations.* 8° 1892
Knighton, William. History of Ceylon, from the Earliest Period to the Present Time, with an Appendix containing an Account of its Present Position. 8° 1845
—— Tropical Sketches, or Reminiscences of an Indian Journalist. 2 vols. 8° 1855
Knipping, E. Bemerkungen zur Kartenskizze des Weges von Tokio bis Yumotto (Nikko-Berge) und zurück bis Matsudo am Yedogawa. *Map.* 4* *Tokio*, N.D.
—— Local-Attraction beobachtet auf dem Gipfel des Futarasan (Nantaisan). *Plate.* 4* *Tokio*, N.D.
—— Einige Angaben ueber die vier letzten starken Erdbeben in Tokio. [1 *sheet.*] 4* *Tokio*, 1880
—— Die Bahnbestimmung der Wirbelstürme durch Normalörter. *Plate.* 8* *Berlin*, 1882
—— Normalörter für die Taifune in den Chinesischen und Japanischen Gewässern des Jahres 1880. *Chart.* Large 8* *Berlin*, 1882
—— Normalörter für die Taifune in den Chinesischen und Japanischen Meeren des Jahres 1881. *Chart.* Large 8* *Berlin*, 1882
Knivet, Anthony. *See* Gottfried; Purchas, Vol. 4, Book 6: Appendix 1.
Knolles, Richard. The Generall Historie of the Turkes, from the First Beginning of that Nation to the Rising of the Othoman Familie, with all the Notable Expeditions of the Christian Princes against them, together with the Lives and Conquests of the Othoman Kings and Emperours, &c. Folio 1603
Knollys, Major Henry. English Life in China. 8° 1885
Knollys, R. J. British Honduras : Outlines of its Geography. 12* N.D.

Knonau, Gerold Meyer von. Erdkunde der Schweizerischen Eidgenossenschaft. 2 vols. *Map.* 8° *Zurich*, 1838-39
Knorr, E. R. Papers on the Eastern and Northern Extensions of the Gulf Stream. From the German of Dr A. Petermann, Dr W. von Freeden, and Dr A. Mühry. Translated in the U.S. Hydrographic Office . . . by E. R. Knorr. *Maps.* 4° *Washington*, 1871
—— Supplements to the same. Vols 1 to 6. 4° *Washington*, 1872-75
Knötel, A. Der Niger der Alten, und andere wichtige Fragen der alten Geographie Afrika's. *Map.* 8* *Glogau*, 1866
Knowles, Commander. *See* West Indies, A : Appendix 2.
Knox, A. A. The New Playground, or Wanderings in Algeria. 8° 1881
Knox, J. New Collection of Voyages, &c.
[For full Title and Contents, *see* Appendix 1, pp. 607-609].
Knox, Robert. A Historical Relation of the Island Ceylon in the East Indies, together with an Account of the Detaining in Captivity the Author and divers other Englishmen now living there, and of the Author's Miraculous Escape. *Map and plates.* Folio 1681
—— *See* Philalethes. The History of Ceylon, &c.; *also* Allgemeine Historie, Vol. 8 : Appendix 1.
Knox, T. W. Overland through Asia : Pictures of Siberian, Chinese, and Tartar Life. *Map and plates.* 8° 1871
Koch, Karl. Crimea and Odessa. Translated by Horner. *Map.* 8° 1855
—— Erläuterungen zu Karte des Kaukasischen Isthmus und Armeniens. 4° *Berlin*, N.D.
—— Der Kaukasus: Landschafts-und Lebens-Bilder. Aus dem Nachlasse von Karl Koch, herausgegeben von Therese Koch. *Portrait.* 8° *Berlin*, 1882
Köchler, Dr F. *See* Dictionary : Appendix 2 (General).
Kœchlin-Schwartz, A. Un Touriste en Laponie : Le Soleil de Minuit, Karasjok, les Lapons, le Fjeld. *Maps.* 12° *Paris*, 1882
—— Un Touriste en Laponie. *Map.* 12° *Paris* [1883]
Koelle, Rev. S. W. Polyglotta Africana, or a Comparative Vocabulary of nearly 300 Words and Phrases in more than 100 distinct African Languages. Folio 1845
—— Outlines of a Grammar of the Vei Language, together with a Vei-English Vocabulary, and an Account of the Discovery and Nature of the Vei Mode of Syllabic Writing. 8° 1854
—— Grammar of the Bornu or Kanuri Language. 8° 1854

Koenig, —. *See* Recueil de Voyages, Vol. 4, p. 611 : Appendix 1.

Koestlin, C. H. Lettres sur l'Histoire Naturelle de l'Isle d'Elbe. [Zoological Appendix.] *Map.* 12° *Vienna*, 1780

Kohl, J. G. Russia : St Petersburg, Moscow, Kharkoff, Riga, Odessa, the German Provinces on the Baltic, the Steppes, the Crimea, and the Interior of the Empire. *Map.* 8° 1843
—— Austria : Vienna, Prague, Hungary, Bohemia, and the Danube ; Galicia, Styria, Moravia, Bukovina, and the Military Frontier. 8° 1844
—— Kitchi - Gami : Wanderings round Lake Superior. 8° 1860
—— Travels in Canada, and through the States of New York and Pennsylvania. Translated by Mrs Percy Sinnett. 2 vols. in 1. 8° 1861
—— Geschichte des Golfstroms und seiner Erforschung von den ältesten Zeiten bis auf den grossen Amerikanischen Bürgerkrieg, &c. *Maps.* 8° *Bremen*, 1868
—— Geschichte der Entdeckungsreisen und Schiffahrten zur Magellan's-Strasse und zu den ihr benachbarten Ländern und Meeren. *Maps.* 8° *Berlin*, 1877

Kol, J. C. Statistical Report on the Portuguese Settlements in India, descriptive of the Geographical Position of the Principal Ports, Territorial Divisions, &c., with Notes, and an Account of the Convents suppressed in 1835. Extracted in 1850 from Official Documents, by Captain J. Cicilia Kol. *Table.* [From the India Records, No. 10]
Bombay, 1855

Kolberg, Joseph. Nach Ecuador : Reisebilder. 3rd edition. *Map and illustrations.* 8° *Freiburg im Breisgau*, 1885

Kolb, G. F. The Condition of Nations, Social and Political ; with Complete Comparative Tables of Universal Statistics. Translated, edited, and collated to 1880 by Mrs Brewer ; with Original Notes and Information by Edwin W. Streeter. 8° 1880

Kolben, Peter. The Present State of the Cape of Good Hope, or a Particular Account of the Several Nations of the Hottentots . . together with a Short Account of the Dutch Settlement at the Cape. Translated by — Medley. 2 vols. *Plates.* 8° 1731
—— *See* Astley, Vol. 3 ; New Collection, Vol. 2, p. 608 ; "The World Displayed," Vol. 10 : Appendix 1.

Koldewey, Karl. Die erste Deutsche Nordpolar-Expedition im Jahre 1868, beschrieben von K. Koldewey, mit einem Vorwort von A. Petermann. (Ergänzungsheft, 28—Petermann's Mittheilungen.) *Plate and maps.* 4° *Gotha*, 1871

Koldewey, Karl. Die zweite Deutsche Nordpolarfahrt in den Jahren 1869 und 1870, unter Führung des Kapitän Karl Koldewey. 2 vols. *Maps and plates.* Large 8° *Leipzig*, 1874
—— The German Arctic Expedition of 1869-70, and Narrative of the Wreck of the "Hansa" in the Ice. By Captain Koldewey ; translated and abridged by the Rev. L. Mercier, and edited by H. W. Bates. *Maps and plates.* 8° 1874
—— *See* Kiepert, H. ; *also* Polar Regions, Arctic, H : Appendix 2.

Köler, H. Einige Notizen über Bonny und die Küste von Guinea, seine Sprache und seine Bewohner ; mit einem Glossarium. 8° *Göttingen*, 1848

Kolff, D. H. Reize door den weinig bekenden Zuidelijken Molukschen Archipel en Langs de geheel Onbekende Zuidwest Kust van Nieuw-Guinea, in 1825-26. *Map.* 8° *Amsterdam*, 1828
—— Voyages through the Southern and little - known parts of the Moluccan Archipelago, and along the previously unknown Southern Coast of New Guinea, in 1825-26. Translated by G. W. Earl. *Maps.* 8° 1840

Koner, B. Literature of Anthropology, &c., for 1876. [In Russian.] 8*
St Petersburg, 1878

Koner, W. Vortrag gehalten in der Sitzung der Geographischen Gesellschaft zu Berlin am 19 Januar 1866. 8*
Berlin, 1866
—— Zur Erinnerung an das Fünfzigjährige Bestehen der Gesellschaft für Erdkunde zu Berlin. *Plate.* 8* *Berlin*, 1878

Konstantinidos, G. M. Topographia tes inson Kupron pros chresin ton demotikon scholeion upo G. M. Konstantinidon. Ekdosis deutera. Genomeno epi te basei tes telentaias apographe. 8*
Larnaka, 1893

Koolemans Beynen, L. R. De Reis der "Pandora" naar de Noordpoolgewesten in den Zomer van 1875. *Map.* 4*
Amsterdam, 1876
—— De Reis der "Pandora" in den Zomer van 1876. *Map.* 4°
Amsterdam, 1877
—— *See* Hakluyt Soc. Publ., 54 : Appendix 1.

Köpke, D. *See* Gama, Vasco da.

Kopp, H. F. *See* Leonhard, C. C.

Köppen, A. Zum fünfzigjährigen Jubiläum des Akademikers Gregor von Helmersen. 8* *St Petersburg*, 1878

Köppen, F. T. *See* Helmersen and Schrenck, Vols. 3, 4, 6 ; Schrenck and Maximowicz, Vols. 5, 6.

Köppen, P. von. *See* Baer and Helmersen, Vols. 4, 11, 13.

Köppen, Prof. W. Die Schreibung Geographischer Namen. 8* *Hamburg*, 1893

Koppin, —. Der Memelstrom in hydro-technischer Beziehung. *Maps.* 4*
Berlin, 1861

Kopsch, H. Geographical Notes on the Province of Kiangsi. (From China Review.) 8* N.D.

—— Kiukiang Trade Reports for the years 1871-72 and 1873. *Table.* Small 4* *Kiukiang*, 1873-74

—— The same, for 1874, 1875, 1876, 1877. *Map and tables.* Small 4*
[*Shanghai*, 1875-78]

—— Report on the Trade at the Treaty Ports of China for 1875. Small 4*
Shanghai, 1876

—— Reports on the Trade of Pakhoi for the years 1880, 1881, 1882, 1883. 4*
[*Pakhoi*, 1881-84]

—— The Kaaba, or Great Shrine at Mecca, as described by Chinese ; with Notes on the Old Arab Trade, and Remarks on Mahommedanism in China. 8*
Shanghai, 1884

Korabinsky, Joh. Matthias. Geograph-isch-historisches und Produkten Lexikon von Ungarn. 8° *Pressburg*, 1876

Körber, Ph. Illustrirter Fremdenführer durch die Fränkische Schweiz und das Fichtelgebirge, Bamberg, Bayreuth, Er-langen, und Coburg. *Map and illustra-tions.* 12° *Bamberg*, 1858

Koren, Johan. *See* Norway, A, Nor-wegian North Atlantic Expedition, 1876-78 : Appendix.

Körner, F. Süd-Afrika : Natur- und Kulturbilder, mit einer historischen Ein-leitung und einer ausführlichen Ueber-sicht der neueren Reisen. *Map and plates.* 8° *Leipzig*, 1873

Körösi, J. Vorläufiger Bericht über die Resultate der Pester Volkszählung, 1870. 8* *Budapest*, 1871

—— Die Bauthätigkeit Pest's in den Jahren 1870 und 1871. Large 8* *Budapest*, 1872

—— Ditto ; im Jahre 1872. Large 8*
Budapest, 1873

—— Untersuchungen über die Einkom-mensteuer der Stadt Pest für das Jahr 1870. Large 8° *Budapest*, 1873

—— Statistisches Jahrbuch der Stadt Pest. Erster Jahrgang. Large 8° *Budapest*, 1873

—— Projet d'un Recensement du Monde : Étude de Statistique internationale. 8*
Paris, 1881

—— Die Hauptstadt Budapest im Jahre 1881. Resultate der Volksbeschreibung und Volkszählung. *Maps and plates.* Large 8° *Berlin*, 1881-82

—— Publicationen des statistischen Bur-eaus der Hauptstadt Budapest, XVI. Die öffentlichen Volksschulen der Haupt-stadt Budapest in den Schuljahren 1873-74, 1874-75, 1875-76, und 1876-77. Large 8* *Berlin*, 1883

Körösi, J. The same. XVII. Die öffent-lichen Volksschulen der Hauptstadt Buda-pest in den Schuljahren 1877-78, 1878-79, 1879-1880, und 1880-81. Large 8°
Berlin, 1884

—— The same. XVIII. Die Sterblichkeit der Stadt Budapest in den Jahren 1876 bis 1881, und deren Ursachen. Large 8° *Berlin*, 1885

—— Exposition Nationale de 1885 à Budapest. Catalogue raisonné de l'Ex-position du Bureau de Statistique de la Ville de Budapest. 8* *Berlin*, 1885

—— Die Bauthätigkeit Budapest's in den Jahren 1875-84. 4* *Berlin*, 1886

—— Die Sterblichkeit der Stadt Budapest in den Jahren 1882 bis 1885, und deren Ursachen. 4° *Berlin*, 1888

Koristka, Carl. Die Hohe Tatra in den Central Karpaten. (Ergänzungsheft, 12— Petermann's Mittheilungen). *Plates and map.* 4° *Gotha*, 1864

—— Die Arbeiten der topographischen Abtheilung der Landesdurchforschung von Böhmen in den Jahren 1864-66. *Map and plate.* 4° *Prague*, 1869

Korthals, P. W. Topographische Schets van een Gedeelte van Sumatra. *Plate.* 8* *Leyden*, 1847

Koschïtzky, Max von. Deutche Co-lonialgeschichte. 2 vols. in 1. *Maps.* 8° *Leipzig*, 1887-88

Kostenko, Capt. Description of the Journey of a Russian Mission to Bokhara in 1870. Translated by R. Michell. 8* N.D.

Koster, Henry. Travels in Brazil. *Maps and plates.* 2 vols. 8° 1817

Kosutány, T. Magyarország Jellemzöbb Doházyainak. Pt. 1 *Budapest*, 1877

Koto, Prof. B. On the Cause of the Great Earthquake in Central Japan, 1891. (Reprinted from the *Journal* of the Col-lege of Science, Imperial University, Japan, Vol. 5, Part 4.) *Plates.* Large 8* 1893

Kotschy, Theodor. Reise in den Cili-cischen Taurus über Tarsus. Vorwort von C. Ritter. *Map and plate.* 8°
Gotha, 1858

—— Die Vegetation und der Canal auf dem Isthmus von Suez. 4* *Vienna*, 1858

—— Der Nil, seine Quellen, Zuflüsse, Länder, und deren Bewohner. *Map.* 8* *Vienna*, 1866

—— **and J. Peyritsch.** Plantes Tin-néennes, ou Description de quelques unes des Plantes recueillies par l'Expédition Tinnéennes sur les bords du Bahr-el-Ghasal et de ses affluents en Afrique Centrale. Published at the cost of Alex-andrine and John A Tinné. *27 coloured plates.* Elph. folio *Vienna*, 1867

Köttstorfer, Dr J. *See* Wolf.

Kotula, B. Distributio Plantarum Vasculosarum in Montibus Tatricis. 4*
　　　　　　　　Cracow, 1889-90
—— Rozmieszczenie roslin naczyniowych w Tatrach. (Ueber die Verbreitung der Gefässpflanzen in der Tatra). 8*
　　　　　　　　Cracow, 1891

Kotzebue, A. von. The most remarkable year in the life of, containing an Account of his Exile into Siberia. Translated by B. Beresford. 3 vols. *Plates.* 12° 1802
—— Travels through Italy in the years 1804 and 1805. 4 vols. 12° 1806
—— *See* Eyriès, Vol. 6 ; Phillips [1], Vols. 1, 4 : Appendix 1.

Kotzebue, Otto von. Narrative of a Journey into Persia in the suite of the Russian Embassy in 1817. Translated from the German. *Plates.* 8° 1819
—— A Voyage of Discovery into the South Sea and Beering's Straits, for the purpose of exploring a North-East Passage, undertaken in the years 1815-18, &c. 3 vols. *Maps and plates.* 8° 1821

Koudelka, Alfred Freiherr von. *See* Dorn, A.

Kouli Khan. The History of the life and surprising Transactions of Thomas Kouli Khan, late Sophi of Persia, including a complete view of all his military exploits, his conquest of India, and deposition and restoration of the Great Moghol. By H. W. Dilworth. *Plates.* 12° 1758

Kouropatkine. *See* Kuropatkin.

Koutorga, Prof. S. Description of a Geological Map of the Province of St Petersburg. MS. N.D.

Kovalefsky, Maxime. Law and Custom in the Caucasus. [In Russian.] 2 vols. 8° *Moscow*, 1890

Kovalevsky, E. de. Les Kourdes et les Jésides, ou les adviateurs du démon. 8° *Brussels*, 1890

Kovalevsky, M. Pshaves: an Ethnographical Sketch. [In Russian.] 8*
　　　　　　　　N.P., N. D.

Krafft, Hugues. Souvenirs de notre Tour du Monde. *Maps and plates.* Small folio *Paris*, 1885

Krafft, Captain J. C. P. de. *See* United States, E, *a* (Navigation) : Appendix 2.

Krahmer, —. Die Russisch-asiatischen Grenzlande. [Translated from the Russian of Venukoff.] *Map.* 8°
　　　　　　　　Leipzig, 1874

Kramer, D. G. *See* Ritter.

Kramer, Gustavus. Commentatio Critica de Codicibus qui Strabonis Geographica continent, Manuscriptis. 4* *Berlin*, 1840

Kranz, M. Natur- und Kulturleben der Zulus, nach vieljährigen Beobachtungen, statistischen und climatischen Berichten geschildert. 12° *Wiesbaden*, 1880

Krapf, J. L. Three Chapters of Genesis translated into the Sooahelee Language. With an Introduction by W. W. Greenough. 8* N.P., N.D.
—— Imperfect Outline of the Elements of the Galla Language ; with Remarks concerning the Nation of the Gallas, by C. W. Isenberg. 12° 1840
—— Vocabulary of the Galla Language. 12° 1842
—— Vocabulary of Six East African Languages (Kisuáheli, Kiníka, Kikámba, Kipokómo, Kihiáu, Kigálla). 4°
　　　　　　　　Tübingen, 1850
—— Outline of the Elements of the Kisuáheli Language, with special reference to the Kiníka Dialect. 8°
　　　　　　　　Tübingen, 1850
—— Vocabulary of the Engútuk Eloi-Kôb, or of the Language of the Wakuafi Nation in the interior of Equatorial Africa. 8° *Tübingen*, 1854
—— Travels, Researches, and Missionary Labours, during an Eighteen Years' Residence in Eastern Africa ; with an Appendix respecting the Snow-capped Mountains, the Sources of the Nile, the Languages and Literature of Abessinia and Eastern Africa, and a concise Account of Geographical Researches in Eastern Africa up to the Discovery of the Uyenyesi by Dr Livingstone, by E. G. Ravenstein. *Portrait, maps, and plates.* 8° 1860
—— A Dictionary of the Suahili Language; with Introduction, containing an Outline of a Suahili Grammar. *Portrait.* Large 8° 1882
—— *See* Isenberg ; Mayer, J.

Krarup, F. Zeniernes Rejse til Norden, et Tolknings Forsög. *Maps.* 12*
　　　　　　　　Copenhagen, 1878

Krasheninnikov, Stefan Petrovich. The History of Kamtschatka and the Kurilsky Islands, with the Countries adjacent. . . Translated into English by James Grieve. *Maps and plates.* 4° *Gloucester*, 1764
——Beschreibung des Landes Kamtschatka. *Maps and plates.* 4° *Lemgo*, 1766

Krause, Dr Arthur, and Dr Aurel Krause. Katalog ethnologischer Gegenstände aus dem Tschaktschenlande und dem Südöstlichen Alaska. 8° *Bremen*, 1882

Krause, Dr Aurel. Die Tlinket Indianer. Ergebnisse einer Reise nach der Nordwest Küste von Amerika und der Beringstrasse ; ausgeführt im Auftrage der Bremer Geographisches Gesellschaft in den Jahren 1880-81, durch die Doctoren Arthur und Aurel Krause, geschildert von Dr Aurel Krause. *Map and illustrations.* 8° *Jena*, 1885

Krause, F. M. *See* Victoria, B : Appendix 2.

Krause, Gottlob Adolf. Mittheilungen der Rieheek'schen Niger - Expedition. 1. Ein Beitrag zur Kenntniss der Fulischen Sprache in Afrika. *Map.* 8° *Leipzig,* 1884
—— The same. 2. Proben der Sprache von Gbāt in der Sáhārā mit Haussanischer und Deutscher Uebersetzung. *Map.* 8° *Leipzig,* 1884
Kreeft, Chr. First Russian Railroad, from St Petersburg to Zarscoe-selo and Pawlowsk. Translated from the German. 8* 1837
Kreil, Karl. Magnetische und Geographische Ortsbestimmungen an den Küsten des Adriatischen Golfes im Jahre 1854. *Plate.* 4* 1855
—— Anleitung zu den magnetischen Beobachtungen. 8° *Vienna,* 1858
Kreitner, G. Report of the Third International Geographical Congress, Venice, September 1881. 8* 1882
—— Im fernen Osten, Reisen des Grafen Bela Széchenyí in Indien, Japan, China, Tibet, und Birma in den Jahren 1877-1880. *Maps and illustrations.* 8° *Vienna,* 1881
Krempelhuber, J. See "Novara."
Krenner, J. A. Die Eishöhle von Dobschau. *Plates.* Folio *Budapest,* 1874
Kretschmann, E. See Verestchagin.
Kretschmer, Konrad. Die physische Erdkunde im Christlichen Mittelalter. (Penck's Geographische Abhandlungen, Band IV.,Heft 1.) Royal 8° *Vienna,* 1889
—— Die Entdeckung Amerika's in ihrer Bedeutung für die Geschichte des Weltbildes. Large 4°, with Atlas, folio *Berlin,* 1892
Kriegk, Georg Ludwig. Kurze physisch - geographische Beschreibung der Umgegend von Frankfurt am Main, oder der Ebene des unteren Mains und des anstossenden Taunus. Imp. 8* *Frankfort,* 1839
—— Schriften zur allgemeinen Erdkunde. 8° *Leipzig,* 1840
Krishna, Pundit (A—K). See Hennessy, J. B. N.
Kromer, E. To the Top of Roraima. [Newspaper Cuttings.] 8* N.D.
Krones, Dr F. von. See Germany, C: Appendix 2.
Kropotkin, P. Orographical Sketch of the Districts of Minusinsk and Krasnoyarsk. [In Russian.] *Map.* 8* *St Petersburg,* 1873
—— General Orographical Sketch of Eastern Siberia [In Russian.] *Map and tables.* 8* *St Petersburg,* 1875
—— Researches on the Glacier Period. [In Russian.] *Maps and plates.* Small folio *St Petersburg,* 1876
—— What Geography ought to be. (From the *Nineteenth Century.*) 8* 1885

Kruijt, J. A. Atjeh en de Atjehers. Twee jaren Blokkade op Sumatra's· Noordoost-Kust. *Maps and plates.* 8° *Leyden,* 1877
Krümmel, Professor Otto. Versuch einer vergleichenden Morphologie der Meeresräume. 8° *Leipzig,* 1879
—— Bemerkungen über die Meeresströmungen und Temperaturen der Falklandsee. *Maps.* 4* *Hamburg,* 1882
—— Der Ozean. Eine Einführung in die allgemeine Meereskunde. *Illustrations.* 12° *Leipzig,* 1886
—— Die Temperaturverteilung in den Ozeanen. 1. Die Oberflächentemperaturen. *Maps.* Large 8* [*Weimar,* 1887]
—— Reisebeschreibung der Plankton-Expedition. *Maps and illustrations.* 4° *Kiel,* 1892
—— Geophysikalische Beobachtungen der Plankton-Expedition. *Maps.* 4° *Kiel,* 1893
—— See Boguslawski ; Peschel.
Kruse, C. Kurze Anzeigen und Erläuterungen über meinen Atlas zur Geschichte aller Europäischen Länder und Staaten. 12° *Halle,* 1812
Kruse, Dr F. See Seetzen.
Krusenstern, Adam John de. Voyage round the World, 1803-6, on board the ships "Nadeshda" and "Neva." Translated from the German by R. B. Hoppner. 2 vols. *Maps and plates.* 4° 1813
—— Recueil de Mémoires Hydrographiques pour servir d'analyse et d'explication à l'Atlas de l'Océan Pacifique. 2 vols. 4° *St Petersburg,* 1824-27
—— Précis du Système, &c., de l'Instruction publique en Russie. 8° *Warsaw,* 1837
—— (the first Russian Circumnavigator). Memoir of. Translated from the German by his daughter Madame Charlotte Bernhardi, and edited by Adm. Sir John Ross. *Portrait.* 8° 1856
—— Admiral J. A. von Krusenstern. [A biography in German.] 8* *St Petersburg,* 1869
—— See Eyriès, Vol. 6 : Appendix 1.
Krusenstern, Paul von. Wissenschaftliche Beobachtungen auf einer Reise in das Petschora-Land, im Jahre 1843. *Maps and plates.* 4° *St Petersburg,* 1846
Krusinski, Father Jude. The History of the Revolution of Persia ; taken from the Memoirs of Father Krusinski, Procurator of the Jesuits at Ispahan, who lived Twenty Years in that Country. Done into English, from the Original, with Additions by Father Du Cerceau. 8° *Dublin,* 1729
Kugelberg, O. F. See Sweden, A (Geologiska Undersökning) : Appendix 2.

Kügelgen, P. von. *See* Schrenck and Maximowicz, Vol. 2.

Kuhn, Carl. Ueber das Klima von München. 4*   *Munich*, 1854

Kulczycki, A. Détermination des Longitudes au Moyen des Chronomètres. Observations pour la détermination des Longitudes des îles Taiti, Ana, Faarava, Taroa, Manihi, Auura, Rairoa. Discussion par M. V. Dumoulin. 8°
Paris, 1851

Kumlien, L. Contributions to the Natural History of Arctic America, made in connection with the Howgate Polar Expedition, 1877-78. 8°   *Washington*, 1879

Kunstmann, Friedrich. Afrika vor den Entdeckungen der Portugiesen. 4°
Munich, 1853

Kuntze, C. E. O. Zur ältesten Geschichte der Pflanzen. 4*   N.P., N.D.

—— Die Schutzmittel der Pflanzen gegen Thiere und Wetterungunst, und die Frage vom salzfreien Urmeer. Studien über Phytophylaxis und Phytogeogenesis. 8°   *Leipzig*, 1877

—— Monographie der Gattung Cinchona, L. 8*   *Leipzig*, 1878

—— Cinchona Arten, Hybriden und Cultur der Chininbäume. Monographische Studie nach eigenen Beobachtungen in den Ampflanzungen auf Java und im Himalaya. *Photographs.* 8° *Leipzig*, 1878

Kuntze, Dr Otto. Um die Erde. Reiseberichte eines Naturforschers. 8°
Leipzig, 1881

Künzel, Heinrich. Ober - Californien : eine geographische Schilderung für den Zweck Deutscher Auswanderung und Ansiedelung. *Maps.* 12* *Darmstadt*, 1848

Kupffer, A. T. Voyage dans les Environs de Mont Elbrouz, dans le Caucase, en 1829. *Plate.* 4° *St Petersburg*, 1830

—— Travaux de la Commission pour fixer les Mesures et Poids de Russie. 2 vols. 4°   *St Petersburg*, 1841

——. Résumés des Observations Météorologiques . . . dans Russie. 4*
St Petersburg, 1846

—— Recherches Expérimentales sur l'Elasticité des Métaux, faites à l'Observatoire Physique Central de Russie. Vol. 1 [wants sheet 52.] *Plates St Petersburg*, 1860

Kuropatkin, A. N. Les Confins Anglo-Russes dans l'Asie Centrale. Étude Historique, Géographique, Politique, et Militaire sur la Kachgarie. Traduite par G. Le Marchand. 12° *Paris*, 1879

—— Kashgaria, Eastern or Chinese Turkistan : Historical and Geographical Sketch of the Country, its Military Strength, Industries, and Trade. Translated from the Russian by Walter E. Gowan. Large 8° *Calcutta*, 1882

Kurz, S. Report on the Vegetation of the Andaman Islands. *Map.* Folio* [1867]

Kuscinski, A. *See* Piassetsky.

Küttner, C. Gottlob. *See* Phillips [1], Vol. 1 : Appendix 1.

Kwast, Capt. Matthys. *See* Burney, Vol. 3 : Appendix 1.

Kyle, Capt. H. D. Three MS. Copies of his Memoranda respecting Expeditions to Nodwenga, Fort Hare, and the Ambaca Country.

L

L——, H. A. "The Old Shekarry." *See* Levison.

L——, G. C. Useful Instructions for Travellers. 8°   1793

L——, W. Minicoy, the Island of Women. (From *Blackwood's Magazine*.) 8* 1889

L——, W. B. The Key to Fortune in New Lands. 12°   1868

—— Diamonds and Gold : The Three Main Routes to the South African Ophir, and how to Equip for the Journey. By W. B. L. *Map.* Small 8*   1871

Labanoff, Prince Alexandre. Catalogue des Cartes Géographiques, Topographiques, et Marines, de la Bibliothèque du Prince Alexandre Labanoff de Rostoff, à Saint-Petersbourg. Suivi d'une Notice de Manuscrits. 8°   *Paris*, 1823

Labat, Jean-Baptiste. Nouvelle Relation de l'Afrique Occidentale. 5 vols. *Maps and illustrations.* 12°   *Paris*, 1728

—— Relation Historique de l'Ethiopie Occidentale. 5 vols. *Maps and illustrations.* 12°   *Paris*, 1732

—— *See* Allgemeine Historie, Vol. 3 : Appendix 1.

Labillardiére, ——. Voyage in Search of La Pérouse, performed by order of the Constituent Assembly, during the years 1791-94. Translated from the French. *Map and plates.* 4°   1800

—— Account of a Voyage in Search of La Perouse, 1791-93, in the "Recherche" and "Espérance," under the command of Rear-Adm. Bruni d'Entrecasteaux. Translated from the French. 2 vols. 8°. *Maps and plates* 4°   1802

—— *See* Pelham, Vol. 2 : Appendix 1.

Lablache, P. Vidal. *See* Vidal : Appendix 1.

"La Bonite" Voyage. *See* Vaillant.

Labonne, Dr Henry. L'Islande et l'Archipel des Færœr. *Maps and illustrations.* 12°   *Paris*, 1888

Laborde, Comte Alex. de. Histoire abregée de la Mer du Sud. 3 vols. *Maps.* 8°   *Paris*, 1791

—— A View of Spain, comprising a Descriptive Itinerary of each Province, and a General Statistical Account of the Country. Translated from the French. 5 vols. *Maps.* 8°   1809

Laborde, Comte Alex de. Itinéraire descriptif de l'Espagne. Troisième édition, revue, corrigée, et considérablement augmentée ; précédé d'une Notice sur la Configuration de l'Espagne et son climat, par M. de Humboldt ; d'un Aperçu sur la Géographie Physique, par M. le Col. Bory de Saint-Vincent ; et d'un Abrégé Historique de la Monarchie Espagnole et des invasions de la Péninsule jusqu'à nos jours. 6 vols. *Plates.* 8° *Paris,* 1827-30

Laborde, Léon de. Voyage de l'Arabie Pétrée, par Léon de Laborde et Linant. *Plates.* Folio *Paris,* 1830

—— Journey through Arabia Petræa to Mount Sinai and the excavated City of Petra, the Edom of the Prophecies. *Map and plates.* 8° 1836

Labre, A. R. P. Itinerario de Exploração do Amazonas á Bolivia. 8* *Belem,* 1887

Lacaille, Louis. Connaissance de Madagascar. 8° *Paris,* 1863

Lacassagne, Dr. Société d'Anthropologie de Lyon. L'Homme Criminel comparé a l'Homme primitif. 8* *Lyon,* 1882

Lacaye, Dr H. Souvenirs de Madagascar. Voyage à Madagascar : Histoire, Population, Mœurs, Institutions. *Map and plate.* 8° *Paris,* 1881

Lacerda, F. J. M. de. Journey to Cazembe in 1798. Translated and annotated by Captain R. F. Burton. Also, Journey of the Pombeiros, P. J. Baptista and Amaro José, across Africa, from Angola to Tette on the Zambeze ; translated by B. A. Beadle ; and a résumé of the Journey of MM. Monteiro and Gammitto, by Dr C. T. Beke. *Map.* 8° 1873

Lacerda, José de. Examen das Viagens do Dr Livingstone. *Maps.* 8° *Lisbon,* 1867

—— Portuguese African Territories. 8* 1865

Lacharme, L. de. Inter-Oceanic Canal Route of Paya. *Map.* 8* *New York,* 1874

Lachlan, Major R. On the Establishment of a System of Simultaneous Meteorological Observations, &c., throughout the British North American Provinces. 4* *Toronto,* 1854

—— On the Periodical Rise and Fall of the Great Canadian Lakes. 4* *Toronto,* 1854

—— A Paper and Resolutions in Advocacy of the Establishment of a Uniform System of Meteorological Observations throughout the whole American Continent. 8* *Cincinnati,* 1859

Lacouperie, Prof. A. Terrien de. The Old Numerals, the Counting-Rods, and the Swan-Pan in China. 8* 1883

—— The Yueh-ti and the Early Buddhist Missionaries in China. 12* 1887

—— The Miryeks or Stone-Men of Corea. 8* *Hertford,* 1887

Lacouperie, Prof. A. Terrien de. The Languages of China before the Chinese : Researches on the Languages spoken by the pre-Chinese Races of China proper, previously to the Chinese Occupation. 8° 1887

—— Formosa ; Notes on MSS., Languages and Races (including a Note on Nine Formosan MSS. by E. Colborne Baber). *Plates.* 8* *Hertford,* 1887

—— The Sinim of Isaiah not the Chinese. 8* [1887]

—— The Old Babylonian Characters and their Chinese Derivates. 8* 1888

—— Did Cyrus introduce Writing into India ? 8* N.D.

—— *See* Colquhoun.

La Croix. *See* Pinkerton.

Lacroix, Léon. Projet d'Exploration dans l'Afrique Centrale par l'Ouellé. *Map.* 8* *Lille,* 1881

Lacrole, Frederico and Julio. Proyecto presentado a las Honorables Cámaras Legislativas sobre el Establecimiento de un Ferrocarril. 8* *Buenos Ayres,* 1866

Lacrole, Julio. Los Ferro-Carriles económicos y el Porvenir de la Republica Argentina. 8* *Buenos Ayres,* 1866

—— Estudio sobre la distribucion de Agua en las Ciudades. 12* *Buenos Ayres,* 1866

Lacroze, V. Histoire du Christianisme des Indes. 2 vols. *Maps and plates.* 12° *The Hague,* 1757-58

Lacy, John. *See* Hakluyt, Vol. 2 : Appendix 1.

Ladichère, A. M. Uriage et ses environs ; Guide pittoresque et descriptif. 2nd edition. *Plates.* Oblong 8° *Uriage,* N.D.

Ladislaus Magyar. *See* Magyar ; Rónay.

Ladrilleros, Juan. *See* Burney, Vol. 1 ; Callander, Vol. 1 : Appendix 1.

Laestadius, L. L. *See* Gaimard, Paul.

Laërne, C. F. Van Delden. Brazil and Java : Report on Coffee Culture in America, Asia, and Africa, to H.E. the Minister of the Colonies. *Plates, maps, and diagrams.* 8° 1885

Laet, Joannes de. Hispania sive de Regis Hispaniæ regnis et opibus Commentarius. 16° *Leyden,* 1629

—— Belgii Confœderati Respublica : seu Gelriæ. Holland. Zeland. Traject. Fris. Transisal. Groning. chorographica Politicaque descriptio. 16° *Leyden,* 1630

—— Persia, seu Regni Persici status, variaque itinera in atque per Persiam, cum aliquot iconibus incolarum. *Plates.* 16° *Leyden,* 1633

Lafitau, Père. Mœurs des Sauvages Ameriquains, comparées aux Mœurs des premier temps. 2 vols. *Plates.* 4° *Paris,* 1724

Lafitau, Père. Histoire des Découvertes et Conquestes des Portugais dans le Nouveau Monde. 2 vols. *Map and plates.* 4°   *Paris*, 1733

Lafitte, J. Le Dahomé : Souvenirs de voyage et de Mission. 3rd edition. *Map and plate.* 8°   *Tours*, 1874

Lafond de Lurcy, Capt. Gabriel. Quinze Ans de Voyages autour du Monde. 2 vols. 8°   *Paris*, 1840
—— Voyages autour du Monde, et Naufrages célébres. 8 vols. *Portrait and plates.* Royal 8°   *Paris*, 1844
[For Contents of these volumes, *see* Appendix 1.]

Lafone y Quevedo, Samuel A. Lóndres y Catamarca. *Frontispiece, map, and plan.* 8°   *Buenos Aires*, 1888

Lafont, J. *See* Ward, C. Y.

Lago, A. P. B. do. Survey of the Coast of the Province of Maranham, from Jericoacoara to the Island of St John, and of the Entrance of the Bay of St Marcos. 4°   1821
—— Estatistica Historica-Geografica da Provincia do Maranhão. *Tables.* 8°   *Lisbon*, 1822

Lagrange, C. Observatoire Royal de Bruxelles. Exposition critique de la Méthode de Wronski pour la Résolution des Problèmes de Mécanique céleste. 1ère Partie. 4°   *Brussels*, 1882

Lagus, W. Quelques Remarques et une proposition au sujet de la première Expédition Russe au Japon. 8* *Leyden*, 1878
—— Numi Cufici aliaque Orientis monumenta vetera in Finlandia reperta. 8*   *Leyden*, 1878

Laharpe, Col. F. C. La Neutralité des Gouvernans de la Suisse, 1789. 12°   *Paris*, 1797

Laharpe, J. F. Abrégé de l'Histoire Générale des Voyages. 24 vols. 8°   *Paris*, 1816
[For full Title and Contents of these volumes, *see* Appendix 1.]

Lahontan, Baron. New Voyages to North America, containing an Account of the several Nations of that vast Continent, their Customs, Commerce, and Way of Navigation upon the Rivers ; a Geographical Description of Canada, &c. ; with an Account of the Author's Retreat to Portugal and Denmark, and his Remarks on these Courts ; to which is added a Dictionary of the Algonquin Language. 2 vols. *Maps and plates.* 8°   1703
—— The same. 2nd edition. Vol. 2. 1735
—— *See* Pinkerton, Vol. 13 ; Allgemeine Historie, Vol. 16 : Appendix 1.

Lahovari, George Joan. Dictionar Geografic al Judetului Arges. 8°   *Bucharest*, 1888

Laing, Major Gordon A. Travels in the Timannee, Kooranko, and Soolima Countries in Western Africa. *Map and plates.* 8°   1825
—— *See* Morocco : Appendix 2.

Laing, J. A Voyage to Spitzbergen, containing an Account of that Country, of the Zoology of the North, of the Shetland Isles, and of the Whale Fishery ; with an Appendix containing an Historical Account of the Dutch, English, and American Whale Fisheries, &c. 12°   *Edinburgh*, 1822

Laing, Samuel. Journal of a Residence in Norway during the years 1834, 1835, and 1836. 8°   1836
—— The same. New edition. 12°   1851
—— Tour in Sweden in 1838 ; comprising Obervations on the Moral, Political, and Economical State of the Swedish Nation. 8°   1839
—— Notes of a Traveller on the Social and Political State of France, Prussia, Switzerland, Italy, and other parts of Europe. First series. 12°   1854

Laird, Lieut. C. *See* United States, E, *a* : Appendix 2.

Laird, E. K. The Rambles of a Globe Trotter in Australia, Japan, China, Java, India, and Cashmere. 2 vols. *Map and photographs.* 8°   1875

Laird, Macgregor. Central Africa Company "Limited." [Prospectus.] *Map.* 4*   [1858]
—— Statement made to the Central African Company. *Map.* Folio*   1858
—— **and R. A. K. Oldfield.** Narrative of an Expedition into the Interior of Africa, by the River Niger, in 1832-34. 2 vols. *Map and plates.* 8°   1837

Laird, William. Letters on the Export Coal Trade of Liverpool. *Map and plates.* 8*   *Liverpool*, 1850

Lakey, Dr James. *See* Delafield.

La Lande. *See* De la Lande.

Lalanne, L., and G. Lemoine. Sur les dernières crues de la Seine. 4*   *Paris*, 1879

Lal, Mohan. Travels in the Punjab, Afghanistan, and Turkistan, to Balk, Bokhara, and Herat ; and a Visit to Great Britain and Germany. 8°   1846

Lallemand, Charles. Tunis et ses Environs. *Coloured illustrations.* 4°   *Paris*, 1890
—— La Tunisie, Pays de Protectorat Français. *Illustrations.* 4° *Paris*, 1892

Lalor, J. Papers connected with a Report on the Hill Districts to the South-West of Mehur, in Sind. [From India Records, No. 58.] Royal 8° *Bombay*, 1860

Lamalle, Dureau de. Géographie Physique de la Mer Noire, de l'Intérieur de l'Afrique, et de la Méditerranée. *Maps.* 8°   *Paris*, 1807

Lamalie, Dureau de. Climatologie comparée de l'Italie et de l'Andalousie Anciennes et Modernes. 8*
Paris, 1849

Lamansky, Eugène. Esquisse Géographique du Bassin de la Mer d'Aral, et quelques Traits des Mœurs des Habitants de Boukhara, Khiva, et Kokan. 8*
Paris, 1858

Lamarck, C. C. *See* Pallas.

Lamarck, J. B. *See* Thunberg.

Lamarck, J. P. A. de M. de. Histoire Naturelle des Animaux sans Vertèbres, &c. Vols. 5, 6, 7. 8° *Paris*, 1811-22

Lamartine, Alphonse de. A Pilgrimage to the Holy Land in 1832-33. 3 vols. *Portrait.* 8° 1835

—— De quelques faits Bibliques, retrouvés dans les Hiéroglyphes Chinois, et Réfutation de quelques Assertions de M. Renan, suivi de Remarques sur quelques erreurs sur la Chine et Confucius. 8*
Versailles, 1859

Lambert, C. and S. The Voyage of the "Wanderer." From the Journals and Letters of C. and S. Lambert. Edited by Gerald Young. *Chart and illustrations.* Large 8° 1883

Lambert, Gustave. Projet de Voyage au Pole Nord ; Note lue à la Société de Geographie, . . 1866. 8* *Paris*, 1866

—— Stand des Nordpolaren Erforschungsprojektes ganz besonders in Bezug auf Betheiligung Preussens, Englands, Frankreichs. 4* *Gotha*, 1867

—— La Question du Pole Nord. Lettres adressées à M. Jules Duval. 8*
Paris, 1867

—— L'Expédition au Pole Nord. 8°
Paris, 1868

—— *See* Malte-Brun.

Lambert, J. Travels through Canada and the United States of North America, in the years 1806, 1807, and 1808 ; to which are added Biographical Notices and Anecdotes of some of the Leading Characters in the United States. 3rd edition. 2 vols. *Map and plates.* 8° 1816

Lambert, Paul. Notice sur la Ville de Maroc. *Plan.* 8* [*Paris*, 1868]

Laming, James. Steam Communication with Australia: a Letter addressed to the Lord Mayor of London. *Map.* 8* 1856

Lamiral, ——. Affrique et le Peuple Affriquain, considérés sous tous leurs rapports avec notre Commerce et nos Colonies. *Map and plates.* 8° *Paris*, 1789

Lamont, J. Untersuchungen über die Richtung und Stärke des Erdmagnetismus an verschiedenen Puncten des südwestlichen Europa. *Plates.* 4°
Munich, 1858

Lamont, James. Seasons with the Sea-Horses ; or, Sporting Adventures in the Northern Seas. *Map and plates.* 8° 1861

—— Meteorological Register, s.s. Yacht "Diana," 4th May to 12th Sept. 1869, and 22nd April to 24th Aug. 1870. MS. *Chart.* Small 4°

—— Yachting in the Arctic Seas ; or, Notes of Five Voyages of Sport and Discovery in the Neighbourhood of Spitzbergen and Novaya Zemlya. *Map and plates.* 8° 1876

Lamouroux, J. V. F. Résumé d'un Cours Elémentaire de Géographie Physique ; augmentée d'une Table Analytique et d'une Table Alphabétique des Matières, précédée d'un Notice Biographique. *Portrait.* 8° *Paris*, 1829

Lamprey, Jones. Further Remarks on the Ethnology of the Chinese. 8* 1867

—— Notes of a Journey in the North-West Neighbourhood of Pekin. 8* [1867]

Lamprey, J. H. On certain Antiquities found in the Islands of the Pacific and South Seas. 8* N.D.

Lancaster, Sir James. *See* Astley, Vol. 1 ; Burney, Vol. 2 ; Gottfried ; Hakluyt's Voyages, Vols. 2, 4 ; Hakluyt Soc. Publ., Vol. 56 ; Kerr, Vol. 8 ; Knox's New Collection, Vol. 2 ; Purchas, Vol. 1 ; Allgemeine Historie, Vol. 1 ; "The World Displayed," Vol. 8 : Appendix 1.

Lanckoróncki, Comte Charles. Les Villes de la Pamphylie et de la Pisidie. Ouvrage publié avec le concours de G. Niemann et E. Petersen, par le Comte Charles Lanckoróncki. Tome premier : La Pamphylie. *Maps, plans, and illustrations.* Large 4° *Paris*, 1890

—— The same. Tome second. La Pisidie. *Illustrations.* Large 4° *Paris*, 1893

Landau, Baron Wilhelm von. Travels in Asia, Australia, and America, comprising the period between 1879 and 1887. Part 1. 12° *New York*, 1888

—— Reisen in Asien, Australien, und Amerika. 12° *Berlin*, 1889

Lander, Richard. Records of Captain Clapperton's Last Expedition to Africa, with the subsequent Adventures of the Author. 2 vols. *Portrait.* 8° 1830

—— **and John Lander.** Journal of an Expedition to Explore the Course and Termination of the Niger, with a Narrative of a Voyage down that River to its Termination. 3 vols. *Maps and plates.* 18° 1833

Landmann, Abbé. Mémoires au Roi sur la Colonisation de l'Algérie. 8°
Paris, 1845

Landor, A. H. Savage. Alone with the Hairy Ainu, or 3,800 Miles on a Packsaddle in Yezo, and a Cruise to the Kurile Islands. *Maps and illustrations.* 8° 1893

—— A Journey round Yezo and up its larger Rivers. Roy. Geog. Soc. Suppl. Papers, Vol. 3. *Map.* Large 8° 1893

Landor, Edward Wilson. Adventures in the North of Europe illustrative of the Poetry and Philosophy of Travel. 2 vols. *Plates.* 8° 1836

Landor, J. W. Savage. *See* Casati.

Landsborough, W. Journal of an Expedition from Carpentaria in Search of Burke and Wills. *Map and portraits.* 8° *Melbourne,* 1862

—— Newspaper Cuttings, containing the Journal of his Expedition to Carpentaria in 1866. Folio* 1866

—— *See* Westgarth.

Landseer, John. Sabæan Researches, in a Series of Essays and Lectures, on the Engraved Hieroglyphics of Chaldea, Egypt, and Canaan ; illustrations of Babylonian Cylinders and other Inedited Monuments of Antiquity. 4° 1823

Landt, Rev. G. Description of the Feroe Islands. Translated from the Danish. *Map and plates.* 8° 1810

Lane, E. W. An Account of the Manners and Customs of the Modern Egyptians, written in Egypt during the years 1833-35. 2 vols. *Woodcuts.* 8° 1836

—— The same. 5th edition. 2 vols. Small 8° 1871

—— *See* Poole.

Lane, Henrie. *See* Purchas, Vol. 3, Book 2 : Appendix 1.

Lane, James C. Report of the Surveys of the Rivers Atrato, Pata, and Baudo, showing the Practicability of Constructing a Ship Canal connecting the Atlantic and Pacific Oceans ; also the Act to incorporate the Atlantic and Pacific Canal Company passed by the Legislature of New York. *Maps.* 8* *New York,* 1856

Lane-Poole, Stanley. Cairo : Sketches of its History, Monuments, and Social Life ; with numerous illustrations by G. L. Seymour, Harry Fenn, J. D. Woodward, and others. Square 8° 1892

Lanessan, J. L. de. L'Expansion Coloniale de la France. Étude Économique, Politique, et Géographique sur les Établissements Français d'Outre-Mer. *Maps.* 8° *Paris,* 1886

—— La Tunisie. *Map.* 8° *Paris,* 1887

—— L'Indo-Chine Français. Étude Politique, Économique, et Administrative sur la Cochin Chine, le Cambodge, l'Annam, et le Tonkin. *Maps.* 8° *Paris,* 1889

Lanfranconi, E. Koyép. Europa viziutai és a Dunafolyam Szabályozásának fontosságáról különös tekintettel a Dévény és Gönyökoyti vorrabra. Small folio *Pressburg,* 1880

—— Ueber die Wasserstrassen Mittel-Europa's und die Wichtigkeit der Regulirung des Donaustromes, mit besonderer Berücksichtigung der Strecke zwischen Theben-Gönyö. Small folio *Pressburg,* 1880

—— Des Voies de Communication par Eau de l'Europe centrale, et de l'Importance de la Régularisation au Danube, spécialement du Passage entre Thèbes et Gönyö. *Atlas of plates.* Folio *Vienna,* 1881

—— Rettung Ungarns vor Ueberschwemmungen. *Maps.* Folio *Budapest,* 1882

Lang, Andrew. *See* Romilly.

Lang, J. Dunmore. View of the Origin and Migrations of the Polynesian Nation, demonstrating their Ancient Discovery and Progressive Settlement of the Continent of America. 8° 1834

—— An Historical Account of New South Wales to the close of 1836, both as a Penal Settlement and as a British Colony. 2 vols. *Map.* 8° 1837

—— The same, from the Founding of the Colony in 1788 to the present day. 2 vols. *Map and plate.* Small 8° 1875

Lang, R. H. Cyprus, its History, its Present Resources, and Future Prospects. *Maps and plates.* 8° 1878

Lang, Lieut.-Col. W. Names, Titles, &c., of the Principal Chiefs of Kattywar, with brief Historical Notices of some of them. List of Fortified Places in the Province of Kattywar. [From the India Records, No. 37.] *Large map separate.* Royal 8° *Bombay,* 1856

Langdon, W. B. A Descriptive Catalogue of the Chinese Collection, now exhibiting at St George's Place, Hyde Park Corner, London ; with Condensed Accounts of the Genius, Government, History, Literature, Agriculture, Arts, Trades, Manners, Customs, and Social Life of the People of the Celestial Empire. *Illustrations.* 8° 1842

Lange, Sir Daniel A. The Isthmus of Suez Canal Question, viewed in its Political bearings. 8* 1859

—— Reflections in the Egyptian Desert. 12* 1862

—— Sir Daniel Lange and the Suez Canal : Debates in Parliament. Large 8* 1890

Lange, Dr Henry. Südbrasilien, die Provinzen São Pedro do Rio Grande do Sul-Santa Catharina und Paraná mit Rück, sicht auf die Deutsche Kolonisation. 2nd edition. *Maps and illustrations.* 8° *Leipzig,* 1885

Lange, H. M. Het Eiland Banka en zijne Aangelegenheden. *Maps and table.* 8° *'sHertogenbosch*, 1850

Lange, Laurence. *See* Astley, Vol. 3 : Appendix 1.

Langegg, F. A. *See* Junker von Langegg.

Langen, L. *See* Allgemeine Historie, Vol. 5 : Appendix 1.

Langenbeck, Dr R. Die Theorieen über die Entstehung der Koralleninseln und Korallenriffe und ihre Bedeutung für geophysische Fragen. 8° *Leipzig*, 1890

Langeveldt van Hemert, A. J. *See* Robidé Van der Aa.

Langler, J. R. The Main Facts of Popular Astronomy and Mathematical Geography : a Manual for Students. 12° 1871

—— Pictorial Geography for Young Beginners. *Woodcuts.* Small 4° 1874

Langlès, L. Mémoire sur les Oasis. *See* Horneman, F.

—— *See* Mengin ; Norden ; Pallas ; Thunberg.

Langley, S. P. *See* United States, H, *b* : Appendix 2.

Langlois, Victor. Voyage dans la Cilicie et dans les Montagnes du Taurus, exécuté pendant les années 1852-53. *Plates.* 8° *Paris*, 1861

—— *See* Ptolemy.

Langsdorff, G. H. von. Voyages and Travels in various Parts of the World, 1803-7. 2 vols. *Portrait and plates.* 4° 1813

—— *See* Eyriès, Vol. 6 : Appendix 1.

Lanier, Alejo Helvecio. Geografia de la Isla de Pinos ó notas Hidrograficas, Topograficas, &c. Small 4* *Havana*, 1836

Lanier, Sydney. Florida, its Scenery, Climate, and History ; with an Account of Charleston, Savannah, Augusta, and Aiken ; and a Chapter for Consumptives : being a complete Handbook and Guide. *Illustrations.* 12° *Philadelphia* [1875]

Lankenau, H. von, and L. v. d. Oelsnitz. Das heutige Russland. 2 vols. *Plates.* 8° *Leipzig*, 1877

Lankester, Edwin, M.D., and Peter Redfern, M.D. Reports made to the Directors of the London (Watford) Spring Water Company, on the Results of Microscopical Examinations of the Organic Matters and Solid Contents of Waters supplied from the Thames and other Sources ; with a Chemical Report on the Quality of various Specimens of Water from Chalk Springs near Watford, by Thomas Clark, M.D. *Woodcuts and tables.* 8* 1852

Lanman, Charles. Adventures in the Wilds of North America. Edited by C. R. Weld. 12° 1854

Lans, W. H. Bijdrage tot de Kennis der Kolonie Suriname. 8° *The Hague*, 1842

Lansdell, Dr Henry. Russian Central Asia, including Kuldja, Bokhara, Khiva, and Merv. 2 vols. *Frontispiece, maps, and illustrations.* 8° 1885

—— Through Central Asia ; with a Map and Appendix on the Diplomacy and Delimitation of the Russo - Afghan Frontier. *Illustrations.* 8° 1887

—— Diplomacy and Delimitation of the Russo-Afghan Frontier. (Being the Appendix to the Author's work, "Through Central Asia.") 8* 1887

—— Chinese Central Asia : a Ride to Little Tibet. 2 vols. *Maps and illustrations.* 8° 1893

Lanzerota, —. *See* "A General Collection of Voyages," p. 610 : Appendix 1.

Lanzoni, Prof. Primo. Stato Independente del Congo. Compendio di geografia fisica, politica, storica e commerciale. *Map, portrait, and illustrations.* 12° *Florence*, 1888

Lapelin, M. T. de. Reconnaissance Hydrographique des Côtes Occidentales du Centre-Amerique. *Maps and plates.* 8° *Paris*, 1854

La Pérouse, Jean François Galaup de. Voyage de, autour du Monde, 1780-88 ; rédigé par L. A. Milet-Mureau. 2 vols. *Portrait.* 4°, and Atlas folio 1799

—— *See* Lesseps ; *also* Eyriès, Vol. 1 ; Pelham, Vol. 2 : Appendix 1.

Laplace, Capt. Voyage autour du Monde, par les Mers de l'Inde et de Chine, exécuté sur la Corvette de l'état "La Favourite," pendant 1830-32. 4 vols. *Map.* 8° *Paris*, 1833-35

Lapparent, A. de. L'Écorce terrestre et son relief. 4* [*Paris*, 1884]

Lapworth, Prof. C. The Crust of the Earth : Address to the Geological Section of the British Association, Edinburgh. 8* 1892

Larcom, T. A. *See* Petty.

Larfeuil, M. de. Guide du Colon en Algérie, et Description des Productions de ce beau Pays. 8° *Paris*, 1848

"La Recherche." *See* Gaimard ; Laroche-Poncié, J. de.

Larenaudière, — de. *See* Malte-Brun.

Largeau, V. Le Pays de Rirha, Ouargla : Voyage à Rhadamès. *Map and plates.* 12° *Paris*, 1879

—— Le Sahara Algérien, les Déserts de l'Erg. 2nd edition. *Maps and illustrations.* 12° *Paris*, 1881

La Roncière Le Noury. *See* Noury.

Larpent, Sir George. *See* Porter.

La Roque. *See* De la Roque.

Larrabure y Unánue, E. Cañete : Apuntes Geograficos, Historicos, Estadisticos, y Arqueologicos. 12* *Lima*, 1874

Larrañaga, A. E. Curso de Geografia del Peru adoptado para la Enseñanza de los Colegios por la Direccion General de Estudios. 12* *Lima*, 1864

Larrieu, Abbé. La Grande Muraille de Chine, où il est prouvé que cette Muraille telle qu'elle est communément décrite non seulement n'existe pas, mais même n'a jamais existé ; suivi d'un article sur la Barrière de Pieux du Léao Tong. 8* *Paris*, 1887

Lartet, Edouard. Note sur Deux Nouveaux Siréniens Fossiles des Terrains Tertiaires du Basin de la Garonne. *Plate.* 8* *Paris*, 1866

—— **and H. Christy.** Reliquiæ Aquitanicæ : being Contributions to the Archæology and Palæontology of Périgord and the adjoining Provinces of Southern France. Edited by T. Rupert-Jones. *Maps and plates.* 4° 1865-75

Lartet, Louis. Recherches sur les Variations de Salure de l'Eau de la Mer Morte en Divers Points de sa Surface, et à Différentes Profondeurs, ainsi que sur l'Origine probable des sels qui entrent dans sa composition. 8* [*Paris*, 1866]
—— *See* Luynes.

Lartigue, —. Exposition du Système des Vents, ou Traité du Mouvement de l'Air à la Surface du Globe, et dans les Régions élevées de l'Atmosphère. *Maps.* 8° *Paris*, 1855

Lasalle, A. de. *See* Vaillant.

Lasaulx, A. von. Sicilien. Ein geographisches Charakterbild. 8* *Bonn*, 1879
—— Der Aetna. Nach den Manuscripten des verstorbenen Dr Wolfgang Sartorius, Freiherrn von Waltershausen. 2 vols. *Maps, plates, and portrait.* 4° *Leipzig*, 1880

Las Casas. *See* Casas.

Laslett, T. Timber and Timber Trees, Native and Foreign. Small 8° 1875

Lassalle, Charles. La Science Géographique devant le Congrès de la Sorbonne. (In No. 7 of "La Province," July 1886.) Small 8* *Paris*, 1886

Lassen, Christian. Zur Geschichte der Griechischen und Indoskythischen Könige in Baktrien, Kabul, und Indien. 8° *Bonn*, 1838

Lastarria, J. V. Lecciones de Jeografia Moderna . . . Nuevamente añadida por Santos Tornero. 10th edition. 12° *Valparaiso*, 1858
—— Historia Jeneral de la República de Chile desde su Independencia hasta nuestros dias. *Plates.* 8° *Santiago*, 1866

Lastarria, V. A. Represas para Augmentar las Aguas del Rio Rimac. Memoria presentada al Empresario Constructor Sr. D. Dionisio Derteano. *Plans.* 8° *Lima*, 1876

Latham, Robert Gordon. Natural History of the Varieties of Man. 8° 1850
—— The Ethnology of the British Islands. 12° 1852
—— The Ethnology of Europe. 12° 1852
—— On the Subjectivity of certain Classes in Ethnology. 8* 1853
—— The Native Races of the Russian Empire. *Map and plate.* 12° 1854
—— Descriptive Ethnology. 2 vols. 8° 1859
—— Opuscula : Essays, chiefly Philological and Ethnographical. 8° 1860
—— *See* Prichard, J. C.

Latham, Wilfrid. The States of the River Plate. 2nd edition. *Map.* 8° 1868

Latif, Syad Muhammad. History of the Panjáb, from the remotest antiquity to the present time. Large 8° *Calcutta*, 1891

Latimer, Isaac. A Summer Climate in Winter : Notes on Travel in the Islands of Teneriffe and Grand Canary. 2nd edition. *Maps.* 12° *Plymouth*, 1887

Latimer, S. Francis. The English in Canary Isles : being a Journal in Teneriffe and Gran Canaria, with latest information. *Maps and illustrations.* 12° *Plymouth*, 1888

Latreille, —. Familles Naturelles du Règne Animal. 8° *Paris*, 1825

Latrie, L. de Mas. Notice sur la Construction d'une Carte de l'Île de Chypre. 8° *Paris*, 1862
—— L'Île de Chypre, sa Situation Présente et ses Souvenirs du Moyen Age. *Map.* 12° *Paris*, 1879

Latrobe, C. J. Journal of a Visit to South Africa in 1815 and 1816, with some Account of the Missionary Settlements of the United Brethren near the Cape of Good Hope. *Map and plate.* 4° 1818
—— The Rambler in Mexico, 1834. *Map.* 8° 1836
—— Negro Education, Windward and Leeward Islands. [Parliamentary Paper.] Folio* 1838
—— Negro Education, British Guiana and Trinidad. [Parliamentary Paper.] Folio* 1839
—— *See* Eyriès, Vol. 11 : Appendix 1.

Latzina, Francis. The Argentine Republic as a Field for European Emigration : a Statistical and Geographical Review of the Country and its Resources, with all its various features. *Map.* Folio* *Buenos Ayres*, 1883
—— Geografia de la Republic Argentina. *Maps.* 8° *Buenos Ayres*, 1888
—— Diccionario Geográfico Argentino. 4° *Buenos Ayres*, 1891

Laube, G. C. Die Echinoiden der Oesterreichisch-Ungarischen oberen Tertiaerablagerungen. *Plates.* 4* *Vienna*, 1871

Laudonniere, René de. *See* Gottfried ; Hakluyt, Vol. 3 : Appendix 1.

Laughton, J. K. Physical Geography in its Relation to the Prevailing Winds and Currents. Small 8° 1870
—— An Introduction to the Practical and Theoretical Study of Nautical Surveying. 12° 1872
—— An Address delivered at the Annual General Meeting of the Meteorological Society, 17th January 1883. 8* 1883
—— The same. 16th January 1884. 8*

Laugier, E. Usage du Cercle Méridien portatif pour la Détermination des Positions Géographiques. *Plate.* 4°
Paris, 1852

Launay, L. de. *See* Martel, E. A.

Laurent, Peter. Classical Tour through various Parts of Greece, Turkey, and Italy in 1818-19. *Coloured plates.* 4° 1821
—— Manual of Ancient Geography, or the Student his own Instructor, with copious Indexes of Ancient and Modern Names, and an Analysis of the Work, with Questions for Self-Examination. *Map.* 8°
Oxford, 1840

Lauridsen, P. Bibliographia Groenlandica eller Fortegnetse paa Vóerker, Afhandlinger og danske Manuskripter, der handle om Grönland indtil Aaret 1880, incl. Paa Grundlag af C. G. F. Pfaff's Samlinger. 8° *Copenhagen*, 1890
—— Vitus J. Bering og de Russiske Opdagelsesrejser fra 1725-43. *Maps.* 8°
Copenhagen, 1885
—— Meddelelser om Grönland. Trettende hefte. 8° *Copenhagen*, 1890

Laurie, R. H., and J. Whittle. New Piloting Directory for the Different Channels of the River Thames, with the Navigation thence to Yarmouth and to Dover, to which are annexed the New Rates of Pilotage. 8° 1816

Laurie, Colonel W. F. B. Ashé Pyee, the Superior Country, or the Great Attractions of Burma to British Enterprise and Commerce. Small 8° 1882

Lauser, Dr W. Ein Herbstausflug nach Siebenbürgen. *Illustrations.* 8*
Vienna, 1886

Lauterburg, Robert. Versuch zur Aufstellung einer allgemeinen Uebersicht der aus der Grösse und Beschaffenheit der Flussgebiete abgeleiteten Schweizerischen Stromabflussmengen, &c. 2nd edition. 8* *Berne*, 1876

Lauture, Count d'Escayrac de. Le Désert et le Soudan. *Maps and plates.* 8° *Paris*, 1853
—— De l'Influence que le Canal des deux Mers exercera sur le Commerce en général et sur celui de la Mer Rouge en particulier. 8* *Paris*, 1855

s

Lauture, Count d'Escayrac de. Mémoire sur le Soudan : Géographie Naturelle et Politique, Histoire et Ethnographie, Mœurs et Institutions de l'Empire des Fellatas, du Bornou, du Baguermi, du Waday, du Darfour. *Map.* 8°
Paris, 1855-56
—— Mémoire sur le Ragle, ou Hallucination du Désert. 8* *Paris*, 1855
—— La Turquie et les États Musulmans en général. 8° *Paris*, 1858
—— Notice sur le Darfour, et sur le Voyage de M. le Dr Cuny dans cette contrée. 8* *Paris*, 1859
—— Analytic Universal Telegraphy : an International Telegraphic Language. 8* 1862
—— Notice sur les Déplacements des deux Principaux Fleuves de la Chine. *Maps.* 8* *Paris*, 1862
—— On the Telegraphic Transmission of the Chinese Characters. *Plates.* 4* *Paris*, 1862
—— Sketch of Tables for the Analytic Universal Telegraphy. 12* 1863
—— Ditto. A Short Explanation of the same. 12* 1863
—— Mémoires sur la Chine : Histoire, Réligion, Gouvernement, Coutumes. [Title wanting.] *Maps and woodcuts.* 4° *Paris*, 1864
—— *See* Malte-Brun.

Laval, François Pyrard de. *See* Pyrard.

Laval, P., Comp. de Jesus. Voyage de la Louisiane [en Amérique], 1720 ; dans lequel sont Traitées diverses Matières de Physique, Astronomie, Géographie, et Marine. L'on y a joint les Observations sur la Refraction . . . la Correction de la Carte de la Côte de Provence . . . . *Maps, plans, and tables.* 4° *Paris*, 1728

Lavalle, J. A. de. Juan de la Torre (uno de los trece de la isla del Galle). 12* *Lima*, 1885

Lavallée, T. Physical, Historical, and Military Geography. From the French of Th. Lavallée ; edited, with Additions and Corrections, by Captain Lendy. 8° 1868

Lavalley, A. Extrait du Compte rendu des Travaux de la Société des Ingénieurs Civils, Séances des 7 et 21 Septembre 1866. Communication faite par M. A. Lavalley sur les Travaux d'Exécution du Canal Maritime de l'Isthme de Suez. *Map and plates.* 8* *Paris*, 1866

Laveau, G. L. de. *See* Mouraviev.

Laveleye, Émile de. La Péninsule des Balkans : Vienne, Croatie, Bosnie, Serbie, Bulgarie, Roumélie, Turquie, Roumanie. 2 vols. Small 8° *Brussels*, 1886
—— The Balkan Peninsula. Translated by Mrs Thorpe ; edited and revised for the English Public by the Author, with an Introductory Chapter upon the most recent events, &c. *Map.* 8° 1887

Lavellée, Joseph. *See* Phillips [1], Vol. 1 : Appendix 1.

Laverdant, Désiré. Colonisation de Madagascar. *Map.* 8°   *Paris*, 1844

Lavigerie, Cardinal, and the African Slave Trade. Edited by Richard F. Clarke. 8°   1889

—— Documents sur la fondation de l'œuvre Antiesclavagiste. 8°   *St Cloud*, 1889

—— Lettre faisant hommage a Sa Majesté le Roi Leopold II. des documents sur la fondation de l'œuvre antiesclavagiste, publiés a l'occasion de la Conférence de Bruxelles. 8*   *Algiers*, 1889

—— Lettre à M. le Président de la Conférence Internationale de Bruxelles pour l'esclavage relativement aux évènements récents de l'Ouganda. 8* *Algiers*, 1890

Law, William John. Some Remarks on the Alpine Passes of Strabo. 8*   1846

—— Criticism of Mr Ellis's New Theory concerning the Route of Hannibal. *Map.* 8*   1855

—— Reply to Mr Ellis's Defence of his Theory in the *Journal of Classical and Sacred Philology.* 8*   1856

—— The Alps of Hannibal. 2 vols. *Map.* 8°   1866

Lawrence, Edwin. The Progress of a Century, or the Age of Iron and Steam. 8*   1886

Lawrence, Sir John. An Account of the Formal Commencement of the Punjaub Railway at Lahore. *Map.* 8* 1859

Lawrence, J. W. Footprints, or Incidents in early history of New Brunswick, 1783-1883. *Portraits and illustrations.* 8°
                           St John, 1883

Lawrence, R. F. See Sinclair, A. C.

Laws, Dr Robert. Table of Concords and Paradigm of Verb of the Chinyanja Language as spoken at Lake Nyasa. Oblong 12*   *Edinburgh*, 1885

—— and Mrs Laws. The Tshigunda Language of the Lower Zambesi Region, East Africa : Vocabularies. 12°
                           Edinburgh, 1886

Lawson, C. Allen. British and Native Cochin. 8°   1861

Lawson, Capt. J. A. Wanderings in the Interior of New Guinea. *Map and plate.* 8°   1875

Lawson, Thomas, M.D. See United States, H, *c* : Appendix 2.

Lawson, W. Manual of Modern Geography, Physical, Political, and Commercial. *Maps and illustrations.* 12° 1879

Lawson, W. R. Spain of To-day : a Descriptive, Industrial, and Financial Survey of the Peninsula ; with a full Account of the Rio Tinto Mines. Crown 8°   1890

Lay, G. Tradescant. Chinese as they are, their Moral, Social, and Literary Character ; a new Analysis of the Language, with Succinct Views of their principal Arts and Sciences. *Woodcuts.* 8°   1841

Lay, G. Tradescant. *See* Japan : Appendix 2.

Layard, Sir Austen Henry. Nineveh and its Remains ; with an Account of a Visit to the Chaldean Christians of Kurdistan, and the Yezidis or Devil-worshippers ; and an Inquiry into the Manners and Arts of the Ancient Assyrians. 2 vols. *Maps and plates.* 8°   1849

—— Discoveries in the Ruins of Nineveh and Babylon ; with Travels in Armenia, Kurdistan, and the Desert ; being the Result of a Second Expedition. *Maps and plates.* 8°   1853

—— La Première Campagne de la Crimée, ou les Batailles Mémorables de l'Alma, de Balaklava, et d'Inkermann. Traduction par A. E. S. Jervis. Small 8°
                           Brussels, 1855

—— Early Adventures in Persia, Susiana, and Babylonia, including a Residence among the Bakhtiyari and other Wild Tribes before the Discovery of Nineveh. 2 vols. *Maps and illustrations.* 8° 1887

—— *See* Rawlinson, H. C.

Layard, Edgar Leopold. The Birds of South Africa : a Descriptive Catalogue of all the known Species occurring south of the 28th Parallel of South Latitude. 8°   1867

Layard, Mrs Granville. Through the West Indies. 12°   1887

Layfield, Dr Eglambie. *See* Purchas, Vol. 4, Book 6 : Appendix 1.

Lazari, V. *See* Marco Polo.

Lazzaroni, M. A. Cristoforo Colombo : Osservazioni critiche sui punti più rilevanti e controversi della sua vita. 2 vols. 4°   *Milan*, 1892

Lea, J. *See* Carey, H. C.

Lea, Rev. T. S. The Island of Fernando Noronha in 1887. *See* Ridley, H. N.

Leach, Boynton. *See* United States, E, *a* : Appendix 2.

Leahy, Edmund. Report of the Danube Canal. Folio   1855

Leake, Lieut.-Col. William Martin. The Topography of Athens ; with some Remarks on its Antiquities. *Maps and plates.* 8°   1821

—— Journal of a Tour in Asia Minor ; with Remarks on the Ancient and Modern Geography of that Country. *Map.* 8°
                           1824

—— Historical Outline of the Greek Revolution ; with a few Remarks on the Present State of Affairs in that Country. *Map.* 8°   1826

—— Travels in the Morea. 3 vols. *Map and plans.* 8°   1830

—— Travels in Northern Greece. 4 vols. *Maps, plans, and plates.* 8°   1835

—— Peloponnesiaca : a Supplement to Travels in the Morea. *Maps.* 8° 1846

Leake, Lieut-Col. William Martin. On the Claim to the Islands of Cervi and Sapienza. 8* 1850
—— Numismata Hellenica : a Catalogue of Greek Coins ; with Notes, a Map and Index, an Appendix, and Supplement. 2 vols. 4° 1854-59
—— On some Disputed Questions of Ancient Geography. *Map.* 8° 1857
—— Plates of Coins to accompany Notes on Syracuse. 8° N.D.
——*See* Walpole, Travels : Appendix 1.
Leal, Dr Oscar. Viagem ás Terras Goyanas (Brazil Central). 8°
Lisbon, 1892
Léal, F. A. La République Dominicaine, Territoire, Climat, Agriculture, Industrie, Commerce, Immigration, et Annuaire Statistique. 8* *Paris,* 1888
Lear, Edward. Journal of a Landscape Painter in Albania, Illyria, &c. *Map and plates.* Royal 8° 1852
—— Journals of a Landscape Painter in Southern Calabria, &c. *Map and plates.* Royal 8° 1852
Leardo, Giovanni. *See* Berchet.
Leared, Arthur. Morocco and the Moors : being an Account of Travels, with a general Description of the Country and its People. *Plates.* 8° 1876
—— A Visit to the Court of Morocco. *Map and illustrations.* 8° 1879
—— Morocco and the Moors. 2nd edition. Revised and edited by Sir Richard Burton. *Map, plans, and illustrations.* 8° 1891
Le Beau, C. *See* Beau.
Le Blanc, Vincent. *See* Blanc.
Lebon, André, and Paul Pelet. France as it is. Specially written for English Readers, and translated from the French by Mrs William Arnold. *Maps.* 8° 1888
Le Bon, Dr Gustave. *See* Bon.
Lebour, G. A. The Geology of the Redesdale Ironstone District. *Maps.* 8* *Newcastle-upon-Tyne,* 1873
—— On the Limits of the Yoredale Series in the North of England. 8* 1875
—— On the Geological Relations of the Secondary Iron Ores of France. *Map and plate.* 8* *Newcastle-upon-Tyne,* 1876
—— The Carrara Marbles : a Chapter in the History of Continental Geology. 8* 1876
—— Outlines of the Geology of Northumberland and Durham. [2nd edition, as regards Northumberland.] *Maps and plates.* 12° *Newcastle-upon-Tyne,* 1886
Le Brun or Le Bruyn. *See* Brun.
Lechevalier, J. B. Voyage de la Propontide et du Pont-Euxin. 2 vols. *Maps.* 8° *Paris,* 1800

Lecky, Capt. S. T. S. The Danger Angle and Off-Shore Distance Tables. 12° 1882
—— "Wrinkles" in Practical Navigation. Revised edition. *Charts and illustrations.* Large 8° 1884
Leclerc, C. Bibliotheca Americana : Histoire, Géographie, Voyages, Archéologie, et Linguistique des deux Amériques et des Iles Philippines. 8° *Paris,* 1878
Leclerc, F. Le Texas et sa Révolution. *Map.* 8° *Paris,* 1840
Leclerc, Max. Les Peuplades de Madagascar. *Map and illustrations.* 8* *Paris,* 1887
Leclerc, —. *See* Arrian.
Leclercq, Jules. La Terre de Glace : Feroë, Island, les Geysers, le Mont Ilékla. *Map, plan, and plates.* 12° *Paris,* 1883
—— Les Geysers de la Terre des Merveilles. 8* *Brussels,* 1885
—— Voyage au Mexique, de New-York à Vera-Cruz en suivant les Routes de Terre. *Map, &c.* 12° *Paris,* 1885
—— Une Visite au Volcan de Jorullo (Mexique). 8* *Paris,* 1886
—— La Terre des Merveilles, Promenade au Parc National de l'Amerique du Nord. *Maps and illustrations.* 12° *Paris,* 1886
—— Du Caucase aux Monts Alaï, Transcaspie, Boukhari, Ferganah. *Map.* 12° *Paris,* 1890
—— Les Monuments de Samarcande. 8* *Brussels,* 1890
—— Histoire des ascensions de l'Ararat. 8* [1891]
—— Voyage au Mont Ararat. *Map and frontispiece.* 12° *Paris,* 1892
—— Excursion on Mt. Ararat. 8* 1893
Lecomte, Capt. —. Corps expéditionnaire du Tonkin. Marche de Lang-pon à Tuyenquan. *Maps and diagrams.* 8° *Paris,* 1888
Le Compte, Louis. *See* Compte.
Lecoq, H. Élémens de Géographie Physique et de Météorologie, ou Résumé des notions acquises sur les grands Phénomènes et les grandes Lois de la Nature. *Plates.* 8° *Paris,* 1836
—— Élémens de Géologie et d'Hydrographie, ou Résumé des notions acquises sur les grandes Lois de Nature. *Plates.* 8° *Brussels,* 1839
Lecousturier, A. F. Dictionnaire des Postes aux Lettres du Royaume de France, suivie de la Division Territoriale. 8° *Paris,* 1819
—— **and F. Chaudouet.** Dictionnaire Géographique des Postes aux Lettres de tous les Départemens de la République Française. 3 vols. 8° *Paris,* 1802
Ledebour, C. F. von. Reise durch das Altai-Gebirge und die Soongorische Kirgisen Steppe. 2 vols. *Tables.* 8° *Berlin,* 1829

Ledyard, John. Memoirs of the Life and Travels of, from his Journals and Correspondence, by Jared Sparks. 8°   1828
—— Travels and Adventures, comprising his Voyage with Capt. Cook's Third and Last Expedition, his Journey on foot 1300 miles round the Gulf of Bothnia to St Petersburgh, his Adventures and Residence in Siberia, and his Exploratory Mission to Africa. 8°   1834

Lee, —. Catalogue of Oriental Manuscripts, purchased in Turkey. 4°
[1830 and 1840]

Lee, H. Memoirs of the War in the Southern Department of the United States. New Editions, with Revisions, and a Biography of the Author, by Robert E. Lee. *Maps, plates, and plans.* Large 8°   1869

Lee, J. E. *See* Keller, F. ; Merk.

Lee, Lionel. *See* Ceylon : Appendix 2.

Lee, Robert. Last Days of Alexander, and the First Days of Nicholas, Emperor of Russia. 8°   1854

Lee, Robert E. *See* Lee, H.

Lee, Rev. Dr S. *See* Belzoni in Walpole's Travels : Appendix 1.

Lee, Sidney. *See* Biography, General : Appendix 2.

Lee, Lieut. S. P. Report and Charts of the Cruise of the U.S. Brig "Dolphin," made under direction of the Navy Department. 8°   *Washington,* 1854

Leech, Lieut. Vocabularies of Seven Languages spoken in the Countries West of the Indus; with Remarks on the Origin of the Afghans. 8* *Bombay,* 1838

Leech, R. Memoir on the Trade, &c., of the Port of Mandvee in Kutch. [From India Records, No. 15.] 8°   *Bombay,* 1855

Leeds, H. Progress Report of Forest Administration in British Burmah, 1862-63, accompanied by a Memorandum thereon by Dr D. Brandis. [From India Records, No. 40.] *Plate.* 8°   *Calcutta,* 1864

Leem, —. *See* Pinkerton, Vol. 1 : Appendix 1.

Leemans, C. Bôrô-Boedoer op het Eiland Java, afgebeeld door en onder toezigt van F. C. Wilsen, met toelichtenden en venklarenden tekst naar de geschreven en gedrukte verhandelingen van F. C. Wilsen, J. F. G. Brumund en andere Bescheiden bewerkt, en uitgegeven op last van Zijne Excellentie den Minister van Kolonien. 3 vols. 8°, and Atlas folio *Leyden,* 1837
—— Bôrô-Boudour dans l'Ile de Java, dessiné par ou sous la direction de Mr F. C. Wilsen, avec texte descriptif et explicatif; rédigé d'après les mémoires manuscrits et imprimés de MM. F. C. Wilsen, J. F. G. Brumund, et autres Documents, et publié d'après les ordres de son Excellence le Ministre des Colonies. *Plates.* 8°   *Leyden,* 1874

Lees, F. R. Sailing Directions for South Australia. 12°   *Sydney,* 1839

Lees, G. Robinson. Jerusalem Illustrated; with a Preface by the Right Rev. Bishop Blyth of Jerusalem ; and an Appendix illustrating the models of Herr Baurath von Schickritter, with descriptive letterpress, translated by the Rev. J. E. Hanauer. *Illustrations.* 8°   1893

Lees, James. The Six Months' Seasons of the Tropics. 12*   1860

Lees, J. A., and W. J. Clutterbuck. "B.C. 1887."—A Ramble in British Columbia. *Maps and illustrations.* 8°   1888

Lees, W. Nassau. Another Word on Tea Cultivation in Eastern Bengal. 8*   *Calcutta,* 1867

Leete, C. H. *See* Chisholm.

Le Favre, J. *See* Favre.

Lefebvre, A. Mémoire sur les Ouragans de la Mer des Indes au Sud de l'Équateur. *Tables.* 8°   *Paris,* 1852

Lefebvre, Paul. Souvenirs de l'Indo-Chine ; Faces Jaunes, Mœurs, et Costumes de l'Extrême-Orient. 12°   *Paris,* 1886

Lefebvre, Théophile. *See* Abyssinia, Voyage en Abyssinie, &c. ; Appendix 2.

Lefils, Florentin. La Topographie du Ponthieu d'après les anciennes cartes. 8*   N.P., N.D.

Lefroy, Henry Maxwell. Memoir and Journal of an Expedition organised by the Colonial Government of Western Australia for Exploring the Interior of the Colony Eastward. *Map and table.* Folio*   [*Perth, W.A.*] 1863

Lefroy, Sir J. H. Memorials of the Discovery and Early Settlement of the Bermudas or Somers Islands, 1515-1685. Compiled from the Colonial Records and and other Original Sources. Vol 1, 1515-1652. *Map.* Large 8°   1877
—— Ditto, 1511-1687. Vol. 2, 1650-1687. *Map and plates.* Large 8°   1879
—— Diary of a Magnetic Survey of a Portion of the Dominion of Canada, chiefly in the North-Western Territories, executed in the years 1842-44. *Charts and diagrams.* 8°   1883

Le Gentil. *See* Gentil.

Leger, Eugène. Trois mois de séjour en Moldavie. 8°   *Paris,* 1861

Leger, Louis. *See* Nestor.

Legge, Alfred O. Sunny Manitoba, its Peoples and its Industries. *Map and plates.* 8°   1893

Legge, J. The Chinese Classics ; with a Translation, critical and exegetical, Notes, Prolegomena, and Copious Indexes. (In 7 volumes.) Vols. 1, 2, and 3. Large 8°   *Hongkong,* 1861-65

Legge, James. A Record of Bhuddhistic Kingdoms : being an Account by the Chinese Monk Fâ-hien of his Travels in India and Ceylon (A.D. 399-414) in Search of the Bhuddist Books of Discipline. Translated and Annotated, with a Corean Recension of the Chinese Text. *Map and plates.* Small 4° *Oxford,* 1886

Leggett, Eugène. Notes on the Mint-Towns and Coins of the Mohamedans, from the Earliest Period to the Present Time. *Map and table.* 8° 1885

Legh, Thomas. Narrative of a Journey in Egypt and the Country beyond the Cataracts. *Map and facsimile.* 4° 1816

Le Grand, Abbé. *See* Ribeyro.

Legrand, Dr. La Nouvelle Société Indo-Chinoise fondée par M. le Marquis de Croizier et son ouvrage l'Art Khmer. *Illustrations.* 8° *Paris,* 1878

Legrand, Émile. Recueil de Poëmes Historiques en Grec vulgaire relatifs à la Turquie et aux Principautés Danubiennes. Large 8° [Publ. de l'École des Langues Orient Viv., Vol. 5] *Paris,* 1877
—— *See* Dapontès.

Legrand, Marcellin. Spécimen de Caractères Chinois, gravès sur acier et fondus en types mobiles. Royal 8* *Paris,* 1859

Legrand, ——. *See* Lobo.

Le Gras, A. *See* Gras.

Leguat, François. *See* Hakluyt Soc. Publ., Vols. 82, 83 : Appendix 1.

Lehmann, A. *See* Baer and Helmersen, 17.

Lehmann, Johann George. Die Lehre der Situation-Zeichnung, oder Anweisung zum richtigen Erkennen und genauen Abbilden der Erd-Oberfläche, in topographischen Charten und Situation-Planen. Herausgegeben und mit Erläuterungen versehen von G. A. Fischer. 2 vols in 1. Small folio *Dresden,* 1820

Lehmann, Dr Richard. Zur Erweiterung der wissenschaftlichen Stationsbeobachtung in fremden Ländern. 8* *Munich,* 1884
—— Vorlesungen über Hülfsmittel und Methode des geographischen Unterrichts. Vol. 1 (8 parts). *Maps.* Royal 8° *Halle,* 1885-91
—— Anleitung zum Gebrauche der Debes' schen Zeichenatlanten. 8* *Leipzig,* 1888
—— *See* Hage and Tegner ; *also* Germany, C : Appendix 2.

Lehnert, Josef Ritter von. *See* Dorn, A.

Lehninger, J. A. Description de la Ville de Dresde et de ses Environs. *Map.* 12° *Dresden,* 1782

Leichhardt, Ludwig. Journal of an Overland Expedition in Australia, from Moreton Bay to Port Essington, a distance of upwards of 3000 miles, during 1844-45. *Plates.* 8° 1847

Leichhardt, Ludwig. Dr Ludwig Leichhardt's Briefe an seine Angehörigen. Herausgegeben im Auftrage der Geographischen Gesellschaft in Hamburg von Dr G. Neumayer und Otto Leichhardt ; mit einem Anhange ; Dr Ludwig Leichhardt als Naturforscher und Entdeckungsreisender, von Dr G. Neumayer. *Map and portrait.* 8° *Hamburg,* 1881
—— *See* Mueller, F. von ; Zuchold, E. A.

Leidy, Joseph. *See* United States, G, *a* : Appendix 2.

Leigh, Capt. Charles. *See* Gottfried ; Hakluyt, Vol. 3 ; Purchas, Vol. 4, Book 6 : Appendix 1.

Leigh, J. S. *See* Hamel.

Leigh, W. H. Reconnoitering Voyages and Travels ; with Adventures in the New Colonies of South Australia, a particular description of the Town of Adelaide and Kangaroo Island, and an Account of the Present State of Sydney and parts adjacent ; including Visits to Nicobar, and other Islands in the Indian Seas, Calcutta, the Cape of Good Hope, and St Helena, during 1836-38. *Plates.* 8° 1840

Leigh's New Pocket Road-Book of Ireland, on the Plan of Reichard's Itineraries, containing an Account of all the Direct and Cross Roads, &c. *Maps.* 12° 1827

Leipoldt, Dr Gustav. Ueber die mittlere Höhe Europa's. 8° *Plauen,* 1874
—— Die Leiden des Europäers im Afrikanischen Tropenklima und die Mittel zu deren Abwehr. Ein Beitrag zur Förderung der deutschen Kolonisationsbestrebungen. 8° *Leipzig,* 1887
—— *See* Peschel.

Leitner, Dr G. W. The Languages and Races of Dardistan. *Maps in cover, plates, and photographs.* 4° *Lahore,* 1877
—— Section I. of Linguistic Fragments discovered in 1870, 1872, and 1879, by G. W. Leitner, relating to the Dialect of the Magadds and other wandering Tribes ; the Argots of Thieves ; the Secret Trade-Dialects and Systems of Native Cryptography in Kabul, Kashmir, and the Punjab ; followed by an Account of Shawl Weaving, .&c., &c. *Plates.* 4* *Lahore,* 1882
—— The same. Appendix to "Changars" and Linguistic Fragments ; Words and Phrases illustrating the Dialects of the Samé and Mé, as also of Dancers, Mirásis, and Dôrns. 4* *Lahore,* 1882
—— Rough Accounts of Itineraries through the Hindukush and to Central Asia. *Map and plate.* 8* N.D.
—— On the Sciences of Language and of Ethnography, with General Reference to the Language and Customs of Hunza. 8* N.D.

Leitner, Dr G. W. A Collection of Specimens of Commercial and other Alphabets and Handwritings, as also of Multiplication Tables, current in Various Parts of the Panjab, Sind, and the North-West Provinces. Folio*   *Lahore*, N.D.
—— La Langue, la Religion, et les Mœurs des Habitants du Hounza. 8*
                       [*Paris*, 1890]
—— Hunza, Nagyr, and the Pamir Regions. *Map and illustrations.* Large 8*   [1891]
—— Dardistan in 1866, 1886, and 1893 : being an Account of the History, Religions, Customs, Legends, Fables, and Songs of Gilgit, Chilás, Kandiá (Gabriál), Yasin, Chitrál, Hunza, Nagyr, and other parts of the Hindu Kush. . . . *Map and illustrations.* 4°   *Woking*, 1893
—— The Hunza and Nagyr Handbook : being an Introduction to a Knowledge of the Language, Race, and Countries of Hunza, Nagyr, and a part of Yasin. 2nd edition. 4°   *Woking*, 1893
Lejean, Guillaume. La Gaule de l'Anonyme de Ravenne. (Extract from Bulletin de la Société de Géographie, Vol. 12.) 8*   *Paris*, 1856
—— Ethnographie de la Turquie d'Europe. (Ergänzungsheft, 4—Petermann's Mittheilungen.) *Maps.* 4°   *Gotha*, 1861
—— Théodore II., le Nouvel Empire l'Abyssinie, et les intérèts Français dans le Sud de la Mer Rouge. *Portrait.* 12°   *Paris* [1865]
—— Voyage aux Deux Nils (Nubie, Kordofan, Soudan Oriental), exécuté de 1860 à 1864, par ordre de l'Empereur. 4°, and Atlas folio   *Paris*, 1865
—— L'Abyssinie en 1868. 8* *Paris*, 1868
Lelewel, Joachim. Géographie du Moyen Age. 4 vols. *Maps.* 8°, and Atlas
                  Brussels, 1852
Le Long, J. *See* Long.
Lelorrain, —. *See* Phillips [3], Vol. 8 : Appendix 1.
Le Maire, Jacob. *See* Maire.
Le Marchand, G. *See* Kuropatkin.
Le Mascrier. *See* Mascrier.
Lemer, Julien. *See* Bellot.
Le Messurier, Colonel A. From London to Bokhara, and a Ride through Persia. *Maps and illustrations.* 8°   1889
—— A Trip to Bokhara. (From *Journal of the United Service Institution of India*, October 1889.) 8*   *Simla*, 1889
Lemire, C. La Colonisation Française, en Nouvelle-Calédonie et Dépendances. *Maps, plates, and photographs.* Square 8°   *Paris*, 1878
—— L'Indo-Chine : Cochinchine Française ; Royaume de Cambodge, Royaume d'Annam et Tonkin. 3rd edition. *Maps and plates.* 8°   *Paris*, 1884

Lemoine, G. Sur les variations du mode de répartition de la pluie entre les différentes époques de l'année pour une même région. 8*   *Paris*, 1869
—— *See* Lalanne, L
Lemon, W. C. *See* Dalrymple, Repertory, Vol. 1 : Appendix 1.
Le Monnier, Franz, *See* Monnier.
Le Moyne, A. *See* Moyne.
Lempriere, J. Classical Dictionary, containing a copious Account of all the Proper Names mentioned in Ancient Authors, with the Value of Coins, Weights, and Measures used among the Greeks and Romans, and a Chronological Table. 8°   1806
Lempriere, William. Tour from Gibraltar to Tangier, Sallee, Mogodore, Santa Cruz, Tarudant, and thence over Mount Atlas to Morocco. *Map.* 8°
                      1791
—— *See* Pinkerton, Vol. 15 : Appendix 1.
Lendenfeld, R. von. The Glacial Period in Australia. *Map and plates.* 8*
                Sydney, N.D.
—— Der Tasman Gletscher. (Ergänzungsheft, 75—Petermann's Mittheilungen.) *Maps.* 4°   *Gotha*, 1884
—— Forschungsreisen in den Australischen Alpen. (Ergänzungsheft, 87 — Petermann's Mittheilungen.) *Maps.* 4°
              Gotha, 1887
—— Australische Reise. *Illustrations.* Large 8°   *Innsbruck*, 1892
Lendy, Captain. Physical, Historical, and Military Geography. From the French of Th. Lavallée. 8°   1868
Lennep, H. J. van. Travels in little-known parts of Asia Minor ; with illustrations of Biblical Literature, and Researches in Archæology. 2 vols. *Maps and plates.* 8°   1870
Lenormant, François. La Grande-Grèce, Paysages et Histoire : Littoral de la Mer Ionienne. 2 vols. 8°   *Paris*, 1881
—— The same. Tome III. La Calabre. 8°   *Paris*, 1884
Lenthéric, C. Les Villes mortes du Golfe de Lyon : Illiberris, Ruscino, Narbon, Agde, Maguelone, Aiguesmortes, Arles, Les Saintes - Maries. *Maps.* 12°   *Paris*, 1876
—— La Grèce et l'Orient en Provence ; Arles, Le Bas Rhône, Marseille. *Maps.* 12°.   *Paris*, 1876
—— La Provence Maritime, Ancienne et Moderne. *Maps.* 12°   *Paris*, 1880
—— Le Rhone : Histoire d'un fleuve. 2 vols. *Maps.* 8°   *Paris*, 1892
Lenz, Dr Oscar. Skizzen aus Westafrika. *Map.* 8°   *Berlin*, 1878
—— Reise vom Okandeland bis zur Mündung des Schebeflusses. *Maps.* 8*
                Vienna, 1878

Lenz, Dr Oscar. Timbuktu. Reise durch Marokko, die Sahara und den Sudan. Ausgeführt im Auftrage der Afrikanischen Gesellschaft in Deutschland in den Jahren 1879 und 1880. 2 vols. *Maps and plates.* 8° *Leipzig*, 1884
—— Nyassa-Shirē. 4* [*Stutigart*] 1892
Leo Africanus, John (a More borne in Granada, and brought up in Barbarie). Geographical Historie of Africa ; before which, out of the best Ancient and Moderne Writers, is prefixed a generall description of Africa, and also a particular treatise of all the Maine Lands and Isles undescribed by John Leo. Translated and collected by John Pory. *Map.* 4° 1600
—— Africæ Descriptio, ix. lib. absoluta. 24° *Leyden*, 1632
—— *See* Purchas, Vol. 2 ; Ramusio, Vol. 1 : Appendix 1.
Leon, Juan Ponce de. *See* Ponce.
Leonard, Bishop of Sidon. *See* Purchas, Vol. 1, Book 1 : Appendix 1.
Leonard, James. Information on the Discovery and Character of the Tea Plant in Assam. 8° 1839
Leonhard, C. C., J. H. Merz, and K. F. Kopp. Systematischtabellarische Uebersicht und Characteristik der Mineralkörper, in Oryktognostischer und orologischer Hinsicht. Folio *Frankfort*, 1806
Leonhard, Richard. Der Stromlauf der mittleren Oder. Inaugural-Dissertation zur Erlangung der philosophischen Doctorwürde . . . Universität Breslau. *Maps.* 8* *Breslau*, 1893
Lepage, Henri. La Ville de Nancy et ses Environs, Guide du Voyageur. *Plates.* 12° *Nancy*, 1844
Lepe, Diego de. *See* Gottfried : Appendix 1.
Lepechin, Iwan. Tagebuch der Reise durch verschiedene Provinzen des Russischen Reiches in 1768-69, aus dem Russischen uebersetzt von C. H. Hase. 3 vols. *Plates.* 4° *Altenburg*, 1774
Lephay, J. *See* France, B, *a* : Appendix 2.
Le Plongeon, Alice D. Here and There in Yucatan. *Illustrations.* 12° *New York*, [1889]
—— Mayapan and Maya Inscriptions. 8* *Worcester, U.S.*, 1881
Le Plongeon, Augustus. Vestiges of the Mayas, or Facts tending to Prove that Communications and Intimate Relations must have existed, in very remote times, between the Inhabitants of Mayab and those of Asia and Africa. 8° *New York*, 1881
—— Sacred Mysteries among the Mayas and the Quiches 11,500 years ago ; their relation to the Sacred Mysteries of

Le Plongeon, Augustus—*continued.* Egypt, Greece, Chaldea, and India ; Free-Masonry in Times anterior to the Temple of Solomon. *Portrait and illustrations.* 8° *New York*, 1886
Le Prédour, M. *See* Horsburgh, J.
Lepsius, Dr Richard. A Tour from Thebes to the Peninsula of Sinai in 1845. 12° 1846
—— Denkmäler aus Egypten und Ethiopien nach den Zeichnungen der Preussischen Expedition auf Befehl Seiner Majestät des Königs, 1842-45. (Vorläufige Bemerkungen.) 4* *Berlin*, 1849
—— Discoveries in Egypt, Ethiopia, and the Peninsula of Sinai, in 1842-45. Edited, with Notes, by Kenneth R. H. Mackenzie. *Maps and plates.* 8° 1852
—— Briefe aus Aegypten, Aethiopien, und der Halbinsel des Sinai, geschrieben in den Jahren 1842-45, während der auf Befehl S. Maj. d. K. Friedrich Wilhelm IV. von Preussen ausgeführten wissenschaftlichen Expedition. *Plate.* 8° *Berlin*, 1852
—— The XXII. Egyptian Royal Dynasty, with some Remarks on XXVI. and other Dynasties of the New Kingdom. Translated by W. Bell. *Plates.* 4* 1858
—— *See* Germany, C, Forschungen, &c., Vol. 1 ; Handbücher zur Deutschen Landes und Volkskunde, Vol. 1 : Appendix 2.
Lerch, P. Ein Blick auf die Resultate der Hissâr'schen Expedition. 8* [*St Petersburg*, 1875]
Lerio (or Lerius), John. *See* Gottfried ; Purchas, Vol. 4 ; Allgemeine Historie, Vol. 16 : Appendix 1.
Léris, G. de. Le Monde Pittoresque e Monumental : l'Italie du Nord. *Illustrations.* 4° *Paris*, 1889
Le Roux, Hugues. *See* Roux.
Leroy-Beaulieu, Paul. De la Colonisation chez les Peuples Modernes. 3rd edition. 8° *Paris*, 1886
—— L'Algerie et la Tunisie. 8° *Paris*, 1887
—— De la Colonisation chez les Peuples Modernes. 4th edition. 8° *Paris*, 1891
Le Roy, P. L. A Narrative of the Singular Adventures of Four Russian Sailors who were Cast Away on the Desert Island of East-Spitzbergen. *See* Staehlin, J. von. An Account of the New Northern Archipelago, &c.
—— *See* Pinkerton, Vol. 1 : Appendix 1.
Le Roy, Rev. Father. *See* Roy.
Le Sage, H. Notions on the Chorography of Brazil by Joaquim Manoel de Macedo. 8° *Leipzig*, 1873
Lescarbot, Marke. *See* Purchas, Vol. 4 : Appendix 1.
Leslie, A. *See* Nordenskiöld.
Leslie, D. The Native Custom of "Hlonipa." 12* N.D.

Leslie, Robert C. *See* Rogers.

Leslie, Dr Rolph. A Few Practical Hints for Travellers in the Tropics. Small 8*   N.D.

Lespy, V. *See* Molyneux, R. G.

Lesquereux, L. *See* Gwen ; *also* United States, G, *a*, *c*, Geological Survey of the Territories, Vol. 8, Part 3—The Cretaceous and Tertiary Floras : Appendix 2.

Lessar, —. Account of Mr Lessar's Ride from Askhabad to Herat. Russian Abstract, No. 19. (From the *Golos*, Nos. 236 and 239, 1st (13th) and 4th (16th) September.) Translated by Robert Michell. Folio*   1882

Lesseps, Ferdinand de. The Isthmus of Suez Question. *Maps.* 8°   1855

—— Percement de l'Isthme de Suez. Exposé et Documents Officiels. *Maps*   *Paris*, 1855

—— New Facts and Figures relative to the Isthmus of Suez Canal ; with a Reply to the *Edinburgh Review*, by St Hilaire. 8°   1856

—— Percement de l'Isthme de Suez. Rapport et Projet de la Commission Internationale. 3° Serie. 8°   *Paris*, 1856

—— Inquiry into the Opinions of the Commercial Classes of Great Britain on the Suez Ship Canal. *Maps.* 8°   1857

—— Percement de l'Isthme de Suez. Actes Constitutifs de la Compagnie Universelle du Canal Maritime de Suez. 6ᵐᵉ Série. *Maps and plans.* 8°   1866

—— The History of the Suez Canal : a Personal Narrative. Translated by Sir H. Drummond Wolff. 12°   1876

—— Addresses at the De Lesseps Banquet, given at Delmonico's, 1st March 1880. 8*   *New York*, 1880

—— *See* Colombia ; Panama : Appendix 2.

Lesseps, J. B. B. Journal Historique du Voyage de M. de Lesseps, Consul de France, employé dans l'Expedition de M. le Comte de la Pérouse. 2 vols. *Maps.* Small 8°   *Paris*, 1790

—— Travels in Kamtschatka during the years 1787 and 1788. Translated from the French. 2 vols. in 1. 8°   1790

—— *See* Pelham, Vol. 2 : Appendix 1.

Lesson, Dr A. Les Polynésiens, leur Origine, leurs Migrations, leur Langage. Ouvrage rédigé d'après le Manuscrit de l'Auteur, par Ludovic Martinet. 4 vols. *Maps.* 8°   *Paris*, 1880-84

Lester, C. Edwards. Sam Houston and his Republic. *Portrait.* 8° *New York*, 1846

Le Strange, Guy. Palestine under the Moslems : a Description of Syria and the Holy Land, from A.D. 650 to 1500. Translated from the works of the Mediæval Arab Geographers. *Maps, plans, and illustrations.* 8°   1890

Le Strange, Guy. *See* Schumacher ; *also* Turkey in Asia, B : Appendix 2.

Letellier, L. Victor. Vocabulaire Oriental, Français, Italien, Arabe, Turc, et Grec. Composé pour la Conversation usuelles et dans lequel se Trouve Figurée la Prononciation à l'Aide des Lettres Françaises. Oblong 8°   *Paris*, 1838

Lethbridge, Sir Roper. *See* Thornton.

Letourneux, A. *See* Hanoteau ; Playfair.

Letronne, A. Recherches Géographiques et critiques sur le livre De mensura orbis terræ, composé en Irlande au commencement du neuvième Siècle par Dicuil, suivies du texte restitué par A. Letronne. 8°   *Paris*, 1814

—— L'Isthme de Suez. Le Canal de Jonction des deux Mers sous les Grecs, les Romains et les Arabes. 8°   *Paris*, 1841

—— Œuvres Choisies de A. J. Letronne. . . . Par E. Fagnan. Deuxième Série. Geographie et Cosmographie. 2 vols. *Maps and plates.* 8°   *Paris*, 1883

Lettres Édifiantes et Curieuses des Missions Étrangères. 26 vols.   1780-83 [For Contents, *see* Voyages and Travels : Appendix 1.]

Leubel, A. G. El Peru en 1860, ó sea Anuario Nacional. 12°   *Lima*, 1861

Leucander. *See* Whiteman in Hakluyt's Voyages, Vol. 2 : Appendix 1.

Leupe, P. A. De Reizen der Nederlanders naar Nieuw-Guinea en de Papoesche Eilanden in de 17ᵈᵉ en 18ᵈᵉ Eeuw. *Maps.* 8°   *The Hague*, 1875

—— *See* Coen, C. J. ; Vries, M. G.

Leutemann, H. Graphic Pictures of Native Life in Distant Lands, illustrating the Typical Races of Mankind ; with Explanatory Text by Professor A. Kirchoff. Translated from the German by George Philip, jun. *Plates.* 4°   1888

Leutholf, J. Jobi Ludolfi aliàs Leutholf dicti Historia Æthiopica, sive Brevis et Succincta Descriptio Regni Habessinorum, quod vulgó malè Presbyteri Johannis vocatur, &c. *Map and plates.* Folio   *Frankfort-o-M.*, 1681

—— A New History of Ethiopia, being a Full and Accurate Description of the Kingdom of Abissinia . . . called the Empire of Prester John. By the Learned Job Ludolphus. Made English by J. P., Gent. *Plates.* Folio   1682

—— The same. 2nd edition. To which is added . . . a Preface . . . with the Life of Gregorius Abba. Made English by J. P., Gent. *Map and plates.* Folio   1684

Leutholf, J. Jobi Ludolfi, aliàs Leutholf dicti, ad suam Historiam Æthiopicam antehac editam Commentarius. *Maps and plates.* Folio *Frankfort-o-M.*, 1691
—— Psalterium Davidis, Æthiopicè et Latine. . . . Accedunt Æthiopice tantum Hymni et Orationes aliquot Vet. et Novi Testamenti, item Canticum Canticorum. Small 4° *Frankfort-o-M.*, 1701

Levaillant, F. Voyage dans l'Intérieur de l'Afrique, par le Cap de Bonne-Espérance, dans les années 1780-85. 2 vols. in 1. *Plates.* 4° *Paris*, 1790
—— The same. 2 vols. *Illustrations.* 8° *Paris*, 1790
—— Second Voyage dans l'Intérieur de l'Afrique, par le Cap de Bonne-Espérance. 3 vols. in 2. *Plates.* 8° *Paris*, An. III. [1794-95]
—— The same, dans les années 1783-85. 2 vols. *Maps and plates.* 4° *Paris*, An. IV. [1795-96]

Levasseur, Prof. Émile. Inauguration du Buste du Dr Crevaux. 8* *Nancy*, 1885
—— La Statistique Graphique. *Maps and diagrams.* 8° 1885
—— La Statistique Officielle en France; Organisation, Travaux, et Publications des Services de Statistique des différents Ministères précédée d'un aperçu Historique. Large 8* *Nancy*, 1885
—— Statistique de la Superficie et de la Population des Contrées de la Terre. *Maps.* Large 8° *Rome*, 1887
—— Les Alpes et les grandes Ascensions. *Maps and illustrations.* Large 8° *Paris*, 1889
—— Le Brésil. Deuxième édition, illustrée de gravures, cartes, et graphiques, accompagnée d'un Appendice . . et d'un Album de Vues du Brésil. 2 vols. 4° *Paris*, 1889
—— Le Brésil. (Extrait de la Grande Encyclopédie.) *Map and illustrations.* 4* *Paris*, 1889
—— Note sur la valeur de la production Agricole. 8* *Paris*, 1891
—— Note sur la méthode d'Enseignement de la Géographie. 8* [1891?]
—— L'Europe. (Extrait de la Grande Encyclopédie, Tome 16.) Par E. Levasseur, avec la collaboration de MM. Hahn, Trouessart, et Deniker. *Map.* 4* *Paris*, 1892
—— Superficie et Population: les Etats d'Europe; Division de la Terre en Cinq Parties du Monde. 4* [*Paris*] 1892
—— La France et ses Colonies. Geographie et Statistique. New edition. 3 vols. *Illustrations.* 8° *Paris*, 1893

Levchine, Alexis de. Description des Hordes et des Steppes des Kirghiz-Kazaks, ou Kirghiz-Kaïssaks. Traduite du Russe par F. de Pigny. *Map and plates.* 8° *Paris*, 1840

Level, Andres A. Nomenclator de Venezuela, contentivo de su censo en orden Alfabético. 2 vols. Folio *Caracas*, 1883

"Leven" and "Barracouta." *See* Boteler; Owen.

Leverson, Capt. J. J. *See* United Kingdom, G, War Office Publ.: Appendix 2.

Leveson, H. A. The High Lands of the Cameroons and Ambas Bay, giving some Description of this most eligible site for a flourishing European colony, and showing its peculiar natural advantages as a Sanitarium, Trading Settlement, Naval Station, and Coaling Depôt. Folio* 1871

Levesque, Pierre-Charles. Histoire de Russie; nouvelle édition, corrigée et augmentée, et conduite jusqu'à la Mort de l'Impératrice Catherine II. 8 vols. *Maps.* 8° *Hamburg*, 1800

Levey, G. C. A Handy Guide to the River Plate, including the Argentine Republic, Uruguay, and Paraguay, their Physical Features, Resources, Railways, and Finances. *Map.* 12° N.D.

Levieux, Fernand. Considerations Geographiques sur les Centres de Civilisation. *Map.* 8° *Brussels*, 1892

Levison, H. A. ["The Old Shekarry"]: The Projected Sub-Marine Telegraph Cable to India and Australia considered as being the most direct, expeditious, and secure line of communication, . . . and compared with existing land lines. *Map.* 8* 1869
—— Camp Life and its Requirements for Soldiers, Travellers, and Sportsmen. Part 1. *Plates.* 8° 1872

Levy, W. Hanks. Blindness and the Blind; or, A Treatise on the Science of Typhlology. Small 8° 1872

Lewin, F. M. *See* Jochmus.

Lewin, T. The Life and Epistles of St Paul. 2 vols. *Maps and plates.* 4° 1875

Lewin, Thomas. The Invasion of Britain by Julius Cæsar. *Maps.* 8° 1859

Lewin, Col. T. H. The Hill Tracts of Chittagong and the Dwellers therein; with Comparative Vocabularies of the Hill Dialects. 8° *Calcutta*, 1869
—— Wild Races of South-Eastern India. 12° 1870
—— A Fly on the Wheel; or, How I helped to govern India. *Maps and illustrations.* 8° 1884

Lewis, E. W. Physical Geography: a Series of Facts and Theories arranged upon the Basis of Questions set at the Oxford and Cambridge Local Examinations. 12° 1880

Lewis, George. On a Visit to Ceylon, and the Relation of Ceylonese Beetles to the Vegetation there. 8* 1882

Lewis, Prof. H. *See* Turkey in Asia, B: Appendix 2.

Lewis, J. W. *See* South Australia, A: Appendix 2.

Lewis, Matthew Gregory. Journal of a Residence among the Negroes in the West Indies. 12° 1845

Lewis, Hon. Samuel. *See* Blyden.

Lewis, Tayler. State Rights: a Photograph from the Ruins of Ancient Greece; with appended Dissertations on the Ideas of Nationality, of Sovereignty, and the Right of Revolution. 8°
Albany, N. Y., 1865

Lewis and Clarke, Capts. Travels to the Source of the Missouri River, and across the American Continent to the Pacific Ocean, in 1804-6. *Maps.* 4° 1814
—— *See* Coues; *also* Eyriès, Vol. 9; Phillips [1], Collection of Modern and Contemporary Voyages and Travels, Vol. 6: Appendix 1.

Lewis's New Traveller's Guide, or a Pocket Edition of the English Counties, containing all the Direct and Cross Roads in England and Wales. *Maps.* 12° 1819

Ley, W. Clement. Aids to the Study and Forecast of Weather. *Charts.* 8*
1880

Leybold, F. Excursion a las Pampas Arjentinas, 1871. *Map.* 8°
Santiago, 1873

Leycester, Lieut. Greek Inscriptions discovered in the Islands of Santorin and Milo. Edited by John Hogg. 8*
N.P., N.D.

Leyden, John. Historical Account of Discoveries and Travels in Africa; enlarged and completed to the Present Time, with Illustrations of its Geography, Natural History, and the Moral and Social Condition of its Inhabitants, by Hugh Murray. 2 vols. *Maps.* 8°
Edinburgh, 1817
—— *See* Murray, Hugh.

Leyds, J. J. K. "Tellus et Homo": Eenige onderzoekingen op Geophysisch Anthropologisch en aanverwant Gebied. (Stellingen en Desiderata.) 8*
Amsterdam, 1885

Leyland, John. The Peak of Derbyshire, its Scenery and Antiquities; with illustrations by Alfred Dawson and Herbert Railton. 8° 1891
—— The Yorkshire Coast and the Cleveland Hills and Dales; with illustrations by Alfred Dawson and Lancelot Speed. 8° 1892

Leyland, R. W. Round the World in 124 Days. *Map and photographs.* 8°
Liverpool, 1880

Leys, P. Borneo. Despatch from Consul-General Leys to Earl Granville. *Map.* Folio* 1883

Leys, T. W. *See* Sherrin and Wallace.

Leyst, E. Katalog der Meteorologischen Beobachtungen in Russland und Finnland. Vierter Supplement - band zum Repertorium für Meteorologie herausgegeben von der Kaiserlichen Academie der Wissenschaften. 4°
St Petersburg, 1887

L'Heremite, Admiral J. *See* Hermite.

Lhotsky, Dr J. A Journey from Sydney to the Australian Alps: being an Account of the Geographical and Natural Relations of the Country traversed, its Aborigines, &c., together with some General Information respecting the Colony of New South Wales. 8° *Sydney*, 1835

Liagre, J. Cosmographie Stellaire. *Plates.* 12° *Brussels*, 1884

Liais, E. Exploração dos Rios S. Francisco e das Velhas. 4*
[*Rio de Janeiro*, 1863]
—— Climats, Géologie, Faune, et Géographie Botanique du Brésil. *Map.* Large 8° *Paris*, 1872

Lias, Brau de Saint-Pol. Déli et les Colons-Explorateurs Français. 8*
Paris, 1877
—— Exploration et Colonisation. *Maps and plates.* 8° *Paris*, 1878
—— Percement de l'Isthme de Panama. *Maps and plates.* 8* *Paris*, 1879
—— Pérak et les Orangs-Sakèys: Voyage dans l'Intérieur de la Presqu'île Malaise. *Maps and illustrations.* 12° *Paris*, 1883
—— Ile de Sumatra, chez les Atchés, Lohong. *Map and illustrations.* 12°
Paris, 1884
—— De France à Sumatra par Java, Singapour, et Pinang; les Anthropophages. *Maps and plates.* 12° *Paris*, 1884

Libbey, William, junr. *See* Guyot.

Libert, Abbé. Voyage Pittoresque sur le Rhin depuis Mayence jusqu'à Dusseldorf, d'après l'Allemand. *Map and plates.* 8°
Frankfort-o-M., 1807

Lichtenstein, Henry. Travels in Southern Africa in 1803-6. Translated from the German by Anne Plumptre. 2 vols. *Map and plates.* 4° 1812-15
—— *See* Eyriès, Vol. 11: Appendix 1.

Licquet, Théod. Rouen: Précis de son Histoire, son Commerce, son Industrie, ses Manufactures, ses Monumens. 12°
Rouen, 1831

Liddell and Gordon, Messrs. Report on the Proposed Railway between the Danube and the Black Sea (from Tchernavoda to Kustendjie), and the Free Port at Kustendjie. *Map.* 8* 1857

Liddell, H. G. *See* Dictionaries, General: Appendix 2.

Lidsky, S. A. Expedition in Turkestan and Bokhara in 1887. [In Russian.] 8*

Lidstone, W. *See* Brown, C. B.

Lieber, O. M. Notes on the Geology of the Coast of Labrador. 4* *Washington* [1860]

Liebig, J. V. Induction und Deduction. 8* *Munich*, 1865
Liebmann, Prof. J. A. See Chisholm.
Liebschen, Dr G. Japan's landwirthschaftliche und allegemeinwirthschaftliche Verhältnisse. *Maps.* 8° *Jena*,1882
Liechtenstern, J. M. F. von. Handbuch der neuesten Geographie des Oesterreichischen Kaiserstaates. 3 vols. 8° *Vienna*, 1817-18
Liégeard, Stephen. La Côte d'Azur. *Illustrations.* 4° *Paris* [1888]
Lieussou, A. Recherches sur les Variations de la Marche des Pendules et des Chronomètres, suivies d'un Projet d'Organisation du Service des Chronomètres Appartenant à la Marine. 8° *Paris*, 1854
Light, Capt. See Walpole, Turkey: Appendix 1.
Light, Henry. Travels in Egypt, Nubia, Holy Land, Mount Lebanon, and Cyprus, in the year 1814. *Plates.* 4° 1818
Ligon, R. See Recueil de divers Voyages, p. 595: Appendix 1.
Liliencron, R. von. Ueber den Inhalt der allgemeinen Bildung in der Zeit der Scholastik. 4* *Munich*, 1876
Lilliehöök, C. B. See Gaimard, Paul.
Lima, Lopez de. See Santarem.
Linant de Bellefonds. See Bellefonds.
Lincoln, William. History of Worcester, Massachusetts, from its earliest Settlement to September 1836. *Map.* 8° *Worcester*, 1837
Lind, Dr J. See Troil.
Linda, Luca de. Descriptio Orbis et Omnium ejus rerum Publicarum. 8° *Amsterdam*, 1665
Lindahl, Erico. See Ihre.
Lindau, W. A. Vergissmeinnicht. Ein Taschenbuch für den Besuch der Sächsischen Schweiz und der angränzenden Theile Böhmens. *Plate.* [*Map wanting.*] 8° *Dresden*, 1823
—— Merkwürdigkeiten Dresdens und der Umgegend. *Maps.* 24° *Leipzig*, 1832
Lindeman, Moritz. Die arktische Fischerei der deutschen Seestädte, 1620-1868. In vergleichender Darstellung. (Ergänzungsheft, 26 — Petermann's Mittheilungen.) 2 *charts.* 4° *Gotha*, 1869
—— Polar-Nachrichten. 4* *Gotha*, 1879
—— Die Seefischereien, ihre Gebiete, Betrieb und Erträge, 1869-78. (Ergänzungsheft, 60 — Petermann's Mittheilungen.) *Maps.* 4° *Gotha*, 18
—— Der Norddeutsche Lloyd, Geschichte und Handbuch. *Tables, maps, and illustrations.* 8° *Bremen*, 1892
—— See Polar, Arctic, H : Appendix 2.
—— **and O. Finsch.** Die zweite Deutsche Nordpolarfahrt in den Jahren 1869 und 1870 unter Führung des Kapitän Koldewey. Volksausgabe. *Maps and plates.* 8° *Leipzig*, 1875

Lindenberg, Paul. See Schütt.
Linder, M. Étude sur les Terrains de Transport du Département de la Gironde, suivie de Considérations sur la Formation du Terrain Quaternaire en général. 8° *Bordeaux*, 1868
Lindhagen, D. G. Geografiska Ortsbestämningar pa Spetsbergen af Prof. A. E. Nordenskiöld. 4* *Stockholm*, 1863
Lindhagen, G. See Struve, W.
Lindley, John. The Vegetable Kingdom ; or, The Structure, Classification, and Uses of Plants illustrated upon the Natural System. 3rd edition, with corrections and additional Genera. *Illustrations.* 8° 1853
Lindley, Walter, and J. P. Widney. California of the South, its Physical Geography, Climate, Resources, Routes of Travel, and Health-Resorts : being a complete Guide-Book to Southern California. *Maps and illustrations.* 8° *New-York*, 1888
Lindsay, A. W. C. Report on the Mysore General Census of 1871. *Map.* 8° *Bangalore*, 1874
—— Supplement to the same. Appendices A to H. 8° *Bangalore*, 1875
Lindsay, D. See South Australia, A: Appendix 2.
Lindsay, David B. Remarks on the Opening of Trade and Cultivation of Tropical Products in the Kingdom of Usambara, East Africa. 8* 1885
Lindsay, H. H. Report of Proceedings on a Voyage to the Northern Ports of China in the ship "Lord Amherst." 2nd edition. 8° 1834
Lindsay, John. Voyage to the Coast of Africa in 1758, containing an Account of the Expedition to, and taking of the Island of Goree, by the Hon. Aug. Keppel. *Map and plates.* 4° 1759
Lindsay, Lord. Letters on Egypt, Edom, and the Holy Land. 8° 1847
—— See Crawford and Balcarres.
Lindsay, Rev. T. M. See Moir.
Lindsay, W. Lauder. Experiments on the Dyeing Properties of Lichens. 8* *Edinburgh*, 1854
—— The Flora of Iceland. 8* *Edinburgh*, 1861
—— On the Geology of the Gold-Fields of Auckland, New Zealand. 8* 1862
—— On the Geology of the Gold-Fields of Otago, New Zealand. [2 *leaves.*] 8* 1862
—— The Lichen-Flora of Greenland; with Notes of Diatomaceæ from Danish Greenland collected by Robert Brown, by Prof. Dickie. 8* [*Edinburgh*, 1870]
Lindsay, W. S. History of Merchant Shipping and Ancient Commerce. 4 vols. *Maps and illustrations.* 8° 1883

Lindström, A. *See* Sweden, A: Appendix 2.

Lindström, G. Om Trias och Juraförsteningar från Spetsbergen. *Plates.* 4*
Stockholm, 1865
—— *See* Richthofen.

Lindt, J. W. Picturesque New Guinea; with an Historical Introduction, and Supplementary Chapters on the Manners and Customs of the Papuans. Accompanied with Fifty full-page Autotype Illustrations from Negatives of Portraits from Life, and Groups and Landscapes from Nature. 4°   1887

Linet, Ph. *See* Taylor, C. E.

Link, H. F. *See* Pelham, Vol. 2: Appendix 1.

Linna, Nicolaus de. *See* Hakluyt, Vol. 1: Appendix 1.

Linnæus, C. Lachesis Lapponica, or a Tour in Lapland. Now first published from the Original Manuscript Journal of the celebrated Linnæus, by J. E. Smith. 2 vols. 8°   1811
—— *See* Ahrling.

Linnarsson, J. G. O. *See* Sweden, A: Appendix 2.

Linschoten, J. H. van. Discourse of Voyages into the East and West Indies. *Maps.* Folio   1598
[For Contents, *see* Appendix 1.]
—— *See* Hakluyt Soc. Publ., Vols. 70, 71; Astley, Vol. 1; Purchas, Vol. 2, Book 10; Allgemeine Historie, Vol. 1: Appendix 1; *also* India: Appendix 2.

Linth, A. Escher von der. Geologische Bemerkungen über das Nördliche Vorarlberg und einige angrenzende Gegenden. *Plates.* 4°   *Zurich*, 1853

Liorel, Jules. Races Berbères Kabylie du Jurjura. Préface de Émile Masqueray. 12°   *Paris*, N.D.

Liot, Capt. W. B. Panamá, Nicaragua, and Tehuantepec; or, Considerations upon the Question of Communication between the Atlantic and Pacific Oceans. *Plates.* 8°   1849

Lippencott, J. B. A Complete Pronouncing Gazetteer or Geographical Dictionary of the World. Edited by J. Thomas and T. Baldwin. 2 vols. Royal 8°   *Philadelphia*, 1885
—— New edition. Royal 8°
Philadelphia, 1893

Lisiansky, Urey. A Voyage round the World, in the years 1803-4-5-6, performed by order of His Imperial Majesty Alexander the First, Emperor of Russia, in the ship "Neva." *Portrait and maps.* 4°   1814
—— *See* Eyriès, Vol. 6: Appendix 1.

Lisle, A. de. *See* Ducat.

Lisle, — de. *See* Allgemeine Historie, Vol. 19: Appendix 1.

Lissignol, E. *See* Mueller, F. von.

Lista, Ramon. Viaje al País de los Tehuelches. Exploraciones en la Patagonia Austral. *Maps and plates.* 8°
Buenos Ayres, 1879
—— Exploracion de la Costa Oriental de la Patagonia, bajo los auspicios del Gobierno Nacional. *Plate.* 8*
Buenos Ayres, 1880
—— Mis Exploraciones y Descurimientos en la Patagonia, 1877-80. *Maps, portraits, and plates.* Large 8°
Buenos Ayres, 1880
—— El Territorio de las Missiones. *Maps and plates.* Small folio
Buenos Ayres, 1883
—— Viaje al País de los Onas, Tierra del Fuego. *Map and plates.* 8°
Buenos Ayres, 1887

Lister, Christopher. *See* Withrington, R., in Burney, Vol. 2; and Hakluyt, Vol. 4: Appendix 1.

Lithgow, William. Travels and Voyages through Europe, Asia, and Africa for Nineteen Years; containing an Account of the Religion . . . of the several Countries . . and a Description of Jerusalem . . ; also a Narrative of the Tortures he suffered in the Spanish Inquisition, &c. 11th edition. *Plates.* 8°
1770

Little, Archibald John. Through the Yang-tse Gorges; or, Trade and Travel in Western China. *Map.* 8°   1888
—— Notes on Western China and the Opening of Ch'ung-King. 8*   [1890]
—— *See* Hosie.

Little, Lieut. C. B. *See* West.

Little, Rev. Henry W. Madagascar, its History and People. *Map.* 8°   1884

Littlehales, G. W. *See* United States, E, *a*, Hydrographic Office Publs.: Appendix 2.

Littrow, H. von. Ueber Seekarten neuerer Art, und über die Darstellung des Meeresgrundes. Square 8*   *Budapest*, 1874

Littrow, Karl von. Verzeichniss geographischer Ortsbestimmungen nach den neuesten Quellen und mit Angabe derselben. 8°   *Leipzig*, 1844
—— Die Culminationspunkte der Oestlichen Central-Alpen. 8*   *Vienna*, 1853
—— Ueber das allgemeine Niveau der Meere. 8*   *Vienna*, 1853

Liveing, Edward H. Transylvanian Gold Mining. *Map.* 8*
Newcastle-upon-Tyne, 1886

Liversidge, Prof. A. List of Scientific Papers and Reports by Professor Archibald Liversidge. 8*   *Sydney*, N.D.
—— The Minerals of New South Wales. 2nd edition. 4°   [*Sydney*, 1882]
—— The Minerals of New South Wales, &c. *Map and diagrams.* Large 8°   1888
—— *See* New South Wales, B: Appendix 2.

Livingstone, David. South-Central Africa and its Explorer: being the Report of a Meeting held in Cape Town, Nov. 12, 1856, in honour of the Rev. Dr Livingstone; with Notes by the Astronomer-Royal. 8* *Cape Town*, 1856
—— Missionary Travels and Researches in South Africa, including a Sketch of Sixteen Years' Residence in the Interior of Africa, and a Journey from the Cape of Good Hope to Loanda on the West Coast, thence across the Continent, down the River Zambesi, to the Eastern Ocean. *Maps and plates.* 8° 1857
—— Outlines of his Missionary Journeys and Discoveries in Central South Africa. *Map.* 8* 1857
—— Narrative of Discoveries. 12* 1857
—— Analysis of the Language of the Bechuanas. 4* 1858
—— Cambridge Lectures; with a Prefatory Letter by Professor Sedgwick. Edited, with Life, Notes, &c., by W. Monk. *Portrait and map.* 8° 1858
—— The Farewell Livingstone Festival. 8* [1858]
—— Newspaper Cuttings. 8* 1872
—— Report to the Subscribers by the Livingstone Search and Relief Committee. 8* 1872
—— Despatches in 1870-71-72. Folio* 1872
—— The Finding of Dr Livingstone by H. M. Stanley. *Plates.* 8° N.D.
—— The Last Journals of David Livingstone in Central Africa; continued by a Narrative of his Last Moments and Sufferings, obtained from his Faithful servants Chuma and Susi. Edited by Horace Waller. 2 vols. *Plates and loose map.* 8° 1874
—— *See* Blaikie; Johnston; Montefiore; Riso; Stanley, Dean; Stanley, H. M.; Vallat.
—— **and Charles Livingstone.** Narrative of an Expedition to the Zambesi and its Tributaries, and of the Discovery of the Lakes Shirwa and Nyassa, 1858-64. *Map and plates.* 8° 1865
Lizzoli, L. Osservazioni sul dipartimento dell' Agogna. 8° *Milan*, 1802
Ljungstedt, Sir Andrew. An Historical Sketch of the Portuguese Settlements in China, and of the Roman Catholick Church and Mission in China; with a Supplementary Chapter descriptive of the City of Canton. *Maps and plates.* 8° *Boston, Mass.*, 1836
Llauradō, André de. Quatrième Congrès International de Navigation Intérieure, Manchester, 1890. La Navigation Intérieure en Espagne. Folio* 1890
Lloyd, G. T. Thirty-three Years in Tasmania and Victoria: being the actual experience of the Author, interspersed with Historic Jottings, Narratives, and Counsel to Emigrants. *Map.* Sm. 8° 1862

Lloyd, H. E. *See* Orlich.
Lloyd, J. A. Account of Levellings carried across the Isthmus of Panamá to ascertain the relative Height of the Pacific Ocean at Panamá and of the Atlantic at the mouth of the River Chagres; accompanied by Geographical and Topographical Notices of the Isthmus. 4* 1829
Lloyd, L. Scandinavian Adventures, with some Account of the Northern Fauna. 2 vols. *Maps and plates.* Royal 8° 1854
Lloyd, Susette Harriet. Sketches of Bermuda. *Plates.* 8° 1835
Lloyd, Major Sir W. Narrative of a Journey from Caunpoor to the Boorendo Pass in the Himalaya Mountains, viâ Gwalior, Agra, Delhi, and Sirhind; with Capt. A. Gerard's Account of an attempt to penetrate to Garoo and the Lake Manasarowara. 2 vols. *Maps.* 8° 1840
—— *See* Gerard, A.
Loaisa, Garcia de. *See* Loyasa.
Lobate, Jose G. Estudio quimico-industrial de los varios Productos del Maguey Mexicano y Analisis Quimico del Aquaruiel y el Pulque. 12° *Mexico*, 1884
Lobeck, Justo Florian. Ojeada retrospectiva sobre la marcha que, desde los tiempos antiguos hasta nuestros dias, se ha seguido al tratar de la Mitolojía Clásica. Estudio primero. 8* *Santiago*, 1862
Lobley, J. Logan. Mount Vesuvius: a Descriptive, Historical, and Geological Account of the Volcano; with a Notice of the recent Eruption, and an Appendix containing Letters by Pliny the Younger, &c. *Map, plate, and section.* 8* 1868
—— Mount Vesuvius and its surroundings. *Map and illustrations.* 8° 1889
Lobo, Jerome. Voyage Historique d'Abissinie. Traduite du Portugais, continuée et augmentée de plusieurs dissertations, lettres et mémoires, par M. Legrand. *Maps.* 4° *Paris*, 1728
—— Voyage to Abyssinia, containing a Narrative of the dangers he underwent in his attempt to pass from the Indies into Abyssinia; with a Description of the Coasts of the Red Sea, History, Laws, Religion, &c., of the Abyssens; Admission of the Jesuits into Abyssinia in 1622 and Expulsion in 1634; a Description of the Nile; with a Continuation of the History, by Legrand. 8° 1735
—— *See* Gottfried; Pinkerton, Vol. 15; Ray; Thevenot, Vol. 4: Appendix 1.
Lobysévitsch, Théodore. La Ligne Militaire du Syr-Daria. 8* *St Petersburg*, 1865

Loch, H. B. Personal Narrative of Occurrences during Lord Elgin's Second Embassy to China, 1860. *Maps and portrait.* 8° 1869

Lock, Alfred G. Gold, its Occurrence and Extraction, embracing the Geographical and Geological Distribution, and the Mineralogical Characters of Gold-bearing Rocks ; a Bibliography of the subject, and a Glossary of English and Foreign Technical Terms. *Frontispiece, maps, and illustrations.* Large 8° 1882

Lock, C. G. W. The Home of the Eddas. With a chapter on the Sprengisandr, by Dr C. Le Neve Foster. 8° 1879

Locke, John. Meteorology of the Sea : Weather Maps, Storm Telegraphs, and the submarine Atlantic Cable. 8* *Dublin,* 1860

—— Polar Exploration, Arctic and Antarctic. *Diagrams.* 8* *Dublin,* 1861

—— Remarkable Discoveries in Central Australia ; with an Improved Map showing the additional routes of Stuart and Burke: Second Paper. 8* *Dublin,* 1862

—— The same, with Map showing the principal routes, including Stuart's Third and Successful Attempt to reach the Northern Coast : Third Paper. 8* *Dublin,* 1863

Lockhart, William. The Medical Missionary in China, a Narrative of Twenty Years' Experience. *Plate.* 8° 1861

Lockhart, Capt. W. S. A. *See* Mouraviev ; *also* Asia, Central : Appendix 2.

Lockwood, Anthony. A brief Description of Nova Scotia, with Plates of the principal Harbours, including a particular Account of the Island of Grand Manan. *Plates.* 4° 1818

Lockyer, Prof. J. Norman. Outlines of Physiography : the Movements of the Earth. *Illustrations.* 12° 1887

—— *See* Symons.

Locusteanu, C. Dictionar Geografic al Judetului Románati. 8° *Bucharest,* 1889

Loczy, Professor. Rapport de la Commission d'Études du Lac Balaton pour 1891. Large 8* *Budapest,* 1891

Loescher, Abraham. *See* Pausanius.

Loewy, B. *See* Victoria, C : Appendix 2.

Löffler, Prof. Dr. E Forsög paa en geognostisk Tydning af Landenes Overfladeforhold. 8* *Copenhagen,* 1876

—— Haandbog i Geographien. *Maps.* 8° *Copenhagen,* 1866

—— Quelques Réflexions sur les Études Géographiques, leur but et leur situation actuelle. Small 8* *Copenhagen,* 1879

—— The Vineland Excursions of the Ancient Scandinavians. 8° *Copenhagen,* 1883

Löfstrand, G. *See* Sweden, A: Appendix 2.

Loftie, W. J. A History of London. 2 vols. *Maps and illustrations.* 8° 1883

Loftus, A. J. Notes of a Journey across the Isthmus of Kra, made with the French Government Survey Expedition, January to April 1883 ; with Explanatory Map and Sections, and Appendix containing Reprint of Report to the Indian Government by Captains Fraser and Forlong in 1863. 8* *Singapore,* 1883

—— A New Year's Paper on the Development of the Kingdom of Siam. *Map.* 8* 1890

—— The Kingdom of Siam, its Progress and Prospects. *Map and portraits.* 8* 1891

Loftus, W. Kennett. Travels and Researches in Chaldea and Susiana ; with an Account of Excavations at Warka, the " Erech " of Nimrod, and Shúsh, " Shushan the Palace " of Esther, in 1849-52. *Maps and plates.* 8° 1857

Logan, J. Richardson. The Rocks of Pulo Ubin, with some Remarks on the Formation and Structure of the Hypogene Rocks, and on the Metamorphic Theory. 4* *Singapore,* 1846

—— Ethnology of the Indo-Pacific Islands. Part 2. Appendix. The Semitic and African Numerals. 8* *Penang,* 1855-56

Logan, Josias. *See* Purchas, Vol. 3, Book 3 : Appendix 1.

Logan, Capt. P. Journal of a Journey from Brisbane Town to St George's Pass ; with an Account of his Murder by the Natives of New South Wales, by Lieutenant Edwards. Folio *Sydney,* 1826-30

Logan, William. Malabar. 2 vols. *Maps, chart, and plates.* 8° *Madras,* 1887

—— A Collection of Treaties, Engagements, and other Papers of importance relating to British Affairs in Malabar. Edited with Notes by W. Logan. 2nd edition. Large 8° *Madras,* 1891

Logan, Sir William E. Plans of Various Lakes and Rivers between Lake Huron and the River Ottawa, to accompany the Geological Reports for 1853-56. 4° *Toronto,* 1857

Löher F. von. Cypern. Reiseberichte über Natur und Landschaft, Volk und Geschichte. Small 8° *Stuttgart,* 1878

—— Cyprus, Historical and Descriptive. Adapted from the German of Franz von Löher, with much additional matter by Mrs A. Batson Joyner. *Maps.* Square 8° 1878

Lok, Capt. John. *See* Astley, Vol. 1 ; Hakluyt, Vol. 2 ; Kerr, Vol. 7 ; Allgemeine Historie, Vol. 1 : Appendix 1.

Lok, Michael. *See* Burney, Vol. 2 : Appendix 1.

Lollis, Cesare De. Cristoforo Colombo nella Leggenda e nella Storia. 8° *Milan,* 1892

Lomba, Ramon Lopez. La República Oriental del Uruguay. Obra de Estadistica escrita con el fin de hacer conocer bajo todos sus aspectos principales el pais y las incomparables ventajas que ofrece a la Emigracion Europea. *Map.* Large 8° *Montevideo*, 1884

Lombard, H. C. Climatologie Médicale. Atlas de la distribution géographique des maladies dans leurs rapports avec les climats. 4° *Paris*, 1880

Lombardini, Elia. Saggio Idrologico sul Nilo. *Maps.* 4* *Milan*, 1864
—— Essai sur l'Hydrologie du Nil. 2 *maps, 1 diagram.* 4* *Paris*, 1865

Lommel, Eugen. Georg Simon Ohm's wissenschaftliche Leistungen. Festrede gehalten in der öffentlichen Sitzung der K. B. Akademie der Wissenschaften zu München am 28 März 1889. 4* *Munich*, 1889
—— *See* Fraunhofer.

Long, Baron de. Pilote Norvégien d'après les travaux de la direction Hydrographique de Norvége, réunis et traduits. *Plates.* 8° *Paris*, 1858

Long, C. Chaillé. *See* Chaillé-Long.

Long, Major E. H. *See* Eyriès, Vol. 9 : Appendix 1.

Long, Prof. George. *See* Xenophon's " Anabasis."
—— *See* Herodotus ; Trendelenburg.
—— **and G. R. Porter.** The Geography of Great Britain. Part 1. England and Wales ; with Statistics to 1850 by Hyde Clarke. 8° N.D.
—— **G. R. Porter, and G. Tucker.** America and the West Indies Geographically Described. *Maps.* 8° 1845

Long, Henry Lawes. Campaign of Alexander in Affghanistan. *Map.* 8* 1848
—— Survey of the Early Geography of Western Europe, as Connected with the First Inhabitants of Britain, their Origin, Language, Religious Rites, and Edifices. *Map and plates.* 8° 1859

Long, J. le. La République Argentine. Étude sur sa situation économique et son état financier en 1876. 2nd edition. 8* *Bordeaux*, 1876
—— Les Pampas de la République Argentine. 2nd edition. *Map.* 8* *Paris*, 1878

Long, J. Voyages and Travels of an Indian Interpreter and Trader, describing the Manners and Customs of the North-American Indians ; with an Account of the Posts situated on the River Saint Lawrence, Lake Ontario, &c. ; to which is added a Vocabulary of the Chippeway Language . . . a list of words in the Iroquois, Mohegan, Shawanee, and Esquimeaux Tongues, &c. *Map.* 4° 1791

Long, Rev. J. Peeps into Social Life in Calcutta a Century Ago. 8*
Calcutta, 1868

Long, Rev. J. The Social Condition of the Muhammadans of Bengal, and the Remedies. 8* *Calcutta*, 1869
—— Oriental Proverbs and their Uses. 8* 1875
—— On Russian Proverbs, as illustrating Russian Manners and Customs. 8* 1876
—— The Position of Turkey in Relation to British Interests in India. 8* 1876
—— The Eastern Question in its Anglo-Indian Aspect. Small 8* -1877
—— The Slavonic Provinces of Turkey : a Tour in the Autumn of 1875. 8* 1876
—— A Visit to Russia in 1876. 8* N.D.
—— Proverbs, English and Keltic, with their Eastern Relations. 8* N.D.
—— Village Communities in India and Russia. 8* *Calcutta*, N.D.
—— The Russian Bugbear : Turkey, Russia, and India. 8* N.P., N.D.
—— Notes on a Visit to Moscow and Kief in 1873 in Reference to the Russian Church, Bible Circulation, and Social Reform. 8* N.D.

Longman, William. Suggestions for the Exploration of Iceland. *Map.* 8* *[Printed by the Alpine Club]* 1861

Longman's School Geographies. *See* Chisholm.

Longnon, A. Géographie de la Gaule au VIe Siècle. *Maps.* 8° 1878

Longobard, —. *See* Purchas, Vol. 3 : Appendix 1.

Longridge, James Atkinson. The Hooghly and the Mutla. Edited by C. Manby and J. Forrest. *Map.* 8* 1864

Longstaff, G. B. Studies in Statistics, Social, Political, and Medical. *Maps and diagrams.* 8° 1891
—— Rural Depopulation. Read before the Royal Statistical Society, 20th June 1893. 8* 1893

Longstaff, L. W. Notes on the Contents of the Wimbledon Free Public Library (September 1888). 3rd edition. 8* 1888

Loomis, Elias. An Introduction to Practical Astronomy, with a Collection of Astronomical Tables. 8° *New York*, 1863

Lopatinsky, L. Russo - Kabardinian Vocabulary. Published by the Educational Department of the Caucasus. [In Russian.] 8° *Tiflis*, 1890

Lopes de Lima, José Joaquim. Ensaios sobre a Statistica das Possessões Portuguezas na Africa Occidental e Oriental, na Asia Occidental, na China, e na Oceania, e Continuados por Francisco Maria Bordalo. 5 vols. *Maps and tables.* 8° *Lisbon*, 1844-62
Vol. 1.—Das Ilhas de Cabo-Verde no Mar Atlantico e suas Dependencias na Guiné Portugueza ao Norte do Equador.

Lopes de Lima, José Joaquim—*continued.*

Vol. 2.—Das Ilhas de S. Thomé e Principe no Golfo de Guiné, e sua Dependencia o Forte de S. João Baptista d'Ajuda na Costa de Léste, Chamada dos Popós Além da Mina.

Vol. 3.—De Angola e Benguella e suas Dependencias na Costa Occidental d'Africa ao sul do Equador.

Vol. 4.—De Moçambique e suas Dependencias na Costa Oriental da Africa ao sul do Equador.

Vol. 5.—Estado da India, Parte Primeira. Goa, Damão, Diu, e suas Dependencias.

—— *See* Santarem.

Lopez de Legaspi, Michael. *See* Burney, Vol. 1 ; Purchas, Vol. 3 : Appendix 1.

Lopez, Duarte or Edouardo. *See* Pigafetta, F ; *also* Astley, Vol. 3 ; Gottfried ; Purchas, Vol. 2, Book 6 ; Allgemeine Historie, Vol. 4 : Appendix 1.

Lopez, Don Hippolito Ruiz, First Botanist, and Chief of the Expedition to Peru and Chili : Historical Eulogium of. Translated from the Spanish. 8*
Salisbury, 1831

Lopez, Juan Joze. Ueber die ökonomischen und politischen Beziehungen Deutschlands mit den La Plata-Staaten, und Europas mit den übrigen Hispano-Amerikanischen Republiken. 4*
Berlin, N.D.

Lopez y Ramajo, Antonio Maria. Breve Descripcion de las Cosas mas Notables que Existen en la insigne Ciudad de Alcalá de Henares. 4* *Madrid,* 1861

Lopez, Thomé. *See* Ramusio, Vol. 1 ; Collecção de Noticias, p. 610, Vol. 2 : Appendix 1.

Lopez, Vicente F. Historia de la Repùblica Argentina su Origen su Revolucion y su Desarrollo Politico hasta 1852. 2 vols. *Planispheres.* 8° *Buenos Ayres,* 1883

Lorck, Andreas. Hermann von Salza, Sein Itinerar. Inaugural Dissertation zur Erlangung der Doctorwürde der philosophischen Facultat der Universitat zu Kiel. 8* *Kiel,* 1880

Lord, Eliot. *See* United States, G, *c,* Geological Survey [King] Monographs, Vol. 4, Comstock Mining and Miners : Appendix 2.

Lord, Rev. H. *See* Churchill, Vol. 6 : Appendix 1.

Lord, J. K. The Naturalist in Vancouver Island and British Columbia. 2 vols. *Plates.* 8° 1866

Lord, W. B., and T. Baines. Shifts and Expedients of Camp Life, Travel, and Exploration. *Plates.* 8° 1876

Lorenz, Otto. Catalogue Général de la Librairie Française depuis 1840. Table des Matières, 1840-1875. [Vols. 7 and 8 of the whole work.] 2 vols. 8° *Paris,* 1878-80

—— The same. Tome Neuvième. (Tome Premier du Catalogue de 1876-85, A—H.) 8° *Paris,* 1886

—— The same. Tome Dixième. (Tome Second du Catalogue de 1876-85, I—Z.) 8° *Paris,* 1887

—— The same. Tome Onzième. (Table des Matières des Tomes IX. et X., 1876-85.) *Paris,* 1888

—— *See* Jordell.

Lorenzen, Chr. C. Dannevirke og Omegn. *Map.* 12* *Hadersleben,* 1863

Lorentz, Dr Pablo G. *See* Argentine, D : Appendix 2.

Loriol, ——. La France : Description Géographique, Statistique, et Topographique, Alsace, Haut-Rhin et Bas-Rhin, Seine Inférieure et Orne, Eure et Loire, et Puy de Dôme. 3 vols. *Maps.* 8° *Paris,* 1834

Loriol, P. de. *See* Choffat.

Lorne, Marquis of. A Trip to the Tropics, and Home through America. 2nd edition. *Frontispiece.* 8° 1867

—— Canadian Pictures, drawn with Pen and Pencil. *Map and illustrations.* 4° 1885

—— Our Railway to the Pacific. With Illustrations by H. R. H. Princess Louise. Reprinted from *Good Words.* Large 8* 1886

—— Canadian Life and Scenery; with Hints to intending Emigrants and Settlers. *Illustrations.* 12° 1886

Lortet, Dr. La Syrie d'Aujourd 'hui : Voyages dans la Phénicie, le Liban, et la Judée 1875-80. *Maps and illustrations.* Folio *Paris,* 1884

Loti, Pierre. Au Maroc. 12° *Paris,* 1890

Lottin de Laval, ——. Voyage dans la Péninsule Arabique du Sinaï et l'Égypte Moyenne, Histoire, Géographie, Épigraphie. 4° *Paris,* 1855-59

Lottin, Victor. *See* Gaimard, Paul.

Lottner, F. H. Geognostische Skizze des Westfälischen Steinkohlen-Gebirges. 8* *Iserlohn,* 1863

Loughman, T. C., and Lieut. H. B. Sandford. Brief Notes relative to the Satara Jageerdars. [From India Records, No. 41] *Bombay,* 1857

Louis XVIII., King of France. Relation d'un Voyage à Bruxelles et à Coblentz, 1791. *Portrait.* 32° *Paris,* 1823

Louis, J. A. H. A Few Words on the Present State and Future Prospects of Sericulture in Bengal. 8* 1880

Loureiro, J. de. Flora Cochinchinensis, Sistens Plantas in Regno Cochin-China nascentes, quibus accedunt Aliæ Observatæ in Sinensi Imperio, Africa Orientali, Indiæque Locis Variis . . . . 2 vols. in 1. 4° *Lisbon,* 1790

Loutfy Bey, Antoun Youssef. Projet d'une ligne de Chemin de Fer reliant l'Égypte à la Syrie, Note lue à la Société Khédiviale de Géographie du Caire le 20 Mars 1891. *Map.* 8* *Cairo,* 1891

Louw, P. J. F. De Derde Javaansche Successie-Oorlog (1746-1755). Large 8° *Batavia,* 1889

Lovén, S. Om en Märklig i Nordsjön Lefvande Art af Spongia. *Plate.* 8* *Stockholm,* 1868

Lovett, Major. *See* Persia : Appendix 2.

Lovett, Richard. James Gilmour of Mongolia, his Diaries, Letters, and Reports. *Portraits, maps, and illustrations.* 8° 1892
—— *See* Gilmour.

Low, C. R. History of the Indian Navy (1613-1863). 2 vols. 8° 1877

Low, Hugh. Sarawak, its Inhabitants and Productions. *Plates.* 8° 1848

Low, Sampson. *See* Catalogues, A, English Catalogue of Books : Appendix 2.

Lowe, F. *See* Smyth, W.

Lowell, Percival. Chosön, the Land of the Morning Calm : a Sketch of Korea. *Maps and illustrations.* Large 8° [1885]

Löwenberg, J. *See* Peschel.

Löwenörn, P. Beskrivelse til Kaartet over Færöerne. 4* *Copenhagen,* 1805
—— New Sailing Directory for the Cattegat, the Sound, and the Belts ; with Directions for the Belt by Mr John Bain and other British Officers, and Descriptions of the New Lights and Alterations to the present time. 8° 1844
—— *See* Mas.

Löwenstern, Isidore. Les États-Unis et la Havane : Souvenirs d'un Voyageur. 8° *Paris,* 1842
—— Remarques sur la Deuxième Écriture Cunéiforme de Persepolis. 4* *Paris,* 1850

Löwl, Dr Ferdinand. Die Granitkerne des Kaiserwaldes bei Marienbad. Ein Problem der Gebirgskunde. *Maps and profiles.* 4* *Prague,* 1885
—— *See* Germany, C, Forschungen, &c., Vol. 2 : Appendix 2.

Low's Discovery of the Banians. *See* Pinkerton, Vol. 8 : Appendix 1.

Lowth, George T. Wanderer in Arabia, or Western Footsteps in Eastern Tracks. 2 vols. *Plates.* 8° 1855

Löwy, Rev. A. Half a Century of Progress in the Knowledge and Practice of Judaism. 8* 1893

T

Löwy, Rev. A. *See* Catalogues, A : Appendix 2 (General).

Loyasa, Garcia Jofre de. *See* Burney, Vol. 1 ; Callander, Vol. 1 ; Gottfried ; Navaretti, Vol. 5 : Appendix 1.

Loyer, Godfrey. *See* Astley, Vol. 2 ; Allgemeine Historie, Vol. 3 : Appendix 1.

Lozano, Pedro. Descripcion Chorographica del Terreno, Rios, Arboles y Animales de las dilatadissimas Provincias del Gran Chaco, Gualamba, y de los ritos . . . de las . . . Naciones . . . qui le habitan. Con una Cabal Relacion Historica, &c. *Map.* *Cordova,* 1733
—— *See* Angelis, Vol. 1 : Appendix 1.

Luard, C. H. *See* Williams, J. M.

Lubafsky, A. Juridical Monographs and Researches. Vol. 4. [In Russian.] Small 8° *St Petersburg,* 1878

Lubbock, Sir John. Pre-Historic Times, as Illustrated by Ancient Remains and the Manners and Customs of Modern Savages. 2nd edition. *Plates.* 8° 1869
—— The Origin of Civilisation, and the Primitive Condition of Man : Mental and Social Condition of Savages. *Plates.* 8° 1870

Lubbock, Mrs. *See* Galton, F., Vacation Tourists.

Luc, Jean André de. Lettres Physiques et Morales sur l'Histoire de la Terre et de l'Homme. 5 vols. 8° *Paris,* 1779
—— Introduction à la Physique Terrestre par les Fluides Expansibles . . . pour servir de suite et de Développement aux Recherches sur les Modifications de l'Atmosphère. 2 vols. *Tables.* 8° *Paris,* 1805
—— Traité Élementaire de Géologie. 8° *Paris,* 1806
—— Histoire du Passage des Alpes par Annibal, dans laquelle on Détermine d'une manière précise la Route de ce Général, depuis Carthagène jusqu'au Tesin, d'après la Narration de Polybe, comparée aux Recherches Faites sur les Lieux. *Map* *Geneva,* 1825

Luca, Ferdinand de. La Società Geografica Italiana : Memoria. 8* *Naples,* 1861

Luca, Giuseppe de. Carte Nautiche del Medio Evo Disegnate in Italia. *Map.* 4* *Naples,* 1866
—— Storia Concetto Limiti della Geografia. 8° *Naples,* 1881

Luca, Jean de. *See* Gottfried ; Thevenot, Vol. 1 : Appendix 1.

Lucas, C. P. Introduction to a Historical Geography of the British Colonies. *Maps.* 12° *Oxford,* 1887
—— Historical Geography of the British Colonies. 3 vols. *Maps.* 12° *Oxford,* 1888-94

Lucas, Paul. Voyage au Levant. 2 vols. *Maps and plates.* 12° *The Hague*, 1709
—— Voyage dans la Grèce, l'Asie Mineure, la Macédoine, et l'Afrique. 2 vols. *Maps and plates.* 12° *Paris*, 1712
—— Voyage fait en 1714, &c., dans la Turquie, l'Asie, Sourie, Palestine, Haute et Basse Egypt, &c. 2 vols. *Maps and plates.* 12° *Amsterdam*, 1720

Lucca, Gaudentio di. The Adventures of Sig. Gaudentio di Lucca : being the substance of his Examination before the Fathers of the Inquisition at Bologna in Italy. . . . Copied from the Original Manuscript in St Mark's Library at Venice, with Critical Notes of the learned Signor Rhedi. . . . Translated from the Italian. 8°   1774

Lüdde, J. G. Die Methodik der Erdkunde. 8*   *Magdeburg*, 1842
—— Zeitschrift für vergleichende Erdkunde. Vol. 1. *Maps.* 8° *Magdeburg*, 1842
—— Die Geschichte der Methodologie der Erdkunde ; in ihrer ersten Grundlage, vermittelst einer historisch - kritischen Zusammenstellung der Literatur der Methodologie der Erdkunde. 8° *Leipzig*, 1849
—— Die Sonne im Dienste der Kartographie ; kritische Erörterungen zur Geschichte der neueren Kartographie, nach Reliefs von C. Raaz, G. Woldermann, C. Bamberg, Fr. Schilling. New ed. by Franz Matthes. 8* *Weimar*, 1874

Ludlam, A. New Zealand Exhibition, 1865 : Essay on the Cultivation and Acclimatisation of Trees and Plants. 8* *Dunedin*, 1865

Ludlow, J. Malcolm. British India, its Races and its History, considered with Reference to the Mutinies of 1857. 2 vols. 12° *Cambridge*, 1858

Ludolphus, Job. *See* Leutholf.

Ludwig, R. Versuch einer geographischen Darstellung von Hessen in der Tertiärzeit. *Map.* 8° *Darmstadt*, 1855
—— Geologische Skizze des Grossherzogthums Hessen. 4* *Darmstadt*, 1867

Ludwig Salvator, Archduke of Austria. Levkosia. *Plates.* 4° *Prague*, 1872
—— Yacht-Reisen in den Syrten, 1873. *Plates.* 4° *Prague*, 1874
—— Eine Spazierfahrt im Golfe von Korinth. *Map and plates.* 4° *Prague*, 1876
—— Um die Welt ohne zu wollen. 12° *Prague*, 1881
—— Hobartown. *Plates.* 4° *Prague*, 1886
—— Lose Blätter aus Abazia. 4° *Vienna*, 1886
—— Paxos und Antipaxos im Ionischen Meere. *Illustrations.* 4° *Vienna*, 1887
—— Die Kaymenen, Juli 1874. *Plates.* 4* *Prague*, 1875
—— Die Balearen in Wort und Bild. 7 vols. in 9. *Maps and plates.* Folio *Leipzig*, 1869-91
—— Die Liparischen Inseln. 5 parts. *Maps and plates.* Folio *Prague*, 1893-95

Lugard, Capt. F. D. Imperial British East Africa Company : Reports of Capt. Lugard on his Expedition to Uganda. 4 Reports. 4° and Folio*   V.D.
—— The Rise of our East African Empire : Early Efforts in Nyassaland and Uganda. 2 vols. *Maps, portraits, and illustrations.* 8°   1893

Lugrin, Charles H. New Brunswick (Canada), its Resources, Progress, and Advantages. *Maps, &c.* 8°   1886

Lühdorf, Baron von Augustus. Die heissen Quellen am Amur bei Neu-Michailowsk, im Bezirke Nicolajefsk. 8* *Hamburg*, 1882

Luillier, Sieur. Voyage aux Grandes Indes, avec une Instruction pour le Commerce des Indes Orientales. *Plate.* 12° *The Hague*, 1706
—— *See* Allgemeine Historie, Vol. 10 : Appendix 1.

Luks, H. T. Das Reichsland Elsass-Lothringen ; Topographisch-statistisches Handbuch mit kriegsgeschichtlichen Notizen und besonderer Berücksichtigung der Vogesen. Small 8° *Metz*, 1875

Luksch, J. Veröffentlichungen der Commission für Erforschung des östlichen Mittelmeeres. Vorläufiger Bericht über Lothungen und physikalische Beobachtungen im Sommer 1891. *Map.* Large 8*   *Vienna*, 1891
—— Vorläufiger Bericht über die physikalisch-oceanographischen Arbeiten im Sommer 1893. *Map.* 8* *Vienna*, 1893
—— *See* Wolf, Julius.

Luksié, Abel. Neueste Beschreibung und vollständiges Orts-Lexicon von Bosnien und der Herzegovina. 12° *Prague*, 1878

Lull, E. P., and F. Collins. Reports of Explorations and Surveys for the location of Inter-oceanic Ship-canals through the Isthmus of Panama and by the Valley of the River Napipi, by U.S. Naval Expeditions, 1875. *Maps and plans.* 4° *Washington*, 1879

Lullin, E. L'Utilisation des Forces Motrices du Rhone et la Regularisation du Lac Léman. 12* *Geneva*, 1890
—— Institution d'un Méridien Central Unique, et d'une heure universelle avec maintien de l'heure locale. *Maps.* 8* *Geneva*, 1892

Lumholtz, Carl. Blandt Menneskeædere Fire Aars Reise i Australien. *Maps and illustrations.* 8° *Copenhagen*, 1888
—— Among Cannibals : an Account of Four Years' Travels in Australia, and of Camp Life with the Aborigines of Queensland. *Maps and illustrations.* 8°   1889

Lumsden, Gen. Sir H. L. The Mission to Kandahar, with Appendices ; with Supplementary Report on the Expedition into Upper Meeránzye and Koorrum in 1856. *Maps.* 8° *Calcutta*, 1860

Lumsden, J. G. Observations on a Map prepared by him showing the Possessions of His Highness the Rao, and the Dependent Chiefs, &c., in Kutch. [From the India Records, No. 15.] *Map.* Royal 8° *Bombay*, 1855

Lumsden, Lieut.-Gen. Sir Peter. *See* Central Asia, A : Appendix 2.

Lumsden, Col. Thomas. A Journey from Merut in India to London, through Arabia, Persia, Armenia, Georgia, Russia, Austria, Switzerland, and France, during the years 1819 and 1820. *Map.* 8° 1822

Lund, T. W. M. Como and Italian Lake-land. *Maps, plan, and illustrations.* Crown 8° 1887

Lundbohm, H. *See* Sweden, A, Geologiska Undersökning : Appendix 2.

Lundgren, W. T. Hamn-Lexikon. 8° *Stockholm* [1881]

—— *See* Sweden, A : Appendix 2.

Lupton Bey. *See* Buchta.

Luro, E. Le Pays d'Annam : Étude sur l'Organisation Politique et Sociale des Annamites. 8° *Paris*, 1878

Luschan, F. von. *See* Turkey in Asia, A : Appendix 2.

Lush, Charles. *See* India, C, Geological Papers on Western India : Appendix 2.

Lushington, Mrs Charles. Narrative of a Journey from Calcutta to Europe, by way of Egypt, 1827-28. 8° 1829

Lussan, Raveneau de. Journal du voyage fait à la mer du Sud. *See* Oexmelin.

Lutké, Admiral Frederic. Voyage autour du Monde, sur la Corvette " Le Séuia-viue," 1826-29. Traduit du Russe par J. Boyé. 3 vols. *Maps.* 8° *Paris*, 1835-36

Vols. 1 and 2.—Partie Historique.

Vol. 3.—Les Travaux de MM. les Naturalistes, rédigés par Alex. Postels.

—— The same. Partie Nautique. *Maps and plates.* 4° *St Petersburg*, 1836

Lutz, Markus. Geographisch-statistisches Handlexikon der Schweiz, für Reisende und Geschäftsmänner ; nebst einem Wegweiser durch die Eidsgenossenchaft, sammt Nachrichten für Reisende über Postenlauf, Geldeswerth, und Gasthöfe. 8° *Aarau*, 1822

Lux, A. E. Von Loanda nach Kimbundu : Ergebnisse der Forschungsreise im äquatorialen West Afrika, 1875-76. *Maps and plates.* 8° *Vienna*, 1880

—— Die Balkanhalbinsel (mit Ausschluss von Griechenland), physikalische und ethnographische, Schilderungen und Städtebilder. *Map and illustrations.* 8° *Freiburg*, 1887

Luynes, Duc de. Voyage d'Exploration à la Mer Morte, à Petra, et sur la rive gauche du Jourdain. Œuvre posthume publié par ses petits-fils sous la direction

Luynes, Duc de—*continued.*
de M. le Comte de Vogüé. 3 vols. and Atlas. Imperial 4° *Paris*, N.D.
Vol. 1.—Relation du Voyage.
Vol. 2.—De Petra à Palmyre, par M. Vignes ; Voyage de Jérusalem à Karak et à Chaubak, par MM. Mauss et Sauvaire.
Vol. 3.—Géologie, par M. Louis Lartet.

Luze, Edouard de. La Transcription et la Prononciation des Noms Géographiques Étrangers. 8° *Paris*, 1883

Lyall, Sir Alfred. The Rise of the British Dominion in India. *Maps.* 8° 1893

Lyall, R. Travels in Russia, the Krimea, the Caucasus, and Georgia. 2 vols. *Map.* 8° 1825

Lycklama, Chevalier A. Nijeholt T. M. Voyage en Russie au Caucase et en Perse, dans la Mésopotamie, le Kurdistan, la Syrie, la Palestine, et la Turquie, exécuté pendant les années 1866-68. 4 vols. in 2. *Map and plates.* 8° *Paris*, 1872-75

Lyde, Lionel W. The Glasgow Series of Elementary Geography. 4 vols. 12° *Glasgow*, 1892-93

Lydekker, Richard. Catalogue of the Remains of Siwalik Vertebrata contained in the Geological Department of the Indian Museum, Calcutta. Part 1. Mammalia. 8* *Calcutta*, 1885

—— The same. Part 2. Aves, Reptilia, and Pisces. 8* *Calcutta*, 1886

—— Catalogue of the Remains of Pleistocene and Pre-historic Vertebrata contained in the Geological Department of the Indian Museum, Calcutta. 8* *Calcutta*, 1886

—— *See* India, C, Palæontologia Indica : Appendix 2.

Lyell, Sir Charles. Principles of Geology : being an Attempt to explain the former Changes on the Earth's Surface by reference to causes now in operation. 2 vols. *Maps, plates, and woodcuts.* 8° 1830

—— Ditto. 4 vols. 12° 1835

—— Travels in North America, with Geological Observations on the United States, Canada, and Nova Scotia. 2 vols. *Maps and plates.* 8° 1845

—— Second Visit to the United States of North America. 2 vols. 8° 1849

—— Principles of Geology, or the Modern Changes of the Earth and its Inhabitants considered as illustrative of Geology. *Maps and plates.* 8° 1853

—— Ditto. 10th edition. 2 vols. 8° 1868

—— Elements of Geology. 6th edition. 8° 1865

—— The Geological Evidences of the Antiquity of Man ; with an Outline of Glacial and Post-Tertiary Geology, and Remarks on the Origin of Species. 4th edition. *Illustrations.* 8° 1873

Lyman, B. S. Topography of the Punjab Oil Region. *Map.* 4* *Philadelphia*, 1872

Lyman, B. S. *See* Japan : Appendix 2.

Lynch, T. K. A Visit to the Suez Canal. *Plates.* Small 4° 1866

Lynch, Lieut. W. F. Report of an Examination of the Dead Sea. *Map.* 8*   *Washington*, 1849

—— Official Report of the United States Expedition to Explore the Dead Sea and the River Jordan. *Map and plates.* 4° *Baltimore*, 1852

Lyndes, T. *See* Cherry, in Purchas, Vol. 3, Book 4 : Appendix 1.

Lyndon, J. W. *See* Poole, F.

Lyne, Charles. The Industries of New South Wales. *Illustrations.* Large 8° *Sydney*, 1882

—— New Guinea : an Account of the Establishment of the British Protectorate over the Southern Shores of New Guinea. *Illustrations.* 12° 1885

Lynn, Capt. *See* Murray, Hugh.

Lyon, Capt. G. F. Narrative of Travels in Northern Africa in 1818-20, with Geographical Notices of Soudan and the Course of the Niger. *Map and plates.* 4° 1821

—— The Private Journal of Capt. G. F. Lyon during the recent Voyage of Discovery under Capt. Parry. *Map and plates.* 8° 1825

—— A Brief Narrative of an Unsuccessful Attempt to reach Repulse Bay . . . in the year 1824. *Map and plates.* 8° 1825

—— Journal of a Residence and Tour in the Republic of Mexico in 1826, with some Account of the Mines. 2 vols. 12° 1828

Lyon, S. S. L. *See* Owen, D. D.

Lyons, Dr R. D. Forest Areas in Europe and America, and probable Future Timber Supplies. Square 8° 1884

—— *See* Canada, B : Appendix 2.

M

M——, F. B. Die Seen der Vorzeit in Oberkrain und die Felsenschliffe der Save. 8*   *Laibach*, 1863

M——, M. Studii Antropologici di M. M. 16°   *Florence*, 1856

Maack, R. Journey on the Amur in 1855. [In Russian.] *Portrait.* 4° *St Petersburg*, 1859

—— Journey along the Valley of the Ussuri. [In Russian.] 2 vols. in 1. *Maps and plates.* Folio *St Petersburg*, 1861

Macarius, Patriarch of Antioch. The Travels of, written by his attendant Archdeacon, Paul of Aleppo, in Arabic. Translated by F. C. Belfour : Part 1, Anatolia, Romelia, and Moldavia ; 2, Wallachia, Moldavia, and the Cossack Country ; 3, The Cossack Country and

Macarius—*continued.*
Muscovy ; 4, Muscovy ; 5, Muscovy ; 6, Moscow, Novogorod ; 7, Novogorod, Moscow, and the Cossack Country ; 8, Moldavia and Wallachia ; 9, Black Sea, Anatolia, Syria. [Oriental Translation Fund.] 2 vols. 4° 1829-36

MacArthur, W. A British Protectorate in Fiji. 8* 1873

MacArthur, Lieut. W. P., and Lieut. W. A. Bartlett. U.S. Coast Survey : Sailing Directions for the Western Coast of the United States, from Monterey to Columbus River. Folio *Washington*, 1850

MacC——, H. E. Instructions for Royal Engineer Officers at Singapore, by H. E. M'C. 8*   N.D.

MacCarthy, James. Paper on Siam, read before the Geographical Section of the British Association at Manchester, on September 5, 1887. 12* 1887

MacCarthy, John. Commercial and Technical Report on West Indian and British Honduras Products at the Colonial and Indian Exhibition. 8* 1886

MacCartney, Earl of. *See* Vincent (Dean), Vol. 2 : Appendix 1.

MacCartney, John. Memoir of a Map of the Punjab and Countries west of the Indus, extending from the 23rd to the 41st Degrees North Latitude, and from the 60th to the 78th Degrees of East Longitude, constructed chiefly from information collected during the March of the Cabul Embassy in 1809. MS. Folio.

Macaulay, Hugh. *See* Dalrymple, A. (Nautical Memoirs).

Macbrair, Rev. R. Maxwell. Grammar of the Mandingo Language, with Vocabularies. 8°   N.D.

—— Sketches of a Missionary's Travels in Egypt, Syria, Western Africa, &c. 12° 1839

MacCall, Col. George A. Reports on New Mexico. 8*   *Washington*, 1851

MacClellan, G. B. *See* Marcy.

MacClelland, I. Some Inquiries in the Province of Kemaon relative to Geology and other Branches of Natural Science. *Map and plates.* 8°   *Calcutta*, 1835

MacClintock, Sir F. Leopold. Reminiscences of Arctic Ice-Travel in Search of Sir John Franklin and his Companions ; with Geological Notes and Illustrations by the Rev. Samuel Haughton. *Map and plate.* 8*   *Dublin*, 1857

—— The Voyage of the "Fox" in the Arctic Seas : a Narrative of the Discovery of the Fate of Sir John Franklin and his Companions ; with Preface by Sir Roderick I. Murchison. 8° 1859

MacClintock, Sir F. Leopold. Fate of Sir John Franklin: the Voyage of the "Fox" in the Arctic Seas in Search of Franklin and his Companions. 3rd edition. *Maps and plates.* 8° 1869
—— Fate of Sir John Franklin: the Voyage of the "Fox" in the Arctic Seas in Search of Franklin and his Companions. 5th edition; with a Chapter on the Recent Searching Expeditions of Captain C. F. Hall and Lieut. F. Schwatka, U.S.A. *Maps and illustrations.* 8° 1881

MacCluer, John. *See* Dalrymple, A.; *also* Eyriès, Vol. 2: Appendix I.

Maclure, Capt. Robert C. M. *See* Osborn.

MacClymont, James R. The Influence of Spanish and Portuguese Discoveries during the first Twenty Years of the 16th Century on the Theory of an Antipodeal Southern Continent. 8° 1892

MacCoan, J. C. Egypt as it is. *Map.* 8° [1877]

MacConaghey, M. A. Memo. on the Mynpoorie System of Khusrah Survey. [From the Records of India, N.W. Provinces, Vol. 4.] 8° 1870

MacCord, J. S. Meteorological Observations made on the Island of St Helen, in the River St Lawrence, opposite Montreal, Canada. *Plates.* 8° *Montreal,* 1842

MacCormick, R. Narrative of a Boat Expedition up the Wellington Channel in 1852 in H.M.B. "Forlorn Hope," in Search of Sir John Franklin. *Charts, illustrations, and plans.* 4° 1854
—— Voyages of Discovery in the Arctic and Antarctic Seas, and Round the World : being Personal Narratives of Attempts to Reach the North and South Poles, and of an Open Boat Expedition up the Wellington Channel; to which are added an Autobiography, Appendix, portraits, maps, and numerous illustrations. 2 vols. Large 8° 1884

MacCormick, Rev. W. T. A Ride across Iceland in the Summer of 1891. 8° 1892

MacCosh, J. Topography of Assam. *Plates.* 8° *Calcutta,* 1837
—— Advice to Officers in India. *Plan.* 8* 1856
—— A Paper on Assam and an Overland Communication with China. 4* 1873
—— On a new Floating Breakwater. Sm. 8* 1874
—— Nuova Italia ; or, Tours and Retours through France, Switzerland, and Italy : a Poem. 2 vols. 12° 1872, 1875
—— Grand Tours in many Lands: a Poem, in Ten Cantos. 12° 1881
—— A Proposal for a Floating Harbour of Refuge. *Plan.* 12* *Edinburgh,* 1882

Macoun, John. *See* Canada, A, Geol. and Nat. Hist. Survey : Appendix 2.

MacCoy, F. *See* Sedgwick ; *also* Victoria, A, Geological and Natural History Survey : Appendix 2.

MacCrindle, J. W. Ancient India, as described by Megasthenês and Arrian : being a Translation of the Fragments of the Indika of Megasthenês collected by Dr Schwanbeck, and of the first part of the Indika of Arrian. *Map.* Small 8° 1877
—— The Commerce and Navigation of the Erythræan Sea : being a Translation of the Periplus Maris Erythræi, and of Arrian's Account of the Voyage of Nearkhos. Small 8° 1879
—— Ancient India as described by Klêsias the Knidian : being a Translation of the Abridgment of his "Indika" by Photios, and the Fragments of that Work preserved in other writers ; with Introduction, Notes, and Index. 8° 1882
—— Ancient India as described by Ptolemy: being a Translation of the Chapters which describe India, and Central and Eastern Asia, in the Treatise on Geography written by Klaudios Ptolemäios, the celebrated Astronomer ; with Introduction, Commentary, Map of India according to Ptolemy, and a very copious Index. *Map.* 8° *Calcutta,* 1885
—— The Invasion of India by Alexander the Great, as described by Arrian, Q. Curtius, Diodoros, Plutarch, and Justin : being translations of such portions of the works of these and other classical authors as describe Alexander's Campaigns in Afghanistan, the Panjâb, Sindh, Gedrosia, and Karmania ; with an Introduction, containing a Life of Alexander, copious Notes, Illustrations, Maps, and Indices. 8° 1893

MacCulloch, John. Description of the Western Islands of Scotland, including the Isle of Man ; comprising an Account of their Geological Structure ; with Remarks on their Agriculture, Scenery, and Antiquities. 3 vols. *Maps and plates.* Vols. 1 and 2 8°, and Vol. 3. 4° *Edinburgh,* 1819

MacCulloch, J. R. Dictionary, Practical, Theoretical, and Historical, of Commerce and Commercial Navigation. *Maps* 1832
—— Descriptive and Statistical Account of the British Empire, including its Extent, Physical Capacities, Population, &c. 2 vols. 8° 1847
—— Dictionary, Geographical, Statistical, and Historical, of the various Countries, Places, and Principal Natural Objects in the World. New edition, Revised, with a Supplement. Vol. 1. *Maps.* 8° 1854

MacCulloch, J. R. Russia and Turkey. From the "Geographical Dictionary." 12°   1854

—— Dictionary, Practical, Theoretical, and Historical, of Commerce and Commercial Navigation. New edition ; with numerous Corrections and Improvements, and a Supplement. *Maps and plans.* 8°   1859

MacCulloch, Major W. Account of the Valley of Munnipore, and of the Hill Tribes ; with a Comparative Vocabulary of the Munnipore and other Languages. [From the Records of India, No. 27.] Royal 8°   *Calcutta*, 1859

Macdermot, William. The Darien Canal, What shall we do with our Convicts? [*2 leaves.*]   4*   1857

MacDermott, A. *See* Horsey.

MacDermott, P. L. British East Africa, or *Ibea :* a History of the Formation and Work of the Imperial British East Africa Company. Compiled by the authority of the Directors from Official Documents and the Records of the Company. *Map and frontispiece.* 8°   1893

Macdonald, Capt. A. Brief Historical Sketch of the Petty State of Baria, in the Rewa Kanta, prepared in 1819. [From the India Records, No. 23.] Royal 8° *Bombay*, 1856

Macdonald, Charles. *See* Velschow.

Macdonald, Sir Claude. *See* Mockler-Ferryman.

Macdonald, D. *See* Campbell, F. A.

Macdonald, Rev. Duff. Africana ; or, The Heart of Heathen Africa. 2 vols. *Illustrations.* 8°   1882

—— New Hebrides Linguistics, Introductory : Three New Hebrides Languages (Efatese, Eromangan, Santo). 12°   *Melbourne*, 1889

—— South Sea Languages : a Series of Studies on the Languages of the New Hebrides and other South Sea Islands. Vol. 2. Tangoan, Santo, Malo, Malekula, Epi (Baki and Bierian), Tanna, and Futuna. 12°   *Melbourne*, 1891

Macdonald, Duncan G. Forbes. British Columbia and Vancouver's Island : comprising a Description of these Dependencies, their Physical Character, Climate, Natural History, Geology, Ethnology, Gold Fields, &c., also an Account of the Manners and Customs of the Native Indians. *Map.* 8°   1862

Macdonald, James. *See* Phillips, Collection of Modern and Contemporary Voyages and Travels [1], Vol. 11 : Appendix 1.

Macdonald, J. G. Journal . . . on an Expedition from Port Denison to the Gulf of Carpentaria and back. *Map and portrait.* 12°   *Brisbane*, 1865

Macdonell, Arthur A. Camping Voyages on German Rivers. *Frontispiece and maps.* Small 8°   1890

MacDonnell, Sir Richard G. Australia, What it is, and what it may be : a Lecture. *Map.* 12*   *Dublin*, 1863

Macdonell, Thomas. Extracts from his MS. Journals, containing Observations on New Zealand. 8°   1834

Macdouall, John. Narrative of a Voyage to Patagonia and Tierra del Fuego through the Straits of Magellan, in H.M. ships "Adventure" and "Beagle," in 1826-27.   12°   1833

MacDougall George F. The Eventful Voyage of H.M. Discovery Ship "Resolute" to the Arctic Regions in Search of Sir John Franklin and the missing Crews of H.M. ships "Erebus" and "Terror," 1852-54. *Map and plates.* 8°   1857

—— Directions for making the Passage from the Downs to the White Sea ; including a Description of the Harbour of Hammerfest and other Anchorages on the Coast of Norway and Lapland, and of the Ports of Archangel and Onega in the White Sea. 8°   1858

—— Instructions Nautiques pour la Cote Sud-Est de la Nouvelle-Ecosse et la Baie de Fundy. 8°   *Paris*, 1869

—— *See* United Kingdom, A, Admiralty Hydrogr. Off. Publ. : Appendix 2.

MacDougall, G. Gordon. *See* Graah.

Mace, W. *See* Hakluyt, Vol. 4 ; Purchas, Vol. 4, Book 8 : Appendix 1.

Macedo, J. M. de. *See* Le Sage.

Macedo, Mgr. de. Le Christophore : la Civilisation dans l'Amazonie : Conférence faite à Manaos (Bresil). 2nd edition. Large 8*   *Paris*, 1885

MacFarlane, C. Constantinople in 1828. *Plates.* 4°   1829

—— The same. 2nd edition ; to which is added an Appendix containing Remarks and Observations to the Autumn of 1829. 2 vols. *Plates.* 8°   1829

—— Japan : an Account, Geographical and Historical, from the Earliest Period at which the Islands were known to Europeans to the Present Time. *Map and woodcuts.* 8°   1852

—— History of British India, from the Earliest English Intercourse ; with Continuation to the Fall of Delhi and the Relief of Lucknow. *Map and plates.* 12°   1857

MacFarlane, J. The Coal Regions of America, their Topography, Geology, and Development. *Maps.* 8° *New York*, 1873

MacFarlane, P. Antidote against the Unscriptural and Unscientific Tendency of Modern Geology. Small 8°   1871

MacFarlane, R. Notes on, and List of Birds and Eggs collected in Arctic America, 1861-66. 8* *Washington*, 1891

MacFarlane, Rev. S. New Guinea. Parts 1, 2, and 3. (From the *Sunday Magazine*.) Large 8* 1874

—— Among the Cannibals of New Guinea : being the Story of the New Guinea Mission of the London Missionary Society. *Map and illustrations.* 12° 1888

—— *See* Australasia and Polynesia, British New Guinea : Appendix 2.

Macfie, Matthew. Vancouver Island and British Columbia, their History, Resources, and Prospects. *Maps and plate.* 8° 1865

MacGahan, J. A. Campaigning on the Oxus, and the Fall of Khiva. *Map.* 8° 1874

—— Under the Northern Lights. *Map and illustrations.* 8° 1876

MacGeachy, Edward. Suggestions towards a General Plan of Rapid Communication by Steam Navigation and Railways between the Eastern and Western Hemispheres. *Maps.* 8* 1846

Macgill, T. Travels in Turkey, Italy, and Russia ; with an Account of some of the Greek Islands. 2 vols. in 1. 12° 1808

—— A Hand-book or Guide for Strangers visiting Malta. *Map.* 12° *Malta,* 1839

Macgillivray, John. Narrative of a Voyage of H.M.S. "Rattlesnake," commanded by Capt. Owen Stanley, 1846-50 ; including Discoveries and Surveys in New Guinea, the Louisiade Archipelago, &c. ; to which is added the Account of E. B. Kennedy's Expedition for the Exploration of the Cape York Peninsula. 2 vols. *Map and plates.* 8° 1852

Macgillivray, Dr W. The Travels and Researches of Alex. von Humboldt. *Plates.* 8° 1853

—— Natural History of Deeside and Braemar. Edited by E. Lankester. *Maps.* 8° 1855

Macgowan, D. J. The Eagre of the Tsien-Tang River. 8* 1853

MacGregor, Sir Charles Metcalfe. A Military Report on the Country of Bhutan, containing all the Information of Military Importance which has been collected up to date (12th July 1866). *Map.* Small folio *Calcutta,* 1873

—— Narrative of a Journey through the Province of Khorassan and on the N.W. Frontier of Afghanistan in 1875. 2 vols. *Maps and plates.* 8° 1879

—— Wanderings in Balochistan. *Maps, plates, and portrait.* 8° 1882

—— The Defence of India : a Strategical Study. *Map.* 8° *Simla,* 1884

—— The Life and Opinions of Major-General Sir Charles Metcalfe MacGregor, Quartermaster-General in India. Edited by Lady MacGregor. 2 vols. *Maps, portrait, &c.* 8° 1888

—— *See* Central Asia, A : Appendix 2.

MacGregor, Fr. Coleman. Die Canarischen Inseln nach ihrem gegenwärtigen Zustande. *Maps and plates.* 8° *Hanover,* 1831

MacGregor, James. Fifty Facts about Australasia. *Map.* 12° 1883

MacGregor, John. British America. 2 vols. *Maps.* 8° *Edinburgh,* 1832

—— Commercial Statistics : a Digest of the Productive Resources, Commercial Legislation, Customs, Tariffs, Navigation, Port, and Quarantine Laws and Charges ; Shipping, Imports, and Exports ; and the Monies, Weights, and Measures of all Nations ; including all British Commercial Treaties with Foreign States. Vols. 1 and 2. Royal 8° 1844

MacGregor, Dr John. Toil and Travel : being a True Story of Roving and Ranging when on a Voyage homeward bound round the World. *Portrait.* 8° 1892

Macgregor, John. The "Rob Roy" on the Baltic : a Canoe Cruise through Norway, Sweden, Denmark, Sleswig, Holstein, the North Sea, and the Baltic. 2nd edition. *Maps and plate.* Small 8° 1867

—— The Voyage alone in the Yawl "Rob Roy" from London to Paris, and back by Havre, the Isle of Wight, South Coast, &c., &c. 2nd edition. *Plates.* Small 8° 1868

—— The "Rob Roy" on the Jordan, Nile, Red Sea, and Gennesareth, &c. : a Canoe Cruise in Palestine and Egypt, and the Waters of Damascus. *Maps and plates.* 8° 1869

—— A Thousand Miles in the "Rob Roy" Canoe on Rivers and Lakes of Europe. 8th edition. *Map and plates.* Small 8° 1871

Macgregor, Sir William. Report on Visit of Inspection to the Island of Kiwai at mouth of Fly River. Folio* *Brisbane,* 1889

—— Inspection Tour of Fly River. *Map.* Folio* *Brisbane,* 1889

—— Despatch from, giving Details of an Expedition undertaken to Explore the Course of the Fly River and some of its Affluents. *Map and plans.* Folio* 1890

—— Handbook of Information for Intending Settlers in British New Guinea. *Map.* 8* *Brisbane,* 1892

—— Despatch reporting the proceedings in connection with the Delimitation of the Boundary between British and Dutch New Guinea. Folio* 1893

—— *See* Thomson, J. P. ; *also* Australasia and Polynesia, British New Guinea : Appendix 2.

Machado, J. J. *See* Portugal, B : Appendix 2.

Machado, J. J. Relatorio acerca dos Trabalhos para a Fixação da Directriz do Caminho de Ferro projectado entre Lourenço Marques e a Fronteira do Transvaal, apresentado a S. Ex. a o Ministro e Secretario d'Estado dos Negocios da Marinha e Ultramar por Joaquim José Machado, Major de Engenheria. 8*
Lisbon, 1884

Macham, —. *See* Hakluyt, Vol. 2 : Appendix 1.

MacHenry, George. The Cotton Trade, its Bearing upon the Prosperity of Great Britain and Commerce of the American Republics considered in connection with Negro Slavery in the Confederate States.
1803

Machéras, Léonce. Chronique de Chypre. Λεοντιου Μαχαιρα Χρονικον Κυπρου. Texte Grec, par E. Miller et C. Sathas. [Vol. 2, 2nd Series, Publ. de l'Éc. des Langues Orient. Viv.] *Map.* Large 8°
Paris, 1882

—— Chronique de Chypre. Traduction Française, par E. Miller et C. Sathas. [Vol. 3, 2nd Series, Publ. de l'Éc. des Langues Orient. Viv.] Large 8°
Paris, 1882

Machiavelli, Nicolo. Opere. *Portrait and facsimile.* 8° 8 vols. 1813

Macintosh, Major-Gen. A. F. Military Tour in European Turkey, the Crimea, and on the Eastern Shores of the Black Sea. 2 vols. *Maps.* 8° 1854

Macintyre, Major-Gen. Donald. Hindu-Koh : Wanderings and Wild Sport on and beyond the Himalayas. *Illustrations.* 8° 1889

MacIver, Lewis. Imperial Census of 1881 : Opèrations and Results in the Presidency of Madras. 5 vols. *Map and diagrams.* Folio *Madras,* 1883

Mackay, A. The Western World ; or, Travels in the United States in 1846-47, exhibiting them in their latest development, Social, Political, Industrial ; including a Chapter on California. Vol. 3. *Map.* Small 8° 1849

—— Western India. Reports addressed to the Chambers of Commerce of Manchester, Liverpool, Blackburn, and Glasgow. Edited by J. Robertson, with a Preface by T. Bazley. *Maps.* 8° 1853

Mackay, Dr Alexander. Index to Manual of Geography. 12° 1861

—— Outlines of Modern Geography. 16° 1865

—— Facts and Dates, or the Leading Events in Sacred and Profane History, and the Principal Facts in the Various Physical Sciences. 2nd edition. 16° 1870

—— Elements of Modern Geography. 7th edition 1870

Mackay, Dr Alexander. Outlines of Modern Geography : a Book for Beginners. 11th edition. 12° 1871

—— Manual of Modern Geography, Mathematical, Physical, and Political, on a New Plan, embracing a Complete Development of the River Systems of the Globe. 12° 1871

Mackay, A. M. A. M. Mackay, Pioneer Missionary of the Church Missionary Society to Uganda : Biography. By his Sister. *Map and portrait.* 8° 1890

MacKeevor, Thomas. *See* Phillips, New Voyages and Travels [3], Vol. 2 : Appendix 2.

Mackenna, Benjamin Vicuña. Exploracion de las Lagunas Negra i del Encañado en las Cordilleras de San José i del Valle del Yeso. *Maps.* 12° *Valparaiso,* 1874

—— Catalogo del Museo historico del Santa Lucia. Square 8° *Santiago,* 1875

—— Lautaro y sus Campañas contra Santiago, 1553-57. 8° *Santiago,* 1876

—— Le Chili considéré sous le Rapport de son Agriculture et de l'Émigration Européenne. *Map.* 12* *Paris,* 1855

—— La Edad del oro en Chile o sea una Demostracion Histórica de la maravillosa abundancia de oro que ha existido en el pais, con una Reseña de los grandes descubrimientos Argentiferos que lo han enriquecido, principalmente en el presente siglo, i Algunas Recientes Excursiones á los Rejiones Auriferas de Catapilco i quebradas de Alvarado i Malcara. 8° *Santiago,* 1881

—— Juan Fernandez : Historia Verdadera de la Isla de Robinson Crusoe. 8° *Santiago,* 1883

—— A Traves de los Andes : Estudio sobre la Mejor Ubicacion del Futuro Ferrocarril Interoceánico entre el Atlántico i el Pacifico en la América del sur [la República Arjentina i Chile]. *Map.* 12° *Santiago,* 1885

Mackenzie, Alex. Voyages from Montreal, on the River St Laurence, through the Continent of North America, to the Frozen and Pacific Oceans, in 1789 and 1793 ; with a Preliminary Account of the Rise, Progress, and Present State of the Fur Trade of that Country. *Portrait and maps.* 4° 1801

—— *See* Eyriès, Vol. 7 : Appendix 1.

Mackenzie, Alexander. History of the Relations of the Government with the Hill Tribes of the North-East Frontier of Bengal. *Map.* 8° *Calcutta,* 1884

—— Report on the Administration of the Central Provinces for the year 1888-89. *Map.* 4° *Nagpur,* 1889

Mackenzie, Alexander. Descriptive Notes on certain Implements, Weapons, &c., from Graham Island, Charlotte Islands, B.C. ; with an Introductory Note by Dr G. M. Dawson. *Plates.* 4* 1891

Mackenzie, Colin. Brazil : Paper read before the British Association, at Aberdeen. 8* *Aberdeen*, 1885

Mackenzie, Mrs Colin. Life in the Mission, the Camp, and the Zenana ; or, Six Years in India. 2nd edition. 2 vols. in 1. *Map and plate.* 8° 1854

Mackenzie, Donald. North-West Africa : a Lecture on the Project for Opening Central Africa to Commerce and Civilisation. 8* *Liverpool*, 1878

—— The Flooding of the Sahara : an Account of the Proposed Plan for Opening Central Africa to Commerce and Civilisation from the North-West Coast ; with a Description of Soudan and Western Sahara, and Notes on Ancient Manuscripts, &c. *Map and illustrations.* Crown 8° 1877

Mackenzie, G. M., and A. P. Irby. The Turks, the Greeks, and the Slavons : Travels in the Slavonic Provinces of Turkey-in-Europe. *Map and plates.* 8° 1867

—— Travels in the Slavonic Provinces of Turkey-in-Europe ; with a Preface by W. E. Gladstone. 2nd edition. 2 vols. *Map and plates.* 8° 1877

Mackenzie, Sir G. Stewart. Travels in Iceland during 1810. *Map and plates.* 4° *Edinburgh*, 1811

—— The same. With Appendix. 4° *Edinburgh*, 1812

—— *See* Pinkerton, Vol. 3 : Appendix 1.

Mackenzie, John. Ten Years North of the Orange River : a Story of Every-day Life and Work among the South African Tribes from 1859 to 1869. *Map and plates.* Small 8° *Edinburgh*, 1871

—— Austral Africa, Losing it or Ruling it : being Incidents and Experiences in Bechuanaland, Cape Colony, and England. 2 vols. *Maps, portraits, and illustrations.* 8° 1887

Mackenzie, K. R. H. *See* Lepsius.

MacKerrow, J. *See* Hutton and Ulrich ; also New Zealand, B : Appendix 2.

Mackinder, H. J., and M. E. Sadler. University Extension, Past, Present, and Future. *Illustrations.* 12° 1891

Mackie, S. J. Thoughts on the Dover Cliffs. *Map and plate.* 8* 1863

MacKinlay, J. Journal of Exploration in the Interior of Australia (Burke Relief Expedition). *Maps.* 8° *Melbourne*, 1862

—— Journal of Exploring Expedition . . . to Examine the Country of the Northern Territory recently annexed to South Australia, for the Purpose of Ascertaining the general Nature of the Country, &c. *Map.* Folio [*Adelaide*] 1866

—— *See* Westgarth.

MacKinnon, Rev. James. South African Traits. 8° *Edinburgh*, 1887

MacKinnon, L. B. Some Account of the Falkland Islands, from a Six Months' Residence in 1838 and 1839. *Map.* 8* 1840

MacKinnon, W. Alex. History of Civilisation and Public Opinion. 2 vols. 8° 1849

Mackintosh, A. An Account of the Origin and Present Condition of the Tribe of Ramoossies, including the Life of the Chief Oomiah Naik. 8° *Bombay*, 1833

Mackintosh, Dr Andrew William. A Whaling Cruise in the Arctic Regions. 12* 1884

Mackintosh, D. The Scenery of England and Wales, its Character and Origin : being an Attempt to Trace the Nature of the Geological Causes, especially Denudation, by which the Physical Features of the Country have been produced. *Illustrations.* 8° 1869

Maclauchlan, Henry. Memoir written during a Survey of the Watling Street, from the Tees to the Scotch Border, in 1850-51. 8* 1852

Maclean, Arthur John, and William Henry Browne. The Catholicos of the East and his People : being the Impressions of Five Years' Work in the "Archbishop of Canterbury's Assyrian Mission." . . . *Map and illustrations.* 12° 1892

MacLean, John. Notes of a Twenty-five Years' Service in the Hudson's Bay Territory. 2 vols. 8° 1849

MacLean, M. Echoes from Japan. *Map and illustrations.* 12° 1889

MacLean, Walter. *See* Buckingham.

Maclear, Sir Thomas. Astronomical Observations made at the Royal Observatory, Cape of Good Hope, in the year 1834. Vol. 1. 4° *Cape Town*, 1840

—— Contributions to Astronomy and Geodesy. 2 parts. 4° 1851-53

Macleay, Wm. *See* Australasia and Polynesia, New Guinea : Appendix 2.

MacLeod, J. Voyage of H.M.S. "Alceste" to China, Corea, and the Island of Lewchew, with an Account of her Shipwreck. *Map and plates.* 8° 1819

—— A Voyage to Africa, with some Account of the Manners and Customs of the Dahomian People. 12° 1820

MacLeod, J. Memoranda on the Pearl Banks and Pearl Fishery, the Sea Fishery, and the Salt Beds of Sind. [From the India Records, No. 17.] *Bombay*, 1855

Macleod, J. Lyons. Travels in Eastern Africa, with a Narrative of a Residence in Mozambique. 2 vols. *Portrait and map.* 8° 1860

—— Madagascar and its People. *Map.* 8° 1865

Macleod, W. C. Copy of Papers relating to the Route of Captain W. C. MacLeod from Moulmein to the Frontiers of China, and to the Route of Dr Richardson on his Fourth Mission to the Shan Provinces of Burmah, or Extracts from the same. *Map.* Folio   1869

MacMahon, Gen. A. R. The Karens of the Golden Chersonese. *Map and plates.* 8°   1876

—— Karenni and the Red Karens. 8* N.D.

—— Far Cathay and Farther India. *Illustrations.* 8°   1893 [1892]

Macmichael, William. Journey from Moscow to Constantinople, in the years 1817-18. *Plates.* 4°   1819

—— *See* Phillips, New Voyages and Travels [3], Vol. 1 : Appendix 1.

MacMicking, Robert. Recollections of Manilla and the Philippines during 1848-50. 8°   1851

Macmillan, George A. *See* Blackwood, Vol. 2 : Appendix 1.

MacMurdo, Lieut. J. Historical Sketch of the District of Okhamundul, in Kattywar. [From the India Records, No. 37.] Royal 8°   *Bombay*, 1856

—— Memoir on the Province of Kattywar ; accompanied by Remarks on the Runn of Kutch. [From the India Records, No. 37.] Royal 8°   *Bombay*, 1856

MacMurray, T. The Free Grant Lands of Canada : from Practical Experience of Bush Farming in the Free Grant Districts of Muskoka and Parry Sound. *Map.* 8*   *Bracebridge (Ontario)*, 1871

Macnabb, D. J. C. Handbook of the Haka or Baungshe Dialect of the Chin Language. 8°   *Rangoon*, 1891

MacNair, F. Perak and the Malays : "Sárong" and "Krs." *Map and plates.* 8°   1878

MacNair, William Watts. *See* Howard.

Macnamara, F. N. Climate and Medical Topography in their Relation to the Disease-Distribution of the Himalayan and Sub-Himalayan Districts of British India. *Map.* 8°   1880

Macneill, Telford. Water Supply of London, by Means of Natural Filtration of the Waters of the River Thames. *Map.* 8*   1866

Macomb, Lieut. M. M. *See* United States, H, *a* : Appendix 2.

Maconochie, Capt. A. Australiana : Thoughts on Convict Management and other subjects connected with the Australian Penal Colonies. 8°   1839

—— On the Management of Prisoners in the Australian Colonies. 4°   [1840]

Macoun, John. Manitoba and the Great North-West : the Field for Investment, the Home of the Emigrant. *Maps and illustrations.* 8°   1883

Macoun, John. *See* Canada, A, Geological and Natural History Survey : Appendix 2.

MacParlan, Dr James. Statistical Survey of the County of Donegal. *Map.* 8° *Dublin,* 1802

MacPherson, Duncan. Antiquities of Kertch, and Researches in the Cimmerian Bosphorus ; with Remarks on the Ethnological and Physical History of the Crimea. *Maps, plates, and woodcuts.* Folio   1857

Macpherson, W. Memorials of Service in India. From the Correspondence of the late Major Samuel Charters Macpherson, C.B. *Map and plates.* 8° 1865

MacQueen, James. Geographical and Commercial View of Northern Central Africa, containing a Particular Account of the Course and Termination of the Great River Niger in the Atlantic Ocean. *Maps.* 8   *Edinburgh,* 1821

—— West India Colonies vindicated from Calumnies and Misrepresentations. 8° 1824

—— A General Plan for a Mail Communication by Steam between Great Britain and the Eastern and Western parts of the World, also to Canton and Sydney westward by the Pacific ; to which are added Geographical Notices of the Isthmus of Panama, Nicaragua, &c. *Maps.* 8°   1838

—— Geographical Survey of Africa, its Rivers, Lakes, Mountains, Productions, States, Population, &c. ; and a Letter on the Slave Trade and the Improvement of Africa. *Map.* 8°   1840

—— Supplement to the Geographical Survey of Africa, containing further details regarding Southern Africa. 8*   1840

—— The Nile Expeditions and Controversy [from the *Morning Advertiser,* December 2, 1864] : in continuation of Burton and M'Queen's "The Nile Basin." Small 4*   1864

—— The African Slave Trade. [Four Letters addressed to Lord Brougham, cut from Newspapers, together with four pages of MS.] Folio*   [1867]

—— *See* Burton ; Isenberg.

MacSwiney, Capt. E. F. H. *See* Gromchefsky.

Madden, R. R. Travels in Turkey, Egypt, Nubia, and Palestine, in 1824-27. 2 vols. *Portrait.* 8°   1829

—— The Island of Cuba, its Resources, Progress, and Prospects, considered in relation especially to the influence of its prosperity on the interests of the British West India Colonies. 12°   1853

Madden, T. M. The Principal Health Resorts of Europe and Africa for the Treatment of Chronic Diseases. 8° 1876

Madini, Antonio. Il Segistan ovvero il corso del Fiume Hindmend secondo Abu Ishak-el-Farssi-el-Istachri Geographo Arabo. *Plate.* 4° *Milan*, 1842

Madoc, Prince. *See* Stephens, Thomas.

Madox, John. Excursions in the Holy Land, Egypt, Nubia, Syria, &c., including a visit to the District of the Haouran. 2 vols. *Plates.* 8° 1834

Madoz, Don Pascual. Diccionario Geográfico-Estadístico-Histórico de España y sus Posesiones de Ultramar. 16 vols. in 8. 4° *Madrid*, 1846
—— The same. Art. Madrid ; Audiencia, Provincia, Intendencia, Vicaria, Partido y Villa. 4° *Madrid*, 1848-50
—— *See* Walton.

Maeff, N. A., and B. W. Trotzky. Russian Turkestan. [In Russian.] 8° *Moscow*, 1872

Maeso, Justo. *See* Parish.

Maestre, Amaio. Descripcion geológica industrial de la Cuenca carbonifera de San Juan de las Abadesas en la provincia de Gerona, con planos y cortes de dicha cuenca, y un mapa comparativo de proyectos de Ferro-carril. *Maps.* 4* *Madrid*, 1855

Maffeus, J. P. Historiarum Indicarum, libri XVI., selectarum item ex India Epistolarum eodem interprete libri IV., accessit Ignatii Loiolæ Vita postremo recognita. Folio *Florence*, 1588

Magalhães, Couto de. Trabalho preparatorio para aproveitamento do Selvagem e do solo por elle occupado no Brazil. O Selvagem, I. Curso da Lingua geral segundo Ollendorf comprehendendo o Texto original de Lendas Tupis. II. Origens, Costumes, Região Selvagem, methodo a empregar para amansal-os por intermedio das Colonias militares e do interprete militar. 8° *Rio de Janeiro*, 1876

Magalhães, Carlos de. Le Zaire et les Contrats de l'Association Internationale. Conférence faite le 21 Juin 1884, par C. Magalhães. 8* *Lisbon*, 1884

Mage, M. E. Voyage dans le Soudan Occidental (Sénégambie-Niger), 1863-66. *Maps and plates.* 8° *Paris*, 1868

Magellan. *See* Guillemard ; *also* Burney, Vol. 1; Callander, Vol. 1; Dalrymple, Vol. 1; Gottfried ; Hakluyt Soc. Publ., Vol. 52; Harris, Vol. 1 ; Kerr, Vol. 10 ; Laharpe, Vol. 15; Navarette, Vol. 4 ; Purchas, Vol. 1 ; Ternaux-Compans, Vol. 2; Allgemeine Historie, Vol. 11; General Collection, p. 610; Collecçao de Noticlas, Vol. 4, p. 611: Appendix 1.

"Magenta." *See* Giglioli.

Mager, Henri. Atlas Colonial ; avec Notices historiques et géographiques. 4° *Paris* [1886]

Magini, G. A. *See* Ptolemy.

Maguire, T. M. The Strategical Geography of Europe. (From *Proceedings* of the Royal Artillery Institute.) 8* 1893

Magyar, Ladislaus. Délafrika-le-velei es naplókivonatai Kiadta Hunfalvy János. *Map.* 8° *Budapest*, 1857
—— Reisen in Süd-Afrika in den Jahren 1849 bis 1857. Aus dem Ungarischen von Johann Hunfalvy. Vol. 1. *Map and plates.* 8° *Leipzig*, 1859
—— Magyar Laszló Délafrikai Utazásai 1849-57 években. *Map and plates.* 8° *Budapest*, 1859
—— *See* Ronáy, H.

Mahomed Peer. *See* Masoom.

Mahu, Jacob. *See* Burney, Vol. 2: Appendix 1.

M— H—. Report on Explorations in Nepal and Tibet by Explorer M— H— (Season 1885-86). *Map.* Folio* *Dehra Dun*, 1887

Mahaffy, J. P. Rambles and Studies in Greece. 3rd edition. *Map and plates.* Crown 8° 1887
—— **and J. E. Rogers.** Sketches from a Tour through Holland and Germany. *Illustrations.* 8° 1889

Mahlmann, Dr W. Ergänzungen zum 3 Theile (II. Bd.) der Deutschen Ausgabe von A. von Humboldt's Central-Asien. 8° *Berlin*, 1844

Mahmoud-Pacha el Falaki. *See* Ismail.

Maiden, J. H. Wattles and Wattle-Barks: being Hints on the Conservation and Cultivation of Wattles, together with particulars of their value. *Plates.* Large 8* *Sydney*, 1890

Maillard, G. Promenade Historique et Pittoresque sur la Seine de Montereau à Paris et de Paris a Montereau en Bateaux a Vapeur. 2nd edition. *Map.* 16° *Paris* 1837
[Bound up with Montyel's "Pélerinage sur la Soane."]

Maillard, N. Doran. History of the Republic of Texas, from the Discovery of the Country to the Present Time, and the Cause of her Separation from the Republic of Mexico. *Map.* 8° 1842

Maillet, — de. *See* Mascrier.

Mailly, E. Essai sur la vie et les ouvrages de L. A. J. Quetelet. 12° *Brussels*, 1875

Main, Mrs. My Home in the Alps. 12° 1892

Main, Rev. R. *See* Herschell ; Oxford, Radcliffe Observatory: Appendix 2.

Mainberger, Charles. Une Semaine à Nuremberg : Description Précise de la Ville de Nuremberg et de ses Environs, précédée d'une Introduction Historique par Jean Scharrer. *Map.* 12° *Nuremburg*, 1838

Maire, Jacob le. Oost ende West Indische Spieghel waerin Beschreven werden de twee laetste Navigatien ghedaen inde Jaeren 1614, 1615, 1616, 1617, ende 1618. De eene door den vermaerden Zee-Heldt Joris van Spilbergen door de Strate van Magellanes ende soo voudt om den gantschen Aerdt-Kloot met alle de Bataelhen soo te Water als te Lande gheschiet, &c., &c. *Maps and illustrations.* Oblong small 8° *Zutphen,* 1621 —— *See* Burney, Vol. 2 ; Callander, Vol. 2; Churchill, Vol. 8 ; Dalrymple (Pacific), Vol. 2 ; Harris, Vol. 1 ; Kerr, Vol. 10; Laharpe, Vol. 15 ; Allgemeine Historie, Vols. 3, 11 ; " The World Displayed," Vol. 5 : Appendix 1.

Maisey, Lieut. F. *See* Central Asia, A : Appendix 2.

Maitland, A. Gibb. Geology and Mineral resources of the Upper Burdekin. *Map and sections.* Folio* *Brisbane,* 1891 —— Coolgarra Tin Mines and surrounding District. *Map and sections.* Folio* *Brisbane,* 1891 —— The Geology of the Cooktown District. *Map and sections.* Folio* *Brisbane,* 1891 —— The Physical Geology of Magnetic Island, Queensland. *Maps and sections.* Folio* *Brisbane,* 1892

Maitland, C. The Church in the Catacombs : a Description of the Primitive Church of Rome illustrated by its Sepulchral Remains. *Plate.* 8° 1846

Major, Dr C. J. Forsyth. *See* Stefani.

Major, Richard Henry. The Life of Prince Henry of Portugal, surnamed The Navigator, and its Results, &c. *Maps.* 8° 1868 —— *See* Hakluyt Soc. Publ., Vols. 2, 6, 10, 11, 14, 15, 17, 25, 43, 46, 50 : Appendix 1.

Major, J. R. *See* Dictionaries (Greek) : Appendix 2 (General).

Malavialle, L. Le Partage Politique de l'Afrique en Decembre 1891. 8* *Montpellier* [1892]

Malchus, C. A. F. von. Handbuch der Militär-Geographie oder Erd und Staaten-Kunde von Europa. 2 vols. *Map.* 8° *Leipzig,* 1833

Malcolm, Lieut. - Col. Sketch of the Sikhs, a Singular Nation, who Inhabit the Provinces of the Penjab, situated between the Rivers Jumna and Indus. 8° 1812 —— *See* Graham, Major D. C.

Malcolm, Rear-Admiral Sir Charles. Addresses to the Ethnological Society of London. [2 pamphlets.] 8* 1845-46

Malcolm, Sir John. Political History of India, from 1784 to 1823. 2 vols. 8° 1826 —— History of Persia, from the most Early Period to the Present Time. 2 vols. 8° 1829

Malcolm, Sir John. Memoir of Central India, including Malwa and adjoining Provinces ; with the History of the Past and Present Condition of that Country. 2 vols. *Maps.* 8° 1832

Malcolmson, J. G. *See* India, C, Geological Papers : Appendix 2.

Malcom. Rev. Howard. Travels in South-Eastern Asia, embracing Hindustan, Malaya, Siam, and China ; with Notices of numerous Missionary Stations, and a Full Account of the Burman Empire. 2 vols. *Map.* 8° 1839 —— Travels in Hindustan and China. People's edition. *Illustrations.* Large 8° *Edinburgh,* 1840 —— *See* Eyriès, Vol. 14 : Appendix 1.

Maldonado, Lorenzo Ferrer. Viaggio dal Mare Atlantico al Pacifico per la via del Nord-ouest, fatto l'anno 1588. Tradotto da un Manoscritto Spagnuolo inedito da Carlo Amoretti. *Maps.* 4° *Milan,* 1811 —— *See* Navarette ; *also* Burney, Vols. 2, 5 : Appendix 1.

Malet, Arthur. Statement, containing the Names of the Towns and Villages in the Kutch Territory, their estimated Annual Revenue, &c. [From the India Records, No. 15.] 8° *Bombay,* 1855

Malet, Sir C. W. *See* Dalrymple, Repertory, Vol. 1 : Appendix 1.

Malet, Capt. G. G. *See* Masoom.

Malet, H. P. New Pages of Natural History : Meteors and Meteorites— Caves and their Contents—Fossil Fish. 8° 1868 —— Sunlight. 2nd edition. 12° 1887

Malfatti, Bartolomeo. Scritti Geografici ed Etnografici. 8° *Milan,* 1869

Malfroy, Camille. Geyser Action at Rotorua, New Zealand : a Paper read before the Auckland Institute. *Plates.* 8* *Wellington,* 1892

Malgo King. *See* Hakluyt, Vol. 1 : Appendix 1.

Malheiro, Lourenço. Sociedade Propagadora de Contrecimentos Geographico-Africanos. Recepção e Conferencia do Ex^tno Sr. Lourenço Malheiro, Engenheiro de Minas na Sociedade em 29 de Julho de 1881. 8* *Loanda,* 1881

Malkin's Tour in Wales. *See* Pinkerton, Vol. 2 : Appendix 1.

Malleson, Col. G. B. Herat, the Granary and Garden of Central Asia. *Map.* 8° 1880

Mallet, Friedrich. Allgemeine oder mathematische Beschreibung der Erdkugel, auf Veranlassung der Cosmographischen Gesellschaft ; aus dem Schwedischen übersetzt von L. H. Rohl. *Plates.* 8° *Greifswald,* 1774

Mallet, Robert. Account of Experiments made at Holyhead (North Wales) to ascertain the Transit-Velocity of Waves, analogous to Earthquake Waves, through the Local Rock Formations. *Map and plates.* 4* 1861
—— The late Earthquake, and Earthquakes in general. 8* 1864
—— *See* Palmieri.

Mallock, W. H. In an Enchanted Island; or, A Winter's Retreat in Cyprus. *Frontispiece.* 8° 1889

Malosse, P. Monumens Antiques de Saint-Remy. 8° *Avignon, 1818*

Malte-Brun, Conrad. Précis de la Géographie Universelle, ou Description de toutes les Parties du Monde, d'après les Grandes Divisions Naturelles du Globe; précédée de l'Histoire de la Géographie chez les Peuples Anciens et Modernes, et d'une Théorie générale de la Géographie, Mathematique, Physique, et Politique; et accompagnée de Cartes, de Tableaux Analytiques, Synoptiques et Élémentaires, et d'une Table alphabétique des Noms de Lieux. 8 vols. 8°, Atlas folio *Paris, 1812-29*
—— Tableau de la Pologne Ancienne et Moderne. *Maps.* 8° *Brussels, 1830*
—— The same. . . . Nouvelle édition, entièrement refondue, augmentée et ornée de cartes, par L. Chodzko. 2 vols. 8° *Paris, 1830*
—— Traité Élémentaire de Géographie, contenant un Abrégé Méthodique du Précis de la Géographie Universelle, divisé en deux parties, celle des Principes et celle des Descriptions; précédé d'une Introduction Historique, et suivi d'un aperçu de la Géographie Ancienne, Sacrée et Profane; terminé d'après de Plan et les Matériaux de ce célèbre Géographie, par ses collaborateurs MM. Larenaudière, Balbi, et Huot. 2 vols. 8° *Paris, 1830-31*
—— Précis de la Géographie Universelle; revue, corrigée, mise dans un nouvel ordre, et augmentée de toutes les nouvelles Découvertes, par M. J. J. N. Huot. 12 vols. 8°, Atlas folio *Paris, 1836-37*

Malte-Brun, V. A. Coup-d'œil d'ensemble sur les différentes Expéditions Arctiques entreprises à la Recherche de Sir J. Franklin, et sur les Découvertes Géographiques, auxquelles elles ont donné lieu. *Map.* 8* *Paris, 1855*
—— Les Cartes Géographiques à l'Exposition Universelle de 1855. 8* *Paris, 1855*
—— Résumé Historique de la Grande Exploration de l'Afrique Centrale faite de 1850 à 1855, par J. Richardson, H. Barth, A. Overweg. *Map.* 8* *Paris, 1856*
—— Résumé Historique des Explorations faites dans l'Afrique Australe de 1849 à 1856, par le Rév. Docteur David Livingstone. *Map.* 8* *Paris, 1857*

Malte-Brun, V. A. Sur l'Expédition aux Sources du Nil, confiée au commandement de M. le Comte D'Escayrac de Lauture. 8* *Paris, 1857*
—— La France Illustrée : Géographie, Histoire, Administration, et Statistique. *Atlas.* 3 vols. 4° *Paris, 1858*
—— Itinéraire Historique et Archéologique de Philippeville à Constantine. *Map.* 8* *Paris, 1858*
—— Résumé Historique de l'Exploration faite dans l'Afrique Centrale de 1853 à 1856, par le Dr Édouard Vogel. *Map.* 8* *Paris, 1858*
—— Résumé Historique de l'Exploration à la Recherche des Grands Lacs de l'Afrique Orientale, faite en 1857-58, par R. F. Burton et J. H. Speke. *Map.* 8* *Paris, 1859*
—— La Destinée de Sir John Franklin dévoilée; Rapport du Capit. MacClintock, Commandant du yacht " Fox," suivi d'un Résumé analytique de l'Expédition des navires " Erebus " et " Terror." *Map.* 8* 1860
—— Un Coup d'œil sur le Yucatan : Géographie, Histoire, et Monuments. *Map.* 8* *Paris* [1865]
—— Canal Interocéanique du Darien Amérique; Notice Historique et Géographique sur l'état de la question du Canal du Darien. *Map.* 8* *Paris* [1865]
—— Résumé Historique et Géographique de l'Exploration de Gerhard Rohlfs au Touât et à In-çâlah d'après le Journal de ce Voyageur, &c. *Map.* 8* *Paris, 1866*
—— Les trois projets (Anglais, S. Osborn; Allemand, A. Petermann; Français, G. Lambert) d'Exploration au Pole Nord : exposé historique et géographique de la question. *Map.* 8° *Paris, 1868*
—— Notice sur les Voyages et les Travaux de M. le Comte Stanislas d'Escayrac de Lauture. 8* *Paris, 1869*
—— La France Vinicole : Nouveau Carte de la Distribution Topographiquè des Vignobles sur le sol Français. Folio* [*Paris, 1875*]
—— Aperçu de l'État de nos connaissances Géographiques au moment de l'ouverture du Congrès International à Paris. *Map.* 8* *Paris, 1875*
—— L'Expédition polaire Anglaise en 1875. *Map.* 8* *Paris, 1876*
—— Tableau Géographique de la Distribution Ethnographique des Nations et des Langues au Mexique. *Map.* 8* *Nancy, 1878*
—— *See* Kelley, Moure ; Peney.

Malte-Brun and Balbi. System of Universal Geography, founded on the Works of; embracing a Historical Sketch of the Progress of Geographical Discovery, the Principles of Mathematical and Physical Geography, and a Complete Description, from the most recent sources, of the Political and Social Condition of all the Countries in the World. 8°
Edinburgh, 1842

Maltzan, Baron Henri de. Pèlerinage à la Mecque. 8*   [1860]
—— *See* Wrede.

Malvezzi, Giuseppe Maria. Intorno alla Morte delle Conte Ugolino, ed alla retta intelligenza del verso LXXV. del canto XXXIII. della Divina Commedia. 8*   *Venice*, 1860
—— Indice dei Manoscritti di Storia Veneta e d'altre materie posseduti. 8*
Venice, 1861
—— Elogio di Giambattista Torre. *Portrait.* Small folio*   *Venice*, 1863

Man, Colonel Alexander. Formosa, an Island with a romantic history. (Reprinted from the *Asiatic Quarterly Review*.) 8*   1892

Man, E. H. The Lord's Prayer translated into the Bôjingîjîda or South Andaman (Elâkâbëäda) Language. With Preface, Introduction, and Notes by R. C. Temple. 8°   *Calcutta*, 1877
—— On the Aboriginal Inhabitants of the Andaman Islands. With Report of Researches into the Language of the South Andaman Islands, by A. J. Ellis. *Map and plates.* 8°   [1883]
—— **and R. C. Temple.** A Grammar of the Bôjingîjîda or South Andaman Language. 8*   *Calcutta*, 1878

Manby, C. *See* Kelley; Longridge; Murray, John; Peniston; Yates.

Manby, G. W. Journal of a Voyage to Greenland in the year 1821. *Plates.* 4°   1822

Mandane, Comte de. *See* St André, H. P.

Mandat-Grancey, Baron E. de. Cowboys and Colonels: Narrative of a Journey across the Prairie and over the Black Hills of Dakota. From "Dans les Montagnes Rocheuses" of Baron E. de Mandat-Grancey. With additional Notes, not contained in the original edition, by William Conn. *Illustrations.* 8°   1887
—— Souvenirs de la Côte d'Afrique, Madagascar, Saint - Barnabé. *Illustrations.* 12°   *Paris*, 1892

Mandelslo, Jean Albert de. Voyages celèbres et remarquables faits de Perse aux Indes Orientales : contenant une Description nouvelle et très-curieuse de l'Indostan, de l'Empire du Grand-Mogol, des Iles et Presqu'iles de l'Orient, des Royaumes de Siam, du Japon, de la

Mandelslo, Jean Albert de—*continued.*
Chine, du Congo, &c.   Mis en ordre et publiez. . . par le Sr. Adam Olearius. . . . traduits de l'original par le Sr. A. de Wicquefort.   New Edition.   2 vols. in 1. *Maps and plates.* Folio *Amsterdam*, 1727
—— *See* Olearius; *also* Harris, Vol. 1; Allgemeine Historie, Vol. 11 : Appendix 1.

Mandeville, Sir John. The Voiage and Travaile of Sir John Maundevile, Kt., which treateth of the Way to Hierusalem, and of Marvayles of Inde, with other Ilands and Countryes. 8°   1725
—— *See* Nicholson and Yule ; Hakluyt, Vol. 2 ; Kerr, Vol. 1 ; Purchas, Vol. 3, Book 1 : Appendix 1.

Manget, J. L. Chamounix, le Mont Blanc, et les deux St Bernards. *Map.* 12°   *Geneva*, 1843

Mangles, James. *See* Irby.

Mangles, Capt. James. Illustrated Geography and Hydrography. Prospectuses of. *Maps.* 8*   1846
—— The same. Wellington Channel Section. *Map.* 8*   1851
—— Geography, Descriptive, Delineative, and in Detail, and Hydrography in Detail, Combined and Universally Applied. 8*   1849
—— A Few Remarks on the "Illustrated Geography and Hydrography." 8*
N.P., N.D.

Mangourit, M. O. B. *See* Phillips, Collection of Modern and Contemporary Voyages [1.], Vol. 3 : Appendix 1.

Mann, Abbé. Dissertation dans laquelle on tâche de déterminer précisément le port où Jules-César s'est embarqué pour passer dans la Grande-Bretagne, et celui où il y aborda ; ainsi que le jour précis où il fit ce Voyage. 4*   *Paris*, 1778
—— Mémoire dans lequel on examine l'opinion de plusieurs Auteurs anciens et modernes qui soutiennent que les Mers Noire, Caspienne, Baltique, et Blanche, ont anciennement communiqué ensemble. 4*   *Paris*, 1779

Mann, Gustav. *See* India, I (Assam) : Appendix 2.

Mann, Henry. Features of Society in Old and in New England. 12°
Providence, R.I., 1885

Mann, John F. First Report on New Guinea. (Royal Geographical Society of Australasia, New South Wales Branch.) 8*   *Sydney*, 1889

Mann, Robert James. The Colony of Natal : an Account of the Characteristics and Capabilities of this British Dependency. *Map.* 8°   1859
—— Meteorological Observations made at Pietermaritzburg during 1865. Folio*
[1866]
—— The Zulus and Boers of South Africa: a Fragment of recent history. 12*   1879
—— *See* Brooks, H.

Manne, — de. *See* Anville.

Mannering, G. E. With Axe and Rope in the New Zealand Alps. *Maps and illustrations.* Large 8° 1891

Mannert, Konrad. Germania, Rhaetia, Noricum, Pannonia, nach den Begriffen der Griechen und Römer ; zweyte völlig umgearbeitete Auflage. *Maps.* 8° *Leipzig,* 1820
—— Geographie von Afrika. *Maps.* 8° *Leipzig,* 1825

Manning, Thomas. *See* Markham, C. R.

Mannl, Rodolphe. Carlsbad, and its Mineral Springs, Medically, Sociably, and Locally Considered. 8° *Leipzig,* 1847

Mansel, Sir Robert. *See* Purchas, Vol. 2 : Appendix 1.

Mansfield, C. B. Paraguay, Brazil, and the Plate, in 1852-53. With Life by the Rev. C. Kingsley. *Map, portrait, and illustrations.* 8° *Cambridge,* 1856

Mansfield, J. S. Remarks on the African Squadron. 8* 1851

Mansfield, R. B. The Log of the "Water-Lily " (Thames Gig), during Two Cruises, in the Summers of 1851-52, on the Rhine, Neckar, Main, Moselle, Danube, and other streams of Germany. 3rd edition. 12° 1854

Mansvelt, —. *See* Burney, Vol. 4 : Appendix 1.

Mantegazza, P. *See* Giglioli.

Mantell, G. A. Notice of the Discovery by Mr Walter Mantell, in the Middle Island of New Zealand, of a Living Specimen of the Notornis. *Plate.* 4* 1852

Manzoni, Angiolo. *See* Issel.

Manzoni, Renzo. El Yèmen : Tre Anni nell' Arabia Felice, escursioni fatte dal Settembre 1877 al Marzo 1880. *Maps, plan, and illustrations.* Large 8° *Rome,* 1884

Mapother, E. D. Lisdoonvarna Spas, and some other Irish Watering-places. 3rd edition. *Map and plates.* 12* 1876

Marcel, Gabriel. Mémoire inédit de Grossin sur Madagascar et Carte Manuscrite. 8* *Paris,* 1883
—— Cartographie de la Nouvelle France, Supplément à l'Ouvrage de M. Harrisse. 8* *Paris,* 1885
—— Documents pour l'Histoire des Colonies Françaises. 1. Une Lettre inédite de Lescarbot, publiée avec une Notice Bibliographique sur l'Auteur par Gabriel Marcel. 2. Le Surintendant Fouquet, Vice-Roi d'Amérique. 8* *Paris,* 1885
—— Mémoire en requête de Champlain pour la continuation du paiement de sa Pension. 8* *Paris,* 1886
—— Note sur une Carte Catalane de Dulceri antérieure à l'Atlas Catalan de 1375, lue à la Société de Géographie de Paris, 7 Janvier 1887. 8* *Paris,* 1887

Marcel, Gabriel. Une Carte d'Amérique, datée de 1669. 8* *Paris,* 1891
—— Note sur une Sphère terrestre en cuivre faite à Rouen à la fin du XVIᵉ siècle. 4* *Rouen,* 1891

Marcet, Edouard. Australie : un Voyage à travers le Bush. *Photographs.* 8° *Geneva,* 1868

Marchais, Chev. des. *See* Astley, Vol. 2 ; Allgemeine Historie, Vol. 3 : Appendix 1.

Marchand, Étienne. Voyage autour du Monde, 1790-92 ; précédé d'une Introduction Historique, auquel on a joint des Recherches sur les Terres Australes de Drake, et un Examen Critique du Voyage de Roggeween ; avec cartes et figures par C. P. Claret Fleurieu. 5 vols. 8°. Vol. 6, *maps,* 4° *Paris,* 1798-1800
—— A Voyage round the World, performed during the years 1790-92. *See* Fleurieu, C. P. Claret de.
—— *See* Eyriès, Vol. 2 : Appendix 1.

Marchand, G. le. *See* Kuropatkin.

Marche, A. Trois Voyages dans l'Afrique Occidentale, Sénégal, Gambie, Casamance, Gabon, Ogooué. *Map and plates.* 12° *Paris,* 1879
—— Luçon et Palaouan, Six Années de Voyages aux Philippines. *Maps and illustrations.* 12° *Paris,* 1887

"Marchesa." *See* Guillemard.

Marco Polo. Travels of, in the Thirteenth Century : being a Description, by that early Traveller, of Remarkable Places and Things in the Eastern Parts of the World. Translated from the Italian, with Notes, by W. Marsden. *Map.* 4° 1818
—— The Travels of. Greatly amended and enlarged from valuable early MSS., with copious Notes, by Hugh Murray. *Maps.* 12° *Edinburgh,* 1844
—— I Viaggi. Tradotti da Rusticiano di Pisa, e Corredati d' Illustrazioni e di Documenti da Vincenzo Lazari ; pubblicati per cura di Lodovico Pasini. *Map.* 8° *Venice,* 1849
—— The Book of Ser Marco Polo, the Venetian, concerning the Kingdoms and Marvels of the East. Newly translated and edited, with Notes, &c., by Col. Henry Yule. 2 vols. *Maps and plates.* 8° 1871
—— The same. 2nd edition. 2 vols. *Maps and plates.* 8° 1875
—— Le Livre de Marco Polo. Fac-simile d'un Manuscrit du XIVᵉ Siècle conservé à la Bibliothèque Royale de Stockholm. 4° *[Stockholm,* 1882]
—— *See* Amrein ; Urbani de Gheltof; *also* Astley, Vol. 4 ; Harris, Vol. 1 ; Kerr, Vol. 1 ; Purchas, Vol. 3 ; Pinkerton, Vol. 7 ; Ramusio, Vol. 2 ; Allgemeine Historie, Vol. 7 ; Recueil des Voyages, Vol. 1, p. 611 : Appendix 1.

Marcou, Jules. Lettres sur les Roches du Jura, et leur Distribution Géographique dans les Deux Hémisphères. Livre I. Les Monts Jura et l'Angleterre. *Map.* 8° *Paris,* 1857
—— Notes pour servir à une Description Géologique des Montagnes Rocheuses. 8* *Geneva,* 1858
—— Geology of North America; with Reports on the Prairies of Arkansas and Texas, the Rocky Mountains of New Mexico, and the Sierra Nevada of California. *Maps and plates.* 4° *Zurich,* 1858
—— On a Second Edition of the Geological Map of the World. 8* [*Boston, Mass.,* 1873]
—— Origin of the name " America." 8* [*Washington,* 1875]
—— Notes upon the First Discoveries of California and the Origin of its Name. *Map.* 8* *Washington,* 1878
—— **and John Belknap Marcou.** United States Geological Survey, J. W. Powell, Director. Mapoteca Geologica Americana : a Catalogue of Geological Maps of America (North and South), 1752-1881, in Geographic and Chronologic order. 8° *Washington,* 1884
Marcoy, Paul. Voyage à Travers l'Amérique du Sud de l'Océan Pacifique à l'Océan Atlantique, &c. 2 vols. *Maps and plates.* 4° *Paris,* 1869
Marcy, Capt. Randolph B. Prairie Traveller : a Hand-Book for Overland Expeditions. *Maps.* 12° *New York,* 1859
—— Report of his Explorations of the Big Witchita and Head Waters of the Brazos Rivers. 8* *Washington,* 1856
—— *See* United States, K (Texas) : Appendix 2.
—— **and Capt. G. B. M'Clellan.** Exploration of the Red River of Louisiana, in 1852 ; with Reports of the Natural History of the Country. 2 vols. *Maps and plates.* 8° *Washington,* 1854
Marenigh, Jean. Guide de Florence et d'autres Villes principales de Toscane. 2 vols. *Map and plates.* 12° *Florence,* 1822
Marès, Paul. Nivellement Barométrique dans les Provinces d'Alger et de Constantine. *Tables.* 8° *Versailles,* 1864
Margary, Augustus Raymond. The Journey of, from Shanghae to Bhamo, and back to Manwyne . . ; with Concluding Chapter by Sir Rutherford Alcock. *Map and portrait.* 8° 1876
Margerie, E. de, and Dr Albert Heim. Les Dislocations de l'Écorce Terrestre ; Essai de Définition et de Nomenclature ; Die Dislocationen der Erdrinde ; Versuch einer Definition und Bezeichnung. *Figures.* 8° *Zurich,* 1888

Margerie, E. de, and F. Schrader. Aperçu de la Structure Géologique des Pyrénées. *Map and diagrams.* 8* *Paris,* 1892
Margerie, E. de. *See* De la Noë ; Schrader.
Margry, Pierre. Les Navigations Françaises et la Révolution Maritime du XIVᵉ au XVIᵉ Siècle, d'après les Documents inédits, &c. 8° *Paris,* 1867
—— Découvertes et Établissements Français dans l'Ouest et dans le Sud de l'Amérique Septentrionale, 1614-98 ; Mémoires et Documents inédits. 3 vols. *Maps and plates.* 8° *Paris,* 1879
—— The same, 1614-1754. Mémoires et Documents originaux. Vols. 4-6. *Facsimile and portraits.* Large 8° *Paris,* 1881-88
Mariette-Bey, Auguste. Aperçu de l'Histoire d'Égypte depuis les temps les plus reculés jusqu'à la Conquête Musulmane. 3rd edition. 12° *Alexandria,* 1872
—— Notice des Principaux Monuments exposés dans les Galeries Provisoires du Musée d'Antiquités Égyptiennes de S. A. le Khédive à Boulaq. 4th edition. 8° *Paris,* 1872
—— Itinéraire de la Haute-Égypte, comprenant une Description des Monuments Antiques des rives du Nil entre le Caire et la Première Cataracte. 12° *Alexandria,* 1872
—— The Monuments of Upper Egypt. A Translation by Alphonse Mariette of the "Itinéraire de la Haute-Égypte." *Map and plans.* 12° *Alexandria,* 1877
Marignola, Johannes von. Reise in das Morgenland v. J. 1339-53. Aus dem Latein übersetzt, geordnet und erläutert von J. G. Meinert. 8° *Prague,* 1820
—— *See* Hakluyt Soc. Publ., Vol. 7 : Appendix 1.
Marigny, E. Taitbout de. Portulan de la Mer Noire, et de la Mer d'Azov, ou Description des Côtes de ces deux Mers à l'usage des Navigateurs. 12° *Odessa,* 1830
—— Three Voyages in the Black Sea to the Coast of Circassia, including Descriptions of the Ports, and the importance of their trade. *Map and frontispiece.* 8° 1837
—— Pilote de la Mer Noire et de la Mer d'Azov : extrait de l'Hydrographie de la Mer Noire et de la Mer d'Azov, comparée à celles de l'Antiquité et du moyen âge du même auteur. 8° *Constantinople,* 1850
—— Black Sea Pilot. 8° 1855
Marilaun, Ritter Fritz Kerner von. Untersuchungen über die Schneegrenze im Gebiete des mittleren Innthales. *Plates.* 4* *Vienna,* 1887

Marinelli, Prof. Giovanni. La Superficie del Regno d'Italia, secondo i piú recenti studi. Terza ediz. 8* *Rome,* 1884
—— Slavi, Tedeschi, Italiani nel cosiddetto "Litorale" Austriaco (Istria, Trieste e Gorizia). 8* *Venice,* 1885
—— Recenti studi Idrografici e Talasso-grafici nel Mediterraneo. 8* *Padua,* 1885
—— Le Alpi Carniche, Nome, Limiti, Divisioni nella Storia e nella Scienza. *Map.* 8* *Turin,* 1888

Mariner, William. An Account of the Natives of the Tonga Islands, in the South Pacific Ocean ; with an Original Grammar and Vocabulary of their Language, compiled and arranged from the extensive communications of Mr William Mariner by John Martin. 2 vols. *Map and portrait.* 8° 1818
—— See Eyriès, Vol. 5 : Appendix 1.

Markham, Admiral Albert Hastings. The Cruise of the "Rosario" amongst the New Hebrides and Santa Cruz Islands. *Map and plates.* 8° 1873
—— A Whaling Cruise to Baffin's Bay and the Gulf of Boothia, and an Account of the Rescue of the Crew of the "Polaris"; with an Introduction by Rear-Admiral Sherard Osborn. *Map and plates.* 8° 1874
—— The Great Frozen Sea : a Personal Narrative of the Voyage of the "Alert" during the Arctic Expedition of 1875-76. *Maps and plates.* 8° 1878
—— Northward Ho ! . . . ; including a Narrative of Capt. Phipps's Expedition, by a Midshipman. *Illustrations.* Small 8° 1879
—— A Polar Reconnaissance : being the Voyage of the "Isbjörn" to Novaya Zemlya in 1879. *Maps and plates.* 8° 1881
—— Hudson's Bay and Strait. Roy. Geo. Soc. Suppl. Papers, Vol. 2. 8° 1887
—— Life of Sir John Franklin, and the North-West Passage. [The World's Great Explorers and Explorations Series.] *Maps and illustrations.* Crown 8° 1891
—— See Hakluyt Soc. Publ., Vol. 59 : Appendix 1.

Markham, Clements Robert. Franklin's Footsteps : a Sketch of Greenland, along the Shores of which his Expedition passed, and of the Parry Isles where the last traces of it were found. *Map.* 12° 1853
—— Cuzco : a Journey to the Ancient Capital of Peru, with an Account of the History, Language, Literature, and Antiquities of the Incas ; and Lima : a Visit to the Capital and Provinces of Modern Peru. *Map and plates.* 8° 1856
—— Travels in Peru and India while Superintending the Collection of Chinchona Plants and Seeds in South America, and their Introduction into India. *Maps and plates.* 8° 1862
U

Markham, Clements Robert. A List of the Tribes in the Valley of the Amazon, including those on the Banks of the Main Stream and of all its Tributaries. 8* 1864
—— The same. New edition. 8* 1895
—— Contributions towards a Grammar and Dictionary of Quichua, the Language of the Yncas of Peru. 8° 1864
—— Chinchona Cultivation in Travancore and on the Pulney Hills : Expedition across an unfrequented Pass, from Peermede to the Cumbum Valley in Madura. *Map.* Folio * 1865
—— On the Origin and Migrations of the Greenland Esquimaux. *Map.* 8* N.D.
—— On the Best Route for North Polar Expeditions. 8* 1865
—— Further Report on Chinchona Cultivation in India. 4* 1866
—— Report on the Irrigation of Eastern Spain. *Maps and plate.* 8°. [1867]
—— A History of the Abyssinian Expedition . . . ; with a Chapter containing an Account of the Mission and Captivity of Mr Rassam and his Companions, by Lieut. W. F. Prideaux. *Maps.* 8° 1869
—— Letter to the Under-Secretary of State for India on the Marine Surveys of India (with five Enclosures). Folio* 1871
—— A Memoir on the Indian Surveys. *Maps.* 4° 1871
—— The same. 2nd edition 1878
—— Ollanta, an Ancient Ynca Drama. Translated from the original Quichua. Small 8° 1871
—— The Threshold of the Unknown Region. [Arctic Exploration.] *Maps.* 8° 1873
—— The same. 3rd and 4th editions 1875
—— A General Sketch of the History of Persia. *Map.* 8° 1874
—— The Arctic Navy List, or a Century of Arctic and Antarctic Officers, 1773-1873 ; together with a List of Officers of the 1875 Expedition, and their services. *Map.* 8* 1875
—— Commodore J. G. Goodenough : a Brief Memoir. *Plate.* Small 8° 1875
—— Narratives of the Mission of George Bogle to Tibet, and of the Journey of Thomas Manning to Lhasa. Edited, with Notes, an Introduction, and Lives of Mr Bogle and Mr Manning, by C. R. Markham. *Map and plates.* 8° 1876
—— The same. 2nd edition 1879
—— Report on the Geographical Department of the India Office, 1867 to 1877. Small 8* [1877]
—— A Refutation of the Report of the Scurvy Committee. 8* *Portsmouth,* 1877
—— The same. 2nd edition, with additions. 8* *Portsmouth,* 1877

Markham, Clements Robert Peru (in Sampson Low & Co.'s Series, "Foreign Countries and British Colonies"). *Maps and illustrations.* 12° 1880
—— Peruvian Bark : a Popular Account of the Introduction of Chinchona Cultivation into British India, 1860-80. *Maps and illustrations.* Small 8° 1880
—— An Account of the Raleigh, Geographical, and Kosmos Clubs. 8* 1880
—— Fifty Years' Work of the Royal Geographical Society. 8° 1881
—— The War between Peru and Chile, 1879-82. *Maps.* Crown 8° 1882
—— Progress of Discovery on the Coasts of New Guinea, with Bibliographical Appendix by E. C. Rye. Roy. Geo. Soc. Suppl. Paper, Vol. 1, 1882-85. 8° 1885
—— Famous Sailors of Former Times : the Story of the Sea Fathers. 2nd edition. *Frontispiece.* 12° 1886
—— Sul Punto d'Approdo di Cristoforo Colombo. *Map.* Large 8* *Rome,* 1889
—— A Life of John Davis the Navigator, 1550-1605, Discoverer of Davis Straits. [The World's Great Explorers and Explorations Series.] *Maps and illustrations.* Crown 8° 1889
—— Latin-American Republics : a History of Peru. *Maps and illustrations.* 8° 1892
—— Christopher Columbus. [The World's Great Explorers and Exploration Series.] *Maps and illustrations.* Crown 8° 1892
—— *See* Hakluyt Soc. Publ., Vols. 24, 26, 28, 29, 33, 34, 41, 45, 47, 48, 56, 57, 60, 61, 63, 68, 79, 86 : Appendix 1.
Markham, Frederick. Shooting in the Himalayas : a Journal of Sporting Adventures and Travel in Chinese Tartary, Ladac, Thibet, Cashmere, &c. *Plates.* 8° 1854
Marlianus, Bartholomaeus. Urbis Romae Topographia . . . libris quinque comprehensa, &c. *Map and plates.* Folio *Bâle,* 1550
Marlowe, Capt. E. *See* Gottfried ; Kerr, Vol. 9 : Appendix 1.
Marmier, Xavier. *See* Gaimard, Paul ; Rafn and Mohnike.
Marmora, Andrea. Historia di Corfù. *Portrait.* 4° *Venice,* 1672
Marni, N. Barbot de. Beschreibung der Astrachanskischen oder Kalmücken-Steppe. *Map.* 8° *St Petersburg,* 1863
Marno, Ernst. Von Dahbeh nach Omderman durch die westliche Bajuda-Steppe. 8* *Vienna,* [1870]
—— Reisen im Gebiete des blauen und weissen Nil, im Egyptischen Sudan und den angrenzenden Negerländern, in den Jahren 1869 bis 1873. *Maps and plates.* 8° *Vienna,* 1874
—— Reise in der Egyptischen Aequatorial-Provinz und in Kordofan, in den Jahren 1874-76. *Maps and plates.* 8° *Vienna,* 1878

Marquette, Pére, and — Joliet. Voyage et Découverte de quelques Pays et Nations de l'Amerique Septentrionale, par le P. Marquette et Sr. Joliet. [Reprint.] *Map.* 8° *Paris,* 1681
—— *See* Gottfried ; Thevenot, Vol. 4 : Appendix 1.
Marquez, Carlos Cuervo. Tierradentro, Los Paeces, San Agustin, El Llano, &c. *Illustrations.* 8° *Bogotá,* 1893
Marquina, P. R. La Provincia de Tucuman, breves apuntes. 8* *Tucuman,* 1890
Marr, Robert A. Observations on the Mississippi River, at Memphis, Tenn. 4* *Washington,* 1853
Marrée, J. A. de. Reizen op en Beschrijving van de Goudkust van Guinea. 2 vols. *Map and plates.* 8° *The Hague,* 1817-18
Marriott, Saville, and R. H. Showell. Rough Notes connected with the Petty Estate of Jowar, in the Tanna Collectorate. [From the Records of India, No. 25.] *Map.* Royal 8* *Bombay,* 1856
Marriott, William. Hints to Meteorological Observers. 2nd ed. 8* 1887
Marryat, Frank S. Borneo and the Indian Archipelago. *Plates.* 4° 1848
Marryat, Horace. Residence in Jutland, the Danish Isles, and Copenhagen. 2 vols. *Map and plates.* 8° 1860
—— One Year in Sweden, including a Visit to the Isle of Götland. 2 vols. *Map and plates.* 8° 1862
Marsden, Kate. On Sledge and Horseback to Outcast Siberian Lepers. *Illustrations.* 8° [1893]
Marsden, Rev. Samuel. Memoirs of the Life and Labours of the Rev. Samuel Marsden, of Paramatta, Senior Chaplain of New South Wales, and of his early connection with the Missions to New Zealand and Tahiti. Edited by the Rev. J. B. Marsden. *Portrait and illustrations.* 8° N.D.
—— *See* Nicholas, J. L.
Marsden, William. On the Chronology of the Hindoos. Large 8* 1790
—— History of Sumatra, containing an Account of the Government, Laws, Customs, and Manners of the Native Inhabitants ; with a Description of the Natural Productions, and a Relation of the Ancient Political State of that Island. *Map and plates.* 4° 1811
—— Dictionary of the Malayan Language ; to which is prefixed a Grammar, with an Introduction and Praxis. 4° 1812
—— Numismata Orientala Illustrata : The Oriental Coins, Ancient and Modern, of his Collection described and historically illustrated. 2 parts in 1 vol. *Plates.* 4° 1823-25

Marsden, William. Bibliotheca Marsdeniana Philologica et Orientalis : a Catalogue of Books and Manuscripts collected with a view to the General Comparison of Languages, and to the Study of Oriental Literature. 4°
Privately printed, 1827
—— Memoirs of a Malayan Family. Written by Themselves, and translated from the Original by W. Marsden. 8° 1830
—— Miscellaneous Works :— 4° 1834
On the Polynesian, or East-Insular Languages. *Maps and plates.*
On a Conventional Roman Alphabet, applicable to Oriental Languages.
Thoughts on the Composition of a National English Dictionary.
—— Brief Memoir of the Life and Writings of, written by himself, with Notes from his Correspondence. 4°
Privately printed, 1838
—— Rudiments of the Malayu Language, being an Abridgement of Marsden's Malayan Grammar. 12° 1847
—— *See* Marco Polo. Dalrymple, Repertory, Vol. 2 : Appendix 1.

Marsh, Ant. *See* Purchas, Vol. 3, Book 4: Appendix 1.

Marsh, A. E. W. Holiday Wanderings in Madeira. *Illustrations.* 8° 1892

Marsh, Hon. George P. Compendious Grammar of the Old-Northern and Icelandic Language, compiled and Translated from the Grammars of Rask. 12°
Burlington, Vt., 1838
—— Man and Nature, or Physical Geography as Modified by Human Action. 8° 1864
—— Lecture on the Camel. 8*
Washington, N.D.

Marsh, Capt. H. C. A Ride through Islam : being a Journey through Persia and Afghanistan to India, viâ Meshed, Herat, and Kandahar. *Map.* 8° 1877

Marsh, Rev. J. W., and W. H. Stirling. The Story of Commander Allen Gardiner, R.N. ; with Sketches of Missionary Work in South America. 8th edition. 1874

Marsh, O. C. Introduction and Succession of Vertebrate Life in America. 8°
New Haven, Conn., 1877
—— *See* United States, G, *c*, and H, *a*, Geological Exploration of the Fortieth Parallel, Vol. 8: Appendix 2.

Marshall, Capt. *See* Phillip ; *also* Pelham, Vol. 1 : Appendix 1.

Marshall, C. The Canadian Dominion. *Plates.* 8° 1871

Marshall, H. Ceylon : a General Description of the Island and its Inhabitants ; with an Historical Sketch of the Conquest of the Colony by the English. *Map.* 8° 1846

Marshall, Thomas. Statistical Reports on the Pergunnahs of Padshapoor, Belgom, Kalaniddee and Chandgurh, Khanapoor, Bagulkot, Badamy, and Hoondgoond, in the Southern Mahratta Country ; followed by a Letter from William Chaplain, and Observations by St John Thackeray. *Tables.* Folio *Bombay*, 1822

Marshall, W. *See* Galton, Vacation Tourists.

Marsili, A. F. Danubius Pannonico-Mysicus, Observationibus Geographicis, Astronomicis, Hydrographicis, Historicis, Physicis perlustratus. 6 vols. (in 3). *Map and plates.* Folio *Amsterdam*, 1726

Marsilli, L. F. G. van. Naturkundige Beschryving der Zeën. *Plates.* Folio *The Hague*, 1786

Martel, Aline. Sparte et les gorges du Taygète. 8* *Paris*, 1892

Martel, E. A. A Collection of Eleven Pamphlets, mainly relating to Researches in the Cevennes and in the Alps. [One Paper written jointly with L. de Launay.] 8° 1884-88
—— Karl von Sonklar. 8* [1885]
—— Nouvelle Carte d'Italie au 100,000°. 8* [*Paris*, 1885]
—— A Collection of Sixteen Pamphlets, relating to Subterranean Explorations. [One Paper written jointly with G. Gaupillat.] 8° 1885-93
—— Le Gouffre du Puits de Padirac. *Illustrations.* 4* *Paris*, 1890
—— Carte d'Autriche au 75,000°. 8* [*Paris*, 1886]
—— Le Causse Noir et Montpellier-le-Vieux (Aveyron). *Plan and illustrations.* 4* [*Paris*, 1886]
—— Les Cévennes et la Région des Causses (Lozére, Aveyron, Herault, Gard, Ardéche). *Map, plans, and illustrations.* 4° *Paris*, 1890
—— and L. de Launay. L'Homme Paléolithique et la Poterie Paléolithique dans la Lozère. 8* *Paris*, 1886
—— and G. Gaupillat. Sur la Formation des sources dans l'intérieur des plateaux calcaires des Causses. 4* [*Paris*, 1889]
—— Sur l'Exploration et la Formation des Avens des Causses. 4* [*Paris*, 1889]
—— Compte-rendu sommaire de la Cinquième Campagne Souterraine. 8* 1892
—— Le Tindoul de la Vayssière (Aveyron). *Plan.* 8* *Paris*, 1892

Marten, C. R. The Province of Southland, New Zealand : General Description of Country, Climate, Resources, and other particulars. (From *Colonial News*.) *Map.* 12* 1871

Marten, Nathaniel. *See* Astley, Vol. 1 ; Purchas, Vol. 1, Book 3 : Appendix 1.

Martens, E. von. *See* Asia (General); New Zealand, A : Appendix 2.

Martens, F. Vojagie naar Groenland of Spitsbergen, mits gaders een net verhaal der Walvis Vanghst en der zelve behandeling. *Plates.* 12° *Dordrecht,* N. D. —— *See* Vries; *also* Hakluyt Soc. Publ., Vol. 18; "Voyages," 1711 (p. 597): Appendix 1.

Martens, G. von. *See* Asia (General): Appendix 2.

Marthe, F. Was bedeutet Carl Ritter für die Geographie? 8* *Berlin,* 1880

Martial, L. F. *See* France, B, *a* (Cape Horn): Appendix 2.

Martin, Arthur B. *See* Noric.

Martin, Benjamin. The Natural History of England, or a Description of each particular County in regard to the Curious Productions of Nature and Art. 2 vols. *Maps.* 8° 1759-63

Martin, Frederick. The Statesman's Yearbook, Statistical and Historical Annual of the States of the World, for the years 1869-82. 8°

Martin, F. R. En resa i vestra Sibirien utförd år 1891 med understöd af Vegastipendiet. 1. Etnografiska och Arkeologiska forskningar i Surgutska Kretsen. 2. Arkeologiska undersökningar i guvernementet Tomsk. (From *Ymer.*) *Illustrations.* 8* *Stockholm,* 1892

Martin, Isaac. *See* Knox's New Collection, Vol. 5 : Appendix 1.

Martin, James. Explorations in North-Western Australia. 8* [1863] —— Journal of a Voyage to the Glenelg River, North-West Australia, in June and July 1863. Small 4* *Perth,* 1864 —— **and F. K. Panter.** Report for the Information of H.E. the Governor of Western Australia, and the Promoters of the North-Western Expedition of 1864, on the Voyage and the Resources of the Districts explored. Small 4* *Perth,* 1864

Martin, John. *See* Mariner.

Martin, J. M. The Changes of Exmouth Warren. Part II. *Maps.* 8* [1876]

Martin, Josiah. *See* Cowan, F.

Martin, J. Ranald. Official Report on the Medical Topography and Climate of Calcutta, with Notices of its Prevalent Diseases, Endemic and Epidemic. 4° *Calcutta,* 1839

Martin, K. Bericht über eine Reise nach Niederländisch West-Indien und darauf gegründete Studien. Erster Theil. Land und Leute ; Zweiter Theil. Geologie. 2 vols. *Maps and plates.* Large 8° *Leyden,* 1888

Martin, M. A Description of the Western Islands of Scotland, containing a Full Account of their Situation, Extent, Soils, Product, Harbours, Bays, Tides, Anchoring-Places, and Fisheries; the Antient and Modern Government, Religion, and Customs of the Inhabitants ; a particular Account of the Second Sight, &c. *Map and plate.* 8° 1716

Martin, M. *See* Pinkerton, Vol. 3 : Appendix 1.

Martin, Robert Montgomery. History of the British Colonies. Vol. 1, Asia ; Vol. 2, West Indies ; Vol. 3, North America ; Vol. 4, Africa and Australasia ; Vol. 5, Europe. 5 vols. *Maps.* 8° 1834-35 —— Colonial Policy of the British Empire. Part 1, Government. 8* 1837 —— The History, Antiquities, Topography, and Statistics of Eastern India, comprising the Districts of Behar, Shahabad, Bhagulpoor, Goruckpoor, Dinajepoor, Puraniya, Rungpoor, and Assam, in Relation to their Geology, Mineralogy, Botany, Agriculture, Commerce, Manufactures, Fine Arts, Population, Religion, Education, Statistics, &c. 3 vols. *Maps and plates.* 8° 1838 —— History of the Colonies of the British Empire in the West Indies, South America, North America, Asia, Australasia, Africa, and Europe, comprising the Area, Agriculture, &c., of each Colony, with the Charters and the Engraved Seals. From the Official Records of the Colonial Office. *Map.* 8° 1843 —— Reports, Minutes, and Despatches on the British Position and Prospects in China. 8° 1846 —— The Hudson's Bay Territories and Vancouver's Island, with an Exposition of the Chartered Rights, Conduct, and Policy of the Hon. Hudson's Bay Corporation. *Map.* 8° 1849 —— Report to the Shareholders of the Liguanea and General Mining Company of Jamaica, and of the Annotto Bay Mining Association. 8* 1851 —— Report on Hong Kong; Report on Chusan ; and Minute on the British Position and Prospects in China; with Governor Davis's Dispatch. *Maps.* Folio* 1857

Martin, W. Notes on the Cape of Good Hope, its Climate, &c., &c. 8* *Calcutta,* 1856

Martin, Major T. Rough Notes on the City of Poona. [From the India Records, No. 79.] Royal 8° *Bombay,* 1864

Martin, Staff-Commander W. R. A Text-book of Ocean Meteorology, compiled from the Sailing Directories for the Oceans of the World by Alex. George Findlay. *Charts.* 8° 1887

Martineau, Harriet. Eastern Life, Present and Past. 3 vols. 8° 1848 —— British Rule in India, a Historical Sketch. 12° 1857

Martinet, Ludovic. *See* Lesson.

Martinez, Carlos Walker. Pajinas de un Viaje al traves de la America del Sur. 8° *Santiago,* 1876

Martinez, J. J. Un Trou à la Terre. Puits d'Observation, Deuxième Appel. 8* *San Francisco*, 1886

Martinez, Matthia. *See* Iarric.

Martinière, Bruzen la. Le Grand Dictionnaire, Géographique et Critique. 10 vols. Folio *The Hague*, 1726-39
—— *See* Vries.

Martinioni, G. *See* Sansovino.

Martinius, M. De Bello Tartarico Historia. *Plates.* 16° *Amsterdam*, 1655

Martins, Charles. Du Spitzberg au Sahara, Étapes d'un Naturaliste au Spitzberg, en Laponie, en Écosse, en Suisse, en France, en Italie, en Orient, en Égypte, en Algérie. *Plates.* 8° *Paris* [1865]
—— Sur la possibilité d'atteindre le Pole Nord, &c. 8* *Paris*, 1866
—— Les Glaciers actuels et la Periode Glaciaire. 8* *Paris* [1867]
—— *See* Gaimard, Paul.
—— **and B. Gastaldi.** Essai sur les Terrains Superficiels de la Vallée du Pô aux Environs de Turin, comparés à ceux du Bassin Helvétique. *Map.* 4* *Versailles*, N.D.

Martins, J. P. de Oliveira. Les Explorations des Portugais antérieures à la découverte de l'Amérique. . . . Traduite de l'Espagnol par Alexandre Boutroue. *Map.* 8* *Paris*, 1893

Martiny, F. W. Handbuch für Reisende nach dem Schlesischen Riesengebirge und der Grafschaft Glatz. *Map and plates.* 12° *Breslau*, 1812

Martius, Carl Friedrich Philipp von. Von dem Rechtszustande unter den Ureinwohnern Brasiliens. *Map.* 4° *Munich*, 1832
—— Die Vergangenheit und Zukunft der Amerikanischen Menschheit. 8* *Munich*, 1839
—— Versuch eines Commentars über die Pflanzen, in den Werken von Marcgrav und Piso über Brasilien. I. Kryptogamen. 4* *Munich*, 1853
—— Wörtersammlung Brasilianischer Sprachen : Glossaria Linguarum Brasiliensium ; Glossarios de Diversas Lingoas e Dialectos, que Fallão os Indios no Imperio do Brazil ; Beiträge zur Ethnographie und Sprachenkunde Amerika's zumal Brasiliens. II. 8° *Leipzig*, 1867
—— Die Fieber-Rinde, der China-Baum, sein Vorkommen, und seine Cultur. 8* N.P., N.D.
—— Dictionnaire Galibi. Dictionarium Gallice, Latine, et Galibi. 8* N.P., N.D.
—— Das Naturell, die Krankheiten, das Arztthum, und die Heilmittel der Urbewohner Brasiliens. 12° *Munich*, N.D.
—— Die Pflanzen und Thiere des Tropischen America. 4* [*Munich*, N.D.]

Martius, Carl Friedrich Philipp von. *See* Meissner ; Schramm : Spix.

Martus, H. C. E. Astronomische Geographie : ein Lehrbuch angewandter Mathematik. *Illustrations.* 8° *Leipzig*, 1880

Martyn, Henry. *See* Smith, George.

Martyr, Peter. The Decades of the Newe Worlde, or West India : conteyning the Navigations and Conquestes of the Spanyardes, with the particular Description of the Most Ryche and Large Landes and Islandes lately founde in the Weste Ocean, perteyning to the Inheritance of the Kinges of Spayne. From the Latin, by Richard Eden. [*Title and pp.* 226-8 *wanting.*] 4° 1555
—— De Rebus Oceanicis et Novo Orbe, Decades Tres. Item ejusdem de Babylonica Legatione, lib. 3, et Item de Rebus Æthiopicis, Indicis, Lusitanicis, et Hispanicis opuscula. Small 8° *Cologne*, 1574
—— *See* Ramusio, Vol. 3 : Appendix 1.

Marvin, Charles. The Eye-Witnesses' Account of the Disastrous Russian Campaign against the Akhal Tekke Turcomans, describing the March across the Burning Desert, the Storming of Dengeel Tépé, and the Disastrous Retreat to the Caspian. *Maps, plans, and portraits.* 8° 1880
—— Colonel Grodekoff's Ride from Samarcand to Herat, through Balkh and the Uzbek States of Afghan Turkestan ; with his own Map of the March-route from the Oxus to Herat. *Portrait.* Small 8° 1880
—— The Russians at Merv and Herat, and their Power of Invading India. *Maps and illustrations.* 8° 1883
—— The Russian Railway to Herat and India ; with an Introduction by Arminius Vámbéry, and a Facsimile of General Annenkoff's Map of the Projected Route. 8* 1883
—— The Petroleum of the Future. Baku, the Petrolia of Europe : a Historical Sketch, showing the Immense and Inexhaustible Character of the Petroleum Deposits of the Caspian Region, from the Earliest Times. *Map.* 8* [1883]
—— The Russians at the Gates of Herat. *Map and portraits.* 12° [1885]
—— The African Question. English Africa : Shall Boer and German sway it ? *Map.* 8* [1887]
—— The Petroleum Question. Our Unappropriated Petroleum Empire : Oil Discoveries in the Colonies. *Maps.* 8* [1889]

Marzolla, Benedetto. Descrizione dell' Isola Ferdinandea, al Mezzo-giorna della Sicilia. *Plates.* Oblong 12* *Naples*, 1826

Mas, Barlatier de. Instructions Nautiques sur les Côtes d'Islande, rédigées d'après ses Observations pendant cinq Campagnes dans ces Parages et les Notes Manuscrites de M. le Contre-Amiral danois P. de Löwenörn. *Maps and plates.* 8°   *Paris*, 1862

Mascrier, — le. Description de l'Egypte, contenant plusiers Remarques curieuses sur la géographie ancienne et moderne de ce païs, &c. Composé sur les memoirés de M. de Maillet. *Maps and plates.* 4°
                                  Paris, 1735
—— The same. 2 vols. *Maps and plates.* 12°   *The Hague*, 1740

Mas Latrie, L. de. *See* Latrie.

Mason, Dr and Mrs. *See* Phayre.

Mason, G. H. Life with the Zulus of Natal, South Africa. 12°   1855

Mason's Hygrometer : Uses to which it is applicable. [*Two leaves.*] *With Tables.* 8*   N.D.

Masoom, Mahomed. History of Sind, embracing the period from A.D. 710 to A.D. 1590; written in Persia at the close of the 16th Century, and translated into English in 1846 by Captain G. G. Malet, assisted by Peer Mahomed. Edited by R. H. Thomas. [From the India Records, No. 13.] 8°   *Bombay*, 1855

Masqueray, Émile. *See* Liorel.

Massa. *See* Gerritsz.

Massaja, Guglielmo. I miei Trentacinque Anni di Missione nell' alta Etiopia. Vols. 1-11. *Illustrations.* 4° *Rome*, 1885-93

Massalongo, C. *See* France, B, a (Cape Horn) : Appendix 2.

Masselin, J. G. Dictionnaire Universale des Géographies, Physique, Historique, et Politique, du Monde Ancien, du Moyen Age, et des Temps Modernes, comparées. 2 vols. *Maps.* 8° *Paris*, 1827

Masson, Charles. Narrative of various Journeys in Balochistan, Afghanistan, the Panjab, and Kalât ; with an Account of the Insurrection at Kalât, and a Memoir on Eastern Balochistan. 4 vols. *Maps and plates.* 8°   1844
—— *See* Wilson, H. H.

Masterman, G. F. Seven Eventful Years in Paraguay : a Narrative of Personal Experience amongst the Paraguayans. *Map.* 8°   1869

Matani, Antonio. Ragionamento Filosofico Istorico sopra la Figura della Terra. 8*   *Pisa*, 1760

Mateer, S. "The Land of Charity:" a Descriptive Account of Travancore and its People. *Map and plates.* Small 8°
                                       1871

Matelief, C. *See* Allgemeine Historie, Vol. 8 : Appendix 1.

Matham, A. Voyage d'Adrien Matham au Maroc (1640-41). Journal de Voyage, publié pour la première fois ; avec Notice Biographique de l'auteur, Introduction et Notes, par F. de Hellwald. Large 8°
                           The Hague, 1866

Mather, W. W. Second Annual Report on the Geological Survey of the State of Ohio. *Map and plates.* 8° *Columbus*, 1838

Mathers, Edward P. The Gold Fields Revisited, being Further Glimpses of the Gold Fields of South Africa. *Maps.* 8°
                           Durban, 1887
—— Golden South Africa, or the Gold Fields Revisited : being Further Glimpses of the Gold Fields of South Africa. *Maps.* 8°   1888
—— The same. 4th edition. *Maps and plans.* 8°   1889
—— Zambesia, England's El Dorado in Africa : being a Description of Matabeleland and Mashonaland, and the less known adjacent Territories, and an Account of the Gold Fields of British South Africa. *Maps and illustrations.* 8°   [1891]

Mathews, C. E. *See* Dent, C. T.

Mathews, E. D. Report to the Directors of the Madeira and Mamoré Railway Co. "Limited." 8*   1875
—— Up the Amazon and Madeira Rivers, through Bolivia and Peru. *Map and plates.* 8°   1879
—— British Guiana and Venezuela. *Map.* 8*   [1888]

Mathews, H. J. G. Long : In Memoriam. 8*   1879

Mathews, W. The Flora of Algeria, considered in Relation to the Physical History of the Mediterranean Region, and supposed Submergence of the Sahara. *Map.* 8°   1880

Mathiesen, General H. Étude sur les Courants et sur la Température des eaux de la mer dans l'Océan Atlantique. *Map.* 4*   *Christiania*, 1892

Mathison, G. F. Narrative of a Visit to Brazil, Chile, Peru, and the Sandwich Islands during 1821-22. *Maps.* 8° 1825

Matkovic, Dr P. Topographische Karte des Gebietes St Michel di Lemmo in Istrien gezeichnet von Fra Mauro. *Map.* 8*   *Vienna*, 1859
—— Putovanja Po-Balkanskom Poluotoka XVI. Vieka. X. Putopis Marka Antuna Pigafette, ili, drugo putovanje Antuna Vrancicá u Carigrad 1567 godine. Large 8°   *Zagrebu*, 1890

Matters, C. H. From Golden Gate to Golden Horn, and many other Worldwide Wanderings, or 50,000 Miles of Travel over Sea and Land. *Portrait.* 12°   *Adelaide*, 1892

Matteucci, Pellegrino. (Spedizione Gessi-Matteucci.) Sudan e Gallas. *Map.* 12°
                           Milan, 1879

Matthes, Dr B. F. Eenige proeven van Boegineesche en Makassaarsche Poëzie. 8* *The Hague*, 1883

Matthews, J. W. Incwadi Yami; or, Twenty Years' Personal Experience in South Africa. *Illustrations.* 8° 1887

Matthews, Washington. *See* United States, G, a (Miscell.) : Appendix 2.

Mauch, Karl. Reisen im Inneren von Süd-Afrika. *Map.* 4* *Gotha*, 1870
—— Reisen im Inneren von Süd-Afrika, 1865-72. (Ergänzungsheft, 37 — Petermann's Mittheilungen.) *Map.* 4° *Gotha*, 1874

Maucroix, D'Estr. de. Note sur le Banc de Feroë. 8* *Paris*, 1846

Maudru, J. B. Elémens Raisonnés de la Langue Russe, ou Principes Généraux de la Grammaire appliqués à la Langue Russe. *Tables.* 8° *Paris*, 1802

Maudslay, A. P. *See* Central America, A (Biologia Centrali-Americana): Appendix 2.

Mauduit, A. F. Adhésions des Savants Français et Étrangers aux Opinions émises dans de livre "Découverte dans la Troade et dans les Traductions d'Homère." 4* *Paris*, 1842-51

Maunder, Samuel, and William Hughes. The Treasury of Geography, Physical, Historical, Descriptive, and Political; containing a Succinct Account of every Country in the World, preceded by an Introductory Outline of the History of Geography. *Maps and plates.* 12° 1856
—— The same. New edition. 1867

Maundrell, Henry. A Journey from Aleppo to Jerusalem, at Easter, A.D. 1697. *Illustrations.* 8° *Oxford*, 1703
—— The same. 7th edition; to which is now added an Account of the Author's Journey to the Banks of Euphrates at Beer, and to the Country of Mesopotamia, with an Index to the whole work. *Illustrations.* 8° *Oxford*, 1749
—— The same. Also a Journal from Grand Cairo to Mount Sinai and back again. Translated from a MS. by the Prefetto of Egypt, by Bishop R. Clayton. *Plates.* 8° 1810
—— *See* Harris, Vol. 2; Pinkerton, Vol. 10; Knox's New Collection, Vol. 6; "The World Displayed," Vol. 11: Appendix 1.

Maunoir, C. Congrès des Sociétés Savantes : Discours prononcé à la Séancé Générale du Congres le Samedi, 31 Mai 1890. Large 8* *Paris*, 1890
—— *See* France, Transactions, L'Année Géogr., p. 799: Appendix 2.

Maunsell, R. Grammar of the New Zealand Language. 3rd edition. 12° *Melbourne*, 1882

Maupertius. *See* Pinkerton, Vol. 1; "The World Displayed," Vol. 20; Allgemeine Historie, Vol. 17; Knox's New Collection, Vol. 4: Appendix 1.

Maurer, Franz. Die Nikobaren: Colonial-Geschichte und Beschreibung nebst motivirtem Vorschlage zur Colonisation dieser Inseln durch Preussen. *Maps.* 8° *Berlin*, 1867

Maurice, Col. J. F. *See* United Kingdom, G : Appendix 2.

Maurice, Thomas. The History of Hindostan. Part 1. The Indian Cosmogony and Chronology. *Plates.* 4° 1790
—— Indian Antiquities; or, Dissertations relative to the Antient Geographical Divisions, the Pure System of Primeval Theology, the Grand Code of Civil Laws, the Original Form of Government, the widely-extended Commerce, and the various and profound Literature of Hindostan; compared throughout with the Religion, Laws, Government, and Literature of Persia, Egypt, and Greece. . . . 7 vols. (Vol. 1, 1806; 2, 1806; 3, 1794; 4, 1800; 5, 1794; 6 (two parts in one vol.), 1796; 7, 1800.) *Plates.* 8° 1794-1800
—— Observations connected with Astronomy and Ancient History, Sacred and Profane, on the Ruins of Babylon, as recently visited and described by C. J. Rich. *Plates.* 4° 1816

Mauro, Fra. *See* Matkovic.

Maury, Alfred. Notice sur la Vie et les Travaux de J. B. Biot. 12* *Paris*, 1851

Maury, L. F. A. Histoire des Grandes Forêts de la Gaule et de l'Ancienne France, précédée de Recherches sur l'Histoire des Forêts de l'Angleterre, de l'Allemagne, et de l'Italie. 8° *Paris*, 1850

Maury, Lieut. M. F. Abstract Log for the use of American Navigators, prepared under the Direction of Commodore Lewis Warrington. 4° *Washington*, 1848
—— Investigations of the Winds and Currents of the Sea. 4° *Washington*, 1851
—— Explanations and Sailing Directions to accompany the "Wind and Current Charts" approved by Commodore Lewis Warrington. 3rd edition. *Maps and plates.* 4° *Washington*, 1851
—— Another, approved by Commodore Charles Morris. 4th edition. *Maps and plates.* 4° *Washington*, 1852
—— Another edition, enlarged and improved. 7th edition. *Maps and plates.* *Philadelphia*, 1855
—— Another edition, approved by Capt. D. N. Ingraham. 8th edition, enlarged and improved. 2 vols. Vol. 1, 1858; Vol. 2, 1859. *Maps and plates.* 4° *Washington*, 1858-59

Maury, Lieut. M. F. Co-operation of the Principal Maritime Nations in collecting materials for "Wind and Current Charts." [*Two leaves.*] 4* *Washington*, 1852

—— Letter concerning Lanes for the Steamers crossing the Atlantic. *Plans.* 4* *New York*, 1855

—— Physical Geography of the Sea. *Maps.* 8° 1855

—— Observations sur la Navigation des Paquebots qui traversent l'Atlantique ; Routes à suivre pour éviter les Abordages en Mer. *Map and plates.* 8° *Paris*, 1856

—— Résumé de la partie physique et descriptive des Sailing Directions par Mr E. Tricault. *Maps and plates.* 8° *Paris*, 1857

—— Letter to C. W. Field on Nautical Directions for Sailing from Valentia to Newfoundland. 8* *Washington*, 1857

—— Instructions Nautiques destinées à accompagner les Cartes de Vents et de Courants. Traduites par Lieut. Ed. Vaneechout. *Maps and plates.* 4° *Paris*, 1859

—— Astronomical Observations made during the years 1849 and 1850, at the U.S. Naval Observatory, Washington. Vol. 5. 4° *Washington*, 1859

—— Nautical Monographs. No. 1, The Winds at Sea ; No. 2, The Barometer at Sea. 2 parts. *Plates.* 4° *Washington*, 1859-61

—— Physical Geography of the Sea, and its Meteorology : being a Reconstruction and Enlargement of the Eighth Edition of "The Physical Geography of the Sea." *Maps and diagrams.* 8° 1860

—— The Physical Survey of Virginia : Geographical Position ; its Commercial Advantages and National Importance. *Maps.* 8° *Richmond, Va.*, 1868

—— A Life of Matthew Fontaine Maury, U.S.N. and C.S.N., author of " Physical Geography of the Sea, and its Meteorology." Compiled by his daughter Diana Fontaine Maury Corbin. 8° 1888

—— *See* Tricault.

Mauss and Sauvaire. *See* Luynes.

Mauve, Carl. Erläuterungen zu der Flötzkarte des Oberschlesischen Steinkohlengebirges zwischen Beuthen, Gleiwitz Nikolai, und Myslowitz. 8* *Breslau*, 1860

Maver, J. *See* Zuñiga, Martinez de.

Mavidal, J. Le Sénégal, son état présent et son avenir. *Map.* 8° *Paris*, 1863

Mavor, W. The British Tourist's or Traveller's Pocket Companion through England, Wales, Scotland, and Ireland. 6 vols. *Maps and plates.* 12° 1798

Maw, G. On the Disposition of Iron in Variegated Strata. *Plates.* 8* 1868

—— *See* Hooker and Ball.

Maw, Lieut. H. L. Journal of a Passage from the Pacific to the Atlantic, crossing the Andes in the Northern Provinces of Peru, and descending the River Marañon or Amazon. *Map.* 8° 1829

—— A Letter to the Editor of the *Edinburgh Review*, in Answer to his Criticism on a "Journal of a Passage down the River Marañon," &c. 8* N.D.

Mawe, J. Mineralogy of Derbyshire, with a Description of the most interesting Mines in the North of England, Scotland, and Wales ; with a Glossary of the Phrases used by the Miners. *Plates.* 8° 1802

Mawe, John. Travels in the Interior of Brazil, particularly the Gold and Diamond Districts of that Country ; including a Voyage to the Rio de la Plata, and an Historical Sketch of the Revolution of Buenos Ayres. *Map and plates.* 4° 1812

Maxmilian, Prinz zu Wied-Neuwied. *See* Wied-Neuwied.

Maximowicz, —. Scientific Results of Prejevalsky's Travels in Central Asia. Botany. 2 parts. 4° *St Petersburg*, 1889

—— *See* Schrenck.

Maxwell, J. R. The Negro Question ; or, Hints for the Physical Improvement of the Negro Race, with special reference to West Africa. Small 8° 1892

May, C. *See* Churchill, Vol. 6 : Appendix 1.

May, Henry. *See* Purchas, Vol. 4, Book 9 : Appendix 1.

May, John. *See* Gottfried ; Kerr, Vol. 8 : Appendix 1.

Maydell, Baron Gerhard. Reisen und Forschungen im Jakutskischen Gebiet, Ostsibiriens in den Jahren 1861-71. Erster Theil. Band 1, Vierte Folge. Beiträge zur Kenntniss des Russischen Reiches und der angrenzenden Länder Asiens . . . herausgegeben von L. von Schrenck und Fr. Schmidt. Large 8° *St Petersburg*, 1893

Mayer, Brantz. Mexico : Aztec, Spanish, and Republican ; a Historical, Geographical, &c., account of that Country, from the Invasion by the Spaniards to the Present Time ; with a View of the Ancient Aztec Empire and Civilisation, a Historical Sketch of the late War, and Notices of New Mexico and California. 2 vols. *Map and plates.* 8° *Hartford, Conn.*, 1852

Mayer, Friedrich. Nürnberg im neunzehnten Jahrhundert, mit stetem Rückblick auf seine Vorzeit. [*Map and plates wanting.*] 8° *Nuremberg*, 1843

Mayer, J. Kurze Wörter-Sammlung, in Englisch, Deutsch, Amharisch, Gallanisch, Guraguesch ; herausgegeben von Dr L. Krapf. 8° *Bâle*, 1878

Mayer, John. The Engineering and Shipbuilding Industries of Glasgow and the Clyde. [Bound up with other Papers for the British Association Meeting at Glasgow, 1876.] 12° *Glasgow, 1876*

Mayer, Luigi. Views in the Ottoman Empire, chiefly in Caramania, a part of Asia Minor hitherto unexplored, from the original Drawings in the possession of Sir R. Ainslie. The text in English and French. *Coloured plates.* Folio
1803

Mayerberg, Baron Augustus de. Iter in Moschoviam A. L. Baronis de Mayerberg . . . et H. G. Caluuccii . . . ab Augustissimo Romanorum Imperatore Leopoldo, ad Tzarem et Magnum Ducem Alexium Mihalowicz, anno 1661 ablegatorum ; Descriptum ab ipso A. L. Barone de Mayerberg, cum Statutis Moschouiticis ex Russico in Latinum idioma ab eodem translatis. Folio
[*Privately printed*, 1661]

Mayes, C. *See* Victoria, C : Appendix 2.

Mayet, Valéry. Voyage dans le Sud de la Tunisie. Deuxième edition. *Map.* 12° *Paris,* 1887

Mayne, R. C. Four Years in British Columbia and Vancouver Island, &c. *Maps and plates.* 8° 1862

Mayne, Capt. R. C. Practical Notes on Marine Surveying and Nautical Astronomy. *Maps.* Small 8° 1874

Mayo, Charles. *See* Galton, F., Vacation Tourists.

Mayo, Earl of. Proposed Expedition to Ovampo-Land, landing at Mossâmedes, S.W. Coast of Africa. [Printed for private circulation.] *Map.* 8° 1882
—— De Rebus Africanis : the Claims of Portugal to the Congo and adjacent Littoral, with Remarks on the French Annexation. *Map.* 8° 1883

Mayr, Emil. Neu-Süd-Wales im Jahre 1881. *Map.* 8* *Vienna,* 1884

Mayr, G. L. *See* "Novara."

Mayson, John Schofield. The Malays of Capetown. 8* *Manchester,* 1861

Mc. *For Names beginning* Mc— *or* M'—, *see under* Mac—.

Meade, H. A Ride through the Disturbed Districts of New Zealand ; together with some Account of the South Sea Islands. *Maps and plates.* 8° 1870

Meade, Wm. An Experimental Inquiry into the Chemical Properties, &c., of the Mineral Waters of Ballston and Saratoga, in the State of New York. *Plates.* 8°
Philadelphia, 1817

Meadows, Thomas Taylor. The Chinese and their Rebellions, viewed in connection with their National Philosophy, Ethics, Legislation, and Administration ;

Meadows, Thomas Taylor—*continued.* with an Essay on Civilisation in the East and West. *Maps.* 8° 1856

Means, J. O. American Board of Commissioners for Foreign Missions. The Proposed Mission in Central Africa. [A Paper read at the Annual Meeting at Syracuse, N.Y., 8th October 1879.] *Map.* 8* *Cambridge, Mass.,* 1879

Meares, John. Voyages made in the years 1788 and 1789, from China to the North-West Coast of America ; to which are prefixed an Introductory Narrative of a Voyage performed in 1786 from Bengal in the ship "Nootka," Observations on the Probable Existence of a North-West Passage, and some Account of the Trade between the North-West Coast of America and China, and the latter Country and Great Britain. *Maps and plates.* 4°
1790
—— *See* Eyriès, Vol. 1 : Appendix 1.

Measor, H. P. A Tour in Egypt, Arabia Petræa, and the Holy Land, in the years 1841-42. *Plate.* Small 8° 1844

Meath, Earl of. A Britisher's Impressions of America and Australasia. (From the *Nineteenth Century.*) 8* 1893

Mechow, Major von. *See* Hann.

Medhurst, W. H. China, its State and Prospects, with special reference to the Spread of the Gospel. *Map.* 8° 1838

Medhurst, Sir Walter. *See* Hatton, F.

Medina, J. T. Ensayo acerca de una Mapoteca Chilena ó sea de una colección de los titulos de los mapas, planos, y vistas relativos á Chile, arreglados cronológicamente, con una Introducción Historica acerca de la Geografia y Cartografia del pais. 12* *Santiago,* 1889

Medina, Pietro da. L'Arte del Navegar, in laqual si contengono lere gole, dechiarationi, secreti, e avisi, alla bona Navegation necessarii. Tradotta de lingua Spagnola in volgar Italiano. *Diagrams.* Small 4° *Venice,* 1555

Medlicott, H. B. Note on the Rèh Efflorescence of North-Western India, and on the Waters of some of the Rivers and Canals. 8* 1862
—— The Coal of Assam : Results of a Brief Visit to the Coal-Fields of that Province in 1865. 8* 1865
—— **and W. T. Blanford.** A Manual of the Geology of India. 2 vols. *Map.* Small 4° *Calcutta,* 1879
—— *See* India, C : Appendix 2.

"Medusa," Shipwreck of the. 12° N.D.
—— *See* Picard.

Meech, L. W. On the Relative Intensity of the Heat and Light of the Sun upon Different Latitudes of the Earth. *Plates.* 4* *Washington,* 1856

Meek, F. B. *See* United States, G, a ;
K, California, Missouri : Appendix 2.

Megiserus, Hieronymus. An Ancient
Account of Madagascar, A.D. 1609.
Translated from the German of Hier-
onymus Megiserus ; with Introductory
Notice by James Sibree, junr. 8*
                              Antananarivo, N.D.

Meidinger, Henri. Dictionnaire Étymo-
logique et Comparatif, des Langues
Teuto-Gothiques ; avec des racines
Slaves, Romanes, et Asiatiques, qui
prouvent l'origine commune de toutes
ces langues. Traduit de l'Allemand. 8°
                          Frankfort-o-M., 1833
—— Die Deutschen Volksstämme. 8°
                          Frankfort-o-M., 1833
—— Zur Statistik Frankfurts : Wohn-
plätze, Bevölkerung, Brod- und Fleisch-
verbrauch, Gewerb- und Armenwesen.
12°   *Frankfort-o-M.*, 1848
—— Die Deutschen Ströme in ihren
Verkehrs und Handels Verhältnissen.
4 vols in 2. *Maps.* 12° *Leipzig*, 1853

Meijer, J. J. *See* Jacobs.

Meiklejohn, Prof. J. M. D. On the Best
and the Worst Methods of Teaching
Geography : a Short Lecture to School-
masters. 8*   1869
—— A New Geography, on the Comparative Method, with Maps and Diagrams.
8°   1889

Meinardus, Dr W. Klimatischen Verhältnisse des nordöstlichen Theils des
Indischen Ozeans. 4*   *Altona*, 1894

Meinecke, Gustav. Koloniales Jahrbuch,
herausgegeben von Gustav Meinecke,
Zweiter Jahrgang, das Jahr 1889. *Maps.*
8°   *Berlin*, 1890
—— The same. Dritter Jahrgang, das
Jahr 1890. *Map.* 8°   *Berlin*, 1891
—— The same. Vierter Jahrgang, Das
Jahr 1891. *Maps and illustrations.* 8°
                              Berlin, 1892
—— The same. Sechster Jahrgang das
Jahr 1893. 8°   *Berlin*, 1894

Meinert, J. G. *See* Marignola.

Meinicke, Dr Carl E. Die Inseln des
Stillen Oceans, eine geographische Monographie. 2 vols in 1. 8° *Leipzig*, 1875-76
—— Das Festland Australien, eine geographische Monographie. 2 vols in 1.
8°   *Prenzlow*, 1837
—— Die Südseevölker und das Christenthum, eine ethnographische Untersuchung. 8°   *Prenzlow*, 1844
—— Die Insel Pitcairn. 4* *Prenzlow*, 1858
—— *See* Petermann.

Meinshausen, K. *See* Baer and Helmersen, Vol. 26.

Meinsma, J. J. Babad Tanah Djawi
in Proza. Javaansche Geschiedenis
Loopende tot het jaar 1647 der Javaansche Jaartelling. Eerste Stuk : Tekst.
8°   *The Hague*, 1874

Meinsma, J. J. The same. Tweede
Stuk : Aanteekeningen. 8°
                          The Hague, 1877

Meisner, H. *See* Röhricht, R.

Meissner, C. F. Denkschrift auf Carl
Friedr. Phil. von Martius. 4*
                              Munich, 1869

Mejoff, V. J. Catalogue of Russian Litera-
ture, Geography, &c. [In Russian.] 8°
      St Petersburg, 1867-68, 1873, 1874,
                                  1877, 1880
—— Recueil du Turkestan : comprenant
des Livres et des Articles sur l'Asie
Centrale en général et le Province du
Turkestan en particulier. Tomes 1-416.
L'Indicateur Systématique et Alpha-
bétique. 4°   *St Petersburg*, 1878-88

Mela Britannicus. Remarks touching
Geography, especially that of the British
Isles, comprising Strictures on the Hier-
archy of Great Britain. By Mela Britannicus. 12°   1825

Mela, Pomponius. Pomponii Melae de
Chorographia, libri tres . . . Edidit
Notisque Criticis instruxit G. Parthey.
8°   *Berlin*, 1867

Meldrum, Charles. A Meteorological
Journal of the Indian Ocean for March
1853, with a Summary of the Results
of the Observations, &c. *Charts and
diagrams.* 4*   *Mauritius*, 1856
—— On the Hurricane and Weather in
the Indian Ocean, from the 6th to the
18th February 1860. 8*   1860

Melena, Elpis. Erlebnisse und Beobachtungen eines mehr als 20-jährigen Aufenthaltes auf Kreta. *Map and illustrations.* 4°   *Hanover*, 1892 [1891]

Meletii, Archimandrite. *See* Boddy.

Melgunof, G. Das südliche Ufer des
Kaspischen Meeres, oder die Nord-
provinzen Persiens. *Map and plate.* 8°
                              Leipzig, 1868

Melik-Beglaroff, J. D. Archæological
Survey of Bengal : Report, 1887. By
Joseph Daviditch Melik-Beglaroff. *Plate.*
8*   *Calcutta*, 1888
—— The same. Report, 1888. By
Joseph Daviditch Melik - Beglaroff.
Plans. 8*   *Calcutta*, 1888

Melliss, J. C. St Helena : a Physical,
Historical, and Topographical Description of the Island, including its Geology,
Fauna, Flora, and Meteorology. *Map
and plates.* Large 8°   1875

Mello, Carlos de. Geographia Economica
de Portugal. Portugal Maritimo. [Vol.
1 ; Part 1 ?] *Illustrations.* 12* *Lisbon*, 1888

Mello, Gorge de. *See* Gottfried : Appendix 1.

Mello, Homem de. Subsidies to the Formation of the Physical Map of Brazil.
4*   *Rio de Janeiro*, 1876

Melly, George. Khartoum and the Blue
and White Niles. 2 vols. *Map and
plates.* 8°   1851

Melnikow, M. Geologische Erforschung des Verbreitungsgebietes der Phosphorite am Dnjester. *Map.* 8* N.P. [1885]

Melvill of Carnbee, and H. D. A. Smits. Seaman's Guide round Java to the Islands east of Java, and through the Straits of Banca and Gaspar. 1st, 2nd, and 3rd editions. 8° 1850-53
—— *See* Siebold, B. F.

Melville, George W. In the Lena Delta : a Narrative of the search for Lieut.-Commander De Long and his Companions ; followed by an Account of the Greely Relief Expedition, and a proposed method of reaching the North Pole. Edited by Melville Philips. *Maps and illustrations.* 8° 1885

Melville, Henry. The Present State of Australia, including New South Wales, Western Australia, South Australia, Victoria, and New Zealand ; with a Description of the Aborigines and their Habits. *Map and plate.* 8° 1851

Melville, Herman. Typee : a Narrative of a Four Months' Residence among the Natives of a Valley of the Marquesas Islands, or a Peep at Polynesian Life. *Map.* 12° 1847
—— The same. New edition, with a Memoir of the Author, and Illustrations. 8° 1893
—— Omoo : a Narrative of Adventures in the South Seas, being a Sequel to the "Residence in the Marquesses Islands." *Map.* 12° 1847
—— The same. New edition, with a Memoir of the Author, and Illustrations. 8° 1893

Memminger, J. D. G. Kleine Beschreibung von Würtemberg. 12°
Stuttgart, 1826

Menard, ——. Histoire des Antiquités de la Ville de Nismes et de ses Environs. New edition. *Plates.* 8° *Nismes*, 1822
—— Histoire des Antiquités de la Ville de Nismes et de ses Environs. [With which is bound "Le Guide des Étrangers à Vienne (Isère)," by M. Rey, 1819.] *Plates.* 8° *Nismes*, 1826

Ménard, René. Le Monde vu par les Artistes. Géographie Artistique. *Plates.* 8° *Paris*, 1881

Mendana, Alvaro de. *See* Burney, Vols. 1, 2 ; Allgemeine Historie, Vol. 18 : Appendix 1.

Mendelssohn, Dr G. B. Das Germanische Europa. 8° *Berlin*, 1836

Mendenhall, Dr T. C. Measurements of the Force of Gravity at Tokio and on the Summit of Fujinoyama. 4* *Tokyo*, 2541 [1881]
—— *See* United States, F, Coast and Geodetic Survey : Appendix 2.

Mendez, Diego, of Segura. *See* Gottfried : Appendix 1.

Mendez, Julio. Realidad del Equilibrio Hispano-Americano, y Necesidad de la Neutralizacion perpetua de Bolivia. Primera parte. Atacama y El Chaco. 12* *Lima*, 1874

Mendez Pinto. *See* Pinto.

Mendonça, J. de. Colonias e Possessões Portuguezas. 2nd edition. 12° *Lisbon*, 1877

Mendoza, Alvaro de. *See* Allgemeine Historie, Vol. 18 : Appendix 1.

Mendoza, E. Apuntes para un Catalogo Razonado de las palabras Mexicanas Introducidas al Castellano. 4* *Mexico*, 1872

Mendoza, Francis Lopez de. *See* Ternaux-Compans, Vol. 20 : Appendix 1.

Mendoza, G. Las Pirámides de Teotihuacan. *Plates.* 4* *Mexico*, 1878

Mendoza, Juan Gonzales de. Histoire du Grand Royaume de la Chine, situé aux Indes Orientales, Divisée en Deux Parties. Traduite en François par Luc de la Porte. 8° *Paris*, 1588
—— *See* Hakluyt Soc. Publ., Vols. 14, 15 ; Purchas, Vol. 3, Book 2 : Appendix 1.

Mendoza, P. de. *See* Allgemeine Historie, Vol. 16 : Appendix 1.

Mendozza, Ant. di. *See* Ramusio, Vol. 3 : Appendix 1.

Menezes, Duarte de. *See* Gottfried ; Purchas, Vol. 2, Book 9 : Appendix 1.

Menezes, Luiz de. Historia de Portugal Restaurado. 4 vols. in 2. 8° *Lisbon*, 1751

Mengin, Félix. Histoire de l'Égypte sous le Gouvernement de Mohammed-Aly . . . Ouvrage enrichi de Notes par MM. Langlès et Jomard, et précédé d'une Introduction Historique par M. Agoub. 2 vols. 8° *Paris*, 1823

Menon, P. S. A History of Travancore, from the Earliest Times. *Illustrations.* Small 8° *Madras*, 1875

Mense, Dr. Rapport sur l'État Sanitaire de Léopoldville de Novembre 1885 à Mars 1887. (Publications de l'État Indépendant du Congo, No. 1.) 8* *Brussels*

Mentelle, ——. Géographie Comparée, ou Analyse de la Géographie, Ancienne et Moderne, des Peuples de tous les Pays et de tous les Ages : Italie Moderne. 8° *Paris*, 1780
—— The same. Géographie, Physique et Politique. 8° *Paris*, 1783

Menzel, Wolfgang. Europe in 1840. Translated from the German. 8° *Edinburgh*, 1841

Mequet, Eugène. *See* Gaimard, Paul.

Mer, Auguste. Mémoire sur le Périple d'Hannon. *Map.* 8° *Paris*, 1885

Mera, Juan Leon. Catecismo de Geografía de la Republica del Ecuador. Segunda edicion. 12* *Guayaquil*, 1884

Mercator, Bartholomew. *See* Bartholomæus.

Mercator, G. Gérard Mercator : sa Vie et ses Œuvres ; par Raemdonck. *Plates.* Imperial 8° *St Nicolas*, 1869
—— *See* Hakluyt's Voyages, Vol. 1 : Appendix 1.

Mercer, A. History of Dunfermline. 12° *Dunfermline*, 1828

Mercer, Hon. C. Fenton. Report on the Inter-Oceanic Connection of the Atlantic and Pacific Oceans by the way of Lake Nicaragua and the River St Juan. *Maps.* 8° *Washington*, 1839

Mercier, Ernest. Histoire de l'Afrique Septentrionale (Berbérie), depuis les temps les plus reculés jusqu'à la Conquête Française (1830). 3 vols. *Map.* 8° *Paris*, 1888-91

Mercier, Hon. Honoré. General Sketch of the Province of Quebec. 8* *Quebec*, 1890

Mercui. *See* Bissy.

"Mercury" Brig. *See* Mortimer.

Meredith, Mrs Charles. My Home in Tasmania, during a Residence of Nine Years. 2 vols. *Illustrations.* 8° 1852

Meredith, H. *See* Eyriès, Vol. 11 · Appendix 1.

Merensky, A. Wie erzieht man am besten Neger zur Plantagen-Arbeit. 8* *Berlin*, 1886
—— Erinnerungen aus dem Missionsleben in Südost-Afrika (Transvaal), 1859-82. *Map and illustrations.* 8° *Leipzig*, 1888

Merewether, Serjeant. Speech before the Committee of the House of Commons on the Taff Vale Railway Bill. 8* 1840

Merewether, Capt. W. L. Report of, with other Papers relating to, the Enlargement of the Bigaree Canal, in Upper Sind. [From the India Records, No. 42.] *Map.* Royal 8° *Bombay*, 1857
—— Report on Places lately Visited between Aden and Suez. *Map.* Folio° N.D.

Merian, Matthaeus. *See* Eckardt, H.

Merick, Andrew. *See* Burney, Vol. 2 : Appendix 1.

Merin, ——. *See* Churchill, Vol. 4 : Appendix 1.

Merk, Conrad. Excavations at the Kesslerloch near Thayngen, Switzerland, a Cave of the Reindeer Period. Translated by J. E. Lee. *Plates.* 8° 1876

Merleker, Karl Friedrich. Historisch-politische Geographie ; oder allgemeine Länder- und Völkerkunde. Viertes Buch, der historisch-comparativen Geographie. Erster Theil : Die Continente Asien, Afrika, und Australien. 8° *Darmstadt*, 1841

Merolla da Sorrento, Jerome. *See* Astley, Vol. 3 ; Churchill, Vol. 1 ; Pinkerton, Vol. 16 ; Allgemeine Historie, Vol. 4 : Appendix 1.

Merrill, Selah. East of the Jordan : a Record of Travel and Observation in the Countries of Moab, Gilead, and Bashan ; with an Introduction by Professor Roswell D. Hitchcock. *Map and illustrations.* 8° 1881
—— The Jaffa and Jerusalem Railway. (From *Scribner's Magazine.*) *Illustrations.* Large 8* 1893

Merriman, C. C. Lectures, Essays, and Published Articles on Scientific and Literary Subjects, and on Foreign Travel. *Illustrations.* 8° *Rochester, N.Y.*, 1885

Merz, J. H. *See* Leonhard, C. C.

Mesa, P. A. de. Junta General de Estadística. Reconocimiento Hidrológico del Valle del Ebro. 4° *Madrid*, 1865

Mesny, William. Tungking. 12° 1884

Messedaglia, G. B. Diario Storico Militare delle Rivolte al Soudan dal 1878 in poi. *Maps:* 8* *Alessandria*, 1886

Meston, A. Report on the Scientific Expedition to the Bellenden-Ker Range [Wooroonooran], North Queensland. Folio* 1889

Metcalfe, F. Oxonian in Norway. 2 vols. 8° 1856
—— Oxonian in Thelemarken ; or, Notes of Travel in South-Western Norway. 2 vols. 8° 1858
—— The Oxonian in Iceland ; or, Notes of Travel in that Island in the Summer of 1860, with Glances at Icelandic Folklore and Sagas. Small 8° 1861

Metchnikoff, Léon. La Civilisation et les grands Fleuves historiques ; avec une Préface de M. Elisée Reclus. 12° *Paris*, 1889

Meteren, Emanuel Van (Meteranus). *See* Purchas, Vol. 4, Book 10 : Appendix 1.

Methold, William. *See* Gottfried ; Thevenot, Vol. 1 ; Allgemeine Historie, Vol. 10 : Appendix 1.

Methuen, Henry H. Life in the Wilderness ; or, Wanderings in South Africa. *Plates.* 12° 1846

Mettenius, G. *See* "Novara."

Metz, F. The Tribes inhabiting the Neilgherry Hills, their Social Customs and Religious Rites. 12° *Mangalore*, 1864

Metzger, Emil. Beiträge zur Kartographie von Niederländisch Ost-Indien, speziell von Java. [Incomplete.] 4* *[Lahr*, 1882]
—— Notes on the Dutch East Indies, 1888. (Reprinted from the *Scottish Geographical Magazine.*) 8* 1888

Meucci, F. Il Globo Celeste Arabico del Secolo xi. esistente nel Gabinetto degli Strumenti Antichi di Astronomia, di Fisica, e di Matematica del R. Istituto di Studi Superiori. *Map.* 8* *Florence*, 1878

Meurs, John. Creta, Cyprus, Rhodus, sive de Nobilissimarum harum Insularum rebus et Antiquitatibus. Small 8° *Amsterdam*, 1675

Meyen, F. J. F. Grundriss der Pflanzen-geographie, mit ausführlichen Untersuchungen über das Vaterland, den Anbau und den Nutzen der vorzüglichsten Culturpflanzen, welche den Wohlstand der Völker begründen. *Table.* 4°
Berlin, 1836
—— Reise um die Erde, ausgeführt auf dem Schiff "Princess Louise," Commandirt von Capitain W. Wendt, 1830-32. Historischer Bericht. 2 vols. *Maps.* 4°
Berlin, 1834-35

Meyendorff, Baron G. de. Voyage d'Orenbourg à Boukhara fait en 1820, à travers les Steppes qui s'étendent à l'est de la Mer d'Aral et au-delà de l'ancien Jaxartes. *Map, coloured frontispiece, and plates.* 8° *Paris,* 1826
—— Journey of the Russian Mission from Orenbourg to Bokhara. Translated by Col. Monteith. 8° *Madras,* 1840

Meyer, A. B. Einige Bemerkungen über den Werth, welcher im Allgemeinen den Angaben in Betreff der Herkunft menschlicher Schädel aus dem ostindischen Archipel beizumessen ist. 8*
Vienna, 1874
—— Ueber einen bemerkenswerthen Farbenunterschied der Geschlechter bei der Papageien, Gattung Eclectus (Wagler), &c. 8* *Vienna* [1874]
—— Uebersicht der von mir auf Neu Guinea und den Inseln Jobi, Mysore, und Mafoor im Jahre 1873 gesammelten Amphibien. 8* *Berlin,* 1874
—— Ueber drei neue auf Neu Guinea entdeckte Papageien. 8* *Vienna* [1874]
—— Anthropologische Mittheilungen über die Papuas von Neu Guinea. I. Aeusserer physischer habitus. *Plate.* 8*
Vienna, 1874
—— Ueber die Mafoor'sche und einige andere Papúa-Sprachen auf Neu Guinea. 8* *Vienna,* 1874
—— Auszüge aus den auf einer Neu Guinea Reise im Jahre 1873, geführten Tagebüchern von ; als Erläuterung zu den Karten der Geelvink-Bai und des Mac-Cluer-Golfes. Folio *Dresden,* 1875
—— Königliches Ethnographisches Museum zu Dresden. I. Bilderschriften des Ostindischen Archipels und der Südsee. *Plates.* Folio *Leipzig,* 1881

Meyer, C. E. H. von. *See* Zittel.

Meyer, E. G. *See* Gaimard, Paul.

Meyer, Dr Hans. Zum Schneehorn des Kilimandscharo ; 40 Photographien aus Deutsch-Ostafrika mit Text. 4°
Berlin [1888]
—— Across East African Glaciers : an Account of the First Ascent of Kilimanjaro. Translated from the German by E. H. S. Calder. *Maps and illustrations.* 8° 1891

Meyer, Dr H. A. Biologische Beobachtungen bei künstlicher Aufzucht des Herings der westlichen Ostsee. 8°
Berlin, 1878

Meyer, H. A. E, Vocabulary of the Language spoken by the Aborigines of the Southern and Eastern Portions of the Settled Districts of South Australia . . . ; preceded by a Grammar, showing the Construction of the Language as far as at present known. 8ª *Adelaide,* 1843

Meyer, H. J. Meyers Reisebücher : Der Orient, Hauptrouten durch Aegypten, Palästina, Syrien, Türkei, Griechenland. Erster Band : Aegypten. *Maps and plans.* 16° *Leipzig,* 1881
—— Zweiter Band : Syrien, Palästina, Griechenland, und Türkei. *Maps and plans.* 16° *Leipzig,* 1882

Meyer, Dr Hugo. Anleitung zur Bearbeitung meteorologischer Beobachtungen für die Klimatologie. 8° *Berlin,* 1891

Meyers, J. *See* Danckwerth.

Meyers, J. R. *See* Graf.

Meynard. *See* Barbier de Meynard.

Mezö-Kövesd. *See* Ujfalvy.

Mezzabarba, C. A. *See* Astley, Vol. 3 ; Allgemeine Historie, Vol. 5 : Appendix 1.

Miall, L. C. *See* India, C., Palæontologia Indica : Appendix 2.

Miani, G. Memoria dedicata al Sig. Roderick Murchison [On the Nile, and Africa generally]. 12*
Constantinople, 1865
—— Il Viaggio di Giovanni Miani al Monbutto. *Map and plate.* 8* *Rome,* 1875
—— *See* Gilbert, P.

Miansarof, M. Bibliographia Caucasica et Transcaucasica : Essai d'une Bibliographie Systématique relative au Caucase, à la Transcaucasie, et aux Populations des Contrées. 1. 8° *St Petersburg,* 1874-76

Michael, James. Persian Fables from the Anwari Sooheyly of Hussein Väiz Käshify; with a Vocabulary. 4° 1827

Michaelis, E. H. Ueber die Darstellung des Hochgebirges in topographischen Karten. 8* *Berlin,* 1845
—— Barometrische Höhenbestimmungen in Elsass, Rheinbayern, Baden, und Würtemberg. 8* *Berlin,* N.D.

Michaelis, Hermann. Von Hankau nach Sutschou. (Ergänzungsheft, 91 —Petermann's Mittheilungen.) *Maps and sketches.* 4° *Gotha,* 1888

Michael of Tripoli. *See* Ray : Appendix 1.

Michailow, —. *See* Phillips, New Voyages and Travels [3], Vol. 7 : Appendix 1.

Michaud, —. Biographie Universelle, Ancienne et Moderne. Nouvelle édition. 45 vols. Large 8° *Paris,* 1854

Michaux, F. A. *See* Phillips, Collection of Modern and Contemporary Voyages [1], Vol. 1 : Appendix 1.

Michel, — de. *See* Joutel.
Michel, A. F. *See* Rondot.
Michel F. *See* Recueil de Voyages, Vol. 4, p. 611 : Appendix 1.
Michelburne, Sir Edward. *See* Astley, Vol. 1 ; Kerr, Vol. 8 ; Allgemeine Historie, Vol. 1 : Appendix 1.
Michele, G. di. *See* Ramusio, Vol. 2 : Appendix 1.
Michelena y Rojas, Francisco. Viajes Cientificos en Todo el Mundo, 1822-42. *Maps and plates.* Royal 8° *Madrid*, 1843
—— Exploracion Oficial por la primera vez desde el Norte de la America del Sur siempre por Rios, entrando por las bocas del Orinóco, de los Valles de este mismo y del Meta, Casiquiare, Rio-Negro ó Guaynia y Amazónas, hasta Nauta en al alto Marañon ó Amazónas, Arriba de las bocas del Ucayali, Bajada del Amazónas hasta el Atlántico . . . Viaje á Rio de Janeiro desde Belen en el Gran Pará, por el Atlántico . . . en los años de 1855 hasta 1859. *Map.* 8°
Brussels, 1867
Michell, John. Conjectures concerning the Cause and Observations upon the Phænomena of Earthquakes, particularly of that Great Earthquake of November 1755. *Plate.* Small 4°   1760
Michell, J. and R. The Russians in Central Asia, their Occupation of the Kirghiz Steppe and the Line of the Syr-Daria, their Political Relations with Khiva, Bokhara, and Kokan ; also Descriptions of Chinese Turkestan and Dzungaria. By Capt. Valikhanof, M. Veniukof, and other Russian Travellers. Translated from the Russian. *Map.* 8°   1865
Michell, Robert. Account of a Russian Mission to Kashgar in October 1868. Compiled from Captain Reinthal's Report ; with a few Introductory Remarks. Folio*   [1870]
—— Summary of Statistics of the Russian Empire. 8°   1872
—— Memorandum on the Country of the Turkomans, giving an Account of the Russian Occupation of the East Coast of the Caspian. *Map.* Small folio* 1873
—— The same. [Reprinted and amplified.] *Map.* 8*   N.D.
—— Epitome of Correspondence relating to Merv ; with Historical and Geographical Accounts of the Place, and Itineraries. *Map.* Folio*   1875
—— Analysis of Water in the Wells in the Transcaspian Region. (From the Russian *Invalide*). [1 *sheet*.] Folio* 1881
—— Russian Contribution to Central Asian Cartography and Geography. I. 8* N.D.
—— *See* Cherkasski ; Fedchenko ; Grigorief ; Kostenko ; Lessar ; Petrusevitch ; Valikhanof ; *also* Central Asia, B : Appendix 2.

Michelot, Henry. Le Portulan de la Mer Mediterranée, ou le vrai Guide des Pilotes costiers. 4°   *Amsterdam*, 1754
Michelotti, Giuseppe Teresio. Saggio Idrografico del Piemonte. *Maps and plate.* 4°   *Rome*, 1803
Michelsen, E. H. The Merchant's Polyglot Manual in Nine Languages, &c. 8°
1860
Michelson, W. *See* Hakluyt, Vol. 4 : Appendix 1.
Micheovo, Mattheo di. *See* Ramusio, Vol. 2 : Appendix 1.
Michie, A. The Siberian Overland Route from Peking to Petersburg, through the Deserts and Steppes of Mongolia, Tartary, &c. *Maps and plates.* 8°   1864
—— Korea. 8*   [1892]
Michiels, A. V. Neêrlands Souvereiniteit over de Schoonste en Rijkste Gewesten van Sumatra. 8*   *Amsterdam*, 1846
Michow, Dr H. Die ältesten Karten von Russland, eine Beitrag zur historischen Geographie. *Maps.* Large 8*
Hamburg, 1888
—— Die schulgeographische Ausstellung auf dem geographischen Weltkongress zu Bern, 1891. Large 8*   1892
—— Caspar Vopell, ein Kölner Kartenzeichner des 16 Jahrhunderts. Seperatabdruck aus " Festschrift der Hamburgischen Amerika-Feier. *Plates, &c.* 4*   1892
—— Katalog der Bibliothek der Geographischen Gesellschaft in Hamburg. 8°   *Hamburg*, 1893
Michler, Lieut. N. Report of the Survey of an Interoceanic Ship Canal near the Isthmus of Darien. *Maps.* Royal 8°
Washington, 1861
Mickle, William Julius. The Lusiad. Translated by W. J. Mickle. *Map.* 8°   1798
Middendorff, A. T. von. Bericht über die Beendigung der Expedition nach Udskoy Ostrog, auf die Schantaren und durch das östliche Grenzgebirge. 8*
St Petersburg, 1845
—— Geognostische Beobachtungen auf seiner Reise durch Sibirien. Bearbeitet von G. von. Helmersen. 4* N.P., 1840
—— Voyage Scientifique dans la Sibérie-Occidentale. 8*   N.P., 1844
—— Voyage à Oudskoï. 8* N.P., 1844
—— Reise in der äussersten Norden und Osten Sibiriens während die Jahre 1843 und 1844. Vols. 1, 2, and 3. *Plates.* Folio   *St Petersburg*, 1847-48
—— Karten-Atlas zu Dr A. v. Middendorff's Reise in den äussersten Norden und Osten Sibiriens. Folio
St Petersburg, 1859
—— Aníkiev, eine Insel im Eismeere, in der Gegend von Kola. 8*
St Petersburg, 1860

Middendorff, A. T. von. Ueber die Nothwendigkeit von Vorbereitungen für den Empfang vorweltlicher Sibirischer Riesenthiere. 8* N.P., 1860
—— Sibirische Reise. Vol. 4, Part 1. Uebersicht der Natur Nord- und Ost-Sibiriens : Geographie, Hydrographie, Orographie, und Geognosie. Folio
St Petersburg, 1860
—— *See* Baer and Helmersen, Vols. 7, 11.

Middendorff, E. W. Peru: Beobachtungen und Studien über das Land und seine Bewohner während eines 25-jähriger Aufenthalts. I. Band: Lima. *Plates, &c.* Large 8° *Berlin,* 1893
—— Ditto. II. Das Küstenland von Peru. *Plates.* Large 8° *Berlin,* 1894

Middleton, Christopher. A Vindication of the Conduct of Capt. Middleton, in a late Voyage on board H.M.S. the "Furnace" for Discovering a North-West Passage to the Western American Ocean ; in Answer to certain Objections and Aspersions of Arthur Dobbs, Esq. 8° 1743
—— *See* Harris, Vol. 2 : Appendix 1.

Middleton, David. *See* Astley, Vol. 1 ; Gottfried ; Kerr, Vol. 8 ; Purchas, Vol. 1, Book 3 ; Allgemeine Historie, Vol. 1 : Appendix 1.

Middleton, E. E. New Process of Measuring the Height of the Sun ; also a few Remarks on the Transit of Venus and the Law of Attraction. 8* 1874

Middleton, Sir Henry. *See* Astley, Vol. 1 ; Gottfried ; Hakluyt Soc. Publ., Vol. 19 ; Kerr, Vol. 8 ; Purchas, Vol. 1, Book 3 ; Ray, Vol. 2 ; Allgemeine Historie, Vol. 1 ; "The World Displayed," Vol. 9 : Appendix 1.

Middleton, John. View of the Agriculture of Middlesex ; with Observations on the Means of its Improvement, and several Essays on Agriculture in general. *Map.* 8° 1807

Mielberg, J. *See* Russia in Asia, A, Tiflis Observatory : Appendix 2.

Miers, E. J. *See* "Erebus."

Miers, J. Travels in Chile and La Plata, including Accounts respecting the Geography, Geology, Statistics, Government, Finances, Agriculture, Manners and Customs, and the Mining Operations in Chile. 2 vols. *Maps and plates.* 8° 1826

Migault, J. A Narrative of the Sufferings of a French Protestant Family at the period of the Revocation of the Edict of Nantes. 8° 1824

Mignan, Capt. Robert. Travels in Chaldea, including a Journey from Bussorah to Bagdad, Hillah, and Babylon, in 1827; with Observations on the Sites of Babel, Seleucia, and Ctesiphon. *Maps and plates.* 8° 1829

Mignan, Capt. Robert. Notes extracted from a private Journal, written during a Tour through a part of Malabar and among the Neilgherries; including an account of the Topography of Ootakamund, with Observations on its Climate, Inhabitants, and Natural History. 8° *Bombay,* 1834
—— Winter Journey through Russia, the Caucasian Alps, and Georgia, thence across Mount Zagros, &c., into Koordistaun. 2 vols. *Plates.* 8° 1839

Miguel, Gregorio. Estudio sobre las Islas Carolinas, comprende la Historia y Geografía do los 36 grupos que forman el Archipiélago Carolino, seguido de la descripción de todas las islas del Océano Pacífico, situadas entre el Ecuador y el paralelo 10° N. 8°, and Atlas large folio
Madrid, 1887

Miguel, V. T. de San. *See* Tofiño.

Mihailescu, G. Geografia României. 8* *Galatz,* 1878

Mih Lang-tsze. Guide to the Antiquities of the Western Lake, near Hangchow. [In Chinese.] 4 vols. 8° 1750

Mijer, P. Bijdrage tot de geschiedenis der Codificatie in Nederlandsch Indie. 8° *Batavia,* 1839

Miklucho-Maclay, N. von. Ethnologische Excursionen in der Malayischen Halbinsel (Nov. 1874 to Oct. 1875). *Map and plates.* 8* N.P., N.D.
—— An Ethnological Excursion in Johore, 15th Dec. 1874 to 2nd Feb. 1875. (From Journal of Eastern Asia, July 1875.) *Plates.* 8* 1875
—— *See* Thomasson.

Milde, J. *See* "Novara."

Mildenhall, John. *See* Gottfried ; Purchas, Vol. 1, Book 3 : Appendix 1.

Miles, Pliny. Nordurfari ; or, Rambles in Iceland. 12° 1854

Miles, S. E. The Grotto of Neptune ("Antro di Nettuno"), Sardinia: a Poem. [With MS. Poem on the Arctic Expedition under Sir G. Nares.] *Plates.* 4* 1864

Miles, Major W. Memoir on the Edur State. [From the India Records, No. 12.] Royal 8° *Bombay,* 1855

Milet-Mureau, L. A. Voyage de La Pérouse autour du Monde. 4 vols. 8° *Paris,* 1798
—— *See* La Pérouse, L. F. G. de.

Milford, John. Norway and her Laplanders in 1841 ; with a Few Hints to the Salmon Fisher. 8° 1842

Mill, Dr Hugh Robert. Elementary Commercial Geography : a Sketch of the Commodities and the Countries of the World. 12° 1888
—— The same. 2nd edition, enlarged. 1894
—— An Elementary Class-Book of General Geography. *Illustrations.* 8° 1889

Milner, Rev. Thomas. A Universal Geography, in four parts, Historical, Mathematical, Physical, and Political. Revised and brought down to the present time by Keith Johnston. 12° 1876

Milton, Viscount. A History of the San Juan Water Boundary Question, as affecting the Division of Territory between Great Britain and the United States. *Maps.* 8° 1869

—— and Dr W. B. Cheadle. The North-West Passage by Land: being the Narrative of an Expedition from the Atlantic to the Pacific, undertaken with the view of Exploring a Route across the Continent to British Columbia through British Territory by one of the Northern Passes in the Rocky Mountains. *Maps and plates.* 8° [1865]

Miñano, Don Sebastian de. Diccionario Geográfico-Estadistico de España y Portugal. 10 vols. *Maps.* 8° *Madrid*, 1826-28

Minchin, Capt. C. Memorandum on the Beloch Tribes in the Dera Ghazi Khan District. [From the Records of India, No. 3, Punjab.] 8° 1869

Minchin, James George Cotton. The Growth of Freedom in the Balkan Peninsula: Notes of a Traveller in Montenegro, Bosnia, Servia, Bulgaria, and Greece; with Historical and Descriptive Sketches of the People. *Map.* 8° 1886

Minoprio, J. *See* Andree, Karl.

Mircher, H. Mission de Ghadamès, Septembre, Octobre, Novembre, et Décembre 1862: Rapports Officiels et Documents à l'appui. *Maps and illustrations.* Royal 8° *Algiers*, 1863

Miriam. Itinéraires Miriam: Les Causses et les Cañonsdu Tarn. *Maps, plans, and illustrations.* Small 8° *Mende*, 1892

Mirza Abu Taleb Khan. Voyages en Asie, Afrique, et en Europe pendant 1799-1803, suivis d'une Réfutation des idées qu'on a en Europe sur la Liberté des Femmes d'Asie. Ecrits en Persan; traduit en Anglais, par C. Stewart; et de l'Anglais en Français, par M. J. C. J. 2 vols. in 1. 8° *Paris*, 1811

Misrah Mahomed. *See* Phillips, New Voyages and Travels [3], Vol. 9: Appendix 1.

Misson, Maximilian. A New Voyage to Italy; with Curious Observations on several other Countries, as Germany, Switzerland, Savoy, Geneva, Flanders, and Holland; together with Useful Instructions for those who shall Travel thither. 2nd edition. 2 vols. *Plates.* 8° 1699

—— *See* Harris, Vol. 2; "The World Displayed," Vols. 17, 18; Knox's New Collection, Vol. 4: Appendix 1.

x

Mistriot, G. Τα αἰτια του ἀρχαιου και του νεωτερου Ἑλληνικου Πολιτισμου. 8° *Athens*, 1891

Mitchell, L. H. Report on the Seizure by the Abyssinians of the Geological and Mineralogical Reconaissance Expedition attached to the General Staff of the Egyptian Army. 8° *Cairo*, 1878

Mitchell, Mrs Murray. A Missionary's Wife among the Wild Tribes of South Bengal: Extracts from the Journal of Mrs Murray Mitchell; with Introduction and Supplement by Dr George Smith. 12° *Edinburgh*, 1871

Mitchell, O. M. The Orbs of Heaven; or, The Planetary and Stellar Worlds. *Woodcuts.* 12° 1856

Mitchell, S. Augustus. A System of Modern Geography, comprising a Description of the Present State of the World, and its Five Great Divisions, with their several Kingdoms, Empires, States, Territories, &c., adapted to the Capacity of Youth. *Illustrations.* 12° *Philadelphia*, 1839

—— A System of Modern Geography, Physical, Political, and Descriptive. 12° *Philadelphia*, 1870

Mitchell, Sir T. L. Three Expeditions into the Interior of Eastern Australia; with Descriptions of the recently explored Region of Australia Felix, and the present Colony of New South Wales. 2 vols. *Maps and plates.* 8° 1839

—— Journal of an Expedition into the Interior of Tropical Australia, in Search of a Route from Sydney to the Gulf of Carpentaria. *Maps and plates.* 8° 1848

Mitchinson, A. W. The Expiring Continent: a Narrative of Travel in Senegambia, with Observations on Native Character, the Present Condition and Future Prospects of Africa and Colonisation. *Map and illustrations.* 8° 1881

Mitford, Major-Gen. R. C. W. Reveley. Orient and Occident: a Journey East from Lahore to Liverpool; with Illustrations from Sketches by the Author. *Map.* Small 8° 1888

Mitre, Gen. Bartolomé. Viajes inéditos de D. Felix de Azara desde Santa Fé á la Asuncion, al interior del Paraguay, y á los Pueblos Misiones; con una noticia preliminar por el General D. Bartolomé Mitre, y algunas noticias por el doctor D. Juan Maria Gutierrez. 8° *Buenos Ayres*, 1873

Mitterrutzner, J. C. Die Sprache der Bari in Central-Afrika: Grammatik, Text, und Wörterbuch. 8° *Brixen*, 1867

Mizzi, M. A. M. Propaganda per l'Africa : Relazione di M. A. M. Mizzi, Segretario della Societa Internazionale di Esplorazione, Colonizzazione, ed Emigrazione Africana.   8*   *Malta*, 1881
—— Cenni sulla Republica di Liberia. [1 *sheet.*] Royal 8*   *Malta*, 1887
Moberg, J. C. *See* Sweden, A, Geologiska Undersökning : Appendix 2.
Moberly, Walter. The Rocks and Rivers of British Columbia. *Map and illustrations.* 8°   1885
Mockler-Ferryman, Capt. A. F. Up the Niger : Narrative of Major Claude Macdonald's Mission to the Niger and Benue Rivers, West Africa ; to which is added a Chapter on Native Musical Instruments by Captain C. R. Day. *Map, portrait, and illustrations.* 8° 1892
Modera, J. Verhaal van eene Reize naar en Langs de Zuid-West Kust van Nieuw-Guinea in 1828. *Map.*   8°
                                    Haarlem, 1830
Modigliani, Elio. Un Viaggio a Nias. *Map and illustrations.* 4° *Milan*, 1890
—— Fra i Battachi Indipendenti, Viaggio di Elio Modigliani pubblicato a cura della Società Geografica Italiana in occasione del primo Congresso Geografica Italiano. *Maps and illustrations.* 8° *Rome*, 1892
Moffat, John S. The Lives of Robert and Mary Moffat, by their Son. 3rd edition. *Maps and portraits.* 8° 1885
Moffat, Rev. Robert. Missionary Labours and Scenes in Southern Africa. *Map and plates.* 8°   1842
—— Letter to the Rev. A. Tidman, on his Journey to the Chief Moselekatse, in South Africa. [2 *leaves.*] 4* 1855
Mofras, Duflot de. Exploration du Territoire de l'Orégon, des Californies, et de la Mer Vermeille, pendant 1840-42. 2 vols. *Plates.* 8°   *Paris*, 1844
Mogg, Edward. Paterson's Roads in England and Wales. Remodelled, Augmented, and Improved by Ed. Mogg. *Maps.* 8°   1829
Mohan Lál, Munshi. Journal of a Tour through the Punjab, Afghanistan, Turkestan, Khorasan, and part of Persia, in company with Lieut. Burnes and Dr Gerard. *Plate.* 12° *Calcutta*, 1834
Mohn, H. Om Kometbanernes Indbyrdes Beliggenhed. *Maps.* 4*
                                    Christiania, 1861
—— Den Magnetiske Declination i Christiania, udledet af Observationer 1842-62. *Plate.* 8*   N.P. 1863
—— Institut Météorologique de Norvège : Température de la Mer entre l'Islande, l'Écosse, et la Norvége. *Maps.* 8*
                                    Christiania, 1870
—— Norske Fangst-Skipperes Opdagelse af Kong Karl-Land. *Map.* 8*
                                    Christiania, 1872

Mohn, H. "Albert's" Expedition til Spidsbergen i November og December 1872, og dens videnskabelige Resultater. *Map.* 8*   *Christiania*, 1873
—— König-Karl-Land. 4* *Gotha*, 1873
—— Askeregnen den 29de — 30de Marts 1875. *Map*   N.P. [1875]
—— Die Norwegische Nordmeer-Expedition. (Ergänzungsheft, 63—Petermann's Mittheilungen). *Maps and charts.* 4°
                                    Gotha, 1880
—— Grundzüge der Meteorologie : Die Lehre von Wind und Wetter, nach den neuesten Forschungen gemeinfasslich dargestellt. 3rd edition. *Maps and woodcuts.* 8°   *Berlin*, 1883
—— The same. 4th edition. *Maps.* 8°   *Berlin*, 1887
—— Die Strömungen des Europäischen Nordmeers. (Ergänzungsheft, 79—Petermann's Mittheilungen.) *Maps and diagrams.* 4°   *Gotha*, 1885
—— *See* Guldberg ; Nansen ; Petermann ; *also* Norway, A, Norwegian North Atlantic Expedition, 1876-78 : Appendix 2.
—— **and H. Hildebrand Hildebrandsson.** Les Orages dans la Péninsule Scandinave. *Diagrams.* 4*   *Upsala*, 1888
Mohnike, G. C. F. *See* Rafn.
Mohr, E. Nach den Victoriafällen des Zambesi. 2 vols. *Maps and plates.* 8°   *Leipzig*, 1875
Mohr, Johan Mauritz. *See* Veth.
Moir, Jane F. A Lady's Letters from Central Africa : a Journey from Mandala, Shiré Highlands, to Ujiji, Lake Tanganyika, and back ; with an Introduction by Rev. T. M. Lindsay, D.D. *Map and illustrations.* 12° *Glasgow*, 1891
Mojsisovics, E. von. Ueber die Grenze zwischen Ost- und West-Alpen. *Map.* 8*   [*Vienna*, 1873]
—— Die Dolomit-Riffe von Süd Tirol und Venetien. Beiträge zur Bildungsgeschichte der Alpen. *Plates.* 8° *Vienna*, 1879
Mokhtar Pasha, Mohammed. Manual of Arabic Geography. [In Arabic.] Small 8°   N.P., N.D.
—— Notes sur le Pays de Harrar. *Map.* 8*   *Cairo*, 1877
—— Étude sur l'origine des mesures Égyptiennes et leur valeur. 8*
                                    Cairo, 1891
—— *See* Ismail-Bey.
Molera, Eusebius J. The Mexican Calendar or Solar Stone. *Illustrations.* 8*   *San Francisco*, 1883
Moléri, ——. De Paris à Strasbourg à Reims, et à Forbach. *Map and illustrations.* Small 8°   *Paris*, 1854
Molesworth, Lord. *See* Harris, Vol. 2 ; "The World Displayed," Vol. 20, p. 610 ; Knox's New Collection, Vol. 4 : Appendix 1.

Molina, Felipe. Bosquejo de la República de Costa-Rica. *Map.* 8* *Madrid,* 1850
—— Memoria sobre las Cuestiones de Límites que se versan entre la República de Costa-Rica y el Estado de Nicaragua. *Map.* 8* *Madrid,* 1850
—— Costa-Rica y Nueva Granada : Exámen de la Cuestion de Límites que hay pendiente entre las dos Repúblicas mencionadas ; y Testimonios de los Titulos Antiguos de Costa-Rica. *Map.* 8* *Washington,* 1852
—— Costa Rica and New Granada : an Inquiry into the Question of Boundaries which is pending between the two Republics. *Map.* 8* *Washington,* 1853
Molina, G. Ignazio. Saggio sulla Storia Civile del Chili. *Map.* 8° *Bologna,* 1787
Molina, J. The Geographical, Natural, and Civil History of Chili, translated from the Italian ; with Notes from the Spanish and French Versions, and two Appendixes : the first, an Account of the Archipelago of Chiloe, from the Descripcion Historial of P. F. Pedro Gonzalez de Agueros ; the second, an Account of the Native Tribes who inhabit the Southern Extremity of South America, extracted chiefly from Falkner's Description of Patagonia. 2 vols. *Map.* 8° 1809
Moll, L. Colonisation et Agriculture de l'Algérie. 2 vols. 8° *Paris,* 1845
Möllendorff, P. G. and O. F. von. Manual of Chinese Bibliography : being a List of Works and Essays relating to China. 8° *Shanghai,* 1876
Möller, P., G. Pagels, and E. Gleerup. Tre år i Kongo. 2 vols. in 1. *Maps and illustrations.* 8° *Stockholm* [1887-88]
Möller, V. von. Paläontologische Beiträge und Erläuterungen zum Briefe Danilewsky's über die Resultate seiner Reise an den Manytsch. Small 8* *St Petersburg,* 1878
Möllhausen, Baldwin. Diary of a Journey from the Mississippi to the Coasts of the Pacific with a United States Expedition ; with an Introduction by Alex. v. Humboldt. Translated by Mrs P. Sinnett. 2 vols. *Map and plates.* 8° 1858
Mollien, G. Travels in the Interior of Africa to the Sources of the Senegal and Gambia, in 1818. Edited by T. E. Bowditch. *Map and plates.* 4° 1820
—— Travels in the Republic of Colombia, in 1822-23. Translated from the French. *Map and plate.* 8° 1824
—— *See* Eyriès, Vol. 11 : Appendix 1.
Moloney, Sir Alfred. Sketch of the Forestry of West Africa, with particular reference to its present principal Commercial Products. Crown 8° 1887
—— Minute by Governor Moloney in connection with the Visit, in April 1888, to the present Eastern Limit of the Colony

Moloney, Sir Alfred—*continued.*
of Lagos, Benin River, the Rio Formosa or Beautiful River of the Portuguese, discovered 1485. Folio * [*Lagos,* 1888]
Moloney, Joseph A. With Capt. Stairs to Katanga. *Map and illustrations.* 8° 1893
Moltke, Baron von. The Russians in Bulgaria and Rumelia in 1828 and 1829. *Maps.* 8° 1854
Moltke, — von. *See* Kiepert, Dr H.
Molyneux, Edmund. Tour in Sweden. 4* *Liverpool,* 1887
Molyneux, Emery. *See* Hakluyt Soc. Publ., Vol. 79 : Appendix 1.
Molyneux, Roger Gordon. Grammar and Vocabulary of the Language of Bearn, for Beginners. Abridged and translated from the work of V. Lespy. 8° 1888
Molyneux, Lieut. Journal Note-Book referring to Survey of the Dead Sea and Jordan Valley. MS. *Map.* 4°.
Mommsen, Theodor. The History of Rome. Translated with the Author's sanction, and additions by William P. Dickson, D.D. 2 vols. *Maps.* 8° 1886
Monaco, Albert, Prince of. Sur une Expérience entreprise pour déterminer la Direction des Courants de l'Atlantique Nord. Deuxième Campagne de l'Hirondelle. 4* [*Paris*] 1885
—— Sur le Gulf Stream. Recherches pour Établir ses Rapports avec la côte de France. Campagne de l'Hirondelle, 1885. *Maps.* Large 8* *Paris,* 1886
—— Deuxième Campagne Scientifique de l'Hirondelle dans l'Atlantique Nord. *Map.* 8* *Paris,* 1887
—— Sur la Troisième Campagne Scientifique de l'Hirondelle. 4* [*Paris,* 1887]
—— Sur le Quatrième Campagne Scientifique de l'Hirondelle. 4* [*Paris,* 1888]
—— Sur l'alimentation des Naufragés en pleine mer. 4* [*Paris,* 1888]
—— Sur l'emploi de Nasses pour des Recherches Zoologiques en eaux profondes. *Illustrations.* 4* [*Paris,* 1888]
—— Sur un Appareil Nouveau pour la Recherche des Organismes Pélagiques à des Profondeurs déterminées. *Illustrations.* 8* [*Paris*] 1889
—— Sur les Courants Superficiels de l'Atlantique Nord. Large 8* [*Paris,* 1889]
—— Le Dynamomètre à Ressorts emboîtés de l'Hirondelle. Le Sondeur à clef de l'Hirondelle. *Illustrations.* 8* [*Paris*] 1889
—— Congrès International des Sciences Géographiques en 1889. Expériences de Flottage sur les Courants Superficiels de l'Atlantique Nord. 8* *Paris,* 1890
Moncayo, P. Cuestion de Limites entre el Ecuador i el Peru, segun el " Uti Possidetis " de 1810 y los Tratados de 1829. 8* *Santiago,* 1860

Monck, Capt. J. *See* Munk ; *also* Churchill, Vol. 1 : Appendix 1.

Mondevergue, —. *See* Allgemeine Historie, Vol. 8 : Appendix 1.

Monet, H. La Martinique. *Illustrations.* 8° [*Paris*, N.D.]

Moneta, Pompeyo. Informe sobre la Practicabilidad de la Prolongacion del Ferrocarril Central Argentino desde Cordoba hasta Jujuy. *Map.* 8* *Buenos Ayres*, 1867

Money, Edward. Twelve Months with the Bashi-Bazouks. *Coloured plates.* 8° 1857

—— The Cultivation and Manufacture of Tea. 3rd edition. 8° 1878

Money, J. W. B. Java ; or, How to Manage a Colony ; showing a Practical Solution of the Questions now affecting British India. 2 vols. 8° 1861

Monfart, —. *See* Purchas, Vol. 3 : Appendix 1.

Monk, W. *See* Livingstone.

Monnet, —. Atlas et Description Minéralogiques de la France. 4° *Paris*, 1780

Monnier, Franz le. Der Geographische Congress und die Ausstellung in Venedig im September 1881. 8* *Vienna*, 1882

Monnier, Marcel. Un Printemps sur le Pacifique, Iles Hawai. *Map and illustrations.* 12° *Paris*, 1885

—— Des Andes au Para. Équateur—Pérou—Amazone. *Maps and illustrations.* Small 4° *Paris*, 1890

Monnier, P. Description Nautique des Côtes de la Martinique, précédé d'un Mémoire sur les Opérations Hydrographiques et Géodésiques exécutées dans cette île en 1824-25. *Map.* Royal 8° *Paris*, 1828

—— Mémoire sur les Courants de la Manche, Mer d'Allemagne, et Canal de St George. *Map.* 1835. Supplément aux Considérations Générales sur ce sujet, 1839. 8° 1835-39

Monoxe, Edward. *See* Purchas, Vol. 2, Book 10 : Appendix 1.

Monreal y Ascaso, B. Curso elemental de Historia de España. Small 8° *Madrid*, 1867

—— Curso elemental de Geographia Astronómica, Fisica y Politica. 10th edition, 1870 ; and 11th edition, 1872. *Maps.* Small 8° *Madrid*, 1870-72

Monson, Lord. Views of the Department of the Isère and the High Alps, chiefly designed to illustrate the "Memoir of Felix Neff" by Dr Gilby. *Map and plates.* Large folio 1840

Monson, Sir William. *See* Churchill, Vol. 3 : Appendix 1.

Montague, W. E. Campaigning in South Africa : Reminiscences of an Officer in 1879. 8° 1880

Montalbanus, J. B. De Turcarum moribus Commentarius. 16° *Leyden*, 1654

Montano, B. A. *See* Benjamin (Rabbi).

Montano, Dr J. Voyage aux Philippines et en Malaisie. *Map and illustrations.* 12° *Paris*, 1886

Montanus, Arnoldus. Gedenkwaerdige Gesantschappen der Oost-Indische Maetschappy in 'l vereenigde Nederland aen de Kaisaren van Japan. *Maps and plates.* Folio *Amsterdam*, 1668

—— Atlas Japannensis : being Remarkable Addresses, by way of Embassy, from the East India Company of the United Provinces to the Emperor of Japan ; containing a Description of their several Territories, Cities, Temples, and Fortresses ; their Religions, Laws, and Customs ; their Prodigious Wealth and Gorgeous Habits ; the Nature of their Soil, Plants, Beasts, Hills, Rivers, and Fountains ; with the Character of the Ancient and Modern Japanners. English'd by John Ogilby. *Plates.* Folio 1670

—— Atlas Chinensis : being a Second Part of a Relation of Remarkable Passages in Two Embassies from the East India Company of the United Provinces to the Viceroy Singlamong and General Taising Lipovi, and to Konchi, Emperor of China and East Tartary; with a Relation of the Netherlanders assisting the Tartar against Coxinga, &c. English'd by John Ogilby. *Plates.* Folio 1671

—— *See* Astley, Vol. 3 ; Harris, Vol. 1 ; Allgemeine Historie, Vol. 5: Appendix 1.

Montanus, P. *See* Ptolemy.

Montbret, Baron C. de. *See* Recueil de Voyages, Vol. 4, p. 611 : Appendix 1.

Montefiore, Arthur J. Florida and the English. *Map.* 8* 1889

—— David Livingstone, his Labours and his Legacy. *Map and illustrations.* 8° [1889]

—— The same. 2nd edition. *Map and illustrations.* Crown 8° N.D.

—— Henry M. Stanley, the African Explorer. *Map and illustrations.* Crown 8° [1889]

—— The same. 9th edition. *Map and illustrations.* Crown 8° N.D.

—— Leaders into unknown Lands : being Chapters of Recent Travel. *Illustrations.* Crown 8° [1891]

Montefiore, Sir Moses, Bart. Narrative of a Mission to the Empire of Morocco, 1863-64. 8° 1864

—— An Open Letter addressed to Sir M. Montefiore on the day of his arrival in the Holy City of Jerusalem . . . July 25, 1875, by the Rev. Meyer Auerbach . . . and the Rev. Samuel Salant . . ; together with a Narrative of a Forty Days' Sojourn in the Holy Land. *Photograph.* 8° 1875

Monteiro, Joachim John. Angola and the River Congo. 2 vols. *Map and plates.* Small 8° 1875

Monteiro, J. M. C., and A. C. P. Gamitto. Résumé of the Journey of, by Dr C. T. Beke. [In R.G.S. volume on Journeys to the Lands of Cazembe.] *See* Lacerda.

Monteiro, J. M. de Souza. Diccionairo Geographico das Provincias e Possessões Portuguezas no Ultramar. 8° *Lisbon,* 1850

Monteiro, Rose. Delagoa Bay, its Natives and Natural History. *Illustrations.* Crown 8° 1891

Monteith, Lieut.-Gen. William. Notes on Georgia and the New Russian Conquests beyond the Caucasus; also a Description of the Frontier of Russia and Persia as settled by the Commissioners in 1828-29. 8* *Privately printed,* N.D.

—— Narrative of the Conquest of Finland by the Russians in 1808-9. By a Russian Officer; edited by Gen. Monteith. *Map.* 8° 1854

—— Kars and Erzeroum, with the Campaigns of Prince Paskiewitch in 1828-29; and an Account of the Conquests of Russia beyond the Caucasus. *Map and plates.* 8° 1856

—— *See* Meyendorff.

Montémont, Alb. Londres: Voyage à cette Capitale et ses Environs. *Map.* 8° *Paris,* N.D.

—— *See* Phillips, New Voyages and Travels [3], Vol. 9: Appendix 1.

Montesinos, L. Fernando. *See* Ternaux-Compans, Vol. 17: Appendix 1.

Montfaucon, Bernard de. The Travels of the Learned Father Montfaucon, from Paris through Italy. *Plates.* 8° 1712

Montgomerie, John E., and A. F. R. de Horsey. A Few Words collected from the Languages spoken by the Indians in the Neighbourhood of Columbia River and Puget's Sound. 8* 1848

Montgomerie, Col. T. G. *See* Cayley and Reynolds; *also* India, Trigonometrical Surveys: Appendix 2.

Montgomery, Robert. Statistical Report of the District of Cawnpoor, 1848. *Maps.* 4° *Calcutta,* 1849

Monticelli, T. Opere dell'. 2 vols. in 1. 4° *Naples,* 1841

Montjau, E. M. de. De l'Émigration des Chinois au point de vue des intérêts Européens. 8* *Paris,* 1873

Montpéreux, F. Dubois de. Voyage autour du Caucase, chez les Tcherkesses et les Abkhases, en Colchide, Géorgie, Arménie, et en Crimée. 3 vols. 8°, and Atlas folio *Paris,* 1839

Montravel, M. L. de Tardy de. Instructions pour Naviguer sur la Côte Septentrionale du Brésil et le Fleuve des Amazones. 8° *Paris,* 1847

Montravel, M. L. de Tardy de. Instructions Nautiques pour Naviguer sur les Côtes des Guyanes. 8° *Paris,* 1851

—— Instructions sur la Nouvelle-Calédonie suivies de Renseignements Hydrographiques et autres sur la Mer du Japon et la Mer d'Okotsk. *Maps and plates.* 8° *Paris,* 1857

Montriou, Lieut. C. W. Report on the Harbour and Town of Sonmeeance. [From the India Records, No. 17.] Royal 8° *Bombay,* 1855

Montry and Fraissinet. *See* Siebold.

Montulé, Edward de. *See* Phillips, New Voyages and Travels [3], Vols. 5, 9: Appendix 1.

Montyel, Evariste Marandon de. Pelérinage sur la Soane de Lyon à Chalon. *Map.* 16° *Chalon,* 1838

Moodie, Donald. The Record; or, A Series of Official Papers relative to the Condition and Treatment of the Native Tribes of South Africa. Compiled, translated, and edited by D. Moodie. Part 1, 1649-1720. 4° *Cape Town,* 1838

Moodie, Lieut. J. W. D. Ten Years in South Africa, including a Particular Description of the Wild Sports of that Country. 2 vols. 8° 1835

Moodoo Kistnaa. *See* Dalrymple, Tracts, Vol. 1: Appendix 1.

Moon, G. Washington. Men and Women of the Time: a Dictionary of Contemporaries. 13th edition. Large 8° 1891

Moor, J. H. Notices of the Indian Archipelago and Adjacent Countries: a Collection of Papers relating to Borneo, Celebes, Bali, Java, Sumatra, Nias, the Philippine Islands, Sulus, Siam, Cochin China, Malayan Peninsula, &c. *Maps.* 4° *Singapore,* 1837

Moorcroft, W., and G. Trebeck. Travels in the Himalayan Provinces of Hindústan and the Panjáb, in Ladakh and Kashmir, in Peshawar, Kabul, Kunduz, and Bokhara, from 1819 to 1825. 2 vols. *Map.* 8° 1841

Moore, Francis. Travels into the Inland Parts of Africa, containing a Description of the several Nations for the space of 600 miles up the River Gambia; with Capt. Stibbs's Voyage in 1723, and Extracts from the Nubian's Geography, &c., concerning the Niger-Nile, or Gambia. *Map and plates.* 8° 1738

—— Description of Texas, containing Sketches of its History, Geology, Geography, and Statistics. *Map and plates.* 8° *Philadelphia,* 1840

—— *See* Astley, Vol. 2; Knox's New Collection, Vol. 6; "The World Displayed," Vol. 17, p. 609; Allgemeine Historie, Vol. 3: Appendix 1.

Moore, Frederic. *See* Catalogues, C (India Museum): Appendix 2.

Moore, Hon. G. F. Evidences of an Inland Sea [in Australia], collected from the Natives of the Swan River Settlement. 8° *Dublin*, 1837

Moore, H. C. The Tidal Wave in the Wye and Severn. 8* [1893]

Moore, Joseph, junr. Outlying Europe and the Nearer Orient: a Narrative of Recent Travel. 8° *Philadelphia*, 1880
—— The Queen's Empire; or, Ind and her Pearl. *Map and plates.* 8° 1886

Moore, J. M. New Zealand for the Emigrant, Invalid, and Tourist. *Maps and illustrations.* 8° 1890

Moore, J. P. *See* Harkness, H. W.

Moore, Richard. *See* Gottfried: Appendix 1.

Moore, William. Log-Book of the schooner "Eliza Scott," from July 1838 to Sept. 1839, during her Voyage from London to New Zealand, on Discovery to the Southward, and to Madagascar, and Return to London; with Remarks. Kept by W. Moore, Chief Mate. MS. 4° 1838-39

Moraes, J. A. da Cunha. Africa Occidental: Album Photographico e Descriptivo; com uma Introducção de Luciano Cordeiro. Primeira parte. (Do Rio Quillo as Ambriz.) Oblong 8° *Lisbon*, 1885
—— The same. Com uma Introducção: idéas geraes sobre Angola. Segunda parte. (Loanda, Cazengo, Rios Dande, e Quanza.) Oblong 8° *Lisbon*, 1886

Morant, E. W. L. Letters regarding the Subject of Trees, Forests, and Rainfall, and the Natural Irrigation of the Treeless Deccan. 12* *Bombay*, 1877

Morant, G. C. Chili and the River Plate in 1891: Reminiscences of Travel in South America. *Illustrations.* 12° 1891

Morant, P. *See* Falle.

Mordecai, E. R. Food of the Shad of the Atlantic Coast of the United States (Alosa præstabilis, de Kay), and the Functions of the Pyloric Cœca. *Plate.* 12* *Philadelphia*, 1860

Morelet, A. Îles Açores: Notice sur l'Histoire Naturelle des Açores, suivie d'une description des Mollusques terrestres de cet Archipel. *Plates.* Large 8° *Paris*, 1860
—— *See* Squier, M. F.

Morell, J. R. Scientific Guide to Switzerland. 8° 1867

Morelli, Jacopo. Dissertazione intorno ad alcuni Viaggiatori eruditi Veneziani poco noti, pubblicata nelle faustissime nozze del Conte Leonardo Manino con la Contessa Foscarina Giovanelli. *Frontispiece.* 4° *Venice*, 1803
—— *See* Columbus.

Moreno, F. Petroleum in Peru from an industrial point of view. *Map.* 8* *Lima*, 1891

Moreno, F. P. Apuntes sobre las Tierras Patagónicas. 8* *Buenos Ayres*, 1878
—— Viaje á la Patagonia Austral. 1876-77. I. *Map and plates.* 4° *Buenos Ayres*, 1879
—— El orígen del Hombre Sud-Americano; razas y civilizaciones de este Continente. Contribuciones al estudio de las colecciones del Museo Antropológico y Arqueológico. 8* *Buenos Ayres*, 1882

Moreno, J. L. Compendio de Jeografia de Bolivia redactada para el uso de la juventud. Segunda edicion. 12° *Santiago*, 1879
—— Nociones de Geografia de Bolivia. 12* *Sucre*, 1886
—— The same. 12* *Sucre*, 1889
—— Nociones de Geografia de Bolivia: Partes Politica y Descriptiva. 6th edition. 12* *Sucre*, 1891

Moresby, J. Discoveries and Surveys in New Guinea and the D'Entrecasteaux Islands, a Cruise in Polynesia, and Visits to the Pearl-shelling Stations in Torres Straits of H.M.S. "Basilisk." *Map and plates.* 8° 1876

Moresby, Comm. Robert. Nautical Directions for the Maldiva Islands and the Chegos Archipelago. 8° 1840
—— **and T. Elwon.** Sailing Directions for the Red Sea. 8° 1841

Moreton, J. Some Account of the Physical Geography of Newfoundland. *Maps.* 8* [1864]

Moreton, Samuel H. Milford Sound and the Scenery of the West Coast of the Middle Island of New Zealand. 8* *Invercargill*, 1882
——. A Scramble over the Lake Mountains. 8* *Invercargill*, 1885
—— A Scramble over the Mountains. [New Zealand.] From *The Weekly Times*, Invercargill, N.Z., 7th February 1885. 8* *Invercargill*, 1885

Morfill, W. R. Poland. ("Story of the Nations" Series.) *Map.* 8° 1893

Morga, Antonio de. *See* Hakluyt Soc. Publ., Vol. 39; Burney, Vol. 2: Appendix 1.

Morgan, Prof. C. L. *See* Compton, Theodore.

Morgan, D. Lloyd. *See* Nordenskiöld, G.

Morgan, E. Delmar. Notes on the recent Geography of Central Asia from Russian Sources. Roy. Geo. Soc. Suppl. Papers, Vol. 1. *Map.* 8° 1885
—— Remarks on the Early Discovery of Australia. *Maps.* Large 8* 1891
—— *See* Coles; Prejevalsky; *also* Hakluyt Soc. Publ., Vols. 72, 73: Appendix 1.

Morgan, Sir Henry. *See* Sharp, Capt. B., and others; Esquemeling, John; *also* Burney, Vol. 4 : Appendix 1.

Morgan, Henry J. The Dominion Annual Register and Review. *See* Canada, Toronto : Appendix 2.

Morgan, J. A Complete History of Algiers ; to which is prefixed an Epitome of the General History of Barbary from the Earliest Times, interspersed with many Curious Remarks and Passages not touched on by any writer whatsoever. 2 vols. (bound in 1). 4° 1728-29

Morgan, J., de. Mission Scientifique au Caucase: Études Archéologiques et Historiques. Tome 1. Les Premiers Ages des Metaux dans l'Arménie Russe. Tome 2. Recherches sur les Origines des Peuples du Caucase. 2 vols. in 1. *Maps and illustrations.* 4° *Paris,* 1889

Morgan, Lady. Italy. 2 vols. in 1. 4° 1821

Morgen, C. Durch Kamerun von Süd nach Nord : Reisen und Forschungen im Hinterlande 1889 bis 1891. *Map and illustrations.* 8° *Leipzig,* 1893

Morier, James. Journey through Persia, Armenia, and Asia Minor, to Constantinople, 1808-9. *Maps and plates.* 4° 1812

—— A Second Journey through Persia, Armenia, and Asia Minor, to Constantinople, between the years 1810 and 1816 : with a Journal of the Voyage by the Brazils and Bombay to the Persian Gulf, &c. *Maps and plates.* 4° 1818

—— *See* Eyriès, Vol. 14 : Appendix 1.

Morier, Sir R. Copy of a Despatch from Sir R. Morier, and other Correspondence respecting attempts to establish Commercial Relations with Siberia through the Kara Sea. *Map.* Folio* 1888

Moris, H. *See* Purchas, Vol. 1, Book 3 : Appendix 1.

Moris, —. *See* Sidi-Aly.

Moritz, August. Lebenslinien der meteorologischen Stationen am Kaukasus ; eine Uebersicht der Tagebücher, welche in dem meteorologischen Archive des Tiflisschen Observatoriums aufbewahrt werden. *Map and table.* Folio* *St Petersburg,* 1859

—— Rectification d'une Erreur découverte dans la Table de M. Regnault, relative à la force expansive de la vapeur d'eau. Lettre à M. Lenz. 8* 1865

—— The Thermal Springs of Lankeran. [In Russian.] 8* [*Tiflis*] 1865

—— Ueber die Anwendung des Pistor'schen Reflections-Kreises zum Messen von Angular-Distanzen zwischen terrestrischen Objecten. 8* 1865

—— On the Caspian Sea. [In Russian.] *Plate.* 8* *Tiflis,* 1865

—— Schemacha und seine Erdbeben. 8* *Tiflis,* 1872

Moritz, August. Olivet. Reply to M. G. respecting Meteorological Observations. [In Russian.] 8* *Tiflis,* 1876

—— Das Reflexions-Thermometer. *Plate.* 12* *Tiflis,* 1876

—— *See* Stebnetzky.

—— **and H. Abich.** Materials for a Climatology of the Caucausus. Meteorological Observations. Vol. 1 (parts 1 and 3), Vol. 2 (3 parts). [In Russian and German.] 8° *Tiflis,* 1877-80

—— **and H. Kiefer.** Tables for Calculation of Barometric Altitudes. [In Russian and, in part, German.] 4° *Tiflis,* 1870

Moritz, Dr B. *See* Hassan.

Moritz, C. P. *See* Pinkerton, Vol. 2 : Appendix 1.

Morley, Wm. Letter to Maj.-Gen. John Briggs, on the Discovery of Part of the Second Volume of the Jámi' al Tawáríkh of Rashíd al Dín. *Plate.* 8* 1839

Morley, William H. Descriptive Catalogue of the Historical Manuscripts in the Arabic and Persian Languages, preserved in the Library of the Royal Asiatic Society of Great Britain and Ireland. 8° 1854

Morlot, A. von. Erläuterungen zur geologischen Uebersichtskarte der nordöstlichen Alpen. *Map.* 8° *Vienna,* 1847

Moro, Gaetano. Report of the Communication between the Atlantic and Pacific Oceans through the Isthmus of Tehuantepec. *Map.* 8° 1845

—— Communication between the Atlantic and Pacific Oceans through the Isthmus of Tehuantepec. Additional Observations to the Report. *Maps.* 8° 1845

Morrell, Capt. Benj. Narrative of Four Voyages to the South Sea, North and South Pacific Ocean, Chinese Sea, Ethiopic and Southern Atlantic Ocean, Indian and Antarctic Ocean, 1822-31. Comprising Critical Surveys of Coasts and Islands, with Sailing Directions ; and an Account of some new and valuable Discoveries, including the Massacre Islands ; to which is prefixed a brief Sketch of the Author's early life. *Portrait.* 8° *New York,* 1832

Morris, Alex. Nova Brittannia ; or, British North America, its Extent and Future. 8° *Montreal,* 1858

Morris, D. The Colony of British Honduras, its Resources and Prospects, with particular reference to its Indigenous Plants and Economic Productions. *Map.* 8° 1883

—— A Report upon the Present Position and Prospects of the Agricultural Resources of the Island of St Helena. *Map.* 8* 1884

—— Annual Report of the Public Gardens . . . of Jamaica for the year ended 30th September 1884. Folio* *Kingston,* 1885

Morris, D. F. van Braam. Reizen van, naar de Noordkust van Nederlandsch Nieuw-Guinea. Erste vaart op de Amberno, of Rochussen Rivier, medegedeeld door P. J. B. C. Robidé van der Aa. *Maps.* 8*   [*The Hague*, 1885]

Morris, E. E. Cassell's Picturesque Australasia. 4 vols. *Illustrations.*
1889-90

Morris, Henry. A Geography, principally intended for the Use of India. 12°
Madras, 1864

—— A Descriptive and Historical Account of the Godavery District in the Presidency of Madras. *Map in cover.* 8°   1878

Morris, John. *See* India, C. Palæontologia Indica: Appendix 2.

Morris, Prof. J. *See* Murchison.

Morris, J. H. Report on the Administration of the Central Provinces for the year 1867-68 8°   *Nagpore* [1868]

Morris, R. The Etymology of Local Names; with a short introduction to the Relationship of Languages. Teutonic names. 12*   N.D.

Morrison, Walter. The Recovery of Jerusalem: a Narrative of Exploration and Discovery in the City and the Holy Land. By Capt. Wilson, Capt. Warren, &c. With an Introduction by Arthur Penrhyn Stanley; edited by W. Morrison. *Maps and plates.* 8°   1871 [1870]

Morritt. *See* Walpole, Turkey: Appendix 1.

Morrona, Alessandro da. Pisa Antica e Moderna. *Map.* 8°   *Pisa,* 1821

Morse, E. S. Shell Mounds of Omori. *Plates.* 4*   *Tokio,* 1879

—— Ancient and Modern Methods of Arrow-Release. (From the Bulletin of the Essex Institute, Vol. 17.) 8* 1885

—— Japanese Homes and their Surroundings. (Peabody Academy of Science: Memoirs, Vol. 2). *Illustrations.* Small folio   *Boston, Mass.,* 1886

Morse, Jedidiah. Report of the Secretary of War of the United States on Indian Affairs, comprising a Tour in 1820 for the purpose of ascertaining the Actual State of the Indian Tribes in our Country. *Map and portrait.* 8°
New Haven, Conn., 1822

Morse, Sidney E. System of Geography for the Use of Schools. *Maps and woodcuts.* 4°   *New York,* 1845

Morsier, F. de. Expedition au Pole Nord: Esquisse des projets proposés jusqu'à ce jour pour son exécution. 8*
[1867]

Mortillet, Gabriel. Guide du Baigneur et de l'Étranger à Aix-les-Bains (Savoie). (Notes statistiques et historiques sur la Savoie.) 16*   *Chambéry,* 1855

Mortillet, G. de. Collection Préhistorique. [Illustrated Catalogue.] 8°   N.D.

Mortimer, George. Observations and Remarks made during a Voyage to the Islands of Teneriffe, Amsterdam, Maria's Islands near Van Diemen's Land; Otaheite, Sandwich Islands; Owhyhee, the Fox Islands on the North-West Coast of America, Tinian, and from thence to Canton, in the brig "Mercury," &c. *Maps and plate.* 4°   1791

Morton, Alexander. Notes of a Trip to New Guinea. 8*   [*Hobart*, N.D.]

—— Handbook for the Use of the Members of the Australasian Association for the Advancement of Science: Hobart Meeting, 1892. *Map and plan.* 12°
Hobart, 1891

Morton, Samuel G. Crania Americana; or, A Comparative View of the Skulls of various Aboriginal Nations of North and South America, with an Essay on the Varieties of the Human Species. *Map and plates.* Folio   *Philadelphia,* 1839

—— Crania Ægyptiaca; or, Observations on Egyptian Ethnography, derived from Anatomy, History, and the Monuments. *Plates.* 4°   *Philadelphia,* 1844

Morton, W. J. South African Diamond Fields, and the Journey to the Mines. 8°   *New York,* 1877

Mörtsell, E. *See* Sweden, A: Appendix 2.

Mosca-Barzi, Carlo. Saggio di una Nuova Spiegazione del Flusso e Riflusso del Mare. *Plates.* 4°   *Pesaro,* 1764

Moschini, Giann Antonio. Guida per la Città di Padova, all' amico delle Belle Arti. *Map and plates.* 12° *Venice,* 1817

Moseley, Prof. H. N. Oregon, its Resources, Climate, People, and Productions. *Map.* 12°   1878

—— Notes by a Naturalist on the "Challenger": being an Account of various Observations made during the Voyage of H.M.S "Challenger" round the World, in the years 1872-76, under the command of Capt. Sir G. S. Nares and Capt. F. T. Thomson. *Map, coloured plates, and woodcuts.* 8°   1879

—— The same. New edition. 8°   1892

Mosenthal, Julius de, and J. E. Harting. Ostriches and Ostrich Farming. *Plates.* 8°   1877

Moser, Henri. A Travers l'Asie Centrale, la Steppe Kirghize, le Turkestan Russe, Boukhara, Khiva, le Pays des Turcomans et la Perse, Impressions de Voyage. *Map and illustrations.* Large 8°
Paris [1885]

Moser, Louis. The Caucasus and its People; with a brief History of their Wars, and a Sketch of the Achievements of the renowned Chief Shamyl. 8° 1856

Mosquera, Gen. T. C. de. Memoria sobre la Geografía, Física y Política, de la Nueva Granada. *Map.* 8°
New York, 1852

Mosquera, Gen. T. C. de. Memoir of the Physical and Political Geography of New Granada : translated from the Spanish, by Theodore Dwight. *Map.* 8° *New York,* 1853
—— Compendio de Geografia, General, Politica, Fisica, y especial de los Estados Unidos de Colombia. 8° 1866

Moss, Dr. Edward L. Shores of the Polar Sea : a Narrative of the Arctic Expedition of 1875-76. *Map, chromolithographs, and engravings.* Large folio 1878

Moss, Frederick J. Through Atolls and Islands in the Great South Sea. *Map, portrait, and illustrations.* 8° 1889

Mossman, Samuel. Australasia and Australia ; contributed to the *Encyclopædia Britannica.* 4° *Edinburgh,* 1853
—— **and T. Banister.** Australia Visited and Revisited : a Narrative of Recent Travels and Old Experiences in Victoria and New South Wales. *Maps.* 8° 1853

Mott, Albert J. On the Literature of Expeditions to the Nile. 8* [*Liverpool,* 1867]
—— Notes on Easter Island. 8* *Liverpool,* 1881

Mott, F. T. The Fruits of all Countries : a Preliminary Catalogue. Oblong 8* *Leicester,* 1883

Motta, Alexio da. See Thevenot, Vol. 1: Appendix 1.

Motte, Standish. Outline of a System of Legislation for securing Protection to the Aboriginal Inhabitants of all Countries Colonised by Great Britain. 8* 1840

Mouat, Dr Fred. J. Rough Notes of a Trip to Réunion, the Mauritius, and Ceylon ; with Remarks on their Eligibility as Sanitaria for Indian Invalids. *Map and woodcuts.* Royal 8° *Calcutta,* 1852
—— Adventures and Researches among the Andaman Islanders. *Map and illustrations.* 8° 1863

Moubach, A. C. G. Zorgdrager's bloeyende Opkomst der aloude en hedendaagsche Groenlandsche Visscherij, &c., met eene korte Historische Beschryving der Noordere Gewesten, voornamentlyk Groenlandt, Yslandt, Spitsbergen, Nova Zembla, Jan Mayen Eilandt, de Straat Davis, en al't aamerklykste in d'Ontdekking deezer Landen en in de Visscherij voorgevalten, met Byvoeging van de Walvischvangst. *Maps and plate.* 4° *Amsterdam,* 1720

Mouchez, Ernest. Observations Chronométriques faites pendant la Campagne de Circumnavigation de la corvette "La Capricieuse." 8° *Paris,* 1855
—— Nouveau Manuel de la Navigation dans le Rio de la Plata d'après les Documents Français et Espagnols. 8° *Paris,* 1862

Mouchez, Ernest. Longitudes Chronométriques des principaux points de la Côte du Brésil. 8° *Paris,* 1863
—— Recherches sur la Longitude de la Côte Orientale de l'Amérique du Sud. 8* *Paris,* 1866
—— Les Cotes du Brésil, Description et Instructions Nautiques. *Maps.* 8° *Paris,* 1866

Mouette, Sieur. See Tellez ; *also* Gottfried: Appendix 1.

Mouhot, Henri. Travels in the Central Parts of Indo-China (Siam), Cambodia, and Laos during 1858-60. 2 vols. *Map and plates.* 8° 1864

Moulle, A. Mémoire sur la Géologie générale et sur les Mines de Diamants de l'Afrique du Sud. *Maps, plans, and sections.* 8° *Paris,* 1885

Mounsey, A. H. A Journey through the Caucasus and the Interior of Persia. *Map.* 8° 1872
—— The Satsuma Rebellion : an Episode of Modern Japanese History. *Maps.* Small 8° 1879

"Mountaineer." A Summer Ramble in the Himalayas, with Sporting Adventures in the Vale of Cashmere. *Plate.* 8° 1860

Mounteney-Jephson, A. J. See Jephson.

Mouqueron, P. A. See Paz Soldan, M.

Moura, J. Le Royaume du Cambodge. 2 vols. *Maps, plans, and illustrations.* Large 8° *Paris,* 1883

Moura, J. de Santo A. See Ibn Batuta.

Mouravieff and Gladisheff. See Khanikoff, Y. B.

Mouraviev, N. Voyage en Turcomanie et à Khiva, 1819-20 ; contenant le Journal de son Voyage, le Récit de la Mission dont il était chargé, la Relation de sa Captivité dans la Khivie, la Description Géographique et Historique du Pays. Traduit du Russe par M. G. Lacointe de Laveau ; revu par J. B. Eyriès et J. Klaproth. *Map and plate.* 8° *Paris,* 1823
—— Journey to Khiva through the Turcoman Country, 1819-20. Translated from the Russian (1824) by Philipp Strahl, Bonn ; and from the German (1871) by Captain W. S. A. Lockhart. *Map.* 8° *Calcutta,* 1871
—— See Eyriès, Vol. 14 : Appendix 1.

Moure, J. G. Amedeo, and V. A. Malte-Brun. Tratado de Geographia Elementar, Physica, Historica, Ecclesiastica, e Politica do Imperio do Brasil. *Portrait.* 12° *Paris,* 1861

Mousson, Alb. Ein Besuch auf Korfu und Cefalonien im 1858. 8° *Zurich,* 1859

Moussy, V. Martin de. Description Géographique et Statistique de la Confédération Argentine. 3 vols. Royal 8° *Paris,* 1860-64
—— Voyage à la Frontière Indienne de Buenos-Ayres en 1863. 8* [*Paris,* 1864]

Mowry, Sylvester. Geography and Resources of Arizona and Sonora. *Map.* 8° *New York,* 1863

Moxly, Rev. J. H. Sutton. An Account of a West Indian Sanatorium, and a Guide to Barbados. 12° 1886

Moxon, Joseph. A Tutor to Astronomy and Geography, or an Easie and Speedie Way to know the Use of both the Globes, Cœlestial and Terrestrial. 3rd edition. 4° 1674
—— The same. . . . Whereunto is added the Ancient Poetical Stories of the Stars . . . as also a Discourse of the Antiquity, Progress, and Augmentation of Astronomy. 4th edition. *Portrait and illustrations.* Square 8° 1686
—— A Brief Discourse of a Passage by the North Pole to Japan, China, &c., pleaded by three experiments ; and Answers to all Objections that can be urged against a Passage that way. *Map.* Small 4° 1697

Moya y Jimenez, Francisco Javier de. Las Islas Filipinas en 1882 : Estudios históricos, geográphicos, estadísticos, y descriptivos. 8° *Madrid,* 1883

Moyano, Carlos M. A Traves de la Patagonia : Informe del Viage y Exploracion desde Santa Cruz al Chubat, presentado por el Capitan de la Armada D. Carlos M. Moyano, al Sr. Ministro de Guerra y Marina Doctor Don Benjamin Victorica. 8° *Buenos Ayres,* 1881

Moyne, A. le. La Nouvelle-Grenade, Santiago de Cuba, la Jamaique, et l'Isthme de Panama. 2 vols. 12° *Paris,* 1880

Moynier, Gustave. La Question du Congo devant l'Institut de Droit International. 8° *Geneva,* 1883

Moyriac de Mailla, Joseph Anne Marie de. Histoire générale de la Chine, ou Annales de cet Empire. Traduites du Tong-Kien-Kang-Mou. 13 vols. *Maps and plates.* 4° *Paris,* 1777-85

Mtesa, King. Letter from King Mtesa to Sir John Kirk. [Original and Translation.] Folio* N.P., N.D.
—— King Mtesa, of Uganda. Extracts from Letters and Journals of the Missionaries of the Church Missionary Society labouring in Central Africa, received during the years 1877 to 1884. 8° 1885

Muddock, J. E. "The J.E.M." Guide to Switzerland. The Alps, and how to see them. Edited by J. E. Muddock. 4th edition. *Maps, plans, and illustrations.* 12° 1884

Mudge, Capt. W., and Isaac Dalby. Trigonometrical Survey of England and Wales, carried on in 1784 to the end of 1796. 2 vols. *Plates.* 4° 1799-1801

Mudge, Capt. W., and G. A. Frazer. Sailing Directions for the N.E., N., and N.W. Coasts of Ireland. 8° 1842
—— *See* Williams, Lt.-Col. E.

Mueller, Baron Sir Ferdinand von. An Historical Review of the Explorations of Australia. 8* 1857
—— Fragmenta Phytographiæ Australiæ. Vols. 1, 4, 6. 8° *Melbourne,* 1858-68
—— Essay on the Plants collected by Mr Eugène Fitzalan, during Lieut. Smith's Epedition to the Estuary of the Burdekin. Folio* *Melbourne,* 1860
—— The Plants indigenous to the Colony of Victoria. Vol. 1. Thalamifloræ. *Plates.* 4° *Melbourne,* 1860-62
—— The same. Lithograms, viz., plates and descriptions. 4° *Melbourne,* 1864-65
—— A Record of the Plants collected by Mr P. Walcott and Mr M. Brown in 1861, during Mr F. Gregory's Exploring Expedition into North-West Australia. 8* 1863
—— The Vegetation of the Chatham Islands. *Plates.* Royal 8° *Melbourne,* 1864
—— The Fate of Dr Leichardt and a Proposed New Search for his Party : a Discourse, &c. 8* *Melbourne,* 1865
—— Notes sur la Vegetation indigène et introduite de l'Australie . . Traduit de l'Anglais par E. Lissignol. *Plate.* 8* *Melbourne,* 1866
—— On the Application of Phytology to the Industrial Purposes of Life. 8* *Melbourne,* 1870
—— Forest Culture in its Relation to Industrial Pursuits. 8* *Melbourne,* 1871
—— Descriptive Notes on Papuan Plants. Parts 1-6. 8° *Melbourne,* 1875-85
—— Select Plants readily Eligible for Industrial Culture or Naturalisation in Victoria, with Indications of their Native Countries and some of their Uses. 8° *Melbourne,* 1876
—— Addresses on the Development of Rural Industries. 8* [*Melbourne,* 1880]
—— Select Extra-Tropical Plants, readily eligible for Industrial Culture or Naturalization, with Indications of their Native Countries and some of their Uses. New South Wales edition (enlarged). 8° *Sydney,* 1881
—— The same. New edition. 8° *Melbourne,* 1885
—— *See* Campbell, F. A. ; *also* Victoria, A, C, D : Appendix 2.

Mueller, Hans. *See* Wissmann.

Mühry, Dr Adolf. Allgemeine geographische Meteorologie oder Versuch einer übersichtlichen Darlegung des Systems der Erd-Meteoration in ihrer klimatischen Bedeutung. *Maps.* 8° *Leipzig,* 1860

Mühry, Dr Adolf. Klimatographische Uebersicht der Erde, in einer Sammlung authentischer Berichte mit hinzugefügten Anmerkungen, zu wissenschaftlichem und zu praktischem Gebrauch; mit einem Appendix. 8° *Leipzig*, 1862
—— Supplement zur Klimatographischen Uebersicht der Erde ; mit einem Appendix, enthaltend Untersuchungen über das Wind-System, &c. *Maps.* 8° *Leipzig*, 1865
—— Ueber die richtige Lage und die Theorie des Calmengürtels auf den Continenten. 8* *Vienna*, N.D.
—— Ueber die Lehre von den Meeres-Strömungen. *Map.* Small 8* *Göttingen*, 1869
—— Zur orographischen Meteorologie. 8* *Vienna*, N.D.

Muir, Francis. A System of Universal Geography. 8° *Edinburgh*, 1864
Muir, Dr Thomas. On the Territorial Expansion of the British Empire during the last Ten Years. *Map.* 8* *Glasgow*, 1889
Muir, Sir William. *See* Kennedy, James.
Muirhead, W. Te la Chuen-che : Universal Geography, Political, Physical, Mathematical, Historical. [In Chinese.] 3 vols. *Maps.* 8° *Shanghai*, 1853-54
Mukharji, T. N. Art Manufactures of India. Specially compiled for the Glasgow International Exhibition, 1888. *Map and plate.* 8° *Calcutta*, 1888
Mulhall, M. G. Rio Grande do Sul and its German Colonies. Small 8° 1873
—— **and E. T. Mulhall.** Handbook of the River Plate, comprising Buenos Ayres, the Upper Provinces, Banda Oriental, and Paraguay. Vol. 1. Large 8° *Buenos Ayres*, 1869
—— Handbook of the River Plate Republics, comprising Buenos Ayres and the Provinces of the Argentine Republic, and the Republics of Uruguay and Paraguay. Small 8° 1875
—— The River Plate Handbook, Guide, Directory, and Almanac for 1863. Small 8° *Buenos Ayres*, 1863
—— From Europe to Paraguay and Matto-Grosso. *Map.* 8° 1877
—— Handbook of the River Plate : comprising the Argentine Republic, Uruguay, and Paraguay. 5th edition. *Maps.* Small 8° *Buenos Ayres*, 1885
Mullens, Joseph. Missions in South India Visited and Described. *Map.* Royal 8° 1854
Mullens, Rev. J. Twelve Months in Madagascar. *Map and plates.* 8° 1875
Müller, Albert. On the Dispersal of Non-migratory Insects by Atmospheric Agencies. 8* 1871
—— Ein Fund vorgeschichtlicher Steingeräthe bei Basel. *Photograph.* Large 8* *Bâle*, 1875

Müller, Dr August. Orientalische Bibliographie unter Mitwirkung der Herren Prof. Dr A. Bezzenberger, Dr Th. Gleiniger, Dr R. J. H. Gottheil, Dr Joh. Müller, Prof. Dr H. L. Strack, Dr K. Vollers, Dr Th. Ch. L. Wijnmalen, u.a.; und mit Unterstützung der Deutschen Morgenländ. Gesellschaft. Herausgegeben von Prof. Dr A. Müller. Vols. 1 to 5. 8° *Berlin*, 1888-93
[Continued to date under the editorship of Dr E. Kuhn, with the co-operation of Dr Lucian Scherman and others.]

Müller, C. Geographi Græci Minores : e codicibus recognovit, prolegomenis annotatione indicibus instruxit, tabulis æri incisis illustravit. 2 vols. and Atlas. 8° *Paris*, 1855-61

VOL. 1.—Hannonis Carthaginiensis Periplus. Scylacis, ut fertur, Periplus. Dicæarchi, ut fertur, Periegesis. Agatharchidis de Mari Erythræo Libri. Scymni Chii, ut fertur, Periegesis. Dionysii Calliphontis F. Periegesis. Isidori Characeni Mansiones Parthicæ. Anonymi Periplus Maris Erythræi. Arriani Indica et Ponti Periplus. Anonymi Periplus Ponti Euxini. Anonymi Stadiasmus Maris Magni. Marciani Heracleensis Peripli.

VOL. 2.—Dionysii Anaplus Bospori. Dionysii Periegesis. Avieni Paraphrasis. Prisciani Paraphrasis. Eustathii Commentarii. Anonymi Paraphrasis. Scholia in Dionysium. Nicephori Geographia. Agathemeri Geographia. Anonymi Geographia. Anonymi Orbis Descriptio. Chrestomathia Straboniana. Pseudoplutarchi Liber de Fluviis.

—— **and T. Müller.** Fragmenta Historicorum Græcorum. Apollodori Bibliotheca cum Fragmentis. 5 vols. 8° *Paris*, 1874
Müller, Christian. *See* Allgemeine Historie, Vol. 20; Phillips, New Voyages and Travels [3], Vol. 8 : Appendix 1.
Müller, C. O. History and Antiquities of the Doric Race. 2 vols. *Maps.* 8° *Oxford*, 1830
Müller, Ferdinand. Considérations sur la Prévision des Tempêtes, et spécialement sur celles du 1 au 4 Décembre 1863. *Plates.* 4* *St Petersburg*, 1864
—— Unter Tungusen und Jakuten : Erlebnisse und Ergebnisse der Olenék-Expedition der kaiserlich Russischen Geographischen Gesellschaft in St Petersburg. *Map and illustrations.* 8° *Leipzig*, 1882
Müller, F. H. Historisch-geographische Darstellung des Stromsystems der Wolga. 8° *Berlin*, 1839

Müller, Ferdinand Max. Proposals for a Missionary Alphabet, submitted to the Alphabetical Conferences held at the Residence of Chevalier Bunsen, Jan. 1854. *Table.* 8*　　　　1854
—— The Sacred Books of the East. Vols. 1-33, 37, 41. 8°　　*Oxford*, 1879-94

Müller, Dr Friedrich. Die Aequatoriale Sprachfamilie in Central Afrika. 8*
　　　　　　　　　　Vienna, 1892
—— *See* "Novara."

Müller, Dr G. F. H. *See* Ritter ; Seetzen.

Müller, Prof. H. D. *See* Bent.

Müller, Dr Johannes. Die Humboldts-Bai und Cap Bonpland in Neu-Guinea : ethnographisch und physikalisch untersucht durch eine Niederländisch-indische Commission. *Plates.* 4*　　*Berlin*, 1864
—— Die wissenschaftlichen Vereine und Gesellschaften Deutschlands in neunzehnten Jahrhundert. Bibliographie ihren Veröffentlichungen seit ihrer Begründung bis auf die Gegenwart. Erste Lief. 4°
　　　　　　　　　　Berlin, 1883
—— Die wissenschaftlichen Vereine und Gesellschaften Deutschlands, &c. Lieferungen 4-11. 4°　　*Berlin*, 1884-87
—— *See* Müller, Dr A.

Müller, Robert. *See* Dorn, A.

Müller, Salomon. Berigten over Sumatra, &c. *Map.* 8*　　*Amsterdam*, 1837
—— Reizen en Onderzoekingen in den Indischen Archipel, gedaan op last der Nederlandsche Indische Regering, in 1828 en 1836. 2 vols. *Maps and plates.* 8°　　　　*Amsterdam*, 1857
—— Geschiedenis der Noordsche Compagnie. 8°　　*Utrecht*, 1874
—— *See* Gerritsz.

Müller, Willi. Die Umsegelung Afrikas durch Phönizische Schiffer ums Jahr 600 v. Chr. Geb. 8°　*Rathenow*, N.D.

Müller-Beeck, George. Reise-Notizen von Teneriffa. *Chart and illustrations.* Large 8*　　*Frankfort-o-M.*, 1879

Müller-Beeck, F. G. Unsere wissenschaftliche Kenntniss von Korea. Vortrag gehalten am 4 Juli 1882, in der Geographischen Gesellschaft zu Greifswald. *Plate.* 8*　*Greifswald*, 1882
—— Eine Reise durch Portugal. *Map.* 8°　　　　*Hamburg*, 1883

Müller-Simonis, P. Relation des Missions scientifiques de MM. H. Hyvernat et P. Müller-Simonis (1888-89). Du Caucase au Golfe Persique à travers l'Arménie, le Kurdistan, et la Mésopotamie . . . suivie de notices sur la géographie et l'histoire ancienne de l'Arménie, et les inscriptions cunéiformes du bassin de Van, par H. Hyvernat. *Maps and illustrations.* Large 4°
　　　　　　　　　　Paris, 1892

Muller, Frederik. Catalogue de Livres, Atlas, Portraits, et Planches sur la Russie. 8*　　*Amsterdam*, 1870
—— Les Indes Orientales. Catalogue de Livres sur les Possessions Néerlandaises aux Indes. 8°　　*Amsterdam*, 1882

Muller, Dr George A. Laguet or Laghetto : a Historical Sketch of its Shrine. *Illustration.* 12*　*Nice*, 1884

Muller, G. F., and P. S. Pallas. Conquest of Siberia ; and the History of the Transactions, Wars, Commerce, &c., carried on between Russia and China from the Earliest Period. 8°　　1842

Muller, H. C. Færöernes Fuglefauna med Bemærkninger om Fuglefangsten. 8*　　　　*Copenhagen*, 1863

Muller, Hendrik P. N. Een Bezœk aan de Delagoa-Baai en de Lijdenburgsche Goudvelden. *Illustrations.* 8*
　　　　　　　　　　Haarlem, 1887
—— Beknopt Verslag van de Voordracht over Oost-Afrika Gehouden door den Heer Hendrik P. N. Muller, naar Aanleiding Zijner Reizen in Afrïka, op 19 Maart 1887 in het Nederlandsch Aardrijkskundig Genootschap. *Map.* 8*
　　　　　　　　　　Amsterdam [1887]
—— Herinneringen uit Afrika. Fragment van een Reisverhaal. Natal. 12*
　　　　　　　　　　　　1888
—— Zuid-Afrika. *Maps and plates.* 8°
　　　　　　　　　　Leyden [1889]
—— Industrie des Cafres du sud-est de l'Afrique. Collection recueillie sur les lieux, et Notice ethnographique. Description des objets représentés par Joh. F. Snelleman. *Plates.* 4°
　　　　　　　　　　Leyden [1893 ?]

Muller, Jean. Histoire des Suisses. Traduite de l'Allemand. Vols. 1-6. 8°
　　　　　　　　　　Lausanne, 1795-97

Muller, Vsevolod. Ossete Studies. Part 3. [In Russian.] 8°　　*Moscow*, 1887

Müllner, Johann. Die Bevölkerungsdichte Tirols. *Map.* 8* [*Vienna*, 1889]

Mumsen, Dr Jacob. Reise nach Norwegen im 1788. 12°　*Hamburg*, 1789

Mun, T. *See* Purchas, Vol. 1, Book 5 : Appendix 1.

Munch, Peter Andreas. Jus Nauticum Recentius quod inter Norvegos olim valuit. 4*　　*Christiania*, 1838
—— Symbolæ ad Historiam Antiquiorem rerum Norvegicarum. 2 *Facsimiles.* 4*
　　　　　　　　　　Christiania, 1850
—— Aslak Bolts Jordebog. Fortegnelse over Jordegods og Andre Herligheder tilhörende Erkebiskopsstolen i Nidaros, affattet ved Erkebiskop Aslak Bolts foranstaltning, 1432-49. 8°
　　　　　　　　　　Christiania, 1852

Munch, Peter Andreas. Olafs Konungs Tryggvasunar. Kong Olaf Tryggvesöns Saga, forfattet paa Latin henimod Slutningen af det Tolfte Aarhundrede af Odd Snorreson ; udgiven af P. A. Munch. *Facsimile.* 8° *Christiania,* 1853
—— Ved Paul Botten Hansen. 8*
Christiania, 1863
—— **and C. R. Unger.** Saga Olafs Konungs ens Helga. Udförligere Saga om Kong Olaf dén Hellige, efter det ældste fuldstændíge pergaments Haandskrift i det store Kongelige Bibliothek i Stockholm. Udgivet efter faranstaltning af det Akademiske Collegium ved det Kong. Norske Fredericks Universitet. 8° *Christiania,* 1853

Mundella, A. J. *See* Plener.

Mundy, D. L. Rotomahana, and the Boiling Springs of New Zealand. A Photographic Series of Sixteen Views, with Descriptive Notes by F. von Hochstetter. 4° 1875

Mundy, Gen. Godfrey C. Our Antipodes, or a Residence and Rambles in the Australasian Colonies ; with a Glimpse of the Gold Fields. Vols. 1 and 3. *Plates.* 8° 1852
—— Pen and Pencil Sketches in India : Journal of a Tour in India. *Map and plates.* 8° 1858

Mundy, Capt. Rodney. Narrative of the Events in Borneo and Celebes, down to the Occupation of Labuan, from the Journals of James Brooke, Rajah of Saräwak ; with a Narrative of the Operations of H.M.S. "Iris." 2 vols. *Maps and plates.* 8° 1848

Munier, —. Essai d'une Méthode Générale propre à étendre les Connoissances des Voyageurs, ou Recueil d'Observations relatives à l'Histoire, à la Répartition des Impôts, au Commerce, aux Sciences, aux Arts, et à la Culture des Terres ; le tout appuyé sur des faits exacts, et enrichi d'expériences utiles. 2 vols. 8° *Paris,* 1779

Munk, J. *See* Monck ; *also* Allgemeine Historie, Vol. 17 : Appendix 1.

Munro, H. T. *See* Stott.

Munro, J. A. R. *See* Hogarth.

Munster, Sebastian. Cosmographia Universalis. [Title wanting.] *Maps and plates.* Folio *Bâle,* 1550

Münzenberger, E. F. A. Abessinien und seine Bedeutung für unsere Zeit . . . herausgegeben von Joseph Spillmann, S. J. *Map and illustrations.* 8° *Freiburg im Breisgau,* 1892

Munzinger, Werner. Ueber die Sitten und das Recht der Bogos ; mit einem Vorwort von J. M. Ziegler. *Map.* 4* *Winterthur,* 1859

Munzinger, Werner. Ostafrikanische Studien. *Map.* 8° *Schaffhausen,* 1864
—— Bericht an den Schweizerischen Bundesrath vom 27 März, 1863. 12* N.P., 1863
—— Ostafrikanische Studien von [Review]. 12* N.P., N.D.
—— *See* Heuglin ; Wild, G.

Muraviev. *See* Mouraviev.

Murchison, Sir Roderick Impey. Supplementary Remarks on the Strata of the Oolitic Series, and the Rocks associated with them, in the Counties of Sutherland and Ross, and in the Hebrides. *Plate.* 4* 1827
—— On the Relations of the Tertiary and Secondary Rocks forming the Southern Flanks of the Tyrolese Alps near Bassano. *Plate.* 8* 1829
—— Outline of the Geology of the Neighbourhood of Cheltenham. *Plate.* 8* *Cheltenham,* 1834
—— The same. New edition, augmented and revised by J. Buckman and H. E. Strickland. *Map and plates.* 8° *Cheltenham,* 1845
—— The Silurian System, founded on Geological Researches in the Counties of Salop, Hereford, Radnor, Montgomery, Caermarthen, Brecon, Pembroke, Monmouth, Gloucester, Worcester, and Stafford ; with Descriptions of the Coal-Fields and Overlying Formations. *Maps, plates, and woodcuts.* 4° 1839
—— First Sketch of some of the Results of a Second Geological Survey of Russia. 8* [1841]
—— Two Vols. of Geographical Addresses, 1844-61, 1863-71. 8° 1844-71
—— Additional Remarks on the Deposit of Œningen in Switzerland. 8* 1846
—— On the Silurian Rocks and their Associates in Parts of Sweden ; with a Postscript. *Plate.* 8* 1847
—— On the Geological Structure of the Alps, Carpathians, and Apennines. 8* 1849
—— On the Development of the Permian System in Saxony, as communicated by Prof. Naumann. 8* 1849
—— On the Earlier Volcanic Rocks of the Papal States, and the adjacent parts of Italy. 8* 1850
—— On the Vents of Hot Vapour in Tuscany, and their Relations to Ancient Lines of Fracture and Eruption. 8* 1850
—— On the Distribution of the Flint Drift of the South-East of England to the South and North of the Weald, and over the Surface of the South Downs. 8* 1851

Murchison, Sir Roderick Impey. On the Slaty Rocks of the Sichon, and on the Origin of the Mineral Springs of Vichy. (2 papers.) 8* 1851
—— Vol. of Pamphlets on the Geology of Scotland ; with Geological Map of Scotland, and Explanations. *Plates.* 8° 1851-62
—— On the meaning of the term "Silurian System" as adopted by Geologists in various countries during the last ten years. 8* 1852
—— Siluria : the History of the Oldest known Rocks containing Organic Remains ; with a Brief Sketch of the Distribution of Gold over the Earth. *Maps and plates.* 8° 1854
—— Additional Observations on the Silurian and Devonian Rocks near Christiania in Norway. 8* 1855
—— Note on the Relative Position of the Strata, near Ludlow, containing the Ichthyolites described by Sir P. Egerton. *Plates.* 8* 1857
—— The Silurian Rocks and Fossils of Norway, as described by M. T. Kjerulf ; those of the Baltic Province of Russia, by Prof. Schmidt ; and both compared with their British Equivalents. 8* 1858
—— Table showing the Vertical Range of the Silurian Fossils of Britain. 8* 1859
—— Siluria : the History of the Oldest Fossiliferous Rocks and their Foundaitons ; with a Brief Sketch of the Distribution of Gold over the Earth, including "The Silurian System." *Maps, plates, and woodcuts.* 8° 1859
—— On the Commercial and Agricultural Value of certain Phosphate Rocks of the Anguilla Isles, in the Leeward Islands. 8* 1859
—— Supplemental Observations on the Order of the Ancient Stratified Rocks of the North of Scotland. 8* 1860
—— On the Inapplicability of the New Term "Dyas" to the "Permian" Group of Rocks, as proposed by Dr Geinitz. 8* 1861
—— On the Permian Rocks of North-Eastern Bohemia. 8* 1863
—— On the Gneiss and other Azoic Rocks, and on the superjacent Palæozoic Formations of Bavaria and Bohemia. *Woodcuts.* 8* 1863
—— Biographical Notice of. 4* *Geneva,* 1866
—— Siluria : a History of the Oldest Rocks in the British Isles and other Countries ; with Sketches of the Origin and Distribution of Native Gold, the General Succession of Geological Formations and Changes of the Earth's Surface. 4th edition (including "The Silurian System "). *Map and plates.* 8° 1867
—— Review of Professor Alphonse Favre's Geological Researches in the Vicinity of Mont Blanc. 8* 1868

Murchison, Sir Roderick Impey. Letter from Sir R. I. Murchison to the *London Scotsman,* and leader thereon, "Where is Livingstone?" 8* 1869
—— Biographical Notice, by G. von Helmersen. 8* *St Petersburg,* 1871
—— On the Distribution of the Superficial Detritus of the Alps, as compared with that of Northern Europe. 8* N.D.
—— On the Superficial Detritus of Sweden, and on the Probable Causes which have affected the Surface of the Rocks in the Central and Southern Portions of that Kingdom. 8* N.D.
—— Brief Review of the Classification of the Sedimentary Rocks of Cornwall. 8* N.D.
—— Life of Sir Roderick I. Murchison, based on his Journals and Letters ; with Notices of his Scientific Contemporaries, and a Sketch of the Rise and Growth of Palæozoic Geology in Britain, by Archibald Geikie. 2 vols. *Portraits.* 8° 1875
—— *See* MacClintock, F. L. ; Miari ; Sedgwick, A. ; *also* India, C, Geological Papers : Appendix 2.
—— **and Robert Harkness.** On the Permian Rocks of the North-West of England, and their Extension into Scotland. 8* 1864
—— **and Prof. J. Morris.** On the Palæozoic and their associated Rocks of the Thüringerwald and the Harz. 8* 1855
—— **and H. E. Strickland.** On the Upper Formations of the New Red Sandstone System in Gloucestershire, Worcestershire, and Warwickshire. *Map and plate.* 4* 1837
—— **Edouard de Verneuil, and Count Alex. von Keyserling.** On the Geological Structure of the Central and Southern Regions of Russia in Europe, and of the Ural Mountains. Royal 8* 1842
—— The Geology of Russia in Europe and the Ural Mountains. Vol. 1, Geology ; Vol. 2, Paléontologie. 2 vols. *Maps and plates.* 4° 1845
—— Ditto. *Plates and maps.* 4°, in case.

Murphy, B. F. Memoir on the Gold Coast, or a Political Description of the Value, Resources, and Present State of that highly interesting Country, and a Demonstration of the Means whereby it may be completely subjugated. *Maps.* Small 4°. MS. 1831

Murphy, H. C. The Voyage of Giovanni Verrazzano : a Chapter in the Early History of Maritime Discovery in America. *Maps.* 8° *New York,* 1875

Murphy, J. Cavanah. History of the Mahometan Empire in Spain : containing General History of the Arabs. *Map.* 4° 1816

Murphy, J. L. The Figure of the Earth. 8* 1853

Murphy, J. M. Sporting Adventures in the Far West. 8° 1879

Murr, C. G. von. *See* Bayer.

Murray, Alexander. Report upon the Geographical Survey of Newfoundland for the year 1870. *Map and plates.* 8* *St John's,* 1870

—— Copy of Letter respecting the Lumber Capabilities and General Fertility of the Country in the Neighbourhood of the Gander River, Newfoundland. 8* [*St John's,* 1874]

—— Glaciation of Newfoundland. 4* 1882

Murray, Hon. Amelia M. Letters from the United States, Cuba, and Canada. 2 vols. 8° 1856

Murray, Andrew. The Geographical Distribution of Mammals. *Maps and plates.* 4° 1866

Murray, Mrs Elizabeth. Sixteen Years of an Artist's Life in Morocco, Spain, and the Canary Islands. *2 plates.* 8° 1859

Murray, Hon. George. *See* Callander, Vol. 3 : Appendix 1.

Murray, Hon. Henry A. Lands of the Slave and the Free ; or Cuba, the United States, and Canada. *Maps and plates.* 8° 1857

Murray, Hugh. Historical Account of Discoveries and Travels in Africa, from the Earliest Ages to the Present Time ; including the Substance of the late Dr Leyden's Work on that subject. 2 vols. *Maps.* 8° *Edinburgh,* 1818

—— Historical Account of Discoveries and Travels in Asia, from the Earliest Ages to the Present Time. 3 vols. *Maps.* 8° *Edinburgh,* 1820

—— Historical Account of Discoveries and Travels in North America ; including the United States, Canada, the Shore of the Polar Sea, and the Voyages in Search of a North-West Passage. Vol. 1. *Map.* 8° 1829

—— The United States of America, their History from the Earliest Period : their Industry, Commerce, Banking Transactions, and National Works ; their Institutions and Character, Political, Social, and Literary ; and a Survey of the Territory, and Remarks on the Prospects and Plans of Emigration ; with Illustrations of Natural History by James Nicol. 3 vols. *Portraits and plates.* 12° *Edinburgh,* 1844

—— **assisted by W. Wallace, R. Jameson, W. J. Hooker, and W. Swainson.** Encyclopædia of Geography : comprising a Complete Description of the Earth, Physical, Statistical, Civil, and Political ; exhibiting its Relation to the Heavenly Bodies, its Physical Structure, the Natural History of each Country, and the Industry, Commerce, Political

Murray, Hugh, and others—*continued.* Institutions, and Civil and Social State of all Nations. 2 vols. *Maps and woodcuts.* 8° 1834

Murray, Hugh, J. Crawford, P. Gordon, Capt. T. Lynn, W. Wallace, and G. Burnett. Historical and Descriptive Account of China : its Ancient and Modern History, Language, Literature, Religion, Government, Industry, Manners, and Social State ; Intercourse with Europe from the Earliest Ages ; Survey of its Geography, Geology, Botany, and Zoology, &c. 3 vols. *Map and plates.* 12° *Edinburgh,* 1836

—— Historical and Descriptive Account of British America : comprehending Canada (Upper and Lower), Nova Scotia, New Brunswick, Newfoundland, Prince Edward Island ; the Bermudas and the Fur Countries ; their History from the Earliest Settlement, &c. ; also an Account of the Manners and Present State of the Aboriginal Tribes : to which is added a Full Detail of the Principles and best Modes of Emigration ; with Illustrations of Natural History, by J. Wilson, R. K. Greville, and Prof. Traill. 3 vols. *Maps and plates.* 12° *Edinburgh,* 1839

Murray, Hugh, Prof. Jameson, and J. Wilson. Narrative of Discovery and Adventure in Africa, from the Earliest Ages to the Present Time ; with Illustrations of the Geology, Mineralogy, and Zoology. *Maps and woodcuts.* 12° *Edinburgh,* 1840

—— *See* Marco Polo.

Murray, James. Notes on the Climate and Diseases of the Satara Territory. *Table.* [From the India, Bombay Selections, No. 41.] Royal 8° *Bombay,* 1857

Murray, John. Handbooks for Travellers. *Maps and plans.* Post 8°.

—— Travel-Talk : being a collection of Questions, Phrases, and Vocabularies, in English, German, French, and Italian, intended to serve as interpreter to English Travellers abroad or Foreigners visiting England. 16th edition. 1882

[UNITED KINGDOM.]

—— London, as it is. 2nd edition. 1874

—— Surrey, Hampshire, and the Isle of Wight. 2nd and 4th editions. 1865, 1888

—— Kent and Sussex. 3rd edition. 1868

—— Sussex. 4th edition. 1877

—— The same. 5th edition. 1893

—— Kent. 5th edition. 1892

—— Wiltshire, Dorsetshire, and Somersetshire. 2nd and 4th editions. 1869, 1882

—— Westmorland, Cumberland, and the Lakes. 2nd edition. 1869

—— Shropshire, Cheshire, and Lancashire. 1870

Murray, John. Shropshire and Cheshire.
2nd edition. 1879
—— Lancashire. 2nd edition. 1880
—— Essex, Suffolk, Norfolk, and Cambridgeshire. 1870
—— The same. 3rd edition. 1892
—— Devon and Cornwall. 8th edition.
1872
—— Devonshire. 9th and 10th editions.
1879, 1887
—— Cornwall. 9th, 10th, and 11th editions. 1879, 1882, 1893
—— Durham and Northumberland. 2nd edition. 1873
—— The same. New edition. 1890
—— Yorkshire. 2nd and 3rd editions.
1874, 1882
—— Gloucestershire, Worcestershire, and Herefordshire. 2nd and 3rd editions.
1872, 1884
—— Berks, Bucks, and Oxfordshire ; including a particular Description of the University and City of Oxford, and the Descent of the Thames to Maidenhead and Windsor. 2nd and 3rd editions.
1872, 1882
—— Oxfordshire. 1894
—— Derbyshire, Nottinghamshire, Leicestershire, and Staffordshire. 2nd edition.
1874
—— The same. 3rd edition. 1892
—— Northamptonshire and Rutland. 1878
—— England and Wales ; alphabetically arranged for the use of travellers. 1878
—— The same. 2nd edition. 1890
—— Lincolnshire. 1890
—— The English Lakes included in the Counties of Cumberland, Westmorland, and Lancashire. 1889
—— North Wales. 4th and 5th editions.
1874, 1885
—— South Wales and its borders, including the River Wye. 2nd and 4th editions. 1870, 1890
—— Scotland. 3rd and 5th editions.
1873, 1884
—— Ireland. 3rd and 4th editions.
1871, 1878

[EUROPEAN CONTINENT.]
—— The Continent :—Part I. Being a Guide to Holland, Belgium, Rhenish Prussia, and the Rhine from Holland to Mayence. 18th and 19th editions.
1873, 1876
—— The same. Part II. Being a Guide to North Germany from the Baltic to the Black Forest, the Hartz, Thüringerwald, Saxon Switzerland, Rügen, the Giant Mountains, Taunus, Odenwald, and the Rhine Countries from Frankfurt to Basle, &c. 18th and 19th editions.
1874, 1877
—— Paris. 1874, 1879
—— The same. New edition. 1882

Murray, J. France Alsace and Lorraine: being a Guide to Normandy, Brittany; the rivers Seine, Loire, Rhône, and Garonne; the French Alps, Dauphiné, the Pyrenees, Provence, and Nice, &c. ; the railways and principal roads. 12th edition. Parts I. and II. 1873
—— The same. Part I. Containing Artois, Picardy, Normandy, Brittanny, the Seine and Loire, the Garonne, Bordeaux, Limousin, Gascony, the Pyrenees, &c. 15th edition. 1879
—— The same. Part II. 15th edition.
1881
—— The same. Parts I. and II. 16th edition. 1882-84
—— The same. 2 vols. 18th edition. 1892
—— Holland and Belgium. 20th and 21st editions. 1881, 1889
—— North Germany from the Baltic to the Black Forest, and the Rhine from Holland to Basle. 20th edition 1886
—— Southern Germany : being a Guide to Würtemberg, Bavaria, Austria, Tyrol, Salzburg, Styria, &c., the Austrian and Bavarian Alps, and the Danube from Ulm to the Black Sea. 12th and 14th editions. 1873, 1879
—— South Germany and Austria. 14th edition. With a Supplement. 1881
—— The same. 15th edition. 2 parts.
1890
—— Switzerland, and the Alps of Savoy and Piedmont. 15th edition. 1874
—— The same (including the Italian Lakes, and part of Dauphiné). 16th edition. 2 vols. 1879
—— Switzerland. 17th edition. 2 vols. 1886
—— The same. 18th edition. 2 parts.
1891-92
—— Portugal : a Complete Guide for Lisbon, Cintra, Mafra, the British Battlefields, Alcobaça, Batalha, Oporto, &c. 3rd and 4th editions 1864, 1887
—— Spain, by Richard Ford. 2 vols. 1855
Part 1.—Andalucia, Ronda and Granada, Murcia, Valencia, and Catalonia ; the Portions best suited for the Invalid. A Winter Tour.
Part 2.—Estremadura, Leon, Galicia, the Asturias, the Castiles (Old and New), the Basque Provinces, Arragon, and Navarre. A Summer Tour.
—— The same. 4th, 5th, 6th, 7th, and 8th editions. 1869, 1878, 1882, 1888, 1892
—— The Riviera, comprising Provence and Dauphiné, and the Coast line from Marseilles to Genoa. 1890
—— Rome and its Environs. 11th, 13th, and 14th editions. 1873, 1881, 1888
—— Northern Italy : States of Sardinia, Lombardy and Venice, Parma and Piacenza, Modena, Lucca, Massa-Carrara, and Tuscany, as far as the Val d'Arno.
1842

Murray, John. Northern Italy : comprising Turin, Milan, Pavia, Cremona, the Italian Lakes, Bergamo, Brescia, Verona, Mantua, Vicenza, Padua, Venice, Ferrara, Bologna, Ravenna, Rimini, Modena, Parma, Piacenza, Genoa, the Riviera, and the intermediate towns and routes. 13th, 15th, and 16th editions.
1874, 1883, 1891

—— Central Italy, including the Papal States, Rome, and the Cities of Etruria.
1843

—— The same, including Florence, Lucca, Tuscany and its off-lying islands, Umbria, the Marches, and part of the late patrimony of St Peter. 8th, 10th, and 11th editions. 2 vols. 1874, 1880, 1889

—— Southern Italy : being a Guide for the Continental Portion of the Kingdom of the Two Sicilies, including the City of Naples and its Suburbs, Pompeii, Herculaneum, Vesuvius, the Islands of the Bay of Naples, and that portion of the Papal States which lies between the Contorni of Rome and the Neapolitan Frontier. By Octavian Blewitt 1853

—— The same. Part I., comprising the Continental States and Island of Sardinia, Lombardy, and Venice. 1858

—— The same. Part II., Parma, Piacenza, Modena, Florence, Pisa, Lucca, and Tuscany as far as the Val d'Arno. 1858

—— The same. Comprising the Provinces of the Abruzzi, Terra di Lavoro, Naples, the Principati, Benevento, Capitanata, Molise, Basilicata, Terra di Bari, Terra d'Otranto, Calabria, &c. 7th and 8th editions. 1873, 1878

—— The same. 8th edition. 1883

—— The same, and Sicily. 9th edition. 2 parts. 1890

—— The Islands of Corsica and Sardinia.
1868

—— The Mediterranean, its Cities, Coasts, and Islands. By Lieut.-Col. Sir R. L. Playfair. 2nd edition, 2 parts in 1 vol., and 3rd edition. 2 vols. 1882, 1890

—— The Ionian Islands, Greece, Turkey, Asia Minor, and Constantinople, including a Description of Malta. 1840

—— Greece, describing the Ionian Islands, Continental Greece, Athens, and the Peloponnesus, the Islands of the Ægean Sea, Albania, Thessaly, and Macedonia. 4th edition. 1872

—— The same. Including the Ionian Islands, Continental Greece, the Peloponnese, the Islands of the Ægean, Crete, Albania, Thessaly, and Macedonia, and a Detailed Description of Athens, Ancient and Modern, Classical and Mediæval. 2 parts. 5th edition.
1884

—— Northern Europe. Part II., Finland and Russia. 1849

Murray, John. Russia, Poland, and Finland. 2nd and 3rd editions (including the Crimea, Caucasus, and Central Asia).
1868, 1875

—— The same, including the Crimea, Caucasus, Siberia, and Central Asia. 4th edition. 1888

—— The same. 5th edition. 1893

—— Denmark, Norway, and Sweden. 3rd edition. 1871

—— Norway. 5th and 7th editions.
1874, 1880

—— The same. 8th edition. 1892

—— Sweden, Stockholm and its vicinity. 4th and 6th editions. 1875, 1883

—— Denmark, with Sleswig and Holstein. 4th edition. 1875

—— The same, and Iceland. 5th and 6th editions. 1883, 1893

[ASIA.]

—— Syria and Palestine : including an Account of the Geography, History, Antiquities, and Inhabitants of these Countries, the Peninsula of Sinai, Edom, and the Syrian Desert ; with detailed Descriptions of Jerusalem, Petra, Damascus, and Palmyra. 2 vols. 1858

—— Syria and Palestine, including an Account of the Geography, History, Antiquities, and Inhabitants of these countries ; the Peninsula of Sinai, Edom, and the Syrian Desert ; with detailed Descriptions of Jerusalem, Petra, Damascus, and Palmyra. Parts I. and II. 2nd edition. 1868

—— The same. New edition. 1892

—— Turkey in Asia, including Constantinople, the Bosphorus, Dardanelles, Brousa and Plain of Troy. 2nd and 4th editions (including the Isles of Cyprus, Rhodes, &c., Smyrna, Ephesus, and the Routes to Persia, Bagdad, Moosool, &c.)
1871, 1878

—— India : being an Account of the three Presidencies, and of the Overland Route ; intended as a Guide for Travellers, Officers, and Civilians ; with vocabularies and dialogues of the spoken languages of India. Part I. Madras ; Part II. Bombay. 1859

—— The same. The Bengal Presidency ; with an account of Calcutta City. 1882

—— The same. The Bombay Presidency ; with an account of Bombay City. 2nd edition. 1881

—— The same. The Madras Presidency ; with a notice of the Overland Route to India. By E. B. Eastwick. 2nd edition.
1879

—— The same. The Punjab, Western Rajpútáná, Kashmir, and Upper Sindh.
1883

Y

Murray, John. India and Ceylon; including the Provinces of Bengal, Bombay, and Madras (the Panjab, North-West Provinces, Rajputana, Central Provinces, Mysore, &c.), the Native States, and Assam. *Maps and plans*   1891
—— Central and Northern Japan : being a Guide to Tōkiō, Kiōto Ozaka, Hakodate, Nagasaki, and other cities; the most interesting parts of the Main Island; Ascents of the Principal Mountains, Descriptions of Temples, and Historical Notes, &c. By E. M. Satow, C.M.G., and Lieut. A. G. S. Hawes. 2nd edition.   1884
—— Japan. 3rd edition. Revised . . by B. H. Chamberlain and W. B. Mason.   1891

[AFRICA.]

—— Egypt ; including Descriptions of the Course of the Nile through Egypt and Nubia, Alexandria, Cairo, the Pyramids, and Thebes, the Suez Canal, the Peninsula of Mount Sinai, the Oases, the Fyoom, &c. 4th edition.   1873
—— Lower and Upper Egypt, &c. In 2 parts. 6th and 7th editions. 1880, 1888
—— The same. 8th edition.   1891
—— Algeria. By Lieut.-Col. Sir R. L. Playfair.   1874
—— Algeria and Tunis : Algiers, Oran, Constantine, Carthage, &c. 2nd and 3rd editions.   1878, 1887

[AUSTRALASIA.]

—— New Zealand, Auckland, the Hot Lake District, Napier, Wanganui, Wellington, Nelson, the Buller, the West Coast Road, Christchurch, Mount Cook, Dunedin, Otago, the Southern Lakes, the Sounds, &c. By F. W. Pennefather, LL.D. *Maps and plans.*   1893
Murray, John. On the North Sea, with Remarks on some of its Friths and Estuaries. Edited by C. Manby and J. Forrest. *Maps.* 8°   1862
Murray, Dr John. *See* "Challenger."
Murray, Rev. J. H. Travels in Uruguay, South America ; together with an Account of the Present State of Sheep-Farming and Emigration to that Country. *Map and illustrations.* 8°   1871
Murray, Kenric B. Commercial Geography, considered especially in its Relation to New Markets and Fields of Production for British Trade. *Chart.* 12° [1887]
Murray, Hon. R. Dundas. Cities and Wilds of Andalucia. 8°   1853
Murray, Hon. Mrs S. Guide to the Beauties of Scotland, to the Lakes of Westmorland, Cumberland, Lancashire, &c. 2 vols. 8°   1799
Murray, Reginald A. F. Victoria: Geology and Physical Geography. *Map and illustrations.* 8° *Melbourne,* 1887
—— *See* Victoria, B ; Appendix 2.

Murray, R. W. South Africa, from Arab Domination to British Rule. *Maps and illustrations.* 8°   1891
Murray, Rev. T. Boyles. Pitcairn, the Island, the People, and the Pastor ; to which is added a Short Notice of the Original Settlement and Present Condition of Norfolk Island. *Plates.* 12° 1860
—— The same ; revised, and brought up to date, by the Rev. C. C. Elcum. *Chart and illustrations.* 12°   1885
Musæus. *See* Purchas, Vol. 1, Book 1 : Appendix 1.
Musgrave, Capt. Thomas. *See* Norman, W. H. ; Shillinglaw.
Musgrave, G. M. Ramble through Normandy ; or, Scenes, Characters, and Incidents in a Sketching Excursion through Calvados. *Plates.* 8°   1855
Mushketof, J. V. Turkestan : a Geological and Orographical Description, from materials collected during Travels undertaken during the years 1874 to 1880. [In Russian.] Vol. 1. *Map and plates*
                            St Petersburg, 1886
Musschenbroek, S. C. J. W. van. Het vaarwater van de Schipbreukelingen van het stoomschip " Koning der Nederlanden " en de kansen op hun Behoud. *Maps.* 8*   *Amsterdam,* 1881
Musson, Eugène. Letter to Napoleon III. on Slavery in the Southern States, by a Creole of Louisiana. 8*   1862
Musters, Capt. G. C. At Home with the Patagonians : a Year's Wanderings over Untrodden Ground, from the Straits of Magellan to the Rio Negro. *Map and plates.* 8°   1871
Myers, Francis, and Trant Chambers. The Victorian Tourists' Railway Guide. Edited by " Telemachus " (Francis Myers). *Maps.* 8° *Melbourne,* 1892

N

Naber, Prof. S. A. *See* Holland : Appendix 2.
Nachtigal, Dr Gustav. Letter to Chevalier Negri from Boornou. 8*   N.D.
—— Saharâ und Sûdân. Ergebnisse sechsjähriger Reisen in Afrika. 3 vols. *Portrait, maps, and plates.* 8°
                              Berlin, 1879-89
—— Trauerfeier für Gustav Nachtigal, 17 Mai 1885. 8*   *Berlin,* 1885
—— Erinnerungen an Gustav Nachtigal. *Portrait.* 8°   *Berlin,* 1887
Nadar, —. *See* Silas, F.
Nadarov, I. P. The Southern Ussurian District at the Present Time. (Translated by Lieut.-Col. J. C. Dalton from the Proceedings of the Russian Imperial Geographical Society, Vol. 25, 1889, No. 3). *Map.* Folio*   1890

Nagamaiya, V. Report on the Census of Travancore, taken on the 17th February 1881 A.D. (7th Mausy 1056 M.E.), along with the Imperial Census of India. 8° *Trevandrum*, 1884

Nalivkine, V. P. Histoire du Khanat de Khokand. Traduit du Russe par Aug. Dozon. [IIIe Serié, Vol. 4 of Publications de l'École des Langues Orientales Vivantes.] Large 8° *Paris*, 1889

Namur, A. Tables de Logarithmes à 12 décimales jusqu'à 434 Milliards. 8° *Brussels*, 1877

Nansen, Dr Fridtjof. The First Crossing of Greenland. Translated from the Norwegian by Hubert Majendie Gepp. 2 vols. *Maps and illustrations.* 8° 1890

—— Towards the North Pole. (From *Longman's Magazine*.) *Map.* 8° 1890

—— Plan til en ny Polarekspedition. *Map.* 8° [1890]

—— A New Route to the North Pole. (From *The Forum*.) 8° 1891

—— Eskimoliv, med Illustrationes af Otto Sinding. 8° *Christiania*, 1891

—— Eskimo Life. Translated by William Archer. *Illustrations.* 8° 1893

—— *See* Jensen.

—— **and H. Mohn.** Durchquerung von Grönland. (Erganzungsheft, 105 — Petermann's Mittheilungen.) *Maps, &c.* 4° *Gotha*, 1892

Naoroji, Dadabhai. The Financial Administration of India. 8° [1870]

Napier, Col. C. J. The Colonies : treating of their Value generally—of the Ionian Islands in particular. *Plates.* 8° 1833

Napier, E. Remarks on Ancient Troy and the Modern Troad. 8° N.D.

—— Reminiscences of Syria and the Holy Land. 2 vols. *Map and plates.* Small 8° [1847]

Napier, Col. E. Elers. Excursions in Southern Africa, including a History of the Cape Colony, an Account of the Native Tribes, &c. 2 vols. *Plates.* 8° 1850

Napier, G. F. *See* Volschinoff.

Napier, Capt. the Hon. G. C. Collection of Journals and Reports received from Capt. the Hon. G. C. Napier, Bengal Staff Corps, on Special Duty in Persia, 1874. 8° 1876

Napier, Sir William. History of General Sir Charles Napier's Administration of Scinde, and Campaign in the Cutchee Hills. *Maps and plates.* 8° 1851

Napp, R. Die Argentinische Republik. Im Auftrag des Argentin. Central-Comité's für die Philadelphia Ausstellung, und mit dem Beistand mehrerer Mitarbeiter. *Maps.* 8° *Buenos Ayres*, 1876

Narborough, Capt. Sir John. *See* Burney, Vol. 3 ; Callander, Vol. 2 ; Allgemeine Historie, 12 : Appendix 1.

Nardi, Francesco. Del Clima di Gondocoro : Memoria. 4* [*Rome*] 1861

—— Diffusione Geographica della Vite : Memoria. 4* *Rome*, 1862

—— Sui più recenti progressi della Geografia. Parte 1. 4* *Rome*, 1862

—— Sulla Scoperta delle Origini del Nilo fatta da Speke e Grant : Memoria. 4* *Rome*, 1864

—— Ricordi di un Viaggio in Oriente, &c. 8° *Rome*, 1866

—— Sullo stato presente dei lavori pel taglio dell' Istmo di Suez. 4* [*Rome*, 1867]

—— Ricerche sui limiti della vita animale nel mare profondo. 4* 1869

—— Sulle ultime Ricerche nell' Oceano polare artico. *Map.* 8* *Rome*, 1872

—— Europei in America avanti Colombo. 12* *Rome*, 1875

—— Spedizione nell' Africa Equatoriale del Conte Pietro di Brazzà-Savorgnan. 4* *Rome*, 1876

Nares, Sir G. S. Investigations of the Gibraltar Strait Current. *Map and plates.* 8* 1872

—— Narrative of a Voyage to the Polar Sea during 1875-76 in H.M. ships "Alert" and "Discovery," with Notes on the Natural History, edited by H. W. Feilden, Naturalist to the Expedition. 2 vols. *Maps and plates.* 8° 1878

—— *See* "Challenger" ; Moseley ; *also* Arctic, C, *b* : Appendix 2.

Narrien, John. Practical Astronomy and Geodesy ; including the Projections of the Sphere and Spherical Trigonometry. 8° 1845

Narvaes, Pamphilio de. *See* Gottfried ; Kerr, Vol. 5 : Appendix 1.

Nasmyth, J., and J. Carpenter. The Moon considered as a Planet, a World, and a Satellite. *Plates.* Small 4° 1874

"Nassau." *See* Cunningham, R. O.

Nassiri Khosrau. *See* Schefer, C.

Nathorst, A. G. Om Floran i Skånes Kolförande Bildningar. I. (Hefts 1 and 2) and II. *Plates.* 4° *Stockholm*, 1878-79

—— Annexe explicative à la Carte géologique générale de la Suède, publiée par l' Institut Royal Geologique de Suède à l' échelle de 1 : 1,000,000. Feuille méridionale, par A.-G. Nathorst. 8* [*Stockholm*, 1884]

—— *See* Sweden, A, Geologiska Undersökning : Appendix 2.

Naumann, Dr E. Notes on Secular Changes of Magnetic Declination in Japan. *Map and plate.* 8* [*Tokyo*, 1882]

—— Ueber den Bau und die Entstehung der Japanischen Inseln. 8* *Berlin*, 1885

—— Die Japanische Inselwelt : eine geographisch, geologisch Skizze. *Maps.* 8* *Vienna*, 1887

Naumann, Dr E. Die Erscheinungen des Erdmagnetismus in ihrer Abhängigkeit von Bau der Erdrinde. 8*
Stuttgart, 1887
—— Terrestrial Magnetism as Modified by the Structure of the Earth's Crust, and Proposals concerning a Magnetic Survey of the Globe. *Plates*. 8* [1889]
—— Neue Beiträge zur Geologie und Geographie Japans. (Ergänzungsheft, 108—Petermann's Mittheilungen.) *Maps*. 4°
Gotha, 1893
—— Vom Goldnen Horn zu den Quellen des Euphrat. Reisebriefe, Tagebuchblätter und Studien über die Asiatische Türkei und die Anatolische Bahn. *Map and illustrations.* 4° *Munich*, 1893
—— **and M. Neumayr.** Zur Geologie und Paläontologie von Japan. *Maps and plates.* 4* *Vienna*, 1890

Navarette, Don Martin Fernandez de. Coleccion de los Viages y Descubrimientos, que hicieron por Mar los Españoles desde fines del Siglo XV., con varios Documentos inéditos concernientes à la Historia de la Marina Castellana y de los Establecimientos Españoles en Indias. 5 vols. *Maps.* 4°
Madrid, 1825-37
[For Contents, see Appendix 1.]
—— Examination of the Account given by Lorenzo Ferrer Maldonado, of the Discovery of the Strait of Anian, and Notices of the principal Expeditions which have been made in search of that Passage, and of a Communication between the Atlantic Ocean and the South Seas. [MS. in Portuguese.] Small 4°
1792
—— Relations des Quatre Voyages entrepris pour la découverte du Nouveau-Monde de 1492 à 1504, suivies de diverses Lettres et Pièces inédites extraites des Archives de la Monarchie Espagnole. 3 vols. *Maps and portraits.* 8° *Paris*, 1828
—— *See* Astley, Vol. 3; Churchill, Vol. 1; Allgemeine Historie, Vol. 5: Appendix 1.

Nazarov, P. *See* Eyriès, Vol. 14: Appendix 1.

Neale, F. A. Eight Years in Syria, Palestine, and Asia Minor, from 1842-50. 2 vols. 8° 1852
—— Narrative of a Residence at the Capital of the Kingdom of Siam, with a Description of the Manners, Customs, and Laws of the Modern Siamese. *Map and illustrations.* 8° 1852

Neamet Ullah. History of the Afghans. Translated from the Persian of Neamet Ullah, by Bernhard Dorn. 2 parts in 1. [Oriental Translation Fund.] 4° 1829

Nearchus's Voyage. *See* Harris, Vol. 1; Vincent, Dean: Appendix 1.

Nebel, C. Voyage Pittoresque et Archæologique dans la partie la plus intéressante du Mexique. Folio *Paris*, 1836

Neck, J. C. van. *See* Allgemeine Historie, Vol. 8: Appendix 1.

Needham, J. F. Report on the Abor Villages beyond the British Frontier. *Map and plates.* Folio* [*Calcutta*, 1885]
—— Report on his Visit to the Abor Villages outside the British Territory. Folio* [*Calcutta*, 1886]
—— Visit to the Zayul Valley in Eastern Tibet. Folio* [*Calcutta*] 1886
—— Journey along the Lohit Brahmaputra between Sadiya in Upper Assam and Rima in South Eastern Tibet. (Roy. Geo. Soc. Suppl. Papers, Vol. 2.) *Map.* 8° 1889

Neelmeyer-Vukassowitsch, H. Russland. Europäisches und Asiatisches Russland. 8° *Leipzig*, 1887

Neff, Felix. *See* Monson, Lord.

Negri, Cristoforo. Del vario grado d'Importanza degli Stati Odierni. 8°
Milan, 1841
—— Movimento della Navigazione Nazionale ed estera, nei porti dello stato e della Navigazione Nazionale, all' estero. *Plate.* 8° *Turin*, 1851
—— L'Emigrazione Italiana al Plata. 8* 1863
—— La Grandezza Italiana: Studi Confronti e Desiderii. 8° *Turin*, 1864
—— La Storia Antica restituita a verità e raffrontata alla Moderna. 8° *Turin*, 1865
—— Due Mesi di Escursione alle Coste Belgiche, Olandesi, e Germaniche. 8*
Florence, 1871
—— Riflessioni sui progetti ferroviarie fra l'Europa e l'Asia. 8* *Rome*, 1878
—— Spedizione Artica Svedese. 8* [*Rome*, 1878]
—— Discorso Pronunciato nell' Università di Padova in occasione della gita fatta dai Membri del Terzo Congresso Geografico Internazionale da Venezia in quella città. 8* *Venice*, 1881
—— Elenco di Portolani. 8* N.P., N.D.

Negri, Gaetano. *See* Stoppani.

Neil, A. Annual Report on Meteorological Observations registered in the Punjab, 1868. Folio *Lodiana*, 1869
—— Report on the Metcorology of the Punjab for the year 1869. *Charts.* Folio
Lahore, 1870

Neil, Rev. James. Palestine Explored, with a view to its present Natural Features, and to the prevailing Manners, Customs, Rites, and Colloquial Expressions of its People which throw light on the figurative language of the Bible. *Plates.* Small 8° 1882

Nekkeib Khan. *See* Asia, General: Appendix 2.

Nelkenbrecher, J. G. Allgemeines Taschenbuch der Münz-, Maass-, und Gewichtstunde, der Wechsel-, Geld-, und Fondscourse, u. s. w. für Banquiers und Kaufleute. Herausgegeben von F. G. Feller, und mit neuen Münz-Tabellen versehen von H. C. Kandelhardt. 12° *Berlin*, 1848

Nelson, Joseph. Direct Route through the North-West Territories of Canada to the Pacific Ocean : Proposed Hudson's Bay and Pacific Railway and New Steamship Route. *Map.* 8* 1893
—— The North-West of Canada. (From the *Westminster Review*.) Large 8* 1893

Nelson, J. H. The Madura Country : a Manual compiled by order of the Madras Government. *Map in cover.* *Madras*, 1868

Nelson, W. Five Years at Panama : the Trans-Isthmian Canal. *Map and illustrations.* Crown 8° 1891

"Nemesis." *See* Hall, W. H.

Németh, Ladislaus von. *See* Teleki von Szék.

Nerciat, Baron de. *See* Recueil de Voyages, Vol. 2, p. 611 : Appendix 1.

Nerker, Dass Gossein. *See* Dalrymple, Repertory, Vol. 2 : Appendix 1.

Néry, F. J. de Santa Anna. Aux États Unis du Brésil : Voyages de M. T. Durand. *Illustrations.* Imperial 8° *Paris*, N.D.
—— Le Pays des Amazones l'El-Dorado les Terres à Caoutchouc. *Maps and illustrations.* Large 8° 1885
—— La Place de Para. Large 8* *Paris*, 1887
—— L'Emigrazioni Italiana ed Il Nuovo Disegno di Legge. 8* *Paris*, 1888
—— Guide de l'Émigrant au Brésil, publié par les soins du Syndicat du Comité Franco-Brésilien pour l'Exposition Universelle de 1889 et rédigé sous la direction de M. F.-J. De Santa-Anna Néry. 12° *Paris*, 1889
—— Le Brésil en 1889, avec une Carte de l'Empire en Chromolithographie, des tableaux statistiques, des graphiques et des cartes. Ouvrage publié paroles soins du Syndicat du Comité Franco-Brésilien pour l'Exposition Universelle de Paris avec la Collaboration de nombreux Écrivains du Brésil sous la direction de M. F.-J. de Santa-Anna Néry. 8° *Paris*, 1889
—— L'Émigration et l'Immigration pendant les dernières années : Communication faite au premier Congrès Géographique Italien tenu à Gènes du 18 au 25 Septembre 1892. 8* *Paris*, 1892

Nesbit, A. A Treatise on Practical Mensuration, to which is added a Treatise on Levelling. *Woodcuts.* 12° 1864

Nestor. Chronique dite de Nestor. Traduite sur le texte Slavon-Russe, avec Introduction et Commentaire .Critique par Louis Leger. [Publ. de l'Ec. des Langues Orient. Viv., II.e Série, Vol. 13.] Large 8° *Paris*, 1884

Netto, C. On Mining and Mines in Japan. 4* *Tokyo*, 1879

Netto, Ladislau. Investigações Historicas e Scientificas sobre o Museu Imperial e Nacional do Rio de Janeiro. *Plate.* 8° *Rio de Janeiro*, 1870
—— Apuntamentos relativos á Botanica applicada no Brazil. 8* *Rio de Janeiro*, 1871
—— Le Museum National de Rio de Janeiro et son influence sur les sciences naturelles au Brésil. 8* *Paris*, 1889

Neubauer, Adolphe. La Géographie du Talmud. (Études Talmudiques, 1.) 8° *Paris*, 1868

Neufville, Capt. J. B. On the Geography and Population of Assam. [From the India Records, No. 23.] Royal 8° *Bombay*, 1855

Neuman and Baretti. *See* Dictionaries, A, Spanish : Appendix 2.

Neumann, Carl Friedrich. Pilgerfahrten Buddhistischer Priester von China nach Indien. Part 1. 8* *Leipzig*, 1833
—— Grundriss zu Vorlesungen über Länder- und Völkerkunde und allgemeine Statistik. 8* *Munich*, 1840
—— Russland und die Tscherkessen. 8° *Stuttgart*, 1840
—— Geschichte des Englischen Reiches in Asien. 2 vols. 8° *Leipzig*, 1867

Neumann, Dr C., and Dr J. Partsch. Physikalische Geographie von Griechenland, mit besonderer Rücksicht auf das Alterthum. 8° *Breslau*, 1885

Neumann, Gustav. Geographisches Lexikon des Deutschen Reichs. 2 vols. *Plans.* Small 8°, and Atlas folio *Leipzig*, 1883

Neumann, Dr L. *See* Penck's Abhandlungen, 1.

Neumayer, Prof. George. Discussion of the Meteorological and Magnetical Observations made at the Flagstaff Observatory, Melbourne, during .the years 1858-63. *Tables.* 4° *Mannheim*, 1867
—— On the Lunar Atmospheric Tide at Melbourne. 8* 1867
—— On a Scientific Exploration of Central Australia. *Map.* 8* 1868
—— Results of the Magnetic Survey of the Colony of Victoria executed during the years 1858-64. *Maps and plate.* 4° *Mannheim*, 1869
—— Anleitung zu wissenschaftlichen Beobachtungen auf Reisen ; mit besonderer Rücksicht auf die Bedürfnisse der kaiserlichen Marine verfasst von P. Ascherson. A. Bastian, &c. *Maps.* 8° *Berlin*, 1875

Neumayer, Prof. George. The same. In Einzel - Abhandlungen . . . herausgegeben von Dr G. Neumayer. 2nd edition. 2 vols. *Maps and illustrations.* 8° *Berlin*, 1888
—— *See* Leichhardt ; *also* Arctic, G, International Polar Observations : Appendix 2.

Neumayr, M. *See* Holub; Naumann, E.; *also* Victoria, D : Appendix 2.

Neuville, D., and C. Bréard. Les Voyages de Savorgnan de Brazza, 1875-82. *Portrait and map.* 8° *Paris*, 1884

" Neva." *See* d'Albertis ; Lisiansky.

Neves, José Accursio das. Considerações Politicas, e Commerciaes sobre os Descobrimentos, e Possessões dos Portuguezes na Africa e na Asia. 12° *Lisbon*, 1830

New, Rev. C. Life, Wanderings, and Labours in Eastern Africa ; with an Account of the first successful Ascent of the Equatorial Snow Mountain, Kilima Njaro, and Remarks upon East African Slavery. *Portrait, map, and plates.* Small 8° 1873

Newall, Major-General D. J. F. The Highlands of India Strategically Considered, with special reference to their Colonization as Reserve Circles, Military, Industrial, and Sanitary. *Map and illustrations.* 8° 1882
—— The same. Vol. 2 : being a Chronicle of Field Sports and Travel in India. *Illustrations.* 8° 1887

Newberie (or Newbery), John. *See* Gottfried ; Kerr, Vol. 7 ; Purchas, Vol. 2, Book 9 : Appendix 1.

Newberry, J. S. Reports on the Geology, Botany, and Zoology of Northern California and Oregon, made to the War Department. *Plates.* 4° *Washington*, 1857
—— The U.S. Sanitary Commission in the Valley of the Mississippi during the War of the Rebellion 1861-66. Final Report. 8° *Cleveland*, 1871
—— *See* United States, G, *c*, Surveys ; K, Ohio : Appendix 2.

Newbery, J. C. *See* Victoria, B ; Appendix 2.

Newbold, Capt. T. J. Political and Statistical Account of the British Settlements in the Straits of Malacca, viz., Pinang, Malacca, and Singapore ; with a History of the Malayan States of the Peninsula of Malacca. 2 vols. *Maps.* 8° 1839
—— On some Ancient Mounds of Scorious Ashes in Southern India. 8° N.P., N.D.
—— Mineral Resources of Southern India. 8° N.P., N.D.
—— On the Processes prevailing among the Hindus, and formerly among the Egyptians, of Quarrying and Polishing

Newbold, Capt. T. J.—*continued.* Granite, its Uses, &c. ; with a few Remarks on the tendency of this Rock in India to Separate by Concentric Exfoliation. 8° N.P., N.D.
—— On the Site of Hai, or Ai, a Royal City of the Canaanites ; with a Notice of those of Nob, Azmaveth, and other Cities of Benjamin, the "Mount of the Amalekites." &c. 8° N.P., N.D.
—— Visit from Wadi Tor to Gebel Nakus, or the Mountain of the Bell, Peninsula of Mount Sinai. 8° N.P., N.D.
—— *See* India, C, Geological Papers : Appendix 2.

Newcomb, Simon. On the Right Ascensions of the Equatorial Fundamental Stars and the Corrections necessary to Reduce the Right Ascensions of different Catalogues to a Mean Homogeneous System. 4° *Washington*, 1872
—— Researches on the Motion of the Moon. Part 1. Reduction and Discussion of Observations of the Moon before 1750. 4° *Washington*, 1878

Newland, H. Forest Scenes in Norway and Sweden : being Extracts from the Journal of a Fisherman. *Plates.* Small 8° 1854

Newland, S. The Far North Country. 8° *Adelaide*, 1887
—— The Parkengees, or Aboriginal Tribes on the Darling River. 8° *Adelaide*, 1889

Newlands, John A. R. On the Discovery of the Periodic Law, and on Relations among the Atomic Weights. *Tables.* 12° 1884

Newman, F. W. Essay towards a Grammar of the Berber Language. 8° 1836

Newman, J. Instructions necessary to be attended to in using the Standard or Portable Mountain Barometer. 8° 1841

Newport, Capt. Chr. *See* Gottfried ; Hakluyt, Vol. 4 ; Kerr, Vol. 9 : Appendix 1.

Newton, Sir C. T. On the Study of Archæology. 8° 1850
—— Travels and Discoveries in the Levant. 2 vols. *Maps and plates.* Large 8° 1865

Newton, Henry. *See* United States, G, *b*, Surveys : Appendix 2.

Newton, R. B. *See* Baron

Newton, Sir I. *See* Brennecke ; Varenius.

Newton, Professor A. *See* West India Islands : Appendix 2.

Newton, Dr Thomas. Life of himself [bound up with the Lives of Dr Zachary Pearce, Dr E. Pocock, and Rev. P. Skelton] 2 vols. 8° 1816

Ney, Napoléon. *See* Brazza.

Neyrat, Alexandre-Stanislas. L'Athos : Notes d'une excursion à la Presqu'île et à la Montagne des Moines. *Plates.* 12° *Paris*, 1880

Nibby, Antonio. Viaggio Antiquario ne' contorni di Roma. *Maps and plates.* 2 vols. 8° *Rome*, 1819
—— *See* Pausanius.

Nibby, Antoine. Itinéraire de Rome et de ses Environs. 11th edition. *Maps, plans, and plates.* 12° *Rome*, 1876

Niccolini, Ant. Tavola Metrica-Chronologica delle varie Altezze tracciate dalla Superficie del Mare fra la Costa di Amalfi ed il Promontorio di Gaeta, &c. 4* *Naples*, 1849

Nicholas, Sir Harris. The Chronology of History, containing Tables, Calculations, and Statements indispensable for Ascertaining the Dates of Historical Events, &c. New edition. 12° [1838]

Nicholas, J. Liddiard. Narrative of a Voyage to New Zealand in 1814-15, in company with the Rev. S. Marsden. 2 vols. *Maps and plates.* 8° 1817
—— *See* Eyriès, Vols. 5 and 6 : Appendix 1.

Nicholas, W. *See* Victoria Geological Survey : Appendix 2.

Nicholay, N. *See* Purchas, Vol. 2, Book 6 : Appendix 1.

Nicholls, C. F. Probability of a Deep Lead of Gold round Melbourne. 8* *Melbourne*, 1865

Nicholls, Capt. George. *See* Telford.

Nicholls, K., E. Arnold, and Col. J. A. Grant. Remarks on a Proposed Line of Telegraph overland from Egypt to the Cape of Good Hope. 8* ,1876

Nichols, Thomas. *See* Astley, Vol. 1 ; Allgemeine Historie, Vol. 2 : Appendix 1.

Nichols, W. *See* Kerr, Vol. 8 : Appendix 1.

Nicholson, Edward Byron, and Henry Yule. Jehan de Mandeville. 4* *Edinburgh*, 1883

Nicholson, G. Cambrian Traveller's Guide. 8° *Stourport*, 1808

Nicholson, H. A. *See* United States, G, a, Surveys : Appendix 2.

Nicholson, John. An Account of the Establishment of the Fatemite Dynasty in Africa, being the Annals of that Province from the year 290 of the Heg'ra to the year 300. Extracted from an ancient Arabic MS. ascribed to El Mas' ûdi . . . with an Introduction and Notes. 8° . *Bristol*, 1840

Nicholson, Prof. Shield. *See* White.

Nicol, James. *See* Murray, Hugh.

Nicol, James. The Climate of Llandudno. 2nd edition. *Illustrations.* 12* 1886

Nicol, John. *See* Purchas, Vol. 4, Book 6 : Appendix 1.

Nicol, William. On Fossil Woods from Newcastle, New South Wales. *Plate.* 8* *Edinburgh*, 1833
—— Observations on the Structure of Recent and Fossil Coniferæ. *Plates.* 8* *Edinburgh*, 1834

Nicolay, C. G. The Oregon Territory : a Geographical and Physical Account of that Country and its Inhabitants, with Outlines of its History and Discovery. *Map.* 18° 1846
—— Proposal to Establish a Missionary College on the North-West Coast of British America. 8* 1853
—— Principles of Physical Geography : being an Inquiry into Natural Phenomena and their Causes. *Maps and diagrams.* 8° 1858

Nicollet, J. N. Report intended to Illustrate a Map of the Hydrographical Basin of the Upper Mississippi River. 8° *Washington*, 1843

Nicolo, M. M. *See* Purchas, Vol. 3, Book 3 : Appendix 1.

Nicols, A. The Puzzle of Life, and How it has been put together. 2nd edition. *Plates.* Small 8° 1877

Nicolson, —. Essai sur l'Histoire Naturelle de St Domingue. *Plates.* 8° *Paris*, 1776

Nicolson, W. The English Historical Library, in Three Parts, giving a Short View and Character of most of our Historians either in Print or Manuscript ; with an Account of our Records, Law-Books, Coins, and other matters serviceable to the Undertakers of a General History of England. 2nd edition. Folio 1741

Nicuessa (or Nicueza), Diego de. *See* Gottfried ; Allgemeine Historie, Vol. 13 ; General Collection of Voyages, &c.; p. 610: Appendix 1.

Niebuhr, Carsten. Beschreibung von Arabien aus eigenen Beobachtungen und im Lande selbst gesammleten Nachrichten abgefasset. *Maps and plates.* 4° *Copenhagen*, 1772
—— Description de l'Arabie d'après les observations et recherches faites dans le pays même. 4° *Copenhagen*, 1773
—— Reisebeschreibung nach Arabien und andern umliegenden Ländern. *Maps and plates.* 4° *Copenhagen*, 1774
—— Voyage en Arabie et en d'autres pays circonvoisins, traduit de l'Allemand. 3 vols. *Maps and plates.* 4° *Amsterdam*, 1774-80
—— Travels through Arabia, and other Countries in the East. Translated into English by Robert Heron. 2 vols. *Map and plates.* 8° *Edinburgh*, 1792
—— Reisebeschreibung nach Arabien und andern umliegenden Ländern. Vol. 3. Reisen durch Syrien und Palästina, nach Cypern, und durch Kleinasien und die Türkey nach Deutschland und Dännemark ; mit Niebuhr's Astronomischen Beobachtungen und einigen kleineren Abhandlungen herausgegeben von J. R. Glover und J. Olshausen. *Maps and plates.* 4° . *Hamburg*, 1837

Niebuhr, Carsten. *See* Forskal, P.; *also* Pinkerton, Vol. 10 : Appendix 1.

Niederlein, Gustavo. *See* Argentine, D, Patagonia : Appendix 2.

Niel, O. Géographie de l'Algérie. 1. Géographie Physique, Agricole, Industrielle, et Commerciale. 12° *Bona*, 1876

Nielsen, Dr Yngvar. Handbook for Travellers in Norway. Translated from the Original Fourth Edition. *Maps.* 12° *Christiania*, 1886

Niemann, George. *See* Lanckorónski; *also* Turkey in Asia, A : Appendix 2.

Niemann, G. K. Bloemlezing uit Maleische Geschriften. 2 vols. 12° *The Hague*, 1870-71

—— Geschiedenis van Tanette. Boeginesche Tekst met Aanteekeningen . . . Feestgave ter gelegenheid van het zesde Internationale Congres der Orientalisten te Leiden. 8° *The Hague*, 1883

Nieuhoff, Jean. L'Ambassade de la Compagnie Orientale des Provinces Unies vers l'Empereur de la Chine, ou Grand Cam de Tartarie, faite par les Srs. Pierre de Goyer et Jacob de Keyser ; illustrée d'une tres-exacte Description des Villes, Bourgs, Villages, Ports de Mers, et autres Lieux plus considerables de la Chine . . . Mis en François . . . par Jean Le Carpentier. *Maps and plates.* Folio *Leyden*, 1665

—— Legatio Batavica, ad Magnum Tartariæ Chamum Sungteium, modernum Sinæ Imperatorem ; Historiarum Narratione, quæ Legatis in Provinciis Quantung, Kiangsi, Nanking, Xantung, Peking, et Aula Imperatoria ab anno 1655 ad annum 1657 obtigerunt, ut et ardua Sinensium in bello Tartarico fortuna, Provinciarum accurata Geographia, urbium delineatione, per Joannem Nieuhovium. Latinitate donata per G. Hornium. *Map and plates.* Folio *Amsterdam*, 1668

—— Het Gezandtschap der Neêrlandtsche Oost-Indische Compagnie, aan den Grooten Tartarischen Cham, den tegenwoordigen Keizer van China ; waar in de gedenkwaerdigste Geschiedenissen, die onder het Reizen door de Sineesche Landtschappen, Quantung, Kiangsi, Nanking, Xantung en Peking, en aan het Keizerlyke Hof te Peking, zedert den jaare 1655-57. Beneffens een naauwkeurige beschryvinge der Sineesche Steden, Dorpen, Regeering, Weetenschappen, Handwerken, &c., en oorlogen tegen de Tarters. Door Joan Nieuhof. *Plates.* Folio *Amsterdam*, 1693

—— *See* Astley, Vol. 3; Churchill, Vol. 2; Knox's New Collection, Vol. 2 : Pinkerton, Vol. 7; Allgemeine Historie, Vol. 5 : Appendix 1.

Nieuwpoort, C. *See* Newport, Capt. C.

Nikitin, Athanasius. *See* Hakluyt Soc. Publ., Vol. 22 : Appendix 1.

Nilsson, S. Petrificata Suecana Formationis Cretaceæ, descripta et iconibus illustrata. Pars Prior, Vertebrata et Mollusca sistens. *Plates.* Folio *Lund*, 1827

—— Skandinaviska Nordens Urinvånare, &c. *Plates.* 4° *Lund*, 1838-43

—— Report on the Primitive Inhabitants of Scandinavia. Translated from the Swedish, by Dr Norton Shaw. [2 *leaves.*] 8° 1848

Nimmo, J. The Proposed American Inter-oceanic Canal in its Commercial Aspects. 8° *Washington*, 1880

Nino, Alfonso. *See* Gottfried; Allgemeine Historie, Vol. 13; General Collection of Voyages, &c. : Appendix 1, p. 610.

Niox, G. Expédition du Mexique, 1861-67. Récit Politique et Militaire. 8°, and Atlas folio *Paris*, 1874

Nissen, Heinrich. Italische Landeskunde. Erster Band : Land und Leute. 8° *Berlin*, 1883

Nizza (or Nica), Marco da. *See* Pausanias ; *also* Burney, Vol. 1 ; Hakluyt, Vol. 3 ; Purchas, Vol. 4, Book 8 ; Ramusio, Vol. 3 : Appendix 1.

Nobile, Antonio. Modo di determinare le differenze di Longitudini Geografiche per via delle Stelle Cadenti. 4° *Naples*, 1840

—— Memoria sulle Maree del Golfo di Napoli. 4° *Naples*, 1841

—— Memoria sulle Stelle Cadenti. 4° *Naples*, 1841

Nobiling. Nachrichten über den Zustand des Rheinstroms innerhalb des Preussischen Gebietes und über die zu dessen Regulirung und weiterer Schiffbarmachung ausgeführten Bauwerke. *Map.* 4° *Berlin*, 1856

Noble, C. F. *See* Dalrymple, Repertory, Vol. 2.

Noble, Daniel. The Brain and its Physiology, a Critical Disquisition on the Methods of Determining the Relations subsisting between the Structure and Functions of the Encephalon. 8° 1846

Noble, Frederic Perry. Africa at the Columbian Exposition. (From *Our Day.*) 8* 1892

—— The Chicago Congress on Africa. (Extract from *Our Day.*) 8* 1893

Noble, James. Review of his Arabic Vocabulary and Index for Richardson's Arabic Grammar. *See* Miscellaneous, p. 769 : Appendix 2.

Noble, John. Descriptive Handbook of the Cape Colony, its condition and resources. *Map and plates.* 12°
Cape Town, 1875
—— South Africa, past and present; a short History of the European Settlements at the Cape. 12° 1877

—— History, Productions, and Resources of the Cape of Good Hope. *Maps and coloured illustrations.* 8° *Cape Town*, 1886
—— Illustrated Official Handbook of the Cape and South Africa: a *résumé* of the History, Conditions, Populations, Productions, and Resources of the several Colonies, States, and Territories. *Map and illustrations.* 8° *Cape Town*, 1893
—— *See* Fairbridge, C. A.

Nocentini, Lodovico. La Scoperta dell' America, attribuita ai Cinesi. [Extract from Proceedings of the Genoa Geographical Congress.] Large 8* 1892

Nodal, B. Garcia de and Gonçalo de. *See* Burney, Vol. 2; Callander, Vol. 2; Allgemeine Historie, Vol. 18: Appendix 1.

Noel, Hon. R. *See* Galton, Vacation Tourists.

Noel, S. B. J. Premier Essai sur le Département de la Seine Inférieure, contenant les Districts de Gournay, Neufchâtel, Dieppe, et Cany. 8° *Rouen*, 1795

Noël, O. Histoire du Commerce du Monde depuis les temps les plus reculés. 2 vols. *Maps and illustrations.* 4°
Paris, 1891-94

Nogueira, A. F. A Raça Negra. 8°
Lisbon, 1880

Noirot, Ernest. A Travers le Fouta Djallon et le Bambouc (Soudan occidental). Souvenirs de Voyage. *Map and illustrations.* 8° *Paris* [1884]

Nollet, Michael. Geography Epitomiz'd, in French and English: containing the Principles of Geography, the Use of Maps, and the Description of all Countries in the World, &c. 8° 1738

Nolloth, Capt. M. S. Notes during a Cruise in the Mozambique. 8* 1857
—— On the Submergence of the Atlantic Telegraph Cable. 8* 1858

Noort (or Van Noort), Oliver. *See* Burney, Vol. 2; Harris, Vol. 1; Kerr, Vol. 10; Laharpe, Vol. 15; Purchas, Vol. 1, Book 2; Allgemeine Historie, Vols. 11, 12: Appendix 1.

Norden, Fred. Lewis. Travels in Egypt and Nubia; translated and enlarged, with Observations from Ancient and Modern Authors, by P. Templeman. *Map and plates.* 8° 1757
—— Voyage d'Égypte et de Nubie. Nouvelle édition, &c., par L. Langlès. 3 vols. *Maps and plates.* 4° *Paris*, 1795

Nordenskiöld, Baron Adolf Erik. Geografisk och Geognostisk Beskrifning öfver Nordöstra Delarne af Spetsbergen och Hinlopen Strait. *Map.* 4*
Stockholm, 1863
—— Sketch of the Geology of Spitzbergen. 8* *Stockholm*, 1867
—— Redogörelse för en Expedition till Grönland, år 1870. *Maps and plate.* 8*
Stockholm, 1871
—— Redogörelse för den Svenska Polarexpeditionen, år 1872-73. *Maps.* 8*
Stockholm, 1875
—— The Arctic Voyages of, 1858-79. *Maps and illustrations.* 8° 1879
—— Sur la Possibilité de la Navigation Commerciale dans la Mer Glaciale de Sibérie. 8* *Stockholm*, 1880
—— The Voyage of the "Vega" round Asia and Europe; with a Historical Review of previous Journeys along the North Coast of the Old World. Translated by Alexander Leslie. 2 vols. *Portraits, maps, and illustrations.* 8° 1881
—— "Vega"- Expeditionens Vetenskapliga Iakttagelser Bearbetade af Deltagare i resan och andra forskare. Vols. 1-5. *Maps and illustrations.* Large 8°
Stockholm, 1882-87
—— Om Bröderna Zenos Resor och de äldsta Kartor öfver Norden. *Maps and facsimile.* Large 8* *Stockholm*, 1883
—— Den Svenska Expeditionen till Grönland år 1883. 8* *Stockholm*, 1883
—— Om en Märklig Globkarta från början af sextonde seklet. *Facsimiles.* 8° *Stockholm*, 1884
—— Studien und Forschungen veranlasst durch meine Reisen im hohen Norden. Herausgegeben von Adolf Erik Freiherrn von Nordenskiöld. Ein populärwissenschaftliches Supplement zu die Umsegelung Asiens und Europas auf der "Vega." *Maps and illustrations.* 8° *Leipzig*, 1885
—— Grönland. Seine Eiswüsten im Innern und seine Ostküste. Schilderung der zweiten Dicksonschen Expedition ausgeführt im Jahre 1883. *Maps and illustrations.* 8° *Leipzig*, 1886
—— Den första på verkliger iakttagelser Grundade Karta öfver norra Asien. *Maps.* 8* [*Stockholm*, 1887]
—— La Seconde Expédition Suédoise au Grönland (l'Inlandsis et la Côte Orientale). Entreprise aux frais de M. Oscar Dickson, traduite du Suédois avec l'Autorisation de l'auteur par Charles Rabot. *Maps and illustrations.* Large 8°
Paris, 1888
—— Utkast till en Svensk Antarktisk Expedition. 8* 1890
—— *See* Dunér; Rosny; *also* United States, A, e, Navigation: Appendix 2.

Nordenskiöld, G. Redogörelse för den Svenska Expeditionen till Spetsbergen, 1890. *Plates.* 8*   *Stockholm*, 1892
—— The Cliff Dwellers of the Mesa Verde, South-Western Colorado ; their Pottery and Implements. Translated by D. Lloyd Morgan. *Plans, plates, &c..* 4°   *Chicago*, 1893
Nordenskiold, N. Beitrag zur Kenntniss der Schrammen in Finnland. *Map and plate.* 4*   *Helsingfors*, 1863
Nordenskiöld, Otto. *See* Sweden, A, Geologiska Undersökning : Appendix 2.
Nordhoff, C. Northern California, Oregon, and the Sandwich Islands. *Map and plates.* 8°   1874
Nordhoff, J. B. *See* Germany, C, Forschungen, &c., Vol. 4 : Appendix 2.
Norfolk, Duke of. *See* Hakluyt's Voyages, Vol. 2 : Appendix 1.
Norie, J. W. Guide du Marin et du Caboteur sur les Côtes est de la Mer du Nord depuis le Cap Grisnez jusqu'au nord du Danemark, sur les Côtes de la Mer Baltique, sur les Côtes ouest de Norwége et sur celles de la Mer Blanche. Traduit par P. Guéry. 8°   *Paris*, 1863
—— A Complete Epitome of Practical Navigation, containing all necessary Instruction for keeping a Ship's Reckoning at Sea. Augmented and improved, and adapted to the New Nautical Almanac, by Arthur B. Martin. *Maps and plates.* 8°   1864
Norman, B. W. Rambles in Yucatan, or Notes of Travel through the Peninsula, including a visit to the remarkable Ruins of Chi-Chen, Kabah, Zayi, and Uxmal. *Map and plates.* 8°   *New York*, 1843
Norman, C. B. Armenia, and the Campaign of 1877. *Maps and plans.* 8°   [1878]
—— Colonial France. *Map.* 8°   1886
Norman, Henry. The Real Japan : Studies of Contemporary Japanese Manners, Morals, Administration, and Politics. *Illustrations.* 8°   1892 [1891]
Norman, John Henry. A Colloquy upon the Science of Money. 8*   1889
—— Norman's Single Grain System for determining the par value of all Moneys of Account, and Gold and Silver Coins, between all Countries ; also for ascertaining the Comparative Weights of fine Gold or Silver, indicated by relative Prices throughout the World. 8*   1887
—— Local Dual Standards : Gold and Silver Standard Currencies ; the Exchanges brought within the comprehension of all. 4*   N.D.
—— John Henry Norman, Esq. Reprinted (by permission) from the *Bankers' Magazine*, February 1890. *Portrait.* 8*   1890
—— *See* Sharland.

Norman, J. M. Quelques Observations de Morphologie Végétale faites au Jardin Botanique de Christiania. *Plates.* 4*   *Christiania*, 1857
Norman, Capt. W. H., and Capt. Thomas Musgrave. Journals of the Voyage and Proceedings of H.M.C.S. "Victoria" in search of Shipwrecked People at the Auckland and other Islands. *Map.* 8*   *Melbourne* [1865]
Normann, C. Oplyminger om Beseilingen af Arsuk-Fjorden i Syd-Grönland. 8°   *Copenhagen*, 1866
Noronha, Garcia de. *See* Gottfried : Appendix 1.
Norris, Lieut. J. A. *See* United States, E, a, Navigation : Appendix 2.
Nort, Olivier du. Description du Penible Voyage fait entour de l'Univers . . . par Sr. Olivier du Nort d'Utrecht . . . pour traversant le Destroict de Magellanes, descouvrir les Costes de Cica, Chili, et Peru, . . . y puis passant les Molucques, et circomnavigant le Globe du Monde, &c. *Maps and plans.* 4°   *Amsterdam*, 1610
North, Frederic W. *See* British South Africa, E : Appendix 2.
North, Marianne. Recollections of a Happy Life : being the Autobiography of Marianne North. 2nd edition. 2 vols. 8°   1892
North, S. N. D. *See* United States, A, Tenth Census, 1880, Vol. 8 : Appendix 2.
Northleigh, J. Observations made in Two Voyages through most parts of Europe. 8°   1720
—— *See* Harris, Vol. 2 : Appendix 1.
Norton, C. L. A Handbook of Florida. *Maps and plans.* 12°   1891
Norwood, Col. R. *See* Churchill, Vol. 6 : Purchas, Vol. 4, Book 9 : Appendix 1.
Nöschel, A. Bemerkungen über die naturhistorischen, insbesondere die geognostisch-hydrographischen Verhältnisse der Steppe zwischen den Flüssen Or und Turgai, Kumak, und Syr-Darja. Mit einem Vorwort von G. v. Helmersen. *Map.* 8*   *St Petersburg*, 1854
—— *See* Baer and Helmersen, 18.
Nostitz, Countess. *See* Helfer, J. W.
Nott, John. Hafiz : Select Odes, translated into English Verse ; with Notes, Critical and Explanatory. 4°   1787
Nott, Samuel. Slavery and the Remedy; or, Principles and Suggestions for a Remedial Code, with a Reply and Appeal to European Advisers. 8°   *Boston, Mass.*, 1859
Nottage, Charles G. In Search of a Climate. *Illustrations.* Large 8°   1894 [1893]

Nourse, Prof. J. E. The Maritime Canal of Suez : Brief Memoir of the Enterprise from its Earliest Date, and comparison of its probable results with those of a Ship Canal across Darien. *Maps and plate.* 8* *Washington,* 1870

—— Reports of Foreign Societies on awarding Medals to the American Arctic Explorers, Kane, Hayes, Hall. *Plate.* 8* [*Washington*] 1876

—— The Maritime Canal of Suez, from its Inauguration 17th November 1869 to the year 1884. *Charts and plates.* 8° *Washington,* 1884

—— *See* Hall, C. F.

Noury, Vice - Admiral Baron de la Roncière de. Notice Biographique, par Alfred de Jancigny. *Portrait.* 8* *Evreux,* 1881

Nova (or Nueva), Juan de. *See* Astley, Vol. 1 ; Allgemeine Historie, Vol. 1 ; Gottfried : Appendix 1.

"Novara." Reise der Oesterreichischen Fregatte "Novara" um die Erde, in den Jahren 1857, 1858, 1859, unter den Befehlen des Commodore B. von Wüllerstorf-Urbair. 3 vols. *Maps and plates.* Large 8° *Vienna,* 1861-62

—— **Official Publications** connected with the Voyage of the "Novara." 4° Medizinischer Theil. Von Eduard Schwarz. *Map and plates* 1861
Nautisch-Physicalischer Theil. *Plates and charts* 1862-5
Statistisch - commercieller Theil von Dr Karl von Scherzer. Bd. 1. *Maps* 1864

—— The same. Bd. 2. *Maps* 1865
Geologischer Theil. Bd. 1. Abtheilung 1. Geologie von Neu-Seeland. Beiträge zur Geologie der Provinzen Auckland und Nelson, von Dr Ferdinand von Hochstetter. *Map and plates* 1864

—— The same. Abtheilung 2. Paläontologie von Neu-Seeland. Beiträge zur Kenntniss der fossilen Flora und der Provinzen Auckland und Nelson, von F. Unger, Karl Zittel, E. Suess; Felix Karrer, F. Stoliczka, G. Stache, und Gustav Jaeger, redigirt von F. von Hochstetter, Moriz Hörnes, und Franz Ritter von Hauer. *Plates* 1864

—— Bd. 2, von F. von Hochstetter, A. E. Reuss, und C. Schwager. *Plates.* 1866
Linguistischer Theil, von Dr Friedrich Müller. 1867
Anthropologischer Theil. Erste Abtheilung von E. Zuckerkandl. Zweiter Abtheilung. Körpermessungen, an Individuen verschiedenen Menschenracen vorgenommen durch

"Novara." Official Publications—Anthropologischer Theil—*continued.*
Dr Karl Scherzer und Dr E. Schwarz, bearbeitet von Dr A. Weisbach. *Tables.* Dritte Abtheilung. Ethnographie, auf Grund des von Dr Karl Scherzer gesammelten Materials bearbeitet von Dr F. Müller. *Photographs and map* 1868-75
Zoologischer Theil. Bd. 1. (Wirbelthiere.) Säugethiere, von J. Zelebor ; Vögel, von A. v. Pelzeln ; Reptilien und Amphibien, von F. Steindachner; Fische, von R. Kner. *Plates* 1869

—— Bd. 2, Abtheilung 1 :—A. Coleoptera, von L. Redtenbacher ; Hymenoptera, von H. de Saussure und J. Sichel ; Formicidæ, von G. L. Mayr ; Neuroptera, von F. Brauer. *Plates.* 1868. B. Diptera, von J. R. Schiner ; Hemiptera, von G. L. Mayr. *Plates* 1868

—— The same. Abth. 2 :—Lepidoptera, von Cajetan Felder und Rudolf Felder. Text. 1864-67. Atlas, von Cajetan Felder, Rudolf Felder, und A. F. Rogenhofer. 2 vols. 1864-67

—— The same. Abth. 3 :—Crustaceen, von C. Heller. *Plates* 1865
Botanischer Theil. Bd. 1. Sporenpflanzen, von A. Grunow, J. Krempelhuber, H. W. Reichardt, G. Mettenius, J. Milde, redigirt von Eduard Fenzl. *Plates* 1870

—— *See* Scherzer.

Novikoff, Madame Olga. *See* Windt.

Novo y Colson, Pedro de. Historia de las Exploraciones Articas hechas en busca del Paso del Nordeste. *Map and portrait.* 8° *Madrid,* 1880

Nowak, Alois. Offenes Schreiben an den Hon. Captain Wilson, derzeit in Palästina. 8* *Prague,* 1866

Nowel, T. *See* Pelham, Vol. 2 : Appendix 1.

Nowrojee, Jehangeer, and Hirjeebhoy Merwanjee. Journal of a Residence of Two Years and a Half in Great Britain. 8° 1841

Nozhet-Elhâdi. Histoire de la Dynastie Saadienne au Maroc (1511-1670), par Mohammed Esseghir Ben Elhadj Ben Abdallah Eloufrâni. Texte Arabe publié Par O Houdas. (IIIe Series. Vols. 2 and 3 of Publications de l'École des Langues Orientales Vivantes.) 2 vols. Large 8° *Paris,* 1888

Nueva, Juan de. *See* Nova.

Nugent, Dr Thomas. The Grand Tour, or a Journey through the Netherlands, Germany, Italy, and France ; to which is added the "European Itinerary." 4 vols. 12° 1778

Nugent, Dr Thomas. *See* "The Modern Traveller," Vol. 4, p. 610: Appendix 1.
Nugnez von Vela, B. *See* Allgemeine Historie, Vol. 15: Appendix 1.
Nunes, J. C. Formulario dos Medicamentos para os Hospitaes da Provincia de S. Thomé e Principe. 8°
Lisbon, 1874
Nunez, Alvaro. *See* Cabeza de Vaca.
Nuñez, Ricardo, and Henry Jalhay. La République de Colombie : Géographie, Histoire, Organisation Politique, Agriculture, Commerce, Industrie, Statistique, Tarif douanier, Indicateur Commerciel, &c. *Map.* Large 8°
Brussels, 1893
Nunnes (or Nunnez, or Nonius), M. *See* Purchas, Vol. 2, Book 7; Allgemeine Historie, Vol. 13 : Appendix 1.
Nursingrow, A. V. G. V. Juggarow Observatory, Daba Gardens, Vizagapatam. Results of Meteorological Observations, 1887, with an Introduction. *Plates.* 12*   *Calcutta*, 1888
—— The same, 1889, with an Introduction. 12*   *Calcutta*, 1890
—— The same, 1890, with an Introduction. 12*   *Calcutta*, 1891
—— The same, 1891, with an Introduction. *Portraits.* 12*   *Calcutta*, 1892
Nyáry, Báró Albert. A heraldika Vezérfonala. 4°   *Budapest*, 1886
Nylander, Gustavus Reinhold. Grammar and Vocabulary of the Bullom Language. 12°   1814
Nyrén, M. Die Polhöhe von Pulkowa. 4*   *St Petersburg*, 1873
Nystrom, J. G. Informe al Supremo Gobierno del Peru sobre una Espedicion al interior de la República. *Maps.* 8*
Lima, 1868

O

Oakes, Lieut. R. F. Survey Report of the Northern Portion of the Pegu District, 1856. [From the Indian Records, No. 15.] Royal 8°   *Calcutta*, 1856
Oates, Frank. Matabele Land and the Victoria Falls : a Naturalist's Wanderings in the Interior of South Africa. From the Letters and Journals of the late Frank Oates, edited by C. G. Oates. *Maps, portrait, and plates.* 8°   1881
Oband, Nicholas de. *See* Gottfried : Appendix 1.
Ober, Frederick A. Camps in the Caribbees : the Adventures of a Naturalist in the Lesser Antilles. *Illustrations.* 8°
Edinburgh, 1880
—— Travels in Mexico and Life among the Mexicans. 1. Yucatan. 2. Central and Southern Mexico. 3. The Border States. *Maps and illustrations.* 8°
Boston, Mass., 1884

Ober, P. Interlaken et ses Environs. 12°
Berne, 1857
Oberlin, H. G. Propositions Géologiques du Ban de la Roche. *Illustrations.* 4°
Strasburg, 1806
O'Brien, H. de Lacy. Banking in Persia. 8*   1868
—— Ditto. Another edition. 8*   1873
O'Brien, Patrick. Journal of a Residence in the Danubian Principalities, in the Autumn and Winter of 1853. 12°   1854
O'Brien, —. *See* Cameron, V. I.
O'Byrne, William R. A Naval Biographical Dictionary, comprising the Life and Services of every living Officer in H.M. Navy, from the Rank of Admiral of the Fleet to that of Lieutenant inclusive. 8°   1849
O'Callaghan, E. A. Remonstrance of New Netherland, and the Occurrences there : addressed to the High and Mighty Lords States-General of the United Netherlands, on the 28th July 1649; with Secretary Van Tienhoven's Answer. Translated from the Original Dutch MS. by E. A. O'Callaghan. 4°
Albany, N.Y., 1856
O'Callaghan, E. B. Documentary History of the State of New York ; arranged under direction of the Hon. Christopher Morgan. 4 vols. *Maps and plates.* 8°
Albany, N.Y., 1850
Ocampo, Gonzale d', and Sebastian d' Ocampo. *See* Gottfried ; Allgemeine Historie, Vol. 13; "A General Collection of Voyages," p. 610: Appendix 1.
Occum Chamnam. *See* Allgemeine Historie, Vol. 10: Appendix 1.
Ochoa, C. Olloba d'. *See* Pemberton.
Ockley, Simon. An Account of South-West Barbary, containing what is most Remarkable in the Territories of the King of Fez and Morocco ; written by a Person who had been a Slave there a considerable time, and published from an Authentick Manuscript, &c. Two letters. *Map.* 12*   1713
Octher or Othere. *See* Hakluyt, Vol. 1 ; Kerr, Vol. 1 : Appendix 1.
O'Curry, J. E. *See* Popper.
O'Donovan, Edmond. The Merv Oasis : Travels and Adventures east of the Caspian during the years 1879-80-81, including Five Months' Residence among the Tekkes of Merv. 2 vols. *Portrait, map, facsimiles of documents.* 8°   1882
Odoric de Pordenone [or Odoricus Beatus, or Oderic of Portenau, or Oderico de Udine]. Les Voyages en Asie au XIVe Siècle du Bienheureux Frère Odoric de Pordenone, Religieux de Saint-François, publiées avec une Introduction et des Notes par Henri Cordier. [Recueil de Voyages et de Documents pour servir a l'Histoire de la Géographie depuis le

Odoric de Pordenone—*continued.*
XIIIe jusqu'à la fin du XVIe Siècle publié sous la direction de MM. Ch. Schefer et Henri Cordier. 10.] *Facsimiles, &c.* Large 8° *Paris*, 1891
—— *See* Hakluyt, Vol. 2 ; Kerr, Vol. 1 ; Ramusio, Vol. 2 : Appendix 1.

Oehlschlaeger, Emil. Posen : Kurz gefasste Geschichte und Beschreibung der Stadt Posen : ein illustrirter Führer für Einheimische und Fremde. *Plan.* 8° *Posen*, 1866

Oelsnitz. *See* Lankenau.

Œrsted, Prof., Biography of. 8* 1872

Oesterley, Dr Hermann. Historisch-geographisches Wörterbuch des Deutschen Mittelalters. Large 8° *Gotha*, 1883

Oexmelin, Alexandre Olivier. Histoire des Aventuriers Flibustiers, qui se sont signalés dans les Indes, 3 vols. ; Vol. 3 contient Le journal du voyage fait à la Mer du Sud, par le Sieur Raveneau de Lussan. 12° *Lyons*, 1774

Ogawa, K. *See* Milne and Burton.

Ogilby, John. Africa : being an Accurate Description of the Religions of Ægypt, Barbary, Lybia, and Billedulgerid, the Land of Negroes, Guinee, Æthiopia, and the Abyssines, with all the adjacent Islands, either in the Mediterranean, Atlantick, Southern, or Oriental Sea, &c. *Maps and plates.* Folio 1670
—— America : being the latest and most Accurate Description of the New World, containing the Original of the Inhabitants, and the remarkable Voyages thither ; the Conquest of the vast Empires of Mexico and Peru, and other large Provinces and Territories, with the several European Plantations in those parts . . . and a Survey of what hath been discovered of the Unknown South-Land and the Arctick Region. *Maps and plates.* Folio 1671
—— Asia : the first part, being an Accurate Description of Persia and the several Provinces thereof, the vast Empire of the Great Mogol, and other parts of India, &c. *Plates.* Folio 1673
—— Britannia, or the Kingdom of England and Dominion of Wales actually surveyed, with a Geographical and Historical Description of the Principal Roads. 100 *Maps.* Folio 1698
—— *See* Montanus ; Owen, J.

Ogilvie, Dr Maria M. Contributions to the Geology of the Wengen and St Cassian Strata in Southern Tyrol. (From *Journal Geological Society*, Vol. 49.) *Maps and sections.* 8* 1893

Ogilvie, William. Exploratory Survey of Part of the Lewes, Tat-on-duc, Porcupine, Bell, Trout, Peel, and Mackenzie Rivers, 1887-88. 8* *Ottawa*, 1890

Ogilvy, John. An Account of Bermuda, Past and Present. Compiled and summarised from numerous sources, with Original Observations. 8* *Hamilton, Bermuda*, 1883

Ogilvy, T. Miscellaneous Information relative to Kutch, furnished by his Highness the Rao. [Bombay Records, No. 15, N.S.] Royal 8° *Bombay*, 1855
—— Statement showing the Names of the Rewa Kanta Tributaries and the Fortified Places. [Bombay Records, No. 23, N.S.] *Map.* Royal 8° *Bombay*, 1856
—— Report on the Revenue, Resources, &c., of the lapsed Satara Territory, with Extracts from Reports on the same subject, by Lieuts. H. B. Sandford and A. C. Parr ; to which is added a Report, dated August 1851, by Mr George Vary, of the Measures adopted by him for improving the Cleaning of Native Cotton, and for introducing the Cultivation of New Orleans Cotton into the Satara Districts. [Bombay Records, No. 41, N.S.] Royal 8° *Bombay*, 1857
—— Memoir on the Satara Territory. [Bombay Records, No. 41, N.S.] Royal 8° *Bombay*, 1857

Ogle, Nathaniel. The Colony of Western Australia : a Manual for Emigrants to that Settlement or its Dependencies, with an Appendix. *Map and plates.* 8° 1839

Ohrling, Joh. *See* Ihre.

Ohrwalder, Father Joseph. *See* Wingate.

O'Jeda, Alonso d'. *See* Gottfried ; Allgemeine Historie, Vol. 13 ; A General Collection of Voyages, &c. : Appendix 1.

Olafsen and Povelsen. *See* Phillips, Collection of Modern and Contemporary Voyages [1], Vol. 2 : Appendix 1.

Olascoago, M. J. Estudio Topografico de la Pampa y Rio Negro : comprende el itinerario de todas las columnas de operaciones que ocuparon el Desierto y clevaron la línea de frontera sobre dicho Rio. *Map and plates.* 4° *Buenos Ayres*, 1880
—— La Conquête de la Pampa : Recueil des documents relatifs à la Campagne du Rio Negro. . . . Précéde d'une Étude Topographique par Manuel J. Olascoaga ; suivi du Rapport du Général Villegas sur l'Expédition à Nahuel-Huapi, et d'une Notice sur l'importance des territoires de la Pampa et du Limay. *Map.* Large 8° *Buenos Ayres*, 1881

Olaus Magnus. *See* Brenner, O.

Oldfield, Capt. J. R. Letters on the Breakwater in the Jumna, at Agra, 1847 and 1848. [From the India Records, Vol 2, N.W. Prov.] Folio 1855

Oldfield, R. A. K. *See* Laird, M.

Oldham, C. F. Notes on the lost River of the Indian Desert. *Map.* 8* [1874]

Oldham, H. Yule. The Discovery of the Cape Verde Islands. (Reprint from the von Richthofen Festschrift.) 4* 1892

Oldham, R. D. On Probable Changes in the Geography of the Punjab and its Rivers: an Historico - Geographical Study. *Map.* 8* *Calcutta*, 1887

—— A Bibliography of Indian Geology : being a List of Books and Papers relating to the Geology of British India and adjoining Countries published previous to the end of 1887. 8* *Calcutta*, 1888

—— A Manual of the Geology of India, chiefly compiled from the Observations of the Geological Survey. Stratigraphical and Structural Geology. 2nd edition. *Map and plates.* Large 8° *Calcutta*, 1893

Oldham, T. *See* India, C, Palæontologia Indica : Appendix 2.

Oldham, W. Historical and Statistical Memoir of the Ghazeepoor District. Part 1. *Maps and plates.* Folio *Allahabad*, 1870

"Old Shekarry." *See* Levison.

Olearius, Adam. The Voyages and Travels of the Ambassadors sent by Frederick Duke of Holstein to the great Duke of Muscovy and the King of Persia, begun in the year MDCXXXIII. and finished in MDCXXXIX., containing a compleat History of Muscovy, Tartary, Persia, and other adjacent countries . . ; whereto are added the Travels of John Albert de Mandelslo from Persia into the East Indies, containing a Particular Description of Indosthan, the Mogul's Empire, the Oriental Islands, Japan, China, &c., . . . faithfully rendered into English by John Davies of Kidwelly. *Maps and plates.* Small folio 1662

—— Voyages très-curieux et très-renommez faits en Moscovie, Tartarie, et Perse . . . Traduits de l'Original et Augmentez par le Sr. de Wicquefort. . . . [New edition.] 2 vols. in 1. *Maps and plates.* Folio *Amsterdam*, 1727

—— *See* Mandelslo.

Oliff, A. S. *See* New South Wales, B : Appendix 2.

Oliphant, J. E. Notes connected with the Estate of Cambay, in the Kaira Collectorate. *Map.* [From the India Records, No. 26.] Royal 8° *Bombay*, 1856

Oliphant, Laurence A Journey to Katmandu, the Capital of Nepaul, with the Camp of Jung Bahadoor ; including a Sketch of the Nepaulese Ambassador at Home. *Map.* 8° 1852

—— The Russian Shores of the Black Sea in 1852 ; with a Voyage down the Volga, and a Tour through the Country of the Don Cossacks. *Maps and plates.* 8° 1854

—— The Coming Campaign. 8* 1855

—— Minnesota and the Far West. *Maps and woodcuts.* 8° 1855

Oliphant, Laurence. The Trans-Caucasian Campaign of the Turkish Army under Omer Pasha. *Maps and plates.* 8° 1856

—— Narrative of the Earl of Elgin's Mission to China and Japan in 1857-59. 2 vols. *Maps and plates.* 8° *Edinburgh*, 1859

—— On the Bayanos River, Isthmus of Panama. *Map.* 8* 1865

—— African Explorers. *Maps.* 8* *Boston, Mass.*, 1877

—— The Land of Gilead, with Excursions in the Lebanon. *Maps and plates.* 8° 1880

—— The Land of Khemi : Up and Down the Middle Nile. *Plates.* 8° 1882

—— Haifa ; or, Life in Modern Palestine. 8° 1887

—— Episodes in a Life of Adventure ; or, Moss from a Rolling Stone. 8° 1887

—— *See* Schumacher ; *also* Blackwood, Vols. 1, 2, and 6 : Appendix 1.

Oliphant, Mrs. *See* Blackwood, Vol. 6 : Appendix 1.

Oliveira, Benjamin. A Few Observations upon the Works of the Isthmus of Suez Canal made during a Visit in 1863. 8* 1863

—— Letters upon the Capabilities of the Island of Teneriffe as a Winter Residence, and the Climate and General History of the Island of Madeira. 8* 1864-65

—— A Visit to the Spanish Camp in Morocco during the late War. 8* *Privately printed*, 1865

Oliver, D. Flora of Tropical Africa : Vol. 1. Ranunculaceæ to Connaraceæ ; Vol. 2. Leguminosæ to Ficoideæ ; Vol. 3. Umbelliferæ to Ebenaceæ. 8° 1868-77

Oliver, Edward E. Across the Border ; or, Pathân and Biloch. *Maps and illustrations.* 8° 1890

Oliver, Lieut.-Col. J. R. A Course of Practical Astronomy for Surveyors ; with the Elements of Geodesy. 8° *Kingston*, 1883

Oliver, Capt. S. P. Madagascar and the Malagasy ; with Sketches in the Provinces of Tamatave, Betanimena, and Ankova. *Plates.* 8° [1865]

—— Les Hovas et autres Tribus caractéristiques de Madagascar. 8* *Guernsey*, 1869

—— The Dolmen-Mounds and Amorpholithic Monuments of Brittany. 8* 1872

—— The True Story of the French Dispute in Madagascar. *Map.* 8° 1885

—— Madagascar, an Historical and Descriptive Account of the Island and its Former Dependencies. 2 vols. *Maps and plates.* 8° 1886

—— Madagascar ; or, Robert Drury's Journal, during Fifteen Years' Captivity on that Island ; and a Further Description of Madagascar by the Abbé Alexis

Oliver, Capt. C. P.—*continued.*
Rochon. Edited, with an Introduction and Notes, by Captain Pasfield Oliver, R.A. *Maps and illustrations.* 8° 1890
—— *See* Hakluyt Soc. Publ., Vols. 82, 83: Appendix 1.
Oliver and Boyd's Pronouncing Gazetteer of the World, Descriptive and Statistical, with Etymological Notices ; being a Geographical Dictionary for Popular Use ; with Atlas of 32 maps. Small 8°
Edinburgh, 1879
Olivier, Aimé, Vicomte de Sanderval. De l'Atlantique au Niger par le Foutah-Djallon. *Map and plates.* 8° *Paris*, 1882
Olivier, J. Taereelen en Merkwaardigheden uit Oost-Indië. Deel I. *Plates.* 8°
Amsterdam, 1836
Olivier, ——. *See* Eyriès, Vol. 14 : Appendix 1.
Ollive, C. Climat de Mogador et de son Influence sur la Phthisie. 8* *Paris*, 1875
Olmsted, Denison. Address on the Scientific Life and Labours of William C. Redfield. *Portrait.* 8*
New Haven, Conn., 1857
Olmsted, Fred. Law. Journey in the Seaboard Slave States ; with Remarks on their Economy. 8° 1856
—— A Journey in the Back Country. 8° 1860
—— Journeys and Explorations in the Cotton Kingdom,&c. 2vols. in 1. 8° 1861
Olsen, O. T. The Fisherman's Practical Navigator. *Map and plates.* 8°
Grimsby, 1878
—— The Fisherman's Nautical Almanac, 1880, 1881, 1882, 1885, 1888, 1890, 1892, and 1893. *Map.* Small 8°
Olshaussen, J. *See* Niebuhr, C.
Olsvig, V. *See* Beyer's Guide to Western Norway.
Oltmanus, Jabbo. *See* Humboldt and Bonpland.
Omārah Al-Hakami, Najm Ad-Din. Yaman, its Early Mediæval History; also the Abridged History of its Dynasties by Ibn Khaldūn, and an Account of the Karmathians of Yaman by Abu 'Abd Allah Baha Ad-din Al-Janadi. The Original Texts, with Translation and Notes, by Henry Cassels Kay. *Map.* 8° 1892
Ommanney, Admiral Sir E. Hydrographical Remarks on the White Sea, in the Summer of 1854. 8* 1855
Ommanney, Lieut. ——. Synopsis of the Cruises of H.M.S. "Espiegle," for 1881 to 1885. 8* *Devonport*, N.D.
Onate, Juan de. *See* Toletus, in Purchas, Vol. 4, Book 8 : Appendix 1.
O'Neill, Henry E. Letter to Earl Granville regarding a Visit to the District of Angoche, Mozambique. Folio* 1881
—— The Mozambique and Nyassa Slave Trade. 8* 1885

O'Neill, T. Sketches of African Scenery from Zanzibar to the Victoria Nyanza : being a Series of Coloured Lithographic Pictures from Original Sketches, by the late Mr Thomas O'Neill, of the Victoria Nyanza Mission of the Church Missionary Society. 4* 1878
Ong-tae-hae. The Chinaman Abroad, or a Desultory Account of the Malayan Archipelago, particularly of Java. By Ong-tae-hae. Translated from the Original. [No. 2 of the *Chinese Miscellany.*] *Map.* Small 8* *Shanghai*, 1849
Onwhyn's Guide to North and South Wales and the Wye. *Plates.* 12° 1853
Oppel, Dr A. Terra incognita : eine kurzgefasste Darstellung der stufenweisen Entwickelung der Erdkenntnis vom Ausgange des Mittelalters bis zur Gegenwart und der derzeitigen Ausdehnung der unerforschten Gebiete. *Maps.* 8* *Bremen*, 1891
Oppelt, Gustave. Navigation aérienne par les Ballons ; Point d'appui, Appareil de direction, Système Oppelt. 8*
Brussels, 1882
Oppert, E. A Forbidden Land : Voyages to the Corea ; with an Account of its Geography, History, Productions, and Commercial capabilities, &c. *Charts and plates.* 8° 1880
Oppert, Gustav. Der Presbyter Johannes in Sage und Geschichte : ein Beitrag zur Voelker- und Kirchenhistorie und zur Heldendichtung des Mittelalters. 8°
Berlin, 1864
Oppert, J. Les Inscriptions Assyriennes des Sargonides et les Fastes de Ninive. 8* *Versailles*, 1862
Orbegozo, Juan de. Reconocimiento del Istmo de Tehuantepec en 1825. 12*
Jalapa, 1831
Orbigny, A. d'. *See* D'Orbigny.
Orcutt, Rev. J. African Colonisation. 8*
New York, N.D.
Ord, H. St. G. Report on Condition of the British Settlements on the West Coast of Africa. [Parly. Rep.] *Maps.* Folio* 1865
Ordoñez y Aguiar, Ramon de. Historia de la Creacion del Cielo, y de la Tierra conforme al Sistema de la Gentilidad Americana ; Theologia de los Culebras, Figurada en ingeniosos Geroglíphicos, Simbolos, Emblemas, y Metaphoras ; Diluvio Universal, Dispersion de las Gentes, verdadéro orígen de los Indios, su salida de Chaldea, su transmigracion á estas partes Septentrionales. . . . MS. Folio 1796
O'Reilly, Comm. Twelve Views in the Black Sea and the Bosphorus, from Sketches made on the spot during the period of service of H.M.S. "Retribution," with a short Account of each Drawing. Folio 1856

O'Reilly, J. P. Explanatory Notes and Discussion of the Nature of the Prismatic Forms of a Group of Columnar Basalts, Giant's Causeway. *Plates.* 4* *Dublin*, 1879

—— On the Correlation of Lines of Direction on the Earth's Surface. 4* *Dublin*, 1879

Orellana, Franciso de. *See* Hakluyt Soc. Publ., Vol. 24 : Appendix 1.

O'Riley, E. Journal of a Tour east from Tounghoo to the Salween River. [From the India Records, No. 20.] Royal 8° *Calcutta*, 1856

—— Notices on Karen Nee, the Country of the "Kaya," or Red Karens, 1857. [From the India Records, No. 24.] Royal 8° *Calcutta*, 1858

Orléans, Prince Henri d'. De Paris au Tonkin par terre. (From *Revue des Deux Mondes*.) *Map.* 8* 1891

—— *See* Bonvalot.

Orléans, Père Pierre Joseph d'. *See* Hakluyt Soc. Publ., Vol. 17 ; Allgemeine Historie, Vol. 18 : Appendix 1.

Orlich, Capt. Leopold von. Travels in India, including Sinde and the Punjab. Translated by H. E. Lloyd. 2 vols. *Illustrations.* 8° 1845

Orme, Robert. A History of the Military Transactions of the British Nation in Indostan, from the year 1745 ; to which is prefixed a Dissertation on the Establishments made by Mahommedan Conquerors in Indostan. 4th edition. Vols. 1 and 2. 8° *Madras*, 1861

—— A Collection of Maps and Plans to accompany above, being Vol. 3 of the new edition of that work, &c. 8° *Madras*, 1862

Ormiston, Thomas. Report on Improvements proposed at the Harbour of Famagousta, Cyprus, dated 10th January 1880. *Maps.* Folio* 1880

Ormsby, John. Autumn Rambles in North Africa. *Plates.* 8° 1864

Oropeza, Samuel. Intereses Nacionales : Cuestion de Limites entre las Republicas de Bolivia y del Perù. 8* *Sucre*, 1888

—— Limites entre la República de Bolivia y la República Argentina. 8° *Sucre*, 1892

Orozco y Berra, Juan. Apuntes sobre Cayo Arenas. *Maps.* 12* *Mexico*, 1886

Orozco y Berra, Manuel. Geografía de las Lenguas y Carta Etnográfica de México, precedidas de un ensayo de Clasificacion de las mismas Lenguas y de apuntes para las Inmigraciones de las Tribus. *Map.* 8° *Mexico*, 1864

—— Memoria para el Plano de la Ciudad de México, formada de órden del Ministerio de Fomento. *Plan.* 12° *Mexico*, 1867

—— Materiales para una Cartografia Mexicana. 4° *Mexico*, 1871

Orozco y Berra, Manuel. Apuntes para la Historia de la Geografia en Mexico. 8° *Mexico*, 1881

Orpen, G. H. The Song of Dermot and the Earl : an old French Poem, from the Carew Manuscript, No. 596, in the Archiepiscopal Library at Lambeth Palace. Edited, with literal Translation and Notes, a facsimile, and a map, by Goddard Henry Orpen. 12° *Oxford*, 1892

Orpen, J. M. Some Principles of Native Government illustrated ; and the Petitions of the Basuto Tribe regarding Land, Law, Representation, and Disarmament to the Cape Parliament considered. *Maps.* 8° *Cape Town*, 1880

Orr, Lieut. R. H. *See* United States, E, *a*, Navigation : Appendix 2.

Orsolle, E. Le Caucase et la Perse. *Map and plan.* 12° *Paris*, 1885

Orsted, A. S. Centralamerikas Rubiaceer. (Bestemmelser og Beskrivelser mestendeels af G. Bentham.) 8* 1852

Orsted, H. C. *See* Forchhammer, G.

Orsua, P. de. *See* Ursua.

Ortelius, Abraham. Theatrum Orbis Terrarum : The Theatre of the Whole World set forth. *Maps.* Folio 1606

—— Ecclesiæ Londino-Batavae Archivum, Tomus Primus. Abrahami Ortelii [Geographi Antuerpiensis] et Virorum Eruditorum ad eundem et ad Jacobum Colium Ortelianum [Abrahami Ortelii Sororis Fileum.] Epistolæ. cum aliquot aliis Epistolis et Tractatibus quibos dam ab utroque Collectis [1524-1628]. Ex Autographis mandante Ecclesia Londino Batava edidit Joannes Henricus Hessels. 4° *Cambridge*, 1887

Orth, Albert. Pamphlets, 8° ; containing :—

　Bericht über die Bodenarten, Bodenkarten und bes. Geologischen Karten auf der Weltausstellung zu Wien 1873.

　Landwirthschaftliche Beziehungen Geographischen Ausstellung zu Paris vom 15 Juli bis 15 August 1875.

　Ueber Untersuchung und kartographische Aufnahme des Bodens und Untergrundes grosser Städte.

　Die naturwissenschaftlichen Grundlagen der Bodenkunde.

　Landwirthschaft.

　Die Schwarzerde und ihre Bedeutung für die Kultur.

　Beiträge zur Meereskunde. *Map.*

　Ueber einige Aufgaben der wissenschaftlichen Meereskunde.

—— Ueber die Anforderungen der Geographie und der Land- und Forstwirthschaft an die geognostische Kartographie des Grund und Bodens. 8* [*Berlin*, 1877]

Ortolani, G. E. Nuovo Dizionario, Géografico, Statistico, e Biografico della Sicilia, Antica e Moderna. *Map.* 8° *Palermo*, 1819

Orton, James. The Andes and the Amazon, or Across the Continent of South America. *Map and plates.* 8°
1870
—— The same. 3rd edition. 8°
New York, 1876
Ortroy, F. van. Esquisse Géographique de l'Afghanistan. 8° *Brussels,* 1888
Orueta y Duarte, Domingo de. Informe sobre los Terremotos Ocurridos en el Sud de España en Diciembre de 1884, y Enero de 1885. *Map and photographs.* Small folio *Malaga,* 1885
Orville, Père de. *See* Thevenot, Vol. 4 : Appendix 1.
Osbeck, Peter. A Voyage to China and the East Indies. Together with a Voyage to Suratte, by Olof Toreen ; and an Account of the Chinese Husbandry, by Captain Charles Gustavus Eckeberg. Translated from the German, by John Reinhold Forster. To which are added, a Faunula and Flora Sinensis. 2 vols. 8° 1771
—— *See* "The Modern Traveller," Vol. 4, p. 610 : Appendix 1.
Osborn, Admiral Sherard. Stray Leaves from an Arctic Journal, or Eighteen Months in the Polar Regions in search of Sir John Franklin's Expedition, in the years 1850-51. *Map and coloured plates.* Small 8° 1852
—— The same. New edition (including the Career, Last Voyage, and Fate of Captain Sir John Franklin). Small 8° 1865
—— The Discovery of the North-West Passage by H.M.S. "Investigator," by Capt. R. M'Clure, 1850-54. Edited by Comm. S. Osborn. (From the Logs and Journals of Capt. M'Clure.) Illustrated by Comm. S. G. Cresswell. *Map and plates.* 8° 1856
—— The same. 4th edition. 8° 1865
—— Quedah, or Stray Leaves from a Journal in Malayan Waters. *Map and plates.* 8° 1857
—— Cruise in Japanese Waters. 8° 1859
—— The Career, Last Voyage, and Fate of Capt. Sir John Franklin. *Map and plates.* 12° 1860
—— The Past and Future of British Relations in China. *Maps.* 8° 1860
—— Japanese Fragments, with Facsimiles of Illustrations by Artists of Yedo. *Plates.* Small 8° 1861
—— On the Exploration of the North Polar Region. 8* 1865
—— Quedah ; a Cruise in Japanese Waters ; the Fight on the Peiho. *Map.* Small 8° 1865
—— On the Exploration of the North Polar Basin. 8* 1872
—— *See* Markham, A. H. ; *also* Blackwood, Vol. 3 : Appendix 1.

Osborne, T. *See* Churchill, Vol. 7 : Appendix 1.
Osburn, Wm. Account of an Egyptian Mummy ; with an Appendix containing the Chemical and Anatomical details of the Examination of the Body, by E. S. George, T. P. Teale, and R. Hey. *Plates.* Royal 8* *Leeds,* 1828
Osculati, Gaetano. Note d'un Viaggio nella Persia e nelle Indie Orientali negli 1841-42. *Plate.* 8* *Monza,* 1844
—— Esplorazione delle Regioni Equatoriali lungo il napo ed il fiume delle Amazzoni : Frammento di un Viaggio fatto nelle due Americhe negli anni 1846-48. *Maps and coloured plates.* Royal 8° *Milan,* 1850
Osgood, Charles S., and H. M. Batchelder. Historical Sketch of Salem, 1626-1879. 4° *Salem, Mass.,* 1879
Osgood's Handbooks for Travellers. 12° *Boston, Mass.*
A Guide to the Chief Cities and Popular Resorts of New England, . . . with the Western and Northern Borders from New York to Quebec. *Maps and plans.* [Two editions.] 1873 and 1875
A Guide to the Chief Cities and Popular Resorts of the Middle States, and to their Scenery and Historic Attractions : with the Northern Frontier from Niagara Falls to Montreal ; also Baltimore, Washington, and Northern Virginia. *Maps and plans* 1874
A Guide to the Chief Cities, Coasts, and Islands of the Maritime Provinces of Canada, and to their Scenery and Historic Attractions ; with the Gulf and River of St Lawrence to Quebec and Montreal, also Newfoundland and the Labrador Coast. *Maps and plans* 1875
Osorio, Jerome. History of the Portuguese, during the Reign of Emmanuel ; containing all their Discoveries, from the Coast of Africk to the farthest parts of China ; their Battles by Sea and Land, their Sieges, and other Memorable Exploits ; with a Description of those Countries, and a particular Account of the Religion, Government, and Customs of the Natives ; including also their Discovery of the Brazils, and their Wars with the Moors. Translated by J. Gibbs. 2 vols. 8° 1752
Ostani, Luciano. Note di Viaggio e cenni di Statistica dell' America Meridionale Conferenza tenuta ad Udine e Venezia, 1886-87. 8* *Venice,* 1887
Osten-Sacken, C. R. On the so-called *Bugonia* of the Ancients, and its relation to *Eristalis tenax,* a two-winged insect. 8* *Florence,* 1893

z

Osten-Sacken, Baron F. von der. Ueber-sicht der geographischen Leistungen in Russland während der Regierung Kaiser Alexander II. 8* *St Petersburg*, 1880

—— **and F. J. Ruprecht.** Sertum Tian-schanicum, Botanische Ergebnisse einer Reise im mittleren Tian-schan. 4* *St Petersburg*, 1869

Ostroumoff, N. V. A Geography of the Turkestan Country; with a short Account of the Khanates of Bokhara and Khiva, and a map of the country. Compiled by N. V. Ostroumoff, Samarkand, 1891. Translated by Staff-Lieutenant E. Peach. (From the *Journal* of the United Service Institution of India.) *Map.* 8* 1893

O'Sullivan, D. R. Tierra del Fuego. (From the *Fortnightly Review*, January 1893.) Large 8* 1893

Oswald, F. L. Streifzüge in den Urwäldern von Mexico und Central-Amerika. *Illustrations.* 8° *Leipzig*, 1881

Othere or Octher. See Hakluyt, Vol 2; Kerr, Vol. 1: Appendix 2.

Otis, F. N. Illustrated History of the Panama Railroad, together with a Traveller's Guide and Business Man's Hand-Book for the Panama Railroad and its Connections. *Map and plates.* 8° *New York*, 1862

Otondo, Isidro. See Burney, Vol. 4: Appendix 1.

Otté, E. C. See Humboldt, Alex. von; Quatrefages.

Otter, Capt. H. C. Scotland: North-West Coast. Little Minch. 8* 1859

—— *See* United Kingdom, A, Hydrogr. Off. Publ.: Appendix 2.

—— **and W. Stanton.** Western or Outer Hebrides. Sailing Directions for the Sound of Harris. *Plates.* 8* 1859

Oudemans, J. A. C. Verslag van de Bepaling der Geographische Ligging van Punten op of nabij de Oostkust van Celebes, verrigt in September-December 1864. *Map.* 8* [*Batavia*, 1865]

—— Die Triangulation von Java, ausge-führt vom Personal des geographischen Dienstes in Niederländisch Ost-Indien. Erste Abtheilung. Vergleichung der Maasstäbe des Repsold'schen Basis-Mess-Apparates mit dem Normalmeter. *Plates.* 4° *Batavia*, 1875

—— The same. Zweite Abtheilung. 4° *The Hague*, 1878

—— Die Triangulation von Java. Dritte Abtheilung. *Plans and plates.* 4° *The Hague*, 1891

Oudiette, Charles. Dictionnaire Géographique et Topographique des Treize Départemens qui composaient les Pays-Bas Autrichiens, Pays de Liège et de

Oudiette, Charles—*continued.* Stavelo, les Électorats de Trèves, May-ence, et Cologne, et les Duchés de Juliers, Gueldre, Clèves, &c., réunis à la France. 2 vols. *Maps.* 8° *Paris*, 1804-5

Ouseley, Sir William. Epitome of the Ancient History of Persia: Extracted and Translated from the "Jehan Ara," a Persian Manuscript. [Persian and English.] *Map and plate.* 12° 1799

—— Travels in various Countries of the East, more particularly Persia, in 1810-12. *Maps and plates.* 3 vols. 4° 1819-23

—— *See* Ebn Haukal; Sádik Isfáháni; *also* Eyriès, Vol. 14: Appendix 1.

Outhier, Abbé. Journal d'un Voyage au Nord en 1736 and 1737. *Maps and plates.* 4° *Paris*, 1744

—— *See* Pinkerton, Vol. 1; Allgemeine Historie, Vol. 17: Appendix 1.

Outram, F. B. Note on Native Perio-dicals and Presses, 1858. [India Records, No. 33.] Large 8° *Allahabad*, 1860

Outram, Sir James. Rough Notes of the Campaign in Sinde and Affghanistan in 1838-39. *Plans.* 12° 1840

—— Narrative of a Journey from Khelat to Sonmeeanee, with a Description of the Route traversed. [From the India Records, No. 17.] Royal 8° *Bombay*, 1855

—— *See* Goldsmid, F. J.

Outram, Joseph. A Hand-Book of Information for Emigrants to Nova Scotia. 12* *Halifax, N.S.*, 1864

Ovalle, Alonso de. *See* Churchill, Vol. 3; Pinkerton, Vol. 14: Appendix 1.

Overbury, Sir Thomas. *See* Churchill, Vol. 7: Appendix 1.

Overweg, A. *See* Petermann.

Ovieda, Andrea. *See* Purchas, Vol. 2, Book 7: Appendix 1.

Oviedo, alias de Valdès, Gonçalo Fernandez de. "Breve sumario," "General i Natural Historia de Indias." [*Title lost.*] Folio N.P. [1526?]

—— *See* Purchas, Vol. 3, Book 5; Ramusio, Vol. 3; Ternaux-Compans, Vol. 14: Appendix 1.

Ovington, J. *See* Allgemeine Historie, Vol. 10: Appendix 1.

Owen, David Dale. Reports of a Geological Reconnoisance of the Chippewa Land District of Wisconsin and the Northern Part of Iowa. *Maps.* 8° *Washington*, 1848

—— Report of a Geological Survey of Wisconsin, Iowa, and Minnesota, and incidentally of a Portion of Nebraska Territory. Made under Instructions from the U.S. Treasury Department. *Maps and plates.* 4° *Philadelphia*, 1852

—— *Illustrations* to the same. 4°

Owen, David Dale. Second and Third Reports of the Geological Survey in Kentucky, made during 1856-57. Assisted by R. Peter, S. S. Lyon, L. Lesquereux, and E. T. Cox ; with *maps and illustrations* separate. 2 vols. Imperial 8° *Frankfort, Kentucky,* 1857

—— First and Second Reports of a Geological Reconnoissance of the Northern and Middle and Southern Counties of Arkansas, made during 1857-60. 2 vols. *Plates.* Royal 8° *Philadelphia,* 1858-60

Owen, E. Observations on the Earths, Rocks, Stones, and Minerals about Bristol. 12° 1754

Owen, John. Britannia Depicta, or Ogilby Improved : being an actual Survey of all the Direct and Principal Cross Roads of England and Wales, compiled from the best Authorities. *Maps.* Small 4° 1764

Owen, Capt. R. Nautical Memoir, descriptive of the Surveys made in H.M. Ships "Blossom" and "Thunder," from 1829 to 1837 ; to which is appended an Essay on the Management and Use of Chronometers. 8° N.D.

Owen, Sir Richard. Anatomy of the King-Crab. *Plates.* 4* 1873

—— *See* India, C (Geological Papers) : Appendix 2.

Owen, Capt. W. F. W. Tables of Latitudes and Longitudes by Chronometer of Places in the Atlantic and Indian Oceans, principally on the West and East Coasts of Africa. From the Observations of H.M.S. "Leven" and "Barracouta" in 1820 to 1826. 4° 1827

—— Narrative of Voyage to Explore the Shores of Africa, Arabia, and Madagascar, performed in H.M. ships "Leven" and "Barracouta." 2 vols. *Maps and plates.* 8° 1833

Oxley, John. Journals of Two Expeditions into the Interior of New South Wales in 1817-18. *Maps and plates.* 4° 1820

—— *See* Wallis ; *also* Eyriès, Vol. 5 : Appendix 1.

Oxnam, John. *See* Burney, Vol. 1 ; Hakluyt, Vol. 4 : Appendix 1.

Ozanne, J. W. Three Years in Roumania. Small 8° 1878

—— *See* Stumm.

Ozell, J. *See* Tournefort.

P

P——, M. de. An Historical Account of the Present Troubles of Persia and Georgia. In a Continuation of Mr Hanway's History to the end of 1753, by M. de P. Translated. 4* 1756

P. A. *See* India, F, *c* : Appendix 2.

Pacheco. *See* Astley, Vol. 1 : in Appendix 1.

Pacht, R. *See* Baer and Helmersen, 21.

Packard, Dr A. S. Notes on the Physical Geography of Labrador. *Maps.* 8* [*New York,* 1887]

—— Who first saw the Labrador Coast ? Geographical Evolution of Labrador. 8* [*New York,* 1888]

—— The Labrador Coast : a Journal of Two Summer Cruises to that region ; with Notes on its Early Discovery, on the Eskimo, on its Physical Geography, Geology, and Natural History. *Maps and illustrations.* 8° *New York,* 1891

Packe, Charles. A Guide to the Pyrenees. 2nd edition. *Maps, diagrams, and tables.* 12° 1867

Padilla, D. Matius de la Mota. Historia de la Conquista de la Provincia de la Nueva-Galicia, escrita . . . en 1742. 4° *Mexico,* 1870

Paez, P. *See* Cooley, W. D.

Paez, Ramon. Travels and Adventures in South and Central America. First series: Life in the Llanos of Venezuela. *Map and plates.* 8° 1868

Paganini, Luigi Pio. La Fototopografia in Italia. *Maps and illustrations.* Large 8* *Rome,* 1889

Page, Dr David. Advanced Text-Book of Physical Geography. 12° 1864

—— Handbook of Geological Terms, Geology, and Physical Geography. 2nd edition. Small 8° 1865

Page, Frederick. The Principle of the English Poor Laws illustrated and defended, by an Historical View of Indigence in Civil Society. 8° 1830

Page, T. Report on the proposed Harbour of Refuge, New Basin, and Dock, at Maryport. 4* 1865

—— Report of the Exploration and Survey of the River La Plata and Tributaries. 8* *Washington,* 1856

—— La-Plata, the Argentine Confederation, and Paraguay. New edition, containing further explorations in La Plata, made during the years 1859 and 1860, under the orders of the United States Government. *Map and plates.* 8° *New York,* 1873

Pagel, Lieut. Louis. La Latitude par les Hauteurs hors du Méridien, Methode facile et courte pour déterminer la Position de l'Observateur par les Hauteurs ; Aperçu sur les Distances Lunaires, &c. 8* *Paris,* 1847

Pagels, G. *See* Möller, P.

Pagenstecher, H. A. Die Insel Mallorka. Reiseskizze. *Woodcuts.* 8° *Leipzig,* 1867

Pagès, — de. Voyages autour du Monde, et vers les deux Poles, par terre et par mer, pendant les années 1767, 1768, 1769, 1770, 1771, 1773, et 1774, 1776. *Maps and illustrations.* 8° *Paris,* 1782

Pagés, Léon. Histoire de la Religion Chrétienne au Japon depuis 1598 jusqu'à 1651. 8° *Paris,* 1869
—— *See* Dictionaries, B, Japanese-French : Appendix 2.

Paget, J. Hungary and Transylvania ; with remarks on their condition, social, political, and economical. 2 vols. *Map and plates.* 8° 1839
—— The same. New edition. 2 vols. *Map and plates.* 8° 1855

Paget, Lieut.-Col. W. H., and Lieut. A. H. Mason. A Record of the Expeditions against the North-West Frontier Tribes, since the Annexation of the Punjab ; compiled from Official Sources, by Lieut.-Col. W. H. Paget, in 1873. Revised and brought up to date by Lieut. A. H. Mason, in 1884. *Maps.* 8° [1885]

Pagliardini, Tito. Essays on the Analogy of Languages. Second Essay : The International Alphabet, or a Plea for Phonetic Spelling. 12° 1864

Paijkull, C. W. En Sommer i Island. *Map and plates.* 8° *Copenhagen,* 1867
—— Bidrag till Kännedomen om Islands Bergsbyggnad. *Map.* 4° *Stockholm,* 1867
—— *See* Sweden, A (Geologiska Undersökning) : Appendix 2.

Paine, Nathaniel. *See* Salisbury, S.

Paiva Manso, Visconde de. Historia do Congo. 8° *Lisbon,* 1877

Pajér, Rudolf. *See* Dorn, A.

Pajot, Élie. Simples renseignements sur l'Ile Bourbon. 12° *Paris,* 1887

Pakington, John Slaney. The Ground we Tread : an Elementary Lecture on Geology. *Plate.* 8* 1854

Palacky, Dr Jan. Zmepeis vseobecný vedécký srovnávací. Vol. 1, Part 1. Berbersko. (Marokko, Alzírsko, Tunissko.) 8° *Prague,* 1857

Palafos, Joan de. *See* Thevenot, Vol. 4 : Appendix 1.

Palander, Lieut. *See* Blackwood, Vol. 2 : Appendix 1.

Palassou, —. Mémoires pour servir à l'Histoire Naturelle des Pyrénées et des Pays adjacents. 8° *Pau,* 1815

Paléocapa, P. Observations sur le Discours prononcé par M. Stephenson de l'Isthme de Suez. 8* *Paris,* 1857

Palgrave, W. C. *See* British South Africa, C : Appendix 2.

Palgrave, William Gifford. Narrative of a Year's Journey through Central and Eastern Arabia, 1862-63. 2 vols. *Map.* 8° 1865
—— The same. 3rd edition. 2 vols. 8°

Palgrave, William Gifford. Notes d'un Voyage au travers de l'intérieur de l'Arabie, de Gaza à El-Khatif, sur le Golfe Persique, en 1862-63, par G. Palgrave. [A Review.] *Map.* 8* 1866
—— Dutch Guiana. *Map and plan.* 8° 1876
—— Report on the General Condition of the Oriental Republic of Uruguay ; its Population, Productions, Trade, Commerce, and Finance for the year 1884. Folio* [1885]
—— Ulysses, or Scenes and Studies in many Lands. 8° 1887

Pallas, P. S. Voyages en différentes Provinces de l'Empire de Russie, et dans l'Asie Septentrionale ; traduits de l'Allemand, par G. de la Peyronie. 5 vols., and Atlas (forming Vol. 6). *Maps and plates.* 4° *Paris,* 1789-93
—— Voyages . . . traduits de l'Allemand par le C. Gauthier de la Peyronie ; revus et enrichis de Notes par les C. C. Lamarck, Langlès, et Billecocq. Appendix, contenant les Descriptions des Animaux et des Végéteaux observés dans les Voyages, avec des Notes et Observations par C. C. Lamarck. New edition. 8 vols. 8°, *and plates* 4° (forming Vol. 9) *Paris,* 1793
—— Tableaux Physiques et Topographiques de la Tauride : tirés du Journal d'un Voyage fait en 1794. 4° *St Petersburg,* 1795
—— Second Voyage de Pallas, ou Voyages entrepris dans les Gouvernemens Méridionaux de l'Empire de Russie, pendant les années 1793 et 1794, par M. le Professeur Pallas. Traduit de l'Allemand par MM. de la Boulaye et Tonnelier. 4 vols. *Plates.* 8°, and Atlas 4° *Paris,* 1811

Pallegoix, Mgr. Déscription du Royaume Thai ou Siam, comprenant la Topographie, Histoire Naturelle, Mœurs et Coutumes, Législation, Langue, &c. 2 vols. *Map and plates.* 12° *Ligny,* 1854

Palliser, Capt. John. The Solitary Hunter, or Sporting Adventures in the Prairies. *Plates.* 12° 1857
—— Papers relative to the Exploration of that Portion of British North-America which lies between the Northern Branch of the River Saskatchewan and the Frontier of the United States, and between the Red River and the Rocky Mountains. [Parly. Paper] *Maps and plates.* Folio 1859
—— Journals, Detailed Reports, and Observations relative to the Exploration of that Portion of British North-America which, in Latitude, lies between the British Boundary Line and the Height of Land or Watershed of the Northern or Frozen Ocean respectively ; and in

Palliser, Capt. John—*continued.*
Longitude, between the Western Shore of Lake Superior and the Pacific Ocean, 1857-60. [Parly. Paper.] Folio 1863

Pallme, Ignaz. Beschreibung von Kordofan und einigen angränzenden Ländern, nebst einen Ueberblick über den dasigen Handel, die Sitten und Gebräuche der Einwohner, und die unter der Regierung Mehemed Ali's stattgefundenen Sklavenjagden. 8° *Stuttgart*, 1843

Pallu, Francesco. Breve, e compendiosa Relatione de' Viaggi de tre Vescovi Francesi, che dalla S. Mem. di Papa Alessandro VII. furono mandati Vicarij Apostolici à i Regni della Cina, Cocincina, e Tonchino, con il racconto di quanto hanno operato per lo stablimento delle loro Missioni. Tradotta dalla Francese in lingua Italiana. 12° *Rome*, 1669

Palmarts, J. Projet d'Exploration au Pole Nord. 8* *Brussels*, 1880

Palmer, Aaron Haight. Memoir, Geographical, Political, and Commercial, on the Present State, Productive Resources, and Capabilities for Commerce of Siberia, Manchuria, and the Asiatic Islands of the Northen Pacific Ocean. *Maps.* 8* *Washington*, 1848
—— Letter to the Hon. J. M. Clayton, enclosing a Paper, Geographical, Political, and Commercial, on the Independent Oriental Nations. 8* *Washington*, 1849
—— Documents and Facts illustrating the Origin of the Mission to Japan authorised by the Government of the United States, May 1851. 8* *Washington*, 1857

Palmer, Prof. E. H. The Desert of the Exodus: Journeys on Foot in the Wilderness of the Forty Years' Wanderings, undertaken in Connection with the Ordnance Survey of Sinai and the Palestine Exploration Fund. 2 vols. *Maps.* 8° 1871
—— *See* Besant ; *also* Dictionaries, B : Appendix 2.

Palmer, F. J. Floods in the Thames Valley, and the Relief of London Bridge and its Approaches. *Maps and plates.* 8° 1877

Palmer, G. Kidnapping in the South Seas : being a Narrative of a Three Months' Cruise of H. M. S. "Rosario." *Plates.* 8° *Edinburgh*, 1871

Palmer, Major H. Spencer. On a Determination of Latitude at Mount Elgin, in the Kan-Lung Peninsula. Folio* *Hong Kong*, 1882

Palmer, J. Linton. On some Tablets found in Easter Island. *Plate.* 8* *Liverpool*, 1876

Palmgren, L. *See* Sweden, A : Appendix 2.

Palmieri, Luigi, and Arcangelo Scacchi. Della Regione Vulcanica del Monte Vulture e del Tremuoto ivi avvenuto nel di 14 Agosto 1851. *Maps and plates.* 4° *Naples*, 1852

Palmieri, Luigi. The Eruption of Vesuvius in 1872; with Notes by R. Mallet. *Plates.* 8° 1873

Palomino, P. Alvares. *See* Gottfried, Appendix 1.

Palyakoff, J. S. Travels in the Valley of the Obi. [In Russian.] 8° *St Petersburg*, 1877

Pananti, Filippo. Avventure e Osservazioni sopra le Coste di Barbeira. *Plates.* 8° *Mendrisio*, 1841

Pancrazi, D. G. M. Antichita Siciliane spiegate. 2 vols. *Map and plates.* Folio *Naples*, 1751-52

Pancritius, A. Hägringar. Reise durch Schweden, Lappland, Norwegen, und Dänemark im Jahre 1850. 8° *Königsberg*, 1852

"Pandora." *See* Hamilton, G. : Koolemans Beynen ; Young, Sir A.

Panet, —. Instructions rédigées par une Commission de la Société de Géographie pour le Voyage de M. Panet du Sénégal en Algérie. 8* *Paris*, 1849

Pansch, —. *See* Arctic, H. : Appendix 2.

Panter, F. K. *See* Martin.

Pantussof, N. N. On the Kuldja Region. [In Russian.] 8° *Kazan*, 1881
—— War of the Mussulmans against the Chinese. Part 1, Text [in Taranchi dialect]. Part 2, Appendices [in Russian]. 8* *Kazan*, 1881
—— Ferghana, according to the Memoirs of Sultan Baber. [In Russian.] 8* *St Petersburg*, 1884

Pappe, L. Floræ Capensis Medicæ Prodromus ; or, An Enumeration of South African Plants used as Remedies by the Colonists of the Cape of Good Hope. *Map.* 8* *Cape Town*, 1857

Paquier, J. B. Le Pamir : Étude de Géographie Physique et Historique sur l'Asie Centrale. *Maps.* 8° *Paris*, 1876

Paradis, Venture de. Grammaire et Dictionnaire abrégés de la Langue Berbère. Revus par P. A. Jaubert. 8° *Paris*, 1844
—— Notice Biographique, par Jomard. 4* *Paris*, 1844

Paravey, Chevalier de. Réponse à l'Article de M. Riambourg sur l'Antiquité Chinoise. 8* *Epernay*, 1836
—— Dissertation sur les Amazones dont le Souvenir est conservé en Chine ; ou Comparaison de ce que nous apprennent les Monumens Indiens et les Livres Chinois, sur les Niu-Mou-Yo, avec les Documens que nous ont laissés les Grecs. *Plate.* 8° *Paris*, 1840
—— Nouvelles Preuves que le Pays du Fou-Sang mentionné dans les livres Chinois est l'Amérique. *Plate.* 8* [*Paris*, 1847]
—— Réfutation de l'Opinion émise par M. Jomard que les Peuples d'Amérique n'ont jamais eu aucun rapport avec ceux de l'Asie. 8* *Paris*, 1849

Paravey, Chevalier de. Mémoire sur la découverte trés ancienne en Asie et dans l'Indo-Perse, de la Poudre à Canon et des Armes à Feu. Royal 8* *Paris*, 1850

—— Des Traces de la Bible, retrouvées dans les Livres Indous, et spécialement d'Abel, type du sacrifice sans tache. 8* *Paris*, 1851

—— Recherches sur le Népenthès des Grecs, dans les Livres Botaniques Chinois. 8* *Versailles*, 1860

—— De l'origine Orientale des Polonais et d'un usage ancien de ce Peuple célèbre et guerrier par excellence. *Plate*. 8* *Paris*, 1861

—— Du Signe Interrogatif des divers Peuples, et des fausses idées de l'Europe sur les Hiéroglyphes. Dissertation. 8* *Lyons*, 1865

—— Du Planisphère de Dendérah et des Zodiaques anciens. 8* [*Paris*, 1866]

—— Recherches sur les Noms primitifs de Dieu. 12* [*Roanne*, N.D.]

—— Dissertation sur les Centaures et les Amazones. 8* *Roanne*, N.D.

Parbury, George. Hand-Book for India and Egypt, comprising the Narrative of a Journey from Calcutta to England, by way of the River Ganges, the North-West of Hindostan, the Himalayas, the Rivers Sutledge and Indus, Bombay, and Egypt ; and Hints for the Guidance of Passengers by that and other Overland Routes to the Three Presidencies of India. *Map*. 8° 1841

Parchappe, ——, and —— de la Marck. Observations Chronométriques et autres faites en 1853, dans l'Archipel des Pomotous. 8° *Paris*, 1857

Pardoe, Miss. The City of the Sultan, and Domestic Manners of the Turks in 1836. 2 vols. *Plates*. 8° 1837

—— The River and the Desert, or Recollections of the Rhône and the Chartreuse. 2 vols. 12° 1838

Paris, C. Voyage d'Exploration de Hué en Cochinchine par la Route Mandarine. *Maps and illustrations*. 8° *Paris*, 1889

Paris, Matthew. See Purchas, Vol. 2, Book 8 ; Vol. 3, Book 1 : Appendix 1.

Paris, T. Clifton. Letters from the Pyrenees, during Three Months' pedestrian wanderings amidst the Wildest Scenes of the French and Spanish Mountains, in 1842. *Woodcuts*. 8° 1843

Parish, John. Translation of " A Voyage to the Island of Mauritius, or Isle of France, the Isle of Bourbon, the Cape of Good Hope, &c." By a French Officer. 8° 1775

Parish, Sir Woodbine. Analysis of the " Coleccion de Obras y Documentos relativos á la Historia Antigua y Moderna de las Provincias del Rio de la Plata ;

Parish, Sir Woodbine—*continued*. ilustrados con notas y Disertaciones, por Pedro de Angelis." Buenos Aires, 1836. 8* [1837]

—— Buenos Ayres and the Provinces of the Rio de la Plata, their Present State, Trade, and Debt ; with some Account of the Progress of Geographical Discovery in those parts of South America during the last Sixty Years. *Maps and plates*. 8° 1838

—— The same, from their Discovery and Conquest by the Spaniards to the Establishment of their Political Independence ; with some Account of their Present State, Trade, Debt, &c. ; an Appendix of Historical and Statistical Documents, and a Description of the Geology of the Pampas. 2nd edition. *Map and illustrations*. 8° 1852

—— Buenos Aires y las Provincias de Rio de la Plata. Traducido y Aumentado con notas y Apuntes por Justo Maeso. *Map and plates*. 8° *Buenos Ayres*, 1853

—— See Cox, G. ; Dalrymple, A. ; Pentland.

Parisot, V. See Vosgien.

Park, A. How I Teach Geography. 12* 1883

Park, Mungo. Travels in the Interior Districts of Africa, performed under the Direction and Patronage of the African Association in the years 1795, 1796, and 1797 ; with an Appendix, containing Geographical Illustrations of Africa, by Major Rennell. *Maps and plates*. 4° 1799

—— The same. 4th edition. *Map, portrait, and plates*. 8° 1800

—— The same ; with an Account of a subsequent Mission to that Country in 1805, to which is added an Account of the Life of Mr Park. A new edition [Vol. 2 only]. Last Journey and Life. *Map*. 8° 1816

—— The Journal of a Mission to the Interior of Africa in the year 1805 ; together with other Documents, Official and Private, relating to the same Mission ; to which is prefixed an Account of the Life of Mr Park. *Map*. 4° 1815

—— Papers in MS. on 3 slips. [*Slip A*. On this is written " Crescent Transport," the name of the vessel that conveyed Mungo Park and party from Portsmouth to Goree ; Register of Observations for Longitude ; no date (about 1805). *Slip B*. MM. On the Rate of the Watch during the Passage to Goree. *Slip C*. A Rough Register of Observations for Longitude made during the Passage to Goree.]

—— See Rios ; Thomson ; also Eyriès, Vol. 11 ; Pelham, 1 ; Pinkerton, 16 : Appendix 1.

Parke, Lieut. J. G. Report of Explorations for that Portion of a Railway Route, near the thirty-second Parallel of Latitude, lying between Dona Ana on the Rio Grande, and Pimas Villages on the Gila. *Maps.* 8° *Washington*, 1854

Parke, Dr T. H. My Personal Experiences in Equatorial Africa as Medical Officer of the Emin Pasha Relief Expedition. *Map and illustrations.* 8° 1891
—— Guide to Health in Africa, with Notes on the Country and its Inhabitants; with Preface by H. M. Stanley. 12° 1893

Parker, E. H. Report on Annam. *Map.* Folio* 1892

Parker, Francis W. How to Study Geography. 12° *New York*, 1889

Parker, Gilbert. Round the Compass in Australia. *Illustrations.* 8° 1892

Parker, P. Journal of an Expedition from Singapore to Japan; with a Visit to Loo-Choo. 12° 1838

Parker, T. Jeffery. The Skeleton of the New Zealand Crayfishes. No. 4 of Studies in Biology for New Zealand Students. *Diagrams.* Large 8* *Wellington, N.Z.*, 1889

Parker, William. *See* Hakluyt, Vol. 4; Purchas, Vol. 4, Book 6: Appendix 1.

Parkes, W. Euphrates Valley Railway: Report on the Ports of the Persian Gulf. *Charts.* 8* 1872

Parkin, George R. Round the Empire; with a Preface by the Earl of Rosebery. *Maps and illustrations.* 12° 1892

Parkinson, J. C. The Ocean Telegraph to India, a Narrative and a Diary. *Map, plates, and tables.* Small 8° 1870

Parkinson, R. Im Bismarck-Archipel, Ergebnisse und Beobachtungen auf der Insel Neu-Pommern (Neu-Britannien). *Map and illustrations.* 8° *Leipzig*, 1887

Parkinson, Sydney. A Journal of a Voyage to the South Seas, in His Majesty's ship "The Endeavour." *Map and illustrations.* 4° 1773

Parkman, F. The Discovery of the Great West. *Map.* 8° *Boston, Mass.*, 1869
—— *See* Horsford.

Parkyns, Mansfield. Life in Abyssinia: being Notes collected during Three Years Residence and Travels in that Country. 2 vols. *Map and plates.* 8° 1853

Parlatore, P. Études sur la Géographie Botanique de l'Italie. 8* *Paris*, 1878

Parlby, Major Samuel. Rational Theory as to the Cause of the Varieties of Temperature in the different Latitudes of the Earth's Surface, and according to the Scriptural Account of the Creation. 8* 1854

Parmentier, Jean and Raoul. Le Discours de la Navigation de Jean et Raoul Parmentier de Dieppe, Voyage à Sumatra en 1529. Description de l'isle de Sainct-

Parmentier, Jean and Raoul—*contd.* Dominigo. Publiée par C. Schefer. [Vol. 4 of Recueil de Voyages, &c.] *Map.* Large 8° *Paris*, 1883

Paroletti, Modeste. Turin et ses Curiosités, ou Description Historique de tout ce que cette Capitale offre de remarquable dans ses Monumens, ses Édifices et ses Environs. *Map.* 8° *Turin*, 1819
—— Turin, à la portée de l'Étranger, ou Description des Palais, Édifices, et Monumens de Science et d'Art, &c. *Map and plates.* Small 8° *Turin*, 1838

Parr, A. C. *See* Ogilvy, T.

Parrot, Friedrich. Reise zum Ararat. 2 parts. *Map and plates.* 8° *Berlin*, 1834
—— Journey to Ararat, translated by W. D. Cooley. *Map and woodcuts.* 8° 1845
—— *See* Engelhardt.

Parry, Francis. The Sacred Maya Stone of Mexico, and its Symbolism. *Plates and illustrations.* Imperial 4° 1893

Parry, Admiral Sir William Edward. Journal of a Voyage for the Discovery of a North-West Passage from the Atlantic to the Pacific, performed in 1819-20 in H.M. ships "Hecla" and "Griper"; with an Appendix containing the Scientific and other Observations. *Charts and plates.* 4° 1821
—— Journal of a Second Voyage for the Discovery of a North-West Passage from the Atlantic to the Pacific in 1821-23, in H.M. ships "Fury" and "Hecla." *Maps and plates.* 4° 1824
—— Appendix to the Second Voyage. *Plates.* 4° 1825
—— Journal of a Third Voyage for the Discovery of a North-West Passage to the Pacific, performed 1824-25, in H.M. ships "Hecla" and "Fury." *Charts and plates.* 4° 1826
—— Narrative of an Attempt to Reach the North Pole, in Boats fitted for the purpose, and attached to H.M. ship "Hecla," in 1827. *Charts and plates.* 4° 1828
—— Brief Memoir of. 8* 1855
—— Memoirs, by the Rev. Edward Parry. *Portrait.* Crown 8° 1857
—— *See* Huish, R.; *also* Eyriès, Vol. 8; Phillips, New Voyages and Travels [3], Vol. 5: Appendix 1.

Parsons, Abraham. Travels in Asia and Africa: including a Journey from Scanderoon to Aleppo, and over the Desert to Bagdad and Bussora; a Voyage from Bussora to Bombay, and along the Western Coast of India; a Voyage from Bombay to Mocha and Suez in the Red Sea; and a Journey from Suez to Cairo and Rosetta. *Plates.* 4° 1808

Parsons, J. West India Directory: Sailing Directions from Puerto Escocés to Sasardi, and for Boca Chica and Bay of Cartagena. 8° 1857

Parsons, Hon. J. L. The Northern Territory, with a Glance at the East : a Lecture delivered . . . 19th May 1887. 8*   *Adelaide*, 1887

Parsons, R. M. Observations made while proceeding from New Westminster to Lake La Hache. *Maps*. 8* *New Westminster, B.C.*, 1862

Parthey, G., and M. Pinder. Itinerarium Antonini Augusti et Hierosolymitanum. *Map*. [1 sheet of Codices.] 8° *Berlin*, 1848

Parthey, G. *See* Mela, Pomponius.

Parthey, H. Ueber den Oberlauf des Nil nach Ptolemæus. *Map*. 8* *Berlin*, 1864

Partsch, Dr Joseph. Die Insel Korfu. (Ergänzungsheft, 88 — Petermann's Mittheilungen.) *Maps*. 4° *Gotha*, 1887 —— Die Insel Leukas. (Ergänzungsheft, 95—Petermann's Mittheilungen.) *Map*. 4° *Gotha*, 1889 —— Kephallenia und Ithaka. (Ergänzungsheft, 98 — Petermann's Mittheilungen.) *Map, plans, and sketches*. 4° *Gotha*, 1890 —— *See* Neumann, C.

Pasco, Capt. Crawford. Presidential Address: Section E, Geography. Australian Assoc. Advancement of Science. 8* *Hobart*, 1892

Pashino, Petr Ivanovich. Turkistan in 1866. [In Russian.] *Map and plates*. 4° *[St Petersburg]* 1868

Pashley, R. Travels in Crete. 2 vols. *Map and illustrations*. 8° *Cambridge*, 1837

Pasini, L. *See* Marco Polo.

Pasius. *See* Purchas, Vol. 3: Appendix 1.

Paske, Major Edward H. Tea Cultivation in the Kangra District. [From the India Records.] 8° *Lahore*, 1869

Pasos, I. de. *See* Angelis, Vol. 4: Appendix 1.

Paspati, A. G. Études sur les Tchinghianés, ou Bohémiens de l'Empire Ottoman. 8° *Constantinople*, 1870

Passarge, Louis. Aus Baltischen Landen; Studien und Bilder. 12° *Glogau*, 1878

Passos, F. P. Estrada de Ferro D. Pedro II. (parte em trafego). Relatorio do anno de 1878. 4° *Rio de Janeiro*, 1879 —— The same. Relatorio do anno de 1879. 4° *Rio de Janeiro*, 1880

Passy, F. *See* Saillens.

Pasumot, F. Voyages Physiques dans les Pyrénées, en 1788 et 1789: Histoire Naturelle d'une partie de ces Montagnes. *Maps*. 8° *Paris*, 1797

Paterson, William. A Narrative of Four Journeys into the Country of the Hottentots and Caffraria, in the years 1777-78-79. *Map and plates*. 4° 1789 —— Central America. [From an MS. in the British Museum, 1701.] *Map*. 8° 1857

Paterson's Roads in England and Wales. *See* Mogg.

Paton, A. A. Servia, the Youngest Member of the European Family ; or, a Residence in Belgrade, and Travels in the Highlands and Woodlands of the Interior, during the years 1843 and 1844. 8° 1845 —— Highlands and Islands of the Adriatic, including Dalmatia, Croatia, and the Southern Provinces of the Austrian Empire. 2 vols. *Map and plates*. 8° 1849 —— The Goth and the Hun ; or, Transylvania, Debreczin, Pesth, and Vienna in 1850. 8° 1851

Paton, James. The Textile Industries of Glasgow and the West of Scotland. [Bound with other Papers, by St John V. Day, John Mayer, and James Paton, for the British Association Meeting at Glasgow, 1876.] 12° *Glasgow*, 1876

Paton, Walter B. The Handy Guide to Emigration to the British Colonies. New edition. *Maps*. 12° 1886

Paton, William Agnew. Down the Islands: a Voyage to the Caribees ; with *illustrations* from drawings by M. J. Burns. Large 8° 1888

Patrick, S. *See* Cellarius, C.

Patten, Robert. Report of the Locating Survey of the St Croix and Lake Superior Railroad. *Map*. 8* *Madison*, 1856

Patterson, A. J. The Magyars, their Country and Institutions. 2 vols. *Map*. Small 8° 1869

Patterson, Carlisle P. *See* United States, F : Appendix 2.

Patterson, William J. The Dominion of Canada : with particulars as to its Extent, Climate, Agricultural Resources, Fisheries, Mines, Manufacturing and other Industries; also Details of Home and Foreign Commerce; including a Summary of the Census of 1881. 8° *Montreal*, 1883

Patton, Jacob Harris. Natural Resources of the United States. 8° 1888

Paul, B. H. *See* Humboldt, Alex. von.

Paul of Aleppo. *See* Macarius.

Paula. Pilgrimage of the holy Paula. *See* Turkey in Asia, B : Appendix 2.

Paulet, Lord George. *See* Simpson.

Paulitschke, Dr Philipp. Die Afrika Literatur in der Zeit von 1500 bis 1750 n. Ch., ein Beitrag zur Geographischen Quellenkunde. 8° *Vienna*, 1882 —— Ueber die Etymologie und Schreibweise einiger geographischer Namen Ost-Afrika's. 8* *Vienna*, 1884 —— Die geographische Erforschung der Adâl-Länder und Harârs in Ost-Afrika; mit Rücksicht auf die Expedition des Dr. Med. Dominik Kammel, Edlen von Hardegger. Large 8° *Leipzig*, 1884

Paulitschke, Dr Philipp. Die Sudânländer nach dem gegenwärtigen Stande der Kenntnis. *Map.* 8° *Freiburg*, 1885
—— Dr D. Kammel von Hardegger's Expedition in Ost-Afrika : Beiträge zur Ethnographie und Anthropologie der Somâl, Galla, und Hararî. *Maps and plates.* Folio *Leipzig*, 1886
—— Harar : Forschungsreise nach den Somâl- und Galla-Landern Ost-Afrikas. Ausgeführt von Dr Kammel von Hardegger, und Prof. Dr Paulitschke. Nebst Beiträgen von Dr Günther Ritter von Beck, L. Ganglbauer, und Dr Heinrich Wichmann. *Maps.* 8° *Leipzig*, 1888
—— Die Wanderungen der Oromó oder Galla Ost-Afrika's. *Plate.* 4*
Vienna, 1889
—— Ethnographie Nordost - Afrikas : die Materielle Cultur der Danakil, Galla, und Somal. *Map and plates.* 8° *Berlin*, 1893
Pauly, F. Topographie von Dännemark, einschlieszlich Islands, und der Färöer. 12° *Altona*, 1828
Pausanias. Pausaniae de tota Græcia libri decem. . . . Abrahamo Loeschero interprete. Folio *Basle*, 1550
—— Viaggio Istorico della Grecia. 5 vols. 4° *Rome*, 1792
—— Pausaniae Græciæ Descriptio. Græce Recensuit ex Codd. et aliunde Emendavit, Explanavit, J. F. Facius; Romuli Amasæi Interpretationem Latinam Continens. 4 vols. 8° *Leipzig*, 1794-96
—— Descrizione della Grecia. Tradotta da A. Nibby. 4 vols. in 2. *Map.* 8° *Rome*, 1817
—— The Description of Greece by Pausanias. Translated from the Greek, with Notes. 3 vols. *Maps and plates.* 8° 1824
Pauthier, G. Mémoire sur l'Origine et la Propagation de la Doctrine du Tao, fondée par Lao-tseu, &c.: Critique littéraire. 8* *Paris*, 1831
—— Réponse à l'Examen Critique de M. S. Julien. 8* *Paris*, 1842
—— Vindiciæ Sinicæ : Dernière Réponse à M. S. Julien ; suivie d'un Parallèle de sa Nouvelle Traduction de Lao-Tseu, avec une traduction précédente, et avec Supplément. 8* *Paris*, 1842-43
—— Vindiciæ Sinicæ Novæ. No. 1. J. P. Abel-Rémusat. 8* *Paris*, 1872
—— *See* Julien ; Khanikoff, N.
Pavet de Courteille, A. Mirâdj-Nâmeh d'après le manuscrit Ouigour de la Bibliothèque nationale. *Illustrations.* 8° *Paris*, 1882
Paxton, J. D. Letters from Palestine, during a Residence there, 1836-38. 12° 1839
Payer, Julius von. Die Adamello - Presanella-Alpen, nach den Forschungen und Aufnahmen von —. (Ergänzungsheft, 17 — Petermann's Mittheilungen.) *Coloured plate and map.* 4° *Gotha*, 1865

Payer, Julius von. Die Ortler-Alpen (Sulden-Gebiet, · und Monte Cevedale), nach den Forschungen und Aufnahmen von —. (Ergänzungsheft, 18 — Peter-mann's Mittheilungen.) *Coloured plate and map.* 4° *Gotha*, 1867
—— Die westlichen Ortler-Alpen (Trafoier Gebiet), nach den Forschungen und Aufnahmen von —. (Ergänzungsheft, 23— Petermann's Mittheilungen.) *Coloured plate and map.* 4° *Gotha*, 1868
—— Die südlichen Ortler-Alpen, nach den Forschungen und Aufnahmen von —. (Ergänzungsheft, 27—Petermann's Mittheilungen.) *Map and coloured plate.* 4° *Gotha*, 1869
—— Die centralen Ortler-Alpen (Gebiete: Martell, Laas, und Saent), nebst einem Anhange zu den Adamello-Presanella-Alpen. (Ergänzungsheft, 31 — Petermann's Mittheilungen.) *Plate and map.* 4° *Gotha*, 1872
—— Die österreichisch-ungarische Nordpol-Expedition in den Jahren 1872-74, nebst einer Skizze der zweiten deutschen Nordpol-Expedition 1869-70, und der Polar-Expedition von 1871. *Maps and plates.* 8° *Vienna*, 1876
—— New Lands within the Arctic Circle: Narrative of the Discoveries of the Austrian ship "Tegetthoff" in the years 1872-74. 2 vols. *Maps and plates.* 8° 1876
—— *See* Weyprecht ; *also* Arctic, B : Appendix 2.
Payne, Edward John. History of European Colonies. *Maps.* 12° 1877
—— History of the New World called America. Vol. 1. Royal 8° *Oxford*, 1892
Payne, F. F. Eskimo of Hudson's Strait. 8* *Toronto*, 1889
—— A few Notes upon the Eskimo of Cape Prince of Wales, Hudson's Strait. 8* [1889]
Payne, J. A. O. Lagos and West African Almanack and Diary for 1894. *Illustrations.* Large 8° 1893
—— Table of Principal Events in Yoruba History, with certain other matters of general interest. Large 8° *Lagos* [1893]
Payne, Rt. Rev. John. Grebo Grammar : for the use of the Protestant Episcopal Mission at Cape Palmas and parts adjacent, West Africa. Small 8° *New York*, 1882
Pays, A. J. du. *See* Joanne.
Payton, E. W. Round about New Zealand: being Notes from a Journal of Three Years' Wanderings in the Antipodes. *Map and illustrations.* 8° 1888
Paz Soldan, Manuel Rouaud y. Nota pasada al Sr. Comisario de Limites . . sobre la Exploracion del Rio Yavari, por el Secretario de la Comision. 4* *Pará*, 1867

Paz Soldan, Manuel Rouaud y. Dos Ilustres Sabios [Lorente et Raimondi] vindicados. 4* *Lima,* 1868
—— Estudio sobre la Altura de las Montañas, aplicado especialmente al Misti o Volcan de Arequipa. 4* *Lima,* 1868
—— Ensayo de una teoria del Magnetismo terrestre en el Peru. 8* *Lima,* 1869
—— Resumen de las Observaciones Meteorologicas hechas en Lima durante el Año de 1869, accompañado de dos Memorias: 1° Adiciones y Correcciones al Estudio de la Altura de la Montañas; y, 2° Sobre la Posicion geografica de Lima. 8* *Lima,* 1870
Paz Soldan, Mariano Felipe. Historia del Perú Independiente. Primer periodo 1819-22. Large 8° *Lima,* 1868
—— The same. Segundo periodo, 1822-27. II. Large 8° *Lima,* 1874
—— Diccionario Geográfico, Estadístico del Peru, contiene ademas la Etimologia Aymara y Quechua de las principales Poblaciones, Lagos, Rios, Cerros, &c. Folio *Lima,* 1877
—— Geografia Argentina, Orografia, Hidrografia, Limites. 8*
Buenos Ayres, 1885
Paz Soldan, Mateo. Geografia del Peru, obra postuma; corregida y aumentada por su Hermano Mariano F. Paz Soldan. Vol. I. *Portrait.* 4° *Paris,* 1862
—— Géographie du Pérou. . . Corrigée et augmentée par . . Mariano F. Paz Soldan. . . Traduction Française par P. Arsène Mouqueron, avec la collaboration de Manuel Rouaud y Paz Soldan. Large 8° *Paris,* 1863
Peace, Walter. Notes on Natal. 8* 1893
Peach, Lieut. E. *See* Ostroumoff.
Peach, B. N. *See* Tudor.
Peacock, D. M. A System of Conic Sections, adapted to the study of Natural Philosophy. 8° 1817
Peacock, D. R. Original Vocabularies of Five West Caucasian Languages. (From the *Journal* of the Royal Asiatic Society, Vol. 19, Part 1.) 8* [1887]
Peacock, Capt. G. On the Supply of Nitrate of Soda and Guano from Peru, with the history of their first introduction into this country, &c. *Map.* 8*
Exeter, 1878
—— Notes on the Isthmus of Panama and Darien, also on the River St Juan, Lakes of Nicaragua, &c., with reference to a Railroad and Canal for joining the Atlantic and Pacific Oceans. *Maps and plans.* 8° *Exeter,* 1879
—— The Guinea or Gold Coast of Africa, formerly a Colony of Axumites, or ancient Abyssinians, in the reign of King Solomon, and the veritable Ophir of Scripture, now an undisputed Colony of Great Britain. *Map and plans.* 8* 1880

Peacock, Capt. G. *See* Colombia (Panama): Appendix 2.
Peacock, R. A. On Steam as the Motive Power in Earthquakes and Volcanoes, and on Cavities in the Earth's Crust. 8* *Jersey,* 1866
—— Physical and Historical evidences of vast Sinkings of Land on the North and West Coasts of France, and South-Western Coasts of England, within the Historical Period. *Maps.* 8° 1868
Peal, S. E. A Peculiarity of the River Names in Asam and some of the countries adjoining. 8*
[*Calcutta,* 1879]
—— The Communal Barracks of Primitive Races. (Extract from the Journal of the Asiatic Society.) 8* 1892
—— *See* India, I (Assam): Appendix 2.
Pearce, J. A. Speech on the Coast Survey of the United States. 8*
Washington, 1849
Pearce, Nathaniel. The Life and Adventures of N. Pearce, written by himself, during a residence in Abyssinia from. . . 1810 to 1819. Together with Mr Coffin's account of his Visit to Gondar. Edited by J. J. Halls. 2 vols. 8° 1831
Pearce, Dr Zachary. Life of Himself [bound up with the Lives of Dr Pocock, Dr Thomas Newton, and Rev. P. Skelton]. 2 vols. 8° 1816
Pearse, E. A. Plans and Details of a Machine for Aerial Navigation, to be called an Aerial Carriage; also a Scheme for an Expedition to the North Pole, to be done in Three Months, at a Cost of Two Thousand Pounds. Folio* 1880
Pearson, A. N. Brief Sketch of the Meteorology of the Bombay Presidency in 1881. *Plates.* 8* [*Bombay,* 1882]
Pearson, C. H. Historical Maps of England during the First Thirteen Centuries; with Explanatory Essays and Indices. 2nd edition. Folio 1870
Pearson, Charles H. National Life and Character: a Forecast. 8° 1893
Pearson, John B. A Series of Observed Lunar Distances, with Explanations and Analysis. Oblong 8° *Cambridge,* 1879
Pearson, W. H. *See* Canada, A: Appendix 2.
Peary, Mrs Josephine Diebitsch. My Arctic Journal: a Year among Icefields and Eskimos; with an Account of the Great White Journey across Greenland, by Robert E. Peary. *Illustrations.* 8° 1893
Pease, Alfred E. Biskra and the Oases and Desert of the Zibans, with Information for Travellers. *Maps and illustrations.* 12° 1893
Pebrer, P. Taxation, Revenue, Expenditure, Power, Statistics, and Debt of the whole British Empire, &c. 8° 1833

Peche, Thomas. *See* Burney, Vol. 3 : Appendix 1.

Pechuel-Loesche, Dr. Kongoland : 1. Amtliche Berichte und Denkschriften über das Belgische Kongo-Unternehmen ; 2. Unterguinea und Kongostaat als Handels- und Wirtschaftsgebiet, nebst einer Liste der Faktoreien bis zum Jahre 1887. 8° *Jena,* 1887

Peck, Rev. E. J. Portions of the Book of Common Prayer, together with Hymns, Addresses, &c., for the use of the Eskimo of Hudson's Bay. 12° 1881

Peck, J. M. Guide for Emigrants to the West ; containing Sketches of Ohio, Indiana, Illinois, Missouri, Michigan, with the Territories of Wisconsin and Arkansas, and the adjacent parts. 18° *Boston, Mass.,* 1836

Peck, William. A Popular Handbook and Atlas of Astronomy, designed as a Complete Guide to a Knowledge of the Heavenly Bodies, and as an Aid to those possessing Telescopes. *Plates, illustrations, diagrams, &c.* 4° 1890

Peckham, S. F. *See* United States, A (Tenth Census, Vol. 10): Appendix 2.

Pécoul, Capt. A. Account and Description of the Sounding-Log, serving to Sound without entirely Stopping the Vessel, &c. 8° *Marseilles,* 1855

Pector, Désiré. Indication Approximative de Vestiges laissés par les Populations Précolombiennes du Nicaragua. Deuxième edition. 8* *Paris,* 1889

—— The same. 2ᵐᵉ partie. *Map and plates.* 8* *Paris,* 1889

—— Aperçu des principales communications relatives à la Linguistique faites au Congrès International des Americanistes. (Huitième Session, Paris, 1890.) 8* *Paris,* 1891

—— Exposé sommaire des voyages et travaux géographiques au Nicaragua dans le cours du XIXᵉ Siècle. (Congrès Internationale Géographique, Paris, 1889.) Large 8* *Paris,* 1891

—— Considérations sur quelques Noms Indigènes de localités de l'Isthme Centre-Americain. Large 8* *Paris,* 1892

—— Notice sur l'Archéologie du Salvador pré-Colombien. 4* *Paris,* 1892

—— Étude économique sur la République de Nicaragua. *Maps.* 8° *Neuchatel,* 1893

Peek, C. E. *See* United Kingdom, Rousdon Observatory, p. 827 : Appendix 3.

Peel, Capt. W. A Ride through the Nubian Desert. *Map.* 8° 1852

Peet, —. Letter from, on a New Chinese Geography. (*Missionary Herald,* July 1850.) 8* *Boston, Mass.,* 1850

Peez, Carl. Mostar und sein Culturkreis. Ein Stadtebild aus der Hercegovina. *Plan and illustrations.* 8° *Leipzig,* 1891

Pegoletti (or Pegolotti), F. B. *See* Kerr, Vol. 1 : Appendix 1.

Peiffer, E. Légende Territoriale de la France, pour servir à la Lecture des Cartes Topographiques. *Maps.* 8° *Paris,* 1877

Peirce, Benjamin. The Latitude of the Cambridge Observatory, in Massachusetts, determined from Transits of Stars over the Prime Vertical, observed during the months of December 1844 and January 1845, by W. C. Bond, Major J. D. Graham, and G. P. Bond. 4*

—— Tables of the Moon, constructed for the use of the American Ephemeris and Nautical Almanac. 4° *Washington,* 1865

Peirce, H. A. Early Discoveries of the Hawaiian Islands in the North Pacific Ocean ; evidences of Visits by Spanish Navigators during the 16th Century. Ethnologically considered, by Charles Wolcott Brooks. 8* *San Francisco,* 1880

Pelagius Cambrensis. *See* Hakluyt, Vol. 2 : Appendix 1.

Pelet, Paul. *See* Lebon.

Pelham, Cavendish. The World, or the Present State of the Universe : being a General and Complete Collection of Modern Voyages and Travels, Selected, Arranged, and Digested from the Narratives of the latest and most Authentic Travellers and Navigators. 2 vols. *Maps and plates.* 4° 1808-10 [For Contents of the two vols., *see* Appendix 1.]

Pelham, Edward. *See* Hakluyt. Soc. Publ., Vol. 18 ; Churchill, Vol. 4 : Appendix 1.

Pélion, M. D. Considérations Politiques et Militaires sur l'Algérie. 8° *Paris,* 1838

Pellegrini, Giuseppe. Elogio di G. Segato da Belluno. 8* *Florence,* 1836

Pelleschi, Giovanni. Eight Months on the Gran Chaco of the Argentine Republic. Crown 8° 1886

Pelletreau, A. Le Chemin de Fer Trans-Saharien : Étude des divers Tracés proposés. 8° *Constantine,* 1879

Pellicer de Tovar, Joseph. Mission Evangelica al Reyno de Congo par la Serafica Religion de los Capuchinos. 8° *Madrid,* 1649

Pellissier, E. *See* Algeria, A : Appendix 2.

Pellow, Thomas. *See* Brown, R.

Pelly, Sir Lewis. Memoir on the Khypoor State in Upper Sind, with Notes. [From the India Records, No. 17.] Royal 8° *Bombay,* 1855

—— Remarks on a Recent Journey to Shiraz ; with an Account of the Country between Bushire and Shirauz, and a Brief Account of the Province of Fars. *Map.* Folio* *Bombay,* 1863

Pelly, Sir Lewis. Visit to Lingah, Kishm, and Bunder Abbass. 8* 1864
—— Report on Route from Bushire to Shiraz, *via* Geesekan and Feroozabad. *Map and plates.* Small folio* 1864
—— Report of Journey from Bunder Abbass to Cape Jashk. *Map.* Folio* 1864
—— Remarks concerning the Pearl Oysterbeds of the Persian Gulf. Folio* 1865
Pelsart (or Pelsaert), Capt. Francis. *See* Hakluyt Soc. Publ., Vol. 25; Callander, 2; Harris, 1: Pinkerton, 11; Allgemeine Historie, 12: Appendix 1.
Pelt, Daniel van. *See* Tollens.
Pelzeln, A. von. Ueber die Malayische Säugethier-Fauna. *Map.* 4*
Vienna, 1876
—— *See* Holub; "Novara."
Pemberton, Capt. R. Boileau. Report on the Eastern Frontier of British India; with an Appendix; and a Supplement by Dr Bayfield on the British Political Relations with Ava. *Maps.* 8°
Culcutta, 1835
—— Report on Bootan; with an Appendix, 1838. *Maps.* Royal 8°
Calcutta, 1838
—— Ambassade au Boutan: Journal abrégé du Voyage en 1837-38. Rédigé par M. Griffith; accompagné de Notes par Ch. Olloba d'Ochoa. *Map.* 8*
Paris, 1840
—— *See* India, I, Assam: Appendix 2.
Pena, Carlos Maria de, and Honoré Roustan. The Oriental Republic of Uruguay at the World's Columbian Exhibition, Chicago, 1893. Geography, Rural Industries, Commerce, General Statistics. Translated into English by J. J. Rethore. *Map.* Large 8°
Montevideo, 1893
Peñafiel, Dr Antonio. *See* Mexico: Appendix 2.
Penck, Dr Albrecht. Mensch und Eiszeit. *Maps.* 4* *Brunswick,* 1884
—— Der Alte Rheingletscher auf dem Alpenvorlande. 8* *Munich,* 1886
—— Der Brenner. 8* [*Munich*] 1887
—— Ueber Denudation der Erdoberfläche. 12* *Vienna,* 1887
—— Die Höttinger Breccie. 8* *Vienna,* 1887
—— Die Ueberschwemmungen des Jahres 1888. 12* 1888
—— Die Bildung der Durchbruchthäler. 12* *Vienna,* 1888
—— Das Endziel der Erosion und Denudation. Vortrag gehalten auf dem VIII. Deutschen Geographentage zu Berlin. 8* *Berlin,* 1889
—— Die Gletscher der Ostalpen. 12* 1889
—— Theorien über das Gleichgewicht der Erdkruste. 12* *Vienna,* 1889
—— Ziele der Erdkunde in Oesterreich. 8* *Vienna,* 1889

Penck, Dr Albrecht. Geographische Bildersammlungen. Vortrag gehalten auf dem VIII. Deutschen Geographentage zu Berlin. 8* *Berlin,* 1889
—— Der Flächeninhalt der österreichisch-ungarischen Monarchie. 8*
Vienna, 1889
—— Die Glacialschotter in den Ostalpen; mit einem Anhange enthaltend die Hauptergebnisse der von A. Penck, E Brückner, und Böhm, bearbeiteten Preisaufgabe über "die Vergletscherung der Ostalpen." 12* *Vienna,* 1890
—— Noës geologische Uebersichtskarte der Alpen. 12* *Vienna,* 1890
—— Der Ausbruch des Tarawera und Rotomahana auf Neu-Seeland. 8*
[*Vienna,* N.D.]
—— Die Donau. *Plates.* 12* *Vienna,* 1891
—— Der Neunte Deutsche Geographentag in Wien. 8* *Vienna,* 1891
—— Die Geographie an der Wiener Universität. 8* *Vienna,* 1891
—— Die Formen der Landoberfläche, ein Vortrag gehalten auf dem 9 Deutschen Geographentage in Wien im Jahre 1891. 8* *Berlin,* 1891
—— Die Erdkarte im Massstabe von 1 : 1,000,000. 4* *Munich,* 1891
—— Bericht der Central-Kommission für Wissenschaftliche Landeskunde von Deutschland über die zwei Geschäftsjahre von Ostern, 1891, bis Ostern 1893. (Sonder-Abdruck aus den Verhandlungen des X Deutschen Geographentages in Stuttgart, 1893.) 8* *Vienna,* 1893
—— Bericht über die Exkursion des X Deutschen Geographentages nach Ober-Schwaben und dem Bodensee, 10-14 April 1893. 8* *Berlin,* 1893
—— *See* Kirchhoff.
—— **A. Böhm, and A. Rodler.** Bericht über eine gemeinsame Excursion in den Böhmerwald. 8* [*Vienna,* 1887]
Penck's Geographische Abhandlungen. Band I., 1886. Large 8° *Vienna,* 1887
　　Heft 1.—Brückner, Dr E. Die Vergletscherung des Salzach - Gebietes nebst Beobachtungen über die Eiszeit in der Schweiz. *Map and plates* 1886
　　Heft 2.—Neumann, Prof. Dr Ludwig. Orometrie des Schwarzwaldes. *Map and plate.* Large 8° 1886
　　Heft 3.—Böhm, Dr A. Eintheilung der Ostalpen. *Map* 1887
—— The same. Band II., 1887. Large 8° *Vienna,* 1888
　　Heft 1.—Geiger, Dr Wilhelm. Die Pamir - Gebiete; eine geographische Monographie. *Map* 1887
　　Heft 2.—Hann, Dr Julius. Die Vertheilung des Luftdruckes in Mittel- und Südeuropa. *Maps* 1887
　　Heft 3.—Soyka, Dr Isidor. Die Schwankungen des Grundwassers 1888

Penck's Geographische Abhandlungen. Band III. Large 8° *Vienna*, 1889 Heft 1.—Sievers, Dr W. Die Cordillere von Mérida, nebst Bemerkungen über das karibische Gebirge. Ergebnisse einer . . . 1884-85 ausgeführten Reisen. *Map* 1888 Heft 2.—Günther, Dr S. Johannes Kepler und der tellurisch-kosmische Magnetismus. 1888 Heft 3.—Woeikof, Dr A. Der Einfluss einer Schneedecke auf Boden, Klima, und Wetter. 1889 —— The same. Band IV. Heft 1.—Kretschmer, Konrad. Die physische Erdkunde im Christlichen Mittelalter. 1889 —— The same. Band V. Heft 1.—Arbeiten des Geographischen Institutes der k.k. Universität Wien. (Heiderich, Karowski, Swarowsky.) *Plates* 1891 Heft 3.—Cvijic, Dr Jovan. Das Karstphänomen. 1893 Heft 4. — Forster, Dr A. E. Die Temperatur fliessender Gewässer Mitteleuropas. *Diagram* 1894

Pendleton, N. G. On Military Posts from Council Bluffs to the Pacific Ocean. *Map.* 8* *Washington*, 1842

Peney, Alfred. Les dernières Explorations dans la Région du Haut Fleuve Blanc. Extraits de ses Papiers et de son Journal de Voyage ; mis en Ordre, accompagnés de Notes, par Malte-Brun. *Map.* 8* *Paris*, 1863

Penington, John. Scraps Osteologic and Archaiological. 8* *Philadelphia*, 1841

Peniston, William Michael. Public Works in Pernambuco, in the Empire of Brazil. Edited by C. Manby and J. Forrest. 8* 1863

Penn, J. *See* United Kingdom, A, Hydrogr. Off. Publ. : Appendix 2.

Pennant, T. A Tour in Scotland, 1769. 3rd edition. *Plates.* 4° *Warrington*, 1774 —— A Tour in Scotland, and Voyage to the Hebrides, 1772. Parts 1 and 2. *Plates.* 4° 1774-76 —— A Journey from London to the Isle of Wight. 2 vols. (in 1). *Maps and plates.* 4° 1801 —— Tours in Wales. 3 vols. *Plates.* 8° 1810 —— The Journey from Chester to London, with Notes. *Plates.* 8° 1811 —— *See* Pinkerton, Vol. 3 ; Appendix 1.

Pennazzi, Luigi. La Grecia Moderna. *Illustrations.* 8° *Milan*, 1879

Pennefather, Captain C. Explorations in the Gulf of Carpentaria, and Surveys in the Vicinity of Point Parker. *Map.* Folio* [*Brisbane*] 1880

Pennefather, Captain C. Cruise of the Queensland Government schooner "Pearl" in the Gulf of Carpentaria. [Report of the Exploration of the Coen, Archer, and Batavia Rivers.] *Plan.* Folio* [*Brisbane*] 1880 —— Report on Further Survey of Point Parker, Gulf of Carpentaria. *Chart.* Folio* *Brisbane*, 1882

Pennefather, F. W. *See* Murray's Handbooks. New Zealand.

Pennesi, Giuseppe. Pietro della Valle e i suoi viaggi in Turchia, Persia, e India. *Map.* 8* *Rome*, 1890 —— Tunisi e il suo nuovo porto (Estratto dalla Rassegna Navale, Anno I. No. 7). 8* [*Palermo*, N.D.] —— L'impresa del Panama. 8* *Florence*, 1893

Penney, Stephen. Concise Navigating Directions for the River Thames ; including all the Pools, Reaches, and Channels, from London Bridge to the South Foreland and Orfordness, and for the English Channel to Beachy Head ; also for the Port of Dunkerque, and the approaches to the Scheldt. *Charts.* Oblong 12° 1892

Penning, W. Henry. A Guide to the Gold Fields of South Africa. *Map.* 12* *Pretoria*, 1883 —— The Geology of the Southern Transvaal. 8° 1893

Penny, Rev. Alfred. Ten Years in Melanesia. *Chart and illustrations.* 12° [1887]

Penny, Capt. *See* Sutherland, P. C.

Penny, William. *See* Franklin, Sir John.

Penrose, F. C. On Certain Anomalies in the Construction of the Parthenon, Athens. 4* 1847

Pentland, J. B., and Sir Woodbine Parish. Notices on the Bolivian Andes and Southern Affluents of the Rivers Amazons and Beni. *Map.* 8* 1835

Pepe, Lieut.-Gen. Scenes and Events in Italy from 1847 to 1849, including the Siege of Venice. 2 vols. 12° 1850

Pepe, José. Espedicion a Bariloche : Apuntes de Viaje. 12* *Valparaiso*, 1885

Pequito, R. A. A Sociedade de Geographia de Lisboa e o Marquez de Sá de Bandeira. 8* *Lisbon*, 1877

Peragallo, P. L'Autenticità delle Historie di Fernando Colombo, e le Critiche del Signor Enrico Harrisse, con ampli frammenti del testo Spagnuolo di D. Fernando. Large 8° *Geneva*, 1884 —— Riconferma dell' Autenticità delle Historie di Fernando Colombo. Risposta alle osservazione dell' Uff. Prof. Dottore Pietro Arata. 8° *Geneva*, 1885 —— Cristoforo Colombo e la sua Famiglia. Rivista generale degli errori del Sig. E. Harrisse, Studi Storico-critici. Large 8° *Lisbon*, 1888

Peralta, Manuel M. de. Costa Rica, its Climate, Constitution, and Resources. 8* 1873

—— Costa-Rica, Nicaragua, y Panamá, en el Siglo XVI. ; su Historia y sus Limites segun los Documentos del Archivo de Indias de Sevilla del de Simancas, &c., recogidos y Publicados con Notas y Aclaraciones Históricas y Geográficas. *Map.* 8° *Madrid,* 1883

—— Francisco Drake en el mar del sur. 8* [*Madrid*] 1883

—— El' Canal Interoceanico de Nicaragua y Costa-Rica en 1620 and en 1887. Relaciones de Diego de Mercado y Thos. C. Reynolds, con otros Documentos Recogidos y Austados. 8* *Brussels,* 1887

Perceval, A. Caussin de. See Bocthor.

Perceval, Westby Brook. New Zealand : a Paper read before the Royal Colonial Institute. 8* 1892

Percher, Hyppolite. See under *nom de plume* Alis, Harry.

Percival, James G. Annual Report of the Geological Survey of the State of Wisconsin. 8* *Madison,* 1856

Percival, Robert. Account of the Island of Ceylon, containing its History, Geography, Natural History, with the Manners and Customs of its various Inhabitants ; with the Journal of an Embassy to the Court of Candy. *Maps.* 4° 1803

—— See Eyriès, Vol. 13 : Appendix 1.

Percival, William Spencer. The Land of the Dragon : my Boating and Shooting Excursions to the Gorges of the Upper Yangtze. *Plan and frontispiece.* 8° 1889

Percy, George. See Purchas, Vol. 4, Book 9 : Appendix 1.

Peredolsky, V. S. Remains of the Stone-Age Inhabitants of the Shores of Lake Ilmeñ, the Banks of the Volkhov, and the Territory of Novgorod Veliky. [In Russian.] 8* *St Petersburg,* 1893

Peregrinus, Gulielmus. See Hakluyt, Vol. 2 : Appendix 1.

Pereira, Father. See Hakluyt Soc. Publ., Vol. 17 : Appendix 1.

Pereira, Feliciano Ant. Marques. Viagem da Corveta "Dom João I.," á Capital do Japão, 1860. *Map.* 8° *Lisbon,* 1863

Pereira, F. F. Taboa Geografico-Estatistica Luzitana, ou Diccionario abreviado de todas as Cidades, Villas, e Freguezias de Portugal ; com o Appendix d'uma breve Noticia das actuaes Possessoens de Portugal no ultramar. 4° *Oporto,* 1839

Pereira, F. M. E. Historia de Minás 'Además Sagad Rei de Ethiopia. Texto Ethiopico. 8* *Lisbon,* 1888

Pereira, Ricardo S. Les États-Unis de Colombie, Précis d'Histoire et de Géographie, Physique, Politique, et Commerciale. *Maps.* 8° *Paris,* 1883

Perelaer, M. T. H. Een Kwart eeuw tusschen de Keerkringen. 4 vols. 8° *Rotterdam,* 1884-85
1. Naar den Equator met een voorspel: van Pastoor Soldaat.
2. In het land der zon.
3. Op sneê verguld.
4. Naar den eindpaal eener Loopbaan.

Perera, Galeotta. See Purchas, Vol. 3, Book 1 : Appendix 1.

Peretti, Abbé J. Christophe Colomb, Français, Corse, et Calvais : Étude Historique sur la Patrie du Grand Amiral de l'Océan. 12° *Paris,* 1888

Pereyaslawzewa, Dr Sophie. Monographie des Turbellariés de la Mer Noire. *Plates.* 8° *Odessa,* 1892

Perez, Felipe. Geografia General, fisica y politica de los Estados Unidos de Colombia, y Geografia particular de la Ciudad de Bogota. Tomo Primero. 8° *Bogota,* 1883

—— Geografia General del Nuevo Mundo y particular de cada uno de los paises y Colonias que lo conponen. 12° *Bogota,* 1888

Perez, Martin. See Purchas, Vol. 4, Book 8 : Appendix 1.

Perez-Rosales, Vicente. Essai sur le Chili. *Maps and table.* 8° *Hamburg,* 1857

Perkins, Emma R. See Diehl.

Perkins, George J. Mackay : an Essay upon the Rise, Progress, Industries, Resources, and Prospects of the Town and District of Mackay. 8* *Mackay,* 1888

Perkins, Guillermo. Las Colonias de Santa Fé, su Origen, Progreso, y actual Situacion ; con Observaciones generales sobre la Emigracion á la Repùblica Argentina. [Spanish and English.] 8° *Rosario,* 1864

—— Relacion de la Espedicion á el Rey en el Chaco. *Map.* 8* *Rosario,* 1867

Perkins, James. A Tour round the Globe. Letters to the *City Press.* 12° 1891

Perley, M. H. Hand-book of Information for Emigrants to New Brunswick. *Map.* 12* *St John's, N.B.,* 1854

Péron, M. F., and Louis Freycinet. Voyage de Découvertes aux Terres Australes, sur les corvettes le "Géographe," le "Naturaliste," et la goelette le "Casuarina," pendant 1800-4. 3 vols. *Plates* 4°, and *Maps* large 4°, 2 vols. *Paris,* 1807-16

—— See Pinkerton, Vol. 11 ; Phillips, Collection of Modern and Contemporary Voyages [1], Vol. 11 : Appendix 1.

Pérouse, Comte de la. See La Pérouse.

Péroz, Étienne. Au Soudan Français. Souvenirs de Guerre et de Mission. *Map.* 8° *Paris,* 1889

Perret, Paul. Les Pyrénées Françaises. Première Partie : Lourdes — Argelés — Cauterets — Luz — Saint Sauveur — Barèges. II. Le Pays Basque et la Basse-Navarre. III. L'Adouri, la Garonne et le Pays de Foix. 3 vols. *Maps and illustrations.* Large 8°
Paris, 1881-84

Perrey, Alexis. Circulaire relative à l'Observation des Tremblements de Terre. 8*   *Paris*, 1854
—— Documents relatifs aux Tremblements de Terre au Chili. Royal 8*
Lyons, 1854
—— Bibliographie Seismique. 8°
Dijon, 1855
—— Note sur les Tremblements de Terre en 1858, avec Suppléments pour les années antérieures. 8* *Brussels*, 1860
—— The same, 1859. 8* *Brussels*, 1861
—— The same, 1860. 8* *Brussels*, 1862
—— Documents sur les Tremblements de Terre et les Phénomènes Volcaniques au Japon. 8*   *Lyons*, 1862
—— Propositions sur les Tremblements de Terre et les Volcans. 8* *Paris*, 1863
—— Documents sur les Tremblements de Terre et les Phénomènes Volcaniques dans l'Archipel des Kouriles et au Kamtschatka. 8*   *Lyons*, 1863
—— Note sur les Tremblements de Terre en 1861, avec Suppléments pour les années antérieures. 8° *Brussels*, 1863-66
—— The same, 1862. 8° *Brussels*, 1864
—— The same, 1863. 8° *Brussels*, [1865]
—— The same, 1864. 8* *Brussels*, 1866
—— Documents sur les Tremblements de Terre et les Phénomènes Volcaniques des îles Aleutiennes, de la Péninsule d'Aljaska et de la Côte Nord d'Amérique. 8°
Dijon, 1866
—— *See* Barbiani.

Perrier, Amelia. A Winter in Morocco. *Plates.* Small 8°   1876

Perrin, F. *See* Conway and Coolidge.

Perron, A. du. Zend-Avesta : Ouvrage de Zoroastre, contenant les Idées Théologiques, Physiques, et Morales de ce Législateur, les Cérémonies du Culte Religieux qu'il a établi, et plusieurs traits importans relatifs à l'ancienne Histoire des Perses. Traduit en François, avec des Remarques ; et accompagné de plusieurs Traités propres à éclaircir les Matières qui en sont l'objet, par M. Anquetil du Perron. 3 vols. *Plates.* 4°   *Paris*, 1771

Perron, E. [Jean Vénéor]. In Memoriam Tschingel. 8*   1892
—— *See* Algeria, A (Exploration, Vol. 10, &c.) : Appendix 2.

Perrot, A. M. Rapport sur le Plan des îles Wanikoro, ou de la Pérouse ; gravé par M. Caplin. 8*   *Paris*, N.D.

Perrot, A. M., and Alex. Aragon. Dictionnaire Universel de Géographie Moderne : Description Physique, Politique, et Historique, de tous les Lieux de la Terre. 2 vols. *Maps.* Small folio
Paris, 1837

Perrot, Georges. Souvenirs d'un Voyage en Asie Mineure. 8°   *Paris*, 1864

Perry, Sir Erskine. On the Geographical Distribution of the Principal Languages of India, and the feasibility of introducing English as a Lingua Franca. *Map.* 8*
1852
—— A Bird's-Eye View of India ; with Extracts from a Journal kept in the Provinces, Nepal, &c. 12°   1855

Perry, Commodore M. C. The Enlargement of Geographical Science, a consequence to the Opening of New Avenues to Commercial Enterprise. Paper read before the American Geographical and Statistical Society, 6th March 1856. 8*   *New York*, 1856
—— Narrative of the Expedition of an American Squadron to the China Seas and Japan, performed in the years 1852, '53, and '54, by order of the Government of the United States. Compiled from the Original Notes and Journals of Commodore Perry and his Officers, at his request and under his supervision, by Francis L. Hawks. 3 vols. in 4. *Maps and plates.* 4°   *Washington*, 1856
Vol. 1.—Narrative. Vol. 2.—Plates and Maps, in two parts. Vol. 3.—United States Japan Expedition.—Observations on the Zodiacal Light, from 2nd April 1853 to 22nd April 1855, made chiefly on board the United States steam-frigate "Mississippi" during her late cruise in Eastern Seas, and her voyage homeward ; with conclusions from the data thus obtained, by the Rev. George Jones.

Persoz, J. *See* Rondot.

Pert, Sir Thomas. *See* Hakluyt, Vol. 3 ; Kerr, Vol. 6 ; Purchas, Vol. 4, Book 6 : Appendix 1.

Perthes, Justus. Justus Perthes in Gotha, 1785-1885 *Portraits.* 4°   N.D.
—— Katalog der Atlanten, Karten und Periodischen Schriften aus dem Verlage von Justus Perthes Geographische Anstalt. 4°   *Gotha*, 1886

Pertuiset, E. Expédition Pertuiset à la Terre de Feu : Rapport envoyé aux Sociétés géographiques. Small 8*
Paris, 1874

Pertusier, C. La Bosnie, considéré dans ses rapports avec l'Empire Ottoman. *Frontispiece.* 8°   *Paris*, 1822
—— *See* Phillips, New Voyages and Travels [3], Vol. 8 : Appendix 1.

Pertz, G. H. Der älteste Versuch zur Entdeckung des Seeweges nach Ostindien im Jahre 1291. 4° *Berlin,* 1859
Pertz, Karolvs Avgvstvs Fridericvs. De Cosmographia Ethici, liber tres. 8° *Berlin,* 1853
Perucca, Aristide. In Birmania. *Portrait, map, and plates.* 8° 1886
Pery, G. A. Geographia e Estatistica Geral de Portugal e Colonias. *Maps.* 8° *Lisbon,* 1875
Peschel, Oscar. Geschichte des Zeitalters der Entdeckungen. 8° *Stuttgart,* 1858
—— Geschichte der Erdkunde bis auf A. v. Humboldt und Carl Ritter. *Maps.* 8° *Munich,* 1865
—— Neue Probleme der vergleichenden Erdkunde als Versuch einer Morphologie der Erdoberfläche. *Map.* 8° *Leipzig,* 1870
—— Völkerkunde. 3rd edition. 8° *Leipzig,* 1876
—— The Races of Man and their Geographical Distribution. Small 8° 1876
—— The same. 3rd edition. *Plates.* 8° *Leipzig,* 1878
—— Abhandlungen zur Erd- und Völkerkunde; herausgegeben von J. Löwenberg. 3 vols. 8° *Leipzig,* 1877-79
—— Europäische Staatenkunde mit einen Anhang; Die Vereinigten Staaten von Amerika. Mit Benutzung der hinterlassenen Manuscripte Oscar Peschel's nach den Originalquellen bearbeitet von Otto Krümmel. Erster Band. Allgemeiner Theil; Das Russische Reich, Skandinavien, Dänemark, Das Britische Reich. [*No more published.*] 8° *Leipzig,* 1880
—— Physische Erdkunde. Nach den hinterlassenen Manuskripten Oscar Peschel's selbständig bearbeitet und herausgegeben von Gustav Leipoldt. Zweite . . Auflage. 2 vols. *Maps and illustrations.* 8° *Leipzig,* 1884-85
—— *See* Bianco.
Pestalozzi, John Henry. *See* Raumer.
Pet, Arthur. *See* Hakluyt, Vol. 1 : Appendix 1.
"Pet," Cruises of the. *See* Hughes, R. E.
Petachia, Rabbi, of Ratisbon. Travels of, who in the latter end of the Twelfth Century visited Poland, Russia, Little Tartary, the Crimea, Armenia, Assyria, Syria, the Holy Land, and Greece. Hebrew and English, with Explanatory Notes by the Translator, Dr A. Benisch, and W. F. Ainsworth. 12° 1856
Petelin, Evesko. *See* Gottfried : Appendix 1.
Peter, Bruno. *See* Reiss and Stühel.
Peter, R. *See* Owen, D. D.

Petermann, Dr Augustus. Statistical Notes to the Cholera Map of the British Isles, 1831-33. 8* 1849
—— Sir John Franklin, the Sea of Spitzbergen, and Whale Fisheries in the Arctic Regions. 8* 1852
—— Historical Summary of the Five Years' Search after Sir John Franklin, from 1st January 1848 to 1st January 1853. 8* N.D.
—— An Account of the Progress of the Expedition to Central Africa performed by order of Her Majesty's Foreign Office, under Messrs Richardson, Barth, Overweg, and Vogel, in the years 1850-51-52-53, consisting of Maps and Illustrations, with Descriptive Notes. Constructed and compiled from official and private materials by Augustus Petermann. Folio 1854
—— Spitzbergen und die arktische Central-Region. (Ergänzungsheft, 16—Petermann's Mittheilungen.) *Maps.* 4° *Gotha,* 1865
—— Erforschung der arktischen Central-Region durch eine Deutsche Nordfahrt. *Map.* 4* [*Gotha,* 1865]
—— Das nördlichste Land der Erde. *Map.* 4* [*Gotha,* 1867]
—— Die Deutsche Nordpol-Expedition, 1868. 4* [*Gotha,* 1868]
—— Eine Kartenskizze von Dr Livingstone's neuen Forschungen. *Maps.* 4* [*Gotha,* 1870]
—— Australien nach dem Stande der geographischen Kenntniss in 1871, mit geographisch-statistischem Kompendium von C. E. Meinicke. (Ergänzungsheft, 29 — Petermann's Mittheilungen.) 4 *coloured maps.* 4° *Gotha,* 1871
—— The same. (Ergänzungsheft, 30—Petermann's Mittheilungen.) *Maps.* 4° *Gotha,* 1871
—— Die neue Oesterreichische Nordpolar Expedition unter dem Commando von Weyprecht und Payer. 4* *Gotha,* 1872
—— Die Süd-Amerikanischen Republiken Argentina, Chile, Paraguay und Uruguay nach dem Stande der geographischen Kenntniss in 1875. Nach originalen und offiziellen Quellen kartographisch dargestellt von A. Petermann. Nebst einem geographisch-statistischen Compendium von Prof. Dr H. Burmeister. (Ergänzungsheft, 39—Petermann's Mittheilungen.) *Map.* 4° *Gotha,* 1875
—— Dr Livingstone's Erforschung des oberen Congo. 4* [*Gotha,* 1872]
—— Geographie und Erforschung der Polar Regionen [Nordenskiöld, Finsch, Nares]. *Maps.* 4* [*Gotha,* 1876]
—— The Expedition to the North Pole. Letter to the President of the R.G.S., 8th December 1876. MS. 8* *Gotha,* 1876

Petermann, Dr Augustus. *See* Malte-Brun ; Koldeway ; *also* Arctic, H, Appendix 2 ; Germany, Gotha : Appendix 3.

—— **and Bruno Hassenstein.** Inner-Afrika, nach dem Stande der geographischen Kenntniss im Jahre 1861 nach den Quellen bearbeitet. Erste Abtheilung : Nubische Wüste, Bajuda-Steppe, Darfur, Kordofan, und Takale, Land der Dinka und Nuehr, Dar Fertit, u.s.w. (Ergänzungsheft, 7—Petermann's Mittheilungen.) 2 *coloured maps.* 4°
Gotha, 1862

—— Inner-Afrika. Dr E. Behm's Land und Folk der Tebu ; M. von Beurmann's Travels in 1862. (Ergänzungsheft, 8—Petermann's Mittheilungen.) *Maps.* 4°
Gotha, 1862

—— Inner-Afrika. Antinori's Reise, 1860 und 1861 ; Beurmann's Reise. (Ergänzungsheft, 10 — Petermann's Mittheilungen.) *Maps.* 4° *Gotha*, 1862

—— Inner - Afrika. Memoire zu den Karten : Reisen von Heuglin, Morlang, Harnier. (Ergänzungsheft, 11 — Petermann's Mittheilungen.) 4°
Gotha, 1862

Peters, Dr Carl. Stanley and Emin Pasha. (From *Contemporary Review*.) 8* 1890

—— New Light on Dark Africa : being the Narrative of the German Emin Pasha Expedition, its Journeyings and Adventures among the Native Tribes of Eastern Equatorial Africa, on the Lake Baringo and the Victoria Nyanza. Translated from the German by H. W. Dulcken, Ph.D. *Map and illustrations.* 8° 1891

Peters, C. H. F. Report on the Determination of the Longitude of Elmira. 8°
Albany, N.Y., 1864

—— Report on the Longitude and Latitude of Ogdensburgh. 8° 1865

Peters, J. C. A Treatise on the Origin, Nature, Prevention, and Treatment of Asiatic Cholera. 12° *New York*, 1866

Peters, C. T. Medico-topographical Report on Muscat. Folio* 1875

Peters, W. *See* Rohlfs.

Petersen, Carl. Erindringer fra Polarlandene Optegnede af, 1850-55. Udgivne af Lieut. L. B. Deichmann. *Map.* 12°
Copenhagen, 1857

—— Den sidste Franklin-Expedition med "Fox," Capt. M'Clintock. *Portrait, maps, plates, and facsimiles.* 8°
Copenhagen, 1860

Petersen, W. *See* Schrenck and Maximowicz, Beiträge zur Kenntniss des Russischen Reiches, &c., 4.

Peterson, E. *See* Lanckoronski ; *also* Turkey-in-Asia, A : Appendix 2.

2 A

Petherick, John. Egypt, the Soudan, and Central Africa, with Explorations from Khartoum on the White Nile to the Regions of the Equator. *Map.* 8°
1861

—— Land Journey westward of the White Nile, from Abu Kuka to Gondokoro. *Map.* 8* [1864]

Petit, P. *See* France, B, *a* : Appendix 2.

Petit, V. Cannes : Promenades des Étrangers dans la Ville et ses Environs. Crown 8° *Cannes* [1866]

Petit-Thouars. *See* Du Petit-Thouen.

Petitot, Émile. Dictionnaire de la Langue Dènè-Dindjie, dialectes Montagnais ou Chippewayan, Peaux de Lièvre et Loucheux ; renfermant en outre un grand nombre de termes propres a sept autres Dialectes de la même Langue ; précédé d'une Monographie des Dènè-Dindjie d'une Grammaire, et de tableaux Synoptiques des Conjugaisons. [Bibliothêque de Linguistique et d'Ethnographie Americaines, publiée par Alph. L. Pinart, Vol. 2.] 4° *Paris*, 1876

—— Vocabulaire Français - Esquimaux. Dialecte des Tchiglit des bouches du Mackenzie et de l'Anderson ; précédé d'une Monographie de cette tribu et de notes grammaticales. [Bibliothèque de Linguistique et d'Ethnographie Americaines, publiée par M. Alph. L. Pinart, Vol. 3.] 4° *Paris*, 1876

—— Traditions Indiennes du Canada Nord-Ouest. [Les Littératures Populaires de toutes les Nations, Tome 23.] 12°
Paris, 1886

—— Traditions Indiennes du Canada Nord-Ouest. Textes Originaux et Traduction Littérale. 8° *Alençon*, 1887

—— En Route pour la Mer Glaciale. *Illustrations.* 12° *Paris* [1887]

—— Les Grands Esquimaux. *Map and illustration.* 12° *Paris*, 1887

—— La Femme aux Métaux. Legende Nationale des Dènè Couteaux-Jaunes du Grand Lac des Esclaves, Canada Nord-Ouest. 8* *Meaux*, 1888

—— Quinze ans sous le Cercle polaire. Mackenzie, Anderson, Youkon. *Map and illustration.* 12° *Paris*, 1889

—— Autour du Grand Lac des Esclaves. *Map and portrait.* 12° *Paris*, 1891

Petley, E. W. Notes on Marmagao (Goa), Portuguese India. 8* N.D.

Petri, Dr E. *See* Jadrinzew ; Javorskij.

Petrie, W. M. Flinders. Tell el Hesy (Lachish). *Illustrations.* 4° 1891

Petroff, Ivan. Department of the Interior, Census Office : Report on the Population, Industries, and Resources of Alaska. *Maps and plates.* 4°
Washington, 1884

—— *See* United States, A (Tenth Census, 1880, Vol. 8) : Appendix 2.

Petrusevitch, Major-Gen. Nicholas. The Turcomans : Part 1. The Turcomans inhabiting the Country between the Uzboi (ancient bed of the Oxus) and the Northern confines of Persia ; Part 2. The North-eastern Provinces of Khorassan ; Part 3. Routes from Astrabad to Meshed ; Part 4. Critique on Sir Henry Rawlinson's " Roads to Merv." (From the *Journal of the Caucasus Branch of the Imperial Russian Geographical Society*, Vol. 11, No. 1, for 1880.) Translated by Robert Michell. Folio* [1879]

Pettersen, Karl. Lofoten og Vesteraalen. *Map.* 8* *Tromsö*, 1880
—— Om Internationela Polarexpeditioner. 8* *Stockholm*, 1883
—— Det Europæiske Polarhav i Sommeren 1885. *Map.* 8* *Stockholm*, 1886

Petterson, A. L. F. *See* Sweden, A : Appendix 2.

Petty, William. History of the Survey of Ireland, commonly called " The Down Survey," A.D. 1655-56. Edited by T. Aiskew Larcom. Small 4° *Dublin*, 1851

Petzholdt, A. Turkestan : auf Grundlage einer im Jahre 1871, unternommenen Bereisung des Landes. *Map.* Small 8* *Leipzig*, 1874

Peuchet, J. Dictionnaire Universel de la Géographie Commerçante. 5 vols. 4° *Paris*, 1799-1800
—— Statistique Elémentaire de la France. 8° *Paris*, 1805

Peucker, Dr Karl. Ueber Geländedarstellung auf Schulkarten. Ein Vortrag gehalten auf dem X. Deutschen Geographentag in Stuttgart im Jahr 1893. 8* *Berlin*, 1893

Peyer, Gustav. Geschichte des Reisens in der Schweiz ; eine Culturgeschichtliche Studie. 12° *Bâle*, 1885

Peyret, Alejo. Cartas sobre Misiones. 8° *Buenos Ayres*, 1881

Peyrère, Isaac de la. *See* De la Peyrère.

Peyssonnel, — de. Observations Historiques et Géographiques sur les Peuples Barbares qui ont habité les bords du Danube et du Pont-Euxin. *Maps and plates.* 4° *Paris*, 1765

Peyssonnel, J. A., and L. R. Desfontaines. Voyages dans les Régences de Tunis et d'Alger. Publiés par Dureau de la Malle. 2 vols. *Maps and plates.* 8° *Paris*, 1838

Peyton, John Lewis. The Adventures of my Grandfather ; with Extracts from his Letters, and other Family Documents, &c. 8° 1867
—— The American Crisis, or Pages from the Note-Book of a State Agent during the Civil War. 2 vols. 8° 1867
—— History of Augusta County, Virginia. 8° *Staunton*, 1882
—— *See* Blundell.

Peyton, Capt. Walter. *See* Gottfried ; Kerr, Vol. 9 ; Purchas, Vol. 1, Book 4 : Appendix 1.

Pezzana, Angelo. L'Antichita del Mappamondo de' Pizigani, fatto nel 1367, vendicata dalle accuse del Padre Pellegrini. 12* *Parma*, 1807

Pezzi, C. B. Di Giovanni Cabotta rivelatore del settentrionale emisfero d'America con documenti inediti. *Plate.* 8° *Venice*, 1881

Pezzl, Johann. Beschreibung der Haupt und Residenz-Stadt Wien. 5th edition. 12° *Vienna*, 1824
—— Beschreibung von Wien ; verbessert und vermehrt von Franz Ziska. 18° *Vienna*, 1826

Pfaff, C. G. F. *See* Lauridsen.

Pfeiffer, Ida. A Lady's Voyage round the World. A selected Translation by Mrs Percy Sinnett. 12° 1851
—— Journey to Iceland, and Travels in Sweden and Norway. From the German, by Charlotte Fenimore Cooper. 8° 1852
—— A Woman's Journey round the World, from Vienna to Brazil, Chili, Tahiti, China, Hindostan, Persia, and Asia Minor. Translated from the German. *Plates.* 8° 1852
—— Visit to the Holy Land, Egypt, and Italy. Translated from the German, by H. W. Dulcken. *Plates.* 8° 1853

Pfeil, Joachim, Graf. Vorschläge zur praktischen Kolonisation in Ost-Afrika. 8* *Berlin*, 1888
—— Account of Travels in East Africa ; Journeys through Kutu and Exploration of the Ulanga. MS. 4° 1888

Pfeil, L., Graf. von. Ein Beitrag zur Geschichte unserer Erde. *Map.* 8* *Berlin*, 1853
—— Cometen und Meteore, die Haupt-Ursachen der Erd-Revolutionen. 8* *Berlin*, 1854
—— Kometische Strömungen auf der Erdoberfläche. *Maps and plates.* Small 8* *Berlin*, 1879

Pfoundes, C. The Folk-Lore of Old Japan. 8* *Birmingham* [1880]
—— Notes on the History of " Old Japan," and the History of Eastern Adventure, Exploration, and Discovery, and Foreign Intercourse with Japan. 8* 1882

Pfund, J. Essai Météorologique. 12° *Cairo*, 1877
—— *See* Zarb.

Phayre, Lieut.-Col. R. Report on the Subject of his Tour among the Karen Mountain Tribes (East India), and the Efforts of the Rev. Dr and Mrs Mason for the Spread of Education and Civilization among them. [Parly. Rep.] Folio 1861

Phayre, Lieut.-Col. R. Report on the Road to Mahabuleshwur, viâ Ambur Khind and Mundur Dew. *Maps.* [From the India Records, No. 65.] Royal 8° *Bombay*, 1862
—— *See* Yule, Sir H.

Phelps, Thomas. *See* Churchill, Vol. 8 : Appendix 1.

"Philalethes." The History of Ceylon, from the Earliest Period to the year MDCCCXV. . . . By Philalethes, A.M. Oxon. To which is subjoined, R. Knox's Historical Relation of the Island, with an Account of his Captivity, &c. *Map and plates.* 4° 1817

Philebert, Gen. C. La Conquête pacifique de l'Intérieur Africain, Nègres, Musulmans, et Chrétiens. *Maps and illustrations.* 8° *Paris*, 1889

Philigret, Capt. Canal Maritime de Suez : Observations Hydrographiques dans la Baie de Péluse. 8* *Paris*, 1857

Philip, George, junr. *See* Leutemann.

Philipos, E. The Syrian Christians of Malabar, otherwise called the Christians of S. Thomas. Edited by the Rev. G. B. Howard. 12° 1869

Philippe, Charles. *See* Possot.

Philippi, Dr R. A. Reise durch die Wüste Atacama auf Befehl der Chilenischen Regierung im Sommer 1853-54. *Maps and plates.* 4° *Halle*, 1860
—— Jeografia. La Isla de Pascua i sus habitantes. Large 8* *Santiago de Chile*, 1873
—— Descripcion de algunos Idolos Peruanos del Museo Nacional de Chile. *Plates.* Large 8* *Santiago*, 1891

Philipps, Thomas. Advantages of Emigration to Algoa Bay and Albany, South Africa. 12* 1864

Philippson, Dr Alfred. Zur Ethnographie des Peloponnes. *Map.* 4° [*Gotha*] 1880
—— Studien über Wasserscheiden. 8* *Leipzig*, 1886
—— Bericht über eine Reise durch Nord- und Mittel-Griechenland. *Map.* 8* *Berlin*, 1890
—— Der Isthmos von Korinth. Eine geologisch-geographische Monographie. *Map and illustrations.* 8* *Berlin*, 1890
—— Peloponnesische Bergfahrten. *Illustrations.* 8* *Vienna*, 1891
—— Der Peloponnes, Versuch einer Landeskunde auf geologischer Grundlage. Large 8° *Berlin*, 1892
—— *See* Galle.

Philips, Melville. *See* Melville, G. W.

Philips, Miles. *See* Hakluyt, Vol. 3 : Appendix 1.

Phillip, Governor Arthur. Voyage to Botany Bay, with an Account of the Establishment of the Colonies of Port Jackson and Norfolk Island, compiled from authentic papers ; to which are

Phillip, Governor Arthur—*continued.* added the Journals of Lieuts. Shortland, Watts, Ball, and Capt. Marshall, with an Account of their New Discoveries. *Map and plates.* 4° 1789
—— *See* Pelham, Vol. 1 : Appendix 1.

Phillippo, James M. The United States and Cuba. 8° 1857

Phillipps-Wolley, Clive. Sport in the Crimea and Caucasus. 8° 1881
—— Savage Svânetia. 2 vols. *Illustrations.* Crown 8° 1883
—— A Sportsman's Eden. 8° 1888

Phillips, H. A Brief Account of the Earthquake at Aix-la-Chapelle (Aachen), on Monday, 26th August 1878. 8* 1879

Phillips, J. The Rivers, Mountains, and Sea-Coast of Yorkshire; with Essays on the Climate, Scenery, and Ancient Inhabitants of the County. *Plates.* 8° 1853
—— Vesuvius. *Map and plates.* Small 8° *Oxford*, 1869

Phillips, Major J. Scott. Interpretations, showing Scriptural Reasons for the Study of Prophecy ; the Re-Settlement of the Seed of Abraham in Syria and Arabia Scripturally explained ; with Geographical Proofs and Maps. 12° 1860

Phillips, Capt. T. *See* Astley, Vol. 2 ; Churchill, Vol. 6 ; Allgemeine Historie, Vol. 3 : Appendix 1.

Phillips, Sir Richard. New Voyages and Travels, consisting of Originals and Translations. 9 vols. *Maps and plates.* 8° 1819-23
[For Contents, *see* Appendix 1.]

Phipps, Capt. Constantine John. A Voyage towards the North Pole undertaken by His Majesty's command, 1773. *Maps, plates, and tables.* 4° 1774
—— Voyage au Pole Boréal, fait en 1773, par ordre du Roi d'Angleterre. Traduit de l'Anglois. *Maps.* 4° *Paris*, 1775
—— *See* Markham, A. H ; *also* Pinkerton, Vol. 1 : Appendix 1.

Phrysius, Gemma. De Principiis Astronomiæ et Cosmographiæ, deque usu Globi ab eodem editi ; item, de Orbis Divisione, et Insulis rebusque nuper inventis. 12° *Antwerp*, 1553

Phythian, J. C. Scenes of Travel in Norway. Small 8° [1877]

Piaggia, C. Dell' Arrivo fra i Niam-Niam, e del Seggiorno sul lago Tzana in Abissinia. 8* *Lucca*, 1877

Piassetsky, P. Voyage à travers la Mongolie et la Chine [with Sosnofsky]. Traduit du Russe, . . . par Aug. Kuscinski. *Map and illustrations.* Large 8° *Paris*, 1883
—— Russian Travellers in Mongolia and China. Translated by J. Gordon-Cumming. 2 vols. *Illustrations.* Small 8° 1884

Piat, Alfred. Projet de Création au moyen de Ressources d'execution à tirer de l'œuvre même d'un Port de Guerre et de Commerce en eau profonde à Cabourg (Calvados), pour suppléer à l'insuffisance irrémédiable de Cherbourg et du Havre. *Map and plans.* 4*   *Paris,* 1887

Picard, Charlotte. La Chaumière Africaine. [Shipwreck of the "Medusa."] *Map.* 12°   *Dijon* [? 182-]

Piccone, Antonio. *See* Issel.

Pichardo, Don Estéban. Diccionario Provincial Casi-Razonado de Voces Cubanas. 8°   *Havana,* 1849
—— Geografía de la Isla de Cuba. Royal 8°   *Havana,* 1854
—— Nueva Carta Geotopografica de la Isla de Cuba. 8*   *Havana,* 1870
—— Memoria Justificativa de la Carta Geo-Coro-Topo-Grafica del Departamento Occidental de la Isla de Cuba hasta el límite Oriental de Nueva Filipina. 4 parts. 8*   *Havana,* N.D.

Pichat, A. Géographie Militaire du Bassin du Rhin. *Map and plans.* 8° *Paris,* 1876

Pichon, Dr Louis. Un Voyage au Yunnan. *Map.* 12°   *Paris,* 1893

Pickering, C. *See* Wilkes.

Pickering, John. A Lecture on Telegraphic Language. 8* *Boston, Mass.,* 1833
—— Remarks on the Indian Languages of North America. Royal 8*   1836
—— Eulogy on Nathaniel Bowditch, President of the American Academy of Arts and Sciences; including an Analysis of his Scientific Publications. 8*
                      Boston, Mass., 1838
—— Memoir on the Language and Inhabitants of Lord North's Island. 4*
                Cambridge, Mass., 1845

Picking, Capt. H. F. *See* United States, E, a, Hydrographic Office Publications : Appendix 2.

Picot, E. *See* Uréchi.

Picquet, Charles. Table Alphabétique en forme d'Itinéraire, des Rues, Ruelles, Culs-de-Sac, &c., &c., qui se trouvent dans le Plan Routier de la Ville de Paris et de ses Faubourgs. 8° *Paris,* 1805
—— Catalogue Méthodique d'un choix de Globes et Sphères, d'Atlas et de Cartes, Astronomiques, Géographiques, Topographiques, &c. 8°   *Paris,* 1837

Pictet, Camille, and Maurice Bedot. Compte Rendu d'un voyage scientifique dans l'archipel Malais. 8* *Geneva,* 1893

Pictet, J. P. Itinéraire des Vallées autour du Mt.-Blanc. *Map.* 12° *Geneva,* 1818

Piddington, Henry. Researches on the Gale and Hurricane in the Bay of Bengal, 3rd to 5th June 1839. *Maps.* 8*
                            Calcutta, 1839

Piddington, Henry. Ten Memoirs on the Law of Storms as applying to the Tempests of the Indian and Chinese Seas, 1839-42. *Maps.* 8° *Calcutta,* 1839-43
—— The Horn-Book of Storms for the Indian and China Seas. *Diagram.* 8°
                            Calcutta, 1845

Piedrahita, L. F. de. Historia General de las Conquistas del nuevo reyno de Granada. Folio *Amberes* [N.D. ? 1688]

Pieraggi, E. *See* Scrope.

Pierce, Josiah, junr. The Economic Use of the Plane-Table in Topographical Surveying ; with an Abstract of the Discussion upon the Paper. *Plate.* 8* 1888

Pierling, P. L'Italie et la Russie au XVIᵉ siècle : Voyages de Paoletto Centurione à Moscow, Dmitri Guérasimov à Rome, Gian Francesco Citus à Moscow. 12°   *Paris,* 1892

Pierotti, Ermete. Une Caravane pour la Syrie, la Phénice, et la Palestine. 12*
                            Lausanne, 1869

Pierrepont, Edward. Fifth Avenue to Alaska. *Maps.* Small 8°   1884

Piesse, Louis. Vichy et ses Environs. *Plan.* Small 4°   *Paris,* 1855
—— Guide aux Eaux Thermales du Mont Doré, de Sainte Alyre, de Royat, de la Bourboule, et de Saint Nectaire, avec la Description du Clermont Farrand. 12°
                            Paris, 1856
—— *See* Joanne.

Pigafetta, Antonio. Primo Viaggio intorno al Globo Terracqueo ossia Ragguaglio della Navigazione alle Indie Orientali per la via d'Occidente fatta dal Cavaliere Antonio Pigafetta . . 1519-22. Ora pubblicato per la prima volta . . . e corredato di note da Carlo Amoretti. Con un Transunto del Trattato di Navigazione dello stesso autore. *Maps.* 4°
                            Milan, 1800
—— Premier Voyage autour du Monde, par le Chevᵣ. Pigafetta, sur l'escadre de Magellan . . . 1519-22 ; suivi de l'Extrait du Traité de Navigation du même auteur ; et d'une Notice sur le Chevalier Martin Behaim, &c. *Maps and plates.* 8°   *Paris,* An. 9 [1801]
—— *See* Matkovic ; *also* Hakluyt Soc. Publ., Vol. 52 ; Pinkerton, Vol. 11 ; Purchas, Vol. 1, Book 2 ; Ramusio, Vol. 1 : Appendix 1.

Pigafetta, Filippo. Relatione del Reame di Congo et delle circonvicine contrade. Tratta dalli Scritti et Ragionamenti di Odoardo Lopez, Portoghese, per Filippo Pigafetta, con dissegni vari di Geografia, di piante, d'habiti, d'animali, e altro. *Maps and plates.* Small square 8°
                            Rome, 1591

Pigafetta, Filippo. A Report of the Kingdom of Congo, a Region of Africa, and of the Countries that border rounde about the same. Drawen out of the Writinges and Discourses of Odoardo Lopez a Portingall, by Philippo Pigafetta. Translated out of Italian by Abraham Hartwell. *Plates.* Small 4° 1597

—— A Report of the Kingdom of Congo, and of the Surrounding Countries: Drawn out of the Writings and Discourses of the Portuguese Duarte Lopez, by Filippo Pigafetta, in Rome, 1591. Newly translated from the Italian; and edited, with Explanatory Notes, by Margarite Hutchinson; with *facsimiles of the original maps*, and a Preface by Sir Thomas Fowell Buxton. 8° 1881

—— *See* Churchill, Vol. 8; Purchas, Vol. 2, Book 7 : Appendix 1.

Piggot, J. Persia, Ancient and Modern. 8° 1874

Pigou, F. *See* Dalrymple, Repertory, Vol. 2 : Appendix 1.

Pijnappel, Dr J. Geographie van Nederlandsch-Indie. 8°
The Hague, 1868

Pike, Nicholas. Sub-tropical Rambles in the Land of the Aphanapteryx : Personal Experiences, Adventures, and Wanderings in and around the Island of Mauritius. *Map and plates.* 8° 1873

Pike, Zebulon, M. Exploratory Travels through the Western Territories of North America : comprising a Voyage from St Louis, on the Mississippi, to the Source of that River, and a Journey through the Interior of Louisiana and the North-Eastern Provinces of New Spain, in 1805-7. *Maps.* 4° 1811
—— *See* Eyriès, Vol. 9 : Appendix 1.

Pike, Warburton. The Barren Ground of Northern Canada. *Map.* 8° 1892

Pilkington, C. *See* Dent, C. T.

Pilkington, J. View of the Present State of Derbyshire, with an Account of its most remarkable Antiquities. 2 vols. *Map and plates.* 8° *Derby,* 1789

Pilling, James Constantine. Bibliography of the Siouan Language. 8*
Washington, 1887
—— Bibliography of the Eskimo Language. 8° *Washington,* 1887
—— Bibliography of the Iroquoian Languages. Large 8° *Washington,* 1888
—— Bibliography of the Muskhogean Languages. Large 8° *Washington,* 1889
—— Bibliography of the Algonquian Languages (Smithsonian Institution, Bureau of Ethnology). *Facsimiles.* 8°
Washington, 1891
—— Ditto. Bibliography of the Athapascan Languages. 8°
Washington, 1892

Pilling, James Constantine. Ditto. Bibliography of the Salishan Languages. 8° *Washington,* 1893
—— Ditto. Bibliography of the Chinookan Languages (including the Chinook Jargon). 8* *Washington,* 1893

Pillsbury, J. E. *See* United States, E, *a,* Hydrographic Office Publications, No. 41a : Appendix 2.

Pilot, Rev. W. Geography of Newfoundland, for the use of Schools. *Map.* 12* N.D.

Pim, Bedford. An Earnest Appeal to the British Public on behalf of the missing Arctic Expedition. 8* 1857
—— Notes on Cherbourg. *Map.* 8* 1858
—— The Gate of the Pacific. *Maps and plates.* 8* 1863
—— The Negro and Jamaica. 8* 1866
—— An Essay on Feudal Tenures. 8* 1871

Pimenta, Nicholas. *See* Purchas, Vol. 2, Book 10 : Appendix 1.

Pimodan, Capt. de. De Goritz à Sofia : Istrie, Dalmatie, Monténégro, Grèce, Turquie, Bulgarie. 8° *Paris,* 1893

Piña, A. de. Deux Ans dans le Pays des Épices. (Iles de la Sonde.) 12° *Paris,* 1880

Pinart, A. L. Les Aléoutes et leur Origine. 8* *Paris* [1872]
—— Catalogue des Collections Rapportées de l'Amerique Russe (aujourd'hui Territoire d'Aliaska). 8* *Paris,* 1872
—— Eskimaux et Koloches : Idées Religieuses et Traditions des Kaniagmioutes. 8* *Paris,* 1873
—— Notes sur les Koloches. 8* *Paris,* 1873
—— Voyage à la Côte Nord-ouest d'Amerique d'Ounlashka à Kadiak (Îles Aléoutiennes et Péninsule d'Aliaska). *Map.* 8* *Paris,* 1874
—— Sur les Atnahs. 8* *Paris,* 1875
—— La Caverne d'Aknañh, Île d'Ounga (Archipel Shumagin, Alaska). *Plates.* Large 4* *Paris,* 1875
—— Voyages à la Côte Nord-ouest de l'Amérique, exécutés durant les années 1870-72. Vol. 1, Part 1. (Histoire naturelle.) *Plates.* Large 4° *Paris,* 1875
—— La Chasse aux Animaux Marins et les Pêcheries chez les indigènes de la Côte Nord-ouest d'Amérique. 8*
Boulogne, 1875
—— Bibliothèque de Linguistique et d'Ethnographie Américaines. Vol. 1. 4°
Paris, 1875
—— *See* Petitot.

Pinchot, Gifford. Biltmore Forest, the property of Mr George W. Vanderbilt : an account of its treatment, and the results of the first year's work. *Map and illustrations.* 8* *Chicago,* 1893

Pinckard, G. Notes on the West Indies, written during the Expedition under the command of the late General Sir Ralph Abercromby ; including Observations on

Pinckard, G.—*continued.*
the Island of Barbadoes, and the Settlements captured by the British Troops upon the Coast of Guiana. 3 vols. 8° 1806

Pindar, Sir Paul. *See* Purchas, Vol. 2, Book 9 : Appendix 1.

Pinder, M. *See* Parthey, G.

Pinder, W. *See* Purchas, Vol. 2, Book 10 : Appendix 1.

Pingle, R. *See* Hakluyt, Vol. 1 : Appendix 1.

Pingré, Canon —. *See* Verdun.

Pingré, R. Russia ; or, Miscellaneous Observations on the Past and Present State of that Country and its Inhabitants. *Plates.* 8° 1833

Pinkas, Julio. Commissão de Estudos da Estrada de Ferro do Madeira e Mamore. Relatorio apresentado a S. Ex. o Sr. Conselheiro Joãs Ferreira de Moura, Ministro e Secretario de Estado dos Negolios da Agricultura, Commercio e Obras Publicas. *Maps and photographs.* 4° Rio de Janeiro, 1885

Pinkerton, John. Modern Geography : a Description of the Empires, Kingdoms, States, and Colonies, with the Oceans, Seas, and Isles, in all Parts of the World, including the most Recent Discoveries and Political Alterations ; the Astronomical Introduction by the Rev. S. Vince. 2 vols. *Maps.* 4° 1802
—— Another edition. The Astronomical Introduction by M. la Croix. Translated by J. Pond. 2 vols. *Maps.* 4° 1811
—— A General Collection of the Best and Most Interesting Voyages and Travels in all Parts of the World, many of which are now first translated into English. 17 vols. *Maps and plates.* 4° 1808-14 [For Contents of these volumes, *see* Appendix 1.]

Pinteado, A. A. *See* Astley, Vol. 1 ; Kerr, Vol. 7 : Appendix 1.

Pinto, A. de Serpa. How I Crossed Africa, from the Atlantic to the Indian Ocean, through unknown Countries, Discovery of the Great Zambesi, &c. Translated from the Author's manuscript, by Alfred Elwes. 2 vols. *Maps and illustrations.* 8° 1881

Pinto, Fernan Mendez. Historia Oriental de las Peregrinaciones de Fernan Mendez Pinto, Portugues, adonde se escriven muchas, y muy estrañas cosas que vio, y oyò en los Reynos de la China, Tartaria, Sornao, que vulgarmente se llama Siam, Calamiñam, Peguu, Martauan, y otros muchos de aquellas partes Orientales, de que en estas nuestras de Occidente ay muy poca, o ninguna noticia. . . . Traduzido de Portugues en Castellano por . . . Francisco de Herrera Maldonado, &c. Folio Madrid, 1627

Pinto, Fernan Mendez. Les Voyages advantureux de Fernand Mendez Pinto. Fidellement traduits de Portugais en François par le Sieur Bernard Figuier. Small 4° Paris, 1645
—— The Voyages and Adventures of Ferdinand Mendez Pinto, the Portuguese. Done into English by Henry Cogan. With an Introduction by Arminius Vambéry. (The Adventure Series.) *Map and illustrations.* 8° 1891
—— *See* Laharpe, Vol. 4 ; Purchas, Vol. 3 ; Allgemeine Historie, Vol. 10 : Appendix 1.

Pinzas, J. M. *See* Wertheman.

Pinzon, Vincent Yanes. *See* Gottfried ; Allgemeine Historie, Vol. 13 ; General Collection of Voyages and Travels, p. 610 : Appendix 1.

Piotrowski, Rufin. My Escape from Siberia. [Translated.] *Portrait and map.* 8° 1863

Piry, A. Theophile. Le Saint Edit : Etude de Littérature Chinoise. 4° Shanghai, 1879

Pisonis, Gulielmi, Medici Amstelædamensis, de Indiæ utriusque re naturali et medica, Libri quatuordecim. *Plates.* Folio Amsterdam, 1658

Pissis, A. Geografia fisica de la República de Chile. Small 8°, and Atlas oblong 4° Paris, 1875

Pitcairn, W. D. Two Years among the Savages of New Guinea ; with Introductory Notes on North Queensland. *Map.* Crown 8° 1891

Pitfield, Alex. *See* Waller, Richard.

Pitman, C. B. *See* Bonvalot.

Pitman, Sir Isaac. Manual of Phonography, or Writing by Sound : a Natural Method of Writing by Signs that represent Spoken Sounds, adapted to the English Language as a Complete System of Phonetic Shorthand. 12* 1860
—— The Phonographic Teacher : a Guide to a Practical Acquaintance with the Art of Phonetic Short-hand. 12* 1860
—— The Phonographic Reader : . . . Lessons in Phonetic Short-hand. 12* 1860

Pitman, R. B. On the Practicability of Joining the Atlantic and Pacific Oceans by a Ship Canal across the Isthmus of America. *Map.* 8° 1825

Pittakys, K. S. L'Ancienne Athènes, ou la Description des Antiquités d'Athènes. *Plates.* 8° Athens, 1835

Pittier, H. Apuntaciones, sobre el clima y geografia de la República de Costa Rica. Resultados de las Observaciones practicadas en el año de 1889. (De los Anales d. Instit. fisico geográf. nacional. Tomo 2, 1889.) 12* San José, 1890
—— Viaje de Exploracion al Valle del Rio Grande de Térraba. *Map.* 12* San José, 1891

Pitts, Joseph. *See* "The World Displayed," Vol. 17 : Appendix 1.

Pitzipios, Prince. The Eastern Question Solved, in a Letter to Lord Palmerston. 8* 1860

Pizarro, Francisco. *See* Hakluyt Soc. Publ., Vol. 47; Gottfried; Kerr, Vol. 4; Laharpe, Vol. 10; Purchas, Vol. 4, Book 7; Ramusio, Vol. 3; Allgemeine Historie, Vol. 15; Knox's New Collection, Vol. 1; "The World Displayed," Vol. 3 : Appendix 1.

Pizarro, Gonzalo. *See* Hakluyt Soc. Publ., Vol. 24; Kerr, Vol. 4; Allgemeine Historie, Vol. 15 : Appendix 1.

Pizarro, Hernando. *See* Hakluyt Soc. Publ., Vol. 47; Burney, Vol. 1; Ramusio, Vol. 3; Ternaux-Compans, Vol. 4: Appendix 1.

Pizarro, J. *See* Allgemeine Historie, Vol. 18 : Appendix 1.

Pizigani. *See* Pezzana.

Plaisted, Barthol. Journal from Calcutta in Bengal, by Sea to Busserah, from thence across the Great Desart to Aleppo, and from thence to Marseilles, and through France to England in 1750; to which are added Capt. Elliot's Directions for Passing over the Little Desart, from Busserah, by the way of Bagdad, Mousul, Orfa, and Aleppo; an Account of the Countries, Cities, and Towns adjacent to Bengal; with a Journal of the Proceedings of the "Doddington" East Indiaman, till she was unfortunately wrecked on the East Coast of Africa, by Mr Webb. *Map.* 12° 1758

Planche, J. R. Descent of the Danube, from Ratisbon to Vienna, during 1827; with Anecdotes and Recollections, Historical and Legendary. . . . *Map and plate.* 8° 1828

Planci, Jani. De Conchis Minus Notis liber; cui accessit specimen Æstus reciproci Maris superi ad Littus Portumque Arimini. *Plates.* 4° *Rome,* 1760

Plänckner, J. von. Der Inselsberg und seine Aussicht, dargestellt durch ein 90 Zoll langes Panorama und erläutert durch ein Winkelblatt und eine kurze Beschreibung. *Diagram and coloured plate.* Large 8* *Gotha,* 1839

Plate, William. Ptolemy's Knowledge of Arabia, especially of Hadhramaut and the Wilderness El-Ahkaf. *Map.* 8* 1845

Plateau, F. Les Voyages des Naturalistes Belges. 8* *Brussels,* 1876

Platzmann, J. Aus der Bai von Paranagua. 8* *Leipzig,* 1866

Playfair, G. M. H. The Cities and Towns of China : a Geographical Dictionary. 8° *Hongkong,* 1879
—— The Mystery of Ta-Ts'in. 8* N.D.

Playfair, Sir R. Lambert. History of Arabia Felix, or Yemen, from the Commencement of the Christian Era to the Present Time, including an Account of the British Settlement of Aden. [From the India Records, No. 49, Bombay.] *Map.* Royal 8° *Bombay,* 1859
—— A Paper on Irrigation in the Deccan and Southern Maratha Country. [From the India Records, No. 5, Irrigation Series.] *Maps.* Royal 8° *Bombay,* 1866
—— Travels in the Footsteps of Bruce in Algeria and Tunis, illustrated by Facsimiles of the Original Drawings. *Plates.* 4° 1877
—— The Scourge of Christendom : Annals of British Relations with Algiers prior to the French Conquest. *Plans and illustrations.* 8° 1884
—— Tunis. Report of a Consular Tour in 1885. *Maps.* 8* 1885
—— The Bibliography of the Barbary States. Part I. Tripoli and the Cyrenaica. Roy. Geog. Soc. Suppl. Papers, Vol. 2. *Map.* 8° 1887
—— A Bibliography of Algeria. Roy. Geog. Soc. Suppl. Papers, Vol. 2. 8° 1889
—— *See* Murray, J. ; Handbooks, Africa.
—— **and Dr Robert Brown.** A Bibliography of Morocco from the Earliest Times to the end of 1891. Roy. Geog. Suppl. Papers, Vol. 3, Part 3. *Map.* Large 8° 1893
—— **and — Letourneux.** Memoir on the Hydrographical System and the Freshwater Fish of Algeria. 8* 1871

Playfair, William. The Commercial and Political Atlas, representing, by means of stained copperplate Charts, the Progress of the Commerce, Revenues, Expenditure, and Debts of England, during the whole of the Eighteenth Century. 3rd edition. 4° 1801

Playse, J. *See* Purchas, Vol. 3, Book 4 : Appendix 1.

Pleasanton, A. J. On the Influence of the Blue Colour of the Sky in developing Animal and Vegetable Life. 8* *Philadelphia,* 1871

Plener, Ernst von. The English Factory Legislation. Translated by F. L. Wienmann, with Introduction by A. J. Mundella. 8° 1873

Pleschééf, Capt. Sergey. Survey of the Russian Empire, according to its present newly regulated State, divided into different Governments. Translated from the Russian, with Additions, by J. Smirnove. *Map and plate of arms and uniforms.* 8° 1792

Pleske, T. *See* Helmersen and Schrenck, 4, 7.

Pliny. The Natural History of. Translated, with copious Notes and Illustrations, by John Bostock and H. T. Riley. 6 vols. 12°   1855-57

Pliny the Younger. *See* Lobley.

Plowden, Walter Chichele. Travels in Abyssinia and the Galla Country, with an Account of a Mission to Ras Ali in 1848 . . . Edited by Trevor Chichele Plowden. *Maps.* 8°   1868

Plumtre, Anne. *See* Pouqueville.

Plunkett, Capt. G. T. The Conversation Manual : a Collection of 670 useful Phrases in English, Hindustani, Persian, and Pashtù, with Summaries of the Grammars of these Languages, and a Vocabulary of nearly 1,500 words, for the use of Engineer Officers and others on the North-West Frontier and in India. 8°   1875
—— English - Arabic Vocabulary, compiled for the use of Residents and Travellers in Egypt. 12°   *Cairo* [1886]
—— Walks in Cairo : a Guide to the most Picturesque Streets and Buildings in the Capital of Egypt. 2nd edition. *Map.* 12*   1889

Plymley, Joseph. General View of the Agriculture of Shropshire, with Observations. *Map and plates.* 8°   1803

Pocock, Edward. Specimen Historiæ Arabum . . . accessit Historia Veterum Arabum ex Abu'l Feda : cura Antonii I. Sylvestre de Sacy. Edidit Josephus White. *Portrait.* 4°   *Oxford,* 1806
—— *See* Twells, Dr.

Pococke, Richard. Description of the East and some other Countries ; containing Observations on Egypt, Palestine, Syria, Mesopotamia, Cyprus, Candia, the Islands of the Archipelago, Asia Minor, Thrace, Greece, and some other parts of Europe. 2 vols. *Maps and plates.* Folio   1743-45
—— *See* Pinkerton, Vols. 10, 15 ; Knox's New Collection, Vol. 6 ; "The World Displayed," Vols. 12, 13 : Appendix 1.

Podiebrad, David J. Alterthümer der Prager Josefstadt : Israelitischer Friedhof, Alt-Neu-Schule, und andere Synagogen, &c. *Plates.* 16° *Prague,* 1855

Poeppig, E. Reise in Chile, Peru, und auf dem Amazonstrome, während der Jahre 1827-32. 2 vols. 4°, Atlas folio
Leipzig, 1835-36

Poestion, J. C. Island : Das Land und seine Bewohner nach den neuesten Quellen. *Map.* 8°   *Vienna,* 1885

Poey, Andres. Sur les Tempètes Électriques, et la Quantité de Victimes que la foudre fait Annuellement aux États-Unis d'Amérique et à l'île de Cuba. Royal 8*   *Versailles,* 1855

Poey, Andres. Mémoire sur la Fréquence des Chutes de Grêles à l'île de Cuba, des cas qui eurent lieu de 1784 à 1854, et des Températures minima de la Glace et de la Gelée Blanche observées dans cette île. 8*   *Paris,* 1855
—— Météorologie : des Caractères Physiques des Éclairs en Boules et de leur affinité avec l'état sphéroidal de la matière. 8*   *Paris,* 1855
—— Tableau Chronologique des Tremblements de Terre ressentis à l'île de Cuba de 1551 à 1855 ; avec Supplément. 2 parts. 8*   *Paris,* 1855
—— The same. Supplément. Accompagné d'une Note additionnelle sur la force ascensionelle qu'exercent les Ouragans, &c. 8*   *Paris,* 1855
—— Couleur des Étoiles et des Globes filants observés en Angleterre de 1841 à 1855. 4*   *Paris,* 1856
—— Couleurs des Étoiles et des Globes filants observés en Chine pendant vingt-quatre Siècles, depuis le VIIe Siècle avant Jésus-Christ jusqu'au milieu du XVIIe Siècle de notre Ère. 4* *Paris,* 1856
—— Analyse des Hypothèses Anciennes et Modernes qui ont été émises sur les Éclairs sans Tonnerre. 2 parts. Royal 8*   *Versailles,* 1856-57
—— Considérations Philosophiques sur un Essai de Systématisation Subjective des Phénomènes Météorologiques. 8*
Lyons, 1857
—— Couleurs des Globes filants observés à Paris de 1841 à 1853, avec l'Indication des Traînées, des Fragments, &c., diversement colorés, observés tant en Chine qu'en Angleterre. 4* *Paris,* 1857
—— Relacion de los Trabajos Físicos y Meteorológicos, destinada para servir de Introduccion á las futuras Tareas del Observatorio Meteorológico de Aquella Ciudad, redactada por Don Ramon de la Sagra. 8*   *Paris,* 1858
—— Catalogue Chronologique des Tremblements de Terre, ressentis dans les Indes-Occidentales de 1530 à 1858 ; suivi d'une Bibliographie Séismique concernant les travaux relatifs aux Tremblements de Terre des Antilles. Royal 8*
Versailles, 1858
—— Répartition Géographique de l'Universalité des Météores en Zones Terrestres, Atmosphériques, Solaires, ou Lunaires, et de leurs Rapports entres elles. 8*   *Paris,* 1858
—— Couleurs des Globes filants observés à Paris de 1853 à 1859. 4* *Paris,* 1859
—— Description de deux magnifiques Aurores Boréales observées à la Havane. [2 *leaves.*] Royal 8*   *Versailles,* 1859
—— Constitution des Halos observés à la Havane, et de leur rapport avec les Phases de la Lune. Royal 8* *Versailles,* 1859

Poey, Andres. Aurore Boréale-orientale observée à la Havane dans la nuit du 24 au 25 Mars 1860. 4* *Versailles*, 1860
—— Loi de la Coloration et de la Décoloration des Étoiles, du Soleil et des Planètes. Royal 8* *Versailles*, 1860
—— Sur les Éclairs sans Tonnerre, observées à la Havane, pendant l'année 1859 dans le Sein des Cumulo Stratus isolés de l'Horizon. [2 *leaves*.] Royal 8* *Versailles*, 1860
—— Expériences sur les Ombres Prismatiques, observées à la Havane, en rapport avec la Déclinaison du Soleil et l'état atmosphérique. Royal 8* *Versailles*,1861
—— Table Chronologique de quatre cents Cyclones qui ont sévi dans les Indes Occidentales et dans l'Océan Atlantique Nord. 8* *Paris*, 1862
—— Relation Historique et Théorie des Images Photo-Électriques de la Foudre, observées depuis l'an 360 de notre Ère jusqu'en 1860. 16° *Paris*, 1864
—— *See* France, B, *b*, Dépôt des Cartes et Plans de la Marine, No. 513 : Appendix 2.

Poey, Felipe. Compendio de la Geografia de la Isla de Cuba. Parte I. Topografia. 12* *Havana*, 1836
—— The same, 3rd edition. 8* *Havana*, 1842

Pogge, Paul. Im Reiche des Muata Jamwo. Tagebuch meiner im Auftrage der Deutschen Gesellschaft zur Erforschung Aequatorial-Afrika's in die Lunda-Staaten unternommenen Reise. *Map and plates.* 8° *Berlin*, 1880
—— *See* Wissmann.

Pogodin, —. *See* Baer and Helmersen, 10.

Pogson, Norman Robert. Report of the Government Astronomer upon the Proceedings of the Observatory, in connexion with the Total Eclipse of the Sun on 18th August 1868, as observed at Masulipatam, Vunpurthy, Madras, and other Stations in Southern India. *Plates.* 8° 1868
—— Telegraphic Determinations of the Difference of Longitude between Karachi, Avanashi, Roorkee, Pondicherry, Colombo, Jaffna, Muddapur, and Singapore, and the Government Observatory, Madras. 8° *Madras*, 1884
—— *See* India, N, Madras Observations : Appendix 2.

Pogson, Captain W. R. A History of the Boondelas. *Map and plates.* 4° *Calcutta*, 1828
—— Narrative during a Tour to Chateegaon, 1831. *Map and plate.* 8° *Serampore*, 1831

Pohl, John Emanuel. Reise im innern von Brasilien : auf allerhöchsten Befehl seiner Majestät des Kaisers von Oesterreich, Franz des Ersten, in 1817-21. Vol. 1. 4° *Vienna*, 1832

Pohl, J. J., and J. Schabus. Tafeln zur Reduction der in Millimetren abgelesenen Barometerstände auf die Normaltemperatur von 0° Celsius. 8* *Vienna*, 1852
—— Tafeln zur Vergleichung und Reduction der in verschiedenen Längenmassen abgelesenen Barometerstände. 8* *Vienna*, 1852

Pointis, M. de. A Genuine and Particular Account of the Taking of Carthagena by the French and Buccaniers in the year 1697 . . . By the Sieur Pointis ; with a Preface giving an Account of the Original of Carthagena in 1532, &c. Small 8° [1740]
[Bound with a " Journal of the Expedition to La Guira and Porto Cavallos "; and " Original Papers relating to the Expedition to Cuba."]
—— *See* Burney, Vol. 4 : Appendix 1.

Poiré, Eugène. La Tunisie Française. 12° *Paris*, 1892

Poiret, Abbé. Voyage en Barbarie, ou Lettres écrites de l'Ancienne Numidie pendant 1785-86, sur la Religion, les Coutumes, et les Mœurs des Maures et des Arabés-Bédouins ; avec un Essai sur l'Histoire Naturelle de ce pays. 2 vols. 8° *Paris*, 1789

Pokorny, Dr A. *See* Kirchhoff.

Polack, J. S. New Zealand : being a Narrative of Travels and Adventures during a Residence in that Country between 1831-37. 2 vols. *Map and plates.* 8° 1838

Polak, Dr J. E. Persien : das Land und seine Bewohner. Ethnographische Schilderungen. 2 vols. in 1. 8° *Leipzig*, 1865

" Polaris." Narrative of the North Polar Expedition, U.S. ship " Polaris," Capt. Charles Francis Hall commanding. Edited under the direction of the Hon. G. M. Robeson, Secretary of the Navy, by Rear-Admiral C. H. Davis, U.S.N., U.S. Naval Observatory, 1876. *Maps and plates.* 4° *Washington*, 1876
—— Scientific Results of the United States Arctic Expedition, steamer " Polaris," C. F. Hall commanding. Vol. 1. Physical Observations. By Emil Bessels. *Map and plates.* 4° *Washington*, 1876
—— *See* Markham, A. H.

Poli, Baldassare. Sull' insegnamento dell' Economia Politica o Sociale in Inghilterra. 8* *Milan* [1862]

Poljakow, J. S. Journey to the Island of Sakhalin, 1881-82. [In Russian.] *Map.* 8* *St Petersburg*, 1883
—— Reise nach der Insel Sachalin in den Jahren 1881-82. Aus dem Russischen übersetzt von Dr A. Arzruni. 8* *Berlin*, 1884

Pollen, J. H. A Description of the Trajan Column. *Plate.* 8° 1874

Pollexfen, Lieut. J. J. Report on the Rajpeepla and adjoining Districts, surveyed 1852 to 1855. *Map.* Statistical Return of the Rajpeepla Districts. Disputes within the Rajpeepla Territory, and between that Territory and the adjoining. [From the India Records, No. 23.] Royal 8° *Bombay,* 1856

Pollington, Viscount. Half round the Old World. Being some account of a Tour in Russia, the Caucasus, Persia, and Turkey, 1865-66. *Map.* 8° 1867

Pollnitz, Charles Lewis, Baron de. Memoirs: being the Observations he made in his late Travels from Persia through Germany, Italy, France, Flanders, Holland, England, &c.; discovering not only the Present State of the Chief Cities and Towns, but the Characters of the Principal Persons at the Several Courts. 4 vols. 8° 1537

Pollock, Sir F. *See* Dent, C. T.

Pollock, Major.-Gen. F. L. *See* Bellew.

Polo, Marco. *See* Marco Polo.

Polybius. The General History of Polybius, translated from the Greek by Mr Hampton. 4th edition. 3 vols. 8° 1809

Pomba, C. Notizie Sopra una Nuova Carta d'Italia in rilievo a superficie curva nella scala di 1 : 1,000,000 tanto per le altezze come per le distanze. Large 8* *Turin,* 1884

Pombeiros, Journey of the. *See* Lacerda.

Pompe van Meerdervoort, J. L. C. Vijf Jaren in Japan (1857-63). Bijdragen tot de Kennis van het Japansche Keizerrijk en zijne Bevolking. 2 vols. *Map and plates.* 8° *Leyden,* 1867-68

Ponceau, Peter du. *See* Gutzlaff.

Ponce, John (Juan Ponce de Leon). A Voyage to Æthiopia, made in the years 1698, 1699, and 1700; describing particularly that famous Empire, likewise the kingdoms of Dongola, Sennar, part of Egypt, &c., with the Natural History of those Parts. Faithfully translated from the French original. 8° 1709
—— *See* Gottfried; Kerr, Vol. 5; Pinkerton, Vol. 15; Allgemeine Historie, Vol. 13; A General Collection of Voyages and Travels, p. 610: Appendix 1.

Ponce, Jules. Le Fleuve Blanc: Notes Géographiques et Ethnologiques et les Chasses à l'Éléphant dans le Pays des Dinka et des Djour. *Map.* 8° *Paris,* 1863

Pond, J. *See* Pinkerton.

Pontanus, J. J. *See* Pinkerton, Vol. 1: Appendix 1.

Ponte, G. M. da. Osservazioni sul Dipartimento del Serio. 8° *Bergamo,* 1803

Ponte, G. M. da. Dizionario Odeporico o sia Storico- Politico-Naturale della Provincia Bergamasca. 3 vols. *Map.* 8° *Bergamo,* 1819

Pontoia, Diego. *See* Purchas, Vol. 3, Book 2: Appendix 1.

Pontoppidan, Bishop Erich. Natural History of Norway. Translated from the Danish. *Map and plates.* Folio 1755
—— *See* "The World Displayed," Vol. 20: Appendix 1.

Ponz, Jean de Leon. *See* Ponce.

Ponzi, Giuseppe. Sulle correnti di lava scoperte dal taglio della ferrovia di Albano. 4* [*Rome,* 1859]
—— Storia naturale dell' Agro Pontino. 8* *Rome,* 1865

Pool, Garrit Thomasz. *See* Hakluyt Society's Publications, Vol. 25; Callander, Vol. 2: Appendix 1.

Poole, F. Queen Charlotte Islands: a narrative of discovery and adventure in the North Pacific. Edited by J. W. Lyndon. *Maps and plates.* 8° 1872

Poole, Henry. On the Meteorology of the Albion Mines, Nova Scotia. 8* 1854

Poole, Jonas. *See* Purchas, Vol. 3, Book 3: Appendix 1.

Poole, Reginald Stuart. *See* Diehl.

Poole, Sarah. The Englishwoman in Egypt: Letters from Cairo, written during a Residence there in 1842-44, with E. W. Lane. 2 vols. in 1. 18° 1851

Poorun, Geer Goosain. *See* Dalrymple, Repertory, Vol. 2: Appendix 1.

Pope, C. W. The Dehra Dun Forests. (From the *Calcutta Review.*) 8* 1893

Pope, Capt. John. Report of an Exploration of the Territory of Minnesota. *Map.* 8* *Washington,* 1850
—— Report of Exploration of a Route for the Pacific Railroad, near the thirty-second parallel of latitude, from the Red River to the Rio Grande. *Maps.* 8° *Washington,* 1854

Popoff, Constantine. *See* Tolstoi.

Popowski, Josef. The Rival Powers in Central Asia, or the struggle between England and Russia in the East. Translated from the German . . . by Arthur Baring Brabant, and edited by Charles E. D. Black. *Map.* 8° 1893

Popper, Julius. The Popper Expedition, Tierra del Fuego. A lecture delivered at the Argentine Geographical Institute, 5th March 1887. (Translated from the Bulletin of the Institute by J. E. O'Curry.) *Map.* 8* *Buenos Ayres* [1887]

Porcacchi, Thomaso. L'isole piu famose del Mondo descritte, e Intagliate da Girolamo Poro. *Maps.* Folio *Padua,* 1620

Porcher E. A. *See* Smith, R. M.

Porcheron, D. P. Ravennatis Anonymi, qui circa Sæculum vii., vixit de Geographia, lib. v. Ex MS. Codice Bibliothecæ Regiæ eruit et Notis illustravit D. P. Porcheron. Small 8° *Paris*, 1688

"Porcupine" and "Lightning." *See* Thomson, Sir C. Wyville.

Porena, Filippo. La Scienza Geografica secondo le più recente dottrine. 8° *Rome*, 1885

Poro, G. *See* Porcacchi.

Porras, Franciscus de. *See* Gottfried : Appendix 1.

Porta, Antonio. Relacion del Reconocimiento de la Costa de Guatemala desde Omoa hasta la Punta de Manabique, y desde la Barra del Rio de Montagua hasta donde se la une el de Chicosapote, a 14 leguas de la Ciudad de Guatemala. Folio* N.P., 1792

Portal, Sir Gerald H. Correspondence respecting his Mission to Abyssinia. *Folio** 1888

—— My Mission to Abyssinia. *Map and illustrations.* 8° 1892 [1891]

Porte, L. de la. *See* De la Porte.

Portenger H. *See* Phillips, New Voyages and Travels [3], Vol. 2 : Appendix 1.

Porter, G. R. *See* Long, G.

Porter, Sir James. Turkey, its History and Progress ; continued to the present time, with Memoir, by Sir George Larpent. 2 vols. *Portraits.* 8° 1854

Porter, J. L. Five Years in Damascus ; including an Account of the History, Topography, and Antiquities of that City ; with Travels and Researches in Palmyra, Lebanon, and the Hauran. 2 vols. *Maps and plates.* 8° 1855

—— The same, with Travels and Researches in Palmyra, Lebanon, the Giant Cities of Bashan, and the Haurân. 2nd edition. *Map and plates.* 8° 1870

Porter, Sir Robert Ker. Travelling Sketches in Russia and Sweden during 1805-8. 2 vols. in 1. *Plates.* 4° 1809

—— Travels in Georgia, Persia, Armenia, Ancient Babylonia, &c., during the years 1817-20. 2 vols. *Maps and plates.* 4° 1821-22

—— *See* Eyriès, Vol. 14 : Appendix 1.

Porter, Robert P. *See* United States, A, Tenth Census, 1880, Vol. 7 : Appendix 2.

—— **H. Gannett, and W. P. Jones.** The West, from the Census of 1880 : a History of the Industrial, Commercial, Social, and Political Development of the States and Territories of the West from 1800 to 1880. *Map and diagrams.* Large 8° *Chicago*, 1882

Porter, Thomas C. *See* United States, G, a, Surveys : Appendix 2.

Porter, Major W. Life in the Trenches before Sebastopol. 12° 1856

Portlock, J. E. Report on the Geology of the County of Londonderry, and of parts of Tyrone and Fermanagh. *Map and plates.* 8° *Dublin*, 1843

Portlock, Capt. Nathaniel. Voyage round the World, but more particularly to the North-West Coast of America, 1785-88. *Maps and plates.* 4° 1789

—— *See* Pelham, Vol. 2 : Appendix 1.

Portlock, and Dixon. *See* Eyriès, Vol. 1 : Appendix 1.

Portman, M. V. A Manual of the Andamanese Languages. 12° 1887

Portus, Æmilius. Lexicon Ionicon Hellenorromaicon : hoc est Dictionarium Ionicum Græco-latínum, quod indicem in omnes Herodoti libros continet, &c. (ed. nov.) 8° 1823

Pory, John. *See* Leo Africanus.

Posade, Clemente Barrial. Historia Geologico-Geografica de la Republica Oriental del Uruguay, Relacionada con la Industria, la Agricultura, y la Ganadería. [Newspaper Cuttings from *La Democracia*, Montevideo, 27th November 1875 *et seq.*] Large 8* 1875-76

Posewitz, Dr Theodor. Borneo : Entdeckungsreisen und Untersuchungen, gegenwärtiger Stand der geologischen Kenntnisse, Verbreitung der nutzbaren Mineralien. *Maps.* Large 8° *Berlin*, 1889

—— Borneo, its Geology and Mineral Resources. Translated from the German by Frederick H. Hatch, Ph.D. *Maps.* Royal 8° 1892

Possart, P. A. F. K. Handbuch für Reisende in Schweden. 12° *Pforzheim*, 1841

—— Statistik und Geographie von Kurland. 8° *Stuttgart*, 1843

Possot, Denis, and Charles Philippe. Le Voyage de la Terre Sainte. Composé par Maitre Denis Possot, et Achevé par Messire Charles Philippe, 1532. Publié et annoté par Ch. Schefer. [Recueil de Voyages et de Documents pour servir a l'Histoire de la Géographie, Depuis le XIIIe jusqu'à la fin du XVIe siècle. Publié sous la direction de MM. Ch. Schefer et Henri Cordier, XI.] *Maps and plates.* Large 8° *Paris*, 1890

Postans, Marianne. Cutch ; or, Random Sketches taken during a Residence in one of the Northern Provinces of Western India, interspersed with Legends and Traditions. *Plates.* 8° 1839

Postans, T. Personal Observations on Sindh, the Manners and Customs of its Inhabitants, and its Productive Capabilities ; with a Sketch of its History. *Map and illustrations.* 8° 1843

—— Memorandum relative to the Trade in Indigo carried on by the Countries bordering on the Indus ; Report on the Munchur Lake, and Arul and Naru Rivers ; Mis-

Postans, T.—*continued*.
cellaneous Information relative to the Town of Shikarpoor, the Trade carried on between that Town and Kandahar, and the Silk-trade between Shikapoor and Khorasan. [From the India Records, No. 17.] Royal 8° *Bombay*, 1855

Postel, Raoul. A Travers la Cochin-Chine. *Map and plan.* 12° *Paris*, 1887

Postels, Alex. *See* Lutké.

Postlethwayt, Malachy. Universal Dictionary of Trade and Commerce, adapting the same to the Present State of British Affairs in America, since the last Treaty of Peace in 1763; with great variety of new remarks and illustrations, together with everything essential that is contained in Savary's Dictionary; also all the Material Laws of Trade and Navigation relating to these Kingdoms, and the Customs and Usages to which all Traders are subject. 2 vols. *Maps.* Folio 1766

Postolacca, Achilles. Synopsis Nvmorvm Vetervm qvi in Mvseo Nvmismatico Athenarvm Pvblico adservantvr. 4°
Athens, 1878

Poston, C. D. Arizona. 8* N.D.

Potanin, G. N. Sketches of North-Western Mongolia. [In Russian.] 4 vols. in 3. *Maps and plates.* 8°
St Petersburg, 1881-83

—— The Tanguto-Tibetan Borderland of China and Central Mongolia: Journey of G. N. Potanin, 1884-1886. [In Russian.] Vols. 1 and 2. *Maps and plates.* 4° *St Petersburg*, 1893

Pote, R. G. Nineveh: a Review of its Ancient History and Modern Explorers. *Illustrations.* 12° N.D.

Potenti de Pistoia, Giuseppe. Légende des Matières contenues dans la Carte Itinéraire, Historique et Statistique, des Chemins de Fer, et des autres voies de communication à vapeur de l'Europe Centrale. 8* *Brussels*, 1846

Potiche, Vicomte de. La Baie du Mont Saint-Michel et ses approches. Création historique de la Baie établie par l'Archéologie, la Géographie, l'Histoire, la Géologie ainsi que par les voies Romaines et les Iles de la Manche. *Maps.* 4°
Paris, 1891

Potocki, Comte Jean. Mémoire sur un Nouveau Péryple du Pont Euxin. *Map.* 4° *Vienna*, 1796

—— Voyage dans les Steps d'Astrakhan et du Caucase, Histoire Primitive des Peuples qui ont habité anciennement ces Contrées. Notes et Tables par Klaproth. 2 vols. *Maps and plates.* 8° *Paris*, 1829

"**Potomac**" **Frigate.** *See* Reynolds.

Potter, John, Archbishop of Canterbury. Archæologia Græca; or, The Antiquities of Greece. 2 vols. *Plates.* 8° 1751

Pottier, E. *See* Gaimard, Paul.

Pottinger, Lieut. Henry. Travels in Beloochistan and Sinde; with a Geographical and Historical Account. *Map.* 4° 1816

—— *See* Eyriès, Vol. 14: Appendix 1.

Poucel, Benjamin. Mes Itinéraires dans les Provinces du Rio de la Plata, 1854-57. Province de Catamarca. 8*
Paris, 1864

—— La Province de Catamarca. 8*
[*Paris*, 1864]

—— Rapport sur le Rejistro Estadistico de la République Argentine. *Maps.* 8°
Marseilles, 1868

—— A propos de la Guerre du Paraguay. [Criticism of Hutchinson's *Parana*.] 4*
Marseilles [1869]

Pouchet, Georges. De la Pluralité des Races Humaines: Essai Anthropologique. 8° *Paris*, 1858

—— Programme d'une Géographie Nosologique, à propos du Traité de Géographie et de Statistique Médicales du Dr Boudin. 8* *Paris*, 1859

—— The Plurality of the Human Race. Translated and edited by Hugh J. C. Beavan. 8° 1864

Pouchet, J., and G. Sautereau. Canal Interocéanique Maritime de Nicaragua. Notes et Documents présentés au Congrès de Géographie de Paris du 15 Mai 1879 à l'appui de Projet de M. Ar.-P. Blanchet. *Map.* 4° *Paris*, 1879

Pouqueville, F. C. Travels in the Morea, Albania, and other Parts of the Ottoman Empire, comprehending . . . an Historical and Geographical Description of the Ancient Epirus. Translated by Anne Plumptre. *Maps and plates.* 4°
1813

—— *See* Phillips, Collection of Modern and Contemporary Voyages [1], Vol. 3: Appendix 1.

Poussié, Dr E. Manuel de Conversation en Trente Langues. 3rd edition. Oblong 12° *Paris*, 1891

Poussin, G. T. Travaux d'Améliorations Interieures Etats-Unis d'Amerique, 1824-31. 4° *Paris*, 1834

Poussin, J. de la Vallée. Les Voyages d'Exploration sur l'Inlandsis du Groenland. 8* *Brussels*, 1893

Pouyanne, J. Note sur l'Établissement de la Carte au 1 : 2,000,000ᵉ de la Région comprise entre le Touat et Timbouktou. *Map.* 8° *Algiers*, 1883

Powell, Rev. Baden. The Order of Nature considered in Reference to the Claims of Revelation. 8° 1859

Powell, David. *See* Galton, F., Vacation Tourists.

Powell, F. T., and R. Ethersay. Memoir on the Survey of Paumben Pass and Adam's Bridge. 8* 1837

Powell, Major J. W. Exploration of the Colorada River of the West and its Tributaries. Explored in 1869, 1870, 1871, and 1872; issued under the direction of the Secretary of the Smithsonian Institution. *Maps and illustrations.* 4° *Washington,* 1875

—— Outlines of the Philosophy of the North American Indians. 8* *New York,* 1877

—— Report on the Lands of the Arid Region of the United States; with a more Detailed Account of the Lands of Utah. 2nd edit. *Maps.* 4° *Washington,* 1879

—— Introduction to the Study of Indian Languages, with Words, Phrases, and Sentences to be collected. 2nd edition. *Charts.* 4° *Washington,* 1880

—— First Annual Report of the Bureau of Ethnology to the Secretary of the Smithsonian Institution, 1879-80. *Maps and plates.* 4° *Washington,* 1881

—— Second do., 1880-81. *Maps and plates.* 4° *Washington,* 1883

—— Third do., 1881-82. *Map and illustrations.* Folio *Washington,* 1884

—— Fourth do., 1882-83. *Illustrations.* 4° *Washington,* 1886

—— Fifth do., 1883-84. *Maps and illustrations.* 4° *Washington,* 1887

—— Sixth do., 1884-85. *Maps and illustrations.* 4° *Washington,* 1888

—— Seventh do., 1885-86. *Maps and plates.* 4° *Washington,* 1891

—— Eighth do., 1886-87. *Plates.* 4° *Washington,* 1891

—— Ninth do., 1887-88. *Maps, plates, and illustrations.* 4° *Washington,* 1892

—— Second Annual Report of the United States Geological Survey to the Secretary of the Interior, 1880-81. *Maps and plates.* 4° *Washington,* 1882

—— Third do., 1881-82. *Maps and plates.* 4° *Washington,* 1883

—— Fourth do., 1882-83. *Maps and illustrations.* 4° *Washington,* 1884

—— Fifth do., 1883-84. *Maps and illustrations.* 4° *Washington,* 1885

—— Sixth do., 1884-85. *Maps and plates.* 4° *Washington,* 1885

—— Seventh do., 1885-86. *Maps and plates.* 4° *Washington,* 1888

—— Eighth do., 1886-87. 2 parts. *Maps and plates.* 4° *Washington,* 1889

—— Ninth do., 1887-88. *Maps and illustrations.* 4° *Washington,* 1889

—— Tenth do., 1888-89. 2 parts. Geology. *Maps and plates.* 4° *Washington,* 1890

—— Eleventh do., 1889-90. 2 parts. *Plates.* 4° *Washington,* 1891

—— Twelfth do., 1890-91. 2 parts. *Maps and plates.* 4° *Washington,* 1891

—— Thirteenth do., 1891-92. 3 parts. *Maps and plates.* 4° *Washington,* 1892-93

Powell, Major J. W. *See* United States, B, c; G, a, Geographical and Geological Surveys: Appendix 2.

Powell, Wilfred. Wanderings in a Wild Country; or, Three Years amongst the Cannibals of New Britain. *Map and illustrations.* 8° 1883

Power, E. R. On the Agricultural, Commercial, Financial, and Military Statistics of Ceylon. 8* 1863

Power, Hon. L. G. The Whereabouts of Vinland. (From the *New England Magazine.*) *Illustrations.* 4* 1892

Power, John. Description of the Province of Sancto Domingo del Darien in South America . . . in the year 1754. Translated from the Original in the National Archives of Bogotá, for the *Panama Star and Herald.* . . . Extracted and arranged by J. Power. [*Title in MS.*] 12* *Panama,* 1868

Power, W. Tyrone. Sketches in New Zealand, with Pen and Pencil; from a Journal kept from July 1846 to June 1848. *Plates.* 8° 1849

—— Recollections of a Three Years' Residence in China; including Peregrinations in Spain, Morocco, Egypt, India, Australia, and New Zealand. *Plate.* 12° 1853

Powles, J. D. New Granada, its Internal Resources. *Maps.* 8° 1863

Powles, L. D. The Land of the Pink Pearl; or, Recollections of Life in the Bahamas. *Map and frontispiece.* 8° 1888

Prado Angelo, Sarrea de Souza. Africa Occidental Portugueza: Angola Caminho de ferro entre Loanda e Ambaco, primeiros estudos technicos; Memoria descriptiva e planta topographica. 8° *Lisbon,* 1877

Prance, R. H. Australian Agricultural Company: Letter to the Shareholders. 8* 1877

Pratt, A. E. To the Snows of Tibet through China. *Map and illustrations.* Large 8° 1892

Prandi, F. *See* Ripa.

Pratt, Rev. G. A Comparison of the Dialects of East and West Polynesian, Malay, Malagasy, and Australian. 8* [*Sydney,* 1886]

Pratt, James Jerram. Sheep and Stock Farming; or, Where to Go. Remarks on the South African or Transvaal Republic, with Information relative to the Settlement of New Scotland. 8* [1867]

Pratt, Peter. *See* Quintus Curtius.

Pratz, Le Page du. Histoire de la Louisiane. 3 vols. *Maps and illustrations.* 12° *Paris,* 1875

Prax, M. Instructions pour le Voyage de, dans le Sahara Septentrional. 8*
Paris, 1847

Prazmovski, A. Rapport sur les Travaux de l'Expédition de Bessarabie en 1852, pour terminer les Opérations de la Mesure de l'Arc du Méridien. 8* 1853

Préandeau, A de. Ministère des Travaux Publics, Ponts et Chaussées : Direction des Routes et de la Navigation, Service Hydrométrique du Bassin de la Seine, Manuel Hydrologique du Bassin de la Seine. *Maps and plates.* 4° *Paris*, 1884

Preece, J. R. Journey from Shiraz to Jashk. Roy. Geog. Soc. Suppl. Papers, Vol. I. *Map.* 8° 1885

Preedy, Capt. H. W., Capt. A. B. Rathbone, and Major P. Goldney. List of, and brief Information in regard to, all Chiefs and Persons of Importance residing within the Kurrachee, Hyderabad, and Shikarpoor Collectorates. [From the India Records, No. 17.] Royal 8°
Bombay, 1855

—— Report on the Hilly Region forming the Western Part of the Kurrachee Collectorate. [From the India Records, No. 35.] Royal 8° *Bombay*, 1856

Prejevalsky, Col. N. M. Mongolia and the Country of Tangut. [In Russian.] Vol. I. Large 8° *St Petersburg*, 1875

—— Mongolia, the Tangut Country, and the Solitudes of Northern Tibet, being a Narrative of Three Years' Travel in Eastern High Asia. Translated by E. Delmar Morgan, with Introduction and Notes by Col. Henry Yule. 2 vols. *Maps and plates.* 8° 1876

—— De Kouldja par le Tian-Schan jusqu'au Lob Nor. (From *Journal de St Pétersbourg.*) Folio* 1878

—— Reise an den Lob Nor und Altyn Tag, 1876-77. (Ergänzungsheft, 53— Petermann's Mittheilungen). 2 *maps.* 4° *Gotha*, 1878

—— From Kulja, across the Tian Shan to Lob-Nor. Translated by E. D. Morgan ; including Notices of the Lakes of Central Asia ; with Introduction by Sir T. Douglas Forsyth. *Maps.* 8° 1879

—— Third Journey to Central Asia from Zaisan viâ Hami to Tibet and the Headwaters of the Yellow River. [In Russian.] *Maps and plates.* 4° *St Petersburg*, 1883

—— Reisen in Tibet und am oberen Lauf des Gelben Flusses in den Jahren 1879 bis 1880 ; aus dem Russischen frei in das Deutsche übertragen und mit Anmerkungen versehen von Stein-Nordheim. *Map and illustrations.* 8° *Jena*, 1884

—— Fourth Journey to Central Asia, 1883-85. [In Russian.] *Maps and plates.* 4° *St Petersburg*, 1888

Prejevalsky, Col. N. M. Scientific Results of the Travels of N. M. Prejevalsky in Central Asia. Botany, 2 parts. [In Russian.] 4° *St Petersburg*, 1889

—— Nikolai Mikhailovitch Prejevalsky. Biographical Sketch by I. F. Dubrovin. [In Russian.] *Map, portraits, and plates.* Large 8° *St Petersburg*, 1890

Prentiss, Henry M. The North Pole and the South Pole. (From the *Overland Monthly.*) 8* *San Francisco*, 1890

Prescott, William H. History of the Conquest of Mexico, with a Preliminary View of the Ancient Mexican Civilisation, and the Life of the Conqueror Hernando Cortés. 2nd edition. 3 vols. *Map and portraits.* 8° 1844

—— See Barca.

Preston, Sir Amias. See Hakluyt, Vol. 4 : Appendix 1.

Preston, T. R. Three Years' Residence in Canada from 1837-39 ; with Notes on a Winter Voyage to New York, and Journey thence to the British Possessions. 2 vols. 8° 1840

Preston, W. See Wallis.

Prestwich, Prof. J. Tables of Temperatures of the Sea at Different Depths beneath the Surface, reduced and collated from the various Observations made between the years 1749 and 1868, discussed. *Map and sections.* 4* 1875

Pretty, Francis. See Purchas, Vol. I, Book 2 : Appendix 1.

Prévost, Abbé A. F. Histoire Générale des Voyages. 20 vols. *Paris*, 1746-89 [For full Title, see Appendix 1.]

Prévost, Constant. Notes sur l'Île Julia, pour servir à l'Histoire de la Formation des Montagnes Volcaniques. *Plates.* 4* N.D.

—— Notice sur, par M. de la Roquette. 8* *Paris*, 1856

Prévost, Florent. See Abyssinia : Appendix 2.

Preyer, W., and F. Zirkel. Reise nach Island im Sommer 1860. Mit wissenschaftlichen Anhängen. *Map and plates.* 8° *Leipzig*, 1862

Price, Major David. Essay towards the History of Arabia prior to the Birth of Mahommed. 4° 1824

—— See Asia, General, Oriental Languages : Appendix 2.

Price, Edward. Norway. Views of Wild Scenery, and Journal. *Plates.* 4° 1834

Price, F. G. H. See Hamilton, Charles.

Price, John Edward. A Descriptive Account of the Guildhall of the City of London, its History and Associations, compiled from Original Documents. *Facsimile charters, maps, and other illustrations.* Folio 1886

Price, John Spencer. The Early History of the Suez Canal. 8* N.D.

Price, Julius M. From the Arctic Ocean to the Yellow Sea : the Narrative of a Journey in 1890 and 1891 across Siberia, Mongolia, the Gobi Desert, and North China. *Portrait, map, and illustrations.* 8° 1892

Price, Rev. Roger. Report of his visit to Zanzibar and the Coast of Eastern Africa. *Map.* 8° 1876

Price, Sir Rose L. The Two Americas : an Account of Sport and Travel, with Notes on Men and Manners, in North and South America. *Plates.* 8° 1877

Price, William. Journal of Travels of the British Embassy to Persia, through Armenia and Asia Minor to Constantinople and Smyrna, with the Voyage back to England ; also a Dissertation upon the Antiquities of Persepolis. 2 vols. in 1. *Plates.* Oblong folio 1833

Price, Rev. W. Salter. My Third Campaign in East Africa : a Story of Missionary Life in troublous times. 2nd edition. *Map and illustrations.* 8° 1891
—— *See* Taylor, Rev. W. E.

Prichard, James Cowles. Researches into the Physical History of Mankind. 4 vols. *Map and plates.* 8° N.D.
—— The same. 3rd edition. 4 vols. *Plates.* 8° 1836
—— The Eastern Origin of the Celtic Nations proved by a comparison of their Dialects with the Sanskrit, Greek, Latin, and Teutonic Languages. Forming a Supplement to " Researches into the Physical History of Mankind." 8° *Oxford*, 1831
—— The same. Edited by R. G. Latham. 8° 1857
—— On the Extinction of Human Races. 8* 1839
—— On the Relations of Ethnology to other Branches of Knowledge. 8* *Edinburgh*, 1847

Prichard, J. T. The Inaugural Lecture of the London Association in aid of Social Progress in India. 8* 1871

Pricket, Abacuck. *See* Purchas, Vol. 3, Book 3 : Appendix 1.

Prickett, M. History of the Priory Church of Bridlington, in the East Riding of the County of York. *Plates.* 8° *Cambridge*, 1836

Prida y Arteaga, F. de. Le Mexique tel qu'il est aujourd' hui. 2nd edition. *Map and portraits.* 8° *Paris*, 1891

Prideaux, Lieut. W. F. *See* Markham, C. R.

Pridham, Charles. Historical, Political, and Statistical Account of Ceylon and its Dependencies. 2 vols. *Map.* 8° 1849

Primisser, Alois. Die kaiserlich-königliche Ambraser-Sammlung. 8° *Vienna*, 1819

Pring, Capt. Martin. *See* Gottfried ; Kerr, Vol. 9 ; Purchas, Vol. 1, Book 5, and Vol. 4, Book 8 : Appendix 1.

Pringle, M. A. Towards the Mountains of the Moon : a Journey in East Africa. *Maps.* 8° 1884

Pringle, Thomas. Narrative of a Residence in South Africa. New edition, with a Biographical Sketch of the Author by Josiah Conder. 8° 1848

Prinsep, E. A. Sealkote, Punjab : Statistical Account of the Sealkote District, geographically sketched, in the years 1855 to 1860. Folio N.P., N.D.
—— Report on the revised Settlement of Sealkote District in the Amritsur division. Small folio *Lahore*, 1865

Prinsep, G. A. An Account of Steam Vessels and of Proceedings connected with Steam Navigation in British India. *Map and plates.* 4° *Calcutta*, 1830
—— Sketch of the Proceedings and Present Position of the Saugor Island Society and its Lessees. *Map.* 8° *Calcutta*, 1831

Prinsep, Henry T. History of the Political and Military Transactions in India during the Administration of the Marquess of Hastings, 1813-23. Enlarged from the Narrative published in 1820. 2 vols. *Maps.* 8° 1825
—— Tibet, Tartary, and Mongolia, their Social and Political Condition, and the Religion of Boodh as there existing . . . 2nd edition. 12° 1852
—— The India Question in 1853. 8° 1853

Prior, James. *See* Phillips, New Voyages and Travels [3], Vols. 1, 2 : Appendix 1.

Prisse, E. Oriental Album : Characters, Costumes, and Modes of Life in the Valley of the Nile, illustrated from Designs taken on the spot ; with Descriptive Letterpress by James A. St John. Large folio 1848

Pritchett, George J. Ecuador Waste Lands. 8* 1858
—— Report of his Mission to the Republic of Ecuador. *Map.* 8* 1858

Pritchett, Morris. Some Account of the African Intermittent Fever which occurred on board H. M. steam-ship "Wilberforce," in the River Niger, . . . comprising an Inquiry into the Causes of Disease in Tropical Climates. *Map and plate.* 8° 1843

Proaño, Victor. Carta en Defensa de la Ciencia Geografica, de la Honra Nacional, de la Propiedad Moral, y de la " Via Proaña." 8* *Quito*, 1884

Procopius. *See* Turkey in Asia, B : Appendix 2.

Procter, John R. Information for Emigrants: the Climate, Soils, Timbers, &c., of Kentucky, contrasted with those of the North-west. *Map.* 8*
Frankfort, Ky., 1881

Proctor-Sims, R. Bhavnagar State Railway: Reports, with General Plan and Section. *Map.* Folio* N.P., N.D.

Prokesch, Anton von. Erinnerungen aus Ægypten und Kleinasien. 2 vols. 8° *Vienna*, 1829-30
—— Land zwischen den Katarakten des Nil. *Map.* 8° 1831
—— Reise ins Heilige Land in 1829. 12° *Vienna*, 1831

Proskowetz, Dr Max von. Vom Newastrand nach Samarkand, durch Russland, auf neuen Geleisen nach Inner-Asien; init einer Einleitung von H. Vambéry. *Maps and illustrations.* 8° *Vienna*, 1889
—— Eine Fahrt nach Russisch-Asien. 8* *Vienna*, 1890
—— La Moravie. (Extrait du Bulletin de la Société de Géographie de Lyon.) 8* *Lyons*, 1892

Proudfoot, W. Jardine. Barrow's Travels in China: an Investigation into the Origin and Authenticity of the "Facts and Observations" related in the work. 8° 1861

Prout, Major H. G. Rapport de sa Reconnaissance entre Khartoum et Obeiyad. (*Moniteur Egyptien*, 19th and 20th September 1875.) Large 8* 1875
—— General Report on the Province of Kordofan, submitted to General C. P. Stone, Chief of the General Staff, Egyptian Army, by Major H. G. Prout, Corps of Engineers, commanding Expedition of Reconnaissance made at El-Obeiyad (Kordofan), 12th March 1876. *Maps and plates.* 8° *Cairo*, 1877

"Providence." See Broughton, W. R.

Proyart, Abbé. Histoire de Loango, Kakongo, et autres Royaumes d'Afrique; redigée d'après les Mémoires des Préfets Apostoliques de la Mission Françoise. *Map.* 12° *Paris*, 1776
—— See Pinkerton, Vol. 16: Appendix 1.

Prschewalsky (or Przewalsky). See Prejevalsky.

Pruen, S. T. The Arab and the African: Experiences in Eastern Equatorial Africa during a Residence of Three Years. *Portrait and illustrations.* Crown 8° 1891

Prunelli, Domenico. Almanacco Marittimo ad uso di tutte le Classi de' Naviganti, 1842. Part 2, e 1846. *Ancona*, 1845-46

Prus, Madame. Residence in Algeria. 8° 1852

Pryer, W. B., and F. Witti. Diaries of Messrs Pryer and Witti. *Map and plate.* [Bound with other papers of the Brit. N. Borneo Assoc.] 4* [1881]

Ptolemy, Claudius. Liber Quadripartiti Ptolomei id est quattuor tractatuum: in radicanti discretione per stellas, de futuris et id hoc Mundo constructionis et destructionis contingentibus. [*Blackletter.*] Small 4° *Venice*, 1484
[Bound with 4° "Tabule Astronomice illustrissimi Alfonsii Regis Castelli." *Venice*, 1483.]
—— Geographicæ Enarrationis Libri octo, Bilibaldo Pirckeymhero interprete, annotationes Joannis de Regio Monte in errores commissos a Jacobo Angelo in translatione sua. Folio *Strasburg*, 1525
—— Geographiæ Claudii Ptolemæi, libri VIII., partim à Bilibaldo Pirckheymero translati ac commentario illustrati, partim etiam Græcorum antiquissimorumque exemplariorum collatione emendati atque in integrum restituti. *Maps.* Folio. *Bâle*, 1552
—— Geographiæ vniversae tvm veteris, tvm novae absolvtissimvm opus, duobus voluminibus distinctum, in quorum priore habentur Cl. Ptolemæi Pelvsiensis Geographicæ enarrationis libri octo: Quorum primus, qui præcepta ipsius facultatis omnia complectitur, commentarijs vberrimis, illustratus est à Io. Antonio Magino Patavino. In secundo volumine insunt Cl. Ptolemæi, antiquæ orbis tabulæ XXVII. ad priscas historias intelligendas summè necessariæ. Et tabulæ XXXVII. recentiores, quibus vniuersi orbis pictura, ac facies, singularumq; eius partium regionum, ac prouinciarum ob oculos patet nostro sæculo congruens. Vnà cum ipsarum tabularum copiosissimis expositionibus, quibus singulæ orbis partes, prouinciæ, regiones, imperia, regna, ducatus, & alia dominia, prout nostro tempore se habent, exactê describuntur. Auctore eodem Io. Ant. Magino Patavino, Mathematicarum in Almo Bononiensi Gymnasio Publico Professore, 1597. 4° *Cologne and Arnheim*, 1597
—— Geografia cioè Descrittione vniversale della Terra, partita in due volumi; nel Primo de' quali si contengono gli otto Libri della Geografia di Cl. Tolomeo; nel secondo vi sono poste XXVII. tavole antiche di Tolomeo, e XXXVII. altre Moderne, tutte reviste e in alcuni luoghi accresciute e illustrate da ricchissimi Commentarii dal Sig. Gio. Ant. Magini. Opera utilissima e specialmente necessaria allo studio dell' Historie, dal Latino nell' Italiano tradotta dal R. D. Leonardo Cernoti. *Maps.* Folio *Venice*, 1598
—— Geographiæ, libri octo, Græco-Latino. Latine primum recogniti et emendati, cum tabulis geographicis ad mentem auctoris restitutis per G. Mercatorem; jam vero ad Gr. et Lat. exemplaria a P. Montano iterum recogniti, et pluribus locis castigati. *Maps.* Folio *Frankfort and Amsterdam*, 1605

Ptolemy, Claudius. Géographie de Ptolémée, reproduction photolithographique du Manuscrit Grec du Monastère de Vatopédi au Mont Athos, exécutée d'après les clichés obtenus sous la direction de M. Pierre de Séwastianoff, et précédée d'une Introduction Historique sur le Mont Athos, les Monastères, et les dépôts littéraires de la presqu'île sainte, par Victor Langlois. Folio *Paris*, 1867
—— Κλανδιου Πτολεμαιου Γεωγραφικη Ὑφηγησις. Claudii Ptolemæi Geographia: E codicibus recognovit, prolegomenis, annotatione, indicibus, tabulis instruxit, Carolus Miillerus. Voluminis Primi Pars Prima. Large 8° *Paris*, 1883
—— A List of Editions of Ptolemy's Geography, 1475-1730. 8* *New York*, 1886
—— *See* Plate, William ; Rylands.
Puchstein, Dr Otto. Bericht über eine Reise in Kurdistan. *Map and plan.* Large 8* *Berlin*, 1883
—— *See* Humann.
Pudsey, ——. *See* Hakluyt, Vol. 4 : App. 1.
Puggaard, C. Deux Vues Géologiques pour servir à la Description Géologique du Danemark. *Plates.* Folio* *Copenhagen*, 1853
—— Description Géologique de la Péninsule de Sorrento dans le Royaume de Naples ; contenant de Nouvelles Observations sur les Dolomies. *Map.* 8* *Copenhagen*, 1858
—— Notice sur les calcaires plutonisés de la Péninsule de Sorrento. 8* *Paris*, 1859
—— Mémoire sur les calcaires plutonisés des Alpes Apuennes et du Monte Pisano. 8* *Paris*, 1860
Pugh, Theophilus P. Brief Outline of the Geographical Position, Population, Climate, Resources, Capabilities, Form of Government, Land Laws, Trade, Revenue, &c., of the Colony of Queensland. 12° *Brisbane*, 1861
—— Queensland Almanac, Directory, Law Calendar, Gazetteer, &c., from 1862 to 1893. *Maps and plates.* 12° *Brisbane*
Pullan, R. Popplewell. The Principal Ruins of Asia Minor, &c. *See* Texier, Charles.
Pullan, Lieut. W. J. L. *See* Kellet, Capt. H.
Pulli, Pietro. Tratta Teorico-Practico su la Raccolta del Nitro di Napoli. 2 vols. *Plates.* 8° *Naples*, 1813-17
Pumpelly, Raphael. Notice of an Account of Geological Observations in China, Japan, and Mongolia. (From the *American Journal of Science and Arts*, Vol. 41). 8* 1866
Pumpelly, Raphael. Northern Transcontinental Survey: First Annual Report of Raphael Pumpelly, Director of the Survey, September 1882. 12* *New York*, 1882

Pumpelly, Raphael. *See* United States, A, Tenth Census, 1880, Vol. 15 : Appendix 2.
Purchas, Samuel, his Pilgrimage, or Relátions of the World and the Religions observed in all Ages. 3rd edition. Folio 1617
—— His Pilgrimes, in Five Books. . . . *Maps and illustrations.* 4 vols. Folio 1625
[For full Title and Contents, *see* Appendix 1. *Also see* Thevenot, Vol. 1 in same Appendix.]
Purdy, Col. E. S. Psychrometrical Observations taken at Fascher, Darfour, 1876. 8* *Cairo*, 1877
Purdy, John. Memoir, Descriptive and Explanatory, to accompany the New Chart of the Atlantic Ocean, and comprising Instructions, General and Particular, for the Navigation of that Sea. 8° 1817
—— New Sailing Directory for the Ethiopic, or Southern Atlantic Ocean, to the Rio de la Plata and the Cape of Good Hope, &c., including the Islands between the two Coasts. 8° 1829
—— Second edition. 8° 1837
—— Third edition, Revised and Corrected by A. G. Findlay. 8° 1845
—— New Sailing Directory for the Strait of Gibraltar and the Western Division of the Mediterranean Sea. 8° 1832
—— New Sailing Directory for the Gulf of Venice, and the Eastern or Levantine Division of the Mediterranean Sea ; together with the Sea of Marmora and the Euxine or Black Sea. 8° 1834
—— Brasilian Navigator ; or, Sailing Directory for all the Coasts of Brasil, &c., from the River Para to the Rio de la Plata, including General Instructions for the Routes both from England and from North America, with Descriptions and Directions for the Madeira, Canary, and Cape Verde Islands, Fernando Noronha, &c. 8° 1844
—— Sailing Directions for the Strait of Gibraltar and the Mediterranean Sea. 8° 1846
—— *See* Huddart ; White, Capt. M.
—— **and Alex. G. Findlay.** Memoir, Descriptive and Explanatory, to accompany the Charts of the Northern Atlantic Ocean ; and comprising Instructions, General and Particular, for the Navigation of that Sea. Corrected, &c., by A. G. Findlay. 9th edition. 8° 1845
—— Eleventh edition. Materially improved by A. G. Findlay. *Maps.* 8° 1861
—— New Piloting Directory for the Different Channels of the Thames and Medway, with the Navigation between Orfordness and Folkestone . . . Revised, &c., by A. G. Findlay. 8° 1846

Purdy, John, and A. G. Findlay. British American Navigator : Sailing Directory ·for the Island and Banks of Newfoundland, the Gulf and River of St Lawrence, Breton Island, Nova Scotia, the Bay of Funday, and the Coasts thence to the River Penobscot, &c. 2nd edition. 8° 1847

—— Colombian Navigator. Vol. 1. Sailing Directory for the Bermuda Islands, the Eastern and Southern Coasts of the United States, and the States of Texas. Improved by A. G. Findlay. 2nd edition. *Map.* 8° 1847

—— The same, Vol. 2. Sailing Directory for the Northern Part of the West Indies and the Mexican Sea, . . . including the Description of the Florida or Gulf Stream. Improved by A. G. Findlay. 4th edition. 8° 1848

—— Sailing Directory for the Windward and Gulf Passages, the Bahama Islands and Channels, the Islands of Hayti, Jamaica, and Cuba, the Coast of Florida, the Martyrs, &c., and the Florida or Gulf Stream. Revised and Corrected by A. G. Findlay. 4th edition. 8° 1848

—— Sailing Directory for the English Channel and Southern Coasts of Ireland. Revised, &c., by Alex. G. Findlay. 8° 1849

—— Memoir, Descriptive and Explanatory, of the Northern Atlantic Ocean. 12th edition. By A. G. Findlay. *Charts and woodcuts.* 8° 1865

Pursglove, W. *See* Purchas, Vol. 3, Book 3 : Appendix 1.

Purves, J. *See* General, International Geological Congress : Appendix 2.

Purvis, Comodoro. Sobre los Avances del, en el Rio de la Plata. 8* *Buenos Ayres,* 1843

Puseley, D. The Rise and Progress of Australia, Tasmania, and New Zealand ; in which will be found the Increase and Habits of Population, Table of Revenue and Expenditure, Commercial Growth, and Present Position of each Dependency, &c. 8° 1858

Putiata, D. V. Expedition to Khingan in 1891 : a Description of the Route taken. [In Russian.] *Maps and plans.* 8* *St Petersburg,* 1893

Puydt, Lucien de. La Vérité sur le Canal Interocéanique de Panama. 8* *Paris,* 1879

Pycroft, J. W. The Claim to the Foreshores of the Sea Coast and Tidal Rivers in . . . Devon and Cornwall by Her Majesty's Commissioners of Woods and Forests examined and considered. 4* 1854

—— Arena Cornubiæ ; or, The Claims of the Commissioners of Woods and Forests to the Sea-Coast and Banks of Tidal Rivers in Cornwall and Devon examined. 4° 1856

Pyrard de Laval, Francois. *See* Gray, A. ; *also* Harris, Vol. 1 ; Hakluyt Soc. Publ., Vols. 76, 77, 80 ; Laharpe, Vol. 3 ; Purchas, Vol. 2, Book 9 ; Allgemeine Historie, Vol. 8 ; "The World Displayed," Vol. 10 : Appendix 1.

Q

Quadri, Antoine. Huit Jours à Venise. *Plates.* 12° *Venice,* 1825

—— Otto Giorni a Venezia. *Map and plates.* 12° *Venice,* 1830

—— The same. Seconda Edizione. Parte Seconda. Compendio della Storia Veneta diviso in otto epoche, dalle origione di Venezia nell' anno 421 sino alla caduta della Repubblica nell' anno 1797. 12° *Venice,* 1826

Quatrefages, A. de. The Rambles of a Naturalist on the Coasts of France, Spain, and Sicily. Translated by E. C. Otté. 2 vols. 8° 1857

—— Les Polynésiens et leurs Migrations. *Maps.* 4° *Paris* [1865 ?]

—— Discours prononcé à l'ouverture de l'Assemblée Générale du 19 Décembre 1890. (Compte Rendu, Société de Géographie.) 8* *Paris,* 1890

Quatrelles, —. Un Parisien dans les Antilles : Saint-Thomas—Puerto-Rico—La Havane —La vie de Province sous les Tropiques. *Plates.* 12° *Paris,* 1883

Quentin,. Ch. An Account of Paraguay, its History, its People, and its Government. From the French. 8* 1865

Quesada, V. G. La Patagonia y las Tierras Australes del Continente Americano. Large 8° *Buenos Ayres,* 1875

Quetelet, L. A. J. Éclipse de Soleil du 15 Mars 1858 : Notice. 8* *Brussels,* 1858

—— Bolide observé dans· la soirée du 4 Mars 1863. 8* *Brussels,* 1863

—— Sur les Étoiles filantes périodiques du mois d'Août 1867, et sur les Orages observés en Belgique pendant l'été de 1867, &c. 8* *Brussels* [1867]

—— Étoiles filantes du milieu de Novembre 1867 et État de l'Atmosphère à la même époque. 8* *Brussels* [1867]

—— Sur la Loi Statistique des tailles humaines, et sur la régularité que suit cette loi dans son développement à chaque age. 8* *Brussels,* 1868

—— Physique Sociale, ou Essai sur le Développement des Facultés de l'Homme. Vol. 2. 8° *Brussels,* 1869

—— Notice sur Charles Babbage. 12* *Brussels,* 1873

—— Unité de l'Espèce Humaine. 8* N.P., N.D.

Quetelet, Ernest. Sur l'état de l'Atmosphère à Bruxelles pendant l'année 1865. 8* *Brussels,* N.D

—— *See* Mailly.

Quétin, —. Guide du Voyageur en Algérie, Itinéraire du Savant, de l'Artiste, de l'Homme du Monde, &c. 2nd edition, to which is added a French-Arabic Vocabulary. 12° *Paris*, 1847
Quiggin's Guide through the Isle of Man. *Map and plates.* 12° *Douglas*, 1842
Quijarro, Dr Antonio. Los Territorios del Noroeste de Bolivia: Vias de Comunicacion que les Corresponden. *Map.* 8* *Buenos Ayres*, 1892
—— Propuestas de Ferro-Carriles para los Departamentos del sud y del Oriente de Bolivia. 8* *Buenos Ayres*, 1893
—— *See* Bach, M.
Quin, Michael J. Steam Voyages on the Seine, the Moselle, and the Rhine; with Railroad Visits to the Principal Cities of Belgium. 2 vols. 8° 1843
Quintus Curtius. The History of Alexander the Great. Translated, with Original Notes, by Peter Pratt. 2 vols. *Map.* 8° 1821
—— Alexander in India : a portion of the History of Quintus Curtius. Edited for Schools and Colleges by W. E. Hartland and E. Raven. *Map.* 12° *Cambridge*, 1879
Quirini (or Quirino), Piero. *See* Kerr, Vol. 1 ; Purchas, Vol. 3, Book 3 ; Ramusio, Vol. 2 : Appendix 1.
Quiroga, Don Francisco. Apuntes de un Viage por el Sáhara occidental. *Plate.* 8* [1886]
Quiroga, P. *See* Allgemeine Historie, Vol. 16 : Appendix 1.
Quirós (or Quir, or Giros), Pedro Fernandez de. Historia del Descubrimiento de las Regiones Australes. Publicada por Don Justo Zaragoza. 3 vols. *Maps and plan.* 8° *Madrid*, 1876-82
—— *See* Gerritz ; *also* Burney, Vol. 2 ; Callander, Vol. 2 ; Harris, Vol. 1 ; Purchas, Vol. 4, Book 7 ; Allgemeine Historie, Vol. 18 : Appendix 1.
Quoy, J. R. C. *See* Freycinet.

R

R——. How about Fiji? or Annexation *versus* Non-Annexation; with an Account of the various Proposals for Cession, and a Short Sketch of the Natural Aspects of the Group. By "R." 8* 1874
R——, V. P. Memoria sobre Emigracion, Inmigracion, i Colonizacion, por V. P. R. 8° *Santiago*, 1854
Rabaud, Alfred. Zanzibar : La Côte orientale d'Afrique et l'Afrique équatoriale. *Maps.* 8° *Marseilles*, 1881
Rabot, Charles. *See* Nordenskiöld.
Raconis, J. B. de *See* Varthema.
Rada, Dr Emeteris Villamil de. La Lengua de Adan y el Hombre de Tiahnanaco; con una indroduccion del Doctor Nicolás Acosta. 8° *La Paz*, 1888

Radau, R. La Géographie de Précision en Afrique. 8* *Paris* [? 1886]
—— *See* Abbadie.
Radcliff, Rev. T. On the Agriculture of Eastern and Western Flanders. *Map and plates.* 8° 1819
Radcliffe, William. The Natural History of East Tartary, traced through the three Kingdoms of Nature ; rendered into English from the French Translation. 8° 1789
Raddatz, Dr H. Das Kaffernland des untern Olifant. *Map.* 4* *Gotha*, 1886
Radde, Dr Gustav. Reisen im Süden von Ost-Sibirien in den Jahren 1855-59. 2 vols. *Maps and plates.* 4° *St Petersburg*, 1862-63
—— Berichte über die biologisch-geographischen Untersuchungen in den Kaukasusländern, im Auftrage der Civil-Hauptverwaltung der Kaukasischen Statthalterschaft ausgeführt. Jahrgang 1. Reisen im Mingrelischen Hochgebirge und in seinen drei Längenhochthälern, Rion, Tskenis-Tsquali, und Ingur. *Maps and plates.* 4° *Tiflis*, 1866
—— Vier Vorträge über den Kaukasus gehalten im Winter 1873-74 in den grösseren Städten Deutschlands. (Ergänzungsheft, 36 — Petermann's Mittheilungen). *Maps.* 4° *Gotha*, 1874
—— Die Chews'uren und ihr Land (ein monographischer Versuch) untersucht im Sommer 1876. *Map and plates.* 8° *Cassel*, 1878
—— The Ornithological Fauna of the Caucasus : a Systematic and Biologico-geographical description of Caucasian birds. [In Russian.] *Maps and plates.* 4° *Tiflis*, 1884
—— Reisen an der Persisch-Russischen Grenze. Talysch und seine Bewohner. *Map and illustrations.* 8° *Leipzig*, 1886
—— Die Fauna und Flora des südwestlichen Caspi Gebietes ; wissenschaftliche Beiträge zu den Reisen an der Persisch-Russischen Grenze. *Plates.* 8° *Leipzig*, 1886
—— Sendschreiben an Herrn Prof. Dr Liebe, zweitem Vorsitzenden des Deutschen Vereins zum Schutze der Vogelwelt. 8* *Tiflis*, 1889
—— Aus den Dagestanischen Hochalpen, vom Schah-dagh zum Dulty und Bogos. (Ergänzungsheft, 85—Petermann's Mittheilungen). *Maps and illustrations.* 4° *Gotha*, 1887
—— Karabagh. Bericht über die im Sommer 1890 im Russischen Karabagh von Dr Gustav Radde und Dr Jean Valentin ausgeführte Reise. (Ergänzungsheft, 100—Petermann's Mittheilungen.) *Map.* 4° *Gotha*, 1890
—— *See* Baer and Helmersen, 23.

Raders, Baron R. F. van. De Vestiging van Nederlanders te Surinam aanbevolen. 8* *The Hague,* 1854

Radford, A. Jottings on the West Indies and Panama. 12° 1886

Radiot, Paul. Le Transsaharien transatlantique. 8* *Paris,* 1891

Radius, J. S. C. de. Characteristic Features of Russian and Slavic Poetry, with specimens, translated by English Authors. 12° 1854

Radlinsky, Prof. A. G. Alessandro Magno; influenza delle sue Conquiste sull' Asia e sull' Europa. 8* *Mantua,* 1857
—— L'America prima di Cristoforo Colombo. 8* *Mantua,* 1857

Radloff, Dr Wilhelm. Aus Sibirien : Lose Blätter aus dem Tagebuche eines reisenden Linguisten. 2 vols. *Map and illustrations.* Small 8° *Leipzig,* 1884
—— Die Hausthiere der Kirgisen. 8*
N.P., N.D.

Rae, Edward. The Land of the North Wind, or Travels among the Laplanders and the Samoyedes. *Maps and plates.* Small 8° 1875
—— The Country of the Moors : a Journey from Tripoli in Barbary to the City of Kairwân. *Map and plates.* 8° 1877
—— The White Sea Peninsula : a Journey in Russian Lapland and Karelia. *Map and illustrations.* 8° 1881

Rae, Dr John. Narrative of an Expedition to the Shores of the Arctic Sea in 1846 and 1847. *Maps.* 8° 1850
—— Voyages and Travels of, in the Arctic Regions. Copy of a Letter from Dr Rae, Feb. 1856. 8* 1856
—— On some physical properties of ice ; on the transposition of Boulders from below to above the Ice ; and on Mammoth-remains. 8* 1874
—— Snow-huts, Sledges, and Sledge Journeys. 8* 1875
—— Arctic and Sub-Arctic Life. 8* 1877

Rae, John. *See* New South Wales, D : Appendix 2.

Raemdonck, Dr J. van. Gerard Mercator : sa Vie et ses Œuvres. *Plates.* Imp. 8° *St Nicolas,* 1869
—— La Géographie Ancienne de la Palestine : Lettre de Gérard Mercator à André Masius, datée de Duisbourg 22 Mai 1567. *Map.* 4* *St Nicolas,* 1884
—— Relations Commerciales entre Gérard Mercator et Christophe Plantin à Anvers. 4* *St Nicolas,* 1884
—— Les Sphères Terrestre et Céleste de Gérard Mercator (1541 et 1551). 8* *St Nicolas,* 1885

Raffenel, Anne. Nouveau Voyage dans le Pays des Nègres, suivi d'études sur la Colonie du Sénégal, et de documents historiques, géographiques et scientifiques. Tome 1. *Plates.* Large 8° *Paris,* 1856

Raffenel, —. *See* Jomard.

Raffles, Sir Thomas Stamford. Substance of a Minute recorded in 1814 on the Introduction of an Improved System of Internal Management, and the Establishment of a Land Rental, on the Island of Java. 4° [*Privately printed*] 1814
—— History of Java. 2 vols. 8°, and separate volume of *Plates* 4° 1830
—— Memoir of the Life and Public Services of, particularly in the Government of Java, 1811-16, and of Bencoolen and its Dependencies, 1817-24 ; with details of the Commerce and Resources of the Eastern Archipelago, and Selections from his Correspondence. By his Widow. With Appendix. *Portrait, maps, and plates.* 4° 1830

Raffray, Achille. Afrique Orientale : Abyssinie. *Map and plates.* 12° *Paris,* 1876

Rafinesque, C. S. The Ancient Monuments of North and South America. 8* *Philadelphia,* 1838

Rafn, Prof. Charles Christian. Færeyínga Saga, eller Færöboernes Historie, i den Islandske Grundtext, med Færöisk og Dansk Oversættelse. *Map and facsimile.* Royal 8° *Copenhagen,* 1832
—— Færeyínga Saga, oder Geschichte der Bewohner der Färöer im Islandischen Grundtext mit Färöischer, Dänischer, und Deutscher Uebersetzung. Herausgegeben von C. C. Rask und G. C. F. Mohnike. *Map and facsimile.* Royal 8° *Copenhagen,* 1833
—— Antiquitates Americanæ, sive Scriptores Septentrionales rerum Ante-Columbianarum in America. Samling af dei nordens Oldskrifter indeholdte Efterretninger am de gamle Nordboers Opdagelsesreiser til America fra det 10de til det 14de Aarhundrede. Imperial 4° *Copenhagen,* 1837
—— Wiadomosc o odkryciu Ameryki Wdziesiatym Wieku; na Francuzkie przelozyl, Ksawery Marmier; na Niemieckie G. Mohnike; a Podlug tych przekladów na Polskie przetlumaczyl, J. K. Trojanski. 12° *Cracow,* 1838
—— Mémoire sur la Découverte de l'Amérique au dixième siècle. Traduit par Xavier Marmier. 8* *Paris,* 1838
—— Memoria sulla scoperta dell' America nel secolo decimo, dettata in Lingua Danese, e tradotta da J. Gräberg da Hemsö. 8* *Pisa,* 1839
—— Americas Opdagelse i det tiende Aarhundrede. *Maps and plates.* 8° *Copenhagen,* 1841
—— Supplement to the Antiquitates Americanæ. *Maps and plates.* 8° *Copenhagen,* 1841
—— Americas Arctiske Landes gamle Geographie efter de nordiske Oldskrifter. *Maps and plates.* 8* *Copenhagen,* 1845

Rafn, Prof. Charles Christian. Antiquités Américaines d'après les Monuments Historiques des Islandais et des Anciens Scandinaves. *Map.* 4°
Copenhagen, 1845
—— Aperçu de l'Ancienne Géographie des Régions Arctiques de l'Amérique. *Maps.* 8* *Copenhagen,* 1847
—— Remarks on a Danish Runic Stone, from the eleventh century, found in the central part of London. *Plates.* 8°
Copenhagen, 1854
—— Antiquités de l'Orient, Monuments Runographiques. 8* *Copenhagen,* 1856
—— Inscription Runique du Pirée, interprétée. [French and Danish.] *Plates.* 8° *Copenhagen,* 1856
—— Cabinet d'Antiquitiés Américaines à Copenhague. Rapport Ethnographique. *Maps.* 8° *Copenhagen,* 1858
—— Inscriptions Runiques du Slesvig Méridional, interprétées. *Map.* 8*
Copenhagen, 1861
—— Renseignements sur les premiers Habitants de la Côte Occidentale du Groenland. Traduits en Groenlandais par Samuël Kleinschmidt. *Map and plate.* 4* 1864
—— Notices of the Life and Writings of, by L. E. Borring. 8*
Copenhagen, 1864
—— The Discovery of America by the Northmen : Connection of the Northmen with the East. [2 *leaves.*] 8* N.D.

Rafn, Prof. C. C., and Jon Sigurdsson. Saga Játvardar Konúngs hins Helga udgiven efter Islandske Oldböger af det Kongelige Nordiske Oldskrift-selskab. 8* *Copenhagen,* 1852

Ragazzi, Dr Vincenzo. Da Antoto ad Harar. Note di Viaggio . . . con prefazione e carta del Prof. G. Dalla Vedova. 8* *Rome,* 1888

Ragosin, V. Volga. Vol. 1 [in Russian.] *Plates.* 8°, and Atlas (Vol. 1) folio
St Petersburg, 1880

Raikes, —. *See* Walpole, Travels: Appendix 1.

Raikes, Charles. Notes on the North-Western Provinces of India. 8° 1852

Raikes, Stanley Napier. Memoir and Brief Notes relative to the Kutch State. [From the India Records, No. 15.] *Portrait and map.* Royal 8° *Bombay,* 1855
—— Memoir on the Thurr and Parkur Districts of Sind, 1856. [From the India Records, No. 54.] *Map and plate.* Royal 8° *Bombay,* 1859

Raikes, T. A Visit to St Petersburg in the winter of 1829-30. 8° 1838

Raimondi, Antonio. Analisis de las Aguas Termales de Yura, Aguas minerales de Jesus, y Aguas potables de Arequipa. *Table.* 8* *Arequipa,* 1864

Raimondi, Antonio. Apuntes sobre la Provincia Litoral de Loreto (Peru). *Maps.* 12* *Lima,* 1862
—— El Departamento de Ancachs y sus Riquezas Minerales. 4° *Lima,* 1873
—— El Peru. 2 vols. *Map, plan, and plates.* 4° *Lima,* 1874-76

Rainaud, Armand. Le Continent Austral; hypothèses et découvertes. Large 8°
Paris, 1893

Rainolds, R. *See* Astley, Vol. 1; Hakluyt, Vol. 3; Kerr, Vol. 7: Appendix 1.

Rainy, W. The Censor Censured; or, The Calumnies of Capt. Burton on the Africans of Sierra Leone refuted, &c.; with some Remarks on the Sierra Leone Exhibition. 8° 1865

Raisin, Miss Catharine A. *See* Elliot, G. F. S.

Raleigh, Sir Walter. History of the World; with Life by Oldys, also his Trial. 2 vols. *Portrait and maps.* Folio 1736
—— Life of Sir Walter Raleigh, by Arthur Cayley. 2 vols. *Portrait.* 8° 1806
—— *See* Whitehead; *also* Hakluyt Soc. Publications, Vol. 3; Astley, Vol. 1; Gottfried; Hakluyt's Voyages, Vols. 2, 4; Kerr, Vol. 7; Pinkerton, Vol. 1; Allgemeine Historie, Vols. 1, 16: Appendix 1.

Ramage, G. A. *See* Ridley.

Rambaud, Alfred. La France Coloniale, Histoire—Géographie—Commerce. Par Alfred Rambaud, avec la collaboration d'une Société de Géographes et de Voyageurs. 6th edition. *Maps.* 8°
Paris, 1893

Rambert, Eugène. Les Alpes Suisses: Études d'Histoire Naturelle, les Plantes Alpines, la Question du Fœhn, le Voyage du Glacier, la Flore Suisse et ses Origines. 12° *Lausanne,* 1888

Ramchundra. Treatise on Problems of Maxima and Minima, solved by Algebra. Reprinted under the Superintendence of Augustus de Morgan. 8° 1859

Ramé, Alfred. Note sur le Manoir d Jacques Cartier. *See* Cartier, J.

Ramirez, Santiago. Noticia Historica de la Requeza Minera de Mexico y de su actual estado de Explotacion. 8°
Mexico, 1884

Ramón, L. P. de. *See* Bartoli.

Ramond, L. Observations faites dans les Pyrénées pour servir de suite à des Observations sur les Alpes. *Maps.* 8°
Paris, 1789
—— Voyages au Mont-Perdu, et dans la partie adjacente des Hautes-Pyrénées. *Plates.* 8° *Paris,* 1801

Ramond, L. Travels in the Pyrenees, containing a Description of the Principal Summits, Passes, and Vallies. Translated from the French, by F. Gold. 8° 1813
—— *See* Pinkerton, Vol. 4 : Appendix 1.

Ramos-Coelho, José. Historia do Infante D. Duarte, irmão de El-Rei D. João IV. 2 vols. *Plates.* 8° *Lisbon,* 1889-90

Ramsay, Sir Andrew C. The Physical Geology and Geography of Great Britain. 3rd edition. *Map.* Small 8° 1872
—— New edition. *Map and plates.* 8° 1894
—— *See* Stanford, E.

Ramsay, E. P. *See* New South Wales, A, Australian Museum Publications : Appendix 2.

Ramsay, J. The Vascular Flora of the West of Scotland. Published for the British Association Meeting, 1876. 12° *Glasgow,* 1876

Ramsay, Prof. W. M. The Historical Geography of Asia Minor. Roy. Geo. Soc. Suppl. Papers, Vol. 4. *Maps and tables.* Large 8° 1890

Ramusio, Gio. Battista. Delle Navigationi et Viaggi. 3 vols. *Maps.* Folio *Venice,* Vol. 1, 1613 ; Vol. 2, 1583 ; Vol. 3, 1606
[For Contents, *see* Appendix 1.]
—— Il Viaggio di Giovan Leone e le Navigazioni di Alvise de ca Da Mosto, di Pietro di Cintra, di Annone, di un piloto Portoghese e di Vasco di Gama ; quali si leggono nella raccolta di Giovambattista Ramusio. *With portrait of Ramusio.* Large 8° *Venice,* 1837

Rance. *See* De Rance.

Rancy, M. de. Description, Géographique, Historique, et Statistique de la Navarre. 8° *Toulouse,* 1817

Rand, M'Nally & Co.'s Handy Guide to Chicago and World's Columbian Exposition. *Plan and illustrations.* 12° *Chicago,* 1892

Rand, Rev. Silas Tertius. Dictionary of the Language of the Micmac Indians who reside in Nova Scotia, New Brunswick, Prince Edward Island, Cape Breton, and Newfoundland. 4° *Halifax, N.S.,* 1888

Randel, J. F. *See* Hunt, R. S.

Rands, William H. The Paradise Gold Field. *Plan and sketch.* Folio* *Brisbane,* 1891
—— The Cape River Gold Field. *Map, diagram, and sections.* Folio* *Brisbane,* 1891
—— The Styx River Gold Field. *Map and plate.* Folio* *Brisbane,* 1892
—— Geological Observations in the Cooktown District. *Map.* Folio* *Brisbane,* 1893

Rang, Sander, and Ferdinand Denis. Fondation de la Régence d'Alger, Histoire des Barberousse, Chronique Arabe du

Rang, Sander, and F. Denis—*contd.* XVIᵉ Siècle, publié sur un Manuscrit de la Bibliothèque Royale, avec un Appendice et des Notes ; Expédition de Charles-Quint ; Aperçu historique et statistique du Port d'Alger. 2 vols. 8° *Paris,* 1837

Ranke, Johannes. *See* Switzerland, B : Appendix 2.

Ranke, Leopold. History of Servia and the Servian Revolution. Translated by Mrs A. Kerr. *Map.* 8° 1847

Rankin, Daniel J. The Portuguese in East Africa. (From the *Fortnightly Review,* February 1890.) 8* 1890
—— Arab Tales : translated from the Swahíli Language into the Túgulu Dialect of the Mákua Languages, as spoken in the immediate vicinity of Mozambique ; together with comparative Vocabularies of Five Dialects of the Mákua Language. *Map.* 12° [N.D., 1891 ?]
—— The Discovery of the Chinde Entrance to the Zambesi River. (From the *Fortnightly Review,* December.) 8* 1892
—— The Zambesi Basin and Nyasaland. *Map and illustrations.* 8° *Edin.,* 1893

Ranking, J. Historical Researches on the Conquest of Peru, Mexico, Bogota, Natchez, and Talomeco, in the 13th Century, by the Mongols, accompanied with Elephants ; and the local agreement of history and tradition with the remains of Elephants and Mastodontes found in the New World, &c. *Maps and plates.* 8° 1827

Ransome, J. Leslie. The Eruptive Rocks of Point Bonita. Bulletin of the Department of Geology of the University of California, Vol. 1, No. 3. Large 8* *Berkeley, Cal.,* 1893

Ranuzzi, Annibale. Saggio di Geografia Pura, ovvero Primi Studi sull' Anatomia della Terra. 8* *Bologna,* 1840
—— Notizia sullo stato attuale degli Studi Geografici in Italia. 12* *Bologna,* 1843
—— Annuario Geografico Italiano, 1844-45. 2 vols. · 12° and 8° *Bologna,* 1844-45

Raper, Lieut. Henry. The Practice of Navigation and Nautical Astronomy. 2nd edition. 8° 1842
—— The same. 5th edition. 8° 1854
—— The same. 6th edition. 8° 1857
—— The same. 10th edition. 8° 1870
—— The same. 12th edition. 8° 1877
—— The same. 19th edition. 8° 1881
—— Supplement to the First Edition of the Practice of Navigation. 8° 1842
—— Maritime Positions, constituting Table 10 of the Practice of Navigation. 8° 1850
—— Rules for Finding Distances and Heights at Sea. 8* 1831, 1859, and 1866
—— Tables of Logarithms to six places : containing Logarithms of Numbers from 1 to 10,000 ; and of Sines, Tangents, and Secants for every half-minute ; with proportional parts for Seconds. 8° 1846

Raper, Lieut. Henry. *See* United Kingdom, A, Hydrogr. Off. Publ.: Appendix 2.

Rapier R. C. Remunerative Railways for
New Countries ; with some Account of
the First Railway in China. *Plates.* 4°
1878

Rask, Rasmus. Singalesisk Skriftlære.
8* *Colombo*, 1821
—— Vejledning til Akra-Sproget paa
Kysten Ginea, med et Tillæg om Akvam-
buisk. 12* *Copenhagen*, 1828
—— A Grammar of the Anglo-Saxon
Tongue; with a Praxis. . . . Translated
from the Danish by B. Thorpe. 8°
Copenhagen, 1830
—— Ræsonneret Lappisk Sproglære, efter
den Sprogart, som Bruges af Fjældlap-
perne i porsangerfjorden i Finmarken ;
en Omarbejdelse af Prof. Knud Leems
Lappiske Grammatica. 12°
Copenhagen, 1832

Rassam, Hormuzd. Narrative of the
British Mission to Theodore, King of
Abyssinia ; with Notices of the Countries
traversed from Massowah, through the
Soodân, the Amhâra, and back to
Annesley Bay, from Mágdala. 2 vols.
Map and plates. 8° 1869
—— *See* Markham, C. R.

Rat, J. Numa. The Elements of the
Hausa Language, or a Short Introductory Grammar of the Language. 16*
1889

Rath, G. vom. *See* Dechen ; Rein.

Rathbone, A. B. *See* Preedy.

Rathbun, Richard. *See* Hartt.

Ratte, A. Felix. *See* New South Wales,
A, Australian Museum Publications :
Appendix 2.

Ratti, C. G. Instruzione di quanto
puo' vedersi di piu' bello in Genova. *Map
and plates.* 8° *Genoa*, 1780

"Rattlesnake," H.M.S. *See* Macgillivray, John.

Rattray, Alex. Vancouver Island and
British Columbia : where they are, what
they are, and what they may become.
Maps and plates. 8° 1862

Ratzel, Dr Friedrich. Aus Mexico,
Reiseskizzen aus den Jahren 1874 und
1875. *Map.* 8° *Breslau*, 1878
—— Anthropo-Geographie oder Grundzüge
der Anwendung der Erdkunde auf die
Geschichte. 8° *Stuttgart*, 1882
—— The same. Zweiter Teil : Die geo-
graphische Verbreitung des Menschen.
Maps. 8° *Stuttgart*, 1891
—— Völkerkunde. 3 vols. *Maps and
illustrations* *Leipzig*, 1887-88
Vol. 1.—Die Naturvölker Afrikas.
Vol. 2.—Die Naturvölker Ozeaniens,
Amerikas, und Asiens.
Vol. 3.—Die Kulturvölker der Alten
und Neuen Welt.

Ratzel, Dr Friedrich. Die Vereinigten
Staaten von Amerika. 1. Physikalische
Geographie und Naturcharacter. *Maps.*
8° *Munich*, 1878
—— Ditto. 2. Politische und Wirtschafts-
Geographie. *Map.* 8° *Munich*, 1893
—— *See* Emin Pasha ; *also* Germany, C,
Forschungen zur Deutschen Landes, &c.,
Vol. 4 : Appendix 2.

Raulin, V. Description Physique et Naturelle de l'Ile de Crète. 2 vols. 8°
Paris, 1869

Raumer, Karl von. Lehrbuch der allge-
meinen Geographie. 8° *Leipzig*, 1835
—— Palästina. *Maps.* 8° *Leipzig*, 1850
—— Life and System of J. H. Pestalozzi.
Translated by J. Tilleard. 8° 1855

Rauwolf, Leonhart. *See* Ray : Appendix 1.

Raven, T. E. *See* Quintus Curtius.

Ravenstein, Augustus. Die vierte Stadt-
Erweiterung. *Map.* 8*
Frankfurt-a-M., 1857

Ravenstein, E. G. Statistic View of the
Population, the Religions, and Languages
of Europe in 1855. *Maps.* 4* 1855
—— A Concise Account of Geographical
Discovery in Eastern Africa. *Map.* 8* 1860
—— The Russians on the Amur, its Dis-
covery, Conquest, and Colonisation.
Maps and plates. 8° 1861
——Geographie und Statistik des Britischen
Reichs. 8° *Leipzig*, 1863
—— Denominational Statistics of England
and Wales. 8* 1870
—— Reisehandbuch für London, England,
und Schottland. *Maps and plates.* 8°
Hildburghausen, 1870
—— London, England, Schottland, und
Irland. Meyer's "Reisebücher." 3rd ed.
Maps and plates. 12° *Leipzig*, 1876
—— Census of the British Isles, 1871 :
The Birthplaces of the People and the
Laws of Migration. *Maps.* 12* 1876
—— Population of Russia and Turkey.
8* 1877
—— Cyprus, its Resources and Capabilities;
with Hints for Tourists. *Maps.* 12* 1878
—— Celtic Languages in the British Isles.
Maps. 8* 1879
—— Somal and Galla Land. 8* 1884
—— Bathyhypsographical Maps. *Maps.*
8* 1886
—— Livingstone and Lake Bangweola.
8* 1889
—— Geographical Co-ordinates in the
Valley of the Upper Nile. 8* 1889
—— The Laws of Migration. 2nd paper.
Maps. 8* 1889
—— Lake Regions of Central Africa. 8*
1891
—— Rivers, Plains, and Mountains. 8* 1891
—— The Field of Geography. 8* 1891
—— Lands still available for European
Settlement. *Maps.* 8* 1891

Ravenstein, E. G. Report on Meteorological Observations in British East Africa for 1893. Large 8*   1893
—— *See* Johnston; Krapf, J. L.; Reclus, É.; Stanford, E.

Raverty, Major H. G. Dictionary of the Puk'hto, Pus'hto, or Language of the Afghans. 4°   1860
—— Grammar of the Puk'hto, Pus'hto, or Language of the Afghans ; in which the Rules are illustrated by Examples . . . together with Translations from the Articles of War, &c.   4°   1860
—— The Gulshan-I-Roh ; being Selections, Prose and Poetical, in the Pus'hto or Afghan Language.   4°   1860
—— The Gospel for the Afghans ; being a Short Critical Examination of a Small Portion of the New Testament in the Pus'hto or Afghan Language, and a Comparison between it and the Original Greek from which it is said to have been made.   8°   1864
—— Muscovite Proceedings on the Afghan Frontier. (From the *United Service Gazette.*) *Map.* Small 4*   1885
—— Notes on Afghánistán and part of Balúchistán, Geographical, Ethnographical, and Historical, extracted from the Writings of little known Afghán and Tájzík Historians, Geographers, and Genealogists ; the Histories of the Ghúris, the Turk Sovereigns of the Dilhí Kingdom, the Mughal Sovereigns of the House of Tímúr, and other Muhammadan Chronicles ; and from Personal Observations.   Folio   [1880-] 1888
—— The Mihrán of Sind and its Tributaries : a Geographical and Historical Study. (Reprinted from *Journal of the Asiatic Society of Bengal.*]   8*   1892

Ravinet, Théodore. Dictionnaire Hydrographique de la France, contenant la Description des Rivières et Canaux flottables et navigables dépendans du Domaine Public ; suivi de la Collection complète des Tarifs des Droits de Navigation.   2 vols.   *Map.*   8°   *Paris*, 1824

Rawley, William. *See* Verulam.

Rawlings, Thomas. The Confederation of the British North American Provinces, their Past History and Future Prospects, including also British Columbia and Hudson's Bay Territory. *Plates.* 8* 1865
—— What shall we do with the Hudson's Bay Territory? Colonize the "Fertile Belt," which contains Forty Millions of Acres.   8*   1866

Rawlins, John. *See* Purchas, Vol. 2, Book 6 : Appendix 1.

Rawlinson, George. The Five Great Monarchies of the Ancient Eastern World ; or, The History, Geography, and Antiquities of Chaldæa, Assyria, Babylon, Media, and Persia. 4th ed. 3 vols. *Maps and illustrations.* 8° 1879

Rawlinson, George. History of Phœnicia. *Maps and illustrations.*   8°   1889
—— *See* Herodotus.

Rawlinson, Gen. Sir Henry C. Notes on the Direct Overland Telegraph from Constantinople to Kurrachi. *Map.* 8* 1861
—— Outlines of Assyrian History, collected from the Cuneiform Inscriptions ; some Remarks by Layard. Report of the Royal Asiatic Society, 1852. 8* 1852
—— England and Russia in the East : a Series of Papers on the Political and Geographical Condition of Central Asia. 2nd edition.   *Map.*   8°   1875
—— Biography, with portrait. (From *Leisure Hour*, August 1877.) 8* 1877
—— *See* Herodotus.

Rawson, Sir Rawson W. Report on the Bahamas for the year 1864. 8° 1866
—— Report upon the Rainfall of Barbados, and upon its Influence on the Sugar-Crops, 1847-71 ; with two Supplements, 1873-74.   4°   *Barbados*, 1874
—— Synopsis of the Tariff and Trade of the British Empire.   *Tables.*   8°   1888
—— Sequel to do.   *Tables.*   8°   1889
—— Analysis of the Maritime Trade of the United Kingdom, 1889-91, with special reference to Proposals for the Establishment of a British Zollverein.   8*   1892

Ray, John. Collection of Curious Travels and Voyages.   2 vols.   8°   1738
[For Contents, *see* Appendix 1.; *also* Harris, Vol. 2, in same Appendix.]

Ray, P. H. *See* United States, K, Alaska : Appendix 2.

Ray, R. C. *See* United States, E, *a*, Navigation : Appendix 2.

Raymond, Captain G. *See* Astley, Vol. 1 ; Kerr, Vol. 8 : Appendix 1.

Raymond, Walter. Saldanha Bay Harbour, its Special Capabilities for Colonisation.   *Map.*   8*   1867

Raynal, F. E. Les Naufragés, ou Vingt Mois sur un Récif des îles Auckland. *Map and plates.* Large 8° *Paris*, 1870

Raynal, Guillaume Thomas. Histoire Philosophique et Politique des Établissemens et du Commerce des Européens dans les deux Indes.   10 vols.   *Plates and tables.*   8°   *Geneva*, 1781
—— A Philosophical and Political History of the Settlements and Trade of the Europeans in the East and West Indies . . . Newly translated from the French, by J. O. Justamond. 8 vols. *Maps.* 8°   1788

Razoumowsky, Comte Grégoire de. Œuvres : contenant Voyage Minéralogique et Physique de Bruxelles à Lausanne, Luxembourg, Lorraine, Champagne, Franche-Comté, Aigle, &c. *Map.* 8°   *Lausanne*, 1784
—— Voyages Minéralogiques dans le Gouvernement d'Aigle, et une partie du Vallais. *Map.* 8°   *Lausanne*, 1784

Read, John Meredith. A Historical Inquiry concerning Henry Hudson, his friends, relatives, and early life, in connection with the Muscovy Company and discovery of Delaware Bay. 8°
Albany, N. Y., 1866

Read, W. T. Navigation and Nautical Astronomy, with special table, diagram, and rules adapted for navigating iron ships. 8° 1869

Reade, E. A. Memorandum upon the Improvement of the Navigation of the Ganges between Allahabad and Revelgunge. [From the Indian Records, N. W. Provinces, Vol. 2.] *Plates.* Large 8° *Agra*, 1855

Reade, Winwood. The Martyrdom of Man. Small 8° 1872
—— The African Sketch-Book. 2 vols. *Maps and plates.* Small 8° 1873
—— The Story of the Ashantee Campaign. Small 8° 1874
—— *See* Rohlfs ; Schweinfurth.

Reade, T. Mellard. The Origin of Mountain Ranges considered experimentally, structurally, dynamically, and in relation to their Geological History. *Plates.* 8° 1886

Rebello, Gabriel. *See* Colleccão de Noticias, Vol. 6 : Appendix 1.

"Recherche." *See* Gaimard.

Reclus, Armand. Panama et Darien. Voyages d'Exploration (1876-78). *Maps and illustrations.* 12° *Paris*, 1881
—— *See* Wyse.

Reclus, Élie. Ethnography and Ethnology. (From Vol. 8 of the "Encyclopædia Britannica," 9th edition.) 4* *Edinburgh*, 1878

Reclus, Élisée. La Terre : Description des Phénomènes de la Vie du Globe. 2 vols. *Maps and plates.* 8° *Paris*, 1868-69
—— La Terre : Description des Phénomènes de la Vie du Globe. I. Les Continents. Deuxième édition. *Maps and illustrations.* Large 8° *Paris*, 1870
—— The Earth : a Descriptive History of the Phenomena of the Life of the Globe. Translated by B. B. Woodward. 3rd edition. *Maps.* 8° 1877
—— The Earth : a Descriptive History of the Phenomena of the Life of the Globe. Edited by Prof. A. H. Keane. *Maps.* Large 8° 1886
—— The Ocean, Atmosphere, and Life : a Descriptive History of the Life of the Globe. Edited by Prof. A. H. Keane. *Maps.* Large 8° 1887
—— Nouvelle Géographie Universelle : la Terre et les Hommes. 19 vols. *Maps and illustrations.* Large 8° *Paris*, 1876-94

Reclus, Élisée —*continued.*
Vol. 1.—L'Europe Méridionale (Grèce, Turquie, Roumanie, Serbie, Italie, Espagne, et Portugal) 1876
Vol. 2.--La France 1877
Vol. 3.—L'Europe Centrale (Suisse, Austro-Hongrie, Allemagne) 1878
Vol. 4.—L'Europe du Nord - Ouest (Belgique, Hollande, Îles Britaniques) 1879
Vol. 5.—L'Europe Scandinave et Russe 1880
Vol. 6. —L'Asie Russe 1881
Vol. 7.—L'Asie Orientale 1882
Vol. 8.—L'Inde et l'Indo-Chine 1883
Vol. 9.—L'Asie Anterieure 1884
Vol. 10. — L'Afrique Septentrionale : Première partie, Bassin du Nil, Soudan Égyptien, Éthiopie, Nubie, Égypte 1885
Vol. 11. — L'Afrique Septentrionale : Deuxième partie, Tripolitaine, Tunisie, Algérie, Maroc, Sahara 1886
Vol. 12.—L'Afrique Occidentale. Archipels Atlantiques, Sénégambie, et Soudan Occidental 1887
Vol. 13.—L'Afrique Méridionale. Iles de l'Atlantique Austral, Gabonie, Congo, Angola, Cap, Zambèze, Zanzibar, Côte de Somal 1888
Vol. 14.—Océan et Terres Océaniques. Iles de l'Océan Indien, Insulinde, Philippines. Micronésie, Nouvelle-Guinée, Melanesie, Nouvelle - Calédonie, Australie, Polynésie 1889
Vol. 15.—Amérique Boréale, Groenland, Archipel Polaire, Alaska, Puissance du Canada, Terre-Neuve 1890
Vol. 16. —Les États-Unis 1892
Vol. 17.—Indes Occidentales : Mexique, Isthmes Americains, Antilles 1891
Vol. 18.—Amérique du Sud : Les Régions Andines, Trinidad, Vénézuela, Colombie, Écuador, Pérou, Bolivie, et Chili 1893
Vol. 19.—Amérique du Sud : L'Amazonie et La Plata, Guyanes, Brésil, Paraguay, Uruguay, République Argentine 1894
—— The Earth and its Inhabitants. The Universal Geography, edited by E. G. Ravenstein and A. H. Keane. Vols. 1-14. *Maps and illustrations.* Large 8° N.D.
Vol. 1. — Southern Europe (Greece, Turkey in Europe, Roumania, Servia, Italy, Spain, and Portugal).
Vol. 2.—France and Switzerland.
Vol. 3.--Austria - Hungary, Germany, Belgium, and the Netherlands.
Vol. 4.—The British Isles.
Vol. 5.—The North - East Atlantic, Islands of the North Atlantic, Scandinavia, European Islands of the Arctic Ocean, Russia in Europe.

Reclus, Élisée. The Earth and its Inhabitants—*continued.*
Vol. 6.—Asiatic Russia.
Vol. 7.—East Asia.
Vol. 8.—India and Indo-China.
Vol. 9.—South-Western Asia.
Vol. 10.—North-East Africa.
Vol. 11.—North-West Africa.
Vol. 12.—West Africa.
Vol. 13.—South and East Africa.
Vol. 14.—Australasia.
—— Voyage à la Sierra-Nevada de Sainte-Marthe. Paysages de la Nature tropicale. Seconde edition. *Map and illustrations.* 12°   *Paris,* 1881
—— East and West. Large 8*   N.D.
—— **and F. J. Vergara.** Colombia. Traducida y anotada con autorizacion del autor por F. J. Vergara y Velasco. 8°   *Bogota,* 1893
—— *See* Metchnikoff.

Recupero, G. Discorso storico sopra l'acque vomitate da Mongibello e suoi ultimi fuochavvenuti nel mese di Marzo del corrento anno MDCCLV. 8*
                              Catania, 1755

Reden, Freiherr Fr. von. Das König-reich Hannover statistisch beschrieben, zunächst in Beziehung auf Landwirth-schaft, Gewerbe und Handel. 2 vols. 8°   *Hanover,* 1839

Redfern, Dr Peter. *See* Lankester, Edwin.

Redfield, William C. On the Courses of Hurricanes, with Notices of the Tyfoons of the China Sea and other Storms. 8*
                              New York, 1838
—— Letter to the Secretary of the Treasury on the History and Causes of Steamboat Explosions, and the Means of Prevention. 8*   *New York,* 1839
—— Whirlwinds excited by fire, with further Notices of the Tyfoons of the China Sea. 8* .   1839
—— Remarks relating to the Tornado which visited New Brunswick (in New Jersey), June 19, 1835. *Map.* 8*
                              New York, 1841
—— Replies to Dr Hare's Objections to the Whirlwind Theory of Storms; with some evidence of the Whirling Action of the Providence Tornado of Aug. 1838. 8*   *New York,* 1842
—— On Three several Hurricanes of the Atlantic, and their relations to the Northers of Mexico and Central America, with Notices of other Storms. *Maps.* 8*   *New Haven, Conn.,* 1846
—— Cape Verde and Hatteras Hurricane, of Aug.-Sept. 1853, with a Hurricane Chart, and notices of various Storms in the Atlantic and Pacific Oceans, North of the Equator. 8*
                        New Haven, Conn., 1854

Redfield, William C. Observations in relation to the Cyclones of the Western Pacific. *Map.* 4*   *Washington,* 1857
—— Cursory Remarks and Suggestions on various topics in Meteorology. By an Amateur Observer. 8*   N.P., N.D.
—— On the Gales and Hurricanes of the Western Atlantic. *Map.* 8* N.P., N.D.

Redhouse, J. W. On the significations of the term "The Turks." 8*   1878
—— *See* General, Dictionaries, A : Appendix 2.

Redman, J. B. Thames Tides. (Cuttings from *Engineering.*) 4*   1878

Redway, Jacques W. Climate and the Gulf Stream. (Reprinted from *The Forum* for October.) Large 8*   1890
—— The Influence of Rainfall on Commercial Development : a Study of the Arid Region. (Reprinted from the *Proceedings of the Engineers' Club of Philadelphia,* October.) 8*   1892
—— Text-Books of Geography. (From the *Educational Review* for February.) 8*   *New York,* 1893

Reed, A. *See* Gutzlaff.

Reed, Sir E. J. Japan, its History, Traditions, and Religions ; with the Narrative of a Visit in 1879. 2 vols. *Map and plates.* 8°   1880

Reed, Lieut. H. A. Photography applied to Surveying. 2nd edition. *Plates.* 4°
                              New York, 1889

Reed, J. *See* Burney, Vol. 4 : Appendix 1.

Reed, J. W., and J. W. King. *See* United Kingdom, A., Hydrogr. Off. Publ. : Appendix 2.

Reehorst, K. P. (tertius). New Dictionary of Technical Terms, &c. 8° 1841

Reenen, Jacob van. A Journal of a Journey from the Cape of Good Hope, undertaken in 1790 and 1791, in search of the Wreck of the Hon. E.I.C. ship the " Grosvenor," with additional Notes by Capt. Edw. Riou. *Map.* 4*   1792

Rees, J. D. Notes of a Journey from Kasveen to Hamadan, across the Kara-ghan Country. *Map.* 8* *Madras,* 1885
—— Seventh Tour of Lord Connemara. Malabar, South Canara, Goa, Bellary, Cuddapah, North Arcot, and Nellore. *Map.* Folio*   [*Madras,* 1888]
—— Tenth Tour. Calcutta, Darjeeling, Allahabad, Simla, Quetta, Kurrachee, and Bombay. *Map.* Folio*   [1889]
—— Eleventh Tour. Coconada, Raja-mundry, Ellore, Bezwada, Singareni, and Hyderabad. *Map.* Folio* [1890]
—— Visit to the Eurasian Settlements of Whitefield and Sansmond by Lord Connemara, Governor of Madras. *Map.* Folio*   [1890]
—— A Fortnight in Finland. (From the *National Review,* October 1893.) 8* 1893

Rees, L. E. Runtz. Personal Narrative of the Siege of Lucknow, from its Commencement to its Relief by Sir Colin Campbell. *Map and portrait.* 8° 1858

Rees, O. van. Overzight van de Geschiedenis der Preanger-Regentschappen. 8° *Batavia,* 1877

Rees, P. van. Quelques Erreurs de MM. Maurice d'Argout et La Place relevées et réfutées. 8° *Utrecht,* 1843

Reeve, Edward. *See* St Julian.

Reeve, L. *See* Jephson, J. M.

Reeves, A. M. The Finding of Wineland the Good : the History of the Icelandic Discovery of America. Edited and Translated from the Earliest Records. *Plates.* 4° 1890

Régamy, F. *See* Guimet.

Regel, Dr Fritz. Die Entwickelung der Ortschaften im Thüringerwald. (Ergänzungsheft, 76 — Petermann's Mittheilungen.) *Map.* 8° *Gotha,* 1884

Regis, Jean Baptiste. *See* Astley, Vol. 4 : Appendix 1.

Regnard, P. Sur un dispositif destiné à éclairer les eaux profondes. [Bound with the Prince of Monaco's "Sur l'emploi de nasses," &c., &c.] *Illustration.* 4° *Paris,* 1888

Regnard, —. Vol. 4 of his works. 12° *Paris,* 1818

—— *See* Pinkerton, Vol. 1 ; Allgemeine Historie, Vol. 17 : Appendix 1.

Reichardt, C. A. L. Grammar of the Fulde Language ; with an Appendix of some Original Traditions and portions of Scripture translated into Fulde ; together with Eight Chapters of the Book of Genesis translated by the late Dr Baikie. 8° 1876

Reichardt, H. W. *See* "Novara."

Reichenbach, O. On Some Properties of the Earth. *Plate.* 8° 1880

—— On Some of the Remarkable Features in the Evolution of the Earth. 8* 1884

—— Colonel Clark's Determination of the Eccentricity of the Equator. Letter to Dr A——, March 1887. 8* 1887

—— Law in the Face of the Earth. 8* 1889

—— Supplements to " On Some Properties of the Earth." 8* N.P., N.D.

Reid, Surg.-Lieut.-Col. A. S. Chin-Lushai Land : including a description of the various Expeditions in the Chin-Lushai Hills, and the final annexation of the country. *Maps and illustiations.* 8° *Calcutta,* 1893

Reid, G. H. An Essay on New South Wales, the Mother-Colony of the Australias. *Map.* 8° *Sydney,* 1876

—— Five Free Trade Essays. 8° *Melbourne,* 1877

Reid, Lieut.-Col. W. An Attempt to Develop the Law of Storms by means of Facts arranged according to Place and Time, and hence to point out a Cause for the Variable Winds, with the view to Practical Use in Navigation. *Charts and woodcuts.* 8° 1838

—— The Progress of the Development of the Law of Storms and of the Variable Winds, with the Practical Application of the subject to Navigation. *Maps and woodcuts.* 8° 1849

—— *See* United Kingdom, B, Meteorological Office Publications : Appendix 2.

Reiff, C. P. *See* General, Dictionaries, A : Appendix 2.

Reille, G. *See* Horsburgh, J.

Rein, Prof. Dr J. J. Gerhard vom Rath, Ein kurzes Lebensbild. (Aus der Sitzung der Niederrheinischen Gesellschaft für Natur und Heilkunde zu Bonn, am 7 Mai 1888.) 8* 1888

—— Der Nakasendô in Japan. (Ergänzungsheft, 38 — Petermann's Mittheilungen.) *Maps.* 4° *Gotha,* 1880

—— Japan : Travels and Researches undertaken at the Cost of the Prussian Government. Translated from the German. *Maps, photographs, and illustrations.* Large 8° 1884

—— Japan, nach Reisen und Studien im Auftrage der königlich preussischen Regierung dargestellt. Zweiter Band, Land und Forstwirthschaft, Industrie und Handel. *Maps and plates* *Leipzig,* 1886

—— The Industries of Japan, together with an Account of its Agriculture, Forestry, Arts, and Commerce. From Travels and Excursions undertaken at the Cost of the Prussian Government. *Maps and illustrations.* Large 8° 1889

—— Columbus und seine vier Reisen nach dem Westen. Natur und hervorragende Erzeugnisse Spaniens. *Illustrations and maps.* 8° *Leipzig,* 1892

—— *See* Kirchhoff.

Reinach, Solomon. *See* Tissot.

Reinaud, J. T. Relation des Voyages faits par les Arabes et les Persans dans l'Inde et à la Chine dans le IXe Siècle. 2 vols. 24° 1845

—— Mémoire Géográphique, Historique, èt Scientifique sur l'Inde antérieurement au milieu du XIe Siècle . . . . . d'après les Écrivains Arabes, Persans, et Chinois. *Map.* 4° *Paris,* 1849

—— Rapport sur le Tableau des Dialectes de l'Algérie et des Contrées voisines, de M. Geslin. 8* *Paris,* 1856

—— Question Scientifique et Personelle, au sujet des dernières Découvertes sur la Géographie et l'Histoire de l'Inde. 8* *Paris,* 1859

Reinaud, J. T. Mémoire sur le Commencement et la Fin du Royaume de la Mésène, et de la Kharacène, et sur l'Époque de la Rédaction du Périple de la Mer Érythrée, d'après les témoignages Grecs, Latins, Arabes, Persans, Indiens, et Chinois. 8° *Paris*, 1861
—— Another edition. 4* *Paris*, 1864
—— Relations Politiques et Commerciales de l'Empire Romain avec l'Asie Orientale (l'Hyrcanie, l'Inde, la Bactriane, et la Chine) pendant les cinq premiers Siècles de l'Ère Chrétienne, d'après les témoignages, Latins, Grecs, Arabes, Persans, Indiens, et Chinois. *Maps.* 8°
Paris, 1863
—— *See* Aboulfeda.

Reinbeck, G. *See* Phillips, Collection of Modern and Contemporary Voyages and Travels [1], Vol. 6 : Appendix 1.

Reineggs, Dr J. Allgemeine historisch-topographische Beschreibung des Kaukasus. Herausgegeben von Friedrich Enoch Schröder. *Plates.* Small 8°
Gotha, 1776
—— **and Marshal Bieberstein.** General, Historical, and Topographical Description of Mount Caucasus; with a Catalogue of Plants indigenous to the Country. Translated by C. Wilkinson. 2 vols. *Map and plates.* 8° 1807

Reinéke, M. Déscription Hydrographique des Côtes Septentrionales de la Russie, Côte de la Laponie et Mer Blanche. Traduction du Russe par H. de la Planche. 2 parts. 8° *Paris*, 1860-62

Reiner, Ignatius. Sailing Directions for, and Remarks on, the Tides and Currents of the Strait of Gibraltar. 8° 1826

Reinthal, Capt. *See* Michell.

Reinwardt, Caspar George Carl. Reis naar het Oostelijk Gedeelte van den Indischen Archipel, in 1821. Uit zijne nagelaten Aanteekeningen Opgesteld, met een Levensberigt en Bijlagen vermeerderd, door W. H. de Vriese. *Plates.* Royal 8° *Amsterdam*, 1858
—— Waarnemingen aangaande de gestelheid van den Grond van het Eiland Aruba, en het goud Aldaar Gevonden. *Map.* 4* N.P., N.D.
—— *See* Veth.

Reiss, W. Tenerife geologisch-topographisch dargestellt. *See* Fritsch, K. von, and others.
—— **and A. Stübel.** Alturas principales tomadas en la Republica del Ecuador, en los años de 1870 y 1871. 4°
Quito, 1871
—— Alturas tomadas en la Republica de Colombia, en los años de 1868 y 1869. 4° *Quito*, 1872
—— Peruvian Antiquities. The Necropolis of Ancon in Peru. [Part 1.] A series of Illustrations of the Civilisation and In-

Reiss, W., and A. Stübel—*continued.*
dustry of the Empire of the Incas, being the results of Excavations made on the spot. *Plates.* Folio 1891
—— Reisen in Sud - Amerika. Geologische Studien in der Republik Colombia. III. Astronomische Ortsbestimmungen bearbeitet von Bruno Peter. 4°
Berlin, 1893

Reiter, Dr Hanns. Die Südpolarfrage und ihre Bedeutung fur die genetische Gliederung der Erdoberfläche. *Map.* 4*
Weimar, 1886

Relandus, Hadrianus. Hadriani Relandi Palaestina ex monumentis veteribus illustrata. 2 vols. *Maps.* 4° *Utrecht*, 1714

Remelé, P. *See* Rohlfs.

Remington, A. Statement relative to the Names of the Towns and Villages in the Province of the Rewa Kanta. [From the India Records, No. 33.] Royal 8°
Bombay, 1856

Remon, Capt. T. Report on Bassadore, situated on the North-Western Side of the Island of Kishm, in the Persian Gulf, with a Plan of the Roads by Midshipman H. H. Hewett. [From the India Records, No. 24.] Royal 8° *Bombay*, 1856
—— *See* Grubb.

Remondino, P. C. The Mediterranean Shores of America. Southern California, its Climatic, Physical, and Meteorological Conditions. *Maps and illustrations.* Large 8° *Philadelphia*, 1892

Rémusat, J. P. Abel. Recherches sur les Langues Tartares, ou Mémoires sur différens points de la Grammaire et de la Littérature des Mandchous, des Mongols, des Ouigours et des Tibetains. Vol. 1. 4° *Paris*, 1820
—— Nouveaux Mélanges Asiatiques, ou Recueil de Morceaux de Critiques et de Mémoires relatifs aux Religions, aux Sciences, aux Coutumes, à l'Histoire et à la Géographie des Nations Orientales. 2 vols. *Map.* 8° *Paris*, 1829
—— *See* Fa Hian; Pauthier.

Remy, Jules. Ka Mooolelo Hawaii : Histoire de l'Archipel Havaiien (Îles Sandwich). Texte et Traduction, précédés d'une Introduction sur l'état physique, moral et politique du pays. 8°
Paris, 1862

—— Ascension de MM. Brenchley et Remy au Maunaloa, Polynésie. Extrait du Journal de M. Jules Remy. 8*
Chalons-sur-Marne, 1892

—— **and Julius Brenchley.** Journey to Great-Salt-Lake City ; with a Sketch of the History, Religion, and Customs of the Mormons, and an Introduction on the Religious Movement in the United States. 2 vols. *Map and plates.* Royal 8° 1861

Renaud, G. L'Afrique centrale d'après Cameron. *Map.* 4* *Paris,* 1876

Renaud, J. Les Ports du Tonkin. 8* *Paris,* 1886

—— La Question des Ports du Tonkin, Haï-Phong, Quang-yen, Honegac. *Map.* 8* *Paris,* 1887

Renaudot, Eusebius. Ancient Accounts of India and China, by two Mahommedan Travellers, who went to those parts in the 9th century; translated from the Arabic, by . . . E. Renaudot, with Notes, Illustrations, &c. 8° 1733

—— *See* Harris, Vol. 1 : Appendix 1.

Rencke, Karl Chr. Breslau : ein Wegweiser für Fremde und Einheimische. *Map.* 12° *Breslau,* 1808

Renefort, Souchu de. Relation du premier Voyage de la Compagnie des Indes Orientales en l'Isle de Madagascar ou Dauphine. 16° *Paris,* 1668

—— *See* Allgemeine Historie, Vol. 8 : Appendix 1.

Rengger, J. R. Reise nach Paraguay in den Jahren 1818 bis 1826. Aus des Verfassers handschriftlichem Nachlasse, herausgegeben von A. Rengger. *Map and plates.* 8° *Aarau,* 1835

—— and — **Longchamps.** The Reign of Dr Joseph G. R. de Francia in Paraguay, being an Account of a Six Years' Residence in that Republic, from July 1819 to May 1825. 8° 1827

Reniger, R. *See* Hakluyt, Vol. 4 : Appendix 1.

Rennell, Major James. Roads in Bengal and Bahar. *Map.* 12° 1778

—— Memoir of a Map of Hindoostan, or the Mogul's Empire; with an Examination of some Positions in the former System of Indian Geography, and some Illustrations of the present one; with a complete Index of Names to the Map. 2nd edition. *Maps.* 4° 1785

—— The same; with an Introduction illustrative of the Geography and Present Division of that Country. . . 1st ed. 1788

—— The same. 3rd edition. 1793

—— Memoir of a Map of the Peninsula of India . . . ; with . . . an Account of the Site and Remains of the Ancient City of Beejanaggur. 4° 1793

—— Illustrations (chiefly Geographical) of the history of the expedition of Cyrus from Sardis to Babylonia, and the retreat of the ten thousand Greeks from thence to Trebisonde and Lydia; with an Appendix containing an inquiry into the best method of improving the Geography of the Anabasis, &c., explained by three maps. *Map.* 4° 1816

—— The Geographical System of Herodotus Examined and Explained, by a comparison with those of other Ancient Authors and with Modern Geography. . . . 2 vols. *Portrait and maps.* 8° 1830

Rennell, Major James. Treatise on the Comparative Geography of Western Asia. 2 vols. 8°, and Atlas large folio 1831

—— An investigation of the Currents of the Atlantic Ocean, and of those which prevail between the Indian Ocean and the Atlantic. *Map and charts.* 8° 1832

—— *See* Hornemann, F. ; Park, Mungo ; Yule, H. ; *also* Phillips, New Voyages and Travels [3], Vol. 9 : Appendix 1.

Renneville, R. A. C. de. Recueil des Voyages qui ont servi à l'Establissement et aux Progrez de la Compagnie des Indes Orientales, &c. 10 vols. *Plates.* 12° *Rouen,* 1725

[For Contents, *see* Appendix 1.]

Rennie, Dr D. F. Peking and the Pekingese during the first year of the British Embassy at Peking. 2 vols. *Plates.* Small 8° 1865

—— Bhotan and the Story of the Dooar War, including Sketches of Three Months' Residence in the Himalayas, and Narrative of a Visit to Bhotan in May 1865. *Map and plates.* 8° 1866

Rennie, George. On the Quantity of Heat developed by Water when rapidly agitated ; with a Continuation of Experiments to determine the Resistances of Screwpropellers when revolving in Water at different Depths and Velocities. *Plate.* 8* 1857

Rennie, G. B. Suggestions for the Improvement of the River Danube, between Isatcha and the Sulina entrance. *Plans.* 8* 1856

Rennie, Sir John. An Account of the Drainage of the Level of Ancholme, Lincolnshire. *Map.* 8* 1845

—— An Historical, Practical, and Theoretical Account of the Breakwater in Plymouth Sound. *Portrait and plates.* Large folio 1848

Repetti, Emanuele. Dizionario Geografico, Fisico, Storico della Toscana ; contenente la Descrizione di tutti i Luoghi del Granducato, Ducato di Lucca, Garfagnana e Lunigiana ; con Supplemento. 6 vols. [Vols. 2 and 3 imperfect.] *Maps and tables.* 8° *Florence,* 1833-45

Reresby, Sir John. The Travels and Memoirs of Sir John Reresby ; the former (now first published) exhibiting a View of the Governments and Society in the principal States of Europe during the time of Cromwell's usurpation ; containing a multiplicity of facts not generally known, with Anecdotes and Secret History of the Courts of Charles II. and James II. 3rd edition. 8° 1831

"**Research.**" Auriferous Drifts in Australasia, or the Cause and its Continuity of the great Geological Convulsions, and the Theory of the Origin and Position of Auriferous Drifts. By "Research." 8* *Melbourne,* 1868

Restrepo, V. Estudio sobre las Minas de Oro y Plata de Colombia. 2nd edition. 8° *Bogota*, 1888
—— Le Miniere d'Oro e d'Argento dello Republica di Colombia. 8*
Rome, 1890
Rethore, J. J. *See* Pena and Roustan.
Retzius, G. Finska Kranier jämte några Natur- och Literatur-Studier inom andra områden af Finsk Antropologi. *Plates.* Folio *Stockholm*, 1878
Reuilly, J. Voyage en Crimée et sur les bords de la Mer Noire, pendant l'année 1803 ; suivi d'un Mémoire sur le Commerce de cette Mer, &c. *Maps and plates.* 8° *Paris*, 1806
—— *See* Phillips, Collection of Modern and Contemporary Voyages and Travels [1], Vol. 5 : Appendix 1.
Reunert, Theodore. Diamonds and Gold in South Africa.' *Maps and illustrations.* 8° 1893
Reusch, Dr Hans. Kortfattet Geografi. *Maps and illustrations.* 8*
Christiania, 1886
—— Bömmelöen og Karmöen med omgivelser. [An English Summary of the Contents.] Udgivet af den geologiske undersögelse. *Maps and illustrations.* 4° *Christiania*, 1888
Reuss, A. E. *See* "Novara."
Reuter, E. De l'Industrie Agricole dans la Province de Luxembourg, et renseignements divers sur le Grand-Duché de Luxembourg. 8° *Luxembourg*, 1875
—— Projet de Création d'une Colonie Agricole Belge dans l'Afrique Centrale, ou Manuel du Colon Belge. 12*
Brussels, 1877
—— Colonies Nationales dans l'Afrique Centrale sous la Protection de Postes Militaires. 8* *Brussels*, 1878
Revett, Nicholas. *See* Stuart, J.
Révoil, Georges. Voyages au Cap des Aromates (Afrique Orientale). *Map and plates.* Small 8° *Paris*, 1880
—— Faune et Flore des Pays Somalis (Afrique Orientale). *Plate.* 8°
Paris, 1882
—— La Vallée du Darror : Voyage aux Pays Somalis (Afrique Orientale). *Maps and illustrations.* Large 8° *Paris*, 1882
Révy, J. J. Hydraulics of Great Rivers : The Paraná, the Uruguay, and the La Plata Estuary. *Chart and plates.* Large 4° 1874
Rey, —. Le Guide des Étrangers à Vienne (Isère). [Bound with Histoire des Antiquités de Nismes.] *Plate.* 8°
Lyons, 1819
Rey, Capt. *See* Phillips, New Voyages and Travels [3], Vol. 4 : Appendix 1.
Rey, Dr H. Le Tonkin. 8° *Paris*, 1888
Rey, W. Les Grisons et la Haute Engadine. 8° *Geneva*, 1850

Reyer, Dr E. Allgemeine Geschichte des Zinnes. 8* *Vienna*, 1880
—— Zinn : eine geologisch-montanistisch historische Monografie. 8* *Berlin*, 1881
—— Bewegungen in losen Massen. Large 8* [*Vienna*] 1881
—— Studien über das Karst-Relief. *Map.* 8* *Vienna*, 1881
—— Geologie des Zinnes. 8* *Vienna*, 1881
—— Aus Toskana : geologisch-technische und kultur-historische Studien. *Plates.* 8° *Vienna*, 1884
—— Kupfer in den Vereinigten Staaten. 4* *Vienna*, 1886
—— Die Eisenindustrie der Vereinigten Staaten. 4* 1887
—— Theoretische Geologie. *Maps and illustrations.* 8° *Stuttgart*, 1888
—— Zwei Profile durch die Sierra Nevada. *Profiles.* 8* N.D.
—— Geologische und geographische Experimente. 2. Heft.—Vulkanische und Massen-Eruptionen. *Plates.* 8*
Leipzig, 1892
—— Ursachen der Deformationen und der Gebirgsbildung. *Plates.* 8* *Leipzig*, 1892
—— Colonisation tropischer Länder ; Ueberwindung der Sanitären Hindernisse. 8* *Vienna*, N.D.
Reyes, Rafael. Apuntamientos Estadisticos sobre la República del Salvador. 8* *San Salvador*, 1888
Reynolds, J. N. Voyage of the U.S. Frigate "Potomac," under the command of Comm. John Downes, during the Circumnavigation of the Globe, 1831-34 ; including a Particular Account of the Engagement at Quallah-Battoo, on the Coast of Sumatra, with all the Official Documents relating to the same. *Plates.* 8° *New York*, 1835
—— Address on the Subject of a Surveying and Exploring Expedition to the Pacific Ocean and South Seas ; with Correspondence and Documents. 8° *New York*, 1836
Reynolds, T. C. *See* Peralta.
Reynolds, W. H. *See* Cayley, H.
Rhedi, Signor. *See* Lucca, G. di.
Rhodes, A. Jerusalem as it is. *Plates.* Small 8° 1865
Rhodes, Alessandro de. Relazione de' felici successi della Santa Fede Predicata da' Padri della Comp. di Giesu nel Regno di Tunchino. 8° *Milan*, 1651
—— Voyages et Missions du Pere A. de Rhodes, S.J., en la Chine et autres Royaumes de l'Orient, avec son retour en Europe par la Perse et l'Arménie. Nouvelle édition, conforme à la première de 1653 ; Annotée par le Pere H. Gourdin, de la même Compagnie, et ornée d'une carte de tous les Voyages de l'auteur. 8° 1884
—— *See* Allgemeine Historie, Vol. 10 : Appendix 1.

Rhodes, Major Godfrey. Tents and Tent-Life, from the Earliest Ages to the Present Time ; to which is added the Practice of Encamping an Army in Ancient and Modern Times ; with a Supplement. *Plates.* 8° 1859

Rhodes, Thomas. Rhodes' Steamship Guide and Holidays Afloat : a Complete Handbook of Coasting Trips and Ocean Voyages. *Map and portrait.* 12° 1889-90

Rialle, Girard de. Mémoire sur l'Asie Centrale, son Histoire et ses Populations. 8* *Paris*, 1874

Ribáry, F. *See* Bonaparte, Prince L. L.

Ribault, Capt. J. *See* Hakluyt Soc. Publ., Vol. 7 ; Hakluyt's Voyages, Vol. 3 ; Gottfried ; Ternaux-Compans, Vol. 20 : Appendix 1.

Ribeiro, C. Estudos Prehistoricos em Portugal : Noticia de Algumas Estações e Monumentos Prehistoricos. *Map and plates.* 4° *Lisbon*, 1878-80
—— Des Formations Tertiaires du Portugal. 8* *Paris*, 1880

Ribeiro. *See* Ribeyro.

Ribeiro, J. S. Historia dos Estabelecimentos Scientificos, Litterarios e Artisticos de Portugal, nos successivos Reinados da Monarchia, Vols. 1-18. 8° *Lisbon*, 1871-93

Ribeiro, M. F. Relatorio ácerca do Serviço de Saude Publica na Provincia de S. Thomé e Principe no anno de 1869. 8° *Lisbon*, 1871
—— A Provincia de S. Thomé e Principe suas Dependencias. *Plates.* 8° *Lisbon*, 1877
—— As Conferencias e o Itinerario do Viajante Serpa Pinto atravez das terras da Africa Austral nos Limites das Provincias de Angola e Moçambique Biè a Shoshong ; Junho a Dezembro de 1878. Estudo Critico e Documentado. *Maps.* 8° *Lisbon*, 1879
—— A Colonisação Luso - Africana zona Occidental. *Diagrams.* 8° *Lisbon*, 1884

Ribeyro, Capt. Joãs. Histoire de l'Isle de Ceylan. Traduite du Portugais, par Monsr. l'Abbé Le Grand. *Maps and plates.* 12° *Amsterdam*, 1701
—— *See* Colecção de Noticias, Vol. 5 : Appendix 1.

Riccardi, G. Ricerche Istoriche e Fisiche sulla Caduta delle Marmore. *Maps.* 8° *Rome*, 1825

Ricci, J. H. de. Fiji : Our New Province in the South Seas. *Maps.* Small 8° 1875
—— British Trade and English Ports. *Maps.* 8* 1889

Ricci, R. H. de. Rambles in Istria, Dalmatia, and Montenegro. 8° 1875

Ricciolio, Giovanni Battista. Geographiæ et Hydrographiæ Reformatæ, nuper recognitæ, et auctæ, libri duodecim. Folio *Venice*, 1672

Riccius, Matthieu. Histoire de l'Expedition Chrétienne au Royaume de la Chine entreprinse par les PP. de la Compagnie de Jesus . . . Tirée des Commentaires du P. Matthieu Riccius par le P. Nicolas Trigault . . . Traduicte par le Sr. D. F. de Riquébourg-Trigault. 12° *Lyons*, 1616

Rice, Lewis. Mysore and Coorg. A Gazetteer compiled for the Government of India. Vols. 1-3. *Maps.* 8° *Bangalore*, 1876-78

Rice, W. Notes on the Geography of Europe, Physical and Political, intended to Serve as a Text-Book for the use of Elementary Classes, and as a Hand-Book to the Wall-Map. 12* 1877

Rich, C. J. Memoir on the Ruins of Babylon. 3rd edition. *Plates.* 8° 1818
—— Narrative of a Residence in Koordistan, and on the Sites of Ancient Nineveh ; with Journal of a Voyage down the Tigris to Bagdad, and an account of a Visit to Shiraz and Persepolis. 2 vols. *Maps and plates.* 8° 1836

Richard, —. Guide du Voyageur en Italie. 8° *Paris*, 1833

Richard, Achille. Tentamen Floræ Abyssinicæ, &c. 2 vols. [1845]. *See* Abyssinia, Voyage en Abyssinie, &c., Part 3 : Appendix 2.

Richard, L. Ilmu Sarfu dan Nahu deri Bhāsa Jāwi, Atau Malayū. Cours Théorique et Pratique de la Langue Commerciale de l'Archipel d'Asie dite Malaise, &c. 8° *Bordeaux*, 1872
—— Kitāb Pada Meniatā - Kan Bhāsa Jāwi, Atau Malayū. Dictionnaire de la Langue Commerciale de l'Archipel d'Asie [dite Malaise], telle qu'elle se parle à Sumatra, Singapour, Borneo, les Célébes, les côtes de Chine, du Cambodge [Säigon], de Siam, de Java, &c. 8° *Bordeaux*, 1873

Richard the First. *See* Hakluyt, Vol. 2 : Appendix 1.

Richarderie, G. B. de la. *See* De la Richarderie.

Richards, Admiral Sir G. H. Vancouver Island Pilot : Sailing Directions for the Coasts of Vancouver Island and British Columbia, from the entrance of Juan de Fuca Strait to Burrard Inlet and Naniamo Harbour. 8°. 1861
—— A Memoir of the Hydrographical Department of the Admiralty. Folio* 1868
—— The Arctic Expedition of 1875-76 : a Reply to its Critics. 8* 1877
—— Memorandum to the Royal Society [on the subject of Antarctic Expedition]. [1 *sheet.*] 4* 1887

Richards, Admiral Sir G. H. Report on the Present State of the Navigation of the River Mersey (1888). *Plan and chart.* 8*   1889
—— The same (1889). *Maps.* 8*   1890
—— The same (1890). *Map and appendix.* Large 8*   1891
—— The same (1891). *Map and appendix.* 8*   1892
—— The same (1892). *Map and appendix.* 8*   1893
—— The same (1893), with Appendix. 8*   1893
—— *See* United Kingdom, A, Hydrogr. Off. Publ. : Appendix 2.
—— **and General Sir Andrew Clarke.** Report on the Maritime Canal connecting the Mediterranean at Port Said with the Red Sea at Suez. *Maps and plans.* Folio*   1870
—— **and F. J. Evans.** New Zealand Pilot. 8°   1859
Richards, John. China : Harbours of Kok-si-Kon and Takau-Kon, at the South-West End of Taï-Wan or Formoza. 8*   1855
—— China Pilot. Appendix 13, 14, 16, 17, 18. Gulf of Siam, La Pérouse Strait, Gulf of Tartary, Kuril Islands, and Sea of Okhotsk, Yang-tse-Kiang, East Coast. 8°   1856-57
—— China Pilot. Appendix No. 1. Gulf of Siam. (From the Surveys made in H.M.S. "Saracen," between the years 1856-58.) 8°   1858
—— The Jersey Island Pilot, comprising the Coast of Jersey and Outlying Reefs ; with Directions for the Violet and other Channels and Passages into the Bays and Harbours. 8°   1866
—— Routier de l'Ile Jersey. . . . Traduit de l'Anglais par M. Jules Vavin. 8°
                                   Paris, 1866
—— *See* United Kingdom, A, Hydrogr. Off. Publ. : Appendix 2.
Richards, Thomas. New South Wales in 1881 ; being a Brief Statistical and Descriptive Account of the Colony up to the end of the year. Extracted chiefly from Official Records. 2nd issue. *Map and diagram.* 8°   *Sydney*, 1882
Richards, —. History of Tonquin. *See* Pinkerton, Vol. 9 : Appendix 1.
Richardson, Dr. *See* Macleod, W. C.
Richardson, James. Touariek Alphabet, with the Corresponding Arabic and English Letters ; Vocabularies of the Ghadamsee and Touarghee Languages, by Taleb Ben Mousa Ben El-Kasem. Folio   1847
—— Mons. Caillié's Account of Timbuctoo compared with the Information procured by Mr James Richardson during his late Tour through the Great Desert. MS. Folio*   1847

Richardson, James. Travels in the Great Desert of Sahara, in 1845-46 ; containing Adventures amongst the Touaricks and other Tribes of Saharan People, including a Description of the Oases and Cities of Ghat, Ghadames, and Mourzak. 2 vols. *Map and plates.* 8°   1848
—— Decline of Geographical Discovery, being an Appeal to the British Public on behalf of Geographical Science. 8*
                                        1849
—— Narrative of a Mission to Centra Africa, in 1850-51. 2 vols. 8°   1853
—— Travels in Morocco. Edited by his Widow. 2 vols. *Plates.* 8°   1860
—— Tour of Nine Months through the Heart of the Great Desert of Sahara. MS. Folio, pp. 20, and Second Notice, "The Touaricks," pp. 18   N.D.
—— "Aheer." MS. Folio*   N.D.
Richardson, Sir John. Report on North American Zoology. 8°   1837
—— On the Frozen Soil of North America. 8*   *Edinburgh*, 1841
—— Arctic Searching Expedition : a Journal of a Boat Voyage through Rupert's Land and the Arctic Sea in Search of the Discovery Ships under command of Sir John Franklin ; with an Appendix on the Physical Geography of North America. 2 vols. *Map and plates.* 8°   1851
—— Polar Regions. (Article from the "Encyclopædia Britannica.") *Map.* 4*
                                Edinburgh, 1859
—— The Polar Regions. *Map.* 8°
                                Edinburgh, 1861
—— *See* 'Erebus " ; Franklin ; Seemann.
Richardson, Sir James, W. Swainson, and Rev. W. Kirby. Fauna Boreali Americana ; or, The Zoology of the Northern Parts of British America, containing Descriptions of the Objects of Natural History collected on the late Northern Land Expeditions under command of Sir John Franklin. 4 vols. *Plates.* 4°   *Norwich*, 1829-37
     Part 1.—Quadrupeds, by Richardson
                                        1829
     Part 2. — Birds, by Swainson and Richardson   1831
     Part 3.—Fish, by Richardson   1836
     Part 4.—Insects, by Kirby   1837
Richardson, Rev. J. Lights and Shadows : or Chequered Experiences among some of the Heathen Tribes of Madagascar. *Map and plate.* 8*   *Antananarivo*, 1877
Richardson, J. A Smaller Manual of Modern Geography, Physical and Political. 12°   1880
—— *See* Malte-Brun, V. A.

Richardson, Ralph. The Ice Age in Britain considered in relation to the Depth of the North Atlantic Ocean as determined by recent and earlier Deep-Sea Soundings. 8* *Edinburgh*, 1876

Richardson, Robert. Travels along the Mediterranean and Parts adjacent, . . . 1816-17-18, extending as far as the Second Cataract of the Nile, Jerusalem, Damascus, Balbec, &c. 2 vols. *Plates.* 8° 1822

Richardson, William. A Catalogue of 7,385 Stars, chiefly in the Southern Hemisphere, prepared from Observations made in 1822-26 at the Observatory at Paramatta, New South Wales. *Plate.* 4° 1835

Richter, Dr E. Geschichte der Schwankungen der Alpengletscher. *Plate.* 8* *Vienna*, 1891

—— *See* Germany, C; Handbücher zur Deutschen Landes- und Volkskunde, Vol. 3 : Appendix 2.

Richter, G. Manual of Coorg : a Gazetteer of the Natural Features of the Country and the Social and Political Condition of its Inhabitants. *Map and plates.* 8° *Mangalore*, 1870

Richter, R. Das Thüringische Schiefergebirge. *Map and plate.* 8* 1869

Richthofen, Ferdinand, Freiherr von. Geognostische Beschreibung der Umgegend von Predazzo, Sanct Cassian und der Seisser Alpe in Süd Tyrol. *Map and plates.* 4° *Gotha*, 1860

—— Die Metallproduktion Californiens und der angrenzenden Länder. (Ergänzungsheft, 14 — Petermann's Mittheilungen). 4° *Gotha*, 1864

—— The Comstock Lode, its Character, and the probable mode of its continuance in depth. 8* *San Francisco*, 1866

—— Letters (and Report) : 1. On the Province of Hunan, 1870 ; 2. On the Province of Hupeh, 1870 ; 3. On the Provinces of Honan and Shansi, 1870 ; 4. On the Provinces of Chekiang and Nganhwei, 1871 ; 5. On the Regions of Nanking and Chinkiang, 1871 ; 6. From Singan-fu, on the Rebellion in Kansu and Shensi, 1872 ; 7. On the Provinces of Chili, Shansi, Shensi, Sz'chwan, with Notes on Mongolia, Kansu, Yünnan, and Kwei-chau, 1872. Folio *Shanghai*, 1870-72

—— Ueber die centralasiatischen Seidenstrassen his zum 2 Jahrhundert n. Chr. 8* *Berlin*, 1877

—— China : Ergebnisse eigener Reisen und darauf gegründeter Studien. Erster Band : Einleitender Theil. *Maps.* 4° *Berlin*, 1877

—— The same. Zweiter Band. Das nördliche China. *Maps and illustrations.* 4° *Berlin*, 1882

2 C

Richthofen, Ferdinand, Freiherr von. The same. Vierter Band : Palæontologischer Theil. Enthaltend Abhandlungen von Dr Wilhelm Dames, Dr Emanuel Kayser, Dr G. Lindström, Dr A. Schenk, und Dr Conrad Schwager. *Plates.* 4° *Berlin*, 1883

—— Aufgaben und Methoden der heutigen Geographie : Akademische Antrittsrede, gehalten in der Aula der universität Leipzig am 27 April 1883. 8* *Leipzig*, 1883

—— Führer für Forschungsreisende : Anteilung zu Beohachtungen über Gegenstände der Physischen Geographie und Geologie. 8° *Berlin*, 1886

Richthofen Testimonial. Festschrift Ferdinand Freiherrn von Richthofen zum sechzigsten Geburtstag am 5 Mai, 1893 dargebracht von seinen Schülern. *Portrait and maps.* 4° *Berlin*, 1893

Rickard, Major F. Ignacio. The Mineral and other Resources of the Argentine Republic (La Plata) in 1869. 8° 1870

Ricketts, H. Report on the Forays of the Wild Tribes of the Chittagong Frontier. [From the India Records, Bengal, No. 11.] *Map.* 8° *Calcutta*, 1853

—— Papers relating to the South-West Frontier : comprising Reports on Purulia or Maubhoom, Chota Nagpore, Sub-Division of Kornda, Hazareebaugh, Sumbhulpore, and South-West Frontier Agency. [From the India Records, Bengal, No. 20.] *Maps and plans.* 8° *Calcutta*, 1855

—— Reports on the Districts of Pooree and Balasore. [From the India Records, Bengal, No. 30.] 8° *Calcutta*, 1859

Ricour, Capt. La Carte du Maroni. *Map.* 8* *Paris*, 1892

Ricketts, L. D. *See* United States, K, Wyoming : Appendix 2.

Riddel, A. A Grammar of the Chinyanja Language as spoken at Lake Nyassa, with Chinyanja-English and English-Chinyanja Vocabularies. 16° *Edinburgh*, 1880

Riddell, R. A. *See* Wilson, Joseph.

Riddle, J. A Treatise on Navigation and Nautical Astronomy, especially adapted for the Use of Students. 9th edition. Revised by Albert Escott. 8° 1871

—— Tables to do. 9th edition. 8° 1877

Ridgway, Robert. *See* United States, H, *a* : Appendix 2.

Ridley, Henry Nicholas, and G. A. Ramage. Notes on the Botany of Fernando Noronha. (Extracted from the Linnæan Society's Journal, Vol. 27.) With a Paper on some Geographical Details of the Island, by Rev. T. S. Lea. *Maps, photographs, &c.* 8* 1890

Riebeck, Dr Emil. The Chittagong Hill Tribes; Results of a Journey made in the year 1882 by Emil Riebeck. Translated by Prof. A. H. Keane. *Map and plates.* Large folio   1885
—— *See* Krause.

Riedel, Dr J. G. F. Inilah Kitab Taman-Wandji namanja jah itu babarapa hhikajat Orang-Orang jang ampunja tjeritra. 8*
Ujong Padang, 1862
—— Inilah pintu gerbang pengatahuwan itu apatah dibukakan guna Orang-Orang padudokh tanah Minahasa ini. Small 4*   *Batavia,* 1862
—— Die Landschaft Dawan oder West-Timor. *Maps.* 8*   [*Bremen,* 1887]
—— De Eedaflegging bij de Tooe-oen-boeloe in de Minahasa, *and* De Tiwoekar of Steenen graven in de Minahasa. *Plate.* 8*   N.P., N.D.
—— De Uitbarsting van den Awoeh-Taroena in 1856. 8*   N.P., N.D.
—— Note sur l'Île Rote. 4*   N.D.

Riedesel, Baron. Travels through Sicily and that part of Italy formerly called Magna Græcia. Translated by J. R. Forster. 8°   1773

Riemann, O. Rectifications au Texte des Cartes des Îles Ioniennes. 8°
Paris, 1880

Rienzi, G, L. Domeny de. Océanie, ou Cinquième Partie du Monde: Revue Géographique et Ethnographique de la Malaisie, de la Micronésie, de la Polynesie, et de la Mélanésie. 3 vols. *Maps and plates.* 8°   *Paris,* 1836

Riesbeck, ——. *See* Pinkerton, Vol. 6: Appendix I.

Rigaud, S. P. On the Relative Quantities of Land and Water on the Surface of the Terraqueous Globe. 4*
Cambridge, 1837

Rigby, Lieut.-Col. C. P. Report on the Zanzibar Dominions. [From the India Records, No. 59.] Roy. 8° *Bombay,* 1861

Riggenbach, Dr A. Was man aus den täglichen Wetterkarten der Schweizer. Meteorologischen Centralanstalt ersieht. *Maps.* 12°   *Bâle,* 1882

Riley, Athelstan. Narrative of a Visit to the Assyrian Christians in Kurdistan, undertaken at the request of the Archbishop of Canterbury, in the autumn of 1884. 8*   N.D.
—— Athos, or the Mountain of the Monks. *Map and illustrations.* 8° 1887

Riley, Gen. B. *See* Smith, Gen. P. F.

Riley. H. T. *See* Pliny.

Riley, James. Loss of the American brig "Commerce," wrecked on the Western Coast of Africa in August 1815; with an Account of Tombuctoo, and of the hitherto undiscovered Great City of Wassanah. *Map.* 4°   1817

Ringgold, Cadwalader. A Series of Charts, with Sailing Directions, embracing Surveys of the Farallones, Entrance to the Bay of San Francisco, Bays of San Francisco and San Pablo, &c., and Sacramento River. 4° *Washington,* 1851

Rink, Dr Hendrik. Om den Geographiske Beskaffenhed af de danske Handelsdistrikter i Nordgrönland tilligemed en Udsigt over Nordgrönlands Geognosi. *Map.* 4*   *Copenhagen,* 1852
—— De danske Handelsdistrikter i Nordgrönland, deres Geographiske Beskassenhed og produktive Erhvervskilder. *Map.* 8°   *Copenhagen,* 1852-55
—— Grönland Geographisk og Statistisk beskrevet. Söndre Inspecktorat. *Maps and plates.* 8°   *Copenhagen,* 1857
—— Om den formeentlige Opdagelse af Grönlands Nordkyst og et aabent Polarhav, om den saakaldte Humboldts-Gletscher og andet, Grönlands Iisdannelser vedkommende, som findes beskrevet i Reise-værket: "Arctic Explorations, 1853-55, by E. K. Kane." 8* N.D.
—— On the Supposed Discovery by Dr E. K. Kane, U.S.N., of the North Coast of Greenland, and of an Open Polar Sea, as described in "Arctic Explorations in the years 1853, 1854, 1855." Condensed from the Danish by Dr Shaw. *Map.* 8*   1858
—— Om Eskimoernes Herkomst. 8*
Copenhagen, 1871
—— Tales and Traditions of the Eskimo; with a Sketch of their Habits, Religion, Language, and other Peculiarities. Translated from the Danish by the Author; edited by Dr Robert Brown. *Illustrations.* 8°   1875
—— Danish Greenland, its People and its Products. Edited by Robert Brown. *Map and plates.* Small 8°   1877
—— The Eskimo Tribes, their Distribution and Characteristics, especially in regard to Language; with a Comparative Vocabulary. *Map.* 8°   1887

Rio, J. M. del. Cuadro Sinóptico Cronologico de las Naciones Antiquas. [1 sheet.] 4*   [*Lima,* 1885]

Rios, Joseph de Mendoza. Complete Collection of Tables for Navigation and Nautical Astronomy. [Imperfect.] 4°   1805
[*This copy belonged to Mungo Park, and was recovered at the Town of Lome, in Nuphi, Central Africa, and conveyed thither from the Town of Boussa, when that place was destroyed, about 1842. It was presented to Lieut. J. H. Glover, attached to the Niger Expedition under Dr Baikie, Jan. 21, 1858; with three slips of Paper in MS. by Mungo Park.*]

Riou, Capt. E. *See* Reenen, J. Van.

Ripa, Father. Memoirs of, during Thirteen Years' Residence at the Court of Peking in the Service of the Emperor of China. Translated from the Italian, by F. Prandi. 12° 1844

Riquebourg-Trigault, D. F. de. *See* Riccius.

Risley, H. H. The Tribes and Castes of Bengal : Anthropometric data. 2 vols. Large 8° *Calcutta*, 1891

Riso, J. de. Le ultime Scoperte di Sir Samuele Baker e del Rev. Dottore David Livingston sulle sorgenti del Nilo. 8* *Florence*, 1873

—— La Ferrovia dell' Eufrate. 8* *Florence*, 1873

Ritchie, Archibald Tucker. The Dynamical Theory of the Formation of the Earth. 2 vols. 8° 1850

Ritchie, J. Ewing. To Canada with Emigrants : a Record of Actual Experiences. *Illustrations.* Crown 8° 1885

Ritter, Carl. Die Erdkunde im Verhältniss zur Natur und zur Geschichte des Menschen : oder Allgemeine vergleichende Geographie, als sichere Grundlage des Studiums und Unterrichts in physikalischen und historischen Wissenschaften. Parts 1 and 2. 8° *Berlin*, 1817-18

—— The same. 2nd edition. 21 vols. 8° *Berlin*, 1822-58

Contents.

I. Thl. 1 Buch. Afrika 1822
II. Thl. 2 Buch. Die Erdkunde von Asien. Bd. I. Der Norden und Nord-Osten von Hoch-Asien 1832
III. Thl. 2 Buch. Ditto. Bd. II. Der Nord-Osten und der Süden von Hoch-Asien 1833
IV. Thl. 2 Buch. Ditto. Bd. III. Der Süd-Osten von Hoch-Asien ; dessen Wassersysteme und Gliederungen gegen Osten und Süden 1834
V. Thl. 2 Buch. Ditto. Bd. IV. 1 Abtheil. Die Indische Welt 1835
VI. Thl. 2 Buch. Ditto. Bd. IV. 2 Abtheil. Die Indische Welt 1836
VII. Thl. 3 Buch. Ditto. Bd. V. West-Asien, Uebergang von Ost- nach West-Asien 1837
VIII. Thl. 3 Buch. Ditto. Bd. VI. 1 Abtheil. West-Asien, Iranische Welt 1838
IX. Thl. 3 Buch. Ditto. Bd. VI. 2 Abtheil. West Asien 1840
X. Thl. 3 Buch. Ditto. Bd. VII. 1 Abtheil. Das Stufenland des Euphrat- und Tigrissystems
XI. Thl. 3 Buch. Ditto. Bd. VII. 2 Abtheil. Euphrat- und Tigrissystems 1844
XII. Thl. 3 Buch. Ditto. Bd. VIII. 1 Abtheil. Die Halbinsel Arabien 1846
XIII. Thl. 3 Buch. Ditto. Bd. VIII. 1 Abtheil. Forsetzung 1847

Ritter, Carl—*continued.*
XIV. Thl. 3 Buch. Ditto. Bd. VIII. 2 Abtheil. Die Sinai-Halbinsel, Palästina, und Syrien. 1 Abschnitt. Die Sinai-Halbinsel 1848
XV. Thl. 3 Buch. The same. 2 Abschnitt. 1 Abth. Palästina und Syrien 1850
XVI. Thl. 3 Buch. The same. 2 Absch. 2 Abth. Fortsetzung, Palästina, und Syrien. *Map and plan* 1852
XVII. Thl. 3 Buch. The same. 3 Abschnitt. Syrien 1854
XVIII. Thl. 3 Buch. Ditto. Bd. IX. Klein-Asien. Theil I. *Plates* 1858
XIX. Thl. 3 Buch. Ditto. Bd. IX. Klein-Asien. Theil. II. 1859

Ideler, J. L. Namen- und Sach-Verzeichniss zu Carl Ritter's Erdkunde von Asien. I. Bd. Ost-Asien. (Zu Band II. bis VI. des ganzen Werkes.) 8° *Berlin*, 1841

Müller, G. F. H. The same. II. Bd. West Asien. (Zu Band VII. bis XI. des ganzen Werkes.) 8° *Berlin*, 1849

—— Ueber das historische Element in der geographischen Wissenschaft. 4* *Berlin*, 1834

—— Géographie Générale Comparée ; ou, Étude de la Terre dans ses Rapports avec la Nature et avec l'Histoire de l'Homme. Afrique. Traduit par Buret et Desor. 3 vols. 8° *Paris*, 1836

—— Die Stupas (Topes) oder die architectonischen Denkmäler an der Indo-Baktrischen Königsstrasse, und die Colosse von Bamiyan. *Map.* 8° *Berlin*, 1838

—— Ueber die geographische Verbreitung des Zuckerrohrs. *Map.* 4° *Berlin*, 1840

—— The Colonisation of New Zealand. Translated from the German. Small 8* 1842

—— Ueber die Asiatische Heimat und die Asiatische Verbreitungsphäre der Platane, des Olivenbaums, des Feigenbaums, der Granate, Pistacie, und Cypresse. 8° [*Berlin*, 1844]

—— Blick in das Nil Quell-land. *Map.* 8* *Berlin*, 1844

—— Der Jordan und die Beschiffung des Todten Meeres. *Map.* 8* *Berlin*, 1850

—— Ueber räumliche Anordnungen auf der Aussenseite des Erdballs, und ihre Functionen im Entwicklungsgange der Geschichten. 8* *Berlin*, 1850

—— Einleitung zur allgemeinen vergleichenden Geographie, und Abhandlungen zur Begründung einer mehr wissenschaftlichen Behandlung der Erdkunde. 8° *Berlin*, 1852

Ritter, Carl. Ueber die geographische Verbreitung der Baumwolle, und ihr Verhältniss zur Industrie der Völker alter und neuer Zeit. Part 1. Antiquarischer Theil. 4* *Berlin*, 1852
—— Geschichte der Erdkunde, und der Entdeckungen : Vorlesungen an der Universität zu Berlin gehalten. Herausgegeben von H. A. Daniel. *Portrait*. 8° *Berlin*, 1861
—— Allgemeine Erdkunde : Vorlesungen an der Universität zu Berlin gehalten. Herausgegeben von H. A. Daniel. 8° *Berlin*, 1862
—— Geography of Asia. Translated into Russian from the German of Carl Ritter by V. V. Grigor'ev. [In Russian.] *Map and plate*. 8° [*St Petersburg*, 1869]
—— Geographisch-Statistisches Lexikon. 2 vols. Large 8° *Leipzig*, 1864-65
—— The same. Other editions 1874, 1883, 1894
—— Die Stupas oder die architektonischen Denkmale an der grossen Königsstrasse zwischen Indien, Persien, und Baktrien. 8* *Berlin*, N.D.
—— Die Heuschreckenplage der Länder der alten Welt. 8* N.P., N.D.
—— Der Indische Feigenbaum, Asvattha ; die Banjane (Ficus Indica). Ihre Verbreitung um die Indischen Gestade von dem Sunda-Archipel bis Afrika ; der Pagodenbaum . . . der Buddhabaum (Ficus religiosa), &c. 8* *Berlin*, N.D.
—— Der Elephant Indiens, nach seiner Verbreitungssphäre und seinen Einfluss auf das Leben des Orients. 8* [*Berlin*, N.D.]
—— Löwen- und Tiger-Land in Asien ; der Bengalische Tiger (Felis Tigris) in Indien und seine Verbreitungssphäre durch Ostasien ; der Guzuratisch Löwe (Felis Leo Goojeratensis) in Indien und seine Verbreitungssphäre durch Westasien. 8° *Berlin*, N.D.
—— Die Opium Cultur und die Mohnpflanze. 8* [*Berlin*, N.D.]
—— Ueber Ausbreitung der Seidenzucht in Asien. 8* N.P., N.D.
—— Carl Ritter, ein Lebensbild nach seinem handschriftlichen Nachlass, dargestellt von D. G. Kramer. Zweite durchgesehene und mit einigen Reisebriefen vermehrte Ausgabe. Erster Theil. Nebst einen Bildniss Ritters. Zweiter Theil. Die Reisebriefe enthaltend. 8° *Halle*, 1875
—— *See* Jomard ; Werne ; Wrangell ; Zimmerman, Carl.

Rittich, A. F. Die Ethnographie Russlands. (Ergänzungsheft, 54 — Petermann's Mittheilungen.) *Maps*. 4° *Gotha*, 1878

Rivera, Carlo A. de. Tavole di Riduzione dei Pesi e delle Misure delle due Sicilie in 1840. 8° *Naples*, 1841

Rivero, F. de. Memoria o sean Apuntamientos sobre la Industria Agricola del Peru, y sobre algunos medios que pudieran adoptarse para remediar su decadencia. 4* *Lima*, 1845

Rivett-Carnac. *See* India, G, Cotton Reports : Appendix 2.

Rivière, É. Voyage dans l'Asie Centrale. Collections d' histoire naturelle et d' ethnographie. 4* N.D.

Rivoli, J. Die Serra da Estrella. (Ergänzungsheft, 61 — Petermann's Mittheilungen.) *Map*. 4° *Gotha*, 1880

Rivoyre, Denis de. Obock, Mascate, Bouchire, Bassorah. *Maps and illustrations*. 12° *Paris*, 1883
—— Les Français à Obock. *Map and illustrations*. 8° *Paris*, N.D.

Riza, Qouly Khan. Relation de l'Ambassade au Kharaezm. Traduite et annotée par Charles Schefer. [No. IV. Publ. de l'Éc. des Langues Orient. Viv.] *Map*. Large 8° *Paris*, 1879

Robb, Dr J. Old Calabar : Inland Tribes and Regions. *Map*. 8* 1872
—— Notes on the Meteorology of Zanzibar, East Africa. 8* 1880

Robecchi - Bricchetti, Captain Luigi. All' oasi di Giove Ammone. *Portrait, map, and illustrations*. 4° *Milan*, 1890
—— Itinerario del viaggio da Obbia ad Alula. *Maps*. 4* [*Rome*, 1891]
—— Tradizione Storiche dei Somali Miguirtini Raccolta in Obbia. 4* *Rome*, 1891

Robelo, Cecilio A. Nombres Geograficos Mexicanos del Estado de Morelos. 8* *Cuernavaca*, 1887
—— Vocabulario Comparativo Castellano y Nahuatl. 2nd edition. 8* *Cuernavaca*, 1889

Robert, Eugéne. *See* Gaimard, Paul.

Robert, Fritz. Senegambien. 4* *St Gallen*, N.D.
—— Afrika als Handelsgebiet : West-, Süd-, und Ost-Afrika. 8° *Vienna*, 1883

Robert of Normandy. *See* Hakluyt, Vol. 2 ; Purchas, Vol. 2, Book 8 : Appendix 1.

Robert of St Remigius. *See* Purchas, Vol. 2, Book 8 : Appendix 1.

Robert, Lieut.-Col. Henry M. *See* United States, H, a, Analytical and Topical Index to the Reports of the Chief of Engineers, &c. : Appendix 2.

Roberts, A. A. Memorandum regarding the Bridge of Boats at Delhi. [From the India Records, N.W. Provinces, Vol. 1.] *Plates*. 8° *Agra*, 1855

Roberts, C. The South-African Traveller's Handbook, containing Zulu Kafir, Xosa Kafir, and Dutch . . . for the use of the Army, &c. 12° 1879

Roberts, C. G. D. The Canadian Guide-Book. The Tourists' and Sportsman's Guide to Eastern Canada and Newfound-

Roberts, C. G. D.—*continued.*
land, including full descriptions of routes, cities, points of interest, summer resorts, fishing places, &c., in Eastern Ontario, . . . the Lake St John country, the Maritime Provinces, Prince Edward Island, and Newfoundland. *Maps, plans, and illustrations.* 12°   1892

Roberts, E. *See* Baird, A. W. ; Rogers, M. W.

Roberts, Emma. Scenes and Characteristics of Hindostan, with Sketches of Anglo-Indian Society. 2 vols. 8° 1837

Roberts, Capt. G. *See* Astley, Vol. 1 ; Allgemeine Historie, Vol. 2 ; Knox's New Collection, Vol. 2 ; "The World Displayed," Vol. 10 : Appendix 1.

Roberts, Dr G. De Dehli à Bombay : fragment d'un Voyage dans les Provinces Intérieures de l'Inde en 1841. 8*
Paris, 1843

Roberts, George. Social History of the People of the Southern Counties of England in past centuries. 8°   1856

Roberts, H. *See* Hakluyt, Vol. 2 ; Kerr, Vol. 7 : Appendix 1.

Roberts, Rev. J. *See* Asia, General, Oriental Languages : Appendix 2.

Roberts, Morley. The Western Avernus, or Toil and Travel in Further North America. *Map.* 8°   1887

Roberts, N. *See* Hacke ; Purchas, Vol. 2, Book 9 : Appendix 1.

Roberts, Orlando W. Narrative of Voyages and Excursions on the East Coast and in the Interior of Central America ; describing a Journey up the River San Juan, and Passage across the Lake of Nicaragua to the City of Leon ; pointing out the Advantages of a direct Commercial Intercourse with the Natives ; with Notes and Observations by Edward Irving. *Map.* 12°   *Edinburgh*, 1827

Roberts, Dr R. D. The Earth's History : an Introduction to Modern Geology. *Maps and illustrations.* 8°   1893

Roberts, W. Milnor. Note on the São Francisco River, Brazil. Small 8* 1880

Robertson, Sir Daniel Brooke. Report respecting his Visit to Haiphong and Hansi in Tonquin. [Parly. Rep.] Folio*
1876

Robertson, George. On the Mud Banks of Narrakal and Allippey, two Natural Harbours of Refuge on the Malabar. Coast. 8*   *Edinburgh*, 1873

Robertson. David. *See* Armstrong, James.

Robertson, Lieut. H. D. Historical Narrative of the City of Cambay, from Sanskrit and Persian Books and Oral Tradition, comprising a brief Sketch of the Province of Guzerat at various periods. [From the India Records, No. 26.] *Table.* Royal 8°   *Bombay*, 1856

Robertson, J. *See* Mackay, A.

Robertson, J. A. *See* Johnston, T. B.

Robertson, J. P. A Political Manual of the Province of Manitoba and the North-West Territories. *Map and illustrations.* 8°   *Winnipeg*, 1887

Robertson, J. P. and W. P. Letters on Paraguay : comprising an Account of a Four Years' Residence in that Republic under the Government of the Dictator Francia. 3 vols. [Title of 3rd volume : " Francia's Reign of Terror," being the continuation of "Letters on Paraguay"]. *Plates.* 8°   1839

—— Letters on South America : comprising Travels on the Banks of the Paraná and Rio de la Plata. 3 vols. 8°   1843

Robertson, Dr Milne. Report upon certain Peculiar Habits and Customs of the Aborigines of Western Australia. 12*   *Perth, W.A.*, 1879

Robertson, R. B. *See* Adams, F. O.

Robertson, —. Copy of Mr Robertson's Report of his Tour in Coimbatore. [Parly. Rep.] Folio   1878

Robertson, W. History of Ancient Greece, till it became a Roman Province. *Map.* 8°   *Edinburgh*, 1793

Robertson, W. Parish. Visit to Mexico, by the West India Islands, Yucatan, and United States, with Observations and Adventures on the Way. 2 vols. *Map and plates.* 8°   1853

Robertson, —. Tour in the Isle of Man. *See* Pinkerton, Vol. 2 : Appendix 1.

Robida, A. La Vieille France : Texte, Dessins, et Lithographes. 4° *Paris* [1893]

Robidé van der Aa, P. J. B. C. Reizen naar Nederlandsch Nieuw-Guinea, ondernomen op Last der Regeering van Nederlandsch-Indie in de Jaren 1871, 1872, 1875-76, door de Heeren P. Van der Crab en J. E. Teysmann, J. G. Coorengel, en A. J. Langeveldt van Hemert en P. Swaan, met geschied en aardrijkskundige Toelichtingen. *Maps.* 8°
The Hague, 1879

—— *See* Bock ; Morris.

Robin, C. C. Voyages dans l'Intérieur de la Louisiane, de la Floride Occidentale, et dans les Isles de la Martinique et de Saint-Dominique, pendant les années 1802-6 . . . suivie de la Flore Louisianaise. 3 vols. *Map and plate.* Small 8°   *Paris*, 1807

Robinson, Capt. Queensland. Extracts from the Correspondence respecting the Proposed Station near Cape York ; with additional Correspondence by Capt. Robinson. 4*   *Brisbane*, 1863

Robinson, C. New South Wales, the Oldest and Richest of the Australian Colonies. *Maps.* 8°   *Sydney*, 1873

—— The Progress and Resources of New South Wales. 8*   *Sydney*, 1877

Robinson, Dr Edward. Biblical Researches in Palestine, Mount Sinai, and Arabia Petræa, 1838. 3 vols. *Maps.* 8° 1841

—— Topography of Jerusalem. From the Bibliotheca Sacra. 8° *New York,* 1846

—— Biblical Researches in Palestine and adjacent Regions: a Journal of Travels, in 1838 and 1852, by E. Robinson, Eli Smith, and others. 3 vols. *Maps.* 8° 1856

Robinson, Frederick. Refutation of Lieut. Wellsted's Attack upon Lord Valentia's Work upon the Red Sea, with Comparative Diagrams showing the Inventions of Bruce. *Maps.* 4* 1842

Robinson, George. Travels in Palestine and Syria. 2 vols. *Maps.* 8° 1837

Robinson, Commr. G. T., and C. and F. Chambers. Magnetical and Meteorological Observations made at the Government Observatory, Bombay, in the years 1865 to 1870. 4° *Bombay,* 1872

Robinson, Sir Hercules. Despatch with Report of the Resident Commissioner of Basutoland, for the year ending 30th June 1887, and Secretary of State's reply thereto. Folio* 1887

Robinson, H. J. Colonial Chronology: a Chronology of the Principal Events connected with the English Colonies and India, from the Close of the Fifteenth Century to the Present Time. *Maps.* 4° 1892

Robinson, Sir John. Notes on Natal: an Old Colonist's Book for New Settlers. 12° 1872

Robinson, John. Check List of the Ferns of North America, North of Mexico. 8° *Salem,* 1873

Robinson, J. H. Journal of an Expedition 1,400 miles up the Orinoco and 300 up the Arauca. *Plates.* 8° 1822

—— *See* Eyriès, Vol. 9 : Appendix 1.

Robinson, P. Cyprus, its Physical, Commercial, Economical, Historical, and Social Aspects. *Map.* 8* 1878

Robinson, Sara T. L. Kansas, its Interior and Exterior Life. *Plates.* 8° *Boston, Mass.,* 1856

Robinson, Thomas. Natural History of Westmoreland and Cumberland. 8° 1709

Robinson, William. Descriptive Account of Asam, with a Sketch of the Local Geography, and a Concise History of the Tea-plant of Asam ; to which is added a short Account of the Neighbouring Tribes, exhibiting their History, Manners, and Customs. *Maps.* 8° *Calcutta,* 1841

—— Report on the Laccadive Islands, dated 19th May 1848. 8° *Madras,* 1841

Robinson, Sir William. Prince Edward Island. Report to accompany the Blue Book of Prince Edward Island for the year 1870, by Lieut.-Governor Robinson. 8° *Charlottetown,* 1871

Robinson, Sir William. Tobacco, its Ups and Downs in England, and How to Cultivate and Cure it in the West Indies. 8* *Port-of-Spain,* 1886

Robinson, Sir W. C. F. The Physical Geography of the South-West of Western Australia. *Map.* 8* *Adelaide,* 1886

Robson, Thomas Charles. A Treatise on Marine Surveying. *Plates.* 8° 1834

Roca, General J. A. *See* Argentine, D, Patagonia : Appendix 2.

Rochas, A. Beau de. Oasis et Soudan. La Pénétration du Soudan considérée dans ses Rapports avec la création de Grandes Oasis Sahariennes. 8* *Paris,* 1888

Roche, W. M. Oliver's Shipping Law Manual. 8° 1879

Rochelle, Roux de. États-Unis d'Amérique ; Histoire et Description des Peuples, de leurs Religions, Mœurs, Coutumes, &c. *Plates.* 8° *Paris,* 1837

Rocher, Émile. La Province Chinoise du Yün-nan. 2 vols. *Maps.* Large 8° *Paris,* 1879-80

Rochet d'Héricourt, C. E. X. Voyage sur la Côte Orientale de la Mer Rouge dans le pays d'Adel et le Royaume de Choa. *Map and plates.* 8* *Plates,* 1841

—— Considérations géographiques et commerciales sur le Golfe Arabique, le pays d'Adel, et le royaume de Choa. *Map and plates.* 8° *Paris,* 1841

—— Second Voyage sur les deux rives de la Mer Rouge dans le pays des Adels et le royaume de Choa. *Map and plates.* Royal 8° *Paris,* 1846

Rochon, A. Voyages à Madagascar, à Maroc, et aux Indes Orientales. [2 vols. only.] *Map.* 12° *Paris,* An. x., 1801

—— A Voyage to Madagascar and the East Indies. Translated from the French . . . to which is added a Memoir on the Chinese Trade. *Map.* 8° 1792

—— *See* Oliver, S. P. ; *also* Pelham, Vol. 2 ; Pinkerton, Vol. 16 : Appendix 1.

Rockhill, W. Woodville. Udânavarga : a Collection of Verses from the Buddhist Canon, compiled by Dharmatrâta. Translated from the Tibetan. 8° 1883

—— The Life of the Buddha, and the Early History of his order : derived from Tibetan works in the Bkah-hgyur and Bstan-hgyur ; followed by Notices on the Early History of Tibet and Khoten. Translated by W. Woodville Rockhill. 8° 1884

—— Through Northern China to the Koko-Nor. (From the *Century Magazine.*) *Maps and illustrations.* 8* 1890

—— The Land of the Lamas : Notes of a Journey through China, Mongolia, and Tibet. *Maps and illustrations.* 8° 1891

Rockhill, W. Woodville. Tibet: a Geographical, Ethnographical, and Historical Sketch, derived from Chinese sources. (From the *Journal of the Royal Asiatic Society*.) 8° N.D.
—— The same. Art. 2. 8° 1891

Rockstroh, E. Informe de la Comision Cientifica del Instituto Nacional de Guatemala, nombrada por el Sr. Ministro de Instruccion Pública para el estudio de los fenómenos volcanicos en el Lago de Ilopango de la Republica del Salvador. *Plan.* 8* *Guatemala*, 1880

Rockwell, John A. Report on Canal and Railway Routes between the Atlantic and Pacific Oceans. *Maps.* 8° *Washington*, 1849

Rodd, Rennell. The Customs and Lore of Modern Greece; with 7 *full-page illustrations* by Tristram Ellis. 8° 1892

Rodenbough, T. F. Afghanistan and the Anglo-Russian Dispute: an account of Russia's Advance towards India, based upon the Reports and Experiences of Russian, German, and British Officers and Travellers, with a description of Afghanistan and of the Military Resources of the Powers concerned. *Maps and illustrations.* 8° 1885

Rödiger, E. Ueber zwei altäthiopische Inschriften. 4* *Halle*, 1839
—— Versuch über die Himjaritischen Schriftmonumente, mit einem Vorwort an Gesenius. 8° *Halle*, 1841

Rodler, Dr A. Bericht über eine Geologische Reise im westlichen Persien. 8* *Vienna*, 1889
—— *See* Penck, A.

Rodman, Hugh. *See* United States, E, *a*, Hydrographic Office Publications, No. 93 : Appendix 2.

Rodrigues, João Barboza. Rio Janapery : Pacificação dos Crichanás. *Map and plate.* 8° *Rio de Janeiro*, 1885

Rodrigues, J. C. The Panama Canal, its History, its Political Aspects, and Financial Difficulties. 12° 1885

Rodriguez, A. Coleccion de Leyes, Decretos del Gobierno, Tratados internacionales, y Acuerdos del Superior Tribunal de Justicia de la Republica Oriental del Uruguay. Large 8° *Montevideo*, 1856
—— The same. Part 2. Large 8° *Montevideo*, 1859
—— The same. Part 3. Large 8° *Montevideo*, 1866

Rodriguez, J. I. *See* Zeledón.

Rodriguez, Manuel. El Marañon y Amazonas. Historia de los descubrimientos, entradas y reduccion de Naciones, . . en las dilatadas montañas y mayores rios de la America. Small folio *Madrid*, 1684

Rodriguez, Maximo. Relacion Diaria, Viage de la Isla de Amat, alias Otagiti, 1774. MS. Square 8° 1774

Rodwell, G. F. Etna : a History of the Mountain and its Eruptions. *Maps and plates.* Small 8° 1878

Roe, Sir Thomas. *See* Churchill, Vol. 1 ; Kerr, Vol. 9 ; Laharpe, Vol. 4 ; Pinkerton, Vol. 8 ; Purchas, Vol. 1, Book 4 ; Thevenot, Vol. 1 ; Allgemeine Historie, Vol. 11 ; Knox's New Collection, Vol. 6 : Appendix 1.

Roebuck, J. A. The Colonies of England : a plan for the government of some portion of our Colonial possessions. 8° 1849

Rœdiger, E. *See* Rödiger.

Roepstorff, F. A. de. Vocabulary of dialects spoken in the Nicobar and Andaman Isles, with a short account of the natives, their customs and habits, and of previous attempts at Colonisation. 8° *Calcutta*, 1875
—— Notes on the Inhabitants of the Nicobars. (From the Proc. Asiatic Soc. of Bengal for January and June 1881.) 8* 1881
—— *See* General, Dictionaries, B : Appendix 2.

Roesler, R. Die Aralseefrage. 8* *Vienna*, 1873

Roger, Baron. Recherches Philosophiques sur la Langue Ouolofe, suivies d'un Vocabulaire abrégé Français-Ouolof. 8° *Paris*, 1829
—— *See* Recueil de Voyages, Vol. 2, p. 611 : Appendix 1.

Roger, J. C. Celticism a Myth. 2nd edition. 1889

Roger, P. Percement de l'Isthme Américain par un Canal Interocéanique : Journal des Voyages, Explorations, et Travaux relatifs à la Ligne du Darien. Large 8* *Paris*, 1864

Rogers, Major B. On the Prevention of Crime. 8* 1874

Rogers, Rev. Charles. Monuments and Monumental Inscriptions in Scotland. Vol. 1. [*Grampian Club Publications.*] *Frontispiece.* 8° 1871
—— Estimate of the Scottish Nobility during the minority of James the Sixth, with preliminary observations. [*Grampian Club Publications.*] 8° 1873
—— The Scottish House of Roger, with notes respecting the families of Playfair and Haldane of Bermony. 2nd edition. 8° *Edinburgh*, 1875
—— *See* Bain, J. ; James the First ; Scot.

Rogers, Capt E. Campaigning in Western Africa and the Ashantee invasion. *Map.* Small 8° 1874

Rogers, Henry D. Report on the Geological Survey of the State of New Jersey. *Map.* 8° *Philadelphia*, 1836

Rogers, Henry D. Geology of the State of New Jersey : being a final Report. *Maps*. 8° *Philadelphia*, 1840
—— Geology of Pennsylvania. First to Sixth Annual Reports. *Maps*. 8° *Harrisburg*, 1836-42
—— On the Laws of Structure of the more disturbed Zones of the Earth's Crust. 4* *Edinburgh*, 1856
Rogers, J. E. *See* Mahaffy.
Rogers, M. E. Domestic Life in Palestine. 8° 1862
Rogers, Major M. W., and E. Roberts. Tide Tables for the Indian Ports for the year 1883 (also January 1884). 12° [1882]
—— The same, for the year 1890 (also January 1891). Parts 1 and 2. 12° [1883]
—— *See* Baird ; Hill.
Rogers, Capt. Woodes. Life aboard a British Privateer in the time of Queen Anne : being the Journal of Captain Woodes Rogers, Master Mariner. With Notes and Illustrations by Robert C. Leslie. 8° 1889
—— *See* Burney, Vol. 4 ; Callander, Vol. 3 ; Harris, Vol. 1 ; Kerr, Vol. 10 ; Laharpe, Vol. 15 ; Allgemeine Historie, Vol. 12 ; Knox's New Collection, Vol. 3 ; "The World Displayed," Vol. 6 : Appendix 1.
Rogge, Dr H. C. *See* Holland : Appendix 2.
Roggewein, Jacob. *See* Burney, Vol. 4 ; Callander, Vol. 3 ; Dalrymple, Pacific, Vol. 2 ; Harris, Vol. 1 ; Kerr, Vol. 11 ; Allgemeine Historie, Vol. 18 ; "The World Displayed," Vol. 9 : Appendix 1.
Rogozinski, S. S. Pod Równikiem. Odczyty S. S. Rogozinskiego wypo wiedziane w Sali Radnej miasta krakowa. [Near the Equator : Lectures in Cracow.] 8* *Cracow*, 1886
Rohl, L. H. *See* Mallet, F.
Rohlfs, Dr Gerhard. Tagebuch seiner Reise durch Marokko nach Tuat, 1864. 4* *Gotha*, 1865
—— Neueste Briefe von, und Rückblick auf seine bisherigen Reisen in Afrika in den Jahren 1861 bis 1865 ; *and* Tagebuch seiner Reise von Tuat nach Ghadames, 1864. *Map*. 4* [*Gotha*, 1866]
—— Neueste Nachrichten aus dem Inneren Afrika's. 4* [*Gotha*] 1867
—— Reise durch Nord-Afrika vom Mittelländischen Meere bis zum Busen von Guinea, 1865-67. 1. Hälfte : Von Tripoli nach Kuka (Fesan, Sahara, Bornu). (Ergänzungsheft, 25—Petermann's Mittheilungen.) *Map*. 4° *Gotha*, 1868
—— Reise durch Nord-Africa, vom Mittelländischen Meere bis zum Busen von Guinea, 1865 bis 1867. 2. Häfte : Von Kuka nach Lagos. (Ergänzungsheft, 34—Petermann's Mittheilungen). 4° *Gotha*, 1872

Rohlfs, Dr Gerhard. Reise durch Marokko, Uebersteigung des grossen Atlas, Exploration der Oasen von Tafilet, Tuat und Tidikelt und Reise durch die grosse Wüste über Rhadames nach Tripoli. *Map and portrait*. 8° *Bremen*, 1868
—— Im Auftrage Sr. Majestät des Königs von Preussen mit dem Englischen Expeditionscorps in Abessinien. *Map, portrait, and tables*. 8° *Bremen*, 1869
—— Land und Volk in Afrika. Berichte aus den Jahren 1865-70. 8° *Bremen*, 1870
—— Von Tripolis nach Alexandrien. Beschreibung der im Auftrage Sr. Majestät des Königs von Preussen in den Jahren 1868 und 1869 ausgeführten Reise. 2 vols. (in 1). *Maps, plates, and photograph*. Small 8° *Bremen*, 1871
—— Mein erster Aufenthalt in Marokko und Reise südlich vom Atlas durch die Oasen Draa und Tafilet. Small 8° *Bremen*, 1873
—— Expedition nach der Libyschen Wüste, 1873-74, in Photographien von P. Remelé. [Album of fifty Photographs.]
—— Adventures in Morocco and journeys through the Oases of Draa and Tafilet ; with an Introduction by Winwood Reade. 8° 1874
—— Quer durch Afrika : Reise vom Mittelmeer nach dem Tschad-See und zum Golf vom Guinea. 8° *Leipzig*, 1854-75
—— Expedition zur Erforschung der Libyschen Wüste unter der Auspicien Sr. Hoheit des Chedive von Aegypten Ismail-Pascha im Winter 1873-74 ausgeführt. I. Reisebericht. *Maps, plates, and photographs*. 8° *Cassel*, 1875
—— The same. II. Physische Geographie und Meteorologie : Bearbeitet von W. Jordan. *Maps and tables*. 4° *Cassel*, 1876
—— Die Bedeutung Tripolitaniens an sich und als Ausgangspunkt für Entdeckungsreisende. *Map*. 8* *Weimar*, 1877
—— Neue Beiträge zur Entdeckung und Erforschung Africas. 8° *Cassel*, 1881
—— Kufra : Reise von Tripolis nach der Oase Kufra ; ausgeführt im Auftrage der Afrikanischen Gesellschaft in Deutschland, nebst Beiträgen von P. Ascherson, J. Hann, F. Karsch, W. Peters, A. Stecker. *Maps and plates*. 8° *Leipzig*, 1881
—— Meine Mission nach Abessinien, auf Befehl Sr. Majestät des Deutschen Kaisers im Winter 1880-81, unternommen von Gerhard Rohlfs. *Map and plates*. 8° *Leipzig*, 1883
—— Quid novi ex Africa ? 8° *Cassel*, 1886

Röhricht, Reinhold. Bibliotheca Geographica Palaestinae. Chronologisches Verzeichniss der auf die Geographie des Heiligen Landes bezüglichen Literatur von 333 bis 1878 und Versuch einer Cartographie. 8° *Berlin,* 1890

—— **and Heinrich Meisner.** Deutsche Pilgerreisen nach dem Heiligen Lande. 8° *Berlin,* 1880

Roissard de Bellet, Baron. La Sardaigne à vol d'oiseau en 1882, son Histoire, ses Mœurs, sa Géologie, ses richesses métallifères et ses productions de toute sorte. *Maps and illustrations.* Large 8° *Paris,* 1884

Rojas, E. Philosophie de la Morale. Traduit par V. Touzet. 8° *St Germain-en-Laye,* 1870

Rokh, Shah. *See* Astley, Vol. 4; Kerr, Vol. 1; Allgemeine Historie, Vol. 7: Appendix 1.

Rolamb, Nicholas. *See* Churchill, Vol. 5: Appendix 1.

Rolland, Georges. La Région de Ouargla. *Map.* 4* [*Paris,* 1883]

—— Chemin de Fer Transsaharien : Géologie du Sahara Algérien et aperçu Géologique sur le Sahara de l'Océan Atlantique à la Mer Rouge. Texte, Extrait des Documents relatifs à la Mission de Laghouat-El-Goléa-Ouargla-Biskra, publiés par le Ministère des Travaux publics (Rapport Géologique). Folio *Paris,* 1890

—— The same. Géologie et Hydrologie du Sahara Algérien. Planches accompagnant les deux volumes de Texte, Extrait des Documents, &c. (Rapports Géologique et Hydrologique.) Folio *Paris,* 1890

—— Le Transsaharien : Réponse à M. Duponchel. 4* N.D.

Romanovski, M. Notes on the Central Asiatic Question. 8° *Calcutta,* 1870

Romer, Mrs. Pilgrimage to the Temples and Tombs of Egypt, Nubia, and Palestine in 1845-46. 2 vols. *Plates* 8° 1846

Romilly, H. H. Report on the Labour Trade in New Britain and New Ireland. Folio* [1884]

—— The Western Pacific and New Guinea : Notes on the Natives, Christian and Cannibal, with some Account of the old Labour Trade. *Map.* Crown 8° 1886

—— From my Verandah in New Guinea : Sketches and Traditions ; with an Introduction by Andrew Lang. *Map.* 8° 1889

Rónay, H. Abstracts of the Travels of Ladislaus Magyar in South Africa, 1849-57. MS. Square 8* N.D.

Rónay, Jáczint. Jellemisme, vagy az Angol, Franczia, Magyar, Német, Olasz, Orosz, Spanyol, Nemzet, Nö, Férfiu és életkorok Jellěmzése lélektani szempontból. 8° *Györött,* 1847

Rónay, W. A Tuzimádó Bölcs az Ös-Világok, Emlékeirol. [History of the Development of the Globe.] *Plates.* 8° *Budapest,* 1860

Rondot, M. Natalis. Notice du Vert de Chine, et de la Teinture en Vert chez les Chinois ; suivie d'une Étude des Propriétés Chimiques et Tinctoriales du Lo-Kao, par M. J. Persoz ; et de Recherches sur la Matière Colorante des Nerpruns Indigènes, par M. A. F. Michel. *Plates.* Royal 8° *Paris,* 1858

—— Commerce de la France avec la Chine. Royal 8* *Lyons,* 1860

—— Pé-King et la Chine : Mésures, Monnaies et Banques Chinoises. Royal 8* *Paris,* 1861

Roon, Albrecht von. Grundzüge der Erd- Völker- und Staatenkunde ; mit einem Vorwort von Carl Ritter. Zweite Abtheil ; Physische Geographie. 8° *Berlin,* 1838

Roorda, T. De Wajangverhalen van Pălă-Sârâ, Pandoe en Raden Pandji, in het Javaansch, met aanteekeningen. [*Javanese.*] 8° *The Hague,* 1869

—— *See* Veth.

Roos, Hon. Fred. Fitzgerald de. Personal Narrative of Travels in the United States and Canada in 1826. *Plates.* 8° 1827

Roque. *See* De la Roque.

Roquefeuil, Camille de. *See* Phillips, New Voyages and Travels [3], Vol. 9: Appendix 1.

Roquette, — de la. *See* De la Roquette.

Roosevelt, T. Hunting Trips of a Ranchman : Sketches of Sport on the Northern Cattle Plains. *Illustrations.* Large 8° 1886

—— Ranch Life and the Hunting-Trail. *Illustrations.* 4° 1888

Rosales, H. *See* Victoria, C: Appendix 2.

Rosales, Manuel Landeata. Recopilacion Geografica, Estadistica, e Historica de Venezuela. 2 vols. Oblong 4° *Caracas,* 1889

Roscher, Albrecht. Ptolemœus und die Handelsstrassen in Central-Africa. *Maps.* 8* *Gotha,* 1857

Roscher, W., and R. Jannasch. Kolonien : Kolonial Politik und Auswanderung. 8° *Leipzig,* 1885

Roscoe, Thomas. Wanderings and Excursions in North Wales. *Map and plates.* 8° 1853

—— Wanderings and Excursions in South Wales, with the Scenery of the River Wye. *Map and plates.* 8° 1854

Rose, G. Reise nach dem Ural, dem Altai, und dem Kaspischen Meere von A. von Humboldt, G. Ehrenberg, und G. Rose. Mineralogisch-geognosticher Theil und historischer Bericht der Reise. 2 vols. *Maps and plates.* 8° *Berlin*
Vol. 1.—Reise nach dem nördlichen Ural und dem Altai 1837
Vol. 2.—Reise nach dem südlichen Ural und dem Kaspischen Meere 1842

Rose, H. J. Untrodden Spain and her Black Country : being Sketches of the Life and Character of the Spaniard of the Interior. 2 vols. 8° 1875

Rose, J. *See* Graham, D. C.

Rose, W. S. *See* Phillips [3], Vol. 1 : Appendix 1.

Roscbery, Earl of. *See* Parkin.

Rosen, G. Das Haram von Jerusalem und der Tempelplatz des Moria. *Maps.* 8* *Gotha*, 1866

Rosén, P. G. Die astronomisch-geodätischen Arbeiten der topographischen Abtheilung des Schwedischen Generalstabes. Erster Band. Heft 2, 3. 4° *Stockholm*, 1885, 1890
—— Die astronomisch-geodätischen Arbeiten der topographischen Abtheilung des Schwedischen Generalstabes. Zweiter Band. Heft 1. *Plates.* 4° *Stockholm*, 1888
—— Projet de mesure d' un arc du méridien de 4° 20' au Spitzberg. *Map.* Large 8* *Stockholm*, 1893

Rosén, Baron Victor. Les Manuscrits Arabes de l'Institut des Langues Orientales. 8° *St Petersburg*, 1877

Rosenberg, C. B. H. von. Reistogten in de Afdeeling Gorontalo gedaan op last der Nederlandsch Indische Regering. *Plates and maps.* 8° *Amsterdam*, 1865
—— Reis naar de Zuidoostereilanden. *Plates.* 8° *The Hague*, 1867
—— Reistochten naar de Geelvinkbai op Nieuw-Guinea in de Jahren 1869 en 1870, ambtenaar belast met wetenschappelijke onderzoekingen in Nederlandsch-Indië. *Maps and plates.* 4° *The Hague*, 1875
—— Der Malayische Archipel. Land und Leute in Schilderungen, gesammelt während eines dreissigjährigen Aufenthaltes in den Kolonien. (Vorwort von Professor P. J. Veth.) *Plates.* 8° *Leipzig*, 1878-79

Rosencoat, — de. Reconnaissance Hydrographique des Côtes Occidentales du Centre Amérique, Province de Veraguas (Nouvelle-Grenade). 8° *Paris*, 1857

Rosenheyn, Max. Die Marienburg, das Haupthaus der deutschen Ordens-Ritter. *Plates and plan.* 16° *Leipzig*, 1858

Rosenwall, P. Bemerkungen eines Russen eber Preussen und dessen Bewohner, desammelt auf einer im Jahr 1814 durch dieses Land unternommenen Reise. Small 8° *Mayence*, 1817

Rosetti, Emilio. Ferrovia Trasandina. Relazione sulla practicabilità di una Stra-la Ferrata attraverso le Ande nella direzione del Passo chiamato del Planchon nel Sud della Provincia di Mendoza. Traduzione Italiana. *Map.* Folio* *Buenos Ayres*, 1870

Rosier, J. *See* Purchas, Vol. 4, Book 8 : Appendix 1.

Rosiwal, A. *See* Höhnel.

Roskoschny, Dr Hermann. Europas Kolonien. Das Kongogebiet und seine Nachbarländer. Nach den neuesten Quellen geschildert. *Maps and illustrations.* 4° *Leipzig*, N.D.
—— The same. West-Africa von Senegal zum Kamerun. Nach den neuesten Quellen geschildert. Dritte Auflage. *Maps and illustrations.* 4° *Leipzig*, N.D.
—— Die Wolga und ihre Zuflüsse : Geschichte, Ethnographie, Hydro- und Orographie nebst Mitteilungen· über das Klima des Wolga-gebietes. 9° *Leipzig*, 1887

Rosny, Léon de. L'Orient. 8* *Paris*, 1860
—— Discours prononcé à l'ouverture du Cours de Japonais. 8* *Paris*, 1863
—— Variétés Orientales, historiques, géographiques, scientifiques, bibliographiques et littéraires. 12° *Paris*, 1872
—— Les documents écrits de l'Antiquité Américaine. Compte-rendu d'une Mission Scientifique en Espagne et en Portugal. (No. 3 of Mémoires de la Société d'Ethnographie.) *Map and plates.* 4* *Paris*, 1882
—— Bibliothèque Royale de Stockholm : Catalogue de la Bibliothèque Japonaise de Nordenskiöld, coordonné, revu, annoté et publié par Léon de Rosny, et précédé d'une Introduction par le Marquis d'Hervey de Saint Denys. 8° *Paris*, 1883
—— Kami yo-no maki : Histoire des Dynasties Divines. Publiée en Japonais, traduite pour la Première fois sur le Texte Original, accompagnée d'une glose inédite composée en Chinois et d'un Commentaire perpétuel rédigé en Français par Léon de Rosny. (Vol. 1. IIe Série. Vol. 16 of Publications de l'École des Langues Orientales Vivantes.) Large 8° *Paris*, 1884 and 1887
—— Les Religions de l'Extrême Orient. Leçon d'ouverture faite à l'École pratique des Hautes-Études. 8* *Paris*, 1886
—— Miscellaneous Pamphlets. 8° *Paris*
—— Chan-hai-king. Antique Géographie Chinoise traduite pour la première fois sur le texte original. Tome I. 8° *Paris*, 1891
—— *See* Cortambert.

Rosny, Lucien de. Les Antilles : Étude d'Ethnographie et d'Archéologie Américaines. (Mémoires de la Société d'Ethnographie.) *Paris*, 1886

Ross, A. Adventures of the First Settlers on the Oregon or Columbia River : being a Narrative of the Expedition fitted out by J. J. Astor. *Map.* 8° 1849

Ross, A., and A. Sinclair. The Peruvian Corporation, Limited. Report on Land in Peru suitable for Agriculture. 4* 1893

Ross, Dr A. M. The Birds of Canada ; with Descriptions of their Habits, Food, Nests, Eggs, Times of Arrival and Departure. *Plates and woodcuts.* Small 8° *Toronto*, 1871

—— U.S. Centennial Exhibition. Catalogue to illustrate the Animal Resources of the Dominion of Canada : list of Fur-bearing, Useful, and Injurious Animals, and the Native and Migratory Birds. 8° *Toronto*, 1876

—— Catalogue of Mammals, Birds, Reptiles, and Fishes of the Dominion of Canada. 8° *Montreal*, 1878

Ross, David. The Land of the Five Rivers and Sindh : Sketches, Historical and Descriptive. *Map.* 8° 1883

—— Military Transport by Indian Railways. *Map and plates.* 8° *Lahore*, 1883

Ross, Lieut.-Col. E. C. Report on a Visit to Kej, and Route through Mekran from Gwadur to Kurrachee. Folio* 1865

—— Notes on Mekran. *Map.* Folio* 1865

—— Report on the Coast of Mekran from Cape Jask to Gwadur. *Map.* Folio* 1867

—— Report of a Tour from Shiraz to Bushire, with *route map.* Folio* 1875

—— Memorandum descriptive of the Route between Sohar and El Bereymee in Oman. Folio* 1876

—— Memorandum on Tribal Divisions in the Principality of Omân. To accompany Table of Tribes. *Tables.* Folio* N.D.

Ross, J. South Australia. Mr J. Ross's Explorations, 1874. Journal and Map. Folio* N.P. [1875]

Ross, Sir James Clark. The Position of the North Magnetic Pole. 4* 1834

—— A Voyage of Discovery and Research in the Southern and Antarctic Regions, 1839-43. 2 vols. *Maps and plates.* 8° 1847

—— *See* "Erebus" and "Terror."

Ross, John. History of Corea, Ancient and Modern, with Description of Manners and Customs, Language and Geography. *Maps and plates.* 8° *Paisley* [1880]

Ross, Adm. Sir John. Voyage of Discovery made in H.M.'s ships "Isabella " and "Alexander," for the purpose of exploring Baffin's Bay and inquiring into the probability of a North-West Passage. *Charts and plates.* 4° 1819

Ross, Adm. Sir John. Narrative of a Second Voyage in Search of a North-West Passage, and of a Residence in the Arctic Regions during 1829-33, including the Reports of Capt. J. C. Ross, and the Discovery of the Northern Magnetic Pole. *Portrait, charts, and plates.* 4° 1835

—— Appendix to do. *Coloured plates.* 4° 1835

—— Explanation and Answer to Mr Braithwaite. 4* 1835-36

—— *See* Huish, R. ; Krusenstern ; *also* Eyriès, Vol. 7 : Appendix 1.

Ross, Ludwig. On the Topography of Halicarnassus, with Guichard and Dalechamp's Account of the Final Destruction of the Mausoleum ; translated, with Notes, by John Hogg. 8° *Cambridge*, 1854

Ross, Malcolm. A Complete Guide to the Lakes of Central Otago, the Switzerland of Australasia. *Maps and illustrations.* 8° *Wellington*, 1889

—— Aorangi ; or, The Heart of the Southern Alps, New Zealand. *Maps and plates.* 8* *Wellington*, 1892

Ross, Mars, and H. Stonehewer-Cooper. The Highlands of Cantabria ; or, Three Days from England. *Map and illustrations.* 8° 1885

Ross, Thomasina. *See* Humboldt and Bonpland ; Tschudi.

Ross, W. A. Yacht Voyage to Norway, Denmark, and Sweden. 8° 1849

Ross, Col. W. A. Pyrology, or Fire Analysis. 8* 1872

Rosser, W. H. Notes on the Physical Geography and Meteorology of the South Atlantic ; together with Sailing Directions for the Principal Ports of Call and for the Islands : to which is appended a Catalogue of all the doubtful Islands, Rocks, and Shoals. *Maps and plates.* 8° 1862

—— A Ship's Position at Sea : Practical Methods of Finding the Latitude and Longitude by two Altitudes of the Sun, or other celestial objects, and of Determining the bearing of the Land from a single Altitude. *Chart.* 8° 1862

—— The Stars : how to know them and how to use them. *Plates.* 8° 1865

—— The Seaman's Guide to the Islands of the North Pacific. *See* United Kingdom, A, North Pacific Pilot, Part 2 : Appendix 2.

—— A Self-Instructor in Navigation and Nautical Astronomy, for the Local Marine Board Examinations and for use at Sea. 2nd edition. *Plates.* 8° 1868

—— Lunars and Lunar Tables : being various Methods of Finding the true Lunar Distance, and thence the Longitude. 8° 1875

Rosser, W. H. A Self-Instructor in Navigation and Nautical Astronomy, for the Local Marine Board Examinations and for use at Sea. 3rd edition. *Plates.* 8° 1876

—— Stellar Navigation, with New A, B, and C Tables for finding by easy methods Latitude, Longitude, and Azimuths ; Latitudes and Declinations ranging to 68° N. or S. 4° 1883

—— *See* Imray ; *also* United Kingdom, North Pacific Pilot : Appendix 2.

Rosset, C. W. The Máldive Islands. (From the *Graphic*, 16th October 1886.) *Illustrations.* Folio* 1886

Rossi, Stefano de. *See* Issel.

Roth, Abraham. The Doldenhorn and Weisse Frau ascended for the first time, by Abraham Roth and Edmund von Fellenberg. *Map and plates.* 8° *Coblentz,* 1863

Roth, H. Ling. Franco-Swiss Dairying. 8* 1885

—— Further Remarks on the Roots of the Sugar-Cane. *Plates.* 8* 1885

—— Arbère : a Short Contribution to the Study of Peasant Proprietorship. 8* 1885

—— Bibliography and Cartography of Hispaniola. (Roy. Geog. Soc. Suppl. Papers, Vol. 2.) 8° 1887

—— *See* Crozet's Voyage.

Roth, J. F. Nürnbergs neueste Beschreibung und Verfassung, nebst einem Verzeichniss der Kaufleute, &c. *Plates.* 12° *Nuremberg,* 1813

Roth, Prof. J. R. Schilderung der Naturverhältnisse in Süd-Abyssinien. 4* *Munich,* 1851

Rothpletz, A. Das Karwendelgebirge. *Map, plates, and sections.* 8* *Munich,* 1888

Rottiers, Colonel. Itinéraire de Tiflis à Constantinople. *Maps and plates.* 8° *Brussels,* 1829

Rotzmital und Blatna, L. von. *See* Horky.

Roudaire, Capt. Rapport à M. le Ministre de l'Instruction Publique sur la Mission des Chotts. Études relatives au Projet de Mer Intérieure. *Map.* 8° *Paris,* 1877

Rougé, Vicomte J. de. Géographie Ancienne de la Basse-Égypte. *Map.* 8° *Paris,* 1891

Rouhaud, Hippolyte. Les Régions Nouvelles : Histoire du Commerce et de la Civilisation au Nord de l'Océan Pacifique. 8° *Paris,* 1868

Rouire, Dr —. L'Emplacement de la Mer Intérieure d'Afrique. *Map.* 8* *Paris,* 1884

—— La découverte de la Mer Intérieure Africaine. 4* [*Paris,* 1884]

—— Des divers Systèmes Modernes ayant assimilé le pays de Gabès à la Région de Triton. *Map.* 8* *Tours,* 1886

Rouire, Dr —. Sur les Dolmens de l'Enfida. Large 8* [*Paris,* 1887]

—— La découverte du Bassin Hydrographique de la Tunisie Centrale et l'Emplacement de l'Ancien Lac Triton (ancienne Mer Intérieure d'Afrique). *Maps.* 8° *Paris,* 1887

Roujouz, H. de. Essai sur l'Atterage et l'Entrée de la Rade de Brest par Temps Brumeux, avec un Batiment à Vapeur. *Plates.* 8° *Paris,* 1868

Rousseau, Alphonse. Géographie Générale de la Bosnie et de l'Herzégovine. 8° 1868

Rousset, L. A Travers la Chine. *Map.* 12° *Paris,* 1878

Roussillon, Duc du. Origines, Migrations, Philologie, et Monuments Antiques. Parts 1, 2. 8* 1867

Roussin, Amiral le Baron. Memoir on the Navigation of the West Coast of Africa, from Cape Bojador to Mount Souzos, 1817-18. Translated from the French by Lieut. J. Badgley. 4° 1827 [Bound up with Capt. Owen's Tables of Latitudes and Longitudes.]

—— Pilote du Brésil, ou Description des Côtes de l'Amérique Méridionale ; comprises entre l'île Santa-Catarina et celle de Maranaõ, avec les Instructions nécessaires pour attérir et Naviguer sur ces Côtes, 1819-20. 8° *Paris,* 1827

Roustan, Honoré. La République de l'Uruguay à l'Exposition Universelle de Paris, 1889. *Map.* 4° *Montevideo,* 1889

—— *See* Pena.

Routier, Gaston. L'Agriculture, la Flore, les Mines, et la Faune de Madagascar. 4* *Rouen,* 1890

Rouvier, C. Cartes du Congo Français : Note sur la Construction des Cartes levées pendant le cours d'une Mission au Congo en 1885-86. *Map.* 8* *Paris,* 1887

Rouwolf, Leendert. *See* Gottfried : Appendix 1.

Roux, Hugues le. Au Sahara. *Illustrations.* 12° *Paris,* N.D.

Roux, Jules Ch. Le Canal de Panama en 1886. *Map, plans, and plates.* 4° *Marseilles,* 1886

Rouzier, S. Dictionnaire géographique et administratif universel d'Haïti illustré . . . ou Guide Général en Haïti. Vol. 1, A—F. *Maps and illustrations.* 8° *Paris* [1891]

—— Vol. 2, G—H. *Map and illustrations.* 8° *Paris,* 1894

Rowan, J. J. The Emigrant and Sportsman in Canada : some Experiences of an old Country Settler, with Sketches of Canadian Life, Sporting Adventures, and Observations on the Forests and Fauna. *Map.* 8° 1876

Rowe, G. S. *See* Williams and Calvert.

Rowell, G. A. On the Change of Temperature in Europe, and the Variation of the Magnetic Needle. *Map.* 8* 1853

Rowlands, C. Henry M. Stanley : The Story of his Birth in 1841 to his Discovery of Livingstone in 1871. *Plates.* Small 8° 1872

Rowlands, Rev. Daniel. The Fishguard Invasion by the French in 1797. Some passages taken from the diary of the late Reverend Daniel Rowlands, some time Vicar of Llanfiangelpenybont. *Illustrations.* 8° 1892

Rowles, Richard. *See* Astley, Vol. 1 ; Gottfried ; Kerr, Vol. 8 ; Purchas, Vol. 1, Book 3 ; Allgemeine Historie, Vol. 1 : Appendix 1.

Rowley, Henry. The Story of the Universities' Mission to Central Africa, from its commencement, under Bishop Mackenzie, to its withdrawal from the Zambesi. *Maps and plates.* 8° 1866

Roxas, S. A. de. *See* Angelis, Vol. 1 : Appendix 1.

Roxburgh, Dr Wm. *See* Dalrymple, Repertory, Vol. 1 : Appendix 1.

Roy, Rev. Father Le. A Travers le Zanguebar. *Map and illustrations.* 8° Paris, 1884

Roy, Josef Jansz. *See* Gottfried : Appendix 1.

Royle, John F. Essay on the Productive Resources of India. Royal 8° 1840

Ruard de Card, E. El Arbitraje Internacional en el pasado, en el presente i en el porvenir. (Traducido del francés.) 8* Santiago de Chile, 1877

Rubriques, William de. Ambassadeur de Saint Louis en Orient. Récit de son Voyage. Traduit de l'Original Latin et Annoté par Louis de Backer. 12° Paris, 1877

—— *See* Astley, Vol. 4 ; Gottfried ; Hakluyt, Vol. 1 ; Harris, Vol. 1 ; Kerr, Vol. 1 ; Pinkerton, Vol. 7 ; Purchas, Vol. 3, Book 1 ; Allgemeine Historie, Vol. 7 : Appendix 1.

Rucellai, G. *See* Alamanni.

Rudge, Thomas. General View of the Agriculture of the County of Gloucester. *Maps.* 8° 1807

Rudinger, N. Ueber die Wege und Ziele der Hirnforschung. 4° Munich, 1893

Rudler, F. W. *See* Stanford.

Ruelens, C. *See* Eredia.

Ruge, Dr Sophus. Ueber Compas und Compaskarten. *Map.* 8* Dresden [1868]

—— Geschichte des Zeitalters der Entdeckungen. *Maps and illustrations.* 8° Berlin, 1881-83

—— Abhandlungen und Vorträge zur Geschichte der Erdkunde. 8° Dresden, 1888

Ruge, Dr Sophus. Christoph Columbus. (Fuhrende Geister. Eine Sammlung von Biographieen. Herausgegeben von Dr Anton Bettelheim. Vierter Band.) *Map and portrait.* 12° Dresden, 1892

Rugendas, M. Malerische Reise in Brasilien. *Plates.* Folio Paris, 1835

Ruggerius. *See* Purchas, Vol. 3, Book 2 : Appendix 1.

Ruidiaz y Caravia. Eugenio. La Florida. 2 vols. *Maps and illustrations.* 8° Madrid, 1893-94

Ruis, Augustin. *See* Hakluyt, Vol. 3 : Appendix 1.

Rumbold, Sir Horace. The Great Silver River : Notes of a Residence in Buenos Ayres in 1880 and 1881. *Illustrations.* 8° 1887

Rukt, Shah. *See* Rokh.

Rumford, Count. The Complete Works of. 4 vols. 8° Boston, Mass., 1870-75
—— *See* Ellis, G. E. [additional volume].

Rumsey, Commr. R. Murray. Report on Survey of the Ancobra River, and on the Axim Gold Region, West Africa. *Sketch maps.* Folio* 1882

Rundall, Major F. M. Manual of the Siyin Dialect spoken in the Northern Chin Hills. 8° Rangoon, 1891
—— The Siyin Chins. Roy. Geog. Soc. Suppl. Papers, Vol. 3. *Map.* Large 8° 1893

Rundall, Thomas. *See* Hakluyt Soc. Publ., Vols. 5, 8 : Appendix 1.

Rupibus, Petrus de. *See* Hakluyt, Vol. 2 : Appendix 1.

Rüppel, Eduard. Reisen in Nubien, Kordofan und dem peträischen Arabien, vorzüglich in geographisch - statistischer Hinsicht. 8° 1829
—— Reise in Abyssinien. 2 vols. 8° Frankfort-o-M., 1838-40

Ruschenberger, Dr W. S. W. Narrative of a Voyage round the World during the years 1835, 1836, and 1837 ; including a Narrative of an Embassy to the Sultan of Muscat and the Kingdom of Siam. 2 vols. *Plates.* 8° 1838

Rusden, G. W. The Discovery, Survey, and Settlement of Port Phillip. *Maps.* 8* 1872
—— History of Australia. 3 vols. *Map.* 8° 1883
—— History of New Zealand. 3 vols. *Map, plans, and plates.* 8° 1883
—— Aureretanga : Groans of the Maoris. 8* 1888
—— The Great Refusal, by Vindex. 8* 1890
—— The Law of Libel. 8* 1890

Rush, George. Accounts of Ascents in the Nassau and Victoria Balloons, 1838, 1849, and 1850 ; with a Description of Rush's Registered Dials for the Improved Aneroid Barometer, and Appendix by W. H. Jones. 8* 1851

Ruskin, John. The Future of England. [A Paper read at the R.A. Institution.] 8* 1869

Russegger, Joseph. Beiträge zur Physiognomik, Geognosie, und Geographie des Afrikanischen Tropenlandes. 8* 1840
—— Reisen in Europa, Asien, und Africa; mit besonderer Rücksicht auf die naturwissenchaftlichen Verhältnisse der betreffenden Länder, in 1835-41. Vol. 1. 8° *Stuttgart*, 1841

Russell, Alexander. The Natural History of Aleppo and Parts adjacent; together with an Account of the Climate, Inhabitants, and Diseases, particularly of the Plague. *Coloured plates.* 4° 1756
—— The same. 2nd edition. Notes by P. Russell. 2 vols. 4° 1794
—— *See* "The World Displayed," Vol. 13, p. 609: Appendix 1.

Russell, Dr. *See* Purchas, Vol. 4, Book 9: Appendix 1.

Russell, Hon. F. A. Rollo. *See* Symons, G. J.

Russell, Major Frank S. *See* United Kingdom, G, War Office Publications: Appendix 2.

Russell, G. *See* Phillips, Voyages and Travels [3], Vol. 1: Appendix 1.

Russell, Count Henry. Biarritz and Basque Countries. *Map.* Small 8° 1873
—— Souvenirs d'un Montagnard (1858-88). Small 8° *Pau*, 1888

Russell, H. C. Abstract of Meteorological Observations made in New South Wales, up to the end of 1869; with Remarks on the Climate. 8* *Sydney*, 1871
—— Results of Meteorological Observations made in New South Wales, during the years 1872-84. 4 vols. *Diagrams.* 8° 1873-92
—— Climate of New South Wales, Descriptive, Historical, and Tabular. *Diagrams.* 8° *Sydney*, 1877
—— Storms on the Coast of New South Wales. *Maps.* 8* 1878
—— Results of Rain Observations made in New South Wales during 1878. *Map.* 8* *Sydney*, 1879
—— Results of Rain and River Observations made in New South Wales during 1879. 8* *Sydney*, 1880
—— Papers read before the Astronomical Section of the Royal Society of New South Wales, 1878-79. 8* [*Sydney*, 1879-80]
—— The "Gem" Cluster in Argo. *Plate.* 8* [*Sydney*, 1880]
—— The Wentworth Hurricane. *Map.* 8* [*Sydney*, 1880]
—— Note upon a Sliding-Scale for correcting Barometer Readings to 32° F. and Mean Sea-Level. *Diagram.* 8* [*Sydn v*, 1880]

Russell, H. C. Some New Double Stars and Southern Binaries. *Diagrams.* 8* [*Sydney*, 1880]
—— Recent Changes in the Surface of Jupiter. *Diagrams.* 8* [*Sydney*, 1881]
—— Thunder and Hail Storms in New South Wales. *Diagram.* 8* [*Sydney*, 1881]
—— Results of Rain and River Observations made in New South Wales, during 1880. *Map and diagram.* 8* [*Sydney*, 1881]
—— Results of Double Star Measures made at the Sydney Observatory, New South Wales, 1871-81. *Diagrams.* 8* *Sydney*, 1882
—— Transit of Mercury, 8th November 1881. 8* [*Sydney*, 1882]
—— Results of Rain and River Observations made in New South Wales, during 1881. *Map and diagrams.* 8* *Sydney*, 1882
—— The same, during 1883 and 1884. *Maps and diagrams.* 8* *Sydney*, 1884-85
—— The same, during 1885. *Map and diagrams.* 8* *Sydney*, 1886
—— Anniversary Address. (Delivered to the Royal Society of N.S.W., 6th May 1885.) 8* 1885
—— Local Variations and Vibrations of the Earth's Surface. *Diagrams.* 8* [*Sydney*, 1886]
—— Notes upon the History of Floods in the River Darling. *Diagram.* 8* [*Sydney*, 1887]
—— Notes upon Floods in Lake George. *Diagrams.* 8* [*Sydney*, 1887]
—— Results of Rain and River Observations made in New South Wales, and part of Queensland, during 1886. *Maps and diagrams.* 8* *Sydney*, 1887
—— Results of Meteorological Observations, 1885-1889. *Diagrams.* 8° *Sydney*, 1887-91
—— On the New Self-Recording Thermometer. 8* [1888]
—— Astronomical and Meteorological Workers in New South Wales, 1778 to 1860. 8* [*Sydney*, 1888]
—— Proposed Method of Recording Variations in the direction of the Vertical. 8* [*Sydney*, 1888]
—— The Source of the Underground Water in the Western Districts. 8* [1889]
—— Results of Rain, River, and Evaporation Observations made in New South Wales, during 1887 and 1888. *Map and diagrams.* 8° *Sydney*, 1888-89
—— Results of Rain, River, and Evaporation Observations made in New South Wales, during 1889. *Maps and diagrams.* 8° *Sydney*, 1890
—— Preparations now being made in Sydney Observatory for the Photographic Chart of the Heavens. *Plate.* 8* 1891

Russell, H. C. Hail Storms. *Chart.* 8*
Sydney, 1892
—— Physical Geography and Climate of New South Wales. 2nd edition. *Maps.* 8*
Sydney, 1892
—— Results of Meteorological Observations made in New South Wales during 1890, under the direction of H. C. Russell. *Map.* 8° Sydney, 1892
—— Diagram of Isothermal Lines of New South Wales. Large 8* Sydney, 1892
—— Results of Rain, River, and Evaporation Observations made in New South Wales, 1890-92. *Maps.* 8°
Sydney, 1891-93
—— Pictorial Rain Maps. *Map.* 8*
Sydney, 1893
—— Moving Anticylones in the Southern Hemisphere. (From the *Quarterly Journal* of the Royal Meteorological Society, Vol. 19, No. 85, January 1893.) *Diagrams.* Large 8* 1893
—— On Meteorite No. 2 from Gilgoin Station. 8* Sydney, 1893
—— President's Address at the First Meeting of the Australian Association for the Advancement of Science. 8* N.D.
Russell, Henry Stuart. The Genesis of Queensland: an Account of the First Exploring Journeys to and over Darling Downs; the Earliest Days of their Occupation . . ; a Resumé of the Causes which led to Separation from New South Wales. *With portrait and maps.* Large 8° Sydney, 1888
Russell, Israel C. An Expedition to Mount St Elias, Alaska. *Maps and plates.* Large 8° Washington, 1891
—— *See* United States, G, *c*, Surveys: Appendix 2.
Russell, Bishop Michael. Palestine, or the Holy Land, from the earliest period to the present time. 3rd edition. *Map and plates.* 8° Edinburgh, 1832
—— View of Ancient and Modern Egypt, with an Outline of its Natural History. *Map and plates.* 12° Edinburgh, 1832
—— Nubia and Abyssinia; comprehending their Civil History, Antiquities, Arts, Religion, Literature, and Natural History. *Map and plates.* 12° Edinburgh, 1833
—— History of the Present Condition of the Barbary States; comprehending a View of their Civil Institutions, Antiquities, Arts, Religion, Literature, Commerce, Agriculture, and Natural Productions. *Map and plates.* 12° Edinburgh, 1835
—— History of Ancient and Modern Egypt, its Temples and Monuments. *Map and plates.* 12° 1852
Russell, Robert. Natal, the Land and its Story: a Geography and History for the use of Schools. *Map.* 12°
Pietermaritzburg, 1891
—— The same. 3rd edition. *Map*
Pietermaritzburg, 1894

Russell, Dr W. H. A Visit to Chile and the Nitrate Fields of Tarapacá, &c. *Maps and illustrations.* 4° 1890
Rust, —. Die deutsche Emin Pascha-Expedition. *Map.* 8° Berlin, 1890
Rütimeyer, L. Beiträge zu einer Palæontologischen Geschichte der Wiederkauer zunächst an Linné's Genus Bos. 8*
Bâle, 1865
—— Ueber Thal- und See-Bildung. Beiträge zum Verständniss der Oberfläche der Schweiz. *Map.* 4* Bâle, 1869
Rutter, W. See Kerr, Vol. 7; Allgemeine Historie, Vol. 1 : Appendix 1.
Ruxton, George F. Adventures in Mexico and the Rocky Mountains. Small 8° 1847
—— The Oregon Question, &c. *See* United States, K, Oregon Question: Appendix 2.
Ryan, P. *See* Sadlier.
Ryan, W. Redmond. Personal Adventures in Upper and Lower California in 1848-49. 2 vols. *Plates.* 8° 1851
Ryder, C. Forslag og Plan til en Undersögelse af Grönlands östkyst fra 66° til 73°. N. Br. 8* Copenhagen, 1890
—— Den Ostgrönlandske Expedition. *Maps.* 4* Copenhagen, 1892
Rye, E. C. New Guinea Bibliography. (Extracted from the Royal Geographical Society's Supplementary Papers, Vol. 1.) 8* 1884
Rykatschew, M. Ueber den Auf- und Zugang der Gewässer des Russischen Reiches; Zweiter Supplementband zum Repertorium für Meteorologie herausgegeben von der Kaiserlichen Academie der Wissenschaften. *Maps.* 4°
St Petersburg, 1887
—— Results with Monro's Anemograph, 1883-85. [In Russian]
St Petersburg, 1889
Rylands, Thomas Glazebrook. The Geography of Ptolemy Elucidated. *Maps and illustrations.* 4° Dublin, 1893
"**Rynda.**" *See* Tilley.

S

S——, V. de. Zambesi : the Anglo-Luso-African Difficulty Explained. By V. de S. 8* 1890
Sá, G. de. *See* Portuguese Voyages, &c., p. 612 : Appendix 1.
Sa, Pedro de. *See* Churchill, Vol. 8 : Appendix 1.
Saabye, Hans Egede. Bruchstükke eines Tagebuches gehalten in Grönland in 1770 bis 1778, aus dem Dänischen übersetzt von G. Fries. *Map.* 8° Hamburg, 1817
—— *See* Egede, Hans.
Saavedra, A. *See* Burney, Vol. 1; Callander, Vol. 1; Navarette, Vol. 5; Allgemeine Historie, Vol. 18 : Appendix 1.

Sabatier, Camille. Touat, Sahara, et Soudan. Étude gèographique, politique, èconomique, et militaire. *Map.* 8° *Paris*, 1891

Sabine, Gen. Sir Edward. Account of Experiments to Determine the Figure of the Earth by means of the Pendulum vibrating Seconds in different Latitudes, as well as on various other subjects of Philosophical Inquiry. (Also containing a Brief Account of Capt. Clavering's Voyage to the Arctic Regions.) *Maps.* 4° 1825

—— Report on the Phænomena of Terrestrial Magnetism : being an Abstract of the "Magnetismus der Erde" of Prof. Ch. Hansteen. *Maps.* 8° 1836

—— Report of the Variations of the Magnetic Intensity observed at different points of the Earth's Surface. *Maps.* 8* 1838

—— Discussion of Magnetic Observations made during the Voyages of H.M. ships "Adventure" and "Beagle," 1826-36. 8° 1838

—— Report on the Magnetic Isoclinal and Isodynamic Lines in the British Islands. *Plates.* 8* 1839

—— Observations made at the Magnetic Observatories of Toronto in Canada, Trevandrum in the East Indies, and St Helena, during a remarkable Magnetic Disturbance on the 25th and 26th of September 1841. 8° 1841

—— Observations made at the Magnetical and Meteorological Observatory at Toronto, in Canada, 1840-48 ; with Abstracts of Observations to 1855 inclusive. *Plates.* 4° 1845-57

—— Observations made at the Magnetical and Meteorological Observatory at Hobarton, in Van Diemen Island, and by the Antarctic Naval Expedition, 1841-48; with Abstracts of the Observations from 1841 to 1848 inclusive. 3 vols. *Plates.* 4° 1848-53

—— Observations on Days of Unusual Magnetic Disturbance, made at the British Colonial Magnetic Observatories under the Departments of the Ordnance and Admiralty, 1840-44. Vol. 1. 4° 1851

—— Some of the Results obtained at the British Colonial Magnetic Observatories. 8* 1854

—— On the Magnetic Variation in the Vicinity of the Cape of Good Hope. 8* 1855

—— Results of the Magnetic Observations at the Kew Observatory from 1857 and 1858 to 1862 inclusive. Nos. 1 and 2. *Plates.* 4° 1863

—— Note on a Correspondence between Her Majesty's Government and the President and Council of the Royal Society regarding Meteorological Observations to be made by Sea and Land. 8* 1866

—— *See* Wrangell.

Sabir, C. de. Esquisse Ethnographique des Manègres. 8* *Paris*, 1861

Sachau, Dr Edward. Reise in Syrien und Mesopotamien. *Maps and plates.* 8° *Leipzig*, 1883

—— *See* Alberuni.

Sachs, C. Aus den Llanos : Schilderung einer naturwissenschaftlichen Reise nach Venezuela. *Map and plates.* 8° *Leipzig*, 1879

Sachs, Capt. H. *See* Stumm.

Sacken. *See* Osten Sacken.

Sacy, Baron de. *See* Walckenaer.

Sádik Isfaháni. The Geographical Works of, translated by J. C. from original Persian MSS. in the Collection of Sir William Ouseley, the Editor ; also, "A Critical Essay on various manuscript works, Arabic and Persian, illustrating the History of Arabia, Persia, Turkomania, India, Syria, Egypt, Mauritania, and Spain," translated by J. C. from a Persian manuscript in the same collection. [Oriental Translation Fund.] 8° 1832

Sadler, M. E. *See* Mackinder.

Sadlier, Capt. G. Forster. Diary of a Journey across Arabia, from El Khatif in the Persian Gulf to Yambo in the Red Sea, during the year 1819. Compiled from the Records of the Bombay Government, by P. Ryan. *Map.* 8° *Bombay*, 1866

Sæwulf, Relation des Voyages de, à Jerusalem et en Terre-Sainte, 1102-3. 4° *Paris*, 1839

—— *See* Recueil de Voyages, Vol. 4, p. 611 : Appendix 1.

Safařík, Pawel Josef. Slowansky Národopis. 12° *Prague*, 1849

Safford, James M. Geological Reconnoissance of the State of Tennessee : First Report. 8° *Nashville, Tenn.*, 1856

Sagot, —. Catalogue des Dessins et Plans sur le Mont Saint-Michel. Folio* N.D.

Saillens, R. Nos droits sur Madagascar et nos griefs contre les Hovas examinés impartialement, par R. Saillens ; avec une Préface de M. Frédéric Passy, et un Appendice contenant des Documents Officiels inédits. 8° *Paris*, 1885

Sainsbury, W. Noël. Calendar of State Papers : Colonial Series—East Indies, China, and Japan, 1513-1616, preserved in Her Majesty's Public Record Office and elsewhere. Royal 8° 1862

St André, D. de. Renseignements Nautiques sur les Côtes de Patagonie. 8° *Paris*, 1862

St André, H. Pouget de. La Colonisation de Madagascar sous Louis XV., d'après la Correspondance inédite du Comte de Mandane. 12° *Paris*, 1886

St Bris, Thomas de. Discovery of the Origin of the Name of America. *Illustrations.* 8°   *New York*, 1888

Sainte - Croix, —. Examen Critique des Anciens Historiens d'Alexandre-le-Grand. 2nd edit. *Maps.* 4°   *Paris*, 1810

Saint-Denys, Baron Juchereau de. Considérations Statistiques, Historiques, Militaires, et Politiques, sur la Régence d'Alger. *Map.* 8°   *Paris*, 1831

Saint-Denys, Marquis d'Hervey de. *See* Rosny.

Saint - Hilaire, A. de. Voyages dans l'Intérieur du Brésil. 2 vols. in 4. *Plate.* 8°   *Paris*, 1833

Saint-Hilaire, J. Barthélemy. Egypt and the Great Suez Canal : a Narrative of Travels. 8°   1857

Saint-Hilaire, I. G. *See* Greece, Morea : Appendix 2.

—— L'Inde Anglaise, son état actuel— son avenir ; précédée d'une Introduction sur l' Angleterre et la Russie. 8°   *Paris*, 1887

Sainthill, Richard. An Olla Podrida ; or, Scraps, Numismatic, Antiquarian, and Literary. 2 vols. *Portraits, plates, and facsimiles.* Royal 8°   *Privately printed*, 1844-53

—— Numismatic Crumbs. *Plate.* Royal 8*   1855

St John, Bayle. Village Life in Egypt, with Sketches of the Saïd. 2 vols. 8° 1852

—— Travels of an Arab Merchant in Soudan . . . Abridged from the French. 8°   1854

—— Subalpine Kingdom ; or, Experiences and Studies in Savoy, Piedmont, and Genoa. 2 vols. 8°   1856

Saint John, Earl of. Life and Correspondence. By Capt. E. P. Brenton. 2 vols. *Portrait and map.* 8° · 1838

St John, H. C. Notes and Sketches from the Wild Coasts of Nipon ; with Chapters on Cruising after Pirates in Chinese Waters. *Maps and plates.* Small 8°   *Edinburgh*, 1880

St John, Horace Roscoe. A Life of Christopher Columbus. *Plate.* 16° 1850

—— The Indian Archipelago, its History and Present State. 2 vols. 8° 1853

St John, J. A. History of the Manners and Customs of Ancient Greece. 3 vols. *Maps.* 8°   1842

St John, J. Augustus. Journal of a Residence in Normandy. 8° *Edinburgh*, 1831

St John, James A. *See* Prisse.

St John, O. Notes on the Geology of North-Eastern New Mexico. *Plates.* 8* [*Washington*] 1876

St John, Sir Spenser. Life in the Forests of the Far East. 2 vols. *Maps and plates.* 8°   1862

—— Hayti, or the Black Republic. *Map.* 8°   1884

2 D

St Julian, Charles. Official Report of Central Polynesia ; with a Gazetteer of Central Polynesia, by Edward Reeve, and other documents appended. Folio* *Sydney*, 1857

Saint-Martin, Vivien de. Histoire des Découvertes Géographiques des Nations Européennes dans les Diverses Parties du Monde . . . d'après les sources originales pour chaque Nation, &c. Vols. 2 and 3 : Asie Mineure. *Map.* 8°   *Paris*, 1845-46

—— Recherches sur les Populations Primitives et les plus Anciennes Traditions du Caucase. 8°   *Paris*, 1847

—— Mémoire Historique sur la Géographie Ancienne du Caucase, depuis l'époque des Argonautes jusqu'aux Guerres de Mithridate. 8°   *Paris*, 1847

—— Les Huns Blancs, ou Ephthalites des Historiens Byzantins. 8°   *Paris*, 1849

—— Étude sur la Géographie Grecque et Latine de l'Inde, et en particulier sur l'Inde de Ptolémée. *Maps.* 4° *Paris*, 1858

—— The same. 3ᵐᵉ Mémoire. Le Bassin du Gange. 4°   *Paris*, N.D.

—— Mémoire Analytique sur la Carte de l'Asie Centrale et de l'Inde, construite d'après le Si-yu-ki, &c., pour les Voyages de Hiouen-Thsang, 629-645. *Map.* 8° *Paris*, 1858

—— Étude sur la Géographie et les Populations Primitives du Nord-Ouest de l'Inde, d'après des Hymnes Védiques ; précédé d'un Aperçu de l'état actuel des études sur l'Inde Ancienne. 8° *Paris*, 1860

—— Sur les Anciens Sites de la Tripolitaine. 8*   *Paris*, 1861

—— Le Nord de l'Afrique dans l'Antiquité Grecque et Romaine. Étude Historique et Géographique. *Maps.* Royal 8° *Paris*, 1863

—— Histoire de la Géographie et des Découvertes Geographiques depuis les temps les plus reculés jusqu'à nos jours. Large 8°   *Paris*, 1873

—— Atlas accompanying the same. Folio *Paris*, 1874

—— Nouveau Dictionnaire de Géographie Universelle. 1 (A-C), 2 (D-J), 3 (K-M), 4 (N-Q), 5 (R-S), 6 (SO-Z). 6 vols. 4° ·   *Paris*, 1879-95

—— L'Année Géographique. *See* France, Paris : Appendix 3.

St Matthew. Issal'-Anjilo, kila Matti ye men safè. Mandinga Kangoto. 12° 1837

Saint-Méry, L. E. Moreau de. Description Topographique et Politique de la partie Espagnole de l'île Saint-Domingue, avec des Observations Générales sur le Climat, Population, Productions, &c. 2 vols. 8°   *Philadelphia*, 1796

—— *See* Braam.

Saint Pierre, J. H. B. de. A Voyage to the Isle of France, the Isle of Bourbon, and the Cape of Good Hope. Translated from the French. 8°   1800

Saint-Pol-Lias, Brau de. See Lias.

Saint-Priest, — de. Mémoires sur l'Ambassade de France en Turquie, et sur le Commerce des Français dans le Levant. [No. 7 of Publ. de l'Éc. des Langues Orient. Viv.] 8°   Paris, 1877

Saint-Sauveur, André Grasset, jeune. Voyage Historique, Littéraire, et Pittoresque dans les Isles et Possessiones ci-devant Vénitiennes du Levant; savoir: Corfou, Paxo, Bucintro, Parga, Prevesa, Vonizza, Sainte-Maure, Thiaqui, Céphalonie, Zante, Strophades, Cérigo, et Cérigotte. 3 vols. 8°   Paris, 1810
—— See Phillips, Collection of Modern and Contemporary Voyages and Travels [1], Vol. 8 : Appendix 1.

St Vincent, J. B. G. M. Bory de. Essais sur les Iles Fortunées et l'Atlantique Atlantide, ou Précis de l'Histoire Générale de l'Archipel des Canaries. *Maps.* 4°   *Paris* [1803]
—— Voyage dans les quatre principales Iles des Mers d'Afrique pendant 1801 ; avec l'Histoire de la Traversée du Capit. Baudin jusqu'au Port-Louis de l'Ile Maurice. 3 vols. 8° *Maps and plates.* 4°   *Paris*, 1804
—— See Greece (Morea): Appendix 2; also Phillips [1], Vol. 2 : Appendix 1.

Saker, A. Dualla Lesson Book. No. 2. Cameroons River. 16° *Bimbia*, 1847

Sala, G. Augustus. Journey due North, being Notes of a Residence in Russia in 1856. 8°   1859

Saladin, E. See Fuchs.

Salant, Rev. S. See Montefiore, Sir M.

Salazer, Domingo. See Cartas de Indias: Appendix 1.

Salbanke, Joseph. See Purchas, Vol. 1, Book 3 : Appendix 1.

Saldamando, Enrique Torres. See Eguiluz.

Saldanha da Gama, A. de. Memoria sobre as Colonias de Portugal, situadas na Costa Occidental d'Africa. 8° *Paris*, 1839

Sale, George. The Koran, commonly called the Alkoran of Mohammed. Translated into English from the Original Arabic, with Explanatory Notes taken from the most approved Commentators, to which is prefixed a Preliminary Discourse by George Sale. 8°   N.D.

Salêl-Ibn-Razik. See Hakluyt Soc. Publ., Vol. 44 : Appendix 1.

Salis, A. de. La Correction des Torrents en Suisse : Exposé raisonné d'ouvrages exécutés. Rédigé par ordre du Département Fédéral de l'Intérieur. Première Livraison. *Maps and plates.* 4° *Berne*, 1891

Salis, A. de. Ditto. Deuxième Livraison. *Plates.* 4°   *Berne*, 1892

Salis, C. U. de. Travels through various Provinces of the Kingdom of Naples in 1789. Translated by A. Aufrere. Conchological Appendix. *Maps and plates.* 8°   1795

Salisbury, Stephen, junior. A Partial Index to the Proceedings of the American Antiquarian Society from its Foundation in 1812 to 1880; to which is added a Table of Contents of all the Publications and Reprints of the Society to April 1883, . . . by Nathaniel Paine. 8°
Worcester, Mass., 1883

Salmoiraghi, A. Aperçu sur les Nouveaux Tacheomètres dits les cleps. *Illustrations.* Small folio   *Milan*, 1884

Salmon, N. See Purchas, Vol. 1, Book 4 : Appendix 1.

Salmon, William. A Table for finding the Latitude from the Altitude of the Polar Star, observed at any hour in the Northern Hemisphere. Royal 8*   1850

Salot des Noyers, M. Instructions sur les Iles et les Passages du grand Archipel d'Asie, &c. 5 vols. *Maps.* 8°
Paris, 1867-68
—— Pilote de la Manche. . . Traduit de l'Anglais.
—— See King, J. W.

Salt, Henry. Voyage to Abyssinia, and Travels into the Interior of that Country in 1809-10, in which are included an Account of the Portuguese Settlements on the East Coast of Africa, a Narrative of late events in Arabia Felix, and some particulars respecting the Aboriginal African Tribes extending from Mosambique to the Borders of Egypt, with Vocabularies of their respective Languages. *Maps and plates.* 4°   1814
—— Voyage en Abyssinie, entrepris par ordre du Gouvernement Britannique en 1809-10 ; traduit par F. Henry. 2 vols. 8°, and Atlas oblong 8°   *Paris*, 1816
—— See Eyriès, Vol. 14 : Appendix 1.

Saltijkov, N. Du niveau moyen de la mer Baltique à Cronstadt. [In Russian.] Large 8°   [*St Petersburg*, 1888]

Salvatierra, P. P. See Burney, Vol. 4 : Appendix 1.

Salvator, Archduke Ludwig. See Ludwig.

Salvin, H. Journal written on board His Majesty's ship "Cambridge," from January 1824 to May 1827. *Plate.* Small 8°   *Newcastle*, 1829

Salvin, O. See Central America, A, Biologia Centrali-Americana : Appendix 2.

Salvo, Marquis de. See Phillips, Collection of Modern and Contemporary Voyages and Travels [1], Vol. 6 : Appendix 1.

Salvolini, François. Traduction et Analyse Grammaticale des Inscriptions sculptées sur l'Obélisque Egyptien de Paris. *Plates.* 4° *Paris*, 1837

Salza, Hermann von. *See* Lorck.

Samanez y Ocampo, Jose B. Exploracion de los Rios Peruanos Apurimac, Eni, Tambo ; Ucayali y Urubamba . . . en 1883 y 1884, Diario de la Expedicion. *Map.* 8* *Lima*, 1885

"Samarang." *See* Belcher.

Sampaio, Fr. Xavier R. de. *See* Coleccão de Noticias, Vol. 6, p. 611: Appendix 1.

Sampayo, Lopo Vaz de. *See* Gottfried : Appendix 1.

Samper, José M. Note sur les Sociétés ou Entreprises fondées à Paris pour la Colonisation ou la Canalisation de l'Isthme du Darien. 8* *Paris*, 1862

Sampson, G. Vaughan. Statistical Survey of the County of Londonderry, with Observations of the Means of Improvement. *Maps and plates.* 8° *Dublin*, 1802

Samuelson, James. Roumania, Past and Present. *Maps and illustrations.* 8° 1882

—— Bulgaria, Past and Present : Historical, Political, and Descriptive. *Map and illustrations.* 8° 1888

—— India, Past and Present : Historical, Social, and Political. *Map and illustrations.* 8° 1890

San Bartolomeo. *See* Bartolomeo.

Sancho, Pedro. *See* Hakluyt Soc. Publ., Vol. 47 ; Purchas, Vol. 4 : Appendix 1.

Sandeman, Major. Transliteration of Burmese Words into English. Folio* 1881

Sandeman, Patrick. Monthly Tables of Daily Means of Meteorological Elements, deduced from Observations taken at the Observatory at Georgetown, Demerara, British Guiana, . . . during eleven years commencing 1846. 4° *Greenock*, 1857

Sanderson, G. P. Thirteen Years among the Wild Beasts of India : their Haunts and Habits from Personal Observation ; with an Account of the Modes of Capturing and Taming Elephants. *Maps and plates.* Square 8° 1878

Sanderson, John. *See* Purchas, Vol. 2, Book 9 : Appendix 1.

Sanderson, Percy. Report on the Foreign Trade of Roumania during the year 1883. Folio* 1885

Sandford, H. B. *See* Ogilvy, T. ; Loughman, T. C.

Sandford, Dr H. H., Bishop of Tasmania. A Mutton Bird Island. (From the *New Review*.) 8* 1892

Sands, J. Out of the World ; or, Life in St Kilda. *Plates.* 12° *Edinburgh*, N.D.

Sandwich, John, Earl of. Voyage round the Mediterranean in 1738-39, written by himself ; to which are prefixed Memoirs

Sandwich, John, Earl of—*continued.* of the Noble Author's Life. *Portrait and plates.* 4° 1799

Sandwith, Humphry. A Narrative of the Siege of Kars, and of Travels and Adventures in Armenia and Lazistan ; with Remarks on the Present State of Turkey. 3rd edition. *Frontispiece, map, and plan.* 8° 1856

Sandys, George. A Relation of a Journey begun An. Dom. 1610, containing a Description of the Turkish Empire, Egypt, the Holy Land, the remote parts of Italy and Ilands adjoining. *Map and illustrations.* Folio 1615

—— *See* Purchas, Vol. 2, Book 8 : Appendix 1.

Sandys, John Edwin. An Easter Vacation in Greece ; with Lists of Books on Greek Travel and Topography, and Time-tables of Greek Steamers and Railways. *Map and plan.* 12° 1887

Sanford, H. S. The Different Systems of Penal Codes in Europe ; also a Report on the Administrative Changes in France since the Revolution of 1848. 8° *Washington*, 1854

Sanford, Major —. *See* Jones, Major H.

Sangermano, Rev. Father. Description of the Burmese Empire, compiled chiefly from Native Documents ; translated from the MS. by W. Tandy. (Oriental Translation Fund.) 4° *Rome*, 1833

Sanguinetti, Dr B. R. *See* Ibn Batuta.

Sanjana, Darab Dastur Peshotan. The Position of Zoroastrian Women in Remote Antiquity, as illustrated in the Avesta, the Sacred Books of the Parsees : being a Lecture delivered at Bombay on the 18th of April 1892. 12° *Bombay*, 1892

San Januario, Viscount. Missão do Visconde de San Januario nas Republicas da America do Sul, 1878 e 1879. 8° *Lisbon*, 1880

—— Mission of Viscount San Januario to the Republics of South America, 1878 and 1879. 8* *Buenos Ayres*, 1881

Sans, R. Monner. El Reino de Hawaii : apuntes Geográficos, Historicos, y Estadisticos. *Plan and portrait.* 8° *Barcelona*, 1883

—— Liberia : apuntes Historicos, Geográficos, y Estadisticos. 8* *Barcelona*, 1884

—— Importancia y Necesidad del Estudio de la Geografia : Discurso leido ante la Sociedad Barcelonesa de Amigos de la Instruccion en la recepción pública del socio D. R. Monner Sans. Large 8* *Barcelona*, 1887

Sans, Rafael. Biblioteca Boliviana de Geografia e Historia. II. Memoria Histórica del Colegio de Misiones de San José de la Paz. *Map and plates.* 8° *La Paz*, 1888

Sanson, Joseph. *See* Phillips, New Voyages and Travels [3], Vol. 3: Appendix 1.

Sanson, N. Géographie de l'Europe. *Maps.* 4° *Paris*, N.D.

Sansovino, Francesco. Venetia Città nobilissima et singolare descritta, con aggiunta da G. Martinioni. Small 4° *Venice*, 1663

Santarem, Vicomte de. L'Introduction des Procédés relatifs à la Fabrication des Étoffes de Soie dans la Péninsule Hispanique, sous la Domination des Arabes. 8* *Paris*, 1838

—— Analyse du Journal de la Navigation de la Flotte qui est allée à la Terre du Brésil en 1530-32, par Pedro Lopes de Sousa. 8* 1840

—— Memoria sobre a Prioridade dos Descobrimentos Portuguezes na Costa d'Africa Occidental. 8° *Paris*, 1841

—— Recherches sur la Priorité de la Découverte des Pays situés sur la Côte Occidentale d'Afrique, au-delà du Cap Bojador, et sur les Progrès de la Science Géographique après les Navigations des Portugais au XVᵉ Siècle. 8° *Paris*, 1842

—— Sur la Véritable Date des Instructions données à un des Premiers Capitaines qui sont allés dans l'Inde après Cabral. 8* *Paris*, 1846

—— Rapport sur un Mémoire de M. de Silveira, relativement à la Découverte des Terres du Prêtre Jean et de la Guinée par les Portugais. 8* *Paris*, 1846

—— Rapport sur l'Ouvrage de M. Lopes de Lima, "Essais Statistiques sur les Possessions Portugaises en Outre-Mer." 8* *Paris*, 1846

—— Examen des Assertions contenues dans un Opuscule, intitulé, "Sur la Publication des Monuments de la Géographie," 1847. 8* *Paris*, 1847

—— Mémoire sur la question de savoir à quelle Époque l'Amérique Méridionale a cessé d'être représentée dans les Cartes Géographiques comme une île d'une grande étendue. 8* *Paris*, 1847

—— Notice sur la Vie et les Travaux de Da Cunha Barbosa. 8* *Paris*, 1847

—— Essai sur l'Histoire de la Cosmographie et de la Cartographie pendant le Moyen-Age, et sur les Progrès de la Géographie après les grandes Découvertes du XVᵉ Siècle, pour servir d'Introduction et d'Explication à l'Atlas composé de Mappemonde et de Portulans, et d'autres Monuments Géographiques, depuis le VIᵉ Siècle de notre ère jusqu'au XVIIᵉ. 3 vols. 8° *Paris*, 1849-52

—— Statement of Facts, proving the Right of the Crown of Portugal to the Territories situated on the Western Coast of Africa lying between the fifth degree and twelve minutes, and the

Santarem, Vicomte de—*continued.* eighth degree of South latitude. Translated from the Portuguese. 8° 1856

—— Quadro Elementar das Relações Politicas e Diplomaticas de Portugal, com as diversas Potencias do Mundo, desde o principio do XVI. Seculo da Monarchia Portugueza ate 'aos nossos dias ; continuado e dirigido pelo Socio da Academia Real das Sciencias de Lisboa Luiz Augusto Rebello da Silva. Vols. 1, 2 (1842) ; Vols. 3, 4 (1843) ; Vol. 4 pte. 2ª (1844) ; Vol. 5 (1845) ; Vols. 6 (1850) and 7 (1851) in one ; Vol. 8 (1853) ; Vol. 9 (1854) ; Vol. 15 (1854) ; Vol. 16 (1858) ; Vol. 17 (1859) ; Vol. 18 (1860). 8° *Paris and Lisbon*

—— Memoria sobre o Estabelecimento de Macau. 8° *Lisbon*, 1879

—— Recherches Historiques, Critiques, et Bibliographiques sur Améric Vespuce et ses Voyages. 8° *Paris*, N.D.

—— Notice sur Plusieurs Monuments Géographiques inédits du Moyen Age et du XVIᵉ Siècle que se Trouvent dans quelques Bibliothèques de l'Italie, avec Notes. 8* *Paris*, N.D.

Sante, Gerret van. Alphabetische Naam-Lyst van alle de Groenlandsche en Straat-Davissche Commandeurs, die zedert het Jaar 1700 op Groenland, en zedert het Jaar 1719 op de Straat-Davis, voor Holland en andere Provincien hebben gevaaren. *Plate.* 4° *Haarlem*, 1770

Santesson, Henrik. *See* Sweden, A : Appendix 2.

Santos, João dos. Ethiopia Oriental, e varia Historia de coosas notaucis do Oriente. Small folio *Evora*, 1609

—— Ethiopia Oriental. [Reprint in the Bibliotheca de Classicos Portuguezes.] 12° *Lisbon*, 1891

—— *See* Pinkerton, Vol. 16 ; Purchas, Vol. 2, Book 9 : Appendix 1.

Santvoort, J. Schouw. Plan van een Onderzoekingstocht in Midden-Sumatra. [Tijds. Aardrijks. Genoots. Biibladen. Eerste Deel. 1.] *Maps.* 4* *Amsterdam*, 1876

Sapeto, Prof. Guiseppe. Viaggio e Missione Cattolica fra i Mensâ i Bogos e gli Habab, con un cenno geografico e storico dell'Abissinia. 8° *Rome*, 1857

—— Etiopia. *Map.* 12° *Rome*, 1890

Sapunov, Y. The River Western Duna : historical and geographical sketch. [In Russian.] *Maps.* *Vitebsk*, 1893

Sarauw, C. von. *See* Central Asia, B : Appendix 2.

Sarbadhicary, S. A Sojourn in India : her Manners, Customs, Religion and its Origin. 12° 1890

Sargeaunt, Lieut.-Col., R. A. Administration Report on the Railways in India for 1892-93. *Maps.* Folio 1893

Sargent, Charles S. *See* United States, A (Tenth Census, Vol. 9) : Appendix 2.

Sargent, Winthrop. Plan of an Ancient Fortification at Marietta, Ohio ; with Introduction by H. I. Bowditch. [2 *leaves, and plans.*] 4* N.P., N.D.

Saris, John. *See* Astley, Vol. 1 ; Gottfried ; Kerr, Vol. 8 ; Purchas, Vol. 1 ; Allgemeine Historie, Vol. 1 : Appendix 1.

Saritschev, —. *See* Sarychef,

Sarmento, Dr F. M. *See* Portugal, Lisbon : Appendix 3.

Sarmento, Affonso de Moraes. Chemin de Fer du Zambèze. *Map and tables.* 4* *Lisbon,* 1889

Sarmiento, P. *See* Burney, Vol. 2 ; Callander, Vol. 1 ; Gottfried ; Laharpe, Vol. 15 ; Allgemeine Historie, Vol. 12 : Appendix 1.

Sars, Prof. Georg Ossian. Norges Ferskvandskrebsdyr. Förste Afsnit. Branchiopoda. 1 Cladocera Ctenopoda, &c. *Plates.* 4* *Christiania,* 1865
—— *See* Norway, North Atlantic Expedition ; United Kingdom, H, Challenger Reports : Appendix 2.

Sars, Michael. Om Siphonodentalium Vitreum, en ny slægt og art af dentalidernes familie. *Plates.*
Christiania, 1861
—— Beskrivelse over Lophogaster Typicus, en Mærkværdig form af de Lavere Tiföddede Krebsdyr. *Plates.* 4*
Christiania, 1862
—— Om de i Norge forekommende fossile Dyrelevninger fra quartærperioden, et Bidrag til vor Faunas Historie. *Plates.* 4* *Christiania,* 1865
—— Mémoires pour servir à la connaissance des Crinoïdes Vivants. *Plates.* 4* *Christiania,* 1868
—— Michael Sars. Nogle Træk af en Naturforskers Levnet og Arbeider. Biografi af P. Chr. Asbjörnsen. Small 8* *Copenhagen,* 1870
—— **and T. Kjerulf.** Jagttagelser over den Postpliocene eller Glaciale Formation i en del af det sydlige Norge. *Map.* 4* *Christiania,* 1860

Sartori, Fr. Naturwunder des Oesterreichischen Kaiserthumes. 4 vols. *Plates.* 12° *Vienna,* 1810

Sartorius, C. Importancia de México para la Emigracion Alemana, traducida del Aleman por Augustin S. de Tagle. *Map.* 8* *Mexico,* 1852
—— Mexico and the Mexicans : Landscapes and Popular Sketches. *Plates.* 4° 1859

Sarychef or (Sarytschew), Capt. Voyages along the N.E. Coast of Siberia, and Arctic and Pacific Oceans, during eight years with the Geographical and Astronomical Expedition under the command

Sarychef (or Sarytschew), Capt.—*contd.* of Capt. Billings from 1785 to 1793. [In Russian.] 2 vols. *Maps and plates.* 4° *St Petersburg,* 1802
—— *See* Phillips, Collection of Modern and Contemporary Voyages and Travels [1], Vol. 5 : Appendix 1.
—— **and Billings.** *See* Eyriès, Vol. 6 : Appendix 1.

Sass, H. A Journey to Rome and Naples, performed in 1817 ; giving an account of the present state of Society in Italy, and containing Observations on the Fine Arts. 8° 1818

Sathas, C. *See* Machéras.

Satow, Sir Ernest Mason. Essay towards a Bibliography of Siam. 8° *Singapore,* 1886
—— The Jesuit Mission Press in Japan, 1591-1610. *Plates.* 4° 1888
—— *See* Murray's Handbook for Japan ; *also* Siam : Appendix 2.
—— **and Lieut. A. G. S. Hawes.** A Handbook for Travellers in Central and Northern Japan : being a Guide to Tōkiō, Kiōto, Ozaka, and other cities, the most interesting parts of the main island between Kōbe and Awomari ; with ascents of the principal mountains, and descriptions of Temples, Historical Notes and Legends. *Maps and plans.* 12° *Yokohama,* 1881
—— A Review and Supplement to Messrs Satow and Hawes' Handbook for Travellers in Central and Northern Japan. Reprinted from the *Japan Daily Herald,* November 1884. 12* [N.P., 1884]
—— **and Ishibashi Masakata.** *See* Dictionaries, B, Japanese : Appendix 2.

Sauer, Martin. Account of a Geographical and Astronomical Expedition to the Northern parts of Russia for ascertaining the degrees of Latitude and Longitude of the mouth of the River Kolima, of the Coast of the Tshutski to East Cape, and of the Islands in the Eastern Ocean, stretching to the American Coast. *Map and plates.* 4° 1802

Saugnier, —. Relations de plusieurs voyages à la Cote d'Afrique, à Maroc, au Sénégal, à Gorée, à Galam, &c. Tirée des Journaux de M. Saugnier, &c. 8° *Paris,* 1792
—— **and — Brisson.** Voyages to the Coast of Africa : containing an account of their shipwreck on board different vessels, and subsequent slavery. Translated from the French. *Map.* 8° 1792

Saulcy, F. de. Narrative of a Journey round the Dead Sea and in the Bible lands in 1850 and 1851. Edited with Notes by Count Edward de Warren. 2 vols. *Map and plate.* 8° 1853

Saulcy, F. de. The same, including an account of the Discovery of the Sites of Sodom and Gomorrah. Edited by Count Edward de Warren. New edition. 2 vols. *Map and plate.* 8°   1854
—— Jérusalem. *Plan and plates.* Large 8°   *Paris*, 1882
Saulnier, —. *See* Phillips, New Voyages and Travels [3], Vol. 8 : Appendix 1.
Saunders, Forster C. G. Beneath Parnassian Clouds and Olympian Sunshine. Crown 8°   1887
Saunders, R. *See* Turner, S.
Saunders, Trelawny W. The Asiatic Mediterranean and its Australian Port : the Settlement of Port Flinders, and the Province of Albert, in the Gulf of Carpentaria, practically proposed. *Maps and plates.* Small 8°   1853
—— A Sketch of the Mountains and River Basins of India ; in two Maps, with Explanatory Memoirs. 8*   1870
—— *See* Hassenstein ; *also* Turkey in Asia, B : Appendix 2.
Saunders, W. Through the Light Continent, or the United States in 1877-78. 8°   1879
Sauseuil, Chevalier de. *See* Villehuet.
Saussure, H. de. Coup d'œil sur l'Hydrologie du Mexique, principalement de la partie Orientale, accompagné de quelques Observations sur la Nature Physique de ce pays. 8°   *Geneva*, 1862
—— La Suisse à l'Exposition de Géographie de Paris. 8*   *Geneva*, 1876
—— *See* "Novara."
Saussure, Horace Benedict de. Voyages dans les Alpes, précédés d'un Essai sur l'Histoire Naturelle des Environs de Genève. 4 vols. *Map and plates.* 4°   *Neuchâtel*, 1786-96
—— Observations Meteorologiques faites au Col du Géant du 5 au 18 juillet 1788. *Portrait and plate.* 4*   *Geneva*, 1891
—— *See* Pinkerton, Vol. 4 : Appendix 1.
Saussure, L. A. N. de. *See* Phillips, New Voyages and Travels [3], Vols. 6, 8 : Appendix 1.
Sauter, E. *See* Hochstetter, F. von.
Sauvage, —. *See* Milliroux.
Savary, M. Letters on Egypt ; with a Parallel between the Manners of its Ancient and Modern Inhabitants, &c., and an Account of the Descent of St Lewis at Damietta. Extracted from Joinville, and Arabian authors. 2 vols. *Maps.* 8°   1786
Savile, Capt. A. R. *See* United Kingdom, G, War Office Publications : Appendix 2.
Saville, Marshall H. The Ruins of Labna, Yucatan. (From No. 12, Vol. 1, of "The Archæologist.") *Plate.* 8*   *Waterloo, Ind.*, 1893
Saville-Kent, W. The Great Barrier Reef of Australia, its Products and Potentialities ; containing an account,

Saville-Kent, W. —*continued.*
with copious coloured and photographic illustrations, of the corals and coral reefs, pearl and pearl shell, bêche-de-mer, other fishing industries, and the marine fauna of the Australian Great Barrier region. *Map and plates.* 4°   [1893]
Sawkins, J. G. *See* Wall, G. P.
Sawyer, Lieut. F. E. *See* United States, E, *a* : Appendix 2.
Sawyer, Major H. A. Report of a Reconnaissance in the Bakhtiari country, South-West Persia. *Maps, sections, &c.* 8°   *Simla*, 1891
Sax, C. Ethnographische Karte der Europäischen Türkei und ihrer Dependenzen zur Zeit des Kriegsausbruches im Jahre 1877. 8°   *Vienna*, 1878
Saxe - Weimar - Eisenach, Bernard, Duke of. Précis de la Campagne de Java en 1811. *Maps and plans.* 8°   *The Hague*, 1834
Say, Thomas. Descriptions of New Species of Heteropterous Hemiptera of North America ; and a Correspondence relative to the Insect which destroys the Cotton Plant. 8*   N.P., N.D.
—— *See* James, E. J.
Sayce, Prof. A. H. *See* Schliemann.
Sayer, H. *See* Astley, Vol. 1 ; Allgemeine Historie, Vol. 1 : Appendix 1.
Scacchi, Arcangelo. Sopra le Specie di Silicati del Monte di somma e del Vesuvio, le taluni casi sono state prodotte per effetto di sublimazioni. 4*   *Naples*, 1852
—— *See* Palmieri.
Scandrett, W. B. Southland and its Resources : being a Paper on the Resources of the District of Southland, Otago. 8*   *Invercargill, N.Z.*, 1883
Scarabelli - Gommi - Flaminj, G. Sulla probabilità che il sollevamento delle Alpi siasi effettuato sopra una linea curva. *Map.* 8*   *Florence*, 1866
Scaramucci, Francesco, and Enrico H. Giglioli. Notizie sui Danakil e più Specialmente su quelli di Assab. 8* 1884
Scarlett, Hon. P. Campbell. South America and the Pacific : comprising a Journey across the Pampas and the Andes, from Buenos Ayres to Valparaiso, Lima, and Panama ; with Remarks upon the Isthmus. 2 vols. *Maps and plates.* 8°   1838
Scarpellini, E. F. Memorandum di la Scienza l'Istmo di Suez : Il Sommo Pontefice Pio IX. visitando nel 1857 i suoi Dominii ; il Nuovo Porto di Roma. *Plates.* 4*   *Rome*, 1858
Schabus, J. *See* Pohl.
Schacht, Theodor. Lehrbuch der Geografie alter und neuer Zeit, mit besonderer Rücksicht auf Politische und Kulturgeschichte. *Maps and plates.* 8°   *Mayence*, 1841

Schaep, H. C. *See* Burney, Vol. 3 : Appendix 1.

Schafhäutl, Karl. Die Geologie in ihrem Verhältnisse zu den übrigen Naturwissenschaften. 4* *Munich*, 1843
—— Geognostische Untersuchungen des Südbayerischen Alpengebirges. *Maps and plates.* 8° *Munich*, 1851

Schalow, H. *See* Böhm.

Scharenberg, W. Handbuch für Sudeten-Reisende. *Maps.* 12° *Breslau*, 1850

Scharf, G. *See* Wordsworth.

Scharrer, Jean. *See* Mainberger.

Schaub, Ch. Réfutation de l'Ouvrage de M. Jacques Replat, intitulé "Note sur le Passage d'Annibal, et Défense de l'Opinion de De Luc, d'après lequel Annibal a franchi le petit Saint-Bernard." *Map.* 12* *Geneva*, 1854
—— Excursion en Morée en 1840. 8° *Geneva*, 1859

Schaub, F. Magnetische Beobachtungen im östlichen Theile des Mittelmeeres, ausgeführt im 1857. 4° *Trieste*, 1858

Schauenburg, Ed. Reisen in Central-Afrika, von Mungo Park bis auf Dr H. Barth und Dr Ed. Vogel. Vol. 1—Park, Clapperton, und Lander. *Map and portraits.* 8° *Lahr*, 1859

Schefer, Charles. Histoire de l'Asie Centrale, par Mir Abdoul Kerim Boukhary. . . . Texte Persan et Traduction Français. 2 vols. [L'Ec. Langues Orient. Viv.] Large 8° *Paris*, 1876
—— Relation du Voyage de Nassiri Khosrau en Syrie, en Palestine, en Égypte, en Arabie, et en Perse, pendant les Années de l'Hégire 437-444. *Illustrations.* Large 8° *Paris*, 1881
—— La Voyage de la Saincte Cyté de Hierusalem, avec la Description des Lieux, Portz, Villes, Citez, et aultres Passaiges fait l'an mil quatre cens quatre vingtz ; estant le siege du grant Turc à Rhodes et regnant en France Loys unziesme de cenom. Large 8° *Paris*, 1882
—— Chrestomathie Persane, 2 vols. [Vols. 7 and 8, 2nd Series Publ. de l'Ec. des Langues Orient. Viv.] Large 8° *Paris*, 1883 and 1885
—— *See* Odoric de Pordenone ; Parmentier ; Possot ; Riza, Qouly Khan ; Thenaud ; Varthema.

Scheffer, John. The History of Lapland. *Plates.* Folio *Oxford*, 1674

Schele, Aug. Das Aufnehmen des Terrains und dessen Darstellung durch Projection Horizontaler Flächen. 8° *Stuttgart*, 1852

Schellong, Dr O. Die Jābim-Sprache der Finschhafener Gegend. N.O. Neu-Guinea, Kaiser Wilhelmsland. 8° *Leipzig*, 1890
—— Beiträge zur Anthropologie der Papuas. *Plates.* Large 8° 1891

Schenk, Dr A. *See* Richthofen.

Schermerhorn, Louis Y., and B. Holden. *See* United States, H, *a* : Appendix 2.

Scherzer, Karl von. Travels in the Free States of Central America : Nicaragua, Honduras, and San Salvador. 2 vols. *Maps.* 8° 1857
—— Narrative of the Circumnavigation of the Globe by the Austrian frigate "Novara" (Commodore B. von Wüllerstorf-Urbair), . . . in the years 1857-59. 3 vols. *Maps and woodcuts.* Royal 8° 1861
—— Aus dem Natur- und Völkerleben im tropischen Amerika. Skizzenbuch. 8° *Leipzig*, 1864
—— Fachmännische Berichte über die österreichisch - ungarische Expedition nach Siam, China, und Japan, 1868-71. *Map and diagrams.* Large 8° *Stuttgart*, 1872
—— La Province de Smyrne, considérée au point de vue Géographique, Économique, et Intellectuel ; traduit de l'Allemand par Ferdinand Silas. *Maps, &c.* 8° *Vienna*, 1873
—— Die wirthschaftlichen Zustände Smyrna's im Jahre 1874. 8* *Vienna*, 1875
—— Das wirthschaftliche Leben der Völker : ein Handbuch über Production und Consum. Large 8° *Leipzig*, 1885
—— *See* "Novara ;" Wagnerm ; Wüllerstorf ; Ximenez.
—— **and Eduard Bratassevic.** Der wirthschaftliche Verkehr der Gegenwart. 8° *Vienna*, 1891
—— **and Ed. Schwarz.** On Measurements as a Diagnostic Means for distinguishing the Human Races. 4* *Sydney*, 1858

Scheuchzer, J. G. *See* Kaempfer.

Scheuchzer, J. J. Ouresiphoites Helveticus, sive Itinera per Helvetiæ Alpinas Regiones facta annis 1702-11. 4 vols. in 2. *Map and plates.* 4° *Leyden*, 1723

Schickritter, B. von. *See* Lees, G. R.

Schiern, F. De la notion des lacs du Nil chez les Anciens. 8* *Copenhagen*, 1866
—— Sur l'Origine de la Tradition des Fourmis qui ramassent l'Or. [Also in Danish and German.] 8* *Copenhagen*, 1873
—— Le Pays des Plumes : Remarques sur quelques passages du 4° livre d'Hérodote. [Also in Danish.] 8* *Copenhagen*, 1875
—— Sur l'Origine de quelques Traditions Ottomanes. [Also in Danish.] 8* *Copenhagen*, 1878

Schiffner, Albert. Beschreibung von Sachsen, und der Ernestinischen, Reussischen und Schwarzburgischen Lande. *Maps and plates.* 8° *Stuttgart*, 1840

Schildtberger, John. *See* Hakluyt Soc. Publ., Vol. 58 ; Kerr, Vol. 1 : Appendix 1.

424   SCH.

Schill, Julius. Geologische Beschreibung der Umgebungen von Ueberlingen. *Map and plate.* 4° *Carlsruhe,* 1859

Schillemans, L. Notice sur l'Annam. 4* [*Paris*] 1885

Schilling, Andrew. See Gottfried: Appendix 1.

Schimidel, Hulderico. *See* Schmidel.

Schiner, —. Description du Départment du Simplon, ou de la ci-devant République du Valais. 8° *Sion,* 1812

Schiner, J. L. *See* "Novara," Official Publications, Zoology.

Schinz, Dr Hans. Deutsch- Südwest-Afrika. Forschungsreisen durch die deutschen Schutzgebiete Gross- Nama-und Hereroland, nach dem Kunene, dem Ngamisee und der Kalahari, 1884-1887. *Map and illustrations.* 8° *Oldenburg* [1891]

Schio, A. da. Di due Astrolabi in caratteri cufici occidentali trovati in Valdagno (Veneto). *Plates.* 4° *Venice,* 1880

Schippan, H. A. Vorlegeblätter zur Belehrung im Situationzeichnen und als Vorbereitung zum Aufnehmen. *Maps and plates.* 4° *Freiberg,* 1819

Schirlitz, S. C. Handbuch der alten Geographie für Schulen. *Maps.* 8° *Halle,* 1837

Schirmer, Dr Henri. Le Sahara. *Maps and illustrations.* 8° *Paris,* 1893

Schirren, C. Der Niandsha und die hydrographischen Merkmale Afrika's. *Map.* Royal 8° *Riga,* 1856

Schläfli, Alexander. Mittheilungen Schweizerischer Reisender. Part 2. Reisen in den Orient. *Map.* Royal 8° *Winterthur,* 1864

Schlagintweit, Adolph and Hermann. Untersuchungen über die physicalische Geographie der Alpen, in ihren Beziehungen zu den Phaenomenen der Gletscher, zur Geologie, Meteorologie, und Pflanzengeographie. *Maps and plates.* Large 8° *Leipzig,* 1850

—— Hypsometrische Bestimmungen in den östlichen Alpen. 4* *Leipzig,* 1850

—— Observations sur la Hauteur du Mont-Rose, et des points principaux de ses Environs. *Plates.* 4* *Turin,* 1853

—— Épreuves de Cartes Géographiques produites par la Photographie d'après les Reliefs du Mont-Rose et de la Zugspitze. *Plates.* 4* *Leipzig,* 1854

—— Hypsometrische Bestimmungen in den westlichen Alpen. 4* *Leipzig,* 1854

—— Ueber die Temperatur des Bodens und der Quellen in den Alpen. 8* N.D.

—— **Adolph, Hermann, and Robert.** Results of a Scientific Mission to India and High Asia, undertaken between the years 1854 and 1858 by Order of the Court of Directors of the Hon. East

Schlagentweit, Adolph, Hermann, and Robert—*continued.* India Company. 4 vols. 4°; Atlas, 3 parts imperial folio *Leipzig and London,* 1861-66

CONTENTS.

Vol. 1.—Astronomical Determinations of Latitudes and Longitudes, and Magnetic Observations.

Vol. 2.—General Hypsometry of India, the Himalaya, and Western Tibet, with Sections across the Chains of the Karakorum and Kuenluen.

Vol. 3.—Route-Book of the Western Parts of the Himalaya, Tibet, and Central Asia; and Geographical Glossary from the Languages of India and Tibet, &c.

Vol. 4.—Meteorology of India. First part.

Schlagintweit, Emil. Buddhism in Tibet, illustrated by Literary Documents and Objects of Religious Worship; with an Account of the Buddhist Systems preceding it in India. *Plates.* Royal 8° *Leipzig,* 1863

—— Indien in Wort und Bild: eine Schilderung des Indischen Kaiserreiches. 2 vols. *Map and plates.* Folio *Leipzig,* 1880-81

—— Ueber den Namen des höchsten Berges der Erde. 4* [*Gotha*] 1888

Schlagintweit, Hermann. Untersuchungen über die Vertheilung der Mittleren Jahres-Temperatur in den Alpen. 4* *Munich,* 1850

—— Neue Daten über den Todestag von Adolph v. Schlagintweit, nebst Bemerkungen über Mussàlmàn'sche Zeitrechnung. 8* *Munich,* 1869

—— Bericht über Anlage des Herbariums während der Reisen, nebst Erläuterung der topographischen Angaben. 4° *Munich,* 1876

—— Ueber das Auftreten von Bor-Verbindungen in Tibet. 8* *Munich,* 1878

—— Meteorologische Untersuchungen. Dritter Theil. 4* N.P., N.D.

—— Ueber Messinstrumente, mit constanten Winkeln (Linsen und Prismenporrhometer). *Plate.* 8* N.P., N.D.

Schlagintweit, Robert von. Die Pacifischen Eisenbahnen in Nord Amerika. (Ergänzungsheft, 82—Petermann's Mittheilungen). *Map.* 4° *Gotha,* 1886

Schlegel, Gustave. Atlas Céleste Chinois et Grec, d'après le Tien-Youen-Li-li. *Plates* 1 to 7. Oblong 4° *The Hague,* 1875

—— "Sing Chin Khao Youen." Uranographie Chinose, ou preuves directes que l'Astronomie primitive est originaire de la Chine, et qu'elle a été empruntée par les anciens peuples occidentaux à la sphère Chinoise. Parts 1 and 2. *Table.* 4° *The Hague,* 1875

Schlegel, Gustave. Problèmes Géographiques. Les Peuples Étrangers chez les Historiens Chinois. II. Wen-Chin Kouo, Le Pays des Tatoués. III. Niu Kouo, Le Pays des Femmes. Small 4* *Leyden*, 1892
—— Ditto. IV. Siao-jin Kouo: Le Pays des Petits Hommes. V. Ta-han-Kouo: Le Pays de Tahan (de l'Est). VI. Ta-jin-Kouo, ou Tchang-jin-kouo: Le Pays des Hommes grands ou longs. VII. Kium-tsze-Kouo: Le Pays des Gentils-hommes. VIII. Pêh-min-Kouo: Le Pays du peuple Blanc. Small 4* *Leyden*, 1893
—— Ditto. IX. Ts'ing-K'ieou Kouo: Les Pays des Collines vertes. X. Heh-Tchi-Kouo: Le Pays aux Dents Noires. XI. Hiouen-Kou-Kouo: Le pays des Cuisses noires. XII. Lo-min Kouo, ou Kiao-min Kouo: Le pays du peuple Lo, ou du peuple Kiâo. Small 4* *Leyden*, 1893
—— La Stèle Funéraire du Teghin Giogh et ses Copistes et traducteurs Chinois, Russes, et Allemands. *Facsimile plate.* Large 8° *Helsingfors*, 1892
Schleicher, A. W. Afrikanische Petrefakten. Ein Versuch die grammatischen Bildungen und Formwurzeln der Afrikanischen Sprachen durch Sprachvergleichung. 8* *Berlin*, 1891
Schleinitz, Freiherr von. See "Gazelle."
Schleisner, P. A. Island undersögt fra et Lægevidenskabeligt Synspunkt. *Plates.* 8° *Copenhagen*, 1849
Schlenker, C. F. Collection of Temné Traditions, Fables, and Proverbs, with an English Translation; to which is appended a Temné-English Vocabulary. 8° 1861
—— Grammar of the Temné Language. 8° 1864
Schlesinger, Dr L. See Germany, C (Forschungen, Vol. 2): Appendix 2.
Schley, Commander W. S., and Prof. J. R. Soley. The Rescue of Greely. *Maps and illustrations.* 8° [1885]
Schlichthorst, Hermann. Geographia Africæ Herodotea. 8° *Gottingen*, 1788
Schliemann, H. Troy and its Remains: a Narrative of Researches and Discoveries made on the site of Ilium and in the Trojan plain. Edited by Philip Smith. *Maps, plans, and plates.* 8° 1875
—— Mycenæ: a Narrative of Researches and Discoveries at Mycenæ and Tiryns. Preface by W. E. Gladstone. *Maps and plates.* 8° 1878
—— Ilios: the City and Country of the Trojans; the Results of Researches and Discoveries on the Site of Troy and throughout the Troad in the years 1871-72-73-78-79; including an Autobiography of the Author; with a Preface, Appendices, and Notes. *Maps, plans, and plates.* 8° 1880

Schliemann, H. Troja: Results of the Latest Researches and Discoveries on the Site of Homer's Troy, and in the Heroic Tumuli and other sites, made in the year 1882; and a Narrative of a Journey in the Troad in 1881. Preface by Prof. A. H. Sayce. *Maps and illustrations.* 8° 1884
—— Tiryns: the Prehistoric Palace of the Kings of Tiryns; the Result of the Latest Excavations. The Preface by Dr Wm. Dörpfeld. *Map, plans, and illustrations.* Crown 4° 1886 [1885]
Schmarda, Ludwig K. Die geographische Verbreitung der Thiere. *Map.* 8° *Vienna*, 1853
Schmelck, Ludwig. See Norway, A, North Atlantic Expedition: Appendix 2.
Schmeller, Dr. Ueber Valentin Fernandez Alemaõ und seine Sammlung von Nachrichten über die Entdeckungen, und Besitzungen der Portugiesen in Afrika und Asien bis zum Jahre 1508. 4° *Munich*, N.D.
Schmick, H. Zur Frage der Meeres-Circulation. 8* N.P., N.D.
Schmid, — von. Hydrotechnische Beschreibung des Weichselstroms, vornehmlich innerhalb des Preussischen Gebiets bis Montauer Spitze. *Maps and plates.* Folio* *Berlin*, 1858
—— Der Elbing-Oberländische Canal. *Map.* 4* *Berlin*, 1861
Schmeltz, J. D. E., and Dr R. Krause. Die Ethnographisch - Anthropologische Abtheilung des Museum Godeffroy in Hamburg. *Map and plates.* 8° *Hamburg*, 1881
Schmidel (or Schmidt), Ulrich. Historia y descubrimiento de el Rio de La Plata, y Paraguay. Folio N.P., N.D.
—— See Gottfried; Hakluyt Soc. Publ., Vol. 81; Purchas, Vol. 4, Book 7; Ternaux-Compans, Vol. 5: Appendix 1.
Schmidl, Adolf A. Der Schneeberg in Unter Oesterreich. *Plate Vienna*, 1831
—— Rudolph von Jenny's Handbuch für Reisende in dem Oesterreichischen Kaiserstaate. 4 vols. in 3. 12° *Vienna*, 1834-36
—— Wien's Umgebungen auf zwanzig Stunden im Umkreise; nach eigenen Wanderungen geschildert. 3 vols. *Map and plates.* 12° *Vienna*, 1835
—— Das Kaiserthum Oesterreich: I. Die Alpenländer; 1. Die gefürstete Grafschaft Tirol mit Vorarlberg. *Plates.* 8* *Stuttgart*, 1837
—— The same. 3. Das Herzogthum Steiermark. 8* *Stuttgart*, 1839
—— Wien und seine nächsten Umgebungen in malerischen Original-Ansichten, nach der Natur aufgenommen und in Stahl gestochen von verschiedenen Künstlern. *Plates.* 8° *Vienna*, 1847
—— Ueber Begriffsbestimmungen in der Geographie. 8* 1849

Schmidl, Adolf A. Reise-Notizen zu Kunst und Altherthum. 8* *Vienna*, 1850
—— Handbuch der Geographie des Oesterreichischen Kaiserstaates. 8°
Vienna, 1850
—— Ueber den unterirdischen Lauf der Recca. *Map.* 8* 1851
—— Die Grotten und Höhlen von Adelsberg, Lueg, Planina, und Laas. 8°
Vienna, 1854
—— Guide du Voyageur dans la Grotte d'Adelsberg et les Cavernes Voisines du Karst. Traduit par Obermayer. *Maps.* 12* *Vienna*, 1854
—— Der Mons Cetius des Ptolemäus. 8*
Vienna, 1856
—— Die Baradla-Höhle bei Aggetelek und die Lednica-Eishöhle bei Szilitze im Gömörer Comitate Ungarns. 8*
Vienna, 1857
—— Die Höhlen des Oetscher. *Plates.* 8* *Vienna*, 1857
—— Wegweiser in die Adelsberger Grotte und die benachbarten Höhlen des Karstes. *Maps.* 12* *Vienna*, 1858
—— Wien und seine nächsten Umgebungen mit besonderer Berücksichtigung wissenschaftlicher Anstalten und Sammlungen. *Map.* 12° *Vienna*, 1858
—— Die Oesterreichischen Höhlen; eine geographische Skizze. 8* *Budapest*, 1858
Schmidt, A. Meine Reise in Usaramo und den Deutschen Schutzgebieten Central Ostafrikas. 8* *Berlin*, 1886
Schmidt, Prof. Dr Carl. Das Wasser des Baikal-Sees. 8* *St Petersburg*, 1877
—— Boden- und Wasser-Untersuchungen aus dem Ferghana- und Ssyr-Darja-Gebiete. 4* *St Petersburg*, 1881
——Hydrologische Untersuchungen. XLIV. Die Thermalwasser Kamtschatkas. *Map.* 4* *St Petersburg*, 1885
—— **and F. Dohrandt.** Wassermenge und Suspensionsschlamm des Amu-Darja in seinem Unterlaufe. *Plate.* 4* *St Petersburg*, 1877
Schmidt, F. Einige Bemerkungen zu Prof. A. v. Nordenskjöld's Reisewerk, die Umsegelung Asiens und Europa's auf der Vega, 1878-80; mit besonderer Beziehung auf die Geschichte der Russischen Entdeckungsreisen im und am Sibirischen Eismeer. 8°
St Petersburg, 1883
—— *See* Helmersen and Schrenck, 6; Schrenck and Schmidt.
—— **P. v. Glehn, and A. D. Brylkin.** Reisen im Gebiete des Amurstromes und auf der Insel Sachalin. [Dupl. of Baer and Helmersen, 25.] *Maps.* 8° *St Petersburg*, 1868
Schmidt, Felix. *See* Faber.
Schmidt, Dr J. C. E. Lehrbuch der mathematischen und physischen Geographie. 2 vols. Small 8° *Göttingen*, 1829-30

Schmidt, J. F. Julius. Beiträge zur physikalischen Geographie von Griechenland. 4° *Athens*, 1861
Schmidt, Dr Karl Wilhelm. Sansibar, ein Ostafrikanisches Culturbild. *Plan and illustrations.* 8° *Leipzig*, 1888
Schmidt, Nicolaus. *See* Gottfried: Appendix 1.
Schmidt, Rochus. Geschichte des Araberaufstandes in Ost-Afrika. Seine Entstehung, seine Niederwerfung und seine Folgen. *Map.* 8°
Frankfurt-o-O. [1892]
Schmidt, Ulrich. *See* Schmidel.
Schmidtmeyer, Peter. Travels into Chile, over the Andes, in the years 1820 and 1821, &c. *Maps, plates, and plans.* 4° 1824
—— *See* Eyriès, Vol. 9: Appendix 1.
Schneider, Dr J. R. Das Seeland der Westschweiz und die Korrectionen seiner Gewässer. Eine Denkschrift von Dr Johann Rudolf Schneider; als Commentar: Hydrotechnisch-finanzielle Baubeschreibung der Juragewässer-Korrektion von Oberst R. la Nicca. *Map, plans, and portraits.* 4° *Berne*, 1881
Schneider, O., and H. Haas. Von Algier nach Oran und Tlemcen. 12°
Dresden, 1878
Schnell, Paul. Das marokkanische Atlasgebirge. Erster Teil. *Map.* 4°
Gotha, 1891
—— The same. (Ergänzungsheft, 103 —Petermann's Mittheilungen.) *Map*
Gotha, 1892
Schnitzler, J. H. Statistique et Itinéraire de la Russie. *Tables.* 12° *Paris*, 1829
—— Moscou: Tableau Statistique, Géographique, Topographique, et Historique de la Ville et du Gouvernement de ce Nom. *Map.* 8* *St Petersburg*, 1834
—— Russie, la Pologne, et la Finlande: Tableau Statistique, Géographique, et Historique. *Maps.* 8° *Paris*, 1835
Schoenlein, P. *See* Klotzsch.
Scholl, H. von. Abriss der Geschichte des Krieges 1840-41 in Syrien. *Maps.* 8* *Vienna*, 1866
Scholz, J. M. A. *See* Phillips, New Voyages and Travels, Vol. 8: Appendix 1.
Schomburgk, Richard. Reisen in Britisch-Guiana in 1840-44; nebst einer Fauna und Flora Guiana's nach Vorlagen von Johannes Müller, Ehrenberg, Erichson, &c. Mit Abbildungen und einer Karte von Britisch-Guiana aufgenommen von Sir Robert Schomburgk. 3 vols. *Map and plates.* Royal 8° *Leipzig*, 1847-48
—— Botanical Reminiscences in British Guiana. 8* *Adelaide*, 1876
Schomburgk, Sir Robert H. Description of British Guiana, Geographical and Statistical. *Map.* 8° 1840

Schomburgk, Sir Robert H. The History of Barbadoes; comprising a Geographical and Statistical Description of the Island, a Sketch of the Historical Events since the Settlement, and an Account of its Geology and Natural Productions. *Plates.* 8° 1848
—— The Peninsula and Bay of Samaná, in the Dominican Republic. *Map.* 8* 1853
—— *See* Adalbert.

Schön, J. F. Vocabulary of the Hausa Language . . to which are prefixed the Grammatical Elements of the Hausa Language. 12° 1843
—— Oku Ibo : Grammatical Elements of the Ibo Language. 12° 1861
—— Grammar of the Hausa Language. 8° 1862
—— Dictionary of the Hausa Language, with Appendices of Hausa Literature. 8° 1876
—— **and Bishop Samuel Crowther.** Journals relating to the Expedition up the Niger in 1841. *Map.* 8° 1842

Schönberg, Baron Erich von. Travels in India and Kashmir. 2 vols. 8° 1853

Schöner, Johann. A Reproduction of his Globe of 1523 long lost ; his Dedicatory Letter to Reymer von Streytperck, and the " De Molvccis " of Maximilianus Transylvanus, with new Translations and Notes on the Globe by Henry Stevens of Vermont. Edited, with an Introduction and Biography, by C. H. Coote. *Plates.* Small 8° 1888

Schoolcraft, Henry R. Travels in the Central Portions of the Mississippi Valley, comprising Observations on its Mineral Geography, Internal Resources, and Aboriginal Population in 1821. *Map and plates.* 8° *New York*, 1825
—— Notes on the Iroquois, or Contributions on the Statistics, Aboriginal History, Antiquities, and General Ethnology of Western New York. Royal 8° *New York*, 1846
—— Historical and Statistical Information respecting the History, Condition, and Prospects of the Indian Tribes of the United States, collected and prepared under the direction of the Bureau of Indian Affairs. 3 vols. *Maps and plates.* 4° *Philadelphia*, 1851-53
—— Summary Narrative of an Exploratory Expedition to the Sources of the Mississippi River in 1820, resumed and completed by the Discovery of its Origin in Itasca Lake in 1832. *Maps.* 8° *Philadelphia*, 1855
—— *See* Phillips, New Voyages and Travels [3], Vol. 4 : Appendix 1.

Schopen, J. History of Armenia at the time of its Annexation to Russia. [In Russian.] 8° *St Petersburg*, 1852

Schot, Apol. *See* Purchas, Vol. 1, Book 2 : Appendix 1.

Schott, A. Andreæ Schotti Itinerarium Italiæ. *Plans.* 16° N.D.
—— *See* Japan : Appendix 2.

Schott, C. A. On the Secular Change of Magnetic Declination in the United States and other parts of North America. 4° *Washington*, 1874
—— *See* Kane.

Schott, W. Versuch über die Tatarischen Sprachen. 4* *Berlin*, 1836

Schouten, Wm. Corn. *See* Burney, Vol. 2 ; Callander, Vol. 2 ; Dalrymple, Pacific, Vol. 2 ; Harris, Vol. 1 ; Kerr, Vol. 10 ; Purchas, Vol. 1, Book 2 ; " The World Displayed," Vol. 5 : Appendix 1.

Schouten, Gautier. Voyage de, aux Indes Orientales, commencé l'an 1658 et fini l'an 1665. Traduit du Hollandois. 2 vols. *Plates.* 12° *Rouen*, 1725
—— *See* Thevenot, Vol. 1 ; Allgemeine Historie, Vol. 12 : Appendix 1.

Schouw, J. F. Grundtræk til en almindelig Plantegeographie. 8° *Copenhagen*, 1822
—— Beiträge zur vergleichenden Klimatologie. Part 1. 8° *Copenhagen*, 1827
—— Specimen Geographiæ Physicæ Comparativæ. *Plates.* 4° *Copenhagen*, 1828
—— Europa, en latfattelig Naturskildring. 12° *Copenhagen*, 1832
—— Tableau du Climat et de la Végétation de l'Italie : Vol. 1. Température et Pluies de l'Italie. 8° *Copenhagen*, 1839
—— De Italienske Naaletræers geographiske og historiske Forhold. *Map.* 4* *Copenhagen*, 1844
—— Ege- og Birke-Familiens geographiske og historiske Forhold i Italien. *Map.* 4* *Copenhagen*, 1847
—— Proben einer Erdbeschreibung mit einer Einleitung über die geographische Methode. Aus dem Dänischen übersetzt von Dr H. Sebald. *Maps.* 8° *Berlin*, 1851

Schow, J. C. L'Europa Quadro Fisiografico facilmente inteso ; notomizzata da J. Graberg da Hemso. 8* *Milan*, 1839

Schrader, F. *See* Margerie.
—— **and Emm. de Margerie.** Aperçu de la forme et relief des Pyrénées. *Map.* 8* *Paris*, 1892

Schram, Dr Robert. Adria-Zeit. 12* *Vienna*, 1889
—— Ueber des Stundenzonen-System der Amerikanischen Eisenbahnen. Large 8* [*Vienna*, 1890]
—— *See* Weiss, Dr E.

Schramm, Hugo. C. F. Ph. v. Martius. Sein Lebens- und Characterbild, insbesondere seine Reiseerlebnisse in Brasilien. 2 vols. 16° *Leipzig*, 1869

Schübeler, F. C. Die Pflanzenwelt Norwegens : ein Beitrag zur Natur- und Culturgeschichte Nord-Europas. *Maps and plates.* 4° *Christiania,* 1873-75
—— Vœxtlivet i Norge, med Sœrligt Hensyn til Plantegeographien. *Maps and illustrations.* 4° *Christiania,* 1879
—— Norges Vœxtrige : et Bidrag til Nord-Europas, Natur- og Culturhistorie. 3 vols. *Portrait, maps, and illustrations.* 4° *Christiania,* 1886-89
—— Tillæg til Viridarium Norvegicum. I. 8° *Christiania,* 1891

Schubert, E. Tables of Melpomene. Computed for the "American Ephemeris and Nautical Almanac," under the superintendence of Commander Charles Henry Davis. 4° *Washington,* 1860
—— Tables of Eunomia. Computed for the "American Ephemeris and Nautical Almanac." 4° *Washington,* 1866
—— Tables of Harmonia. Computed for the "American Ephemeris and Nautical Almanac." 4° *Washington,* 1869
—— Tables of Parthenope. Computed for the "American Ephemeris and Nautical Almanac." 4° *Washington,* 1871

Schubert, F. W. *See* Kant.

Schubert, G. H. von. Reise in das Morgenland in 1836-37. 3 vols. *Map.* 8° *Erlangen,* 1858

Schück, Kapitän A. Die Wirbelstürme oder Cyclonen mit Orkangewalt, nach dem jetzigen Standpunkt unserer Kenntniss derselben in Form eines Handbuches gemeinfasslich dargestellt. *Plates.* 8° *Oldenburg* [1881]
—— Beobachtungen der Missweisung, Inklination, Schwingungszeit der Magnetnadel auf der Elbe und der Nordsee zwischen Hamburg und Rouen, 1884 und 1885; London und Hamburg, 1886. *Tables.* 4° *Hamburg,* 1886

Schück, Dr Richard. Brandenburg-Preussens Kolonial - Politik unter dem grossen Kurfürsten und seinen Nachfolgern, 1647-1721 ; mit einer Vorrede von Dr Paul Kayser. 2 vols. Large 8° *Leipzig,* 1889

Schulthess, F. Expéditions Suédoises de 1876 au Yénisséi. *Maps.* 8° *Upsala,* 1877

Schultz, Friedrich. Ueber den allgemeinen Zusammenhang der Höhen. *Map.* 4° *Weimar,* 1803

Schultz, Woldemar. Studien über agrarische und physikalische Verhältnisse in Südbrasilien, in Hinblick auf die Colonisation und die freie Einwanderung. *Map.* 8*, and Atlas folio *Leipzig,* 1865

Schultze, Dr E. *See* Germany, C : Appendix 2.

Schultzen, Walter. Ost-Indische Reyse. *Plates.* Small folio *Amsterdam,* 1676

Schulz, G. Descripcion Geognóstica del Reino de Galicia. *Map.* Small 8* *Madrid,* 1835

Schulz, K. *See* Zsigmondy.

Schulze, F. W. On Periodical Change of Terrestrial Magnetism. 8* 1879

Schulze, J. M. F. Kleines Lehrbuch der natürlichen Gränz- und Länderkunde, nebst einer vorhergehenden Abhandlung über Geographie und geographische Lehrmethode. 12° *Halle,* 1787

Schumacher, Gottlieb. Across the Jordan: being an Exploration and Survey of part of Hauran and Jaulan ; with Additions by Laurence Oliphant and Guy le Strange. *Maps and illustrations.* Crown 8° 1886
—— Der Dscholan. *Map.* 8° *Leipzig,* 1886
—— The Jaulân. With all the original *maps and illustrations.* 8° 1888
—— Pella. *Plan and illustrations.* 12° 1888
—— Northern 'Ajlûn "Within the Decapolis." *Maps, plans, and illustrations.* 8° 1890

Schumann, Dr Carl. Kritische Untersuchungen über die Zimtländer. (Ergänzungsheft, 73 — Petermann's Mittheilungen.) *Map.* 4° *Gotha,* 1883

Schürmann, C. W. Vocabulary of the Parnkalla Language, spoken by the Natives inhabiting the Western Shores of Spencer's Gulf; with a Collection of Grammatical Rules. 8° *Adelaide,* 1844
—— *See* Teichelmann.

Schütt, Otto H. Reisen im südwestlichen Becken des Congo, nach den Tagebüchern und Aufzeichnungen des Reisenden ; bearbeitet und herausgegeben von Paul Lindenberg. [Forms Part 4 of "Beiträge zur Entdeckungsgeschichte Afrika's.] *Maps.* 8° *Berlin,* 1881

Schuver, Juan Maria. Reisen im oberen Nilgebiet. (Ergänzungsheft, 72—Petermann's Mittheilungen.) *Map.* 4° *Gotha,* 1883

Schuyler, E. Turkestan: Notes of a Journey in Russian Turkestan, Khokand, Bukhara, and Kuldja. 2 vols. *Maps and plates.* 8° 1876

Schvarcz, Gyula. A Fajtakérdés Szinvonala három év elött. 8° *Budapest,* 1861

Schwab, M. le. Bibliographie de la Perse. 8° *Paris,* 1875

Schwager, Dr Conrad. *See* Richthofen; "Novara."

Schwanbeck, Dr. *See* M'Crindle, J. W.

Schwaner, C. A. L. M. Borneo, beschrijving van het Stroomgebied van den Barito en Reizen langs eenige voorname Rivieren van het Zuid-Oostelijk gedeelte van dat eiland, in 1843-47. 2 vols. *Map and plates.* Royal 8° *Amsterdam,* 1853

Schwartner, M. von. Statistik des Königreichs Ungarn. 2 vols. 8° *Budapest,* 1809-11

Schwarz, Adolf. *See* Dorn, A.

Schwarz, Dr Bernhard. Montenegro : Schilderung einer Reise durch das Innere, nebst Entwurf einer Geographie des Landes. *Map and illustrations.* 8°
Leipzig, 1883
—— Die Erschliessung der Gebirge von den ältesten Zeiten bis auf Saussure (1787). Nach Vorlesungen an der königlichen Bergakademie zu Freiberg i. S. für Geographen, Kulturhistoriker und Militärs. 8° *Leipzig*, 1885
—— Kamerun. Reise in die Hinterlande der Kolonie. *Map.* 8° *Leipzig*, 1886
—— Quer durch Bithynien, ein Beitrag zur Kenntniss Kleinasiens. *Map.* 8°
Berlin, 1889

Schwarz, Christopher Gottlieb. Untersuchungen vom Meere, die auf Veranlassung einer Schrift, De Columnis Herculis, welche . . . Herr C. G. Schwarz herausgegeben, . . . von einem Liebhaber der Naturlehre und der Philologie vorgetragen werden. Small 4° *Leipzig*, 1750

Schwarz, Eduard. Reine natürliche Geographie von Würtemberg. *Map.* 8°
Stuttgart, 1832
—— *See* " Novara ; " Scherzer.

Schwarz, T. Ueber Fels und Firn : die Bezwingung der mächtigsten Hochgipfel der Erde durch den Menschen. Nach Berichten aus früherer und späterer Zeit für junge wie alte Freunde der Berge. 8° *Leipzig*, 1884

Schwarzenberg, F. A. Alexander von Humboldt ; or, What may be accomplished in a Lifetime. 8° 1866

Schwarzott, J. G. Die Hercules-Bäder bei Mehadia. 12° *Vienna*, 1831

Schwatka, Lieut. Search for Franklin Remains. (Cuttings from *New York Herald*.) *Map.* Small 4° 1880
—— Along Alaska's Great River : a Popular Account of the Travels of the Alaska Exploring Expedition of 1883, along the Great Yukon River, from its Source to its Mouth. *Maps and illustrations* *New York*, [1885]
—— Wonderland, or Alaska and the Inland Passage ; with a Description of the Country traversed by the Northern Pacific Railroad, by John Hyde. *Map and illustrations.* Small 4° *St Paul*, 1886
—— *See* M'Clintock, Sir F. L.

Schweder, E. Ueber die Weltkarte des Kosmographen von Ravenna : Versuch einer Rekonstruction der Karte. *Maps.* 8* *Kiel*, 1886

Schweiger-Lerchenfeld, A. von. Bosnien, das Land und seine Bewohner : geschichtlich, geographisch, ethnographisch, und social-politisch geschildert. 2nd edition. *Map and plates.* 8°
Vienna, 1879
—— Die Adria : Land und Seefahrten im Bereiche des Adriatischen Meeres. *Map, plans, and illustrations.* 8° *Vienna*, 1883

Schweiger-Lerchenfeld, A. von. Das Mittelmeer. *Map and illustrations.* 8°
Freiburg in Breisgau, 1888
—— *See* Kirchner.

Schweinfurth, Dr G. Pflanzengeographische Skizze des gesammten Nil-Gebiets und der Uferländer des Rothen Meeres. [*Incomplete.*] *Map.* 4* [*Gotha*, 1868]
—— The Heart of Africa : Three Years' Travels and Adventures in the Unexplored Regions of Central Africa, from 1868 to 1871. Translated by Ellen E. Frewer ; with an Introduction by Winwood Reade. 2 vols. *Maps and plates.* 8° 1873
—— Linguistische Ergebnisse einer Reise nach Centralafrika. 8* *Berlin*, 1873
—— The same. 2nd edition. 1874
—— Artes Africanæ : Illustrations and Descriptions of Productions of the Industrial Arts of Central African Tribes. [In German and English.] *Plates.* 4° N.D.
—— Ueber die Art des Reisens in Afrika. 8° *Berlin*, 1875
—— La Terra incognita dell' Egitto propriamente detto. *Map.* 8* *Milan*, 1878
—— Ueber die geologische Schichtengliederung des Mokattam bei Cairo. *Map, plate, and sections.* 8* 1883
—— Das Volk von Socotra. 8*
Leipzig, 1883
—— Alte Baureste und hieroglyphische Inschriften im Uadi Gasūs ; mit Bemerkungen von Prof. A. Erman. *Map and plate.* 4* *Berlin*, 1885
—— Sur une Ancienne digue en pierre aux environs de Hélouan. *Maps.* 8*
N.P. [1885]
—— Les Ateliers des Outils en Silex dans le Désert Oriental de l'Égypte ; sur la découverte d'une faune paléozoïque dans le grès d'Égypte ; la vraie Rose de Jéricho (Asteriscus Pygmæus Coss. et Dur). Les dernières dècouvertes Botaniques dans les Anciens tombeaux de l'Égypte. 8* [*Cairo*, 1886]
—— Reise in das Depressionsgebiet im Umkreise des Fajūm im Januar 1886. *Map.* 8* *Berlin*, 1886
—— Zur Topographie der Ruinenstätte des alten Schet (Krokodilopolis-Arsinoë). Nebst Zusätzen von U. Wilcken. *Map.* 8* *Berlin*, 1887
—— Sur une récente Exploration Géologique de l'Ouadi Arabah. 8* *Cairo*, 1888
—— Sur la Flore des Anciens Jardins Arabes d'Égypte. 8* *Cairo*, 1888
—— Le Piante Utili dell' Eritrea. 8*
Naples, 1891
—— Ægyptens auswärtige Beziehungen hinsichtlich der Culturgewächse. 8*
Berlin, 1891
—— Erinnerungen von einer Fahrt nach Sokotra. (From *Westermann's Illustr. Monatshefte.*) *Illustrations.* 8* [1891]

Schweinfurth, Dr G. Abyssinische Pflanzennamen : eine alphabetische Aufzählung von Namen einheimischer Gewächse in Tigrinja, sowie in anderen Semitischen und Hamitischen Sprachen von Abyssinien unter Beifügung der Botanischen Artbezeichnung. 4* *Berlin*, 1893

—— Translation of a Note by Dr Schweinfurth on the Salt in the Wady Rayan. 4* [*Cairo*, 1893]

—— Ueber Balsam und Myrrhe. Sonderabdruck aus den Berichten der pharmaceutischen Gesellschaft. 8* *Berlin* [1893]

—— **and P. Ascherson.** Primitiæ Floræ Marmaricæ, mit Beiträgen von P. Taubert. *Plate.* 8° *Rome*, 1893

—— *See* Beyrich ; Emin Pasha.

Schwöy, F. J. Topographie vom Markgrafthum Mähren. 3 vols. 8° *Vienna*, 1793-94

Schynse, August Wilhelm. Zwei Jahre am Congo. Erlebnisse und Schilderungen. Herausgegeben von Karl Hespers. *Illustrations.* 8° *Cologne*, 1889

—— Mit Stanley und Emin Pascha durch Deutsch Ost-Africa. Herausgegeben von Karl Hespers. 8° *Cologne*, 1890

—— A Travers l'Afrique avec Stanley et Emin Pacha : Journal de Voyage du Père Schynse, publié par Charles Hespers. 12° *Paris*, 1890

Scidmore, Miss E. Ruhamah. Alaska, its Southern Coast and the Sitkan Archipelago. *Map and illustrations.* Crown 8° *Boston, Mass.* [1885]

—— Jinrikisha Days in Japan. *Illustrations.* 8° *New York*, 1891

Sclater, P. L. *See* Galton, Vacation Tourists ; *also* West Indies, A : Appendix 2.

Scobel, A. Die geographischen und Kultur-Verhältnisse Mexicos. *Map.* 8* *Leipzig*, 1883

—— Die Verkehrswege Mexicos und ihre wirtschaftliche Bedeutung. *Map.* 8* *Bremen*, 1887

Scoresby, William. Account of the Arctic Regions ; with a History and Description of the Northern Whale Fishery. 2 vols. *Maps and plates.* 8° *Edinburgh*, 1820

—— Journal of a Voyage to the Northern Whale Fishery ; including Researches and Discoveries on the Eastern Coast of West Greenland, made in 1822. *Maps and plates.* 8° *Edinburgh*, 1823

—— The Franklin Expedition ; or, Considerations on Measures for the Discovery and Relief of our absent Countrymen in the Arctic Regions. *Maps.* 8° 1850

—— The Life of William Scoresby ; by his nephew R. E. Scoresby - Jackson. *Portrait, map, and plates.* 12° 1861

Scoresby-Jackson, Dr R. E. On the Influence of Weather upon Disease and Mortality. *Map and plates.* 4* *Edinburgh*, 1863

—— *See* Scoresby.

Scot, Edmund. *See* Astley, Vol. 1 ; Kerr, Vol. 8 ; Purchas, Vol. 1, Book 3 ; Allgemeine Historie, Vol. 1 : Appendix 1.

Scot, Sir John, of Scotstarvet. The staggering state of Scottish Statesmen from 1550 to 1650 ; with a Memoir of the Author and Historical Illustrations by the Rev. Charles Rogers. 8° *Edinburgh*, 1872

Scot, W. L. *See* Purchas, Vol. 2, Book 10 : Appendix 1.

Scott, Alexander. Remarks on the Natural History of Socotra : being an Account of the Expedition to the Island under the auspices of the Royal Society of London, in February and March 1880. 8* 1881

Scott, Alexander. *See* Phillips [3], Vol. 9 : Appendix 1.

Scott, Arthur, and Lewis Atkinson. A Short History of Diamond Cutting ; with a Preface by Edwin W. Streeter. 12* N.D.

Scott, Charles H. The Baltic, the Black Sea, and the Crimea : comprising Travels in Russia, a Voyage down the Volga to Astrachan, and a Tour through Crim Tartary. 8° 1854

—— The Danes and the Swedes : being an Account of a Visit to Denmark, including Schleswig - Holstein and the Danish Islands, with a Peep into Jutland. 8° 1856

—— **Colonel.** A Journal of a Residence in the Esmailla of Abdel-Kader, and of Travels in Moroco and Algiers. *Portrait.* 8° 1842

Scott, Rev. D. C. A Cyclopædic Dictionary of the Mang'anja Language spoken in British Central Africa. Crown 8° *Edinburgh*, 1892

Scott, G. B. *See* Blackwood, Vol. 3 : Appendix 1.

Scott, H. J. South Australia in 1887. 8° *Adelaide*, 1887

Scott, James George (Shway Yoe). France and Tonking : a Narrative of the Campaign of 1884 and the Occupation of Further India. *Map and plans.* 8° 1885

—— Burma as it was, as it is, and as it will be. Small 8° 1886

—— The British Shan States. (*The Asiatic Quarterly Review*, July 1889.) 8* 1889

Scott, Hon. J. R., and C. P. Sprent. Reports on the Western Country of Tasmania. Folio* *Hobart*, 1877

Scott, Robert. *See* Dictionaries, A : App. 2.

Scott, Robert H. Report of an Inquiry into the connection between Strong Winds and Barometrical differences. 8* 1868

Scott, Robert H. Barometer Manual. Board of Trade. 8*   1871

—— The History of the Kew Observatory, Richmond, Surrey. 8°   1885

—— *See* Symons, G. J. ; *also* United Kingdom, B, Appendix 2.

—— **and Richard H. Curtis.** On the Working of the Harmonic Analyser at the Meteorological Office. 8°   1886

Scott-Moncrieff, Sir Colin. *See* Brown, Major R. H.

Scrafton, Luke. Reflections on the Government of Indostan ; with a Short Sketch of the History of Bengal from 1739 to 1756, and an Account of the English Affairs to 1758. 8°   1770

Scratchley, Sir P. *See* Cooke, C. K.; Fort.

Scribner, G. Hilton. Where did Life Begin ? a Brief Inquiry as to the Probable Place of Beginning, and the Natural Courses of Migration therefrom, of the Flora and Fauna of the Earth. Small 8°   *New York*, 1883

Scroggs, —. *See* Allgemeine Historie, Vol. 17 : Appendix 1.

Scrope, G. Poulett. Considerations on Volcanos, the Probable Causes of their Phenomena, &c., leading to the Establishment of a New Theory of the Earth. *Map and plates.* 8°   1825

—— The Geology and Extinct Volcanoes of Central France. 2nd edition. *Maps and plates.* 8°   1858

—— Mémoire sur le Mode de Formation des Cones Volcaniques et des Cratères. Traduit de l'Anglais, par E. Pieraggi. *Plate and woodcuts.* 8*   *Paris*, 1860

Scudder, S. H. Revision of the Stylated Fossorial Crickets. 4* *Salem, Mass.,* 1869

—— A Year of Exploration in North America : President's Address before the Appalachian Mountain Club, 9th January 1878. 8*   *Boston, Mass.,* 1878

—— Description of an Articulate of Doubtful Relationship of the Tertiary Beds of Florissant, Colorado. 4* 1882

—— Nomenclator Zoologicus : an Alphabetical List of all Generic Names that have been employed by Naturalists for Recent and Fossil Animals from the earliest times to the close of the year 1879. 2 parts. 1st, Supplemental List ; 2nd, Universal Index. 8°
      Washington, 1882

—— Dr John Lawrence Le Conte : a Memoir read to the National Academy of Science ; with an Appendix on the Ancestry of the Family. *Portrait.* 8*   N.P., 1884

—— *See* Harris, C. W.

Scully, William. Brazil, its Provinces and Chief Cities, the Manners and Customs of the People, &c. *Map.* 8° 1866

Sealsfield, Charles. *See* Blackwood, Vol. 3 : Appendix 1.

Seaman, William. Grammatica Linguæ Turcicæ. Small 4°   *Oxford,* 1670

Sebald, Dr H. *See* Schouw.

Secchi, A. Escursione Scientifica fatta a Norcia ad Occasione dei Terremoti del 22 Agosto 1859. 4°   *Rome,* 1860

Secchi, P. A. Misura della Base Trigonometrica eseguita sulla Via Appia, 1854-55. *Plates.* Folio *Rome,* 1858

Sedgwick, Adam. A Synopsis of the Classification of the British Palæozoic Rocks ; with a Detailed Systematic Description of the British Palæozoic Fossils in the Geological Museums of the University of Cambridge, by Frederick McCoy. Fasc. 2. *Plates.* 4°   1852

—— **and Sir Roderick I. Murchison.** On the Structure and Relations of the Deposits contained between the Primary Rocks and the Oolitic Series in the North of Scotland. *Maps and plates.* 4° 1828

—— A Sketch of the Structure of the Eastern Alps ; with Sections through the Newer Formations on the Northern Flanks of the Chain, and through the Tertiary Deposits of Styria, &c. ; with Supplementary Observations by Sir R. I. Murchison. *Maps and plates.* 4° 1831

—— Description of a Raised Beach in Barnstaple or Bideford Bay, on the North-west Coast of Devonshire. *Woodcuts.* 4°   1836

—— On the Physical Structure of Devonshire, and on the Subdivisions and Geological Relations of its Older Stratified Deposits, &c. *Map and plates.* 4* 1837

—— Classification of the Older Stratified Rocks of Devonshire and Cornwall. 8*
                                        1839

—— On the Distribution and Classification of the Older or Palæozoic Deposits of the North of Germany and Belgium, and on their Comparison with Formations of the same Age in the British Isles ; followed by a Description of the Fossil Mollusca by M. E. de Verneuil and Viscount D'Archiac. 4°   1842

Sedgwick, James. The True Principle of the Law of Storms, practically arranged for both Hemispheres. *Diagrams.* Royal 8*   1852

Sedgwick, Professor. *See* Livingstone.

Sédillot, —. Notice sur une Carte Routière de Mesched à Bokhara et de Bokhara à Balkh, d'après la Traduction de M. Garcin de Tessy. *Maps.* 8* *Paris,* 1852

—— *See* Hansteen.

Seebohm, F. The Crisis of Emancipation in America. 8*   1865

Seebohm, Henry. Siberia in Europe : a Visit to the Valley of the Petchora in North-east Russia ; with Descriptions of the Natural History, Migration of Birds, &c. *Map and illustrations.* 8°   1880

Seebohm, Henry. Siberia in Asia: a Visit to the Valley of the Yenesay in East Siberia; with Description of the Natural History, Migration of Birds, &c. *Map and illustrations.* Crown 8° 1882

Seeley, H. G. The Fresh-water Fishes of Europe: a History of their Genera, Species, Structure, Habits, and Distribution. *Illustrations.* Large 8° 1886

Seeley, J. R. *See* Trendell.

Seemann, Berthold. Narrative of the Voyage of H.M.S. "Herald," 1845-51, under the command of Capt. Henry Kellett: being a Circumnavigation of the Globe, and Three Cruises to the Arctic Regions in search of Sir John Franklin. 2 vols. *Maps and plates.* 8° 1853

—— The Zoology of the Voyage of H.M.S. "Herald" . . . Edited by Prof. Edward Forbes; Vertebrals, including Fossil Mammals, by Sir John Richardson. *Plates.* 4° 1854

—— Viti: an Account of a Government Mission to the Vitian or Fijian Islands in the years 1860-61. *Map and plates.* 8° 1862

—— *See* Galton, Vacation Tourists; Kittlitz.

Seetzen, Ulrich Jasper. Brief Account of the Countries adjoining the Lake of Tiberias, the Jordan, and the Dead Sea. *Map.* 4° *Bath,* 1810

—— Reisen durch Syrien, Palästina, Phönicien, die Transjordan-Länder, Arabia Petraea, und Unter-Aegypten. Herausgegeben und commentirt von Prof. Dr F. Kruse in Verbindung mit Prof. Dr Hinrichs, Dr G. F. H. Müller, und mehreren andern Gelehrten. Vols. 1 and 2 in one. 8° *Berlin,* 1854

Seguin, J. Les Antiquitez d'Arles, traitées en manière d'entretien et d'Itinéraire. Small 4° *Arles,* 1687

Segura, José C., and Manuel D. Cordero. Reseña sobre el cultivo de algunas Plantas industriales que se explotan en la República. *Plates.* 8° *Mexico,* 1884

Seillière, Ernest. Une Excursion à Ithaque: Dessins de Pierre Vignal d'après les photographies de l'auteur. 4° *Paris,* 1892

Seidel, Ludwig. Untersuchungen über die Lichtstärke der Planeten Venus, Mars, Jupiter, und Saturn. 4° *Munich,* 1859

Sein-ko. *See* Taw Sein-ko.

Selberg, Eduard. Reis naar Java en Bezoek op het Eiland Madura; vrij vertaald, naar het Hoogduitsch . . . door W. L. de Sturler. *Map.* 8° *Amsterdam,* 1846

Selby, W. B. Memoir on the Ruins of Babylon. [From the India Records, No. 51.] *Plans.* Royal 8° *Bombay,* 1859

2 E

Selby, W. B. Directions for approaching Bombay. 8* N.P., N.D.

Seler, Dr Edward. Reisebriefe aus Mexiko. *Illustrations.* 8° *Berlin,* 1889

Selfridge, T. O. Reports of Explorations and Surveys to ascertain the Practicability of a Ship-Canal between the Atlantic and Pacific Oceans by the way of the Isthmus of Darien. *Maps and plates.* 4° *Washington,* 1874

Selim, Capt. Premier Voyage à la recherche des Sources du Bahr-el-Abiad ou Nil-Blanc. 8* *Paris,* 1840

Sella, V., and D. Vallino. Monte Rosa and Gressoney. *Illustrations.* Oblong 8° [1890]

—— Nel Caucaso Centrale. Note di Escursioni colla Camera oscura. *Map and illustrations.* 8° *Turin,* 1890

Selous, Frederick Courteney. A Hunter's Wanderings in Africa: being a Narrative of Nine Years spent amongst the Game of the Far Interior of South Africa, containing Accounts of Explorations . . ; with full Notes upon the Natural History and Present Distribution of all the large Mammalia. 2nd edition. *Map and illustrations.* 8° 1890

—— Travel and Adventure in South-east Africa: being the Narrative of the last Eleven Years spent by the Author on the Zambesi and its Tributaries; with an Account of the Colonisation of Mashunaland, and the progress of the Gold Industry of that Country. *Map and illustrations.* 8° 1893

Selwyn, Alfred R. C. *See* Stanford, E.; *also* Victoria, D: Appendix 1.

—— **and George H. F. Ulrich.** Intercolonial Exhibition Essays, 1866. Notes on the Physical Geography, Geology, and Mineralogy of Victoria. *Map and plates.* 8* *Melbourne,* 1866

—— **and G. M. Dawson.** Descriptive Sketch of the Physical Geography and Geology of the Dominion of Canada. *Map.* 8° *Montreal,* 1884

Selwyn, Capt. J. H. Explanation of the Floating Cylinders for Laying Telegraphic Submarine Cables. *Plate.* 4* N.D.

Semenoff, P. Geographico - Statistical Lexicon of the Russian Empire. [In Russian.] 5 vols. Large 8° *St Petersburg,* 1863-85

Semmes, Raphael. My Adventures Afloat: a Personal Memoir of My Cruises and Services in "The Sumter" and "Alabama." Vol. 2. 8° 1869

Semper, Dr Karl. Die Philippinen und ihre Bewohner. Sechs Skizzen. *Maps.* 8° *Würzburg,* 1869

—— Die Palau-Inseln im Stillen Ocean. 8° *Leipzig,* 1873

Semple, R. *See* Phillips, Collection of Modern and Contemporary Voyages and Travels [1], Vol. 8 : Appendix 1.

Sené, —. Le Relief du Mont-Blanc et des Sommités Environnantes. 8*
Geneva, 1844

—— *See* Jomard.

Senhouse, Humphrey le Fleming. Graham Island. [Copy of a Letter dated 5th August 1831.] 8* [1831]

Senillosa, Don F. Programa de un Curso de Geometria. 8* *Buenos Ayres,* 1825

—— Memoria sobre los Pesos y Medidas. 8* *Buenos Ayres,* 1835

Senior, N. W. A Journal kept in Turkey and Greece in the Autumn of 1857 and the beginning of 1858. *Maps and plates.* 8° 1859

" Senjawin." *See* Kittlitz.

Seoane, Guillermo A. Tribunales de Arbitraje : Contra-Memorándum sobre algunas Reclamaciones Francesas presentado al Tribunal Franco-Chileno. 8°
Santiago, 1885

Sepp, Ant. *See* Churchill, Vol. 4 : Appendix 1.

Sequeira, Diego Lopez de. *See* Gottfried : Appendix 1.

Sequeira, Gonsalo de. *See* Gottfried : Appendix 1.

Séréna, Carla. Mon Voyage : Souvenirs personnels—1. De la Baltique à la Mer Caspienne ; 2. Une Européenne en Perse. *Portrait and frontispiece.* 12°
Paris [1881]

—— Hommes et Choses en Perse. *Portrait and plates.* 12° *Paris,* 1883

Serrano, M. Ramon. Derrotero del Estrecho de Magallanes, Tierra del Fuego i Canales de la Patagonia. Desde el Canal de Chacao hasta el Cabo de Hornos. *Plates.* Large 8° *Santiago de Chile,* 1891

Serrant, Émile. Le Bispain pour l'Alimentation du Soldat en Campagne et du Marin. 8* *Paris,* N.D.

—— Les Mines d'Or du Bambouk. 8*
Paris, 1888

Serrurier, L. Professor Schlegel's zoogenaamde Kritiek van het Japansch-Nederlandsch en Japansch- Engelsch Woordenboek. Deel 3. 8* *Leyden,* 1893

Sessions, Frederick. The Gonds of Central India, their Country, Religion, and Customs. (Reprinted from *The Friends' Quarterly Examiner.*) 8* N.D.

Sesti, Don Battista G. Piante delle Città, &c., di Milano. 4° *Milan,* 1707

Seton, G. St Kilda, Past and Present. *Map and plates.* 8° 1878

Seton-Karr, H. W. Shores and Alps of Alaska. *Maps and illustrations.* 8° 1887

—— Ten Years' Wild Sports in Foreign Lands, or Travels in the Eighties. 8° 1889

Settimanni, Cesare. D'une nouvelle Méthode pour déterminer la Parallaxe du Soleil. 8* *Florence,* 1869

—— D'un seconde Nouvelle Méthode pour déterminer la Parallaxe du Soleil. 8*
Florence, 1870

Seue, C. de. La Névé de Justedal et ses Glaciers. *Map and plates.* 4*
Christiania, 1870

—— Windrosen des südlichen Norwegens. *Tables.* 4* *Christiania,* 1876

—— Historisk Beretning om Norges Geografiske Opmaaling fra den Stiftelse i 1773 indtil Udgangen af 1876. *Maps.* 8° *Christiania,* 1876

Seume, G. J. A Tour through Part of Germany, Poland, Russia, Sweden, Denmark, &c., during the summer of 1805. Translated from the German. *Plates.* 8° 1807

—— *See* Phillips [1], Vol. 7 : Appendix 1.

Sève, Edouard. La Patria Chilena : le Chili tel qu'il est. I. 8° *Valparaiso,* 1876

Seward, A. C. Fossil Plants as Tests of Climate : being the Sedgwick Prize Essay for the year 1892. 8° 1892

Seward, William. Journal of a Voyage from Savannah to Philadelphia, and from Philadelphia to England, 1740. 8° 1740

Séwastionoff, Pierre de. *See* Ptolemy.

Sewell, Robert. *See* Weber, A.

Sewerzow, N. Travels in Turkestan and Researches in the Thian-Shan. [In Russian.] *Maps and illustrations.* 8°
St Petersburg, 1873

—— Erforschung des Thian-Schan-Gebirgs-Systems, 1867. (Ergänzungsheft, 42 and 43 — Petermann's Mittheilungen.) *Coloured map.* 4° *Gotha,* 1875

Sexe, S. A. Mærker efter en Iistid i Omegnen af Hardangerfjorden. *Map.* 4* *Christiania,* 1866

—— Boiumbræen, 1 Juli 1868. Universitets-Program for Förste Semester 1869. *Plate.* 4* *Christiania,* 1869

Seyd, Ernest. California and its Resources : a Work for the Merchant, the Capitalist, and the Emigrant. *Maps and plates.* 8° 1858

Seymour, G. L. *See* Lane-Poole, S.

Seymour, H. D. Russia on the Black Sea and Sea of Azof : being a Narrative of Travels in the Crimea and bordering Provinces. *Maps.* 8° 1855

Shabeeny, —. *See* Jackson, J. G.

Shadwell, C. F. A. Tables for Facilitating the Approximate Prediction of Occultations and Eclipses for any particular place. *Diagrams.* 8° 1847

—— Tables for Facilitating the Determination of the Latitude at Sea by the Simultaneous Altitudes of two Stars. 8° 1849

—— Tables for Facilitating the Determination of the Latitude and Time at Sea by Observations of the Stars. 8° 1854

Shadwell, C. F. A. Formulæ of Navigation and Nautical Astronomy, on 12 Cards, in case. 12° 1856 and 1859
—— Tables for Facilitating the Reduction of Lunar Observations. 8° 1860
—— Notes on the Management of Chronometers and the Measurement of Meridian Distances. 8° 1855 and 1861
—— Notes on Interpolation, Mathematical and Practical. 8° 1879

Shaffner, Tal. P. The Telegraph Manual: a Complete History and Description of the Semaphoric, Electric, and Magnetic Telegraphs of Europe, Asia, Africa, and America, Ancient and Modern. *Portraits and illustrations.* 8° *New York,* 1859

Shahamet Ali. The Sikhs and Afghans, in connection with India and Persia, immediately before and after the death of Ranjeet Singh. 8° 1847

Shakespear, A. Memoir of the Statistics of the North-Western Provinces of the Bengal Presidency. Royal 8° *Calcutta,* 1848

Shakespear, John. Muntakhabāt-i-Hindī: or Selections in Hindustani, with Verbal Translations or particular Vocabularies, and a Grammatical Analysis of some parts. Vol. 1. 4° 1824

Shakespear, Capt. Sir Richmond. *See* Blackwood, Vol. 2 : Appendix 1.

Shaler, Prof. N. S. Aspects of the Earth : a Popular Account of some familiar Geological Phenomena. *Illustrations.* 8° 1890
—— Nature and Man in America. Crown 8° 1892

Share, James M. Great Circle Tables for the North Atlantic, by which the Great Circle and Mercator Courses, &c., may be easily found ; together with Short Practical Rules and Corresponding Examples in Great Circle Sailing. 4° 1852
—— The Lee Shore, or Loss of H.M.S. "Warrior," and other Poems. 12° 1856
—— Tables for Ascertaining a Ship's Distance from the Summit of High Land, having taken its Altitude above the Sea Horizon with a Sextant ; with a Short Distance Table. 4° 1857

Sharland, Emily Cruwys. Coin of the Realm ; what is it ? or Talks about Gold and Silver Coins . . . ; also, as an Appendix, an Exchange Calculus (Five Papers), and a Memorandum on Money, with Valuable and Original Tables by John Henry Norman. 8° 1888

Sharp, Capt. Bartholomew, and others. Voyages and Adventures in the South Sea ; also Capt. Van Horn with his Buccanieres surprizing of la Vera Cruz ; to which is added the true Relation of Sir Henry Morgan his Expedition against the Spaniards in the West Indies, and

Sharp, Capt. B., &c.—*continued.* his taking Panama, together with the President of Panama's Account of the same Expedition ; and Col. Beeston's adjustment of the Peace between the Spaniards and English in the West Indies. 8° 1684
—— *See* Callander, Vol. 2 ; Hacke : Appendix 1.

Sharp, David. An Address read before the Entomological Society of London. 8* 1889

Sharp, Samuel. *See* "The Modern Traveller," Vol. 4, p. 610 : Appendix 1.

Sharpe, R. B. *See* "Erebus" and "Terror."

Sharpe, Reginald R. Calendar of Letters from the Mayor and Corporation of the City of London, circa A.D. 1350-70, enrolled and preserved among the Archives of the Corporation at the Guildhall. Edited [with an Introduction] by Reginald R. Sharpe, D.C.L. 8° 1885

Sharpe, Samuel. History of Egypt, from the Earliest Times till the Conquest by the Arabs, A.D. 640. 8° 1846

Sharpe, A. Report, dated from Sumbo, S.W. corner of Tanganyika, 8th September 1890, and addressed to Consul-General Johnston. Folio* 1892

Sharpey, Alex. *See* Astley, Vol. 1 ; Gottfried ; Kerr, Vol. 8 ; Purchas, Vol. 1, Book 3 ; Allgemeine Historie, Vol. 1 : Appendix 1.

Shaw, Barnabas. Memorials of South Africa. *Map and plate.* 8° 1840

Shaw, Miss Flora L. Letters from Queensland. By *The Times* Special Correspondent. 12° 1893
—— Letters from South Africa. By *The Times* Special Correspondent. Reprinted from *The Times* of July, August, September, and October 1892. Crown 8° 1893

Shaw, George A. Madagascar and France : with some Account of the Island, its People, its Resources, and Development. *Map and illustrations.* Crown 8° 1885
—— Madagascar of To-day : an Account of the Island, its People, Resources, and Development. *Illustrations.* 32° 1886

Shaw, Dr J. Ramble through the United States, Canada, and the West Indies. 8° 1856

Shaw, J. The Geography of South Africa, Physical and Political. 12° 1878

Shaw, Dr Norton. Introductory Notice to Dr Isaac I. Hayes's "Boat Journey," with Lists of Arctic Expeditions and Works. 12* 1860
—— *See* Hayes ; Jackson, Col. J. R. ; Nilsson ; Rink.

Shaw, Peter. *See* Varenius.

Shaw, R. Visits to High Tartary, Yârkand, and Kâshghar [formerly Chinese Tartary], and Return Journey over the Karakóram Pass. *Maps and plates.* 8° 1871

Shaw, Thomas. Travels, or Observations relating to several parts of Barbary and the Levant. *Maps and plates.* 4° 1757

—— Travels, with some Account of the Author. 2 vols. *Maps and plates.* 8° *Edinburgh*, 1808

—— *See* Pinkerton, Vol. 15; Knox's New Collection, Vol. 6; "The World Displayed," Vols. 11, 17, 18 : Appendix 1.

Shaw, William. *See* Dictionaries, A, Gaelic : Appendix 2.

Shaw's Tour in the West of England. *See* Pinkerton, Vol. 2 : Appendix 1.

Sheafer, Messrs. *See* United States, K, Pennsylvania : Appendix 2.

"Shearwater." *See* Carpenter, W. B.

Shedden, Robert. Nautical Obervations, &c., taken during the Voyage of the "Nancy Dawson" to Behring Strait, &c. 3 vols. MS. Folio 1848-49

Sheepshanks, R. Reply to Mr Babbage's Letter "On the Planet Neptune and the Royal Astronomical Society's Medal." 8* 1847

Sheil, Lady. Glimpses of Life and Manners in Persia. *Plates.* 8° 1856

Shelbourne, Major Sidney F. Interoceanic Ship Canal : San Blas Route. *Map.* 8* *New York*, 1880

—— Comparative View of the Panama and San Blas Routes for an Interoceanic Canal. 8* *New York*, 1880

Sheldon, J. P. To Canada and through it with the British Association. *Map and illustrations.* 8° *Ottawa*, 1885

Sheldon, Mrs M. French. Sultan to Sultan : Adventures among the Masai and other Tribes of East Africa. *Map, portrait, and illustrations.* Small 4° 1892

Shelley, G. E. A Handbook to the Birds of Egypt. *Plates.* Large 8° 1872

Shelvocke, George. A Voyage round the World by the way of the Great South Sea, performed in the years 1719-20-21-22, in the "Speedwell" of London . . . till she was cast away on the Island of Juan Fernandes, in May 1720; and afterwards continu'd in the "Recovery," the "Jesus Maria," and "Sacra Familia," &c. *Map and plates.* 8° 1726

—— The same, in the year 1718. 2nd. edition. *Maps and plates.* 8° 1757

—— *See* Burney, Vol. 4; Callander, Vol. 3; Harris, Vol. 1; Kerr, Vol. 10 : Appendix 1.

Shepard, J. S. Over the Dovrefjelds. *Plate.* Small 8° 1873

Shepherd, C. W. The North-West Peninsula of Iceland : being the Journal of a Tour in Iceland in the Spring and Summer of 1862. *Map and plates.* 8° 1867

Shepherd, W. Homeward through Mongolia and Siberia. *Map.* 8* 1880

Shepherd, Major W. Prairie Experiences in handling Cattle and Sheep. *Map and illustrations.* 8° 1884

Sheridan, Lieut.-General P. H. Report, dated 20th September 1881, of his Expedition through the Big Horn Mountains, Yellowstone National Park, &c.; together with Reports of Lieut.-Col. J. F. Gregory, Surgeon W. H. Forwood, and Capt. S. C. Kellogg. *Maps.* 8* *Washington*, 1882

—— Report of an Exploration of Parts of Wyoming, Idaho, and Montana, in 1882; with the Itinerary of Col. Jas. F. Gregory, and a Geological and Botanical Report by Surgeon W. H. Forwood. *Map.* 8* *Washington*, 1882

—— and **W. T. Sherman.** Reports of Inspection made in the summer of 1877 of country north of the Union Pacific Railroad. *Maps and plates.* 8° *Washington*, 1878

Sherley, Sir A. *See* Shirley.

Sherman, O. T. *See* United States, H, *b*, Signal Service : Appendix 2.

Sherman, W. T. *See* Sheridan.

Sherriff, William. Report on the Northern Shan States. *Map and illustration.* Folio* *Rangoon*, 1889

Sherrin, R. A. A., and J. H. Wallace. Brett's Historical Series. Early History of New Zealand : From Earliest Times to 1840, by R. A. A. Sherrin ; from 1840 to 1845, by J. H. Wallace. Edited by Thomson W. Leys. *Illustrations.* 4° *Auckland*, 1890

Sherwill, Capt. W. S. Report on the Rivers of Bengal. *Maps.* Papers of 1856, '57, and '58, on the Damoodah Embankments, &c. *Maps.* [From India Records, No. 29.] Royal 8° *Bengal*, 1858

Shields, G. O. The Big Game of North America, its Habits, Habitat, Haunts, and Characteristics; How, when, and where to Hunt it. . . . Edited by G. O. Shields ("Conquina"). *Illustrations.* 8° 1890

Shillibeer, Lieut. J. Narrative of the "Briton's" Voyage to Pitcairn's Island, including a Sketch of the Present State of the Brazils and Spanish South America. *Plates.* 8° 1818

—— *See* Eyriès, Vol. 6 : Appendix 1.

Shillinglaw, John J. Narrative of Arctic Discovery, from the Earliest Period to the Present Time ; with Details of Measures adopted for the Relief of Sir John Franklin. *Maps and portrait.* 8° 1850

Shillinglaw, John J. Cast away on the Auckland Isles: a Narrative of the Wreck of the "Grafton," and of the Escape of the Crew after twenty months' suffering, from the Private Journals of Capt. Thos. Musgrave; with a Map, and some Account of the Auck-lands. 8°				*Melbourne*, 1865
—— Historical Records of Port Phillip: the First Annals of the Colony of Victoria. *Map and plates.* 8°
Melbourne, 1879
Shipley, John B. The Full Significance of 1492. 12°			*New York*, 1890
—— **and Marie A. Shipley.** The Eng-lish Re-discovery and Colonisation of America. Crown 8°			[1890]
Shipley, Mrs John B. Suppressed His-torical Facts: Roman Catholic Evidence confirming Leif Erikson's Discovery of America. 12°			*New York*, 1890
Shipp, Barnard. The History of Hernando de Soto and Florida, or Record of the Events of Fifty-six Years, from 1512 to 1568. *Maps.* Large 8°
Philadelphia, 1881
Shirley (or Sherley), Sir Anthony. Voyages to the West Indies, Central America, Newfoundland, and Persia. *See* Gottfried; Hakluyt, Vol. 4; Purchas, Vol. 2, Book 9: Appendix 1.
Shirley, William. Letter to the Duke of Newcastle; with a Journal of the Siege of Louisburg, and other Operations of the Forces during the Expedition against the French Settlements on Cape Breton. 8*				1746
Sholl, T. C. The North-West Settle-ments. [Cuttings from a Newspaper, containing an Account by T. C. Sholl of a North Australian Exploring Expedi-tion.] Folio*		N.P., 1866
Shoolbred, J. N. On the Changes in the Tidal Portion of the River Mersey and in its Estuary. *Maps.* 8*		1876
Shooter, Joseph. The Kafirs of Natal and the Zulu Country. *Map and plates.* 8°				1857
Shore, Hon. Henry Noel. The Flight of the Lapwing: a Naval Officer's jottings in China, Formosa, and Japan. *Map and illustrations.* 8°		1881
Shortland, Edward. Maori Religion and Mythology, illustrated by Translations of Traditions, Karakia, &c.; to which are added Notes on Maori Tenure of Land. Small 8°				1882
Shortland, Lieut. *See* Phillip, Governor Arthur; *also* Pelham, Vol. 1: Appendix 1.
Shortland, P. F. Bay of Fundy: Re-marks for Sailing Directions, made be-tween the years 1850-55. 8°		1856
—— Bay of Fundy Pilot, from Baccaro Point to Quoddy Head, including the Grand Manan Island. 8°		1857

Shortland, P. F. Sounding Voyage of Her Majesty's ship "Hydra," 1868. *Plates.* Square 8°			1869
Shortrede, Robert. Compendious Loga-rithmic Tables, embracing Logarithms to Numbers and Numbers to Logarithms, with Logarithmic Sines and Tangents to every Five Minutes of the Quadrant. 8°
Edinburgh, 1844
—— Logarithmic Tables, to Seven Places of Decimals, containing Logarithms to Numbers from 1 to 120,000. . . . Royal 8°				*Edinburgh*, 1844
Shortt, J. Topographical Report on the Political Districts of Raigurh, Sarungurh, Sonepore, and Sumbulpore. [From the India Records, No. 23] Royal 8°
Calcutta, 1855
Showell, R. H. Rough Notes on the Petty Estate of Jowar. *See* Marriott.
Shreeve, W. Whitaker. Sierra Leone, the Principal British Colony on the Western Coast of Africa. 8°		1847
Shuck, J. L. Portfolio Chinensis, or a Collection of authentic Chinese State Papers illustrative of the History of the Present Position of Affairs in China; with a Translation, Notes, and Introduc-tion. 8°			*Macao*, 1840
Shufeldt, R. W. Reports of Explorations and Surveys to ascertain the Practica-bility of a Ship-Canal between the Atlantic and Pacific Oceans by the way of the Isthmus of Tehuantepec. *Maps, plates, and profiles.* 4°	*Washington*, 1872
Shumard, B. F. Report on the Geo-logical Survey of the State of Missouri. *See* United States, K (Missouri): Ap-pendix 2.
—— **and G. C. Swallow.** Descriptions of New Fossils from the Coal Measures of Missouri and Kansas. 8*
St Louis, 1858
Shurtleff, Nath. B. Records of the Colony of New Plymouth, in New Eng-land, 1633-89. 8 vols. in 6. 4°
Boston, Mass., 1855-57
Shway Yeo. *See* Scott, J. G.
Sibree, James, junr. Madagascar and its People: Notes of a Four Years' Resi-dence; with a Sketch of the History, Position, and Prospects of Mission Work amongst the Malagasy. 8°		[1870]
—— South-East Madagascar: being Notes of a Journey through the Tanala, Tai-moro, and Taisaka Countries, in June and July 1876. *Map.* 12* *Antananarivo*, N.D.
—— The Great African Island: Chapters on Madagascar, a Popular Account of Recent Researches, &c. *Maps and plates.* 8°				1880
—— A Madagascar Bibliography: includ-ing Publications in the Malagasy Lan-guage and a List of Maps of Madagascar. 8*			*Antananarivo*, 1885

Sibree, James, junr. *See* Megiserus.

Sibley, Dr. *See* Phillips [1], Vol. 6: Appendix 1.

Sibthorp, Dr. *See* Walpole, Turkey: Appendix 1.

Sibthorpe, A. B. C. The Geography of Sierra Leone. Revised, corrected, and enlarged. 2nd edition. 16* N.D.
—— The Geography of the Surrounding Territories of Sierra Leone. 16* 1892

Sicé, Eugène. Traité des Lois Mahométanes, ou Recueil des Lois, Usages, et Coutumes des Musulmans du Décan. 8° *Paris,* 1841

Sichel, J. *See* "Novara."

Sickler, F. K. L. Handbuch der alten Geographie fuer Gymnasien und zum Selbstunterricht, mit steter Ruecksicht auf die Numismatische Geographie, &c. 2 vols. 8° *Cassel,* 1822

Sidenbladh, Elis. *See* Sweden, A (Geologiska Undersökning): Appendix 2.

Sidi-Aly. Relation des Voyages de Sidi-Aly fils d'Houtian, nommé ordinairement Katibi Roumi, Amiral de Soliman II. Écrite en Turk; traduite de l'allemand, sur la version de M. de Diez, par M. Moris. 8° *Paris,* 1827

Sidney, Samuel. The Three Colonies of Australia—New South Wales, Victoria, South Australia, their Pastures, Copper Mines, and Gold Fields. *Map and illustrations.* 8° 1853

Sidoti, Jean Baptiste. *See* Burney, Vol. 5: Appendix 1.

Siebold, C. Th. E. Ueber Parthenogenesis. 4* *Munich,* 1862

Siebold, Carl Theodor von. *See* Hertwig.

Siebold, Ph. Fr. de. Voyage au Japon pendant 1823-30. Édition Française, rédigée par Montry et Fraissinet, Vols. 1 and 5. 8° *Paris,* 1838 and 1840
—— Lettre sur l'utilité des Musées Ethnographiques, et sur l'importance de leur création dans les États Européens qui possèdent des Colonies, ou qui entretiennent des Relations Commerciales avec les autres parties du Monde. Royal 8* *Paris,* 1843
—— Nippon. Archiv zur Beschreibung von Japan und dessen Neben- und Schutzländern; Jezo mit den Südlichen Kurilen, Krafto, Kooraï, und den Liukiu-Inseln, &c. Vols. 1-6. *Maps and plates.* Folio *Leyden,* 1852
—— *See* Vries.
—— **and P. Melvill de Carnbee.** Le Moniteur des Indes-Orientales et Occidentales, recueil de Mémoires et de Notices Scientifiques et Industriels, de Nouvelles et de Faits importants concernant les Possessions Néerlandaises d'Asie et d'Amérique, 1846-49. 3 vols. *Maps and plates.* 4° *The Hague,* 1847-49

Sieger, Dr Robert. Die Schwankungen der hocharmenischen Seen seit 1800 in Vergleichung, mit einigen verwandten Erscheinungen. *Diagrams.* 8* *Vienna,* 1888
—— Gletscher- und Seespiegelschwankungen. 12* *Munich,* 1888
—— Neue Beiträge zur Statistik der Seespiegelschwankungen. 8* *Vienna,* 1888
—— Schwankungen der innerafrikanischen Seen. 8* *Vienna,* N.D.
—— Seenschwankungen und Strandverschiebungen in Skandinavien. (Sonderabdruck aus der Zeitschrift der Gesellschaft für Erdkunde zu Berlin XXVIII. Band 1893. No. 1 und 6.) 8* *Berlin,* 1893

Sievers, Dr W. Ueber die Abhängigkeit der jetzigen Confessionsverteilung in Südwestdeutschland von den früheren Territorialgrenzen. (Inaugural dissertation zur Erlangung der Philosophischen Doctorwürde an der Universität Göttingen.) 4° *Hamburg,* 1883
—— Reise in der Sierra Nevada de Santa Marta. *Illustrations.* 8° *Leipzig,* 1887
—— Venezuela, mit einer Karte der Venezolanischen Cordillere, bearbeitet und gezeichnet auf Basis der Sievers'schen Forschungen von L. Friederichsen. 8° *Hamburg,* 1888
—— *See* Penck, Geographische Abhandlungen, Band 3.

Siewers, Carl. *See* Tromholt.

Sighelmus, —. *See* Hakluyt, Vol. 2; Kerr, Vol. 1; Purchas, Vol. 1, Book 3: Appendix 1.

Sigismund, Reinhold. Die Aromata in ihrer Bedeutung für Religion, Sitten, Gebräuche, Handel, und Geographie des Altertums bis zu den ersten Jahrhunderten unserer Zeitrechnung. 8° *Leipzig,* 1884

Sigsbee, C. D. *See* United States, F, Coast and Geodetic Survey: Appendix 2.

Sigurdsson, Jon. *See* Rafn.

Silas, Ferdinand. The Giant Balloon; an Account of its Construction, and of the Two Ascents made by Nadar, together with various Scientific Notices respecting the Helice, or Screw, applied to Aerial Navigation; compiled from the French of MM. Babinet, Barral, and Nadar. 8* 1863

Silas, F. *See* Scherzer.

Siljeström, P. A. *See* Gaimard, Paul.

Silliman, Benjamin. *See* Phillips, New Voyages and Travels [3], Vol. 7: Appendix 1.

Silva, A. C. da. *See* Portugal, Lisbon: Appendix 2.

Silva Figueroa, Garcia. *See* Purchas, Vol. 2, Book 9: Appendix 1.

Silva, J. M. Pereira da. Christovam Columbo e o descobrimento da America. 8° *Rio de Janeiro*, 1892

Silva, Luiz A. Rebello da. *See* Santarem.

Silva, Nuno da. *See* Callander, Vol. 1 ; Hakluyt, Vol. 4 ; Kerr, Vol. 10: Appendix 1.

Silveira, — de. *See* Santarem.

Silver, J. M. W. Sketches of Japanese Manners and Customs. Illustrated by native drawings reproduced in . . . chromo-lithography. 4° 1867

Silver, S. W. Handbook to South Africa. *Map.* Small 8* 1872
—— The same, including the Cape Colony, Natal, the Diamond Fields, the Trans-Orange Republics, &c., also a Gazetteer. 2nd edition. *Plates.* Small 8° 1876
—— The same, 3rd edition, including the Transvaal, Orange Free State, &c. *Map and plates.* Small 8° 1880
—— Handbook for Australia and New Zealand, with Seasons' Chart of the World. Small 8° 1874
—— The same, 3rd edition, including the Fiji Islands. *Map.* Small 8° 1880
—— The same, with New Map of the Colonies. 5th edition. 1886
—— Handbook to the Transvaal, British South Africa : its natural features, industries, population, and gold-fields. *Map.* Small 8° 1877
—— Handbook to Canada : a Guide for Travellers and Settlers in the Provinces of Ontario, Manitoba, Quebec, Nova Scotia, New Brunswick, British Columbia, Prince Edward Island, North - West Territories, &c. 2nd edition. *Map.* Crown 8° 1884
—— Handbook to South Africa : including the Cape Colony, the Diamond Fields, Natal, British Bechuanaland, Bechuanaland Protectorate, Zambesia and its Gold Fields, the Transvaal and its Gold Fields, Orange Free State, &c. *Also a Gazetteer and map.* 4th edition. *Illustrations.* 12° 1891
—— *See* Buller, W. L.

Silvestre, J. L'Empire d'Annam et le Peuple Annamite ; Aperçu sur la Géographie, les Productions, l'Industrie les Mœurs et les coutumes de l'Annam, *Map.* 12° *Paris*, 1889

Silvestri, Carlo. Istorica e geografica descrizione delle antiche paludi Adriane, ora chiamate Lagune di Venezia . . . con notizie della citta di Adria, e Gavello . . . di Rovigo . . . e delle terre di Lendinara e Badia. *Maps.* Small 4° *Venice*, 1736

Sime, James. Geography of Europe. *Illustrations.* 12° 1890

Simler, Josias. Iosiæ Simleri Vallesiæ et Alpium descriptio. 8° *Leyden*, 1633

Simmonds, P. L. The Commercial Products of the Vegetable Kingdom, considered in their various uses to Man and in their relation to the Arts and Manufactures, forming a Practical Treatise and Handbook of Reference for the Colonist, Manufacturer, Merchant, and Consumer. 8° 1854
—— Waste Products and Undeveloped Substances : a Synopsis of progress made in their economic utilisation during the last quarter of a century at home and abroad. 3rd edition. 12° 1876
—— Tropical Agriculture : a Treatise on the culture, preparation, commerce, and consumption of the principal products of the Vegetable Kingdom. 8° 1877
—— The Commercial Products of the Sea ; or, Marine Contributions to Food, Industry, and Art. 8° 1879

Simms, F. W. A Treatise on the Principal Mathematical and Drawing Instruments employed by the Engineer, Architect, and Surveyor ; with a Description of the Theodolite, together with Instructions in Field-work. *Woodcuts.* 12° 1847
—— A Treatise on the Principal Mathematical Instruments employed in Surveying, Levelling, and Astronomy, explaining their Construction, Adjustments, and Use ; with an Appendix and Tables. *Diagrams.* 8° 1850
—— The Sextant and its Applications ; including the Correction of Observations for Instrumental Errors, and the Determination of Latitude, Time, and Longitude, by various methods, on Land and Sea, with Examples and Tables. 8° 1858

Simon, Gabriel. Voyage en Abyssinie et chez les Gallas-Raias : L'Éthiopie, ses mœurs, ses traditions, le Négouss Johannès, les Églises monolithes de Lalibéla. *Map and illustrations.* 8° *Paris*, 1885

Simon, G. E. China : its Social, Political, and Religious Life. From the French of G. Eug. Simon. 8° 1887

Simon, Pedro. *See* Hakluyt Soc. Publ., Vol. 28 : Appendix 1.

Simond, L. Journal of a Tour and Residence in Great Britain, during the years 1810 and 1811. 2nd edition. 2 vols. *Plates.* 8° *Edinburgh*, 1817
—— Switzerland in 1817-19 ; with an Historical Sketch of the Manners and Customs of Ancient and Modern Helvetia. 2 vols. 8° 1823
—— *See* Phillips, New Voyages and Travels [3], Vol. 7 : Appendix 1.

Simonin, L. La Toscane et la Mer Tyrrhénienne : Études et Explorations. 12° *Paris*, 1868

Simonoff, L. J. Description of an Astronomical Observatory of the Imperial Kazan University. [In Russian.] *Plates.* 8*   *St Petersburg,* 1838

Simonsen, Vedel. Biedrag til Danske Slottes og Herreborges . . . Historie. 12°   *Odense,* 1840
—— Biedrag til Odense Byes Aeldre Historie. Vol. I. 12°   *Odense,* 1842
—— Samlinger til Hagenskov Slots, nuvaerende Frederiksgaves, Historie. 12*
                               Odense, 1842

Simony, Dr Friedrich. Das Dachsteingebiet, ein geographisches Charakterbild aus den Österreichischen Nordalpen. Erste Lieferung. *Photographs, &c.* 4°
                               Vienna, 1889
—— Das Schwinden des Karlseisfeldes nach 50 jährigen Beobachtungen und Aufnahmen. *Photographs.* 8°
                               Vienna, 1891
—— Begleitwort zur zweiten Lieferung des Werkes das Dachsteingebiet. *Plates.* 4°   *Vienna,* 1893
—— Verzeichniss der in Druck veröffentlichten Arbeiten von Friedrich Simony, von Dr A. E. Forster. Large 8°
                               Vienna, 1893

Simpson, Alex. The Sandwich Islands : Progress of Events since their Discovery by Capt. Cook, their Occupation by Lord George Paulet, their Value and Importance. *Maps.* 8°   1843
—— The Oregon Territory, &c. *See* United States, K (Oregon) : Appendix 2.

Simpson, Edward. *See* United States, E, *a*, Hydrographic Office Publications, No. 92 : Appendix 2.

Simpson, Sir George. Narrative of a Journey round the World during 1841-42. 2 vols. *Map and portrait.* 8° 1847

Simpson, Capt. James H. Report of the Route from Fort Smith, Arkansas, to Santa-Fé, New Mexico. *Maps.* 8*
                               Washington, 1850
—— Report of Wagon Road Routes in Utah Territory. 8* *Washington,* 1859

Simpson, John. Results of Thermometrical Observations made at the "Plover's" Wintering - place, Point Barrow. *Plate.* 8*   1857

Simpson, J. H. *See* United States, K (Texas) : Appendix 2.

Simpson, Thomas. Narrative of the Discoveries on the North Coast of America effected by the Officers of the Hudson's Bay Company during 1836-39. *Map.* 8°   1843

Simpson, W. A Private Journal kept during the Niger Expedition, from the commencement in May 1841 until the recall of the Expedition in June 1842. 8°   1843

Sims, A. A Vocabulary of Kibangi, as spoken by the Babangi (commonly called Bayansi) on the Upper Congo, from Kwa Mouth (Kasai) to Liboko (Bangala). English-Kibangi. 12°   1886
—— A Vocabulary of the Kiteke, as spoken by the Bateke (Batio) and kindred Tribes on the Upper Congo. English-Kiteke. 12°   1886

Simson, Alfred. Travels in the Wilds of Ecuador and the Exploration of the Putumayo River. *Map.* Crown 8° 1886

Simson, Robert. Account of the Life and Writings of, by W. Trail. *Portrait and plate.* 4°   *Bath,* 1812

Sinclair, A. *See* Ross, A.

Sinclair, A. C., and R. Fyfe Lawrence. The Handbook of Jamaica for 1883, comprising Historical, Statistical, and General Information concerning the Island. 8°   1883
—— The same, for 1884-85. 8° 1884
—— The same, for 1885-86. 8° 1885
—— The same, for 1886-87. *Map.* 8°   1886
—— The same, for 1887-88. *Map.* 8°   1887
—— The same, for 1888-89. *Map.* 8°   1888

Sinclair, Catherine. Shetland and the Shetlanders. 8°   *Edinburgh,* 1840

Sinclair, Sir John. The Statistical Account of Scotland, drawn up from the Communications of the Ministers of the different Parishes. 21 vols. 8°
                         Edinburgh, 1791-99
—— Analysis of the Statistical Account of Scotland, with a General View of the History of that Country. Part 2. 8°
                               1826
—— The Correspondence of the Right Honourable Sir J. Sinclair. . . . Illustrated by Facsimiles of Two Hundred Autographs. 2 vols. *Map and portrait.* 8°   1831

Sinding, Otto. *See* Nansen.

Sinkel, E. Ma Vie de Marin. Vol. I. Small 8°   *Brussels,* 1872

Sinnett, Mrs Percy. *See* Huc ; Mollhausen ; Pfeiffer.

Sintra, Pedro di. *See* Cintra.

Sionita, Gabriel. *See* Purchas, Vol. 2, Book 9 : Appendix 1.

Sipière, Clément. Le Cinquième Congrès National des Sociétés Françaises de Géographie à Bordeaux. Compte Rendu. 8°   *Toulouse,* 1882

Sirotka, Prince Radwil. Journey to the Holy Land, 1582-84. [In Russian.]
                         St Petersburg, 1879

Sirr, Henry Charles. China and the Chinese : their Religion, Character, Customs, and Manufactures, and the Evils arising from the Opium Trade. 2 vols. 8°   1849

Sitgreaves, Capt. L. Report of an Expedition down the Zuni and Colorado Rivers. *Maps and plates.* 8°
Washington, 1854

Siu, Paul. Dissertation on the Silk Manufacture and the Cultivation of the Mulberry. Translated from the works of Tseu-Kwang-K'he, called also Paul Siu. *Plates.* 8° *Shanghai*, 1849

Skalkofsky's Russian Trade in the Pacific Ocean : Economic Investigations of the Russian Trading and Sea Routes on the Coasts of Eastern Siberia, Korea, China, Japan, and California. [In Russian.] 8° *St Petersburg*, 1883

Skeen, W. Adam's Peak : Legendary, Traditional, and Historic Notices of the Samanala and Sri-pada ; with a Descriptive Account of the Pilgrim's Route from Colombo to the Sacred Foot-print. *Map.* Square 8° 1870

Skelton, Rev. P. *See* Burdy.

Skertchly, J. A. Dahomey as it is : being a Narrative of Eight Months' Residence in that Country . . ; also an Appendix on Ashantee. *Map and plates.* 8° 1874

Skertchly, S. B. J. *See* Miller, S. H.

Skinner, A. M. Geography of the Malay Peninsula. Part I. *Maps.* 8*
N.P., N.D.

Skinner, J. E. Hilary. Roughing it in Crete in 1867. *Map.* 8° 1868

Skinner, Joseph. The Present State of Peru ; comprising its Geography, Topography, Natural History, &c. 4° 1805

Skinner, Major Thomas. Excursions in India, including a Walk over the Himalaya Mountains to the Sources of the Jumna and the Ganges. 2 vols. 8° 1832

—— Adventures during a Journey overland to India by way of Egypt, Syria, and the Holy Land. [Vol. 2 only.] 8° 1837

Skinner, Walter R. The Mining Manual for 1888, containing full Particulars of Mining Companies, and of all those registered from June 1887, together with a List of Mining Directors. 8°

Skippon, Sir Philip. *See* Churchill, Vol. 6 ; Harris, Vol. 2 : Appendix 1.

Skrine, Henry. A General Account of all the Rivers of Note in Great Britain, with their several Courses, their peculiar Characters, and the Countries through which they flow, and the entire Sea Coast of our Island. *Maps.* 8° 1801

Skrine's Tour in Wales. *See* Pinkerton, Vol. 2 : Appendix 1.

Slack, Captain Charles. Tourists' and Students' Manual of Languages. 4th edition. 12° 1891

—— Introduction to Swahili : for the use of Travellers, Students, and others. *Map.* 12° 1891

Slade, Adolphus. Turkey, Greece, and Malta. 2 vols. *Plates.* 8° 1837

Slade, John. Narrative of the late Proceedings and Events in China. 8°
Canton, 1839

Sladen, Sir E. B. Trade through Burmah to China : an Address read to the Glasgow Chamber of Commerce, on 14th November 1870. *Map.* 8*
Glasgow, 1870

—— Copy of Major Sladen's Report on the Bhamo Route : Official Narrative of the Expedition to explore the Trade Routes to China viâ Bhamo, under the guidance of Major E. B. Sladen, Political Agent, Mandalay ; with connected Papers. *Map.* [Parly. Rep.] Folio 1871

—— *See* Anderson, John.

Sladen, W. P. *See* India, C (Palæontologia Indica) ; United Kingdom, H, "Challenger" Reports : Appendix 2.

Slafter, Rev. Edmund F. History and Causes of the Incorrect Latitudes as recorded in the Journals of the Early Writers, Navigators, and Explorers, relating to the Atlantic Coast of North America, 1535-1740. *Illustrations.* 8*
Boston, Mass., 1882

—— Reconnaissance of the Defences of Norumbega. *See* Horsford.

Sleeman, Major-Gen. Sir W. H. Rambles and Recollections of an Indian Official. 2 vols. *Plates.* Royal 8° 1844

—— Journey through the Kingdom of Oude in 1849-50, with Private Correspondence relative to the Annexation of Oude to British India. 2 vols. *Map.* 8° 1858

—— Rambles and Recollections of an Indian Official. A new edition. Edited by Vincent Arthur Smith. (No. 5 of Constable's Oriental Miscellany.) 2 vols. 8° 1893

Sleeman, Lucy. *See* Blennerhassett.

Slevin, T. E. The Magnetic Pole. *Figures.* 8* *San Francisco*, 1882

Sloane, Hans. Voyage to the Islands Madera, Barbados, Nieves, S. Christophers, and Jamaica, with the Natural History of the last of these islands . . ; with some Relations concerning the neighbouring Continent and Islands of America. 2 vols. *Maps and plates.* Folio 1707

Small, H. B. Canadian Forests, Forest Trees, Timber, and Forest Products. 8°
Montreal, 1884

Smart, Dr T. William Wake. *See* Warne.

Smeaton, Donald Mackenzie. The Loyal Karens of Burma. Crown 8° 1887

Smellie, Thomas D. Ocean and Air Currents. 8* *Glasgow*, 1885

Smirnove, J. *See* Pleschééf.

Smishlyaer, D. The Perm Region (Perm-skiy Krai). A collection of information on the Government of Perm, published by the Local Statistical Committee. 2 vols. [In Russian.] *Perm*, 1892-93

Smit, J. *See* Hudson.

Smith, A. *See* United Kingdom, A (Hydrogr. Off. Publ.) : Appendix 2.

Smith, Agnes. Through Cyprus. *Map and illustrations.* 8° 1887

Smith, Albert. Month at Constantinople. *Illustrations.* 8° 1850

—— Mont Blanc ; with a Memoir by Edmund Yates. *Woodcuts.* 12° 1860

—— *See* Blackwood, Vol. 4 : Appendix 1.

Smith, Dr Andrew. Report of the Expedition for Exploring Central Africa from the Cape of Good Hope, 1834. 8°
Cape Town, 1836

Smith, Dr Archibald. Peru as it is : a Residence in Lima and other parts of the Peruvian Republic, comprising an Account of the Social and Physical Features of that Country. 2 vols. in 1. 8° 1839

Smith, Archibald. Instructions for the Construction of the Best Table of the Deviations of a Ship's Compass, from Deviations observed on 4, 8, 16, or 32 Points ; and for the Adjustment of the Table on a change of Magnetic Latitude. 8* 1850

—— Practical Rules for Ascertaining and Applying the Deviations of the Compass caused by the Iron in a Ship ; with Supplement, being Instructions for the Computation of a Table of the Deviations of a Ship's Compass, from Observations made on 4, 8, 16, or 32 points, and a Graphic Method of Correcting the Deviations of a Ship's Compass. 8* 1855-59

—— Instructions for Correcting the Deviation of the Compass. 8* 1857

—— A Graphic Method of Correcting the Deviations of a Ship's Compass, from Observations made on 4 or more Points. *Diagrams.* 8* 1859

Smith, A. R. Bibliotheca Americana : a Catalogue of . . . Books and Pamphlets illustrating the History and Geography of North and South America and the West Indies. 8° 1874

Smith, Cecil. The Ruins of Persepolis. (From *Macmillan's Magazine*, Feb. 1893.) 8* 1893

Smith, Charles. *See* Fuchs and Saladin.

Smith, C. H. M. Road report from Vador to the Chamalang Valley by the Mawáriki Mountain, and back to Saki Sarwar by the Shahidáni Pass. *Maps and plates.* Large 8* *Calcutta*, 1883

Smith, C. I. Statistical Report on the Mysore. *Map.* 8° *Edinburgh*, 1854

Smith, C. Michie. Results of Observations of the Fixed Stars, made with the

Smith, C. Michie—*continued.*
Meridian Circle, at the Government Observatory, Madras, in the years 1861-90. *See* India, N (Madras Astronomical Observations) : Appendix 2.

Smith, Charles Roach. Notes on some of the Antiquities of France, made during a Fortnight's Excursion in 1854. *Plate.* 8* 1855

Smith, Lieut. Charles Stewart. Explorations in Zanzibar Dominions. (Roy. Geog. Soc. Suppl. Papers, Vol. 2.) *Map.* Large 8° 1887

Smith, D. A True Key to the Assyrian History, Sciences, and Religion : being an Introduction to the History of the Remarkable Discovery of the Primitive Alphabet. 8° 1869

Smith, Edward. Account of a Journey through North-Eastern Texas, in 1849, for the purposes of Emigration. *Maps.* 12° 1849

Smith, E. A. *See* "Erebus" and "Terror."

Smith, Eli. *See* Robinson, E.

Smith, E. R. The Araucanians, or Notes of a Tour among the Indian Tribes of Southern Chili. Small 8°
New York, 1855

Smith, Sir C. Euan. *See* Persia : Appendix 2.

Smith, Capt. Francis. An Account of a Voyage for the Discovery of a North-West Passage by Hudson's Straits to the Western and Southern Ocean of America, in 1746 and 1747, in the ship "California." By a Clerk of the "California." 2 vols. *Maps.* 8° 1748

Smith, F. Harrison. Through Abyssinia : an Envoy's Ride to the King of Zion. *Map and illustrations.* 8° 1890

Smith, F. Hopkinson. A White Umbrella in Mexico. *Illustrations.* 12° 1889

Smith, F. Porter. A Vocabulary of Proper Names, in Chinese and English, of Places, Persons, Tribes, and Sects in China, Japan, Corea, Annam, Siam, Burmah, the Straits, and adjacent Countries. Large 8* *Shanghai*, 1870

—— The Oils of Chinese Pharmacy and Commerce. 8* 1874

Smith, Bishop George. Narrative of an Exploratory Visit to each of the Consular Cities of China, and to the Islands of Hong-Kong and Chusan, in 1844-46. 2nd edition. *Map and plates.* 8° 1847

—— Narrative of a Visit to Lewchew, or Loo Choo, in 1850 ; with the Report of the Loochoo Mission Society for 1851-52, and Extracts from the Journal of Dr Bettelheim, 1850-52. *Map.* 12° 1853

Smith, George. The Chaldean Account of Genesis : containing the description of the Creation, the Fall of Man, the Deluge, the Tower of Babel, the Times of the Patriarchs, and Nimrod ; Baby-

Smith, George—*continued.*
Ionian Fables, and Legends of the Gods ; from the Cuneiform Inscriptions. *Plates.* 8° 1876
—— Assyrian Discoveries: an Account of Explorations and Discoveries on the Site of Nineveh, during 1873 and 1874. *Map and plates.* 8° 1876
Smith, Dr George. The Life of John Wilson, for fifty years Philanthropist and Scholar in the East. *Maps and plates.* 8° 1878
—— Fifty Years of Foreign Missions, or the Foreign Missions of the Free Church of Scotland in their year of Jubilee, 1879-80. 14th edition. *Maps and illustrations.* 8° *Edinburgh,* 1880
—— The Students' Geography of India : the Geography of British India, Political and Physical. *Maps.* Crown 8° 1882
—— Short History of Christian Missions, from Abraham and Paul to Carey, Livingstone, and Duff. Small 8° *Edinburgh,* 1884
—— The Life of William Carey, D.D. *Portrait and illustrations.* 8° 1885
—— Stephen Hislop, Pioneer Missionary and Naturalist in Central India from 1844 to 1863. *Map, portrait, and illustrations.* 8° 1888
—— A Modern Apostle, Alexander N. Somerville, D.D., 1813-1889, in Glasgow, Scotland, and Ireland ; India and America ; Australasia and Austral-Africa; Spain, France, and Italy ; Germany and Russia ; Greece and Turkey ; Austro-Hungary and Slavonia. *Map, portrait, and illustrations.* 8° 1890
—— Henry Martyn, Saint and Scholar, First Modern Missionary to the Mohammedans, 1781-1812. *Portrait and illustrations.* 8° 1892
—— The Conversion of India, from Pantænus to the Present Time, A.D. 193-1893. *Illustrations.* 8° 1893
—— *See* Mitchell, Mrs M.
Smith, G. A. The Advantages of the Far West of America as compared with other fields of Emigration. 8° 1870
Smith, Prof. George Adam. On some Unpublished Inscriptions from the Hauran and Gilead. (From the *Critical Review,* January 1892.) *Plates.* 8° *Edinburgh,* 1892
Smith, Rev. G. Furness. Uganda : its Story and its Claim. Illustrated by Lancelot Speed. Oblong 12° [1892]
Smith, Col. H. *See* Blackwood, Vol. 5 : Appendix I.
Smith, H. H. Brazil, the Amazons, and the Coast. *Map and woodcuts.* 8° 1879
Smith, Col. Sir Holled. Report on the Beni Amer Country. *Map.* Folio *Suakin,* 1892

Smith, James. Voyage and Shipwreck of St Paul, with Dissertations on the Writings of St Luke, and the Ships and Navigation of the Antients. *Maps.* 8° 1848
Smith, Mrs James. The Booandik Tribe of South Australian Aborigines: a Sketch of their Habits, Customs, Legends, and Language ; also an account of the efforts made by Mr and Mrs James Smith to Christianise and civilise them. *Illustrations.* 12° *Adelaide,* 1880
Smith, Captain John. The True Travels, Adventures, and Observations of Captaine John Smith in Europe, Asia, Affrica, and America, from Anno Domini 1593 to 1629 ; his accidents and sea-fights in the Straights ; his service and stratagems of warre in Hungaria, Transilvania, Wallachia, and Moldavia . . . Tartaria . . . Cambia . . . Together with a continuation of his generall History of Virginia, Summer-Isles, New England, and their proceedings since 1624 to this present 1629 ; as also of the new Plantations of the great river of the Amazons, the Iles of St Christopher, Meirs, and Barbados in the West Indies. *Plate.* 4° 1630
—— The True Travels, Adventures, and Observations of Capt. Iohn Smith, in Europe, Asia, Africka, and America, beginning about the yeere 1593 and continued to this present 1629 [from edition of 1629] ; The General Historie of Virginia, New-England, and the Summer Isles [from the edition of 1627]. 2 vols. *Portrait, maps, and plates.* 8° *Richmond, Va.,* 1819
—— *See* Churchill, Vol. 2 ; Gottfried ; Pinkerton, Vol. 13 ; Purchas, Vols. 2, Book 8, and 4, Books 9, 10: Appendix I.
Smith, J. Calvin. *See* Haskel.
Smith, Dr J. E. A Sketch of a Tour on the Continent in the years 1786 and 1787. 3 vols. 8° 1793
—— *See* Linnæus.
Smith, J. L. Clifford. Narrative of the discovery of the Great Central Lakes of Africa: Tanganyika, Victoria Nyanza, Albert Nyanza, and Nyassa. *Map.* Small 8° *Halifax,* 1877
Smith, J. W. Report to the Mexican Gulf Railway Company. *Map.* 8° *Liverpool,* 1847
Smith, Joseph W., and G. E. Dalrymple. Report of the Proceedings of the Queensland Government schooner " Spitfire " in search of the Mouth of the River Burdekin, on the North-Eastern Coast of Australia ; and of a portion of that Coast extending from Gloucester Island to Halifax Bay. 8° *Brisbane,* 1860
Smith, Lieut. Explorations on the Victoria Nyanza. (From *The Church Missionary Intelligencer and Record.*) 8° 1878

Smith, Mary H. The Earth and its Inhabitants : Common School Geography. (Guyot's Geographical Series.) *Maps.* 4° *New York,* 1870

Smith, M. L., and E. L. F. Hardcastle. Survey of the Valley of Mexico. [Congress Report.] *Map.* 8* *Washington,* 1849

Smith, Gen. Persifor F., and Gen. B. Riley. Report on the Geology and Topography of California. *See* United States, K, California : Appendix 2.

Smith, Philip. *See* Schliemann.

Smith, R. B. Italian Irrigation : being a Report on the Agricultural Canals of Piedmont and Lombardy. 2nd edition. 2 vols. 8°, and Atlas 1855

Smith, R. Bosworth. Mohammed and Mohammedanism. 2nd edition. Small 8° 1876

—— Carthage and the Carthaginians. *Maps and plates.* Small 8° 1878

—— Uganda. Two Letters to the *Times.* 8* 1882

Smith, Sir R. Murdoch. Persian Art. *Plate.* 8° [1876]

—— and Comm. E. A. Porcher. History of the Recent Discoveries at Cyrene, made during an Expedition to the Cyrenaica in 1860-61, under the auspices of H.M. Government. *Map and plates.* 4° 1864

Smith, Robert. *See* Purchas, Vol. 1, Book 5 : Appendix 1.

Smith, Lieut. R. S. A Manual of Topographical Drawing. *Plates.* Royal 8° *New York,* 1854

Smith, S. Percy. The Eruption of Tarawera : a Report to the Surveyor-General. *Maps and plates.* 8° *Wellington,* 1886 [1887]

—— The Kermadec Islands, their Capabilities and Extent. *Map and illustrations.* 8* *Wellington,* 1887

—— *See* New Zealand, B : Appendix 2.

Smith, Thomas. De Republica Anglorum. 16° *Leyden,* 1641

Smith, Thomas. The Wonders of Nature and Art, or a Concise Account of whatever is Curious and Remarkable in the World. 11 vols. [Vol. 3 missing.] *Plates.* 18° 1803-4

Smith, Capt. Thomas. Narrative of a Five Years' Residence at Nepaul, from 1841 to 1845. 2 vols. 8° 1852

Smith, Thomas. *See* Boldakoff ; *also* Ray : Appendix 1.

Smith, Vincent Arthur. *See* Sleeman ; *also* India, A, Archæological Survey : Appendix 2.

Smith, Sir Wm. Dictionary of Greek and Roman Geography. 2 vols. *Woodcuts.* 8° 1856

—— The Student's Manual of Ancient Geography. *See* Bevan, W. L.

Smith, William. A New Voyage to Guinea : Describing the Customs, Manners, Soil, Climate . . . and whatever else is Memorable among the Inhabitants, &c. *Plates.* 8° 1745

—— *See* Astley, Vol. 3 ; Laharpe, Vol. 2 ; Allgemeine Historie, Vol. 3 : Appendix 1.

Smith, W. Anderson. Benderloch, or Notes from the West Highlands. 2nd edition. *Map.* Crown 8° *Paisley,* 1883

—— Loch Creran : Notes from the West Highlands. 8° 1887

Smith, W. F. *See* United States, K, Texas : Appendix 2.

Smith, W. H. Birmingham and its Vicinity, as a Manufacturing and Commercial District. *Map and plates.* 8° 1836

Smith, W. H. Canada, Past, Present, and Future : being a Historical, Geographical, Geological, and Statistical Account of Canada West. 2 vols. *Maps.* 8° *Toronto,* 1851

Smith, William R. History of Wisconsin, in three parts,—Historical, Documentary, and Descriptive. Vols. 1 and 3. 8° *Madison, Wis.,* 1854

Smith, W. Wilson Hind. A Boy's Scrambles, Falls, and Mishaps in Morocco. *Illustrations.* Small 8° N.D.

Smith-Delacour, E. W. Shironga Vocabulary, or Word Book on the Language of the Natives of Delagoa Bay, South-East Coast of Africa. *Map.* 8° 1893

Smits, D. H. A. *See* Melvill.

Smollett, Dr. *See* "The Modern Traveller," Vol. 4, p. 610 : Appendix 1.

Smoult, W. H. *See* Baikie, R.

Smucker, Samuel M. Arctic Explorations and Discoveries during the Nineteenth Century, being Detailed Accounts of the several Expeditions to the North Seas, both English and American, by Ross, Parry, Back, Franklin, M'Clure, &c., including the First Grinnell Expedition. *Woodcuts.* 12° *New York,* 1857

—— *See* Fremont.

Smyth, Prof. Charles Piazzi. Report to the Principal Secretary of State for the Home Department on the Royal Observatory of Edinburgh, 1846. 4° *Edinburgh,* 1846

—— Contributions to a Knowledge of the Phenomena of the Zodiacal Light. *Plate.* 4* *Edinburgh,* 1852

—— On the Total Solar Eclipse of 1851. *Plate.* 4* *Edinburgh,* 1852

—— Report to the Board of Visitors of the Royal Observatory of Edinburgh, November 1852. 4° *Edinburgh,* 1852

—— On Raising Water for the Purposes of Irrigation in the Colonies. *Woodcuts.* 8* 1853

Smyth, Prof. Charles Piazzi. Description of New and Improved Instruments for Navigation and Astronomy. [Paris Universal Exhibition of 1855.] Royal 8° *Edinburgh,* 1855

—— Experiences with a Free-Revolver Stand for a Telescope at Sea during a Voyage to Teneriffe in 1856. 8° 1856

—— Astronomical Observations made at the Royal Observatory, Edinburgh. Vols. 11 (1849-54) and 12 (1855-59). *Plates.* Oblong 4° *Edinburgh,* 1857-63

—— Extracts from the Letterpress of the Astronomical Observations made at the Royal Observatory, Edinburgh. Vols. 11 and 12 (1849-54.) *Plates.* 4° *Edinburgh,* 1857

—— Report on the Teneriffe Astronomical Experiment of 1856. *Plates.* 4° 1858

—— Teneriffe: an Astronomer's Experiment, or Specialities of a Residence above the Clouds. *Photo-stereograph plates.* 8° 1858

—— Three Cities in Russia. 2 vols. *Maps and illustrations.* 8° 1862

—— Report read to the Special Meeting of H.M. Government Board of Visitors of the Royal Observatory, Edinburgh, 11th November and 4th December 1864. 2 parts. 4* *Edinburgh,* 1864

—— On an Equal-surface Projection for Maps of the World, and its Application to certain Anthropological Questions. *Maps.* 8* *Edinburgh,* 1870

—— A Poor Man's Photography at the Great Pyramid in . . . 1865, compared with that of the Ordnance Survey Establishment subsidised by London Wealth . . . at the same place four years afterwards : a Discourse, &c. 8° 1870

—— Our Inheritance in the Great Pyramid. Fourth and much enlarged edition, including all the most important Discoveries up to the time of publication. *Plates.* 8° 1880

—— Madeira Spectroscopic : being a Revision of 21 Places in the Red Half of the Solar Visible Spectrum at Madeira during the Summer of 1881. *Plates.* 4° *Edinburgh,* 1882

—— Astronomical Observations made at the Royal Observatory, Edinburgh, being Vol. 15 for 1878 to 1886, containing only the remainder of the Star Catalogue, Discussion, and Ephemeris for 1830 to 1890, of which the first four hours appeared in Vol. 14. 4° *Edinburgh,* 1886

Smyth, R. Brough. Mining and Mineral Statistics, with Notes on the Rock Formations of Victoria ; to which is added a Sketch of a new Geological Map of Victoria. 8° *Melbourne,* 1873

Smyth, R. Brough. The Aborigines of Victoria, with Notes relating to the Habits of the Natives of other parts of Australia and Tasmania. 2 vols. *Maps and plates.* 4° 1878

—— *See* Victoria, B : Appendix 2.

Smyth, Lieut. W., and F. Lowe. Narrative of a Journey from Lima, Para, across the Andes and down the Amazon, undertaken with a View of Ascertaining the Practicability of a Navigable Communication with the Atlantic by the Rivers Pachitea, Ucayali, and Amazon. *Maps and plates.* 8° 1836

Smyth, Admiral Wm. Henry. Memoir descriptive of the Resources, Inhabitants, and Hydrography of Sicily and its Islands. *Maps and plates.* 4° 1824

—— Sketch of the Present State of the Island of Sardinia. *Map and plates.* 8° 1828

—— Account of a Private Observatory recently erected at Bedford. 4* 1831

—— Some Remarks on an Error respecting the Site and Origin of Graham Island. *Map.* 4* 1832

—— Descriptive Catalogue of a Cabinet of Roman Imperial Large Brass Medals. 4° *Bedford,* 1834

—— Observations of Halley's Comet. *Plate.* 4* 1836

—— Nautical Observations on the Port and Maritime Vicinity of Cardiff. *Map.* 8° *Cardiff,* 1840

—— The Mediterranean : a Memoir, Physical, Historical, and Nautical. 8° 1844

—— On some Roman Vestigia recently found at Kirkby Thore, in Westmoreland. *Woodcuts.* 4* 1845

—— Descriptive Catalogue of a Cabinet of Roman Family Coins, belonging to the Duke of Northumberland. 4° *Privately printed,* 1856

—— Notice of Certain Relics found near Aylesbury, with Further Remarks on Rubbings. 8* 1859

—— The Cycle of Celestial Objects continued at the Hartwell Observatory to 1859 ; with a Notice of Recent Discoveries, including Details from the Ædes Hartwellianæ. *Map, plates, facsimile, and woodcuts.* 4° *Privately printed,* 1860

—— Letter on a "Double-Faced" Brass in Stone Church ; with a Few Remarks on the Desecration and Robberies in Sacred Edifices. 8* 1860

—— A Word More on the "Double-Faced" Brass in Stone Church, with a Few Particulars respecting that Edifice, &c. *Plate.* 8* 1861

—— Sidereal Chromatics : being a Reprint, with Additions, from the "Bedford Cycle of Celestial Objects," and its "Hartwell Continuation," on the Colours of Multiple Stars. *Plate.* Royal 8° *Privately printed,* 1864

Smyth, Admiral Wm. Henry. The Sailor's Word-Book : an Alphabetical Digest of Nautical Terms . . . Revised for the Press by Vice-Admiral Sir E. Belcher. 8°   1867
—— *See* Campana.

Smyth, W. W. A Year with the Turks, or Sketches of Travel in the European and Asiatic Dominions of the Sultan. *Map.* 8°   1854

Smythe, Mrs. Ten Months in the Fiji Islands ; with an Introduction and Appendix by Colonel W. J. Smythe. *Maps and plates.* 8°   1864

Smythies, Right Rev. C. A. Mission Work on Lake Nyassa. [Cuttings from *Manchester Guardian.*]   N.D.
—— A Journey from Matope on the Upper Shire to Newala on the Rovuma . . . in 1885. 12*   *Zanzibar,* 1885
—— A Journey to Lake Nyassa, and Visit to the Magwangwara and the Source of the Rovuma. 8*   *Zanzibar* [1887]

Snelgrave, Capt. W. A New Account of some Parts of Guinea and the Slave Trade. *Map.* Small 8°   1734
—— *See* Astley, Vol. 2 ; Laharpe, Vol. 2 ; Allgemeine Historie, Vol. 3 : Appendix 1.

Snellemann, J. F. Daniel David Veth. *Portrait.* 8*   *Haarlem,* 1885
—— *See* Muller, H. P. N. ; Veth, P. J.

Snider, A. La Création et ses Mystères Dévoilés : Ouvrage où l'on expose clairement la Nature de tous les Etres, les Éléments dont ils sont composés, et leurs Rapports avec le Globe et les Astres ; la Nature et la Situation du Feu du Soleil ; l'Origine de l'Amérique et de ses Habitants Primitifs ; la Formation forcée de Nouvelles Planètes ; l'Origine des Langues, et les Causes de la Variété des Physionomies ; le Compte courant de l'Homme avec la Terre, &c. *Plates.* 8°   *Paris,* 1858
—— Les Émanations : Recherches sur l'Origine et la Formation forcée et perpétuelle des Mondes. [2nd edition.] 8*
                                           Paris, 1860
—— Nouvelle Théorie sur la formation des Comètes et leur raison d'être. 8*
                                           Paris, 1861

Snider-Pellegrini, A. Du Développement du Commerce de l'Algérie avec l'Intérieur de l'Afrique, et d'une Route par Terre d'Alger au Sénégal par Tombouctou ; précédé d'Observations sur l'Algerie et le Maroc. 8*   *Paris,* 1857
—— Storia della Casa d'Austria dalla sua origine sino al giorno d'oggi. 8°
                                           Turin, 1861

Snodgrass, Major. Narrative of the Burmese War, detailing the Operations of Major-General Campbell's Army, from its Landing at Rangoon in 1824 to the Conclusion of a Treaty of Peace at Yandaboo in 1826. *Map and plates.* 8°   1827

Snow, Robert. Observations of the Aurora Borealis, from September 1834 to September 1839. 12*   1842

Snow, W. Parker. Voyage of the "Prince Albert" in Search of Sir John Franklin : a Narrative of Every-day Life in the Arctic Seas. *Map and plates.* 8° 1851
—— Two Years' Cruise off Tierra del Fuego, the Falkland Islands, Patagonia, and in the River Plate. 2 vols. *Maps and plates.* 8°   1857
—— On the Lost Polar Expedition and Possible Recovery of its Scientific Documents ; with an Introduction and Supplementary Remarks, containing an Analysis and Critical Examination of Facts and Opinions on the Subject, demonstrating the Probability of Survivors yet being found. 8*   1860
—— Ocean Relief Dépôts, and Exploring in the Far North. 8*   [*Edinburgh*] 1880
—— Character Sketch of W. Parker Snow, Sailor, Explorer, and Author. 4* N.D.

Soares, Joaquim Pedro Celestino. Bosquejo das Possessões Portuguezas no Oriente ou resumo de algumas derrotas da India e da China. [Vol. 1.] *Plans, plates, and tables.* 8°   *Lisbon,* 1851
—— Documentos Comprovativos do Bosquejo das Possessões Portuguezas no Oriente. Vol. 3. [Goa.] *Tables.* 8°
                                           Lisbon, 1853
—— Quadros Navaes, ou Collecção dos Folhetins Maritimos do Patriota seguidos de huma Epopeia Naval Portugueza. 3 vols. 8°   *Lisbon,* 1861-63

Soares, Lopez. *See* Astley, Vol. 1 ; Gottfried : Appendix 1.

Soares, Dr S. F. Estatistica do Commercio maritimo do Brazil do exercicio de 1872-73. (2a Parte. Commercio maritimo geral, Importação e Exportação. Organizada pela Commissão dirigida pelo Dr Sebastião Ferreira Soares.) Vol. 2. 8°   *Rio de Janeiro,* 1882
—— The same. (3a Parte. Commercio de longo curso por provincias. Organizada, &c.) Vol. 3. 8°
                                 Rio de Janeiro, 1882
—— The same. (4a Parte. Commercio de Cabotagem por Provincias. Generos nacionaes. Organizada, &c.) Vol. 5. 8°   *Rio de Janeiro,* 1884

Soetbeer, Dr Adolf. Edelmetall-Produktion. (Ergänzungsheft, 57—Petermann's Mittheilungen.) 3 *coloured tables.* 4°
                                           Gotha, 1879

Solander, Dr Daniel. *See* Tröil.

Solander, E. Observations du Magnétisme Terrestre faites à Upsala. 4 *charts.* 4°   *Stockholm,* 1893

Soldan. *See* Paz Soldan.

Soldner, J. Bestimmung des Azimuths von Altomünster, und dadurch der Lage des Meridians, auf dem nördlichen Frauen-Thurme zu München. 8°
Munich, 1813

Soleillet, Paul. Exploration du Sahara Central : Avenir de la France en Afrique. 8* *Paris*, 1876
—— L'Afrique Occidentale : Algérie, Mzab, Tildikelt. *Map.* Small 8°
Avignon, 1877
—— Voyage à Ségou, 1878-79 ; rédigé d'après les Notes et Journaux de Voyage de Soleillet, par Gabriel Gravier. *Map and portrait.* 8° *Paris*, 1887

Soleymân, Pasha. See Astley, Vol. 1 ; Kerr, Vol. 6 ; Allgemeine Historie, Vol. 1 : Appendix 1.

Solinus, C. Julius. Polyhistor, Rerum toto Orbe Memorabilium thesaurus locupletissimus ; huic ob argumenti similitudinem Pomponii Melæ de Situ Orbis, libros tres, fide diligentiaque summa recognitos, adjunximus ; cum Indice rerum atque verborum. *Maps.* Folio
Bâle, 1538

Solis, Don Antonio de. Historia de la Conquista de Méjico, Poblacion y Progresos de la América Septentrional conocida por el nombre de Nueva España. 2 vols. 18° *Paris*, 1827

Solis, G. C. de. L'Origine di molte Citta del Mondo et particularmente di tutta Italia . . . col principio del Regno de Longobardi, &c. 8° *Venice*, 1592

Solis, Juan (or Jean Dias) de. See Burney, Vol. 1 ; Gottfried ; Allgemeine Historie, Vol. 13 ; A General Collection of Voyages and Travels, p. 610 : Appendix 1.

Solms, Marie de. Nice. 12° *Florence*, 1854

Solomon, George. Population and Prosperity, or Free *versus* Slave Production. 8* *Kingston, Jamaica*, 1859

Solomon, Job Ben. See Astley, Vol. 2 ; Knox's New Collection, Vol. 6 ; Allgemeine Historie, Vol. 3 : Appendix 1.

Soltera, Maria. A Lady's Ride across Spanish Honduras. *Illustrations.* 8°
Edinburgh, 1884

Soltykoff, Prince Alexis. Voyages dans l'Inde. 2nd edition. 2 vols. *Map.* 8°
Paris, 1851

Solvyns, F. Baltazard. Les Hindoûs, ou Description de leurs Mœurs, Coutumes, et Cérémonies. Vols. 2, 3, 4. *Plates.* Folio *Paris*, 1810-12

Somera, Josef. Voyage to the Palaos or Pelew Islands. See Burney, Vol. 5 : Appendix 1.

Somerville, Alexander N. See Truter and Somerville, in Vol. 11 of Eyriès : Appendix 1.

Somerville, Lieut. Boyle T. A Vocabulary in various Dialects used in some Islands of the New Hebrides, South Pacific. Oblong 8° 1892

Somerville, Mary. On the Connexion of the Physical Sciences. *Plates.* 12° 1836
—— Physical Geography. 2 vols. *Portrait.* 12° 1848
—— The same. 6th edition, thoroughly revised by H. W. Bates. *Portrait.* 8° 1870

Sommer, Jean Adolphe. Répertoire Analytique et Descriptif pour la Carte d'Athènes et ses Environs publiée en 1841. 4° *Munich*, 1841

Sommer, Joh. Gottfr. Das Kaiserthum Oesterreich, geographisch-statistisch dargestellt. 8° *Prague*, 1839
—— Taschenbuch zur Verbreitung Geographischer Kenntnisse, 1841. *Plates.* 12° *Prague*, 1841

Sommers, Sir G. See Summers.

Sommier, S. Fra i Basckiri (Capitolo di un Libro inedito). 8* [*Florence*] N.D.
—— Un' Estate in Siberia fra Ostiacchi, Samoiedi, Siriéni, Tatári, Kirghísi, e Baskíri. *Maps and illustrations.* Large 8° *Florence*, 1885
—— Prima Ascensione Invernale al Capo Nord e ritorno attraverso la Lapponia e la Finlandia. *Map and illustrations.* 8* *Rome*, 1886
—— Due Communicazioni fatte alla Società d'Antropologia sui Lapponi e sui Finlandesi Settentrionali. 8* 1886
—— Siriéni Ostiacchi e Samoiedi dell' Ob. Prima parte. *Map and illustrations.* 4° *Florence*, 1887
—— Una Genziana Nuova per l'Europa. 8* 1888
—— Note di Viaggio. 1. Esposizione Uralo-Siberiana di Ekaterinburg, Ceremissi degli Urali e del Volga. 2. Mordvá —Popolazione di Astrakan—Kalmucchi. *Illustrations.* 4* *Florence*, 1889
—— and E. H. Giglioli. Il Dottor Finsch alla Nuova Guinea. 8*
[*Florence*, 1889]

Sommières, Col. L. C. V. de. See Phillips, New Voyages and Travels [3], Vol. 4 : Appendix 1.

Sonklar, Carl A. von. Ein Condensations Hygrometer. *Plate.* 8* *Vienna*, 1856
—— Der neuerliche Ausbruch des Suldnergletschers in Tirol. *Map.* 8* *Vienna*, 1857
—— Ueber den Zusammenhang der Gletscherschwankungen mit den meteorologischen Verhältnissen. 8* *Vienna*, 1858
—— Grundzüge einer Hyetographie des Oesterreichischen Kaiserstaates. *Map and tables.* Royal 8* *Vienna*, 1860
—— Die Oetzthaler Gebirgsgruppe, mit besonderer Rücksicht auf Orographie und Gletscherkunde. *Plate.* 8°
Gotha, 1860

Sonklar, Carl A. von. Von den Glets-
chern der Diluvialzeit. Royal 8*
                                Vienna, 1862
—— Von den Alpen. 2 parts. (Oesterr.
Revue, 3 band, 1864.) *Maps.* 8* [1864]
—— Die Gebirgsgruppe der Hohen-Tauern,
mit besonderer Rücksicht auf Orographie,
Gletscherkunde, Geologie, und Meteor-
ologie. *Maps.* 8°   *Vienna*, 1866
—— Die Zillerthaler Alpen, mit besonderer
Rücksicht auf Orographie, Gletscher-
kunde und Geologie. (Ergänzungsheft,
32 — Petermann's Mittheilungen.)   3
maps. 4°   *Gotha*, 1872
—— Leitfaden der Geographie von Europa,
für höhere Lehranstalten. 2nd edition.
8°   *Vienna*, 1876
—— Lehrbuch der Geographie für die k. k.
Militär-, Real-, und Kadeten-Schulen.
Maps. 8°   *Vienna*, 1877
—— The same. 2nd edition. 8°   1880
—— Von den Ueberschwemmungen. Ent-
haltend: Allgemeine Beschreibung,
Chronik der Ueberschwemmungen und
Mittel der Abwehr. 8°   *Vienna*, 1883
—— *See* Martel ; *also* Switzerland, B, Alps :
Appendix 2.

Sonnenschein, A. *See* Kirchhoff.

Sonnenstern, M. von. *See* Central
America, Nicaragua : Appendix 2.

Sonnerat, M. Voyage à la Nouvelle
Guinée, dans lequel on trouve la Descrip-
tion des Lieux, des Observations Phy-
siques et Morales, et des détails relatifs
à l'Histoire Naturelle dans le Regne
Animal et le Regne Végétal. *Plates.* 4°
                                Paris, 1776
—— Voyage aux Indes Orientales et à la
Chine, 1774-81. 2 vols. *Plates.* 4°
                                Paris, 1782

Sonnini, C. S. Travels in Upper and
Lower Egypt, undertaken by order of the
old Government of France. Translated
by Henry Hunter. 3 vols. *Maps and
plates.* 8°   1799
—— Travels in Upper and Lower Egypt.
Translated from the French. *Map and
plates.* 4°   1800
—— Travels in Greece and Turkey. 2 vols.
Map and plates. 8°   1801
—— The same. 4°   1801
—— The same. Collection of plates. 4°
                                    1801
—— Voyage dans la Haute et Basse Égypte.
Illustrations. 3 vols. Small 8°, and
vol. of plates 4°   *Paris*, 1798
—— *See* Pelham, Vol. 1 : Appendix 1.

Sonnleithner, H. von. Skizze über den
Oesterreichischen Reisenden, Virgil von
Helmreichen. 8°   *Vienna*, 1852

Sonora, Marqués de. Informe General
que en virtud de Real Orden instruyó y
entregó el Excmo. Sr. Marqués de Sonora
siendo visitador General de este Reyno

Sonora, Marqués de—*continued.*
al Excmo. Sr. Virrey Frey D. Antonio
Bucarely y Ursua con fecha de 31 de
Diciembre de 1771. 8°   *Mexico*, 1867

Sopwith, T. Notes of a Visit to Egypt,
by Paris, Lyons, Nismes, Marseilles, and
Toulon. *Plates.* 12°   1857

Soraluce y Zubizarreta, Nicolás de.
Las Excmas, juntas y diputaciones de
Guipúzcoa y Juan Sebastian del Cano
inmortal Protorodeador del Mundo ante
la Historia. 8*   *Vitoria*, 1883

Sorby, Dr H. C. On the Motions of
Waves as illustrating the Structure and
Formation of Stratified Rocks. 8* 1855
—— On the Terraces in the Valley of the
Tay north of Dunkeld. 8*
                            Edinburgh, 1856
—— On the Physical Geography of the
Tertiary Estuary of the Isle of Wight.
Map. 8*   *Edinburgh*, 1857

Sörensen, N. G. *See* Sweden, A, Geologiska Undersökning : Appendix 2.

Soria, Pablo. Informe del Comisionado
de la Sociedad del Rio Bermejo, á los
Señores Accionistas. Small 4°
                            Buenos Ayres, 1831

Sosa, P. *See* Wyse.

Sosnoffsky, Col. J. Russian Scientific-
Commercial Expedition to China in 1874-
75. [In Russian.] 8° *St Petersburg*, 1876
—— *See* Clarke, F. C. H. ; Piassetsky.

Sotheby, S. Leigh. Principia Typo-
graphica : on the Block-Books, or Xylo-
graphic Delineations of Scripture History issued in Holland, Flanders, and
Germany during the 15th Century ;
on their Connexion with the Origin of
Printing ; and on the Character of the
Water-marks in the Paper of the Period.
3 vols. in 1. *Plates.* Folio   1858

Soto, Fernando de. *See* Gottfried ;
Hakluyt Soc. Publ., Vol. 9 ; Kerr, Vol.
5 ; Purchas, Vol. 4, Book 8 ; Ternaux-
Compans, Vol. 20 ; Allgemeine Historie,
Vol. 16 : Appendix 1.

Soubeiran, J. Léon. L'Afrique Australe
Tempérée. *Map.* 8* [*Montpellier*, 1882]
—— L'Observatoire de l'Aigoual. 8*
                            [*Montpellier*, 1883]

Souleyet, L. *See* Vaillant.

Sousa, Francisco de. Tratado das Ilhas
Novus e dos Portuguezes que forão de
Viana, e das Ilhas dos Açores a povoar
a Terra Nova do Bacalháo. 2nd edition.
Map. 8*   *Ponta Delgada*, 1884

Sousa. *See* Faria y Sousa.

Sousa, Pedro Lopes de. Diario da Nave-
gação da Armada que foi á Terra do Brasil,
em 1530, sob a Capitania-Mor Martim
A. de Sousa. Publicado por F. A. de
Varnhagen. *Portrait.* 8° *Lisbon*, 1839
—— *See* Santarem.

Southam, T. *See* Hakluyt, Vol. 1 : Appendix 1.

Southesk, Earl of. Saskatchewan and the Rocky Mountains : a Diary and Narrative of Travel, Sport, and Adventure during a Journey through the Hudson's Bay Company's Territories in 1859 and 1860. *Maps and plates.* 8° 1875

Sowerby, J. The Forest Cantons of Switzerland, Lucerne, Schwyz, Uri, Unterwalden. *Map.* 12° 1892

Sowerby, W. Reports on the Survey of the Mineral Deposits in Kumaon, and on the Iron Smelting Operations experimentally conducted at Dechouree. [India Records, No. 17.] *Map and plates* *Calcutta,* 1856

—— Report on the Government Iron Works at Kumaon, with Plans, Specifications, and Estimates . . . and Remarks on the Iron Deposits of the Himalayas. [India Records, No. 26.] *Map and plates* *Calcutta,* 1859

Soyaux, Herman. Deutsche Arbeit in Afrika : Erfahrungen und Betrachtungen. 8° *Leipzig,* 1888

Soyka, Dr Isidor. *See* Penck's Abhandlungen.

Spaight, A. W. The Resources, Soil, and Climate of Texas. *Map.* 8° *Galveston,* 1882

Spalding, H. Khiva and Turkestan. Translated from the Russian. *Map.* Small 8° 1874

Spalding, J. W. Japan, and Around the World : an Account of Three Visits to the Japanese Empire. *Plates.* 8° 1856

Spallanzani, Abbe Lazzaro. Travels in the Two Sicilies and some parts of the Apennines. Translated from the Italian. 4 vols. *Plates.* 8° 1798

Spanberg, ——. *See* Allgemeine Historie, Vol. 17 : Appendix 1.

Spankie, R. *See* Hammond, H. W.

Spark (or Sparke), J. *See* Hakluyt, Vol. 1 : Appendix 1.

Sparks, Jared. Life and Travels of John Ledyard. 8° 1828

—— American Biography : Lives of Robert Cavelier de la Salle and Patrick Henry. 12° *Boston, Mass.,* 1844

Sparrey, Francis. *See* Purchas, Vol. 4, Book 6 : Appendix 1.

Sparrman, Andrew. Voyage to the Cape of Good Hope, towards the Antarctic Circle, and round the World, but chiefly into the Country of the Hottentots and Caffres, from 1772-76. Translated from the Swedish. 2 vols. *Plates.* 4° 1785

Speed, John. A Prospect of the most famous parts of the World . . . with these kingdoms therein contained, Grecia . . . &c. ; together with all the provinces, counties, and shires contained in that large theater of Great Brittaine's Empire. [Imperfect copy.] *Maps and plates.* Folio 1631

2 F

Speed, Lancelot. *See* Leyland, John ; Smith, Rev. G. F.

Speedy, Mrs. My Wanderings in the Soudan. 2 vols. *Map and illustrations.* Crown 8° 1884

Speedy, T. C. S. Report on the Province of Larut in Perak, Straits Settlements. 4* *Singapore,* 1875

Speir, Mrs. Life in Ancient India. *Map and illustrations.* 8° 1856

Speke, Capt. John Hanning. Journal of the Discovery of the Source of the Nile. *Portraits, maps, and plates.* 8° 1863

—— What led to the Discovery of the Source of the Nile. *Map and frontispiece.* 8° *Edinburgh,* 1864

—— An octavo Pamphlet of 43 pages, containing water-colour drawings of parts of various African Mammals, taken out by Capts. Speke and Grant, with interpolated original drawings by both those travellers. 8* N.D.

—— An octavo Pamphlet, originally containing coloured lithographs of African Birds, and a Report on a Zoological Collection from the Somali country by Edward Blyth, 1860, with interpolated original drawings by Capts. Speke and Grant. 8* N.D.

—— *See* Malte-Brun ; Nardi ; Swayne, G. C. ; *also* Blackwood, Vol. 1 : Appendix 1.

Spelman, Edward. The Expedition of Cyrus into Persia, and the Retreat of the Ten Thousand Greeks. Translated from the original Greek of Xenophon. 8° 1812

Spence, J. M. Primera Ascension al Pico de Naiguata. 8* *Caracas,* 1872

—— Illustrations of Venezuela : Catalogue of Works of Art, &c., collected during eighteen months' travel in that Republic, 1871-72. 8* *Manchester,* 1873

—— Venezuela : its people and its products. 8* *Manchester,* 1874

—— The Land of Bolivar ; or, War, Peace, and Adventure in the Republic of Venezuela. 2 vols. *Maps and plates.* 8° 1878

Spence, Lancelot M. Dalrymple. The Civil Service Geography . . . arranged especially for Examination Candidates and the Higher Forms of Schools. Revised throughout by T. Gray. *Maps.* 16° 1867

Spence, William. The Radical Cause of the Present Distresses of the West-India Planters pointed out ; with Remarks on the Publications of Sir W. Young, C. Bosanquet, and J. Lowe, relative to the Value of the West-India Trade. 8° 1807

Spencer, Capt. Edmund. Travels in Circassia, Krim Tartary, &c., including a Steam Voyage down the Danube from Vienna to Constantinople, and round the Black Sea, in 1836. 2 vols. *Map and plates.* 8° 1837

—— Travels in the Western Caucasus, including a Tour through Imeritia, Mingrelia, Turkey, Moldavia, Galicia, Silesia, and Moravia in 1836. 2 vols. *Plates.* 8° 1838

—— Travels in European Turkey in 1850, through Bosnia, Servia, Bulgaria, Macedonia, Thrace, Albania, and Epirus ; with a Visit to Greece and the Ionian Isles, and a Homeward Tour through Hungary and the Slavonian Provinces of Austria on the Lower Danube. 2 vols. *Map and plates.* 8° 1851

—— Tour of Inquiry through France and Italy, illustrating their present Social, Political, and Religious Condition. 2 vols. 8° 1853

—— Turkey, Russia, the Black Sea, and Circassia. *Map and illustrations, some coloured.* 8° 1854

Spencer, Herbert. On alleged "Spontaneous Generation," and on the hypothesis of physiological units. 8* 1868

Spencer, J. A. The East : Sketches of Travels in Egypt and the Holy Land. *Map and plates.* 8° 1850

Spener, Jacobus Carolus. Notitia Germaniæ Antiquæ, ab ortu Reipublicæ ad Regnorum Germanicorum in Romanis Provinciis stabilimenta, Germaniæ et Germanicarum Civitatum statum et conditionem plene declarans ; ex fide dignis monumentis argumentum perfecit et Novis Tabulis Geographicis instruxit, accessit conspectus Germaniæ Mediæ, qualis seculo VI. et post paulo sequentibus seculis fuit. *Maps.* Small 4° *Halle*, 1717

Spice, R. P. A Brief Account of a Tour from Westminster to the extreme North of Norway. 8* 1878

Spiers, R. Phené. *See* Fergusson, James.

Spilbergen, Admiral George. *See* Burney, Vol. 2 ; Callander, Vol. 2 ; Harris, 1 ; Kerr, 10 ; Laharpe, 15 ; Allgemeine Historie, 8, 12 : Appendix 1.

Spillman, Joseph. *See* Münzenberger.

Spilman, James. A Journey through Russia into Persia, by two English Gentlemen, . . . 1739, from Petersburg, in order to make a discovery how the Trade from Great Britain might be carried on from Astracan over the Caspian. 8* 1742

Spilsbury, F. B. *See* Phillips [1], Vol. 6 : Appendix 1.

Spinola, Dr A. de Souza. *See* Jardim.

Spittel. Der Weichselstrom von Montauerspitze bis zur Mündung. *Maps and plates.* 4* *Berlin*, 1862

Spittler, L. T. Geschichte des Fürstenthums Hannover seit den Zeiten der Reformation bis zu Ende des Siebenzehnten Jahrhunderts. 2 vols. 8° *Hanover*, 1798

Spix, J. B. von, and C. F. P. von Martius. Reise in Brasilien auf Befehl Sr. Majestät Maximilian Joseph I., Königs von Baiern, in den Jahren 1817 bis 1820. 3 vols. 4° Atlas eleph. folio *Munich*, 1823-31

—— Travels in Brazil in 1817-20, undertaken by command of the King of Bavaria. 2 vols. *Plates.* 8° 1824

Spörer, J. Novaja Semlä in geographischer, naturhistorischer, und volkswirthschaftlicher Beziehung. (Ergänzungsheft, 21—Petermann's Mittheilungen.) *Map.* 4° *Gotha*, 1867

—— *See* Polar Regions, Arctic, H : Appendix 2.

Spottiswoode, G. A. *See* Galton, Vacation Tourists.

Spottiswoode, W. A Tarantasse Journey through Eastern Russia in 1856. *Map and plates.* 8° 1857

—— On a Method for determining Longitude by means of Observations on the Moon's greatest Altitude. 4* 1860

Spratt, Admiral T. A. B. Report of Deep Soundings between Malta and the Archipelago in 1856-57, with Remarks on the best Means of obtaining Deep Soundings. *Map.* 8° 1857

—— Report on the Delta of the Danube, with Plans and Sections. Folio* 1857

—— Remarks on the Comparative Conditions of the different Mouths and Branches of the Danube. *Maps and plans.* [Parly. Rep.] Folio* 1858

—— An Investigation on the Effect of the Prevailing Wave Influence on the Nile's Deposits. *Maps.* Folio* 1859

—— A Dissertation on the True Position of Pelusium and Farama. *Maps.* Folio* 1859

—— Sailing Directions for the Island of Crete or Candia. 8* 1861

—— Instructions sur l'île de Crète ou Candie. Traduction par A. le Gras. 8* *Paris*, 1861

—— Travels and Researches in Crete. 2 vols. *Maps and plates.* 8° 1865

—— On the Evidences of the rapid Silting in progress at Port Said, the entrance to the Suez Canal. *Maps.* 8* 1870

—— A Suggestion for the Improvement of the Entrance to the Mersey. *Map.* 8* 1880

—— Report on the Present State of the Navigation of the River Mersey, 1880. *Plans.* 8* 1881

—— The same, 1882. *Plan.* 8* 1883

Spratt, Admiral T. A. B. The same, 1883. *Chart and plans.* 8*   1884
—— The same, 1884. *Plan.* 8*   1885
—— The same, 1885. *Plan.* 8*   1886
—— Remarks on the Dorian Peninsula and Gulf; with Notes on the Temple of Latona there. *Map.* 4*   1886
—— *See* United Kingdom, A, Hydrogr. Off. Publ.: Appendix 2.
—— **and Prof. E. Forbes.** Travels in Lycia, Milyas, and the Cibyratis. 2 vols. *Map and plates.* 8°   1847

Sprecher von Bernegg, Hektor. Die Verteilung der bodenständigen Bevölkerung im Rheinischen Deutschland im Jahre 1820. Ein Beitrag zur Methodik der Dichtigkeitskarten und zur Anthropogeographie des südwestlichen und westlichen Deutschland. *Map.* 8*
Göttingen, 1887

Sprengel, M. C. Geschichte der wichtigsten geographischen Entdeckungen bis zur Ankunft der Portugiesen in Japan, 1542. 12°   *Halle*, 1792
—— *See* Ehrmann.

Sprent, C. P. *See* Scott, J. R.

Sproat, Gilbert Malcolm. Scenes and Studies of Savage Life. *Plate.* 8° 1868

Spruce, Richard. Report on the Expedition to procure Seeds and Plants of the Cinchona Succirubra, or Red Bark Tree [in Ecuador]. 8°   1861
—— Notes on the Valleys of Piura and Chira in Northern Peru, and on the Cultivation of Cotton therein. 8* 1864
—— On the River Purús, a tributary of the Amazon. 8*   1864
—— Palmæ Amazonicæ, sive Enumeratio Palmarum in itinere suo per regiones Americæ æquatoriales lectarum. 8°[1871]

Spry, W. J. J. The Cruise of Her Majesty's ship "Challenger": Voyages over many Seas, Scenes in many Lands. *Map and plates.* 8°   1876

Sprye, Capt. Richard. Commerce with Western and Interior China, Thibet and Tartary, across British Pegue from the Port of Rangoon to Esmok on the South-Western Frontier of China Proper; with Introduction and Notices by the Press. Royal 8* [*Privately printed*] 1860
—— The Western - Inland-Provinces of China Proper, Geographically and Commercially considered in connection with British-Eastern-Pegue and the Port of Rangoon. *Map.* 8*
[*Privately printed*] 1862
—— Commerce with Western and Central China, Thibet, and Tartary. Introduction to Notices by the Press [and various Press Notices.] 4*   [1868]
—— The Sprye Route to Western China. [A Cutting from *The Engineer* of 24th December 1869.] *Map.* Small 8* 1869

Sprye, Captain Richard, and R. H. F. Sprye. Aërial Telegraph to Hong-Kong and the Open Ports of China, and a New Commerce with the vast West of that Empire across Eastern-Pegue from Rangoon. 8* [*Privately printed*] 1862

Sprye, R. H. F. and C. H. F. The British and China Railway, from H. M. Port of Rangoon, in the Bay of Bengal, through Pegue and Burmah to the Yunnan Province of China, with Loop-Lines to Siam and Cambogia, Tonquin and Cochin-China. *Map.* Royal 8* 1858

Spurway, Thomas. *See* Gottfried; Purchas, Vol. 1, Book 5: Appendix 1.

Squier, E. G. Antiquities of the State of New York. Being the Results of Extensive Original Surveys and Explorations, with a Supplement on the Antiquities of the West. *Plates.* 8°
Buffalo, N. Y., 1851
—— Travels in Central America, particularly in Nicaragua; with Descriptions of its Aboriginal Monuments, Scenery, and People, their Languages, Institutions, Religions, &c. 2 vols. *Maps and coloured plates.* 8°   *New York*, 1853
—— Honduras Interoceanic Railway: Preliminary Report. *Maps.* 8*
New York, 1854
—— Do. Supplementary Report. 8* 1856
—— Notes on Central America, particularly the States of Honduras and San Salvador, their Geography, Topography, Climate, &c., and the proposed Honduras Inter-Oceanic Railway. *Maps and plates.* 8°   *New York*, 1855
—— Collection of Rare and Original Documents and Relations concerning the Discovery and Conquest of America, chiefly from the Spanish Archives; published in the Original, with Translations, Illustrative Notes, Maps, and Biographical Sketches. No. 1. Square 8°
New York, 1860
—— Honduras: Descriptive, Historical, and Statistical. *Map.* 8°   1870
—— The Primeval Monuments of Peru compared with those in other parts of the World. 8*   1870
—— Observations on the Geography and Archæology of Peru. 8*   1870
—— Peru. Incidents of Travel and Exploration in the Land of the Incas. *Plates.* 8°   1877
—— Nicaragua: its People, Scenery, Monuments, Resources, Condition, and Proposed Canal. *Map and illustrations.* 8°   *New York*, 1860

Squier, M. F. Travels in Central America, including Accounts of some Regions unexplored since the Conquest. From the French of the Chevalier Arthur Morelet; Introduction and Notes by E. G. Squier. *Map and plates.* 8° 1871

Squire, Col. *See* Walpole, Turkey, Appendix 1.

Squire, Jane. Proposal to determine our Longitude. Small 4° 1742

Stache, G. Die projectirte Verbindung des Algerisch-tunesischen Chott-Gebietes mit dem Mittelmeere. 8* *Vienna*, 1875
—— *See* " Novara."

Stack, E. Six Months in Persia. 2 vols. *Maps.* 12° 1882

Stade, Hans. *See* Hakluyt Soc. Publ., Vol. 51 ; Gottfried ; Ternaux-Compans, Vol. 3 : Appendix 1.

Stæhlin, J. von. An Account of the New Northern Archipelago lately discovered by the Russians in the Seas of Kamtschatka and Anadir. Translated from the German Original : *also* a Narrative of the Singular Adventures of Four Russian Sailors who were cast away on the Desert Island of East-Spitzbergen. By P. L. Le Roy. Translated from the German original. 8° 1774

Stahlberger, E. Die Ebbe und Fluth in der Rhede von Fiume. *Diagrams.* 4° *Budapest*, 1874

Stainbank, H. E. Coffee in Natal, its Culture and Preparation. Small 8* 1874

Stairs, Capt. *See* Moloney.

Stallibrass, E. On Deep-Sea Sounding in connection with Submarine Telegraphy. *Plates.* 8* 1887

Stanford, C. Catalogue of the Geological Maps, Sections, and Memoirs of the Geological Survey of Great Britain and Ireland, under the Superintendence of Sir Roderick I. Murchison. 8° N.D.

Stanford, E. Stanford's Compendium of Geography and Travel, based on Hellwald's " Die Erde und ihre Völker." *Maps and plates.* 8°
Europe. By F. W. Rudler and Geo. G. Chisholm. Edited by Sir Andrew C. Ramsay ; with Ethnological Appendix by A. H. Keane. 1885
Asia. With Ethnological Appendix by Augustus H. Keane ; edited by Sir Richard Temple. 1882
The same. 2nd edition 1886
Africa. Edited and extended by Keith Johnston ; with Ethnological Appendix by A. H. Keane. 1878
The same, by the late Keith Johnston. Revised and corrected by E. G. Ravenstein ; with Ethnological Appendix by A. H. Keane. 4th edition 1884
North America. Edited and enlarged by Prof. F. V. Hayden and Prof. A. R. C. Selwyn. 1883
Central America, the West Indies, and South America. Edited and extended by H. W. Bates, with Ethnological Appendix by A. H. Keane. 1878
The same. 3rd edition 1885

Stanford E.—*continued.*
Australasia. Edited and extended by Alfred R. Wallace . . . ; with Ethnological Appendix by A. H. Keane. 1879
The same. 4th edition. 1884
The same. (New issue.) Australasia, Vol. 1 ; Australia and New Zealand. By Alfred R. Wallace. 1893
—— A Catalogue of Maps, Atlases, Books, and other Publications issued or sold by Edward Stanford. 8° 1890

Stanley, Arthur Penrhyn. Sinai and Palestine in connection with their History. 4th edition. *Maps.* 8° 1857
—— The Mission of the Traveller. [Funeral Sermon on Dr Livingstone : from *Good Words.*] 8* 1874
—— *See* Morrison ; Whitty.

Stanley, Bishop Edward. Heads for the Arrangement of Local Information in every Department of Parochial and Rural Interest. 8* 1848

Stanley, H. Chinese Manual, with Commentary or Explication : Recueil de Phrases Chinoises, composées de quatre Caractères, et dont les Explications sont rangées dans l'ordre Alphabétique Français. Chinese, French, and English. Folio 1854

Stanley, Hon. H. E. J. *See* Stanley of Alderley, Lord.

Stanley, H. M. How I found Livingstone : Travels, Adventures, and Discoveries in Central Africa ; including Four Months' Residence with Dr Livingstone. *Maps and plates.* 8° 1872
—— The same. 2nd edition 1873
—— Coomassie and Magdala : the Story of Two British Campaigns in Africa. *Maps and plates.* 8° 1874
—— Through the Dark Continent ; or, The Sources of the Nile around the great Lakes of Equatorial Africa, and down the Livingstone River to the Atlantic Ocean. 2 vols. *Maps and plates.* 8° 1878
—— The same. Small 8° 1880
—— The Congo, and the Founding of its Free State : a Story of Work and Exploration. 2 vols. *Maps and illustrations.* 8° 1885
—— The Story of Emin's Rescue as told in H. M. Stanley's Letters. Published with Mr Stanley's permission, and edited by J. Scott Keltie. *Map.* 12° 1890
—— In Darkest Africa ; or, The Quest, Rescue, and Retreat of Emin, Governor of Equatoria. 2 vols. *Maps and illustrations.* 8° 1890
—— The same. 2 vols. 4° 1890

Stanley, H. M. Mr H. M. Stanley's March through the Great Forest Region of Central Africa, from the Congo to the Nile Lakes ; with Sketches and Descriptions by Officers of the Emin Relief Expedition. Special Number of the *Illustrated London News*. Folio 1890

—— Slavery and the Slave Trade in Africa. (From *Harper's Magazine*, March 1893.) *Illustrations.* 8* 1893

—— *See* Casdagli ; Glave ; Jephson ; Montefiore ; Parke, T. H. ; Peters ; Rowlands ; Schynse ; Troup ; Wauters ; Werner ; Yule and Hyndman.

Stanley, J. M. Catalogue of the Portraits of North American Indians, with his Sketches of Scenery, &c. 8°
Washington, 1852

Stanley of Alderley, Lord. *See* Hakluyt Soc. Publ., Vols. 35, 39, 42, 49, 52, 64 : Appendix I.

Stanley, William Ford. Experimental Researches into the Properties and Motions of Fluids, with Theoretical Deductions therefrom. *Illustrations.* 8° 1881

Stansbury, Howard. Exploration and Survey of the Valley of the Great Salt Lake of Utah, including a Reconnoissance of a New Route through the Rocky Mountains. *Maps and plates.* 8°
Philadelphia, 1852

Stanton, R. B. Availability of the Cañons of the Colorado River of the West for Railway purposes. *Map and plates.* 8* [1892]

Starke, Mariana. Information and Directions for Travellers on the Continent. 8° 1829

Statkowski, B. Problèmes de la Climatologie du Caucase. 8° *Paris*, 1879

Statter, Dover. The Decimal System as a whole in its relation to Time, Measure, Weight, Capacity, and Money in unison with each other. *Diagram.* 8* 1856

Stauber, Anton. Das Studium der Geographie in und ausser der Schule. 8°
Augsburg, 1888

Staudinger, Paul. Im Herzen der Haussaländer : Reise im westlichen Sudan nebst Bericht über den Verlauf der Deutschen Niger-Benue Expedition, sowie Abhandlungen über klimatische, naturwissenschaftliche, und ethnographische Beobachtungen in den eigentlichen Haussaländern. *Map.* Large 8°
Berlin, 1889

—— The same. 2nd edition. *Map.* Large 8° *Leipzig*, 1891

Staunton, Sir George Thomas. An Authentic Account of an Embassy . . . to the Emperor of China ; including cursory Observations made, and Infor-

Staunton, Sir Geo. Thos.—*continued.*
mation obtained, in Travelling through that Ancient Empire, and a small part of Chinese Tartary ; together with a Relation of the Voyage . . . to the Yellow Sea and Gulf of Pekin. 2 vols. *Portrait.* 4°, and folio Atlas 1797

—— Narrative of the Chinese Embassy to the Khan of the Tourgouth Tartars, 1712-15. By the Chinese Ambassador, and published, by the Emperor's authority, at Pekin. Translated from the Chinese, and accompanied by an Appendix of miscellaneous translations. *Map.* 8° 1821

—— Miscellaneous Notices relating to China, and on Commercial Intercourse with that Country. 8° 1822-50

—— Notes of Proceedings and Occurrences during the British Embassy to Pekin in 1816. 8°
[*Privately printed*], *Havant*, 1824

—— *See* Pelham, Vol. 1 : Appendix I.

Stavorinus, J. S. Voyage par le Cap de Bonne-Espérance et Batavia, à Samarang, à Macassar, à Amboine, et à Surate, en 1774-78. 3 vols. *Maps and plates.* 8° *Paris*, 1800

—— *See* Pinkerton, Vol. 11 : Appendix I.

Stebnitzky, J. Ueber die geographische Lage und die absolute Höhe der Stadt Teheran. [Translated from the Russian, by A. Moritz.] 4* N.P., N.D.

Stecker, A. *See* Rohlfs.

Stedman, Capt. J. G. Narrative of a Five Years' Expedition against the Revolted Negroes of Surinam, in Guiana, on the Wild Coast of South America, from 1772 to 1777 ; elucidating the History of that country and describing its Productions, with an Account of the Indians of Guiana and Negroes of Guinea. 2 vols. *Maps and plates.* 4° 1796

Steedman, Andrew. Wanderings and Adventures in the Interior of South Africa. 2 vols. *Maps and plates.* 8° 1835

Steel, R. *See* Kerr, Vol. 9 ; Purchas, Vol. 1, Book 4 : Appendix I.

Steel, W. G. A Visit to Crater Lake, the Proposed National Park. (From *The West Shore* for March 1886.) 8*
Portland, Or., 1886

—— The Mountains of Oregon. *Plates.* 8° *Portland, Or.*, 1890

Steen, Aksel S. *See* Polar, Arctic, G : Appendix 2.

Steenis, Hendrik Cornelis. Journaal wegens de . . . Reys-tocht met het Oorlogschip Het Huys en't Bosch, 1751. Small 4° *Amsterdam*, N.D.

Steenstrup, Japetus. Zeni'ernes Reiser i Norden. En Kritisk Fremstilling af det sidste tiaars vigtige bidrag til Forstaaelsen af Venetianerne Zeni's ophold i Norden fra 1391 til 1405. *Map and facsimiles.* 8° *Copenhagen*, 1883

Steenstrup, Japetus. Les Voyages des Frères Zeni dans le Nord. *Facsimiles.* 8* *Copenhagen*, 1884

Steenstrup, J. J. S. Et Blik paa Natur-og Oldforskningens Forstudier til Bes-varelsen af Spörgsmaalet om Menneskes-lægtens tidligste Optræden i Europa. *Plate.* 8* *Copenhagen*, 1865

Steenstrup, K. J. V. Om de Kulförende Dannelser paa Öen Disko, Hareöen, og Syd - Siden af Nûgssuak's Halvöen i Nord-Grönland. *Map and plates.* 8* *Copenhagen*, 1874

—— Ur Kongliga Bibliotekets Handskrift-samling : 2. Bemærkninger til et gam-melt Manuskriptkaart over Grönland. *Plate.* 8* [*Stockholm*, 1887]

Steere, Bishop E. A Walk to the Nyassa Country. 12* *Zanzibar*, 1876

—— Swahili Exercises. Compiled for the Universities Mission to Central Africa. 12° 1882

—— *See* Heanley.

Stefani, Prof. Carlo de, Dr C. J. Forsyth Major, and William Barbey. Samos : Étude géologique, paléonto-logique, et botanique ; avec treize planches par Ch. Cuisin. 4° *Lausanne*, 1891

Stefano, Hieronomo di Santo. *See* Hakluyt Soc. Publ., Vol. 22 ; Ramusio, Vol. 1 : Appendix 1.

Stein, Christian G. D. Handbuch der Geographie und Statistik für die gebildeten Stände ; nach den neueren Ansichten, bearbeitet von F. Hörschel-mann. 3 vols. 8° *Leipzig*, 1833-34

—— **and F. Hörschelmann.** Handbuch der Geographie und Statistik für die gebildeten Stände. Neu arbeitet unter Mitwirkung mehrerer Gelehrten, von Dr J. E. Wappäus. 7th edition. 4 vols. (11 parts) in 9. 8° *Leipzig*, 1855-68

Stein, —. *See* Choroschchin.

Steinberger, A. B. Report upon Samoa or the Navigator's Islands. 8* *Washington*, 1874

Steindachner, F. *See* " Novara."

Steinen, Karl von den. Durch Central-Brasilien : Expedition zur Erforschung des Schingú im Jahre 1884. *Maps and illustrations.* Large 8° *Leipzig*, 1886

—— Zweite Schingú Expedition, 1887-88. Die Bakaïrí-Sprache . . . Mit Beit-rägen zu einer Lautlehre der Karai-bischen Grundsprache. *Frontispiece.* 8° *Leipzig*, 1892

Steiner, J. Der Reise-Gefährte durch die Oesterreichische Schweiz, oder das Ober-Ennsische Salzkammergut. 12° *Linz*, 1829

Steinschneider, M. Die Hebraeischen Handschriften der K. Hof- und Staats-bibliothek in Muenchen. 8° *Munich*, 1875

Steinthal, H. Die Mande-Neger-Spra-chen, psychologisch und phonetisch betrachtet. 8° *Berlin*, 1867

Steinwenter, A. Versuch einer zusam-menhängenden Darstellung des Strom-systems des obern Nil. *Map.* 8* *Marburg*, 1875

Stellers, Georg Wilhelm. Beschreibung von dem Lande Kamtschatka, dessen Einwohnern, deren Sitten, Nahmen, Lebensart, und verschiedenen Gewohn-heiten, herausgegeben von J. B. S. *Map and plates.* 8° *Frankfurt*, 1774

Stendhall, Count de. Rome, Naples, and Florence in 1817. 8° 1818

Stephen, Leslie. *See* General, Biography : Appendix 2.

Stephen, Rev. Leslie. *See* Galton, Vacation Tourists.

Stephens, John L. Incidents of Travel in Egypt, Arabia Petræa, and the Holy Land. 8° [? 1836]

—— The same. (" By George Stephens.") New edition. 2 vols. 8° 1838

—— Incidents of Travel in Central America, Chiapas, and Yucatan. 2 vols. *Map and plates.* 8° 1842

—— Incidents of Travel in Yucatan. 2 vols. *Map and plates.* 8° 1843

Stephens (or Stevens), Sacheverel. *See* Knox's New Coll., Vol. 5, p. 608 ; " The World Displayed," Vol. 19 : Ap-pendix 1.

Stephens, Thomas. Madoc : an Essay on the Discovery of America by Madoc ap Owen Gwynedd, in the 12th Century. 8° 1893

Stephens, Thomas. *See* Stevens.

Stephenson, Sir Macdonald. Railways in China. Report upon the Feasibility and most effectual means of introducing Railway Communication into the Empire of China. *Map.* Folio 1864

Stern, Henry A. Wanderings among the Falashas in Abyssinia ; together with a Description of the Country and its various Inhabitants. *Map and plates.* 8° 1862

Sternberg, C. G. von. Reise durch Tyrol in die Oesterreichischen Provinzen Italiens. *Plates.* 4° *Vienna*, 1811

Sterndale, R. A. Seonee, or Camp Life on the Satpura Range, a Tale of Indian Adventure. *Map and plates.* 8° 1877

Sterrett, J. R. Sitlington. An Epi-graphical Journey in Asia Minor. [Archæological Institute of America : Papers of the American School of Classi-cal Studies at Athens, Vol. 2, 1883-84.] *Maps.* 8° *Boston, Mass.*, 1888

—— The Wolfe Expedition to Asia Minor. The same. Vol. 3, 1884-85. *Maps.* 8° *Boston, Mass.*, 1888

Stetson, G. R. The Liberian Republic as it is. 8* *Boston, Mass.*, 1881

Steuart, Lieut. C. J. A Short Account of the Chootas, a Tribe inhabiting portions of the Valley of the Hubb and of the Country adjacent to the Western Frontier of Scinde. *Map and plates.* [Bombay Records, No. 5, N.S.] Royal 8° *Bombay*, 1854

Steuart, James. Notes on Ceylon and its Affairs, with Observations on the Antiquity of Point de Galle, and on the Pearl Fishery. *Map and plate.* 8° *Privately printed*, 1862

Steub, Ludwig. Ueber die Urbewohner Rätiens und ihren Zusammenhang mit den Etruskern. 8° *Munich*, 1843

Steudner, —. *See* Heuglin.

Steveni, W. Barnes. Colonel Grambcheffsky's Pamir Explorations and the Indian Government. *Portrait.* Large 8* N.D.

—— Colonel Grambcheffsky's Expeditions in Central Asia, and the Recent Events on the Pamirs. *Map.* Large 8* N.D.

—— *See* Gromchefsky.

Stevens, B. F. *See* Columbus.

Stevens, C. Ellis. The City, a Study, with practical bearings. 2nd edition. 8* *New York*, N.D.

Stevens, G. S. Report: Aden, 20th February 1880. *Map.* Folio* 1880

—— The same. 27th September 1880. *Maps.* Folio* 1880

Stevens, Henry. Historical and Geographical Notes, 1453-1530. *Maps.* 8° *New Haven, Conn.*, 1869

—— Sebastian Cabot—John Cabot=o. 12* *Boston, Mass.*, 1870

—— Bibliotheca Geographica et Historica; or, A Catalogue . . . of rare and valuable Ancient and Modern Books, Maps . . . &c., illustrative of Historical Geography and Geographical History, &c. Part 1. *Frontispiece.* 8° 1872

—— The Dawn of British Trade to the East Indies, as Recorded in the Court Minutes of the East India Company, 1599-1603. Containing an Account of the Formation of the Company ; the First Adventure, and Waymouth's Voyage in Search of the North-West Passage. Now first printed from the Original Manuscript, by Henry Stevens of Vermont. With an Introduction by Sir George Birdwood. 8° 1886

—— *See* Schöner.

Stevens, John. *See* Herrera, A. de

Stevens, J. J. Report of Exploration of a Route for the Pacific Railroad, near the Forty-seventh and Forty-ninth Parallels, from St Paul to Puget Sound. *Maps.* 8° *Washington*, 1854

—— *See* United States, II, *c* : Appendix 2.

Stevens, Sacheverel. *See* Stephens.

Stevens, Samuel. Directions for Collecting and Preserving Specimens of Natural History in Tropical Climates. 8* N.D.

Stevens, S. The New Route of Commerce by the Isthmus of Tehuantepec. *Maps.* 8* 1871

—— The New Route of Commerce by the Isthmus of Tehuantepec : Argument demonstrating the advantages which the Tehuantepec possesses over all other Routes across the American Isthmus. 8* [*New York*] 1872

Stevens, Thomas. Around the World on a Bicycle, from San Francisco to Teheran. *Illustrations.* 8° 1887

—— Around the World on a Bicycle, from Teheran to Yokohama. *Illustrations.* 8° 1888

Stevens, Thomas. *See* Astley, Vol. 1 ; Hakluyt, Vol. 2 ; Kerr, Vol. 7 ; Purchas, Vol. 1, Book 3, Vol. 2, Book 9 : Allgemeine Historie, Vol. 1 : Appendix 1.

Stevenson, James. Notes on the Country between Kilwa and Tanganika. *Maps.* 8* *Glasgow*, 1877

—— The Civilisation of South-Eastern Africa, including remarks on the approach to Nyassa by the Zambesi, and Notes on the Country between Kilwa and Tanganika. 3rd edition. *Maps.* 8* *Glasgow*, 1877

—— The Water Highways of the Interior of Africa, with Notes on Slave-Hunting and the Means of its Suppression. *Maps.* 8* *Glasgow*, 1883

—— The Arabs in Central Africa and at Lake Nyassa, with Correspondence with H.M. Secretary of State for Foreign Affairs on the attitude of Portugal. *Maps.* 8* *Glasgow*, 1888

—— The Arab in Central Africa. *Map.* 8* *Glasgow*, 1888

Stevenson, William. General View of the Agriculture of the County of Surrey. *Map.* 8° 1809

Stevenson, W. *See* Kerr, Vol. 18 : Appendix 1.

Stevenson, W. B. Historical and Descriptive Narrative of Twenty Years' Residence in South America. 3 vols. *Plates.* 8° 1825

Stewardson, Henry C. *See* Turkey in Asia, B, Palestine : Appendix 2.

Stewart, Charles. History of Bengal, from the first Mohammedan Invasion until the virtual Conquest by the English, A.D. 1757. *Map.* 4° 1813

—— *See* Timûr.

Stewart, C. *See* Mirza Abu Taleb Khan.

Stewart, C. S. A Visit to the South Seas, in the United States ship "Vincennes," during the years 1829 and 1830 ; including Scenes in Brazil, Peru, Manilla. the Cape of Good Hope, and St Helena, 2 vols. *Plates.* 8° 1832

Stewart, Lieut-Col. D. H. Report on the Soudan. [Parly. Rep.] *Map.* Folio* 1883

Stewart, Dr James. *See* Africa, General, D: Appendix 2.

Stewart, J. On the Zambesi. 8* N.D.

Stibbs, Capt. Bartholomew. *See* Astley, Vol. 2; Allgemeine Historie, Vol. 3: Appendix 1.

Stier, H. C. G. *See* Gama, Vasco da.

Stierlin, R. Alpen-Ansieht vom Gurten bei Bern. 8* *Berne*, 1868

Stiffe, Capt. A. W. Survey of the Mouth of the Indus, in March 1867. Folio* N.D.
—— The same. Folio* 1877
—— Baluchistan Provinee of Las Baila: Journal of a Visit to Baila *via* Soumiyáni, in March 1878. Folio* [1885]
—— *See* United Kingdom, A, Hydrogr. Off. Publ. ; and India Return of Wrecks, &c. : Appendix 2.

Stillman, J. D. B. Seeking the Golden Fleece: a Record of Pioneer Life in California ; to which is annexed Footprints of Early Navigators, other than Spanish, in California; with an Account of the Voyage of the schooner "Dolphin." *Plates.* 8* *San Francisco*, 1877

Stirling, A. An Account, Geographical, Statistical, and Historical, of Orissa Proper, or Cuttack. In Two Parts : Part 1—General Description, Boundaries (Ancient and Modern), Soil, Productions, Geology, Rivers, Towns, &c.; Part 2—Chronology and History. MS. Folio
—— The same. Letterpress copy. *Plates.* 4° N.P., N.D.

Stirling, V. H. *See* Marsh, J. W.

Stirton, Dr J. Cryptogamic Flora of the West of Scotland. Published for the British Association Meeting, 1876. 12° *Glasgow*, 1876
—— *See* United Kingdom, K : Appendix 2.

Stizenberger, E. Index Lichenum Hyperboreorum. 12° *St Gall*, 1876

Stockdale, F. W. L. A Concise Historical and Topographical Sketch of Hastings, Winchelsea, and Rye, including also several other places in the vicinity of those ancient towns. *Plates.* 8° 1817

Stocks, J. E. Practical Remarks on the Plants of Sind, and the uses of certain Wild Plants in Medicine, the Arts, and Domestic Economy. [Bombay Records, No. 17, N.S.] Royal 8* *Bombay*, 1855
—— *See* Burton, R. F.

Stockwell, G. S. The Republic of Liberia, its Geography, Climate, Soil, and Productions, with a History of its Early Settlement. 12° *New York*, 1868

Stocqueler, J. H. Fifteen Months' Pilgrimage through Untrodden Tracts in Khuzistan and Persia, in 1831-32, in a Journey from India to England through parts of Turkish Arabia, Armenia, Russia, and Germany. 8° 1832
—— The Overland Companion, being a Guide for the traveller to India *via* Egypt. 12° 1850

Stoddart, J. The Meteorology of Ceylon in 1883, and Average Results from 1869. 4° [1884]

Stoddart, Col. *See* Wolff, J.

Stoffel, Col. Baron. *See* United Kingdom, G, War Office Publications : Appendix 2.

Stok, J. P. van der. *See* Van der Stok.

Stokes, Prof. G. G. *See* Symons, G. J.

Stokes, H. J. An Historical Account of the Belgaum District in the Bombay Presidency. [Bombay Records, No. 115, N.S.] Royal 8* *Bombay*, 1870

Stokes, Capt. J. Lort. Discoveries in Australia, with an Account of the Coasts and Rivers Explored and Surveyed during the Voyage of H.M.S. "Beagle" in 1837-43; also a Narrative of Capt. Owen Stanley's Visits to the Islands in the Arafura Sea. 2 vols. *Maps and plates.* 8° 1846

Stokes, Robert. Regulated Slave Trade : Evidence given before the Select Committee of the House of Lords in 1849. *Plate.* 8° 1851

Stolberg, F. L. Graf zu. Reise in Deutschland, der Schweiz, Italien, und Sicilien. 3 vols. 8° *Leipzig*, 1794
—— *See* Pelham, Vol. 2: Appendix 1.

Stoliczka, F. A Brief Account of the Geological Structure of the Hill Ranges between the Indus Valley in Ladak and Shah-i-dula on the Frontier of Yarkand Territory. 8* *Calcutta*, 1874
—— Geological Notes on the Route traversed by the Yarkand Embassy from Shah-i-dula to Yarkand and Kashgar. 8* *Calcutta*, 1874
—— Geological Observations made on a Visit to the Chaderkul, Thian Shan Range. 8* *Calcutta*, 1874
—— *See* "Novara ;" *also* India, C, Palæontologia Indica : Appendix 2.

Stoll, Otto. Zur Ethnographie der Republik Guatemala. *Map.* 8° *Zürich*, 1884
—— Guatemala, Reisen und Schilderungen aus den Jahren 1878-83. *Maps and illustrations.* 8° *Leipzig*, 1886

Stolpe, M. *See* Sweden, Geologiska Undersökning : Appendix 2.

Stolpyanski, N. "Narodnaya Azbuka." [*Russian Primer.*] 12* *St Petersburg*, 1872

Stolze, F., and F. C. Andreas. Die Handelsverhältnisse Persiens. (Ergänzungsheft, 77 — Petermann's Mittheilungen). *Map.* 4° *Gotha*, 1885

Stone, Octavius C. A Few Months in New Guinea. *Maps and plates.* 8° 1880

Stone, Olivia M. Tenerife and its Six Satellites ; or, The Canary Islands, Past and Present. 2 vols. *Maps and illustrations.* 8° 1887

Stonehewer-Cooper, H. Coral Lands. 2 vols. *Photographs.* 8° 1880

—— *See* Ross, Mars.

Stoneman, John. *See* Purchas, Vol. 4, Book 10 : Appendix 1.

Stone's Dunedin and Invercargill Commercial, Municipal, and General Directory ; Otago and Southland Gazetteer, Almanac, and Companion for 1886. *Maps.* Small 8° *Dunedin, N.Z.,* 1886

Stoney, Capt. H. Butler. Residence in Tasmania ; with a Descriptive Tour through the Island, from Macquarie Harbour to Circular Head. *Map and plates.* 8° 1856

—— Victoria ; with a Description of its principal cities Melbourne and Geelong, and Remarks on the Present State of the Colony, including an Account of the Ballarat Disturbances. *Maps and plates.* 8° 1856

Stoppani, Antonio. Carattere Marino dei grandi Anfiteatri Morenici dell' alta Italia. Estratto dall' opera Geologia d'Italia per A. Stoppani e Gaetano Negri compresa nella grande publicazione : L'Italia sotto l'aspetto Fisico, Storico, Letterario, Artistico, ecc.: Opera divisa in tre parti : Il dizionario corografico dell' Italia, 1 trattate scientifici sull' Italia, e l'Atlante Geografico, Storico, ecc., dell' Italia. *Maps and illustrations.* Large 8* *Milan,* 1877

Story, John. *See* Churchill, Vol. 7 : Appendix 1.

Story, W. *See* Victoria, C : Appendix 2.

Stott, J. G. The Killin Hills, by J. G. Stott. Tables giving all the Scottish Mountains exceeding 3,000 feet in height, by H. T. Munro. 8* N.D.

Stout, B. Narrative of the Loss of the ship "Hercules," on the Coast of Caffraria, the 16th of June 1796 ; also a Circumstantial Detail of his Travels through the Southern Deserts of Africa and the Colonies, to the Cape of Good Hope ; with an Introductory Address to the Rt. Honourable John Adams. 8° 1798

Stow, G. W. *See* Jones, T. Rupert.

Stow, John. A Hermit's Idea that the Stars are the Homes of the Heavenly Hosts, &c., &c. 4* 1862

Stow, J. P. South Australia, its History, Productions, and Natural Resources. *Maps, plan, and illustrations.* 8° *Adelaide,* 1883

—— The same. 2nd edition. 8° *Adelaide,* 1884

Strabo. Strabonis de Situ Orbis. Vol. I. 24° *Leyden,* 1557

—— Strabonis Rerum Geographicarum, Libri XVII.; accedunt huic editioni, ad Casaubonianam iii expressæ, notæ integræ G. Xylandri, Is. Casauboni, F. Morellii, J. Palmerii; selectæ vero ex scriptis P. Merulæ, J. Meursii, P. Cluverii, L. Holstenii, C. Salmasii, S. Bocharti, Is. Vossii, E. Spanhemii, C. Cellarii aliorumque; subjiciuntur Chrestomathiæ Græc. et Lat. 2 vols. Folio *Amsterdam,* 1707

—— Strabonis Rerum Geographicarum, Libri XVII., Graece et Latine, cum variorum, præcipue Casauboni, animadversionibus, juxta Editionem Amstelodamensem. Codicum MSS. collationem, Annotationes, et Tabulas Geographicas, adjecit T. Falconer ; subjiciuntur Chrestomathiæ Gr. et Lat. 2 vols. *Maps.* [Large paper.] Folio *Oxford,* 1807

—— Strabon's Erdbeschreibung in siebenzehn Büchern . . . Verdeutscht von Christoph Gottlieb Groskurd. 4 vols. 8° *Berlin and Stettin,* 1831-34

—— Strabonis Geographica, recensuit, Commentario Critico instruxit, Gustavus Kramer. 3 vols. 8° *Berlin,* 1844

—— Geography of Strabo. Literally translated, with Notes, by H. C. Hamilton and W. Falconer. 3 vols. 12° 1854-57

—— *See* Dubois ; Tozer.

Strachan, Capt. John. Explorations and Adventures in New Guinea. *Portrait, maps, and illustrations.* 8° 1888

Strachan, R. Principles of Weather Forecasts and Storm Prevision. 2nd edition. 8* 1868

—— On the Weather of Thirteen Autumns, Winters, Springs, and Summers ; and on the Annual Means of Thirteen Years' Observations at London. [Extract from *Quarterly Journal of Meteorological Society,* ii.] *Chart.* 8* N.D.

—— Results of Meteorological Observations made at Asuncion, Paraguay. 8* [1885]

Strachey, Capt. Henry. Narrative of a Journey to the Lakes Cho-Lagan or Rákas Tal, and Cho-Mapan or Mánasarówar, and the Valley of Pruang, in Tibet, in 1846. *Map.* 8° *Calcutta,* 1848

—— Physical Geography of Western Tibet. *Map.* 8* 1854

Strachey, John. Observations on the different Strata of Earths and Minerals, more particularly of such as are found in the Coal Mines of Great Britain. *Plate.* Small 4° 1727

Strachey, J. Notes regarding the trade of the Moradabad District. [Records, N.W. Prov., Part 22.] Royal 8* *Agra,* 1855

Strachey, Sir John. India. *Map.* 8° 1888

Strachey, Gen. R. Introductory Lecture on Scientific Geography. 8* 1877
—— Lectures on Geography, delivered before the University of Cambridge, during the Lent Term 1888. Crown 8° 1888
Strachey, William. See Hakluyt Soc. Publ., Vol. 6 ; Purchas, Vol. 4, Book 9 : Appendix 1.
Strahan, G. See India, F, c, Trigonometrical Survey : Appendix 2.
Strahl, Philipp. See Mouraviev.
Strahlenberg, Philipp Johann von. Das nord- und ostliche Theil von Europa und Asia, in so weit solches das gantze Russische Reich mit Siberien und der grossen Tatarey in sich begreiffet, in einer historisch-geographischen Beschreibung der alten und neuern Zeiten . . . vorgestellet. Nebst einer. . . . Tabula Polyglotta von zwey und dreissigerley Arten Tatarischer Völcker Sprachen und einem Kalmuckischen Vocabulario, &c. Map and plates. 4° Stockholm, 1730
—— An Historico-Geographical Description of the North and Eastern Parts of Europe and Asia ; but more particularly of Russia, Siberia, and Great Tartary, . . . with Table of the Dialects of thirty-two Tartarian Nations, and a Vocabulary of the Kalmuck-Mungalian Tongue, &c. Square 8° 1738
Strahorn, R. E. To the Rockies and Beyond, or a Summer on the Union Pacific Railroad and Branches : Saunterings in the popular Health, Pleasure, and Hunting Resorts of Nebraska, Dakota, Wyoming, Colorado, Utah, Idaho, Oregon, Washington, and Montana, &c. Plates. 8° Omaha, 1879
Stralisky, J. Account of the Survey of the Russian Empire during the Reign of the Emperor Alexander II. [In Russian.] 4° St Petersburg, 1874
Strangford, Viscountess. The Eastern Shores of the Adriatic in 1863 ; with a Visit to Montenegro. Plates. 8° 1864
Strauss, Johann Jansen. Reise durch Italien, Griechenland, Liefland, Moskau, die Tatarei, Medien, Persien, die Türkei, Japan, und Ostindien ; worin ausser den Schicksalen des Verfassers, die Merkwürdigkeiten, Lebensarten, Sitten, und Gebräuche der durchreis'ten Länder beschrieben werden ; angefangen im 1647 und beendigt 1673. 8° Gotha, 1832
Strecker, Wilhelm. Topographische Mittheilungen über Hoch - Armenien. Map. 8* Berlin, 1861
Streeter, Edwin W. Precious Stones and Gems, their History and distinguishing Characteristics. Plates. 8° 1877
—— The Great Diamonds of the World. Edited and annotated by Joseph Hatton and A. H. Keane. 8° [1882]
—— See Scott and Atkinson.

Street's Indian and Colonial Mercantile Directory for 1888-89. Maps. Large 8° 1888
Strehler, Dr. Bijzonderheden wegens Batavia en deszelfs omstreken ; uit het Dagboek, gedurende twee Reizen derwaarts in 1828-30. . . . Uit het Hoogduitsch. 8° Haarlem, 1833
Streich, Victor. Scientific Results of the "Elder" Exploring Expedition : Geology and Meteorology. Map and illustrations. 8* [Adelaide, 1893]
Strelbitsky, J. Superficie de l'Europe. Publication du Comité Central Russe de Statistique. Maps. 4° St Petersburg, 1882
Stretch, Richard H. Illustrations of the Zygænidæ and Bombycidæ of North America : Vol. 1, Parts 1 to 9. 8° 1872-93.
Streyc, Daniel. Beskrivelse over den ö Islandia, fra Polsk oversat af E. M. Thorson ; med Anmærkninger af S. Jonasson. 8° Copenhagen, 1859
Strickland, H. E. On the True Method of Discovering the Natural System in Zoology and Botany. 8* 1840
—— Report on the Recent Progress and Present State of Ornithology. 8* 1845
—— On Geology in relation to the Studies of the University of Oxford. 8* Oxford, 1852
—— See Jardine, W. ; Murchison.
Stringer, C. E. W. Report of a Journey to the Laos State of Nan, Siam. Map. Folio* 1888
Stringer, M. Opera Mineralia Explicata ; or, The Mineral Kingdom within the Dominions of Great Britain display'd : being a compleat History of the Ancient Corporations of the City of London, of and for the Mines, the Mineral and the Battery Works. 8° 1713
Strobl, Heinrich. Kreta : eine geographisch-historische Skizze. Map. 4° Munich, 1875-76
Ström, Hans. Physisk og Oeconomisk Beskrivelse over Fogderiet Söndmör, beliggende i Bergens Stift i Norge. 2 parts. Plates. 4° Soröe, 1762
Strong, Fred. Greece as a Kingdom, or a Statistical Description of that Country, from the arrival of King Otho, in 1833, down to the present time. 8° 1842
Strong, Capt. John. See Burney, Vol. 4 : Appendix 1.
Strover, G. A. Memorandum on the Metals and Minerals of Upper Burmah. Folio* 1873
Stroza, Peter. See Purchas, Vol. 1, Book 1 : Appendix 1.
Struckmann, C. Ueber die Veranderungen in der geographischende, Verbreitung der höheren wildlebenden.

Struckmann, C.—*continued.*
Tiere im mittleren Europa und Speciell in Deutschland seit deralten Quartärzeit bis zur Gegenwart. [Incomplete.] Large 8*   [*Lahr*, 1882]

Struve, F. G. W. Table des Positions Géographiques principales de la Russie. 4*   *St Petersburg*, 1843
—— Resultate der in den Jahren 1816 bis 1819 ausgeführten, astronomisch-trigonometrischen Vermessung Livlands. *Maps.* 4°   *St Petersburg*, 1844
—— Description de l'Observatoire du Poulkowa. *Plates.* 4° *St Petersburg*, 1845
—— Astronomische Ortsbestimmungen in der Europäischen Türkei, in Kaukasien, und Klein-Asien. 4° *St Petersburg*, 1845
—— Ueber den Flächeninhalt der 37 westlichen Gouvernements und Provinzen des Europäischen Russlands. *Plate.* 4*   *St Petersburg*, 1845
—— Rapport fait à l'Académie Impériale des Sciences sur une Mission Scientifique dont il fut chargé en 1847. 4*
                    St Petersburg, 1849
—— Exposé Historique des Travaux exécutés jusqu'à la fin de l'Année 1851, pour la Mesure de l'Arc du Méridien, entre Fuglenæs 70° 40' et Ismaïl 45° 20' ; suivi de deux Rapports de M. G. Lindhagen sur l'Expédition de Finnmarken, et sur les Opérations de Lapponie. *Maps.* 4*   *St Petersburg*, 1852
—— Sur la Jonction des Opérations Géodésiques Russes et Autrichiennes, exécutée par ordre des deux Gouvernements. 8*   *St Petersburg*, 1853
—— Arc du Méridien de 25° 20' entre le Danube et la Mer Glaciale, mesuré, depuis 1816 jusqu'en 1855, sous la Direction de C. de Tenner, N. H. Selander, Chr. Hansteen, et F. G. W. Struve. 2 vols. *Maps and plates.* 4°
                    St Petersburg, 1857-60
—— Vergleichungen der Wiener Masse mit mehreren auf der Kaiserl. Russischen Hauptsternwarte zu Pulkowa befindlichen Masseinheiten. 8° *Vienna*, 1861
—— **and O. W.** Expédition Chronométrique entre Altona et Greenwich, pour la Détermination de la Longitude Géographique de l'Observatoire Central de Russie. *Plates.* 4° *St Petersburg*, 1846

Struve, H. Landkarten; ihre Herstellung und ihre Fehlergrenzen. 8* *Berlin*, 1887

Struve, Otto W. Détermination des Positions Géographiques de Novgorod, Moscou, Riazan, Lipetsk, Voroneje, et Toula. 4°   *St Petersburg*, 1843
—— Résultats Géographiques du Voyage en Perse en 1838-39. 4*
                    St Petersburg, 1851
—— Expéditions Chronométriques de 1845 et 1846. 2 parts. 4°
                    St Petersburg, 1853-54

Struve, Otto W. Positions Géographiques déterminées en 1847, par le Lieut.-Col. Lemm dans le Pays des Cosaques du Don. *Map.* 4°
                    St Petersburg, 1855
—— Recueil de Mémoires présentés à l'Académie des Sciences, par les Astronomes de Poulkova, ou offerts à l'Observatoire Central par d'autres Astronomes du Pays. Vol. 2. *Map and plates.* 4°
                    St Petersburg, 1859
—— Librorum in Bibliotheca Speculæ Pulcovensis anno 1858 exeunte contentorum Catalogus Systematicus. Royal 8°   *St Petersburg*, 1860
—— Ueber einen vom General Schubert an die Akademie gerichteten Antrag, betreffend die Russisch-Scandinavische Meridian-Gradmessung. 8°   1861
—— Uebersicht der Thätigkeit der Nicolai-Hauptsternwarte. *Portrait.* 4°
                    St Petersburg, 1865
—— Tabulæ auxiliares ad Transitus per Planum primum verticale reducendos inservien es. 4* *St Petersburg*, 1868
—— Tabulae Quantitatum Bessebianarum, pro annis 1875-79. 8° *St Petersburg*, 1871
—— Die Beschlüsse der Washingtoner Meridian Conferenz. 8* *St Peterburg*, 1885

Struys, Jean. Les Voyages de Jean Struys en Moscovie, en Tartarie, en Perse, aux Indes, et en plusieurs autres pais étrangers, &c. 4° *Amsterdam*, 1681
—— The same. Par M. Glanius. 3 vols. *Plates.* 12°   *Rouen*, 1724
—— The same. Vols. 1 and 3. *Plates.* 18°   *Lyons*, 1782

Strzelecki, P. E. de. Physical Description of New South Wales and Van Diemen's Land. *Maps and plates.* 8° 1845

Stuart, James, and Nicholas Revett. The Antiquities of Athens, and other places in Greece; with the Supplementary Volume by C. Cockerell, W. Kinnard, &c. ; together with the Uncdited Antiquities of Attica, comprising the Architectural Remains of Eleusis, Rhamnus, Sunium, and Thoricus, by the Society of Dilettanti. 5 vols. *Maps and plates.* Folio   1825-33

Stuart, J. M'Douall. Journal of an Expedition into the Unexplored Country to the North-West and South-West of Port Augusta, South Australia. *Map.* Folio*   1858
—— Explorations across . . . Australia, 1861-62. *Map.* 8* *Melbourne*, 1863
—— Journals of Explorations in Australia, 1858-62, when he fixed the Centre of the Continent and successfully crossed it from Sea to Sea. Edited from Mr Stuart's MS. by W. Hardman. *Portrait, maps, and plates.* 8°   1864
—— *See* Westgarth.

Stuart, J. M. The Ancient Gold Fields of Africa: from the Gold Coast to Mashonaland. *Maps and plates.* 4° N.D.

Stuart, Lieut.-Col. Journal of a Residence in Northern Persia and the Adjacent Provinces of Turkey. 8° 1854

Stuart, Villiers. Nile Gleanings concerning the Ethnology, History, and Art of Ancient Egypt, as revealed by Egyptian Paintings and Bas-Reliefs ; with Descriptions of Nubia and its great rock temples to the Second Cataract. *Map and plates.* 8° 1879

—— Egypt after the War : being the Narrative of a Tour of Inspection (undertaken last autumn), including experiences among the Natives, with descriptions of their Homes and Habits; in which are embodied Notices of the latest Archæological Discoveries, and a revised account of the Funeral Canopy of an Egyptian Queen. *Maps and plates.* Large 8° 1883

Stübel, A. W. Reiss und A. Stübel, Reisen in Süd-Amerika. Skizzen aus Ecuador dem 6. Deutschen Geographentage ; gewidmet von Alphons Stübel. *Illustrations.* Folio *Berlin*, 1886

—— *See* Reiss.

Stucklé, Henri. Le Commerce de la France avec le Soudan. 12* *Paris*, 1864

Studer, B. Ueber die natürliche Lage von Bern. *Map.* 4° *Berne*, 1859

—— Geschichte der physischen Geographie der Schweiz bis 1815. 8° *Berne*, 1863

Studley, T. *See* Purchas, Vol. 4, Book 9: Appendix 1.

Stukeley, T. *See* Hakluyt, Vol. 2 : Appendix 1.

Stumm, H. Der russische Feldzug nach Chiwa. 1 Theil. Historische und militär-statistische Uebersicht des russischen Operationsfeldes in Mittelasien. *Maps.* Large 8° *Berlin*, 1875

—— Russia in Central Asia : Historical Sketch of Russia's progress in the East up to 1873, and of the Incidents which led to the Campaign against Khiva ; with a Description of the Military Districts of the Caucasus, Orenburg, and Turkestan. Translated into English by J. W. Ozanne and Captain H. Sachs. *Maps.* 8° 1885

—— *See* Vincent, C. E. H.

Stumpf. J. *See* Switzerland,B: Appendix 2.

Stur, D. Geologie der Steiermark. 4° *Graz*, 1871

Sturge, Edmund. West India: "Compensation" to the Owners of Slaves, its History and its Results. 8* 1893

Sturge, Mrs George. *See* Helfer.

Sturgis, William. The Oregon Question. *Map.* 8* *Boston, Mass.*, 1845

Sturler, W. L. de. Proeve eener Beschrijving van het Gebied van Palembang, &c. *Map.* 8° *Groningen*, 1843

—— Redevoering over de natuurlijke Voordeelen van Bodem en Luchtstreek op Java, &c. 8* *Groningen*, 1847

—— *See* Selberg.

Sturt, Capt. Charles. Two Expeditions into the Interior of Southern Australia during 1828-31 ; with Observations on the Soil, Climate, and General Resources of New South Wales. 2 vols. *Maps and plates.* 8° 1834

—— Narrative of an Expedition into Central Australia during 1844-46 ; together with a Notice of the Province of South Australia in 1847. 2 vols. *Map and plates.* 8° 1849

Sturz, J. J. German Emigration to British Colonies. Small 8° 1860

—— Der Nord- und Ostsee Kanal durch Holstein; Deutschlands Doppelpforte zu seinen Meeren und zum Weltmeere. *Map.* 8* *Berlin*, 1864

—— Schafzucht und Wollproduction für deutsche Rechnung in Uruguay, als Grundlage für deutsche Ansiedelungen in La Plata-Flussgebiete. 8* *Berlin*, 1864

—— Neue Beiträge über Brasilien und die La Plata-Länder. 8* *Berlin*, 1865

—— Die deutsche Auswanderung und die Verschleppung deutscher Auswanderer ; mit speciellen Documenten über die Auswanderung nach Brazilien zur Widerlegung falscher Angaben. 8* *Berlin*, 1868

—— Circular [in German] relative to Emigration to Paraguay. 4* *Berlin*, 1869

Stutfield, Hugh E. M. El Maghreb : 1,200 Miles' Ride through Morocco. *Map.* Crown 8° 1886

Stüwe, F. Die Handelszüge der Araber unter den Abbassinden durch Afrika, Asia, und Osteuropa. *Map.* 8° *Berlin*, 1836

Suchet, Maréchal. Mémoires sur ses Campagnes en Espagne depuis 1808 . jusqu'en 1814. 2 vols. *Portrait.* 8° *Paris*, 1828

Sucksbich, R. *See* Purchas, Vol. 2, Book 9: Appendix 1.

Suess, Eduard. Das Antlitz der Erde. Erster Band. *Maps and illustrations.* Large 8° *Leipzig*, 1885

—— Ditto. Zweiter Band. *Maps.* Large 8° *Leipzig*, 1888

—— *See* Höhnel ; "Novara."

Sulaka, Simon. *See* Purchas, Vol. 1, Book 1 : Appendix 1.

Suleiman Pasha. *See* Soleyman.

Sulivan, B. J. Derrotero de las islas Malvinas. 8** *Santiago*, 1883

Sulivan, Capt. G. L. Dhow chasing in Zanzibar Waters and on the Eastern Coast of Africa : Narrative of five years' experiences in the suppression of the Slave Trade. *Map.* 8° 1873

Sullivan, Edward. The Bungalow and the Tent; or, A Visit to Ceylon. 8° 1854

Sullivan, John T. Report of Historical and Technical Information relating to the Problem of Interoceanic Communication by Way of the American Isthmus. *Maps, plans, and profiles.* 4° *Washington,* 1883

Sullivan, Robert. Geography Generalised; or, An Introduction to the Study of Geography on the Principles of Classification and Comparison. *Maps and illustrations.* 8° 1863

Summers, James. Lecture on the Chinese Language and Literature, delivered in King's College, London, 13th April 1853. 12* 1853

Sumner, Hon. Charles. Speech . . . on the Cession of Russian America to the United States. 8* *Washington,* 1867

Supan, Dr Alexander. Archiv für Wirtschaftsgeographie. (Ergänzungsheft, 84 —Petermann's Mittheilungen). *Maps.* 4° *Gotha,* 1886
—— *See* Wagner and Supan.

Surrè, Herbert. *See* Blackwood, Vol. 4 : Appendix 1.

"Susan," Ship. *See* Hakluyt, Vol. 2 : Appendix 1.

Sutcliffe, Thomas. The Earthquake of Juan Fernandez, as it occurred in 1835 ; with a Refutation of several Misstatements that have been published in the *Nautical Magazine* of 1837 and the Public Papers. *Plates.* Royal 8* *Manchester,* 1839
—— Sixteen Years in Chile and Peru from 1822 to 1839. By the retired Governor of Juan Fernandez. 8° [1841]

Sutherland, Alexander. . Geography of Victoria. 12° 1893
—— *See* Dawson, G. M.

Sutherland, D. A Tour up the Straits from Gibraltar to Constantinople ; with the Leading Events in the Present War between the Austrians, Russians, and the Turks, to the commencement of the year 1789. 8° 1790

Sutherland, Lieut.-Col. J. Original Matter contained in Lieut.-Colonel Sutherland's Memoir on the Kaffers, Hottentots, and Bosjemans, of South Africa : Heads 1st and 2nd, Commentaries and Notes on the Text used in the compilation of the Memoirs. 8° *Cape Town,* 1847

Sutherland, Peter C. Journal of a Voyage in Baffin's Bay and Barrow Straits in 1850-51, performed by H.M. ships "Lady Franklin" and "Sophia," under the Command of Capt. Penny, in Search of the Missing Crews of H.M. ships "Erebus" and "Terror"; with a Narrative of Sledge Excursions on the Ice of Wellington Channel, &c. 2 vols. *Maps and plates.* 8° 1852

Sutro, A. The Sutro Tunnel to the Comstock Lode in the State of Nevada, Importance of its Construction, and Revenue to be derived therefrom. *Map.* 8* *New York,* 1866

Svanberg, Jöns. Exposition des Opérations faites en Lapponie, pour la détermination d'un Arc du Méridien, en 1801-3 ; par Öfverbom, Svanberg, Holmquist, et Palander. 8° *Stockholm,* 1805

Svedmark, E. *See* Sweden, A, Geologiska Undersökning : Appendix 2.

Svenonius, F. V. *See* Sweden, A, Geologiska Undersökning : Appendix 2.

Svoboda, Alexander. The Seven Churches of Asia, as seen in their Present Condition, and other Eastern Subjects. [Descriptive Catalogue of Paintings.] 8* 1869

Svoboda, Dr. Futschau-fu am Minflusse. 8* [*Vienna,* 1888]
—— Annam und das französische Cochinchina. *Maps.* 8* [*Vienna,* 1888]
—— Ein kurzer Besuch auf den Nicobaren. *Map and plates.* 8* *Vienna,* 1888
—— Die Nikobaren-Inseln und ihre Bewohner. *Maps and plates.* 8* *Vienna,*1889

Swaan, P. *See* Robidé van der Aa.

Swain, G. F. Statistics of Water Power employed in manufacturing in the United States. (Publ. of the American Statistical Association, N S., No. 1, March 1888.) 8* *Boston,* 1888

Swainson, W. A Treatise on the Geography and Classification of Animals. 12° 1835
—— Observations on the Climate of New Zealand, principally with reference to its Sanative character. 8* 1840
—— *See* Murray, Hugh; Richardson, Sir J.

Swallow, G. C. Geological Report of the Country along the Line of the South-Western Branch of the Pacific Railroad, State of Missouri ; with Memoir of the Pacific Railroad. *Map.* 8° *St Louis,* 1859
—— *See* Shumard.

Swan, C. A. Letters and Diary of C. A. Swan, of Garenganze, September 1888 to May 1889. 12* 1890
—— Notes on the Grammatical Construction of Chiluba (the language of the Luba people), as spoken in Garenganze, Central Africa ; with brief Vocabularies in Luba-English and English-Luba, and six chapters in Chiluba from the Gospel of John. 12° *Bath* [1892]

Swan, R. *See* Burney, Vol. 4 ; Kerr, 9 ; Purchas, Vol. 1, Book 5 : Appendix 1.

Swan, R. M. W. *See* Bent, J. T.

Swank, James M. Department of the Interior : Tenth Census of the United States. Francis A. Walker, Superintendent. Statistics of the Iron and Steel Production of the United States. *Maps.* 4° *Washington,* 1881

Swanus. *See* Hakluyt, Vol. 2; Kerr, Vol. 1 : Appendix 1.

Swart, Jacob. Vernieuwde Uitgave van Douwes Zeeman's Tafelen, of Grond-beginselen der dadelijke Zeevart Kunde. Vierde Druk. 8° *Amsterdam*, 1844
—— *See* Schröder, J. F. L. ; Tasman.

Swayne, Lieut. E. J. E. Expedition to the Nogal Valley. R.G.S. Suppl. Papers, Vol. 3. *Map.* Large 8° 1893
—— *See* Swayne, Capt. H. G. C.

Swayne, George C. Lake Victoria : a Narrative of Explorations in Search of the Source of the Nile, compiled from the Memoirs of Captains Speke and Grant. *Map and plates.* 8° 1868

Swayne, Capt. H. G. C. Journal of two Expeditions across Somali-land to the Webbe Shabeyli River. *Map.* Folio 1893
—— **and Lieut. E. J. E. Swayne.** Report on the Reconnaissance of Northern Somali-land, February to November 1891. Folio *Bombay*, 1892

Sweetser, M. F. King's Handbook of the United States. Planned and edited by Moses King. Text by M. F. Sweetser. *Maps and illustrations.* 8° 1891

Swettenham, F. A. Journal kept during a Journey across the Malay Peninsula. 8* [*Pahang*, 1885]

Swift, Jonathan. *See* Craik.

Swinburne, Henry. Travels in the Two Sicilies, 1777-80. 2 vols. *Map and plates.* 4° 1783-85
—— The same. 2nd edition. 4 vols. *Plates.* 8° 1790
—— Travels through Spain in the years 1775 and 1776, in which several Monuments of Roman and Moorish Architecture are illustrated by accurate Drawings taken on the spot. 2nd edition, to which is added a Journey from Bayonne to Marseilles. 2 vols. *Plates.* 8° 1787

Swindells, R. A Summer Trip to the Island of St Michael, the Azores. *Map and plates.* 12°
[*Privately printed*], *Manchester*, 1877

Swinhoe, Robert. Narrative of the North China Campaign of 1860, containing personal experiences of Chinese character, and of the moral and social condition of the country, together with a description of the interior of Pekin. *Map and plates.* 8° 1861
—— Notes on the Island of Formosa. *Map and coloured plates.* 8° 1863
—— On the Chinese Dialect spoken in Hainan. 4* 1870
—— Reports of Special Mission to the Vang-tsze-Kiang, &c. Folio* 1870
—— A Revised Catalogue of the Birds of China and its Islands, &c. 8* 1871
—— The Natural History of Hainan. *Plates.* Small 8° 1871

Swire, H. *See* Blackwood, Vol. 6 : Appendix 1.

Sydow, E. von. Begleitworte zum Wand-Atlas über alle Theile der Erde. 8° *Gotha*, 1839
—— Ein Nachruf. 8° *Berlin*, 1873

Sykes, Col. W. H. On a portion of Dukhun, East Indies. *Map.* 4* 1836
—— Discussion of Meteorological Observations taken in India, at various heights, embracing those at Dodabetta on the Neelgherry Mountains, at 8,640 feet above the level of the Sea. *Plates.* 4° 1850
—— Traits of Indian Character. 8* 1859
—— Notes on the Progress of the Trade of England with China since 1833, and on its present condition and prospects. 8* 1861
—— The Taeping Rebellion in China, its Origin, Progress, and Present Condition. 8* 1863
—— *See* India, C, Geological Papers : Appendix 2.

"Sylvanus." Rambles in Sweden and Gottland ; with Etchings by the Wayside, by Sylvanus. *Plates.* 8° 1847

Symes, Major Michael. Account of an Embassy to the Kingdom of Ava in 1795. *Maps and plates.* 4° 1800
—— *See* Eyriès, Vol. 13 ; Pelham, Vol. 2 ; Pinkerton, Vol. 9 : Appendix 1.

Symington, Andrew James. Pen and Pencil Sketches of Faröe and Iceland ; with Translations from the Icelandic. *Woodcuts.* 8° 1862

Symonds, Admiral Thomas W. C. Our Great Peril, if War overtake us with our Fleet deficient in Number, Structure, and Armament. 8*
Newton Abbot, N.D.

Symons, G. J. Rainfall Tables of the British Isles for 1866-80. 8° 1883
—— The Eruption of Krakatoa, and subsequent Phenomena. Report of the Krakatoa Committee of the Royal Society, viz. :—Hon. R. Abercromby, E. D. Archibald, Prof. T. G. Bonney, Sir F. J. Evans, Dr A. Geikie, Prof. J. W. Judd, J. N. Lockyer, Hon. F. A. R. Russell, R. H. Scott, Prof. G. G. Stokes, Lieut.-Gen. Strachey, G. J. Symons, Capt. W. J. L. Wharton. Edited by G. J. Symons. *Maps and illustrations.* 4° 1888

Symons, Lieut. Thomas W. Report of an Examination of the Upper Columbia River and the Territory in its vicinity in September and October 1881, to determine its navigability, and adaptability to Steamboat transportation. *Maps and illustrations.* 4°
Washington, 1882

Synge, Capt. Millington H. Great Britain one Empire : on the Union of the Dominions of Great Britain by inter-communication with the Pacific and the East *via* British North America. *Map.* 8° 1852

Szabad, E. Hungary, Past and Present, embracing its History from the Magyar Conquest to the present time. 8° *Edinburgh*, 1854

Szászky, J. Tomka. Introductio in Orbis hodierni Geographiam, ad ad-curatissimas quasque Calcographorum Tabulas, Methodo quantum ejus fieri licuit facili, directoque ordine, adnexa simul naturalis atque Civilis Regnorum habitus, descriptione ; Præfatus est, de fatis Geographiæ priscis ac recentioribus M. Belius. 8° *Presburg*, 1748

Széchenyi, Count Béla. Die wissens-chaftlichen Ergebnisse der Reise des Grafen Béla Széchenyi in Ostasien 1877-80. Erster Band. Die Beobach-tungen während der Reise. *Map, plates, &c.* 4°, and Atlas large 4° *Vienna*, 1893

Szék. *See* Teleki.

T

T——, Comte — de. Sur les routes du Danube à Constantinople. 8* *Paris*, 1828

Tachard, Guy. Second Voyage du Père Tachard et des Jesuites envoyez par le Roy au Royaume de Siam, contenant diverses remarques d'Histoire, de Phy-sique, de Géographie, et d'Astronomie. *Plates.* Square 8° *Paris*, 1686

—— *See* Laharpe, Vol. 5 ; Allgemeine Historie, 10 : Appendix 1.

Tafel, Theophilus Luc. Frid. De Thessalonica ejusque Agro : Dissertatio Geographica. 8° *Berlin*, 1839

—— De Via Militari Romanorum Egnatia, qua Illyricum, Macedonia, et Thracia jungebantur : Dissertatio Geographica. 4° *Tubingen*, 1842

Tagle, A. S. de. *See* Sartorius.

Tagliabue, E. Dieci Anni a Massaua. Considerazioni politico coloniali. 8* *Milan*, 1888

Taine, H. Voyage aux Pyrénées. Troisième édition, illustrée par Gustave Doré. 8° *Paris*, 1860

Taintor, E. C. Geographical Sketch of the Island of Hainan. *Map.* 4* *Canton*, 1868

—— The Aborigines of Northern Formosa. 8* *Shanghai*, 1874

Taiso, ——. *See* Purchas, Vol. 3, Book 2 : Appendix 1.

Tait, M. Yorkshire, its Scenes, Lore, and Legends, elaborated from a Prize Essay written for the Bradford Geo-graphical Exhibition, 1887 ; with maps by F. D. King. Square 12° *Leeds*, 1888

Talbot, Thorp. The New Guide to the Lakes and Hot Springs, and a Month in Hot Water. *Illustrations.* 8° *Auckland, N.Z.*, 1882

Tallenay, Jenny de. Souvenirs de Vene-zuela : Notes de Voyage. *Illustrations.* 12° *Paris*, 1884

Tamborrel, Joaquin de Mendizabul. Tesis leida en el examen profesional de Ingeniero Géografo sustentado en la escuela nacional de Ingenieros. *Plate.* 8° *Mexico*, 1884

Tancoigne, ——. A Narrative of a Journey into Persia, and Residence at Teheran, containing a Descriptive Itinerary from Constantinople to the Persian Capital . . . *Map and frontispiece.* 8° 1820

Tandy, W. *See* Sangermano.

Tanner, Prof. Henry. The Canadian North-West, and the advantages it offers for Emigration purposes. [2nd edition.] *Map and illustrations.* 8* 1886

—— Successful Emigration to Canada. Revised edition. *Map.* 8* *Ottawa*, 1886

—— British Columbia, its Agricultural and Commercial capabilities, and the advantages it offers for Emigration pur-poses. *Illustrations.* 8* 1887

Tanner, H. S. American Traveller, or Guide through the United States. *Maps.* 12° *Philadelphia*, 1840

—— Description of the Canals and Rail-roads of the United States, compre-hending Notices of all the Works of Internal Improvement throughout the several States. *Maps.* 8° *New York*, 1840

—— The Traveller's Handbook for the State of New York and the Province of Canada. *Maps.* 12° *New York*, 1844

Tappenbeck. Lieut. —— Bericht von Lieutenant Tappenbeck. [On a Journey on the Congo.] 8* [*Berlin*, 1886]

Tarducci, T. R. Di Giovanni e Sebas-tiano Caboto : Memorie raccolte e docu-mentate. Large 8° *Venice*, 1892

Tarnovski, Lieut. G. Review of the Trans-Caspian Region for 1891 and 1892. [In Russian.] 8° *Askhabad*, 1893

Tasman, Abel Jansz. Journaal van de Reis naar het Onbekende Zuidland, 1642, met de Schepen "Heemskerck" en de "Zeehaen." Medegedeeld en met eenige Aanteekeningen voorzien door Jacob Swart. *Map.* 8° *Amsterdam*, 1860

—— *See* Burney, Vol. 3 ; Callander, Vol. 2 ; Dalrymple, Pacific, Vol. 2 ; Harris, Vol. 1 ; Pinkerton, Vol. 11 ; Allgemeine Historie, Vol. 12 ; "Voyages," p. 597 : Appendix 1.

Tassy, Garcin de. Les Auteurs Hin-doustanis et leurs Ouvrages. 8* *Paris*, 1868

Tassy, Garcin de. Bag o Bahar, Le Jardin et le Printemps : Poëme Hindoustani. Traduit en Français. [No. 8 of Publ. de l'Éc. des Langues Orient. Viv.] 8° *Paris*, 1878

Tate, T. Notes on a Voyage to the Arctic Seas in 1863. 12° *Alnwick*, 1864

Tattam, Henry. Compendious Grammar of the Egyptian Language, as contained in the Coptic and Sahidic Dialects ; with Observations on the Bashmuric ; . . . with an Appendix consisting of the Rudiments of a Dictionary of the Ancient Egyptian Language in the Enchorial Character, by Thomas Young. 8° 1830

Tatton, J. *See* Astley, Vol. 1 ; Purchas, Vol. 1, Book 3 : Appendix 1.

Taubert, P. *See* Schweinfurth and Ascherson.

Taubman-Goldie. *See* Goldie.

Taunt, Emory H. Report of Lieutenant Taunt of a Journey on the River Congo. 8° *Washington*, 1887

Tavara, Santiago. Memoria de la Constitucion Médica del Callao en el Año 1877. 12* *Callao*, 1878

Tavares Bastos. A livre Navegacão do Amasonas. [*Journal do Pará*, Nos. 22, 23, e 24 ; Jan. 28, 29, 30, 1864.] 3 Nos. Folio* *Para*, 1864

Tavernier, John Baptista. The Six Voyages of John Baptista Tavernier . . . through Turkey into Persia and the East Indies, finished in the year 1670 . . . made English by J. P. *Plates*. Small folio 1678

—— Recueil de Plusieurs Relations et Traitez singuliers et curieux de J. B. Tavernier.

[For full Titles and Contents, *see* Appendix 1.]

—— *See* Ball, V. ; *also* Harris, Vol. 1 ; Pinkerton, Vol. 8 ; Allgemeine Historie, Vols. 10, 11 : Appendix 1.

Taw Sein-ko. A Preliminary Study of the Kalyani Inscriptions of Dhammachetti, 1476 A.D. *Plates*. 4* *Bombay*, 1893

—— Notes on an Archæological Tour through Ramannadesa (the Talaing country of Burma). Reprinted from the *Indian Antiquary. Plate*. 4* *Bombay*, 1893

Taylor, A. Dundas. On the Harbours of India. 8* *Liverpool*, 1870

—— The Indian Directory, for the Guidance of Commanders of Steamers and Sailing Vessels, founded upon the work of the late Captain James Horsburgh : Part the First, containing the East Indies and interjacent parts of Africa and South America. Revised, extended, and illustrated, with Charts of Winds, Currents, Passages, Variation, and Tides. Small 4° 1874

—— *See* United Kingdom, A, Admiralty Publ. ; India, D, Marine Surveys and Returns of Wrecks : Appendix 2.

Taylor, A. J. Imperial Federation *versus* Australian Independence. 8* *Hobart*, 1889

—— A Chat about the Aborigines of Tasmania. With some Reflections on the subject, . . also some Notes on the Shell-Mounds at Little Swanport. 8* *Hobart* [1891]

Taylor, Annie R. An Englishwoman in Thibet. (From the *National Review* for September 1893.) 8* 1893

Taylor, Bayard. Visit to India, China, and Japan in 1853. 8° 1855

Taylor, C. E. Leaflets from the Danish West Indies, descriptive of the Social, Political, and Commercial Condition of these Islands ; with a *Portrait* of the Author, and a Biographical Sketch written by Ph. Linet. *Illustrations*. 8° 1888

Taylor, Elizabeth I. *See* Tiele, C. P.

Taylor, Ellen M. Madeira, its Scenery, and how to see it ; with Letters of a Year's Residence, and Lists of the Trees, Flowers, Ferns, and Seaweeds. *Frontispiece, map, and plan.* Crown 8° 1882

—— The same. 2nd edition. *Frontispiece, map, and plan.* Crown 8° 1889

Taylor, G. A Ramble through Southern Formosa. (From *The China Review*.) *Sketches.* 8* N.P. [1888]

Taylor, G. Cavendish. Adventures with the British Army, from the Commencement of the War to the Taking of Sebastopol. 2 vols. 8° 1856

Taylor, J. Words and Places ; or, Etymological Illustrations of History, Ethnology, and Geography. 3rd edition. *Maps.* 12° 1873

Taylor, Major John. Travels from England to India, in 1789, by the way of the Tyrol, Venice, Scandaroon, Aleppo, and over the Great Desart to Bussora ; with Instructions for Travellers, and an Account of the Expense of Travelling, &c. 2 vols. *Maps.* 8° 1799

Taylor, J. E. *See* Adalbert.

Taylor, J. G. Travels in Kurdistan, with Notices of the Sources of the Eastern and Western Tigris, and Ancient Ruins in their Neighbourhood. 8* [1865]

Taylor, Mrs. Lunar Tables, by which the True Distance is obtained from the Apparent Altitudes, and the usual tedious preparations avoided previous to clearing a Lunar Distance. 8° 1835

Taylor, N. *See* Victoria, B : Appendix 2.

Taylor, Capt. R. Historical and other Information connected with the Province of Oman, Muskat, and the adjoining Country ; the Islands of Bahrein, Ormus, Kishm, and Karrack ; and other Ports and Places in the Persian Gulf : prepared in 1818. [From the India Record, No. 24.] *Maps.* Royal 8° *Bombay*, 1856

Taylor, Capt. R. Report on the Navigation of the River Gogra. *Plans.* [India Records, Part 31, N.W. Provinces.] Large 8* *Calcutta*, 1858

Taylor, Rev. Richard. Te Ika a Maui; or, New Zealand and its Inhabitants, illustrating the Origin, Manners, Customs, . . . and Language of the Natives; together with the Geology, Natural History, Productions, and Climate of the Country, &c. *Map and plates.* 4° 1855
—— The same. 2nd edition. *Plates.* 8° 1870

Taylor, Richard C. Two Reports on the Coal Lands, Mines, and Improvements of the Dauphin and Susquehanna Coal Company, and of the Geological Examinations, Present Condition, and Prospects of the Stony Creek Coal Estate, Pennsylvania; with an Appendix containing tables and statistical information. *Maps.* 8° *Philadelphia*, 1840

Taylor, T. G. Meteorological Observations made at the Meteorological Bungalow on Dodabetta, 8,640 feet above the level of the sea, in 1847-48. 8* *Madras*, 1848
—— *See* India, N, Madras Observations : Appendix 2.
—— **and J. Caldecott.** Observations on the Directions and Intensity of the Terrestrial Magnetic Force in Southern India, *Map.* 8* *Madras*, 1839

Taylor, Rev. W. E. African Aphorisms, or Saws from Swahili-Land; with a Preface by the Rev. W. Salter Price. 12° 1891

Taysen, F. *See* Blackwood, Vol. 3 : Appendix 1.

Tchernycheff, T. Hauteurs absolues déterminées dans l'Oural Meridional en 1882-85, calculées sans la direction du Gén. A. de Tillo. 4° *St Petersburg*, 1886
—— Notes sur les Travaux exécutés par l'Expedition de Timane en 1890. [In Russian.] *Map.* Large 8° [*St Petersburg*, 1891]

Tchihatcheff, P. de. Voyage Scientifique dans l'Altaï Oriental et les parties adjacentes de la Frontière de Chine. *Plates.* Large 4° *Paris*, 1845
—— Mémoire relatif à la Constitution Géologique de l'Altaï. 4* *Paris*, 1845
—— Notice of Researches in Asia Minor. 8° 1849
—— " Miscellanea.' 8° *Paris, &c.*
Including: Notice of Researches in Asia Minor. 1849
Mémoire sur les Terrains Jurassique, Crétacé, et Nummulitique de la Bithynie, de la Galatie, et de la Paphlagonie. 1851
Dépôts Nummulitiques et Diluviens de la Presqu'île de Thrace. *Map* 1851
Le Paix de Zurich et le nouveau Congrès Européen. 1859
2 G

Tchihatcheff, P. de.—*continued.*
Italie et Turquie. 1859
Lettres sur la Turquie. 1859
—— L'Asie Mineure et l'Empire Ottoman : État Actuel et Richesses Naturelles de l'Asie Mineure, situation Politique, Militaire, et Financière de la Turquie. 8° *Paris*, 1850
—— Asie Mineure : Description Physique, Statistique, et Archéologique de cette contrée. 8 vols. Royal 8°, and Atlas 4° *Paris*
Iᵉ Partie—Géographie Physique comparée. *Plates* 1853
IIᵉ Partie—Climatologie et Zoologie. *Plates* 1856
IIIᵉ Partie—Botanique. 2 vols. 1860
IVᵉ Partie—Géologie. 3 vols. Vol. 1, 1857 ; Vols. 2 and 3, 1869. *Map and plate.*
—— Paléontologic. *Atlas of plates,* 1860 (par A. D'Archiac, P. Fischer, and E. de Verneuil). 1866
—— Dépôts Tertiaires d'une partie de la Cilicie Trachée, de la Cilicie Champêtre, et de la Cappadoce ; Dépôts Tertiaires du Midi de la Carie et d'une partie septentrionale de la Pisidie ; Dépôts Paléozoïques de la Cappadoce et du Bosphore. *Map.* 8° *Paris*, 1854
—— Lettre sur les Antiquités de l'Asie Mineure, addressée à M. Mohl. 8* *Paris*, 1854
—— Considérations Historiques sur les Phénomènes de Congélation constatés dans le Bassin de la Mer Noire. Large 8* *Versailles* [1855]
—— Études sur la Végétation des Hautes Montagnes de l'Asie - Mineure et de l'Arménie. 8* *Paris*, 1857
—— Le Bosphore et Constantinople ; avec Perspectives des Pays Limitrophes. *Maps and plates.* Royal 8° *Paris*, 1864
—— Reisen in Kleinasien und Armenien, 1847-63. (Ergänzungsheft, 20—Petermann's Mittheilungen.) *Map.* 4° *Gotha*, 1867
—— Une Page sur l'Orient. 12° *Paris*, 1868
—— Espagne, Algérie, et Tunisie : Lettres à Michel Chevalier. *Map.* 8° *Paris*, 1880
—— Préface de la nouvelle édition de " l'Asie Centrale " de Humboldt. 8* N.P., N.D.
—— Klein-Asien. *Map and illustrations.* 12° *Leipzig*, 1887
—— Études de Géographie et d'Histoire Naturelle. 8° *Florence*, 1890
—— *See* Grisebach.

Tchirikoff, Gen. E. I. *See* Gamazoff.

Tchirikow. *See* Allgemeine Historie, Vol. 17: Appendix 1.

Teale, T. P. *See* Osburn, W.

Tebbutt, John. Meteorological Observations made at the Private Observatory of J. Tebbutt, Jun., Windsor, N.S.W., 1863-66. 8° *Sydney*, 1868

Tebbutt, John. The same, 1867-68-69-70. Folio   *Sydney*, 1874
—— The same, 1871-76. Folio
                                       Sydney, 1877
Techo, F. Michel del. *See* Churchill, Vol. 4 : Appendix 1.
Tecla, Maria. *See* Purchas, Vol. 1, Book 1 : Appendix 1.
Teenstra, M. D. Beknopte Beschrijving van de Nederlandsche Overzeesche Be-zittingen . . . in Oost- en West-Indien, &c. *Map and plate.* 8° *Groningen*, 1846
Teetzmann, F. *See* Baer and Helmer-sen, 11.
"**Tegetthoff.**" *See* Payer.
Tegg, James. New South Wales Pocket Almanac and Remembrancer for 1840. 18°   *Sydney*, 1840
Tegner, H. *See* Hage.
Tegoborski, M. L. de. Commentaries on the Productive Forces of Russia. 2 vols. 8°   1855
Teichelmann, C. G., and C. W. Schür-mann. Outlines of a Grammar, Voca-bulary, and Phraseology of the Aboriginal Language of South Australia spoken by the Natives in and for some distance around Adelaide. 8°   *Adelaide*, 1840
Teignmouth, Lord. Sketches of the Coasts and Islands of Scotland, and of the Isle of Man. 2 vols. *Maps.* 8° 1836
Teixeira, P. *See* Tellez ; *also* Allge-meine Historie, Vol. 16 : Appendix 1.
Teleki von Szék, D. Reisen durch Ungern und einige angränzende Länder ; aus dem Ungrischen übersetzt durch Ladislaus v. Németh. *Portrait.* 8°
                                       Pesth, 1825
Telfer, Capt. J. Buchan. The Crimea and Transcaucasia : being a Narrative of a Journey in the Kouban, in Gouria, Georgia, Armenia, Ossety, Imeritia, Swannety, and Mingrelia, and in the Tauric range. 2 vols. *Maps and plates.* 8°   1876
—— Armenia and its People. Large 8*
                                       1891
—— *See* Hakluyt Soc. Publ., 58 ; Ap-pendix 1.
Telford, Thomas, and Capt. George Nicholls. Ship Canal for the Junction of the English and Bristol Channels : Reports, with an Appendix. 8* 1824
Tellez, Balthazar. The Travels of the Jesuits in Ethiopia . . . Travels of the Sieur Mouette in the Kingdoms of Fez and Morocco [1670] ; Travels of Peter Teixeira from India to Italy, by land [after 1600] ; Voyage to Madagascar, the adjacent Islands, and Coast of Africk, by F. Cauche [after 1638]. *Maps.* Small 4°   1710
—— *See* Thevenot, Vol. 4 ; Recueil de divers Voyages, p. 595 : Appendix 1.

Tellier, J. Essai d'Étude positiviste sur le Sud Algérien. 8*   *Brussels*, 1878
Temminck, C. J. Coup d'œil général sur les possessions Néerlandaises dans l'Inde Archipélagique. 3 vols. 8°
                                       Leyden, 1846-49
Temple, Edmond. Travels in various parts of Peru, including a Year's Resi-dence in Potosi. 2 vols. *Map and plates.* 8°   1830
Temple, Sir Grenville T. Excursions in the Mediterranean, Algiers, and Tunis. 2 vols. *Maps, plates, and facsimiles.* 8°   1835
—— Travels in Greece and Turkey, being the Second Part of Excursions in the Mediterranean. 2 vols. *Plates.* 8° 1836
—— Sketch of the Campaign of Kostan-tinah, in 1837. 8*   1839
Temple, Lieut. G. T. Hydrography, Past and Present. *Map.* 8*   1879
—— Statement in Vindication of Com-mander T. A. Hull, R.N., Superin-tendent of Charts at the Admiralty. 8*
                                       1880
—— Pleasure Cruise to the Land of the Midnight Sun, in the Orient Company's s.s. "Chimborazo." *Map and illustra-tions.* 4*   [1889]
—— Notes on a Winter Cruise in the West Indies by the Orient Company's s.s. "Garonne," November 1893. *Map and illustrations.* 4*   1893
—— *See* United Kingdom, A, Sailing Directions : Appendix 2.
Temple, Sir Richard. Report on the Moquddumee Biswahdaree Settlement of Pergunnah Barrah, Zillah Allahabad. [From the India Records, Part 27, N.W. Provinces.]   *Agra*, 1856
—— Report showing the Relations of the British Government with the Tribes, Independent and Dependent, on the N.W. Frontier of the Punjab, from annexation in 1849 to the close of 1855. [From the India Records, No 12.] Royal 8°   *Calcutta*, 1856
—— Report on the Mahanuddy and its Tributaries, and the Resources and Trade of the adjacent countries. [From the India Records, No. 43, Public Works Department.] Royal 8° *Calcutta*, 1864
—— India in 1880. *Maps.* 8°   1880
—— Men and Events of My Time in India. 8°   1882
—— Journals kept in Hyderabad, Kash-mir, Sikkim, and Nepal. Edited, with Introductions, by his son Richard Carnac Temple. 2 vols. *Maps and illustrations.* 8°   1887
—— Palestine. *Illustrations.* 4° 1888
—— *See* Stanford, E.
Temple, Richard Carnac. Notes on the Transliteration of the Burmese Alpha-bet into Roman Characters ; to which is

Temple, Richard Carnac—*continued.*
attached a Note on the Vocal and Consonantal Sounds of the Peguan or Talaing Language. Folio* *Rangoon,* 1876
—— Notes on the Formation of the Country passed through by the 2nd Column, Tal Chotiali Field Force, during its march from Kala Abdullah Khán in the Khójak Pass to Lugárí Bárkhán, Spring of 1879. *Map.* 8* *Calcutta,* 1879
—— Rough Notes on the Distribution of the Afghan Tribes about Kandahar. *Maps.* 8* 1879
—— Remarks on the Afgháns found along the Route of the Tal Chotiali Field Force, in the Spring of 1879. Parts 1 and 2. *Maps and plates.* 8*
[*Calcutta,* 1880]
—— The Legends of the Punjab. 8*
Bombay, N.D.
—— *See* Man.
Templeman, P. *See* Norden.
Templeton, Frederick. Statement made to the Directors of the British American Land Company, on the Eastern Townships of Lower Canada. 8° 1836
Tempsky, G. F. von Mitla. A Narrative of Incidents and Personal Adventures on a Journey in Mexico, Guatemala, and Salvador, in 1853-55. Edited by J. S. Bell. *Map and plates.* 8° 1858
Tenison-Woods, Rev. J. E. *See* Woods.
Ten Kate, Dr H. F. C. Reizen en Onderzoekingen in Noord Amerika. *Maps and plates.* 8° *Leyden,* 1885
—— Sur les Cranes de Lagoa-Santa. 8*
Paris, 1885
—— Legends of the Cherokees. (Reprinted from *Journal of American Folk-Lore,* Vol. 2, No. 4.) 8* N.P. N.D.
—— Zuni Fetiches. *Plate.* 4* 1890
Tennant, Lieut.-Col. J. F. Report on Observations of the Total Eclipse of the Sun on 11th and 12th December 1871, made by order of the Government of India, at Dodabetta, near Ootacamund. *Plates.* 4* 1875
Tennant, Robert. Sardinia and its Resources. *Map and illustrations.* Large 8° 1885
Tennent, Sir James Emerson. Ceylon: an Account of the Island, Physical, Historical, and Topographical, with Notices of its Natural History, Antiquities, and Productions. 2 vols. *Maps and plates.* 8° 1860
—— Sketches of the Natural History of Ceylon, with Narratives and Anecdotes, &c. *Illustrations.* 8° 1861
Tenore e Gussoni. Viaggio alla Meta, al Morrone, ed alla Maïella [Abruzzo]. 4° N.D.
Ten Rhyne, —. *See* Churchill, Vol. 4: Appendix 1.

Teran, Ignacio. Teoria de la Lluvia ó sea ; un ensayo de razones sobre el modo como se verifica el fenómeno de la lluvia. 12* *Sucre,* 1890
Ternant, Victor de. L'Exposition des Colonies and de l'Inde à Londres, 1886 : Rapport présenté à la Société des Études Coloniales et Maritimes, par son délégué à l'Exposition. 8* *Paris,* 1887
Ternaux - Compans, H. Bibliothèque Asiatique et Africaine, ou Catalogue des Ouvrages relatifs à l'Asie et à l'Afrique qui ont paru depuis la Découverte de l'Imprimerie jusqu'en 1700. 8°
Paris, 1841
—— Essai sur l'Ancien Cundinamarca. 8*
Paris, N.D.
—— Voyages, Relations, et Memoires Originaux, pour servir à l'Histoire de la Découverte de l'Amérique. 20 vols. in 10. 8° *Paris,* 1837-41
[For Contents of these volumes, *see* Appendix 1.]
Terry, Charles. New Zealand, its Advantages and Prospects as a British Colony; with an Account of the Aborigines, &c. *Map and plates.* 8° 1842
Terry, Edward. Voyage to East India . . . Reprinted from the edition of 1655. *Map and plates.* 8° 1777
—— *See* Gottfried ; Kerr, Vol. 9 ; Purchas, Vol. 2 ; Thevenot, Vol. 1 : Appendix 1.
Tessan, U. de. Rapport verbal sur un Ouvrage imprimé de M. Cialdi intitulé " Sul moto ondoso del Mare, &c." 4*
Paris, 1866
—— *See* Du Petit-Thouars.
Tessy, Garcin de. *See* Sédillot.
Tevet, Andrea. Historia dell' India America, detta altramente Francia Antarctica. Tradotta di Francese, da G. Horologgi. 12° *Venice,* 1561
Texeira, Peter. *See* Teixeira.
Texier, C. Description de l'Arménie, la Perse, et la Mésopotamie. 2 vols. *Plates.* Folio *Paris,* 1842
—— and R. Popplewell Pullan. The Principal Ruins of Asia Minor illustrated and described. *Map and plates.* Folio 1865
Teysmann, J. E. *See* Robidé van der Aa.
Thackeray, Col. E. T. From Assam to Kashmir : Notes on Sport and Travel. *Illustrations.* 8* N.D.
Thackeray, St John. *See* Marshall, T.
Thayer, Russell. Earthquakes : a Scientific Investigation of the Method of Action of these Terrestrial Phenomena, and a Theory of their Primary Cause. *Plan.* 8* *Philadelphia,* 1886
Theal, G. M'Call. Compendium of the History and Geography of South Africa. 3rd edition. 8° 1878

Theal, G. M'Call. History of the Boers in South Africa; or, The Wanderings and Wars of the Emigrant Farmers from their leaving the Cape Colony to the acknowledgment of their Independence by Great Britain. *Maps.* 8°   1887
—— History of South Africa. [1486-1691.] *Maps.* 8°   1888
—— The same. [1691-1795.] *Maps and frontispiece.* 8°   1888
—— The same. [1795-1834.] *Maps.* 8°   1891
—— The same. The Republics and Native Territories from 1854 to 1872. *Map.* 8°
1889

Thebæus. *See* Purchas, Vol. 1, Book 1: Appendix 1.

Thenaud, Jean. Le Voyage d'outremer (Egypte, Mont Sinay, Palestine) de Jean Thenaud Gardien du couvent des Cordeliers d'Angoulême; suivi de la Relation de l'Ambassade de Domenico Trevisan auprès du Sudan d'Egypte, 1512. Publié et annoté par Ch. Schefer. [Recueil de Voyages et de Documents pour servir à l'Histoire de la Géographie depuis le XIIIᵉ jusqu'à la fin du XVIᵉ Siècle. Publié sous la direction de MM. Ch. Schefer et Henri Cordier. Vol. 5.] *Plate.* Large 8° *Paris,* 1884

Theodoricus, Sebastianus. Novæ Questiones Sphæræ, hoc est, de Circulis Cœlestibus et primo mobili, in gratiam studiosæ inventutis scriptæ. *Woodcut diagrams (some movable).* 12°
Wittenberg, 1567
[Bound up with other works and entitled "Cosmographia."]

Thevenot, J. P. E. Traité des Maladies Européens dans les Pays Chauds, et spécialement au Sénégal; ou Essai Statistique, Médical, et Hygiénique sur le Sol, le Climat, et les Maladies de cette partie de l'Afrique. 8° *Paris,* 1840

Thévenot, Jean de. Troisième partie des Voyages de, contenant la Relation de l'Indostan, des Nouveaux Mogols, et des autres Peuples et Pays des Indes. 4° *Paris,* 1684
—— Travels into the Levant, viz., Turkey, Persia, the East Indies. *Portrait and plates.* Folio   1687
—— *See* Harris, Vol. 2; "The World Displayed," Vols. 11, 12; Knox's New Collection, Vol. 6: Appendix 1.

Thevenot, Melchizedec. Relation de divers Voayges [sic] curieux qui n'ont point esté publiées . . .
[For full Title and Contents, *see* Appendix 1.]

Thévoz, F. and E. *See* Turkey in Asia, B, Palestine: Appendix 2.

Thibaut, —. Journal de l'Expédition à la Recherche des Sources du Nil, 1839-40. 8* *Paris,* 1856

Thiébaut de Berneaud, Arsenne. *See* Berneaud.

Thielmann, Max von. Streifzüge im Kaukasus, in Persien, und in der Asiatischen Türkei. *Map and plates.* 8°
Leipzig, 1875
—— Journey in the Caucasus, Persia, and Turkey in Asia. Translated by Charles Heneage. 2 vols. *Map and plates.* Small 8°   1875
—— Vier Wege durch Amerika. *Maps and plates.* 4°   *Leipzig,* 1879

Thoemmel, Gustav. Geschichtliche, Politische und Topografisch-statistische Beschreibung des Vilajet Bosnien, das ist das eigentliche Bosnien, nebst türkisch Croatien, der Hercegovina und Rascien. 8°   *Vienna,* 1867

Thom, Alex. Inquiry into the Nature and Course of Storms in the Indian Ocean South of the Equator. *Maps and diagrams.* 8°   1845

Thomä, Dr C. Das unterirdische Eisfeld, bei der Dornburg, am südlichen Fusse des Westerwaldes. *Map.* 12°
Wiesbaden, 1841

Thoman, Fedor. Métrologie Espagnole. 8*   *Paris* [1870]

Thomas, A. Etymologisches Wörterbuch geographischer Namen, namentlich solcher aus dem Bereiche der Schul Geographie. 8°   *Breslau,* 1886

Thomas, Charles ap. To the Summit of the Andes by Rail. 12*
Gravesend, N.D.

Thomas, Cyrus. A Study of the Manuscript Troano; with an Introduction by D. G. Brinton, M.D. [From "Contributions to North American Ethnology," Vol. 5.] *Plates.* 4° *Washington,* 1882
—— Work in Mound Exploration of the Bureau of Ethnology. 8*
Washington, 1887
—— The Circular, Square, and Octagonal Earthworks of Ohio. *Illustrations.* 8*
Washington, 1886
—— The Problem of the Ohio Mounds. *Illustrations.* 8*   *Washington,* 1889
—— Catalogue of Prehistoric Works east of the Rocky Mountains. Large 8°
Washington, 1891
—— *See* United States, G, *a* (Surveys): Appendix 2.

Thomas, E. Early Armenian Coins. 8*
1867

Thomas, Edward. The Indian Balhará, and the Arabian Intercourse with India in 9th and following Centuries. 4* 1882

Thomas, H. T. Untrodden Jamaica. *Map and illustrations.* 8*
Kingston, Jamaica, 1890

Thomas, Isaiah. History of Printing in America, with a Biography of Printers and an Account of Newspapers; to which is prefixed a Concise View of the Discovery and Progress of the Art in other Parts of the World. 2 vols. *Facsimiles.* 8° *Worcester, Mass.,* 1810

Thomas, J., and T. Baldwin. Complete Pronouncing Gazetteer. *See* Lippincott.

Thomas, J. *See* Astley, Vol. 1: Appendix 1.

Thomas, Julian. Cannibals and Convicts: Notes of Personal Experiences in the Western Pacific. *Map and portraits.* 8° 1886

Thomas, of Woodstock. *See* Gloucester, Duke of.

Thomas, P. U. Essai de Statistique de l'île de Bourbon: suivi d'un projet de Colonisation de l'Intérieur de cette île. 2 vols. 8° *Paris,* 1828

Thomas, R. H. *See* Graham, D. C.; Keily.

Thomas, Commr. T. E. L. *See* Kellet, Capt.; *also* India: Appendix 2.

Thomas, T. M. Eleven Years in Central South Africa. *Map and plates.* 8° [1872]

Thomason, A. Men and Things in America. 12° 1838

Thomason, Hon. James. Despatches and Minutes, Vol. 2. [From the India Records, Part 41.] Royal 8° *Calcutta,* 1858

Thomassen, E. S. Biographical Sketch of Nicholas de Miklouho-Maclay. *Plate and portraits.* 8° 1882

Thomassy, M. R. Note sur l'Hydrologie Maritime et sur les Lignes d'Équisalure de l'Océan Atlantique. 8° *Paris,* 1860

Thompson, C. W. Report on Route Survey: Accra to Prahsue. *Sketch map.* Folio* [*Elmina,* 1882]
—— Manual of the Sextant, containing Instructions for its Use in determining Time, Latitude, Longitude, and the Variation of the Compass. 8° 1887

Thompson, David. *See* Tyrrell.

Thompson, Edward H. Explorations at Labna, Yucatan. *Plan.* 8* 1887
—— Extracts from Letters on Explorations in Yucatan. 8* 1888
—— The Ancient Structures of Yucatan not Communal Dwellings, and Yucatan at the Time of its Discovery. (From *Proceedings of the American Antiquarian Society,* 21st October 1892.) *Plates.* 8* *Worcester, Mass.,* 1893

Thompson, George. Travels and Adventures in Southern Africa, comprising a View of the Present State of the Cape Colony. 2 vols. *Map and plates.* 8° 1827
—— The War in Paraguay, with a Historical Sketch of the Country and its People, and Notes upon the Military Engineering of the War. *Maps.* 8° 1869

Thompson, G "Confederation in South Africa," and "Delagoa Bay." [Extracts from the *Empire* newspaper] N.P., 1874

Thompson, G. A. Narrative of an Official Visit to Guatemala from Mexico. *Map.* 12° 1829

Thompson, J. G. Complete Phonetic Alphabet, based upon Lepsius's Standard Alphabet. 8* *Bombay,* 1859
—— Pointed and Unpointed Romanic Alphabets compared, in Six Versions of Luke xiv. 18-20. 8* *Mangalore,* 1859

Thompson, Robert, and John Hogg. Sketches of Kertch, its larger Tumuli, and some other Remains. *Map and plates.* 8* 1857

Thompson, R. Report on Forests of Tuppehs Doodhee, Bara and Pulwa, Pergunnah Singrowlee, District Mirzapoor, 1869. [Records, Vol. 2, Part 2, 2nd Series, N.W. Prov.] 8° *Allahabad,* 1869

Thompson, William Mann. Improved Systems of Chaining for Land and Engineering Surveys. 8* 1888

Thomson, Arthur S. Story of New Zealand, Past and Present, Savage and Civilised. 2 vols. *Maps and plates.* 8° 1859

Thomson, Sir C. Wyville. The Depths of the Sea: an Account of the General Results of the Dredging Cruises of H.M. ships "Porcupine" and "Lightning" during the Summers of 1868, 1869, and 1870. *Maps and plates.* 8° 1873
—— The Voyage of the "Challenger." The Atlantic: a Preliminary Account of the General Results of the Exploring Voyage of H.M.S. "Challenger" during the year 1873 and the early part of the year 1876. 2 vols. *Maps and plates.* 8° 1877
—— *See* "Challenger" Voyage.

Thomson, David. Lunar and Horary Tables, &c. 51st edition. 8° 1856

Thomson, Capt. F. T. *See* "Challenger."

Thomson, Dr James. On the Grand Currents of Atmospheric Circulation. 4* 1892

Thomson, John. The Antiquities of Cambodia: a series of Photographs taken on the spot, with Letterpress description. Oblong 4° *Edinburgh,* 1867
—— Notes on Cambodia and its Races. 8* 1867
—— Illustrations of China and its People: a series of two hundred Photographs, with Letterpress descriptive of the places and people represented. 4 vols. Folio 1873-74
—— The Straits of Malacca, Indo-China, and China; or, Ten Years' Travels, Adventures, and Residence abroad. *Plates.* 8° 1875
—— The Land and the People of China. *Map and plates.* 12° 1876

Thomson, John. Through Cyprus with the Camera in the Autumn of 1878. 2 vols. *Photographs.* 4° 1879

Thomson, Joseph. To the Central African Lakes and back: the Narrative of the Royal Geographical Society's East Central African Expedition, 1878-80 ; with short Biographical Notice of the late Mr Keith Johnston. *Maps and portraits.* Small 8° 1881
—— Through Masăi Land: a Journey of Exploration among the Snowclad Volcanic Mountains and Strange Tribes of Eastern Equatorial Africa, being the Narrative of the Royal Geographical Society's Expedition to Mount Kenia and Lake Victoria Nyanza, 1883-84. 3rd edition. *Maps and illustrations.* 8° 1885
—— Up the Niger to the Central Sudan. [Cuttings from *Good Words*, January, February, April, and May 1886.] *Map and illustrations.* Large 8* 1886
—— Travels in the Atlas and Southern Morocco: a Narrative of Exploration. *Maps and illustrations.* 8° 1889
—— Mungo Park and the Niger. *Maps and illustrations.* Crown 8° 1890

Thomson, J. P. The Island of Kadavu. *Map.* 8* [*Edinburgh*, 1889]
—— Sir William MacGregor's Upper Fly River Exploration, British New Guinea. 8* [*Brisbane*, 1890]
—— Notes on the Brisbane River Floods. 8* [*Brisbane*, 1890]
—— British New Guinea. *Map and illustrations.* Royal 8° 1892
—— Exploration and Discoveries in British New Guinea since the Proclamation of Sovereignty. 8* [*Hobart*, 1892]
—— Practical Suggestions to Travellers. 8* [*Sydney*, 1892]

Thomson, J. Turnbull. Sketch of the Province of Otago. 8* *Dunedin*, 1858
—— *See* New Zealand, B: Appendix 2.

Thomson, Thomas. Travels in Sweden in 1812. *Maps and plates.* 4° 1813

Thomson, Dr Thomas. Western Himalaya and Tibet: a Narrative of a Journey through the Mountains of Northern India in 1847-48. *Maps and plates.* 8° 1852
—— *See* Hooker, Sir J. D.

Thomson, William. New Methods of finding the Apparent Time and the Sun's Altitude for any given place and time; and finding the Latitude by Double Altitudes, and also by a single Altitude of the Sun. 8° *Bombay*, 1848

Thomson, Sir William (Lord Kelvin). Polar Icecaps and their Influence in changing Sea Levels. 8* [*Glasgow*, 1888]

Thomson, W. M. The Land and the Book ; or, Biblical Illustrations drawn from the Manners and Customs, Scenes and Scenery, of the Holy Land. 2 vols. *Maps and plates.* 8° 1859

Thorburn, John. Struggles in Africa, and how I transported a steam-boat on wheels 1,600 miles across the country. 12* N. D.

Thorburn, S. S. Bannú, or our Afghan Frontier. *Map.* 8° 1876

Thorden, K. M. Om Telefonen. 8* [*Upsala*, 1884]
—— Verlds telegrafnätet, betraktadt hufvudsakligen från geografisk synpunkt. 8* [*Upsala*, 1884]
—— De Telegrafiska Undervaltensledningarna. 8* [*Stockholm*, 1885]
—— Den Elektriska Telegrafen, dess Utveckling och nuvarande tillstånd. 8* [*Stockholm*, 1885]

Thoreau, Henry D. A Week on the Concord and Merrimack Rivers. 12° *Boston, Mass.*, 1849

Thorel, C. Notes Médicales du Voyage d'Exploration du Mékong et de Cochinchine. 8° *Paris*, 1870

Thoresby, R. *See* Kirk, T.

Thorn, F. M. *See* United States, F: Appendix 2.

Thorne, James. Rambles by Rivers: the Duddon, the Mole, the Adur, Arun, and Wey, the Lea, the Dove. *Woodcuts.* 18° 1844
—— The same. The Avon. *Woodcuts.* 18° 1845
—— Handbook to the Environs of London, alphabetically arranged, containing an Account of every Town and Village, and of all places of interest within a circle of twenty miles round London. 2 vols. Small 8° 1876

Thorne, Robert. *See* Kerr, Vol. 6; Purchas, Vol. 3, Book 4 ; Hakluyt Soc. Publ., Vol. 7 : Appendix 1.

Thornton, Bertram. The Comparative Climatology of London and the chief English Health Resorts. *Map.* 12* 1891

Thornton, Edward. Chapters of the Modern History of British India. 8° 1840
—— History of the British Empire in India. 6 vols. *Maps.* 8° 1841-45
—— Gazetteer of the Countries adjacent to India on the North-West, including Sinde, Afghanistan, Beloochistan, the Punjab, &c. 2 vols. 8° 1844
—— A Gazetteer of the Territories under the Government of the East-India Company, and of the Native States on the Continent of India. 4 vols. *Map.* 8° 1854
—— A Gazetteer of the Territories under the Government of the Viceroy of India. Revised and edited by Sir Roper Lethbridge and Arthur N. Wollaston. 8° 1886

Thornton, John. Advanced Physiography. *Map and illustrations.* 12° 1890

Thornton, J. W. The Landing at Cape Anne; or, The Charter of the first Permanent Colony on the Territory of the Massachusetts Company. From the original MS.; with an inquiry into its authority, and a history of the Colony, 1624-28. *Plate.* 8° *Boston, Mass, 1850*

Thornton, Thomas. The Present State of Turkey; or, A Description of the Political, Civil, and Religious Constitution, Government, and Laws of the Ottoman Empire; together with the Geographical, Political, and Civil State of the Principalities of Moldavia and Wallachia. 4° 1807

Thornton, W. T. Indian Public Works and cognate Indian Topics. *Map.* Small 8° 1875

Thoroddsen, Th. Oversight over de Islandske Vulkaners Historie. (Avec un résumé en français.) *Map.* 8° *Copenhagen, 1882*
—— Fra Islands indre Höjland, en Rejseberetning fra Sommeren 1889. *Map.* 4* [*Copenhagen*] N.D.
—— De varme Kilder paa Hveravellir i Island. *Map.* 8* [*Stockholm*] 1889
—— Nogle Bemáerkninger om de Islandske Findesteder for Dobbelspath. *Figures.* 8* [*Stockholm*, 1890]
—— Reisen in Island und einige Ergebnisse seiner Forschungen. 8* *Berlin, 1892*
—— Rejse i Vester-Skaptafells Syssel paa Island i Sommeren 1893. (From the *Tidskrift* of the Royal Danish Geographical Society, 1893-94.) *Map.* 4* *Copenhagen, 1893*
—— *See* Boehmer.

Thorp, Robert. Cashmere Misgovernment. 8* 1870

Thorpe, B. *See* Rask.

Thorpe, W. G. Ipplepen; Round and About an Old Devon Village. 8* 1889

Thorpe, Mrs. *See* Laveleye.

Thorson, E. M. *See* Streyc.

Thouar, A. A la recherche de la mission Crevaux. [Cutting from the *Revue Occidentale* (3), IV., No. 7.] 4* [*Paris*, 1884]
—— Explorations dans l'Amérique du Sud. *Maps and illustrations.* 12° *Paris, 1891*

Thoulet, J. Océanographie Statique. *Illustrations.* 8° *Paris, 1890*
—— Les Courants de la Mer et le Gulf-Stream. [Reprint from the publication of the French Association for the Advancement of Science.] 8* 1893
—— Introduction à l'Étude de la Géographie Physique. 8° *Paris, 1893*

Thoyon, —. Renseignements sur quelques Mouillages de la Côte d'Islande et de Norvége. *Plates.* 8° *Paris, 1865*

Threlkeld, L. E. Australian Grammar, comprehending the Principles and Natural Rules of the Language as spoken by the Aborigines in the vicinity of Hunter's River, Lake Macquarie, &c., New South Wales. 8° *Sydney, 1834*
—— An Australian Language as spoken by the Awabakal, the People of Awaba or Lake Macquarie (near Newcastle, New South Wales), being an Account of their Language, Traditions, and Customs. Rearranged, condensed, and edited, with an Appendix, by John Fraser. *Map and plates.* 8° *Sydney, 1892*

Thrum, T. G. Hawaiian Almanac and Annual for 1890: a Handbook of Information on Interesting Matters relating to the Hawaiian Islands. 8° *Honolulu, 1889*

Thrupp, Joseph Francis. Antient Jerusalem: a new Investigation into the History, Topography, and Plan of the City, Environs, and Temple, &c. *Map and plates.* 8° *Cambridge, 1855*

Thrupp, J. Godfrey. *See* James, F. L.

Thucydides. *See* Wheeler, J. T.

Thuillier, Sir H. L. General Reports on the Topographical Surveys of India. *See* India, F, *b*: Appendix 2.
—— and R. Smyth. A Manual of Surveying for India, detailing the mode of operations on the Trigonometrical, Topographical, and Revenue Surveys of India. 3rd edition. *Maps, plates, &c.* 8° *Calcutta, 1875*

Thunberg, Carl. P. Reisen in Europa, Afrika, und Asien, vorzüglich in Japan, während der Jahre 1770 bis 1779, übersetzt von K. Sprengel, und mit Anmerkungen begleitet von J. R. Forster, aus dem Schwedischen frey übersetzt von C. H. Groskurd. 2 vols. in 1. *Plates.* 8° *Berlin, 1792-94*
—— Travels in Europe, Africa, and Asia, made between the years 1770 and 1779. Vol. 3, containing a voyage to Japan and travels in different parts of that Empire in the years 1775 and 1776. 3rd edition. 8° 1796
—— The same. Vol. 4, containing travels in the Empire of Japan, and in the Islands of Java and Ceylon, together with the voyage home. *Plates.* 8° 1795
—— Voyages au Japon, par le Cap de Bonne-Espérance, les îles de la Sonde, &c., 1770-78. Traduits, rédigés, et augmentés de notes considérables sur la Religion, le Gouvernement, le Commerce, l'Industrie, et les Langues de ces différentes contrées, particulièrement sur le Javan et le Malai, par L. Langlés; et revus, quant á la partie de l'Histoire naturelle, par J. B. Lamarck. 2 vols. *Plates.* 4° *Paris, 1796*

Thunberg, Carl P. The same. 2 vols. 8° *Paris*, 1796
—— *See* Pinkerton, Vol. 16 : Appendix 1.
Thurn. *See* Im Thurn.
Thwaites, R. G. Epochs of American History : The Colonies, 1492-1750. *Maps.* 12° 1891
Thys, Capt. —. Au Congo et au Kassai : Conférences données à la Société Belge des Ingénieurs et des Indnstriels. [Bound with maps entitled " Le Kassai et la Louloa de Kwamouth à Louèbo levés à bord du Steamer 'Stanley.'"] 8° *Brussels*, 1888
Tiarks, J. L. Report on Capt. Foster's Chronometrical Observations in H.M.S. "Chanticleer." 8° N.D.
Tickell, Major R. Reports on River Breakwaters. [India Records, Vol. 2, N.W. Prov.] *Plate.* Large 8° *Agra*, 1855
Tiedemann, Adolf von. Tana-Baringo-Nil. Mit Karl Peters zu Emin Pascha. 2nd edition. *Map, portrait, and illustrations.* 8° *Berlin*, 1892
Tiedemann, B. von. *See* United Kingdom, War Office : Appendix 2.
Tieffenthaler, J. *See* Bernoulli.
Tiele, C. P. Western Asia, according to the most recent discoveries. Rectorial address on the 318th anniversary of the Leyden University, Feb. 8, 1893. Translated by Elizabeth J. Taylor. 8° 1893
Tiele, P. A. Mémoire Bibliographique sur les Journaux des Navigateurs Néerlandais réimprimés dans les collections de De Bry et de Hulsius et dans les collections Hollandaises du XVIIᵉ siècle, et sur les anciennes éditions Hollandaises des Journaux de Navigateurs étrangers ; la plupart en la possession de Frederick Muller à Amsterdam. *Plate.* 8° *Amsterdam*, 1867
—— Nederlandsche Bibliographie van Land en Volkenkunde. Large 8° *Amsterdam*, 1884
—— *See* Hakluyt Soc. Publ., Vol. 71 : Appendix 1.
Tietkens, W. H. An Account of the latest Exploring Expedition across Australia. 12* [1877]
—— Journal of the Central Australian Exploring Expedition, 1889, under the command of W. H. Tietkens. *Map.* Small 8* *Adelaide*, 1891
—— *See* South Australia, A: Appendix 2.
Tighe, William. Statistical Observations relative to the County of Kilkenny, made in 1800 and 1811. *Maps and plates.* 8° *Dublin*, 1802
Tilleard, J. *See* Pestalozzi.
Tilley, H. A. Japan, the Amoor, and the Pacific ; with Notices of other places, comprised in a voyage of circumnavigation in the Imperial Russian corvette " Rynda " in 1858-60. *Plates.* 8° 1861

Tillinghast, William H. Notes on the Historical Hydrography of the Handkerchief Shoal in the Bahamas. Large 8* *Cambridge, Mass.* 1881
Tillo, Alexis de. Terrestrial Magnetism in Orenburg, 1830-70. [In Russian.] *Maps.* 4° *St Petersburg*, 1872
—— Notice sur le Congrès des Géographes Allemands à Halle [12-14 Avril 1882.] 8* [*Leipzig*, 1882]
—— *See* Tchernycheff.
Timberlake, Lieut. Henry, who accompanied the Three Cherokee Indians to England in 1762, Memoirs of ; containing whatever he observed remarkable, or worthy of public notice, during his Travels to and from that Nation ; wherein the Country, Government, Genius, and Customs of the Inhabitants are authentically described. *Map and plate.* 8° 1765
Timberley, H. *See* Purchas, Vol. 2, Book 9 : Appendix 1.
Timkovski, J. Voyage à Péking à travers la Mongolie, in 1820 et 1821. . . . Traduit du Russe. . . . Publié, avec des Corrections et des Notes, par M. J. Klaproth, &c. 2 vols. 8°, and Atlas folio *Paris*, 1827
—— Travels of the Russian Mission through Mongolia to China, and Residence in Pekin in 1820-21 ; with Corrections and Notes by J. von Klaproth. 2 vols. *Maps and plates.* 8° 1827
Timūr. The Mulfuzāt Timūry, or Autobiographical Memoirs of the Moghul Emperor Timūr. Written in the Jagtay Tūrky Language, turned into Persian by Abu Talib Hussyny, and translated into English by Major Charles Stewart. [Oriental Translation Committee publication.] *Map.* 4° 1830
Tindal, J. G. A. *See* Schröder, J. F. L.
Tinne, John A. Geographical Notes of Expeditions in Central Africa, by three Dutch Ladies. *Maps.* 8° *Liverpool*, 1864
Tinter, Prof. Dr W. Publication für die Internationale Erdmessung. Astronomische Arbeiten der Oesterreichischen Gradmessungs-Commission. Large 4° *Vienna*, 1891
Tippenhauer, L. Gentil. Die Insel Haiti. *Maps and plates.* Folio *Leipzig*, 1893
Tippoo, Sultan. *See* Dalrymple, Repertory, Vol. 1 : Appendix 1.
Tischner, August. The Sun changes its Position in Space, therefore it cannot be regarded as being " in a condition of rest." *Portrait.* 16° *Leipzig*, 1883
—— The Fixed Idea of Astronomical Theory. *Plates.* 8° *Leipzig*, 1885
Tison, Thomas. *See* Hakluyt, Vol. 3 ; Kerr, Vol. 6 : Appendix 1.

Tissandier, Albert. Voyage autour du Monde : Inde et Ceylan, Chine et Japon, 1887-90-91. *Illustrations.* 4° *Paris,* 1892

Tissanier, Joseph. Relation du Voyage du P. Joseph Tissanier, de la Compagnie de Jesus, depuis la France, jusqu'au Royaume de Tunquin ; avec ce qui s'est passé de plus memorable dans cette Mission durant les années 1658-59-60. [Bound up with Jacques Le Favre's Letter upon China.] 12° *Paris,* 1663

Tissot, Charles. Recherches sur la Géographie comparée de la Maurétanie Tingitane. *Maps and plates.* 4° *Paris,* 1877
—— Le Bassin du Bagrada et la Voie Romaine de Carthage à Hippone par Bulla Regia. *Maps and plates.* 4° *Paris,* 1881
—— Exploration Scientifique de la Tunisie, Géographie comparée de la Province Romaine d'Afrique. Tome Premier. Géographie Physique—Géographie Historique — Chorographie. *Maps, plans, and plates.* 4° *Paris,* 1884
—— The same. Tome Second. Chorographie—Réseau Routier. Ouvrage publié d'après le Manuscrit de l'Auteur ; avec des Notes, des Additions, et un Atlas, par Salomon Reinach. 4° *Paris,* 1888

Tissot, E. *See* Bernard, H.

Tissot, M. A. Mémoire sur la Représentation des Surfaces et les Projections des Cartes Géographiques. 8° *Paris,* 1881

Tissot, Victor. Unknown Switzerland. Translated from the 12th edition, by Mrs Wilson. 12° 1889

Tizard, T. H. Contribution to the Meteorology of Japan. 4* 1876

Tobler, Titus. Dritte Wanderung nach Palästina in 1857 ; Ritt durch Philistäa, Fussreisen in Gebirge Judäas und Nachlese in Jerusalem. *Map.* 8° *Gotha,* 1859
—— Bibliographia Geographica Palaestinae : Zunächst kritische Uebersicht gedruckter und ungedruckter Beschreibungen der Reisen ins Heilige Land. 8* *Leipzig,* 1867
—— Bibliographia Geographica Palaestinae ab anno CCCXXXIII. usque ad annum M. 8° *Dresden,* 1875
—— Itinera et Descriptiones Terræ Sanctæ, lingua latina sæc. 4-11, exarata I. 8° *Geneva,* 1877
—— **and A. Molinier,** Itinera Hierosolymitana et Descriptiones Terræ Sanctæ bellis sacris anteriora. 8° *Geneva,* 1879

Tod, Lieut.-Col. J. Annals and Antiquities of Rájastihán, or the Central and Western Rajpoot States of India. 2 vols. *Map and plates.* 4° 1829
—— Travels in Western India, embracing a Visit to the Sacred Mounts of the Jains and the most celebrated Shrines of Hindu Faith between Rajpootana and the Indus ; with an Account of the ancient City of Nehrwalla. *Plates.* 4° 1839

Todd, Charles. Rainfall in South Australia and the Northern Territory during 1887 ; with Weather Characteristics of each Month. *Map.* Folio* *Adelaide,* 1888
—— *See* South Australia, A : Appendix 2.

Todd, D. P. A Continuation of De Damoiseau's Tables of the Satellites of Jupiter to the year 1900. [Published for the *American Ephemeris and Nautical Almanac.*] 4* *Washington,* 1876

Todkill, Anas. *See* Purchas, Vol. 4, Book 9 : Appendix 1.

Toeppen, Dr Hugo. Die Doppelinsel Nowaja Semlja. Geschichte ihrer Entdeckung. *Map.* 8° *Leipzig,* 1878
—— Hundert Tage in Paraguay. Reise in's Innere. Paraguay im Hinblick auf Deutsche Kolonisations - Bestrebungen. *Map.* 8° *Hamburg,* 1885

Tofiño de San Miguel, Vicente. Derrotero de las Costas de España en el Mediterraneo, y su Correspondiente de Africa, para Inteligencia y uso de las Cartas Esféricas. Descripciones de las islas Pithiusas y Baleares. Small 4° *Madrid,* 1787
—— Derrotero de las Costas de España en el Océano Atlantico y de las Islas Azores ó Terceras, para Inteligencia y uso de las Cartas Esféricas. 4° *Madrid,* 1789
—— España Maritima, or Spanish Coasting Pilot, containing Directions for Navigating the Coasts and Harbours of Spain, in the Atlantic, with the Coast of Portugal. Translated by John Dougall. 2 vols. *Charts and plans.* 4° 1814

Toletus, L. T. *See* Purchas, Vol. 4, Book 8 : Appendix 1.

Tolhausen. *See* General ; Dictionaries, A : Appendix 2.

Toll, Baron Eduard. *See* Schrenck and Maximowicz : Beiträge zur Kenntniss des Russischen Reiches, &c., Vol. 3.

Tollens, Hendrik. The Hollanders in Nova Zembla [1596-97]. An Arctic Poem, translated from the Dutch of Hendrik Tollens by Daniel van Pelt ; with a Preface and a Historical Introduction by Samuel Richard van Campen ; including Notes. *Frontispiece.* 12° *New York and London,* 1884

Tolmie, W. Fraser. *See* Canada, A, Geological and Natural History Survey : Appendix 2.

Tolstoi, Graf D. A. *See* Schrenck and Maximowicz : Beiträge zur Kenntniss des Russischen Reiches, &c., Vols. 1, 2 ; Helmersen and Schrenck, Vol. 8.

Tolstoi, Leon. What I Believe. Translated from the Russian, by Constantine Popoff. 8° 1885

Tolstoy, G. The First Forty Years of Intercourse between England and Russia, 1553-93. [In Russian.] Crown 8° *St Petersburg,* 1875

Tomalin, Lewis R. S. *See* Jaeger.

Tomaschek, Wilhelm. Die vorslawische Topographie der Bosna, Herzegowina, Crnagora und der angrenzenden Gebiete. 8* *Vienna*, 1880
—— Centralasiatische Studien. 2. Die Pamir-Dialekte. 8* *Vienna*, 1880
—— Zur Kunde der Hämus-Halbinsel : Topographische, Archäologische, &c., Miscellen. 8* *Vienna*, 1882
—— The same. 2. Die Handelswege im 12 Jahrhundert nach den Erkundigungen des Arabers Idrîsî. 8* *Vienna*, 1887
—— Zur historischen Topographie von Persien. 1. Die Strassenzüge der Tabula Peutingerana. 8* *Vienna*, 1883
—— The same. 2. Die Wege durch die Persische Wüste. *Map*. 8* *Vienna*, 1885
—— Topographische Erläuterung der Küstenfahrt Nearchs vom Indus bis zum Euphrat. 8* *Vienna*, 1890

Tombleson, W. Tombleson's Views of the Rhine, edited by W. G. Fearnside. 8° 1832
—— Tombleson's Upper Rhine. *Map and plates*. 8° [1840 ?]

Tomlinson, Thomas. The Congo Treaty. *Map*. 8* 1884

Tomson, R. *See* Hakluyt, Vol. 3 : Appendix 1.

Tonnelier. *See* Pallas.

Tönsberg, C. Norway: Illustrated Handbook for Travellers. *Maps and plates*. 12° *Christiania*, 1875

Tooke, W. *See* Pelham, Vol. 2 : Appendix 1.

Tootal, A. *See* Hakluyt Soc. Publ., 51 : Appendix 1.

Topinard, Dr Paul. La Société, l'École, le Laboratoire, et le Musée Broca. Large 8* *Paris*, 1890
—— De la Notion de Race en Anthropologie. 8* N.P., N.D.

Topley, William. Notes on the Physical Geography of East Yorkshire. 8* *Hertford*, 1866
—— On the Lower Cretaceous Beds of the Bas-Boulonnais, with Notes on their English equivalents. 8* 1868
—— On the Comparative Agriculture of England and Wales. 8* 1871
—— Geology of the Straits of Dover. *Map and plates*. 8* 1872
—— On the Agricultural Geology of the Weald. *Map*. 8* 1872
—— The National Geological Surveys of Europe. 8* 1885
—— Report of the Committee on the Erosion of the Sea-Coasts of England and Wales. *Map*. 8* 1886
—— Geology in its Relation to Hygiene. 8* 1890
—— *See* General, International Geological Congress : Appendix 2.

Topping, M. *See* Dalrymple, Repertory, Vol. 1 : Appendix 1.

Toreen, Olof. A Voyage to Suratte, China, &c., 1750-52. *See* Osbeck, P. A Voyage to China, &c.
—— *See* "The Modern Traveller," Vol. 4 : Appendix 1.

Torell, Otto. On the Causes of the Glacial Phenomena in the North-Eastern portion of North America. *Map*. 8* *Stockholm*, 1878
—— *See* Sweden, A : Appendix 2.

Torelli, Luigi. Carta della Malaria dell' Italia. *Map*. 4* *Florence*, 1882

Torlonia, Prince D. A. Prosciugamenta del Lago Fucino. *Diagrams*. 8° *Florence*, 1871
—— *See* Brisse and Rotrou.

Törnebohm, A. E. *See* Sweden, A : Appendix 2.

Tornero, R. S. Chile ilustrado : Guia descriptivo del Territorio de Chile, de las capitales de provincia, de los puertos principales. *Plates*. 4° *Valparaiso*, 1872

Tornöe, H. *See* Norway, A, Norwegian North Atlantic Expedition, 1876-78 : Appendix 2.

Törnquist, S. L. *See* Sweden, A : Appendix 2.

Torquemada, F. Juan de. Primera (Segunda y Tercera) parte de los Veinte i un libros i rituales Monarchia Indiana, con el origen y guerras de los Indios occidentales, de sus Poblaçones, Descubrimiento, Conquista, Conversion, y otras cosas maravillosas de la mesma tierra. 3 vols. *Map*. Folio *Madrid*, 1723

Torre, Bertrand de la. *See* De la Torre.

Torre, Count Raymonde de la. *See* De la Torre.

Torrend, J. A Comparative Grammar of the South-African Bantu Languages, comprising those of Zanzibar, Mozambique, the Zambesi, Kafirland, Benguela, Angola, the Congo, the Ogowe, the Cameroons, the Lake Region, &c. *Map*. Large 8° 1891

Torrens, H. On the Greek Legends of the Coins of the Indo-Scythian Princes of Cabul. 8* N.D.

Torrens, Henry D. Travels in Lâdak, Tartary, and Kashmir. *Plates*. 8° 1862

Torrente, Mariano. Geografía Universal, Física, Política, é Histórica. 2 vols. *Maps*. Folio *Madrid*, 1827-28

Torres, Louis Vaez de. *See* Hakluyt Soc. Publ., 25, 39 ; Burney, Vol. 2 : Appendix 1.

Torres, Simon Perez de. Viaje del Mundo. Folio N.P., N.D.

Toscanelli, Paolo dal Pozzo. Paolo dal Pozzo Toscanelli e la Circumnavigazione dell' Africa secondo la testimonianza di un contemporaneo. 8* *Florence*, 1891
—— *See* Uzielli ; V., B. A.

Totten, G. M. Communication of the Board of Directors of the Panama Railroad Company to the Stockholders; with an Appendix, containing Tables of the Grades, Tangents, and Curves of the Panama Railroad, and Observations upon the Levels of the Atlantic and Pacific Oceans. *Map.* 8* *New York,* 1855
—— *See* United States, E, *a*, Hydrogr. Off. Publ., Nos. 50 and 52 : Appendix 2.
—— **and S. Schroeder.** *See* United States, E, *a*, Hydro. Off. Publ., No. 60.

Toula, Franz. Eine geologische Reise in den westlichen Balkan und in die benachbarten Gebiete. *Map.* 8*
Vienna, 1876
—— Reisen und geologische Untersuchungen in Bulgarien : Vortrag gehalten den 19 März 1890. *Map and illustrations.* 12* *Vienna,* 1890
—— Der Stand der Geologischen Kenntnis der Balkanländer. *Map.* 8* *Berlin,* 1891
—— *See* Höhnel.

Tournefort, Pitton de. Relation d'un Voyage du Levant, fait par ordre du Roi, contenant l'Histoire Ancienne et Moderne de plusieurs Iles de l'Archipel, de Constantinople, des Côtes de la Mer Noire, de l'Armenie, de la Georgie, des Frontieres de Perse et de l'Asie Mineure ; avec les Plans des Villes et des Lieux considerables ; le Genie, les Meurs, le Commerce, et la Religion des differens Peuples qui les habitent ; et l'Explication des Medailles et des Monumens Antiques. *Maps and plates.* 4° *Amsterdam,* 1718
—— A Voyage into the Levant, &c. 2 vols. *Maps and plates.* 4° 1718
—— The same. Translated by J. Ozell. 3 vols. *Maps and plates.* 8° 1741

Toussaint, —. Indicateur complet de la Ville de Caen : Guide des Etrangers. 18* *Caen,* 1835

Touzet, V. *See* Rojas, E.

Towerson, W. *See* Towrson.

Townley, —. *See* Burney, Vol. 4 : Appendix 1.

Townsend, F. T. Wild Life in Florida, with a Visit to Cuba. *Map and plates.* 8° 1875

Townsend, Horatio. Statistical Survey of the County of Cork, with Observations on the Means of Improvement. 8°
Dublin, 1810

Townsend, Joseph. A Journey through Spain in 1786-87 ; and Remarks in passing through a part of France. 3 vols. *Map and plates.* 8° 1792

Townsend, J. K. Narrative of a Journey across the Rocky Mountains to the Columbia River, and a Visit to the Sandwich Islands, Chili, &c. ; with a Scientific Appendix. 8°
Philadelphia, 1839

Townshend, S. Nugent. Our Indian Summer in the Far West : an Autumn Tour of Fifteen Thousand Miles in Kansas, Texas, New Mexico, Colorado, and the Indian Territory. Illustrated by J. G. Hyde. *Photographs.* 4° 1880

Townson, Robert. Travels in Hungary; with a Short Account of Vienna in 1793. *Map and plates.* 4° 1797

Towrson, W. *See* Astley, Vol. 1 ; Hakluyt, Vol. 2 ; Kerr, Vol. 7 ; Allgemeine Historie, Vol. 1 : Appendix 1.

Towson, John Thomas. Tables to facilitate the Practice of Great Circle Sailing and the Determination of Azimuths. *Chart.* 8° 1854
—— On Ice Impediments in Australian Voyages. 8* 1855
—— The Principles of Great Circle and Composite Sailing, with Observations made from more recent Voyages. *Chart.* 8* *Liverpool,* 1855
—— Tables for the Reduction of the Ex-Meridian Altitudes. 8° 1856
—— *See* United Kingdom, A, Admiralty : Appendix 2.

Toynbee, Capt. Henry. On the Normal Circulation and Weight of the Atmosphere in the North and South Atlantic Oceans, so far as it can be proved by a steady Meteorological Registration during five voyages to India. *Map.* 8* 1865
—— Report . . . on the Meteorology of the North Atlantic, between the parallels of 40° and 50° N. . . . ; with Remarks on the difference in the Winds and Weather experienced, according as the ship's course is Westerly or Easterly, &c. *Tables.* 8° 1869
—— Report to the Committee of the Meteorological Office on the use of Isobaric Curves, and a line of greatest Barometric change in attempting to foretell Winds ; with some Practical Suggestions for Seamen, and a few Remarks on Buys Ballot's Law. *Charts.* 8* 1869
—— On the Physical Geography of the part of the Atlantic which lies between 20° N. and 10° S., and extends from 10° to 40° W. *Tables.* 8* 1876
—— On the Great Hurricane, the Tracks of American Storms, and the Ordinary Winds of the N. Atlantic, in August 1873. *Maps.* 8* 1877
—— Report of the Gales experienced in the Ocean District adjacent to the Cape of Good Hope, &c. *Plates.* 4° 1882
—— Weather Forecasting for the British Islands by means of a Barometer, the Direction and Force of Wind and Cirrus Clouds. *Diagrams.* 12* 1890

Tozer, Henry Fanshawe. Researches in the Highlands of Turkey, including Visits to Mounts Ida, Athos, Olympus, and Pelion . . . ; with Notes on the

Tozer, Henry Fanshawe—*continued.*
Ballads, Tales, and Classical Superstitions
of the Modern Greeks. 2 vols. *Map
and plates.* 8° 1869
—— Lectures on the Geography of Greece.
Map. Small 8° 1873
—— Turkish Armenia and Eastern Asia
Minor. *Map and plates.* 8° 1881
—— The Islands of the Aegean. *Maps.*
Small 8° *Oxford*, 1890
—— Selections from Strabo; with an In-
troduction on Strabo's Life and Works.
Maps and plans. 8° *Oxford*, 1893
—— *See* Galton, Vacation Tourists.
Tozetti, J. T. Voyage Minéralogique,
Philosophique, et Historique en Toscane.
2 vols. 8° *Paris*, 1792
Tracey, Capt. Notes on the Antechamber
of the Great Pyramid. 8* *Edinburgh*, 1871
Trafford, F. W. C. Amphiorama, ou
La Vue du Monde des Montagnes de la
Spezia. *Map.* 8* *Zürich*, 1874
—— The same. 2me Notice. 8*
Zürich, 1875
—— The same. 8* *Lausanne*, 1875, 1877
—— Souvenir de l'Amphiorama, ou la Vue
du Monde pendant son passage dans une
Comète. 8* *Zürich*, 1880-81
Trail, W. Account of the Life and
Writings of Robert Simson. *Portrait
and plate.* 4° *Bath*, 1882
Traill, G. W. An Elementary Treatise
on Quartz and Opal, including their
varieties; with a Notice of the principal
Foreign and British localities in which
they occur. 12° *Edinburgh*, 1867
—— Statistical Report on the Bhotia
Metals of Kamaon. 4* N.D.
Traill, Dr T. S. Physical Geography.
Plates. 8° *Edinburgh*, 1838
—— *See* Murray, Hugh.
Tramezzino, Michele. Diversi avisi
particolari dall' Indie di Portogallo
ricevuti, dall'· anno 1551 fino al 1558,
dalli Reverendi Padri della Compagnia di
Giesu . . . Tradotti nuovamente dalla
lingua Spagnuola nella Italiana. 12°
N.P., N.D.
Trap, J. P. Statistik-Topographisk
Beskrivelse af Kongeriget Danmark.
5 vols. *Maps and plates.* 8°
Copenhagen, 1858-60
Trask, Dr John B. Report on the
Geology of the Coast Mountains, and
part of the Sierra Nevada, embracing
their industrial Resources in Agriculture
and Mining. 8* 1854
—— Report on the Geology of Northern
and Southern California, embracing the
Mineral and Agricultural Resources of
those Sections. 8* *Washington*, 1856
**Traubenberg, Dr Paul Freiherr Rausch
von.** Hauptverkehrswege Persiens. Ver-
such einer Verkehrsgeographie dieses
Landes. *Maps and profiles.* 8°
Halle a S., 1890

Trautwein, Th. Register Oesterr. Deutsch.
Alpenvereins, 1863-86. [*See* Austria-
Hungary, Vienna, in Appendix 3.] 8°
Munich, 1887
—— Bibliographie der Alpinen Literatur,
1871. 8* N.P., N.D.
Trautwine, John C. Rough Notes of an
Exploration for an Inter-Oceanic Canal
Route by way of the Rivers Atrato and
San Juan, in New Granada, South
America. *Map.* 8° *Philadelphia*, 1854
Travers, H. De La Cour. Letter to Sir
Bartle Frere on Development of Trade
on the East Coast of Africa. 8*
Cape Town, 1877
Travers, W. T. L. *See* New Zealand,
D : Appendix 2.
Travideani, —. *See* Aveiro.
Treacher, Governor. Handbook of
British North Borneo. Compiled from
Reports received from Governor Treacher
and other Officers in the British North
Borneo Company's Service; with an
Introduction by Sir Rutherford Alcock.
Maps. 8° 1886
Trebeck, —. *See* Moorcroft.
Tregear, Edward. The Maori in Asia.
8* *Wellington*, 1885
—— The Aryan Maori. *Plate.* 8°
Wellington, 1885
—— The Maori-Polynesian Comparative
Dictionary. Large 8° *Wellington*, 1891
—— A Paumotuan Dictionary. (From
the *Journal of the Polynesian Society*). 4
parts. Large 8* N.D.
—— **and H. Williams.** Description and
Vocabulary of Niue, or Savage Island.
(From *Journ. Polynes. Soc.*) 8* N.D.
Tréhouart, —. *See* Gaimard.
Trémeaux, —. Voyage au Soudan
Oriental et dans l'Afrique Septentrionale
pendant 1847-48. 12* *Paris*, 1853
Tremenheere, Col. C. W. On a Coast
Current from the Mouths of the Indus
towards Kurrachee Harbour. Folio* 1865
Trench, F. The Russo-Indian Question
historically, strategically, and politically
considered; with a Sketch of Central
Asiatic Politics. *Maps.* 8° 1869
Trendelenburg, Frederick A. The Life
and Writings of Aristotle. Translated
from the German, by G. Long. 8* N.D.
Trendell, A. J. R. Her Majesty's
Colonies : a Series of Original Papers
issued under the Authority of the Royal
Commission. Compiled and edited by
A. J. R. Trendell ; with Introduction by
J. R. Seeley. 2nd edition. *Maps.* 8° 1886
—— The Colonial Year Book for the year
1890; with Introduction by J. R. Seeley.
Maps. 8° 1890
Tresilian, F. H. Remarks on Christmas
Island. 8* 1838
Trevelyan, Arthur. Notice regarding
some Experiments on the Vibration of
Heated Metals. 4* *Edinburgh*, 1831

Trevelyan, Sir W. C., Bart. Notions of the Americans, picked up by a Travelling Bachelor. 2 vols. 8° 1828
—— Vegetation and Temperature of the Faröe Islands. 8* *Edinburgh*, 1835
—— The same. 4* *Florence*, 1837

Trevisan, D. *See* Thenaud.

Tricault, E. Explication et usage des "Wind and Current Charts." Extrait des "Sailing Directions" du Lieut. Maury. *Plates.* 8* *Paris*, 1857
—— *See* Maury, M. F.

Trigault, Nicholas (Trigantius). *See* Riccius; *also* Purchas, Vols. 2, Book 10; 3, Book 2: Appendix 1.

Trinius, August. Thüringer Wanderbuch. 2 vols. 8°
Minden in Westf., 1886-88

Triplett, Robert. Bon Harbour (on the Ohio River), its Advantages for Manufacturing. [The *Western Journal*, Feb. 1849.] 8* *St Louis*, 1849

Tripp, W. B. Rainfall in South Africa. *Map.* 8* [1886]
—— Rainfall of South Africa, 1842-86. (From *Quarterly Journal Royal Meteorological Society*, Vol. 14.) *Maps.* 8* [1888]

Tristram, H. B. The Great Sahara: Wanderings South of the Atlas Mountains. *Maps and plates.* 8° 1860
—— The Land of Israel: a Journal of Travels in Palestine, undertaken with special reference to its physical character. *Map.* 8° 1865
—— The Land of Moab: Travels and Discoveries on the east side of the Dead Sea and the Jordan; with a Chapter on the Persian Palace of Mashita, by Jas. Fergusson. *Map and plates.* 8° 1873
—— The same. 2nd edition. 1874
—— *See* Galton, Vacation Tourists.

Trivier, E. Mon Voyage au Continent Noir. La "Gironde," en Afrique. *Maps and portrait.* 12° *Paris*, 1891

Tróil, Uno von. Letters on Iceland, containing Observations on the Natural History of the Country, Antiquities, Manners and Customs of the Inhabitants, &c. &c., made during a Voyage undertaken in 1772 by Sir Joseph Banks, assisted by Dr Solander, Dr J. Lind, and other Literary and Ingenious Gentlemen; with Notes and Additions by the Translator; the whole revised and corrected by E. Mendes da Costa. *Map.* 8° 1783
—— *See* Pinkerton, Vol 1: Appendix 1.

Trojanski, J. K. *See* Rafn and Mohnika.

Trollope, Anthony. The West Indies and the Spanish Main. *Map.* 8° 1859
—— Australia and New Zealand. 2 vols. *Maps.* 8° 1873
—— South Africa. 2 vols. *Map.* 8° 1878

Trollope, T. Adolphus. A Summer in Brittany. Edited by F. Trollope. 2 vols. *Plates.* 8° [1840]

Tromholt, Sophus. Under the Rays of the Aurora Borealis in the Land of the Lapps and Kvæns. Original edition, edited by Carl Siewers. 2 vols. *Map and illustrations.* 8° 1885

Trommsdorff, J. B. Pharmacopœa Austriaca. 8° *Vienna*, 1818

Tromp, S. W. *See* Bock.

Tronson, J. M. Narrative of a Voyage to Japan, Kamtschatka, Siberia, Tartary, and various parts of the Coast of China. *Maps and plates.* 8° 1859

Trotter, Coutts. Among the Islands of the South Pacific, Fiji. (From *Blackwood's Magazine*, April 1888.) 8* 1888
—— The same. Tonga and Samoa. (From *Blackwood's Magazine*, June 1888.) 8* 1888
—— Impressions of Australia; with an Account of the Fish River Caves. (From *Blackwood's Magazine*, July 1888.) 8* 1888
—— Memoir of Colonel Sir Henry Yule. 8* [*Edinburgh*, 1891]

Trotter, Lieut.-Col. H. Account of the Survey Operations in connection with the Mission to Yarkand and Kashgar in 1873-74. *Maps [one in cover].* 4° *Calcutta*, 1875
—— *See* India, F, *c*, Surveys, Trigonometrical: Appendix 2.

Trotter, Capt. H. D. *See* Wilson, J. L.

Trotter, Lieut-Col. J. K. *See* United Kingdom, G, War Office: Appendix 2.

Trotter, Capt. J. M. *See* Asia, Central: Appendix 2.

Trotter, Lieut.-Col. P. D. Our Mission to the Court of Marocco in 1880 under Sir John Drummond Hay. *Map and illustrations.* 8° *Edinburgh*, 1881
—— *See* De la Martinière.

Trouessart, —. *See* Levasseur.

Troup, J. Rose. With Stanley's Rear Column. *Map and illustrations.* 8° 1890

Troutbeck, J. Survey and Present State of the Scilly Islands. 8° *Sherborne*, N.D.

Trow, J. Manitoba and North-West Territories. *Map.* Small 8° *Ottawa*, 1878

Trowbridge, T. C. Pamphlets: including—1. The Physical Geography of Turkey (from the *Transatlantic*, November 1872); 2. Proposals for establishing a Christian College and Medical School in Central Turkey, 1873. Education in Turkey (from the *Princeton Theological Review*, October 1870); 3. The Americans in Turkey (from the *Nonconformist*, 23rd April 1873); 4. Robert College, Constantinople. Large and small 8* V.P., V.D.

Trowbridge, Prof. W. P. *See* United States, A, Tenth Census, 1880, Vols. 16 and 22: Appendix 2.

Trow, —. New York City Directory. See Wilson, H.

Troyon, F. Monuments de l'Antiquité dans l'Europe Barbare. 8°
Lausanne, 1868

Trübner's Catalogue of Dictionaries and Grammars of the Principal Languages and Dialects of the World. 2nd edition. 8°   1882

Truilhier, Capt. Mémoire descriptif de la Route de Téhran à Meched et de Meched à Iezd, reconnue en 1807; avec Observations dans son Voyage en Perse, par M. Daussy. *Maps.* 8° *Paris*, 1841

Trumpp, Ernest. Sindhi Reading-Book, in the Sanscrit and Arabic Characters. 8°   1858
—— Grammar of the Sindhi Language compared with the Sanskrit-Prakrit and the cognate Indian Vernaculars. 8° 1872
—— Nānak, der Stifter der Sikh Religion. 4*   *Munich*, 1876

Trutch, Joseph W. British Columbia: Overland Coach Road. Minute of the Chief Commissioner of Lands and Works, 1868. Folio* *New Westminster*, 1868

Truter and Somerville. See Eyriès, Vol. 11 : Appendix 1.

Tschernyschew, Th. Notes sur les Travaux, executés par l'Expedition de Timane en 1890. [In Russian.] *Map.* Large 8°   [*St Petersburg*, 1891]
—— *See* Tchernichef.

Tschihatscheff, P. von. *See* Tchihatcheff.

Tschudi, Johann Jacob von. Travels in Peru during 1838-42, on the Coast, in the Sierra, across the Cordilleras and the Andes into the Primeval Forests. Translated from the German, by T. Ross. *Frontispiece.* 8°   1847
—— Reise durch die Andes von Süd-Amerika, von Cordova nach Cobija, im Jahre 1858. (Ergänzungsheft, 2—Peter-mann's Mittheilungen.) *Illustrations and maps.* 4°   *Gotha*, 1860
—— Reisen dürch Südamerika. 5 vols. in 3. *Maps and plates.* 8° *Leipzig*, 1866-69
—— Der Tourist in der Schweiz, und dem angrenzenden Süd-Deutschland, Oher-Italien, und Savoyen. 25th edition. *Maps, plans, &c.* 12° *St Gallen*, 1883

Tseu-Kwang-K'he. *See* Siu.

Tucker, Luther H. American Glimpses of Agriculture in Great Britain. 8*
Albany, N. Y., 1860

Tuckey, Capt. James Kingston. Maritime Geography and Statistics, or a Description of the Ocean and its Coasts, Maritime Commerce, Navigation, &c. 4 vols. 8°   1815
—— Narrative of an Expedition to Explore the River Zaire, usually called the Congo, in South Africa, in 1816 ; to which is

Tuckey, Capt. Jas. Kingston—*contd.* added the Journal of Professor Smith, some general Observations on the Country and its Inhabitants, and an Appendix on the Natural History of Congo. *Map and plates.* 4°   1818
—— *See* Eyriès, Vols. 4, 11 ; Phillips, Collection of Modern and Contemporary Voyages and Travels [1], Vol. 1 : Appendix 1.

Tudor, John R. The Orkneys and Shetland, their Past and Present State ; with chapters on Geology by Benjamin W. Peach and John Horne, and Notes on the Flora of the Orkneys by William Irvine Fortescue, and Notes on the Flora of Shetland by Peter White. *Maps, plans, and illustrations.* 8°   1883

Tuke, G. P. *See* Haig.

Tullberg, S. A. *See* Sweden, A : Appendix 2.

Tully, Richard. Narrative of a Ten Years' Residence at Tripoli, in Africa. From the Original Correspondence in the possession of the family of the late Richard Tully, Esq., the British Consul. 2nd edition. *Map and plates.* 4° 1817

Tuma, Anton. Griechenland, Makedonien und Süd-Albanien, oder : Die südliche Balkan-Halbinsel. 8° *Hanover*, 1888

Tupac Amaru. *See* Angelis, Vol. 5 ; Kerr, Vol. 5 : Appendix 1.

Tupper, M. F. A Hymn for all Nations, 1851; translated into Thirty Languages [upwards of Fifty Versions]; the Music composed expressly by S. Sebastian Wesley. 8°   1851

Turenne, Cte. Louis de. Quatorze Mois dans l'Amérique du Nord (1875-76). 2 vols. *Map.* 12°   *Paris*, 1879

Turnbull, David. Travels in the West : Cuba, with Notices of Porto Rico and the Slave Trade. *Map.* 8°   1840

Turnbull, John. Voyage round the World in 1800-1804, in which the Author visited the principal islands in the Pacific Ocean, and the English Settlements of Port Jackson and Norfolk Island. 3 vols. 12°   1805
—— *See* Eyriès, Vol. 3 ; Phillips, Collection of Modern and Contemporary Voyages [1], Vol. 3 : Appendix 1.

Turnbull, M. A Manual of the improved Newtonian Astronomical Globe. 2nd edition. *Illustrations.* 4* *Toronto*, 1887

Turnbull, William. Elements of Spherical Astronomy, comprising the Stereographic Projection of the Sphere; with Tables of Formulæ, and Rules for Calculating the Declinations, &c., of the Heavenly Bodies, the Times of their Rising, Setting, and Culminating. *Diagrams.* 8°   1849

Turnbull, William. Treatise on Trigonometrical Surveying, comprising full and detailed Solutions of all the most Important Cases of Triangulation that usually occur in the Surveying of a Country or a Sea Coast. 8° 1849

—— Key to the Exercises of Spherical Astronomy, comprising full Solutions of all the Examples, &c. 8° 1850

—— A New Practical System of Spherical Trigonometry, comprising the Stereographic Projection of the Circles of the Sphere, together with the Construction and Calculation of all the cases of Right and Oblique Angled Spherical Triangles. *Diagrams.* 8° 1850

—— Key to the Exercises of Spherical Trigonometry, comprising Solutions in full of all the Examples, &c. 8° 1850

—— The Mariner's Daily Assistant, comprising the Principles of Plane, Traverse, Parallel, Middle Latitude, Mercator's, Oblique and Current Sailing, with Rules for finding the Latitude; with the Journal of a Voyage from London to Madeira, and an Appendix. *Map and plates.* 8° 1854

Turneham, Robert. *See* Hakluyt, Vol. 2: Appendix 1.

Turner, D. Account of a Tour in Normandy, undertaken chiefly for the purpose of investigating the Architectural Antiquities of the Duchy; with Observations on its history, on the country, and on the inhabitants. 2 vols. in 1. *Plates.* 8° 1820

Turner, Rev. George. Nineteen Years in Polynesia: Missionary Life, Travels, and Researches in the Islands of the Pacific. *Map and plates.* 8° 1861

—— Samoa a Hundred Years ago, and long before; together with Notes on the Cults and Customs of twenty-three other Islands in the Pacific; with a Preface by E. B. Tylor. *Maps and illustrations.* Small 8° 1884

Turner, George. "Under Canvas," or Tents, their early origin, construction, and uses. Small 8* 1878

Turner, M. The Beverley Guide: being a Description of whatever is curious in the Town. 12° *Beverley,* 1830

Turner, Capt. Samuel. Account of an Embassy to the Court of the Teshoo Lama, in Tibet, containing a Narrative of a Journey through Bootan, and part of Tibet; Views by Lieut. S. Davis; and Observations, Botanical, Mineralogical, and Medical, by R. Saunders. *Map and plates.* 4° 1806

—— *See* Eyriès, Vol. 14: Appendix 1.

Turner, Thomas. *See* Purchas, Vol. 4, Book 6: Appendix 1.

Turner, Thomas A. Argentina and the Argentines: Notes and Impressions of a Five Years' Sojourn in the Argentine Republic, 1885-90. *Illustrations.* 8° 1892

Turner, W. Journal of a Tour in the Levant. 3 vols. *Map and plates.* 8° 1820

—— *See* Dalrymple, Repertory: Appendix 1.

Turner, William. *See* Purchas, Vol. 4, Book 6: Appendix 1.

Turner, Prof. W. *See* Whipple, A. W.

Turner-Turner, J. Three Years' Hunting and Trapping in America and the Great North-West. Illustrated by Constance Hoare. *Maps and illustrations.* 4° 1888

Turnour, Hon. George. The Mahawanso, in Roman Characters, with the Translation subjoined; and an Introductory Essay on Páli Budhistical Literature. Vol. 1. 4° *Ceylon,* 1837

Turpin, —. *See* Pinkerton, Vol. 9: Appendix 1.

Turquand, W. J. Historical, Statistical, and other Notes, connected with the Penth Estate, in the Nasik Sub-Collectorate. *Map.* Proceedings connected with the Succession to the Penth Estate, in consequence of the Death, in 1837, of Dulput Rao, Raja of that Estate. *Table.* [Bombay Records, No. 26, N.S.] Royal 8° *Bombay,* 1856

Türr, —. Szegedin et les Inondations de la Tisza. Les Portes de Fer du Danube. 4* *Paris,* 1879

Türst, C. *See* Switzerland, B: Appendix 2.

"Tuscarora." *See* United States, E, *a*, Hydrogr. Off. Publ., No. 54: Appendix 2.

Tutschek, Charles. Dictionary of the Galla Language, published by L. Tutschek. Part I. Galla-English-German. 8° *Munich,* 1844

Tvethe, M. B. Norges Statistik. 8° *Christiania,* 1848

Twells, Dr. The Life of Dr Edward Pocock. [Bound up with the lives of Dr Pearce, Dr Newton, and Rev. Philip Skelton.] 2 vols. 8° 1816

Twining, Thomas. Travels in India a Hundred Years ago, with a Visit to the United States: being Notes and Reminiscences by Thomas Twining, a Civil Servant of the Honourable East India Company. Preserved by his son Thomas Twining, of Twickenham, and edited by the Rev. William H. G. Twining. *Map and portrait.* 8° 1893

Twiss, Sir Travers. On Consular Jurisdiction in the Levant, and the Status of Foreigners in the Ottoman Law Courts. 8* 1880

—— An International Protectorate of the Congo River. 8* 1883

Twiss, Sir Travers. Sir Travers Twiss et le Congo: Réponse à la Revue de Droit international et de Législation comparée et au Law Magazine and Review, par un Membre de la Société Royal de Géographie d'Anvers. 8° *Brussels*, 1884

Twynam, E. District Surveyor Twynam to the Surveyor General, transmitting Memorandum of Measurement of Base line at Newcastle, with Field Notes, &c. *Diagrams and sections.* Folio*
Goulburn, 1879

Tyler, Major. See United Kingdom, G; War Office Publications: Appendix 2.

Tylor, Alfred. On the Formation of Deltas, and on the evidence and cause of great changes in the sea-level during the Glacial Period, with the laws of denudation and river levels. *Plate.* 8*
1872

Tylor, Charles. A Historical Tour in Franconia in the Summer of 1852. *Map and plates.* 8° *Brighton*, 1852

Tylor, Prof. Edward B. Anahuac, or Mexico and the Mexicans, Ancient and Modern. *Map and plates.* 8° 1861

—— Researches into the Early History of Mankind and the Development of Civilization. 8° 1865

—— Anthropology: an Introduction to the Study of Man and Civilization. *Illustrations.* Small 8° 1881

—— See Turner, George.

Tyndale, John Warre. The Island of Sardinia, including Pictures of the Manners and Customs of the Sardinians, and Notes on the Antiquities and Modern Objects of Interest in the Island; to which is added some Account of the House of Savoy. 3 vols. *Map and plates.* 8° 1849

Tyndall, Prof. John. On the Physical Phenomena of Glaciers. On the Veined Structure of Glaciers. 4* 1859

—— Remarks on Ice and Glaciers. 8* 1859

—— Glaciers of the Alps: being a Narrative of Excursions and Ascents, an Account of the Origin and Phenomena of Glaciers, and an Exposition of the Physical Principles to which they are related. 8° 1860

—— On Faraday as a Discoverer. 8° 1868

—— Hours of Exercise in the Alps. *Plates.* Small 8° 1871

—— The Forms of Water in Clouds and Rivers, Ice and Glaciers. *Illustrations.* 9th edition. 8° 1885

—— New Fragments. Small 8° 1892

—— See Galton, Vacation Tourists.

Tyrrell, J. B. Notes to accompany a preliminary Map of the Duck and Riding Mountains in North-Western Manitoba. *Map.* 8* *Montreal*, 1888

Tyrrell, J. B. A Brief Narrative of the Journeys of David Thompson, in North-Western America. 8* *Toronto*, 1888

—— Post-Tertiary Deposits of Manitoba and the adjoining Territories of North-Western Canada. Large 8*
Washington, 1890

Tyrwhitt, Rev. R. St John. See Galton, Vacation Tourists.

Tyson, E. The Cruise of the "Florence;" or, Extracts from the Journal of the preliminary Arctic Expedition of 1877-78. (Edited by Capt. H. W. Howgate.) 12°
Washington, 1879

Tyson, J. R. Discourse on the Surviving Remnant of the Indian Race in the United States. 8* *Philadelphia*, 1836

Tyson, Philip T. Report upon the Geology of California. *See* United States, K, California: Appendix 2.

U.

Ubicini, A., and Pavet de Courteille. État présent de l'Empire Ottoman, Statistique, Gouvernement, Administration, Finances, Armée, Communautés non Musulmanes, &c., d'après le Salnâmêh (Annuaire Impérial), pour l'année 1293 de l'Hégire (1875-76), et les documents officiels les plus récents. 8°
Paris, 1876

U. G. [Lama]. *See* India, F, *c*: Appendix 2.

Uggeri, Ange. Journée Pittoresque des Édifices de Rome Ancienne. [Text in French and Italian.] 3 vols. in 2. *Map and plates.* Oblong 4° *Rome*, 1800

Uhde, Adolph. Die Länder am untern Rio Bravo del Norte. *Map.* 8°
Heidelberg, 1861

Uhle, J. P. Der Winter in Oberägypten als klimatisches Heilmittel. *Plates.* 12°
Leipzig, 1858

Ujfalvy-Bourdon, Marie de. De Paris à Samarkand, le Ferghanah, le Kouldja et la Sibérie Occidentale: Impressions de Voyage d'une Parisienne. *Portrait, maps, and plates.* 4° *Paris*, 1880

Ujfalvy de Mezö-Kövesd, C. E. de. Les Migrations des Peuples, et particulièrement celle des Touraniens. *Maps.* Large 8° *Paris*, 1873

—— Leçon d'Ouverture d'un Cours de Géographie Historique et Politique de l'Asie Centrale, à l'École des Langues Orientales Vivantes. 8* *Paris*, 1878

—— Expédition Scientifique Française en Russie, en Sibérie, et dans le Turkestan. *Maps, plates, and tables.* Large 8° *Paris* Vol. 1.—Le Kohistan, le Ferghanah, et Kouldja, avec un Appendice sur la Kachgharie. 1878

Ujfalvy de Mezö - Kövesd, C. E. de.
Expédition Scientifique Française en Russie, en Sibérie, et dans le Turkestan —*continued.*
Vol. 2.—Le Syr-Daria, le Zérafchâne, le pays des Sept-rivières, et la Sibérie Occidentale.   1879
Vol. 3.—Les Bachkirs, les Vêpses, et les Antiquités Finno-Ougriennes et Altaïques, précédés des Resultats Anthropologiques d'un Voyage en Asie Centrale.   1880
Vol.—4. Atlas Anthropologique des Peuples de Ferghanah.   1879
Vol. 5.—Atlas des Étoffes, Bijoux, Aiguières, Émaux, &c., de l'Asie Centrale.   1880
Vol. 6.—Atlas Archéologique des Antiquités Finno-Ougriennes et Altaïques de la Russie, de la Sibérie, et du Turkestan.   1880
—— Résultats Anthropologiques d'un Voyage en Asie Centrale, communiqués au Congrès Anthropologique de Moscou. 8*   *Paris*, 1880
—— Aus dem westlichen Himalaja, Erlebnisse, und Forschungen. *Maps and illustrations.* 8°   *Leipzig*, 1884

Ukert, F. A. Ueber die Art der Griechen und Römer die Entfernungen zu bestimmen und über das Stadium. 12°
                     Weimar, 1813

Ulloa, Antonio de. Mémoires Philosophiques, Historiques, Physiques, concernant la Découverte de l'Amérique, ses anciens habitans, leurs mœurs, leurs usages, leur connexion avec les nouveaux habitans, &c. Traduit par M. 2 vols. *Plates.* 8°   *Paris*, 1787
—— *See* Juan, Don Jorge ; *also* Callander, Vol. 3 ; Pinkerton, Vol. 14 ; Allgemeine Historie, Vol. 15 ; Knox's New Collection, Vol. 1 : Appendix 1.

Ulloa, Capt. Francesco. *See* Burney, Vol. 1 ; Callander, Vol. 1 ; Hakluyt, Vol. 3 ; Ramusio, Vol. 3 : Appendix 1.

Ulrich, G. H. F. *See* Hutton ; Selwyn ; *also* South Australia, A : Appendix 2.

Ulrich, Melchior. Die Seitenthäler des Wallis und der Monterosa. 8*
                     Zürich, 1850
—— Das Lötschenthal, der Monte Leone, der Portiengrat, und die Diablerets. 8*
                     Zürich, 1851
—— Der Geltengrat, das Heremence- und Bagnethal, das Einfischthal und der Weissthorpass. *Map.* 8* *Zürich*, 1853

Ulrichs, H. N. Topography of the Harbours, and Position of the Long Walls, of Athens. Translated from the Modern Greek, by Ewing Pye Colquhoun. *Map.* 8°   1847

Umfreville, Edward. The Present State of Hudson's Bay and of the Fur Trade ; the Present State of Nova Scotia ; with

Umfreville, Edward—*continued.*
a Brief Account of Canada and the British Islands on the Coast of North America. 2nd edition. *Map.* 8° *Edinburgh*, 1887

Umlauft, Dr Friedrich. Afrika in kartographischer Darstellung von Herodot bis heute. *Maps.* 8°   *Vienna*, 1887
—— Die Alpen, Handbuch der gesammten Alpenkunde. *Maps and illustrations.* 8°   *Vienna*, 1887
—— The Alps. Translated by Louisa Brough. *Map and illustrations.* 8°
                     1888-89

Underhill, E. Bean. The West Indies, their Social and Religious Condition. 8°   1862
—— and Rev. J. T. Brown. Two Addresses on Emancipation in the West Indies. 8*   1861

"Undine." Our Cruise in the "Undine," the Journal of an English Pair-oar Expedition through France, Baden, Rhenish Bavaria, Prussia, and Belgium. By the Captain. *Map and plates.* 8°   1854

Ungár, Ad. Central-Afrika, ein neuer und wichtiger Ansiedlungspunkt für deutsche Colonisten. 2 parts. 8*
                     Stuttgart, 1850

Unger, F. Die Insel Cypern einst und jetzt. 8*   *Vienna*, 1866
—— and T. Kotschy. Die Insel Cypern : ihrer physischen und organischen Natur, mit Rücksicht auf ihre frühere Geschichte. *Map and plates.* 8°   *Vienna*, 1865

Upham, Edward. The Mahávansi, the Rájá-Ratnácari, and the Rájá-Vali, forming the Sacred and Historical Books of Ceylon ; also a Collection of Tracts illustrative of the Doctrines and Literature of Buddhism. 3 vols. 8° 1823

Upham, Warren. *See* Wright, G. F.

Upton, Col. *See* Dalrymple, Repertory, Vol. 1 : Appendix 1.

"Uranie" and "Physicienne." *See* Freycinet.

Urban. *See* D'Urban.

Urbani de Gheltof, G. M. Terzo Congresso Geografico Internazionale in Venezia. La Collezione del Doge Marino Faliero e i tesori di Marco Polo. 8*
                     Venice, 1881
—— The same. Le Scoperte Americane di Amerigo Vespucci negli anni 1504 e 1505. Small 8*   *Venice*, 1881
—— The same. Lettera inedita di Cristoforo Colombo ai Signori Venitiani. 12*   *Venice*, 1881

Urcullu, José de. Tratado Elementar de Geografia, Astronómica, Fizica, Histórica, ó Politica, Antiga e Moderna. 3 vols. *Plates.* 8°   *Oporto*, 1835
—— Grammatica Inglesa, reducida á viente y siete Lecciones. 8°   *Cadiz*, 1845

2 H

Uréchi, Grégoire. Chronique de Moldavie depuis le milieu du XIVe siècle jusqu'à l'an 1594. Avec traduction par Émile Picot. [No. 9 of Publ. de l'Éc. des Langues Orient. Viv.] 8° *Paris*, 1878-86

Urmston, Sir J. Brabazon. Observations on the China Trade, and on the Importance and Advantages of removing it from Canton to some other part of the Coast. 8° [*Privately printed*] 1833

Urquhart, David. Exposition of the Causes and the Consequences of the Boundary Differences between Great Britain and the United States, subsequently to their adjustment by arbitration. *Map.* 4°
　　[*Privately printed*] *Liverpool*, 1839
—— The Spirit of the East. 2 vols. *Map.* 8° 1839
—— The Pillars of Hercules; or, A Narrative of Travels in Spain and Morocco in 1848. 2 vols. 8° 1850
—— The Lebanon (Mount Souria): a History and a Diary. 2 vols. 8° 1860

Ursino, Alex. Relation concerning the Coast of Terra Firma, &c. *See* Purchas, Vol. 4, Book 7 : Appendix 1.

Ursua, Pedro de. Expedition in Search of El Dorado. *See* Allgemeine Historie, Vol. 16; Hakluyt Soc. Publ., Vol. 28 : Appendix 1.

Urville. *See* D'Urville.

Uslar, Baron P. K. The Ethnography of the Caucasus. Philology. The Abkhasian Language. [In Russian.] *Portrait.* 8° *Tiflis*, 1887
—— Ethnography of the Caucasus. Philology, Part 2. The Language of the Chechens. [In Russian.] 8° *Tiflis*, 1888
—— The same. Philology. The Avar Language. [In Russian.] 8° *Tiflis*, 1889
—— The same. Philology. Part 4. The Lak Language. [In Russian.] 8° *Tiflis*, 1890

Ussher, Archbishop. *See* Churchill, Vol. 7 : Appendix 1.

Ussher, John. A Journey from London to Persepolis; including Wanderings in Daghestan, Georgia, Armenia, Kurdistan, Mesopotamia, and Persia. *Plates.* 8° 1865

Ussing, T. Algreen, and P. S. Ussing. Den legale Medicins Grundsœtninger og Resultater. 8° *Copenhagen*, 1834

Utiesenovic, O. Die Naturschätze im nördlichen Croatien. *Map.* 8° *Vienna*, 1879

Uzielli, Gustavo. Ricerche intorno a Leonardo da Vinci. Serie Seconda. *Plate.* 8° *Rome*, 1884
—— Paolo dal Pozzo Toscanelli Iniziatore della Scoperta d'America : Ricordo del Solstizio d'Estate del 1892. *Florence*, 1892
—— *See* Dati ; Issel.

Uztariz, Geronymo de. The Theory and Practice of Commerce and Maritime Affairs. Translated from the Spanish by John Kippax. 2 vols. 8° 1751

V.

V——, B. A. Qui a imprimé la première lettre de Christoph Colomb? 8* *Leipzig*, 1892
—— Christophe Colomb et Toscanelli. 8* *Paris*, 1893

V——, G. D. La Spedizione Bòttego. Relazione sommaria di G. D. V. *Map.* 8* *Rome*, 1893

Vaca, Cabeza de (or Vacca, Capo di). *See* Cabeza de Vaca.

Vacani, Baron Camillo. Della Laguna di Venezia e dei Fiumi nelle attigue Provincie. *Map.* 8° *Florence*, 1867

Vaccarone, Luigi. Statistica delle Prime Ascensioni nelle Alpi Occidentali. Terza edizione. 12° *Turin*, 1890

Vahl, J. *See* Gaimard, Paul.

Vail, E. A. Notice sur les Indiens de l'Amérique du Nord. *Maps and plates coloured.* 8° *Paris*, 1840

Vaillant, Admiral A. N. Voyage autour du Monde, exécuté pendant les années 1836 et 1837 sur la Corvette "La Bonite," commandée par M. Vaillant. 15 vols. 8°; 3 vols. eleph. folio *Paris*, 1841-52
Lasalle, A. de. Relation du Voyage. 3 vols. (Vol. 1 with *plates*.) 8° 1845, 1851, 1852
Darondeau, B., and E. Chevalier. Physique.
　Observations météorologiques. Vol. 1, 1840 ; Vol. 2, 1841. 8°
　Observations magnétiques. Vol. 1, 1842 ; Vol. 2, 1846. 8°
Laurent, —. Zoophytologie. 8° 1844
Gaudichaud, G. Botanique. 8°
　Introduction. Vols. 1 and 2, 1851.
　Cryptogames cellulaires et vasculaires, par Montagne, Léveillé, and Spring. Vol. 1, 1844-46.
　Explication des Planches de l'Atlas, par C. d'Alleizette. 8° 1866
Eydoux, —, and L. Souleyet. Zoologie. Vol. 1, 1841 ; Vol. 2, 1852. 8°
Album Historique. *Plates.* Eleph. folio N.D.
Atlas (Zoologie). Eleph. folio N.D.
Atlas (Botanique). Eleph. folio N.D.

Valbezen, E. de. Les Anglais et l'Inde. 2 vols. 8° *Paris*, 1875

Valderrama, Adolfo. Bosquejo Histórico de la Poesía Chilena. 8° *Santiago*, 1866

Valdés, G. F. de. *See* Oviedo.

Valdés, Julio Cesar. La Paz de Ayacucho. Relacion Historica, Descriptiva, y Commercial. 8* *La Paz*, 1890

Valdés, Julio Cesar. Rectificaciones Geográficas a un Dictionario Espagnol. Small 8* *La Paz,* 1891

Valdez, Francisco Travassos. Six Years of a Traveller's Life in Western Africa. 2 vols. *Plates.* 8° 1861
—— Africa Occidental : Noticias e Considerações. Vol. 1. *Portrait and plates.* 8° *Lisbon,* 1864
—— Da Oceania a Lisboa Viagem. 8° *Rio de Janeiro,* 1866

Valente, A. J. Sous do Combate Anglo-Luzo, ou Ó Sonho de John Bull Bully pelo auctor da Historia "Angola e Congo." 4° *Lisbon,* 1890

Valentia, Viscount. Voyages and Travels to India, Ceylon, the Red Sea, Abyssinia, and Egypt, in 1802-6. 4 vols. 3 vols. 8°, Vol. 4 (*plates*) 4° 1811
—— *See* Robinson, F. ; *also* Phillips [1], Vol. 11 : Appendix 1.

Valentin, Dr Jean. *See* Radde.

Valentini, Baron de. Description of the Seat of War in European Turkey. Translated by Montague Gore. 8° 1854

Valentyn, François. Oud en Niew Oost-Indiën. 8 vols. Folio *Dordrecht,* 1724-26
[For full Title and Contents, *see* Appendix 1.]

Valesio, H. *See* Ramusio, Vol. 2 : Appendix 1.

Valguanera, Mariano. Origine ed Antichità di Palermo. Small 8° *Palermo,* 1614

Valignanus. *See* Purchas, Vol. 3, Book 2 : Appendix 1.

Valikhanof, Captain. A Journey to Kashgar in 1858. Translated from the Russian, by Robert Michell. Folio* [1868]
—— *See* Michell.

Vallat, Gustave. Livingstone. Poème, par Gustave Vallat. 8* *Moulins,* 1876

Valle, P. della. *See* Della Valle.

Vallée, E. J. C. Exploração do Rio Araguaya. 4* *Rio de Janeiro* [1864]

Vallée, Léon. Essai d'une Bibliographie de la Nouvelle-Calédonie et Dependances. 12* *Paris,* 1883

Vallentin, Florian. Les Alpes Cottiennes et Graies, Geographie Gallo-Romaine. *Map.* 8° *Paris,* 1883

Vallin, Acisclo Fernández. Discursos leidos ante la Real Academia de ciencias exactas, fisicas, y naturales en la Reception Publica. *Portrait.* Large 8° *Madrid,* 1893

Vallino, D. *See* Sella.

Vallon, A. Influence des Courants sur la Navigation à la Côte Occidentale d'Afrique. 8° *Paris,* 1860

Vallot, J. L'Observatoire du Mont Blanc. 4* [*Paris*] 1891

Valois, Alfred de. Mexique, Havane, et Guatemala : Notes de Voyage. 12° *Paris* [1862]

"Valorous." H.M.S. "Valorous:" Deep-Sea Soundings and Temperatures, North Atlantic Ocean, 1875. *Chart.* Folio 1875

Vambéry, Arminius. Travels in Central Asia : being the Account of a Journey from Teheran across the Turkoman Desert on the Eastern Shore of the Caspian to Khiva, Bokhara, and Samarcand, performed in . . . 1863. *Map and plates.* 8° 1864
—— History of Bokhara, from the Earliest Period down to the Present, composed for the first time after Oriental known and unknown Historical Manuscripts. 8° 1873
—— Centralasien und die Englisch-Russische Grenzfrage. 8° *Leipzig,* 1873
—— Central Asia and the Anglo-Russian Frontier Question : a Series of Political Papers. Translated by F. E. Bunnett. Small 8° 1874
—— Arminius Vambéry, his Life and Adventures, written by Himself. 3rd edition. *Portrait and plates.* 8° 1884
—— *See* Marvin ; Pinto, F. M.

Vambéry, Hermann. Cagataische Sprachstudien, enthaltend grammatikalischen Umriss, Chrestomathie, und Wörterbuch der Cagataischen Sprache. 4° *Leipzig,* 1867
—— Die Sarten und ihre Sprache. 8* [*Leipzig,* 1890]
—— *See* Proskowetz.

Van Braam, A. E. *See* Braam.

Van Bruyssel, Ernest. *See* Bruyssel.

Van Campen, Samuel Richard. *See* Campen.

Vancouver, Charles. General View of the Agriculture of the County of Devon, with Observations on the Means of its Improvement. *Maps and plates.* 8° 1808

Vancouver, Capt. George. Voyage of Discovery to the North Pacific Ocean, and Round the World ; in which the Coast of North-West America has been carefully examined and accurately surveyed, principally with a view to ascertain the existence of any navigable communication between the North Pacific and North Atlantic Oceans, 1790-95. 3 vols. *Plates.* 4° 1798
—— *See* Eyriès, Vol. 2 ; Pelham, Vol. 1 : Appendix 1.

Van den Berg, H. P. J. Brieven aan een Suikerfabrikant over de Muntkwestie in verband tot de Landbouw-Nijverheid. 8° *Batavia,* 1888

Van den Berg, L. W. C. Le Hadhramout et les Colonies Arabes dans l'Archipel Indien. *Map and plates.* Large 8° *Batavia,* 1886

Van den Bosch, J. Nederlandsche Bezittingen, in Azie, Amerika, en Afrika, in derzelver toestand en aangelegenheid voor dit Rijk, Wysgeerig, Staatshuis-

Van den Bosch, J.—*continued.*
houdkundig en Geographisch beschouwd,
met byvoeging der noordige Tabellen,
en eenen Atlas nieuwe Kaarten. 2 vols.
Vignettes. 8°, Atlas folio (1817)
Amsterdam, 1818
Van den Broeck, Ernest. Étude sur le
Dimorphisme des Foraminifères et des
Nummulites en Particulier. 8*
Brussels, 1893
—— *See* General, International Geological
Congress : Appendix 2.
Van den Broek, Peter. *See* Allgemeine
Historie, Vols. 3, 8, 18 : Appendix 1.
Van den Gheyn, J. Le Plateau de Pamir
d'après les Récentes Explorations. *Map.*
8*   *Brussels*, 1883
Van den Hagen, S. *See* Allgemeine His-
torie, Vol. 8 : Appendix 1.
Van den Heuvel, Dr. Débarquement des
Éléphants. *Plates.* 8* [*Brussels*] 1879
Van de Putte, S. *See* Veth, P. J.
Van der Aa, A. J. Nederlands Oost-
Indië, of Beschrijving der Nederlandsche
Bezittingen in Oost-Indië, &c. Eerste
deel. *Maps and plates.* 8° *Amsterdam*, 1846
—— The same. Tweede deel., pp. 1-192.
8°   *Amsterdam*, 1846
Van der Aa, Pieter. Naaukeurige Ver-
sameling der gedenk-waardigste Zee- en
Land- Reysen na Oost- en West-Indiën,
mitsgaders andere Gewesten, ter eerster
Ontdekking en soo vervolgens van ver-
scheyde Volkeren, meerendeels door
Vorsten, of Maatschappyen derwaarts
gesonden, gedaan, . . . 1246-1670. 27
vols. *Maps and plates.* 12° *Leyden*, 1707
[For Contents, *see* Appendix 1, p. 595.]
Van der Aa. *See* Robidé Van der Aa.
Van der Broek, W. Palmer. Javaansche
Vertellingen, bevattende de Lotgevallen
van een Kantjil, en Reebok, en andere
Dieren. [*In Javan, with Dutch notes.*]
8°   *The Hague*, 1878
Van der Chijs, J. A. Neêrlands Streven
tot openstelling van Japan voor den
Wereldhandel, &c. 8° *Amsterdam*, 1867
—— Nederlandsch - Indisch Plakaatboek,
1602-1811. 8°   *Batavia*
  1 deel., 1602-42.   1885
  2 deel., 1642-77.   1886
  3 deel., 1678-1709.   1886
  4 deel., 1709-43.   1887
  5 deel., 1743-50.   1888
  6 deel., 1750-54.   1889
  7 deel., 1755-64.   1890
  8 deel., 1765-75.   1891
  9 deel. Nieuwe Statuten van Batavia.
                                          1891
 10 deel., 1776-87.   1892
 11 deel., 1788-94.   1893
—— Catalogus der Numismatische Verzameling van het Bataviaasch Genootschap van Kunsten en Wetenschappen.
Tweede en Derde druk. 8°
Batavia, 1877-86

Van der Chijs, J. A. De Vestiging van
het Nederlandsche Gezag over de Banda-
Eilanden (1599-1621). *Map.* Large 8°
Batavia, 1886
—— Dagh-Register gehouden int Casteel
Batavia vant passerende daer ter plaetse
als over geheel Nederlandts-India, anno
1640-41. Imperial 8°
Batavia and the Hague, 1887
—— The same. Anno 1653.   1888
—— The same. Anno 1661.   1889
—— The same. Anno 1663.   1891
—— The same. Anno 1664.   1893
Van der Hart, C. Reize rondon het
Eiland Celebes en naar eenige der
Moluksche Eilanden, in 1850. *Maps
and plates.* 8°   *The Hague*, 1853
Van der Kemp, P. H. Billiton-Opstellen.
Nos. 3, 4, 5, 6. 4*   *Batavia*, 1886
—— Resumé van gewestelijke rapporten
over de Kunstnijverheid in Nederlandsch-
Indie. 8°   *Batavia*, 1889
Van der Maelen, Ph. Dictionnaire Géo-
graphique de la Province de Liége,
précédé d'un Fragment du Mémorial de
l'Établissement Géographique de Brux-
elles, fondé par Ph. Van der Maelen.
Plates and tables. 8°   *Brussels*, 1831
—— Ditto, de la Province de Namur.
Maps and tables. 8°   *Brussels*, 1832
—— Ditto, de la Province de Hainaut.
Tables. 8°   *Brussels*, 1833
—— Ditto, de la Province d'Anvers.
Tables. 8°   *Brussels*, 1834
—— Ditto, de la Flandre Orientale. 8°
Brussels, 1834
—— Ditto, du Limbourg. 8°
Brussels, 1835
—— Ditto, de la Flandre Occidentale. 8°
Brussels, 1836
—— Ditto, du Luxembourg. 8°
Brussels, 1838
—— L'Établissement Géographique de
Bruxelles. 8°   *Brussels*, 1831
—— Lettre sur l'Établissement Géogra-
phique de Bruxelles, fondé en 1830. 8*
Brussels, 1836
Van der Stell, S. *See* British South
Africa, A : Appendix 2.
Van der Stok, Dr J. P. Rainfall in the
East Indian Archipelago : Fourth year,
1882. 8°   *Batavia*, 1883
Van der Tuuk, H. N. Les Manuscrits
Lampongs, en possession de M. le Baron
Sloet van de Beele. 4°   *Leyden*, 1868
—— Maleisch Leesboek. 8*   1868
Van de Velde, C. W. M. Toelichtende
Aanteekeningen behoorende bij de Kaart
van het Eiland Java. 8° *Leyden*, 1847
—— Narrative of a Journey through Syria
and Palestine in 1851 and 1852. 2 vols.
Map and plates. 8°   1854
—— Memoir to accompany the Map of the
Holy Land. 8°   *Gotha*, 1858

Van de Velde, C. W. M. Discours sur la Palestine. 8* *Geneva*, 1864
—— Notes on the Map of the Holy Land. 2nd edition. 8* *Gotha*, 1865
Vaneechout, E. *See* Maury.
Van Egmont. *See* Egmont.
Van Hasselt, A. L. *See* Veth, P. J.
Van Hoorn, Lord. *See* Hoorn.
Van Kampen, N. G. *See* Kampen.
Van Linschoten. *See* Linschoten.
Van Noort, Oliver. *See* Noort.
Van Pelt, Daniel. *See* Tollens.
Van Reenen, Jacob. *See* Reenen.
Vanrenen, D. C. *See* India, F, *a* ; F, *d* : Appendix 2.
Vansleb, —. *See* Ray : Appendix 1.
Van Slyke, L. L. *See* Emersons.
Varenius, B. Geographia Generalis, in quâ Affectiones Generales Telluris explicantur. *Plates.* 16° *Amsterdam*, 1671
—— Bernhardi Vareni Med. D. Descriptio Regni Japoniæ et Siam ; Item de Japoniorum Religione et Siamensium ; De Diversis omnium Gentium Religionibus ; Quibus, præmissâ Dissertatione de variis Rerum publicarum generibus, adduntur quædam de Priscorum Afrorum fide excerpta ex Leone Africano. 12° *Cambridge*, 1673
—— Geographia Generalis, in quâ Affectiones Generales Telluris explicantur, summa cura quam plurimis in locis emendata, et XXXIII. schematibus novis, ære incisis, una cum Tabb. Aliquot quæ desiderabantur ; aucta et illustrata ab Isaaco Newton. *Plates.* 8° *Cambridge*, 1681
—— Complete System of General Geography, explaining the Nature and Properties of the Earth ; improved and illustrated by Sir Isaac Newton and Dr Jurin. Translated, with Notes, by Dugdale, and revised by Peter Shaw. 2 vols. *Maps and plates.* 8° 1765
Varnhagen, Francisco Ad. de. Reflexões Criticas sobre o Escripto do Seculo XIV. impresso com o titulo de Noticia do Brasil, no tomo 3°. da Collecção de Not. Ultr. 8° *Lisbon*, 1839
—— Vespucc et son premier Voyage : ou Notice d'une Découverte et Exploration primitive du Golfe du Mexique et des États-Unis en 1497 et 1498. 8° *Paris*, 1858
—— Examen de quelques points de l'Histoire Géographique du Brésil, ou Analyse Critique du Rapport de M. d'Avezac, sur la Récente Histoire Générale du Brésil. *Map.* 8* *Paris*, 1858
—— La Verdadera Guanahani de Colon : Memoria communicada á la Facultad de Humanidades. *Map.* Royal 8* *Santiago*, 1864

Varnhagen, Francisco Ad. de. Amerígo Vespucci, son Caractère, ses écrits (même les moins authentiques), sa vie, et ses navigations, avec une Carte indiquant les routes. Folio *Lima*, 1865
—— Sull' Importanza d'un Manoscritto inedito della Biblioteca Imperiale di Vienna, per verificare quale fu la prima Isola scoperta dal Colombo, ed anche altri punti della Storia della America. Discorso. *Map.* 8° *Vienna*, 1869
—— Das wahre Guanahani des Columbus. Uebersetzung von * * *Maps.* 8° *Vienna*, 1869
—— *See* Sousa, P. L. de.
Varthema (or Verthema), Ludovico di [sometimes called Barthema, and Vertomoman or Vertomanus]. The Navigation and Vyages of Lewis Wertomannus, Gentelman of the Citie of Rome, to the Regions of Arabia, Egypte, Persia, Syria, Ethiopia, and East India, both within and without the Ryuer of Ganges, &c., in the Yeere of our Lorde 1503 ; conteyning many notable and straunge thinges, both hystoricall and naturall. Translated out of Latine into Englyshe by Richard Eden, in the yeere of our Lord 1576. [*Privately printed for the Aungervyle Society.*] 8° *Edinburgh*, 1884
—— Les Voyages de Ludovico di Varthema, ou le Viateur en la plus grande partie d'Orient. Traduits de l'Italien en Français par J. Balarin de Raconis ; publiés et annotés par M. Ch. Schefer. [Recueil de Voyages . . .], Vol. 9. *Maps.* Large 8° *Paris*, 1888
—— *See* Hakluyt, Vol. 4 ; Hakluyt Soc. Publ., Vol. 32 ; Kerr, Vol. 7 ; Purchas, Vol. 2 ; Ramusio, Vol. 1 : Appendix 1.
Vary, George. *See* Ogilvy, T.
Vasco Nunes (or Nunez), de Balboa. *See* Gottfried.
Vasconcellos, J. L. de. *See* Portugal, B ; Appendix 2.
Vasey, Dr J. The Grasses of the United States : being a Synopsis of the Tribes and Genera, with Descriptions of the Genera, and a List of the Species. 8* *Washington*, 1883
Vasi, Mariano di. Itinerario Instruttivo da Roma a Napoli e delle sue Vicinanze. *Map and plates.* 12° *Rome*, 1816
—— Itinerario di Roma, antica e moderna. 2 vols. *Map and plates.* 12° 1819-20
Vasquez de Coronado, Francesco. *See* Purchas, Vol. 4, Book 8 ; Ramusio, Vol. 3 : Appendix 1.
Vatslik, J. Y. *See* Gowan.
Vaughan, Lieut. H. B. Report of a Journey through Persia. *Map and plates.* 8° *Calcutta*, 1890
—— A Journey through Persia. With Notes by Sir Frederick Goldsmid. [Roy. Geog. Soc. Suppl. Papers, Vol. 3.] Large 8° 1892

Vaughan, William. Memoir of William Vaughan ; with Miscellaneous Pieces relative to Docks, Commerce, &c. *Portrait.* 8° 1839

Vaugondy, Robert de. Institutions · Géographiques. *Plates.* 8° *Paris*, 1766

Vauhello, Le Saulnier de. Mémoire sur les Attérages des Côtes Occidentales de France, et Précis des Opérations Hydrographiques et Astronomiques, faites en 1828 et '29 sur les Bricks " la Badine " et " l'Alsacienne." 4° *Paris*, 1833

Vause, R. Notes from the East, descriptive of a Trip to Zanzibar and back. 12* *Natal*, 1877

Vautibault, Gazeau de. Le Trans-Saharien. 12* *Paris*, N.D.

Vaux, H. del. Dictionnaire Géographique et Statistique de la Province de Liége. 8° *Liége*, 1835

Vaux, W. S. W. Nineveh and Persepolis : an Historical Sketch of Ancient Assyria and Persia, with an Account of the recent Researches in those Countries. *Plates.* 8° 1851

Vavin, Jules. *See* Richards, John.

Vayrac, Abbé de. État présent de l'Espagne. 3 vols. 12° *Amsterdam*, 1719

Vayssières, A. Souvenirs d'un Voyage en Abyssinie. 32° *Brussels*, 1857

Vaz, Lopez. *See* Callander, Vol. 1 ; Purchas, Vol. 4, Book 7 ; General Collection, p. 610 : Appendix 1.

Vea, Anto de. Burney, Vol. 4 : Appendix 1.

Veaux, S. de. The Traveller's Own Book to Saratoga Springs, Niagara Falls, and Canada ; containing Routes, Distances, Conveyances, Expenses, Use of Mineral Waters, Baths, Description of Scenery, &c. *Maps and plates.* 18° *Buffalo*, 1841

Vedova, G. Dalla. *See* Dalla Vedova.

Veer, Gerrit de. Tre Navigationi fatte dagli Olandesi e Zelandesi, al Settentrione nella Norvegia, Moscovia, e Tartaria verso il Catai, e Regno de' Sini, doue scopersero il Mare di Veygatz, la Nuova Zembla, et un Paese nell Ottantesimo grado creduto la Groenlandia. Small 4° *Venice*, 1599
—— *See* Hakluyt Soc. Publ., Vols. 13, 54 ; Purchas, Vol. 3, Book 3 : Appendix 1.

Veer, Gustav de. Prinz Heinrich der Seefahrer und seine Zeit ; mit einer Einleitung über die Geschichte des Portugiesischen Handels und Scewesens bis zum Anfange des 15 Jahrhunderts. *Portrait.* 8° *Danzig*, 1864

Vega, Garcilaso de la. *See* De la Vega.

Vega, Luis Salinas. Catálogo General de Archivos o' Sea. Doumentos relativos á Bolivia encontrados en el archivo de Indias y en el de la Real Académia de la Historia. 8* *La Paz*, 1889

Veitch, S. F. T. Views in Central Abyssinia, with Portraits of the Natives of the Galla Tribes. By a German Traveller ; with Descriptions by S. F. T. Veitch. *Plates.* Oblong 8° 1868

Vekeman, G. Voyages au Canada. *Plates.* 8° *Namur*, 1885

Vélain, C. Description Géologique de la presqu'île d'Aden, de l'île de la Réunion, des îles Saint-Paul et Amsterdam. *Map, plates, and photographs.* 4° *Paris*, 1878
—— Passage de Vénus sur le Soleil (9 Décembre 1874) : Expédition Française aux Iles Saint Paul et Amsterdam ; Observations générales sur la Faune des deux Iles suivies d'une Description des Mollusques. [From " Archives de Zoologie Expérimentale et Générale," T. 6, 1877.] *Maps and plates.* 8* *Paris*, 1877

Velasco, Juan de. *See* Ternaux-Compans, Vols. 18, 19 : Appendix 1.

Velasques, Diego. *See* Gottfried : Appendix 1.

Velschow, Franz A. On the Cause of Trade Winds ; with Discussion by Charles Macdonald. *Maps.* 8° [1890]

Venedey, I. Römerthum, Christenthum, und Germanenthum, und deren wechselseitiger Einfluss bei der Ungestaltung der Sclaverei des Altherthums, in die Leibeigenschaft des Mittelalters. 8° *Frankfurt*, 1840

Venegas, Miguel. A Natural and Civil History of California, containing an accurate Description of that Country, &c. Translated from the original Spanish. 2 vols. *Map and plates.* 8° 1759

Vénéon, Jean. [E. Perrin.] In Memoriam, Tschingel. 8* [1892]

Veness, W. T. El Dorado ; or, British Guiana as a Field for Colonisation. *Maps.* 8° 1867

Venezia, Baldassare. Dizionario Statistico dei Paesi del Regno delle Due Sicilie. 8° *Naples*, 1818

Venukoff, M. Travels on the Confines of Russian Asia, &c. [In Russian.] Small 8° *[St Petersburg]* 1868
—— Sketch of the Japanese Archipelago. [In Russian.] Parts 1 and 2. *Map.* 8° *St Petersburg*, 1871
—— Attempt at a Military Sketch of the Russian Frontiers in Asia. [In Russian.] *Map.* 8° *St Petersburg*, 1873
—— Die Russisch-Asiatischen Grenzlande, aus dem Russischen übersetzt von — Krahmer. 8° *Leipzig*, 1874
—— On the Geographical Conditions of the Existence and the Progress of the Russian People. [In Russian.] 8* *[St Petersburg]* N.D.
—— Russia and the East. [In Russian.] Small 8° *St Petersburg*, 1877

Venukoff, M. Aperçu Sommaire de la partie méridionale de la Province Littorale de la Sibérie. *Map.* 8*
[Paris, 1884]
—— Du Dessèchement des Lacs dans l'Asie Centrale. *Map.* 8* *[Paris]* 1886
—— The Canal of Panama. [In Russian.] 8* [1887]
—— Progrès de la Cartographie dans l'Empire Russe. 8* *[Paris,* 1889]
—— Les Voyageurs Russes en Asie depuis 20 ans, 1854-74. [*Table* in Russian and French.] 8* N.P., N.D.
—— Liste des Voyageurs Russes en Asie depuis l'occupation par les Russes du bassin de l'Amour et du Sémirétchié : 1854-80. [Also in Russian.] 12* N.P., N.D.
—— On Geographical Discoveries in Asiatic Russia, 1577-1877. [In Russian.] 8* N.P., N.D.
—— Aperçu Historique des Découvertes Géographiques faites dans la Russie d'Asie depuis les temps les plus reculés jusqu'à nos jours. *Map.* 8*
Paris [1879 ?]
—— La Tunisie contemporaine (fevrier 1893). [In Russian.] 8* 1893
—— The Indian Ocean. [In Russian.] Large 8* [1893]
—— *See* Michell ; *also* Central Asia, A : Appendix 2.
"**Vénus.**" Voyage autour du monde. *See* Du Petit-Thouars.
Venuti, Ridolfino. Descrizione Topografica delle Antichita di Roma. 2 vols. *Map and plates.* 4° *Rome,* 1824
Vera, Gerardo di. *See* Veer, Gerrit de.
Verbeek, R. D. M. Krakatau. 8°. *Maps, plates, &c.,* in separate case, 4° *Batavia,* 1886
—— Notice jointe aux Cartes de l'edition Française de Krakatau. 4* N.P., N.D.
Verbiest, Ferdinand. *See* Hakluyt Soc. Publ., Vol. 17 ; Allgemeine Historie, Vol. 7 : Appendix 1.
Verdan, D. Guide Historique et Descriptif de Wiesbade et de ses Environs. 12* *Wiesbaden* [1860]
Verdun de la Crenne, — de, Le Chevalier de Borda, and le Chanoine Pingré. Voyage fait par ordre du Roi en 1771 et 1772 en diverses parties de l'Europe, de l'Afrique, et de l'Amérique ; pour vérifier l'utilité de plusieurs méthodes et instrumens, servant à déterminer la Latitude et la Longitude, tant du vaisseau que des côtes, Isles, et Écueils qu'on reconnoît : suivi de recherches pour rectifier les cartes hydrographiques. 2 vols. *Maps and plates.* 4° *Paris,* 1778
Vereker, Hon. H. P. British Shipmasters' Hand-Book to Rio Grande do Sul. *Plates.* 12° 1860

Verestchagin, V. Skizzen und Erinnerungen, aus dem Russischen übersetzt von E. Kretschmann. *Illustrations.* 8° *Leipzig,* 1885
—— Vassili Verestchagin, Painter—Soldier —Traveller : Autobiographical Sketches. Translated from the German and the French by F. H. Peters. 2 vols. *Illustrations.* 8° 1887
—— **und Frau Verestchagin.** Reiseskizzen aus Indien. 1. Bändchen, Ost-Himalaya ; 2. Bändchen, Kaschmir, Ladak. *Illustrations.* 12° *Leipzig,* 1882-85
Vergara, José Ignacio. Anuario de la Oficina Central Meteorolójica de Santiago de Chile. 8° *Santiago,* 1879
—— Observaciones Meteorolójicas hechas en el Observatorio Astronómico de Santiago, 1873-81. *Diagrams.* Small 4° *Santiago,* 1884
—— The same. 1882-84. *Diagrams.* 8° *Santiago,* 1885
Vergara, R. G. Noticias sobre las Provincias del litoral correspondiente al Departamento de Lima, i de la Provincia constitucional del Callao, por la Oficina Hidrográfica. *Map.* 8° *Santiago,* 1879
—— Los Descubridores del Estrecho de Magallanes i sus primeros Exploradores. 1553-84. *Map.* 8° *Santiago,* 1880
Vergara y Velasco, F. J. *See* Reclus.
Vergers, A. Noel des. Histoire de l'Afrique. *See* Ebn-Khaldoun.
Vernazani, Miguel. *See* Angelis, Vol. 5 : Appendix 1.
Verneuil, E. de. *See* Sedgwick, A. ; Tchihatchef.
Verney, Sir Harry. A Route from the Atlantic to the Pacific through British Territory. (From *Fraser's Magazine.*) 8* 1869
Vernon, Francis. *See* Ray : Appendix 1.
Verrazzano, Giov. *See* Murphy ; *also* Gottfried ; Hakluyt Voyages, Vol. 3 ; Hakluyt Soc. Publ., Vol. 7 ; Ramusio, Vol. 3 ; Allgemeine Historie, Vol. 15 : Appendix 1.
Verrier, J. le. *See* Hakluyt Soc. Publ., Vol. 46 : Appendix 1.
Verteuil, L. A. A. de. Trinidad, its Geography, Natural Resources, Administration, Present Condition, and Prospects. 8° 1858
—— The same. 2nd edition. *Map.* 8° 1884
Verthema, Ludovico. *See* Varthema.
Verulam, Francis, Lord. Sylva Sylvarum, or a Natural History, in Ten Centuries ; whereunto is newly added the History Naturall and Experimentall of life and death, or of the prolongation of life. Published after the author's death by Wm. Rawley. 6th edition. Small folio 1651

Vespucci, Amerigo (or Vespucis, or Vespucius, Americus). *See* Hugues ; Santarem ; Urbani de Gheltof; Varnhagen ; *also* Burney, Vol. 1 ; Callander, Vol. 1 ; Gottfried ; Kerr, Vol. 3 ; Navarette, Vol. 3 ; Ramusio, Vol. 1; Allgemeine Historie, Vols. 13, 18, &c. ; Colecção de Noticias, Vol. 2, p. 610 ; General Collection of Voyages, p. 610 ; Cartas de Indias, p. 612 : Appendix 1.

Vessélowsky, C. Du Climat de la Russie. 8* *St Petersburg,* 1855
—— Époques des Débâcles et de la Prise par les Glaces de la Dwina, à Arkhangel. 8* *St Petersburg,* 1856

Vetch, Capt. James. Inquiry into the Means of Establishing a Ship Navigation between the Mediterranean and the Red Seas. *Map.* 8* 1843
—— On Havens of Safety. *Map and plates.* 4* 1844
—— Plans and Papers on the subject of a Harbour at Port Natal, South Africa. *Plates.* Folio* 1859

Vetch, Capt. *See* India, I : Appendix 2.

Veth, D. D. Daniel David Veth, door Prof. P. J. Veth. *Portrait.* 8* N.P., 1885
—— *See* Snellemann ; Veth, P. J., Midden-Sumatra.

Veth, P. J. Borneo's Wester-Afdeeling : Geographisch, Statistisch, Historisch voorafgegaan door eene algemeene Schets des ganschen Eilands. 2 vols. *Plates.* 8° *Zaltbommel,* 1854 *and* 1856
—— Het Eiland Flores. 8*
[*Amsterdam,* 1855]
—— Over de Physische Geographie van den Indischen Archipel. [Translated from A. R. Wallace.] 8* *Zaltbommel,* 1865
——Geographische Aanteekeningen betrekkelijk het Eiland Flores. *Map.* 4* *Amsterdam,* 1876
—— Geographische Aanteekeningen betreffende de Kei-Eilanden. *Map.* 4* *Amsterdam,* 1877
—— Het Landschap Deli op Sumatra. *Map.* 4* *Amsterdam,* 1877
—— Het Landschap Aboeng en de Aboengers op Sumatra. *Map.* 4* *Amsterdam,* 1877
—— Beccari's Reis van Makasser naar Kendari. 4* *Amsterdam,* 1877
—— Een Woord bij de Kaart van Diëng-Gebergte. *Map.* 4* *Amsterdam,* 1877
—— Geographische Aanteekeningen omtrent de Oostkust van Atjeh. 4* *Amsterdam,* 1877
—— Notizia su Selajar e isole adiacenti. *Map.* 8* *Tui in,* 1880
—— Midden-Sumatra : Reizen en Onderzoekingen der Sumatra-Expeditie, uitgerust door het Aardrijkskundig Genootschap, 1877-79; beschreven door de

Veth, P. J.—*continued.*
Leden der Expeditie onder Toezicht van Prof. P. J. Veth. 4 vols. in 3. *Plates.* 4° *Leyden*

CONTENTS.

Eerste Deel. Reisverhaal. Eerste Gedeelte, door A. L. van Hasselt en Joh. F. Snelleman. *Plates* 1881
—— 2 Gedeelte, door C. H. Cornelissen, A. L. van Hasselt, en J. F. Snelleman. *Map and plates* 1882
Tweede Deel. Aardrijks kundige Beschrijving, met Atlas, door D. D. Veth. *Plate* 1882
Derde Deel. Volksbeschrijving en Taal, door A. L. van Hasselt. 1 Gedeelte, 1 Afdeeling. *Plate.* 1882. 2 Afdeel. Ethnographische Atlas, met Verklarenden Tekst. 1881
—— 2 Gedeelte. De Talen en Letterkunde van Midden-Sumatra, door A. L. van Hasselt. *Plate* 1881
Vierde Deel. Natuurlijke Historie ; Eerste Gedeelte, Fauna, door Joh. F. Snelleman. 2 vols. *Plates* 1887-92
—— 2 Gedeelte. Flora, door A. L. van Hasselt en Dr J. G. Boerlage. *Plates* 1884
—— Ontdekkers en Onderzoekers. Zevental Levensschetsen, ter tweede verbeterde en vermeerderde Uitgave bijeenverzameld. 8° *Leyden,* 1884
1. Philippus Baldaeus ; 2. Samuel van de Putte ; 3. Caspar George Carl Reinwardt ; 4. Jan Frederik Gerrit Brumund ; 5. Taco Roorda ; 6. Wolter Robert van Hoëvell ; 7. Jan Karl Jacob de Jonge.
—— Johan Mauritz Mohr. [From *De Gids,* 1885, No. 7.] *Plate.* 8* 1885
—— Hendrik Adriaan van Reede tot Drakestein. 8* [1887]
—— De Nederlanders in Afrika. 8* *Leyden,* 1893
—— *See* Rosenberg ; *also* Dutch East Indies : Appendix 2.
—— **and C. M. Kan.** Bibliografie van Nederlandsche Boeken, Brochures, Kaarten, &c., over Afrika. 8° *Utrecht,* 1876

Viani, P. *See* Astley, Vol. 3: Appendix 1.

Vibe, A. Höidemaalinger i Norge fra Aar 1774 til 1860. 8° *Christiania,* 1860
—— Küsten und Meer Norwegens. Mit einer Karte von Dr A. Petermann, und zwei original Ansichten, in chromolith. Ausgeführt von Bernatz. (Ergänzungsheft, 1 — Petermann's Mittheilungen.) *Coloured map and plates.* 4° *Gotha,* 1860

Vicary, Capt. *See* India, C (Geological Papers) : Appendix 2.

Vicentius Beluacensis. *See* Purchas, Vol. 3, Book 1 : Appendix 1.

"**Victoria**," **Ship.** *See* Norman, W. H.

Victorica, Dr Don Benjamin. *See* Moyano.

Vidal, E. E. Picturesque Illustrations of Buenos Ayres and Monte Video, with Descriptions of the Scenery, and of the Costumes, Manners, &c., of the Inhabitants of those Cities and their Environs. 24 *coloured plates.* 4° 1820

Vidal-Lablache, P. Des Divisions Fondamentales du sol Française. 8* *Paris*, 1888

Viedma, Don Francisco de. Informe general de la Provincia de Santa Cruz, de la Sierra, cuya capital es la Ciudad de Cochabamba, comprehend la Descripcion Geografica de toda ella con sus verdadera latitudes, y longitudes, frutos, y comercios, demostrando su estado en la Balanza del interno y externo, asi entre la misma Provincia, como en las de este Reyno, y los de España, y se proponen los medios mas adaptados à su prosperidad, conciliando el libre comercio con las misiones de Moxos y Chiquitos. Lo dirige el Gobernador Intendente de ella Don Francisco de Viedma. [With this is a Report by Don Alvarez de Sotomayer.] MS. Folio 1793

Viele, E. L. The Topography and Physical Resources of the State of New York. 8* [*New York*, 1875]

Vignal, Pierre. *See* Seillière.

Vigne, G. T. Personal Narrative of a Visit to Ghuzni, Kabul, and Afghanistan, and a Residence at the Court of Dost Mohamed. *Map and plates.* 8° 1840

Vignes, —. *See* Luynes.

Vignoles, Charles. International Exhibition of 1862 . . : Model of the Passage of the Tudela and Bilbao Railway across the Chain of the Cantabrian Pyrenees, through the Basque Provinces in the North of Spain. *Map and table.* 8* 1862

Vignon, Louis. La France dans l'Afrique du Nord, Algérie, et Tunisie. *Map.* 8° *Paris*, 1887

Vigoni, Pippo. Abissinia : Giornale di un Viaggio. *Map and plates.* 8° *Milan*, 1881

Viguier, Maurice. La Géographie dans les Chaires de l'Université. 8* *Avignon*, 1893

Villafañe, J. A. de. Quilatador de la Plata, Oro, y Piedras. Small 8° *Valladolid*, 1572

Villalobos, Ruy Lopez de. *See* Burney, Vol. 1 : Appendix 1.

Villaneuva, A. Salitres i Guanos del Desierto de Atacama : Clasificacion i Analisis de varias plantas halladas en el Desierto. 8* *Santiago*, 1878

Villaret, E. de. Dai Nippon (le Japon). *Maps.* 8° *Paris*, 1889

Villarino, Don Basilio. No. 1. Don Basilio Villarino's Survey and Diary of his Exploration of the great River Negro in Patagonia, to its Sources in the Cordillera of the Andes, 1782. [MS. in Spanish.] *Map.* No. 2. Diary of his Voyage from the Rio Negro to Examine the Coasts, the Bay of All Saints, the Isles of Buen Success, and to verify the Mouth of the Rio Colorado, and to ascend it, 1787. (The original paper.) [MS. in Spanish.] Folio N.P., V.D.

Villault, Sieur. *See* Astley, Vol. 2 ; Laharpe, Vol. 2 ; Allgemeine Historie, Vol. 3 : Appendix 1.

Villaumez. *See* Bouet-Villaumez.

Villavicencio, Enrique. Republica de Costa-Rica : Historia, Geografía, &c. 12* 1886

Villavicencio, Manuel. Geografia de la Republica del Ecuador. *Maps and plates* [*maps separate*]. 8° *New York*, 1858

Villavicencio, Dr R. La Republica de Venezuela bajo el punto de vista de la Geografia y Topografia Medicus y de la Demografia. 8° *Caracas*, 1880

Villegagnon. *See* Callander, Vol. 1 : Appendix 1.

Villehuet, Bourdé de. The Manœuverer, or Skilful Seaman : being an Essay on the Theory and Practice of the various Movements of a Ship at Sea, as well as of Naval Evolution in general. Translated by the Chevalier de Sauseuil. *Plates.* 4° 1788

Vilovo, J. S. von. Die Felsengen des Kazan und die Donau- und Theiss-Regulirung. *Maps.* 8° *Vienna*, 1879

Vince, Rev. S. *See* Pinkerton.

Vincendon-Dumoulin, C. A., and C. Desgraz. Iles Marquises ou Nouka-Hiva, histoire, géographie, mœurs, et considérations générales. *Maps.* 8° *Paris*, 1843

—— **and C. P. de Kerhallet.** Description Nautique de la Côte N. du Maroc. *Plates.* 8° *Paris*, 1857

—— Manuel de la Navigation dans le Détroit de Gibraltar. *Map and plates.* 8° *Paris*, 1857

Vincent, Benjamin. *See* Haydn ; *also* Catalogues, A (Royal Institution) : Appendix 2.

Vincent, C. E. H. Russia's Advance Eastward : based on the Official Reports of Lieutenant Hugo Stumm, to which is appended other information on the subject, and a minute Account of the Russian Army. *Map.* 12° 1874

Vincent, F. The Land of the White Elephant : Sights and Scenes in South-Eastern Asia, a Personal Narrative of Travel and Adventure in Farther India, embracing the Countries of Burma, Siam, Cambodia, and Cochin-China (1871-72). *Maps and plates.* 8° 1873

Vincent, Frank. In and Out of Central America, and other Sketches and Studies of Travel. *Maps and illustrations.* Crown 8° *New York,* 1890
—— Around and About South America : Twenty Months of Quest and Query. *Map, plan, and charts.* 8° *New York,* 1890
Vincent, J. E. Matthew. Problems of Australian Colonization. 12* 1892
Vincent, Prof. M. C. Report on the St Genevieve Glass-Sand Property of Southern Missouri. 8* 1869
Vincent, Dean William. The Commerce and Navigation of the Ancients in the Indian Ocean. 2 vols. *Portrait and maps.* 4° 1807
[For Contents of Volumes, *see* Appendix 1.]
Vinci, Leonardo da. *See* Uzielli.
Vincke, V. *See* Kiepert.
"Vindex." *See* Rusden.
Vines, —. Report on the Trade and Navigation of the Port of Islay, for the years 1870 and 1871, and touching the Resources, Traffic, Communications, and General Condition of Southern Peru. 8* 1872
Vining, Edward P. An Inglorious Columbus, or Evidence that Hwui Shăn and a party of Buddhist Monks from Afghanistan discovered America in the 5th Century A.D. *Map.* 8° *New York,* 1885
Vink, —. *See* Callander, Vol. 2 ; Allgemeine Historie, Vol. 18 : Appendix 1.
Vinson, A. Voyage à Madagascar au Couronnement de Radama II. *Plates.* Large 8° *Paris,* 1865
Vinson, J. *See* Bonaparte, Prince L. L.
Viquesnel, A. Coup d'Œil sur quelques points de l'Histoire générale des peuples Slaves et de leurs voisins les Turcs et les Finnois. 4° *Lyons,* 1865
Virgin, C. A. Kongliga Svenska Fregatten Eugenies Resa omkring Jorden under Befäl af C. A. Virgin, åren 1851-53, Vetenskapliga Iakttagelser. 4° *Stockholm*
Vol. 1.—Botanik. Andersson, N. J. Om Galapagos - öarnes Vegetation. *Plates* [1857]
Vol. 2.—Zoologi. 1. Insecta. *Plates* 1858-68
The same. Annulata. *Plates* N.D.
Vol. 3.—Fysik. [Also in French.] *Maps* 1858-74
Virlet d'Aoust. *See* Aoust, V. d'.
Virlet, Theodore. *See* Greece (Morea) : Appendix 2.
Viscaino, Sebastian. *See* Burney, Vol. 2 : Appendix 1.
Visconti, Ferd. Sistema Metrico della Città di Napoli. 8° *Naples,* 1838

Vissering, S. Handleiding tot wetenschappelijke Waarnemingen ten Behoeve van Reizigers, Koloniale Ambtenaren, Consuls, en andere Residenten in vreemde Gewesten. Small 8° *Utrecht,* 1875
Vivaldi, —. *See* Avezac.
Vivien, M. Recherches sur l'Histoire de l'Anthropologie. 8* *Paris,* N.D.
Vlamingh, Willem de. *See* Hakluyt Soc. Publ., Vol. 25 ; Callander, Vol. 3 ; Allgemeine Historie, Vol. 18 : Appendix 1.
Voeikoff, —. *See* Woeikof.
Vogel, Dr E. *See* Malte-Brun ; Petermann ; Schauenburg.
Vogel, Hermann. Beobachtungen von Nebelflecken und Sternhaufen am sechsflüssigen Refractor und zwölfflüssigen Aequatoreal der Leipziger Sternwarte ausgeführt. 8* *Leipzig,* 1867
Vogel, Sir Julius. The Official Handbook of New Zealand : a Collection of Papers by experienced Colonists on the Colony as a whole, and on the several Provinces. *Plates.* 8° 1875
—— New Zealand and the South Sea Islands, and their Relation to the Empire. 8* 1878
Vogt, Carl. Lectures on Man, his place in Creation, and in the History of the Earth. Edited by J. Hunt. 8° 1864
—— Su alcuni antichi Cranii Umani rinvenuti in Italia. Lettera . . . al Signor B. Gastaldi. 8* 1866
Vogüé, Vicomte E. M. de. Syrie, Palestine, Mont Athos: Voyage aux pays du passé. *Plates.* 12° *Paris,* 1876
—— *See* Luynes.
Volkersen, Capt. S. *See* Hakluyt Soc. Publ., Vol. 25 : Appendix 1.
Volkmann, Johann Jacob. Neueste Reisen durch die Vereinigten Niederlande, vorzüglich in Absicht auf die Kunstsammlungen, Naturgeschichte, Oekonomie und Manufacturen. *Map.* 8° *Leipzig,* 1783
Vollers, Dr K. *See* Müller, A.
Volney, C. F. Voyage en Syrie et en Égypte pendant les années 1783-85. 2nd edition [*Large paper*]. 2 vols. *Maps and plates.* 4° *Paris,* 1787
—— Tableau du Climat et du Sol des États-Unis d'Amérique ; suivi d'Éclaircissemens sur la Floride, sur la Colonie Française au Scioto, sur quelques Colonies Canadiennes, et sur les Sauvages. 2 vols. *Maps and plates.* 8° *Paris,* 1803
—— *See* Pelham, Vol. 2 : Appendix 1.
Volschinoff, N. A. The Siberian Railway. Translated by G. F. Napier. (From the Journal of the U.S. Institution of India, No. 91.) 8* 1892

Völter, Daniel. Die Grundlinien der mathematischen Geographie und die physikalische Beschreibung von Afrika und Asien. 8° *Esslingen*, 1841
—— Lehrbuch der politischen Geographie. 8° *Esslingen*, 1845
Von den Steinen, K. *See* Steinen.
Von der Decken, Baron Carl Claus. Reisen in Ost-Afrika in den Jahren 1859-65. Vols 1, 2, 3 (in 3 parts), 4. *Map, plates, and tables.* 4° *Leipzig*, 1869-79
—— Abridged Translation of Von der Decken's Journey up the River Juba (1865). MS. 4° N.D.
Von der Gabelentz, Prof. Georg. The Languages of Melanesia. (From the Journal of the Royal Asiatic Society of Great Britain and Ireland, Vol. 18, Part 4.) 8° [1886]
Von der Horck, Alexander Humboldt v. H. The Question of Arctic Discovery, and its Valuable Results ; with an Account of the Author's Recent Explorations in the Spitzbergen Seas, and a Boat Journey through Russian and Finnish Lapland. Address delivered before the American Geographical Society, 29th November 1876. 8° *New York*, 1876
—— Meine Expedition nach dem Polarmeer und die Rückreise von Vadsö durch Lappland und Finnland. 8° *Berlin*, 1876
—— Meine Reise nach dem Polarmeer und über die Bewohner der Nordküiste. *Plate.* 8° *Berlin*, 1876
—— The Physical Condition and Psychical Characteristics of the Races inhabiting the North Coast of Europe. 8° *Berlin*, 1876
—— The Physical Condition and Distinctive Characteristics of the Lapplanders and the Races inhabiting the North Coast of Europe. 8° [1877]
—— Auszug aus der von der medicinischen Facultät der Friedrich-Wilhelms-Universitat zu Berlin gekrönten Preisschrift. Small 8° *Berlin*, N.D.
Von der Linth, A. E. *See* Bürkli.
Von Orlich, Capt. L. *See* Orlich.
Von Siebold, C. T. *See* Hertwig.
Von Troil. *See* Troil.
Vopell, Caspar. *See* Michow, H.
"Voringen." *See* Norway, Norwegian North Atlantic Expedition, 1876-78 : Appendix 2.
Vos, J. Zeevaartkundige Beschrijving van de Kust van Guyana tusschen Cayenne en Demerary, behoorende bij de Kaart dezer Kust. *Chart.* 8° *Amsterdam*, 1854
"Vosgien" Dictionnaire Géographique Universel ; avec un Tableau Synoptique par département, et Appendices, par V. Parisot. *Maps.* 8° *Paris*, 1836
"Vossenbosch," **Ship.** *See* Hakluyt Soc. Publ., Vol. 25 : Appendix 1.

Vossion, Louis. Rapport sur la possibilité d'établir des relations Commerciales entre la France et la Birmanie. 8° *Paris*, 1879
—— Le Commerce de l'Ivoire à Khartoum et au Soudan Egyptien. 8° *Paris*, 1892
Vossius, Isaacus. De Nili et aliorum fluminum origine. *Maps.* 8° *The Hague*, 1666
Voyages and Travels, Collections of. *See* Appendix 1.
Voysey, Dr. *See* India, C (Geological Papers) : Appendix 2.
Vretos, A. P. La Bulgarie ancienne et moderne, sous le rapport Géographique, Historique, Archéologique, Statistique, et Commercial. 8° *Saint-Petersburg*, 1856
Vries, G. de. De Zeeweringen en Waterschappen van Noord-Holland. 8° *Haarlem*, 1864
Vries, M. G. Reize van Maarten Gerritsz Vries in 1643 naar het Noorden en Oosten van Japan, volgens het Journal gehouden door C. J. Corn, op het schip "Castricum." . . . vermeerderd door P. A. Leupe ; met . . . geographische en ethnographische Aanteekeningen, tevens dienende tot een Zeemansgids naar Jezo, Krafto en de Kurilen, en stukken over de Taal en Voortbrengselen der Aino-Landen, van P. F. von Siebold. *Map.* 8° *Amsterdam*, 1858
—— *See* Burney, Vol. 3, Appendix 1.
Vries, S. de. De Noordsche Weereld ; vertoond in twee nieuwe aenmercklijcke derwaerts gedaene Reysen : d'eene van de Heer Martiniere, door Norweegen, Lapland, Boranday, Siberien, Samojessie, Ys-land, Groenland, en Nova-Zembla, &c. ; d'andere van de Hamburger Frederick Martens, verright nae Spitsbergen of Groenland in't jaer 1671, &c. *Plates.* Square 8° *Amsterdam*, 1685
Vsévolojsky, N. S. Dictionnaire Géographique Historique de l'Empire de Russie. 2 vols. 8° *Moscow*, 1813
—— The same. [3rd edit.], augmentée d'un Supplement . . . par Maurice Allart. 2 vols. in 1. 8° *St Petersburg*, 1833
Vyse, Griffin W. Report on the Irrigation and Inundation of the Nile. 8° 1878
Vyse, Col. Howard. Operations carried on at the Pyramids of Gizeh in 1837 ; with an Account of a Voyage into Upper Egypt, and an Appendix. 3 vols. *Maps, plans, and plates.* Imperial 8° 1840-42

W

W——, C. M. Colonel C. G. Gordon, C.B., and Abyssinia. 8° 188–
Waagen, W. Ueber die geographische Vertheilung der Fossilen Organismen in Indien. *Map.* 4° *Vienna*, 1878
—— *See* India, C, Palæontologia Indica : Appendix 2.

Waddell, Dr L. A. On some New and Little-Known Hot Springs in South Bihar. (Reprinted from the *Journal of the Asiatic Society of Bengal*, Vol. 59, Part 2, No. 3.) 8* *Calcutta*, 1890
—— Place- and River-Names in the Darjiling District and Sikhim. (From the *Journal of the Asiatic Society of Bengal*, Vol. 60, Part 1, No. 2, 1891.] 8* 1891
—— Discovery of the exact Site of Asoka's Classic Capital of Pataliputra, the *Palibothra* of the Greeks, and Description of the Superficial Remains. *Map, plate, and plans.* 4* *Calcutta*, 1892
—— Identification of the Old Orissan port of Chitratala, the Che-li-ta-lo of Hieun Tsiang. (From the *Proceedings of the Asiatic Society of Bengal*, December 1892.) 8* 1892
—— A List of Sikhim Birds, showing their Geographical Distribution. [*Proof.*] 4* 1893

Waddington, Alfred. Overland Communication by Land and Water through British North America. 8* *Victoria, B.C.*, 1867
—— Overland Route through British North America, or the Shortest and Speediest Road to the East. *Map.* 8* 1868
—— Sketch of the proposed Line of Overland Railroad through British North America. 8* 1869

Waddington, G., and B. Hanbury. Journal of a Visit to some parts of Ethiopia. *Maps and plates.* 4° 1822

Wade, Sir Thomas Francis, and Walter Caine Hillier (Yü Yen Tzu Erh Chi). A Progressive Course, designed to assist the Student of Colloquial Chinese as spoken in the Capital and the Metropolitan Department. 3 vols. 4° *Shanghai*, 1886

Wadstrom, C. B. An Essay on Colonisation, particularly applied to the Western Coast of Africa, &c. *Maps and plate.* 4° 1794

Wafer, Lionel. New Voyage and Description of the Isthmus of America, with an Account of the Form and Make of the Country, the Coasts, Hills, Rivers, &c.; to which are added the Natural History, by a F.R.S., and Davis's Expedition to the Gold Mines in 1702. *Map and plates.* 8° 1704
—— *See* Callander, Vol. 2 ; Knox's New Collection, Vol. 2 : Appendix 1.

Wagener, G. On a New Seismometer. Folio* . [*Kioto*] 1880

Wagener, Z. *See* Churchill, Vol. 2 : Appendix 1.

Waghorn, Lieut. Thomas. Two Letters on the Extension of Steam Navigation from Singapore to Port Jackson, Australia. 8* 1846-47

Wagner, Prof. Hermann. Patrokles am Kara Bugas ? 8* *Göttingen*, 1885
—— Bericht über die Entwickelung der Methodik und des Studiums der Erdkunde. 8* *Gotha*, 1888
—— Festrede im Namen der Georg-Augusts-Universität zur Akademischen Preisverteilung am 4, Juni 1890. 4* *Göttingen*, 1890
—— Hermann Berghaus. 4* *Göttingen*, 1890
—— Ueber das von S. Günther 1888, herausgegebene Spätmittelalterliche Verzeichnis geographischer Koordinatenwerte. 8* *Göttingen*, 1891
—— Die dritte Weltkarte Peter Apians v. J. 1530, und die Pseudo-Apianische Weltkarte von 1551. 4* *Göttingen*, 1892
—— Geographische Jahrbuch. 1881 and onwards. 8°
—— *See* Guthe ; *also* Germany, Gotha: Appendix 3.
—— **and E. Behm** (subsequently **H. Wagner and A. Supan**). Die Bevölkerung der Erde. Nos. I.-IX. (Ergänzungshefte, 33, 35, 41, 49, 55, 62, 69, 101, 107—Petermann's Mittheilungen.) *Gotha*, 1872-93
—— **and H. Wichmann.** Geographische Gesellschaften, Congresse, und Zeitschriften. 12* *Gotha*, 1880

Wagner, Johann Christoph. Das mächtige Kayser-Reich Sina, und die Asiatische Tartarey vor Augen gestellet, in aussführlicher Beschreibung der Königreiche, Provinzien, Landschafften, Städte. Flüsse, Berge, Gewächse, Bäume, Früchte, Thiere, Gevögel, Fische, &c., so in diesen weit-entlegenen Welt-Gegenden sich finden ; wie auch solcher Völcker Landes-Regierung, Ehren-Stellen, Götzen-Dienst . . . neben vielen andern wunderseltsamen Merckwürdigkeiten. *Map and plates.* Folio *Augsburg*, 1688

Wagner, Dr Moritz. Der Kaukasus und das Land der Kosaken in der Jahren 1843 bis 1846. 12° *Leipzig*, 1850
—— Travels in Persia, Georgia, and Koordistan, with Sketches of the Cossacks and the Caucasus. From the German. 3 vols. 8° 1856
—— Beiträge zu einer physisch-geographischen Skizze des Isthmus von Panama. Mit einer Karte. [Ergänzungsheft, 5 —Petermann's Mittheilungen.] *Map.* 4° *Gotha*, 1861
—— Naturwissenschaftliche Reisen im Tropischen Amerika. 8° *Stuttgart*, 1870
—— **and Carl Scherzer.** Die Republik Costa Rica in Central-Amerika, mit besonderer Berücksichtigung der Naturverhältnisse und der Frage der Deutschen Auswanderung und Colonisation. Reisestudien und Skizzen aus den Jahren 1853 und 1854. *Map.* 8° *Leipzig*, 1856

Wagner, S. C. Natur-Wunder und Länder-Merkwürdigkeiten. 6 vols. 12°
Berlin, 1802-11

Wahl, F. S. Günther. Altes und neues Vorder- und Mittel-Asien, oder Pragmatisch - Geografische, Fysische, und Statistische Schilderung und Geschichte des Persischen Reichs, von den ältesten Zeiten bis auf diesen Tag. Vol. 1. 8°
Leipzig, 1795

Wahl, Maurice. L'Algérie. 2nd edition. 8° *Paris*, 1889 [1888]

Wahlén, E. Wahre Tagesmittel und tägliche Variation der Temperatur an 18 Stationen des Russischen Reiches. Dritter Supplementband zum Repertorium für Meteorologie. 4°
St Petersburg, 1886

Wahlenberg, G. De Vegetatione et Climate in Helvetia Septentrionali inter Flumina Rhenum et Arolam, &c. *Map.* 8° *Zurich*, 1813

Wahlquist, A. H. *See* Sweden, A (Geologiska Undersökning): Appendix 2.

Wahlstedt, L. J. Exposition Internationale d'Amsterdam en 1883: Catalogue de la Collection des Semences Suédoises, avec une Introduction Topographique Climatologique, &c. *Map.* 8° *Lund*, 1883

Waitz, T. Introduction to Anthropology. Edited by J. T. Collingwood. 8° 1863

Wakefield, E. Jerningham. Adventure in New Zealand, from 1839 to 1844, with some Account of the Beginning of the British Colonisation of the Islands. 2 vols. 8° 1845

Wakefield, Rev. M. Vocabulary of the Kavirόndo Language. 12° 1887

Wakefield, Thomas. Footprints in Eastern Africa, or Notes of a Visit to the Southern Galas. 8* 1866

Wakhoucht, Tsarévitch. *See* Brosset.

Walch, Garnet. Victoria in 1880. Illustrated by Charles Turner. 4°
Melbourne [1881]

Walckenaer, Baron C. A. Dicuili liber de mensura orbis terræ. 8° *Paris*, 1807

—— Le Monde Maritime, ou Tableau Géographique et Historique de l'Archipel d'Orient, de la Polynésie, et de l'Australie, &c. 2 vols. *Map and plates.* 8°
Paris, 1819

—— Recherches Géographiques sur l'Intérieur de l'Afrique Septentrionale, comprenant l'Histoire des Voyages entrepris ou exécutés jusqu'à ce jour pénétrer dans l'Intérieur du Soudan; l'exposition des Systèmes Géographiques qu'on a formés sur cette Contrée; l'Analyse de divers Itinéraires Arabes pour déterminer la position de Timbouctou; et l'examen des connaissances des Anciens relativement à l'Intérieur de l'Afrique;

Walckenaer, Baron C. A.—*continued.* suivies d'un Appendice, contenant divers Itinéraires, traduits de l'Arabe par M. le Baron de Sacy, et M. de la Porte. *Map.* 8° *Paris*, 1821

—— Géographie Ancienne, Historique et Comparée des Gaules Cisalpine et Transalpine; suivie de l'Analyse Géographique des Itinéraires Anciens. 3 vols. 8°, and Atlas 4° *Paris*, 1839

—— Notice Biographique, par M. Cortambert. 8* *Paris*, 1853

—— **and Jomard.** Rapport sur un Pied Romain trouvé dans la Forêt de Maulevrier (près de Caudebec). *Plate.* 4°
Paris, 1839

Walcott, Charles D. *See* United States, G, *c*, Surveys: Appendix 2.

Walcott, P. *See* Mueller, F. von.

Waldo, Frank. *See* United States, H, *b* (Signal Service): Appendix 2.

Wales, Prince George of (Duke of York). *See* "Bacchante."

Wales, William. Remarks on Mr Forster's Account of Captain Cook's last Voyage round the World in the years 1772, '73, '74, and '75. 8° 1778

—— *See* Vincent, Vol. 1: Appendix 1.

Walford, Edward. Hardwicke's Annual Biography for 1857, containing Original and Selected Memoirs of Celebrated Characters who have died during the year 1856. 12° 1857

Walker, Col. Alex. Reports :—

Reports on the Resources, &c., of the Districts of Noriad, Matur Mondeh, Beejapoor, Dholka, Dundooka, and Gogo, the Tuppa of Napar, and the Kusba of Ranpoor, in Guzerat; with brief Notes relative to the Fort of Kaira, the Chouth of Cambay, the former Condition of Guzerat, &c., to the close of the last Century.

Proceedings adopted in 1804 and 1807, consequent on an application from certain Chiefs in the Province of Kattywar, soliciting the Protection of the British Government, &c.

Report on the Districts of Jhalawar, Muchoo Kanta, Nowanuggur, Gohelwar, Poorbunder, Soruth, Hallar, and Kattywar Proper, in Kattywar.

Review of the Proceedings (to May 1808) of the Hon. East India Company's Government in the Western Peninsula of Guzerat; accompanied by Miscellaneous Information connected with the Province of Kattywar.

Transfer from the Gaekwar State to the British Government of the Annual Tribute payable by the Thakoor of Bhownuggur; negotiated in 1808. [Bombay Records, No. 39, Part 1, N.S.] Large 8° *Bombay*, 1856

Walker, F. A. *See* United States, A, Census Reports: Appendix 2.

Walker, Rev. F. A. L'Orient, or a Journal of my Tour in the East, 1st March to 30th June 1882. 8° 1882
—— Nine Hundred Miles up the Nile, 3rd November to 9th February 1884. 8° 1884
—— The Botany and Entomology of Iceland. 8* N.D.

Walker, J. B. Notes illustrating Charts of the Cross and Old Calabar Rivers, June 1871 ; and Notes of a Visit to the Old Calabar and Qua Rivers, the Ekoi Country, and the Qua Rapids, 14th May 1875. (From the *United Presbyterian Missionary Record*, Sept. 1872, March and April 1876.) *Maps.* 8*

Walker, Captain J. G. *See* United States, E, *a*: Appendix 2.

Walker, James J. A Year's Insect-Hunting at Gibraltar. (From the *Entomologist's Monthly Magazine*, Jan. 1888.) 8* 1888

Walker, Gen. J. T. Explorations of the Great Sanpo River of Tibet during 1877, in connection with the operations of the Survey of India. *Maps.* 8*
[*Calcutta*, 1879]
—— Captain Henry John Harman, Royal Engineers. 12* [1883]
—— *See* India, F, *c* and *d* : Appendix 2.

Walker, Mrs. Untrodden Paths in Roumania. *Illustrations.* 8° 1888

Walker, Robert. The Five Threes, 33,333 Miles by Land and Sea : Holiday Notes. *Illustrations.* 8° 1884

Walker, Samuel Abraham. Missions in Western Africa among the Soosoos, &c., being the first undertaken by the Church Missionary Society for Africa and the East. *Map.* 8° *Dublin*, 1845

Walker, William. On the Social and Economic Position and Prospects of the British West India Possessions. 8° 1873
—— British Guiana at the Paris Exhibition : Catalogue of Exhibits ; to which are prefixed some Illustrative Notices of the Colony. Edited by Wm. Walker. *Map and plate.* 8° 1878

Walker, W. B. Cyclical Deluges : an Explication of the chief Geological Phenomena of the Globe by proofs of Periodical Changes of the Earth's Axis . . . 12° 1871

Walker, Walter Frederick. The Azores, or Western Islands : a Political, Commercial, and Geographical Account. *Maps and illustrations.* 8° 1882

Wall, G. P., and J. G. Sawkins. Report on the Geology of Trinidad, &c. *Maps and plates.* 8° 1860

Wall, H. Beresford de la Poer. Manual of Physical Geography of Australia. *Plates.* 12° *Melbourne*, 1883

Wallace, Albert. Jottings referring to the Early Discovery of Gold in Australia, and some Remarks relative to the Veteran Gold Miner, John Calvert. *Sydney*, N.D.

Wallace, Capt. A. The Occupation of the Southern Shan Country at the commencement of 1887. (From the J. United Service of India, Vol. 18, No. 75, Simla.) 8* 1889

Wallace, Dr Alfred Russel. Narrative of Travels on the Amazon and Rio Negro ; with an Account of the Native Tribes, and Observations on the Climate, Geology, and Natural History of the Amazon Valley. *Map and plates.* 8° 1853
—— The same. 2nd edition. [The Minerva Library of Famous Books.] *Map, portrait, and illustrations.* Crown 8° 1889
—— Palm Trees of the Amazon and their uses. *Map and plates.* 8° 1853
—— On the Law which has regulated the Introduction of New Species. 8* 1855
—— The Malay Archipelago, the Land of the Orang-Utan and the Bird of Paradise : a Narrative of Travel, with Studies of Man and Nature. 2 vols. *Maps and plates.* 8° 1869
—— Another edition. *Maps and plates.* Small 8° 1872
—— Another edition 1886
—— The Geographical Distribution of Animals, with a Study of the Relations of Living and Extinct Faunas as elucidating the Past Changes of the Earth's Surface. 2 vols. *Maps and plates* 1876
—— Island Life, or the Phenomena and Causes of Insular Faunas and Floras, including a Revision and attempted Solution of the Problem of Geological Climates. *Maps.* 8° 1880
—— The same. 2nd edition. *Maps, diagrams, &c.* Small 8° 1892
—— Inaccessible Valleys : a Study in Physical Geography. (From the *Nineteenth Century*, March 1893.) 8* 1893
—— The Ice Age and its Work. Part 1. Erratic Block and Ice Sheets. (From the *Fortnightly Review*, November.) 8* 1893
—— *See* Stanford.

Wallace, Sir Donald Mackenzie. Russia. 2 vols. *Maps.* 8° 1877
—— Egypt and the Egyptian Question. 8° 1883

Wallace, E. A. The Guahivos. 8*
Demerara, 1887

Wallace, Edward J. The Oregon Question determined by the Rules of International Law. 8* 1846

Wallace, J. H. *See* Sherrin and Wallace.

Wallace, Prof. Robert. India in 1887 as seen by Robert Wallace. *Maps and illustrations.* 8° *Edinburgh*, 1888
—— The Rural Economy and Agriculture of Australia and New Zealand. *Maps and illustrations.* 8° 1891

Wallace, Major R. Historical Sketch of the Native States under the Control of the Political Agent in the Rewa Kanta, prepared in 1854. [Records, Bombay, No. 23, N.S.] *Map.* Royal 8° *Bombay,* 1856

Wallace, W. *See* Murray, Hugh.

Wallach, H. *See* Kaufmann.

Waller, Rev. Horace. Remarks on the Bilious Intermittent Fever of Africa, its treatment, and precautions to be used in dangerous localities. 8* 1873
—— The Title-Deeds to Nyassa-Land. *Map.* 8* 1887
—— Trafficking in Liquor with the Natives of Africa. 8* [1887]
—— On some African Entanglements. 8* [1888]
—— Nyassaland : Great Britain's Case against Portugal. *Maps.* 8* 1890
—— "Ivory, Apes, and Peacocks:" an African Contemplation. 12° 1891
—— Health Hints for Central Africa; with Remarks on "Fever," its treatment, and Precautions to be used in dangerous localities. 5th edition. 16* 1893
—— Heligoland for Zanzibar, or One Island full of Freemen for Two full of Slaves. 8* 1893
—— *See* Livingstone ; Young, E. D.

Waller, J. A. *See* Phillips, New Voyages and Travels [3], Vol. 3: Appendix 1.

Waller, Richard. Memoirs for a Natural History of Animals, containing the Anatomical descriptions of several Creatures dissected by the Royal Academy of Sciences at Paris. Englished by Alex. Pitfield. [Bound with the following book.] Folio 1688
—— The Measure of the Earth : being an Account of several Observations made for that purpose by divers Members of the Royal Academy of Sciences at Paris. Translated out of the French by Richard Waller, Fellow of the Royal Society. *Plates.* Folio 1688

Wallich, G. C. Notes on the Presence of Animal Life at Vast Depths in the Sea, with Observations on the Nature of the Sea-Bed, as bearing on Submarine Telegraphy. 8* [*Privately printed*] 1860
—— The North-Atlantic Sea-Bed : comprising a Diary of the Voyage on board H.M.S. "Bulldog" in 1860, and Observations on the Presence of Animal Life, and the Formation and Nature of Organic Deposits, at great Depths in the Ocean. Part 1. *Map and plates.* 4° 1862
—— The Atlantic Deep-Sea Bed and its Inhabitants. (*Quarterly Journal of Science*, No. 1.) *Plate.* 8* 1864

Wallis, Capt. James. An Historical Account of the Colony of New South Wales and its dependent Settlements, in illustration of Twelve Views from Drawings taken on the spot by Capt. Wallis,

Wallis, Capt. James—*continued.*
engraved by W. Preston, a convict; with a Map of Port Macquarie by J. Oxley. Folio 1821

Wallis, Capt. S. *See* Hawkesworth ; Kerr, Vol. 12 ; Laharpe, Vol. 18 ; "The Modern Traveller," Vol. 4 : Appendix 1.

Walraff, W. J. Geographische Verbreitung, Geschichte, und kommerzielle Bedeutung der Halfa (*Stipa tenacissima, L.*), nebst Karte des Verbreitungsgebietes. 8° *Bonn,* 1890

Walpole, Lieut. Hon. Fred. Four Years in the Pacific in H.M.S. "Collingwood," from 1844 to 1848. 2 vols. *Frontispiece.* 8° 1849
—— The Ansayrii and the Assassins, with Travels in the Further East in 1850-51, including a Visit to Nineveh. 3 vols. *Portrait.* 8° 1851

Walpole, Robert. Memoirs relating to European and Asiatic Turkey, edited from Manuscript Journals. *Map and plates.* 4° 1817
—— Travels in various Countries of the East. *Maps, &c.* 4° 1820
[For Contents, *see* Appendix 1.]

Walpole, Thomas. Journal of the late Campaign in Egypt : including Descriptions of that Country, and of Gibraltar, Minorca, Malta, Marmorice, and Macri; with an Appendix containing official papers and documents. *Maps and plates.* 4° 1803

Walras, Léon. Théorie de la Monnaie. *Plates.* 8° *Lausanne,* 1886

Walsh, R. Narrative of a Journey from Constantinople to England. 3rd edition. *Maps.* 8° 1829
—— Journey from Constantinople to England. 12° 1831

Waltenberger, A. Die Rhätikonkette, Lechthaler- und Vorarlberger Alpen. (Ergänzungsheft, 40—Petermann's Mittheilungen.) *Maps.* 4° *Gotha,* 1875

Walter, Capt. Charles. Historical Sketch of Kutch. [Bombay Records, No. 15, N.S.] Royal 8° *Bombay,* 1855

Walter, Rev. Richard. *See* Anson.

Walters, H. Journey across the Pandua Hills, near Silhet, in Bengal. *Plates.* 4° N.D.

Waltershausen, W. Sartorius von. *See* Lasaulx.

Waltham, Edward. Our Journey to Fez. 8* 1882

Walther, Dr Johannes. Allgemeine Meereskunde. *Map and illustrations.* 12° *Leipzig,* 1893

Walton, William. Letter relating to the Affairs of Portugal. 8* 1829
—— Sketch of the River Ebro, showing its course through Spain . . . from the Spanish of Don Pascual Madoz. 8° 1852

Waltzemüller, Martin. [Hylacomylus.]
Ses Ouvrages et ses Collaborateurs . . .
par un Géographe Bibliophile. 8°
Paris, 1867
"Wanderer," Voyage of. *See* Lambert.
"Wanderer." Notes on the Caucasus.
By Wanderer. 8°   1883
Wangemann, Dr. *See* Jeppe.
Wappäus, Dr J. E. Die Republiken von
Südamerika. Part 1. Venezuela. 8°
Göttingen, 1843
—— Deutsche Auswanderung und Colonisa-
tion. 8°   *Leipzig*, 1846
—— *See* Stein and Hörschelmann.
Warburg, Dr Charles. Fever Tincture
and Tonic Medicine. *Portrait.* 12* N.D.
Warburton, Eliot. Darien, or the Mer-
chant Prince : a Historical Romance.
3 vols. 8°   1852
Warburton, George. Conquest of Canada.
2 vols. *Portraits.* 8°   1850
—— Hochelaga, or England in the New
World. Edited by Eliot Warburton.
4th edition. 2 vols. *Plate.* 8° 1851
Warburton, Col. P. Egerton. Journey
across the Western Interior of Australia ;
with an Introduction and Additions by
C. H. Eden. Edited by H. W. Bates.
Map and plates. 8°   1875
Warburton, Piers Eliot. Florida, Past,
Present, and Future : being a Lecture on
Florida, delivered in the Albert Hall,
Edinburgh, on 24th March 1885. 12* 1885
Ward, Lieut. Aaron. *See* United States,
E *a*, Hydrographic Office Publications,
No. 94 : Appendix 2.
Ward, C. S. "Thorough Guide" Series.
Maps and plans. 12°
—— North Devon and North Cornwall,
from Exmoor to the Land's End. 3rd
edition.   1885
—— The Eastern Counties, their Watering-
Places, Cathedral Cities, together with
the approaches from London. 2nd and
3rd editions.   1886 and 1892
—— Surrey and Sussex, including Tun-
bridge Wells.   1890
—— *See* Baddeley.
Ward, C. Y. Pilote du Golfe d'Aden,
Sokotra, et îles adjacentes ; Côtes de
Somáli et d'Arabie dans le Golfe d'Aden ;
Côte Est d'Arabie et îles adjacentes . . .
Traduit par M. J. Lafont. 8° *Paris*, 1866
—— *See* United Kingdom, A : App. 2.
Ward, E. Knapsack-Manual for Sports-
men on the Field. 8°   1872
Ward, Hon. Elijah. Atrato Ship-Canal,
its Importance to the Commerce of the
United States and other Nations. 8*
Washington, 1859
Ward, F. O. Sur l'Adoucissement, la
Purification, et l'Aération Artificielle de
l'Eau des Grandes Villes, d'après de
nouveaux procédés Anglais. 8*
Brussels, 1857

Ward, Herbert. Five Years with the
Congo Cannibals. *Illustrations.* Large
8°   1890
Ward, H. G. Mexico in 1827. 2 vols.
Maps and plates. 8°   1828
Ward, Luke. *See* Burney, Vol. 2 ; Hak-
luyt, Vol. 4 : Appendix 1.
Ward, Thomas Humphry. The Reign of
Queen Victoria : a Survey of Fifty Years
of Progress. 2 vols. *Maps.* 8° 1887
Warden, D. B. A Chorographical and
Statistical Description of the District of
Columbia, the seat of the General Go-
vernment of the United States. *Map,
plate, and tables.* 8°   *Paris*, 1816
Warden, Francis. Historical Sketches,
&c. [Bombay Records, No. 24, N.S.]
Large 8°   *Bombay*, 1850
Brief Notes relative to the Province of
Oman, prepared in 1819. Historical
Sketch of the Joasmee Tribe of Arabs
from 1747 to 1819 ; with continuations
from 1819 to 1853 by Lieuts. S. Hennell,
A. B. Kemball, and H. F. Disbrowe.
Historical Sketch of the Uttoobee
Tribe of Arabs (Bahrein) from 1716 to
1817 ; with continuations from 1817 to
1853 by Lieuts. Hennell, Kemball, and
Disbrowe.
Historical Sketch of the Wahabee
Tribe of Arabs from 1795 to 1818 ; with
continuations from 1819 to 1853 by Lieuts.
Hennell, Kemball, and Disbrowe. Notes
relative to the Rise and Progress of the
Arab Tribes of the Persian Gulf. His-
torical Sketch of the Rise and Progress
of the Government of Muskat, commenc-
ing with the year 1694-95 and continued
to 1819 ; to which is added a Narrative
of Events connected with that Govern-
ment from 1819 to 1831, by Lieut. S.
Hennell ; from 1832 to 1844, by Lieut.
A. B. Kemball ; from 1844 to 1853, by
Lieut. H. F. Disbrowe.
Warden, M. *See* Recueil de Voyages,
Vol. 2, p. 611 : Appendix 1.
Wardrop, Oliver. The Kingdom of
Georgia : Notes of Travel in a Land of
Women, Wine, and Song ; to which
are appended Historical, Literary, and
Political Sketches, Specimens of the
National Music, and a compendious
Bibliography. *Maps and illustrations.*
8°   1888
Warelius, A. *See* Baer and Helmersen, 13.
Waring, Edward Scott. A Tour to
Sheeraz by the Route of Kazroon and
Feerozabad ; with Remarks on the
Manners, Customs, Laws, Language,
and Literature of the Persians ; to which
is added a History of Persia from the
death of Kureem Khan to the subver-
sion of the Zund Dynasty. *Plates.* 4°
1807

Waring, Edward Scott. *See* Phillips, Collection of Modern and Contemporary Travels [1], Vol. 6: Appendix 1.

Waring, George E., jun. *See* United States, A, Tenth Census, Vol. 18, 1880: Appendix 2.

Warne, Charles. The Celtic Tumuli of Dorset: an Account of Personal and other Researches in the Sepulchral Mounds of the Durotriges. *Plates.* Large folio 1866

—— Ancient Dorset: the Celtic, Roman, Saxon, and Danish Antiquities of the County, including the Early Coinage, illustrated with plates and woodcuts; also an Introduction to the Ethnology of Dorset, and other Archæological Notices of the County, by Dr T. William Wake Smart. Large folio *Bournemouth,* 1872

Warren, Sir Charles. Underground Jerusalem: an Account of some of the principal difficulties encountered in its Exploration, and the results obtained; with a Narrative of an Expedition through the Jordan Valley, and a Visit to the Samaritans. *Plates and photographs.* 8° 1876

—— *See* Morrison; *also* Turkey in Asia, B; South Africa, B: Appendix 2.

Warren, Comte Edouard de. L'Inde Anglaise en 1843. [A Review.] 12* *Paris,* 1844

—— *See* Saulcy.

Warren, George. *See* Churchill, Vol. 8: Appendix 1.

Warren, Lieut. G. K. Explorations in the Dacota Country in 1855. *Maps.* 8° *Washington,* 1856

—— Letter to the Hon. G. W. Jones, relative to Explorations of Nebraska Territory. *Map.* 8* *Washington,* 1858

—— Memoir to accompany the Map of the Territory of the United States, from the Mississippi River to the Pacific Ocean, giving an Account of each of the Exploring Expeditions since A.D. 1800; with a detailed description of the method adopted in compiling the general Map. *Maps.* 4° *Washington,* 1859

—— An Essay concerning Physical Features exhibited in the Valley of the Minnesota River, and upon their signification. *Maps.* 8* *Washington,* 1874

—— *See* United States, H, *u,* Surveys: Appendix 2.

Warren, Lieut.-Col. J. Kala Sankalita: a Collection of Memoirs on the Various Modes according to which the Nations of the Southern parts of India divide Time. 4° *Madras,* 1825

Warren, W. W. Life on the Nile, and Excursions on Shore between Cairo and Asouan; also a Tour in Syria and Palestine in 1866-67. 12° *Paris,* 1867

2 I

Warrington, Lewis. *See* Maury, M. F.

"Warrior," H.M.S. *See* Share.

Warwick, W. Van. *See* Allgemeine Historie, Vol. 8: Appendix 1.

Washington, Major F. P. Lecture on the Methods and Processes of the Ordnance Survey, delivered at the Royal Engineer Institute, Chatham. 8* 1890

Washington, Capt. John. Eskimaux and English Vocabulary, for the use of the Arctic Expeditions. Oblong 12° 1850

"Washington," Ship. *See* Giglioli.

Wassa, Effendi. The Truth on Albania and the Albanians, Historical and Physical. Translation by Edward St John Fairman. 8* 1879

Waterhouse, Col. J. Report on the Operations connected with the Observation of the Total Solar Eclipse of 6th April 1875 at Camorta in the Nicobar Islands. Folio *Calcutta,* 1875

—— The Application of Photography to the Reproduction of Maps and Plans by the Photomechanical and other processes. *Maps.* 8° *Calcutta,* 1878

—— Notes on the Survey Operations in Afghanistan in connection with the Campaign of 1878-79 *Map.* 8* [*Calcutta,* 1879]

—— Annual Address and Review, Asiatic Society of Bengal. 8* *Calcutta,* 1889

—— The same. 8* *Calcutta,* 1890

"Water Lily." Cruises of the "Water Lily." *See* Mansfield.

Waterton, Charles. Wanderings in South America, the North-West of the United States, and the Antilles, in 1812-16-20 and 1824; with original Instructions for the perfect Preservation of Birds, &c., for Cabinets of Natural History. 8° 1828

Wathen, George H. The Golden Colony, or Victoria in 1854; with Remarks on the Geology of the Australian Gold-Fields. *Maps and illustrations.* Small 4° 1855

Watkis, Capt. H. B. B. The Anglo-Russian Question in Central Asia, and the Defence of India. (From the *Journal,* United Service Institution of India, Vol. 20, No. 88.) 8* [*Simla,* 1891]

Watson, Col. C. M. The Campaign of Gordon's Steamers. *Maps.* 8* 1888

—— Comparative Vocabularies of the Languages spoken at Suakin: Arabic, Hadendoa, Beni-Ameer. 8* 1888

Watson, G. C. The Gregory South and Warrego Districts: Report on the Physical Features of the Country. *Map.* Folio* *Brisbane,* 1882

Watson, H. C. Topographical Botany: being Local and Personal Records towards showing the Distribution of British Plants traced through the 112 Counties

Watson, H. C.—*continued.*
and Vice-Counties of England and Scot-
land. *Map.* 8° *Thames Ditton*, 1873-74
Part 1.—Ranunculaceæ—Coniferæ.
Part 2.—Orchidaceæ—Equisetaceæ.
Watson, J. Forbes. Classified and De-
scriptive Catalogue of the Indian Depart-
ment in the International Exhibition,
1862. Imperial 8°   1862
Watson, R. S. The Villages around
Metz. 8* *Newcastle-upon-Tyne,* 1870
—— A Visit to Wazan, the Sacred City of
Morocco. *Map and illustrations.* 8°
                                         1880
Watson, Sereno. *See* United States,
H, *a*: Appendix 1.
Watson, T. Letter to Sir Bartle Frere on
Telegraphic Communication in Africa.
8*   *Cape Town,* 1877
Watson, William. A Philosophical
Treatise on the Earth and its Satellites.
MS. Folio*   1866
Watt, Alexander. Scientific Industries
Explained, showing how some of the
important articles of commerce are
made. Small 8°   *Edinburgh,* 1888
Watt, George. The Aboriginal Tribes
of Manipur. *Plates.* 8*   1887
—— A Dictionary of the Economic Pro-
ducts of India. By George Watt, M.B.,
assisted by numerous Contributors. 6
vols. (in 9). Large 8° *Calcutta,* 1889-93
Watt, Hugh. British Guiana and Vene-
zuela: Two Lectures. 8* 1887 and 1888
Watt, —, and W. Winterbottom. *See*
Eyriès, Vol. 10: Appendix 1.
Watteville, Baron de. Rapport à M.
Waddington, Ministre de l'Instruction
Publique et des Beaux-Arts, sur le service
des Missions et Voyages Scientifiques en
1876. 8°   *Paris,* 1877
Watts, John. Self-Made Men, or Sketches
of those who have distinguished them-
selves in Life by Industry and Self-
Culture, &c. 8*   *Port of Spain,* 1867
Watts, Lieut. *See* Phillip ; *also* Pelham,
Vol. 1 : Appendix 1.
Watts, W. L. Snioland ; or Iceland, its
Jokulls and Fjalls. 12°   1875
—— Across the Vatna Jökull, or Scenes in
Iceland ; being a Description of hitherto
Unknown Regions. *Plates.* 12° 1876
Watts, W. W. *See* Whitaker.
Waugh, Gen. Sir A. Scott. Instructions
for Topographical Surveying. *Diagrams.*
8*   *Roorkee,* 1861
—— *See* India, F, *c*, Surveys, Trigono-
metrical : Appendix 2.
Wauters, Alphonse. Atlas Pittoresque
des Chemins de Fer de la Belgique.
Maps and plates. Oblong 8°
                               Brussels, 1840
—— Guide Pittoresque du Voyageur à la
Grotte de Han-sur-Lesse. *Plates.* 4*
                               Brussels, 1841

Wauters, A. J. L'Afrique Centrale en
1522 : Le Lac Sachaf d'après Martin Hy-
lacomilus et Gerard Mercator ; quelques
mots à propos de la doctrine Portugaise
sur la Découverte de l'Afrique Centrale
au XVIᵉ siècle. *Map.* 8* *Brussels,* 1879
—— Les Belges au Congo. [Numéro Extraordinaire du Mouvement Géographique.] *Maps, portraits, and illustrations.* Folio*   1885
—— Bibliothèque Géographique: Le Congo
au Point de Vue Économique. *Maps
and illustrations* 12° *Brussels,* 1885
—— Stanley's Emin Pasha Expedition.
Maps and illustrations. Small 8° 1890
—— Stanley au secours d'Emin-Pacha.
Map, portrait, and illustrations. 12°
                                Paris, 1890
—— L'Orthographie des Noms Géogra-
phiques au Congo. *Map.* 8*
                               Brussels, 1892
Wauwermans, Colonel. Libéria: His-
toire de la Fondation d'un État Nègre
Libre. *Maps.* 12°   *Brussels,* 1885
Wawn, William T. The South Sea
Islanders and the Queensland Labour
Trade : a Record of Voyages and Expe-
riences in the Western Pacific from 1875
to 1891. *Illustrations.* Large 8° 1893
**Waymouth (or Weymouth), Capt.
George.** *See* Gottfried ; Hakluyt Soc.
Publ., Vol. 5 ; Purchas, Vol. 3 ; Allge-
meine Historie, Vol. 17: Appendix 1.
Weakley, R. H. Narrative of a Journey
into the Interior of Asia Minor. *Plate.*
4*   1867
Wears, W. G. The Prospects of Gold
Mining in Venezuela. *Plan.* 8* [1888]
—— The same, and a Guide to the Guayana
Gold-Fields. Revised edition. *Plan.*
8*   1888
Weatherhead, Geo. Hume. An Account
of the Beulah Saline Spa at Norwood,
Surrey. *Plate.* 8°   1832
Webb, Filippo Barker. Osservazioni
intorno allo stato antico e presente dell'
Agro Trojano. *Map.* 8° *Milan,* 1821
Webb, F. C. Up the Tigris to Bagdad.
Plates. 8°   1870
Webb, P., and S. Berthelot. Histoire
Naturelle des Iles Canaries. 3 vols.
Plates. Large 4°, and folio Atlas
                              Paris, 1836-50
CONTENTS.
Vol. 1.—Part 1. L'Ethnographie et les
Annales de la Conquête   1842
Part 2. Les Miscellanées Canariennes
                                        1839
Vol. 2.—Part 1. La Géographie Descrip-
tive, la Statistique, et la Géologie 1839
Part 2. La Zoologie   1836-44
Vol. 3.—Part 1. La Géographie Botan-
ique   1840
Part 2. Phytographia Canariensis
                                     1836-50

Webb, W. W. The Currencies of the Hindu State of Rájputána. *Map and plates.* Large 8° 1893

Webb, —. *See* Plaisted.

Webb —. *See* Eyriès, Vol. 14 : Appendix 1.

Webber, Lieut.-Col. British Guiana : The Essequibo and Potaro Rivers, with an Account of a Visit to the recently discovered Kaieteur Falls. *Maps and photographs.* Large 8° 1873

Webber, V. A. Journal of a Voyage round Cape Horn. 8° *Swansea*, 1859

Weber, Albrecht. Indische Skizzen : Vier bisher in Zeitschriften zerstreute Vorträge und Abhandlungen. *Table.* 8° *Berlin*, 1857
—— India and the West in the Old Days. Translated from the German by Emily Hawtrey ; edited by Robert Sewell. 8° *Madras*, 1887

Weber, Max Maria von. Die Wasserstrassen Nord-Europa's. Ergebnisse von im Auftrage des Herrn Königl. Preuss. Ministers für öffentliche Arbeiten unternommenen Studienreisen. *Map and plans.* 8° *Leipzig*, 1881

Webster, Daniel. *See* Gallatin.

Webster, David. Topographical Dictionary of Scotland. *Map.* 8° *Edinburgh*, 1817

Webster, Lieut. J. D. Report of a Survey of the Gulf Coast at the Mouth of the Rio Grande. *Map.* 8° *Washington*, 1850

Webster, W. D. *See* British South Africa, A : Appendix 2.

Webster, W. H. B. Narrative of a Voyage to the Southern Atlantic Ocean in 1828-30, in H.M. sloop "Chanticleer," under the command of Capt. Henry Foster. 2 vols. *Maps and plates.* 8° 1834
—— The Recurring Monthly Periods and Periodic System of the Atmospheric Actions, with Evidences of the Transfer of Heat and Electricity, and géneral Observations on Meteorology. *Chart.* 8° 1857

Weddell, H. A. Aperçu d'un Voyage dans le Nord de la Bolivie, et dans les parties voisines du Pérou. *Map.* 8° *Paris*, 1852
—— Voyage dans le Nord de la Bolivie, et dans les parties voisines du Pérou, ou Visite au District aurifère de Tipuani. *Map and plates.* 8° *Paris*, 1853

Weddell, James. Voyage towards the South Pole, 1822-24, containing an Examination of the Antarctic Sea to the 74th degree of latitude, and a Visit to Tierra del Fuego, with a particular Account of the Inhabitants ; to which is added much useful Information on the Coasting Navigation of Cape Horn and the adjacent Islands ; with Observations on the probability of reaching the South

Weddell, James—*continued.* Pole, and an Account of a Second Voyage by Capt. Brisbane to the same Seas. *Maps and plates.* 8° 1827

Wedderburn, Alex. Statistical and Practical Observations relative to the Province of New Brunswick. 4° *St John*, 1835

Weeks, Joseph D. *See* United States, A, Tenth Census, 1880, Vols. 10 and 20 : Appendix 2.

Ween, C. van. *See* Allgemeine Historie, Vol. 8 : Appendix 1.

Weert, Sibald de. *See* Harris, Vol. 1 ; Kerr, Vol. 10 ; Laharpe, Vol. 15 ; Purchas, Vol. 1, Book 2 : Appendix 1.

Weetman, Sydney. Notes on the Great Barrier Island. 8* [*Auckland*, 1889]

Wegener, Dr Georg. Versuch einer Orographie des Kwen-Lun. *Maps.* 8* *Marburg*, 1891
—— *See* Himly.

Weidmann, F. C. Darstellungen aus dem Steyermärkischen Oberlande. *Map.* 8° *Vienna*, 1834

Weigand, Dr Gustav. Von Berat über Muskopolje nach Gjordscha. *Illustrations.* 4* *Brunswick*, 1892

Weigel, T. O. T. O. Weigel's Systematisches Verzeichniss der Hauptwerke der Deutschen Literatur aus den Gebieten der Geschichte und Geographie von 1820-82. Bearbeitet von Dr E. Fromm. 4° *Leipzig*, 1887

Weihrauch, K. Zehnjährigen Mittelwerthe (1865 bis 1875) nebst neunjährigen Stundenmitteln (1867 bis 1875) für Dorpat. *Tables.* 8* *Dorpat*, 1877

Weinhold, Dr K. *See* Germany, C : Appendix 2 ; Forschungen, &c., Vol. 2.

Weininger, H. Fremdenführer durch Regensburg und dessen nächste Umgebung. 16* *Ratisbon*, 1863

Weir, A. *See* Galton, Vacation Tourists.

Weisbach, Dr A. *See* "Novara."

Weise, Arthur James. The Discoveries of America to the year 1525. *Maps.* 8° 1884

Weiskern, F. W. Topographie von Niederösterreich. 3 vols. *Map.* 8° *Vienna*, 1770

Weiss, Prof. Dr Edmund, und Dr Robert Schram. Publicationen für die Internationale Erdmessung. Astronomische Arbeiten des k. k. Gradmessungs Bureau. 5 vols. 4° *Vienna*, 1889-93

Weiss, Friedrich. Die Gesetze der Satellitenbildung. Einleitung zur Geschichte der Erde. *Plates.* 8° *Gotha*, 1860

Weiss, Kurt. Meine Reise nach dem Kilima-Ndjarogebiet im Auftrage der Deutsch Ostafrikanischen Gesellschaft. *Map.* 12* *Berlin*, 1886

Weisse, J. A. To the English-speaking Populations in Europe, America, Asia, Africa, Australia, and Polynesia. 8* *New York*, 1873

Weissenborn, Herm. J. Chr. Ninive und sein Gebiet, mit Rücksicht auf die neuesten Ausgrabungen im Tigristhale. *Plates.* 4* *Erfurt*, 1851

Welbe, John. See Burney, Vol. 4: Appendix 1.

Weld, Charles Richard. History of the Mace given to the Royal Society by King Charles the Second. *Plate.* Royal 8* 1846

—— A History of the Royal Society, with Memoirs of the Presidents; compiled from authentic documents. 2 vols. *Plates.* 8° 1848

—— A Vacation Tour in the United States and Canada. *Map.* Small 8° 1855

—— A Vacation in Brittany. *Illustrations.* 8° 1856

—— The Pyrenees, West and East. *Plate.* 8° 1859

Weld, I., jun. Travels through the States of North America and the Provinces of Upper and Lower Canada, during the years 1795, '96, and '97. 3rd edition. 2 vols. *Plates.* 8° 1800

Weldon's Guide to Epping Forest, with a concise history of the Forest by Frederic Johnson. (Map missing.) *Illustrations.* 8* [1882]

Wellesley, Capt. the Hon. W. Private Letter-Box (from November 1830 to June 1833) of H.M.S. "Sapphire," during her Voyage from Portsmouth to Bermuda, Gulf of St Lawrence, Halifax, Maranham, Para, La Guayra, Vera Cruz, &c.; with some Account of the Indiarubber Tree, and Remarks made concerning the Passage to and Navigation upon the Northern Coast of Brazil; and of H.M.S. "Winchester" from Port Royal to Chatham. MS. Folio 1830-33

Wellesley, Marquis. Despatches, Minutes, and Correspondence of Marquess Wellesley during his Administration in India. Edited by Mr Montgomery Martin. 5 vols. *Portrait and maps.* 8° 1836-37

Wellington, Duke of. Despatches of Field-Marshal the Duke of Wellington during his various Campaigns in India, Denmark, Portugal, Spain, the Low Countries, and France, from 1799 to 1818. Compiled from official and authentic documents; with Index. 13 vols. 8° 1837-39

Wells, J. C. The Gateway to the Polynia: a Voyage to Spitzbergen. *Map and plates.* 8° 1873

Wells, James W. Exploring and Travelling Three Thousand Miles through Brazil from Rio de Janeiro to Maranhão; with Appendix containing Statistics, &c. 2 vols. *Maps and illustrations.* 8° 1886

—— A Sketch of Brazil. [Supplement to *Chamber of Commerce Journal.*] 4* 1887

—— A Survey journey in Santo Domingo, West Indies. Roy. Geog. Soc. Suppl. Papers, Vol. 3. *Map.* Large 8° 1893

—— See Dinarte.

Wells, R., jun., and J. W. Kelly. English - Eskimo and Eskimo - English Vocabularies; preceded by Ethnographical Memoranda concerning the Arctic Eskimos in Alaska and Siberia. *Maps.* 8* *Washington*, 1890

Wells, William Henry. Geographical Dictionary, or Gazetteer of the Australian Colonies, their Physical and Political Geography, together with a brief Notice of all the Capitals, Principal Towns, and Villages; also of Rivers, Bays, Gulfs, Mountains, Population, and General Statistics. *Maps and plates.* 8° *Sydney*, 1848

Wells, William V. Explorations and Adventures in Honduras, comprising Sketches of Travel in the Gold Regions of Olancho, and a Review of the History and General Resources of Central America. *Maps and plates.* 8° *New York*, 1857

Wellsted, Lieut. J. R. Travels in Arabia. 2 vols. *Maps and plates.* 8° 1838

—— Travels to the City of the Caliphs, along the Shores of the Persian Gulf and the Mediterranean, including a Voyage to the Coast of Arabia and a Tour on the Island of Socotra. 2 vols. *Map.* 8° 1840

—— See Robinson, F.

Welsh, James. See Astley, Vol. 1; Hakluyt's Voyages, Vol. 2; Kerr, Vol. 7; Allgemeine Historie, Vol. 1; Appendix 1.

Welz, G. de. Saggio su i mezzi da moltiplicare prontamente le ricchezze della Sicilia. *Maps and tables.* 4° *Paris*, 1822

Wende, G. Deutschland's Kolonien. See Frenzel.

Wendover, Roger. See Purchas, Vol. 3, Book 1: Appendix 1.

Wenger, J. A Catalogue of Sanscrit and Bengalee Publications printed in Bengal. [From the India Records, No. 41.] 8° *Calcutta*, 1865

Wentworth, W. C. Statistical, Historical, and Political Description of the Colony of New South Wales and its dependent Settlements in Van Diemen's Land. 8° 1819

Wereschagen, W. W. *See* Verestchagen.

Werne, Ferdinand. Expedition zur Entdeckung des Weissen Nil. Mit einem Vorworte von Carl Ritter. 8° *Berlin*, 1848

—— Feldzug von Sennaar nach Taka, Basa, und Beni-Amer, mit besonderem Hinblick auf die Völker von Bellad-Sudan. *Map and portraits.* 8°
Stuttgart, 1851

—— African Wanderings, or an Expedition from Sennaar to Taka, Basa, and Beni-Amer, with a particular glance at the Races of Bellad Sudan. Translated by Johnson. *Map.* 12° 1852

—— Reise durch Sennaar nach Mandera, Nasub, Cheli, im Lande zwischen dem blauen Nil und dem Atbara. *Map and plates.* 8° *Berlin*, 1852

Werner, B. von. Ein Deutsches Kriegsschiff in der Südsee. Zweite Auflage. *Maps and illustrations.* 8°
Leipzig, 1889

Werner, J. R. A Visit to Stanley's Rear-Guard at Major Barttelot's Camp on the Aruhwimi, with an Account of River-Life in the Congo. *Maps, portraits, and illustrations.* 8° 1889

—— Major Barttelot's Camp on the Aruhwimi. (From *Blackwood's Magazine*, Feb. 1889.) *Maps.* 8* 1889

Wert, Sebald de. *See* Weert.

Wertheman, Arthur. Informe de la Exploracion de los Rios Pereno y Tambo. *Map.* 8* *Lima*, 1877

—— Iquitos, the River Perené, and Huánuco. [Newspaper Cuttings from *El Nacional* and *El Peruano*, September and November 1870, of Reports by Arthur Wertheman, B. Bermudes, José Cárdenas, and José Manuel Pinzas. 8* 1870

Wertomannus, Lewis. *See* Varthema.

Wesley, S. B. *See* Tupper.

Wesseling, Peter. Vetera Romanorum Itineraria, sive Antonini Augusti Itinerarium, cum integris Jos. Simleri, Hieron. Suritae, et And. Schotti Notis. Itinerarium Hierosolymitanum ; et Hieroclis Grammatici Synecdemus Curante Petro Wesselingio, qui et suas addidit Adnotationes. *Frontispiece.* 4° *Amsterdam*, 1735

Wesselowsky, C. Tabellen über mittlere Temperaturen im Russischen Reiche. 8° [*St Petersburg*, 1856]

—— *See* Baer and Helmersen, 18.

West, Edward W. A Memoir of the States of the Southern Maratha Country. [From the India Records, No. 113.] *Map.* Royal 8° *Bombay*, 1869

West, Lieut. J., and Lieut. C. B. Little. Gazetteer of Manipur, the country between it and Ava, and some of the adjacent Hill tracts. [No map.] 8° *Calcutta*, 1884

Westgarth, William, Tracks of M'Kinlay and Party across Australia, by John Davis, one of the Expedition. Edited from Mr Davis's Manuscript Journal ; with an introductory view of the recent Australian Explorations of M'Douall Stuart, Burke and Wills, Landsborough, &c. *Map and plates.* 8° 1863

—— The Colony of Victoria, its History, Commerce, and Gold Mining, its Social and Political Institutions, down to the end of 1863 ; with Remarks, incidental and comparative, upon the other Australian Colonies. *Map.* 8° 1864

—— Half-a-Century of Australasian Progress : a Personal Retrospect. Part 1, Itinerary of the Tour of a Revisit; Part 2, A Series of Articles on General Questions of Australasia, the Colonies, and the Empire generally. *Maps.* 8° 1889

Westgarth Prize Essays. Essays on the Street Re-alignment, Reconstruction, and Sanitation of Central London, and on the Re-Housing of the Poorer Classes, to which Prizes offered by William Westgarth were awarded by the Society of Arts, 1885. *Plans.* 8° 1886

Westmacott, R. M. Sketches in Australia. 18 *Plates.* Folio
Privately printed, Exeter, N.D.

Weston, A. Report on the Sugar Industry on the Clarence and Richmond Rivers. Folio* [*Brisbane*] 1882

Weston, Comm. Henry Burton. Tables for Finding the Longitude by Chronometer at Sunrise and Sunset. 8° 1856

Wetmore, Alphonso. Gazetteer of the State of Missouri ; with an Appendix containing Frontier Sketches and Illustrations of Indian Character. *Frontispiece.* 8° *St Louis, Miss.*, 1837

Wettstein, H. Die Strömungen des Festen, Flüssigen und Gasförmigen, und ihre Bedeutung für Geologie, Astronomie, Klimatologie, und Meteorologie. *Maps.* 8° *Zürich*, 1880

Wex, Gustav von. Zweite Abhandlung über die Wasserabnahme in den Quellen, Flüssen und Strömen bei gleichzeitiger Steigerung der Hochwässer in den Culturländern. 4* *Vienna*, 1879

Wey, William. The Itineraries of William Wey, Fellow of Eton College, to Jerusalem A.D. 1458 and A.D. 1462 ; and to Saint James of Compostella, A.D. 1456. From the original Manuscript in the Bodleian Library. Large square 8° [*Roxburghe Club*] 1857

—— Map illustrating the Itineraries of 1458 and 1462. In facsimile, from the original in the Bodleian Library. Large square 8° 1867

Weymouth, George. Voyage to the North-West. *See* Waymouth.

Weyprecht, Carl. Grundprincipien der arktischen Forschung. 4*
[*Triest*, 1875]
—— An Address delivered by Carl Weyprecht before the 48th Meeting of German Naturalists and Physicians at Graz, on the 18th September 1875 : Fundamental Principles of Scientific Arctic Investigation. 4* *Vienna*, 1875
—— Die Metamorphosen des Polareises. *Map and plate.* 8° *Vienna*, 1879
—— **and J. Payer.** Berichte des Oesterreichisch-ungarischen Nordpol-Expedition, 1872 bis 1874. 8* *Vienna*, 1874
—— La Spedizione Austro-Ungarica al Polo Nord, 1872-74 : Rapporti ufficiali dell imperiale regia Marina al Comitato della Spedizione, &c. *Map.* 8*
Rome, 1874
—— *See* Wüllerstorf-Urbair, Wiggins ; *also* Polar Regions, Arctic, B, German and Austrian Exped. : Appendix 2.

Whall, W. B. Handy-Book of the Tides, with Twelve Charts showing the State of the Tide at every hour at Dover. Oblong 8* N.D.
—— The same, with Fifteen Charts. 4th edition. Oblong 8* N.D.

Wharton, Adm. W. J. L. Hydrographical Surveying : a Description of the Means and Methods employed in constructing Marine Charts. 8° 1882
—— Orthography on Admiralty Charts. Folio* 1884
—— Captain Cook's Journal during his First Voyage round the World, made in H.M. bark "Endeavour," 1768-71. A literal transcription of the original MS., with Notes and Introduction. *Maps and facsimiles.* 4° 1893
—— *See* Freshfield ; Symons ; *also* United Kingdom, A, Admiralty [Hydrogr. Off. Publ.] : Appendix 2.

Wheatstone, Charles. The Universal Telegraph, invented 1839, improved 1858. 8* *Glasgow*, N.D.

Wheeler, Daniel. Extracts from the Letters and Journals of Daniel Wheeler, now engaged in a Religious Visit to some of the Islands of the Pacific Ocean, Van Diemen's Land, and New South Wales, accompanied by his son C. Wheeler. 8° 1839

Wheeler, Sir George. *See* Ray : Appendix 1.

Wheeler, Capt. George M. Report upon the Third International Geographical Congress and Exhibition at Venice, Italy, 1881 ; accompanied by data concerning the principal Government Land and Marine Surveys of the World. *Maps.* 4° *Washington*, 1885
—— *See* United States, H, *a* : Appendix 2.

Wheeler, J. Talboys. An Analysis and Summary of Thucydides ; with a Chronological Table of Principal Events, Money, Distances, &c., reduced to English Terms, a Skeleton Outline of the Geography, Abstracts of all the Speeches, &c. 12° *Oxford*, 1850
—— An Analysis and Summary of Herodotus ; with a Synchronistical Table of Principal Events, Tables of Weights, Measures, Money, and Distances, an Outline of the History of Geography, and the Dates completed from Gaisford, Baehr, &c. ; with explanatory Notes, including Histories of Assyria, Babylonia, Egypt, Ethiopia, Scythia, &c., digested from other Ancient Writers and Modern Researches. 2nd edition. 12° 1852
—— An Analysis and Summary of Old Testament History and the Laws of Moses, with a Connexion between the Old and New Testaments. 12°
Oxford, 1852
—— An Analysis and Summary of New Testament History, including the Four Gospels, harmonized into one continuous Narrative, the Acts of the Apostles, and continuous History of St Paul, an Analysis of the Epistles and Book of Revelation, the Critical History, Geography, &c. ; with Copious Notes, Historical, Geographical, and Antiquarian. 12° *Oxford*, 1852
—— Popular Abridgment of the Old and New Testament History, for Schools, Families, and General Reading. *Maps.* 18° 1854
—— The Geography of Herodotus developed, explained, and illustrated, from Modern Researches and Discoveries. *Maps.* 8° 1854
—— Journal of a Voyage up the Irrawaddy to Mandalay and Bhamo. 8*
Rangoon, 1871

Wheeler, O. E. Gazetteer of Arabia. Part 4. Aden. *Map.* Large 8*
Simla, 1884
—— Somali-land, or the North-East Horn of Africa, from the Gulf of Tajourah to the Equator. *Maps and illustrations.* Large 8° *Simla*, 1884

Wheelwright, W. Statements and Documents relative to the Establishment of Steam Navigation in the Pacific, with Copies of the Decrees of the Governments of Peru, Bolivia, and Chile, granting exclusive privileges to the undertaking. *Map.* 8° 1838
—— Report on Steam Navigation in the Pacific, with an Account of the Coal Mines of Chile and Panama. 8* 1843
—— Introductory Remarks on the Provinces of La Plata, and the Cultivation of Cotton ; Parana and Cordova Rail-

Wheelwright, W.—*continued.*
way, Report of Allan Campbell ; Proposal for an Inter - oceanic Railway between the Rio de la Plata and Pacific. *Map.* 8* 1861
—— Ferro-Carril a la Ensenada. 8*
Buenos Ayres, 1870
—— La Vida y los Trabajos Industriales de W. Wheelwright en la América del Sud, por J. B. Alberdi. 8° *Paris,* 1876
Wheler, George. A Journey into Greece. *Plates.* Small folio 1682
Whetham. *See* Boddam-Whetham.
Whewell, Dr William. Address delivered at the Anniversary Meeting of the Geological Society. 8* 1839
—— Researches on the Tides, Additional Note to the Eleventh Series of. 4* 1840
—— The same. Thirteenth Series : On the Tides of the Pacific, and on the Diurnal Inequality. *Map.* 4* 1848
—— Astronomy and General Physics, considered with reference to Natural Theology. (Bridgewater Treatise.) 12° 1847
Whiddon, Capt. *See* Kerr, Vol. 7 ; Allgemeine Historie, Vol. 1 : Appendix 1.
Whipple, Lieut. A. W. Report of an Expedition from San-Diego to the Colorado ; with a Vocabulary of the Yuma (or Cuchan) Language. 8°
Washington, 1851
—— Report of Explorations for a Railway Route near the Thirty-fifth Parallel of Latitude, from the Mississippi River to the Pacific Ocean. *Maps.* 8°
Washington, 1854
—— T. Ewbank, and Prof. W. Turner. Report upon the Indian Tribes, with Vocabularies of North American Languages. *Illustrations.* 4°
Washington, 1855
Whipple, G. M. On the Relation between the Height of the Barometer, the Duration of Sunshine, and the Amount of Cloud, as observed at the Kew Observatory. 8* 1879
—— On the Relation existing between the Duration of Sunshine, the Amount of Solar Radiation, and the Temperature indicated by the Black-Bulb Thermometer *in vacuo.* 8* 1879
—— On the Rate at which Barometric Changes traverse the British Isles. 8*
1880
Whishaw, Fred. J. Out of Doors in Tsarland : a Record of the Seeings and Doings of a Wanderer in Russia. 8° 1893
Whitaker, Alex. *See* Purchas, Vol. 4, Book 9 : Appendix 1.
Whitaker, W. List of Works on the Geology, &c., of Cornwall. 8*
Truro, 1875
—— A List of Works relating to the Geology of Cumberland and Westmoreland. 8* N.D.

Whitaker, W. List of Works on the Geology, Mineralogy, and Palæontology of Cheshire. 8* *Liverpool,* 1876
—— List of Works on the Geology of Hertfordshire. 8* [1876]
—— List of Works on the Geology, Mineralogy, and Palæontology of Wales (to the end of 1873). 8* [1880]
—— List of Works on the Geology and Palæontology of Oxfordshire, of Berkshire, and of Buckinghamshire. 8*
[1882]
—— Easter Excursion, 1887 : Preliminary Excursion to Southampton, in conjunction with the Hampshire Field Club. (Reprinted from *Proceedings of the Geologists' Association.*) 8* 1887
—— and W. H. Dalton. List of Works on the Geology, &c., of Essex. 8*
[1889]
—— and W. W. Watts. List of Works on the Geology, Mineralogy, and Palæontology of Shropshire. 8*
Oswestry, 1889
Whitbourne, Capt. R. *See* Purchas, Vol. 4, Book 10 : Appendix 1.
White, Arnold. Recent Experiments in Colonisation. (From *Contemporary Review.*) 8* 1890
White, A. Silva. On the Achievements of Scotsmen during the 19th Century in the Fields of Geographical Exploration and Research : a Report to the Paris Geographical International Congress of 1889. 8* *Edinburgh,* 1889
—— The Development of Africa. *Maps.* 8° 1890
—— The same. 2nd edition. *Maps.* Crown 8° 1892
—— Britannic Confederation : a Series of Papers by Admiral Sir John Colomb, Prof. E. A. Freeman, G. G. Chisholm, Prof. Shield Nicholson, M. H. Hervey, and Lord Thring. Edited, with Introduction, by A. Silva White. 8° 1892
White, C. A. *See* United States, G, *c,* Surveys : Appendix 2.
White, F. W. Notes on the Province of Chêkiang. *Map.* Small 8* *Bath,* 1875
White, Gilbert. Natural History of Selborne. 2 vols. *Plates.* 8° 1813
White, John. Journal of a Voyage to New South Wales. *Plates.* 4° 1790
White, Joseph. *See* Pocock.
White, Capt. Martin. Sailing Directions for the English Channel, including a General Description of the South Coasts of England and Ireland, and a Detailed Account of the Channel Islands. 8° 1850
—— and John Purday. Portulan des Côtes de la Manche, du Canal de Bristol, et de la Côte sud d'Irlande, traduit des Instructions Anglaises. *Illustrations.* 8° *Paris,* 1855
White, Peter. *See* Tudor.

Whitney, J. D. The Yosemite Guide-Book : a description of the Yosemite Valley and the adjacent region of the Sierra Nevada, and of the Big Trees of California. *Maps and plates.* 4° *Cambridge, Mass.,* 1869
—— The same. 2nd edition. 12° *Cambridge, Mass.,* 1871
—— The same. A new edition. 1874
—— Geographical and Geological Surveys. 8* *Cambridge, Mass.,* 1875
—— Are we Drying up? 8* *Cambridge, Mass.,* 1876
—— The Auriferous Gravels of the Sierra Nevada of California. (Vol. 1 of "Contributions to American Geology.") *Maps and plates.* 4° *Cambridge, Mass.,* 1880
—— The Climatic Changes of later Geological Times : a Discussion based on Observations made in the Cordilleras of North America. 4° *Cambridge, Mass.,* 1882
—— Names and Places : Studies in Geographical and Topographical Nomenclature. 12° *Cambridge, Mass.,* 1888
—— The United States : Facts and Figures illustrating the Physical Geography of the Country and its Material Resources ; written for, and published in part in the "Encyclopædia Britannica," 9th edition. 8° *Boston, Mass.,* 1889
—— Ditto. Supplement 1 : Population, Immigration, Irrigation. 8° *Boston, Mass.,* 1894
Whitney, J. P. Colorado, in the United States of America : Schedule of Ores contributed by sundry persons to the Paris Universal Exposition of 1867; with some information about the Region and its Resources. *Maps.* 4* 1867
Whitney, Milton. *See* United States, C : Appendix 2.
Whitney, W. N. A Concise Dictionary of the Principal Roads, Chief Towns, and Villages of Japan, with Populations, Post Offices, &c.; together with Lists of Ken, Kuni, Köri, and Railways. Compiled from Official Documents. *Map.* 12° *Tokyo,* 1889
Whittle, J. *See* Laurie, R. H.
Whittington, Nicholas. *See* Kerr, Vol. 9 ; Purchas, Vol. 1, Book 4 : Appendix 1.
Whitty, John Irwine. Proposed Water Supply and Sewerage for Jerusalem; with Description of its Present State and Former Resources, . . . and an Introduction by Canon Stanley. *Maps and plate.* 8° 1863
—— Water Supply of Jerusalem, Ancient and Modern. *Map.* 8* 1864
Whitworth, R. P. Bailliere's New South Wales Gazetteer and Road Guide, containing the most recent and accurate information as to every place in the Colony. *Map.* 8° *Sydney,* 1866

Whymper, E. Scrambles amongst the Alps in the years 1860-69. 2nd edition. *Maps and plates.* 8° 1871
—— The same, 4th edition. *Maps and illustrations.* 8° 1893
—— The Ascent of the Matterhorn. *Maps and plates.* 8° 1880
—— How to Use the Aneroid Barometer. Large 8° 1891
—— Travels amongst the Great Andes of the Equator. *Maps and illustrations.* Large 8° 1892
—— The same. Supplementary Appendix. *Illustrations.* Large 8° 1891
—— Ascents in the Himalayas. (From the *Leisure Hour* for January and February 1893.) 4* 1893
Whymper, Frederick. Travel and Adventure in the Territory of Alaska, . . . and in various other parts of the North Pacific. *Map and plates.* 8° 1868
Whyte, W. A. A Land Journey from Asia to Europe : being an Account of a Camel and Sledge Journey from Canton to St Petersburg through the Plains of Mongolia and Siberia. *Maps and plate.* 8° 1871
Wichmann, Dr H. Stanley's Zug zu Dr Emin-Pascha. *Map.* 4* [*Gotha*] 1889
—— *See* Paulitschke; *also* General, Miscellaneous : Appendix 2.
Wickersham, Hon. James. Is it "Mount Tacoma" or "Rainier"? What do History and Tradition say? 12* *Tacoma,* 1893
Wickham, H. A. Rough Notes of a Journey through the Wilderness, from Trinidad to Pará, Brazil, by way of the Great Cataracts of the Orinoco, Atabapo, and Rio Negro. *Plates.* 8° 1872
Widdicombe, John. Fourteen Years in Basutoland : a Sketch of African Mission Life. *Illustrations.* 12° [1891]
Widdrington, Capt. S. E. Spain and the Spaniards in 1843. 2 vols. 8° 1844
Widney, J. P. California of the South. *See* Lindley.
Wiebe, E. Ueber die Reinigung und Entwässerung der Stadt Berlin. 8° *Berlin,* 1861
Wiebel, K. W. M. Die Insel Helgoland : Untersuchungen über deren Grösse in Vorzeit und Gegenwart, vom Standpunkte der Geschichte und Geologie. *Maps and plate.* 4° *Hamburg,* 1848
Wied-Neuwied, Maxmilian, Prinz zu. Reise nach Brasilien in den Jahren 1815 bis 1817. *Plates and maps.* 2 vols. 4°; and Atlas, 2 vols. folio *Frankfort o. M.,* 1821
—— Voyage dans l'Intérieur de l'Amérique du Nord pendant 1832-34. Vol. 1, part 1 ; and Vol. 2. *Map and plates.* 8° *Paris,* 1840-41

Wiener, C. Pérou et Bolivie : Récit de Voyage, suivi d'Études Archéologiques et Ethnographiques, et de Notes sur l'Écriture et les Langues des Populations Indiennes. *Maps and plates.* 4° *Paris*, 1880
—— Chili and Chiliens. *Illustrations.* 8° *Paris*, 1888

Wienmann, F. L. *See* Plener.

Wieser, Dr Franz. Magalhâes-Strasse und Austral-Continent, auf den Globen des Johannes Schöner. *Maps.* 8° *Innsbruck*, 1881
—— Die Karte des Bartolomeo Colombo über die vierte Reise des Admirals. *Plates.* 8° *Innsbruck*, 1893

Wiggins, Capt. J. The Austro-German Polar Expedition, under the command of Lieut. Weyprecht. Translated from the German. 8* *Bishopswearmouth*, 1875
—— Newspaper Extracts descriptive of Voyages to the Obi and Yennesei Rivers, North Siberia. 8* N.D.

Wijkander, A. Observations Météorologiques de l'Expedition Arctique Suédoise, 1872-73. *Plate.* 4* *Stockholm*, 1875

Wilbraham, Ed. B. Ascent of Mont Blanc in 1830. 8* 1832

Wilbraham, Capt. Richard. Travels in the Trans-Caucasian Provinces of Russia, and along the Southern Shore of the Lakes of Van and Urumiah, in 1837. *Map and plates.* 8° 1839

Wilcken, U. *See* Schweinfurth.

Wilcocke, S. Hull. History of the Viceroyalty of Buenos Ayres, containing the most accurate details relative to the Topography, History, &c., of that valuable Colony. *Map and plates.* 8° 1807

Wilcocks, Alexander. Thoughts on the Influence of Ether in the Solar System, its relations to the Zodiacal Light, Comets, the Seasons, and Periodical Shooting Stars. *Plate.* 4° *Philadelphia*, 1864

Wilcox, Lieut. R. Memoir of a Survey of Assam and the Neighbouring Countries, executed in 1825-6-7-8. *Map.* 4° [*Calcutta*, 1832]
—— Memoir of a Survey of Assam and the Neighbouring Countries, executed in 1825-28. [From the India Records, No. 23] *Calcutta*, 1855
—— *See* India, I, Assam : Appendix 2.

Wild, G. Von Kairo nach Massaua, eine Erinnerung an Werner Munzinger ; mit einem Vorwort über das Leben Munzinger's, von Peter Dietschl. *Map and plates.* 12* *Olten*, 1879

Wild, Heinrich. Die Temperatur-Verhältnisse des Russischen Reiches. 4°, and folio Atlas . *St Petersburg*, 1881
—— Bericht über eine neue Verification der Schwingungszahl der Normal-Stimmgabel Russlands im physikalischen Central-Observatorium. 8* *St Petersburg*, 1885

Wild, Heinrich. Die Regen-Verhältnisse des Russischen Reiches. 5.—Supplementband zum Repertorium für Meteorologie herausgegeben von der kaiserlichen Academie der Wissenschaften. 4°, and folio Atlas *St Petersburg*, 1887
—— Annalen des Physikalischen Central-Observatorinms, and Repertorium für Meteorologie. *See* Russia, St Petersburg : Appendix 2.
—— Mittheilungen der Int. Polar Commission. *See* Polar Regions, Arctic, G : Appendix 2.

Wild, John James. Letter to Lord Brougham, containing Proposals for a Scientific Exploration of Egypt and Ethiopia. *Plates.* 8° 1850

Wild, John James. Thalassa : an Essay on the Depth, Temperature, and Currents of the Ocean. *Charts and diagrams.* 8° 1877
—— At Anchor: a Narrative of Experiences Afloat and Ashore during the Voyage of H.M.S. "Challenger," from 1872 to 1876. *Map and plates.* 4° 1878

Wilde, Dr Éduardo. Arrendamiento de las Obras de Salubridad de la Capitol. 12° *Buenos Ayres*, 1887

Wilde, Henry. On the Causes of the Phenomena of Terrestrial Magnetism, and on some Electro-mechanism for exhibiting the Secular Changes in its Horizontal and Vertical Components. [In English and French.] *Maps and plate.* 4* 1890

Wilde, R. T. Remarks Introductory and Explanatory on his Topographic Model of the City and Peninsula of Aden. 12* 1844

Wilde, W. R. Narrative of a Voyage to Madeira, Teneriffe, and along the Shores of the Mediterranean, including a Visit to Algiers, Egypt, Palestine, Tyre, Rhodes, Telmessus, Cyprus, and Greece. *Maps and woodcuts.* 8° *Dublin*, 1852
—— Descriptive Catalogue of the Antiquities of Stone, Earthen, and Vegetable Materials, in the Museum of the Royal Irish Academy. *Woodcuts.* 8° *Dublin*, 1857

Wiley, William H., and Sara King. The Yosemite, Alaska, and the Yellowstone. Reprinted from *Engineering. Illustrations.* 4° [1893]

Wilkes, Capt. Charles. Narrative of the United States Exploring Expedition, 1838-42. 5 vols. *Maps and illustrations.* 8° *Philadelphia*, 1845
—— The same. 5 vols. and Atlas. *Maps, portraits, and illustrations.* Imperial 8° *Philadelphia*, 1845
—— The same. Vol. 7. Ethnography and Philology. By Horatio Hale. 4° *Philadelphia*, 1846
—— The same. Condensed and abridged. Royal 8° 1845

Wilkes, Capt. Charles. The same. Vol.
15, The Geographical Distribution of
Animals and Plants; Part 1, Chronological Observations on introduced
Animals and Plants. By C. Pickering.
8°   1854
—— Theory of the Winds; to which is
added Sailing Directions for a Voyage
round the World. *Map.* 8°
                        Philadelphia, 1856
—— See Biot, J. B.
Wilkins, Colonel H. St Clair. Recon-
noitring in Abyssinia: a Narrative of the
Proceedings of the Reconnoitring Party,
prior to the arrival of the main body of
the Expeditionary Field Force. *Maps
and coloured plates.* 8°   1870
Wilkins, Jacob. See Purchas, Vol. 2,
Book 10: Appendix 1.
Wilkins, W. Atheniensia, or Remarks
on the Topography and Buildings of
Athens. *Map and plate.* 8°   1816
Wilkins, W. The Geography of New
South Wales, Physical, Industrial, and
Political. 16°   *Sydney*, 1863
—— Australasia: a Descriptive and Pic-
torial Account of the Australian and
New Zealand Colonies, Tasmania, and
the adjacent Lands. *Maps and illustra-
tions.* Crown 8°   1888
Wilkinson, C. See Reineggs.
Wilkinson, C. S. See New South Wales,
B: Appendix 2.
Wilkinson, George Blakiston. South
Australia, its Advantages and its Re-
sources, &c. 12°   1848
Wilkinson, Sir J. Gardner. Topography
of Thebes, and General View of Egypt:
being a Short Account of the Principal
Objects worthy of Notice in the Valley
of the Nile to the Second Cataract and
Wadee Samneh, with the Fyoom, Oases,
and Eastern Desert, from Sooez to Bere-
nice; with Remarks on the Manners
and Customs of the Ancient Egyptians
and the Productions of the Country.
Plates. 8°   1835
—— Manners and Customs of the Ancient
Egyptians, including their Private Life,
Government, Laws, Arts, Manufactures,
&c. 3 vols. *Plates.* 8°   1837
—— A second series of the Manners and
Customs of the Ancient Egyptians, in-
cluding their Religion, Agriculture, &c.
2 vols. and vol. of Plates, &c. 8° 1841
—— Dalmatia and Montenegro; with a
Journey to Mostar in Herzegovina, and
Remarks on the Slavonic Nations, the
History of Dalmatia and Ragusa, the
Uscocs, &c. Vol. 2. *Map and plates.*
8°   1848
—— Popular Account of the Ancient
Egyptians. Vol. 1. *Woodcut illustra-
tions.* 12°   1854

Wilkinson, Sir J. Gardner. The Egyp-
tians in the Time of the Pharaohs: being
a Companion to the Crystal Palace
Egyptian Collections; to which is added
an Introduction to the Study of the
Egyptian Hieroglyphs, by S. Birch.
Plates and woodcuts. 12°   1857
—— See Herodotus.
Wilkinson, J. J. G. The African, and
the True Christian Religion his Magna
Charta. 12°   1892
Wilkinson, T. The Trip from Tama-
tave to the Capital. [Cuttings from a
Newspaper, describing a Journey in
Madagascar.] 4*   [1867]
Willard, Emma. Ancient Geography, as
connected with Chronology, and pre-
paratory to the Study of Ancient History;
to which are added Problems on the
Globes, and Rules for the Construction
of Maps. 12°   *Hartford, Conn.*, 1831
Wille, C. See Norway, A, Norwegian
North Atlantic Expedition, 1876-78:
Appendix 2.
Wille, C. F. See Norway, A, Norway
Pilot: Appendix 2.
"Willem Barents." See Polar Regions,
Arctic, D: Appendix 1.
Willer, T. J. Het Eiland Boeroe. Uit-
gegeven door J. P. Cornets de Groot van
Kraaijenburg. *Map.* 8°
                        Amsterdam, 1858
Willett, Mark. History, Antiquities, and
Scenery of Monmouthshire, with Glossary.
12°   *Chepstow*, 1813
William of Tyre. See Hakluyt, Vol. 2;
Purchas, Vol. 2, Book 8: Appendix 1.
William I. See Hakluyt, Vol. 2: Appen-
dix 1.
Williams, Albert, jun. See United States
Surveys, G, c: Appendix 2.
Williams, B. On the Land of Ditmarsh
and the Mark Confederation. 4° 1858
Williams, C. The Armenian Campaign:
a Diary of the Campaign of 1877 in
Armenia and Koordistan. *Maps.* Square
8°   1878
Williams, Clement. Memorandum on the
Question of British Trade with Western
China *via* Burmah. [*Lithographed.*]
Map. 4*   1864
—— Through Burmah to Western China:
being Notes of a Journey in 1863 to
Establish the Practicability of a Trade-
Route between the Irawaddi and the
Yang-tse-Kiang. *Map and plates.* 8°
                                     1868
Williams, Lieut.-Col. Edward, Capt.
W. Mudge, and I. Dalby. An Ac-
count of the Trigonometrical Survey in
England and Wales, carried on in 1791
to 1794. *Plates.* 4°   1795
Williams, Lieut. E. C. S. Geography
of the Province of Pegu, and on the
working of the Topographical Survey.

Williams, Lieut. E. C. S.—*continued.*
[From the India Records, No. 20, Foreign
Department.] Royal 8° *Calcutta,* 1856
Williams, George. Historical and De-
scriptive Memoir on the Town and
Environs of Jerusalem. 8° 1849
—— The Holy City : Historical, Topo-
graphical, and Antiquarian Notices of
Jerusalem. 2nd edition, with additions,
including an Architectural History of the
Church of the Holy Sepulchre by R.
Willis. 2 vols. *Plates.* 8° 1849
Williams, G. H., and W. B. Clark.
Outline of the Geology and Physical
Features of Maryland. *Maps and plates.*
4° *Baltimore,* 1893
Williams, Hon. George W. A Report,
upon the Congo-State and Country, to
the President of the U.S. of America.
8* N.P., 1890
—— An Open Letter to His Serene
Majesty Leopold II., King of the Bel-
gians and Sovereign of the Independent
State of Congo. 8* N.P., 1890
—— A Report upon the Proposed Congo
Railway. 8* N.P., 1890
Williams, Helen M. *See* Humboldt and
Bonpland.
Williams, J. Observations of Comets,
from B.C. 611 to A.D. 1640, extracted
from the Chinese Annals. Translated,
with Introductory Remarks, and an
Appendix comprising the Tables neces-
sary for reducing Chinese Time to
European Reckoning, and a Chinese
Celestial Atlas. 4° 1871
Williams, Rev. John. Two Essays on the
Geography of Ancient Asia, intended
partly to illustrate the Campaigns of
Alexander and the Anabasis of Xenophon. *Maps.* 8° 1829
—— Narrative of Missionary Enterprises
in the South Sea Islands ; with Remarks
on the Natural History of the Islands,
and the Origin, Languages, Traditions,
and Usages of the Inhabitants. *Map
and plates.* 8° 1837
Williams, Jonathan. Thermometrical
Navigation : being a Series of Experiments and Observations tending to prove
that, by ascertaining the Relative Heat
of the Sea-Water from time to time, the
Passage of a Ship through the Gulf
Stream, and from Deep Water into
Soundings, may be Discovered in Time
to avoid Danger. . . . *Map.* 8°
Philadelphia, 1799
Williams, J. Butler. Practical Geodesy,
comprising Chain Surveying and the use
of Surveying Instruments, Levelling, and
Tracing of Contours ; together with
Sanitary Surveys of Towns, Trigono-
metrical, Colonial, Mining, and Maritime
Surveying. *Plate and woodcuts.* 8° 1855
Williams, J. F. *See* Hughes, W.

Williams, J. J. Report upon the Location of the Tehuantepec Railway and
Carriage Road across the Isthmus of
Tehuantepec; with the Map and Profiles as approved by the Government of
Mexico, 1st July 1870, and his Report
on the subject of a Ship Canal across
the Isthmus of Tehuantepec to unite the
Atlantic and Pacific Oceans. 8*
[New York] 1870
Williams, J. M. Memorandum on Rail-
way Communication with Western China
and the intermediate Shan States from
the Port of Rangoon in British Burma.
Map. Folio* 1865
—— **and C. H. Luard.** Copies of the
Survey Report, dated the 15th June
1867, and of the Journals, Maps, Sec-
tions, &c., attached thereto, respecting
Rangoon and Western China, &c. Folio*
1867
Williams, Ralph C. British South-
Central Africa. Vol. 2. [Magazine
Article.] 8* N.P., N.D.
Williams, S. Wells. The Middle
Kingdom : a Survey of the . . . Chinese
Empire and its Inhabitants. 2 vols.
Map and plates. Small 8° 1848
—— The same. Revised edition. 2 vols.
Map and illustrations. 8° 1883
Williams, T. *See* Phillips [1], Vol. 8 :
Appendix 1.
Williams, T., and J. Calvert. Fiji and
the Fijians. Edited by Geo. Stringer
Rowe. *Map and plates.* 12° 1870
Williams, Dr Theodore. The Value of
Meteorological Instruments in the Selec-
tion of Health Resorts. 8* 1892
Williams, T. C. An Appeal on behalf
of the Ngatiraukawa Tribe. 8°
Wellington, 1873
Williams, W. Traveller's and Tourist's
Guide through the United States of
America, Canada, &c. *Map.* 18°
Philadelphia, 1851
Williams, William. Vocabulary of the
Languages of the Aborigines of the
Adelaide District, and other Friendly
Tribes of the Province of South Australia.
8* *Adelaide,* 1839
Williams, William. Climbing Mount St
Elias. (From *Scribner's Magazine.*) *Map
and illustrations.* 8* 1889
Williamson, Alexander. Notes on the
North of China, its Productions and
Communications. 8* 1867
—— Journeys in North China, Manchuria,
and Eastern Mongolia, with some Account
of Corea. 2 vols. *Maps and plates.* 8°
1870
Williamson, Isabelle. Old Highways in
China. *Map and illustrations.* 8° 1884
Williamson, Lieut. R. S. Report of a
Reconnaisance and Survey in California,
in connection with Explorations for a

Williamson, Lieut. R. S.—*continued.*
Practicable Railway Route from the
Mississippi River to the Pacific Ocean
in 1853. *Maps.* 8° *Washington*, 1854

Willich, Charles M. Popular Tables,
with additional Tables of Natural or
Hyperbolic Logarithms, Trigonometry,
Astronomy, Geography, &c. 12° 1853

Willinck, T. P. M. Reize om de Wereld
gedaan in de Jaren 1823-24, met Z.M.
Korvet "Lynx." *Plate.* 8° *Breda*, 1836

Willink, H. G. *See* Dent, C. T.

Willis, N. P. *See* Bartlett, W. H.

Willis, Robert. Architectural History of
the Church of the Holy Sepulchre. *See*
Williams, G.

Willkomm, Moritz. Die Halbinsel der
Pyrenäen, eine geographisch-statistische
Monographie, nach den neuesten Quellen
und nach eigener Anschauung. 8°
Leipzig, 1855

Willmott, C. *See* Bilgrami.

Willoughby, Francis. *See* Harris, Vol. 2;
Ray: Appendix 1.

Willoughby, Sir Hugh. *See* Hakluyt,
Vol. 1; Purchas, Vol. 3, Book 2; Pinkerton, Vol, 1: Appendix 1.

Willoughby, Major Sir J. C. East
Africa, its Big Game : the Narrative of
a Sporting Trip from Zanzibar to the
Borders of the Masai; with Postscript by
Sir Robert G. Harvey. *Maps and illustrations.* 8°
—— A Narrative of further Excavations
at Zimbabye (Mashonaland). *Illustrations.* 12° 1893

Willoughby, J. P. Historical Sketch of
the Petty State of Baria, in the Rewa
Kanta; with Information relative to the
Mineral and Vegetable Productions, and
Notices of the various Tribes, &c.
[From the India Records, No. 23.]
Royal 8° *Bombay*, 1889

Wills, Alfred. Wanderings among the
High Alps. *Plates.* Post 8° 1856

Wills, C. J. In the Land of the Lion and
Sun, or Modern Persia : being Experi-
ences of Life in Persia during a Residence
of Fifteen Years in various parts of that
Country, from 1866 to 1881. *Frontis-
piece.* 8° 1883
—— Persia as it is : being Sketches of
Modern Persian Life and Character.
Crown 8° 1886

Wills, J. T. Emin Bey, Gordon's Lieutenant. *Map.* 8° [1886]

Wills, Mr Justice. *See* Dent, C. T.

Wills, W. John. Successful Explorations
through the Interior of Australia, from
Melbourne to the Gulf of Carpentaria.
Map and portraits. 8° 1863

Willson, J. *See* India, I; Assam: Appendix 2.

Willson, Thomas B. The Handy Guide
to Norway; with Maps, and an Appendix
on the Flora and Lepidoptera of Norway
by R. C. R. Jordan, M.D. 12° 1886
—— The Handy Guide to Norway. 3rd
edition. 1891

Willson, W. G. The Cyclone in the
Bay of Bengal in June 1872. 8*
[*Calcutta*, 1872]
—— Report to the Government of Bengal:
Meteorological Abstract for the year
1874. Folio *Calcutta*, 1875
—— Administration Report to the Govern-
ment of Bengal for the year 1874-75.
Folio [*Calcutta*, 1875]

Willughby, Francis. *See* Willoughby.

Wilmot, A. History of the Zulu War.
Map and portrait. 8° 1880
—— Geography of South Africa, for the
use of Higher Classes in Schools. 3rd
edition. *Map.* 12° *Cape Town*, 1883
—— and J. C. Chase. History of the
Colony of the Cape of Good Hope,
from its Discovery to the year 1819
by A. Wilmot, and from 1820 to 1868
by the Hon. John Centlivres Chase. 8°
Cape Town, 1869

Wilsen, F. C. *See* Leemans, C

Wilson, Andrew. The " Ever-Victorious
Army : " a History of the Chinese Cam-
paign under Lt.-Colonel C. G. Gordon,
and of the Suppression of the Tai-ping
Rebellion. *Map.* 8° *Edinburgh*, 1868
—— The Abode of Snow : Observations
on a Journey from Chinese Tibet to
the Indian Caucasus, through the Upper
Valleys of the Himalaya. *Plate.* 8°
Edinburgh, 1875
—— *See* Blackwood, Vols. 2, 3, 5, 6 : Ap-
pendix 1.

Wilson, Rev. C. T., and R. W. Felkin.
Uganda and the Egyptian Soudan. 2
vols. *Maps and illustrations.* Crown
8° 1882

Wilson, Maj.-Gen. Sir Charles W.
The Euphrates Valley Railway. By an
Austrian Officer. Translated by Capt.
C. Wilson. *Map.* 8* 1872
—— From Korti to Khartum : a Journal
of the Desert March from Korti to Gubat,
and of the Ascent of the Nile in General
Gordon's Steamer. *Maps.* Crown 8°
1885
—— Extracts from a Paper on the Utilisa-
tion of the Ordnance Survey Maps, with
special reference to Local Administration
and the Sale and Transfer of Land, read
at the Meeting of the British Association
at Manchester. 8* 1887
—— Picturesque Palestine, Sinai, and
Egypt. Edited by Colonel Wilson,
assisted by the most eminent Palestine
Explorers, &c. In 4 vols. Vol. 1.
Illustrations. 4* N.D.
—— *See* Morrison.

Wilson, Sir Daniel. Pre-historic Man : Researches into the Origin of Civilisation in the Old and New World. 2 vols. *Plates*. 8°   1862

Wilson, D. Bishop Wilson's Journal Letters, addressed to his family, during the First Nine Years of his Indian Episcopate. 8°   1863

Wilson, Erasmus. Cleopatra's Needle ; with brief Notes on Egypt and Egyptian Obelisks. *Plates*. Small 8°   [1878]

Wilson, H. Trow's New York City Directory . . . 1st May 1868. *Map*. 8°
New York, 1868

Wilson, Horace H. Ariana Antiqua: a Descriptive Account of the Antiquities and Coins of Afghanistan ; with a Description of the Buildings called Topes, by C. Masson. *Maps and plates*. 4°   1841
—— Description of Select Coins, from Originals or Drawings in the possession of the Asiatic Society. *Plates*. 4* N.D.
—— *See* Mill, James.

Wilson, J. *See* Murray, Hugh.

Wilson, John. *See* Purchas, Vol. 4, Book 6 : Appendix 1.

Wilson, John. *See* Smith, George.

Wilson, John. Indian Caste. 8° 1877

Wilson, Capt. J. A Missionary Voyage to the Southern Pacific Ocean, performed in the years 1796-97-98, in the ship "Duff." Compiled from Journals of the Officers and the Missionaries, &c.; with a preliminary discourse on the Geography and History of the South Sea Islands, and an Appendix on the Natural and Civil State of Otaheite. *Maps and plates*. 4° 1799
—— *See* Eyriès, Vol. 3 ; Appendix 1.

Wilson, J. A. Remarks on Australian and New Zealand Climatology, relative to our Droughts, Rains, and Hot Winds. [Cuttings from the *Daily Southern Cross*.] 4*   1864
—— The Story of Te Waharoa : a Chapter in early New Zealand History. 8*
Auckland, 1866

Wilson, Hon. J. Bowie. Report on the Present State and Future Prospects of Lord Howe Island. *Maps and photographs*. 4*   *Sydney*, 1882

Wilson, James Harrison. China : Travels and Investigations in the "Middle Kingdom ;" a Study of its Civilisation and Possibilities, with a Glance at Japan. *Map*. 8°   *New York*, 1887

Wilson, James S. On the Gold Regions of California. 8*   1854

Wilson, Joseph. History of Mountains, Geographical and Mineralogical, to accompany a Picturesque View of the Principal Mountains of the World in their respective proportions of height above the level of the sea painted by Robert Andrew Riddell. 3 vols. 4° 1807-10

Wilson, J. Leighton. The British Squadron on the Coast of Africa ; with Notes by Capt. H. D. Trotter. *Map*. 8°   1851
—— Western Africa, its History, Condition, and Prospects. *Map and plates*. 8°   1856

Wilson, J. Spottiswoode. Geological Mechanism, or an Epitome of the History of the Earth. *Frontispiece*. 12°

Wilson, Mrs. *See* Tissot, V.

Wilson, Ralph. Voyage to the East Indies. *See* Gottfried; Purchas, Vol. 1, Book 4 : Appendix 1.

Wilson, Robert Anderson. Mexico and its Religion ; with Incidents of Travel in that Country during . . . 1851-54, and Historical Notices, &c. *Illustrations*. 8°   1856
—— A New History of the Conquest of Mexico, &c. 8°   1859

Wilson, R. T. History of the British Expedition to Egypt ; to which is subjoined a Sketch of the Present State of that Country and its Means of Defence. 2nd edition. *Maps and plates*. 4°   1803

Wilson, Sir Samuel. Salmon at the Antipodes : being an Account of the Successful Introduction of Salmon and Trout into Australian Waters. *Map and photograph*. Small 8°   1879

Wilson, Thomas. Nozrāni in Egypt and Syria. *Maps*. 12°   1846

Wilson, T. B. Narrative of a Voyage round the World ; comprehending an Account of the Wreck of the ship "Governor Ready" in Torres Straits, and Description of the British Settlements on the Coasts of New Holland, more particularly Raffles Bay, Melville Island, Swan River, and King George's Sound. *Map and plates*. 8°   1835

Wilson, T. Letter to Sir J. Wolstenholme on the Ormuz War. *See* Purchas, Vol. 2, Book 10 : Appendix 1.

Wilson, Thomas W. The Island of Cuba in 1850 : being a Description of the Island, its Resources, Productions, Commerce, &c. Royal 8*
New Orleans, 1850

Wilson, W. *See* Pelham, Vol. 1 : Appendix 1.

Wilson, William Rae. Travels in Norway, Sweden, Denmark, Hanover, Germany, Netherlands, &c. *Plates*. 8°   1826

Winchester, Earl of. *See* Hakluyt, Vol. 2 : Appendix 1.

Winchester, J. W. Topographical Report on the City of Tatta and its Environs. [From the India Records, No. 17.] Royal 8°   *Bombay*, 1855

Winchell, N. H. and H. W. *See* United States, K, Minnesota : Appendix 2.

Winchell, N. H., and Arthur Winslow. The Size and Scale of Maps : a Discussion. 8* [1893]

Winderlich, C. Das deutsche Land und seine Bewohner. 8° *Leipzig*, 1852

Windham, Capt. T. *See* Astley, Vol. 1 ; Hakluyt, Vol. 2; Kerr, Vol. 7; Allgemeine Historie, Vol. 1: Appendix 1.

Windisch, K. G. von. Geographie des Königreichs Ungarn, und Siebenbürgen. 3 vols. 8° *Pressburg*, 1780-90

Windsor. The Royal Windsor Guide ; with a Brief Account of Eton, Virginia Water, and the Surrounding Neighbourhood. 12° *Windsor*, N.D.

Windt, H. de. From Pekin to Calais by Land. *Map and illustrations.* 8° 1889
—— Siberia as it is ; with an Introduction by Her Excellency Madame Olga Novikoff ("O. K."). *Illustrations.* 8° 1892

Windus, John. Journey to Mequinez, the Residence of the present Emperor of Fez and Morocco, on the occasion of Comm. Stewart's Embassy thither for the Redemption of the British Captives in 1821. [*Large paper.*] *Plates.* 8° 1825
—— *See* Knox's New Collection, Vol. 6 ; Pinkerton, Vol. 15 ; "The World Displayed," Vol. 17 : Appendix 1.

Wines, Frederick Howard. *See* United States, A, Tenth Census, 1880, Vol. 21 · Appendix 2.

Wingate, Major F. R. Chronological Index of the Events in the Sudan for the years 1881-89 inclusive. Prepared . . . for the Intelligence Division of the War Office. 12* 1890
—— Mahdiism and the Egyptian Sudan : being an Account of the Rise and Progress of Mahdiism, and of subsequent Events in the Sudan to the present time. *Maps and plans.* 8° 1891
—— Ten Years' Captivity in the Mahdi's Camp, 1882-92. From the Original Manuscripts of Father Joseph Ohrwalder ; with Maps and Illustrations by Walter C. Horsley. 8° 1892
—— The Sudan, Past and Present. (From *Proceedings*, Royal Artillery Institution, Vol. 19.) *Map and plan.* 8* [1892]

Wingfield, Col. Anthony. *See* Hakluyt, Vol. 2 ; Purchas, Vol. 4, Book 10 : Appendix 1.

Wingfield, C. J. Report on the Trade of Nujeebabad, Keerutpoor, &c. [From the India Records, N.W. Provinces, Part 22.] *Map* *Agra*, 1855

Wingfield, W. F. Tour in Dalmatia, Albania, and Montenegro, with an Historical Sketch of the Republic of Ragusa. 8° 1859

Winkler, G. G. Island, seine Bewohner, Landesbildung und vulcanische Natur. *Map and woodcuts.* 8° *Brunswick*, 1861

Winkler, T. C. Musée Teyler : Catalogue systématique de la Collection Paléontologique. 8° *Haarlem*, 1866

Winkopp, P. A. Neuestes Staats-Zeitungs- Reise- Post- und Handlungs-Lexikon, oder Geographisch, Historisch, Statistisches Handbuch von allen fünf Theilen der Erde. Vol. 1, A bis D. 4° *Leipzig*, 1804

Winlock, Joseph. Tables of Mercury, for the use of the American Ephemeris and Nautical Almanac. 4* *Washington*, 1864

Winnecke, C. *See* South Australia, A : Appendix 2.

Winser, Henry J. The Yellowstone National Park : a Manual for Tourists ; with an Appendix containing Railroad Lines and Rates, &c. *Maps and illustrations.* 12° *New York*, 1883

Winslow, Arthur. *See* Winchell ; *also* United States, K, Missouri : Appendix 2.

Winslow, E. *See* Purchas, Vol. 4, Book 10: Appendix 1.

Winsor, Dr Justin. A Bibliography of Ptolemy's Geography. Large 8* *Cambridge, Mass.*, 1884
—— Narrative and Critical History of America. Vols. 1 to 8. *Maps, portraits, and illustrations.* 4° 1886-1889

CONTENTS.

Vol. 1—Aboriginal America.
Vol. 2.—Spanish Explorations and Settlements in America from the 15th to the 17th Century 1886
Vol. 3.—English Explorations and Settlements in North America, 1497-1689 1886
Vol. 4. — French Explorations and Settlements in North America, and those of the Portuguese, Dutch, and Swedes, 1500-1700 1886
Vol. 5.—The English and French in North America, 1689-1763 1887
Vol. 6.—The United States of North America. Part 1 1888
Vol. 7.—The same. Part 2 1888
Vol. 8.—The Later History of British, Spanish, and Portuguese America 1889

—— Christopher Columbus, and how he received and imparted the spirit of Discovery. *Maps, portraits, &c.* 8° [1891]
—— The Pageant of Saint Lusson, Sault Ste. Marie, 1671. 8* *Ann Arbor, Mich.*, 1892
—— The Results in Europe of Cartier's Explorations, 1542-1603. 8* *Cambridge, Mass.*, 1892
—— The Anticipations of Cartier's Voyages, 1492-1534. *Facsimiles* of the Maillo maps. 8° *Cambridge, Mass.*, 1893
—— America Prefigured : an Address at Howard University, 21st October 1892. Small 4* *Cambridge, Mass.*, 1893
—— *See* Horsford.

Winstanley, W. A Visit to Abyssinia : an Account of Travel in Modern Ethiopia. 2 vols. Small 8° 1881

Winter, C. F. Het Boek Adji-Sâkâ, oude fabelachtige geschiedenis van Java, van de Regering van Vorst Sîndoelâ te galoeh tot aan de Stichting van Mâdjâ-Paït, door Vorst Soesoeroeh ; met een uitvoerig Bijvoegsel tot het Javaansche woordenboek van Gericke en Roorda. 8° *Amsterdam*, 1857

Winter, Christopher T. Six Months in British Burmah, or India beyond the Ganges, in 1857. *Plates.* 8° 1858

Winter, John. *See* Callander, Vol. 1 ; Hakluyt, Vol. 4 ; Kerr, Vol. 10 : Appendix 1.

Winter, J. W. "Gigantic Inhumanity": South African Notes on Woman Slavery in Natal, Confederation, and the Diamond and Gold Fields. *Plate.* 8* 1877

Winterberg, A. Malta : Geschichte und Gegenwart. *Map.* 12° *Vienna*, 1879

Winterbotham, W. Historical, Geographical, Commercial, and Philosophical View of the American United States, and of the European Settlements in America and the West Indies. 4 vols. *Plates.* 8° 1795

Winterbottom, W. *See* Eyriés, Vol. 10 : Appendix 1.

"Winterton." A Narrative of the Loss of the "Winterton," East Indiaman, wrecked on the Coast of Madagascar in 1792, . . . to which is subjoined a Short Account of the Natives of Madagascar, with Suggestions as to their Civilisation. By a Passenger in the Ship. *Map and plates.* 8° *Edinburgh*, 1820

Winthrop, T. The Canoe and the Saddle : Adventures among the North-Western Rivers and Forests, and Isthmiana. 5th edition. Small 8° *Boston, Mass.*, 1863

Wise, Henry. Analysis of One Hundred Voyages to and from India, China, &c., performed by ships in the Honourable East India Company's Service ; with Remarks on the Advantages of Steam Power. *Plates.* Royal 8° 1839

Wisely, Lieut. *See* United Kingdom, G, War Office Publications : Appendix 2.

Wislicenus, Dr W. F. Handbuch der geographischen Ortsbestimmungen auf Reisen zum Gebrauch für Geographen und Forschungsreisende. 8° *Leipzig*, 1891

Wislizenus, A. Memoir of a Tour to Northern Mexico, connected with Col. Doniphan's Expedition, in 1846 and 1847 ; with a Scientific Appendix. *Maps.* Royal 8° *Washington*, 1848

Wisotzki, Dr Emil. Hauptfluss und Nebenfluss : Versuch einer begrifflichen Nachbildung derselben. 8° *Stettin*, 1889

Wissmann, Hermann von. Unter Deutscher Flagge quer durch Afrika von West nach Ost, von 1880 bis 1883, ausgeführt von Paul Pogge und Hermann Wissmann. 2 Auflage. *Maps, portraits, and illustrations.* 8° *Berlin*, 1889

—— Meine zweite Durchquerung Aequatorial-Afrikas vom Congo zum Zambesi während der Jahre 1886 und 1887. *Maps and illustrations.* 8° *Frankfurt-a-O.* [1890]

—— My Second Journey through Equatorial Africa, from the Congo to the Zambesi, in the years 1886 and 1887. Translated from the German, by Minna J. A. Bergmann. *Map and illustrations.* 8° 1891

—— **Ludwig Wolf, Curt von François, and Hans Mueller.** Im Innern Afrikas ; die Erforschung des Kassai während der Jahre 1883-84-85. *Maps and illustrations.* 8° *Leipzig*, 1888

Wither. *See* Bigg-Wither.

Withrington, R. *See* Burney, Vol. 2 ; Hakluyt, Vol. 4 : Appendix 1.

Witte, Dr Hans. *See* Germany, C : Appendix 2.

Witti, F. *See* Pryer.

Wittington, Nicholas. *See* Whittington.

Witsen, Burgomaster. *See* Hakluyt Soc. Publ., Vol. 25 : Appendix 1.

Witt, Georgius. Disputatio Medica Inauguralis : De Cholera epidemica Indiæ Orientalis. 4° *Leyden*, 1830

Wittman, W. Travels in Turkey, Asia Minor, Syria, and across the Desert into Egypt, during the years 1799, 1800, and 1801, in company with the Turkish Army and the British Military Mission. *Map and plates.* 4° 1803

Wlangali, —. Reise nach der östlichen Kirgisen Steppe. *Map.* 8° *St Petersburg*, 1856

—— *See* Baer and Helmersen, 20.

Woeikof, Dr Alexander von. Die Atmosphärische Circulation. Verbreitung des Luftdruckes, der Winde und der Regen auf der Oberfläche der Erde. (Ergänzungsheft, 38—Petermann's Mittheilungen.) 3 *maps.* 4° *Gotha*, 1874

—— Gletscher und Eiszeiten in ihrem Verhältnisse zum Klima. 8* *Berlin*, 1881

—— Flüsse und Landseen als Produkte des Klima's. 8* *Berlin*, 1885

—— Die Klimate der Erde, nach dem Russischen, vom Verfasser besorgte, bedeutend veränderte Deutsche Bearbeitung. 2 vols. *Diagrams.* 8° *Jena*, 1887 [1886]

—— *See* Penck's Abhandlungen, 3.

Woerl's Reisehandbücher : West Indien zur Reise und zum Aufenthalt. *Map and plates.* 12° *Vienna*, 1887

Wohlgemuth, Emil Edler von. *See* Polar Regions, Arctic, G : Appendix 1.

Woldt, A. Capitain Jacobsen's Reise an der Nordwestkuste Amerikas, 1881-83, zum Zwecke ethnologischer Sammlungen und Erkundigungen, nebst Beschreibung persönlicher Erlebnisse; für den Deutschen Leserkreis bearbeitet von A. Woldt. *Maps and illustrations.* 8° *Leipzig*, 1884

Wohltmann, Dr F. Die natürlichen Faktoren der tropischen Agrikultur und die Merkmale ihrer Beurteilung. (Handbuch der Tropischen Agrikultur für die Deutschen Kolonieen in Afrika auf wissenschaftlicher und praktischer Grundlage. Erster Band.) Large 8° *Leipzig*,1892

Wolf, Heinrich. Die barometrischen Höhenbestimmungen der k. k. Geologischen Reichsanstalt, 1858-60. Royal 8° *Vienna*, 1863

Wolf, P. P. Geschichte, Statistik und Topographie von Tirol. 8° *Munich*, 1880

Wolf, Julius, and Josef Luksch. Bericht an die königlich Ungarische Seebehörde in Fiume über die von Professor Emil Stahlberger, und den Berichterstattern am Bord des Dampfbootes "Nautilus," im Sommer 1874, ausgeführte Vorexpedition zum Zwecke physikalischer Untersuchungen längs der Ostküste des Adriatischen Meeres, Fiume 1875. (1 Bericht.) *Map and plates.* Large 8* *Fiume*, 1877

—— and Dr J. Köttstorfer. Ditto, über die am Bord der Dampfyacht "Deli," und des Dampfbootes "Nautilus," während des Sommers 1875, durchgeführten physikalischen Untersuchungen im Nordbecken der Adria, Fiume 1876. (2 Bericht.) *Map and plates.* 8* *Fiume*, 1877

—— Ditto, über die am Bord der Dampfyacht "Deli," während des Sommers 1876, durchgeführten physikalischen Untersuchungen im Adriatischen Meere, Fiume 1877. (3 Bericht.) *Map and plates.* Large 8* *Fiume*, 1878

—— Ditto, über die am Bord der Dampfyacht "Deli," und des Dampfbootes "Nautilus," im Zeitraume von 1875 bis 1877, durchgeführten physikalischen Untersuchungen im Quarnero, Fiume 1878. (4 Bericht.) *Map and plates.* Large 8* *Fiume*, 1878

—— Physikalische Untersuchungen in der Adria. *Map.* 8* *Vienna*, 1887

Wolf, Dr Ludwig. Volksstämme Central-Afrikas. (Verhandl. der Berlin anthropol. Gesell.) 8* [*Berlin*] 1886

—— Die Erforschung des Sankuru. *Map.* 4* [*Gotha*] 1888

—— Dr Ludwig Wolf's letzte Reise nach der Landschaft Barbar (Bariba) oder Borgu; die Höhenmessungen Dr L. Wolf's auf seiner letzten Reise nach Barbar oder Borgu. *Map.* 8* [*Berlin*, 1891]

—— *See* Wissmann.

2 K

Wolf, Prof. O. *See* Fellenberg.

Wolf, Theodor. Geografia y Geologia del Ecuador. *Map and illustrations.* Large 8° *Leipzig*, 1872

—— Ein Besuch der Galápagos-Inseln. *Maps.* Small 8* *Heidelberg*, 1879

Wolfe, Commr. James. Sailing Directions for the Lower Shannon and for Lough Derg. 8° 1843

—— Sailing Directions, &c., with some Hydrographic Notices of Lough Ree and Lough Erne. 8° 1850

Wolff, Sir H. D. Reports by Sir H. Drummond Wolff on the Administration of Egypt. [Foreign Office Report, No. 5, 1887.] Folio 1887

Wolff, Henry W. Rambles in the Black Forest. 8° 1890

—— The Country of the Vosges. *Map.* 8° 1891

Wolff, Joseph. Journal of, in a Series of Letters to Sir Thomas Baring, containing an Account of his Missionary Labours from 1827-31 and 1835-38. 8° 1839

—— Narrative of a Mission to Bokhara in 1843-45, to ascertain the fate of Colonel Stoddart and Captain Conolly. 8° 1846

—— Travels and Adventures. 2 vols. *Portrait.* 8° 1860

Wolff, Dr Willy. Von Banana zum Kiamwo, eine Forschungsreise in West Afrika, im Auftrage der Afrikanischen Gesellschaft in Deutschland. *Map.* 8° *Leipzig*, 1889

Wolkenhauer, Dr W. Geographische Nekrologie für die Jahre 1888-89-90. 8* *Gotha*, 1891

—— Ditto, 1891 und 1892. 8* *Gotha*, 1893

—— Zeittafel zur Geschichte der Kartographie. 8* *Bremen*, 1893

Wollaston, A. N. *See* Thornton, E.

Wollzogen, Baron von, and — von Wurmb. Briefe auf ihren Reisen nach Afrika und Ostindien in den Jahren 1774 bis 1792. *Plate.* 12° *Gotha*, 1794

Wolseley, General Viscount. Narrative of the Red River Expedition. *See* Blackwood, Vol. 1: Appendix 1.

Wolstans, ——. *See* Hakluyt, Vol. 1: Appendix 1.

Wonner, E. De las Industrias y del Desarrollo Industrial en la República Oriental del Uruguay, especialmente en Montevideo. 4° *Montevideo*, 1889

Wood, ——. *See* Knox's New Collection, Vol. 6: Appendix 1.

Wood, Capt. Benjamin. Voyage towards the East Indies. *See* Astley, Vol. 1; Gottfried; Hacke; Kerr, Vol. 8; Purchas, Vol. 1, Book 3: Allgemeine Historie, Vol. 1: Appendix 1.

Wood, C. *See* India, F, c, Trans-Himalayan Explorations: Appendix 2.

Wood, C. F. A Yachting Cruise in the South Seas. *Photographs.* 8° 1875

Wood, Charles W. Through Holland. *Illustrations.* 8° 1877

—— Letters from Majorca. *Illustrations.* 8° 1888

Wood, Harrie. *See* New South Wales, B : Appendix 2.

Wood, Herbert. Notice sur une cause probable du changement de direction survenu dans le cours de l'Amou-Daria par lequel son embouchure a été transportée de la Caspienne à l'Aral. 8* *Geneva,* 1875

—— The Shores of Lake Aral. *Maps.* 8° 1876

Wood, Capt. J. *See* Account of several late Voyages," p. 599 ; Allgemeine Historie, Vol. 17 : Appendix 1.

Wood, Capt. John. Personal Narrative of a Journey to the Source of the River Oxus, by the Route of the Indus, Kabul, and Badakhshan. *Map.* 8° 1841

—— Twelve Months in Wellington, Port Nicholson ; or Notes for the Public and the New Zealand Company. Small 8* 1843

—— New Zealand and its Claimants ; with some Suggestions for the Preservation of the Aborigines, briefly considered in a Letter to the Premier. 8* 1845

—— Report on the River Indus. [Records, No. 17, Bombay, N.S.] *Woodcuts.* Royal 8° *Bombay,* 1855

—— A Journey to the Source of the River Oxus ; with an Essay on the Geography of the Valley of the Oxus, by Col. H. Yule. New edition. *Maps and frontispiece.* 8° 1872

Wood, J. Walter, jun. *See* Davis, W. M.

Wood, Robert. The Ruins of Palmyra, otherwise Tedmor, in the Desart. *Plates.* Large folio 1753

—— The Ruins of Balbec, otherwise Heliopolis, in Cœlo Syria. *Plates.* Large folio 1757

Woodard (or Woodward), Capt. David. The Narrative of Capt. David Woodard, and Four Seamen, who lost their Ship while in a Boat at Sea, and surrendered themselves up to the Malays in the Island of Celebes ; with an Account of the Manners and Customs of the Country, and a Description of the Harbours and Coasts. *Maps.* 8° 1805

—— *See* Phillips, Modern and Contemporary Voyages [1], Vol. 1 : Appendix 1.

Woodbridge, W. Channing. System of Universal Geography, on the Principles of Comparison and Classification. *Maps and woodcuts.* 12° *Hartford, Conn.,* 1831

—— Report on the Navigation of the Great Lakes, and the Construction and Completion of Harbour Improvements, &c. 8* *Washington,* 1843

Woodcock, W. J. Scripture Lands : being a Visit to the Scenes of the Bible. *Plates.* 8° 1849

Woodford, C. M. A Naturalist among the Head-Hunters : being an Account of Three Visits to the Solomon Islands in the years 1886, '87, and '88. *Maps and illustrations.* Crown 8° 1890

Woodley, Capt. William. The System of the Universe, with Diagrams showing the Daily Motion of the Sun, Moon, &c., round the Earth . . . *Plates.* 8° 1832

—— Treatise on the Divine System of the Universe . . . ; with an Introduction refuting the Solar System of Copernicus, the Newtonian Philosophy, and Mathematics. *Plate.* 8° 1834

—— The Descriptive Use of the Universal Time-piece, exhibiting the Universal Method for finding the Longitude by the apparent true place of the Moon, and for determining correctly the Greenwich Time at Sea. 8° 1834

—— The Practical Almanac and Astronomical Ephemeris for 1840, with a Treatise. 12° 1840

Woods, Henry. Elementary Palæontology for Geological Students. 12° *Cambridge,* 1893

Woods, Rev. Julian E. Tenison. North Australia, its Physical Geography and Natural History. 8* *Adelaide,* 1864

—— A History of the Discovery and Exploration of Australia, or an Account of the Progress of Geographical Discovery in that Continent from the earliest period to the present day. 2 vols. *Map and frontispiece.* 8° 1865

—— Fish and Fisheries of New South Wales. *Illustrated.* Large 8° *Sydney,* 1882

—— *See* New Zealand, A : Appendix 2.

Woodstock, Thomas of. *See* Gloucester, Duke of.

Woodthorpe, Col. R. G. The Lushai Expedition, 1871-72. *Frontispiece.* 8° 1873

—— The Aka Expedition. (From the *Journal of the United Service Institution of India,* Oct. 1889.) *Maps and plates.* 8* [*Simla,* 1889]

—— The Lushai Country. *Map and illustrations.* 8* [1889]

Woodward, A. S. *See* New South Wales, B : Appendix 2.

Woodward, B. B. *See* Reclus, Élisée.

Woodward, D. *See* Woodard.

Woodward, Henry. On Volcanoes. 8* 1871

Woodward, Horace B. The Geology of England and Wales : a Concise Account of the Lithological Characters, Leading Fossils, and Economic Products of the Rocks ; with Notes on the Physical Features of the Country. *Map and plates.* 8° 1876

Woodward, Horace B. The same. 2nd edition. *Map and illustrations.* 8° 1887
—— The Scenery of Norfolk. 8*
[*Norwich*] 1882
Woodward, H. P. *See* Western, Australia: Appendix 2.
Woodward, Rev. H. W. Collections for a Handbook of the Boondéi Language. 12° [1882]
Woodward, R. S. On the Form and Position of the Sea Level. (Geological Survey Bulletin.) 8° *Washington,* 1888
—— Latitudes and Longitudes of certain Points in Missouri, Kansas, and New Mexico. (Geological Survey Bulletin.) 8° *Washington,* 1889
Woodward, Samuel. Descriptive Outline of the Roman Remains in Norfolk. *Map.* 4* 1831
Woolhouse. W. S. B. Tables of Continental Lineal and Square Measures. 8* 1836
—— The Measures, Weights, and Moneys of all Nations, and an Analysis of the Christian, Hebrew, and Mahometan Calendars. 12° 1863
Worcester, Joseph E. Elements of Geography, Modern and Ancient. 12° *Boston, Mass.,* 1839
—— *See* General, Dictionaries, A : Appendix 2.
Wordsworth, Christopher. Greece : Pictorial, Descriptive, and Historical ; and a History of the Characteristics of Greek Art illustrated by G. Scharf. *Plates.* Imperial 8° 1853
Worms, Henry. The Earth and its Mechanism : being an Account of the various Proofs of the Rotation of the Earth, with a Description of the Instruments used in the Experimental Demonstrations ; to which is added the Theory of Foucault's Pendulum and Gyroscope. *Woodcuts.* 8° 1862
Worsaae, J. J. A. Account of the Danes and Norwegians in England, Scotland, and Ireland. *Woodcuts.* 8° 1852
Worsfold, W. B. A Visit to Java ; with an Account of the Founding of Singapore. *Illustrations.* 8° 1893
Wortabet, Gregory M. Syria and the Syrians, or Turkey in the Dependencies. 2 vols. *Portrait.* 8° 1856
Worth, R. N. Tourist's Guide to Somersetshire, Rail and Road. *Map and plan.* Small 8° 1881
Wrag, R. *See* Hakluyt's Voyages, Vol. 2 : Appendix 1.
Wragge, Clement L. Remarks on the "Red Glow." (From the Transactions of the Royal Society of South Australia.) 8* 1884

Wrangell, Adm. Ferdinand von. Reise längs der Nordküste von Sibirien und auf dem Eismeere in 1820-24 ; nach den handschriftlichen Journalen und Notizen bearbeitet von G. Engelhardt ; herausgegeben nebst einem Vorwort von C. Ritter. 2 vols. in 1. *Map.* 8° *Berlin,* 1839
—— Statistische und Ethnographische Nachrichten über die Russischen Besitzungen an der Nordwestküste von Amerika. *Map.* 8° *St Petersburg,* 1839
—— Narrative of an Expedition to the Polar Sea in 1820-23. Edited by Major E. Sabine. *Map.* 8° 1840
—— Another edition, with additions. *Map and portrait.* 12° 1844
—— *See* Baer and Helmersen, 1.
Wraxall, N. A Tour through some of the Northern parts of Europe, particularly Copenhagen, Stockholm, and St Petersburgh. 3rd edition. *Map.* 8° 1776
—— A Tour round the Baltic, through the Northern Counties of Europe, particularly Denmark, Sweden, Finland, Russia, and Prussia. 4th edition. 8° 1807
Wray, L., jun. Notes on Perak ; with a Sketch of its Vegetable, Animal, and Mineral Products. *Map.* 8* 1886
Wrede, Adolph von. Reise in Hadramaut, Beled Beny 'Yssà und Beled el Hadschar ; herausgegeben mit einer Einleitung, Anmerkungen und Erklärung der Inschrift von 'Obne versehen von Heinrich Freiherr von Maltzan. *Map and facsimile.* 8° *Brunswick,* 1870
Wren, Walter. *See* Astley, Vol. 1 : Appendix 1.
Wrenne, G. *See* Hakluyt, Vol. 1 : Appendix 1.
Wright, —. *See* Recueil de Voyages, Vol. 4, p. 611 : Appendix 1.
Wright, Bryce. Description of the Collection of Gold Ornaments from the "Huacas" or Graves of some Aboriginal Races of the North-Western Provinces of South America, belonging to Lady Brassey. *Illustrations.* 8* 1884
—— A Catalogue *raisonné* of the Natural History, Ethnological Specimens, and Curiosities collected by Lady Brassey during the Voyages of the "Sunbeam," 1876-83. *Illustrations.* 8° 1885
Wright, C. Darwinism : being an Examination of Mr St George Mivart's "Genesis of Species." 8* 1871
Wright, Edward. *See* Astley, Vol. 1 ; Allgemeine Historie, Vol. 1 : Appendix 1.
Wright, G. Frederick. The Ice Age in North America and its bearings upon the Antiquity of Man ; with an Appendix on the Probable Cause of Glaciation, by Warren Upham. *Maps and illustrations.* 8° *New York,* 1889

Wright, G. N. Guide to the Giant's Causeway. *Map and plates.* 12° 1823

Wright, Rev. G. N. The Shores and Islands of the Mediterranean, drawn from Nature by Sir G. Temple, Leitch, Major Irton, and Lieut. Allen; with an Analysis of the Mediterranean, and Description of the Plates by the Rev. G. N. Wright. 4° 1843

Wright, J. O. *See* General, Catalogues, A, Barlow's American Library: Appendix 2.

Wright, Philip B. *See* Bristowe.

Wright, Col. Richard. A Brief Sketch of the Lands and Mines of the Republic of the Equator, with a few observations. *Maps.* 12* 1838

Wright, Thomas. Essay on the State of Literature and Learning under the Anglo-Saxons. 8° 1839
—— Lecture on the Antiquities of the Anglo-Saxon Cemeteries of the Ages of Paganism. 8* *Liverpool*, 1854
—— Early Christianity in Arabia: an Historical Essay. 8° 1855
—— On the Early History of Leeds, in Yorkshire, and on some Questions of Præhistoric Archæology agitated at the present time. 8* *Leeds*, 1864

Wright, Col. — von. *See* United Kingdom, G, War Office: Appendix 2.

Wronski, —. *See* Lagrange.

Wrottesley, Lord. Speech in the House of Lords, on Lieut. Maury's Plan for Improving Navigation. 8* 1853

Wroughton, Major R. Memoranda on the Mode of Surveying adopted in the Revenue Surveys. [Records, N.W. Prov., Vol. 2.] Large 8° *Agra*, 1856

Wulfstein, —. *See* Kerr, Vol. 1: Appendix 1.

Wüllerstorf-Urbair, Baron B. von. Zur wissenschaftlichen Verwerthüng des Aneroides. 4* *Vienna*, 1871
—— Die Meteorologischen Beobachtungen und die Analyse des Schiffcurses während der Polarexpedition unter Weyprecht und Payer, 1872-74. 4* *Vienna*, 1875
—— Bernhard Freiherr v. Wüllerstorf. Ein Blatt pietätvoller Erinnerung von Dr Karl v. Scherzer. 8* *Munich*, 1883
—— *See* "Novara"; Scherzer.

Wurmb, — von. *See* Wollzogen.

Wüstenfeld, F. Die Strasse von Baçra nach Mekka mit der Landschaft Dharîja. *Map.* 4* *Göttingen*, 1871
—— Das Gebiet von Medina: nach arabischen Geographen beschrieben. *Map.* Square 8* *Göttingen*, 1873

Wuttke, Heinrich. Die Kosmographie des Istrier Aithikos im lateinischen Auszuge des Hieronymus aus einer Leipziger Handschrift zum erstenmale besonders herausgegeben. *Map and plate.* 8° *Leipzig*, 1853

Wundt, Theodor. Die Besteigung des Cimone della Pala; ein Album für Kletterer und Dolimiten Freunde. 2nd edition. *Plates.* Oblong 8° *Stuttgart* [1893]

Wyche, Sir P. *See* Egypt, B, Short Relation of the River Nile: Appendix 2.

Wyld, James. Gold Fields of Australia: Notes on the Distribution of Gold throughout the World, including Australia, California, and Russia. 3rd edition; to which is added a Gazetteer of the Gold Diggings of Australia. 8* 1853
—— Geographical and Hydrographical Notes to accompany Mr Wyld's Maps of the Ottoman Empire and the Black Sea. *Map.* 12° 1854
—— Index to Map of India, alphabetically arranged, with Geographical Positions correctly ascertained. *Maps.* 8° N.D.
—— Notes on Map of Afghanistan, Punjaub, &c. 8* N.D.
—— The same. Oblong 8* N.D.

Wylde, A. B. '83 to '87 in the Soudan; with an Account of Sir William Hewett's Mission to King John of Abyssinia. 2 vols. *Map.* 8° 1888

Wylie, A. Notes on Chinese Literature; with Introductory Remarks on the progressive advancement of the Art, and a list of Translations from the Chinese into various European Languages. 4° *Shanghai*, 1867

Wyse, Lucien Napoleon Bonaparte. Canal Interocéanique, 1876-77: Rapport sur les Études de la Commission Internationale d'Exploration de l'Isthme du Darien. 4° *Paris*, 1877
—— Canal Interocéanique, 1877-78: Rapport sommaire de la Commission Internationale d'Exploration. 4* *Paris*, 1878
—— Le Canal de Panama; l'Isthme Americain; Explorations, Comparaison des tracés Études, Negociations, état des Travaux. *Map, plan, and illustrations.* Small folio *Paris*, 1886
—— Canal Interocéanique de Panama: Mission de 1890-91 en Colombie: Rapport général. *Plan.* Small folio *Paris*, 1891
—— **A. Reclus, and P. Sosa.** Canal Interocéanique 1877-88: Rapports sur les études de la Commission Internationale d'Exploration de l'Isthme Américain, par L. N.-B. Wyse, A. Reclus, et P. Sosa. *Maps.* 4° *Paris*, 1879

Wyse, Sir T. An Excursion in the Peloponnesus in the year 1858. Edited by Winifrede M. Wyse. 2 vols. *Plates.* Large 8° 1865

X.

Xavier, Francis. *See* Purchas, Vol. 3, Book 2: Appendix 1.

Xenophon's Anabasis [Greek]. Edited by Professor George Long. 8° 1831

Xenophon. *See* Spelman.

Xerez, Francisco de. Conquista del Peru. Folio N.P., N.D.
—— *See* Hakluyt Soc. Publ., Vol. 47; Purchas, Vol. 4, Book 7; Ramusio, Vol. 3; Ternaux-Compans, Vol. 4: Appendix 1..

Ximenez, R. P. F. Francisco. Las Historias del Origen de los Indios de esta Provincia de Guatemala; exactamente segun el Texto Español del MS. Original, y aumentado con una Introduccion y Anotaciones por el Dr C. Scherzer. 8° 1857

Y.

Yarnall, Professor M. *See* United States, Naval Observatory, D: Appendix 2.

Yaschenko, —. On the Amu - Daria, between Chardjui and Kelif. [In Russian.] *Plates.* 8* *St Petersburg,* 1891

Yate, Capt. A. C. England and Russia Face to Face in Asia : Travels with the Afghan Boundary Commission. *Maps, portraits, and plates.* 8° 1887
—— Notes on a Journey to Tashkent and back in September-October 1890. 8*
—— The same. (From the *Journal of the United Service Institution of India*, Vol. 20, No. 88.) 8* [*Simla*, 1891]
—— The Transcaspian Railway, and the power of Russia to occupy Herat. 8*
 Simla, 1891

Yate, Col. C. E. Northern Afghanistan, or Letters from the Afghan Boundary Commission. *Maps.* 8° 1888

Yates, Edmund. *See* Smith, Albert.

Yates, James. Remarks on "Gesenius' paläographische Studien über phönizische und punische Schrift." 8* N.D.
—— On the Limes Rhæticus and Limes Transrhenanus of the Roman Empire. *Map and woodcuts.* 8* 1852
—— On the French System of Measures, Weights, and Coins, and its adaptation to general use; with an Abstract of the Discussion upon the Paper. Edited by C. Manby. 8* 1854
—— Narrative of the Origin and Formation of the International Association for obtaining a Uniform Decimal System of Measures, Weights, and Coins. 8* 1856
—— What is the Best Unit of Length? 8* 1858
—— On the Excess of Water in the Region of the Earth about New Zealand, its Causes and its Effects. 8* 1862
—— Some Account of a Volume containing portions of Ptolemy's Geography, and of the "Geographi Græci Minores." 8* 1864
—— **and Alfred Barrett.** Improvements in Arithmetic, with a Vindication of the Decimal Principle. 8* 1860

Ydiaquez, A. de. Le Pérou en 1889 : Notice Géographique, Statistique, et Commerciale à l'usage des Emigrants, Capitalistes, Industriels, et Explorateurs. *Map.* Large 8° *Havre,* 1890

Yeates, Thomas. Dissertation on the Antiquity, Origin, and Design of the Principal Pyramids of Egypt, particularly of the Great Pyramid of Ghizeeh, with its Measures, as reported by various authors. *Plates.* 4* 1833
—— Remarks on the History of Ancient Egypt, from Mizraim to Cambyses the Son of Cyrus, and to the end of the Persian Government in that Country. 8° 1835

Yeats, Dr John. Technical, Industrial, and Trade Education : a Manual of recent and existing Commerce, from the year 1789 to 1872. Small 8° 1872
—— The Growth and Vicissitudes of Commerce, from B.C. 1500 to A.D. 1789. *Map and chart.* Small 8° 1872
—— On Commercial Training. Small 8° 1873
—— The Natural History of the Raw Materials of Commerce, illustrated by Synoptical Tables and a folio Chart; a copious List of Commercial Products, and their Synonymes in the principal European and Oriental Languages; a Glossary and an Index; with an Industrial Map, printed in colours. 3rd edition. Crown 8° 1887
—— The Technical History of Commerce, or the Progress of the Useful Arts. 3rd edition. *Map.* Crown 8° 1887
—— The Growth and Vicissitudes of Commerce in all Ages : an Historical Narrative of the Industry and Intercourse of Civilised Nations; with Charts of Caravan Routes, and Appendix. 3rd edition. Crown 8° 1887
—— Recent and Existing Commerce; with Statistical Supplement, Maps showing Trade-Areas, and Tabulated List of Places important in Business or Trade. 3rd edition. Crown 8° 1887
—— The Golden Gates of Trade with our Home Industries : introductory to a Study of Mercantile Economy and of the Science of Commerce. *Map.* 8° 1890
—— Map Studies of the Mercantile World, auxiliary to our Foreign and Colonial Trade, and illustrative of part of the Science of Commerce. 8° 1890

Yepes, Joaquim Lopez. Catecismo y Declaracion de la Doctrina Cristiana en Lengua Otomí, con un Vocabulario del mismo Idioma. Square 8° *Mexico,* 1826

"Yittadairn." Moyarra, an Australian Legend, in Two Cantos. *Frontispiece.* 12° 1891

Yolland, Capt. William. Ordnance Survey: an Account of the Measurement of the Lough Foyle Base in Ireland, with its Verification and Extension by Triangulation; together with the various Methods of Computation followed on the Ordnance Survey, and the Requisite Tables. *Plates.* 4° 1847
—— Ordnance Survey: Astronomical Observations made with Airy's Zenith Sector, from 1842 to 1850, for the Determination of the Latitudes of various Trigonometrical Stations used in the Ordnance Survey of the British Isles. *Map and plates.* 4° 1852

York, Duke of. *See* "Bacchante."

Young, Sir Allen. Remarks on Korea. *Map.* 8° 1865
—— Cruise of the "Pandora." (From the private Journal kept by Allen Young, Commander of the Expedition.) *Map and photographs.* 8° 1876

Young, Arthur. Six Weeks' Tour through the Southern Counties of England and Wales. 8° 1768
—— Six Months' Tour through the North of England. 4 vols. *Plates.* 8° 1770
—— Travels during the years 1787, '88, and '89, undertaken more particularly with a view of ascertaining the Cultivation, Wealth, Resources, and National Prosperity of the Kingdom of France. *Maps.* 4° *Bury St Edmunds*, 1792
—— General View of the Agriculture of the County of Norfolk. *Map and plates.* 8° 1804
—— *See* Pinkerton, Vols. 3, 4: Appendix 1.

Young, C. *See* Galton, Vacation Tourists.

Young, Charles A. A Text-book of General Astronomy for Colleges and Scientific Schools. *Illustrations.* 8° *Boston, Mass.*, 1889
—— The Elements of Astronomy. 8° *Boston, Mass.*, 1890

Young, E. D. The Search for Livingstone: a Diary kept during the investigation of his reported murder. Revised by Rev. Horace Waller. *Map and plates.* 16° 1868
—— Nyassa: a Journal of Adventures whilst exploring Lake Nyassa, Central Africa, and establishing the Settlement of "Livingstonia." Revised by Horace Waller. *Maps.* 12° 1877

Young, E. R. Stories from Indian Wigwams and Northern Camp-Fires. *Illustrations.* 8° 1893

Young, Frederick. Transplantation the True System of Emigration. 2nd edition. 8° 1869

Young, F. Imperial Federation of Great Britain and her Colonies. 8° 1876

Young, Sir Frederick. A Winter Tour in South Africa. *Maps and photographs.* 8° 1890

Young, G. A History of Whitby and Streoneshalh Abbey; with a Statistical Survey of the Vicinity to the distance of twenty-five miles. 2 vols. *Maps and plates.* 8° *Whitby*, 1817

Young, Gerald. *See* Lambert, C. and S.

Young, J. Physical Geography. Small 8° 1874

Young, Jess. Recent Journey of Exploration across the Continent of Australia, its Deserts, Native Races, and Natural History. 8° *New York*, 1878

Young, Prof. John. *See* Armstrong, J.; *also* United Kingdom, K: Appendix 2.

Young, Robert. The Martyr Islands of the New Hebrides and adjacent groups. *Map.* 12° *Edinburgh*, 1889
—— The Success of Christian Missions: Testimonies to their Beneficial Results. 8° 1890
—— Trophies from African Heathenism. *Map.* Crown 8° 1892

Young, Thomas. An Account of some Recent Discoveries in Hieroglyphical Literature and Egyptian Antiquities, including the Author's Original Alphabet, as extended by M. Champollion, with a Translation of five unpublished MSS. 8° 1823
—— *See* Tattam.

Young, Sir W. The West-India Commonplace Book, compiled from Parliamentary and Official Documents, showing the Interests of Great Britain in its Sugar Colonies. &c. *Map.* 4° 1807
—— *See* Edwards, B.; Spence, Wm.

Younghusband, Capt. F. E. A Journey through Manchuria, Mongolia, and Chinese Turkestan. 8° *Lahore*, 1888

Younghusband, Captain G. J. Eighteen Hundred Miles on a Burmese Tat through Burmah, Siam, and the Eastern Shan States. *Map and illustrations.* 8° 1888
—— The Invasion of India by Russia. (From the *Nineteenth Century*.) 8° 1893

Yovnani, F. Paul, and J. Mekhitarist. Concise Geography of the Whole Earth; with the New Arrangements of Kingdoms. [In the Armenian Language.] 12° *Vienna*, 1835

Yoxall, J. H. The Pupil-Teachers' Geography, Political, Physical, and Physiographical. Crown 8° N.D.

Yriarte, C. Bosnie et Herzégovine: Souvenirs de Voyage pendant l'Insurrection. *Map and plates.* 12° *Paris*, 1876

Ysbrant-Ydes. *See* Ides.

Yule, Charles B. Routier de l'Australie (Cotes Nord, N.O. et Ouest . . .) Traduit de l'Anglais par M. Besson. Vol. 3. 8° *Paris*, 1866

Yule, Charles B. *See* United Kingdom, A, Admiralty; the Australia Directory: Appendix 2.

Yule, Col. Sir Henry. The African Squadron Vindicated. 8* 1850
—— Narrative of Major Phayre's Mission to the Court of Ava; with Notices of the Country, Government, and People; and Notes on the Geological Features of the Banks of the River Irawadee, and of the Country North of the City of Amarapoora, by Thomas Oldham. *Maps and plates.* 4° *Calcutta*, 1856
—— Narrative of the Mission sent by the Governor-General of India to the Court of Ava in 1855; with Notices of the Country, Government, and People. *Map and plates.* 4° 1858
—— Notes on Hwen Thsang's Account of the Principalities of Tokháristán. *Map.* 8* 1872
—— Sketch of the Geography and History of the Upper Amu-Daria. Translated by O. Fedchenko; with Supplementary Matter and Notes by A. Fedchenko, N. Khanikoff, and the Author. [In Russian.] *Map.* 8° *St Petersburg*, 1873
—— Afghânistan. [Article in the "Encyclopædia Britannica," 9th edition.] 4* *[Edinburgh*, 1875]
—— Major James Rennell, F.R.S. 8* [1881]
—— *See* Cordier; Gill, Capt. W.; Marco Polo; Nicholson, E. B.; Prejevalsky; Trotter, C.; Wood, J.; *also* Hakluyt Soc. Publ., Vols. 31, 36, 37, 74, 75, 78: Appendix 1.
—— **and Arthur Coke Burnell.** Hobson-Jobson: being a Glossary of Anglo-Indian Colloquial Words and Phrases, and of Kindred Terms, Etymological, Historical, Geographical, and Discursive. 8° 1886
—— **and H. M. Hyndman.** Mr Henry M. Stanley and the Royal Geographical Society: being the Record of a Protest. 8* 1878

Yule, Major P. Remarks on the disputed North-Western Boundary of New Brunswick, bordering on the United States of North America; with an Explanatory Sketch. *Map.* 8* 1838

Z.

Zabala, Amado Osorio. Vocabulary of the Fan Language in Western Africa, south of the Equator, with Spanish interpretation, prepared on the spot. 12° 1887

Zachariæ, G. *See* Hovgaard.

Zacharias, Dr O. *See* Germany, C, Forschungen zur Deutschen Landes-, &c. Vol. 4: Appendix 2.

Zagursky, L. Note on the Investigation of Caucasian Languages. [In Russian.] 4* *Moscow*, 1880

Zahn, F. M. Nochmals sechs Jahre Missions - Arbeit in Westafrica. Vier. Freistätten im Sclavenlande. *Map.* 8* *Bremen*, 1870

Zahrtmann, Vice-Admiral C. C. Danish Pilot. 8° 1853
—— Remarks on the Voyages to the Northern Hemisphere ascribed to the Zeni of Venice. 8* 1835

Zamacola, D. J. A. Historia de las Naciones Bascas, de una y otra parte del Pirineo Septentrional y costas del Mar Cantabrico. 3 vols. 8° *Auch*, 1818

Zannetti, A. *See* Giglioli; Issel.

Zaragoza, Justo. *See* Quirós.

Zarate, Augustin de. Historia del Déscubrimiento y Conquista de la Provincia del Peru. Folio *Ambers*, 1555
—— *See* Kerr, Vols. 4 and 5: Appendix 1.

Zarb, J. H. Rapport fait à S.E. le Général Stone Pacha . . . sur les Spécimens Botaniques . . . colligés pendant les Expéditions Egyptiennes au Kordofan et au Darfour en 1875 et 1876 par le D^r. Pfund. Par J. H. Zarb. Small 4° *Cairo*, 1875

Zarco, Gonzalez. *See* General Collection of Voyages and Travels, p. 610: Appendix 1.

Zaremba, C. W. The Merchants' and Tourists' Guide to Mexico. *Maps.* 8° *Chicago*, 1883

Zeballos, E. S. La Conquista de Quince Mil Leguas: Estudio sobre la Translacion de la Frontera Sud de la Republica al Rio Negro. *Maps and plans.* 8° *Buenos Ayres*, 1878
—— The same, 2nd edition. *Maps.* 8° *Buenos Ayres*, 1878
—— Congreso Cientifico Internacional Sud-Americano. 8° *Buenos Ayres*, 1878
—— Descripcion Amena de la República Argentina. Tomo 3.—A Traves de las Cabañas. *Illustrations.* Large 8° *Buenos Ayres*, 1888

Zehden, Dr Karl. *See* Dorn, A.

Zeilderus, Martinus. Itinerarium Germaniæ et Regnorum vicinorum. 18° *Ulm*, 1653
—— Regnorum Daniæ et Norwegiæ ut et Ducatuum Slesvici et Holsatiæ, Regionumque ad ea spectantium, Descriptio Nova. *Plans.* 16° *Amsterdam*, 1655

Zeithammer, A. O. Ideen zur Begründung eines Oesterreichischen Ethnographischen Museums. Royal 8* *Vienna*, 1860

Zeleber, J. *See* "Novara."

Zeledón, Pedro Pérez. Argument on the Question of the Validity of the Treaty of Limits between Costa-Rica and Nicaragua, and other Supplementary Points connected with it, submitted to the Arbi-

Zincken, C. F. Das Vorkommen der natürlichen Kohlenwasserstoff und der anderen Erdgase. *Plate.* 4° *Halle,* 1890

Zinkel, Ferdinand. *See* United States, H, *a*: Appendix 2.

Zirkel, A. *See* Preyer.

Zittel, Carl A. Denkschrift auf C. E. H. von Meyer. 4* *Munich,* 1870

—— Ueber den geologischen Bau der Libyschen Wüste. *Map.* 4* *Munich,* 1880

Zöller, Hugo. Das Batanga-Land. 8* *Berlin,* 1885

—— Die Deutschen Besitzungen an der westafrikanischen Küste. 1. Das Togoland und die Sklavenküste, Leben und Sitten der Eingebornen, Natur, Klima und kulturelle Bedeutung des Landes, dessen Handel und die deutschen Faktoreien auf Grund eigner Anschauung und Studien geschildert. *Maps and illustrations.* Small 8° *Berlin,* 1885

—— The same. 2, 3, 4. Die deutsche Colonie Kamerun; Forschungsreisen in der deutschen Colonie Kamerun. 3 vols. *Maps and illustrations.* 12° *Berlin,* 1885

—— Deutsch-Neuguinea und meine Ersteigung des Finisterre Gebirges; eine Schilderung des ersten erfolgreichen Vordringens zu den Hochgebirgen Inner-Neuguineas, der Natur des Landes, der Sitten der Eingeborenen, &c., in Kaiser-Wilhelms-Land, Bismarck- und Salomon-Archipel, nebst einem Wortverzeichnis von 46 Papua-Sprachen. *Portrait, maps, and illustrations.* Large 8° *Stuttgart,* 1891

Zograf, N. Les types Anthropologiques des Grands-Russes des Gouvernements du centre de la Russie. [A French abstract accompanying a 4° volume in Russian, descriptive of the types of inhabitants in Great Russia, and illustrated by numerous portraits and statistical diagrams.] Large 8° *Moscow,* 1892

Zollikofer, T. von, and J. Gobanz. Höhen-bestimmungen in Steiermark. 8* *Gratz,* 1864

Zöppritz, Prof. Dr K. Pruyssenaere's Reisen im Nilgebete. Parts 1 and 2. (Ergänzungshefte, 50 and 51 — Petermann's Mittheilungen.] 2 *maps.* 4° *Gotha,* 1877

—— *See* Boguslawski; Hirschfeld.

Zorgdrager, C. G. *See* Moubach.

Zornlin, Rosina M. Recreations in Physical Geography, or the Earth as it is. *Maps and plates.* 12° 1840

"Zrinyi" Voyage. *See* Benko.

Zschokke, H. Reisebilder aus Finnland und Russland. 8° *Vienna,* 1878

Zsigmondy, Dr Emil. Im Hochgebirge; mit Abbildungen von G. T. Compton herausgegeben von K. Schulz. 4° *Leipzig,* 1889

Zucchinetti, Dr. Souvenirs de mon séjour chez Emin Pasha el Soudani. 4* *Cairo,* 1890

Zuchold, Ernst Amandus. Dr Ludwig Leichhardt: eine biographische Skizze. Nebst einem Berichte über dessen zweite Reise im Innern des Austral-Continents nach dem Tagebuche seines Begleiters, des Botanikers Daniel Bunce. *Portrait and facsimile.* 8° *Leipzig,* 1856

Zuckerkandl. *See* "Novara."

Zückert, J. F. Die Naturgeschichte und Bergwercksverfassung des Ober Hartzes. Small 8° *Berlin,* 1762

Zucoli, Luigi. Descrizione di Milano. *Map.* 16° *Milan,* 1841

Zumarraga, Juan de. *See* Ternaux-Compans, Vol. 16: Appendix 1.

Zuñiga, Martinez de. Historical View of the Philippine Islands, exhibiting their Discovery, Population, Government, Language, &c. Translated by J. Maver. 2 vols. *Map.* 8° 1814

Zurita, Alonzo de. *See* Ternaux-Compans, Vol. 11: Appendix 1.

Zurla, Placido. Sulle Antiche Mappe Idro-Geografiche lavorate in Venezia, Commentario. *Maps.* 4° *Venice,* 1818

Zwack, D. C. F. Magazin von Natur- und Ländermerkwürdigkeiten, und wunderbaren Ereignissen. 3 vols. *Plates.* 12° *Stadt-am-Hof,* 1806

APPENDIX I.

COLLECTIONS OF VOYAGES AND TRAVELS

GIVING THE CONTENTS OF THE VOLUMES.

APPENDIX I.

COLLECTIONS OF VOYAGES AND TRAVELS.

Allgemeine Historie. *See* pp. 598-607.

Angelis, Pedro de. Colleecion de Obras y Documentos relativos á la Historia, Antigua y Moderna, de las Provincias del Rio de la Plata, illustrados con Notas y Disertaciones. 6 vols. Folio
Buenos Ayres, 1836-37

CONTENTS.
VOLUME I.

Guzman, Rui Diaz de. Historia Argentina, del Descubrimiento, Poblacion, y Conquista de las Provincias del Rio de la Plata, 1612.

Cruz, Luis de la. Viage desde el Fuerte de Ballenar, hasta la Ciudad de Buenos Aires.

—— Descripcion de la naturaleza de los Terrenos, que se comprenden en los Andes, poseidos por los Peguenches; y los demas espacios hasta el Rio de Chadileubu.

Falkener, Tomas. Descripcion de Patagonia, y de las partes adyacentes de la America Meridional. Escrita en Ingles.

Derroteros y Viages a la Ciudad Encantada, ó de los Césares ; que se creia existiese en la Cordillera, al Sud de Valdivia :—

Roxas, Silvestre A. de. Viage desde Buenos Aires á los Césares, por el Tandil y el Volcan, rumbo de Sud Oeste, 1707.

Cardiel, P. Jesuita José. Carta, sobre los Descubrimientos de las Tierras Patagónicas, en lo que toca á los Césares, 1746.

Lozano, P. Pedro. Carta, sobre los Césares que dicen están poblados en el estrecho de Magallanes.

Falkner, T. Derrotero desde la Ciudad de Buenos Aires hasta la de los Césares, que por otro nombre llaman la Ciudad Encantada, 1760.

Pinuer, Ignacio. Relacion de las Noticias adquiridas sobre una Ciudad grande de Españoles, que hay entre los Indios, al Sud de Valdivia, 1774.

Angelis, Vol. 1—*continued.*

Jauregui, Augustin de, Presidente de Chile. Carta escrita al Virey del Peru sobre los Césares, 1774.

Nuevo Descubriniento preparado por el Gobernador de Valdivia, 1777.

Villagran, Capit. D. Fermin. Declaracion sobre la Ciudad de los Césares, 1781.

Uriondo, Perez de. Informe y dictámen del Fiscal de Chile, sobre las Ciudades de los Césares, y los arbitrios que se deberian emplear para descubrir-las, 1782.

Lozano, P. Pedro. Diario de un Viage a la Costa de la Mar Magallanica, en 1745, desde Buenos Aires hasta el Estrecho de Magallanes ; formado sobre las Observaciones de los P.P. Cardiel y Quiroga.

Undiano y Gastelu, Sebastian. Proyecto de traslacion de las fronteras de Buenos Aires, al Rio Negro y Colorado ; al que se agrega el Itinerario de un Camino, desde Buenos Aires hasta Talca, por José Santiago Cerro y Zamudio.

Viedma, Francisco de. Memoria sobre los obstaculos que han encontrado, y las ventajas que prometen los establecimientos proyectados en la Costa Patagonica.

VOLUME 2.

Manrique, Juan del Pino. Descripcion de la Villa de Potosi, y de los partidos sugetos á su Intendencia, 1787.

Guevara, P. Historia del Paraguay, Rio de la Plata, y Tucuman.

Bautista, P. Série de los Gobernadores del Paraguay, de Buenos Aires, y de los Vireyes del Rio de la Plata, 1512-1810.

Barco Centenera, Martin del. La Argentina, o la Conquista Del Rio de la Plata, Poema Histórico.

Quiroga, P. Jose. Descripcion del Rio Paraguay, desde la Boca del Xaurù, hasta la Confluencia del Parana.

Angelis, Vol. 2—*continued.*

Azara, Felix de. Diario de la Navegacion y Reconocimiento del Rio Tebicuari, 1785.

VOLUME 3.

Viedma, D. Francisco de. Descripcion Geografica y Estadistica de la Provincia de Santa Cruz de la Sierra.

Garay, D. Juan de. Fundacion de la Ciudad de Buenos Aires, con otros documentos de aquella epoca.

Actas Capitulares desde el 21 hasta el 25 de Mayo de 1810, en Buenos Aires.

Garcia, D. Pedro Andres. Memoria sobre la navegacion del Tercero y otros rios que confluyen al Parana.

Zavala, Gen. D. Bruno Mauricio. Fundacion de la Ciudad de Montevideo ; con otros documentos relativos al Estado Oriental.

Doblas, D. Gonzalo de. Memoria Historica, Geografica, Politica y Economica, sobre la Provincia de Misiones de Indios Guaranis.

Garcia, P. A. Diario de un Viage á Salinas Grandes, en los Campos del Sud de Buenos Aires.

Manrique, D. Juan del Pino. Descripcion de la Provincia y Ciudad de Tarija, 1785.

Schmidel, Ulderico. Viage al Rio de la Plata y Paraguay.

VOLUME 4.

Tratado firmado en Madrid á 13 de enero de 1750, para determinar los limites de los Estados pertenecientes á las Coronas de España y Portugal, en Asia y América.

Tratado Preliminar sobre los Limites de los Estados pertenecientesá las Coronas de España y Portugal, en la América Meridional ; ajustado y concluido en San Lorenzo, 1777.

Flores, D. Manuel A. de. Carta al Marques de Valdelirios, para la egecucion del Tratado de Limites celebrado en Madrid, en 1750.

Arredondo, Virey D. Nicolas de. Informe del, á su sucesor Melo de Portugal, sobre el estado de la cuestion de Limites, en 1795.

Azara, D. Felix de. Correspondencia Oficial e Inedita sobre la Demarcacion de Límites entre el Paraguay y el Brasil, 1784-95.

Apuntes Históricos sobre la Demarcation de Límites de la Banda Oriental y el Brasil, 1777-1801.

Alvear, D. Diego de. Relacion Geográfica é Histórica de la Provincia de Misiones.

Angelis, Vol. 4—*continued.*

Pasos, D. Ignacio de. Diario de una Navegacion y Reconocimiento del Rio Paraguay, desde la Ciudad de la Asumpcion, hasta los Presidios Portugueses de Coimbra y Albuquerque.

Cabrer, D. Jose Maria. Reoonocimiento del Rio Pepiri-Guazú.

Azara, Felix de. Informes sobre varios Proyectos de Colonizar el Chaco, 1799.

Garcia de Solalinde, D. Antonio. Proyecto de Colonizacion del Chaco, 1799.

Cornejo, D. Adrian F. Expedicion al Chaco, por el Rio Bermejo, 1790.

—— Descubrimiento de un Nuevo Camino, desde el Valle de Centa, hasta la Villa de Tarija, 1791.

Garcia, D. Pedro A. Diario de la Expedicion de 1822 á los Campos del Sud de Buenos Aires, desde Moron hasta la Sierra de la Ventana ; con las Observaciones, Descripciones y demas Trabajos cientificos, egecutados por D. José Maria de los Reyes.

Tabla Corográfica de los treinta pueblos de las Misiones de los Jesuites, sobre los rios Paraná y Uruguay.

VOLUME 5.

Tamajuncosa, Fray Antonio. Descripcion de las Misiones, al Cargo del Colegio de Nuestra Señora de los Angeles, de la Villa de Tarija, 1800.

Henis, P. Tadeo Xavier. Diario Hitsórica de la Rebelion y Guerra de los Pueblos Guaranís, situados en la Costa Oriental del Rio Uruguay, 1754.

Tupac-Amaru, José Gabriel, Relacion Histórica de los Sucesos de la Rebelion de, en las Provincias del Peru, 1780.

—— Documentos para la História de la Sublevacion de, Cacique de la Provincia de Tinta, en el Peru.

Colleccion de Viages y Expediciones á los Campos du Buenos Aires y á las Costas de Patagonia :—

1. Cardiel, P. José, Extracto ó resúmen del Diario del, en el Viage que hizo desde Buenos Aires al Volcan, y de este siguiendo la Costa Patagónica, hasta el Arroyo de la Ascension, 1747.

2. Barne, Jorge. Viage que hizo el San Martin, desde Buenos Aires al Puerto de San Julian, 1752.

   Relacion que ha hecho el Indio Paraguay, nombrado Hilario Tapary, que se quedó en el Puerto de San Julian, desde donde se vino por Tierra á esta Ciudad de Buenos Aires, 1753-55.

3. Vernazani, Miguel. Observaciones extraidas de los Viages que al Estrecho de Magallanes han egecutado en diferentes años los Almirantes y Capitanes, O. de

Angelis, Vol. 5—*continued.*

Noort, S. de Cordes, J. Spilberg, F. Drake, J. Childey, T. Candish, J. Narborough, &c.

4. Hernandez, Capit. D. Juan A. Diario de la Expedicion contra los Indios Teguelches, 1770.

Calidades y condiciones mas caracteristicas de los Indios Pampas y Aucaces.

5. Pabon, D. Pedro Pablo. Diario, que contiene la explicacion exacta de los rumbos, distancias pastos, bañados y demas particularidades que hemos hallado en el reconocimiento del Campo y Sierras, 1772.

6. Eguia, Ramon-Pedro Ruiz. Relacion individual que dan los dos Pilotos comisionados al reconocimiento de la Campaña, de los parages que contemplan mas al propósito para fortificar y poblar.

7. Extracto resumido de lo que ha ocurrido en la Expedicion de descubrimiento de la Bahía sin Fondo, en la Costa Patagónica.

8. Noticia de la Expedicion y destacamento, que por órden del Virey D. T. J. de Vertiz, marchó al campo del enemigo, reconociéndolo hasta llegar á las Salinas, que se hallan en las campañas yermas del sud.

9, 10. Sá y Farias, Custodia. Informe sobre al Puerto de San José, 1779 e 1786.

11. Casas, Diego de las. Noticia individual de los Caciques, ó Capitanes Peguenches y Pampas que residen al Sud, circunvecinos á las fronteras de la Punta del Sauce, Tercero y Saladillo, jurisdiccion de la Ciudad de Córdoba, &c., 1779.

12. Amigorena, José Fr. de. Diario de la Expedicion, contra los Indios Barbaros Peguenches, 1780.

13. Villarino, D. Basilio Piloto. Informe sobre los Puertos de la Costa Patagónica, 1782.

14. Vertiz, Virey Juan José de. Informe, para que se abandonen los establecimientos de la Costa Patagónica, 1783.

VOLUME 6.

Hernandez, D. Estevan. Diario de un Viage desde el Fuerte de San Rafael del Diamante, hasta el de San Lorenzo, en las Puntas del Rio Quinto, 1806.

Zamudio, D. José S. de Cerro y. Diario formado en el viage para el descubrimiento de camino sin Cordillera, desde el reino de Chile á la Ciudad de Buenos Aires, 1802.

Cruz, D. Luis de la, Exámen Crítico del Diario de, por una Comision del Consulado de Buenos Aires, y Defensa del Autor, 1807.

Malaspina, D. Alejandro. Tablas de Latitudes y Longitudes de los Principales

Angelis, Vol. 6—*continued.*

Puntos del Rio de la Plata, nuevamente arregladas al Meridiano que pasa por lo mas Occidental de la Isla de Ferro.

Azara, D. Feliz de. Diario de un Reconocimiento de las Guardias y Fortines, que guarnecen la línea de frontera de Buenos Aires, 1796.

Rosas, D. Juan M. de. Diario de la Comision nombrada para establecer la nueva línea de frontera, al Sud de Buenos Aires, 1826.

Matorras, D. Geronimo. Diario de la expedicion hecha en 1774, á los paises del Gran Chaco, desde el Fuerte de Valle.

Cornejo, D. Juan A. F. Diario de la primera expedicion al Chaco, emprendida, en 1780.

Azara. Diario inédito de Viage al Rio Pilcomayo.

Morillo, Fray Francisco. Diario del Viage al Rio Bermejo, 1780.

Zizur, D. Pablo. Diario de una Expedicion á Salinas, 1786.

Souillac, J. S. de. Descripcion Geográfica de un Nuevo Camino de la Gran Cordillera, para facilitar las comunicaciones de Buenos Aires con Chile, 1805.

—— Itinerario de Buenos Aires á Córdoba.

Garcia, D. Pedro Andres. Nuevo plan de fronteras de la provincia de Buenos Aires, proyectado en 1816.

Villarino, D. Basilio. Diario de la Navegacion emprendida en 1781, desde el Rio Negro, para reconocer la Bahia de Todos los Santos, las Islas del Buen Suceso, y el desagüe del Rio Colerado:

Arias, D. Fr. Gavino de. Diario de la Expedicion Reduccional de 1780, al Gran Chaco.

Discurso preliminar del editor ; con la Bibliografia del Chaco, un Cotejo de ocho idiomas Indios, etc.

Viedma, D. Antonio de. Diario de un Viage á la costa de Patagonia, para reconocer los puntos en donde establecer poblaciones ; con una descripcion de la naturaleza de los terrenos, de sus producciones y habitantes ; desde el Puerto de Santa Elena hasta la boca del Estrecho de Magallanes.

Discurso preliminar del editor ; al que se añde un Vocabulario de los Patagones, con varios apuntes sobre la Isla Pepys, yuna lámina.

Villarino, D. Basilio. Diario del reconocimiento que hizo del Rio Negro, en la Costa Oriental de Patagonia, 1782.

Cramer, D. Ambrosio. Reconocimiento del Fuerte del Carmen del Rio Negro, y de los puntos adyacentes de la costa Patagonica, 1882.

Anonymous. For Anonymous Collections, see pp. 595-612.

Astley, Thomas. New General Collection of Voyages and Travels, consisting of the most Esteemed Relations which have been hitherto Published in any Language, comprehending Everything Remarkable in its Kind, in Europe, Asia, Africa, and America, with respect to the Several Empires, Kingdoms, and Provinces, their Situation, Extent, Bounds, and Division, Climate, Soil, and Produce, their Lakes, Rivers, Mountains, Cities, Principal Towns, Harbours, Buildings, &c., and the Gradual Alterations that from Time to Time have happened in each; also, the Manners and Customs of the Several Inhabitants, their Religion and Government, Arts and Sciences, Trades and Manufactures, so as to Form a Complete System of Modern Geography and History of all Nations. 4 vols. *Maps and plates.* 8°　　　　　1745-47

CONTENTS.

VOLUME I.

Of the Rise and Progress of Navigation and Commerce in Several Parts of the World.

Voyages to the South-East and East Indies, till the Europeans settled there:—

Voyages and Discoveries of the Portuguese along the Coast of Africa, as far as the Cape of Good Hope, Collected from De Faria y Sousa, Juan de Barros, A. Galvano, and other Authors.

Portuguese Sent to Discover the East Indies by Land, with an Account of Mandinga, Guinea, and Kongo.

Vasco de Gama's Voyage to India, round Africa, 1497.

Voyage of Pedro A. Cabral in 1500 to India.

Voyage of Juan de Nueva to the East Indies.

Vasco de Gama's Second Voyage to the East Indies in 1502.

Voyages and Transactions of the Portuguese in India from 1503-7, with the Exploits of Pacheco.

Exploits of the Portuguese, in 1507-10, under Don Francisco de Almeyda.

Exploits of Albuquerque from 1510-16.

Account of the Portuguese Transactions in India from 1516-21, under Lopez Soarez.

Transactions and Discoveries of the Portuguese from 1521-42.

Account of the Portuguese Possessions from the Cape of Good Hope to China.

Voyage of Soleymân Bashâ from Suez to India, in his Expedition against the Portuguese at Diu in 1539.

Astley, Vol. 1—*continued.*

Voyage of Don Stefano de Gama from Goa to Suez in 1540, with Intent to burn the Turkish Galleys, by Juan de Castro.

Description of the Sea of Kolzum, commonly called the Arabic Gulf or Red Sea, from Abû'lfeda's Geography.

The Second Siege of Diu, by Mahmud, King of Kambaya in 1545.

The First Voyages of the English to Guinea and the East Indies.

Thomas, J. Second Voyage to Barbary in 1552, by Captain T. Windham.

Voyage to Guinea and Benin in 1553, by Captains T. Windham and A. A. Pinteado.

Lok, Captain J. Second Voyage to Guinea.

Towrson, W. Three Voyages to Guinea, and the Castle Del Mina, in 1555-57.

Voyages to Guinea in 1561-66.

Wren, Walter. Voyage of Captain G. Fenner to the Islands of Cape Verde in 1566.

Stephens, Thomas. Voyage in the Portuguese Fleet to Goa in 1579.

Naval Expeditions and Cruising Voyages against the Spaniards and Portuguese.

Welsh, J. Two Voyages to Benin, beyond Guinea, in 1588 and 1590.

Wright, Edw. Cruising Voyage to the Azores in 1589, by the Earl of Cumberland.

Ralegh, Sir Walter. Fight between the "Revenge" Man-of-War, commanded by Sir R. Grenville, and 15 Armadas of Spain, in 1591.

Flicke, Captain Robert. Cruising Voyage to the Azores in 1591 with a Fleet of London Ships; with an Account of the West India Fleet, expected in Spain the same year, and the number of Ships lost or taken.

Exploits of the English in several Expeditions and Cruising Voyages from 1589-92. Extracted from J. H. van Linschoten's Voyage from Goa to Portugal.

Barker, Edmund. Report of a Voyage to the East Indies in 1591, by Capts. G. Raymond and J. Lancaster.

Voyages of R. Rainolds and T. Dassel to the Rivers of Senega and Gambra, adjoining on Guinea, 1591.

Burrough, Sir John. Cruising Voyage to the Azores in 1592, in order to intercept the East India Caraks.

Two remarkable Sea-fights; one in 1592, wherein two Assogue Ships were taken; the other in 1593, when a large East India Carak was burned.

Unfortunate Voyage of Capt. B. Wood toward the East Indies in 1596.

Astley, Vol. 1—*continued.*

Davis, Capt. John. Voyage to the East Indies in 1598.

First Voyages of the English to the East Indies, set forth by the Company of Merchants:—

Voyage of Capt. J. Lancaster in 1600.

Voyage of Capt. Sir Henry Middleton in 1604.

Scot, Edm. Account of Java and the First Settlement of the English at Bantam, with a Journal of occurences there, 1602-5. Abridged.

Voyage of Sir Edward Michelburne to Bantam in 1604.

Keeling, Capt. W. Voyage to Bantam and Banda in 1607, abbreviated.

Voyage of Capt. D. Middleton to Bantam and the Molukkos in 1607.

Coverte, Capt. R. Voyage of Capt. A. Sharpey in 1608.

Jones, Thomas. Voyage of the "Ascension."

Voyage of Capt. R. Rowles to Priaman, in the "Union."

Voyage of Capt. D. Middleton to Java and Banda in 1609.

Middleton, Sir H. Voyage to the Red Sea and Surat in 1610.

Dounton, Lieut.-Gen. N. Journal of, in a Voyage to the Red Sea and Surat in 1610.

Marten, Nath. Voyage of Capt. A. Hippon to the Coast of Koromandel, Bantam, and Siam in 1611.

Floris, P. W., Journal of, in the same Voyage of Capt. Hippon. Translated from the Dutch.

Tatton, J. Voyage of Capt. S. Castleton to Priaman in 1612.

Saris, Capt. J. Voyage to the Red Sea, the Molukkos, and Japan in 1611.

—— Occurrences at Bantam and other parts of the East Indies, 1605-9; with an Account of the Marts and Commodities of those parts.

Cocks, R. Relation of what passed at Firando in the General's absence at the Emperor's Court.

—— Some Particulars relating to the Affairs of Japan from 1614-20; with the Substance of Two Letters from Mr Sayer, and a Letter from the Emperor of Japan to the Prince of Orange.

Adams, W. Voyage to Japan, with his Adventures and Promotion there.

Voyages to several parts of Africa and the Islands adjacent ; with particular Descriptions of the respective Countries and their Inhabitants:—

Nichols, T. Description of the Canary Islands and Madeira, with their remarkable Fruits and Commodities ; also a further Account from later Authors.

Astley, Vol. 1—*continued.*

Cada Mosto, Aluise da. Two Voyages to and along the Coast of Africa as far as Rio Grande, in which the Cape de Verde Islands were discovered, 1455-56.

—— Voyage of Capt. Piedro de Cintra to Sierra Leone.

Roberts, Capt. G. Account of a Voyage to the Islands of the Canaries, Cape de Verde, and Barbadoes in 1721.

Description of the Cape de Verde Islands.

VOLUME 2.

Voyages and Travels along the Western Coast of Africa from Cape Blanco to Sierra Leona ; containing a Description of the several Countries and their Inhabitants within that Division, more particularly an Account of the Rivers Sanaga and Gambra or Gambia, and of the French and English Settlements :—

Account of the French Settlements between Cape Blanco and Sierra Leona.

Jannequin, Claude. Abstract of a Voyage to Libya, particularly to the Kingdom of Sanaga on the River Niger.

Brue, Sieur André. Voyages and Travels along the Western Coast of Africa on account of the French Commerce.

—— Description of the River Sanaga, with an Enquiry whether it be the Niger or a Branch thereof.

—— First Voyage up the Sanaga in 1697.

—— Second Voyage up the Sanaga to the Kingdom of Galam in 1698.

Differences between the English and French about the Trade of the River Gambra.

Brue, Sieur. Journey from Albreda to Kachao by Land in 1700.

—— Voyage to the Isles of Bissao and Bissagos, with his Negotiations in these parts in 1700.

—— Attempt for a Discovery of the Lake of Kayor in 1714 ; with an Account of the Trade carried on from Goree.

—— Third Voyage up the Sanaga in 1715 on account of the Gum Trade.

Account of the Country to the North of the Sanaga, where the Gum is gathered, its Inhabitants and Productions.

Campagnon, Sieur. Account of the Discovery of the Kingdom of Bambûk and its Gold Mines in 1716, with a Description of the Country and its Inhabitants.

Account of the Rise and Progress of the English Royal African Company.

A General Description of the River Gambia, with an Account of the European Settlements, particularly the English.

Astley, Vol. 2—*continued.*

Jobson, Capt. R. Voyage for the Discovery of the River Gambra, and the Golden Trade of Tombûto, in 1620-21.

Letter concerning the Discovery of the Gold Mines in a Voyage up the Gambra.

Stibbs, Capt. Bartholomew. Voyage up the Gambra in 1724, for making Discoveries and Improving the Trade of that River.

Moore, Francis. Travels into the Inland Parts of Africa, containing a Description of the Countries and their Inhabitants for 600 miles up the River Gambra.

The Remarkable Captivity and Deliverance of Job ben Solomon, a Mohammedan Priest of Bûnda, near the Gambra, in 1732, with some Remarks relating to the Kingdom of Fûta.

Of the Trade carried on by Europeans in the river Gambra, particularly by the English.

Two Voyages to Cape de Verde and the Neighbouring Coast of Africa. Translated from the French.

Account of the Jalofs, particularly those Inhabiting towards the Gambra.

Of the Fûli Inhabiting along the Gambra.

Account of the Mandigos.

The Customs and Rites common to the Inhabitants of Bûlmberre or Sierra Lione.

Of the Trees, Fruits, Vegetables, Animals, Insects, Reptiles, Birds, Fish, and Amphibious Animals in this part of Africa.

Voyages and Travels to Guinea and Benin, comprehending the Coast from Sierra Leona to Cape Lope Gonsalvo:—

Villault, Sieur. Abstract of a Voyage to the Coast of Africa and Guinea in 1666.

Phillips, Capt. T. Abstract of a Voyage along the Coast of Guinea to Whidah, the Island of St Thomas, and thence to Barbadoes, in 1693.

Loyer, Godfrey. Abstract of a Voyage to Issini on the Gold Coast in 1701, with a Description of the Country and its Inhabitants.

Atkins, John. Voyage to Guinea, Brazil, and the West Indies, in 1721.

Marchais, Chev. des. Voyage to Guinea and the adjacent Islands in 1725.

Smith, W. Voyage to Guinea in 1726.

Snelgrave, Capt. W. A New Account of some Parts of Guinea, and the Slave Trade, in 1730.

A Description of Guinea, including the Geography, with the Natural and Civil History.

Astley, Vol. 2—*continued.*

The Malaghetta, Grain or Pepper Coast.

Account of the Inland Countries between Sierra Leona and Rio Sextos, or Sestro.

Of the Ivory Coast.

Gold Coast, its Discovery and Settlements made there by Europeans, with its Geography.

Inland Countries behind the Gold Coast.

Of the Gold Coast Negroes, their Persons, Character, and Dress.

Natural History of the Gold Coast.

VOLUME 3.

Voyages and Travels to Guinea, containing a Description of the Coast from Rio da Volta to Benin :—

The Kingdoms of Koto and Popo.

The Kingdom of Whidah ; with an Account of the Natives, their Marriages, Diversions, Diseases and Funerals, Religion, Government, and Natural History.

D'Elbée, Sieur. Voyage to Ardrah, and Travels to the Capital Assem in 1669-70. To which is added an Embassy from the King of Ardrah to Louis XIV.

Voyages and Travels to Benin, containing a Description of that Country, and the Coast as far as Congo :—

An Account of the Kingdom of Benin.

Barbot, J., and J. Grazilhier. Abstract of a Voyage to New Kalabar, Bandi, and Doni Rivers in 1699.

The Coast from Old Kalabar River to Cape Lope Gonsalvo.

Voyages and Travels to Congo and Angola :—

Voyages of Edw. Lopez and And. Battel.

Voyage to Kongo in 1666-67 by Michael Angelo and Denis de Carli, Capauchin Missionaries.

Voyage to Kongo and several other Countries in the South Part of Africa in 1682, by J. Merolla de Sorrento.

Abstract of a Voyage to Kongo River and Kabinda in 1700, by J. Barbot and J. Casseneuve.

A Description of the Kingdoms of Loango, Kongo, Angola, Benguela, and the adjacent Countries, with an Account of the Inhabitants and Natural Productions.

A Description of the Countries along the Eastern Coast of Africa, from the Cape of Good Hope to Cape Guarda Fuy, containing more particularly an Account of the Hottentots and the Empire of Monomotapa.

Kolben. Account of the Country of the Hottentots, and the several Nations inhabiting the same.

Astley, Vol. 3—*continued*.

Description of the Dutch Possessions at the Cape.

Hamilton, Capt. Alex. Remarks on the Maritime Countries and Islands between the Capes of Good Hope and Guarda Fuy.

Account of the Empire of Monomopata, from De Faria y Sousa.

Voyages and Travels in the Empire of China :—

Nieuhoff, John. Embassy of Peter de Goyer and Jacob de Keyzer from the Dutch East India Company to the Emperor of China in 1655.

Montanus, A. Embassy of J. Van Campen and C. Noble to Sing la mong, Viceroy of Fo Kyen.

Expedition of the Dutch for Recovering Formosa, in conjunction with the Tartars.

Embassy of the Lord van Hoorn to Kang hi, Emperor of China and Eastern Tartary.

Narrative of the Dutch Embassy in 1655, with the Arts used by the Jesuits to defeat it.

The First Attempts of the Dutch to Trade to China, and Settlement at Tay Wan.

Navarette's Travels through China in 1658.

Travels of Five French Jesuits from Ning po fû to Peking in 1687.

Journey of Jean de Fontancy, Jesuit, from Peking Kyang chew, in the Province of Shan si, and thence to Nanking in 1688.

Journey of Joachim Bouvet, Jesuit, from Peking to Kanton, when sent by the Emperor Kang hi into Europe in 1693.

Travels of Dr J. F. Gemelli Careri in China in 1695.

Travels of Everard Isbrand Ides, the Russian Ambassador, in China in 1693.

Travels of Laurence Lange, the Russian Envoy, in China in 1717.

Journey of Anthony Gaubil, Jesuit, from Kanton to Peking in 1722.

Viani, P. Legation of C. A. Mezzabarba, titular Patriarch of Alexandria, from the Pope to the Emperor Kang hi in 1720.

VOLUME 4.

Description of China, containing the Geography, with the Civil and Natural History.

Description of Korea, Eastern Tartary, and Tibet.

Regis, Jean Baptiste, Jesuit. Geographical Observations and History of Korea.

Hamel, H. Travels of Some Dutchmen in Korea, with an Account of the Country

Astley, Vol. 4—*continued*.

and their Shipwreck on the Island of Quelpaert.

Description of Tartary, subject to China of Tibet, or Tibbet, of the Kingdom of Karazm, of Great Bukhâria, of Little Bukhâria, or the Kingdom of 'Kâshgar, and of the Country of Turkestân.

Travels through Tartary, Tibet, and Bukhâria, to and from China :—

Travels of John de Plano Carpini, and other Friars, into Tartary in 1246.

Travels of Friar W. de Rubruquis into the Eastern Parts of the World in 1253.

Travels of Marco Polo into Tartary in 1272.

Embassy of Shâh Rokh, son of Tamerlan, and other Princes, to the Emperor of Katay, or China, in 1419. Translated from the Persian.

Voyage and Travels of A. Jenkinson from Russia to Boghâr, or Bokhâra, in 1557; to which are added some Information of others concerning the Road thence to Katay or China.

Travels of Benedict Goëz, Jesuit, from Lahor, in the Mogol's Empire, to China in 1602.

Travels through Tibet, to and from China, by several Missioners.

Gerbillon, J. F., Jesuit. Travels into Western Tartary, by order of the Emperor of China, between 1688 and 1698.

Bates, H. W. Illustrated Travels. *See* Appendix 3.

Blackwood — Travel, Adventure, and Sport. From *Blackwood's Magazine*. 6 vols. 12°   *Edinburgh*, V.D.

Vol. 1.—Speke, Capt. : The Discovery of the Victoria N'Yanza [*Maga*, Oct., Nov. 1859.] Oliphant, Laurence : My Home in Palestine [*Maga*, Feb. 1883]. A Sketch in the Tropics, from a Supercargo's Log [*Maga*, Sept. 1843]. Wolseley, Gen. Viscount : Narrative of the Red River Expedition [*Maga*, Dec. 1870-Feb. 1871]. A Ride to Babylon [*Maga*, June 1863]. The King of Tristan d'Acunha, a Forgotten Monarch [*Maga*, Dec. 1818].

Vol. 2.—The North-East Passage : Narrative of Lieut. Palander [*Maga*, March 1880]. Two Nights in Southern Mexico [*Maga*, April 1844]. Macmillan, George A. : A Ride Across the Peloponnese [*Maga*, May 1878]. Shakespear, Capt. Sir Richmond : A Personal Narrative of a Journey from Herat to Orenburg on the Caspian, in 1840 [*Maga*, June 1842]. Wilson, Andrew : The Inland Sea of Japan

Blackwood, Vol. 2—*continued.*

[*Maga*, Nov. 1861]. Oliphant, Laurence : A Ride to Nicaragua [*Maga*, May 1857]. Up Stream on the Red River [*Maga*, Nov. 1844].

Vol. 3.—Taysen, Frederick : A Reindeer Ride through Lapland [*Maga*, Aug. 1880]. Wilson, Andrew : The Valley of the Shadow of Death [*Maga*, Nov. 1874]. Osborn, Admiral Sherrard : A Cruise up the Yangstze in 1858-59 [*Maga*, June 1861]. Scott, G. B. : Among the Afghans, a Surveyor's Narrative [*Maga*, Nov. 1879]. The Americans and the Aborigines : Scenes in the Short War, from the German of Charles Sealsfield [*Maga*, May-July 1846], &c.

Vol. 4 [No. 7].—Albert Smith's Ascent of Mont Blanc [*Maga*, Jan. 1852]. Surrè, Herbert : Summer Sport in Nova Zemla [*Maga*, Sept. 1883]. A Ride to Magnesia [*Maga*, Feb.-March 1847]. Hamley, Colonel Charles : Aland—the Baltic in 1854 [*Maga*, June 1855].

Vol. 5.—Crosse, Landor R. : The Destruction of Szegedin [*Maga*, June 1879]. Smith, Lieut.-Col. H. : Reminiscences of a Ross-shire Forest [*Maga*, Aug. 1883 and Feb. 1884]. Wilson, Andrew : A Run through Kathiawar [*Maga*, Aug., Oct., and Nov. 1876], &c.

Vol. 6.—Clerk, Capt. Claud : Shiraz to Bushire [*Maga*, September 1862]. Oliphant, Mrs : Life in an Island [*Maga*, Jan. 1865]. A Recent Ride to Herat [*Maga*, Aug. 1885]. Swire, H. : In Search of the Eira [*Maga*, Nov. 1882]. Adventures in Louisiana [*Maga*, July-Aug. 1843]. Wilson, Andrew : Kashmir [*Maga*, April-May, 1875]. Oliphant, Laurence : Travels in Circassia [*Maga*, June-July, 1856].

Burney, Capt. James. Chronological History of the Discoveries in the South Sea or Pacific Ocean. 5 vols. *Maps and plates.* 4°   1803-17

CONTENTS.

VOLUME I.

Commencing with an Account of the Earliest Discovery of that Sea by Europeans, and terminating with the Voyage of Sir Francis Drake. 1579 :—

A Brief Account of the Discoveries made in the South Sea, previous to the Voyage of Magalhanes. Columbus, the Cabots, Americus Vespucius, Juan de Soils.

Magalhanes, F. de. Voyage, 1517-21.

Burney, Vol. 1—*continued.*

Sequel of the Voyage after the Death of Magalhanes, 1521-22.

Progress of Discovery on the Western Coast of America, 1522-24. Hernandez Cortez, Pizzaro, Gomara. Attempt to Discover a Strait near the Isthmus of Darien.

Loyasa, Garcia Jofre de. Voyage from Spain to the Moluccas, 1525-27.

Discovery of the North Coast of Papua, by the Portuguese.

Saavedra, Alvaro de. Voyage from New Spain to the Moluccas, 1527-29.

Expeditions between 1526 and 1833. Discoveries on the Western Coast of America. Discovery of California, 1533. S. Cabot, Villegagnon, Mendoza, Grijalva.

Alcazova, Simon de. Expedition to the South from Peru, 1534-35.

Cortes, Marquis del Valle. Sails to California, 1536.

Grijalva, H. de, and Alvarado. Voyage from Peru to the Moluccas, 1537.

Camargo, Alonzo de. Voyage from Spain to Peru, 1539.

Niza, Marcos de. Journey to Cevola, 1539.

Ulloa, F. de. Voyage, and Discovery that California was part of the Continent. 1539-40.

Alarcon, Hernando de. Voyage to the North of Mexico, 1540.

Vasquez de Cornado, F. Expedition to the North of Mexico, 1540.

Cabrillo, J. Rodrigues. Voyage to the North of California, 1542.

Villalobos, Ruy Lopez de. Voyage from New Spain to Mindanao, Las Philippinas, and the Moluccas, 1542-45.

Ladrilleros, Juan. Voyage from Valdivia to the Strait of Magalhanes 1557-58.

Lopez de Legaspi, Miguel. Expedition from New Spain to the Philippine Islands, 1564-65.

Of the Islands discovered near the Continent of America in the Pacific Ocean.

Mendana, Alvaro de. Discovery of the Salomon Islands, 1567.

Oxnam, John. Enterprise in the South Sea, 1575.

Reports concerning a Discovery of a Southern Continent.

Drake, Sir Francis. Voyage Round the World, 1577-80.

VOLUME 2.

From 1579 to 1620 :—

Sarmiento de Gamboa, Pedro. Voyage from Peru to the Strait of Magalhanes, and thence to Europe, 1579-86.

—— Expedition to Fortify the Strait of Magalhanes.

Burney, Vol. 3—*continued.*

Attempts of the Portuguese to Renew their Trade with Japan, 1685.

The name Carolinas given to Islands Southward of the Marianas, 1686.

First Mission of the French Jesuits to China, 1687.

Islas de 1688. Island Donna Maria de Lajara.

Memoir Explanatory of a Chart of the Coast of China, and the Sea Eastward, from the River of Canton to the Southern Islands of Japan.

VOLUME 4.

From 1688 to 1723, including a History of the Buccaneers of America :—

Considerations on the Rights Acquired by the Discovery of Unknown Lands, and on the Claims advanced by the Spaniards.

Review of the Dominion of the Spaniards in Hayti or Hispaniola, 1492-1519.

Ships of Different European Nations frequent the West Indies. Opposition Experienced by them from the Spaniards. Hunting of Cattle in Hispaniola. 1518-86.

Iniquitous Settlement of the Island Saint Christopher by the English and French. Tortuga seized by the Hunters, 1625-30.

Origin of the name Buccaneer ; the name Filibustier. Customs Attributed to the Buccaneers.

Increase of English and French in the West Indies, 1630-33. Tortuga Surprised by the Spaniards, 1638.

Mansvelt attempts to Form an Independent Buccaneer Establishment, 1664.

Morgan succeeds Mansvelt as Chief of the Buccaneers, 1665.

Treaty of America, 1670.

Expedition of the Buccaneers against Panama, 1670.

Exquemelin's History of the American Sea Rovers.

Peche, Thomas. Voyage, 1673.

La Sound attempts to Cross the Isthmus of America, 1675.

De Vea, Ant. Voyage to the Strait of Magalhanes, 1676.

Various Adventures of the Buccaneers in the West Indies, to 1679.

Meeting of Buccaneers at the Samballas, and Golden Island, 1680.

Account of the Mosquito Indians.

Journey of the Buccaneers across the Isthmus of America, 1680.

First Buccaneer Expedition to the South Sea, 1680-82.

Disputes between the French Government and their West India Colonies, 1680.

Burney, Vol. 4—*continued.*

Morgan, Sir Henry, becomes Deputy Governor of Jamaica, 1680.

Van Horn, Granmont, and De Graaf, go against La Vera Cruz, 1683.

Circumstances which preceded the Second Irruption of the Buccaneers into the South Sea.

Cook, John, Buccaneers under, Sail from Virginia, stop at the Cape de Verde Islands, Sierra Leone, Pepys' Island, Juan Fernandez, the Galapagos Islands, thence to the Coast of New Spain, 1683-1684.

Davis, Edw. On the Coast of New Spain and Peru, the Cocos and Galapagos Islands, 1684-85.

—— Third Visit to the Galapagos, sailing Southward discovers an Island, arrives in the West Indies, 1687-88.

Swan and Townley's Adventures on the Coast of New Spain, until their Separation, 1685.

Swan, Captain, and J. Reed. The "Cygnet" and her Crew on the Coast of Nueva Galicia, and at the Tres Marias Islands ; Passage across the Pacific Ocean, at the Ladrones, Mindanao, Ponghou Isles, Five Islands, Philippines, Celebes, and Timor, on the Coast of New Holland ; end of the "Cygnet," 1686-88.

French Buccaneers under François Grogniet and Le Picard, to the Death of Grogniet, 1685-87.

Retreat of the French Buccaneers across New Spain to the West Indies. All the Buccaneers quit the South Sea, 1687-90.

Pointis, M. de. Siege and Plunder of the City of Carthagena on the Terra Firma, by an Armament from France, in Conjunction with the Filibustiers of Saint Domingo, 1686-97.

Second Plunder of Carthagena. Peace of Ryswick, 1697. Entire Suppression of the Buccaneers and Filibustiers, 1697-1722.

Strong, Capt. John. Voyage to the Coast of Chili, 1689-91.

Gennes, M. de. Voyage to the Strait of Magalhanes, 1695-97.

Careri, Gemelli. Passage from Manilla to New Spain, 1697.

Of the Expeditions of the Spaniards in California, to their First Establishment in 1697.

Otondo, Don Isidro. Expedition, 1683-85.

Salvatierra goes to California, 1697.

Kino, and Salvatierra, P. P., Doubt concerning the Junction of California with the Continent verified by.

Callander, Vol. 1—*continued.*
to Polynesia.—Sir Thomas Cavendish to
Magellanica for the second time.

VOLUME 2.

Sir Richard Hawkins to Magellanica, in
1593. — Fernand de Quiros to Poly-
nesia and Australasia.—George Spilberg
to Magellanica and Polynesia.—James
Le Maire and William Schouten to
Magellanica, Polynesia, and Australasia.
—Garcia De Nodal to Magellanica.—
Account of the Dutch Navigations to the
Terris Australis, from 1616 to the end of
the 17th century.—Jacques Le Hermite
to Polynesia and Australasia.—Francis
Pelsart to Australasia.—Gerard Pool to
Australasia.—Abel Tasman to Australasia.—Henry Brewer to Magellanica.—
A Dutch Frigate to the Isle of Tristan
d'Acunha, in 1643.—Vink to Australasia.—Sir John Narborough to Magellanica, in 1670.—Keyts to Australasia,
in 1678.—Bartholemew Sharp to Magellanica, in 1680.—Cowley to Magellanica
and Polynesia, in 1683.—William Dampier to Magellanica and Polynesia.—
Lionel Wafer to Magellanica.

VOLUME 3.

De Gennes to Magellanica.—Vlaming to
the East Indies by the Cape of Good
Hope.—History of the New Philippine
Islands.—Antony Cantova to the Caroline
Islands.—Manners and Customs of the
Inhabitants of the Marion or Ladrone
Islands.—Beauchesne Gouin to Magel-
lanica.—Dampier's last Voyage Round
the World.—Funnell's Voyage Round the
World.—Fouquet and Peree to the South
Seas.—Captain Woodes Rogers's famous
Voyage Round the World.—Louis Feuil-
lée to the South Seas. — Monsieur
Frezier's curious and useful Journal of his
Voyage to Magellanica.—La Barbinais's
Voyage Round the World.—Clipperton's
Voyage to the South Seas and East
Indies. — Shelvocke's Voyage Round
the World.—Commodore Roggewein's
Voyage Round the World, with a full
Account of the Dutch Settlements in
India.—Lozier Bouvet to Magellanica.—
Commodore Anson's Voyage Round the
World. — The Hon. George Murray,
Esq., his Account of the Separation of
the ships "Severn" and "Pearl" from
Anson's Squadron.—Don Antonio Ulloa
to the South Seas.—Hen Brignon to
Magellanica.—Commodore Byron to the
South Seas.—Of the Method of Forming
Colonies in the Terra Australis, and the
advantages that may be expected to result
to Great Britain from such Establish-
ments in that Hemisphere.

Churchill, A. and J. Collection of Voyages
and Travels: some now first Printed from
Original Manuscripts ; others Translated
out of Foreign Languages, and now first
Published in English ; to which are added
some few that have formerly appeared in
English, but do now for their Excellency
and Scarceness deserve to be Reprinted ;
with a General Preface, giving an Account of the Progress of Navigation,
from its Beginning to the Perfection it is
now in. Also a Collection compiled
from the Curious and Valuable Library
of the late Earl of Oxford [the Harleian
Collection]. 8 vols. *Maps and plates.*
Folio   1707-47

CONTENTS.

VOLUME I.

Navarette, D. F. Account of the Empire of China, Historical, Political,
Moral, and Religious.

Baumgarten, M. Travels through Egypt,
Arabia, Palestine, and Syria ; with the
Author's Life.

Brawern, H., and E. Herckemann. Voyage to the Kingdom of Chili in America.

Candidius, G. Account of the Island of
Formosa in the East Indies.

Japan. Curious Remarks on the Empire
of Japan. From the High-Dutch.

Monck, Capt. J. Account of a most
Dangerous Voyage to Hudson's Straits,
in order to Discover a Passage that way
to the West Indies ; with a Description
of Old and New Greenland.

Beauplan, Sieur de. Description of Ukraine, with the Customs, Manner of
Living, and of Managing the Wars of
those People.

Angelo, M., and D. Carli. Curious and
Exact Account of a Voyage to Congo in
1666-67.

Merolla da Sorrento, Jerom. Voyage to
Congo and several other Countries in
the Southern Africk.

Roe, Sir Thomas. Journal of his Voyage
to the East Indies, and Observations
there during his Residence at the
Mogul's Court, as Ambassador from
England.

VOLUME 2.

Nieuhoff, J. Voyages and Travels into
Brazil, and the best parts of the East
Indies.

Smith, Capt. J. True Travels and Adventures in Europe, Asia, Africa, and
America, from 1592 to 1629.

Greenland and Spitzbergen. Two Journals : The First kept by Seven Sailors,
in the Isle of S. Maurice in Greenland, in 1633-4, who passed the winter,
and all died in the Island : The Second,
kept by Seven other Sailors, who in
1633-4 wintered at Spitzbergen.

Churchill, Vol. 2—*continued.*

Spitzbergen. A True and Short Account of Forty-two Persons who Perished by Shipwreck near Spitzbergen in 1646.

Peyrere, La. Account of Iceland, sent to M. de la Mothe de Vayer.

—— Account of Greenland.

James, Capt. T. Strange and Dangerous Voyage in his intended Discovery of the North-West Passage into the South-Sea, in 1631-32; with curious Observations.

Backhoff, F. Iskowitz, Muscovite Envoy. Voyage into China.

Wagener, Z. Voyage through a great part of the World into China.

Columbus, Christopher. Life, and the History of his Discovery of the West Indies, by his son D. F. Columbus.

Greaves, John. Pyramidographia ; or, A Description of the Pyramids of Egypt.

—— Discourse of the Roman Foot and Denarius, from whence, as from Two Principles, the Measures and Weights used by the Ancients may be deduced.

Borri, R. F. Chr. Account of Cochinchina, in two Parts.

VOLUME 3.

Ovalle, Alonso de. Historical Relation of the Kingdom of Chili.

Monson, Sir William. Naval Tracts. Treating of all the Actions of the English by Sea, under Queen Elizabeth and King James I.; the Office of High Admiral and his Inferior Officers; Discoveries and Enterprises of the Spaniards and Portugueses ; Projects and Stratagems ; and of Fish and Fishery.

Baldæus, Philip. A True and Exact Description of the most Celebrated East-India Coast of Malabar and Coromandel, and of the Island Ceylon, with all the adjacent Countries.

VOLUME 4.

Careri, J. F. Gemelli. Voyage Round the World, containing the most Remarkable Things in Turkey, Persia, India, China, the Philippine Islands, and New Spain.

Corea. An Account of the Shipwreck of a Dutch Vessel on the Coast of the Isle of Quelpaert, together with the Description of the Kingdom of Corea.

Sepp, F. F. Ant., and Ant. Behme. Account of a Voyage from Spain to Paraquaria.

Salomon. A Fragment concerning the Discovery of the Islands of Salomon.

Techo, F. Nich. del. History of the Provinces of Paraguay, Tucuman, Rio de la Plata, Parana, Guaira, and Urvaica,

Churchill, Vol. 4—*continued.*

and something of the Kingdom of Chile, in South America.

Pelham's Preservation of Eight Men in Greenland, nine months and twelve days.

Merin's Journey to the Mines in Hungary.

Ten Rhyne's Account of the Cape of Good Hope and the Hottentotes, the Barbarous Natives of that Country.

Boland's Observations on the Streights of Gibraltar and the Tides and Currents.

VOLUME 5.

Barbot, J. Description of the Coasts of North and South Guinea and of Ethiopia Inferior, vulgarly Angola, being a New and Accurate Account of the Western Maritime Countries of Africa; with a New Relation of the Province of Guiana, and of the Rivers of Amazons and Oronoque in South America; and an Account of the First Discoveries of America in the 14th Century. From Herrera's History of the West Indies.

Rolamb, Nicholas. Relation of a Journey to Constantinople.

VOLUME 6.

Baron, S. Description of the Kingdom of Tonqueen.

Careri, J. G. Travels through Europe.

Norwood, Col. Voyage to Virginia.

Phillips, Capt. Journal of his Voyage from England to Cape Mounseradoe in Africa, and along the Coast of Guiney to Whidaw, the Island of St Thomas, and so forward to Barbadoes.

Gatonbe, J. Voyage into the North-West Passage by Sir George Lancaster and others.

Everard, Rob. Relation of Three Years' Sufferings upon the Coast of Assada, near Madagascar, in a Voyage to India.

Mosquito. A Familiar Description of the Mosqueto Kingdom in America, with a Relation of their Strange Customs, Religion, Wars, &c.

Lord, Rev. H. Discovery of Two Foreign Sects in the East Indies, viz., the Sect of the Banians, the Ancient Natives of India ; and the Sect of the Persees, the Ancient Inhabitants of Persia, with the Religion and Manners of each Sect.

May, C. Account of the Wonderful Preservation of the Ship " Terra Nova " of London, Homeward Bound from Virginia.

Mocha. Account of the King of Mocha, and of his Country.

Bombay. Some Reasons for the Unhealthiness of the Island of Bombay.

Skippon, Sir Philip. Journey through Part of the Low Countries, Germany, Italy, and France.

Churchill—*continued*.

VOLUME 7.

Osborne, T. Introductory Discourse concerning Geography, Navigation, Government, Commerce, Religion, Travel, and a Geographical Description of Europe.

Gonzales, Manuel. Voyage to Great Britain, containing an Historical, Geographical, Topographical, Political, and Ecclesiastical Account of England and Scotland.

Story, John. Travels through Sweden, with a Brief Description of all its Provinces.

Muscovy. A Description of Muscovy, containing its Ancient and Modern State, Situation, Extent, Latitude, &c.

Overbury, Sir Thomas. Observations in his Travels upon the State of the Seventeen Provinces, as they stood A.D. 1609.

France and Italy, a Tour in, made by an English Gentleman, 1675.

Davis, William. A True Relation of the Travels and Captivity of, under the Duke of Florence, wherein is truly set down the Manner of his Taking, Time of Slavery, and the Means of Delivery, after Eight Years and Ten Months' Captivity in the Gallies; with a Description of Civita Vecchia, Algier, Tunis, Leghorn, Naples, the River of Amazons, the Islands of Malta and Cyprus.

Ussher, Abp. J. Geographical and Historical Disquisition touching the Asia properly so called, the Lydian Asia (which is the Asia mentioned in the New Testament), the Proconsular Asia, and the Asian Diocese.

Turkey. A General Account of the Turkish Empire.

Blount, Henry. Voyage into the Levant.

Daulphinois, Nicholas N., Lord of Arfeuile. Navigations, Peregrinations, and Voyages made into Turkey.

Cartwright, John. The Preacher's Travels to the Confines of the East Indies, through the Great Countries of Syria, Mesopotamia, Armenia, Media, Hyrcania, and Parthia, with the Author's Return by the way of Persia, Susiana, Assyria, Chaldea, and Arabia; with a Survey of the Kingdom of Persia, a Relation of Sir A. Sherley's Entertainment, and a Description of a Port in the Persian Gulf.

Biddulph, W. Travels of Four Englishmen, and a Preacher, into Africa, Asia, Troy, Bythinia, Thracia, the Black Sea, Syria, Cilicia, Pisidia, Mesopotamia, Damascus, Canaan, Galilee, Samaria, Judea, Palestina, Jerusalem, Jericho, and the Red Sea, in 1600 and 1611.

Churchill, Vol. 7—*continued*.

Dandini, Father Jerom. Voyage to Mount Libanus, wherein is an Account of the Customs and Manners of the Turks; also a Description of Candia, Nicosia, Tripoli, &c.

VOLUME 8.

Baudier, M. History of the Court of the King of China.

Bernardine of Escalanta. Account of the Empire of China, with a Discourse of the Navigation which the Portugueze do make to the Realms and Provinces of the East Parts of the World. Translated by Frampton.

Sa, Pedro de. Description of Siam.

Siam. A Full and True Relation of the Great and Wonderful Revolution in the Kingdom of Siam, in the East Indies; also an Account of the Expulsion of all the Jesuits, &c., of the French Nation out of that Kingdom.

Bernier, F. Voyage to Surat, containing the History of the late Revolution of the Empire of the Great Mogul, with a Letter to Lord Colbert touching the Extent of Indostan, and a Description of Delhi and Agra; together with the Emperor's Voyage to Kachemire in 1644, commonly called the Paradise of the Indies.

Coverte, Capt. Rob. True and almost Incredible Report of an Englishman, that (being cast away in Cambaya, the farthest part of the East Indies) Travelled by Land through many Unknown Kingdoms and Great Cities; with a Description of all those Kingdoms, Cities, and Peoples, and a Discovery of the Great Mogul; to which is prefixed an Account of India Proper.

Bruton, W. News from the East Indies; or, A Voyage to Bengalla, one of the Greatest Kingdoms under the Great Mogul, with the State and Magnificence of the Court of Malcandy, kept by the Nabob, or Vice-King, under the aforesaid Monarch; also their Detestable Religion, Wicked Sacrifices, and Impious Customs.

East Indies. A True Relation of the Unjust, Cruel, and Barbarous Proceedings against the English, at Amboyna, in the East Indies, by the Netherlandish Governor and Council there.

—— A True Declaration of the News that came out of the East Indies, concerning a Conspiracy discovered in the Island of Amboyna, and the Punishment following thereon, in 1624.

—— An Answer unto the Dutch Pamphlet, made in Defence of the Unjust and Barbarous Proceedings against the English at Amboyna by the Hollanders there.

Churchill, Vol. 8—*continued.*

East Indies. A Remonstrance of the Directors of the Netherlands East India Company, in Defence, touching the Bloody Proceeding against English Merchants, executed at Amboyna ; with the Acts of the Process, and Reply of the English East India Company.

Galvano, Ant. Discoveries of the World, from their first Original unto 1555. Corrected, Quoted, and Published in English by R. Hakluyt.

East Indies. Description of a Voyage made by certain Ships of Holland into the East Indies, with their Adventures and Successes, in 1595-97 ; to which is added the Sea Journal of the Hollanders into Java, &c.

Drake, Sir Francis. The World Encompassed : Collected out of the Notes of Mr Francis Fletcher, and Compared with Divers other Notes of others that went in the same Voyage.

Knight, Francis. Relation of Seven Years' Slavery under the Turks of Algier, suffered by an English Captive Merchant ; with a Description of Algier.

Dunton, John. True Journal of the Sallee Fleet, with the Proceedings of the Voyage.

Phelps, Thomas. True Account of the Captivity of, at Machiness, in Barbary, in 1684-85.

Guinea. A True Relation of the Inhuman and Barbarous Murders of Negroes or Moors, committed on Three Englishmen in Old Calabar in Guiney.

Pigafetta, Philippo. Report of the Kingdom of Congo, a Region in Africa, and of the Countries that border round about the same, drawn out of the Writings of Odoardo Lopez.

Froger. Relation of a Voyage made in 1695-97, on the Coasts of Africa, by a Squadron of French Men-of-War, under the Command of M. de Gennes.

Le Maire, Sieur. Voyages of, to the Canary Islands, Cape Verde, Senegal, and Gambia.

Boothby, Richard. A Brief Discovery or Description of the most Famous Island of Madagascar, or St Laurence, in Asia, near unto the East Indies.

Castle, W. A Short Discovery of the Coast and Continent of America, from the Equinoctial Northward, and of the Adjacent Isles ; with Sir Benj. Rudger's Speech, Jan. 1644, concerning America.

King Charles I. : Commission for the Well-governing of our People Inhabiting in Newfoundland, or Trafficking in Bays, Creeks, or Fresh Rivers there.

Geare, Allen. Ebenezer ; or, A Monument of Thankfulness, being a True

Churchill, Vol. 8—*continued.*

Account of the Preservation of Nine Men in a Small Boat, Inclosed within Islands of Ice, about Seventy Leagues from Land, and Continued in Distress Twenty-eight Days; with Considerations of the Trade of Newfoundland.

Nova Francia ; or, The Description of that part of New France, which is one Continent with Virginia, Described in the Voyages made by MM. de Monto, du Pont-Gravé, and de Poutrincourt, into La Cadia, lying to the South-West of Cape Breton.

Warren, George. Description of Surinam, upon the Continent of Guiana, in America.

Clarke, E. D. Travels in Various Countries of Europe, Asia, and Africa. 5 vols. *Maps and plates.* 4°
Part 1. Russia, Tartary, and Turkey. 1810
Part 2. Sect. 1-3. Greece, Egypt, and the Holy Land. 1812-16
Part 3. Sect. 1. Scandinavia. 1819
—— The same. 11 vols. *Portraits, maps, and woodcuts.* 8° 1816-24
Vols. 1 and 2. Russia, Tartary, and Turkey.
Vols. 3-8. Greece, Egypt, and the Holy Land, with a Journey from Constantinople to Vienna, and an Account of the Gold Mines of Transylvania and Hungary.
Vols. 9-11. Scandinavia.
—— Travels in Various Countries of Scandinavia, including Denmark, Sweden, Norway, Lapland, and Finland. 2 vols. *Maps and plates.* 4° 1838

Dalrymple, A. Historical Collection of the several Voyages and Discoveries in the South Pacific Ocean. 2 vols. in 1. *Maps.* 4° 1770-71

CONTENTS.

VOLUME I.

Being chiefly a Literal Translation from the Spanish Writers :—

Account of some Natural Curiosities at Sooloo.
Enquiry into the Formation of Islands.
Of the Salomon Islands.
Magalhane's Voyage, 1520.
Grijalva, Ferdinand, and Alvarado's Voyage, 1537.
Spanish Discoveries before 1595.
Fernandez, Juan. Voyage, 1576.
Mendana de Neyra, Alvaro. Voyage, 1595.
Quiros, P. F. de. Voyage, 1606, with a Relation of a Memorial presented to His Majesty, about the Discovery of the Southern Continent.

Dalrymple, Pacific, Vol. 1—*continued.*

Figueroa, Christoval Suarez. Additions and Elucidations to the Voyage of A. Mendano de Neyra, 1595.

VOLUME 2.

Containing the Dutch Voyages :—

Le Mair, James, and W. Schouten. Voyage, 1616.

Tasman, A. J. Voyage, 1642-43.

Roggewein, Jacob. Voyage, 1722.

Conduct of the Discoverers in the Tracks they made choice of.

Investigation of what may be farther expected in the South Sea.

Vocabulary of Languages in some of the Islands visited by Le Maire and Schouten.

Dalrymple, A. Tracts, from 1764 to 1808. 3 vols. 8°

CONTENTS.

VOLUME I.

An Account of the Discoveries made in the South Pacific Ocean previous to 1764. *Map and plates* 1767

A General View of the East India Company, 1769, with some Observations on the Present State of their Affairs. 1772

A Paper concerning the General Government of India.

The Rights of the East India Company. 1773

An Account of what has passed between the India Directors and A. Dalrymple; intended as an Introduction to a Plan for Extending the Commerce of this Kingdom by an Establishment at Balambangan. 1769

A Plan for Extending the Commerce of this Kingdom, and of the East India Company. *Map* 1769

A Letter to the Proprietors of East India Stock concerning the proposed Supervisors. 1769

Considerations on a Pamphlet entitled "Thoughts on our Acquisitions in the East Indies, particularly respecting Bengal." 1772

A Full and Clear Proof that the Spaniards can have no Claim to Balambangan. 1774

Considerations on the Present State of Affairs between England and America. 1778

Considerations on the East India Bill now depending in Parliament. 1779

State of the East India Company. 1780

Heads of an Agreement between Parliament and the East India Company. 1780

Reflections on the Present State of the East India Company. 1783

A Short Account of the Gentoo Mode of Collecting the Revenues on the Coast of Coromandel. 1783

Dalrymple, Tracts, Vol. 1—*continued.*

Postscript to Mr Dalrymple's Account, being Observations made on a Perusal of it, by Moodoo Kistna. 1785

VOLUME 2.

A Retrospective View of the Ancient System of the East India Company, with a Plan of Regulation. 1784

An Account of the Loss of the "Grosvenor" Indiaman, commanded by Capt. John Coxon, on 4th August 1782 (inferred to have happened between 28° and 29° S.), with a Relation of Events which befel the Survivors. 1785

A Fair State of the Case between the East India Company and the Owners of Ships now in their Service ; with Considerations on Mr Brough's Pamphlet concerning the East India Company's Shipping. 1786

A Serious Admonition to the Public on the Intended Thief-Colony at Botany Bay. 1786

Review of the Contest, concerning four new Regiments graciously offered by His Majesty to be sent to India, on the late Apprehension of War. 1788

A Letter to a Friend on the Test Act, by a Christian Believer, Philanthropist, and North Briton.

The Spanish Pretensions fairly discussed. *Maps* 1790

The Spanish Memorial of 4th June considered. 1790

Parliamentary Reform Improper in the Present State of this Country. 1792

Mr Fox's Letter to his Worthy and Independent Electors of Westminster considered. 1793

Observations on the Copper Coinage wanted for the Circars. 1794

The Poor Man's Friend. 1795

A Fragment on the Indian Trade, written in 1791. 1797

VOLUME 3.

Memorial to the Proprietors of India Stock, 1768.

An Account of what has passed between the India Directors and A. Dalrymple, &c. 1768

Considerations on a Pamphlet, &c. 1772

Thoughts of an Old Man, &c. 1800

Longitude. 1806

Case of A. Dalrymple, late Hydrographer to the Admiralty. 1808

[For Tracts, from 1769 to 1793, *see* Dalrymple in Authors' Catalogue].

Dalrymple, A. Oriental Repertory : Vol. 1. From April 1791 to January 1793 ; Vol. 2. Concluded in 1808. *Maps and plates.* 4° 1793-1808

De la Richarderie—*continued.*

Eyriès, J. B. B. Abrégé des Voyages Modernes depuis 1780 jusqu'à nos jours, contenant ce qu'il y a de plus remarquable, de plus utile et de mieux avéré dans les pays ou les voyageurs ont pénétré; les mœurs des habitans, la religion, les usages, arts et sciences, commerce et manufactures. 14 vols. in 7. 8° *Paris*, 1822-24

Eyriès, Vol. 2—*continued.*

Eyriès, Vol. 6—*continued.*

Billings et Saritchev. Voyage dans le Grand Océan boréal, 1785-94.
Krusenstern. Voyage autour du Monde, 1803-6.
Lisiansky. Voyage autour du Monde, 1803-6.
Langsdorff, G. H. de. Voyage aux îles Aléoutiennes, et à la côte de l'Amérique septentrionale, 1805-8.
Kotzebue. Voyage autour du Monde, 1815-18.

VOLUME 7.

Hooker. Voyage en Islande, 1809.
Henderson, E., D.D. Voyage en Islande, 1814-15.
Hearne. Voyage dans la partie boréale de l'Amerique, 1769-72.
Mackenzie. Voyages dans l'Amérique septentrionale, du Fort Chipiouyan aux côtes du Grand Océan, 1789-93.
Ross. Voyage dans la Mer de Baffin, 1818.

VOLUME 8.

Parry, W. E. Voyage à la mer Glaciale au nord de l'Amérique, 1819-20.
Franklin, Capt. John. Voyage aux côtes de la mer Polaire, fait par terre, à travers l'Amérique septentrionale, 1819-21.
Harmon de Montreal, D. W. Voyage aux côtes nord-ouest de l'Amerique.
Terre de Labrador.
Canada.
États-Unis.

VOLUME 9.

Suite des États Unis d'Amérique.
Lewis et Clarke. Voyage aux sources du Missouri et à l'embouchure de la Columbia dans le Grand Océan, 1804-6.
Pike. Voyage aux sources du Mississippi, 1805-6.
——— Voyage dans l'ouest de la Louisiane, aux sources de l'Arkansa, du Kansès, de la Platte et de la Pierre-Jaune, suivi d'une excursion au Nouveau Mexique, 1805-7.
Brackenbridge. Voyage au Missouri, 1811.
Long, Major E. H. Voyage de Pittsbourg aux Monts Rocailleux.
Robinson, J. H. Voyage à l'Orénoque, 1818-19.
Schmidtmeyer, P. Voyage au Chili, à travers la chaîne des Andes, 1820-21.
Brésil.
Guyane.

VOLUME 10.

Antilles.
Iles Lucayes.
Voyages en Africa. — Sahara.—Naufrage de Saugnier, Follie, Brisson, Padock, Adams, Riley, Cochelet.
Sénégambie.—Iles Saint-Louis et Gorée.

Eyriès, Vol. 10—*continued.*

Galam.
Houghton. Voyage dans l'intérieur de l'Afrique.
Watt et Winterbottom. Voyage à Timbou, 1794.

VOLUME 11.

Park, Mungo. Voyage dans l'interieur de l'Afrique.
Mollien, M. Voyage aux sources du Sénégal et de la Gambie, 1818.
Meredith, H. Description de la Côte d'Or.
Bowdich, M. Voyage dans le pays d'Achanti, 1817.
Hutton, M. Voyage en Achanti, 1820.
Tuckey. Voyage au Zaïre ou fleuve du Congo, 1816.
Barrow, M. Voyages au Cap de Bonne Espérance, 1797.
Truter et Somerville. Voyage au pays des Betjouanas, 1801.
Lichtenstein, M. Voyage au Cap de Bonne Espérance, 1803-6.
Latrobe. Voyage au Cap de Bonne Espérance, 1805.
Campbell, M. Voyages au Cap de Bonne Espérance, 1812-21.

VOLUME 12.

Sumatra. Java. Borneo. Célébes. Mindanao. Soulou.
Camper, M. de Nourquer du. Remarques sur les Philippines, les Moluques, et plusieurs établissemens des Européens dans l'Asie Orientale, 1821-25.
Voyages en Asie. Japon.
Chine. Ambassade des Anglais, 1792 et 1816.

VOLUME 13.

Iles Lieou-Kieou.
Cochin-chine.
Empire Burman. Symes. Cox.
Ceylan. Percival. Boyd. Davy.
Hindoustan.
Forster, G. Voyage à Cachemir et dans l'Afghanistan.

VOLUME 14.

Tibet et Boutan—Bogle. Turner.
Duvaucel, A. Voyage dans le Silhet.
Népal. Kirkpatrick. Hamilton.
Voyages au travers de l'Himalaya et aux sources des rivières de l'Hindoustan. Hardwicke. Webb. Moorcroft. Fraser.
Elphinstone. Voyage dans l'Afghanistan, 1808.
Sindhy.
Beloutchistan — Pottinger. Christie.
Boukharie.
Nazarov, P. Voyage dans le Khokhan, 1813-14.
Mouraviev, N. Voyage en Turcomie et à Khiva.

Eyriès, Vol. 14—*continued.*

Perse—Olivier. Malcolm. Morier. Jaubert. Ker-Porter. Sir W. Gore Ouseley. Drouville. Dupré, &c.
Asie Turque. Syrie et Palestine. Arabie.
Voyages dans l'est et dans le nord de Afrique : Mozambique—Thoman [Thouman or Thomas]. Salt.
Abyssinie. Voyage au Darfour, par Browne, 1793-99.
Egypte. Nubie.
Siouah, Fezzan, et Intérieur de l'Afrique.

Gottfried, Johan Lodewyk. De Aanmerkenswaardigste en alomberoemde Zee- en Landreizen der Portugeezen, Spanjaarden, Engelsen, en allerhande natiën : zoo van Fransen, Italiaanen, Deenen, Hoogh- en Neder-Duitsen als van veele andere Volkeren. Voornaamenlyk ondernomen tot Ondekking van de Oost- en West - Indiën, midsgaders andere verafgelegene Gewesten des Aardryks. 8 vols. *Maps and plates.* Folio *Leyden*, 1727 [*The secondary titles are dated* 1706].

Contents.

[A.] *De doorlugtige Scheeps-togten der Portugyzen na Oost-Indiën.*
VOLUME I.
De alder-eerste Scheeps-togten der Portugyzen, 1419-1490 ; Voyagien van Vasco da Gamma, Pedralvarez Cabral en Joan da Nova, Francisco D'Albuquerque en Lopo Soares, Francisco D'Almeida, Pedro da Nhaya, Tristano d'Acunha, Alfonso d'Albuquerque, Jorge de Mello en Jorge d'Aguilar, Fernando Coutinho, Gonsalo de Sequeira en Garcia de Noronha, Fernando Perez d'Andrade.

VOLUME 2.
Voyagien van Diego Lopez de Sequeira, Duarte de Menezes, Vasco da Gamma, Lopo Vaz de Sampayo, Nuno da Cunha.

[B.] *De gedenkwaardige en alomberoemde Voyagien der Spanjaarden na West-Indiën.*
VOLUME I.
Voyagien van Christoffel Kolumbus, Alonso d'Ojeda, Amerikus Vespútius, Christoffel Guerre, Pero Alonso Nino, Vincent Yanes Pinzon, Diego de Lepe, Peralvarez de Kabral, Rodriguez de Bastidas, Nikolaas de Obando, Diego Mendez de Segura, Bartolemi Fiesco, Franciscus de Porras, Ferdinandes Cortes, Jean Dias de Solis, Sebastiaan D'Ocampo, Jean Ponze de Leon, Diego de Nicueza, Jean de Ezquebel, Vasco Nunes de Balboa, Diego Velasques, Pamphilio de Narvaes, Vasco Nunez, Pedrarias Davila, Franciscus Hernandez de Cordua, Jean de Gryalva.

Gottfried [B.]—*continued.*
VOLUME 2.
Voyagien van Ferdinandes Cortes, Alonso d'Ojeda, Ferdinandes Magelanes, Gonzale d'Ocampo, Panfilio de Narvaez, Lucas Vasquez d'Ayllon, Gil Gonzales Davila, Stephan Gomez, Franciscus de Garay, Pedro d'Alvarado, Diego de Godoy, Garcia Jofre de Loyasa, Rodrique de Bastidas, P. Alvares Palomino, Sebastiaan Gaboto, Diego Garcia.

[C.] *De wijd-bersemde Voyagien na Oost en West-Indiën mitsgaders andere Gedeeltens des Werelds gedaan door de Engelsen.*
VOLUME I.
Voyagien van Anthony Jenkinson, Martin Frobisher, Franciscus Draak, Joan Haukins, Pieter Carder, Johan Newberie, Petro Sarmiento, Ralph Fitch, Georg, Graf van Cumberland, Thomas Candisch, Andries Battel, Antoni Knivet, Ellis, Hendrik May, Richard Moore, Johan Smith, Walther Ralegh, Benjamin Wood, Johan Davis, William Adams, Antony Sherley, Johan Mildenhal, Johan Cartwright, James Lancaster, David Middleton, Georg Weymouth, Bartholomeus Gosnol, Martin Pringe, Bartholomeus Gilbert, Hendrik Middelton, Charles Leig, Johan Saris, Willem Keeling, Roberte Coverte, William Hawkins, William Finch.
VOLUME 2.
Voyagien van Robert Harcourt, Alexander Sharpey en Richard Rowles, David Middleton, Hendrik Middelton, Nicolaas Dounton, Antony Hippon, Pieter Williamson Floris, Joan Saris, Edmund Marlow, Thomas Best, Ralph Wilson, Samuel Castelton, Christoffel Nieuwpoort, Nicolaas Dounton, Johan Milward, Johan Smith, Thomas Coryat, Walter Peyton, Edward Terry, Roger Hawes, Alexander Childe, Thomas Spurway, Martin Pring, Edward Heynes, William Hoare, William Methold, Andrew Schilling, Richard Jobson, Anthony Chester, Hendrik Blunt, T. S. (een Engels Koopman), Francoys Brooks, Jonathan Dickenson.

[D.] *De aanmerkenswaardige Voyagien door Francoisen, Italiaanen, Deenen, Hoogduytsen en andere Vreemde Volkeren gedaan na Oost- en West-Indiën, mitsgaders door andere Gewesten.*
VOLUME I.
Voyagien van Johan du Plan Carpin, Broeder Ascelin, Willem de Rubruquis, Joseph den Indiaan, Johan de Verrazano, Franciscus Pizarrus, and Didacus Almagrus, Nicolaas Clenard, Pedro de Mendosa, Ulrich Schmidt, Ferdinand de Soto, Johan de Castro, Hieronymus Benzo, Jan Staden, Johannes Lerius,

Gottfried [D], Vol. 1—*continued.*
Johannes Pontius, Johan Ribald, Renatus de Laudonniere, Dominicus Gourgues, Cæsar Frederik, Dithmar Bleikenius, Leendert Rouwulf.

VOLUME 2.

Voyagien van Eduard Lopez, Caspar Balby, Michiel Heberer, Joseph d'Acosta, Benedictus Goes, Nicolaus Schmidt, Antonio Fernandez, Evesko Petelin, Jan de Luca, &c., Hieronymus Lobo, Manuel d'Almeida, Saedor Jacowits Boicoof, Mouette, Gallonye, Marqnette en Joliet, Otho Fridrich van der Greuben, Jacob Jansz de Roy.

Hacke, William. A Collection of Original Voyages, containing—1, Captain Cowley's Voyage round the Globe ; 2, Captain Sharp's Journey over the Isthmus of Darien, and Expedition into the South Seas, written by himself ; 3, Captain Woods' Voyage through the Streights of Magellan ; 4, Mr Roberts's Adventures among the Corsairs of the Levant, his Account of their way of living, Description of the Archipelago Islands, Taking of Scio, &c. *Maps.* 12° 1699

Hakluyt, Richard. The Principall Navigations, Voiages, and Discoveries of the English Nation made by Sea or ouer Land to the most remote and farthest distant quarters of the Earth at any time within the compasse of these 1500 yeeres ; Deuided into three seuerall parts, according to the position of the Regions to which they were directed. 4° 1589
—— Principal Navigations, Voyages, Traffiques, and Discoveries of the English Nation. Blackletter. Vol. 2. Folio 1599
—— The Principal Navigations, Voyages, Traffiqves, and Discoveries of the English Nation, made by Sea or ouerland, to the remote and farthest distant quarters of the Earth, at any time within the compasse of these 1600 yeres ; Diuided into three seuerall Volumes, &c. 3 vols. in 2. Small folio 1599-1600
—— The Principal Navigations, Voyages, Traffiques, and Discoveries of the English Nation, made by Sea or Overland, to the remote and farthest distant quarters of the Earth, at any time within the compasse of these 1600 yeres, divided into severall volumes, according to the positions of the Regions, whereunto they were directed ; with additions. 5 vols. Folio 1809

CONTENTS.

[*As in the* 1809 *edition, omitting the illustrative notes, documents, &c., interspersed.*]

VOLUME I.

Arthur, King. Voyage to Island, and the most North-Eastern Parts of Europe, 517.

2 M

Hakluyt, Vol. 1—*continued.*
Malgo, King. Voyage to Island, Gotland, Orkney, Denmark, and Norway, 580.
Edwin, the Saxon King of Northumberland. Conquest of the Isles of Anglesey and Man, 624.
Bertus. Voyage into Ireland, 684.
Octher. Voyage to the North Parts beyond Norway, about 890.
—— Second Voyage, into the Sound of Denmarke.
Wolstans. Navigation into the East Sea, or the Sound of Denmarke.
Edgar, King. Voyage with 4000 shippes round about his large Monarchie, 973.
Edmund and Edward, the Sonnes of King Edmund Ironside. Voyage into Hungary, 1017.
The Marriage of the Daughter of Harald unto Ieruslaus Duke of Russia in his owne Countrey, 1067.
Voyage of a certaine Englishman into Tartaria, and from thence into Poland and Hungary, 1243.
Carpini, Frier John de Plano. Long and Wonderfull Voyage, 1246.
Rubricis, Frier W. de. Journall, 1253.
Nicolaus de Linna, a Franciscan Frier. Voyage to all the Regions situate under the North Pole, 1360.
Henry IV., King. Voyage into Prussia and Letto, 1390.
Thomas of Woodstock, Duke of Glocester. Voyage into Prussia, 1391.
Willoughby, Sir Hugh. Voyage, wherein he unfortunately perished at Arzina Reca in Lapland, 1553.
Chanceller, Richard, Pilote Major, the first Discoverer by Sea of the Kingdome of Moscovia, Voyage of, 1553.
Burrough, Stephen. Voyage towards the River of Ob, intending the Discovery of the North-East Passage, 1556.
Johnson, R. Landing among the Samoeds, 1556.
Burrough, S. Voyage from Colmogro in Russia to Wardhouse, in search of certain English Ships not heard of the yeere before, 1557.
Jenkinson, Anthony. Voyage into Russia, wherein Osep Napea, first Ambassador from the Emperour of Moscovia to Queene Mary, was transported into his Countrey, 1557.
—— Voyage from the City of Mosco in Russia to Boghar in Bactria, 1558.
—— Voyage through Russia, and over the Caspian Sea into Persia, 1561.
Alcock, T., G. Wrenne, and R. Cheyney. Voyage into Persia, 1563.
Johnson, R., A. Kitchin, and A. Edwards. Voyage into Persia, 1565.

Hakluyt, Vol. 2—*continued.*

Rainulph Glanville, Earle of Chester. Voyage to the Holy Land, and to Damiata in Ægypt, 1218.

Petrus de Rupibus, Bp. of Winchester. Voyage to Jerusalem, 1231.

The honourable Voyage of Richard, Earle of Cornwall, with William Long-espee, Earl of Salisburie, &c., into Syria, 1240.

Voyage of William Long-espee into Ægypt with Lewis, the French King, 1248.

Edward, Prince. Voyage into Syria, 1270.

Turneham, Robert. Voyage into Syria, 1270.

Mandevil, Sir John. Voyage from England to Judea, and from thence to India, China, Tartarie, and as farre as 33 deg. to the South of the Equinoctiall, from 1322 to 1355.

Odoricus, Frier Beatus. Voyage to Asia Minor, Armenia, Chaldæa, Persia, India, China, and other remote parts, &c., about 1325.

Gurney, Matthew. Voyage against the Moores of Alger to Barbary, and Spaine.

Henry IV. Voyage, with an Armie of Englishmen, to Tunis in Barbary.

Hawkwood, John. Travailes and Memorable Victories, in diverse places of Italy.

Lord John of Holland, Earle of Huntington. Voyage to Jerusalem, and S. Katherins Mount, 1394.

Mowhrey, Thomas Lord, Duke of Norfolk. Voyage to Jerusalem, 1399.

Voyage of the Bishop of Winchester to Jerusalem, 1417.

Voyage intended by Henry IV. to the Holy Land, against the Saracens and Infidels, 1413.

Voyage made with two ships, the "Holy Crosse" and the "Mathew Gunson," to the Isles of Candia and Chio, about 1534.

Another Vovage unto Candia and Chio, made by the "Matthew Gunson," 1535.

Head, Peter. Voyage to Tunis, 1538.

Chaloner, Sir Thomas. Voyage to Algier, 1541.

Bodenham, Roger. Voyage to Candia and Chio, 1550.

Lok, John. Voyage to Jerusalem, 1553.

Foxe, John. Voyage to the Streit of Gibraltar, 1563, and his worthy enterprise in delivering 266 Christians from the Captivitie of the Turkes at Alexandria, 1577.

Aldersey, Laurence. Voyage to the Cities of Jerusalem and Tripolis, 1581.

Hakluyt, Vol. 2—*continued.*

Voyage of the "Susan" to Constantinople ; wherein M. W. Hareborne was sent first Ambassador unto Zuldan Murad Can, the Great Turke, 1582.

Voyage of a Ship, called "The Jesus," to Tripolis in Barbary, 1583.

Austel, H. Voyage by Venice to Ragusa, and thence overland to Constantinople; and through Moldavia, Polonia, Silesia, and Germany into England, 1586.

Voyage of Master Cesar Frederick into the East India and beyonde the Indies, 1563.

Fitch, Ralph. The long, dangerous, and memorable Voyage of, by the way of Tripolis in Syria, to Ormuz, Goa in the East Indies, Cambaia, the River Ganges, Bengala, Bacola, Chonderi, Pegu, Siam, &c., begunne in 1583 and ended in 1591.

Eldred, John. Voyage to Tripolis in Syria by sea, and from thence by land and river to Babylon and Balsara, 1583.

Evesham, John. Voyage by sea into Ægypt, 1586.

Aldersey, L. Voyage to the Cities of Alexandria and Cairo in Ægypt, 1586.

Voyage of five Marchant Ships of London into Turkie ; and their valiant Fight in their returne with 11 Gallies and two Frigats of the King of Spaine, at Pantalarea, within the Streits of Gibraltar, 1586.

Hareborne, W. Voyage overland from Constantinople to London, 1588.

Wrag, R. Description of a Voyage to Constantinople and Syria, 1593-95 ; wherein is shewed the manner of delivering the Second Present by M. Ed. Barton, Her Majestie's Ambassadour, to Sultan Murad Can, the Emperour of Turkie.

Voyages made without the Straight of Gibraltar to the South and South-East Quarters of the World, wherein also mention is made of certaine Sea-fights, and other Memorable Acts performed by the English Nation :—

Voyage of Macham, the First Discoverer of the Isle of Madera, 1344.

First Two Voyages to Barbary, 1551-52.

Windam, T. Voyage to Guinea and Benin, 1553.

Lok, J. Voyage to Guinea, 1554.

Towrson, W. Three Voyages to Guinea, the Castle of Mina, and the River Sestos, 1555-57.

Voyage made to Guinea at the charges of Sir W. Gerard, Sir W. Chester, &c., 1562.

Baker, Rt. Two Voyages to Guinea, 1562-63.

Hakluyt, Vol. 2—*continued.*

The success of another Voyage to Guinea, at the direction of Sir W. Gerard and others, 1564.

Fenner, Geo. Voyage to Guinea and the Isles of Capo Verde, 1566.

Hogan, Edm. Voyage and Ambassage to the Emperour of Marocco, 1577.

Stukeley, T. Voyage into Barbary, 1578.

Stevens, T. Voyage about the Cape of Buona Esperanza unto Goa, in the East India, 1579.

Lancaster, J. Memorable Voyage about the Cape of Buona Esperanza, along the Easterne Coast of Africa, beyond Cape Comori, as far as the maine land of Malacca, and thence home again, begun 1591.

Roberts, H. Voyage and Ambassage to Mully Hamet, Emperor of Marocco, 1585.

Evesham, John. Voyage of two of Sir W. Raleghs pinases to the Azores; which tooke the Governour of the Isle of S. Michael, and Pedro Sarmiento, Governour of the Streights of Magellan, in 1586.

Drake, Sir Francis. Voyage to Cadiz, and the Memorable Exploits and Services performed by him as well there as at diverse other places upon the Coast of Spaine and Portugale, and his taking the great East Indian Carak, called the "Sant Philip," neere the Isle of S. Michael, 1587.

Welsh, James. Two Voyages to Benin, beyond the Countrey of Guinea, in Africa, 1588-90.

Voyage to Spaine and Portugale, written (as it is thought) by Colonel Anthonie Wingfield, 1589.

Cumberland, Earle of. Voyage to the Azores, 1589.

Fight performed by ten marchants Ships of London against 12 Spanish Gallies in the Streit of Gibraltar, 1590.

The Valiant Fight performed in the Streit of Gibraltar by the "Centurion" of London against five Spanish Gallies, 1591.

True Report of the Fight about the Isles of the Azores between H.M.S. the "Revenge," under Sir Richard Grinvile, and an Armada of the King of Spaine, 1591.

Voyage of certaine Ships of London to the Coast of Spaine and the Azores, 1591. Reported by Robert Flick.

VOLUME 3.

Relation concerning the Estate of the Island and Castle of Arguin, and touching the rich and secret Trade from the inland of Africa thither, written in 1491.

Hakluyt, Vol. 3—*continued.*

Rainolds, R., and T. Dassell. Voyage to the Rivers Senega and Gambra, neere the Coast of Guinea, 1591.

Two Briefe Relations concerning the Cities and Provinces of Tombuto and Gago, and the Conquest by the King of Marocco, written in 1594.

White, T. The taking of two Spanish Ships, laden with Quicksilver and with the Pope's Bulles, bound for the West Indies, 1592.

The taking of the Mightie and Rich Carak called the "Madre de Dios," and of the "Santa Clara," a biskaine of 600 tunnes, as likewise the firing of another Great Carak called the "Santa Cruz," 1592.

The firing and sinking of the Stout and Warlike Carak called the "Cinquo Chaguas," 1592.

Report of the casting away of the Ship "Tobie," neere Cape Espartel, on the Coast of Barbary, 1593.

Voyages to America.

The most ancient Voyage and Discovery of the West Indies, performed by Madoc, the sonne of Guined, Prince of North Wales, 1170.

Columbus, Christopher. Offer of the Discovery of the West Indies to King Henry VII., with the King's acceptance of the said offer.

Voyages undertaken for the Finding of a North-West Passage to the North parts of America, to Meta Incognita, and the backeside of Groenland, as farre as 72 deg. 12 min. :—

Sebastian Cabota. Voyage to the North part of America, for the Discovery of a North-West Passages as far as 58 deg. of lat., and from thence back againe all along the Coast till he fell with some part of Florida, 1497.

A Briefe Extract concerning the Discovery of Newfoundland.

Gilbert, Sir Humfrey. Discourse to Prove a Passage by the North-West to Cataya and the East Indies.

Frobisher, M. Voyages of Discovery to the West and North-West, in Search for a Passage to China, 1576-78.

A Generall and Briefe Description of the Country and Condition of the People which are found in Meta Incognita.

Davis, John. Voyages for the Discovery of a North-West Passage, 1585-86.

Voyage and Course of which the Ships "Sunshine" and "Northstarre" held, after M. John Davis had sent them from him to Discover a Passage betweene Groenland and Iseland, 1587.

Hakluyt, Vol. 3—*continued.*

Zeno, Nicholas and Anthony. Voyage to the Yles of Frisland, Island, Engronland, Estotiland, Drogeo, and Icaria, begun 1380.

Voyages made to Newfoundland, to the Isles of Ramea, and the Isle of Assumption, otherwise called Natiscotec, as also the Coasts of Cape Briton and Arambec :—

Voyage of two Ships, whereof one was called the " Dominus vobiscum," for the Discovery of the North Parts, 1527.

Hore, M. Voyage to Newfoundland and Cape Briton, in 1536.

Gilbert, Sir Humfrey. Voyage to Newfoundland, 1583.

The First Discovery of the Isle of Ramea, made by ——, in the Ship " Bonaventure," 1591.

Fisher, R. Voyage of the Ship " Marigold " unto Cape Briton, and beyond, to latitude 44 deg. and a halfe, 1593.

Drake, Geo. Voyage to the Isle of Ramea, 1593.

Voyage of the " Grace" of Bristoll up the Gulfe of S. Laurence to the North-West of Newfoundland, as far as the Isle of Assumption or Natiscotec, 1594.

Leigh, C. Voyage to Cape Briton and the Isle of Ramea, 1597.

Voyages made for the Discovery of the Gulfe of Saint Laurence, to the West of Newfoundland, and from thence up the River of Canada to Hochelaga, Saguenay, and other places :—

Cartier, Jacques. Voyages to Newfoundland, the Gulfe of Saint Laurence and the Grand Bay, up the River of Canada to Hochelaga and Saguenay, 1534, 1540.

Roche, John Francis de la. Voyage with three Ships to the Countries of Canada, Hochelaga, and Saguenay, 1542.

Voyages and Navigations of the English to Virginia, and of the severall Discoveries thereof, chiefly at the charges of Sir Walter Ralegh :—

First Voyage, made to the Coast of Virginia, by Philip Amadas and A. Barlow, 1584.

Second Voyage, made by Sir R. Grinvile, 1585, at what time the First Colonie was there left under M. Ralfe Lane.

Third Voyage, made in 1586, for the Reliefe of the Colonie.

Fourth Voyage, made in 1587, wherein was transported the Second Colonie.

Fifth Voyage, made by John White in 1590.

Hakluyt, Vol. 3—*continued.*

Voyages to the Coast and Inland of Florida :—

Verazzono, John de, a Florentine. Voyage to the Coast of Florida, sailing from thence northerly to the latitude of 50 deg., 1524.

Ribault, John. Voyages to Florida, 1562 and 1565.

Laudonniere, Capt. René. Voyage to Florida, 1564.

Gourgues, Capt. Dominique. Voyage to Florida, 1567.

Description of the West Indies in general, but more particularly of Florida.

Voyages made from Nueva Galicia and Nueva Biscaya, in New Spaine, to New Mexico, Cibola, and Quivira :—

Marco de Nica, Friar. Voyage from the town of S. Michael in Culiacan, to the Kingdome of Ceuola, or Cibola, situate about 30 deg. of latitude to the North of Nueva Espanna, 1539.

Vasquez de Coronado, Francis. Voyage from Nueva Galicia to Cibola, Acuco, Tiguex, Quivira, and to the Westerne Ocean, 1540.

Ruis, Frier Augustin. Voyage to the 15 Provinces of New Mexico, 1581.

Espejo, Ant. de. Voyage from the Valley of S. Bartholomew, in Nueva Galicia, to New Mexico, 1582.

Voyages made for the discovery of the Gulf of California, &c.:—

Ulloa, Francisco de. Voyage by the Coasts of Nueva Galicia, and Culiacan, into the Gulfe of California, called El mar vermejo, as also on the backside of Cape California, as far as 30 deg., 1539.

Alarchon, Fernando. Voyage and Discovery, to the bottome of the Gulfe of California, and 85 leagues up the River Buena Guia, 1540.

Drake, Sir Francis. Voyage and Course held from the haven of Guatulco, on the backside of Nueva Espanna, to the North-West of California, as far as 43 deg., and backe again to 38 deg., where he entrenched himselfe on land, called the Countrey Nova Albion, and tooke possession on behalfe of Her Majestie.

Gualle, Francis. Voyage from the haven of Acapulco in New Spaine, to the Islands of the Luçones, or the Philippinas, the haven of Manilla, and to Macao, in China ; and from Macao by the Lequeos, the Isles of Japan, and by the North-West part of America in 37½ deg. backe againe to Acapulco, 1582-84.

Hakluyt, Vol. 3—*continued.*

*Voyages to Mexico and to all the Prin-
cipal Provinces thorowout the Great
and Large Kingdome of New Spaine,
even as farre as Nicaragua and
Panama, and from thence to Peru,
&c. : —*

Tomson, R.   Voyage into New Spaine,
1555.

Bodenham, Roger.   Voyage to Sant
Juan de Ullua, in the Bay of Mexico,
and to the City of Mexico, 1564.

Chilton, John.   Voyage to all the principall parts of Nueva Espanna, and to
divers places in Perú, 1568.

Hawks, H.   Voyage to Nueva Espanna,
in which countre he travelled for five
yeres, 1572.

Philips, Miles.   Voyage, 1568, a little to
the North of Panuco, from whence he
travelled to Mexico, and afterward to
sundry other places.

Hortop, Job.   Travels to the North of
Panuco, 1586.

Relation of the Haven of Tecuanapa, a
most convenient Place for Building
Ships, situate upon the South Sea,
not farre from Nicaragua.

Pert, Sir Thomas, and Sebastian Cabot.
Voyage to Brasil, Santa Domingo, and
Sant Juan de Puerto Rico, 1516.

Tison, Thomas.   Voyage to the West
Indies, before 1526.

Hawkins, Sir John.   Voyages to the
West Indies, the Coast of Guinie, the
Isle of Dominica, the Coast of Tierra
Firma, Nueva Espanna, the Cape of
S. Anton, upon the West end of Cuba,
and thorow the Chanel of Bahama,
1562-68.

VOLUME 4.

Drake, Sir Francis.   Voyages to Nombre
de Dios and Dariene, about 1572.

Oxnam, J.   Voyage to the West India,
and over the Streight of Dariene into
the South Sea, 1575.

Barker, And.   Voyage to the Coast of
Tierra Firma, and the Bay of the
Honduras, in the West Indies, 1576.

Drake, Sir Francis.   Expedition to the
West Indies, wherein were taken the
Cities of Saint Jago, S. Dominigo,
Cartagena, with the Fort and Towne
of S. Augustin in Florida, 1585-86.

Michelson, W., and W. Macc.   Voyage
to the Bay of Mexico, 1589.

Carey, Sir George.   Relation of a
Memorable Fight, made the 13th June
1591, against certain Spanish Ships
and Gallies in the West Indies.

Newport, Chr.   Voyage to the Isles of
Dominica, S. Juan de Puerto Rico,
Hispaniola, and to the Bay of the
Honduras, 1591.

Hakluyt, Vol. 4—*continued.*

King, Captain W.   Voyage to the Bay
of Mexico, 1592.

May, Henry.   Voyage to the East
Indies, who in his return homeward
by the West Indies, suffered shipwracke upon the Isle of Bermuda,
1591-93.

Duddeley, Sir Robert.   Voyage to the
Isle of Trinidad and the Coast of
Paria ; with his returne homeward by
the Isles of Granata, Santa Cruz,
Sant Juan de Puerto Rico, Mona,
Zacheo, the sholdes called Abreojos,
and the Isle of Bermuda, 1594-95.

Preston, Sir Amias.   Voyage to the
West Indies, 1595.

Drake, Sir Francis, and Sir John Hawkins.
Last Voyage to the Islands and Maine
of the West Indies, 1595, in which
Voyage both died.

Sherley, Sir Antony.   Voyage to S.
Jago, Dominica, Margarita, along the
Coast of Tierra Firma, to the Isle of
Jamaica, the Bay of the Honduras, thirty
leagues up Rio Dolce, and Newfound-
land, 1596.

Parker, W.   Voyage to Margarita,
Jamaica, Truxillo, Puerto de Cavallos,
&c., with his surprize of Campeche,
the chief town of Jucatan, 1596-97.

*Voyages made for the Discovery of the
Empire of Guiana :—*

Ralegh, Sir Walter.   Voyage, 1595.

*Voyages to the Coast of Brasills, &c.,
and the River of Plate :—*

Keymis, L.   The Second Voyage, 1596.

Masham, T.   Account of the Third
Voyage in the " Wat," begun 1596.

Hawkins,W.   Voyages to Brasil,1530-32.

Reniger, R., and T. Borey.   Voyage to
Brasil, 1540.

Pudsey.   Voyage to Baya, in Brasil, 1542.

Hare, S.   Voyage to Brasil, 1580.

Lancaster, James.   Voyage to the Towne
of Fernambuck in Brasil, 1594.

Voyage of two Englishmen to the River
Plate, 1527.

Drake, John.   Voyage up the River
Plate, 1582.

A Ruttier which declareth the situation
of the Coast of Brasil, from the Isle
of Santa Catelina unto the mouth of
the River of Plate, and all along up
within the said River, as farre as it is
navigable with small barkes.

*Voyages to the Streights of Magellan,
the South Sea along the Coasts of
Chili, Peru, Nicaragua, and Nueva
Galicia, to the Headland of California, and to the North-West as far
as 43 deg., likewise to Isles of the Ladrones, the Philippinas, the Malucos,
and the Javas; and from thence by*

Hakluyt, Vol. 4—*continued.*

the Cape of Buena Esperanza, and the Isle of S. Helena, the whole Globe being circompassed :—

Drake, Sir Francis. Voyage into the South Sea, and about the Globe of the whole Earth, 1577.

Voyage of Nunno de Silva, a Portugal Pilot, taken by Sir Francis Drake at the Isles of Cabo Verde, and caried along with him as far as the Haven of Guatulco upon the Coaste of New Spaine, with his Confession to the Viceroy of Mexico.

Winter, John. Voyage into the South Sea by the Streight of Magellan, 1577.

Fenton, Edw., and L. Ward. Voyage to the Coast of Brasil, as far as 33 deg. South Latitude, 1582.

Withrington, and Chr. Lister. Voyage to South Latitude of 44 deg., 1586.

Çandish, T. Voyages into the South Sea, and so round the circumference of the whole Earth, 1586-91.

Voyage of the " Delight," a Ship of Bristol, to the Streights of Magellan, 1589.

Supplement.

Galvano's Discoveries of the World, from the first original unto 1555, corrected and published in English by R. Hakluyt.

Davis, J. The Worldes Hydrographical Description.

Bertrandon de la Brocquière. Voyage d'Outremer et Retour de Jérusalem en France par la Voie de Terre, pendant 1432-33.

Vertomannus, Lewes. Navigation and Voyages to the Regions of Arabia, Egypte, Persia, Syria, Ethiopia, and East India, both within and without the River of Ganges, in 1503.

CONTENTS OF VOL. 5.

Voyage made by certaine Ships of Holland into the East Indies, 1595-97.

The Prosperous and Speedy Voyage to Java in the East Indies, performed by eight Ships of Amsterdam, from Texell, in Holland, whereof four went forward from Java for the Moluccas, 1598-99.

Bruton, W. Newes from the East Indies, or a Voyage to Bengalla, one of the greatest Kingdoms under the Great Mogull, with their detestable Religion, mad and foppish Rites, wicked Sacrifices, and impious Customes, 1638.

The Fardle of Facions, conteining the Aunciente Maners, Customes, and Lawes of the Peoples enhabiting the two partes of the Earth, called Affricke and Asie, 1555.

Hakluyt, Vol. 5—*continued.*

The Conquest of the Grand Canaries, by 73 Saile of Shippes, sent forth at the Command of the States Generall to the Coast of Spanie and the Canarie Isles, 1599.

Hakluyt, R. Historie of the West Indies, containing the Actes and Adventures of the Spaniards, which have Conquered and Peopled those Countries, translated from the Latin by M. Lok.

Virginia Richly Valued, by the Description of the Maine Land of Florida, her next Neighbour, translated out of the Portuguese by Hakluyt, 1609.

Jourdan, Sil. Discovery of the Barmudas, otherwise called the Isle of Divels; by Sir T. Gates, Sir G. Sommers, and Captain Newport, 1610.

True Coppie of a Discourse written by a Gentleman, employed in the late Voyage of Spaine and Portingale, 1589.

The Omissions of Cales Voyage, Stated and Discussed by the Earl of Essex.

Hakluyt Society Publications—

VOLUME 1.

Hawkins, Sir Richard, Knight. Observations in his Voyage into the South-Sea, 1593. Reprinted from the edition of 1622. Edited by Capt. C. R. Drinkwater Bethune. 8°   1847

VOLUME 2.

Columbus, Christopher. Select Letters, with other Original Documents, relating to his Four Voyages to the New World. Translated and edited by R. H. Major. 8°   1847

VOLUME 3.

Ralegh, Sir W., Knight. The Discovery of the Large, Rich, and Beautiful Empire of Guiana, with a Relation of the great and golden City of Manoa (which the Spaniards call El Dorado), &c., performed in 1595. Reprinted from the edition of 1596, with some Unpublished Documents relative to that Country. Edited, with Notes and a Biographical Memoir, by Sir R. H. Schomburgk. *Map.* 8°   1848

VOLUME 4.

Drake, Sir Francis. His Voyage, 1595, by Thomas Maynarde, together with the Spanish Account of Drake's Attack on Puerto Rico. Edited from the Original Manuscripts by W. D. Cooley. 8°   1849

VOLUME 5.

Rundall, Thomas. Narratives of Voyages towards the North-West in search of a Passage to Cathay and India, 1496 to 1631 ; with Selections from the

Hakluyt Soc. Publ., Vol. 5—*contd.*
early Records of the Hon. E. I. Company, and from MSS. in the British Museum. *Maps.* 8°   1849
Cabota, Sebastian. Voyage, 1496.
Frobisher, Sir Martin. Voyages, 1576-81.
Davis, John. Voyages, 1585-87.
Waymouth, Capt. George. Voyage, 1602.
Knight, John. Voyage, 1606.
Hudson, Henry. Voyage, 1610.
Button, Sir Thomas. Voyage, 1612.
Hall, James. Voyage, 1612.
Bylot and Baffin. Voyage, 1615-16.
Hawkridge, Capt. Voyage, 1619.
Fox, Capt. Luke. Voyage, 1631.
James, Capt. Voyage, 1631.

VOLUME 6.
Strachey, William. The Historie of Travaile into Virginia Britannia; expressing the Cosmographie and Commodities of the Country, together with the Manners and Customs of the People. Edited from the Original MS. by R. H. Major. 8°   1849

VOLUME 7.
Hakluyt, Richard. Divers Voyages touching the Discovery of America and the Islands adjacent. Edited, with Notes and an Introduction, by J. Winter Jones. *Maps and facsimile.* 8°   1850
A Verie Late and Great Probabilitie of a Passage by the N.W. Part of America in 58 deg. of N. latitude.
Fabian, R. Note of S. Cabotes Voyage of Discoverie, 1498.
Thorne, R. Declaration of the Indies and Landes Discovered and Subdued unto the Emperour and King of Portugale.
—— Information of the Parts of the World Discovered by the Emperour Charles and the King of Portugale, and also of the Way to the Moluccaes by the North. 1527.
Verarzanus, John. Relation of the Lande by him Discovered. [Morum Bega.] 1524.
Ribault, Capt. J. True and Last Discoverie of Florida. 1562.

VOLUME 8.
Rundall, Thomas. Memorials of the Empire of Japon in the 16th and 17th Centuries, with Notes. *Map and facsimiles.* 8°   1850
Description of the Empire in the 16th Century.
Adams, William. Letters of, 1611-17.

VOLUME 9.
Soto, Don Fernando de. The Discovery and Conquest of Florida by, and 600 Spaniards his Followers; written by

Hakluyt Soc. Publ., Vol. 9—*contd.*
Gentleman of Elvas, and translated by R. Hakluyt. Reprinted from the edition of 1611. Edited, with Notes and Introduction, and a Translation of a Narrative of the Expedition by Luis H. de Biedma, Factor of the same, by W. B. Rye. *Map.* 8°   1851

VOLUMES 10 and 11.
Herberstein, Baron Sigismund von. Notes upon Russia : being a Translation of the Earliest Account of that Country, entitled Rerum Moscoviticarum Commentarii. Translated and edited, with Notes and an Introduction, by R. H. Major. 2 vols. *Maps and portraits.* 8°   1851-52

VOLUME 12.
Coats, Capt. W. Geography of Hudson's Bay: being the Remarks of, in many Voyages to that Locality between 1727-1751 ; with an Appendix containing Extracts from the Log of Capt. Middleton on his Voyage for the Discovery of the North-West Passage in 1741-42. Edited by John Barrow. 8°   1852

VOLUME 13.
Veer, Gerrit de. True Description of Three Voyages by the North-east towards Cathay and China, undertaken by the Dutch in 1594-96 ; with their Discovery of Spitzbergen, their Residence of Ten Months in Novaya Zemlya, and their Safe Return in Open Boats. Translated by W. Philip, 1609. Edited by C. T. Beke. *Maps and plates.* 8°   1853

VOLUMES 14 and 15.
Mendoza, Padre Juan Gonzalez de. History of the Great and Mighty Kingdom of China, and the Situation thereof. Reprinted from the Early Translation of R. Parke. Edited by Sir George T. Staunton, Bart., with an Introduction by R. H. Major. 2 vols. 8°   1853

VOLUME 16.
Drake, Sir Francis. The World Encompassed ; being his next Voyage to that to Nombre de Dios. Collated with an unpublished Manuscript of Francis Fletcher, with Appendices illustrative of the same Voyage, and Introduction, by W. S. W. Vaux. 8°   1854

VOLUME 17.
D'Orléans, Père Pierre Joseph. History of the Two Tartar Conquerors of China, including the Two Journeys into Tartary of Father Ferdinand Verbiest, in the Suite of the Emperor Kang-Hi ; to which is added Father Pereira's Journey into Tartary in the Suite of the same Emperor, from the Dutch of N. Witsen.

Hakluyt Soc. Publ., Vol. 17—*contd.*
Translated and edited by the Earl of
Ellesmere ; with an Introduction by R.
H. Major. 8°   1854

VOLUME 18.

Collection of Documents on Spitsbergen
and Greenland. Edited, with Notes, by
Adam White. *Maps and plates.* 8°
                                      1855
Marten, F. Voyage into Spitzbergen
and Greenland, with some Account
of the Weather, 1671.
Peyrère, Isaac de la. Histoire du
Groenland, 1663. Translated.
Pellham, Edward. God's Power and
Providence shewed in the Miraculous
Preservation and Deliverance of
Eight Englishmen, in Green-land,
nine moneths and twelve dayes,
anno 1630.

VOLUME 19.

Middleton, Sir Henry. Voyage to Bantam and the Maluco Islands. From
the edition of 1606. Annotated and
edited by Bolton Corney. *Maps and
plates.* 8   1855

VOLUME 20.

Russia at the Close of the Sixteenth Century. Edited by E. A. Bond. 8° 1856
Fletcher, Giles. Treatise "Of the
Russe Common Wealth."
Horsey, Sir Jerome. Travels ; now
for the first time printed entire from
his MS.

VOLUME 21.

Benzoni, Girolamo. History of the New
World, showing his Travels in Ame-
rica, from 1541 to 1556 ; with some
Particulars of the Island of Canary.
Translated and edited by Rear-Admiral
W. H. Smyth. *Woodcuts.* 8°   1857

VOLUME 22.

India in the Fifteenth Century : being a
Collection of Narratives of Voyages to
India in the Century preceding the Por-
tuguese Discovery of the Cape of Good
Hope, from Latin, Persian, Russian, and
Italian sources, translated into English.
Edited, with an Introduction, by R. H.
Major. 8°   1857
Abd-er-Razzak. Narrative of my Voy-
age into Hindoostan, 1442.
Conti, Nicolò. Travels in the East in
the early part of the 15th century.
Nikitin, Athanasius. Travels to India.
Stefano, Hieronimo di Santo. Account
of the Journey of, from Cairo to
India, 1499.

VOLUME 23.

Champlain, Samuel. Narrative of a Voyage to the West Indies and Mexico
in 1599-1602. Translated from the

Hakluyt Soc. Publ., Vol. 23—*contd.*
Original MS., with a Biographical
Notice and Notes, by Alice Wilmere.
Edited by Norton Shaw. *Maps and
plates.* 8°   1859

VOLUME 24.

Expeditions into the Valley of the Amazons, 1539, 1540, 1639. Translated and
edited, with Notes, by Clements R.
Markham. *Map.* 8°   1859

Pizarro, Gonzalo. Expedition to the
Land of Cinnamon, 1539-42. By G.
Inca de la Vega.
Orellana, Francisco de. Voyage down
the River of the Amazons, 1540-41.
By A. de Herrera.
Acuña, Father Christopher de. New
Discovery of the Great River of
the Amazons, 1639.
List of the Principal Tribes of the
Valley of the Amazons.

VOLUME 25.

Early Voyages to Terra Australis, now
called Australia ; a Collection of Documents and Extracts from early MS. Maps,
illustrative of the History of Discovery on
the Coast of that Island, from the Beginning of the 16th Century to the Time of
Capt. Cook. Edited, with an Introduction and a Supplement, by R. H. Major.
Maps. 8°   1859
Arias, Juan Luis. Memorial respecting the Exploration, Colonization,
and Conversion of the Southern Land.
Torres, Luis Vaez de. Relation concerning the Discoveries of Quiros, as
his Almirante, 1607.
Extract from the Book of Dispatches
from Batavia, 1644.
Pelsart, Capt. Francis. Voyage and
Shipwreck on the Coast of New Hol-
land, and his succeeding Adventures,
1628.
Pool, Gerrit Thomasz. Voyage to the
South Land, 1629.
Account of the Wreck of the Ship
"De Vergulde Draeck" on the
South Land, and the Expeditions
undertaken, both from Batavia and
the Cape of Good Hope, in Search
of the Survivors, 1655-59.
Volkersen, Capt. S. Description of
the West Coast on the South Land,
1658.
Witsen, Burgomaster. Extract [on
New Guinea] translated from his
"Noord en Oost Tartarye."
Dampier, Capt. W. Observations on
the Coast of New Holland in 1687-88.
—— Adventures of, who, with others,
1686-87, left Capt. Sherpe in the
South Seas, and travelled back over
Land through the Country of Darien.

Hakluyt Soc. Publ., Vol. 25—*contd.*

Vlamingh, Willem de. Some Particulars relating to the Voyage to New Holland, 1696.

Extract from the Journal of a Voyage made to the Unexplored South Land, by Order of the Dutch East India Company, 1696-97. Translated from the Dutch.

Dampier, Capt. W. Observations on the Coast of New Holland, 1699.

Detail of the Discoveries and Noticeable Occurrences in the Voyage of the Fluyt "Vossenbosch," &c., Despatched by the Goverment of India, 1705, from Batavia by way of Timor to New Holland. Translated from the Dutch.

The Houtman's Abrolhos in 1727. Translated.

Major, R. H. Supplement, on the Discovery of Australia by the Portuguese in 1601.

VOLUME 26.

Clavijo, Ruy Gonzalez de. Narrative of the Embassy of, to the Court of Timour, at Samarcand, 1403-6. Translated, with Notes, a Preface, and an Introductory Life of Timour Beg, by Clements R. Markham. *Map.* 8° 1859

VOLUME 27.

Hudson, Henry, the Navigator. The Original Documents, in which his Career is Recorded. Collected, partly Translated, and Annotated, with an Introduction, by George Asher. 8° 1860

VOLUME 28.

Ursua, Pedro de, and Lope de Aguirre. Expedition of, in Search of El Dorado and Omagua. Translated from Fray Pedro Simon's "Conquest of Tierra Firme," by W. Bollaert; with an Introduction by C. R. Markham. *Map.* 8° 1861

VOLUME 29.

Guzman, Don Alonzo Enriquez de. Life and Acts of, 1518 to 1543. Translated from an Original and Inedited MS. in the National Library at Madrid; with Notes and an Introduction by C. R. Markham. 8° 1862

VOLUME 30.

Galvano, Antonio. Discoveries of the World, from the First Original unto 1555; corrected, quoted, and published in England by R. Hakluyt (1601). Now reprinted, with the Original Portuguese Text, and edited by Vice-Admiral Bethune. 8° 1862

Hakluyt Soc. Publ.—*continued.*

VOLUME 31.

Jordanus, Friar (circa 1330). Mirabilia Descripta. The Wonders of the East. Translated from the Latin, with a Commentary, by Col. Henry Yule. 8° 1863

VOLUME 32.

Varthema, Ludovica di. Travels in Egypt, Syria, Arabia Deserta and Arabia Felix, in Persia, India, and Ethiopia, 1503 to 1508. Translated from the Italian edition of 1510, with a Preface by J. Winter Jones, and edited, with Notes and an Introduction, by G. Percy Badger. *Map.* 8° 1863

VOLUME 33.

Cieza de Leon, Pedro de. The Travels of, A.D. 1532-50, contained in the First Part of his Chronicle of Peru. Translated and edited, with Notes and an Introduction, by C. R. Markham. *Map.* 8° 1864

VOLUME 34.

Narrative of the Proceedings of Pedrarias Davila in the Provinces of Tierre Firme or Castilla del Oro, and of the Discovery of the South Sea and the Coasts of Peru and Nicaragua, written by Pascual de Andagoya. Translated and edited, with Notes and an Introduction, by C. R. Markham. *Map.* 8° 1865

VOLUME 35.

A Description of the Coasts of East Africa and Malabar in the beginning of the Sixteenth Century, by Duarte Barbosa, a Portuguese. Translated from an early Spanish Manuscript in the Barcelona Library, with Notes and a Preface, by the Hon. Henry E. J. Stanley. 8° 1866

VOLUMES 36 and 37.

Cathay and the Way thither: being a Collection of Medieval Notices of China. Translated and edited by Col. H. Yule . . . ; with Essay on the Intercourse between China and the West previous to the Discovery of the Cape Route. 2 vols. 8° 1866

[Contains Travels of Oderic, Marignolli, Ibn Batuta, Goes, &c.]

VOLUME 38.

The Three Voyages of Martin Frobisher in Search of a Passage to Cathaia and India by the North-West, A.D. 1576-78. Reprinted from the first edition of Hakluyt's Voyages, with Selections from Manuscript Documents in the British Museum and State Paper Office, by Rear-Admiral Richard Collinson. *Portrait and maps.* 8° 1868

VOLUME 39.

The Philippine Islands, Moluccas, Siam, Cambodia, Japan, and China, at the Close of the Sixteenth Century, by

Hakluyt Soc. Publ., Vol. 39—*contd.*

Antonio de Morga. Translated from the Spanish, with Notes and a Preface, and a Letter from Luis Vaez de Torres describing his voyage through the Torres Straits, by the Hon. Henry E. J. Stanley. *Maps and plate.* 8° 1868

VOLUME 40.

The Fifth Letter of Hernan Cortes to the Emperor Charles V., containing an Account of his Expedition to Honduras. Translated from the original Spanish by Don Pascual de Gayangos. 8° 1868

VOLUME 41.

First Part of the Royal Commentaries of the Yncas, by the Ynca Garcilasso de la Vega. Translated and edited, with Notes and an Introduction, by Clements R. Markham. Vol 1. 8° 1869

VOLUME 42.

The Three Voyages of Vasco da Gama and his Viceroyalty, from the Lendas da India of Gaspar Correa. Accompanied by Original Documents. Translated from the Portuguese, with Notes and an Introduction, by the Hon. Henry E. J. Stanley. *Portrait, plate, &c.* 8° 1869

VOLUME 43.

Select Letters of Christopher Columbus, with other Original Documents, relating to his Four Voyages to the New World. Translated and edited by R. H. Major. 2nd edition. *Maps and plate.* 8° 1870

VOLUME 44.

History of the Imâms and Seyyids of 'Omân, by Salîl-Ibn-Razîk, from A.D. 661-1856. Translated from the Original Arabic, and edited, with Notes, Appendices, and an Introduction, continuing the History down to 1870, by George Percy Badger. *Map.* 8° 1871

VOLUME 45.

First Part of the Royal Commentaries of the Yncas, by the Ynca Garcilasso de la Vega. Translated and edited, with Notes, an Introduction, and an Analytical Index, by Clements R. Markham. Vol. 2 (containing Books 5, 6, 7, 8, and 9). *Maps.* 8° 1871

VOLUME 46.

The Canarian, or Book of the Conquest and Conversion of the Canarians in the year 1402, by Messire Jean de Bethencourt. Composed by Pierre Bontier and Jean le Verrier. Translated and edited, with Notes and an Introduction, by R. H. Major. *Map and portrait.* 8° 1872

VOLUME 47.

Reports on the Discovery of Peru. 1. Report of Francisco de Xeres, Secretary to Francisco Pizarro; 2. Report of

Hakluyt Soc. Publ., Vol. 47—*contd.*

Miguel de Astete on the Expedition to Pachacamac; 3. Letter of Hernando Pizarro to the Royal Audience of Santo Domingo; 4. Report of Pedro Sancho on the Partition of the Ransom of Atahuallpa. Translated and edited, with Notes and an Introduction, by Clements R. Markham. *Map.* 8° 1872

VOLUME 48.

Narratives of the Rites and Laws of the Yncas. Translated from the original Spanish Manuscripts, and edited, with Notes and an Introduction, by Clements R. Markham. 8° 1873

VOLUME 49.

Travels to Tana and Persia, by Josafa Barbaro and Ambrogio Contarini. Translated from the Italian, and edited, with an Introduction, by Lord Stanley of Alderley. 8° 1873

VOLUME 50.

The Voyages of the Venetian brothers Nicolò and Antonio Zeno to the Northern Seas, in the Fourteenth Century, &c. Translated and edited, with Notes and an Introduction, by Richard Henry Major. *Maps.* 8° 1873

VOLUME 51.

The Captivity of Hans Stade of Hesse, in A.D. 1547-55, among the Wild Tribes of Eastern Brazil. Translated by Albert Tootal, Esq., of Rio de Janeiro, and annotated by R. F. Burton. 8° 1874

VOLUME 52.

The First Voyage round the World by Magellan. Translated from the Accounts of Pigafetta and other contemporary writers, accompanied by Original Documents, with Notes and an Introduction, by Lord Stanley of Alderley. *Portrait, map, &c.* 8° 1874

VOLUME 53.

The Commentaries of the Great Afonso Dalboquerque, second Viceroy of India. Translated from the Portuguese edition of 1774, with Notes and an Introduction, by Walter de Gray Birch. Vol. 1. *Maps and plate.* 8° 1875

VOLUME 54.

The Three Voyages of William Barents to the Arctic Regions (1594, '95, and '96), by Gerrit de Veer. Second Edition, with an Introduction, by Lieutenant Koolemans Beynen. *Map and plates.* 8° 1876

VOLUME 55.

The Commentaries of the Great Afonso Dalboquerque. Vol. 2. *Map and plates.* 8° 1877

Hakluyt Soc. Publ.—*continued.*

VOLUME 56.

The Voyages of Sir James Lancaster, Kt., to the East Indies, with Abstracts of Journals of Voyages to the East Indies during the Seventeenth Century, preserved in the India Office ; and the Voyage of Capt. John Knight (1606) to seek the North-West Passage. Edited by Clements R. Markham. 8° 1877

VOLUME 57.

The Hawkins' Voyages during the Reigns of Henry VIII., Queen Elizabeth, and James I. Edited, with an Introduction, by Clements R. Markham. *Portrait.* 8° 1878

VOLUME 58.

The Bondage and Travels of Johann Schiltberger, a native of Bavaria, in Europe, Asia, and Africa, 1396-1427. Translated from the Heidelberg MS. edited in 1859 by Professor Karl Friedrich Neumann, by Commander J. Buchan Telfer ; with Notes by Professor P. Brunn ; and a Preface, Introduction, and Notes by the Translator and Editor. *Map.* 8° 1879

VOLUME 59.

The Voyages and Works of John Davis the Navigator. Edited, with an Introduction and Notes, by Albert Hastings Markham. *Map, &c.* 1880
The Map of the World, A.D. 1600. Called by Shakspere "The New Map, with the Augmentation of the Indies." To illustrate the Voyages of John Davis. [In cover.] 1880

VOLUME 60.

The Natural and Moral History of the Indies, by Father Joseph de Acosta. Reprinted from the English translated edition of Edward Grimston, 1604, and edited, with Notes and an Introduction, by Clements R. Markham. Vol. 1. The Natural History (Books 1, 2, 3, and 4). Issued with this work is also a "Map of Peru ; to illustrate the Travels of Cieza de Leon, in 1532-50 ; the Royal Commentaries of Garcilasso de la Vega (1609) ; and the Natural and Moral History of the Indies, by Father Joseph de Acosta (1608)." 8° 1880

VOLUME 61.

The Natural and Moral History of the Indies, by Father Joseph de Acosta. Edited by Clements R. Markham. Vol. 2. The Moral History (Books 5, 6, and 7). 8° 1880

VOLUME 62.

The Commentaries of the Great Afonso Dalboquerque. Vol. 3. *Maps and portraits.* 8° 1880

Hakluyt Soc. Publ.—*continued.*

VOLUME 63.

The Voyages of William Baffin, 1612-22. Edited, with Notes and an Introduction, by Clements R. Markham. *Maps and frontispiece.* 8° 1881

VOLUME 64.

Narrative of the Portuguese Embassy to Abyssinia during the years 1520-27. By Father Francisco Alvarez. Translated from the Portuguese, and edited, with Notes and an Introduction, by Lord Stanley of Alderley. *Map.* 8° 1881

VOLUME 65.

The Historye of the Bermudaes or Summer Islands. Edited, from a MS. in the Sloane Collection, British Museum, by General Sir J. Henry Lefroy. *Map, plate, and portraits.* 8° 1882

VOLUMES 66 and 67.

Diary of Richard Cooks, Cape-Merchant in the English Factory in Japan, 1615-22, with Correspondence. Edited by Edward Maunde Thompson. 2 vols. 8° 1883

VOLUME 68.

The Second Part of the Chronicle of Peru. By Pedro de Cieza de Leon. Translated and Edited, with Notes and an Introduction, by Clements R. Markham. 8° 1883

VOLUME 69.

The Commentaries of the Great Afonso Dalboquerque. Vol. 4. *Plates.* 8° 1884

VOLUMES 70 and 71.

The Voyage of John Huyghen Van Linschoten to the East Indies. From the Old English Translation of 1598. The First Book, containing his Description of the East. Edited, the first volume by the late Arthur Coke Burnell, Ph.D., the second volume by Mr P. A. Tiele. 2 vols. *Frontispiece.* 8° 1885

VOLUMES 72 and 73.

Early Voyages and Travels to Russia and Persia, by Anthony Jenkinson, and other Englishmen ; with some Account of the First Intercourse of the English with Russia and Central Asia by way of the Caspian Sea. Edited by E. Delmar Morgan and C. H. Coote. 2 vols. *Maps, frontispiece, &c.* 8° 1886

VOLUME 74.

The Diary of William Hedges, Esq. (afterwards Sir William Hedges), during his Agency in Bengal, as well as on his Voyage out and return overland (1681-87). Transcribed for the press, with Introductory Notes, &c., by R. Barlow, Esq., and illustrated by copious extracts from Unpublished Records, &c., by Colonel Henry Yule. Vol. 1. The Diary, with Index. 8° 1887

Hakluyt Soc. Publ. - *continued.*

VOLUME 75.

The same. Vol. 2. Containing Notices regarding Sir William Hedges, Documentary Memoirs of Job Charnock, and other Biographical and Miscellaneous Illustrations of the Time in India. *Portraits.* 8° 1888

VOLUME 76.

The Voyage of François Pyrard of Laval to the East Indies, the Maldives, the Moluccas, and Brazil. Translated into English from the Third French Edition of 1619, and edited, with Notes, by Albert Gray, assisted by H. C. P. Bell. Vol. 1. *Map and illustrations.* 8° 1887

VOLUME 77.

The same. Vol. 2. Part 1. *Illustrations.* 8° 1888

VOLUME 78.

Diary of W. Hedges. Vol. 3. Containing Documentary Contributions to a Biography of Thomas Pitt, Governor of Fort St George; with Collections on the Early History of the Company's Settlement in Bengal, and on Early Charts and Topography of the Húglí River. *Map and portraits.* 8° 1889

VOLUME 79.

Tractatus de Globis et eorum usu. A Treatise descriptive of the Globes constructed by Emery Molyneux, and published in 1592. By Robert Hues. Edited, with Annotated Indices and an Introduction, by Clements R. Markham. *Map and frontispiece.* 8° 1889

VOLUME 80.

The Voyage of François Pyrard of Laval to the East Indies, the Maldives, the Moluccas, and Brazil. Vol. 2. Part 2. *Charts and plates.* 8° 1890

VOLUME 81.

The Conquest of the River Plate (1535-1555). 1. Voyage of Ulrich Schmidt to the Rivers la Plata and Paraguai, from the Original German Edition, 1567. 2. The Commentaries of Alvar Nuñez Cabeza de Vaca, from the Original Spanish Edition, 1855. With Notes and Introduction by Luis S. Dominguez. *Map.* 8° 1891

VOLUMES 82 and 83.

The Voyage of François Leguat of Bresse to Rodriguez, Mauritius, Java, and the Cape of Good Hope. Transcribed from the First English Edition. Edited and Annotated by Captain Pasfield Oliver. 2 vols. 8° 1891

VOLUMES 84 and 85.

The Travels of Pietro Della Valle in India, from the Old English Translation of 1664 by G. Havers. Edited, with a

Hakluyt Soc. Publ., Vol. 85—*contd.*

Life of the Author, and Introduction and Notes, by Edward Grey. 2 vols. 8° 1892

VOLUME 86.

The Journal of Christopher Columbus (during his First Voyage, 1492-93), and Documents relating to the Voyages of Gaspar Corte Real. Translated, with Notes and an Introduction, by C. R. Markham. *Facsimile maps.* 8° 1893

VOLUME 87.

Early Voyages and Travels in the Levant. 1. The Diary of Master Thomas Dallam, 1599-1600. 2. Extracts from the Diaries of Dr John Covel, 1670-79. Edited, with an Introduction and Notes, by J. Theodore Bent. *Portrait.* 8° 1893

Harris, John. Navigantium atque Itinerantium Bibliotheca; or, a Compleat Collection of Voyages and Travels, consisting of above four hundred of the most Authentick Writers; beginning with Hackluit, Purchass, &c., in English; Ramusio in Italian; Thevenot, &c., in French; De Bry, and Grynæi Novus Orbis, in Latin; the Dutch East India Company, in Dutch; and continued with others of note, &c. 2 vols. *Maps, portraits, and plates.* Folio 1705

—— Another edition of the same, consisting of above 600 of the most Authentic Writers, beginning with Hackluit, Purchass, &c., in English; Ramusio, Alamandini, Carreri, &c., in Italian; Thevenot, Renaudot, Labat, &c., in French; De Brye, Grynæus, Maffeus, &c., in Latin; Herrera, Oviedo, Coreal, &c., in Spanish; and the Voyages under the Direction of the East-India Company in Holland, in Dutch; together with such other Histories, Voyages, Travels, or Discoveries, as are in general esteem; containing whatever has been observed worthy of notice in Europe, Asia, Africa, and America; in respect to the extent and situation of Empires, Kingdoms, Provinces, &c., with an Introduction, comprehending the Rise and Progress of the Art of Navigation, and its successive improvements, together with the Invention of the Loadstone, and its Variation. Carefully revised, with large additions, and continued down to the present time; including Particular Accounts of the Manufactures and Commerce of each Country. 2 vols. in 4. *Maps, portraits, and plates.* Folio London, 1744-48

CONTENTS.

VOLUME I [*a*].

The History of the Circumnavigators:—
The superiority of the Moderns over the Ancients in the Art of Navigation

Harris, Vol. 1—*continued.*

explained, and the causes of that superiority assigned.

Columbus, Christopher. Voyages, 1493-1506.

Maglianes, or Magellan, Ferdinand. Voyage from the South Seas to the East Indies, 1519-22.

Drake, Sir Francis. Voyage round the Globe, 1577-80.

Candish, or Cavendish, Sir Thomas. Voyage round the World, 1585-88.

Van Noort, Oliver. Voyage (the first attempted by the Dutch) round the World, 1598-1601.

Weert, Capt. Sebald de. Remarkable Voyage to the South Seas and the Streights of Magellan, 1598-1600.

Spilbergen, George. Voyage round the World, 1614-17.

Schouten, W. C., and Jacques le Maire. Remarkable Voyage round the World by a New Passage into the South Seas, 1615-17.

Quiros, Don Pedro F. de. Voyage for the Discovery of the Southern Continental Islands, about 1600.

Hermite, Jacques le. Voyage of the Nassau Fleet round the Globe, 1623-26.

Cowley, Capt. Voyage round the World, 1683-86.

Dampier, Capt. William. First Voyage round the World, collected from his own Account, 1683-91.

—— Voyage to New Holland and New Guiney, from his own Account, 1699-1701.

Funnell, William. Voyage round the World, 1703-6.

Rogers, Capt. Woodes, and Capt. S. Courtney. Voyage round the World, 1708-11.

Clipperton, Capt. John. Voyage round the World, 1719-22.

Shelvocke, Capt. George. Voyage round the World, 1719-22.

Betagh, Capt. Observations on the Country of Peru and its Inhabitants during his Captivity, 1720.

Roggewein, Comm. Account of his Expedition, with three Ships, for the Discovery of Southern Lands, 1721-33.

Pelsart, Capt. Francis. Voyage and Shipwreck of, on the Coast of New Holland, and his succeeding Adventures, 1628.

Tasman, Capt. Abel Jansen. Voyage for the Discovery of Southern Countries, 1642-43.

Anson, Comm. Account of the Expedition of, round the World, 1740-44.

The Discovery, Settlement, and Commerce of the East Indies:—

The History of India in the Earliest Ages.

Harris, Vol. 1 [*a*]—*continued.*

The History of this Commerce in the hands of the Idumeans, Israelites, Tyrians, &c., with some Account of its Profits.

Of the Indian Commerce under the Persian Empire.

An Exact Account of Alexander's Conquest of the Persian Empire, and more particularly of his Indian Expedition, and the Consequences he intended to have drawn from thence.

Nearchus. Voyage from the Mouth of the River Indus up the Persian Gulph, for the Discovery of the Coasts and their Inhabitants.

The History of the Seleucidæ, Kings of of Syria, who were the immediate possessors of Alexander's Indian Conquests.

The History of the Greek Empire in Egypt, under the Ptolemies ; the Establishment of the Indian Commerce at Alexandria, and the Consequences of that establishment, to the Reduction of Egypt into a Province by the Romans.

The History of the Indian Trade, as carried on through Egypt by the Red Sea, under the Romans, the Manner of its Establishment, the Profits drawn therefrom, and the Discoveries made in consequence of this Commerce.

An Account of the Affairs of Egypt, and of the Commerce carried on by the Romans through that country to the East, till the Seat of the Empire was transferred from Rome to Constantinople.

An Account of the Religion, Government, Laws, Customs, and Manners of the Indians, as they are recorded in the Works of ancient Authors.

The Learning, Discipline, Office, Manner of Living, and Privileges of the Brachmans, including an Account of their peculiar Doctrines in Theology.

Of the Land Animals in the East Indies, as described by antient Authors, compared with modern Authors.

An Account of the most remarkable Fish and Fowl in the East Indies, as described by ancient and modern Authors.

VOLUME 1 [*b*].

An Account of the Descriptions left us by the Ancients of the Eastern and Northern Parts of the Indies, the notions they had of their Riches, with Enquiry into the Reasons which hindered the extending their Discoveries on that side.

History of the Rise, Progress, and Decline of the Constantinopolitan Empire, together with the Commerce of its Subjects in the East ; also a brief Detail of the Rise of the Arabian Empire, the

Harris, Vol. 1 [b]—*continued.*

Recovery of the Indian Commerce in Egypt, and the Reviving the Trade of Alexandria.

An Account of the several Passages to the Indies, both by Sea and Land, that have been Attempted, Discovered, or Practised by the Antients.

An Account of the Travels of Two Mahommedans through India and China in the Ninth Century. Translated from the Arabic by the Abbé Renaudot.

Benjamin, Rabbi, the son of Jonas of Tudela. Travels through Europe, Asia, and Africa, from Spain to China, 1160-1173. From the Latin of Montanus.

Rubruquis, William de. The remarkable Travels of, in the East, particularly into Tartary and China, 1253.

Marco Polo. The curious and remarkable Voyages and Travels of, in the middle of the XIIIth century ; through a great part of Asia, all the Dominions of the Tartars, and home by sea through the Islands of the East Indies.

History of the Empire of the Great Mogul, from its foundation by Timur-Bec, or Tamerlane, to the present time.

History of the Rise and Progress of the Portuguese Empire in the East Indies; their Discoveries set forth in their natural Order ; the form of their Government in those parts explained ; the causes of the Declension of their Power examined ; and the present Posture of their Affairs in this part of the World truly stated.

Pirard de Laval, Francis. Voyage to the East Indies ; his Shipwreck amongst the Maldives, and his copious Account of that Archipelago, 1601-11.

Beaulieu, Comm. Augustin de. Expedition to the East Indies, containing a curious Description of the Sea-Coasts and Commerce, as also curious Observations on the Manners of the People, and the means of establishing Colonies among them, 1619-22.

Mandelsloe, John Albert de. Remarks and Observations made in his Passage from the Kingdom of Persia through several Countries of the Indies, 1638.

—— The remaining Voyages through the Indies, including his Descriptions of Countries, Historical Remarks upon several Nations, and his Observations on the Commerce of the Portuguese, English, and Dutch at that time, 1639.

Tavernier, J. B. Account of the Commodities, Manufactures, and the Produce of the several Countries of the East Indies.

—— An Account of the different Routes to all the great Cities and chief Marts in the Indies.

Harris, Vol. 1 [b]—*continued.*

Tavernier, J. B. Remarks and Observations in his Travels through the Indies, together with his Account of the Dutch Settlement, and of his Voyage on board a Dutch Ship from Batavia to Europe.

Cunningham, James. Observations and Remarks made during his Residence on the Island of Chusan, on the Coast of China, 1701.

Adams, William. Account of the Adventures of, who resided many years in the Empire of Japan, 1609-31.

An Historical Account of the Intercourse between the Inhabitants of Great Britain and the People in the East Indies, containing likewise a Compleat History of the East India Company from its Erection under Queen Elizabeth, and of the several Alterations that have been made therein.

History of the Rise, Progress, and Establishment of the Dutch East India Company.

History of the French East India Commerce from its first Original, together with a clear and concise Account of the several Alterations it has undergone, and a full and plain Description of its present Circumstances at Home and Abroad, 1741.

History of the Rise, Progress, and Suppression of the Imperial Company of the Indies, established at Ostend by the Emperor Charles V.

History of the Danish Commerce to the East Indies, their Establishments there, the Decay of the Old Company, and the Motives which induced them to set up a New One.

History of the Swedish East India Company.

VOLUME 2 [a].

The Discovery, Settlement, and Commerce of the West Indies :—

Of the Importance of the new-discovered Continent of America, the nature of the Discovery, the felicities attending it, the advantages derived from thence to the Art of Navigation, &c.

Columbus Chr. First Voyage, in which he Discovered the Lucayan Islands, and afterwards Cuba and Hispaniola, which opened a Passage from Europe to America, with his return to Spain, 1492-93.

—— Second Voyage, to the West Indies, including an Account of all the Discoveries made in that Voyage, 1493-96.

—— Third Voyage, to the West Indies, in which he first saw the Continent of America, 1498-1500.

—— Fourth Voyage : his Discoveries on the Continent, and of the Islands in America, 1502-5.

Harris, Vol. 2 [*a*]—*continued.*

Cortes, Hernan. The History of the several Discoveries, Settlements and Conquests made by the Spaniards, in the West Indies, after the Death of Chr. Columbus.

—— Expedition for the Reduction of New Spain, 1518.

The Progress of this Expedition from the Time of the Spaniards embarking for New Spain, to the first Message sent by Cortes to Mōtezuma, Emperor of Mexico, 1519.

The Continuation of the Expedition, his Alliances with several Indian Nations, his success in quelling various Seditions in his own Army, and his preparations for his March to Mexico by burning his whole Fleet, 1519.

The History of the War of Tlascala, from its breaking out to Cortes's concluding a Peace with that Republic; and his taking them into the Confederacy against the Indian Emperor Montezuma, 1519.

The March of the Spaniards to Mexico, the Reception given to Cortes by Montezuma, his Imprisonment and other Transactions to the Time of his ordering the Spaniards to quit his Dominions, 1519.

The History of Cortes's Expedition continued to the Death of Montezuma, and the Spaniards being forced to abandon the City of Mexico, 1520.

The Conclusion of Hernan Cortes's Expedition, including the History of the remaining part of the War, to the Reduction of the City and Empire of Mexico, 1520-21.

The Discoveries made by the Spaniards in the Province called Golden Castile; their first knowledge of the South Sea, and their Establishment of Panama, by which a Passage was opened to the Discovery and Conquest of the Empire of Peru, 1513-26.

Pizarro, Francis. The History of the Discovery and Conquest of the Empire of Peru, 1524, together with the Discovery of Chili, and the Conquest of that Country, 1535.

History of the Discovery, Settlement, and Cultivation of Brazil by the Portuguese; the Conquest of the greatest part of that Country by the Dutch; the Recovery thereof by the Portuguese, and the vast advantages that have accrued to them from this noble Colony, 1500-1709.

The Discoveries and Settlements made by the English. in different parts of America, from the Reign of Henry VII. to the Close of the Reign of Queen Elizabeth, 1495-1603.

Harris, Vol. 2 [*a*]—*continued.*

The History of the Discoveries, Settlements, and other Transactions of the English Nation in America, from the Accession of James I. to the Restoration, 1603-60.

An Historical Account of the British Settlements in America, from the Restoration of Charles II. to the Revolution, 1660-88.

The History of the British Colonies in America, from the Revolution to the Death of George I.

The History of the Rise, Progress, and Present State of the Colony of Georgia, 1732-42.

History of the Discoveries, Settlements, and Conquests of the French in America, 1523-1713.

The Discoveries, Conquests, Settlements, and Present State of the Dutch Colonies in America, with an Account of the Danish Settlement, 1642-1714.

Discoveries towards the North and through most of the Countries of Europe :—

History of the Countries lying round the North Pole, their Climate, Soil, and Produce: Greenland, Spitzbergen, Mayen Island, Nova Zembla, Yedzo, &c., 1585-1746.

Philosophical Motives for seeking a Passage into the South Seas, by the North-West, examined and explained, together with the History of the Attempts made with that view, for the space of 130 years.

James, Capt. Thomas. Voyage for the Discovery of a Passage into the South Seas, by the North-West, his wintering in Charlton Island, and return to England, 1631-33.

Middleton, Capt. Chr. Attempts made for the Discovery of a Passage into the South Seas, from Hudson's Bay, with Orginal Papers by Dobbs, 1725-42.

Account of the Grounds upon which a North-East Passage into the Sea of Japon has been sought for; the Attempts of the English and Dutch on that side.

A Voyage to the North, containing an Account of the Sea Coasts and Mines of Norway, the Danish, Swedish, and Muscovite Laplands; Borandia, Siberia, Samojedia, Zembla, and Iceland, with some curious Remarks on the Norwegians, Laplanders, Russians, Poles, Circassians, Cossacks, and other Nations; extracted from the Journal of a Gentleman employed . by the North-Sea Company at Copenhagen, and from the Memoirs of a French Gentleman.

Harris, Vol. 2 [*a*]—*continued.*

An Impartial Account of the Kingdom of Sweden, with respect to its Climate, Soil, and Produce, &c., collected from the Writings of an English Minister residing there.

Molesworth and others. The Present State of the Dominions of the Crown of Denmark, and of its Subjects, in respect to their Manners, Customs, &c.

Connor, Bernard. A Comprehensive Account of the Kingdom of Poland, the Situation, &c.

Beauplan, Mr. A Short Account of the Ukrain, and of its Inhabitants the Cossacks.

VOLUME 2 [*b*].

Misson, Maximilian. Travels through part of Holland, the Spanish Low Countries, Germany, Tyrol, and the Bishoprick of Trent, on his way to Italy, 1687-88.

—— Travels through a great part of Italy, with Observations on the Manners, Customs, &c., of the Inhabitants.

—— Arrival at Rome, to his Departure out of Italy.

Burnet, Bishop Gilbert. Travels through Switzerland, part of Italy, some Provinces of Germany, and the Low Countries, 1685-86.

Ray, John. Travels through the Low Countries and Germany, towards Italy, 1663.

—— Travels through the Dominions of the State of Venice, Lombardy, Tuscany, the Kingdom of Naples, the Islands of Sicily and Malta, the Ecclesiastical State, the Bishoprick of Trent, the Country of the Grisons, Switzerland, &c.

Willoughby, Francis. Travels through Spain, 1664.

Travels through Portugal and Spain, with a distinct Description of the Principal Cities in both Kingdoms, particularly Lisbon, Coimbra, Porto, and Braga, Madrid, Valentia, Alicant, &c., by an English Gentleman, 1693.

Skippon, Sir Philip, and John Ray. Travels through the best part of the Kingdom of France, 1664.

Northleigh, John. Travels through France, 1702.

Browne, Edward. Voyage from England to Holland, with a Journey from thence, by Land, through the Electorates of Cologne, Treves, and Mentz, the Lower and Upper Palatinate, Bavaria, and Austria to Vienna; from thence through Moravia, Bohemia and Saxony to Hamburgh, 1668.

2 N

Harris, Vol. 2 [*b*]—*continued.*

Browne, Edward. Description of the Noble Kingdom of Hungary, interspersed with a Variety of Geographical, Historical, Physical, &c., Remarks.

—— Travels through Hungary into Thessaly; a Description of the City of Larissa, &c.

—— Journey from Vienna to Venice by Land, with an Account of the Quicksilver Mines in Friuli, including Observations in his Passages through Styria, Carinthia, and Carniola.

Thevenot, John. Voyages and Travels from Italy to Constantinople, 1655.

—— Account of the Customs and Manners of the Turks, &c.; also an Account of the Christians and Jews inhabiting Countries that are Subject to the Grand Signior.

—— Account of several of the most remarkable Cities in Asia, of various Islands in the Archipelago, intermixed with Accounts from Wheeler and Lebrun, 1656.

Maundrell, Henry. Journey from Aleppo to Jerusalem, 1696.

Chardin, Sir John. Travels by way of the Black Sea, through the Countries of Circassia, Mingrelia, the Country of the Abcas, Georgia, Armenia, and Media, into Persia Proper, 1672.

Description of the Great Empire of Persia; its Situation, Extent, Distribution into Provinces, &c., collected from the Writings of Herbert, Chardin, Tavernier, Thevenot, Le Brun, and others.

View of the Persian History, from the earliest Accounts down to the Present Time, collected from Oriental Writers, and from Greek and Latin Historians.

Yshrants Ides, E. Travels from Muscovy through Great Ustiga, Siriana, Permia, Siberia, Daour, &c., to the Frontiers of China; through the Countries of the Mongul Tartars, lying between the Russian and Chinese Empires, the Passage through the Famous Wall, and from thence to the City of Peking, the Capital of China; with an Account of Peking, and Return from China by Land, 1692-95.

—— Description of Siberia.

Kao, Dionysius. A Geographical Description of the Extensive Empire of China, and of the Sixteen Provinces into which it is divided.

—— An Authentick Account of whatever is most remarkable in regard to persons or things throughout the whole Empire of China, with a Description of Japan, Corea, Formosa, Tunkin, and Laos, &c.

Harris, Vol. 2 [*b*]—*continued*.

Description of the Country, History of the Inhabitants, and Account of the present state of the Kingdom of Corea.

Account of Part of the North-east Frontier of the Russian Empire, commonly called the Country of Kamschatka or Kamschatska.

Behring, Capt. Voyages for Discovery towards the East, 1725-26.

Retrospective View of this whole Collection, in which its particular Advantages are explained, and an Account given of the Uses to which the Contents may be applied.

Hawkesworth, John. An Account of the Voyages undertaken by the Order of His Present Majesty for making Discoveries in the Southern Hemisphere, and successively performed by Comm. Byron, Capt. Wallis, Capt. Carteret, and Capt. Cook, in the "Dolphin," the "Swallow," and the "Endeavour." Drawn up from the Journals which were kept by the several Commanders, and from the Papers of Joseph Banks, Esq. 3 vols. *Maps and plates.* 4°   1773

CONTENTS.

VOLUME I.

Byron, Comm. Voyage from the Downs to Rio de Janeiro, Port Desire, Patagonia, up the Streight of Magellan to Port Famine and back to Falkland's Islands, Cape Monday, Islands of Disappointment, King George's Islands, Islands of Saypan, Tinian, Aguigan, and Timoan, Batavia, Cape of Good Hope to England ; with Descriptions of the various Islands, 1764-66.

Wallis, Capt. Voyage to the Coast of Patagonia, Otaheite, Tinian, Batavia, and the Cape of Good Hope, with Tables of Latitudes and Longitudes West of London, 1766-68.

Carteret, Capt. Voyage from Plymouth to Madeira, from thence through the Streight of Magellan to Masafuero, Queen Charlotte's Islands, Egmont Island, Nova Britannia, Mindanao, Celebes, to Batavia, round the Cape of Good Hope to England, with a Table of the Variation of the Compass, 1766-69.

VOLUMES 2 AND 3.

Cook, Capt. Voyage round the World, 1768-71.

Kerr, Robert. A General History and Collection of Voyages and Travels, arranged in Systematic Order ; forming a complete History of the Origin and Progress of Navigation, Discovery, and

Kerr—*continued*.

Commerce, by Sea and Land, from the earliest ages to the present time.   18 vols. *Maps and charts.*   8°
Edinburgh, 1811-24

CONTENTS.

VOLUME I.

Voyages and Travels of Discovery, from the Era of King Alfred, in the Ninth Century, to the Era of Don Henry, Prince of Portugal, at the commencement of the Fifteenth Century :—

Discoveries in the Time of Alfred.

Discovery of Iceland by the Norwegians, in the ninth century.

Ohthere, Voyages of, to the White Sea and the Baltic, in the ninth century.

Forster, J. R. Remarks on the Situation of Sciringes-heal and Hæthum.

Wulfstein. Voyage in the Baltic, as related to King Alfred.

Sighelm. Voyage to India, in the reign of Alfred.

Erigena, John. Travels to Athens, in the ninth century.

Alfred, King. Geography of the Known World.

Leucander, And. Travels to Jerusalem, in the eleventh century.

Swanus. Voyage to Jerusalem, 1052.

Voyage of three Ambassadors from England to Constantinople, about 1056.

Alured. Pilgrimage to Jerusalem, 1058.

Ingulphus. Pilgrimage to Jerusalem, 1064.

Original Discovery of Greenland by the Icelanders, in the ninth century.

Early Discovery of Winland, or America, by the Icelanders, 1001.

Travels of two Mahometans into India and China, in the ninth century.

Benjamin, Rabbi. Travels from Spain to China, in the twelfth century.

Travels of an Englishman in Tartary, 1242.

Sketch of the Revolutions in Tartary.

Carpini, John de Plano. Travels in Tartary, 1246.

Rubruquis, W. de. Travels in Tartary, about 1253.

Haitho, Prince of Armenia. Travels in Tartary, 1254.

Marco Polo. Travels into China and the East, from 1260 to 1295.

Oderic of Portenau. Travels into China and the East, 1318.

Mandeville, Sir John. Travels into the East, 1322.

Pegoletti. Itinerary between Azof and China, 1355.

Zeno, Nicolo and Antonio. Voyages, 1380.

Kerr, Vol. 1—*continued.*

Schildtberger, John. Travels into Tartary, 1394.

Travels of the Ambassadors of Mirza Shah Rokh, King of Persia, from Herat to Khanbalek, in Kathay, 1419.

Quirini, Pietro. Voyage and Travels into Norway, 1431.

Barbaro, Josaphat. Travels from Venice to Tanna, now called Asof, 1436.

VOLUME 2.

Account of various early Pilgrimages from England to the Holy Land, between 1097 and 1107.

Discovery of Madeira.

Account of the Discovery and Conquest of the Canary Islands.

General Voyages and Travels, chiefly of Discovery, from 1412 to 1760 :—

Galvano, Ant. Summary of the Discoveries of the World, from their first original to 1555.

Contarini, Ambrose. Journey from the Republic of Venice to Uzun-Hassan, King of Persia, 1473-76.

Voyages of Discovery by the Portuguese along the Western Coast of Africa, during the Life, and under the direction of Don Henry.

Cada Mosto and Pedro de Cintra. Original Journals of the Voyages of, to the Coast of Africa, 1455-56.

Portuguese Discoveries along the Coast of Africa, from the Death of Don Henry in 1463, to the Discovery of the Cape of Good Hope, 1486.

Castaneda, Hernan Lopez de. History of the Discovery and Conquest of India by the Portuguese, 1497-1505.

Letters from Lisbon in the beginning of the Sixteenth Century, respecting the recent Discovery of the Route by Sea to India, and the Indian Trade.

VOLUME 3.

History of the Discovery of America, and of some of the early Conquests in the New World :—

Columbus, Christopher. History of the Discovery of America, by Ferdinand Columbus.

—— Account of the Discovery of America, by Antonio de Herrera.

Vespucius Americus. Voyages to the New World.

Summary of the Discoveries and Settlements of the Spaniards in the West Indies, from the Death of Columbus to the Expedition of Hernando Cortes against Mexico.

Diaz del Castillo, Capt. Bernal. History of the Discovery and Conquest of Mexico, written in 1568.

Kerr—*continued.*

VOLUME 4.

Diaz del Castello. History of the Discovery and Conquest of Mexico, continued.

Zarate, Augustino. History of the Discovery and Conquest of Peru, by Francisco Pizarro.

—— Early History of Peru, after the Death of F. Pizarro, to the Defeat of Gonzalo Pizarro, and the re-establishment of tranquility in the Country.

VOLUME 5.

Zarate, A. Early History of Peru, continued.

De la Vega, Garcilasso. Early History of Peru, from the restoration of tranquility by Gasca in 1549, to the Death of the Inca Tupac Amaru.

History of the Discovery and Conquest of Chili.

Discovery of Florida, and Account of the several ineffectual Attempts to Conquer and Settle that Country by the Spaniards, under Juan Ponce de Leon, Panfilo de Narvaez, Cabeza de Vaca, and Ferdinand de Soto, from Herrera's History of America.

VOLUME 6.

Early English Voyages of Discovery to America :—

Cabot, Sebastian. Discovery of Newfoundland, 1479.

Butrigarius, G. Discourse respecting the Discoveries in America by S. Cabot.

Thorne, Robert. Brief Notice of the Discovery of Newfoundland.

Pert, Sir Thomas, and S. Cabot. Voyage to Brazil, St Domingo, and Porto Rico, about 1516.

Tison, T. Brief Note of a Voyage to the West Indies, before 1526.

Cartier, Jacques. Voyages from St Maloes to Newfoundland, Canada, Hochelaga, Saguenay, and New France, 1534-37.

Continuation of the Discoveries and Conquests of the Portuguese in the East ; together with some Account of the Voyages of other European Nations to India :—

Discoveries, &c., of the Portuguese, 1505-1539 : F. de Almeyda, Albuquerque, and others. With observations on early Indian trade, &c.

Particular Relation of the Expedition of Solyman Pacha from Suez to India, against the Portuguese at Diu, by a Venetian Officer.

Kerr, Vol. 17—*continued.*
ing a faithful Narrative of the Loss of
H.M.S. the "Wager."

VOLUME 18.

Stevenson, W. Historical Sketch of the
Progress of Discovery, Navigation, and
Commerce, from the earliest Records
to the beginning of the Nineteenth
Century.
Catalogue of Voyages and Travels.

Knox, J. New Collection. *See* p. 607.

Lafond de Lurcy, Capt. Gabriel. Voyages autour du Monde, et Naufrages
célèbres. 8 vols. *Portraits and plates.*
Royal 8°   *Paris*, 1844
CONTENTS.

Vols. 1, 2.—Voyages dans l'Amérique
Españole pendant les Guerres de
l'Indépendance.

Vol. 3.—Voyages dans les îsles Marquises
et dans celles de la Société.

Vol. 4.—Voyages dans les îsles Sandwich,
dans celles des Philippines, et en Chine.

Vol. 5.—Voyages en Chine, dans la
Malaisie et les îles Moluques.

Vol. 6.—Naufrage de Drury à Madagascar ; Naufrage de "l'Arabe" et
Aventures d'un Jeune Parisien.

Vol. 7.—Description de l'Afrique Méridionale ; Naufrage des Navires "l'Aber-
crombie-Robinson " et le " Waterloo "
dans la rade du Cap de Bonne-Espérance : George Barlow, Sarah Macfarlane, et John Murray ; Histoire de
Naufrage du Brick " la Nossa-Senhora-
da-Conceiçao," sur les Côtes du Sahara ;
Résidence et Excursions dans l'Empire
du Maroc.

Vol. 8.—Naufrage sur les Côtes du
Sahara, continué ; Voyage et Naufrage
du " Candide " dans la Polynésie.

Laharpe, J. F. Abrégé de l'Histoire Générale des Voyages [Prévost's], contenant ce
qu'il y a de plus remarquable, de plus utile
et de mieux avéré dans les pays où les
Voyageurs ont pénétré ; les Mœurs des
Habitans, la Religion, les Usages, Arts
et Sciences, Commerce et Manufactures.
24 vols. 8°   *Paris*, 1816

CONTENTS.
VOLUME I.

Afrique. Découvertes et Conquêtes des
Portuguais. Gama, Cabral, Albuquerque.
Voyages des Anglais sur les Côtes
d'Afrique, dans les Indes, et dans la
Mer Rouge ; de les Iles Canaries.
Voyages au Sénégal et sur les Côtes
d'Afrique jusqu'à Sierra-Léone. Cadamosto, André Brue.

Laharpe—*continued.*
VOLUME 2.

Afrique. Voyages au Sénégal jusqu'à
Sierra Leone.
Voyages sur la Côte de Guinée. Con-
quêtes de Dahomey. Villault, Atkins,
Smith, Snelgrave.

VOLUME 3.

Afrique. Congo. Cap de Bonne-Espér-
ance ou Hottentots. Monomotapa.
Asie. Iles de la Mer des Indes. Voyage
et Infortunes de F. Pyrard. Iles
Maldives, Ceylan, Sumatra, Java,
Batavia, Bornéo, Moluques, Timor,
Célèbes, Philippines, Marianes.

VOLUME 4.

Asie. Voyages et Aventures de Mendez-
Pinto.
Naufrage de G. Bontekoë.
Continent de l'Inde. Côte de Malabar,
Surate, Goa, Golconde, Coromandel,
Guzarate, Cambaye, et Visapour. Voy-
age de T. Rhoé dans l'Indostan.

VOLUME 5.

Continent de l'Inde. Voyage de Taver-
nier dans l'Indostan. Voyage de
Bernier à Cachemire.
Partie Orientale des Indes. Arrakan,
Pégu, Boutan, Azem, Cochinchine,
Tonquin.
Voyage du Père Tachard à Siam.
Observations sur la royaume de Siam,
tirées des Mémoires de Forbin.
Voyage d'Occum Chamnam.

VOLUME 6.

Partie Orientale des Indes, Siam.
Histoire naturelle des Indes.
Précis de différens Voyages à la Chine,
depuis le treizième siècle jusqu'à nos
jours.
Voyages, Négociations et Enterprises des
Hollandais à la Chine.
Voyages de Navarrette ; Missions de
Jésuites. Ambassade Russe. Observa-
tions tirées de Gémelli Carreri et autres
voyageurs.
Description des quinze provinces de la
Chine.

VOLUME 7.

Mœurs des Chinois ; Division de la
Nation en différentes classes, Com-
merce, Arts, Sciences, Histoire, Morale,
Langage ; Confucius ou Konfut-tsée,
Religion, Gouvernement, &c.

VOLUME 8.

Histoire Naturelle de la Chine. De la
Corée.
Tartarie Chinoise, Tartares Mantchous ;
Mogols noirs, Mogols jaunes ou Kalkas.
Tartarie Indépendante. Tartares Eleuths
ou Kalmouks. Thibet. Pays des
Usbecks, Turkestan.

Laharpe, Vol. 8—*continued.*
Sibérie. Voyage de Gmelin.
Samoïèdes et Ostiaks, par un Anonyme.
Voyage de M. l'Abbé Chappe.
Japon. Voyage de Kæmpfer, Gouvernement, Mœurs, Religion, et Histoire naturelle des Japonais.

VOLUME 9.

Amérique. Prémières Découvertes et Prémiers Etablissemens Espagñols dans le Nouveau-Monde. Christophe Colomb.
Nouvelles Découvertes et nouveaux Crimes ; Vasco Nugnez, Las Casas.
Mexique. Hernandez de Cordove, Découverte de l'Yucatan.
Fernand Cortez. Découverte du Mexique.

VOLUME 10.

Amerique.—Mexique. Prise de Mexico. Nouvelle-Espagne, ou Description du Mexique. Pérou. Découverte et Conquête du Pérou par F. Pizarre et Don Diègue d'Almagro, avec Description.

VOLUME 11.

Amerique.—Pérou. Origine des Incas, Mœurs des Péruviens modernes et des Créoles. Détails sur les Anciens Péruviens. Mines et Montagnes. Voyage des Mathématiciens Français et Espagnols aux Montagnes de Quito. Retour de M. de La Condamine par la Rivière des Amazones.
Amérique Meridionale.—Tierra-Firme, Rio de la Plata, Guiane, Histoire Naturelle, depuis l'Isthme de Panama jusqu'au Brésil.

VOLUME 12.

Amerique.—Brésil. Etablissemens, Description, et Histoire Naturelle du Brésil.
Amérique Septentrionale. — Floride. Colonies Anglaises. Nouvelle-Angleterre, Nouvelle - York, Caroline, Géorgie.

VOLUME 13.

Amerique.—Colonies Françaises. Baie d'Hudson, Ile Royale, Canada ou Nouvelle-France. Caractère, Usages, Religion, Mœurs, des Habitans, et Histoire Naturelle de l'Amérique Septentrionale. Observations particulières sur les Pays les plus éloignés vers le Nord.

VOLUME 14.

Amerique.—Antilles. Mœurs des Caraïbes. Saint-Domingue, La Martinique, La Guadeloupe, La Grenade, Sainte-Lucie. Commerce des îles Francaises. Saint-Christophe, Jamaique, Barbade, Antigoa, Montserrat, Nevis, La Barboude, Anguilla. Histoire Naturelle des Antilles.

Laharpe—*continued.*

VOLUME 15.

Voyages autour du Monde et aux Poles.
Voyages au Sud-Oüest. Magellan, Drake, Sarmiento, Candish, Sebald de Weert, Spilberg, Noort, Le Maire, Wood Rogers, Dampier, Gemelli-Carréri, La Barbinais le Gentil, Anson.
Voyages au Nord-Ouest et au Nord-Est.

VOLUME 16.

Islande. Iles de Jean Mayen. Nouvelle-Zemble. Kamschatka, climat, minéraux, animaux.

VOLUME 17.

Kamschatka. Habitans. Découverte et Conquête par les Russes, leur Commerce avec ce pays, Vocabulaire.
Groenland. Glaces, Climat, Minéraux, Végétaux, Bêtes, Oiseaux, Poissons, et Habitans.

VOLUME 18.

Annales, ou Histoire civile du Groenland. Prémiers établissemens Danois, jusqu'à 1740.
Nouveaux Voyages dans la Mer du Sud. Byron, Carteret, Wallis, Bougainville.

VOLUME 19.

Nouveaux Voyages dans la Mer du Sud. Cook.

VOLUME 20.

Cook. Second Voyage.

VOLUME 21.

Cook. Second Voyage continué. Extrait de l'Ouvrage de J. R. Forster, intitulé "Observations faites pendant un Voyage autour du Monde," &c.

VOLUMES 22-24.

Cook. Troisième Voyage.

Linschoten, John Hughen van. Discourse of Voyages into the East and West Indies. [Wants general title.] *Maps.*
Folio 1598
First Booke.—Travailles into the East or Portingales Indies, The Ile Madagascar, Mossambique, Arabia Felix, Ormus, Cambaia, of the Coast of India, from Goa to the Cape de Comoriin, Malabar, the Islands called Maldyua, Seylon, the Coast of Choramandel, Bengalen and the River Ganges, the Coasts and Lands of Aracan, Pegu and Sian to the Cape of Singapura, and the towne of Malacca, the Islands of Sumatra, Java Major, Maluco, Borneo, Manillios or Philippinas, China, Japan, a Description of the Ilands of St Helena, Ascention, the Canaria, and the Acores.
Second Booke.—The true and perfect Description of the whole Coast of Guinea, Manicongo, Angola, Monomotapa, and right over against them the Cape of S. Augustin in Brasilia, with

Linschoten, Book 2—*continued.*

the compasse of the whole Ocean Seas, together with the Ilands, as S. Thomas, S. Helena, and the Ascension, &c.

Thirde Booke.—The Navigation of the Portingales into the East Indies, containing their Travels by Sea, into East India, and from the East Indies into Portingall, also from the Portingall Indies to Malacca, China, Japon, the Ilands of Java and Sunda, both to and fro, and from China to the Spanish Indies, as also of the Coast of Brasilia, and the Havens thereof.

Fourth Booke.—A most true and certaine extract and summarie of all the Rents, Demaines, Tolles, Taxes, Impostes, Tributes, Tenthes, third-pennies, and incommings of the King of Spain.

Navarette, Don Martin Fernandez de. Coleccion de los Viages y Descubrimientos, que hicieron por Mar los Españoles desde fines del Siglo XV., con varios Documentos inéditos concernientes á la Historia de la Marina Castellana y de los Establecimientos Españoles en Indias. 5 vols. *Maps.* Small 4° *Madrid*, 1825-37

Vol. 1.—Colon, Almir. D. Cristobal. Relaciones, Cartas, y otros Documentos, concernientes a los cuatro Viages para el Descubrimiento de las Indias Occidentales.

Vol. 2.—Documentos de Colon y de las Primeras Poblaciones, años 1474-1515.

Vol. 3.—Viages Menores, 1495-1595. Las Cuatro Navegaciones de Américo Vespucio. Establecimientos de los Españoles en el Darien. Suplemento al Tomo 2.

Vol. 4.—Expediciones al Maluco. Viage de Magallanes y de Elcano, años 1518-24.

Vol. 5.—Expediciones al Maluco. Viages de Loaisa, y de Saavedra, años 1522-1537.

—— French Translation of the part relating to the Voyages of Columbus. 3 vols. 8° *Paris*, 1828

Pelham, Cavendish. The World, or the Present State of the Universe : being a General and Complete Collection of Modern Voyages and Travels, selected, arranged, and digested from the Narratives of the latest and most Authentic Travellers and Navigators. 2 vols. *Maps and plates.* 4° 1808-10

CONTENTS.

VOLUME 1.

Sonnini, C. S. Travels in Upper and Lower Egypt, abridged.

Park, Mungo. Travels into the Interior Districts of Africa, in 1795-97.

Pelham, Vol. 1—*continued.*

Cook, Capt. James. Strictures on the Life of, and on his First and Second Voyages to the Southern Hemisphere.

Cooke, Clerke, and Gore, Captains. Voyage to the Pacific Ocean for making Discoveries in the Northern Hemisphere, in 1776-80.

Vancouver, Capt. George. Voyage of Discovery of the North Pacific Ocean, and round the World, in 1790-95.

Wilson, W. Missionary Voyage to the South Pacific Ocean, in 1796-98, in the ship " Duff."

Staunton, Sir George. Account of the Earl of Macartney's Embassy from the King of Great Britain to the Emperor of China.

Philip, Governor. Voyage to Botany Bay, with an Account of the Establishment of the Colonies of Port Jackson and Norfolk Island ; to which are added the Journals of Lieuts. Shortland, Watts, Ball, and Capt. Marshall.

Hodges, William. Travels in India during 1780-83.

VOLUME 2.

La Pérouse. Voyage round the World during 1785-88.

Labillardière, M. Voyage in Search of La Pérouse, in 1791-93.

Lesseps, M. de. Travels in Kamtschatka, in 1787-88.

Portlock, Capt. Nathaniel. Voyage round the World, but more particularly to the North-West Coast of America, in 1786-88, abridged.

Rochon, Abbé. Voyage to Madagascar and the East Indies.

Volney, C. F. Travels through Syria and Egypt, in 1783-85.

Dillon, J. Talbot. Travels through Spain, with Notes and Observations from a Tour through Spain and Portugal in 1803, by C. A. Fischer.

Link, H. F. Travels in Portugal.

Stolberg, Count F. L. Travels through Germany, Switzerland, Italy, and Sicily.

Brie, J De. Appendix to Stolberg's Travels, extracted from a Journey in Moravia and Bohemia, in 1804.

Dutens, J. V. Travels in Upper and Lower Hungary, Transylvania, Sclavonia, Croatia, and Morlachia, in 1806.

Coxe, W. Travels in Poland.

Nowel, T. Travels in Denmark, Norway, and Sweden, in 1801.

Tooke, W. View of the Russian Empire.

Symes, M. Account of an Embassy to the Kingdom of Ava, in 1795.

Pelham, Vol. 2—*continued.*

Franklin, W. Observations made on a Tour from Bengal to Persia, in 1786-87, with an Account of the Remains of the Palace of Persepolis.

Jackson, J. Journey from India towards England in 1797, through Curdistan, Diarbekr, Armenia, and Natolia, in Asia ; and Romelia, Bulgaria, Wallachia, Transylvania, &c., in Europe. General Geographical Description of the World.

Phillips, Sir Richard. A Collection of Modern and Contemporary Voyages and Travels, containing : — 1. Translations from Foreign Languages of Voyages and Travels never before translated ; 2. Original Voyages and Travels never before published ; 3. Analysis of New Voyages and Travels published in England. [*1st Series.*] 11 vols. *Maps and plates.* [Published by Sir Richard Phillips.] 8°   1805-10

CONTENTS.

VOLUME 1.

Cassas, L. F. Travels in Istria and Dalmatia, 1702, drawn up from the Itinerary by Joseph Lavellée. Translated from the French.

Küttner, C. Gottlob. Travels through Denmark, Sweden, Austria, and part of Italy, 1798-99. Translated from the German.

Michaux, F. A. Travels to the Westward of the Allegany Mountains, in the States of the Ohio, Kentucky, and Tennessee, 1802. Translated from the French.

An Itinerary from London to Constantinople, in 60 days, taken in the suite of the British Ambassador to the Ottoman Porte, 1794.

Woodward, Capt. David. Narrative of the Sufferings of, and four Seamen, who lost their ship while in a boat at sea, and surrendered themselves to the Malays, in the Island of Celebes, 1804.

Kotzebue, Aug. Von. Journey from Berlin through Switzerland to Paris, 1804.

Tuckey, J. H. Account of a Voyage to establish a Colony at Port Philip, in Bass's Strait, on the South Coast of New South Wales, 1802-4.

VOLUME 2.

Olafsen and Povelsen. Travels in Iceland, 1800-1. Translated from the Danish.

St Vincent, J. B. G. M. Bory de. Voyage to, and Travels through the Four Principal Islands of the African Seas[Canaries, Teneriffe, Isle of France, Isle of Bourbon], 1801-2; with a Narrative of the Passage of Capt. Baudin to Port Louis in the Mauritius.

Phillips [1], Vol. 2—*continued.*

Gleanings of a Wanderer in various parts of England, Scotland, and North Wales, made during an Excursion in 1804.

Holcroft, Thomas. Travels from Hamburgh, through Westphalia, Holland, and the Netherlands, to Paris.

VOLUME 3.

Pouqueville, F. C. H. L. Travels through the Morea, Albania, and several other parts of the Ottoman Empire to Constantinople, 1798-1801. Translated from the French.

Mangourit, M. O. B. Travels in Hanover, 1803-4, containing an Account of the Form of Government, Religion, Agriculture, Commerce, and Natural History of the country.

Fischer, Christian Aug. Letters written during a Journey to Montpellier, 1804.

Spain and Portugal, A Tour through the Principal Provinces of, 1803 ; with cursory Observations on the Manners of the Inhabitants.

Journal of a Tour in Ireland, 1804 ; with Remarks on the Character, Manners, and Customs of the Inhabitants.

Carr, John. A Northern Summer ; or, Travels round the Baltic, through Denmark, Sweden, Russia, Prussia, and part of Germany, 1804.

Turnbull, John. Voyage round the World, 1800-4.

VOLUME 4.

Durand, J. P. L. Voyage to Senegal ; or, Historical, Philosophical, and Political Memoirs relative to the Discoveries, Establishments, and Commerce of Europeans in the Atlantic Ocean, from Cape Blanco to the River of Sierra Leone ; to which is added an Account of a Journey from Isle St Louis to Galam, 1785-86.

Depons, F. Travels in parts of South America, 1801-4.

A Tour in Wales, and several Counties of England, including both the Universities, 1805.

Kotzebue, Aug. v. Travels through Italy, 1804-5.

VOLUME 5.

Sarytschew, Gawrila. Account of a Voyage of Discovery to the North-East of Siberia, the Frozen Ocean, and the North-East Sea, 1785. Translated from the Russian.

Reuilly, J. Travels in the Crimea, and along the Shores of the Black Sea, 1803. Translated from the French.

Fischer, C. A. Travels to Hyères, in the South of France, 1806. Translated from the German.

Phillips [1], Vol. 5—*continued.*

A Tour through the Island of Rügen, in the Baltic, 1805. By a Temporary Inhabitant. Translated from the German.

Helms, Anthony Z. Travels from Buenos Ayres, by Potosi to Lima ; with Notes by the Translator.

An Account of a Voyage to India, China, &c., in H.M.S. " Caroline," 1803-5, with Descriptive Sketches and cursory remarks. By an Officer of the " Caroline."

Carr, John. Stranger in Ireland, or a Tour in the Southern and Western Parts of that country, 1805.

VOLUME 6.

Du Lac, Perrin. Travels through the Two Louisianas, and among the Savage Nations of the Missouri ; also in the United States, along the Ohio, and the adjacent Provinces, 1801-3. Translated from the French.

Sarytschew, G. Voyage of Discovery to the North-East of Siberia. Vol. 2.

Reinbeck, G. Travels from St Petersburgh through Moscow, Grodno, Warsaw, Breslaw, &c., to Germany, 1805. Translated from the German.

Lewis and Clark, Captains, Dr Sibley, and Mr Dunbar. Travels in the Interior Parts of America, communicating Discoveries made in exploring the Missouri, Red River, and Washita ; with a Statistical Account of the Countries adjacent, 1805.

Spilsbury, F. B. Account of a Voyage to the West Coast of Africa by H.M. Sloop " Favourite," 1805.

Waring, Edw. Scott. Tour to Sheeraz, by the Route of Kazroon and Feerozabad, 1802 ; with Remarks on the Manners, &c., of the Persians.

Salvo, Marquis de. Travels from Italy to England, through the Tyrol, Styria, Bohemia, Gallicia, Poland, and Livonia, 1806.

VOLUME 7.

Millin, A. L. Travels through the Southern Departments of France, 1804-5.

Seume, J. G. Tour through part of Germany, Poland, Russia, Sweden, Denmark, &c., 1805. Translated from the German.

Heriot, George. Travels through the Canadas, containing a Description of the Scenery on some of the Rivers and Lakes, &c. ; to which is subjoined a comparative view of the Manners and Customs of several of

Phillips [1] Vol. 7—*continued.*

the Indian Nations of North and South America.

VOLUME 8.

St Sauveur, A. G. de. Travels through the Balearic and Pithiusian Islands, 1801-6. Translated from the French.

Campenhausen, Baron. Travels through several Provinces of the Russian Empire, with an Historical Account of the Zaporog Cossacks, and of Bessarabia, Moldavia, Wallachia, and the Crimea, about 1805.

Carr, Sir John. Tour through Holland, along the right and left banks of the Rhine, to the South of Germany, 1806.

Williams, T. Travels through France during 1802-6.

Semple, R. Observations on a Journey through Spain and Italy to Naples, 1805.

VOLUME 9.

Bourgoing, J. F. Travels in Spain, containing a New, Accurate, and Comprehensive View of the State of that country, down to 1806.

Travels from Paris through Switzerland and Italy, 1801-2 ; with Sketches of the Manners and Characters of the respective Inhabitants. By a Native of Pennsylvania.

VOLUME 10.

Bolingbroke, Henry. Voyage to the Demerary, containing a Statistical Account of the Settlements there, and of those on the Essequebo, the Berbice, and other contiguous rivers of Guyana, 1799.

Ashe, Thomas. Travels in America, 1806, for the purpose of Exploring the Rivers Alleghany, Monongahela, Ohio, and Mississippi.

Collins, Francis. Voyages to Portugal, Spain, Sicily, Malta, Asia Minor, Egypt, &c., 1796-1801, with an Historical Sketch, and occasional reflections.

Journal of a Tour to the Western Counties of England, 1807. By the Author of "A Tour in Ireland."

VOLUME 11.

Peron, M. F. Voyage of Discovery to the Southern Hemisphere, 1801-4.

Valentia, Viscount. Voyages and Travels to India, Ceylon, the Red Sea, Abyssinia, and Egypt, 1802-6.

Keith, Sir G. M., Bart. Voyage to South America and the Cape of Good Hope, 1805-6.

Macdonald, James. Travels through Denmark and part of Sweden, 1809.

Phillips, Sir Richard. A Collection of Modern and Contemporary Voyages and Travels. [*2nd Series.*] 6 vols. *Maps and plates.* 8°   1810

CONTENTS.

VOLUME I.

Durand, J. P. L. Voyage to Senegal, 1785-86.

Depons, F. Travels in Parts of South America, 1801-4.

A Tour in Wales, and through several Counties of England, 1805.

VOLUME 2.

Travels from Paris through Switzerland and Italy, 1801-2. By a Native of Pennsylvania.

Bourgoing, J. F. Travels in Spain, 1806.

VOLUME 3.

Campenhausen, Baron. Travels through several Provinces of the Russian Empire.

St Sauveur, A. G. de. Travels through the Balearic and Pithiusian Islands, 1801-6.

Carr, Sir John. Tour through Holland, 1806.

Williams, T. Travels through France, 1802-6.

VOLUME 4.

Peron, M. F. Voyage of Discovery to the Southern Hemisphere, 1801-4.

Valentia, Viscount. Voyages and Travels to India, Ceylon, the Red Sea, Abyssinia, and Egypt, 1802-6.

VOLUME 5.

Bolingbroke, Henry. Voyage to the Demerary, 1799.

Ashe, T. Travels in America, 1806.

Journal of a Tour in the Western Counties of England, 1807. By the Author of "A Tour in Ireland."

VOLUME 6.

Macdonald, J. Travels through Denmark and part of Sweden, 1809.

Seume, J. G. Tour through part of Germany, Poland, Russia, Sweden, Denmark, &c., 1805.

Sarytschew, G. Voyage of Discovery to the North-East of Siberia, 1785.

A Tour through the Island of Rügen, in the Baltic, 1805. By a Temporary Inhabitant.

Mangourit, M. O. B. Travels in Hanover, 1803-4.

Spain and Portugal, A Tour through the Principal Provinces of, 1803.

Collins, F. Voyages to Portugal, Spain, Sicily, Malta, Asia Minor, Egypt, &c., 1796-1801.

Semple, R. Journey through Spain and Italy.

Phillips, Sir Richard. New Voyages and Travels, consisting of Originals and Translations. [*3rd Series.*] 9 vols. *Maps and plates.* 8°   1819-23

CONTENTS.

VOLUME I.

Fisher, Alex. Journal of a Voyage of Discovery to the Arctic Regions, 1818, in H.M.S. "Alexander," W. E. Parry, Commander.

Prior, James. Voyage in the Indian Seas, in the "Nisus" Frigate, to the Cape of Good Hope, Isles of Bourbon, France, and Seychelles, to Madras, and the Isles of Java, St Paul, and Amsterdam, 1810-11.

Chateauvieux, F. Lillin de. Travels in Italy, descriptive of the Rural Manners and Economy of that country, 1812-13.

Forbin, Count de. Travels in Greece, Turkey, and the Holy Land, 1817-18.

Fitzclarence, Lt.-Col. Journal of a Route across India, through Egypt to England, 1817-18. Abridged.

Bowdich, T. E. Mission from Cape Coast Castle to Ashantee, 1817. Abridged.

Rose, W. S. Letters from Italy. Abridged.

Macmichel, W. Journey from Moscow to Constantinople, 1817-18. Abridged.

Hoare, Sir R. C. Classical Tour through Italy and Sicily, 1790. Abridged.

Baillie, Marianne. First Impressions, or a Tour upon the Continent, 1818. Abridged.

Russell, G. Tour through Sicily, 1815. Abridged.

VOLUME 2.

Forbin, Count de. Travels in Egypt: being a continuation of the Travels in the Holy Land, 1817-18.

M'Keevor, Thomas. Voyage to Hudson's Bay, 1812 ; containing a particular Account of the Icebergs and other phenomena which present themselves in those Regions, also a Description of the Esquimeaux and North American Indians.

Freminville's Voyage towards the North Pole, 1806.

Dumont, P. J. Narrative of Thirty-Four Years' Slavery and Travels in Africa. Collected from the account delivered by himself, by J. S. Quesne.

Portenger, Henderick. Narrative of the Sufferings and Adventures of a Private Soldier of the late Swiss Regiment de Mueron, who was wrecked on the Shores of Abyssinia, in the Red Sea, 1802. By R. de May.

Burckhardt, M. Some Account of the Travels of, in Egypt and Nubia. From the *Calcutta Journal.*

Phillips [3], Vol. 2—*continued.*

Prior, James. Voyage along the Eastern Coast of Africa to Mosambique, Johanna, and Quiloa, to St Helena; to Rio de Janeiro, Bahia, and Pernambuco, in Brazil, in the "Nisus" frigate, 1813.

Cordova, Adm. Don A. de. Voyage of Discovery to the Strait of Magellan; with an Account of the Manners and Customs of the Inhabitants, and of the Natural Productions of Patagonia. Translated from the Spanish.

VOLUME 3.

Sanson, Joseph. Travels in Lower Canada, 1817; with Recollections of the Soil and Aspect, the Morals, Habits, and Religious Institutions of that country.

Cornelius, Elias. Tour in Virginia, Tennessee, &c., 1818.

Graham, William. Travels through Portugal and Spain during the Peninsular War, 1812-14.

Bowring, J. Observations on the State of Religion and Literature in Spain, made during a Journey through the Peninsula in 1819.

Castellan, A. L. Letters on Italy, 1820.

Brackenridge, H. M. Voyage to Buenos Ayres, 1817-18.

Waller, John Augustine. Voyage in the West Indies; containing various Observations made during a Residence in Barbadoes and several of the Leeward Islands; with some Notices and Illustrations relative to the city of Paramarabo, in Surinam, 1807.

VOLUME 4.

Gourbillon, M. Travels in Sicily and to Mount Etna, 1819.

Sommières, Col. L. C. Vialla de. Travels in Montenegro, containing a Topographical, Picturesque, and Statistical Account of that hitherto undescribed Country, 1806.

Pouqueville, F. C. H. L. Travels in Epirus, Albania, Macedonia, and Thessaly, 1805.

Schoolcraft, Henry R. Journal of a Tour into the Interior of Missouri and Arkansaw, from Potosi, or Mine à Burton, in a south-west direction toward the Rocky Mountains, 1818-19.

Rey, Capt. Voyage from France to Cochin China, 1819-20.

Kellsall, Charles. Classical Excursion from Rome to Arpino, 1820.

VOLUME 5.

Hallberg, Baron von. Sentimental Sketches, written during a Journey through the North of Germany, Denmark, Sweden, and Norway, about 1820. Translated from the German.

Phillips [3], Vol. 5—*continued.*

Madras. A Visit to Madras: being a Sketch of the Local and Characteristic Peculiarities of that Presidency, 1811.

Travideani, or Aveiro, Signor. Letters from Africa, to Canova, 1818-20.

Friedländer, Herman. Views in Italy, during a Journey in 1815-16.

Montulé, Edward de. Travels in Egypt, 1818-19.

Parry, Capt. Voyage of Discovery in the Western Arctic Sea, 1819-20. Letters written by an Officer of the Expedition.

Haafner, J. Travels on foot through the Island of Ceylon. Translated from the Dutch.

VOLUME 6.

Kotzebue, Otto von. Voyage of Discovery in the South Sea, and to Behring Straits, in search of a North-East Passage, 1815-18.

Saussure, L. A. Necker de. Travels in Scotland, descriptive of the State of Manners, Literature, and Science. Translated from the French.

Switzerland and France, Letters from, written during a Residence of between two and three years in different parts of those countries.

Diary of a Journey Overland through the Maritime Provinces of China, from Manchao, on the South Coast of Hainan, to Canton, 1819-20.

VOLUME 7.

Michailow, a Russian captive. Adventures among the Kalmucs, Kirghiz, and Kiwenses.

Voyage to St Petersburg in 1814, with Remarks on the Imperial Russian Navy. By a Surgeon in the British Navy.

Cailliaud, M. Frederic. Travels in the Oasis of Thebes, and in the Deserts situated East and West of the Thebaid, 1815-18. Edited by M. Jomard. Translated from the French.

Drovetti, Chev. Itinerary of an Excursion to the Valley of Dakel, 1818, with a previous Itinerary from Syout to Dongolah and Darfour.

Simond, L. Travels in Switzerland, 1817-19. Translated from the French.

Silliman, Benj. Tour to Quebec, 1819.

Dupin, Charles. Tour through the Naval and Military Establishments of Great Britain, 1816-20. Translated from the French.

VOLUME 8.

Pertusier, Charles. Picturesque Promenades in and near Constantinople, and on the Waters of the Bosphorus, 1820.

Müller, Christian. Journey through Greece and the Ionian Islands, 1821.

Phillips [3], Vol. 8—*continued.*

Lelorrain, M. Journey in Egypt, 1821, and Observations on the Circular Zodiac of Denderah, by M. Saulnier.

Saussure, L. A. Necker de. Voyage to the Hebrides, or Western Isles of Scotland; with Observations on the Manners and Customs of the Highlanders, 1822.

A Sketch of Old England, by a New England Man, 1822.

Scholz, J. M. A. Travels in the Countries between Alexandria and Parætonium, the Lybian Desert, Siwa, Egypt, Palestine, and Syria, 1821.

VOLUME 9.

Roquefeuil, Camille de. Voyage round the World, 1816-19.

Montule, E. Voyage to North America and the West Indies, 1817.

Cochelet, Charles. Narrative of the Shipwreck of the "Sophia," 1819, on the Western Coast of Africa, and of the Captivity of a part of the Crew in the Desert of Sahara.

Montèmont, Albert. Tour over the Alps, and in Italy, 1820.

Misrah, Mahomed. Narrative of a Journey from Egypt to the Western Coast of Africa, 1821.

Scott, Alex. Account of the Captivity of, among the Wandering Arabs of the Great African Desert, for a Period of nearly Six Years, 1810-16.

Rennell, Major J. Observations on the Geography of Mr Scott's Routes in North Africa.

Cramp, W. B. Narrative of a Voyage to India; of a Shipwreck on Board the "Lady Castlereagh"; and a Description of New South Wales, 1815-21.

Forbin, Count de. Recollections of Sicily, 1820.

Pinkerton, John. A General Collection of the best and most interesting Voyages and Travels in all Parts of the World, many of which are now first translated into English. 17 vols. *Maps and plates.* 4° 1808-14

CONTENTS.

VOLUME 1.—EUROPE.

Willoughby, Sir Hugh, and others. Voyages to the Northern Parts of Russia and Siberia.

Three Voyages of the Dutch to the North of Europe.

Pontanus, J. I. Dissertation concerning the North-East Passage.

Regnard's Journey to Lapland, &c.

Maupertius's Journey to the Polar Circle.

Outhier's Journal of a Voyage to the North.

Pinkerton, Vol. 1—*continued.*

Ehrenmalm, M. Arwid. Travels into Western Nordland, &c.

Leems's Account of Danish Lapland.

Allison's Voyage from Archangel.

Samoiedia, A New Account of, and the Samoiedes.

Spitsbergen, Journal of Seven Seaman left at.

Phipps's Journal of a Voyage to the North Pole.

Le Roy's Narrative of four Russian Sailors cast upon the Island of East Spitsbergen.

Backstrom's Voyage to Spitsbergen.

Von Troil's Letters on Iceland.

Kerguelen's Voyage to the North.

Cumberland, Earl of. Voyage to the Azores.

Raleigh's Report of an Engagement near the Azores.

De Chaste's Voyage to Tercera.

VOLUME 2.—EUROPE.

Gonzales. Voyage to England and Scotland.

Shaw's Tour to the West of England.

Bray, W. Sketch of a Tour into Derbyshire.

Ferber's Oryctography of Derbyshire.

Moritz, C. P. Travels through several parts of England.

Skrine's Tour through Wales.

Malkin's Tour through Wales.

Hassell's Tour to the Isle of Wight.

Heath's Account of the Islands of Scilly.

Robertson's Tour through the Isle of Man.

VOLUME 3.—EUROPE.

Pennant, T. Two Tours in Scotland.

Garnet's Account of the Drosacks.

Martin's Description of the Western Islands.

Martin's Voyage to St Kilda.

Mackenzie, Sir Geo. Account of Hirta and Rona.

Brand's Description of the Orkneys and Shetland.

Young's Tour in Ireland, An Abstract of.

Hamilton's Letters on the Northern Coast of Ireland.

VOLUME 4.—EUROPE.

Lister's Journey to Paris, 1698.

Young's Travels in France.

Saussure's Attempts to reach the Summit of Mont Blanc.

Ramond's Journey to the Summit of Mount Perdu.

VOLUME 5.—EUROPE.

Spallanzani's Travels in Italy.

Dolomieu's Account of the Earthquakes of Calabria in 1783.

Bourgoanne's Travels in Spain.

Coxe's Travels in Switzerland.

Pinkerton, Vol. 16—*continued.*

Battel, Andrew, Strange Adventure of, sent by the Portuguese Prisoner to Angola.

Bonnan's Description of the Coast of Guinea.

Proyart's History of Loango, Kakonga, and other Kingdoms in Africa.

Adanson's Voyage to Senegal, the Island of Goree, and the River Gambia.

Santos' History of Eastern Ethiopia.

Rochon's Voyage to Madagascar.

Glas's History of the Canary Islands.

Park's Travels in Africa.

VOLUME 17.

Retrospect of the Origin and Progress of Discovery, by Sea and Land, in Ancient, Modern, and most Recent Times.

Critical Catalogue of Books of Voyages and Travels.

General Index.

Prévost, Abbé. Histoire générale des Voyages, ou Nouvelle Collection de toutes les relations de Voyages par Mer et par Terre, qui ont été publiées jusqu'à présent dans les differentes Langues de toutes les Nations connues, &c. 20 vols. [No. 17 is a Supplement, printed in Amsterdam in 1761; and Nos. 18, 19, and 20 are in continuation of the work.] *Maps and plates.* 4° *Paris*, 1746-89 [*The first 7 vols. are practically a translation of Astley's Voyages. For contents of the whole see those of the " Allgemeine Historie" (p. 598), which is a German translation of the above, with a few additions.*]

Purchas, Samuel. Purchas his Pilgrimage, or Relations of the World and the Religions observed in al Ages and Places^ discovered, from the Creation unto this Present. Folio 1617

ASIA— CONTENTS.

Of the first beginning of the World and Religion ; and of the Regions and Religions of Babylonia, Assyria, Syria, Phœnicia, Palestina.

Of the Hebrew Nation and Religion.

Of the Arabians, Saracens, Turkes, and of the Ancient Inhabitants of Asia Minor, and of their Religions.

Of the Armenians, Medes, Persians, Parthians, Scythians, Tartarians, Chinois, and of their Religions.

Of the East Indies, and of the Seas and Ilands about Asia, with their Religions.

AFRICA—

Of Ægypt, Barbary, Numidia, Libya, &c., and of their Religions.

Of Æthiopia, and the African Ilands, and of their Religions.

Purchas, Pilgrimage —*continued.*

AMERICA—

Of New France, Virginia, Florida, New Spaine, with other Regions of America Mexicana, and of their Religions.

Of Cumana, Guiana, Brasil, Chica, Chili, Peru, and other Regions of America Peruviana, and of their Religions.

Purchas, Samuel. Purchas his Pilgrimes. [Each vol.] in 5 Bookes. 4 vols. (parts). *Map and illustrations.* Folio 1625 [*Vols.* 1 *and* 2 *comprise the* 10 *Books of Part* 1, *Vols.* 3 *and* 4 *the* 10 *Books of Part* 2, *the general contents of the books being given on the respective title-pages.*]

CONTENTS.

PART I.—VOLUME I.

BOOK I.

Salomons, King. Navie sent from Ezion-geber to Ophir, the Voyage largely discussed out of Divine, Ecclesiasticall, and Humane Testimony.

The Commendations of Navigation, as an Art worthy of the care of the most Worthie ; the Necessitie, Commoditie, Dignitie thereof.

Of Ezion Geber, Eloth, and the Red Sea ; that of Edom it received that name, and communicated it to the Indian Ocean, by the Phœnician Navigations frequent in those times to India.

Of Ophir, divers opinions weighed and censured ; whether the Compas was knowne to the Old World ; that the remote parts were lately inhabited, the New World but newly, and a great part thereof not yet.

Joctans posteritie seated in the East parts of Asia, amongst them, Ophir in India ultra Gangem, where Chryse was of old, and now is the Kingdome of Pegu, and the Regions adjoining.

Of the Gold, Silver, Gemmes, Ivorie, Almug Trees, Apes and Peacockes, which Salomon's Fleet brought from Ophir.

Probable conjectures of the course taken in the Ophirian Voyage, and account given of the three yeeres time spent there ; also of the course taken in like Voyages by the Romans, and the divers Ports whereto the Spices and Riches of India have in divers Ages been brought, and thence dispersed to the several parts of Europe.

Of Tharsis, or Tharshish, whether it be the same with Ophir, and both, some indefinite remoter Countrie, whether it be the Sea, or Tartessus, or any place in Spaine. Of the Ancient Navigations about Africa, and of the Phœnician Antiquities.

Man's Life a Pilgrimage. The Peregrinations of Christ, and the first encompassing the habitable or then inhabited World by the Holy Apostles and first Planters of the Gospell.

The Peregrination of St Peter, St Andrew, John, the two Jacobi, Philip, Simon Zelotes, Thomas, Bartholomew, Matthew, Jude, Matthias, and of counterfeit Writings in the Apostles' names.

Of S. Paul; of Apostolicall Assistants.

Of America, whether it were then peopled.

The glorie of Apostolicall Conquests; the hopes of enlarging the Church in this last Age, by knowledge of Arts and Languages, through the benefit of Printing and Navigation.

Of divers other principall Voyages and Peregrinations mentioned in Holy Scripture. Of the travels and dispersions of the Jewes, and of National Transmigrations.

Fabulous Antiquities of the Peregrinations and Navigations of Bacchus, Osiris, Hercules, the Argonauts, Cadmus, the Græcian Navie to Troy, Menelaus, Ulysses, Æneas, and others.

A Briefe Recital of the Famous Expeditions mentioned in Ancient Histories, of the Assyrians, Egyptians, Scythians, Ethiopians, Persians, and others.

Travels of the Antient Philosophers and learned men briefly mentioned.

Phœnician Voyages, and especially that of Hanno, a Carthaginian Captaine.

Iambulus, his Navigation to Arabia and Ethiopia, and thence to a strange Iland, from whence he sailed to Palimbothra in India.

Alexander the Great; Life, Acts, Peregrinations, and Conquests briefly related.

Travels of Musæus, Thebæus, and others mentioned by S. Ambrose; of others also mentioned in the Ecclesiastical Histories of Eusebius, Ruffinus, Socrates, and Sozomen.

A Briefe and General Consideration of Europe compared with the other parts of the World; the Names, Quantitie, Bounds, Qualitie, Excellencies, and Languages of Europe.

Brerewood, Edw. Enquiries of Languages.

—— Enquiries of the Religions professed in the World, with other Philosophical Speculations, and divers Annotations added.

Relations of divers Travellers, touching the Diversities of Christian Rites and Tenents in divers parts of the World.

2 O

Tecla Maria, an Abassine. Answeres to questions touching the Religion of the Abassines and Cophti.

Leonard, Bp. of Sidon. Relations of the Jacobites and Armenians.

Of Simon Sulaka, a Papal Easterne Patriarke, amongst the Chaldæans; and of divers others thither sent. Of Abdesu, Aatalla, Donha, his successors.

Of the Cophti, their Synode at Cairo, the Jesuites being the Pope's Agents, and of Stephen Colinzas Message to the Georgians, and two Jesuites sent to the Maronites.

Errores ex libris Maronitarum excerpti.

Angelos, Chr. Of the Condition of Life in which the Greeks now live, and of their Rites of Fasts, Feasts, and other Observations.

Stroza, Peter. Treatise of the Opinions of the Chaldeans, touching the Patriarke of Babylon, and the Nestorians in Asia.

A Briefe Survey of the Ecclesiasticall Politie, Ancient and Moderne, or of the severall Patriarchs, Archbishops, and Bishops' Sees thorow the Christian World; also of the Jesuites' Colledges and Numbers, and of other Monastical Orders.

A Discourse of the Diversitie of Letters used in divers Nations of the World; the Antiquitie, manifold use and varietie thereof, with exemplarie descriptions of very many strange Alphabets.

BOOK 2.

Of the Improvement of Navigation in later Times.

Of Magnetical and Astronomical Instruments, first applied to Navigation.

Henrie, Prince; son of John, King of Portugal. Discoveries, and of the helps both against the Moores, and in their Discoveries which the Portugals have received of our Nation.

John, King. Second Discoveries, and Advancement of the Art of Navigation, 1481-87.

Columbus, Chr. Conjectures touching a New World.

—— First Voyage, and Improvements therein of the Mariner's Art, 1492.

Alexander VI., Pope. Bull made to Castile touching the New World, 1493, with Animadversions.

The Portugals Discontent and Compromise with the Spaniard, and the First Discoveries of the East Indies, 1493-94.

Gama's Acts at Calicut, and his Return, 1499.

Purchas, Vol. 1, Book 2—*continued.*

The Second Fleet sent to the East Indies; their Discoverie of Brazil, and other acts, 1500.

Albuquerque's Exploits, and the first knowledge of the Moluccas.

Magalianes, F. The occasion of his Voyage, and the particulars of the same, with the Compassing of the World; gathered out of Ant. Pigafetta, who was in the said Circumnavigation, as also from divers other authors, 1519-22.

Drake, Sir Francis. Circumnavigation of the Earth, 1577-80.

Pretty, Francis. Voyage of Thomas Candish into the South Sea, and from thence round about the Circumference of the whole Earth, 1586-88.

Candish, Thomas. Letter to Lord Hunsdon, touching the successe of his Voyage about the World, 1588.

Noort, Oliver. Voyage round about the Globe, 1598-1601.

Sebald de Wert. Voyage to the South Sea, and Miserie in the Streights nine months, 1598-99.

Spilbergen, George. Voyage of, which passed by the Magellane Streights, and South Sea, unto the East Indies, and thence (having encompassed the whole circumference of the Earth) home, 1614-17.

Schot, Apol. Discourse of the Present State of the Moluccas.

Spilbergen, G. Brief Description of the Forts, Souldiers, and Militarie Provision, as also of their Trade and Shipping in the East Indies, under the States of the United Provinces, 1616.

Schouten, W. C., Circumnavigation by; who, Southwards from the Streights of Magellan in Terra del Fuego, found and discovered a new passage through the great South Sea, and that way sayled round about the World, 1615-17.

BOOK 3.

Of the First English Voyages to the East Indies, before the establishment of the East Indian Companie :—

Sighelmus, Mandevile, Stevens, Fitch, and divers other Englishmen, their Indian Voyages.

Wood, Benj. Voyage into the East Indies, 1596-1601.

Mildenhall, John. Travailes into the Indies, and in the Countries of Persia, and of the Great Mogul, 1599.

—— Second Letter to Master R. Staper, from Casbin in Persia, 1606.

Davis, Capt. John. Voyage to the Easterne India, 1598-1600.

Adams, W. Voyage by the Magellan Streights to Japon, 1598-1611.

Purchas, Vol. 1, Book 3—*continued.*

Davis, Capt. J. Third Voyage, with Sir E. Michelborne to the East Indies, 1604-6.

A Priviledge for fifteene yeeres granted by Her Majestie to certaine Adventurers, for the Discoverie of the Trade for the East Indies, Dec. 30, 1600.

First Voyage made to East India by Sir John Lancaster, 1600, with four ships. The preparation to this Voyage, and what befell them in the Way till they departed from Saldania to Achen in Sumatra, with their trading at Saint Maries, Antongill, Nicubar; the strange plant of Sombrero, and other occurrents. Their entertainment and Trade at Achen, and Q. Elizabeth's Letter to that King; their presents to and from the King, his letters to Q. Elizabeth, their departure from Priaman and Bantam, and settling a Trade there, with their departure for England. Portugall Wiles discovered, with a Prize taken neere Malacca.

Scot, Edmund. Discourse of Java, and of the First English Factorie there, with divers Indian, English, and Dutch occurrents, 1602-5.

Clayborne, Thomas. Discourse of a Second Voyage to the East Indies under Sir H. Middleton, 1604-6, with 4 ships.

Keeling, W. Journal of third Voyage to the East Indies, 1607-10, with 3 ships. Their disasters and putting back for Sierra Leona ; what happened till they departed from Saldania. Instructions learned at Delisa of the Moores and Gusarates touching the Monsons ; coming to Priaman and Bantam, with their Voyage to Banda.

Hawkins, Capt. W. Relation of the occurrents which happened in the time of his residence in India, in the Countie of the Great Mogoll ; and of his departure from thence, 1608-13. A briefe discourse of the strength, wealth, and government, with some Customs of the Great Mogoll.

Middleton, David. Voyage from Tilburie Hope, 1606-8.

A briefe narration of the Fourth Voyage to the East Indies under Alex. Sharpey, and R. Rowles, with the Discoverie of the Red Sea.

Report of W. Nicols, which travelled by land from Bramport to Masulipatan, written at Bantam by H. Moris, 1612.

The unhappie Voyage of the "Union," till she arrived at Priaman, 1609, reported by a Letter sent by S. Bradshaw ; written by H. Moris, 1610.

Purchas, Vol. 1, Book 3—*continued*.

Salbanke, Joseph. Voyage through India, Persia, part of Turkie, the Persian Gulfe, and Arabia, 1609.

Middleton, David. Voyage to Java and Banda, 1609.

Middleton, Sir Henrie. Sixth Voyage, set forth by the East Indian Companie in 3 ships, 1610-12. The Proceeding of his Voyage till he came to Moha in the Red Sea. Turkish treacherie at Moha and Aden with the English. Sir H. Middleton and 34 others sent to the Basha at Zenan ; Description of the Countrie, and occurrents till their returne. Indian shipping at Moha ; Sir H. Middleton's escape from the Turkes. Departure from Surat, and what happened there with the Cambayans and Portugals, going to Dabul, and thence to the Red Sea, and enforced trade with the Guzerates.

Dounton, Capt. Nich. Journal, or certain extracts thereof, 1611-12. Their coming to Saldania, and thence to Socatora. Of Abba del Curia, Arabia Felix, Aden and Moha, and the treacherous dealing of both places. Their departure from Moha to Assab, and after that, higher into the Red Sea, thence to Socatora, and after that Surat.

Marten, Nath. Seventh Voyage into East India, under Capt. Anth. Hippon, 1610-15.

Floris, P. Williamson. Extracts of his Journal, for the Seventh Voyage, 1610-15. Voyage to Paleacatte, Petapoli, Masulipatan, Bantam, Patania, and Siam. Relations of strange occurrents in Pegu, Siam, Joor, Patane, and the Kingdoms adjacent.

Tatton, John. Journal of a Voyage made by Capt. S. Castleton to the East Indies, 1612-13.

BOOK 4.

Saris, John. Eighth Voyage set forth by the East Indian Societie, wherein were employed three ships, under the command of Capt. John Saris. His course and acts to and in the Red Sea, Java, Moluccas, and Japan (by the inhabitants called Neffoon, where also he first began and settled an English Trade and Factorie), with other remarkable rarities, 1611-14.

—— Observations of occurrents which happened in the East Indies during his abode at Bantam, 1605-9.

Cockes, R. Relation of what passed in the General's absence going to the Emperour's Court. Whereunto are added divers Letters of his and others, for the better knowledge of Japonian affaires.

Purchas, Vol. 1, Book 4—*continued*.

Finch, W. Observations taken out of his large Journall, touching Sierra Leona, in 1607 ; S. Augustine and Socotora ; Occurrents in India ; Journey to Agra ; Description of Fetipore, Byana, Lahore, &c.

Davy, John. Journal of the Ninth Voyage to the East Indies, under Capt. E. Marlowe, 1611-15.

Davis, John. A Ruter, or briefe direction for readie sayling into the East India, digested into a plaine methode, upon experience of the five voyages thither, and home again.

Best, Thomas. Journal of the tenth Voyage to the East India, 1611-14, with 2 ships. Observations in their way to Surat, their Acts with the Mogol's subjects, and Fights against the Portugals, setling a Factorie, and departure to Achen, Trade to Tecoo and Passaman, their going to Bantam, and thence home.

Copland, Rev. P. Remembrances taken out of a Tractate written by, on the former Voyage [Best]. King of Achen's Letter to His Majestie ; and Notes of N. Salmon's Journal.

Boner, Robert. Notes taken out of the Journal of; who was then Master in the "Dragon" [Capt. Best].

Extracts of a Tractate, written by Nich. Withington, which was left in the Mogul's Countrey by Capt. Best, a Factor ; his Adventures, and Travels therein.

Wilson, Ralph. Journal of the eleventh Voyage to the East Indies, 1611-13.

Payton, Walter. Journal of all the principal matters passed in the Voyage to the East India, 1612-14.

Downton, Captain Nic. Extracts of the Journal of a Voyage to the East Indies ; wherein is related their happy successe against the Vice-Roy, and all the Indian Sea Forces of the Portugals, 1613-15.

Elkington, Captain T. Collections taken out of the Journal of a Voyage to the East Indies, 1613-15.

Dodsworth, Edw. Briefe Memorialls observed by, during a Voyage to the East Indies, 1613-15.

Francisco, Domingo. Examination of, taken in Swally Roade, East India, aboord the "Gift," Feb. 20, 1614.

Steel, R., and J. Crowther. Journal of a Journey from Azmere, in India, to Spahan, in Persia, 1615-16.

Millward, John. Memorials of a Voyage to the East Indies, 1614-15.

Peyton, Captain Walter. Second Voyage to the East Indies, 1614-16. A Briefe Declaration of the Ports, Cities,

Purchas, Vol. 1, Book 4—*continued*.

and Towns, inhabitated and traded unto by the Portugalls, betwixt the Cape of Good Hope and Japan.

Roe, Sir Thomas. Observations Collected out of his Journal, of matters occurring worthy memorie in the way, and in the Mogol's Court, his customs, cities, countries, subjects, and other Indian Affaires, 1614-17.

Coryat, Thomas. Letter from Jerusalem to the Court of the Great Mogol, 1615-16, with Observations.

BOOK 5.

Hawes, Roger. Memorialls taken out of the Journal of, touching the Proceedings of the Factorie of Cranganor under the Great Samorine, 1615.

Childe, Alex. Journal from England to Surat, and thence to Jasques, in Persia, 1616.

Spurway, Thomas. Letter touching the Wrongs done at Banda to the English by the Hollanders, 1617.

Hatch, John. Relations and Remembrances of a Voyage, set forth by the East Indian Societie, 1616-21.

Heynes, Edw. Voyage from Surat to Moha, in the Red Sea, for setling an English Trade in those parts, 1618.

Pring, Captain Martin. Brief Notes of two Voyages into the East Indies, 1614-16 and 1616-21 :—Occurrents in the way, at Surat, Bantam, Jacatra, Coromandel, and Teco. Voyage from Bantam to Patania, and thence to Japan and Jacatra, set by itself for the use of Mariners.

Hores, W. Discourse of his Voyage from Surat to Achen, Teco, and Bantam, 1618-19.

Courthop, Nath. Journal of his Voyage from Bantam to the Ilands of Banda, with his Residence in Banda and Occurrents there, 1616-20, with the Surrender of Poolaroone by the Dutch.

Hayes, Rt. Continuation of the former Journal, containing the Death of Capt. Courthop, Surrender of Lantore, News of the Peace, and after the Peace Lantore and Poolaroone seized by the Dutch, 1620-21.

Letter written to the East India Companie in England, from their Factors, 1621.

The Hollanders Declaration of the Affaires of the East Indies; written in an Answere to the former Reports, touching Wrongs done to the English in the Islands of Banda, 1622.

An Answer to the Hollanders Declaration concerning the Occurrents of the East India.

Purchas, Vol. 1, Book 5—*continued*.

Relations and Depositions touching the Hollanders brutish and cruel usage of the English, 1621.

Fitz-Herbert, Captain Humphrey. Pithy Description of the chiefe Ilands of Banda and Moluccas, 1621.

Middleton, Sir H. Voyage to the Moluccas; with three severall surrenders of certaine of the Banda Islands to the King of England, 1620.

Dutch Navigations to the East Indies, out of their own Journals and other Histories.

Swan, R. Extract of a Journal of a Voyage to Surat and to Jasques, in the Persian Gulfe, with four Ships.

Relation of the Fight of four English Ships with foure Portugall Ships, two Galliots, and ten Frigates in the Gulfe of Persia, 1620.

Smith, Rt. Letter to his Brother, relating of a Rare Attempt and Exploit of a small English Pinnasse, in taking a Portugall Ship.

Hobbs, Giles. Travaile from Musco to Spahan, 1620.

Mun, T. Discourse of Trade from England unto the East Indies, answering to divers objections which are usually made against the same.

PART I.—VOLUME 2.
BOOK 6.

Leo, John. Observations of Africa, and a Description of the Kingdomes of Bugia and Tunis, the Land of Negroes, and of the Confines of Egypt; with an Account of the People, Tribes, Languages, Seasons, Vertues, Vices, and other more general considerations of Africa.

Collections of things most remarkable in the Historie of Barbarie, by Ro. C.

The Trading of the Moores into Guinee and Gago for Gold Ore, or Sandie Gold.

African Possessions of the King of Spain, and the Turke.

Nicholay, Nich. Description of the City of Alger, and how it came into the Possession of Barbarossa, and also of Malta and Tripolie.

Journal of all Occurrents hapning in the Fleet of Ships sent out by the King, as well against the Pirats of Algiers as others, 1620, under Sir Robert Mansel.

Relation of the "Jacob," a Ship of Bristoll, which was in 1621 taken by the Turkish Pirats of Argier, and within five days after, four English youths overcame thirteen of the Turkes, and brought the ship to St Lucas, in Spaine, where they sold nine for Gallie-slaves, 1621.

Purchas, Vol. 2, Book 6—*continued*.

Rawlins, John. Wonderfull Recovery of the " Exchange," of Bristow, from the Turkish Pirats of Algier.

Sandys, George. Relations of Africa, his Voyage from Rhodes to Alexandria, Observations of Egypt and of Nilus, Journey to Cairo and Gaza, 1610.

BOOK 7.

Jobson, R. True Relation of a Voyage for the Discovery of Gambra, in which they passed 960 miles up the River into the Continent.

Guinea. A Description and Historicall Declaration of the Kingdom of Guinea, otherwise called the Golden Coast of Myna, in Africa, showing their beliefe, opinions, traffiquing, bartering, and manner of speech, together with the situation of the Country, Townes, Havens, and Rivers, as they are now found out and discovered. Translated out of Dutch.

The Passage from the Golden Coast to the Kingdome of Benni, or Rio de Benni, and Rio Floreado, the Citie, Court, Gentry, Apparell, and other places described. .

Battell, And. Voyage to the River of Plate ; who being taken on the Coast of Brasil, was sent a prisoner to Angola ; Discovery of the Gagas, and escape to Loango.

Pigafetta, P. Report of the Kingdom of Congo, gathered out of the Discourses of Ed. Lopes, translated by A. Hartwell.

Alvarez, Sir Francis. Voyage unto the Court of Prete Janni, the Great Christian Emperour of Ethiopia, 1520-33.

Castro, Don John. Voyage which the Portugals made from India to Zoez,1540-41.

Brief Relation of the Embassage which the Patriarch Don John Bermudez brought from the Emperour of Ethiopia to Don John, King of Portugal ; in the which he reciteth the death of Don Christopher of Gama, and the Successes of the Portugals that went in his Companie.

Nunnez (or Nonius) Baretus, John, and Andrea Ovieda. Relations of the State and Religion in Ethiopia, 1555-77. Description of the Countries, and the severall Regions, Religions, and Abassine Opinions.

An Armenian his Report of Sussinus, the Emperor of the Abaxins, by us vulgarly called Prester John.

BOOK 8.

The Historie of the first Expedition to Jerusalem, by Godfrey of Bullen, Robert of Normandie, and other Christian Princes, written by Robert, a Monk of S. Remigius, 1095.

Purchas, Vol. 2, Book 8—*continued*.

Fulcherius Carnotensis. Acts of the Pilgrimes in their Expedition to Jerusalem, before and after the taking thereof, 1095-1124.

Supplement of the Holy Land Storie, gleaned out of the large Historie of William, Archbishop of Tyrus, 1126-78.

Continuation of the Jerusalem Expedition and other additions, gathered out of Matthew Paris, chiefly relating the Acts of English Pilgrimes in that employment, 1118-1292.

Pilgrimage to Jerusalem, written in very old English Rime.

The Churches Peregrination by the Holy Land way, and warre into Mystical Babylon, or a Mysterie of Papal Iniquitie revealed, how the Papal Monarchie in and over Christendome was advanced in that age and the following, and principally by this Expedition into the Holy Land.

The History of the Normans and their Proceedings. Of Urban and Boamund's Policie, &c.

Monuments of Antiquitie, taken out of Ancient Records, to testifie the quondam Commerce betwixt our Kings and their Subjects, and those Easterne Princes.

Sandys, George. Relation of a Journey to the Holy Land, begun 1610. Constantinople described.

Biddulph, W. Part of a Letter from Aleppo.

—— Part of a Letter from Jerusalem.

Glover, Sir Thomas. Account of the Journey of Ed. Barton, Esq., Ambassador with the Grand Signior in Constantinople, 1596.

Barton, Ed. Two Letters to G. Sanderson and G. Sandy from Agria, 1596.

Smith, Captain John. Travels and Adventures in divers Parts of the World, thorow France, Italie, and on the Sea Coasts of Europe, Africa, and Asia, with his Transylvanian Acts ; begun about 1596.

Osman, Sultan. The Death of, and the setting up of Mustafa, his uncle.

Mount Sinai, Oreb, and the adioining parts of Arabia, described out of the four Journals of Breidenbach, Baumgarten, Bellonius, and Chr. Furer.

BOOK 9.

Sherley, Sir Anthonie. Travels into Persia, and employed thence Ambassadour to the Christian Princes, 1599.

—— Voyage over the Caspian Sea, and thorow Russia, from W. Parry's Discourse of the whole Voyage of Sir A. Sherley, 1601.

Purchas, Vol. 2, Book 9—*continued.*

Newberie, John. Two Voyages. One into the Holy Land, 1578-79; the other to Balsara, Ormus, Persia, and back thorow Turkie, 1580-82.

Cartwright, John. Observations in his Voyage from Aleppo to Hispaan, and backe again, about 1603.

Benjamin, the Son of Jonas, a Jew. Peregrination of, discovering both the State of the Jews and of the World, about 460 yeeres since.

Terry, Edward. Relation of a Voyage to the Easterne India, 1615. A Description of the Mogols Empire, the People of Indostan, and the Gentile Sects.

Sultan Achmet Chan, Letter to King James I.

Barthema, or Vertoman, Lewis. Travels into Egypt, Syria, Arabia, Persia, and India, 1503. His travel thorow the Desart of Medina and Mecha, passage by the Red Sea to Aden, imprisonment and escape, visiting other parts of Arabia, Zeila, Cambia.

Collections of Asia, especially of Arabia, gathered out of an Arabike booke of Geographie, written by a Nubian, 470 yeeres ago, translated into Latin by Gabriel Sionita, and J. Hesronita.

Collections of divers Mahumetan authors in their Arabicke Bookes, by G. Sionita and J. Hesronita, touching the most remarkable things in the East, especially of the Mosleman superstitions and rites, and the places of chiefe note.

Duart de Meneses, Don. Tractate of the Portugall Indies [Goa], containing the Laws, Customes, Revenues, Expenses, and other matters, remarkable therein.

Silva Figueroa, Don Garcia, ambassador from the King of Spain to the Persian. Letter written at Hispahan, to the Marquesse of Bedmar, touching matters of Persia, 1619.

João dos Sanctos, Friar. Collections out of the Voyage and Historie of his Æthiopia Orientalis, et Varia Historia, and out of other Portugals, for the better knowledge of Africa and the Christianitie therein.

Gramaye, J. B. Relations of the Christianitie of Africa, and especially of Barbarie and Algier, 1619.

Jobson, Richard. Observations touching the River Gambra, with the people, merchandise, and creatures of those parts.

Letter containing the admirable escape and glorious victorie of N. Roberts, T. Stevens, and R. Sucksbich, taken by Algier Pyrates.

Purchas, Vol. 2, Book 9—*continued.*

Withers, Robert. Description of the Grand Signior's Seraglio.

Letter sent by Sultan Osman, to His Majestie, by Husein Chiaus.

Letter written by Halil Bashaw, Chief Vizier and Generall in the Persian Expedition, to Sir Paul Pindar, April 1618.

Sanderson, John. Voyages to Constantinople, Cairo, and Tripoli, with an Historical Description of Constantinople, 1584-1602.

—— Pilgrimage from Constantinople to the Holy Land, and so to Tripolie in Syria, 1601.

Timberley, H. Report of the Voyage from Cairo in Egypt, to Jerusalem, 1601.

Newbery, John. Letters relating to his third and last Voyage into the Easterne parts of the World, Aleppo, Balsara, and Ormus, 1583.

Eldred, J., and W. Shales. Letters from Bagdet and Balsara, 1583.

Pyrard de Laval, Francois. Voyage to the East Indies, and especially his observations of the Maldives, where, being ship-wracked, hee lived five yeeres, 1601-11.

BOOK 10.

Briefe collections of Voyages, chiefly of Spaniards and Portugals, taken out of Antonie Galvano's Book of the Discoveries of the World.

Trigautius, Nic., a Jesuite. Letter touching his Voyage to India, and of the state of Christianitie in China and Japan, 1618.

Cocke, R. Letter concerning later occurrents in Japon, 1622.

Hatch, Arthur. Letter touching Japon, with the Government affaires and later occurrents, 1623.

Frederike, Cæsar. Extracts of his eighteen yeeres Indian observations, 1563-81.

Balbi, Gasparo. Voyage to Pegu, and observations there, 1579-83.

Fitch, Ralph. Voyage to Ormus, and so to Goa, in the East Indies, to Cambaia, Ganges, Bengala; to Bacola, and Chonderi to Pegu, to Jamahay in the Kingdom of Siam, and backe to Pegu, and from thence to Malacca, Zeilan, Cochin, and all the Coast of the East Indias, 1583-91.

Pimenta, Nicholas. Indian Observations, written from divers Indian Regions, principally relating the Countries and accidents of the Coast of Coromandel and Pegu, 1597-99.

Linschoten, John Huighen van. Voyage to Goa, and observations of the East Indies, 1483.

Purchas, Vol. 3, Book 2—*continued.*

Riccius and Trigautius. Discourse of China, contayning the Country, people, government, religion, rites, sects, characters, studies, arts, acts, and a Map, taken out of a China Map, illustrated with notes.

Monfart. Continuation of the Jesuites Acts and observations in China, till the death of Riccius and some yeeres after. Of Hanceu or Quinsay. Cir. 1618.

BOOK 3.

Fletcher, Giles. Treatise of Russia and the adjoining Regions, 1588.

Edge, Thomas. Northerne Discoveries of Seas, Coasts, and Countries, in order as they were hopefully begun and happily continued by the Societie of Muscovia Merchants of London ; with a Description of Greenland, 1553-1622.

Veer, Gerart de. Voyages of W. Barents, alias Bernards, into the North Seas ; behind Norway, Muscovia, and Tartaria, and to the Kingdoms of Cathaia and China, 1594-96.

Iver Boty, a Gronlander. Treatise of the Course from Island to Groneland, 1608.

Description of the Countries of Siberia, Samoieda, and Tingoesia ; together with the Journeyes leading unto the same Countries toward the East and North-east, as they are daily frequented by the Moscovites, 1612.

Gourdon, William. Voyage made to Pechora, 1611.

Finch, Richard. Letter to Sir Thomas Smith touching the former Voyage, and other observations.

Names of the Places that the Russes sayle by, from Pechorskoie Zauorot to Mongozey, with the manner of their travell.

Logan, Josias. Voyage to Pechora and his wintering there, 1611.

Pursglove, W. Voyage to Pechora and his wintering there, 1611.

—— Travell from Pechora to Permia, Ougoria, and to the River Ob, and the Townes situated thereupon, over Land. Commodities for Pechora, Siberia, Permia, Ougoria, and among the Tingussies.

Gourdon, W. Later Observations, in his wintering at Pustozera, 1614-15, with a description of the Samoyeds.

Poole, Jonas. Voyages to Cherie Iland, 1604-9.

Hudson, Henrie. Discoverie toward the North Pole, 1607 ; written by J. Playse and H. Hudson.

—— Second Voyage for finding a passage to the East Indies by the North-West, written by H. Hudson, 1608.

Purchas, Vol. 3, Book 3—*continued.*

Hudson, Henry. Third Voyage toward Nova Zembla, and at his returne, his passing from Farre Ilands to New-found-Land, and along to 44 deg. 10 min., and thence to Cape Cod, and so to 33 deg. and along the Coast to the Northward, and up the River neere to 43 deg., 1609, written by R. Juet.

—— Abstract of his Journall for the Discoverie of the North-west passage, 1610.

Pricket, Abacuk. Larger Discourse of the same Voyage, and the successe thereof, 1610.

Nicolo, M. M., and A. Zeni. Discoveries in Iseland and Friesland, gathered out of their Letters, 1380.

Quirino, Piero. Shipwracke of, on the Coast of Norway, 1431.

Ancient Commerce betwixt England and Norway, and other Northerne Regions.

Barkley, George. Travels by Sea and Land, in Europe, Asia, Africa, and America, and their Ilands, 1605.

Broniouis de Biezerfedea, Martin. Description of Tartaria, or Chersonesus Taurica, and the Regions subject to the Perecop or Crim Tartars, with their customs, private and publicke, in peace and warre.

Blefkens, Dithmar. Voyages and History of Island and Groenland, 1563.

Jonas, Arngrim, an Islander. Chrymogoea or History of Island, 1609.

BOOK 4.

Poole, Jonas. Voyages set forth by Sir Thomas Smith and the Muscovie Company, to Cherry Island, Greenland, for a further discoverie to be made towards the North Pole, and also the West, for the likelihood of a Trade or a passage that way, 1610-12.

Baffin, W. Journall of the Voyage made to Greeneland, 1613.

Fotherbye, R. Voyage of Discovery to Greeneland, 1614.

—— True Report of a Voyage for Discoverie of Seas, Lands, and Ilands to the Northwards, 1615.

Heley, W. Divers Voyages to Greenland, with Letters of those which were there employed, 1617-23.

Russia. The late changes and manifold alterations in Russia since Ivan Vasilowich to this present, gathered out of many letters and observations of English Embassadours and other Travellers in those parts, 1570-1615.

—— A briefe Copie of the points of the Contracts between the Emperour and the King of Sweden, 1616.

Relation of two Russe Cossacks Travailes out of Siberia to Catay, and other Countries adjoining, 1619.

Purchas, Vol. 4, Book 6—*continued*.

Relation of the Habitations and other Observations of the River of Marwin, and the adjoining Regions.

Rivers from Brabisse to the Amazones.

Davies, William. Description and Discoverie of the River of Amazons.

BOOK 7.

A Treatise of Brasill, written by a Portugall which had long lived there.

Lerius, John. Extracts out of the Historie of Brasill, 1558.

Schnirdel, Hulderike. Travels, from 1534-54. His Voyage up the River Plate, Foundation of Townes, their Expedition up the River of Parana and Parabol ; the people of these parts ; and a Long March from Assumption into Peru.

Hawkins, Sir Richard. Observations in his Voyage into the South Sea, 1593.

Ellis, John, A Brief Note written by, in his Voyage through the Strait of Magelan, concerning the said Strait, and certain places on the Coast and Inland of Peru, 1593.

A Briefe Relation of an Englishman which had been 13 yeeres Captive to the Spaniards in Peru, &c., 1603.

Ursino, Alex. Relation concerning the Coast of Terra Firma, and the secrets of Peru and Chili, 1581.

Giros, or de Quir, P. F. Relation of the New Discoverie in the South Sea, 1609.

—— Petition presented to the King of Spaine, touching the Discoverie of the fourth part of the World, called Terra Australis Incognita, and of the great riches and fertilitie of the same, 1610.

Vaz, Lopez. Historie of (taken by Capt. Withrington at the River of Plate, 1586, with this Discourse about him), touching American places, discoveries and occurents.

Benzo, Jerom. Briefe extracts translated out of his three books of the New World, touching the Spaniards cruell handling of the Indians, and the effects thereof, 1641.

De la Vega, Inca Garcilasso. Observations of things most remarkable, collected out of the first part of the Commentaries of ; of the originall Lives, Conquests, Lawes, and Idolatries of the Incas, or Ancient Kings of Peru.

—— Suppliment of the Historie of the Incas, collected out of the second part, or Generall Historie of Peru.

Pizarro, Francis. Brief Notes of his Conquest of Peru, 1531-34.

Xeres, Francisco de. Conquest of Peru and Cusco, called New Castile, 1524-33.

Purchas, Vol. 4, Book 7—*continued*.

Sancho, Pedro. Relations of Occurrents in the Conquest of Peru after F. Pizarro's departure, 1534.

BOOK 8.

Nunez, Alvaro, called Capo di Vacca. A true Relation concerning that which happened to the Fleet in India, from 1527 to 1536.

Soto, F. de. Voyage to Florida, and Discoverie of the Regions in that Continent, with the Travels of the Spaniards four yeeres together therein, and the accidents which befell them, 1539-43.

Gusman, Nunno di. Relation of New Spaine, 1530.

Voyages of Frier Marco de Niça, Don F. Vasquez de Coronado, Don Ant. de Espeio, &c., into New Mexico and the adjoining Coasts and Lands, 1539-90.

Perez, Martin. Extracts out of certain Letters of, from the New Mission of the Province of Cinoloa, to the Fathers of Mexico, 1591. With a Letter added, of later Discoveries, 1605.

Toletus, L. T. Letter written from Valladolid to R. Hakluyt, touching Juau de Onate his Discoveries in New Mexico, 500 leagues from the old Mexico, 1605.

Las Casas, Bartholomew de. Briefe Narration of the Destruction of the Indies by the Spaniards, 1542. Of the Iles of Hispaniola, S. John, Jamaica, Cuba, Terra Firma, Nicaragua, New Spaine, Guatimala, Panuco, Xalisco, Yucatan, S. Martha, Carthagene, the Coast of Pearles, the River Vuia pari : of Venesuela, Florida, the River La Plata, Peru, and Granada.

Notes of Voyages and Plantations of the French in the Northerne America, both in Florida and Canada, 1524-82.

Champlaine, S. Voyage made unto Canada, 1603.

Lescarbot, Marke. Voyage of M. de Monts into New France, Canada, &c., 1603-9.

Collections out of a French Booke, called additions to Nova Francia ; containing the accidents there, from 1607-11.

The First Plantation of English Colonies in Virginia, briefly mentioned, 1514-90.

Gosnol, Capt. Voyage to the North part of Virginia, 1602.

Notes of same Voyage, and of Mace's Voyage to Virginia, 1602.

Pringe, Martin. Voyage for the Discovery of the North part of Virginia, 1603.

Canner, Thomas. Relation of the Voyage made to Virginia by Capt. B. Gilbert, 1603.

Ramusio, Vol. 1—*continued.*

Barros, Giovan di. Della Historia, con alcuni Capitoli estratti appartenenti alla Cosmografia.

VOLUME 2.

Marco Polo. Delle cose de' Tartarie e dell' Indie Orientali, 1250, con Prefatione di Ramusio, ed Espositione sopra le prime Parole del libro di M. Marco.

Hayton Armeno. Dell' origine e successione de' Gran Cani Imperadori Tartari, 1253-1303.

Angiolello, G. M. Della vita e fatti d' Ussuncassan Re di Persia, che altrimenti era chiamato Assambei; e delle guerre da lui fatte con Mahometo Gran Turco, 1462-1524.

Viaggio d'un Mercante, che fu nella Persia, 1507-20.

Barbaro, Josafa. Viaggio della Tana, e nella Persia, 1436-87.

Contarino, Ambrosio. Viaggio nella Persia, 1473-77.

Campense, Alberto. Lettera intorno le Cose di Moscovia.

Jovio, Paolo. Delle cose della Moscovia.

Sigismondo, Barone in Herberstain. Commentari della Moscovia et della Russia, 1559.

Arriano. Lettera, della sua Navigatione d'intorno al Mar Maggiore.

Giorgio interiano Genovese della Vita de Zychi, altrimenti Circassi.

Hippocrate. Parte del Trattato, dell' aere e dell' acqua nella quale si Ragiona de gli Scithi.

Quirino, Pietro. Viaggio e Naufragio, 1431.

Fiorauante, C., e G. di Michele. Descritto Naufragio del sopra detto P. Quirino.

Cabota, Sebastiano. Navigatione nelle Parte Settentrionali, 1556-57.

Zeno, Caterino. Viaggio in Persia, e delle Guerre fatte nell' Imperio Persiano dal tempo di Ussuncassano, 1450.

—— Nicolò e Antonio. Dello scoprimento dell' Isola Frislanda, Eslanda, fatto sotto il Polo Artico.

Due Viaggi in Tartaria par alcuni frate, 1247.

Odorico da Udine, Beato. Due Viaggi, 1318.

Guagnino, Alessandro. Descrittione della Sarmatia Europea.

Valesio, H. Compendio delle Chroniche di Polonia.

Mattheo di Micheovo. Descrittione delle due Sarmatie.

VOLUME 3.

Martire, Pietro. Sommario cavato della sua Historia del Nuovo Mondo, scoperta da C. Colombo, poi detto Indie Occidentali, 1492-1515.

Oviedo, G. F. d'. Sommario da lui stesso

Ramusio, Vol. 3—*continued.*

levato della sua Historia Naturale e Generale, dell' Indie Occidentali, scoperte da C. Colombo.

—— Historia Generale et Naturale dell' Indie Occidentali, in Lib. xx.

Cortese, Fernando. Relationi Seconda, Terza, e Quarta, delle sue grandi imprese, con l' acquisto della gran Città del Temistitan Messico, dove hora è detto la Nuova Spagna, 1519-24.

Alvarado, Pietro d'. Lettere due à F. Cortese, del discoprimento nella Nuova Spagna.

Godoi, Diego. Lettera à F. Cortese, del discoprimento nella Nuova Spagna.

D' un gentil' huomo del F. Cortese, Relatione della gran Città del Temistitan Messico, e d' altre Cose della Nuova Spagna.

Nunez, Alvaro, detto Capo di Vacca. Relatione delle Indie, e della Nuova Galitia, 1527-36.

Gusman, Nunno di. Relatione dell' imprese fatte in acquistare molte Provincie e Città nella Maggior Spagna, 1530.

Ulloa, Capit. Francesco d'. Navigatione per discoprire l' Isole delle Specierie fino al mare detto Vermeio, 1532-39.

Vasquez di Coronado, F. Sommario di due sue Lettere, del Viaggio fatto da Fra Marco da Nizza alle sette Città di Cevola, 1539.

Mendozza, Antonio di. Lettera del discoprimento della Terra Ferma della Nuova Spagna verso Tramontana, 1539.

Nizza, Marco da. Relatione del Viaggio fatto per terra à Cevola Regno delle sette Città, 1539.

Vasquez di Coronado, Francesco. Relatione del Viaggio alle dette sette Città, 1540.

Alarchon, Fernando. Navigatione con l'armata di A. di Mendozza, quale andò per mare à scoprire il Regno delle sette Città, 1540.

Relatione d'un Capitano Spagnuolo del discoprimento e conquista del Perù fatta da F. ed H. Pizarro, 1531.

Xerez, Francesco. Relatione della Conquista fatta da F. Pizarro del Perù e Provincia del Cuscho, chiamata la Nuova Castiglia, 1532-33.

Relatione d' un Secretario di F. Pizarro, della Conquista fatta della Provincia del Perù, con la Descrittione della gran Città del Cuscho, 1534.

Oviedo, Gonzalo F. d'. Relatione della Navigatione per il grandissimo Fiume Maragnon, posto sopra la Terra Ferma dell' Indie Occidentali, 1543.

Ramusio. Discorso sopra la Terra Ferma dell' Indie Occidentali, detta del Lavorador de los Baccalaos, et della Nuova Francia.

Ramusio, Vol. 3—*continued*.

Verrazzano, Giov. Relatione della terra per lui scoperta al Rè Christianissimo, 1524.

Discorso d' un gran Capitano di Mare Francese, sopra le Navigationi fatte alla Nuova Francia, e sopra la terra del Brasil, Guinea, Isola di San Lorenzo, e quella di Summatra.

Carthier, Jacques. Prima Relatione della Terra Nuoua detta la Nuoua Francia, 1534.

—— Seconda Relatione, della Navigatione per lui fatta all' Isole di Canada, Hochelaga, Saguenai, etc., al presente dette la Nuoua Francia, 1535.

Cesare de' Federici. Viaggio nell' India Orientale, ed oltra l' India, per via di Soria, 1563-69.

Navigationi fatte da gli Olandesi e Zelandesi al Settentrione, nella Noruegia, Moscovia, e Tartaria verso il Catai, e Regno de' Sini, dove scopersero il Mare di Veygatz, e la Nuoua Zembla. Et un pæse nell' ottantesimo grado creduto la Groenlandia, 1594-97.

Ray, John. Travels. 2 vols. 8° 1738

Vol. 1. — Travels through the Low-Countries, Germany, Italy, and France, with curious observations; also, a Catalogue of Plants, and an account of the travels of Francis Willughby through great part of Spain.

Vol. 2.—A Collection of curious Travels and Voyages.

CONTENTS.

Rauwolf, Leonhart. Journey into the Eastern Countries, viz., Syria, Palestine, Armenia, Mesopotamia, Assyria, Chaldea, &c.

Belon, Mr. Remarks in the Island of Creta or Candy; Description of Mount Athos, commonly called Monte Santo; Journey from Mount Athos to Constantinople, wherein the Gold and Silver Mines of Macedonia, &c., are described.

Vernon, Francis. Travels from Venice through Istria, Dalmatia, Greece, and the Archipelago to Smyrna.

Wheeler, Sir George. Plants observed in his Voyage to Greece and Asia Minor.

Smith, Thomas. Historical Observations relating to Constantinople; and an Account of the City of Prusa in Bithynia.

Greaves, John. Account of the Latitude of Constantinople and Rhodes.

Belon, Mr. Observations made in a Voyage to Egypt.

Greaves, John. Description of the Pyramids in Egypt, 1638-39.

Ray, Vol. 2—*continued*.

Vansleb, Father. Of the Pyramids, Sphynx, Mummies, &c., of Egypt.

Huntingdon, R. Letter concerning the Porphyry Pillars in Egypt.

Journey from Grand Cairo to Mecca.

Middleton, Sir Henry. Observations in Arabia Felix.

Michael of Tripoli. Of Ethiopia.

Lobo, Father. Observations of Ethiopia.

Renneville, R. A. Constantin de. Recueil des Voyages qui ont servi à l'Establissement et aux Progrez de la Compagnie des Indes Orientales, formée dans les Provinces-Unies des Païs-Bas. Nouvelle edition. 10 vols. *Plates.* 12°

Rouen, 1725

CONTENTS.

Vol. 1.—Trois Voyages des Hollandois et des Zélandois par le Nord.—Description de la Siberie, de la Samoyede, et de la Tingeese.—Jean Isaac Pontanus: Dissertation, pour aller à la Chine par le Nord.—Premier Voyage des Hollandois aux Indes Orientales.

Vol. 2.—Premier Voyage, &c. (Suite).—Second Voyage. — Voyage de cinq Vaisseaux de Rotterdam au Détroit de Magellan.

Vol. 3.—Voyage d' Olivier de Noort autour du Monde.—Voyages de Paul van Caerden et J. van Neck aux Indes Orientales.—Mémoires touchant les Indes Orientales.—Voyage d' Etienne van der Hagen. — Voyage de deux Vaisseaux Hollandois au Roiaume d' Achin, 1600-1; de Wolphart Harmansen, 1601-8; de Corneille de Veen, 1602.

Vol. 4.—Premier Voiage de G. Spilberg, 1601-4.—Description de Java, tirée de J. I. Pontanus.—Voyage de Wybrandt van Waarwyk, 1602-7.

Vol. 5.—Second Voyage d' Etienne van der Hagen, 1603-8.—Voyage de Corneille Matelief le Jeune, 1605-8.

Vol. 6.—Voyage de Matelief (Suite).—Second Voiage de Paul van Caerden, 1606-9.

Vol. 7.—Voyage de Pierre Willemsz Verhoeven, aux Indes Orientales, au Japon, &c., 1607 *et seq.*—Mémoires touchant les Isles de Banda, Borneo, Moluques, Solor et Timor, Amboine, &c., et des Forts que la Compagnie possédoit dans les Indes Orientales, 1616. — Voyage de Pierre van der Broeck au Cap Vert, Angola, et aux Indes Orientales.

Vol. 8.—Voyage de George Spilberg aux Isles Moluques, 1614. — Navigation Australe de Jacques le Maire et Willem Cornelisz Schouten, 1615-17.—Voyage de Guillaume Isbrandtsz Bontekou, 1618.

Renneville—*continued.*
Vol. 9.—Voyage de la Flote de Nassau sous Jacques l'Hermite. —Description du Pérou. —Voyage de Sayger van Rechteren, 1628-33 ; de Henry Hagenaar, 1631-38.
Vol. 10.—Voyage de Hagenaar (Suite). Histoire d'un Persécution, faite aux Chrétiens du Japon.—Visit du Daïro à l'Empereur du Japon.—Lettre d'un Magistrat du Japon.—Lettre et Mémoire touchant le Commerce du Japon. —Prise de Formosa par les Chinois.

Tavernier, John Baptista. The Six Voyages of John Baptista Tavernier . . . through Turky into Persia and the East-Indies, finished in the year 1670 . . . Made English by J. P. ; to which is added a description of all the Kingdoms which encompass the Euxine and Caspian Seas, by an English Traveller. *Plates.* Small folio 1678
—— Recueil de plusieurs Relations et Traitez singuliers et curieux de J. B. Tavernier, Escuyer, Baron d'Aubonne, qui n'ont point esté mis dans ses six premiers voyages. *Maps and plates.* 4°
Paris, 1679
Contents.
1. Une relation du Japon, et de la cause de la persecution des Chrestiens dans ses Isles ; avec la carte du pais.
2. Relation de ce qui c'est passé dans la Negociation des Deputez qui ont esté en Perse et aux Indes, tant de la part du Roy, que de la Compagnie Françoise, pour l'établissement du Commerce.
3. Observations sur le Commerce des Indes Orientales, et sur les fraudes qui s'y peuvent commettre.
4. Relation nouvelle et singuliere du Royaume de Tunquin ; avec plusieurs figures et la carte du pais.
5. Histoire de la Conduite des Hollandois en Asie.
—— Les Six Voyages de Jean - Baptiste Tavernier, Chevalier, Baron d'Aubonne, qu'il fait en Turquie, en Perse, et aux Indes. Nouvelle edition. 3 vols. *Illustrations.* 4° *Paris,* 1681
—— Les Six Voyages de Jean-Baptiste Tavernier, Chevalier Baron d'Aubonne, qu'il a fait en Turquie, en Perse, et aux Indes. 2 vols. *Plates (and water-colour drawing by Svindler).* 4° *Paris,* 1682

Ternaux - Compans, H. Voyages, Relations, et Mémoires Originaux, pour servir à l'Histoire de la Découverte de l'Amérique. 20-vols in 10. 8°
Paris, 1837-41
Contents.
Vol. 1.—Federmann le Jeune, d'Ulm, Nicolas. Narration du Premier Voyage aux Indes de la Mer Océane, 1529-32.

Ternaux-Compans—*continued.*
Vol. 2.—Magalhanes de Gandavo, Pero de. Histoire de la Province de Sancta-Crux, que nous nommons ordinairement le Brésil, 1576.
Vol. 3.—Staden de Homberg, Hans. Véritable Histoire et Description d'un Pays habité par des Hommes Sauvages, nus, féroces et anthropophages, situé dans le Nouveau Monde, nommé Amérique, 1547-55.
—— Relation véridique et précise des Mœurs et Coutumes des Tuppinambas.
Vol. 4.—Xérès, François. Relation véridique de la Conquête du Pérou, et de la Province de Cuzco nommée Nouvelle-Castille, 1524-33.
—— Relation du Voyage fait par le Seign. Capit. Ferdinand Pizarre, 1533-1534.
Vol. 5.—Hulsius, Levinus. Histoire véritable d'un Voyage Curieux, fait par Ulrich Schmidel de Straubing, dans l'Amérique ou le Nouveau Monde, par le Brésil, et le Rio de la Plata, 1534-54.
Vol. 6.—Cabeça de Vaca, Alvar Nuñez, Adelantade et Gouverneur du Rio de la Plata. Commentaires de ; rédigés par Pero Hernandez, 1555.
Vol. 7.—Cabeça de Vaca, Alvar.Nuñez. Relation et Naufrages, 1527-37.
Vol. 8. — Ixtlilxôchitl, Don Fernando d'Alva. . Cruautés Horribles des Conquérants du Mexique, Mémoire, 1519-1524.
Vol. 9.—Castañeda de Nagera, Pédro de. Relation du Voyage de Cibola, en 1540.
Vol. 10.—Recueil de Pièces relatives à la Conquête du Mexique, 1518-87.
Vol. 11.—Zurita, Alonzo de. Rapport sur les différentes classes de Chefs de la Nouvelle-Espagne.
Vols. 12 and 13.—Ixtlilxôchitl, F. d'Alva. Histoire des Chichimèques, ou des Anciens Rois de Tezcuco ; traduite sur le Manuscrit Espagnol. 2 vols.
Vol. 14. —Oviedo y Valdés, Gonzalo Fernandez. Histoire du Nicaragua.
Vol. 15.—Balboa, Miguel Cavello. Histoire du Pérou.
Vol. 16.—Second Recueil de Pièces sur le Mexique. Lettres de Don Juan de Zumarraga, Évêque élu de Mexico, &c.
Vol. 17. — Montesinos, L. Fernando. Mémoires Historiques sur l'Ancien Pérou.
Vols. 18 and 19.—Velasco, Don Juan de. Histoire du Royaume de Quito. 2 vols.
Vol. 20.—D'Escalante Fontanedo, Hernando. Mémoire sur la Floride, ses Côtes et ses Habitants.
—— Soto, Hernando de. Lettre écrite par, au Corps Municipal de la ville de Santiago, de l'Ile de Cuba, 1539.

Ternaux-Compans—*continued.*

Vol. 20.—Biedma, Luis H. de. Relation de ce qui arriva pendant le Voyage du Soto, 1544.

—— Beteta, Frère Gregorio de. Relation de la Floride, 1549.

—— Guido de las Bazares. Voyage sur la Côte de la Floride, 1559.

—— Lopez de Mendoza, Francisco. Voyage de Pero M. de Abiles à la Côte et dans la Province de la Floride, 1565.

—— Velasquez, Luis de. Lettre sur les affaires de la Floride.

—— Ribaut, Capit. Jean. Histoire Mémorable du dernier Voyage aux Indes, lieu appelé la Floride, en 1565.

—— Gourgue, Capit. La Reprinse de la Floride.

Thevenot, Melchisedec. Relation de divers Voayges [*sic*] curieux qui n'ont point esté publiées ; ou qui sont esté traduites d'Hacluyt, de Purchas, et d'autres Voyageurs Anglois, Hollandois, Portugais, Allemands, Espagnols ; et de quelques Persans, Arabes, et autres Auteurs Orientaux, &c. 4 vols. in 2. *Maps and plates.* Folio *Paris*, 1683 [*The secondary titles bear earlier dates.*]

• Contents.
VOLUME I.

Des Cosaques, avec la vie de Kmielniski, tirée d'un manuscrit des Tartares du Crime, des Nogais, des Circasses, et des Abassas, par Jean de Luca.

De la Colchide ou Mengrelie.

Informatione della Georgia di Pietro della Valle, tirée d'un manuscrit, avec l'Oraison funebre de Sitti Maani sa femme, qu'il recita luy-mesme.

Voyage d'Antoine Jenkinson au Cathay.

Extrait de la Relation de l'Ambassade que les Hollandois envoyerent en 1656 et 1657, au Tartare, qui est presentement Maistre de la Chine.

Relation de la prise de l'Isle Formosa par les Chinois le 5 Juillet 1661.

Relation de la Cour du Mogol par la Captaine Haukins.

Mémoires de Thomas Rhoë Ambassadeur du Roy d'Angleterre près du Mogol, traduits du Recüeil Anglois de Purchas.

Voyage de Edoüard Terry aux Etats du Mogol, traduits du Recüeil Anglois de Purchas.

Description des Plantes et des Animaux des Indes Orientales, par Cosmas, Monachos autrement Indopleustes.

Les Climats Alhend et Alsend de la Géographie d'Abulfeda. [Wanting.]

Relation des Antiquitez de Persepolis, traduite d'Herbert. [Wanting.]

Commencement d'un Livre des Chaldéens de Bassora, autrement appellez les Chrétiens de S. Jean, écrit en caractères

Thevenot, Vol. 1—*continued.*

tres-anciens non encore vûs en Europe, avec l'alphabet de ces mêmes caractères et une Carte Arabe du païs. [Wanting.]

Relation des Royaumes de Golconda, Tannassari, Arecan, par Wilhem Methold, President de la Compagnie Angloise.

Relation de Floris Villiamson du Golfe de Bengale.

Relation du Royaume de Siam par Schouten, traduit de l'Hollandois.

Voyages aux Indes Orientales de Bontekoüe, traduit de l'Hollandois.

Découverte de la Terre Australe, traduite aussi de l'Hollandois, avec une carte de cette cinquième partie du Monde.

Routier des Indes Orientales par Aleixo da Motta, traduit d'un manuscrit Portugais.

Description des Pyramides d'Egypte, par Jean Greaves, traduite de l'Anglois.

VOLUME 2.

Avis d'un des Facteurs de la Compagnie Hollandoise sur le commerce des Indes.

Autre avis sur le commerce du Japon.

Le Routier d'Alaixo da Motta, traduit du Portugais.

Carte Portugaise de la Carrea, ou Navigation des Indes Orientales.

Veües des principales costes des Indes Orientales.

Voyage de Beaulieu aux Indes Orientales.

Trois Relations des Isles Philippines.

Relation du Japon. Martyrs du Japon.

Relation de la découverte de la terre de Ieso.

Briefve Relation de la Chine, . . . par le tres R. P. Michel Boym, [including] Flora Sinensis, ou description des Plantes et Fleurs de la Chine, . . . avec figures.

Voyage des Hollandois à Pekin.

VOLUME 3.

Ambassade des Hollandois à la Chine.

Description Geographique de l'Empire de la Chine, par le Pere Martin Martinius.

Grammaire de la Langue des Tartares Mogols.

Rapport que les Directeurs de la Compagnie Hollandoise des Indes Orientales ont fait de l'état de leurs affaires aux Indes, en l'an 1664.

VOLUME 4.

L'Indien, ou Portrait au naturel des Indiens, par Dom Joan de Palafos, Evêque de la Puebla de los Angeles.

Relation des Voyages du Sieur Acarete sur la Riviere de la Platte, et de là par terre jusqu'au Perou et au Potosi.

Voyage à la Chine des Peres Grueber et d'Orville . . . le mesme en Italien.

Thevenot, Vol. 4—*continued.*
La science morale des Chinois, ou le second livre de Confussius, traduit de la langue Chinoise par le Pere Introcetta.
Histoire de la Haute-Ethiopie écrite sur les lieux par le Pere Manuël d'Almeïda, Jesuite, extraite et traduite de la copie Portugaise du Pere Balthazar Tellez.
Remarques sur les Relations de l'Ethiopie des Peres ·Jeronimo Lobo et de Balthazar Tellez, Jusuites.
Relation du Pere Jeronimo Lobo de l'Empire des Abyssins, des sources du Nil, de Licorne, &c.
Découverte de quelques païs qui sont entre l'Empire des Abyssins et la coste de Melinde.
Relation du Voyage du Zaid ou de la Thebaïde fait en 1668, par les Capucins Missionaires en Egypte.
Histoire de l'Empire Mexicain representée par figures.
Relation du Mexique, avec l'Histoire de la Nouvelle Espagne, par Thomas Gages.
Voyage et découverte du P. Marquette et Sieur Iolliet dans l'Amerique Septentrionale.
Ambassade des Moscovites à la Chine, ou Voyage de Moskou à Peguin par terre, traduit du Muscovite.
Discours sur l'Art de Navigation, avec quelques Problèmes pour y servir de supplément.
Supplément de l'Histoire naturelle de l'Ephemere.

Valentyn, François. Oud en Nieuw Oost-Indiën, vervattende een Naaukeurige en Uitvoerige verhandeling van Nederlands Mogentheyd in die Gewesten, benevens eene wydluftige Beschryvinge der Moluccos, Amboina, Banda, Timor, en Solor, Java, en alle de Eylanden onder dezelve Landbestieringen behoorende ; het Nederlands Comptoir op Suratte, en de Levens der Groote Mogols ; als ook een Keurlyke verhandeling van 't wezentlykste, dat men behoort te weten van Choromandel, Pegu, Arracan, Bengale, Mocha, Persien, Malacca, Sumatra, Ceylon, Malabar, Celebes of Macassar, China, Japan, Tayouan of Formosa, Tonkin, Cambodia, Siam, Borneo, Bali, Kaap der Goede Hoope, en van Mauritius. Te zamen dus behelzende niet alleen eene zeer nette Beschryving van alles, wat Nederlands Oost-Indiën betreft, maar ook 't voornaamste dat eenigzins tot eenige andere Europeërs, in die Gewesten, betrekking heeft. 8 vols. *Maps, portraits, and plates.* Folio *Dordrecht*, 1724-26
CONTENTS.
Vol. 1.—Oud en Nieuw Oost-Indiën, of Nederlands Mogentheid aldaar. Beschryving der Moluccos. Molukse Zaaken.
2 P

Valentyn—*continued.*
Vol. 2.—Beschryving van Amboina. Ambonsche Zaaken.
Vol. 3.—Ambonsche Zaaken van den Godsdienst. Beschryving der Boomen, Planten Heesters en Gewassen van Amboina. Verhandeling der Dieren, Vogelen, Water-Dieren, Visschen van Amboina.
Vol. 4.—Verhandeling der Zee-Horenkens en Schelpen ofte Dubbletten van Amboina. Beschryvinge van Banda, Solor en Timor, Macassar, Borneo, Bali, Tonkin, Cambodia, Siam.
Vol. 5.—Beschryvinge van Groot Java, Bantam, Batavia, benevens de Levens der Opper-land Voogden.
Vol. 6.—Zaaken van den Gods-dienst op Java. Beschryving van Suratte en de Levens der Groote Mogols. Beschryvinge van Tsjina, Tayouan of Formosa. Des Schryvers Uyt en T'Huys-Reyze, 1685-1714.
Vol. 7.—Beschryving van Choromandel, Pegu, Arrakan, Bengale, Mocha, in Persien. Beschryvinge van Malakka, Sumatra, Ceylon.
Vol. 8.—Beschryvinge van Malabar, Japan, Kaap der Goede Hoope.

Van der Aa, Pieter. *See* Naaukeurige Versameling, p. 595.

Vincent, Dean William. The Commerce and Navigation of the Ancients in the Indian Ocean. 2 vols. *Portrait and maps.* 4° 1807
CONTENTS.
VOLUME 1.
Arrian's Voyage of Nearchus, from the Indus to the Euphrates. Illustrated by authorities, ancient and modern.
Sequel to the Voyage of Nearchus.
On the Site of Opis.
Wales, W. On the Rising of the Constellations.
Horsley, Bp. S. On the Rising of the Constellations.
De la Rochette, M. On the First Meridian of Ptolemy.
VOLUME 2.
The Periplus of the Erythrean Sea. Part the First, containing an account of the Navigation of the Ancients, from the Sea of Suez to the Coast of Zanguebar.
Sequel to the Periplus of the Erythrean Sea.
Dissertations.
On the Adulitick Inscription, collected from Chishull, Montfaucon, Melchisedeck Thevenot, and other authors.
OnEITENHDIOMMENOUTHESIAS
On the Ancient Maps of the World.
On the Sinæ, the Seres, and the Termination of Ancient Geography on the East.

Vincent, Dissertations—*continued.*
On the Twenty-Seventh Chapter of Ezekiel.
On the Navigation and Compass of the Chinese, by the Right Hon. the Earl Macartney.
On the Map of Fra Mauro, in the Monastery of St Michael di Murano, at Venice, so far as it relates to the Circumnavigation of Africa.
A Catalogue of the Articles of Commerce in the Periplus, corrected, enlarged, and compared with the Articles enumerated in the Digest of the Roman Law, relating to the Imports and Exports at Alexandria.

Vincent, Dean William. The Voyage of Nearchus and the Periplus of the Erythrean Sea. Translated from the Greek. *Plate.* 4° *Oxford*, 1809

Walpole, Robert. Memoirs relating to European and Asiatic Turkey. Edited from Manuscript Journals. *Map and plates.* 4° 1817
CONTENTS.
Walpole, R. The Causes of the Weakness and Decline of the Turkish Monarchy.
Morritt, Mr. Account of a Journey through the District of Maina, in the Morea, 1795.
Sibthorp, Dr. Parnassus, and the neighbouring District, 1794.
—— Observations on Natural History, relating to parts of Greece and to the Island of Cyprus.
Hunt, Dr. Journey from Parium to the Troad ; Ascent to the Summit of Ida ; the Salt Springs of Tousla ; Ruins of Assos, 1799.
Sibthorp, Dr. Remarks respecting Attica.
Carlyle, Professor J. D. Letters during his Residence in Turkey.
Hunt, Dr. Mount Athos. An Account of the Monastic Institutions, and the Libraries on the Holy Mountain.
Walpole, R. Remarks on the Sepulchres of the European and Asiatic Greeks.
Hume, Dr. Plants collected in Cyprus.
Sibthorp, Dr. Birds, Quadrupeds, and Fishes of Greece and Cyprus.
Raikes, Mr. Journal through parts of Bœotia, Phocis, Rhamnus, Ascent to the Corycian Cave, &c.
Squire, Col. Remarks relating to the Military Architecture of the Ancient Greeks.
—— The Plain of Marathon, the Isthmus of Corinth, &c.
Davison, Mr. Observations relating to some of the Antiquities of Egypt.
Walpole, R. The Catacombs of Alexandria.

Walpole, Turkey—*continued.*
Hume, Dr. Remarks on the Manners and Customs of the Modern Inhabitants of Egypt.
Light, Capt. Journal of a Voyage up the Nile into part of Nubia, May 1814.
Walpole, R., and the Earl of Aberdeen. On the Mines of Laurium. —Gold and Silver Coinage of the Athenians.—Revenue of Attica.
Aberdeen, The Earl of. Remarks on two Sculptured Marbles brought from Amyclæ.
Hawkins, Mr. On the Topography of Athens, the Vale of Tempe, the Syrinx of Strabo, and the Bridge over the Euripus.
Haygarth, W. Panoramic View of Athens illustrated.
Walpole, R. Remarks on the Thesauri of the Greeks.
—— Remarks on the Demetrian System of the Troad.
Morritt, Mr. Remarks on the Troad, in a Letter to Dr Clarke.
Wilkins, Mr. Remarks on the Architectural Inscription brought from Athens, and now preserved in the British Museum.

Walpole, Robert. Travels in Various Countries of the East, being a Continua- tion of Memoirs relating to European and Asiatic Turkey, &c. *Maps and plates.* 4° 1820
CONTENTS.
Hawkins, Mr. On the Tar Springs of Zante.
Sibthorp, Dr. Voyage in the Grecian Seas, Princes' Islands, Dardanelles, Cyprus, Islands of Lero, Patmos, Stenosa, Argentiera, Eubœa, Mount Athos, Isthmus of Corinth.
Whittington, Mr. Discovery of the Remains of the Acropolis of Patmos.
Sibthorp, Dr. Second Voyage in the Grecian Seas.
Hunt, Dr. Lemnos.
Sibthorp, Dr. Journal relating to Parts of the ancient Elis, Arcadia, Argolis, Laconia, Messenia, and the Islands on the Western Shores of Greece.
Brown, William George. Journey from Constantinople through Asia Minor, with Miscellaneous Remarks written at Constantinople, 1802.
—— Letter to Smithson Tennant, Esq., dated Tabriz (on the frontiers of Persia), July 16, 1813.
—— Price of Commodities at Smyrna, in 1780, 1790, 1800, and 1812.
—— Biographical Memoir of.
Leake, Col. Journey through some Provinces of Asia Minor, in 1800.
Hume, Dr. Extracts from the Journals relating to Parts of Cyprus, and a De-

Walpole, Travels—*continued.*

scription of the Bay of Marmorice, on the Coast of Caramania.

Leake, Col. Remarks on the Ancient and Modern Geography of parts of Asia Minor.

Hawkins, Mr. Some Particulars respecting the Police of Constantinople.

—— An Account of the Discovery of a very Ancient Temple on Mount Ocha, in Euboea.

Squire, Col. Travels through part of the Ancient Coele-Syria, and Syria Salutaris.

Clarke, Edw. Daniel. Letter on a remarkable Egyptian Bas - Relief, inscribed with Greek Characters ; together with a Postscript, containing observations upon other Egyptian Antiquities.

Fazakerley, J. N. Journey from Suez to Mount Sinai.

Hawkins, Mr. On a Law of Custom which is peculiar to the Islands of the Archipelago.

Cockerell, Mr. On the Labyrinth of Crete.

Wilkins, Mr. On the Sculptures of the Parthenon.

Notice of some remarkable Monuments of Antiquity discovered on the Site of the Ancient Susa, in Persia.

Sibthorp, Dr. Remarks relating to the Natural History of parts of European Turkey.

Belzoni, M. The Arabic Inscription discovered in the Pyramid of Chephrenes, and a Translation by the Rev. S. Lee.

Whittington, Mr. Account of a Journey through part of Little Tartary, and of some Armenian, Greek, and Tartar Settlements.

Hawkins, Mr. On the Site of Dodona.

Aberdeen, Earl of. Letter relating to some Statements made by M. R. Rochette in his Work on the Authenticity of the Inscriptions of Fourmont.

Leake, Col. Inscriptions copied in various parts of Greece.

Cockerell, Mr. Letter respecting the very singular Sepulchral Monuments and Inscriptions discovered by him on the Southern Coast of Asia Minor.

Walpole, R. Inscriptions copied in different parts of Asia Minor, Greece, and Egypt, illustrated.

ANONYMOUS.

[In Chronological Order.]

Recueil de divers Voyages faits en Afrique et en l'Amérique qui n'ont point esté encore publiez . . ; avec des Traitez curieux touchant la Haute Ethy-

Recueil de divers Voyages—*continued.*

opie, le débordement du Nil, la mer Rouge, et le Prete-Jean. *Maps and plates.* 4° *Paris,* 1684

CONTENTS.

Ligon, R. Histoire de l'isle des Barbades.

Relation de la Riviere du Nil, &c.

Telles, B. Extrait del'histoire d'Ethiopie.

Description de l'Empire du Prete-Jean.

Relation du Voyage fait sur les costes d'Afrique . . . 1670, 1671, commençant au Cap Verd.

De la Borde, —. Relation de l'origine, moeurs, coustumes, &c., des Caraibes sauvages des isles Antilles de l'Amérique.

Relation de la Guiane.

Description de l'isle de Jamaique.

Relation de l'isle des Barbades.

Description de l'isle de Saint Christophe.

Naaukeurige Versameling der Gedenkwaardigste Zee en Land-Reysen na Oost en West-Indiën, mitsgaders andere Gewesten, ... Beginnende met her Jaar 1246, en eyndigende op dese tijd, &c. &c. 27 vols. *Maps and plates. Leyden,* 1707

[*This collection is by the same publisher (P. Van der Aa) as that edited by Gottfried* (q.v.). *The contents are on the whole the same, but are arranged chronologically instead of according to the nationality of the Travellers.*]

CONTENTS.

Vol. 1.—Johan du Plan Carpin en Broeder Ascelin, 1246-47.—Willem de Rubriquis, 1253.—Scheeps-Togten der Portgysen (26), 1419-90.

Vol. 2.—Christoffel Columbus, 1492-93, — Vasco da Gamma, 1497. — Chr. Columbus, 1498.—Alonso d'Ojeda en Americus Vesputius, 1499.—Christoffel Guerre en Pero Alfonso Nino, 1499.

Vol. 3.—Pedralverez Cabral, Joan da Nova, Vincent Yanes Pinzon, Diego de Lepe, Rodriquez de Bastidas, Alonso d'Ojeda en Am. Vesputius, 1500-1.—Joseph den Indiaan (Oost-Indiën), 1501. — Vasco da Gamma, 1502. — Antonius de Torres, Nicolaus d'Obando (West Indiën), 1502.— Chr. Columbus, 1502.—Diego Mendez de Zigura en Bartelemi de Fiesco (West Indiën), 1503. — F. d'Albuquerque (Oost Indiën), 1503.—Lopo Soares (Oost Indiën), 1504.

Vol. 4.—Franciscus de Porras, Ferdinandes Cortes en Alonzo Quintero (West Indiën), 1504.—Francisco d'Almeida, Pero da Nhaya (Oost Ind.), 1505.— Jean Dias de Solis en Vincent Yanes

Naaukeurige Versameling—*contd.*

Pinzon (Yucatan), 1506. — Tristano d'Acunha (Oost Ind.), 1506, *et seq.*

Vol. 5.—Alfonso d'Albuquerque (Roode Zee en Oost Ind.), 1506.—Jorge de Mello (Oost Ind.), 1507. — Jorge d'Aguiar (Oost Ind.), 1508.

Vol. 6.—D'Ocampo, Ponze de Leon, Solis en Pinzon, d'Ojeda (West Ind.), 1508-9. — Fernando Coutinho (Oost Ind.), 1509. — Jean de Ezquebel (Jamaica), 1510. — Vasco Nunes en Diego Velasquez, 1511.—Gonzalo de Sequeira (Oost Ind.), 1510.—Garcia de Noronha (Oost Ind.), 1511.—Jean Ponze de Leon, Pamphilio de Narvaas (Florida, &c.), 1512-13.

Vol. 7. — Pedrarius Davila (Darien), 1514.—Jean Diaz de Solis en Jean Ponze de Leon (Karibanen), 1515.—Lopo Soares d'Albegeria (Oost Ind.), 1515. — Fernando Perez d'Andrade (Sumatra, Ternate, China), 1516.—Franciscus Hernandez de Cordua, Jean de Gryalva (Yucatan en Nieuw Spanjen), 1517-18.

Vol. 8.—Diego Lopez de Sequeira (Oost Ind.), 1518. — Jorge d'Albuquerque (Oost Ind.), 1519.—Ferdinand Magellanes, 1521. — Simon d'Andrade (China), 1518. — Ferdinand Cortes (Nieuw Spanje), 1518.

Vol. 9. — Ferdinand Cortes (Nieuw Spanje), 1519.—Alonso d'Ojeda (Chiribichi), Ferdinand Magellanes, Gonzale d'Ocampo (Chiribichi en Cubagua), Panfilio de Narvaez (Nieuw Spanje), Lucas Vasquez d'Ayllon (Chicora), 1520.—Duarte de Menezes en Diego Lopez de Sequeira (Oost Ind.), 1521.

Vol. 10.—Cortes, 1521. — Magellaan, 1521.—Gil Gonzales Davila (Zuyd-Zee en Nicaragua), 1522.—Stephen Gomes (Toeleg om een Straat uyt de Noord in de Zuyd-Zee t'ontdekken), 1523.—Franciscus de Garay (Panuco), Pedro d'Alvarado (Guatemala), Diego de Godoy (Mexico, &c.), 1523.—Johann de Verazzano (Florida), 1524.

Vol. 11.—Gil Gonzales Davila (Honduras), 1524. — Vasco da Gamma, 1524. — Garcia Jofre de Loyasa (Specery-Eylanden), 1525.—Rodrigue de Bastidas (St Martha, &c.), 1525.—Stephan Gomes (ter ontdekking van eene nieuwe Straat ten Noorden na Cataya, &c.), 1525.—Lucas Vasquez d'Ayllyon (Florida), 1525.—Sebastiaan Gaboto (Rio de Plata), 1526. — F. Cortes (Weder-komst in Mexico), 1526.—Diego Garcia (Americaanse Kusten), 1526.—Het bestuur van Niew-Spanjen, 1526.

Vol. 12.—Franciscus Pizarrus en Didacus Almagrus (Peru), 1526.—Lopo Vaz

Naaukeurige Versameling—*contd.*

de Sampayo (Oost Ind.), 1526.—Het Koninkrijk Zunda met dat van Java. —Jorge de Menezes (Borneo en Moluccos), 1527.—Vincent de Fonseca (Banda), 1528.—Lopo Vaz de Sampayo en Martin Alfonso de Mello (Oost Ind.), 1529.—Simon de Souza Galvaon (Achem), 1529.

Vol. 13 en Vervolg.—Nunho da Cunha (Gouverneur Generaal in Oost Ind.), 1529, *et seq.*—Voyagien Van Diogo Botello, Manuel Pacheco, Martin Alfonso de Souza, Martin Alfonso de Mello, Estevan de Gama, Antonio Galvaon, Garcia de Noronha.

Vol. 14.—Nicolaas Clenard (Vraukrijk, Spanjen en Portugal, en Africa), 1535. —Pedro de Mendosa en Ulrich Schmidt (R. de la Plata), 1535. — Ferdinand de Soto (Florida), 1539.—Johan de Castro (verhaal van een Reys door Portugijsen uyt Indiën na Soez), 1540-41. — Hieronymus Benzo (West Ind.), 1541.

Vol. 15.—Jan Staden van Homberg in Hessen (Brazil), 1547-9.—Johannes Lerius (Brazil), 1556.

Vol. 16.—Anthony Jenkinson (Tartarie), 1558.—Pontius, Ribald, Laudonnière, Gourgues, &c. (Florida), 1562. — Cæsar Frederik (Oost Ind.), 1563, *et seq.*

Vol. 17.—Dithmar Blefkenius (Ysland en Groenland), 1563.—Leendert Rouwolf (Syrien, Arabien, Assyrien, &c.), 1573.—Martin Frobischer, 1576-84.

Vol. 18.—Franciscus Drake, 1577.—Pieter Carder (Reys met F. Drake), 1578.—Eduard Lopez (Congo), 1579. — Johan Newberie (Heylig Land, Persiën, &c.), 1579. — Caspar Balby (Oost Ind.), 1579-88.

Vol. 19.—Michiel Herberer (Asia en Africa), 1582, *et seq.*—Ralph Fitch (Oost Ind.), 1583-91.—Georg, Graf van Cumberland (West Ind., &c.), 1586-98.

Vol. 20.—Thomas Candish, 1586.—Andries Battel (Brazil en Angola), 1589.—Antony Knivet (Zuyd Zee), 1591.—Joseph d'Acosta (Ontdekking von West Indiën), 1592.

Vol. 21.—Ellis (Straat van Magellanes en Peru), 1593.—Engelse Reysen na de Bermudas, 1593-1612. — Johan Smith (Verscheyde Gedeelten des Werelds), 1593, *et seq.* — Walther Ralegh (Guiana), 1595-97.—Benjamin Woods (Oost Ind.), 1596.—Johan Davis (Oost Ind.), 1598-1604. — William Adams (Oost Ind.), 1598, *et seq.* — Berigt van een Mohometaans Koopman, 1598. — Benedict Goes (door Tartaryen na China), 1598, *et seq.*—Antony Sherley (Persiën), 1599.

Naaukeurige Versameling—*contd.*

—John Mildenhall en Johann Cartwright (Landen van Persien en den Grooten Mogol), 1599.

Vol. 22.—James Lancaster (Oost Ind.), 1601.—David Middelton en Michael Geare (West Ind.), 1601.—Georg Weymouth (Noord-West), 1601.—Bartholomeus Gosnol (Virginien), 1602.— Martin Pringe (Virginien), 1603.— Bartholmeus Gilbert (Virginien), 1603. —Hendrik Middelton (Oost Ind.), 1604.—Charles Leig (Guiana), 1604.— Nicolaus Schmidt (Constantinopolen en Egypten), 1605, *et seq.* — Johan Saris (Oost Ind.), 1605.

Vol. 23.—Johann Smith (Virginien), 1606, *et seq.*—Willem Keeling (Oost Ind.), 1607-10.—Robert Coverte (Oost Ind., Persien, Arabien, &c.), 1607-11. —William Hawkins (Oost Ind.), 1607-8.

Vol. 24.—Robert Harcourt (Guiana), 1608.—Alexander Sharpey en Richard Rowles (Oost Ind.), 1608. — David Middelton (Oost Ind.), 1609.—Hendrik Middelton en Nicolaas Dounton (Oost Ind.), 1610.—Antony Hippon en Pieter Williamson Floris (Oost Ind.), 1611.—Joan Saris (Oost Ind.), 1611.

Vol. 25.—Edmund Marlow, Thomas Best, Ralph Wilson (Oost Ind.), 1611. —Samuel Castelton (Oost Ind.), 1612. —Christoffel Nieuwpoort (Oost Ind.), 1613.—Antonio Fernandez (Gingiro, Africa), 1613. — Nicolaas Dounton (Oost Ind.), 1614.—Johan Wilward, (Oost Ind.), 1614.—Johan Smith (Nieuw Engeland), 1614-15.—Walter Peyton (Oost Ind.), 1615.—Thomas Coryat (Ajmere), 1615. — Edward Terry (Oost Ind.), 1615. — Roger Hawes, Alexander Childe (Oost Ind.), 1616.

Vol. 26.—Thomas Spurway (Banda), 1616. — Martin Pring (Oost Ind.), 1617.—Edward Heynes (Oost Ind.), 1618.—William Hoare (Achen, Bantam), 1618.—William Methold (Oost Ind.), 1619.—Evesko Petelin en Andrasko (Tartarye en Cathay), 1619.— Andrew Schilling (Oost Ind.), 1620.— Richard Jobson (Gambra), 1620.— Anthony Chester (Virginia), 1620.— De Landschappen der Percoptize en Nogaize Tartars. &c., 1633.—Hendrik Blunt (Levant), 1634.

Vol. 27.—Hieronymus Lobo (Abyssinien), 1636. — Manuel d'Almeda (Opper Ethiopien), 1336.—T. S., een Engels Koopman (Algiers), 1648. — Saedor Jacowitz Boicoof (China), 1653. — Moüette (Slavernye in Marocco), 1670. —Gallonye (Eyland St Christoffel: Slavernye te Salée in Africa), 1670.

Account of several late Voyages and Discoveries; with a large Introduction and Supplement. *Maps and plates.* 8°
1711

CONTENTS.

Introduction. Navigations towards the South and North; with the Observations and Discoveries by Captains Fox, J. Gillam, and others, of the North-East and North-West Passages.

Narbrough, Sir John. Voyages to the South Sea, by the command of King Charles II.; and his Instructions for settling a Commerce in those parts; with a Description of the Capes, Harbours, Rivers, Customs of the Inhabitants, and Commodities in which they trade.

Tasman, Captain J. Discoveries on the Coast of the South Terra Incognita.

Wood, Captain J. Attempt to Discover a North-East Passage to China and Japan.

Marten, F. Observations made in Spitzbergen, Greenland, and other Northern Countries.

Flawes, Captain W. Journal of a Voyage from Nova Zembla to England.

Supplement. Description of Cherry and other Islands, John Mayen's Island, Groenland or Engroenland, the Discovery of Freezland or Friseland.

Recueil de Voiages au Nord, contenant divers Mémoires tres utiles au Commerce et à la Navigation. 10 vols. *Maps and plates.* 12°
Amsterdam, 1715-38

CONTENTS.

Vol. 1.—Discours Preliminaire. — Instructions pour Voiager utilement.— Relation de l'Island.—Memoires pour la pêche de la Baleine.—Relation du Groenland.

Vol. 2.—F. Martens. Voyage au Spitzbergen.—Description de Spitzberguen, ses Animaux et Plantes.—Wood, Capt. Discours sur le passage sur le Nord-Est, et Journal de son Voyage.

Vol. 3.—White. Relation de Terre-Neuve.—De l'Ile. Lettre sur le Japon.—Découverte de Jesso.—Caron. Relation concernant le Japon.—Martini. Relation de la Tartarie Orientale. — Delile. Lettres touchant le Mississippi et la Californie.—Memoire touchant la Californie.—Relation d'une descente des Espagnols dans la Californie.—Verbiest. Voyage de l'Empereur de la Chine dans la Tartarie Orientale.

Recueil de Voiages au Nord—*contd.*

Vol. 4.—Relation du Roiaume de Corée.
—Jartroux. Lettre touchant le Ginseng.—Jenkinson, Antoine. Voiage pour découvrir le chemin de Catay.—Ferrand. Relation de la Tartarie Krimée et des Tartares Nogais.

Vol. 5.—Relation de la Louisiane, par un Officier de Marine.—Relation de la Louisianne et du Fleuve Mississippi.—Hennepin. Voyage entre la mer glaciale et le Nouveau Mexique.—Gosnol, Pringe et Gilbert. Voyage aux Côtes de la Virginie.—Relation du Détroit et de la Baye de Hudson.—Frobisher, Martin. Trois Navigations.

Vol. 6.—Monier. Relation de l'Armenie [Missing.]—Histoire de la Conqueste de la Chine par les Tartares.

Vol. 7.—Père d'Orleans. Histoire des deux Conquerans Tartares qui' ont subjugué la Chine.—De Luca. Relations des Tartares Percopites, Nogaies, Circassses, &c., et addition tirée de Beauplan.—Lamberti et Zampi. Relations de la Mingrelie. — Perry. Ecrits pour l'intelligence des Nouvelles Cartes de la mer Caspienne, &c.—Duplan Carpin, J. Voyage en Tartarie.

Vol. 8.—Isbrands Ides, Evert. Voyage de Moscou à la Chine.—Lange. Négociations à la Chine, &c.—Müller. Moeurs et Usages des Ostiackes.

Vol. 9.—Relation des Natchez. — Raisons qui ont porté le Gouvernement d'Angleterre à établir une Colonie dans la Georgie.—Hennepin. Découverte d'un Païs plus grand que l'Europe, dans l'Amérique Septentrionale.

Vol. 10.—Relation de la grande Tartarie, dressée sur les mémoires des Suedois Prisonnières en Siberie.—D'Entrecolles. Lettre sur la Porcelaine.—Lettre sur le nouvel Etablissement de la Mission des Peres Jésuites dans la Krimée.—Tartares Cirkasses. —Ferrand. Voyage de Krimée en Cirkassie par le pays des Tartares Nogaïs.

Dutch East India Company. A Collection of Voyages undertaken by the Dutch East India Company, for the Improvement of Trade and Navigation ; containing an Account of Several Attempts to find out the North-East Passage, and their discoveries in the East Indies and the South Seas ; together with an Historical Introduction giving an Account of the Rise, Establishment, and Progress of that great body. Translated into English. *Maps.* Small 8°   1730

Dutch East India Company—*contd.*

CONTENTS.

The First and Second North Voyages of the Hollanders and Zelanders along the Coasts of Norway, Muscovy, and Tartary, in quest of a Passage to the Kingdoms of Cathai and China.

The Third North Voyage of the Dutch, through the Seas of Muscovy and Tartary, to find a passage that way to the Kingdoms of Cathai and China, by the permission of the Town-Council of Amsterdam, in the year 1596.

Other Voyages (Hudson) in quest of a Passage to China by the North.

A Description of Siberia.

A Short Account of the Roads and Rivers to be met with in going from Muscovy to the East and East-North-East, according to the course the Muscovites observe, &c.

A Dissertation of Isaac Pontanus, wherein he answers Objections against a Passage by the North, &c.

Relations of the First (1595) and Second (1598) Voyages of the Dutch into the East Indies.

An Account of the Voyage of five Rotterdam ships which sailed the 27th June 1598 to the Streight of Magellan.

Voyages faits principalement en Asie dans les XII., XIII., XIV., et XV. siecles, par Benjamin de Tudele, Jean du Plan-Carpin, N. Ascelin, Guillaume de Rubruquis, Marc Paul Venitien, Haiton, Jean de Mandeville, et Ambroise Contarini ; accompagnés de l'histoire des Sarasins et des Tartares, et precedez d'une introduction concernant les Voyages et les nouvelles découvertes des principaux Voyageurs, par Pierre Bergeron. 2 vols. *Maps.* 4°
                    The Hague, 1735

Histoire générale des Voyages. *See* Prévost.

Allgemeine Historie der Reisen zu Wasser und Lande ; oder Sammlung aller Reisebeschreibungen, welche bis itzo in verschiedenen Sprachen von allen Völkern herausgegeben worden, und einen vollständigen Begriff von der neuern Erdbeschreibung und Geschichte machen ; Worinnen der wirkliche Zustand aller Nationen vorgestellet, und das Merkwürdigste, Nützlichste, und Wahrhaftigste in Europa, Asia, Africa, und America, in Ansehung ihrer verschiedenen Reiche und Länder ; deren Lage, Grösse, Grenzen, Eintheilungen, Himmelsgegenden, Erdreichs, Früchte, Thiere, Flüsse, Seen, Gebirge, grossen, und kleinen Städte, Hafen, Gebäude, u. s. w., wie auch der Sitten und Gebräuche der Einwohner,

Allgemeine Historie—*continued.*

ihrer Religion, Regierungsart, Künste und Wissenschaften, Handlung und Manufacturen, enthalten ist, &c.   21 vols. *Maps and plates.* 4° *Leipzig,* 1747-77

[*Virtually a translation of the French "Histoire Générale des Voyages," by the Abbé Prévost, of which the first seven volumes were translated, with some alterations, from Astley's Voyages.*]

CONTENTS.

VOLUME I.

Von dem Ursprunge und Fortgange der Schiffahrt und Handlung in verschiedenen Theilen der Welt.

BOOK 1.—*Die ersten Reisen der Portugiesen nach Ostindien :—*

Reisen und Entdeckungen der Portugiesen längst den Küsten von Africa bis an das grüne Vorgebürge ; aus dem Faria y Sousa, Juan de Barros, Antonio Galvano, und andern zusammengetragen.

Fortsetzung der Entdeckungen der Portugiesen von dem grünen Vorgebürge bis an Cabo de Buena Esperanza, oder das Vorgebürge der guten Hoffnung, aus eben den Schriftstellern.

Die Portugiesen wollen Ostendien zu Lande entdecken, nebst einer umständlichen Nachricht von den ersten Neiderlassungen in Mandinga, Guinea, und Kongo.

Vasco de Gama. Reise nach Indien, im Jahre 1497 ; die erste welche die Portugiesen um Africa herum vollführet.

Cabral, Pedro Alvarez. Reise im Jahre 1500 ; die zweyte welche die Portugiesen nach Indien gethan, vornehmlich aus dem Castanneda genommen.

Juan de Nueva, Reise von ; die dritte welche die Portugiesen nach Ostindien gethan ; vornehmlich aus dem Castanneda genommen.

Vasco de Gama's zweyte Reise, in Jahre 1502 ; die vierte welche die Portugiesen nach Ostindien gethan.

Reisen und Verrichtungen der Portugiesen in Indien, vom Jahre 1503 bis 1507, mit den Thaten des Pacheco. Aus dem Castanneda, de Barros, und de Faria y Sousa genommen.

Thaten der Portugiesen im Jahre 1507, unter Don Francisco de Almeyda, erstem Viceköäge von Indien ; aus eben denselben Schriftstellern gezogen.

Fortsetzung der Thaten der Portugiesen unter den Viceköäge Almeyda, vom Jahre 1508 bis 1510.

Albuquerque's Verrichtungen als Vicekönig von Indien, vom Jahre 1510 bis 1516.

Allgemeine Historie, Vol. 1—*contd.*

Kurze Nachricht von der Portugiesen Thaten in Indien, von dem Jahre 1516 bis 1521, unter dem Statthalter Lope Soarez.

Verrichtungen und Entdeckungen der Portugiesen vom Jahre 1521 bis 1537.

Fortsetzung der Portugiesischen Verrichtungen und Entdeckungen, vom Jahre 1537 bis 1542.

Nachricht von allem dem, was die Portugiesen von dem Vorgebürge der guten Hoffnung an bis nach China besitzen.

Des Soleyman Bascha Reise von Suez nach Indien, bey seinem Feldzuge wider die Portugiesen in Diu, vom Jahre 1537 ; beschrieben von einem Officier der venetianischen Galeeren, welcher zu dem Türkischen Dienste gezwungen worden ; jetzo zuerst aus dem Italienischen übersetzet.

Die Belagerung von Diu, durch Soleyman Bascha von Aegypten.

Don Stephano de Gama. Reise aus Goa nach Suez, in der Absicht, die türkischen Schiffe in diesem Hafen zu verbrennen, beschrieben durch Don Juan de Castro, damaligen Schiffshauptmann auf der Flotte, nach der Zeit Statthalter und Vicekönig von Indien ; aus dem Portugiesischen übersetzt und zusammengezogen.

Eine Beschreibung der See von Kolzum, welche gemeiniglich der arabische Meerbusen, oder das Rothe Meer genannt wird, aus Abulfeda's Geographie.

Die zweyte Belagerung der Stadt Diu von Mahmud, Könige von Kambaja, im Jahre 1545, unter des Don Juan de Castro Statthalterschaft.

Book 2.—*Die ersten Reisen der Engländer nach Guinea und Ostindien :—*

Windham, Thomas. Die zweyte Reise nach der Barbarey, im Jahre 1552, beschrieben von James Thomas.

—— und Antonio Anes Pinteado. Eine Reise nach Guinea und Benin, im Jahre 1553.

Lok, Johann. Die zweyte Reise nach Guinea, im Jahre 1554 ; beschrieben von einem der vornehmsten Lootsen.

Towrson, William. Erste Reise nach der Küste von Guinea, im Jahre 1555.

—— Zweyte Reise nach den Küsten von Guinea und dem Castelle del Mina, im Jahre 1556.

—— Dritte und letzte Reise nach der Küste von Guinea und dem Castelle del Mina, im Jahre 1557.

Reisen nach Guinea, in den Jahren 1561, 1562, 1563, und 1564.

1. Reise nach Guinea, im Jahre 1561, welche Johann Lok unternommen, aber wieder aufgegeben hat, nebst den Ursachen, die er deswegen anführet.

Allgemeine Historie, Vol. 1—*contd.*

2. Eine Reise nach Guinea, im Jahre 1562, von Wilh. Ruttern beschrieben.

3. Ergänzung zu der vorhergehenden Reisebeschreibung, die aus Bakers Beschreibung in Versen gezogen ist.

4. Baker, —. Die 2te Reise nach Guinea und dem Flusse Sestos im Jahre 1563.

5. Carlet, David. Eine Reise nach Guinea, im Jahre 1564.

Fenner, Georg. Reise in die Inseln des grünen Vorgebürges, im Jahre 1566 mit dreyen Schiffen und einer Pinnasse; beschrieben durch Walter Wreen.

Stephens, Thomas. Reise auf der portugiesischen Flotte nach Goa, im Jahre 1579.

Einige Seefahrten und Capereyen gegen die Spanier und Portugiesen.

1. Verrichtungen der "Schlüsselblume" von London.

2. Whiddon, —. Reise mit zwoen Pinassen 1586 an die Azorischen Inseln; beschrieben durch Joh. Evescham.

3. Drake, Sir Franz. Reise nach Cadix und den Azorischen Inseln, in welcher auf hundert Schiffe zu Grunde gerichtet, und eine grosse Caracke aus Ostindien nebst andern Fahrzeugen erobert worden.

Zwey Reisen nach Benin hinter Guinea, im Jahre 1588 und 1590; beschrieben von James Welsch.

Georg von Cumberland, Graf. Reise nach den Azorischen Eylanden, im Jahre 1589; beschrieben von Eduard Wright.

Das Gefecht zwischen dem Kriegesschiffe "Die Rache," welches Hr. Richard Greenville geführet, und funfzehen Armadas des Königs in Spanien, im Jahre 1591, von dem Herrn Walter Ralegh, Ritter, beschrieben.

Erzählung der Reise einer Flotte londonscher Schiffe, unter dem Hauptmanne Robert Flicke, welcher bey den Azorischen Inseln 1591 gekreuzet, und dem Lord Thomas Howard zur Hülfe bestimmt ward; von dem Hauptmanne selbst beschrieben. Wozu eine Nachricht von der westindischen Flotte, die selbiges Jahr in Spanien ewartet wurde, und der Zahl der verlohrnen oder genommenen Schiffe gesetzt ist.

Die Thaten der Engländer bey verschiedenen Schiffahrten und kreuzenden Seereizen, vom Jahre 1589 bis 1592; aus Joh. Huighen van Linschoten's Reise von Goa nach Portugall gezogen.

Eine Reise nach Ostindien, im Jahre 1591; die erste, welche die Engländer in diese Gegenden gethan, von dem Hauptm. Georg Raymond angefangen, und von dem Hauptm. James Lan-

Allgemeine Historie, Vol. 1—*contd.*

caster geendigt. Nach der Erzählung Edmund Barker's, Lieutenant's von dem "Bonaventure," aufgesetzt.

Rainolds, Richard, und Thomas Dassels. Reisen nach den Flüssen Senega und Gambra, im Jahre 1591.

Burrough, Johann. Eine kreuzende Reise nach den Azorischen Inseln, im Jahre 1592, in der Absicht, die ostindischen Caracken aufzufangen.

Zwey merkwürdige Seegefechte; das eine im Jahre 1592, in welchem zwey Assogueschiffe erobert worden; das andere 1593, in welchem eine grosse ostindische Caracke im Rauche aufgegangen.

Wood, Benjamin. Die unglückliche Reise des Hauptmanns, nach Ostindien, im Jahre 1596.

Davis, Johann. Reise des Hauptmanns, damaligen Lootsmannes auf einem holländischen Schiffe nach Ostindien, im Jahre 1598; beschrieben von ihm selbst.

BOOK 3.—*Die ersten Reisen der Engländer nach Ostindien welche eine Gessellschaft von Kaufleutern angestellt :—*

Lancaster, James. Reise im Jahre 1600, welche die erste ist, die auf Rechnung der ostindischen Compagnie gethan worden.

Middleton, Heinrich. Reise im Jahre 1604, welches die zweyte ist, die von der ostindischen Compagnie angestellt worden.

Nachricht von Java, und wie sich die Engländer das erstemal zu Bantam festgesetzet; nebst einem Tagebuche von den dasigen Begebenheiten, besonders was zwischen ihnen und sowohl den Niederländern, als den Eingebohrnen von 1602 bis zu Ende des Jahres 1605 vorgegangen. Aus einer weitläuftigen Erzählung des Oberfactors Edmund Scot gezogen.

Michelburn, Eduard. Reise nach Bantam, im Jahre 1604.

Keeling, William. Reise vom Jahre 1607, nach Bantam und Banda; die dritte, welche von der ostindischen Compagnie ausgeführet worden; von dem Hauptmanne selbst beschrieben, und hier abgekürzet.

Middleton, David. Reise nach Bantam und den Molukken, im Jahre 1607.

Scharpey, Alexander. Reise im Jahre 1608; die vierte, welche von der ostindischen Gesellschaft ausgeführet worden; vom Hauptmanne Robert Coverte beschrieben.

Jones, Thomas. Kurze Nachricht von eben der Reise der "Himmelfahrt."

Allgemeine Historie, Vol. 1—*contd.*

Rowles, Richard. Reise nach Priaman in der "Vereinigung"; als eine Fortsetzung der vierten Reise.

Middleton, David. Reise nach Java und Banda, im Jahre 1609; die fünfte, welche von der Gesellschaft vollstreckt worden; aus einem Briefe ausgezogen, den er selbst an die Kaufleute abgelassen.

Middleton, Heinr. Fahrt nach dem rothen Meere und Surat, im Jahre 1610; die sechste, welche von der ostindischen Gesellschaft ausgeführet worden; von ihm selbst beschrieben.

Dounton, Niklas. Tagebuch von eben dieser Reise des Hrn. Heinr. Middletons.

Hippon, Anton. Reise nach der Küste Koromandel, Bantam, und Siam, im Jahre 1611; die siebente, die auf Veranstaltung der ostindischen Compagnie geschehen; beschrieben durch den Unterschiffer, Nathanael Marten.

Floris, Peter Williamson. Tageregister des, Oberkaufmanns bey eben der Reise des Hauptmanns Hippon; aus dem Holländischen übersetzt, und zusammengezogen.

Castleton's Fahrt nach Priaman, im Jahre 1612; vom Steuerm. Joh. Tatton aufgesetzt.

Saris, Johann. Reise nach dem rothen Meere, den Molukken und Japan, im Jahre 1611; die achte, welche von der ostindischen Gesellschaft ausgeführet worden; aus des Hauptmanns eigenem Tageregister gesammlet.

—— Begebenheiten zu Bantam und an andern Orten in Ostindien, von dem Weinmonate 1605 bis zu dem Weinmonate 1609, nebst einer Nachricht von den Marktplätzen und Waaren daselbst.

Cocks, Richard. Nachricht von dem, was zu Firando in des Generals Abwesenheit an dem kaiserlichen Hofe zu Japan vorgefallen.

Einige Umstände von den Sachen in Japan, von 1614 bis 1620, aus den Briefen des Herrn Cocks, welchem der Inhalt zweener Briefe des Herrn Sayers, und ein Schreiben des Kaisers von Japan an den Prinzen von Oranien beygefüget ist.

Adams, Wilhelm. Reise nach Japan, und Begebenheiten daselbst; von ihm selbst beschrieben.

VOLUME 2.

BOOK 4. — *Reisen nach verschiedenen Theilen von Africa:*—

Nicols, Thomas. Beschreibung der Canarischen Eylande und Madera nebst ihren merkwürdigen Früchten · und Waaren, 1560.

Allgemeine Historie, Vol. 2—*contd.*

Cada Mosto, Aluise da. Reise des, längst der Africanischen Küste bis Rio Grande, 1455-56.

Cintra, Piedro de. Reise des nach Sierra Leona, 1462.

Roberts, G. Bericht von einer Reise nach den Canarieninseln, dem grünen Vorgebirge und Barbados, 1721.

Beschreibung der Eylande des grünen Vorgebirges.

BOOK 5.—*Reisen längst der Westlichen Küste von Africa:*—

Nachricht, wie sich die Franzosen, zwischen Capo Blanco und Sierra Leona niedergelassen.

Jannequin, C. Auszug von einer Reisebeschreibung nach Lybia, vornehmlich nach dem Königreiche Sanaga an dem Nigerflusse, 1637.

Brüe, And. Reisen zu Wasser und Lande längst den Westlichen Küsten von Africa, 1697.

—— Beschreibung des Flusses Sanaga, nebst einer untersuchung, ob es der Niger selbst oder nur ein Arm davon sey.

—— Reise auf der Sanaga, 1697.

—— Andere Reise den Sanagastrom hinauf in das Königreich Galam, 1698.

—— Reise von Albreda an dem Flusse Gambra nach Kachao zu Lande, 1700.

—— Reise nach Inseln Bissao und Bissagos, 1700.

—— Versuch die See Kayor zu entdecken, 1714, nebst einer Nachricht, wie die Handlung von Gorea geführet wird.

—— Dritte Reise die Sanaga, 1715.

Eine Nachricht von dem Lande gegen Norden von Sanaga wo der Gummi gesammelt wird, dessen Einwohnern und Früchten.

Compagnon, Herr. Eine Nachricht von der Entdeckung des Königreichs Bambuk und dessen Goldadern, 1716, nebst einer Beschreibung des Landes und dessen Einwohner.

VOLUME 3.

BOOK 6.—*The same.*

Eine kurze Nachricht von dem Ursprunge und Fortgange der Königlichen Englischen Africanischen Compagnie.

Eine allgemeine Beschreibung von dem Flusse Gambra oder Gambia.

Jobson, R. Reise sur Entdeckung des Flusses Gambra, und des Goldhandels in Tombuto, 1620-21.

Stibbs, B. Reise auf der Gambra, 1724.

Moore, F. Reisen in die Inländischen Theile von Africa, welche eine Beschreibung der verschiedenen Landschaften und deren Einwohner auf sechshundert meilen an der Gambra.

Allgemeine Historie, Vol. 3—*contd.*

Solomon, Job ben. Die merkwürdige Gefangenschaft und Befreyung, eines muhammedanischen Priesters von Bunda, nahe bey der Gambra, 1732.

Broek, Peter van den. Reise nach dem grünen Vorgebirge und der Küste von Africa, 1606.

Le Maire, Herr. Reise nach den Canarieninseln, dem grünen Vorgebirge, der Sanaga und Gambra, 1682.

Beschreibung von den Jalofern, besonders von denen, die gegen die Gambra zu wohnen, von den Fuliern, und der Mandingoern.

Finch, W. Beobachtungen über Sierra Leona, 1607.

Villault de Bellefond. Beschreibung von Sierra Leona, 1666.

Barbot, J. Beschreibung von Sierra Leona, 1678.

Atkins, H. Beschreibung von Sierra Leona, 1721.

Labat. Beschreibung von Sierra Leona, 1728.

Von den Bäumen, Thieren, Vogeln, &c., dieses Theils von Africa.

BOOK 7.—*Reisen nach Guinea und Benin:*—

Villault, Ritter. Auszug aus einer Reise nach den Küsten von Africa und Guinea, 1666.

Phillips, T. Beschreibung einer Reise längst der Küste von Guinea nach Whidaw, dem Eylande St Thomas, und von da nach Barbadoes, 1693.

Loyer, G. Kurze Nachricht von einer Seefahrt nach Issini auf der Goldküste, 1701.

Atkins, J. Reise nach Guinea, Brasilien, und Westindien, 1721.

Marchais, Ritter des. Eine Fahrt nach Guinea und den anliegenden Eylanden, 1725.

Smith, W. Eine Reise nach Guinea, 1726.

Snelgrave, W. Neue Nachricht von einigen Theilen von Guinea und dem Sklavenhandel, 1730.

BOOK 8. — *Beschreibung von Guinea, nebst der Erdbeschreibung, der Natur- und politischen Geschichte.*

VOLUME 4.

Beschreibung von Guinea, fortlaufend.

BOOK 9.—*Beschreibung der Küsten von Rio da Volta bis an das Vorgebirge Lope Gonsalvo.*

BOOK 10.—*Schiffahrten und Reisen nach Guinea und Benin, welche eine Beschreibung von Benin und der Küste bis nach Kongo in sich enthalten:*—

Barbot, J., und J. Grazilhier. Beschreibung von einer Seefahrt nach den Flüssen Neu-Kalabar, Bandi und Doni, 1699.

Allgemeine Historie, Vol. 4—*contd.*

BOOK 11.—*Reisen nach Congo und Angola:*—

Lopez, Ed. Die Reise nach Kongo, 1578.

Battels, And. Die Reisen und Begebenheiten in Angola, 1589.

Angelo, M. Reise nach Kongo, 1666.

Carli, D. Reisen der Missionarien in Kongo, 1667.

Merolla, Hieron. Eine Reise nach Kongo und verschiedenen andern Ländern in den südlichen Theilen von Africa, 1682-88.

Barbot, Jac., und J. Casseneuve. Auszug aus einer Reise an den Fluss von Kongo und nach Kabinda, 1700.

BOOK 12.—*Beschreibung der Königreiche Loango, Kongo, Angola, Benguela, und den angränzenden Ländern.*

VOLUME 5.

BOOK 12, *continued.*

BOOK 13.—*Beschreibung der Länder längst der ostlichen Küste von Africa:*—

Hamilton, Alex. Einige Anmerkungen über die Küsten und Inseln zwischen dem Vorgebirge der guten Hoffnung und Capo Guarda Fuy.

BOOK 14.—*Reisen nach dem Reich China:*—

Nieuhoff, J. P. von Goyer's und J. von Keyser's Gesandtschaft von der Holländischen Ostindischen Compagnie an den Kaiser in China, 1655.

Montanus, A. Die Gesandtschaft J. von Campen und C. Nobles, an den Unterkönig von Fokyen Sing la mong, 1662.

—— Der Seezug der Holländer, das Eyland Formosa in Vereinigung mit den Tartarn wieder zu erobern, 1663-64.

—— Die Gesandtschaft des Herrn van Hoorn an Kanghi, Kaiser in China und der ostlichen Tartarey, 1666-67.

Eine Erzählung von der Gesandtschaft der Holländer im 1655, und von denen Kunstgriffen, welche die Jesuiten gebraucht haben die Absichten derselben zu hintertreiben.

Van Rechteren, S. Erste Versuche der Holländer, nach China zu handeln, und ihr Handelssitz zu Taywan.

Navarette, F. Reisen des, durch China, 1658.

Fünf Französischer Jesuiten Reisen von Ning po fu nach Peking, 1687.

Comte et Fontaney. Reise von Siam nach Ning po fu, Ching hyen fu, Tay ngan chew, und Peking.

Fontaney, J. Reise von Peking nach Kyangchew in der Provinz Shan si, und von dar nach Nan king, 1688.

Bouvet, J. Reise von Peking nach Kanton, 1693.

Allgemeine Historie, Vol. 5—*contd.*

Careri, J. F. Gemelli. Reise in China, 1695. Nanking, Peking, Kanton.

Isbrand Ides, E. Reise nach China, 1693.

Langen, L. Reise nach China, 1717.

Gaubil, A. Reise von Kanton nach Peking, 1722.

Mezzabarba, C. A., Titularpatriarch von Alexandria. Legation im Namen des Pabstes an den Kaiser Kang hi, im China, 1720.

VOLUME 6.

BOOK 15.—*Beschreibung von China.*

BOOK 16.—*Beschreibung von Korea, der westlichen Tartarey und Tibet:*—

Regis, J. B. Geographische Beobachtungen und Geschichte von Korea, 1720.

Hamel, H. Reisen einiger Holländer nach Korea, nebst einer Nachricht von dem Lande und von ihrem Schiffbruche an der Insel Quelpaert, 1658-68.

VOLUME 7.

Verbiest, Ferd. Reise in die östliche Tartarey, 1682.

BOOK 17.—*Reisen durch die Tartarey, Tibet und Bucharey, nach und von China:*—

Carpini, J. de Plano. Reisen nach der Tartarey, 1246.

Ascelin, Mönch. Reisen zu den Tartarn, 1247.

Rubruquis, W. Reisen in die Östlichen Gegenden der Welt, 1253.

Marco Polo. Reisen in die Tartarey, 1272.

Gesandtschaft des Sohnes Tamerlans, Schach Rokh und anderer Fürsten an den Kaiser in Katay oder China, 1419-22.

Jenkinson, A. Reise aus Russland nach Boghar oder Bokhara, 1557.

Goez, B. Reisen in des Mongols Reiche nach China, 1602.

Gruber, J. Reisen von China nach Europa, 1661.

Desiderius. H. Reisen nach Tibet, 1714.

Horaz della Penna, Bruder. Nachricht vom Anfange und itzigen Zustande der Kapucinermission in Tibet, 1741.

Gerbillon, J. F. Reisen in die westliche Tartarey auf Befehl des Kaisers von China, 1688-98.

[*Astley's collection ends here.*]

VOLUME 8.

BOOK 1.—*Reisen der Holländer nach Ostindien:*—

Erste Reise nach Ostindien von C. Houtmann, 1595.

Zweyte Reise, des J. C. van Neck und W. van Warwick, nach Insel Java, 1598-1600.

Allgemeine Historie, Vol. 8—*contd.*

Andere Reisen des P. van Caerden, und J. van Neck nach Achin, 1600-1602.

Van der Hagen, S., W. Hermansen, und C. van Ween. Reisen nach Bantam, 1599-1602.

Pyrard, F. Reise, welche die erste der Franzosen nach Ostindien ist, 1601-10. Fahrt und Begebenheiten bis an die Inseln Comorres, Schiffbruch und Gefangenschaft ankunft zu Goa, und Rückreise nach Europa.

Spilberg, G. Reise nach Ostindien, 1601-3. Fahrt bis zu den Comorrischen Inseln. Reise nach der Insel Ceylan und Verrichtungen daselbst.

Warwyck, W. van. Reise nach Ostindien, 1602-4,

Van der Hagen, S. Zweyte Reise nach Ostindien, 1604-5.

Matelief, C. Reise nach Ostindien, 1605-8. Seefahrt bis nach Malacca, Verrichtungen zu Johor, und Reise nach China.

Beschreibung der Moluckischen Insel.

Caerden, P. van. Zweyte Reise nach Ostindien, 1607-11.

Verhoeven, P. W. Reise nach Ostindien, 1607-11. Verrichtungen und Fahrt bis nach Johor, und Ermordung. Fernere Reise nach Japon.

Bontekoe, W. I. Reise nach Ostindien, 1618-25.

Broeck, P. van den. Reise nach Ostindien, 1613-27. Reisen und Verrichtungen bis zur Niederlassung der Holländer in Mocka, Nachricht von dem Ursprunge der Stadt Batavia.

Knoxen, R. Reise nach der Insel Ceylan, 1657-79.

BOOK 2.—*Reisen der Franzosen und anderer nach Ostindien:*—

Renneforts Reise nach der Insel Madagascar, 1665-66.

Mondevergue. Reise, oder Anhang zu Renneforts Reisebeschreibung, 1666-71.

De la Haie. Reise nach Ostindien, 1670-72. Fahrt nach Ceylan und Verrichtungen zu St Thomä.

VOLUME 9.

[*Not in the French edition.*]

Juan, Georg, und A. de Ulloa. Reise nach dem Königreiche Peru.

VOLUME 10.

BOOK 2—*continued.*

Carre. Reise nach Ostindien, 1668-71.

L'Estra. Reise nach Ostindien, 1671-75.

Ovington, J. Reise nach Surate und andern in Africa und Asia gelegenen Orten, 1690-93.

Allgeimene Historie, Vol. 10—*contd.*

Floris, W. Reise nach dem Bengalischen
Meerbusen, 1611-13.

Ovington, J. Beschreibung des König-
reiches Arrakan.

Rhodes, Alex. Reise nach Ostindien,
1619-49.

—— Reise nach Cochinchina, nach
Tunkin, den Philippinen und Malacca,
nach Batavia, Bantam, Macassar, und
Surate.

Baron. Beschreibung von Tunkin, 1685.

Tachard, Guido. Reise nach Siam, 1685.

Chaumont, Ritter von. Reise nach Siam,
1685.

Tachard, G. Zweyte Reise nach Ostindien, 1687.

Fontenay, Peter von. Reise von Siam
nach China, 1686.

Occum Chamnam. Reise nach Siam
und Portugall, 1684-86. Abschickung
aus Siam, Schiffbruch und Reise zu
den Hottentotten.

Beschreibung des Königreichs Siam.

Beaulieu, Aug. von. Reise nach Ostindien,
1619-21. Fahrt bis nach dem Vorgebirge Comorin. Reise nach Achem
und Aufenthalt daselbst. Beschreibung
der Insel Sumatra.

Pinto, F. Mendez. Reisen nach Indien,
&c.

Dellon. Reise nach den Französischen
Handelsplätzen auf der Malabarischen
Küste. 1670-72.

Methold, W. Reise nach den Diamant-
gruben in Golkonda, Visapur, und
Bengalen, 1622.

Tavernier. Reisen nach den Diamant-
gruben. Die Königreiche Butan, Tipra
und Asem, 1652.

Beschreibung der Königreiche Golkonda
und Pegu.

Graaf, N. Reise auf dem Ganges, 1668-
73.

Luillier. Reise nach dem Bengalischen
Seebusen, 1722-23. Niederlassung der
Franzosen zu Pondichery.

Zusätse zu der Beschreibung der Eylande
Bourbon und Frankreich.

VOLUME 11.

——Rhoe, T. Reise nach Indostan, 1615-17.

Mandelslo, J. A. Reise nach Indostan,
1638-39.

Bernier, Herr. Reise in das Königreich
Kachemir, 1664.

Tavernier. Reisen im Indostanischen,
1665-66. Reise nach Indostan, von
Surata nach Goa, nach Java, nach
Europa.

Beschreibung von Indostan.

Erste Reisen der Franzosen nach dem
glücklichen Arabien durch das Morgenländische Meer, 1708. Beobachtungen
von den Caffeebaume.

Allgemeine Historie, Vol. 11—*contd.*

Nachrichten von Carnate, durch einige
Jesuiten-Missionarien.

Von den Münzen oder verschiedenen Arten
von Metallenen Stücken, Muschel-
schaalen und Mandeln, die für Münzen
gehalten werden.

Magalhanes, oder Magellan, F. Reise
nach Ostindien durch Südwest, 1519.

Noort, O. von. Reise nach Ostindien
durch Südwesten, 1598-1601.

Beschreibung der Marianischen Inseln.

Beschreibung der Philippinischen Inseln.

Le Maire, J. Reise, eine neue Durchfahrt
Südwärts unter der Magellanischen
Strasse zu entdecken, 1615-16.

Beschreibung der Insel Celebes oder
Macassar.

Kämpfer, E. Reise nach Japon, von
Batavia, 1690-91.

Beschreibung der Japonischen Inseln.

VOLUME 12.

Drake, Ritter F. Reise, 1577-79.

Sarmiento, P. Reise, 1580.

Verschiedene Reisen nach Ostindien
durch die Magellanische Strasse.

Candish, T. Reise, 1586.

Noort, O. von, und S. von Weert.
Reisen, 1598-99.

Spilberg, G. Reise, 1614.

L'Hermite, J., und Schapenham. Reise,
1624.

Narborough, J. Reise, 1669-71.

Frogers Reise, oder Nachricht von des
Herrn von Genes Reise nach der
Magellanischen Strasse, 1695-96.

Rogers, W. Reise nach Ostindien durch
Südwesten, 1708-10.

Wood, H. Reise durch die Magellanische Strasse.

Frezier. Riese durch die Strasse des le
Maire, 1711-14.

Anson, Lord. Reise um die Welt durch
Südwest, 1740-44.

BOOK 3. — *Reisen nach den Südländern:* —

Pelsart, F. Reise nach den Südländern,
1629.

Tasmann, A. J. Reise nach den Südländern, 1642-43.

Dampier, W. Reise nach den Südländern, 1699-1700.

Beschreibung des Eylandes Timor.

Reise zweyer Französischen Schiffe nach
den Südländern.

BOOK 4.—*Irrende Reisen, oder Solche
die kein gewisses vorgesetztes Ziel
haben :*—

Schouten, G. Reisen nach Batavia,
Arrakan, China, Malabarischen Küste,
Mataram, und nach Norwegen, 1658-65.

Dampier, W. Reise um die Welt,
1683-89.

Allgemeine Historie, Vol. 12—*contd.*
Beschreibung der Malabarischen Küste.
Careri, G. Reise um die Welt, 1695-97.
Gentil, Barbinais le. Reise um die Welt, 1714-17.
Naturgeschichte von Ostindien.

VOLUME 13.

BOOK 5.—*Entdeckungen und Nieder-lassungen der Europäer in America:—*
Columbus, Christoph. Reisen, 1492-1505.
Reise des A. Ojeda, J. de la Cosa, und Americus Vesputius.
Reise des A. Nino und der beyden Guerren.
Y. Pinzons Reise.
Reise des Diego de Lopez.
Reise des Alvarez von Cabral.
Reise des Gaspard von Corte Real.
J. Cabots und seiner drey Söhne Reise.
Verfolg der dritten Reise des C. Columbus.
Zustand und Fortgang der Entdeckungen nach Chr. Columbens Tode, 1506.
Solis, Diaz de, und des Y. Pinzon. Reise, 1507.
Ocampo. Reise um die Insel Cuba, 1508.
Ponce, J. Reise nach Borriquen oder Portorico und Errichtung eines Wohn-platzes daselbst, 1508-9.
Ojeda, A., und Nicuessa. Reisen, 1510.
Entdeckung des Landes Darien und anderer Länder.
Nugnez Balboa, Entdeckungen, welche den Weg nach Peru bahneten, 1510.
Weitere Eroberungen der Castilianer in den Inseln Jamaica, Hispaniola, und Cuba, 1511.
Ponce de Leon. Reise und Entdeckung von Florida, 1512.
Nugnez de Balboa, Folge der Indian-ischen Begebenheiten und Entdeckung des Süd-meeres, 1512-13.
Fernere Folge der Westindischen Ent-deckungen und Begebenheiten, 1514-16.
Solis, J. Diaz de. Letzte Reise und Entdeckungen nach Süden, 1516.
Beschreibung der Insel Hispaniola, insgemein St Domingo genannt.
Cordua, H. von. Reise und Entdeckung des Landes Yucatan, 1517.
Grijalva, J. Reise und allererste Ent-deckung Neuspaniens, 1517-18.
Cortez, F. Reise, Entdeckung und Eroberung des Reiches Mexico, 1518-22.
Beschreibung von Mexico oder Neu-spanien.

VOLUME 14.

[*Not in the French edition.*]
Charlevoix, P. F. Xavier. Beschreibung von Neu-Frankreich; worinnen alles dasjenige enthalten ist, was die Entdeckungen und Eroberungen der Franzosen in dem Nordlichen America betrifft.

Allgemeine Historie—*continued.*

VOLUME 15.

BOOK 6.—*The same.*
Las Casas, B. de. Reise und Nieder-lassung an der Küste von Cumana, 1520-21.
Verazzani, J. Reise und Entdeckungen von Nord-America, 1523-24.
Cartier, J., und Roberval. Reisen, 1534-42.
Pizarro, F. Reisen und Entdeckung und Eroberung von Peru, Niederlassung an der Küste von St Martha, Venezuela und Coro, 1524-41.
Almagro, Don Diego von. Entdeckung von Chili.
Castro, Vacco von. Reise, 1541-42.
Nugnez von Vela, B. Reise, 1543-44.
Pizarro, G. Statthalterschaft des, 1544-46.
Gasca, P. de la. Reise, 1546-50.
Beschreibungen der erstern entdeckten Länder in dem mittäglichen America: Terra Firma, Carthagena, Peru, Lima, Cuzco, Quito, Chili, und Sant Jago.
Juan, G., und A. von Ulloa. Reisen.
Correal, F. Reisen nach Peru, 1692-95.
Frezier. Reise an den Küsten von Peru, 1713.
Condamine, Herr de la. Reise, 1735-42.
Ursprung, Regierung, Religion, Sitten, Gebräuche, Wissenschaften, Denk-maale Merkwürdigkeiten, u. d. gl. des alten Reiches Peru.

VOLUME 16.

Reisen auf dem Maranjon oder Amazonen-flusse: Orsua, 1560; Carvallo, 1633; Texeira, 1637; Acunja und Artieda, 1639-40; De la Condamine, 1743-45.
Reisen auf dem Flusse de la Plata und an der Magellanischen Küste: Cabot, S., 1526-27; Mendoza, P. von., 1535-36; Cabrera, Alf. von., 1538; Bes-chreibung von Chaco, und der Stadt Buenos Ayres; Quiroga, P., Reise nach der Küste des Magellanischen Landes, 1745-46; Küste Der Stat-thalterschaft, Rio de la Plata bis nach Brasilien.
Naturgeschichte der Spanischen Land-schaften in dem Südlichen America; des Landes Guayaquil, von Peru.
Reisen und Niederlassungen der Portu-giesen Franzosen und Holländer in Brasilien: J. von Lery, Reise, 1556-58; Beschreibung von Brasilien, der Insel Marignan, der Provinz Guayra und anderer Völkerschaften in Brasilien.
Reisen auf dem Orinoko und weiter an den Küsten von Süd America. Raleigh, Sir W.: Reise in Guiana, 1595. Keymis, L.: Reise nach Guiana, 1596. Französisches Guiana. Niederlassun-gen in Neuandalusien von dem Orinoko

Allgemeine Historie, Vol. 16—*contd.*
bis an Rio de la Hacha. Statthalter-
schaften Rio de la Hacha und St
Martha. Neues Königreich Grenada.
Reisen und Niederlassungen in dem
Nordlichen America. Soto, F. von :
Reise nach Florida, der Provinz Apa-
lache, &c., 1537-43.
Reisen, Entdeckungen und Niederlas-
sungen der Engländer in dem Nord-
lichen America, in Virginien, Maryland,
Neuengland, Newyork, Newyersey,
Pensylvanien, Carolina, Spanisches
Florida, und Neugorgien.
Fortsetzung der Reisen, Entdeckungen
und Niederlassungen der Franzosen in
Nord - America. Beschreibung der
Hudsonshay und dasiger Wilden, von
Canada oder Neufrankreich. Charle-
voix, P. de : Reisen und Beobach-
tungen, 1720-21. La Hontan, Baron
de : Reise auf dem langen Flusse,
1688. Charlevoix, P. de : Reise nach
Luisiana auf dem Mississippi, 1721-22.

VOLUME 17.

Von den Gebräuchen, Sitten und der
Gemüthsart der Indianer in dem
Nordlichen America.
Reisen gegen Nordwest und Nordost zur
Entdeckung einer Fahrt nach Ostindien.
Cabot, 1497 ; Frobisher, 1579 ; Davis,
1585-87; Barentz, 1594-95; Heems-
kerke, 1596-97 ; Weimouth, 1602 ;
Hudson, 1607-10 ; Button, 1612 ;
Baffin, 1616 ; Fox, 1631 ; James, 1631,
&c.; J. Munk, 1619 ; D'Aguilar, 1602;
Adm. De Fonte, 1640 ; Woods, 1676;
Beerings, 1725 ; Spanberg, 1739 ;
Tchirikow, 1741 ; Gillam ; Barlow,
1719; Scroggs, 1722; Middleton, 1737 ;
Ellis, 1746.
Naturgeschichte von Nord-America.
Beschreibung und natürliche Eigen-
schaften von Spitzbergen.
Regnard. Reise nach Lappland, 1681.
Maupertuis, Herm. von. Reise nach
Lappland, 1736-37.
Outhier, Ab. Reise nach Lappland,
1737.
BOOK 7.—*Reisen und Niederlassungen
auf den Antillen :—*
Niederlassung der Franzosen in der
Insel Hispaniola oder St Domingo,
1630-92.
Von den Reisen nach den Antillen und
den Niederlassungen daselbst über-
haupt, 1635-63.
Reisen und Niederlassungen in der Insel
St Christoph, 1627.
Ursprung, Gemüthsart und Gebräuche
der Caraiben.
Reisen nach Martinique.
Reisen nach Guadeloupe, Insel Granada,
Insel St Lucia oder Sainte Alousie.

Allgemeine Historie, Vol. 17—*contd.*
Handlung auf den Französischen Inseln.
Engländische Inseln. Reisen und Nieder-
lassungen in Jamaica, Barbadoes,
Antigo, Montserrat, Nevis, Barbuda,
und Anguilla.
Reisen und Niederlassungen auf den
Inseln Bermudas oder den Com-
mereylanden.
Reisen und Niederlassungen auf den
Lucayischen Eylanden.
Reisen und Neiderlassungen in der Insel
Neuland.
Zusatz zu den Reisen und Niederlassungen
auf den Antillen.

VOLUME 18.

Anmerkungen, welche zur Verbindung
des Fortganges der Holländer in
Ostindien dienen.
Broeck, Van den. Stiftung der Stadt
Batavia, 1618-19.
Belagerung der Stadt Batavia von dem
Kaiser in Java, 1628-29.
Zusatz zur Beschreibung der Moluckischen
Inseln and Amboina.
Zusatz zu der Beschreibung der Insel
Banda.
Zusatz zur Beschreibung der Insel Ceylan,
welcher die Holländischen Nieder-
lassungen auf diesem Eylande enthält.
Forbin, Graf. von. Auszug aus der Reise-
beschreibung in Siam, 1685-88.
Des Farges. Bericht von denen 1688 in
Siam vorgefallenen Reichsveränder-
ungen.
D'Orleans. Zusätze zu der vorherge-
henden Erzählung, 1688.
De Challes. Letzte Nachricht von dem
Schicksale der Franzosen zu Siam,
1690-91.
Beschreibung der Königreiche Laos und
Camboja, 1691.
Beaulieu, A. v. Reise der Insel Sumatra.
Weg, welchen man nehmen muss, um
durch die Strassen von Malaca und
Gobernadur zu kommen.
Zusatz zu der letzten Regierungsänderung
in Golkonda.
Genealogisches Verzeichniss der grossen
Mogole, 1370-1723.
Zusatz zu der Nachricht von Carnate,
1703-36.
Zusatz zu der Französischen Nieder-
lassung in Pondichery seit 1741-55.
Zustand der Franzosen in Indien bis 1755.
Beschreibung der Küste Coromandel.
Beschreibung der Königreiche Tanjur,
Marava, Madure, Maissur, Gingi, und
Carnate.
Neue und nähere Beobachtungen über
den Bau des Caffees.
Zusatz zu der Entdeckung der Palaos oder
neuen Philippinischen Inseln, 1710.

Allgemeine Historie, Vol. 18—*contd.*

Neue Erläuterungen über die Insel Palaos, 1721-32.

Zweytes Unternehmen der Holländer wider die Insel Celebes oder Macassar, und Einnahme derselben, 1666-69.

Beschreibung der Insel Borneo.

Cowley. Reise um die Welt, 1684.

Anson, Herr. Zusatz zu der Reise ins Stille Meer, 1741-45.

Pizarre, J., Geschichte des Spanischen Geschwaders unter, 1740-45.

Vesputius, Americus. Erste Entdeckung der Südlichen Welt, 1502.

Gonneville, B. P. Erste Entdeckung der Südlichen Welt, 1504.

Savedra, Don A. Reise nach Mexico, 1526.

Gaetan, J., und B. Della Torre. Reise, 1542-43.

Mendoce, Alvare de, und A. de Mindana. Reise nach Peru, 1567.

Mindana, Alvare von. Andere Reise nach die Südsee, 1595-96.

Quiros, F. Reise nach Peru, &c., 1606.

Nodal, Garcie de. Reise nach Rio Janeiro, &c., 1618.

Entdeckungen der Holländer, in den Südländern, 1616-44.

Vink. Reise nach Neuguinea, 1663.

Keyts, J. Reise nach Neuguinea, 1678.

Vlaming, W. Reise nach den Südländern, 1696.

Benachbarte Eylande um Timor und Solor.

Eylande, die unter der Regierung zu Banda stehen.

Eylande der Papue bey Neuguinea.

Geographische Beschreibung einer Küste von Neuguinea, 1705.

Roggeveen, Adm. Reise nach den Südländern, 1722.

Beobachtungen wegen des Eises in denen Meeren, welche an die Pole gränzen.

Untersuchung der Frage, ob es in den Südländern Riesen gebe.

Zusatz zu der Beschreibung von Malabar.

VOLUME 19.

Besondere Geschichte von Island.

Beschreibung der Insel Jean Mayen oder der Dreyeinigkeits-Insel.

Von dem Russischen Neulande oder Nova Semlia.

Reise nach Kamtschatka durch Sibirien.

Gmelin, Herr. Reise in Sibirien, 1733-43.

Reisen, welche von den Russen versuchet worden, durch die Lena in das Eismeer und durch Nordosten nach Kamtschatka zu gehen.

Neue Nachricht von Samojedien und den Samojeden.

Besondere Nachricht von den Ostiaken.

Lisle, Herr de. Auszug aus der Beschreibung einer Reise nach Beresow in Sibirien, 1740.

Allgemeine Historie—*continued.*

VOLUME 20.

Crantz, D. Historie und Beschreibung von Grönland und dasigen Missionen. Von der Lage und Beschaffenheit des Landes. Von den Thieren, Vögeln, und Fischen. Von den Einwohnern. Bürgerliche Geschichte von Grönland.

Geschichte von Kamtschatka. Von dem Lande. Von den Einwohnern. Politische und bürgerliche Geschichte. Von den nahe bey Kamtschatka liegenden Ländern und Völkern.

Müller, Herr. Auszug aus den Reisen und Entdeckungen längst den Küsten des Eismeeres und auf dem Morgenländischen Meere, so wohl gegen Japon als gegen America zu.

Castell, P. Abhandlung über die berühmten Länder Kamtschatka und Jesso, oder über die Gemeinschaft des festen Landes von Asien und America und die durchfahrt aus dem oestlichen in das Nördliche Meer.

Engel, Herr. Nachrichten und Geographischkritische Beobachtungen über die Lage der mitternächtlichen Länder von Asien und America. Nebst einem Versuche über den Weg nach Indien durch den Norden.

Chappe d'Auteroche, Ab. Auszug aus Reise nach Sibirien, 1760-61.

Högström, Peter. Historische Beschreibung des Schwedischen Lapplandes.

Ehrenmalm, Arwid. Reise durch Westnordland nach der Lappmark Asele, 1741.

VOLUME 21.

Kerguelen Tremarec, Herr von. Nachricht von seiner Reise in die Nordsee, von Brest nach Island, &c. 1767-68

Alphabetisches Verzeichniss der Reisen.

Geographisches Verzeichniss der Länder, &c.

A New Collection of Voyages, Discoveries, and Travels, containing whatever is worthy of notice in Europe, Asia, Africa, and America, &c. 7 vols. *Maps and plates.* 8° [Printed for J. Knox.] 1767

CONTENTS.

Vol. 1.—The four Voyages of Columbus to America. — Discoveries of the Spaniards, from the death of Columbus to the expedition of Hernando Cortes. —The Conquest of Mexico by Hernando Cortes. — The Discovery of Golden Castile. — The Conquest of Peru, by Francis Pizarro.—A Voyage to South America, by John George Juan and Don Antonio de Ulloa.—Remarks on the Trade between Spain and the West Indies.—Some Particulars relating to the Inhabitants of Patagonia.

New Collection—*continued.*

Vol. 2.—Mr John Nieuhoff's Voyage to, and account of, Brazil in South America.—Modern state of Brazil.—Memoir concerning the Settlements of the Jesuits in Paraguay.—Mr Lionel Wafer's Journey over the Isthmus of Darien.—A brief Account of North America, from Major Rogers and others, with Particulars relating to the Indian Natives.—An Abstract of the Account of Colonel Bouquet's Expedition against the Ohio Indians in 1764. ·—Reflections on the War with the Savages of North America.—A short Account of the American Islands.—The Proclamation for regulating the Cessions made to us by the last Treaty of Peace. — Conclusion to the Discoveries, Voyages, and Descriptions relating to America.—The first Voyage to the East Indies by Vasquez de Gama.—The first Voyage to the East Indies, on the Account of the English East India Company, under the command of Captain James Lancaster.—A Voyage to the Cape de Verde Islands, by Captain George Roberts.—Mr Peter Kolben's Voyage to the Cape of Good Hope, containing an Account of the Dutch Settlement and the Hottentot Natives.—Mr John Nieuhoff's Voyages to the East Indies, containing an Account of the Dutch Settlements, particularly Batavia on the Island of Java.— Narrative of Cruelties exercised by the Dutch on the English at Amboyna.—Mr Grosse's Voyage to the East Indies, &c.

Vol. 3.—The Voyage of Sir Francis Drake round the Globe.—The Voyage round the World performed by Captain William Dampier.—The Voyage of Captain Woodes Rogers in the "Duke" and Captain Stephen Courtney in the "Duchess" round the World, including the account of their finding Alexander Selkirk on the Island of Juan Fernandez.—The Voyage round the World, by George Anson.

Vol. 4.—Travels through the most northern parts of Europe, particularly Norway, Danish, Swedish, and Muscovite Lapland, Borandia, Samojedia, Zembla, and Iceland ; extracted from the journal of a Gentleman employed by the North-Sea Company of Copenhagen, to make discoveries. — The Travels of Maupertuis and his associates to determine the figure of the earth at the Polar circle.—Natural history of Norway, by Erick Pontoppidan.—Account of Sweden, from the writings of an English minister residing there.—The present state of Denmark, from

New Collection, Vol. 4—*continued.*

the writings of Lord Molesworth and others.—Account of Poland, from the writings of Dr Bernard Connor, physician to King John Sobieski.—Account of the Ukrain and the Cossacks, from the writings of Mr Beauplan and others.—A description of the seven United Provinces of the Low Countries, from Misson, Hanway, and others.—Travels through Germany, Hungary, Bohemia, Switzerland, Italy, and Lorrain, by John George Keysler, &c.

Vol. 5. — Continuation of Keysler's Travels. — Travels through France, by Sacheverel Stephens. — Travels through and an account of the kingdoms of Spain and Portugal, from the remarks of the Reverend Mr Clarke, chaplain to the Earl of Bristol, Ambassador at Madrid in 1760, including an authentic narrative of the suffering of Isaac Martin in the Inquisition at Granada.—Account of the Empire of Russia, from the observations of Mr Hanway, &c.—Account of the Kingdom of Prussia.

Vol. 6.—The Voyage and Travels of Mr John Thevenot from Italy to Constantinople. — Mr Wood's Journey to Palmyra, or Tedmor in the Desart.—Mr Wood's Account of the Ruins of Balbec, the ancient Heliopolis, in Coelosyria.—A Description of Judea, or the Holy Land, and particularly of Jerusalem, from Maundrell, Shaw, and other Travellers.—The Travels of Dr Pococke through Egypt, with occasional Extracts from Mr Norden.—Dr Shaw's Travels through Barbary.—A Journey to Mequainez, by Mr Windus.—Travels into the inland parts of Africa, by Francis Moore, including an Account of the Adventures of Job Ben Solomon, son of the High Priest of Bundo. — The Travels of Sir John Chardin through Mingrelia and Georgia into Persia.—An Account of Indostan, interspersed with the Observations of Sir T. Roe, &c.—A Journey from St Petersburg to Pekin, with an Embassy from his Imperial Majesty Peter the First, to Kamhi, Emperor of China, by J. Bell, Esq.

Vol. 7. — An Account of the Country and Constitution of Great Britain in general, and of England in particular.—A short general Description of the City of London, &c.—An Account of the Kingdom and Laws of Scotland, with the general Articles of its Union with that of England.—A Short View of the Naval Transactions of Britain : Elizabeth to Peace of Versailles, 1763.

New Collection, Vol. 7—*continued.*
—A List of the Royal Navy of Great Britain at the close of 1762.

The World Displayed ; or, A Curious Collection of Voyages and Travels, selected from the Writers of all Nations, &c. 2nd [partly 3rd] edition. Vols. 1 to 20. 8°
1767-68
Vol. 1.—The Voyages of Christopher Columbus to America.
The Discoveries of the Spaniards, from the Death of Columbus to Cortes's Expedition.
Vol. 2.—The Conquest of Mexico, by Hernando Cortes. 1518.
Vol. 3. — The Discovery of Golden Castile. 1513.
The Conquest of Peru, by Francis Pizarro. 1524.
The Settlement of Brasil by the Portuguese, and its several Revolutions. 1500.
Vol. 4.—The Discoveries of the English in America.
Vol. 5.—The Discoveries and Settlements of the French in America.
The Discoveries and Settlements of the Dutch in America.
A Danish Settlement in America.
The Voyage of Sir Francis Drake round the World.
The Voyage of Schouten and Le Maire round the World.
Vol. 6.—The Voyage of Capt. William Dampier round the World. 1684.
The Voyage of Capt. Woodes Rogers round the World. 1708.
Vol. 7.—Commodore Anson's Voyage round the World. 1740.
Vol. 8.—The Voyage of Vasco de Gama to India. 1497.
The Voyage of Pedro Alvarez de Cabral to the East Indies. 1500.
The Voyage of Capt. James Lancaster to the East Indies. 1600.
The Expedition of Commodore Beaulieu to the East Indies. 1619.
Vol. 9.—The Voyage of Sir Henry Middleton to the East Indies. 1610.
The Voyage of Mr Grose to the East Indies. 1750.
The Voyage of Commodore Roggewein for the Discovery of Southern Lands. 1721.
Vol. 10.—Pirard de Laval, Francis. A Description of the Maldiva Islands. 1601.
Kolben, Peter. Voyage to the Cape of Good Hope. 1705.
A Voyage to the Cape de Verd Islands, by Capt. George Roberts. 1721.
The Voyage of Capt. Thomas James for the Discovery of a North-West Passage to the South Seas. 1631.
2 Q

The World Displayed, Vol. 10—*contd.*
Ellis, Henry. Voyage for the Discovery of a North-West Passage to the South Seas. 1746.
Vol. 11.—Maundrell, Henry. Travels from Aleppo to Jerusalem. 1696.
An Account of the Ruins of Balbec, the ancient Heliopolis, in Cœlosyria.
Shaw, Thomas. Travels into Syria and the Holy Land.
The Travels of Mr John Thevenot in the Levant. 1655.
Vol. 12.—The Travels of Mr John Thevenot (continued).
Pococke, Richard. Travels through Egypt. 1737.
Vol. 13.—Pococke, Richard. Travels (continued).
A Journey to Palmyra, or Tedmor in the Desart.
Russel, Alexander. A Description of Aleppo and the adjacent parts.
The Travels of the Ambassadors from the Duke of Holstein into Moscovy, Tartary, and Persia. 1635.
Vol. 14.—The Travels of the Ambassadors, &c. (continued).
The Travels of Mr Jonas Hanway, Merchant, through Russia into Persia, and back through Russia, Germany, and Holland. 1743.
Vol. 15.—The Travels of Mr Jonas Hanway (continued).
Chardin, Sir John. Travels through Mingrelia and Georgia into Persia. 1671.
Vol. 16.—Chardin, Sir John. Travels (continued).
A New History of the East-Indies.
Le Compte, Louis, and P. A. Du Halde. Description of China. 1685.
Vol. 17.—A Description of Guinea.
Moore, Francis. Travels into the Inland Parts of Africa. 1730.
A Description of the Country up the Senegal.
Windus, Mr. A Journey to Mequinez in the Kingdom of Morocco. 1720.
Pitts, Joseph. Of the Religion of the Mahometans, with a Description of Mecca and Medina. 1678.
Shaw, T. Travels through Barbary.
Vol. 18.—Shaw, T. Travels (continued).
Misson, Maximilian. Travels through Germany and Italy.
Vol. 19.—Misson, Maximilian. Travels (continued).
Addison, Joseph. Travels through Italy and Swisserland. 1699.
Keysler, John George. Travels through Swisserland, Germany, and Hungary. 1729.
Stevens, Sacheverell. Travels through France. 1738.

The World Displayed—*continued.*
Vol. 20.—A Description of Spain and
Portugal.
A Description of Sweden.
Molesworth, Lord. An Account of
Denmark.
Pontoppidon, Erich. The Natural
History of Norway.
—Travels through the most Northern
parts of Europe, particularly Norway,
Danish, Swedish, and Muscovite Lap-
land, Borandia, Samojedia, Zembla,
and Iceland. Extracted from the
Journal of a Gentleman employed by
the North Sea Company of Copen-
hagen to make discoveries. 1653.
Maupertuis, Monsieur. Travels made
by order of the French King to
determine the figure of the Earth at
the Polar Circle. 1736.

The Modern Traveller : being a Collection of useful and entertaining Travels,
lately made into various Countries,
the whole carefully abridged ; exhibiting a view of the Manners, Religion,
Government, Arts, Agriculture, Manufactures, and Commerce of the known
World. *Maps and illustrations.* 12°
1776

[*Of this work there is only the Fourth
Volume, which contains :*—]
Peter Osheck's Voyages from Sweden to
China, 1750-52.
Olof Toreen's Voyage to Surat, China,
&c., 1750-52.
Capt. C. G. Eckeberg's Account of
Chinese Husbandry.
Captain Edward Thompson's Sailor's
Letters, from 1754 to 1759.
S. Joseph Baretti's Travels through Spain
and Portugal in 1760.
The Rev. Mr Clark's Journey to Madrid
in 1760.
The Abbé Chappe's (d'Auterouche)
Travels through Russia and Siberia,
1761.
Dr Smollett's Travels through France
and Italy, 1765.
Mr Samuel Sharp's Letters from Italy in
1765-66.
Monsieur Grosley's Observations made in
Italy, 1758-59.
Commodore Byron's Voyage round the
World, 1764, 1765, 1766.
M. de Bougainville's Voyage round the
World, 1766, 1867, 1768, 1769.
Dr Thomas Nugent's Travels through
Germany, 1766.
Capt. Wallis's Voyage round the World,
1766-68.
Capt. Carteret's Voyage round the World,
1766-69.
Capt. Cook's Voyage round the World,
1768-71.

Lettres, édifiantes et curieuses, écrites
des Missions Étrangères. 26 vols.
Maps and plates. 12° *Paris*, 1780-83
Vols. 1-5. Levant.
,, 6-9. Amérique.
,, 10-15. Indes.
,, 16-24. Chine.
,, 25-26. Indes et la Chine.

**A General Collection of Voyages and
Discoveries** made by the Portuguese and
the Spaniards during the Fifteenth and
Sixteenth Centuries : containing the
interesting and entertaining Voyages of
the celebrated Gonzalez and Vaz, Gon-
zalez Zarco, Lanzerota, Diogo Gill, Cada
Mosto, Pedro di Sintra, Diogo d'Azam-
buza, Bartholomew Dias, Vasco de Gama ;
Voyages to the Canary Islands, Voyages
of Columbus, Nino and Guierra, Ojeda
and Vespusius, Cortereal, Alvarez Cabral,
Francis Almeed, Albuquerque, Andrea
Corsali, Voyage to St Thomas, Voyage
of De Solis, Pinzon, &c. ; Voyage of
John Ponce, Grijalva, Nicuessa, Cortes,
Ojeda and Ocampo, Magellan ; with
other Voyages to the East Indies, the
West Indies, round the World, &c.
Map and plates. 4° 1789

Collecção de Noticias para a Historia e Geografia das Nações Ultramarinas, que vivem nos Dominios
Portuguezes, ou lhes são visinhas. Publicada pela Academia Real das Sciencias.
7 vols. Small 4° *Lisbon*, 1812-41

CONTENTS.

VOLUME 1.
Breve Relação das Escrituras dos Gentios
da India Oriental, e dos seus Costumes.
Noticia summaria do Gentilismo da Asia.
Joseph de Anchieta. Epistola quam-
plurimarum rerum Naturalium, quæ
S. Vincentii (nunc S. Pauli) Pro-
vinciam incolunt, sistens descriptionem.
Memorias para a Historia da Capitania
do Maranhão (Brazil), 1614.

VOLUME 2.
Cadamosta, Luiz de. Navegaçòes a que se
ajuntou a Viagem de Pedro de Cintra.
Navegação de Lisboa á Ilha de S. Thomé,
escrita por hum Piloto Portuguez, e
mandada ao Conde Raymundo de la
Torre.
Cabral, Pedro Alvares. Navegação,
escrita por hum Piloto Portuguez.
Vespucio, Americo. Cartas sobre duas
Viagens, 1501.
Lopes, Thomé. Navegação a's Indias
Orientaes, 1502.
Empoli, João de. Viagem a's Indias
Orientaes, 1503.
Barbosa, Duarte. Livro de. 1516.

Collecção de Noticias—*continued.*
VOLUME 3.
Noticia do Brazil. Descripção Verdadeira da Costa daquelle Estado que pertence á Coroa do Reino de Portugal, sitio da Bahia de Todos os Santos.
Catalogo dos Governadores do Reino de Angola, con huma previa noticia do Principio da sua Conquista, e do que nella obrarão os Governadores dignos de Memoria.

VOLUME 4.
Fonseca, Jose Gonsalves da. Navegação feita da Cidade do Gram Pará, até á Bocca do Rio da Madeira, 1749.

VOLUME 5.
Magalhães, Fernam de. Roteiro da Viagem.
Caminha, P. V. de. Carta a el rei D. Manoel.
Magalhães, Pero de. Tratado do Brazil.
Ribeiro, Capt. João. Fatalidade Historica da Ilha de Ceilão. 1685.

VOLUME 6.
Roteiro da Viagem da Cidade do Pará até a's ultimas Colonias dos Dominios Portuguezes em os Rios Amazonas e Negro.
Appendix ao Diario da Viagem, que em Visita, e Correição das Povoações da Capitania de S. José do Rio Negro, fez o Ouvidor, e Intendente Geral da mesma, Fr. Xavier Ribeiro de Sampaio, 1774-1775.
Rebello, Gabriel. Informação das Cousas de Maluco.

VOLUME 7.
Tratado sobre a Demarcação dos Limites na America Meridional.
Folque, Filippe. Reflexões acerca de algumas irregularidades, inadvertencias, e inexactidões, que se encontrão no Diario dos Trabalhos da Demarcação dos Limites dos Dominios de Portugal e Hespanha na America Meridional.

Recueil de Voyages et de Mémoires publié par la Société de Geographie. 7 vols. *Maps and plates.* 4°
Paris, 1824-44
CONTENTS.
VOLUME 1.
Voyage de Marc Pol.
Peregrinatio Marci Pauli, ex MS. Bibliothecæ Regiæ.
Glossaire des Mots hors d'Usage, avec des Noms Propres et des Noms de Lieux.
VOLUME 2.
Relation de Ghanat, et des Coutumes de ses Habitants. Traduite de l'Arabe par M. A. Jaubert.

Recueil de Voyages, Vol. 2—*contd.*
Cervelli, M. Aug. Relations inédites de la Cyrénaïque. Extrait du Journal d'une Expédition faite en 1811-12, de Tripoli à Derne; rédigé par M. Delaporte.
Monte Cassiano, le R. P. Pacifique de. Relation succincte de la Pentapole Libyque. Traduite par M. Delaporte.
Caraboeuf, M. Notice sur une mesure géométrique de la hauteur, au-dessus de la mer, de quelques sommités des Alpes.
Résultat des questions adressées au nommé Mbouia, Marabou maure, de Tischit, et à un nègre de Walet. Par M. le Baron Roger.
Réponses aux questions proposées par la Société de Géographie sur l'Afrique Septentrionale. Par M. Delaporte.
Itinéraire de Constantinople à la Mecque. Extrait de l'ouvrage Turc intitulé Kitab Menassik el-Hadj; traduit par M. Bianchi.
Warden, M. Description des Ruines découvertes près de Palenquè, suivie de Recherches sur l'Ancienne Population de l'Amérique.
Notice sur la Carte générale des Paschaliks de Hhaleb, Orfa, et Baghdad, et sur le plan de Hhaleb par M. Rousseau (article de M. J. G. Barbié du Bocage).
Extrait de la Traduction faite par M. le Baron de Nerciat, d'un Mémoire de M. de Hammer, sur la Perse, pour ce qui concerne la partie géographique.
Warden, M. Recherches sur les Antiquités des États-Unis de l'Amérique Septentrionale.

VOLUME 3.
Bruguière, M. Louis. Orographie de l'Europe.
VOLUME 4.
Jordan (ou Jourdain) Catalani, Père. Description des Merveilles d'une partie de l'Asie; éclaircissements préliminaires, par M. le Baron Coquebert de Montbret; Note sur les Chrétiens de Saint-Thomas.
Relation d'un Voyage à l'île d'Amat ou Taiti et aux îles voisines. Rédigé par Don José de Andia y Varela; Note préliminaire, par M. D'Avezac.
Vocabulaires appartenant à diverses Contrées ou Tribus de l'Afrique, par M. Koenig; Observations Préliminaires, par M. Jomard.
Relations des Voyages de Guillaume de Rubruk, Jean du Plan de Carpin, Bernard, Sæwulf, &c. Note préliminaires par M. d'Avezac.
Voyage en Orient du Frère G. de Rubruk, 1253. Notice par MM. F. Michel et Wright.

Recueil de Voyages, Vol. 4—*contd.*

Carpin, Frère Jean du Plan de. Relation des Mongols ou Tartares, pendant 1245-47 ; précédée d'une Notice sur les Anciens Voyages de Tartarie en générale, et sur celui de Jean de Carpin en particulier, par M. d'Avezac.

Voyage de Bernard et de ses Compagnons en Égypt et en Terre-Sainte ; avec Notice sur Bernard-le-Sage par M. F. Michel.

Relation des Voyages de Sæwulf, à Jérusalem, et en Terre-Sainte, pendant 1102-3 ; avec Note préliminaire par M. d'Avezac.

VOLUMES 5 AND 6.

Géographie d'Édrisi. Traduite de l'Arabe en Français d'après deux MSS. de la Bibliothèque du Roi, et accompagnée de Notes, par P. Amédée Jaubert.

VOLUME 7.

Paradis, Venture de : Grammaire et Dictionnaire abrégés de la langue Berbère.

Khanikoff, Nicolas de : Mémoire sur la partie Méridionale de l'Asie Centrale.

Poulain de Bossay, P. A. : Recherches sur Tyr et Palætyr.

Collecção de Monumentos ineditos para a Historia das Conquistas dos Portuguezes em Africa, Asia, e America. Ser. I. Historia da Asia. 11 vols. in 15. *Plates and maps.* 4° *Lisbon*, 1858-93

CONTENTS.

Vol. 1.—Lendas da India, por Gaspar Correa. Livro 1. Acçoens de Vasca da Gama, Pedralvares Cabral, João da Nova, Francisco de Alboquerque, Vicente Sodre', Duarte Pacheco, Lopo Soares, Manuel Telles, D. Francisco d'Almeida ; Lenda de 13 annos, desde o primeiro Descobrimento da India, até o anno de 1510.   1858-59

Vol. 2.—The same. Livro 2. Em que se recontão os famosos feitos d'Afonso d'Alboquerque, Lopo Soares, Diogo Lopes de Sequeira, D. Duarte de Menezcs, D. Vasco da Gama Visorey, D. Anrique de Menezes ; Lenda de 17 annos, acabados no anno de 1526.
                                1860-61

Vol. 3.—The same. Livro 3. Que conta dos feitos de Pero Mascarenhas, e Lopo Vaz de Sampayo, e Nuno da Cunha ; em que se passarão 17 annos.
                                1862-63

Vol. 4.—The same. Livro 4. A Quarta Parte da Cronico dos feytos que se passarão na India do ano de 1583 até

Collecção de Monumentos, Vol. 4—*contd.*

o ano de 1550, em que residerão seis Gouernadores (D. Gracia de Noronha, D. Esteuão da Gama, Martim Afonso de Sousa, D. João de Crasto, Gracia de Sá, e Jorge Cabral).   1864-66

Vol. 5.—Subsidios para a Historia de India Portugueza. . . . 1. O livro dos Pesos, Medidas, o Moedas, por Antonio Nunes ; 2. O Tombo do Estado da India, por Simão Botelho ; 3. Lembrancas das cousas da India ec 1525.
                                1868

Vol. 6.—Decada 13 da Historia da India, composta por Antonio Boccaro. Parts 1 and 2   1876

Vols. 7, 8, 9, 11. — Documentos Remettidos da India, ou Livres das Monções publicados de ordem da Classe de Sciencias Moraes, Politicas, Bellas-Lettras da Academia Real das Sciencias de Lisboa, e soh a direcção de Raymundo Antonio de Bulhão Pato. Vols. 1-4   1880-93

Vol. 10.—Cartas de Affonso de Albuquerque seguidas de Documentos que as elucidam publicadas de ordem, &c. Vol. 1   1884

Cartas de Indias. Publicalas por Primera Vez el Ministerio de Fomento. *Facsimiles and maps.* Folio
                                Madrid, 1877

CONTENTS.

Christóbal Colon, Amerrigo Vespucci, Fray Bartolomé de las Casas, y Bernal Dias del Castillo.

Nueva España. Religiosos, Prelados, Clérigos. Vireyes, Gobernadores, Caciques, Justicias y Regimientos, Particulares.

América Central. Prelados de Guatemala y Chiapa.

Peru. Gobernaciones de Cristóbal Vaca de Castro y de Pedro de la Gasca.

Rio de la Plata. Gobernacion de Domingo Martinez de Irala.

Islas Filipinas. El Obispo Fray Domingo Salazar.

Recueil de Voyages et de Documents pour servir à l'Histoire de le Géographie depuis le XIIIᵉ. jusqu'à la fin du XVIᵉ. Siècle publié sous la direction de MM. Ch. Schefer et Henri Cordier : I. [*see* Cabot]; II. [*see* Schefer]; III. [*see* Harrisse]; IV. [*see* Parmentier]; V. [*see* Thenaud]; VI. [*see* Harrisse]; VIII. [*see* Aramon]; IX. [*see* Varthema]; X. [*see* Odoric de Pordenone]; XI. [*see* Possot et Philippe]. Large 8°
                                Paris, 1882-91

APPENDIX II.

GOVERNMENT, ANONYMOUS, AND OTHER
MISCELLANEOUS PUBLICATIONS.

CONTENTS OF APPENDIX II.

APPENDIX II.

AFRICA.

GENERAL.

A. Parliamentary Reports.

Africa. No. 8 (1888). Correspondence respecting the Expedition for the Relief of Emin Pasha, 1886-87. Folio 1888
—— No. 9 (1888). Paper respecting the Reported Capture of Emin Pasha and Mr Stanley. Folio 1888
—— No. 4 (1890). Correspondence respecting Mr Stanley's Expedition for the Relief of Emin Pasha. Folio 1890
—— No. 6 (1890). Correspondence respecting the Anglo-German Agreement relative to Africa and Heligoland. Folio 1890
—— No. 9 (1890). Declarations exchanged between the Government of Her Britannic Majesty and the Government of the French Republic with respect to Territories in Africa. Signed at London, August 5, 1890. Folio 1890
Anglo - Portuguese Convention, Papers relating to the, signed at Lisbon, June 11, 1891. Folio 1891

B. International Conferences, &c.

Association Internationale Africaine. Rapports. 8° *Brussels*
No. 1. Rapports sur les Marches de la Première Expédition 1879
No. 2. Journal et Notes de Voyage de la Première Expédition 1879
Nos. 3 and 4. Extraits des Rapports des Voyageurs de l'Association 1880
—— Comité National Belge. Seance Publique du 1° Mars, 1880. *Maps.* Folio *Brussels*, 1880
—— — et le Comité d' Études, Haut Congo. Travaux et Résultats, 1877-82. 8° *Brussels*, 1882
Berlin. Conférence Africaine de Berlin. Reconnaisssance par la Belgique de l'Association Internationale du Congo. Communication faite à la Chambre des représentants par M. le Ministre des Affaires étrangères. (Séance du 10 mars 1885.) 4° 1885

GENERAL.—B.

Berlin. The same. Communication faite au Sénat par M. le Ministre des Affaires étrangères. (Séance du 24 mars 1885.) 4° 1885
—— (No. 90.) Chambre des Représentants. Séance du 10 mars 1885. Acte Générale de la Conférence de Berlin, date du 26 Février 1885. 4°
—— Africa. No. 3 (1885). Correspondence with Her Majesty's Ambassador at Berlin respecting West African Conference. Folio 1885
—— No. 3 (1885). Further Correspondence respecting the West African Conference. Folio 1885
—— No. 4 (1885). Protocols and General Act of the West African Conference. Folio 1885
—— No. 3 (1886). General Act of the Conference of Berlin. Signed February 26, 1885. Folio 1886
Brussels. Actes de la Conférence de Bruxelles, 1889-90. Folio *Brussels*, 1890
—— La Conférence de Bruxelles et les Pays Bas. Par un Ami de la Verité. 8° *Antwerp*, 1890

C. Slave Trade.

A Concise Statement of the Question regarding the Abolition of the Slave Trade. 8° 1804
Resolutions of the Select Committee of the House of Lords in 1849 to consider the means to adopt for the Final Extinction of the African Slave Trade, 1849 ; with Report, 1850. 8° 1849-50
Extracts from the Evidence taken before Committees in Parliament relative to the Slave Trade. By a Barrister of the Inner Temple. 8° 1851
African Squadron. 8° 1851
Papers relative to Free Labour and the Slave Trade. 8° 1861
Correspondence respecting the Slave Trade and other matters, Jan. to Dec. 1869. [Parly. Rep.] Folio 1870
Slave Trade Report. [Parly. Rep.] Folio 1871

GENERAL—C.

Report from the Select Committee on Slave Trade, with the Proceedings of the Committee. [Parly. Rep.] Folio 1871
Recent Correspondence respecting the Slave Trade. [Parly. Rep.] Folio 1871
Africa. No. 1 (1883). Correspondence with British Representatives and Agents Abroad, and Reports from Naval Officers and the Treasury, relative to the Slave Trade, 1882-83. Folio 1883
—— No. 1 (1884). The same, 1883-84. Folio 1884
—— Mémoire sur l'abolition de l'esclavage et de la traite des Noirs sur le territoire Portugais. Large 8° *Lisbon*, 1889
—— La Traite des Esclaves en Afrique. Renseignements et documents recueillis pour la Conférence de Bruxelles (1840 á 1890). *Map*. Folio *Brussels*, 1890

D. Miscellaneous and Anonymous.

Collection of Pamphlets (in 1 vol.) relating to the Royal African Company. *Map*. Small 4° 1667-1748
New Sailing Directions for the Coast of Africa, extending from Cape Spartel, in lat. 34° 48′ North, to the Cape of Good Hope, in lat. 34° 31′ South; and of the African Islands, situate in the Atlantic and Ethiopic Oceans. From the Journals, Manuscripts, Remarks, and Draughts of Archibald Dalzel, Norris, Woodville, Capt. Glas, Maxwell, Fisher, &c. *Portrait*. 8° 1799
Historical and Philosophical Sketch of the Discoveries and Settlements of the Europeans in Northern and Western Africa at the close of the Eighteenth Century. 8° *Edinburgh*, 1799
Narrative of Discovery and Adventure in Africa, from the Earliest Ages to the Present Time; with Illustrations of the Geology, Mineralogy, and Zoology; by Professor Jameson, James Wilson, and Hugh Murray. *Map and plates*. 16° 1830
Queries relative to the State of the Slave-Trade, Agriculture, Commerce, and Manufactures, Geography, Natural Productions, Political Institutions, General Character, Habits, Disposition, Health, and Religious Instruction. Folio N.D.
African Languages. Dialogues, and a Small Portion of the New Testament, in the English, Arabic, Haussa, and Bornu Languages. Oblong folio 1853
German Society for the Exploration of Equatorial Africa. Album der Deutschen Gesellschaft zur Erforschung Aequatorial-Afrikas, landschaftlicher und anthropologischer Theile . . . herausgegeben von der Kommission Dr Max

GENERAL—D.

Boehr, Dr Robert Hartmann, Dr Henry Lange. *Photographs*. Oblong 4° *Berlin*, 1876
Royal Geographical Society's African Exploration Fund Circular. *Map*. 8° 1877
Africa, Past and Present: a Concise Account of the Country, its History, Geography, Explorations, Climates, Productions, Resources, Population, Tribes, Manners, Customs, Languages, Colonization, and Christian Missions. By an Old Resident. *Map and plate*. Small 8° 1879
African Papers, No. 1. Edited by James Stewart, M.D. *Map*. 8° *Edinburgh*, 1879
Minutes of Conferences held at 1 Savile Row, respecting the Feasibility of a Line of Overland Telegraph through Africa to connect the Lines in South Africa with those of Egypt. 4°. And of "The Conference." Folio [1879]
Possedimenti e Protettorati Europei in Africa, 1889. Raccolta di Notizie Geografiche, Storiche, Politiche e Militari sulle regioni Costiere Africane. *Maps*. 8° *Rome*, 1889
—— The same, 1890. 2nd edition. *Maps*. 8° *Rome*. 1890
The Anglo-Luso Difficulty Explained. By V. de S. 8° 1890
The Anglo-Portuguese Convention. Cuttings from the *Times*, Aug. 22nd. 1890
Die neuesten Reisen und Entdeckungen in Inner-Afrika. *Map and plate*. 8° *Winterthur*, N.D.
English and French Rivalry in Eastern Africa. [An Article or Review, so named.] 8° N.D.

ABYSSINIA.

Further Correspondence respecting the British Captives in Abyssinia. [Parly. Rep.] Folio 1866
See Portal.
Africa. No. 1 (1888). Correspondence respecting Mr Portal's Mission to Abyssinia. Folio 1888
Voyage en Abyssinie exécuté pendant les années 1839, 1840, 1841, 1842, 1843, par une Commission Scientifique . . . Publié par ordre du Roi, &c. 6 vols. in 8, 8°; and 3 vols. in 2, folio *Paris* [1845]
 Pt. 1.—Relation Historique, par M. Théophile Lefebvre. 2 vols. in 4.
 Pt. 2.—Itinéraire. — Description et Dictionnaire géographiques.—Physique et Météorologie. — Statistique, Ethnologie, Linguistique. — Archéologie. Par M. Théophile Lefebvre.

Abyssinia.

Voyage en Abyssinie—*continued.*

Pt. 3.—Histoire Naturelle: Botanique, par M. A. Richard. 2 vols.

Pt. 4.—Histoire Naturelle : Zoologie, par MM. O. Des Muss, Florent Prévost, Guichenot, et Guerin-Menneville.

Album Historique, Ethnologique et Archéologique. Atlas, Histoire naturelle, Zoologie ; Do. Botanique. 3 vols. in 2. Folio.

Abyssinian War. Newspaper Cuttings.

———

ALGERIA AND TUNIS.

A. Government Publications.

Aperçu Historique, Statistique et Topographique, sur l'état d'Alger, à l'usage de l'Armée Expéditionnaire d'Afrique. [*No plates.*] 8° *Paris*, 1830

Tableau de la Situation des Etablissements Française dans l'Algérie, 1837-49, 1852-54. 11 vols. 4° *Paris*, 1839-55

Exploration Scientifique de l'Algérie pendant les années 1840, 1841, 1842, publiée par ordre du Gouvernement, et avec le concours d'une Commission Académique. *Paris*

Sciences Historiques et Géographiques. 8° :—

Vol. 1.— Carette, E. Étude des Routes suivies par les Arabes dans la partie Méridionale de l'Algérie et de la Régence de Tunis. *Map* 1844

Vol. 2.—Carette, E. Recherches sur la Géographie et le Commerce de l'Algérie Méridionale, suivies d'une Notice Géographique sur une partie de l'Afrique Septentrionale, par E. Renou. *Maps* 1844

Vol. 3.—Carette, E. Recherches sur l'origine et les Migrations des Principales Tribus de l'Afrique septentrional et particulièrement de l'Algérie. 8° 1853

Vols. 4 and 5.—Carette, E. Études sur la Kabilie proprement dite. 8° 1849 and 1848

Vol. 6. — Pellissier, E. Mémoires Historiques et Géographiques sur l'Algérie. 1844

Vol. 7. — Pellissier and Rémusat. Historie de l'Afrique de Moh'ammed-Ben-Abi-El-Raini-El-K'airouâni. Traduite de l'Arabe. 1845

Vol. 8.— Renou, Emilien. Description Géographique de l'Empire de Maroc, suivie d'Itinéraires et Renseignements sur le Pays de Sous et autres parties Méridionales du Maroc recucillis, par M. Adrien Berbrugger. *Map* 1846

Vol. 9.—Berbrugger, A. Voyages dans le Sud de l'Algérie et des Etats Barbaresques de l'ouest et de la est, par

Algeria and Tunis—A.

Exploration de l'Algérie—*continued.*

El-'Aïachi et Moula Ah'med; traduits sur deux manuscrits Arabes de la Bibliothèque d'Alger, suivis d'Itinéraires et Renseignements fournis par Sid-Ahmed-Oulid - Bon - Mezrag et du Voyage par terre, de T'aza a Tunis, par M. Fabre. 1846

Vols. 10-15.—Perron, E. Précis de Jurisprudence Musulmane, ou Principes de Législation Musulmane Civile et Réligieuse selon le rite Mâlékite, par Khalîl-Ibn-Ish'âk. Traduit de l'Arabe. 1848, 1849, 1851, 1852

Vol. 16.—Pellissier, E. Description de la Régence de Tunis. 8° 1853

Physique Générale. Folio :—

Vol. 1.—Aimé, G. Recherches de physique sur la Méditerranée. *Plates* 1844

Vol. 2.—Aimé, G. Observations sur la Magnétisme terrestre. *Plates* 1846

Sciences Médicales. Vols. 1 and 2 in 1 vol.

Suivi d'un Mémoire sur la Peste en Algérie. Par A. Berbrugger. 1847

Annuaire de l'Algérie et des Colonies, 1859. 8° *Paris*, 1859

Observatoire d'Alger. 1re Partie. Panorama Meteorologique du Climat d'Alger. Observations Meteorologiques, Janvier 1872. *Tables.* Folio N.D.

Gouvernement Général Civil de l'Algérie. Statistique Générale de l'Algérie, années 1867 à 1872, 1873 à 1875. Large 4° *Paris*, 1874-77

Gouvernement de M. le Maréchal Duc D'Isly en Algérie. 8°

B. Miscellaneous and Anonymous.

Itinéraire du Royaume d'Alger. Par J. M., H. B. 8° *Toulon*, 1830

De la Fausse Direction donnée aux Affaires d'Alger par le Système d'Expéditions. 8° *Paris*, 1836

Excursions dans l'Afrique Septentrionale, par la Société pour l'Exploration de Carthage, accompagnées d'inscriptions. *Plates.* 8° *Paris*, 1838

Notes sur le Théâtre des Opérations Militaires dans le Centre de l'Algérie. 8° *Paris*, 1840

La France en Afrique. 8° *Paris*, 1846

De la Colonisation de l'Algérie. 8° *Paris*, 1847

L'Algérie et l'Opinion. 8° *Paris*, 1847

Barbary, Leaves from a Lady's Diary of her Travels in. 2 vols. 8° 1850

Le Pays du Mouton. Des conditions d'existence des troupeaux sur les Hauts-Plateaux et dans le Sud de l'Algérie. *Maps and illustrations.* 4° *Algiers*, 1893

ALGERIA AND TUNIS—B.

Bizerta und seine Zukunft. *Map and illustrations*. 16° *Prague*, 1881

Constantine. Expédition de, par un Officier de l'Armée d'Afrique. *Plates.* 8° *Brussels*, 1838

Kabyles. Recherches sur l'Origine des Kabyles. 8° *Geneva*, 1871

Oran. Association Française pour l'Avancement des Sciences. Congrès d'Oran, 1888 ; Oran et Algérie en 1887. Notices Historiques, Scientifiques, et Economiques. 2 vols. *Maps, plans, and illustrations.* 12° *Oran*, 1888

Tunis. Exposition Internationale et Coloniale d'Amsterdam, 1883. Section Tunisienne. 8° *Tunis*, 1883

Syrtes. Yacht-Reise in den Syrten, 1873. *Plates.* 4° *Prague*, 1874

BRITISH CENTRAL AFRICA.

[*See also* British South Africa ; Portuguese East Africa.]

Slave-Raiding. Africa, No. 5 (1892). Papers relative to the Suppression of Slave-Raiding in Nyassaland. Folio 1892

Livingstonia : Central Africa. *Map.* 8° *Edinburgh* [1875]

—— The Mission of the Free Church of Scotland to Lake Nyassa. 2nd edition. *Map.* 8° *Edinburgh*, 1876

—— The Free Church "Livingstonia" Mission, Lake Nyassa. Newspaper Cuttings. 8° N.D.

—— The Livingstonia Mission of the Free Church of Scotland in Nyassa-land. Third Quinquennial Narrative. *Map.* 8° *Edinburgh*, 1891

Newspaper Cuttings on the Nyassa region of East Africa. 4° [1888]

Fighting on Lake Nyassa. Cuttings from the *Manchester Guardian*. N.D.

Anglo-Portuguese Boundary. *See* Africa, General.

BRITISH EAST AFRICA.

Africa. No. 2 (1892). Papers respecting Proposed Railway from Mombasa to Lake Victoria Nyanza. Folio 1892

—— No. 4 (1892). Papers relating to the Mombasa Railway Survey and Uganda 1892

—— *See* United Kingdom : War Office Publ.

Commercial Prospects in East Africa. Cuttings from *Manchester Guardian*.

Church Missionary Society. Letters from the Members. Newspaper Cuttings. Folio 1876

—— The Story of the Uganda Mission and the Church Missionary Society's Work in Eastern Equatorial Africa. *Map and illustrations.* 4° N.D.

BRITISH EAST AFRICA.

Church Missionary Society. A Brief Account of the Church Missionary Society's Mission to Central Africa; with Extracts from the Missionaries' Letters, and *New Map.* 12° N.D.

Uganda. "Philo - Africanus." (From *Imp. and Asiat. Quart. Rev.*) 8° 1893

Correspondence respecting Sir Bartle Frere's Mission to the East Coast of Africa, 1872-73. [Parly. Rep.] Folio 1873

Zanzibar. No. 1 (1876). Treaty between Her Majesty and the Sultan of Zanzibar, Supplementary to the Treaty for the Suppression of the Slave Trade of June 5, 1873. Folio 1876

—— No. 1 (1886). Correspondence relating to Zanzibar. Folio 1886

—— No. 1 (1888) Further Correspondence relating to Zanzibar. Folio 1888

—— Ditto, respecting Germany and Zanzibar. Folio 1888

Report on the Spice and other Cultivation of Zanzibar and Pemba Islands. (Foreign Office Misc. Series, No. 266.) 8° 1892

Swahili Version of the Book of Common Prayer. 12° 1893

BRITISH SOUTH AFRICA.

A. General.

· **Report** of Inquiry relating to the Condition of the Hottentots, Bushmen, Caffres, and other Native Tribes of South Africa, and of the Missionary Institutions. [Parly. Rep.] Folio 1830

Further Correspondence relative to the Affairs of South Africa. [In continuation of c.—1401 of February 1876.] Folio 1876

Further Correspondence respecting the Proposed Bill for Enabling the South African Colonies and States to unite under one Government. Folio 1877

Further Correspondence respecting the War between the Transvaal Republic and Neighbouring Native Tribes, and generally with reference to Native Affairs in South Africa. Folio 1877

South African Blue-Book, Feb. 1880. Papers connected with John Dunn and Missionaries. Also Settlement of Basuto Land. Folio [1879]

Further Correspondence respecting the Affairs of South Africa. *Map.* Folio 1879

Extracts from Further Papers respecting the Affairs of South Africa. [Parly. Rep.] *Maps.* Folio 1879

Further Correspondence and Extracts respecting the Affairs of South Africa. [Parly. Rep.] *Maps.* Folio 1880

BRITISH SOUTH AFRICA—A.

Further Correspondence respecting the Affairs of South Africa. September 1880. *Maps.* Folio 1880

Further Correspondence respecting the Affairs of South Africa. *Map and sketches.* Folio 1881

Correspondence relating to the High Commissionership in South Africa. and its Separation from the Governorship of the Cape. *Map.* Folio 1888

South African Quarterly Journal. [Incomplete.] 8° *Cape Town* [1830]
CONTENTS.
Smith, A. A Description of the Birds inhabiting the South of Africa.
—— Observations relative to the Origin and History of the Bushmen.
Buchenroder, W. L. von. An Account of the Earthquakes which occurred at the Cape of Good Hope during the month of December 1809; with a Meteorological Table from the 4th to the 27th; and an Appendix containing Notices of Shocks which have occurred at various other periods.
Webster, W. D. A Description of Two Supposed Undescribed Species of Fishes from Table Bay.
Bowie, J. Sketches of the Botany of South Africa.
Van der Stell, S. Diary of a Journey made to the Country of the Amaquas in the year 1685. Translated from the Dutch by W. L. von Buchenroder.

Gold. Newspaper Cuttings relating to Karl Mauch's Discovery of Gold in South Africa [1867-68]
—— Newspaper Cuttings relating to the South African Gold Fields. *Map* 1868

South Africa and its Resources, being Parts V. and VI. of the Appendix to the "Key to Fortune in New Lands." *Map.* 8° 1870

Report of Dr Bleek concerning his Researches into the Bushman Language. Folio 1873

The Cape and South Africa. Small 8° 1879

The Cave Cannibals of South Africa. By W. H. I. B. 8° N.D.

Prospectus of an Expedition into the Interior of South Africa from Delagoa Bay. *Map* N.D.

B. Bechuanaland.

Reports, by Colonel Warren, R.E., C.M.G., and Captain Harell (late 89th Regiment), on the Affairs of Bechuanaland, dated 3rd April 1879 and 27th April 1880. *Map.* Folio 1883

Further Correspondence respecting the Affairs of Bechuanaland and Adjacent Territories. Feb., June, and Sept. 1887; Apr. and Aug. 1888; and 1890. Folio 1887-90

[*See also* United Kingdom: War Office.]

2 R

C. Mashonaland, &c.

South Africa Company, The. General Information of the Country, and Press Notices. 4° 1889

Africa. No. 2 (1890). Correspondence respecting the Action of Portugal in Mashonaland, and in the Districts of the Shiré and Lake Nyassa. Folio 1890

Special Number of "South Africa," containing Accounts of Matabeleland and Mashonaland. *Illustrations.* 4° 1891

Review of "The Ruined Cities of Mashonaland." (From the *Edinburgh Review*.) 8° 1893

Anglo-Portuguese Boundary. *See* Africa: General.

D. Various.

Basutoland. Despatch from Sir H. Robinson, with Report of the Re-ident Commissioner, Basutoland, &c. Folio 1887
—— *See* United Kingdom: War Office.

Pondoland. Correspondence respecting the Affairs of Pondoland. Folio 1885
—— Further Correspondence respecting the Affairs of Pondoland. *Map.* Folio 1888
—— *See* United Kingdom: War Office.

Swaziland. Correspondence respecting. Folio 1887

Zululand. Further Correspondence respecting the Affairs of Zululand and adjacent Territories, from 1887 to 1890. *Maps.* Folio.
—— The Zulus. By an Ex-Colonial Chaplain. 12° N.D.

———

CAMEROONS.

Africa. No. 1 (1885). Correspondence respecting Affairs in the Cameroons. *Map.* Folio 1885

Newspaper Cuttings. The Cameroon Country:—1 and 2: The German Annexation. 3 and 4: The Land of the Duallas. 5: The New Colony. 6: The Duallas. 7: Sketches of Dualla Life. 8: Dualla Customs; Germany and the Cameroons. 8° V.D.

Dualla. Ikwala ya Bwam. F. Tatilabe na Mattiyu. Bwambu Bwa Dualla. [Proofsheet of a Dualla Translation of St Matthew.] 16° *Bethel, Cameroons,* 1848

———

CAPE COLONY.

Extracts of Correspondence relative to the Condition and Treatment of Slaves and Hottentots at the Cape of Good Hope, 1819-24; Account of Grants of Land made to Hottentots or Bonshmen, 1817-24; Accounts of all the Commandos

CAPE COLONY.

or Expeditions against the Bonshmen since 1797; Census of the Population since 1797. [Parly. Rep.] Folio 1827

Reports of the Commissioners of Inquiry : —1. Upon the Administration of the Government at the Cape of Good Hope ; 2. Upon the Finances of the Cape of Good Hope. [Parly. Report.] Folio 1827

Report of Inquiry upon the Trade of the Cape of Good Hope, the Navigation of the Coast, and the Improvement of the Harbours of that Colony. [Parly. Rep.] Folio 1829

Zenith Distances observed with the Mural Circle, at the Royal Observatory, Cape of Good Hope, and the Calculation of the Geocentric South Polar Distances, 1836 and 1837. 4° 1837

Correspondence relative to the Establishment of a Representative Assembly at the Cape of Good Hope. [Parly. Rep.] Folio 1850

Despatches relative to the Reception of Convicts at the Cape of Good Hope. Folio 1850

Correspondence with the Governor of the Cape of Good Hope, relative to Assumption of Sovereignty over the Territory between the Vaal and Orange Rivers. [Parly. Rep.] Folio 1851

Correspondence with the Governor of the Cape of Good Hope, relative to the State of the Kafir Tribes and to the Recent Outbreak on the Eastern Frontier of the Colony. Folio 1851

Further Papers relative to the Establishment of a Representative Assembly at the Cape of Good Hope. [Parly. Rep.] Folio 1852

Kaffraria. Correspondence relative to the Annexation of British Kaffraria to the Colony of the Cape of Good Hope. [Parly. Rep.] *Map.* Folio 1865

Correspondence respecting the Affairs of the. [Parly. Rep.] *Map.* Folio 1871

Further Correspondence respecting. [Parly. Rep.] *Map.* Folio 1872

Ministerial Department of Native Affairs. Report of W. Coates Palgrave, Esq., Special Commissioner to the Tribes north of the Orange River, of his Mission to Damaraland and Great Namaqualand in 1876. *Map.* 8° *Cape Town,* 1877

Report on the Division of Oudtshoorn, by John G. Gamble, Hydraulic Engineer to the Colony. *Map and plates.* Folio *Cape Town,* 1877

Report and Proceedings of the Commission appointed by His Excellency the Governor, to Collect, Examine, Classify, and Index the Archives of the Colony of the Cape of Good Hope. Folio *Cape Town,* 1877

CAPE COLONY.

Blue-Books for the Colony of the Cape of Good Hope, for the years 1878, 1879, 1880, 1885, 1888. Folio *Cape Town,* 1879-89

Report on the Blue-Book for 1879, 1880, and 1881. Folio *Cape Town,* 1880-82

Despatches. Correspondence and Papers, &c., relative to Proposed Constitution of the Trigonometrical Survey of the Cape Colony in connection with the Adjacent Territories. *Maps.* Folio *Cape Town,* 1880

Acts of the Cape Parliament, 1880, 1881, and 1887. Folio *Cape Town,* 1880-87

Ministerial Department of Native Affairs. Blue-Book on Native Affairs, 1880-82 and 1884-88. Vol. 1. (Part 1 and 2.) Appendix to the same, 1883. *Maps.* Folio *Cape Town,* 1880-88

Correspondence between the Government of the Colony and Commandant General of Colonial Forces on the subject of the Position of Affairs in Bashutoland and other Native Territories and the Reorganisation of the Colonial Forces. *Maps.* Folio 1883

Cape Colony. Further Correspondence respecting the Claims of British Subjects in the German Protectorate. Folio 1887

Cape of Good Hope Civil Service List for 1887 and 1888. 8° *Cape Town,* 1887-88

Sources of Revenue of the Colony, with Tariffs, &c. 8° *Cape Town,* 1887

Statistical Register of the Colony of the Cape of Good Hope for the years 1890, 1891, and 1892. *Cape Town,* 1891-93

Census. Results of a Census of the Colony of the Cape of Good Hope, as on the night of Sunday, 5th April 1891. Folio *Cape Town,* 1892

Imperial Federation Series of Colonial State-Paper Catalogues. Edited by F. Campbell. No. 1. Cape of Good Hope, 1892 (Preliminary Issue). 8° 1893

Agricultural and Live-Stock Returns for 1893-94. Folio *Cape Town,* 1894 [*See also* United Kingdom, Emigrants' Handbooks ; War Office.]

South African Directory Advertiser for 1831. *Map and plates.* 8° *Cape Town,* 1830

Kaffir War, Summary of the, 1834-35 ; with Notes by the Editor of the *Zuid Afrikaan.* 8° *Cape Town,* 1836

Cape of Good Hope. Universal Exhibition, 1855 : Vade-Mecum. 8° *Cape Town,* 1855

The Hot Springs at the Cape of Good Hope : a Sanatorium for Persons suffering from Consumption, Chronic Rheumatism, Gout, Sciatica, &c. *Illustration.* 12° 1884

CENTRAL AFRICA.

Spedizione. Geografica Italiana nell' Africa Equatoriale. 8°   *Rome,* 1876
West Central. The Mission of the American Board to West Central Africa. Pioneer Work, 1881. *Map.* 12°
Boston, 1882
The Critical Position of Europeans in Central Africa. (From *Blackwood's Magazine.*) 8°   1889

CONGO STATE.

Congo. No. 92. Chambre des Représentants. Séance du 10 Mars 1885. Déclarations du 23 Février 1885, relatives à la Reconnaissance de l'Association Internationale du Congo par la Belgique. Folio   1885
Compagnie du Congo pour le Commerce et l'Industrie (Société Anonyme). The Congo Railway from Matadi to the Stanley Pool. Results of Survey. First Draft ; Conclusions, with 24 schedules. Several Notes. *Maps, plans, and estimates.* 8°   *Brussels,* 1889
—— Exposition de Photographies représentant des Vues et Types du Congo ouverte au Cercle Artistique et Littéraire. Catalogue. *Map.* 8°
Bruxelles, 1890
L'État Indépendant du Congo et la Compagnie de Rotterdam. Replique de " Un Ami de la Verité." 8°
Antwerp, 1890
Congo Question. Meeting tenu à Londres 4 Nov. 1890. 8°   *Brussels,* 1890
[*See also* Africa : General.]

EGYPT.

A. Government Publications.

Ministère de l'Intérieur. Statistique de l'Egypte, Ann. 1873. (1290 de l'Hégire.) 8°   *Cairo,* 1873
—— Direction du Recensement. Récensement Général de l'Égypte. 15 Gamad Akher 1299—3 Mai 1882. Tome Ier. 4°   *Cairo,* 1884
Correspondence relative to the question of the Suez Canal dues, together with the Procès-verbaux of the Meetings held by the International Commission at Constantinople. [Parly. Rep.] Folio 1874
Egyptian General Staff Publications— Rapport fait à S.E. Général Stone Pacha . . . sur les Spécimens Botaniques . . . colligés pendant les Expéditions Égyptiennes au Kordofan et au Darfour en 1875 et 1876 par le D^r. Pfund. Par J. H. Zarb. Small 4°   1875

Egyptian General Staff Publications— Journal of the March of an Expedition in Nubia between Assouan and Abouhamid, executed by Eugène Fechet. 8°
1878
Report on the Seizure by the Abyssinians of the Geological and Mineralogical Reconnaissance Expedition attached to the General Staff of the Egyptian Army. By L. H. Mitchell. 8°
1878
Provinces of the Equator. Summary of Letters and Reports of His Excellency the Governor-General. Part 1. Year 1874. 8°   1877
—— *See also* Prout ; Purdy, E. S.
Egypt. No. 5. 1887. Reports by Sir H. Drummond Wolff, on the Administration of Egypt. Folio   1887
—— No. 1. 1888. Correspondence respecting the Proposed International Convention for Securing the Free Navigation of the Suez Canal. Folio   1888
—— No. 6. 1888. Copy of a Despatch from Sir E. Baring, inclosing a Report on the Condition of the Agricultural Population in Egypt. Folio   1888
—— No. 1. 1889. Further Correspondence respecting Affairs at Suakin. *Plans.* Folio   1889
Convention between Great Britain, Germany, Austria-Hungary, Spain, France, Italy, the Netherlands, Russia, and Turkey, respecting the Free Navigation of the Suez Maritime Canal. Folio 1889
Returns of Shipping and Tonnage, 1886, 1887, and 1888. Folio   1889
Ville d'Alexandrie. Municipalité Rapport sur l'Assainissement de la Ville. Presenté à la Commission Municipale (par L. Dietrich Bey). Parties 1, 2, 3. Roy 8°
Alexandria, 1892-93
[*See also* United Kingdom : War Office.]

B. Miscellaneous and Anonymous.

A Short Relation of the River Nile, of its Source and Current, of its Overflowing the Campagnia of Ægypt till it runs into the Mediterranean, and of other Curiosities. [Translated by Sir P. Wyche.] 12°   1673
—— Ditto. Another edition. 8°   1791
Relation de l'Expédition Scientifique des Français en Egypte en 1798. [Extr. de l'Encyclop. des Gens du Monde.] 8°.
Dongola and Sennaar. Narrative of the Expedition to Dongola and Sennaar, under the Command of his Excellency Ismael Pasha. By an American in the Service of the Viceroy. 8°   1822
Rosetta Stone. Nouvelles Recherches sur l'Inscription en Lettres Sacrées du Monument de Rosette. *Plate.* 8° *Florence,* 1830

EGYPT—B.

The Antiquities of Egypt, with a particular Notice of those that illustrate the Sacred Scriptures. *Plates.* 8° 1841

Notes from a Private Journal of a Visit to Egypt and Palestine by way of Italy and the Mediterranean. [Not published.] 12° 1844

Société d'Études de l'Isthme de Suez. Travaux de la Brigade Française. Rapport de l'Ingénieur. *Map.* 8° *Paris,* 1847

Outline of the Plan for the proposed Navigation through the Isthmus. *Map.* 8° 1850

The Present Crisis in Egypt, in Relation to our Overland Communication with India. No. 1. 8° 1851

Suez Canal. Compagnie Universelle du Canal Maritime de Suez. Firman de Concession et Cahier des Charges Statuts. 8° *Paris,* 1856

—— Assemblée générale des Actionnaires (8e Réunion, 1er Août 1866). Rapport de M. F. de Lesseps. Rapport de la Commission de Vérification des Comptes. Resolutions de l'Assemblée Générale. 8° *Paris,* 1866

Caravan Routes. Die Karawanen-Strasse von Aegypten nach Syrien. *Plates.* Square 8° *Prague,* 1879

Hebrew Migration from Egypt, The. *Maps.* 8° 1879

ERITREA.

Assab et les Limites de la Souveraineté Turco-Egyptienne dans la Mer Rouge. Mémoire du Gouvernement Italien. Mars 1882. *Maps.* 4° *Rome,* 1882

Provvedimenti per la Costituzione e l'Ordinamento di una Colonia Italiana in Assab. Relazione Ministeriale e Disegno di Legge presentati al Parlamento Italiano dal Ministro degli Affari Esteri (Mancini) nella tornata del 12 Giugno 1882. *Maps.* 4° *Rome,* 1882

Possessi e Protettorati in Africa. (Estr. dell' Annuario Statistico, Anno 1890 : Ministero di Agricultura, &c.) 4° *Rome,* 1891

[*See also* Italy.]

FRENCH CONGO.

Loango Expedition. Die Loango-Expedition ausgesandt von der Deutschen Gesellschaft zur Erforschung Aequatorial-Africas, 1873-76. Ein Reisewerk in drei Abtheilungen, von Paul Güssfeldt, Julius Falkenstein, Eduard Pechuël-Loesche. Erste und zweite Abtheilungen ; Dritte Abtheilungun, Erste Hälfte. *Maps and plates.* 4° *Leipzig,* 1879-82

FRENCH CONGO.

Gabon-Congo à l'Exposition, 1889. *Illustrations.* 12° *Paris*

GAMBIA.

Correspondence respecting the Limits of British Jurisdiction in the River Gambia. [Parly. Rep.] Folio 1877

Correspondence relating to the Recent Expedition to the Upper Gambia under Administrator V. S. Gouldsbury. *Maps.* Folio 1881

Report on Blue-Book for 1885. 8° *Bathurst,* 1886

GERMAN EAST AFRICA.

Bekleidungs - Bestimmungen für die Schutztruppe für Deutsch - Ostafrika. Uniform - Bestimmungen für die Civil Beamten in Deutsch-Ostafrika. (Beilage Deutsch-Kolonialblatt.) 12° 1891

Gogo Version of the " Peep of Day." 12° 1893

GERMAN SOUTH-WEST AFRICA.

Angra Pequena. Correspondence respecting the Settlement at Angra Pequena, on the S.W. Coast of Africa. *Map.* Fol. 1884

Further Correspondence respecting the Settlement at Angra Pequena, on the S.W. Coast of Africa. *Map.* Folio 1884

Copy of a Despatch from the Right Hon. the Earl of Derby, K.G., to Her Majesty's High Commissioner in South Africa, relative to the Establishment of a German Protectorate at Angra Pequena and along the neighbouring Coast. Folio 1884

Claims of British Subjects. *See* Cape Colony.

GOLD COAST.

[*See also* West Africa.]

Affairs of the Gold Coast, and threatened Ashanti Invasion. *Maps.* Folio 1881

Further Correspondence regarding Affairs of the Gold Coast. *Maps.* Folio 1882

—— The same. *Maps.* Folio 1883

Further Correspondence respecting the Affairs of the Gold Coast. *Maps.* Folio 1885

—— The same. *Maps.* Folio 1888

—— The same. *Maps.* Folio 1888

Cape Coast Castle. Letters of Advice and Instructions to the Governors, Council, &c., of Cape Coast Castle, by the Committee of the Company of Merchants trading to Africa, from 21st August 1751 to 10th November 1768. MS. Folio.

LAGOS.

[*See also* West Africa.]

Correspondence respecting the War between Native Tribes in the Interior and the Negotiations for Peace conducted by the Government of Lagos, February 1887. *Maps.* Folio 1887
—— The same. *Maps.* Folio 1887
Repatriation of Natives. Folio 1890
Circular - letter, dated 24th September 1890, on the Advisability of Securing for Examination and Report suitable Samples of the Valuable Timbers of Yoruba. Folio 1890
Circular Correspondence on the subject of the Ficus Elastica of Asia. Folio
Lagos, 1890
Yoruba. A Vocabulary of the Yoruba Language. 8° N.D.

MADAGASCAR.

Madagascar. No 1 (1883). Correspondence respecting Madagascar relating to the Mission of Hova Envoys to Europe in 1882-83. Folio 1883
[*See also* United Kingdom: War Office.]

MOROCCO.

Grammatica Linguæ-Mauro-Arabicæ juxta vernaculi idiomates usum. Small 4° 1800
Observations on the Western Coast of the Morocco State during my Journey from Mogador to Tangier, in July and August 1830. Memorandum respecting the Foundation of Mogador, its Trade, Description of the Bay, &c. ; with a Description of Santa Cruz, Ceuta, Tetuan, and other Ports of the State of Morocco ; with an Account of the Death of Major Laing, &c. Folio MS.
Mogador. Our Ports. v. Mogador. (From the *Times of Morocco*, 11th Aug. 1888.) 8°.

NATAL.

Emigration to Natal, and Conditions of Government Land Grants. 8° 1868
Emigration to Natal, and Conditions of Government Land Grants ; with Full Description of the Colony and its Industries. *Map.* 8°
Pietermaritzburg, 1870
Correspondence relative to Military Affairs in Natal and the Transvaal. [Parly. Rep.] *Maps.* Folio 1879
Department of Mines. Report upon the Coal-Fields of Klip River, Weenan, Umuoti, and Victoria Counties ; together with Tabulated Statement of Results obtained from a Series of Trials of

NATAL.

Department of Mines—*continued.*
Colonial Coal upon the Natal Government Railways, by Frederic W. North. *Maps, sections, &c.* Folio 1881
Correspondence relating to the Proposal to establish Responsible Government in Natal 1891
[*See also* United Kingdom, H, Emigrants' Handbooks.]

Natal Land and Colonization Company, Limited : Correspondence in reference to the Prospects of New Settlers in Natal ; the Amount of Capital required ; with Hints as to the Mode of Procedure in selecting Land, &c. 8° 1869
Colony of Natal. [A collection of letters.] 8° 1869
The Natal Almanac, Directory, and Yearly Register. 12° 1871

NIGER DISTRICT.

Papers relative to the Expedition to the River Niger. [Parly. Rep.] *Map.* Folio 1843
Journals and Notices of the Native Missionaries on the River Niger, 1862. 12° 1863
Copy of Correspondence on the Subject of an Application from the Company of African Merchants (Limited) for a Subsidy towards establishing Steamers on the River Niger. Folio 1864

NYASALAND. *See* British Central Africa.

PORTUGUESE EAST AFRICA.

Portugal. No. 1 (1875). Delagoa Bay. Correspondence respecting the Claims of Her Majesty's Government. *Maps.* Folio 1875
—— No. 1 (1890). Correspondence respecting the Action of Portugal in regard to the Delagoa Bay Railway. Folio 1890
Delagoa Bay. Remarks on Delagoa Bay, a large Harbour situated on the South-East Coast of Africa, and on the Country and Nations adjoining it. 8° N.D.
Umzila's Kingdom. Explorations for the Mission to Umzila's Kingdom, South-Eastern Africa. *Map.* 8°
Boston, Mass., 1882
Matope to Newala. A Journey from Matope on the Upper Shire to Newala on the Rovuma, by the Right Rev. the Bishop, in 1885. Corrected edition. 12°
Zanzibar, 1858

PORTUGUESE EAST AFRICA.

A Journey to Lake Nyassa, and Visit to the Magwangwara and the Source of the Rovuma, in the year 1886, by the Bishop of the Universities' Mission to Central Africa. 8° *Zanzibar* [1887]
Africa Oriental. Caminho de Ferro da Beira a Manica. Excursões e estudos effectuados em 1891. *Maps and plates.* 4° *Lisbon*, 1892

PORTUGUESE WEST AFRICA.

Renseignements sur la partie de la Côte entre le Cap Négro et le Cap Lopez. *Chart.* 8° *Paris*, 1850
Angola. Observatorio do Infante D. Luiz. Provincia de Angolo. Resumo das Observações Met orologicas feitas no anno de 1880. Resulta io das observações do Magnetismo Terre-tre feitas nos annos de 1877 a 1881. *Plate.* Folio *Lisbon*, 1881
St Thomas. *See* African Islands.
Loanda. Observatorio Meteorologico de Loanda. Volume Primeiro. Observações Meteorologicas e Magneticas, 1879-81. Folio *Lisbon*, 1882
Benguella. Summary of an Article, written in the *Gazeta de Portugal*, 4th March 1888, prompted in view of the probability of a Submarine Cable being laid to the Southward of Loanda. MS. Folio.

SENEGAL.

Annuaire du Sénégal et Dépendances pour l'année 1865. Suivi d'une notice sur les Serières par Pinet-Laprade, et d'une étude sur leur langue par Faidherbe. 12° *Saint-Louis*, 1865
Ministère de la Marine et des Colonies. Sénégal et Niger. La France dans l'Afrique Occidentale 1879-83. Text and Atlas. 8° *Paris*, 1884
Annales Sénégalaises de 1854 à 1885, suivies des Traités passés avec les Indigènes. 12° *Paris*, 1885

SIERRA LEONE.

Report from the Select Committee on the Settlements of Sierra Leone and Fernando Po. [Parly. Rep.] *Maps.* Folio 1830
Papers relating to the Colony of Sierra Leone. [Parly. Rep.] Folio 1830
Addresses, Petitions, &c., from the Chiefs of Sudan and the Inhabitants of Sierra Leone to His Majesty William IV. and Lieut.-Governor H. D. Campbell. 8° *Privately printed*, 1838

SIERRA LEONE.

Papers relating to Her Majesty's Possessions in West Africa, Sierra Leone, and Gold Coast Colony, including Lagos. Folio 1876
—— The same. (In continuation of c.— 1343 of 1875). *Maps.* Folio 1876
Correspondence respecting the Proceedings at the Jong River in May 1882. *Map.* Folio 1882
Further Correspondence respecting the Disturbances in the neighbourhood of British Sherbro in April and May 1883. Folio 1884
Despatch from the Administrator-in-Chief enclosing Information regarding the different Districts and Tribes of Sierra Leone and its Vicinity. *Map.* Folio 1887
Correspondence respecting the Recent Expedition against the Yonnie Tribe adjacent to Sierra Leone. *Maps.* Folio 1888
Gazetteer of Places in and adjacent to the Colony of Sierra Leone. 12° 1889

SOMALI-LAND.

European Captives among the Somali Tribes of Eastern Africa. *Map.* 8° 1869

SOUTH AFRICA. *See* Brit. S. Africa.

SOUTH AFRICAN REPUBLIC (TRANSVAAL).

Transvaal-boundary. [Parliamentary Papers]. *Maps.* Folio 1876
Transvaal Royal Commission. Report of the Commissioners appointed to Inquire into the Report upon all Matters relating to the Settlement of the Transvaal Territory. Part I. *Maps.* Folio 1882
A Convention between Her Majesty the Queen of the United Kingdom of Great Britain and Ireland and the South African Republic. Folio 1884
Correspondence respecting the Convention concluded with the South African Republic on the 27th February 1884. *Map.* Folio 1884
Further Correspondence respecting the Affairs of the Transvaal and adjacent Territories. *Maps.* Folio 1884
Further Correspondence respecting the Affairs of the Transvaal and adjacent Territories. *Map.* Folio 1885

WEST AFRICA.

[See also Senegal; Gambia; Gold Coast; Sierra Leone; Lagos; Niger.]

Papers respecting the Danish Possessions on the West Coast of Africa. [Parl. Rep.] *Map.* Folio 1850

Papers relating to H.M. Possessions in West Africa, Sierra Leone, and Gold Coast Colony, including Lagos. Folio 1876

—— Continuation of the same 1876

Africa. No. 2 (1883). Correspondence respecting the Territory on the West Coast of Africa lying between 5° 12' and 8° of South Latitude, 1845-77. Folio 1882

Gulf of Guinea. Supplementary Arrangement between England and Germany relative to their respective spheres of action in the Gulf of Guinea. Folio 1886

No. 2 (1888). Papers relative to King Ja Ja of Opobo, and to the Opening of West African Markets to British Trade. Folio 1888

Mandingo Language. Vocabulary of the Mandingo Language. MS. Folio 1837

Outline of a Vocabulary of a few of the Principal Languages of Western and Central Africa, compiled for the Use of the Niger Expedition. Oblong 12° 1841

Narrative in the Vai Character of Western Africa. A Negro's Life. 12° 1851

ZANZIBAR. *See* British East Africa.

AFRICAN ISLANDS.

Cape Verde Islands. Posto Meteorologico da Cidade da Praia da Ilha de S. Thiago de Cabo Verde. Resumos das Observações feitas nos annos de 1875 a 1879. Folio *Lisbon*, 1881

Mauritius. Report of the Commissioners appointed to take a Census of the Island of Mauritius and its Dependencies, April 1861. Folio *Port Louis*, 1862

Journal of Five Months' Residence in the Mauritius. 8° *Calcutta*, 1838

Procès-verbaux de la Société d'histoire naturelle de l'île Maurice, du 6 Octobre 1842 au 28 Août 1845. Large 8° *Mauritius*, 1846

A Transport Voyage to the Mauritius and back, touching at the Cape of Good Hope and St Helena. 8° 1851

Geography of Mauritius; with an Abstract of its History. 12° *Mauritius*, 1874

Mauritius as it was before the Cyclone. From *Blackwood's Magazine.* 8° 1892

St Thomas. Observatorio do Infante D. Luiz. Ilha de S. Thomé. Resumo das Principaes Observações Meteorologicas executadas durante o Periodo de 9 Annos de corridos desde 1872 a 1880. Elementos magneticos observados em 1881. Folio *Lisbon*, 1881

AMERICA, NORTH.

GENERAL.

An Account of the European Settlements in America. 2 vols. *Map.* 8° 1757
Anecdotes Américaines, ou Histoire abrégée des principaux événements arrivés dans le Nouveau Monde, depuis sa découverte. 12° *Paris*, 1776
Descriptive Catalogue of Indian Gallery; containing Portraits, Landscapes, Costumes, &c., and Representations of the Manners and Customs of the North American Indians. Small 4° 1840
Pacific Railway. Imperial Atlantic and Pacific Railroad. 8° [1851]
Discovery of America. (Estratto dal Bollettino della Societa Geografica Italiana, July 1886.) 8° 1886
Quatrième Centenaire de la Découverte de l'Amérique. Catalogue des Documents Géographiques exposés à la Section des Cartes et Plans de le Bibliothèque Nationale *Paris*, 1892
Time Standards. Standard Time for the United States of America, Canada, and Mexico. *Diagrams.* 8°
[*See also* General Catalogues.]

BRITISH NORTH AMERICA— CANADA.

A. Geological and Natural History Survey.

Reports of Progress, for 1853-58. *Maps.* 8° *Toronto*, 1857-59
Plans of various Lakes and Rivers between Lake Huron and the River Ottawa, to accompany the Geological Reports for 1853-54-55-56. 4° *Toronto*, 1857
—— The same, from Commencement of the Survey to 1863. Atlas of Maps and Sections, with an Introduction and Appendix. 8° *Montreal*, 1865
—— The same, from 1863 to 1866. 8° *Ottawa*, 1866
—— The same, from 1866 to 1869. 8° *Montreal*, 1870
—— The same, for 1870-71. 8° *Ottawa*, 1872
—— The same, for 1871-72, 1872-73, 1873-74, 1875-76, 1876-77, 1878-79, 1879-80, 1880-81-82, 1882-83-84. *Plates and maps (some separate).* 8° *Montreal*, 1872-85

BRITISH NORTH AMERICA—CANADA, A.
Annual Report. New Series. Vol. 1, 1885. *Maps and plates.* 8°.
—— Vol. 2, 1886. *Maps, plates, and sections.* 8°.
—— Vol. 3, 1887-88. In 2 parts. *Illustrations and maps (separate).*
—— Vol. 4, 1888-89. *Maps.*
—— Vol. 5 (2 parts, and maps separate), 1890-91 *Ottawa*, 1893
Report on the Fossil Plants of the Lower Carboniferous and Millstone Grit Formations of Canada. By J. W. Dawson. 8° *Montreal*. 1873
Palæozoic Fossils. Vol. 2. Part 1. By E. Billings. 8° *Montreal*, 1874
Mesozoic Fossils. Vol. 1. Parts 1 and 2. By J. F. Whiteaves. *Plates.* 8° *Montreal*, 1876-79
Catalogue of Canadian Plants. Parts 1, 2, 4, 5. By John Macoun. 8° *Montreal*, 1883-90
Part 1.—Polypetalæ.
Part 2.—Gamopetalæ.
Part 4.—Endogens.
Part 5.—Acrogens
—— Part 6.—Musci. By J. Macoun and Prof. N. C. Kindberg 1892
Comparative Vocabularies of the Indian Tribes of British Columbia, with a Map illustrating Distribution. By W. Fraser Tolmie and G. M. Dawson. *Map.* 8° *Montreal*, 1884
Contributions to Canadian Palæontology. By J. F. Whiteaves. Vol. 1, Parts 1 and 2. *Plates.* 8° *Montreal*, 1885-89
Summary Report of the Operations of the Geological and Natural History Survey to 31st December 1885, being Part 3—Annual Report of the Department of the Interior, 1885. 8° *Ottawa*, 1886
—— The same, to 31st December 1887, being Part 3—Annual Report of the Department of the Interior, 1887. 8° *Ottawa*, 1888
—— The same, to 31st December 1890. 8° *Ottawa*, 1891
List of Canadian Hepaticæ. By W. H. Pearson. *Plates.* 8° *Montreal*, 1890
Report on N.W. Manitoba, with parts of Assiniboia and Saskatchewan. By J. R. Tyrrell. *Maps and plates* Large 8° *Ottawa*, 1892

BRITISH NORTH AMERICA—CANADA, A.

Catalogue of a Stratigraphical Collection of Canadian Rocks, prepared for the World's Columbian Exposition, Chicago, 1893. By W. F. Ferrier. Large 8°
Ottawa, 1893

Catalogue of Section 1 of the Museum of the Geological Survey, embracing the Systematic Collection of Minerals and the Collections of Economic Minerals, and Rocks and Specimens illustrative of Structural Geology. By G. C. Hoffmann. *Plan.* Large 8° *Ottawa*, 1893

List of Publications of the Geological and Natural History Survey of Canada. 8° *Ottawa*, 1884

B. Various Government Publications.

Water Communications in Canada. Estimates of the Expense of the Construction of Water Communications in the Canadas. [Parly. Rep.] Folio 1827

Estimates of the Expense of the Construction of Water Communications in the Canadas, between Montreal and the Ottawa, from the Ottawa to Kingston, and from Lake Erie to Lake Ontario. [Parly. Rep.] *Map.* Folio 1828

Copies of Two Despatches upon the subject of the Welland Canal. [Parly. Rep.] Folio 1828

Report of the Court of Directors of the Canada Company to the Proprietors. *Map.* 8° 1831

Reports of the Committee of Roads and Public Improvements. Folio
Quebec, 1831

To take into consideration the Accounts and Papers relating to the Rideau Canal. [Parly. Rep.] Folio 1831

Report from the Select Committee appointed to take into consideration the Accounts and Papers relating to the Canal Communications in Canada, 1832. [Parly. Rep.] *Map.* Folio 1832

Extracts of Correspondence between the Board of Ordnance and Officers under their Orders in Canada, respecting the Progress of the Canal Communications. [Parly. Rep.] Folio 1832

Copy of Letter from the Secretary of the Ordnance respecting the Expenditure upon the Works of the Rideau Canal in Canada ; with a Copy of the Treasury Minute thereon. [Parly. Rep.] Folio 1832

An Estimate of the Expense of Rideau Canal for 1833. [Parly. Rep.] Folio 1832

Copy of the Report of Mr Richards to the Colonial Secretary, respecting the Waste Lands in the Canadas, and Emigration. [Parly. Rep.] Folio 1832

BRITISH NORTH AMERICA—CANADA, B.

Appendix to Report of the Commissioner of Crown Lands. Part 2. *Maps of Canada.* 4° *Toronto*, 1857

Remarks on Upper Canada Surveys. Huron and Ottawa Territory. (Appendix No. 36 to the Report of the Commissioner of Crown Lands for 1860.) 8° *Quebec*, 1861

General Report of the Commissioner of Public Works, for the year ending 30th June 1867. *Maps.* 8°
Ottawa, 1868

Second Report of the Standing Committee on Immigration and Colonisation. *Map.* 8° *Ottawa*, 1869

Reports of Surveyor-General of Dominion Lands. 8° *Ottawa*, 1874-80

Paris Universal Exhibition, 1878. Handbook and Official Catalogue of the Canadian Section. Published under the direction of T. C. Keefer. *Maps in cover.* 8° 1878

Report of the Select Standing Committee on Immigration and Colonisation. *Map.* 8° *Ottawa*, 1878

Telegraphy with the Coasts and Islands of the Gulf and Lower River St Lawrence, and the Coasts of the Maritime Provinces. *Maps.* 8° *Quebec*, 1879

Transit of Venus. Report of the Canadian Observations of the Transit of Venus, 6th December 1882. *Plan.* 8°.

Annual Report of the Department of the Interior for the year ended 30th June 1881. 8° *Ottawa*, 1882
— The same, for the years 1882-91-92. 8° *Ottawa*, 1883-93

Census of Canada, 1880-81. Recensement du Canada. 4 vols. 8°
Ottawa, 1882-85

Mineral Resources of Canada. 8°
Ottawa, 1882

Eastern Townships. Information for intending Settlers. *Map.* 8°
Ottawa, 1883

Dominion Land Surveys. Manual showing the System of Survey of the Dominion Lands, with Instructions to Surveyors. 8° *Ottawa*, 1883

A Guide Book containing information for intending Settlers. 5th, 6th, and 7th editions. *Maps and illustrations.* 8°
Ottawa, 1884-86

Reports on the Forests of Canada. With Précis by Dr Lyons, M.P., of certain Papers submitted therewith. *Map.* Folio 1885

Canada, its History, Products, and Natural Resources. 2 *maps.* 8°
Ottawa, 1886

Geodetic Levelling. *Diagrams.* Large 8° *Ottawa*, 1886

BRITISH NORTH AMERICA—CANADA, B.

A Memorial Volume. A Statistical and Descriptive Handbook of the Dominion. Prepared under the authority of the Government of the Dominion and the various Provincial Administrations. Edited and published by E. B. Biggar, Montreal. *Maps and illustrations.* 8°
1889

Time Standard. Documents relating to the Fixing of a Standard of Time, and the Legalisation thereof. *Map.* Large 8°
Ottawa, 1891
[*See also* United Kingdom, H, Emigrants' Handbooks.]

Canada and United States.

North American Boundary. Part 2. Correspondence relating to the Boundary between the British Possessions in North America and the United States of America under the Treaty of 1783, (with) Report of the British Commissioners appointed to Survey the Territory in dispute between Great Britain and the United States of America, on the North-Eastern Boundary of the United States, with an Appendix. [Parly. Rep.] *Maps.* Folio
1840

North-West American Water Boundary. Parliamentary Reports A–G, with reference to the Case submitted to the arbitration of H.M. the Emperor of Germany. *Maps.* Folio
1873

Correspondence respecting the determination of the North-Western Boundary between Canada and the United States. [Parly. Rep.] Folio
1875

Bering Sea. Correspondence relative to the Seizure of British American Vessels, in Behring Sea, by the United States Authorities. *Map.* 8° *Ottawa*, 1887

—— Behring Sea Arbitration. Case presented on the part of the Government of H.B.M. (U.S. No. 1, 1893.) Folio.

—— Report of the Behring Sea Commission, and of the British Commissioners, June 1892. *Maps and diagrams.* (U.S. No. 2, 1893.) Folio.

Further Correspondence respecting North American Fisheries, 1887-88; with Despatch enclosing Treaty signed at Washington, Feb. 15, 1888. Folio.
[*See also* United States, J, and K, Oregon.]

C. Miscellaneous and Anonymous.

British Colonies in America. Canada. Published by the Society for Promoting Christian Knowledge. *Maps.* 18° 1847

Petition of the Hon. Augustin N. Morin and others, praying for a Charter, by the name of "The Northern Pacific Railway Company," &c. &c. 8°
Quebec, 1854

BRITISH NORTH AMERICA—CANADA, C.

Canada West and the Hudson's Bay Company: a Political and Humane Question, of vital Importance to the Honour of Great Britain, to the Prosperity of Canada, and to the Existence of the Native Tribes; with an Appendix. 8°
1856

Directory for 1857-58 : containing Names of Professional and Business Men and of the Principal Inhabitants in the Cities, Towns, and Villages throughout the Province, Alphabetical Directories, &c., and Railway and Steamboat Routes throughout Canada. *Map.* Royal 8°
Montreal, 1857

Relations des Jésuites : contenant ce qui s'est passé de plus remarquable dans les Missions des Pères de la Compagnie de Jésus, dans la Nouvelle-France, 1611 à 1672. 3 vols. *Maps.* Royal 8°
Quebec, 1858

The Grand Trunk Railway Company of [Canada,] its Present Position and Future Prospects. Large 8° 1873

Institut Canadien-Français d'Ottawa, 1852-1877. Célébration du 25° Anniversaire. 8° *Ottawa*, 1879

Canada under the National Policy. Arts and Manufactures, 1883. *Illustrations.* 4° *Montreal*, 1883

By the West to the East. Memorandum on some Imperial Aspects of the Completion of the Canadian Pacific Railway. 12° 1885

Canadian Economics: being Papers prepared for Reading before the Economical Section (British Association for the Advancement of Science, Montreal Meeting, 1884.) With an Introductory Report. 8° *Montreal and London*, 1885

A Canadian Tour. A Reprint of Letters from the Special Correspondent of the *Times.* 4° 1886

Great Mackenzie Basin. Minutes of Proceedings of the Senate of Canada, Wednesday, 2nd May 1888. Large 8°

—— Report of the Select Committee of the Senate appointed to Inquire into the Resources of the Great Mackenzie Basin. Session 1888. *Maps.* *Ottawa*, 1888

—— Rapport du Comité Sénatorial Chargé de faire une Enquête sur les Ressources au Grand Bassin du Mackenzie. Session de 1888. *Maps.* 8° *Ottawa*, 1888

Star Almanac, The: a Canadian Cyclopedia of Facts and Figures; with a Calendar for 1893, and 6 *coloured maps.* 8° *Montreal*

Pleasant Places by the Shore, and in the Forests of Quebec, and the Maritime Provinces *via* the Intercolonial Railway. *Map and illustrations.* Large 8° N.D.

BRITISH NORTH AMERICA—CANADA, C.

Traité sur la Culture du Tabac Canadian. 8° N.D.

D. British Columbia Province.

Papers relative to the Affairs of British Columbia. Parts I., II., and III. (Relative to the Government of the Colony and Revocation of Hudson Bay Co.'s exclusive Trading Rights.) [Parly. Rep.] *Maps*. Folio 1859 and 1860
Information for Emigrants. *Map*. 8° 1875
Information for Intending Settlers. *Map*. 8° *Ottowa*, 1884
—— The same. *Maps*. 8° *Ottawa*, 1886
British Columbia Illustrated. The West Shore. *Illustrated*. 8° *Portland, Oregon*, 1887
Prize Essay and Poem on. 8° *Victoria, B.C.*, 1868
Reply to Letter of " Old Settler," published in the *Times* newspaper, on the Selection of a Terminus on the Pacific Coast for the proposed Canadian Pacific Railway. By a British North American. 8° 1877

E. Manitoba Province.

A Year in Manitoba, 1880-81 : being the experience of a retired officer in settling his sons. *Illustrations*. 12° 1882
Extracts from Surveyors' Reports of Townships in Manitoba and the North-West Territories. 8° 1884
Report of the Select Committee of the Legislative Assembly of the Province of Manitoba, appointed to procure evidence as to the practicability of the establishment of a System of Communication with this Province *via* Hudson's Bay. 8° *Winnipeg*, 1884
Manitoba and the North-West Territories. A General Description of the Resources and Capabilities of the Canadian North-West, as well as some Experiences of Men and Women Settlers. *Map and illustrations*. 4° 1886
Albany Settlement, qu'Appelle Valley, North-West Territory, Canada. *Plates and diagram* 1886
Census of Manitoba, 1885-86. Recensement de Manitoba. 8° *Ottawa*, 1887
A Few Facts respecting the Regina District in the great Grain-Growing and Stock-Raising Province of Assiniboia, North-West Territories, Canada. *Map*. 8° *Regina*, 1889
Winnipeg. Souvenir of the City of Winnipeg, presented to the Members of the British Association for the Advancement of Science, 1884. *Illustrations*. 8° *Winnipeg*

BRITISH NORTH AMERICA—CANADA, F.

F. New Brunswick Province.

Practical Information to Emigrants, including Details collected from the most Authentic Accounts relative to the Soil, Climate, Natural Productions, Agriculture, &c., of the Province of New Brunswick. *Maps*. 8° 1832
Report of the Directors of the New Brunswick and Nova Scotia Land Company. *Maps*. 8° 1832
Eastern Provinces Guides. St John and the Provinces of New Brunswick : a Handbook for Travellers, Tourists, and Business Men. 3rd edition. *Maps and illustrations*. 12° [1884]
New Brunswick as a Home for the Farmer Emigrant. 8° *Ottawa*, 1884
[*See also* Nova Scotia.]

G. Nova Scotia Province.

Copies of Communications between the Lords of the Treasury, the Lords of the Admiralty, and the Secretary of State for the Colonies, on the subject of the Shubenaccadie in Nova Scotia. [Parly. Rep.] *Map*. Folio 1830
Record of the Proceedings of the Halifax Fisheries Commission. *Maps*. Folio 1877
Information for Intending Settlers. 8° *Ottawa*, 1884
Information for intending Emigrants. Small 8° *Halifax*, 1886
Les Mines d'Or de la Nouvelle Écosse : Revue Statistique, 1862-66. 12° *Halifax, N.S.*, 1867
The Maritime Provinces of Canada, Nova Scotia, New Brunswick, Prince Edward Island. A Handbook of General Information, including the Report of Mr Thomas Davey . . . ; an Extract from Paper by Dr Fraser . . . ; Letters from Residents in the Provinces, &c. *Map and illustrations* 1892

H. Ontario Province.

Letters from Settlers in Upper Canada to their Friends here, containing Important Practical Information relating to that Country, for the Guidance of Emigrants. 8° 1831
Report on the Indians of Upper Canada. By a Sub-Committee of the Aborigines Protection Society. 8° 1839
Ottawa, the Future Capital of Canada : a Description of the Country, its Resources, Trade, Population, &c. ; Hints to Emigrants. *Plate*. 8° 1858
Annual Report of the Normal, Model, Grammar, and Common Schools in Upper Canada, for 1858. By E. Ryerson. Royal 8° *Toronto*, 1859
The Immigrant in Ontario, the Premier Province of Canada. *Map*. 8° *Brantford, Ont.*, 1884

BRITISH NORTH AMERICA—CANADA, H.

Ontario as a Home for the British Tenant Farmer who desires to become his own Landlord. *Map.* 8°   *Toronto*, 1886

Ontario Boundary Act, 1889. Large 8°.

Welland. A Historical and Descriptive Sketch of the County of Welland, in the Province of Ontario, Canada. 8°
Welland, 1886

Report of the Royal Commission on the Mineral Resources of Ontario, and Measures for their Development. *Map.* 8°   *Toronto*, 1890

I. Quebec Province.

St Lawrence. Report of the Chief Engineer of Public Works on the Navigation of the River St Lawrence between Lake Ontario and Montreal.   *Ottawa*, 1875

—— Report on the Advantages and Necessity of Establishing a Submarine Telegraphic System for the River and Gulf of St Lawrence. *Map.* 8° *Ottawa*, 1876

Hints for Entering the River Saguenay. 8°   1840

Anticosti. The Island of Anticosti, its Geographical Position, Extent, Resources, &c. *Map.* 8°   1867

Temiskaming Lake. Au Lac Temiskaming. *Maps.* 8°   *Ottawa*, 1885

BRITISH NORTH AMERICA— NEWFOUNDLAND.

Reports of Progress of the Geological Survey for the years 1874, 1876, 1881. *Illustrations and maps.* 8°
St John's, 1875-82

Ministère des Affaires Etrangères. Documents Diplomatiques. Affaires de Terre-Neuve. *Map.* Folio   *Paris*, 1891

Labrador. Facsimile of a part of a MS. found on the Coast of Labrador. 4°.

MEXICO.

Diario del Gobierno de la República Mejicana. [Odd numbers] 1839 and 1840

Memoria presentada á S. M. el Emperador por el Ministro de Fomento Luis Robles Pezuela, de los Trabajos ejecutados en su Ramo el año de 1865. *Maps and plates.* 8°   1866

Memoria que el Secretario de Estado y del Despacho de Fomento, Colonizacion, Industria, y Comercio de la Republica Mexicana presenta al Congreso de la Union. Correspondiente al año trascurrido de 1° de Julio de 1868 al 30 de Junio de 1869. *Maps.* 8°   *Mexico*, 1870

The same. Conteniendo Documentos hasta el 30 de Junio de 1873. *Map.* 8°
Mexico, 1874

MEXICO.

Anales del Ministerio de Fomento de la República Mexicana, año de 1877. Tomo 1, 2. *Maps.* 8°   *Mexico*, 1877

Estudio sobre las aguas Medicinales di la Republica Mexicana.   *Mexico*, 1884

Nombres Géographicos de Mexico : Catálogo Alfabético de los Nombres de Lugar Pertenecientes al idioma " Nahnatl." Estudio Jeroglifico de la Matrícula de los Tributos del Códice Mendocino, por el Dr Antonio Peñafiel. 4°, with Atlas   *Mexico*, 1885

Informes y Documentas Relations à Comercio Interior y Exterior Agricultura e Industrias. (Estados Unidos Mexicanos, No. 13, Julio 1886.) 8°
Mexico, 1886

República Mexicana : Casas de Moneda. Noticias de Acuñacion é Introduccion de Metales en el año fiscal de 1884 á 1885. Folio   *Mexico*, 1886

Codigo de Mineria de la República Mexicana. 12° *Paris and Mexico*, 1889

[*See also* United States, I, Bureau of the American Republics.]

Journey from Acapulco to the Capital of Mexico, by way of Tasco, Summer 1849. (*Hutchings' California Magazine.*) *Illustrations.* 8° [*San Francisco*, 1858]

The Republic of Mexico Restored. 8°
Mexico, 1867

La Ramirita.   *Mexico*, 1885

Popocatepetl. Ascensione al Volcano Popocatepetl. 8°   *Turin*, 1856

Tehuantepec Railway, its Location, Features, and Advantages under the La Sere Grant of 1869. 8°   1869

Geographical Positions in Mexico. In MS. 4°   N.D.

UNITED STATES.

A. Census Reports.

Seventh Census. Report of the Superintendent of the Census for December 1852, to which is appended the Report for December 1851. 8° *Washington*, 1853

—— Statistical View of the United States . . . : being a Compendium of the Seventh Census, &c., by J. D. B. de Bow. 8°   *Washington*, 1854

Eighth Census. Preliminary Report on the Eighth Census, 1860. By J. C. G. Kennedy. 8°   *Washington*, 1862

—— Eighth Census of the U.S., 1860. Population. Compiled from the orginal returns by J. C. G. Kennedy. 4°
Washington, 1864

—— The same. Statistics of the U.S. 4°
Washington, 1866

Ninth Census. Compiled by F. A. Walker. 3 vols. *Maps.* 4°
Washington, 1872

UNITED STATES—A.

Tenth Census of the United States; Francis A. Walker, Superintendent. The History and Present Condition of the Fishery Industries, prepared under the direction of Professor S. F. Baird, by G. Brown Goode. *See* Elliott, H. W. ; Ingersoll, E.

—— Department of the Interior. Compendium of the Tenth Census (1st June 1880). 2 parts. 8° *Washington*, 1883

—— Tenth Census of the United States, 1880. Vols. 1 and 2, 4-13, 15-22. 4° *Washington*

Vol. 1. Statistics of Population. *Maps and diagrams* 1883

Vol. 2. Report on the Manufactures of the United States. *Maps and plates* 1883

Vol. 4. Report on the Agencies of Transportation in the United States. *Map* 1883

Vol. 5. Report on Cotton Production in the United States. Eugene W. Hilgard, Ph.D., . . . Special Agent in charge. Part 1, Mississippi Valley and South-Western States. *Maps* 1884

Vol. 6. Ditto. Part 2, Eastern Gulf, Atlantic, and Pacific States. *Maps* 1884

Vol. 7. Report on Valuation, Taxation, and Public Indebtedness in the United States. Compiled under the direction of Robert P. Porter, Special Agent. *Plans and plates* 1884

Vol. 8. The Newspaper and Periodical Press, by S. N. D. North. Its Population, Industries, and Resources, by Ivan Petroff. The Seal Islands of Alaska, by Henry W. Elliott. Ship Building Industry in the United States, by Henry Hall. *Maps, coloured plates, and illustrations* 1884

Vol. 9. Report on the Forests of North America, exclusive of Mexico, by Charles S. Sargent. *Maps* 1884

Vol. 10. Production, Technology, and Uses of Petroleum and its Products, by S. F. Peckham. The Manufacture of Coke, by Joseph D. Weeks. Building Stones of the United States, and Statistics of the Quarry Industry for 1880. *Maps, charts, and plates* 1884

Vol. 11. Report on the Mortality and Vital Statistics of the United States, by John S. Billings. Part 1. *Plates and diagrams* 1885

Vol. 12. Ditto. Part 2. *Maps, plates, and diagrams* (some separate) 1886

Vol. 13. Statistics and Technology of the Precious Metals. Prepared under the Direction of Clarence King, by S. F. Emmons and G. F. Becker. *Plates* 1885

UNITED STATES—A.

Tenth Census—*continued.*

Vol. 15. Report on the Mining Industries of the United States (exclusive of the Precious Metals), with Special Investigations into the Iron Resources of the Republic, and into the Cretaceous Coals of the North-West, by Raphael Pumpelly. *Maps, plates, and diagrams* 1886

Vols. 16 and 17. Statistics of Power and Machinery employed in Manufactures, by Prof. W. P. Trowbridge. Reports on the Water-Power of the United States. Parts 1 and 2. *Illustrations, maps, and plates* 1885-87

Vols. 18 and 19. Report on the Social Statistics of Cities. Compiled by George E. Waring, jun. Part 1, The New England and the Middle States ; Part 2, The Southern and the Western States. Parts 1 and 2. *Maps, plans, &c.* 1886-87

Vol. 20. Report on the Statistics of Wages. In Manufacturing Industries ; with Supplementary Reports on the Average Retail Prices of Necessaries of Life, and on Trades Societies and Strikes and Lock-Outs. By Jos. D. Weeks. 1886

Vol. 21. Report on the Defective, Dependent, and Delinquent Classes of the Population of the United States, by Frederick Howard Wines. 1888

Vol. 22. Report on Power and Machinery employed in Manufactures, by Professor W. P. Trowbridge. Also Report on the Ice Industry of the United States, by Henry Hall. *Plates and figures* 1888

—— *See* Swank, J. M. ; King, C.

B. Consular Reports.

Reports from the Consuls of the United States on the Commerce, Manufactures, &c., of their Consular Districts. Vols. 1-43 ; Nos. 1-159 *Washington*, 1890-93

Vol.	Nos.	Vol.	Nos.	Vol.	Nos
1...	1- 3	16...	53	56	30...105-107½
2...	4- 8	17...	57	59	31...108-111
3...	9-11	18...	60	62	32...112-115
4	..12-14	19...	63	68	33...116-119
5...	15-18	20...	68½- 72	34...120-123
6...	19-22	21...	73	75	35 ..124-127
7...	23-24½	22...	76	80	36...128-131
8...	25-26½	23...	81	84	37...132-135
9...	27-30	24...	85	87	38...136-139
10...	31-34	25...	88 - 91	39...140-143
11...	35-38	26...	92	94	40...144-147
12...	39-41½	27...	95	97	41...148-151
13...	42-44	28...	98 -100	42...152-155
14...	45-48	29...	101 -104	43...156-159
15...	49-52				[158 missing]

—— Indices to the above. Nos. 1-59, and 60 to 111. 8° 1887-90

UNITED STATES—B.

Reports, Miscellaneous. 8° *Washington*
Declared Exports for the U.S., 1883.
(2 parts) 1883-84
Trade Guilds of Europe. Cholera in
Europe in 1884. The Liquorice Plant.
Pounding and Polishing Rice. 1885
Forestry in Europe. 1887

Special Reports. Vols. 1-9. 8° 1890-93
Vol. 1. Cotton Textiles Files in Spanish
America. Carpet Manufacture. Malt
and Beer in Spanish America. Fruit
Culture in Foreign Countries.
Vol. 2. Refrigerators and Food Preserva-
tion. European Emigration. Olive
Culture in the Alpes Maritimes. Beet
Sugar Industry and Flax Cultivation.
Vol. 3. Streets and Highways in Foreign
Countries.
Vol. 4. Port Regulations in Foreign
Countries.
Vol. 5. Canals and Irrigation in Foreign
Countries.
Vol. 6. Coal in Spanish America. Gas
in Foreign Countries. India-rubber.
Vol. 7. The Slave Trade. Tariffs in
Foreign Countries.
Vol. 8. Fire and Building Regulations in
Foreign Countries.
Vol. 9. Australasian Sheep and Wool.
Vagrancy and Public Charities in
Foreign Countries.

C. **Department of Agriculture.**

a. Weather Bureau.

Reports for 1891, 1892, and 1893. By
Mark W. Harrington. Also Special
Report for 1891. 8°
Washington, 1891-94
Monthly Weather Review, 1891-94 (M.
W. Harrington, Director). 4 vols. *Maps
and plates.* 4° *Washington*, 1892-94
Circular of Information. Protection from
Lightning. By A. M'Adie. 8°
Washington, 1894
The Climatology and Physical Features
of Maryland. First Biennial Report of
the Maryland State Weather Service for
the years 1892 and 1893. *Maps and
diagrams.* Large 8° *Baltimore*, 1894

Bulletins. *Maps and diagrams.* 8°
Washington
No. 1. Climate and Meteorology of
Death Valley, California. By Mark
W. Harrington. 1892
No. 2. New Method for the Discussion
of Magnetic Observations. By F. H.
Bigelow. 1892
No. 3. Report on the Relations of Soil
to Climate. By E. W. Hilgard. 1892
No. 4. Some Physical Properties of Soils
in their Relation to Moisture and Crop
Distribution. By Milton Whitney.
1892

UNITED STATES—C—*a.*

Bulletins—*continued.*
No. 5. Observations and Experiments
on the Fluctuations in the Level of
Ground-water. By Franklin H. King.
1892
No. 6. The Diurnal Variation of Baro-
metric Pressure. By Frank N. Cole.
1892
No. 8. Report on the Climatology of the
Cotton Plant. By P. H. Mell. 1893
[*See also* Maryland ; Finley, in Authors'
Catalogue ; and for other Meteoro-
logical Papers, *see* War Department, *b.*]

b. Division of Statistics.

Report of the Statistician, Jan.-Feb. 1893.
8° *Washington*, 1893
Production and Distribution of the Princi-
pal Agricultural Products of the World.
[Misc. Series, No. 5.] 8°
Washington, 1893

c. Miscellaneous.

Entomological Commission. Third Re-
port. *Maps and plates.* 8°
Washington, 1883
—— See G, *a*, Unclassed, *infra.*
Special Report. *See* Vasey.
Agricultural Report. Meteorology in its
connection with Agriculture. By Prof.
Joseph Henry. 8° N.D.

D. **Naval Observatory Publications.**

Astronomical and Meteorological Observations made during the year 1871 1873
Ditto, 1872 1874
Ditto, 1873 1875
Ditto, 1874 1877
Ditto, 1875 1878
Observations made during the year 1884
at the United States Naval Observatory.
4° 1889
—— The same, during the years 1886-89.
4° 1891-93
Washington Observations for 1868.
Appendix 1. A Catalogue of 1963 Stars
reduced to the beginning of the year
1850 . . . from Observations made . . .
by the U.S. Naval Astronomical Ex-
pedition to the Southern Hemisphere.
1870
—— Ditto for 1871. Appendix 3. Cata-
logue of Stars observed at the United
States Naval Observatory during the
years 1845 to 1871. By Prof. M. Yarnall.
1873
—— Ditto for 1871. Appendix 4. Memoir
of the Founding and Progress of the U.S.
Naval Observatory. Prepared by Prof.
J. E. Nourse 1873.
—— Ditto for 1872. Appendix 2. *See*
Eastman.

UNITED STATES—D.

Washington Observations for 1884. Appendix 1. Catalogue of Stars observed at the United States Naval Observatory during the years 1845 to 1877, and prepared for publication by Prof. M. Yarnall, U.S.N. 3rd edition . . . with Renumbering of the Stars by Prof. Edgar Frisby, U.S.N. 4° 1889
—— Ditto for 1886. Appendix 1. Magnetic Observations at the United States Naval Observatory, 1888 and 1889. By Ensign J. A. Hoogewerff, U.S. Navy. *Plates.* 4° *Washington,* 1890
——— Ditto for 1887. Appendix 1. Report upon some of the Magnetic Observatories of Enrope. By C. C. Marsh. 4° 1891
—— Ditto for 1887. Appendix 2. Observations at the U.S. Naval Observatory, 1890. By J. A. Hoogewerff. 4° 1891
—— Ditto for 1887. Appendix 3. Meteorological Observations and Results, 1883-87. 4° 1891
—— Ditto for 1888. Appendix 2. Magnetic Observations at the U.S. Naval Observatory, 1891. By J. A. Hoogewerff. 4° 1892
—— Ditto for 1889. Appendix 1. Magnetic Observations, 1892. By Stimson J. Brown. 4° 1893
Report of Superintendent of the United States Naval Observatory for the year to June 30, 1889. 8° *Washington,* 1889
—— The same, 1890-93 (4 Reports). 8°
Instructions for Observing the total Solar Eclipse of July 29, 1878 1878

E. Navy Department—Bureau of Navigation.

a. Hydrographic Office Publications.

A List of the Reported Dangers to Navigation in the Pacific Ocean, whose positions are doubtful, or not found in the Charts in general use. 8° 1866
Tables to facilitate the Reduction of Places of the Fixed Stars. For the use of the American Ephemeris and Nautical Almanac. 2nd edition 1873
Catalogue of Charts, Plans, and Views published by the United States Hydrographic Office, with a List of Books sold to Agents. 8° 1876
—— Ditto. 8° 1881
Catalogue of Charts, Plans, and Sailing Directions, published by the United States Hydrographic Office, July 1884. 8° *Washington,* 1884
Catalogue of Charts, Plans, Sailing Directions, and other Publications of the United States Hydrographic Office, 1st July 1891.
Telegraphic Measurement of Differences of Longitude by Officers of the U.S. Navy in 1878 and 1879. Greenwich, Lisbon,

UNITED STATES—E—*a.*

Telegraphic Longitudes *—continued.*
Funchal, Porto Grande, Pernambuco, Bahia, Rio de Jaheiro, Monte Video, Buenos Ayres. Pernambuco—Para 1880
—— *See below,* Nos. 65 B, 76.
A List of Geographical Positions for the use of Navigators and others. Compiled . . . by Lt.-Commander F. M. Green, U.S.N. 4° *Washington,* 1883
The International Code of Signals for the Use of all Nations. Large 8° 1894
General Instructions for Hydrographic Work 1883. *Illustrations.* 8° *Washington,* 1883

Numbered Series :—
No. 7. An Observing List of Stars selected for the Determination of Time with the Portable Meridian Transit in the Southern Hemisphere. 8° 1877
No. 30. (No. 1.) List of Lights of North and South America (East and West Coasts). Seven issues. 8° and 4° 1877 94
No. 31. (No. 2) List of Lights of South and East Coast of Africa and the East Indies, including the East India Islands, China, Japan, Australia, Tasmania, and New Zealand. Six issues. 8° and 4° 1877-92
No. 32. (No. 3.) List of Lights of the West Coast of Africa and the Mediterranean Sea. Six issues. 8° and 4° 1877-94
No. 33. (No. 4.) List of Lights of the Atlantic Coast of Europe, the English Channel, and North Sea. Four issues. 8° 1877-85
No. 33 A. (No. 5.) List of Lights of the North, Baltic, and White Seas. Three issues. 8° 1877-84
No. 33 B. (No. 6.) List of Lights of the British Islands. Three issues. 8° 1877-84 [*See* Nos. 74, 75.]
[No. 34. English Channel, Part 1, missing.]
—— Supplement, No. 2 1891
——— Supplement. 3rd edition 1893
No. 35. Sailing Directions for the English Channel. Part 2. North Coast of France and Channel Islands. By Asher C. Baker. *Map.* 8° 1877
—— Supplement, No. 2 1892
—— Supplement. 3rd edition 1893
No. 37. Coasts of the Mediterranean Sea. Part 1. S. and S.E. Coasts of Spain, from Mala Bahia to Cape Creux, Balearic Islands, and N. Coast of Africa from Ceuta to La Cala. By H. H. Gorringe. 8° 1875
—— Supplement. 1892 and 1894
No. 38. Coasts and Ports of the Gulf of Lyons and Gulf of Genoa ; Cape Creux to Piombino Headland. By H. H. Gorringe. 8° 1877

UNITED STATES—E—*a*.

Numbered Series—*continued.*

No. 38.   Coasts and Islands of the Mediterranean Sea. Part 2. By H. H. Gorringe and S. Schroeder. 8° 1878
—— Supplement.   3rd edition   1892
No. 41 A.   Reported Dangers to Navigation in the Pacific Ocean, inclusive of Australia and the East India Archipelago. By J. E. Pillsbury. Part 2. South of the Equator.   *Chart in cover.* 8°   1879
—— Supplement.   1891
No. 41 B.   Supplement to First Edition of Reported Dangers to Navigation in the North Pacific Ocean, inclusive of the China and Japan Seas and the East India Archipelago. By Commander William Gibson. 8°   1880
—— Supplement, No. ? to No. 41. Edition of 1871.   1891
No. 42.   Coasts and Islands of the Mediterranean Sea. Part 3. By H. H. Gorringe and S. Schroeder. 8° 1879
—— Supplement.   3rd edition   1892
No. 43.   The Coast of Brazil from Cape Orange to Rio Janeiro. By H. H. Gorringe.   *Profiles.* 8°   1873
No. 45.   Navigation of the Atlantic Ocean. (Labrosse.) By J. B. Coghlan. 8°   1873
No. 46.   The West Coast of Africa. Part 1.   From Cape Spartel to Sierra Leone. By H. H. Gorringe. *Profiles.* 8°   1873
No. 47.   The West Coast of Africa. Part 2.   From Sierra Leone to Cape Lopez. By Leonard Chenery. *Profiles.* 8°   1875
No. 48.   The West Coast of Africa. Part 3.   Cape Lopez to the Cape of Good Hope, including the islands in the Bight of Biafra, and Ascension and St Helena Islands. By Lieut.-Comm. J. R. Bartlett.   *Profiles.* 8°   1877
—— Supplement. 2nd edition   1892
No. 50.   The Azores or Western Islands (Kerhallet, with Additions). By Lieut. G. M. Totten. 8°   1874
No. 51.   Madeira, the Salvages, and the Canary Islands (Kerhallet and Le Gras, with Additions). 8°   1874
No. 52.   The North-West and West Coast of Spain and the Coast of Portugal, from Point Estaca to Cape Trafalgar. By Lieut. G. M. Totten. 8°   1874
No. 54.   Deep-Sea Soundings in the North Pacific Ocean, obtained in the United States steamer "Tuscarora." By Comm. G. E. Belknap. *Plates and profiles.* 8°   1874
No. 56.   Remarks on the Coasts of Lower California and Mexico. By Comm. George Dewey. 8°   1874

UNITED STATES—E—*a*.

Numbered Series—*continued.*

No. 57.   Tables for finding the Distance of an Object by Two Bearings. 8° 1874
No. 58.   The Navigation of the Pacific Ocean, China Seas, &c. (Labrosse). By J. W. Miller. 8°   1875
No. 59.   The Coasts of Chile, Bolivia, and Peru.   *Profiles.* 8°   1876
No. 60.   Coasts and Ports of the Bay of Biscay. By Lieuts. G. M. Totten and S. Schroeder. 8°   1876
—— Supplement.   3rd edition   1892
No. 61.   The Rio de la Plata.   By Lieut.-Comm. H. H. Gorringe. *Charts, plates, &c.* 8°   1875
No. 63.   The Navigation of the Carribean Sea and Gulf of Mexico. Vol. 1. The West India Islands, including the Bahama Banks and Islands, and the Bermuda Islands. By Lieut.-Comm. F. M. Green. 8°   1877
No. 64.   The Navigation of the Caribbean Sea and Gulf of Mexico. Vol. 2. 2nd edition. The Coast of the Mainland, from the Rio Grande del Norte, Mexico, to Cape Orange, Brazil, with the adjacent Islands, Cays, and Banks. Revised by R. C. Ray. Large 8° 1890
—— Supplement, No. 1. 1st, 2nd, and 3rd editions   1891-94
—— Supplement, No. 2. Prepared by Lieut. W. S. Hughes. Large 8° 1891
—— Supplement, No. 3   1895
No. 65.   Report on the Telegraphic Determination of Differences of Longitude in the West Indies and Central America. By Lieut.-Comm. F. M. Green. 4°   1877
No. 65 B.   Telegraphic Determination of Longitudes in Japan, China, and the East Indies, embracing the Meridians of Yokohama, Nagasaki, Wladiwostok, Shanghai, Amoy, Hong-Kong, Manila, Cape St James, Singapore, Batavia, and Madras, with the Latitude of the several Stations, by Lieut.-Commanders F. M. Green and C. H. Davis and Lieut. J. A. Norris, U.S.N., in 1881 and 1882. Published by order of Captain J. G. Walker, U.S.N. *Chart.* 8°   1883
No. 70.   Sailing Directions for the Kattegat Sound, and Great and Little Belts, to the Baltic Sea. Compiled from Danish and Swedish Surveys. Bureau of Navigation, Navy Department, Captain J. C. P. de Krafft, U.S.N., Hydrographer to the Bureau. 8°   1881
[No. 73.   Newfoundland and Labrador, &c., missing]
—— Supplement, No. 2   1891

UNITED STATES—E—*a*.
Numbered Series—*continued.*

No. 74. (No. 5.) List of Lights of the North, Baltic, and White Seas, corrected to July 1885. 8°   1885
—— List of Lights of the World. Vol. 5. North, Baltic, and White Seas. Revised and corrected to March 1890. By Boynton Leach.   1890
No. 75. (No. 6.) List of Lights of the British Islands, corrected to July 1885. 8°   1885
No. 76. Telegraphic Determination of Longitudes in Mexico and Central America, and on the West Coast of South America, embracing the Meridians of Vera Cruz, Guatemala, La Libertad, Salvador, Paita, Lima, Arica, Valparaiso, and the Argentine National Observatory at Cordoba, with the Latitudes of the several Sea-Coast Stations. By Lieut. - Comm. C. H. Davis, and Lieuts. J. A. Norris and C. Laird, U.S.N., &c. *Plates.* 4°.
No. 77. Practical Hints in regard to West Indian Hurricanes. Translated from the Spanish by Lieut. George L. Dyer, U.S.N. 8°   1885
No. 84. The West Coast of Mexico and Central America, from the Boundary Line between the United States and Mexico to Panama, including the Gulf of California. Large 8°   1887
No. 85. Sailing Directions of the Indian Ocean, the Winds, Monsoons, Currents, and Passages, including also the Java Sea, Sulu Sea, Afuera Sea, and the Philippine Islands. Compiled by Lieut. F. E. Sawyer. Large 8°   1887
—— Supplement, No. 3. Large 8°   1892
No. 86. The Navigation of the Caribbean Sea and Gulf of Mexico. Vol. 1. The West India Islands, including the Bahama Banks and Islands, and the Bermuda Islands. Revised and Compiled by Lieutenant S. L. Graham and Lieutenant F. E. Sawyer. Large 8°   1888
—— Supplement. 3rd edition   1894
No. 88. The East Coast of South America, from Cape Orange to Cape Virgins, including Falkland, South Georgia, Sandwich and South Shetland Islands. Compiled by Lieut. J. C. Fremont and R. H. Orr. Large 8°   1889
—— Supplement. 1st and 2nd editions   1891-93
No. 89. The West Coast of South America, comprising Magellan Strait, Tierra del Fuego, and the outlying islands. Revised . . . by R. C. Ray. Large 8°   1890
—— Supplement. 1st, 2nd, and 3rd editions   1892-93

UNITED STATES—E—*a*.
Numbered Series—*continued.*

No. 92. Report of Ice and Ice Movements in Bering Sea and the Arctic Basin. By Ensign Edward Simpson, U.S.N. *Map.* 8°   1890
No. 93. Report of Ice and Ice Movements in the North Atlantic Ocean. By Ensign Hugh Rodman, under the direction of Capt. Henry F. Picking. *Charts.* 8°   1890
No. 94. Report of the International Meteorologic Congress at Paris, France, September 19–26, 1889. By Lieut. Aaron Ward, U.S.N., under the direction of Capt. Henry F. Picking, U.S.N., Hydrographer. 8°   1890
No. 95. The Average Form of Isolated Submarine Peaks, and the interval which should obtain between Deep-Sea Soundings taken to disclose the character of the bottom of the ocean. By G. W. Littlehales. *Plates.* 8°   1890
No. 96. The Coast of British Columbia, including the Juan de Fuca Strait, Puget Sound, Vancouver, and Queen Charlotte Islands. Compiled by R. C. Ray, under the direction of Richardson Clover, Hydrographer. *Chart.* 8°   1891
—— Supplement. 1st and 2nd editions. Large 8°   1891-94
No. 97. Telegraphic Determination of Longitudes in Mexico, Central America, the West Indies, and on the North Coast of South America, 1888-89-90 ; with the latitudes of the several stations. By Lieuts. J. A. Norris and Charles Laird. Also Magnetic Observations by Lieut. C. Land and Ensigns J. H. L. Holcombe and L. M. Garrett. *Charts.* 4°   1891
No. 98. Report on Uniform System for Spelling Foreign Geographic Names.   1891
No. 99. Nova Scotia, Bar of Fundy, and South Shore of Gulf of St Lawrence. Compiled by R. H. Orr. 1891
—— Supplement.   1894
No. 100. Gulf and River St Lawrence and Cape Breton Island. Compiled by R. H. Orr.   1894
—— Supplement.   1891
No. 101. The Methods and Results of the Survey of the West Coast of Lower California. By the Officers of the "Ranger," 1889-90   1892
No. 102. The Azores, Madeiras, Salvages, Canaries, and Cape Verde Islands. 2nd edition   1892
No. 105. West Coast of Africa, from Cape Spartel to Cape Agulhas, with Islands. 2nd edition   1892

UNITED STATES—E—*a*.

Nautical Monographs. No. 5. The Great Storm off the Atlantic Coast of the United States, March 11-14, 1888. By Everett Hayden. *Charts.* 4°
Washington, 1888

b. Miscellaneous.

Report of the Secretary of the Navy relative to the Naval Expedition to Japan. 8°   *Washington,* 1855

Annual Reports of the Secretary of the Navy on the Operations of the Department for 1871 and 1873. 8°
Washington, 1871-73

Jeannette. Proceedings of a Court of Inquiry, convened at the Navy Department, Washington, D.C., October 5, 1882, in pursuance of a Joint-Resolution of Congress . . . to investigate the circumstances of the loss in the Arctic Seas of the exploring steamer "Jeannette," &c. *Plates and charts.* 8° *Washington,* 1883

Annual Reports of the Hydrographer to the Bureau of Navigation, for the fiscal years ending June 30, 1884-94. 11 Reports. 8°   *Washington,* 1884-94

Reports of Observations of the Total Eclipse of the Sun, August 7, 1869, made by parties under the general direction of Prof. J. H. C. Coffin. *Plates.* 4°   *Washington,* 1877

Publications of the Office of Naval Intelligence (War Series). No. 3. Report of the British Naval and Military Operations in Egypt, 1882. By Lieut.-Commander Caspar F. Goodrich. *Maps and plates.* 8°   *Washington,* 1883

F. Surveys : Coast and Geodetic.

Coast Survey.

Reports of the Superintendent of the Coast Survey for the years 1844-45 and 1847-51. 8°; and volume of *maps* to accompany for 1851, 4° *Washington,* 1845-52

—— The same, showing the Progress of the Survey during the years 1852-75. 24 Reports. *Text and maps.* 4°
Washington, 1853-78

—— The same, for the fiscal years ending with June 1876, and June 1877. *Text and maps.* 4°   *Washington,* 1879-80

—— Report, 1874. Appendix. Tidal Researches. By W. Ferrel. 4°
Washington, 1874

Sailing Directions to accompany the New Chart of the Western Coast of the United States   1850

Report on Mt. St Elias. By W. H. Dall. From Appendix to Report for 1875. 4°. [*See also* Bache.]

UNITED STATES—F.

Coast and Geodetic Survey.

Reports of the Superintendent of the U.S. Coast and Geodetic Survey, showing the Progress of the work during the fiscal years ending with June 1878-90. *Maps and illustrations.* 4°
Washington, 1881-91

—— The same, ending June 1891 and 1892. Part 2. *Maps, &c.* 8°
Washington, 1892-94

Methods and Results. Report on Telegraphic Longitudes. Appendix No. 6— Report for 1880. *Diagram.* 4°
Washington, 1882

—— Explanation of Apparatus for Observation of Telegraphic Longitudes. Appendix No. 7—Report for 1880. *Plates.* 4°   *Washington,* 1882

—— Report on Geodetic Leveling on the Mississippi River. Appendix No. 11— Report for 1880. *Plates.* 4°
Washington, 1882

—— A Treatise on the Plane Table and its use in Topographical Surveying. Appendix No. 13—Report for 1880. *Illustrations.* 4°   *Washington,* 1882

—— Determination of Time, Longitude, Latitude, and Azimuth. 3rd edition. Appendix No. 14—Report for 1880. *Plates.* 4°   *Washington,* 1882

—— A Review of various Projections for Charts in connection with the Polyconic Projection used in the Coast and Geodetic Survey. Appendix No. 15— Report for 1880. *Maps.* 4°
Washington, 1882

—— The Currents and Temperatures of Bering Sea. Appendix No. 16—Report for 1880. Carlile P. Patterson, Superintendent. *Charts.* 4° *Washington,* 1882

—— An Account of a Perfected Form of the Contact-Slide Base Apparatus used in the Coast and Geodetic Survey. Appendix No. 17—Report for 1880. *Plate.* 4°   *Washington,* 1882

—— An Attempt to solve the Problem of the first Landing-Place of Columbus in the New World. Appendix No. 18— Report for 1880. Carlile P. Patterson, Superintendent. *Chart.* 4°
Washington, 1882

—— An Enquiry into the Variation of the Compass off the Bahama Islands at the time of the Landfall of Columbus in 1492. Appendix No. 19—Report for 1880. Carlile P. Patterson, Superintendent. *Chart.* 4° *Washington,* 1882

—— General Index of Scientific Papers contained in the Annual Reports of the U.S. Coast and Geodetic Survey, from 1845 to 1880 inclusive. Appendix No. 6—Report for 1881. 4°
Washington, 1882

UNITED STATES—F.
Methods and Results—*continued.*

—— Directions for Measurement of Terrestrial Magnetism. 3rd edition. Appendix No. 8—Report for 1881. *Plates.* 4° *Washington,* 1882

—— Terrestrial Magnetism: Collection of Results for Declination, Dip, and Intensity, from Observations made by the United States Coast and Geodetic Survey between 1833 and July 1882. Appendix No. 9—Report for 1881. 4° *Washington,* 1882

—— On the Length of a Nautical Mile. Appendix No. 12—Report for 1881. 4° *Washington,* 1882

—— Pendulum Experiments. Appendices Nos. 14, 15, 16, and 17—Report for 1881. 4° *Washington,* 1882

—— A new Compensation Primary Base-Apparatus, including the Determination of the Length of the corresponding Five-Metre Standard Bars. Appendix No. 7—Report for 1882. *Plates.* 4° *Washington,* 1883

—— Measurement of the Yolo Base, Yolo County, California. Appendix No. 8—Report for 1882. *Plates.* 4° *Washington,* 1883

—— Field Work of the Triangulation. Appendix No. 9—Report for 1882. 4° *Washington,* 1883

—— On the Construction of Observing Tripods and Scaffolds. Appendix No. 10—Report for 1882. *Plates.* 4° *Washington,* 1883

—— Results of the Transcontinental Line of Geodetic Spirit Leveling near the Parallel of 39°. Appendix No. 11—Report for 1882. *Map.* 4° *Washington,* 1883

—— Secular Variation of the Magnetic Declination in the United States and at some Foreign Stations. 5th edition. Appendix No. 12—Report for 1882. *Plates.* 4° *Washington,* 1883

—— Distribution of the Magnetic Declination in the United States at the epoch January 1885. Appendix No. 13—Report for 1882. *Charts and plate.* 4° *Washington,* 1883

—— Study of the Effect of River Bends in the Lower Mississippi. Appendix No. 16—Report for 1882. *Plate.* 4° *Washington,* 1883

—— Discussion of the Tides of the Pacific Coast of the United States. Appendix No. 17—Report for 1882. *Maps.* 4° *Washington,* 1883

—— Report on the Siemens Electrical Deep-Sea Thermometer. Appendix No. 18—Report for 1882. *Plates.* 4° *Washington,* 1882

UNITED STATES—F.
Methods and Results—*continued.*

—— A new reduction of La Caille's Observations of Fundamental Stars in the Southern Heavens, 1749-57. Appendix No. 21—Report for 1882. 4° *Washington,* 1883

—— Report of a Conference on Gravity Determinations. Appendix No. 22—Report for 1882. 4° *Washington,* 1883

—— Descriptive Catalogue of Publications. Appendix No 6—Report for 1883. 4° *Washington,* 1884

—— Table for Depths of Harbours on the Coasts of the United States. Appendix No. 7—Report for 1883. 4° *Washington,* 1883

—— The Estuary of the Delaware. Appendix No. 8—Report for 1883. *Map.* 4° *Washington,* 1884

—— Tides at Sandy Hook. Appendix No. 9—Report for 1883. *Map.* 4° *Washington,* 1884

—— Maxima and Minima Tide-Predicting Machine. Appendix No. 10—Report for 1883. *Plates.* 4° *Washington,* 1884

—— On the Length of the Yolo Base Line, California. Appendix No. 11—Report for 1883. *Diagram.* 4° *Washington,* 1884

—— Results for Atmospheric Refraction from Hypsometric Measures made in California in 1888. Appendix No. 12—Report for 1883. *Diagram.* 4° *Washington,* 1884

—— Report upon Magnetic Observations made at the U.S. Polar Station, Ooglamie, Point Barrow, Alaska, 1881-82-83. Appendix No. 13 — Report for 1883. *Map.* 4° *Washington,* 1884

—— Standard Topographical Drawings. First and Second Series. Appendix No. 14—Report for 1883. *Plates.* 4° *Washington,* 1884

—— Field Catalogue of Time and Circumpolar Stars for 1885. Appendix No. 18—Report for 1883. 4° *Washington,* 1884

—— Determinations of Gravity at Stations in Pennsylvania, 1879-80. Appendix No. 19—Report for 1883. 4° *Washington,* 1884

—— Tables for the Projection of Maps on a Polyconic Development. Appendix No. 6—Report for 1884. 4° *Washington,* 1885

—— Formulæ and Factors for the Computation of Geodetic Latitudes, Longitudes, and Azimuths. 3rd edition. Appendix No. 7—Report for 1884. 4° *Washington,* 1885

UNITED STATES—F.

Methods and Results—*continued*.

—— Junction of the Triangulations of the Lake Survey and Coast and Geodetic Survey at Lake Ontario. Appendix No. 9—Report for 1884. *Map*. 4°
Washington, 1885

—— Heights of the Stations of the Davidson Quadrilaterals from Trigonometrical Determinations. Appendix No. 10— Report for 1884. 4° *Washington*, 1885

——- Longitudes determined by Electric Telegraph between 1846 and 1885. Appendix No. 11 — Report for 1884. *Map and diagram*. 4°
Washington, 1885

—— Physical Hydrography of Delaware River and Bay. Comparison of recent with former Surveys. Appendix No. 12—Report for 1884. *Maps*. 4°
Washington, 1885

—— Determinations of Gravity with the Kater Pendulums. Appendix No. 14— Report for 1884. 4° *Washington*, 1885

—— Gravity Research. Use of the Noddy for Measuring the Swaying of a Pendulum Support. Appendix No. 15— Report for 1884. 4° *Washington*, 1885

—— Gravity Research. Effect of the Flexure of a Pendulum upon its Period of Oscillation. Appendix No. 16 — Report for 1884. 4° *Washington*, 1885

—— Description of a Model of the Depths of the Sea in the Bay of North America and Gulf of Mexico. Appendix No. 17—Report for 1884. *Map*. 4°
Washington, 1885

—— Voyages of Discovery and Exploration on the North - West Coast of America, from 1539 to 1603. Appendix No. 7—Report for 1886. F. M. Thorn, Superintendent. *Chart*. 4°
Washington, 1887

—— A Bibliography of Geodesy. By J. Howard Gore, B.S., Ph.D. Appendix No. 16—Report for 1887. F. M. Thorn, Superintendent. 4°
Washington, 1889

—— Geodesy. Determinations of Latitude and Gravity for the Hawaiian Government. By E. D. Preston. Appendix No. 14—Report for 1888. *Plates*. 4° *Washington*, 1890

—— Geographical Explorations. Early Expeditions to the Region of Bering Sea and Strait. From the Reports and Journals of V. I. Bering. Translated by W. H. Dall. Appendix No. 19— Report for 1887. 4° 1891

—— Determinations of Gravity with half-second Pendulums in Alaska, at Washington, and Hoboken, N. J. By T. C. Mendenhall. Appendix No. 15—Report for 1891. 4° 1892

UNITED STATES—F.

Atlantic Coast Pilot. Eastport to Boston. *Charts, &c.* 4° *Washington*, 1879

—— Ditto. Boston to New York. 2nd edition. *Charts, &c.* 4°
Washington, 1880

Pacific Coast Pilot. Coasts and Islands of Alaska. Second Series. *Maps and plates*. 4° *Washington*, 1879

—— The same. Alaska. Part 1. *Maps, &c.* 4° *Washington*, 1883

—— The same. Coast of California, Oregon, and Washington. By George Davidson. 4th edition. *Plates*. 4°
Washington, 1889

Deep-Sea Sounding and Dredging. A Description and Discussion of the Methods and Appliances used on Board the Coast and Geodetic Survey steamer "Blake." By Charles D. Sigsbee. *Plates*. 4°
Washington, 1880

Laws and Regulations relating to the Coast and Geodetic Survey of the United States. 8° *Washington*, 1881

A Treatise on Projections. By Thomas Craig. 4° *Washington*, 1882

Tide-Tables for the Atlantic Coast of the United States for the years 1884 and 1886 1883-85

Tide-Tables for the Pacific Coast of the United States, together with a few Stations in Lower California, British Columbia, and Alaska Territory, for the years 1884 and 1886. 12°
Washington, 1883-85

The late Attacks upon the Coast and Geodetic Survey. 8° *Philadelphia*, 1884

Bulletins, Nos. 3–24 (No. 13 missing). 4° 1888-93

—— Nos. 26, 27, 29. 8° 1893

G. Surveys : Geological and Geographical.

a. Geological (and Geographical) Survey of the Territories.

Annual Reports :—

First, Second, and Third Annual Reports of the United States Geological Survey of the Territories for the years 1867, 1868, and 1869, under the Department of the Interior. 8° *Washington*, 1873

Preliminary Report of the Survey of Wyoming and portions of contiguous territories [practically the 4th Annual Report]. 8° *Washington*, 1871

Preliminary Report of the Survey of Montana and portions of adjacent Territories, being a Fifth Annual Report. *Maps and plates*. 8° *Washington*, 1872

Supplement to Fifth Annual Report. Report on Fossil Flora. By Leo Lesquereux. 8° *Washington*, 1872

UNITED STATES—G—*a.*
Annual Reports—*continued.*

Sixth Annual Report, embracing portions of Montana, Idaho, Wyoming, and Utah, for the year 1872. *Plates.* 8°
Washington, 1873
Seventh Annual Report, embracing Colorado, for the year 1873. *Maps and plates.* 8° 1874
Eighth Annual Report, embracing Colorado and parts of adjacent Territories, for the year 1874. *Maps and plates.* 8°
Washington, 1876
Ninth Annual Report, embracing Colorado and parts of adjacent Territories, for the year 1875. *Maps and plates.* 8°
Washington, 1877
Tenth Annual Report, embracing Colorado and parts of adjacent Territories, for the year 1876. *Maps.* 8° *Washington,* 1878
Preliminary Report of the Field Work for the season of 1877. 8° *Washington,* 1877
Eleventh Annual Report, embracing Idaho and Wyoming, for the year 1877. *Maps and plates.* 8° *Washington,* 1879
Preliminary Report of the Field Work for the season of 1878. 8° *Washington,* 1878
Twelfth Annual Report. Report of Progress of Exploration in Wyoming and Idaho for the year 1878. In two parts. By F. V. Hayden, United States Geologist. *Maps and plates (some coloured), also maps and panoramic views in separate cover.* 8°
Washington, 1883

Bulletins of the Survey. Vols. 1-6. *Maps and illustrations.* 8°
Washington, 1875-82
[For other Series of Bulletins, *see* Geological Survey, *infra.*]

Final Reports of the Geological Survey of the Territories. 4° *Washington*
Vol. 1. Fossil Vertebrates. Part 1. Contributions to the Extinct Vertebrate Fauna of the Western Territories. By J. Leidy. *Plates* 1873
Vol. 2. The Vertebrata of the Cretaceous Formations of the West. By E. D. Cope. *Plates* 1875
Vol. 3. The Vertebrata of the Tertiary Formations of the West. Book 1. By Edward D. Cope. *Plates* 1884
Vol. 5. Zoology and Botany. Part 1. Synopsis of the Acrididæ of North America. By Cyrus Thomas. Part 2. Acrididæ of North America not found in the United States. *Plate* 1873
Vol. 6. Contributions to the Fossil Flora of the Western Territories. Part 1. The Cretaceous Flora. By Leo Lesquereux. *Plates* 1874
Vol. 7. Contributions to the Fossil Flora of the Western Territories. Part 2. The Tertiary Flora. By Leo Lesquereux. *Plates* 1878

UNITED STATES—G—*a.*
Final Reports—*continued.*

Vol. 8. Preliminary issue of Plates only. Illustrations of Cretaceous and Tertiary Plants of the Western Territories of the United States. *Plates.* 4° 1878
Vol. 8. Contributions to the Fossil Flora of the Western Territories. Part 3. The Cretaceous and Tertiary Floras. By Leo Lesquereux. *Plates.* 4°
Washington, 1883
Vol. 9. The Invertebrate Cretaceous and Tertiary Fossils of the Upper Missouri Country. By F. B. Meek. *Plates* 1876
Vol. 10. A Monograph of the Geometrid Moths, or Phalænidæ, of the United States. By A. S. Packard, jun. *Plates* 1876
Vol. 11. Monographs of North American Rodentia. By Elliott Coues and J. A. Allen 1877
Vol. 12. Fresh-water Rhizopods of North America. By Joseph Leidy. *Plates* 1879

Report on the Geology of the Eastern Portion of the Uinta Mountains and a region of country adjacent thereto. By J. W. Powell. *Plates.* 4°, with Atlas
Washington, 1876

Miscellaneous Publications *Washington*
No. 1. Lists of Elevations and Distances in that portion of the United States West of the Mississippi River. Collated and arranged by Prof. C. Thomas, under Dr F. V. Hayden. 12°
1872
—— Ditto. Collated and arranged by Henry Gannett. 8° 1873
—— Ditto. 3rd and 4th eds. 1875, 1877
No. 2. Meteorological Observations, during the year 1872, in Utah, Idaho, and Montana. By Henry Gannett. 8° 1873
No. 3. Birds of the North-West : a Handbook of the Ornithology of the region drained by the Missouri River and its tributaries. By Elliot Coues. 8° 1874
No. 4. Synopsis of the Flora of Colorado. By Thomas C. Porter and John M. Coulter. 8° 1874
No. 5. Descriptive Catalogue of the Photographs of the U.S. Geological Survey of the Territories for the years 1869 to 1875 inclusive. 2nd edition. W. H. Jackson, photographer. *Plates.* 8° 1875
No. 6. Meteorological Observations, 1873-74, in Colorado and Montana. By G. B. Chittenden. 8° 1874
No. 7. Ethnography and Philology of the Hidatsa Indians. By Washington Matthews. 8° 1877

UNITED STATES—G—a.

Miscellaneous Publications—*continued.*

No. 8. Fur-bearing Animals : a Monograph of North American Mustelidæ . . . by Elliott Coues. *Plates.* 8° 1877

No. 9. Descriptive Catalogue of Photographs of North American Indians. By W. H. Jackson. 8° 1877

No. 10. Bibliography of North American Invertebrate Paleontology. By C. A. White and H. A. Nicholson. 8° 1878

No. 11. Birds of the Colorado Valley. By E. Coues. Part 1. 8° 1878

No. 12. History of North American Pinnipeds : a Monograph of the Walruses, Sea-Lions, Sea-Bears, and Seals of North America. By J. A. Allen. 8° 188o

Unclassed :—

Final Report of the United States Geological Survey of Nebraska and portions of the adjacent Territories, made under the direction of the Commissioner of the General Land Office. *Maps.* 8° *Washington,* 1872

Profiles, Sections, and other Illustrations, designed to accompany the Final Report of the Chief Geologist of the Survey, and sketched under his directions by Henry W. Elliott. 4° *New York,* 1872

Account of Photographs of 1873. 8° *Washington,* 1873

Twenty-five Photographic Views.

Catalogue of the Publications of the U.S. Geological and Geographical Survey of the Territories. 8° *Washington,* 1874 —— Ditto. 3rd edition, revised to Dec. 31, 1878. 8° *Washington,* 1879

The Grotto Geyser of the Yellowstone National Park ; with Descriptive Note. *Map and illustration.* Atlas folio 1876

Sketch of the Origin and Progress of the United States Geological and Geographical Survey of the Territories. 8° *Washington,* 1877

Bulletin of the Entomological Commission, Nos. 1 and 2. *Washington,* 1877

First and Third Reports of the United States Entomological Commission for the years 1877 and 1883, relating to the Rocky Mountain Locust. *Maps and plates.* 8° *Washington,* 1878-83

Hayden, F. V. Surveys West of the Mississippi. [Congress Rep.] 8° *Washington,* 1874

Summary of the Field Work of the Hayden Geological Survey during the season of 1875. 8° *Washington* [1876]

Explorations made under the direction of Prof. F. V. Hayden in 1876 N.P., N.D. [*See also* Hayden.]

UNITED STATES—G—b.

b. Geographical and Geological Survey of the Rocky Mountain Region. J. W. Powell in charge.

Preliminary Report on the Palæontology of the Black Hills. By R. P. Whitfield. 8° *Washington,* 1877

Report on the Geology of the Henry Mountains. By G. K. Gilbert. *Maps and plates.* 4° *Washington,* 1877

Report on the Geology and Resources of the Black Hills of Dakota ; with Atlas. By Henry Newton and Walter P. Jenney. *Plates.* 4° *Washington,* 188o

Contributions to North American Ethnology. Vol. 1. *Maps in cover.* 4° *Washington,* 1877 —— Ditto. Vol. 3. *Maps and plates.* 4° *Washington,* 1877 —— Ditto. Vol. 4. *Coloured frontispiece and illustrations* *Washington,* 1881 —— Ditto. Vol. 5. *Coloured plates, &c.* 4° *Washington,* 1882 —— Ditto. Vol. 6 *Washington,* 1890 —— Ditto. Vol. 7. A Dakota-English Dictionary. By Stephen Return Riggs ; edited by James Owen Dorsey. 4° *Washington,* 1890

c. U. S. Geological Survey.

Annual Reports. *See* King, C. ; Powell, J. W.

Monographs of the United States Geological Survey. J. W. Powell and Clarence King, Directors.

Vol. 1. Lake Bonneville. By G. K. Gilbert. *Maps and plates.* 4° *Washington,* 1890

Vol. 2. Tertiary History of the Grand Cañon District ; with Atlas. By Clarence E. Dutton. *Maps and plates* *Washington,* 1882

Vol. 3. Geology of the Comstock Lode and the Washoe District ; with Atlas. By George F. Becker. *Plates* 1882

Vol. 4. Comstock Mining and Miners. By Eliot Lord. *Maps* 1883

Vol. 5. The Copper-Bearing Rocks of Lake Superior. By Roland Duer Irving. *Maps and plates* 1883

Vol. 6. Contributions to the Knowledge of the Older Mesozoic Flora of Virginia. By William Morris Fontaine. *Plates.* 4° *Washington,* 1883

Vol. 7. Silver-Lead Deposits of Eureka, Nevada. By Joseph Storey Curtis. *Plates.* 4° *Washington,* 1884

Vol. 8. Palæontology of the Eureka District. By Charles Doolittle Walcott. *Plates.* 4° *Washington,* 1884

Vol. 9. Brachiopoda and Lamellibranchiata of the Raritan Clays and Marls of New Jersey. By Robert P. Whitfield. *Maps and plates.* 4° *Washington,* 1885

Monographs—*continued.*

Vol. 10. Dinocerata: a Monograph of an Extinct Order of Gigantic Mammals. By Othniel Charles Marsh. *Plates.* 4° *Washington,* 1886

Vol. 11. Geological History of Lake Lahontan, a Quaternary Lake of North-Western Nevada. By Israel Cook Russell. *Maps and plates.* 4° *Washington,* 1885

Vol. 12. Geology and Mining Industry of Leadville, Colorado ; with Atlas. By Samuel Franklin Emmons. *Plates* 1886

Vol. 13. Geology ot the Quicksilver Deposits of the Pacific Slope; with an Atlas. By George F. Becker. *Maps and plates.* 4° *Washington,* 1887-88

Vol. 14. Fossil Fishes and Fossil Plants of the Triassic Rocks of New Jersey and the Connecticut Valley. By John S. Newberry. *Plates.* 4° *Washington,*1888

Vol. 15. Text and Plates. The Potomac, or Younger Mesozoic Flora. By W. M. Fontaine. 4° *Washington,* 1889

Vol. 16. The Paleozoic Fishes of North America. By J. S. Newberry. *Plates.* 4° *Washington,* 1889

Vol. 17. The Flora of the Dakota Group. By L. Lesquereux. *Plates.* 4° *Washington,* 1891

Vol. 18. Gasteropoda and Cephalopoda of the Raritan Clays and Greensand Marls of New Jersey. By Robert Parr Whitfield. *Plates.* 4° *Washington,* 1891

Vol. 19. The Penokee Iron-bearing series of Michigan and Wisconsin. By Roland Duer Irving and C. R. Van Hise. *Maps and plates.* 4° *Washington,* 1892

Vol. 20. Geology of the Eureka District, with Atlas. By Arnold Hague. *Plates.* 4° *Washington,* 1892

Vol. 21. Tertiary Rhyncophorous Coleoptera of the U.S. By S. H. Scudder. *Plates.* 4° *Washington,* 1893

Vol. 22. A Manual of Topographic Methods. By Henry Gannett. *Plates.* 4° *Washington,* 1893

Bulletins of the Survey. 8° *Washington*

1. On Hypersthene-Andesite and on Triclinic Pyroxene in Augitic Rocks, by Whitman Cross ; with a Geological Sketch of Buffalo Peaks, Colorado ; by S. F. Emmons. *Plates* . 1883

2. Gold and Silver Conversion Tables, giving the coining values of troy ounces of fine metal, &c. Computed by Albert Williams, jun. 1883

3. On the Fossil Faunas of the Upper Devonian, along the meridian of 76°30', from Tompkins County, New York, to Bradford County, Pennsylvania. By Henry S. Williams. 1884

Bulletins—*continued.*

4. On Mesozoic Fossils. By Charles A. White. *Plates* 1884

5. A Dictionary of Altitudes in the United States. Compiled by Henry Gannett 1884

6. Elevations in the Dominion of Canada. By J. W. Spencer 1884

7. Mapoteca Geologica Americana. A Catalogue of Geological Maps of America (North and South), 1752-1881, in Geographic and Chronologic order. By Jules Marcou and John Belknap Marcou 1884

8. On Secondary Enlargements of Mineral Fragments in Certain Rocks. By R. D. Irving and C. R. Van Hise. *Plates* 1884

9. A Report of Work done in the Washington Laboratory during the fiscal year 1883-84. F. W. Clarke, Chief Chemist ; T. M. Chatard, Assistant Chemist 1884

10. On the Cambrian Faunas of North America. Preliminary studies. By Charles Doolittle Walcott. *Plates* 1884

11. On the Quaternary and Recent Mollusca of the Great Basin; with Descriptions of New Forms. By R. Ellsworth Call. Introduced by a sketch of the Quaternary Lakes of the Great Basin, by G. K. Gilbert. *Plates* 1884

12. A Crystallographic Study of the Thinolite of Lake Lahontan. By Edward S. Dana. *Plates* 1884

13. Boundaries of the United States and of the several States and Territories, with a Historical Sketch of the Territorial Changes. By Henry Gannett 1885

14. The Electrical and Magnetic Properties of the Iron Carburets. By Carl Barus and Vincent Strouhal 1885

15. On the Mesozoic and Cenozoic Paleontology of California. By Charles A. White 1885

16. On the Higher Devonian Faunas of Ontario County, New York. By John M. Clarke. *Plates* 1885

17. On the Development of Crystallisation in the Igneous Rocks of Washhoe, Nevada, with Notes on the Geology of the District. By Arnold Hague and Joseph P. Iddings 1885

18. On Marine Eocene, Fresh-water Miocene, and other Fossil Mollusca of Western North America. By Charles A. White. *Plates* 1885

19. Notes on the Stratigraphy of California. By George F. Becker 1885

20. Contributions to the Mineralogy of the Rocky Mountains. By Whitman Cross and W. F. Hillebrand. *Plate* 1885

UNITED STATES—G—*c.*
Bulletins—*continued.*

56. Fossil Wood and Lignite of the Potomac Formation. By Frank Hall Knowlton. *Plates* 1889
57. A Geological Reconnaissance in South-western Kansas. By Robert Hay. *Plates* 1890
58. The Glacial Boundary in Western Pennsylvania, Ohio, Kentucky, Indiana, and Illinois. By George Fred. Wright. With an Introduction by Thomas Chrowder Chamberlin. *Plates* 1890
59. The Gabbros and Associated Rocks in Delaware. By Frederick D. Chester. *Plate* 1890
60. Report of Work done in the Division of Chemistry and Physics, mainly during the fiscal year 1887-88. F. W. Clark, Chief Chemist 1890
61. Contributions to the Mineralogy of the Pacific Coast. By William Harlow Melville and Waldemar Lindgren. *Plates* 1890
62. The Greenstone Schist Areas of the Menominee and Marquette Regions of Michigan : a Contribution to the subject of Dynamic Metamorphism in Eruptive Rocks. By George Huntington Williams ; with an Introduction by Roland Duer Irving. *Plates* 1890
63. A Bibliography of Paleozoic Crustacea from 1698 to 1889, including a list of North American species and a systematic arrangement of genera. By Anthony W. Vogdes 1890
64. A Report of Work done in the Division of Chemistry and Physics, mainly during the fiscal year 1888-89. F. W. Clarke, Chief Chemist 1890
65. Stratigraphy of the Bituminous Coal Field of Pennsylvania, Ohio, and West Virginia. By Israel C. White. *Plates* 1891
66. On a Group of Volcanic Rocks from the Tewan Mountains, New Mexico, and on the occurrence of Primary Quartz in certain Basalts. By Joseph Paxson Iddings 1890
67. The Relations of the Traps of the Newark System in the New Jersey Region. By Nelson Horatio Darton 1890
68. Earthquakes in California in 1889. By James Edward Keeler 1890
69. A Classed and Annotated Bibliography of Fossil Insects. By Samuel Hubbard Scudder 1890
70. Report on Astronomical Work of 1889 and 1890. By Robert Simpson Woodward 1890
71. Index to the known Fossil Insects of the World, including Myriapods and Arachnids. By Samuel Hubbard Scudder 1891

UNITED STATES—G—*c.*
Bulletins – *continued.*

72. Altitudes between Lake Superior and the Rocky Mountains. By Warren Upham 1891
73. The Viscosity of Solids. By Carl Barus. *Plates* 1891
74. The Minerals of North Carolina. By Frederick Augustus Genth 1891
75. Record of North American Geology for 1887 to 1889 inclusive. By Nelson Horatio Darton 1891
76. A Dictionary of Altitudes in the United States. 2nd edition. Compiled by Henry Gannett, Chief Topographer 1891
77. The Texan Permian and its Mesozoic Types of Fossils. By Charles A. Whyte. *Plates* 1891
78. A Report of Work done in the Division of Chemistry and Physics, mainly during the fiscal year 1889-90. F. W. Clarke, Chief Chemist 1891
79. A Late Volcanic Eruption in Northern California and its peculiar Lava. By J. S. Diller. *Plates* 1891
80. Correlation Papers—Devonian and Carboniferous. By Henry Shaler Williams 1891
81. Correlation Papers—Cambrian. By Charles Doolittle Walcott. *Plates* 1891
82. Correlation Papers—Cretaceous. By Charles A. Whyte. *Plates* 1891
83. Correlation Papers — Eocene. By William Bullock Clark. *Plates* 1891
84. Correlation Papers—Neocene. By W. H. Dall and G. D. Harris. *Plates* 1892
85. Correlation Papers — The Newark System. By Israel Cook Russell. *Plates* 1892
86. Correlation Papers — Archean and Algonkian. By C. R. Van Hise. *Plates* 1892
90. A Report of Work done in the Division of Chemistry and Physics, mainly during the fiscal year 1890-91. F. W. Clarke, Chief Chemist 1892
91. Record of North American Geology for 1890. By Nelson Horatio Darton 1891
92. The Compressibility of Liquids. By Carl Barus. *Plates* 1892
93. Some Insects of special interest from Florissant, Colorado, and other points in the Tertiaries of Colorado and Utah. By Samuel Hubbard Scudder. *Plates* 1892
94. The Mechanism of Solid Viscosity. By Carl Barus 1892
95. Earthquakes in California in 1890 and 1891. By Edward Singleton Holden 1892
96. The Volume Thermodynamics of Liquids. By Carl Barus 1892

UNITED STATES—G—*c.*

Bulletins—*continued.*

97. The Mesozoic Echinodermata of the United States. By William Bullock Clark. *Plates* 1893

98. Flora of the Outlying Carboniferous Basins of South-western Missouri. By David White. *Plates* 1893

99. Record of North American Geology for 1891. By Nelson Horatio Darton 1892

100. Bibliography and Index of the Publications of the U.S. Geological Survey, 1879-92. By Philip Creveling Warman 1893

101. Insect Fauna of the Rhode Island Coal Field. By Samuel Hubbard Scudder. *Plates* 1893

102. A Catalogue and Bibliography of North American Mesozoic Invertebrata. By Cornelius Breckinridge Boyle 1893

103. High Temperature Work in Igneous Fusion and Ebullition, chiefly in relation to Pressure. By Carl Barus. *Plates* 1893

104. Glaciation of the Yellowstone Valley north of the Park. By Walter Harvey Weed. *Plates* 1893

105. The Laramie and the overlying Livingston Formation in Montana. By Walter Harvey Weed. With Report on Flora, by Frank Hall Knowlton. *Plates* 1893

106. The Colorado Formation and its Invertebrate Fauna. By T. W. Stanton. *Plates* 1893

107. The Trap Dykes of the Lake Champlain Region. By James Furman Kemp and Vernon Freeman Marsters. *Plates* 1893

108. A Geological Reconnoissance in Central Washington. By Israel Cook Russell. *Plates* 1893

109. The Eruptive and Sedimentary Rocks on Pidgeon Point, Minnesota, and their contact phenomena. By William Shirley Bayley. *Plates* 1893

110. The Paleozoic Section in the vicinity of Three Forks, Montana. By Albert Charles Peale. *Plates* 1893

111. Geology of the Big Stone Gap Coal Field of Virginia and Kentucky. By Marius R. Campbell. *Plates* 1893

112. Earthquakes in California in 1892. By Charles D. Perrine 1893

113. A Report of Work done in the Division of Chemistry during the fiscal years 1891-92 and 1892-93. F. W. Clarke, Chief Chemist 1893

114. Earthquakes in California in 1893. By Charles D. Perrine 1894

115. A Geographic Dictionary of Rhode Island. By Henry Gannett 1894

UNITED STATES—G—*c.*

Bulletins—*continued.*

116. A Geographic Dictionary of Massachussets. By Henry Gannett 1894

117. A Geographic Dictionary of Connecticut. By Henry Gannett 1894

Statistical Papers :—

Mineral Resources of the United States. Albert Williams, jr. 8° *Washington,* 1883

—— Ditto, Calendar years 1883 and 1884. Albert Williams, jr. 8° *Washington,* 1885

—— Ditto. Calendar year 1885. Division of Mining Statistics and Technology. 8° *Washington,* 1886

—— Ditto. Calendar years 1886-93. David T. Day, Chief of Division of Mining Statistics and Technology. 8° *Washington,* 1887-94

A New Method of Measuring Heights by means of the Barometer. By G. K. Gilbert. *Table.* Folio *Washington,* 1882

Geological Exploration of the Fortieth Parallel, Reports of. See below, H, Army Engineer Department, Professional Papers, &c.

H. War Department.

a. Engineer Department, U.S. Army.

Preliminary Report of Explorations in Nebraska and Dakota, in the years 1855-56-57. By G. K. Warren. *Map.* 8° *Washington,* 1875

Annual Report of the Chief of Engineers to the Secretary of War for the year 1879. In 3 parts. *Maps, tables, &c.* 8° *Washington,* 1879

—— Ditto, for the year 1880. In 3 parts. *Maps, tables, &c.* 8° *Washington,* 1880

—— Ditto, for the year 1881. In 3 parts. *Maps, &c.* 8° *Washington,* 1881

—— Ditto, for the year 1882. In 3 parts. *Maps, plates, &c.* *Washington,* 1882

—— Ditto, for the year 1883. In 3 parts. *Maps and plates* *Washington,* 1883

—— Ditto, for the year 1884. In 4 parts. *Maps, &c.* *Washington,* 1884

—— Ditto, for the year 1885. In 4 parts. *Charts, plans, &c.* 8° *Washington,* 1885

—— Ditto, for the year 1888. 4 parts. *Maps and plates.* 8° *Washington,* 1888

—— Ditto, for the year 1889. 4 parts. *Maps and plates.* 8° *Washington,* 1889

—— Ditto, for the year 1890. 4 parts. *Maps.* 8° *Washington,* 1890

—— Ditto, for the year 1891. 6 parts. *Maps.* 8° *Washington,* 1891

—— Ditto, for the year 1892. 4 parts. 8°, and Atlas 4° *Washington,* 1892

—— Ditto, for the year 1893. 6 parts. *Maps and plates.* 8° *Washington,* 1893

UNITED STATES—H—*a.*

Analytical and Topical Index to the Reports of the Chief of Engineers and the Officers of the Corps of Engineers, United States Army, upon Works and Surveys for River and Harbor Improvement. Vol. 2, 1880-87. Compiled, under the direction of Lieut.-Col. Henry M. Robert, Corps of Engineers, by Louis Y. Schermerhorn, C.E., and Holden B. Schermerhorn. 8° *Washington*, 1889

Appendices to Annual Reports. Report of the Commission of Engineers upon the Reclamation of the Alluvial Basin of the Mississippi River. [Appendix O, 1875.] *Diagram and charts.* 8° *Washington*, 1875

Report on the Transportation Route along the Wiseonsin and Fox Rivers, in the State of Wisconsin, between the Mississippi River and Lake Michigan. [Appendix T (Part 2), 1876.] *Plates.* 8° *Washington*, 1876

Report of the Surveys and Examinations of the Connecticut River between Hartford, Conn., and Holyoke, Mass., made since 1867. [Appendix B 14, 1878.] *Maps, diagrams.* 8° *Washington*, 1878

Annual Report upon the Improvement of Rivers and Harbours on the Coast of S. Carolina, Georgia, and the Atlantic Coast of Florida, in charge of Q. A. Gilmore. [Appendix J, 1880] *Washington*, 1880

Annual Report upon the Geographical Explorations and Surveys West of the 100th Meridian, in California, Nevada, Nebraska, Utah, Arizona, Colorado, New Mexico, Wyoming, and Montana. By George M. Wheeler. [Appendix LL, 1875.] *Maps and plates.* 8° *Washington*, 1875

Topographical Atlas aceompanying.
—— The like Report and Topographical Atlas for 1876. [Appendix JJ, 1876.] *Maps.* 8° *Washington*, 1876

Surveys W. of 100th Meridian.
Report upon United States Geographical Surveys West of the 100th Meridian, in charge of First Lieut. Geo. M. Wheeler. 4° *Washington*
Vol. 1. Geographical Report. *Maps and plates* 1889
Vol. 2. Astronomy and Barometric Hypsometry 1877
Vol. 3. Geology. *Plates and photographs* 1875
Vol. 3. Supplement—Geology. *Maps and plates.* 4° *Washington*, 1881
Vol. 4. Paleontology. *Plates* 1877
Vol. 5. Zoology. *Plates* 1875
Vol. 6. Botany. *Plates* 1875
Vol. 7. Archæology. *Maps and plates.* 4° *Washington*, 1879

UNITED STATES—H—*a.*

Surveys W. of 100th Meridian—*contd.*
List of Reports and Maps of the United States Geographical Surveys West of the 100th Meridian. George M. Wheeler. 2nd edition. *Map.* 8° *Washington*, 1881

Tables of Geographie Positions, Azimuths, and Distances ; together with Lists of Barometric Altitudes, Magnetic Declinations, and Itineraries of Important Routes. Prepared principally by First Lieut. M. M. Macomb, 4th U.S. Artillery, Assistant, from data gathered by parties of the United States Geographical Surveys West of the 100th Meridian, operating in the States and Territories of California, Colorado, Nebraska, Nevada, Oregon. Arizona, Idaho, Montana, New Mexico, and Wyoming ; under the direction of Capt. Geo. M. Wheeler, Corps of Engineers, U.S. Army, in charge. 1883. Folio *Washington*, 1885

Professional Papers of the Corps of Engineers.
No. 18. Report of the Geological Exploration of the Fortieth Parallel . . . By Clarence King, U.S. Geologist. 4° *Washington*
Vol. 1. Systematic Geology. By Clarence King. *Plates* 1878
Vol. 2. Descriptive Geology. By Arnold Hague and S. F. Emmons. *Plates* 1877
Vol. 3. Mining Industry. By J. D. Hague ; with Geological Contributions by Clarence King. *Plates.* Atlas to ditto 1870
Vol. 4. Part 1. Palæontology. By F. B. Meek. Part 2. Palæontology. By James Hall and R. P. Whitfield. Part 3. Ornithology. By Robert Ridgway. *Plates* 1877
Vol. 5. Botany. By Sereno Watson, D. C. Eaton, and others. *Map and plates* 1871
Vol. 6. Microseopieal Petrography. By Ferdinand Zinkel. *Plates* 1877
Vol. 7. Odontornithes : a Monograph on the Extinct Toothed Birds of North America. By Othniel Charles Marsh. *Plates* 1880
No. 24. Report upon the Primary Triangulation of the United States Lake Survey. By Lieut.-Col. C. B. Comstock, Corps of Engineers, aided by the Assistants on the Survey. *Plates.* 4° *Washington*, 1882

b. Signal Service.

Annual Reports of the Chief Signal Officer to the Secretary of War for the years 1871, 1872, 1879, 1880, and 1883-1890. (1880, 1885, and 1887, in 2 parts.) *Maps, &c.* 8° *Washington*, 1872

UNITED STATES—H—*b.*

Annual Reports—*continued.*

Part 2 (1885) consists of : Recent Advances in Meteorology, systematically arranged in the form of a Text-Book, designed for use in the Signal Service School of Instruction of Fort Myer, Va., and also for a Hand-Book in the Office of the Chief Signal Officer. Prepared, under the direction of Brigadier and Brevet Major-Gen. W. B. Hazen, by William Ferrel, M.A., Ph.D.

Professional Papers of the Signal Service.

No. 1. Report on the Solar Eclipse of July 1878. By Cleveland Abbe. *Maps, diagrams, and plates.* 4°
Washington, 1881

No. 2. Isothermal Lines of the United States, 1871-80. By First-Lieutenant A. W. Greely. *Maps.* 4° 1881

No. 3. Chronological List of Auroras observed from 1870 to 1879. Compiled by First-Lieutenant A. W. Greely. 4° 1881

No. 4. Report of the Tornadoes of May 29 and 30, 1879, in Kansas, Nebraska, Missouri, and Iowa. By Sergeant J. P. Finley. *Maps.* 4°
Washington, 1881

No. 5. Information relative to the Construction and Maintenance of Time-Balls. 4° 1881

No. 6. The Reduction of Air-Pressure to Sea-level, at Elevated Stations West of the Mississippi River. By Henry A. Hazen, A.M. *Maps.* 4°
Washington, 1882

No. 7. Report on the Character of Six Hundred Tornadoes. Prepared . . . by Sergeant J. P. Finley. *Maps.* 4°
Washington, 1882

No. 8. Recent Mathematical Papers concerning the Motions of the Atmosphere. Part 1. The Motions of Fluids and Solids on the Earth's Surface. By Professor William Ferrel. Reprinted, with Notes, by Frank Waldo. 4°
Washington, 1882

No. 9. Charts and Tables showing Geographical Distribution of Rainfall in the United States. Prepared . . . by H. H. C. Dunwoody. 4°
Washington, 1883

No. 10. Signal Service Tables of Rainfall and Temperature compared with Crop Production. Prepared . . . by H. H. C. Dunwoody. 4°
Washington, 1882

No. 11. Meteorological and Physical Observations on the East Coast of British America. By Orray Taft Sherman. *Chart.* 4°
Washington, 1883

UNITED STATES—H—*b.*

Professional Papers—*continued.*

No. 12. Popular Essays on the Movements of the Atmosphere. Compiled . . . by Professor William Ferrel. 4°
Washington, 1882

No. 13. Temperature of the Atmosphere and Earth's Surface. Prepared . . . by Professor William Ferrel. 4° 1884

No. 14. Charts of Relative Storm Frequency for a portion of the Northern Hemisphere. Prepared . . . by John P. Finley. 4° *Washington,* 1884

No. 15. Researches on Solar Heat and its Absorption by the Earth's Atmosphere : a Report of the Mount Whitney Expedition. Prepared . . by S. P. Langley. *Maps and plates.* 4°
Washington, 1884

No. 16. Tornado Studies for 1884. Prepared . . . by John P. Finley. *Maps.* 4° *Washington,* 1885

No. 17. *See* Ferrel.

No. 18. Thermometer Exposure. Prepared . . . by Henry A. Hazen. 4°
Washington, 1885

Signal Service Notes. No. 5. Work of the Signal Service in the Arctic Regions. *Chart.* 8° *Washington,* 1883
—— No. 10. *See* Garlington.

Bulletin of International Meteorological Observations taken simultaneously, Dec. 26, 1878. 4° *Washington,* 1878

Mean Temperatures and their Corrections in the United States. By Alexander M'Adie. 4° *Washington,* 1891
[For other Meteorological papers, *see* Department of Agriculture, *a.*]

c. Miscellaneous.

Meteorological Register for the years 1826-42. From Observations made by the Surgeons of the Army and others. Prepared under the direction of Thomas Lawson. 2 vols. in 1. 8°
Philadelphia, 1840 ; *Washington,* 1851
—— Army Meteorological Register, for twelve years 1843-54. Compiled from Observations made by the Officers of the Medical Department. 4°
Washington, 1855

Reports of Explorations and Surveys to ascertain the most Practicable and Economical Route for a Railroad from the Mississippi to the Pacific Ocean, made under the direction of the Secretary of War, the Hon. Jefferson Davis, Gen. J. S. Jessup, Govr. J. J. Stevens, &c. &c., in 1853-54. According to Acts of Congress. 12 vols. in 13. *Maps and plates.* 4° *Washington,* 1855-60

War Department Circular. The Practical Use of Meteorological Reports and Weather-maps. *Plates.* 8°
Washington, 1871

UNITED STATES—I.

I. Various Government Publications.

Message from the President of the U.S. concerning the Boundary between the U.S. and the Republic of Mexico. 8° *Philadelphia*, 1837

Report of the Commissioner of General Land Office, accompanying the Annual Report of the Secretary of the Interior, for 1837, 1839, 1848, and 1860. *Maps* *Washington*, 1837-60

Report of the Committee on Roads and Canals (Mount Carmel and New Albany Railroad). 8° *Washington*, 1839

Report of the Secretary of the Treasury, of the Commerce and Navigation of the United States for 1839, 1856, 1857, 1858, 1860. 4 vols. 8° *Washington*, 1839-60

Messages from the Presidents of the United States to the Two Houses of Congress, at the Commencement of the Session, with Documents and Diplomatic Correspondence, 1839, 1847, 1849-50 (3 parts), 1850-51 (2 parts), 1851-52 (2 parts), 1853 (Part 1), 1854 (2 parts), 1855 (3 parts), 1856 (2 vols.), 1862 (2 vols.) 18 vols. 8° *Washington*, 1839-62

Commerce and Navigation. 8° *Washington*, 1840

Message of the President of the U.S. in Relation to the Boundary between the United States and the Republic of Texas. *Maps*. 8° *Washington*, 1842

Annual Report of the Commissioner of the General Land Office. 8° *Washington*, 1848

—— Ditto, for the year 1867 [in German, French, and Swedish]. 8° *Washington*, 1868

—— Ditto, for the years 1868, 1869, and 1871. 8° *Washington*, 1868-71

Table of Post Offices in the U.S., arranged in alphabetical order, with an Appendix. 8° *Philadelphia*, 1851

Official Report to the American Congress on the Communications between the Atlantic and Pacific Oceans. 8° *Washington*, 1850

Report of the Lighthouse Board *Washington*, 1852

The American Ephemeris and Nautical Almanac for the years 1855 to date. Large 8° *Washington*, 1852

Ship-Canal Question. State of the Great Ship Canal Question : Convention between Great Britain and the United States. 8° 1860

Results of Meteorological Observations made under the Direction of the United States Patent Office and the Smithsonian Institution, from 1854 to 1859 inclusive. Vol. 1. 4° *Washington*, 1861

Sanitary Commission. Reports *Washington*, 1867

UNITED STATES—I.

Lists of Distances, compiled for the Information and Guidance of Officers doing duty in the Quartermaster's Department in making Payments for Mileage. 8° *Washington*, 1868

Handbook for Immigrants to the United States. *Maps*. Small 8° *New York*, 1871

Transit of Venus. Papers relating to the Transit of Venus in 1874 : Parts 1 and 2. *Charts*. 4° *Washington*, 1872

Tables to Facilitate the Reduction of Places of the Fixed Stars. Prepared for the use of the American Ephemeris and Nautical Almanac. 2nd edition. Large 8° *Washington*, 1873

Report of the Superintendent of the Yellowstone National Park for the year 1872. 8° *Washington*, 1873

Report of the Superintendent of the Yellowstone National Park to the Secretary of the Interior, 1887. 8° *Washington*, 1887

Report of the Select Committee on Transportation. Routes to the Seaboard, with Appendix and Evidence. Parts 1 and 2. 8° *Washington*, 1874

Progress Report of the Mississippi River Commission. *Plates* 1882

Emigration and Immigration. Reports of the Consular Officers of the United States. 8° *Washington*, 1887

Commercial Relations of the United States with Foreign Countries during the years 1885 and 1886. 2 vols. *Chart, plans, and illustrations*. 8° *Washington*, 1887

Further Correspondence as to North American Fisheries, 1887-88 ; with Despatch enclosing Treaty signed at Washington, 15th February 1888. Folio.

Fish Commission. Extract from the Bulletin, giving Account of the Explorations of the Fishing Grounds of Alaska, Washington Territory, and Oregon, during 1888, by the U.S. Fish Commission Steamer "Albatross." *Illustrations*. Large 8° *Washington*, 1889

Board on Geographic Names. Bulletins Nos. 1-3. 8° *Washington*, 1890-91

Bureau of the Statistics of Labour. 22nd Annual Report, March 1892. 8° *Boston*, 1892

Bureau of American Republics. Bulletin. No. 2. Handbook of the American Republics. Enlarged and revised edition. 1 vol. *Maps and plates*. 8° *Washington, Feb.* 1891

—— Ditto. No. 7. Brazil. 1 vol. *Map and plates*. 8° *Washington, June* 1891

—— Ditto. No. 9. Mexico. Prepared by Arthur W. Ferguson. 1 vol. *Plates*. 8° *Washington, July* 1891

UNITED STATES —I.

Bur. Amer. Republics—*continued.*
—— Special Bulletin. Coffee in America : Methods of Production and Facilities for Successful Cultivation in Mexico, the Central States, Brazil, and other South American Countries, and the West Indies. 8° *Washington, Oct.* 1893
Bureau of Ethnology. *See* Henshaw ; Pilling ; Powell.

J. Miscellaneous and Anonymous.

General Outline of the U.S. of North America, her Resources and Prospects ; with a Statistical Comparison. *Map.* 8° *Philadelphia*, 1824
Inquiries respecting the History, Present Condition, and Future Prospects of the Indian Tribes of the United States. 4°
A Connected View of the whole Internal Navigation of the United States, Natural and Artificial, Present and Prospective. By a Citizen of the United States. *Maps.* 8° *Philadelphia*, 1830
Account of the Conduct of the Religious Society of Friends towards the Indian Tribes in the Settlement of East and West Jersey and Pennsylvania, to 1843. Published by the Aborigines Protection Society. *Maps.* 8° 1844
Economical Causes of Slavery in the United States, and Obstacles to Abolition. By a South Carolinian. 8° 1857
Rockford, Rock Island, and St Louis Rail-Road Company. Circular. *Map.* 8° *New York*, 1868
Union Pacific Railroad Company, chartered by the United States : Progress of their Road west from Omaha, Nebraska, across the Continent. 8° *New York*, 1868
Letters on the Necessity of Cheapening Transport between the West and the Ocean, addressed to the *Milwaukee Sentinel* and *Chicago Tribune*, by " A Western Trader." 8° *Milwaukee*, 1868
Reports of Observations of the Total Eclipse of the Sun, August 7, 1869, made by Parties under the General Direction of Prof. J. H. C. Coffin, U.S.N. *Plates.* 4° [*Washington*]
Hiawatha : the Story of the Iroquois Sage. 12° *New York*, 1873
The Englishman's Illustrated Guide-Book to the United States and Canada, especially adapted to the use of British Tourists and Settlers, &c. 3rd edition, with Appendix containing a Description of the International Exhibition of 1876 at Philadelphia. *Plates.* 12° 1876
—— Ditto, with an Appendix of the Shooting and Fishing Resorts of North America. Edition of 1884. 12° *London and New York*
—— Ditto. Edition of 1885. 12°

UNITED STATES —J.

The Total Eclipse of the Sun, Jan. 1, 1889 : Report of Washington University Eclipse Party (Acad. Sci., St Louis) *Cambridge*, 1891

K. States and Territories.

Alaska.

Cruise of the Revenue steamer "Corwin" in Alaska and the N.W. Arctic Ocean in 1881. Notes and Memoranda : Medical and Anthropological ; Botanical ; Ornithological. *Plates.* 4° *Washington*, 1883
—— *See also* Hooper.
Alaska. A Sketch of the Country and its People. *Map.* 8° [1883]
Report of the International Polar Expedition to Point Barrow, Alaska. [Lieut. P. H. Ray, Commanding.] *Map and plates.* 4° *Washington*, 1885
St Elias. Up the Saint Elias Alps. [Cuttings from the *New York Times*.] *Map.* Folio 1886
Report of the Governor of Alaska for the fiscal year 1888. *Map.* 8° *Washington*, 1889
Alaska and Passamaquoddy Bay. Convention between Great Britain and the United States of America respecting the Boundary between the two countries, signed at Washington, July 22, 1892. 8°

California.

California Claims. Report on Memorial of John Charles Fremont. 8° *Washington*, 1848
Geological Survey. J. D. Whitney, State Geologist. *Plates.* 4° [*Philadelphia and Cambridge, Mass.*,] 1865-76
Geology.—Vol. 1. Report of Progress and Synopsis of the Field-work, from 1860 to 1864, by J. D. Whitney 1865
Palæontology.—Vol. 1. Carboniferous and Jurassic Fossils, by F. B. Meek ; Triassic and Cretaceous Fossils, by W. M. Gabb, 1864.—Vol. 2. Cretaceous and Tertiary Fossils, by W. M. Gabb 1869
Ornithology.--Vol. 1. Land Birds ; edited by S. F. Baird, from the MS. and Notes of J. G. Cooper 1870
Botany.—Vol. 1. Polypetalæ, by W. H. Brewer and Sereno Watson ; Gamopetalæ, by Asa Gray, 1876.—Vol. 2. By Sereno Watson 1880
Contributions to Barometric Hypsometry ; with Tables for use in California 1874
State Mining Bureau. Third Annual Report of the State Mineralogist, for the year ending 1st June 1883. *Map and illustrations.* 8° *Sacramento*, 1883

UNITED STATES—K.

State Mining Bureau—*continued.*

—— Fourth, and Seventh to Tenth Annual Reports of the State Mineralogist, for the years ending 15th May 1884, 1st October 1887 and 1888, 1st December 1889 and 1890. *Maps and plates.* 8°
Sacramento, 1884-90

—— Eleventh Report of the State Mineralogist (First Biennial). Two years ending 15th September 1892. *Maps and plates.* 8° *Sacramento,* 1893

California Academy of Sciences. Occasional Papers. 4 vols. 8°
San Francisco, 1890-93
1. A Revision of the South American Nematognathi or Cat Fishes. By C. H. and R. S. Eigenmann. 1890
2. Land Birds of the Pacific District. By Lyman Belding. 1890
3. Evolution of the Colours of North American Land Birds. By C. A. Keeler. 1893
4. Bibliography of the Palæozoic Crustacea, 1698-1892, with Catalogue of N. American Species. By A. W. Vogdes. 1893

Eine Blume aus dem Goldenen Lande, oder Los Angeles. *Plates.* 12° *Prague,* 1878

Carolina, South.

A Sketch of the Resources and Industries of South Carolina. *Maps and illustrations.* 8° *Charleston, S.C.,* 1888

Columbia, District of.

Statistical Information concerning. 4° N.D.

Dakota.

Resources of Dakota. *Maps and illustrations.* 8° *Sioux Falls, Dakota,* 1887

An Act to provide for the Division of Dakota into two States, &c. 8° 1889

A Dictionary of Dakota, conveniently arranging a multitude of facts about the Resources and Capabilities of the Great Territory soon to become two States. 8° *Aberdeen, S.D.,* N.D.

The Year of Statehood, 1889. Dakota: Official Guide, containing useful information in handy form for Settlers and Homeseekers concerning North and South Dakota. *Maps.* 8° *Aberdeen, S.D.,* N.D.

Dakota, South.

Facts about South Dakota : an Official Encyclopedia containing useful information in handy form for Settlers, Homeseekers, and Investors, in regard to Soil, Climate, Productions, Advantages, and Development—Agricultural, Manufacturing, Commercial, and Mineral; the Great Sioux Reservation recently opened for Settlement ; the Government Land Laws,&c. 8° *Aberdeen, S.D.,* 1890

UNITED STATES—K.

Florida.

Description of the Windward Passage and Gulf of Florida, with the Course of the British Trading-Ships to and from the Island of Jamaica ; also an Account of the Trade Winds, &c. *Map.* 4° 1739

Orange County, Zellwood. *Maps and illustrations.* 12°
Philadelphia and Zellwood, 1885

Georgia.

A State of the Province of Georgia, attested upon Oath in the Court of Savannah, 10th Nov. 1740. 8° 1742

De Præstantia Coloniæ Georgico-Anglicanæ præ Coloniis aliis. *Maps.* Square 8° *Aug. Vindel.,* 1747

North Georgia Gazette and Winter Chronicle. 4° N.P., 1821

Illinois.

Chicago Exhibition. Royal Commission for the Chicago Exhibition, 1893. Handbook of Regulations and General Information. 1st edition. 12° 1892

Kentucky.

Kentucky Towns and Counties : being Reports of their Growth, Natural Resources, and Industrial Improvement, made to the State Industrial and Commercial Conference at Louisville, 4th, 5th, and 6th October 1887. 8°
Frankfort, Ky., 1887

Louisiana.

The Present State of the Country and Inhabitants, Europeans and Indians, of Louisiana, on the North Continent of America. By an Officer at New Orleans. 8° N.P., 1744

Maine.

Message from the President of the United States upon the State of Affairs between the State of Maine and the British Province of New Brunswick. 8°
Washington, 1839

Plan for Shortening the Time of Passage between New York and London. Printed by order of the Legislature of Maine. 8° 1850

Maryland.

Message from the Governor of Maryland, transmitting the Reports of the Joint Commissioners, and of Lieut.-Colonel Graham, in Relation to the Intersection of the Boundary Lines of the States of Maryland, Pennsylvania, and Delaware. *Map.* 8° *Washington,* 1850

State Weather Service. [In Co-operation with the U.S. Dep. Agr., Weather Bureau.] Monthly Reports. Parts of Vols. 2, 3, and 4 (incomplete). 4° 1892-94

—— *See* U.S. : Department of Agriculture.

UNITED STATES—K.

Massachusetts.

The Illustrated Pilgrim Memorial. Published in Aid of the Monument Fund. 4° *Boston*, 1863

Michigan.

The Sault Ste. Marie Canal and Hay Lake Channel : Necessity of their Speedy Improvement. Proceedings of the Waterways Convention held at Sault Ste. Marie, Michigan, 20th July 1887. *Map and diagrams* *Duluth*, 1887

Minnesota.

The State of Minnesota, its Agricultural, Lumbering, and Mining Resources, Manufacturing and Commercial Facilities, Railroads, Pleasure Resorts, Fish, Game, &c. *Illustrations.* 8° *St Paul, Minn.*, 1885

Geological and Natural History Survey of : First, Seventh, and Tenth to Twentieth Annual Reports, for the years 1872-91. *Maps and plates.* 8° *Minneapolis and St Paul*, 1884-90
—— Bulletins of the Survey (Nos. 1-5). *Plates.* Large 8° *St Paul*, 1887-89
—— The same. No. 6. The Iron Ores of Minnesota. By N. H. and H. W. Winchell *St Paul*, 1891
—— The same. No. 7. The Mammals of Minnesota : a Scientific and Popular Account of their Features and Habits. By C. L. Herrick. Large 8° *Minneapolis*, 1892

Missouri.

Geological Survey. Reports on the Geological Survey of the State of Missouri, 1855-71. By G. C. Broadhead, F. B. Meek, and B. F. Shumard. *Maps and plates.* 8° *Jefferson City*, 1873
—— The same, including Field Work of 1873-74. *Plates.* 8°, and Atlas 4° *Jefferson City*, 1874
—— Preliminary Report on the Iron Ores and Coalfields, from the Field Work of 1872. *Maps and plates.* Large 8°, and Atlas oblong folio *New York*, 1873
—— Bulletins (Nos. 1-5). *Maps and plates.* Large 8° *Jefferson City*, 1890-91
—— Preliminary Report on the Coal Deposits of Missouri, from Field Work prosecuted during the years 1890 and 1891. By Arthur Winslow. *Illustrations.* Large 8° *Jefferson City*, 1891
—— Biennial Report of the State Geologist transmitted . . . to the Thirty-sixth General Assembly. *Diagrams.* 8° *Jefferson City*, 1891

Nebraska.

Quadrennial Report of the Freedmen's Aid and Southern Education Society to the General Conference of the Methodist Episcopal Church, held in Omaha, Nebraska, May 1892. 8° *Omaha*, 1892

UNITED STATES—K.

New Jersey.

Annual Report of the State Geologist of New Jersey for 1869. *Plans.* 8° *Trenton, N.J.*, 1870

Statistical Information concerning New Jersey. 4° N.P., N.D.

New York.

Communications from the Governor relative to the Geological Survey of the State of New York, 1838, 1839, and 1840. 8° *New York*, 1838-40

On the Longitudes of the Dudley Observatory, the Hamilton College Observatory, the City of Buffalo, the City of Syracuse. *Plates.* 8° *Albany, N.Y.*, 1862

Reports of Dr Peters on the Longitude of Elmira, and on the Longitude and Latitude of Ogdensburgh. 8° *Albany, N.Y.*, 1864-65

State Survey. Report of the Board of Commissioners of the State Survey. *Map.* 8° *Albany, N.Y.*, 1877
—— Reports of, for the years 1877 and 1878. *Maps.* 8° *Albany, N.Y.*, 1878-79
—— Special Report of, on the Preservation of the Scenery of Niagara Falls ; and Fourth Annual Report on the Triangulation of the State for the year 1879. *Maps and plates.* 8° *Albany, N.Y.*, 1880
—— Reports of, for the years 1880 to 1883. *Maps and sections.* 8° *Albany, N.Y.*, 1881-84

New York and Pennsylvania Boundary. Report of the Regents' Boundary Commission upon the New York and Pennsylvania Boundary ; with the Final Report of Major H. W. Clarke, Surveyor for the Commission. *Maps and sketches.* 8° *Albany, N.Y.*, 1886

Report on the Progress of the State of New York. *Maps and plates.* 8° *Albany*, 1891

Niagara. Engineers' Opinion of the Marine Railway around the Falls of Niagara. 8° *New York*, 1865
—— Water-Power at Niagara Falls to be successfully Utilized. *Plates.* Large 8° 1886
—— Annual Reports, 6th, 7th 9th, and 10th, of the Commissioners of the State Reservation at Niagara, for the fiscal years 1888-89, 1889-90, 1891-92, and 1892-93. *Maps and illustrations.* 8° *Albany, N.Y.*, 1890-94

Erie Campaigns in 1868 ; or, How they Manage things on the New York Exchange. 8°.

"Farewell." An Oil-Painting : Account of its presentation to Kane Lodge, No. 454, F. and A. M. Masonic Hall, New York, Tuesday Evening, 4th June 1889. *Plates.* 12°.

UNITED STATES—K.

Ohio.

Geological Survey. Report of Progress in 1870. By J. S. Newberry. *Sections.* 8° *Columbus*, 1871

Oregon.

The Oregon Question, &c. [Pamphlets by T. Falconer, A. Simpson, and G. F. Ruxton; together with Extracts from Reviews and Newspaper Cuttings on the subject.] 8° 1845-46

Pennsylvania.

Report of the Board of Canal Commissioners. 8° *Harrisburg*, 1838

Lehigh Coal and Navigation Company, History of the. *Maps.* 8° *Philadelphia*, 1840

Diagram of the Progress of the Anthracite Coal Trade of Pennsylvania to and including the year 1879; with Statistical Tables by Messrs Sheafer. 4° *Pottsville, Pa.*, 1880

Handbook of Christchurch, Philadelphia. *Plates and portraits.* 8° 1892

Geological Survey. *See* Rogers, H. D.

Texas.

A Visit to Texas: being the Journal of a Traveller through those parts most interesting to American Settlers. 18° *New York*, 1836

Western Texas. Reports of the Secretary of War, with Reconnaissances of Routes from San Antonio to El Paso, by J. E. Johnston, W. F. Smith, F. T. Bryan, N. H. Michler, and S. G. French; also the Report of Capt. R. B. Marcy's Route from Fort Smith to Santa Fé; and the Report of Lieut. J. H. Simpson of an Expedition into the Navajo Country; and the Report of Lieut. W. H. C. Whiting's Reconnaissance of the Western Frontier of Texas. *Maps.* 8° *Washington*, 1850

Utah.

Utah Epitomized: a Brief Compendium of the Resources, Attractions, Advantages, Possibilities, Mineral, Industrial, and Agricultural, of Utah and her Capital. *Illustrations.* 8° N.D.

UNITED STATES—K.

Salt Lake City. A Sketch of Utah's Wonderful Resources. *Illustrations.* Small 4° *Salt Lake*, 1888

Virginia.

A Geographical and Political Summary, embracing a Description of the State, its Geology, Soils, Minerals, and Climate; its Animal and Vegetable Productions, Manufacturing and Commercial Facilities, Religious and Educational Advantages, Internal Improvements, and Form of Government. Prepared and published under the supervision of the Board of Immigration. *Maps.* 8° *Richmond, Va.*, 1876

Tobacco in Virginia and North Carolina. *Map.* 8° *Richmond, Va.*, 1877

A Synopsis of the Geology, Geography, Climate, and Soil of the State; together with its Resources of Mines, Forests, and Fields, its Flocks and its Herds. *Map.* 8° *Richmond, Va.*, 1889

Wisconsin.

Geological Survey of Wisconsin, 1873-79. Vol. 1. *Maps and illustrations.* Large 8° [*Madison*] 1883

Vol. 2. *Plates.* Large 8° [*Madison*] 1877

Vol. 3. *Maps and plates.* Large 8° [*Madison*] 1880

Vol. 4. *Maps and plates.* Large 8° [*Madison*] 1882

Folio Atlas accompanying Vols. 2, 3, and 4 1882

Madison. Charter of the City of Madison, Wisconsin. 8° *Madison*, 1856

Watertown, Wisconsin, City of: its Manufacturing and Railroad Advantages and Business Statistics. *Map.* 12° *Watertown*, 1856

Wyoming.

Annual Report of the Territorial Geologist to the Governor of Wyoming, January 1888. Louis D. Ricketts, D.Sc., Territorial Geologist. 8° *Cheyenne, Wyo.*, 1888

Resources of Wyoming, 1889. *Map.* 8° *Cheyenne, Wyo.*, 1889

AMERICA, CENTRAL, AND WEST INDIES.

CENTRAL AMERICA.

A. General.

Brief Statement, supported by Original Documents, of the Important Grants conceded to the Eastern Coast of Central America Commercial and Agricultural Company by the State of Guatemala. *Maps.* 8° 1831

Tigre Island and Central America. Message from the President of the United States, transmitting Documents, &c. 8° [*Washington*] 1850

Description of the Facilities and Advantages which a Road across Central America, from Admiral's Bay, or Chiriqui Lagoon, on the Atlantic, to Chiriqui Bay, on the Pacific, would afford to the Commerce of the World. *Plate.* 8° *Philadelphia,* 1852

Biologia Centrali-Americana ; or, Contributions to the Knowledge of the Fauna and Flora of Mexico and Central America. Edited by F. Ducane Godman and Osbert Salvin. Archæology by A. P. Maudslay. Parts 1-4. *Text (illustrations)* 4°; *and atlas, Parts* 1-4, oblong 4° 1889-90

B. Costa Rica.

Documentos que dan á Conocer el Estado actual de la Sociedad Itineraria del Norte. Small 4° *Costa Rica,* 1882

Informe de Hacienda en 1853. 4° *San José,* 1853

Account of the Costa Rica Railway. *Map.* 8° *Liverpool,* 1855

Decretos y Constitucion Politica de la Republica de Costa-Rica eimtida en 1871 y adoptada el 26 de Abril de 1882. 16° *San José,* 1882
[*See* Nicaragua.]

C. Guatemala.

Censo General de la Republica de Guatemala, levantado el año de 1880. 4° *Guatemala* [1881]

Movimiento de Poblacion habido en los Pueblos de la Republica de Guatemala durante el año de 1881. 4° *Guatemala,* 1882
[Continued as]—

Anales Estadisticos de la Republica de Guatemala, año de 1882. Tomo 1. 4° *Guatemala* [1883]

—— The same. Año de 1883. Tomo 2. 4° *Guatemala* [1884]

CENTRAL AMERICA—C.

Directorio de la Ciudad de Guatemala, compilado por la Direccion General de Estadistica, año de 1886. 8° *Guatemala,* N.D.

—— Informe de la Direccion General de Estadistica, 1886-88. 8° *Guatemala,* N.D.

Exposition Universelle Internationale, Paris, 1889. République de Guatémala, Amérique Centrale. Catalogue des Exposants, avec une Introduction par le Dr Gustave E. Guzman, suivi d'une Notice sur certains produits spéciaux exposés par Adolphe Boucard. *Portrait.* 8° *Tours,* N.D.

Demarcación politica de la República de Guatemala, compilada por la Oficina de Estadistica, 1892. Large 8° *Guatemala,* 1893

Memoria con que el Secretario de Estado en el Despacho de Hacienda y Credito de Publico da cuenta á la Asamblea Nacional Legislativa de los trabajos effectuados durante el año de 1892. Royal 8° *Guatemala,* 1893

Memoria presentada por la secretario de relationes exteriores de la Republica de Guatemala á la Asamblea National Legislativa en 1893. Royal 8° *Guatemala,* 1893

D. Honduras.

Report of the Commissioners of Legal Inquiry on the Case of the Indians at Honduras. [Parl. Rep.] Folio 1828

Primer Anuario Estadistico correspondiente al año de 1889. Por Antonio R. Vallejo. Large 4° *Tegucigalpa,* 1893

E. Nicaragua.

Nicaragua, and Costa Rica. 8° 1850

Nicaragua Route for an Inter-Oceanic Ship Canal. Report by Max. von Sonnenstern to the Minister of Public Works, Nicaragua. 4° *Washington,* 1874

Nicaragua, No. 1 (1881). Arbitration : Mosquito Coast. Papers relating to the Arbitration of His Imperial Majesty the Emperor of Austria in the Differences between the Government of Her Britannic Majesty and the Government of the Republic of Nicaragua respecting the Interpretation of Certain Articles of the Treaty of Managua signed on the 28th of January 1860. *Map.* Folio 1881

CENTRAL AMERICA—E.

The Case of the Republic of Nicaragua submitted to His Excellency Hon. Grover Cleveland, President of the United States, Arbitrator, under the Treaty of Guatemala of 24th December 1886. 8° *Washington,* 1888

The Interoceanic Canal of Nicaragua, its History, Physical Condition, Plans, and Prospects. Published by the Nicaragua Canal Construction Company. *Chart and illustrations.* 4° *New York,* 1891 [*See also* Colombia : Panama Canal.]

Mosquitoland. Bericht über die . . . ; Untersuchung einiger Theile des Mosquitolandes erstattet von der dazu ernannten Commission. *Maps and plates.* 8° *Berlin,* 1845

F. Salvador.

Apuntamientos Estadisticos sobre la República del Salvador (Reyes) *San Salvador* [1889]

Notice sur le Salvador. Exposition Universelle de Paris en 1889. 8° *Paris,* 1889

WEST INDIES.
A. General.

Journal of the Expedition to La Guira and Porto Cavallos in the West Indies, under the command of Commodore Knowles. 12° 1744

An Account showing the Rates and Amount of Duties, levied under British Acts of Parliament, on British West India Products, imported into the British North American Colonies of Nova Scotia, New Brunswick, Upper and Lower Canada, Newfoundland and Prince Edward's Islands, distinguishing such Products under the heads of Sugar, Rum, Molasses, Coffee, &c., also of the above Articles of Foreign Growth, for 1829. [Parly. Rep.] Folio 1830

Accounts showing the Rates and Amount of Duties levied in each of the British West India Colonies on Goods, Wares, and Merchandise ; of the Quantities of Sugar, Rum, Coffee, and Molasses exported ; Comparative Statement of the Quantities of the different Productions of the United States of America imported into the West India Colonies, &c. [Parly. Rep.] Folio 1830

Observations relative to the Establishment of the West India Agricultural Company. 8° 1836

The Lighthouses of the West India Islands and the adjacent Coasts. Corrected to 1848, 1853, 1858, 1859. 4 parts. 8° 1848-59

WEST INDIES—A.

The West India Labour Question : being Replies to Inquiries instituted by the Committee of the British and Foreign Anti-Slavery Society. 8° 1858

Report of the Committee, consisting of Mr Thiselton Dyer (Secretary), Professor Newton, Professor Flower, Mr Carruthers, and Mr Sclater, appointed for the purpose of reporting on the present state of our knowledge of the Zoology and Botany of the West India Islands, and taking steps to investigate ascertained deficiencies in the Fauna and Flora. 8° [1888] [*See also* Atlantic.]

B. Bahamas.

Fisheries. Official Introduction to Bahamas Fisheries, with a Description of the Islands. By Rebus. 8° 1883

C. Cuba.

Original Papers relating to the Expedition to the Island of Cuba. Small 8° 1744

Guia de Forasteros, en la siempre fiel Isla de Cuba para el año de 1842. *Plans.* 18° *Havana,* 1842

Cuadro Estadistico de la siempre fiel Isla de Cuba, correspondiente al año de 1846. 4° *Havana,* 1847

Cuba in Revolution: a Statement of Facts. 8° 1871

Habana. Balanza Mercantil de la Habana, correspondiente al año de 1837 e 1840. 2 parts. 4° *Havana,* 1838-41

D. Jamaica.

Public Gardens, &c. *See* Morris, D.

Blue-Book. Island of Jamaica, 1887-88. Folio *Kingston,* 1889

E. San Domingo.

Report of the Commission of Inquiry to Santo Domingo, with the Introductory Message of the President, Special Reports made to the Commission, State Papers furnished by the Dominican Government, and the Statements of over Seventy Witnesses. *Map.* 8° *Washington,* 1871

Decree annulling the agreement of Dec. 28, 1872, by which the Peninsula and Bay of Samana were leased to an American Company. [Parly. Rep.] Folio 1874

La République Dominicaine à l'Exposition Universelle de Paris. 8° *Havre,* 1889

F. Windward Islands.

St Lucia and St Vincent. A Relation of the late intended Settlement of the Islands of St Lucia and St Vincent in America, in right of the Duke of Montagu, . . . 1722. *Maps.* 12° 1725

AMERICA, SOUTH.

GENERAL.

Outline of the Revolution in Spanish America, or an Account of the Origin &c., of the War carried on between Spain and Spanish America. By a South-American. 8° 1817

Rays of Sunlight in Darkest South America, or God's Wondrous Working on Southern Shores and Seas. 3rd edition N. D.

ARGENTINE REPUBLIC.

A. Government Publications.

Registro Estadistico de la Provincia de Buenos Aires. Nos 1-16. 8°
Buenos Ayres, 1822-24

Reglamentos de Policia Maritima en los puertos y rios de la Nacion Arjentina. 8° *Buenos Ayres*, 1863

Código Rural de la Provincia de. 8°
Buenos Ayres, 1865

Rejistro estadistico de la República Arjentina. 1864-65. 2 vols. 4°
Buenos Ayres, 1865-67

La Republica Argentina, sus Colonias Agrícolas, Ferro-Carriles, Navegacion, Comercio, Riqueza Territorial, &c., &c. Por la Comision de Inmigracion de Buenos Aires. *Maps and plates.* 8°
Buenos Ayres, 1866

Terrenos cedidos por el Exmo. Gobierno de la Provincia al Exmo. Gobierno Nacional con destino a la venta o permuta de los que han de expropiarse para ceder a la Empresa del Ferro-Carril Central Argentino, &c. 8° *Buenos Ayres*, 1866

Ultimas Leyes y Decretos sobre Tierras públicas. 12° *Buenos Ayres*, 1867

Anuario de Correos de la Republica Arjentina. Novena publicacion. 8°
[*Buenos Ayres*] 1867

Datos Oficiales. La Republica Arjentina. Poblacion — Immigracion — Colonias Agricolas—Concessiones de Terrenos—Ferro-Carriles, &c. 8° *Paris*, 1867

Memorias de los diversos Departamentos de la Provincia de Buenos Aires y de las Municipalidades de Campaña. Part 1. 8° *Buenos Ayres*, 1867

Documentos Relativos a la Esposicion de Productos Argentinos en Paris, 1867. 8° *Buenos Ayres*, 1867

Correspondence respecting Hostilities in the River Plate. In continuation of Papers presented to Parliament in 1867. *Map.* Folio 1868

La Esposicion Nacional, año 1871. Publication autorizada por la Comission directiva de la Exposicion. Folio
Cordova, 1871-72

Censo Escolar Nacional. Resúmenes Generales y Preliminares en Cifras Absolutas y Relativas del Censo Escolar Nacional Levantado a fines de 1883 y Principios de 1884. *Plate.* Large 8°
Buenos Ayres, 1884

—— The same. Correspondiente a Fines de 1883 y principios de 1884 (F. Latzina). Vols. 1-3. *Plates and plans.* Royal 8° *Buenos Ayres*, 1885

Estadistica del Comercio y de la Navegacion de la Republica Argentina correspondiente al año 1885. *Diagram.* Large 8° *Buenos Ayres*, 1886

——The same. 1892. *Buenos Ayres*, 1893

Senado Argentino. Arrendamiento de las Obras de Salubridad de la Capital. Discurso Pronunciado, por el Dr Eduardo Wilde, Ministro del Interior en Sessiones 6, 7, y 8 de Julio 1887. 12°
Buenos Ayres, 1887

Consejo Escolar del 11° Distrito de la Capital (Parroquia de Monserrat). Organizacion y Disciplina. Large 8°
Buenos Ayres, 1888

B. Miscellaneous and Anonymous.

La Plata States. Noticias Históricas, Políticas, y Estadísticas, de las Provincias Unidas del Rio de la Plata, con un Apendice sobra la Usurpacion de Montevideo por los Gobiernos Portugues y Brasilero. *Map.* 8° N.P., 1825

An Account, Historical, Political, and Statistical, of the United Provinces of Rio de la Plata, with an Appendix concerning the Usurpation of Monte Video by the Portuguese and Brazilian Governments. Translated from the Spanish. *Map.* 8° 1825

Campagnie de Navigation à Vapeur du Rio Salado, Republique Argentine. (Prospectus.) *Map.* Small 8°
Paris [? 1859]

Central Argentine Railway, from Rosario to Cordova. Concession and Official Documents relating to this undertaking. 8° 1863

Nuestra Industria Rural. 8°
Buenos Ayres, 1866

ARGENTINE REPUBLIC—B.

The River Plate (South America) as a Field for Emigration, its Geography, Climate, &c. 2nd edition. *Maps.* 8° [1866]

Sociedad Rural Argentina. Bases y Reglamento de la Soc., &c. 16° *Buenos Ayres*, 1866

Report of the Proceedings at the Second Ordinary General Meeting of the Central Argentine Railway Company. 8° 1866

Central Argentine Railroad. Report, &c. 8° 1867

Letters Concerning the Country of the Argentine Republic (South America), being suitable for Emigrants and Capitalists to settle in, 1869. Second issue. 8° 1869

Exposicion Nacional en Córdoba. Boletin. Tom. I.-III. *Plates.* 8° *Buenos Ayres*, 1869-72

—— La Exposicion Nacional, año 1871. Publicacion autorizada por la Comision directiva de la Exposicion. Folio *Cordova*, 1871-72

—— Catalogos de los Productos Nacionales y Estranjeros. Tom. IV. 8° *Buenos Ayres*, 1872

—— Boletin Oficial. Série de Memorias 1-18. Tom. V.-VII. Royal 8° *Buenos Ayres*, 1875

Argentine Exhibition. Katalog der Argentinischen Ausstellung veranstaltet von der Geographischen Gesellschaft in Bremen im Tivoli-Saale. Mai-Juni 1884. *Map.* 8° *Bremen*, 1884

—— Catalogue de l'Exposition Argentine, arrangée par la Société de Géographie de Brême dans la Salle du Tivoli. Mai-Juin 1884. *Map.* 8° *Bremen*, 1884

C. Provinces.

Buenos Ayres.

Censo general de la Provincia de Buenos Aires demográfico, agrícola, industrial, comercial, etc., verificado el 9 de Octubre de 1881, bajo la Adminstracion del Doctor Don Dardo Rocha. *Maps and plates.* 4° *Buenos Ayres*, 1883

Censo General de Poblacion, Edificacion, Comercio é Industrias de la Ciudad de Buenos Aires, Capital Federal de la República Argentina. Levantado en los dias 17 de Agosto, 15 y 30 de Setiembre de 1887 bajo la administracion del Dr Don Antonio F. Crespoy compilado por una Comision, compuesta de los Señores Francisco Latzina, Presidente. Manuel C. Chueco y Alberto B. Martinez, Vocales. Dr Don Roberto Perez., Secretario. 2 vols. *Map, plans, and plates.* Large 8° *Buenos Ayres*, 1889

ARGENTINE REPUBLIC—C.

Annuaire Statistique de la Province de Buénos Ayres, publié sous la direction du Docteur Emile R. Coni, Quatrième Année, 1884. *Maps and plans.* Small folio *Buenos Ayres*, 1885

—— The same. Huitième Année, 1888. *Map.* Large 8° *La Plata*, 1889

Anuario Estadistico de la Ciudad de Buenos Aires. Año I., 1891. 4° *Buenos Ayres*, 1892

Mensaje del Gobernador de la Provincia de Buenos Aires. (Julio A. Costa.) Royal 8° *La Plata*, 1892

Ministerio de Gobierno, Oficina de Estadistica general. Reseña Estadistica y Descriptiva de la Plata, capital de la Provincia de Buenos Aires. Publicada bajo la direccion del Doctor Emilio R. Coni. *Plans and plates.* Large 8° *Buenos Ayres*, 1885

Entre Rios.

Coleccion de Leyes, Decretos y Acuerdos sobre las Tierras de Pastereo de la Provincia de Entre Rios. 8° *Buenos Ayres*, 1864

Santa Fé.

Registro Oficial de la Provincia de Santa Fé, 1862 y 1863. 8° *Santa-Fé*, 1863

—— The same. 2. Semestre. Año de 1863. 8° *Santa-Fé*, 1864

Reglamento de Policia Urbana y Rural para la Provincia de Santa-Fé. 8° *Rosario*, 1866

Coleccion de las Leyes de Tierras Sancionadas en la Provincia de Santa-Fé bajo la Administracion del Exmo Señor D. Nicasio Oroño. *Maps.* 8° *Buenos Ayres*, 1866

Compilacion de Leyes, Decretos, y demas Disposiciones que sobre Tierras Públicas se han dictado en la Provincia de Santa-Fé desde 1853 hasta 1866. 8° *Buenos Ayres*, 1867

Exposicion y Féria de la Provincia de Santa-Fé, 1887. *Plan.* 8° *Santa-Fé*, 1887

Primer Censo General de la Provincia de Santa Fé (Republica Argentina, América del Sud), Verificado bajo la Administración del Doctor Don José Galvez el 6, 7, y 8 de Junio de 1887. Gabriel Carrasco, Director y Comisario General del Censo. Libro I. Censo de la Poblacion. *Plans and plates.* Folio *Buenos Ayres*, 1888

—— The same. Libros II. a VIII. Agricultura, Ganaderia, Industria, Comercio, Vias de Comunicacion y Trasporte, Rentas, Instituciones Administrativas y Sociales, Leyes, Procedimientos y Formularios del Censo. *Maps and plates.* Folio *Buenos Ayres*, 1888

ARGENTINE REPUBLIC—C.

Primer Censo—*continued*.

—— The same. Libros IX. á XI. Sinopsis Fisica, Politica, Administrativa é Histórica. *Maps and plates*. Folio
Buenos Ayres, 1888

Tucuman.

Memoria Histórica y Description de la Provincia de Tucuman. *Plates*. Small folio *Buenos Ayres*, 1882

D. Patagonia.

Informe Oficial de la Comision Cientifica agregada al Estado Mayor General de la Expedicion al Rio Negro (Patagonia), realizada en los meses de Abril, Mayo, y Junio de 1879, Vajo las órdcnes del General D. Julio A. Roca. 4°
Buenos Ayres
Entrega I. Zoologia. *Plates* 1881
Entrega II. Botanica, por Pablo G. Lorentz, Dr., y Gustavo Niederlein. *Plates* 1881
Entrega III. Geologia, por el Dr D. Adolfo Doering. 1882
Cape Horn Mission. *See* France : Ministère de la Marine, &c.

———

BOLIVIA.

Notizen über den Minenbetrieb in Bolivien un den brasilianischen Mittel-Provinzen Matto Grosso und Goyaz im Gegensatze zu dem im Westen der Union. 8° *Berlin* [1867]
Biblioteca Boliviana. Catálogo del archivo de Mojos y Chiquitos. 8°
Santiago de Chile, 1888
Colonizacion del Territorio de Otuquis en el Departamento de Santa Cruz. 8°
La Paz, 1890
Fronteras de Bolivia en el Departamento del Beni por Pedro Suarez S. 8°
Santa-Cruz, 1892

———

BRAZIL.

Observatory. Annales de l'Observatoire Impérial de Rio de Janeiro. Tome 1er Description de l'Observatoire. *Illustrations*. 4° *Rio de Janeiro*, 1882
—— The same. Publiées par L. Crules. Tome 2me Observations et Mémoires, 1882. *Plates*. 4° *Rio de Janeiro*, 1883
National Library. Guia da Exposição Permanente da Bibliotheca Nacional. 12° *Rio de Janeiro*, 1885
—— Catalogo da Exposição Permanente dos Cimelios da Bibliotheca Nacional, publicado sob a direcção do Bibliothecario João de Saldanha da Gama. *Plates*. 8° *Rio de Janeiro*, 1885
[*See also* United States : Bureau of the American Republics.]

BRAZIL.

Brasilianische Zustände und Aussichten in 1861. Mit Belegen nebst einem Vorschlag zur Aufhebung der Sklaverei und Entfernung der Schwarzen aus Nord-Amerika. Folio
Berlin, 1862
La Politique du Brésil, ou la fermeture des Fleuves sous prétexte de l'ouverture de l'Amazone. Traduit de l'Espagnol. *Map*. 8° *Paris*, 1867
The Empire of Brazil at the Paris International Exhibition of 1867. *Map*. 8° *Rio de Janeiro*, 1867
L'Empire du Brésil à l'Exposition Universelle de Vienne en 1873.
Rio de Janeiro, 1873
The Empire of Brazil at the Vienna Universal Exhibition of 1873.
Rio de Janeiro, 1873
L'Empire du Brésil à l'Exposition Universélle de 1876 à Philadelphie. *Maps*. 8° *Rio de Janeiro*, 1876
The Empire of Brazil at the Universal Exhibition of 1876 at Philadelphia. 8° *Rio de Janeiro*, 1876
Railway Reports. *See* Passos.
Impressões de uma Viagem do Pará do Recife. Passando Por S. Miguel E. Teneriffe, a Bordo da Corvetta "Tragano." Por A. A. C. Large 8° *Rio de Janeiro*, 1879
Bibliotheca Brasilica. Catalogue of an Extensive Collection of Ancient and Modern Books, relating to the Brazilian Empire, from its First Discovery in 1500 to the Present Time ; and to the neighbouring South American States. 8° 1879
Lettres Sur le Brésil. Réponse au *Times*. 8° *Paris*, 1881
Katalog der Brasilianischen Ausstellung des Centralvereins für Handelsgeographie und Förderung deutscher Interessen im Auslande. 8° *Berlin*, 1882

———

CHILE.

A. Government Publications.

Lei de Presupuestos de los Gastos Jenerales de la Administracion Pública para el año de 1855. Small folio
Santiago, 1854
Lei sobre la Organizacion i Atribuciones de las Municipalides. Small folio
Santiago, 1854
Memoria del Ministro de Estado en el Departamento de Hacienda, 1854. Small folio *Santiago*, 1854
Memoria del Interior. 1854. Small folio
Santiago, 1854
Memoria de Justicia, Culto e Instruccion Pública, 1854. Small folio
Santiago, 1854

CHILE—A.

Memoria de Relaciones Exteriores, 1854. Small folio *Santiago*, 1854

Cuenta de los Ingresos i Gastos que tuvo la República de Chile, en el año de 1853. Small folio *Santiago*, 1854

Sessiones del Congreso Nacional, 1854. Nos. 1, 2, 3. Small folio
Santiago, 1854

Estadística Comercial de la República de Chile del año 1854, 1858. 2 parts. Folio *Valparaiso*, 1854-59
—— The same, 1879.

Censo Jeneral de la República de Chile, levantado en Abril de 1854. Large oblong folio *Santiago*, 1858

Memoria que el Ministro de Estado en el Departamento de Marina presenta al Congreso Nacional de 1871. 8°
Santiago, 1871
—— The same, and Conclusion. 2 vols. 8° *Santiago*, 1872
—— The same, for 1873. *Plans.* 8°
Santiago, 1873

Ministerio del Interior. Recopilación de Leyes y Decretos de interés general vigentes en 21 de Mayo de 1888. 8°
Santiago, 1888

Documentos para la Historia de la Nautica en Chile. *Map.* 8° *Santiago*, 1889

Sesto Censo General de la Poblacion de Chile levantado el 26 de Noviembre de 1885. 2 vols. 4°
Valparaiso, 1889-90

Strait of Magellan. Relacion del Ultimo Viage al Estrecho de Magallanes de la Fragata de S.M. Santa Marí de la Cabeza, en los Años de 1785 y 1786; y Noticia de los Habitantes, Suelo, Clima, y Producciones del Estrecho. Appendice, que contiene el de los paquebotes "Santa Casilda" y "Santa Eulalia," para completar el Reconocimiento del Estrecho en 1788 y 1789. *Maps and portrait*
Madrid, 1788-93

Journey from Valparaiso to Santiago, across the Andes to Mendoza, to San Luis, and over the Pampas to Buenos Ayres, in January 1822 [in company with Lord H. Thynne]. MS.

Notice sur le Chile, par un Voyageur Français. 8° *Paris*, 1844

Description of the Country of Chili. MS. Folio N.D.

Nitrate and Guano Deposits in the Desert of Atacama : an Account of the Measures taken by the Government of Chile to facilitate the Development thereof. *Map.* 8° 1878

Chile and Peru. Narrative of the Events which led to the Declaration of War by Chili against Bolivia and Peru. Small 8° 1879

CHILE—A.

Patagonia, Western. Estudios Hydrograficos sobre la Patagonia Occidental ejecutados, por el Comandante i Oficiales de la Real corbeta Italiana "Caracciolo" en 1882. Traduccion de la Oficina Hydrografica. *Charts.* 8° *Santiago*, 1883

The Transandine Railway. *Map and illustrations.* 8° 1892

COLOMBIA.

Colombia : being a Geographical, Statistical, Agricultural, Commercial, and Political Account of that Country. *Map and portraits.* 2 vols. 8° 1822

The Present State of Colombia ; containing an Account of the Principal Events of its Revolutionary War, its Constitution, Mines, &c. By an Officer late in the Columbian Service. *Map.* 8° 1827

Noticia sobre la Geografia Política de Colombia. 18° *Caracas*, 1830

New Granada and Costa Rica. The Boundary Question carefully Examined and Defined from Authentic Documents. *Map.* 8° 1852

New Granada as a Field for Emigration. *Maps.* 8° 1859
—— The same. 2nd edition. *Map.* 8° 1860

Foreign Debt of New Granada : Report of the Special Committee appointed by the Bondholders at their Meeting on the 20th of March 1861. 8° [1861]

Catálogo de los objetos enviados por la Sociedad de Naturalistas Colombianos á la Exposicion del 20 de Julio de 1871. 8° *Bogota*, 1871

Esploracion Minera practicada en el Estado del Magdalena (Estados Unidos de Colombia) del 9 de Febrero al 21 de Abril de 1876. Con un apéndice sobre Minos situadas en los territorios nacionales de la nevada i Motilones. *Map.* 8° *Cartagena*, 1876

Descripcion Historia, Geografica, y Politica de la Republica de Colombia. 12° *Bogota*, 1887

Carthagena. An Account of the Expedition to Carthagena. Small 8° 1743
—— Original Papers relating to the Expedition to Carthagena. [Bound up with other papers.] *Map.* Small 8° 1744

Darien. Memoirs of Darien, giving a short Description of that Country, with an Account of the Attempts of the Company of Scotland to Settle a Colonie in that place. 12° *Glasgow*, 1715
—— The Isthmus of Darien in 1852. (*Colonial and Asiatic Review*, March 1853.) 8° 1853

COLOMBIA.

Panamá. Contract between the Republic of New Granada and the Panamá Railway Company. 8° *New York,* 1850

Panama Canal. The Nicaragua and Darien Ship-Canal Routes. (*Colonial and Asiatic Review*, March 1853.) 8° 1853

—— The Practicability and Importance of a Ship Canal to connect the Atlantic and Pacific Oceans; with a History of the Enterprise from its first Inception to the Completion of the Surveys. *Maps.* 8° *New York,* 1855

—— International Company of the Columbian Canal, founded in Paris, 9th of March 1864, for the purpose of Cutting a Ship Canal across the Columbian Isthmus, and Securing the Necessary Concession. *Map.* 8° *Privately printed, Paris,* 1867

—— Canal Interocéanique sans Écluses, ou Tunnels à travers le Territoire du Darien, entre les Golfes d'Uraba et de San Miguel (États-Unis de Colombie). *Maps.* 8° *Paris,* 1876

—— Inter-Oceanic Canal Projects, Discussions on. 8° [1880]

—— Le Canal de Panama: l'Action Panama valant quatre fois l'Action Suez. 4° [*Paris,* 1880]

—— The Isthmus of Panama Inter-Oceanic Canal. M. le Comte de Lesseps at Liverpool; with the Address of the Count, and the Speech of Captain Peacock, as to the Feasibility of Uniting the Atlantic with the Pacific Ocean, &c., &c. *Map.* 8° *Exeter,* 1880

—— The Water Supply of the Panama Canal; The Nicaraguan Canal Surveys; What the Slaven Dredges are doing at Panama; The Actual Status of the Panama Canal; More Light on the Panama Canal Question. [Cuttings from the *Engineering News*, June 16, 1888.] 4° 1888

San Martin. Informe de los Esploradores del Territorio de San Martin. 8° *Bogotá,* 1871

[*See also* Venezuela.]

————

ECUADOR.

Quito. Memoria sobre las Oscilaciones de la Brujula en Quito, consideradas en su relacion con los Temblores de Tierra y seguidas en su marcha paralela con las Fluctuaciones del Barometro; Añadese un breve resumen de los Principales Fenomenos que accompañaron al Terremoto del 16 de Agosto de 1868, &c. 8° *Quito,* 1868

Ecuador Land Company, Limited. [A Prospectus.] 8° [1861?]

ECUADOR.

Ecuador und die Ecuador-Land Compagnie. *Maps.* 8° *Mannheim,* 1862 [*See also* Venezuela.]

————

GUIANA, BRITISH.

Papers relative to the Affairs of British Guiana. [Parly. Rep.] *Map.* Folio 1840

Catalogue of Contributions transmitted from British Guiana to the Paris Universal Exhibition of 1867. *Map.* 8° 1867

Reports of the Geological Survey, taken from the *Colonist* newspaper, December 1869. 8° *Demerara,* 1870

Correspondence arising out of Complaints of Portuguese Residents in British Guiana. Folio 1871

Case for Including the Yuruari Valley within the Boundary of British Guiana. Folio [1887]

Latest Correspondence on the Question of Limits of Guiana. *Map.* 4° *Caracas,* 1887

Reports of the Government Agent of the N.W. District of British Guiana for 1890-91 and 1893-94. Folio *Georgetown,* 1891-94

————

GUIANA, DUTCH.

Aanteekeningen, betrekkelyk de Colonie Suriname. *Maps.* 8° *Arnhem,* 1826

Verzameling van Stukken aangaande de Surinaamsche Aangelegenheden, thans aanhangig bij de Tweede Kamer der Staten-Generaal. 1 and 2. 8° *The Hague,* 1845-46

————

PARAGUAY.

Description de la Provincia del Paraguay-Conquista. MS. Folio N.D.

La Guerra del Paraguay. 8° *Buenos Ayres,* 1867

The Republic of, its Constitution. 8° *Edinburgh,* 1871

A Note on its Position and Prospects. *Map.* 4° 1871

Guide de l'Immigrant au Paraguay. 12° *Asuncion,* 1889

————

PERU.

Peru-Bolivian Confederation. Pacto y Ley Fundamental de la Confederacion Perú-Boliviana. 24° 1837

Ministerio de Hacienda. Arancel de la Republica del Peru, que debe regir en los años de 1852 y 1853. Small folio *Lima,* 1852

PERU.

Memorias de los Vireyos que han gobernado el Perú durante el Tiempo del Coloniaje Espñaol. 6 vols. Imp. 4°
Lima, 1859
Vol. 1.   Juan de Mendoza y Luna, Francisco de Borja y Aragon, Baltasar de la Cueva, Melchor de Liñan y Cisneros.
Vol. 2.   Melchor de Navarra y Rocaful.
Vol. 3.   José Armendaris, J. A. de Mendoza.
Vol. 4.   Francisco Gil de Taboada y Lemos.
Vol. 5.   Teodoro de Croix.
Vol. 6.   José Antonio Manso de Velasco, Manuel Amat y Yunient.
Documentos encontradòs ultimamente en el Archivo Oficial de la Sub-prefectura de Moyobamba, que acreditan la posesion del Peru sobre los Territorios de Quijos y Canelos y que forman el complemento de los publicados anteriormente.   Folio   *Lima,* 1860
Reports to Admiralty, &c., relative to Guano deposits in Peru. [Parly. Rep.] Folio   1874
Report on the Guano deposits on the islands of Lobos de Tierra, Lobos de Afuera, Macabi, and Guanape. [Parly. Rep.] Folio   1874
Demarcacion politica del Peru : Edicion Oficial de la Direccion de Estadistica. Oblong 4°   *Lima,* 1874
Informe sobre las Minas de la Sociedad Carbonifera denominada " La Union," situados en el departamento de Ancachs. 12°   *Lima,* 1875
Coleccion de los Tratados del Peru.   8°
Lima, 1876
Lima. A True and Particular Relation of the Dreadful Earthquake which happened at Lima, the Capital of Peru, and the neighbouring Port of Callao, on the 28th October 1746 ; with a Description of Callao and Lima before their Destruction, and of the Kingdom of Peru in general, with its Inhabitants.   Translated from the Spanish, by a Gentleman who resided many years in those Countries.   *Maps and plates.* 8°   1848
Paucarpata.   An Exposé on the Treaty of Paucarpata, in Peru, and the Events connected with it.   8°   *Andover,* 1838
Compañia Anonima (limitada) " Huacas del Inca." 12°   *Lima,* 1887
The Amazon Provinces of Peru as a field for English Enterprise : Letter from Mr Charles H. Dolby-Tyler Iquitos.   An English Lady's Journey down the Amazon across the Andes to Peru.   12°   1890

URUGUAY.

Estadistica de Advana, año 1864.   Folio
Montevideo, 1866
Memoria de la Comision extraordinaria . . . 31 Marzo 1865-31—Deciembre 1866.   8°   *Montevideo,* 1867
De Republiek Oriental del Uruguay (Zuid Amerika) op de Amsterdamsche Tentoonstelling 1883.   La République Orientale de l'Uruguay à l'Exposition d'Amsterdam 1883.   8°   1883
The Republic of Uruguay.   The Country in the Paris Exhibition.   General Description and Statistical Data, 1888-89. *Maps, plans, and illustrations.*   4°
Liverpool, 1889
——— International Exhibition of Mining and Metallurgy, Crystal Palace, London, 1890 *Maps.* 8°   *London,* 1890
Rosario.   Breve Noticia y documentos relativos a la Colonia Agricola del Rosario Oriental, &c.   *Map.*   8°
Montevideo [1859]

VENEZUELA.

Exposicion que dirige al Congreso de Venezuela en 1841, el Secretario de Guerra y Marina.   Royal 8°
Caracas, 1841
Exposicion que dirige al Congreso en 1833, 1841, and 1843, el Secretario de Hacienda. *Tables.*   Royal 8°   *Caracas,* 1833-43
Memoria que presente a la Legislatura de 1847 el Ministro de Relaciones Exteriores del Gobierno de Venezuela.   Royal 8°
Caracas, 1847
A Descriptive Catalogue of the Venezuela Department at the Philadelphia International Exhibition, 1876.   Compiled by Dr Adolphus Ernst.   12°
Philadelphia, 1876
Tropical Information : a Treatise on the History, Climate, Soil, Productions, &c., of Venezuela ; with like Notices of New Granada and Ecuador, and a slight glance at Bolivia and Peru.   12°   1846
The Emigrant's Vade-Mecum, or Guide to the " Price Grant " in Venezuelan Guayana.   8°   1868
The London Venezuelan Guyana Mutual Emigration Society.   Prospectus, with Code of Laws, &c., in the Settlement and Colony of Pattisonville.   12° [1869]
Notice Politique, Statistique, Commerciale, &c., sur les États-Unis du Vénézuéla, contenant les renseignements les plus utiles et les plus précis sur ce pays.   En Français, Anglais, Espagnol, Allemand, et Italien.   *Map.*   12°   *Paris,* 1889

ASIA.

GENERAL.

Jesuits. Lettere dell' India Orientale, scritte da' Reurendi Padri della Compagnia di Giesù.   12°   *Venice*, 1580
Travels of several Learned Missioners of the Society of Jesus into divers parts of the Archipelago, India, China, and America. Containing a General Description of the Most Remarkable Towns, with a particular Account of the Customs, Manners, and Religion of those several Nations, interspersed with Philosophical Observations, and other curious Remarks. Translated from the French. *Plates.* 8°   1714
Biblical Geography. Observations on divers passages of Scripture . . . grounded on Circumstances incidentally mentioned in Books of Voyages and Travels into the East.   8°   1764
Eastern Nations. Dictionary of the Religious Ceremonies of the Eastern Nations, with Historical and Critical Observations, some Account of their Learned Men and most Remarkable Places in Asia; to which is added a Medical Vocabulary. 4°   *Calcutta*, 1787
Oriental Languages. Miscellaneous Translations from Oriental Languages. Vol. 1.   8°   1831
  1. Notes of a Journey into the Interior of Northern Africa. By Hadji Ebned-din El Eghwhati; translated from the Arabic by W. B. Hodgson.
  2. Extracts from the Sakaa Thevan Saasteram, or Book of Fate. Translated from the Tamul by Rev. Jos. Roberts.
  3. The Last Days of Krishna and the Sons of Pandu. Translated from the Persian of Neikkeib Khan by Major David Price.
  4. The Vedala Cadai. Translated by B. G. Babington.
  5. Indian Cookery. Translated by Sandford Arnot.
List of Russian Travellers in Asia, 1854-74. [In Russian and French.]. Single sheet
                                      ? 1874
Rough Notes of Journeys made in the years 1868, 1869, 1870, 1871, 1872, and 1873, in Syria, down the Tigris, India, Kashmir, Ceylon, Japan, Mongolia, Siberia, the United States, the Sandwich Islands, and Australasia.   8°   1875

GENERAL.

Report on the Geodetical and Topographical Explorations of Russians in Asia, in 1888. [In Russian.] (From *Russian Invalide.*)   8°   1889
Geography of Asia. [*Proof.*]   2 parts. *Incomplete*   N.D.
Eastern Asia. Die Preussische Expedition nach Ost-Asien. Nach amtlichen Quellen.   7 vols. *Maps and plates.* Small 4°   *Berlin*, 1864-73
  Botanischer Theil. Die Tange, von Georg v. Martens.   1866
  Zoologischer Theil. I. Allgemeines und Wirbelthiere, von Eduard v. Martens.   1876
  —— II. Die Landschnecken, von Eduard v. Martens.   1867

ARABIA.

Moka. Notes Instructives sur le Commerce de Moka en 1787. MS. 4°.
Arabic Grammar, compiled for the use of Travellers.   8°   *Bombay*, 1834

CENTRAL ASIA.
[*See also* Russia in Asia.]
A. Official Publications.

Central Asia. Part 1. A Contribution towards the better Knowledge of the Topography, Ethnography, Statistics, and History of the North-West Frontier of British India. Compiled (for Military and Political Reference) by Lieut.-Col. C. M. MacGregor.   3 vols.   8°
                                      Calcutta, 1873
—— Part 3. A Contribution towards the better Knowledge of the Topography, Ethnology, Resources, and History of Belochistan. Compiled (for Political and Military Reference) by Capt. W. S. A. Lockhart.   8°   *Calcutta*, 1875
—— Part 4. A Contribution towards the better Knowledge of the Topography, Ethnology, Resources, and History of Persia. Compiled (. . .) by Lieut.-Col. C. M. MacGregor. [*Without map*]
                                      Calcutta, 1871
—— Part 5. A Contribution towards the better Knowledge of the History, Ethnography, Topography, and Resources of Part of Asiatic Turkey and Caucasia. Compiled by Lieut.-Col. C. M. MacGregor.   8°   *Calcutta*, 1872

Central Asia. Part 6, Section 1. A Contribution towards the better Knowledge of the Topography, Ethnography, Resources, and History of the Khanat of Khiva. Compiled (. . .) by Capt. H. Collett. *Maps.* 8° *Calcutta,* 1873

—— Part 6, Section 2. A Contribution towards the better Knowledge of the Topography, &c., of the Khanat of Bokhara. Compiled (. . .) by Capt. John Moubray Trotter. 8° *Calcutta,* 1873

—— Part 7, Section 1. A Gazetteer of Kashmir and the adjacent Districts of Kishtwár, Badrawár, Jamú, Naoshera, Púnch, and the Valley of the Kishen Ganga. Compiled (. . .) by Charles Ellison Bates. *Maps.* 8° *Calcutta,* 1873

—— Part 7, Section 2. A Contribution towards the better Knowledge of the Topography, Ethnology, Resources, and History of Ladak. Compiled (. . .) by Lieut. F. Maisey. 8° *Calcutta,* 1878

Correspondence with Russia respecting Central Asia. Folio 1873

Russian Advances in Asia. (Continuation No. 2.) *Maps.* Folio.

Papers relating to Central Asia and Quetta. Folio 1879

Further Correspondence respecting Affairs in Central Asia, 1879. Folio 1880

Foreign Office Reports. No. 1 (1882). Correspondence respecting the Affairs of Central Asia. *Map.* Folio 1882

—— No. 1 (1885). Telegram from Lieut.-General Sir Peter Lumsden relative to the Fight between the Russians and Afghans at Ak Tépé. Folio 1885

—— No. 2 (1885). Further Correspondence respecting Central Asia. Folio 1885

—— No. 3 (1885). Maps to accompany "Central Asia" Nos. 2 and 4 (1885).

—— No. 4 (1885). Further Correspondence respecting Central Asia. *Maps.* Folio 1889

—— No. 5 (1885). Further Correspondence respecting the Affairs of Central Asia. Folio 1885

—— No. 1 (1887). Correspondence respecting the Affairs of Central Asia. *Maps.* Folio 1887

—— No. 2 (1887). Further Correspondence respecting the Affairs of Central Asia. *Maps.* Folio 1887

—— No. 1 (1888). Further Correspondence respecting the Affairs in Central Asia. *Map.* Folio 1888

—— No. 2 (1888). Further Correspondence respecting the Affairs of Central Asia. *Map.* Folio 1888

Delimitation Afghane. Négociations entre la Russie et la Grande Bretagne 1872-1885. Edition du Ministère des Affaires étrangères. (With a Memoir in Russian by M. Venukoff.) *Maps.* 4° *St Petersburg,* 1886

B. Miscellaneous and Anonymous.

Recueil d'Itinéraires et de Voyages dans l'Asie Centrale et l'extrême Orient. ["Publications de l'École des Langues Orient. Viv., vii."] *Map.* 8° *Paris,* 1878

CONTENTS.

Journal d'une Mission en Corée.
Mémoires d'un Voyageur Chinois dans l'Empire d' Annam.
Itinéraires de l'Asie Centrale.
Itinéraire de la Valée du Moyen Zerefchan.
Itinéraires de Pichaver à Kaboul, de Kaboul à Qandahar, et de Qandahar à Hérat.

From Orsk to Khiva and back. Journey performed in 1740 by Gladishef and Muravief. *Resumé* by R. Michell. *Map.* Folio N.D.

Central Asia and British India. By a British Subject. 8° 1865

The Central Asian Question, from an Eastern Stand-point. 8° 1869

Russia's Commercial Mission in Central Asia. [A translation of a Pamphlet on that subject by Christian von Sarauw, Captain in the Danish Army, Leipzig, 1871.] Large 8° *Simla,* 1872

A Journey in Khorassan and Central Asia, March and April 1890. *Map.* 12° 1890

CEYLON.

Ceylon. Report of Lieut.-Col. Colebrook upon the Administration of the Government of Ceylon, 24th Dec. 1831, with *map.* Report of the same upon the Revenues of Ceylon, 31st Jan. 1832. Report of Charles Hay Cameron upon the Judicial Establishments and Procedure in Ceylon, 31st Jan. 1832. [Parly. Rep.] Folio 1832

—— Correspondence relating to the Deepening of the Paumben Channel; Further do., and Further Report respecting the Paumben Ship Canal. [Parly. Rep.] *Map.* Folio 1872-73

—— Correspondence respecting the Improvement of Colombo Harbour. *Map.* [Parly. Rep.] Folio 1874

—— Census of Ceylon, 1891 . . . Compiled by Lionel Lee. 3 vols. *Map.* Folio *Colombo,* 1892

CHINESE EMPIRE.

A. Government Publications.

Memorials, &c., on the Subject of Opening up a Direct Commerce with the West of China from the Port of Rangoon. [Parly. Rep.] Folio 1864

Report upon the Feasibility and most effectual means of introducing Railway Communication into the Empire of China. By Sir Macdonald Stephenson. *Map.* Folio 1864

Correspondence respecting the Woosung Bar near Shanghae. [Parly. Rep.] Folio 1874

Reports on Trade at the Treaty Ports in China for the years 1871, '72, '73, '76, '77. 4° *Shanghai,* 1874-78

Commercial Reports by Her Majesty's Consuls in China, 1877. *Map.* 8° 1878

—— The same, 1877-78. 8° 1879

China. No. 1 (1883). Despatch from Her Majesty's Chargé d'Affaires at Peking, forwarding a Report by Mr A. Hosie, Student Interpreter in the China Consular Service, of a Journey through the Provinces of Kueichow and Yünnan. Folio 1883

—— No. 3 (1885). Report by Mr L. C. Hopkins, on the Island of Formosa, dated 12th October 1884. *Map.* 8° 1885

—— No. 1 (1886). Correspondence respecting the French Treaty with Annam, and Negotiations between France and China. Folio 1886

—— No. 3 (1886). Agreement between the Governments of Great Britain and China for the Settlement of the Yünnan Case, Official Intercourse, and Trade between the two Countries; Signed in the English and Chinese Languages, at Chefoo, 13th September 1876. With an Additional Article thereto for Regulating the Traffic in Opium; Signed in London, 18th July 1885. Folio 1886

—— No. 2 (1887). Despatch from Her Majesty's Minister at Peking, forwarding a Report by Mr H. E. Fulford, Student Interpreter in the China Consular Service, of a Journey in Manchuria. *Map.* Folio 1887

—— No. 1 (1888). Report by Mr F. S. A. Bourne, of a Journey in South-Western China. *Maps.* Folio 1888

Imperial Maritime Customs :—

1. *Statistical Series—*

Nos. 3 and 4. Returns of Trade at the Treaty Ports, and Trade Reports, for years 1884, 1885. *Diagrams.* 4° *Shanghai,* 1885-86

—— The same, for the years 1887-93, each year in 2 parts. *Maps and diagrams.* 4° *Shanghai,* 1888-94

CHINESE EMPIRE—A.

Imperial Maritime Customs :—

2. *Special Series—*

No. 3. Silk. *Illustrations.* 4° *Shanghai,* 1881

No. 9. Native Opium, 1887. With an Appendix : Native Opium, 1863. 4° *Shanghai,* 1888

No. 10. Opium : Crude and Prepared. 4° *Shanghai,* 1888

No. 17. Ichang to Chungking, 1890 *Shanghai,* 1892

3. *Miscellaneous Series—*

No. 5. Catalogue spécial de la Collection Exposée au Palais du Champ de Mars. Exposition Universelle, Paris, 1878. 4° *Shanghai,* 1878

No. 6. List of the Chinese Lighthouses, Light - Vessels, Buoys, and Beacons, for the years 1881-93. *Charts and diagrams.* 4° *Shanghai,* 1881-93

Formosa. Correspondence respecting the Settlement of the Difficulty between China and Japan in regard to the Island of Formosa. [Parly. Rep.] Folio 1875

Yarkand Mission. Progress and Route Report. Folio 1873

Yunnan and Western China. *See* Burma ; *also* Indo-China.

B. Miscellaneous and Anonymous.

Mémoires concernant l'Histoire, les Sciences, les Arts, les Mœurs, les Usages, &c., des Chinois, par les Missionaries de Pekin. *Portrait.* 4° *Paris,* 1776

Description of the Empire of China. [In the Chinese character.] *Maps.* 8°

Hints for Collecting Information, compiled for the Expedition to China. *Plate.* 8° *Calcutta,* 1840

Chinese Topography, being an Alphabetical List of the Provinces, Departments, and Districts in the Chinese Empire, with their Latitudes and Longitudes. 8° *Canton,* 1844

—— The same, interleaved with MS. Additions. 8° *Canton,* 1844

A Glance at the Interior of, obtained during a Journey through the Silk and Green Tea Districts, 1845. [No. 1 of the *Chinese Miscellany*]. *Maps and plans.* Small 8° *Shanghai,* 1849

Relation de l'Expédition de Chine en 1860. 4° *Paris,* 1862

China in 1863. [In Chinese.] 2 vols. *Woodcuts.* 8°

Topography of China and Neighbouring States ; with Degrees of Longitude and Latitude. 8° *Hongkong,* 1864

CHINESE EMPIRE—B.

Statistics of Trade at the Ports of Newchang, Tientsin, Cheefoo, Hankow, Kiukiang, Chinkiang, Shanghai, Ningpo, Foochow, Tamsu (Formosa), Takow (Formosa), Amoy, Swatow, and Canton, for the period 1863-72. Compiled for the Austro-Hungarian Exhibition, &c. 14 vols. 4° *Shanghai*, 1873

Port Catalogues of the Chinese Customs Collection at the Austro-Hungarian Universal Exhibition, Vienna, 1873, to illustrate the International Exchange of Products. 4° *Shanghai*, 1873

Sosnovsky Expedition. Catalogue of Photographs, Models, Pictures, and Articles of Commercial and Industrial Use brought from China by the Russian Scientific-Commercial Expedition. [In Russian.] 3 parts in 2. 8° *St Petersburg*, 1876

The Colquhoun and Wahab Expedition through Southern China into Burma. Opinions of the Press. 12° 1882

Formosa and the Gospel. 8° N.P., N.D.

Macao *See* Portuguese Asia.

Mongolia. Voyages de Bruxelles en Mongolie et Travaux des Missionnaires de la Congrégation de Scheutveld (lez Bruxelles). 2 vols. *Maps and illustrations.* 8° *Brussels*, 1873-77

Peking. Descriptive Notes on Peking, written to accompany a large Map of that City, compiled from Native Authorities. 4° *Shanghai*, 1866

Shanghae, General Description of, and its Environs. [No. 4 of the *Chinese Miscellany.*] *Maps.* Small 8° *Shanghai*, 1850

Yangtsze (Upper). Report of the Delegates of the Shanghai General Chamber of Commerce on the Trade of the Upper Yangtsze, and Report of the Naval Surveyors on the River above Hankow. *Map.* Folio *Shanghai*, 1869

CYPRUS.

Reports made to the Admiralty on the Anchorages, &c., of the Island of Cyprus. *Maps and plan.* Folio 1879

Report by Her Majesty's High Commissioner for the year 1879. 8° 1880

Census of Cyprus, 1881. Report on the Census of Cyprus, 1881 ; with Appendix by Frederick W. Barry, M.D., Sc.D. Folio 1884

DUTCH EAST INDIES.

Dutch E. I. Co. Ambassades de la Compagnie Hollandoise des Indes d'Orient, vers l'Empereur du Japon, divisées en trois parties ; ornées de figures en taille douce ; avec une relation exacte des guerres civiles de ce pays là. 12° *Paris*, 1722

DUTCH EAST INDIES.

Dutch E. I. Co. Staat der generale Nederlandsche Oost-Indische Compagnie. 8° *Amsterdam*, 1722

—— *See also* Renneville : Appendix 1.

Handleiding tot de Aardrijkskunde van Nederlands Oost-Indische Bezittingen. Vitgegeven door Maatschappij. *Map.* 8° *Leyden, Deventer, & Groningen*, 1843

Aardrijkskundig en Statistisch Woordenboek van Nederlandsch Indië, bewerkt naar de jongste en beste Berigten. Met eene Voorrede van Prof. P. J. Veth. 3 vols. 8° *Amsterdam*, 1869

Catalogue de livres sur les possessions Néerlandaises aux Indes, avec des divisions sur les Indes Anglaises, la Chine et le Japon, Siam, la Perse, Siberie, l'Afrique, spèciallement la côte de Guinée et le Cap de Bonne Esperance, Surinam, Guana, et l'Australie. A la fin un Atlas. 8° *Amsterdam*, 1882

Bibliotheca Neerlando-Indica. Catalogue de livres et de quelques manuscrits concernant les Indes-Occidentales Néerlandaises, l'Empire Indo-Brittannique, l'Inde Française, les îles Philippines, la Chine, le Japon, et l'Australie, en ordre systematique, et avec quelques notes bibliographique. 8° *The Hague*, 1883

Bijdrajen tot de Taal- Land- en Volkenkunde van Nederlandsch-Indië. Uitgegeven vanwege het Koninklijk Instituut voor de Taal- Land- en Volkenkunde van Nederlandsch-Indië ter gelegenheid van het yesde Internationale Congres der Orientalisten te Leiden. Land- en Volkenkunde. *Maps.* 8° *The Hague*, 1883

—— Ditto. Taal- en Letterkunde. *Plate.* 8° *The Hague*, 1883

Report. Holland, East Indies, Colonial Possessions, 1887. *Maps and plans.* Folio.

Handboek voor Cultuuren Handels ondernemingen in Nederlandsch-Indië. Erste jaargang. 8° *Amsterdam*, 1888

Achin. Correspondence relative to Relations between Great Britain and Achin. [Parly. Rep.] Folio 1873

Batavia. Realia. Register op de Generale Resolutiën van het Kasteel Batavia, 1632-1805. Uitgegeven door het Bataviaasch Genootschap van Kunsten en Wetenschappen. 3 vols. 4° *The Hague and Batavia*, 1886

Deli. De Tabakscultuur in Deli. *Plates.* 4° *Amsterdam*, 1890

Java. Reglement voor de Schutterijen op Java. 8° [1838]

—— Zeilaanwijzingen van Java naar het Kanaal. Uitgegeven door het Koninklijk Nederlandsch Meteorologisch Instituut. 2 Deel. Folio and 4° *Utrecht*, 1868-70

DUTCH EAST INDIES.

Kei Islands. Verslag van het Vooige vallene in zake de ontworpen Expeditie naar de Kei-eilanden en van de voorberei dende Maatregelen, te dien spyichte genomen. Voorstellen van hit Huishondelijk Bestnur. 8°   [1887]

Krakatao. Les Premières Nouvelles concernant l'Eruption du Krakatau en 1883 dans les Journaux de l'Insulinde. Large 8°   *Paris*, 1884

Neiuw Guinea, Ethnographisch en Natuurkundig onderzocht en Beschreven in 1858 door een Nederlandsch Indische commissie; uitgegeven door het Koninklijk Institut voor taal- land- en volkenkunde van Nederlandsch Indië. *Plates.* 8°, and Atlas small 4° *Amsterdam*, 1862

Palembang. De Heldhaftige Bevreding van Palembang, het aldaar sints 1810 voorafgebeurde, wederlegging van Raffles en Court, en voorloopige korte beschrijving van Palembang, Banca, enz. *Maps.* 8°   *Rotterdam*, 1822

Torres Strait. Naam der Straat tusschen Nieuw-Holland en Nieuw-Guinea. 8°
N.D.

FRENCH INDO-CHINA.

Tonkin. Rapports adressés à M. le Ministre de la Marine et des Colonies par M. le Résident Général a Hué sur la Situation Agricole industrielle et commerciale au Tonkin. [2 pamphlets.] 4°
[1885]

HONG-KONG.

A Letter from Hong-Kong, descriptive of that Colony. By a Resident. 8° 1845

Directions for Making the Passage from England to Hong-Kong through Sunda Strait. Compiled from Various Authorities. 8°   1857

Hong-Kong Observatory. *See* Doberck.

INDIAN EMPIRE.

A. Archæological Survey.

Archæological Survey of India. 6 vols. *Plates, maps.* 8°
Simla and Calcutta, 1871-78

Vols. 1 and 2. Four Reports made during 1862, -63, -64, and -65, by Alexander Cunningham.

Vols. 3 and 4. Report for 1871-72, by A. Cunningham.

Delhi, by J. B. Beglar.

Agra, by A. C. L. Carlleyle.

INDIAN EMPIRE—A.

Vol. 5. Report for 1872-73, by A. Cunningham.

Vol. 6. Report of a Tour in Eastern Rajputana in 1871-72 and 1872-73, by A. C. L. Carlleyle.

—— The same. Vol. 23. Report of a Tour in the Punjâb and Râjpûtâna in 1883-84, by Mr H. B. W. Garrick. *Map and plates.* 8°   *Calcutta*, 1887

—— General Index to the Reports of the. Volumes 1 to 23, with a Glossary and General Table of Contents by V. A. Smith. 8°   *Calcutta*, 1887

Southern India. Archæological Survey of Southern India. Vol. 4. Tamil and Sanskrit Inscriptions, with some Notes on Village Antiquities collected chiefly in the South of the Madras Presidency. By Jas. Burgess, C.I.E., &c.; with Translations by S. M. Nātēsa Sastrī Pandit. 4°   *Madras*, 1886

—— The same. [Vol. 1.] The Buddhist Stupas of Amaravati and Jaggayyapeta in the Krishna District, Madras Presidency, Surveyed in 1882 by Jas. Burgess, LL.D.; with Translations of the Asoka Inscriptions at Jangada and Dhauli, by Georg Bühler, Ph.D. *Map, plates, and woodcuts.* 4°   1887

Archæological Survey of India. New Series. Vol. 1. The Shargi Architecture of Jaunpur; with Notes on Zafarabad, Sahet-Mahet, and other places in the North-Western Provinces and Oudh. By A. Führer, Ph.D. With Drawings and Architectural Descriptions by Ed. W. Smith. Edited by Jas. Burgess, LL.D. 4°   *Calcutta*, 1889

—— The same. Vol. 2 (North - West Provinces and Oudh. Vol. 2). The Monumental Antiquities and Inscriptions in the N.W. Prov. and Oudh. By A. Führer. 4°   *Allahabad*, 1891

—— The same. Vol. 3 (Southern India. Vol. 2). South - Indian Inscriptions, Tamil and Sanskrit, from Stone and Copperplate Edicts at Mamallapuram, Kanchipuram, in the North Arcot District, and other parts of the Madras Presidency, chiefly collected in 1886-87. Edited and translated by E. Hultzsch, Ph.D. Vol. 1. 4°   *Madras*, 1890

—— The same. [Vol. 4.—South India, Vol. 3.] South Indian Inscriptions. Vols. 2, Parts 1 and 2. Tamil Inscriptions of Rajaraja, Rajendra-Chola and others in the Rajarajesvara Temple at Tanjavur. Edited and Translated by E. Hultzsch. *Plates.* 4° *Madras*, 1891-92

INDIAN EMPIRE—A.

Epigraphia Indica, and Record of the Archæological Survey of India. Edited by Jas. Burgess, LL.D. Parts i.-xvi. (Vols. 1 and 2). *Plates.* 4°
Calcutta, 1888-94

Western India. Archæological Survey of Western India. 5 vols. *Plates, photographs.* 4° 1874-83

Vol. 1. Report of the First Season's Operations in the Belgâm and Kaladgi Districts, January to May 1874.

Vol. 2. Report on the Antiquities of Kâthiâwâd and Kachh, being the Result of the Second Season's Operations, 1874-75.

Vol. 3. Report on the Antiquities in the Bidar and Aurungabad Districts, in the Territories of his Highness the Nizam of Haidarabad, being the Result of the Third Season's Operations, 1875-76.

Vol. 4. Report on the Buddhist Cave Temples and their Inscriptions, being part of the Results of the Fourth, Fifth, and Sixth Seasons' Operations of the Archæological Survey of Western India, 1876-77, 1877-78, 1878-79; supplementary to the Volume on the Cave Temples of India. By Jas. Burgess. *Plates and woodcuts.* 4° 1883

Vol. 5. Report on the Elura Cave Temples and the Brahmanical and Jaina Caves in Western India, completing the Results of the Fifth, Sixth, and Seventh Seasons' Operations of the Archæological Survey, 1877-78, 1878-79, 1879-80; supplementary to the Volume on the Cave Temples of India. By Jas. Burgess. *Plates and woodcuts.* 4° 1883

—— The same. No. 11. Lists of the Antiquarian Remains in the Bombay Presidency; with an Appendix of Inscriptions from Gujarat, compiled from information supplied by the Revenue, Educational, and other Government Officers. By Jas. Burgess. *Plates.* 4° *Bombay,* 1885

—— The same. No. 12. The Caves at Nadsur and Karsambla. By H. Cousens. *Plates.* 4° *Bombay,* 1891 [*See also* Dr J. Burgess.]

B. Census Reports.

Census of 1881. 3 vols. *Diagrams.* Folio *London and Calcutta,* 1883

Census of India, 1891.

General Report. By J. A. Baines. Folio *London,* 1893

INDIAN EMPIRE—B.

General Tables. 2 vols. Folio
London, 1892-93

Provincial Reports and Tables.
Shillong, Calcutta, &c. &c., 1892-94
Vols. 1, 2. Assam. By E. A. Gait.
Vols. 3, 4, 5. Lower Provinces of Bengal, &c. By C. J. O'Donnell. (*See below.*)
Vol. 6. Berar. By W. Hastings.
Vols. 7, 8. Bombay. By W. W. Drew.
Vols. 9, 10. Burma. By H. L. Eales.
Vols. 11, 12. Central Provinces, &c. By B. Robertson.
Vols. 13, 14, 15. Madras. By H. A. Stuart.
Vols. 16, 17, 18. N.-W. Provinces and Oudh. By D. C. Baillie.
Vols. 19, 20, 21. Punjab, &c. By E. D. Maclagan.
Vol. 27. Central India. By R. H. Gunion.
—— Assam. Provincial Tables 1892
—— Lower Provinces of Bengal. Provincial Tables 1893
—— Districts of Ajmere - Merwara. By B. Egerton 1893
—— Coorg. By H. A. Stuart 1893
—— Report on the Census of Calcutta. By H. F. J. T. Maguire. Folio
Calcutta, 1891

C. Geological Survey, &c.

Memoirs of the Geological Survey of India. 23 vols. *Maps and plates.* Royal 8° *Calcutta,* 1859-91

VOLUME 1.

On the Coal and Iron of Cuttack—Structure and Relations of the Tálchir Coal-field—Gold Deposits in Upper Assam—Gold and Gold-dust from Shue-Gween—Geology of the Khasi Hills—The Nilghiri Hills—Geology of Bankoorah, Midnapore, and Orissa — Laterite of Orissa—Fossil Teeth of Ceratodus. 1859

VOLUME 2.

Report on the Vindhyan Rocks and their Associates in Bundelkand—Geological Structure of the Central Portion of the Nerbudda District—Tertiary and Alluvial Deposits of the Nerbudda Valley—Geological Relations and Probable Geological Age of the Several Groups of Rocks in Central India and Bengal. 1859

VOLUME 3.

Report on the Ranigunj Coal-field—Additional Remarks on the Geological Age of Indian Rock Systems—On the Sub-Himalayan Ranges between the Ganges and Sutlej. 1863-64

INDIAN EMPIRE—C.
Palæontologia Indica—*continued.*
VOLUME 2.
The Gastropoda, by F. Stoliczka, 1867-68.
VOLUME 3.
The Pelecypoda; with a Review of all known genera of this Class, fossil and recent, by F. Stoliczka, 1870-71.
VOLUME 4.
The Brachiopoda, Ciliopoda, Echinodermata, Anthozoa, Spongozoa, Foraminifera, Arthrozoa, and Spondylozoa, by F. Stoliczka, 1872-73.
SERIES 2, 11, 12: THE FOSSIL FLORA OF THE GONDWANA SYSTEM.
VOLUME 1.
Part 1. The Fossil Flora of the Rájmáhal Series, Rájmáhal Hills, Bengal, by T. Oldham and J. Morris, 1863. Part 2. Jurasssic (Liassic) Flora of do., by Ottokar Feistmantel, 1877. Part 3. Do. from Golapilli (near Ellore), South Godaveri district, by O. Feistmantel, 1877. Part 4. Outliers on the Madras Coast, by O. Feistmantel, 1879.
VOLUME 2.
Part 1. Jurassic (Oolitic) Flora of Kach, by O. Feistmantel, 1876. Part 2. Flora of the Jabalpur Group, in the Son-Narbada Region, by O. Feistmantel, 1878.
VOLUME 3.
Part 1. Lower Gondwanas, by Ottokar-Feistmantel, 1879; and Supplement (1881), The Flora of the Talchirr Kaharbari Beds. Part 2 (1880). The Flora of the Damuda-Panchet Divisions (first half). Part 3 (1881). The same (conclusion).
VOLUME 4.
Part 1 (1882). The Fossil Flora of the South Rewah Gondwana Basin, by O. Feistmantel. Part 2 (1886). The Fossil Flora of some of the Coalfields in Western Bengal, by O. Feistmantel.
SERIES 9: JURASSIC FAUNA OF KACH.
VOLUME 1.
The Cephalopoda, by W. Waagen, 1873-76.
VOLUME 2.
Part 1 (1893). The Echinoidea of Cutch. By J. W. Gregory.
SERIES 4: INDIAN PRETERTIARY VERTEBRATA.
VOLUME 1.
Part 1. On Vertebrate Fossils from the Panchet Rocks, near Ranigunj, Bengal, by T. H. Huxley, 1865. Part 2. On some Remains of Ganoid Fishes from the Deccan, by Sir Philip de M. Grey

2 U

INDIAN EMPIRE—C.
Palæontologia Indica—*continued.*
Egerton, Bart.; On the Genus Ceratodus, with Special Reference to the Fossil Teeth found at Maledi, Central India, by L. C. Miall; On the Stratigraphy and Homotaxis of the Kota-Maledi Deposits, by W. T. Blanford, 1878. Part 3. Fossil Reptilia and Batrachia, by R. Lydekker, 1879. Part 5. The Reptilia and Amphibia of the Maleri and Denwa Groups, by R. Lydekker, 1885.
SERIES 10: INDIAN TERTIARY AND POST-TERTIARY VERTEBRATA.
VOLUME 1.
Part 1. Rhinoceros Deccanensis, by R. B. Foote, 1874. Part 2. Molar Teeth and other Remains of Mammalia, by R. Lydekker, 1877. Parts 3 and 4. Crania of Ruminants, by R. Lydekker, 1878-80. Part 5. Siwalik and Narbada Proboscidia, by R. Lydekker, 1880.
VOLUME 2.
Part 1. Siwalik Rhinocerotidæ, by R. Lydekker, 1881. Part 2. Supplement to Proboscidia, by R. Lydekker, 1881. Part 3. Siwalik and Narbada Equidæ, by R Lydekker, 1882. Part 4. Siwalik Camelopardalidæ, by R. Lydekker, 1882. Part 5. Siwalik Selenodont Suina, by R. Lydekker, 1883. Part 6. Siwalik and Narbada Carnivora, by R. Lydekker, 1884.
VOLUME 3.
Part 1. Additional Siwalik Perissodactyla and Proboscidea, by R. Lydekker, 1884. Part 2. Siwalik and Narbada Bunodont Suina, by R. Lydekker, 1884. Part 3. Rodents, Ruminants, and Synopsis of Mammalia, by R. Lydekker, 1884. Part 4. Siwalik Birds, by R. Lydekker, 1884. Part 5. Mastodon Teeth from Perim Island, by R. Lydekker, 1884. Part 6. Siwalik and Narbada Chelonia, by R. Lydekker, 1885. Part 7. Siwalik Crocodilia, Lacertilia, and Ophidia, by R. Lydekker, 1886. Part 8. Tertiary Fishes, by R. Lydekker, 1886.
VOLUME 4.
Part 1. Siwalik Mammalia; Supplement 1, by R. Lydekker, 1886. Part 2. The Fauna of the Karnul Caves (and Addendum to Part 1), by R. Lydekker, 1886. Part 3. Eocene Chelonia from Salt-Range, by R. Lydekker, 1887.
SERIES 7, 14: TERTIARY AND UPPER CRETACEOUS FAUNA OF WESTERN INDIA.
VOLUME 1.
Part 1. On some Tertiary Crabs from Sind and Kutch, by F. Stoliczka, 1871. Part 2 [in error, 1]. Sind Fossil Corals and Alcyonaria, by P. Martin Duncan,

INDIAN EMPIRE—C.

Palæontologia Indica—*continued.*
1880. Part 3. Fossil Echinoidea of West-
ern Sind and the Coast of Biluchestan
and of the Persian Gulf, from the Tertiary
Formations, by P. Martin Duncan and
W. Percy Sladen, 1882-86. Part 4. The
Fossil Echinoidea of Kachh and Katty-
war, by P. Martin Duncan and W. Percy
Sladen, with an Introduction by W. T.
Blanford, 1883.

SERIES 13 : SALT-RANGE FOSSILS.

VOLUME 1.
Productus-Limestone Group. By W.
Waagen. Part 1. Pisces—Cephalopoda,
1879. Part 2. Supplement to do. and
Gastropoda, 1880. Part 3. Pelecypoda,
1881. Part 4. Brachiopoda (fas. 1, 2, 5),
1885. Part 5. Bryozoa—Annelida—
Echinodermata, 1885. Part 6. Cœlen-
terata, 1886. Part 7. Cœlenterata—
Amorphozoa—Protozoa, 1887.

VOLUME 4.
Parts 1 and 2. Geological Results, by
W. Waagen, 1889-91.

INDEX.
Index to the Genera and Species
described in the Palæontologia Indica up
to the year 1891. By W. Theobald. 4°
                                Calcutta, 1892

Geological Papers on Western India,
including Cutch, Scinde, and the South-
East Coast of Arabia ; with a Summary
of the Geology of India generally. Edited
by H. J. Carter. *Maps and plates.*
Royal 8°   *Bombay*, 1857
CONTENTS.
Malcolmson, John G. On the Fossils
of the Eastern Portion of the Great
Basaltic District of India.
Voysey, Dr. Extracts from the Private
Journal of, on the Survey in Southern
and Central India, from Secunderabad to
Beeder.
Newbold, Capt. Notes, chiefly Geo-
logical, across the Peninsula, from
Masulipatam to Goa, comprising Re-
marks on the Origin of the Regur and
Laterite, &c.
Voysey, H. W. On some Petrified
Shells found in the Gawilgerh Range of
Hills, in April 1823.
Sykes, Lieut.-Col. W. H. On the Geo-
logy of a Portion of Dukhun, East Indies.
Carter, H. J. Geology of the Island
of Bombay.
Buist, G. Geology of the Island of
Bombay.
Coulthard, Capt. S. The Trap For-
mation of the Sagar District, and of those
Districts westward of it as far as Bhopal-
pur, on the Banks of the River Newas,
in Omatwara.

INDIAN EMPIRE—C.

Geological Papers—*continued.*
Dangerfield, Capt. On the Geology
of Malwa.
Hislop, S., and R. Hunter. On the
Geology and Fossils of the Neighbour-
hood of Nágpur, Central India.
Owen, Prof. Description of the
Cranium of a Labyrinthodont Reptile,
Brachyops Laticeps, from Mangali, Central
India.
Hislop, S. On the Connexion of the
Umreh Coal-beds of Nágpur, and of both
with those of Burdwan.
Sykes, Col. On a Fossil Fish from
the Table-land of the Deccan, in the
Peninsula of India ; with a Description
of the Specimens by Sir P. de M. G.
Egerton.
Bell, Thomas L. On the Geology of
the Neighbourhood of Kotab, Deccan.
Newbold, Capt. Notes, principally
Geological, on the Tract between Bellary
and Bijapore.
Notes, principally Geological, from
Bijapore to Bellary, *via* Kannighirri.
Christie, Alex. Turnbull. Sketch of
the Geology of the Southern Mahratta
Country.
Newbold, Capt. Notes, principally
Geological, on the South Mahratta
Country ; Falls of Gokauk ; Classifica-
tion of Rocks.
Aytoun, Lieut. Geological Report on
the Bagulkot and part of the adjoining
Talooks of the Belgaum Collectorate.
Geological Structure of the Basin
of the Mulpurba, in the Collectorate of
Belgaum, including the Gold-district.
Grant, Capt. C. W. Memoir to Illus-
trate a Geological Map of Cutch.
Sykes, Lieut.-Col. W. H. A Notice
respecting some Fossils collected in
Cutch by Captain Smee.
Finnis, Lieut. John. Summary De-
scription of the Geology of the Country
between Hoshungabad, on the Nerbudda,
and Nágpoor, by the direction of Baitool.
Ethersey, Lieut. R. Note on Perim
Island, in the Gulf of Cambay.
Falconer, H. Description of some
Fossil Remains of Dinotherium, Giraffe,
and other Mammalia, from the Gulf of
Cambay, Western Coast of India.
Copland, John. Account of the Cor-
nelian Mines in the Neighbourhood of
Baroach.
Lush, Charles. Geological Notes on
the Northern Concan, and a small por-
tion of Guzerat and Kattywar.
Abbott, Capt. Account of certain
Agate Splinters in the Clay bordering
the Nerbudda.
Granite in the Nerbudda.

INDIAN EMPIRE—C.

Geological Papers—*continued.*

Malcolmson, J. G. Notes on Lacustrine Tertiary Fossils from the Vindyah Mountains, near Mandoo.

Fulljames, Capt. G. A Visit, in Dec. 1832, to the Cornelian Mines situated in the Rajpipla Hills to the eastward of Baroach.

Note on the Discovery of Fossil Bones of Mammalia in Kattyawar.

Vicary, Capt. N. Notes on the Geological Structure of Parts of Scinde.

Murchison, Sir R. I. Introduction to a Second Memoir of Capt. Vicary on the Geology of Parts of Scinde.

Vicary, Capt. N. Geological Report on a Portion of the Beloochistan Hills.

Fleming, A. On the Geology of Part of the Sooliman Range.

Frere, H. B. E. On the Geology of a part of Sinde.

Carter, H. J. Descriptions of some of the Larger Forms of Fossilized Foraminifera in Sinde, with Observations on their Internal Structure. *Plate.*

Memoir on the Geology of the South-East Coast of Arabia. *Plates.*

Summary of the Geology of India, between the Ganges, the Indus, and Cape Comorin. *Plate.*

Egerton, Sir P. de M. Grey. On Two New Species of Lepidotus, from the Deccan.

Atlas to Geological Papers on Western India ; to which is appended a Summary of the Geology of India. Edited by H. J. Carter. Oblong folio *Bombay*, 1857

Manual of the Geology of India. Part 1. Peninsular Area ; Part 2. Extra Peninsular Area. By H. B. Medlicott and W. T. Blanford. With separate *map.* Small 4° *Calcutta*, 1879

—— The same. Part 3. Economic Geology. By V. Ball. *Maps and plates.* Small 4° *Calcutta*, 1881

—— The same. Part 4. Mineralogy (mainly Non - Economic). By F. R. Mallet. *Plates.* Large 8° *Calcutta*, 1887

—— New edition. *See* Oldham.

D. Marine Department.

Memoir to accompany the Chart of the Arabian Sea 1853

Marine Survey. Dispatch from the Secretary of State to the Governor-General, with Enclosures. Folio 1871

—— General Report of the Operations of the Marine Survey of India, from the commencement in 1874 to the end of the official year 1875-76. Prepared by Commander A. Dundas Taylor. *Maps.* Folio 1876

INDIAN EMPIRE—D.

Marine Survey. The same, for the years 1876-77, 1877-78, 1878-79, and 1880-81 1878-81

—— Administration Reports of the Marine Survey of India for the official years 1889-90, 1891-92, 1892-93, 1893-94. Folio 1890-94

Hydrographic Notices :—

No.

17. Ratnagiri, Rajapur Bay, and Viziadurg. 8° 1879

18. Bay of Bengal—Siam Coast. 8° 1879

— The same. 2nd edition. 8° 1880

19. Africa East Coast, Pemba Island, and adjacent coast. 8° 1879

20. India—West Coast. The coast from Kundari Island to Chaul, and the harbours of Dabhol and Jaygad. 8° 1880

Bay of Bengal—Coast of Orissa. 8° [1886]

List of Light-houses and Light-vessels in British India, including the Red Sea and Coast of Arabia (Suez to Singapore), corrected to January 1 in the years 1878-82. By R. C. Carrington. *Chart.* Oblong 8° *Calcutta*, 1878-82

Returns of Wrecks and Casualties in Indian Waters for the years 1878-93 (1883 missing). Prepared under the superintendence of R. C. Carrington, A. D. Taylor, J. M. Brebner, A. W. Stiffe, E. W. Petley, and B. P. Creagh. *Charts.* Folio *Calcutta*, 1879-94

Tide Tables for Indian Ports for the years 1881-95 ; from 1889 onward two Parts annually. Part 1, Western Ports (Aden to Paumbem Pass) ; Part 2, Eastern and Burma Ports (Negapatam to Port Blair). 12° *See* Baird ; Hill, J. ; Rogers, M. W.

E. Meteorological.

Abstracts of the Results of the Hourly Meteorological Observations taken at the Surveyor General's Office, Calcutta, 1869 (incomplete), 1870-76, 1877 (incomplete). 8° *Calcutta*

Indian Meteorological Memoirs, relating to India and the Neighbouring Countries. Vol. 1. *Plates, plans, and tables.* 4° *Calcutta*, 1876-81

The same. Vol. 2. *Maps, charts, and plates.* 4° *Calcutta*, 1882-85

The same. Vol. 3, Parts 1 and 2. *Maps, plates, and charts.* 4° *Calcutta*, 1886-87

The same. Vol. 4, Parts 1 to 4. *Plates and diagrams.* 4° *Calcutta*, 1886-87

Reports on the Administration of the Meteorological Department of the Government of India, in the years 1880-87. 4°.

INDIAN EMPIRE—E.

Reports on the Meteorology of India for the years 1879-85 (5th to 11th years). By H. F. Blanford. 7 vols. *Maps.* 4° 1881-87

F. Surveys.

[*See also* Archæological and Geological Surveys.]

a. Revenue Surveys.

Reports. Folio *Calcutta*

Thuillier, H. L. General Report on the Revenue Surveys of the Bengal Presidency, for the seasons 1858-59, 1859-60, and 1860-61 1863

Vanrenen, Col. D. C. Report on the Revenue Survey Operations of Lower Provinces, for seasons 1868-69 and 1869-70 1869-71

Gastrell, Col. J. E. General Report on the Revenue Survey Operations of the Bengal Presidency, Upper Circle, for season 1868-69 1870

Vanrenen, Col. D. C. General Report on the Revenue Survey Operations of the Bengal Presidency, Upper Circle, for season 1869-70 1871

Gastrell, Col. J. E., and Major J. Macdonald. General Report on the Revenue Survey Operations of the Upper and Lower Provinces in Bengal (including Boundary Commissioner's Report), for season 1870-71 1872

—— and Col. D. C. Vanrenen. General Report of the Revenue Survey Operations of the Upper and Lower Circles (including Boundary Commissioner's Report), for season 1871-72. *Map* 1873

—— The same, 1872-73, 1873-74, and 1874-75 1874-76

b. Topographical Surveys.

Reports. *Calcutta*

Depree, G. C. Report, Geographical and Statistical, on that Part of the Chota Nagpore Division which has come under the Operations of the Topographical Survey. *Plates.* 4° 1868

General Report of the Topographical Surveys of the Bengal Presidency, and of the Surveyor-General's Offices, for seasons 1862-63 and 1867-68. Folio 1864-69

Thuillier, Lieut.-Col. H. L. General Report on the Topographical Surveys of India, and of the Surveyor-General's Department, Head-Quarter establishment, for season 1868-69. Folio 1870

The same, 1869-70 (1871), 1870-71 (1872), 1871-72 (1873), 1872-73 (1874), 1873-74 (*Maps*, 1875), 1874-75 (1876), 1875-76 (*Maps*, 1877).

INDIAN EMPIRE—F.

c. Trignometrical Surveys.

Report on the Survey of India for the Three Years ending 1858-59. By Lieut.-Col. Sir A. S. Waugh. Folio 1861

Report of the Operations of the Great Trigonometrical Survey of India, during 1862-63. By Major J. T. Walker. Folio *Dehra Dun*, 1863

Extracts from General Report on the Operations of the Great Trigonometrical Survey of India, during 1866-67. By Col. J. T. Walker. Folio *Dehra Dun*, 1867

General Report on the Operations of the Great Trigonometrical Survey of India, during 1867-68, 1868-69, and 1869-70, by Col. J. T. Walker; and during 1870-71 and 1871-72, by Major T. G. Montgomerie; during 1872-73, 1873-74, and 1874-75, by Col. J. T. Walker; during 1875-76, by J. B. N. Hennessey; and during 1876-77, by Col. J. T. Walker. *Maps.* Folio *Dehra Dun, Roorkee, and Calcutta*, 1868-78

[*For later years see below—United Surveys.*]

Trans-Himalayan Explorations.

Reports on the Trans-Himalayan Explorations in connection with the Great Trigonometrical Survey of India, during 1865-67, 1869, and 1871. By Major T. G. Montgomerie. *Map.* Folio *Dehra Dun*, 1867-72

—— The same, during 1873-74-75. Drawn up from the Original Records by Capt. H. Trotter. Folio *Calcutta*, 1876

Report on Explorations in Nepal and Thibet, by Explorer M— H (season 1885-86). Prepared in the Office of the Trizon Branch, Survey of India ... by C. Wood. *Map.* Folio *Dehra Dun*, 1887

Report on the Explorations of Lama Serap Gyatsho, 1856-68; Explorer K—P., 1880-84; Lama U. G., 1883; Explorer R. N., 1885-86; Explorer P. A., 1885-86; in Sikkim, Bhutan, and Tibet. Prepared in the office of the Trigonometrical Branch Survey of India. *Maps.* Folio *Dehra Dun*, 1889

Spirit-Levelling Operations.

Tables of Heights, in Sind, the Punjab, N.W. Provinces, and Central India, determined by the Great Trigonometrical Survey of India . . . in May 1862. *Map.* 8° *Calcutta*, 1863

Tables of Heights in N.W. Provinces and Bengal, determined by the Great Trigonometrical Survey of India by Spirit-levelling Operations to May 1865. 8° *Roorkee*, 1866

Spirit-levels taken in the Punjab since 1862. 8° *Dehra Dun*, 1869

INDIAN EMPIRE—F—c.

Spirit-Levelling—continued.

Spirit-levels taken in the N.W. Provinces and Oude; seasons 1867-58-69. 8°   Dehra Dun, 1869
Spirit - levelled Heights. Section 7; seasons 1868-69-70. Lucknow to Dildernugger. Map. 8° Dehra Dun, 1871
The same. Season 1869-70. Tutukudi to Parmespuran. 8° Dehra Dun, 1872
The same. Section 8; season 1870-71. Goruckpore to Parsurman. 8°
Dehra Dun, 1872
The same. Section 9; season 1871-72. Map. 8°   Dehra Dun, 1873
The same. No. 1, Madras Presidency, 1869-85; No. 2, 1885-86; No. 3, 1886-87; No. 4, 1887-88; No. 5, 1888-89; No. 6, 1888-89 and 1889-90. Maps. 8°
Dehra Dun, 1886-90
The same. Bombay Presidency, Nizam's Dominion, and Central India Agency. Nos. 2 and 3, 1877-80. Revised edition. No. 4, 1877-78, 1881-84; No. 5, 1889-90; No. 7, 1890-92, Maps. 8°   Dehra Dun, 1886-93
The same. Spirit-levelled Heights in Cuttack, Balasore, Midnapore, Howrah, 24 Pergunnahs, the Sundarbans, Hooghly, and Nuddea Districts of Bengal. Bengal Presidency; seasons 1881-82-83 and 1887-88. Map. 8°
Dehra Dun, 1884 and 1889

Introductory Account of the Operations of the Great Arc Meridional Series. 4°   N.D.

Account of the Operations of the Great Trigonometrical Survey of India.

Vol. 1. The Standards of Measure and the Base-Lines. Also an Introductory Account of the Early Operations of the Survey during the period 1800-1830. Map and plates. 4° Dehra Dun, 1870
Vol. 2. History and General Description of the Principal Triangulation, and of its Reduction. Chart and plans. 4°
Dehra Dun, 1879
Vol. 3. Do. The Base-Line Figures, the Karachi Longitudinal, N.W. Himalaya, and Great Indus Series of the North-West Quadrilateral. Chart and plates. 4° Dehra Dun, 1873 [Issued in 1879]
Vol. 4. Do. The Great Arc-section 24°-30°, Rahun, Gurhagarh, and Jogi-Tila Meridional Series, and the Sutlej Series of the North-West Quadrilateral. Chart and plates. 4° Dehra Dun. 1876 [Issued in 1879]
Vol. 4a. General Description of the Principal Triangulation of the Jodhpore and the Eastern Sind Meridional Series of the North-West Quadrilateral, with the Details of their Reduction and the Final Results. Charts and plates. 4°
Dehra Dun, 1886

INDIAN EMPIRE—F—c.

Account of Operations—continued.

Vol. 5. Details of the Pendulum Operations by J. P. Basevi, R.E., and W. J. Heaviside, R.E., and of their Reduction. Maps and plates. 4°   Calcutta, 1879
Vol. 6. The Principal Triangulation of the South-East Quadrilateral, including the Great Arc-section 18° to 24°, the East Coast Series, the Calcutta and the Bider Longitudinal Series, the Jabalpur and the Bilaspur Meridional Series, and the Details of their Simultaneous Reduction. Maps and plates. 4°
Dehra Dun, 1880
Vol. 7. Do., of the North-East Quadrilateral, including the Simultaneous Reduction, and the Details of Five of the Component Series:—The North-East Longitudinal, the Budhon Meridional, the Rangir Meridional, the Amua Meridional, the Karara Meridional. Charts and plates. 4° Dehra Dun, 1882
Vol. 8. Do., of Eleven of the Component Series of the North-East Quadrilateral, including the Gurwani Meridional, the Gora Meridional, the Hurilaong Meridional, the Chendwar Meridional, the North Parasnath Meridional, the North Maluncha Meridional, the Calcutta Meridional, the East Calcutta Longitudinal, the Brahmaputra Meridional, the Eastern Frontier, Sec. 23° to 26°, the Assam Longitudinal. Charts and plates. 4° Dehra Dun, 1882
Vol. 9. Electro-Telegraphic Longitude Operations, executed during 1875-77 and 1880-81, by Lieut.-Col. W. M. Campbell and Major W. J. Heaviside. Charts and plates. 4°   Dehra Dun, 1883
Vol. 10. Electro-Telegraphic Longitude Operations executed during the years 1881-82, 1882-83, 1883-84, by Major G. Strahan, R.E., and Major W. J. Heaviside, R.E. Diagram and charts. 4°   Dehra Dun, 1887
Vol. 11. Astronomical Observations for Latitude made during the period 1805 to 1885, with a General Description of the Operations and Final Results. Chart and plates. 4°   Dehra Dun, 1890
Vol. 12. General Description of the Southern Trigon., including the Simultaneous Reduction, and the Details of Two of the Component Series—the Great Arc Meridional, Sec. 8° to 18°, and the Bombay Longitudinal. Charts and plates. 4°   Dehra Dun, 1890
Vol. 13. Do. of Five of the Component Series of the Southern Trigon., including the following series:—the South Konkan Coast, the Mangalore Meridional, the Madras Meridional and Coast, the South-East Coast, the Madras Longitudinal. Chart and plates. 4° Dehra Dun, 1890

INDIAN EMPIRE—F—*c.*
Account of Operations—*continued.*

Vol. 14. Do., of the South-West Quadrilateral, including the Simultaneous
Reduction, and the Details of its Com-
ponent Series. *Chart and plates.* 4°
Dehra Dun, 1890
Vol. 15. Electro-Telegraphic Longi-
tude Operations during 1885-86, 1887-88,
1889-90, and 1891-92, &c. 4°
Dehra Dun, 1893
Synopsis of the Results of the Opera-
tions of the Great Trigonometrical
Survey of India. *Diagrams and charts.*
4° *Dehra Dun*
Vol. 1. Descriptions and Co-ordinates
of the Principal and Second Stations
and other fixed Points of the Great Indus
Series 1874
Vol. 2. The great Arc-section 24° to
30° 1874
Vol. 3. The Karachi Longitudinal
Series 1874
Vol. 4. The Gurhagarh Meridional
Series 1875
Vol. 5. The Rahun Meridional Series
1875
Vol. 6. The Joga-Tila Meridional
Series, and the Sutlej Series 1875
Vol. 7. The North-West Himalaya
Series, and the Triangulation of the
Kashmir Survey 1879
Vol. 7*a.* The Jodhpore Meridional
Series and the Eastern Sind Meridional
Series 1887
Vol. 8. The Great Arc-section 18° to
24° 1878
Vol. 9. The Jabalpur Meridional Series
1878
Vol. 10. The Bider Longitudinal Series
1880
Vol. 11. The Bilaspur Meridional
Series 1880
Vol. 12. The Calcutta Longitudinal
Series 1880
Vol. 13. The East Coast Series 1880
Vol. 13*a.* Account of the Final Reduc-
tions, with the Details of the South Paras-
mata and South Maluncha Meridional
Series of the South-East Quadrilateral
1885
Vol. 14. Descriptions and Co-ordinates
of the Principal and Secondary Stations
and other Fixed Points of the Budhon
Meridional Series 1883
Vol. 15. The Rangir Meridional Series,
or Series K of the North-East Quad-
rilateral 1883
Vol. 16. The Amu Meridional Series
and the Karara Meridional Series 1883
Vol. 17. The Gurwani Meridional
Series and Gora Meridional Series 1883
Vol. 18. The Hurliaong Meridional
Series and the Chendwar Meridional
Series 1883

INDIAN EMPIRE—F—*c.*
Synopsis of Results—*continued.*

Vol. 19. The North Parasnath Meri-
dional Series and the North Maluncha
Meridional Series 1883
Vol. 20. The Calcutta Meridional
Series and the Brahmaputra Series 1883
Vol. 21. The East Calcutta Longi-
tudinal Series and the Eastern Frontier
Series, Sec. 23° to 26° 1883
Vol. 22. The Assam Valley Triangula-
tion 1891
Vol. 23. The South Konkan Coast
Series 1891
Vol. 24. The Mangalore Meridional
Series 1891
Vol. 25. The S.-E. Coast Series 1891
Vol. 26. The Bombay Longitudinal
Series 1892
Vol. 27. The Madras Longitudinal
Series 1892
Vol. 28. The Madras Meridional and
Coast Series 1892
Vol. 30. The Abu Meridional Series,
and the Gujarat Longitudinal Series 1892
Vol. 31. The Khanpisura Meridional
Series 1893
Vol. 32. The Singi Meridional Series
1893
Vol. 34. The Cutch Coast Series 1893
Catalogue of Stars for the Epoch, Jan. 1,
1892. From Observations by the Gt.
Trig. Surv. Compiled by Col. G.
Strahan. 4° *Dehra Dun,* 1893
d. United Surveys.
Extracts from the Reports of the
Trigonometrical, Topographical, and
Revenue Surveys of India, for 1871-72.
8° 1873
Abstract of the Reports of the Surveys
and of other Geographical Operations in
India, for 1869-70, 1870-71, 1871-72,
1872-73, 1873-74, 1874-75, 1876-77,
1877-78. Small 4° 1871-76, 1878-79
General Report on the Operations of the
General Report on the Operations of the
Survey of India, comprising the Great
Trigonometrical, the Topographical, and
the Revenue Surveys under the Govern-
ment of India, during 1877-78. By
Major-Generals J. T. Walker and D. C.
Vanrenen. *Maps.* Folio 1879
The same, for each year from 1878-79
to 1892-93. *Maps, charts, and plates.*
Folio 1880-94
Catalogue of Manuscript and Printed
Reports, Field-books, Memoirs, Maps,
&c., of the Indian Surveys, in the Map-
room of the India Office. 8° 1878

G. Various Government Publications.

Copies of Treaties, Agreements, &c.,
concluded by the Hon. East India
Company with the Sawunt Waree State,
between 1730 and 1843.

INDIAN EMPIRE—G.

Selections from Records—*continued.*

No.

43. Administrative	1864
44. The same	1864
45. The same	1864
47. Forests, Central	1864

—— Maps and Plans to accompany Government Record No. 53, or Annual Progress Reports of the Executive Engineers in the Southern, Central, and Northern Provinces for 1857-58, also in Sind for 1856-57 and 1857-58. Oblong folio

MILITARY DEPARTMENT.

No.

2. Sanitary　　　　　　　　　　　1861

Statistical Papers relating to India. *Maps.* Folio　　　　　　　　　　　　　　1853

Reports with Proceedings and Appendix of the Committee appointed by Government to Inquire into the State of the River Hooghly. *Maps.* Folio　*Calcutta,* 1854

Copies of Treaties, Engagements, &c., entered into by the Hon. East India Company with the Kutch State, between 1809 and 1851　　　　　　　　　1855

—— of Treaties, Agreements, &c., concluded between Great Britain and Portugal, between 1661 and 1850. From the India Records　　　　　　　　1855

Maps and Statistics : Copy of Maps and Statistical Information with reference to India. Folio　　　　　　　　　　1869

Progress and Condition. Statement exhibiting the Moral and Material Progress and Condition of India during the years 1867-68, 1869-70, 1871-72, 1873-74, 1874-75, 1875-76, 1882-83 (Parts 1 and 2), 1887-88, 1888-89. [Parly. Rep.] *Maps.* Folio　　　　　　　1869-90

Abstract of Letters received from India, 11th March 1871 (Cinchona Plantations, &c.). Folio　　　　　　　　　1871

Copy of Further Correspondence on the Subject of the Looshai Raids, and the Consequent Hostilities (Cachar). [Parly. Rep.] Folio　　　　　　　　　1872

Cotton Reports. Copy of the Reports of Mr H. Rivett-Carnac, Commissioner for the Central Provinces and the Berars, for the year 1868-69. *Maps.* Folio　1871

Reports on the Tea and Tobacco Industries in India. [Parly. Rep.] 4°　　1874

—— on Trade Routes and Fairs on the Northern Frontiers of India. [Parly. Rep.] Folio　　　　　　　　　1874

East India Railway Communication. Report from the Select Committee on East India Railway Communication ; together with the Proceedings of the Committee, Minutes of Evidence, and Appendix. Folio　　　　　1884

INDIAN EMPIRE—G.

Statement of the Trade of British India with British Possessions and Foreign Countries, for the five years 1884-85 to 1888-89. Folio　　　　1890

List of the Principal Indian Government Publications, on sale in this country and at the various Government Presses in India. Folio　　　　　　　1891

Botanical Survey of India. Records, Vol. I. (Nos. 1-4). *Map.* 8°　　　　　*Calcutta,* 1893-94

Gazetteer of India. *See* Hunter, W. W.

India Museum. *See* Catalogues.

Dictionary of Economic Products. *See* Watt.

H. Miscellaneous and Anonymous.

East India Company. The History and Management of the East India Company, from its Origin in 1600 to the Present Time. Vol. 1. *Map.* 8°　　1782

—— A General View of the Variations which have been made in the Affairs of the East India Company, from the conclusion of the War in India in 1784 to the commencement of the present hostilities. 8°　　　　　　1792

—— A Demonstration of the Necessity and Advantage of a Free Trade to the East Indies, and of a Termination to the Present Monopoly of the East India Company. 8°　　　　　1807

Voyage dans l'Inde [1789-90]. Vol. 2. 8°　　　　　　　　　N.D.

Fifteen Years in India, or Sketches of a Soldier's Life. From the Journal of an Officer in His Majesty's Service. 8° 1823

East and West India Trade. Five Accounts of the Real and Official Value of Exports to the East Indies, and to the British West Indies ; of Imports from the East Indies, and from the British West Indies ; and of Duties Received, 1814-26. [Parly. Rep.] Folio　　　　　　　　　　1827

A Further Enquiry into the Expediency of applying the Principles of Colonial Policy to the Government of India, and of effecting an essential Change in its Landed Tenures and in the Character of its Inhabitants. 8°　　　　1828

Anglo-Eastern Empire. The Political, Commercial, and Financial Condition of, in 1832. 8°　　　　　　1832

An Historical Sketch of the Princes of India, Stipendiary, Subsidiary, Protected, Tributary, and Feudatory ; with a Sketch of the Origin and Progress of British Power in India. 8°　*Edinburgh,* 1833

Thugs of India. Ramaseeana ; or, A Vocabulary of the Peculiar Language used by the Thugs ; with an Introduction and Appendix. [Imperfect copy.] *Plates.* 8°　　　*Calcutta,* 1836

INDIAN EMPIRE—II.

Thugs of India. Review of the above. 8° Calcutta, 1836

—— Illustrations of the History and Practices of the Thugs, and Notices of some of the Proceedings of the Government of India for the Suppression of the Crime of Thuggee. 8° 1837

Afghan War. Report of the East India Committee of the Colonial Society on the Causes and Consequences of the Afghan War 1842

The Results of Missionary Labour in India. 8° 1852

Ganges Canal, Short Account of the. [English. Sanscrit, and Hindustani.] Map and plate. 4° 1853

Indian Officers. Grievances and Present Condition of our Indian Officers, considered with a View to Improvement and Redress under Future Indian Administration. 8° Bombay, 1853

Sir Mordaunt Wells, and Public Opinion in India. 8° Calcutta, 1863

Scinde Railway. The Indus Steam Flotilla ; the Punjab Railway; the Delhi Railway ; Reports of the Directors, September 1863. Folio 1863

Early Travels in India : being Reprints of Rare and Curious Narratives of Old Travellers in India, in the 16th and 17th Centuries. First Series, comprising "Purchas's Pilgrimage" and the "Travels of Van Linschoten." 8° Calcutta, 1864

Indus Route. The Route of the Indus, and the Advance of Russia towards India : a Letter to W. P. Andrew on the Importance and Necessity of placing Delhi and Lahore in Railway Communication with Kurrachee on the Arabian Sea. 8° 1865

Report of the Ethnological Committee on Papers laid before them, and upon Examination of Specimens of Aboriginal Tribes brought to the Jubbulpore Exhibition of 1866-67. 8° Nagpore, 1868

The English Press on the Proposed Construction of Railways in India by Government Agency. 8° 1869

Geography of India, comprising an Account of British India, and the various States enclosed or adjoining. 12° 1870

The Indian Treaty. 12° Lisbon, 1879

A Few Hints to Travellers to India. By an Anglo-Indian. 12° 1889

Indian Words. Report of the Sub-Committee of the Madras Literary Society, and Auxiliary of the Royal Asiatic Society, on Writing Indian Words in Roman Characters. 8°

Opium. Anti-opium ; or, Things to think on . . on India, Opium, and China. 8° N.D.

INDIAN EMPIRE—H.

Instructions for Navigating the Gulf of Manaar and Palk's Bay. 8° N D.

I. Assam—

Selections of Papers regarding the Hill Tracts between Assam and Burmah, and on the Upper Brahmaputra. Large 8° Calcutta, 1873

CONTENTS.

Vol. 1.—Memoir of a Survey of Assam and the Neighbouring Countries, executed in 1825-6-7-8. By Lieut. R. Wilcox.

Vol. 2.—Abstract of the Journal of a Route travelled by Capt. S. F. Hannay, in 1835-36, from the Capital of Ava to the Amber Mines of the Hookoong Valley, on the South-East Frontier of Assam. By Capt. R. B. Pemberton.

Vol. 3.—Journal of a Trip to the Mishmi Mountains, from the Debouching of the Lohit to about Ten Miles East of the Ghalums. By W. Griffith.

Vol. 4.—Journey from Upper Assam towards Hookhoom, Ava, and Rangoon. By W. Griffith.

Vol. 5.—Narrative of a Journey from Ava to the Frontiers of Assam, and back, performed between December 1836 and May 1837. By G. T. Bayfield.

Vol. 6.—Notes on a Trip across the Patkoi Range from Assam to the Hookoong Valley. By H. L. Jenkins, in 1869-70.

Vol. 7.—Notes on the Burmese Route from Assam to Hookoong Valley. By H. L. Jenkins. Map.

Vol. 8.—Report of a Visit by Capt. Vetch to the Singpho and Naga Frontier to Luckimpore, 1842.

Vol. 9.—Reports of Lieut. Brodie's Dealings with the Nagas on the Seebsaugor Frontier, 1841-46.

Vol. 10.—Notes on a Visit to the Tribes inhabiting the Hills South of Seebsaugor, Assam. By S. E. Peal.

Annual Reports, &c.

Report on the Administration of the Province of Assam for the years 1888-89, 1889-90, 1890-91, 1891-92, and 1892-93. Maps. Folio Shillong, 1889-93

Progress Report of Forest Administration of the Province of Assam for the year 1889-90, by Gustav Mann ; and for 1891-92 and 1892-93, by J. M'Kee. Maps. Folio Shillong, 1890-93

General Report on Public Instruction in Assam for the years 1889-90, 1890-91, 1891-92, and 1892-93. By J. Willson and M. Prothero. Maps. Folio Shillong, 1890-94

INDIAN EMPIRE—I. ASSAM.
Annual Reports—*continued*.
Annual Sanitary Report of the Province of Assam for the year 1889, by C. P. Costello; and for 1893, by W. P. Warburton. *Maps*. Folio
Shillong, 1890-94
Annual Report of the Department of Land Records and Agriculture, Assam, for 1889-90, 1891-92, and 1892-93, by H. Z. Darrah; and for 1893-94, by A. E. Gait. *Maps*. Folio *Shillong*, 1890-94
Report on Tea Culture in Assam for 1889, 1891, 1892, and 1893. Folio
Shillong, 1890-94
Annual Report on Labour Immigration into Assam for the years 1889, 1891, 1892, and 1893. *Maps*. Folio
Shillong, 1890-93
Report on the Trade between Assam and the adjoining Foreign Countries for the periods of three years ending 31st March 1890 and 1893. By H. Z. Darrah. *Maps*. Folio *Shillong*, 1890-93
Annual Note on Crop Experiments carried out during 1891-92 and during 1892-93. Folio *Shillong*, 1892-93
Assam: Sketch of its History, Soil, and Productions, with the Discovery of the Tea-Plant, and of the Countries adjoining Assam. *Maps*. 8°   1839
Tea Company. Report of the Provincial Committee of the Assam Company, made on the 31st January 1840, with an Abstract of the Deed of Settlement of the Company. 8°   1840
Report of the Directors and Auditors, made . . . 7th May 1841, with Appendix. 8°   1841
The same, 6th May 1842, with Appendix. 8°   1842
The same, 5th May 1843, with Appendix. 8°   1843
The same (Circular Report &c. 1844)
The same, 2nd May 1845. *Map*. 8°
1845
The same, 11th November 1845. 8°
1845
The Tea of Assam. 8°   N.P., N.D.
The Assam Association. Memorial to the Right Hon. Viscount Cranbrook, and Report of the Deputation to his Lordship, 31st July 1878. 8°   1878

J. Bengal—

Selections from the Records of the Bengal Government. Royal 8°
Calcutta, 1853-73
No.
11. Administrative   1853
15. Embankments   1854
17. Administrative   1854
18. The same   1854
19. Water Communications   1854

INDIAN EMPIRE—J. BENGAL.
Selections from the Records of the Bengal Government—*continued*.
No.
20. Administrative   1855
21. The same   1855
22. Vernacular Education   1855
23. Geography and Survey of Assam
1855
24. Administrative   1856
26. The same   1857
27. Geography, &c., Himalayas   1857
28. Administrative   1858
29. Rivers and Embankments   1858
30. Administrative   1859
31. The same   1859
32. Vernacular Press   1859
33. Indigo Cultivation   1860
34. Administrative   1860
35. Cuttack Rivers   1860
36. Irrigation   1861
37. Tea Cultivation   1861
38. Sanitary   1861
39. Administrative   1863-64
40. Embankments   1863
41. Sanscrit and Bengalee Publications
1865
42. Administrative   1866

Reports of the Meteorological Reporter to the Government of Bengal, 1867-70, and 1872-74. 2 vols. Small folio
Calcutta, 1868-75
Papers regarding the Village and Rural Indigenous Agency employed in taking the Bengal Census of 1872. 8°   1873
Calcutta Botanical Garden. Annual Report (and Resolution) of the Royal Botanical Garden, Calcutta, for 1880-81. Folio   1881
—— Annual Report of the Royal Botanic Garden, Calcutta, for 1884-85. Folio
Calcutta, 1885
Bay of Bengal. Cyclone Memoirs. Part 1. Bay of Bengal Cyclone of May 20th —28th, 1887. *Plates*. 8°
Calcutta, 1888
Asiatic Society of Bengal. Extra No. to Part 1, Vol. 47. A Sketch of the Turki Language as spoken in Eastern Turkistan. By R. B. Shaw. Appendix by J. Scully.

K. Bombay—

Observations made at the Magnetical and Meteorological Observatory at Bombay; under the Superintendence of A. B. Orlebar, Comm. C. W. Montriou, Lieut. E. F. T. Fergusson, and Lieut. P. W. Mitcheson, 1846-62. 18 vols. Large 4°   *Bombay*, 1849-63
—— Ditto, in the years 1871-78, under the superintendence of Charles and F. Chambers. Folio   *Bombay*, 1881

INDIAN EMPIRE—K. BOMBAY.

Observations. Magnetic and Meteorological Observations made at the Government Observatory, Bombay, in the years 1884, '86, '87, '88-89, '90, '91, '92, and '93. Folio   *Bombay*, 1885-94

Selections from the Records of the Bombay Government. New Series. Royal 8°   *Bombay*, 1854-77

INDIAN EMPIRE—K. BOMBAY.

Selections from the Records of the Bombay Government—*continued*.

INDIAN EMPIRE—K. BOMBAY.

Selections from the Records of the Bombay Government—*continued*.

No.
127. Calendar for 1870 (Report)   1872
128. Administrative   1872
129. The same   1872
130. Assessments   1872
131. Police Reports for 1870   1873
132. Suam Commission   1873
133. Police Reports, 1871   1873
135. City Surveys, Gujarat   1873
136. Administrative   1873
139. Survey Rates, Sind   1874
140. Revenue   1874
141. Administrative   1874
142. Sind Police Report for 1873   1874
143. Police Reports for 1873   1874
144. Assessments   1874
145. The same   1875
146. Survey, Guzerat   1875
147. Administrative   1875
148. Assessments   1875
149 [in error 148]. Surat City Survey 1877

IRRIGATION SERIES.

No.
1. Bombay Presidency   1866
2. Water Supply of Poona and Kirkee   1866
3. Bombay Presidency   1866
4. S. Maratha Country   1866
5. The same, and Deccan   1866

Census of the Island of Bombay, taken 2nd February 1864. 8°   *Bombay*, 1864

Census of the Bombay Presidency, 21st Feb. 1872. General Report and Tables. 2 parts. Folio   *Bombay*, 1875
—— The same. Maps of Different Collectorates in the Bombay Presidency (Part 4). *Maps*. Folio *Bombay*, 1876

Selections from the Letters, Despatches, and other State Papers preserved in the Bombay Secretariat. Marátha Series, Vol. 1. Edited by George W. Forrest. 4° *Bombay*, 1885
—— The same. Home Series, Vols. 1 and 2. Edited by George W. Forrest. 4°   *Bombay*, 1887

Royal Asiatic Society. Bombay Branch. Extra numbers of Journal. Reports of Operations in search of Sanskrit MSS. in the Bombay Circle. By G. Bühler and Prof. P. Peterson. (4 Reports.) 8°   *Bombay*, 1877-94

Places and Common Official Words. Folio   N. P., N. D.

Historical Account of the Settlement and Possession of Bombay by the English East India Company, and of the Rise and Progress of the War with the Mahratta Nation. 8°   1781

The Riots in 1874. Large 8°   *Bombay*, 1874

INDIAN EMPIRE—L.

L. Burma—

Public Works Department. Reclamation of Waste Land and Improvement of Communications. Part 1, 1867-68, and 1868-69. Folio   *Rangoon*, 1868

Census. Report on the Census of British Burma taken in August 1872. Folio   *Rangoon*, 1875

Trade with Western China. Direct Commerce with the Shan States and West of China, by Railway from Rangoon to Kian-Hung, on the Upper Kamboja River, on the South-West Frontier of China. Memorial from the Wakefield Chamber of Commerce to the Lords of Her Majesty's Treasury. 8°   1869
—— Papers connected with the Development of Trade between British Burmah and Western China, and with the Mission to Yunnan of 1874-75. Folio   1876
—— Railway Connections a Pressing Necessity ; with a few Remarks on Communications in and with Burmah, Past and Present. *Map*. 12°   1888
—— *See* Colquhoun and Halkett.

Annual Reports, &c.

Report on the Administration of British Burma during 1882-83. Folio   *Rangoon*, 1883
Report on the Administration of Lower Burma during 1885-86, and on the Administration of Upper Burma during 1886. Folio   *Rangoon*, 1887
Report on the Administration of Burma during 1888-89 and 1889-90. Folio   *Rangoon*, 1889-90
Note on the Progress made in the Settlement of Upper Burma from April 1887 to August 1889. Folio   *Simla*, 1889
Reports on the Department of Land Records and Agriculture, Burma, for the years 1888-89 and 1889-90. *Maps*. Folio   *Rangoon*, 1889-90
Reports on Public Instruction in Lower Burma for the years 1888-89 and 1889-90. Folio *Rangoon*, 1889-90
Reports on the Revenue Administration of Burma for the years 1888-89 and 1889-90. *Maps*. Folio   *Rangoon*, 1889-90
Report on the Trade and Navigation of Burma for the year 1888-89, with Memorandum on the Inland Trade. Folio   *Rangoon*, 1889
The same, for the year 1889-90. Folio   *Rangoon*, 1890
Report on the Frontier Affairs of Burma in 1889-90. *Maps*. Folio   *Rangoon*, 1890

INDIAN EMPIRE—L. BURMA.

Annual Reports—*continued.*

Report on the Trade between Burma and the adjoining Foreign Countries for the Three Years ending the 31st March 1890. *Map.* Folio *Rangoon,* 1890

Report (or Memorandum) on the Internal Trade of Burma for the years 1889-90, 1891-92, 1892-93, and 1893-94. Folio *Rangoon,* 1890-94

Gazetteer. The British Burma Gazetteer. 2 vols. *Photographs.* 8° *Rangoon,* 1879-80

Transliteration. Memorandum on the Transliteration of Burmese Words into English. Folio N.D.

Surveys. Brief Instructions for the Lower Burma Field-to-Field Survey, 1891 *Rangoon,* 1892

—— List and Specimens of Forms in ordinary use in the Lower Burma Field-to-Field Survey.

—— *See also* Clancey.

Ava. Two Years in Ava, from May 1824 to May 1862. By an Officer on the Staff of the Quartermaster - General's Department. *Maps and plate.* 8° 1827

Shan States.

Shan Names. Tables for the Translation of Shan Names into English. 8° *Rangoon,* 1882

Report on the Shan States, 1887-88. Folio *Rangoon,* 1889

Report on the Administration of the Shan States for 1888-89. Folio *Rangoon,* 1889

—— Ditto (Northern) for 1890-91 and 1891-92. Folio *Rangoon,* 1891-92

—— Ditto (Southern) for 1891-92. Folio *Rangoon,* 1892

—— *See* Daly, Hildebrand, Sherriff.

M. Central Provinces—

Reports, &c. *See* Dods, Grant, Mackenzie.

N. Madras—

Selections from the Records of the Madras Government. Royal 8° *Madras,* 1855-77

No.
1. Medical 1855
2. Public Instruction 1855
3. Navigation of the Godavery 1857
4. Administrative 1855
6. The same 1855
7. Medical 1855
9. Revenue 1855
11. Water Supply 1855
13. Roads 1855
14. Medical Topography 1855
16. Salt 1855
20. Medical 1855
21. The same 1855

INDIAN EMPIRE—N. MADRAS.

Selections from the Records of the Madras Government—*continued.*

No.
24. Administrative 1856
26. Village Vernacular Schools 1856
27. Public Works 1856
28. The same 1856
29. The same 1856
30. District Roads 1856
31. Commutation Rates 1856
32. Sanitary 1856
33. Agricultural Exhibitions 1856
34. Medical 1856
35. Public Instruction, 1855-56 1856
36. Medical College 1856
37. Railways, Fares, &c. Part 2 1856-57
38. Public Works 1857
39. Museums 1857
40. Railway Report, 1855 1857
41. Educational Grants in Aid 1857
42. Medical 1857
43. Railways, Fares, &c. Vol. 2 1857
44. Railway Report, 1856 1857
45. Agricultural Exhibitions. Vol. 2 1858
46. Medical 1857
47. Roads 1857
48. Medical College 1858
49. Public Instruction, 1855-57 1858
49A Land Holdings and Tenancies, Malabar 1858
50. Agricultural Exhibitions, 1857 1858
51. Medical 1858
52. Educational Grants in Aid 1858
53. Revenue Survey 1858
53A Railway Report, 1857 1878
54. Public Works 1858
55. Medical 1858
56. Public Instruction, 1857-58 1858
57. Medical College 1859
66. The same 1860
67. Medical 1860
68. The same 1861
69. Public Instruction, 1859-60 1861
69A Medical College 1862
70A Medical 1862
71A Medical College 1862
72. Medical 1862
73. The same 1862
73A The same 1863
74. Revenue Survey 1863
 Vaccination 1863
75. Medical College 1863
76. Public Instruction 1863
77. Medical 1864
78. The same 1864
79. Medical College 1864
80. Public Instruction 1864
81. Jeypore. *Map* 1864
82. Grants in Aid 1865
83. C. S. Examinations 1865
84. Medical 1865
85. The same 1865

—— Ditto. Folio.
Memoir of the Survey of Travancore and Cochin, 1816-20. By Lieut. B. S. Ward. Folio   *Madras*, 1891
Geographical and Statistical Memoir of the Survey of the Travancore and Cochin States, under Lieuts. Ward and Conner, 1810-21. Vol. 4. *Map.* Folio
                                Madras, 1893

Astronomical Observations made at the E. I. Co.'s Observatory at Madras, 1843-47, &c. By T. G. Taylor. Large 4°   1848

INDIAN EMPIRE—N. MADRAS.

Astronomical Observations. Results of Observations of the Fixed Stars made with the Meridian Circle at the Government Observatory, Madras, in the years 1862, 1863, and 1864, under the direction of Norman Robert Pogson. 4°
                                Madras, 1887
—— The same, 1865, 1866, and 1867, &c. 4°   *Madras*, 1888
—— The same, 1868, 1869, and 1870, &c. 4°   *Madras*, 1890
—— The same, 1871, 1872, and 1873, under the direction of N. R. Pogson. By C. Michie Smith. 4° *Madras*, 1892
—— The same, 1874, 1875, and 1876, &c. 4°   *Madras*, 1892
—— The same, 1877, 1878, and 1879, &c. Vol. 6. 4°   *Madras*, 1893
—— The same, 1880, 1881, and 1882, &c. 4°   *Madras*, 1894
—— The same, 1883-87, &c. Vol. 8. 4°
                                Madras, 1894
—— Results of the Observations made at the Government Observatory, Madras, during the years 1861-1890 . . . Edited by C. Michie Smith. 4° *Madras*, 1892
Census of the Town of Madras, 1871. *Maps.* Folio   *Madras*, 1873
—— *See also* Cornish, MacIver.
Alphabetical Lists of the Names of Places in the Madras Presidency, (1) in which the popular Spelling has been retained, (2) in which the system of Transliteration has been followed. Folio
                                Madras, 1879
Routes in the Madras Presidency, completed in the Office of the Quartermaster-General of the Madras Army. Revised edition. Large 8°   *Madras*, 1879
Report on the Administration of the Madras Presidency during the years 1888-89, 1889-90, 1890-91, 1891-92, and 1892-93. Folio. *Maps and diagrams*
                                Madras, 1889-93
Manual of Standing Information for the Madras Presidency, 1893. *Map.* 4°
                                Madras, 1893
Meteorological Observations. Hourly Meteorological Observations made at the Madras Observatory from January 1856 to February 1861. 4° *Madras*, 1893
Neilgherry Mountains. Geographical and Statistical Memoir of a Survey of the Neilgherry Mountains. 8°
                                Madras, 1848

O. North - West Provinces and Oudh—

Official Reports on the Province of Kumoan ; with a Medical Report on the Mahamurree in Gurhwal in 1840-50. Edited by J. H. Batten. *Maps.* 8°
                                Agra, 1851

INDIAN EMPIRE—O. N.W. PROVINCES.

Selections from the Records of Government : North-Western Provinces. Royal 8° and folio
Agra, Calcutta, and Allahabad, 1855-73

VOLUME 1.
Judicial, Fiscal, and Miscellaneous.

VOLUME 2.
Irrigation, Bridges, Roads, Miscellaneous Works. (Continued in Parts 22, 23, 24, 25, 26, 27, 28, 29, 31, 32, 33, 34, and 43.)

SECOND SERIES.

VOLUME 1.
No.
1. Miscellaneous   1870
2. Irrigation, Forestry   1870
3 and 4. Miscellaneous Works   1870

VOLUME 2.
No.
1. Sanitary   1870
2. Forestry, Agriculture   1870
3. Publications Registered   1870
4. Cotton Crops, Miscellaneous 1870

VOLUME 3.
Meteorological, Archæological, Educational, Forestial, Miscellaneous
                                1870

VOLUME 4.
No.
1. Agricultural, Forestial, Miscellaneous   1870
2. Miscellaneous   1870
3. The same, and Educational   1870
4. Public Instruction   1870

VOLUME 5.
No.
1. Judicial   1870
2. The same   1870

VOLUME 6.
No.
1. Miscellaneous   1870
2. The same   1870
3. The same   1870
4. Administrative, Educational, Agricultural, and Miscellaneous 1870

Census. Report on the Census of Oudh. 2 vols. Folio   *Lucknow*, 1869

Statistical, Descriptive, and Historical Account of the North-Western Provinces of India. Vols. I.-IV. edited and prepared by Edwin T. Atkinson; Vol. V. compiled by H. C. Conybeare, and edited by E. T. Atkinson; Vol. VI. by F. N. Wright, E. B. Alexander, and H. C. Conybeare, edited by E. T. Atkinson; Vol. VII. chiefly compiled by H. C. Conybeare, and edited by E. T. Atkinson and F. H. Fisher; Vol. VIII. by H. C. Conybeare, F. H. Fisher, and J. P. Hewett; Vol. IX. by F. H. Fisher; Vols. X.-XII. The Himálayan

INDIAN EMPIRE—O. N.W. PROVINCES.

Districts of the North-Western Provinces of India, by E. T. Atkinson; Vol. XIII. by F. H. Fisher; Vol. XIV. by F. H. Fisher and J. P. Hewett. *Maps and plans.* Large 8°   *Allahabad*, 1874-86

Report on the Administration of the N.-W. Provinces and Oudh, for the years ending 31st March 1889, '90, '91, '92, '93. Folio   *Allahabad*, 1890-94

Progress Reports of the Epigraphical and Architectural Branches of the N.-W. Provinces and Oudh for 1891-92. *Plan.* Folio   *Allahabad*, 1892

Lucknow. The Lucknow Album, containing a Series of Fifty Photographic Views of Lucknow and its Environs, together with a large-sized Plan of the City executed by Darogha Ubbas Alli, Assistant Municipal Engineer. 8°
                                Calcutta, 1874

P. Punjab—

General Report upon the Administration of the Punjab Proper, for 1849-51, being the two first years after Annexation ; with a Supplementary Notice of the Cisand Trans-Sutlej Territories. *Maps and tables.* Folio   1854

Report on the Sanitary Administration of the Punjab, 1869. *Map.* 4°
                                Lahore, 1870

Reports on the Administration of the Punjab and its Dependencies, for the years 1882-83, 1888-89, 1889-90, 1890-91, 1891-92, and 1892-93. *Maps and diagrams.* Folio   *Lahore*, 1884-94

Selections from the Records of the Government of the Punjab and its Dependencies. Public Works Department, No. 1. Vol. VI., No. 2. New Series : Nos. 1, 2, 3, 5, 6, 7, 9, 10, 12, and 13. Administration and Miscellaneous
                                1868-76

—— *See also* Leitner (Linguistic Fragments).

Census. Report on the Census of the Punjab taken on 10th January 1868. 4°   *Lahore*, 1870

—— Report on the Census of the Punjab taken on the 17th February 1881. By C. J. Ibbetson. 3 vols. *Map.* Folio
                    Calcutta and Lahore, 1883

District Gazetteers compiled and published under the Authority of the Punjab Government, for 1883-84 (31 vols.), 1888-89 (4 vols.), 1891-92 (1 vol.), 1892 (1 vol.), 1892-93 (3 vols.), 1893 (1 vol.), and 1894 (1 vol.). 8°
                    Calcutta and Lahore

Original Sketches in the Punjab. Oblong 4°   1854

Delhi Railway. Opening of the Meerut and Umballa Section of the Delhi Railway, on the 14th November 1868, &c. 8°   1869

INDIAN EMPIRE.

Q. Various—

Aden. Indian Papers. Correspondence relating to Aden. [Parly. Rep.] *Map.* Folio   1839

Ajmere and Mhairwarra, Report upon the Census of. Folio   *Simla*, 1877
—— *See* India Selections, For. Dep. No. 122.

Andaman Islands : with Notes of Barren Islands. From Indian Records, No. 45. *Maps and plates.* Royal 8°
         Calcutta, 1857

Berar. Census Report. *See* Kitts.

Bootan. Political Missions to Bootan, comprising the Reports of the Hon'ble Ashley Eden, 1864 ; Capt. R. B. Pemberton, 1837-38 ; with Dr W. Griffiths's Journal, and the Account by Baboo Kishen Kant Bose. 8°   *Calcutta,* 1865

Dardistan. Account of Dardistan, with Map of the Country, surveyed during 1882-83 in connection with the Trigonometrical Branch, Survey of India. Folio
         Dehra Dun, 1884

Minicoy. The Island of Women. (From *Blackwood's Magazine.*) 8°   1889

Mysore. Census Report. *See* Lindsay.

Nicobar Islands; Some Old Pages relating to the. [*Incomplete.*] 8°   1858

Quetta. The Quetta Directory for 1893.
8°   *Quetta,* 1893

Rajputana. The Rajputana Gazetteer. 3 vols. 8°   *Calcutta,* 1879-80

Travancore. Report on the Administration of Travancore for the year M.E. 1058 (1882-83). *Diagram.* 8°
         Trevandrum, 1884

JAPAN.

Reports and Official Letters to the Kaitakushi, by Horace Capron, Commissioner and Adviser, and his Foreign Assistants. 8°   *Tokyo,* 1875

Geological Survey of Japan. Reports of Progress for 1878 and 1879, by Benjamin Smith Lyman. 8°
         Tokyo, 1879

Japan. No. 2 (1883). Memorandum respecting the Trade between Japan and Corea. 8°.

Tokyo University. Memoirs of the Science Department. Earthquake Measurement. By J. A. Ewing. Small 4°   *Tokyo,* 1883
[*See also* Morse, E. S. ; Netto, C.]

Tenth Annual Report of the Minister of Education for the Fifteenth Year of Meiji (1882). 8°   *Tokyo,* 1886

JAPAN.

Jesuit Letters. Nuovi Avvisi del Giapone con alcuni altri della Cina del LXXXIII. et LXXXIV. Cavati dalle Lettere della Compagnia di Giesù. Ricevute il mese di Decembre Prossimo Passato MDLXXXV. 8°   *Venice,* 1586
Lettera Annale del Giapone scritta al Padre Generale della Compagnia di Giesu, 1588. 12°   *Rome,* 1590
Litteræ Societatis Jesu, anno MDCII. et MDCIII., e Sinis, Molucis, Japone, datæ. 12°   *Mayence,* 1607
Litteræ Japonicæ annorum M. DC. IX. et X. ad R. admodum piæ mem. P. Claudium Aquavivam Generalem Præpositum Societatis Jesu a R. P. Provinciali eiusdem in Japone Societ. missæ. Ex Italicis Latinæ factæ ab And. Schotto. 8°   *Antwerp,* 1615

The Claims of Japan and Malaysia upon Christendom, exhibited in Notes of Voyages made in 1837, from Canton, in the ship " Morrison " and brig " Himmaleh," under direction of the owners. 2 vols. *Maps.* 12°   *New York,* 1839

CONTENTS.

Vol. 1. Notes of the Voyage of the " Morrison " from Canton to Japan. By C. W. King.
Vol. 2. Notes made during the Voyage of the " Himmaleh " in the Malayan Archipelago. By C. Tradescant Lay.

Manners and Customs of the Japanese in the Nineteenth Century. 8°   1841

Handy Guide Book to the Japanese Islands. *Maps.* 12°   N.D.

Night Record of a Visit to East Yesso [in Japanese]. *Woodcuts.* 8°   [1865]

Kioto. Stray Notes on Kioto and its Environs. 2nd edition, revised. Small 8°   *Hiogo,* 1878

The Morse Collection of Japanese Pottery. Reprinted from the *American Architect* of May 28, 1887. 4°
      Salem, Mass., 1887

Ainu. Baptismal Services in the Ainu Language. 12°   1891

Seismological Society of Japan : Earthquake Observation. [Note - Book.] Oblong 12°   N.D.

KOREA.

Reports on Corean Mines. 8°   1883.

Despatch from H.M. Minister in Japan forwarding a Report on Corea. [Japan, No. 1, 1883.] 8°.
—— The same, forwarding Reports on Mines in Corea. [Japan, No. 3, 1883.] 8°   1883

Corea, No. 1 (1885.) Commercial Reports by H.M. Consul-General, 1882-83 ; and Report of a Journey from Soul to Songdo, in August 1884. 8°   1885.

KOREA.

Annual Reports on the Trade of Corea in Foreign Vessels. No. 1 (year 1885). 4°
Shanghai, 1886

MALAY ARCHIPELAGO.

[*See also* Dutch East Indies.]
Sentences in English and Malay. Printed for the Borneo Mission. 12° 1847

British North Borneo.

Borneo and Sulu. Spain, No. 1 (1882). (Borneo and Sulu.) Papers relating to the Affairs of Sulu and Borneo, and to the grant of a Charter of Incorporation to the " British North Borneo Company." Part I.—Correspondence respecting the Claims of Spain. *Map.* Folio 1882
—— Netherlands, No. 1 (1882). (Borneo and Sulu.) Papers relating to the Affairs of Sulu and Borneo, and to the grant of a Charter of Incorporation to the " British North Borneo Company." Part II.—Correspondence respecting the Claims of Holland. *Maps.* Folio 1882
—— Handbook of British North Borneo. Compiled from Reports received from Governor Treacher and other Officers in the British North Borneo Company's Service. With an Introduction by Sir Rutherford Alcock. *Maps.* 8° 1886
The same. Compiled from Reports of the Governor and Officers of the Residential Staff in Borneo, and other sources of information of an authentic nature. With an Appendix of Documents, Trade Returns, &c., showing the Progress and Development of the Company's Territory to the latest date. *Maps and illustrations.* 8° 1890
[*See also* Leys.]

Philippines.

Manila. Provincia de Tondo (incomplete), Provincia de Bulacan (*map*), and Provincia de Pangasinan [Nos. 2, 3, and 5 of a Survey of Manila]. Small 8°
Manila, 1819
Philippines. Estados de la Poblacion de Filipinas correspondiente a el año de 1818. Small 8° *Manila*, 1820
Philippine Islands. Informe sobre el Estados de la Islas Filipinas en 1842. Por el Autor del Aristodemo. 2 vols.
Madrid, 1843
Das Datum, wie solcher auf den Philippinen gezählt wird. 8° N.D.

PERSIA.

Eastern Persia. An Account of the Journeys of the Persian Boundary Commission, 1870-71-72 : Vol. 1. The
2 X

PERSIA.

Geography, with Narratives by Majors St John, Lovett, and Euan Smith, and an Introduction by Major-General Sir Frederic John Goldsmid ; Vol. 2. The Zoology and Geology, by W. T. Blanford. *Maps and tables.* 8° 1876
Bakhtiari Region. Survey of the Bakhtiari Region. 8° [*Simla*, N.D.]
Khorasan. *See* Central Asia.
Sketches of Persia, from the Journals of a Traveller in the East. 2 vols. 8°
1827
The River Karun, an opening to British Commerce. *Map.* 12° 1890

Persian Gulf.

Geology. Reprint of two papers on the Geology of the Persian Gulf. 8°
Calcutta, 1859-60

PORTUGUESE ASIA.

Goa. Relation de l'Inquisition de Goa. 16° *Leyden*, 1687
Macao. Relatorio e Documentos sobre a abolição da Emigração de Chinas contrados em Macau apresentado as Cortes na sessão legislativa de 1874. (Pelo ministro e secretario d'estado dos negocios da marina e ultramas.) Folio
Lisbon, 1874

RUSSIA IN ASIA.

A. Caucasus, &c.

Memoir of a Map of the Countries comprehended between the Black Sea and the Caspian ; with an Account of the Caucasian Nations, and Vocabularies of their Languages. *Map.* 4° 1788
Description des Pays situés entre la Mer Noire et la Mer Caspienne. *Map.* Mémoire sur le Cours de l'Araxe et du Cyrus, et sur les Pyles Caucasiennes. Par St Croix. *Map.* Extrait du Journal d'un Voyage fait 1784 dans la Partie Méridionale de la Russie. 4°
Paris, 1793
Tiflis Observatory. Beobachtungen der Temperatur des Erdbodens im Tifliser Physikalischen Observatorium im Jahre 1884, nebst Anhang: Beobachtungen am Radiations-Thermometer in den Jahren 1881-84. 8° *Tiflis*, 1886
—— The same, 1885. 8° *Tiflis*, 1891
—— Meteorologische Beobachtungen des Tifl. Phys. Observ. in den Jahren 1887-88, 1889, herausgegeben von J. Mielberg. 8° *Tiflis*, 1889-90
—— Magnetische Beobachtungen des Tifl. Phys. Observ. im Jahre 1888-89, herausgegeben von J. Mielberg. 8°
Tiflis, 18—

RUSSIÆ IN ASIA—A.

Collection of Materials for the Description of Localties and Tribes of the Caucasus. Published by the Education Department of the Caucasus. Parts 10, 12-18
Tiflis, 1890-94
Notes on the Caucasus. By Wanderer. 8° 1883

B. Russian Turkistan.

[*See also* Central Asia.]
Russia and Persia. Histoire des Découvertes faites par divers Savans Voyageurs, dans plusieurs contrées de la Russie et de la Perse, relativement à l'Histoire civile et Naturelle, à l'Economie Rurale, au Commerce, &c. 3 vols. *Maps and plates.* Small 4° *Berne,* 1779-87
—— The same. 6 vols. *Maps and plates.* 8° *Lausanne,* 1784
Treaty between Russia and Bokhara. Folio 1869
Russian Turkestan. Collection of Articles published with reference to the Polytechnic Exhibition. [In Russian.] 2 parts. 8° *Moscow,* 1872
Scientific Expeditions in Turkistan during 1878. [In Russian.] Small 8°
Tashkent, 1879
Amu and Usboi. Descriptive History of, since 1716. [In Russian.] *Map and plate.* Small 8° *Samara,* 1879
Transcaspian Expedition. Wissenschaftliche Ergebnisse der im Jahre 1886. Allerhöchst befohlenen Expedition nach Transcaspien. Band 1. Zoologie. *Map and plates.* 8° *Tiflis,* 1890
Report on the Trans-Caspian Triangulation. [In Russian.] *Maps.* Folio N.D.
Oxus. Fall and Rapidity of the Oxus and of other Rivers compared with it. MS. 4°.
Is Russia Vulnerable in Central Asia? From the *Asiatic Quarterly Review.* 8° 1889
Russians in the East. 8° [Review. ?1865]
Expedition against the Tekke Turkomans. *See* United Kingdom, War Office Pub.

C. Siberia.

Results of the Siberian Expedition of the Imperial Russian Geographical Society. [In Russian.]
Vol. 1. Historical Reports on Physical Geographical Researches. By T. B. Schmidt and P. P. Glen. *Maps.* 4° *St Petersburg,* 1866
Vol. 2. Botany. By F. B. Schmidt. *Plates.* 4° *St Petersburg,* 1874
Vol. 3. Geognosy. Part 1. Fossils of the Cretaceous Formation in Sakhalin. By F. B. Schmidt. *Map and plates.* 4° *St Petersburg,* 1873

RUSSIA IN ASIA—C.

Report on the Survey of the Country between the Mouth of River Korotaika and Possl-Cort Tents, on the Obi River, for the projected Obi Railway . . . in August 1886, by J. M. Vorspay. *Map.* Folio 1886
A New Trade Route to connect Europe with Western Siberia and China. By A. D. Golokwastoff. Folio. [Bound up with preceding] 1887
Russia. No. 1 (1888). Copy of a Despatch from Sir R. Morier, and other Correspondence respecting Attempts to Establish Commercial Relations with Siberia through Kara Sea. *Map.* Folio 1888
Die Wissenschaftliche Thätigkeit der Ost-Sihirischen Section der Kaiserlichen Russischen Geographischen Gesellshaft in Jahre 1891. 8° N.D.

SIAM.

Copies of Treaty between the Government of India and the King of Siam, Papers, &c. [Parly. Rep.] Folio 1874
Report on the Country traversed by Mr Satow in his Journey to Chiengmai (in Siam) in December 1885 and January 1886. [Foreign Office Paper.] *Map.* Folio 1886
Voyage de Siam, des Pères Jesuites ; avec leurs Observations Astronomiques, et leurs Remarques de Physique, de Géographie, d'Hydrographie, et d'Histoire. *Plates.* Small 4° *Paris,* 1686
Bangkok Calendar, 1859, 1864; corresponding to the Siamese Civil Era 1220-1, 1225-6, and nearly so to the Chinese Cycle Era, 4496, 4501. 8°
Bangkok, 1859, 1864
The Directory for Bangkok and Siam for 1892. *Plan.* Small 4° 1892
Mekong Valley. The Truth about the Mekong Valley. 8° *Bangkok,* 1891

STRAITS SETTLEMENTS.

Report of the Committee appointed to consider the adoption of a uniform system of spelling Native Names. Folio
Singapore, 1879
Annual Reports on the State of Selangor for the years 1886, '87, '90, '91, '92, '93. Folio
Singapore and Kuala Lumpur, 1887-94
—— On the States of Sungei Ujong and Jelebu for the years 1891-93. Folio
Singapore and Kuala Lumpur, 1892-94
—— On the State of Perak for the years 1891-93. Folio *Taiping,* 1892-94
—— On the State of Pehang for the years 1891-93. Folio *Kuala Lumpur,* 1892-94

STRAITS SETTLEMENTS.

Annual Reports on the State of Negri Sembilan for the years 1891-93. Folio
Singapore, 1891-94

Native States. Correspondence relative to the Affairs of certain Native States in the Malay Peninsula, in the neighbourhood of the Straits Settlements. [Parly. Rep.] Folio 1874
—— Further Correspondence respecting the Protected Malay States (in continuation of November 1888). Folio 1889

Report on the Botanic and Zoological Gardens, Singapore. By the Superintendent of the Botanic Gardens, for the year 1882. Folio *Singapore,* 1883

Prince of Wales Island. Exposition of the Political and Commercial Relations of the Government of Prince of Wales Island, with the States of the East Coast of Sumatra, from Diamond Point to Siack. 4° *Prince of Wales Island,* 1824

Perak. Copy of the Journal kept by the Officer in Charge of Kinta District, from 14th to 31st August 1878. Square 8°
[*Singapore,* 1878]
—— The Perak Handbook and Civil Service List, 1893; with a new map. Large 8° *Taiping*

The Resources of the Malay Peninsula. [Cuttings from the *Chamber of Commerce Journal.*] *Map.* 4° 1883

Miscellaneous Papers relating to Indo-China. Reprinted for the Straits Branch of the Royal Asiatic Society, from Dalrymple's "Oriental Repertory," and the "Asiatic Researches and Journal" of the Asiatic Society of Bengal. 2 vols. *Map and plan.* 8° 1886
—— The same, and the Indian Archipelago. Reprinted for the Straits Branch of the Royal Asiatic Society, from the "Journals" of the Royal Asiatic, Bengal Asiatic, and Royal Geographical Societies; the "Transactions" and "Journal" of the Asiatic Society of Batavia; and the "Malayan Miscellanies." Second Series. 2 vols. *Map and plates.* 8° 1887

TURKEY IN ASIA.

Travels in the Track of the Ten Thousand Greeks, being a Geographical and Descriptive Account of the Expedition of Cyrus and of the Retreat of the Ten Thousand Greeks. *Map.* 8° 1844

Euphrates Valley Route to India. By a Traveller. *Map.* 8° 1856
—— Reports respecting Communication with India through Turkey, by the Euphrates Valley Route. [Parly. Rep.] *Map.* Folio 1872

TURKEY IN ASIA.

Euphrates. Report from the Select Committee on the Euphrates Valley Railway; together with the Proceedings of the Committee, Minutes of Evidence, &c. [Parly. Rep.] Folio 1872

Statistical Tables of the Vilayets of the Turkish Empire nearest to Trans-Caucasia. [In Russian.] *Map.* 8°
Tiflis, 1889

A. Asia Minor.

Reisen in Südwestlichen Kleinasien. 2 vols. Folio *Vienna,* 1884-89
Vol. 1.—Benndorf, Otto, and George Niemann. Reisen in Lykien und Karien. Ausgeführt im Auftrage des K. K. Ministeriums für Cultus und Unterricht unter dienstlicher Förderung durch seiner Majestät Raddampfer "Taurus," Commandant Fürst Wrede, beschrieben von Otto Benndorf und George Niemann. *Map and plates* 1884
Vol. 2.—Petersen, E., and F. von Luschan. Reisen in Lykien Milyas und Kibyratis. Ausgeführt auf Veranlassung der Oesterreichischen Gesellschaft für Archæologische Erforschung Kleinasiens, unter dienstlicher Förderung durch seiner Majestät Raddampfer "Taurus," Commandant Baritz von Ikafalva, beschrieben und im Auftrage des K. K. Ministeriums für Cultus und Unterricht herausgegeben von Eugen Petersen und Felix von Luschan. *Plates* 1889

B. Palestine.

Palestine Exploration Fund.

Survey of Western Palestine. An Introduction to the Survey of Western Palestine. By Trelawney Saunders. 8° 1881
—— Special Papers on Topography, Archæology, Manners and Customs, &c., contributed by Lieut.-Colonel Sir Charles Wilson, Lieut.-Colonel Warren, Lieut. Conder, Lieut. Kitchener, Prof. E. H. Palmer, Mr George Smith, Rev. Greville Chester, M. Clermont-Ganneau, &c., for the Committee of the Palestine Exploration Fund. *Map.* 4° 1881
—— Arabic and English Name Lists, collected during the Survey of Lieuts. Conder and Kitchener. Transliterated and explained by E. H. Palmer, for the Committee of the Palestine Exploration Fund. 4° 1881
—— Memoirs of the Topography, Orography, Hydrography, and Archæology. By Lieut. C. R. Conder and Lieut. H. H. Kitchener. Edited, with additions, by E. H. Palmer and Walter Besant, for the Committee of the Palestine Exploration Fund. Vol. 1. Sheets 1-6: Galilee. *Illustrations.* 4° 1881

Survey. The same. Vol. 2. Sheet 7-16:
Samaria. *Illustrations.* 4° 1882
—— The same. Vol. 3. Sheets 17-26:
Judæa. *Plans and illustrations.* 4°
1883
—— Jerusalem. By Col. Sir Charles
Warren and Capt. Claude Reigner
Conder. *Plans and illustrations.* 4°
1884
—— The Fauna and Flora of Palestine.
By H. B. Tristram. *Plates.* 4° 1884
—— Memoir on the Physical Geology
and Geography of Arabia Petræa,
Palestine, and adjoining Districts; with
Special Reference to the Mode of Forma-
tion of the Jordan-Arabah Depression
and the Dead Sea. By Edward Hull.
Maps and sections. 4° 1886
—— A General Index to—1. The Memoirs,
Vols. 1-3; 2. The Special ·Papers; 3.
The Jerusalem Volume; 4. The Flora
and Fauna of Palestine; 5. The Geo-
logical Survey; and to the Arabic and
English Name Lists. Compiled by
Henry C. Stewardson. 4° 1888
Survey of Eastern Palestine: Memoirs
of the Topography, Orography, Hydro-
graphy, Archæology, &c. Vol. 1. The
Adwân Country. By Major C. R.
Conder. *Map in cover, plans and illus-
trations.* 4° 1889
Twenty-one Years' Work in the Holy
Land (a Record and a Summary), 22nd
June 1865 to 22nd June 1886. *Plans
and illustrations.* 8° 1886
[*See also* Conder; Hart; Hull; Morri-
son; Warren, C.]

Palestine Pilgrims' Text Society.

Of the Holy Places visited by Antoninus
Martyr. Translated by Aubrey Stewart,
and annotated by Sir C. W. Wilson.
Map. Crown 8° 1885
The Pilgrimage of the Holy Paula. By
St Jerome. Translated by Aubrey
Stewart, and annotated by Sir C. W.
Wilson. *Map.* Crown 8° 1885
Of the Buildings of Justinian. By Pro-
copius. Translated by Aubrey Stewart,
and annotated by Sir C. W. Wilson
and Prof. H. Lewis. *Map and plates.*
Crown 8° 1886
Description of Syria, including Palestine.
By Mukaddasi. Translated from the
Arabic, and annotated by Guy Le
Strange. *Map and plans.* Crown 8°
1886
Itinerary from Bordeaux to Jerusalem.
"The Bordeaux Pilgrim." Translated by
Aubrey Stewart, and annotated by Sir
C. W. Wilson. *Plans.* Crown 8° 1887

La Palestine Illustrée: Collection de
Vues recueillies en Orient, par F. et E.
Thévoz, de Genève, reproduites par la
phototypie. Texte explicatif par Philippe
Bridel, pasteur à Lausanne. 1. De Jaffa
à Jérusalem; 2. De Jérusalem à Hébron.
Oblong 4° *Lausanne* [1889]
—— The same. 3. Samarie et Côte
maritime; 4. Galilée et Liban. Oblong
4° *Lausanne* [1890-91]

Anonymous.

Alphabethum Samaritanum. *A Fragment,
pp.* 5-100. 4°.
Relation nouvelle et exacte d'un Voyage
de la Terre Sainte. 12° *Paris,* 1688
Three Weeks in Palestine and Lebanon.
Plates. 12° 1836
An Excursion from Jericho to the Ruins
of the Ancient Cities of Geraza and
Amman in the Country east of the River
Jordan. 8° 1852
Two Months in Palestine; or, A Guide
to a Rapid Journey to the Chief Places
of Interest in the Holy Land. 2nd
edition. *Map and plates.* Small 8°
1871
Helps to the Study of the Bible, including
Introductions to the several Books, the
History and Antiquities of the Jews,
the results of Modern Discoveries, and
the Natural History of Palestine; with
copious tables, concordance, and indices,
and a series of maps. Small 8° *Oxford*
Viaggio da Gerusalemme per le coste
della Sorla. 2 vols. Small 8°
Leghorn, 1887

Jerusalem. Jerusalem Water Relief So-
ciety, established 1864. [Prospectus.]
8° [1864]
—— Note sur quelques Déterminations de
Coordonnées Géographiques. 8°
Paris, 1864
—— An Eastern Vacation in Jerusalem.
12° 1890

C. Syria.

Notes Géographiques pour servir d'Index
à la Carte de Syrie, relative à l'Histoire
de l'Expédition de Bonaparte en Orient.
8° *Paris,* 1803
Rambles in the Deserts of Syria and
among the Turkomans and Bedaweens.
8° 1864
Journey from Aleppo to Damascus; with
a Description of those two Capital Cities,
and the neighbouring parts of Syria;
to which is added an Account of the
Maronites inhabiting Mount Libanus,
&c. *Map.* 8° 1737

AUSTRALASIA AND PACIFIC ISLANDS.

AUSTRALIA, GENERAL.

The **Official** Directory and Year-Book of Australia for 1884. 8°.

The **Year-Book** of Australia for 1885. *Maps.* 8°.

Australian Museum. *See* New South Wales.

Auriferous Drifts in Australasia, or the Cause and its Continuity of the great Geological Convulsions, and the Theory of the Origin and Position of Auriferous Drifts. By " Research." 8°
Melbourne, 1868

The **Friend** of Australia ; or, A Plan for Exploring the Interior and for carrying on a Survey of the whole Continent. By a Retired Officer. *Map and plates.* 8° 1830

Aborigines of Australia. Extract from a Letter, dated Perth, Swan River, W. Australia, 1836. Letter from the Rev. Joseph Orton, dated Hobart Town, Van Dieman's Land, 1836. 8° [1836]

Competence in a Colony contrasted with Poverty at Home ; or, Relief to Landlords and Labourers held out by Australian Colonisation and Emigration. *Map.* 8° 1848

Report of Proceedings adopted for the Establishment of Steam Communication with the Australian Colonies and New Zealand. 8° 1850

Further Papers relative to the Discovery of Gold in Australia. Folio 1855

Sketches in Pencil and Ink of Australian Scenery, &c. [? Babbage's Expedition, 1858]. Oblong crown 8° N.D.

South Sea Bubbles. By "The Earl and the Doctor." 8° 1872

Report of the Sub-Committee of the Aborigines Protection Society. 8° N.D.

Australian Bibliography (in three parts). Catalogue of Books in the Free Public Library, Sydney, relating to, or published in, Australasia. 4° *Sydney,* 1893

BRITISH NEW GUINEA.

[Including also neighbouring Islands of the Western Pacific.]

Further Correspondence respecting New Guinea. Folio 1883
—— The same. Folio 1883

Correspondence respecting New Guinea and other Islands, and the Convention at Sydney of Representatives of the Australasian Colonies. Folio 1884

BRITISH NEW GUINEA.

Further Correspondence respecting New Guinea and other Islands in the Western Pacific Ocean. Folio 1885
—— The same. Folio 1885

Arrangement between Great Britain and Germany relative to their respective Spheres of Action in Portions of New Guinea. No. 1 (1885). Folio 1885

Correspondence respecting the Return of the New Guinea Islanders. *Chart.* Folio
Brisbane, 1885

Copies of certain Correspondence in reference to a Claim made by Mr Theodore Bevan for a Grant of Land in New Guinea. Folio [1888]

Report for the year 1888. By Her Majesty's Special Commissioner for the Protected Territory ; with Appendices. *Maps.* Folio *Sydney,* 1889

Correspondence by Administrator Macgregor on his Visits to Parts of British New Guinea. Two Colonial Office Papers, 11th Feb. and 2nd April 1889. Folio.

Despatch reporting Tour of Inspection made by His Honour the Administrator of British New Guinea, extending from Manu Manu on the Coast of the Possession to the Owen Stanley Range in the Interior. Folio 1889

Annual Report on British New Guinea, from 4th Sept. 1888 to 30th June 1889, with Appendices. *Map.* Folio *Brisbane,* 1890
—— The same, from 1st July 1889 to 30th June 1890, with Appendices. *Maps.* Folio *Brisbane,* 1890

Further Correspondence respecting New Guinea. *Maps.* Folio 1890

Annual Report on British New Guinea, from 1st July 1890 to 30th June 1891 ; with Appendices. *Maps.* Folio *Brisbane,* 1892

Handbook of Information for intending Settlers in British New Guinea. Published by authority. 8° *Brisbane,* 1892

Copies of Letters relating to the Proceedings of the Administrator of British New Guinea and the Dutch Resident of Ternate for the Rectification of the Dutch and British Borders in New Guinea. Folio [1893]

Exploration of New Guinea : an Inland Trip. 12° *Mackay,* 1886

The **Voyage** of the "Chevert," by Wm. Macleay ; Exploration of a New River, named the Baxter, by S. McFarlane ; D'Albertis's Account, &c. [Letters in the *Sydney Morning Herald* of 22nd October 1875.] Small 8° *Sydney,* 1875

BRITISH NEW GUINEA.

British New Guinea, with Illustrations of Scenery. Issued by Burns, Philip, & Co. 4°   *Sydney*, 1886
—— Position and Description. Folio 1889
Among the Islands : Explorations by the Administrator : Habits and Customs of the Natives ; Prospecting for Gold. [Newspaper Cuttings.] Folio   1889
Vocabulary of the Kiwai Language, British New Guinea. Folio
                                        [*Brisbane*] 1889

NEW SOUTH WALES.

A. Australian Museum.

Report of the Trustees for 1881. Folio
                                        Sydney, 1882
Descriptive Catalogue (with Notes) of the General Collection of Minerals in the Australian Museum. By A. Felix Ratte. 8°   *Sydney*, 1885
Catalogue of the Echinodermata in the Australian Museum. By E. P. Ramsay. Part 1. Echini Desmosticha and Petalosticha. *Plates.* 8°   *Sydney*, 1885
Memoirs, No. 2. Lord Howe Island, its Zoology, Geology, and Physical Characters. *Maps and plates.* 8°
                                        Sydney, 1889
Records of the Australian Museum. Edited by the Curator. Vol. 1, Nos. 1, 2, 4, 5. *Plates.* 8°   *Sydney*, 1890
Catalogue of the Marine Shells of Australia and Tasmania. Part 2. Pteropoda. By John Brazier. 8°   *Sydney*, 1892
—— *See also* Haswell, W. A.; Bale, W. M.

B. Department of Mines and Agriculture.

Mines and Mineral Statistics of New South Wales, and Notes on the Geological Collection of the Department of Mines. *Maps.* 8°   *Sydney*, 1875
Annual Report of the Department of Mines, New South Wales, for the years 1876-81, 1885-88, 1890 (of Mines and Agriculture), 1891-93. *Map, sections, &c.* 4°   *Sydney*, 1876-94
Mineral Products of New South Wales, by Harrie Wood ; Notes on the Geology of New South Wales, by C. S. Wilkinson— with Description of the Minerals of New South Wales, by Archibald Liversidge. Also Catalogue of Works, Papers, Reports, and Maps on the Geology, Palæontology, Mineralogy, &c., of the Australian Continent and Tasmania, by R. Etheridge, junr., and R. L. Jack. 4°   *Sydney*, 1882
—— The same, with Description of the Seams of Coal worked in New South Wales, by John Mackenzie. *Maps, plans, &c.* 4°   *Sydney*, 1887

NEW SOUTH WALES—B.

Geological Survey of New South Wales, by C. S. Wilkinson ; Geology of the Vegetable Creek Tin-Mining Field, New England District, with Maps and Sections, by T. W. Edgeworth David. 4°   *Sydney*, 1887
Memoirs of the Geological Survey of New South Wales, by C. S. Wilkinson. Palæontology, No. 1. The Invertebrate Fauna of the Hawkesbury, Wianamatta Series. (Beds above the productive Coal Measures.) By Robert Etheridge, junr. *Plates.* 4°   *Sydney*, 1888
—— Palæontology, No. 2. Contributions on the Tertiary Flora of Australia. By D. Constantin, Baron von Ettingshausen. *Plates.* 4°   *Sydney*, 1888
—— Palæontology, No. 3. Geological and Palæontological Relations of the Coal and Plant Bearing Beds of Palæozoic and Mesozoic Age in Eastern Australia and Tasmania, with special reference to the Fossil Flora . . . By Ottokar Feistmantel, M. D.,&c. *Plates.* 4° *Sydney*, 1890
—— Palæontology, No. 4. The Fossil Fishes of the Hawkesbury Series at Gosford. By Arthur Smith Woodward. *Maps.* 4°   *Sydney*, 1890
—— Palæontology, No. 5. A Monograph of the Carboniferous and Permo-Carboniferous Invertebrata of New South Wales. Part 1. Coelenterata. By R. Etheridge, junr. *Plates.* 4°   *Sydney*, 1891
—— The same, Part 2. Echinodermata, Annelida, and Crustacea. By R. Etheridge, junr. *Plates.* 4°   *Sydney*, 1894
—— Palæontology, No. 7. The Mesozoic and Tertiary Insects of New South Wales. By R. Etheridge, junr., and A. Sidney Olliff. *Plates.* 4° *Sydney*, 1890
—— Palæontology, No. 8. Contributions to a Catalogue of Works, Reports, and Papers on the Anthropology, Ethnology, and Geological History of the Australian and Tasmanian Aborigines. Parts 1 and 2. By R. Etheridge, junr. 4° *Sydney*, 1890-91
—— Geology, No. 5. Geology of the Broken Hill Lode and Barrier Ranges Mineral Field. By J. B. Jaquet. *Maps, plans, and sections.* 4°   *Sydney*, 1894
Records of the Geological Survey of New South Wales, Vol. 1, 1889-90. *Plates.* Small 4°   *Sydney*, 1890
—— Vol. 2, 1890-92   1892
—— Vol. 3, 1892-93   1894
—— Vol. 4, Parts 1 and 2   1894
Alphabetical List of Mineral Localities
                                        N.P., N.D.

C. Results of Observations.

Astronomical. Results of Astronomical Observations made at Sydney Observatory, 1877-78, under the direction of H. C. Russell. 8°   *Sydney*, 1881

NEW SOUTH WALES—C.

Astronomical. The same, in the years 1879, 1880, and 1881, under the direction of H. C. Russell. 8° *Sydney*, 1893
—— Observations of the Transit of Venus, 9th December 1874, made at Stations in New South Wales; illustrated with Photographs and Drawings, under the direction of H. C. Russell. 4° *Sydney*, 1892

Meteorological. Results of Meteorological Observations made in New South Wales during the years 1872-90, under the direction of H. C. Russell. *Maps and diagrams.* 8° *Sydney*, 1873-92 [*Note.* — Those for 1880-81-82 and 1883-84 not published till 1892.]

Rain and River (and Evaporation). Results of Rain and River Observations made in New South Wales during the years 1879-81, 1883-92. *Maps and diagrams.* 8° *Sydney*, 1880-93

D. Various Government Publications.

Report of the Commissioner of Inquiry into the State of the Colony of New South Wales. [Parly. Rep.] Folio 1822
—— The same, on the State of Agriculture and Trade in the Colony of New South Wales. [Parly. Rep.] Folio 1823
—— The same, on the Judicial Establishments of New South Wales and Van Diemen's Land. [Parly. Rep.] Folio 1823

Copies of the Royal Instructions to the Governors of New South Wales, Van Diemen's Land, and Western Australia, as to the Mode to be adopted in Disposing of Crown Lands. [Parly. Rep.] Folio 1831

Copies of Instructions given by His Majesty's Secretary of State for the Colonies, for promoting the Moral and Religious Instruction of the Aboriginal Inhabitants of New Holland or Van Diemen's Land. [Parly. Rep.] Folio 1831

Land Regulations: Copies of the Royal Instructions issued to Sir Thomas Brisbane and Lieut.-Gen. Darling respecting the Establishment and Duties of the Commissioners for Apportioning the Territory of New South Wales. [Parly. Rep.] Folio 1832

Debate in the Legislative Council of New South Wales, and other Documents on the subject of Immigration to the Colony, October 1840. 8° *Sydney*, 1840

Map of New South Wales, to accompany "Correspondence respecting Emigration," presented to both Houses of Parliament by Command, 1st May 1871. Folio 1871

Financial Statement of the Treasurer. Folio [*Sydney*] 1873

NEW SOUTH WALES—D.

Search for Leichardt's Party. Papers connected with Andrew Hume. Folio *Sydney*, 1874

Ways and Means: the Financial Statement of the Hon. Alexander Stuart, Colonial Treasurer of New South Wales made 24th January 1877. Small 8° *Sydney*, 1877

Railways of New South Wales: Report on their Construction and Working during 1876, by John Rae. *Maps and plans.* Folio *Sydney*, 1877

Lord Howe Island. Report on Present State and Future Prospects of. *Maps.* Folio *Sydney*, 1882

Royal Commission, Conservation of Water: First, Second, and Third (Final) Reports of the Commissioners. *Plans.* Folio *Sydney*, 1885-87
—— Diagrams and Plans to accompany First Report of the Commissioners. Folio.
—— The same, to accompany Final Report of Commissioners. Folio.

Stations determined Astronomically in connection with Trigonometrical Survey, 1891. Department of Lands, Sydney, N.S.W. *Map.* Large 8° *Sydney*, 1892

Reports of Departments of Lands, Public Works, Public Instruction, Forest Administration, &c. Folio *Sydney*, V.D.

Sydney Observatory: History and Progress. 8° N.D.

E. Miscellaneous and Anonymous.

Narrative of the Melancholy Wreck of the "Dunbar," Merchant Ship, on the South Head of Port Jackson, 20th August 1857. *Illustrations.* 8° *Sydney*, 1857

London International Exhibition, 1862: Catalogue of the Natural and Industrial Products of New South Wales; with a Map, and Introductory Account of its Population, Commerce, and General Resources. Small 4° 1862

Gazetteer of New South Wales. *Map.* 12° *Sydney* [1863]

Industrial Progress of New South Wales: being a Report of the Intercolonial Exhibition of 1870, at Sydney; together with a Variety of Papers illustrative of the Industrial Resources of the Colony. 8° *Sydney*, 1871

Railways. New South Wales Railway Guide. *Illustrations.* 4° *Sydney*, 1881
—— The same. For the use of Tourists, Excursionists, and others. *Containing various maps and numerous illustrations.* 3rd edition. 4° *Sydney*, 1886

New South Wales in 1881. Large 8° *Sydney*, 1881

New South Wales. Map, Illustrations, and Text. 4° *Sydney*, 1884

New South Wales—E.

New South Wales. Physical Geography and Climate. *Map and diagrams.* 8°
　　　　　　　　　　　　[*Sydney*, 1884]
Year-Book of New South Wales for 1885. *Map and illustrations.* 8°.
Melbourne Centennial International Exhibition, 1888. New South Wales Mineral Court: Descriptive Catalogue of Exhibits of Metals, Minerals, Fossils, and Timbers. Large 8° *Sydney*, 1889
Statistical Register of New South Wales for the year 1891. Compiled from Original Returns, by J. A. Coghlan. Folio　　　　　　　*Sydney*, 1892

———

Sydney. Visitors' Guide to Sydney, comprising Description of the City, &c., and Information respecting the Resources of New South Wales. *Plan.* 12°
　　　　　　　　　　　　Sydney, 1872

———

NEW ZEALAND.

A. Colonial Museum and Geological Survey.

Geological Survey of New Zealand: First General Report on the Coal Deposits of New Zealand. By James Hector. 8°
　　　　　　　　　Wellington, 1866
　　Abstract Report on the Progress of the Geological Survey of New Zealand during 1868-69 ; together with Reports on Barrier Island, Okarita District, East Cape, Thames Gold Fields, and Kawau Island. *Maps.* 8° *Wellington*, 1869
　　Second Report on the Thames Gold Fields, Province of Auckland ; together with Maps and Plans showing the position of some of the most important Claims, and Analysis of the Rock Specimens. *Maps.* 8° *Wellington*, 1869
　　Reports of Geological Explorations during 1870-71, 1871-72, 1873-74, 1874-76, 1876-77, 1877-78, 1878-79, 1879-80, 1881, 1882, 1883-84, 1885, 1886-87, 1887-88, 1888-89, 1890-91. *Maps, sections, and plates* *Wellington*, 1871-92
　　Maps of the Buller Coal Field, to illustrate Reports by Mr Cox and Mr Denniston. Geological Reports, 1874-77.
　　Index to Reports of the Geological Survey of New Zealand from 1866 to 1885 inclusive. 8° *Wellington*, 1887
Zoology, &c. 8° *Wellington*
　　Catalogue of the Birds of New Zealand, with Diagnoses of the Species. By F. W. Hutton　　　　　　　1871
　　Catalogue of the Echinodermata of New Zealand, with Diagnoses of the Species. By the same　　　1872
　　Catalogue of the Marine Mollusca of New Zealand, with Diagnoses of the Species. *Plate.* By the same　1873

New Zealand—A.

Zoology, &c.—*continued.*
　　Catalogue of the Tertiary Mollusca and Echinodermata of New Zealand, in the Collection of the Colonial Museum. By the same　　　　　　　　1873
　　Critical List of the Mollusca of New Zealand contained in European Collections. By E. von Martens　　1873
　　Catalogue of the Land Mollusca of New Zealand, with Descriptions of the Species. From various Authors 1873
　　Manual of the Indigenous Grasses of New Zealand. By John Buchanan. *Plates*　　　　　　　　1880
　　Palæontology of New Zealand. Part 4. Corals and Bryozoa of the Neozoic Period in New Zealand. By the Rev. J. E. Tenison-Woods. *Plates*　　　1880
　　Manual of the New Zealand Coleoptera. By Capt. T. Broun　1880-93
　　Manual of the New Zealand Mollusca: a Systematic and Descriptive Catalogue of the Marine and Land Shells, and of the Soft Mollusks and Polyzoa of New Zealand and the adjacent Islands. By F. W. Hutton　　　　　　1880
　　Catalogues of the New Zealand Diptera, Orthoptera, Hymenoptera ; with Descriptions of the Species. By F. W. Hutton. 8°　　　　　　1881
　　Manual of the Birds of New Zealand. By W. L. Buller. *Plates.* 8°　1882
　　Studies in Biology for New Zealand Students. No. 3. The Anatomy of the Common Mussels (Mytilus latus, edulis, Magellanicus). By Alex. Purdie, M.A. *Plates.* 8°　　　　　　1887
　　Phormium Tenax as a Fibrous Plant. Edited by Sir J. Hector. *Plates* 1889

Annual Reports [some missing] on the Colonial Museum and Laboratory; together with Lists of Donations and Deposits　　　　　　1868-93

Meteorological Report, 1873 ; including Returns for 1871-72, and averages for previous years　　　　　　1874
　　The same, 1875; including Returns for 1873-74, &c.　　　　　　1877
　　The same, 1877; including Returns for 1875-76, &c.　　　　　　1878
　　The same, 1880; including Returns for 1877-78-79, &c. 8°　　1881
　　The same, 1883 ; including Returns for 1880-81-82, &c. *Diagrams.* 8° 1884
　　The same, 1885 ; including Returns for 1883 and 1884, and Averages for previous years. *Diagrams.* 8° [1885]

Handbook of New Zealand. By Sir J. Hector. *Maps and diagrams.* 3rd and 4th editions. 8°　　　　1883-86

Catalogue of the Colonial Museum and Library. Large 8° *Wellington*, 1890

NEW ZEALAND.

B. Survey Department.

Two Reports by the Surveyor-General (J. T. Thomson) on the Surveys of New Zealand. *Plans.* Folio
Wellington, 1877

Reports for the years 1881-82, 1882-83, 1883-84, 1885-86, 1886-87, and 1887-88, by J. M'Kerrow ; and for 1888-89, 1889-90, 1890-91, 1891-92, 1892-93, by S. Percy Smith. *Maps and plans, &c.*
Wellington, 1882-93

C. Various Government Publications.

Statistics of New Zealand for 1853-62, compiled from Official Records, including the Results of a Census of the Colony taken 16th December 1861. 7 vols. *Tables.* Folio *Auckland,* 1858-63
—— Statistics of the Colony of New Zealand for 1869, '70, '72, '74, '76, '77, and '78. Folio *Wellington,* 1870-79
—— Appendix to the Statistics of New Zealand for the year 1884 : a Series of Diagrams, showing the Progress of the Colony by increase of Population, Trade, Live Stock, Cultivation, Occupied Holdings, Deposits in Banks, Revenue, Railways, Telegraph Lines, Shipping Inwards and Outwards ; and the Ages of the People, Birthplaces, Religious Denominations, Education, Industries, as at the Census of April 1881. Folio
Wellington, 1886
—— Statistics of the Colony of New Zealand for the year 1885 ; with Abstracts from the Agricultural Statistics of 1886. Folio *Wellington,* 1886
—— Statistics of the Colony of New Zealand for the years 1890 to 1892, with Abstracts from the Agricultural Statistics, &c. *Wellington,* 1891-93
—— Report on the Statistics of New Zealand, 1890 *Wellington,* 1892

Papers relating to the Recent Disturbances in New Zealand. [Parly. Rep.] *Maps.* Folio 1861

Report on the Geological Formation of the Timaru District in reference to obtaining a Supply of Water. By Julius Haast. *Sections.* Folio
Christchurch, 1865

New Zealand Exhibition, 1865 : Reports and Awards of the Jurors, and Appendix. 8° *Dunedin,* 1866

Extract from Parliamentary Debates : Second Session of the Fourth Parliament, Legislative Council, 6th September 1867. 8° *Chester,* 1867

New Zealand Court: International Exhibition, Sydney, 1879. Appendix to Official Catalogue. 8° *Wellington,* 1880

Results of a Census of the Colony of New Zealand, taken for the night of the 3rd April 1881. Folio *Wellington,* 1882

NEW ZEALAND—C.

Results of a Census of New Zealand, taken for the night of the 28th March 1886. Folio *Wellington,* 1887
—— Ditto. Taken for the night of the 5th April 1891. Folio *Wellington,* 1892

New Zealand Thermal - Springs Districts : Papers relating to the Sale of the Township of Rotorua ; together with information relating to the Hot-Springs Districts, and a Report on the Mineral Waters. *Maps and plans.* 4°
Wellington, 1882

Crown Lands Guide. Nos. 5 and 10. *Maps.* 8° *Wellington,* 1883-90

Recent Volcanic Eruptions, Preliminary Report on. By Dr Hector. *Map and diagram.* Folio [*Wellington*] 1886

Exhibition. New Zealand Industrial Exhibition, 1885 : The Official Record. *Plan.* 8° *Wellington,* 1886

Waitomo Caves, King Country, Report on. *Plans and illustrations.* Folio
[*Wellington*] 1886

Mining Machinery and Treatment of Ores in Australian Colonies. Reports on Machinery exhibited at the Melbourne Exhibition : on Mining, and Plants for the Reduction and Treatment of Ores . . . ; on Processes adopted in America, &c. *Plates.* Folio *Wellington,* 1889

Report on the Mining Industry of New Zealand *Wellington,* 1891

The Cheviot Estate. Particulars, Terms, and Conditions of Disposal and Occupation of 33,474 acres, open on 13th and 17th November 1893. *Maps and illustrations.* 8° *Wellington,* 1893
[*See also* United Kingdom, H, Emigrants' Handbooks ; I, Colonial and Indian Exhibition.]

D. Miscellaneous and Anonymous.

Grammar and Vocabulary of the Language of New Zealand. Published by the Church Missionary Society. 12° 1820

British Colonisation of New Zealand : being an Account of the Principles, Objects, and Plans of the New Zealand Association ; with particulars concerning the Position, Extent, Soil, and Climate, Natural Productions, and Native Inhabitants of New Zealand. *Maps and plates.* 12° 1837

Twelfth Report of the Directors of the New Zealand Company, held 26th April 1844, with Documents appended. 2 parts. 8° 1844

On the British Colonisation of New Zealand. By the Committee of the Aborigines' Protection Society. 8° 1846

Sketch of the present Position of the Province of Auckland, Statistically and Financially. *Map.* 8° 1863

NEW ZEALAND—D.

The New Zealand Government and the Maori War of 1863-64, with especial reference to the Confiscation of Native Lands, and the Colonial Ministry's Defence of their War Policy. 8°   1864

New Zealand, Graphic and Descriptive. The illustrations by C. D. Barraud; edited by W. T. L. Travers. *Coloured plates.* Atlas folio   1877

Sutherland Fall, the Highest Waterfall in the World. [Cuttings from the *Nelson Evening Mail*, Jan. 16, 1889.] 8°

Some particulars concerning New Zealand. 8°   N.D.

Early History of New Zealand. (Brett's Historical Series.) 4°   *Auckland*, 1890

QUEENSLAND.

Report of the Proceedings of the Government schooner "Spitfire," in search of the mouth of the River Burdekin, and Exploration of a portion of the Coast of N.E. Australia. By G. E. Dalrymple. 8°   *Brisbane*, 1860

Review of Works on Queensland. 8°   [*Edinburgh*, 1863]

Report from the Joint Select Committee on Existing and Proposed Lines of Steam Communication, together with the Proceedings of the Committee and Minutes of Evidence. Folio   *Brisbane*, 1865

On the New Settlement in Rockingham Bay, and advance of Colonisation over North-Eastern Australia, including Mr J. E. Dalrymple's Report on his Journey from Rockingham Bay to the Valley of Lagoons. 8°   1865

Queensland as a Field for Emigration. 8°   1868

Handbook for Emigrants to Queensland, Australia. 8°   [1870]

Census of 1871, taken on the 1st day of September, being the fourth taken in the Colony. Folio   *Brisbane*, 1872

—— Eighth Census of the Colony of Queensland, taken on April 5, 1891. *Map and diagram.* Folio   *Brisbane*, 1892

Narrative and Reports of the Queensland North-East Coast Expedition, 1873. Folio   [*Brisbane*, 1874]

Geological Features of part of the Coast Range between the Dalrymple and Charters Towers Roads [Preliminary Report relating to]. Folio   [*Brisbane*] 1879

—— Survey of Northern Queensland : Further Reports on the Progress of the Gold-Prospecting Expedition in Cape York Peninsula. *Map.* Folio   [*Brisbane*] 1881

QUEENSLAND.

Geological Survey. Annual Progress Reports for the years 1889-92. *Maps, &c.*   *Brisbane*, 1890-93

Cultivation of Kaurie Pine on Fraser Island [Papers in connection with the]. Folio   [*Brisbane*] 1882

Report on the Sugar Industry on the Clarence and Richmond Rivers. By A. Meston. Folio   [*Brisbane*] 1882

Meteorological Reports for 1881, 1887-91. *Maps and diagrams*   *Brisbane*, 1882-92

Report on Proposed Railway, Cloncurry Mines to Gulf of Carpentaria. *Map.* Folio   *Brisbane*, 1884

Oyster Fisheries of Moreton Bay. Report on the. *Map.* Folio   *Brisbane*, 1884

—— The same. *Maps.* Folio   [*Brisbane*, 1886]

Management of the Public Gardens and Reserves of the Colony. Folio   *Brisbane*, 1884

Reports upon Sundry Rivers and Harbours in the Gulf of Carpentaria. *Charts.* Folio   [*Brisbane*] 1884

The Return of the New Guinea Islanders, Correspondence respecting. *Chart.* Folio   *Brisbane*, 1885

Queensland. Essays on its Resources and Institutions. *Plates.* 8°   1886

Report on Harbours and Lighthouses. Folio   *Brisbane*, 1887

Report on the Geology and Mineral Resources of the Districts of Kilkivan and Black Snake. By the Assistant Government Geologist. *Maps and plans.* Folio   *Brisbane*, 1886

The Survey of the Queensland Coast. Surveying services performed by the "Paluma" during 1885 and 1886   *Brisbane*, 1887

Styx River Coal Fields (Report on, by William H. Rands)   1892

[*See* United Kingdom, H, Emigrants' Handbooks; *also* Coode; Cullen; Hodgkinson; Jack; Maitland; Meston; Watson.]

SOUTH AUSTRALIA.

A. Government Publications.

Survey of Northern Territory. Folio   *Adelaide*, 1869

Report on Anglo-Australian Telegraph (C. Todd). *Map.* Folio   *Adelaide*, 1869

Report on the Mineral Resources lying within 250 Miles of Port Augusta (G. H. F. Ulrich). *Map and plates.* Folio   *Adelaide*, 1872

Colonel Warburton's Explorations. Folio   *Adelaide*, 1873

W. C. Gosse's Explorations, 1873. *Maps.* Folio   *Adelaide*, 1874

SOUTH AUSTRALIA—A.

Lieut. Goalen's Survey of Port Adelaide. *Map.* Folio [*Adelaide*, 1875]

Report on the Lake Eyre Expedition (J. W. Lewis). *Map.* Folio [*Adelaide*, 1875]

E. Giles's Explorations, 1873-74. *Map.* Folio N.D.

E. Giles's Explorations, 1875-76. Proceedings of the Hon. Thomas Elder's Expedition, under the Command of Ernest Giles, from Perth to Adelaide. *Maps.* Folio *Adelaide*, N.D.

E. Giles's Explorations, 1875-76. *Map.* Folio *Adelaide*, 1876

Statistical Register for 1875. Folio *Adelaide*, 1876

Navigability of Murray Mouth. (Return by Robert Hickson.) *Maps.* Folio *Adelaide*, 1876

Sections of Port Adelaide Creek. (Report by Lieut. Goalen). *Maps.* Folio *Adelaide*, 1876

Australian Coastline and Ports. (Report by F. Howard). Folio *Adelaide*, 1876

Improvement of Semaphore Harbour. Folio *Adelaide*, 1876

Report from the Public Works Department for 1875. Folio *Adelaide*, 1876

Progress of South Australia, 1870 to 1875. Folio *Adelaide*, 1876

Journal of Mr Henry Barclay's Exploration, 1878. *Plan.* Folio *Adelaide*, 1878

Meteorological Observations made at the Adelaide Observatory during the years 1878-79-80. *Map.* Folio *Adelaide*, 1879-82

Meteorological Observations made at the Adelaide Observatory, and other places in South Australia and the Northern Territory, during the years 1881-82-83, 1884-85, 1886-87, and 1888-90, under the direction of Charles Todd. Folio *Adelaide*, 1884-93

Examination of Country North-east of Eucla. *Plan.* Folio *Adelaide*, 1880

Woods and Forests. Annual Report of the Forest Board, with Conservator's Progress Report, and Appendices, for 1880-81. *Plans.* Folio *Adelaide*, 1881

—— Annual Progress Report upon State Forest Administration in South Australia for the year 1881-82, by J. Ednie Brown. 4° *Adelaide*, 1882

Diary of Northern Exploration Party under the Leadership of Mr Charles Winnecke. Folio [*Adelaide*, 1884?]

Mr D. Lindsay's Explorations through Arnheim's Land. *Map.* Folio 1884

Work in Progress in Geological Department. Folio *Adelaide*, 1884

SOUTH AUSTRALIA—A.

Government Geologist's Report *re* Visit to Far North. Folio [*Adelaide*, 1884]

—— The same, on a Journey from Adelaide to Hale River. *Map and section.* Folio [1889]

Quarterly Report on the Northern Territory. Folio 1884

Report on Telegraphic Determination of Australian Longitudes. Folio 1886

Report on Nullabor Plain and Fowler's Bay Country. Folio *Adelaide*, 1887

Final Report of Commission on Transcontinental Railway; together with Minutes of Proceedings and Appendices. *Illustrations and map.* Folio *Adelaide*, 1887

Journal of Mr W. H. Tietkens' Central Australian Exploring Expedition. *Map and plate* Folio [*Adelaide*] 1890

[*See* United Kingdom, H, Emigrants' Handbooks : I. Colonial Exhibition.]

B. Miscellaneous and Anonymous.

Plan of a Company to be Established for the Purpose of Founding a Colony in Southern Australia. *Map.* 8° 1832

Summary of Geographical Discoveries during 1857, to the Westward and Northward of Eyria (the Port Lincoln Peninsula), South Australia, abridged from the *South Australian Register* and the *Adelaide Observer.* [1 *leaf.*] Folio *Derby*, 1858

Handbook of South Australia. *Plan and illustrations.* 8° 1886

Prospectus of the Northern Territory Pastoral Company Limited, the Property of W. F. & N. Buchanan, on the Victoria River and Stuarts Creek, Northern Territory of South Australia. *Map.* 8° 1887

TASMANIA.

Copies of all Correspondence between Lieut.-Gov. Arthur and His Majesty's Secretary of State for the Colonies on the subject of the Military Operations lately carried on against the Aboriginal Inhabitants of Van Diemen's Land. [Parly. Rep.] Folio 1831

The Van Diemen's Land Almanack for the year 1832. 12° 1832

Statistical Returns of Van Diemen's Land, from 1824 to 1835 and 1839. Folio *Hobart*, 1836-39

Sketches of Tasman's Peninsula. 8° *Tasmania*, 1837

Mount Bischoff, Mr Sprent's Report on Country round. Folio *Hobarttown*, 1876

Hobbarttown oder Sommerfrische in den Antipoden. *Map and illustrations.* 4° *Prague*, 1886

[*See also* United Kingdom, H, Emigrants' Handbooks.]

VICTORIA.

A. Geological Survey, &c.

Prodromus of the Palæontology of Victoria; or, Figures and Descriptions of Victorian Organic Remains. Decades i., iii. By Frederick M'Coy. *Plates.* 8°
Melbourne, 1874-76

Prodromus of the Zoology of Victoria ; or, Figures and Descriptions of the Living Species of all Classes of the Victorian Indigenous Animals. By Frederick M'Coy. Vols. 1 and 2. *Plates.* Imperial 8°
Melbourne and London, 1885-90

Observations on New Vegetable Fossils of the Auriferous Drifts. By Baron Ferdinand von Mueller. *Plates.* Large 8°
Melbourne, 1883

B. Department of Mines.

Reports of the Mining Surveyors and Registrars. Quarters ending September and December 1867 ; March and September 1868 ; June and December 1869, 1870, 1871 ; March 1872, 1873-76 ; March and September 1877 ; June and September 1878 ; March and September 1879 ; March and September 1887. Folio   *Melbourne*, 1867-80
—— The Gold Fields of Victoria. Reports of the Mining Registrars for the quarters ended March and June 1885 and 1886, September and December 1886, and June 1887.

Mineral Statistics of Victoria for the years 1867-78, 1880, 1885. Folio
Melbourne, 1868-86

Reports of the Chief Inspector of Mines to the Honourable the Minister of Mines, for the years 1874-79. Folio
Melbourne, 1875-80

Report of Progress by R. Brough Smith, Secretary for Mines, &c. . . ; with Reports on the Geology, Mineralogy, and Physical Structure of various parts of the Colony, by F. M. Krausé, R. A. F. Murray, A. M. Howitt, N. Taylor, T. Cowan, W. Nicholas, and J. C. Newbery. *Maps and plates.* 8°
Melbourne, 1876
—— The same, 1877-78-80 and 1884
Melbourne and London, 1877-84

Annual Report of the Secretary for Mines and Water Supply on the Workings of the Regulation and Inspection of Mines and Mining Machinery Act during the year 1885. *Plates.* Folio
Melbourne, 1886
Ditto, during the years 1887 and 1888-89. *Plans and plates.* Folio
Melbourne, 1888-90

Annual Reports of the Secretary for Mines for the years 1889-92. Folio
Melbourne, 1890-93

C. Various Government Publications.

Report of Commander Norman, of H.M.C.S. "Victoria," together with copy of his Journal on the late Expedition to the Gulf of Carpentaria
Melbourne [1842]

The Victorian Government Prize Essays, 1860. 8°   *Melbourne*, 1861
Acheson, F. Essay on the Collection and Storage of Water in Victoria.
Mayes, C. On the Manufactures more immediately required for the Economical Development of the Resources of the Colony, with special reference to those Manufactures, the Raw Materials of which are the Produce of Victoria. *Map.*
Rosales, H. On the Origin and Distribution of Gold in Quartz Veins, and its Association with other Minerals ; and on the best improved methods of excavating Gold from its matrices.
Story, W. Upon the Agriculture of Victoria, with reference to its Climate Advantages, and the Geological and Chemical Character of the Soils. *Plan.*

Report of the Government Botanist and Director of the Botanic and Zoological Garden. [F. Mueller.] Folio
Melbourne, 1861

Report of the Commissioners appointed to Enquire into and Report upon the Circumstances connected with the Sufferings and Death of Robert O'Hara Burke and William John Wills, the Victorian Explorers. Folio   *Melbourne* [1862]

Progress Reports and Final Report of the Exploration Committee of the Royal Society of Victoria. Folio   1872

Report on the Physical Character and Resources of Gippsland. By the Surveyor-General and Secretary of Mines. *Map and geological sections.* 8°
Melbourne, 1874

Census of Victoria, 1871. Parts 1 to 9 (B) ; with Preliminary Report. Ditto, Part 9 (B)—Occupations of the People : Detailed Tables. Ditto, General Report and Appendices. Folio *Melbourne*, 1874
—— Ditto, 1881. Approximate Returns. Folio   *Melbourne*, 1881
—— The same. [*Single sheet*]
—— The same. *Tables.* Folio
Melbourne, 1892

Statistics of Friendly Societies for the years 1873-76, 1878 ; with Reports by the Government Statist, and Annual Reports of the Proceedings of the Government Statist in connection with Friendly Societies, 1879-80. Folio
Melbourne, 1874-80

VICTORIA—C.

Australasian Statistics for the years 1873-76, 1879-81; with Reports by the Government Statist of Victoria. Folio
Melbourne, 1874-82
Agricultural Statistics, 1875-76, 1876-77, 1879-80. Folio *Melbourne*
—— Ditto, for the year ended 1st March 1885. Folio.
Report of the Conference of Government Statists held in Tasmania, 1875; with Introductory Letter by the Government Statist of Victoria. Folio *Melbourne*, 1875
[*See also* United Kingdom, H, Emigrants' Handbooks.]

D. Miscellaneous and Anonymous.

Gipps' Land. Progress of Discovery in Gipps' Land, between the Australian Alps and the Eastern Coast. 12° 1840
Catalogue of the Victorian Exhibition, 1861; with Prefatory Essays indicating the Progress, Resources, and Physical Characteristics of the Colony. By Archer, Mueller, Smyth, Neumayer, M'Coy, Selwyn, Birkmyre. 8° *Melbourne*, 1861
Essais Divers, servant d'Introduction au Catalogue de l'Exposition des produits de la Colonie de Victoria : mettants en Relief les Progrès, Ressources, et Caractère physique de la Colonie. (Par W. H. Archer, F. Mueller, R. B. Smyth, Neumayer, F. M'Coy, A. R. C. Selwyn, W. Birkmyre.) 8° *Melbourne*, 1861
Die Colonie Victoria in Australien ; ihr Fortschritt, ihre Hilfsquellen, und ihr physikalischer Charakter. (Translated by B. Loewy.) 8° *Melbourne*, 1861
Illustrated Handbook of Victoria, Australia. Large 8° *Melbourne*, 1886
The Victorian Tourist's Railway Guide
Melbourne, 1892
Columbus Jubilee, Melbourne Town Hall, 12th October 1892. [From the *Proceedings*, Victorian Branch, R.G.S. Austr.]
" **Through Gipps' Land.** " Cutting from *Melbourne Argus* of 14th Feb. 1874.

WESTERN AUSTRALIA.

Report of the Committee, appointed 3rd August 1838, to take into Consideration the Present State and Condition of the Colony of Western Australia, embodying a Statistical Report to the end of June 1837, with a Supplement to the close of the year, hy Sir James Stirling. Royal 8° *Perth*, 1838
Geological Exploration S. of the Murchison River. *Map.* Folio *Perth*, 1873
Special Settlement of that part of the Territory of Western Australia which is North of the 19th Parallel of South Latitude. Folio *Perth*, 1878

WESTERN AUSTRALIA.

Instructions Issued to Alexander Forrest, Esq., Commander of the Northern Exploring Expedition: and Progress Reports of Expedition from De Grey River to Beagle Bay, and from Beagle Bay to Port Darwin, by A. Forrest. *Map.* Folio
Perth, 1879
Crown Lands and Surveys. Report for the year 1878. *Maps.* Folio *Perth*, 1879
A Brief Account of the Natives of Western Australia, their Character, Manners, and Customs; prepared . . . to illustrate the Collection of Weapons, Implements, &c., sent to the Exhibition at Sydney, N.S.W., 1879. *Diagram and map.* 8° *Perth*, 1879
Report by the Director of Public Works, on the Public Works of the Colony, for the year 1885. *Map.* Folio *Perth*, 1886
Blue-Book for 1887. Folio *Perth*, 1888
Annual General Report for 1888-89. By Henry Page Woodward, Government Geologist. 8° *Perth*, 1890
Annual General Report for the year 1890. By H. P. Woodward *Perth*, 1891
Report on the Goldfields of Kimberley District. By H. P. Woodward *Perth*, 1891

Second Report of the Western Australian Association. *Map.* 8° 1837
Journals and Reports of Two Voyages to the Glenelg River and the North-West Coast of Australia, 1863-64. *Maps.* 8° *Perth*, 1864
Notes of Travel in the Far North of West Australia : a Visit to Beagle Bay Mission
N.D.
[*See* United Kingdom, H, Emigrants' Handbooks.]

PACIFIC ISLANDS.

South Sea Company. A View of the Coasts, Countries, and Islands within the limits of the South Sea Company : containing an Account of the Discoveries, Settlements, Progress, and Present State ; with the Bays, Ports, Harbours, and Rivers, &c., the various Winds and Soundings ; the Product, People, Manufactures, Trade, and Riches of the several places ; from the River Aranoca to Terra del Fuego, and through the South Sea to the farthest bounds of the late Act of Parliament. Collected from the best Authors. 8° 1711
An Account of the Discoveries made in the South Pacifick Ocean previous to 1764. Part 1. *Plates* 1767
Three Years in the Pacific : containing Notices of Brazil, Chile, Bolivia, Peru, &c., in 1831-34. By an Officer in the U.S. Navy. 2 vols. 8° 1835

EUROPE.

GENERAL.

Correspondence respecting the European Commissions appointed for the Demarcation of Frontiers under the Treaty of Berlin. [Parly. Rep.] Folio 1879
Further Correspondence respecting the European Commissions appointed for the Demarcation of Frontiers under the Treaty of Berlin. [Parly. Rep.] *Map and plan.* Folio 1880

Prospetto Geographico-Statistico degli Stati Europei. Oblong 8° *Milan,* 1802
An Enquiry into the Primeval State of Europe. Small 8° 1864
Die Grundzüge im geologischen Bau Europa's. *Map.* 8° *Gotha,* 1881
The Hotels of Europe, 1885, with Maps, and Railway and Steamship Routes, and Appendix of Foreign Hotels. Large 8°.
The Picturesque Mediterranean. 2 vols. *Coloured and other illustrations.* 4° 1890-91

Illustrated Europe.—Europäische Wanderbilder.—L'Europe Illustrée. *Maps and illustrations.* 12° *Zurich,* N.D.

English Edition.

No. 1. The Arth-Rigi Railway. No. 3. The Vitznau-Rigi-Rail, by August Feierabend. No. 9. Zurich and its Environs. No. 10. Constance and its Environs. No. 11. Nyon and its Environs, by Aug. Testury. No. 12. Thusis, by A. Rumpf. No. 13. Lucerne and its Environs. No. 14. Florence, by S. H. M. Byers. Nos. 15, 16. Milan, by J. Hardmeyer. No. 17. Schaffhausen and the Falls of the Rhine. No. 18. Ragaz-Pfäfers. No. 19. Vevey, its Environs and Climate, by Alfr. Ceresole. No. 20. The Baths of Kreuth (Bad Kreuth) in the Bavarian Alps, by Dr May. No. 21. Davos. No. 22. The Baths of Reinery, by P. Dargler. No. 23. The Gruyère, the new Mountain Road from Vevey to Interlaken by Bulle-Boltigen. Nos. 24, 25, 26. The St Gothard Railway. Nos. 27, 28. Freiburg (Baden) and its Environs, by L. Neumann. Nos. 29, 30. Görbersdorf, Dr Brehmer's Sanatorium for Consumptives, by R. Ortmann. Nos. 31, 32. Chaux-de-Fonds, Locle, Brenets, and their Environs. No. 33. From Froburg to Waldenburg, an Excursion among

GENERAL.

Illustrated Europe —*continued.*
the Mountains of Soleure and Basle. Nos. 34, 35. The Bürgenstock, Lake of Lucerne, by Dr W. Cubasch. Nos. 36, 37. Neuchatel and its Environs, by A. Bachelin. Nos. 38, 39. Battaglia, near Padua, by Edward Mautner. Nos. 40,41. Coire and its Environs, by Dr E. Killias. Nos. 48, 49, 50. From the Danube to the Adriatic : Vienna, Semmering, Trieste, Abbazia, by Dr Henry Noé. Nos. 51, 52. Graz. Nos. 53, 54. From Paris to Berne *via* Dijon and Pontarlier. Nos. 55, 56. The Lake of Lucerne, by I. Hardmeyer. No. 57. The Bergstrasse from Jugenheim to Auerbach, by Ernest Pasqué. Nos. 58, 59. Aix-les-Bains and its Environs, by V. Barbier. Nos. 60, 61. Heidelberg, by Carl Pfaff. Nos. 62, 63,64. Budapest, by Edmund Steinacker. No. 65. Montreux (Lake of Geneva), from the French of Alfred Ceresole. Nos. 69, 70, 71, 72. Canton Glarus and the Lake of Walenstadt, by Ernest Buss. Nos. 73, 74, 75, 76. From Paris to Milan *via* Mont Cenis (Fréjus), by V. Barbier. Nos. 77, 78, 79. The Black Forest Railway (Grand-Duchy of Baden), by J. Hardmeyer.

German Edition.

No. 2. Die Vetliberg-Bahn, von J. J. Binder, 2 aufl. No. 5. Der Wallgahrtsort Einseedeln. No. 14. Das Tössthal, von Dr G. Geilfus. No. 25. Eisenerz in der obern Steiermark, von J. Krainz. No. 28. Pyrmont, von R. Geissler. No. 29. Villach in Kärnten, und seine Umgebung, von H. Noé. Nos. 38, 39. Bad Krankenheil-Tölz im Bayerischen Hochlande, von G. Schäfer. Nos. 42, 43. Das Vorchristliche Rom, von Dr O. Henne-Amrhyn. Nos. 44, 45, 46. Ajaccio als Winterkurort, und die Insel Corsica, von R. Gerber. Nos. 47, 48. Augsburg, von A. Buff. Nos. 49, 50. Bonn und seine Umgebung, von L. Lorbach. Nos. 71,72. Durch den Arlberg, von Ludwig von Hörmann. Nos. 77, 78, 79, 80. Konstantinopel und Umgebung, von P. Leowhardi. Nos. 81, 82. Wallis und Chamonix, von der Furka bis Brig. von F. O. Wolf. No. 83. Das National-Denkmal am Niederwald, von Josef Schrattenholz. Nos. 92, 93. Bad Driburg, aus dem Tagebuche eines Hypochonders, von Dr

GENERAL.

Illustrated Europe—*continued.*

Theodor Riefenstahl. Nos. 94, 95.
Wallis und Chamonix, II. Heft : Brig
und der Simplon, von F. O. Wolf.
Nos. 99, 100, 101, 102. Wallis und Chamonix, III. Heft : die Visperthäler, von
F. C. Wolf. Nos. 103, 104. Murten,
von Dr F. Stock. Nos. 105, 106, 107.
Wallis und Chamonix, IV. Heft : Löt-
schen und Leukerbad, von F. C. Wolf.
Nos. 108, 109, 110. Wallis und Chamonix, V. Heft : die Thäler von Turt-
man und Eifisch, von F. O. Wolf. Nos.
114, 115, 116. Lugano und die Verbind-
ungslinie zwischen den drei oberitalien-
ischen See'n, von J. Hardmeyer. Nos.
121, 122. Bad Cudowa (Provinz Schlesien): von F. L. Martieb. Nos. 123,
124. Die Höllenthalbahn, von Sieg-
fried Bodenheimer. No. 125. Fried-
richshafen am Bodensee.

French Edition.

No. 140. Le Chemin de Fer du Monte
Generoso, par J. Hardmeyer.

Picturesque Europe; with Illustrations
on Steel and Wood by the most Eminent
Artists. 5 vols. 4°　　　　　　N.D.

AUSTRIA-HUNGARY.

A. Official Reports.

Statistischen Bureau der kön. Freistadt
Pest. Publicationen, Nos. 3, 7, 9, 11,
13, 54, 63, 69, 71, 77, 83, 89, 90, 101,
125, 127. [III., V.-VIII., XV. (Band
i.-iii.), XVI.-XX., XXII.-XXV. (Band
i.) Medium and royal 8°
　　　　　Budapest and Berlin, 1871-94
[*See* Körösi.]
Bericht über die " Nautilus " Expedition.
See Wolf, J.
Astronomische, Magnetische, und Meteoro-
logische Beobachtungen an der K. K.
Sternwarte zu Prag im Jahre 1881.
　　　　　　　　　Prague, N.D.
Verhandlungen der Oesterreichischen
Gradmessungs Commission. Protokolle
über die Sitzungen, 1885-94. 8°
　　　　　　　　Vienna, 1889-94
Mediterranean. Berichte der Commission
für Erforschung des Oestlichen Mittel-
meeres. Erste Reihe. *Maps and illus-
trations.* 4°　　　　*Vienna* [1893 ?]
—— Ditto. Zweite Reihe. *Maps and
plates.* 4°　　　　　*Vienna* [1893]
—— Ditto. Dritte Reihe. *Maps and
plates.* 4°　　　　　*Vienna* [1894]
[Aus den Denkschriften der Kais.
Akad. der Wissenschaften, Band 59, 60,
61.]

AUSTRIA-HUNGARY.

B. Miscellaneous Publications.

Adriatic. Erster Bericht der ständigen
Commission für die Adria an die kais.
Akademie der Wissenschaften. *Tables.*
8°　　　　　　　　*Vienna*, 1869
Oesterreichischer Ingenieur und Archi-
tekten Verein. II. Bericht des Hydro-
technischen Comité's über die Wasser-
abnahme in den Quellen, Flüssen, und
Strömen in den Culturstaaten. *Plates.*
8°　　　　　　　　*Vienna*, 1881
Festschrift aus Veranlassung der Fün-
fundzwanig Jährigen Jubelfeier der K. K.
Geographischen Gesellschaft in Wien im
December 1881. Small 4° *Vienna*, 1881
Bericht über das X. Vereinsjahr (15
November 1883 bis 6 December 1884)
erstattet vom Vereine der Geographen an
der Universitat Wien. 8° *Vienna*, 1885
*Publications of the National Hungarian
Academy of Science.*
Acsády, Ignácz. Magyarorszag pén-
zügyei I. Ferdinánd uralkodása alatt,
1526-64. 8°　　　　*Budapest*, 1888
Ballagi, Aladar. Colbert. Parts 1 and
2. 8°　　　　　*Budapest*, 1887-90
Beke, Antal, and Barabas Samu. I.
Rákoczy György és a porta. Levelek és
ikiratok. 8°　　　　*Budapest*, 1888
Coloman, Szily. Rapport sur les Travaux
de l'Academie des Sciences de Hongrie
en 1892 8°　　　　*Budapest*, 1893
Csánki, Dezsö. Hunyadiak kora Mag-
yarországon. Vol. 6.—Magyarorszag
történelmi földrajza a hunyadiak korában.
Vol. 1. 8°　　　　*Budapest*, 1893
Czadeczky, Lajos. Báthory istvan
lengyel királylyá válastása, 1574-1576.
8°　　　　　　*Budapest*, 1887
Dankó, József. A franczia könyvdisz a
renaissance korban. *Plates.* 8°
　　　　　　　　Budapest, 1886
Deák, Farkas. A bujdosók levéltára.
A gróf teleki-csalad mados-vásárhelyi
levéltárából. 8°　　*Budapest*, 1883
Demkó, Kálman. Felsö-magyarországi
Városok életerol a XV.-XVII. szazadban.
8°　　　　　　*Budapest*, 1890
Fejérpataky, László. A királyi kanczel-
lária a z árpádok korában. 8° *Budapest*, 1885
—— Magyarorszagi városok regi szama-
daskönyvei. Selmecz-bánya, Pozsony,
Beszterczebánia, Nagyszombat, Sopron,
Bartfa és Körmöczbánya városok levél-
taraiból. 8°　　　　*Budapest*, 1885
Finaly, Henrik. Az ókori súlyokról és
mértékekröl. 8°　　*Budapest*, 1883
Gelcich, József. Raguza és Magyarország
összeköttetéseinek oklevéltára. A ragu-
zai allami, a bécsi cs. és kir. titkos és
egyéb levéltárakban levö okiratokból
összeállitotta — Bevezetéssel és jegyze-
tekkel elatti Strallóczy Lajos. 8°
　　　　　　　　Budapest, 1887

Ipolyi, Arnold. Alsó-sztregovai és rimai Rimay János államiratai és levelezése. 8° *Budapest*, 1887

Kállay, Béni. Magyarorszag a kelet és a nyugot határán. 8° *Budapest*, 1883

Karácsonyi, János. Szent-istván Kiraly Oklevelei a Szilveszter—Bulla diplomatikai tanulmány. 8° *Budapest*, 1891

Károlyi, Arpád. Illéshazy istván hütlenségi pöre. 8° *Budapest*, 1883

Kerpely, Antal. Magyarorszag Vaskövei, &c. *See* Authors' Catalogue.

Kiss, Károly. Hunyadi Janos utolsó hadjárata bolgár es szerborszag-aban 1454 ben, és Nandorféjer-rar fölmentise, a török töboretástöl 1456. 8° *Budapest*, 1859

Knauz, Nándor. Az országos tanács es országgyülések története, 1445-1452. 8° *Budapest*, 1859

—— Kortan (Chronologia) hazai történelmünkhöz alkalmazva. 4° *Budapest*, 1877

Kolozsvari, S., and K. Ovari. A Magyar törvényhatóságok jogszabályainak gyüjteménye. Magyarországi jogtörténete emlékek. (Monumenta Hungariae Juridicó - Historika. Corpus Statutorum Hungariae Municipalium.) Vols. 1-3. 8° *Budapest*, 1885-92

Kőrösi, József. Budapest nemzetiségi állapota és magyarosodása az 1881-diki népszámlálás eredményei szerint. 8° *Budapest*, 1882

—— **and others.** Megyei Monografiák. Magyarország közgazdasági és közmüvelödési állapota a XIX. czazag végén. 8° *Budapest*, 1891

Kovács, Nandor. Betürendes névmutató Wenzel Gusztav árpádkori új okmánytarához. Index alphabeticus codicis diplomatici arpadiani continuati. 8° *Budapest*, 1889

Lászlófalvi, V. A., and E. Kammerer. Magyarországi török kinestári desterek. Vol. 1, 1543-1635. 8° *Budapest*, 1886

Ortvay, Tivadar. Magyarország régi vizrajza u XIII-ik század végeig. Vols. 1 and 2. 8° *Budapest*, 1882

Ovary, Lipot. Oklevéltár Bethlen Gábor Diplomacziai összeköttetései történetéhez. Diplomatarium relationum Gabrielis Bethlen cum Venetorum republica. A valenezei állami levéltárban Mircse János által eszközölt mázolatokból szerkesztette. 8° *Budapest*, 1886

—— A Magyar Tud. Akadémia történelmi bizottságának Oklevel-Másolatai. Part I. 8° *Budapest*, 1890

Péch, Antal. Alsó Magyarország bányamivelésének története. Vols. 1 and 2. *Map.* 8° *Budapest*, 1884-87

2 Y

Pesty, Frigyes. A szörényi bánzág és szörény vácmegye története. Vols. 1-3. 8° *Budapest*, 1877-78

—— A Magyarországi várispánságok története különösen a XIII. században. 8° *Budapest*, 1882

—— Az eltünt régi vármegyék. 2 vols. 8° *Budapest*, 1880

—— Magyarorszag helynevei történeti, &c. Vol. 1. 8° *Budapest*, 1888

Pisztóry, Mór. A nemzetgazdaságtan haladása és iranya az utolsó tizenöt év alatt. 8° *Budapest*, 1888

Rentmeister, Antal. Lex Falcidia és Quarta Falcidia. (Ertekezés a pandektajog köréböl.) 8° *Budapest*, 1888

Rupp, Jakab. Magyarország helyrajzi története fő tekintettel az egyházi intezetekre vagyis nevezetesb városok helységek, s azokban létezett egyházi intézetek, püspökmegyék szerint rendezve. Vol. I. Parts 1 and 2. 8° *Budapest*, 1870

Szádeczky, Lajos. Izabella és János Zsigmond Lengyelországban, 1552-1556. 8° *Budapest*, 1888

Szentkláray, Jeno. A dunai hajóhadak története. 8° *Budapest*, 1886

Szilágyi, Sándor. Bethlen gábor és a svéd diplomaczia. (A Stockholmi kir. svéd államleveltárban s az Upsalai egyetemi könyvtárban örzött adatok alapjan.) 8° *Budapest*, 1882

—— Levelek és okiratok I. Rakoczy György keleti összeköttetései történetéhez. 8° *Budapest*, 1883

—— Transsylvania et bellum boreoorientale acta et documenta. Erdély és az északkeleti háború levelek és okiratok. Vol. 2. 8° *Budapest*, 1891

Szinnyei, Jozsef. Hazai és külföldi folyóiratok Magyar Tudományos Repertóriuma. 2 vols. 8° *Budapest*, 1874-85

Thaly, Kálmán. A székesi gróf Bercsénvi család, 1525-1706. Vols. 1-3. *Plates.* 8° *Budapest*, 1885-92

Torma, Károli. Repertorium ad literaturam Daciae archaeologicam et epigraphicam. [In Hungarian.] 8° *Budapest*, 1880

Vámbéry, Armin. A Magyarok eredete. Ethnologiai tanulmány. 8° *Budapest*, 1882

Vass, Jozsef. Hazai és külföldi iskolázás az Arpád-korszak alatt. A gorove dijjal jutalmazott pályamunka. 8° *Budapest*, 1862

Vécsey, Tamás. Aemilius Papinianus pályaja és müvei. 8° *Budapest*, 1884

Wenzel, Gusztáv. A Fuggerek jelentösége Magyarország történetében. 8° *Budapest*, 1882

—— Magyarorszag mezögazdaságának története. 8° *Budapest*, 1887

AUSTRIA-HUNGARY—B.

Hungarian Academy—*continued.*

Wlassigs, Gyula. A bünkisérlet és bevégzett büncselekmeny. A tettesség és részesség tana. Vols. 1 and 2. 8°
Budapest, 1885-87

Történettudományi Pályamunkák. Kiadja A Magyar Tudós Társaság. Vols. 1 and 2. 8° *Budapest,* 1841-42
A Magyar Nyelv Rendszere. Kozre bocsátá A Magyar Tudos Társasag. Második kiadas. 8° *Budapest,* 1847
Monumenta Hungariæ Archæologica ævi Præhistorici. Lipp, Vilmos. A keszthelyi sirmezók. *Plates.* Royal 4° *Budapest,* 1884
—— Nyary, Jenö. Az aggteleki barlang öskori tementö. *Plates.* Royal 4°
Budapest, 1881
Monumenta Hungariæ Archæologica ævi Medii. Reisenberger, L. és J. Henszlmann. A nagyszebeni és a székesfehérvári régi templom. *Plates.* Royal 4° *Budapest,* 1883
—— Puszky, Ferencz. A rézkor magyarországban. *Plates.* Royal 4°
Budapest, 1883

C. Anonymous.

Poland. Nachrichten über Polen.
Salzburg, 1793
Umriss von der Oesterreichischen Monarchie, nebst einer ethnographischen Karte. 8° *Leipzig,* 1834
Carlsbad. Der Führer in Carlsbad und der Umgebung. *Plate.* 16°
Carlsbad, 1853
Piski - Zsilthal Railway. Gesuch um Bewilligung der Staats-Garantie für die Piski-Zsilthaler Eisenbahn. 8°
Vienna, 1864
Buccari. Der Golf von Buccari-Porto Rè. *Maps and plates.* 4° *Prague,* 1871
Magyarland : being the Narrative of our Travels through the Highlands and Lowlands of Hungary. By a Fellow of the Carpathian Society. 2 vols. *Illustrations.* Large 8° 1881
Abazia. Lose Blätter aus Abazia. *Illustrations.* 4° *Vienna,* 1886
Pola. Seine Vergangenheit, Gegenwart und Zukunft. Eine Studie. *Plans and plates.* Large 8° *Vienna,* 1886
Hungary. Les Roumains Hongrois et la Nation Hongroise. Réponse au Mémoire des Étudiants Universitaires de Roumanie. 8° *Budapest,* 1891
Bosnia - Herzegowina. Von der Adria bis Sarajevo. *Illustrations.* 12°
Vienna, N.D.
Die Donau von Passau bis Linz und Wien. *Map.* 12° *Leipzig,* N.D.

BELGIUM.

Ministère de la Guerre. Communications de l'Institut Cartographique Militaire, No. 19. Conférence sur l'Application du Mouvement de la Mer. *Plates.* 8°
Brussels, 1881
—— Notice sur les Cartes, Documents, et Objets exposés au Grand Concours International de Bruxelles en 1888. Large 8° *Brussels,* 1888
Spa. Le Guide des Curieux qui visitent les Eaux de Spa. 8° *Verviers,* 1814
—— Guide aux Eaux et aux Jeux de Spa. *Map.* 8° *Spa,* 1865
Education. Réglement sur l'Organisation de l'Enseignement Supérieur dans les Provinces Méridionales du Royaume des Pays-Bas. 18° *Louvain,* 1816
Livre de Poste de la Belgique. 8°
Brussels, 1833
Receuil de Documens Statistiques de la Belgique. 8° N.P., 1833
African Association. *See* Africa : General.
Antwerp and its Exhibition. A Holiday in Belgium, including Brussels and Waterloo, Mechlin, Ghent, and Bruges. *Illustrations.* 8° N.D.

DENMARK.

Den Danske Lods, beskrivelse over de Danske Fárvande. 8° 1843-60 and 1866
—— Tillæg og Rettelser. No. 1. 8° 1872
—— The same. Maj 1888. Large 8°

Danorum Regum heroumque Historiæ,stilo elegantia, Saxone Grammatico, natione Sialandico. [Blackletter.] Folio
Paris, 1514
Sokartet offuer Oster oc Wester Söen. Small 4° *Copenhagen,* 1568
Meddelelser om Gronland. *See* Polar, Arctic, I.
An Account of Denmark as it was in the year 1692 ; an Account of Sweden as it was in the year 1688; with several Pieces relating to those Accounts. 8° 1738
—— The same. 4th edition. 8° 1738
Iceland. An Historical and Descriptive Account of Iceland, Greenland, and the Faroe Islands, with Illustrations of their Natural History. *Map and plates.* 12°
Edinburgh, 1840
The New Sailing Directory for the Cattegat, the Sound, and the Belts. To accompany the Chart published by R. H. Laurie. 3rd edition. 8° 1844

FRANCE.

A. Ministère de la Guerre.

Dépôt de la Guerre.

Mémorial Topographique et Militaire rédigé au Dépôt Général de la Guerre. No. 5. Topographie, IIIe Trimestre de l'an XI. 8° *Paris,* 1803

FRANCE—A.

Mémorial du Dépôt Général de la Guerre, imprimé par ordre du Ministre. Vol. 3. 8° 1825
—— The same, Vols. 1, 3-7. [Vols. 6 and 7 contain the "Description Géométrique de la France," Parts 1 and 2.] 4°
Paris, 1829-40

Service Géographique de l'Armée.

Exposition Universelle de 1889. Notice sur les objets exposés : Instruments, Cartes. *Maps.* 8° *Paris*, 1889
Sous Commission du Serv. Géogr. de l'Armée. Rapport de la Commission chargé de recherches et d'étudier à l'Exposition Universelle de 1889 les objets, produits, appareils, et procédés pouvant interesser l'Armée. Fascicule No. 1. Large 8° *Paris*, 1890
Catalogue des Cartes, Plans, et autres ouvrages, publiés par le Serv. Géogr. de l'Armée. 8° 1892
Rapport sur les Travaux exécutés en 1892. 8° *Paris*, 1893

B. Ministère de la Marine et des Colonies.

a. Miscellaneous.

Annales Maritimes et Coloniales. *See* Appendix 3.
Notices Statistiques sur les Colonies Françaises. Parts 1, 2, and 4. 3 vols. 8° *Paris*, 1837-40
Part 1.—Martinique, Guadeloupe, et Dépendances.
Part 2.—Bourbon, Guyane Française.
Part 4.—Madagascar, Saint-Pierre, et Miquelon.
Tableaux de Population, de Culture, de Commerce, de Navigation, &c. ; la Suite des Tableaux insérés dans les Notices Statistiques sur les Colonies Françaises, 1839, '41, '42, '45, '46, '49, '50-'75. 24 vols. in 14. 8° *Paris*, 1842-78
—— The same, 1876-77, 1879-81. 5 Nos. 8° *Paris*, 1878-83
Notices Statistiques sur les Colonies Françaises. 8° *Paris*, 1883
Notices Coloniales publiées à l'occasion de l'Exposition Universelle d'Anvers en 1885. 3 vols. *Maps.* 8° *Paris*, 1885
Les Colonies Françaises : Notices Illustrées, publiées par ordre du Sous-Secrétaire d'État des Colonies. 20 vols. *Maps and illustrations.* 12°
Paris [1889-90]
Notices sur Annam, Cambodge, Cochinchine, l'Inde Française, Tonkin, le Soudan Français, le Gabon-Congo, le Sénégal, la Guinée, Obock, Mayotte, les Comores, Nossé-Bé, Diego-Suarez, Sainte-Marie de Madagascar, la Réunion, Madagas-

FRANCE—B—*a*.

Les Colonies—*continued.*
car, Saint-Pierre et Miquelon, La Guyane, la Martinique, les Wallis, Futuna, Kerguelen, la Guadeloupe, Tahiti, Iles-sous-le-vent, les Nouvelles-Hébrides, la Nouvelle-Calédonie.
Cape Horn. Ministères de la Marine et de l'Instruction Publique. Mission Scientifique du Cap Horn (1882-83). 7 vols. *Maps and plates.* 4° *Paris*, 1885-92
Tome 1.—Histoire du Voyage, par L. F. Martial 1888
Tome 2.—Météorologie, par J. Lephay 1885
Tome 3.—Magnétisme Terrestre. Recherches sur la Constitution Chimique de l'Atmosphère 1886
Tome 4.—Géologie, par le Dr Hyades 1887
Tome 5.—Botanique, par P. Hariot, P. Petit, J. Muller d'Argovie, E. Bescherelle, C. Massalongo, et A. Franchet 1889
Tome 6.—Zoologie 1887-91
Tome 7. — Anthropologie, Ethnographie, par P. Hyades et J. Deniker 1891

b. Dépôt des Cartes et Plans de la Marine.

Annales Hydrographiques. *See* Transactions : Appendix 3.
Annuaire des Marées des Côtes de France, 1836, 1839, and 1849-94 (1856, '73, '89, and '91 missing). 16° *Paris* [*Later numbers included in series below.*]

Unnumbered Series. 8° *Paris*

Pilôte de Brézil. *See* Roussin 1827
Côtes de la Martinique. *See* Monnier 1828
Reconnaissance Hydrographique des Côtes de France, sur le Passage entre Bréhat et les Roches Douvres. *Map*
Paris, 1832
Courants de la Manche, &c. *See* Monnier 1835-39
Description Nautique des Côtes de l'Algérie. Par — de Tessan 1837
Mélanges Hydrographiques. *See* Darondeau 1846
Côtes de l'Afrique Occidentale. *See* Bouet-Villaumez 1846
Emploi des Chronomètres à la Mer. *See* Givry 1846
Côte Sept. du Brésil, &c. *See* Montravel 1847
La Latitude par les Hauteurs Hors du Méridien. *See* Pagel 1847
Golf de Venise. *See* Beautemps-Beaupré 1849
Phares de Hollande et de Belgique. *See* Darondeau 1849

France—B—*b*. Marine.

Unnumbered Series.

Bayonne, Barre De. Instruction pour aborder et franchir la Barre de Bayonne. 8°　　　　　　　　　　　*Paris*, 1850

Description Nautique du Détroit de la Sonde. Par M. Melvill de Carnbee 1850

Océan Pacifique. *See* Kerhallet 1851

Côtes des Guyanes. *See* Montravel 1851

Azores. *See* Kerhallet 1851

Côte Occidentale de l'Afrique. *See* Kerhallet 1851

Détermination des Longitudes. *See* Kulczycki 1851

Phares de l'Amérique du Nord. *See* Darondeau 1851

Phares de la Méditerranée, &c. *See* Darondeau 1852

Ouragans de la Mer des Indes. *See* Lefebvre 1852

Cercle Méridien Portatif. *See* Laugier 1852

Golfe de Finlande, Côtes de l'Esthonie, &c. *See* Hjorth 1854-5

Considérations Générales sur l'Océan Atlantique. *See* Kerhallet 1854

Variations des Pendules et des Chronomètres. *See* Lieussou 1854

Mer Adriatique. *See* Gras 1855

Régime des Courants. *See* Keller 1855

Portulan des Côtes de la Manche, &c. Par V. A. Moulac 1855

Pilote Danois. Trad. du Danske-Lods 1855

Routier de l'Australie. *See* Gras 1855-61

Observations sur la Navigation des Paquebots qui traversent l'Atlantique 1856

Mer d'Azof. *See* Cloué 1856

Océan Pacifique. *See* Kerhallet 1856

Mer Baltique. *See* Klint 1856

Phares des Mers du Globe, &c. *See* Gras ; *also infra*, No. 216, *et seq.* 1856-78

Côte N. du Maroc ; Detroit de Gibraltar. *See* Vincendon-Dumoulin 1857

Nouvelle Calédonie. *See* Montravel 1857

Résumé de la partie Physique et Descriptive des "Sailing Directions" du Lieut. Maury. Par E. Tricault 1857

Erreurs des Compas. *See* Darondeau 1858

Pilote Norvègien. *See* Long, Baron de 1858

Mer du Nord. 1ʳᵉ Partie. Les Iles Shetland et les Iles Orcades. Trad. de l'Anglais 1858

Instructions Nautiques. *See* Maury 1859

Longitudes Chronométriques des principaux points de la Côte du Brésil. Par E. Mozichzez 1863

France—B—*b*. Marine.

Numbered Series. 8°　　　　　　*Paris*

No. 216.—Phares de la Mer du Nord, la Mer Baltique, et la Mer Blanche. Par A. Le Gras. 8°　　　　　　　　　　1877

No. 217.—Phares des Côtes des iles Britanniques. Par A. Le Gras. 8° 1876, 1877

No. 218.—Phares des Côtes nord et ouest de France, et des côtes ouest d'Espagne et de Portugal. 8° 1874, 1877

No. 219.—Phares de la Mer Méditerranée, de la Mer Noire, et de la Mer d'Azof. Espagne, France, Italie, États de l'Église, Autriche, Grèce, Turquie, et Russie. Par A. Le Gras. 8° 1875, 1877

No. 220.—Phares des Côtes orientales de l'Amérique Anglaise et des États-Unis. Par A. Le Gras. 8° 1875, 1877

No. 221.—Phares de la Mer des Antilles et du Golfe du Mexique. Par A. Le Gras. 8°　　　　　1872, 1874

No. 222.—Phares des Côtes Ouest, Sud et Est d'Afrique, et des îles éparses de l'Océan Atlantique. Par A. Le Gras. 8°　　　　　　1869, 1876

No. 223.—Phares des Côtes orientales de l'Amerique du Sud. Par A. Le Gras. 8°　　　　　　1874, 1876

No. 224.—Phares des Mers des Indes et de Chine, de l'Australie, Terre de Van-Diemen et Nouvelle-Zélande, 1872, 1877 ; Do., de l'Australie, de la Tasmanie, de la Nouvelle-Zélande, et des Côtes Sud et Est d'Afrique, 1878. Par A. Le Gras. 8°　　1872, 1877, 1878

No. 225.—Phares du grand Océan. Côtes occidentales d'Amérique et îles éparses. 8°　　　　　　　　1878

No. 230.—Manuel de la Navigation dans le Rio de la Plata. Par A. Boucarut 1857

No. 237.—*See* Klint.

No. 249.—Côtes Occid. du Centre Amérique. *See* Rosencoat 1857

No. 262.—Instructions à donner aux batiments venant en Nouvelle Calédonie par le Cap de Bonne Espérance 1858

Nos. 275, 278, 281, 327, 338, 384, 398, 505, 556, 561, 588, 671, 698.—Recherches sur les Chronomètres et les Instruments Nautiques. Parts 1-14 (part 4 missing) 1859-87

No. 277.—Formose, Corée, &c. *See* Gras 1859

No. 278.—*See* No. 275.

No. 280.—Nouvelle - Calédonie, &c. *See* Grimoult 1859

No. 281.—*See* No. 275.

No. 291.—Courants de la Côte Occid. d'Afrique. *See* Vallon 1860

No. 295.—Note sur l'Évaluation des Distances en Mer. Par — de la Roche-Poncié 1860

FRANCE—B—*b*. MARINE.
Numbered Series.

296.—Détroit de Banka. Nouvelle Passe pour donner dans le détroit en venant du Sud. Position de quelques Écueils dans la Mer de Corail. 8° 1860

Nos. 303, 337.—Côtes N. de la Russie, &c. *See* Reinèke 1860

No. 307. — Environs de Cherbourg. *See* Keller 1861

No. 308.—Instructions nautiques sur les traversées d'aller et de retour de la Manche à Java. Traduit sous la direction de C. Le Helloco. 4° 1861

No. 309.—Océan Indien—Ile de Ceylan. Description des Basses et des dangers qui sont près de la Côte S.E. de l'Ile de Ceylan. 8° 1861

No. 312.—Routier d'Australie. Vol. 2. *See* Gras 1861

No. 314.—Routier de Baie de Fundy et de la Nouvelle-Ecosse. Par A. Le Gras 1861

No. 315. — Instructions sur l'Ile de Crète ou Candie. Trad. par A. le Gras 1861

No. 326.—Ouragans. *See* Keller 1861

No. 327.—*See* No. 275.

No. 329.—Description Hydrographique de la Côte Orientale de la Corée, et du Golfe d'Osaka. Par H. de la Planche 1861

No. 330. — La Vrai Principe de la Loi des Ouragans. Trad. de l'Anglais. 8° 1861

No. 334.—Renseignements Nautiques sur les Côtes de Patagonie 1862

No. 335.—Côtes d'Islande. *See* Mas 1862

No. 337.—*See* No. 303.

No. 338.—*See* 275.

No. 339.—Instructions Nautiques sur le Sound de Harris et le Petit Minch. Par A. le Gras 1862

Nos. 340, 351.—Mer des Antilles, &c. *See* Kerhallet 1862-63

No. 342.—G. de Guinée, Vents et Courants. *See* Capello, Brito 1862

No. 343.—Côte de Syrie. *See* Desmoulins 1862

No. 346.—R. de la Plata. *See* Mouchez 1862

No. 347.—Campagne de la Cordeliére. Études sur l'Océan Indien. Par le Vicomte Fleuriot de Langle. 8° 1862

No. 348.—Table de Cyclones. *See* Poey 1862

No. 351.—*See* No. 340.

No. 352.—Routier de la Côte Sud et Est d'Afrique 1863

No. 353.—Golfe S. Laurent. *See* Bayfield 1863

No. 354.—Mer du Nord, Baltique, Mer Blanche, &c. *See* Norie 1863

FRANCE—B—*b*. MARINE.
Numbered Series.

No. 357.—Renseignements sur la Mer Rouge. Par — Lapierre. 8° 1863

No. 358. — Formule générale pour trouver la Latitude et la Longitude par les hauteurs hors du Méridien. Par Louis Pagel. 8° 1863

No. 359.—Mer de Chine. Route de Singapour à Saigon. 8° 1863

No. 361.—Instructions Nautiques sur les Côtes orientales de l'Amérique du Sud comprises entre La Plata et le Détroit de Magellan. Par E. Hamelin. 8° 1863

No. 362.—Sur l'Emploi du Compas étalon, &e. Par B. Darondeau 1863

No. 363.—Instructions Nautiques sur les Côtes Occid. d'Amérique, de la Rivière Trembez à Panama. Traduit de l'Anglais par A. MacDermott 1863

No. 364.—Instructions Nautiques sur les Côtes de Patagonie. Par P. Martin 1863

No. 365.—Instruction pour aller chercher La Barre de Bayonne et entrer dans la rivière, ou pour relacher ou mouiller dans les environs. 8° 1863

No. 367.—Les Côtes du Brésil, Description et Instructions Nautiques. Par E. Mouchez. 2me Sect. De Bahia à Rio Janeiro. *Charts.* 8° 1864

No. 368.—Rapport sur une nouvelle Route pour doubler le Cap de Bonne-Espérance, de l'Est à l'Ouest, pendant la saison d'hiver, de Mai à Septembre. Par — Bridet. *Chart.* 8° 1863

No. 370.—Météorologique Nautique. Vents et Courants, Routes Générales (Maury). Par E. Ploix. *Plates and charts.* 4° 1863

No. 371.—Instructions Nautiques sur les Côtes occidentales de l'Amerique, du Golfe de Peñas à la rivière Tumbez. Par — MaeDermott. 8° 1863

No. 372.—Instructions Nautiques sur la Mer Baltique 1864

No. 373.—Instructions Nautiques sur les Côtes Est de la Chine, la Mer Jaune, les Golfes de Pe-Chili et de Liau-Tung, et la Côtes Ouest de la Corée (China Pilot). Par — de Vautré et A. Le Gras. 8° 1863

No. 376.—Pilote de l'île Guernsey. Trad. de l'Anglais par M. Massias 1863

No. 378.—Routier de la Côte Nord d'Espagne. Trad. de l'Espagnol par A. le Gras 1864

No. 379.—Instructions Nautiques pour les principaux ports de la Côte Est de l'Amérique du Nord. Par — MacDermott. 8° 1864

No. 380.—Manuel de la Navigation dans la Mer des Antilles et dans le Golfe du Mexique. Par C. P. de Kerhallet. 3me Ptie. 2me éd. *Maps, &c.* 8° 1864

FRANCE—B—b. MARINE.
Numbered Series.

No. 382.—Mer du Nord. 4ᵐᵉ Ptie.
Par A. Le Gras. 8° 1864
No. 383.—La Loi des Tempêtes considérée dans ses Rapports avec les Mouvements de l'Atmosphère (Dove). Par A. Le Gras. *Plates and charts.* 8° 1864
No. 384.—Recherches sur les Chronomètres et les Instruments Nautiques. 7ᵐᵉ Cahier. 8° 1864
No. 385.—Madagascar (Côte orientale), Partie comprenant l'île Fong, Tamatave, Foulepointe, Mahambo, Fénérive, Sainte-Marie et Tintingue. Par — Germain. 8° 1861
No. 387.—Instruction pour le Micromètre Lugeol à Cadran Lorieux. Par J. Bosc. *Plates.* 8° 1864
No. 389.—Instructions Nautiques sur les Côtes de Corse. Par — Sallot des Noyers. 8° 1865
No. 390.—Annuaire des Marées des Côtes de France pour l'an 1866. Par — Gaussin et E. Ploix. 16° 1865
No. 393.—Pilote de la Mer Noire. Par H. de la Planche. Côte d'Asie. *Plans and profiles.* 8° 1865
No. 394. — Pilote du Golfe Saint-Laurent. Trad. de l'Anglais 1865
No. 395.—Mer de Chine. 1ᵉʳᵉ Ptie. Instructions Nautiques sur la Côte Est de la Malaisie, le Golfe de Siam, les Côtes de la Cochinchine, le Golfe de Tonquin, et la Côte Sud de la Chine. Par A. Le Gras. 8° 1865
No. 396.—Renseignements sur la Navigation des Côtes et des Rivières de la Guyane Française. Par E. Gouy. 8° 1865
No. 398.—Recherches sur les Chronomètres et les Instruments Nautiques. 8ᵐᵉ Cahier. 8° 1865
No. 399.—Mouillages d'Islande et de Norvège. *See* Thoyon 1865
No. 400.—Supplément au Routier de l'Australie, 2. Côte Est, Détroit de Torrès, et Mer de Corrail. 8° 1865
No. 403.—Routier de l'île Aubigny. Trad. par J. Varin 1865
No. 404. — Supplément aux Instructions (No. 373) sur la Mer de Chine. 2ᵐᵉ Ptie. Contenant des Instructions sur les Côtes Est de Chine, la Mer Jaune, les Golfes de Pe-Chili et de Lia-Tong et la Côte Ouest de la Corée (China Pilot). Par — Costa. 8° 1865
Nos. 406 and 407.—Le Pilote de la Nouvelle-Zélande (Richards et Evans). Par A. Jouan, revue par Sallot des Noyers. 1ᵉʳᵉ and 2ᵐᵉ Pties. *Maps.* Oblong 12° 1865
Nos. 411-12. — Golfe Persique. *See* Constable 1866
No. 415.—Golfe d'Aden, &c. *See* Ward, C. Y. 1866

FRANCE—B—b. MARINE.
Numbered Series.

No. 415.—Annuaire des Marées des Côtes de France pour l'an 1867. Par — Gaussin et E. Ploix. 16° 1866
No. 417. — Mer Méditerranée. *See* Gras 1866
No. 418. — Routier de l'île Jersey. Trad. de l'Anglais 1866
No. 420.—Routier de l'Australie, Côtes Nord, N.O., et Ouest (Yule). Par — Besson. 8° 1866
No. 421.—Côtes S. S. E. et E. d'Afrique. *See* Horsey, de 1866
Nos. 422, 428, 433, 437, 442.—Archipel d'Asie. *See* Sallot des Noyers 1867-68
No. 423.—Note sur les Traversées de Retour du Golfe du Mexique en France. Par B. F. Grasset. Route d'Europe au Mexique. 8° 1866
No. 424.—Ports de l'Océanie, &c. *See* Foy 1866
No. 426.—Mer de Chine. 3ᵐᵉ Ptie. Instructions Nautiques sur les îles et les Passages entre les Philippines et le Japon et les îles du Japon. Par A. Le Gras. 8° 1867
No. 428.—*See* No. 422.
No. 430.—Annuaire des Marées des Côtes de France p ur l'an 1868. Par — Gaussin. 16° 1867
No. 432.—Mer de Chine. 5ᵐᵉ Ptie. Instructions Nautiques sur la Mer du Japon, la Côte Ouest du Nippon, la Côte Est de la Corée et la Côte de Tartarie, la Manche de Tartarie, le Détroit de Tsugar, les îles Kouriles, le Détroit de La Pérouse, la Mer d'Okhotsk, et la Kamschatka. Par A. Le Gras. 8° 1867
Nos. 433, 437, 442.—*See* No. 422.
No. 434.—2ᵐᵉ Supplément aux Instructions (No. 373) sur la Mer de Chine. 2ᵐᵉ Ptie. Contenant des Renseignements Nautiques sur la Côte Ouest de la Corée et la Rivière de Séoul, recueillis pendant l'Exploration faite en Septembre et Octobre 1866, par la Division Navale de Chine sous les ordres du C. A. Roze. *Maps.* 8° 1867
No. 435.—Instructions Nautiques sur la Côte occidentale d'Afrique, comprenant le Maroc, le Sahara, et la Sénégambie. Par C. P. de Kerhallet, revues par Le Gras et Vallon. *Profiles.* 8° 1867
No. 438.—Pilote de l'île Vancouver (Richards). Par — Hocquart. 8° 1867
No. 439.—Annuaire des Marées des Côtes de France pour l'an 1869. Par — Gaussin. 16° 1868
No. 440.—Pilote de la Côte occidentale de l'Hindostan, comprenant la Golfe de Manar, les îles Maldives et Laquedives (Taylor). Par J. Lafont. 8° 1868

FRANCE—B—b. MARINE.
Numbered Series.

No. 443.—Côte occidentale d'Amérique. Baie de San Francisco et Côte au Nord. 8° 1868

No. 444.—Instruction pour entre dans le Port d'Alexandrie, Égypte. Par A. Bouquet de la Grye. 8° 1867

No. 447.—Mer de Chine. 4me Ptie. Instructions Nautiques pour naviguer sur les Côtes Ouest et N.-O. de Borneo, les détroits de Balabac, les Côtes Ouest et Est de Palawan, les îles Calamianos, le détroit de Mindoro, et les Côtes S.-O. et Ouest de l'île Luçon, suivies d'une Description des Bancs de la Mer de Chine. Par A. Le Gras. 8° 1868

No. 447b. — Îles Philippines. Renseignements sur les îles de Manille à Ilo-Ilo, à Zebu, et à Samboangon. 8° 1879

No. 448.—Rade de Brest. *See* Roujoux 1868

No. 449.—Pilote de la Manche. *See below*, No. 636 1869

No. 451.—Annuaire des Marées des Côtes de France pour l'an 1870. Par — Gaussin. 16° 1869

No. 452.—Description des Côtes du Royaume de Portugal. Par A. Le Gras. *Profiles.* 8° 1869

No. 454.—Instructions Nautiques pour la Côte S.E. de la Nouvelle Écosse et la Baie de Fundy. Trad. de l'Anglais par J. Lafont 1869

No. 455. — Côtes du Brésil. *See* Mouchez 1869

No. 456.—Note sur les Sondes faites par de grandes profondeurs (Davis), et détermination du diamètre de la meilleure ligne de sonde. Par A. Bouquet de la Grye. 8° 1869

No. 458. — Nouvelle - Écosse. *See* Chambeyron 1869

No. 461. Pilote de la Mer Noire. Par H. de Laplanche. Côte d'Europe. *Plans and profiles.* 8° 1869

No. 462.—Côte Ouest d'Écosse. *See*. Frickmann 1869

No. 463.—Côtes d'Espagne. *See* Gras 1869

No. 464.—Pilote des Côtes Ouest de France. Par A. Bouquet de la Grye. I. Partie comprise entre Penmarc'h et la Loire. *Plans, &c.* 8° 1869

Nos. 468,469.—Pilote de Terre-Neuve. *See below*, Nos. 646, 647.

No. 470.—Étude sur les Ouragans de l'Hémisphère Austral. Par M. Bridet. 8° 1869

No. 470.—Instructions Nautiques sur la Côte occidentale d'Afrique, comprenant la Côte de Libéria, la Côte d'Ivoire, la Côte d'Or, la Côte de Batonga, et la Côte du Gabon. Par C. P. de Kerhallet, revues et corrigées par A. Le Gras. *Profiles.* 8° 1870

FRANCE—B—b. MARINE.
Numbered Series.

No. 473.—Annuaire des Marées des Côtes de France pour l'an 1871. Par — Gaussin et — Bouillet. 16° 1870

No. 474.—Instructions pour Naviguer dans le Canal de Bristol (Bedford). Par Paul Martin. 8° 1870

No. 477.—Tables pour l'Évaluation des Distances en Mer. 8° 1870

No. 478.—Terre Neuve. Supplément aux Instructions No. 468 et 469. 8° 1870

No. 479.—Côte Est d'Angleterre. 8° 1870

No. 480.—Instructions Nautiques pour la Côte d'Irlande (Hoskin). Par J. Lafont. 8° 1870

No. 481.—Pilote de la Manche. Côtes Nord de France. Vol. I. De la Pointe de Penmarc'h à l'île de Bas. Par — Thomassin. 8° 1870

No. 482.—Instructions pour Naviguer dans la Mer Rouge. (Moresby et Elwon.) Par A. Le Gras. 8° 1870

No. 485.—Instructions Nautiques sur le Côte occidentale d'Afrique, comprenant la Côte de Congo, la Côte d'Angola, la Côte de Benguela, et la Colonie du Cap. Par C. P. de Kerhallet et A. Le Gras. *Profiles.* 8° 1871

No. 486.—Routier de l'Australie. 1ère Ptie. Côte Sud et partie de la Côte Est, Détroit de Bass et Tasmanie. Par A. Frickmann. I. Comprenant du Cap Leeuwin au Cap Schanck. 8° 1871

No. 488.—Mer de Chine. 4me Ptie. Supplément No. 3 à l'Instruction No. 447. 8° 1871

No. 489.—Mer de Chine. 3me Ptie. Supplément No. 8 à l'Instruction No. 426. Îles du Japon. 8° 1871

No. 490.—Annuaire des Marées des Côtes de France pour l'an 1872. Par — Gaussin et — Bouillet. 16° 1871

No. 491.—Instructions Nautiques pour la Côte d'Irlande. 1ère Ptie. Par H. de Laplanche. 8° 1871

No. 493.—Océan Pacifique Nord. Renseignements sur les îles Havaii ou Sandwich, et le Groupe d'îlots et Rochers qui est dans le N.-O. Par A. Frickmann. 8° 1871

No. 494.—Routier de l'Australie. 1ère Ptie. Côte Sud et partie de la Côte Est, détroit de Bass et Tasmanie. Par É. Frickmann. II. Comprenant du Cap Schanck au Port Jackson. 8° 1871

No. 495.—Étude sur les Embouchures du Nil et sur les Changements qui s'y sont produits dans les derniers Siècles, d'après une Reconnaissance Hydrographique exécutée en 1860. Par E. Larousse. *Charts.* 8° 1871

No. 496. — Route des Batiments à vapeur dans l'Océan Indien d'Aden au détroit de la Sonde, et retour. *Charts* 1872

FRANCE—B—*b.* MARINE.
Numbered Series.

No. 499.—Instructions Nautiques sur la Côte du Pérou. Par F. Chardonneau. 8°   1872

No. 500.—Instructions pour Naviguer dans le Détroit de Magellan et les Canaux conduisant au Golfe de Peñas (Mayne). Par E. Talpomba et E. de Lapierre. 8°   1872

No. 501.—Côte occidentale de l'Amérique du Nord. Côtes de Californie. Instructions pour la Navigation sur la Côte de Californie, de la Baie San Diego à la Baie San Francisco. Par A. Frickmann. 8°   1872

No. 502.—Côtes de l'Orégon et du Territoire de Washington, de la Baie Pélican à l'entrée du Détroit de Juan de Fuca. Par A. Frickmann. 8°   1872

No. 505.—Recherches sur les Chronomètres et les Instruments Nautiques. 9me Cahier. 8°   1872

No. 506.—Mémoire sur les Marées de la Basse Cochinchine. Par G. Héraud. *Plate.* 8°   1873

No. 508.—Le Kattegat, le Sund, et les Belts. Par A. Le Gras. *Profiles.* 8°   1873

No. 509.—Instructions pour naviguer sur les Côtes de l'île Reine-Charlotte et d'Alaska, dans les îles Aléoutiennes, la Mer de Behring, et le Détroit de Behring. Par le Vicomte De la Tour du Pin. 8° 1873

No. 510.—Instructions pour naviguer sur la Côte occidentale d'Angleterre, de Milford Haven à la Mull of Galloway, y compris l'île de Man. Par A. Frickmann. 8°   1873

No. 511.—Pilote des Côtes Ouest de France. Par A. Bouquet de la Grye. II. Partie comprise entre la Loire et la Bidassoa ; et Côte Nord d'Espagne jusques et y compris Saint-Sébastien. *Plans, &c.* 8°   1873

No. 513.—Nouvelle Classification des Nuages, suivie d'Instructions pour servir à l'Observation des Nuages et des Courants Atmosphériques. Par A. Poey. 8°   1873

No. 515.—Catalogue Chronologique des Cartes, Plans, Vues de Côtes, Mémoires, Instructions Nautiques, &c., qui composent l'Hydrographie Française. 8°   1873

No. 515-*bis.*—Supplement   1880

No. 516.—Des Vents et des Coups de Vent observés dans l'Atlantique Nord sur les Routes des Bâtiments à Vapeur, allant de La Manche à New York et vice versâ. Par le Vicomte De la Tour du Pin. 8° 1873

No. 518.—Annuaire des Marées des Côtes de France pour l'an 1874. Par — Gaussin. 16°   1873

FRANCE—B—*b.* MARINE.
Numbered Series.

No. 519.—Annuaire des Marées de la Basse Cochinchine pour l'an 1874. Par G. Héraud. 16°   1873

No. 521.—Routier de l'Australie, Côte Est d'Australie. Pt. 2. Vol. 1. Par A. Le Gras. 8°   1873

No. 522.—Instructions Nautiques sur les Côtes du Chili et de la Bolivie. Par F. Chardonneau. 8°   1873

No. 524.—Les Côtes du Brésil, Description et Instructions Nautiques. 1ère Section : Du Cap San Roque à Bahia. Par E. Mouchez. 8°   1874

No. 525.—Pilote de la Manche. Côtes Nord de France. Par — Thomassin. 2me Ptie. De l'île de Bas aux Héaux de Bréhat. 8°   1874

No. 526.—Note sur la Régulation des Compas par des Observations de Force Horizontale. Par E. Caspari. 8° 1873

No. 528.—Instructions Nautiques sur les Côtes de l'Équateur et des États-Unis de Colombie, d'après les Capitaines Kellett et de Rosencoat. Par F. Chardonneau. 8°   1874

No. 529.— Recherches Hydrographiques sur la Régime des Côtes. 1er Cahier (1838-1858). 4°   1874

No. 530.—Notes sur la Forme des Cyclones dans l'Océan Indien, &c. (Meldrum.) 8°   1874

No. 531.—Annuaire des Marées des Côtes de France pour l'an 1875. Par — Gaussin. 16°   1874

No. 532. — Météorologie Nautique. Vents et Courants, Routes Générales, extrait des Sailing Directions de Maury et des Travaux les plus récents. Par C. Ploix et E. Caspari. 4°   1874

No. 534. — Instructions Nautiques : Côte Ouest d'Écosse; traduit de l'Anglais, &c. 2me Ptie. Par L. de la Chauvinière. 8°   1874

No. 535.—Routier de l'Australie, Côte Est d'Australie, Détroit de Torrès, et Mer de Corail, revu et complété jusqu'en 1874. 2me Ptie. 2. Comprenant le Détroit de Torrès, la Mer de Corail, la Côte Sud de la Nouvelle-Guinée, et l'Archipel de la Louisiade. Par A. Le Gras. 8°   1874

No. 537.—Pilote de la Guadeloupe. Par E. Ploix. *Charts and profiles.* 8°   1875

No. 538. — Océan Pacifique. Renseignements sur les Archipels Marshall et Gilbert. Par A. Le Gras. 8° *Paris,* 1875

No. 541.—Annuaire des Marées des Côtes de France pour l'an 1876. Par — Gaussin. 16°   1875

No. 542.—Mer des Antilles et Golfe du Mexique. 2me Ptie. Comprenant les

FRANCE—B—*b*. MARINE.
Numbered Series.

petites Antilles, les grandes Antilles, les îles et les bancs de Bahama, les Récifs de la Floride et les Bermudes. 2ᵉ et 3ᵉ parties du Manuel de la Navigation dans la Mer des Antilles, par A. Le Gras. 8° *Paris*, 1875

No. 546.—Mer Méditerranée, Côtes Sud et Sud-est d'Espagne, îles Baléares. 8° 1875

No. 547.—Annuaire des Marées de la Basse Cochinchine pour l'an 1876. 16° 1875

No. 548.—Mer Baltique. Côte de Prusse, de Memel à Darscrort. *Plates.* 8° 1875

No. 549.—Mer de Chine. 3ᵐᵉ Ptie. Le Séto Utchi, Mer intérieure du Japon et ses approches. Par A. Banaré. 8° 1876

No. 550.—Pilote des Côtes Sud de France. Par A. Germain. 8° *Plates.* Oblong 8° 1876

No. 552.—Pilote de la Manche, Côtes Nord de France. 3ᵐᵉ Ptie. Des Iléaux de Bréhat au Cap de la Hague. Par — Thomassin. 8° 1875

No. 553.—Supplément à l'Instruction No. 421. Afrique. Côte Sud et Est. 8° 1875

No. 554.—Pilote des Côtes Nord de France. I. Cherbourg au Havre. Par — Estignard. *Plates.* 8° 1875

No. 555.—Annuaire des Marées des Côtes de France pour l'an 1877. Par — Gaussin. 16° 1876

No. 556.—Recherches sur les Chronomètres et les Instruments Nautiques. 10ᵐᵉ Cahier. 8° 1876

No. 558.—Mer du Nord. 3ᵐᵉ Ptie. Côtes Est d'Angleterre. 8° 1876

No. 560.—Annuaire des Marées de la Basse Cochinchine pour l'an 1877. 16° 1876

No. 561.—Recherches sur les Chronomètres et les Instruments Nautiques. 11ᵐᵉ Cahier. 8° 1876

No. 563.—Mer Méditerranée. Par J. S. Bayot. 8° 1876

No. 564.—Mer des Antilles et Golfe du Mexique. 1ᵉʳᵉ Ptie. Par A. Sallot des Noyers. 8° 1876

No. 565.—Supplément à l'Instruction No. 352, Côtes Sud et Est d'Afrique. 8° 1876

No. 566.—Supplément à l'Instruction No. 353, Labrador, Côte Nord-Est. 8° 1876

No. 568.—Supplément aux Instructions No. 468 et 469, Terre-Neuve, Côtes Est et Sud. 8° 1876

No. 569. — Recherches Météorologiques. No. 1. Géographie physique de la partie équatoriale de l'Océan Atlantique (Toynbee). Par C. Ploix. *Charts.* 4° 1877

FRANCE—B—*b*. MARINE.
Numbered Series.

No. 570.—Annuaire des Marées des Côtes de France pour l'an 1878. Par — Gaussin et — Hatt. 16° 1877

No. 572.—Recherches hydrographiques sur le Régime des Côtes. 2ᵐᵉ Cahier (1858-63). *Maps.* 4° 1877

No. 573.—Supplément à l'Instruction No. 361. Renseignements sur la Côte Nord du Golfe Saint-Georges (Patagonie). Par J. B. Olry. 8° 1877

No. 574.—Guyane Française et Fleuve des Amazones. 8° 1877

No. 575.—Supplément aux Instructions Nos. 521, 535, 420, 486, Côtes Est, Nord, Nord-Ouest, et Sud de l'Australie. 8° 1877

No. 576.—Recherches hydrographiques sur le Régime des Côtes. 7ᵐᵉ Cahier. Rapport sur la reconnaissance de Boulogne. Par E. Ploix (1876). *Charts and plates.* 4° 1877

No. 578.—Recherches hydrographiques sur le Régime des Côtes. 3ᵐᵉ Cahier (1864-66). 4° 1877

No. 579.—Recherches hydrographiques sur le Régime des Côtes. 6ᵐᵉ Cahier. Étude hydrographique de la Baie de la Rochelle, &c. Par A. B. de la Grye. *Maps and plates.* 4° 1877

No. 580.—Annuaire des Marées des Côtes de France pour l'an 1878. Basse Cochinchine et du Tong-Kin pour l'an 1878. 16° 1877

No. 582.—Recherches hydrographiques sur le Régime des Côtes. 4ᵐᵉ Cahier (1867-70). *Charts.* 4° 1877

No. 583.—Océan Indien. Golfe du Bengale, depuis la Pointe de Galle jusqu'à la Tête d'Achem. Par — Weyl. 8° 1877

No. 584.—Mer de Chine. 3ᵐᵉ Ptie. Instructions Nautiques pour les Iles et les Passages entre les Philippines et le Japon, et les îles du Japon, comprenant Formose, les îles Low Chow, les Mariannes, les Pelew, les îles Bonin, les Côtes Sud, Est, et Ouest des îles Kinsiu et Nipon. Par A. Le Gras. 8° 1877

No. 585.—Annuaire des Marées des Côtes de France pour l'an 1879. Par — Gaussin et — Hatt. 16° 1878

No. 586.—Mer Méditerranée. Golfe de Gênes, Côtes Ouest et Sud d'Italie (de la frontière de France à Brindisi). 8° 1878

No. 588.—Recherches sur les Chronomètres et les Instruments Nautiques. 12ᵐᵉ Cahier. 8° 1878

No. 589.—Annuaire des Marées de la Basse Cochinchine et du Tong-Kin pour l'an 1879. 16° 1878

FRANCE—B—*b*. MARINE.
Numbered Series.

No. 591.— Recherches hydrographiques sur le régime des Côtes. 8me Cahier. Rapport sur la reconnaissance hydrographique de 1875 à l'embouchure de la Seine. Par — Estignard. *Charts.* 4° 1878

No. 592.—Instruction sur les Cartes pour la Navigation par l'arc de grand Cercle. Par — Hilleret. 8° 1878

No. 593.—Instructions sur les Côtes d'Espagne et de Portugal, de la Corogne au Cap Trafalgar. Par A. Le Gras. 8° 1878

No. 597.—Annuaire des Marées des Côtes de France pour l'an 1880. Par — Gaussin et — Hatt. 16° 1879

No. 598. — Recherches hydrographiques sur le régime des Côtes. 9me Cahier. Reconnaissance de l'embouchure de la Gironde en 1874. Per L. Manen, E. Larousse, E. Caspari, et — Hanusse. 4°, and folio Atlas 1878

No. 599.—Instructions Nautiques sur les Côtes Ouest du Centre-Amérique et du Mexique. Par A. Pailhès. 8° 1879

No. 600.—Annuaire des Courants de Marée de la Manche pour l'an 1879. Par — Gaussin. 16° 1879

No. 602*b*.—Océan Pacifique Sud, Les îles Salomon ; No. 602*c*.—Nouvelles Hébrides, îles Bangs et Archipel de Santa Cruz ; No. 602*d*.—Îles Wallis. 8° 1879

No. 602*l*.—Notice Hydrographique, No.6,1884. Océan Pacifique Sud [Notice, No. 12]. Îles Samoa—Souwarov, Keppel, et Boscawen. Large 8° 1884

No. 603.—Instructions Nautiques sur les îles du Cap Vert. Par C. P. de Kerhallet et A. Le Gras. *Profiles.* 8° 1879

No. 604.—Annuaire des Marées de la Basse Cochinchine et du Tong-Kin pour l'an 1880. 16° 1879

No. 606.— Patagonie. Détroit de Magellan et Canaux latéraux, Cap Horn et Terre de Feu. Par P. Cave. 8° 1879

No. 607.—Renseignements Nautiques sur quelques îles éparses de l'Océan Indien Sud, Prince Édouard, Crozet, Kerguelen, MacDonald, Rodriguez, Maurice, La Réunion, Saint-Paul et Amsterdam, Les Seychelles, Madagascar et Mayotte. 8° 1879

No. 608.—Instructions Nautiques sur les Côtes l'Algérie. Par M. le Contre-Amiral Mouchez. 8° 1879

No. 609.—Notice Météorologique sur les Mers comprises entre la Chine et le Japon. Par J. Revertégat. *Charts.* 4° 1879

No. 615.—Annuaire des Courants de Marée de la Manche pour l'an 1880. Par — Gaussin. 16° 1880

FRANCE—B—*b*. MARINE.
Numbered Series.

No. 616.—Annuaire des Marées des Côtes de France pour l'an 1881. Par — Gaussin. 16° 1880

No. 617.—Annuaire des Marées de la Basse Cochinchine et du Tong-Kin pour l'an 1881. Par G. Héraud. 16° 1880

No. 619.—Pilote de la Manche. Côtes Nord de France. Par E. de Courthille et F. Hédouin. 1. 8° 1880

No. 622.—Bassin oriental de la Mer Méditerranée. 2me Ptie. Tripoli, Égypte (de l'île Djerbah á El-Arish). 8° 1880

No. 623.—Pilote de la Manche. Côtes Nord de France. 2. 8° 1880

No. 628.—Madère, les îles Salvages, et les îles Canaries. Instructions Nautiques rédigées par M. C. Philippe de Kerhallet, et complétées par le Service des Instructions Nautiques. *Plates.* 8° 1888

No. 629.—Annuaire des Marées des Côtes de France pour l'an 1882. Par — Gaussin et — Hatt. 16° 1881

No. 631.—Annuaire des Courants de Marée de la Manche pour l'an 1881. Par — Gaussin. 12° 1881

No. 633.—Instructions Nautiques sur les Côtes Sud et Est d'Afrique. De Table Bay à Guardafui. Traduit et collationné par — Loizillon. 8° 1881

No. 634.—Description Nautique des Açores, rédigée par Charles Philippe de Kerhallet, et complétée par le Service des Instructions Nautiques. 4me édition. 8° 1881

No. 636.—Pilote de la Manche. Instructions Nautiques sur les Côtes Sud et S.-O. d'Angleterre du Cap Trévose à North Foreland. Traduit de la Première édition du "Channel Pilot" par M. Sallot Des Moyers, et mis à jour d'après la dernière édition Anglaise et les documents les plus récents, par M. Loizillon. Large 8° 1881

No. 637.—Côte Est d'Australie : Vues de Côtes. Par M. Wallut. Large 8° 1882

No. 638.—Mer du Nord. Quatrième Partie. Instructions Nautiques de Dunkerque jusqu'au Cap Skagen. Collationné et revisé d'après les documents les plus récents, par M. Frickmann. Large 8° 1881

No. 639.—Annuaire des Courants de Marée de la Manche pour l'an 1882. Par M. Gaussin, publié sous le Ministère de M. Gougeard. 12° 1882

No. 641*a*.—Traité d'Hydrographie. Levé et construction des Cartes Marines. Par A. Germain. Large 8° 1882

No. 641*b*.—The same. Tables. Large 8° 1882

No. 643.—Annuaire des Marées des Côtes de France pour l'an 1883. Par M. Gaussin et M. Hatt. 12° 1882

FRANCE—B—b. MARINE.
Numbered Series.

No. 644.—Algérie. Vues de Côtes.
Par M. Le Contre-Amiral Mouchez et
M. Turquet De Beauregard. Large 8°
1882

Nos. 646 and 647.—Pilote de Terre-
Neuve, par le Vice-Amiral G. Cloué.
2nd edition. 2 vols. *Maps and plates.*
Large 8° 1882

No. 648.—Stations de Signaux horaires
établis sur le littoral des diverses nations
maritimes pour le Réglage des Chronomètres des bâtiments, 1er Juillet 1882.
8° 1882

No. 652. — Recherches hydrograph-
iques sur le régime des Côtes. Onzième
Cahier. Rapport sur le régime de la Loire
Maritime. Par M. A. Bouquet de la
Grye. *Charts.* 4° *Paris,* 1882

No. 653.—Annuaire des Courants de
Marée de la Manche pour l'an 1883. Par
M. Gaussin. 12° 1883

No. 655.—Annuaire des Marées des
Côtes de France pour l'an 1884. Par M.
Gaussin et M. Hatt. 16° 1883

No. 656.—Annuaire des Marées de la
Basse Cochinchine et du Tong-kin pour
l'an 1884. Par M. G. Héraud. 16° 1883

No. 657.—Catalogue par ordre géographique des Cartes, Plans, Vues de
Côtes, Mémoires, Instructions Nautiques,
&c., qui composent l'Hydrographie
Française. 8° 1883

No. 658.—Instructions Nautiques sur
la Côte occidentale d'Afrique, de Sierra
Leone au Cap Lopez y compris les îles
du Golfe de Biafra. Par feu M. Charles
Philippes de Kerhallet, complétés par M.
François. Large 8° 1883

No. 661.—Instructions Nautiques sur
les Mers de Chine. Introduction;
Navigation générale. *Maps.* Large 8°
1883

No. 662.—Instructions Nautiques sur les
Côtes Ouest de Norvège. De Lindesnæs
à la Rivière Jacob. Traduites de
l'Anglais "Norway Pilot" par M.
Martial, et complétées à l'aide du
"Norske Lods" par M. Frickmann.
Large 8° 1883

No. 664.—Annuaire des Marées des
Côtes de France pour l'an 1885. Par M.
Hatt. 16° 1884

No. 666.—Instructions Nautiques sur
les Mers de Chine. Tome 2. Du
Détroit de Singapour aux atterrages de
Canton et de Hong-Kong. Collation-
nées . . . par M. Dartige Du Fournet.
Large 8° 1884

No. 668.—Pilote des Côtes Nord de
France. Second Volume. Du Havre à
la Frontière, de Belgique. Par M. X.
Estignard, avec le concours de MM.
G. Héraud, et F. Bouillet. Large 8° 1884

FRANCE—B—b. MARINE.
Numbered Series.

No. 669.—Entrées de la Mer Baltique
de l'extrémité sud du Kattegat au Sund
de Fehmarn. Vues de Côtes, extraites
des documents Danois et Allemands.
Large 8° 1884

No. 670.—Instructions Nautiques sur
les Mers de Chine. Tome 3. Des
atterrages de Canton et de Hong-Kong
à l'île Quelpaert. Large 8° *Paris,* 1884

No. 671.—Dépôt général des Cartes
et Plans de la Marine. Recherches
sur Chronomètres et les Instruments
Nautiques. 13e Cahier. *Diagrams.* 8°
1885

No. 672.—Notions sur le Phénomène
des Marées. Par M. P. Hatt. *Plates.*
8° 1885

No. 674.—Instructions Nautiques sur
les Mers de Chine. Tome premier.
Entrées occidentales de la Mer de Chine,
Sumatra, et canaux avoisinants. Large
8° 1885

No. 675.—Annuaire des Marées des
Côtes de France pour l'an 1886. Par M.
Hatt. 16° 1885

No. 677.—Instructions Nautiques sur
les Côtes Sud de France. Par M. A.
Germain. 2nd edition. Large 8° 1885

No. 678.—Mer Baltique. Côte Nord
de Prusse (de Pelzerhaken à la frontière
Russe). Vues de Côtes extraites des
documents Allemands. Large 8° 1885

No. 680.—Instructions Nautiques sur
le Grand Archipel d'Asie. Large 8°
1885

No. 681.—Instructions Nautiques sur
la Mer Rouge et le Golfe d'Aden.
Large 8° 1885

No. 682.—Océan Indien. Instructions Nautiques sur Madagascar et les
îles de l'Océan Indien méridional.
Large 8° 1885

No. 683.—Annuaire des Marées des
Côtes de France pour l'an 1887. Par M.
Hatt. 16° 1886

No. 684.—Marine et Colonies. Service hydrographique. Catalogue chronologique des Cartes, Plans, Vues de
Côtes, Mémoires, Instructions, Nautiques, &c., qui composent l'Hydrographie
Française. 8° 1886

No. 685.—Service hydrographique de
la Marine. Annuaire des Marées de la
Basse Cochinchine et du Tonkin pour
l'an 1887. Par M. G. Héraud. 12°
1886

No. 687.—The same. Instruction
pour aller chercher la Barre de Bayonne,
entrer dans la rivière ou mouiller dans
les environs (extrait du Pilote des Côtes
ouest de France). Par M. Bouquet de la
Grye. Large 8° *Paris,* 1886

FRANCE—B—*b*. MARINE.
Numbered Series.

No. 689.—Océan Pacifique Sud. Instructions Nautiques sur la Nouvelle-Calédonie et ses Dépendances. Par MM. Chambeyron et Banaré. 3rd edition, . . . par M. Banaré. Large 8°　1886
No. 690.—Océan Pacifique Sud. Instructions Nautiques sur les Nouvelles-Hébrides, les îles, Banks, Torrès, et l'Archipel de Santa-Cruz. Collationnées par le Service des Instructions Nautiques.　Large 8°　　　　　1886
No. 691.—Mer Méditerranée. Instructions Nautiques sur les îles Ioniennes, les Côtes de Grèce et de Turque, l'Archipel, le Détroit des Dardanelles, la Mer de Marmara et le Bosphore. . . . Par M. A. François.　Large 8°　1886
No. 692.—Annuaire des Marées des Côtes de France pour l'an 1888. Par M. Hatt.　12°　　　　　　　1887
No. 694.—Service hydrographique de la Marine. Annuaire des Marées de la Basse Cochinchine et du Tonkin pour l'an. 1888.　Par M. G. Héraud.　12°
　　　　　　　　　　　　　　　1887
No. 695.—The same. Recherches hydrographiques sur le régime des Côtes.　Douzième Cahier (1878-79).
Maps.　4°　　　　　*Paris*, 1887
No. 698.—Service hydrographique de la Marine. Recherches sur les Chronomètres et les Instruments Nautiques.　8°
　　　　　　　　　　　　　　　1887
No. 708.—Annuaire des Marées de la Basse Cochinchine et du Tonkin pour l'an. 1890.　Par M. G. Héraud.　12°
　　　　　　　　　　　　　　　1889
No. 709.—Annuaire des Marées des Côtes de France pour l'an 1890. Par M. Hatt.　16°　　　　　　　1889
No. 729.—Catalogue, par Ordre Géographique　　　　　　　　　1892
No. 742.—Annuaire des Marées de la Basse Cochin Chine et du Tonkin pour l'an 1894　　　　　　　1893

C. Various Government Publications.

Liste Générale des Postes de France, dressée par ordre de Voyer de Paulmy, Chevalier Comte D'Argenson, &c.　12°
　　　　　　　　　　　Paris, 1749
Livre de Poste, ou État général des Postes aux Chevaux du Royaume de France, des Relais des Routes desservies en Poste, conduisant des Frontières de France aux principales Capitales de l'Europe ; . . . pour l'an. 1833. *Map*. Small 8°　　　　　*Paris*, 1833

Bureau des Longitudes.

Annuaire du Bureau des Longitudes, 1820-87.　68 vols.　16°·　*Paris*, 1820-87

FRANCE—C.
Le Connaissance des Tems ou des Mouvements Célestes à l'usage des Astronome, et des Navigateurs, pour les ans. 1838, '39, '43, '44, '45, '58, '61-68, '70-73, '76-80, '83-87, '89-97. 37 vols.　8°
　　　　　　　　　　　Paris, 1835-94

Ministère du Commerce de l'Industrie.

Statistique Générale de la France.

Resultats Statistiques du Dénombrement de 1886.　1ʳᵉ Partie. France. *Maps*. Large 8°　　　*Paris and Nancy*, 1888
—— The same.　Dénombrement de 1891. Large 8°　　　　　　*Paris*, 1894
Annuaire Statistique de la France.　Large 8°　　　　　　　　　*Paris*, 1890

Statistique Municipale.

Annuaire de la Ville de Paris.　IXᵉ Annee, 1888.　Large 8°　　*Paris*, 1890

Ministère de l'Intérieur.

Statistique de la France.　6 vols.　8°
　　　　　　　　　　　Paris, 1801
Dénombrement de la Population, 1886. 8°　　　　　　　　*Paris*, 1887

Ministère des Travaux Publiques.

Direction des Routes, de la Navigation et des Mines.

Voies Navigables ; Manuel des Distances comprises entre les principaux points de chaque voie (Annexe à la Circulaire du 31 Août 1881). *Map*.　12°　*Paris*, 1882
Guide Officiel de la Navigation Intérieure, avec itinéraires Graphiques des principales Signes de Navigation et Carte générale des Voies Navigables de la France. 5th edition.　12°　*Paris*, 1891

Ponts et Chaussées : Service Hydrometrique du Bassin de la Seine.

Resumé des Observations Centralisées . . . pendant les années 1871-73, 1881, 1883-92. [*Accompanied in each case by separate lithographic folio plates.*] Large 8°　　　　　*Versailles*, 1883-93
[*See also* Courtin ; Préaudaux.]

D. École des Langues Orientales Vivantes : Publications.

Mélanges Orientaux.　Textes et traductions publiés par les Professeurs de l'École Spéciale des Langues Orientales Vivantes à l'occasion du Sixième Congrès International des Orientalistes réuni à Leyde, Septembre 1883.　2nd Series, Vol. 9. *Plates and facsimiles*. Large 8°
　　　　　　　　　　　Paris, 1883
Nouveaux Mélanges Orientaux.　Mémoirs, Textes et Traductions, publiés par les Professeurs de l'École Spéciale

FRANCE—D.

Nouveaux Mélanges Orientaux—*contd.*
des Langues Orientales Vivantes à l'occasion du Septiéme Congres International des Orientalists réuni à Vienne, Septembre 1886. 2nd Series, Vol. 19. *Map.* Large 8° *Paris*, 1886

Recueil de Textes et de Traductions publié par les Professeurs de l'École des Langues Orientales Vivantes, à l'occasion du VIII. Congrés International des Orientalistes tenu à Stockholm en 1889. [3rd Series, Vols. 5 and 6.] 2 vols. Large 8° *Paris*, 1889
[*See* Asia, Central. *Also,* Barbier de Meynard; Bretschneider; Cordier; Dapontès; Daron; Derenbourg; Des Michels; Devéria; Ezziani; Imbault-Huart; Leger; Legrand; Machéras; Nalivkine; Nozhet-Elhadi; Pavet de Courteille; Riza Qouly-Khan; Rosny; Saint-Priest; Schefer; Tassy; Urechi; in Authors' Catalogue. For summary of volumes, *see* France: Appendix 3.]

E. Anonymous and Miscellaneous.

Voyages en France. Tom. 4, Provence, Chantilly, Normandie, Beaune, Havre-de-Grace. *Plates.* 12° *Paris*, 1768
Géographie de la France. 2 vols. *Map.* 8° *Paris*, 1802
Statistique générale et particulière de la France et de ses Colonies, par une Société de Gens de Lettres. [J. Peuchet, Sonnini, Herbin, &c.] 7 vols. 8° *Paris*, 1803
Dictionnaire Général des Communes de France, et des Principaux Hameaux en Dépendant, indiquant les Départemens, les Bureaux de Poste, la Distance des Communes aux chefs-lieux d'Arrondissement, et de ceux-ci à Paris. 8° *Paris*, 1818
Itinéraire de la France. *Map.* 8° *Paris*, 1823
—— The same. *Map and plates.* 12° *Paris*, 1824
Mont Blanc, and the Valley of Chamonix. *Plate.* 12° *Geneva*, 1855
—— Topography of the Chain of Mont Blanc. 8° 1865
Four Years in France; or, Narrative of an English Family's Residence there during that period; preceded by some account of the Conversion of the Author to the Catholick Faith. 8° 1826
Instruments. Notice sur les Instruments Enregistreurs Construits par Richard, Frères. 4° *Paris*, 1886
The Colonial Policy of France. From the *Edinburgh Review*, April 1893.
Société Ethnologique. Instruction Générale, adressée aux Voyageurs, &c. 8° *Paris*, N.D.

FRANCE—E.

Bordeaux. Catalogue Spécial des objets composant l'Exposition Géographique, 1882. (Société de Géographie Commercial de Bordeaux) *Bordeaux*, 1882
—— Notice sur les Vins de Bordeaux. Extrait de la 3mo édition du Guide de l'Étranger à Bordeaux. 18° *Bordeaux*, 1834
—— Nouveau Conducteur de l'Étranger à Bordeaux. *Plan and views.* 12° *Bordeaux*, 1861
Chambery. Notice sur les Charmettes et sur les Environs de Chambery. 3rd edition, &c. 8° *Chambery*, 1824
Chamouni, The Peasants of; containing an attempt to reach the Summit of Mont Blanc, and a Delineation of the Scenery among the Alps. 12° 1823
Corsica. A New Description, Geographical and Historical, of the Island of Corsica; also Memoirs of Theodore Baron de Neuhoff. *Map.* 8° 1739
—— Guide du Voyageur en Corse. *Maps.* 16° *Ajaccio*, 1868
Drome. Le Petit Guide de l'Étranger dans le Département de la Drome. Par la Société des Petits Guides. 32° *Valence*, 1863
Grenoble. Le Petit Guide de l'Étranger à Grenoble. Par la Société des Petits Guides. 32° *Grenoble*, 1863
Nice. Account by Mediterranean Hotel Company. 8° 1866-67
Paris. View of Paris, and Places adjoining. 8° 1701
—— **Geographical Congress.** *See* General, International Congresses.
—— **Geographical Society.** Notice sur la Société de Géographie fondée en 1821, Reconnue d'utilité Publique en 1827. *Plates.* 8° *Paris*, 1886
Provence, Voyage en. *Plates.* 12° *Paris*, 1798
Pyrénées. Essai sur la Minéralogie des Monts Pyrénées. *Maps and plates.* 4° *Paris*, 1784
—— Explorations Pyrénéennes. 8° *Bagnères-de-Bigorre*, 1866
Seine. Itinéraire des Bateaux à Vapeur de Paris au Havre, avec une Description Statistique et Anectdotique des Bords de la Seine, suivi d'un Guide du Voyageur; précédé d'une Notice Historique sur le Chemin de Fer de Paris à Saint-Germain. *Maps and plates.* 18° *Paris*, N.D.
—— **Notice Historique** sur le Monument érigé par la Ville de Paris aux sources de la Seine en 1867. *Maps and plans.* 8° *Paris*, 1868
Toulouse. L'Indicateur Toulousain, ou le Guide du Voyageur dans Toulouse. 12° *Toulouse*, 1822
Vichy. On the Medicinal Properties of the Mineral Waters of Vichy. Small 8° 1857
—— its Mineral Waters, Salts, and Lozenges. 16° *Paris* [1870]

GERMAN EMPIRE.

A. Prussian Geodetic Institute.

Publicationen des Konigl. Preuss. Geodätischen Institutes. Astronomisch-Geodätische Ortsbestimmungeni m Harz. Bestimmung der Polhöhen und der geodätischen Lage der Stationen Blankenburg, Hüttenrode, Hasselfelde, und der Polhöhe von Nordhausen. Im Jahre 1881—ausgeführt von Dr Moritz Löw. 4° *Berlin*, 1882

—— Astronomisch - Geodätische Arbeiten in den Jahren 1881 und 1882. Instruction für die Polhöhen- und Azimuthbestimmungen der Astronomischen Section des Geodätischen Institutes. Bestimmung der Polhöhe und des Azimuthes auf den Stationen : Gottenberg, Thurmberg, Goldaper Berg, Springberg, Moschin, Schönsee, und Jauernick. 4° *Berlin*, 1883

—— The same. In den Jahren 1883 und 1884. Bestimmung der Längen-differenzen Berlin-Swinemünde, Kiel-Swinemünde, Swinemünde-Königsberg, Königsberg-Warschau, und Berlin-Warschau. Bestimmung der Polhöhe des Zeitballes in Swinemünde. 4° *Berlin*, 1885

—— Das Mittelwasser der Ostsee bei Travemünde. Bearbeitet von Prof. Dr Wilhelm Seibt. *Plan and plates.* 4° *Berlin*, 1885

—— Uebersicht der Arbeiten des Königl. Geodätischen Instituts unter Generallieutenant Z. D. Dr Baeyer, nebst einem allgemeinen Arbeitsplane des Instituts für das nächste Decennium. *Maps.* 4° *Berlin*, 1886

—— Lothabweichungen. Heft 1. Formeln und Tafelen sowie einige numerische Ergebnisse für Norddeutschland. Der Allgemeinen Konferenz der Internationalen Erdmessung im Oktober 1886 zu Berlin gewidmet. *Plates.* 4° *Berlin*, 1886

—— Präcisions Nivellement der Elbe. Dritte Mittheilung. Auf Veranlassung der Elbstrom-Baubehörden von Preussen, Mecklenburg, und Anhalt, im Auftrage des Königlichen Geodätischen Instituts ausgeführt und bearbeitet von Prof. Dr Wilhelm Seibt. *Plate.* 4° *Berlin*, 1887

—— Astronomisch-Geodätische Arbeiten I. Ordnung. Telegraphische Längenbestimmungen in den Jahren 1885 und 1886. 4° *Berlin*, 1887

—— Gradmessungs-Nivellement, zwischen Anclam und Cuxhaven. Nebst einem Anhange. Höhen über M. N. von Festpunkten der früheren Gradmessungs-Nivellements des Geodätischen Institutes. *Map and plate.* 4° *Berlin*, 1888

Publicationen, &c. Das Märkisch-Thüringische Dreiecksnetz. *Map.* 4° *Berlin*, 1889

—— Astronomisch-Geodätische Arbeiten, I. Ordnung. Telegraphische Längenbestimmungen im Jahre 1887. Bestimmung der Polhöhe und des Azimutes auf den Stationen Rauenberg und Kiel in den Jahren 1886 und 1887. 4° *Berlin*, 1889

—— Lotabweichungen in der Umgebung von Berlin. *Plates.* 4° *Berlin*, 1889

—— Gewichtsbestimmungen für Seitenverhältnisse im schematischen Dreiecksnetzen, von Dr Paul Simon. 4° *Berlin*, 1889

—— Polhöhen - Bestimmungen aus dem Jahre 1886 für zwanzig Stationen nahe dem Meridian des Brockens vom Harz bis zur Dänischen Grenze. Gelegentlich ausgeführte Polhöhen- und Azimutbestimmungen aus den Jahren 1878 bis 1884. 4° *Berlin*, 1889

—— Astronomisch-Geodätische Arbeiten I. Ordnung. Telegraphische Längenbestimmungen in dem Jahren 1888 und 1889. Bestimmung der Polhöhe und des Azimutes auf der Schneekoppe im Jahre 1888. Bestimmung des Azimutes auf Station Trockenberg im Jahre 1888. *Plan and plates.* 4° *Berlin*, 1890

—— Das Mittelwassers der Ostsee bei Swinemünde. Zweite Mittheilung. *Plates.* 4° *Berlin*, 1890

—— Das Berliner Basisnetz, 1885 - 87. *Plates.* 4° *Berlin*, 1891

—— The same. (Und Central-Bureaus der Internationalen Erdmessung.) Die Schwerkraft im Hochgebirge, insbesondere in den Tyroler Alpen in geodätischer und geologischer Beziehung, von F. R. Helmert. *Plates.* 4° *Berlin*, 1890

—— Die Europäische Längengradmessung in 52 Grad Breite von Greenwich bis Warschau. I. Heft. Hauptdreiecke und Grundlinien-anschlüsse von England bis Polen. Herausgegeben von F. R. Helmert. *Plates.* 4° *Berlin*, 1893

—— Jahresbericht des Direktors des königlichen Geodätischen Instituts für die Zeit von April 1887 bis April 1888. 8° *Berlin*, 1888

—— The same. 1888-89, 1889-90, 1891-92, 1892-93, 1893-94. 8° *Berlin*, 1889-94

B. Various Government Publications.

General Staff. Registrande der Geographisch - Statistischen Abtheilung des Grossen Generalstabes ; Neues aus der Geographie, Kartographie, und Statistik Europa's und seiner Kolonien. Vols. 1-13. *Maps* *Berlin*, 1869-83

GERMANY—B.

Meterological Institute. Das Königlich Preussische Meteorologische Institut in Berlin, und dessen Observatorium bei Potsdam. Aus amtlichem Anlass herausgegeben von Wilhelm von Bezold. *Plan.* 4° *Berlin,* 1890

North Sea. Die Ergebnisse der Untersuchungsfahrten S. M. Knbt. "Drache," Kommandant Korvetten-Kapitän Holzhauer, in der Nordsee in den Sommern 1881, 1882, und 1884. Veröffentlicht von dem Hydrographischen Amt der Admiralität. *Maps, &c.* 4° *Berlin,* 1886

Repertorium aller Oerter und Anderer Gegenstände in der Topographisch-Militarischen Charte von Deutschland, in 204 Blättern. 2 vols. *Tables.* 8° *Weimar,* 1812-13

Rivers. Die Stromgebiete des Deutschen Reichs, hydrographisch und orographisch dargestellt mit beschreibendem Verzeichniss der deutschen Wasserstrassen. Theil I. Gebiet der Ostsee. Herausgegeben vom Kaiserlichen Statistischen Amt.—Statistik des Deutschen Reichs. N. F. Band 39. Erster Theil. *Maps.* 4° *Berlin,* 1891

Sailing Directions. Deutsche Seewarte Segelhandbuch für den Atlantischen Ozean. Mit Atlas von 36 Karten. *Maps and diagrams.* Large 8° *Hamburg,* 1885

—— The same. Atlas folio *Hamburg,* 1882

Weissbuch. Vorgelegt dem Deutschen Reichstage. Large 8° *Berlin*

1 Theil.—Afrika, Südsee, &c. 1885
2 Theil.—Fidji, Südsee, 2 1885
3 Theil.—Congo-frage, Aegypten 1885
4 Theil.—Aufstand in Ostafrika, 1 1889
5 Theil.—Samoa, 1 1889
6 Theil.—Samoa, 2. Aufstand in Ostafrika, 2 1889
7 Theil.—Nigergebiete. Aufstand in Ostafrika, 3 1889
8 Theil.—Aufstand in Ostafrika, 4. Samoa, 3 1890
9 Theil.—Witu. Aufstand in Ostafrika, 5. Regelung der Verhältnisse in Ostafrika 1891
11, 12 Theil.—Vorgänge in Chili 1891
13 Theil.—Samoa, 4 1893

Bavaria. Gesetzblatt für das Königreich Bayern. VIII. Stück. München. 4° *Munich,* 1828

—— Die Forstverwaltung Bayerns beschrieben nach ihrem dermaligem Stande vom Königlich Bayerischen Ministerial-Forstbureau. *Map.* Royal 8° *Munich,* 1861

—— Steuer-Kataster zugleich Grund-Taal- und Lagerbuch der Gemeinde Sieglizhof. *Map.* Folio *Erlangen,* 1837-38

GERMANY—B.

Frankfort-on-Main. Statistische Beschreibung der Stadt Frankfurt am Main und ihrer Bevölkerung. I. Theil. Die aussere Vertheilung der Bevölkerung. *Plans.* Large 8° *Frankfort-on-Main,* 1892

—— The same. Zweites Heft 1893

Rhine. Der Rheinstrom und seine wichtigsten Nebenflüsse von dem Quellen bis zum Austritt des Stromes aus dem Deutschen Reich. Eine hydrographische, wasserwirthschaftliche und wasserrechtliche Darstellung mit vorzugsweise eingehender Behandlung des Deutschen Stromgebietes. Im Auftrag der Reichskommission zur Untersuchung der Rheinstromverhältnisse herausgegeben von dem Centralbureau für Meteorologie und Hydrographie im Grossherzogthum Baden. 4° *Berlin,* 1889

—— The same. Atlas accompanying. Oblong 4° *Berlin,* 1889

Saxony. Resultate aus den Meteorologischen Beobachtungen an den 25 Konigl. Sächsischen Stationen, 1868-71. (4 Parts in 1 vol.) 4° *Dresden and Leipzig,* 1870-74

C. Miscellaneous.

Forschungen zur Deutschen Landes- und Volkskunde im Auftrage der Centralkommission für wissenschaftliche Landeskunde von Deutschland. 8° *Stuttgart,* 1886-94

CONTENTS.

Vol. 1.—Herausgegeben von Dr Richard Lehmann 1889
Geinitz, Dr E. Der Boden Mecklenburgs 1885
Lepsius, Dr Richard. Die oberrheinische Tiefebene und ihre Randgebirge. *Map* 1885
Hahn, Dr F. G. Die Städte der Norddeutschen Tiefebene in ihrer Beziehung zur Bodengestaltung 1885
Gruber, C. Das Münchener Becken. Ein Beitrag zur physikalischen Geographie Südbayerns. *Map and profiles* 1885
Geinitz, Dr E. Die Mecklenburgischen Höhenrucken (Geschiebestreifen), und ihre Beziehungen zur Eiszeit. *Maps and profiles* 1886
Assmann, R. Der Einfluss der Gebirge auf das Klima von Mitteldeutschland. *Maps and profiles* 1886
Bidermann, Dr H. J. Die Nationalitäten in Tirol und die wechselnden Schicksale ihrer Verbreitung 1886
Jansen, Prof. Dr K. Paleographie der cimbrischen Halbinsel, ein Versuch die Ansiedlungen Nordalbingiens in ihrer Bedingtheit durch Natur und Geschichte nachzuweisen 1886

GERMANY—D.

D. Anonymous.

Baden. Festschrift für die Mitglieder der XXI. Versammlung deutscher Land- und Forstwirthe. Beiträge zur Kenntniss der Land- und Forstwirthschaft im Grossherzogthum Baden. *Map and plates.* Royal 8°　　　　*Heidelberg,* 1860

Berlin. Guide de Berlin, de Potsdam et des Environs. *Map.* 12° *Berlin,* 1793

Bremen. Die Freie Hansestadt Bremen und ihre Umgebungen. Festgabe, den Teilnehmern an der 63te. Versammlung der Gesellschaft deutscher Naturforscher und Aerzte gewidmet vom Aerztlichen Vereine, Naturwissenschaftlichen Vereine, und der Geographischen Gesellschaft zu Bremen. *Plans, portraits, and illustrations.* 8°　　*Bremen,* 1890

Colonies. Die Entwickelung unserer Kolonien. Sechs Denkschriften. 4°
Berlin, 1892

Danzig. A Particular Description of the City of Dantzick. . . . By an English Merchant, lately resident there. 8°
1734

Frankfort-on-Main. Tableau Historique et Topographique de Francfort sur Main. 13°　　　　　*Frankfort,* 1828

Hamburg Commercial Library. *See* Catalogues, A.

Harz Mountains. The Hartz Mountains. Holiday Handbook, No. 5, edited by Percy Lindley. *Illustrations.* 8°　　　　　　　　　　N.D.

Munich. A Guide to Munich, its Buildings, Institutions, and Environs. *Map and plates.* 12°　　　　1870

Posen. A Narrative of Recent Occurrences in Posen. 8°　　　　1848

Prussia. Erläuterungen zu der Karte über die Production, Consumtion, und Circulation der mineralischen Brennstoffe in Preussen in 1862. 4°　*Berlin,* 1863

Rhine. An Autumn near the Rhine ; or, Sketches of Courts, Society, and Scenery in Germany, with a Tour in the Taunus Mountains, in 1820. 2nd edition, to which are added Translations from Schiller, Goethe, and other German Poets. *Plate.* 8°　　　　1821

Rhine and Danube. The Theatres of War of the Rhine and Danube, prepared to accompany a Map of the Basins of the Rhine and Danube. 12°　　　1891

Routen-Aufnahme-Buch *Berlin,* 1893

Saxony. Dresden und die umliegende Gegend bis Elsterwerda, Baussen, Herrnhut, Rumburg, Aussig, Täpliss, Frenberg, und Hubertsburg. Eine Darstellung für Natur- und Kunstfreunde. 2 vols. 8°　　　*Dresden,* 1804

—— Alphabetisches Orts-Verzeichniss des Königreichs Sachsen. 4° *Dresden,* 1837
2 Z

GERMANY—D.

Schleswig. On Nationality and Language in the Duchy of Sleswick, or South Jutland. 8°　　　*Copenhagen,* 1848

Schwetzingen. Description du Jardin de Schwetzingen. *Map and plates.* 12°

GREECE.

Correspondence respecting the Rectification of the Greek Frontier. Greece, No. 1 (1882). *Maps.* Folio　　　1882

Ministère des Finances. Bureau de Statistique. Commerce de la Grèce avec les pays Étrangers, 1887, '88, '89, '92. [In Greek and French.] 4° *Athens,* 1888-92

—— Bulletin Mensuel du Commerce Spécial de la Grèce avec les pays Étrangers. Odd numbers, 1888-94. 4° *Athens,* 1888-94

—— Tarif des Douanes. 4° *Athens,* 1890

Ministry of Foreign Affairs. Correspondence relating to the Mines of Laurium. [In Greek and French.] 4° 1873 [*See also* Catalogues.]

Athens. The British School of Archæology at Athens : Report of Committee and of the First Meeting of Subscribers, 1885. 8°

Corinth. Eine Spazierfahrt im Golfe von Korinth. *Map in cover. Plates.* 4°
Prague, 1876

Morea. Memorie Istorico Geografiche della Morea, riacquistata dall' Armi Venete dal Regno di Negroponte, e degli altri luoghi circonuicini, e di quelli c' hanno sotomesso nella Dalmacia, e nell' Epiro dal principio della Guerra intimata al Turco in Constantinopoli nel 1684-87. Colla Descrizione delle Fortezze di Castel Nuovo, e Chnin. *Plates and plans.* Folio　　　　*Venice,* 1687

—— Expedition Scientifique de Morée. Section des Sciences Physiques. 4 vols. 4°, Atlas folio (1831-35)　　*Paris*

Vol. 1.—Relation, par Bory de Saint-Vincent. 1836.

Vol. 2. Part 1.—Géographie, par Bory de Saint-Vincent. 1834.

Vol. 2. Part 2.—Géologie et Minéralogie, par E. Puillon de Boblaye et Théodore Virlet. 1833.

Vol. 3. Part 1.— Zoologie. Sect. 1. Mammifères et Oiseaux, par Isidore Geoffrey Saint-Hilaire, 1833 ; Sect. 2. Animaux articulés, par Brullé (Crustacés, par Guérin), 1832.

Vol. 4. Part 2.—Botanique, par Fauché, Ad. Brongniart, Chaubard, et Bory de Saint Vincent. 1832. [This vol. also includes—Recherches Géographiques sur les Ruines de la Morée, par E. Puillon de Boblaye.]

Santorin. Einige Worte über die Kaymenen, July 1874. *Plates.* 4° *Prague,*1875

HOLLAND.

Koninklijk Nederlandsch Meteorologisch Instituut.

Onderzoekingen met den Zeethermometer, als uitkomsten van Wetenschap en Ervaring. 4° *Utrecht*, 1861
Reizen van Australie naar Java. 4° *Utrecht*, 1862
Zeilaanwijzingen van Java naar het Kanaal. Erste en Tweede Deelen. Oblong folio *Utrecht*, 1868-70
Temperatuur van het Zeewater aan de Oppervlakte van het gedeelte van den Noorde Atlantischen Oceaan, tusschen 30°-52° Norderbreedte en 0°-50° Westerlengte. Oblong folio *Utrecht*, 1872
Marche Annuelle du Thermomètre et du Baromètre en Néerlande, déduite d'Observation simultanées de 1843 à 1875. 4° *Utrecht*, 1876
De Stroomen op de Nederlandsche Kust. 4° *Utrecht*, 1890

Nederlandsch Aardrifkskundig Genootschap.

Nomina Geographica Neerlandica. Geschiedkundig Onderzoek der Nederlandsche Aardrijkskundige Namen, on der redactie van Dr J. Dornseiffen, Prof. J. H. Gallée, Prof. H. Kern, Prof. S. A. Naber, en Dr H. C. Rogge. 1ste Deel. 8° *Amsterdam and Utrecht*, 1885

Miscellaneous.

Atlas. Nieuwe Zak-Atlas voor de Reizigers door de gezamentlyke Nederlanden. *Frontispiece and coloured maps.* Small 8° *Amsterdam*, 1739
—— Compleete Zak-Atlas van de Zeventien Nederlandsche Provinciën. *Coloured maps.* Small 8° *Amsterdam*, 1786
Colonies. Catalogus der Afdeeling Nederlandsche Koloniën van de Internationale Koloniale en Uitvoerhandel Teutomstelling van 1 Mei tot ult°. October 1883, te Amsterdam. Groeps 1, 2, 3. 3 vols. *Maps, plan, and plates.* Large 8° *Leyden*, 1883
—— The same. French édition. 3 vols. *Maps, &c.* Large 8° *Leyden*, 1883

ITALY.

A. Government Publications.

Ministero di Agricoltura, Industria, e Commercio.

Direzione Generale della Statistica.

Carte Topografiche, Idrografiche, e Geologiche annesse alla Monografia Statistica della città di Roma e Campagna Romana, presentata all' Esposizione Universale di Parigi, 1878. Large folio.

ITALY—A.

Monografia della Città di Roma e della campagna romana. 2 vols. *Plans and diagrams.* Large 8° *Rome*, 1881
—— Appendice. Bibliografia Storica di Roma antica di Ruggero Bonghi. Large 8° *Rome*, 1881
—— Appendice. Note alla carta agronomica dei dintorni di Roma per Raffaello Canevari. Large 8° *Rome*, 1881
—— Appendice. Indice Bibliografico delle opere publicate in Roma da qualunque autore cd anche fuori di Roma da persone residenti nella Capitale dal 1870 a tutto il 1877, per Gustavo Uzielli. Large 8° *Rome*, 1881
Notizie sulle Condizione Industriali della provincia di Genova, con una carta stradale e industriale. Pubblicate della Direzione generale della Statistica. 8° *Rome*, 1892
Annuario Statistico Italiano, anno 1886. 8° *Rome*, 1887

Direzione Generale dell' Agricultura.

Bollettino di Notizie Agrarie. Anno XV. (II. semestre). Nos. 25, 26, and 28. 8° *Rome*, 1893

[*See* Africa ; Eritrea.]

Ministero per gli Affari Esteri.

Bollettino Consolare pubblicato per cura del Ministero per gli Affari Esteri d'Italia. Vols. 1-23. *Plates, &c.* Large 8° *Turin*, 1861-87
—— del Ministero degli Affari Esteri [12 vols.], 1888-93. *Maps, &c.* Large 8° *Rome*, 1888-93
—— The same. New Series. Nos. 1-8, 22, 23, 33-40. 8° *Rome*, 1894-95
Parliamentary Reports. Atti Parlamentari, XVI. Legislatura—Quarta Sessione 1889-90. Camera dei Deputate. No. 15 (Documenti). Documenti Diplomatici presentati al Parlamento Italiano del Presidente del Consiglio Ministro ad interim degli Affari Esteri (Crispi). Etiopia. 4° *Rome*, 1890
—— The same. Sessione 1890. Camera dei Deputati. No. 14 (Documenti). Documenti presentati al Parlamento Italiano del Presidente del Consiglios Ministro ad interim degli Affari esteri (Crispi), di Concerto col Ministro della Guerra (Bertolè Viale). L'Occupazione di Keren e dell Asmara. 4° *Rome*, 1890
Documenti Diplomatici presentati al Parlamento Italiano. Missione Antonelli in Etiopia. 4° *Rome*, 1891

B. Geographical Congress and Exhibition.

Relazioni su alcune Tesi e Communicazioni da presentarsi alla Sezione Prima del Congresso, Autori Bianchi, Botto, Dohrn, Fiorini, Grablovitz, Marinelli, Paganini, Roncagli, Sergi. 8° *Rome*, 1892

ITALY—B.

Relazioni su alcune Tesi e Communicazioni da presentarsi alla Sezione Prima del Congresso. Sezione Seconda. Autori Carerji, Corte, Magliano, Rossi, Scalabrini, Sitta, Vedovelli, Volpe-Landi.
—— The same. Sezione Terza. Autori Bertacchi, Canevello, Marinelli, Pennesi Porena.

Catalogo Generale della Prima Mostra Geografica Italiana. 7-30 Settembre 1892. [Società Geografica Italiana.] *Plan.* 8° *Genoa*, 1892

Atti del Primo Congresso Geografico Italiano, tenuto in Genova, 1892. Vol. 1, and Vol. 2, Parts 1 and 2. Large 8° *Genoa*, 1894

C. Anonymous.

De Principibus Italiæ Commentarius, ex Italico in Lat. versus à **T.** Segetho. 18° *Leyden*, 1631

Itinéraire d' Italie. 2nd edition. *Maps.* 8° *Florence*, 1801
—— 5th edition. *Maps.* 12° *Milan*, 1814

Itinerario Italiano. *Maps.* 8° *Milan*, 1822

Itinéraire Classique d'Italie. *Maps.* 12° *Paris*, 1823

Poems. Raccolta di Poesie Satiriche. *Portrait.* 8° *Milan*, 1808

Calendario Generale Pe' Regii Stati. 8° *Turin*, 1828

Studi Bibliografici e Biografici sulla Storia della Geografia in Italia. *Maps and photographs.* 4° *Rome*, 1875
—— sulla Geografia Naturale e Civile dell' Italia. *Map.* 4° *Rome*, 1857

Studi Biografici e Bibliografici sulla Storia della Geografia in Italia, pubblicati in occasione of III. Congresso Geografico Internazionale. Vol. 1. Biografia dei Viaggiatori Italiani colla Bibliografia delle loro opere, per P. Amat di S. Filippo. Vol. 2. Mappamondi, Carte Nautiche, Portolani, ed Altrimonumenti Cartografici Specialmente Italiani dei Secoli XIII.-XVII., par G. Uzielli e P. Amat di S. Filippo. 2nd edition. [Società Geografica Italiana.] *Maps.* 8° *Rome*, 1882

——

Alps. Dei Passaggi Alpini, sulle Rivoluzioni delle Alpi. 8° *Milan*, 1804
—— Le Alpi che cingono l' Italia. Parte prima. *Maps.* 8 *Turin*, 1845

Calabria. Istoria de' Fenomeni del Tremoto avvenuto nel Calabrie, e nel Valdemone nell' anno 1783, posta in luce dalla Realle Academia della Scienze, e delle Belle Lettere di Napoli. 4° *Naples*, 1784
—— Calabria during a Military Residence of Three Years, in a Series of Letters by a General Officer of the French Army, &c. *Plate.* 8° 1832

ITALY—C.

Catania. Su' Lavori pel Molo di Catania, negli 1843-46. Terza Lettera di un Catanese al Signor N. N. 8° *Catania*, 1846

Florence. Guida di. *Maps and plates.* 2 vols. 12° *Florence*, 1820
—— Guide de Florence at d'autres villes principales de Toscane. 2 vols. *Plates.* 16° 1822
—— Guida della Città di Firenze. *Map and plates.* 12° *Florence*, 1833
—— **National Central Library.** Elenco delle Pubblicazioni Periodiche Italiane ricevute dalla Biblioteca nel 1891. 8° *Florence*, 1891

Genoa. Description des Beautés de Gênes et de ses Environs. *Map and plates.* 8° *Genoa*, 1819
—— Nouvelle Description de Gênes. *Map and plates.* 18° *Genoa*, 1826

Liguria. Descrizione delle Rivière delle Stato Ligure. 8° *Genoa*, 1780

Lombardy. Elenco Alfabetico dei Comuni Denominativi e delle frazioni aggregate appartenenti al Regne Lombardo-Veneto. 8° *Milan*, 1819

Lucca. Guida del Forestiere per la Città di Lucca. 12° *Lucca*, 1829

Naples. Delle Istorie della Chiesa Greca in Napoli Esistente. 4° *Naples*, 1790

Rome in the Nineteenth Century. 3 vols. 8° *Edinburgh*, 1826

Varallo. Guida al Sacro Monte di Varallo. 12° *Varallo*, N.D.

Venice. Guida per l'Arsenale di Venezia. *Plan and plates.* 12° *Venice*, 1829
—— Venezia e le sue lagune. 2 vols. (in 3). 4° *Venice*, 1847
—— Saggio di Cartografia della Regione Veneta. Large 8° *Venice*, 1881

Vesuvius. The Natural History of Mount Vesuvius. 12° 1743

——

NORWAY.

A. Government Publications.

Geodetic Commission. Publication der Norwegischen Commission der Europäischen Gradmessung. Udgivet af den Norske Gradmaalingskom mission.

Geodetische Arbeiten. Heft 1-7. 4° *Christiania*, 1882-90

Vandstands observationer. Heft 1, 3-5. 4° *Christiania*, 1882-93

Geographiske Opmaaling.

Beskrivelse til Kaartet over den Norske Kyst. 14 Nos. in 1 vol. 4° *Christiania*, 1835-57

Den Norske Lods, udgiven af den Geografiske Opmaaling. *Profiles.* 8° *Christiania*
1ste Hefte.—Kyststrækningen fra Idefjorden til Jomfruland, udarbejdet efter de Hydrografiske Undersøgelser 1863 til 1870, ved C. F. Wille 1871

NORWAY—A.

Den Norske Lods—*continued.*

2^{dte} Hefte.— . . . fra Jomfruland til Kristiansand, omarbeidet efter de ældre Beskrivelser og Hydrografiske Undersågelser 1853 til 1855, ved J. S. Fabricius 1880

3^{die} Hefte.—. . . . fra Kristiansand til Stavanger, udarbeidet . . . ved C. Wille 1867

4de Hefte.— . . . fra Stavanger til Bergen udarbeidet . . . ved C. F. Wille 1868

5te Hefte.— . . . fra Korsfjord og Bergen til Utvær tilligemed leden fra Sognesåen til Alden, udarbeidet efter de Hydrografiske Undersågelser, 1863-67, ved J. S. Fabricius 1883

6te Hefte.— . . . fra Sognesjåen til Aalesund med Undtagelse af beden fra Sognesjåen til Alden (beskrevet i 5te Hefte), ved R. M. Petersen 1885

8de Hefte.— . . . fra Trondhjemsleden til den Russiske Grændse . . . ved J. S. Fabricius 1870 and 1885

Reisekart over Norges 5 sydlige Stifter, udgivet i 2 Blade af den Geografiske Opmaaling. [2 pamphlets.] 12°
Christiania, 1873

Beskrivelse af Tromso Amt efter de i anledning af ordningen af forholdet Mellem flytlapperne og de fastboende i aarene 1869, 1870, og 1872 unförte Krokeringer M. M. Udgivet af den geografiske Opmaaling. *Maps.* 8°
Christiania, 1874

Meteorologisch Institut.

Nedbör-höiden i Norge, beregnet efter observationer 1867 til 1891.

Beitrag zur Climatologie. Novaja Semlja's. Von Aksel S. Steen. 4°
Christiania, 1878

Norwegian North-Atlantic Expedition, 1876-78 [the "Voringen," Capt. Wille], General Report of the (in Norwegian and English). Imperial 4° *Christiania,* 1880
Part 1.—Chemistry.—1. On the Air in Sea-water; 2. On the Carbonic Acid in Sea-water; 3. On the Amount of Salt in the Water of the Norwegian Sea. By Hercules Tornöe. *Maps and woodcuts.*
Part 2.—Zoology.—Fishes. By Robert Collett. *Maps, plates, and woodcuts.*
Part 3.—Zoology.—Gephyrea. By D. C. Danielssen and Johan Koren. *Map and plates* 1881
Part 4.—1. Historical Account; with one *map.* 2. The Apparatus and How used; with a *frontispiece and illustrations.* By C. Wille 1882
Part 5.—1. Astronomical Observations: H. Mohn. 2. Magnetical Observations: C. Wille. 3. Geography and Natural History: H. Mohn. *Maps, chromo-l'²-graphs, &c.*

NORWAY—A.

Norwegian North-Atlantic Expedition —*continued.*

Part 6. — Zoology. — Holothurioidea. By D. C. Danielssen and Johan Koren. *Map and plates* 1882
Part 7.—Zoology.—Annelida. By G. Armauer Hansen. *Map and plates* 1882
Part 8.—Zoology.—Mollusca. 1. Buccinidæ. By Herman Friele. *Map and plates* 1882
Part 9.—Chemistry.—1. On the Solid Matter in Sea-water. 2. On Oceanic Deposits. By Ludwig Schmelck. *Maps and woodcut* 1882
Part 10.—Meteorology. By H. Mohn. *Map, plates, and woodcuts* 1883
Part 11.—Zoology.—Asteroidea. By D. C. Danielssen and Johan Koren. *Map and plates* 1884
Part 12.—Zoology.—Pennatulida. By D. C. Danielssen and Johan Koren. *Map and plates* 1884
Part 13.—Zoology.—Spongiadæ. By G. Armauer Hansen, M.D. *Map and plates* 1885
Part 14. — Zoology. — Crustacea. I.^a and I.^b By G. O. Sars. *Maps and plates* 1885
Part 15. — Zoology. — Crustacea. II. By G. O. Sars. *Map* 1886
Part 16. — Zoology. — Mollusca. II. By Herman Friele. *Plates* 1886
Part 17. — Zoology. — Alcyonida. By D. C. Danielssen. *Map and plates* 1887
Part 18^a and 18^b.—The North Ocean, its Depths, Temperature, and Circulation. By H. Mohn. *Maps, plates, and woodcuts* 1887
Part 19.—Zoology.—Actinia. By D. C. Danielssen. *Map and plates* 1890
Part 20. — Zoology. — Pycnogonidea. By G. O. Sars. *Map and plates* 1891
Part 21. — Zoology. — Crinoida and Echinida. By D. C. Danielssen. *Map and plates* 1892
Part 22.—Zoology.—Ophiuridea. By James A. Grieg. *Map and plates* 1893

Polar Observations. *See* Polar Regions, Arctic, G, International.

B. Anonymous.

Archaeology. Nordiske Fortidsminder. Udgivne af det Kgl. Nordiske Oldskriftselskab. Avec des Résumés en Français. Hefte 1, 2. *Plates.* 4°.

Beretning om Kongeriget Norges ökonomiske Tilstand, 1846-55. 2 vols. *Tables.* Folio *Christiania,* 1853-58

Den Norske Turistforenings Årbog, 1873-74-75. *Plates.* 8° *Christiania*

Tromsö. Beretning om den almindelige Udstilling for Tromsö Stift. *Plate.* 8°
Christiania, 1872

NORWAY—B.

Statistics. Résumé de Renseignements Statistiques sur la Norvège. 8°
Christiania, 1875

PORTUGAL.

A. Various.

Relatorios do Ministro e Secretario d'Estado dos Negocios da Marina e Ultramar, Janeiro de 1864. 8°
Lisbon, 1864
La Population du Département de Lisbonne, d'après les recensements opérés à 1864 et à 1878. 4° *Lisbon,* 1878
Portugallia, sive de Regis Portugalliæ regnis et opibus Commentarius. 8°
Leyden, 1641
Mappa Chronologico do Reino de Portugal, e seus Dominios, por L. M. P. S. M. C. 18° *Lisbon,* 1815
Portugal and Gallicia : with a Review of the Social and Political State of the Basque Provinces, and a few Remarks on Recent Events in Spain. 2nd edition. 2 vols. 8° 1837
Portuguese Colonies. Diccionario Geografico das Colonias Portuguezas. 8°
Oporto, 1842
Manual do Viajante, por G. A. de S. C. 12° *Lisbon,* 1845
Portugaliæ Monumenta Historica, a sæculo octavo post Christum usque ad quintumdecimum, jussu Academiæ Scientiarum Olisiponensis edita. *Facsimiles.* Folio *Lisbon,* 1856-63
Leges et Consuetudines. Vol. 1. Parts 1, 2, 3.
Scriptores. Vol. 1. Parts 1, 2, 3.
Descripção e Roteiro da Costa occidental de Africa. Por A. Magno de Castilho. 2 vols. Large 8° *Lisbon,* 1866-67
Commissaõ Geologica de Portugal : Estudos Geologicos. Da Existencia do homen no nosso solo em tempos mui remotos provada pelo estudo das Cavernas. 4°.
Opusc. 1. Delgado, J. F. N. Noticia ácerca das Grutas da Cesareda, com a versao em Francez por M. Dalhunty
Lisbon, 1867
—— *See* Costa, P. da.
L'Instruction Primaire au Département de Lisbonne. 4° *Lisbon,* 1878
Portugal in 1872. Constitutional Life of a Nation of the Latin Race. 8°
Lisbon, 1873
Estatistica Medica dos Hospitaes das Provincias Ultramarinas, 1871-72-73. 4°
Lisbon, 1873-75
Commerce. Tableaux Statistiques : Le Commerce du Portugal (1866-75). 4°
Lisbon, 1878

PORTUGAL—A.

Portugal and the Congo : a Statement prepared by the African Committee of the Lisbon Geographical Society, Luciano Cordeiro, Recording Secretary. *Maps.* 8° 1883
Memorandum concerning the Portuguese Rights and Pretensions to Sovereignty on the West Coast of Africa. *Map.* 8° 1883

B. Geographical Society of Lisbon.

Exploration Géographique et Commerciale de la Guinée Portugaise. 8° 1878
Tableaux Statistiques. Le Commerce du Portugal (1866-75) ; La Population du Département de Lisbonne (1864 et de 1878) ; L'Instruction primaire obrigatoire et gratuite au Département de Lisbonne. 4° *Lisbon,* 1878
African Committee. The Geographical Society of Lisbon and Mr Stanley. 12° *Lisbon,* 1878
De l'Enseignement de la Géographie. Projet de Reforme présenté au Govt. Portugais, par la Soc. de Geogr. de Lisbonne. Traduction. 12° *Lisbon,* 1878
L'Enseignement Commercial en Portugal. 12° *Lisbon,* 1878
Expédition Portugaise à l'Afrique Centrale (Serpa Pinto, Brito Capello, et R. Ivens). 12° *Lisbon,* 1878
Expedição Scientifica ao Interior de Africa. Observações Meteorologicas e Magneticas feitas pelos Exploradores Portuguezes Hermenegildo de Brito Capello e Roberto Ivens. Folio 1879
Bases d'un plan d'Études Commerciales présentées au Congrès International de Géographie Commerciale (Bruxelles, 1879) par la Société de Geogr. de Lisbon. 8° 1879
O districto de Lourenço Marques no presente e no futuro (por A. de Castilho). Sess. 14 April 1880. 8° *Lisbon,* 1880
O Zambeze. Apontamentos de duas Viagens (por A. de Castilho). Sess. 27 Jul. 1880. 8° *Lisbon,* 1880
Questões Africanas. Proposta . . . pela Commissão Nacional Portugueza de Exploração e Civilisação d'Africa. 8° *Lisbon,* 1880
—— Representação ao Governo Portuguez. Sess. 10 Jul. 1880.
Commissão Africana. Sess. 12 Feb. 1880
Mozambique. Communição à Sociedade de Geographia de Lisboa nas Sessões de 6, 13, e 22 de Decembro de 1880 (por Joaquim Jose Machado). 8° *Lisbon,* 1881
A Questão do Transvaal. Documentos colligidos, tradusidos e communicados a Sociedade de Geographia de Lisboa em 24 de Fevereiro de 1881 (por Augusto de Castilho). 8° *Lisbon,* 1881

PORTUGAL—B.

Explorações Geologicas e Mineras nas Colonias Portuguezas (por Lourenço Malheiro). 8°   *Lisbon*, 1881

Stanley's First Opinions. Portugal and the Slave Trade. 8°   *Lisbon*, 1883

La Question du Zaire. Droits du Portugal. 8°   *Lisbon*, 1883

A Questão do Meridiano Universal (por J. B. Ferreira D'Almeida). 8° *Lisbon*, 1883

Les Institutions de Prévoyance du Portugal (par Costa Godolphin). 8°
Lisbon, 1883

La Question du Zaire : Suum Cuique (par M. Luciano Cordeiro). 8° *Lisbon*, 1883

Reposta a Sociedade Anti-Esclavista de Londres (por J. A. Corte Real). 8°
Lisbon, 1884

Le Congo. Communication à la Société (par G. Arthur). 8°   *Lisbon*, 1886

Elogio Historico do Presidente Honorario e effectivo da Sociedade de Geographia de Lisboa. O Conselheiro Antonio Augusto D'Aguiar (por Gomes de Brito). 8°   *Lisbon*, 1887

Importation Abusive en Afrique par des sujets Anglais d'armes perfectionnées. Protestation présentée au Gouvernement Portugais par la Société de Geographie de Lisbonne. 8°   *Lisbon*, 1889

L'Incident Anglo-Portugais. Motion votée à la séance de la Société de Géographie de Lisbonne le 2 Decembre 1889. 8°
Lisbon, 1889

Descobertas e Descobridores. Diogo d'Azambuja. Memoria apresentada à 10ᵃ Sessão do Congresso International dos Orientalistas (por Luciano Cordeiro). *Plates.* 8°   *Lisbon*, 1892

—— De como e quando foi feito conde Vasco da Gama. Memoria apresentada a 10ᵃ Sessão do Congresso Internacional dos Orientalistas (por Luciano Cordeiro). *Plates.* 8°   *Lisbon*, 1892

La responsabilité qui revient au Portugal dans la convocation du 10ᵉᵐᵉ Congrés des Orientalistes. Rapport par G. de Vasconcellos Abreu. 8°   *Lisbon*, 1892

Dos Primeiros Trabalhos dos Portuguezes no Monomotapa. O Padre D. Gonçalo da Silveira, 1560. Memoria apresentada à 10ᵃ Sessão Congresso International dos Orientalistas (por A. P. de Paiva E. Pona). 8°   *Lisbon*, 1892

Sociologia Chinesa. O Homem como medicamento superstiçoes medicas e religiosas que victimam o homem offindade d'estas crenças com as crises Anti-Europeias de 1891, pelo Dr Macgovan. Nota destinada à 10 Sessão do Congresso International dos Orientalistas, pelo traductor Demetrio Cinatti. 8°
Lisbon, 1892

PORTUGAL.—B.

Deux Faits de l'honologie Historique Portugaise. Mémoire présentè à la 10ᵉᵐᵉ Session Congrès International des Orientalistes (par A. R. Gonçalves Vianna). 8°   *Lisbon*, 1892

Sur le Dialecte Portugais de Macao. Exposé d'un mémoire destiné à la 10ᵉᵐᵉ Session du Congrès International des Orientalistes (par J. Leite de Vasconcellos). 8°   *Lisbon*, 1892

La Connaissance de la Peninsule Espagnole par les hommes du nord. Mémoire destiné a la 10ᵉᵐᵉ Session du Congrès International de Orientalistes (par Adam Kristoffer Fabricius). 8° *Lisbon*, 1892

Sur les Amulettes Portugaises. Résumé d'un mémoire destiné à la 10ᵉᵐᵉ Session du Congrès International des Orientalistes (par J. Leite de Vasconcellos). 8°
Lisbon, 1892

La première Invasion des Normands dans l'Espagne Musulmane en 844. Mémoire destiné à la 10ᵉᵐᵉ Session du Congrès International des Orientalistes (par Adam Kristoffer Fabricius). 8° *Lisbon*, 1892

Sur les Religions de la Lusitanie. Abrégé d'un mémoire destiné à la 10ᵉᵐᵉ Session du Congrès International des Orientalistes (par J. Leite de Vasconcellos). 8°
Lisbon, 1892

Les Collections Minéralogique et Géologique installées à la Société de Géographie de Lisbonne (par J. M. D. Rego Lima). 8°   *Lisbon*, 1892

[*See also* Catalogues ; and Aranha, B.; Cordeiro, L. ; Edwards, E. M. ; Guedes, O. ; Magalhães, C. ; Pequito, R. A.]

RUMANIA.

Danube. Advantages likely to accrue to the Trade of the Danube from the Canal and Establishment of a Free Port on the Black Sea. Folio   1855

—— Mémoire sur le Régime Administratif établi aux embouchures du Danube, par la Commission Européenne chargée d'en améliorer la navigabilité, &c. 4°
Galatz, 1867

—— Mémoire sur les travaux d'amélioration exécutés aux embouchures du Danube par la Commission Européenne instituée en vertu l'article 16 du Traité de Paris du 30 Mars 1856. Accompagné d'un Atlas. *Plans.* 8°   *Galatz*, 1867

—— Mémoire sur les Travaux d'amélioration du cours du Bas-Danube, exécutés pendant la période 1873-86 par la Commission Européenne. *Maps.* 4°
Galatz, 1888

—— The same. Atlas accompanying. Folio
Leipzig, 1887

RUSSIA.

[*See also* Russia-in-Asia.]

A. Government Publications.

Chronometrical Expedition made by order of the Emperor of Russia, 1833. By Lieut.-Gen. Schubert. [In Russian.] 4°   *St Petersburg*, 1836

Catalogue of Trigonometrical and Astronomical Positions determined in the Russian Empire . . . up to 1860. By Lieut.-Gen. Blaraemberg. (Memoirs of Russian Topogr. Dépot.) [In Russian.] 4°
                         St Petersburg, 1863

Marine Hydrographic Department. Catalogue of Atlases, Maps, Plans, &c., issued by. 8°   *St Petersburg*, 1872

Military-Topographical Department of the General Staff. Auxiliary Tables of Trigonometrical Functions for small arcs. By D. Oblomievsky. [In Russian.] 8°   *St Petersburg*, 1875

Posting Directory of the Russian Empire. [In Russian.] 8°   *St Petersburg*, 1875

Meteorological Observations taken on ships of the Russian Navy. Issued by the Marine Meteorological Section of Central Physical Observatory, and Hydrographic Dept., Ministry of Marine. [In Russian.] Vol. I. 4° *St Petersburg*, 1883
—— The same. (Appendix to Parts 1 and 2 of "Hydrographical Memoirs.") Issued by the Ministry of Marine. [In Russian.] Large 8°   *St Petersburg*, 1887

Nicolai-Hauptsternwarte. Jahresbericht für 1882-83 und 1883-84 dem Comité . . . abgestaltet vom Director. Aus dem Russischen übersetzt. 8° *St Petersburg*, 1884
—— The same, 25 Mai 1885. 8°
                         St Petersburg, 1885
—— Bericht fur die Periode 1887, 1 Mai (13) bis 1889, : November (13). 8°
                         St Petersburg, 1890
—— *See* Struve, Otto.

Museum. [Report of the] Annual Session of the Committee for arranging a Museum of Applied Sciences, 30th November 1887 (15th year). [In Russian.] Large 8°   *Moscow*, 1888

Polar Observations. *See* Polar Regions, Arctic, G, International.

B. Imperial Russian Geographical Society.

Pocket-Book for Amateurs of Geography. Published by the Russian Geographical Society. [In Russian.] 12°
                         St Petersburg, 1849

Der Nördliche Ural und das Küstengebirge Pai-Choi, untersucht und beschrieben von einer in 1847-1850 durch die Kaiserlich-Russische Geographische Gesellschaft ausgerüsteten Expedition. 2 vols. *Maps and plates.* 4°
                         St Petersburg, 1853-56

RUSSIA—B.

Year-Book of Observations on Russian Climate made in 1851. (Issued by the Imp. Russ. Geogr. Soc.) [In Russian.] 4°   *St Petersburg*, 1854

Geographical-Statistical Dictionary of the Russian Empire, published by the Imperial Geographical Society. [In Russian.] 5 vols. Royal 8°
                         St Petersburg, 1865

Review of the most important Geographical work performed in Russia in 1865, 1866, and 1867-68. (From the *Izvestia* of the Imp. Russ. Geogr. Soc.) [In Russian.] Large 8°   *St Petersburg*, 1866-70

Essay towards a Scheme for Researches into the Agrarian Commune. Published by order of the Imp. Russ. Geogr. Soc. [In Russian.] 8°   *St Petersburg*, 1878

Programme for the Collection of National Juridical Customs. (Imp. Russ. Geogr. Soc.) [In Russian.] 8°
                         St Petersburg, 1889

C. Anonymous.

Kola Peninsula. Wissenschaftliche Ergebnisse der Finnischen Expeditionen nach der Halbinsel Kola in den Jahren 1887 - 92. Eine Sammlung Separat-Abdrücke A. Kartographie, Geologie, Klimatologie. I. and II. *Maps and illustrations.* Large 8°
                         Helsingfors, 1890-94
—— The same. B. Botanik, Zoologie. I. and II. *Map and plates.* Large 8°
                         Helsingfors, 1890-92

Catalogue and Report of the Geographical Exhibition at Moscow, 1892. [In Russian.] *Plates.* 8°   *Moscow*, 1893

Tableaux des Longeurs du Pendule aux différentes Stations de l'Empire Russe et de l'Etranger, observées par les Savants Russes. 8°   *St Petersburg*, 1893

Russia seu Moscovia itemque Tartaria, Commentario Topographicoatque Politico Illustratæ. 16°   *Leyden*, 1530

Authentic Narrative of the Russian Expedition against the Turks by Sea and Land. *Plans.* 8°   1772

Hydrographie de l'Empire de Russie. *Lithograph.* Folio *St Petersburg*, 1833

Black Sea. A Geographical, Statistical, and Commercial Account of the Russian Ports of the Black Sea, the Sea of Asoph, and the Danube. *Map.* 8°   1837

Sketch Map of the acquisitions of Russia, in Europe and Central Asia, since the Accession of Peter I. to the Throne. New edition.

Revelations of Russia, or the Emperor Nicholas and his Empire in 1844. 2 vols. *Map and plates.* 8°   1844

Explanation of the Agricultural and Statistical Atlas of European Russia. [In Russian.] 8°   *St Petersburg*, 1851

Russia—C.

Russo-Turkish War. The Present Crisis ; or, The Russo-Turkish War and its Consequences to England and the World. 8°   1853
Russia. By a Recent Traveller. *Plates.* 8°   1859
Six Years' Travels in Russia. By an English Lady. 2 vols. *Frontispiece.* 8°   1859
Das Russische Reich in Europa : Eine Studie. 8°   *Berlin*, 1884
The Penury of Russia. (Review of a Report by E. J. F. Law, from the *Edinburgh Review*, January 1893.) 8° 1893

SPAIN.

Ordenanza General de Correos, Postas, Caminos y Demas Ramos agregados á la Superintendencia General. 8°
                              Madrid, 1794
Hydrographical Office. Idea General del Discurso y de las Memorias publicadas por la Direccion Hidrográfica, sobre los fundamentos que ha tenido para la Construccion de las Cartas de Marear, que ha dado à luz desde 1897. 8° *Madrid*, 1810
—— See Tofiño de San Miguel.
Almanaque Naútico y Efemérides Astronomicas para el año de 1835. Calculadas . . . para el Observatorio Real de Marina de la ciudad de San Fernando. 12°
                              Madrid, 1832
Censo de la Poblacion de España 1857, por la Comision de Estadística General del Reino. Folio   *Madrid*, 1858
Nomenclátor de los Pueblos de España, formado por la Comision de Estadística General del Reino. Folio *Madrid*, 1858
Depósito de la Guerra. Cuerpo de Estado Mayor del Ejercito. Itinerario Descriptivo Militar de España, formado y publicado por el Dep. de la Guerra. 8 vols. Oblong 12°   *Madrid*, 1866-67
Colonies. Exposicion Colonial de Amsterdam en 1883 : Catalogo correspondiente á las Provincias Ultramarinas de España. Publicado por la Comision Central Española. 8°   *Madrid*, 1883
Congreso Español de Géografia Colonial y Mercantil celebrado en Madrid en los dias 4, 5, 6, 7, 8, 9, 10, y 12 de Noviembre de 1883. Actas. Vols. 1 and 2. 8°   *Madrid*, 1884
Reseña Geográfica y Estadística de España, por la Direccion General del Instituto Geográfico y Estadístico. *Map.* 4°
                              Madrid, 1888
Descripción Universal de los Indios y Demarcación de los reyes de Castilla en declaración de la tabla precedente. Issued with Bol. Soc. Geogr.   *Madrid*, N.D.

Spain.

Diccionario Geográfico - Histórico de España. 2 vols. *Map.* 4°
                              Madrid, 1802
Voyage Pittoresque et historique de l'Espagne. *Plates and plans.* Large 4°
                              Paris, 1806
Atlas del Itinerario Descriptivo de España.
                              Valencia, 1826
Memoir annexed to an Atlas containing Plans of the Principal Battles, Sieges, and Affairs, in which the British troops were engaged, in the Spanish Peninsula and South of France, 1808-14. 4° 1841
Border Lands of Spain and France, with an Account of a Visit to the Republic of Andorre. 8°   1856
A Winter Tour in Spain. By the author of "Dacia Singleton," &c. *Plate.* 8°
                                        1868
Gibraltar. Cuttings from the *Times* relative to the proposed Cession to Spain of Gibraltar in exchange for Ceuta.
                                        1868-69
Viaje de España. Por un Anónimo (1446-48). Traducido directamente del Aleman por E. G. R. *Illustrations.* 4°
                              Madrid, 1883

SWEDEN.

A. Government Publications.

General Staff Publications. *See* Rosén.
Geological Survey. Sveriges Geologiska Undersökning, pa offentlig bekostnad utförd under ledning af A. Erdmann.
                                        Stockholm
Ser. Aa. Kartblad i skalan 1 : 50,000 *med beskrigningar. Maps.* 8°.
—— No. 1. Karlsson, V. Några Ord till upplysning om Bladet "Westerås." *Plate.* 8°   1862
—— No. 2. Sidenbladh, Elis. Några, &c. Bladet "Arboga." *Plates.* 8°
                                        1862
—— No. 3. Kugelberg, O. F. Några, &c. Bladet "Skultuna." *Plate.* 8°
                                        1862
—— No. 4. Törnebohm, A. E. Några, &c. Bladet "Södertelge." *Plate.* 8°
                                        1862
—— No. 5. Karlsson, V. Några, &c. Bladet "Eskilstuna." *Plate.* 8° 1863
—— No. 6. Fries, J. O., A. H. Wahlquist, och A. E. Törnebohm. Några, &c. Bladet "Stockholm." *Plates.* 8°
                                        1863
—— No. 7. Kugelberg, O. F. Några, &c. Bladet "Enköping." *Plate.* 8°
                                        1863
—— No. 8. Törnebohm, A. E. Några, &c. Bladet "Fânö." *Plate.* 8° 1863

SWEDEN—A.
Geological Survey. *Ser. Aa.—contd.*
—— No. 9. Sidenbladh, Elis. Några, &c. Bladet "Säfstaholm." *Plates.* 8° 1864
—— No. 10. Fries, J. O., och V. Karlsson. Några, &c. Bladet "Angsö." *Plate.* 8° 1864
—— No. 11. Karlsson, V. Några, &c. Bladet "Köping." *Plate.* 8° 1864
—— No. 12. Kugelberg, O. F. Några, &c. Bladet "Hellefors." *Plate.* 8° 1864
—— No. 13. Paijkull, C. W. Några, &c. Bladet "Lindholm." *Plate.* 8° 1864
—— No. 14. Erdmann, E. Några, &c. Bladet "Lindsbro." *Map.* 8° 1865
—— No. 15. Hummel, David. Några, &c. Bladet "Skattmanso." *Map.* 8° 1865
—— No. 16. Gumælius, O., och C. W. Paykull. Några, &c. Bladet "Sigtuna." 8° 1865
—— No. 17. Törnebohm, A. E. Några, &c. Bladet "Malmköping." 8° 1865
—— No. 18. Karlsson, V., och J. O. Fries. Några, &c. Bladet "Strengnäs." 8° 1865
—— No. 19. Stolpe, M. Några, &c. Bladet "Ramnäs." 8° 1866
—— No. 20. Fries, J. O. Några, &c. Bladet "Wårgårda." 8° 1866
—— No. 21. Törnebohm, A. E. Några, &c. Bladet "Ulricehamn." 8° 1866
—— No. 22. Hummel, D. Några, &c. Bladet "Eriksberg." 8° 1867
—— No. 23. Erdmann, E. Några, &c. Bladet "Nyköping." 8° 1867
—— No. 24. Sidenbladh, E. Några, &c. Bladet "Tärna." 8° 1867
—— No. 25. Fries, J. O. Några, &c. Bladet "Sämsholm." 8° 1867
—— No. 26. Gumælius, O. Några, &c. Bladet "Sala." 8° 1868
—— No. 27. Sidenbladh, E. Några, &c. Bladet "Kånäs." 8° 1868
—— No. 28. Stolpe, M. Några, &c. Bladet "Borås." 8° 1868
—— No. 29. Wahlqvist, A. H. Några, &c. Bladet "Leufsta." 8° 1868
—— No. 30. Wahlqvist, A. H. Några, &c. Bladet "Eggegrund." 8° 1868
—— No. 31. Stolpe, M. Några, &c. Bladet "Upsala." 8° 1869
—— No. 32. Stolpe, M. Några, &c. Bladet "Orbyhus." 8° 1869
—— No. 33. Karlsson, V. Några, &c. Bladet "Svenljunga." 8° 1870
—— No. 34. Törnebohm, A. E. Några, &c. Bladet "Åmål." 8° 1870
—— No. 35. Hummel, D., och E. Erdmann. Några, &c. Bladet "Baldersnäs." 8° 1870

SWEDEN—A.
Geological Survey. *Ser. Aa.—contd.*
—— No. 36. Törnebohm, A. E. Några, &c. Bladet "Wingershamn." 8° 1870
—— No. 37. Törnebohm, A. E. Några, &c. Bladet "Upperud." 8° 1870
—— No. 38. Karlsson, V. Några, &c. Bladet "Degelberg." 8° 1870
—— No. 39. Karlsson, V., och A. H. Wahlqvist. Några, &c. Bladet "Rådanefors." 8° 1870
—— No. 40. Sidenbladh, E. Några, &c. Bladet "Wenersborg." 8° 1870
—— No. 41. Fries, J. O. Några, &c. Bladet "Wiskafors." 8° 1870
—— Börtzell, A. Rättelser till Höjdmälningarne å Bladen "Wårgårda" och "Sämshohm." 8° 1870
—— No. 42. Gumælius, Otto. Några ord till upplysning om bladet "Engelsberg." 8° 1871
—— No. 43. Pettersson, A. L. T. Några ord till upplysning om bladet "Salsta." 8° 1871
—— No. 44. Erdmann, E. Några ord till upplysning om bladet "Rydboholm." 8° 1871
—— No. 45. Stolpe, M. Några ord till upplysning om bladet "Hörningsholm." 8° 1871
—— No. 46. Karlsson, V. Beskrifning till Kartbladet "Riddarhyttan." 8° 1873
—— No. 47. Hummel, D. Beskrifning till Kartbladet "Linde." 8° 1873
—— No. 48. Gumælius, O. Beskrifning till Kartbladet "Örebro." 8° 1873
—— No. 49. Karlsson, V. Beskrifning till Kartbladet "Segersjo." 8° 1873
—— No. 50. Palmgren, L. Beskrifning till Kartbladet "Ärsta." 8° 1874
—— No. 51. —— Beskrifning till Kartbladet "Nynäs." 8° 1874
—— No. 52. Hummel, David. Beskrifning till Kartbladet "Trosa." *Plates.* 8° 1874
—— No. 53. Stolpe, M. Beskrifning till Kartbladet "Björksund." 8° 1874
—— No. 54. Stolpe, M. Beskrifning till Kartbladet "Riseberga." 8° 1875
—— No. 55. Linnarsson, G. Beskrifning till Kartbladet "Latorp." 8° 1875
—— No. 56. Gumælius, Otto. Beskrifning till Kartbladet "Nora." 8° 1875
—— No. 57. Nathorst, A. G. Beskrifning till Kartbladet "Stafsjo." *Plate.* 8° 1876
—— No. 58, 59. —— Beskrifning till Kartbladen "Sandhamn" och "Tärnskär." 8° 1877
—— No. 60. Hummel, David. Beskrifning till Kartbladet "Båstad." *Map.* 8° 1877
—— No. 61. Lindström, Axel. Beskrifning till Kartbladet "Hessleholm." 8° 1877

SWEDEN—A.

Geological Survey. *Ser. Aa.—contd.*

—— No. 62. Karlsson, V. Beskrifning till Kartbladet "Claestorp." 8° 1877
—— No. 63. Erdmann, E. Beskrifning till Kartbladet "Brefven." *Plate.* 8° 1878
—— No. 64. Nathorst, A. G. Beskrifning till Kartbladet "Gottenvik." 8° 1873
—— Nos. 65 and 66. Nathorst, A. G. Beskrifning till Kartbladen "Landsort" och "Källskären." 8° 1878
—— No. 67. Lindström, Axel. Beskrifning till Kartbladet "Herrevadskloster." 8° 1878
—— No. 68. Karlsson, V. Beskrifning till Kartbladet "Linderöd." 8° 1879
—— No. 69. Blomberg, A. Beskrifning till Kartbladet "Hjulsjö." 8° 1879
—— No. 70. Stolpe, M. Beskrifning till Kartbladet "Tjällmo." 8° 1881
—— No. 71. Stolpe, M. Beskrifning till Kartbladet "Norrköping." 8° 1879
—— No. 72. Holst, N. O. Beskrifning till Kartbladet "Möja." 8° 1879
—— No. 73. Nathorst, A. G. Beskrifning till Kartbladet "Gustafsberg." 8° 1881
—— No. 74. Erdmann, E. Beskrifning till Kartbladet "Helsingborg." *Plates.* 8° 1881
—— No. 75. ——. Beskrifning till Kartbladet "Landskrona." 8° 1881
—— No 76. Lindström, Axel. Beskrifning till Kartbladet "Engelholm." *Plate.* 8° 1880
—— Nos. 77 and 78. ——. Beskrifning till Kartbladen "Kullen" och "Höganäs." 8° 1880
—— No. 79. Carlsson, G. A. Beskrifning till Kartbladet "Norsholm." 8° 1880
—— Nos. 80 and 81. Holst, N. O. Beskrifning till Kartbladen "Dalarö" och "Utö." *Plate.* 8° 1882
—— No. 82. Stolpe, M. Beskrifning till Kartbladet "Finspång." 8° 1881
—— No. 83. Linnarsson, G., and Tullberg, S. A. Beskrifning till Kartbladet "Vreta Kloster." *Plate.* 8° 1882
—— No. 84. Erdmann, E. Beskrifning till Kartbladet "Askersund." *Plate.* 8° 1889
—— No. 85. Nathorst, A. G. Beskrifning till Kartbladet "Kristianstad." 8° 1882
—— No. 86. Tullberg, S. A. Beskrifning till Kartbladet "Ovedskloster." *Plate.* 8° 1882
—— No. 87. Nathorst, A. G. Beskrifning till Kartbladet "Trollcholm." *Plates.* 8° 1885

SWEDEN—A.

Geological Survey. *Ser. Aa.—contd.*

—— Nos. 89 and 90. Holst, N. O. Beskrifning till Kartbladen "Svenska Stenarne" och "Svenska Högarne." 8° 1883
—— No. 91. Jönsson, J. Beskrifning till Kartbladet "Malmö." 8° 1884
—— No. 92. Geer, G. de. Beskrifning till Kartbladet "Lund." *Plate.* 8° 1887
—— No. 93. Svedmark, E. Beskrifning till Kartbladet "Furnsund." 8° 1885
—— No. 94. Svedmark, E. Beskrifning till Kartbladet "Norrtelge." *Maps.* 8° 1887
—— No. 95. ——. Beskrifning till Kartbladet "Rådmansö." 8° 1885
—— No. 96. Svenonius, F. Beskrifning till Kartbladet "Grundkallegrundet." *Plate.* 8° 1885
—— No. 97. Holst, N. O. Beskrifning till Kartbladet "Svartklubben." *Map.* 8° 1887
—— Nos. 98 and 99. Svenonius, F. Beskrifning till Kartbladen "Forsmark" och "Björn." 8° 1887
—— No. 100. Blomberg, A. Beskrifning till Kartbladet "Penningby." *Map.* 8° 1889
—— No. 101. Blomberg, A. Beskrifning till Kartbladet "Öregrund." *Map.* 8° 1886
—— No. 102. Jönsson, J. Beskrifning till Kartbladet "Motala." *Maps.* 8° 1887
—— No. 103. Geer, G. de. Beskrifning till Kartbladet "Bäckasko." *Maps.* 8° 1889
—— No. 104. Blomberg, A. Beskrifning till Kartbladet "Alunda." *Map.* 8° 1889
—— No. 105, 106, and 107. Geer, G. de. Beskrifning till Kartbladen Vidtsköfle, Karlshamn (Skånedelen) och Sölvesborg (Skånedelen). *Maps.* 8° 1889
—— No. 108. Beskrifning till Kartbladet "Glimakra," af Abert Blomberg. *Map.* 8° *Stockholm,* 1892
—— No. 109. Holst, N. O. Beskrifning till Kartbladet "Simrishamn," af N. O. Holst. *Maps.* 8° *Stockholm,* 1892

Ser. Ab. Kartblad i skalan 1 : 200,000 med beskrifningar.

—— No. 1. Hummel, D. Beskrifning till Kartbladet "Huseby." 8° 1877
—— No. 2. —— Beskrifning till Kartbladet "Ljungby." 8° 1877
—— No. 3. —— Beskrifning till Kartbladet "Vexiö." *Plate.* 8° 1877
—— No. 4. Holst, N. O. Beskrifning till Kartbladet "Lessebo." 8° 1879
—— No. 5. Blomberg, A. Beskrifning till Kartbladet "Ölmestad." *Map.* 8° 1879

SWEDEN—A.

Geological Survey. *Ser. Ab.—contd.*

—— No. 6. ——. Beskrifning till Kartbladet "Nissafors." *Map.* 8° 1880

—— No. 7. Lindström, A. Beskrifning till Kartbladet "Borås." *Maps.* 8° 1883

—— No. 8. Holst, N. O. Beskrifning till Kartbladet "Hvetlanda." *Maps and plate.* 8° 1885

—— No 9. Blomberg, A. Beskrifning till Kartbladet "Särö." *Maps.* 8° 1883

—— No. 10. ——. Beskrifning till Kartbladet "Kungsbacka." *Maps.* 8° 1883

—— No. 11. Lindström, A. Beskrifning till Kartbladet "Venersborg." *Maps.* 8° 1887

—— No. 12. Lundbohm, H. Beskrifning till Kartbladet "Halmstad.' *Maps.* 8° 1887

—— No. 13. Beskrifning till Kartbladet "Varberg," af Eugène Svedmark. *Maps.* 8° *Stockholm,* 1893

—— No. 14. Beskrifning till Kartbladet "Nydala," af M. Stolpe. *Maps and illustrations.* 8° *Stockholm,* 1892

—— No. 15. Beskrifning till Kartbladet "Lenhofda," af Nils Olof Holst. *Maps.* 8° *Stockholm,* 1893

Ser. Ba. Cartes générales avec descriptions.

—— No. 4. Annexe explicative a la Carte Géologique Générale de la Suède publiée par l'Institut Royal Géologique de Suède à l'échelle de 1 : 1,000,000. Feuille Méridionale. par A. G. Nathorst. 8° [1884]

Ser. Bb. Specialkartor och beskrifningar.

—— Nos. 1 and 2. Lindström, A. Beskrifning till de Agronomiskt Geologiska Kartorna öfver Skottorp och Dömmestorp i Hollands Län. 8° 1881

—— No. 3. Beskrifning till Karta öfver Berggrunden inom de Malmförande Trakterna i norra delen af Örebro Län. I. Allmän Geologisk Beskrifning utarbetad af Henrik Santesson under medverkan af Alb. Blomberg och Birger Santesson. *Map.* 4° 1883

—— No. 4. Ditto. II. Geognostiska Kartor och Beskrifningar öfver de vigtigare Grufvefälten af Birger Santesson. *Plates.* 4° 1889

—— No. 5. Jönsson, J. Beskrifning till Agronomiskt Geologisk Karta öfver Egendomen Svalnäs i Roslagen. *Map.* 8° 1887

—— No. 6. ——. Beskrifning till Praktiskt Geologisk Karta öfver Farsta och Gustafsberg med Utgårdar, Torp och Lägenheter i Stockholms Län. 8° 1890

SWEDEN—A.

Geological Survey. *Ser. Bb.—contd.*

—— No. 7. Beskrifning till Agronomiskt Geologisk Karta öfver Iorreby, på Bekostnad af Grosshandlaren N. G. Sörensen, upprättad af J. Jönsson. 8° *Stockholm,* 1892

Ser. C. Afhandlingar och uppsatser.

—— No. 26. Torell, O. On the Causes of the Glacial Phenomena in the North-Eastern portion of N. America. *Map.* 8° 1877

—— No. 28. Linnarsson, G. De Paleozoiska Bildningarna vid Humlenäs i Småland. *Map.* 8° 1878

—— No. 29. Nathorst, A. G. Om Floran i Skånes Kolförande Bidningar. 2. Floran vid Höganäs och Helsingborg. *Plates.* 4° 1878

—— No. 31. Linnarsson, G. Jakttagelser öfver de Graptolitförande Skifrarne i Skåne. *Map.* 8° 1879

—— No. 32. Blomberg, A., and A. Lindström. Praktiskt Geologiska Undersökningar inom Herjedalen och Jemtland, utförda sommaren, 1876. *Maps.* 8° 1879

—— No. 34. Lindström, A. Praktiskt Geologiska Jakttagelser under Resor på Gotland, 1876-78. *Map.* 8° 1879

—— No. 35. Linnarsson, G. Om fannan i Kalken med Conocoryphe exsulans ("Coronatuskalken"). *Plates.* 8° 1879

—— No. 36. Nathorst, A. G. Om Spirangium och dess förekomst i Skånes Kolförande Bildningar. *Plates.* 8° 1879

—— No. 37. Linnarsson, G. Om Gotlands Graptoliter. *Plate.* 8° 1879

—— No. 38. Nathorst, A. G. Om de Svenska Urbergens Sekulära Forvittring. 8° 1880

—— No. 39. ——. Om de Äldre Sandstens- och Skifferbildningarne vid Vettern. *Map.* 8° 1880

—— No. 40. Törnquist, S. L. Några Iakttagelser öfver Dalarnes Graptolitskiffrar. 8° 1880

—— No. 41. Tullberg, S. A. Om Lagerföljden i de Kambriska och Siluriska Aflagringarne vid Röstånga. *Map.* 8° 1880

—— No. 43. Linnarsson, G. Om Försteningarne i de Svenska lagren med Peltura och Sphærophthalmus. *Plates.* 8° 1880

—— No. 44. Nathorst, A. G. Om de Växtförande Lagren i Skånes Kolförande Bildningar och deras plats i lagerföljden. 8° 1880

—— No. 45. Svenonius, F. Om "Sevegruppen" i nordligaste Jemtland och Ångermanland samt dess Förhällande till Fossilförande lager. *Maps.* 8° 1881

SWEDEN—A.
Geological Survey. *Ser. C.—contd.*
—— No. 115. Mörtsell, E. Resenotiser från det fossilförande Kambrisk-siluriska området af Vesterbottens lappmark.—Holm, G. Försteningar från Lappland, insamlade af E. Mortsell.—Holm, G. Om förekomsten af en Caryocrinus i Sverige. 8° 1890
—— No. 116. Om Kvartsit-Sparagmit-området i Sveriges Sydliga Fjelltrakter, af A. G. Högbom. *Diagrams.* 8° *Stockholm*, 1891
—— No. 117. Bidrag till Kännedomen om de Glaciala Företeelserna i Norrbotten, af K. A. Fredholm. *Map.* 8° *Stockholm*, 1892
—— No. 118. Skotska Byggnadssätt för Naturlig Sten, af Hjalmar Lundbohm. *Plate and diagrams.* 8° *Stockholm*, 1891
—— No. 119. Agronomiskt-Botaniska Studier i Norra Dalarne åren 1890 och 1891, af A. G. Kellgren. 8° *Stockholm*, 1892
—— No. 120. Untersuchungen über Fossile Hölzer Schwedens, von H. Conwentz. *Plates.* 4° *Stockholm*, 1892
—— No. 121. Om Mynningen Ilos Situites, af Gerhard Holm. 8° *Stockholm*, 1892
—— No. 122. Meddelanden om Jordstötar i Sverige, af E. Svedmark. II. 8° *Stockholm*, 1892
—— No. 123. Anteckningar från en i Praktiskt syfte foretagen Geologisk resa i Vesterbottens Län, af Alber Blomberg. *Map.* 8° *Stockholm*, 1892
—— No. 124. Studier öfver de Glaciola Aflagringarna i Upland af A. G. Högbom. *Map.* 8° *Stockholm*, 1892
—— No. 125. Moberg, J. C. Om Skiffern med Clonograptus tenellus dess fauna veb geologiska ålder, med 1 tafla. Om on nyupptackt fauna i block af Kambrisk sandsten. Med en tafla. Om några nya graptoliter från Skanes undre graptolitskiffer, med en tafla. Till frågan om pygidiets byggnad hos Ctenopyge pecten. Om un af Trinucleus cosinorrhinus ang. karakteriserade kalkens geologiska Ålder. *Plates.* 8° *Stockholm*, 1892
—— No. 126. Om Berggrunden i Norrbottens Län och utsigterna till Brytvärda Apatitförekomster Derstädes, af Fredr. Svenonius. *Map and illustrations.* 8° *Stockholm*, 1892
—— No. 127. Apatitförekomster i Norrbottens Malmberg, af Hjalmar Lundbohm. *Diagrams.* 8° *Stockholm*, 1892
—— No. 128. Högbom, A. G. Om Märken efter Isdämda Sjoar i Jemtlands Fjelltrakter med Två Ta˜

SWEDEN—A.
Geological Survey. *Ser. C.—contd.*
Aftryck nr Geol. Fören i Stockholm Forhandl. Bd. 14, H. 7, 1892. Om Interglaciala Aflagringar i Jemtland Aftryck ur Geol. Fören i Stockholm Forhandl. Bd. 15, H. 1, 1893. *Map and illustrations.* 8° *Stockholm*, 1893
—— No. 129. Om Stenindustrien i Förenta Staterna, åf Hjalmar Lundbohm. 8° *Stockholm*, 1893
—— No. 130. Bidrag till Kännedomen om Lagerföljden inom den Kambriska Sandstenen, af Nils Olof Holst. 8° *Stockholm*, 1893
—— No. 131. Praktiskt Geologiska undersökningar inom Hallands Län med bidrag af Länets Hushållningssällskap utforda Genom Sveriges Geologiska undersökning åren 1882-91, I.-II. *Map.* 4° *Stockholm*, 1893
—— No. 132. Hjalmar Lundbohm om Berggrunden i Vesternorrlands Kustrakter.—A. G. Högbom : Om Postarkäiska Eruptiver inom det Svenskfinsks Urberget. Meden Tafla. — A. G. Högbom : Om de S. K. Urgraniterna i Upland. *Plate.* 8° *Stockholm*, 1893
—— No. 133. Om de Porfyriska Gångbergarterna i Östra Småland, af Otto Nordenskjöld. 8° *Stockholm*, 1893
—— No. 134. Om Hasselns Forntida och Nutida Urtredning i Sverige, af Herman Hedström. *Map.* 8° *Stockholm*, 1893

Miscellaneous Works.

Erdmann, E. Description de la formation carbonifère de la Scanie. (Traducteur J. H. Kramer.) Abridged edition. *Maps and plates.* 8° 1873 [Including the original Swedish work, "Beskrifning öfver Skånes Stenkolsförande formation, af Edvard Erdmann."] [*F. of the series.*] 1872
Börtzell, A. Beskrifning öfver Besier-Ecksteins Kromolitografi och Litotypografi använda vid tryckningen af Geologisk Öfversigtskarta öfver Skåne. *Coloured diagrams.* 4° [G.] 1872
Törnebohm, A. E. En geognostisk profil öfver den Skandinaviska Fjällryggen mellan östersund och Levanger. *Plate.* 8° [H.] 1872
Gumælins, O. Bidrag till kännedomen om Sveriges Erratiska Bildningar, samlade à Geologiska Kartbladet "Orebro." 8° [I.] 1872
Hummel, D. Öfversigt af de Geologiska Förbälla ndenen vid Hallands Ås. 8° [J.] 1873
Törnebohm, A. E. Ueber die Geognosie der schwedischen Hochgebirge. *Map.* 8° [K.] 1872

Sweden—A.

Geological Survey. *Miscellaneous—contd.*

Linnarsson, J. G. O. Om några För-
steninger från Sveriges och Norges
" Primordialzon." 8° [L.] 1873

Gumælius, O. Om mellersta Sveriges
glaciala Bildningar. *Plate* 8° [M.]
1874

—— 2. Om rullstensgrus. *Map.* 8° 1876

Hummel, D. Om Rullstensbildningar.
Maps. 8° [N.] 1874

Gumælius, O. Om Malmlagrens Ålders-
följd och deras användande såsom
ledlager. *Map.* 8° [O.] 1875

Törnebohm, A. E. Geognostisk Beskrifning öfver Persbergets Grufvevält.
Map and plates. 4° [P.] 1875

Hummel, D. Om Sveriges lagrade Ur-
berg jemförda med sydvestra Europas.
Map. 8° [Q.] 1875

Santesson, Henrik. Kemiska bergarts-
analyser. I. Gneis, Hälleflintgneis
(" Eurit ") och Hälleflinta. Large 8°
[R.] 1877

Torell, Otto. Sur les traces les plus
anciennes de l'existence de l'homme
en Suède. 8° [T.] [1876]

Nathorst A. G. Om en cycadékotte
från den rätiska formationens lager vid
Tinkarp i S. Kåne. *Plate.* 8° [U.]
[1876]

Nathorst, A. G. Nya Fyndorter för
arktiska växtlemningar i Skåne. 8°.
[V.] 1877

Linnarsson, G. Ofversigt af Nerikes
öfvergångsbildningar. *Map.* 8°. [X.]
1875

Linnarsson, G. Om faunan i Lagren
med Paradoxides Olandicus. *Plates.*
8° 1877

Svedmark, E. Halle och Hunnebergs
Trapp. 8° 1878

Svenonius, F. V. Bidrag till Norrbottens
Geologi. *Plates.* 8° 1880

Löfstrand, G. Om apatitens förekomst
satt i Norrbottens lan jemfördt med
dess uppträdande i Norge. 8° 1890

Systematisk Fortckning öfver offent-
liggjorda arbeten, 1862-1893. *Maps.*
8° *Stockholm,* 1894

Die Ausstellung der geologischen Landes-
Untersuchung Schwedens auf der
Weltausstellung in Wien, 1873. 8° 1873

Nautisk Meteorologiska Byrån, Stockholm *Stockholm*

No. 1. Instruktion för Meteorologisk
loggboks förande. *Plates.* 8° 1879

No. 3. Väderleksbok. Small 8°

No. 4. Instruktion för Meteorologiska
Observationers utförande vid Svenska Fyrstationer. *Plates.* 8° 1879

No. 5. Instruktion för Hydrografiska
Observationers utförande vid Svenska
Fyr- och Lots-stationer. *Plates.* 8°
1879

Sweden.

B. Anonymous.

Svecia, sive de Suecorum Regis Dominiis
et opibus Commentarius Politicus. 8°
1631

Guide through Sweden. 12°
Gothenburg, 1824

Topographiska och Statistisa Uppgifter.
[Reports on various districts, 8 numbers]
viz.:—1842, 1844, 1845, 1849, 1850,
1857, 1859, and 1860. 12° and 8°
Stockholm, 1842-60

Upplysningar till Geologisk Kartan (af
E. W. Olbers). Bohns Län (7 pamphlets). 12° *Gotsburg,* 1859-66

Upprättad i Rikets ekonomiska Karteverk.
Beskrifning till Kartans, &c. . . . Upsal
Län och Orebro Län. Åren, 1860-68
(18 parts). 4° *Stockholm,* 1860-68

Guide du Voyageur en Suède et en Norvège. 3rd edition. *Maps.*
Stockholm, 1874

The Traveller's Illustrated Guide for
Sweden, Stockholm, and the principal
pleasure routes in the interior. *Maps
and plates.* 12° *Stockholm,* 1875

Underdanig Berättelse om en på Nådig
befallning år 1875 företagen Undersökning af Malmfyndigheter inom Gellivare
och Jukkasjärvi soknar af Norbottens län.
Maps. 4° 1877

SWITZERLAND.

A. Government Publications.

Bibliographie Nationale Suisse. Reper-
toire Méthodique de ce qui a été publié
sur la Suisse et ses Habitants. Fasc 2ª,
2ᵇ, 2ᶜ. 8° *Berne*

Fasc 2ª. Géodésie et cartes de la Suisse,
des Régions et Cantons. Publié par
le Bureau Topographique Fédéral.
Rédigé par le Prof. Dr J. H. Graf
1892

Fasc 2ᵇ. Cartes de Parcelles plus ou
moins grandes du Territoire Suisse.
Rédigé par le Prof. Dr J. H. Graf
1892

Fasc 2ᶜ. Plans de Villes et de Lieux-
Habités, Reliefs et Panoramas. Rédigé
par le Prof. Dr J. H. Graf 1893

Census of Switzerland, 1st of December
1870. MS. Folio.

—— Les Résultats du Recensement
Fédéral du 1ᵉʳ Décembre 1888. Vols.
1 and 2. *Maps.* 4° *Berne,* 1892-93

Statistical Bureau. Statistischer Jahr-
buch der Schweiz. Jahrgang I.-III.
Maps and plates. Small 4°
Berne, 1891-93

—— Statistique de la Suisse. Livraisons
87, 90, 92, 94, 95-98. (1891-93.)
Maps. 4° *Berne,* 1893-94

SWITZERLAND—A.

Survey. Ergebnisse der Trigono-
metrischen Vermessung in der Schweiz.
Von J. Eschmann. 4°   *Zurich,* 1840

Geodetic Commission.

Europäische Gradmessung, Das Schweizer-
ische Dreieck-netz herausgegeben von der
Schweizerischen geodätischen Commis-
sion, Erster Band. Die Winkelmes-
sungen und Stationsausgleichungen. 4°
Zurich, 1881
—— Ditto. Zweiter Band. Die Netzaus-
gleichung und die Anschlussnetze der
Sternwarten und astronomischen Punkte.
Figures. 4°   *Zurich,* 1884
—— Ditto. Vierter Band. Die Ansch-
lussnetze der Grundlinien. 4°
Zurich, 1889
—— Ditto. Fünfter Band. Astronomische
Beobachtungen im Tessiner Basisnetze,
auf Gähris und Simplon ; definitive
Dreieckseitenlängen ; geographische Co-
ordinaten. *Map.* 4°   *Zurich,* 1890
—— Ditto. Sechster Band. Lotabwei-
chungen in der Westschweiz. Bear-
beitet von Dr J. B. Messerschmitt.
Map. 4°   *Zurich,* 1894
Le Réseau de Triangulation Suisse,
publié par la Commission Géodésique
Suisse.' 3 vols. La Mensuration des
Bases par A. Hirsch et J. Dumur. *Plates.*
Large 4°   *Lausanne,* 1888
Nivellement de Précision de la Suisse,
exécuté par la Commission Géodésique
Fédérale, sous la direction de M.M.
Hirsch et Plantamour. Vol. 1 (Livr.
1-4, 6, 7, 9.) *Map and plate.* 4°
Geneva and Bâle, 1867-91
—— Ditto. Vol. 2 (Livr. 10). Catalogue
des Hauteurs Suisses. *Map.* 4°
Geneva, &c., 1891

B. Anonymous and Miscellaneous.

Helvetiorum Respublica. 16°
The Hague, 1627
Gemälde der Schweiz. Zürich, Uri,
Thurgau, Schwyz, Unterwalden, Frei-
burg, Solothurn, Schaffhausen, Appen-
zell, Graubünden, Tessin. 11 vols. 8°
Berne, 1834-38
Practical Swiss Guide: a Complete
Itinerary of Switzerland. 12°   1859
Brussels Conference. Gutachten über
den Anschluss der Schweiz au die
Bestrebungen der Internat. Afrik. Gesell-
schaft in Brüssel, vom Initiativ-Comité
in St Gallen. 8°   1877
Alps. Anleitung zu wissenschaftlichen Beo-
bachtungen auf Alpenreiseu. Heraus-
gegeben vom Deutschen und Oesterreichischen Alpenverein. 2 vols. in 1.
Map and illustrations. 12°
Vienna, 1882

SWITZERLAND—B.

Vol. 1. Sonklar, C. von. Orographie und
Topographie, Hydrographie, Glets-
cherwesen.
Gümbel, C. W. Kurze Anleitung
zu Geologischen Beobachtungen in
den Alpen.
Hann, J. Einführung in die
Meteorologie der Alpen.
Ranke, Johannes. Anleitung zu an-
thropologisch-vorgeschichtlichen Beo-
bachtungen im Gebiet der Deutschen
und Osterreichischen Alpen.
Vol. 2. Dalla Torre, K. W. V. Anlei-
tung zur Beobachtung der Alpinen
Thierwelt.
Anleitung zum Beobachten und
zum Bestimmen der Alpenpflanzen.
—— Die Wissenschaftlichen Arbeiten des
D. u Ol. Alpenvereins. (From the
Mitteilungen.) 12°   *Vienna,* 1891
Quellen zur Schweizer Geschichte, heraus-
gegeben von der Allgemeinem Geschicht-
forschenden Gesellschaft der Schweiz.
Sechster Band. Conradi Türst De Situ
Confoederatorum Descriptio. Balci De-
scriptio Helvetiæ. Fratris Felicis Fabri
Descriptio Sveviæ. Reisebericht von
Johannes Stumpf, 1544. *Map.* 8°
Bâle, 1884
Annuaire de la Suisse Pittoresque et
Hygiénique. Stations Climatériques,
Bains, Belles Excursions, Villes d'Hiver
de la Mediterranée. *Maps and illus-
trations.* 12°   *Lausanne,* 1890
—— Ditto. 3rd edition. *Maps and illus-
trations.* 12° *Paris and Lausanne,* 1891
—— Ditto. 4th edition.
Lausanne and Paris, 1892-93
Central Kommission für Schweizer
Landeskunde. IV. Mittheilung. Bericht
der Central Kommission über den Stand
der Arbeit an der Bibliographie der
Schweizerischen Landeskunde, Ende
März 1892, &c. 8°   *Berne,* 1892
Statistique de la Suisse. 90°, 95°, and
96° Livr. 4°   *Berne,* 1893-94
Berne. Hand Atlas für Reisende in das
Berner Oberland. *Maps and plates.* 8°
Berne, 1816
—— Nouvelle Description de l'Oberland
Bernois, à l'usage des Voyageurs. *Maps.*
8°   *Berne,* 1838
—— Arbeiten aus dem Geographischen
Institut der Universität Bern. Th. Steck:
Die Wassermassen des Thuner- und des
Brienzersees. Th. Steck : Die Denuda-
tion im Kandergebiet. R. Zeller : Die
Schneegrenze im Triftgebiet. (Aus dem
XI. Jahresbericht der Geogr. Gesellsch.
von Bern.) Large 8°   *Berne,* 1893
Davos-Platz : a New Alpine Resort for
Sick and Sound in Summer and Winter.
Map. 12°   1878

3 A

UNITED KINGDOM—A.
Admiralty Publications—*continued.*
Catalogues of Charts, Plans, and Sailing Directions. 8° 1885-95
[*See also* Burdwood ; Evans; Weston.]

Sailing Directions. Large 8°
The Norway Pilot. Part 1. From the Naze to the Kattegat. 1854
—— Part 1. From the Naze to Christiania ; thence to the Kattegat. 2nd edition. Compiled by Lieut. G. T. Temple, R.N. 1888
—— Part 2. From the Naze to North Cape ; thence to Jacob River. Compiled by Lieut. G. T. Temple, R.N. 1880
—— Supplement, 1893. 2nd edition 1894
Sailing Directions for the Baltic Sea and the Gulf of Finland. By Adm. Gustav Klint 1854
Views in the Baltic to accompany Klint's Sailing Directions 1854
The Baltic Pilot : comprising directions for the Baltic Sea, Gulf of Finland, and Gulf of Bothnia. 2nd edition 1888
—— Supplement, 1893.
The Danish Pilot. Originally compiled by the late Vice-Admiral Zahrtmann. 2nd edition 1885
Supplement 1890, and Revised ditto, 1892.
The Færöe Islands Pilot. Compiled by the Royal Chart Department, Copenhagen 1891
Information relating to Currents, Ice and Magnetism, with general remarks on the Navigation on the Coast of Iceland. By Lieut. C. F. Wandel, Royal Danish Navy, 1879. Also information relating to Harbours, Tides, and Weather in the Færöe Islands. By the Rev. G. Landt, Gov. Chaplain, 1872 1891
The Bothnia Pilot. By Adm. Gustavus Klint 1855
—— Supplementary Sailing Directions 1856
North Sea Pilot. Part 1. 2nd edition. *Map* 1876
—— Part 2. 3rd edition. *Map* 1875
—— Part 3. 3rd edition. *Map* 1874
—— Part 4. 3rd edition. *Map* 1878
—— Part 1. Shetland and Orkneys. 3rd and 4th editions 1887-94
—— Part 2. North and East Coasts of Scotland. 4th edition 1885
—— Part 3. East Coast of England. 5th edition 1889
—— Supplement 1894
—— Part 4. Rivers Thames and Medway, and the Shores of the North Sea from Calais to the Skaw. 4th edition 1887

UNITED KINGDOM—A.
Admiralty Publications—*continued.*
North Sea Pilot. Supplement, 1890. Part 4. 4th edition, 1887 (corrected to 3rd July 1890) 1890
Directions for making the passage from the Downs to the White Sea. Compiled by George F. M'Dougall 1858
The White Sea Pilot : Coast of Russian Lapland and the White Sea 1887
Sailing Directions for the Bristol Channel. Compiled by Capt. E. J. Bedford. *Map* 1872
Sailing Directions for the West Coast of England. Compiled by Capt. E. J. Bedford. 2nd edition. *Map* 1876 ; and 4th edition, 1891
Sailing Directions for the West Coast of Scotland. Part 1. Hebrides or Western Isles. By Capt. H. C. Otter. 2nd edition 1874
—— Part 2. Cape Wrath to the Mull of Galloway. By G. F. M'Dougall. 2nd edition 1877
—— Part 1. 3rd edition. *Diagram and illustrations* 1885
—— Part 2. 3rd edition 1886
Sailing Directions for the Coast of Ireland. Parts 1 and 2. By Staff-Commander Richard Hoskyn 1866-68
Sailing Directions for the Coast of Ireland. Part 1. South, East, and North Coasts of Ireland. Compiled . . . by Staff-Commander Richard Hoskyn, R. N. 3rd edition 1885
—— Part 2. South-West, West, and North-West Coasts. Originally compiled . . . by Capt. Richard Hoskyn, R.N. 3rd edition 1887
The Irish Coast Pilot. 4th edition. [Both Parts in 1 vol.] 1893
The Channel Pilot. Part 1. South-West and South Coasts of England. Compiled by Staff-Commander John W. King, R.N. 7th edition 1886
—— Supplement 1891
—— Part 2. Coast of France and the Channel Islands. Originally compiled by Staff-Commander John W. King, R.N. 5th edition 1888
—— Supplement 1892
—— Part 1. 8th edition 1893
The Guernsey Island Pilot 1863
The Jersey Island Pilot. By Staff-Commander J. Richards 1866
The Alderney Island Pilot 1864
The Channel Islands Pilot. By Staff-Commander J. Richards 1870
Sailing Directions for the West Coasts of France, Spain, and Portugal. Compiled by Staff-Commander James Penn. 2nd edition 1873
—— 5th edition 1891

Admiralty Publications—*continued.*

Directions for entering the River Tagus. By G. Biddlecombe 1854

Directions for the River Douro. By Commander E. Belcher. 2nd edition 1833

The Mediterranean Pilot. Vol. 1. Comprising Gibraltar Strait, Coast of Spain, African Coast from Cape Spartel to Gulf of Kabes, together with the Balearic, Sardinian, Sicilian, and Maltese Islands. 2nd and 3rd editions 1885-94

—— Revised Supplement 1891

—— Vol. 2. Comprising Coast of France, and of Italy to the Adriatic ; African Coast from Jerbah to El Arish ; Coasts of Karamania and Syria; together with the Tuscan Archipelago, and Islands of Corsica and Cyprus. 2nd edition 1885

—— Supplement 1891

—— Vol. 3. Comprising the Adriatic Sea, Ionian Islands, the Coasts of Albania and Greece to Cape Malea, with Cerigo Island ; also the Gulfs of Patras and Corinth. 2nd edition 1890

—— Supplement 1894

—— Vol. 4. Comprising the Archipelago, with the adjacent Coasts of Greece and Turkey, including also the Island of Candia or Crete. 2nd edition 1892

Sailing Directions for the Island of Candia or Crete. By Capt. T. Spratt. 2nd edition 1866

The Black Sea Pilot. 2nd edition 1871

-- — 3rd edition 1884

—— Supplement, 1890. 3rd edition, 1884 (corrected to 27th October 1890) 1890

Report on the Currents of the Dardanelles and Bosphorus. By W. J. L. Wharton. *Map and sections* 1872

Sailing Directions for Dardanelles, Sea of Marmora, Bosphorus, and Black Sea. 4th edition 1893

The Gulf of 'Aden Pilot. Sokótra and adjacent Islands ; the Somáli and Arabian Coasts in the Gulf of 'Aden ; the East Coast of Arabia, and off-lying Islands. Compiled originally by Commander C. Y. Ward. 3rd edition 1887

The Red Sea Pilot. From Suez and from 'Akabah to the Straits of Báb-el-Mandeb, and the Arabian Coast thence to 'Aden; also directions for the Navigation of the Suez Canal. 3rd edition 1883

—— Revised Supplement 1889

The Red Sea and Gulf of Aden Pilot. Superseding 3rd edition of the Red Sea Pilot, and 3rd edition of the Gulf of Aden Pilot. 4th edition 1892

Admiralty Publications—*continued.*

The Persian Gulf Pilot, including the Gulf of Omman. Compiled by Capt. C. G. Constable and Lieut. A. W. Stiffe. (With Hydrographic Notice, No. 15) 1870

—— Supplement. Coast of Balúchistán, from Karáchi to Rás-al-Kúh, or Makrán Coast. By Lieut. A. W. Stiffe 1875

—— Comprising the Persian Gulf, Gulf of 'Omman, and Makrán Coast. Originally compiled by Capt. C. G. Constable and Lieut. A. W. Stiffe, late Indian Navy. 3rd edition 1890

The West Coast of Hindostan Pilot, including the Gulf of Manar, the Maldivh and the Lakadivh Islands. Compiled by Commander A. D. Taylor 1866

—— 3rd edition 1891

The Bay of Bengal Pilot, including South-west Coast of Ceylon, North Coast of Sumatra, Nicobar, and Andaman Islands 1887

—— Supplement 1889

—— 2nd edition 1892

The China Pilot. By Staff-Commander J. W. King. 4th edition 1864

—— Appendix, No. 2. General Observations on the Coasts of Borneo, the Sulu and Mindoro Seas, with Sailing Directions for Palawan Passage and Island 1859

—— No. 13. Gulf of Siam 1856

—— No. 14. La Pérouse Strait, Gulf of Tartary, Kuril Islands, and Sea of Okhotsk 1855-56

—— Nos. 16 and 17. Yang-tse-Kiang 1857

—— No. 18. East Coast 1859

The China Sea Directory. Vol. 1, containing Directions for the Approaches to the China Sea and to Singapore, by the Straits of Sunda, Banka, Gaspa, Carimata, Rhio, Varella, Durian, and Singapore. 1st, 2nd, and 3rd editions 1867-86

—— Supplement to 3rd edition 1890

—— Vol. 2, Containing Directions for the Navigation of the China Sea, between Singapore and Hong Kong. By J. W. Reed and J. W. King. 1st, 2nd, and 3rd editions 1868-89

—— Supplement to 3rd edition 1893

—— Vol. 3, Comprising the Coasts of China from Hong Kong to the Korea ; North Coast of Luzon, Formosa Island and Strait ; the Babuyan, Bashee and Meiaco Sima Groups ; Yellow Sea, Gulfs of Pe-Chili and Liau-Tung ; also the Rivers Canton, West, Min, Yung, Yangste, Yellow, Pei Ho, and Liau Ho, and Pratas Island. By C. J. Bullock. 1st, 2nd, and 3rd editions 1874-94

UNITED KINGDOM—A.
Admiralty Publications—*continued.*

The China Sea Directory. Vol. 4, Comprising the Coasts of Korea, Russian Tartary, the Japan Isl·nds, Gulfs of Tartary and Amur, and the Sea of Okhotsk; also the Meiaco, Liu-Kiu, Lin·choten, Mariana, Bonin, Saghalin, and Kuril Islands. By F. W. Jarrad. 1st, 2nd, and 3rd editions   1873-94
Sailing Directions for the Arafura Sea. Compiled G. W. Earl   1837
Eastern Archipelago. Part 1. (Eastern Part). Comprising the Philipines, Sulu Sea, Sulu Archipelago, N.E. Coast of Borneo, Celebes Sea, N.E. Coast of Celebes, Molucca and Gillolo Passages, Banda and Arafura Seas, N.W. and West Coasts of New Guinea, and North Coast of Australia. Compiled . . . by Capt. J. P. Maclear, R.N. Large 8° 1890
—— Supplement   1893
Eastern   Archipelago.   Part   2. (Western Part). Comprising the S.E. Coast of Samatra, Java, The Islands East of Java, The South and East Coasts of Borneo, and Celebes Island. Compiled by Rear-Adm. J. P. Maclear
                                    1893
Islands in the Southern Indian Ocean Westward of Long. 80° E., including Madagascar. 1st edition   1891
The Africa Pilot. By Capt. Algernon F. R. De Horsey. For the South and East Coasts of Africa, from the Cape of Good Hope to Cape Guardafui, including the Islands in the Mozambique Channel. 2nd edition   1865
—— Part 1, Or Sailing Directions for the Western Coast of Africa; comprising the Azores, Madeira, Canary, and Cape Verde Islands, and from Cape Spartel to the River Cameroon. 2nd edition 1873
—— Part 2, From the River Cameroon to the Cape of Good Hope. Including Ascension, St Helena, Tristan da Cunha, and Gough Islands. 2nd edition
                                    1884
—— Part 3, South and East Coasts of Africa, from the Cape of Good Hope to Cape Guardafui; including the Islands in Mozambique Channel. Originally compiled by Capt. Algernon F. R. De Horsey. 3rd edition. *Map*   1878
—— Part 1. 5th edition. Large 8° 1890
—— Part 2. 4th edition   1893
—— Part 3. 5th edition   1889
—— Supplement, 1890; and Revised ditto   1892
Remarks on Baffin Bay. By R. C. Allen, W. P. Snow, and Comm. E. A. Inglefield   1853
Remarks on Davis Strait, Baffin Bay, Smith Sound, and the Channels thence northward to 82¼° N. Large 8° 1875

UNITED KINGDOM—A.
Admiralty Publications—*continued.*

Newfoundland: East and South Coasts. Bonavista Bay to Placentia Harbour. 8°   1868
The Newfoundland and Labrador Pilot, comprising also the Strait of Belle Isle, the North-East and part of the North Coast of Labrador. Originally compiled by Staff-Commander W. F. Maxwell. 2nd edition. Large 8° 1887
—— Supplement, 1891; and Revised ditto   1892 and 1894
The St Lawrence Pilot, comprising Sailing Directions for the Gulf and River. Originally compiled by Rear-Admiral H. W. Bayfield. 5th edition. 2 vols. Large 8°   1881-82
—— Vol. 1.   6th edition   1894
The Nova Scotia Pilot. S.E. Coast from Mars Head to Cape Canso. By Rear-Adm. H. W. Bayfield   1860
Sailing Directions for the South-East Coast of Nova Scotia and Bay of Fundy. By Staff-Com. G. F. M'Dougall 1867
Sailing Directions for the Principal Ports of the East Coast of North America to 1858   1863
—— 3rd and 4th editions. Large 8°
                                  1885-94
—— 3rd edition. Large 8°   1882
The Vancouver Island Pilot, containing Sailing Directions for the Coasts of Vancouver Island and part of British Columbia. From the Surveys of Capt. G. H. Richards   1864
The British Columbia Pilot, including the Coast of British Columbia, from Juan de Fuca Strait to Portland Canal, together with Vancouver and Queen Charlotte Islands. Large 8°   1888
The West Indian Pilot. Vol. 1. Compiled by Capt. E. Barnett   1872
—— Vol. 2.   2nd edition. Compiled by Capt. E. Barnett, 1866; and 3rd edition. *Map*   1876
—— Vol. 1. From Cape North of the Amazons to Cape Sable in Florida, with the adjacent Islands. Originally compiled by Capt. E. Barnett, 1829. 4th and 5th editions. Large 8° 1883-93
—— Revised Supplement   1889
Vol. 2. The Caribbean Sea, from Barbadoes to Cuba; with Florida Strait, Bahama and Bermuda Islands. Originally compiled by Capt. E. Barnett. 4th edition. Large 8°   1887
—— Revised Supplement   1894
The South America Pilot. Part 1. The East Coast of South America, from Cape St Roque to Cape San Antonio, Rio de la Plata; and the North Coast, from Cape St Roque to the Rio Maroni in French Guayana. By Staff-Commander J. Penn   1864

UNITED KINGDOM—A.

Admiralty Publications—*continued.*

The South America Pilot. Part 2. The South-East and West Coasts of South America, from the Rio de la Plata to the Bay of Panama, including Magellan Strait, the Falkland and Galapagos Islands. By Capts. Philip Parker King and Robert Fitzroy. 6th edition 1865

—— Part 1. 3rd edition. Large 8° 1885

—— Supplement, corrected to 24th October 1890. Large 8° 1890

—— Part 2. 8th edition. Large 8° 1886

The Australia Directory. Vol. 1. South and East Coasts, Bass Strait, and Tasmania. Compiled by Capt. Charles B. Yule. 6th edition 1868

—— Vol. 2. Comprising the East Coast, Torres Strait, and the Coral Sea. 2nd edition 1864

—— Vol. 3. North, North-West, and West Coasts 1863

—— Vol. 1. 8th edition. Large 8° 1884

—— Revised Supplement, corrected to 21st June 1889. Large 8° 1889

—— Vol. 2. Comprising the East Coast from Port Jackson to Cape York, Torres Strait and Approaches, the Coral Sea, and part of Carpentaria Gulf. 4th edition. Large 8° 1889

—— Supplement 1892

—— Vol. 3. North, North-West, and West Coasts, from the Gulf of Carpentaria to Cape Leeuwin, with Directions for Passages through the Neighbouring Seas. 2nd edition. Large 8° 1881

—— Supplement, corrected to January 1885. Large 8° 1885

North-Eastern Australia. Coast-views between Sandy Cape and Endeavour Strait for the Navigation of the Inner Passage to Torres Strait. *Plates.* Oblong 8° N.D.

The New Zealand Pilot, including also the Chatham Islands and the off-lying Islands southward of New Zealand. Compiled by Capts. G. H. Richards and F. J. Evans. 4th edition. *Map* 1875

—— 6th edition 1891

North Pacific Pilot. Part 1. Sailing Directions for the West Coast of North America, between Panama and Queen Charlotte Islands. By James F. Imray. 2nd edition. *Maps.* Part 2. The Seaman's Guide to the Islands of the North Pacific, with an Appendix on the Winds, Weather, Currents, &c., of the North and South Pacific. By W. H. Rosser. *Maps.* 8° 1870

—— *See* Rosser.

UNITED KINGDOM—A.

Admiralty Publications—*continued.*

Pacific Islands Pilot. Vol. 1. (Western Groups). 2nd edition 1890

—— Supplement 1894

—— Vol. 1. Part 2. Western Groups, comprising New Caledonia and the Loyalty Islands. Also Supplementary Information respecting the New Hebrides, Banks, Tores, and Santa Cruz Groups. Compiled . . . Capt. H. A. Moriarty 1893

—— Vol. 2. (Central and Eastern Groups.) Containing former Vols. 2, 3, and Fiji Islands. 2nd edition 1891

Sailing Directions for the South-East, North-East, and North Coasts of New Guinea, Louisiade, d'Entrecasteaux, New Hebrides, Solomon, New Ireland, New Britain, Admiralty, and Caroline Islands. Large 8° 1890

B. Board of Trade Publications.

Meteorological Papers, published by authority of the Board of Trade. Nos. 1-4. 4° 1857-60

—— The same. Nos. 5-10. 4° and 8° 1861

—— The same. Nos. 10, 11. 8° 1861

Report of a Committee appointed to consider certain questions relating to the Meteorological Department of the Board of Trade. *Map.* Folio 1866 [*See also* Fitzroy ; Scott, R. H.]

Meteorological Committee. Publications issued by :—

Official.

Nos. 5, 17, 22, 26, 29, 31, 35, 41, 64, 75, 79, 84, 91, 99, 104. Annual Reports, 1868-92 [wanting those for '69-71, '75, '76, '79, '81-83, '85, '86]. 8° 1869-93

Nos. 7 (parts 1, 3, 4), 9 (part 4), 14, 16, 19, 25, 30, 33 (part 1), 49 (part 4), 50 (parts 1, 3, 4). Quarterly Weather Report, 1869-80 [wanting 1869, part 2 ; 1870, parts 1-3 ; 1876, parts 2, 3, 4 ; 1877-78 ; 1879, parts, 1-3 ; 1880, part 2]. 4° 1870-91

No. 18.—Contributions to our knowledge of the Meteorology of the Antarctic Regions. 4° 1873

No. 20.—Remarks to accompany the Monthly Charts of Meteorological data for square 3. 4° 1874

No. 21.—Report of the Proceedings of the Meteorological Congress at Vienna. 8° 1874

No. 23.—Report of the Proceedings of the Conference on Maritime Meteorology held in London, 1874. 8° 1875

No. 24.—Instructions in the Use of Meteorological Instruments. Compiled by R. H. Scott. 8° 1880

UNITED KINGDOM—B.

Board of Trade Publications—*contd.*

No. 27.—Remarks to accompany the Monthly Charts of Meteorological data for nine 10° squares of the Atlantic. 4° 1876

No. 37.—Report on the Meteorology of Kerguelen Island. By the Rev. S. J. Perry. 4° 1879

Nos. 39, 45, 57, 66, 73, 78, 82, 88, 95, 101, 108.—Meteorological Observations at Stations of the Second Order, for the years 1878-89 [1882 wanting. First 4 Nos. bound in 1 vol.] 1880-93

No. 46.—Report on the Storm of October 13-14, 1881. 8° 1882

No. 47.—*See* Symons, G. J.

No. 51.—Hourly Readings, 1881, part 4. 4° 1883

No. 56.—Sunshine Records of the United Kingdom for 1881. 8° 1883

No. 60.—*See* Abercromby, R.

No. 61.—A Barometer Manual for the Use of Seamen. 8° 1884

No. 70.—Hourly Readings, 1884, part 3. 4° 1887

No. 89. — Meteorological Observations made at Sanchez (Samana Bay), St Domingo, 1886-88. By the late W. Reid. 4° 1890

No. 93.—Harmonic Analysis of Hourly Observations of Air Temperature and Pressure at British Observatories. 4° 1891

Nos. 94, 97.—Hourly Means at Four Observatories, 1887-88. 4° 1891

No. 98.—Ten Years' Sunshine in the British Isles, 1881-90. 8° 1891

No. 102.—Report of the International Meteorological Conference at Munich, 1891. 8° 1893

Non-Official.

No. 2.—*See* Toynbee.

No. 6.—Report of the Proceedings of the Meteorological Conference at Leipzig. 8° 1873

No. 7.—Notes on the Form of Cyclones in the Southern Indian Ocean. By C. Meldrum. 8° 1873

No. 8.—Report on Weather Telegraphy and Storm-Warnings, presented to the Meteorological Congress at Vienna. 8° 1874

No. 9.—Report of the Permanent Committee of the First International Meteorological Congress at Vienna, for the year 1874. Meeting at Vienna and Utrecht, 1873-74. 8° 1875

No. 11.—The same. Meeting at London, 1876. 8° 1876

—— Supplement 1877

No. 12.—Reports to the Permanent Committee, &c., on Atmospheric Electricity, Maritime Meteorology, Weather Telegraphy. 8° 1878

UNITED KINGDOM—B.

Board of Trade Publications—*contd.*

No. 13.—Report of the Permanent Committee, &c., Meeting at Utrecht. 8° 1879

No. 14.—Report of the Int. Met. Committee Meeting at Berne, 1880. 8° 1881

No. 15.—Report of the Second Meeting of the Int. Met. Committee, Copenhagen, 1882. 8° 1883

No. 16.—Report of the Third Meeting of the same, Paris, 1885. 8° 1887

No. 17.—Report of the Fourth Meeting of the same, Zürich, 1888. 8° 1889

Report by Mr Hawkshaw and Sir A. Clarke on Dover Harbour. Folio 1873

Additions and Corrections to Dock Book, 1890. Folio 1893

The Mercantile Navy List, and Annual Appendage to the Commercial Code of Signals for all Nations. 1857-62, edited by J. H. Brown ; 1863-64, edited by J. J. Mayo. 8 vols. Large 8° 1857-64

C. Colonial Office Publications.

Colonial Reports. Annual—

Europe.—Gibraltar, No. 75 ; Malta, No. 79.

Asia.—Ceylon, Nos. 60, 90 ; Hongkong, No. 85 ; Labuan, No. 93 ; Straits Settlements, Nos. 59, 81.

Africa.—Basutoland, Nos. 62, 89 ; Bechuanaland, No. 47 ; Gambia, No. 80 ; Gold Coast, No. 88 ; Lagos, No. 95 ; Mauritius, No. 57 ; Natal, No. 61 ; Rodrigues, No. 70 ; Sierra Leone, No. 64.

America.—Newfoundland, No. 67 ; British Honduras, Nos. 73, 94 ; West Indies, Nos. 52, 53, 65, 66, 74, 76-78, 82-84, 86.

Atlantic.—St Helena, No. 63 ; Bermuda, No. 71 ; Falkland Is., No. 87.

Australasia.—British New Guinea, No. 68 ; Fiji, No. 72 ; Victoria, No. 69.

Miscellaneous.—No. 2, Zululand ; No. 3, Sierra Leone.

—— Her Majesty's Colonial Possessions—

Asia.—Ceylon, No. 78 ; Hongkong, No. 77.

Africa. — Basutoland, No. 70 ; Gold Coast, Nos. 12, 74, 76 ; Lagos, No. 40 ; Sierra Leone, No. 75.

America.—British Guiana, No. 72 ; Brit. Honduras, No. 71.

Australasia.—Fiji, No. 79 ; W. Australia, No. 73.

The Colonial Office List for 1891, comprising Historical and Statistical Information respecting the Colonial Dependencies of Great Britain. *Maps.* 8° 1891

UNITED KINGDOM—D.

Foreign Office Publications—*contd.*

NORTH AMERICA.

United States.—A.S., Nos. 718, 1157, 1164, 1176, 1181, 1203, 1205, 1233, 1251, 1274, 1285, 1319; M.S., Nos. 277, 280, 289, 292, 314.

Mexico.—A.S., Nos. 322, 357, 396, 637, 786, 1150, 1218, 1301; M.S., Nos. 116, 133, 136, 138, 170, 284, 302, 309.

CENTRAL AMERICA AND WEST INDIES.

Costa Rica.—A.S., Nos. 317, 694, 1219.

Cuba [Spain].—A.S., Nos. 205, 609, 779, 1132, 1213; M.S., Nos. 59, 115, 177.

Guatemala.—A.S., Nos. 600, 763, 1070, 1096, 1245.

Hayti and San Domingo.—A.S., Nos. 729, 902, 1240; M.S., No. 52.

Honduras.—A.S., No. 1314.

Porto Rico [Spain].—A.S., Nos. 628, 816, 1306.

San Salvador.—A.S., Nos. 749, 1281.

SOUTH AMERICA.

Argentine Republic.—A.S., Nos. 111, 654, 660, 1147, 1161, 1178, 1283, 1303; M.S., Nos. 165, 172, 186, 298.

Brazil.—A.S., Nos. 216, 323, 693, 702, 715, 793, 807, 1141, 1160, 1263, 1290, 1321; M.S., Nos. 45, 178.

Chile.—A.S., Nos. 310, 369, 385, 407, 634, 685, 743, 1311; M.S., Nos. 61, 157.

Colombia.—A.S., Nos. 253, 626, 804, 1148; M.S., No. 103.

Ecuador.—A.S., Nos. 805, 811, 951, 1146, 1171; M.S., No. 273.

Guiana, Dutch.—A.S., Nos. 410, 583, 737, 1307.

Paraguay.—A.S., No. 792.

Peru.—A.S., Nos. 118, 728, 806, 1053, 1185, 1318; M.S., No. 167.

Uruguay.—A.S., Nos. 129, 794, 1294.

Venezuela.—A.S., Nos. 138, 723, 912, 1207.

OCEANIA.

Hawaii.—A.S., No. 738.

New Caledonia [France].—A.S., Nos. 335, 521, 758, 909.

New Hebrides.—A.S., No. 666.

Samoa.—A.S., Nos. 831, 1064, 1065, 1262.

Tahiti [France].—A.S., Nos. 319, 602, 635, 759, 904, 1210; M.S., No. 308.

Tonga [Fiji].—A.S., Nos. 158, 569, 601, 1137.

Index to Consular Reports, 1886-92. 8°   1892

—— Ditto, 1886-93. 8°   1893

—— Ditto, 1886-94. 8°   1894

The Foreign Office List, 1892, forming a Complete British Diplomatic and Consular Handbook. *Maps.* 8°   1892

UNITED KINGDOM.

E. Ordnance Survey.

Astronomical Observations made with Ramsden's Zenith Sector; together with a Catalogue of the Stars which have been observed, and the Amplitudes of the Celestial Arcs, deduced from Observations at the different Stations. 4° 1842

Ordnance Maps, Correspondence, &c., respecting the adoption of the 6-inch Scale in 1840, and respecting the relative advantages of that Scale, and a still larger one. [Parly. Rep.] Folio 1853

Ireland. Abstracts of Principal Lines of Spirit Levelling in Ireland, 1839-43, under the direction of the late Major-General Colby. 4°   1855

Scotland. Book of Reference to the Plan of the Parish of Stow (part of), in the County of Selkirk. *Map.* Oblong 8°   1859

Domesday Book, or the Great Survey of England of William the Conqueror, A.D. MLXXXVI., in Facsimile, viz., Yorkshire, Kent, Surrey, Sussex, Berkshire, Hampshire, Wiltshire, Dorsetshire, Devonshire, Cornwall, Lincolnshire, Cambridgeshire, Norfolk, Suffolk, Essex, Cheshire and Lancashire, Shropshire, Herefordshire, Gloucestershire, Somersetshire, Staffordshire, Derbyshire, Nottinghamshire, Leicestershire and Rutland, Warwickshire, Worcestershire, Oxfordshire, Buckinghamshire, Middlesex, Hertfordshire, Bedfordshire, Huntingdonshire, Northamptonshire. 33 vols. 4°   1861-63

Report of the Progress of the Ordnance Survey and Topographical Depôt to 31st December 1860, 1863, and 1866. 3 parts. [Parly. Rep.] *Maps.* Folio 1861-67

—— The same, to 31st December 1886. *Maps.* Folio   1887

Catalogues of Maps, &c. 8°   1862-69

Extension of the Triangulation of the Ordnance Survey into France and Belgium, with the Measurement of an Arc of Parallel in Lat. 52° N. By Col. Sir H. James. *Plates.* 4°   1863

European Arc. Determinations of the Positions of Feaghmain and Haverfordwest, Longitude Stations on the Great European Arc of Parallel. By Capt. A. R. Clarke. *Plates.* 4°   1867

Report of the Departmental Committee appointed by the Board of Agriculture to inquire into the present condition of the Ordnance Survey. Folio   1893

[*See also* James, Sir H.; Mudge; Williams, E.; Yolland.]

UNITED KINGDOM.

F. Parliamentary Papers.

[See also under the various Countries dealt with.]

Colonies. Return from each Colony or Foreign Possession of the British Crown, stating the date at which each Colony or Possession was Captured, Ceded, or Settled ; the Number of the Population, and the Manner of Government ; stating also the Value of Exports and Imports, &c., in 1829. Folio   1831

—— Extracts of Reports from the Governors or Lieut.-Governors of British Possessions in North America, and of the Answers thereto as may throw light on the state of the Aboriginal Tribes in North America, or in any adjacent Territories ; and also the state of the Indian Department in Upper and Lower Canada, New Brunswick, Nova Scotia, New South Wales, Van Diemen's Land, and the British Guiana Indians. Folio   1834

—— Papers presented to Parliament in Explanation of the Measures adopted by Government for giving effect to the Act for the Abolition of Slavery throughout the British Colonies. Part 2. West India Islands and Cape of Good Hope, 1833-35. Folio   1835

Dover Harbour. Copy Report by Mr Hawkshaw and Sir Andrew Clarke upon the possibility of combining Naval and Military Requirements with the objects of Dover Harbour Bill. *Map.* Folio 1873

Emigration. Reports from the Select Committee on Emigration from the United Kingdom. *Maps.* Folio 1826

—— Reports from the Commissioners for Emigration, addressed to the Secretary of State for the Colonial Department. Folio   1832

—— Correspondence respecting Emigration. Folio   1871

Norwich and Lowestoft Navigation Bill. Minutes and Evidence taken before the Committee on the Bill for Making and Maintaining a Navigable Communication for Ships and other Vessels between the City of Norwich and the Sea at or near Lowestoft, in the County of Suffolk. Folio   1826

Ordnance. Estimates of the Office of Ordnance ; including Barracks, Surveys of the United Kingdom, Commissariat, and Military and Civil Superannuations, 1840-41. *Maps.* Folio   1840

Parliamentary Divisions. An Act to Settle and Describe the Divisions of Counties, and the Limits of Cities and Boroughs in England and Wales, in so far as Respects the Election of Members to Serve in Parliament. Folio   1832

UNITED KINGDOM—F.

Parliamentary Reports from Commissioners on Proposed Division of Counties and Boundaries of Boroughs. Parts 1 to 8. 4 vols. *Maps.* Folio   1832

—— Reports on the Proposed Divisions of the Counties mentioned in Schedule (F) of the Reform Bill [England]. *Maps* 1832

Statistical Abstract for the several Colonial and other Possessions of the United Kingdom in each year from 1875 to 1889, and from 1877 to 1891 (27th and 29th Nos.). 8°   1890, 1892

—— The same. For the Principal and other Foreign Countries in each year from 1878 to 1887-88 (16th No.). 8°   1890

Sugar. An Account of the Quantity of British Plantation, Mauritius, and other Sugar, on which Duty has been paid, in 1828-30. Folio   1830

Telegraph Cables. Report of the Joint Committee appointed by the Lords of the Committee of Privy Council for Trade, and the Atlantic Telegraph Company, to inquire into the Construction of Submarine Telegraph Cables ; with the Minutes of Evidences, and Appendix. *Plans and plates.* Folio   1861

Trade. General Statement of Imports and Exports of the Principal Articles of Merchandize between the United Kingdom and the several Foreign Countries and British Possessions Abroad, in 1830. Folio   1832

—— Accounts of the Official and Declared Value of the Imports to and Exports from the United Kingdom from and to each of the British Colonies and Possessions, and Amount to Foreign Countries, for the year ending Jan. 5, 1831. Folio   1832

—— Accounts relating to Trade and Navigation of the United Kingdom, for each month during the year 1891. 8°   1891

Uninhabited Islands. Correspondence in regard to Her Majesty's Ships visiting groups of uninhabited islands lying on the tracks of vessels between Great Britain and the Australasian Colonies. Folio   1877

G. War Office.

Publications of the Topographical, Statistical, and Intelligence Branches : Quarter-Master-General's Department :—
Venetia with the Quadrilateral, a Military Geographical Sketch. By M. Biffart ; translated by Lieut.-Col. A. C. Cooke. *Maps.* 8°   1866
Ideas on our Military Position in a War with Russia. By an Austrian Officer. [Translated from the German.] 8°   1870

UNITED KINGDOM—G.

War Office Publications—*continued.*

The Campaign of 1866 in Germany. Compiled by the department of Military History of the Prussian Staff. Translated by Col. Von Wright and Captain H. M. Hozier. *Plans.* 8° 1872

—— Atlas of Plans separate. Folio.

Military Reports. addressed to the French War Minister by Colonel Baron Stoffel, French Military Attaché in Prussia, 1866-60. Translated by Captain Home. 8° 1872

Reforms in the French Army. Part 1. The Law of Recruiting. Translated by Captain Home. 8° 1872

—— Part 2. General Organisation. By Major C. B. Brackenbury. 8° 1875

National Assembly : Committees on the Re-organisation of the Army, and on Contracts. Précis of the Speech of the Duke d'Audiffret Pasquier. 8° 1874

The Armed Strength of Italy. Translated from the German by Lieut. W. A. H. Hare. 8° 1875

The Armed Strength of the German Empire. Part 1. Organisation and Administration. Compiled by Capt. F. C. H. Clarke. *Map.* 8° 1876

—— 2nd edition. *See below* (1888).

The Ottoman Empire and its tributary States (excepting Egypt), with a Sketch of Greece. Compiled by Capt. W. S. Cooke. *Maps.* 8° 1876

The Armed Strength of France. By Major C. J. East. *Map.* 8° 1877

The Siege Operations in the Campaign against France, 1870-71. By B. von Tiedemann ; translated by Major Tyler. *Plans.* 8° 1877

A Précis of Modern Tactics, compiled from the Works of recent Continental Writers. By Major Robert Home. *Maps and plates.* 8° 1873

The Armed Strength of Russia. [Translated.] 8° 1873

—— *See below* (1882).

The New Law regulating Military Service in Russia. 8° N.D.

Steppe Campaigns. Translated from the Russian by Capt. F. C. H. Clarke. 8° 1874

Statistics and Geography of Russian Turkestan. By Brevet-Major F. C. H. Clarke. Folio 1879

The Armed Strength of Austria. Compiled by Capt. W. S. Cooke. Parts 1 and 2. *Map and tables.* 8° 1873-74

The Armed Strength of Denmark. Compiled by Capt. W. S. Cooke. 8° 1874

The Armed Strength of Sweden and Norway. Compiled by Capt. W. S. Cooke. 8° [1874]

UNITED KINGDOM—G.

War Office Publications—*continued.*

The Armed Strength of the Netherlands. By Capt. F. C. H. Clarke. *Map.* 8° 1876

The Franco-German War, 1870-71. Translated from the German Official Account by Capt. F. C. H. Clarke. First Part—History of the War to the Downfall of the Empire : Vol. 1, From the Outbreak of Hostilities to the Battle of Gravelotte. 1874

—— First Part. Vol. 2, From the Battle of Gravelotte to the Downfall of the Empire. *Maps in pocket.* 8° 1876

—— Second Part. History of the War against the Republic : Vol. 1, From the Investment of Paris to the Re-occupation of Orleans by the Germans. *Maps* separate. *Maps.* 8° 1880

—— Second Part. Vol. 2, Events in Northern France from the end of November, in the North-West from the beginning of December, and the Siege of Paris from the commencement of December to the Armistice ; Operations in the South-East from the middle of November to the middle of January. *Maps, and maps in case.* 8° 1883

—— Second Part. Vol. 3, Events in South-East France from the middle of January to the Termination of Hostilities ; Rearward Communications ; The Armistice ; Homeward March and Occupation ; Retrospect. *Maps, and maps in case.* 8° 1884

—— Index. *See* Hale.

Cyprus. By Captain A. R. Savile. *Map.* 8° 1878

The Anglo-Afghan War of 1878. First Section, 20th Nov. to 20th Dec. Folio 1878

The Anglo-Afghan War of 1878-79. Second Section, 21st Dec. 1878 to 31st Jan. 1879. Third Section, From 1st Feb. 1879 to the Close of the War. *Maps.* Folio 1879

Memorandum on Afghanistan with Reference to the Probable British Operations consequent on the Murder at Kabul of the Resident and Escort, on 3rd September 1879. *Maps.* Folio 1879

The Anglo-Afghan War of 1879-80. First Section, From the Kabul Massacre on 3rd Sept. 1879 to 25th Nov. 1879. Second Section, From 26th Nov. 1879 to 31st Dec. 1879. *Maps.* Folio 1879

Précis of Information concerning the Colony of Natal, corrected to June 1879. *Map.* 8° 1879

Précis of Information concerning the Zulu Country. *Map.* 8° 1879

UNITED KINGDOM—G.

War Office Publications—*continued.*

Chár Asiäb. [1 *sheet*] 1879

The Armed Strength of Switzerland. Compiled by Major Frank S. Russell. *Map.* 8° 1880
—— *See below* (1889).

Notes on the Russian Expedition against the Tekke Turkomans, 1879. *Map.* Folio.

The Armed Strength of Belgium, 1882. *Maps.* 8° 1882

The Armed Strength of Russia. *Maps.* 8° 1882

Report on Egypt. *Map and sections.* 8° 1882

The Armed Strength of Spain. *Map.* 8° 1883

Annam and Tong-King. *Maps.* Folio [1883]

Bechuanaland, 1883. *Maps.* Fol. [1883]

Précis of Information concerning the Straits Settlements and the Native States of the Malay Peninsula. *Map.* 8° 1883
—— *See below* (1891).

The Insurrection of the False Prophet. Compiled in the Intelligence Branch, Quarter-Master-General's Department, Horse Guards, War Office. Folio 1883
—— Part 2. From General Hicks' Departure from Khartoum (9th Sept. 1883) to Baker Pasha's Defeat at Et-Tib (4th February 1884). Compiled, &c., by Capt. J. J. Leverson, R.E. Folio 1884
—— Part 3. British Expedition to the Red Sea : from Baker Pasha's Defeat at Et-Teb (4th February 1884) to the Capture of Tokar (1st March 1884). Compiled, &c., by J. J. Leverson, R.E. Folio 1884
—— Part 4. British Expedition to the Red Sea : from the Battle of Et-Teb (29th January 1884) to the Departure of Major-General Graham from Suakin (3rd April 1884). Compiled, &c., by Capt. J. J. Leverson, R.E. Folio 1884

Report on the Egyptian Provinces of the Sûdan, Red Sea, and Equator. Compiled in the Intelligence Branch, Quartermaster General's Department, Horse Guards, War Office. Revised up to July 1884. *Map.* Small 8° 1881

Griqualand, West. Road Reports. 8° 1884

Précis of Information concerning Zululand. *Map.* 8° 1885

Table of Distances in Russia, Central Asia, and India. (Compiled at the Intelligence Branch of the War Office, May 1875, by Lieutenant Wisely, R.E., under the Direction of Col. Cameron, V.C.) Folio.

UNITED KINGDOM—G.

War Office Publications—*continued.*

French Operations in Madagascar, 1882-1886. Prepared by Major W. S. Cooke, February 1886. *Map.* Folio 1886

Short History of Basutoland. Chiefly compiled from Blue Books. Prepared in the Intelligence Branch, War Office, by Captain L. Darwin, R.E. *Map.* 8° 1886

Précis of Information concerning Pondoland, including Port St John's. Prepared in the Intelligence Branch, War Office. Corrected to February 1886. *Map.* 8° 1886

The Armed Strength of Japan, by Capt. J. M. Grierson. *Map and plates.* 8° 1886

The Armed Strength of the Netherlands and their Colonies, by Major J. K. Trotter. *Map.* 8° 1887

Military History of the Campaign of 1882 in Egypt. Prepared in the Intelligence Branch of the War Office, by Colonel J. F. Maurice, Royal Artillery. *Maps.* 8° [1887]

The Armed Strength of Portugal, by Lieutenant Count Gleichen. *Map.* 8° [1887]

The Armed Strength of Roumania, by Captain C. E. Callwell. *Map.* 8° 1888

The Armed Strength of the German Empire. Parts 1 and 2, by Captain J. M. Grierson, and edited by Colonel C. W. Bowdler Bell. 2nd edition. *Map.* 8° 1888

The Armed Strength of Switzerland. Prepared in the Intelligence Division of the War Office, by Colonel C. W. Bowdler Bell. *Map.* 8° 1889

Colville, Col. H. E. History of the Sudan Campaign. 2 parts, with a Case of Maps. Compiled in the Intelligence Division of the War Office. 8° [1889]

Sudan Almanac for 1889, '90, '91, and '93. Compiled at the Intelligence Division, War Office. 12°.

Précis of Information concerning the Straits Settlements, &c. New edition. 1891

Notes on the Geography, Government, and Inhabitants of Uganda, with a Sketch of its History to 1892. Prepared in the Intelligence Division of the War Office by Capt. Hubert Foster. Folio 1892

Handbook of British East Africa, including Zanzibar, Uganda, and the Territory of the Imperial British East Africa Company. *Maps.* 8° 1893

Hints on Reconnaisance Mapping for Explorers in Unsurveyed Countries. Folio.

[*See* Catalogues ; *also* Haly ; Wingate.]

UNITED KINGDOM.

H. Various Government Publications.

Births, Deaths, and Marriages. 7th, 13th, 16th, 17th, and 18th Annual Reports of the Registrar-General (years 1843-44, 1850, 1853-55). 8° and large 8° 1846-57

Census of England and Wales, 1891. Preliminary Report, and Tables of the Population and Houses enumerated in England and Wales, and in the Islands in the British Seas, on 6th April 1891. Folio 1891

—— Ditto. Area, Houses, and Population. Vol. 1. Administrative and Adjacent Counties. Folio 1893

—— Ditto. The same. Vol. 2. Registration Areas and Sanitary Districts. Folio 1893

—— Ditto. Ages, Condition as to Marriage, Occupation, Birthplaces, and Infirmities. Vol. 3. Folio 1893

—— Ditto. Vol. 4. General Report, with Summary Tables and Appendices. Folio 1893

—— Ditto. Index to the Population Tables of England and Wales. Folio 1893

Emigrants' Handbooks. Emigrants' Information Office Handbooks, 1890, consisting of the following 12 Handbooks —1. Canada ; 2. New South Wales ; 3. Victoria ; 4. South Australia ; 5. Queensland ; 6. Western Australia ; 7. Tasmania ; 8. New Zealand ; 9. Cape Colony and British Bechuanaland ; 10. Natal ; 11. Professional Handbook ; 12. Emigration Statutes and General Handbook. *Maps.* 8° 1890

Education. Reports of the Committee of Council on Education (England, Wales, and Scotland). 8° 1870-93

Greenwich Observatory. Description of the Altitude and Azimuth Instrument erected at the Royal Observatory, Greenwich, in 1847. [Greenwich Astronomical Observations.] 4° 1847

—— Description of the Instruments and Process used in the Photographic Self-Registration of the Magnetical and Meteorological Instruments at the Royal Observatory, Greenwich. [Exts. from Greenwich Magnetical and Meteorological Observations, 1847.] 4° 1849

—— Results of the Magnetical and Meteorological Observations made at the Royal Observatory, Greenwich, in the year 1880. . . . Edited by W. H. M. Christie. 4° 1882

—— Rates of Chronometers on Trial, 1869, '73, '74, '77, '83-87, '89-93 ; of Deck-Watches, 1889-93. 4°

Kew Gardens. Royal Gardens, Kew : Official Guide to the Museums of Economic Botany. No. 3. Timbers. 12° 1886

UNITED KINGDOM—H.

Kew Museums. A Handbook to the Museums of Economic Botany of the Royal Gardens, Kew. By D. Oliver. 6th edition ; with additions by J. R. Jackson. 12° 1875

Kew Observatory. Report of the Incorporated Kew Committee for the year ending 31st December 1893. [From the Proc. R.S.] 8° 1894

Nautical Almanac. Tables requisite to be used with the Astronomical and Nautical Ephemeris, published by order of the Commissioners of Longitude. 8° 1766

—— Ditto. 2nd edition 1781

—— Ditto. 3rd edition 1802

—— Circular, No. 15. Local Particulars of the Total Eclipse of the Sun, Aug. 8-9 1896. Large 8° 1893

Transit of Venus, 1882. Report of the Committee appointed by the British Government to Superintend the Arrangements to be made for the sending of Expeditions at the Government expense, and securing co-operation with the Government Expeditions, for the Observation of the Transit of Venus, 6th December 1882. Folio.

"Challenger" Expedition. Report on the Scientific Results of the Voyage of H.M.S. "Challenger," 1873-76. . . . Prepared under the superintendence of the late Sir C. Wyville Thomson, and now of John Murray. *Charts and plates.* 4°.

—— Zoology. 1880-89

Vol 1.—1. Brachiopoda, by T. Davidson ; 2. Pennatulida, by A. v. Kölliker ; 3. Ostracoda, by G. S. Brady ; 4. Bones of Cetacea, by W. Turner ; 5. Green Turtle, by W. K. Parker ; 6. Shore Fishes, by A. Günther.

Vol. 2.—7. Corals, by H. N. Mosely ; 8. Birds, by P. L. Sclater.

Vol. 3.—9. Echinoidea, by A. Agassiz ; 10. Pycnogonida, by P. P. C. Hoek.

Vol. 4.—11. Anatomy of the Petrels, by W. A. Forbes ; 12. Deep-sea Medusæ, by E. Haeckel ; 13. Holothurioidea (Elasipoda), by H. Théel.

Vol. 5.—14. Ophiuroidea, by T. Tyman ; 16. Marsupialia, by D. J. Cunningham.

Vol. 6.—15. Actiniaria, by R. Hertwig ; 17. Tunicata (Ascidiæ Simplices), by W. A. Herdman.

Vol. 7.—18. Anatomy of Spheniscidae, by M. Watson ; 19. Pelagic Hemiptera, by F. B. White ; 20. Hydroida (Plumularidæ), by G. J. Allman ; 21. Orbitolites, by W. B. Carpenter.

Vol. 8.—23. Copepoda, by G. S. Brady ; 24. Calcarea, by N. Poléjaeff ; 25. Cirripedia (Systematic), by P. P. C. Hoek.

I. Miscellaneous.

Alpine Club. Provisional Report of the Special Committee on Equipment for Mountaineers. 8° 1891

UNITED KINGDOM—I.

South Kensington Museum. Conferences held in connection with the Special Loan Collection of Scientific Apparatus, 1876 : Chemistry, Biology, Physical Geography, Geology, Mineralogy, and Meteorology. 8° N.D.
—— Ditto. Physics and Mechanics. 8°
—— *See* Catalogues, C.

J. Anonymous.

Descriptio Britanniæ, Scotiæ, Hyberniæ, et Orchodvm, ex Libro Paoli Jovii, Episcopi Nvcer. De Imperiis, et Gentibvs cogniti Orbis, com eivs operis prohœmis, ad Alexandrvm Farnesivm Card. Am pliss. 8°.
Magna Britannia et Hibernia, Antiqua et Nova, or a New Survey of Great Britain, &c. Vols. 1, 2, 5, 6. *Maps.* Small 4° 1730
The Geography of England and Wales : done in the Manner of Gordon's Geographical Grammar. *Maps.* 8° 1744
Rivers. Historical Account of the Navigable Rivers, Canals, and Railways of Great Britain, as a Reference to Nichols, Priestly, and Walker's new Map of Inland Navigation. *Maps.* 8° 1831
—— The Rivers of Great Britain, Descriptive, Historical, Pictorial : Rivers of the East Coast. *Illustrations.* 4° 1889
—— Industrial Rivers of the United Kingdom, namely, the Thames, Mersey, Tyne, Tawe, Clyde, Wear, Taff, Avon, Southampton Water, the Hartlepools, Humber, Neath, Port Talbot, and Caermarthen, the Liffey, Usk, Tees, Severn, Wyre, and Lagan. By various well-known Experts. *Illustrations.* 8° 1888
Canals and Railways : Observations on the Comparative Merits of; occasioned by the Reports of the Committee of the Liverpool and Manchester Railway. *Plate.* 8° 1832
England and America : a Comparison of the Social and Political State of both the Nations. 2 vols. 8° 1833
Lifeboats. Report of the Committee on Lifeboat Models for premium offered by Duke of Northumberland. Long 4° 1851
The Colonies : a Synopsis of their Agricultural, Financial, Commercial, and Social Condition ; Tabular Historical Summary of the effect of Treaties on the Partition of Europe ; Tabular View of the Indian Territories ; War and Finance ; Tables of the Revenue and Expenditure of all Nations ; War Force of different Nations ; Abstract of the Losses of the Allies in the late War with Russia. 3 *sheets and map in case* *Edinburgh,* 1857
Facts and Observations with reference to Masters R.N. ; with a plan for the removal of their disabilities. 8° 1858

UNITED KINGDOM—J.

The Report of the Royal Commissioners on Lights, Buoys, and Beacons, 1861, examined and refuted. By an Englishman. 8° 1861
Great Britain and Ireland in 1886. 8°.
The Imperial Gazetteer of England and Wales [Fullarton's]. 6 vóls. 4° ; and Index to Atlas N.D.

Birmingham, Handbook of. Prepared for the Members of the British Association, 1886. *Map.* 12° *Birmingham,* 1886
Bridlington, Opening of Barrows near. 8° 1868
Canterbury Guide, The ; containing a Concise Account of that Ancient City and its Suburbs. *Plates.* 12° *Canterbury,* 1830
Cornwall. An Unsentimental Journey through Cornwall. By the Author of "John Halifax, Gentleman." With illustrations by C. Napier Henry. 4° 1884
Liverpool, The Stranger in : an Historical and Descriptive View of the Town of Liverpool and its Environs. *Map.* 12° *Liverpool,* 1831
—— Meteorological Results deduced from Observations taken at the Liverpool Observatory, 1889-91. Published by order of the Mersey Docks and Harbour Board. 8° 1893
London. London's Roll of Fame : being Complimentary Notes and Addresses from the City of London, on presentation of the Honorary Freedom of that City, and on other occasions, to Royal Personages, Statesmen, Patriots, Warriors, Arctic Explorers, Discoverers, Philanthropists, and Scientific Men ; with their Replies and Acknowledgments. From the close of the Reign of George II., A.D. 1757, to 1884. With a Critical and Historical Introduction. *Illustrations.* 4°.
—— London Illustrated : a complete Guide to the Places of Amusement, &c. &c. Large 8° 1885
Oxford University and City Guide : to which is added a Description of Blenheim, Nuneham, the Roman Villa, &c. *Map and plates.* 12° *Oxford,* 1831
Ripon. The Tourist's Companion : being a Concise Description and History of Ripon, Studley Park, Fountains Abbey, Hackfall, Brimham Crags, Newby Hall, Knaresborough, Harrogate, Bolton Priory, &c. *Plates.* 12° *Ripon,* 1828
Southport Meteorological Department. Report and Results of Observations for the year 1893 ; with 2 Appendices. By Joseph Baxendell. 8° *Southport,* 1893
Wales. History and Geography of Wales for the Young. Compiled by an Owner of Welsh land. 12° N.D.

K. Scotland.

First, Second, Third, and Fifth Annual Reports of the Board of Education for Scotland, to the Right Hon. the Lords of Committee of the Privy Council on Education in Scotland. 8°
Edinburgh, 1874-78

The Traveller's Guide through Scotland and its Islands. *Maps and plates.* 12°
Edinburgh, 1811

Journal of a Tour through the Highlands of Scotland during the Summer of 1829. 12° *Norton Hall,* 1830

Scottish Tourist and Itinerary; or, A Guide to the Scenery and Antiquities of Scotland and the Western Islands. *Maps and plates.* 12° *Edinburgh,* 1834

Gazetteer. Topographical, Statistical, and Historical Gazetteer of Scotland. 2 vols. *Maps and plates.* Royal 8°
Glasgow, 1842

—— Ordnance Gazetteer of Scotland : a Survey of Scottish Topography, Statistical, Biographical, and Historical. Edited by Francis H. Groome. 3 vols. *Map, plates, and plans.* Imperial 8°
Edinburgh, 1885

Letters on the Ordnance Survey of Scotland. By a Practical Surveyor. 8°
1853

Notices of some of the Principal Manufactures of the West of Scotland : The Iron and Steel Industries, by St John V. Day ; the Engineering and Shipbuilding Industries, by John Mayer ; the Textile Industries, by James Paton ; Chemical Manufactures, by John Ferguson. *Map.* 12° *Glasgow,* 1876

Catalogue of the Western Scottish Fossils, compiled by James Armstrong, John Young, and David Robertson ; with Introduction on the Geology and Palæontology of the District by Professor Young. *Map and plates.* 12°
Glasgow, 1876

Notes on the Fauna and Flora of the West of Scotland : Mammalia, by E. R. Alston ; Birds, by R. Gray ; Insects, by P. Cameron ; Vascular Flora, by J. Ramsay ; Cryptogamic Flora, by J. Stirton. 12° *Glasgow,* 1876

Missions. Fifty Years of Foreign Missions, or the Foreign Missions of the Free Church of Scotland in the Year of Jubilee 1879-80. *Maps and plates.* 8°
Edinburgh, 1880

Scotland—*continued.*

Ben Nevis Meteorological Observatory : an Account of its Foundation and Work. *Map and illustrations.* 8°
Edinburgh, 1885

Scottish Hills. Our Western Hills : How to reach them, and the Views from their Summits. By a Glasgow Pedestrian. 12° *Glasgow,* 1892

Orkney. Handbook to the Orkney Islands. *Plates.* 12° *Kirkwall* [1868]

L. Ireland.

Reports of the Commissioners appointed to Inquire into the Nature and Extent of the several Bogs in Ireland, and the Practicability of Draining and Cultivating them. *Maps and plate.* [4 Reports in 3 vols.] Folio 1810-14

Markree Observatory. Catalogue of Stars near the Ecliptic observed at Markree during the years 1854-55-56. Vol. I. 1856

—— Vol. II., during 1851-52 1853

—— Vol. III., during 1852-53-54 1854

—— Vol. IV., during 1854-55-56 1856

Cork Harbour. Correspondence in Reference to Removal or Lighting of Daunts Rock, &c. [Parly. Rep.] Folio 1874

A Geographical Description of the Kingdom of Ireland, newly corrected and improved by actual observations, &c. *Maps.* Oblong 12° 1728

Killarney, A Description of. 4° 1776

Dublin. Memorandum of Objects of Geological Interest in the Vicinity of Dublin. *Map.* 8° *Dublin,* 1835

A Plan for the Improvement of Ireland, by the Union of English and Irish Capital, and the Co-operation of the People in both Countries; with an Appendix. *Map.* 8° 1844

Parliamentary Gazetteer of Ireland, adapted to the New Poor Law, as existing in 1844-45, presenting the results, in detail, of the Census of 1841, compared with that of 1831. 3 vols. in 10 parts. *Maps and plates.* Royal 8°
Dublin, London, and Edinburgh, 1846

Post-Chaise Companion, or Traveller's Directory through Ireland, to which is added a Travelling Dictionary. *Map and plates.* 8° *Dublin,* N.D.

OCEANIC ISLANDS, &c.

ATLANTIC.

Azores. History of the Azores or Western Islands; containing an Account of the Government, Laws, and Religion; the Manners, Ceremonies, and Character of the Inhabitants; and Demonstrating the Importance of these valuable Islands to the British Empire. *Maps and plates.* 4° 1813

Bermuda, a Colony, a Fortress, and a Prison; or, Eighteen Months in the Somers Islands. By a Field Officer. *Map and plates.* 8° 1857

Fernando de Noronha. The Natural History of the Island of Fernando de Noronha based on the Collections made by the British Museum Expedition in 1887. From the *Journal of the Linnean Society*, 1890. *Map, photographs, &c.* 8°

Madeira. The Traveller's Guide to Madeira and the West Indies : being a Hieroglyphic Representation of Appearances and Incidents during a Voyage out and homewards. By a Young Traveller. *Map and plates.* 8° *Haddington,* 1815

Telegraph. Great North Atlantic Telegraph Route. *Map and plate.* 8° 1866

INDIAN AND PACIFIC.

Kerguelen Island. Note on the Report on the Meteorology of Kerguelen Island, published by the Meteorological Council, 1879. 4°.

Report on the Zoological Collections made in the Indo-Pacific Ocean during the Voyage of H.M.S. "Alert," 1881-82. *Plates.* 8° 1884

POLAR REGIONS.

ARCTIC.

A. American Expeditions.

Instructions for the Expedition toward the North Pole, from Hon. George M. Robeson, Sec. of the Navy, with an Appendix from the National Academy of Sciences. 8°   *Washington*, 1871
Reports of Foreign Societies on awarding Medals to the American Arctic Explorers, Kane, Hayes, Hall. *Plate.* 8°
            U.S. Naval Observatory, 1876
Report to the Congress from Committee on Naval Affairs to whom was referred a Bill to Authorise and Equip an Expedition to the Arctic Seas. 8°
                            1877
Report to the President of the United States of Action of the Navy Department in the Matter of the Disaster to the United States Exploring Expedition ["Polaris"] toward the North Pole, accompanied by a Report of the Examination of the Rescued Party, &c. *Map.* 8°   [*Washington*, N.D.]
Report on Substituted Expedition to the Arctic Seas. 8°   [*Washington*, 1880]
United States, Arctic Colonisation, and Exploration in 1881.   8°
                    [*Kansas City*] 1881
[*See also* United States. Signal Service Notes, No. 5.]

B. Austrian Expeditions.

Polar-Expedition von K. Weyprecht und J. Payer im Jahre 1871. [Mitt. Geogr. Ges.] 8°   *Vienna*, 1872
—— The same. Fuller reports   1874
Programme des travaux d'une Expédition Polaire Internationale, proposé par le Comte Wilezek et Charles Weyprecht. 4°   *Vienna*, 1877
Resultate der Osterreichisch-ungarischen Arctischen Expedition, 1872-74. *Plates.* 4°   *Vienna*, 1878

C. British Expeditions.

a. Franklin Search.

A **Collection** of eight bound folio volumes [presented by Mr J. Barrow] of Parliamentary Papers relating to the Search for Sir John Franklin and the Officers and Crews of H.M. Ships "Erebus" and "Terror" :—

ARCTIC—C—*a. Franklin Search.*
            CONTENTS.
Vol. 1. 1848-50.—(1.) Copies of Instructions to Captain Sir John Franklin, in reference to the Arctic Expedition of 1845, and to the Officers who have been appointed to Command Expeditions in Search of Sir John Franklin ; Proposed Plans for Relief of the Arctic Expedition ; Copies and Extracts of Correspondence and Proceedings of the Admiralty in reference to the Arctic Expedition. (2.) Copy of the Orders from the Lords Commissioners of the Admiralty, under which Capt. Sir J. C. Ross, R.N., has proceeded on an Expedition in Search of Capt. Sir J. Franklin, R.N. (3.) Extracts of Proceedings or Correspondence of the Admiralty, in reference to the Arctic Expeditions. (4.) Return of the Opinions of the most Experienced Officers [Sir W. E. Parry, Sir G. Back, Capt. Beechey, Colonel Sabine, and Sir E. Belcher] connected with the Arctic Expeditions, on the necessity of sending a Ship to the Entrance of Lancaster Sound with Supplies for Sir J. Ross's Expedition ; and their Joint Opinion as to certain Measures proposed to be adopted.   (5.) Copies of Reports or Statements from the Officers employed in the Arctic Expeditions or from any other Persons, &c., in respect to the Resumption of the Search ; of Plans of Search ; of Orders issued by the Board of Admiralty to Captains Collinson, Kellett, and Moore, and Lieut. Pullen ; of Instructions to Dr Rae ; and of Chart of the Polar Sea. (6.) Orders to Capt. Penny, "Lady Franklin," and Mr Saunders, "North Star." (7.) Orders to Captain Austin, "Resolute." (8.) Proceedings of Dr Rae, and of Lieut. Pullen, " Plover ; " also copies of Arctic Reward and other Bills.
Vol. 2. 1851.—Report of the Committee appointed by the Lords Commissioners of the Admiralty to Inquire into and Report on the recent Arctic Expeditions in search of Sir J. Franklin, together with the Minutes of Evidence taken before the Committee, and Papers connected with the subject.
Vol. 3. 1851. —Additional Papers relative to the Arctic Expedition under the Orders of Captain Austin and Mr William Penny.

ARCTIC—C—*a. Franklin Search.*

Collection, &c.—*continued.*

Vol. 4. 1852-53.—(1.) Copies and Extracts and Correspondence or Proceedings, of Instructions to Officers, and of Correspondence or Communications from the Government of the United States or H.M. Minister at Washington, in relation to Search made on the part of the United States or from its Territory for the Franklin Expedition. (2.) Further Correspondence and Proceedings. (3.) Correspondence between Capt. Penny and the Admiralty, Rumours at Byron's Bay, Adam Beck's Deposition. (4.) Track Chart of the American Expedition. (5.) Communications in reference to certain Vessels observed on an Iceberg in the N. Atlantic in 1851.

Vol. 5. 1853-54.—(1.) Copies of Correspondence from Sir E. Belcher's Squadron, from Mr Kennedy of the "Prince Albert," from Commander Inglefield of the "Isabel," and Plans and Suggestions of Search and further Correspondence. (2.) Papers relative to the Recent Arctic Expeditions in Search of H.M.S. "Erebus" and "Terror." (3.) Dr M'Cormick's Expedition up the Wellington Channel in the year 1852, Commanding H.M. Boat "Forlorn Hope" in Search of Sir John Franklin. (4.) Copy of Lady Franklin's Letter to Lords Commissioners of the Admiralty [with MS. Autograph Letter from Lady Franklin to Mr Barrow]. (5.) Sir John Richardson on Equipments for Arctic Travelling. (6.) Sir W. Parry on Equipments for Arctic Travelling. (7.) Sir J. C. Ross on same subject. (8.) Colonel Sabine on same subject.

Vol. 6. 1854-55. — Further Papers relative to the recent Arctic Expeditions, &c. Photograph of Sir Robert M'Clure, and Autographs.

Vol. 7. 1855-56.—(1.) Report from the Select Committee on Arctic Expedition ; together with the Proceedings of the Committee, Minutes of Evidence, and Appendix. (2.) Further Papers relative to the Recent Arctic Expeditions in Search of Sir J. Franklin and the Crews of Her Majesty's Ships "Erebus" and "Terror," including the Report of Dr Kane and Messrs Anderson and Stewart, and Correspondence relative to the Adjudication of £10,000 as a Reward for Ascertaining the Fate of the Crews of Her Majesty's Ships "Erebus" and "Terror."

Vol. 8.—Charts.

ARCTIC—C—*a. Franklin Search.*

A Collection made by Mr J. Barrow of Eight 8° vols. of Pamphlets connected with the Search for Sir John Franklin, containing :—

VOLUME I.

Osborn, S. Letters on the Relief of Sir John Franklin's Expedition 1850
Weld, C. R. A Lecture on Arctic Expeditions. *Map* 1850
Scoresby, W. The Franklin Expedition 1850
Weld, C. R. The Search for Sir John Franklin, a Lecture delivered at the Russell Institution. *Map* 1851
O'Byrne, W. R. The Arctic Council: Descriptive Key to the Historical Picture by S. Pearce 1851
Farrar, F. W. The Arctic Regions, and the Hopes of Discovering the Lost Adventurers: Prize Poem (Cambridge, Chancellor's Medal) 1852
Petermann, A. The Search for Sir John Franklin, a suggestion submitted to the British Public. *Chart* 1852
Mangles, J. Papers and Despatches relating to the Arctic Searching Expeditions of 1850-51-52. Collected and Arranged. 2nd edition. *Maps* 1852

VOLUME 2.

De la Roquette,—. Régions Arctiques: Terre Grinnell, Mont Franklin: Question de priorité de découverte. *Map* *Paris*, 1852
Kane, E. K. Access to the Open Polar Sea in connection with the Search after Sir John Franklin and his Companions. *Map* *New York*, 1853
Allen, R. C., Snow, W. P., and Inglefield, E. A. Remarks on Baffin Bay 1853
Petermann, A. Historical Summary of the Search for Sir John Franklin, reprinted from Seemann's Narrative of the Voyage of H.M.S. "Herald," and Notes on the Distribution of Animals available as Food in the Arctic Regions 1852
The Search for Sir John Franklin [N.D. ; Chambers's Tracts.]
The Arctic Dispatches, containing an Account of the Discovery of the North-West Passage by Capt. Robert Maclure, with Narrative of Proceedings of H.M.S. "Resolute," Capt. Kellett, and the Dispatches of Capt. Sir E. Belcher, Capt. Inglefield, and Comm. Pullen. *Map* 1853
The North - West Passage : Capt. M'Clure's Despatches from Her Majesty's Discovery Ship "Investigator," off Point Warren and Cape Bathurst. *Map* 1853
Jago, E., and Seemann, B. The History of the Poetical Assembly (on board H.M.S. "Herald") *Hanover*, 1852
Prospectus of Portrait of Capt. Penny.

ARCTIC—C—_a._

Further Papers relative to the Recent Arctic Expeditions in Search of Sir John Franklin and the Crews of Her Majesty's ships "Erebus" and "Terror." Folio 1855
—— The same, including the Reports of Dr Kane and Messrs Anderson and Stewart. Folio 1856

b. Nares Expedition.

Arctic Geography and Ethnology. _See_ Transactions, Royal Geographical Society: Appendix 3.

Manual of the Natural History, Geology, and Physics of Greenland and the Neighbouring Regions, prepared for the use of the Arctic Expedition of 1875, under the direction of the Arctic Committee of the Royal Society, and edited by T. Rupert Jones ; together with Instructions suggested by the Arctic Committee of the Royal Society for the use of the Expedition. 8° 1875

Report of Proceedings. Folio 1876

Papers and Correspondence relating to the Equipment and Fitting out of the Arctic Expedition of 1875, including Report of the Admiralty Arctic Committee. [Parly. Rep.] Folio 1875

Journals and Proceedings of the Arctic Expedition, 1875-76, under the Command of Capt. Sir George S. Nares, R.N., K.C.B. _Maps._ Folio 1877

Results derived from the Arctic Expedition, 1875-76. 1. Physical Observations by Capt. Sir Georges Nares and Capt. Feilden, &c. 2. Medical Report on the Eskimo Dog Disease, by Fleet-Surgeon B. Ninnis. _Plates._ Folio 1878

D. Dutch Expeditions.

Meteorologische Waarnemingen en Diepzeeloodingen gedaan aan Boord van "de Willem Barendsz," Kommandant A. de Bruijne in de Spitzbergen- en Barendszee in den zomer van 1878. _Coloured plate._ 4° _Utrecht,_ 1879
—— The same, in 1879 _Utrecht,_ 1880

De Verslagen omtrent den Tocht met de Willem Barents naar en in de Ijszee in den zomer van 1878, uitgebracht door A. de Bruijne, L. R. Koolemans-Beijnen, J. H. M. Speelman, C. P. Sluyter, en P. J. H. van Anrooy. [Bijblad No. 5, Aardrijksk. Genootschap.] 4°
Amsterdam and Utrecht, 1879
—— The same, en den zomer van 1879. [Bijblad, No. 6.] 4°
Amsterdam and Utrecht, 1880

Verslagen omtrent den vierden Tocht van de Willem Barents naar de Ijszee in den zomer van 1881, uitgebracht aan het Comité van uitvoering. _Maps and plates._ 8° _Haarlem,_ 1882

ARCTIC—D.

Dutch Expeditions —_continued._

Verslag van den vijfden Tocht van de Willem Barents naar de Noordelijke Ijszee in den zomer van 1882, nitgebracht aan het Bestuwo der Vereeniging Willem Barents. _Maps and plates._ 8° _Haarlem,_ 1883

Verslag van den Zesden Tocht van de Willem Barents naar de Noordelijke Ijszee in den zomer van 1883, uitgebracht van het Bestuwo der Vereeniging Willem Barents. _Charts and illustrations._ 8° _Haarlem,_ 1884

Verslag van den Zevenden Tocht van de Willem Barents naar de Noordelijke Ijszee in den zomer van 1884, &c. _Map and illustrations._ 8° _Haarlem,_ 1885

E. German Expeditions.

Die zweite deutsche Nordpolar-Expedition. Officielle Mittheilungen des Bremischen Comité's. _Plates._ 8° _Brunswick,_ 1870

Die zweite deutsche Nordpolarfahrt, 1869-70. _Map._ 8° _Berlin,_ 1871

F. Swedish Expedition.

Nordenskjöld's Voyage, 1878. _Map._ 8° 1879

G. International Polar Research.

International Polar Conference. Bericht über die Verhandlungen und die Ergebnisse der internationalen Polar-Konferenz, abgehalten in Hamburg in den Tagen vom 1 bis 5 October 1879. Rapport des Discussions et des Résolutions de la Conférence Polaire Internationale, tenue à Hambourg du 1er au 5me Octobre 1879. 4° _Hamburg,_ 1880
—— The same, der zweite internationalen Polar-Konferenz, abgehalten in Bern in den Tagen vom 7 bis 9 August 1880. Rapport sur les Actes et Resultats de la deuxième Conférence Polaire Internationale, tenue à Berne du 7 au 9 Août 1880. 4° _Hamburg,_ 1881
—— The same, der dritte internationalen Polar-Konferenz, abgehalten in St Petersburg in den Tagen vom 1 bis 6 August 1881. Rapport sur les Actes et Resultats de la troisième Conférence Polaire Internationale, tenue à St Petersbourg pendant les jours du 1er au 6 Août 1881. 4°[1881]
—— Protocols of the Proceedings of the Second Conference at Bern, from the 7th to 9th August 1880. [In German.] Folio _Berne,_ 1880
—— Mittheilungen der Internationalen Polar Commission. [_Ed._ H. Wild.] 7 parts. 4° _St Petersburg,_ 1882-91

Arctic—G.

International Observations, 1882-83.

Austrian. Bericht des Leiters der Oesterreichischen Arktischen Beobachtungs-Station auf Jan Mayen K. K. Linienschiffs-Lieutenant Emil Edler von Wohlgemuth. 8° *Pola,* 1883

—— Die Oesterreichische Polarstation Jan Mayen ausgerüstet durch Seine Excellencz Graf Hanns Wilczek geleitet von K. K. Corvetten-Capitän Emil Edlen von Wohlgemuth. Beobachtungs-Ergebnisse herausgegeben von der Kaiserlichen Akademie der Wissenschaften. 1 Band. *Maps and plates.* 4° *Vienna,* 1886

—— The same. 2. Band I. und II. Abtheil. *Plates and diagrams.* 4° *Vienna,* 1886

—— The same. 3. Band. *Plates.* 4° *Vienna,* 1886

[*British.*] Fort Rae. *Plates.* 4° 1886

Danish. Expédition Danoise, Observations faites à Godthaab sous la direction de Adam F. W. Paulsen. Publiées par l'Institut Météorologique de Danemark. Tome 1. Première liv. *Plates.* 4° *Copenhagen,* 1893

—— Tome 1. 2 livr. 1894
—— Tome 2. 1 livr. 1886
—— Tome 2. 2 livr. 1889

German. Die Beobachtungs-Ergebnisse der Deutschen Stationen. Band 1. Kingua-Fjord und die Meteorologischen Stationen II. Ordnung in Labrador ; Hebron, Okak, Nain, Zoar, Hoffenthal, Rama, sowie die Magnetischen Observatorien in Breslau und Göttingen. Band 2. Süd-Georgien und das Magnetische Observatorium der Kaiserlichen Marine in Wilhelmshaven. Herausgegeben im Auftrage der Deutschen Polar-Kommission von Prof. Dr Neumayer und Prof. Dr Börgen. *Maps, diagrams, &c.* 4° *Berlin,* 1886

—— Die Deutschen Expeditionen und ihre Ergebnisse. Band 1. Geschichtlicher Theil und in einem Anhange mehrere einzelne Abhandlungen physikalischen und sonstigen Inhalts ; herausgegeben im Auftrage der Deutschen Polar-Kommission von deren vorsitzendem Dr G. Neumayer. *Maps and plates.* Imperial 8° *Berlin,* 1891

Norwegian. Beobachtungs-Ergebnisse der Norwegischen Polarstation Bossekop in Alten. Im Auftrage des Königl. Norwegischen-Cultus- Ministeriums herausgegeben von Aksel S. Steen. *Plates.* 4° *Christiania* [1887-] 1888

Russian. Beobachtungen auf Nowaja Semlja. 1 Theil. Meteorologische Beobachtungen bearbeitet von K. Andrejeff. [In German and Russian.] *Maps and plates.* 4° 1891
—— 2 Theil 1886

Arctic—G.

International Observations—*contd.*

Russian. Beobachtungen der Russischen Polar-station an der Lenamündung. 2 Theil. Meteorologische Beobachtungen bearbeitet von A. Eigner : 1. Lieferung. Beobachtungen vom Jahre 1882-83. *Map and plates.* 4° 1886

—— The same. 2. Lieferung. Beobachtungen vom Jahre 1883-84. *Plates.* 4° 1887

Swedish. Observations faites au Cap Thordsen, Spitzberg, par l'Expédition Suedoise. Publiées par l'Académie Royale des Sciences de Suède. 2 vols. *Plates.* 4° *Stockholm,* 1887-92

United States. See Greeley.

H. Miscellaneous.

Vorstellungen des Norden, oder Bericht von einigen Nordländern, und absonderlich von dem so genannten Grünlande, &c. 8° *Hamburg,* 1675

Voyage to Davis Strait, by David Duncan, Master of the ship "Dundee." *Plate.* 8° 1827

Arctic Expeditions from England, from 1497 to 1833. *Map.* 8° 1834

Eskimaux and English Vocabulary for the use of the Arctic Expeditions. Published by Order of the Lords Commissioners of the Admiralty. 8° 1850

Greenland-Eskimo Vocabulary, for the use of the Arctic Expeditions. Published by Order of the Lords Commissioners of the Admiralty. 8° 1853

Arctic Rewards, and their Claimants. 1856

Petermann's Arctic Papers. 4° 8° *Gotha,* 1867-71

CONTENTS.

Spörer, J. Nowaja Semlä in geographischer, naturhistorischer und volkswirthschaftlicher Beziehung. *Maps* 1867

Petermann, A. Die Deutsche Nordpol-Expedition, 1868. *Map* 1868

—— Das neu entdeckte Polar-Land und die Expeditionen im Eismeere nördlich der Bering-Strasse von 1648-1867. *Map* 1869

Freeden, W. von. Die wissenschaftlichen Ergebnisse der ersten Deutschen Nordfahrt, 1868. *Map* 1869

Lindeman. Die Arktische Fischerei der Deutschen Seestädte, 1620 - 1868. *Maps* 1869

Payer, J. Die zweite Deutsche Nordpolar-Expedition, 1869-70 1871

Petermann, A. Instruktion für die zweite Deutsche Nordpolar-Expedition, 1869-70 1869

Arctic—H.

Petermann's Arctic Papers—*contd.*

Die zweite Deutsche Nordpolar-Expedition, 1869-70, Stand der Publikationen. Dr Pansch über das Klima, Pflanzen- und Thierleben auf Ostgrönland. Neue Expeditionen in 1871. Russische Nordpolar Expedition. Kapitän E. H. Johannesen's Umfahrung von Nowaja Semlä im September 1870. *Map* 1871

Th. v. Heuglin's Aufnahmen in Ost-Spitzbergen, 1870. *Map.*

Payer, J. Die zweite Deutsche Nordpolar-Expedition, 1869-70 (Schlittenreise an der Küste Grönlands nach Norden, 8 März, 27th April 1870, and Die Entdeckung des Kaiser Franz Josef-Fjordes in Ost-Grönland, Aug. 1870). *Map* 1871

Petermann, A. Die Erschliessung eines Theiles des Nördlichen Eismeeres durch die Fahrten und Beobachtungen der Norwegischen Seefahrer Torkildsen, Ulve, Mack, Qvale, und Nedrevaag im Karischen Meere, 1870. *Maps* 1871

Koldewey, K. Die erste Deutsche Nordpolar - Expedition im Jahre 1858 (preface by Petermann). *Maps and plate* 1871

Arctic Land Discoveries. (Newspaper Cuttings, 1867.) 8°

—— The same (from *Honolulu Advertiser*, 9th November 1867).

The Literature of the Polar Regions of the Earth, by Dr J. Chavanne, Dr A. Karpf, and F. Chevalier de Le Monnier. 8°   *Vienna*, 1878

Arctic Regions and Arctic Explorations. 12°.

Contributions to our Knowledge of the Meteorology of the Arctic Regions. Vol. 1. *Charts and diagram.* 4°   1885
—— The same. Part 5. 4°   1888

Arctic—II.

Extract of a Letter from an Officer in the Arctic Expedition. 8°   N. D.

I. Greenland.

Relation de Groenland. *Map and plates.* 8°   *Paris*, 1663

Kaladlit Assilialiait, or Woodcuts drawn and engraved by Greenlanders. 4°   *Godthaab*, 1860

Meddelelser om Grönland, udgivne af Commissionen for Ledelsen af der Geologiske og Geographiske Undersögelser i Grönland. Förste Hefte. *Maps and plates.* 8°   *Copenhagen*, 1879
—— The same. Andet Hefte. 8°   1881
—— The same. Tredie Hefte. 8°   1880
—— The same. Tredie Hefte. Fortsættelse. 8°   1887
—— The same. Fjerde Hefte. *Maps and plates.* 8°   1883
—— The same. Femte Hefte. *Maps and plate.* 8°   1883
—— The same. Tillæg til Femte Hefte. *Map and plates.* 4°   1883
—— The same. Sjette Hefte. *Maps and plates.* 8°   1883
—— The same. Ellevte Hefte. *Map.* 1887; and bound with Supplement, or Vol. 2. *Plate*   1891
—— The same. Trettende Hefte. 8° 1890
—— The same. Supplement, or Vol. 2.

ANTARCTIC.

Antarctic Discovery. A. Z.'s Letter to Royal Geographical Society. *Map.* 8°   N.D.

Report of the Committee of Physics, and Meteorology of the Royal Society, relative to the Observations to be made in the Antarctic Expedition and in the Magnetic Observatories. *Plates.* 8° 1840

GENERAL.

BIOGRAPHY.

Dictionaries.

Dictionary of National Biography. Edited by Leslie Stephen and Sidney Lee. Vols. 1-42. Abbadie—Owen. Large 8° 1885-95

Imperial Dictionary of Universal Biography : comprising a Series of Original Memoirs of Distinguished Men of all Ages and all Nations, by Writers of Eminence in the various branches of Literature, Science, and Art. 3 vols. *Portraits.* Imperial 8° *Glasgow*, N.D.

Biographie Universelle (Michaud). Ancienne et Moderne. Nouvelle edition. 45 vols. Large 8° *Paris*, 1854 *et seq.*

Miscellaneous.

Biography. The Lives of Dr Pocock, Dr Zachary Pearce, Dr Thomas Newton, and Rev. Philip Skelton. 2 vols. 8° 1816

Livingstone, Dr. MS. Address from the German Society for the Exploration of Equatorial Africa to the Royal Geographical Society on the occasion of the death of Dr Livingstone. Signed by A. Bastian and Dr Neumayer *Berlin*, 1874

Cook, Captain. Centenaire de la Mort de Cook, célébré le 14 Février 1879, à l'hôtel de la Société de Géographie. 8° *Paris*, 1879

Chevreul, Centenaire de M. Discours prononcés au Muséum d'Histoire Naturelle. 4° *Paris*, 1886

Yakhchitch, V. Jubilé Cinquantenaire de l'activité littéraire de Vladimir Yakhchitch. [In Russian] *Belgrade*, 1890

CATALOGUES.

A. Books.

Belgium.

Catalogue des Livres de la Bibliothèque de l'Acad. R. Belgique. Second partie (3e fasc. Nos. 10,908-15,545). Sciences, Morales, et Politiques, Beaux-Arts *Brussels*, 1890

France.

Catalogue Général de la Librairie Française depuis 1840, par O. Lorenz. Vols. 7-12. *Paris*, 1878-92

Ministère de la Guerre. Bibliothèque du Dépôt de la Guerre. Catalogue, Vols. 1-7. 8° *Paris*, 1883-90

Catalogues—*continued.*

Société d'Anthropologie de Paris. Catalogue de la Bibliothèque à la date du 31st Décembre 1890, 1ere Pte. and 2 Pte. *Paris*, 1891

Germany.

Academy of Naturalists. Katalog der Bibliothek der K. Leopoldinisch-Carolinischen Deutschen Akademie der Naturforscher. Lieferung 1-4. 8° *Halle*, 1887-93

Hamburg Commercial Library. Katalog der Commerz-Bibliothek in Hamburg, 1864 ; Erste Fortsetzung, 1864-67 ; Zweite Fortsetzung, 1868-71 ; Dritte Fortsetzung, 1872-78; Vierte Fortsetzung, 1879-85. 8° *Hamburg* [1864]-1886

Munich Royal Library. Catalogus Codicum Manuscriptorum Bibliothecae Regiæ Monacensis. Tomi primi, pars secunda, Codices Arabicos complectens. Die Arabischen Handschriften der K. Hof und Staatsbibliothek in München, beschrieben von Joseph Aumer. 8° *Munich*, 1866

—— Catalogus Codicum Latinorum Bibliothecæ Regiæ Monacensis (Halm, C., Laubmann, G., Meyer, G., Keinz, F., Thomas, G.) I. Parts 1 and 2. II. Parts 2, 3, and 4. IV. Part 1. 8° *Munich*, 1868-81

—— Verzeichniss der Orientalischen Handschriften der K. Hof und Staatsbibliothek in München, mit Ausschluss der Hebræischen, Arabischen und Persischen. Nebst Anhang zum Verzeichniss der Arabischen und Persischen Handschriften. 8° *Munich*, 1875

Uebersicht über die auf dem Gebiete der Geographie erschienenen Bücher,Aufsätze und Karten, 1871-85. [Extracted from the Zeitschrift der Ges. für Erdk.] 3 vols. 8°.

Greece.

Καταλογος των βιβλιων της Εθνικης Βιβλιοθηκης της Ελλαδος, τμημα δ', Γλωσσολογια. 4° *Athens*, 1891

Holland.

Catalogus der Bibliotheek van het Indisch Genootschap te 's Gravenhage. Door J. Boudewijnse. 8° *The Hague*, 1869

Catalogues—*continued.*

Italy.

Catalogo Ragionato delle più rare o più importanti opere Geografiche a Stampa che si Conservano nella Biblioteca del Collegio Romano, compilato da Carlo Castellani. 8°   *Rome*, 1876

Malta.

Catalogo dei Libri esistenti nella Publica Biblioteca de Malta. (Theology and Jurisprudence.) 8°   *Valletta*, 1843
—— Ditto. (History.) 8°   *Valletta*, 1844
Index Librorum Orientalium et Latinorum Publicæ Bibliothecæ Melitensis Ordine Alphabeti. 8°   *Malta*, 1857
Catalogue of English Books in the Public Library of Malta. 8°   *Valletta*, 1857
Catalogue Alphabetique des livres en langue Francais de la Bibliothèque de Malte. 8°   *Valletta*, 1857

Portugal.

Sociedade de Geographia de Lisboa, Catalogos e Indices. As Publicaçoes. Por L. Cordeiro. 8°   *Lisbon*, 1889
—— A Bibliotheca.   1. Obras Impressos. Por A. C. Borges de Figueiredo. 8°
                                           Lisbon, 1890
—— The same. Primeiro Annexo. 8°
                                           Lisbon, 1893
—— Catalogo dos Periodicos Politicos e Noticiosas e das Revistas Literarias e Scientificas. 16°   *Lisbon*, 1893
Ministerio da Marinha e Ultramar, Commissão de Cartographia. Relação de diversos Mappas, Cartas, Plantas, e Vistas pertencentes a este ministerio. Por Ernesto Julio de Carvalho e Vasconcellos. 1892. 8°   *Lisbon*, 1892

Russia.

Catalogue of the Library of the Russian Geographical Society. [In Russian.] Large 8°   *St Petersburg*, 1878
List of Publications of the Imperial Russian Geographical Society relating to Asia (from the Catalogue of the Society's Library). [In Russian.] 8°
                                      St Petersburg, N.D.

Sweden.

Sveriges Offentliga Bibliotek. Accessions-Katalogue, 1-8, 1886-93. 8°
                                       Stockholm, 1887-94

United Kingdom.

Admiralty. Catalogue of the Books in the Admiralty Library. 8°   1858
—— Catalogue of the Admiralty Library. By R. Thorburn. 4°   1875
Alpine Club, Catalogue of Books in the Library of the.   1888
America. A Catalogue of Books, relating principally to America, arranged under the years in which they were printed. 8°   1832

Catalogues—*continued.*

America. Bibliotheca Americana Nova, or a Catalogue of Books in various Languages, relating to America, printed since the year 1700. Compiled . . . by O. Rich.
8°   *London and New York*, 1835
British Museum. Catalogue of Printed Books in the British Museum. Vol. 1 1841
—— Librorum Impressorum qui in Museo Britannico adservantur Catalogues. Folio.
—— A Subject Index to the Modern Works added to the Library of the British Musenm in the years 1880-85. Compiled by G. K. Fortescue. 4°   1886
City Liberal Club, Catalogue of the Library of the. In two parts: Part I., Authors; Part II., Subjects. (Corrected to 21st August 1889.) Large 8°   1890
Corporation of the City of London, Catalogue of Hebraica and Judaica in the Library of the. With a Subject Index by the Rev. A. Löwy. Large 8°
                                                 1891
Foreign Office, Catalogue of Printed Books in the Library of the, 31st December 1885. Large 8°   1886
Geological Society. Catalogue of the Library of the Geological Society of London. Compiled under the direction of the Assistant Secretary by James Dallas. 8°   1881
India Office, Catalogue of the Library of the. Vol. 1, and Index. 8°   1888
Inst. Civil Engineers. Catalogue of the Library of the Institution of Civil Engineers, corrected to 1850. 8° 1851
—— Supplement to the 2nd edition, containing the Additions from 1st January 1866 to 31st October 1870. 8°   1870
London Catalogue of Books, with their Sizes, Prices, and Publishers; containing the Books published in London, and those altered in Size or Price, since 1814 to December 1834. 8°   1835
—— Published in Great Britain, 1831 to 1855   1855
—— The English Catalogue of Books. Compiled by Sampson Low. (The Old London Catalogue, together with the British Catalogue, are merged in this work.) 4 vols., 1835-89. 8°   1864-91
—— Indices to the above. 3 vols., 1837-80. 8°   1858-84
—— The English Catalogue of Books for 1890, 1891, and 1892   1893
London Library. Catalogue of the London Library, 12 St James's Square, S.W. . . . ; with Classified Index of Subjects. By Robert Harrison. 4th edition. Large 8°   1875
—— Supplemental Volume.   1875-80. Large 8°   1881
—— 5th edition. [With Appendix.] 2 vols. Large 8°   1888

Catalogues—*continued.*

Museum of Practical Geology. A Catalogue of the Library of the Museum of Practical Geology and Geological Survey. Compiled by Henry White and Thomas W. Newton. 8°   1878

Oriental Manuscripts, Catalogue of, purchased in Turkey. 4°   1830

Reference Catalogue of Current Literature, containing the Full Titles of Books now in Print and on Sale, with the Prices at which they may be obtained of all Booksellers, and an Index to nearly 30,000 Works. 8°   1877

Royal Society, Catalogue of the Scientific Books in the Library of the. Transactions—Journals—Observations and Reports—Surveys—Museums. 8°   1881
—— Catalogue of Scientific Papers. *See* Appendix 3.

Royal Asiatic Society, Catalogue of Printed Books in the Library of the. 4°   1830

Royal Colo:.ial Institute, Catalogue of the Library of the, to October 1881. 8°.
—— Ditto   1886

Royal Engineers, Catalogue of the Royal Engineer Corps Libraries (except Chatham and Dublin). Compiled by Lieut. J. J. Curling, and edited by Capt. C. E. Luard. Royal 8°   1876

Royal Geographical Society. *See* Transactions : Appendix 3.

Royal Institution. New Classified Catalogue of the Library of the Royal Institution of Great Britain ; with Indexes of Authors and Subjects, and a List of Historical Pamphlets chronologically arranged. 8°   1857
—— The same. By Benjamin Vincent. Vol. 2. Including the Additions from 1857 to 1882. 8°   1882

Royal Scottish Geographical Society: Catalogue of the Library, 31st March 1891   *Edinburgh,* 1891

Royal United Service Institution, Catalogue of the Library of the. 8°   1865

Statistical Society, Catalogue of the Library of the. Large 8°   1884
—— Index to the Subject-Matter of the Works contained in the Catalogue of the Statistical Society, completed to 31st December 1883. Large 8°   1886

War Office Library Catalogue Index. 8°   1868-69
—— Catalogue of Books in the Library of the War Office. 1st January 1878. Part 1. Nominal Order. 8°   1878
—— Ditto. 1st Jan. 1883. Part 2. Classification. 4°   1883

York Gate Library. Catalogue of the York Gate Geographical and Colonial Library. 2nd edition. Large 8° 1886

Catalogues—*continued.*

Zoological Society, Catalogues of the Library of the. 8°   1872 and 1880
—— Supplement, Additions to 30th August 1883. 8°   1883

China.

Catalogue of the Library of the North China Branch of the Royal Asiatic Society. By H. Cordier. 8°   *Shanghai,* 1872

India.

Classified Catalogue of English Books in the Shri Sayaji Library of Sampatrao K. Gaekad, Baroda. 8°   *Bombay,* 1891

Tasmania.

Catalogue of the Library of the Royal Society of Tasmania. 8° *Hobart,* 1885

United States.

Catalogue of the American Philosophical Society Library. Parts 2 and 3. Large 8°   *Philadelphia,* 1866, 1878

Catalogue of the American Library of the late Samuel Latham Mitchell Barlow. Prepared by James Osborne Wright. Large 8°   *New York,* 1889

British Guiana.

Catalogue of the Library of the Royal Agricultural Society of British Guiana. 8°   1868

B. Maps.

Austria.

Verzeichniss der Karten der K. K. Familien- Fideicommiss- Bibliothek. Large 4°   *Vienna,* 1882

France.

Catalogue Chronologique des Cartes, Plans, Vues de Côtes, Mémoires, Instructions Nautiques, &c., qui composent l'Hydrographie Française. 8°   1860

Russia.

Catalogue of the Geographical Depôt of the General Staff. 8° *St Petersburg,* 1865

Library of the Moscow Archives. List of Atlases, Maps, Plans, and Views of Battlefields. Drawn up in 1816 ; with Additions to 1877. 8°   *St Petersburg,* 1877

United Kingdom.

British Museum. Catalogue of Maps, Prints, Drawings, &c., Presented by King George IV. Folio   1829
—— Catalogue of the Printed Maps, Plans, and Charts in the British Museum. 2 vols. 4°   1885

Ordnance Survey. Catalogue of the Maps and Plans and other Publications of the Ordnance Survey of England and Wales, and the Isle of Man, to 1st January 1890. 8°   1890

CATALOGUES—B.

War Office. Catalogue of Maps in the Intelligence Division, War Office. Compiled in the Intelligence Division, War Office. 4 vols. 1890-91. Large folio.
—— Accessions, Jan. to June 1894.

List of Maps exhibited by Foreign Governments at the Paris Geographical Congress, selected as Specimens of Cartography for the Royal Geographical Society by Mr Galton and Major Wilson. MS. Small 4°   [1875]

Dutch East Indies.

Catalogus der Archeologische Verzameling van het Bataviaasch Genootschap van Kunsten en Wetenschappen. Door W. P. Groeneveldt. 8°   1887

India.

Catalogue of Maps, Plans, &c., of India and Burma, and other parts of Asia. Folio   1891

C. Miscellaneous.

France.

Catalogue des Portraits de Voyageurs et de Géographes qui se trouvent dans les albums de la Société de Géographie à la date du 22 Novembre 1885 *Paris*, 1885

United Kingdom.

British Association for the Advancement of Science. Catalogue of Stars. 4° 1845
British Museum. List of Additions made to the Collections in 1831-35. 5 vols. Royal 8°   1833-39
—— Guide to the Christy Collection of Prehistoric Antiquities and Ethnography. 12°   1868
Indian Gallery, Descriptive Catalogue of; containing Portraits, Landscapes, Costumes, &c., and Representations of the Manners and Customs of the North American Indians. Small 4°   1840
Indian Department in the International Exhibition, 1862, Classified and Descriptive Catalogue of. By J. Forbes Watson. Imperial 8°   1862
Museum, E. I. Co. A Catalogue of the Mammalia in the Museum of the Hon. East India Company. 8°   1851
—— A Catalogue of the Birds in ditto. By Thomas Horsfield and Frederic Moore. 2 vols. (in 1). 8°   1856-58
—— A Catalogue of the Lepidopterous Insects in ditto. By Thomas Horsfield and Frederic Moore. 2 vols. *Plates.* 8°   1857-59
S. Kensington Museum. Catalogue of the Objects of Indian Art exhibited in the South Kensington Museum. By H. H. Cole. *Map and plates.* 8°   1874
—— Catalogue of Persian Objects in the South Kensington Museum. 8° 1876

CATALOGUES—C.

S. Kensington Museum. Catalogue of the Educational Division of the South Kensington Museum. 9th edition. 8°   1876
—— Catalogue of the Special Loan Collection of Scientific Apparatus at the South Kensington Museum. 2nd and 3rd editions. 8°   1876-77

DICTIONARIES.

A. European Languages.

Greek. Dictionarium Græcum cum interpretatione Latina, omnium quæ hactenus impressa sunt, copiosissimum. Folio
                                         Venice, 1524
—— Schrevelius's Greek Lexicon, translated into English, with many new words added, and a copious English and Greek Lexicon. Edited by J. R. Major. 8°
                                                  1831
—— A Greek-English Lexicon. Compiled by Henry George Liddell, D.D., and Robert Scott, D.D. 7th edition. 4°
                                       Oxford, 1890
Danish. A New Pocket Dictionary of the English and Danish Languages. 12°
                                     Leipzig, 1875
Dutch. Nieuw volledig Nederlandsch-Engelsch en Engelsch - Nederlandsch Woordenhoek, door J. M. Calisch. 2 vols. 8°   *Tiel,* 1875
English. Dictionary of the English Language. By J. E. Worcester. 4°
                                 Boston, Mass., 1860
German. Dictionary of the English and German Languages. By Friedrich Köhler. 13th edition. 8°   *Leipzig,* 1875
French. The International English and French Dictionary. By L. Smith and H. Hamilton. New edition. Large 8°
                                        Paris, 1878
—— Dictionnaire International Français-Anglais. Par MM. H. Hamilton et E. Legros.   *Paris,* 1879
—— Royal Dictionary, English and French, and French and English, &c. By Professors Fleming and Tibbins. 2 vols. 4°   *Paris,* 1863-65
French-German : Technological. Dictionnaire Technologique, dans les langues Française, Anglaise, et Allemande, renfermant les termes techniques usités dans les Arts et Métiers et dans l'Industrie en général. 1st part, French, German, English, 1873; 2nd part, English, German, French, 1874 ; 3rd part, German, English, French, 1876. By A. and L. Tolhausen. 3 vols. 12°   *Leipzig*
Gaelic. Galic and English, and English and Galic Dictionary ; containing all the words in the Scotch and Irish Dialects of the Celtic, that could be collected from

Dictionaries, Gaelic—*continued.*

the voice and old Books and MSS.; and the most useful and necessary words in the English Language, explained by the correspondent words in the Galic. By the Rev. William Shaw. 2 vols. in I. 4° 1780

—— Dictionarium Scoto - Celticum: a Dictionary of the Gaelic Language, comprising an ample Vocabulary of Gaelic Words, with their Signification and various Meanings in English and Latin, and Vocabularies of Latin and English Words, with their Translation into Gaelic; to which is prefixed a Compendium of Gaelic Grammar. Compiled and published under the direction of the Highland Society of Scotland. 2 vols. 4° *Edinburgh*, 1828

Italian. A New Dictionary of the Italian and English Languages, based upon that of Baretti . . . Compiled by J. Davenport and G. Comelati. 2 vols. 8° 1873

Portuguese. *See* Canto, J. D. do.

Russian. Le Cellarius François, ou méthode tres facile pour apprendre sans peine et en peu de tems les mots les plus necessaires de la Langue Françoise, avec un Registre Alphabétique de Mots Russes. [French and Russian, and Russian only.] 8° *Moscow*, 1782

—— Nouveau Dictionaire de Poche Français-Russe et Russe-Français. Par A. Oldecop, revue . . . par X. Polévoï. *St Petersburg*, 1854

—— New Parallel Dictionaries of the Russian, French, German, and English Languages: First part, Russian, with Explanation in French, German, and English, 1876; Fourth part, English, with Explanation in Russian, French, and German. By C. P. Reiff. 3rd edition. 2 vols. Small 8°. *Carlsruhe*

—— New Pocket Dictionary of the English and Russian, and of the Russian and English Languages. 18° *Leipzig*, N.D.

Spanish. A Dictionary of the Spanish and English Languages (originally compiled by Neuman and Baretti), . . . By M. Seoane. New edition. 2 vols. 8° N.D.

Swedish. A New Pocket Dictionary of the English and Swedish Languages. 12° *Leipzig*, 1875

Turkish. English and Turkish Dictionary, in 2 parts, English and Turkish, and Turkish and English . . . By J. W. Redhouse. 8° 1856

—— *See* Barbier de Meynard; Kieffer.

B. Asiatic Languages.

Japanese. Dictionnaire Japonais-Français. . . . Traduit du dictionnaire Japonais-Portugais composé par les Missionnaires de la Compagnie de Jésus, et imprimé

Dictionaries, Japanese—*continued.*

en 1603 a Nangasaki . . . et revu sur la traduction Espagnole du même ouvrage rédigée par un Père Dominicain, et imprimée en 1630, a Manille, &c.; publié par Léon Pagés. 8° *Paris*, 1868

—— Japanese, English, French, and Dutch Vocabulary. Royal 8°

—— Japanese English and English-Japanese Dictionary. By J. C. Hepburn. 12° *New York*, 1873

—— English-Japanese Dictionary of the Spoken Language. By Ernest Mason Satow and Ishibashi Masa Kata. 2nd edition. 12° 1879

Nicobarese. A Dictionary of the Nancowry Dialect of the Nicobarese Language; in two parts, Nicobarese-English and English-Nicobarese. By the late F. A. de Roepstorff; edited by Mrs de Roepstorff. *Plate*. 8° *Calcutta*, 1884

Persian. A Concise Dictionary of the Persian Language. By E. H. Palmer. 12° 1877

C. African Languages.

Berber. Dictionnaire Français-Berbère; Dialecte écrit et parlé par les Kabaïles de la Division d'Alger. Royal 8° *Paris*, 1844

D. Australian Languages.

New Zealand. A Dictionary of the New Zealand Language; to which is added a Selection of Colloquial Sentences. By the Right Rev. William Williams, D.C.L. 3rd edition, with numerous Additions and Corrections, and an Introduction by the Venerable W. L. Williams, B.A. 8° 1871

Dictionaries, Biographical. *See* Biography.
Dictionaries, Geographical. *See* Gazetteer.

ENCYCLOPÆDIAS.

Encyclopédie Méthodique—
Mentelle, M. Géographie Ancienne. 3 vols. in 6. 4° *Paris*, 1787-92
Robert, M. M. Masson de Morvilliers, et M. Mentelle. Géographie Moderne, 3 vols. 4° *Paris*, 1782-88

Penny Cyclopædia of the Society for the Diffusion of Useful Knowledge. Vols. I.-XXVII. *Illustrated.* 4° *London*, 1833-43

Encyclopædia Britannica, or Dictionary of Arts, Sciences, and General Literature. 8th edition, with extensive improvements and additions, and numerous engravings. 8th edition. Vols. I.-XXI. *Illustrations.* Index to same. 4° *Edinburgh*, 1840-60

Encyclopædia Britannica—*contd.*

—— The .same. 9th edition. Vols. I.-XXIV. (and Index vol., with List of Contributors and Key to their Initials). 25 vols. *Maps, plates, and woodcuts.* 4° *Edinburgh,* 1875-89
—— Extra vol. of Geographical Articles from. 8th edition.

Cyclopædia, Imperial. Subdivision Cyclopædia of the British Empire. *Maps and plates.* Vol. 1, A to G. Royal 8°. ' Published by Charles Knight
1852

Encyclopædia Americana, The : a Supplemental Dictionary of Arts, Sciences, and General Literature, Illustrated. Vols. I.-IV. *Maps and woodcuts.* 4°
New York and Philadelphia, 1883-89

Chambers's Encyclopædia : a Dictionary of Universal Knowledge. New edition. Vols. I.-X. *Maps, plates, and woodcuts.* Royal 8° *Edinburgh,* 1888-95

GAZETTEERS AND GEOGRAPHICAL DICTIONARIES.

England's Gazetteer, Vol. 3 : being a New Index Villaris, or Alphabetical Register of the less-noted Villages, with their Distance or Bearing from the next Market-Town or well-known Place. 12° 1751

A New Geographical Dictionary : containing a full and accurate account of the several parts of the known World, as it is divided into Continents, Islands, Oceans, Seas, Rivers, Lakes, &c. The situation, extent, and boundaries of all the Empires, Kingdoms, States, Provinces, &c., in Europe, Asia, Africa, and America ; their Constitutions, Revenues, Forces, &c., &c. To which is prefixed an introductory dissertation explaining the Figure and Motion of the Earth, &c., &c. 2 vols. *Maps and plates.* Folio 1759-60

Compendious Geographical Dictionary, containing a Concise Description of the most Remarkable Places, Ancient and Modern, in Europe, Asia, Africa, and America, interspersed with Historical Anecdotes ; with a Chronological Table from the Creation to the Present Time, &c., and an Introduction exhibiting a View of the Newtonian System of the Planets, &c. *Maps.* 18° 1795

Historical Anecdotes, Tables of Population of England and Wales, Coins, Introduction on Newtonian System, &c. 3rd edition. *Maps.* 18° 1804

Gazetteers—*continued.*

Edinburgh Gazetteer, or Geographical Dictionary ; containing a Description of the various Countries, Kingdoms, States, Cities, Towns, Mountains, &c., of the World ; an Account of the Government, Customs, and Religion of the Inhabitants; the Boundaries and Natural Productions of each Country, &c. ; forming a complete body of Geography, Physical, Political, Statistical, and Commercial. 6 vols. 8° *Edinburgh,* 1822

Dictionnaire Géographique Universel, conténant la Description de tous les Lieux du Globe intéressans sous le Rapport de la Géographie Physique et Politique, de l'Histoire, de la Statistique, du Commerce, de l'Industrie, &c. Par une Société de Géographes. 10 vols. 8°
Paris, 1823-33

Parliamentary Gazetteer of England and Wales, adapted to the New Poor-Law, Franchise, Municipal, and Ecclesiastical arrangements, and compiled with a special reference to the Lines of Railroad and Canal Communication, as existing in 1840-43 ; with an Appendix, containing the results in detail of the Census of 1841. 4 vols. *Maps and plates.* 8° 1843

Gazetteer of the World, or Dictionary of Geographical Knowledge ; compiled from the most recent Authorities, and forming a Complete Body of Modern Geography, Physical, Political, Statistical, Historical, and Ethnographical. Edited by a Member of the Royal Geographical Society. 7 vols. *Maps, plates, and woodcuts.* Royal 8°. Published by A. Fullarton & Co.
Edinburgh, 1850-56

Cabinet Geographical Gazetteer : a Popular Exposition of the Countries of the World ; with Brief Notices of their History and Antiquities, from the Latest Authorities. By the Author of the "Cabinet Lawyer." *Map.* 12° 1853

Dictionnaire de Géographie Ancienne et Moderne à l'usage du Libraire et de l'Amateur de Livres. 4° *Paris,* 1870

Dictionar Geografic. Vols. I.-VIII. 1888-91. 8° *Iasi and Bucharest,* 1888-91
See Authors' Catalogue for separate contributors, viz. — Antonescu-Remusi, Chirita, Condrea, Condurateanu, Filipescu-Dubau, Lahovari, and Locusteanu.

GENERAL GEOGRAPHY.

Cosmographiæ Introductio ; cum quibusdam Geometriæ ac Astronomiæ Principiis ad eam rem necessariis. *Diagram and woodcuts.* 12° *Ingoldstadt,* 1529

General Geography—*continued.*

Atlas Geographus; or, A Compleat System of Geography, Ancient and Modern; containing what is of most use in Bleau, Varienius, Cellarius, Cluverius, Baudrand, Brietius, Sanson, &c., with the Discoveries and Improvements of the best Modern Authors to this time. 5 vols. *Maps* by Herman Moll, *and plates.*
4° 1711-17

The Compleat Geographer, or the Chorography and Topography of all the Known Parts of the Earth, to which is premis'd an Introduction to Geography, and a Natural History of the Earth and the Elements, &c. &c. 4th edition. *Maps and frontispiece.* Folio 1723

A Compendious Geographical and Historical Grammar, exhibiting a Brief Survey of the Terraqueous Globe . . . ; and also a Concise View of the Political History of the several Empires, Kingdoms, and States. *Maps.* 16° 1795

Critical Researches in Philology and Geography. 8° *Glasgow*, 1824

Collection of 16 vols. 8° and 2 vols. 4°, containing 202 Miscellaneous Articles on Geography and Allied Subjects, in Different Languages and of Various Dates, from 1835 to 1864.

Popular Statistics and Universal Geography: a Perpetual Companion to all the Almanacs, containing the Length, Breadth, Population, Chief Cities, Produce, Government, Revenue, Military and Naval Strength, Arts, Religion, &c., of every State in the World. *Map.*
12° 1835

Manual of Mathematical, Physical, Historical, and Descriptive Geography. 2 vols. *Illustrations.* 8° 1852-59
CONTENTS.

Vol. 1. O'Brien, Rev. M. Mathematical Geography.
Ansted, D. T. Physical Geography.
Jackson, J. R. Chartography.
Nicolay, Rev. C. G. Theory of Descriptive and Geographical Terminology.

Vol. 2. Bevan, Rev. W. L. Ancient Geography.
Nicolay, Rev. C. G. Maritime Discovery and Modern Geography.

Progressive Geography for Children. By the Author of "Stories for Children." 5th edition, revised. 12° 1856

Die Erde in Karten und Bildern. Hand Atlas in 63 Karten, nebst 125 bogen Text mit 1,000 illustrationen. Folio
Vienna, 1889

California State Series of School Text-Books: Advanced Geography. Compiled under the direction of the State Board of Education. *Maps and illustrations.* 4° *Sacramento* [1893]

INTERNATIONAL CONGRESSES.

African. *See* Africa : General.

Americanists. Congrès International des Américanistes. Compte - rendu de la Cinquième Session, Copenhague, 1883. *Plate, maps, and facsimiles.* 8°
Copenhagen, 1884
—— The same, de la Huitième Session tenue à Paris en 1890. 8° *Paris*, 1892

Anthropology. Int. Congress of Anthropology, Chicago. Address by the President. The "Nation as an Element in Anthropology." By Dr Daniel G. Brinton. (Reprinted from the Memoirs of the Congress.) 8° N.D.

Archæology, &c. Congrès International d'Archéologie et d'Anthropologie Préhistoriques. Deuxième Session, à Moscou, Août 1892. 2 vols. *Moscow*, 1893

Colonial. Institut Colonial International. Compte - Rendu des Séances tenues à Bruxelles, Mai 1894, précédé des Statuts et Règlement. 8° *Brussels*, 1894

Geodetic. Comptes Rendus, &c. *See* Switzerland : Appendix 3.

Geographical. Paris, 1875. Congrès International des Sciences Géographiques, Paris, 1875. Catalogue des Produits Exposés, 3rd and 5th editions. *Plans.* 8° *Paris*, 1875
—— Berichte über den Internationalen Geographischen Congres und die damit verbunbene Geographische Aufstellung zu Paris, 1875 *Vienna*, 1875
—— Compte rendu des Séances. 2 vols. *Maps and plates.* 8° *Paris*, 1878-80
—— **Venice,** 1881. Terzo Congresso Geografico Internazionale, Venezia, 1881. 8° *Rome*, 1881
—— The same. Vol. 2. *Maps and plates.* 8° *Rome*, 1884
—— The same. Note préliminaire sur le 2me volume des Actes du 3me Congrès International de Géographie. 8°
[*Rome*, 1884]
—— *See* Kreitner ; Wheeler, G. M.
—— **Paris,** 1889. IVe Congrès International des Sciences Géographiques á Paris en 1889. 2 vols. Compte rendu publié par le Secrétariat Général du Congrès. *Maps.* Large 8°
Paris, 1890-91
—— *See* France, A.
—— **Bern,** 1891. Compte rendu du Vme Congrès International des Sciences Géographiques tenu à Berne du 10 au 14 Août 1891. *Plans, &c.* 8° *Berne*, 1892
—— Catalogue de l'Exposition Internationaler Geographischer Kongress in Bern, 1891. Katalog der Ausstellung. *Plans.* 8° *Berne*, 1891

International Congresses—*continued.*

Geological. Congrès Géologique International, 4me Session, Londres, 1888. Études sur les Schistes Cristallins. *Profiles.* 8° 1888
—— Explications des Excursions. Rédigés par W. Topley, Secretaire Général du Congrès, avec la collaboration de E. Van den Broeck et J. Purves. *Maps, &c.* 8° 1888

Maritime. Maritime Conference held at Brussels for Devising a Uniform System of Meteorological Observations at Sea. 4° *Brussels,* 1853
—— International Marine Conference at Washington, Oct. to Dec. 1889. Summary of the Protocols and Final Act. Folio 1890

Meteorologic. *See* United States Hydrographic Office Publications, No. 94.

Polar. *See* Polar Regions, Arctic, G.

Prime Meridian, &c. International Conference held at Washington for Fixing a Prime Meridian and a Universal Day, October 1884. Protocols of the Proceedings. Large 8° *Washington,* 1884

Orientalists. Third International Congress of Orientalists, held at St Petersburg, August 1876. 8°.
—— Travaux de la Troisième Session du Congrès International des Orientalistes, St Pétersbourg, 1876. Vol. 2. *Plates.* 8° *St Petersburg and Leyden,* 1879
—— Verhandlungen des Fünften Internationalen Orientalisten Congresses gehalten zu Berlin im September 1881. Erster Theil, Bericht über die Verhandlungen. Zweiter Theil (in 2 vols.) Abhandlungen und Vorträge. 8° *Berlin,* 1881-82
—— *See* France: Publ. de l'École des Langues Orient. Viv.

Photography. Exposition Universelle de 1889. Congrès International de Photographie. Rapports et Documents, publiés par les soins de M. S. Pector, Secrétaire Général. *Illustrations.* 8° *Paris,* 1890

MISCELLANEOUS.

Highways. The General History of the Highways in all Parts of the World, more particularly in Great Britain. Small 8° 1712

Le Jardin des Racines Grecques, mises en vers François, &c. 12° *Paris,* 1719

Astronomy. Description and Use of a New Astronomical Instrument for taking Altitudes of the Sun and Stars at Sea, without an Horizon; together with an Easy and Sure Method of Observing the Eclipses of Jupiter's Satellites, with Tables. *Plate.* 4° 1735

Miscellaneous—*continued.*

Instructions for Travellers. Useful Instructions for Travellers: a Dissertation on the Most Common Accidents that may happen in Travelling, with the Means to be Used for Preventing Them. By an Experienced Traveller. 8° 1793

Ship-Building. Observations on Ship-Building. [First inserted on the Cover of the *European Magazine* for January 1795.] 8° 1795

Critical Researches in Philology and Geography. 8° *Glasgow,* 1824 [Reviews of Works by Lee and Noble on Persian and Arabic Grammar, &c.]

Directions for Collecting and Preserving Animals, addressed by the Board of Curators of the Museum of the Royal College of Surgeons in London. Small 4° 1835

Shipping. The Conservation of our Wooden Walls and Shipping against any Enemies whatever, Russian, French, Steamers, or Rockets. 8° 1837

Ethnology. A Manual of Ethnological Inquiry, being a Series of Questions concerning the Human Race, prepared by a Sub-Committee of the British Association for the Advancement of Science, 1851. 8° 1852

Cartography. Voorschrift ter Vervaardiging van Kaarten, vastgesteld bij Koninklijk Besluit van den 21e Junij 1856. Oblong 12° N.P.

Bible of Every Land, The. A History of the Sacred Scriptures in every Language and Dialect into which Translations have been made; illustrated by Specimen Portions in Native Characters; Series of Alphabets; Tables, Indexes, &c. *Coloured ethnographical maps.* 4° 1860

Account of Total Eclipse of the Sun, 18th August 1868, as Observed on Barram Point, N.W. Borneo. [Newspaper Cutting.] 8°.

Civil Engineers. The Education and Status of, in the United Kingdom and in Foreign Countries. Compiled from Documents supplied to the Council of the Institution of Civil Engineers, 1868 to 1870. 8° 1870

Languages, The Treasury of: a Rudimentary Dictionary of Universal Philology. Small 8° 1873

Anthropology. Notes and Queries on Anthropology, for the use of Travellers and Residents in Uncivilized Lands. [British Association Committee] 12° 1874

Numerical Language. International Correspondence by means of Numbers; an easy method whereby people of different nations may readily communicate with each other. 16° 1874

Miscellaneous—*continued*.

Times, The. A Reprint from *The Times*. The Annual Summaries for a Quarter of a Century. 12° 1876

—— *The Times* Register of Events in 1884. 8° 1885

Grumpel's Patent Rudder. Small 8° 1875

Round the World in 320 days, including Six Months of Inland Excursions. Programme of the First Voyage. *Plan and chart.* 12° 1877

The Tides. A Theory thereof. 8° 1883

Geographische Gesellschaften, Zeitschriften, Kongresse und Ausstellungen. I. Die Geographischen Gesellschaften, von H. Wichmann; II. Geographische Zeitschriften, von H. Wichmann; III. Geographische Kongresse und Austellungen, von H. Wagner. 12° *Gotha,* 1885

India Rubber, Gutta Percha, and Telegraph Works Company Limited. Soundings taken, 1885-87:—Havanakey West Expedition, 1885; Second West-African Expedition, 1885-86; Havanakey West Expedition, 1886; Congo Repairs Expedition, 1887. 8°.

Medical Guide. The Traveller's Medical Guide: a Brief Manual for Explorers, Missionaries, Colonists, and Ship Captains. By a Physician. 2nd edition. 12° 1888

On the Organisation of Science: being an Essay towards Systematisation. By a Free Lance. 12° 1892

Miscellaneous—*continued*.

Hints for Collecting Geographical Information. 8° N.D.

Société Ethnologique. Instruction Générale addressée aux Voyageurs. 8° N.P., N.D.

Société de Géographie. Questions et Instructions pour les Voyageurs. 8° *Paris,* N.D.

Directions for the Use of Berger's Patent Sphereometer. 8° N.D.

Un Mot touchant les Questions relatives à l'Enseignement Supérieur, et en Particulier l'Usage du Latin dans les Leçons Académiques. 8° N.D.

Illustrated Guide of the Orient Line of Steamers between England and Australia. *Maps, plans, and illustrations.* Oblong 4°

Handbook for the Weldon Range-finder. 8° N.D.

Urdu. An Urdu Translation of Mrs C. D. Francis' "Questions on the Order for Morning and Evening Prayer, and on the Litany." 12° N.D.

Addenda to Professor Rhys David's Translation of the Jàtakas, 1-40, to supply certain omissions. (Translated by T. B. Pànabokka.) 8° N.D.

Translations from the Pasi of Jàtakas, 41-50, by the Lord Bishop of Colombo. Small 8° N.D.

Oriental Languages, Translations from. *See* Asia, General.

3 C

APPENDIX III.

LIST OF PERIODICALS

INCLUDING

PROCEEDINGS AND TRANSACTIONS OF ACADEMIES AND SCIENTIFIC SOCIETIES.

COMPILED BY JAMES MURIE, M.D., LL.D.

APPENDIX III.

AFRICA.

ALGERIA.

ALGIERS.

Association Française pour l'Avancement des Sciences. Compte Rendu de la
10ᵉ Sess. *Maps and illustrations.* 8° *Algiers*, 1881 [*Paris*, 1882]
École Supérieure des Lettres d'Alger. Bulletin de Correspondance Africaine.
Ann. III., fasc. 2. Royal 8° *Algiers*, 1884
Annuaire d'Algerie. *See* Appendix 2 : Algeria.
Société Historique Algérienne. Revue Africaine : Journal des Travaux de la Société
Historique Algeriénne, par les Membres de la Société, et sous la Direction du
Président. Tom. VII., XI., XIII. 8° *Algiers*, 1863-69

CONSTANTINE.

Société de Géographie de Constantin. Bulletin Mensuel. Nos. 1-6 (Tom. I. , 1883.
Bull. Trimestriel 1. Jan.-Mars. 1884 ; et 1. 2. Jan.-Jul. 1885. 8°
Constantine, 1883-85

ORAN.

Société de Géographie et d'Archéologie de la Province d'Oran. Bulletin Trimestriel
de Géographie et d'Archéologie. Tom. I.-XI [imperfect set]. *Maps and plates.* 8°
Oran, 1878-91

CAPE COLONY.

CAPE TOWN.

South African Literary and Philosophical Institution, Report of the Meteorological
Committee of the. 8° *Cape Town*, 1836-37
[Continued as]
South African Philosophical Society, Transactions of the. Vols. I.-III., Sess.
1877-85. Small 8° (Vol. IV. wanting) *Cape Town*, 1880-84
—— Vol. V., VI., VII. (pt. 1), and VIII. (pt. 1), 1886 to 1892. *Plates.* Royal 8°
Cape Town, 1888-93
South African Quarterly Journal. Vol. I. (Nos. 1 and 2). 8° *Cape Town* [1829-30]
[For Articles contained, *see* Appendix 2 : British South Africa.]
University, Cape of Good Hope. Calendar for 1880. 12° *Cape Town*, 1880

PORT ELIZABETH.

Annual Reports of the Committee of the Port Elizabeth Chamber of Commerce. For 1891 and 1892 (27th and 28th Annual Reports). 8°
Port Elizabeth, 1892-93

EGYPT.

ALEXANDRIA.

Association Littéraire d'Égypte. Ægyptiaca Consociatio Litteraturæ. Miscellanea
Ægyptiaca. 1 Part. Super royal 8° *Alexandria*, 1842
Ville d'Alexandrie Municipalité. Rapport. *See* Appendix 2.

CAIRO.

Egyptian General Staff, Publications of the. *See* Egypt : Appendix 2.
Institut Égyptien. Bulletin, No. 12. (Année 1872-73.) 8° *Alexandria*, 1873
—— (Ser. 2.) Nos. 1-5. (Années 1880-84.) 8° *Cairo*, 1882-85
—— Statuts. 8° *Cairo*, 1885
Société Khédiviale de Géographie du Caire. Bulletin (Trimestrial) Ser. 1. Nos. 1-12.
2 vols. *Maps* 1876-81
—— Ser. 2. Nos. 1-12. 2 vols. *Maps and plates* 1881-88
—— Ser. 3. Nos. 1-12. 2 vols. *Maps and plates* 1888-93
—— Total. Tom. I.-VI. *Maps and plates.* 8° *Cairo*, 1876-93
[For Extra Bull. Biographie Mahmoud Pasha, *see* Egypt : Appendix 2.]
Sudan Almanac. *See* Appendix 2 : United Kingdom, War Office Publications.

BRITISH CENTRAL AFRICA.

BLANTYRE.

Nyasa News, The. No. 1. Aug. 1893. Small 4°   [*Blantyre, Nyasa Land*, 1893]

LIBERIA.

MONROVIA.

Liberia Herald. Vol. I.-III. [imperfect set]. Small 4° and folio   *Monrovia*, 1830-32
Liberia [Quarterly Bulletins], &c.   *See* under American Colonisation Society, Washington (D.C.), United States, *postea*.

PORTUGUESE EAST AFRICA.

MOÇAMBIQUE.

Sociedade de Geographiæ de Moçambique. Boletim, 1st Ser., Nos. 2-6. 8°
Moçambique, 1881

PORTUGUESE WEST AFRICA.

LOANDO.

Observatorio do Infante Don Luiz. Provincia de Angolo. Resumo Meteorol. &c., Magnet. Obs. &c. *See* Appendix 2 : Portug. W. Africa ; also St Thomas. *See* Appendix 2 : African Islands.
Sociedade Propagadora de Conhecimentos Geographico-Africanos. Sess. Julho 1881. (Recepção e Conferencia do Exmo. Sr. Lourenço Malheiro, Engenheiro de Minas.) [Pamph. 14 pp.] Small 8°   *Loando*, 1881

SENEGAL.

ST LOUIS.

Annales Sénégalaises. *See* Appendix 2.
Annuaire du Sénégal et Dépendances pour les années 1864 et 1865. Suivi d'une notice sur les Serrères par M. Pinet-Laprades et d'une étude sur leur langue par M. Faidherbe. 8° and 12°   *St Louis*, 1865

SOUTH AFRICAN REPUBLIC : TRANSVAAL.

JOHANNESBURG.

Witwatersrand Mining and Metallurgical Review. A Monthly Journal devoted to the Interests of the South African Gold Fields. Vols. I. and II. [imperfect, Nos. 3, 7-21]. *Plates.* Small 4°   *Johannesburg*, 1890-91

AFRICAN ISLANDS.

MADAGASCAR.

ANTANANARIVO.

Antananarivo Annual and Madagascar Magazine. (*Eds.* J. Sibree and R. Baron.) Vol. I.-V. [Vols 1, 2, and 5 imperfect]. *Maps and plates.* 8°
Antananarivo (*and London*), 1875-93
Madagascar News, The. Vols. I.-V. [an imperfect set]. 4° and folio
Antananarivo, 1890-94
Observatoire Royal de Madagascar. Observations Meteorologiques faites à Tananarive, par R. P. E. Colin, 1889 and 1890. Vols. I.-II. 8°   *Antananarivo*, 1890-91

MAURITIUS.

PORT LOUIS.

Meteorological Society of Mauritius, Proceedings and Transactions of the. Vols. V. and VI. (part ?) Sess. 1859-62. 8°   *Port Louis*, 1861-62
—— *See* Meldrum, C. : Author's Catalogue.
Société d'Histoire Naturelle de l'Ile Maurice. Rapport Annuel sur les Travaux de la Soc., par M. Julien Desjardins. 8°   *Port Louis*, 1835
——- Procès Verbaux, Oct. 1842 to Aout 1845. Small folio or 4°   *Port Louis*, 1846

AMERICA, NORTH.

DOMINION OF CANADA.

HALIFAX (NOVA SCOTIA).

Nova Scotian Institute of Science. Proceedings and Transactions, Sess. 1890-93.
Ser. 2., Vol. I., pts. 1-3. *Map and plate.* 8° *Halifax, N.S.*, 1891-93

HAMILTON (ONTARIO).

Hamilton Association (for the Cultivation of Literature, Science, and Art). Journal
and Proceedings. Vol. I. (pts. 1, 2), 1882-85. 8° *Hamilton (Ont.)*, 1884-85

MONTREAL (QUEBEC).

Canadian Record, The, &c. Vol. I. (No. 1). 8° *Montreal*, 1884
Canadian Naturalist. Summary, Contents. Ser. 1, 2 (Pamph.) 8° *Montreal* [N.D.]
Royal Society of Canada. Proceedings and Transactions. Vol. III.-XI., 1885-93.
Maps and plates. 4° *Montreal and Ottawa*, 1886-94
—— Mémoires et Comptes Rendus de la Soc. Roy. du Canada. [The French version
contained in the above volumes. The two sets, in English and French, are bound
together in the same volumes ; but with different title and pagination.]

OTTAWA.

Association of Dominion Land Surveyors. Proceedings (3rd Ann. Meeting, 1886).
Map. 8° *Ottawa*, 1886
Geological Survey of Canada, Publications of. *See* Appendix 2.
Institut Canadien-Français d'Ottawa, 1852-77. Celebration du 25e Anniversaire.
8° *Ottawa*, 1879
Statistical Year-Book of Canada, for 1890. (6th year.) 8° *Ottawa*, 1891

QUEBEC.

Geographical Society of Quebec, Constitution and By-Laws of the. 12° *Quebec*, 1878
—— Transactions. Bulletin de la Société de Géographie. Vols. I.-II. *Maps and plates.*
Royal 8° *Quebec and Joliette*, 1880-92
  Vol. I. contains Sessions 1880-89 } [as bound the Society's Vols. I., II. corre-
  „ II. „ „ 1889-92 } spond to Vol. I. opposite.]
Literary and Historical Society of Quebec, Transactions of the. Sessions 1824-28.
(Vol. I.) *Map and plates.* 8° *Quebec*, 1829
—— The same. Sessions 1882-83. [New Series ?] 8° *Quebec*, 1883

TORONTO (ONTARIO).

Canadian Journal: a Repertory of Industry, Science, and Art, and a Record of the
Proceedings of the Canadian Institute. Edited by Henry Youle Hind. *Maps and
plates.* 1852-54. Vols. I. and II. (bound in 1 vol.). 4° *Toronto*, 1853-54
  [Continued as]
Canadian Journal of Industry, Science, and Art; conducted by the Editing Com-
mittee of the Canadian Institute. New Series. Vols. I.-XI. *Maps and plates.* 8°
Toronto, 1856-68
  [Title altered to]
The Canadian Journal of Science, Literature, and History. Vols. XII.-XV.
Toronto, 1870-78
  Continued as]
Proceedings of the Canadian Institute. Third Series. Vols. I.-VII. *Plates.* 8°
Toronto, 1879-90
  [Continued as]
Transactions of the Canadian Institute. Fourth Series. Vols. I.-IV. (pt. 1), (1889-94).
Maps and plates. Royal 8° *Toronto*, 1891-94
Annual Reports of the Canadian Institute : being part of Appendix to the Report of
the Minister of Education, Ontario. Sess. 1886-87 to 1893-94. I.-VII. Ann. Reps.
Woodcuts. Royal 8° *Toronto*, 1888-94
Dominion Annual Register and Review, The. For the 17th and 18th year of the
Canadian Union, 1883 and 1884. Edited by Henry J. Morgan. 8° *Toronto*, 1884-85

WINNIPEG (MANITOBA).

Historical and Scientific Society of Manitoba, Transactions and Proceedings of the [Vol. I.], from its organisation in 1879 till the close of the Society's year 1888-89: being Trans. Nos. 1-34, and Annual Reports for the years 1880 to 1888. *Illustrations.* 8° *Winnipeg*, 1889
—— [Vol. II.] Trans. and Proc., No. 35-47, and Ann. Reps. 1889-93. *Maps and plates.* 8° *Winnipeg,* 1889-94
   [Each paper is issued in special wrapper, and with separate title-page and pagination.]

MEXICO.

MEXICO AND TACUBAYA.

Memoria del Ministerio de Fomento, de la Republica Mexicana. Años 1865,⁣1868-69, y 1873. 3 vols. *Maps and plates.* Royal 8° *Mexico,* 1866-73
   [Continued as]
Anales del Ministerio de Fomento, de la Republica Mexicana. 1877 y 1887. Tom. I., II., and VIII. *Maps and plates.* 8° *Mexico,* 1877-87
Observatorio Astronomico Nacional de Tacubaya. Boletin, Tom. I. 4° [*Mexico*] *Tacubaya,* 1890-93
—— Annuario, Años VI.-XIV. (A. Anguiano). *Plates.* 12° *Mexico,* 1885-93
Observatorio Meteorológico-Magnético Central de México. Boletin Mensual, Tom. I. (No. 6-12, Suppl., Resum. 1888, y Indice); II. and III. (No. 1-3). 4° *Mexico,* 1888-90
Sociedad Cientifica "Antonio Alzate." Memorias, Tom. III. and IV. (imperfect). *Maps and illustrations.* 8° *Mexico,* 1889-91
Sociedad Mexicana de Geografia y Estadistica. Boletin de la Soc., Tom. IX.-XI., XII. (Nos. 1 and 2). *Maps and plates.* 4° *Mexico,* 1863-66
—— 2ª Epoca (Ser. 2), Tom. I.-IV. (1 and 2 imperfect). 4° *Mexico,* 1869-72
—— 3ª Epoca (Ser. 3), Tom. I., II., and III. (imperfect); IV., V., and VI. (imperfect). Royal 8° *Mexico,* 1873-87
—— 4ª Epoca (Ser. 4), Tom. I. and II. (I. imperfect). 8° *Mexico,* 1888-93
   [*See* Arroyo, Orozco y Berra, and Padilla: Authors' Catalogue.]

UNITED STATES.

CALIFORNIA.

SACRAMENTO.

California State Mining Bureau. Annual Reports, 3rd, 4th, 7th, 11th. *Maps and plates.* 8° *Sacramento,* 1883-93

SAN FRANCISCO.

California Academy of Natural Sciences, Proceedings of the. Vols. I.-VII. (2 ed., 1854-57). *Maps and plates.* 8° *San Francisco,* 1858-77
—— 2 Ser. Vols. I.-IV. 8° [*See* Brooks, C. W.: Auth. Cat.] *San Francisco,* 1888-94
—— Memoirs presented to the. Vol. I. (pt. 1, 2), II. (No. 1, 2) [imperfect set]. *Plates.* Royal 4° *San Francisco,* 1868 and 1888
—— Bulletin. Vols. I., II. (1884-87). *Maps and plates.* 8° *San Francisco,* 1886-87
—— Occasional Papers. Vols. I.-IV. *Maps and plates.* 8° *San Francisco,* 1890-93
California Geological Survey, Publications of. *See* Appendix 2.
Geographical Society of California. Special Bulletin (*Calif. Illus. Mag.,* 1892). *Illustrations.* 8° [*See* T. C. Johnston: Authors' Catalogue.] *San Francisco,* 1892
—— Bulletin I. (pt. 1), II. *Maps and plates.* 8° *California,* 1893-94
Geographical Society of the Pacific. San Francisco. Transactions and Proceedings, Vols. I., II., III. [imperfect set]. *Maps.* 8° and Royal 8° *San Francisco,* 1881-92
   [*See* C. W. Brooks, Geo. Davidson, C. L. Hooper, and J. H. Slevin: Authors' Catalogue.]
—— Constitution and By-Laws of the [pamph., 21 pp.]. 12° *San Francisco,* 1881
Hutching's California Magazine. *See* Appendix 2, under Mexico.
Kosmos : an Eclectic Monthly Journal of Nature, Science, and Art. Vol. I. (Nos. 1-4.) 4° *San Francisco,* 1887
Sierra Club, The. Articles of Association, By-Laws, and List of Members [pamph. 20 pp.]. 12° *San Francisco,* 1892
—— Bulletin. Vol. I. (Nos. 1-9.) *Maps and illustrations.* 12° and 8° *San Francisco,* 1893-93

COLUMBIA, DISTRICT OF.

WASHINGTON, D.C.

American Colonization Society. Annual Reports of the Amer. Soc. for Colonizing the Free People of Colour of the United States (with Appendices). 6th to 14th Rep., 1823-31 ; 35th and 36th Rep., 1852-53; [77th and 78th Rep., 1894, *infra* "Liberia"]. *Map.* 8° *Washington, 1823-53*

[For Auxiliary Soc. of Pensylv., *see* Trans. Philadelphia. This is bound with the above, together as one vol.]

[The Amer. Coloniz. Soc. publs. continued as]

Liberia. [Quarterly Bulletins.] Bull. Nos. 3-6. *Map, plates, and portraits.* Royal 8° *Washington, 1893-94*

[Nos. 4 and 6 contain the 77th and 78th Ann. Rep. of Amer. Coloniz. Soc., *supra.*]

American Ephemeris and Nautical Almanac. For the years 1855 to 1896. 42 vols. Royal 8° *Washington, 1852-93*

See Authors' Catalogue, under Hill, G. W. ; Schubert, E. ; Todd, D. P. ; Peirce, B. ; and Winlock, J.

Anthropological Society of Washington (D.C.). Abstracts of Transactions for 1st and 2nd years, 1880-81. 1 vol. [150 pp.]. 8° *Washington, 1881*

—— Transactions. Vol. III. (1883-85). *Woodcuts.* 8° *Washington, 1885*

Bureau of American Republics. Bulletins, Nos. 2, 7, and 9, and Special Bull. [pamph.]. 3 vols. and part. *Maps, plates, and woodcuts.* 8° *Washington, 1891 and 1893* [*See* Appendix 2 : United States, I.]

Census Bulletin. For 1892-93. Nos. 193-376 (imperfect series). Small 4° *Washington, 1892-93*

—— Extra Census Bulletin. For 1892-94. Nos. 24-70 (imperfect series). 4° *Washington, 1892-94*

Geological Society of America, Bulletin of the. Vols. I., II. (4 odd parts). *Plates.* Royal 8° *Washington and Rochester, 1889-91* [*See* Authors' Catalogue: R. Bell, G. M. Dawson, W. M. Davis, and J. B. Tyrrell.]

Geographical and Geological Surveys, U.S.A., Annual Reports, Bulletins, &c., of. [*See* Appendix 2 : United States Surveys.]

National Geographic Magazine, The. Vols. I.-V. (1889-1893). *Maps and plates.* 8° *Washington, 1889-94*

National Institute for the Promotion of Science, Bulletin of the Proceedings of the, 1840-45. (3 parts.) *Plates.* 8° *Washington, 1841-45*

Naval Observatory Publications, Washington. *See* Appendix 2 : United States.

Smithsonian Institution, for the Increase and Diffusion of Knowledge among Men. Annual Reports of the Board of Regents of the Smithsonian Institution, showing the Operations, Expenditure, and Condition of the Institution. For 1853-92. 43 vols. *Plates and cuts.* 8° *Washington, 1854-93*

—— Bureau of Ethnology: J. W. Powell, Director. 15 Numbers. Separate Papers and Vols., viz., Bibliographies, N. Amer., Indian Languages, Mound Explor., Ohio, and others. 8° *Washington, 1887-93* [*See* Authors' Catalogue: Dorsey, J. O. ; Henshaw, H. W. ; Holmes, W. H. ; Pilling, J. C. ; and Thomas, C.]

—— Smithsonian Contributions to Knowledge. Vols. I.-XXIX. (27 and 29 imperfect). *Maps and plates.* 4° *Washington, 1848-92*

—— Smithsonian Miscellaneous Collections. Vols. I.-XXXVI. (Vol. 35 wanting). 8° *Washington, 1862-93*

—— List of Foreign Correspondents of the Smithsonian Institution, corrected to January 1882. 8° *Washington, 1882*

—— Check List of Publications. [Pamphlet.] 8° *Washington, 1890*

United States National Museum, Washington (D.C.), Bulletin of the.   Vols. I.-III.
(Nos. 1-16; [followed by Nos. 17-32 not in Library] and continued separate, Nos.
33-42).   *Plates.*   8°   *Washington,* 1875-92
   [Of this 8° series, the first sixteen numbers were reprinted in Vols. XIII. (Nos.
   1-10), XXIII. (Nos. 11-15), and XXIV. (No. 16) of "Miscellaneous Collec-
   tions of the Smithsonian Institution," and were distributed in this form to the
   Institutions and Libraries.   Afterwards from No. 17 onwards each number
   was printed in separate pamphlet form, and thus distributed.]
—— Proceedings of the.   Vol. I.-XV.   *Plates and text-figures.*   8°
                                                             Washington, 1878-92
   [Of this 8° series, Vols. I.-II. were reprinted in Vol. XIX., and Vols. III.-IV. in
   Vol. XXII. of the "Miscellaneous Collections of the Smithsonian Institution."
   From Vol. V. onwards they were printed as separate volumes.   Each article
   in the series has its special number, Nos. 1-1000 having been published up to
   1st August 1894.   Since beginning of Vol. XII. (No. 761), each paper, printed
   separately, has been distributed to specialists in advance of its vol.]
Weather Bureau.   Bulletins.   Nos. 1-6, 8, 11.   8°: and Monthly Weather Review.
   4 vols.   4°   *Washington,* 1891-93
   [For other Bureau Publications, *see* Appendix 2.]

CONNECTICUT.

MERIDEN (Conn.).

Meriden Scientific Association.   Transactions.   Vol. V.   *Plate.*   8°
                                                     Meriden, Conn., 1894

NEW HAVEN (Conn.).

Connecticut Academy of Arts and Sciences, Transactions of the.   Vols. I.-III.,
   IV. and V. (imperfect).   *Plates.*   8°   *New Haven,* 1866-80
American Journal of Science and Arts, The (Silliman's).   Ser. 1.   Vols. I.-XXXIX.
   Maps and plates.   8°   *New York and New Haven,* 1819-40
—— Ser. 2.   Vols. V., XIV.-XIX., XXI.-XXII., and XXIII. (imperfect), XXVII.-L.
   Plates.   8°   *New Haven,* 1848-70
—— Ser. 3.   Vols. I.-XLVII.   *Plates.*   8°   *New Haven,* 1871-93
—— General Index of Third Series.   For Vols. I. to X., bound up with Jour. Vol. X.
   8°.   *Philadelphia,* 1875.   For Vols. XXI. to XL., bound up with Vol. XL.   8°
                                                             New Haven, 1891

GEORGIA.

North Georgia Gazette.   *See* Appendix 2 : United States (K).

ILLINOIS.

CHICAGO.

Journal of Geology, The: a Semi-Quarterly Magazine of Geology and Related
   Sciences.   Vols I. and II.   *Maps and plates.*   Royal 8°   *Chicago,* 1893-94

IOWA.

DAVENPORT.

Davenport Academy of Natural Sciences, Proceedings of the.   Vol. I. (1867-76).
   Plates.   8°   *Davenport, Iowa,* 1876

MAINE.

BANGOR.

Travel (various numbers), with Index to "Travel."   Nos. 1-60 (pamph. 130 pp.)   8°.
   [Pub. by W. M. Griswold]   *Bangor, Maine* [N.D.]

MASSACHUSETTS.

BOSTON, Mass.

American Almanac, The, and Repository of Useful Knowledge.   For 1830-61 [1851
   missing], in 17 vols.   *Maps.*   12°   *Boston,* 1833-61
American Statistical Association, Publications of the.   New Series.   Nos. 1-3.
   Maps.   8°   *Boston,* 1888
Appalachia.   The Journal of the Appalachian Mountain Club.   Vol. I.-VII. (1876-93).
   Maps and plates.   8°   *Boston,* 1879-93

Boston Society of Natural History. Boston Journal of Natural History, containing Papers and Communications read to the Boston Society of Natural History. Vols. I.-VII. (1834-63). *Plates.* 8°   *Boston,* 1837-63
[Continued as]
—— Memoirs read before the Boston Society of Natural History ; being a new series of the Boston Journal of Natural History. Vols. I.-IV. (1852-92). *Plates.* 4°
                                                                                      Boston, 1866-93
—— Proceedings. Vols. I.-XXV. (1841-92). *Maps and plates.* 8°   *Boston,* 1844-92
—— Occasional Papers of the [by T. W. Harris, N. M. Hentz, and W. O. Crosby]. Vols. I.-IV. *Plates.* 8°   *Boston,* 1869-93
Boston University Year Book. Vol. XII. 8°   *Boston,* 1885
Records, Colony of New Plymouth. *See* N. B. Shurtleff : Authors' Catalogue.

CAMBRIDGE, Mass.

American Academy of Arts and Sciences, Memoirs of the.   New Ser., Vol. I.-XII. *Maps and plates.* 4°   *Cambridge and Boston,* 1833-93
—— Proceedings of the.   Vol. I.-VIII. (1846-73). *Plates.* 8°
                                                         Cambridge and Boston, Mass., 1848-73
—— New Ser., Vol. I.-XX. (1873-93). *Plates.* 8°   *Boston, Mass.,* 1874-93
American Board of Commissioners for Foreign Missions. The Missionary Herald, containing the Proceedings of the Amer. B. of C. for For. Miss., with a View of other Benevolent Operations. Vols. LXXVI.-XC. *Maps and illustrations.* 8° ·   *Cambridge and Boston,* 1890-94
—— Annual Reports.   70th to 83rd [71st and 81st missing].   8°   *Boston,* 1880-93
[*See* Means, J. O. : Authors' Catalogue.]
Harvard University Bulletin. (*Ed.* Justin Winsor). Vols. II. and III. (imperfect) and IV.-VII. 8°   *Cambridge, Mass.,* 1880-94
Science : an Illustrated Journal. Vols. I.-XXII. and XXIII. (Nos. 570-581). *Maps and plates.* 4° (2 sizes).   *Cambridge, Mass., and New York,* 1883-94

SALEM, Mass.

American Association for the Advancement of Science, Proceedings of the. 21 vols. *Maps and plates.* 8°   *Boston, Washington, Cambridge, and Salem,* 1849-82

2nd Meeting—Cambridge (Mass.), 1849			18th Meeting—Salem (Mass.), 1869		
4th	,,	New Haven (Conn.), 1850	19th	,,	Troy (N. York), 1870
9th	,,	Providence (R.I.), 1855	20th	,,	Indianopolis (Indiana), 1871
10th	,,	Albany (N. York), 1856	21st	,,	Dubuque (Iowa), 1872
11th	,,	Montreal (Canada), 1857	24th	,,	Detroit (Mich.), 1875
12th	,,	Baltimore (Maryland), 1858	25th	,,	Buffalo (N. York), 1876
13th	,,	Springfield (Mass.), 1859	26th	,,	Nashville (Tenn.), 1877
14th	,,	Newport (R.I.), 1860	27th	,,	St Louis (Missouri), 1878
15th }	{	Buffalo (N. York), 1866	29th	,,	Boston (Mass.), 1880
16th }	"	{ Burlington (Vermont), 1867	30th	,,	Cincinnati (Ohio), 1881
17th	,,	Chicago (Illinois), 1868	31st	,,	Montreal (Canada), 1882

American Naturalist : a Popular Illustrated Magazine of Natural History. (*Ed.* A. S. Packard, jun., and others).   Vols. I.-XVIII. (after Vol. XI., with addition of " Geography and Travels "). *Maps and plates.* 8°
                                                    Salem, Mass., Boston, and Philadelphia, 1868-94
Essex Institute, Proceedings of the.   Vol. IV.   1864, 1865. *Plates.* 8°
                                                                                      Salem, Mass., 1866
—— Bulletin of the.   Vols. I.-XXV. and XXVI. (Nos. 1-3).   1869-94. *Woodcuts.* (Vols. 9 and 10 wanting.) 8°   *Salem, Mass.,* 1870-94
—— Charter and By-Laws, and List of Members. (Pamphlet.) 8°   *Salem,* 1889
—— Rough Subject Index to the Publications of the E. Instit., viz.—Proceedings, Vols. I.-VI. ; Bulletin, Vols. I.-XXII. ; Historical Collections, Vols. I.-XXVII. (by G. M. Jones). [Pamphlet, 29 pp.] 8°   *Salem,* 1892
Peabody Academy of Sciences, Annual Report of the Trustees of the.   4th to 17th, and 19th Reps. 8°   *Salem, Mass.,* 1872-87
—— Memoirs.   Vol. I. (Nos. 2-6). *Plates.* Royal 8°   *Salem, Mass.,* 1871-81

WORCESTER, Mass.

Antiquarian Society. Archæologia Americana : Transactions and Collections of the American. *Maps.* Vols. I., II., and III., Part 1.
                                                         Worcester, Mass., and Cambridge, 1820-50

American Antiquarian Society, Proceedings of the.   New Ser.   Vols. II.-IV.
    1882-87.   Royal 8°   *Worcester, Mass.*, 1883-88
—— A Partial Index to the Proc. of the Amer. Antiq. Soc., from the foundation in 1812
    to 1890 (by S. Salisbury and Nat. Paine).   Royal 8°   *Worcester, Mass.*, 1883
Worcester Magazine and Historical Journal.   Vols. I. and II., Oct. 1825 to Oct.
    1826.   8°   *Worcester, Mass.*, 1826

MICHIGAN.
HOUGHTON.

Michigan Mining School, Catalogue of the, for 1892-94.   *Maps and plates.*   Small
    8vo   *Houghton, Mich.*, 1894

MINNESOTA.
MINNEAPOLIS AND ST PAUL.

Geological and Natural History Survey of Minnesota.   [For Annual Reports,
    Bulletins, &c., *see* Appendix 2 : United States, Minnesota.]

MISSOURI.
ST LOUIS.

Academy of Science of St Louis, Transactions of the.   Vols. I.-VI. (1856-94).   *Maps
    and plates.*   8°.   [*See* Appendix 2 : United States (J.)]   *St Louis*, 1860-94
—— Charter and By-Laws (pamph.).   8°   *St Louis*, 1890
Missouri Geological Survey.   *See* Appendix 2 : United States.
Missouri Historical Society.   Publications, Nos. 4-7.   *Plate and cuts.*   8°
                                                                        St Louis, 1880-83
Western Journal, of Agriculture, Manufactures, Mechanic Arts, Internal Improvement,
    Commerce, and General Literature.   (*Eds.* M. Tarver and T. F. Risk.)   Vol. II.
    (No. 14).   8°   *St Louis*, 1849

NEBRASKA.
LINCOLN.

University of Nebraska.   University Studies, published by the.   Vol. I. (No. 1).   8°
                                                                    Lincoln, Nebraska, 1888

NEW JERSEY.
VINELAND, N.J.

African News, The.   Bishop Taylor's Magazine.   Vols. II. and III. (both imperfect).
    Map and illustrations.   8°   *Vineland, N.J.*, 1890-91
    [Continued as]—
The African.   (*Ed.* C. E. Welch).   New Series, Nos. 1-3.   8°   *Vineland, N.J.*, 1891

NEW YORK.
ALBANY, N.Y.

American Institute of the City of New York.   Annual Report, 1871-72.   *Plates.*   8°
                                                                            Albany, 1872
New York State Agricultural Society.   Transactions of the.   (With an Abstract
    of the Proceedings of the County Agricultural Societies.)   Vols. XIII., XV.-XXI.,
    XXIII., XXVII. (2 vols.), and XXXI.—in all 12 vols.   *Maps and plates.*   8°
                                                                        Albany, 1854-73
Survey of the State of New York, Reports of the Geologists.   4 vols., 1837, 1838,
    1839, and 1840.   *Woodcuts.*   8°   *Albany*, 1838-40
—— Topographical Survey—viz., On the Adirondack Wilderness of New York.   Reports
    for 1872, 1873, and 1891.   *Maps and plates.*   8°   *Albany*, 1873-91
——— Reports of the New York State Survey for 1876 to 1883.   (8 Reports.)   *Maps and
    plates.*   8°.   [*See also* Appendix 2 : United States (K.)   *Albany*, 1877-84
University of the State of New York.   New York State Library.   Annual Reports,
    74th, 75th, and 76th, for 1891, 1892, and 1893.   *Plates.*   8°   *Albany*, 1893-94
—— State Library Bulletin.   4 Numbers.   Royal 8   *Albany*, 1891-94

BUFFALO, N.Y.

Buffalo Historical Society.   Annual Reports, 1885-93.   (5 Reps., imperfect Ser.)
    Plate.   8°   *Buffalo*, 1885-94

NEW YORK.

American Ethnological Society. Constitution and List of Officers (pamph. 4 pp.)
8° *New York*, 1878
—— Transactions of the. Vols. I., II., and III., Part 1. *Maps and plates.* 8°
New York, 1845-53
American Geographical [and Statistical] Society of New York, Bulletin of the.
1852-57, 1873-77. Bound in 4 vols. *Maps and plates.* 8° *New York*, 1852-77
—— Journal of the Geographical and Statistical Society. Vols. I. and II. (1859-70);
continued as Annual Report of the American Geographical Society of New York
(Vol. III.) for 1870-71 (Albany, 1872); and as Journal (Vol. IV. to XXVI.),
1873-94. *Maps and plates.* 8° *New York*, 1859-94
—— Proceedings of the. Sess. 1862-63, 1863-64, and 1864-65, viz., 3 years, bound in
1 vol. *Maps and plates.* 8° *New York*, 1862-65
—— Statement of the Objects and Organisation of the. With a Copy of its Charter,
By-Laws, &c. [Pamph.] 8° *New York*, 1856
—— Report of the Committee on Recent Discoveries, and Publications on Sub-Oceanic
Geography, Jan. 1857. 8° *New York*, 1857
—— Annual Report of the Council and Officers (Geographical and Statistical Society),
with Appendix, for 1857. 8° *New York*, 1858
[The above Society, originally Amer. Geogr. and Statist. Soc., founded 1854,
about 1870 changed its title to Amer. Geogr. Soc. of New York, but continued
to use the old seal to 1878.]
American Oriental Society, Journal of the. Vols. I. (Nos. 1 and 3), II.-V. *Maps.*
8° *New York and Boston*, 1843-56
Cooper Union for the Advancement of Science and Art, Annual Report of the
Trustees of the. 29th Report, 1888. [Pamph.] 8° *New York*, 1888
Goldthwaite's Geographical Magazine. Vols. I.-V. *Maps and plates.* Royal 8°
New York, 1891-93
Historical Magazine, and Notes and Queries concerning the Antiquities, History, and
Biography of America. Vol. III. (Nos. 1-8). Small 4° *New York*, 1859
Linnæan Society of New York, Abstract of the Proceedings of the. 1888-89, 1890,
1892-93, 1893-94 [Nos. 1, 2, 5, and 6]. 8° *New York*, 1889-94
—— Transactions. Vols. I.-II. *Plates.* Royal 8° *New York*, 1882-84
Lyceum of Natural History of New York, Annals of the. Vol. IV. (Nos. 5-12)
and V. *Plates.* 8° *New York*, 1846-52
New York Historical Society, Collections of the. Second Series. Vol. I. *Maps
and plates.* 8° *New York*, 1841
—— Proceedings of the. 1844-45. 8° [Bound in 1 vol.] *New York*, 1845-46
—— An Address delivered before the N.Y. Hist. Soc. at its 40th Anniversary.
By John Romeyn Bromhead. 8° [Bound up with Proc., 1844-45.] *New York*, 1844

OHIO.

CINCINNATI.

Cincinnati Society of Natural History, Journal of the. Vol. I. (Nos. 1 and 2), III.
(No. 1), and XI. (No. 4). *Plates.* 8° *Cincinnati*, 1878-89

PENNSYLVANIA.

PHILADELPHIA.

Academy of Natural Sciences of Philadelphia, Proceedings of the, 1859 to 1893.
(Bound in 33 vols.) *Plates.* 8° *Philadelphia*, 1860-93
American Philosophical Society for Promoting Useful Knowledge, Laws and
Regulations of the, together with the Charter of the Society. 8° *Philadelphia*, 1860
—— Early Proceedings, from the Manuscript Minutes of its Meetings from 1744 to 1838.
1 vol. *Plates.* 8° *Philadelphia*, 1884
—— Proceedings. Vols. I.-XXXI., 1838-93. *Maps and Plates.* 8° *Philadelphia*, 1840-93
—— Transactions. New Series. Vols. I.-XVI. and XVIII. (Pt. 1). *Maps and plates.*
4° *Philadelphia*, 1818-93
Franklin Institute of the State of Pennsylvania, Journal of the. Total number of
vols. 134, viz.—
(*New.*) Ser. 2. Vols. I.-XXVI. *Plates and cuts.* 8° *Philadelphia*, 1828-40
,, Ser. 3. Vols. I.-CVII. *Maps and plates.* 8° *Philadelphia*, 1841-93

Geographical Club of Philadelphia. Bulletin. Vol. I. *Maps and plates.* 8°
Philadelphia, 1893-94
—— Charter, By-Laws, and List of Members. [Pamph.] 8°   *Philadelphia*, 1894
Geological Society of Pennsylvania, Transactions of the. Vol. I. (Part I). *Plates.*
8°   *Philadelphia*, 1834
Numismatic and Antiquarian Society of Philadelphia, Report of the Proceedings of
the, 1887-89. *Plates.* 8°   *Philadelphia*, 1891
Pennsylvania Colonization Society. Reports of the Board of Managers of the Penns.
Col. Soc.; with an Introduction and Appendix (pamph. 48 pp.) 8°
Philadelphia (and London), 1831
[This Auxiliary State Soc. of Pennsyl. was connected with the Amer. Coloniz.
Soc. *See* Trans., Washington. It is bound up with vol. of same.]
University of Pennsylvania, Contributions from the Botanical Laboratory of. Vol. I.
(No. 2). *Plates and map.* Royal 8°   *Philadelphia*, 1893
Wagner Free Institute of Science of Philadelphia. Transactions. Vol. I. *Plates.*
Royal 8°   *Philadelphia*, 1887

TEXAS.

AUSTIN.

Texas Academy of Science. Transactions. Vol. I. (Nos. 1 and 2). Royal 8°
Austin, 1892-93

VIRGINIA.

BALTIMORE.

John Hopkin's University, Publications of.
—— J. H. U. Circulars published with the approbation of the Board of Trustees.
Vols. XII. and XIII. 4°   *Baltimore*, 1893-94
—— J. H. U. Studies. Ser. IV. (No. 6), X. (No. 12), XI.-XII. 8° *Baltimore*, 1892-94

WISCONSIN.

MADISON, MILWAUKIE.

Geological Survey of the State of Wisconsin. Annual Report, 1856. (2nd Report.)
J. G. Percival. 8°   *Madison*, 1856
[For Annual Reports 1873, '74, '75, *see* "Geol. of Wisconsin," *infra*, Vol. II., 1877,
pp. 5-89.]
—— Geology of Wisconsin : Survey of, 1873-79. By T. C. Chamberlin and others. Vols.
I.-IV. *Sketch-map and plates.* Royal 8°   [*Madison (Beloit)*], 1877-83
—— Atlas of 45 plates. Elephant folio   *Milwaukee, Wis.*, 1882
State Historical Society of Wisconsin, First and Second Annual Reports and Col-
lections of the, for the years 1854 and 1855. Vols. I., II. 8°   *Madison*, 1855-56
Wisconsin Academy of Sciences, Arts, and Letters, Transactions of the. Vol. VII.
(1883-87). *Plates and cuts.* 8°   *Madison (Wis.)*, 1889

AMERICA, CENTRAL.

COSTA RICA.

SAN JOSE.

Instituto Fisico-Geografico y del Museo Nacional de Costa Rico. Boletin
trimestral del Instituto Meteorologico Nacional, Nos. 1-4, 1888. Tom. I., de los
Anales del Inst. Fis. Geogr. Nacion. Royal 4°   *San Jose*, 1888-89
[Continued as]—
—— Anales, del Instituto Fisico-Geografico y del Mus. Nacion de Costa Rica. Tom.
II., III., and IV., 1889-91. *Maps and plates.* Royal 4°   *San Jose*, 1890-93

GUATEMALA.

GUATEMALA.

Anales Estadisticos de Guatemala. *See* Appendix 2.
Sociedad Guatemalteca de Ciencias. Revista Mensual. Tom. I.-II. (imperfect). 8°
Guatemala, 1893-94

HONDURAS.

TEGUCIGALPA.

Republica de Honduras. Primer Anuario Estadistico correspondiente al año de 1889. Con *illustraciones.* Por Antinio R. Vallejo. Royal 4° *Tegucigalpa*, 1893

WEST INDIES.

JAMAICA.

Institute of Jamaica, Journal of the. Vol. I. (No. 4). *Plates.* Royal 8°
Kingston, Jamaica, 1892

SAN DOMINGO.

Resena General. *See* J. R. Abad : Authors' Catalogue.

AMERICA, SOUTH.

ARGENTINE REPUBLIC.

BUENOS AYRES AND CORDOBA.

Academia Nacional de Ciencias de la Republica Argentina en Cordoba. Actas. Tom. II. (pt. 1), IV. (pt. 1), V. (pts. 1-3). *Plates.* Royal 4° *Buenos Ayres*, 1882-86
—— Boletin. Tom. III.-XII. and XIII. (Entrega 1). *Maps and plates.* Small and royal 8° *Cordoba and Buenos Ayres*, 1881-89
—— Indice de los Tomos I. and X. [as Append. to Vol. 10].
Anuario Bibliográfica de la República Argentina. Año II.-V., VII.-IX. (1880-87). 12° *Buenos Ayres*, 1881-88
Estadistica Municipal de la Ciudad de Buenos Aires, Boletin Mensual de. Año (I.) 1887, 1888, and 1889. *Plates, plans, &c.* Royal 8° *Buenos Ayres*, 1887-90
—— Boletin Trimestral de. Año 1890 (2 parts). Royal 8° *Buenos Ayres*, 1890
[Continued as]—
—— Anuario Estadistico de. Años I.-II. (1891 and 1892). Royal 8°
Buenos Ayres, 1892-93
Instituto Geografica Argentina. (Publicado bajo la Direccion do su Presidente, D. E. S. Zeballos ; L. A. Huergo ; A. Sorondo.) Boletin del. Tom. I. (II., IV., and V. imperfect), VI.-XIV. *Maps and plates.* Royal 8° *Buenos Ayres*, 1879-93
Museo Público de Buenos Aires. Anales del (por German Burmeister). Vols. I.-III. *Plates.* Royal 4° *Buenos Ayres*, 1864-93
Oficina Meteorologica Argentina, Anales de la. Tom. VII. and VIII. (G. G. Davis.) 4° *Buenos Ayres*, 1889-90
—— Ligeros Apuntes sobre el Clima de la Republica Argentina. (G. G. Davis.) *Maps and plates.* 4° *Buenos Ayres*, 1889
Revista Argentina de Historia Natural. (Publicacion Bimestral dirijida por Florentino Ameghino.) Tom. I. *Woodcuts.* 8° *Buenos Ayres*, 1891
Revista del Centro Boliviano, Geografia Colonizacion, Ciencias. Tom. I. (Entregas 3-6 and 9). Royal 8° *Buenos Ayres*, 1886-92
Sociedad Científica Argentina, Anales de la. Tom. VIII., Entrega 2. 8°
Buenos Ayres, 1879
Sociedad Geográfica Argentina (D. Ramon Lista), Revista de la. Tom. I. (Entregas 3-5). *Map.* Royal 8° *Buenos Ayres*, 1881-82
Sociedad Rural Argentina. Bases y Reglamento. 16° *Buenos Ayres*, 1866
—— Anales. Vol. I. (No. 12). 4° *Buenos Ayres*, 1867

LA PLATA.

Museo de la Plata. Materiales para la Historia Fisica y Moral del Continente Sud-Americano. (Dir. Francisco P. Moreno.) Anales del Museo. Entregas 1, 2. *Map and plates.* Folio *La Plata*, 1892
—— Revista del Museo. Tom. I.-IV. *Maps and plates.* Small 4° *La Plata*, 1890-93

BOLIVIA.

LA PAZ.

Sociedad Geografica de la Paz. Boletin. "Numero I., 16 Julie de 1889," pp. 1-10. 12° *La Paz*, 1889

BRITISH GUIANA.

GEORGETOWN (*Demerara*).

Institute of Mines and Forests [of British Guiana]. Report of the Secretary, for
    year ending 1892. 12°   *Georgetown,* 1892
Timehri, being the Journal of the Royal Agricultural and Commercial Society of British
    Guiana. Vols. I.-V. *Plates.* 8°   *Demerara,* 1882-86
—— New Ser. Vols. I.-VIII. *Plates.* 8°   *Demerara,* 1887-94
—— [*See* Roy. Agric. and Com. Soc. Brit. Guiana.   Under London, *postea.*]

BRAZIL.

CEARA (*or Fortaleza*).
Instituto do Ceará. Revista Trimensal do. Tomo V. (4 Trimest.), VIII. (3, 4 Trimest).
    8°   *Fortaleza [or Ceara],* 1891-94
PERNAMBUCO (*or Recife*).
Instituto Archeologico e Geographico Pernambucano. Revista. Nos. 41 and 42.
    Square 8°   *Recife [or Pernambuco],* 1891
RIO DE JANEIRO.
Estatistica do Commercio Maritimo do Brazil (1872-73). Tom. II., III., V. 8°
                                                            Rio de Janeiro, 1881-84
Instituto Historico, Geographico, e Ethnographico do Brazil. Revista Trimensal,
    Tom. XLIV. (pt. 1), XLVI., XLIX.
    [Title changed to]—
Instituto Historico e Geographico Brazileiro. Tom. LII. (pt. 2), LIII.-LV.
    and LVI. (pt. 1). 8°   *Rio de Janeiro,* 1881-93
—— Homenagem do Inst., &c. . . . Sessão extraordinaria em commemoraçao do
    fallecimento de S.M.O. Snr. D. Pedro II. celebrada a 4 de Março de 1892. *Plate.*
    [Pamph.] 8°   *Rio de Janeiro,* 1892
L'Observatoire Imperial de Rio de Janeiro. Annales de ——. Tom. I.-II. *Plates*
    and illustrations. 4°   *Rio de Janeiro,* 1882-83
—— Bulletin Astronomique et Météorologique de, 1881-82-83. *Plates.* Royal 4°
                                                            Rio de Janeiro, 1882-83
—— Revista do Observatorio (Publicação Mensal). No. 2. Anno III. Royal 8°
                                                            Rio de Janeiro, 1888
Museu Nacional do Rio de Janeiro. Archivos. Vols. I. (Trimestres 1-3), VII., and
    VIII. *Plates.* 4°   *Rio de Janeiro,* 1876-92
Secção da Sociedade de Geographia de Lisboa no Brazil. Revista Mensal.
    Tom. I.-III. (imperfect). 8°   *Rio de Janeiro,* 1881-85
—— Revista. 2 Ser. 1885-86. Nos. 1-4. 8°   *Rio de Janeiro,* 1885-86
Sociedade de Geographia do Rio de Janeiro. Boletim. Tom. I. 8°
                                                            Rio de Janeiro, 1885
—— Revista (Boletin). Tom. II., III., VII. (complete), and IV., V., VI., VIII.,
    and IX. (imperfect). *Maps.* 8°   *Rio de Janeiro,* 1886-93

SAN PAULO.
Commissão Geographica e Geologica da Provincia de S. Paulo. Boletim. Nos.
    1-9 and extra Nos. 8*a*, 8*b*. *Maps and plates.* 8°   *S. Paulo,* 1889-93

CHILE.

SANTIAGO.
Anuario Hidrográfico, de la Marina de Chile. Anos I.-VIII., XV., and XVI. *Maps*
    and plates. 4°   *Santiago,* 1875-92
Deutschen Wissenschaftlichen Verein zu Santiago. Verhandlungen. Vols. I.-II.
    Maps and plates. 8°   *Santiago, Valparaiso, and Valdivia,* 1886-93
La Libertad. Nos. 5, 12, 26, 27 de Enero de 1868. [Each number contains a geo-
    graphical article.] Folio   *Santiago,* 1868
Observatorio Astronomico de Santiago and Oficina Cent. Meteorol. *See* J. I.
    Vergara : Authors' Catalogue.
Oficina Central de Estadistica en Santiago. Anuario Estadistico de la Republica
    de Chile, correspondiente a los años 1860-64, 1877-78, 1883-85. Tom. II., IV., VI.,
    XX., and XXIV. Royal 4°   *Santiago and Valparaiso,* 1861-90

CHILE.

SANTIAGO—*continued*.

Revista de la Direcçión de Obras Públicas de Chile. Memorias é Informes sobre construcçiones Civiles Ferrocarriles, Arquitectura, Minas, Industria, y Geografía. (*Ed.* Francisco J. San Román.) Año I. No. 1-3. *Maps.* Royal 8° *Santiago*, 1890

Sinopsis Estadístico y Geographica de Chile. Anos 1880-81, 1885, 1886, 1892-93. (5 numbers.) 8° *Santiago*, 1882-94

Société Scientifique du Chili. Actes. Tomes II.-IV. (imperfect). *Plates.* Small 4° *Santiago*, 1892-94

Universidad de Chile, Anales de la. [Total representing 40 vols. and odd parts.] *Maps, plates, and tables.* 8° *Santiago*, 1846-80
   Viz. :—Años de 1843-44, 1848-57 (10 vols.); 1858-69 (18 vols., viz., Tom. XV.-XXXIII.); 1871-72 (5 vols., viz., Tom. XXXVIII.-XLII.); imperfect vol., viz., Nov. 1875, pp. 651-705 ; 1878-80 (6 vols., viz., Tom. LIII.-LVIII, 2 imperfect).

—— Reseña de los Trabajos de la Universidad, desde 1855 hasta el presente. (Memoria, por I. Domeyko.) 8° *Santiago*, 1872

VALPARAISO.

Estadística Comercial de la República de Chile. Años 1854, 1858 (small folio), y Año 1879. 8° *Valparaiso*, 1854-79

COLOMBIA.

BOGOTA.

Anales de la Instrucçion Publica en la Republica de Colombia. Tom. X., XI., XII., XIII. (imperfect set). *Plates.* Royal 8° *Bogota*, 1887-88

Revista de Minas. (Organo de la Casa " Muñoz y de la Torre," y de la " Agencia de Minas " de R. Espinosa G.) Nos. 2-8 and 11-12. Año I. 8° *Bogota*, 1888

ECUADOR.

QUITO.

Alturas Tomadas, &c. *See* W. Reiss and A. Stübel: Authors' Catalogue.

PARAGUAY.

ASUNCION.

Anuario Estadistica, de la República de Paraguay (Oficina Gen. de Estadistica). Año 1887. (Libro segundo del anuario.) 4° *Asuncion*, 1889

Revue du Paraguay. (Publication Officielle.) 12 numbers in irregular sequence, 1st to 6th year. Royal 8° *Asuncion*, 1889-92

PERU.

LIMA.

Peruano, El. Publicacion Oficial. [Viz.—Reports on the Exploration of the Rivers Ucayali, Pachitea, Palcazu, Yavari, and Morona.] No. 14, 30 Marzo ; 4 Junio; 26, 31 Octubre ; 19, 21 Diciembre de 1867. Folio *Lima*, 1867

Sociedad Carbonifera. Lima. *See* Peru : Appendix 2.

Sociedad Geográfica de Lima. Boletin. Tom. I.-III. Royal 8° *Lima*, 1892-93

URUGUAY.

MONTEVIDEO.

Anuario Estadístico de la República Oriental del Uruguay. Años 1887, 1888. *Maps, plates, and plans.* 4° *Montevideo*, 1888-89

Observatorio Meteorológico del Colegio Pio de Villa Colon Montevideo. Boletin Mensual, del Año I. Nos. 1, 2. Royal 8° *Montevideo*, 1888

VENEZUELA.

CARACAS.

Anuario Estadistico de los Estados Unidos de Venezuela. Ann. 1884, 1889, and 1891. *Maps and plans.* Folio and 8° *Caracas*, 1884-91
   [There are copies of the 1889 statistical annual in French and German, and 1884 is in English.]

Vargasia. Boletin de la Sociedad de Ciencias Fisicas y Naturales de Caracas. Tomo I. *Map.* 8° *Caracas*, 1868

3 D

ASIA.

CEYLON.

COLOMBO.

Ceylon Branch of the Royal Asiatic Society. Journal and Proceedings. Vols. IV., VII., VIII., X., and XIII. (1865-93) [imperfect set]. *Plates.* Small 8°
[For Addenda, *see* Appendix 2 : General, Miscell.] *Colombo*, 1866-94

CHINA.

CANTON.

Canton Register, The. Vols. I.-X. ; bound in 3 vols. [wherein Vols. VI.-X. have imperfections]. 4° *Canton*, 1827-37
Chinese Repository, The. Vols. I.-V., VII.-XV., and XVI., XVII., XIX., and XX. imperfect. (1833-51.) *Maps and plates.* 8° *Canton*, 1834-51

SHANGHAI.

China Review, The. *See* G. Taylor : Authors' Catalogue.
Chinese Miscellany, The. Designed to illustrate the Government, Philosophy, Religion, Arts, Manufactures, Trade, Manners, Customs, History, and Statistics of China. Nos. 1, 2, and 4—3 vols. *Maps and plates.* 8° *Shanghai*, 1849-50
Cycle, The. Vol. I. (No. 25). Folio *Shanghai*, 1870
Shanghai Literary and Scientific Society, Journal of the. No. 1 (June 1858). *Maps and plates.* 8° *Shanghai*, 1858
[Title of Soc. altered to and continued as]—
North China Branch of the Royal Asiatic Society, Journal of the. Vols. I. and II. (1858-60). *Maps and plates.* 8° *Shanghai*, 1858-60
—— New Series. Vols. I.-XXVI. (1864-90-92). *Maps and plates* *Shanghai*, 1865-94
[Vol. I. contains No. 1 of Jour. Shanghai Lit. and Sci. Soc., *supra* ; also Nos. 2 and 3 of Jour. N. China Br. R. Asiat. Soc.]

HONGKONG.

VICTORIA.

Hongkong Observatory, Observations and Researches made at the. Years 1884 and 1885 (by W. Doberck). Folio *Hongkong*, 1885-86
Notes and Queries on China and Japan. (A Monthly Medium of Intercommunication for Professorial and Literary Men, Missionaries, and Residents in the East generally.) Vols. I.-III. (*Ed.* N. B. Dennys). *Illustrations.* Royal 8°
Hongkong, 1867-69
—— New Series (*Ed.* C. Landon Davis, and with addition to title of " with which is incorporated ' Papers on China ' ' '). Vol. IV. (Nos. 1-5, Feb. to Aug.). Royal 8°
Hongkong, 1870

EAST INDIAN ARCHIPELAGO.

See Malay Archipelago, *postea.*

FRENCH INDO-CHINA.

SAIGON.

Societé des Études Indo-Chinoises de Saigon. Bulletin. Ann. 1883, 1º Fasc. ; Ann. 1886, 1º Semestre. 8° *Saigon*, 1883 and 1886
Excursions et Reconnaissances. (Cochinchine Française.) Tom. II. (Nos. 5, 6), III.-XIV., and XV. (No. 33). *Maps, &c.* Royal 8° *Saigon*, 1880-89

INDIA.

ALLAHABAD.

Panjab Notes and Queries : a Monthly Periodical devoted to the Systematic Collection of Authentic Notes and Scraps of Information regarding the Country and the People. (*Ed.* Capt. R. C. Temple.) Vol. I. (No. 1 to 6). Oct. 1883 to March 1884. 4°
Allahabad, 1883-84

BOMBAY.

Bombay Branch of the Royal Asiatic Society, Journal of the (including Proceedings). Vols. I.-XVIII (1841-94). *Maps and plates.* 8° *Bombay,* 1844-94
—— Supplementary parts and vols., viz., Reports on Search for Sanskrit MSS., by G. Buhler and P. Peterson. Extra No. Vol. XII., 1877; XVI., 1884; XVII., 1886; XVIII., 1894. [For Index, Vols. 1-17, *see* Literary Soc., Bombay.]
[The Bombay Geographical Society, 1873, merged into the above Soc. *See infra.*]

Bombay Geographical Society, Proceedings of the. 1837 and 1838. *Maps.* 8° *Bombay,* 1837-38
—— Report by the Secretary on the Proceedings of the, for 1849-50. 8° *Bombay,* 1850
—— Transactions of the. Vols. I.-XIX., 1836 to 1873. *Maps and plates.* 8° *Bombay,* 1844-74
—— Index to the first seventeen volumes, with Catalogue of the Library, and Catalogue of Charts, Maps, Sketches, and Views. (*Ed.* D. J. Kennelly.) 8° *Edinburgh,* 1866
—— Catalogue of the Library. (Compiled by D. J. Kennelly.) 8° *Bombay,* 1862
[The Bombay Geographical Society afterwards (Jan. 1873) amalgamated with the Bombay Branch of the Royal Asiatic Soc.]

Indian Antiquary, The: a Journal of Oriental Research in Archæology, Epigraphy, Ethnology, Geography, History, Folklore, Languages, Literature, Numismatics, Philosophy, Religion, &c. 11 vols. Vols. VII.-IX. (incomplete), (*ed.* J. Burgess); Vols. XVI.-XX. (*eds.,* R. C. Temple and J. F. Fleet); Vols. XXI.-XXII. (*ed.,* R. C. Temple). *Plates.* Small 4° *Bombay,* 1878-93

Literary Society of Bombay, Index to the Transactions of the, Vols. I. to III.; and to the Journals of the Bombay Branch of the Royal Asiatic Society, Vols. I. to XVII., with a Historical Sketch of the Society. By Ganpatrao Krishna Tivarekar. 8° *Bombay,* 1886

[For Transactions of the, *see* London, *postea.*]

CALCUTTA.

Asiatic Society of Bengal. Asiatic Researches; or, Transactions of the Society, instituted in Bengal, for inquiring into the History, Antiquities, Arts, Sciences, and Literature of Asia. Vols. I.-XX. *Maps and plates.* 4° *Calcutta,* 1788-1836
—— Index to the First Eighteen Volumes. 4° *Calcutta,* 1835
—— Index to Vols. XIX. and XX. of the Asiatic Researches, and to Vols. I. to XXIII. of the Journal, &c. 8° *Calcutta,* 1856
—— Journal of the. Vols. I.-LXII., and LXIII. (incomplete). *Maps and plates.* 8° *Calcutta,* 1832-94
—— Extra number to Pt. 1 of Vol. XLVII. (viz., A Sketch of the Turki Language, by R. B. Shaw, and Appendix by J. Scully.) 8° *Calcutta,* 1880
—— Extra numbers to Pt. 1 of Vol. XLIX. for 1880, and Pt. 1 of Vol. LVII. for 1889. 8° [*See* G. A. Grierson: Authors' Catalogue.] *Calcutta,* 1881 and 1889
—— Proceedings of the. Vols. for 1865 to 1893 (29 vols; that for 1865 and 1893 defective). *Maps and plates.* 8° *Calcutta,* 1866-94
—— Centenary Review of the Asiatic Society of Bengal, from 1784 to 1883. [This contains a History of the Soc., Indexes of its Publications classified, &c.] 1 vol. 8° *Calcutta,* 1885

[For Branches of Roy. Asiat. Soc., *see* under Shanghai, Hongkong, Bombay, Madras, Ceylon, Japan, and Straits Settlements.]

Buddhist Text Society of India, Journal and Text of the. (*Ed.* Sarat Candra Dās.) Vol. I. (pt. 4), II. (pts. 1-3). *Plates.* 8° *Calcutta,* 1893-94

Indian Forester, The: a Quarterly Magazine of Forestry. (*Ed.* J. S. Gamble.) Vol. IV. (Nos. 3 and 4.) 8° *Calcutta,* 1879

Indian Meteorological Memoirs. *See* Appendix 2.

Records and Reports of the Geological Survey of India, and other Indian Government Publications. *See* Appendix 2.

Juggarow (G. V.) Observatory, Daba Gardens, Vizagapatam. Results of Meteorological Observations for 1887, 1889-91 (4 vols. bound in 2). By A. V. Nursingrow. *Plates and meteorological diagrams.* 12° *Calcutta,* 1889-92

LAHORE.

Punjab Magazine, The. The Organ of Punjab Asssociation. Nos. 1, 2, 3, for April, July, and October 1887. Royal 8° *Lahore,* 1887

MADRAS.

Madras Journal of Literature and Science, The. Published under the auspices of the
  Madras Literary Society, and Auxiliary of the Royal Asiatic Society. Ser. 1, Vols.
  I.-XVI. (1833-50).   *Maps and plates.* 8°   *Madras,* 1834-51
—— Ser. 2, Vols. I.-VI. (1856-61). *Maps and plates.* 8°   *Madras,* 1857-61
—— Ser. 3, Vol. I. (1864). 8°   *Madras,* 1864
—— [Ser. 4?] (*Ed.* G. Oppert), Vols. 1878 and 1879. *Plates*   *Madras,* 1879-80
Maine Historical Society (Madras), Proceedings of the. Pt. 1. Small 4° *Madras,* 1890
Royal Asiatic Society of Madras, Journal of the.   1866. 8°   *Madras,* 1866

JAPAN.

TOKYO.

Eastern Asiatic Society (Japan), Report of the.   Vol. If. [In Japanese.] Royal 8°
                                                                           Tokyo [1891]
Tokyo Geographical Society.   Regulations of the Toukiyau Geographical Society.
  [In English.]   12°.   N.P. [? 1879.]   22 small 8° and 2 12° numbers [in Japanese] of
  the Society's Publications.
—— Journal of the.   Vols. III. (Nos. 4-10), IV.-XV., 1881-93 (14th to 26th year
  Meiji). [In Japanese.]   *Maps and plates.*   12°   *Tokyo,* 1891-93
—— Reports of the Annual Meetings, 3rd, 4th, 5th, and 6th (? 1881-84). [Separate
  pamphlets, those of 7th to 11th being published in Journals 1886-90.] [In Japanese.]
  12°   *Tokyo,* 1881-90
Tokio Daigaku.   Imperial University of Japan. Calendar of the Department of Law,
  Sicence, and Literature, for 1879-80, 1881-82, and 1889 to 1894.   6 vols.   12°
                                                                           Tokyo, 1890-94
—— Memoirs of the Science Department. Nos. 1, 2, 4, 5 (with Append. 5*a*, 5*b*, 5*c*),
  and 9.   1 vol.   *Plates.*   Small 4°   *Tokyo,* 1879-85
  [*See* Appendix 2 : Tokio University, J. A. Ewing.]
  [Followed by]—
—— Journal of the College of Science, The.   Vols. I.-VIII. *Maps and plates.* Small 4°
                                                                           Tokyo, 1887-94
—— Memoirs of the Literature College, The.   No. 1.   Small 4°   *Tokyo,* 1886
  [*See* Chamberlain, B. H. : Authors' Catalogue.]

YOKOHAMA.

Asiatic Society of Japan, Transactions of the. Vols. I.-XV., XIX.-XXII, 1872-93.
  Maps and plates. 8°   *Yokohama,* 1874-94
—— Supplements to Vol. XX (Parts 1, 2, 3 [sect. 1], and 5).   8°   *Yokohama,* 1892
Deutsche Gesellschaft für Natur- und Völkerkunde Ostasiens in Tokio. Mitteil-
  ungen, Bände I.-V. (and Append.), VI. (Hefte 51, 52, 53, and Append.) ; Suppl.
  zu Bd. V. (Hefte 1-3, April 1889 and Oct. 1892) ; and zu Bd. VI. (Heft 1, Jul. 1894).
  Maps and plates. 4°   *Yokohama and Tokyo,* 1873-94
Seismological Society of Japan, Transactions of the. Vols. I.-XVI. [bound in 7 vols.]
  Maps and plates. 8°   *Yokohama,* 1890-92
  [Followed by]—
The Seismological Journal of Japan. Vols. I.-III. [XVII. of entire series; the 3 vols.
  bound in 1]. *Maps and plates.* 8°   *Yokohama,* 1894

MALAY ARCHIPELAGO.

JAVA.

BATAVIA.

Bataviaasch Genootschap van Kunsten en Wetenschappen. Verhandelingen van
  het.   Deel. XX. and XXI. (in 2 parts), 3 vols., 8°, 1844-47 ; XXII.-XXIV., 3 vols.,
  4°, 1849-52; XXXIX. (2ᵉ stuk), XL.-XLVI., and XLVII. (1ᵉ stuk), royal 8°, 1879-
  92—Total 15 vols.   *Plates.*   8°, royal 8°, and 4°
                                         Batavia, The Hague, and Leyden, 1844-92
—— Notulen van Algemeene en Bestuurs-Vergaderingen van het. Deel. XVI.-XXXI.
  8°   *Batavia,* 1878-93
—— Register op de Notulen over de Jaren 1867-78 and 1879-88. (J. A. Van der Chijs.)
  (2 pamphs.) 8°   *Batavia,* 1879 and 1889
—— Realia. Register, &c.   *See* Appendix 2 : Dutch E. Indies, Batavia.

Bataviaasch Genootschap van Kunsten en Wetenschappen Tijdschrift voor Indische Taal-, Land-, en Volkenkunde, uitgegeven door het genootschap. Deel. XXV.-XXXVI. *Maps and plates.* 8° *Batavia*, 1878-93
—— Catalogus der Numismatische Afdeeling van het Museum van. J. A. Van der Chijs. 2 and 3 Druk. 8° *Batavia*, 1877 and 1886
—— Algemeen Reglement en Reglement van Orde. 8° *Batavia*, 1889
[*See* Holle, K. F. : Authors' Catalogue.]
Batavian Magnetical and Meteorological Observatory (Published by order of the Government of Netherlands, India), Observations made at the. Vols. V. and VI., 1879 and 1880. (P. A. Bergsma and J. P. van der Stok.) Folio *Batavia*, 1882-85
Nederlandsch-Indische Maatschappij van Nijverheid en Landbouw. Tijdschrift. Deel. XXXI. (Aflev. 6, 1885), XXXII.-XLVII. [Vols. 31, 33, 39, and 45 imperfect]. *Plates and tables.* 8° *Batavia*, 1885-94
Regeeringsalmanak voor Nederlandsch-Indië, 1892. Vols. I.-II. 8° *Batavia*, 1892
Regenwaarnemingen in Nederlandsch-Indië. Iᵉ.-VIIᵉ. Jaargang (1879-85). 8° *Batavia*, 1880-86

SAMARANG AND JOGJAKARTA.

Indisch Aardrijksundkig Genootschap. (Redaktie van A. J. Ten Brink.) Deel. I. (1-4 aflevering). *Maps and plates.* Small 4° *Samarang and Jogjakarta*, 1880-83

BORNEO, BRITISH.

SANDAKAN.

British North Borneo Herald and Official Gazette, The. Vols. VI., X.-XIII. (5 imperfect vols.) Folio *Sandakan*, 1888-93

PHILIPPINES.

MANILA.

Observatorio Meteorologico de Manila. Bajo la Direccion de los P. P. de la Compañia de Jesus. (1.) Observaciones verificadas durant Años 1890-94. 5 vols. *Plates and diagrams.* Folio *Manila*, 1890-94
—— (2.) El Magnetismo Terrestre en Filipinas (por Ricardo Cirera). *Maps and plates.* Folio *Manila*, 1893

STRAITS SETTLEMENTS.

SINGAPORE.

Journal of Eastern Asia, The. (*Ed.* James Collins.) Vol. I., No. 1 [all published]. 8° *Singapore*, 1875
Journal of the Indian Archipelago and Eastern Asia. (*Ed.* J. R. Logan.) Vols. I.-IX. *Maps and plates.* 8° *Singapore*, 1847-55
—— New Ser. Vol. I., II., and III. (pt. 1). 8° *Singapore*, 1856-59
Straits Branch of the Royal Asiatic Society, Journal of the. Nos. I.-XXIV. [bound in 16 vols.] *Maps and plates.* 8° *Singapore*, 1878-91
—— Notes and Queries. (*Ed.* Hon. Sec.). Nos. 1-4. 8° *Singapore*, 1885-87

TAIPING (PERAK).

Perak Government Gazette, The. Vols. V. and VI. (imperfect set). Folio *Taiping*, 1892-93

Perak Museum Notes. Nos. 1-3. *Maps and plates.* 8° *Taiping, Perak*, 1893

AUSTRALASIA.

AUSTRALIA.

NEW SOUTH WALES.

MAITLAND.

Annuaire de la Delegation Générale de l'Océanie. *See under* Societé d'Ethnographie, Paris, in France, *postea.*

SYDNEY.

Australian Museum (Sydney, N.S.W.), Records of the. Vol. I. (No. 3 wanting). *Plates.* Royal 8° *Sydney*, 1890-91
—— Memoirs. Royal 8° *Sydney*, 1889
[*See* Appendix 2 : New South Wales, A.

Linnean Society of New South Wales. Proceedings. Vol. I. (Pts. 2 and 3). *Plates.* Small 8°   *Sydney*, 1876
Royal Geographical Society of Australasia, New South Wales Branch, Proceedings of the. Vols. I.-V. Sess. 1883-84 to 1891-92. *Maps and plates.* 8°   *Sydney*, 1885-92
—— Special Vol. of Proceedings of Soc. *Map and plates.* 8°   *Sydney*, 1885
—— Special Record. . . Exped. to N. Guinea. (Pamph.) 8°   *Sydney*, 1885
Royal Society of New South Wales. Philosophical Society of New South Wales, Transactions of the. For 1862-65. 1 vol. 8°   *Sydney*, 1866
      [Continued as Roy. Soc., N.S.W.]—
—— Transactions and Proceedings of the Roy. Soc., N.S.W. Vols. I., VI.-VIII. (1867, 1872-74). *Maps and plates.* Small 8°   *Sydney*, 1868-75
—— Journal and Proceedings of the. Vols. X.-XXVII. (in 18 vols). 1876-93. *Plates and tables.* 8°   *Sydney*, 1877-94

   [The *Royal Society of New South Wales* originated in 1821 as the *Philosophical Society of
   Australia.* After an interval of inactivity it was resuscitated in 1850, under the name of the
   Australian Philosophical Society, by which title it was known until 1856, when the name
   was changed to the *Philosophical Society of New South Wales.* In 1866 it assumed its
   present title, *Royal Society of New South Wales.*]

QUEENSLAND.

BRISBANE.

Acclimatisation Society of Queensland. Report of the Council (21st Rep. 1886). 8°   *Brisbane*, 1887
Philosophic Society of North Queensland, Proceedings of the. Vol. I. (1 part, 1889-90.) *Plates.* 8°   *Brisbane*, 1891
Pugh's Queensland Almanac, Law Calendar, Directory, Coast Guide, and Gazetteer. For 1862 and 1863, and for 1878-94 (with Vols. 1884 and 1887 missing). Total, 16 vols; these comprise the 4th and 5th and 20th to 36th years of publication. *Maps.* 16° and 12°   *Brisbane*, 1862-94
      [Vols. 1885 and 1886 have addition to sub-title, " and of Men of the Time"; and in Vols 1888-94 the title is shortened to "Pugh's Almanack and Queensland Directory."]
Queensland Branch of the Royal Geographical Society of Australasia. Proceedings and Transactions. Vols. I.-IX. (Sess. 1885-86 to 1893-94.) *Maps and plates.* 8°   *Brisbane*, 1886-94
Royal Society of Queensland. Proceedings. Vols. I., V. (pt. 4); VI. (pts. 2, 3, and 5); IX. (part). *Maps and plates.* 8°   *Brisbane*, 1884-93
—— [Report.] Annual Meeting, July 1889. (Pamph.) 8°   *Brisbane*, 1889

SOUTH AUSTRALIA.

ADELAIDE.

Meteorological Society of Australia, The. History, Rules and Regulations, List of Members (pamph. 18 pp.). 8°   *Adelaide*, 1886
Royal Agricultural and Horticultural Society of South Australia, Proceedings of the. 1880, 1881. 8°   *Adelaide*, 1881
Royal Society of South Australia, Transactions, Proceedings, and Reports of the. Vols. IX., XI.-XVIII. (9 and 16 imperfect). 1885-94. *Maps and plates.* Small 8°   *Adelaide*, 1887-94
South Australian Branch of the Royal Geographical Society of Australasia. Transactions and Proceedings. Vols. I. and II. (Sess. 1885-86 to 1887-88). *Maps.* 8°   *Adelaide*, 1886-90
South Australian Institute. Annual Report, 1877-78, and Appendices A to D. Small 4°   *Adelaide*, 1878

VICTORIA.

MELBOURNE.

Australian Scientific Magazine, The. Vol. I., No. 1. 8°   *Melbourne*, 1885
Geological Society of Australia (R. T. Litton), List of Members of the. Also a Catalogue of Works in the Library of the Society. 12°   *Melbourne*, 1886
—— Transactions. Vol. I. (pts. 1, 3, and 4). *Illustrations.* Small 4° *Melbourne*, 1886
Geological Survey of Victoria. *See* Appendix 2.
Philosophical Society of Victoria, Transactions of the. Including the Papers and Proceedings of the Society, ending July 1855. Vol. I. *Plates.* 8° *Melbourne*, 1855
      [Title of Society altered to]—

Philosophical Institute of Victoria, Transactions of the. (*Ed.* J. Macadam.) Vol.
II.-IV., and Appendix. *Maps and plates.* 8°   *Melbourne,* 1858-60
    [Title of Society altered to]—
Royal Society of Victoria, Transactions of the. (*Ed.* J. Macadam.) Vol. V. *Plates.*
8°   *Melbourne,* 1860
    [Continued as]—
—— Transactions and Proceedings of the. Vols. VI.-XXIV. (1861-87). *Maps and
plates.* 8°   *Melbourne,* 1865-88
    [When division of publications followed, viz.]—
—— Transactions. New Ser. Vols. I., II., and III. (pt. 1). *Plates.* 4° *Melbourne,* 1888-91
—— Proceedings of the. New Ser. Vols. I.-VI. *Plates.* 8°   *Melbourne,* 1889-94
Royal Geographical Society of Australasia, Victorian Branch, Transactions and
Proceedings of the. Vols. I.-XI. (Sess. 1885-86 to 1893-94.) *Maps and plates.*
8°   *Melbourne,* 1885-94
    [Vols. I.-II. were printed in Sydney, and correspond to same vols. N.S. Wales
    Branch ; as also the special vol., *supra*].
Victoria Mining Surveyors' Reports. Furnished by the Mining Surveyors of
Victoria to the Board of Science. Nos. 9-15. 8°   *Melbourne,* 1860
Victorian Year Book, containing a Digest of the Statistics of the Colony. (*Ed.* H. H.
Hayter.) For the years 1873-93 (bound in 19 vols.) [1884 and 1885 missing]. *Maps
and plates.* 8°   *Melbourne,* 1874-93

TASMANIA, *formerly* VAN DIEMEN'S LAND.

HOBART (*formerly* HOBART TOWN).

Australian Association for the Advancement of Science, Transactions of the. 4th
Meeting (Hobart), 1892 ; Sect. Geography, &c. (Pamphs.) *Plate.* 8° *Hobart,* 1892
Royal Society of Van Diemen's Land, Papers and Proceedings of the. Vols. I.,
II., and III. (pts. 1 and 2). *Plates.* 8°   *Tasmania,* 1851-59
    [Continued as]—
—— Monthly Notices of Papers and Proceedings (including Reports). Vols. I.-III.,
viz., for years 1863 and 1864, 1 vol. ; and 1868-74, 2 vols. *Plates.* Small 8°
                                                                    Hobart, 1863-75

    [Again continued as]—
—— Papers, Proceedings, and Reports of the Roy. Soc. of Tasmania. For years 1875-93
(1887 missing). *Maps and plates.* Small 8°   *Hobart,* 1876-94
—— Reports of the. For years 1848, 1852, 1859, 1860, 1864, and 1865. *Plates.* 8°
                                                                    Hobart, 1849-66
                                                                    Hobart, 1848
—— Rules of the. (Pamph.) 8°
—— Catalogue of the Library of the Roy. Soc. of Tasmania (by Alex. Morton).
(Pamph.) Royal 8°   *Tasmania,* 1885
Tasmanian Journal of Natural Science, Agriculture, Statistics, &c. Vols. I. and II.
(imperfect, viz., Nos. 2, 5, 6, 7). *Maps and plates.* 8°   *Hobart,* 1841-43

NEW ZEALAND.

CHRISTCHURCH AND DUNEDIN.

New Zealand Alpine Club. The New Zealand Alpine Journal : a Record of Mountain Exploration and Adventure, by Members of the N.Z. Alp. Club. Vol. I. (Nos.
1-6). *Map and plates.* 8°   *Christchurch and Dunedin,* 1892-94

WELLINGTON.

New Zealand Institute, Transactions and Proceedings of the. (*Ed.* J. Hector.) Vols.
I.-XXV. *Plates.* 8°, two sizes   *Wellington,* 1869-93
    [These vols. contain the Proceedings of various N.Z. branch or affiliated Societies
    and Institutes, viz., Auckland, Canterbury, Otago, &c.)
Polynesian Society, The Journal of the, containing the Transactions and Proceedings
of the. Vols. I. and II. 8°   *Wellington,* 1892-93

PACIFIC ISLANDS.

HAWAII : HONOLULU.

Hawaiian Historical Society. *See* Authors' Catalogue, under Alexander, W. D., and
Atkinson, A. T.

EUROPE.

AUSTRIA-HUNGARY—AUSTRIA.

VIENNA.

Commission für Erforschung des Oestlichen Mittelmeers, Berichte der. Reihe I.-II. *Maps and plates.* 4° *Vienna*, 1892-93

Deutsche Rundschau für Geographie und Statistik. (*Eds.* Drs C. Arendts and F. Umlauft). Jahrg. I.-XVI. *Maps and plates.* Royal 8° *Vienna and Leipzig*, 1879-94

Gesellschaft der Freunde der Naturwissenschaften (Wien). Berichte über die Mittheilungen von. (W. Haidinger). 7 vols. in 5. 8° *Vienna*, 1847-51

—— Naturwissenschaftliche Abhandlungen, gesammelt, und durch Subscription herausgegeben von Wilhelm Haidinger. Bände I.-IV. *Maps and plates.* 4° *Vienna*, 1847-52

Kaiserlichen Akademie der Wissenschaften (Wien). Sitzungsberichte der Mathematisch - Naturwissenschaftlichen Classe. Bände I.-XXVII., XXX.-CII. (Total bound in 152 vols.), 1847-93. *Plates and maps.* 8° *Vienna*, 1848-93

[From Vol. XLIV. to XCVI. inclusive 2 vols. were issued annually, and from XCVII. to CII. inclusive 3 vols. annually have been published. . . . . These constitute 3 separate sections, viz. :—1. Biology and Geography ; 2. Mathematics and Physics ; 3. Chemistry.]

—— Register (or Gen. Index to Sitzb.). Bände I.-XC., Jahre 1848-84. 8°

[These were issued at intervals in separate parts, as follows :—

Bdr. I.-X..	..	..	..	in 1854	Bdr. LXI.-LXIV...	..	..	in 1872
„ XI.-XX.	..	..	..	„ 1856	„ LXV.-LXXV.	..	..	„ 1878
„ XXI.-XXX...	..	..	„ 1859	„ LXXVI.-LXXX.	..	..	„ 1880
„ XXXI.-XLII.	..	..	,. 1862	„ LXXXI.-LXXXV.	..	..	„ 1882
„ — missing	..	..	„ —	„ LXXXVI.-XC.	..	..	„ 1885
„ LI.-LX.	..	..	..	„ 1870			

—— Denkschriften (Mathemat.-naturwissen Classe). Bd. XII. *Plates.* 4° *Vienna*, 1856

K. K. Central-Anstalt für Meteorologie und Erdmagnetismus. Jahrbücher. Neue Folge. Bände I.-XXIX. Jahrg. 1864-92. *Maps and plates.* 4° *Vienna*, 1866-94

K. K. Geographischen Gesellschaft (Wien). Mittheilungen. Bänder I.-XXXVII. (entire series). Ser. 1. Bände I.-X. *Maps and plates.* Royal 8° *Vienna*, 1857-68

—— Ser. 2 (Neue Folge.) Bände I.-XXVI. *Maps and plates.* 8° *Vienna*, 1868-93

K. K. Militär-Geographischen Institutes in Wien. Mittheilungen. (Herausgegeben auf Befehl des K. K. Reichs-Kriegs ministeriums.) Bände V.-XII., 1885-92. *Maps and plates.* 8° *Vienna*, 1885-93

—— Die Astronomisch-Geodätischen Arbeiten des. Bände I.-II. *Maps and plates.* 4° *Vienna*, 1871-92

K. K. Geologischen Reichsanstalt. Abhandlungen. Bände I.-V., VI. (Hefte 1, 2), VII.-XI. (Abtheil 1), XII. (Hefte 1-3). *Maps and plates.* Royal 4° *Vienna*, 1852-85

—— Jahrbuch. Bände I.-XXXIV. *Maps and plates.* Small 4° and royal 8° *Vienna*, 1850-84

—— Gen. Register der Bände I-X., 1850-59. Royal 8° *Vienna*, 1863

—— Gen. Register der Bände XI.-XX., 1860-70. Royal 8° *Vienna*, 1872

—— Gen. Register der Bände XXI.-XXX., 1871-80. Royal 8° *Vienna*, 1881

—— Verhandlungen. Jahrg. 1867-84. 18 vols. Royal 8° *Vienna*, 1867-84

—— Gen. Register, 1860-70 and 1871-1880 ; combined with Gen. Reg. Jahrb., published (*supra*) in 1872 and 1881.

—— Geologische Uebersichtskarte der Oesterreichischen Monarchie nach dem Aufnahmen der . . . (von Franz Ritter von Hauer.) Blatt I.-V., VII., and X. [An imperfect irregular set.] Royal 8° *Vienna*, 1867-73

K. K. Naturhistorischen Hofmuseums (Wien). Annalen des. (*Ed.* Franz Ritter von Hauer.) Band I. Nos. 1 and 2. (Jahresbericht, 1885, und Notizen), Bd. V. *Plates.* Imp. 8° *Vienna*, 1886 and 1890

Mittheilungen der Prähistorischen Commission, der Kais. Akad. der Wissenschaften. Band I. (Nos. 2, 3). *Plates and illustrations.* 4° *Vienna*, 1890-93

Oesterreichischen Alpen-Vereins, Jahrbuch des. Bände I.-IX. (1863 to 1873).
Maps and plates. [*See* Remarks *infra.*] 8° *Vienna,* 1865-73

—— Mittheilungen des. (*Ed.* E. V. Mjsisovics and P. Grohman.) Bände I.-II. *Maps and plates.* 12° *Vienna,* 1863-64
[Society continued as]—

Deutschen und Oesterreichischen Alpen-Vereins, Zeitschrift des. Bände I.-XXV. (1869-94). *Maps and plates.* 8° *Munich and Berlin,* 1870-94

—— Beilage zur Zeitsch. des Deutsch und Oester. Alp.-Ver. (1878). Abtheil I.
Munich, 1878

—— Anleitung zu wissenschaftlichen Beobachtungen auf Alpenreisen (herausgegeben von Deutsch. and Oester. Alpen-Verein). Bände I.-II. *Maps and plates.* 12° *Vienna,* 1882
[Vol. III. of Zeitsch. d. Deutsch. Alp.-Ver. is equivalent to Vol. VIII. of Jahrb. Oesterr. Ver. ; in other words, they are the same vol., with different title, issued separately by the two societies, which thereafter amalgamated, their united publication becoming Zeitsch. d. Deutsch. und Oesterr. Alp. Ver.]

—— Register zu den Publicationen des :—(*a*) Oesterreichischen Alpenvereins, 1863 bis 1873 ; des (*b*) Deutschen Alpenvereins, 1869 bis 1872 ; und des (*c*) Deutschen und Oesterreichischen Alpenvereins, 1873 bis 1886. (Von Th. Trautwein.) 8°
[*See* " Deutschen Alpenvereins," Munich, Germany.] *Munich,* 1887

Oesterreichische Monatsschrift für den Orient. (Herausgegeben vom Orientalischen Museum in Wien.) Jahrg. I.-XIX. [20 vols.] *Maps and plates.* Small 4° *Vienna,* 1875-93

Oesterreichischen Gesellschaft für Meteorologie, Zeitschrift der. (C. Jelinek and J. Hann). Bände I.-XX. *Maps and plates.* 8° and small 4° *Vienna,* 1866-85
[Continued as]—

Meteorologische Zeitschrift. (Herausgegeben von der Oesterreichischen Gesellschaft für Meteorologie und der Deutschen Meteorologischen Gesellschaft, — Hann, Höppen, and Hellmann). 1886-92. (Vols. XXI.-XXVIII., entire series.) *Maps and plates.* Small 4° *Berlin and Vienna,* 1886-93

Publicationen für die Internationale Erdmessung. Astronomische Arbeiten, &c. Bände I.-V. *Woodcuts.* 4° *See* Appendix 2 : Austria Hungary (A).
Vienna, 1889-93

—— der Oesterreichischen Gradmessungs Commission. (By W. Tinter.) 4°
Vienna, 1891

Sonnblick-Verein. Jahresbericht. Vol. I. 1892. *Plates.* Royal 8° *Vienna,* 1893

Verein der Geographen an der Universitat Wien. Bericht 9, 10, 11, and 13. Vereinsjahr 1883-87 8° *Vienna,* 1884-87
—— Jahrsbericht des. Erster u. Zweiter (pamph.). 8° *Vienna,* 1875-76

Wissenschaftlichen Club, Wien. Jahresbericht [I.] 1876-77. 8° *Vienna,* 1877

AUSTRIA-HUNGARY—HUNGARY.

BUDAPEST.

Budapesti Szemle. [Budapest Review.] (Szerkeszti és Kiadja Csengery Antal.) Kötet (Vol.) XIII.-XVIII. [bound in 3 vols.] *Maps and plates.* Royal 8°
Budapest, 1861-63
—— Uj Folyam. (New Ser.). Vols. XIII. (imperfect), XIV., XV. 8° *Budapest,* 1869

Ethnologische Mitteilungen aus Ungarn. Zeitschrift für die Volkskunde der Bewohner Ungarns und seinen Nebenländer. (Dr Anton Hermann.) Jahrg. I. (Hefte 1 and 3). 4° *Budapest,* 1887-89

MAGYAR TUDOMÁNOS AKADÉMIA.

(*Hungarian Academy of Sciences.*)

I. Academical Records, &c.

Almanach polgári és csillagászati naptárral. Mag. Tud. Akad. 1867, 1870-90, 1892-1893 (23 vols.) 8° *Budapest,* 1867-93

A Magyar Földrajzi Társaság tisztikaránk és tagjainak Névjegyzéke az 1893 év elején. [Liste générale des Membres de la Société Hongroise de Géographie.] 8°
[*See* Földrajzi Közlemények, p. 795.] *Budapest,* 1893

Értesitöje. Mag. Tud. Akad. [*Compte-Rendu of Proceedings of the Hungarian Academy of Science.*] (Szerkeszti a Fötitkár.) Kötet. (Vol.) I.-XXIII. [2 vols. missing and several imperfect.] 8° *Budapest*, 1867-90
—— Subject Index to Vols. I.-VIII. (1867-74), " Nev-es Tárgymutató." 8°
Budapest, 1875
Jegyzéke a Mag. Tud. Ak. Altal kiadott Könyveknek jelentékenyen leszallitott Arakon. [*General Catalogue of Works published by the Hungarian Academy of Sciences.*] (Pamph.) 8° *Budapest*, 1875
Mag. Tud. Akademiai Jegyzökönyvei, MDCCCLXVI. Parts 1 and 2. 12°
Budapest, 1866
Munkák és Folyóiratok Betürendes Czim és Tartalomjegyzéke.—Mag. Tud. Akad. Kiadásában Megjelent, 1830-89. Small 8° *Budapest*, 1890
[*Catalogue of Periodicals and Separate Works* issued under the authority of the Academy between 1830-89].
Rapport sur les Travaux de l'Academie des Sciences de Hongrie en 1892. Par Coloman Szily. (Pamph.) 8° *Budapest*, 1893
Vázlatok a Mag. Tud. Akad. Félszázados Történetéböl, 1831-1881. 8° *Budapest*, 1881

II. History, Archæology. Philosophy, and Statistical Science.

Historiæ Hungaricæ Fontes Domestici. Chronica Minora. (M. Florianus). Vol. IV. Royal 8° *Budapest*, 1885
Magyar Történelmi Tár. [*Hungarian Historical Documents.*] A Történeti kútfök Ismeretének elömozdítására. Kiadja a Mag. Tud. Akad. Történelmi bizottmánya. Kötet. (Vol.) I.-XII. and XIV.-XXV., 1854-57. *Plates.* 8° *Budapest*, 1855-78
Monumenta Hungariæ Historica. Diplomataria. Magyar Történelmi Emlékek. Mag. Tud. Akad. Tört. Bizottmánya. Okmánytárak. Kötet. (VoL) I.-IX., XII.-XXV. (bound in 19 vols.). 8° *Budapest*, 1857-73
[There are 2 extra vols., viz., 15th, 1887, and Vol. " *Okirattár, Strassburg Pál*," by Szilágyi Sándor, 1882.]
Monumenta Hungariæ Historica. Scriptores. Magyar Történelmi Emlékek. Mag. Tud. Akad. Tört. Bizottmánya. Második Osztaly: Irók. Kötet. (Vol.) I.-VI., IX., XIV., XV., XX.-XXII., XXV.-XXXII. [With 2 Append. to Vol. XXX. Total, 20 vols.] 8° *Budapest*, 1857-75
Monumenta Hungariæ Historica. Codex Diplomataria Hungaricus Andegavensis. Magyar Történelmi Emlékek [1301-1357]. Mag. Tud. Akad. Tört. Bizottsága. Megbizásából. Anjoukori Okınánytár. (Szerkesztette Nagy Imre.) Kötet. (Vol.) I.-VI. 8° *Budapest*, 1878-91
Monumenta Comitialia Regni Hungariæ. Magyar Országgyülési Emlékek. Történeti Bevezetésekkel. [1598-1604.] A Mag. Tud. Akad. Tört. Bizottsága. (Dr Fraknói Vilmos es Dr Károlyi Árpád.) Kötet. (Vols.) IX.-X. 8° *Budapest*, 1885-90
Monumenta Comitialia Regni Transylvaniæ. Erdélyi Országgyülési Emlékek. Történeti Bevezetésekkel. [1637-1674.] Mag. Tud. Akad. Tört. Bizottsága (Szilágyi Sándor). Kötet. (Vols.) X.-XV. 8° *Budapest*, 1884-92
Archæologiai Értesitö. Mag. Tud. Archæol. Bizottságának Közlönye. [*Journal of the Archæological Commission.*] Kötet. (Vols.) X.-XII. *Woodcuts.* 8°
Budapest, 1876-78
—— Uj Folyam. [New Ser.] Kötet. (Vol.) I.-XIII. (a few imperfect). *Plates, plans,* &c. Royal 8° *Budapest*, 1881-93
Archæologiai Közlemények. A Hazai Müemlékek Ismertetésének Elömozdítására. [*Memoirs of the Archæological Commission.*] Mag. Tud. Akad. Archæol. Bizottmánya. Kötet. (Vols.) I.-II. *Maps and plates.* ("Képatlasz" or *Atlas* to Vol. II. fol. 1861.) 8° *Budapest*, 1859-61
—— . . . Bizottsága. Uj Folyam. (New Ser.) Kötet. (Vols.) VIII.-XI., XIV., XV. (or Vols. VI.-IX., XII., and XIII. of Ser. 2—some imperfect). *Maps and plates.* Folio *Budapest*, 1870-86
Magyarországi Régészeti Emlékek. (Mag. Tud. Akad. Archæologiai Bizottsága.) Vol. I. (pt. 2), II. (pt. 2), III. and IV. (pts. 1 and 2). *Plates and plans.* Folio
Budapest, 1869-80
A Philosophiai Törvény-és Történettudományi Osztályok Közlönye. (Szerkeszti, Csengery Antal). [*Bulletin, section of Philosophy of Acad.*] Kötet. (Vols.) I.-III. 8° *Budapest*, 1860-63
Értekezések a Bölcseleti Tudományok Köréböl. Mag. Tud. Akad. A III. Osztály Rendeletéböl. (Szerkeszté, Pesty Frigyes.) Kötet. (Vol.) III. Füzet (pts.) 1, 2. 8° *Budapest*, 1889

Történelmi Emlékek. Török Magyarkori. Mag. Tud. Akad. Tört. Bizottmánya.
Elsö Osztály (Sect. 1): Okmánytár. Kötet. (Vol.) I., II., IV.-VII., and IX.
(7 vols.) 8° *Budapest*, 1863-72
—— Hakodik Osztály (Sect. 2): Irók. Kötet. (Vol.) I. 8° *Budapest*, 1893
Történettudományi Pályamunkák. Kiadja a Magyar Tudós Társaság. Kötet. (Vols.)
I. and II. 8° *Budapest*, 1841-42
Értekezések a Nemzetgazdaságtan és Statisztika Köréböl. Mag. Tud. Akad.
[*Memoirs Statistical Commission of Hungarian Acad.*] A Nemzetgazdasági-Statisztikai állandó Bizottságnak Rendeletéböl. (Szerkeszti, Földes Béla). Kötet. (Vols.)
I. II. (imperfect), 1882-85. 8° *Budapest*, 1883-85
Publicationen des statistischen Bureaus der kön. Friestadt Pest. Nos. 3, 5-8.
Large 8° *Budapest*, 1871-73
See Append. 2 : Austria-Hungary.
Statisztikai Közlemények [*Statistical Proceedings*]. A hazai Allapotok Ismeretének
Elömozdítására. Kiadja a Mag. Tud. Akad. Statisztikai Bizottmánya. (*Ed.*
Hunfalvy János es Keleti Károly.) Vols. I.-VIII. [bound in 6 vols.] *Diagrams
and tables.* 8° *Budapest*, 1861-72
Statisztikai es Nemzetgazdasági Közlemények [*Statistical and Political Economical
Review*]. Vols. V.-VIII. 8° *Budapest*, 1869-72

III. *Mathematical and Natural Sciences.*

A Magyar Tudós Társaság' Évkönyvei. Vols. I.-X. and XII.-XVII. (1831-1889).
[Some incomplete.] *Plates.* 4° *Budapest*, 1833-89
Emlékbeszédek a Mag. Tud. Akad. Tagjai Fölött. (Szerkeszti a fötitkár.) Kötet.
(Vols.) I.-VI., 1882-90. (Vols. II. and III. defective.) 8° *Budapest*, 1884-90
Értesitö.—A Mathematikai és Természettudományi Osztályok Közlönye. (Szerkesti,
Györy Sándor.) [Bulletin, Mathematical and Natural Science Section of Acad.]
Kötet. (Vol.) I. *Plates.* 8° *Budapest*, 1860
Mathematische und Naturwissenschaftliche Berichte aus Ungarn. (Mit Unterstützung der Ungarischen Akademie der Wissenschaften und der Könglich Ungarischen Naturwissenschaftlichen Gesellschaft). [J. Frölich and others]. Vol. I.-VII.,
IX. and X. *Maps and plates.* 8° *Budapest and Berlin*, 1882-93
Földrajzi Közlemények . . . kiadja a Magyar Földrajzi Társulat. [*Journal and
Proceedings of the Hungarian Geographical Society.*] Kötet (Vols.) I.-III., X.-
XXIII. (some incomplete). *Maps and plates.* 8° *Budapest*, 1873-95
—— Abrégé du Bulletin de la Société Hongroise de Géographie. Tom. X.-XXIII.
[A few imperfect ; each French Abstract bound with its corresponding vol. of
"Földrajzi."] 8° [For List of Members, see p. 793] *Budapest*, 1882-95

IV.—*Philology and Belle Lettres.*

Archivum Rákócziánum. II. Rákóczy Ferencz Levéltára. Bel-és Külföldi Irattárakból Bövitve. A Mag. Tud. Akad. :—
1. Oszotály (Sect. 1) Had-és Belügy. Kötet. (Vol.) II.-X. [The last contains an
Index to the 10 vols.] 8° *Budapest*, 1873-89
2. Osztály (Sect. 2) Diplomatia. Kötet. (Vol.) I.-III. 8° *Budapest*, 1872-71
Értekezések a Társadalmi Tudományok Köréböl. Mag. Tud. Akad. Kötet. (Vol.)
III.-XI. (some imperfect). 8° *Budapest*, 1875-92
Értekezések a Történelmi Tudományok Köréböl. Mag. Tud. Akad. A II.
Osztály Rendeletéböl. Kötet. (Vol.) IV.-XIV. (2 imperfect). 8° *Budapest*, 1874-90
Értekezések a Történeti Tudományok Köréböl. Mag. Tud. Akad. A II. Osztály
Rendeletéböl. Kötet. (Vol.) I.-III., XV.-XVI. (imperfect set). 8° *Budapest*, 1869-93
Értekezések a Természettudományok Köréböl. Mag. Tud. Akad. A III.
Osztály Rendeletéböl. Kötet. (Vol.) I. (füzet (parts) 1-4 and 14-19), II. 8°
Budapest, 1867-71
Értesitö. Mag. Tud. Akad. Nyelv-és Széptudományi Osztály Közlönye. (Szerkeszti,
Toldy Ferencz.) [Bulletin, Section of Philology of Acad.] Kötet. (Vol.) I. 8°
Budapest, 1860
Közlemények. Nyelvtudományi. Mag. Tud. Akad. [Memoirs Philological Section of
Hungarian Acad.]. (Szerkeszti Hunfalvy Pál.) Kötet. (Vols.) V. and VII. (imperfect set). 8° *Budapest*, 1866 and 1869
Ungarische Revue, mit Unterstützung der Ungarischen Akademie der Wissenschaften.
Jahrg. 1881-93 (13 vols. ; 1890, '91, and '93 imperfect). *Plates.* 8° and royal 8°
Budapest, 1881-93

CRACOW.

Akademija Umiejetnosci w Krakowie. [*Academy of Sciences, Cracow.*] Sprawozdanie Komisyi Fizograficznej . . . Materyjaly do Fizjografii Galicyi. Tom. II.-XXVIII. *Maps and plates.* 8°   *Cracow*, 1868-93
    [Report of Physiographical Commission . with Materials of Galician Physiography.]
—— Rozprawy i Sprawozdania z Posiedzén Wydzialu Historyczno-Filozoficznego. Tom. XIX. and XX. *Maps.* 8°   *Cracow*, 1887
    [Historical and Philosophical Memoirs ; contains Articles on Ancient Geography, with Maps.]
—— Rocznik Zarzadu (Akad. Umiej. w. Krak.). Rok 1886 and 1887. 12°
    [Annual of Acad. Sci., Cracow.]   *Cracow*, 1887-88
—— Bulletin International de l'Acad. des Sciences de Cracovie. Comptes Rendus des Séances de l'Ann 1889 and 1895, part 1 (8 parts). 8°   *Cracow*, 1889
    [Anzeiger der Akad. der Wissenschaft *supra*.]

IGLÓ.

Ungarischen Karpathen - Verein. (Magyarországi Kárpátegyesület). Jahrbuch [Vol.] XV.-XIX. Jahrg. 1888-1892 and 1894. (Deutsche Ausgabe.) *Plates.* 8°
    Igló, 1888-93

BELGIUM.

ANTWERP.

Société Royale de Géographie d'Anvers. Bulletin. Tom. I.-XVIII. *Maps and plates.* 8°   *Antwerp*, 1877-93
—— Memoires. Tom. I.-III. *Maps and plates.* 8°   *Antwerp*, 1879-86

BRUSSELS.

Académie Royale des Sciences et Belle-Lettres de Belgique. Annuaire de l'.—
Ann. LVI.-LIX. *Portraits.* 12°   *Brussels*, 1890-93
—— Bulletins des Séances de la Classe des Sciences. (2 vols.) *Plates.* 8°
    Brussels, 1863-64
—— Bulletin de l'Academie. *Plates.* 8°   *Brussels*, 1870-80
—— Ser. 2. Tom. XIX.-L. (32 vols.). Ann. 34 to 50. *Plates.* 8° *Brussels*, 1865-80
—— Ser. 3. Tom. I.-XXV. (25 vols.). Ann. 50 to 63. *Plates.* 8° *Brussels*, 1881-93
—— Tables Générales du Recueil des Bulletins. 2ᵉ Ser. Tomes XXI.-L. (1867-1880). 8°   *Brussels*, 1883
—— Centième Anniversaire de Fondation (1772-1872). Tom. I.-II. Royal 8°
    Brussels, 1872
—— Mémoires couronnés et autres Mémoires, publiés par l'Academie. Tom. XXII.-XLVI. *Plates.* 8°   *Brussels*, 1872-92
—— Mémoires couronnés et Mémoires des savants étrangers, publiés par l'Academie. Tom. XXXIII.-LII. 1865-67 to 1890-93 (20 vols.) *Plates.* 4° *Brussels*, 1867-93
—— Mémoires de l'Academie. Tom. XXXV.-XLIX. et L. (1 fasc.). [Bound in 15 vols.] *Plates.* 4°   *Brussels*, 1865-93
—— Notices Biographiques et Bibliographiques, concernant les Membres, les Correspondants, et les Associés. Ann. 1866. *Portraits.* 12°   *Brussels*, 1887
—— Tables des Mémoires des Membres, &c., 1816-57, 1858-78. 12° *Brussels*, 1858-79
Association Internationale Africaine. Rapports, &c. See Appendix 2 : Africa, General.
Missions en Chine et au Congo. Annales des années 1889-94. 6 vols. (bound in 2).
Plates. Small 4°   *Brussels*, 1889-94
Mouvement Antiesclavagiste Belge, Le. Revue Mensuelle Internationale Illustrée. Ann. V. (No. 9 and 12), VI. *Plates.* Royal 8°   *Brussels*, 1894
Observations Météorologiques faites aux Stations Internationales de la Belgique et des Pays-Bas. Parts II. and III., 1878, 1879. 4°   *Brussels*, 1879-80
Publications de l'Etat Independant du Congo. See Etienne, E., and Mense, Dr : Authors' Catalogue.
Observatoire Royale de Bruxelles, L. Annales (Nouv. Ser.) Tom. V. (1 fasc.) *Plates.* 4°   *Brussels*, 1882
—— Astronom. Append. 8°. See Houzeau, J. C. : Authors' Catalogue.

Société Belge de Géographie.   Bulletin.   Tom. I.-XVIII.   *Maps and plates.*   8°
                                                                    Brussels, 1877-94
—— Compte-Rendu des Actes de la Société.   Tom. I.-XVIII.   8°   *Brussels,* 1877-94
   [The Compte-Rendu is bound with the Bulletin.]

BRITISH ISLES : ENGLAND.

[*See under* United Kingdom, *postea.*]

DENMARK.

COPENHAGEN.

Annales de l'Observatoire Magnetique de Copenhague.   Publiées par Adam
Paulsen.   Année 1892.   Folio   *Copenhagen,* 1893
Danske Meteorologiske Institut, Meteorologisk Aarbog, udgivet af.   För 1886-93,
   8 vols.   *Maps.*   4° [Title-page also given in French]   *Copenhagen,* 1887-94
K. Danske Geografisk Selskab.   Geografisk Tidskrift, udgivet af Bestyrelsen for det
   K. D. G. Selsk.   Vols. I.-XII., 1877-93 (some incomplete).   *Maps and plates.*   4°
                                                                  Copenhagen, 1877-94
Kongelige Danske Videnskabernes Selskabs.   Historiske og Philosophiske
   Afhandlinger.   Vol. VII.   *Plate.*   Small 4°   *Copenhagen,* 1845
—— Naturvidenskabelige og Mathematiske Afhandlinger.   *Map and plates.*   Vols. XI.
   and XII.   4°   *Copenhagen,* 1845-46
—— Skrifter.   Naturvidenskabelig og Mathematisk Afdeling.   Ser. 5.   Vols. I.-XII.
   Maps and plates.   4°   *Copenhagen,* 1849-80
—— Ser. 6.   Vol. I.-VII. (6-7 imperfect).   *Maps and plates.*   4°   *Copenhagen,* 1880-93
—— Oversigt over det K. dansk. Vidensk. Selsk., Forhandlinger og dets Medlemmers
   Arbeider i Aaret, 1844-93 (bound in 19 vols.)   *Plates.*   8°   *Copenhagen,* 1845-93
—— [Classified Gen. Index.]   Fortegnelse over de Af. det Kongelige Danske Videnska-
   bernes Selskab i Tidsrummet 1742-1891.   Udgivne Videnskabelige Arbejder
   [pamph. 136 pp.]   8°   *Copenhagen,* 1892
K. Nordiske Oldskrift-Selskab.   Aarböger for Nordisk Oldkyndighed og Historie,
   udgivne af det K. Nord. Oldsk. Selsk.   Ser. 1—Aargang, 1866-85, 20 vols. ; Ser.
   2—Aargang, 1886-94, 8 vols.   *Plates.*   8°   *Copenhagen,* 1866-94
—— Tillæg til Aarböger.   Aarg. 1866-85 (18 parts, bound in 2 vols.)   8°
                                                                  Copenhagen, 1867-86

—— Annaler for Nordisk Oldkyndighed.   Aarg. 1836-37, 1840-41, 3 vols. ; 1847-50,
   4 vols. ; 1856 and 1859, 2 vols.—Total of 9 vols.   *Maps and plates.*   8°
                                                                  Copenhagen, 1837-59
—— Antiquarisk Tidskrift.   Aarg. 1843-45, 1855-60, 4 vols.   *Plates.*   8°
                                                                  Copenhagen, 1845-61
Société Royale des Antiquaires du Nord.   Mémoires de la, 1836-60.   4 vols. bound
   in 3.   *Maps and plates.*   8°   *Copenhagen,* 1836-61
—— Nouvelle Série, 1866-92, 5 vols. (2 incomplete).   *Maps and plates.*   8°
                                                                  Copenhagen, 1866-92

—— Cinquantième Anniversaire de la Fondation de la Société.   Discours prononcé par
   J. J. A. Warsaae.   8°   *Copenhagen,* 1875
—— Reports of the General Anniversary Meetings of the Royal Society of Northern
   Antiquaries, 1834-43.   *Plates.*   8°   *Copenhagen,* 1834-43
—— Report Addressed to the Royal Society of Northern Antiquaries by its British and
   American Members.   *Plates.*   8°   *Copenhagen,* 1836
—— Works Presented to the Society, 1855-57.   [Critical Remarks on, &c.]   1 vol.
   Woodcuts.   8°   *Copenhagen* [1860 ?]

FRANCE.

BORDEAUX.

Société de Géographie Commerciale de Bordeaux (Group Régional Girondin).   Bul-
   letin.   Ser. 1.   No. 2, 1875-76.   8°   *Bordeaux,* 1877
—— Bulletin.   Ser. 2.   Ann. I.-XVI., 1878-93 (16 tom.).   *Maps and plates.*   8°
                                                                  Bordeaux, 1878-93
—— Règlement.   [Pamph.]   8°   *Bordeaux,* 1877

DIJON.

Académie des Sciences, Arts, et Belle Lettres de Dijon, Mémoires de. *Plates.*
8° *Dijon*, 1830-50
—— 1e Ser. Année 1830-50. 8 vols.
—— 2e Ser. Tom. I.-XVI. (1851-70). [Bound in 11 vols.] *Plates.* 8° *Dijon*, 1852-71
—— 3e Ser. Tom. I. and IV.-X. (1871-87). [In 8 vols.] *Plates.* 8° *Dijon*, 1873-88
—— 4e Ser. Tom. I.-III. (1888-92). *Plates.* 8° *Dijon*, 1889-92
Journal d'Agriculture de la Côte d'Or, publié par la Société d'Agriculture et d'Industrie Agricole du Département. Vol. XXIV. 8° *Dijon*, 1862

HAVRE.

Société de Géographie Commerciale du Havre. Annuaire, 1886-93. 8 Reports.
8° *Havre*, 1886-93
—— Bulletin, 1884-93. *Maps and plates.* 8° *Havre*, 1884-93

LILLE AND DOUAI.

Bulletin Scientifique du Départment du Nord et des Pays Voisins. (Pas de Calais, Somme, Aisne, Ardennes, Belgique.) [A. Giard et J. de Guerne.] Tom. XI. Ser. 2. Ann. 2, 1879. *Plates.* 8° *Lille*, 1880
Société de Geographie de Lille, Bulletin de la, 1889. Tom. XI. (No. 5). *Plate.*
Royal 8° *Lille*, 1889
Union Géographique du Nord de la France. Bulletin. Vols. I.-XIII. and XIV. (incomplete). *Maps and plates.* Large and small 8° *Lille and Douai*, 1880-93

LYONS.

Les Missions Catholiques. *See* Paris, *infra.*
Société d'Anthropologie de Lyon. Bulletin. Vols. I.-XI. (1881-91). *Plates.* 8°
Lyons, 1882-91
Société de Géographie de Lyon. Bulletin. Vols. I.-XI. *Maps.* 8° *Lyons*, 1875-92
[Sep. vol. " Lyon et la Région lyonnaise."]
—— Rapport Annuel Séance Solennelle, 23rd Dec. 1880. [Pamph.] 8° *Lyons*, 1881
—— Procés-Verbaux. No. 1. Nov. 1881. [Pamph. 4 pp.] Small 4° *Lyons*, 1881

MARSEILLES.

Société de Géographie de Marseilles. Bulletin. Vols. I.-XVII. *Maps.* 8°
Marseilles, 1877-93

MONTPELLIER.

Société Languedocienne de Géographie. Bulletin. Vols. I.-XVI. *Maps and plates.* 8° *Montpellier*, 1878-93

NANCY.

Société de Géographie de l'Est. Publié par les soins et sous le Contrôle du Comité de Redaction. Bulletin de la, 1885. 2e Trimestre. 8° *Nancy*, 1885
Société des Sciences de Nancy. [Bulletin published at Paris. *See* Paris.]

NANTES.

Société de Géographie Commerciale de Nantes. Bulletin. Ann. 1885-86 et 1886. (3 parts). *Map.* 8° *Nantes*, 1885-86
—— Exposition de Géographie Commerciale, organisée sous le patronage de la Ville par la Soc. G. C. N. (Pamph.) 8° *Nantes*, 1886

PARIS.

Académie des Sciences Paris. Comptes Rendus Hebdomadaires des Séances de l', par MM. les Secrétaires Perpétuels. Tom. IV.-CXVIII. 4° *Paris*, 1837-93
—— Table Générale des Comptes Rendus des Séances. Tomes LXII.-XCL. (1866-1880). 4° *Paris*, 1888
Alliance Scientifique Universelle. *See under* " Institution Ethnogr.," and " Soc. Ethnographique," *postea.*
Annales de Géographie. [P. Vidal de la Blache et Marcel Dubois.] Tom. I.-II. (1891-92, 1892-93). *Maps.* 8° *Paris*, 1891-93
Annales de l'Agriculture des Colonies, et des Régions Tropicales. Publiées sous la Direction de M. Paul Madinier. Vols. I.-III. 8° *Paris*, 1860-61
Annales de l'Extréme Orient. *See* Soc. Acad. Indo-Chinoise, *infra.*

Annales Hydrographiques. Recueil de Documents et Mémoires relatifs à l'Hydrographie et à la Navigation publié au Depôt des Cartes et Plans de la Marine par le Service des Instructions. Ser. 1. Tom. I.-XLI. 1848-78. *Maps and plates.* 8°
Paris, 1849-79
—— Ser. 2. Tom. I.-XV. 1879-93. *Maps and plates.* 8° *Paris*, 1879-93
—— Index Alphabetique des Noms de Lieux contenus dans les Tomes I.-XXVIII. et XXIX.-XLI. 8° *Paris*, 1870-79
Annuaire des Marées des Côtes de France. *See* Appendix 2 : France (B).
Annuaire du Bureau des Longitudes, 1820-87. 68 vols. 16° *Paris*, 1820-87
Annales Maritimes, &c. *See* Ministère de Marine, *infra*.
Archives des Mission Scientifiques et Litteraires. [Publiées sous les auspices dé Ministère de l'Instruction Publique et des Cultes.] 33 vols. 1° Ser. Tom. I.-VI.
Plates. 8° *Paris*, 1855-57
—— 2° Ser. Tom. I.-VII. *Plates.* 8° *Paris*, 1864-72
—— 3° Ser. Tom. I.-XV. *Plates.* 8° *Paris*, 1873-89
—— 4° Ser. Tom. I.-IV. *Plates.* 8° *Paris*, 1891-93
—— Table Générale des Archives des Miss. Sci. et Lit., comprenant les trois Series jusqu' au Tom. XV. [et XV. *bis.*] 8° *Paris*, 1890
Association Internationale des Hommes de Science. *See under* Institution Ethnographique, *infra*.
Association de la Propagation de la Foi. Annales . . Recueil Périodique des Lettres des Évêques et des Missionaires des Missions des Deux Mondes, et de tous les Documens Relatifs aux Missions et à l'Association. Collection Faisant Suite à toutes les Éditions des Lettres Édifiantes. Tom. I.-XXIII. *Maps and plates.* 8°
See "Lettres Édifiantes," &c., *infra* *Paris, Lyons*, 1825-51
Association Française pour l'Avancement des Sciences. *See under* Algiers, *antea*.
Bulletin de Géographie Historique et Descriptive. *See* Comité des Travaux, &c., *infra*.
Bulletin des Sciences Géographiques, &c., Economie Publique : Voyages. [6 Sect. Bull. Universel des Sciences et de l'Industrie. Dir. De Férussac.] Tom. I.-XXVIII. (bound in 13 vols.) 8° *Paris*, 1824-31
Bulletin du Comité de l'Afrique Française. [Publication Mensuelle.] Ann. I°. to Vᵃ. and Supplements. *Maps and woodcuts.* 4° *Paris*, 1891-94
Canal de Suez, Le. Bulletin Décadaire de la Compagnie Universelle du Canal Maritime de Suez. [Commencing] No. 492, 22nd Aug. 1885. [Imperfect set.] 4°
Paris, 1885-93
Canal Interocéanique, Bulletin du. Année I.-IX. [or Nos. 1-225, imperfect set].
Maps. 4° *Paris*, 1879-89
Club Alpin Francais, Annuaire du. Ann. I.-XX (1874-93). *Maps and plates.* 8°
Paris, 1875-94
Comité des Travaux Historiques et Scientifiques. (Ministère de l'Instruction Publique et des Beaux Arts.) Bulletin de Géographie Historique et Descriptive.
Ann. 1886. (Nos. 1 and 2.) 8° *Paris*, 1886
Institution Ethnographique (Paris). "Alliance Scientifique Universelle," Association Internationale des Hommes de Science," comprise "Societé d'Ethnographie," "Soc. Americaine de France," "Soc. Sinico-Japanaise,"—Soc. des Etudes, Jap., &c. (With Sections, Orient. et Africaine, Amer. et Orient., and Oceanique.)
—— *See under* Soc. d'Ethnographie, *postea*.
La Clef du Cabinet des Princes de l'Europe, ou Recueil Historique et Politique sur les matières du tems, Juillet 1704—Dec. 1713. 23 vols. 12°. Imprimé chez Jacques le Sincère, à l'Enseigne de la Verité *Paris*, 1704-15
L'Année Géographique. Revue Annuel des Voyages de Terre et de Mer, &c. Ser. 1. Tom. II.-XIII., 1863-75 (par Vivien de Saint Martin). 12° *Paris*, 1864-76
—— Ser. 2. Tom. I.-II., 1876-77 (par C. Maunoir et H. Duveyrier). 12°
Paris, 1878-79
La Géographie. Revue Générale des Science Géographiques. (Dir. Léon Frémont, Redact. Gaston Dujarric.) Ann. VI. (imperfect). 4° *Paris*, 1893
Lettres Édifiantes et Curieuses Écrites des Missions Étrangers. Nouv. ed.
Tom. I.-XXVI. *Maps and plates.* 12° *Paris*, 1780-83
—— *See* [Append. 1 : " *Letters*," &c., p. 610, for regional divisions of vols.]
[Continued as]—
Nouvelles Lettres Édifiantes les Missions de la Chine et des Indies Orientales.
[*See* Note below.] Tom. I.-VIII. 12° *Paris*, 1818-23
[Continued as]—

Annales de l'Association de la Propapation de la Foi. Tom. I.-XXIII. *Maps and plates.* 8° *Paris (and Lyons)* 1825-51
[*See* "Assoc. Propagation de la Foi," *supra.*]

Les Missions Catholiques. Bulletin Hebdomadaire de l'Œuvre de la Propagation de la Foi. Tom. I.-XXV. *Maps, woodcuts, &c.* 4° [*Lyons and*] *Paris,* 1868-93
[The volume "*Nouvelles des Missions Orientales,*" published in London, 1797 (*see* under United Kingdom, *postea*), seems partly to fill the gap between "Lettres Edif." and "Nouv. Lettres," *supra.* The turmoil in France about the period in question might account for temporary cessation of Jesuitical periodicals in Paris.]

L'Explorateur, Journal Géographique et Commerciale. (Hebdomadaire, avec illustrations Cartes et Planches sous le patronage de la Soc. de Géogr. Comm. Déléguée par la Soc. . . . sous la direction de C. Hertz et A. Puissant.) Tom. I.-III. (and all issued of IV.). *Maps and illustrations.* Folio *Paris,* 1875-76
[Continued as]—

L'Exploration : Journal des Couquêtes de la Civilisation sur tous les points du Globe. (*Éds.* C. Hertz, H. Capetaine, and P. Tournaford.) Tom. I.-XVII., Dec. 1876 to 1884. *Maps and plates.* 8° *Paris,* 1877-84
[*See* "La Géogr. Contemporaine," &c., by C. Hertz : Authors' Catalogue.]
[Continued as]—

La Gazette Géographique et Exploration. Nouv. Ser. Année 1885 to 1887. 6 vols. *Maps and plates.* Small 4° *Paris,* 1885-87
[Followed by]—

Revue Française, de l'Étranger et les Colonies, et Exploration : Gazette Géographique. Tom. IV.-XV. (1885-93). *Maps and plates.* Royal 8° *Paris,* 1886-93

Magasin Asiatique, ou Revue Géographique et Historique de l'Asie Centrale et Septentrionale (par J. Klaproth). Tom. I.-II. (bound in 1 vol.). *Maps.* 8° *Paris,* 1825
[*See* "Asiatisches Magazin," Weimar (Germany), 1802, *postea.*]

Ministère de la Marine et des Colonies. Annales Maritimes et Coloniales, ou Recueil des Lois et Ordonnances Royales, Règlemens et Décisions Ministérielles, Mémoires, Observations, et Notices particulières, et généralement de tout ce qui peut intéresser la Marine et les Colonies, sous les Rapports Militaires, Administratifs, Judiciaires, Nautiques, Consulaires, et Commerciaux, 1829. (By M. Bajot.) 1 tom. in 2 parts (2 vols.). *Maps and plates.* 8° *Paris,* 1829

Ponts et Chaussées. Service Hydrometrique, &c. For publications of, *see* Append. 2.

Publications de l'École des Langues Orientales Vivantes. Ser. 1. Tom. I.-XX. *Maps.* Royal 8° *Paris,* 1876-85
—— Ser. 2. Tom. I.-XVII. *Plates.* Royal 8° *Paris,* 1881-86
—— Ser. 3. Tom. I.-VI. *Maps and plates.* Royal 8° *Paris,* 1886-89
[Total 43 vols. of the 47 published, those wanting in Soc. Library being Vols. 11, 17, and 20 of Ser. 2, and Vol. 7 of Ser. 3. For titles and subjects contained in separate vols. *see* Appendix 2 : France (D) ; and Authors' Catalogue.]

Revue Algerienne et Coloniale, No. de Septembre. Annuaire de l'Algérie et des Colonies, 1859. 1 vol. 8° *Paris,* 1859

Revue de Géographie. (Dirigée par Ludovic Drapeyron.) Tom. I.-XXXIV. *Maps and plates.* 8° *Paris,* 1877-93

Revue Géographique Internationale. Journal Mensuel Illustrée des Sciences Géographiques. [Vols. VI.-XVIII.] Ann. 1881-93. *Maps and plates.* (Imperfect set.] 4° *Paris,* 1881-93

Revue Maritime et Coloniale. (Ministère de la Marine et des Colonies.) Vols. I.-LV., LXXIII.-CXXII. (Total 105 vols., 6 incomplete.) *Maps and plates.* 8° *Paris,* 1861-93
—— Table Alphabétique et Analytique des Matières contenus dans les 40 volumes de la Rev. Mar. et Colon. de 1879-88. 8° *Paris,* 1889
[*See* Annales Maritimes (1829), *supra*; *also* Notices Statist. Colon. France, and Tableaux, &c. ; Appendix 2 : France (B).]

Societé Academique Indo-Chinoise. Revue Asiatique et Oceanique (*Ed.* C. Meyners D'Estrey). Annales de l'Extreme Orient. (Bull. de la Soc.). Tom. L.-XIV. *Maps and plates.* Royal 8° and 8° *Paris,* 1878-90
—— Bulletin de la Soc. (*Ed.* M. de Crozier). 2nd Ser. Tom. I.-III. *Maps and plates.* 8° *Paris,* 1882-90
—— Mémoires de la Soc. Tom. I, Ann. 1877 to 1878. *Plates.* 4° *Paris,* 1879

Societé Americaine de France. *See* under Soc. d'Ethnographie, *infra*.

Société Asiatique, Journal Asiatique Nouveau, ou Recuei lde Memoires, d'Extraits, et de Notices relatif à l'Histoire, à la Philosophie, aux Langues, et à la Litterature des Peuples Orientaux, publié par la Soc. Asiat. Total 126 vols. *Maps and plates.* 8°
Paris, 1831-94

Ser. 2.—10 Tomes (VII.-XVI)	1831-35	Ser. 6.—20 Tomes (I.-XX.)	1863-72
Ser. 3.—14 Tomes (I.-XIV.)	1836-42	Ser. 7.—20 Tomes (I.-XX.)	1873-82
Ser. 4.—20 Tomes (I.-XX.)	1843-52	Ser. 8.—20 Tomes (I.-XX.)	1883-93
Ser. 5.—20 Tomes (I.-XX.)	1853-62	Ser. 9.—2 Tomes (I.-II.)	1893

Société d'Anthropologie de Paris. Bulletin. 3° Ser. Tom. V.-XII (11 incomplete). *Plates.* 8°
Paris, 1882-89
—— 4° Ser. Tom. I.-IV. *Plates.* 8°
Paris, 1890-93
—— Mémoires. 2° Ser. Tom. III. (fasc. 3, 4) and IV. *Plates.* 8° *Paris*, 1888-93
—— 3° Ser. Tom. I. (fasc. 1-3). Royal 8°
Paris, 1893-94
—— Catalogue de la Bibliothèque. Pts. I. and II., 2 vols. 8°
Paris, 1891

Société d'Encouragement pour l'Industrie Nationale, Bulletin de la. Tom. XI. 4°
Paris,, 1864-65

Société d'Ethnographie (Paris).

I. *Américaine et Orientale.*

Comptes-Rendus des Séances de la Soc. Tom. I. and II. (2 pts.). 8° *Paris*, 1860
Rapport Annuel, . . . sur la Progrès (Ethnog.), &c. . . . pendant les Années 1858-59 and 1863 [*see* E. Cortambert : Authors' Catalogue.] 8° *Paris*, 1860 and 1864
Revue Orientale et Americaine (Rédigée par Léon de Rosny). Nouv. Ser. (2) I.-III. (5 Nos.). *Plates.* 8°
Paris, 1877-79

II. *Ethnographie Générale.*

Actes de la Soc. Ser. 2. Tom. I. (and Append.), II., VII.-X., 1865-85 [total 20 Nos.].
[Imperfect set in vols. and continuity of numbers. Append., Vol. I., "*Notice Descriptive de l'Exposition Ethnographique*," &c.] 8° *Paris*, 1867-86
Annuaire de la Soc., Sess. 1861, 1862 (2° and 3° Ann.), 1874 (8°), 1877, 1878 and bis, 1882-86 and 1888 [total 12 pts.]. 12° *Paris*, 1861-88
[The extra "Annuaire," 1878 contains "Résumé Historique," 1859-75.]
Memoires de la Soc. [8° SER.] *Sect. Orientale.* Revue Orient. 2° Ser. Tom. I. (No. 1), 1867, and Tom. XII. (No. 2), 1873. *Plate.* 8° *Paris*, 1867 and 1873
—— *Sect. Mem. et Travaux.* Revue Ethnographique. Ann. I. (Nos. 1, 2). *Plates.* 8°
Paris, 1869
—— [4° SER.] Tom. I. (Nos. 2, 3). *Map and plates.* 4° *Paris*, 1881-82
[For No. 3 *see* Léon de Rosny : Authors' Catalogue.]

III. *Société Americaine de France.*

Annuaire de la Soc., 1873 (1868-73), 1875 (1874-75), and 1881. 8° and 12° *Paris*, 1873-81
Archives de la Soc., Nouv. (2°) Ser. Tom. I. *Plates.* 8° *Paris*, 1875
Compte-Rendu des Séances (Actes de l'Institution Ethnographique). Sess. 1878. *Plates.* 8°
Paris, 1879

IV. *Société des Études Japonaises, Chinoises, &c.*

Annuaire de le Soc., 1873 (1° Ann.). 8° *Paris*, 1873
Memoires de la Soc., 1885 (pt. Tom. IV.). 8° *Paris*, 1885
Compte-Rendu des Séances de la Soc. 1877 (included in Tom. VIII., 1878, of Actes de l'Institution Ethnographique, *supra*).

V. *Institution Ethnographique.*

Bulletins. Ser. 1—Nos. 2 (1878), 41, 45, 48, 49 (1882), and 51, 52, 53 (1883) ; Ser. 2—Nos. 1-7 (1887), 21-24 (1888). [Total 21 Nos.] 8° *Paris*, 1878-88
[The 1st Ser. bears title " Bull. Instit. Ethnog.," the 2nd Ser. "Bull. Soc. Ethnog.," and extra heading " Alliance Scientifique Univcrselle."]
Rapport Annuel sur les Récompenses, &c. 1883-86 (4 Nos.). 8° *Paris*, 1883-86
[Extra heading " Alliance Sci. Univ."]
Annuaire de la Délégation Générale de l'Oceanie, 1884-85. 16°
Maitland (*N.S. Wales, Australia*), 1885

3 F

Société de Géographie (Paris), Bulletin de la. Total, 128 vols, bound in 91 vols. 8°
Paris, 1822-94

Ser. 1.—20 Tomes (in 20)	..	1822-33	Ser. 5.—20 Tomes (in 10) ..	1861-70
Ser. 2.—20 Tomes (in 10)		1834-43	Ser. 6.—20 Tomes (in 19) ..	1871-80
Ser. 3.—14 Tomes (in 7)	..	1844-50	Ser. 7.—15 Tomes (in 15) ..	1881-93
Ser. 4.—20 Tomes (in 10)		1851-60		

—— Bull. Table Alphabétique et Raisonnée des Matières contenues dans les deux premières Series, 1822-43. (E. de Froberville.) 8° *Paris*, 1845
—— Ditto. 3° and 4° Ser., 1844-61. (V. A. Barbié du Bocage.) 8° *Paris*, 1866
—— Compte-Rendu des Séances de la Soc. de Géogr. et de la Commission Centrale. Année, 1882-93 (12 tomes). *Maps.* 8° *Paris*, 1883-93
    [The Compt. Rend, Lists of Members, and other Notices prior to 1882, are bound up with the vols. of Bulletin.]
—— Notice sur la Soc., &c. *See* Appendix 2 : France (E.), Anonymous.
Société de Géographie Commerciale (de Paris), Bulletin de la. Tom. V., VII.-XIV., XV. [incomplete], 1882-93. *Maps.* 8° *Paris*, 1883-93
Société des Études Japonaises, Chinoises, Tartares, et Indo-Chinoises (fondée 1873). *See under* Institution Ethnogr. and Soc. d'Ethnographie, *antea*.
Société des Sciences de Nancy, Bulletin de la. Tom. I.-VIII. (18 fasc.). Ann. 1875-86. Nov. Ser. (loose), Nos. 2-5, Mai-Aout. 1889. [Imperfect set.] *Maps and plates.* 8° *Paris*, 1876-89
Société de Topographie de France. Bulletin. Ann. VII., Nos. 10-12 (1883) ; XVII., Nos. 1-3 and 7-12 (1893). *Plates*. Small 8° *Paris*, 1883-93
Société Ethnologique de Paris, Mémoires de la. Tom. I.-II. *Maps and plates.* 8° [*See* Appendix 2 : France (E.), Anonymous]. *Paris*, 1841-45
—— Bulletin de la. Ann. 1846-47 (2 parts, 1 vol.) 8° *Paris*, 1846-47
Société Français de Statistique Universelle, Bulletin de la. Ann. 1830-31. 2 tomes (in 1 vol). *Tables.* 4° *Paris*, 1831
Société Geologique de France, Bulletin de la. Vol. I. 8° *Paris*, 1830
Soc. Histor. et Archéolog. du Perigord. *See* Esperandieu, F. : Authors' Catalogue.
Société Météorologique de France, Annuaire de la. (2° Partie, Bulletin des Séances). Tom. XIII. Feuilles 1-22, 3 Nos. *Woodcuts.* Royal 8° *Paris*, 1865
Société Sinico-Japonaise. *See under* Institution Ethnographique and Soc. d'Ethnogr.
Tour du Monde, Le. Nouveau Journal des Voyages, fondé par Édouard Charton. Tom. I.-LXV. *Maps and plates.* 4° *Paris*, 1860-93
—— Table des Matières. Vols. I.-XX. (1860-70, bound with Tom. XXI.). 4°
Paris, 1870
Tour du Monde, Le. Nouvelles Geographiques (F. Schrader and H. Jacottet). Ann. I.-III. (1891-93). *Illustrations.* 4° [Also an 8° edition of Ann. I.] *Paris*, 1891-94

ROCHEFORT.

Société de Géographie de Rochefort. Bulletin. Tom. I. and XII. (imperfect, 2 Nos., 1879 and 1890-91), and Tom. XIV., XV., and XVI. (1892-94). Royal 8°
Rochefort and Paris, 1879-94

ROUEN.

Société Normande de Géographie. Bulletin. Tom. I.-XV. (Ann. 1879-94). *Maps.* Small 4° *Rouen*, 1879-94

SAINT-NAZAIRE.

Société de Géographie et du Musée Commercial de Saint-Nazaire. Bulletin. I.-IV., VI., VIII., et X. (7 parts). 8° *Saint-Nazaire*, 1886-93

TOULOUSE.

Société Académique Franco-Hispano-Portugaise de Toulouse. Annuaire, 1884-85 and 1887-88. 8° *Toulouse*, 1884-87
—— Bulletin. Tom. I.-XI. 8° *Toulouse*, 1880-93
    [Imperfect. The Bull., Tom. I., was issued under the title " Soc. Acad. Hispano-Portugaise," the " Franco " being added from Tom. II. onwards. From Tom. VI. (1885), the additional separate heading " Union Latine" is affixed.]
—— Statuts et Règlements (pamph. 30 pp.). 8° *Toulouse*, 1883
Société de Géographie de Toulouse. Annuaire 1890. 8° *Toulouse*, 1890

TOURS.

Union Géographique du Centre. Société de Géographie de Tours : Revue. Ann. III. (Nos. 3-9) [imperfect]. 8° *Tours*, 1886

GERMAN EMPIRE.

ALTENBURG.

Kunst- und Handwerks-Verein : Naturforschende Gesellschaft. Mittheilungen aus dem Osterlande. Gemeinschaftlich herausgegeben vom Kunst und Handwerks Vereine und von der Naturforschenden Gesellschaft zu Altenburg. Bände XV.-XVIII. *Plates.* 8° *Altenburg*, 1861-68
["Nachrichten u. Lebensbilder," &c. (1815-1857), Append. to Bd. XV.]

AUGSBURG.

Das Ausland. Ueberschau der neuesten Forschungen auf dem Gebiete der Natur-, Erd- und Völkerkunde. Jahrg. XXXVIII.-LXVI. (bound in 31 vols.). 4°
Augsburg and Stuttgart, 1865-93
[From 1828 to 1872, 45 vols. were published at Augsburg ; in 1873 the place of publication was changed to Stuttgart ; in 1882 the sub-title was altered to "Wochenschrift für Ländes, und Völkeskunde ;" and at the end of 1893 "Das Ausland" ceased, becoming incorporated with "Globus," published at Brunswick.]

BERLIN.

Archiv für wissenschaftliche Kunde von Russland. (A. Erman.) Band I.-XXV. 8° *Berlin*, 1841-67

Association International du Congo. *See* Danckelman : Authors' Catalogue.

Central-Verein für Handelsgeographie, und Förderung deutscher Interessen in Auslande (zu Berlin). Geographische Nachrichten für Welthandel und Volkswirthschaft. Organ für Auswanderungs- und Colonisationswesen. . . . Jahrg. I., II. (Hefte 1, 2), III. (Hefte 1-3), 1879, 1880, and 1881. *Maps.* 8° *Berlin*, 1879-81
[Continued as]—
—— Export, Organ des Central Vereins für Handelsgeographie, &c., Jahrg. IV.-XV., and XVI. (incomplete), 1882-93. 4° *Berlin*, 1882-93

Commission zur wissenschaftlichen Untersuchung der Deutsche Meere in Kiel, Jahresberichte der . . . Jahrg. I.-VI. für 1871-76. *Maps and plates.* Folio *Berlin*, 1873-78
—— Ergebnisse, der Beobachtungsstationen an dem Deutschenküsten über die Physikalischen Eigenschaften der Ost See und Nord See und die Fischerei. Jahrg. 1890, 1891, 1892 (3 Bände). Oblong 8° *Berlin*, 1891-93

Deutsche Geographentages, Verhandlungen des. Jahren 1881-93, 10 vols. *Maps and plates.* 8° *Berlin*, 1892-93

Erste.	D. Geogr. zu Berlin	1881	Sechsten.	D. Geogr. zu Dresden	1886
Zweiten.	„ zu Halle	1882	Siebenten.	„ zu Karlsruhe	1887
Dritten.	„ zu Frankfort	1883	Achten.	„ zu Berlin	1889
Vierten.	„ zu Munich	1884	Neunten.	„ zu Vienna	1891
Fünften.	„ zu Hamburg	1885	Zehnten.	„ zu Stuttgart	1893

—— Bericht über die Ausstellung des IX. Deutsch. Geographentages zu Wien, 1891. Nebst Ausstellungskatalog. 8° *Vienna*, 1891

Dentsche Gesellschaft zur Enforschung Æquatorial Afrikas. [A title altered to]—
Africanische Gesellschaft, Correspondenzblatt der. (W. Koner und R. Hartmann.) Band I. (Nos. 1-20), 1873-76. *Maps.* Small 8° *Berlin*, 1877
—— Band II. (Nos. 21, 24-29), 1877-78 (imperfect) 7 Nos., Herausgegeben von dem Obmann des Ausschusses). Small 8° *Dresden*, 1877-78
[*See* Appendix 2 : Africa, General, Miscellaneous.]
[Soc. Title again altered to]—
Afrikanischen Gesellschaft in Deutschland. Bände I.-V., 1878-89. (Dr W. Erman.) *Maps.* 8° *Berlin*, 1879-89

Deutsches Kolonialblatt. Amtsblatt für die Schutzgebiete des Deutschen Reichs, herausgegeben in der Kolonial-Abtheilung des auswärtigen Amts. Jahrg. I.-IV. *Maps and plates.* Small 4° *Berlin*, 1890-93

Deutschen Kolonial-Gesellschaft. Jahresbericht. 1892. Royal 8° *Berlin*, 1893

Deutsche Kolonialzeitung, Organ der Deutschen Kolonialvereins. (*Eds.* R. Lesser and G. Meinicke.) Bände I.-IV. *Maps.* 8° (*Frankfurt-a-M. and*) *Berlin*, 1884-87
—— Neue Folge. Jahrgang I.-VI. *Maps.* 4° *Berlin*, 1888-93

Export, &c. *See* Central-Verein, *supra.*

Geographische Nachrichten, &c. *See* Central-Verein, *supra*.

Gesellschaft für Erdkunde zu Berlin. Monatsberichte über die Verhandlungen der Jahrg. I.-IV. (in 1 vol.), Ser. 1 (1839-43). *Maps and plates.* 8° *Berlin*, 1840-43

—— Ser. 2. Bände I.-X. (in 5 vols.) *Maps and plates.* 8° *Berlin*, 1844-53
[Followed by]—

—— Zeitschrift für allgemeine Erdkunde. Bände II.-VI. (Ser. 1, T. E. Gumprecht). *Maps and plans.* 8° *Berlin*, 1854-56

—— The same. Neue Folge. Bände I.-XIX. (Ser. 2, K. Neumann and W. Koner). *Maps and plates.* 8° *Berlin*, 1856-65
[Continued as]—

—— Zeitschrift der Gesellschaft für Erdkunde. Bände I.-XXVIII. (W. Koner, A. von Danckelman, and G. Kollm). *Maps and plates.* 8° *Berlin*, 1866-93

—— Verhandlungen der. Bände I.-XX. (1873-94). *Maps.* 8° *Berlin*, 1875-94

—— Bibliothek der Gesell. f. Erdk. zu Berlin. Verzeichniss der Bücher. 1 Bd. 8° *Berlin*, 1888

Hydrographischen Amt der Admiralität, Reichs-Marine Amts, und der Deutschen Seewarte in Hamburg. Annalen der Hydrographie und Maritimen Meteorologie. Jahrg. XV. (Heft 6), XVI. (Hefte 1-6), XVII. (Hefte 1-6), XVIII., XIX. (Hefte 7-12), XX.-XXII. *Maps and plates.* Royal 8° *Berlin*, 1887-94

Koloniales Jahrbuch. (*Ed.* Gustav Meinicke.) Jahrg. II.-VI., 1889 to 1894. *Maps and woodcuts.* 8° *Berlin*, 1890-94

Kolonial Politische Correspondenz. Jahrg. I.-III. (1 and 2 slightly imperfect). Small 4° *Berlin*, 1885-87

Königliche Akademie der Wissenschaften (Berlin), Abhandlungen der. Jahren 1822-1893 (bound in 75 vols). *Maps, plates, and tables.* 4° *Berlin*, 1825-93

—— The same. Verzeichniss der Abhandlungen, von 1710-1870, in Alphabetischer Folge der Verfasser. 8° *Berlin*, 1871

—— The same. Inhaltsverzeichniss der Abhandl., 1822-72, nach den Klassen geordnet. 8° *Berlin*, 1873

—— Berichte über die zur Bekanntmachung geeigneten Verhandlungen der. Jahren 1839-55 (17 vols. bound in 16). *Maps and plates.* 8° *Berlin*, 1839-55
[Continued as]—

—— Monatsberichte der. Jahren 1856-81 (26 vols.) *Maps and plates.* 8° *Berlin*, 1860-82

—— Register für die Monatsb. 1836-73 (2 vols. bound in 1). 8° *Berlin*, 1860-75
[Continued as]—

—— Sitzungberichte der. Jahrgang 1882-94 [2 vols. annually=26 vols. total]. *Maps and plates.* Royal 8° *Berlin*, 1882-95

Königlichen Geodätischen Instituts (Berlin). Jahresbericht des Direktors, 1887-88 and 1893-94. (7 Jahresb.) 8° *Berlin*, 1888-94
[For other Publications of Preuss. Geodet. Instit., *see* Appendix 2 : Germany.]

Königliche Museum zu Berlin. *See* Ehrenreich, P. . Authors' Catalogue.

Königlich Preussischen Meteorologischen Instituts, Abhandlungen der. Band I. (Nos. 1-5). *Illustrations.* Royal 4° *Berlin*, 1890-92

—— Bericht über die Thätigkeit des. 1891-93 (3 parts). (Wilhelm von Bezold.) 8° *Berlin*, 1893-94

—— Ergebnisse (Stationen II.-III. Ordnung). 3 hefts. Royal 8° *Berlin*, 1893-94

—— The same, der Niederschlags, &c. Jahren 1891-92. Royal 4° *Berlin*, 1893-94

—— The same, der Meteorologischen Beobachtungen. (W. von Bezold.) Jahren 1886-1892 (7 vols.) *Maps.* Royal 4° *Berlin*, 1888-93

Kritischer Wegweiser im Gebiete der Landkarten-Kunde nebst andern Nachrichten zur Beförderung der Mathematisch-Physikalischen Geographie und Hydrographie. Bände I.-III. *Maps and plates.* 8° *Berlin*, 1829-32

Magazin von Natur und Ländermerkwurdigkeiten, &c. Theil I.-III. (3 vols.) *Plates.* 12° *Stadt-am-hof* [*Berlin*], 1806

Mittheilungen von Forchungsreisenden und Gelehrten aus den Deutschen Schutzgebieten. (Mit Benutzung amtlicher Quellen). Von Dr Freiherr v. Danckelman. Bände I.-VI. *Maps and plates.* Royal 8° *Berlin*, 1883-89

Natur-Wunder und Länder-merkwürdigkeiten. (Ein Beitrag zur Verdrängung Unnützer und Schädlicher Romane.) Von S. C. Wagner. Bande I.-VI. *Plates.* 16° *Berlin*, 1802-11
Neu Guinea Compagnie zu Berlin. Nachrichten über Kaiser Wilhelms-Land und den Bismarck-Archipel. Jahrg. I.-IX., 1885-93. *Maps and plates.* 8° *Berlin*, 1886-93
—— Beiheft zu. I vol. (viz.—Die Flora von Kaiser Wilhelms-Land. Von K. Schumann und M. Hollrung). 8° *Berlin*, 1889
Orientalische Bibliographie. *See* Dr Aug. Müller: Authors' Catalogue.
Publicationen für die Internationale Erdmessung. Bericht der Verhandlungen (und Abhang, &c.) 14 bände (1867-93). *Maps and plates.* 4°
(*Neuchatel and*) *Berlin*, 1868-94
[*See under* Florence, Neuchatel, and Zurich, *postea.*]
Registrande, Geogr.-Statist, Gross.-Generalstabes. *See* Appendix 2 : Germany (B).
Repertorium der Naturwissenschaften. Monatliche Uebersicht der neusten Arbeiten auf dem Gebiete der Naturwissenschaften. Herausgegeben von der Redaction des Naturforscher. Jahrg. I., 1875. 4° *Berlin*, 1875
Zeitschrift für Ethnologie und ihre Hülfswissenschaften als Lehre vom Menschen in seinen Beziehungen zur Natur und zur Geschichte. (A. Bastian und R. Hartmann.) Jahrg. I., Heft I. Royal 8° *Berlin*, 1869

BREMEN.

Geographischen Gesellschaft in Bremen. Verein für die deutsche Nordpolarfahrt. Berichte über die Sitzungen nebst Anlagen. [Vol. I.] Small 8° *Bremen*, 1870-76
[Publication succeeded by the]—
—— Deutsche geographische Blätter. (Herausgegeben von der geographischen Gesellschaft in Bremen durch deren Schriftführer Dr M. Lindeman.) Jahrgang I.-XVI. *Maps and plates.* Royal 8° *Bremen*, 1877-93
—— Jahresberichte des Vorstandes der Geogr. Gesel. in Bremen. Nos. I, 3-10. 8° *Bremen*, 1878-89
[*See* O. Finsch : Authors' Catalogue ; *also* Appendix 2 : Germany (D), Anon., Bremen.]
Naturwissenschaftlichen Verein zu Bremen. Abhandlungen, herausgegeben vom. Band I., 1866-68. *Plates.* 8° *Bremen*, 1868
[Bound with the]—
—— Jahresbericht, 1-3. (1864-66 to 1867-68.) 8° *Bremen*, 1866-68

BRUNSWICK.

Globus. *See* Hildburghausen, *infra.*

DARMSTADT (HESSE).

Mittelrheinischen Geologischen Verein. Karten und Mittheilungen des Mit. Geol. Ver. Geologische Specialkarte des Grossherzogthums Hessen und der Angrenzenden Landesgebiete (im Maasstabe von 1 : 50,000.) [Mittheilungen issued in 17 " Hefte " or Geolog. Sects., with accompanying maps and plates, of which there are in the Library the undermentioned :—]
Hefte II.-IX., XI.-XII., XIV.-XVI. 13 Hefte. *Maps and plates.* 8°
Darmstadt, 1856-72

Heft 2. Sect. Giessen, von E. Dieffenbach	1856
Heft 3. Sect. Budingen, von R. Ludwig	1857
Heft 4. Sect. Offenbach, von G. Theobald and R. Ludwig. 1 *plate*	1858
Heft 5. Sect. Scholten, von H. Tasche	1859
Heft 6. Sect. Dieburg (Darmstadt), von F. Becker and R. Ludwig	1861
Heft 7. Sect. Herbstein-Fulda, von H. Tasche and W. C. J. Gutberlet	1863
Heft 8. Sect. Erbach, von P. Seibert and R. Ludwig	1863
Heft 9. Sect. Darmstadt, von R. Ludwig	1864
Heft 11. Sect. Mainz., von A. Groos	1867
Heft 12. Sect. Lauterbach, von H. Tasche, W. C. J. Gutberlet, and R. Ludwig	1869
Heft 14. Sect. Allendorf, von E. Dieffenbach and R. Ludwig	1870
Heft 15. Sect. Gladenbach, von R. Ludwig. 5 *plates*	1870
Heft 16. Sect. Budenkapf, von R. Ludwig	1871

Maps accompany, in elephant fol. (Darmstadt), 1855-71 Index Map (Ludwig), 1867 ; Sect. I, Friedburg (Ludwig), 1855 ; Sects. 2-9, *supra ;* Sect. 10 Alzey (Ludwig), 1866 ; Sects. 11, 12, and 14-16, *supra.*

Vereine fur Erdkunde und verwandte Wissenschaft zu Darmstadt, Statuten des. Mit allerhöchster handsherrlichen Genehmigung bestehenden. 8° *Darmstadt*, 1845
—— Beiträge zur Landes- Volks- und Staatskunde des Grossherzogthums Hessen. 2 Hefte in 1 vol. *Maps and plates*. 8° *Darmstadt*, 1850-53
[Followed by the]—
—— Notizblatt des Vereins für Erdkunde und verwandte Wissenschaften zu Darmstadt. Ser. 1. Nos. 1-46, Band I. Oct 1854 to May 1857. *Maps*. 8° *Darmstadt*, 1857
[Amalgamation of Socs., and title altered to]—
—— Notizblatt des Ver. f. Erdk. . . . und des Mittelrheinischen Geological Vereins. Ser. 2. Jahrg. I. (Bd. I), Nos. 1-20. May 1857 to May 1858. *Plates and diagrams*. 8° *Darmstadt*, 1858
—— Jahrg. II. (Bd. II.), Nos. 21-40. Jan. 1859 to Feb. 1860. *Plates and diagrams*. 8° *Darmstadt*, 1860
—— Jahrg. III. (Bd. III.), Nos. 41-60. April 1860 to June 1861. *Plates and diagrams*. 8° *Darmstadt*, 1861
[The above 3 Jahrg. bound in 1 vol., along with Beiträge, *infra*.]
—— Appendix, viz. :—Beiträge zur Geologie des Grossherzogthums Hessen und der angrenzenden Gegenden. Ergänzungsblätter zur Notizblatt, &c. Heft I. 8°, *Darmstadt*, 1858
[Again amalgamation of Socs., and title altered to]—
—— Notizblatt des Ver. f. Erdk. . . . und des Mittelrhein. Geolog. Ver. Nebst Mittheilungen aus des Grossh. Hessischen Centralstelle für die Landesstatistik. (L. Ewald.)
Ser. 3. Hefte I.-XVIII., Nos. 1-216 Blätter [some missing, or 192 Nos. bound in 5 vols.]. *Plates and diagrams*. 8° *Darmstadt*, 1862-79
Ser. 4. Hefte I.-VII., IX., XII.-XIV. (9 sep. vols.) *Tables and plate*. 8° *Darmstadt*, 1880-92
[In Hefte I. and II. of Ser. 4 there are Nos. 1-15, after which numbers cease.]
—— Mittheilungen des Grossherzoglich Hessischen Centralstelle für die Landesstatistik. Bände I.-XXII. [From I.-X. (1871-80) they are incorporated with the Notizblatt without separate pagination ; from 1891-92 as Bds. XI.-XII. they appear in Notizblatt, with separate pagination.]

DRESDEN.

Kalender und Statistisches Jahrbuch für das Königreich Sachsen nebst Marktverzeichnissen für Sachsen und die Nachbarstaaten auf das Jahren 1888, 1889, 1893, and 1894. 8° *Dresden*, 1887-93
Königreich Sächsischen Statischen Bureau, Zeitschrift des. Bände XXXVII., XXXVIII. 4° *Dresden*, 1891-93
Naturwissenschaftlichen Gesellschaft Isis in Dresden, Sitzungs-Berichte der. Jahrg. 1866. *Map and plate*. 8° *Dresden*, 1866-67
Verein fur Erdkunde zu Dresden. Jahresberichte. I.-XXIII. (No. 21 missing). *Map and plates*. Small 8° *Dresden*, 1865-93

FRANKFORT-ON-MAIN.

Frankfürter Verein für Geographie und Statistik. Jahresberichte. 1872-73 to 1891-92 (9 pts), Jahrg. 37-65. *Maps*. 8° *Frankfort-a-M.*, 1875-93

GIESSEN.

Oberhessischen Gesellschaft fur Natur und Heilkunde. Bericht 7 and 8, 1858-59. *Maps and plates*. 8° *Giessen*, 1859-60

GOTHA.

Geographisches Jahrbuch. Bande I.-VII., von Dr E. Behm ; and VIII.-XVII., H. Wagner. Bände I.-XVII. 8° *Gotha*, 1866-94
Petermann's Mittheilungen aus Justus Perthes' Geographischer Anstalt über wichtige neue Erforschungen, auf dem Gesammtgebiete der Geographie. (*Eds*. Dr A. Petermann, I.-XXIV. ; Drs E. Behm and M. Lindeman, XXV. ; Dr E. Behm, XXVI.-XXX. ; Dr A. Supan, XXX.-XL. Bände I.-XL. *Maps*. 4° *Gotha*, 1855-94
[Inhaltsverzeichniss for Vols. I.-X., XI.-XX., XXI.-XXX., bound with 1864, 1874, and 1884.]
—— Ergänzungshände. Bände I.-XXV. *Maps and plates*. 4° *Gotha*, 1861-94
Monatliche Correspondenz zur Beförderung der Erd- und Himmels-Kunde (F. von Zach). Bänd. I.-XXVIII. _ _ _ *Gotha*, 1800-13

Geographischen Gesellschaft zu Greifswald. Jahresbericht 1882-83. *Plate.* 8°
Greifswald, 1883

HALLE AM SAALE.

Kaiserliche Leopoldino - Carolinische Deutsche Akademie der Naturforscher.
—Leopoldina. Jahrgang 1878-93. Heft XIV., XVI.-XXIX. 15 vols. 4°
Halle, 1878-93
—— Nova acta. Physico-Medica (Verhandlungen). Bände XL.-LX. (22 vols.) *Plates.*
4° *Dresden and Halle*, 1878-94
——— Geschichte der Kaiserlichen Leopoldinisch-Carolinischen Deutschen Akademie der
Naturforscher während der Jahre 1852-87, mit einem Rückblick auf die frühere
Zeit ihres Bestehens im Auftrage des Präsidenten Herrn Geheimenrathes Professors
Dr Hermann Knoblauch, verfasst von Dr Phil. Wille Ule. 1 vol. 4° *Halle*, 1889
Verein für Erdkunde zu Halle. Zugleich Organ des Thüringisch-Sächsischen
Gesamtvereins für Erdkunde. Mittheilungen des. Jahre 1877-94 (18 Jahre). *Maps
and plates.* 8° *Halle*, 1877-94

HAMBURG.

Journal des Museum Godeffroy. Geographische, ethnographische, und naturwissenschaftliche Mittheilungen. Heft I.-XV. (imperfect set). *Maps and coloured plates.*
4° *Hamburg*, 1873-81
Geographischen Gesellschaft in Hamburg. Jahresbericht. Bände I.-II. (1873-74
and 1874-75). *Maps and plans.* Royal 8° *Hamburg*, 1874-75
[Followed by]—
—— Mittheilungen der. [Bände I.-IX.] Jahres, 1876-77, 1891-92. *Maps and plates.*
8° *Hamburg*, 1878-91
—— Katalog der Bibliothek. 8° *Hamburg*, 1893
Mittheilungen aus der Nordeutschen Seewarte. Hefte II. und IV., 1860-67 und
1860-69. *Maps.* 4° *Hamburg*, 1870-72
—— Jahresbericht der Norddeutschen Seewarte. Jahr 1870 und 1874. 8° [*See* Freeden,
W. von : Authors' Catalogue.] *Hamburg*, 1870-74

HANOVER.

Geographischen Gesellschaft zu Hanover. Jahresbericht, I., 1879. *Maps.* Small 8°
Hanover, 1879

HEIDELBERG.

Naturhistorisch-Medecinischen Verein zu Heidelberg. Verhandlungen. Neue Folge.
Bände I., II., and III. (Heft I). *Maps and plates.* 8° *Heidelberg*, 1877-81

HILDBURGHAUSEN.

Globus. Illustrirte Zeitschrift für Länder und Volkerkunde, Chronik der Reisen und
Geographische Zeitung. (K. and R. Andree, and R. Kiepert.) Bände I.-LXIV.
Maps and plates. 4° *Hildburghausen and Brunswick*, 1862-93
[In 1893 "*Das Ausland*" was amalgamated with "*Globus*." *See* remarks under
Augsburg, *antea.*]
Jahresbericht des Vereins für Erdkunde in Dresden. 4° *Hildburghausen*, 1864

JENA.

Geographischen Gesellschaft (für Thüringen) zu Jena. Mitteilungen, Bände I., II.
(Hefte 1-2), XI. und XII. *Maps.* 8° *Jena*, 1882-93
——; [Gen. Index.] Inhaltsübersicht zu Bänden I.-XII. (1882-1893), &c. 8° *Jena*, 1894

KARLSRUHE.

Badischen Geographischen Gesellschaft zu Karlsruhe, Verhandlungen der. 1880-
82, 1882-83, 1883-84, 1884-86. *Maps and plates.* 8° *Karlsruhe*, 1883-86
—— Beiträge zur Statistik der inneren Verwaltung des Grossherzogthums Baden ;
herausgegeben von dem Handels-Ministerium. Parts I to 14. 4° *Karlsruhe*, 1855-63

KIEL.

Universität zu Kiel. Schriften der. Bände I.-XXVII. (1854-81). *Maps and plates.*
4° *Kiel*, 1855-81
Jahresbericht der Commission zur wissenschaftlichen Untersuchung der Deutsche
Meere in Kiel. *See under* Berlin, *antea* Commission, &c.

KÖNIGSBERG.

K. Physikalisch. Oekonomischen Gesellschaft zu Königsberg, Schriften der. Jahrg.
I.-VII., 1860-66 [bound in 2 vols.]. *Plates.* 4°   *Königsberg*, 1861-6(

LAHR.

Zeitschrift für wissenschaftliche Geographie. Lahr. (J. T. Kettler.) Jahrg.
I.-VIII., 1880-91. *Maps.* Small 4°   *Lahr, Vienna, and Wiemar,* 1880-91

LEIPZIG.

Deutschen Morgenländischen Gesellschaft. Abhandlungen für die Kunde des
Morgenlandes ; herausgegeben von der Deutschen Morgenländischen Gesellschaft.
Vols. I.-X., 1857-93. (Vols. IX. and X. imperfect.) *Maps and plates.* 8°
                                                        Leipzig, 1859-94
—— Jahresbericht. für das Jahre 1845 und 1846. [Bound up with Zeitschrift, Vol. I.]
   8°   *Leipzig*, 1846-47
        [Continued as]—
—— Wissenschaftlicher Jahresbericht über die Morgenländischen Studien. Jahre 1859-
   61, 1862-67, and 1876-81. 8°   *Leipzig*, 1868-85
—— Zeitschrift der Deutschen Morgenländischen Gesellschaft ; herausgegeben von den
   Geschäftsführern. Bände I.-XLVIII. (Vols. VIII. and XIX. imperfect.) *Plates.*
   8°   *Leipzig*, 1847-94
—— Register zu Bänden, I.-X. ; XI.-XX. ; und XXI.-XXX. 8°
                                             Leipzig, 1858, 1872, and 1877
Deutschen Palæstina-Vereins, Zeitschrift des. (*Ed.* Lic Hermann Guthe.) Band
   I. (heft. 1). *Maps and plates.* 8°   *Leipzig*, 1878
—— Statuten d. D. Ver. zu Erforschung Palästinas. (Pamph. 4 pp.) 8° *Leipzig*, 1878
Jahrbuch der Deutschen Kolonial-Politik. Bände I.-II. *Maps.* 8°
                                                        Leipzig, 1886-89
        [A vol. with title " Die Deutschen Kolonial Politik " was published at Leipzig in
        1886, and appears to answer to the Vol. I. here given, though differing in
        title.]
Jahrbuch der Astronomie und Geophysik. (Enhaltend die wichtigsten Fortschritt auf
   den Gebieten Astrophysik, Meteorologie, und physikalischen Erdkunde.) Von Dr
   Hermann J. Klein. Jahrg. 1892 and 1893, Band III. *Maps and plates.* 8°
                                                        Leipzig, 1893
Verein von Freunden der Erdkunde zu Leipzig. Jahresberichte I.-XI. (1861-71).
   Maps and plates. 8°   *Leipzig*, 1862-72
        [Continued as]—
—— Mittheilungen des Verein, 1872-93. *Maps and plates.* 8°   *Leipzig*, 1873-94
   [Folio Atlas, with Mitt. Ver. f. Erdk., accompanying Dr Alois Geistbeck's paper
   for 1884. *See* Geistbeck : Authors' Catalogue.]
—— Bücher-Verzeichniss der Bibliothek des Verein. 8°   *Leipzig*, 1887
   [Bound with Mittheilungen, 1886.]
—— Wissenschaftliche Veröffentlichungen. *See* Appendix 2 : Germany (C).

LÜBECK.

Geographischen Gesellschaft in Lübeck. Mitteilungen. Hefte 2 and 3 (1882-83).
   Maps and plates. 8°   *Lübeck*, 1883

MADEBURG.

Zeitschrift für vergleichende Erdkunde. Zur Forderung und Verbreitung dieser
   Wissenschaft für bis Gelehrten und Gebildeten. (Von Johann Gottfried Lüdde.)
   Band I. *Maps and plates*   *Madeburg*, 1842

METZ.

Verein fur Erdkunde zu Metz. Jahresberichte. I.-III., 1878-80. *Maps and plates.*
   8°   *Metz*, 1879-81

MUNICH.

Deutschen Alpenvereins, Zeitschrift des. Band I.-III. (1869 to 1872). *Maps and
   plates.* 8°   *Munich*, 1870-72
        [*See* "Oesterreichischen Alpen-Verein" and "Deutschen und Oesterreichischen
        Alpen-Verein," Wien, Austria-Hungary.]
Geographischen Gesellschaft in München. Jahresbericht für 1871 zu 1890 and 1891.
   (16 Jahrb., oder 14 Hefte.) *Maps and plates.* 8°   *Munich*, 1871-92

Königlich Bayerischen Akademie der Wissenschaften zu München. Abhand-
lungen der Mathematisch-Physikalischen Classe der. Bände I.-XVII., und XVIII.
(1829-93). *Plates.* 4°   *Munich*, 1832-93
—— Sitzungsberichte, Jahrgang 1860-70. (21 vols., bound in 17.) *Plates.* 8°
                                                          Munich, 1860-70
—— Neue Folge. Mathematisch-physikalishen classe. Vol. I.-XXIV. (Jahrg. 1871-94).
Plates. 8°   *Munich*, 1871-94
—— Inhaltsverzeichniss zu Jahrgang 1860-70. 8°   *Munich*, 1872
—— Almanach der K. Akad. für das Jahr. 1855. 12°   *Munich* [1855]
—— Bulletin der K. Akad. Jahren 1852 and 1853. 4°   *Munich*, 1852-53

STETTIN.

Verein für Erdkunde zu Stettin. Jahresbericht, 1883-89 (4 Nos.). *Maps and plates.*
  8°   *Stettin*, 1885-89

STUTTGART.

Allgemeine Länder und Volkerkunde. Bände I.-VI. *Plates.* 8° *Stuttgart*, 1837-44
  [*See* Berghaus, H. ; Authors' Catalogue.]
Almanach, Genealogisch-historisch, Statistischen. (Sub-title altered to "Den Freunden
  der Erdkunde Gwidmet"—Von H. Berghaus). 4 vols. *Maps and plates.* 16° and
  12° [Forerunner of the Almanach de Gotha]   *Stuttgart*, 1838-40
Das Ausland, &c. [*See under* Augsburg, *antea.*]
Forschungen zur Deutschen Landes- und Volkskunde, &c. . . . *See* Appendix 2 :
  Germany, C, Miscellaneous.
Geographische Abhandlungen, aus den Reichslanden Elsass-Lothringen. (Mit Unter-
  stützung der Kaiserl. Regierung zu Strassburg.) G. Gerland. 1 Heft. *Plates and
  plans.* 8°   *Stuttgart*, 1892
Hertha. Zeitschrift für Erd- Völker- und Staatenkunde. (Besorgt von Heinrich Berghaus
  in Berlin und Karl Friederich Vollrath Hoffmann in Stuttgart.) Bände I.-XIV.
  [Vol. VII. missing, and VI., X., and XIII. wanting parts.] *Maps and plates.* 8°
                                              Stuttgart und Tübingen, 1825-29
       [Continued as]—
Annalen der Erd- Völker- und Staatenkunde. (*Ed.* H. Berghaus.) Bände IV.-IX.
  Maps and plates. 8°   *Berlin*, 1837-40
       [These vols. are marked on binding as XVI. (1837) to XXI. (1839-40), evidently
       the running numbers from "Hertha."]
Wirtembergisches Urkundenbuch (herausgegeben von dem k. Staatsarchiv in Stutt-
  gart). Vol. V. 4°   *Stuttgart*, 1889
Wurttembergischen Verein für Handelsgeographie, und Förderung Deutscher
  Interessen in Auslande. Jahresberichte I.-VI. (1882-84 to 1886-88). *Woodcuts.* 8°
                                                          Stuttgart, 1884-88

WEIMAR.

Asiatisches Magazin. Verfasst von einer Gesellschaft Gelehrten und herausgegeben von
  Julius Klaproth. *Map and plates.* 2 vols. 8°   *Weimar*, 1802
  [*See* "Magasin Asiatique," Paris, 1825, *antea.*]
Zeitschrift für wissenschaftliche Geographie. (Herausgegeben von J. I. Kettler :
  Geographisches Institut, Weimar.) Ergänzungsheft No. 2. *Map.* Royal 8°. [Die
  Orientfahrt des Ritter A. von Harff. Beiträge zu einer Kritik seiner Reise Besch-
  reibung von R. Frhr. v. Seydlitz.]   *Weimar*, 1890

GREECE.

ATHENS.

Athenaion Syngramma Periodicon. Vols. I.-II. [In Greek.] 8° *Athens*, 1873-74
Archæological Society of Athens. Archæological Ephemeris (Periodos B' Teuchos
  Iz'). [In Greek.] *Plate.* 4°   *Athens*, 1874
—— Proceedings of the. 1872-73. [In Greek.] 8°   *Athens*, 1873

HOLLAND OR NETHERLANDS.

AMSTERDAM.

Aardrijkskundig Weekblad (Nieuwe Serie). Redact. van Dr G. J. Dozy. Vols. I. and II. *Plates.* Royal 8°   *Amsterdam*, 1879-80

Koninklijke Akademie van Wetenschappen. Verhandelingen der. Deel. I.-XXIX. *Maps and plates.* 4°   *Amsterdam*, 1854-92
[Afterwards divided into two sections, viz. :—]
—— [Sect. I.] Wiskunde, Naturkunde Scheikunde, Kristallenleer, Storrenkunde, Weerkunde, en Ingenieurswetenschappen. Deel. I.-II. *Maps and plates.* Royal 8°
Amsterdam, 1893-94
—— [Sect. II.] Plantkunde, Dierkunde, Aardkunde, Deftstokunde, Ontleedkunde, Physiologie, Gezondheidsleer, en Ziektekunde. Deel. I.-III. *Map and plates.* Royal 8°   *Amsterdam*, 1892-94
—— Verslagen en Mededeelingen der. Afdeeling [Section] Natuurkunde.
Ser. 1.   [Vols. I.-XVII.] 1853-64.   *Maps and plates.*   8°   *Amsterdam*, 1853-65
Ser. 2.   [Vols. I.-XX.] 1866-84.   *Maps and plates.*   8°   *Amsterdam*, 1866-84
Ser. 3.   [Vols. I.-IX.] 1884-91.   *Maps and plates.*   8°   *Amsterdam*, 1885-92
—— Naam-en Zaakregister [Ser. 1].   Deel. I.-XVII., 1853-64.   8°   *Amsterdam*, 1880
—— [Ser. 2.]   Deel. I.-XX., 1866-84.   8   *Amsterdam*, 1884
—— [Ser. 3.]   Deel. I.-IX., 1884-91.   8°   *Amsterdam*, 1893
—— Processen-Verbaal van de Gewone Vergaderingen der K. Akad. Afdeel [Sect.] Natuurkunde.   Nos. 1-10.   8°   *Amsterdam*, 1880-81
—— Afdeeling [Section] Letterkunde. Ser. 2, Deel. IX., and Ser. 3, Deel. I. *Plates.* 8°   *Amsterdam*, 1881
—— Jaarboek der. Deel. 1857-93 (— vols.).   8° and royal 8°   *Amsterdam*, 1858-94
—— Overzigt van de Boeken, Kaarten, Penningen Enz., ingekomen bij de Koninklijke Akademie van Wetenschappen, te Amsterdam, van Junij 1857 tot April 1860, Julij 1861 tot Mei 1862.   8°   *Amsterdam*, 1860-62

Nederlandsche Aardrijkskundig Genootschap. Nomina Geographica Neerlandica. *See* Appendix 2 : Holland.
—— Tidschrift van het Aardrijkskundig Geenootschap. (*Redact.* van C. M. Kan, N. W. Posthumus, en J. Æ. C. A. Zimmerman.) 35 vols., with Appendix. *Maps and plates.* 4° and 8°   *Amsterdam and Leyden*, 1876-93
Ser. 1.   Vols. I.-VIII. (1876-83).   *Maps and plates.*   4°   *Amsterdam*, 1876-83
—— Bijbladen [Appendix]. Vols. I.-III.   *Maps and plates.*   4°
Amsterdam, 1879-83
Ser. 2.   Afdeeling [Sect. 1] : Verslagen en Aardrijkundige Mededeelingen. Vols. I.-VI.   *Maps and plates.*   8°   *Amsterdam and Leyden*, 1884-89
—— Afdeeling [Sect. 2] : Meer Uitgebreide Artikelen. Vols. I.-VI. *Maps and plates.* 8°   *Amsterdam and Leyden*, 1884-89
—— The same. Vol. VII.-X.   *Maps and plates.*   8°   *Leyden*, 1890-94
[From Vols. VII. to X., two vols. have been issued annually, the pagination in these running continuously—the vols. being marked respectively (*) and (**), equal to parts 1 and 2.]

Revue Coloniale Internationale, fondée par l'Association Colonial Nederlandaise à Amsterdam. (Drs C. M. Kan, P. A. van de Lith, D. J. Jitta, and H. C. Rogge.) 1885-87, 5 tomes (2 annually). *Maps and plates.* Royal 8°   *Amsterdam*, 1885-87

Verhandelingen en Berigten over eenige Onderwerpen der Zeevaartkunde. (*Redact.* J. F. L. Schroder, J. G. A. Tindal, en J. Swart.) Jaargang 1837-64. Nieue Volgarde, Deel. I.-XIII., XV.-XXIV.   *Maps and plates.*   8°   *Amsterdam*, 1837-64

THE HAGUE.

Koninklijk Institut voor de Taal- Land- en Volkenkunde van Neêrlandsch Indië. Bijdragen tot de Taal- Land- en Volk. van Neêrl. Ind.; Tijdschrift van het Konink. Inst. v.d. Taal-Land, &c. [Total 43 vols. bound in 39.] *Maps and plates.* 8°
The Hague and Amsterdam, 1853-94
[Ser. 1.]   Vols. I.-IV.   1853-55
[Ser. 2.]   Nieuwe Volgreeks.   Vols. I.-VIII.   1856-64
[Ser. 3.]   Derde Volgreeks. Vols. I.-XI.   1866-76
[Ser. 4.]   Vierde Volgreeks. Vols. I.-X.   1877-85
[Ser. 5.]   Vijfde Volgreeks. Vols. I.-X.   1886-94
[Vol. IX. of Ser. 5 deficient, its issue being delayed. *See under* Dutch East East Indies : Appendix 2.]

HARLEM.

Annalen der Sternwarte in Leiden. Herausgegeben von Dr F. Kaiser. Bd. 1. 4°
Harlem, 1868

LEYDEN.

De Indische Bij, Tijdschrift ter bevordering van de Kennis der Nederlandsche Volkplantingen en derzelver belang en, uitgegeven door C. L. Blume. *Plates.* 8°
Leyden, 1843

UTRECHT.

Bijdragen tot de Kennis der Nederlandsche en vreemde Koloniën, bijzonder Betrekkelijk de Vrijlating der Slaven. [Nederlandsch Guyana.] Jaarh. 1844 and 1845, 2 vols. [No. 4 in Vol. 1845 missing.] 8° *Utrecht,* 1844-46
Koninlijk Nederlandsch Meteorologisch Instituut (Utrecht), Publications of the. *See* Holland : Appendix 2.

ITALY.

BOLOGNA.

Nuovi Annali delle Scienze Naturali. Anno. 2-5. Vols. III. (part 2), IV.-IX. *Plates.* 8° *Bologna,* 1840-43
Annuario Geografico Italiano, 1844-45. [*See* Ranuzzi, A. . Authors' Catalogue.]

GENOA.

Museo Civico di Storia Naturale di Genova. (G. Doria e R. Gestro.) Annali, Vols. I.-XXXIII. (Ser. 1. Vols. I.-XX, 1870-84 ; and Ser. 2. Vols. I.-XIII., 1884-93.) *Maps and plates.* Royal 8° *Genoa,* 1879-93
Pubblicazioni del Comitato Centrale per la Spedizione Antartica Italiana. Fasc. 1. *Map.* 8° *Genoa,* 1880

FLORENCE.

Association Geodésique Internationale. Supplementary vols., viz., "Rapports sur les Triangulations." 3 vols. *Maps and plates.* 4° *Florence and Lausanne,* 1887-93
Biblioteca Nazionale Centrale di Firenze. Bollettino delle Pubblicazione Italiane (ricevute per diritto di Stampa), 1891, 1892, 1893, and 1894. 8° *Florence,* 1891-94
—— Elenco delle Pubblicazioni Periodiche Italiane, ricevuto dalla Biblioteca nel 1891. 8° *Florence,* 1891
Bollettino Italiano degli Studii Orientali. Anno I. (Nos. 2, 3). 8° *Florence,* 1876
Bulletins de l'Académie Nationale Hongroise des Sciences. I.-V. 8° *Florence,* 1884-86
Società Africana d'Italia, Bullettino della Sezione Fiorentina della. Anno. 1. Vol. I. Fasc. 1° e 2°. 8° *Florence,* 1885
Società Geografica Italiana, Bollettina della. Vols. I.-XXXIX. Anni 1-28. *Maps and plates.* 8° *Florence and Rome,* 1868-94
[The First Series in part (Vols. I.-VII., 1868-72,) was published at Florence ; thereafter the seat of publication was transferred to Rome, where appeared the Second Series (1876-87), and the Third Series (1888-94) now in progress. *See under* Rome, *postea.*]

MILAN.

Reale Instituto Lombardo di Scienze e Lettere ed Arti, Giornale dell.' Ser. 1. Tom. I.-VIII. *Plates.* 8° *Milan,* 1841-47
—— Ser. 2. Tom. I.-IX. *Maps and plates.* 4° *Milan,* 1847-56
—— Atti, dell'. Tom. I.-III. *Maps and plates.* Royal 4° *Milan,* 1858-62
—— Annuario dell'. 12° *Milan,* 1864
—— Memorie (Regno Lombardo-Veneto). Vols. I.-V. (Anni 1812 to 1836). *Plates.* Royal 4° *Milan,* 1819-38
—— The same. Ser. 1 and 2 (Nov. Ser.). Vols. I.-IX. *Maps and plates.* Royal 4° *Milan,* 1843-63
—— The same. Ser. 3 (Classe di Scienze, Matematiche, e Naturali). Vols. I.-VII. (fasc. 1, 2) ; Vols. X. to XVI. of entire Ser. *Maps and plates.* Royal 4° *Milan,* 1867-88
—— The same. Ser. 3 (Classe di Lettere e Scienze Morali e Storiche). Vols. VI.-IX. *Plates.* Royal 4°. Vols. XV.-XVIII. of entire Series *Milan,* 1885-91
—— Rendiconti (Classe di Scienze, Matematiche, e Naturali). Vols. I.-IV. *Plates.* 8° *Milan,* 1864-67
—— The same (Classe di Lettere e Scienze, Morali, e Politiche). Vols. I.-IV. 8° [These two Ser. are bound together as one set in 4 vols.] *Milan,* 1864-67

Reale Instituto Lombardo di Scienze e Lettere ed Arti. Rendiconti.   Ser. 2. Vols.
I.-XXIII. (bound in 25 vols.)   *Plates.*   8°   *Milan and Naples*, 1868-90
   [In this Series a "Bulletino Bibliografico" is contained in each vol., and is
   separately paged from Vol. VII. onwards.]

Società d'Esplorazione Comerciale in Africa.   L'Esploratore, Giornale di Viaggi e
   Geografia Commerciale, diretto dal Capitano Manfredo Camperio.   Organo Ufficiale
   della Soc.   Vols. I.-IX. [incomplete].   *Maps and plates.*   4°   *Milan*, 1877-85
        [Continued as]—
—— L'Esplorazione Commerciale.   (Dir. Dr N. Bolognini.)   Vols. I.-III. and IV. (fasc.
   1, 2, 6, 7, 8), IX. and X. (parts), and Suppl. Bollettino, May 1887 and Jan. 1888.
Maps and plates.   Small 4°   *Milan*, 1886-94

Annali Civili del Regno delle due Sicilie.   Tom. I.-XIV.   *Plates and tables.*   4°
                                                              Naples, 1833-46
Calendario Napoli.   6 vols.   *Maps.*   12° and 16°   *Naples*, 1819-24
L'Esplorazione Rassegna Quindicinale, delle Conquiste Geografiche e degl' Interessi
   Italiani in Tutti i Punti del Globo.   (Direttori : G. B. Licati e Ferd. Borsari.)
   Vol. I.   8°   *Naples*, 1883
Regale Academia Ercolanese di Archeologia.   Vols. I.-VIII. [in 9 vols.]   *Maps
   and plates.*   4°   *Naples*, 1822-56
Società Africana d'Italia, Bollettino della.   Ann. I. (1882) ; VII. fasc. 5, 6 (1888) ;
   IX. fasc. 1-4 (1890).   8°   *Naples*, 1882-90
Società Americana d'Italia.   Programma e Statuto.   Royal 8°   *Naples*, 1890

Academia di Scienzi e Lettre di Palermo, Atti della.   4°   *Palermo*, 1866
R. Associazione dei Benemeriti Italiani, Statuto ed Elenco dei Soci della.   (Sede
   Centrale in Palermo 5ᴿ ed.)   [Pamph.]   8°   *Palermo*, 1879
Reale Osservatorio di Palermo, Bulletino Meteorologico del.   Anno VIII.-XV. (1872-
   79, or 7 vols. bound in 1.)   4°   *Palermo*, 1873-81

Biblioteca Nazionale Centrale Vittorio Emanuele di Roma.   Bolletino della Opere
   Moderne Straniere Aquistate dalle Biblioteche pubbliche Governative del Regno
   d'Italia.   Vol VII., 1892.   (Index Alfabetico.)   8°   *Rome*, 1893
Bolletino Consolare Italia.   Ser. 1, 23 vols. ; Ser. 2, 12 vols. ; [Ser. 3], 18 Nos.   8°
   [*See* Appendix 2 : Italy (A), Govt. Pubs.]   (*Turin and*) *Rome*, 1861-95
Bulletino Nautico e Geografico di Roma (diretto da E. Fabri-Scarpellini).   Appendice
   alla Corrispondenza Scientifica di Roma.   Vol. I.   4°   *Rome*, 1862
Bolletino di Notizie Agrarie (Roma).   *See* Appendix 2 : Italy, (A) Govt. Pubs.
Instituto Cartografico Italiano, Annuario dell'.   Anno I., III., and IV.   *Maps.*   8°
                                                              Rome, 1885-89
Institut International de Statistique, Bulletin de.   Tom. I. (3 and 4 livraisons), II.
   and IV. (livrais. 1).   [Bound as 4 vols.]   *Maps and plates.*   Small 4°   *Rome*, 1886-89
Reale Academia dei Lincei.   Ser. 1. Atti dell Acad. Pontificia dei Nuovi Lincei.
   Tom. X., XVII.-XXIII., 8 vols (1856-57 to 1869-70).   *Plates.*   4°   *Rome*, 1856-69
—— Ser. 2. Atti della Reale Acad. dei Lincei.   Tom. I.-VIII. (1873-74 to 1876-77).
   Maps and plates.   4°   *Rome*, 1875-83
—— Ser. 3. Memorie (Classe de Scienze, Fisiche, Mathematiche, e Naturali).   Tom.
   I.-XIX. [bound in 13 vols.] (1876-77 to 1883-84).   *Maps and plates.*   4°
                                                              Rome, 1877-84
—— Ser. 4. —— Tom. I.-VI. [bound in 5 vols.] (1884-85 to 1889).   *Maps and plates.*
   4°   *Rome*, 1885-90
—— Ser. 3. —— (Classe di Scienze Morali, Storichi, e Filologie.)   Tom. I.-XIII.
   (1876-77 to 1883-84).   *Maps and plates.*   4°   *Rome*, 1877-84
—— Ser. 4. —— Tom. I.-X. [latter incomplete] (1884-85 to 1892).   *Maps and plates.*
   4°   *Rome*, 1885-93
—— Ser. 5. —— Tom. I. (incomplete).   4°   *Rome*, 1893
—— Ser. 3. Transunte.   Tom. I.-VIII. (1876-77 to 1883-84).   4°   *Rome*, 1877-84
—— Ser. 4. Rendiconti.   Tom. I.-VII. [bound in 13 vols., viz., 2 volumes annually]
   (1884-85 to 1891).   4°   *Rome*, 1885-91
—— Ser. 5. —— Tom. I.-III. [bound in 6 vols.]   4°   *Rome*, 1892-94

Revista Geografica Italiana. Ann. I. (fasc. 1-10). *Maps and plates.* 8° *Rome,* 1893-94
Rivista Marittima. Vols. XII. and XIII. *Plates and charts.* 8° *Rome,* 1879-80
Societa Geografica Italiana, Bollettino della. (Total 39 vols. bound in 30)—
   Ser. 1. Vols. I.-XII., anni 1-9 (1868-75). *Maps and plates.* 8°
                                    (Florence and) Rome, 1868-75
   Ser. 2. Vols. I.-XII., anni 10-21 (1876-87). *Maps and plates.* 8° *Rome,* 1876-87
   Ser. 3. Vols. I.-VII., anni 22-28 (1888-94). *Maps and plates.* 8° *Rome,* 1888-94
—— Indice Generale della Serie 1ᵃ (anni 1867-75, Vols. I.-XII.). 8° *Rome,* 1882
   [*See* Remarks Soc. Geogr. Ital., under Florence, *antea.*]
—— Memorie della Società. Vols. I.-III. *Maps.* 8° *Rome,* 1878-81

ROVERETO.

Societa degli Alpinista Tridentini. Annuario XIV. Anno Sociale 1888. *Plates.* 8°
                                                  Rovereto, 1889

TURIN.

Circolo Geografico Italiano. Pubblicazioni del Circ. Geogr. Ital., sotto gli Auspizi di
   S.A.R. il Principe Eugenio di Savoja Carignano. Fasc. Dec. 1868 [pamph. 78 pp.]
   8° *Turin,* 1868
      [Continued as]—
Periodico bimestrale di Geografia, Etnografia, e Scienze affini. Año I.-III. and IV.
   [incomplete]. *Plates.* 8° *Turin,* 1872-76
      [Followed by]—
Società di Geografia ed Etnografia Torino. Circolare Statuto Provvisiori [pamph.].
   Royal 8° *Turin,* 1884
Club Alpino Italiano. Revista Mensile. Vol. IV. (No. 11, 12). 8° *Turin,* 1885
Cosmos: Communicazioni sui progressi più recenti e notevoli della Geografia e delle
   Scienze affini, di Guido Cora. Vols. I.-XI. *Maps and plates.* 4° *Turin,* 1873-93

MALTA.

VALLETTA.

Società Geografica Maltese. Monitore Geografico e Scientifico de Malta. Fasc. 1.
   (Nuova Serie.) Anno I. 8° *Valetta,* 1887
—— Programma e Regolamenti. (Pamph. 8 pp.) 8° *Malta,* 1887

NORWAY.

CHRISTIANIA.

Geografiske Opmaaling, Den Norske Lods, udgiven, af. . . Hefte I.-VIII.
   (8 vols.) *Maps and plates.* 8° *Christiania,* 1871-85
Kgl. Nordiske Oldskriftselskab (Christiania). *See* Appendix 2: Norway (B) Anon.
Kongelige Norske Frederiks Universitets, Det. Aarsberetning for Aaret 1866-69,
   med Bilage. 8° *Christiania,* 1869
—— Statistics and Reports (Christiania University) *Christiania,* 1868-69
Norske Geografiske Selskabs. Aarbog. I.-V. (1889-90 to 1893-94). *Maps and
plates.* 8° *Christiania,* 1891-94
Norske Gradmaalings Kommission, Udgivet af den. Vanstandsobservationer. Hefte
   I.-IV., fra 1872-86. 4° *Christiania,* 1882-92
Norske Meteorologiske Institut. Norsk Meteorologisk Aarbog. Aargang I.-VII.,
   1867-73 (7 parts bound in 1 vol.). Oblong 8° *Christiania,* 1868-74
      [Followed by]—
—— Jahrbuch des Norwegischen Meteorologischen Instituts (von Dr H. Mohn) für
   1874-90. (Total, 17 parts, of which 7 are bound in 1 vol.) *Maps.* 4°
                                            Christiania, 1877-92
   [For other pubs. of the Institut., *see* Appendix 2: Norway (A), Govt. Pubs.]
Christiania Observatorium, Meteorologiske Iagttagelser paa. 4°
                                              Christiania, 1868-69
Norwegischen Commission der Europaischen Gradmessung, Publication der
   Geodätische Arbeiten. Heft I.-VII. *Geod. maps.* 4° *Christiania,* 1882-90

TROMSÖ.

Tromsö Museums Aarshefter.   III.   *Map.*   (Pamph.)   8°   *Tromsö,* 188

PORTUGAL.

LISBON.

Academia Real das Sciencias de Lisboa.   Memorias.   Ser. 1.   Tom. I.-XII. (178(
1837).   *Plates.*   4°   *Lisbon,* 1797-183
     [Continued as]—
—— Ser. 2. Historia e Memorias da.   1843-56.   Tom. I.-III.,   1838-56.   *Plates an*
     map.   4°   *Lisbon,* 1843-5
     [Continued as]—
—— Ser. 3. Memorias da.   (Nova Serie.)   4°   *Lisbon,* 1854-8
     a. Classe de Sciencias Mathematicas, Physicas e Naturaes.   Tom. I.-V]
        (bound in 10 vols.), 1854-87.   *Plates and maps.*   4°   *Lisbon,* 1854-8
     b. Classe de Sciencias Moraes, Politicas e Bellas Lettras.   Tom. I.-II]
        (1854-63).   *Illus.*   4°   *Lisbon,* 1854-6
—— Annaes das Sciencias e Lettras (publicados debaixo dos auspicios da Academi
     Real das Sciencias).
     a. Sciencias Mathematicas, Physicas, Historico-Naturaes, e Medicas.   Ann.]
        (Tom. I.)   8°   *Lisbon,* 185
     b. Sciencias Moraes, Politicas, e Bellas Lettras.   Ann. I.-II. (Tom. I.-II.)   8°
                                                                    Lisbon, 1857-5
—— Jornal de Sciencias Mathematicas, Physicas e Naturaes.
     Ser. 1. Tom. I.-XII. (1866-89).   *Maps and plates.*   8°   *Lisbon,* 1868-8
     Ser. 2. Tom. I.-III. [latter imperfect], 1889-93.   *Maps and plates.*   8°
                                                                    Lisbon, 1890-9
—— Conferencias celebradas na Academia.   Acerca dos De-cobrimentos e Colonisaçõe
     dos Portuguezes na Africa.   I.-IV.   8°   *Lisbon,* 1877-8
—— Sessão publica da Academia, 1875, 1877, 1880, and 1893.   8°   *Lisbon,* 1875-9
Annaes Maritimos e Coloniaes; publicação mensal redigida sob a Direcção d
     Associação Maritima e Colonial.   Tom. I., III.-V., and VI. (Nos. 1-4), Ser. 1-€
     Maps and plates.   8°   *Lisbon,* 1840-4
Annaes e Boletim do Conselho Ultramarino, Boletim do.   Legislação antiga.   Tom.]
     (1446-1754); II. (1755-1834) [wanting pp. 1-24].   Small folio   *Lisbon,* 186
—— Boletim do.   Legislação novissima.   Tom. I. (1834-51); II. (1852-56) [wantin
     pp. 1-48]; III. (1857-62); IV. (1863).   Small folio   *Lisbon,* 1867-6
—— Annaes do.   Parte oficial.   Tom. I.-VIII., Ser. 1 (1854-58; Ser. 2 (1859-61
     [wanting pp. 1-32]; Ser. 3-6 (1862-65); Ser. 7-8 (1866-67).   Small folio
                                                                    Lisbon, 1867-6
—— Annaes do.   Parte não oficial.   Tom. I.-VIII.   Ser. 1 (1854-58).   *Maps an*
     plates.   Ser. 2 (1859-61) [wanting pp. 1-30]; Ser. 3-6 (1862-65); Ser. 7-8 (186€
     67).   Small folio   *Lisbon,* 1867-6
Annaes da Commissão Central Permanente de Geographia (Ministro dos Negocic
     da Marina e Ultramar).   Nos. 1 and 2.   *Map.*   8°   *Lisbon,* 1876-7
—— Constituição e Regulamento Geral [pamph. 19 pp.].   12°   *Lisbon,* 187
—— Organisation et Règlement [pamph. 12 pp.].   8°   *Lisbon,* 187
—— Expedição Scientifica a Serra da Estrella en 1881.   5 parts or memoirs.   *Maps an*
     plates.   Royal 4°   *Lisbon,* 188
     Archeologio por F. M. Sarmento: Botanica, J. A. Henriques; Ethnographia
     L. F. M. Ferreira; Medicina, F. L. da Fonseca, Jr.; Meteorologia, A. C. d
     Silva.
Observatorio do Infante Don Luiz.   Provincia de Angola.   Resume Meteorol. an
     Magnet Obs., &c.   [*See* Appendix 2: Portuguese W. Africa.]   *Lisboa,* 188

Sociedade de Geographia de Lisboa (fundada em 1875), Boletim da. Nos. 3 and
4. 8° *Porto*, 1878-79
—— Actas das Sessões da Soc. Tom. I.-XIII., 1876 to 1893. 8° *Lisbon*, 1881-93
—— Actas das Sessões da Soc. Ser. 2 to Ser. 12. 11 vols., each containing 12 num-
bers. *Maps and plates.* 8° *Lisbon*, 1880-93
   For another set of Publications issued as Series of separate papers, with special
   titles, in 8° pamphlet form, &c. (some 46 in all), *see* Appendix 2 : Portugal
   (B.), Geogr. Soc., Lisbon.
—— Seccao da Soc. de Geogr. de Lisboa No Brazil. *See under* Trans. Brazil, Rio de
Janeiro, *antea*.
Quadro Elementar das Relacões, Politicas, &c., de Portugal. Tom. I.-IX., XV.-
XVIII. 8° *Lisbon*, 1842-64
Associação Commercial do Porto. Relatorio dos Actos da Direcção da, 1891-93.
3 vols. *Plates.* 8° *Oporto*, 1892-94

OPORTO.

Sociedade Carlos Ribeiro [Oporto]. Revista de Sciencias Naturaes e Sociaes, Orgão dos
Trabalhos do Soc. Publicação Trimestral. Vol. I., No. 2. 8° *Oporto*, 1889
Sociedade de Geographia Commercial do Porto, Boletim da. Tom. I., No. 1
(1880). Royal 8° *Oporto*, 1881
Sociedade Portuense de Geographia. Estatutos [Pamph. 14 pp.] 12° *Oporto*, 1880

RUMANIA.

BUCHAREST.

Buletin Statistic General al Romaniei. Ministerul Agriculturei, Industriel, i
Domenielor (Roumania). (C. E. Crupenski.) Anul I.-II. 8° and royal 8°
Bucharest, 1892-94
Institutului Meteorologic al Romaniei (*Ed.* S. C. Hepites). Analele Tom. I., II.,
IV.-VI. (1885-90). *Plates.* Royal 4° *Bucharest*, 1886-93
Societătii Geografice Române. Buletinul. Ann. I.-XIV. [Vol. 2 imperfect ; the
whole bound in 10 vols.] *Maps and plates.* 8° *Bucharest*, 1876-93

RUSSIAN EMPIRE.

RUSSIA IN EUROPE.

FINLAND : HELSINGFORS.

Fennia. Bulletin de la Société de Géographie de Finlande. Vols. I.-IX. et XII.
Maps and plates. Royal 8° *Helsingfors*, 1889-94
Finska Vetenskaps Societeten. Bidrag, till Kännedom af Finlands Natur och
Folk, Utgifna af. Häftet XLVIII.-LI. *Maps and plates.* 8° *Helsingfors*, 1889-92
—— Översigt, af Finsk. Vet. Soc. Förhandlingar, XXXI.-XXXIV. (1888-89 to
1891-92). *Plates.* 8° *Helsingfors*, 1889-92
Geografiska Föreningens Tidskrift. (Dr R. Hult). Årgången III.-IV. (1891-92).
Maps and plates. 8° *Helsingfors*, 1891-93
Institut Météorologique Central de la Societé des Sciences de Finlande. Obser-
vations Météorologiques (*publiées par*), from 1881-88 (4 vols.). Folio
Kuopio, 1893-94
—— Observations Météorologiques "*faites à Helsingfors*," en 1887-89, 1890, et en 1892
(3 parts, or Vols. 6, 7, 8, 9, and 11). Royal 4° *Helsingfors*, 1891-93
Societatis Scientiarum Fennicæ. Acta. Tom. XV.-XVIII. *Maps and plates.* 4°
Helsingfors, 1888-91

KIEF.

Zapiski Kievskago Obshchest. Yestyestvoispytateley. [Memoirs of the Society of
Naturalists of Kief.] Vols. X., XI., and XII. *Kief*, 1889-92

MOSCOW.

Imp. Soc. of Friends of Natural Science, &c., Moscow University, Trudy
[Transactions of the Anthropological Sect. of the]. Vols. XIII., XV., XVII.
[Vols. 71, 76, 83, and 88 of *Izvestiya*]. *Plates.* Folio *Moscow*, 1893-94
Société Impériale des Naturalistes de Moscou, Bulletin de. Années 1864 and 1891
(Nos. 1 and 4, in 2 vols.). *Plates.* 8° *Moscow*, 1864 and 1892

ODESSA.

Zapiski Novorossiiskago Obshchestva Yestyestvoispytateley. [Memoirs of the Society of Naturalists of New Russia.] Vols. I. and Append. II. (pt. 1), XVI., XVII. (pts. 2 and 3), and XVIII. (pt. 2). *Map and plates.* 8°   *Odessa*, 1872-94
—— Mathemat. Sect. Vols. XII. and XIII.   *Odessa*, 1891-92

ST PETERSBURG.

L'ACADÉMIE IMPÉRIALE DES SCIENCES DE ST PETERSBOURG.

Mémoires, présentés a l'Académie . . . par divers Savants et lus dans ses Assemblées. Tom. I.-IX., 1821 to 1858 (Vol. 7 missing). *Maps and plates.* 4°
                                                                St Petersburg, 1831-59
—— (Ser. 6.) Sciences Mathématiques, Physiques et Naturelles. Tom. I.-IX, 1826 to 1858. [Vol. 5 wanting and 3 in 2 parts ; total bound in 9 vols.] *Plates.* 4°
                                                                St Petersburg, 1831-59
—— (Ser. 7.) Tom. I.-XL., 1854 to 1892 [Vols. 39 and 40 incomplete]. *Plates.* Large 4°   *St Petersburg*, 1859-92
—— Sciences Politiques, Histoire, Philologie. *Plates.* Vols. VIII. and IX. 4°
                                                                St Petersburg, 1855-59
Bulletin Scientifique, publié par l'Acad. Tom. I.-X. (7, 8, and 9 imperfect), 1835 to 1842 [bound in 4 vols.]. *Plates.* 4°   *St Petersburg*, 1836-42
—— [Ser. 2.] Bulletin de l'Acad. Tom. I.-XXXII., 1859-93. *Maps and plates.* Royal 4°   *St Petersburg*, 1860-88
—— [Ser. 3.] Nouv. Ser. Tom. I.-IV., equal to Tom. I., XXXIII.-XXXVI. of entire Series. *Map and plates.* 4°   *St Petersburg*, 1890-94
—— Recueil des Actes de la Séance publique de l'Acad. 1837 to 1844. [7 parts bound in 1 vol.] *Portraits.* 4°   *St Petersburg*, 1838-44
—— Compte Rendu de l'Acad. Ann. 1852-57 (6 years, bound in 2 vols.). *Portraits.* 8°   *St Petersburg*, 1853-58
—— Acad. Imp. de St Pétersb., Mélanges Physiques et Chimiques, tirés du Bulletin Physico-Mathématique de l'. 8°   *St Petersburg*, 1868-69
—— Tableau général, méthodique et alphabétique des matières contenues dans les publi- cations de l'Académie . . . depuis sa fondation. 1ʳᵉ Partie et Suppl. Publi- cations en Langues étrangères. 8°   *St Petersburg*, 1872
Biblioteki Moskovskago Glavnago Arkhiva Min. Inostr. Dyel. [Register of Atlases, Maps, Plans, &c., in the Library of the Moscow Principality—Archives of the Ministry of Foreign Affairs.] 8°   *St Petersburg*, 1877

IMP. RUSS. GEOGRAPHICAL SOC. ST PETERSBURG.

Zapisky Russkago Geogr. Obshchesta. Memoirs Imp. Russ. Geogr. Soc. [In Russian.] [Ser. 1.] Vols. I.-XIII. *Maps and plates.* 8° *St Petersburg*, 1849-59
    [The first issue of Vols. 1 and 2 was in 1846-47. Those in Soc. Library are the 2nd issue or reprint, dated 1849. Also *see* Denkschrift, printed at Weimar, *infra*.]
—— [Ser. 2.] Vols. for 1861, 1862, 1863, and 1864 (Vols. I.-IV.). *Maps and plates.* 8°   *St Petersburg*, 1861-64
—— [Ser. 3.] Zapisky, &c., divided into Sections, viz.—
    General Geography. Vols. I.-XXVI. *Maps and plates.* 8° *St Petersburg*, 1867-93
    [Append. Atlases fol. to Vol. 9 and Vol. 21 ; Kaulbars' and Tillo's papers.]
    Ethnography. Vols. I.-XVI., XVII. (pt. 1), XIX., XX., XXI. (pt. 1), XXII. (pt. 1), and XXIII, (pt. 1 and 2). *Maps and plates.* 8° *St Petersburg*, 1867-94
    Statistics. Vols. I.-VII. *Maps and plates.* 8°   *St Petersburg*, 1876-93
Denkschrift der Russischen Geographischen Gesellschaft zu St Petersburg. Band I. *Maps.* 8°   *Weimar*, 1849
    [This is a German Translation of the 1st issue, 1846-47, of Vols. 1 and 2 of Zapisky, *supra*.]
Izvestiya Imp. Russk. Geogr. Obshchest., Transactions of the. [In Russian.] 1848-50 [in 1 vol.]. *Maps and plates.* 8°   *St Petersburg*, 1848-50
Otchót Imp. Russk. Geogr. Obshchest. [Reports of the Soc.] For 1848-54, 1856, 1857, 1862, 1866-71, 1873-77, 1879, 1881-90, 1892, 1893 (34 Reps.). 8°
                                                                St Petersburg, 1849-94
Compte Rendu de la Soc. (Traduit du Russe.) Ann. 1850-64 (13 years, bound in 4 vols.). *Maps.* 8°   *St Petersburg*, 1851-65

Vestnik Imp. Russk. Geogr. Obshchest, Proceedings of the. [In Russian.] Vols. I.-XXX., 1851-60. *Maps.* 8° *St Petersburg*, 1851-60
Yejegodnik Imperatorskago Geographicheskago Obshchestva. [Annuary Imp. Russ. Geogr. Soc.] Vols. I.-III. *Geodetic maps.* 8° and royal 8° *St Petersburg*, 1890-94
Extraits des Publications de la Soc. Imp. Géogr. de Russie, en 1856 et 1857. Royal 8° *St Petersburg*, 1859
Katalog. Biblioteki Imp. Russk. Geogr. Obshchest. [Catalogue of the Library of the Russ. Geogr. Soc.] 8° *St Petersburg*, 1878
Ukazatel K. Izdaniyam Imp. Russk. Geogr. Obshchest. i yego Otdielov. [Index to the publications of the Russ. Geogr. Soc. and its Branches, 1846-75.] 8° *St Petersburg*, 1886
Ethnographicheskii Sbornik. [Collection of the Ethnography of Russian Districts.] Parts I.-IV. [in 2 vols.] *St Petersburg*, 1853-58
Literatura Russkoi Geographii Statisitki i Ethnographii. Tom. I.-IX., 1864 to 1880. 8° *St Petersburg*, 1865-83
—— [*See* Mejoff, V. I. : Authors' Catalogue.]
Sbornik Statis. Svedenii o Rossii. [Statistical Compendium for Russia, published by the Soc.] [In Russian.] Vols. I.-III. *Tables.* Royal 8° *St Petersburg*, 1851-58
Repertorium für Meteorologie. (K. Geogr. Gesell. St. Petersburg.)
[Ser. 1.] Bände I.-III. (2 and 3 incomplete). (Redig. L. F. Kamtz.) 4° *Dorpat*, 1860-63
[Ser. 2.] Bände I.-XIV. [Redig. H. Wild.] *Maps and plates.* Royal 4° *St Petersburg*, 1870-91
Jahresbericht des Physikalischen Central-Observatoriums für 1869-72 [4 parts bound in 1 vol.], und Beilage (von H. Wild). 4° *St Petersburg*, 1870-73
Trudy. [Transactions of the *Geological Sect.* Imp. Russ. Geogr. Soc., St Petersb.] Vols. I.-XI. and XIII. [some vols. imperfect]. 4° *St Petersburg*, 1883-92
Izvestiya Geologicheskago Komiteta. [Proceedings of Geological Commmittee of Imp. Russ. Geogr. Soc.] Vols. I.-X., XI., and XII. (pts.). 8° *St Petersburg*, 1882-92
[With Appendices, viz. :—]
—— Russk. Geologich. Biblioteka. [Catalogue of the Geolog. Library of Imp. Russ. Geogr. Soc.] 1885-92 (7 pts.). 8° *St Petersburg*, 1885-92
Trudy Expeditsii snaryajonnoi Imp. Volnym Ekonomicheskim I. Russ. Geogr. Obshch., dlya Izslédovaniya Khlébnoi Torgovli i Proizvoditelnosti v. Rossii. [Works of the Expedition equipped by the Imp. Free Economical and Russ. Geogr. Societies for the enquiry into the Corn Trade and Production in Russia.] Vol. II. *Map and plates.* Royal 8° *St Petersburg*, 1870
Internationalen Polar-Commission, Mittheilungen der. (*Ed.* H. Wild.) Hefte I.-VII. Royal 8° *St Petersburg*, 1882-91
Russische Revue : Monatsschrift für die Kunde Russlands. Jahrg. I.-XXIII. (C. Röttger) ; XXIV.-XXXI. (R. Hammerschmidt). 8° *St Petersburg*, 1872-91
University of St Petersburg. [Council Minutes in Russian.] Nos. 1-11, 1870-75. 8° *St Petersburg*, 1870-75
Zapiski Voienno-Topographicheskago Depo [Memoirs of the Military-Topographical Bureau].
[Continued as]—
Zapiski Voienno-Topographicheskago Otdiela Glavnago Shtaba [Memoirs of the Military-Topographical Section of the General Staff]. Pts. XXIV.-XLVII. [bound in 17 vols.]. *Maps and plates.* 4° *St Petersburg*, 1863-91

RUSSIA IN ASIA.

CAUCASUS : TIFLIS.

IMP. RUSS. GEOGR. SOC.—CAUCASUS SECTION.

Otchot Kavkaz Otd. [Reports of Caucasus Section], 1870 and 1879. 8° (2 sizes) *Tiflis*, 1871 and 1879
Izvestiya Kavkazkago Otd. Imp. Russk. Geogr. Obshchestva. [Proceedings or Bulletin of Caucasus Sect., &c.] Vols. I.-X. (8th with Appendix, and 1, 2, 5 incomplete). *Maps and plates.* Royal 8° *Tiflis*, 1872-91
[*See* "Ukazatel," &c., *infra.*]
Kavkazkii Otdiel Imp. Russk. Geogr. Obshchest. [Review of 25 years in the Caucasus Sect. of the Imp. Russ. Geogr. Soc.] 1851-76. 8° *Tiflis*, 1876
Zapiski Kavkazkago Otd. Imp. Russk. Geogr. Obshchest. [Memoirs of Caucasus Sect.] Vols. IX.-XVI. *Maps and plates.* 8° *St Petersburg and Tiflis*, 1875-94

3 F

Materialui dlya Sostavleniya Climatologii Kavkaza [Data upon the climate of the Caucasus]. Vols. I., II. *Maps and plates.* 8° *Tiflis*, 1871-80
Observatoire Physique Central de Russie, Annales de. Ann. 1852-63 [12 tomes, A. T. Kupffer]; 1864 [1 tom., L. F. Kamtz]; 1865-90 [26 tomes, H. Wild]. [Total 39 vols.] 4° *St Petersburg*, 1855-91
—— Beobachtungen der Temperatur des Erdbodens; Meteorol. Beobacht. u. Magnetische Beobacht. *See* Appendix 2 : Russia in Asia (A).
Sbornik Materiala dlya Opisaniye Mestnosti i plemion Kafkaza. [Materials for the Topography and Ethnology of the Caucasus : in Russian.] Vols. X., XII.-XVIII. (8 vols.). 8° *Tiflis*, 1890-94
Ukazatel Geogr. Materiala v. Kubanskikh Viedomostiakh. [Index to Geogr. Material contained in the *Kuban Times.*] Append. Izvest. Caucasus Sect. of Imp. Russ. Geogr. Soc. Za 1863, 1866, 1867-74. 8° *Tiflis*, 1874-75

IMPER. RUSS GEOGRAPHICAL SOC.—SIBERIAN SECT.
IRKUTSK.

Zapiski Sibirskago Otdyela Imp. Russk. Geogr. Obshchestva [Memoirs of the Siberian Section of the Soc. : in Russian]. Vol. II. *Maps.* [Section afterwards divided into East and West Siberian Sections.] Royal 8° *St Petersburg*, 1856
Izvestiya Vostotchno-Sibirskago Otdyela Imp. Russk. Geogr. Soc. [Proceedings of the *East* Siberian Section of Imp. Russ. Geogr. Soc. : in Russian.] Vols. XII. (Nos. 1-5), XIII. (Nos. 1-3), XIV. (Nos. 1-5), XV. (Nos. 1, 2, 5, 6). 4° *Irkutsk*, 1881-85
—— The same. Vols. XVI., XVII. (Nos. 1-4), XVIII., XIX. (Nos. 1, 3, 5), XX., XXI., XXII. (Nos. 1-3), XXIII. (Nos. 2-5), XXIV. (Nos. 1-4), XXV. (No. 1). *Maps and plates.* 8° *Irkutsk*, 1886-94
Zapiski Vostotchno-Sibirskago Otdyela, Imp. Russk. Geogr. Obshch. [Memoirs of *East* Siberian Sect. Imp. Russ. Geogr. Soc. : in Russian.] Vol. XII. 8° *Irkutsk*, 1886
Otchot Vostotchno-Sibirskago Otdyela Imp. Russk. Geogr. Obshch. [Reports of the *East* Siberian Section] 1879, 1882, 1891, and 1892. 8° *St Petersburg*, 1879-92

OMSK.

Zapiski, Zapadno, v Sibirskago Otdyela Imp. Russk. Geogr. Obshch. [Memoirs of the *West* Siberian Section of Imp. Russ. Geogr. Soc.] Vols. XIV. and XV. 8° *Omsk*, 1893

VLADIVOSTOK.

Zapiski, Obshchestva Izucheniya Amurskago Kraya, pod redakziei predsedatelya Obshchestva. [Memoirs of Society for Study of Amur Region.] Tom. I. (No. 1). *Map and plates.* 8° *Vladivostok*, 1888

SPAIN.
BARCELONA.

Ambos Mundos. Revista dedicada al cuerpo Consular, al Comercio y à la industria de España. (D. R. Monner Hans.) Año I. Nos. 2 and 5. 12° *Barcelona*, 1886

CADIZ.

Real Academia Gaditana de Ciencias y Letras (Cadiz), Estatutos y Reglamento de la. (Pamph.) Small 8° *Cadiz*, 1876
—— Acto Solemne Celebrado por la Acad. . . . con motivo de la visita Hecha a Esta Ciudad por el Rey D. Alfonso XII. el 23 de Marzo de 1877. Small 8° *Cadiz*, 1877
—— Inauguracion del Año Académico, 1876, 1878 a 1879, y 1880 a 1881. [3 parts.] Small 8° *Cadiz*, 1876-80
—— Sesion Extraordinaria, Pública y Solemne, Celebrada en Honor de Don Pedro Calderon de la Barca el 26 de Mayo de 1881, con la Recepcion del Académico Numerario D. Julian de Vargas. Small 8° *Cadiz*, 1881

MADRID.

El Centenario, Revista Illustrada. Vol. IV. (Nos. 1-37). *Plates.* 4° *Madrid*, 1892
Instituto Geográfico y Estadistica de España, Resena geográfica y Estadistica de España por la direccion general del. (Dir. Carlos Ibáñez). 1 vol. *Maps.* 4° *Maarid*, 1888
Real Academia de Ciencias. Memorias de la Real Academia de Ciencias Exactas, Físicas, y Naturales de Madrid. Tom. I.-VI., XI.-XIII., and XV. *Plates and maps.* 4°. [*See* A. F. Vallins : Authors' Catalogue] *Madrid*, 1850-90
—— Resúmen de las Actas. Años 1847-48, 1856-57; 10 ses. Small 4° *Madrid*, 1848-58

Real Academia de la Historia (Madrid), Memorias. Tom. X. Small 4° *Madrid,* 1885
Real Observatorio de Madrid. Annuario. Años I., IV.-VI. 12° *Madrid,* 1862-65
Revista de los Progressos de las Sciencias, Exactas, Fisicas, y Naturales, Tom.
XXI., XXII. [both imperfect]. 8° *Madrid,* 1886-89
Revista General de Marina. Vols. III., VI., and VII. [incomplete]. *Maps and plates.* 8° *Madrid,* 1878-80
Sociedad Antropologica Española. Revista de Antropologia. Organo Oficial de la
Sociedad Antropológica Española. Tomo I. (Cuadermo 1°-6°). 8° *Madrid,* 1874
Sociedad Española de Geografía Comércial (antes de Africanistas y Colonistas).
Revista de Geografía Comercial Organo de la. Tom. I. (Nos. 1-13), II. (Nos. 25-
30), V. (Nos. 1-4). *Maps and plans.* 4° *Madrid,* 1885-94
Sociedad Geográfia de Madrid. Boletin. Vols. I.-XXXV., and XXXVI. (Nos. 1-6)
[Vols. 26, 28, and 33 imperfect]. *Maps and plates.* 8° *Madrid,* 1876-93
—— Indice de Authores, de los 20 Primeros Tomos (viz., 1876-86 *supra*). 8° *Madrid,* 1890
—— Reglamento de la Sociedad. (Pamph. 9 pp.) 8° *Madrid,* 1876

VITORIA.

Associacion Euskara para la Exploracion y Civilizacion del Africa Central.
Boletín de la Exploradora. Año I., Tom. I.-II. *Maps.* 8°
Vitoria and Madrid, 1880-81

SWEDEN.

STOCKHOLM.

Anthropologiska Sällskapet i Stockholm. Tidskrift för Anthropologi och Kultur-
historia uitgven af Soc. Band I., 3 Haftet, 1873-77. *Plates and cuts.* 8° *Stockholm,* 1875-82
[Title of Society altered to]—
Svenska Sällskapet för Anthropologi och Geografi. Tidskrift Anthropologiska
Sektionens. Band I. *Plates and cuts.* 8° *Stockholm,* 1878-81
—— Tidskrift Geografiska Sektionens. Band I. *Maps and plates.* 8° *Stockholm,* 1878-80
—— Forhandlingar vid Sällskapet Sammankomster, 1878-80. 8° *Stockholm,* 1882
[The Tidskrifts and Forhandlingar together form 1 vol., and are bound as such.]
"Ymer." Tidskrift uitgifven af Svensk. Sällsk för Antrop. o Geogr. Årgängen, 1881-
92. Vols. I.-XI. and XII. (incomplete). *Maps and plates.* 8° *Stockholm,* 1882-93
Astronomisch-Geodätischen Arbeiten. *See* P. G. Rosén : Authors' Catalogue.
Astronomiska Iakttagelser och Undersökningar anställda på Stockholms Observatorium.
(H. Gylden.) Bands I. (2 häftet), II. (häft. 2 and 4), III. and IV. (9 Nos.)
Small 4° *Stockholm,* 1880-91
Kongliga Svenska Vetenskaps-Akademie. Der Konigl. Schwedischen Akademie
der Wissenschaften. Abhandlungen, aus der Naturlehre, Haushaltungskunst und
Mechanik, 1755, '56, '57, '59-66, aus dem Schwedischen übersetzt, von A. G.
Kästner. *Plates.* 11 vols. 8° *Hamburg and Leipzig,* 1757-68
—— Öfversigt af Kongl. Vetensk.-Akad. Förhandlingar. Vols. I.-L. (in 40 vols., 1844-
93). *Maps and plates.* 8° *Stockholm,* 1845-94
—— Appendix to Vol. XXI., viz. :—Kritisk Förteckning öfver de I. Riks. Museum
Befintliga Salmonider (af F. A. Smit). Atlas folio. [Bound separately from Series]
Stockholm, 1887
—— Förteckning Öfver innehället i Kongl. Svenska Vetensk.-Akad. Skrifter 1826-83
(af E. W. Dahlgren). 12° *Stockholm,* 1884
—— Handlingar Kongl. Vetensk.-Akad., 1847-54. 8 vols. in 4. *Maps and plates.* 8° *Stockholm,* 1849-56
—— Handlingar Ny Följd. Vols. I.-XXV. (1855-93). *Maps and plates.* 4° *Stockholm,* 1858-93
—— Bihang. Vols. I.-XIX. *Maps and plates.* 8° *Stockholm,* 1872-93
—— Lefnadsteckningar öfver Kongl. Svenska Vetensk.-Akad. efter är 1854 affinda
Ledamöter. Vols. I., II., and III. 8° *Stockholm,* 1869-94
—— Meteorolgiska Iakttagelser i Sverge utgivna af. . . . Anställda och utarbetade under
inseende af Meteorologiska Central-Anstalten. Entire Ser. Vols. XV., XVII.-
XXXII. ; equal to Ser. 2. Vols. I., III.-XVIII., viz., 1873, 1875 to 1890. *Maps.* 4° *Stockholm,* 1876-94
—— Meddelanden, &c. *See* Upsal Univ., *infra.*
—— Svenska, Norske och Utländske Ledamoter. 8° *Stockholm,* 1885-89

Sveriges Geologiska Undersökning. [Of these Publications the Soc. Library possesses 260 numbers, the majority in 8° and some (irregularly distributed in the series) in 4°.] *Maps and plates*   *Stockholm*, 1862-93
Ser. A. *a.* Kartblad med beskrifningar- i skalan 1 : 50,000, Nos. 1-109. 8° (1862-92.)
    Ser. A. *b.* —— 1 : 200,000, Nos. 1-15. 8°. (1877-93.)
    Ser. B. *a.* Öfversigtskartor, No. 1. 8°. (1884.)
    Ser. B. *b.* Specialkartor med beskrifningar, Nos. 1-7. 8° and 4°. (1881-92.)
    Ser. C. Afhandlingar och uppsatser, Nos. 26-134 (105 Nos.). 8° and 4°. (1877-93.)
    Ser. (Miscellaneous, some with temporary lettering F. to X.). Total, 23 numbers.
        8°. (1872-90.) [*See* under Sweden : Appendix 2, for separate titles, &c.]

UPSALA.

Upsala Universitets. Årsskrift. Mathematik och Naturvetenskap.   1870-74 (4 parts).
  Maps. 8°   *Upsala*, 1870-74
—— Årsskrift. Medicin. 1884-85 och 1893 (2 parts). 8°   *Upsala*, 1885-95
—— Meddelanden, frän U. Univ. Mineralog.—Geologiska Instit. Nos. 1-13. *Maps
  and plates.* 8°   *Stockholm*, 1891-94

SWITZERLAND.

AARAU.

Mittelschweizerischen Geographisch-Commerciellen Gesellschaft in Aarau. Ethnologisches Gewerbemuseum in Aarau. Aufruf der Mittelschweizerischen Geographisch-Commerciellen Gesellschaft in Aarau an ihre Mitglieder, Freunde, und Gönner in der Heimat und in fernen Landen. (Pamph. 16 pp.) 8°   *Aarau*, 1886
—— Fernschau. Jahrbuch der Gesellschaft. Bände I.-II. *Woodcuts.* 8° *Aarau*, 1886-88

BERNE.

Geographische Gesellschaft von Bern. Jahresberichte I.-XII. and XIII. (heft. 1), 1878-94. *Maps and plates.* 8°   *Berne*, 1879-94
Schweizer Alpen Club, Jahrbuch des. Jahrg. I.-XXIX., 1864 to 1893. *Maps and
  plates.* (From 1 to 25 vols. in 12°, and 26 to 28 vols. in 8°)   *Berne*, 1864-93
—— Beilagen des Schweizerischen Alpen Club. Jahrg. III.-IV., VII., VIII., X.-XXVIII.
  22 bänder [viz.—Maps, &c., in cases, of various sizes and shapes, oblong 8°, 4°, &c.]
                                                   Berne, 1866-93
—— Repertorium und Ortsregister für die Jahrbücher I. bis XX. des Schw. Alp. Clubs.
  (Zusammengestellt und den Mitglieder des S.A.C., Gewidmet von Otto von Bulow.)
  Map. 12°   *Berne*, 1886
—— Die Ersten 25 Jahre des Schw. Alp. Club. (Denkschrift im Auftrag des Central-comite verfasst von Dr Ernst Buss.) (Pamph.) 12°   *Glarus*, 1889

GENEVA.

Archives des Sciences Physiques et Naturelles. Total, 60 vols., bound in 36 as follows :—[2°] Nouvelle Période. Tom. IV., V., VII.-XII., XV.-XVIII. (12 vols.)
  Maps and plates. 8° [Bound with " Bibl. Univ."]   *Geneva*, 1859-63
—— The same. Tom. XXV.-LXIV. *Maps and plates.* 8° [Separately bound,
  2 vols. in 1.]   *Geneva*, 1866-78
—— 3° Période. Tom. I.-IV. *Maps and plates.* 8°   *Geneva*, 1878-80
Association des Sociétés Suisses de Géographie, Trauvaux de l'. Deuxième Session
  à Genève, Août 1882. *Maps.* (Pamph.) 8°   *Geneva*, 1883
Bibliothèque Universelle de Genève. Nouvelle Série. Tom. I.-XLII. (10 missing—
  41 vols.). 8°   *Geneva*, 1836-42
    [Followed by]—
Bibliothèque Universelle, revue Suisse et Étrangère. Nouvelle Période. Tom. IV.,
  V., VII.-XII., XV.-XVIII. (12 vols.). *Maps and plates.* 8°   *Geneva*, 1859-63
    [Followed by]—
Globe, Le. *Infra,* Soc. Geogr. Genev.
L'Afrique Explorée et Civilisée. Journal Mensuel. Tom. I.-XV. (1879-94). *Maps.*
  8°   *Geneva*, 1879-94
Société de Géographie de Genève. Bulletin. Vols. I.-XI. *Maps.* 8° *Geneva*, 1860-72
—— Memoires. Vols. I.-XI. *Maps.* 8°. [Bull. and Mém. bound together] *Geneva*, 1860-72
    [Continued as]—
—— Le Globe : Journal Géographique. Organe de la Société de Géographie de Genève
  pour ses Mémoires et Bulletin.
—— Bulletin. Vols. XII.-XXXIII. *Maps.* 8°   *Geneva*, 1873-94

Sociéte de Géographie de Genève. Mémoires. Vols. XII.-XXXIII. *Maps.* 8°
Geneva, 1873-94
[These publications of the Society, though issued in volumes having successive
numbers as above, are also subdivided into Series, viz. :—1st Ser., Vols I.-
XIII. ; 2nd Ser., XIV.-XVI. ; 3rd Ser., XVII.-XX. ; 4th Ser., XXI.-
XXVIII. ; 5th Ser., XXIX. onwards. The Mémoires and Bull. are bound
together.]
Société de Physique et d'Histoire Naturelle de Genève. Memoires. Tom. I.-
XXXI. (T. XIII. pt. 1 missing). *Plates.* 4° *Geneva*, 1821-93
—— The same. Tom. Supplementaire : Centenaire de la Fondation de la Societe.
Plates. 4° *Geneva*, 1891
Societe Suisse de Topographie, Bulletin de la. Année I. (livr. Jan. et Feb.)
Plate. 12° *Geneva*, 1880

LAUSANNE.

Societé d'Agriculture et d'Économie du Canton du Vaud, Feuilles d'Agriculture
et d'Économie Generale publie par la. Tom. I.-VII. *Plates.* 8° *Lausanne*, 1812-20
[Continued as]—
Feuille du Canton de Vaud, ou Journal d'Agriculture Pratique, des Sciences Naturelles
et d'Économie Publique. Tom. VIII.-XV. *Plates.* 8° *Lausanne*, 1821-28

NEUCHATEL.

Association Géodèsique Internationale. Comptes Rendus des Conferences (Geod.
Internat. pour la Mesure des Degrés en Europe). 14 vols. and supplements. *Maps
and plates.* 4° *Neuchatel and Berlin*, 1868-94
Places of meetings and dates as follows :—

Berlin	..	..	..	1867	Stuttgart ..	.. ..	1877	Berlin	.. .. ..	1886
Vienna	..	..	1871	Munich	.. ..	1880	Nice	.. .. ..	1887
Dresden	..	..	1874	Rome	..	1883		

Supplementary Reports of Conferences, by General A. Ferrero, held at :—

Salzburg	..	..	1883	Fribourg ..	.. ..	1890	Bruxelles ..	.. ..	1892
Paris	..	..	1889	Florence ..	.. ..	1891	Genéve	.. ..	1893

[The above contains Reports of the Ordinary Meetings and of those of the Per-
manent Commission of the European Gradmessung and of the International
Erdmessung. as the title of the former was changed to. *See under* Florence,
Zürich, and Berlin.]
Commission Géodesique Suisse. Procès-verbal de la séance de la Commission
Géodesique Suisse. XVIII. 12° *Neuchatel*, 1878
Société Neuchateloise de Géographie, Bulletin de la. Tom. I.-VII. (1865 to 1893).
Maps and plates. 8° *Neuchatel*, 1886-93

ST GALLEN.

Ostschweizerischen Geographisch-Commerciellen Gesellschaft in St Gallen.
Jahresbericht pro 1879. Small 8° *St Gallen*, 1880
—— The same, 1881-82. *Plates.* Royal 8° *St Gallen*, 1882
[Continued as]—
—— Mitteilungen. 1883-91, 13 hefte. *Map.* Royal 8° and 8° *St Gallen*, 1883-91
—— Katalog der Geographischen Ausstellung veranstaltet von der Gesellschaft. 16°
[Pamph.] [*St Gallen*, 1879]
—— Publication. (Dr J. A. Kaiser.) [Pamph. 17 pp.] 8° *St Gallen*, 1882
—— Statuten der Geogr.-Commerc. Ges. (4 pp.). 8° [N.D.]

WINTERTHUR.

Schweizerische Polytechnische Zeitschrift. Unter Mitwirkung mehrerer Professoren
des Schweiz. Polytechnikums und anderer Fachmänner ; herausgegeben von Dr P.
Bolley und J. H. Kronauer. Vols. I.-XV. (Vol. 4 missing). *Maps and plates.* 4°
[Bound in 7 vols.] *Winterthur*, 1856-70

ZÜRICH.

Antiquarische Gesellschaft in Zürich. Berichte über die Verrichtungen der Antiquar-
ischen Gesellschaft in Zürich, vom Juli 1844 bis November 1862. Nos. 1 to 18. 4°
Zürich, 1845-63
—— Denkschrift zurfunfzigjähr Stiftungsfeir der Antiq. Ges. *Plates.* 4° *Zurich*, 1882
—— Mittheilungen der Antiquarischen Gesellschaft (der Gesellschaft für Vaterländische
Alterthümer) in Zürich. Bände IX. (Abtheil. II., heft 3), XII. (heft 3), XVI.,
XVII. (hefte 5-8), XIX.-XXIII. *Maps and plates.* 4° *Zürich*, 1854-94

Naturforschenden Gesellschaft in Zürich, Mitteilungen der.   Vols. I.-III. (1847-55).
Maps and plates.   8°   *Zürich,* 1849-55
—— Vierteljahrsschrift.   Jahrg. I., II., III. (hefte 1, 2), VI.-XXXVIII.   [Jahrg. 3,
   34, and 36 imperfect.] *Maps and plates.*   Small 8°   *Zürich,* 1856-93
—— Generalregister der Publikationen der Naturforschenden Gesellschaft in Zürich und
   Uebersicht ihres Tauschverkehres.   [Pamph.]   Small 8°   *Zürich,* 1892
Publicationen für die Internationale Erdmessung Europäische Gradmessung.   Das
   Schweizerische Dreiecknetz (herausgegeben von der Schwezerischen Géodetische
   Commission).   Bände I.-VI.   *Plates.*   4°   *Zürich,* 1881-94
   [From Vol. III. onwards the title is altered to Internationale Erdmessung.   *See
   also* Neuchatel, *supra.*]

UNITED KINGDOM OF GREAT BRITAIN AND
IRELAND.

A. ENGLAND.

BATH.

Echoes of Service : a Record of Labour in the Lord's name in many Lands.   Vols. 1891
   (imperfect) and 1892-93, 3 vols.   Small 4°   *Bath,* 1891-93

BIRMINGHAM.

Birmingham Philosophical Society. Proceedings.   Vols. III.-VIII. (1881-93).   *Plates.*
   8°   *Birmingham,* 1883-93
—— Annual Report and List of Members (pamph.).   8°   *Birminghm,* 1893

CHESTER.

Architectural, Archæological, and Historic Society for the County, City, and
   Neighbourhood of Chester.   Journal Parts 2 and 3, July 1850 to December 1852.
   Plates.   8°   *Chester,* 1852-54

FALMOUTH.

Royal Cornwall Polytechnic Society, Annual Reports of.   1835-53, 3rd to 21st Rep.
   Bound in 4 vols.   *Maps and plates.*   8°   *Falmouth,* 1835-53

GRIMSBY.

The Fisherman's Nautical Almanack and Tide-Tables.   For the years 1880-85,
   1885-95 (14 vols.).   *Maps and illustrations.*   12°   *Grimsby,* 1880-94

LIVERPOOL.

Historic Society of Lancashire and Cheshire, Proceedings and Papers of the.   Sess.
   VI., 1853-54.   *Maps and plates.*   8°   *Liverpool,* 1854
—— Transactions.   Vols. VII.-XII.   Sess. 1854-60.   *Maps and plates.*   8°
                                                                       Liverpool, 1855-60
—— New. Ser.   Vols. I.-IX.   Sess. 1860-70 (Vols. XIII.-XXII., Entire Series).
   Maps and plates.   8°   *Liverpool,* 1860-70
—— 3rd Ser.   Vols. I.-VIII.   Sess. 1872-80 (Vols. XXV.-XXXII., Entire Series).
   Maps and plates.   8°   *Liverpool,* 1873-80
—— Index to the First and Second Series, Vols. I.-XXIV.   8°   *Liverpool,* 1874
Literary and Philosophical Society of Liverpool.   Proceedings.   Vols. XII.-XLIII.
   (Sess. 1857-58 to 1888-89.)   *Maps and plates.*   8°   *Liverpool,* 1858-89
Liverpool Geographical Society.   Report of the Council, 1892-94 (II.-III. ann.).
   Small 8°   *Liverpool,* 1893-94

LONDON.

Aborigines' Protection Society. The Colonial Intelligencer or Aborigines' Friend : comprising the Transactions of the Aborigines' Protection Society ; Interesting Intelligence concerning the Aborigines of Various Climes, and Articles upon Colonial Affairs ; with Comments upon the Proceedings of Government and of Colonists towards Native Tribes. Vols. I.-IV. (1847-54). *Illustrations.* 8°   1848-55
—— The same. New. Ser. Vol. I. (1855-58). *Map.* 8°   1858
—— Annual Reports. 1st, 4th (1838-41), 13th and 14th (1850-51), and 19th to 21st (1856-58). 8°   1838-58
—— Extracts from the Papers and Proceedings of the. Vols. I. (Nos. 1-6), 1839 ; II. (Nos. 1-6), 1841. 8°   1839-41

Academy, The : a Weekly Review of Literature, Science, and Art. 37 vols., viz., Vols. VII.-XLIII. 4°   1875-93

Admiralty Publications, Hydrographic Office. *See* Nautical Almanac, *postea ; also under* Hydrographic Office : Appendix 2, United Kingdom.

African Civilization Society, Report of the Committee of the, 1842 ; with an Appendix. *Map.* 8°   1842

Africa. Quarterly Review and Journal. Vols. I.-II. (1883-84). *Maps and plates.* Small 4°   1883-84

Alpine Journal, The : a Record of Mountain Adventure and Scientific Observation (by Members of the Alpine Club). Vols. I.-XVI. (1863-93). *Maps, plates, and portraits.* 8° [*See* Appendix 2 : United Kingdom, Miscell. (I.)]   1864-93
—— Index to the Alpine Journal (including Peaks, Passes, and Glaciers), for Vols. I.-XV. (1863-91). *Map.* 8°   1892

Anglo-Jewish Association, in connection with the Alliance Israelite Universelle, Annual Reports of the. 7th to 21st (1877-92). 8°   1878-92

Anglo-Saxon, The. Vols. I.-II. *Maps and plates.* 8°   1849-50

Annual Index of Periodicals and Photographs, The, for 1890. Small 4°   1891
[Title altered to]—
Index to the Periodical Literature of the World, for 1891 and 1892. Small 4° 1892-93

Anthropological Review, &c., *infra,* and Appendix 2 : Gen. Miscell.

Anthropological Society of London. Anthropological Review* and Journal of the Anthrop. Society of London. Vols. I.-VIII. *Plates.* 8°   1863-70
—— Memoirs* read before the Anthrop. Society of London. Vols. I.-III. (1863-69). *Maps and plates.* 8°   1865-70
[Title of Society altered to]—
Anthropological Institute of Great Britain and Ireland, Journal* of the. Vols. I.-XXIII. and XXIV. (pts. 1 and 2). *Maps and plates.* 8°   1872-94
—— List of Members. [Pamphs.] 8°   1875 and 1881
—— * Index to the Publications of the Soc. [1843-91], including the Jour. and Trans. of the Ethnological Society [1843-71] and of the Anthropol. Review. By George Bloxam. 8°   1893
[For separate volumes issued by the Anthrop. Soc., *see under* Broca, P. ; Pouchet, G. ; and Waitz, T. : Authors' Catalogue.]

Anthropology, Journal of. Vol. I. [all published]. *Map and plates.* 8°   1870-71

Anthropology, Popular Magazine of. Vol. I. [all published]. 8°   1866

Artizan, The : a Monthly Record of the Progress of Civil and Mechanical Engineering, Shipbuilding, Steam Navigation, the Application of Chemistry to the Industrial Arts, &c. Vols. XVI.-XXIX. (13 vols.) *Plates.* 4°   1858-71

Asiatic Journal, The. Vol. XXI. *Map.* 8°   1836

Association for Promoting the Discovery of the Interior Parts of Africa, Proceedings of the. Vol. I. *Map.* 4°   1790
—— Reissue of ; with continuations and additional papers. In 2 vols. 8°   1810

Athenæum, The : Journal of Literature, Science, and the Fine Arts. 2 vols. annually ; set bound in 103 vols. 4°   1831-93

Atlantis, The : a Register of Literature and Science. Conducted by Members of the Catholic University of Ireland. Vols. I.-II. and IV. *Maps and plates.* 8° 1858-63

Baptist Missionary Society. Missionary Herald of the B.M.S. for 1885-94. 10 vols.
1885 [incomplete]. *Maps and plates.* 8° 1885-94
Board of Trade Journal, of Tariff and Trade Notices, and Miscellaneous Commercial
Information. Vols. XIV.-XVI. (imperfect). 8° 1883-93
—— Index to the, for Vols. I.-XIV. 8° 1893
Bookseller, The : a Handbook of British and Foreign Literature, with which is
incorporated "Bent's Literary Advertiser." 1891 and 1892. Royal 8° 1891-92
British and Foreign Anti-Slavery Society. The Anti-Slavery Reporter.
—— Ser. 3, Vols. I.-VII. and IX. Royal 8° 1853-61
—— Ser. 4, Vols. II., VII., and VIII.-XIII. (1882-88 imperfect). 8° 1882-93
British Association for the Advancement of Science, Reports of the Meetings of the,
including its Proceedings, Recommendations, and Transactions. Total 62 vols.,
1831-93. *Maps, plates, and tables.* 8° 1833-94
York, 1831 ; Oxford, 1832 ; Cambridge, 1833 ; Edinburgh, 1834 ; Dublin, 1835 ;
Bristol, 1836 ; Liverpool, 1837 ; Newcastle, 1838 ; Birmingham, 1839 ;
Glasgow, 1840 ; Plymouth, 1841 ; Manchester, 1842 ; Cork, 1843 ; York,
1844 ; Cambridge, 1845 ; Southampton, 1846 ; Oxford, 1847 ; Swansea, 1848 ;
Birmingham, 1849 ; Edinburgh, 1850 ; Ipswich, 1851 ; Belfast, 1852 ; Hull,
1853 ; Liverpool, 1854 ; Glasgow, 1855 ; Cheltenham, 1856 ; Dublin, 1857 ;
Leeds, 1858 ; Aberdeen, 1859 ; Oxford, 1860 ; Manchester, 1861 ; Cambridge,
1862 ; Newcastle-upon-Tyne, 1863 ; Bath, 1864; Birmingham, 1865 ; Notting-
ham, 1866 ; Dundee, 1867 ; Norwich, 1868 ; Exeter, 1869 ; Liverpool, 1870 ;
Edinburgh, 1871 ; Brighton, 1872 ; Bradford, 1873 ; Belfast, 1874 ; Bristol,
1875 ; Glasgow, 1876 ; Plymouth, 1877 ; Dublin, 1878 ; Sheffield, 1879 ;
Swansea, 1880 ; York, 1881 ; Southampton, 1882 ; Southport, 1883 ; Montreal,
1884 ; Aberdeen, 1885 ; Birmingham, 1886 ; Manchester, 1887 ; Bath, 1888 ;
Newcastle-upon-Tyne, 1889 ; Leeds, 1890 ; Cardiff, 1891 ; Edinburgh, 1892 ;
Nottingham, 1893.
—— Index to Reports and Transactions of the. 2 vols., viz., from :—
1831 to 1860 ; 1861 to 1890 inclusive. 2 vols. 8° 1864 and 1893
[The Reports for 1831 and 1832 were published in one volume.]
British Commercial Geographical Society. Objects and Proposed Rules, &c.
[Pamph., 2 editions, all published by Lieut. V. L. Cameron.] 8° 1884
British South Africa Co. Annual Reports. *Maps.* 4° 1891-94
China Inland Mission. China's Millions. [11 vols.], Vols. VII.-X. (imperfect), XI.-
XVI. *Illustrations.* Small 4° 1882-93
—— New Ser. Vols. I. and II. (incomplete). *Illustrations.* Small 4° 1893-94
Chronological Institute of London, Transactions of the. Vols. I., II. (pts. 3 and 4),
III. (pt. 1). 8° 1858-66
Church Missionary Intelligencer : a Monthly Journal of Missionary Information. 45
vols. in all. [1 Ser.] Vols. I.-XV. *Maps and plates.* Royal 8° 1850-64
—— The same. [2 Ser.] Vols. I.-XI. *Maps and plates.* Royal 8° 1865-75
[Continued as]—
Church Missionary Intelligencer and Record, The. [3 Ser.] Vols. I.-XVIII. *Maps
and plates.* 8° and royal 8° 1876-93
Church Missionary Society for Africa and the East, Proceedings of the, and Annual
Report, 1888-89 to 1890-92. 90th to 94th year. *Maps.* 8° 1888-93
Colonial Book Circular, The, and Biographical Record.
[Title altered to]—
The Torch, and Colonial Book Circular, including Classified Lists of New English
Books, and of Publications relating to, or issued in, the British Colonies. (*Ed.* E. A.
Petherick.) Vols. I.-V., Nos. 1-18 (8, 9, and 12 missing). Small 4° 1887-92
Colonial and Consular Reports. *See* Appendix 2 : United Kingdom (C) (D).
Colonial Magazine and Foreign Miscellany. (*Ed.* P. L. Simmonds.) Vols. I.-XIV.
Illustrations. 8° 1844-48
Colonies and India, The : a Weekly Journal of General Information, with especial
reference to Colonial and Indian Interests, for 1888 to 1893. 13 vols. (some numbers
missing). *Illustrations.* 4° 1888-93
Commerce : an Illustrated Weekly Journal ; with which is officially incorporated "The
Chamber of Commerce Journal." Vol. I. (imperfect). Folio 1893

County of Middlesex Natural History and Science Society, Transactions of the. Sess. 1886-87. 8°   1887

Eastern and Western Review, The : a Monthly Magazine of Political Literature and Science. Vols. I.-III. *Plates.* Small 4° and royal 8°. [All issued]   1892-93

East India Association. Journal. Vols. XXIV.-XXVI. (imperfect). *Maps and plates.* 8°   1892-94

Education. Vols. I.-II. 4°   1890-91
    [Continued as]—

Educational Review, The. Vols. I.-VII. (New Series.) *Plates.* 8° and royal 8°   1891-94

Ethnological Society of London, Journal of the. Vols. I.-IV. *Maps and plates.* 8°   1848-56

—— New Ser., Vols. I.-II. *Maps and plates.* 8°   1869-70

—— Transactions of the. New Ser., Vols. I. (pt. 2) -VII. *Plates.* 8°   1861-69
    [For Classified Index of Journ. and Trans., *see* Anthropol. Inst. of Gt. Brit. and Ireland, *supra.*]

Folk Lore : a Quarterly Review of Myth, Tradition, Institution, and Custom (incorporating the "Archæological Review and Folk Lore Journal"). Vols. I.-III. and IV. (No. 1). 8°   1890-93

Geological Magazine, The ; or, Monthly Journal of Geology; with which is incorporated "The Geologist." (*Eds.* T. Rupert Jones, H. Woodward, and others.)
    Decade 1. Vols. I.-X.   1864-73 ⎫
         " 2. Vols. I.-X.   1874-83 ⎬ Total 28 vols. *Maps and plates.* 8° 1864-89
         " 3. Vols. I.-VIII. 1884-89 ⎭

Geological Record, The : an Account of Works on Geology, Mineralogy, and Palæontology during the year (with Supplements). Vols. for 1874 to 1879 (*Eds.* W. Whitaker and W. H. Dalton); Vols. for 1880 to 1884 (*Eds.* W. Topley and C. D. Sherborn); and with addition to subtitle of—"Together with certain deficiencies omitted from previous volumes." Total of 8 vols. 8°   1875-89

Geological Society of London, Transactions of the. [1st Ser.] Vols. I.-V. (and 2 vols. Plates and Maps to same). 7 vols. 4°   1811-21

—— [2nd Ser.] Vols. I.-VII. (and 1 vol. Plates and Maps to accompany Vol. IV.) 8 vols. 4°   1824-56

—— Proceedings of the. Vols. I.-IV., 1826-45. *Maps and plates.* 8°   1834-46

—— Quarterly Journal of the. Vols. I.-XLIX., 1845-93. *Maps and plates.* 8° 1845-93

—— A Classified Index to the Transactions, Proceedings, and Quarterly Journal. 2nd edition, including all the Memoirs and Notices to the end of 1868. (By G. W. Ormerod.) 8°   1870

—— Lists of the Geological Society, 1885, '87, '88, '91-94 (6 Nos.). 8°   1885-94

—— Charter and Bye-Laws of the. 8°   1845

Geologists' Association, Proceedings of the. Vols. X.-XII. (imperfect set). *Maps and plates.* 8°   1887-92

—— Annual Report, together with List of Members, &c., 1871 and 1892. 8° 1872-92

Horological Journal : the Special Organ of the British Horological Institute. Vol. II. to date. Royal 8°   1860-65

Horticultural Society of London, Journal of the. Vols. I.-IX. [bound in 5 vols.] *Plates.* 8°   1846-55
    [Afterwards the]—

Royal Horticultural Society, Proceedings of the. Vols. I.-II. (1859-62). 8° 1861-62

Illustrated Travels : a Record of Discovery, Geography, and Adventure. (*Ed.* H. W. Bates.) Vols. I.-VI. *Maps and plates.* 4°   [1869-72 ?]

Imperial Institute of the United Kingdom, the Colonies, and India, The Work of the . . . [*See* Abel, Sir Fred. : Authors' Catalogue.] *Map.* Small 8° 1887

—— Annual Report for 1892 and 1893. 8°   1893

—— Charter of Incorporation of. [Pamph.] Small 8°   1888

—— "The Imperial Institute" (Account of). 2nd ed. *Plates and woodcuts.* 8° 1893

—— Year Book. 1892 and 1894. Royal 8°   1892-94

Indian Review, The : containing the Cream of Current Literature. Vol. III. (Nos. 17 and 22). Royal 8°   . 1885

Institution of Civil Engineers. Proceedings. Total 118 vols., viz. :—
  Minutes of Proceedings of the Institution of Civil Engineers : containing Abstracts
    of Papers and of Conversations, for the Sessions 1837-47. Vols. I.-VI., or 6 vols.
    Sub-title altered to—" With Abstracts of the Discussions." Vols. VII.-XXXVIII.,
    or 32 vols. Sub-title again altered to—" With other Selected and Abstracted Papers."
    Vols. XXXIX.-CXVIII., or 80 vols. (*Ed.* J. Forrest). *Maps and plates.* 8° 1837-93
  —— Transactions of the. Vols. I.-III. *Plates.* 4°   1836-42
  —— Charter, Bye-Laws, and Regulations, and List of Members. 1879, 1881-1885,
    1887, and 1889. 6 vols. 8°   1879-89
  —— General Index, Vols. I. to XX. (1837-61), XXI.-XXX. (1861-70). 2 vols. 8°
                                                                              1865-71
  —— Name Index, Vols. I. to LVIII. (Sess. 1837-79). 1 vol. 8°   1885
  —— Subject Index, Vols. I. to LVIII. (Sess. 1833-79), and Vols. LIX. to CXVIII.
    (Sess. 1879-94). 2 vols. 8°   1880-94
  —— Education and Status of Civil Engineers. [*See* Appendix 2 : Gen. Miscel.]
Journal of Travel and Natural History, The. (*Ed.* A. Murray.) Vol. I. [all pub-
  lished]. *Plates.* 8°   1868
Lagos and West African Almanack. *See* Payne, J. A. O. ; Authors' Catalogue.
Literary Society of Bombay, Transactions of the. Vols. I.-III. *Plates.* 4° 1819-23
Linnean Society of London, Transactions of the. Vols. XVI.-XXX., 1826 to 1874.
  Plates. 4°   1833-75
  —— Ser. 2. Zoology. Vol. I., 1875 to 1879. *Plates.* 4°   1879
  —— Ser. 2. Botany. Vol. I. (parts 1-6), 1875-79. *Plates.* 4°   1879
  —— General Index to the First Series of Trans., viz., to Vols. I.-XXV., 1867, and to
    Vols. XXVI.-XXX. 4°   1876
  —— Proceedings of the. Sessions 1838 to 1893. [As bound equal to 8 vols.] 1849-94
    [Continued as]—
  —— Journal of the Proceedings o fthe. [Sect.] Botany, Vols. I.-VIII., 1856-65 ; [Sect.]
    Zoology, Vols. I.-VIII., 1856-1865. *Plates.* 8°   1857-65
    [Continued as]--
  —— Journals of the. [Sect.] Botany, Vols. IX.-XXIX., 1865-93 ; [Sect.] Zoology,
    Vols. VIII.-XXIV., 1862-94. *Maps and plates.* 8°   1862-94
    [The Proceedings. Sess. 1838-55. 2 vols., as issued by Linn. Soc. From 1856
      to 1865, as Jour. of Proc., with sub-divisions in the same volumes of Proc.
      Records of other business, Botany and Zool., 8 vols. were issued. Thereafter
      the Botanical and Zoological Journals were published independently and with
      separate titles, and the Proceedings, &c., were issued by themselves in
      numbers both sessionally and at irregular intervals.]
  —— List of Fellows, &c., 1888-89 to 1893-94. 2 parts.   1888-94
London Missionary Society. The Chronicle of the London Missionary Society for the
  years 1878-91, 14 vols. (and odd numbers, 1874-77.) *Maps and plates.* 8° 1874-91
  —— New Ser. 1892-93. 2 vols. *Maps and plates.* Small 4°   1892-93
  —— 83ᵈ Report of the, 1877. (Pamph. 103 pp.) 8°   1877
  —— Mission in Central Africa (Thomson, Dodgshun, Hore, and Hutley). *Map.* 8° 1879
  —— Mission in New Guinea, The. From the Letters and Journals of the Revs. S.
    Macfarlane and James Chalmers. (*Map,* Eastern N.G.) 8°   1879
Mercantile Marine Magazine, The, and Nautical Record. Vols. I.-XX. (Vol. 18
  missing.) *Maps.* 8°   1854-73
    [From Vol. 12 onwards secondary title altered to " *and Record of the Royal Naval
      Reserve.*"]
Mercantile Navy List, The, and Annual Appendage to the Commercial Code of
  Signals for all Nations. (*Ed.* J. H. Brown.) For 1857 to 1864. 8 vols. *Plates
  and cuts.* 8°   1857-64
Missionary Register, The : Containing the Principal Transactions of the various
  Institutions for Propagating the Gospel, with the Proceedings at large of the Church
  Missionary Society, for 1837 to 1843. 7 vols. *Plates.* 8°   1837-43
Moravian Foreign Missions. Periodical Accounts relating to the Foreign Missions of
  the Church of the United Brethren. 2nd century. Vols. I. and II. (6 numbers).
  Maps and plates. 8°   1890-94
National Association for the Promotion of Social Science, Transactions of the.
  London Meeting, 1862. (*Ed.* G. W. Hastings.) 8°   1863

Natural Science: a Monthly Review of Scientific Progress. Vols. I.-II. *Maps and plates.* Royal 8° *London and New York*, 1892-93

Nature: a Weekly Illustrated Journal of Science. Vols. I.-XLIX. *Maps and illustrations.* Small 4° 1870-93

Nautical Almanac and Astronomical Ephemeris, The. From the Commencement, 1767, to present date, 1896. Total 180 vols. [1852, 1865, and 1866 missing.] 8° 1776-94

Nautical Magazine and Naval Chronicle, The: a Journal of Papers on Subjects connected with Maritime Affairs. [Total 61 vols.] Vols. I.-XL. *Maps and plates.* 8° 1832-71

—— New Ser., for years 1872 to 1890. 19 vols. 8° 1872-90

—— (New Ser.), Enlarged, for years 1891 to 1892. 2 vols. Royal 8° 1891-92

Naval Chronicle, The. (Containing a General Biographical History of the Royal Navy of the United Kingdom ; with a variety of Original Papers on Nautical Subjects.) Vols. I.-XXXIV. [Vol. 28 missing.] *Maps and plates.* 8° 1799-1815

Naval Science: a Quarterly Magazine for Promoting the Improvement of Naval Architecture, Marine Engineering, Steam Navigation, and Seamanship. (*Ed.* E. J. Reed.) Vols. I.-IV. (1872 to 1875, latter imperfect). *Maps and plates.* 8° 1872-75

Nouvelles des Missions Orientales. Reçus à Londres par les Directeurs du Seminaire des Missions Etrangers, en 1793, 1794, 1795, and 1796. Pouvant servir de suite aux Lettres Édifiantes des missionaires de la Compagnie de Jesus. 1 vol. 12° 1797
[*See* " Lettres Édifiantes, &c.," under Paris, *antea.*]

Observatory, The: a Monthly Review of Astronomy. (*Eds.* Turner, Lewis, and Hollis.) Nos. 194, 207, 215. 8° 1892-93

Oriental Herald, and Colonial Review. Vols. I.-XXIII. (4 vols. annually.) 8° 1824-29

Our Ocean Highways. The Monthly Geographical Record and Travellers' Register. Title altered in 2nd vol. to " Ocean Highways : The Geographical Record." Vols. I.-II. [Vol. I. imperfect and 2 copies Vol. 2.] *Maps.* Small folio 1870-73
[Continued as]—

Ocean Highways: The Geographical Review. (*Ed.* Clements R. Markham.) New Ser. Vol. I. (1873-74). [2 copies.] *Maps.* 8° 1874
[Continued as] —

Geographical Magazine, The. (*Ed.* C. R. Markham.) Vols. I.-V. [2 sets.] *Maps.* Small folio 1874-78

Palestine Exploration Fund. Volume of Preliminary Reports, &c., by Capt. C. W. Wilson, Lieut. Warren, and E. H. Palmer. Prospectuses, Catalogues of Photographs, &c. *Plans.* Small 8° 1834-70

—— Quarterly Statement, 1869-80 (wants No. for January 1872). *Maps and plates.* 12°. 1869-93, 20 vols. *Maps and plates.* Small 8° 1869-93
[*See* under Turkey in Asia, Palestine : Appendix 2.]

Palestine Pilgrims' Text Society. Vols. I.-V. *Maps and plates.* 8° 1885-87
[For articles in numbers (vols.), *see* Appendix 2 : Palestine.]

Philosophical Magazine and Journal of Science. (*The Lond., Edinb., and Dublin.*) 4th Ser. Vols. XXX.-XXXIV., XXXVI.-XL. (July 1865 to Dec. 1870). *Plates.* 8° 1865-70

Phoenix, The : a Monthly Magazine for China, Japan, and Eastern Asia. (*Ed.* Rev. J. Summers.) Vols. I.-II. Small 4° 1870-72

Proceedings of the General Conference on Foreign Missions. Held, &c. . . . Oct. 1878. 1 vol. 8° 1879

Quarterly Review. (Total 143 vols.) Vols. I.-LXXIX., LXXXI.-XCIX., CI.-CXXXIX., CXLI.-CLIX., CLXI.-CLXXVII. (Vols. 1-3 later eds.) 8° 1809-93

Regions Beyond. (*Ed.* H. Grattan Guiness.) For 1891-93. 3 vols., and odd numbers of years 1882, '84, '85. *Maps and plates.* 8°, small 4°, and royal 8° 1882-93

Rousdon Observatory, Devon. (Supt. Cuthbert E. Peek.) Meteorological Observations. [Vol. I.] for years 1884 to 1893. *Plates and diagrams.* 4° 1885-94
[Each yearly vol. is under 50 pages, the entire series being bound in 1 vol.]

Royal Agricultural and Commercial Society of British Guiana.
—— Catalogue of the Library of the. 1 vol. 8° 1868
—— Catalogue of Contrib. from Guiana to Paris Exhib. [*See* Append. 2 : Guiana, Brit.]

Royal Agricultural Society of England, Journal of the. [First Series.] Vols. I.-XXV. (1840-64). *Plates.* 8° 1843-64
—— Second Series. Vol. I.-XXV. (1864-89). *Plates.* 8° 1865-89
—— Third Series. Vols. I.-IV. *Plates.* 8° 1890-93
—— General Index. Second Series, Vols. I.-X. (for 1865-74). 8° 1875

Royal Asiatic Society of Great Britain and Ireland. Transactions. Vols. I.-III.
  Plates. 4°   1827-35
    [Followed by]—
—— Journal. Total 45 vols. [First Series.] Vols. I.-XX., 1834-63. [Second] New
    Series. Vols. I.-XX., 1865-88. [Third] New Series. Vols.   1889-94. (6
    vols.) *Plates.* 8°   1889-93
—— General Index of Transactions, Vols. I.-III., and of Journal, 1st and 2nd Series,
    (bound up with Vol. XX. of Second Series)   1834-88
Royal Astronomical Society of London, Memoirs of the. (Vols. I.-L., 1821 to
    1890-91) [Vols. XXV. and XLVIII. missing.] *Plates.* 4°   1822-92
—— Monthly Notices of. Containing Papers, Abstracts of Papers, and Reports of the
    Proceedings of the Society. Vols. IX.-XXXI. (1848-71). *Plates.* 8° and 4° 1849-71
    [Vols. XIX. to XXVII. inclusive, in 4°, are bound up with the Memoirs, Vols.
    XXVI. to XXXVI.]
—— A General Index to the first twenty-nine volumes of the Monthly Notices of the
    Astronomical Society. Comprising the Proceedings of the Society from February 9,
    1827, to the end of the Session 1868-69. 8°   1870
Royal Colonial Institute, Proceedings of the. Vols. I.-XXIV. (Sess. 1879-70 to 1893-94;
    Vols. 1 and 2 bound together). 8°   1870-94
—— Journal of the. Vols. XXIV., XXV. (incomplete). 8°   1892-93
    [The *Proceedings* are issued only in annual vols., but the *Journal* is published
    monthly.]
Royal Gardens, Kew. Bulletin of Miscellaneous Information. For 1887-94, 8 vols.
  8°   1887-94
Royal Geographical Society, Journal of the. Vols. I.-L., Sess. 1830-80. *Maps and
  plates.* 8°   1832-80
—— General Index to the Contents of the First 10 vols., 1832-41. (J. R. Jackson.)
    1 vol. 8°   1844
—— General Index to the Second 10 vols., 1841-50. (G. S. Brent.) 1 vol. 8°   1853
—— General Index to the Third 10 vols, 1851-60. (Col. H. Yule.) 8°   1867
—— General Index to the Fourth 10 vols., 1861-70. (Norton Shaw.) 8°   1881
—— General Index to the Fifth 10 vols., 1871-80. 8°   1884
—— Proceedings of the. [Ser. 1.] Vols. I.-XXII. Sess. 1855-56, 1877-78. *Maps.* 8°
    [Continued as]—   1865-78
—— Proceedings of the R.G.S., and Monthly Record of Geography. New Monthly
    Series. [Ser. 2.] Vols. I.-XIV., 1879-92. *Maps and illustrations.* Royal 8° 1879-82
    [Continued as]—
—— The Geographical Journal; including the Proceedings of the Roy. Geogr. Soc.
    Vols. I.-V. (2 vols. annually). *Maps and illustrations.* Royal 8°   1893-94
—— List of Maps and other Illustrations contained in the Journal and Proceedings, to
    December 1880. 8°   1881
—— Roy. Geogr. Soc., Supplementary Papers. Vols. I.-IV., 1881-93. *Maps and
  plates.* 8°   1866-93
—— Narrative of an Expedition to the East Coast of Greenland, &c. 1 vol. 8° 1837
    See Graah, W. A.: Authors' Catalogue.
—— The Lands of Cazembe, &c. 1 vol. 8° [*See* Lacerda: Authors' Catalogue.] 1873
—— Arctic Geography and Ethnology. A Selection of Papers reprinted and presented
    to the Arctic Expedition of 1875 by the President, Council, and Fellows of the
    R.G.S. 1 vol. *Maps and plates.* 8°   1875
—— Hints to Travellers. [Ed. 1.] From Jour. R.G.S. Vol. XXIV. 8°   1854
—— [Ed. 2.] Revised edition. *Woodcuts.* 8°   1865
—— [Ed. 3.] Revised edition. 8°   Dec. 1871
—— [Ed. 4.] (*Ed.* by Francis Galton.) *Woodcuts.* 12°   1878
—— [Ed. 5.] (*Ed.* by H. H. Godwin-Austen, J. K. Laughton, and D. W. Freshfield.)
  Maps and plates. 12°   1883
—— [Ed. 6.] (*Ed.* by D. W. Freshfield and W. J. L. Wharton.) *Maps.* 12° 1889
—— [Ed. 7.] (*Ed.* by D. W. Freshfield and W. J. L. Wharton.) *Maps.* 12° 1893
    [The 5th, 6th, and 7th editions have a secondary title of "*Scientific and General.*"]
—— The Fifty Years' Work of the Roy. Geogr. Soc. (By Clements R. Markham.) 1
  vol. 8°   1881
—— Review of British Geographical Work during the hundred years 1789-1889.
    Bibliography. 8° [Unpublished.]   1893
—— Report of the Proceedings of the Society in reference to the Improvement of
    Geographical Education. [And Exhibition Educational Appliances, &c.] (J. Scott
    Keltie.) 1 vol. 8°   1886

Royal Geographical Society, Catalogue of the Library, corrected to May 1851. (Compiled by Norton Shaw.) 1 vol. 8°   1852

—— Do., to May 1865. 1 vol. 8°   1865

—— Supplement to the Alphabetical Catalogue . . containing the additions from 1865 to December 1870. 1 vol. 8°   1871

. —— Classified Catalogue . . . to December 1870. (G. M. Evans.) 1 vol. 8° 1871

—— Second Supplement to the Alphabetical Catalogue . . . containing additions from December 1870 to December 1880. (E. C. Rye.) 1 vol. 8°   1882

—— Catalogue of Map-room of the R.G.S. to March 1881. (J. Coles.) 1 vol. 8° 1882

—— Presidents' Addresses, 1836-74. 4 vols. and 3 separate Addresses, viz.: 1876, 1877, and 1878. 8°   1836-78
[The Annual Presidental Address was afterwards printed in the Journal.]

—— African Exploration Fund Circular. *Map.* (Pamph.) 4°   1877

—— Charter and Regulations of the Roy. Geogr. Soc., Established 1830, as amended up to 21st May 1892. 8°   *London*, 1894

Royal Historical Society, Transactions of the. (*Ed.* by the Rev. C. Rogers.) Vols. I. (2nd ed.), 1875, New Ser.; II., 1873; III., 1874; IV., 1876. 8°   1873-76

Royal Institute of British Architects, Kalendar of the. 57 to 59 Sess. 8°   1891-93

—— Journal of Proceedings. New Ser. Vol. IX. 4°   1892

—— Transactions. New Ser. Vols. IV.-VIII. (54th to 58th year). Sess. 1887-88 to 1891-92. *Plates.* 4°   1888-92

Royal Institution of Great Britain, Notices of the Proceedings at the Meetings of the Members of the. With Abstracts of the Discourses delivered at the Evening Meetings. Vols. I.-XII. and XIII. (pts. 1 and 2), 1851-91. *Maps and plates.* 8°
                                                                                 1854-92
—— General Index. Vols. I.-XII. (bound up with Proc. XII.). 8°   1889

—— List of Members. 1885, 1890, and 1891. 8°   1886-92

Royal Society of Literature of the United Kingdom, Transactions of the. Vols. I.-III. (1825-39). *Plates.* 4°   1829-39

—— 2nd Ser. Vols. I.-XII., XIII. (pt. 1), XV. (pt. 1), 1840-93. *Maps and plates.* 8°
                                                                                 1843-93
—— Report of the, for 1891. (Pamph.) 8°   1891

Royal Society of London, Philosophical Transactions of the, from their Commencement in 1665 to 1800, *abridged*, with Notes and Biographic Illustrations. (By C. Hutton, G. Shaw, and R. Pearson.) Vols. I.-XVIII., and 1 vol. *Plates* (accompanying Vol. XVI.), viz., 19 vols. 4°   1809

Vol. I.		1665-72	Vol. VII.		1724-34	Vol. XIII.			1770-76
„ II.		1672-83	„ VIII.		1735-43	„ XIV.			1776-80
„ III.		1683-94	„ IX.		1744-49	„ XV.			1781-85
„ IV.		1694-1702	„ X.		1750-55	„ XVI.			1785-90
„ V.		1703-12	„ XI.		1755-63	„ XVII.			1791-96
„ VI.		1713-23	„ XII.		1763-69	„ XVIII.			1796-1800

—— Philosophical Transactions (entire). Vols. CXX.-CLXXVIII., 1830-88. *Maps and plates.* 4°   1830-88

—— Proceedings of the. Vols. I.-LVI. (1800-94). *Plates.* 8°   1832-94

—— Royal Society, Catalogue of Scientific Papers. Compiled and published by the Roy. Soc., Lond. Vols. I.-X. for 1800 to 1883. 4°   1867-94

—— Catalogues of the Scientific Books in the Library. 2 parts. 8°   1883

—— Meteorological Committee of (Govt. Com.). For Reports and other Publications of, *see* Appendix 2 : United Kingdom, (B) Board of Trade.

Royal United Service Institution, Journal of the. Vols. I.-XXXVII. (1857 to 1893). *Maps and plates.* 8°   1858-93

—— Index of the Lectures and Papers contained in Vols. XI.-XX. 8°. 1878 : and of Vols. XXI.-XXX. 8°   1887

—— List of Members to Jan. 1892. 8°   1892

Selborne Society. Nature Notes. (The Selborne Society's Magazine, with which is incorporated "The Field Club.") Vols. I.-IV. *Illustrations.* 8°. *London*, 1890-93

Society of Antiquaries of London. Archæologia ; or, Miscellaneous Tracts relating to
Antiquity.   Published by the Soc.   Vols. I., II., VI., XI.-XIV., XV.-XXXI.,
XXXIII.-LIII.   (Each vol. consists of parts 1 and 2, 2 vols., or a total of 58 vols.,
and containing material from 1749 to 1892.)   *Maps and plates.* 4°   1804-93
—— Index to Archæologia, from Vol. XVI.-XXX. 4°   1844
—— The same, from Vol. I.-L.   4°   1889
—— Proceedings of the Soc. [Ser. 1.] Vols. I.-IV. (1843-59). *Plates.* 8°   1849-59
—— The same. Ser. 2. Vols. I.-XIV. (1859-93). *Plates.* 8°   1861-93
   [General Index to Proc., Vols. I.-IV., bound up with Vol. IV. of 2nd Ser.]

Society of Biblical Archæology. Transactions. Vols. I.-IX. *Maps and plates.* 8°
                                                                           1872-93
—— Proceedings. Vols. I.-XVI. *Plates.* 8°   1879-94
   [Alphabetical Index of Contents of Vols. I.-X. of Proceedings, 1878-88, bound
   with Vol. X.)

Society of Hebrew Literature.   Miscellany of Hebrew Literature.   (*Ed.* Rev. A.
Löwy.)   Ser. 2. Vol. II. 8°   1877

Society for the Encouragement of Arts, Manufactures, and Commerce (Lond.
Instituted 1783), Transactions of the.   Vols. I.-LV. (1754-83). [4th vol. missing.]
Plates. 8°   1806-45
   [Title altered to]—

Society of Arts (and of the Institutions in Union), Journal of the.   Vols. I.-XLI. [2nd
vol. missing] (1852-93). *Plates and cuts.* Royal 8°   1853-93
—— General Index to Vols. I.-X. (1852-62) ; XI.-XX. (1862-72) ; XXI.-XXX. (1872-82),
   [all bound in 1 vol.] ; XXXI.-XL. (1882-92), separate. Small 4°   1873-94
—— List of Council and Officers. Sess. 1885-86. Royal 8°   1885
—— Programme of Soc. Examinations for 1892-94. Royal-8°   1891-93

Society for the Extinction of the Slave Trade, and for the Civilisation of Africa.
The Friend of Africa, by the Soc., &c.   Vols. I.-II. *Maps.* 8°   1841-42

Society for the Propagation of the Gospel.   The Mission Field. Vols. XXXIV. and
XXXV. (imperfect), XXXVI. and XXXVII. (complete), and XXXVIII. (imperfect).
Illustrations. Royal 8°   1889-93
—— Reports for the years 1889-93. *Maps.* 8°   1889-93

South American Journal, and Brazil and River Plate Mail. Vol. XXII. Folio 1885

South American Missionary Society.   South American Missionary Magazine. Vols.
II.-V. and XX.-XXIV. and XXV.-XXVI. (imperfect). *Illustrations.* 8° 1868-92

Statistical Society of London, Journal of the.   Vols. I.-LVI. (1838-93). *Maps and
plates.* 8°   1839-93
—— General Index to :—

                Vols.   I.- XV. (1839-52) | Vols. XXVI.-XXXV. (1863-72)
                 „ XVI.-XXV. (1853-62) | „ . XXXVI.-L.   (1873-87)
        These four parts 8°, issued respectively 1854, 1863, 1874, and 1889.

Syro-Egyptian Society of London, Original Papers read before the.   Vol. I. (pts. 1
and 2). *Plates.* 8°   1845-50
—— Transactions of the. Sess. 1867-68. *Plate.* 8°   1868

Universities' Missions to Central Africa.   Central Africa : a Monthly Record of the
Work of the U.M. to C.A. Vols. I.-XII. [imperfect set]. *Illustrations.* 8° 1883-94
—— Annual Reports. 1868-93, 25 Reps. *Maps and illustrations.* 12°   1868-93
—— Occasional Papers. Nos. 3-19. *Maps and illustrations.* 16°   1869-82

Vacation Tourists and Notes of Travel.   (*Ed.* F. Galton.) Vols. I.-III. (1860,
1862-63). *Maps.* 8° [For Contents, *see* Galton, F. : Authors' Catalogue] 1861-64

Victoria Institute, or Philosophical Society of Great Britain, Journal of the Transactions
of the.   Vols. XXII. (incomplete), XXIII.-XXVI., and XXVII. (No. 106). *Maps
and plates.* 8°   1888-92

Wesleyan Missionary Notices (relating principally to the Foreign Missions under the
Direction of the Methodist Conference), for 1886-91, 8 vols. Also odd numbers, viz.,
No. 13, 1840 ; No. 17, 1842 ; and No. 58, 1843. *Maps and plates.* 8° and small 4°
                                                                           1886-94

Year Book of Australia.   For 1884-86 and 1889-90 (5 vols., viz., III., IV., V., VIII.,
and IX.) *Maps.* 8°   1884-90

Zoological Society of London, Transactions of the.　Vols. I.-XII. and XIII. (parts), 1833 to 1887.　*Maps and plates.*　4°　　　　　　　　　　　　　　　1835-90
—— General Index to the Trans.　1835 to 1879, or Vols. I.-X.　4°　　　1881
—— Proceedings of the.　From 1830-32 to 1893, bound in 46 vols.　*Plates.*　8°　1830-93
—— Index of Proceedings as undermentioned :—

1830-47. 8°	1866	1871-80. 8°	1882
1848-60. 8°	1863	1881-90. 8°	1892
1861-70. 8°	1872		

—— List of the Vertebrated Animals now or lately living in the Gardens of the Zoological Society of London. 8th edition, with first Supplement.　*Woodcuts.*　8°　　1882
—— Catalogue of the Library.　1880.　8°, and Supplement　　　　　　1883

MANCHESTER.

Literary and Philosophical Society of Manchester.　Memoirs.　Second Series. | -- Vol. XV. (pts. 1 and 2).　Sess. 1857-59.　8°　　(*London and*) *Manchester*, 1858-60
—— The same.　Third Series.　Vols. I.-X.　Sess. 1859-86.　*Plates.*　8°
　　　　　　　　　　　　　　　　　　　(*London and*) *Manchester*, 1862-87
—— The same.　Fourth Series.　Vols. I.-VIII. (No. 1 and 2).　Sess. 1887-88 to 1893-94. *Plates.*　8°　　　　　　　　　　　　　　　*Manchester*, 1888-94
—— Proceedings.　Vols. I.-XXVI.　Sess. 1857-60 to 1886-87.　*Plates.*　8°
　　　　　　　　　　　　　　　　　　　　　　　　Manchester, 1861-87
　　[From 1887 the Proceedings were issued along with the Memoirs, under the title "Memoirs and Proceedings of the Manchester Literary Philosophical Society."]

Manchester Geographical Society, Journal of the.　Vols. I.-IX.　*Maps and plates.*　8°
　　　　　　　　　　　　　　　　　　　　　　　Manchester, 1885-93
—— Report of the Education Committee to the Council of the M.G.S. on the subject of Geographical Education.　8°　　　　　　　　　*Manchester*, 1886
—— Catalogue of Exhibition of Appliances used in Geographical Education. (From the Roy. Geogr. Soc. Exhib., with additions.)　8°　　　　*Manchester*, 1886

Manchester Geological Society.　Transactions.　Vol. XX., pts. 18 and 19.　*Plate.*　8°
　　　　　　　　　　　　　　　　　　　　　　　Manchester, 1890

NEWCASTLE-ON-TYNE.

Tyneside Geographical Society (Newcastle-on-Tyne), Journal of the.　Vols. I., II., and III. (No. 1).　*Maps and plates.*　8°　　　*Newcastle-on-Tyne*, 1889-94
　　[No. 1, Vol. I., comprises Report, Prospectus, and Rules, and the Title-page comes in No. 2.]

OXFORD.

Radcliffe Observatory, Oxford.　Astronomical Observations made at the Radcliffe Observatory, Oxford, for 1840-52, 13 vols.
　　[Continued as]—
—— Astronomical and Meteorological Obs., &c.　1853-64, 11 vols.
　　[Continued as]—
—— Results of Astronomical and Meteorological Obs., &c. (under R. Main).　1865 to 1867 ; and 1869, 1882, 1884 to 1887, 9 vols.　Total 33 vols.　8°　*Oxford*, 1842-91
—— The Radcliffe Catalogue of 6317 Stars, chiefly Circumpolar, &c. (for Epoch 1845). Royal 8°　　　　　　　　　　　　　　　　*Oxford*, 1860
—— Second Radcliffe Catalogue, containing 2386 Stars (for Epoch 1860).　Royal 8°
　　　　　　　　　　　　　　　　　　　　　　　Oxford, 1870

TRURO.

Royal Institution of Cornwall, Journal of.　Vol. IX. (pts. 1-3).　*Maps and plates.*　8°
　　　　　　　　　　　　　　　　　　　　　　　Truro, 1886-88

WOKING.

Imperial and Asiatic Quarterly Review, and Oriental and Colonial Review, The. 2 Ser.　Vols. V.-VIII.　*Plates.*　Royal 8°　　　*Woking* [*Surrey*] 1893-94

SCOTLAND.

Dun Echt (Aberdeen).

Dun Echt Observatory Publications. Vol. III. (Divis. 1) Mauritius Expedition, 1874; (Divis. 2) Determinations of Longitude and Latitude. *Map and diagram.* 4°
Dun Echt, Aberdeen, 1885

Edinburgh.

Edinburgh Geological Society, Transactions of the. Sessions 1866-94. Vols. I.-VI. *Maps and plates.* 8° *Edinburgh,* 1870-93
—— Catalogue of the Library. 8° *Edinburgh,* 1887
—— Roll of the, and List of Corresponding Societies and Institutions. [Pamph.] 8° *Edinburgh,* 1893

Edinburgh Journal of Natural and Geographical Science, The. (*Ed.* W. Ainsworth and W. Cheek.) Vols. I. to III. *Maps and plates.* 8° *Edinburgh,* 1830-31

Edinburgh Philosophical Journal, The: exhibiting a View of the Progress of Discovery in Natural Philosophy, Chemistry, Natural History, Practical Mechanics, Geography, Statistics, and the Fine and Useful Arts, conducted by Dr Brewster and Prof. Jameson. Vols. I.-XIV. *Maps and plates.* 8° *Edinburgh,* 1819-26
[Continued as]—

Edinburgh New Philosophical Journal, The: exhibiting a View of the Progressive Discoveries and Improvements in the Sciences and the Arts. Conducted by Robert and Laurence Jameson. Vols. XV., XIX., L.-LVII. (10 vols.). *Maps and plates.* 8° *Edinburgh,* 1826-54

Free Church of Scotland, The Home and Foreign Missionary Record of the, for 1878 to 1888 (10 vols.). Small 4° *Edinburgh,* 1879-89
—— Reports on Foreign Missions to the General Assembly of the Free Church of Scotland. 49th to 63rd Reports, 1879 to 1893. *Maps.* 8° *Edinburgh,* 1880-93

Edinburgh Review, or Critical Journal. (Total 115 vols. and 3 Gen. Indexes.) Vols. I.-CXIV., and CXXIV. [some of early vols. later editions]. 8° *Edinburgh,* 1802-66
—— Gen. Index to Vols. 1 to 80. 3 vols. 8° *Edinburgh,* 1813, 1832, and 1850

Royal Scottish Geographical Society. The Scottish Geographical Magazine. Vols. I.-X. (1885-94). *Maps and plates.* 8° *Edinburgh,* 1885-94

Royal Society of Edinburgh. Transactions. Vols. IV.-XXXVI. and XXXVII. (pts. 1 and 2). *Maps and plates.* 4° *Edinburgh,* 1798-1893
—— Gen. Index to first Thirty-four Vols. (1873-88), with History of the Institution of the Society, Royal Charters, List of the Contents of each Vol., &c. &c. 4° *Edinburgh,* 1890
—— Proceedings. Vols. I.-XIX. (1832-92). *Plates.* 8° *Edinburgh,* 1845-93
—— Catalogue of the Library to March 1891; and Accessions to October 1893. 8° *Edinburgh,* 1891-93

Scottish Meteorological Society, Journal of the. Ser. 2, New Ser., Vols. I.-V. (Vol. 6 missing); Ser. 3, New Ser., Vols. VII.-IX. *Maps, charts, &c.* Royal 8° *Edinburgh,* 1866-93

Wernerian Natural History Society, Memoirs of the, for 1831-37. Vol. VII. *Map and plates.* 8° *Edinburgh,* 1838

Glasgow.

Natural History Society of Glasgow, Proceedings of the. [1st Ser.] Vols. I.-V. (1858-83). *Plates.* 8° *Glasgow,* 1869-84
—— Index to the Proceedings. Vols. I.-V., 1851-83. 8° *Glasgow,* 1885
—— 2nd, New Ser. Vols. I.-III. (1883-92). *Plates.* 8° *Glasgow,* 1885-92

Philosophical Society of Glasgow, Proceedings of the. Vols. XIII.-XXV. (1881-82 to 1893-94). *Maps and plates.* 8° *Glasgow,* 1882-93

IRELAND.

Dublin.

Geological Society of Dublin, Journal of the. Vols. III.-X. (1844-64). *Plates.* 8° *Dublin,* 1849-64

[Title of Soc. altered to]—

Royal Geological Society of Ireland, Journal of the. New Series. Vols. I.-VIII. [with imperfections] (1864-87). *Plates.* 8° (Entire Ser. I.-XVIII). *Dublin,* 1867-87
Royal Dublin Society, Journal of the. Vols. I.-VII. (1856-77). *Maps and plates.* 8°
Dublin, 1858-78
—— Scientific Proceedings of the. New Series. Vols. I.-VII., and VIII. (pts. 1 and 2), 1877-93. *Maps and plates.* 8° *Dublin,* 1878-93
—— Scientific Transactions of the. New Series. Vols. I. (pts. 1-24), II. (pts. 1-2), 1877-82. *Plates.* 4° *Dublin,* 1877-83
—— Series 2. Vols. I.-IV. and V. (pts. 1-4), 1881-93. *Plates.* 4° *Dublin,* 1882-93
Royal Irish Academy. Proceedings. [1st Ser.] Vol. VI.-X. (1853-69). *Maps and plates.* 8° *Dublin,* 1858-70
—— 2nd Ser. Science. Vols. I.-IV. (1869-86). *Maps and plates.* 8° *Dublin,* 1879-88
—— The same. Polite Literature and Antiquities. Vols. I.-II. (1870-86). *Plates.* 8°
Dublin, 1879-88
—— The same. Appendix to 2nd Series. Minutes of Academy. (Sess. 1869-77.) 8°
Dublin, 1878
—— 3rd Ser. I., II., and III. (No. 1, 2) (1879-93). *Plates.* 8° *Dublin,* 1889-94
—— List of the Council and Officers and Members of the Roy. Irish Acad., Dublin, to Aug. 1874. 8° *Dublin,* 1874
—— Transactions. Science. Vols. XXIII.-XXVI., XXVIII., XXIX., and XXX. (Parts 1-14), 1849-93. *Plates.* 4° *Dublin,* 1856-94
—— Science, Polite Literature, Antiquities. Vols. XXIII. (Part 2). *Maps and plates.* 4° *Dublin,* 1859
—— Polite Literature and Antiquities. Vols. XXIV. and XXVII. (Pts. 1, 2, 4-8), 1862-86. *Plates.* 4° *Dublin,* 1873-86
—— "Cunningham Memoirs." Nos. 1-5, 7 (1879-92) *Plates.* 4° *Dublin,* 1880-92
—— Irish Manuscript Series. Vol. I. (pt. 1, 1871). 4° *Dublin,* 1880
—— List of the Papers published in the Transactions, Cunningham Memoirs, and Irish Manuscript Series, of the Royal Irish Academy, between the years 1786 and 1886. With an Appendix, giving the names of the Officers of the Academy, from 1785 to 1887, and of those to whom the Academy's Cunningham Gold Medals have been awarded. 4° *Dublin,* 1887

ATLANTIC ISLANDS.

AZORES: SAN MIGUEL.

Archivo dos Açores. Publicação Periodica Destinada a Vulgarisação des Elementos indispensaveis para Todos os Ramos, da Historia Açoriana. Vols. V.-X. (Nos. 28-58), &c. *Map.* 8° *Ponta Delgada, Ilha de S. Miguel*